China Markets Yearbook 2004
中国市场年鉴 2004

(Reports on 500 Markets)
（500 行业报告）

All China Marketing Research Co., Ltd.
北京华通人市场信息有限责任公司

FOREIGN LANGUAGES PRESS
外 文 出 版 社

ISBN: 7-119-03448-0

Editorial Committee: Gao Yu-xian, David K Tse, Jiang Xing-rong, Tony Lin, Hongfang Tang, Lina Cao

Technical Support: Eric Liu

Published by: All China Marketing Research Co., Ltd.
7/F, Jingrun Building, No.28 Jia, Fuchengmen Wai,
Xicheng, Beijing, China
Tel: (86-10) 68032288
Fax: (86-10) 68012338
E-mail: cdc@acmr.com.cn
Website: www.acmr.com.cn

All data are exclusively provided by the National Bureau of Statistics of China.

国际标准书号：7-119-03448-0

出版 ：北京华通人市场信息有限责任公司

北京市西城区阜成门外大街甲 28 号京润大厦 7 层

电话：（86-10）68032288

传真：（86-10）68012338

电邮：cdc@acmr.com.cn

网址：www.acmr.com.cn

本年鉴数据资料由中国国家统计局独家提供。

Contents

Section 1 Description

Section 2 Summary Report by Industry

（Complete list on page xviii）

Mining and Forestry

Manufacturing

Electricity, Gas and Water Production and Supplies

Index

目录

第一部分

第二部分

500行业总览

（详细行业分类表载于第xxxiv页）

采掘业

制造业

索引

Preface

China Markets Yearbook is a collection of all the main industry markets in China. Since its first publication in 1997, we got great supports of most of our readers. Now it has become the indispensable reference for enterprises and research institutions so as to identify and pursue business opportunities in China and bring them to a successful conclusion.

All data of *China Markets Yearbook* derived from National Bureau of Statistics of China. We still have made extra effort to further reduce the errors. We hope we can provide the most abundant, exact information to our readers.

China Markets Yearbook 2004 mainly consists of:

1. 9 different indicators showing each industry on total number of firms, total number of employees, total revenue, total profit, return on assets, return on equity, labor productivity, debts/assets, and total assets.
2. The 9 indictors also showing the ownership of firm: state-owned, collective-owned, foreign & overseas Chinese funded and the economic situation in different provinces and areas.
3. Changing of each industry's scale in the latest three years: total number of firms, total number of employees, total revenue, total profit.
4. The company sizes and other basic conditions of the top 10 corporations.
5. The top 10 cities' production volume.
6. The contact details of the 10 major wholesalers.

前言

《中国市场年鉴》是一本涵盖中国主要工业行业的资料性年刊，自一九九七年开始出版以来，深得广大读者好评，成为密切关注市场的商家和研究者了解各行业发展状况不可或缺的参考资料。

《中国市场年鉴》中所有资料均来自于中国国家统计局，为保证质量，我们对原始资料进行了精心的筛选和复查，力争将更加丰富、准确的资料提供给读者。

《中国市场年鉴 2004》的主要内容包括：

- 以 9 种指标显示每个行业的总体经营状况：企业总数、职工总数、总销售收入、总利润、资产利润率、权益利润率、劳动生产率、资产负债率、总资产。
- 9 种经营指标分别按所有权、地区、省份列示。
- 全国销售收入最高的 10 家企业的规模及基本情况。
- 销售收入排名前 10 位的城市。
- 全国 10 家主要批发商的联络方式。

Explanation of Terms

The coverage of all the statistical data in the yearbook is as follows:
All state-owned industrial enterprises and non-state-owned industrial enterprises with an annual sales of over RMB 5 Million yuan.

Industry Overall	All the relevant "Industry Overall" figures are calculated using the unit of the measurement for the indicator. For example, "Return on assets" is calculated by dividing "the total profits" of the industry by "the total assets" of the industry. (Note: firms with large assets will have a larger weight.)
No. of Employees	Number of employees
Revenue	Revenues in units of 1,000 Renminbi (RMB).
Profit	Profit in units of 1,000 RMB.
Return on Assets	Profit divided by total assets: (profit) / (total assets).
Return on Equity	Profit divided by equity, which is total assets less total debts: (profit) / [(total assets) - (total debts)].
Labour Productivity	Value added of industry/Average number of staff and workers
Debts/Assets	Debts to assets ratio
Total Assets	The sum of fixed assets and current assets (including all debts).
Rate of Change	from year *t* to year *t+1*: {[(year *t+1* figure)-(year *t* figure)]/(year *t* figure)} x 100%
Major Wholesalers	To facilitate the reader to contact wholesalers which carry the products of an industry. Please note that wholesalers listed here may carry not only the specific products of an industry, but also products of other industries.

Market Share (A region's revenue in an industry)/ (Total revenue of the industry)

Ownership

State-Owned. Firms owned by different level of governments such as the central government, the provincial government, or the local government.

Collectively-Owned. Firms owned by a collective body, such as a village, a township [town and village enterprises (TVEs)], all workers of a firm, or individuals who give up their private ownership. Collective-ownership is considered "public-ownership".

Privately-Owned. Firms owned by individuals.

Domestic Joint Ventures (JVs). This category includes firms that are joint ventures (JVs) between domestic firms with different ownership types. For example, JVs between state- and collectively owned, or JVs between state- and privately owned.

Joint Stock. This category refers to all companies with limited liabilities, including (1) companies that explicitly issue stock certificates which may be traded publicly and (2) companies that have two or more shareholders with limited liabilities.

Foreign-Funded. "Foreign" is defined as foreign investors excluding Chinese outside China (overseas Chinese and Chinese from Taiwan, Hong Kong, and Macao). This category includes three types of "foreign-funded" firms: (1) Foreign-invested equity JVs; (2) foreign-involved contractual JVs; (3) foreign wholly-owned firms.

Overseas Chinese-Funded. "Overseas Chinese "includes all Chinese outside China, including Chinese from Taiwan, Hong Kong, Macao, and other countries. This category includes three types of firms: (1) equity JVs by Overseas Chinese, (2) contractual JVs by Overseas Chinese, and (3) firms wholly owned by Overseas Chinese.

指标解释

本书中数据的统计范围是：

全部国有工业企业及年产品销售收入 500 万元人民币以上的非国有工业企业。

行业总体 此栏的平均值是根据行业总体、行业总人数、总资本和总利润计算的，并没用（企业数）作加权计算。如甲行业有 10,000 人员，30,000 元销售收入，则人均销售收入为 30,000/10,000=30

职工数 职工人数

销售收入 以人民币为单位

利润 以人民币为单位的利润

资产利润率 （利润）/（总资产）

权益利润率 （利润）/（净资产），即（利润）/[（总资产）-（总负债）]

劳动生产率 工业增加值/平均职工人数

资产负债率 总负债/总资产

总资产 净资产+总负债

变化率 {（今年比去年的增长）/（去年总值）} x 100%

主要批发商 为方便用户，我们列出经销本行业（但不限于本行业）的最大的批发商

地区的市场份额 （甲行业在本地区的销售收入）/（甲行业的总销售收入）

产业所有权 **国有**：生产资料归国家所有的企业

集体：生产资料归公民集体所有的企业，包括城乡使用集体投资举办的企业

私有：包括各种生产资料归公民私人所有的企业

联营：国内不同所有制（国有、集体、私有）的企业以各种形式联营的企业

股份制：指由股东出资，以股份形式投资举办的企业，包括各种有限责任公司和发行股票的公司

外商投资：中外合资、合作、以及外国独资企业，但不含由海外华人和港、澳、台投资的企业

港澳台资：由港、澳、台和海外华人投资的合资、合作及独资企业

三资：包括外商投资及港澳台和海外华人投资企业

Selected Socioeconomic Statiastics by Province, 2002

Province or Municipality	Capital	Year-end Population (Million)	GDP growth with Preceding year (%)	Total Imports & Exports of Customs (USD 100 million)	Actually Used Foreign Direct Investment (USD 10 000)	Per capita income (RMB)		Consumer Price Index (preceding year=100)	
						Urban	Rural	Urban	Rural
Beijing	Beijing	1,423	10.2	267.3	172,464	12,464	5,399	99.5	NA
Tianjin	Tianjin	1,007	12.5	227.9	158,195	9,338	4,279	101.1	NA
Hebei	Shijiazhuang	6,735	9.6	68.3	78,271	6,680	2,685	100.3	100.2
Shanxi	Taiyuan	3,294	10.8	35.7	21,164	6,234	2,150	98.9	99.7
Inner Mongolia	Huhhot	2,379	11.6	26.6	17,701	6,051	2,086	100.8	105.4
Liaoning	Shenyang	4,203	10.2	234.3	341,168	6,525	2,751	99.6	100.1
Jilin	Changchun	2,699	9.5	40.8	24,468	6,260	2,301	100.0	100.1
Heilongjiang	Harbin	3,813	10.3	46.8	35,511	6,051	2,405	99.6	100.3
Shanghai	Shanghai	1,625	10.9	727.8	427,229	13,250	6,224	99.2	NA
Jiangsu	Nanjing	7,381	11.6	745.0	1,018,960	8,178	3,980	98.9	99.9
Zhejiang	Hangzhou	4,647	12.3	463.6	307,610	11,716	4,940	99.6	99.8
Anhui	Hefei	6,338	8.9	42.1	38,375	6,032	2,118	99.4	99.1
Fujian	Fuzhou	3,466	10.5	303.3	383,837	9,189	3,539	100.2	100.2
Jiangxi	Nanchang	4,222	10.5	20.0	108,197	6,336	2,307	99.8	99.8
Shandong	Jinan	9,082	11.6	373.7	473,404	7,614	2,948	99.5	100.3
Henan	Zhengzhou	9,613	9.5	37.3	40,463	6,245	2,216	99.4	100.1
Hubei	Wuhan	5,988	9.1	45.3	142,665	6,789	2,444	98.9	101.1
Hunan	Changsha	6,629	9.0	32.7	90,022	6,959	2,398	100.0	102.0
Guangdong	Guangzhou	7,859	10.8	2,254.6	1,133,400	11,137	3,912	99.5	99.2
Guangxi	Nanning	4,822	10.3	26.1	41,726	7,315	2,013	99.8	99.9
Hainan	Haikou	803	9.2	17.9	51,196	6,823	2,423	100.2	98.8
Chongqing	Chongqing	3,107	10.3	20.2	19,576	7,238	2,098	98.7	NA
Sichuan	Chengdu	8,673	10.6	44.6	55,583	6,610	2,108	99.6	99.7
Guizhou	Guiyang	3,837	9.1	9.8	3,821	5,944	1,489	98.3	99.0
Yunnan	Kunming	4,333	8.1	23.3	11,169	7,240	1,609	101.1	100.4
Tibet	Lhasa	267	NA	1.3	NA	8,079	1,462	101.1	100.1
Shaanxi	Xi'an	3,674	9.7	27.8	36,005	6,331	1,596	99.1	102.1
Gansu	Lanzhou	2,593	9.4	10.4	6,121	6,151	1,590	99.6	99.6
Qinghai	Xining	529	12.4	2.3	4,726	6,171	1,669	100.8	104.5
Ningxia	Yinchuan	572	10.2	4.9	2,200	6,067	1,917	100.6	98.8
Xinjiang	Urumqi	1,905	8.1	30.8	1,899	6,890	1,863	97.6	99.4

Note: "NA" means not available

Sources of data:

All data in this table are from *China Statistical Abstract 2003* or National Bureau of Statistics of China.

1. Data for year-end population is gained through the quick collections of 2000 China Population Census at zero hour on the 1st, November.
2. GDP growth is calculated at comparable prices.
3. The data is calculated by places of destination or origin in China.
4. Per capita income of urban households is per capita annual disposable income, that of rural households is per capita annual net income.

2002年各省社会经济状况

省（市）	省会	年底总人口（万人）	GDP比上年增长（%）	海关进出口总额（亿美元）	外商实际直接投资额（万美元）	人均收入（元）		居民消费价格指数（2001年=100）	
						城镇	农村	城镇	农村
北京	北京	1,423	10.2	267.3	172,464	12,464	5,399	99.5	NA
天津	天津	1,007	12.5	227.9	158,195	9,338	4,279	101.1	NA
河北	石家庄	6,735	9.6	68.3	78,271	6,680	2,685	100.3	100.2
山西	太原	3,294	10.8	35.7	21,164	6,234	2,150	98.9	99.7
内蒙古	呼和浩特	2,379	11.6	26.6	17,701	6,051	2,086	100.8	105.4
辽宁	沈阳	4,203	10.2	234.3	341,168	6,525	2,751	99.6	100.1
吉林	长春	2,699	9.5	40.8	24,468	6,260	2,301	100.0	100.1
黑龙江	哈尔滨	3,813	10.3	46.8	35,511	6,051	2,405	99.6	100.3
上海	上海	1,625	10.9	727.8	427,229	13,250	6,224	99.2	NA
江苏	南京	7,381	11.6	745.0	1,018,960	8,178	3,980	98.9	99.9
浙江	杭州	4,647	12.3	463.6	307,610	11,716	4,940	99.6	99.8
安徽	合肥	6,338	8.9	42.1	38,375	6,032	2,118	99.4	99.1
福建	福州	3,466	10.5	303.3	383,837	9,189	3,539	100.2	100.2
江西	南昌	4,222	10.5	20.0	108,197	6,336	2,307	99.8	99.8
山东	济南	9,082	11.6	373.7	473,404	7,614	2,948	99.5	100.3
河南	郑州	9,613	9.5	37.3	40,463	6,245	2,216	99.4	100.1
湖北	武汉	5,988	9.1	45.3	142,665	6,789	2,444	98.9	101.1
湖南	长沙	6,629	9.0	32.7	90,022	6,959	2,398	100.0	102.0
广东	广州	7,859	10.8	2,254.6	1,133,400	11,137	3,912	99.5	99.2
广西	南宁	4,822	10.3	26.1	41,726	7,315	2,013	99.8	99.9
海南	海口	803	9.2	17.9	51,196	6,823	2,423	100.2	98.8
重庆	重庆	3,107	10.3	20.2	19,576	7,238	2,098	98.7	NA
四川	成都	8,673	10.6	44.6	55,583	6,610	2,108	99.6	99.7
贵州	贵阳	3,837	9.1	9.8	3,821	5,944	1,489	98.3	99.0
云南	昆明	4,333	8.1	23.3	11,169	7,240	1,609	101.1	100.4
西藏	拉萨	267	NA	1.3	NA	8,079	1,462	101.1	100.1
陕西	西安	3,674	9.7	27.8	36,005	6,331	1,596	99.1	102.1
甘肃	兰州	2,593	9.4	10.4	6,121	6,151	1,590	99.6	99.6
青海	西宁	529	12.4	2.3	4,726	6,171	1,669	100.8	104.5
宁夏	银川	572	10.2	4.9	2,200	6,067	1,917	100.6	98.8
新疆	乌鲁木齐	1,905	8.1	30.8	1,899	6,890	1,863	97.6	99.4

“NA”即欠缺资料

资料来源说明：
本表中所有资料来源于《中国统计摘要2003》或国家统计局。
1. 年底总人口数据中各省总人口包括外来人口，不包括外出人口，未包括中国人民解放军现役军人数。
2. GDP增长速度按可比价格计算。
3. 按境内目的地、货源地计算的进出口总额。
4. 城镇人均收入是指可支配收入，农村人均收入是指纯收入。

Chinese Industrial Classification Code
国民经济行业分类代码

=== Industry classify ===

Chinese Industrial Classification Code	Industry	Page

Mining and Forestry

Coal Mining and Dressing

Petroleum and Natural Gas Extraction

Ferrous Metal Ores Mining and Dressing

Non-ferrous Ores Mining and Dressing

Non-metal Ores Mining and Dressing

General Machinery Manufacturing

Special Equipment Manufacturing

Electronic and Communication Equipment

Chinese Industrial Classification Code	Industry	Page

Instruments, Meters, Education and Office Equipment

Other Manufacturing

Chinese Industrial Classification Code	Industry	Page

Electricity, Gas and Water Production and Supplies

Electricity, Stream, Hot Water Production and Supplies

Gas Production and Supplies

Tap Water Production and Supplics

=== 行业分类 ===

国民经济行业分类代码	行业名称	页码

采掘业

饮料制造业

烟草加工业

纺织业

化学原料及化学制品制造业

国民经济行业分类代码	行业名称	页码

塑料制品业

非金属矿物制品业

国民经济行业分类代码	行业名称	页码

普通机械制造业

专用设备制造业

国民经济行业分类代码	行业名称	页码

交通运输设备制造业

电气机械及器材制造业

其他制造业

电力、煤气及水的生产和供应业

电力、煤气及水的生产和供应业

煤气生产和供应业

自来水生产和供应业

Reports on 500 Markets

500 行业报告

0610: Coal Mining 煤炭开采业

The industry accounts for 1.698% of the total revenue of China's industrial sector in 2002. The rate of return on assets is 1.72%. 84.70% of all firms in the industry made a profit while 15.30% had negative returns.The top province in terms of the industry's revenue is Shandong, accounting for 19.75% of the total revenue.
2002年本行业收入占全行业的 1.698%，资产利润率为 1.72%。84.70%的企业赢利，15.30%的企业亏损。收入最高的省为山东省，占本行业的19.75%。

	Total number of firms 企业总数	Total number of employees 职工总数	Total revenue (Mil.RMB) 总销售收入（百万元）	Total profit (Mil.RMB) 总利润（百万元）	Return on assets 资产利润率（%）	Return on equity 权益利润率（%）	Labour productivity ('000 RMB/ worker) 劳动生产率（千元/人）	Debts/ assets 资产负债率（%）	Total assets (Mil.RMB) 总资产（百万元）
Industry Overall 行业总体	2556	3,733,939	182,113	7,979	1.72	4.01	23.36	57.18	464,696

	Number of firms 企业个数	Average number of employees 平均职工人数	Average revenue ('000 RMB) 平均销售收入（千元）	Average profit ('000 RMB) 平均利润（千元）	Return on assets 资产利润率（%）	Return on equity 权益利润率（%）	Labour productivity ('000 RMB/ worker) 劳动生产率（千元/人）	Debts/ assets 资产负债率（%）	Average total assets ('000 RMB) 平均总资产（千元）
By ownership 产业所有权									
State-owned 国有	922	1,592	58,200	1,588	0.94	2.48	17.90	62.23	169,198
Collective-owned 集体	925	346	17,801	1,667	9.61	24.12	23.06	60.15	17,338
Foreign & Overseas Chinese Funded 三资	7	493	248,424	11,584	4.68	8.24	181.65	43.17	247,306
By regional distribution 地区分布									
Central-North 华北	758	1,365	73,890	3,224	1.55	3.34	25.60	53.69	208,448
Beijing 北京	17	1,661	104,577	6,547	3.15	4.46	36.63	29.52	208,096
Tianjin 天津									
Hebei 河北	95	2,687	113,166	2,800	0.94	2.13	21.87	55.99	298,196
Shanxi 山西	571	1,091	61,334	2,940	1.74	3.98	25.82	56.40	169,377
Inner Mongolia 内蒙古	75	1,711	112,783	5,176	1.32	2.42	29.54	45.49	392,308
Northeast 东北	153	3,344	107,290	22	0.01	0.02	13.74	63.90	402,932
Liaoning 辽宁	43	3,935	169,540	978	0.17	0.35	17.22	51.57	582,564
Jilin 吉林	49	1,833	35,190	-1,511	-1.10	-5.57	8.33	80.18	136,909
Heilongjiang 黑龙江	61	4,141	121,325	579	0.12	0.40	13.33	70.59	489,996
Central-East 华东	389	2,480	157,699	9,027	2.84	7.23	31.24	60.66	317,466
Shanghai 上海	1	19,008	1,549,316	220,099	10.64	13.77	38.06	22.70	2,068,252
Jiangsu 江苏	13	9,746	490,628	9,859	1.15	2.65	25.75	56.51	856,500
Zhejiang 浙江	2	4,897	427,989	2,087	0.44	1.19	26.13	62.72	470,060
Anhui 安徽	56	4,240	224,069	6,887	1.13	2.96	22.83	61.94	612,078
Fujian 福建	50	448	31,925	1,702	3.84	7.42	32.74	48.21	44,305
Jiangxi 江西	57	1,129	43,041	892	1.00	2.00	19.22	49.92	88,924
Shandong 山东	210	2,310	171,257	12,559	3.89	10.52	38.15	63.03	322,814
Central-South 中南	635	1,000	42,608	2,678	3.08	6.42	21.62	52.10	87,056
Henan 河南	327	1,392	65,643	4,920	3.56	7.15	25.46	50.19	138,180
Hubei 湖北	39	599	15,959	730	2.20	6.01	10.88	63.45	33,204
Hunan 湖南	226	563	17,904	486	1.69	4.07	12.39	58.47	28,776
Guangdong 广东	20	391	15,345	-548	-1.74	-35.77	9.28	95.13	31,472
Guangxi 广西	22	967	27,727	-1,513	-2.08	-4.57	11.07	54.37	72,649
Hainan 海南	1	220	4,892	-2,594	-3.72	-6.20	4.60	40.01	69,765
Southwest 西南	355	917	28,471	-82	-0.10	-0.23	13.88	56.95	82,666
Chongqing 重庆	64	1,065	30,837	-336	-0.44	-0.89	11.96	51.24	76,976
Sichuan 四川	161	897	25,683	478	0.86	2.25	13.97	61.87	55,813
Guizhou 贵州	74	1,067	36,248	969	0.66	1.32	11.83	49.99	146,828
Yunnan 云南	55	617	23,889	-2,870	-3.46	-11.61	22.02	70.17	82,846
Tibet 西藏	1	42	2,587	1,459	11.81	13.11	113.90	9.95	12,356
Northwest 西北	266	984	42,032	1,311	0.94	2.20	20.32	57.05	138,809
Shaanxi 陕西	73	1,357	70,848	1,826	0.85	2.72	20.69	68.78	215,183
Gansu 甘肃	103	635	19,933	1,068	1.27	2.78	14.02	54.18	83,923
Qinghai 青海	10	665	22,487	435	0.79	1.47	15.52	46.24	54,979
Ningxia 宁夏	16	3,094	130,822	1,227	0.28	0.44	24.55	35.69	437,117
Xinjiang 新疆	64	643	25,584	1,273	1.62	3.70	25.12	56.23	78,547

Year 年份	Number of firms 企业个数	Rate of change 变化率 (%)	Number of employees 职工人数 (人)	Rate of change 变化率 (%)	Total revenue (Mil. RMB) 总销售收入 (百万元)	Rate of change 变化率 (%)	Total profit (Mil RMB) 总利润 (百万元)	Rate of change 变化率 (%)
2000	2462		4,076,434		115,916		-123	
2001	2362	-4.06	3,694,639	-9.37	140,514	21.22	3,918	-
2002	2556	8.21	3,733,939	1.06	182,113	29.60	7,979	103.65

Major Products 主要产品	Output 产量	Unit 单位
Raw Coal 原煤	111,293	10,000 Tons 万吨
Soft Coal 烟煤	83,131	10,000 Tons 万吨

10 Main Firms with Maximal Revenue (year founded) 收入最大的十家主要企业（创办年份）	City 城市	Province 省	Telephone/fax 电话/传真	Number of employees 职工人数	Ownership 产业所有权	Revenue ('000 RMB) 销售收入 (千元)	Profit('000 RMB) (rank) 利润(千元)(排名)	Total assets ('000 RMB) 总资产 (千元)	Major products 主要产品
Yanzhou Mine Group Co., Ltd.	Jining	Shandong	(0537)5380666		Joint Stock				Coal
兖矿集团有限公司(1996)	济宁市	山东省	(0537)5313001	101,238	股份制	12,058,983	578,000(1)	25,152,328	煤炭
Datong Coal Mine Group Co. Ltd.	Datong	Shanxi	(0352)7014368		State Enterprises				Raw Coal
大同煤矿集团有限责任公司(1949)	大同市	山西省	(0352)7014803	94,056	国有独资	8,002,020	102,830(15)	15,619,620	原煤
Pingdingshan Coal(Group) Co.,Ltd.	Pingdingshan	Henan	(0375)2921770		State Enterprises				Raw Coal
平顶山煤业（集团）有限责任公司(1957)	平顶山市	河南省	(0375)2921770	124,381	国有独资	5,496,911	93,509(20)	11,751,120	原煤
Xinwen Mining Co., Ltd.	Taian	Shandong	(0538)7872347		State Enterprises				Raw Coal
新汶矿业集团有限责任公司(1956)	泰安市	山东省	(0538)7872531	85,864	国有独资	4,771,770	70,910(29)	7,489,151	原煤
Kailuan (Group) Co.,Ltd.	Tangshan	Hebei	(0315)3022218		State Enterprises				Coal
开滦(集团)有限责任公司(1999)	唐山市	河北省	(0315)2827307	104,094	国有独资	4,318,471	11,837(117)	11,664,297	煤炭
Xuzhou Coal Mining Group Co., Ltd.	Xuzhou	Jiangsu	(0516)5320593		State Enterprises				Raw Coal
徐州矿务集团有限公司(1934)	徐州市	江苏省	(0516)5768590	77,406	国有独资	3,900,000	50,000(39)	5,994,700	原煤
Huaibei Mining (Group) Co.,Ltd.	Huaibei	Anhui	(0561)4951956		State Enterprises				Raw Coal
淮北矿业(集团)有限责任公司(1959)	淮北市	安徽省	(0561)4951959	72,950	国有独资	3,854,970	41,290(45)	10,053,050	原煤
Yangquan Coal Industry (Group) Co.,Ltd.	Yangquan	Shanxi	(0353)7073112		State-owned				Coal
阳泉煤业(集团)有限责任公司(1994)	阳泉市	山西省	(0353)7071144	46,124	国有企业	2,818,230	110,580(13)	9,755,710	煤炭
Zibo Mining Group Co., Ltd.	Zibo	Shandong	(0533)5851173		State-owned				Coal
淄博矿业集团有限责任公司(1953)	淄博市	山东省		33,485	国有企业	2,740,130	94,800(19)	5,556,830	煤炭
Shanxi Luan Mining Group Company	Changzhi	Shanxi	(0355)5921443		State-owned				Raw Coal
山西省潞安矿业集团公司(1959)	长治市	山西省	(0355)5921443	27,004	国有企业	2,286,530	96,700(18)	6,445,270	原煤

Top 10 Cities by Revenue 销售收入排名前10位城市	Province 省	Market share 市场份额 (%)	Number of firms 企业个数
Jining 济宁市	Shandong 山东省	8.41	12
Datong 大同市	Shanxi 山西省	5.58	101
Taian 泰安市	Shandong 山东省	4.56	39
Huainan 淮南市	Anhui 安徽省	3.73	20
Pingdingshan 平顶山市	Henan 河南省	3.35	34
Xuzhou 徐州市	Jiangsu 江苏省	3.31	8
Jincheng 晋城市	Shanxi 山西省	3.30	83
Zaozhuang 枣庄市	Shandong 山东省	3.06	54
Huaibei 淮北市	Anhui 安徽省	3.05	13
Zhengzhou 郑州市	Henan 河南省	2.68	146

10 Major Wholesalers 十家主要批发商	City 城市	Province 省	Telephone/Fax 电话/传真
Shenhua Coal Transport & Sale Company	Beijing	Beijing	(010)64485202
神华煤炭运销公司	北京市	北京市	(010)64485345
China National Coal Group Corp.	Beijing	Beijing	(010)64287188
中国煤炭工业进出口集团公司	北京市	北京市	(010)64287166
Shanxi Coal Import & Export Group Company	Taiyuan	Shanxi	(0351)4043793
山西煤炭进出口集团公司	太原市	山西省	(0351)4043860
Shanghai Fuel General Corporation	Shanghai	Shanghai	(021)63605086
上海市燃料总公司	上海市	上海市	(021)63606224
Yanzhou Coal Co., Ltd.	Chucheng	Shandong	(0537)5383310
兖州煤业股份有限公司	邹城市	山东省	
Guangdong Electric Power Industry Fuel Company	Guangzhou	Guangdong	(020)85122013
广东省电力工业燃料公司	广州市	广东省	(020)85122010
China Coal Import & Export Company	Beijing	Beijing	(010)64287354
中国煤炭进出口公司	北京市	北京市	(010)64287166
Shanghai Datun Energy Co.,Ltd.	Shanghai	Shanghai	(021)68558399
上海大屯能源股份有限公司	上海市	上海市	(021)58513101
Jiangxi Electric Power Fuel Co.,Ltd.	Nanchang	Jiangxi	(0791)8694820
江西省电力燃料有限公司	南昌市	江西省	(0791)8694820
Tianjin Zhongmei Import & Export Co., Ltd.	Tianjin	Tianjin	(022)23112550
天津中煤进出口有限公司	天津市	天津市	(022)23112550

0620: Coal Dressing 煤炭洗选业

The industry accounts for 0.130% of the total revenue of China's industrial sector in 2002. The rate of return on assets is 2.99%. 80.47% of all firms in the industry made a profit while 19.53% had negative returns.The top province in terms of the industry's revenue is Shanxi, accounting for 41.81% of the total revenue.
2002年本行业收入占全行业的 0.130%，资产利润率为 2.99%。80.47%的企业赢利，19.53%的企业亏损。收入最高的省为山西省，占本行业的41.81%。

	Total number of firms 企业总数	Total number of employees 职工总数	Total revenue (Mil.RMB) 总销售收入 (百万元)	Total profit (Mil.RMB) 总利润 (百万元)	Return on assets 资产利润率 (%)	Return on equity 权益利润率 (%)	Labour productivity ('000 RMB/ worker) 劳动生产率 (千元/人)	Debts/ assets 资产负债率 (%)	Total assets (Mil.RMB) 总资产 (百万元)
Industry Overall 行业总体	256	63,113	13,962	503	2.99	6.03	73.91	50.50	16,836

	Number of firms 企业个数	Average number of employees 平均职工人数	Average revenue ('000 RMB) 平均销售收入 (千元)	Average profit ('000 RMB) 平均利润 (千元)	Return on assets 资产利润率 (%)	Return on equity 权益利润率 (%)	Labour productivity ('000 RMB/ worker) 劳动生产率 (千元/人)	Debts/ assets 资产负债率 (%)	Average total assets ('000 RMB) 平均总资产 (千元)
By ownership 产业所有权									
State-owned 国有	25	525	140,820	232	0.07	0.12	108.32	40.60	333,637
Collective-owned 集体	70	276	31,940	1,607	5.56	12.60	44.78	55.89	28,895
Foreign & Overseas Chinese Funded 三资	9	107	41,292	612	0.65	3.05	196.64	78.52	93,448
By regional distribution 地区分布									
Central-North 华北	127	272	78,782	3,008	2.97	5.72	96.11	48.07	101,297
Beijing 北京	4	29	837,076	59,172	40.41	64.77	5,183.66	37.60	146,422
Tianjin 天津	2	35	93,400	43	0.01	0.07	2,000.43	81.28	345,101
Hebei 河北	11	611	21,560	551	2.40	18.38	16.10	86.95	22,958
Shanxi 山西	98	251	59,569	1,074	1.03	1.85	90.38	44.41	104,368
Inner Mongolia 内蒙古	12	253	32,942	2,826	3.06	7.26	81.36	57.85	92,354
Northeast 东北	31	310	31,402	1,439	3.32	6.84	49.62	51.49	43,349
Liaoning 辽宁	10	572	19,216	-1,849	-5.08	-19.80	14.37	74.37	36,420
Jilin 吉林	3	164	52,872	6,545	10.68	17.87	184.26	40.26	61,310
Heilongjiang 黑龙江	18	189	34,594	2,414	5.46	9.69	89.28	43.61	44,205
Central-East 华东	26	100	33,205	2,219	28.08	72.87	119.11	61.47	7,903
Shanghai 上海									
Jiangsu 江苏									
Zhejiang 浙江									
Anhui 安徽									
Fujian 福建									
Jiangxi 江西	2	55	7,415	112	3.48	30.94	56.59	88.77	3,223
Shandong 山东	24	103	35,354	2,395	28.88	73.26	121.88	60.58	8,293
Central-South 中南	36	192	33,246	221	0.56	1.70	46.88	66.93	39,216
Henan 河南	29	150	25,568	483	1.64	6.16	51.01	73.45	29,547
Hubei 湖北									
Hunan 湖南	7	364	65,055	-868	-1.09	-2.54	39.82	56.87	79,273
Guangdong 广东									
Guangxi 广西									
Hainan 海南									
Southwest 西南	29	299	21,220	193	0.84	1.88	20.73	55.26	22,891
Chongqing 重庆	6	188	8,098	-15	-0.15	-0.21	12.48	27.96	9,599
Sichuan 四川	14	366	25,022	634	3.88	11.08	21.40	64.99	16,334
Guizhou 贵州	3	69	6,287	-29	-0.45	-0.94	38.16	52.40	6,541
Yunnan 云南	6	371	32,937	-516	-0.87	-1.86	21.77	53.59	59,659
Tibet 西藏									
Northwest 西北	7	109	43,934	690	1.39	3.04	70.43	54.20	49,501
Shaanxi 陕西	1	450	202,361	2,017	0.91	1.78	69.76	48.96	222,269
Gansu 甘肃									
Qinghai 青海	1	9	1,120	-45	-0.74	-0.80	10.11	7.48	6,084
Ningxia 宁夏	4	72	25,443	642	2.30	6.88	73.68	66.54	27,914
Xinjiang 新疆	1	15	2,284	288	4.43	12.62	64.93	64.91	6,503

0620: Coal Dressing 煤炭洗选业

Year 年份	Number of firms 企业个数	Rate of change 变化率 (%)	Number of employees 职工人数 (人)	Rate of change 变化率 (%)	Total revenue (Mil. RMB) 总销售收入 (百万元)	Rate of change 变化率 (%)	Total profit (Mil RMB) 总利润 (百万元)	Rate of change 变化率 (%)
2000	204		46,120		5,461		173	
2001	241	18.14	58,442	26.72	9,801	79.47	265	53.18
2002	256	6.22	63,113	7.99	13,962	42.45	503	89.81

Major Products 主要产品	Output 产量	Unit 单位
Coal Washing 洗煤	22,343	10,000 Tons 万吨
Fine Coal Washing 洗精煤	13,751	10,000 Tons 万吨

10 Main Firms with Maximal Revenue (year founded) 收入最大的十家主要企业（创办年份）	City 城市	Province 省	Telephone/fax 电话/传真	Number of employees 职工人数	Ownership 产业所有权	Revenue ('000 RMB) 销售收入 (千元)	Profit('000 RMB) (rank) 利润(千元) (排名)	Total assets ('000 RMB) 总资产 (千元)	Major products 主要产品
Pingshuo Coal Industry Company 平朔煤炭工业公司(1990)	Shuozhou 朔州市	Shanxi 山西省	(0349)2054455 (0349)2055488	7,950	State-owned 国有企业	2,878,965	11,521(6)	7,020,697	Coal 煤炭
Hunan Gaoxi Group Company 湖南高溪集团公司(1993)	Loudi 娄底市	Hunan 湖南省	(0738)8617273 (0738)8614742	1,017	Collective-owned 集体企业	256,800	9,330(7)	234,300	Fine Coal Washing 洗精煤
Shanxi Lingshi Tongyu Coal Transport Co., Ltd. 山西省灵石通宇煤运有限公司(2001)	Jinzhong 晋中市	Shanxi 山西省	(0354)7614507	901	Limited-Liability 有限公司	220,469	412(124)	165,205	Coke 焦炭
Hancheng Mining Developing Co., Ltd. 韩城市矿业开发有限责任公司(1997)	Weinan 渭南市	Shannxi 陕西省	(0913)5218618 (0913)5207133	450	Private Owned 私营企业	202,361	2,017(45)	222,269	Raw Coal 原煤
Shanxi Hongdong ZhaoCheng Coking Industrial Group 洪洞县赵城焦化实业集团(1989)	Linfen 临汾市	Shanxi 山西省	(0357)6564125 (0357)6564666	420	Collective-owned 集体企业	138,965	6,946(14)	139,855	Fine Coal Washing 洗精煤
Yunnan Dongyuan Industrial Group Co., Ltd. 云南东源实业股份有限公司(1999)	Qujing 曲靖市	Yunnan 云南省	(0874)4635867 (0874)4638517	919	Joint Stock 股份制	131,265	252(138)	274,613	Fine Coal Washing 洗精煤
Jeneral Nice (TianJing) Industry Co.,Ltd. 俊安(天津)实业有限公司(1997)	Tianjin 天津市	Tianjin 天津市	(022)25290191 (022)25325776	53	Overseas Chinese-funded 港澳台资	127,809	603(104)	344,365	Coke 焦炭
Shanxi Hongxin Coking Co.,Ltd. Xiangfen Coal Dressing & Coking Factory山西鸿昕焦化有限公司襄汾选煤焦化厂(1996)	Linfen 临汾市	Shanxi 山西省	(0357)3639009 (0357)3639160	113	Collective-owned 集体企业	123,647	2,269(37)	56,420	Fine Coal Washing 洗精煤
Hongdong Yuanzhong Coking Co.,Ltd. 洪洞县远中焦化有限公司(1995)	Linfen 临汾市	Shanxi 山西省	(0357)6564633 (0357)6566888	220	Private Owned 私营企业	116,800	8,773(8)	86,095	Fine Coal Washing 洗精煤
Tengzhou Zhongfutianchen Mine Coal Washing Factory 滕州市中福田陈矿区洗煤厂(1993)	Zaozhuang 枣庄市	Shandong 山东省	(0632)2809168 (0632)2809168	58	Collective-owned 集体企业	109,133	20,029(3)	29,867	Fine Coal Washing 洗精煤

Top 10 Cities by Revenue 销售收入排名前10位城市	Province 省	Market share 市场份额 (%)	Number of firms 企业个数
Beijing 北京市	Beijing 北京市	23.98	4
Shuozhou 朔州市	Shanxi 山西省	21.74	2
Linfen 临汾市	Shanxi 山西省	5.82	22
Lvliang 吕梁地区	Shanxi 山西省	4.72	15
Zaozhuang 枣庄市	Shandong 山东省	4.66	18
Jinzhong 晋中市	Shanxi 山西省	3.86	19
Pingdingshan 平顶山市	Henan 河南省	3.11	16
Taiyuan 太原市	Shanxi 山西省	2.65	14
Loudi 娄底市	Hunan 湖南省	2.20	2
Jixi 鸡西市	Heilongjiang 黑龙江省	2.12	7

10 Major Wholesalers 十家主要批发商	City 城市	Province 省	Telephone/Fax 电话/传真
Shenhua Coal Transport & Sale Company 神华煤炭运销公司	Beijing 北京市	Beijing 北京市	(010)64485202 (010)64485345
China National Coal Group Corp. 中国煤炭工业进出口集团公司	Beijing 北京市	Beijing 北京市	(010)64287188 (010)64287166
Shanxi Coal Import & Export Group Company 山西煤炭进出口集团公司	Taiyuan 太原市	Shanxi 山西省	(0351)4043793 (0351)4043860
Shanghai Fuel General Corporation 上海市燃料总公司	Shanghai 上海市	Shanghai 上海市	(021)63605086 (021)63606224
Yanzhou Coal Co., Ltd. 兖州煤业股份有限公司	Chucheng 邹城市	Shandong 山东省	(0537)5383310
Guangdong Electric Power Industry Fuel Company 广东省电力工业燃料公司	Guangzhou 广州市	Guangdong 广东省	(020)85122013 (020)85122010
China Coal Import & Export Company 中国煤炭进出口公司	Beijing 北京市	Beijing 北京市	(010)64287354 (010)64287166
Shanghai Datun Energy Co.,Ltd. 上海大屯能源股份有限公司	Shanghai 上海市	Shanghai 上海市	(021)68558399 (021)58513101
Jiangxi Electric Power Fuel Co.,Ltd. 江西省电力燃料有限公司	Nanchang 南昌市	Jiangxi 江西省	(0791)8694820 (0791)8694820
Tianjin Zhongmei Import & Export Co., Ltd. 天津中煤进出口有限公司	Tianjin 天津市	Tianjin 天津市	(022)23112550 (022)23112550

0710: Crude Petroleum Extraction 天然原油开采业

The industry accounts for 2.380% of the total revenue of China's industrial sector in 2002. The rate of return on assets is 21.60%. 93.33% of all firms in the industry made a profit while 6.67% had negative returns.The top province in terms of the industry's revenue is Heilong Jiang, accounting for 28.63% of the total revenue.
2002年本行业收入占全行业的2.380%，资产利润率为21.60%。93.33%的企业赢利，6.67%的企业亏损。收入最高的省为黑龙江省，占本行业的28.63%。

	Total number of firms 企业总数	Total number of employees 职工总数	Total revenue (Mil.RMB) 总销售收入(百万元)	Total profit (Mil.RMB) 总利润(百万元)	Return on assets 资产利润率(%)	Return on equity 权益利润率(%)	Labour productivity ('000 RMB/ worker) 劳动生产率(千元/人)	Debts/ assets 资产负债率(%)	Total assets (Mil.RMB) 总资产(百万元)
Industry Overall 行业总体	75	535,220	255,308	90,237	21.60	33.16	353.34	34.85	417,696

	Number of firms 企业个数	Average number of employees 平均职工人数	Average revenue ('000 RMB) 平均销售收入（千元）	Average profit ('000 RMB) 平均利润(千元)	Return on assets 资产利润率(%)	Return on equity 权益利润率(%)	Labour productivity ('000 RMB/ worker) 劳动生产率(千元/人)	Debts/ assets 资产负债率(%)	Average total assets ('000 RMB) 平均总资产(千元)
By ownership 产业所有权									
State-owned 国有	29	5,387	939,651	73,630	3.99	7.19	68.21	44.50	1,845,300
Collective-owned 集体									
Foreign & Overseas Chinese Funded 三资	2	752	5,689,979	2,690,925	51.50	57.27	7,090.61	10.08	5,225,199
By regional distribution 地区分布									
Central-North 华北	9	8,296	3,146,861	897,022	16.61	25.52	213.60	34.91	5,400,549
Beijing 北京	1	30	11,366	1,208	11.33	19.67	90.77	42.38	10,659
Tianjin 天津	4	14,328	4,985,726	1,422,817	16.57	25.22	171.63	34.31	8,587,608
Hebei 河北	2	7,598	3,683,300	1,178,800	19.42	32.23	350.97	39.74	6,069,270
Shanxi 山西									
Inner Mongolia 内蒙古	2	1,064	500,442	11,562	1.10	1.32	364.66	16.86	1,052,655
Northeast 东北	21	8,530	4,878,079	2,397,965	35.36	47.17	515.27	25.04	6,782,363
Liaoning 辽宁	2	35,912	11,737,762	2,616,975	13.15	22.30	213.17	41.06	19,906,712
Jilin 吉林	17	981	345,912	83,429	8.61	16.48	283.88	47.78	969,205
Heilongjiang 黑龙江	2	45,319	36,541,822	21,852,510	50.74	58.51	797.22	13.29	43,069,856
Central-East 华东	5	20,080	7,627,725	2,329,652	19.59	27.29	281.03	28.20	11,890,031
Shanghai 上海									
Jiangsu 江苏	2	10,804	1,092,830	156,600	4.97	6.68	74.86	25.53	3,150,251
Zhejiang 浙江									
Anhui 安徽									
Fujian 福建									
Jiangxi 江西									
Shandong 山东	3	26,264	11,984,321	3,778,353	21.33	29.84	337.57	28.52	17,716,551
Central-South 中南	8	10,089	3,605,929	797,324	13.82	22.42	220.91	38.37	5,770,032
Henan 河南	4	15,233	3,240,495	239,263	3.90	7.00	92.11	44.33	6,140,192
Hubei 湖北	1	18,255	4,423,494	-12,112	-0.11	-0.23	82.25	52.12	11,011,400
Hunan 湖南									
Guangdong 广东	2	752	5,689,979	2,690,925	51.50	57.27	7,090.61	10.08	5,225,199
Guangxi 广西									
Hainan 海南	1	20	82,002	51,799	37.62	47.95	2,902.00	21.54	137,691
Southwest 西南	1	94	14,710	4,085	12.77	19.62	71.50	34.93	32,000
Chongqing 重庆									
Sichuan 四川	1	94	14,710	4,085	12.77	19.62	71.50	34.93	32,000
Guizhou 贵州									
Yunnan 云南									
Tibet 西藏									
Northwest 西北	31	3,233	1,856,323	444,375	11.38	22.01	347.37	48.29	3,903,826
Shaanxi 陕西	17	2,226	1,206,966	326,986	13.20	25.47	288.69	48.15	2,476,310
Gansu 甘肃	5	1,816	1,472,367	210,501	11.49	15.73	448.73	26.93	1,831,996
Qinghai 青海	3	6,825	1,814,358	209,300	5.13	24.23	112.32	78.81	4,076,376
Ningxia 宁夏									
Xinjiang 新疆	6	5,470	4,037,112	1,089,406	11.36	20.77	533.64	45.30	9,588,704

0710: Crude Petroleum Extraction 天然原油开采业

Year 年份	Number of firms 企业个数	Rate of change 变化率(%)	Number of employees 职工人数(人)	Rate of change 变化率(%)	Total revenue (Mil. RMB) 总销售收入(百万元)	Rate of change 变化率(%)	Total profit (Mil RMB) 总利润(百万元)	Rate of change 变化率(%)
2000	67		716,251		283,669		114,121	
2001	80	19.40	575,481	-19.65	257,742	-9.14	96,871	-15.12
2002	75	-6.25	535,220	-7.00	255,308	-0.94	90,237	-6.85

Major Products 主要产品	Output 产量	Unit 单位
Crude Petroleum 天然原油	16,887	10,000 Tons 万吨
Natural Gas 天然气	326	100,000,000 Stere 亿立方米

10 Main Firms with Maximal Revenue (year founded) 收入最大的十家主要企业（创办年份）	City 城市	Province 省	Telephone/fax 电话/传真	Number of employees 职工人数	Ownership 产业所有权	Revenue ('000 RMB) 销售收入(千元)	Profit('000 RMB) (rank) 利润(千元)(排名)	Total assets ('000 RMB) 总资产(千元)	Major products 主要产品
Daqing Oilfield Co., Ltd.	Daqing	Heilongjiang	(0459)5994050		Joint Stock				Crude Petroleum
大庆油田有限责任公司(1999)	大庆市	黑龙江省	(0459)5994050	90,436	股份制	72,843,340	43,595,800(1)	85,808,770	天然原油
SINOPEC Shengli Oilfield Co., Ltd.	Dongying	Shandong	(0546)8711103		Limited-Liability				Crude Petroleum
中国石化胜利油田有限公司(2000)	东营市	山东省	(0546)8221719	75,800	有限公司	34,539,137	10,822,174(2)	49,984,532	天然原油
PetroChina Liaohe Oilfield Branch	Panjin	Liaoning	(0427)7820090		Joint Stock				Crude Petroleum
中国石油天然气股份有限公司辽河油田分公司(1999)	盘锦市	辽宁省	(0427)7822545	29,438	股份制	16,216,443	4,807,859(3)	31,241,603	天然原油
PetroChina Changqing Oilfield Branch	Xi'an	Shannxi	(029)6592380		Joint Stock				Crude Petroleum
中国石油长庆油田分公司(1999)	西安市	陕西省	(029)6599999	12,209	股份制	14,263,010	4,286,440(5)	29,393,800	天然原油
PetroChina Xinjiang Oilfield Company	Kelamayi	Xinjiang	(0990)6888135		Joint Stock				Crude Petroleum
中国石油天然气股份有限公司新疆油田分公司(1999)	克拉玛依市	新疆	(0990)6887790	16,002	股份制	11,824,500	2,854,220(6)	32,706,330	天然原油
Liaohe Petroleum Exploration Bureau	Panjin	Liaoning	(0427)7821325		State-owned				Petroleum Natural Gas
辽河石油勘探局(1972)	盘锦市	辽宁省	(0427)7821325	42,386	国有企业	7,259,080	426,090(18)	8,571,820	石油天然气
PetroChina Talimu Oilfield Branch	Bayinguoleng	Xinjiang	(0996)2171744		Joint Stock				Crude Petroleum
中国石油天然气股份公司塔里木油田分公司(1989)	巴音郭楞州	新疆		9,744	股份制	6,669,070	1,799,540(10)	13,377,750	天然原油
PetroChina Hua Bei Oilfield Branch	Cangzhou	Hebei	(0371)2725215		Joint Stock				Crude Petroleum
中国石油天然气股份有限公司华北油田分公司(1975)	沧州市	河北省	(0371)2725397	13,434	股份制	6,437,200	2,140,370(9)	10,646,310	天然原油
SINOPEC Center Plain Oilfield Company	Puyang	Henan	(0393)4819493		Joint Stock				Petroleum Natural Gas
中国石油化工股份有限公司中原油田分公司(2000)	濮阳市	河南省	(0393)4819563	26,436	股份制	6,352,880	221,219(21)	11,477,941	石油天然气
Henan Petroleum Prospecting Bureau	Nanyang	Henan	(0377)3830011		State-owned				Crude Petroleum
河南石油勘探局(1970)	南阳市	河南省		27,700	国有企业	4,814,861	180,203(26)	9,066,693	天然原油

Top 10 Cities by Revenue 销售收入排名前10位城市	Province 省	Market share 市场份额(%)	Number of firms 企业个数
Daqing 大庆市	Heilongjiang 黑龙江省	28.53	1
Dongying 东营市	Shandong 山东省	14.08	3
Panjin 盘锦市	Liaoning 辽宁省	9.19	2
Tianjin 天津市	Tianjin 天津市	7.81	4
Xi'an 西安市	Shannxi 陕西省	5.59	1
Kelamayi 克拉玛依市	Xinjiang 新疆	4.65	3
Puyang 濮阳市	Henan 河南省	3.19	2
Bayinguoleng 巴音郭楞州	Xinjiang 新疆	2.61	1
Cangzhou 沧州市	Hebei 河北省	2.52	1
Songyuan 松原市	Jilin 吉林省	2.29	14

10 Major Wholesalers 十家主要批发商	City 城市	Province 省	Telephone/Fax 电话/传真
HLJ Petroleumchemical Marketing Corp.	Haerbin	Heilongjiang	(0451)84612530
黑龙江省石油化工销售总公司	哈尔滨市	黑龙江省	(0451)84610195
PetroChina Northeast Sale Company Daqing Filiale	Daqing	Heilongjiang	(0459)6215380
石油天然气股份有限公司东北销售大庆分公司	大庆市	黑龙江省	(0459)6215361
China Railway Goods & Materials Shanghai Company	Shanghai	Shanghai	(021)56309366
中国铁路物资上海公司	上海市	上海市	(021)56632150
SINOPEC Hubei Petroleum General Company	Wuhan	Hubei	(027)83601087
中国石化集团湖北石油总公司	武汉市	湖北省	(027)83601075
South China Bluesky Aviation Oilseed Co.,Ltd.	Guangzhou	Guangdong	(020)86120888
华南蓝天航空油料有限公司	广州市	广东省	(020)86650789
Guangdong Petroleum Enterprise Group Company	Guangzhou	Guangdong	(020)81298040
广东省石油企业集团公司	广州市	广东省	(020)81298098
Shenzhen Huaan Liuefied Petroleum Gas Co.,Ltd.	Shenzhen	Guangdong	(0755)84231898
深圳华安液化石油气有限公司	深圳市	广东省	(0755)82461896
SINOPEC Sale Southwest Company	Maoming	Guangdong	(0668)2868292
中国石化销售西南公司	茂名市	广东省	(0668)2868278
Guangdong Dongguan Petroleum Company	Dongguan	Guangdong	(0769)2258741
广东省东莞市石油公司	东莞市	广东省	(0769)2506290
PetroChina Sichuan Sale Company	Chengdu	Sichuan	(028)86520001
中国石油天然气股份有限公司四川销售公司	成都市	四川省	(028)86520001

0810: Iron Ores Mining and Dressing 铁矿采选业

The industry accounts for 0.188% of the total revenue of China's industrial sector in 2002. The rate of return on assets is 3.10%. 85.37% of all firms in the industry made a profit while 14.63% had negative returns.The top province in terms of the industry's revenue is Hebei, accounting for 34.20% of the total revenue.
2002年本行业收入占全行业的 0.188%，资产利润率为 3.10%。85.37%的企业赢利，14.63%的企业亏损。收入最高的省为河北省，占本行业的34.20%。

	Total number of firms 企业总数	Total number of employees 职工总数	Total revenue (Mil.RMB) 总销售收入 (百万元)	Total profit (Mil.RMB) 总利润 (百万元)	Return on assets 资产利润率 (%)	Return on equity 权益利润率 (%)	Labour productivity ('000 RMB/ worker) 劳动生产率 (千元/人)	Debts/ assets 资产负债率 (%)	Total assets (Mil.RMB) 总资产 (百万元)
Industry Overall 行业总体	615	226,004	20,165	1,084	3.10	5.79	35.62	46.48	34,969

	Number of firms 企业个数	Average number of employees 平均职工人数	Average revenue ('000 RMB) 平均销售收入 (千元)	Average profit ('000 RMB) 平均利润 (千元)	Return on assets 资产利润率 (%)	Return on equity 权益利润率 (%)	Labour productivity ('000 RMB/ worker) 劳动生产率 (千元/人)	Debts/ assets 资产负债率 (%)	Average total assets ('000 RMB) 平均总资产 (千元)
By ownership 产业所有权									
State-owned 国有	68	1,251	74,766	3,780	1.30	2.06	27.51	37.04	291,747
Collective-owned 集体	202	276	25,485	1,542	8.27	26.29	31.59	68.55	18,648
Foreign & Overseas Chinese Funded 三资	11	106	16,957	551	3.48	7.35	50.56	52.57	15,814
By regional distribution 地区分布									
Central-North 华北	270	264	30,157	1,774	6.08	17.50	47.41	65.27	29,184
Beijing 北京	3	661	56,012	-2,156	-1.92	-6.01	17.32	68.08	112,319
Tianjin 天津									
Hebei 河北	205	269	33,645	2,051	6.75	20.10	51.07	66.45	30,409
Shanxi 山西	50	222	16,165	886	5.22	12.75	33.90	59.05	16,965
Inner Mongolia 内蒙古	12	271	22,412	1,720	4.48	10.87	50.09	58.78	38,371
Northeast 东北	85	433	23,965	888	2.63	5.78	16.79	54.43	33,740
Liaoning 辽宁	73	373	19,844	836	3.41	11.43	15.11	70.18	24,516
Jilin 吉林	11	839	52,490	1,291	1.33	1.84	21.92	27.83	97,250
Heilongjiang 黑龙江	1	300	11,019	279	3.30	27.65	11.41	88.05	8,443
Central-East 华东	83	763	57,743	4,796	2.35	3.34	32.90	29.65	204,307
Shanghai 上海									
Jiangsu 江苏	8	1,458	119,245	2,305	0.94	3.24	35.05	71.08	245,773
Zhejiang 浙江	3	673	46,537	429	0.32	0.53	30.49	39.29	134,317
Anhui 安徽	17	1,581	91,405	14,585	2.17	2.60	28.34	16.43	672,165
Fujian 福建	21	134	18,274	847	4.00	9.44	58.94	57.67	21,198
Jiangxi 江西	4	109	6,542	168	0.70	2.71	16.40	74.31	24,074
Shandong 山东	30	650	57,845	3,732	4.27	8.27	34.74	48.33	87,335
Central-South 中南	104	303	32,147	1,133	3.01	7.86	40.34	61.67	37,620
Henan 河南	25	133	10,952	396	5.54	10.86	25.90	48.99	7,146
Hubei 湖北	39	336	51,043	2,022	10.62	20.97	45.79	49.36	19,040
Hunan 湖南	14	78	9,879	134	1.31	8.08	40.51	83.74	10,185
Guangdong 广东	20	278	33,013	2,464	3.38	8.96	68.28	62.31	72,984
Guangxi 广西	5	56	1,879	65	0.89	1.99	7.14	55.33	7,350
Hainan 海南	1	8,160	270,829	-22,420	-1.66	-5.06	19.54	67.25	1,352,259
Southwest 西南	29	533	38,655	-210	-0.34	-0.92	26.41	62.84	61,675
Chongqing 重庆	1	3,929	236,704	-1,212	-0.26	-0.40	15.45	35.11	468,615
Sichuan 四川	18	393	25,952	661	1.69	4.78	30.14	64.60	39,045
Guizhou 贵州	2	163	20,885	-2,430	-8.66	-141.28	30.63	93.87	28,075
Yunnan 云南	6	648	62,119	-2,113	-2.29	-12.47	31.67	81.62	92,220
Tibet 西藏	2	120	1,338	380	9.89	11.37	5.00	13.01	3,842
Northwest 西北	44	171	16,568	451	1.27	3.44	37.85	63.11	35,515
Shaanxi 陕西	6	184	8,654	-177	-1.06	-37.70	19.17	97.18	16,614
Gansu 甘肃	22	98	4,607	-56	-0.48	-1.41	26.60	65.90	11,632
Qinghai 青海	3	189	20,699	2,676	18.42	29.83	42.78	38.24	14,529
Ningxia 宁夏									
Xinjiang 新疆	13	285	39,510	1,083	1.21	3.07	49.17	60.51	89,498

0810: Iron Ores Mining and Dressing 铁矿采选业

Year 年份	Number of firms 企业个数	Rate of change 变化率 (%)	Number of employees 职工人数 (人)	Rate of change 变化率 (%)	Total revenue (Mil. RMB) 总销售收入 (百万元)	Rate of change 变化率 (%)	Total profit (Mil RMB) 总利润 (百万元)	Rate of change 变化率 (%)
2000	507		217,913		14,019		612	
2001	563	11.05	224,654	3.09	16,639	18.69	883	44.28
2002	615	9.24	226,004	0.60	20,165	21.19	1,084	22.76

Major Products 主要产品	Output 产量	Unit 单位
Crude Iron Ore 铁矿石原矿量	23,143	10,000 Tons 万吨
Finished Iron Ore 铁矿石成品矿	11,678	10,000 Tons 万吨

10 Main Firms with Maximal Revenue (year founded) 收入最大的十家主要企业（创办年份）	City 城市	Province 省	Telephone/ fax 电话/ 传真	Number of employees 职工人数	Ownership 产业所有权	Revenue ('000 RMB) 销售收入 (千元)	Profit('000 RMB) (rank) 利润(千元) (排名)	Total assets ('000 RMB) 总资产 (千元)	Major products 主要产品
Ma'anshan Iron & Steel Corperation (Group)Control Stock Co.,Ltd. 马钢(集团)控股有限公司(1993)	Maanshan 马鞍山市	Anhui 安徽省	(0555)2883492 (0555)2884350	22,189	State-owned 国有企业	1,368,405	241,381(1)	11,130,909	Iron Ore 铁矿石
Daye Chengui Mining Group Co. Ltd. 大冶市陈贵矿业集团有限责任公司(1996)	Huangshi 黄石市	Hubei 湖北省	(0714)8996010 (0714)8996878	3,803	Limited-Liability 有限公司	640,634	33,097(3)	266,028	Iron Ore 铁矿石
Shanghai Meishan Mining Co., Ltd. 上海梅山矿业有限公司(1961)	Nanjing 南京市	Jiangsu 江苏省	(025)4084205 (025)2803235	5,433	State-owned 国有企业	520,900	1,320(146)	1,295,400	Iron Ore 铁矿石
Daye Hualing Group Mining Co., Ltd. 大冶市华灵集团矿业责任有限公司(1997)	Huangshi 黄石市	Hubei 湖北省	(0714)8473789 (0714)8472524	1,668	Collective-owned 集体企业	351,120	13,660(11)	109,220	Iron Ore 铁矿石
Luzhong Metallurgical Mining Group 鲁中冶金矿山公司(1970)	Laiwu 莱芜市	Shandong 山东省	(0634)6811012 (0634)6811316	7,821	State-owned 国有企业	319,360	2,600(104)	968,356	Iron Ore 铁矿石
Chongqing Iron & Steel Company Mineral Industry Co.Ltd. 重庆钢铁集团矿业有限公司(1996)	Chongqing 重庆市	Chongqing 重庆市	(023)68843436 (023)68844119	3,929	Limited-Liability 有限公司	236,704	-	468,615	Iron Ore 铁矿石
Guangdong Dading Iron Mine Group Co., Ltd. 广东大顶铁矿集团有限公司(1991)	Heyuan 河源市	Guangdong 广东省	(0762)3314831 (0762)3314831	783	Joint Stock 股份制	228,452	43,875(2)	609,044	Iron Ore 铁矿石
Guangdong Dabaoshan Mining Co., Ltd. 广东省大宝山矿业有限公司(1966)	Shaoguan 韶关市	Guangdong 广东省	(0751)6618799 (0751)6618321	3,384	State-owned 国有企业	217,800	1,038(164)	629,730	Iron Ore 铁矿石
Shandong JinLing Iron Ore 山东金岭铁矿(1949)	Zibo 淄博市	Shandong 山东省	(0533)3081201 (0533)3081263	3,762	State-owned 国有企业	211,920	450(240)	501,900	Iron Ore 铁矿石
Daye Lingxiang ChangPing Group 大冶市灵乡镇长坪集团(1998)	Huangshi 黄石市	Hubei 湖北省	(0714)8474288 (0714)8474288	835	Collective-owned 集体企业	180,060	9,710(20)	23,460	Iron Ore 铁矿石

Top 10 Cities by Revenue 销售收入排名前10位城市	Province 省	Market share 市场份额 (%)	Number of firms 企业个数
Tangshan 唐山市	Hebei 河北省	15.05	98
Maanshan 马鞍山市	Anhui 安徽省	7.14	6
Huangshi 黄石市	Hubei 湖北省	7.03	14
Handan 邯郸市	Hebei 河北省	6.21	14
Xingtai 邢台市	Hebei 河北省	5.71	20
Zibo 淄博市	Shandong 山东省	4.51	13
Chengde 承德市	Hebei 河北省	3.72	39
Liaoyang 辽阳市	Liaoning 辽宁省	3.37	18
Nanjing 南京市	Jiangsu 江苏省	3.31	5
Ezhou 鄂州市	Hubei 湖北省	2.09	12

10 Major Wholesalers 十家主要批发商	City 城市	Province 省	Telephone/Fax 电话/传真
China Railway Materials Beijing Company 中国铁路物资北京公司	Beijing 北京市	Beijing 北京市	(010)63602299 (010)63601722
Shanghai BM Import & Export Co., Ltd. 上海宝矿进出口有限公司	Shanghai 上海市	Shanghai 上海市	(021)50320000 (021)50326700
Citic Trading Co.,Ltd. 中信贸易公司	Beijing 北京市	Beijing 北京市	(010)84865638 (010)84865271
Qingdao Iron And Steel Import & Export Corp. 青岛钢铁进出口公司	Qingdao 青岛市	Shandong 山东省	(0532)5798210 (0532)5798069
Guangzhou Metals and Minerals Import & Export .Ltd. 广州五金矿产进出口有限公司	Guangzhou 广州市	Guangdong 广东省	(020)81082026 (020)81084886
Shanghai Foreign Economics Trading Development Company 上海外经贸发展公司	Shanghai 上海市	Shanghai 上海市	(021)62719538 (021)62729625
China Nonferrous Metal Import & Export Jiangsu Company 中国有色金属进出口江苏公司	Nanjing 南京市	Jiangsu 江苏省	(025)4400366 (025)4400773
China Hardware Minerals Import & Export Shenzhen Branch Company 中国五金矿产进出口深圳分公司	Shenzhen 深圳市	Guangdong 广东省	(0755)82388365 (0755)82388335
Guangdong Dongfang Import & Export Corp. 广东省东方进出口公司	Shenzhen 深圳市	Guangdong 广东省	(0755)25950270 (0755)25950220
Shannxi Import & Export Corp. 陕西省进出口公司	Xi'an 西安市	Shannxi 陕西省	(029)6520075 (029)6511071

0821: Manganese Ores Mining and Dressing 锰矿采选业

The industry accounts for 0.011% of the total revenue of China's total industrial sector in 2002. The rate of return on assets is 0.32%. 63.38% of all firms in the industry made a profit while 36.62% had negative returns.The top province in terms of the industry's revenue is Guangxi, accounting for 21.96% of the total revenue.
2002年本行业收入占全行业的0.011%，资产利润率为0.32%。63.38%的企业赢利，36.62%的企业亏损。收入最高的省为广西，占本行业的21.96%。

	Total number of firms 企业总数	Total number of employees 职工总数	Total revenue (Mil.RMB) 总销售收入（百万元）	Total profit (Mil.RMB) 总利润（百万元）	Return on assets 资产利润率 (%)	Return on equity 权益利润率 (%)	Labour productivity ('000 RMB/ worker) 劳动生产率（千元/人）	Debts/ assets 资产负债率 (%)	Total assets (Mil.RMB) 总资产（百万元）
Industry Overall 行业总体	71	18,879	1,151	10	0.32	1.03	27.06	69.35	3,039

	Number of firms 企业个数	Average number of employees 平均职工人数	Average revenue ('000 RMB) 平均销售收入（千元）	Average profit ('000 RMB) 平均利润（千元）	Return on assets 资产利润率 (%)	Return on equity 权益利润率 (%)	Labour productivity ('000 RMB/ worker) 劳动生产率（千元/人）	Debts/ assets 资产负债率 (%)	Average total assets ('000 RMB) 平均总资产（千元）
By ownership 产业所有权									
State-owned 国有	30	330	18,814	-291	-0.36	-1.29	22.10	71.74	80,080
Collective-owned 集体	15	194	10,891	309	4.55	11.61	15.03	60.81	6,799
Foreign & Overseas Chinese Funded 三资	2	433	14,877	569	4.58	7.85	13.57	41.69	12,419
By regional distribution 地区分布									
Central-North 华北	4	341	23,924	895	3.41	11.60	43.70	70.60	26,236
Beijing 北京									
Tianjin 天津									
Hebei 河北									
Shanxi 山西	4	341	23,924	895	3.41	11.60	43.70	70.60	26,236
Inner Mongolia 内蒙古									
Northeast 东北	3	429	11,687	-20	-0.21	-0.28	8.42	27.08	9,816
Liaoning 辽宁	3	429	11,687	-20	-0.21	-0.28	8.42	27.08	9,816
Jilin 吉林									
Heilongjiang 黑龙江									
Central-East 华东	3	296	13,671	723	6.95	8.45	17.44	17.79	10,397
Shanghai 上海									
Jiangsu 江苏									
Zhejiang 浙江									
Anhui 安徽	1	205	14,600	582	17.85	38.65	19.73	53.82	3,261
Fujian 福建	1	482	20,363	593	2.36	2.77	17.32	14.74	25,131
Jiangxi 江西	1	200	6,050	993	35.46	36.64	15.37	3.21	2,800
Shandong 山东									
Central-South 中南	37	198	12,731	-123	-0.22	-0.74	23.90	70.30	55,805
Henan 河南	1	70	22,982	1,260	24.83		122.47	111.49	5,075
Hubei 湖北									
Hunan 湖南	14	206	12,635	-323	-0.31	-1.20	23.57	74.26	104,526
Guangdong 广东	2	159	9,128	41	0.21	0.28	28.01	24.47	19,709
Guangxi 广西	20	202	12,646	-69	-0.25	-0.66	22.10	62.78	27,845
Hainan 海南									
Southwest 西南	18	386	26,803	530	1.28	4.45	34.46	71.32	41,510
Chongqing 重庆	7	274	15,267	658	2.47	5.44	40.31	54.60	26,638
Sichuan 四川	3	362	33,014	887	1.82	3.68	46.40	50.54	48,697
Guizhou 贵州	4	197	10,217	87	0.59	1.65	18.91	64.06	14,627
Yunnan 云南	4	790	58,916	481	0.54	5.30	30.66	89.79	89,028
Tibet 西藏									
Northwest 西北	6	180	4,373	-179	-1.75	-4.15	9.97	57.72	10,189
Shaanxi 陕西	4	228	6,488	-295	-1.97	-4.62	9.81	57.31	14,958
Gansu 甘肃	2	85	143	55	8.38	35.62	10.79	76.48	651
Qinghai 青海									
Ningxia 宁夏									
Xinjiang 新疆									

0821: Manganese Ores Mining and Dressing 锰矿采选业

Year 年份	Number of firms 企业个数	Rate of change 变化率 (%)	Number of employees 职工人数 (人)	Rate of change 变化率 (%)	Total revenue (Mil. RMB) 总销售收入 (百万元)	Rate of change 变化率 (%)	Total profit (Mil RMB) 总利润 (百万元)	Rate of change 变化率 (%)
2000	77		16,780		973		-5	
2001	68	-11.69	16,810	0.18	962	-1.13	-4	20.00
2002	71	4.41	18,879	12.31	1,151	19.65	10	-

Major Products 主要产品	Output 产量	Unit 单位
Finished Manganese Ore 锰矿石成品矿	227	10,000 Tons 万吨

10 Main Firms with Maximal Revenue (year founded) 收入最大的十家主要企业（创办年份）	City 城市	Province 省	Telephone/fax 电话/传真	Number of employees 职工人数	Ownership 产业所有权	Revenue ('000 RMB) 销售收入 (千元)	Profit('000 RMB) (rank) 利润(千元) (排名)	Total assets ('000 RMB) 总资产 (千元)	Major products 主要产品
Yunnan Wenshan Dounan Manganese Industry Co.Ltd.	Wenshan	Yunnan	(0876)3882649		State-owned				Manganese Ore
云南文山斗南锰业有限责任公司(1973)	文山州	云南省	(0876)3880152	1,099	国有企业	101,418	-	153,865	锰矿石
Guangxi Daxin Manganese Mine	Chongzuo	Guangxi	(0771)3783338		State-owned				Manganese Ore
广西壮族自治区大新锰矿(1963)	崇左市	广西	(0771)3783899	1,360	国有企业	95,160	806(13)	166,289	锰矿石
Yunnan Jianshui Ferromanganese	Honghe	Yunnan	(0873)7686601		State-owned				Discharge Manganese Powder
云南建水锰矿(1958)	红河州	云南省	(0873)7686838	981	国有企业	79,686	53(33)	117,842	放电锰粉
Shanxi Lingqiu County Mine Industry Co.,Ltd.	Datong	Shanxi	(0352)8522076		Limited-Liability				Manganese Ore
山西省灵丘县矿业有限公司(1992)	大同市	山西省	(0352)8526699	380	有限公司	64,064	4,121(2)	56,164	锰矿石
Sichuan Hanyuan Manganese Mine	Yaan	Sichuan	(0835)4222871		State-owned				Manganese Ore
四川省汉源锰矿(1958)	雅安市	四川省	(0835)4222856	514	国有企业	50,079	2,069(4)	97,374	锰矿石
Sichuan Pingwu Manganese Industry (Group) Co., Ltd.	Mianyang	Sichuan	(0816)8832388		Limited-Liability				Electrolytic Metal Manganese电
四川省平武锰业（集团）有限公司(2000)	绵阳市	四川省	(0816)8832388	509	有限公司	42,024	192(26)	46,494	解金属锰
Yunnan Heqing Manganese Industry Group Co., Ltd.	Dali	Yunnan	(0872)4125034		Limited-Liability				Manganese Ore
云南省鹤庆锰业集团有限责任公司(1974)	大理州	云南省	(0872)4123932	684	有限公司	39,926	4,931(1)	76,221	锰矿石
Hunan Chenzhou Agate Mountain Mine	Chenzhou	Hunan	(0735)2602184		State-owned				Manganese Ore
湖南郴州玛瑙山矿(1965)	郴州市	湖南省	(0735)2602267	833	国有企业	39,598	606(16)	72,794	锰矿石
Youyang Tianxiong Manganese Industry Co., Ltd.	Chongqing	Chongqing	(023)75310225		Joint Stock				Electrolytic Metal Manganese电
酉阳县天雄锰业有限公司(2001)	重庆市	重庆市	(023)75310225	400	股份制	33,600	1,597(6)	75,850	解金属锰
Chengkou County Mine Resources Development Company	Chongqing	Chongqing	(023)59501191		Private Owned				Manganese Ore
城口县矿资源开发公司(1997)	重庆市	重庆市	(023)59222129	450	私营企业	32,589	1,304(7)	62,990	锰矿石

Top 10 Cities by Revenue 销售收入排名前10位城市	Province 省	Market share 市场份额 (%)	Number of firms 企业个数
Chongzuo 崇左市	Guangxi 广西	11.27	4
Chongqing 重庆市	Chongqing 重庆市	9.28	7
Wenshan 文山州	Yunnan 云南省	8.81	1
Datong 大同市	Shanxi 山西省	8.31	4
Honghe 红河州	Yunnan 云南省	8.19	2
Chenzhou 郴州市	Hunan 湖南省	6.66	3
Baise 百色市	Guangxi 广西	4.76	4
Yaan 雅安市	Sichuan 四川省	4.35	1
Mianyang 绵阳市	Sichuan 四川省	3.65	1
Dali 大理州	Yunnan 云南省	3.47	1

10 Major Wholesalers 十家主要批发商	City 城市	Province 省	Telephone/Fax 电话/传真
China Railway Materials Beijing Company	Beijing	Beijing	(010)63602299
中国铁路物资北京公司	北京市	北京市	(010)63601722
Shanghai BM Import & Export Co., Ltd.	Shanghai	Shanghai	(021)50320000
上海宝矿进出口有限公司	上海市	上海市	(021)50326700
Citic Trading Co.,Ltd.	Beijing	Beijing	(010)84865638
中信贸易公司	北京市	北京市	(010)84865271
Qingdao Iron And Steel Import & Export Corp.	Qingdao	Shandong	(0532)5798210
青岛钢铁进出口公司	青岛市	山东省	(0532)5798069
Guangzhou Metals and Minerals Import & Export .Ltd.	Guangzhou	Guangdong	(020)81082026
广州五金矿产进出口有限公司	广州市	广东省	(020)81084886
Shanghai Foreign Economics Trading Development Company	Shanghai	Shanghai	(021)62719538
上海外经贸发展公司	上海市	上海市	(021)62729625
China Nonferrous Metal Import & Export Jiangsu Company	Nanjing	Jiangsu	(025)4400366
中国有色金属进出口江苏公司	南京市	江苏省	(025)4400773
China Hardware Minerals Import & Export Shenzhen Branch Company	Shenzhen	Guangdong	(0755)82388365
中国五金矿产进出口深圳分公司	深圳市	广东省	(0755)82388335
Guangdong Dongfang Import & Export Corp.	Shenzhen	Guangdong	(0755)25950270
广东省东方进出口公司	深圳市	广东省	(0755)25950220
Shannxi Import & Export Corp.	Xi'an	Shannxi	(029)6520075
陕西省进出口公司	西安市	陕西省	(029)6511071

0911: Copper Ores Mining and Dressing 铜矿采选业

The industry accounts for 0.037% of the total revenue of China's industrial sector in 2002. The rate of return on assets is 1.53%. 86.54% of all firms in the industry made a profit while 13.46% had negative returns.The top province in terms of the industry's revenue is Yunnan, accounting for 26.72% of the total revenue.
2002年本行业收入占全行业的 0.037%，资产利润率为 1.53%。86.54%的企业赢利，13.46%的企业亏损。收入最高的省为云南省，占本行业的26.72%。

	Total number of firms 企业总数	Total number of employees 职工总数	Total revenue (Mil.RMB) 总销售收入 (百万元)	Total profit (Mil.RMB) 总利润 (百万元)	Return on assets 资产利润率 (%)	Return on equity 权益利润率 (%)	Labour productivity ('000 RMB/ worker) 劳动生产率 (千元/人)	Debts/ assets 资产负债率 (%)	Total assets (Mil.RMB) 总资产 (百万元)
Industry Overall 行业总体	104	52,304	3,930	108	1.53	4.89	25.24	68.79	7,052

	Number of firms 企业个数	Average number of employees 平均职工人数	Average revenue ('000 RMB) 平均销售收入 (千元)	Average profit ('000 RMB) 平均利润 (千元)	Return on assets 资产利润率 (%)	Return on equity 权益利润率 (%)	Labour productivity ('000 RMB/ worker) 劳动生产率 (千元/人)	Debts/ assets 资产负债率 (%)	Average total assets ('000 RMB) 平均总资产 (千元)
By ownership 产业所有权									
State-owned 国有	37	796	55,136	1,016	0.83	3.54	19.63	76.46	122,029
Collective-owned 集体	20	305	28,093	872	4.56	8.59	31.82	46.95	19,138
Foreign & Overseas Chinese Funded 三资	1	56	12,200	330	8.46	10.52	56.82	19.54	3,900
By regional distribution 地区分布									
Central-North 华北	11	544	19,731	-961	-1.10		15.15	117.16	87,447
Beijing 北京									
Tianjin 天津									
Hebei 河北	1	1,453	3,380	-10,259	-23.39		-0.09	254.56	43,854
Shanxi 山西	5	231	21,705	-490	-0.78	-3.65	38.85	78.65	62,893
Inner Mongolia 内蒙古	5	675	21,028	427	0.35		13.60	127.25	120,721
Northeast 东北	6	1,327	73,819	5,572	4.35	15.13	23.16	71.26	128,180
Liaoning 辽宁	2	1,974	133,223	1,425	0.94	2.41	31.62	61.00	151,305
Jilin 吉林	1	62	24,520	10	0.03	0.19	52.58	83.57	32,017
Heilongjiang 黑龙江	3	1,318	50,649	10,191	7.04	31.28	14.26	77.50	144,817
Central-East 华东	17	543	38,776	664	1.20	4.78	21.90	74.88	55,338
Shanghai 上海									
Jiangsu 江苏									
Zhejiang 浙江	2	648	107,348	2,972	2.67	6.86	42.12	61.06	111,210
Anhui 安徽	11	576	34,660	501	1.17	2.84	19.47	58.77	42,813
Fujian 福建									
Jiangxi 江西	2	502	19,722	41	0.15	0.39	18.70	62.10	27,436
Shandong 山东	2	301	11,893	-123	-0.13		9.31	133.89	96,258
Central-South 中南	28	366	31,337	1,594	3.88	8.27	28.04	53.14	41,112
Henan 河南	1	692	25,609	-1,532	-2.88	-7.01	16.66	59.00	53,282
Hubei 湖北	20	352	35,717	1,398	4.02	8.72	29.98	53.87	34,747
Hunan 湖南	3	327	18,171	215	0.69	1.13	14.64	38.57	31,055
Guangdong 广东	2	402	23,407	7,983	6.61	14.71	40.81	55.08	120,798
Guangxi 广西	2	365	18,071	796	2.34	5.09	24.09	54.07	34,081
Hainan 海南									
Southwest 西南	20	719	64,582	994	0.79	1.77	33.02	55.19	125,309
Chongqing 重庆									
Sichuan 四川	9	422	26,644	1,539	1.74	3.04	49.37	42.87	88,467
Guizhou 贵州	1	3						86.76	8,521
Yunnan 云南	8	1,311	131,257	809	0.38	0.97	27.12	60.72	212,111
Tibet 西藏	2	48	901	-224	-9.78	-77.24	30.33	87.34	2,290
Northwest 西北	22	204	20,085	407	1.24	3.64	17.91	65.94	32,877
Shaanxi 陕西	4	356	39,206	-462	-0.78	-2.94	-14.18	73.49	59,230
Gansu 甘肃	12	99	6,114	156	1.95	3.89	27.17	49.84	7,999
Qinghai 青海	3	116	16,364	-124	-1.63	-2.61	66.37	37.63	7,608
Ningxia 宁夏									
Xinjiang 新疆	3	510	54,194	3,102	2.53	7.68	29.57	67.03	122,524

0911: Copper Ores Mining and Dressing 铜矿采选业

Year 年份	Number of firms 企业个数	Rate of change 变化率 (%)	Number of employees 职工人数 (人)	Rate of change 变化率 (%)	Total revenue (Mil. RMB) 总销售收入 (百万元)	Rate of change 变化率 (%)	Total profit (Mil RMB) 总利润 (百万元)	Rate of change 变化率 (%)
2000	112		76,822		3,616		24	
2001	95	-15.18	59,630	-22.38	3,411	-5.67	-34	-
2002	104	9.47	52,304	-12.29	3,930	15.22	108	-

Major Products 主要产品	Output 产量	Unit 单位
Copper Concentrate 铜精矿含铜量	55	10,000 Tons 万吨

10 Main Firms with Maximal Revenue (year founded) 收入最大的十家主要企业（创办年份）	City 城市	Province 省	Telephone/fax 电话/传真	Number of employees 职工人数	Ownership 产业所有权	Revenue ('000 RMB) 销售收入 (千元)	Profit('000 RMB) (rank) 利润(千元) (排名)	Total assets ('000 RMB) 总资产 (千元)	Major products 主要产品
Fushun Hongtoushan Copper Mine 抚顺红透山铜矿(1948)	Fushun 抚顺市	Liaoning 辽宁省	(0413)3368212 (0413)3265924	3,835	State-owned 国有企业	251,857	649(33)	291,915	Crude Copper 铜矿石
Yunnan Dayao Copper Mine 大姚铜矿(1976)	Chuxiong 楚雄州	Yunnan 云南省	(0878)6386306 (0878)6386308	2,776	State-owned 国有企业	205,380	740(29)	314,030	Copper Mine 铜矿
Pingshui Copper Mine 平水铜矿(1967)	Shaoxing 绍兴市	Zhejiang 浙江省	(0575)5767111 (0575)5767412	831	State-owned 国有企业	190,083	5,074(8)	129,350	Copper Concentrate 铜精矿
Yunnan Jinsha Mining Co.,Ltd. 云南金沙矿业股份有限公司(2001)	Kunming 昆明市	Yunnan 云南省	(0871)2135682 (0871)2135682	2,012	Joint Stock 股份制	189,542	1,560(18)	105,295	Copper Concentrate 铜精矿
Tongcheng Longda Group Company 桐城市龙达集团公司(1996)	Anqing 安庆市	Anhui 安徽省	(0556)6202888 (0556)6202888	2,120	Collective-owned 集体企业	125,267	4,877(9)	58,303	
Harbin Songjiang Copper Trade Co.,Ltd. 哈尔滨松江铜业（集团）有限公司(1998)	Harbin 哈尔滨市	Heilongjiang 黑龙江省	(0451)2686464 (0451)2933284	3,013	State-owned 国有企业	113,968	32,575(1)	276,841	Copper Concentrate Powder 铜精矿粉
Jinduicheng Huaguang Industrial General Company 金堆城华光实业总公司(1988)	Weinan 渭南市	Shannxi 陕西省	(0913)4089995 (0913)4089994	717	State-owned 国有企业	102,890	67(58)	50,462	Copper Concentrate 铜精矿
Sichuan Liwu Copper Industry Co.,Ltd. 四川省里伍铜业股份有限公司(1995)	Ganzi 甘孜州	Sichuan 四川省	(0836)3326008 (0836)3326006	661	State Enterprises 国有独资	62,290	8,316(4)	240,526	Copper Mine 铜矿
Anqing Yueshan Copper Mine 安庆市月山铜矿(1970)	Anqing 安庆市	Anhui 安徽省	(0556)4051081 (0556)4051081	972	State-owned 国有企业	50,394	-	122,715	Copper Concentrate 铜精矿
Tongling Shida Industrial Company 铜陵市狮达实业公司(1983)	Tongling 铜陵市	Anhui 安徽省	(0562)6821146 (0562)6826348	695	Collective-owned 集体企业	48,984	250(47)	65,960	Copper Concentrate 铜精矿

Top 10 Cities by Revenue 销售收入排名前10位城市	Province 省	Market share 市场份额 (%)	Number of firms 企业个数
Huangshi 黄石市	Hubei 湖北省	16.75	16
Yuxi 玉溪市	Yunnan 云南省	13.46	1
Fushun 抚顺市	Liaoning 辽宁省	6.78	2
Anqing 安庆市	Anhui 安徽省	6.21	5
Kunming 昆明市	Yunnan 云南省	5.61	2
Chuxiong 楚雄州	Yunnan 云南省	5.43	2
Shaoxing 绍兴市	Zhejiang 浙江省	4.84	1
Liangshan 凉山州	Sichuan 四川省	4.31	7
Aletai 阿勒泰地区	Xinjiang 新疆	3.13	1
Harbin 哈尔滨市	Heilongjiang 黑龙江省	2.90	1

10 Major Wholesalers 十家主要批发商	City 城市	Province 省	Telephone/Fax 电话/传真
China Railway Materials Beijing Company 中国铁路物资北京公司	Beijing 北京市	Beijing 北京市	(010)63602299 (010)63601722
Shanghai BM Import & Export Co., Ltd. 上海宝矿进出口有限公司	Shanghai 上海市	Shanghai 上海市	(021)50320000 (021)50326700
Citic Trading Co.,Ltd. 中信贸易公司	Beijing 北京市	Beijing 北京市	(010)84865638 (010)84865271
Qingdao Iron And Steel Import & Export Corp. 青岛钢铁进出口公司	Qingdao 青岛市	Shandong 山东省	(0532)5798210 (0532)5798069
Guangzhou Metals and Minerals Import & Export .Ltd. 广州五金矿产进出口有限公司	Guangzhou 广州市	Guangdong 广东省	(020)81082026 (020)81084886
Shanghai Foreign Economics Trading Development Company 上海外经贸发展公司	Shanghai 上海市	Shanghai 上海市	(021)62719538 (021)62729625
China Nonferrous Metal Import & Export Jiangsu Company 中国有色金属进出口江苏公司	Nanjing 南京市	Jiangsu 江苏省	(025)4400366 (025)4400773
China Hardware Minerals Import & Export Shenzhen Branch Company 中国五金矿产进出口深圳分公司	Shenzhen 深圳市	Guangdong 广东省	(0755)82388365 (0755)82388335
Guangdong Dongtang Import & Export Corp. 广东省东方进出口公司	Shenzhen 深圳市	Guangdong 广东省	(0755)25950270 (0755)25950220
Shannxi Import & Export Corp. 陕西省进出口公司	Xi'an 西安市	Shannxi 陕西省	(029)6520075 (029)6511071

0912: Lead and Zinc Ores Mining and Dressing 铅锌矿采选业

The industry accounts for 0.072% of the total revenue of China's industrial sector in 2002. The rate of return on assets is 3.37%. 82.41% of all firms in the industry made a profit while 17.59% had negative returns.The top province in terms of the industry's revenue is Hunan, accounting for 14.62% of the total revenue.
2002年本行业收入占全行业的0.072%，资产利润率为3.37%。82.41%的企业赢利，17.59%的企业亏损。收入最高的省为湖南省，占本行业的14.62%。

	Total number of firms 企业总数	Total number of employees 职工总数	Total revenue (Mil.RMB) 总销售收入（百万元）	Total profit (Mil.RMB) 总利润（百万元）	Return on assets 资产利润率（%）	Return on equity 权益利润率（%）	Labour productivity ('000 RMB/ worker) 劳动生产率（千元/人）	Debts/ assets 资产负债率（%）	Total assets (Mil.RMB) 总资产（百万元）
Industry Overall 行业总体	324	93,278	7,725	386	3.37	8.29	30.73	59.30	11,449

	Number of firms 企业个数	Average number of employees 平均职工人数	Average revenue ('000 RMB) 平均销售收入（千元）	Average profit ('000 RMB) 平均利润（千元）	Return on assets 资产利润率（%）	Return on equity 权益利润率（%）	Labour productivity ('000 RMB/ worker) 劳动生产率（千元/人）	Debts/ assets 资产负债率（%）	Average total assets ('000 RMB) 平均总资产（千元）
By ownership 产业所有权									
State-owned 国有	64	561	34,098	1,519	2.44	5.78	22.10	57.84	62,277
Collective-owned 集体	103	166	13,337	645	4.93	12.05	30.66	59.12	13,088
Foreign & Overseas Chinese Funded 三资	8	133	12,080	1,419	8.25	28.85	37.00	71.40	17,199
By regional distribution 地区分布									
Central-North 华北	19	389	22,209	2,247	3.50	5.77	28.28	39.47	64,278
Beijing 北京	1	13	441	-386	-2.77	-4.55	19.92	39.12	13,923
Tianjin 天津									
Hebei 河北	4	160	16,090	1,286	5.23	10.74	34.43	51.31	24,585
Shanxi 山西	1	430	38,206	1,950	4.21	7.99	74.92	47.33	46,310
Inner Mongolia 内蒙古	13	485	24,535	2,768	3.39	5.46	24.49	38.03	81,747
Northeast 东北	15	506	28,713	282	0.87	2.69	18.55	67.68	32,522
Liaoning 辽宁	11	533	33,286	1,091	3.90	7.04	21.00	44.69	28,015
Jilin 吉林	3	56	11,781	504	10.01	12.70	83.16	21.14	5,033
Heilongjiang 黑龙江	1	1,555	29,206	-9,283	-5.64		2.27	115.01	164,571
Central-East 华东	33	219	21,173	908	3.37	11.09	33.41	69.65	26,975
Shanghai 上海									
Jiangsu 江苏	2	740	70,267	1,445	1.00	3.35	32.29	70.12	144,302
Zhejiang 浙江	8	161	18,892	372	2.08	6.01	32.44	65.38	17,862
Anhui 安徽	4	388	29,116	468	1.37	4.49	20.93	69.44	34,072
Fujian 福建	13	129	16,397	1,648	13.97	44.53	58.22	68.62	11,794
Jiangxi 江西	6	203	12,906	134	0.47	1.80	17.50	73.55	28,179
Shandong 山东									
Central-South 中南	120	288	22,997	588	2.13	4.43	28.25	51.77	27,565
Henan 河南	22	76	14,465	1,761	27.08	77.40	54.91	65.02	6,502
Hubei 湖北	1	140	46,390	1,572	8.82	52.05	23.41	83.06	17,830
Hunan 湖南	60	263	18,819	80	0.35	0.66	24.84	46.07	22,589
Guangdong 广东	10	511	61,080	2,992	3.44	8.31	55.25	58.56	86,871
Guangxi 广西	27	440	24,262	-164	-0.48	-0.98	17.49	51.10	34,178
Hainan 海南									
Southwest 西南	54	365	25,805	1,671	5.17	14.49	32.22	64.30	32,289
Chongqing 重庆									
Sichuan 四川	20	276	18,840	771	4.31	8.78	33.66	50.92	17,891
Guizhou 贵州	12	276	7,068	-61	-0.67	-2.21	8.27	69.54	9,031
Yunnan 云南	21	510	43,883	3,480	5.82	18.61	38.86	68.73	59,797
Tibet 西藏	1	150	10,314	2,450	11.32	11.56	33.19	2.11	21,650
Northwest 西北	83	203	24,349	1,790	3.91	11.66	39.53	66.44	45,762
Shaanxi 陕西	24	190	17,576	929	3.27	11.33	27.62	71.13	28,398
Gansu 甘肃	52	142	13,153	1,336	5.13	11.69	42.85	56.14	26,060
Qinghai 青海	5	932	179,552	11,337	3.26	11.80	46.11	72.36	347,478
Ningxia 宁夏									
Xinjiang 新疆	2	95	8,712	73	0.60	4.31	34.96	85.96	12,068

0912: Lead and Zinc Ores Mining and Dressing 铅锌矿采选业

Year 年份	Number of firms 企业个数	Rate of change 变化率 (%)	Number of employees 职工人数 (人)	Rate of change 变化率 (%)	Total revenue (Mil. RMB) 总销售收入 (百万元)	Rate of change 变化率 (%)	Total profit (Mil RMB) 总利润 (百万元)	Rate of change 变化率 (%)
2000	356		95,239		7,732		362	
2001	336	-5.62	96,512	1.34	6,914	-10.58	292	-19.34
2002	324	-3.57	93,278	-3.35	7,725	11.73	386	32.19

Major Products 主要产品	Output 产量	Unit 单位
Zinc Concentrate 锌精矿含锌量	146	10,000 Tons 万吨
Lead Concentrate 铅精矿含铅量	54	10,000 Tons 万吨

10 Main Firms with Maximal Revenue (year founded) 收入最大的十家主要企业（创办年份）	City 城市	Province 省	Telephone/fax 电话/传真	Number of employees 职工人数	Ownership 产业所有权	Revenue ('000 RMB) 销售收入 (千元)	Profit('000 RMB) (rank) 利润(千元) (排名)	Total assets ('000 RMB) 总资产 (千元)	Major products 主要产品
Yunnan Lanping Nonferrous Metal Co., Ltd.	Nujiang	Yunnan	(0886)3221330		Limited-Liability				Zinc Ingot
云南兰坪有色金属有限责任公司(1998)	怒江州	云南省	(0886)3221352	1,598	有限公司	212,252	36,419(2)	410,639	锌锭
Siding plumbum-zinc Mine	Liuzhou	Guangxi	(0772)8372101		State-owned				Zinc Mine
泗顶铅锌矿(1960)	柳州市	广西	(0772)8372029	2,664	国有企业	170,921	1,099(82)	192,296	锌矿
Chifeng Baiyin Nuoer Plumbum-zinc Mine	Chifeng	Inner Mongolia	(0476)7782378		State-owned				Concentrated Lead
赤峰市白音诺尔铅锌矿(1979)	赤峰市	内蒙古	(0476)7782223	2,939	国有企业	152,165	24,039(4)	499,159	精铅
Hunan Huangshaping Plumbum-Zinc Mine	Chenzhou	Hunan	(0735)4572224		State-owned				Lead Mine
湖南黄沙坪铅锌矿(1958)	郴州市	湖南省	(0735)4572275	3,212	国有企业	140,062	6,032(18)	264,406	铅矿
Yunnan Wenshanzhou Dulong Zinc-Tin Co., Ltd.	Wenshan	Yunnan	(0876)7361100		State-owned				Concentrate Zinc
云南省文山州都龙锌锡有限责任公司(1958)	文山州	云南省	(0876)7361686	912	国有企业	135,761	13,864(8)	145,739	精矿含锌
Hunan Metals And Stones Mine Industry Co., Ltd.	Huaihua	Hunan	(0745)4551708		Limited-Liability				Zinc Mine
湖南金石矿业有限公司(2001)	怀化市	湖南省	(0745)4551088	850	有限公司	128,781	-	234,526	锌矿
Huili Zinc Mine	Liangshan	Sichuan	(0834)5648166		State-owned				Zinc Mine
会理锌矿(1951)	凉山州	四川省	(0834)5648001	1,760	国有企业	125,421	2,522(42)	93,434	锌矿
Mengzi Ore Smelting Co., Ltd.	Honghe	Yunnan	(0873)3727070		Limited-Liability				Zinc Concentrate
蒙自矿冶有限责任公司(1996)	红河州	云南省	(0873)3726983	800	有限公司	102,515	21,648(5)	135,929	锌精矿
Youxi Mining Group Co., Ltd.	Sanming	Fujian	(0598)6326091		Joint Stock				Copper Concentrate
尤溪矿业集团有限公司(1995)	三明市	福建省	(0598)6330288	497	股份制	96,268	11,188(11)	66,899	铅精矿
Huanren Mining Company	Benxi	Liaoning	(0414)8174541		Limited-Liability				
桓仁满族自治县矿业有限公司(1951)	本溪市	辽宁省	(0414)8172545	1,616	有限公司	94,708	2,170(50)	36,300	

Top 10 Cities by Revenue 销售收入排名前10位城市	Province 省	Market share 市场份额 (%)	Number of firms 企业个数
Haixi 海西州	Qinghai 青海省	11.54	2
Chenzhou 郴州市	Hunan 湖南省	11.03	38
Longnan 陇南地区	Gansu 甘肃省	8.34	50
Shaoguan 韶关市	Guangdong 广东省	6.98	6
Nujiang 怒江州	Yunnan 云南省	4.93	8
Baoji 宝鸡市	Shannxi 陕西省	3.73	11
Chifeng 赤峰市	Inner Mongolia 内蒙古	3.01	5
Sanmenxia 三门峡市	Henan 河南省	2.74	13
Hechi 河池市	Guangxi 广西	2.52	7
Yaan 雅安市	Sichuan 四川省	2.35	11

10 Major Wholesalers 十家主要批发商	City 城市	Province 省	Telephone/Fax 电话/传真
China Railway Materials Beijing Company	Beijing	Beijing	(010)63602299
中国铁路物资北京公司	北京市	北京市	(010)63601722
Shanghai BM Import & Export Co., Ltd.	Shanghai	Shanghai	(021)50320000
上海宝矿进出口有限公司	上海市	上海市	(021)50326700
Citic Trading Co.,Ltd.	Beijing	Beijing	(010)84865638
中信贸易公司	北京市	北京市	(010)84865271
Qingdao Iron And Steel Import & Export Corp.	Qingdao	Shandong	(0532)5798210
青岛钢铁进出口公司	青岛市	山东省	(0532)5798069
Guangzhou Metals and Minerals Import & Export .Ltd.	Guangzhou	Guangdong	(020)81082026
广州五金矿产进出口有限公司	广州市	广东省	(020)81084886
Shanghai Foreign Economics Trading Development Company	Shanghai	Shanghai	(021)62719538
上海外经贸发展公司	上海市	上海市	(021)62729625
China Nonferrous Metal Import & Export Jiangsu Company	Nanjing	Jiangsu	(025)4400366
中国有色金属进出口江苏公司	南京市	江苏省	(025)4400773
China Hardware Minerals Import & Export Shenzhen Branch Company	Shenzhen	Guangdong	(0755)82388365
中国五金矿产进出口深圳分公司	深圳市	广东省	(0755)82388335
Guangdong Dongfang Import & Export Corp.	Shenzhen	Guangdong	(0755)25950270
广东省东方进出口公司	深圳市	广东省	(0755)25950220
Shannxi Import & Export Corp.	Xi'an	Shannxi	(029)6520075
陕西省进出口公司	西安市	陕西省	(029)6511071

0915: Tin Ores Mining and Dressing 锡矿采选业

The industry accounts for 0.016% of the total revenue of China's industrial sector in 2002. The rate of return on assets is -9.88%. 68.29% of all firms in the industry made a profit while 31.71% had negative returns.The top province in terms of the industry's revenue is Guangxi, accounting for 56.68% of the total revenue.
2002年本行业收入占全行业的 0.016%，资产利润率为 -9.88%。68.29%的企业赢利，31.71%的企业亏损。收入最高的省为广西，占本行业的56.68%。

	Total number of firms 企业总数	Total number of employees 职工总数	Total revenue (Mil.RMB) 总销售收入 (百万元)	Total profit (Mil.RMB) 总利润 (百万元)	Return on assets 资产利润率 (%)	Return on equity 权益利润率 (%)	Labour productivity ('000 RMB/ worker) 劳动生产率 (千元/人)	Debts/ assets 资产负债率 (%)	Total assets (Mil.RMB) 总资产 (百万元)
Industry Overall 行业总体	41	30,290	1,763	-389	-9.88	-60.16	15.10	83.58	3,932

	Number of firms 企业个数	Average number of employees 平均职工人数	Average revenue ('000 RMB) 平均销售收入 (千元)	Average profit ('000 RMB) 平均利润 (千元)	Return on assets 资产利润率 (%)	Return on equity 权益利润率 (%)	Labour productivity ('000 RMB/ worker) 劳动生产率 (千元/人)	Debts/ assets 资产负债率 (%)	Average total assets ('000 RMB) 平均总资产 (千元)
By ownership 产业所有权									
State-owned 国有	8	279	7,538	-2,141	-7.60		8.87	104.60	28,161
Collective-owned 集体	14	624	35,035	1,229	4.87	10.26	17.27	52.56	25,228
Foreign & Overseas Chinese Funded 三资									
By regional distribution 地区分布									
Central-North 华北									
Beijing 北京									
Tianjin 天津									
Hebei 河北									
Shanxi 山西									
Inner Mongolia 内蒙古									
Northeast 东北									
Liaoning 辽宁									
Jilin 吉林									
Heilongjiang 黑龙江									
Central-East 华东	1	347	28,800	1,127	2.16	4.41	35.65	51.03	52,203
Shanghai 上海									
Jiangsu 江苏									
Zhejiang 浙江									
Anhui 安徽									
Fujian 福建									
Jiangxi 江西	1	347	28,800	1,127	2.16	4.41	35.65	51.03	52,203
Shandong 山东									
Central-South 中南	32	663	42,570	-11,695	-11.34	-75.63	15.65	85.01	103,134
Henan 河南									
Hubei 湖北									
Hunan 湖南	26	230	13,948	688	5.83	12.34	18.87	52.77	11,795
Guangdong 广东	1	6	535	-52	-4.75		44.00	100.00	1,094
Guangxi 广西	5	3,046	199,811	-78,415	-13.10	-112.02	14.37	88.30	598,510
Hainan 海南									
Southwest 西南	8	1,092	46,464	-1,931	-2.66	-12.31	12.96	78.36	72,497
Chongqing 重庆									
Sichuan 四川									
Guizhou 贵州									
Yunnan 云南	8	1,092	46,464	-1,931	-2.66	-12.31	12.96	78.36	72,497
Tibet 西藏									
Northwest 西北									
Shaanxi 陕西									
Gansu 甘肃									
Qinghai 青海									
Ningxia 宁夏									
Xinjiang 新疆									

0915: Tin Ores Mining and Dressing 锡矿采选业

Year 年份	Number of firms 企业个数	Rate of change 变化率 (%)	Number of employees 职工人数 (人)	Rate of change 变化率 (%)	Total revenue (Mil. RMB) 总销售收入 (百万元)	Rate of change 变化率 (%)	Total profit (Mil RMB) 总利润 (百万元)	Rate of change 变化率 (%)
2000	41		34,384		2,391		165	
2001	34	-17.07	29,615	-13.87	2,224	-6.98	42	-74.55
2002	41	20.59	30,290	2.28	1,763	-20.73	-389	-

Major Products 主要产品	Output 产量	Unit 单位
Stannum Concentrate 锡精矿含锡量	4	10,000 Tons 万吨

10 Main Firms with Maximal Revenue (year founded) 收入最大的十家主要企业（创办年份）	City 城市	Province 省	Telephone/ fax 电话/传真	Number of employees 职工人数	Ownership 产业所有权	Revenue ('000 RMB) 销售收入（千元）	Profit('000 RMB) (rank) 利润(千元)(排名)	Total assets ('000 RMB) 总资产（千元）	Major products 主要产品
Liuzhou Huaxi Group Co.,Ltd.	Liuzhou	Guangxi	(0772)2610111		State Enterprises				Tin Mine
柳州华锡集团有限责任公司(1953)	柳州市	广西	(0772)2612186	13,585	国有独资	915,309	-	2,643,121	锡矿
Gejiu Xidu Industrial General Company	Honghe	Yunnan	(0873)2125200		Collective-owned				Tin Concentrate
个旧锡都实业总公司(1979)	红河州	云南省	(0873)2132099	5,915	集体企业	279,877	5,885(1)	216,338	锡精矿
Guangxi Gaofeng Mining Co.,Ltd.	Hechi	Guangxi	(0778)7577054		Limited-Liability				Tin Concentrate
广西高峰矿业有限责任公司(1985)	河池市	广西	(0778)7577545	1,069	有限公司	68,603	-	282,319	锡精矿
Jiangxi Huichang Jinlong Tin Industry Co.,Ltd.	Ganzhou	Jiangxi	(0797)5589002		Private Owned				Tin Concentrate
江西省会昌金龙锡业有限公司(1999)	赣州市	江西省	(0797)5589010	347	私营企业	28,800	1,127(5)	52,203	锡精矿
Gejiu Xinjian Mining Co.,Ltd.	Honghe	Yunnan	(0873)2752238		Limited-Liability				Tin Concentrate
个旧市新建矿业有限责任公司(1999)	红河州	云南省	(0873)2752238	428	有限公司	20,186	-	58,832	锡精矿
Linwu Wangfa Nonferrous Metal Industry & Trade Co.,Ltd.	Chenzhou	Hunan	(0735)6355828		Private Enterprises				Tin-Lead Mine
临武县旺发有色金属有限公司(1999)	郴州市	湖南省	(0735)6355828	130	私营独资	18,800	1,080(6)	6,413	锡铅矿
Linwu County Paojinshan Plumbum-Zinc Mine	Chenzhou	Hunan	(0735)6475188		State-owned				Tin Concentrate
临武县泡金山铅锌矿(1970)	郴州市	湖南省	(0735)6475188	536	国有企业	18,548	197(25)	20,561	锡精矿
Gejiu Redflag Mining Co., Ltd.	Honghe	Yunnan	(0873)2122404		Limited-Liability				Tin Concentrate
个旧市红旗矿业有限责任公司(2000)	红河州	云南省	(0873)2122404	690	有限公司	17,356	-	70,616	锡精矿
Gejiu Cujing Mining Co., Ltd.	Honghe	Yunnan	(0873)2221019		Limited-Liability				Tin Concentrate
个旧市促进矿业有限责任公司(2000)	红河州	云南省	(0873)2221016	392	有限公司	16,273	-	27,055	锡精矿
Yunlong Tin-Electric Co., Ltd.	Dali	Yunnan	(0872)5722181		Limited-Liability				Tin
云龙县锡电有限责任公司(1971)	大理州	云南省	(0872)5722181	289	有限公司	13,367	-	57,592	锡

Top 10 Cities by Revenue 销售收入排名前10位城市	Province 省	Market share 市场份额 (%)	Number of firms 企业个数
Liuzhou 柳州市	Guangxi 广西	51.93	1
Chenzhou 郴州市	Hunan 湖南省	20.05	25
Honghe 红河州	Yunnan 云南省	19.37	5
Hechi 河池市	Guangxi 广西	4.75	4
Ganzhou 赣州市	Jiangxi 江西省	1.63	1
Dali 大理州	Yunnan 云南省	0.76	1
Dehong 德宏州	Yunnan 云南省	0.71	1
Yongzhou 永州市	Hunan 湖南省	0.52	1
Simao 思茅地区	Yunnan 云南省	0.25	1
Yunfu 云浮市	Guangdong 广东省	0.03	1

10 Major Wholesalers 十家主要批发商	City 城市	Province 省	Telephone/Fax 电话/传真
China Railway Materials Beijing Company	Beijing	Beijing	(010)63602299
中国铁路物资北京公司	北京市	北京市	(010)63601722
Shanghai BM Import & Export Co., Ltd.	Shanghai	Shanghai	(021)50320000
上海宝矿进出口有限公司	上海市	上海市	(021)50326700
Citic Trading Co.,Ltd.	Beijing	Beijing	(010)84865638
中信贸易公司	北京市	北京市	(010)84865271
Qingdao Iron And Steel Import & Export Corp.	Qingdao	Shandong	(0532)5798210
青岛钢铁进出口公司	青岛市	山东省	(0532)5798069
Guangzhou Metals and Minerals Import & Export .Ltd.	Guangzhou	Guangdong	(020)81082026
广州五金矿产进出口有限公司	广州市	广东省	(020)81084886
Shanghai Foreign Economics Trading Development Company	Shanghai	Shanghai	(021)62719538
上海外经贸发展公司	上海市	上海市	(021)62729625
China Nonferrous Metal Import & Export Jiangsu Company	Nanjing	Jiangsu	(025)4400366
中国有色金属进出口江苏公司	南京市	江苏省	(025)4400773
China Hardware Minerals Import & Export Shenzhen Branch Company	Shenzhen	Guangdong	(0755)82388365
中国五金矿产进出口深圳分公司	深圳市	广东省	(0755)82388335
Guangdong Dongfang Import & Export Corp.	Shenzhen	Guangdong	(0755)25950270
广东省东方进出口公司	深圳市	广东省	(0755)25950220
Shannxi Import & Export Corp.	Xi'an	Shannxi	(029)6520075
陕西省进出口公司	西安市	陕西省	(029)6511071

0933: Titanium Ores Mining and Dressing 钛矿采选业

The industry accounts for 0.002% of the total revenue of China's industrial sector in 2002. The rate of return on assets is -0.83%. 65.00% of all firms in the industry made a profit while 35.00% had negative returns.The top province in terms of the industry's revenue is Guangdong, accounting for 44.25% of the total revenue.
2002年本行业收入占全行业的0.002%，资产利润率为 -0.83%。65.00%的企业赢利，35.00%的企业亏损。收入最高的省为广东省，占本行业的44.25%。

	Total number of firms 企业总数	Total number of employees 职工总数	Total revenue (Mil.RMB) 总销售收入（百万元）	Total profit (Mil.RMB) 总利润（百万元）	Return on assets 资产利润率（%）	Return on equity 权益利润率（%）	Labour productivity ('000 RMB/worker) 劳动生产率（千元/人）	Debts/assets 资产负债率（%）	Total assets (Mil.RMB) 总资产（百万元）
Industry Overall 行业总体	20	1,393	179	-1	-0.83	-26.07	46.16	96.83	169

	Number of firms 企业个数	Average number of employees 平均职工人数	Average revenue ('000 RMB) 平均销售收入（千元）	Average profit ('000 RMB) 平均利润（千元）	Return on assets 资产利润率（%）	Return on equity 权益利润率（%）	Labour productivity ('000 RMB/worker) 劳动生产率（千元/人）	Debts/assets 资产负债率（%）	Average total assets ('000 RMB) 平均总资产（千元）
By ownership 产业所有权									
State-owned 国有	6	49	2,292	-421	-4.46		6.52	129.08	9,450
Collective-owned 集体	1	360	22,800	1,300	10.74	13.13	18.06	18.18	12,100
Foreign & Overseas Chinese Funded 三资	1	21	9,162	-326	-4.20		14.38	180.73	7,760
By regional distribution 地区分布									
Central-North 华北	1	120	1,970				5.83	101.54	14,720
Beijing 北京									
Tianjin 天津									
Hebei 河北									
Shanxi 山西	1	120	1,970				5.83	101.54	14,720
Inner Mongolia 内蒙古									
Northeast 东北									
Liaoning 辽宁									
Jilin 吉林									
Heilongjiang 黑龙江									
Central-East 华东									
Shanghai 上海									
Jiangsu 江苏									
Zhejiang 浙江									
Anhui 安徽									
Fujian 福建									
Jiangxi 江西									
Shandong 山东									
Central-South 中南	18	68	9,393	-75	-0.96	-146.70	48.84	99.35	7,854
Henan 河南									
Hubei 湖北									
Hunan 湖南									
Guangdong 广东	2	201	39,629	654	2.25	12.35	16.66	81.78	29,064
Guangxi 广西	6	70	9,462	-61	-0.74	-3.91	34.14	81.01	8,148
Hainan 海南	10	41	3,304	-230	-6.69		95.73	155.17	3,435
Southwest 西南	1	45	8,057	-45	-0.34	-0.96	80.31	64.31	13,085
Chongqing 重庆									
Sichuan 四川									
Guizhou 贵州									
Yunnan 云南	1	45	8,057	-45	-0.34	-0.96	80.31	64.31	13,085
Tibet 西藏									
Northwest 西北									
Shaanxi 陕西									
Gansu 甘肃									
Qinghai 青海									
Ningxia 宁夏									
Xinjiang 新疆									

0933: Titanium Ores Mining and Dressing 钛矿采选业

Year 年份	Number of firms 企业个数	Rate of change 变化率(%)	Number of employees 职工人数(人)	Rate of change 变化率(%)	Total revenue (Mil. RMB) 总销售收入(百万元)	Rate of change 变化率(%)	Total profit (Mil RMB) 总利润(百万元)	Rate of change 变化率(%)
2000	28		2,056		134		-3	
2001	21	-25.00	1,515	-26.31	134	0	-3	0
2002	20	-4.76	1,393	-8.05	179	33.58	-1	66.67

Major Products 主要产品	Output 产量	Unit 单位

10 Main Firms with Maximal Revenue (year founded) 收入最大的十家主要企业(创办年份)	City 城市	Province 省	Telephone/fax 电话/传真	Number of employees 职工人数	Ownership 产业所有权	Revenue ('000 RMB) 销售收入(千元)	Profit('000 RMB) (rank) 利润(千元)(排名)	Total assets ('000 RMB) 总资产(千元)	Major products 主要产品
Maoming Ubridge Group Mineral Industry Co., Ltd.	Maoming	Guangdong	(0668)2987766		Limited-Liability				Rutile Concentrate Powder金
茂名市粤桥集团矿业有限公司(2001)	茂名市	广东省	(0668)2286666	41	有限公司	56,458	8(7)	46,028	红石精矿
Huazhou Pingding Town Luojiang Titanium Mine Company	Maoming	Guangdong	(0668)7530388		Collective-owned				Titanium Mine
化州市平定镇罗江钛矿公司(1992)	茂名市	广东省	(0668)7530909	360	集体企业	22,800	1,300(1)	12,100	钛矿
Lingshan Titanium Dioxide Limited Company	Qinzhou	Guangxi	(0777)6211857		Private Owned				Tilanium Dioxide
灵山县钛白粉有限公司(1989)	钦州市	广西	(0777)6211857	147	私营企业	20,883	-	5,920	钛白粉
Qinzhou Chuangda Mining Co.,Ltd.	Qinzhou	Guangxi	(0777)2832617		Private Owned				Titanium Concentrate
钦州市创大矿业有限公司(2000)	钦州市	广西	(0777)2852085	80	私营企业	18,316	94(4)	9,389	钛精矿
Hainan Lingshui Xinhua Mill Running Factory	Hainan	Hainan	(0898)83329812		State-owned				Titanium Concentrate
海南陵水新华选矿厂(1963)	陵水县	海南省	(0898)83329812	11	国有企业	6,907	-	9,713	钛精矿
Cenxi South Mining Co., Ltd.	Wuzhou	Guangxi	(0774)8220708		Limited-Liability				Ferrotitanium Concentrate
岑溪市南方矿业有限责任公司(1996)	梧州市	广西	(0774)8220706	50	有限公司	5,019	25(6)	2,667	钛铁矿
Shanxi Daixian Rutile Mine	Xinzhou	Shanxi	(0350)5203168		State-owned				Rutile Concentrated Powder金红
山西省代县金红石矿(1986)	忻州市	山西省		120	国有企业	1,970	-	14,720	石精矿粉
Hainan Nan'gang Titanium Mine	Hainan	Hainan	(0898)6277016		State-owned				Ferrotitanium Concentrate
海南省南港钛矿(1986)	琼海市	海南省		65	国有企业	1,373	-	6,892	钛铁精矿
Beihai Mill Running Factory	Beihai	Guangxi	(0779)2052291		State-owned				Man made Rutile人
北海选矿厂(1966)	北海市	广西		54	国有企业	16	-	16,069	造金红石
Luchuan Magnetic Separation Factory	Yulin	Guangxi	(0775)7172151		State-owned				Titanium Mine
广西陆川县磁选厂(1977)	玉林市	广西		5	国有企业		-	5,028	钛矿

Top 10 Cities by Revenue 销售收入排名前10位城市	Province 省	Market share 市场份额(%)	Number of firms 企业个数
Maoming 茂名市	Guangdong 广东省	44.25	2
Qinzhou 钦州市	Guangxi 广西	21.89	2
Wanning 万宁市	Hainan 海南省	13.83	5
Guilin 桂林市	Guangxi 广西	7.00	1
Kunming 昆明市	Yunnan 云南省	4.50	1
Lingshui 陵水县	Hainan 海南省	3.86	1
Wuzhou 梧州市	Guangxi 广西	2.80	1
Xinzhou 忻州市	Shanxi 山西省	1.10	1
Qionghai 琼海市	Hainan 海南省	0.77	1
Beihai 北海市	Guangxi 广西	0.01	1

10 Major Wholesalers 十家主要批发商	City 城市	Province 省	Telephone/Fax 电话/传真
China Railway Materials Beijing Company	Beijing	Beijing	(010)63602299
中国铁路物资北京公司	北京市	北京市	(010)63601722
Shanghai BM Import & Export Co., Ltd.	Shanghai	Shanghai	(021)50320000
上海宝矿进出口有限公司	上海市	上海市	(021)50326700
Citic Trading Co.,Ltd.	Beijing	Beijing	(010)84865638
中信贸易公司	北京市	北京市	(010)84865271
Qingdao Iron And Steel Import & Export Corp.	Qingdao	Shandong	(0532)5798210
青岛钢铁进出口公司	青岛市	山东省	(0532)5798069
Guangzhou Metals and Minerals Import & Export .Ltd.	Guangzhou	Guangdong	(020)81082026
广州五金矿产进出口有限公司	广州市	广东省	(020)81084886
Shanghai Foreign Economics Trading Development Company	Shanghai	Shanghai	(021)62719538
上海外经贸发展公司	上海市	上海市	(021)62729625
China Nonferrous Metal Import & Export Jiangsu Company	Nanjing	Jiangsu	(025)4400366
中国有色金属进出口江苏公司	南京市	江苏省	(025)4400773
China Hardware Minerals Import & Export Shenzhen Branch Company	Shenzhen	Guangdong	(0755)82388365
中国五金矿产进出口深圳分公司	深圳市	广东省	(0755)82388335
Guangdong Dongfang Import & Export Corp.	Shenzhen	Guangdong	(0755)25950270
广东省东方进出口公司	深圳市	广东省	(0755)25950220
Shannxi Import & Export Corp.	Xi'an	Shannxi	(029)6520075
陕西省进出口公司	西安市	陕西省	(029)6511071

1011: Limestone Quarrying 石灰石开采业

The industry accounts for 0.034% of the total revenue of China's industrial sector in 2002. The rate of return on assets is 2.48%. 88.42% of all firms in the industry made a profit while 11.58% had negative returns.The top province in terms of the industry's revenue is Guangdong, accounting for 28.60% of the total revenue.
2002年本行业收入占全行业的0.034%，资产利润率为2.48%。88.42%的企业赢利，11.58%的企业亏损。收入最高的省为广东省，占本行业的28.60%。

	Total number of firms 企业总数	Total number of employees 职工总数	Total revenue (Mil.RMB) 总销售收入 (百万元)	Total profit (Mil.RMB) 总利润 (百万元)	Return on assets 资产利润率 (%)	Return on equity 权益利润率 (%)	Labour productivity ('000 RMB/ worker) 劳动生产率 (千元/人)	Debts/ assets 资产负债率 (%)	Total assets (Mil.RMB) 总资产 (百万元)
Industry Overall 行业总体	190	36,279	3,650	113	2.48	3.53	34.79	29.89	4,557

	Number of firms 企业个数	Average number of employees 平均职工人数	Average revenue ('000 RMB) 平均销售收入 (千元)	Average profit ('000 RMB) 平均利润 (千元)	Return on assets 资产利润率 (%)	Return on equity 权益利润率 (%)	Labour productivity ('000 RMB/ worker) 劳动生产率 (千元/人)	Debts/ assets 资产负债率 (%)	Average total assets ('000 RMB) 平均总资产 (千元)
By ownership 产业所有权									
State-owned 国有	26	168	12,603	414	0.91	1.21	27.81	24.78	45,519
Collective-owned 集体	77	204	19,610	858	11.31	25.73	32.94	56.05	7,592
Foreign & Overseas Chinese Funded 三资	1	35	44,109	54	0.27	1.98	42.31	86.52	20,200
By regional distribution 地区分布									
Central-North 华北	14	174	10,062	574	1.94	2.39	18.80	18.90	29,567
Beijing 北京	3	269	16,245	59	0.16	0.23	15.85	30.95	36,988
Tianjin 天津	1	410	21,720	2,560	1.14	1.17	27.03	2.69	224,540
Hebei 河北	6	104	6,595	400	6.70	13.90	21.63	51.77	5,971
Shanxi 山西	2	172	2,574	101	0.70	1.21	5.91	41.57	14,263
Inner Mongolia 内蒙古	2	125	12,847	1,345	19.09	40.56	25.48	52.94	7,043
Northeast 东北	7	195	10,526	643	5.08	9.22	17.44	44.88	12,659
Liaoning 辽宁	4	72	8,018	484	4.63	6.24	34.07	25.73	10,445
Jilin 吉林	3	359	13,869	856	5.48	14.41	12.99	61.97	15,612
Heilongjiang 黑龙江									
Central-East 华东	67	246	24,016	980	3.10	4.62	35.81	33.04	31,658
Shanghai 上海	1	138	5,059	401	6.06	38.26	17.80	84.15	6,614
Jiangsu 江苏	25	281	31,299	886	1.36	1.82	41.18	25.39	65,373
Zhejiang 浙江	13	207	12,690	832	6.46	14.85	24.51	56.48	12,875
Anhui 安徽	6	469	27,694	1,079	5.09	10.99	17.30	53.68	21,206
Fujian 福建	10	182	9,070	140	1.56	4.98	27.63	68.68	8,958
Jiangxi 江西	4	162	6,115	324	7.67	14.52	15.67	47.18	4,226
Shandong 山东	8	172	46,906	2,894	29.29	74.35	90.55	60.60	9,880
Central-South 中南	80	160	20,355	355	1.64	2.13	39.88	23.18	21,660
Henan 河南	9	416	29,305	1,756	42.41	84.44	22.62	49.77	4,139
Hubei 湖北	9	204	17,615	568	5.16		50.16	101.61	11,009
Hunan 湖南	3	345	39,635	2,022	11.22	30.72	35.16	63.46	18,014
Guangdong 广东	55	94	18,975	706	8.09	15.89	54.18	49.11	8,728
Guangxi 广西	4	244	10,893	-9,353	-3.52	-3.56	15.64	1.17	265,608
Hainan 海南									
Southwest 西南	7	299	20,413	116	0.69	3.17	31.24	78.38	16,941
Chongqing 重庆	1	650	33,500	1,800	35.12	37.31	28.92	5.85	5,125
Sichuan 四川	4	348	26,917	-209	-0.77	-4.47	32.84	82.88	27,285
Guizhou 贵州	1	28	1,509	20	0.50	1.07	32.82	53.60	4,011
Yunnan 云南									
Tibet 西藏	1	25	216	-171	-54.29	-63.81	0.72	14.92	315
Northwest 西北	15	73	3,647	361	6.64	16.39	23.95	59.49	5,442
Shaanxi 陕西	2	113	5,430	97	1.01	8.53	19.71	88.14	9,580
Gansu 甘肃	11	44	1,081	83	3.80	8.54	21.22	55.52	2,180
Qinghai 青海	1	264	24,907	4,134	11.01	21.13	38.27	47.89	37,540
Ningxia 宁夏	1	120	7,050	180	18.95	31.58	11.42	40.00	950
Xinjiang 新疆									

1011: Limestone Quarrying 石灰石开采业

Year 年份	Number of firms 企业个数	Rate of change 变化率 (%)	Number of employees 职工人数 (人)	Rate of change 变化率 (%)	Total revenue (Mil. RMB) 总销售收入 (百万元)	Rate of change 变化率 (%)	Total profit (Mil RMB) 总利润 (百万元)	Rate of change 变化率 (%)
2000	207		41,061		3,492		92	
2001	203	-1.93	39,897	-2.83	3,415	-2.21	112	21.74
2002	190	-6.40	36,279	-9.07	3,650	6.88	113	0.89

Major Products 主要产品	Output 产量	Unit 单位

10 Main Firms with Maximal Revenue (year founded) 收入最大的十家主要企业（创办年份）	City 城市	Province 省	Telephone/fax 电话/传真	Number of employees 职工人数	Ownership 产业所有权	Revenue ('000 RMB) 销售收入 (千元)	Profit('000 RMB) (rank) 利润(千元) (排名)	Total assets ('000 RMB) 总资产 (千元)	Major products 主要产品
Jiangsu Chuanshan Group Co.,Ltd.	Zhenjiang	Jiangsu	(0511)5685016		Limited-Liability				Limestone
江苏船山集团有限责任公司(1973)	镇江市	江苏省		1,128	有限公司	211,460	7,580(2)	774,043	石灰石
Xingyang Cuimiao Building Materials Development Co.,Ltd.	Zhengzhou	Henan	(0371)4823183		Joint Stock				Limestone
荥阳市崔庙建材开发有限公司(1999)	郑州市	河南省	(0371)4822003	980	股份制	105,200	9,150(1)	11,200	石灰石
Deqing Luohong Stone Mine Factory	Zhaoqing	Guangdong	(0758)7619463		State-owned				Limestone
德庆县罗洪石矿场(1974)	肇庆市	广东省	(0758)7619701	307	国有企业	87,310	590(66)	43,941	石灰石
Zhangdian Fengshui Town Mine Company	Zibo	Shandong	(0533)2086618		Collective-owned				Limestone
张店区洋水镇矿山公司(1987)	淄博市	山东省		30	集体企业	58,710	3,170(13)	18,503	石灰石
Jurong Xiashu Town Zhenwu Society Mine	Zhenjiang	Jiangsu			Private Partnership				Limestone
句容市下蜀镇镇五村社会矿(1982)	镇江市	江苏省	(0511)7751307	580	私营合伙	57,070	980(47)	21,140	石灰石
Huangshi Tieshan Shizhou Stone Material CO.,Ltd.	Huangshi	Hubei	(0714)5424204		Collective-owned				Stone As Material
黄石市铁山区石洲石材有限公司(1995)	黄石市	湖北省		310	集体企业	55,479	1,721(26)	67,412	石料
Lantian Stone Field	Guangzhou	Guangdong	(020)86712448		Collective-owned				Limestone
蓝田石场(1993)	广州市	广东省	(020)86712448	80	集体企业	47,555	350(89)	3,985	石灰石
Tengzhou Jiehe Quarry	Zaozhuang	Shandong	(0632)2722055		Limited-Liability				Stone As Material
滕州市界河镇采石场(1991)	枣庄市	山东省		212	有限公司	47,000	4,220(7)	5,570	石料
Caohu Sanbing Mine Resources Development Co., Ltd.	Chaohu	Anhui	(0565)8382888		Collective-owned				Stone As Material
巢湖市散兵矿山资源开发有限公司(2001)	巢湖市	安徽省	(0565)8382886	1,065	集体企业	41,411	700(60)	24,200	石料
Anhui Wanbao Mining Co., Ltd.	Chizhou	Anhui	(0566)2043394		Joint Stock				Dolomite
安徽皖宝矿业股份有限公司(1997)	池州市	安徽省	(0566)2038992	429	股份制	41,407	2,023(23)	59,742	白云石

Top 10 Cities by Revenue 销售收入排名前10位城市	Province 省	Market share 市场份额 (%)	Number of firms 企业个数
Guangzhou 广州市	Guangdong 广东省	17.17	38
Zhenjiang 镇江市	Jiangsu 江苏省	14.14	8
Zhaoqing 肇庆市	Guangdong 广东省	6.11	8
Yantai 烟台市	Shandong 山东省	5.98	3
Nanjing 南京市	Jiangsu 江苏省	4.37	10
Huzhou 湖州市	Zhejiang 浙江省	3.61	8
Maoming 茂名市	Guangdong 广东省	3.35	3
Zhengzhou 郑州市	Henan 河南省	2.88	1
Hengyang 衡阳市	Hunan 湖南省	2.87	2
Nanyang 南阳市	Henan 河南省	2.71	4

10 Major Wholesalers 十家主要批发商	City 城市	Province 省	Telephone/Fax 电话/传真
China Railway Materials Beijing Company	Beijing	Beijing	(010)63602299
中国铁路物资北京公司	北京市	北京市	(010)63601722
Shanghai BM Import & Export Co., Ltd.	Shanghai	Shanghai	(021)50320000
上海宝矿进出口有限公司	上海市	上海市	(021)50326700
Citic Trading Co.,Ltd.	Beijing	Beijing	(010)84865638
中信贸易公司	北京市	北京市	(010)84865271
Qingdao Iron And Steel Import & Export Corp.	Qingdao	Shandong	(0532)5798210
青岛钢铁进出口公司	青岛市	山东省	(0532)5798069
Guangzhou Metals and Minerals Import & Export .Ltd.	Guangzhou	Guangdong	(020)81082026
广州五金矿产进出口有限公司	广州市	广东省	(020)81084886
Shanghai Foreign Economics Trading Development Company	Shanghai	Shanghai	(021)62719538
上海外经贸发展公司	上海市	上海市	(021)62729625
China Nonferrous Metal Import & Export Jiangsu Company	Nanjing	Jiangsu	(025)4400366
中国有色金属进出口江苏公司	南京市	江苏省	(025)4400773
China Hardware Minerals Import & Export Shenzhen Branch Company	Shenzhen	Guangdong	(0755)82388365
中国五金矿产进出口深圳分公司	深圳市	广东省	(0755)82388335
Guangdong Dongfang Import & Export Corp.	Shenzhen	Guangdong	(0755)25950270
广东省东方进出口公司	深圳市	广东省	(0755)25950220
Shannxi Import & Export Corp.	Xi'an	Shannxi	(029)6520075
陕西省进出口公司	西安市	陕西省	(029)6511071

1012: Constructing Stone Quarrying 建筑用石开采业

The industry accounts for 0.059% of the total revenue of China's industrial sector in 2002. The rate of return on assets is 9.18%. 91.02% of all firms in the industry made a profit while 8.98% had negative returns.The top province in terms of the industry's revenue is Guangdong, accounting for 19.23% of the total revenue.
2002年本行业收入占全行业的 0.059%，资产利润率为 9.18%。91.02%的企业赢利，8.98%的企业亏损。收入最高的省为广东省，占本行业的19.23%。

	Total number of firms 企业总数	Total number of employees 职工总数	Total revenue (Mil.RMB) 总销售收入 (百万元)	Total profit (Mil.RMB) 总利润 (百万元)	Return on assets 资产利润率 (%)	Return on equity 权益利润率 (%)	Labour productivity ('000 RMB/ worker) 劳动生产率 (千元/人)	Debts/ assets 资产负债率 (%)	Total assets (Mil.RMB) 总资产 (百万元)
Industry Overall 行业总体	323	44,793	6,276	380	9.18	17.56	47.34	47.69	4,133

	Number of firms 企业个数	Average number of employees 平均职工人数	Average revenue ('000 RMB) 平均销售收入 (千元)	Average profit ('000 RMB) 平均利润 (千元)	Return on assets 资产利润率 (%)	Return on equity 权益利润率 (%)	Labour productivity ('000 RMB/ worker) 劳动生产率 (千元/人)	Debts/ assets 资产负债率 (%)	Average total assets ('000 RMB) 平均总资产 (千元)
By ownership 产业所有权									
State-owned 国有	46	160	12,001	233	1.23	2.29	33.07	46.15	18,877
Collective-owned 集体	147	149	21,239	1,352	16.41	28.07	45.99	41.52	8,240
Foreign & Overseas Chinese Funded 三资	17	94	22,670	625	3.41	7.85	77.42	56.51	18,305
By regional distribution 地区分布									
Central-North 华北	37	109	16,884	355	1.52	3.07	61.60	50.44	23,271
Beijing 北京	3	65	8,067	373	22.47	144.70	54.90	84.47	1,662
Tianjin 天津	13	45	6,158	727	51.14	77.71	43.90	34.20	1,422
Hebei 河北	14	124	11,832	143	0.45	1.33	23.14	65.98	31,601
Shanxi 山西	3	262	102,750	-468	-0.41	-0.59	198.57	29.97	113,056
Inner Mongolia 内蒙古	4	182	11,638	489	3.49	7.57	21.22	53.93	14,000
Northeast 东北	30	168	7,591	411	3.77	7.85	17.52	51.96	10,895
Liaoning 辽宁	7	172	8,413	-126	-1.18	-3.74	23.65	68.48	10,712
Jilin 吉林	4	101	1,408	-488	-9.39	-28.90	4.60	67.52	5,201
Heilongjiang 黑龙江	19	180	8,590	798	6.57	11.98	16.89	45.19	12,161
Central-East 华东	108	171	26,364	1,979	14.15	27.51	48.98	48.57	13,992
Shanghai 上海									
Jiangsu 江苏	33	150	24,352	876	10.26	23.96	40.15	57.17	8,533
Zhejiang 浙江	43	178	22,003	1,875	10.33	19.49	43.33	46.98	18,144
Anhui 安徽	6	419	11,095	868	33.50	88.17	7.85	62.01	2,592
Fujian 福建	11	117	24,618	4,959	36.93	57.18	92.94	35.41	13,425
Jiangxi 江西	2	160	153	-91	-4.24	-35.48	0.57	88.06	2,148
Shandong 山东	13	129	58,452	3,435	15.85	31.66	137.85	49.95	21,677
Central-South 中南	131	122	19,266	1,053	10.47	17.46	53.46	40.02	10,050
Henan 河南	21	156	16,612	1,367	18.17	25.57	43.32	28.92	7,521
Hubei 湖北	19	127	12,243	560	9.98	16.93	38.24	41.03	5,610
Hunan 湖南	18	257	35,927	514	4.11	9.38	49.93	56.17	12,502
Guangdong 广东	65	73	18,564	1,317	11.27	18.16	67.66	37.92	11,680
Guangxi 广西	6	90	14,843	617	5.46	8.30	59.20	34.21	11,299
Hainan 海南	2	168					99.85		
Southwest 西南	4	48	2,151	55	0.90	3.61	14.93	75.20	6,111
Chongqing 重庆									
Sichuan 四川	3	60	2,784	25	0.31	1.30	15.45	75.84	8,078
Guizhou 贵州									
Yunnan 云南									
Tibet 西藏	1	12	250	143	68.75	68.75	7.08		208
Northwest 西北	13	92	3,390	176	2.46	42.57	23.37	94.23	7,171
Shaanxi 陕西	3	257	8,171	30	0.15		9.91	108.54	19,908
Gansu 甘肃	9	42	1,101	130	14.82	35.02	22.07	57.67	878
Qinghai 青海									
Ningxia 宁夏									
Xinjiang 新疆	1	49	9,645	1,029	4.02	14.42	245.16	72.12	25,593

1012: Constructing Stone Quarrying 建筑用石开采业

Year 年份	Number of firms 企业个数	Rate of change 变化率(%)	Number of employees 职工人数(人)	Rate of change 变化率(%)	Total revenue (Mil. RMB) 总销售收入(百万元)	Rate of change 变化率(%)	Total profit (Mil RMB) 总利润(百万元)	Rate of change 变化率(%)
2000	351		53,205		5,293		318	
2001	336	-4.27	54,713	2.83	5,664	7.01	327	2.83
2002	323	-3.87	44,793	-18.13	6,276	10.81	380	16.21

Major Products 主要产品	Output 产量	Unit 单位
Granite Slab 花岗石板材	5,688	10,000 Sq.M. 万平方米

10 Main Firms with Maximal Revenue (year founded) 收入最大的十家主要企业（创办年份）	City 城市	Province 省	Telephone/fax 电话/传真	Number of employees 职工人数	Ownership 产业所有权	Revenue ('000 RMB) 销售收入(千元)	Profit('000 RMB) (rank) 利润(千元)(排名)	Total assets ('000 RMB) 总资产(千元)	Major products 主要产品
Zhuhai Wanshan Building Materials Development Company 珠海市万山区建材开发公司(1988)	Zhuhai 珠海市	Guangdong 广东省	(0756)2127359	235	Collective-owned 集体企业	192,121	39,471(2)	135,867	Stone As Material 石料
Zhenjiang Maodi Industrial Co., Ltd. 镇江市茅迪实业有限公司(1997)	Zhenjiang 镇江市	Jiangsu 江苏省	(0511)7426188 (0511)7426112	455	Private Enterprises 私营独资	188,550	1,380(55)	74,230	Basalt 玄武石
Huarong Shengfeng Mine-Stone Building Materials Factory 华容县胜峰乡矿石建材厂(1969)	Yueyang 岳阳市	Hunan 湖南省	(0730)4470389 (0730)4470383	368	Collective-owned 集体企业	185,000	7,240(12)	53,600	Rough Granite Material 花岗岩荒料
Zhaoyuan Stone Material General Company 招远市石材总公司(1986)	Yantai 烟台市	Shandong 山东省	(0535)8342038 (0535)8342038	18	Collective-owned 集体企业	160,800	10,810(6)	8,700	Rough Granite Material 花岗石荒料
Qingdao Leixin Group Co.Ltd. 青岛磊鑫集团有限公司(1997)	Qingdao 青岛市	Shandong 山东省	(0532)7785288 (0532)7785288	260	Joint Stock 股份制	158,128	8,823(8)	100,425	Stone As Material 石料
Jinan Bluestar Materials Industry Development Co., Ltd. 济南蓝星石材矿业发展有限公司(1998)	Jinan 济南市	Shandong 山东省	(0531)3878364 (0531)3861836	81	Foreign Funded 外商投资	88,779	9,500(7)	33,371	Rough Granite Material 花岗石荒料
Deqing Longtou Mountain Stone Material Co., Ltd. 德清县龙头山石料有限公司(2001)	Huzhou 湖州市	Zhejiang 浙江省	(0572)8255745	330	Limited-Liability 有限公司	88,000	10,851(5)	33,395	Stone As Material 石料
Enterprise Office of Chuanshanping In Miluo 汨罗市川山坪镇企业公司(1995)	Yueyang 岳阳市	Hunan 湖南省	(0730)5840020	2,146	Collective-owned 集体企业	68,156	500(129)	13,270	Porous Stone 麻石
Donghai Shilianghe Quarrying Factory 东海县石梁河镇磨山采石厂(1977)	Lianyungang 连云港市	Jiangsu 江苏省	(0518)7368851	173	Collective-owned 集体企业	61,960	980(79)	2,000	Stone for Building 建筑石
Hengyang No.10 Building Materials Co., Ltd. 衡阳县第十建筑有限公司(2001)	Hengyang 衡阳市	Hunan 湖南省	(0734)6021493	145	Collective-owned 集体企业	60,008	1,500(48)	8,045	Granite 花岗石

Top 10 Cities by Revenue 销售收入排名前10位城市	Province 省	Market share 市场份额(%)	Number of firms 企业个数
Huzhou 湖州市	Zhejiang 浙江省	10.21	20
Datong 大同市	Shanxi 山西省	4.91	3
Jinan 济南市	Shandong 山东省	4.75	5
Maoming 茂名市	Guangdong 广东省	4.57	16
Yueyang 岳阳市	Hunan 湖南省	4.35	4
Lianyungang 连云港市	Jiangsu 江苏省	4.29	12
Guangzhou 广州市	Guangdong 广东省	3.87	17
Yantai 烟台市	Shandong 山东省	3.77	4
Hengyang 衡阳市	Hunan 湖南省	3.66	4
Zhenjiang 镇江市	Jiangsu 江苏省	3.29	3

10 Major Wholesalers 十家主要批发商	City 城市	Province 省	Telephone/Fax 电话/传真
China Railway Materials Beijing Company 中国铁路物资北京公司	Beijing 北京市	Beijing 北京市	(010)63602299 (010)63601722
Shanghai BM Import & Export Co., Ltd. 上海宝矿进出口有限公司	Shanghai 上海市	Shanghai 上海市	(021)50320000 (021)50326700
Citic Trading Co.,Ltd. 中信贸易公司	Beijing 北京市	Beijing 北京市	(010)84865638 (010)84865271
Qingdao Iron And Steel Import & Export Corp. 青岛钢铁进出口公司	Qingdao 青岛市	Shandong 山东省	(0532)5798210 (0532)5798069
Guangzhou Metals and Minerals Import & Export .Ltd. 广州五金矿产进出口有限公司	Guangzhou 广州市	Guangdong 广东省	(020)81082026 (020)81084886
Shanghai Foreign Economics Trading Development Company 上海外经贸发展公司	Shanghai 上海市	Shanghai 上海市	(021)62719538 (021)62729625
China Nonferrous Metal Import & Export Jiangsu Company 中国有色金属进出口江苏公司	Nanjing 南京市	Jiangsu 江苏省	(025)4400366 (025)4400773
China Hardware Minerals Import & Export Shenzhen Branch Company 中国五金矿产进出口深圳分公司	Shenzhen 深圳市	Guangdong 广东省	(0755)82388365 (0755)82388335
Guangdong Dongfang Import & Export Corp. 广东省东方进出口公司	Shenzhen 深圳市	Guangdong 广东省	(0755)25950270 (0755)25950220
Shannxi Import & Export Corp. 陕西省进出口公司	Xi'an 西安市	Shannxi 陕西省	(029)6520075 (029)6511071

1013: Refractory Clay and Stone Mining 耐火土石开采业

The industry accounts for 0.014% of the total revenue of China's industrial sector in 2002. The rate of return on assets is 3.03%. 91.84% of all firms in the industry made a profit while 8.16% had negative returns.The top province in terms of the industry's revenue is Guangdong, accounting for 24.43% of the total revenue.
2002年本行业收入占全行业的0.014%，资产利润率为3.03%。91.84%的企业赢利，8.16%的企业亏损。收入最高的省为广东省，占本行业的24.43%。

	Total number of firms 企业总数	Total number of employees 职工总数	Total revenue (Mil.RMB) 总销售收入（百万元）	Total profit (Mil.RMB) 总利润（百万元）	Return on assets 资产利润率（%）	Return on equity 权益利润率（%）	Labour productivity ('000 RMB/ worker) 劳动生产率（千元/人）	Debts/ assets 资产负债率（%）	Total assets (Mil.RMB) 总资产（百万元）
Industry Overall 行业总体	49	14,239	1,480	59	3.03	7.22	32.04	58.07	1,935

	Number of firms 企业个数	Average number of employees 平均职工人数	Average revenue ('000 RMB) 平均销售收入（千元）	Average profit ('000 RMB) 平均利润（千元）	Return on assets 资产利润率（%）	Return on equity 权益利润率（%）	Labour productivity ('000 RMB/ worker) 劳动生产率（千元/人）	Debts/ assets 资产负债率（%）	Average total assets ('000 RMB) 平均总资产（千元）
By ownership 产业所有权									
State-owned 国有	10	528	23,598	356	0.49	1.68	13.28	71.10	73,242
Collective-owned 集体	22	158	36,747	1,793	15.99	35.74	63.81	55.25	11,213
Foreign & Overseas Chinese Funded 三资	1	114	5,745	-36	-0.22	-0.55	3.05	59.64	16,323
By regional distribution 地区分布									
Central-North 华北	8	111	16,022	1,009	4.27	19.49	40.37	78.10	23,651
Beijing 北京	1	88	7,077	9	0.38	1.96	4.73	80.79	2,389
Tianjin 天津									
Hebei 河北	2	128	16,328	2,500	30.15	132.25	42.61	77.20	8,290
Shanxi 山西	4	108	20,674	776	2.02	10.13	56.15	80.11	38,479
Inner Mongolia 内蒙古	1	114	5,745	-36	-0.22	-0.55	3.05	59.64	16,323
Northeast 东北	6	780	30,782	714	0.56	1.69	10.69	66.76	126,955
Liaoning 辽宁	3	1,266	52,789	1,129	0.57	2.01	11.17	71.48	197,469
Jilin 吉林	2	392	10,112	-262	-0.33	-0.67	8.56	51.17	79,736
Heilongjiang 黑龙江	1	100	6,101	1,420	14.41	22.21	9.25	35.09	9,851
Central-East 华东	10	421	33,665	633	0.97	1.68	27.94	42.02	65,028
Shanghai 上海									
Jiangsu 江苏	4	645	50,688	390	0.28	0.44	31.75	36.48	138,070
Zhejiang 浙江	1	36	10,477	859	9.16	59.32	111.47	84.55	9,374
Anhui 安徽									
Fujian 福建									
Jiangxi 江西	1	162	5,561				9.92	105.96	6,725
Shandong 山东	4	359	29,464	977	4.77	15.55	21.06	69.31	20,476
Central-South 中南	16	253	50,513	2,463	12.49	30.66	58.39	59.27	19,723
Henan 河南	9	249	31,329	2,816	11.89	30.05	43.66	60.43	23,683
Hubei 湖北	2	163	8,980	595	19.67	43.59	18.09	54.88	3,025
Hunan 湖南	2	180	73,341	165	2.87	9.45	116.25	69.64	5,751
Guangdong 广东	3	374	120,536	4,181	14.78	33.04	80.98	55.27	28,291
Guangxi 广西									
Hainan 海南									
Southwest 西南	2	58	2,484	7	0.51	1.40	18.52	63.22	1,360
Chongqing 重庆									
Sichuan 四川									
Guizhou 贵州	1	100	4,968	14	0.51	1.40	20.55	63.22	2,719
Yunnan 云南									
Tibet 西藏	1	15					5.00		
Northwest 西北	7	42	2,493	69	3.19	4.80	47.74	33.64	2,153
Shaanxi 陕西									
Gansu 甘肃	7	42	2,493	69	3.19	4.80	47.74	33.64	2,153
Qinghai 青海									
Ningxia 宁夏									
Xinjiang 新疆									

1013: Refractory Clay and Stone Mining 耐火土石开采业

Year 年份	Number of firms 企业个数	Rate of change 变化率 (%)	Number of employees 职工人数 (人)	Rate of change 变化率 (%)	Total revenue (Mil. RMB) 总销售收入 (百万元)	Rate of change 变化率 (%)	Total profit (Mil RMB) 总利润 (百万元)	Rate of change 变化率 (%)
2000	54		17,078		1,213		47	
2001	54	-	18,505	8.36	1,457	20.12	37	-21.28
2002	49	-9.26	14,239	-23.05	1,480	1.58	59	59.46

Major Products 主要产品	Output 产量	Unit 单位

10 Main Firms with Maximal Revenue (year founded) 收入最大的十家主要企业（创办年份）	City 城市	Province 省	Telephone/fax 电话/传真	Number of employees 职工人数	Ownership 产业所有权	Revenue ('000 RMB) 销售收入 (千元)	Profit('000 RMB) (rank) 利润(千元) (排名)	Total assets ('000 RMB) 总资产 (千元)	Major products 主要产品
Gaoyao Hetai Town Kaolin Development Co., Ltd. 高要市河台镇高岭土开发集团有限公司(1993)	Zhaoqing 肇庆市	Guangdong 广东省	(0758)8218582	928	Collective-owned 集体企业	296,630	7,310(2)	58,182	Kaolin 高岭土
Haicheng Magnesium Mine Refractory Materials General Factory海城市镁矿耐火材料总厂(1951)	An'shan 鞍山市	Liaoning 辽宁省	(0412)3772962 (0412)3772360	3,279	State-owned 国有企业	148,990	3030(6)	557,710	Magnesium Sand 镁砂
Yuzhou Changzhuang Bauxite Mining 禹州市苌庄乡铝矾土矿(1972)	Xuchang 许昌市	Henan 河南省	(0374)8761168	615	Collective-owned 集体企业	111,494	11,680(1)	55,600	Bauxite 铝矾土
Yuzhou Changzhuang Bauxite Mining 禹州市苌庄乡铝矾土矿(1972)	Nanjing 南京市	Jiangsu 江苏省	(025)6894301 (025)6894300	1,365	State Enterprises 国有独资	95,670	480(22)	502,280	Dolomite 白云石
Nanjing Huahong (Group) Co., Ltd. 南京华宏(集团)有限公司(1950)	Zhengzhou 郑州市	Henan 河南省	(0371)2922088 (0371)2922018	600	Collective Owned 集体企业	73,053	7,260(3)	41,998	Crude Bauxite 生铝钒土
Zhengzhou Rongda Group Company 郑州市荣达集团公司(1985)	Jinzhong 晋中市	Shanxi 山西省	(0354)2442266 (0354)3069698	122	Private Owned 私营企业	55,842	2,236(10)	83,197	High Bauxite Cushioning Material高铝钒土垫料
Shanxi Yuci Bangli Al-Fa Factory 山西省榆次邦力铝钒土厂(1997)	Zhenjiang 镇江市	Jiangsu 江苏省	(0511)3372862 (0511)3372570	819	Limited-Liability 有限公司	51,411	460(23)	30,906	Finished Dolomite Ore白云石成品矿
Zhenjiang Qinglong Mountain Mining Chemical Industry Co., Ltd. 镇江青龙山矿业化工有限责任公司(1959)	Zaozhuang 枣庄市	Shandong 山东省	(0632)7016098	220	Collective-owned 集体企业	51,100	2,750(8)	4,172	Dolomite 白云石
Dolomite Mine of Yicheng District In Zaozhuang 枣庄市峄城区白云石矿(1994)	Zibo 淄博市	Shandong 山东省	(0533)6686138 (0533)6680174	015	Limited-Liability 有限公司	49,536	612(19)	42,304	Hard Fire-resistant Clay硬质耐火粘土
Shandong Zhongqi Refractory Material Co., Ltd. 山东中齐耐火材料有限公司(2001)	Zhenjiang 镇江市	Jiangsu 江苏省	(0511)3361259 (0511)3361261	207	State-owned 国有企业	42,023	50(32)	7,825	Dolomite 白云石

Top 10 Cities by Revenue 销售收入排名前10位城市	Province 省	Market share 市场份额 (%)	Number of firms 企业个数
Zhaoqing 肇庆市	Guangdong 广东省	20.04	1
Anshan 鞍山市	Liaoning 辽宁省	10.07	1
Yueyang 岳阳市	Hunan 湖南省	9.91	2
Xuchang 许昌市	Henan 河南省	7.53	1
Zhenjiang 镇江市	Jiangsu 江苏省	7.23	3
Nanjing 南京市	Jiangsu 江苏省	6.46	1
Zhengzhou 郑州市	Henan 河南省	5.07	2
Jinzhong 晋中市	Shanxi 山西省	4.93	2
Heyuan 河源市	Guangdong 广东省	4.39	2
Zibo 淄博市	Shandong 山东省	3.90	2

10 Major Wholesalers 十家主要批发商	City 城市	Province 省	Telephone/Fax 电话/传真
China Railway Materials Beijing Company 中国铁路物资北京公司	Beijing 北京市	Beijing 北京市	(010)63602299 (010)63601722
Shanghai BM Import & Export Co., Ltd. 上海宝矿进出口有限公司	Shanghai 上海市	Shanghai 上海市	(021)50320000 (021)50326700
Citic Trading Co.,Ltd. 中信贸易公司	Beijing 北京市	Beijing 北京市	(010)84865638 (010)84865271
Qingdao Iron And Steel Import & Export Corp. 青岛钢铁进出口公司	Qingdao 青岛市	Shandong 山东省	(0532)5798210 (0532)5798069
Guangzhou Metals and Minerals Import & Export .Ltd. 广州五金矿产进出口有限公司	Guangzhou 广州市	Guangdong 广东省	(020)81082026 (020)81084886
Shanghai Foreign Economics Trading Development Company 上海外经贸发展公司	Shanghai 上海市	Shanghai 上海市	(021)62719538 (021)62729625
China Nonferrous Metal Import & Export Jiangsu Company 中国有色金属进出口江苏公司	Nanjing 南京市	Jiangsu 江苏省	(025)4400366 (025)4400773
China Hardware Minerals Import & Export Shenzhen Branch Company 中国五金矿产进出口深圳分公司	Shenzhen 深圳市	Guangdong 广东省	(0755)82388365 (0755)82388335
Guangdong Dongfang Import & Export Corp. 广东省东方进出口公司	Shenzhen 深圳市	Guangdong 广东省	(0755)25950270 (0755)25950220
Shannxi Import & Export Corp. 陕西省进出口公司	Xi'an 西安市	Shannxi 陕西省	(029)6520075 (029)6511071

1019: Other Clay, Sand and Stone Mining 其他土砂石开采业

The industry accounts for 0.055% of the total revenue of China's industrial sector in 2002. The rate of return on assets is 7.83%. 89.67% of all firms in the industry made a profit while 10.33% had negative returns.The top province in terms of the industry's revenue is Jiangsu, accounting for 19.61% of the total revenue.
2002年本行业收入占全行业的 0.055%，资产利润率为 7.83%。89.67%的企业赢利，10.33%的企业亏损。收入最高的省为江苏省，占本行业的19.61%。

	Total number of firms 企业总数	Total number of employees 职工总数	Total revenue (Mil.RMB) 总销售收入 (百万元)	Total profit (Mil.RMB) 总利润 (百万元)	Return on assets 资产利润率 (%)	Return on equity 权益利润率 (%)	Labour productivity ('000 RMB/ worker) 劳动生产率 (千元/人)	Debts/ assets 资产负债率 (%)	Total assets (Mil.RMB) 总资产 (百万元)
Industry Overall 行业总体	368	51,727	5,914	260	7.83	15.44	36.18	49.31	3,317

	Number of firms 企业个数	Average number of employees 平均职工人数	Average revenue ('000 RMB) 平均销售收入 (千元)	Average profit ('000 RMB) 平均利润 (千元)	Return on assets 资产利润率 (%)	Return on equity 权益利润率 (%)	Labour productivity ('000 RMB/ worker) 劳动生产率 (千元/人)	Debts/ assets 资产负债率 (%)	Average total assets ('000 RMB) 平均总资产 (千元)
By ownership 产业所有权									
State-owned 国有	49	106	3,621	-50	-0.39	-0.93	22.38	57.62	12,563
Collective-owned 集体	142	146	16,782	985	17.32	32.11	35.17	46.06	5,685
Foreign & Overseas Chinese Funded 三资	15	83	24,313	-257	-1.00	-2.16	77.06	53.94	25,814
By regional distribution 地区分布									
Central-North 华北	32	89	10,177	855	9.08	20.79	42.02	56.31	9,413
Beijing 北京	5	33	12,680	1,102	31.27	40.00	74.40	21.82	3,523
Tianjin 天津	5	61	4,007	388	4.30	5.82	56.74	26.16	9,033
Hebei 河北	14	80	13,254	1,189	15.83	87.62	60.53	81.93	7,508
Shanxi 山西	3	85	1,840	-497	-4.80	-11.37	7.06	57.75	10,340
Inner Mongolia 内蒙古	5	202	10,231	951	4.65	9.08	20.46	48.81	20,462
Northeast 东北	26	128	9,510	574	8.28	20.13	33.89	58.88	6,936
Liaoning 辽宁	15	137	4,452	-17	-0.32	-0.72	13.91	55.66	5,393
Jilin 吉林	6	164	19,514	1,570	11.10	27.81	68.73	60.08	14,137
Heilongjiang 黑龙江	5	55	12,678	1,153	39.45	130.22	58.73	69.70	2,923
Central-East 华东	123	185	22,938	901	7.47	14.68	36.18	49.12	12,059
Shanghai 上海									
Jiangsu 江苏	41	221	28,288	945	14.37	23.23	35.23	38.14	6,579
Zhejiang 浙江	15	118	10,764	678	6.91	16.31	29.13	57.65	9,811
Anhui 安徽	20	191	14,867	539	5.27	8.60	25.89	38.66	10,228
Fujian 福建	15	96	14,288	161	1.05	1.36	41.19	22.52	15,300
Jiangxi 江西	13	87	9,924	251	1.17	7.47	12.33	84.34	21,494
Shandong 山东	19	290	45,232	2,391	12.87	25.45	50.75	49.42	18,575
Central-South 中南	136	142	16,367	671	7.62	14.25	36.36	46.55	8,807
Henan 河南	31	196	18,426	1,639	20.45	30.60	32.03	33.17	8,014
Hubei 湖北	41	151	14,282	636	7.81	12.35	34.67	36.77	8,143
Hunan 湖南	15	98	14,314	585	14.66	30.90	47.74	52.54	3,990
Guangdong 广东	40	123	20,073	136	1.20	2.92	40.83	59.03	11,360
Guangxi 广西	7	82	3,829	-86	-1.47	-4.63	16.22	68.37	5,888
Hainan 海南	2	65	12,379	377	1.26	2.13	110.35	40.82	29,977
Southwest 西南	9	73	12,240	683	18.86	34.90	57.77	45.94	3,621
Chongqing 重庆	2	140	15,530	397	66.22	108.92	22.31	39.20	600
Sichuan 四川	5	62	13,593	243	5.03	11.81	87.26	57.44	4,841
Guizhou 贵州									
Yunnan 云南	2	33	5,568	2,069	57.55	62.80	70.62	8.35	3,594
Tibet 西藏									
Northwest 西北	42	67	4,364	218	7.54	14.58	26.60	48.30	2,893
Shaanxi 陕西	4	82	5,784	119	3.30	7.26	25.77	54.55	3,616
Gansu 甘肃	38	65	4,214	228	8.11	15.43	26.71	47.45	2,817
Qinghai 青海									
Ningxia 宁夏									
Xinjiang 新疆									

1019: Other Clay, Sand and Stone Mining 其他土砂石开采业

Year 年份	Number of firms 企业个数	Rate of change 变化率 (%)	Number of employees 职工人数 (人)	Rate of change 变化率 (%)	Total revenue (Mil. RMB) 总销售收入 (百万元)	Rate of change 变化率 (%)	Total profit (Mil RMB) 总利润 (百万元)	Rate of change 变化率 (%)
2000	381		47,489		4,852		210	
2001	356	-6.56	49,208	3.62	4,694	-3.26	230	9.52
2002	368	3.37	51,727	5.12	5,914	25.99	260	13.04

Major Products 主要产品	Output 产量	Unit 单位

10 Main Firms with Maximal Revenue (year founded) 收入最大的十家主要企业（创办年份）	City 城市	Province 省	Telephone/ fax 电话/传真	Number of employees 职工人数	Ownership 产业所有权	Revenue ('000 RMB) 销售收入 (千元)	Profit('000 RMB) (rank) 利润(千元) (排名)	Total assets ('000 RMB) 总资产 (千元)	Major products 主要产品
Suyu County Shiling Yellow Sand Managing Station	Suqian	Jiangsu	(0527)4881602		Private Enterprises				Yellow Grit
宿豫县侍岭黄砂管理站(1994)	宿迁市	江苏省		1,800	私营独资	119,600	4,611(9)	6,130	黄砂
Shandong Hongxing General (Group) Corp.	Yantai	Shandong	(0535)2571053		Limited-Liability				Fluorite
山东宏兴集团总公司(1979)	烟台市	山东省	(0535)2571051	438	有限公司	95,760	4,901(8)	62,079	萤石
Zhongmo Zheng'an Moulding Sand Co., Ltd.	Zhengzhou	Henan	(0371)2262026		Private Enterprises				Scrub Grit
中牟县郑庵型砂有限公司(2001)	郑州市	河南省	(0371)2261222	520	私营独资	94,755	3,973(13)	24,311	擦洗砂
Shandong Changyi Quartz Ore Sand Factory	Weifang	Shandong	(0536)7722360		Overseas Chinese-funded				Quartz Grit
山东省昌邑市石英矿砂厂(1994)	潍坊市	山东省	(0536)7722973	250	港澳台资	94,100	8,510(2)	28,330	石英砂
Guangzhou Conghua Ceramics Raw Stuff Co., Ltd.	Guangzhou	Guangdong	(020)87875208		Overseas Chinese-funded				Ceramics Raw Materials
广州市从华陶瓷原料有限公司(1992)	广州市	广东省	(020)87875208	300	港澳台资	79,102	3,322(18)	53,000	陶瓷原料
Jiangning Dongshan Mineral Products Factory	Nanjing	Jiangsu	(025)2741787		Private Enterprises				Clay
江宁区东善矿产制品厂(1958)	南京市	江苏省	(025)2741787	479	私营独资	77,430	1,820(44)	12,260	粘土
Fuzhou Yonghui Sandstone Co., Ltd.	Fuzhou	Fujian	(0591)7617097		Overseas Chinese-funded				River Sand
福州永辉砂石有限公司(1999)	福州市	福建省	(0591)7608717	31	港澳台资	61,796	-	6,430	河沙
Ganyu Chengtou Yellow Sand Company	Lianyungang	Jiangsu	(0518)6561437		Collective-owned				Yellow Grit
赣榆县城头镇黄砂公司(1983)	连云港市	江苏省		325	集体企业	60,160	980(83)	1,730	黄砂
Hukou Rivers and lakes Sand Co., Ltd.	Jiujiang	Jiangxi	(0792)6310518		Limited-Liability				River Sand
湖口县江湖河砂有限责任公司(2001)	九江市	江西省		224	有限公司	46,931	2,326(30)	22,228	河砂
Hailin Xinhai Quartz Sand Factory	Mudanjiang	Heilongjiang	(0453)7235710		Collective-owned				Quartz Grit Power
海林市新海石英砂厂(1995)	牡丹江市	黑龙江省		140	集体企业	43,904	4,064(11)	5,443	石英砂粉

Top 10 Cities by Revenue 销售收入排名前10位城市	Province 省	Market share 市场份额 (%)	Number of firms 企业个数
Lianyungang 连云港市	Jiangsu 江苏省	7.35	11
Guangzhou 广州市	Guangdong 广东省	7.14	22
Suqian 宿迁市	Jiangsu 江苏省	5.86	11
Zhaoqing 肇庆市	Guangdong 广东省	4.75	10
Zaozhuang 枣庄市	Shandong 山东省	4.36	4
Jinan 济南市	Shandong 山东省	4.35	1
Nanjing 南京市	Jiangsu 江苏省	4.25	10
Zhengzhou 郑州市	Henan 河南省	3.86	5
Huanggang 黄冈市	Hubei 湖北省	3.64	16
Xinyang 信阳市	Henan 河南省	3.46	13

10 Major Wholesalers 十家主要批发商	City 城市	Province 省	Telephone/Fax 电话/传真
China Railway Materials Beijing Company	Beijing	Beijing	(010)63602299
中国铁路物资北京公司	北京市	北京市	(010)63601722
Shanghai BM Import & Export Co., Ltd.	Shanghai	Shanghai	(021)50320000
上海宝矿进出口有限公司	上海市	上海市	(021)50326700
Citic Trading Co.,Ltd.	Beijing	Beijing	(010)84865638
中信贸易公司	北京市	北京市	(010)84865271
Qingdao Iron And Steel Import & Export Corp.	Qingdao	Shandong	(0532)5798210
青岛钢铁进出口公司	青岛市	山东省	(0532)5798069
Guangzhou Metals and Minerals Import & Export .Ltd.	Guangzhou	Guangdong	(020)81082026
广州五金矿产进出口有限公司	广州市	广东省	(020)81084886
Shanghai Foreign Economics Trading Development Company	Shanghai	Shanghai	(021)62719538
上海外经贸发展公司	上海市	上海市	(021)62729625
China Nonferrous Metal Import & Export Jiangsu Company	Nanjing	Jiangsu	(025)4400366
中国有色金属进出口江苏公司	南京市	江苏省	(025)4400773
China Hardware Minerals Import & Export Shenzhen Branch Company	Shenzhen	Guangdong	(0755)82388365
中国五金矿产进出口深圳分公司	深圳市	广东省	(0755)82388335
Guangdong Dongfang Import & Export Corp.	Shenzhen	Guangdong	(0755)25950270
广东省东方进出口公司	深圳市	广东省	(0755)25950220
Shannxi Import & Export Corp.	Xi'an	Shannxi	(029)6520075
陕西省进出口公司	西安市	陕西省	(029)6511071

1021: Sulfur Ores Mining and Dressing 硫矿采选业

The industry accounts for 0.005% of the total revenue of China's industrial sector in 2002. The rate of return on assets is 0.41%. 56.25% of all firms in the industry made a profit while 43.75% had negative returns.The top province in terms of the industry's revenue is Tianjin, accounting for 47.05% of the total revenue.
2002年本行业收入占全行业的0.005%，资产利润率为0.41%。56.25%的企业赢利，43.75%的企业亏损。收入最高的省为天津市，占本行业的47.05%。

	Total number of firms 企业总数	Total number of employees 职工总数	Total revenue (Mil.RMB) 总销售收入（百万元）	Total profit (Mil.RMB) 总利润（百万元）	Return on assets 资产利润率（%）	Return on equity 权益利润率（%）	Labour productivity ('000 RMB/ worker) 劳动生产率（千元/人）	Debts/ assets 资产负债率（%）	Total assets (Mil.RMB) 总资产（百万元）
Industry Overall 行业总体	32	11,648	540	7	0.41	1.04	12.56	60.88	1,789

	Number of firms 企业个数	Average number of employees 平均职工人数	Average revenue ('000 RMB) 平均销售收入（千元）	Average profit ('000 RMB) 平均利润（千元）	Return on assets 资产利润率（%）	Return on equity 权益利润率（%）	Labour productivity ('000 RMB/ worker) 劳动生产率（千元/人）	Debts/ assets 资产负债率（%）	Average total assets ('000 RMB) 平均总资产（千元）
By ownership 产业所有权									
State-owned 国有	22	426	10,221	-585	-0.92	-2.08	8.47	56.05	63,884
Collective-owned 集体	5	229	7,075	472	5.01	12.00	11.62	58.27	9,437
Foreign & Overseas Chinese Funded 三资	1	80	14,530	120	1.80	3.29	23.75	45.11	6,650
By regional distribution 地区分布									
Central-North 华北	6	230	42,803	2,875	6.00	70.51	35.12	91.49	47,917
Beijing 北京									
Tianjin 天津	1	820	254,210	18,230	7.24	99.84	57.33	92.75	251,950
Hebei 河北									
Shanxi 山西	5	112	521	-197	-2.76	-15.86	2.54	82.56	7,111
Inner Mongolia 内蒙古									
Northeast 东北	4	390	6,499	-1,449	-3.13	-66.17	6.04	95.27	46,256
Liaoning 辽宁	3	504	7,623	-1,961	-3.25	-102.22	5.63	96.82	60,393
Jilin 吉林	1	50	3,125	90	2.34	3.00	18.50	21.96	3,844
Heilongjiang 黑龙江									
Central-East 华东	5	253	7,486	-166	-0.38	-1.08	11.14	64.59	43,300
Shanghai 上海									
Jiangsu 江苏	1	845	17,730	-720	-0.75	-2.51	6.05	70.18	96,090
Zhejiang 浙江									
Anhui 安徽	3	130	6,458	-37	-0.12	-0.24	22.43	49.85	30,910
Fujian 福建									
Jiangxi 江西	1	28	329				7.00	94.56	27,677
Shandong 山东									
Central-South 中南	10	587	19,796	135	0.14	0.24	11.44	43.27	97,669
Henan 河南	2	60	11,725	790	16.20	23.39	34.75	30.75	4,878
Hubei 湖北									
Hunan 湖南	3	73	3,847	-25	-0.12	-0.21	15.71	45.25	21,734
Guangdong 广东	2	2,649	76,509	128	0.03	0.05	10.76	42.51	442,378
Guangxi 广西	3	78	3,318	-137	-2.42	-13.53	10.83	82.10	5,658
Hainan 海南									
Southwest 西南	6	243	3,600	-759	-4.44	-13.34	4.18	66.74	17,102
Chongqing 重庆									
Sichuan 四川	2	462	8,599	-1,592	-3.50	-8.35	4.89	58.04	45,442
Guizhou 贵州	2	186	1,132	-166	-6.73		1.33	236.00	2,460
Yunnan 云南	1	98	1,163	-1,448	-25.29	-87.12	4.51	70.97	5,725
Tibet 西藏	1	63	976	411	37.85	39.90	10.13	5.16	1,086
Northwest 西北	1	115	486	-144	-0.70	-8.12	9.62	91.42	20,665
Shaanxi 陕西	1	115	486	-144	-0.70	-8.12	9.62	91.42	20,665
Gansu 甘肃									
Qinghai 青海									
Ningxia 宁夏									
Xinjiang 新疆									

1021: Sulfur Ores Mining and Dressing 硫矿采选业

Year 年份	Number of firms 企业个数	Rate of change 变化率 (%)	Number of employees 职工人数 (人)	Rate of change 变化率 (%)	Total revenue (Mil. RMB) 总销售收入 (百万元)	Rate of change 变化率 (%)	Total profit (Mil RMB) 总利润 (百万元)	Rate of change 变化率 (%)
2000	53		25,047		540		-47	
2001	44	-16.98	14,899	-40.52	634	17.41	8	-
2002	32	-27.27	11,648	-21.82	540	-14.83	7	-12.50

Major Products 主要产品	Output 产量	Unit 单位
Sulfuric Acid(Converting into 100%) 硫酸（折１００％）	2,967	10,000 Tons 万吨
Pyrite (Convert into Containing S 35%) 硫铁矿（折含S 35%）	926	10,000 Tons 万吨

10 Main Firms with Maximal Revenue (year founded) 收入最大的十家主要企业（创办年份）	City 城市	Province 省	Telephone/fax 电话/传真	Number of employees 职工人数	Ownership 产业所有权	Revenue ('000 RMB) 销售收入 (千元)	Profit('000 RMB) (rank) 利润(千元) (排名)	Total assets ('000 RMB) 总资产 (千元)	Major products 主要产品
Tianjin Rongcheng Iron And Steel Co.,ltd.	Tianjin	Tianjin	(022)28697317		Private Partnership				Pig Iron
天津市荣程钢铁有限公司(2001)	天津市	天津市	(022)28691473	820	私营合伙	254,210	18,230(1)	251,950	生铁
Yunfu Sulfurous Iron Ore Enterprise Group Corp	yunfu	Guangdong	(0766)8825123		State-owned				Sulfurous Iron Ore
云浮硫铁矿企业集团公司	云浮市	广东省	(0766)8828210	5,287	国有企业	153,018	255(5)	884,434	硫铁矿
Nanjing Yuntaishan Sulfurous Iron Mine	Nanjing	Jiangsu	(025)6161993		State-owned				Sulfurous Iron Ore
南京云台山硫铁矿(1959)	南京市	江苏省	(025)6161992	845	国有企业	17,730	-	96,090	硫铁矿
Tianquan Erlangshan Enterprise Group Company	Yaan	Sichuan	(0835)7222012		State-owned				Sulfurous Iron Ore
四川省天全县二郎山企业集团公司(1994)	雅安市	四川省	(0835)7222012	427	国有企业	15,931	-	75,761	硫铁矿
Fushun Hongtoushan Copper Mine Service Co.	Fushun	Liaoning	(0413)3368429		Collective-owned				Sulfurous Iron Ore
抚顺红透山铜矿服务公司(1978)	抚顺市	辽宁省	(0413)3265524	850	集体企业	15,431	16(9)	28,921	硫铁矿
Lingbao Linghua Group Tonggou Gold Yinjiagou Branch	Sanmenxia	Henan	(0398)6810971		Collective-owned				Sulfur Ore
灵宝市灵化集团桐沟金矿银家沟分矿(2000)	三门峡市	河南省		40	集体企业	8,920	1,460(2)	3,105	硫矿石
Xuanchen City Xuanzhou District Sulfurous Iron Mine	Xuancheng	Anhui	(0563)3418145		State Enterprises				Sulfurous Iron Ore
Co., Ltd.宣城市宣州区硫铁矿有限公司(1957)	宣城市	安徽省	(0563)3418238	165	国有独资	7,883	-	22,259	硫铁矿
Anhui Qingyang Sulfurous Iron Mine	Chizhou	Anhui	(0566)5760209		State-owned				Sulfurous Iron Ore
安徽省青阳县硫铁矿(1980)	池州市	安徽省		98	国有企业	6,443	2(11)	59,541	硫铁矿
Tongling Xinqiao Sulfurous Iron Mine	Tongling	Anhui	(0562)8701441		Collective-owned				Sulfurous Mine
铜陵县新桥硫铁矿(1989)	铜陵市	安徽省		128	集体企业	5,047	355(4)	10,931	硫矿
Dandong Zhangjiagou Pyrites	Dandong	Liaoning	(0415)8591089		State-owned				Sulphuric Acid
丹东张家沟硫化铁矿(1958)	丹东市	辽宁省		340	国有企业	4,271	-	111,660	硫酸

Top 10 Cities by Revenue 销售收入排名前10位城市	Province 省	Market share 市场份额 (%)	Number of firms 企业个数
Tianjin 天津市	Tianjin 天津市	47.05	1
Yunfu 云浮市	Guangdong 广东省	28.32	1
Sanmenxia 三门峡市	Henan 河南省	4.34	2
Nanjing 南京市	Jiangsu 江苏省	3.28	1
Yaan 雅安市	Sichuan 四川省	2.95	1
Fushun 抚顺市	Liaoning 辽宁省	2.86	1
Xuancheng 宣城市	Anhui 安徽省	1.46	1
Baise 百色市	Guangxi 广西	1.24	1
Chizhou 池州市	Anhui 安徽省	1.19	1
Hengyang 衡阳市	Hunan 湖南省	1.15	1

10 Major Wholesalers 十家主要批发商	City 城市	Province 省	Telephone/Fax 电话/传真
China Railway Materials Beijing Company	Beijing	Beijing	(010)63602299
中国铁路物资北京公司	北京市	北京市	(010)63601722
Shanghai BM Import & Export Co., Ltd.	Shanghai	Shanghai	(021)50320000
上海宝矿进出口有限公司	上海市	上海市	(021)50326700
Citic Trading Co.,Ltd.	Beijing	Beijing	(010)84865638
中信贸易公司	北京市	北京市	(010)84865271
Qingdao Iron And Steel Import & Export Corp.	Qingdao	Shandong	(0532)5798210
青岛钢铁进出口公司	青岛市	山东省	(0532)5798069
Guangzhou Metals and Minerals Import & Export .Ltd.	Guangzhou	Guangdong	(020)81082026
广州五金矿产进出口有限公司	广州市	广东省	(020)81084886
Shanghai Foreign Economics Trading Development Company	Shanghai	Shanghai	(021)62719538
上海外经贸发展公司	上海市	上海市	(021)62729625
China Nonferrous Metal Import & Export Jiangsu Company	Nanjing	Jiangsu	(025)4400366
中国有色金属进出口江苏公司	南京市	江苏省	(025)4400773
China Hardware Minerals Import & Export Shenzhen Branch Company	Shenzhen	Guangdong	(0755)82388365
中国五金矿产进出口深圳分公司	深圳市	广东省	(0755)82388335
Guangdong Dongfang Import & Export Corp.	Shenzhen	Guangdong	(0755)25950270
广东省东方进出口公司	深圳市	广东省	(0755)25950220
Shannxi Import & Export Corp.	Xi'an	Shannxi	(029)6520075
陕西省进出口公司	西安市	陕西省	(029)6511071

1022: Phosphorus Ores Mining and Dressing 磷矿采选业

The industry accounts for 0.038% of the total revenue of China's industrial sector in 2002. The rate of return on assets is -0.26%. 64.47% of all firms in the industry made a profit while 35.53% had negative returns.The top province in terms of the industry's revenue is Guizhou, accounting for 56.87% of the total revenue.
2002年本行业收入占全行业的0.038%，资产利润率为-0.26%。64.47%的企业赢利，35.53%的企业亏损。收入最高的省为贵州省，占本行业的56.87%。

	Total number of firms 企业总数	Total number of employees 职工总数	Total revenue (Mil.RMB) 总销售收入(百万元)	Total profit (Mil.RMB) 总利润(百万元)	Return on assets 资产利润率(%)	Return on equity 权益利润率(%)	Labour productivity ('000 RMB/worker) 劳动生产率(千元/人)	Debts/assets 资产负债率(%)	Total assets (Mil.RMB) 总资产(百万元)
Industry Overall 行业总体	76	53,501	4,056	-47	-0.26	-0.64	24.64	59.87	18,181

	Number of firms 企业个数	Average number of employees 平均职工人数	Average revenue ('000 RMB) 平均销售收入(千元)	Average profit ('000 RMB) 平均利润(千元)	Return on assets 资产利润率(%)	Return on equity 权益利润率(%)	Labour productivity ('000 RMB/worker) 劳动生产率(千元/人)	Debts/assets 资产负债率(%)	Average total assets ('000 RMB) 平均总资产(千元)
By ownership 产业所有权									
State-owned 国有	22	1,212	124,738	-751	-0.14	-0.24	28.26	40.79	526,549
Collective-owned 集体	11	300	21,191	1,406	6.46	18.86	21.04	65.73	21,752
Foreign & Overseas Chinese Funded 三资	1	46	9,163	-623	-2.53		99.67	130.53	24,601
By regional distribution 地区分布									
Central-North 华北	1	1,312	105,645	530	0.07	0.09	37.97	19.04	741,688
Beijing 北京									
Tianjin 天津									
Hebei 河北	1	1,312	105,645	530	0.07	0.09	37.97	19.04	741,688
Shanxi 山西									
Inner Mongolia 内蒙古									
Northeast 东北									
Liaoning 辽宁									
Jilin 吉林									
Heilongjiang 黑龙江									
Central-East 华东	4	915	24,985	-837	-1.35	-11.43	11.12	88.20	62,041
Shanghai 上海									
Jiangsu 江苏	2	1,637	47,424	-1,023	-0.97	-5.80	11.80	83.34	105,919
Zhejiang 浙江									
Anhui 安徽	1	48	2,865	-113	-3.25	-62.78	18.77	94.83	3,480
Fujian 福建									
Jiangxi 江西	1	340	2,228	-1,188	-3.62		3.52	118.89	32,845
Shandong 山东									
Central-South 中南	40	519	20,096	-1,613	-1.04	-35.52	18.56	97.08	155,334
Henan 河南									
Hubei 湖北	36	555	21,870	-1,752	-1.05	-40.44	18.99	97.41	167,323
Hunan 湖南	3	222	4,996	-441	-0.71	-5.61	8.92	87.43	62,493
Guangdong 广东									
Guangxi 广西	1	140	1,526	-130	-5.71	-6.13	3.19	6.85	2,276
Hainan 海南									
Southwest 西南	30	914	101,483	811	0.22	0.38	30.64	40.89	365,390
Chongqing 重庆									
Sichuan 四川	8	761	43,514	1,461	1.61	5.25	20.62	69.38	90,859
Guizhou 贵州	13	1,166	177,408	2,536	0.37	0.62	39.87	39.71	678,372
Yunnan 云南	9	688	43,343	-2,259	-1.44	-2.16	17.88	33.59	157,333
Tibet 西藏									
Northwest 西北	1	321	1,841	-3,739	-23.83	-83.27	5.20	71.38	15,691
Shaanxi 陕西	1	321	1,841	-3,739	-23.83	-83.27	5.20	71.38	15,691
Gansu 甘肃									
Qinghai 青海									
Ningxia 宁夏									
Xinjiang 新疆									

1022: Phosphorus Ores Mining and Dressing 磷矿采选业

Year 年份	Number of firms 企业个数	Rate of change 变化率 (%)	Number of employees 职工人数 (人)	Rate of change 变化率 (%)	Total revenue (Mil. RMB) 总销售收入 (百万元)	Rate of change 变化率 (%)	Total profit (Mil RMB) 总利润 (百万元)	Rate of change 变化率 (%)
2000	87		57,233		2,596		-151	
2001	77	-11.49	56,676	-0.97	3,203	23.38	-29	80.79
2002	76	-1.30	53,501	-5.60	4,056	26.63	-47	-62.07

Major Products 主要产品	Output 产量	Unit 单位
Phosphorite Ore(Convert into Containing P2O5 30%) 磷矿石（折含P2O5 30%）	2,301	10,000 Tons 万吨

10 Main Firms with Maximal Revenue (year founded) 收入最大的十家主要企业（创办年份）	City 城市	Province 省	Telephone/fax 电话/传真	Number of employees 职工人数	Ownership 产业所有权	Revenue ('000 RMB) 销售收入 (千元)	Profit('000 RMB) (rank) 利润(千元) (排名)	Total assets ('000 RMB) 总资产 (千元)	Major products 主要产品
Guizhou Hongfu Industrial Development General Co., Ltd.	Qiannan	Guizhou	(0854)2184303		State-owned				Phosphoreted Ore
贵州宏福实业开发有限总公司(1991)	黔南州	贵州省	(0854)2444190	3,386	国有企业	1,226,596	9,775(3)	6,655,879	磷矿石
Guizhou Kai Lin (Group) Co., Ltd	Guiyang	Guizhou	(0851)5868485		State-owned				Phosphoreted Ore
贵州开磷(集团)有限责任公司(1995)	贵阳市	贵州省	(0851)5861104	7,282	国有企业	735,445	11,461(2)	1,809,189	磷矿石
Yunnan Phosphorus Chenicals Group Co., Ltd	Kunming	Yunnan	(0871)7888640		State-owned				Phosphoreted Ore
云南磷化学集团有限公司(1966)	昆明市	云南省	(0871)7896019	4,401	国有企业	222,041	-	1,101,879	磷矿石
Hebei Fanshan Phosphorus Mine	Zhangjiakou	Hebei	(0313)6750015		State-owned				Phosphoreted Ore
河北矾山磷矿(1997)	张家口市	河北省	(0313)6750688	1,312	国有企业	105,645	530(26)	741,688	磷矿石
GPCC Co.,Ltd.	Jingmen	Hubei	(0724)4890378		Limited-Liability				Phosphoreted Ore
湖北荆襄化工（集团）有限责任公司(1958)	荆门市	湖北省	(0724)4890748	12,467	有限公司	97,276	-	5,188,532	磷矿石
Sichuan Jinhe Phosphoreted Mine	Deyang	Sichuan	(0838)8808016		State-owned				Phosphoreted Ore
四川省金河磷矿(1961)	德阳市	四川省	(0838)8806481	1,507	国有企业	95,779	-	183,060	磷矿石
Guizhou Xifeng Phosphoreted Mine	Guiyang	Guizhou	(0851)7781070		State-owned				Phosphoreted Ore
贵州息烽磷矿(1964)	贵阳市	贵州省	(0851)7781077	530	国有企业	84,483	1,556(16)	74,125	磷矿石
Baokang Yaozhi River Phosphoreted Mine Co., Ltd.	Xiangfan	Hubei	(0710)5062018		Limited-Liability				Phosphoreted Ore
保康县尧治河磷矿有限责任公司(1997)	襄樊市	湖北省	(0710)5062157	41	有限公司	78,867	456(30)	25,707	磷矿石
Yichang Taoping River Chemical Industry Co., Ltd.	Yichang	Hubei	(0717)7822130		Limited-Liability				Phosphoreted Ore
宜昌桃坪河化工有限责任公司(1975)	宜昌市	湖北省	(0717)7829004	384	有限公司	70,256	2,602(9)	114,351	磷矿石
Sichuan Qingping Phosphoreted Mine	Deyang	Sichuan	(0838)6373020		State-owned				Phosphoreted Ore
四川省清平磷矿(1966)	德阳市	四川省	(0838)6373088	1,881	国有企业	56,621	501(27)	220,493	磷矿石

Top 10 Cities by Revenue 销售收入排名前10位城市	Province 省	Market share 市场份额 (%)	Number of firms 企业个数
Qiannan 黔南州	Guizhou 贵州省	33.07	5
Guiyang 贵阳市	Guizhou 贵州省	23.56	7
Yichang 宜昌市	Hubei 湖北省	11.98	15
Kunming 昆明市	Yunnan 云南省	9.62	9
Deyang 德阳市	Sichuan 四川省	8.14	5
Xiangfan 襄樊市	Hubei 湖北省	3.91	12
Jingmen 荆门市	Hubei 湖北省	3.14	6
Zhangjiakou 张家口市	Hebei 河北省	2.60	1
Lianyungang 连云港市	Jiangsu 江苏省	2.34	2
Leshan 乐山市	Sichuan 四川省	0.44	3

10 Major Wholesalers 十家主要批发商	City 城市	Province 省	Telephone/Fax 电话/传真
China Railway Materials Beijing Company	Beijing	Beijing	(010)63602299
中国铁路物资北京公司	北京市	北京市	(010)63601722
Shanghai BM Import & Export Co., Ltd.	Shanghai	Shanghai	(021)50320000
上海宝矿进出口有限公司	上海市	上海市	(021)50326700
Citic Trading Co.,Ltd.	Beijing	Beijing	(010)84865638
中信贸易公司	北京市	北京市	(010)84865271
Qingdao Iron And Steel Import & Export Corp.	Qingdao	Shandong	(0532)5798210
青岛钢铁进出口公司	青岛市	山东省	(0532)5798069
Guangzhou Metals and Minerals Import & Export .Ltd.	Guangzhou	Guangdong	(020)81082026
广州五金矿产进出口有限公司	广州市	广东省	(020)81084886
Shanghai Foreign Economics Trading Development Company	Shanghai	Shanghai	(021)62719538
上海外经贸发展公司	上海市	上海市	(021)62729625
China Nonferrous Metal Import & Export Jiangsu Company	Nanjing	Jiangsu	(025)4400366
中国有色金属进出口江苏公司	南京市	江苏省	(025)4400773
China Hardware Minerals Import & Export Shenzhen Branch Company	Shenzhen	Guangdong	(0755)82388365
中国五金矿产进出口深圳分公司	深圳市	广东省	(0755)82388335
Guangdong Dongfang Import & Export Corp.	Shenzhen	Guangdong	(0755)25950270
广东省东方进出口公司	深圳市	广东省	(0755)25950220
Shannxi Import & Export Corp.	Xi'an	Shannxi	(029)6520075
陕西省进出口公司	西安市	陕西省	(029)6511071

1029: Other Chemical Ores Mining and Dressing 其他化学矿采选业

The industry accounts for 0.020% of the total revenue of China's industrial sector in 2002. The rate of return on assets is 4.14%. 89.13% of all firms in the industry made a profit while 10.87% had negative returns.The top province in terms of the industry's revenue is Gansu, accounting for 49.64% of the total revenue.
2002年本行业收入占全行业的0.020%，资产利润率为4.14%。89.13%的企业赢利，10.87%的企业亏损。收入最高的省为甘肃省，占本行业的49.64%。

	Total number of firms 企业总数	Total number of employees 职工总数	Total revenue (Mil.RMB) 总销售收入 (百万元)	Total profit (Mil.RMB) 总利润 (百万元)	Return on assets 资产利润率 (%)	Return on equity 权益利润率 (%)	Labour productivity ('000 RMB/ worker) 劳动生产率 (千元/人)	Debts/ assets 资产负债率 (%)	Total assets (Mil.RMB) 总资产 (百万元)
Industry Overall 行业总体	46	24,857	2,112	251	4.14	8.62	25.91	51.97	6,056

	Number of firms 企业个数	Average number of employees 平均职工人数	Average revenue ('000 RMB) 平均销售收入 (千元)	Average profit ('000 RMB) 平均利润 (千元)	Return on assets 资产利润率 (%)	Return on equity 权益利润率 (%)	Labour productivity ('000 RMB/ worker) 劳动生产率 (千元/人)	Debts/ assets 资产负债率 (%)	Average total assets ('000 RMB) 平均总资产 (千元)
By ownership 产业所有权									
State-owned 国有	11	392	17,605	-26	-0.05	-0.21	18.37	74.82	48,615
Collective-owned 集体	8	210	22,329	3,951	19.41	36.40	43.49	46.66	20,354
Foreign & Overseas Chinese Funded 三资	4	87	7,152	236	0.76	2.01	28.72	61.97	30,906
By regional distribution 地区分布									
Central-North 华北	3	67	3,756	1,185	16.06	56.23	26.27	71.44	7,377
Beijing 北京	1	169	6,061	665	17.05	19.22	14.35	11.28	3,900
Tianjin 天津									
Hebei 河北									
Shanxi 山西									
Inner Mongolia 内蒙古	2	16	2,604	1,445	15.85	101.01	89.25	84.31	9,116
Northeast 东北	1	56						120.00	49,850
Liaoning 辽宁									
Jilin 吉林	1	56						120.00	49,850
Heilongjiang 黑龙江									
Central-East 华东	26	157	22,615	2,359	8.79	20.27	43.56	56.65	26,849
Shanghai 上海									
Jiangsu 江苏	3	351	71,792	18,049	20.18	37.36	75.36	45.98	89,420
Zhejiang 浙江	14	151	22,308	394	1.53	3.88	35.45	60.70	25,802
Anhui 安徽	1	130	4,350	-581	-15.59	-116.20	18.48	86.58	3,727
Fujian 福建	4	26	4,132	-15	-0.21	-0.62	38.74	65.89	6,885
Jiangxi 江西	2	273	14,107	832	5.81	535.05	20.95	98.91	14,318
Shandong 山东	2	58	5,610	328	7.54	11.82	41.37	36.20	4,343
Central-South 中南	10	331	29,190	4,304	4.58	9.76	47.75	53.04	93,929
Henan 河南	3	724	76,400	13,899	5.51	11.94	63.68	53.81	252,055
Hubei 湖北	1	113	14,668	30	0.07	0.07	37.81	4.20	42,974
Hunan 湖南	4	174	5,387	128	0.53	2.45	11.77	78.38	24,137
Guangdong 广东									
Guangxi 广西	2	164	13,246	403	1.85	2.70	21.87	31.65	21,800
Hainan 海南									
Southwest 西南	3	594	57,255	16,624	35.08	68.55	55.70	48.82	47,385
Chongqing 重庆	2	863	84,560	24,950	38.65	72.34	57.51	46.57	64,562
Sichuan 四川									
Guizhou 贵州									
Yunnan 云南	1	57	2,647	-27	-0.21	-0.72	1.07	71.11	13,033
Tibet 西藏									
Northwest 西北	3	5,146	349,814	31,018	2.21	4.44	13.23	50.15	1,401,586
Shaanxi 陕西									
Gansu 甘肃	2	7,690	524,321	46,528	2.21	4.44	13.24	50.15	2,102,380
Qinghai 青海	1	60	800				10.00		
Ningxia 宁夏									
Xinjiang 新疆									

1029: Other Chemical Ores Mining and Dressing 其他化学矿采选业

Year 年份	Number of firms 企业个数	Rate of change 变化率(%)	Number of employees 职工人数(人)	Rate of change 变化率(%)	Total revenue (Mil. RMB) 总销售收入(百万元)	Rate of change 变化率(%)	Total profit (Mil RMB) 总利润(百万元)	Rate of change 变化率(%)
2000	30		26,382		1,418		96	
2001	39	30.00	25,513	-3.29	1,566	10.44	150	56.25
2002	46	17.95	24,857	-2.57	2,112	34.87	251	67.33

Major Products 主要产品	Output 产量	Unit 单位

10 Main Firms with Maximal Revenue (year founded) 收入最大的十家主要企业（创办年份）	City 城市	Province 省	Telephone/fax 电话/传真	Number of employees 职工人数	Ownership 产业所有权	Revenue ('000 RMB) 销售收入(千元)	Profit('000 RMB) (rank) 利润(千元)(排名)	Total assets ('000 RMB) 总资产(千元)	Major products 主要产品
Gansu Yasheng Industrial (Group)Co., Ltd.	Lanzhou	Gansu	(0931)8474092		Joint Stock				Sulfurated Alkali
甘肃亚盛实业(集团)股份有限公司(1995)	兰州市	甘肃省	(0931)8455074	15,334	股份制	1,046,641	92955(1)	4,201,759	硫化碱
Zhejiang Centralflour Industries Group Co., Ltd.	Jinhua	Zhejiang	(0579)2312400		'rivate Owned				Fluorite Concentrated Powder
浙江中萤实业集团有限公司(1996)	金华市	浙江省	(0579)2311213	27	私营企业	121,187	12,286(7)	88,555	萤石精粉
Chongqing Dazu Celestite Mining Company	Chongqing	Chongqing	(023)43451525		Collective-owned				Celestite
重庆市大足天青石矿业公司(1987)	重庆市	重庆市	(023)43451525	928	集体企业	108,456	29,249(4)	74,285	天青石
Shanghai Pacific Ocean Chemical Industry Huai'an Anhydrous Sodium Sulfate Co.Ltd 上海太平洋化工淮安元明粉有限公司(1997)	Huaian	Jiangsu	(0517)4563463		Joint Stock				Anhydrous Sodium Sulfate
	淮安市	江苏省	(0517)4563463	286	股份制	93,690	33,160(3)	130,315	元明粉
Jiangsu Donghai Serpentine Mine	Lianyungang	Jiangsu	(0518)7692221		State-owned				Serpentine
江苏省东海蛇纹石矿(1965)	连云港市	江苏省	(0518)7692222	635	国有企业	61,722	1,315(10)	56,068	蛇纹石
Henan Nanyang Wucheng Saline-alkali Mine	Nanyang	Henan	(0377)8135686		State-owned				Heavy Soda Ash
河南省南阳吴城盐碱矿(1976)	南阳市	河南省	(0377)8135687	1,478	国有企业	61,185	4,850(8)	278,762	重质纯碱
Chongqing Tianqing Strontium Stock Co., Ltd.	Chongqing	Chongqing	(023)45682930		Joint Stock				Celestite
重庆天青锶化股份有限公司(1998)	重庆市	重庆市	(023)45682115	798	股份制	60,663	20,651(5)	54,838	天青石
Nanfeng Group Huai'an Anhydrous Sodium Sulfate Co., Ltd.	Huaian	Jiangsu	(0517)4565366		Joint Stock				Anhydrous Mirabilite
南风集团淮安元明粉有限公司(2001)	淮安市	江苏省	(0517)4565366	133	股份制	59,964	19,673(6)	81,876	无水芒硝
Jinhua Choiceness Mine Industry Co., Ltd.	Jinhua	Zhejiang	(0579)2273500		Private Owned				Fluorite
金华市精选矿业有限公司(1993)	金华市	浙江省	(0579)2273501	54	私营企业	51,682	637(17)	37,903	萤石矿
Fuyang Shunda Refine Mineral Fines Factory	Hangzhou	Zhejiang	(0571)63261117		Collective-owned				Calcite Powder
杭州富阳顺达钢球厂(1999)	杭州市	浙江省	(0571)63261108	70	集体企业	16,655	556(18)	14,314	方解石粉

Top 10 Cities by Revenue 销售收入排名前10位城市	Province 省	Market share 市场份额 (%)	Number of firms 企业个数
Lanzhou 兰州市	Gansu 甘肃省	49.55	1
Nanyang 南阳市	Henan 河南省	10.32	2
Jinhua 金华市	Zhejiang 浙江省	8.72	4
Chongqing 重庆市	Chongqing 重庆市	8.01	2
Huaian 淮安市	Jiangsu 江苏省	7.27	2
Lianyungang 连云港市	Jiangsu 江苏省	2.92	1
Wenzhou 温州市	Zhejiang 浙江省	2.08	1
Hangzhou 杭州市	Zhejiang 浙江省	1.93	4
Lishui 丽水市	Zhejiang 浙江省	1.61	4
Guilin 桂林市	Guangxi 广西	1.25	2

10 Major Wholesalers 十家主要批发商	City 城市	Province 省	Telephone/Fax 电话/传真
China Railway Materials Beijing Company	Beijing	Beijing	(010)63602299
中国铁路物资北京公司	北京市	北京市	(010)63601722
Shanghai BM Import & Export Co., Ltd.	Shanghai	Shanghai	(021)50320000
上海宝矿进出口有限公司	上海市	上海市	(021)50326700
Citic Trading Co.,Ltd.	Beijing	Beijing	(010)84865638
中信贸易公司	北京市	北京市	(010)84865271
Qingdao Iron And Steel Import & Export Corp.	Qingdao	Shandong	(0532)5798210
青岛钢铁进出口公司	青岛市	山东省	(0532)5798069
Guangzhou Metals and Minerals Import & Export .Ltd.	Guangzhou	Guangdong	(020)81082026
广州五金矿产进出口有限公司	广州市	广东省	(020)81084886
Shanghai Foreign Economics Trading Development Company	Shanghai	Shanghai	(021)62719538
上海外经贸发展公司	上海市	上海市	(021)62729625
China Nonferrous Metal Import & Export Jiangsu Company	Nanjing	Jiangsu	(025)4400366
中国有色金属进出口江苏公司	南京市	江苏省	(025)4400773
China Hardware Minerals Import & Export Shenzhen Branch Company	Shenzhen	Guangdong	(0755)82388365
中国五金矿产进出口深圳分公司	深圳市	广东省	(0755)82388335
Guangdong Dongfang Import & Export Corp.	Shenzhen	Guangdong	(0755)25950270
广东省东方进出口公司	深圳市	广东省	(0755)25950220
Shannxi Import & Export Corp.	Xi'an	Shannxi	(029)6520075
陕西省进出口公司	西安市	陕西省	(029)6511071

1031: Sea Salt Mining 海盐业

The industry accounts for 0.042% of the total revenue of China's industrial sector in 2002. The rate of return on assets is -0.09%. 67.54% of all firms in the industry made a profit while 32.46% had negative returns.The top province in terms of the industry's revenue is Shandong, accounting for 54.52% of the total revenue.
2002年本行业收入占全行业的0.042%，资产利润率为 -0.09%。67.54%的企业赢利，32.46%的企业亏损。收入最高的省为山东省，占本行业的54.52%。

	Total number of firms 企业总数	Total number of employees 职工总数	Total revenue (Mil.RMB) 总销售收入 (百万元)	Total profit (Mil.RMB) 总利润 (百万元)	Return on assets 资产利润率 (%)	Return on equity 权益利润率 (%)	Labour productivity ('000 RMB/ worker) 劳动生产率 (千元/人)	Debts/ assets 资产负债率 (%)	Total assets (Mil.RMB) 总资产 (百万元)
Industry Overall 行业总体	114	106,459	4,532	-15	-0.09	-0.25	20.09	63.04	16,243

	Number of firms 企业个数	Average number of employees 平均职工人数	Average revenue ('000 RMB) 平均销售收入（千元）	Average profit ('000 RMB) 平均利润 (千元)	Return on assets 资产利润率 (%)	Return on equity 权益利润率 (%)	Labour productivity ('000 RMB/ worker) 劳动生产率 (千元/人)	Debts/ assets 资产负债率 (%)	Average total assets ('000 RMB) 平均总资产 (千元)
By ownership 产业所有权									
State-owned 国有	66	787	19,991	-256	-0.30	-0.80	14.91	62.86	86,256
Collective-owned 集体	26	184	27,792	2,004	10.36	30.29	62.91	65.81	19,355
Foreign & Overseas Chinese Funded 三资	2	80	5,500	500	3.78	8.71	22.54	56.65	13,240
By regional distribution 地区分布									
Central-North 华北	21	1,479	49,703	-1,806	-0.71	-1.61	22.83	55.63	252,897
Beijing 北京									
Tianjin 天津	3	3,999	146,453	-3,788	-0.55	-1.24	21.69	55.39	683,549
Hebei 河北	18	1,059	33,578	-1,476	-0.81	-1.84	23.55	55.78	181,122
Shanxi 山西									
Inner Mongolia 内蒙古									
Northeast 东北	8	1,375	36,219	-10,005	-6.31	-60.61	9.68	89.58	158,444
Liaoning 辽宁	8	1,375	36,219	-10,005	-6.31	-60.61	9.68	89.58	158,444
Jilin 吉林									
Heilongjiang 黑龙江									
Central-East 华东	67	791	45,783	1,673	1.25	3.45	23.80	63.88	134,281
Shanghai 上海									
Jiangsu 江苏	11	1,920	45,357	-677	-0.41	-1.43	13.49	71.17	164,674
Zhejiang 浙江	5	159	4,754	1,077	3.33	4.77	23.23	30.28	32,380
Anhui 安徽									
Fujian 福建	11	815	6,727	-215	-1.49	-3.54	7.00	57.96	14,477
Jiangxi 江西									
Shandong 山东	40	552	61,769	2,914	1.70	4.57	40.48	62.88	171,607
Central-South 中南	18	635	7,273	-492	-1.33	-3.34	5.49	60.25	37,089
Henan 河南									
Hubei 湖北	1	277	27,847	515	1.51	10.44	49.39	85.51	34,058
Hunan 湖南									
Guangdong 广东	6	873	8,254	-1,002	-2.44	-9.68	4.87	74.83	41,134
Guangxi 广西	5	514	3,796	-666	-2.12	-3.19	4.35	33.60	31,393
Hainan 海南	6	559	5,760	-6	-0.01	-0.04	3.69	59.05	38,296
Southwest 西南									
Chongqing 重庆									
Sichuan 四川									
Guizhou 贵州									
Yunnan 云南									
Tibet 西藏									
Northwest 西北									
Shaanxi 陕西									
Gansu 甘肃									
Qinghai 青海									
Ningxia 宁夏									
Xinjiang 新疆									

Year 年份	Number of firms 企业个数	Rate of change 变化率 (%)	Number of employees 职工人数 (人)	Rate of change 变化率 (%)	Total revenue (Mil. RMB) 总销售收入 (百万元)	Rate of change 变化率 (%)	Total profit (Mil RMB) 总利润 (百万元)	Rate of change 变化率 (%)
2000	112		103,006		3,507		77	
2001	115	2.68	106,833	3.72	3,971	13.23	88	14.29
2002	114	-0.87	106,459	-0.35	4,532	14.13	-15	-

Major Products 主要产品	Output 产量	Unit 单位
Crude Salt 原盐	3,283	10,000 Tons 万吨

10 Main Firms with Maximal Revenue (year founded) 收入最大的十家主要企业（创办年份）	City 城市	Province 省	Telephone/fax 电话/传真	Number of employees 职工人数	Ownership 产业所有权	Revenue ('000 RMB) 销售收入 (千元)	Profit('000 RMB) (rank) 利润(千元) (排名)	Total assets ('000 RMB) 总资产 (千元)	Major products 主要产品
Shandong Haiyuan Salt Chemical Group Co.,Ltd.	Weifang	Shandong	(0536)5221807		Limited-Liability				Crude Salt
山东海源盐化集团有限责任公司(1998)	潍坊市	山东省	(0536)5223393	2,933	有限公司	357,601	10,138(7)	576,881	原盐
Hebei Nanbao Saltern	Tangshan	Hebei	(0315)8327163		State-owned				Crude Salt
河北省南堡盐场(1956)	唐山市	河北省	(0315)8515154	6,439	国有企业	267,339	17,600(2)	1,202,058	原盐
Tianjin Changlu Haijing Group Co.,Ltd.	Tianjin	Tianjin	(022)66887185		State Enterprises				Sea Salt
天津长芦海晶集团有限公司(1942)	天津市	天津市	(022)25895796	4,858	国有独资	244,688	-	1,398,804	海盐
Jiangsu Jinqiao Salt Industry Co., Ltd.	Lianyungang	Jiangsu	(0518)5411116		State Enterprises				Crude Salt
江苏省金桥盐业有限公司(1998)	连云港市	江苏省	(0518)5500426	10,694	国有独资	216,701	-	1,024,576	原盐
Tianjin Changlu Hangu Saltworks Co.,Ltd.	Tianjin	Tianjin	(022)67906509		State Enterprises				Sea Salt
天津长芦汉沽盐场有限责任公司(1948)	天津市	天津市	(022)67114997	6,973	国有独资	182,040	-	591,406	海盐
Wendeng Xiaoguan Saltern	Weihai	Shandong	(0631)8853807		Collective-owned				Sea Salt
文登市小观盐场(1974)	威海市	山东省		104	集体企业	169,120	11,620(5)	23,400	海盐
Jiangsu Yinbao Salt Industry Co., Ltd.	Yancheng	Jiangsu	(0515)8429085		State Enterprises				Crude Salt
江苏省银宝盐业有限公司(1998)	盐城市	江苏省	(0515)8429035	6,474	国有独资	132,060	-	558,430	原盐
Shandong Changyi Salt Chemical (Group) Co.,Ltd.	Weifang	Shandong	(0536)7211854		Limited-Liability				Crude Salt
山东昌邑盐化（集团）有限公司(1995)	潍坊市	山东省	(0536)7211455	943	有限公司	121,428	-	198,356	原盐
Wendeng Houjia Town Maidao Saltern	Weihai	Shandong	(0631)8727057		Collective-owned				Crude Salt
文登市侯家镇麦岛盐场(1975)	威海市	山东省		100	集体企业	114,370	11,710(4)	20,890	原盐
Shandong Caiyangzi Saltern	Weifang	Shandong	(0536)5342555		State-owned				Common Salt
山东菜央子盐场(1959)	潍坊市	山东省	(0536)5342555	913	国有企业	90,750	1,434(18)	178,357	食盐

Top 10 Cities by Revenue 销售收入排名前10位城市	Province 省	Market share 市场份额 (%)	Number of firms 企业个数
Weifang 潍坊市	Shandong 山东省	38.50	21
Tianjin 天津市	Tianjin 天津市	9.69	3
Weihai 威海市	Shandong 山东省	9.55	8
Tangshan 唐山市	Hebei 河北省	8.86	12
Lianyungang 连云港市	Jiangsu 江苏省	5.16	2
Yancheng 盐城市	Jiangsu 江苏省	4.92	6
Cangzhou 沧州市	Hebei 河北省	4.48	6
Yantai 烟台市	Shandong 山东省	3.95	6
Yingkou 营口市	Liaoning 辽宁省	2.91	2
Dalian 大连市	Liaoning 辽宁省	2.63	4

10 Major Wholesalers 十家主要批发商	City 城市	Province 省	Telephone/Fax 电话/传真
Guangdong Foodstuffs Import & Export Group Corporation	Guangzhou	Guangdong	(020)83854888
广东省食品进出口集团公司	广州市	广东省	(020)83856823
Hubei Salt Industry General Company	Wuhan	Hubei	(027)82832190
湖北盐业总公司	武汉市	湖北省	(027)82816030
Henan Provincial Salt Business Administration Bureau (Henan Provincial Salt Industry General Company)	Zhengzhou	Henan	(0371)5907597
河南省盐务管理局(河南省盐业总公司)	郑州市	河南省	(0371)5906346
Sichuan Salt Industry General Company	Chengdu	Sichuan	(028)86652441
四川省盐业总公司	成都市	四川省	(028)86663440
China National Salt Tianjin Changlu Salt Industry Co.,Ltd.	Tianjin	Tianjin	(022)23022160
中盐天津市长芦盐业有限公司	天津市	天津市	(022)23022110
Zhejiang Salt Industry Company	Hangzhou	Zhejiang	(0571)87800292
浙江省盐业公司	杭州市	浙江省	(0571)87800082
Fujian Salt Industry Company	Fuzhou	Fujian	(0591)7534344
福建省盐业公司	福州市	福建省	(0591)7535047
Jiangxi Salt Industry General Company	Nanchang	Jiangxi	(0791)6816695
江西省盐业总公司	南昌市	江西省	(0791)6812316
Hubei Salt Transportation & Sale Company	Xiaogan	Hubei	(0712)3611320
湖北省盐业运销公司	孝感市	湖北省	(0712)3611244
Hunan Salt Industry Group Co.,Ltd.Jinshi Allocation & Transportation Company	Changde	Hunan	(0736)4223817
湖南省盐业集团有限责任公司津市调运公司	常德市	湖南省	(0736)4223817

1032: Lake Salt Mining 湖盐业

The industry accounts for 0.006% of the total revenue of China's industrial sector in 2002. The rate of return on assets is 5.17%. 77.27% of all firms in the industry made a profit while 22.73% had negative returns.The top province in terms of the industry's revenue is Inner mongolia, accounting for 61.79% of the total revenue.
2002年本行业收入占全行业的 0.006%，资产利润率为 5.17%。77.27%的企业赢利，22.73%的企业亏损。收入最高的省为内蒙古，占本行业的61.79%。

	Total number of firms 企业总数	Total number of employees 职工总数	Total revenue (Mil.RMB) 总销售收入 (百万元)	Total profit (Mil.RMB) 总利润 (百万元)	Return on assets 资产利润率 (%)	Return on equity 权益利润率 (%)	Labour productivity ('000 RMB/ worker) 劳动生产率 (千元/人)	Debts/ assets 资产负债率 (%)	Total assets (Mil.RMB) 总资产 (百万元)
Industry Overall 行业总体	22	8,535	624	85	5.17	9.61	51.45	46.26	1,640

	Number of firms 企业个数	Average number of employees 平均职工人数	Average revenue ('000 RMB) 平均销售收入 (千元)	Average profit ('000 RMB) 平均利润 (千元)	Return on assets 资产利润率 (%)	Return on equity 权益利润率 (%)	Labour productivity ('000 RMB/ worker) 劳动生产率 (千元/人)	Debts/ assets 资产负债率 (%)	Average total assets ('000 RMB) 平均总资产 (千元)
By ownership 产业所有权									
State-owned 国有	11	282	14,966	1,304	4.42	13.48	30.48	67.18	29,478
Collective-owned 集体	1	120	2,018	47	0.92	1.59	16.63	42.21	5,129
Foreign & Overseas Chinese Funded 三资									
By regional distribution 地区分布									
Central-North 华北	7	593	55,129	11,439	6.12	10.43	79.11	41.29	186,786
Beijing 北京									
Tianjin 天津									
Hebei 河北									
Shanxi 山西									
Inner Mongolia 内蒙古	7	593	55,129	11,439	6.12	10.43	79.11	41.29	186,786
Northeast 东北									
Liaoning 辽宁									
Jilin 吉林									
Heilongjiang 黑龙江									
Central-East 华东									
Shanghai 上海									
Jiangsu 江苏									
Zhejiang 浙江									
Anhui 安徽									
Fujian 福建									
Jiangxi 江西									
Shandong 山东									
Central-South 中南									
Henan 河南									
Hubei 湖北									
Hunan 湖南									
Guangdong 广东									
Guangxi 广西									
Hainan 海南									
Southwest 西南									
Chongqing 重庆									
Sichuan 四川									
Guizhou 贵州									
Yunnan 云南									
Tibet 西藏									
Northwest 西北	15	292	15,906	310	1.40	4.09	25.27	65.78	22,164
Shaanxi 陕西	1	401	11,663	127	0.42	1.51	23.28	72.21	30,201
Gansu 甘肃	2	68	2,493	60	1.29	3.29	19.10	60.86	4,662
Qinghai 青海	4	527	23,201	-782	-1.70	-4.46	27.10	61.89	45,946
Ningxia 宁夏									
Xinjiang 新疆	8	218	16,142	942	6.90	23.79	23.99	70.98	13,644

Year 年份	Number of firms 企业个数	Rate of change 变化率 (%)	Number of employees 职工人数 (人)	Rate of change 变化率 (%)	Total revenue (Mil. RMB) 总销售收入 (百万元)	Rate of change 变化率 (%)	Total profit (Mil RMB) 总利润 (百万元)	Rate of change 变化率 (%)
2000	21		6,479		504		48	
2001	23	9.52	8,536	31.75	593	17.66	81	68.75
2002	22	-4.35	8,535	-0.01	624	5.23	85	4.94

Major Products 主要产品	Output 产量	Unit 单位
Crude Salt 原盐	3,283	10,000 Tons 万吨

10 Main Firms with Maximal Revenue (year founded) 收入最大的十家主要企业（创办年份）	City 城市	Province 省	Telephone/fax 电话/传真	Number of employees 职工人数	Ownership 产业所有权	Revenue ('000 RMB) 销售收入 (千元)	Profit('000 RMB) (rank) 利润(千元) (排名)	Total assets ('000 RMB) 总资产 (千元)	Major products 主要产品
Inner Mongolia Lantal Industrial Co.,Ltd.	Alashan	Inner Mongolia	(0483)8838044		Joint Stock				Crude Salt
内蒙古兰太实业股份有限公司(1953)	阿拉善	内蒙古	(0483)8838735	2,376	股份制	257,900	55,500(1)	1,043,000	原盐
Sinkiang Yanhu Salt Co., Ltd.	Urumqi	Xinjiang	(0991)5830075		Limited-Liability				Crude Salt
新疆盐湖制盐有限公司(2000)	乌鲁木齐市	新疆	(0991)5830377	637	有限公司	83,164	7,252(3)	49,779	原盐
Inner Mongolia Yili Science & Technology Industrial Co.,Ltd.Fushui	Eerduosi	Inner Mongolia	(0477)6881102		State-owned				Crude Salt
Fushui Branch内蒙古亿利科技实业股份有限公司富水分公司(1950)	鄂尔多斯市	内蒙古	(0477)6881102	87	国有企业	42,000	17,000(2)	70,424	原盐
Inner Mongolia Ya-Bu-Lai Salt Chemical Co., Ltd.	Alashan	Inner Mongolia	(0483)6452317		Joint Stock				Crude Salt
内蒙古雅布赖盐化有限责任公司(1908)	阿拉善	内蒙古	(0483)6452410	781	股份制	41,893	3,201(5)	77,186	原盐
A'zuoqi Hetunchi Salt Industry Co., Ltd.	Alashan	Inner Mongolia	(0483)8838745		Limited-Liability				Crude Salt
阿左旗和屯池盐业有限责任公司(1994)	阿拉善	内蒙古	(0483)8838651	192	有限公司	14,415	3,468(4)	19,297	原盐
Xilinguole Meng Eji'nao'er Saltern	Xilinguole	Inner Mongolia	(0479)3453018		State-owned				Crude Salt
锡盟额吉淖尔盐场(1946)	锡林郭勒	内蒙古	(0479)3453023	312	国有企业	11,696	515(7)	25,427	原盐
Dingbian Great Wall Salt Chemical Co., Ltd.	Yulin	Shannxi	(0912)4290046		State-owned				Lake Salt
定边县长城盐化有限责任公司(1960)	榆林市	陕西省		401	国有企业	11,663	127(12)	30,201	湖盐
Jinghe Jinghe Salt Chemical Co., Ltd.	Boertala	Xinjiang	(0909)5332228		Limited-Liability				Lake Salt
精河县精河盐化有限责任公司(1998)	博尔塔拉州	新疆	(0909)5332228	206	有限公司	9,301	-	16,723	湖盐
Hami Salt Industry Co., Ltd.	Hami	Xinjiang	(0902)2511213		Limited-Liability				Salt
哈密盐业有限责任公司(1995)	哈密	新疆	(0902)2513965	64	有限公司	7,381	295(9)	8,659	盐
Sinkiang Luntai Saltern	Bayinguoleng	Xinjiang	(0996)4698157		State-owned				Salt
新疆轮台县盐厂(1971)	巴音郭楞州	新疆	(0996)4698157	116	国有企业	4,294	56(14)	7,599	盐

Top 10 Cities by Revenue 销售收入排名前10位城市	Province 省	Market share 市场份额 (%)	Number of firms 企业个数
Alashan 阿拉善盟	Inner Mongolia 内蒙古	52.15	4
Haixi 海西州	Qinghai 青海省	14.67	2
Urumuqi 乌鲁木齐市	Xinjiang 新疆	13.32	1
Eerduosi 鄂尔多斯市	Inner Mongolia 内蒙古	7.77	2
Tacheng 塔城地区	Xinjiang 新疆	3.66	1
Xilinguole 锡林郭勒盟	Inner Mongolia 内蒙古	1.87	1
Yulin 榆林市	Shannxi 陕西省	1.87	1
Boertala 博尔塔拉州	Xinjiang 新疆	1.49	1
Hami 哈密地区	Xinjiang 新疆	1.18	1
Bayinguoleng 巴音郭楞州	Xinjiang 新疆	1.00	3

10 Major Wholesalers 十家主要批发商	City 城市	Province 省	Telephone/Fax 电话/传真
Guangdong Foodstuffs Import & Export Group Corporation	Guangzhou	Guangdong	(020)83854888
广东省食品进出口集团公司	广州市	广东省	(020)83856823
Hubei Salt Industry General Company	Wuhan	Hubei	(027)82832190
湖北盐业总公司	武汉市	湖北省	(027)82816030
Henan Provincial Salt Business Administration Bureau (Henan Provincial Salt Industry General Company)	Zhengzhou	Henan	(0371)5907597
河南省盐务管理局(河南省盐业总公司)	郑州市	河南省	(0371)5906346
Sichuan Salt Industry General Company	Chengdu	Sichuan	(028)86652441
四川省盐业总公司	成都市	四川省	(028)86663440
China National Salt Tianjin Changlu Salt Industry Co.,Ltd.	Tianjin	Tianjin	(022)23022160
中盐天津市长芦盐业有限公司	天津市	天津市	(022)23022110
Zhejiang Salt Industry Company	Hangzhou	Zhejiang	(0571)87800292
浙江省盐业公司	杭州市	浙江省	(0571)87800082
Fujian Salt Industry Company	Fuzhou	Fujian	(0591)7534344
福建省盐业公司	福州市	福建省	(0591)7535047
Jiangxi Salt Industry General Company	Nanchang	Jiangxi	(0791)6816695
江西省盐业总公司	南昌市	江西省	(0791)6812316
Hubei Salt Transportation & Sale Company	Xiaogan	Hubei	(0712)3611320
湖北省盐业运销公司	孝感市	湖北省	(0712)3611244
Hunan Salt Industry Group Co.,Ltd.Jinshi Allocation & Transportation Company	Changde	Hunan	(0736)4223817
湖南省盐业集团有限责任公司津市调运公司	常德市	湖南省	(0736)4223817

1033: Well Salt Mining 井盐业

The industry accounts for 0.011% of the total revenue of China's industrial sector in 2002. The rate of return on assets is 3.69%. 85.71% of all firms in the industry made a profit while 14.29% had negative returns.Thc top province in terms of the industry's revenue is Sichuan, accounting for 73.93% of the total revenue.
2002年本行业收入占全行业的0.011%，资产利润率为3.69%。85.71%的企业赢利，14.29%的企业亏损。收入最高的省为四川省，占本行业的73.93%。

	Total number of firms 企业总数	Total number of employees 职工总数	Total revenue (Mil.RMB) 总销售收入（百万元）	Total profit (Mil.RMB) 总利润（百万元）	Return on assets 资产利润率 (%)	Return on equity 权益利润率 (%)	Labour productivity ('000 RMB/ worker) 劳动生产率（千元/人）	Debts/ assets 资产负债率 (%)	Total assets (Mil.RMB) 总资产（百万元）
Industry Overall 行业总体	28	17,822	1,222	91	3.69	11.87	29.46	68.94	2,473

	Number of firms 企业个数	Average number of employees 平均职工人数	Average revenue ('000 RMB) 平均销售收入（千元）	Average profit ('000 RMB) 平均利润（千元）	Return on assets 资产利润率 (%)	Return on equity 权益利润率 (%)	Labour productivity ('000 RMB/ worker) 劳动生产率（千元/人）	Debts/ assets 资产负债率 (%)	Average total assets ('000 RMB) 平均总资产（千元）
By ownership 产业所有权									
State-owned 国有	9	378	13,665	478	1.30		18.71	102.65	36,786
Collective-owned 集体	2	160	9,524	700	5.51	44.40	32.57	87.58	12,696
Foreign & Overseas Chinese Funded 三资									
By regional distribution 地区分布									
Central-North 华北									
Beijing 北京									
Tianjin 天津									
Hebei 河北									
Shanxi 山西									
Inner Mongolia 内蒙古									
Northeast 东北									
Liaoning 辽宁									
Jilin 吉林									
Heilongjiang 黑龙江									
Central-East 华东	3	193	27,889	2,052	2.82	7.66	66.85	63.21	72,837
Shanghai 上海									
Jiangsu 江苏	2	141	29,008	1,264	1.34	3.49	71.04	61.72	94,628
Zhejiang 浙江									
Anhui 安徽									
Fujian 福建									
Jiangxi 江西									
Shandong 山东	1	299	25,652	3,629	12.40	45.59	62.91	72.79	29,256
Central-South 中南	2	252	3,831	-195	-0.95		5.86	104.69	20,595
Henan 河南	1	22	5,315	730	8.19	37.82	59.00	78.34	8,910
Hubei 湖北	1	481	2,346	-1,120	-3.47		3.43	111.96	32,280
Hunan 湖南									
Guangdong 广东									
Guangxi 广西									
Hainan 海南									
Southwest 西南	22	748	51,050	3,878	3.90	12.12	29.15	67.79	99,328
Chongqing 重庆	4	724	54,946	4,099	3.08	6.68	34.21	53.85	132,867
Sichuan 四川	18	753	50,184	3,829	4.17	15.03	28.07	72.27	91,875
Guizhou 贵州									
Yunnan 云南									
Tibet 西藏									
Northwest 西北	1	287	7,474	50	0.18		13.11	151.03	28,071
Shaanxi 陕西									
Gansu 甘肃	1	287	7,474	50	0.18		13.11	151.03	28,071
Qinghai 青海									
Ningxia 宁夏									
Xinjiang 新疆									

1033: Well Salt Mining 井盐业

Year 年份	Number of firms 企业个数	Rate of change 变化率(%)	Number of employees 职工人数(人)	Rate of change 变化率(%)	Total revenue (Mil. RMB) 总销售收入(百万元)	Rate of change 变化率(%)	Total profit (Mil RMB) 总利润(百万元)	Rate of change 变化率(%)
2000	43		29,764		1,261		50	
2001	35	-18.60	22,266	-25.19	1,197	-5.08	36	-28.00
2002	28	-20.00	17,822	-19.96	1,222	2.09	91	152.78

Major Products 主要产品	Output 产量	Unit 单位
Crude Salt 原盐	3,283	10,000 Tons 万吨

10 Main Firms with Maximal Revenue (year founded) 收入最大的十家主要企业（创办年份）	City 城市	Province 省	Telephone/fax 电话/传真	Number of employees 职工人数	Ownership 产业所有权	Revenue ('000 RMB) 销售收入(千元)	Profit('000 RMB) (rank) 利润(千元)(排名)	Total assets ('000 RMB) 总资产(千元)	Major products 主要产品
Sichuan Jiuda Salt Indutry Group Company 四川久大盐业集团公司(1971)	Zigong 自贡市	Sichuan 四川省	(0813)8105828 (0813)8105472	3,510	Limited-Liability 有限公司	326,574	57,165(1)	793,490	Haloid 卤水
Chongqing SOTE Co., Ltd. 重庆索特盐化股份有限公司(1992)	Chongqing 重庆市	Chongqing 重庆市	(023)58960318 (023)58960313	946	Joint Stock 股份制	165,772	19,664(2)	384,513	Well Salt 井盐
Zigong Zhangjiaba Salt Chemical Co., Ltd. 自贡市张家坝盐化有限公司(2000)	Zigong 自贡市	Sichuan 四川省	(0813)5202297 (0813)5205394	1,304	Limited-Liability 有限公司	121,845	2,064(6)	67,860	Refined Salt 精盐
Sichuan Jiuda Da'an Salt Refining Co., Ltd. 四川久大大安制盐有限公司(1957)	Zigong 自贡市	Sichuan 四川省	(0813)5105174 (0813)5100060	1,237	Limited-Liability 有限公司	67,560	1,068(10)	51,668	Salt 盐
Sichuan Penglai Salt Chemical Co.,Ltd. 四川蓬莱盐化有限公司(2001)	Suining 遂宁市	Sichuan 四川省	(0825)7852798 (0825)7851421	958	Limited-Liability 有限公司	56,354	2,310(5)	104,549	Well Salt 井盐
CNSIC Jintan Salt Chemical Co., Ltd. 中盐金坛市盐化有限责任公司(2001)	Changzhou 常州市	Jiangsu 江苏省	(0519)2323778 (0519)2331781	221	Limited-Liability 有限公司	48,060	1,250(9)	172,810	Mine Salt 矿盐
Yibin Sifeng Salt Chemical Industry Co., Ltd. 宜宾四丰盐化工业有限公司(1988)	Yibin 宜宾市	Sichuan 四川省	(0831)4622107 (0831)4622107	344	Limited-Liability 有限公司	31,957	5,333(3)	80,917	Liquid Salt 液体盐
Chongqing Hechuan Salt Chemical Industry Co., Ltd. 重庆合川盐化工业有限公司(1996)	Chongqing 重庆市	Chongqing 重庆市	(023)42727004	475	State-owned 国有企业	29,053	1,930(7)	57,068	Common Salt 食盐
Shandong Tai'an Dongyue Refined Saltern 山东泰安市东岳精制盐厂(1998)	Taian 泰安市	Shandong 山东省	(0538)8811330 (0538)8811229	299	State-owned 国有企业	25,652	3,629(4)	29,256	Well Salt 井矿盐
Sichuan Quxian Saltern 四川省渠县盐厂(1993)	Dazhou 达州市	Sichuan 四川省	(0818)7322951 (0818)7323894	629	State-owned 国有企业	18,020	-	79,028	Well Salt 井盐

Top 10 Cities by Revenue 销售收入排名前10位城市	Province 省	Market share 市场份额(%)	Number of firms 企业个数
Zigong 自贡市	Sichuan 四川省	44.11	6
Chongqing 重庆市	Chongqing 重庆市	17.99	4
Leshan 乐山市	Sichuan 四川省	17.78	6
Suining 遂宁市	Sichuan 四川省	4.61	1
Changzhou 常州市	Jiangsu 江苏省	3.93	1
Yibin 宜宾市	Sichuan 四川省	2.62	1
Taian 泰安市	Shandong 山东省	2.10	1
Nanchong 南充市	Sichuan 四川省	2.01	1
Dazhou 达州市	Sichuan 四川省	1.47	1
Zhenjiang 镇江市	Jiangsu 江苏省	0.81	1

10 Major Wholesalers 十家主要批发商	City 城市	Province 省	Telephone/Fax 电话/传真
Guangdong Foodstuffs Import & Export Group Corporation 广东省食品进出口集团公司	Guangzhou 广州市	Guangdong 广东省	(020)83854888 (020)83856823
Hubei Salt Industry General Company 湖北盐业总公司	Wuhan 武汉市	Hubei 湖北省	(027)82832190 (027)82816030
Henan Provincial Salt Business Administration Bureau (Henan Provincial Salt Industry General Company) 河南省盐务管理局(河南省盐业总公司)	Zhengzhou 郑州市	Henan 河南省	(0371)5907597 (0371)5906346
Sichuan Salt Industry General Company 四川省盐业总公司	Chengdu 成都市	Sichuan 四川省	(028)86652441 (028)86663440
China National Salt Tianjin Changlu Salt Industry Co.,Ltd. 中盐天津市长芦盐业有限公司	Tianjin 天津市	Tianjin 天津市	(022)23022160 (022)23022110
Zhejiang Salt Industry Company 浙江省盐业公司	Hangzhou 杭州市	Zhejiang 浙江省	(0571)87800292 (0571)87800082
Fujian Salt Industry Company 福建省盐业公司	Fuzhou 福州市	Fujian 福建省	(0591)7534344 (0591)7535047
Jiangxi Salt Industry General Company 江西省盐业总公司	Nanchang 南昌市	Jiangxi 江西省	(0791)6816695 (0791)6812316
Hubei Salt Transportation & Sale Company 湖北省盐业运销公司	Xiaogan 孝感市	Hubei 湖北省	(0712)3611320 (0712)3611244
Hunan Salt Industry Group Co.,Ltd.Jinshi Allocation & Transportation Company 湖南省盐业集团有限责任公司津市调运公司	Changde 常德市	Hunan 湖南省	(0736)4223817 (0736)4223817

1034: Underground Salt Mining 矿盐业

The industry accounts for 0.013% of the total revenue of China's industrial sector in 2002. The rate of return on assets is 1.99%. 75.00% of all firms in the industry made a profit while 25.00% had negative returns.The top province in terms of the industry's revenue is Yunnan, accounting for 26.00% of the total revenue.
2002年本行业收入占全行业的0.013%，资产利润率为1.99%。75.00%的企业赢利，25.00%的企业亏损。收入最高的省为云南省，占本行业的26.00%。

	Total number of firms 企业总数	Total number of employees 职工总数	Total revenue (Mil.RMB) 总销售收入（百万元）	Total profit (Mil.RMB) 总利润（百万元）	Return on assets 资产利润率（%）	Return on equity 权益利润率（%）	Labour productivity ('000 RMB/ worker) 劳动生产率（千元/人）	Debts/ assets 资产负债率（%）	Total assets (Mil.RMB) 总资产（百万元）
Industry Overall 行业总体	20	18,146	1,406	54	1.99	4.64	31.18	57.14	2,694

	Number of firms 企业个数	Average number of employees 平均职工人数	Average revenue ('000 RMB) 平均销售收入（千元）	Average profit ('000 RMB) 平均利润（千元）	Return on assets 资产利润率（%）	Return on equity 权益利润率（%）	Labour productivity ('000 RMB/ worker) 劳动生产率（千元/人）	Debts/ assets 资产负债率（%）	Average total assets ('000 RMB) 平均总资产（千元）
By ownership 产业所有权									
State-owned 国有	13	1,053	73,615	832	0.53	1.27	26.89	57.80	155,730
Collective-owned 集体									
Foreign & Overseas Chinese Funded 三资									
By regional distribution 地区分布									
Central-North 华北									
Beijing 北京									
Tianjin 天津									
Hebei 河北									
Shanxi 山西									
Inner Mongolia 内蒙古									
Northeast 东北									
Liaoning 辽宁									
Jilin 吉林									
Heilongjiang 黑龙江									
Central-East 华东	5	1,145	89,261	1,876	1.00	2.10	27.69	52.57	187,928
Shanghai 上海									
Jiangsu 江苏	1	784	109,604	4,552	2.70	8.21	54.63	67.15	168,752
Zhejiang 浙江									
Anhui 安徽	1	2,237	172,421	3,678	1.31	4.63	27.02	71.71	280,640
Fujian 福建									
Jiangxi 江西	3	902	54,760	383	0.23	0.37	20.44	36.59	163,417
Shandong 山东									
Central-South 中南	9	955	66,007	530	0.39	1.06	27.23	63.52	137,204
Henan 河南									
Hubei 湖北	6	909	55,493	-30	-0.02	-0.08	26.01	70.90	123,634
Hunan 湖南	2	1,542	128,319	2,171	0.91	1.95	28.93	53.34	238,772
Guangdong 广东	1	56	4,471	607	3.92	5.17	53.21	24.29	15,493
Guangxi 广西									
Hainan 海南									
Southwest 西南	6	638	60,928	6,572	7.60	15.26	45.27	50.21	86,507
Chongqing 重庆									
Sichuan 四川									
Guizhou 贵州									
Yunnan 云南	6	638	60,928	6,572	7.60	15.26	45.27	50.21	86,507
Tibet 西藏									
Northwest 西北									
Shaanxi 陕西									
Gansu 甘肃									
Qinghai 青海									
Ningxia 宁夏									
Xinjiang 新疆									

Year 年份	Number of firms 企业个数	Rate of change 变化率 (%)	Number of employees 职工人数 (人)	Rate of change 变化率 (%)	Total revenue (Mil. RMB) 总销售收入 (百万元)	Rate of change 变化率 (%)	Total profit (Mil RMB) 总利润 (百万元)	Rate of change 变化率 (%)
2000	21		15,654		717		1	
2001	20	-4.76	17,502	11.81	976	36.12	9	800.00
2002	20	0	18,146	3.68	1,406	44.06	54	500.00

Major Products 主要产品	Output 产量	Unit 单位

10 Main Firms with Maximal Revenue (year founded) 收入最大的十家主要企业（创办年份）	City 城市	Province 省	Telephone/fax 电话/传真	Number of employees 职工人数	Ownership 产业所有权	Revenue ('000 RMB) 销售收入 (千元)	Profit('000 RMB) (rank) 利润(千元) (排名)	Total assets ('000 RMB) 总资产 (千元)	Major products 主要产品
Yunnan Salt Chemiclal Co.,Ltd.	Kunming	Yunnan	(0871)3177615		Joint Stock				Common Salt
云南盐化股份有限公司(2002)	昆明市	云南省	(0871)3177615	1,898	股份制	314,967	40,407(1)	389,848	食盐
Dingyuan Salt Mine	Chuzhou	Anhui	(0550)4480027		State-owned				Refined Salt
定远盐矿(1990)	滁州市	安徽省	(0550)4480028	2,237	国有企业	172,421	3,678(4)	280,640	精制盐
Hunan Xiangli Salt Mine	Changde	Hunan	(0736)4223188		State-owned				Refined Salt
湖南省湘澧盐矿(1969)	常德市	湖南省	(0736)4223106	1,954	国有企业	146,429	514(11)	264,642	精制盐
Jiangxi Salt Mine Co., Ltd	Yichun	Jiangxi	(0795)7372424		State-owned				Refined Salt
江西盐矿有限责任公司(1970)	宜春市	江西省	(0795)7377766	1,425	国有企业	119,793	1,098(8)	367,394	精制盐
Hubei Silver Light Salt Chemiclal Co., Ltd.	Xiaogan	Hubei	(0712)3223713		State-owned				Refined Salt
湖北银光盐化有限公司(1998)	孝感市	湖北省	(0712)3223915	1,844	国有企业	113,500	2,234(5)	318,302	精制盐
Hunan Xiangheng Salt Mine	Hengyang	Hunan	(0734)8302286		State-owned				Crude Salt
湖南省湘衡盐矿(1969)	衡阳市	湖南省	(0734)8301210	1,129	国有企业	110,209	3,827(3)	212,902	原盐
CNSIC Changjiang Salt Chemicals Co.,Ltd.	Xiaogan	Hubei	(0712)3610019		State-owned				Mine Salt
中盐长江盐化有限公司(1970)	孝感市	湖北省	(0712)3611332	781	国有企业	74,354	1,746(6)	101,948	矿盐
Hubei Kaiyuan Making-Salt Co.,Ltd.	Xiaogan	Hubei	(0712)3238124		Joint Stock				Mine Salt
湖北开元制盐股份有限公司(1988)	孝感市	湖北省	(0712)3238004	849	股份制	51,936	-	94,831	矿盐
Zhangshu Fuda Industrial Company	Yichun	Jiangxi	(0795)7372088		State-owned				
樟树富达实业公司(1993)	宜春市	江西省	(0795)7377496	680	国有企业	38,468	1,320(7)	88,220	
Xiaogan Yongxiang Salt Refining Co., Ltd	Xiaogan	Hubei	(0712)3222209		Limited-Liability				Common Salt
孝感市永祥制盐有限责任公司(1997)	孝感市	湖北省		587	有限公司	36,014	356(13)	64,495	食盐

Top 10 Cities by Revenue 销售收入排名前10位城市	Province 省	Market share 市场份额 (%)	Number of firms 企业个数
Xiaogan 孝感市	Hubei 湖北省	23.68	6
Kunming 昆明市	Yunnan 云南省	23.13	2
Chuzhou 滁州市	Anhui 安徽省	12.26	1
Yichun 宜春市	Jiangxi 江西省	11.26	2
Changde 常德市	Hunan 湖南省	10.42	1
Hengyang 衡阳市	Hunan 湖南省	7.84	1
Huaian 淮安市	Jiangsu 江苏省	7.80	1
Simao 思茅地区	Yunnan 云南省	1.56	1
Dali 大理州	Yunnan 云南省	0.78	1
Ganzhou 赣州市	Jiangxi 江西省	0.43	1

10 Major Wholesalers 十家主要批发商	City 城市	Province 省	Telephone/Fax 电话/传真
Guangdong Foodstuffs Import & Export Group Corporation	Guangzhou	Guangdong	(020)83854888
广东省食品进出口集团公司	广州市	广东省	(020)83856823
Hubei Salt Industry General Company	Wuhan	Hubei	(027)82832190
湖北盐业总公司	武汉市	湖北省	(027)82816030
Henan Provincial Salt Business Administration Bureau (Henan Provincial Salt Industry General Company)	Zhengzhou	Henan	(0371)5907597
河南省盐务管理局(河南省盐业总公司)	郑州市	河南省	(0371)5906346
Sichuan Salt Industry General Company	Chengdu	Sichuan	(028)86652441
四川省盐业总公司	成都市	四川省	(028)86663440
China National Salt Tianjin Changlu Salt Industry Co.,Ltd.	Tianjin	Tianjin	(022)23022160
中盐天津市长芦盐业有限公司	天津市	天津市	(022)23022110
Zhejiang Salt Industry Company	Hangzhou	Zhejiang	(0571)87800292
浙江省盐业公司	杭州市	浙江省	(0571)87800082
Fujian Salt Industry Company	Fuzhou	Fujian	(0591)7534344
福建省盐业公司	福州市	福建省	(0591)7535047
Jiangxi Salt Industry General Company	Nanchang	Jiangxi	(0791)6816695
江西省盐业总公司	南昌市	江西省	(0791)6812316
Hubei Salt Transportation & Sale Company	Xiaogan	Hubei	(0712)3611320
湖北省盐业运销公司	孝感市	湖北省	(0712)3611244
Hunan Salt Industry Group Co.,Ltd.Jinshi Allocation & Transportation Company	Changde	Hunan	(0736)4223817
湖南省盐业集团有限责任公司津市调运公司	常德市	湖南省	(0736)4223817

1091: Asbestos Mining 石棉采选业

The industry accounts for 0.005% of the total revenue of China's industrial sector in 2002. The rate of return on assets is 0.92%. 94.29% of all firms in the industry made a profit while 5.71% had negative returns.The top province in terms of the industry's revenue is Gansu, accounting for 47.23% of the total revenue.
2002年本行业收入占全行业的 0.005%，资产利润率为 0.92%。94.29%的企业赢利，5.71%的企业亏损。收入最高的省为甘肃省，占本行业的47.23%。

	Total number of firms 企业总数	Total number of employees 职工总数	Total revenue (Mil.RMB) 总销售收入（百万元）	Total profit (Mil.RMB) 总利润（百万元）	Return on assets 资产利润率 (%)	Return on equity 权益利润率 (%)	Labour productivity ('000 RMB/ worker) 劳动生产率（千元/人）	Debts/ assets 资产负债率 (%)	Total assets (Mil.RMB) 总资产（百万元）
Industry Overall 行业总体	35	14,200	497	12	0.92	2.75	15.72	66.52	1,274

	Number of firms 企业个数	Average number of employees 平均职工人数	Average revenue ('000 RMB) 平均销售收入（千元）	Average profit ('000 RMB) 平均利润（千元）	Return on assets 资产利润率 (%)	Return on equity 权益利润率 (%)	Labour productivity ('000 RMB/ worker) 劳动生产率（千元/人）	Debts/ assets 资产负债率 (%)	Average total assets ('000 RMB) 平均总资产（千元）
By ownership 产业所有权									
State-owned 国有	8	1,178	32,103	-1,204	-0.92	-2.84	13.50	67.49	130,501
Collective-owned 集体	15	271	12,023	1,070	12.41	27.62	17.61	55.07	8,627
Foreign & Overseas Chinese Funded 三资									
By regional distribution 地区分布									
Central-North 华北	1	830	921	19	0.16	1.41	0.30	88.65	11,883
Beijing 北京									
Tianjin 天津									
Hebei 河北	1	830	921	19	0.16	1.41	0.30	88.65	11,883
Shanxi 山西									
Inner Mongolia 内蒙古									
Northeast 东北									
Liaoning 辽宁									
Jilin 吉林									
Heilongjiang 黑龙江									
Central-East 华东	1	489	20,966	647	0.79	1.77	29.39	55.51	82,151
Shanghai 上海									
Jiangsu 江苏									
Zhejiang 浙江									
Anhui 安徽									
Fujian 福建									
Jiangxi 江西									
Shandong 山东	1	489	20,966	647	0.79	1.77	29.39	55.51	82,151
Central-South 中南									
Henan 河南									
Hubei 湖北									
Hunan 湖南									
Guangdong 广东									
Guangxi 广西									
Hainan 海南									
Southwest 西南	2	1,969	38,632	26	0.01	0.04	11.58	65.84	173,364
Chongqing 重庆									
Sichuan 四川	2	1,969	38,632	26	0.01	0.04	11.58	65.84	173,364
Guizhou 贵州									
Yunnan 云南									
Tibet 西藏									
Northwest 西北	31	289	12,849	355	1.32	4.08	18.22	67.58	26,888
Shaanxi 陕西									
Gansu 甘肃	25	189	9,398	840	9.35	24.74	20.00	62.21	8,983
Qinghai 青海	4	750	27,370	-3,072	-2.97	-10.38	14.64	71.36	103,302
Ningxia 宁夏									
Xinjiang 新疆	2	610	26,948	1,156	1.18	3.45	20.16	65.76	97,871

1091: Asbestos Mining 石棉采选业

Year 年份	Number of firms 企业个数	Rate of change 变化率 (%)	Number of employees 职工人数 (人)	Rate of change 变化率 (%)	Total revenue (Mil. RMB) 总销售收入 (百万元)	Rate of change 变化率 (%)	Total profit (Mil RMB) 总利润 (百万元)	Rate of change 变化率 (%)
2000	25		18,374		475		8	
2001	35	40.00	13,633	-25.80	475	0	6	-25.00
2002	35	0	14,200	4.16	497	4.63	12	100.00

Major Products 主要产品	Output 产量	Unit 单位
Asbestos 石棉	26	10,000 Tons 万吨

10 Main Firms with Maximal Revenue (year founded) 收入最大的十家主要企业（创办年份）	City 城市	Province 省	Telephone/fax 电话/传真	Number of employees 职工人数	Ownership 产业所有权	Revenue ('000 RMB) 销售收入 (千元)	Profit('000 RMB) (rank) 利润(千元) (排名)	Total assets ('000 RMB) 总资产 (千元)	Major products 主要产品
Mangya Asbestos Mine	Haixi	Qinghai	(0977)8258021		State-owned				Asbestos
茫崖石棉矿(1958)	海西州	青海省	(0977)8258030	2,444	国有企业	83,674	861(6)	275,657	石棉
Sichuan Xinkang Asbestos Mine	Yaan	Sichuan	(0835)8870212		State-owned				Asbestos
四川新康石棉矿(1951)	雅安市	四川省	(0835)8870262	1,870	国有企业	41,427	14(28)	148,741	石棉
Xinjiang Bazhou Asbestos Mine	Bayinguoleng	Xinjiang	(0996)7520014		State-owned				Asbestos
新疆若羌巴州石棉矿(1966)	巴音郭楞州	新疆	(0996)7520003	960	国有企业	39,290	5,034(1)	135,146	石棉
Sichuan Asbestos Mine	Yaan	Sichuan	(0835)8863600		State-owned				Asbestos
四川省石棉矿(1950)	雅安市	四川省	(0835)8863671	2,067	国有企业	35,837	37(25)	197,986	石棉
A'kesai Jianshe Countryside Enterprise Corporation	Jiuquan	Gansu	(0937)8323011		Collective-owned				Asbestos
阿克塞县建设乡企业公司(1992)	酒泉市	甘肃省	(0937)8323011	480	集体企业	22,501	2,321(4)	11,389	石棉
Shandong Rizhao Luda Mining Industry Group Company	Rizhao	Shandong	(0633)2651185		State-owned				Asbestos
山东省日照鲁达矿业集团公司(1958)	日照市	山东省	(0633)2651188	489	国有企业	20,966	647(8)	82,151	石棉
Qi Lianxian Asbestos Industry General Company	Haibei	Qinghai	(0970)8672385		State-owned				Asbestos Fine Hair
祁连县石棉工业总公司(1969)	海北州	青海省	(0970)8673189	507	国有企业	20,106	-	131,849	石棉绒
Jiuquan Sealing Material Industrial Company	Jiuquan	Gansu	(0937)2793002		Collective-owned				Asbestos
酒泉市密封材料实业公司(1993)	酒泉市	甘肃省	(0937)2793005	50	集体企业	5,990	650(7)	7,475	石棉
Qilianxian Xingda Asbestos Co., Ltd.	Haibei	Qinghai	(0970)8672385		Collective-owned				Asbestos Fine Hair
祁连县兴达石棉有限责任公司(1990)	海北州	青海省	(0970)8673189	29	集体企业	3,500	310(14)	2,700	石棉绒
Laiyuan Asbestos Insustry General Company	Baoding	Hebei	(0312)7339182		State-owned				Asbestos
涞源县石棉工业总公司(1949)	保定市	河北省	(0312)7339207	830	国有企业	921	19(27)	11,883	石棉

Top 10 Cities by Revenue 销售收入排名前10位城市	Province 省	Market share 市场份额 (%)	Number of firms 企业个数
Jiuquan 酒泉市	Gansu 甘肃省	47.23	25
Haixi 海西州	Qinghai 青海省	16.82	1
Yaan 雅安市	Sichuan 四川省	15.53	2
Bayinguoleng 巴音郭楞州	Xinjiang 新疆	10.83	2
Haibei 海北州	Qinghai 青海省	5.19	3
Rizhao 日照市	Shandong 山东省	4.21	1
Baoding 保定市	Hebei 河北省	0.19	1

10 Major Wholesalers 十家主要批发商	City 城市	Province 省	Telephone/Fax 电话/传真
Xuzhou New Century Building Materials Decorative City	Xuzhou	Jiangsu	(0516)83666780
徐州市新世纪建材装饰城	徐州市	江苏省	(0516)63804485
Orienthome Co.,Ltd.	Beijing	Beijing	(010)63808294
东方家园有限公司	北京市	北京市	
Shanghai Jinkai Goods & Materials Co.,Ltd.	Shanghai	Shanghai	(021)52193967
上海金凯物资有限公司	上海市	上海市	
Guangzhou Building Materials Development Co.,Ltd.	Guangzhou	Guangdong	(020)83335062
广州市建材发展有限公司	广州市	广东省	(020)83341110
Guangxi Qiaofeng Goods & Materials Trade Co.,Ltd.	Nanning	Guangxi	(0771)2631539
广西侨丰物资贸易有限责任公司	南宁市	广西	(0771)2631539
Gansu Building Materials State-owned Assets Marketing Co.,Ltd.	Lanzhou	Gansu	(0931)8821359
甘肃建材国有资产经营有限责任公司	兰州市	甘肃省	(0931)8960243
Shanghai East Asia United Building Materials Co.,Ltd.	Shanghai	Shanghai	(021)33134520
上海东亚联合建材有限公司	上海市	上海市	(021)63216165
Shanghai Zhuzong Materials General Company	Shanghai	Shanghai	(021)32240030
上海住总物资总公司	上海市	上海市	(021)32240024
Guangdong Building Materials Company	Guangzhou	Guangdong	(020)83802713
广东省建材公司	广州市	广东省	(020)83817640
Guangdong Dongguan Hardware Minerals Import & Export Co.,Ltd	Dongguan	Guangdong	(0769)2227090
广东省东莞五金矿产进出口公司	东莞市	广东省	(0769)2221045

1093: Graphite Mining and Dressing 石墨采选业

The industry accounts for 0.006% of the total revenue of China's industrial sector in 2002. The rate of return on assets is 0.29%. 72.73% of all firms in the industry made a profit while 27.27% had negative returns.The top province in terms of the industry's revenue is Shandong, accounting for 65.18% of the total revenue.
2002年本行业收入占全行业的0.006%，资产利润率为0.29%。72.73%的企业赢利，27.27%的企业亏损。收入最高的省为山东省，占本行业的65.18%。

	Total number of firms 企业总数	Total number of employees 职工总数	Total revenue (Mil.RMB) 总销售收入（百万元）	Total profit (Mil.RMB) 总利润（百万元）	Return on assets 资产利润率（%）	Return on equity 权益利润率（%）	Labour productivity ('000 RMB/ worker) 劳动生产率（千元/人）	Debts/ assets 资产负债率（%）	Total assets (Mil.RMB) 总资产（百万元）
Industry Overall 行业总体	33	9,518	624	2	0.29	0.87	26.04	66.55	764

	Number of firms 企业个数	Average number of employees 平均职工人数	Average revenue ('000 RMB) 平均销售收入（千元）	Average profit ('000 RMB) 平均利润（千元）	Return on assets 资产利润率（%）	Return on equity 权益利润率（%）	Labour productivity ('000 RMB/ worker) 劳动生产率（千元/人）	Debts/ assets 资产负债率（%）	Average total assets ('000 RMB) 平均总资产（千元）
By ownership 产业所有权									
State-owned 国有	5	377	3,986	-3,517	-16.04		4.42	116.31	21,929
Collective-owned 集体	5	102	23,494	1,463	21.70	29.15	82.79	25.57	6,741
Foreign & Overseas Chinese Funded 三资	2	606	14,169	-3,670	-8.92	-36.41	11.98	75.51	41,154
By regional distribution 地区分布									
Central-North 华北	3	378	11,559	113	0.69	1.67	14.04	58.46	16,313
Beijing 北京									
Tianjin 天津									
Hebei 河北	1	207	4,202				14.66	100.64	15,065
Shanxi 山西									
Inner Mongolia 内蒙古	2	464	15,238	170	1.00	1.66	13.90	39.70	16,938
Northeast 东北	9	317	7,505	-1,026	-3.84	-10.84	15.85	64.56	26,699
Liaoning 辽宁									
Jilin 吉林	1	553		-618	-1.43			103.15	43,276
Heilongjiang 黑龙江	8	288	8,444	-1,077	-4.37	-9.96	19.66	56.08	24,627
Central-East 华东	12	298	33,874	1,009	4.09	11.67	35.55	64.92	24,646
Shanghai 上海									
Jiangsu 江苏									
Zhejiang 浙江									
Anhui 安徽									
Fujian 福建									
Jiangxi 江西									
Shandong 山东	12	298	33,874	1,009	4.09	11.67	35.55	64.92	24,646
Central-South 中南	7	234	14,441	-188	-0.86	-3.04	34.77	71.59	21,762
Henan 河南	1	533	56,577	13,840	12.97	29.93	70.75	56.66	106,689
Hubei 湖北									
Hunan 湖南	6	184	7,418	-2,526	-33.20		17.42	106.48	7,607
Guangdong 广东									
Guangxi 广西									
Hainan 海南									
Southwest 西南	2	159	6,925	166	1.23	10.46	8.58	88.28	13,542
Chongqing 重庆									
Sichuan 四川	2	159	6,925	166	1.23	10.46	8.58	88.28	13,542
Guizhou 贵州									
Yunnan 云南									
Tibet 西藏									
Northwest 西北									
Shaanxi 陕西									
Gansu 甘肃									
Qinghai 青海									
Ningxia 宁夏									
Xinjiang 新疆									

1093: Graphite Mining and Dressing 石墨采选业

Year 年份	Number of firms 企业个数	Rate of change 变化率(%)	Number of employees 职工人数(人)	Rate of change 变化率(%)	Total revenue (Mil. RMB) 总销售收入(百万元)	Rate of change 变化率(%)	Total profit (Mil RMB) 总利润(百万元)	Rate of change 变化率(%)
2000	41		15,326		976		26	
2001	30	-26.83	9,316	-39.21	534	-45.29	18	-30.77
2002	33	10.00	9,518	2.17	624	16.85	2	-88.89

Major Products 主要产品	Output 产量	Unit 单位
Graphite 石墨	63	10,000 Tons 万吨

10 Main Firms with Maximal Revenue (year founded) 收入最大的十家主要企业(创办年份)	City 城市	Province 省	Telephone/fax 电话/传真	Number of employees 职工人数	Ownership 产业所有权	Revenue ('000 RMB) 销售收入(千元)	Profit('000 RMB) (rank) 利润(千元)(排名)	Total assets ('000 RMB) 总资产(千元)	Major products 主要产品
Qingdao Graphite Stock Co., Ltd.	Qingdao	Shandong	(0532)3431085		Joint Stock				Squama Graphite
青岛石墨股份有限公司(1943)	青岛市	山东省	(0532)3431082	1,697	股份制	83,553	-	207,692	鳞片石墨
Pingdu Tianzhuang Grathite Co., Ltd.	Qingdao	Shandong	(0532)6383054		Private Owned				
平度市田庄石墨有限公司(2001)	青岛市	山东省	(0532)6383132	310	私营企业	68,290	4,150(3)	16,190	石墨
Xixia Longcheng Group	Nanyang	Henan	(0377)4928358		Private Owned				Graphite
西峡县龙成集团(1978)	南阳市	河南省		533	私营企业	56,577	13,840(1)	106,689	石墨
Pingdu Tianying Graphite Co., Ltd.	Qingdao	Shandong	(0532)6383025		Private Owned				High-carbon Graphite
平度市天英石墨有限公司(1996)	青岛市	山东省	(0532)6383881	150	私营企业	38,900	2,330(4)	22,410	高碳石墨
Xinghe Graphite Group Company	Wulanchabu	Inner Mongolia	(0474)7578001		Joint Owned				Graphite
兴和县石墨集团公司(1972)	乌兰察布	内蒙古	(0474)7578198	820	联营企业	25,429	390(12)	25,214	石墨
Qingdao Pingdu Jianqing Graphite Co., Ltd.	Qingdao	Shandong	(0532)7321064		Private Owned				Graphite
青岛市平度建庆石墨有限公司(1998)	青岛市	山东省	(0532)7328881	178	私营企业	24,380	1,600(6)	2,176	石墨
Pingdu Jinhui Graphite Mine	Qingdao	Shandong	(0532)7389888		Private Enterprises				Graphite
平度市金汇石墨矿(2000)	青岛市	山东省	(0532)7389688	330	私营独资	19,992	193(16)	8,898	石墨
Pingdu Yunxiang Graphite Co., Ltd.	Qingdao	Shandong	(0532)3341236		Private Owned				Graphite
平度市云祥石墨有限公司(1997)	青岛市	山东省		171	私营企业	18,350	780(9)	5,470	石墨
Jixi Hongsheng Graphite Products Co., Ltd.	Jixi	Heilongjiang	(0467)2469192		Private Owned				Graphite
鸡西市宏升石墨制品有限公司(1996)	鸡西市	黑龙江省	(0467)2469192	140	私营企业	9,098	150(17)	22,331	石墨
Jixi Aoyu Graphite Products Co., Ltd.	Jixi	Heilongjiang	(0467)2499997		Private Owned				Squama Graphite
鸡西奥宇石墨制品有限公司(2000)	鸡西市	黑龙江省	(0467)2499256	360	私营企业	8,173	-	62,019	鳞片石墨

Top 10 Cities by Revenue 销售收入排名前10位城市	Province 省	Market share 市场份额(%)	Number of firms 企业个数
Qingdao 青岛市	Shandong 山东省	51.95	11
Jinan 济南市	Shandong 山东省	13.23	1
Nanyang 南阳市	Henan 河南省	9.07	1
Jixi 鸡西市	Heilongjiang 黑龙江省	8.51	6
Chenzhou 郴州市	Hunan 湖南省	7.14	6
Wulanchabu 乌兰察布盟	Inner Mongolia 内蒙古	4.89	2
Hegang 鹤岗市	Heilongjiang 黑龙江省	1.50	1
Bazhong 巴中市	Sichuan 四川省	1.34	1
Panzhihua 攀枝花市	Sichuan 四川省	0.88	1
Mudanjiang 牡丹江市	Heilongjiang 黑龙江省	0.82	1

10 Major Wholesalers 十家主要批发商	City 城市	Province 省	Telephone/Fax 电话/传真
Xuzhou New Century Building Materials Decorative City	Xuzhou	Jiangsu	(0516)83666780
徐州市新世纪建材装饰城	徐州市	江苏省	(0516)63804485
Orienthome Co.,Ltd.	Beijing	Beijing	(010)63808294
东方家园有限公司	北京市	北京市	
Shanghai Jinkai Goods & Materials Co.,Ltd.	Shanghai	Shanghai	(021)52193967
上海金凯物资有限公司	上海市	上海市	
Guangzhou Building Materials Development Co.,Ltd.	Guangzhou	Guangdong	(020)83335062
广州市建材发展有限公司	广州市	广东省	(020)83341110
Guangxi Qiaofeng Goods & Materials Trade Co.,Ltd.	Nanning	Guangxi	(0771)2631539
广西侨丰物资贸易有限责任公司	南宁市	广西	(0771)2631539
Gansu Building Materials State-owned Assets Marketing Co.,Ltd.	Lanzhou	Gansu	(0931)8821359
甘肃建材国有资产经营有限责任公司	兰州市	甘肃省	(0931)8960243
Shanghai East Asia United Building Materials Co.,Ltd.	Shanghai	Shanghai	(021)33134520
上海东亚联合建材有限公司	上海市	上海市	(021)63216165
Shanghai Zhuzong Materials General Company	Shanghai	Shanghai	(021)32240030
上海住总物资总公司	上海市	上海市	(021)32240024
Guangdong Building Materials Company	Guangzhou	Guangdong	(020)83802713
广东省建材公司	广州市	广东省	(020)83817640
Guangdong Dongguan Hardware Minerals Import & Export Co.,Ltd	Dongguan	Guangdong	(0769)2227090
广东省东莞五金矿产进出口公司	东莞市	广东省	(0769)2221045

1094: Gypsum Mining and Dressing 石膏采选业

The industry accounts for 0.012% of the total revenue of China's industrial sector in 2002. The rate of return on assets is 4.49%. 79.75% of all firms in the industry made a profit while 20.25% had negative returns.The top province in terms of the industry's revenue is Shandong, accounting for 55.22% of the total revenue.
2002年本行业收入占全行业的 0.012%，资产利润率为 4.49%。79.75%的企业赢利，20.25%的企业亏损。收入最高的省为山东省，占本行业的55.22%。

	Total number of firms 企业总数	Total number of employees 职工总数	Total revenue (Mil.RMB) 总销售收入 (百万元)	Total profit (Mil.RMB) 总利润 (百万元)	Return on assets 资产利润率 (%)	Return on equity 权益利润率 (%)	Labour productivity ('000 RMB/worker) 劳动生产率 (千元/人)	Debts/assets 资产负债率 (%)	Total assets (Mil.RMB) 总资产 (百万元)
Industry Overall 行业总体	79	24,092	1,270	72	4.49	9.35	19.16	51.93	1,604

	Number of firms 企业个数	Average number of employees 平均职工人数	Average revenue ('000 RMB) 平均销售收入 (千元)	Average profit ('000 RMB) 平均利润 (千元)	Return on assets 资产利润率 (%)	Return on equity 权益利润率 (%)	Labour productivity ('000 RMB/worker) 劳动生产率 (千元/人)	Debts/assets 资产负债率 (%)	Average total assets ('000 RMB) 平均总资产 (千元)
By ownership 产业所有权									
State-owned 国有	12	463	12,245	846	1.68	3.54	12.52	52.52	50,386
Collective-owned 集体	38	269	20,320	1,284	10.76	20.42	23.88	47.28	11,931
Foreign & Overseas Chinese Funded 三资	4	164	13,475	413	3.94	23.36	37.72	83.12	10,472
By regional distribution 地区分布									
Central-North 华北	4	174	8,454	384	1.24	2.29	24.29	45.82	30,869
Beijing 北京									
Tianjin 天津									
Hebei 河北	2	92	8,581	1,118	5.29	9.50	55.99	44.35	21,144
Shanxi 山西	1	498	13,222	-760	-1.01	-1.83	10.84	44.76	75,228
Inner Mongolia 内蒙古	1	13	3,432	58	0.97	3.20	91.08	69.64	5,961
Northeast 东北	6	226	6,743	9	0.06	0.21	11.55	70.58	13,826
Liaoning 辽宁	1	150	12,170	-190	-0.81		34.87	107.93	23,320
Jilin 吉林	5	242	5,658	48	0.40	0.92	8.66	55.97	11,927
Heilongjiang 黑龙江									
Central-East 华东	28	356	27,446	1,605	7.10	15.00	23.69	52.66	22,614
Shanghai 上海									
Jiangsu 江苏	2	694	19,290	-80	-0.11	-0.21	14.25	46.46	70,880
Zhejiang 浙江									
Anhui 安徽	2	322	10,311	311	1.28	7.90	13.40	83.76	24,204
Fujian 福建									
Jiangxi 江西	1	215	8,097	180	2.71	3.32	13.94	18.29	6,644
Shandong 山东	23	335	30,487	1,927	10.15	21.04	26.52	51.75	18,973
Central-South 中南	31	345	13,147	797	3.63	6.46	16.95	43.90	21,995
Henan 河南									
Hubei 湖北	19	341	11,048	244	1.50	4.11	13.46	63.60	16,346
Hunan 湖南	7	271	8,364	294	3.82	15.07	9.88	74.65	7,699
Guangdong 广东	5	466	27,817	3,603	5.68	7.04	32.41	19.41	63,478
Guangxi 广西									
Hainan 海南									
Southwest 西南	5	113	2,084	169	2.67	6.90	7.87	61.29	6,317
Chongqing 重庆	1	216	5,429	164	2.47	4.47	15.39	44.68	6,632
Sichuan 四川	2	82	1,084	-48	-1.69	-4.46	4.31	62.18	2,818
Guizhou 贵州									
Yunnan 云南	1	66	585	-273	-2.36	-14.55	-2.39	83.75	11,546
Tibet 西藏	1	121	2,241	1,047	13.47	23.02	4.84	41.45	7,770
Northwest 西北	5	161	1,803				8.80	128.89	10,204
Shaanxi 陕西									
Gansu 甘肃	5	161	1,803				8.80	128.89	10,204
Qinghai 青海									
Ningxia 宁夏									
Xinjiang 新疆									

1094: Gypsum Mining and Dressing 石膏采选业

Year 年份	Number of firms 企业个数	Rate of change 变化率(%)	Number of employees 职工人数(人)	Rate of change 变化率(%)	Total revenue (Mil. RMB) 总销售收入(百万元)	Rate of change 变化率(%)	Total profit (Mil RMB) 总利润(百万元)	Rate of change 变化率(%)
2000	75		30,354		1,009		63	
2001	79	5.33	24,935	-17.85	1,077	6.74	65	3.17
2002	79	o	24,092	-3.38	1,270	17.92	72	10.77

Major Products 主要产品	Output 产量	Unit 单位
Gypsum Slab 石膏板	17,332	10,000 Sq.M. 万平方米

10 Main Firms with Maximal Revenue (year founded) 收入最大的十家主要企业(创办年份)	City 城市	Province 省	Telephone/fax 电话/传真	Number of employees 职工人数	Ownership 产业所有权	Revenue ('000 RMB) 销售收入(千元)	Profit('000 RMB) (rank) 利润(千元)(排名)	Total assets ('000 RMB) 总资产(千元)	Major products 主要产品
Guangdong Sihui Gypsum Mine	Zhaoqing	Guangdong	(0758)3866268		State-owned				Gypsum
广东省四会石膏矿(1977)	肇庆市	广东省	(0758)3866182	675	国有企业	46,126	13,013(1)	108,638	石膏
Zaozhuang Yicheng Lihua Gypsum Mine	Zaozhuang	Shandong	(0632)7764888		Collective-owned				Gypsum
枣庄市峄城区利华石膏矿(1986)	枣庄市	山东省		300	集体企业	37,560	2,921(7)	6,923	石膏
Foshan Sanshui Qingqi Gypsum Mine Co.,Ltd.	Foshan	Guangdong	(0757)7613388		Collective-owned				Gypsum
佛山市三水青岐矿业有限公司(1981)	佛山市	广东省	(0757)7612211	506	集体企业	36,899	4,492(2)	48,588	石膏
Nanjing Gypsum Mine	Nanjing	Jiangsu	(025)4111928		State-owned				Gypsum
南京石膏矿(1985)	南京市	江苏省	(025)4110270	657	国有企业	32,230	160(49)	125,310	石膏
Shandong Luneng Tai'an Mining Development Co., Ltd.	Taian	Shandong	(0538)8118155		Limited-Liability				Gypsum
山东鲁能泰山矿业开发有限公司(1999)	泰安市	山东省	(0538)8118089	700	有限公司	27,565	982(26)	96,744	石膏
Zaozhuang New Fuyuan Gypsum Co., Ltd.	Zaozhuang	Shandong	(0632)7761086		Limited-Liability				Gypsum
枣庄新富源石膏有限责任公司(1988)	枣庄市	山东省		283	有限公司	26,580	1,470(22)	5,490	石膏
Zaozhuang Yicheng Area Ganlugou Gypsum Mine	Zaozhuang	Shandong	(0632)7761086		Collective-owned				Gypsum
枣庄市峄城区甘露沟石膏矿(1980)	枣庄市	山东省		570	集体企业	23,770	1,240(23)	9,390	石膏
Dangyang Gypsum Mine	Yichang	Hubei	(0717)3350144		Collective-owned				Gypsum
当阳市石膏矿(1977)	宜昌市	湖北省		131	集体企业	23,340	-	5,600	石膏
GuangBang Longyuan Gypsum Co., Ltd.	Jingmen	Hubei	(0724)2440487		Overseas Chinese-funded				Gypsum
光邦龙源石膏有限公司	荆门市	湖北省	(0724)2440827	238	港澳台资	21,500	675(35)	9,847	石膏
Wandong Sanhe Gypsum Development Co., Ltd.	Chuzhou	Anhui	(0550)4968103		Collective-owned				Gypsum
皖东三和石膏开发有限公司(1994)	滁州市	安徽省	(0550)4968102	438	集体企业	16,322	608(36)	31,427	石膏

Top 10 Cities by Revenue 销售收入排名前10位城市	Province 省	Market share 市场份额(%)	Number of firms 企业个数
Zaozhuang 枣庄市	Shandong 山东省	52.02	21
Jingmen 荆门市	Hubei 湖北省	8.13	11
Xiaogan 孝感市	Hubei 湖北省	6.57	7
Foshan 佛山市	Guangdong 广东省	6.12	2
Zhaoqing 肇庆市	Guangdong 广东省	3.63	1
Taian 泰安市	Shandong 山东省	3.20	2
Nanjing 南京市	Jiangsu 江苏省	2.54	1
Yichang 宜昌市	Hubei 湖北省	1.84	1
Loudi 娄底市	Hunan 湖南省	1.80	2
Chuzhou 滁州市	Anhui 安徽省	1.62	2

10 Major Wholesalers 十家主要批发商	City 城市	Province 省	Telephone/Fax 电话/传真
Xuzhou New Century Building Materials Decorative City	Xuzhou	Jiangsu	(0516)83666780
徐州市新世纪建材装饰城	徐州市	江苏省	(0516)63804485
Orienthome Co.,Ltd.	Beijing	Beijing	(010)63808294
东方家园有限公司	北京市	北京市	
Shanghai Jinkai Goods & Materials Co.,Ltd.	Shanghai	Shanghai	(021)52193967
上海金凯物资有限公司	上海市	上海市	
Guangzhou Building Materials Development Co.,Ltd.	Guangzhou	Guangdong	(020)83335062
广州市建材发展有限公司	广州市	广东省	(020)83341110
Guangxi Qiaofeng Goods & Materials Trade Co.,Ltd.	Nanning	Guangxi	(0771)2631539
广西侨丰物资贸易有限责任公司	南宁市	广西	(0771)2631539
Gansu Building Materials State-owned Assets Marketing Co.,Ltd.	Lanzhou	Gansu	(0931)8821359
甘肃建材国有资产经营有限责任公司	兰州市	甘肃省	(0931)8960243
Shanghai East Asia United Building Materials Co.,Ltd.	Shanghai	Shanghai	(021)33134520
上海东亚联合建材有限公司	上海市	上海市	(021)63216165
Shanghai Zhuzong Materials General Company	Shanghai	Shanghai	(021)32240030
上海住总物资总公司	上海市	上海市	(021)32240024
Guangdong Building Materials Company	Guangzhou	Guangdong	(020)83802713
广东省建材公司	广州市	广东省	(020)83817640
Guangdong Dongguan Hardware Minerals Import & Export Co.,Ltd	Dongguan	Guangdong	(0769)2227090
广东省东莞五金矿产进出口公司	东莞市	广东省	(0769)2221045

1097: Talcum Mining and Dressing 滑石采选业

The industry accounts for 0.012% of the total revenue of China's industrial sector in 2002. The rate of return on assets is 8.46%. 87.10% of all firms in the industry made a profit while 12.90% had negative returns.The top province in terms of the industry's revenue is Shandong, accounting for 33.28% of the total revenue.
2002年本行业收入占全行业的 0.012%，资产利润率为 8.46%。87.10%的企业赢利，12.90%的企业亏损。收入最高的省为山东省，占本行业的33.28%。

	Total number of firms 企业总数	Total number of employees 职工总数	Total revenue (Mil.RMB) 总销售收入（百万元）	Total profit (Mil.RMB) 总利润（百万元）	Return on assets 资产利润率（%）	Return on equity 权益利润率（%）	Labour productivity ('000 RMB/ worker) 劳动生产率（千元/人）	Debts/ assets 资产负债率（%）	Total assets (Mil.RMB) 总资产（百万元）
Industry Overall 行业总体	31	10,560	1,299	92	8.46	20.69	42.32	59.12	1,087

	Number of firms 企业个数	Average number of employees 平均职工人数	Average revenue ('000 RMB) 平均销售收入（千元）	Average profit ('000 RMB) 平均利润（千元）	Return on assets 资产利润率（%）	Return on equity 权益利润率（%）	Labour productivity ('000 RMB/ worker) 劳动生产率（千元/人）	Debts/ assets 资产负债率（%）	Average total assets ('000 RMB) 平均总资产（千元）
By ownership 产业所有权									
State-owned 国有	8	392	33,843	3,153	5.42	11.21	32.96	51.65	58,189
Collective-owned 集体	10	317	44,121	1,910	14.20	46.85	49.21	69.69	13,450
Foreign & Overseas Chinese Funded 三资	2	661	56,458	6,581	5.36	14.24	25.38	62.40	122,890
By regional distribution 地区分布									
Central-North 华北									
Beijing 北京									
Tianjin 天津									
Hebei 河北									
Shanxi 山西									
Inner Mongolia 内蒙古									
Northeast 东北	6	549	67,138	5,223	8.50	29.56	37.41	71.23	61,415
Liaoning 辽宁	6	549	67,138	5,223	8.50	29.56	37.41	71.23	61,415
Jilin 吉林									
Heilongjiang 黑龙江									
Central-East 华东	14	238	36,515	1,494	7.37	23.61	52.87	68.80	20,286
Shanghai 上海									
Jiangsu 江苏	1	104	46,743	1,734	29.11	41.75	120.59	30.27	5,956
Zhejiang 浙江									
Anhui 安徽	2	176	9,026	301	3.76	7.83	15.95	52.01	8,000
Fujian 福建									
Jiangxi 江西	1	50	14,215	6	0.13	0.19	128.06	33.77	4,667
Shandong 山东	10	283	43,220	1,858	7.22	25.22	53.63	71.37	25,738
Central-South 中南	11	357	34,973	3,605	9.14	15.89	37.48	42.52	39,460
Henan 河南	3	468	29,607	2,520	16.12	29.18	23.95	44.74	15,629
Hubei 湖北	1	50	6,240	215	4.22	5.00	35.96	15.69	5,100
Hunan 湖南									
Guangdong 广东									
Guangxi 广西	7	354	41,378	4,554	8.34	14.54	45.20	42.60	54,582
Hainan 海南									
Southwest 西南									
Chongqing 重庆									
Sichuan 四川									
Guizhou 贵州									
Yunnan 云南									
Tibet 西藏									
Northwest 西北									
Shaanxi 陕西									
Gansu 甘肃									
Qinghai 青海									
Ningxia 宁夏									
Xinjiang 新疆									

1097: Talcum Mining and Dressing 滑石采选业

Year 年份	Number of firms 企业个数	Rate of change 变化率 (%)	Number of employees 职工人数 (人)	Rate of change 变化率 (%)	Total revenue (Mil. RMB) 总销售收入 (百万元)	Rate of change 变化率 (%)	Total profit (Mil RMB) 总利润 (百万元)	Rate of change 变化率 (%)
2000	32		9,765		1,176		65	
2001	31	-3.13	10,059	3.01	1,152	-2.04	83	27.69
2002	31	o	10,560	4.98	1,299	12.76	92	10.84

Major Products 主要产品	Output 产量	Unit 单位

10 Main Firms with Maximal Revenue (year founded) 收入最大的十家主要企业（创办年份）	City 城市	Province 省	Telephone/fax 电话/传真	Number of employees 职工人数	Ownership 产业所有权	Revenue ('000 RMB) 销售收入 (千元)	Profit('000 RMB) (rank) 利润(千元) (排名)	Total assets ('000 RMB) 总资产 (千元)	Major products 主要产品
Haicheng Pailou Talcum Mine	Anshan	Liaoning	(0412)3772306		Private Enterprises				Talcum
海城市牌楼滑石矿(1971)	鞍山市	辽宁省	(0412)3772288	890	私营独资	285,800	24,800(1)	105,680	滑石
Xixia Xueguang Talcum Powder Co., Ltd	Yantai	Shandong	(0535)5541018		Collective-owned				Talcum Powder
栖霞市雪光滑石粉有限公司(1994)	烟台市	山东省	(0535)5541018	125	集体企业	208,880	7,890(4)	12,830	滑石粉
Guangxi Talcum Industry Company	Guilin	Guangxi	(0773)5592275		State-owned				Talcum Block
广西滑石工业公司(1986)	桂林市	广西	(0773)5592420	911	国有企业	101,498	13,188(2)	149,587	滑石块
Guangxi Longsheng Huamei Talcum Empolder Co.,Ltd.	Guilin	Guangxi	(0773)7432224		Foreign Funded				Talcum Block
中外合资广西龙胜华美滑石开发有限公司(1985)	桂林市	广西	(0773)7432229	387	外商投资	77,196	11,132(3)	76,840	滑石块
Shandong Xixia Huasheng Fine Chemical Industry Co., Ltd.	Yantai	Shandong	(0535)5541346		Limited-Liability				Talcum Powder
山东省栖霞市华盛精细化工有限公司(1998)	烟台市	山东省	(0535)5541888	60	有限公司	51,030	1,870(13)	1,890	滑石粉
Donghai Shuangdian Town Baiyun Talcum Powder Factory	Lianyungang	Jiangsu	(0518)7812005		Collective-owned				Talcum Powder
东海县双店镇白云滑石粉厂(1985)	连云港市	江苏省	(0518)7812071	104	集体企业	46,743	1,734(14)	5,956	滑石粉
Liaoning Aihai Talcum Co.Ltd.	Anshan	Liaoning	(0412)3268999		Foreign Funded				Talcum Powder
辽宁艾海滑石有限公司(1997)	鞍山市	辽宁省	(0412)3269888	935	外商投资	35,720	2,030(12)	168,940	滑石粉
Laizhou Yufeng Talcum Mine Co., Ltd.	Yantai	Shandong	(0535)2321036		Limited-Liability				Talcum
莱州市玉凤滑石矿业有限公司(1949)	烟台市	山东省	(0535)2321035	448	有限公司	28,730	3,587(7)	36,707	滑石
Haicheng Palc Mining Co.Ltd.	Anshan	Liaoning	(0412)3270259		Joint Stock				Talcum
海城市水泉滑石矿矿业有限公司(1995)	鞍山市	辽宁省	(0412)3270925	379	股份制	23,910	2,070(11)	54,720	滑石
Shanglin County Minerals Company	Nanning	Guangxi	(0771)5220570		State-owned				Talcum Mine
上林县矿产公司	南宁市	广西	(0771)5223337	71	国有企业	21,149	435(19)	13,295	滑石矿

Top 10 Cities by Revenue 销售收入排名前10位城市	Province 省	Market share 市场份额 (%)	Number of firms 企业个数
Anshan 鞍山市	Liaoning 辽宁省	29.53	5
Yantai 烟台市	Shandong 山东省	23.63	5
Guilin 桂林市	Guangxi 广西	20.59	4
Nanyang 南阳市	Henan 河南省	6.84	3
Linyi 临沂市	Shandong 山东省	6.37	3
Lianyungang 连云港市	Jiangsu 江苏省	3.60	1
Qingdao 青岛市	Shandong 山东省	3.28	2
Nanning 南宁市	Guangxi 广西	1.71	2
Liaoyang 辽阳市	Liaoning 辽宁省	1.49	1
Shangrao 上饶市	Jiangxi 江西省	1.09	1

10 Major Wholesalers 十家主要批发商	City 城市	Province 省	Telephone/Fax 电话/传真
China Railway Materials Beijing Company	Beijing	Beijing	(010)63602299
中国铁路物资北京公司	北京市	北京市	(010)63601722
Shanghai BM Import & Export Co., Ltd.	Shanghai	Shanghai	(021)50320000
上海宝矿进出口有限公司	上海市	上海市	(021)50326700
Citic Trading Co.,Ltd.	Beijing	Beijing	(010)84865638
中信贸易公司	北京市	北京市	(010)84865271
Qingdao Iron And Steel Import & Export Corp.	Qingdao	Shandong	(0532)5798210
青岛钢铁进出口公司	青岛市	山东省	(0532)5798069
Guangzhou Metals and Minerals Import & Export .Ltd.	Guangzhou	Guangdong	(020)81082026
广州五金矿产进出口有限公司	广州市	广东省	(020)81084886
Shanghai Foreign Economics Trading Development Company	Shanghai	Shanghai	(021)62719538
上海外经贸发展公司	上海市	上海市	(021)62729625
China Nonferrous Metal Import & Export Jiangsu Company	Nanjing	Jiangsu	(025)4400366
中国有色金属进出口江苏公司	南京市	江苏省	(025)4400773
China Hardware Minerals Import & Export Shenzhen Branch Company	Shenzhen	Guangdong	(0755)82388365
中国五金矿产进出口深圳分公司	深圳市	广东省	(0755)82388335
Guangdong Dongfang Import & Export Corp.	Shenzhen	Guangdong	(0755)25950270
广东省东方进出口公司	深圳市	广东省	(0755)25950220
Shannxi Import & Export Corp.	Xi'an	Shannxi	(029)6520075
陕西省进出口公司	西安市	陕西省	(029)6511071

1099: Other Non-metal Ores Mining and Dressing

其他类未包括的非金属矿采选业

The industry accounts for 0.031% of the total revenue of China's industrial sector in 2002. The rate of return on assets is 4.27%. 80.43% of all firms in the industry made a profit while 19.57% had negative returns.The top province in terms of the industry's revenue is Guangdong, accounting for 29.39% of the total revenue.
2002年本行业收入占全行业的0.031%，资产利润率为4.27%。80.43%的企业赢利，19.57%的企业亏损。收入最高的省为广东省，占本行业的29.39%。

	Total number of firms 企业总数	Total number of employees 职工总数	Total revenue (Mil.RMB) 总销售收入(百万元)	Total profit (Mil.RMB) 总利润(百万元)	Return on assets 资产利润率(%)	Return on equity 权益利润率(%)	Labour productivity ('000 RMB/worker) 劳动生产率(千元/人)	Debts/assets 资产负债率(%)	Total assets (Mil.RMB) 总资产(百万元)
Industry Overall 行业总体	235	34,722	3,373	181	4.27	10.04	34.39	57.50	4,235

	Number of firms 企业个数	Average number of employees 平均职工人数	Average revenue ('000 RMB) 平均销售收入（千元）	Average profit ('000 RMB) 平均利润（千元）	Return on assets 资产利润率(%)	Return on equity 权益利润率(%)	Labour productivity ('000 RMB/worker) 劳动生产率(千元/人)	Debts/assets 资产负债率(%)	Average total assets ('000 RMB) 平均总资产（千元）
By ownership 产业所有权									
State-owned 国有	32	334	10,892	687	2.10	5.04	18.00	58.28	32,654
Collective-owned 集体	55	128	19,155	1,305	8.55	17.49	45.85	51.12	15,271
Foreign & Overseas Chinese Funded 三资	27	110	19,313	771	3.53	5.73	55.77	38.48	21,860
By regional distribution 地区分布									
Central-North 华北	11	68	6,195	447	4.94	9.88	35.63	50.01	9,060
Beijing 北京	3	42	9,416	946	13.14	36.54	93.02	64.05	7,202
Tianjin 天津	1	35	4,730	450	37.19	37.19	42.00		1,210
Hebei 河北	4	82	4,698	121	1.40	4.26	18.40	67.14	8,653
Shanxi 山西									
Inner Mongolia 内蒙古	3	86	5,457	383	2.72	3.90	28.43	30.22	14,077
Northeast 东北	26	161	9,669	233	1.32	3.68	26.60	64.12	17,674
Liaoning 辽宁	13	182	13,447	638	2.38	6.38	31.99	62.67	26,806
Jilin 吉林	11	156	5,414	-138	-1.53	-4.97	17.81	69.13	9,017
Heilongjiang 黑龙江	2	59	8,523	-353	-5.95	-17.00	46.09	65.00	5,931
Central-East 华东	89	181	15,540	662	3.05	6.94	30.84	55.99	21,683
Shanghai 上海									
Jiangsu 江苏	4	590	39,905	388	0.60	3.01	24.31	80.02	64,544
Zhejiang 浙江	29	120	16,372	580	2.57	6.11	36.85	57.93	22,573
Anhui 安徽	9	56	8,734	178	4.92	9.39	53.27	47.63	3,623
Fujian 福建	17	71	15,086	1,432	7.98	13.67	115.44	41.63	17,958
Jiangxi 江西	22	333	12,284	222	1.04	2.71	13.15	61.65	21,395
Shandong 山东	8	156	17,910	1,214	4.66	6.63	39.29	29.67	26,047
Central-South 中南	81	130	18,240	1,239	8.12	17.28	43.67	53.00	15,256
Henan 河南	19	116	9,411	805	7.31	24.82	30.10	70.55	11,012
Hubei 湖北	12	138	13,952	718	11.96	24.86	39.54	51.87	5,997
Hunan 湖南	12	150	7,390	171	1.50	3.46	19.23	56.57	11,369
Guangdong 广东	30	137	33,043	2,606	10.46	19.17	66.84	45.45	24,925
Guangxi 广西	6	118	7,444	-197	-2.01	-9.74	24.00	79.33	9,802
Hainan 海南	2	41	3,277	-1,301	-22.56	-49.47	39.98	54.40	5,765
Southwest 西南	10	168	8,179	258	0.85	3.87	22.57	78.00	30,309
Chongqing 重庆									
Sichuan 四川	8	189	8,697	52	0.15	0.66	21.84	77.69	35,225
Guizhou 贵州	1	12	526	-45	-8.91	-36.59	11.33	75.64	505
Yunnan 云南	1	160	11,695	2,211	10.64	59.71	30.33	82.18	20,778
Tibet 西藏									
Northwest 西北	18	78	6,180	439	3.82	8.96	42.38	57.40	11,505
Shaanxi 陕西	3	148	7,866	-4	-0.03	-0.04	37.20	36.97	14,461
Gansu 甘肃	12	41	3,479	-10	-0.18	-0.64	40.36	72.07	5,437
Qinghai 青海									
Ningxia 宁夏									
Xinjiang 新疆	3	152	15,303	2,678	8.16	18.84	49.60	56.68	32,820

1099: Other Non-metal Ores Mining and Dressing

其他类未包括的非金属矿采选业

Year 年份	Number of firms 企业个数	Rate of change 变化率 (%)	Number of employees 职工人数 (人)	Rate of change 变化率 (%)	Total revenue (Mil. RMB) 总销售收入 (百万元)	Rate of change 变化率 (%)	Total profit (Mil RMB) 总利润 (百万元)	Rate of change 变化率 (%)
2000	207		37,870		2,881		144	
2001	241	16.43	38,404	1.41	3,388	17.60	139	-3.47
2002	235	-2.49	34,722	-9.59	3,373	-0.44	181	30.22

Major Products 主要产品	Output 产量	Unit 单位

10 Main Firms with Maximal Revenue (year founded) 收入最大的十家主要企业（创办年份）	City 城市	Province 省	Telephone/fax 电话/传真	Number of employees 职工人数	Ownership 产业所有权	Revenue ('000 RMB) 销售收入 (千元)	Profit('000 RMB) (rank) 利润(千元) (排名)	Total assets ('000 RMB) 总资产 (千元)	Major products 主要产品
Guangzhou Timian Mineral Resources Co., Ltd.	Guangzhou	Guangdong	(020)86851532		Collective-owned				Porcelain Clay
广州市梯面矿产资源有限公司(1978)	广州市	广东省		234	集体企业	148,749	24,660(1)	65,908	瓷土
Zhejiang Huate Industrial Group Co., Ltd.	Hangzhou	Zhejiang	(0571)85774398		Collective-owned				Bentonite In Powder
浙江华特实业集团有限公司(1997)	杭州市	浙江省	(0571)63711398	470	集体企业	120,134	12,618(4)	218,853	膨润土粉
Conghua Youtao Kaolin Co., Ltd.	Guangzhou	Guangdong	(020)87880181		Foreign Funded				Dolomite
从化佑陶高岭土有限公司(1992)	广州市	广东省	(020)87880369	380	外商投资	99,423	4,275(11)	75,200	白石土
China Kaolin Company	Suzhou	Jiangsu	(0512)65391612		State-owned				Porcelain Clay
中国高岭土公司(1955)	苏州市	江苏省	(0512)65391459	1,617	国有企业	87,288	598(64)	215,578	瓷土
Xinhui Jiayao Ceramic Raw Materials Co., Ltd.	Jiangmen	Guangdong	(0750)6455239		Overseas Chinese-funded				Porcelain Clay
新会区嘉窑陶瓷原料有限公司(1994)	江门市	广东省	(0750)6455216	279	港澳台资	86,590	6,380(7)	64,666	瓷坭
Maoming Kaolin Science & Technology Co., Ltd.	Maoming	Guangdong	(0668)2716738		Limited-Liability				Dope Dry Powder
茂名高岭科技有限公司(1994)	茂名市	广东省	(0668)2710211	591	有限公司	77,579	17,558(3)	121,159	涂料干粉
Jiangxi Yongfeng Jinfeng Fluorite Co., Ltd.	Ji'an	Jiangxi	(0796)2351028		Private Owned				Fluorite Concentrated Powder
江西永丰县金丰萤石有限公司(2000)	吉安市	江西省	(0796)2222567	110	私营企业	65,264	782(50)	12,686	萤石精粉
Donghai Qianqiangwei Stone Powder Factory	Lianyungang	Jiangsu	(0518)7328776		Collective-owned				Quartz Sand
东海县前蔷薇石粉厂(1985)	连云港市	江苏省	(0518)7328909	140	集体企业	51,060	1,592(28)	2,897	石英砂
Mianchi Tianma Group Co., Ltd.	Sanmenxia	Henan	(0398)4944629		Limited-Liability				Porcelain Stone Powder
渑池县天马集团有限责任公司(1998)	三门峡市	河南省		136	有限公司	41,390	3,731(12)	24,394	瓷石粉
Maoming Shange Porcelain Clay Company	Maoming	Guangdong	(0668)2711218		Joint Stock				kaolin
茂名市山阁瓷土公司(1987)	茂名市	广东省	(0668)2710017	306	股份制	38,560	2,686(15)	94,517	高岭土

Top 10 Cities by Revenue 销售收入排名前10位城市	Province 省	Market share 市场份额 (%)	Number of firms 企业个数
Zhaoqing 肇庆市	Guangdong 广东省	9.64	5
Guangzhou 广州市	Guangdong 广东省	7.63	3
Hangzhou 杭州市	Zhejiang 浙江省	5.46	7
Maoming 茂名市	Guangdong 广东省	4.99	8
Jiangmen 江门市	Guangdong 广东省	3.87	3
Longyan 龙岩市	Fujian 福建省	2.89	4
Ganzhou 赣州市	Jiangxi 江西省	2.84	6
Suzhou 苏州市	Jiangsu 江苏省	2.74	2
Sanming 三明市	Fujian 福建省	2.73	6
Qingdao 青岛市	Shandong 山东省	2.47	2

10 Major Wholesalers 十家主要批发商	City 城市	Province 省	Telephone/Fax 电话/传真
China Railway Materials Beijing Company	Beijing	Beijing	(010)63602299
中国铁路物资北京公司	北京市	北京市	(010)63601722
Shanghai BM Import & Export Co., Ltd.	Shanghai	Shanghai	(021)50320000
上海宝矿进出口有限公司	上海市	上海市	(021)50326700
Citic Trading Co.,Ltd.	Beijing	Beijing	(010)84865638
中信贸易公司	北京市	北京市	(010)84865271
Qingdao Iron And Steel Import & Export Corp.	Qingdao	Shandong	(0532)5798210
青岛钢铁进出口公司	青岛市	山东省	(0532)5798069
Guangzhou Metals and Minerals Import & Export .Ltd.	Guangzhou	Guangdong	(020)81082026
广州五金矿产进出口有限公司	广州市	广东省	(020)81084886
Shanghai Foreign Economics Trading Development Company	Shanghai	Shanghai	(021)62719538
上海外经贸发展公司	上海市	上海市	(021)62729625
China Nonferrous Metal Import & Export Jiangsu Company	Nanjing	Jiangsu	(025)4400366
中国有色金属进出口江苏公司	南京市	江苏省	(025)4400773
China Hardware Minerals Import & Export Shenzhen Branch Company	Shenzhen	Guangdong	(0755)82388365
中国五金矿产进出口深圳分公司	深圳市	广东省	(0755)82388335
Guangdong Dongfang Import & Export Corp.	Shenzhen	Guangdong	(0755)25950270
广东省东方进出口公司	深圳市	广东省	(0755)25950220
Shannxi Import & Export Corp.	Xi'an	Shannxi	(029)6520075
陕西省进出口公司	西安市	陕西省	(029)6511071

1210: Logging and Transport Of Timber 木材采运业

The industry accounts for 0.089% of the total revenue of China's industrial sector in 2002. The rate of return on assets is 0.68%. 61.02% of all firms in the industry made a profit while 38.98% had negative returns.The top province in terms of the industry's revenue is Heilong Jiang, accounting for 39.08% of the total revenue.
2002年本行业收入占全行业的0.089%，资产利润率为0.68%。61.02%的企业赢利，38.98%的企业亏损。收入最高的省为黑龙江省，占本行业的39.08%。

	Total number of firms 企业总数	Total number of employees 职工总数	Total revenue (Mil.RMB) 总销售收入 (百万元)	Total profit (Mil.RMB) 总利润 (百万元)	Return on assets 资产利润率 (%)	Return on equity 权益利润率 (%)	Labour productivity ('000 RMB/ worker) 劳动生产率 (千元/人)	Debts/ assets 资产负债率 (%)	Total assets (Mil.RMB) 总资产 (百万元)
Industry Overall 行业总体	372	577,796	9,509	276	0.68	2.00	9.62	66.02	40,614

	Number of firms 企业个数	Average number of employees 平均职工人数	Average revenue ('000 RMB) 平均销售收入（千元）	Average profit ('000 RMB) 平均利润 (千元)	Return on assets 资产利润率 (%)	Return on equity 权益利润率 (%)	Labour productivity ('000 RMB/ worker) 劳动生产率 (千元/人)	Debts/ assets 资产负债率 (%)	Average total assets ('000 RMB) 平均总资产 (千元)
By ownership 产业所有权									
State-owned 国有	356	1,573	24,817	567	0.52	1.64	9.18	67.95	108,123
Collective-owned 集体	3	67	7,041	144	2.04	2.22	45.59	8.42	7,055
Foreign & Overseas Chinese Funded 三资									
By regional distribution 地区分布									
Central-North 华北	19	4,386	68,191	3,907	1.04	3.00	10.42	65.33	375,169
Beijing 北京									
Tianjin 天津									
Hebei 河北									
Shanxi 山西									
Inner Mongolia 内蒙古	19	4,386	68,191	3,907	1.04	3.00	10.42	65.33	375,169
Northeast 东北	96	4,682	72,854	2,424	0.88	2.87	8.85	69.30	275,473
Liaoning 辽宁									
Jilin 吉林	36	3,510	91,053	4,866	2.07	5.00	12.32	58.51	234,611
Heilongjiang 黑龙江	60	5,385	61,935	959	0.32	1.25	7.49	74.37	299,990
Central-East 华东	128	205	6,371	-123	-0.40	-0.98	21.28	58.74	30,589
Shanghai 上海									
Jiangsu 江苏									
Zhejiang 浙江									
Anhui 安徽									
Fujian 福建	40	266	14,254	132	0.17	0.40	42.66	55.87	75,812
Jiangxi 江西	88	177	2,787	-240	-2.39	-7.60	6.67	68.59	10,033
Shandong 山东									
Central-South 中南	65	171	4,322	-195	-0.65	-1.10	9.38	41.14	30,194
Henan 河南									
Hubei 湖北	1	241	3,065	890	4.42	7.63	8.95	42.15	20,150
Hunan 湖南	16	230	5,712	-416	-1.66	-5.53	6.89	70.02	25,112
Guangdong 广东	24	124	4,572	-289	-1.36	-2.38	14.24	42.96	21,343
Guangxi 广西	20	131	3,377	48	0.11	0.14	11.99	18.77	43,167
Hainan 海南	4	406	2,293	-236	-0.57	-3.18	2.00	82.06	41,280
Southwest 西南	54	88	1,902	38	0.25	0.68	9.51	63.91	15,597
Chongqing 重庆									
Sichuan 四川	11	1						66.85	34,171
Guizhou 贵州	25	80	1,483	10	0.10	0.23	7.25	56.30	9,785
Yunnan 云南	16	164	3,885	111	0.82	2.55	11.18	67.82	13,546
Tibet 西藏	2	58	1,748	20	0.78	1.42	12.15	45.19	2,506
Northwest 西北	10	289	2,042	-496	-1.55	-3.63	1.72	57.37	31,985
Shaanxi 陕西	3	640	2,831	-1,172	-1.97	-3.27	1.47	39.90	59,586
Gansu 甘肃									
Qinghai 青海									
Ningxia 宁夏									
Xinjiang 新疆	7	139	1,704	-206	-1.02	-4.98	2.20	79.49	20,155

1210: Logging and Transport Of Timber 木材采运业

Year 年份	Number of firms 企业个数	Rate of change 变化率 (%)	Number of employees 职工人数 (人)	Rate of change 变化率 (%)	Total revenue (Mil. RMB) 总销售收入 (百万元)	Rate of change 变化率 (%)	Total profit (Mil RMB) 总利润 (百万元)	Rate of change 变化率 (%)
2000	490		815,015		10,831		115	
2001	420	-14.29	654,274	-19.72	9,417	-13.06	208	80.87
2002	372	-11.43	577,796	-11.69	9,509	0.98	276	32.69

Major Products 主要产品	Output 产量	Unit 单位
Timber 木材	1,875	10,000 stere 万立方米

10 Main Firms with Maximal Revenue (year founded) 收入最大的十家主要企业 (创办年份)	City 城市	Province 省	Telephone/fax 电话/传真	Number of employees 职工人数	Ownership 产业所有权	Revenue ('000 RMB) 销售收入 (千元)	Profit('000 RMB) (rank) 利润(千元) (排名)	Total assets ('000 RMB) 总资产 (千元)	Major products 主要产品
Jilin Linjiang Forest Industry Bureau	Baishan	Jilin	(0439)5216111		State-owned				Timber
吉林省临江林业局(1953)	白山市	吉林省	(0439)5216111	15,672	国有企业	277,743	9,707(13)	365,622	木材
Jilin Forest Industry Group Songjiang River Forestry Co.,Ltd.	Baishan	Jilin	(0439)6320520		State-owned				Timber
吉林森工集团松江河林业有限公司(1958)	白山市	吉林省	(0439)6311115	7,553	国有企业	232,088	10,104(12)	479,702	木材
Jilin Dunhua Danfeng Forestry Co., Ltd.	Yanbian	Jilin	(0433)6209781		State-owned				Timber
吉林敦化丹峰林业有限公司(1957)	延边州	吉林省	(0433)6208020	8,983	国有企业	214,642	4,066(34)	446,209	木材
Jilin Fusong Lushui River Forest Industry Bureau	Baishan	Jilin	(0439)6369104		State-owned				Timber
吉林省抚松县露水河林业局(1970)	白山市	吉林省	(0439)6369104	6,907	国有企业	189,428	8,230(18)	369,482	木材
Daxing'anling No.18 Station Forest Industry Bureau	Daxinganling	Heilongjiang	(0457)3616522		State-owned				Timber
大兴安岭十八站林业局(1974)	大兴安岭	黑龙江省		5,363	国有企业	172,165	13,655(7)	639,887	木材
Jilin Fusong Quanyang Forest Industry Bureau	Baishan	Jilin	(0439)6520016		State-owned				Timber
吉林省抚松县泉阳林业局(1965)	白山市	吉林省	(0439)6511000	5,961	国有企业	156,928	9,657(14)	446,684	木材
Heilong Jiang Langxiang Forest Industry Bureau	Yichun	Heilongjiang	(0458)2586083		State-owned				Timber
黑龙江省朗乡林业局(1953)	伊春市	黑龙江省	(0458)2583770	9,522	国有企业	140,031	12,048(9)	456,509	木材
Songling Forest Industry Bureau	Daxinganling	Heilongjiang	(0457)3322382		State-owned				Timber
松岭林业局(1964)	大兴安岭	黑龙江省	(0457)3321007	6,554	国有企业	138,859	18,352(4)	444,095	木材
Daxing Anling Tahe Forest Industry Bureau	Daxinganling	Heilongjiang	(0457)3609133		State-owned				Timber
大兴安岭塔河林业局(1965)	大兴安岭	黑龙江省	(0457)3662666	8,709	国有企业	137,327	7,872(21)	703,941	木材
Daxing'anling Tuqiang Forestry Co., Ltd.	Daxinganling	Heilongjiang	(0457)2855001		State Enterprises				Timber
大兴安岭图强有限责任公司(1977)	大兴安岭	黑龙江省	(0457)2855001	8,807	国有独资	116,398	3,118(41)	670,760	木材

Top 10 Cities by Revenue 销售收入排名前10位城市	Province 省	Market share 市场份额 (%)	Number of firms 企业个数
Yanbian 延边州	Jilin 吉林省	15.10	13
Daxinganling 大兴安岭地区	Heilongjiang 黑龙江省	13.06	9
Hulunber 呼伦贝尔市	Inner Mongolia 内蒙古	13.05	16
Baishan 白山市	Jilin 吉林省	12.68	9
Yichun 伊春市	Heilongjiang 黑龙江省	7.89	17
Mudanjiang 牡丹江市	Heilongjiang 黑龙江省	6.34	8
Jilin 吉林市	Jilin 吉林省	6.19	13
Harbin 哈尔滨市	Heilongjiang 黑龙江省	5.89	17
Nanping 南平市	Fujian 福建省	2.67	13
Sanming 三明市	Fujian 福建省	2.33	15

10 Major Wholesalers 十家主要批发商	City 城市	Province 省	Telephone/Fax 电话/传真
Shanghai Xinmei (Group) Co.,Ltd.	Shanghai	Shanghai	(021)58120888
上海新美（集团）有限公司	上海市	上海市	(021)67559188
Guangdong Native Products Import & Export (Group) Corporation	Guangzhou	Guangdong	(020)84244025
广东省土产进出口（集团）公司	广州市	广东省	(020)84423070
China Timber Import & Export Co.,Ltd.	Beijing	Beijing	(010)64203414
中国木材进出口股份有限公司	北京市	北京市	(010)64208900
Xiamen Yongquan Group Co.,Ltd.	Xiamen	Fujian	(0592)5161286
厦门涌泉集团有限公司	厦门市	福建省	(0592)5162966
China National Forest Products Marketing Co.	Beijing	Beijing	(010)64228370
中国林产品经销公司	北京市	北京市	(010)64216443
Liaoning Huiming International Trade Co.,Ltd.	Dalian	Liaoning	(0411)3620626
大连市辽宁汇明国际贸易有限公司	大连市	辽宁省	(0411)3636995
Shanghai Senda Wood Industry Co.,Ltd.	Shanghai	Shanghai	(021)54367592
上海森大木业有限公司	上海市	上海市	(021)54360331
Shanghai Timber General Corp.	Shanghai	Shanghai	(021)63230138
上海市木材总公司	上海市	上海市	(021)63236079
Guangdong Nanyou Economic Development Corp.	Guangzhou	Guangdong	(020)87304129
广东南油经济发展公司	广州市	广东省	(020)87756069
Zhuhai S.E.Z.Materials Company	Zhuhai	Guangdong	(0756)2116092
珠海经济特区物资公司	珠海市	广东省	(0756)2116718

1311: Rice Milling 碾米业

The industry accounts for 0.184% of the total revenue of China's industrial sector in 2002. The rate of return on assets is 2.53%. 78.89% of all firms in the industry made a profit while 21.11% had negative returns.The top province in terms of the industry's revenue is Jiangsu, accounting for 25.16% of the total revenue.
2002年本行业收入占全行业的 0.184%，资产利润率为 2.53%。78.89%的企业赢利，21.11%的企业亏损。收入最高的省为江苏省，占本行业的25.16%。

	Total number of firms 企业总数	Total number of employees 职工总数	Total revenue (Mil.RMB) 总销售收入 (百万元)	Total profit (Mil.RMB) 总利润 (百万元)	Return on assets 资产利润率 (%)	Return on equity 权益利润率 (%)	Labour productivity ('000 RMB/ worker) 劳动生产率 (千元/人)	Debts/ assets 资产负债率 (%)	Total assets (Mil.RMB) 总资产 (百万元)
Industry Overall 行业总体	995	82,321	19,715	327	2.53	7.83	64.66	67.65	12,893

	Number of firms 企业个数	Average number of employees 平均职工人数	Average revenue ('000 RMB) 平均销售收入 (千元)	Average profit ('000 RMB) 平均利润 (千元)	Return on assets 资产利润率 (%)	Return on equity 权益利润率 (%)	Labour productivity ('000 RMB/ worker) 劳动生产率 (千元/人)	Debts/ assets 资产负债率 (%)	Average total assets ('000 RMB) 平均总资产 (千元)
By ownership 产业所有权									
State-owned 国有	406	74	10,819	-160	-1.64	-13.67	53.52	87.99	9,727
Collective-owned 集体	90	129	29,009	1,106	12.56	30.09	69.41	58.25	8,802
Foreign & Overseas Chinese Funded 三资	12	72	16,365	-391	-1.19	-2.97	83.54	59.73	32,769
By regional distribution 地区分布									
Central-North 华北	19	34	17,016	761	11.74	33.01	110.86	64.42	6,481
Beijing 北京	2	42	21,932	-479	-1.79	-3.23	30.35	44.70	26,822
Tianjin 天津	3	25	14,298	631	20.24		29.95	109.19	3,116
Hebei 河北	13	35	16,301	991	21.82	92.78	123.91	76.48	4,540
Shanxi 山西									
Inner Mongolia 内蒙古	1	24	24,625	650	57.78	57.78	393.75		1,125
Northeast 东北	88	117	37,646	495	1.09	3.76	77.70	70.98	45,439
Liaoning 辽宁	23	69	27,928	167	0.63	2.52	103.75	74.95	26,510
Jilin 吉林	27	127	12,320	-1,464	-6.41	-31.15	26.19	79.42	22,832
Heilongjiang 黑龙江	38	140	61,522	2,086	2.86	9.00	103.20	68.24	72,959
Central-East 华东	489	73	19,727	311	3.46	9.96	61.33	65.28	9,005
Shanghai 上海	3	104	84,605	1,853	2.68	5.10	111.17	47.53	69,238
Jiangsu 江苏	198	75	25,048	362	5.52	16.37	73.09	66.31	6,563
Zhejiang 浙江	33	26	13,777	197	3.31	13.58	54.36	75.64	5,956
Anhui 安徽	95	113	26,042	707	4.51	10.25	60.01	55.95	15,673
Fujian 福建	15	28	11,011	-3	-0.04	-0.08	101.49	47.22	7,541
Jiangxi 江西	139	58	9,179	-18	-0.24	-1.17	37.62	79.71	7,692
Shandong 山东	6	47	10,548	647	13.58	247.89	77.72	94.52	4,764
Central-South 中南	334	96	17,197	401	3.67	10.17	66.16	63.87	10,926
Henan 河南	34	57	11,362	439	7.54	20.18	67.86	62.62	5,817
Hubei 湖北	169	126	19,473	545	5.25	14.59	71.52	63.98	10,378
Hunan 湖南	87	75	12,778	32	0.30	0.96	45.00	68.39	10,424
Guangdong 广东	32	42	16,318	521	3.87	7.04	92.14	44.99	13,445
Guangxi 广西	10	84	43,047	756	2.15	8.41	54.01	74.47	35,221
Hainan 海南	2	28	1,082	5	0.11		8.04	107.82	4,046
Southwest 西南	55	56	11,680	-123	-1.13	-4.78	46.42	76.46	10,926
Chongqing 重庆	3	100	12,475	-250	-2.94	-15.83	7.93	81.40	8,501
Sichuan 四川	22	72	20,375	190	1.23	7.71	69.10	83.98	15,378
Guizhou 贵州	15	26	5,733	75	1.69	4.41	52.64	61.67	4,426
Yunnan 云南	15	54	4,717	-754	-6.63	-19.81	13.26	66.55	11,381
Tibet 西藏									
Northwest 西北	10	72	4,606	-1,082	-9.20		11.92	118.29	11,763
Shaanxi 陕西	5	92	1,115	-449	-5.64		12.74	126.08	7,962
Gansu 甘肃	1	13	5	2	0.54	0.56	100.08	3.52	369
Qinghai 青海									
Ningxia 宁夏	4	61	10,119	-2,145	-11.08		5.70	114.84	19,362
Xinjiang 新疆									

1311: Rice Milling 碾米业

Year 年份	Number of firms 企业个数	Rate of change 变化率 (%)	Number of employees 职工人数 (人)	Rate of change 变化率 (%)	Total revenue (Mil. RMB) 总销售收入 (百万元)	Rate of change 变化率 (%)	Total profit (Mil RMB) 总利润 (百万元)	Rate of change 变化率 (%)
2000	1181		95,604		14,301		137	
2001	1082	-8.38	86,663	-9.35	15,630	9.29	218	59.12
2002	995	-8.04	82,321	-5.01	19,715	26.14	327	50.00

Major Products 主要产品	Output 产量	Unit 单位
Rice 大米	2,217	10,000 Tons 万吨

10 Main Firms with Maximal Revenue (year founded) 收入最大的十家主要企业（创办年份）	City 城市	Province 省	Telephone/fax 电话/传真	Number of employees 职工人数	Ownership 产业所有权	Revenue ('000 RMB) 销售收入 (千元)	Profit('000 RMB) (rank) 利润(千元) (排名)	Total assets ('000 RMB) 总资产 (千元)	Major products 主要产品
Heilongjiang Beidahuang Rice Industry Co., Ltd. 黑龙江省北大荒米业有限公司(2001)	Harbin 哈尔滨市	Heilongjiang 黑龙江省	(0451)82362205 (0451)82363273	1,073	State Enterprises 国有独资	944,300	20,020(2)	1,749,460	Rice 大米
Guilin Liyuan Grain & Oil Food Co., ltd. 桂林市力源粮油食品有限公司(1953)	Guilin 桂林市	Guangxi 广西省	(0773)2601237 (0773)2605135	490	Limited-Liability 有限公司	384,704	14,521(5)	166,860	Rice 大米
Heilongjiang Jinqiu Enterprise Group Co., Ltd. 黑龙江金秋企业集团有限责任公司(1996)	Qiqihar 齐齐哈尔市	Heilongjiang 黑龙江省	(0452)2523239 (0452)2523229	1,193	Limited-Liability 有限公司	307,073	23,694(1)	73,439	Rice 大米
Anhui Fengda Stock Co., Ltd. 安徽丰大股份有限公司(1997)	Hefei 合肥市	Anhui 安徽省	(0551)4483892	1,862	Joint Stock 股份制	281,655	19,486(4)	277,603	Wheat Flour 小麦粉
Lvdu Group Stock Co., Ltd. 绿都集团股份有限公司(1998)	Jixi 鸡西市	Heilongjiang 黑龙江省	(0467)5831448 (0467)5822622	345	Joint Stock 股份制	273,794	3,548(19)	284,587	Refined Rice 精制米
Anhui Jiaxian Rice Industry Group Co., Ltd. 安徽省稼仙米业集团有限公司(2001)	Anqing 安庆市	Anhui 安徽省	(0556)4618548 (0556)4618548	1,423	State Enterprises 国有独资	269,150	3,650(18)	111,256	Rice 大米
Hubei Yinxin Group Co., Ltd. 湖北银欣集团有限公司(1993)	Jingzhou 荆州市	Hubei 湖北省	(0716)3784388 (0716)3785031	1,200	Private Enterprises 私营独资	262,766	5,063(13)	102,492	Rice 大米
Wuhu Jintian Group Co., Ltd. 芜湖金田集团有限公司(1988)	Wuhu 芜湖市	Anhui 安徽省	(0553)8146152 (0553)8813888	218	Limited-Liability 有限公司	253,720	9,746(8)	362,570	Rice 大米
Anhui Lvyi Grain & Oil Group 安徽绿一粮油集团(1929)	Chuzhou 滁州市	Anhui 安徽省	(0550)3023488 (0550)3020600	600	State-owned 国有企业	239,754	493(161)	90,277	Rice 大米
Shanghai Fuxin Flour Co., Ltd. 上海福新面粉有限公司(1999)	Shanghai 上海市	Shanghai 上海市	(021)64355522 (021)54711020	228	State Enterprises 国有独资	216,193	7,044(10)	189,509	Grain Products 粮食制品

Top 10 Cities by Revenue 销售收入排名前10位城市	Province 省	Market share 市场份额 (%)	Number of firms 企业个数
Lianyungang 连云港市	Jiangsu 江苏省	6.59	23
Suizhou 随州市	Hubei 湖北省	5.70	46
Harbin 哈尔滨市	Heilongjiang 黑龙江省	5.66	7
Huaian 淮安市	Jiangsu 江苏省	4.76	51
Suqian 宿迁市	Jiangsu 江苏省	4.60	43
Chuzhou 滁州市	Anhui 安徽省	3.63	32
Jingzhou 荆州市	Hubei 湖北省	3.12	18
Yancheng 盐城市	Jiangsu 江苏省	2.95	23
Xiaogan 孝感市	Hubei 湖北省	2.76	21
Huanggang 黄冈市	Hubei 湖北省	2.32	26

10 Major Wholesalers 十家主要批发商	City 城市	Province 省	Telephone/Fax 电话/传真
COFCO International (Beijing) Ltd. 中粮国际(北京)有限公司	Beijing 北京市	Beijing 北京市	(010)65268888 (010)65223623
China National Cereals, Oils & Foodstuffs Imp. & Exp. Corp. 中国粮油食品进出口(集团)有限公司	Beijing 北京市	Beijing 北京市	(010)65268888 (010)62578612
China Grains and Oils Group Corp. 中谷粮油集团公司	Beijing 北京市	Beijing 北京市	(010)88518866 (010)68476847
China Tobacco General Company Beijing Company 中国烟草总公司北京市公司	Beijing 北京市	Beijing 北京市	(010)64434106 (010)64418742
Jilin Grain Group Import & Export Ltd. 吉林粮食集团进出口有限公司	Changchun 长春市	Jilin 吉林省	(0431)5598115 (0431)5598118
Zhejiang Cereals, Oils & Foodstuffs Import & Export Co.,Ltd. 浙江省粮油食品进出口股份有限公司	Hangzhou 杭州市	Zhejiang 浙江省	(0571)85779999 (0571)85152514
China Tobacco General Company Shenzhen Company 中国烟草总公司深圳市公司	Shenzhen 深圳市	Guangdong 广东省	(0755)82230333 (0755)82206815
China National Vegetable Oil Corporation 中国植物油公司	Beijing 北京市	Beijing 北京市	(010)68083380 (010)68081127
Beijing Yangu Grain & Oil Purchase & Sale Company 北京市燕谷粮油购销公司	Beijing 北京市	Beijing 北京市	(010)63041782 (010)63034914
Shanghai Good Companion Sea Lion Industrial Co., Ltd Sale Filiale 上海良友海狮油脂实业有限公司销售分公司	Shanghai 上海市	Shanghai 上海市	(021)63321662 (021)54095735

1312: Flour Milling 磨粉业

The industry accounts for 0.329% of the total revenue of China's industrial sector in 2002. The rate of return on assets is 2.13%. 77.65% of all firms in the industry made a profit while 22.35% had negative returns.The top province in terms of the industry's revenue is Henan, accounting for 26.75% of the total revenue.
2002年本行业收入占全行业的0.329%，资产利润率为2.13%。77.65%的企业赢利，22.35%的企业亏损。收入最高的省为河南省，占本行业的26.75%。

	Total number of firms 企业总数	Total number of employees 职工总数	Total revenue (Mil.RMB) 总销售收入(百万元)	Total profit (Mil.RMB) 总利润(百万元)	Return on assets 资产利润率(%)	Return on equity 权益利润率(%)	Labour productivity ('000 RMB/worker) 劳动生产率(千元/人)	Debts/assets 资产负债率(%)	Total assets (Mil.RMB) 总资产(百万元)
Industry Overall 行业总体	1606	148,846	35,271	605	2.13	7.82	58.05	72.74	28,369

	Number of firms 企业个数	Average number of employees 平均职工人数	Average revenue ('000 RMB) 平均销售收入(千元)	Average profit ('000 RMB) 平均利润(千元)	Return on assets 资产利润率(%)	Return on equity 权益利润率(%)	Labour productivity ('000 RMB/worker) 劳动生产率(千元/人)	Debts/assets 资产负债率(%)	Average total assets ('000 RMB) 平均总资产(千元)
By ownership 产业所有权									
State-owned 国有	486	101	13,174	-350	-1.74	-17.56	33.87	90.08	20,110
Collective-owned 集体	256	81	20,755	1,376	12.90	25.72	73.98	49.85	10,669
Foreign & Overseas Chinese Funded 三资	52	146	66,084	-128	-0.17	-0.44	86.85	59.91	73,415
By regional distribution 地区分布									
Central-North 华北	190	85	21,038	162	0.74	3.02	48.73	75.48	21,862
Beijing 北京	13	114	36,704	-1,938	-6.44	-17.66	38.97	63.53	30,091
Tianjin 天津	25	95	35,943	933	2.54	6.94	34.14	63.42	36,768
Hebei 河北	98	79	20,635	427	2.77	14.89	51.42	81.42	15,443
Shanxi 山西	39	74	3,904	-71	-0.43	-2.95	24.57	85.46	16,600
Inner Mongolia 内蒙古	15	111	29,802	-429	-0.94	-3.91	107.20	75.92	45,509
Northeast 东北	53	160	19,604	-1,117	-2.71	-18.19	24.91	85.12	41,272
Liaoning 辽宁	14	170	37,159	-1,939	-3.19	-16.73	25.60	80.94	60,803
Jilin 吉林	13	176	2,144	-3,205	-10.80		2.65	126.90	29,677
Heilongjiang 黑龙江	26	148	18,882	369	1.01	3.59	37.78	71.90	36,552
Central-East 华东	503	107	30,376	603	3.17	12.04	70.06	73.68	19,024
Shanghai 上海	1	33	9,496	-791	-5.01	-71.78	-6.55	93.02	15,786
Jiangsu 江苏	119	114	31,303	-52	-0.30	-2.41	58.35	87.46	17,135
Zhejiang 浙江	13	114	47,107	370	0.77	2.09	69.32	63.25	48,083
Anhui 安徽	63	99	15,265	102	0.67	3.96	46.47	83.11	15,322
Fujian 福建	10	82	52,329	-1,005	-2.46	-5.50	111.41	55.23	40,768
Jiangxi 江西	12	133	10,777	72	0.41	1.50	26.11	72.94	17,630
Shandong 山东	285	105	32,695	1,081	5.81	18.91	81.64	69.29	18,612
Central-South 中南	553	89	21,560	631	3.95	12.85	63.08	69.26	15,987
Henan 河南	454	83	20,783	860	7.07	21.16	66.78	66.56	12,149
Hubei 湖北	50	109	17,575	-173	-1.01	-9.77	65.49	89.66	17,141
Hunan 湖南	10	213	27,699	-110	-0.14	-0.40	25.57	63.74	76,475
Guangdong 广东	31	101	36,608	-429	-0.97	-2.58	48.63	62.58	44,434
Guangxi 广西	6	69	28,332	-67	-0.19	-2.52	46.40	92.61	35,893
Hainan 海南	2	163	13,286	-8,821	-15.97		1.01	121.67	55,246
Southwest 西南	61	69	9,009	-334	-3.30	-12.72	26.61	74.02	10,099
Chongqing 重庆	4	75	7,545	-154	-2.57		21.96	106.82	5,969
Sichuan 四川	25	64	14,094	5	0.07	0.31	53.28	78.15	7,061
Guizhou 贵州	9	104	5,424	-412	-3.21	-8.07	9.68	60.19	12,834
Yunnan 云南	16	78	6,730	-979	-6.04	-28.94	6.75	79.12	16,199
Tibet 西藏	7	24	1,502	-69	-1.17	-2.09	21.56	43.83	5,850
Northwest 西北	246	70	10,094	4	0.04	0.11	39.04	66.94	12,204
Shaanxi 陕西	81	109	12,316	-211	-1.65	-7.74	24.58	78.65	12,791
Gansu 甘肃	117	39	3,946	-12	-0.19	-0.43	59.61	56.35	6,623
Qinghai 青海	4	158	21,696	-1,693	-2.57	-5.76	9.04	55.34	65,837
Ningxia 宁夏	4	82	23,649	2,961	14.99	25.16	74.13	40.41	19,750
Xinjiang 新疆	40	70	21,063	365	1.72	5.44	53.34	68.37	21,220

1312: Flour Milling 磨粉业

Year 年份	Number of firms 企业个数	Rate of change 变化率 (%)	Number of employees 职工人数 (人)	Rate of change 变化率 (%)	Total revenue (Mil. RMB) 总销售收入 (百万元)	Rate of change 变化率 (%)	Total profit (Mil RMB) 总利润 (百万元)	Rate of change 变化率 (%)
2000	1783		210,571		33,025		175	
2001	1680	-5.78	169,110	-19.69	32,961	-0.19	446	154.86
2002	1606	-4.40	148,846	-11.98	35,271	7.01	605	35.65

Major Products 主要产品	Output 产量	Unit 单位
Wheat Flour 小麦粉	2,962	10,000 Tons 万吨

10 Main Firms with Maximal Revenue (year founded) 收入最大的十家主要企业（创办年份）	City 城市	Province 省	Telephone/fax 电话/传真	Number of employees 职工人数	Ownership 产业所有权	Revenue ('000 RMB) 销售收入(千元)	Profit('000 RMB) (rank) 利润(千元)(排名)	Total assets ('000 RMB) 总资产(千元)	Major products 主要产品
Henan Beixu Group 河南省北徐集团(1991)	Luohe 漯河市	Henan 河南省	(0395)8166053 (0395)8169856	2,012	Collective-owned 集体企业	564,427	49,737(2)	378,240	Flour 面粉
Henan Longyun Group 河南省龙云集团(1991)	Luohe 漯河市	Henan 河南省	(0395)8166086	1,840	Collective-owned 集体企业	527,684	50,055(1)	402,574	Flour 面粉
Zhengzhou Jinyuan Flour Industry Co.,Ltd. 郑州金苑面业有限公司(1993)	Zhengzhou 郑州市	Henan 河南省	(0371)3723234 (0371)3757756	800	Private Owned 私营企业	464,500	1,380(168)	156,155	Flour 面粉
Shandong Luwang Group General Company 山东省鲁王集团总公司(1994)	Jining 济宁市	Shandong 山东省	(0537)6151004 (0537)6150422	1,130	Joint Stock 股份制	325,490	8,670(14)	117,020	Flour 面粉
Zhenzhou Haijia Food Co., Ltd. 郑州海嘉食品有限公司(1993)	Zhengzhou 郑州市	Henan 河南省	(0371)6357857 (0371)6316496	316	Overseas Chinese-funded 港澳台资	287,032	12,349(9)	113,375	Special Flour 特一粉
Tianjin Lijin Co., Ltd. 天津利金股份有限公司(2000)	Tianjin 天津市	Tianjin 天津市	(022)27322272 (022)27322272	627	Joint Stock 股份制	277,263	3,633(64)	131,161	Wheat Flour 小麦粉
Inner Mongolia Hengfeng Food Industry (Group) Co., Ltd. 内蒙古恒丰食品工业（集团）股份有限公司(1998)	Bayannaoer 巴彦淖尔	Inner Mongolia 内蒙古	(0478)8244020 (0478)8217522	582	Overseas Chinese-funded 港澳台资	242,286	3,573(65)	308,302	Wheat Flour 小麦粉
Shenyang Xiangxue Flour Holding Co., Ltd. 沈阳香雪面粉股份有限公司(1994)	Shenyang 沈阳市	Liaoning 辽宁省	(024)25874694 (024)25850855	851	Joint Stock 股份制	216,360	-	110,810	Flour 面粉
Shandong Hemisphere Flour Co., Ltd. 山东半球面粉有限公司(2000)	Dongying 东营市	Shandong 山东省	(0546)6916187 (0546)6917105	600	Limited-Liability 有限公司	214,529	5,267(36)	84,143	Flour 面粉
Hebei WudelLi Group Shengzhou Flour Co., Ltd. 河北五得利集团深州面粉有限公司(2001)	Hengshui 衡水市	Hebei 河北省	(0318)3321068 (0318)3311498	310	Private Owned 私营企业	198,355	805(266)	33,825	Flour 面粉

Top 10 Cities by Revenue 销售收入排名前10位城市	Province 省	Market share 市场份额 (%)	Number of firms 企业个数
Dezhou 德州市	Shandong 山东省	9.02	87
Luohe 漯河市	Henan 河南省	5.47	39
Zhengzhou 郑州市	Henan 河南省	3.33	22
Puyang 濮阳市	Henan 河南省	3.31	58
Jining 济宁市	Shandong 山东省	2.64	26
Tianjin 天津市	Tianjin 天津市	2.55	25
Xinxiang 新乡市	Henan 河南省	2.25	32
Nanyang 南阳市	Henan 河南省	2.07	56
Kaifeng 开封市	Henan 河南省	2.02	33
Taizhou 泰州市	Jiangsu 江苏省	1.98	15

10 Major Wholesalers 十家主要批发商	City 城市	Province 省	Telephone/Fax 电话/传真
COFCO International (Beijing) Ltd. 中粮国际(北京)有限公司	Beijing 北京市	Beijing 北京市	(010)65268888 (010)65223623
China National Cereals, Oils & Foodstuffs Imp. & Exp. Corp. 中国粮油食品进出口(集团)有限公司	Beijing 北京市	Beijing 北京市	(010)65268888 (010)62578612
China Grains and Oils Group Corp. 中谷粮油集团公司	Beijing 北京市	Beijing 北京市	(010)88518866 (010)68476847
China Tobacco General Company Beijing Company 中国烟草总公司北京市公司	Beijing 北京市	Beijing 北京市	(010)64434106 (010)64418742
Jilin Grain Group Import & Export Ltd. 吉林粮食集团进出口有限公司	Changchun 长春市	Jilin 吉林省	(0431)5598115 (0431)5598118
Zhejiang Cereals, Oils & Foodstuffs Import & Export Co.,Ltd. 浙江省粮油食品进出口股份有限公司	Hangzhou 杭州市	Zhejiang 浙江省	(0571)85779999 (0571)85152514
China Tobacco General Company Shenzhen Company 中国烟草总公司深圳市公司	Shenzhen 深圳市	Guangdong 广东省	(0755)82230333 (0755)82206815
China National Vegetable Oil Corporation 中国植物油公司	Beijing 北京市	Beijing 北京市	(010)68083380 (010)68081127
Beijing Yangu Grain & Oil Purchase & Sale Company 北京市燕谷粮油购销公司	Beijing 北京市	Beijing 北京市	(010)63041782 (010)63034914
Shanghai Good Companion Sea Lion Industrial Co., Ltd Sale Filiale 上海良友海狮油脂实业有限公司销售分公司	Shanghai 上海市	Shanghai 上海市	(021)63321662 (021)54095735

1313: Rice and Flour Products 面、米制品业

The industry accounts for 0.045% of the total revenue of China's industrial sector in 2002. The rate of return on assets is 0.50%. 71.63% of all firms in the industry made a profit while 28.37% had negative returns. The top province in terms of the industry's revenue is Guangdong, accounting for 22.80% of the total revenue.
2002年本行业收入占全行业的0.045%，资产利润率为0.50%。71.63%的企业赢利，28.37%的企业亏损。收入最高的省为广东省，占本行业的22.80%。

	Total number of firms 企业总数	Total number of employees 职工总数	Total revenue (Mil.RMB) 总销售收入（百万元）	Total profit (Mil.RMB) 总利润（百万元）	Return on assets 资产利润率（%）	Return on equity 权益利润率（%）	Labour productivity ('000 RMB/worker) 劳动生产率（千元/人）	Debts/assets 资产负债率（%）	Total assets (Mil.RMB) 总资产（百万元）
Industry Overall 行业总体	282	32,289	4,873	21	0.50	1.37	38.98	63.25	4,111

	Number of firms 企业个数	Average number of employees 平均职工人数	Average revenue ('000 RMB) 平均销售收入（千元）	Average profit ('000 RMB) 平均利润（千元）	Return on assets 资产利润率（%）	Return on equity 权益利润率（%）	Labour productivity ('000 RMB/worker) 劳动生产率（千元/人）	Debts/assets 资产负债率（%）	Average total assets ('000 RMB) 平均总资产（千元）
By ownership 产业所有权									
State-owned 国有	102	85	7,640	-221	-1.89	-21.76	26.64	91.33	11,715
Collective-owned 集体	36	97	11,998	228	3.58	9.78	41.15	63.37	6,352
Foreign & Overseas Chinese Funded 三资	32	194	40,635	-605	-1.52	-2.85	41.11	46.78	39,907
By regional distribution 地区分布									
Central-North 华北	28	83	12,793	249	3.52	18.96	38.66	81.41	7,064
Beijing 北京	5	80	8,846	64	0.90	2.01	30.35	55.35	7,122
Tianjin 天津	9	51	17,289	764	19.21	61.99	22.19	69.00	3,977
Hebei 河北	10	98	13,185	-32	-0.35	-41.94	36.92	99.18	9,125
Shanxi 山西	3	66	138	-36	-0.64	-3.74	16.14	82.91	5,633
Inner Mongolia 内蒙古	1	286	26,125	196	1.07	3.20	98.52	66.40	18,239
Northeast 东北	12	207	14,603	688	2.53	12.22	15.23	79.28	27,181
Liaoning 辽宁	4	197	34,560	2,161	6.80	11.58	47.12	41.28	31,781
Jilin 吉林	5	258	3,736	-62	-0.19		1.72	115.37	33,173
Heilongjiang 黑龙江	3	135	6,107	-25	-0.23	-0.41	-3.62	44.48	11,059
Central-East 华东	78	133	20,709	-119	-0.69	-1.55	30.17	55.40	17,229
Shanghai 上海	7	183	49,620	-5,709	-9.75	-20.03	31.83	51.33	58,564
Jiangsu 江苏	12	116	28,057	815	3.72	7.28	45.40	48.95	21,921
Zhejiang 浙江	2	246	38,220	3,482	30.10	38.95	41.99	22.71	11,567
Anhui 安徽	10	102	5,507	320	4.34	9.68	12.65	55.13	7,356
Fujian 福建	14	90	7,156	135	2.63	7.84	31.74	66.39	5,105
Jiangxi 江西	24	160	19,046	375	2.31	5.24	23.51	55.95	16,259
Shandong 山东	9	120	26,943	-19	-0.15	-0.90	41.70	83.28	12,495
Central-South 中南	121	114	19,334	277	1.84	4.27	50.96	56.85	15,033
Henan 河南	30	128	16,680	212	1.57	2.76	44.95	43.17	13,531
Hubei 湖北	26	81	15,964	276	3.48	6.22	87.45	44.14	7,938
Hunan 湖南	16	87	7,816	90	0.95	9.66	26.87	90.12	9,379
Guangdong 广东	41	146	27,095	403	1.63	3.90	46.25	58.09	24,668
Guangxi 广西	8	54	23,503	254	4.50	1,087.70	68.97	99.59	5,654
Hainan 海南									
Southwest 西南	36	80	10,337	-435	-4.14	-56.43	34.91	92.67	10,508
Chongqing 重庆	1	105	19,534	620	13.82	43.15	75.43	67.96	4,485
Sichuan 四川	15	101	18,317	188	2.24		52.53	106.88	8,389
Guizhou 贵州	8	81	5,556	-1,473	-10.02		9.17	112.13	14,702
Yunnan 云南	9	59	2,658	-688	-9.82	-51.61	11.53	80.97	7,001
Tibet 西藏	3	28	3,159	-370	-1.65	-2.98	12.51	44.74	22,448
Northwest 西北	7	71	1,836	-448	-6.83		34.05	112.47	6,559
Shaanxi 陕西	1	140	7,880	-50	-0.30	-2.29	96.24	86.69	16,435
Gansu 甘肃	5	52	993	-26	-1.23	-4.19	13.41	70.63	2,146
Qinghai 青海									
Ningxia 宁夏									
Xinjiang 新疆	1	94	5	-2,956	-15.77		-1.28	159.01	18,750

1313: Rice and Flour Products 面、米制品业

Year 年份	Number of firms 企业个数	Rate of change 变化率 (%)	Number of employees 职工人数 (人)	Rate of change 变化率 (%)	Total revenue (Mil. RMB) 总销售收入 (百万元)	Rate of change 变化率 (%)	Total profit (Mil RMB) 总利润 (百万元)	Rate of change 变化率 (%)
2000	357		40,511		4,556		34	
2001	329	-7.84	31,186	-23.02	3,908	-14.22	24	-29.41
2002	282	-14.29	32,289	3.54	4,873	24.69	21	-12.50

Major Products 主要产品	Output 产量	Unit 单位
Wheat Flour 小麦粉	2,962	10,000 Tons 万吨

10 Main Firms with Maximal Revenue (year founded) 收入最大的十家主要企业（创办年份）	City 城市	Province 省	Telephone/fax 电话/传真	Number of employees 职工人数	Ownership 产业所有权	Revenue ('000 RMB) 销售收入 (千元)	Profit('000 RMB) (rank) 利润(千元) (排名)	Total assets ('000 RMB) 总资产 (千元)	Major products 主要产品
Shenzhen South Seas Grain Industries Co., Ltd.	Shenzhen	Guangdong	(0755)26694470		Foreign Funded				Flour
深圳南海粮食工业有限公司(1990)	深圳市	广东省	(0755)26694473	255	外商投资	280,927	13,306(1)	237,079	面粉
Jiangxi Zhangshu Grain & Oil Company	Yichun	Jiangxi	(0795)7340821		State-owned				Rice
江西省樟树粮油公司(1957)	宜春市	江西省	(0795)7349257	720	国有企业	215,242	664(49)	188,393	大米
Hebei Wudeli Group Dongming Flour Co., Ltd.	Heze	Shandong	(0530)7293119		Limited-Liability				Flour
河北五得利集团东明面粉有限公司(2001)	荷泽市	山东省	(0530)7293048	244	有限公司	211,450	311(82)	35,889	面粉
Shanghai Weidan Food Co., Ltd.	Shanghai	Shanghai	(021)57602525		Overseas Chinese-funded				Instant Noodle
上海味丹食品有限公司(1994)	上海市	上海市	(021)57602528	473	港澳台资	127,859	-	201,173	方便面
Shenzhen Flour Co., Ltd.	Shenzhen	Guangdong	(0755)26980333		Limited-Liability				Flour
深圳市面粉有限公司(1991)	深圳市	广东省	(0755)26980251	135	有限公司	116,077	4,724(7)	120,966	面粉
Shunde Beiyao Town Nissin Foods Co., Ltd.	Foshan	Guangdong	(0765)6330489		Foreign Funded				Instant Noodle
顺德市北窖镇日清食品有限公司(1995)	佛山市	广东省	(0765)6652778	440	外商投资	114,363	-	110,653	即食面
Guangzhou Fourgardener Flour Co.. Ltd.	Guangzhou	Guangdong	(020)84630221		Overseas Chinese-funded				Wheat Products
广州市福加德面粉有限公司(2000)	广州市	广东省	(020)84628565	150	港澳台资	110,915	871(34)	79,490	小麦制品
Chengdu Huazhonghua Agriculture Development Co., Ltd.	Chengdu	Sichuan	(028)82411630		Private Owned				Agricultural Products
成都花中花农业发展有限责任公司(2000)	成都市	四川省	(028)82462097	200	私营企业	83,950	3,065(8)	15,447	农产品
Xinxiang Changyuan Industrial Group	Xinxiang	Henan	(0373)8791111		Private Owned				Flour
新乡市长远实业集团(1998)	新乡市	河南省	(0373)8716719	510	私营企业	71,663	-	96,496	面粉
Xixian Grain Bureau Comprehensive Processing Plant	Xinyang	Henan	(0376)5958726		State-owned				Rice
息县粮食局综合加工厂(1985)	信阳市	河南省		375	国有企业	65,980	1,400(20)	11,020	大米

Top 10 Cities by Revenue 销售收入排名前10位城市	Province 省	Market share 市场份额 (%)	Number of firms 企业个数
Shenzhen 深圳市	Guangdong 广东省	9.28	5
Shanghai 上海市	Shanghai 上海市	7.13	7
Yichun 宜春市	Jiangxi 江西省	4.42	1
Heze 荷泽市	Shandong 山东省	4.34	1
Nanning 南宁市	Guangxi 广西	3.84	1
Foshan 佛山市	Guangdong 广东省	3.64	2
Guangzhou 广州市	Guangdong 广东省	3.35	5
Chengdu 成都市	Sichuan 四川省	3.32	6
Tianjin 天津市	Tianjin 天津市	3.19	9
Huanggang 黄冈市	Hubei 湖北省	2.46	5

10 Major Wholesalers 十家主要批发商	City 城市	Province 省	Telephone/Fax 电话/传真
COFCO International (Beijing) Ltd.	Beijing	Beijing	(010)65268888
中粮国际(北京)有限公司	北京市	北京市	(010)65223623
China National Cereals, Oils & Foodstuffs Imp. & Exp. Corp.	Beijing	Beijing	(010)65268888
中国粮油食品进出口(集团)有限公司	北京市	北京市	(010)62578612
China Grains and Oils Group Corp.	Beijing	Beijing	(010)88518866
中谷粮油集团公司	北京市	北京市	(010)68476847
China Tobacco General Company Beijing Company	Beijing	Beijing	(010)64434106
中国烟草总公司北京市公司	北京市	北京市	(010)64418742
Jilin Grain Group Import & Export Ltd.	Changchun	Jilin	(0431)5598115
吉林粮食集团进出口有限公司	长春市	吉林省	(0431)5598118
Zhejiang Cereals, Oils & Foodstuffs Import & Export Co.,Ltd.	Hangzhou	Zhejiang	(0571)85779999
浙江省粮油食品进出口股份有限公司	杭州市	浙江省	(0571)85152514
China Tobacco General Company Shenzhen Company	Shenzhen	Guangdong	(0755)82230333
中国烟草总公司深圳市公司	深圳市	广东省	(0755)82206815
China National Vegetable Oil Corporation	Beijing	Beijing	(010)68083380
中国植物油公司	北京市	北京市	(010)68081127
Beijing Yangu Grain & Oil Purchase & Sale Company	Beijing	Beijing	(010)63041782
北京市燕谷粮油购销公司	北京市	北京市	(010)63034914
Shanghai Good Companion Sea Lion Industrial Co., Ltd Sale Filiale	Shanghai	Shanghai	(021)63321662
上海良友海狮油脂实业有限公司销售分公司	上海市	上海市	(021)54095735

1314: Mixed Feed 配合及混合饲料制造业

The industry accounts for 0.665% of the total revenue of China's industrial sector in 2002. The rate of return on assets is 2.90%. 72.66% of all firms in the industry made a profit while 27.34% had negative returns.The top province in terms of the industry's revenue is Guangdong, accounting for 15.68% of the total revenue.
2002年本行业收入占全行业的 0.665%，资产利润率为 2.90%。72.66%的企业赢利，27.34%的企业亏损。收入最高的省为广东省，占本行业的15.68%。

	Total number of firms 企业总数	Total number of employees 职工总数	Total revenue (Mil.RMB) 总销售收入 (百万元)	Total profit (Mil.RMB) 总利润 (百万元)	Return on assets 资产利润率 (%)	Return on equity 权益利润率 (%)	Labour productivity ('000 RMB/ worker) 劳动生产率 (千元/人)	Debts/ assets 资产负债率 (%)	Total assets (Mil.RMB) 总资产 (百万元)
Industry Overall 行业总体	1595	163,548	71,354	1,166	2.90	7.19	95.90	59.66	40,193

	Number of firms 企业个数	Average number of employees 平均职工人数	Average revenue ('000 RMB) 平均销售收入（千元）	Average profit ('000 RMB) 平均利润 (千元)	Return on assets 资产利润率 (%)	Return on equity 权益利润率 (%)	Labour productivity ('000 RMB/ worker) 劳动生产率 (千元/人)	Debts/ assets 资产负债率 (%)	Average total assets ('000 RMB) 平均总资产 (千元)
By ownership 产业所有权									
State-owned 国有	346	55	13,236	-124	-0.96	-7.10	57.91	86.46	12,889
Collective-owned 集体	114	70	26,864	836	5.04	12.31	98.71	59.07	16,594
Foreign & Overseas Chinese Funded 三资	206	180	108,358	622	0.96	2.24	117.46	57.00	64,687
By regional distribution 地区分布									
Central-North 华北	205	88	35,501	879	5.04	13.10	81.14	61.54	17,449
Beijing 北京	43	67	41,511	2,474	9.35	17.96	105.33	47.93	26,454
Tianjin 天津	26	68	21,493	288	1.78	9.36	99.47	81.02	16,208
Hebei 河北	93	112	38,864	448	3.15	9.85	64.87	68.04	14,226
Shanxi 山西	33	42	13,165	71	0.64	1.68	51.82	62.11	11,159
Inner Mongolia 内蒙古	10	164	88,515	2,242	6.86	15.88	146.79	56.80	32,686
Northeast 东北	152	133	39,434	205	0.80	1.70	62.57	53.08	25,778
Liaoning 辽宁	81	98	45,772	-279	-1.18	-2.79	78.93	57.68	23,654
Jilin 吉林	42	106	34,215	661	2.09	4.02	99.45	48.06	31,694
Heilongjiang 黑龙江	29	271	29,289	897	3.88	7.74	25.18	49.91	23,142
Central-East 华东	470	97	45,658	371	1.51	3.97	100.56	62.03	24,573
Shanghai 上海	26	116	84,359	-5,814	-7.17	-17.80	15.64	59.68	81,043
Jiangsu 江苏	90	86	39,634	385	1.93	4.85	91.30	60.14	19,886
Zhejiang 浙江	88	65	34,543	201	1.12	3.11	80.74	63.81	17,922
Anhui 安徽	35	128	41,184	197	0.68	2.18	77.75	68.77	29,000
Fujian 福建	50	72	44,384	1,736	7.17	12.68	157.89	43.44	24,216
Jiangxi 江西	57	96	41,927	-168	-0.86	-3.89	107.60	77.85	19,436
Shandong 山东	124	127	53,294	1,523	6.89	18.81	119.55	63.37	22,109
Central-South 中南	505	95	50,104	859	2.88	7.39	117.63	61.05	29,820
Henan 河南	137	74	24,563	228	1.76	6.86	83.88	74.39	12,963
Hubei 湖北	53	97	28,510	529	2.96	6.39	100.34	53.72	17,885
Hunan 湖南	88	100	54,068	1,290	2.80	5.22	147.43	46.32	46,001
Guangdong 广东	135	110	82,864	1,698	3.81	10.77	148.21	64.62	44,563
Guangxi 广西	84	98	42,517	377	1.72	5.36	79.92	67.96	21,941
Hainan 海南	8	122	113,806	-7	-0.01	-0.07	142.29	81.34	53,512
Southwest 西南	175	146	51,689	1,720	6.54	14.35	84.27	54.45	26,311
Chongqing 重庆	14	157	99,255	3,531	11.82	29.10	89.40	59.38	29,879
Sichuan 四川	83	228	71,608	2,857	7.19	14.16	96.31	49.19	39,710
Guizhou 贵州	35	43	10,196	-34	-0.56	-2.44	44.47	77.10	6,061
Yunnan 云南	41	72	33,062	379	2.29	7.62	24.02	69.94	16,526
Tibet 西藏	2	9	85	74	32.89	32.89	3.22		225
Northwest 西北	88	65	25,856	523	3.10	7.07	92.55	56.18	16,881
Shaanxi 陕西	33	70	25,658	381	2.16	5.42	81.40	60.15	17,638
Gansu 甘肃	28	38	10,936	93	1.27	2.86	87.35	55.76	7,336
Qinghai 青海	3	26	784	-297	-6.40	-20.20	19.58	68.32	4,635
Ningxia 宁夏	5	79	35,148	957	3.62	7.04	54.75	48.57	26,430
Xinjiang 新疆	19	97	49,701	1,418	4.88	10.54	120.59	53.68	29,053

1314: Mixed Feed 配合及混合饲料制造业

Year 年份	Number of firms 企业个数	Rate of change 变化率 (%)	Number of employees 职工人数 (人)	Rate of change 变化率 (%)	Total revenue (Mil. RMB) 总销售收入 (百万元)	Rate of change 变化率 (%)	Total profit (Mil RMB) 总利润 (百万元)	Rate of change 变化率 (%)
2000	1812		178,330		62,386		914	
2001	1685	-7.01	173,263	-2.84	69,906	12.05	1,066	16.63
2002	1595	-5.34	163,548	-5.61	71,354	2.07	1,166	9.38

Major Products 主要产品	Output 产量	Unit 单位
Mixed Feed 配混合饲料	4,214	10,000 Tons 万吨

10 Main Firms with Maximal Revenue (year founded) 收入最大的十家主要企业（创办年份）	City 城市	Province 省	Telephone/fax 电话/传真	Number of employees 职工人数	Ownership 产业所有权	Revenue ('000 RMB) 销售收入（千元）	Profit('000 RMB) (rank) 利润(千元)(排名)	Total assets ('000 RMB) 总资产（千元）	Major products 主要产品
Shanghai Dajiang (Group)Stock Co., Ltd. 上海大江(集团)股份有限公司(1985)	Shanghai 上海市	Shanghai 上海市	(021)57822480 (021)57820072	1,338	Foreign Funded 外商投资	1,438,925	-	1,694,162	Feedstuff 饲料
Hunan Zhenghong Science & Technology Development Co.,ltd. 湖南正虹科技发展有限公司(1997)	Yueyang 岳阳市	Hunan 湖南省	(0730)5728005 (0730)5728015	1,086	Joint Stock 股份制	1,184,693	43,663(4)	1,465,139	Mingled Feedstuff 配合饲料
Qinhuangdao Chia Tai Co.Ltd. 秦皇岛正大有限公司(1995)	Qinhuangdao 秦皇岛市	Hebei 河北省	(0335)5028516 (0335)5052600	4,180	Foreign Funded 外商投资	1,048,753	-	376,525	Chicken 鸡肉
Great Wall Food (Dalian) Co., Ltd. 大成食品（大连）有限公司(1996)	Dalian 大连市	Liaoning 辽宁省	(0411)5250499 (0411)5250907	2,056	Foreign Funded 外商投资	887,972	-	312,145	Feedstuff 饲料
Mianzhu Lomon Corporation 绵竹龙蟒集团有限责任公司(1984)	Deyang 德阳市	Sichuan 四川省	(0838)6101476 (0838)6101476	5,601	Limited-Liability 有限公司	835,794	95,618(1)	962,147	
Hunan Tangrenshen Group Stock Co., Ltd. 湖南唐人神集团股份有限公司(1993)	Zhuzhou 株洲市	Hunan 湖南省	(0733)8591298 (0733)8513853	751	Joint Stock 股份制	649,345	48,184(3)	390,343	Feedstuff 饲料
Guangzhou Jiang Feng Industrial Co., Ltd. 广州市江丰实业有限公司(1991)	Guangzhou 广州市	Guangdong 广东省	(020)86601868 (020)86602388	793	Limited-Liability 有限公司	530,432	7,027(52)	298,197	Feedstuff 饲料
Zhejiang Yixing Feedstuff Group Co., Ltd. 浙江一星饲料集团有限责任公司(1995)	Jiaxing 嘉兴市	Zhejiang 浙江省	(0573)6026314 (0573)6026314	295	Limited-Liability 有限公司	498,016	5,283(74)	200,885	Feedstuff 饲料
Tongliao Yuetai Co., Ltd. 通辽岳泰股份有限公司(1997)	Tongliao 通辽市	Inner Mongolia 内蒙古	(0475)8502630 (0475)8502630	710	Joint Stock 股份制	491,200	11,789(34)	71,243	Feedstuff 饲料
Fuzhou Hippocampi Feedstuff Co., Ltd. 福州海马饲料有限公司(1998)	Fuzhou 福州市	Fujian 福建省	(0591)3981159 (0591)3681422	446	Overseas Chinese-funded 港澳台资	446,728	38,385(5)	179,622	Mixed Feedstuff 混合饲料

Top 10 Cities by Revenue 销售收入排名前10位城市	Province 省	Market share 市场份额 (%)	Number of firms 企业个数
Foshan 佛山市	Guangdong 广东省	4.43	26
Yueyang 岳阳市	Hunan 湖南省	3.55	17
Shanghai 上海市	Shanghai 上海市	3.07	26
Guangzhou 广州市	Guangdong 广东省	2.70	23
Beijing 北京市	Beijing 北京市	2.50	43
Chengdu 成都市	Sichuan 四川省	2.25	20
Nanning 南宁市	Guangxi 广西	2.17	38
Jiaxing 嘉兴市	Zhejiang 浙江省	1.98	18
Chongqing 重庆市	Chongqing 重庆市	1.95	14
Qingdao 青岛市	Shandong 山东省	1.94	8

10 Major Wholesalers 十家主要批发商	City 城市	Province 省	Telephone/Fax 电话/传真
Ningbo Haitian Group General Company 宁波海田集团总公司	Ningbo 宁波市	Zhejiang 浙江省	(0574)87195360 (0574)87195821
Heilongjiang Agriculture Means Of Production Company 黑龙江省农业生产资料公司	Harbin 哈尔滨市	Heilongjiang 黑龙江省	(0451)88383752 (0451)88382367
Yantai Agriculture Means Of Production General Company 烟台市农业生产资料总公司	Yantai 烟台市	Shandong 山东省	(0535)6216374 (0535)6211348
Guangdong Agriculture Means Of Production General Company 广东省农业生产资料总公司	Guangzhou 广州市	Guangdong 广东省	(020)87773051 (020)87754117
Inner Mongolia Autonomous Region Agriculture & Animal Husbandry Means Of Production Co.,Ltd. 内蒙古自治区农牧业生产资料股份有限公司	Huhhot 呼和浩特市	Inner Mongolia 内蒙古	(0471)6963132 (0471)6964434
Shanghai Agriculture Means Of Production Company 上海市农业生产资料公司	Shanghai 上海市	Shanghai 上海市	(021)63807100 (021)63806807
Ningbo Haitian International Trade Co.,Ltd. 宁波海田国际贸易有限公司	Ningbo 宁波市	Zhejiang 浙江省	(0574)87345251 (0574)87345620
Fujian AMP Incorpration 福建省农资集团公司	Fuzhou 福州市	Fujian 福建省	(0591)7508666 (0591)7614839
Shandong Agricultural Machinery Group General Company 山东省农业机械集团总公司	Jinan 济南市	Shandong 山东省	(0531)8951240 (0531)8951240
Shandong Yantai Agriculture Means Of Production Purchasing Supply Station 山东省烟台市农业生产资料采购供应站	Yantai 烟台市	Shandong 山东省	(0535)6222126 (0535)6216440

1315: Protein Feed 蛋白饲料制造业

The industry accounts for 0.020% of the total revenue of China's industrial sector in 2002. The rate of return on assets is 4.96%. 77.55% of all firms in the industry made a profit while 22.45% had negative returns.The top province in terms of the industry's revenue is Tianjin, accounting for 22.30% of the total revenue.
2002年本行业收入占全行业的0.020%，资产利润率为4.96%。77.55%的企业赢利，22.45%的企业亏损。收入最高的省为天津市，占本行业的22.30%。

	Total number of firms 企业总数	Total number of employees 职工总数	Total revenue (Mil.RMB) 总销售收入(百万元)	Total profit (Mil.RMB) 总利润(百万元)	Return on assets 资产利润率(%)	Return on equity 权益利润率(%)	Labour productivity ('000 RMB/worker) 劳动生产率(千元/人)	Debts/assets 资产负债率(%)	Total assets (Mil.RMB) 总资产(百万元)
Industry Overall 行业总体	49	5,355	2,124	93	4.96	18.04	89.03	72.49	1,869

	Number of firms 企业个数	Average number of employees 平均职工人数	Average revenue ('000 RMB) 平均销售收入(千元)	Average profit ('000 RMB) 平均利润(千元)	Return on assets 资产利润率(%)	Return on equity 权益利润率(%)	Labour productivity ('000 RMB/worker) 劳动生产率(千元/人)	Debts/assets 资产负债率(%)	Average total assets ('000 RMB) 平均总资产(千元)
By ownership 产业所有权									
State-owned 国有	6	36	21,715	-9	-0.06		63.07	102.01	14,531
Collective-owned 集体	9	64	33,200	1,868	28.90	44.32	145.50	34.79	6,465
Foreign & Overseas Chinese Funded 三资	7	166	109,326	11,840	14.15	42.20	130.17	66.47	83,687
By regional distribution 地区分布									
Central-North 华北	10	187	78,914	6,346	8.23	73.08	86.38	88.73	77,091
Beijing 北京	3	60	41,296	364	2.49		120.29	114.44	14,654
Tianjin 天津	3	194	157,821	24,621	19.61	59.88	151.38	67.24	125,539
Hebei 河北	3	366	63,794	-3,829	-3.29		46.82	108.70	116,304
Shanxi 山西	1	8	410	-6	-0.42	-3.51	19.63	87.96	1,420
Inner Mongolia 内蒙古									
Northeast 东北	4	120	45,486	238	0.22	0.52	109.23	58.13	108,580
Liaoning 辽宁	2	103	41,424	-36	-0.07	-0.08	145.93	10.06	49,313
Jilin 吉林									
Heilongjiang 黑龙江	2	137	49,549	512	0.30	1.10	81.67	72.25	167,847
Central-East 华东	10	123	55,085	2,545	10.18	23.75	87.32	57.16	25,011
Shanghai 上海	1	48	26,735	601	6.47	11.14	89.52	41.91	9,291
Jiangsu 江苏	2	94	50,382	1,975	19.76	31.38	138.09	37.04	9,993
Zhejiang 浙江	4	215	69,707	4,428	9.21	23.30	58.72	60.48	48,089
Anhui 安徽									
Fujian 福建	1	30	37,341	705	7.47	13.61	106.70	45.08	9,432
Jiangxi 江西									
Shandong 山东	2	51	53,594	1,241	13.02	31.10	229.36	58.12	9,525
Central-South 中南	21	65	22,065	-47	-0.36	-1.12	103.48	67.85	12,930
Henan 河南	9	72	23,438	816	8.33	19.99	93.92	58.33	9,801
Hubei 湖北	3	45	4,757	222	6.00	18.49	63.02	67.55	3,705
Hunan 湖南	3	46	10,775	275	2.49	9.91	39.27	74.86	11,021
Guangdong 广东	5	80	35,770	-1,981	-7.53	-26.14	152.75	71.19	26,312
Guangxi 广西	1	48	26,981	88	1.16	12.09	118.31	90.39	7,574
Hainan 海南									
Southwest 西南	2	64	10,119	272	0.96	2.30	27.88	58.20	28,288
Chongqing 重庆									
Sichuan 四川	2	64	10,119	272	0.96	2.30	27.88	58.20	28,288
Guizhou 贵州									
Yunnan 云南									
Tibet 西藏									
Northwest 西北	2	144	59,000	1,644	3.85	12.06	38.47	68.11	42,728
Shaanxi 陕西									
Gansu 甘肃									
Qinghai 青海									
Ningxia 宁夏									
Xinjiang 新疆	2	144	59,000	1,644	3.85	12.06	38.47	68.11	42,728

1315: Protein Feed 蛋白饲料制造业

Year 年份	Number of firms 企业个数	Rate of change 变化率 (%)	Number of employees 职工人数 (人)	Rate of change 变化率 (%)	Total revenue (Mil. RMB) 总销售收入 (百万元)	Rate of change 变化率 (%)	Total profit (Mil RMB) 总利润 (百万元)	Rate of change 变化率 (%)
2000	70		7,062		1,666		149	
2001	53	-24.29	5,874	-16.82	2,032	21.97	147	-1.34
2002	49	-7.55	5,355	-8.84	2,124	4.53	93	-36.73

Major Products 主要产品	Output 产量	Unit 单位

10 Main Firms with Maximal Revenue (year founded) 收入最大的十家主要企业（创办年份）	City 城市	Province 省	Telephone/fax 电话/传真	Number of employees 职工人数	Ownership 产业所有权	Revenue ('000 RMB) 销售收入 (千元)	Profit('000 RMB) (rank) 利润(千元) (排名)	Total assets ('000 RMB) 总资产 (千元)	Major products 主要产品
Tianjin Zhengda Feedstuff Science & Technology Co., Ltd. 天津正大饲料科技有限公司(1993)	Tianjin 天津市	Tianjin 天津市	(022)25324550 (022)25328454	482	Foreign Funded 外商投资	462,214	72,764(1)	370,518	Feedstuff 饲料
Xingchang GuoBang Chemicals Industrials Co.,Ltd. 新昌国邦化学工业有限公司(1996)	Shaoxing 绍兴市	Zhejiang 浙江省	(0575)6126511 (0575)6126550	450	Foreign Funded 外商投资	222,143	17257(2)	450	Feedstuff Additive饲料添加剂
Chengde Bishu Shanzhuang Wine-making Industry Co., Ltd. 承德避暑山庄酒业有限责任公司(2002)	Chengde 承德市	Hebei 河北省	(0314)6206904	923	Limited-Liability 有限公司	175,019	-	330,433	Protein Feedstuff 蛋白饲料
Kangyoumei Soybean Co., Ltd. 康尤美大豆有限责任公司(1999)	Yili 伊犁州	Xinjiang 新疆	(0999)5026727 (0999)5029396	198	Limited-Liability 有限公司	104,999	3,287(7)	58,857	Bean Dregs 豆粕
Guangzhou Hope Industrial Co., Ltd. 广州希望实业有限公司(1998)	Guangzhou 广州市	Guangdong 广东省	(020)34991396 (020)34930399	130	Private Owned 私营企业	98,348	-	49,286	Feedstuff 饲料
Henan Yubei Lishi Group 河南豫北立世集团(1987)	Hebi 鹤壁市	Henan 河南省	(0392)5524320 (0392)5522623	190	Collective-owned 集体企业	95,510	5,110(4)	16,800	Protein Feedstuff蛋白质饲料
Beijing Thr-Annulus Feedstuff Factory 北京市三环饲料厂(1976)	Beijing 北京市	Beijing 北京市	(010)89682525	14	State-owned 国有企业	88,900	808(12)	14,735	Mixed Feedstuff配混合饲料
Guangzhou Panyu Lingshan Feedstuff Factory 广州市番禺区灵山饲料厂(1998)	Guangzhou 广州市	Guangdong 广东省	(020)34930312 (020)34930312	140	Private Enterprises 私营独资	66,511	-	16,254	Feedstuff 饲料
Harbin High-Tech Soybean Food Co., Ltd. 哈高大豆食品有限公司(2000)	Harbin 哈尔滨市	Heilongjiang 黑龙江省	(0451)84348037 (0451)84348242	223	Limited-Liability 有限公司	63,406	1,023(11)	308,665	Soybean Separated Protein大豆分离蛋白
Fuzhou Sanshui Aquatic Products Feedstuff Co., Ltd. 福州三水水产饲料有限公司(1995)	Fuzhou 福州市	Fujian 福建省	(0591)3671023 (0591)3671023	30	Private Owned 私营企业	37,341	705(13)	9,432	Protein Feedstuff 蛋白饲料

Top 10 Cities by Revenue 销售收入排名前10位城市	Province 省	Market share 市场份额 (%)	Number of firms 企业个数
Tianjin 天津市	Tianjin 天津市	22.30	3
Shaoxing 绍兴市	Zhejiang 浙江省	10.46	1
Chengde 承德市	Hebei 河北省	8.24	1
Guangzhou 广州市	Guangdong 广东省	7.76	2
Beijing 北京市	Beijing 北京市	5.83	3
Yili 伊犁州	Xinjiang 新疆	4.94	1
Harbin 哈尔滨市	Heilongjiang 黑龙江省	4.67	2
Yancheng 盐城市	Jiangsu 江苏省	4.57	1
Hebi 鹤壁市	Henan 河南省	4.50	1
Weihai 威海市	Shandong 山东省	3.57	1

10 Major Wholesalers 十家主要批发商	City 城市	Province 省	Telephone/Fax 电话/传真
Ningbo Haitian Group General Company 宁波海田集团总公司	Ningbo 宁波市	Zhejiang 浙江省	(0574)87195360 (0574)87195821
Heilongjiang Agriculture Means Of Production Company 黑龙江省农业生产资料公司	Harbin 哈尔滨市	Heilongjiang 黑龙江省	(0451)88383752 (0451)88382367
Yantai Agriculture Means Of Production General Company 烟台市农业生产资料总公司	Yantai 烟台市	Shandong 山东省	(0535)6216374 (0535)6211348
Guangdong Agriculture Means Of Production General Company 广东省农业生产资料总公司	Guangzhou 广州市	Guangdong 广东省	(020)87773051 (020)87754117
Inner Mongolia Autonomous Region Agriculture & Animal Husbandry Means Of Production Co.,Ltd. 内蒙古自治区农牧业生产资料股份有限公司	Huhhot 呼和浩特市	Inner Mongolia 内蒙古	(0471)6963132 (0471)6964434
Shanghai Agriculture Means Of Production Company 上海市农业生产资料公司	Shanghai 上海市	Shanghai 上海市	(021)63807100 (021)63806807
Ningbo Haitian International Trade Co.,Ltd. 宁波海田国际贸易有限公司	Ningbo 宁波市	Zhejiang 浙江省	(0574)87345251 (0574)87345620
Fujian AMP Incorpration 福建省农资集团公司	Fuzhou 福州市	Fujian 福建省	(0591)7508666 (0591)7614839
Shandong Agricultural Machinery Group General Company 山东省农业机械集团总公司	Jinan 济南市	Shandong 山东省	(0531)8931240 (0531)8951240
Shandong Yantai Agriculture Means Of Production Purchasing Supply Station 山东省烟台市农业生产资料采购供应站	Yantai 烟台市	Shandong 山东省	(0535)6222126 (0535)6216440

1317: Aquatic Feed 水产饲料制造业

The industry accounts for 0.044% of the total revenue of China's industrial sector in 2002. The rate of return on assets is 5.62%. 80.00% of all firms in the industry made a profit while 20.00% had negative returns.The top province in terms of the industry's revenue is Guangdong, accounting for 31.47% of the total revenue.
2002年本行业收入占全行业的0.044%，资产利润率为5.62%。80.00%的企业赢利，20.00%的企业亏损。收入最高的省为广东省，占本行业的31.47%。

	Total number of firms 企业总数	Total number of employees 职工总数	Total revenue (Mil.RMB) 总销售收入 (百万元)	Total profit (Mil.RMB) 总利润 (百万元)	Return on assets 资产利润率 (%)	Return on equity 权益利润率 (%)	Labour productivity ('000 RMB/ worker) 劳动生产率 (千元/人)	Debts/ assets 资产负债率 (%)	Total assets (Mil.RMB) 总资产 (百万元)
Industry Overall 行业总体	125	9,784	4,758	204	5.62	11.84	116.16	52.56	3,636

	Number of firms 企业个数	Average number of employees 平均职工人数	Average revenue ('000 RMB) 平均销售收入 (千元)	Average profit ('000 RMB) 平均利润 (千元)	Return on assets 资产利润率 (%)	Return on equity 权益利润率 (%)	Labour productivity ('000 RMB/ worker) 劳动生产率 (千元/人)	Debts/ assets 资产负债率 (%)	Average total assets ('000 RMB) 平均总资产 (千元)
By ownership 产业所有权									
State-owned 国有	11	52	10,896	-25	-0.12	-0.51	13.05	76.15	20,547
Collective-owned 集体	7	55	13,391	623	4.94	11.57	58.20	57.33	12,628
Foreign & Overseas Chinese Funded 三资	30	78	67,839	2,190	3.84	8.16	167.60	52.92	57,001
By regional distribution 地区分布									
Central-North 华北	12	54	13,557	63	0.35	2.42	5.50	85.63	18,003
Beijing 北京	3	70	21,733	185	0.63	1.73	-50.47	63.66	29,408
Tianjin 天津	4	48	14,025	74	0.39	2.02	24.14	80.64	18,873
Hebei 河北	3	32	6,872	424	21.98	128.13	30.77	82.84	1,927
Shanxi 山西	1	82	2,247	-2,130	-5.26		-6.66	154.70	40,496
Inner Mongolia 内蒙古	1	65	18,520	760	12.59	13.73	108.43	8.28	6,036
Northeast 东北	3	49	27,555	1,138	4.81	8.22	121.71	41.51	23,662
Liaoning 辽宁	2	48	30,273	1,077	16.64	31.34	175.11	46.91	6,474
Jilin 吉林									
Heilongjiang 黑龙江	1	51	22,119	1,260	2.17	3.64	22.24	40.30	58,038
Central-East 华东	62	76	38,242	1,443	4.73	9.69	85.22	51.13	30,483
Shanghai 上海	2	92	14,524	-3,858	-10.99	-21.31	-0.32	48.41	35,097
Jiangsu 江苏	8	71	19,295	188	1.20	2.80	43.86	57.00	15,584
Zhejiang 浙江	21	74	28,528	2,279	12.11	23.96	79.45	49.45	18,822
Anhui 安徽									
Fujian 福建	22	63	65,816	2,085	4.70	9.99	153.42	52.95	44,346
Jiangxi 江西									
Shandong 山东	9	113	15,617	218	0.61	1.12	38.80	46.04	36,026
Central-South 中南	45	92	46,794	2,472	7.77	15.52	168.76	49.95	31,820
Henan 河南	4	49	17,174	870	35.62	62.31	62.70	42.82	2,441
Hubei 湖北	6	145	52,673	2,919	16.50	21.53	161.87	23.36	17,692
Hunan 湖南	1	1						50.10	998
Guangdong 广东	25	103	59,899	2,386	5.68	11.47	181.04	50.53	42,047
Guangxi 广西	3	54	11,778	-1,017	-7.93	-71.08	58.91	88.84	12,820
Hainan 海南	6	57	31,368	5,606	14.93	32.08	206.33	53.48	37,556
Southwest 西南	2	59	15,548	-78	-0.77	-1.65	54.66	53.33	10,135
Chongqing 重庆									
Sichuan 四川	1	68	15,260	-112	-3.93	-53.59	43.78	92.66	2,848
Guizhou 贵州	1	50	15,836	-44	-0.25	-0.48	69.46	46.90	17,421
Yunnan 云南									
Tibet 西藏									
Northwest 西北	1	19	5,080	-421	-6.13	-15.90	391.53	61.47	6,870
Shaanxi 陕西									
Gansu 甘肃									
Qinghai 青海									
Ningxia 宁夏									
Xinjiang 新疆	1	19	5,080	-421	-6.13	-15.90	391.53	61.47	6,870

1317: Aquatic Feed 水产饲料制造业

Year 年份	Number of firms 企业个数	Rate of change 变化率 (%)	Number of employees 职工人数 (人)	Rate of change 变化率 (%)	Total revenue (Mil. RMB) 总销售收入 (百万元)	Rate of change 变化率 (%)	Total profit (Mil RMB) 总利润 (百万元)	Rate of change 变化率 (%)
2000	101		6,266		2,415		139	
2001	114	12.87	9,630	53.69	4,003	65.76	210	51.08
2002	125	9.65	9,784	1.60	4,758	18.86	204	-2.86

Major Products 主要产品	Output 产量	Unit 单位

10 Main Firms with Maximal Revenue (year founded) 收入最大的十家主要企业 (创办年份)	City 城市	Province 省	Telephone/fax 电话/传真	Number of employees 职工人数	Ownership 产业所有权	Revenue ('000 RMB) 销售收入 (千元)	Profit('000 RMB) (rank) 利润(千元) (排名)	Total assets ('000 RMB) 总资产 (千元)	Major products 主要产品
Fu Jian Coland Enterprises Co., Ltd.	Fuzhou	Fujian	(0591)3981150		Overseas Chinese-funded				Fish Meal
福建高龙实业有限公司(1995)	福州市	福建省	(0591)3687907	122	港澳台资	377,189	519(55)	179,996	鱼粉
Guangdong Tongwei Feedstuff Co., Ltd.	Foshan	Guangdong	(0757)6667849		Limited-Liability				Feedstuff
广东通威饲料有限公司(1999)	佛山市	广东省	(0757)6666668	250	有限公司	315,000	4,200(13)	88,000	饲料
Xiamen Putou Feedstuff Co.,Ltd.	Xiamen	Fujian	(0592)7029999		Private Owned				Feedstuff
厦门浦头饲料有限公司(1987)	厦门市	福建省	(0592)7127777	128	私营企业	227,564	19,861(3)	85,174	饲料
Zhanjiang Yuehua Aquatic Products Feedstuff Co., Ltd.	Zhanjiang	Guangdong	(0759)3329906		Overseas Chinese-funded				Shrimp Feedstuff
湛江粤华水产饲料有限公司(1999)	湛江市	广东省	(0759)3200006	52	港澳台资	207,550	15,780(6)	162,249	虾饲料
Zhanjiang Yuehai Feedstuff Co., Ltd.	Zhanjiang	Guangdong	(0759)2309799		Overseas Chinese-funded				Prawn Feedstuff
湛江粤海饲料有限公司(1994)	湛江市	广东省	(0759)2305446	230	港澳台资	176,965	17,019(5)	184,377	对虾饲料
Gold Coin Feed Mill (China) Co., Ltd.	Shenzhen	Guangdong	(0755)26691231		Foreign Funded				Marine Lives Feedstuff
金钱饲料（中国）有限公司(1983)	深圳市	广东省	(0755)26692645	111	外商投资	144,285	4,492(11)	75,302	水产饲料
Ningbo Tech_bank Co.,Ltd.	Ningbo	Zhejiang	(0574)62817777		Joint Stock				Soft-shelled Turtle Feedstuff
宁波天邦股份有限公司(1996)	宁波市	浙江省	(0574)62816666	123	股份制	136,404	19,453(4)	125,519	甲鱼饲料
Nanhai Tian_Bank Feedstuff Science & Technology Co.,Ltd.	Foshan	Guangdong	(0757)6681689		Limited-Liability				Soft-shelled Turtle Feedstuff
南海市天邦饲料科技有限公司(2001)	佛山市	广东省	(0757)6681555	79	有限公司	82,074	-	55,384	甲鱼饲料
Hainan Yangpu Duoba Co., Ltd.	Hainan	Hainan	(0898)28821134		Private Partnership				Tortoise Powder
海南洋浦多巴有限公司(2001)	洋浦开发区	海南省	(0898)28821134	13	私营合伙	80,524	29,773(1)	53,873	龟鳖粉
Nanfang Feedstuff Co., Ltd.	Xiantao	Hubei	(0728)2852648		Private Enterprises				Feedstuff
南方饲料有限责任公司(1996)	仙桃市	湖北省	(0728)2852648	213	私营独资	70,468	1,435(31)	20,816	饲料

Top 10 Cities by Revenue 销售收入排名前10位城市	Province 省	Market share 市场份额 (%)	Number of firms 企业个数
Fuzhou 福州市	Fujian 福建省	20.13	13
Zhanjiang 湛江市	Guangdong 广东省	11.70	9
Foshan 佛山市	Guangdong 广东省	8.51	3
Xiamen 厦门市	Fujian 福建省	5.87	3
Ningbo 宁波市	Zhejiang 浙江省	3.84	2
Wenzhou 温州市	Zhejiang 浙江省	3.40	9
Wuhan 武汉市	Hubei 湖北省	3.35	1
Shenzhen 深圳市	Guangdong 广东省	3.03	1
Hainan 海南省	Hainan 海南省	3.00	4
Guangzhou 广州市	Guangdong 广东省	2.57	3

10 Major Wholesalers 十家主要批发商	City 城市	Province 省	Telephone/Fax 电话/传真
Ningbo Haitian Group General Company	Ningbo	Zhejiang	(0574)87195360
宁波海田集团总公司	宁波市	浙江省	(0574)87195821
Heilongjiang Agriculture Means Of Production Company	Harbin	Heilongjiang	(0451)88383752
黑龙江省农业生产资料公司	哈尔滨市	黑龙江省	(0451)88382367
Yantai Agriculture Means Of Production General Company	Yantai	Shandong	(0535)6216374
烟台市农业生产资料总公司	烟台市	山东省	(0535)6211348
Guangdong Agriculture Means Of Production General Company	Guangzhou	Guangdong	(020)87773051
广东省农业生产资料总公司	广州市	广东省	(020)87754117
Inner Mongolia Autonomous Region Agriculture & Animal Husbandry Means Of Production Co.,Ltd.	Huhhot	Inner Mongolia	(0471)6963132
内蒙古自治区农牧业生产资料股份有限公司	呼和浩特市	内蒙古	(0471)6964434
Shanghai Agriculture Means Of Production Company	Shanghai	Shanghai	(021)63807100
上海市农业生产资料公司	上海市	上海市	(021)63806807
Ningbo Haitian International Trade Co.,Ltd.	Ningbo	Zhejiang	(0574)87345251
宁波海田国际贸易有限公司	宁波市	浙江省	(0574)87345620
Fujian AMP Incorpration	Fuzhou	Fujian	(0591)7508666
福建省农资集团公司	福州市	福建省	(0591)7614839
Shandong Agricultural Machinery Group General Company	Jinan	Shandong	(0531)8951240
山东省农业机械集团总公司	济南市	山东省	(0531)8951240
Shandong Yantai Agriculture Means Of Production Purchasing Supply Station	Yantai	Shandong	(0535)6222126
山东省烟台市农业生产资料采购供应站	烟台市	山东省	(0535)6216440

1319: Other Animal Feed 其他饲料制造业

The industry accounts for 0.030% of the total revenue of China's industrial sector in 2002. The rate of return on assets is 3.42%. 81.05% of all firms in the industry made a profit while 18.95% had negative returns.The top province in terms of the industry's revenue is Fujian, accounting for 14.50% of the total revenue.
2002年本行业收入占全行业的0.030%，资产利润率为3.42%。81.05%的企业赢利，18.95%的企业亏损。收入最高的省为福建省，占本行业的14.50%。

	Total number of firms 企业总数	Total number of employees 职工总数	Total revenue (Mil.RMB) 总销售收入（百万元）	Total profit (Mil.RMB) 总利润（百万元）	Return on assets 资产利润率 (%)	Return on equity 权益利润率 (%)	Labour productivity ('000 RMB/ worker) 劳动生产率（千元/人）	Debts/ assets 资产负债率 (%)	Total assets (Mil.RMB) 总资产（百万元）
Industry Overall 行业总体	95	8,471	3,199	58	3.42	7.89	119.14	56.64	1,701

	Number of firms 企业个数	Average number of employees 平均职工人数	Average revenue ('000 RMB) 平均销售收入（千元）	Average profit ('000 RMB) 平均利润（千元）	Return on assets 资产利润率 (%)	Return on equity 权益利润率 (%)	Labour productivity ('000 RMB/ worker) 劳动生产率（千元/人）	Debts/ assets 资产负债率 (%)	Average total assets ('000 RMB) 平均总资产（千元）
By ownership 产业所有权									
State-owned 国有	12	38	10,287	-88	-1.21	-18.79	56.85	93.57	7,302
Collective-owned 集体	12	121	29,979	1,108	8.02	13.36	60.13	40.01	13,824
Foreign & Overseas Chinese Funded 三资	12	80	34,929	-607	-1.58	-3.08	75.82	48.73	38,453
By regional distribution 地区分布									
Central-North 华北	14	80	45,199	1,228	11.55	20.55	127.49	43.78	10,632
Beijing 北京	2	169	71,790	-1,080	-5.15	-34.81	46.41	85.20	20,956
Tianjin 天津	4	63	28,136	1,130	23.48	45.87	58.52	48.82	4,814
Hebei 河北	6	89	62,167	2,473	17.05	21.87	210.75	22.03	14,501
Shanxi 山西	2	2	1,829				232.00	133.04	336
Inner Mongolia 内蒙古									
Northeast 东北	9	53	31,334	-39	-0.32	-0.83	156.14	61.60	12,171
Liaoning 辽宁	4	68	34,183	-432	-2.75	-16.63	75.06	83.48	15,730
Jilin 吉林	2	48	44,274	428	4.93	6.23	447.54	20.89	8,680
Heilongjiang 黑龙江	3	37	18,908	174	1.78	2.91	102.81	38.69	9,753
Central-East 华东	29	100	34,959	833	3.37	7.17	95.11	53.00	24,727
Shanghai 上海	1	31	15,567	2,239	21.85	44.04	100.16	50.39	10,247
Jiangsu 江苏	5	68	26,835	1,260	14.02	25.13	101.89	44.21	8,985
Zhejiang 浙江	8	177	28,295	1,887	15.12	33.53	30.78	54.91	12,481
Anhui 安徽									
Fujian 福建	5	98	92,799	578	0.77	2.10	286.38	63.12	74,565
Jiangxi 江西									
Shandong 山东	10	62	17,373	-236	-1.25	-1.90	87.05	34.28	18,923
Central-South 中南	34	85	28,149	698	5.37	13.96	95.07	61.55	13,012
Henan 河南	15	89	25,412	907	9.57	17.76	77.12	46.10	9,480
Hubei 湖北	3	66	46,125	1,097	6.75	23.76	324.30	71.61	16,258
Hunan 湖南	3	90	12,352	285	3.84	8.38	48.22	54.19	7,419
Guangdong 广东	9	71	31,841	459	2.18	7.27	111.40	70.02	21,039
Guangxi 广西	4	115	28,470	465	4.67	14.70	53.15	68.26	9,955
Hainan 海南									
Southwest 西南	5	57	57,240	-366	-1.90	-21.97	814.90	91.33	19,228
Chongqing 重庆									
Sichuan 四川	2	69	131,819	-98	-0.25	-2.31	1,659.53	89.04	38,687
Guizhou 贵州	2	42	10,948	-143	-2.56	-19.42	19.04	86.80	5,580
Yunnan 云南	1	61	669	-1,349	-17.74		0.03	121.30	7,605
Tibet 西藏									
Northwest 西北	4	200	6,896	-1,177	-2.51	-4.88	12.89	48.54	46,871
Shaanxi 陕西	2	351	11,172	457	1.35	1.97	11.08	31.58	33,889
Gansu 甘肃	2	49	2,620	-2,810	-4.69	-11.22	25.88	58.14	59,853
Qinghai 青海									
Ningxia 宁夏									
Xinjiang 新疆									

Year 年份	Number of firms 企业个数	Rate of change 变化率 (%)	Number of employees 职工人数 (人)	Rate of change 变化率 (%)	Total revenue (Mil. RMB) 总销售收入 (百万元)	Rate of change 变化率 (%)	Total profit (Mil RMB) 总利润 (百万元)	Rate of change 变化率 (%)
2000	86		6,008		2,169		50	
2001	78	-9.30	5,920	-1.46	2,050	-5.49	93	86.00
2002	95	21.79	8,471	43.09	3,199	56.05	58	-37.63

Major Products 主要产品	Output 产量	Unit 单位

10 Main Firms with Maximal Revenue (year founded) 收入最大的十家主要企业（创办年份）	City 城市	Province 省	Telephone/fax 电话/传真	Number of employees 职工人数	Ownership 产业所有权	Revenue ('000 RMB) 销售收入 (千元)	Profit('000 RMB) (rank) 利润(千元) (排名)	Total assets ('000 RMB) 总资产 (千元)	Major products 主要产品
Fujian Kanghong Co., Ltd.	Fuzhou	Fujian	(0591)5588888		Private Enterprises				Bean Dregs
福建康宏股份有限公司(2000)	福州市	福建省	(0591)5588855	186	私营企业	341,347	1438(20)	224,501	豆粕
Sichuan Livestoke Feedstuff Co., Ltd.	Chengdu	Sichuan	(028)4514210		Joint Stock				Feedstuff Additive
四川省畜科饲料有限公司(1999)	成都市	四川省		66	股份制	241,661	-	66,513	料添加剂
Zhongte Science & Technology Co., Ltd.	Cangzhou	Hebei	(0317)4704133		Private Enterprises				Feedstuff
中特科技有限公司(1996)	沧州市	河北省	(0317)4704818	154	私营独资	178,650	7,090(3)	14,239	饲料
Cangzhou Health Protection Feedstuff Development Co.,Ltd.	Cangzhou	Hebei	(0317)4043267		Private Enterprises				Feedstuff
沧州市保健饲料开发有限公司(1995)	沧州市	河北省	(0317)4702288	268	私营企业	168,850	8,070(2)	26,188	饲料
Kangdi Huamei（Wuhan) Feedstuff Co., Ltd.	Wuhan	Hubei	(027)86532790		Foreign Funded				Feedstuff
康地华美（武汉）饲料有限公司(1986)	武汉市	湖北省	(027)86535004	150	外商投资	109,473	2,405(11)	41,574	饲料
Beijing Tongwei Feedstuff Co., Ltd.	Beijing	Beijing	(010)67999597		Joint Stock				Feedstuff
北京通威饲料有限公司(1998)	北京市	北京市	(010)67961484	190	股份制	99,459	-	19,331	饲料
Taian Hongwei Feedstuff Co., Ltd.	Anshan	Liaoning	(0412)4838550		Collective-owned				Feedstuff
台安县宏伟饲料有限责任公司(1999)	鞍山市	辽宁省	(0412)4835000	145	集体企业	87,500	690(32)	7,780	饲料
Wuxi Zhengda Animal & Poultry Co., Ltd.	Wuxi	Jiangsu	(0510)3119904		Private Owned				Feedstuff Additive饲
无锡市正大畜禽有限公司(1998)	无锡市	江苏省	(0510)3109248	119	私营企业	78,147	4,742(4)	19,316	料添加剂
Henan Hongzhan Industrial Co.,Ltd.	Zhengzhou	Henan	(0371)5695953		Private Owned				Feedstuff Additive饲
河南宏展实业有限公司(1999)	郑州市	河南省	(0371)5693932	320	私营企业	77,117	860(20)	13,609	料添加剂
Changchun Tongjiang Feedstuff Industrial Co., Ltd.	Changchun	Jilin	(0431)4523426		Joint Owned				Feedstuff
长春桐江饲料实业有限公司(1999)	长春市	吉林省	(0431)4523426	51	联营企业	75,600	756(30)	7,200	饲料

Top 10 Cities by Revenue 销售收入排名前10位城市	Province 省	Market share 市场份额 (%)	Number of firms 企业个数
Cangzhou 沧州市	Hebei 河北省	11.02	3
Fuzhou 福州市	Fujian 福建省	10.67	1
Chengdu 成都市	Sichuan 四川省	7.55	1
Zhengzhou 郑州市	Henan 河南省	5.41	4
Beijing 北京市	Beijing 北京市	4.49	2
Taizhou 台州市	Zhejiang 浙江省	4.01	2
Anshan 鞍山市	Liaoning 辽宁省	3.70	2
Guangzhou 广州市	Guangdong 广东省	3.67	3
Tianjin 天津市	Tianjin 天津市	3.52	4
Wuhan 武汉市	Hubei 湖北省	3.42	1

10 Major Wholesalers 十家主要批发商	City 城市	Province 省	Telephone/Fax 电话/传真
Ningbo Haitian Group General Company	Ningbo	Zhejiang	(0574)87195360
宁波海田集团总公司	宁波市	浙江省	(0574)87195821
Heilongjiang Agriculture Means Of Production Company	Harbin	Heilongjiang	(0451)88383752
黑龙江省农业生产资料公司	哈尔滨市	黑龙江省	(0451)88382367
Yantai Agriculture Means Of Production General Company	Yantai	Shandong	(0535)6216374
烟台市农业生产资料总公司	烟台市	山东省	(0535)6211348
Guangdong Agriculture Means Of Production General Company	Guangzhou	Guangdong	(020)87773051
广东省农业生产资料总公司	广州市	广东省	(020)87754117
Inner Mongolia Autonomous Region Agriculture & Animal Husbandry Means Of Production Co.,Ltd.	Huhhot	Inner Mongolia	(0471)6963132
内蒙古自治区农牧业生产资料股份有限公司	呼和浩特市	内蒙古	(0471)6964434
Shanghai Agriculture Means Of Production Company	Shanghai	Shanghai	(021)63807100
上海市农业生产资料公司	上海市	上海市	(021)63806807
Ningbo Haitian International Trade Co.,Ltd.	Ningbo	Zhejiang	(0574)87345251
宁波海田国际贸易有限公司	宁波市	浙江省	(0574)87345620
Fujian AMP Incorpration	Fuzhou	Fujian	(0591)7508666
福建省农资集团公司	福州市	福建省	(0591)7614839
Shandong Agricultural Machinery Group General Company	Jinan	Shandong	(0531)8951240
山东省农业机械集团总公司	济南市	山东省	(0531)8951240
Shandong Yantai Agriculture Means Of Production Purchasing Supply Station	Yantai	Shandong	(0535)6222126
山东省烟台市农业生产资料采购供应站	烟台市	山东省	(0535)6216440

1321: Edible Vegetable Oil 食用植物油加工业

The industry accounts for 0.872% of the total revenue of China's industrial sector in 2002. The rate of return on assets is 2.89%. 76.31% of all firms in the industry made a profit while 23.69% had negative returns.The top province in terms of the industry's revenue is Shandong, accounting for 20.02% of the total revenue.
2002年本行业收入占全行业的 0.872%，资产利润率为 2.89%。76.31%的企业赢利，23.69%的企业亏损。收入最高的省为山东省，占本行业的20.02%。

	Total number of firms 企业总数	Total number of employees 职工总数	Total revenue (Mil.RMB) 总销售收入(百万元)	Total profit (Mil.RMB) 总利润(百万元)	Return on assets 资产利润率(%)	Return on equity 权益利润率(%)	Labour productivity ('000 RMB/ worker) 劳动生产率(千元/人)	Debts/ assets 资产负债率(%)	Total assets (Mil.RMB) 总资产(百万元)
Industry Overall 行业总体	1186	164,020	93,530	1,866	2.89	10.88	123.27	73.45	64,575

	Number of firms 企业个数	Average number of employees 平均职工人数	Average revenue ('000 RMB) 平均销售收入(千元)	Average profit ('000 RMB) 平均利润(千元)	Return on assets 资产利润率(%)	Return on equity 权益利润率(%)	Labour productivity ('000 RMB/ worker) 劳动生产率(千元/人)	Debts/ assets 资产负债率(%)	Average total assets ('000 RMB) 平均总资产(千元)
By ownership 产业所有权									
State-owned 国有	299	140	31,800	114	0.32	3.31	44.67	90.47	36,234
Collective-owned 集体	163	145	44,997	1,713	5.80	33.56	76.73	82.70	29,519
Foreign & Overseas Chinese Funded 三资	84	214	431,240	10,178	4.01	11.66	441.76	65.63	253,886
By regional distribution 地区分布									
Central-North 华北	106	184	108,135	3,374	5.33	19.62	46.82	72.82	63,274
Beijing 北京	5	75	46,541	-1,742	-4.55	-7.98	75.78	42.95	38,245
Tianjin 天津	17	289	259,756	8,646	5.36	20.43	-122.19	73.75	161,260
Hebei 河北	50	185	109,751	4,134	8.06	30.28	111.47	73.38	51,282
Shanxi 山西	12	203	45,905	426	0.78	3.19	84.61	75.70	54,851
Inner Mongolia 内蒙古	22	114	35,240	342	1.36	4.95	98.66	72.45	25,096
Northeast 东北	142	185	81,145	1,428	1.76	12.42	90.53	85.81	81,024
Liaoning 辽宁	31	194	204,418	4,357	3.33	15.69	226.73	78.75	130,674
Jilin 吉林	29	169	46,096	1,417	3.23	28.54	80.39	88.69	43,904
Heilongjiang 黑龙江	82	187	46,937	324	0.43	4.24	40.55	89.85	75,381
Central-East 华东	388	152	114,776	2,239	3.39	12.39	166.98	72.60	65,974
Shanghai 上海	16	126	201,956	4,366	4.41	12.25	384.55	63.98	98,960
Jiangsu 江苏	112	143	133,456	2,784	3.51	11.24	219.37	68.79	79,337
Zhejiang 浙江	30	92	132,842	-440	-0.41	-1.80	88.67	77.16	107,320
Anhui 安徽	64	143	36,401	233	0.78	5.14	59.05	84.78	29,740
Fujian 福建	9	115	113,774	-1,825	-2.25	-6.20	140.66	63.65	80,957
Jiangxi 江西	18	84	16,299	-330	-1.79	-15.76	46.83	88.64	18,438
Shandong 山东	139	190	134,693	3,652	5.68	21.68	172.23	73.82	64,356
Central-South 中南	347	119	61,930	1,286	2.69	7.79	142.89	65.43	47,770
Henan 河南	153	113	33,986	873	4.70	39.03	80.58	87.97	18,582
Hubei 湖北	120	117	39,269	1,312	3.01	8.85	110.60	66.03	43,629
Hunan 湖南	40	115	54,045	-1,786	-2.14	-5.01	138.99	57.22	83,368
Guangdong 广东	28	174	334,354	8,263	4.56	10.64	470.26	57.15	181,337
Guangxi 广西	6	70	8,967	-784	-5.50	-60.85	29.94	90.97	14,256
Hainan 海南									
Southwest 西南	100	78	21,950	-164	-0.90	-3.62	79.26	75.22	18,286
Chongqing 重庆	6	108	12,222	-355	-3.50		21.68	104.17	10,138
Sichuan 四川	48	82	30,845	26	0.13	0.37	113.86	65.85	20,752
Guizhou 贵州	37	72	15,916	-107	-0.63	-4.18	48.79	84.82	16,911
Yunnan 云南	7	63	7,137	-1,623	-8.55	-73.97	42.01	88.44	18,981
Tibet 西藏	2	17	1,120	-96	-1.47	-3.72	42.12	60.44	6,528
Northwest 西北	103	101	22,596	71	0.31	1.47	56.95	79.08	22,910
Shaanxi 陕西	22	140	43,704	-179	-0.59	-2.47	77.20	75.90	30,050
Gansu 甘肃	18	91	3,969	-256	-2.60	-12.66	22.75	79.44	9,837
Qinghai 青海	8	94	12,368	-288	-1.98	-16.88	27.64	88.24	14,513
Ningxia 宁夏	1	30	10,854	30	0.51	6.70	90.53	92.39	5,888
Xinjiang 新疆	54	90	21,938	335	1.29	6.37	59.93	79.72	25,917

1321: Edible Vegetable Oil 食用植物油加工业

Year 年份	Number of firms 企业个数	Rate of change 变化率 (%)	Number of employees 职工人数 (人)	Rate of change 变化率 (%)	Total revenue (Mil. RMB) 总销售收入 (百万元)	Rate of change 变化率 (%)	Total profit (Mil RMB) 总利润 (百万元)	Rate of change 变化率 (%)
2000	1321		203,121		69,633		471	
2001	1228	-7.04	180,009	-11.38	75,952	9.07	903	91.72
2002	1186	-3.42	164,020	-8.88	93,530	23.14	1,866	106.64

Major Products 主要产品	Output 产量	Unit 单位
Edible Vegetable Oil 食用植物油	943	10,000 Tons 万吨

10 Main Firms with Maximal Revenue (year founded) 收入最大的十家主要企业（创办年份）	City 城市	Province 省	Telephone/fax 电话/传真	Number of employees 职工人数	Ownership 产业所有权	Revenue ('000 RMB) 销售收入 (千元)	Profit('000 RMB) (rank) 利润(千元) (排名)	Total assets ('000 RMB) 总资产 (千元)	Major products 主要产品
Southseas Oil & Fats Industrial(Chiwan) Co., Ltd.	Shenzhen	Guangdong	(0755)26694322		Overseas Chinese-funded				Edible Oil
南海油脂工业（赤湾）有限公司(1988)	深圳市	广东省	(0755)26674280	630	港澳台资	2,834,765	79,012(4)	889,183	食用油
Qinhuangdao Jinhai Grain & Oil Industry Co., Ltd.	Qinhuangdao	Hebei	(0335)3097133		Foreign Funded				Bean oil
秦皇岛金海粮油工业有限公司(2000)	秦皇岛市	河北省		220	外商投资	2,153,558	70,089(6)	778,717	豆油
Shanghai Kerry Grain & Oils Industrial Co.,Ltd.	Shanghai	Shanghai	(021)68462277		Overseas Chinese-funded				Edible Oil
上海嘉里粮油工业有限公司(1994)	上海市	上海市	(021)68467008	494	港澳台资	1,787,704	70,566(5)	658,416	食用油
Shandong Bohai Oils & Fats Industrial Co.,Ltd.	Binzhou	Shandong	(0543)2325654		Foreign Funded				Salad Oil
博兴县渤海油脂工业有限公司(1995)	滨州市	山东省	(0543)2305440	216	外商投资	1,507,202	34,239(17)	558,544	色拉油
Dalian Huanong Bean Industrial Group Stock Co., Ltd.	Dalian	Liaoning	(0411)7260419		Joint Stock				Food Edible Oil食
大连华农豆业集团股份有限公司(1989)	大连市	辽宁省	(0411)7260282	588	股份制	1,453,439	142,909(2)	854,372	用植物油
Liaoyang Edible Oil Co., Ltd.	Liaoyang	Liaoning	(0419)2268808		Overseas Chinese-funded				Bean Dregs
辽阳食用油品有限公司(1999)	辽阳市	辽宁省	(0419)2268811	1,002	港澳台资	1,452,872	7,691(56)	602,135	豆粕
Shanhe Hopefull Grain & Oil Foods Makeing Co.,Ltd.	Langfang	Hebei	(0316)3311168		Limited-Liability				Salad Oil
三河汇福粮油食品制作有限公司(1999)	廊坊市	河北省		450	有限公司	1,357,308	54,511(11)	422,096	色拉油
Jingguang Foodstuffs (Ningbo) Co.,Ltd.	Ningbo	Zhejiang	(0574)86888188		Foreign Funded				Edible Oil
金光食品(宁波)有限公司(1994)	宁波市	浙江省	(0574)86889902	180	外商投资	1,263,139	-	1,256,444	食用油
Shandong Xiangchi Grain & Oil Co., Ltd.	Binzhou	Shandong	(0543)2510047		Limited Liability				Bean oil
山东香驰粮油有限公司(1990)	滨州市	山东省	(0543)2510047	306	有限公司	1,250,460	30,178(22)	431,362	豆油
Beihai Oils and Grains Industries(Tianjin) Co.,Ltd.	Tianjin	Tianjin	(022)66581818		Overseas Chinese-funded				Refined Oil
北海粮油工业(天津)有限公司(1992)	天津市	天津市	(022)66581858	520	港澳台资	1,114,933	-	633,599	精炼油

Top 10 Cities by Revenue 销售收入排名前10位城市	Province 省	Market share 市场份额 (%)	Number of firms 企业个数
Suzhou 苏州市	Jiangsu 江苏省	6.75	10
Tianjin 天津市	Tianjin 天津市	4.72	17
Shenzhen 深圳市	Guangdong 广东省	4.59	4
Binzhou 滨州市	Shandong 山东省	4.11	20
Shanghai 上海市	Shanghai 上海市	3.45	16
Dalian 大连市	Liaoning 辽宁省	3.14	5
Yantai 烟台市	Shandong 山东省	2.82	9
Guangzhou 广州市	Guangdong 广东省	2.60	9
Jining 济宁市	Shandong 山东省	2.40	18
Qinhuangdao 秦皇岛市	Hebei 河北省	2.34	2

10 Major Wholesalers 十家主要批发商	City 城市	Province 省	Telephone/Fax 电话/传真
COFCO International (Beijing) Ltd.	Beijing	Beijing	(010)65268888
中粮国际(北京)有限公司	北京市	北京市	(010)65223623
China National Cereals, Oils & Foodstuffs Imp. & Exp. Corp.	Beijing	Beijing	(010)65268888
中国粮油食品进出口(集团)有限公司	北京市	北京市	(010)62578612
China Grains and Oils Group Corp.	Beijing	Beijing	(010)88518866
中谷粮油集团公司	北京市	北京市	(010)68476847
China Tobacco General Company Beijing Company	Beijing	Beijing	(010)64434106
中国烟草总公司北京市公司	北京市	北京市	(010)64418742
Jilin Grain Group Import & Export Ltd.	Changchun	Jilin	(0431)5598115
吉林粮食集团进出口有限公司	长春市	吉林省	(0431)5598118
Zhejiang Cereals, Oils & Foodstuffs Import & Export Co.,Ltd.	Hangzhou	Zhejiang	(0571)85779999
浙江省粮油食品进出口股份有限公司	杭州市	浙江省	(0571)85152514
China Tobacco General Company Shenzhen Company	Shenzhen	Guangdong	(0755)82230333
中国烟草总公司深圳市公司	深圳市	广东省	(0755)82206815
China National Vegetable Oil Corporation	Beijing	Beijing	(010)68083380
中国植物油公司	北京市	北京市	(010)68081127
Beijing Yangu Grain & Oil Purchase & Sale Company	Beijing	Beijing	(010)63041782
北京市燕谷粮油购销公司	北京市	北京市	(010)63034914
Shanghai Good Companion Sea Lion Industrial Co., Ltd Sale Filiale	Shanghai	Shanghai	(021)63321662
上海良友海狮油脂实业有限公司销售分公司	上海市	上海市	(021)54095735

1322: Inedible Vegetable Oil 非食用植物油加工业

The industry accounts for 0.009% of the total revenue of China's industrial sector in 2002. The rate of return on assets is 12.06%. 87.50% of all firms in the industry made a profit while 12.50% had negative returns.The top province in terms of the industry's revenue is Tianjin, accounting for 27.08% of the total revenue.
2002年本行业收入占全行业的 0.009%，资产利润率为 12.06%。87.50%的企业赢利，12.50%的企业亏损。收入最高的省为天津市，占本行业的27.08%。

	Total number of firms 企业总数	Total number of employees 职工总数	Total revenue (Mil.RMB) 总销售收入（百万元）	Total profit (Mil.RMB) 总利润（百万元）	Return on assets 资产利润率（%）	Return on equity 权益利润率（%）	Labour productivity ('000 RMB/worker) 劳动生产率（千元/人）	Debts/assets 资产负债率（%）	Total assets (Mil.RMB) 总资产（百万元）
Industry Overall 行业总体	40	2,504	918	53	12.06	31.59	146.34	61.84	441

	Number of firms 企业个数	Average number of employees 平均职工人数	Average revenue ('000 RMB) 平均销售收入（千元）	Average profit ('000 RMB) 平均利润（千元）	Return on assets 资产利润率（%）	Return on equity 权益利润率（%）	Labour productivity ('000 RMB/worker) 劳动生产率（千元/人）	Debts/assets 资产负债率（%）	Average total assets ('000 RMB) 平均总资产（千元）
By ownership 产业所有权									
State-owned 国有	5	22	1,718	-146	-4.47	-12.06	23.58	62.91	3,259
Collective-owned 集体	8	95	35,718	3,166	18.27	45.05	272.87	59.45	17,328
Foreign & Overseas Chinese Funded 三资	3	22	14,111	1,313	10.15	23.98	320.85	57.65	12,933
By regional distribution 地区分布									
Central-North 华北	6	73	45,463	4,277	31.65	90.21	108.52	64.91	13,513
Beijing 北京									
Tianjin 天津	4	93	62,170	6,163	39.67	103.83	113.22	61.79	15,533
Hebei 河北									
Shanxi 山西	2	33	12,050	507	5.35	21.51	81.82	75.15	9,473
Inner Mongolia 内蒙古									
Northeast 东北	5	54	15,285	1,247	17.14	37.79	130.23	54.65	7,276
Liaoning 辽宁	3	43	23,142	2,070	23.40	53.07	148.95	55.91	8,847
Jilin 吉林	2	71	3,500	13	0.25	0.52	113.09	51.24	4,919
Heilongjiang 黑龙江									
Central-East 华东	10	46	24,522	646	6.19	14.35	61.63	56.86	10,434
Shanghai 上海									
Jiangsu 江苏	1	38	16,260	890	11.57	51.74	108.42	77.63	7,690
Zhejiang 浙江	2	33	5,510	647	12.08	24.08	31.83	49.83	5,351
Anhui 安徽									
Fujian 福建									
Jiangxi 江西									
Shandong 山东	7	50	31,134	611	4.97	11.27	62.08	55.87	12,279
Central-South 中南	6	99	33,570	2,236	10.86	26.42	310.69	58.89	20,583
Henan 河南									
Hubei 湖北	1	440	185,320	14,827	16.08	39.01	413.25	58.78	92,210
Hunan 湖南	2	13	1,737	-367	-4.95	-7.37	36.44	32.78	7,398
Guangdong 广东									
Guangxi 广西	3	43	4,210	-227	-4.12	-24.20	16.28	82.96	5,497
Hainan 海南									
Southwest 西南	10	57	10,035	76	1.29	4.16	113.65	68.91	5,864
Chongqing 重庆	1	22	10,508	70	0.81	1.90	130.95	57.04	8,596
Sichuan 四川	3	111	20,262	181	2.14	4.84	164.20	55.74	8,433
Guizhou 贵州	6	36	4,842	24	0.59	4.37	33.08	86.51	4,124
Yunnan 云南									
Tibet 西藏									
Northwest 西北	3	60	7,420	206	1.68	6.67	36.76	74.89	12,292
Shaanxi 陕西	1	135	16,205	340	1.02	4.64	25.60	78.09	33,446
Gansu 甘肃	2	23	3,028	139	8.10	14.40	69.50	43.72	1,716
Qinghai 青海									
Ningxia 宁夏									
Xinjiang 新疆									

1322: Inedible Vegetable Oil 非食用植物油加工业

Year 年份	Number of firms 企业个数	Rate of change 变化率 (%)	Number of employees 职工人数 (人)	Rate of change 变化率 (%)	Total revenue (Mil. RMB) 总销售收入 (百万元)	Rate of change 变化率 (%)	Total profit (Mil RMB) 总利润 (百万元)	Rate of change 变化率 (%)
2000	48		2,287		475		2	
2001	42	-12.50	2,942	28.64	585	23.16	9	350.00
2002	40	-4.76	2,504	-14.89	918	56.92	53	488.89

Major Products 主要产品	Output 产量	Unit 单位

10 Main Firms with Maximal Revenue (year founded) 收入最大的十家主要企业（创办年份）	City 城市	Province 省	Telephone/fax 电话/传真	Number of employees 职工人数	Ownership 产业所有权	Revenue ('000 RMB) 销售收入 (千元)	Profit('000 RMB) (rank) 利润(千元) (排名)	Total assets ('000 RMB) 总资产 (千元)	Major products 主要产品
Hubei Shuangbei Grain & Oil Group	Xiangfan	Hubei	(0710)2871177		Collective-owned				
湖北双北粮油集团(1993)	襄樊市	湖北省	(0710)2871188	440	集体企业	185,320	14,827(2)	92,210	
Tianjin Yongming Oil & Fat Manufacturing Factory	Tianjin	Tianjin	(022)86840251		Private Enterprises				Ink Resin
天津市永明油脂制造厂(1994)	天津市	天津市	(022)86840251	150	私营独资	183,890	16,100(1)	34,640	油墨树脂
Lijin Shunli Oilseed Processing Co., Ltd.	Dongying	Shandong	(0546)5319629		Private Owned				Castor Oil
利津县顺利油料加工有限责任公司(1996)	东营市	山东省	(0546)5319629	30	私营企业	63,830	488(16)	12,543	蓖麻油
Jianyang Jianyuan Oil & Fat Co., Ltd.	Ziyang	Sichuan	(0832)7281959		Joint Stock				Refined Cotton Oil
简阳市建元油脂有限责任公司(1952)	资阳市	四川省	(0832)7281959	152	股份制	52,685	25(27)	11,921	精棉油
Zouping Tianxing Chemical Industry Co., Ltd.	Binzhou	Shandong	(0543)4342171		Private Enterprises				Sebacic Acid
邹平天兴化工有限公司(2000)	滨州市	山东省	(0543)4342039	130	私营独资	42,944	589(14)	38,635	葵二酸
Lijin Dongying Oilseed Processing Co., Ltd	Dongying	Shandong	(0546)5319568		Private Owned				Castor Oil
利津县东营油料加工有限责任公司(1999)	东营市	山东省	(0546)5319568	20	私营企业	39,789	645(13)	9,522	蓖麻油
Shenyang Goerlich Natural Plant Oils Co.,Ltd.	Shenyang	Liaoning	(024)89737455		Foreign Funded				Inedible Vegetable Oil非食
沈阳格力西植物油有限公司(2000)	沈阳市	辽宁省	(024)89737399	25	外商投资	31,825	3,870(4)	21,270	用植物油
Tianjin Hualong Oil & Fat Chemical Industry Company	Tianjin	Tianjin	(022)86848277		Collective-owned				Lipid
天津市华隆油脂化工公司(1994)	天津市	天津市	(022)86841951	77	集体企业	30,220	6,620(3)	13,880	油脂
Zouping Castor Oil Factory	Binzhou	Shandong	(0543)4781328		Private Owned				Castor Oil
邹平县蓖麻油厂(2000)	滨州市	山东省	(0543)4781328	24	私营企业	20,370	250(22)	6,250	蓖麻油
Yuci Jinbei Oil & Fat Factory	Jinzhong	Shanxi	(0354)2523305		Collective-owned				Industry Oil
榆次区晋北油脂厂(1986)	晋中市	山西省	(0354)2523486	29	集体企业	18,889	998(8)	11,366	工业用油

Top 10 Cities by Revenue 销售收入排名前10位城市	Province 省	Market share 市场份额 (%)	Number of firms 企业个数
Tianjin 天津市	Tianjin 天津市	27.08	4
Xiangfan 襄樊市	Hubei 湖北省	20.18	1
Dongying 东营市	Shandong 山东省	15.22	4
Binzhou 滨州市	Shandong 山东省	6.92	2
Ziyang 资阳市	Sichuan 四川省	5.74	1
Anshan 鞍山市	Liaoning 辽宁省	4.09	1
Shenyang 沈阳市	Liaoning 辽宁省	3.47	1
Jinzhong 晋中市	Shanxi 山西省	2.06	1
Changzhou 常州市	Jiangsu 江苏省	1.77	1
Shangluo 商洛市	Shannxi 陕西省	1.76	1

10 Major Wholesalers 十家主要批发商	City 城市	Province 省	Telephone/Fax 电话/传真
COFCO International (Beijing) Ltd.	Beijing	Beijing	(010)65268888
中粮国际(北京)有限公司	北京市	北京市	(010)65223623
China National Cereals, Oils & Foodstuffs Imp. & Exp. Corp.	Beijing	Beijing	(010)65268888
中国粮油食品进出口(集团)有限公司	北京市	北京市	(010)62578612
China Grains and Oils Group Corp.	Beijing	Beijing	(010)88518866
中谷粮油集团公司	北京市	北京市	(010)68476847
China Tobacco General Company Beijing Company	Beijing	Beijing	(010)64434106
中国烟草总公司北京市公司	北京市	北京市	(010)64418742
Jilin Grain Group Import & Export Ltd.	Changchun	Jilin	(0431)5598115
吉林粮食集团进出口有限公司	长春市	吉林省	(0431)5598118
Zhejiang Cereals, Oils & Foodstuffs Import & Export Co.,Ltd.	Hangzhou	Zhejiang	(0571)85779999
浙江省粮油食品进出口股份有限公司	杭州市	浙江省	(0571)85152514
China Tobacco General Company Shenzhen Company	Shenzhen	Guangdong	(0755)82230333
中国烟草总公司深圳市公司	深圳市	广东省	(0755)82206815
China National Vegetable Oil Corporation	Beijing	Beijing	(010)68083380
中国植物油公司	北京市	北京市	(010)68081127
Beijing Yangu Grain & Oil Purchase & Sale Company	Beijing	Beijing	(010)63041782
北京市燕谷粮油购销公司	北京市	北京市	(010)63034914
Shanghai Good Companion Sea Lion Industrial Co., Ltd Sale Filiale	Shanghai	Shanghai	(021)63321662
上海良友海狮油脂实业有限公司销售分公司	上海市	上海市	(021)54095735

1331: Cane Sugar 甘蔗糖业

The industry accounts for 0.238% of the total revenue of China's industrial sector in 2002. The rate of return on assets is 0.73%. 46.49% of all firms in the industry made a profit while 53.51% had negative returns.The top province in terms of the industry's revenue is Guangxi, accounting for 55.79% of the total revenue.
2002年本行业收入占全行业的 0.238%，资产利润率为 0.73%。46.49%的企业赢利，53.51%的企业亏损。收入最高的省为广西，占本行业的55.79%。

	Total number of firms 企业总数	Total number of employees 职工总数	Total revenue (Mil.RMB) 总销售收入 (百万元)	Total profit (Mil.RMB) 总利润 (百万元)	Return on assets 资产利润率 (%)	Return on equity 权益利润率 (%)	Labour productivity ('000 RMB/ worker) 劳动生产率 (千元/人)	Debts/ assets 资产负债率 (%)	Total assets (Mil.RMB) 总资产 (百万元)
Industry Overall 行业总体	271	156,083	25,509	266	0.73	2.42	46.03	69.88	36,396

	Number of firms 企业个数	Average number of employees 平均职工人数	Average revenue ('000 RMB) 平均销售收入 (千元)	Average profit ('000 RMB) 平均利润 (千元)	Return on assets 资产利润率 (%)	Return on equity 权益利润率 (%)	Labour productivity ('000 RMB/ worker) 劳动生产率 (千元/人)	Debts/ assets 资产负债率 (%)	Average total assets ('000 RMB) 平均总资产 (千元)
By ownership 产业所有权									
State-owned 国有	98	455	49,574	-1,943	-2.02	-16.42	28.53	87.70	96,263
Collective-owned 集体	10	300	39,998	-2,623	-3.38	-37.68	43.02	91.03	77,647
Foreign & Overseas Chinese Funded 三资	14	773	372,495	30,028	9.61	19.48	126.15	50.66	312,469
By regional distribution 地区分布									
Central-North 华北	1	20	750	-1,375	-8.12		3.70	106.75	16,936
Beijing 北京									
Tianjin 天津									
Hebei 河北									
Shanxi 山西	1	20	750	-1,375	-8.12		3.70	106.75	16,936
Inner Mongolia 内蒙古									
Northeast 东北									
Liaoning 辽宁									
Jilin 吉林									
Heilongjiang 黑龙江									
Central-East 华东	9	469	41,603	-2,534	-3.12	-5.83	8.79	46.37	81,101
Shanghai 上海									
Jiangsu 江苏									
Zhejiang 浙江									
Anhui 安徽	1	21	1,543	37	1.51	7.01	19.33	78.40	2,444
Fujian 福建	3	722	95,344	-6,133	-3.84	-6.81	9.34	43.61	159,661
Jiangxi 江西	5	407	17,371	-889	-1.79	-3.68	8.10	51.36	49,697
Shandong 山东									
Central-South 中南	179	633	118,581	4,248	2.82	7.69	54.22	63.32	150,687
Henan 河南									
Hubei 湖北	6	441	69,443	-2,350	-5.43	-36.53	24.68	85.12	43,236
Hunan 湖南	11	412	22,500	-181	-0.59	-2.87	13.51	79.42	30,593
Guangdong 广东	47	652	114,914	-3,449	-2.09	-6.29	48.14	66.79	165,007
Guangxi 广西	90	715	158,116	10,215	5.36	13.39	66.72	59.94	190,510
Hainan 海南	25	442	37,217	767	1.30	5.62	22.09	76.86	59,031
Southwest 西南	82	471	47,654	-5,739	-5.42	-69.10	26.07	92.15	105,813
Chongqing 重庆									
Sichuan 四川	8	452	37,301	-2,828	-4.94	-29.06	29.97	82.98	57,196
Guizhou 贵州	4	176	12,012	-135	-0.30	-4.77	26.03	93.66	44,696
Yunnan 云南	70	490	50,873	-6,392	-5.56	-75.60	25.66	92.64	114,862
Tibet 西藏									
Northwest 西北									
Shaanxi 陕西									
Gansu 甘肃									
Qinghai 青海									
Ningxia 宁夏									
Xinjiang 新疆									

1331: Cane Sugar 甘蔗糖业

Year 年份	Number of firms 企业个数	Rate of change 变化率(%)	Number of employees 职工人数(人)	Rate of change 变化率(%)	Total revenue (Mil. RMB) 总销售收入(百万元)	Rate of change 变化率(%)	Total profit (Mil RMB) 总利润(百万元)	Rate of change 变化率(%)
2000	319		201,153		19,110		714	
2001	266	-16.61	159,410	-20.75	20,511	7.33	1,438	101.40
2002	271	1.88	156,083	-2.09	25,509	24.37	266	-81.50

Major Products 主要产品	Output 产量	Unit 单位
Machine-made Sugar 机制糖	915	10,000 Tons 万吨

10 Main Firms with Maximal Revenue (year founded) 收入最大的十家主要企业（创办年份）	City 城市	Province 省	Telephone/fax 电话/传真	Number of employees 职工人数	Ownership 产业所有权	Revenue ('000 RMB) 销售收入(千元)	Profit('000 RMB) (rank) 利润(千元)(排名)	Total assets ('000 RMB) 总资产(千元)	Major products 主要产品
Nanning Sugar Industry Co.,Ltd.	Nanning	Guangxi	(0771)4910567		Joint Stock				Machine-made Sugar
南宁糖业股份有限公司(1999)	南宁市	广西自治区	(0771)4917711	6,681	股份制	1,411,752	111,018(1)	1,355,322	机制糖
Guangxi Guitang(Group) Co.,Ltd.	Guigang	Guangxi	(0775)4262888		Joint Stock				Machine-made Sugar
广西贵糖（集团）股份有限公司(1956)	贵港市	广西自治区	(0775)4260088	3,316	股份制	840,086	20,000(15)	1,294,179	机制糖
Jiangmen Sugarcane Chemical Plant (Group) Co., Ltd.	Jiangmen	Guangdong	(0750)3361611		Joint Stock				Machine-made Sugar
江门甘蔗化工厂(集团)股份有限公司(1959)	江门市	广东省	(0750)3361973	3,580	股份制	798,969	-	1,667,671	机制糖
Dongguan Dongtang Group Company	Dongguan	Guangdong	(0769)8812123		State-owned				Machine-made Sugar
东莞市东糖集团公司(1936)	东莞市	广东省	(0769)8815957	2,435	国有企业	720,924	1,854(64)	1,192,005	机制糖
Guangxi Fengtang Biochemisty Co.Ltd.	Liuzhou	Guangxi	(0772)2362327		State Enterprises				Machine-made Sugar
广西凤糖生化股份有限公司(1958)	柳州市	广西省	(0772)2361140	1,646	国有独资	625,999	38,462(10)	495,358	机制糖
Guangxi Funan East Asia Sugar Co.,Ltd.	Chongzuo	Guangxi	(0771)7538035		Foreign Funded				Machine-made Sugar
广西扶南东亚糖业有限公司(1993)	崇左市	广西自治区	(0771)7531062	1,276	外商投资	479,690	70,119(3)	341,515	机制糖
Guangxi Boqing Food Co., Ltd.	Hechi	Guangxi	(0778)3146691		Foreign Funded				Machine-made Sugar
广西博庆食品有限公司(1975)	河池市	广西自治区	(0778)3146633	1,550	外商投资	429,254	63,654(4)	458,806	机制糖
Guangxi TuoIu East Asia Sugar Co.,Ltd.	Chongzuo	Guangxi	(0771)7950368		Overseas Chinese-funded				Machine-made Sugar
广西驮卢东亚糖业有限公司(1993)	崇左市	广西自治区	(0771)7950369	1,030	港澳台资	383,543	60,552(5)	304,231	机制糖
Guang Xi Chong Zuo East Asia Sugar Co.,Ltd.	Chongzuo	Guangxi	(0771)5536971		Overseas Chinese-funded				Machine-made Sugar
广西崇左东亚糖业有限公司(1993)	崇左市	广西自治区	(0771)7822495	1,056	港澳台资	373,224	49,567(6)	281,126	机制糖
Guangdong Fengshou Sugar Industry Development Co.,Ltd.	Zhanjiang	Guangdong	(0759)8951762		State Enterprises				White Granulated Sugar
广东省丰收糖业发展有限公司(1995)	湛江市	广东省	(0759)8951180	1,615	国有独资	357,325	19,301(17)	192,296	白砂糖

Top 10 Cities by Revenue 销售收入排名前10位城市	Province 省	Market share 市场份额(%)	Number of firms 企业个数
Chongzuo 崇左市	Guangxi 广西	10.91	13
Nanning 南宁市	Guangxi 广西	10.53	12
Fangchenggang 防城港市	Guangxi 广西	10.02	5
Zhanjiang 湛江市	Guangdong 广东省	9.91	22
Liuzhou 柳州市	Guangxi 广西	6.02	10
Laibin 来宾市	Guangxi 广西	5.86	15
Guigang 贵港市	Guangxi 广西	4.02	4
Jiangmen 江门市	Guangdong 广东省	3.23	3
Hainan 海南省	Hainan 海南省	3.17	22
Lincang 临沧地区	Yunnan 云南省	3.12	13

10 Major Wholesalers 十家主要批发商	City 城市	Province 省	Telephone/Fax 电话/传真
Beijing Chaoyang Non-Staple Foodstuffs General Company	Beijing	Beijing	(010)65016285
北京朝阳副食品总公司	北京市	北京市	(010)65016285
Beijing Sugar,Cigarette & Wine Company	Beijing	Beijing	(010)67210304
北京市糖业烟酒公司	北京市	北京市	(010)67210310
Shanghai Sugar Cigarette & Wine (Group) Co.,Ltd.	Shanghai	Shanghai	(021)63224190
上海市糖业烟酒(集团)有限公司	上海市	上海市	(021)63223169
Jiangsu Sutang Sugar & Wine Co.,Ltd.	Nanjing	Jiangsu	(025)6661088
江苏苏糖糖酒食品有限公司	南京市	江苏省	(025)6661088
Fujian Commerce (Group) Co.,Ltd.	Fuzhou	Fujian	(0591)7847148
福建省商业（集团）有限责任公司	福州市	福建省	(0591)7847145
Yantai Changyu Pioneer Winer Co., Ltd.	Yantai	Shandong	(0535)6602730
烟台张裕葡萄酿酒股份有限公司	烟台市	山东省	(0535)6214078
BlueRibbon Beer Sale Co.,Ltd.	Zhaoqing	Guangdong	(0758)2862322
蓝带啤酒销售有限公司	肇庆市	广东省	(0758)2862424
Fujian Shenlong Development Co.,Ltd.	Fuzhou	Fujian	(0591)7503218
福建省神龙发展股份有限公司	福州市	福建省	(0591)7503068
Guangdong Sugar, Cigarette & Wine Group Company	Guangzhou	Guangdong	(020)83566131
广东省糖烟酒集团公司	广州市	广东省	(020)83561421
Shunde Daliang Sugar, Cigarette & Wine Co.,Ltd.	Shunde	Guangdong	(0765)2231804
顺德市大良区糖烟酒有限公司	顺德市	广东省	(0765)2222300

1332: Beet Sugar 甜菜糖业

The industry accounts for 0.032% of the total revenue of China's industrial sector in 2002. The rate of return on assets is 2.20%. 75.00% of all firms in the industry made a profit while 25.00% had negative returns.The top province in terms of the industry's revenue is Xinjiang, accounting for 37.52% of the total revenue.
2002年本行业收入占全行业的0.032%，资产利润率为2.20%。75.00%的企业赢利，25.00%的企业亏损。收入最高的省为新疆，占本行业的37.52%。

	Total number of firms 企业总数	Total number of employees 职工总数	Total revenue (Mil.RMB) 总销售收入（百万元）	Total profit (Mil.RMB) 总利润（百万元）	Return on assets 资产利润率（%）	Return on equity 权益利润率（%）	Labour productivity ('000 RMB/ worker) 劳动生产率（千元/人）	Debts/ assets 资产负债率（%）	Total assets (Mil.RMB) 总资产（百万元）
Industry Overall 行业总体	56	30,494	3,434	159	2.20	5.47	40.29	59.74	7,221

	Number of firms 企业个数	Average number of employees 平均职工人数	Average revenue ('000 RMB) 平均销售收入（千元）	Average profit ('000 RMB) 平均利润（千元）	Return on assets 资产利润率（%）	Return on equity 权益利润率（%）	Labour productivity ('000 RMB/ worker) 劳动生产率（千元/人）	Debts/ assets 资产负债率（%）	Average total assets ('000 RMB) 平均总资产（千元）
By ownership 产业所有权									
State-owned 国有	13	537	49,839	-305	-0.16	-0.46	45.28	64.24	186,980
Collective-owned 集体	2	410	18,130	711	5.90	37.46	42.59	84.26	12,061
Foreign & Overseas Chinese Funded 三资	1	240	1,230	-514	-1.47	-1.70	2.41	13.19	34,920
By regional distribution 地区分布									
Central-North 华北	13	582	68,226	7,936	4.92	7.83	49.89	37.12	161,274
Beijing 北京									
Tianjin 天津									
Hebei 河北	2	269	38,436	5,935	17.19	60.29	52.46	71.48	34,519
Shanxi 山西	1								
Inner Mongolia 内蒙古	10	703	81,006	9,130	4.50	7.03	49.70	35.95	202,753
Northeast 东北	22	595	51,308	626	0.62	1.33	30.40	53.38	100,904
Liaoning 辽宁	4	401	20,216	-362	-0.71	-1.34	21.80	46.79	50,852
Jilin 吉林	3	454	17,926	-500	-0.77		8.10	119.60	65,059
Heilongjiang 黑龙江	15	675	66,275	1,114	0.92	1.73	34.76	47.02	121,421
Central-East 华东	2	104	36,269	3,686	12.32	23.93	61.04	48.52	29,923
Shanghai 上海									
Jiangsu 江苏									
Zhejiang 浙江									
Anhui 安徽									
Fujian 福建									
Jiangxi 江西									
Shandong 山东	2	104	36,269	3,686	12.32	23.93	61.04	48.52	29,923
Central-South 中南	4	228	12,794	233	0.75	3.26	38.01	77.07	31,070
Henan 河南	3	161	13,322	475	2.50	3.77	53.21	33.64	18,974
Hubei 湖北									
Hunan 湖南									
Guangdong 广东									
Guangxi 广西	1	429	11,209	-495	-0.73		20.93	113.77	67,358
Hainan 海南									
Southwest 西南									
Chongqing 重庆									
Sichuan 四川									
Guizhou 贵州									
Yunnan 云南									
Tibet 西藏									
Northwest 西北	15	581	86,328	2,256	1.24	6.83	46.55	81.80	181,390
Shaanxi 陕西	1	340	6,300	-598	-2.49	-2.49	5.61		23,973
Gansu 甘肃									
Qinghai 青海									
Ningxia 宁夏									
Xinjiang 新疆	14	599	92,044	2,459	1.28	7.31	48.21	82.53	192,634

Year 年份	Number of firms 企业个数	Rate of change 变化率(%)	Number of employees 职工人数(人)	Rate of change 变化率(%)	Total revenue (Mil. RMB) 总销售收入(百万元)	Rate of change 变化率(%)	Total profit (Mil RMB) 总利润(百万元)	Rate of change 变化率(%)
2000	59		45,332		2,877		96	
2001	56	-5.08	34,551	-23.78	3,346	16.30	237	146.88
2002	56	-	30,494	-11.74	3,434	2.63	159	-32.91

Major Products 主要产品	Output 产量	Unit 单位

10 Main Firms with Maximal Revenue (year founded) 收入最大的十家主要企业(创办年份)	City 城市	Province 省	Telephone/fax 电话/传真	Number of employees 职工人数	Ownership 产业所有权	Revenue ('000 RMB) 销售收入(千元)	Profit('000 RMB) (rank) 利润(千元)(排名)	Total assets ('000 RMB) 总资产(千元)	Major products 主要产品
Baotou Huazi Industry Co.,Ltd.	Baotou	Inner Mongolia	(0472)4192200		Joint Stock				Machine-made Beet Sugar
包头华资实业股份有限公司(1998)	包头市	内蒙古	(0472)4193504	2,297	股份制	414,768	80,206(1)	1,474,614	机制甜菜糖
Xinjiang Tunhe Xinyuan Sugar Industry Co., Ltd. Branch Company	Yili	Xinjiang	(0999)5022191		State Enterprises				White Granulated Sugar
新疆屯河新源县糖业有限责任分公司(1989)	伊犁州	新疆	(0999)5022191	804	国有独资	176,252	278(28)	368,129	白砂糖
Jiamusi Dongfang Sugar Industry Development Co.,Ltd.	Jiamusi	Heilongjiang	(0454)8556020		Limited-Liability				White Sugar
佳木斯东方糖业发展有限公司(2000)	佳木斯市	黑龙江省	(0454)8555442	733	有限公司	150,269	7,182(8)	53,122	绵白糖
Xinjiang Changji Sugar Factory	Changji	Xinjiang	(0994)2592002		State-owned				White Granulated Sugar
新疆昌吉糖厂(1991)	昌吉州	新疆	(0994)2562014	530	国有企业	126,327	10,117(3)	289,107	白砂糖
Xinjiang Tunhe Group Co., Ltd. Emin Food Branch Company	Tacheng	Xinjiang	(0901)3360808		Limited-Liability				White Granulated Sugar
新疆屯河集团有限责任公司额敏食品分公司(1984)	塔城	新疆		546	有限公司	88,798	3,721(14)	128,422	白砂糖
Xinjiang Tunhe Investment Co.,Ltd. Yanqi Food Branch Company	Bayinguoleng	Xinjiang	(0996)6015070		Limited-Liability				White Granulated Sugar
新疆屯河投资股份焉耆食品分公司(1976)	巴音郭楞州	新疆	(0996)6015070	560	有限公司	84,743	4,362(11)	167,276	白砂糖
Linxi Lengshan Sugar Refining Co.,Ltd.	Chifeng	Inner Mongolia	(0476)5322747		Joint Stock				Beetsugar
林西县冷山制糖有限责任公司(1979)	赤峰市	内蒙古	(0476)5322732	719	股份制	78,961	814(22)	143,090	甜菜糖
Hebei Tian Lu Sugar Industry Co., Ltd.	Zhangjiakou	Hebei	(0313)5233592		Joint Stock				Beetsugar
河北天露糖业有限公司(2001)	张家口市	河北省		487	股份制	76,451	11,853(2)	65,027	甜菜糖
Qiqihar Lvquan Group Baiquan Feixue Sugar Refining Co.,Ltd.	Qiqihar	Heilongjiang	(0452)7322092		Private Owned				Beetsugar
齐齐哈尔绿泉集团拜泉飞雪制糖有限责任公司(1970)	齐齐哈尔市	黑龙江省	(0452)7327734	521	私营企业	57,063	2,844(15)	27,720	甜菜糖
Chifeng Fulong Group Sugar Industry Co., Ltd.	Chifeng	Inner Mongolia	(0476)8410733		Limited-Liability				Beetsugar
赤峰富龙集团糖业有限责任公司(2001)	赤峰市	内蒙古	(0476)5322732	207	有限公司	54,057	4,104(12)	58,308	甜菜糖

Top 10 Cities by Revenue 销售收入排名前10位城市	Province 省	Market share 市场份额 (%)	Number of firms 企业个数
Yili 伊犁州	Xinjiang 新疆	15.04	4
Qiqihar 齐齐哈尔市	Heilongjiang 黑龙江省	14.11	4
Baotou 包头市	Inner Mongolia 内蒙古	12.08	1
Tacheng 塔城地区	Xinjiang 新疆	6.14	2
Bayinguoleng 巴音郭楞州	Xinjiang 新疆	5.61	2
Changji 昌吉州	Xinjiang 新疆	5.23	2
Jiamusi 佳木斯市	Heilongjiang 黑龙江省	4.38	1
Suihua 绥化市	Heilongjiang 黑龙江省	3.99	2
Chifeng 赤峰市	Inner Mongolia 内蒙古	3.87	2
Zhangjiakou 张家口市	Hebei 河北省	2.23	1

10 Major Wholesalers 十家主要批发商	City 城市	Province 省	Telephone/Fax 电话/传真
Beijing Chaoyang Non-Staple Foodstuffs General Company	Beijing	Beijing	(010)65016285
北京朝阳副食品总公司	北京市	北京市	(010)65016285
Beijing Sugar,Cigarette & Wine Company	Beijing	Beijing	(010)67210304
北京市糖业烟酒公司	北京市	北京市	(010)67210310
Shanghai Sugar Cigarette & Wine (Group) Co.,Ltd.	Shanghai	Shanghai	(021)63224190
上海市糖业烟酒(集团)有限公司	上海市	上海市	(021)63223169
Jiangsu Sutang Sugar & Wine Co.,Ltd.	Nanjing	Jiangsu	(025)6661088
江苏苏糖糖酒食品有限公司	南京市	江苏省	(025)6661088
Fujian Commerce (Group) Co.,Ltd.	Fuzhou	Fujian	(0591)7847148
福建省商业(集团)有限责任公司	福州市	福建省	(0591)7847145
Yantai Changyu Pioneer Winer Co., Ltd.	Yantai	Shandong	(0535)6602730
烟台张裕葡萄酿酒股份有限公司	烟台市	山东省	(0535)6214078
BlueRibbon Beer Sale Co.,Ltd.	Zhaoqing	Guangdong	(0758)2862322
蓝带啤酒销售有限公司	肇庆市	广东省	(0758)2862424
Fujian Shenlong Development Co.,Ltd.	Fuzhou	Fujian	(0591)7503218
福建省神龙发展股份有限公司	福州市	福建省	(0591)7503068
Guangdong Sugar, Cigarette & Wine Group Company	Guangzhou	Guangdong	(020)83566131
广东省糖烟酒集团公司	广州市	广东省	(020)83561421
Shunde Daliang Sugar, Cigarette & Wine Co.,Ltd.	Shunde	Guangdong	(0765)2231804
顺德市大良区糖烟酒有限公司	顺德市	广东省	(0765)2222300

1334: Sugar 加工糖业

The industry accounts for 0.011% of the total revenue of China's industrial sector in 2002. The rate of return on assets is 1.18%. 84.38% of all firms in the industry made a profit while 15.63% had negative returns.The top province in terms of the industry's revenue is Jiangsu, accounting for 39.58% of the total revenue.
2002年本行业收入占全行业的0.011%，资产利润率为1.18%。84.38%的企业赢利，15.63%的企业亏损。收入最高的省为江苏省，占本行业的39.58%。

	Total number of firms 企业总数	Total number of employees 职工总数	Total revenue (Mil.RMB) 总销售收入（百万元）	Total profit (Mil.RMB) 总利润（百万元）	Return on assets 资产利润率（%）	Return on equity 权益利润率（%）	Labour productivity ('000 RMB/ worker) 劳动生产率（千元/人）	Debts/ assets 资产负债率（%）	Total assets (Mil.RMB) 总资产（百万元）
Industry Overall 行业总体	32	4,508	1,143	11	1.18	2.83	70.59	58.14	916

	Number of firms 企业个数	Average number of employees 平均职工人数	Average revenue ('000 RMB) 平均销售收入（千元）	Average profit ('000 RMB) 平均利润（千元）	Return on assets 资产利润率（%）	Return on equity 权益利润率（%）	Labour productivity ('000 RMB/ worker) 劳动生产率（千元/人）	Debts/ assets 资产负债率（%）	Average total assets ('000 RMB) 平均总资产（千元）
By ownership 产业所有权									
State-owned 国有	4	236	97,906	85	0.10	0.19	99.95	47.05	82,284
Collective-owned 集体	4	78	17,612	392	2.67	6.89	28.26	61.24	14,680
Foreign & Overseas Chinese Funded 三资	2	171	43,858	1,724	3.74	15.39	59.54	75.67	46,031
By regional distribution 地区分布									
Central-North 华北	7	130	15,298	303	1.77	4.19	21.61	57.66	17,071
Beijing 北京									
Tianjin 天津	4	96	17,505	251	1.37	5.97	22.86	77.12	18,359
Hebei 河北	2	179	15,673	426	2.05	2.58	25.34	20.49	20,745
Shanxi 山西	1	170	5,720	266	5.82	32.84	10.94	82.28	4,570
Inner Mongolia 内蒙古									
Northeast 东北	1	192	5,987	805	0.80	0.81	2.60	1.22	100,882
Liaoning 辽宁									
Jilin 吉林									
Heilongjiang 黑龙江	1	192	5,987	805	0.80	0.81	2.60	1.22	100,882
Central-East 华东	8	130	63,974	1,217	4.64	16.79	140.41	72.37	26,229
Shanghai 上海									
Jiangsu 江苏	4	180	113,077	1,296	2.95	11.59	177.41	74.52	43,915
Zhejiang 浙江	1	25	2,950	-200	-2.33	-4.38	11.68	46.80	8,590
Anhui 安徽									
Fujian 福建									
Jiangxi 江西	1	178	6,390	103	0.76	6.44	13.25	88.19	13,544
Shandong 山东	2	59	25,071	2,322	38.57	65.81	134.00	41.38	6,020
Central-South 中南	12	150	38,522	-256	-0.81	-1.98	82.03	58.96	31,520
Henan 河南	3	203	28,224	1,244	12.15	21.09	42.72	42.40	10,236
Hubei 湖北	1	60	8,900	8	0.08	0.10	26.33	20.39	10,300
Hunan 湖南	1	302	76,857	1,850	5.18	18.53	193.18	72.04	35,700
Guangdong 广东	7	118	41,691	-1,237	-2.87	-7.26	74.48	60.41	43,075
Guangxi 广西									
Hainan 海南									
Southwest 西南	3	184	18,113	365	1.02	5.72	6.62	82.08	35,588
Chongqing 重庆	1	345	6,675	94	2.45	3.19	3.33	22.98	3,830
Sichuan 四川	1	96	35,557	1,000	1.44	9.82	14.15	85.36	69,569
Guizhou 贵州									
Yunnan 云南	1	111	12,107				10.34	82.02	33,364
Tibet 西藏									
Northwest 西北	1	12	1,390	161	14.32	17.06	58.25	16.01	1,124
Shaanxi 陕西									
Gansu 甘肃	1	12	1,390	161	14.32	17.06	58.25	16.01	1,124
Qinghai 青海									
Ningxia 宁夏									
Xinjiang 新疆									

Year 年份	Number of firms 企业个数	Rate of change 变化率 (%)	Number of employees 职工人数 (人)	Rate of change 变化率 (%)	Total revenue (Mil. RMB) 总销售收入 (百万元)	Rate of change 变化率 (%)	Total profit (Mil RMB) 总利润 (百万元)	Rate of change 变化率 (%)
2000	33		3,624		926		1	
2001	31	-6.06	4,096	13.02	1,087	17.39	13	1,200.00
2002	32	3.23	4,508	10.06	1,143	5.15	11	-15.38

Major Products 主要产品	Output 产量	Unit 单位

10 Main Firms with Maximal Revenue (year founded) 收入最大的十家主要企业（创办年份）	City 城市	Province 省	Telephone/fax 电话/传真	Number of employees 职工人数	Ownership 产业所有权	Revenue ('000 RMB) 销售收入(千元)	Profit('000 RMB) (rank) 利润(千元)(排名)	Total assets ('000 RMB) 总资产(千元)	Major products 主要产品
Hai'an Huifeng Sugar Industry Co.,Ltd.	Nantong	Jiangsu	(0513)8711140		Joint Stock				Machining Sugar
海安县汇丰糖业有限责任公司(1979)	南通市	江苏省	(0513)8711140	111	股份制	161,533	419(13)	30,438	加工糖
Jiangsu Huai'an Baimei Sugar Industry Co.,Ltd.	Huaian	Jiangsu	(0517)4923829		State-owned				White Sugar
江苏淮安白玫糖业有限公司(1959)	淮安市	江苏省	(0517)4921151	346	国有企业	148,531	1,721(6)	98,298	绵白糖
Rugao Huashen Sugar Industry Co.,Ltd.	Nantong	Jiangsu	(0513)8591067		Private Owned				Machining Sugar
如皋花神糖业有限责任公司(2001)	南通市	江苏省	(0513)8591066	214	私营企业	134,014	2,905(1)	44,584	加工糖
Hunan Taoyuan Sweetline Co.,Ltd.	Changde	Hunan	(0736)6610732		Limited-Liability				High Barley-sugar Plasm高
湖南省桃源县鲁洲糖业有限公司(2000)	常德市	湖南省	(0736)6610732	302	有限公司	76,857	1,850(5)	35,700	麦芽糖浆
Zhengzhou Gongtai Chemical Industry Co., Ltd.	Zhengzhou	Henan	(0371)4350415		Foreign Funded				Xylose
郑州巩泰化工有限公司(1992)	郑州市	河南省		245	外商投资	52,159	2,447(2)	22,492	木糖
Sichuan Nanbao Bee Products Co.,Ltd.	Chengdu	Sichuan	(028)87181693		Foreign Funded				Nanbao Bees
四川南宝蜂有限公司(1994)	成都市	四川省	(028)87283089	96	外商投资	35,557	1,000(10)	69,569	南宝蜂
Guangrao Huabao Food Factory	Dongying	Shandong	(0546)6511140		Private Enterprises				Suger
广饶县华宝食品厂(1995)	东营市	山东省		72	私营独资	26,596	2,212(4)	4,097	糖
Hebei Suning Tianxiang Food Co., Ltd.	Cangzhou	Hebei	(0317)5041574		Joint Stock				Candy
河北省肃宁县天祥食品有限责任公司(1998)	沧州市	河北省	(0317)5041554	258	股份制	25,380	350(14)	37,490	糖果
Guangdong Xinyi Sugar Industry Co.,Ltd.	Guangzhou	Guangdong	(020)82861237		State Enterprises				Glucose Plasm
广东新怡糖业有限公司(1997)	广州市	广东省	(020)82861237	103	国有独资	21,409	-	52,441	葡萄糖浆
Yunnan Hantai Food Co., Ltd.	Chuxiong	Yunnan	(0878)8321845		Limited-Liability				White Sugar
云南瀚泰食品有限公司(2000)	楚雄州	云南省	(0878)8321557	111	有限公司	12,107	-	33,364	绵白糖

Top 10 Cities by Revenue 销售收入排名前10位城市	Province 省	Market share 市场份额 (%)	Number of firms 企业个数
Nantong 南通市	Jiangsu 江苏省	25.86	2
Guangzhou 广州市	Guangdong 广东省	23.14	3
Huaian 淮安市	Jiangsu 江苏省	13.00	1
Changde 常德市	Hunan 湖南省	6.73	1
Tianjin 天津市	Tianjin 天津市	6.13	4
Zhengzhou 郑州市	Henan 河南省	4.56	1
Dongying 东营市	Shandong 山东省	4.39	2
Chengdu 成都市	Sichuan 四川省	3.11	1
Luohe 漯河市	Henan 河南省	2.46	1
Cangzhou 沧州市	Hebei 河北省	2.22	1

10 Major Wholesalers 十家主要批发商	City 城市	Province 省	Telephone/Fax 电话/传真
Beijing Chaoyang Non-Staple Foodstuffs General Company	Beijing	Beijing	(010)65016285
北京朝阳副食品总公司	北京市	北京市	(010)65016285
Beijing Sugar,Cigarette & Wine Company	Beijing	Beijing	(010)67210304
北京市糖业烟酒公司	北京市	北京市	(010)67210310
Shanghai Sugar Cigarette & Wine (Group) Co.,Ltd.	Shanghai	Shanghai	(021)63224190
上海市糖业烟酒(集团)有限公司	上海市	上海市	(021)63223169
Jiangsu Sutang Sugar & Wine Co.,Ltd.	Nanjing	Jiangsu	(025)6661088
江苏苏糖糖酒食品有限公司	南京市	江苏省	(025)6661088
Fujian Commerce (Group) Co.,Ltd.	Fuzhou	Fujian	(0591)7847148
福建省商业（集团）有限责任公司	福州市	福建省	(0591)7847145
Yantai Changyu Pioneer Winer Co., Ltd.	Yantai	Shandong	(0535)6602730
烟台张裕葡萄酿酒股份有限公司	烟台市	山东省	(0535)6214078
BlueRibbon Beer Sale Co.,Ltd.	Zhaoqing	Guangdong	(0758)2862322
蓝带啤酒销售有限公司	肇庆市	广东省	(0758)2862424
Fujian Shenlong Development Co.,Ltd.	Fuzhou	Fujian	(0591)7503218
福建省神龙发展股份有限公司	福州市	福建省	(0591)7503068
Guangdong Sugar, Cigarette & Wine Group Company	Guangzhou	Guangdong	(020)83566131
广东省糖烟酒集团公司	广州市	广东省	(020)83561421
Shunde Daliang Sugar, Cigarette & Wine Co.,Ltd.	Shunde	Guangdong	(0765)2231804
顺德市大良区糖烟酒有限公司	顺德市	广东省	(0765)2222300

1341: Slaughtering 屠宰业

The industry accounts for 0.262% of the total revenue of China's industrial sector in 2002. The rate of return on assets is 2.69%. 76.82% of all firms in the industry made a profit while 23.18% had negative returns.The top province in terms of the industry's revenue is Shandong, accounting for 12.79% of the total revenue.
2002年本行业收入占全行业的0.262%，资产利润率为2.69%。76.82%的企业赢利，23.18%的企业亏损。收入最高的省为山东省，占本行业的12.79%。

	Total number of firms 企业总数	Total number of employees 职工总数	Total revenue (Mil.RMB) 总销售收入（百万元）	Total profit (Mil.RMB) 总利润（百万元）	Return on assets 资产利润率（%）	Return on equity 权益利润率（%）	Labour productivity ('000 RMB/worker) 劳动生产率（千元/人）	Debts/assets 资产负债率（%）	Total assets (Mil.RMB) 总资产（百万元）
Industry Overall 行业总体	673	148,748	28,124	490	2.69	8.69	47.05	69.06	18,236

	Number of firms 企业个数	Average number of employees 平均职工人数	Average revenue ('000 RMB) 平均销售收入（千元）	Average profit ('000 RMB) 平均利润（千元）	Return on assets 资产利润率（%）	Return on equity 权益利润率（%）	Labour productivity ('000 RMB/worker) 劳动生产率（千元/人）	Debts/assets 资产负债率（%）	Average total assets ('000 RMB) 平均总资产（千元）
By ownership 产业所有权									
State-owned 国有	279	186	22,000	-77	-0.34	-1.41	30.00	75.84	22,794
Collective-owned 集体	95	223	39,408	1,689	17.37	35.13	50.69	50.56	9,724
Foreign & Overseas Chinese Funded 三资	18	1,190	286,157	3,125	1.48	8.03	39.67	81.59	211,472
By regional distribution 地区分布									
Central-North 华北	147	163	35,665	1,481	6.59	15.03	49.62	56.13	22,466
Beijing 北京	19	211	63,981	3,281	5.90	12.23	30.59	51.77	55,620
Tianjin 天津	17	389	52,572	3,288	21.72	80.89	22.61	73.16	15,141
Hebei 河北	51	162	35,393	1,330	5.06	11.84	50.07	57.26	26,285
Shanxi 山西	10	145	6,312	88	0.37	0.60	14.27	39.12	23,854
Inner Mongolia 内蒙古	50	73	25,304	617	7.54	20.30	132.00	62.85	8,184
Northeast 东北	91	360	64,666	516	1.07	4.91	33.23	78.24	48,281
Liaoning 辽宁	47	195	30,370	-141	-0.79	-1.93	34.27	59.18	17,872
Jilin 吉林	20	752	167,003	6,766	6.43	20.39	26.48	68.49	105,272
Heilongjiang 黑龙江	24	356	46,549	-3,406	-5.64		44.01	103.49	60,339
Central-East 华东	185	231	42,504	479	1.68	7.18	45.86	76.58	28,464
Shanghai 上海	13	476	62,073	-564	-0.64	-1.88	16.59	65.98	88,385
Jiangsu 江苏	44	240	48,362	-20	-0.07	-0.58	40.01	87.96	28,394
Zhejiang 浙江	7	112	24,996	345	2.57	11.30	35.52	77.27	13,430
Anhui 安徽	17	316	40,386	136	0.46	1.79	37.40	74.60	29,817
Fujian 福建	14	64	21,459	-168	-1.07	-4.31	148.62	75.28	15,782
Jiangxi 江西	15	211	11,324	-448	-2.50	-12.20	16.02	79.51	17,928
Shandong 山东	75	211	47,953	1,348	5.69	23.39	64.78	75.67	23,691
Central-South 中南	153	184	43,023	828	4.07	10.48	73.23	61.17	20,335
Henan 河南	43	287	65,190	1,616	4.53	11.05	66.42	59.01	35,679
Hubei 湖北	38	217	40,352	966	8.86	38.27	83.33	76.85	10,905
Hunan 湖南	15	74	12,753	17	0.18	2.64	56.72	93.31	9,838
Guangdong 广东	51	115	38,660	384	2.07	4.56	80.38	54.64	18,545
Guangxi 广西	4	109	20,671	146	0.90	1.42	30.22	36.41	16,110
Hainan 海南	2	70	205	-10	-0.39	-0.56	41.21	29.94	2,440
Southwest 西南	54	180	36,517	140	0.62	1.87	50.66	66.75	22,441
Chongqing 重庆	2	358	1,686	-382	-2.00		0.79	136.93	19,057
Sichuan 四川	32	221	52,287	367	1.33	3.46	60.34	61.69	27,688
Guizhou 贵州	14	102	11,488	-261	-1.81	-6.87	36.71	73.74	14,439
Yunnan 云南	4	123	33,546	45	0.21	0.74	25.89	71.74	21,241
Tibet 西藏	2	7	164	20	7.18	7.83	11.36	8.29	272
Northwest 西北	43	265	13,466	71	0.32	0.78	18.09	58.66	22,118
Shaanxi 陕西	9	921	38,034	934	2.80	10.55	16.98	73.44	33,341
Gansu 甘肃	14	128	3,406	-356	-1.63	-4.69	18.26	65.32	21,889
Qinghai 青海	16	65	10,088	-22	-0.12	-0.19	47.72	37.91	18,967
Ningxia 宁夏	2	95	12,552	-26	-0.20	-0.26	-92.82	24.07	13,024
Xinjiang 新疆	2	53	1,278	24	0.32		9.86	106.88	7,520

1341: Slaughtering 屠宰业

Year 年份	Number of firms 企业个数	Rate of change 变化率 (%)	Number of employees 职工人数 (人)	Rate of change 变化率 (%)	Total revenue (Mil. RMB) 总销售收入 (百万元)	Rate of change 变化率 (%)	Total profit (Mil RMB) 总利润 (百万元)	Rate of change 变化率 (%)
2000	609		136,811		20,959		299	
2001	631	3.61	142,373	4.07	23,877	13.92	338	13.04
2002	673	6.66	148,748	4.48	28,124	17.79	490	44.97

Major Products 主要产品	Output 产量	Unit 单位
Fresh & Frozen Animal Meat 鲜、冻畜肉	479	10,000 Tons 万吨

10 Main Firms with Maximal Revenue (year founded) 收入最大的十家主要企业（创办年份）	City 城市	Province 省	Telephone/fax 电话/传真	Number of employees 职工人数	Ownership 产业所有权	Revenue ('000 RMB) 销售收入 (千元)	Profit('000 RMB) (rank) 利润(千元)(排名)	Total assets ('000 RMB) 总资产 (千元)	Major products 主要产品
Henan Huaying Livestock Industry Group Co., Ltd.	Xinyang	Henan	(0376)3931030		Joint Stock				Duck Products
河南华英禽业集团股份有限公司(1991)	信阳市	河南省	(0376)3931030	2,122	股份制	1,039,857	37,482(4)	595,210	鸭产品
Heilongjiang Chia Tai Enter Prise Co., Ltd.	Harbin	Heilongjiang	(0451)7356953		Foreign Funded				Chicken
黑龙江正大实业有限公司(1995)	哈尔滨市	黑龙江省	(0451)7356939	4,807	外商投资	726,608	-	932,200	鸡肉
Beijing Shunxin Agriculture Holding Co.,Ltd.Pengcheng Food	Beijing	Beijing	(010)69471618		Joint Stock				Slaughter
Branch北京顺鑫农业股份有限公司鹏程食品分公司(1976)	北京市	北京市	(010)69474053	1,002	股份制	502,146	36,535(5)	350,536	屠宰
Wuhan Changzheng Meat Co., Ltd.	Wuhan	Hubei	(027)88114003		Collective-owned				Slaughter
武汉长征肉类有限公司(1996)	武汉市	湖北省	(027)88114003	268	集体企业	399,220	11,980(12)	34,633	屠宰
Shanghai Shang Shi Meat Co.,Ltd.	Shanghai	Shanghai	(021)56682219		State-owned				Pig Slaughter
上海上食肉类有限公司(1973)	上海市	上海市	(021)66620014	1,452	国有企业	393,588	9,467(16)	427,935	生猪屠宰
Xianghe Chia Tai Co.,Ltd.	Langfang	Hebei	(0316)8331049		Foreign Funded				Slaughter Duck
香河正大有限公司(1997)	廊坊市	河北省	(0316)8331653	366	外商投资	319,213	-	152,061	屠宰鸭
Dacheng Farming & Animal Husbandry (Yingkou) Co., Ltd.	Yingkou	Liaoning	(0417)5901001		Overseas Chinese-funded				Chicken
大成农牧（营口）有限公司(1997)	营口市	辽宁省	(0417)5901000	771	港澳台资	309,511	864(117)	46,957	鸡肉
Jiangsu Furun Meat Processing Plant Co.,Ltd.	Lianyungang	Jiangsu	(0518)7217328		Limited-Liability				Slaughter
江苏福润肉类加工有限公司(1997)	连云港市	江苏省	(0518)7221094	686	有限公司	303,701	4,349(29)	185,524	屠宰
Sichuan Furun Meat Co., Ltd.	Neijiang	Sichuan	(0832)2191024		Private Owned				Pig Slaughter
四川省福润肉类食品有限公司(2000)	内江市	四川省		812	私营企业	280,677	4,861(20)	195,861	生猪屠宰
Hebei Fucheng Wufeng Food Co., Ltd.	Langfang	Hebei	(0316)3314145		Overseas Chinese-funded				Meats Processing
河北福成五丰食品股份有限公司(1998)	廊坊市	河北省		700	港澳台资	280,031	44,328(3)	308,834	肉制品

Top 10 Cities by Revenue 销售收入排名前10位城市	Province 省	Market share 市场份额 (%)	Number of firms 企业个数
Changchun 长春市	Jilin 吉林省	10.70	3
Xinyang 信阳市	Henan 河南省	4.77	7
Beijing 北京市	Beijing 北京市	4.32	19
Harbin 哈尔滨市	Heilongjiang 黑龙江省	3.41	10
Hebi 鹤壁市	Henan 河南省	3.26	2
Tianjin 天津市	Tianjin 天津市	3.18	17
Langfang 廊坊市	Hebei 河北省	3.10	7
Linyi 临沂市	Shandong 山东省	2.97	24
Shanghai 上海市	Shanghai 上海市	2.87	13
Tongliao 通辽市	Inner Mongolia 内蒙古	2.57	1

10 Major Wholesalers 十家主要批发商	City 城市	Province 省	Telephone/Fax 电话/传真
Shanghai Nanpu Food Co.,Ltd.	Shanghai	Shanghai	(021)50813333
上海市南浦食品有限公司	上海市	上海市	(021)58201748
Shandong Food Import & Export Company	Qingdao	Shandong	(0532)5897888
山东省食品进出口公司	青岛市	山东省	(0532)5897788
Taishan Changjiang Food Co.,Ltd.	Jiangmen	Guangdong	(0750)5668746
台山市长江食品有限公司	江门市	广东省	(0750)5676264
Guangzhou Food Enterprise Group Co.,Ltd.	Guangzhou	Guangdong	(020)81267810
广州食品企业集团有限公司	广州市	广东省	(020)81267255
Guangdong Zhaoqing Food Import & Export Company	Zhaoqing	Guangdong	(0758)2824427
广东省肇庆食品进出口公司	肇庆市	广东省	(0758)2831199
Shanghai Yangpu (Group)Company	Shanghai	Shanghai	(021)65433282
上海阳普(集团)公司	上海市	上海市	(021)65198109
Nanjing Tianhuan Food Group Co.,Ltd.	Nanjing	Jiangsu	(025)8785191
南京天环食品集团有限责任公司	南京市	江苏省	(025)8712979
Hubei Gucheng Food Company	Xiangfan	Hubei	(0710)7232135
湖北省谷城县食品公司	襄樊市	湖北省	
Guangzhou Panyu Food Group Co.,Ltd.	Guangzhou	Guangdong	(020)84669925
广州市番禺食品集团有限公司	广州市	广东省	(020)84669915
Guangxi Guigang Food General Company	Guigang	Guangxi	(0775)4215631
广西贵港市食品总公司	贵港市	广西	(0775)4234980

1342: Meat Products 肉制品加工业

The industry accounts for 0.601% of the total revenue of China's industrial sector in 2002. The rate of return on assets is 4.64%. 80.52% of all firms in the industry made a profit while 19.48% had negative returns.The top province in terms of the industry's revenue is Shandong, accounting for 40.57% of the total revenue.
2002年本行业收入占全行业的0.601%，资产利润率为4.64%。80.52%的企业赢利，19.48%的企业亏损。收入最高的省为山东省，占本行业的40.57%。

	Total number of firms 企业总数	Total number of employees 职工总数	Total revenue (Mil.RMB) 总销售收入（百万元）	Total profit (Mil.RMB) 总利润（百万元）	Return on assets 资产利润率（%）	Return on equity 权益利润率（%）	Labour productivity ('000 RMB/worker) 劳动生产率（千元/人）	Debts/assets 资产负债率（%）	Total assets (Mil.RMB) 总资产（百万元）
Industry Overall 行业总体	991	349,535	64,502	2,255	4.64	11.73	42.41	60.41	48,571

	Number of firms 企业个数	Average number of employees 平均职工人数	Average revenue ('000 RMB) 平均销售收入（千元）	Average profit ('000 RMB) 平均利润（千元）	Return on assets 资产利润率（%）	Return on equity 权益利润率（%）	Labour productivity ('000 RMB/worker) 劳动生产率（千元/人）	Debts/assets 资产负债率（%）	Average total assets ('000 RMB) 平均总资产（千元）
By ownership 产业所有权									
State-owned 国有	225	168	22,220	-55	-0.20	-1.01	36.64	80.47	28,181
Collective-owned 集体	138	364	101,425	5,617	10.45	20.16	71.11	48.17	53,760
Foreign & Overseas Chinese Funded 三资	98	303	80,613	1,818	3.08	7.71	53.25	60.04	59,019
By regional distribution 地区分布									
Central-North 华北	147	199	38,258	1,325	3.04	7.60	43.25	59.97	43,512
Beijing 北京	45	112	19,599	318	1.54	4.13	40.16	62.70	20,658
Tianjin 天津	15	367	71,287	-1,152	-2.75	-12.35	18.99	77.69	41,800
Hebei 河北	43	87	20,943	1,117	5.32	13.83	74.13	61.52	20,997
Shanxi 山西	19	221	32,048	2,045	5.48	11.89	33.13	53.96	37,337
Inner Mongolia 内蒙古	25	430	86,527	4,431	3.43	7.91	50.38	56.63	129,092
Northeast 东北	90	266	60,488	1,700	3.52	10.02	49.49	64.84	48,241
Liaoning 辽宁	55	240	52,948	1,490	3.93	9.46	44.73	58.50	37,929
Jilin 吉林	15	319	93,318	3,307	3.22	11.12	69.49	71.03	102,616
Heilongjiang 黑龙江	20	299	56,600	1,075	3.00	10.00	43.98	69.98	35,817
Central-East 华东	346	669	98,665	3,587	4.90	12.60	35.05	61.11	73,203
Shanghai 上海	29	145	37,014	699	1.63	4.60	53.77	64.48	42,805
Jiangsu 江苏	61	260	68,662	1,845	4.02	10.65	58.43	62.20	45,840
Zhejiang 浙江	31	119	19,136	2,130	8.81	18.43	38.73	52.20	24,173
Anhui 安徽	30	199	33,135	597	2.04	7.09	35.49	71.17	29,220
Fujian 福建	15	306	42,830	1,484	2.94	6.28	37.09	53.14	50,415
Jiangxi 江西	20	209	24,063	688	2.54	5.45	33.74	53.38	27,083
Shandong 山东	160	1,205	163,534	6,176	5.38	13.85	32.62	61.16	114,794
Central-South 中南	241	185	59,057	2,687	7.13	16.68	67.04	57.27	37,692
Henan 河南	144	241	88,330	4,243	8.60	18.86	73.46	54.43	49,364
Hubei 湖北	22	107	8,805	-400	-2.21	-12.99	41.88	83.00	18,126
Hunan 湖南	40	98	15,379	125	0.70	1.63	48.85	57.14	17,884
Guangdong 广东	27	110	22,275	1,669	6.57	21.55	39.30	69.50	25,398
Guangxi 广西	6	96	7,564	-290	-2.71	-11.09	19.26	75.54	10,685
Hainan 海南	2	19	28,767	-1,482	-2.66	-6.94	532.43	61.69	55,709
Southwest 西南	122	138	37,419	213	1.13	2.79	69.66	59.35	18,784
Chongqing 重庆	18	137	23,760	60	0.39	3.31	22.53	88.22	15,302
Sichuan 四川	75	156	52,029	456	2.14	4.78	90.18	55.25	21,325
Guizhou 贵州	21	85	9,936	-338	-3.13	-10.77	26.25	70.97	10,803
Yunnan 云南	5	101	1,770	-686	-12.82		5.47	150.66	5,351
Tibet 西藏	3	117	5,902	394	0.72	0.90	31.79	19.68	54,407
Northwest 西北	45	80	11,074	-156	-0.62	-1.46	29.37	57.55	25,093
Shaanxi 陕西	12	168	32,192	-698	-1.02	-2.70	20.34	62.23	68,350
Gansu 甘肃	23	37	3,126	134	2.12	4.68	54.17	54.76	6,341
Qinghai 青海	5	82	4,279	49	0.20	0.27	25.59	26.78	24,288
Ningxia 宁夏	1	57	36	-1,860	-28.66		0.16	154.74	6,491
Xinjiang 新疆	4	64	4,671	-27	-0.31	-0.60	30.71	48.52	8,807

Year 年份	Number of firms 企业个数	Rate of change 变化率 (%)	Number of employees 职工人数 (人)	Rate of change 变化率 (%)	Total revenue (Mil. RMB) 总销售收入 (百万元)	Rate of change 变化率 (%)	Total profit (Mil RMB) 总利润 (百万元)	Rate of change 变化率 (%)
2000	1022		236,712		47,373		1,387	
2001	1001	-2.05	248,342	4.91	54,611	15.28	1,706	23.00
2002	991	-1.00	349,535	40.75	64,502	18.11	2,255	32.18

Major Products 主要产品	Output 产量	Unit 单位

10 Main Firms with Maximal Revenue (year founded) 收入最大的十家主要企业（创办年份）	City 城市	Province 省	Telephone/fax 电话/传真	Number of employees 职工人数	Ownership 产业所有权	Revenue ('000 RMB) 销售收入 (千元)	Profit('000 RMB) (rank) 利润(千元) (排名)	Total assets ('000 RMB) 总资产 (千元)	Major products 主要产品
Henan Luohe Shineway Group Co., Ltd.	Luohe	Henan	(0395)2622616		Limited-Liability				Ham Sausage
河南省漯河市双汇实业集团有限责任公司(1994)	漯河市	河南省	(0395)2623398	11,830	有限公司	7,810,381	559,523(1)	3,938,168	火腿肠
Shandong Jinluo Enterprise Group Parent Company	Linyi	Shandong	(0539)2977300		Collective-owned				Chicken Products
山东金锣企业集团总公司(1996)	临沂市	山东省	(0539)8692321	15,028	集体企业	5,560,178	390,501(2)	1,856,273	鸡肉产品
Zhucheng Dalong Enterprise Co., Ltd	Weifang	Shandong	(0536)6063672		Limited-Liability				Frozen Chook
诸城市大龙实业有限公司(1999)	潍坊市	山东省	(0536)6051092	6,083	有限公司	4,260,268	81,228(6)	3,870,689	冻鸡
Huasheng Jiangquan Group Co., Ltd.	Linyi	Shandong	(0539)8283669		Collective-owned				Meat Products
华盛江泉集团总公司(1992)	临沂市	山东省	(0539)8241427	16,300	集体企业	2,693,378	152,752(3)	2,269,394	肉制品
Zhucheng Delisi Group Co.,Ltd.	Weifang	Shandong	(0536)6339999		Collective-owned				Low-temperature Meat Products
诸城市得利斯集团公司(1986)	潍坊市	山东省	(0536)6401233	3,350	集体企业	1,620,659	85,236(5)	1,379,127	低温肉制品
Shandong Fengxiang LDC Group Co.,Ltd.	Liaocheng	Shandong	(0635)6779260		Limited-Liability				Meat Products
山东凤祥有限责任公司(1994)	聊城市	山东省	(0635)6779261	101,375	有限公司	1,617,588	61,952(7)	1,368,046	肉制品
Jiangsu Yurun Food Industry Group Co.,Ltd.	Nanjing	Jiangsu	(025)6800888		Private Owned				Meat Products
江苏雨润食品产业集团有限公司(1993)	南京市	江苏省	(025)6802612	5,100	私营企业	1,097,170	53,400(8)	1,480,220	肉食品
Kangdi Wanda (Tianjin) Co., Ltd.	Tianjin	Tianjin	(022)27950535		Foreign Funded				
康地万达(天津)有限公司	天津市	天津市	(022)27950995	2,691	外商投资	702,822	-	288,787	
Qingdao Kangda Foreign Trade Group Co., Ltd.	Qingdao	Shandong	(0532)6164559		Limited-Liability				Aquatic Products
青岛康大外贸集团有限公司(2000)	青岛市	山东省	(0532)6167310	790	有限公司	636,000	5,100(56)	392,628	水产品
Shandong Xinchang Meat Co., Ltd.	Weifang	Shandong	(0536)7216460		Private Owned				Frozen Chook
山东新昌肉食有限责任公司(1988)	潍坊市	山东省	(0536)7126179	540	私营企业	596,518	5,222(54)	533,421	冻鸡

Top 10 Cities by Revenue 销售收入排名前10位城市	Province 省	Market share 市场份额 (%)	Number of firms 企业个数
Weifang 潍坊市	Shandong 山东省	14.67	39
Linyi 临沂市	Shandong 山东省	14.55	25
Luohe 漯河市	Henan 河南省	12.69	23
Nanjing 南京市	Jiangsu 江苏省	3.86	13
Qingdao 青岛市	Shandong 山东省	3.04	19
Liaocheng 聊城市	Shandong 山东省	2.95	9
Chifeng 赤峰市	Inner Mongolia 内蒙古	2.74	4
Shanghai 上海市	Shanghai 上海市	1.66	29
Tianjin 天津市	Tianjin 天津市	1.66	15
Nanyang 南阳市	Henan 河南省	1.52	34

10 Major Wholesalers 十家主要批发商	City 城市	Province 省	Telephone/Fax 电话/传真
Shanghai Nanpu Food Co.,Ltd.	Shanghai	Shanghai	(021)50813333
上海市南浦食品有限公司	上海市	上海市	(021)58201748
Shandong Food Import & Export Company	Qingdao	Shandong	(0532)5897888
山东省食品进出口公司	青岛市	山东省	(0532)5897788
Taishan Changjiang Food Co.,Ltd.	Jiangmen	Guangdong	(0750)5668746
台山市长江食品有限公司	江门市	广东省	(0750)5676264
Guangzhou Food Enterprise Group Co.,Ltd.	Guangzhou	Guangdong	(020)81267810
广州食品企业集团有限公司	广州市	广东省	(020)81267255
Guangdong Zhaoqing Food Import & Export Company	Zhaoqing	Guangdong	(0758)2824427
广东省肇庆食品进出口公司	肇庆市	广东省	(0758)2831199
Shanghai Yangpu (Group)Company	Shanghai	Shanghai	(021)65433282
上海阳普(集团)公司	上海市	上海市	(021)65198109
Nanjing Tianhuan Food Group Co.,Ltd.	Nanjing	Jiangsu	(025)8785191
南京天环食品集团有限责任公司	南京市	江苏省	(025)8712979
Hubei Gucheng Food Company	Xiangfan	Hubei	(0710)7232135
湖北省谷城县食品公司	襄樊市	湖北省	
Guangzhou Panyu Food Group Co.,Ltd.	Guangzhou	Guangdong	(020)84669925
广州市番禺食品集团有限公司	广州市	广东省	(020)84669915
Guangxi Guigang Food General Company	Guigang	Guangxi	(0775)4215631
广西贵港市食品总公司	贵港市	广西	(0775)4234980

1343: Meat By-products 肉类副产品加工业

The industry accounts for 0.032% of the total revenue of China's industrial sector in 2002. The rate of return on assets is 3.33%. 79.26% of all firms in the industry made a profit while 20.74% had negative returns.The top province in terms of the industry's revenue is Jiangsu, accounting for 24.56% of the total revenue.
2002年本行业收入占全行业的0.032%，资产利润率为3.33%。79.26%的企业赢利，20.74%的企业亏损。收入最高的省为江苏省，占本行业的24.56%。

	Total number of firms 企业总数	Total number of employees 职工总数	Total revenue (Mil.RMB) 总销售收入(百万元)	Total profit (Mil.RMB) 总利润(百万元)	Return on assets 资产利润率(%)	Return on equity 权益利润率(%)	Labour productivity ('000 RMB/worker) 劳动生产率(千元/人)	Debts/assets 资产负债率(%)	Total assets (Mil.RMB) 总资产(百万元)
Industry Overall 行业总体	135	15,531	3,395	99	3.33	10.32	51.66	67.76	2,962

	Number of firms 企业个数	Average number of employees 平均职工人数	Average revenue ('000 RMB) 平均销售收入（千元）	Average profit ('000 RMB) 平均利润（千元）	Return on assets 资产利润率(%)	Return on equity 权益利润率(%)	Labour productivity ('000 RMB/worker) 劳动生产率(千元/人)	Debts/assets 资产负债率(%)	Average total assets ('000 RMB) 平均总资产（千元）
By ownership 产业所有权									
State-owned 国有	14	131	10,765	255	0.98	8.46	24.97	88.38	25,962
Collective-owned 集体	11	97	20,271	522	4.36	17.61	58.22	75.27	11,995
Foreign & Overseas Chinese Funded 三资	45	168	36,367	1,409	4.38	10.45	52.12	58.10	32,165
By regional distribution 地区分布									
Central-North 华北	25	98	20,444	81	0.33	2.39	48.74	86.39	25,030
Beijing 北京	2	87	16,910	1,517	8.36	281.35	69.20	97.03	18,151
Tianjin 天津	2	83	36,165	340	1.86	22.08	43.76	91.58	18,285
Hebei 河北	19	104	20,669	-80	-0.29	-1.97	47.42	85.30	27,610
Shanxi 山西									
Inner Mongolia 内蒙古	2	74	6,118	-80	-0.56	-4.07	47.93	86.19	14,147
Northeast 东北	5	141	15,721	602	3.18	6.75	35.34	52.87	18,925
Liaoning 辽宁	2	317	32,524	1,071	2.64	5.93	29.33	55.50	40,537
Jilin 吉林	1	18	128				105.67	3.08	1,170
Heilongjiang 黑龙江	2	27	6,714	435	7.02	11.76	82.28	40.33	6,190
Central-East 华东	61	126	29,759	953	5.16	19.97	52.89	74.13	18,443
Shanghai 上海	7	226	40,394	3,164	17.50	39.54	48.62	55.74	18,078
Jiangsu 江苏	22	125	37,896	927	4.72	22.87	59.60	79.37	19,656
Zhejiang 浙江	9	80	24,646	556	3.88	11.26	58.39	65.56	14,331
Anhui 安徽	3	165	25,762	482	1.80	4.44	33.56	59.47	26,785
Fujian 福建									
Jiangxi 江西	3	59	4,443	457	9.36		13.55	119.62	4,880
Shandong 山东	17	115	22,730	455	2.26	10.79	53.37	79.05	20,121
Central-South 中南	23	142	30,673	1,252	4.30	7.62	57.41	43.58	29,136
Henan 河南	13	68	13,040	149	1.27	3.81	70.31	66.56	11,668
Hubei 湖北									
Hunan 湖南	7	97	16,195	1,691	12.11	25.43	58.14	52.40	13,966
Guangdong 广东	1	1,200	178,991	7,095	8.12	9.19	46.03	11.57	87,340
Guangxi 广西	1	445	35,593	2,747	2.08	9.26	56.21	77.55	132,091
Hainan 海南	1	50	208,015	5,192	2.58	2.98	103.30	13.56	201,253
Southwest 西南	14	66	12,722	295	3.43	8.24	46.91	58.40	8,594
Chongqing 重庆	1	210	40,927	2,487	12.68	28.02	53.35	54.76	19,619
Sichuan 四川	12	59	11,431	136	1.62	3.97	45.01	59.11	8,392
Guizhou 贵州	1								
Yunnan 云南									
Tibet 西藏									
Northwest 西北	7	74	15,192	351	0.75	2.31	41.81	67.47	46,615
Shaanxi 陕西									
Gansu 甘肃	3	60	6,723	32	0.73	3.01	29.52	75.64	4,370
Qinghai 青海									
Ningxia 宁夏									
Xinjiang 新疆	4	85	21,544	590	0.75	2.29	48.30	67.13	78,299

1343: Meat By-products 肉类副产品加工业

Year 年份	Number of firms 企业个数	Rate of change 变化率 (%)	Number of employees 职工人数 (人)	Rate of change 变化率 (%)	Total revenue (Mil. RMB) 总销售收入 (百万元)	Rate of change 变化率 (%)	Total profit (Mil RMB) 总利润 (百万元)	Rate of change 变化率 (%)
2000	108		11,257		2,573		64	
2001	125	15.74	67,834	502.59	2,380	-7.50	19	-70.31
2002	135	8.00	15,531	-77.10	3,395	42.65	99	421.05

Major Products 主要产品	Output 产量	Unit 单位

10 Main Firms with Maximal Revenue (year founded) 收入最大的十家主要企业（创办年份）	City 城市	Province 省	Telephone/fax 电话/传真	Number of employees 职工人数	Ownership 产业所有权	Revenue ('000 RMB) 销售收入 (千元)	Profit('000 RMB) (rank) 利润(千元) (排名)	Total assets ('000 RMB) 总资产 (千元)	Major products 主要产品
Shanghai Fuen Casing Co.,Ltd.	Shanghai	Shanghai	(021)64099220		Foreign Funded				Pig Casing For Sausages
上海富恩肠衣有限公司(1999)	上海市	上海市	(021)64099220	129	外商投资	139,926	5,875(5)	30,732	猪肠衣
Yancheng Lianyi Casing Products Co.,ltd.	Yancheng	Jiangsu	(0515)8660838		Overseas Chinese-funded				Casing For Sausages
盐城联益肠衣制品有限公司(1998)	盐城市	江苏省	(0515)8660019	1,200	港澳台资	119,000	6,320(3)	25,310	肠衣
Jintan Casing Factory	Changzhou	Jiangsu	(0519)2852709		Joint Stock				Casing For Sausages
金坛市肠衣厂(1989)	常州市	江苏省	(0519)2856855	120	股份制	115,640	5,820(6)	75,740	肠衣
Heibei Handan Yahua Casing Co.,Ltd.	Handan	Hebei	(0310)3610168		Overseas Chinese-funded				Goats Casing For Sausages
河北省邯郸市魏县亚华肠衣有限公司(1996)	邯郸市	河北省	(0310)3610068	120	港澳台资	97,983	2,701(13)	89,216	山羊肠衣
Rugao Baxin Casing For Sausages Co., Ltd.	Nantong	Jiangsu	(0513)7532618		Private Owned				Pig Casing For Sausages
如皋市坝新肠衣有限公司(2001)	南通市	江苏省	(0513)7276168	65	私营企业	87,850	1,320(23)	4,310	猪肠衣
Yancheng Huayi Casing Products Co.,Ltd.	Yancheng	Jiangsu	(0515)8452666		Foreign Funded				Salted Pig Casing For Sausages
盐城华意肠衣制品有限公司(1999)	盐城市	江苏省	(0515)8451988	85	外商投资	83,200	3,080(10)	15,200	盐渍猪肠衣
Hangzhou Lide Casing Co.,Ltd.	Hangzhou	Zhejiang	(0571)88586388		Foreign Funded				Casing For Sausages
杭州利德肠衣有限公司(1997)	杭州市	浙江省		122	外商投资	66,500	1,020(29)	24,000	肠衣
Yantai Xinli Biochemistry Products Factory	Yantai	Shandong	(0535)7317858		Private Enterprises				Chondroitin Sulfate
烟台新利生化制品有限公司(1996)	烟台市	山东省	(0535)7319917	35	私营独资	60,438	784(35)	39,950	硫酸软骨素
Shandong Wulian Joint Meatpacking Processing Factory	Rizhao	Shandong	(0633)5572027		State-owned				Fresh Frozen Pork
山东省五莲县肉联加工厂(1978)	日照市	山东省	(0633)5572110	658	国有企业	60,181	-	110,072	鲜冻猪肉
Greatwall Gourmet (Dalian)Co., ltd.	Dalian	Liaoning	(0411)5250032		Foreign Funded				Barbecue Products
大成美食（大连）有限公司(2000)	大连市	辽宁省	(0411)5253650	600	外商投资	59,603	1,680(19)	68,550	烧烤品

Top 10 Cities by Revenue 销售收入排名前10位城市	Province 省	Market share 市场份额 (%)	Number of firms 企业个数
Nantong 南通市	Jiangsu 江苏省	9.29	12
Shanghai 上海市	Shanghai 上海市	8.33	7
Yancheng 盐城市	Jiangsu 江苏省	6.41	3
Wenchang 文昌市	Hainan 海南省	6.13	1
Baoding 保定市	Hebei 河北省	5.53	9
Jieyang 揭阳市	Guangdong 广东省	5.27	1
Hangzhou 杭州市	Zhejiang 浙江省	5.22	5
Yantai 烟台市	Shandong 山东省	3.53	3
Changzhou 常州市	Jiangsu 江苏省	3.41	1
Handan 邯郸市	Hebei 河北省	2.89	1

10 Major Wholesalers 十家主要批发商	City 城市	Province 省	Telephone/Fax 电话/传真
Shanghai Nanpu Food Co.,Ltd.	Shanghai	Shanghai	(021)50813333
上海市南浦食品有限公司	上海市	上海市	(021)58201748
Shandong Food Import & Export Company	Qingdao	Shandong	(0532)5897888
山东省食品进出口公司	青岛市	山东省	(0532)5897788
Taishan Changjiang Food Co.,Ltd.	Jiangmen	Guangdong	(0750)5668746
台山市长江食品有限公司	江门市	广东省	(0750)5676264
Guangzhou Food Enterprise Group Co.,Ltd.	Guangzhou	Guangdong	(020)81267810
广州食品企业集团有限公司	广州市	广东省	(020)81267255
Guangdong Zhaoqing Food Import & Export Company	Zhaoqing	Guangdong	(0758)2824427
广东省肇庆食品进出口公司	肇庆市	广东省	(0758)2831199
Shanghai Yangpu (Group)Company	Shanghai	Shanghai	(021)65433282
上海阳普(集团)公司	上海市	上海市	(021)65198109
Nanjing Tianhuan Food Group Co.,Ltd.	Nanjing	Jiangsu	(025)8785191
南京天环食品集团有限责任公司	南京市	江苏省	(025)8712979
Hubei Gucheng Food Company	Xiangfan	Hubei	(0710)7232135
湖北省谷城县食品公司	襄樊市	湖北省	
Guangzhou Panyu Food Group Co.,Ltd.	Guangzhou	Guangdong	(020)84669925
广州市番禺食品集团有限公司	广州市	广东省	(020)84669915
Guangxi Guigang Food General Company	Guigang	Guangxi	(0775)4215631
广西贵港市食品总公司	贵港市	广西	(0775)4234980

1344: Egg Products 蛋品加工业

The industry accounts for 0.020% of the total revenue of China's industrial sector in 2002. The rate of return on assets is 2.43%. 71.70% of all firms in the industry made a profit while 28.30% had negative returns.The top province in terms of the industry's revenue is Shandong, accounting for 38.06% of the total revenue.
2002年本行业收入占全行业的0.020%，资产利润率为2.43%。71.70%的企业赢利，28.30%的企业亏损。收入最高的省为山东省，占本行业的38.06%。

	Total number of firms 企业总数	Total number of employees 职工总数	Total revenue (Mil.RMB) 总销售收入（百万元）	Total profit (Mil.RMB) 总利润（百万元）	Return on assets 资产利润率（%）	Return on equity 权益利润率（%）	Labour productivity ('000 RMB/ worker) 劳动生产率（千元/人）	Debts/ assets 资产负债率（%）	Total assets (Mil.RMB) 总资产（百万元）
Industry Overall 行业总体	53	8,541	2,106	32	2.43	6.59	96.11	63.13	1,319

	Number of firms 企业个数	Average number of employees 平均职工人数	Average revenue ('000 RMB) 平均销售收入（千元）	Average profit ('000 RMB) 平均利润（千元）	Return on assets 资产利润率（%）	Return on equity 权益利润率（%）	Labour productivity ('000 RMB/ worker) 劳动生产率（千元/人）	Debts/ assets 资产负债率（%）	Average total assets ('000 RMB) 平均总资产（千元）
By ownership 产业所有权									
State-owned 国有	12	111	4,213	-229	-0.75	-2.38	10.90	68.65	30,683
Collective-owned 集体	7	502	127,902	1,661	4.73	12.10	144.91	60.92	35,109
Foreign & Overseas Chinese Funded 三资	7	164	88,707	1,863	3.17	6.50	149.72	51.18	58,747
By regional distribution 地区分布									
Central-North 华北	3	26	10,611	684	16.18	151.62	116.10	89.33	4,228
Beijing 北京	1	27	4,113	-27	-0.27	-93.10	37.04	99.70	9,830
Tianjin 天津	1	15	4,900	350	51.47	70.00	42.67	26.47	680
Hebei 河北	1	35	22,820	1,730	79.54	209.70	208.57	62.07	2,175
Shanxi 山西									
Inner Mongolia 内蒙古									
Northeast 东北	1	40	11,604	102	3.19	4.00	11.50	20.28	3,200
Liaoning 辽宁	1	40	11,604	102	3.19	4.00	11.50	20.28	3,200
Jilin 吉林									
Heilongjiang 黑龙江									
Central-East 华东	28	183	44,107	638	3.90	10.68	113.99	63.49	16,373
Shanghai 上海	1	58	51,434	1,015	8.07	21.40	136.59	62.32	12,585
Jiangsu 江苏	6	138	25,563	20	0.14	1.18	46.65	88.16	14,211
Zhejiang 浙江	4	48	16,458	699	14.54	35.39	62.00	58.91	4,805
Anhui 安徽	3	53	3,824	86	1.23	8.01	16.79	84.62	7,004
Fujian 福建	4	59	17,599	178	1.51	2.76	80.46	45.32	11,775
Jiangxi 江西	5	81	16,170	51	0.74	3.04	56.63	75.58	6,810
Shandong 山东	5	647	160,328	2,545	5.32	11.86	148.34	55.13	47,844
Central-South 中南	19	166	42,571	716	1.69	4.36	69.46	61.16	42,326
Henan 河南	1	32	12,290	490	19.22	46.67	116.25	58.82	2,550
Hubei 湖北	10	195	13,833	224	2.76	7.76	22.90	64.41	8,093
Hunan 湖南	5	76	7,014	-471	-0.73	-1.99	20.49	63.18	64,212
Guangdong 广东	3	262	207,719	4,414	3.31	8.06	207.03	58.89	133,217
Guangxi 广西									
Hainan 海南									
Southwest 西南									
Chongqing 重庆									
Sichuan 四川									
Guizhou 贵州									
Yunnan 云南									
Tibet 西藏									
Northwest 西北	2	82	9,369	-803	-3.94	-57.67	61.87	93.17	20,384
Shaanxi 陕西	1	150	18,317	-1,621	-4.05	-51.06	64.53	92.06	39,983
Gansu 甘肃	1	13	420	15	1.91		31.15	149.68	785
Qinghai 青海									
Ningxia 宁夏									
Xinjiang 新疆									

1344: Egg Products 蛋品加工业

Year 年份	Number of firms 企业个数	Rate of change 变化率 (%)	Number of employees 职工人数 (人)	Rate of change 变化率 (%)	Total revenue (Mil. RMB) 总销售收入 (百万元)	Rate of change 变化率 (%)	Total profit (Mil RMB) 总利润 (百万元)	Rate of change 变化率 (%)
2000	52		8,478		1,029		24	
2001	51	-1.92	8,783	3.60	1,647	60.06	34	41.67
2002	53	3.92	8,541	-2.76	2,106	27.87	32	-5.88

Major Products 主要产品	Output 产量	Unit 单位

10 Main Firms with Maximal Revenue (year founded) 收入最大的十家主要企业（创办年份）	City 城市	Province 省	Telephone/fax 电话/传真	Number of employees 职工人数	Ownership 产业所有权	Revenue ('000 RMB) 销售收入 (千元)	Profit('000 RMB) (rank) 利润(千元) (排名)	Total assets ('000 RMB) 总资产 (千元)	Major products 主要产品
Xiantao Shuangyuan Eggs Co.,Ltd. 仙桃市双圆蛋品有限公司(1995)	Xiantao 仙桃市	Hubei 湖北省	(0728)2782530	651	Collective-owned 集体企业	75,988	1,416(9)	31,238	Preserved Salty Eggs 皮盐蛋
Jiangsu Taizhou No.2 Foodstuff Processing Factory 泰州市第二食品厂(1985)	Taizhou 泰州市	Jiangsu 江苏省	(0523)6223104 (0523)6225514	202	Private Enterprises 私营独资	53,125	379(19)	32,508	Preserved Eggs 松花皮蛋
Shanghai Qingxi Poultry Eggs Foodstuff Co., Ltd. 上海青西禽蛋食品有限公司(1994)	Shanghai 上海市	Shanghai 上海市	(021)59296335 (021)59295516	58	Collective-owned 集体企业	51,434	1,015(11)	12,585	Regenerated Egg 再制蛋
Funing Hongxiang Egg Products Factory 阜宁县宏翔蛋品厂(1999)	Yancheng 盐城市	Jiangsu 江苏省	(0515)7531040 (0515)7531040	70	Private Enterprises 私营独资	47,400	1,030(10)	4,590	Preserved Egg 皮蛋
Yuyao Poultry & Eggs Processing Factory 余姚市禽蛋加工厂(1984)	Ningbo 宁波市	Zhejiang 浙江省	(0574)2154338 (0574)62154039	49	Joint Stock 股份制	34,800	1,570(8)	7,233	Salty Eggs 咸蛋
Liuhe Feedstuff Stock Co., Ltd. 六和饲料股份有限公司(2002)	Qingdao 青岛市	Shandong 山东省	(0532)7922166 (0532)7922226	80	Joint Stock 股份制	33,800	1,618(6)	5,188	Food 食品
Gaoyou Sanhu Eggs Products Co.,Ltd. 高邮市三湖蛋品有限公司(1991)	Yangzhou 扬州市	Jiangsu 江苏省	(0514)4742072 (0514)4745622	280	Private Enterprises 私营独资	31,690	500(16)	23,798	Regenerated Egg 再制蛋
Hunan Xiyang Food Industry Group Co.,Ltd. 湖南喜阳食品工业集团股份公司(1998)	Xiangxi 湘西州	Hunan 湖南省	(0743)7723495 (0743)7726432	315	State-owned 国有企业	30,914	-	306,361	Preserved Eggs 松花皮蛋
Qingdao Da Shui Food Co.,Ltd. 青岛大水食品有限公司(1993)	Qingdao 青岛市	Shandong 山东省	(0532)4936282 (0532)4936184	270	Foreign Funded 外商投资	29,359	2,903(3)	31,696	
Nanchang Meishi Xiangxiang Eggs Products Processing Factory 南昌市梅氏香香禽蛋加工厂(2001)	Nanchang 南昌市	Jiangxi 江西省	(0791)5294306 (0791)5294306	112	Joint Stock 股份制	29,299	43(33)	3,398	Poultry Eggs 禽蛋

Top 10 Cities by Revenue 销售收入排名前10位城市	Province 省	Market share 市场份额 (%)	Number of firms 企业个数
Qingdao 青岛市	Shandong 山东省	36.29	3
Guangzhou 广州市	Guangdong 广东省	29.59	3
Nanchang 南昌市	Jiangxi 江西省	3.60	4
Ningbo 宁波市	Zhejiang 浙江省	3.13	4
Taizhou 泰州市	Jiangsu 江苏省	2.89	2
Shanghai 上海市	Shanghai 上海市	2.44	1
Yancheng 盐城市	Jiangsu 江苏省	2.25	1
Putian 莆田市	Fujian 福建省	1.91	2
Yangzhou 扬州市	Jiangsu 江苏省	1.86	2

10 Major Wholesalers 十家主要批发商	City 城市	Province 省	Telephone/Fax 电话/传真
Shanghai Nanpu Food Co.,Ltd. 上海市南浦食品有限公司	Shanghai 上海市	Shanghai 上海市	(021)50813333 (021)58201748
Shandong Food Import & Export Company 山东省食品进出口公司	Qingdao 青岛市	Shandong 山东省	(0532)5897888 (0532)5897788
Taishan Changjiang Food Co.,Ltd. 台山市长江食品有限公司	Jiangmen 江门市	Guangdong 广东省	(0750)5668746 (0750)5676264
Guangzhou Food Enterprise Group Co.,Ltd. 广州食品企业集团有限公司	Guangzhou 广州市	Guangdong 广东省	(020)81267810 (020)81267255
Guangdong Zhaoqing Food Import & Export Company 广东省肇庆食品进出口公司	Zhaoqing 肇庆市	Guangdong 广东省	(0758)2824427 (0758)2831199
Shanghai Yangpu (Group)Company 上海阳普(集团)公司	Shanghai 上海市	Shanghai 上海市	(021)65433282 (021)65198109
Nanjing Tianhuan Food Group Co.,Ltd. 南京天环食品集团有限责任公司	Nanjing 南京市	Jiangsu 江苏省	(025)8785191 (025)8712979
Hubei Gucheng Food Company 湖北省谷城县食品公司	Xiangfan 襄樊市	Hubei 湖北省	(0710)7232135
Guangzhou Panyu Food Group Co.,Ltd. 广州市番禺食品集团有限公司	Guangzhou 广州市	Guangdong 广东省	(020)84669925 (020)84669915
Guangxi Guigang Food General Company 广西贵港市食品总公司	Guigang 贵港市	Guangxi 广西	(0775)4215631 (0775)4234980

1351: Frozen Aquatic Products 冷冻水产品加工业

The industry accounts for 0.440% of the total revenue of China's industrial sector in 2002. The rate of return on assets is 8.25%. 83.80% of all firms in the industry made a profit while 16.20% had negative returns.The top province in terms of the industry's revenue is Shandong, accounting for 61.82% of the total revenue.
2002年本行业收入占全行业的 0.440%，资产利润率为 8.25%。83.80%的企业赢利，16.20%的企业亏损。收入最高的省为山东省，占本行业的61.82%。

	Total number of firms 企业总数	Total number of employees 职工总数	Total revenue (Mil.RMB) 总销售收入 (百万元)	Total profit (Mil.RMB) 总利润 (百万元)	Return on assets 资产利润率 (%)	Return on equity 权益利润率 (%)	Labour productivity ('000 RMB/ worker) 劳动生产率 (千元/人)	Debts/ assets 资产负债率 (%)	Total assets (Mil.RMB) 总资产 (百万元)
Industry Overall 行业总体	852	176,596	47,218	2,368	8.25	20.12	74.13	59.00	28,696

	Number of firms 企业个数	Average number of employees 平均职工人数	Average revenue ('000 RMB) 平均销售收入 (千元)	Average profit ('000 RMB) 平均利润 (千元)	Return on assets 资产利润率 (%)	Return on equity 权益利润率 (%)	Labour productivity ('000 RMB/ worker) 劳动生产率 (千元/人)	Debts/ assets 资产负债率 (%)	Average total assets ('000 RMB) 平均总资产 (千元)
By ownership 产业所有权									
State-owned 国有	88	301	29,927	277	0.70	2.62	23.47	73.48	39,824
Collective-owned 集体	123	327	121,259	8,321	18.01	42.36	111.21	57.48	46,199
Foreign & Overseas Chinese Funded 三资	217	200	47,370	1,498	4.63	12.91	61.39	64.14	32,347
By regional distribution 地区分布									
Central-North 华北	32	83	12,315	51	0.33	0.71	46.99	54.02	15,551
Beijing 北京	2	22	11,178	1,432	26.18	58.04	98.18	54.89	5,468
Tianjin 天津	12	118	12,589	-330	-1.44	-2.60	43.61	44.72	22,985
Hebei 河北	17	68	12,972	160	1.34	3.95	50.35	66.07	11,971
Shanxi 山西	1	29	151	-10	-0.14	-0.42	0.14	67.78	7,367
Inner Mongolia 内蒙古									
Northeast 东北	68	200	26,527	597	2.20	6.01	32.60	63.39	27,128
Liaoning 辽宁	64	205	27,749	646	2.40	6.57	33.26	63.49	26,902
Jilin 吉林	2	233	12,905	-443	-0.75	-2.10	15.09	64.13	58,837
Heilongjiang 黑龙江	2	13	1,052	61	2.29	2.64	11.81	13.32	2,647
Central-East 华东	640	211	63,495	3,510	9.77	24.36	83.07	59.88	35,909
Shanghai 上海	3	124	18,945	-482	-1.53	-4.94	47.53	69.00	31,466
Jiangsu 江苏	71	111	37,825	690	5.70	24.78	86.50	77.00	12,098
Zhejiang 浙江	235	99	29,700	525	2.40	6.76	61.18	64.47	21,894
Anhui 安徽	4	129	9,648	133	0.52	3.29	19.30	84.15	25,487
Fujian 福建	86	104	19,592	364	2.93	5.89	57.78	50.22	12,404
Jiangxi 江西									
Shandong 山东	241	390	121,128	8,479	13.00	30.88	91.07	57.89	65,206
Central-South 中南	105	237	40,771	761	2.42	4.99	51.80	51.48	31,452
Henan 河南	1	32	17,060	1,192	39.22	40.00	113.88	1.94	3,039
Hubei 湖北	12	684	33,831	1,223	1.53	2.85	17.72	46.14	79,828
Hunan 湖南	2	45	9,145	-20	-0.29	-1.14	29.30	74.53	6,896
Guangdong 广东	68	196	48,363	1,008	3.72	7.95	72.32	53.17	27,079
Guangxi 广西	10	170	15,065	-765	-3.84	-16.70	26.55	77.00	19,920
Hainan 海南	12	126	33,360	270	1.13	1.89	83.99	40.22	23,925
Southwest 西南	3	97	28,193	45	0.48	1.12	77.16	56.86	9,252
Chongqing 重庆									
Sichuan 四川	3	97	28,193	45	0.48	1.12	77.16	56.86	9,252
Guizhou 贵州									
Yunnan 云南									
Tibet 西藏									
Northwest 西北	4	60	4,330	-192	-1.85	-2.81	19.63	34.03	10,352
Shaanxi 陕西	2	72	6,614	-139	-0.75	-1.11	28.98	32.45	18,538
Gansu 甘肃	1	41	1,526	57	9.69	10.04	14.24	3.40	588
Qinghai 青海	1	55	2,568	-546	-14.59	-32.02	-0.82	54.45	3,743
Ningxia 宁夏									
Xinjiang 新疆									

1351: Frozen Aquatic Products 冷冻水产品加工业

Year 年份	Number of firms 企业个数	Rate of change 变化率 (%)	Number of employees 职工人数 (人)	Rate of change 变化率 (%)	Total revenue (Mil. RMB) 总销售收入 (百万元)	Rate of change 变化率 (%)	Total profit (Mil RMB) 总利润 (百万元)	Rate of change 变化率 (%)
2000	695		123,277		32,892		1,269	
2001	760	9.35	133,450	8.25	34,345	4.42	1,577	24.27
2002	852	12.11	176,596	32.33	47,218	37.48	2,368	50.16

Major Products 主要产品	Output 产量	Unit 单位
Processed Aquatic Products 水产加工品	304	10,000 Tons 万吨

10 Main Firms with Maximal Revenue (year founded) 收入最大的十家主要企业（创办年份）	City 城市	Province 省	Telephone/fax 电话/传真	Number of employees 职工人数	Ownership 产业所有权	Revenue ('000 RMB) 销售收入（千元）	Profit('000 RMB) (rank) 利润(千元)(排名)	Total assets ('000 RMB) 总资产（千元）	Major products 主要产品
Wendeng Zeku Aquatic Products Co.,ltd.	Weihai	Shandong	(0631)8781011		Collective-owned				Freezing Aquatic Products
文登市泽库水产总公司(1992)	威海市	山东省	(0631)8781266	397	集体企业	1,248,740	83,380(2)	157,610	冷冻水产品
Shandong Sunjiatuan Aquatic Products Group Company	Weihai	Shandong	(0631)5125176		Collective-owned				Aquatic Products
山东孙家疃水产集团公司(1991)	威海市	山东省	(0631)5125988	1,160	集体企业	1,243,960	80,330(3)	104,670	水产品
Shandong Yuankuang Industrial Group Co., Ltd.	Weihai	Shandong	(0631)7455001		Limited-Liability				Freezing Fish
山东院夼实业集团有限公司(1968)	威海市	山东省	(0631)7455072	350	有限公司	751,630	78,100(4)	86,910	冷冻鱼
Rizhao Aquatic Products Group General Company	Rizhao	Shandong	(0633)8321746		State-owned				Freezing Aquatic Products
日照市水产集团总公司(1992)	日照市	山东省	(0633)8321498	3,807	国有企业	723,093	35,362(15)	659,107	冷冻水产品
Shandong Chishan Aquatic Products Group Co., Ltd.	Weihai	Shandong	(0631)7321100		Collective-owned				Aquatic Products
山东斥山水产集团有限公司(1987)	威海市	山东省	(0631)7323288	2,599	集体企业	721,160	42,190(10)	483,380	水产品
Wendeng Qiandao Fishery Company	Weihai	Shandong	(0631)8787018		Collective-owned				Aquatic Products
文登市前岛渔业公司(1956)	威海市	山东省	(0631)8781968	900	集体企业	633,000	54,630(8)	197,650	水产品
Shandong Qingshun Fishery Co.,Ltd.	Weihai	Shandong	(0631)8781084		Joint Stock				Aquatic Products
山东庆顺渔业股份有限公司(1995)	威海市	山东省	(0631)8781488	800	股份制	602,500	43,650(9)	98,830	水产品
Shandong Jinghai Industrial Co.,ltd.	Weihai	Shandong	(0631)7461082		Joint Stock				Sea-farming
山东靖海实业集团有限公司(2000)	威海市	山东省	(0631)7461084	320	股份制	585,620	40,240(12)	504,050	海水养殖
Zhoushan Industrial Co.,Ltd.	Zhoushan	Zhejiang	(0580)3695888		Foreign Funded				Aquatic Products
舟山兴业有限公司(1994)	舟山市	浙江省	(0580)3695596	2,420	外商投资	564,290	7,080(85)	540,030	水产品
Shandong Xunshan Aquatic Products Group Co., Ltd.	Weihai	Shandong	(0631)7651082		Limited-Liability				Marine Products
山东寻山水产集团有限公司(1965)	威海市	山东省	(0631)7651158	192	有限公司	563,500	40,340(11)	69,780	海产品

Top 10 Cities by Revenue 销售收入排名前10位城市	Province 省	Market share 市场份额 (%)	Number of firms 企业个数
Weihai 威海市	Shandong 山东省	46.19	127
Zhoushan 舟山市	Zhejiang 浙江省	9.07	113
Qingdao 青岛市	Shandong 山东省	6.73	42
Yantai 烟台市	Shandong 山东省	5.73	60
Shantou 汕头市	Guangdong 广东省	3.44	16
Nantong 南通市	Jiangsu 江苏省	2.60	32
Rizhao 日照市	Shandong 山东省	2.50	7
Taizhou 台州市	Zhejiang 浙江省	2.49	71
Zhanjiang 湛江市	Guangdong 广东省	2.37	25
Dalian 大连市	Liaoning 辽宁省	2.18	35

10 Major Wholesalers 十家主要批发商	City 城市	Province 省	Telephone/Fax 电话/传真
Guangdong Zhongshan Food & Aquatic Products Import & Export Group Company	Zhongshan	Guangdong	(0760)8310882
广东省中山食品水产进出口集团公司	中山市	广东省	(0760)8311207
Shenzhen Haishun Aquatic Products Corporation	Shenzhen	Guangdong	(0755)25200854
深圳市海顺水产公司	深圳市	广东省	(0755)25202051
Guangdong Shunde Foodstuffs Import & Export Company	Foshan	Guangdong	(0765)6383348
广东省顺德食品进出口公司	佛山市	广东省	(0765)6681345
Shandong Horizon International Transportation Co.,Ltd.	Qingdao	Shandong	(0532)2661591
山东华鑫国际货运代理有限公司	青岛市	山东省	(0532)2661586
Shenzhen Aquatic Products Company	Shenzhen	Guangdong	(0755)82223281
深圳市水产公司	深圳市	广东省	(0755)82222810
Xi'an Tonghai Aquatic Products & Non-staple Food Square	Xi'an	Shannxi	(029)7215718
西安通海水产副食品广场	西安市	陕西省	
Zhejiang Ocean Fishery Group Co.,Ltd.	Hangzhou	Zhejiang	(0571)87230058
浙江省远洋渔业集团股份有限公司	杭州市	浙江省	(0571)87227956
Shandong Shanhai Fishery Business Center	Jinan	Shandong	(0531)8556615
山东省山海水产贸易中心	济南市	山东省	(0531)8558288
Shandong Sanfod Trading Co.,ltd.	Qingdao	Shandong	(0532)5897888
山东山孚得贸易有限公司	青岛市	山东省	(0532)5895888
Shanwei Municipal Aquatic Products Wholesale Market Management Institute	Shanwei	Guangdong	(0660)3331240
汕尾市城区水产品批发市场管理所	汕尾市	广东省	(0660)3318660

1352: Dry Aquatic Products 干制水产品加工业

The industry accounts for 0.051% of the total revenue of China's industrial sector in 2002. The rate of return on assets is 2.87%. 83.22% of all firms in the industry made a profit while 16.78% had negative returns.The top province in terms of the industry's revenue is Fujian, accounting for 48.27% of the total revenue.
2002年本行业收入占全行业的0.051%，资产利润率为2.87%。83.22%的企业赢利，16.78%的企业亏损。收入最高的省为福建省，占本行业的48.27%。

	Total number of firms 企业总数	Total number of employees 职工总数	Total revenue (Mil.RMB) 总销售收入(百万元)	Total profit (Mil.RMB) 总利润(百万元)	Return on assets 资产利润率(%)	Return on equity 权益利润率(%)	Labour productivity ('000 RMB/worker) 劳动生产率(千元/人)	Debts/assets 资产负债率(%)	Total assets (Mil.RMB) 总资产(百万元)
Industry Overall 行业总体	143	19,820	5,506	124	2.87	6.73	77.08	57.40	4,308

	Number of firms 企业个数	Average number of employees 平均职工人数	Average revenue ('000 RMB) 平均销售收入（千元）	Average profit ('000 RMB) 平均利润（千元）	Return on assets 资产利润率(%)	Return on equity 权益利润率(%)	Labour productivity ('000 RMB/worker) 劳动生产率(千元/人)	Debts/assets 资产负债率(%)	Average total assets ('000 RMB) 平均总资产(千元)
By ownership 产业所有权									
State-owned 国有	6	309	11,495	3	0.01	0.02	15.59	47.63	27,672
Collective-owned 集体	6	84	10,560	199	2.45	30.14	40.40	91.86	8,124
Foreign & Overseas Chinese Funded 三资	81	150	53,742	1,184	3.04	7.71	96.98	60.53	38,940
By regional distribution 地区分布									
Central-North 华北	2	541	7,216	-291	-0.70	-1.17	8.48	39.69	41,311
Beijing 北京									
Tianjin 天津	2	541	7,216	-291	-0.70	-1.17	8.48	39.69	41,311
Hebei 河北									
Shanxi 山西									
Inner Mongolia 内蒙古									
Northeast 东北	10	209	36,450	1,585	4.27	9.43	36.58	54.67	37,083
Liaoning 辽宁	7	269	49,386	2,235	4.88	10.13	29.94	51.82	45,787
Jilin 吉林	3	68	6,264	67	0.40	1.47	97.86	72.85	16,771
Heilongjiang 黑龙江									
Central-East 华东	114	128	39,766	851	3.03	7.93	90.93	61.78	28,075
Shanghai 上海									
Jiangsu 江苏	45	73	21,672	1,068	6.18	13.36	73.71	53.75	17,280
Zhejiang 浙江	11	105	24,632	428	2.72	7.14	51.37	61.95	15,763
Anhui 安徽									
Fujian 福建	42	175	63,280	460	1.10	3.14	113.28	64.91	41,704
Jiangxi 江西	2	192	130,057	2,552	3.76	13.35	185.24	71.86	67,913
Shandong 山东	14	175	26,370	1,414	5.47	13.66	50.51	59.99	25,867
Central-South 中南	16	124	36,687	701	1.74	2.87	56.02	39.54	40,408
Henan 河南									
Hubei 湖北									
Hunan 湖南	1	152	19,700	650	14.19	34.21	42.41	58.52	4,580
Guangdong 广东	14	129	40,051	809	1.78	2.93	57.46	39.37	45,523
Guangxi 广西	1	26	6,577	-760	-16.44	-28.99	35.19	43.27	4,622
Hainan 海南									
Southwest 西南	1	53	6,628	101	1.44	3.27	45.79	56.01	7,015
Chongqing 重庆									
Sichuan 四川									
Guizhou 贵州	1	53	6,628	101	1.44	3.27	45.79	56.01	7,015
Yunnan 云南									
Tibet 西藏									
Northwest 西北									
Shaanxi 陕西									
Gansu 甘肃									
Qinghai 青海									
Ningxia 宁夏									
Xinjiang 新疆									

1352: Dry Aquatic Products 干制水产品加工业

Year 年份	Number of firms 企业个数	Rate of change 变化率 (%)	Number of employees 职工人数 (人)	Rate of change 变化率 (%)	Total revenue (Mil. RMB) 总销售收入 (百万元)	Rate of change 变化率 (%)	Total profit (Mil RMB) 总利润 (百万元)	Rate of change 变化率 (%)
2000	109		14,299		5,695		74	
2001	115	5.50	16,504	15.42	4,800	-15.72	81	9.46
2002	143	24.35	19,820	20.09	5,506	14.71	124	53.09

Major Products 主要产品	Output 产量	Unit 单位
Processed Aquatic Products 水产加工品	304	10,000 Tons 万吨

10 Main Firms with Maximal Revenue (year founded) 收入最大的十家主要企业（创办年份）	City 城市	Province 省	Telephone/fax 电话/传真	Number of employees 职工人数	Ownership 产业所有权	Revenue ('000 RMB) 销售收入 (千元)	Profit('000 RMB) (rank) 利润(千元) (排名)	Total assets ('000 RMB) 总资产 (千元)	Major products 主要产品
Allied Pacific Food (Dalian) Co.,Ltd.	Dalian	Liaoning	(0411)7821188		Overseas Chinese-funded				Shrimp
中联食品(大连)有限公司(2000)	大连市	辽宁省	(0411)7821199	1,069	港澳台资	231,667	6,872(5)	193,829	虾
Ruijin Hongdu Aquatic Products Food Co., Ltd.	Ganzhou	Jiangxi	(0797)2508777		Overseas Chinese-funded				Roast Eel
瑞金市红都水产食品有限公司(1996)	赣州市	江西省	(0797)2508766	210	港澳台资	180,529	6,667(6)	113,013	烤鳗
Putian Dongyuan Aquatic Products Food Co.,ltd.	Putian	Fujian	(0594)3600821		Overseas Chinese-funded				Roast Eel
莆田东源水产食品有限公司(1994)	莆田市	福建省	(0594)3600222	260	港澳台资	176,419	1,602(24)	98,142	烤鳗
Fuzhou Modern Ocean Food Co.,ltd.	Fuzhou	Fujian	(0591)2352599		Overseas Chinese-funded				Roast Eel
福州顺源食品有限公司(2000)	福州市	福建省	(0591)2351599	50	港澳台资	173,491	-	37,676	烤鳗
Fuqing Furong Foods Co.,Ltd.	Fuzhou	Fujian	(0591)5621678		Overseas Chinese-funded				Roast Eel
福清市福荣食品有限公司(1995)	福州市	福建省	(0591)5621518	335	港澳台资	152,636	5,828(7)	98,654	烤鳗
Shunde Baoli Food Co.,Ltd.	Foshan	Guangdong	(0765)7686611		Overseas Chinese-funded				Roast Eel
顺德保利食品有限公司(1994)	佛山市	广东省	(0765)7686616	300	港澳台资	147,494	-	93,960	烤鳗
Fujian Changfeng Frozen Food Co.,Ltd.	Fuzhou	Fujian	(0591)5382841		Overseas Chinese-funded				Roast Eel
福建省昌丰冷冻食品有限公司(1998)	福州市	福建省	(0591)5380351	251	港澳台资	141,224	5,354(8)	51,216	烤鳗
Fuqing Hongsheng Food Co.,Ltd.	Fuzhou	Fujian	(0591)5681608		Overseas Chinese-funded				Roast Eel
福清弘晟食品有限公司(1992)	福州市	福建省	(0591)5682081	367	港澳台资	134,431	-	56,386	烤鳗
Putian Xinghe Food Industry Co.,ltd.	Putian	Fujian	(0594)3299088		Overseas Chinese-funded				Roast Eel
莆田市兴和食品工业有限公司(2001)	莆田市	福建省	(0594)3299288	257	港澳台资	132,112	16,825(1)	77,141	烤鳗
Fujian Yifeng Eel Food Processing Co.,Ltd.	Fuzhou	Fujian	(0591)5381651		Overseas Chinese-funded				Roast Eel
福建益丰鳗业食品有限公司(1993)	福州市	福建省	(0591)5372729	245	港澳台资	128,633	7,382(3)	70,084	烤鳗

Top 10 Cities by Revenue 销售收入排名前10位城市	Province 省	Market share 市场份额 (%)	Number of firms 企业个数
Fuzhou 福州市	Fujian 福建省	34.68	28
Lianyungang 连云港市	Jiangsu 江苏省	9.09	21
Putian 莆田市	Fujian 福建省	7.65	3
Nantong 南通市	Jiangsu 江苏省	6.18	19
Dalian 大连市	Liaoning 辽宁省	5.59	5
Xiamen 厦门市	Fujian 福建省	3.42	3
Ganzhou 赣州市	Jiangxi 江西省	3.28	1
Foshan 佛山市	Guangdong 广东省	2.68	1
Jiangmen 江门市	Guangdong 广东省	2.66	6
Chaozhou 潮州市	Guangdong 广东省	2.66	3

10 Major Wholesalers 十家主要批发商	City 城市	Province 省	Telephone/Fax 电话/传真
Guangdong Zhongshan Food & Aquatic Products Import & Export Group Company	Zhongshan	Guangdong	(0760)8310882
广东省中山食品水产进出口集团公司	中山市	广东省	(0760)8311207
Shenzhen Haishun Aquatic Products Corporation	Shenzhen	Guangdong	(0755)25200854
深圳市海顺水产公司	深圳市	广东省	(0755)25202051
Guangdong Shunde Foodstuffs Import & Export Company	Foshan	Guangdong	(0765)6383348
广东省顺德食品进出口公司	佛山市	广东省	(0765)6681345
Shandong Horizon International Transportation Co.,Ltd.	Qingdao	Shandong	(0532)2661591
山东华鑫国际货运代理有限公司	青岛市	山东省	(0532)2661586
Shenzhen Aquatic Products Company	Shenzhen	Guangdong	(0755)82223281
深圳市水产公司	深圳市	广东省	(0755)82222810
Xi'an Tonghai Aquatic Products & Non-staple Food Square	Xi'an	Shannxi	(029)7215718
西安通海水产副食品广场	西安市	陕西省	
Zhejiang Ocean Fishery Group Co.,Ltd.	Hangzhou	Zhejiang	(0571)87230058
浙江省远洋渔业集团股份有限公司	杭州市	浙江省	(0571)87227956
Shandong Shanhai Fishery Business Center	Jinan	Shandong	(0531)8556615
山东省山海水产贸易中心	济南市	山东省	(0531)8558288
Shandong Sanfod Trading Co.,ltd.	Qingdao	Shandong	(0532)5897888
山东山孚得贸易有限公司	青岛市	山东省	(0532)5895888
Shanwei Municipal Aquatic Products Wholesale Market Management Institute	Shanwei	Guangdong	(0660)3331240
汕尾市城区水产品批发市场管理所	汕尾市	广东省	(0660)3318660

1353: Preserved Aquatic Products 腌制水产品加工业

The industry accounts for 0.004% of the total revenue of China's industrial sector in 2002. The rate of return on assets is 8.52%. 88.00% of all firms in the industry made a profit while 12.00% had negative returns.The top province in terms of the industry's revenue is Guangdong, accounting for 32.20% of the total revenue.
2002年本行业收入占全行业的 0.004%，资产利润率为 8.52%。88.00%的企业赢利，12.00%的企业亏损。收入最高的省为广东省，占本行业的32.20%。

	Total number of firms 企业总数	Total number of employees 职工总数	Total revenue (Mil.RMB) 总销售收入（百万元）	Total profit (Mil.RMB) 总利润（百万元）	Return on assets 资产利润率（%）	Return on equity 权益利润率（%）	Labour productivity ('000 RMB/worker) 劳动生产率（千元/人）	Debts/assets 资产负债率（%）	Total assets (Mil.RMB) 总资产（百万元）
Industry Overall 行业总体	25	2,168	428	26	8.52	20.95	47.20	59.32	308

	Number of firms 企业个数	Average number of employees 平均职工人数	Average revenue ('000 RMB) 平均销售收入（千元）	Average profit ('000 RMB) 平均利润（千元）	Return on assets 资产利润率（%）	Return on equity 权益利润率（%）	Labour productivity ('000 RMB/worker) 劳动生产率（千元/人）	Debts/assets 资产负债率（%）	Average total assets ('000 RMB) 平均总资产（千元）
By ownership 产业所有权									
State-owned 国有	2	14	610	100	4.24		13.81	262.49	2,357
Collective-owned 集体	5	38	7,892	375	10.10	21.38	101.29	52.75	3,711
Foreign & Overseas Chinese Funded 三资	10	64	23,736	1,326	6.45	16.15	64.85	60.04	20,549
By regional distribution 地区分布									
Central-North 华北	1	12	6,150	470	26.55	94.00	679.17	71.75	1,770
Beijing 北京									
Tianjin 天津	1	12	6,150	470	26.55	94.00	679.17	71.75	1,770
Hebei 河北									
Shanxi 山西									
Inner Mongolia 内蒙古									
Northeast 东北	6	29	8,384	164	1.50	6.84	69.44	78.07	10,922
Liaoning 辽宁	6	29	8,384	164	1.50	6.84	69.44	78.07	10,922
Jilin 吉林									
Heilongjiang 黑龙江									
Central-East 华东	7	163	21,973	2,635	14.84	36.78	28.10	59.66	17,757
Shanghai 上海	3	84	20,199	306	2.36	10.91	18.43	78.39	12,980
Jiangsu 江苏									
Zhejiang 浙江	1	42	8,276	525	7.60	18.95	50.55	59.90	6,907
Anhui 安徽									
Fujian 福建	2	382	19,814	2,452	30.24	45.22	14.91	33.12	8,106
Jiangxi 江西									
Shandong 山东	1	81	45,309	12,098	19.44	43.03	171.09	54.83	62,242
Central-South 中南	8	61	20,378	663	7.57	13.60	79.04	44.30	8,758
Henan 河南									
Hubei 湖北									
Hunan 湖南	1	37	25,322	3,609	89.11	130.29	188.49	31.60	4,050
Guangdong 广东	7	64	19,671	242	2.57	4.68	70.06	45.08	9,430
Guangxi 广西									
Hainan 海南									
Southwest 西南	2	165	26,536	422	1.84	4.00	34.34	53.97	22,928
Chongqing 重庆									
Sichuan 四川	2	165	26,536	422	1.84	4.00	34.34	53.97	22,928
Guizhou 贵州									
Yunnan 云南									
Tibet 西藏									
Northwest 西北	1	27	1,220	200	42.55	133.33	13.81	68.09	470
Shaanxi 陕西	1	27	1,220	200	42.55	133.33	13.81	68.09	470
Gansu 甘肃									
Qinghai 青海									
Ningxia 宁夏									
Xinjiang 新疆									

1353: Preserved Aquatic Products 腌制水产品加工业

Year 年份	Number of firms 企业个数	Rate of change 变化率(%)	Number of employees 职工人数(人)	Rate of change 变化率(%)	Total revenue (Mil. RMB) 总销售收入(百万元)	Rate of change 变化率(%)	Total profit (Mil RMB) 总利润(百万元)	Rate of change 变化率(%)
2000	24		1,832		298		-3	
2001	28	16.67	1,733	-5.40	542	81.88	33	-
2002	25	-10.71	2,168	25.10	428	-21.03	26	-21.21

Major Products 主要产品	Output 产量	Unit 单位
Processed Aquatic Products 水产加工品	304	10,000 Tons 万吨

10 Main Firms with Maximal Revenue (year founded) 收入最大的十家主要企业（创办年份）	City 城市	Province 省	Telephone/fax 电话/传真	Number of employees 职工人数	Ownership 产业所有权	Revenue ('000 RMB) 销售收入(千元)	Profit('000 RMB) (rank) 利润(千元)(排名)	Total assets ('000 RMB) 总资产(千元)	Major products 主要产品
Everfresh Agricultural Seafood And Meat Products Co.,Ltd.	Qingyuan	Guangdong	(0763)5819737		Foreign Funded				Roast Eel
清鲜（清新县）农林渔牧副产品有限公司(2000)	清远市	广东省	(0763)5819717	120	外商投资	72,504	-	32,848	烤鳗
Yantai Jiabao Food Co.,Ltd.	Yantai	Shandong	(0535)6378863		Foreign Funded				Sweet Water Chestnut
烟台加宝食品有限公司(1995)	烟台市	山东省	(0535)6378875	81	外商投资	45,309	12,098(1)	62,242	糖水栗肉
Shanghai New Star Natural Food Co.,Ltd.	Shanghai	Shanghai	(021)53960780		Foreign Funded				Salted Aquatic Products腌
上海新星天然食品有限公司(1991)	上海市	上海市	(021)53960921	150	外商投资	45,117	662(8)	27,843	制水产品
Sichuan Zizhou Enterprise Co.,Ltd.	Mianyang	Sichuan	(0816)2275011		Joint Stock				Salted Bacon Foodstuff
四川省梓州企业有限公司(1984)	绵阳市	四川省	(0816)2275011	250	股份制	37,220	780(6)	31,500	腌腊食品
Jinzhou Baihe Food Co.,Ltd.	Jinzhou	Liaoning	(0416)8270027		Foreign Funded				Salted Vegetables
锦州百合食品有限公司(1997)	锦州市	辽宁省	(0416)8270030	58	外商投资	24,233	1,051(4)	16,729	盐渍菜
Wuchuan Aquatic Products Processing Co., Ltd.	Zhanjiang	Guangdong	(0759)5566682		Private Owned				Jellyfish
吴川市水产加工有限公司(1995)	湛江市	广东省	(0759)5571916	120	私营企业	16,060	-	18,262	海蜇
Sichuan Dongyu Food co.,ltd.	Chengdu	Sichuan	(028)85885555		Foreign Funded				Agricultural & Sideline Products
四川东誉食品有限公司(1995)	成都市	四川省	(028)85885557	80	外商投资	15,852	64(19)	14,355	农副产品
Jinzhou Tongya Food Co.,Ltd.	Jinzhou	Liaoning	(0416)8270027		Foreign Funded				Salted Vegetables
锦州通亚食品有限公司(1993)	锦州市	辽宁省	(0416)8270030	59	外商投资	10,274	163(17)	33,806	盐渍菜
Shanhai Shaowansheng Food Company	Shanghai	Shanghai	(021)63782657		Collective-owned				Grains Drink Food
上海邵万生食品公司(1999)	上海市	上海市	(021)63782657	54	集体企业	8,914	176(16)	9,984	糟醉食品
Wenzhou Hengyuan Aquatic Products Co., Ltd.	Wenzhou	Zhejiang	(0577)63438373		Overseas Chinese-funded				Salted Shrimp
温州恒源水产有限公司(1999)	温州市	浙江省	(0577)63438628	42	港澳台资	8,276	525(10)	6,907	盐水虾

Top 10 Cities by Revenue 销售收入排名前10位城市	Province 省	Market share 市场份额(%)	Number of firms 企业个数
Qingyuan 清远市	Guangdong 广东省	16.96	1
Shanghai 上海市	Shanghai 上海市	14.17	3
Yantai 烟台市	Shandong 山东省	10.60	1
Fuzhou 福州市	Fujian 福建省	9.27	2
Maoming 茂名市	Guangdong 广东省	9.13	4
Mianyang 绵阳市	Sichuan 四川省	8.70	1
Jinzhou 锦州市	Liaoning 辽宁省	8.07	2
Zhanjiang 湛江市	Guangdong 广东省	6.12	2
Yueyang 岳阳市	Hunan 湖南省	5.92	1
Chengdu 成都市	Sichuan 四川省	3.71	1

10 Major Wholesalers 十家主要批发商	City 城市	Province 省	Telephone/Fax 电话/传真
Guangdong Zhongshan Food & Aquatic Products Import & Export Group Company	Zhongshan	Guangdong	(0760)8310882
广东省中山食品水产进出口集团公司	中山市	广东省	(0760)8311207
Shenzhen Haishun Aquatic Products Corporation	Shenzhen	Guangdong	(0755)25200854
深圳市海顺水产公司	深圳市	广东省	(0755)25202051
Guangdong Shunde Foodstuffs Import & Export Company	Foshan	Guangdong	(0765)6383348
广东省顺德食品进出口公司	佛山市	广东省	(0765)6681345
Shandong Horizon International Transportation Co.,Ltd.	Qingdao	Shandong	(0532)2661591
山东华鑫国际货运代理有限公司	青岛市	山东省	(0532)2661586
Shenzhen Aquatic Products Company	Shenzhen	Guangdong	(0755)82223281
深圳市水产公司	深圳市	广东省	(0755)82222810
Xi'an Tonghai Aquatic Products & Non-staple Food Square	Xi'an	Shannxi	(029)7215718
西安通海水产副食品广场	西安市	陕西省	
Zhejiang Ocean Fishery Group Co.,Ltd.	Hangzhou	Zhejiang	(0571)87230058
浙江省远洋渔业集团股份有限公司	杭州市	浙江省	(0571)87227956
Shandong Shanhai Fishery Business Center	Jinan	Shandong	(0531)8556615
山东省山海水产贸易中心	济南市	山东省	(0531)8558288
Shandong Sanfod Trading Co.,ltd.	Qingdao	Shandong	(0532)5897888
山东山孚得贸易有限公司	青岛市	山东省	(0532)5895888
Shanwei Municipal Aquatic Products Wholesale Market Management Institute	Shanwei	Guangdong	(0660)3331240
汕尾市城区水产品批发市场管理所	汕尾市	广东省	(0660)3318660

1354: Fish Meat and Fish Meat Products 鱼糜及鱼糜制品加工业

The industry accounts for 0.008% of the total revenue of China's industrial sector in 2002. The rate of return on assets is -1.15%. 60.00% of all firms in the industry made a profit while 40.00% had negative returns.The top province in terms of the industry's revenue is Fujian, accounting for 60.07% of the total revenue.
2002年本行业收入占全行业的 0.008%，资产利润率为 -1.15%。60.00%的企业赢利，40.00%的企业亏损。收入最高的省为福建省，占本行业的60.07%。

	Total number of firms 企业总数	Total number of employees 职工总数	Total revenue (Mil.RMB) 总销售收入（百万元）	Total profit (Mil.RMB) 总利润（百万元）	Return on assets 资产利润率（%）	Return on equity 权益利润率（%）	Labour productivity ('000 RMB/worker) 劳动生产率（千元/人）	Debts/assets 资产负债率（%）	Total assets (Mil.RMB) 总资产（百万元）
Industry Overall 行业总体	25	4,403	860	-10	-1.15	-3.12	51.86	63.12	882

	Number of firms 企业个数	Average number of employees 平均职工人数	Average revenue ('000 RMB) 平均销售收入（千元）	Average profit ('000 RMB) 平均利润（千元）	Return on assets 资产利润率（%）	Return on equity 权益利润率（%）	Labour productivity ('000 RMB/worker) 劳动生产率（千元/人）	Debts/assets 资产负债率（%）	Average total assets ('000 RMB) 平均总资产（千元）
By ownership 产业所有权									
State-owned 国有	2	277	12,261	-418	-0.91	-7.66	25.94	88.05	45,697
Collective-owned 集体									
Foreign & Overseas Chinese Funded 三资	19	160	36,096	-557	-1.94	-5.02	53.78	61.32	28,656
By regional distribution 地区分布									
Central-North 华北									
Beijing 北京									
Tianjin 天津									
Hebei 河北									
Shanxi 山西									
Inner Mongolia 内蒙古									
Northeast 东北	6	100	9,446	-480	-2.56	-4.56	23.94	43.77	18,713
Liaoning 辽宁	6	100	9,446	-480	-2.56	-4.56	23.94	43.77	18,713
Jilin 吉林									
Heilongjiang 黑龙江									
Central-East 华东	14	184	51,923	-574	-1.17	-3.80	88.46	69.17	48,956
Shanghai 上海	1	58	8,503	64	0.77	5.02	8.57	84.55	8,260
Jiangsu 江苏	1	60	7,769	459	4.72	7.11	34.72	33.65	9,732
Zhejiang 浙江	1	116	26,679	1,008	3.58	6.38	54.82	43.95	28,167
Anhui 安徽									
Fujian 福建	5	225	103,333	-56	-0.08	-0.20	145.15	59.40	70,396
Jiangxi 江西									
Shandong 山东	6	204	27,885	-1,548	-3.23	-20.68	46.05	84.37	47,875
Central-South 中南	5	244	15,307	152	0.90	1.49	-11.73	39.85	16,962
Henan 河南									
Hubei 湖北									
Hunan 湖南									
Guangdong 广东	4	299	16,231	78	0.37	0.62	-14.00	40.02	21,113
Guangxi 广西	1	28	11,610	448	124.44	124.44	85.11		360
Hainan 海南									
Southwest 西南									
Chongqing 重庆									
Sichuan 四川									
Guizhou 贵州									
Yunnan 云南									
Tibet 西藏									
Northwest 西北									
Shaanxi 陕西									
Gansu 甘肃									
Qinghai 青海									
Ningxia 宁夏									
Xinjiang 新疆									

1354: Fish Meat and Fish Meat Products 鱼糜及鱼糜制品加工业

Year 年份	Number of firms 企业个数	Rate of change 变化率(%)	Number of employees 职工人数(人)	Rate of change 变化率(%)	Total revenue (Mil. RMB) 总销售收入(百万元)	Rate of change 变化率(%)	Total profit (Mil RMB) 总利润(百万元)	Rate of change 变化率(%)
2000	23		3,265		753		24	
2001	23	-	3,154	-3.40	741	-1.59	30	25.00
2002	25	8.70	4,403	39.60	860	16.06	-10	-

Major Products 主要产品	Output 产量	Unit 单位
Processed Aquatic Products 水产加工品	304	10,000 Tons 万吨

10 Main Firms with Maximal Revenue (year founded) 收入最大的十家主要企业（创办年份）	City 城市	Province 省	Telephone/fax 电话/传真	Number of employees 职工人数	Ownership 产业所有权	Revenue ('000 RMB) 销售收入(千元)	Profit('000 RMB) (rank) 利润(千元)(排名)	Total assets ('000 RMB) 总资产(千元)	Major products 主要产品
Changle Juquan Foodstuff Co.,Ltd. 长乐聚泉食品有限公司(1998)	Fuzhou 福州市	Fujian 福建省	(0591)8955888 (0591)8110036	50	Overseas Chinese-funded 港澳台资	297,350	3,542(1)	43,262	Eel 鳗鱼
Sanfeng Frozen Food Co.,Ltd. 莆田三峰冷冻食品有限公司(1994)	Putian 莆田市	Fujian 福建省	(0594)2022680 (0594)2022686	240	Overseas Chinese-funded 港澳台资	91,769	-	56,323	Roast Eel 烤鳗
Rizhao Yongxing Foodstuff Co.,Ltd. 日照永兴食品有限公司(1997)	Rizhao 日照市	Shandong 山东省	(0633)2881345 (0633)2886659	160	Foreign Funded 外商投资	60,250	580(6)	30,990	Star Eel Sliced Meat 星鳗鱼片
Shenzhen Yu Ben Food Co., ltd. 深圳鱼本食品有限公司(1993)	Shenzhen 深圳市	Guangdong 广东省	(0755)27854090 (0755)27855330	660	Overseas Chinese-funded 港澳台资	40,443	3,008(2)	57,904	Fish Food 鱼类食品
Xiamen Huashun Food Industry Co.,Ltd. 厦门华顺食品工业有限公司(1990)	Xiamen 厦门市	Fujian 福建省	(0592)2089111 (0592)2089110	362	Overseas Chinese-funded 港澳台资	35,483	-	88,692	Aquatic Processing Products水产加工品
Fuzhou Haixin Frozen Food Co., Ltd. 福州海欣冷冻食品有限公司(1996)	Fuzhou 福州市	Fujian 福建省	(0591)3673433 (0591)3673433	156	Private Owned 私营企业	27,467	185(12)	15,692	Frozen Food 冷冻食品
Longsheng (Yuhuan) Aquatic Products Co.,Ltd. 玉环龙生水产制品有限公司(1993)	Taizhou 台州市	Zhejiang 浙江省	(0576)7570506 (0576)7570550	116	Foreign Funded 外商投资	26,679	1,008(5)	28,167	Mince Fish Products 鱼糜制品
Shandong Foodstaff Import and Export Co. Qngdao Deep Frozen Factory山东省食品进出口公司青岛冷藏厂(1967)	Qingdao 青岛市	Shandong 山东省	(0532)2616789 (0532)2616188	505	State-owned 国有企业	22,161	-	88,751	Aquatic Products 水产品
Dianbai Yihun Food Co., Ltd. 电白亿顺食品有限公司(1992)	Maoming 茂名市	Guangdong 广东省	(0668)5602299 (0668)5604397	116	Overseas Chinese-funded 港澳台资	15,320	60(15)	13,643	Fish Plasm 鱼浆
Dalian Youlian Sea Food Co.,Ltd. 大连友联海味品有限公司(1997)	Dalian 大连市	Liaoning 辽宁省	(0411)7820968 (0411)7800333	99	Overseas Chinese-funded 港澳台资	13,500	356(10)	31,622	Imitated Crab Meat 模拟蟹肉

Top 10 Cities by Revenue 销售收入排名前10位城市	Province 省	Market share 市场份额 (%)	Number of firms 企业个数
Fuzhou 福州市	Fujian 福建省	37.76	2
Qingdao 青岛市	Shandong 山东省	12.45	5
Putian 莆田市	Fujian 福建省	10.67	1
Quanzhou 泉州市	Fujian 福建省	7.51	1
Rizhao 日照市	Shandong 山东省	7.00	1
Dalian 大连市	Liaoning 辽宁省	6.59	6
Shenzhen 深圳市	Guangdong 广东省	4.70	1
Xiamen 厦门市	Fujian 福建省	4.13	1
Taizhou 台州市	Zhejiang 浙江省	3.10	1
Maoming 茂名市	Guangdong 广东省	2.06	2

10 Major Wholesalers 十家主要批发商	City 城市	Province 省	Telephone/Fax 电话/传真
Guangdong Zhongshan Food & Aquatic Products Import & Export Group Company 广东省中山食品水产进出口集团公司	Zhongshan 中山市	Guangdong 广东省	(0760)8310882 (0760)8311207
Shenzhen Haishun Aquatic Products Corporation 深圳市海顺水产公司	Shenzhen 深圳市	Guangdong 广东省	(0755)25200854 (0755)25202051
Guangdong Shunde Foodstuffs Import & Export Company 广东省顺德食品进出口公司	Foshan 佛山市	Guangdong 广东省	(0765)6383348 (0765)6681345
Shandong Horizon International Transportation Co.,Ltd. 山东华鑫国际货运代理有限公司	Qingdao 青岛市	Shandong 山东省	(0532)2661591 (0532)2661586
Shenzhen Aquatic Products Company 深圳市水产公司	Shenzhen 深圳市	Guangdong 广东省	(0755)82223281 (0755)82222810
Xi'an Tonghai Aquatic Products & Non-staple Food Square 西安通海水产副食品广场	Xi'an 西安市	Shannxi 陕西省	(029)7215718
Zhejiang Ocean Fishery Group Co.,Ltd. 浙江省远洋渔业集团股份有限公司	Hangzhou 杭州市	Zhejiang 浙江省	(0571)87230058 (0571)87227956
Shandong Shanhai Fishery Business Center 山东省山海水产贸易中心	Jinan 济南市	Shandong 山东省	(0531)8556615 (0531)8558288
Shandong Sanfod Trading Co.,ltd. 山东山孚得贸易有限公司	Qingdao 青岛市	Shandong 山东省	(0532)5897888 (0532)5895888
Shanwei Municipal Aquatic Products Wholesale Market Management Institute 汕尾市城区水产品批发市场管理所	Shanwei 汕尾市	Guangdong 广东省	(0660)3331240 (0660)3318660

1359: Other Aquatic Products 其它水产品加工业

The industry accounts for 0.031% of the total revenue of China's industrial sector in 2002. The rate of return on assets is 3.26%. 86.00% of all firms in the industry made a profit while 14.00% had negative returns.The top province in terms of the industry's revenue is Jiangsu, accounting for 54.74% of the total revenue.
2002年本行业收入占全行业的0.031%，资产利润率为3.26%。86.00%的企业赢利，14.00%的企业亏损。收入最高的省为江苏省，占本行业的54.74%。

	Total number of firms 企业总数	Total number of employees 职工总数	Total revenue (Mil.RMB) 总销售收入 (百万元)	Total profit (Mil.RMB) 总利润 (百万元)	Return on assets 资产利润率 (%)	Return on equity 权益利润率 (%)	Labour productivity ('000 RMB/ worker) 劳动生产率 (千元/人)	Debts/ assets 资产负债率 (%)	Total assets (Mil.RMB) 总资产 (百万元)
Industry Overall 行业总体	50	9,381	3,376	121	3.26	8.25	97.90	60.48	3,718

	Number of firms 企业个数	Average number of employees 平均职工人数	Average revenue ('000 RMB) 平均销售收入 (千元)	Average profit ('000 RMB) 平均利润 (千元)	Return on assets 资产利润率 (%)	Return on equity 权益利润率 (%)	Labour productivity ('000 RMB/ worker) 劳动生产率 (千元/人)	Debts/ assets 资产负债率 (%)	Average total assets ('000 RMB) 平均总资产 (千元)
By ownership 产业所有权									
State-owned 国有	4	259	12,042	-1,533	-3.04	-6.36	39.79	52.25	50,504
Collective-owned 集体	8	484	245,872	10,923	3.61	11.13	137.63	67.62	302,969
Foreign & Overseas Chinese Funded 三资	17	87	50,711	996	2.89	7.39	140.89	60.89	34,491
By regional distribution 地区分布									
Central-North 华北									
Beijing 北京									
Tianjin 天津									
Hebei 河北									
Shanxi 山西									
Inner Mongolia 内蒙古									
Northeast 东北	5	81	12,945	520	5.15	10.43	31.10	50.67	10,108
Liaoning 辽宁	5	81	12,945	520	5.15	10.43	31.10	50.67	10,108
Jilin 吉林									
Heilongjiang 黑龙江									
Central-East 华东	30	240	86,014	3,590	3.57	10.07	91.55	64.54	100,502
Shanghai 上海									
Jiangsu 江苏	9	262	205,334	6,727	2.75	8.49	213.72	67.66	244,883
Zhejiang 浙江	3	47	10,835	1,644	12.46	18.03	85.29	30.88	13,188
Anhui 安徽									
Fujian 福建	8	166	29,080	338	1.17	3.17	16.67	63.02	28,827
Jiangxi 江西									
Shandong 山东	10	337	46,727	3,952	7.31	16.22	35.81	54.96	54,094
Central-South 中南	15	118	48,713	730	1.68	2.92	139.07	42.43	43,474
Henan 河南									
Hubei 湖北	1	250	6,300	96	0.79	0.91	198.34	12.69	12,140
Hunan 湖南									
Guangdong 广东	7	64	77,865	1,007	2.95	9.20	233.83	67.92	34,120
Guangxi 广西	1	425	22,639	540	0.94	2.84	83.11	66.99	57,515
Hainan 海南	6	109	26,118	545	0.95	1.22	87.91	21.65	57,269
Southwest 西南									
Chongqing 重庆									
Sichuan 四川									
Guizhou 贵州									
Yunnan 云南									
Tibet 西藏									
Northwest 西北									
Shaanxi 陕西									
Gansu 甘肃									
Qinghai 青海									
Ningxia 宁夏									
Xinjiang 新疆									

1359: Other Aquatic Products 其它水产品加工业

Year 年份	Number of firms 企业个数	Rate of change 变化率(%)	Number of employees 职工人数(人)	Rate of change 变化率(%)	Total revenue (Mil. RMB) 总销售收入(百万元)	Rate of change 变化率(%)	Total profit (Mil RMB) 总利润(百万元)	Rate of change 变化率(%)
2000	47		10,919		2,771		115	
2001	44	-6.38	8,677	-20.53	2,706	-2.35	121	5.22
2002	50	13.64	9,381	8.11	3,376	24.76	121	o

Major Products 主要产品	Output 产量	Unit 单位
Processed Aquatic Products 水产加工品	304	10,000 Tons 万吨

10 Main Firms with Maximal Revenue (year founded) 收入最大的十家主要企业（创办年份）	City 城市	Province 省	Telephone/fax 电话/传真	Number of employees 职工人数	Ownership 产业所有权	Revenue ('000 RMB) 销售收入(千元)	Profit('000 RMB) (rank) 利润(千元)(排名)	Total assets ('000 RMB) 总资产(千元)	Major products 主要产品
Chaozhou Huahai Aquatic Products Co.,ltd.	Chaozhou	Guangdong	(0768)6961212		Overseas Chinese-funded				Roasted Eel
潮州市华海水产有限公司(1999)	潮州市	广东省	(0768)6960388	160	港澳台资	466,232	1,802(11)	186,302	烤鳗
Shandong Shenghai Group Company	Weifang	Shandong	(0536)5342493		Collective-owned				Marine Products
山东圣海集团公司(1953)	潍坊市	山东省	(0536)5342218	2,300	集体企业	260,013	33,017(2)	295,307	海产品
Xiamen Xing Village Eel Industry Co., Ltd.	Xiamen	Fujian	(0592)6070692		Overseas Chinese-funded				Roasted Eel
厦门杏村鳗业有限公司(1994)	厦门市	福建省	(0592)6072788	124	港澳台资	159,821	2,301(7)	100,963	烤鳗
Weihai Hongqiao Aquatic Products Co., Ltd.	Weihai	Shandong	(0631)7831143		Joint Stock				Marine Products
威海市宏桥水产有限公司(1972)	威海市	山东省		204	股份制	120,900	5,900(3)	25,280	海产品
Qidong Huanghai Beach Development Group Co., Ltd.	Nantong	Jiangsu	(0513)3755657		Private Partnership				Aquatic Products
启东市黄海滩涂开发有限公司(1995)	南通市	江苏省	(0513)3755657	450	私营合伙	95,958	3,617(6)	12,217	水产品
Nikou Sizhou (Shandou) Co., Ltd.	Shantou	Guangdong	(0754)8115519		Overseas Chinese-funded				Food
你口四洲（汕头）有限公司(1997)	汕头市	广东省	(0754)8115523	108	港澳台资	37,758	4,461(4)	34,712	食品
Dalian Xingyang Marine Products Co., Ltd.	Dalian	Liaoning	(0411)7804082		Foreign Funded				Aquatic Products
大连兴洋海产有限公司(1991)	大连市	辽宁省	(0411)7810099	120	外商投资	32,000	1,060(17)	20,220	水产品
Rizhao Sanhua Marine Foodstuff Co., ltd.	Rizhao	Shandong	(0633)8655608		Foreign Funded				Imitated Crab Meat
日照三华海产食品有限公司(2000)	日照市	山东省	(0633)2611666	46	外商投资	23,660	1,080(16)	31,109	模拟蟹肉
Beihai Guofar Marine Biological Industry Co., Ltd.	Beihai	Guangxi	(0779)2079623		State-owned				
北海国发海洋生物产业股份有限公司(1950)	北海市	广西	(0779)2079623	425	国有企业	22,639	540(24)	57,515	
Dycolor Seaweed Industrial (Lianyungang) Co., ltd.	Lianyungang	Jiangsu	(0518)6736588		Foreign Funded				Seaweed
达柯拉海藻工业（连云港）有限公司(2002)	连云港市	江苏省	(0518)6736827	130	外商投资	22,360	1,600(14)	6,880	海藻

Top 10 Cities by Revenue 销售收入排名前10位城市	Province 省	Market share 市场份额(%)	Number of firms 企业个数
Zhenjiang 镇江市	Jiangsu 江苏省	48.55	1
Chaozhou 潮州市	Guangdong 广东省	13.81	1
Weifang 潍坊市	Shandong 山东省	7.70	1
Xiamen 厦门市	Fujian 福建省	5.12	2
Hainan 海南省	Hainan 海南省	4.35	3
Weihai 威海市	Shandong 山东省	4.01	3
Nantong 南通市	Jiangsu 江苏省	3.63	3
Dalian 大连市	Liaoning 辽宁省	1.80	4
Shantou 汕头市	Guangdong 广东省	1.29	2
Suzhou 苏州市	Jiangsu 江苏省	1.17	1

10 Major Wholesalers 十家主要批发商	City 城市	Province 省	Telephone/Fax 电话/传真
Guangdong Zhongshan Food & Aquatic Products Import & Export Group Company	Zhongshan	Guangdong	(0760)8310882
广东省中山食品水产进出口集团公司	中山市	广东省	(0760)8311207
Shenzhen Haishun Aquatic Products Corporation	Shenzhen	Guangdong	(0755)25200854
深圳市海顺水产公司	深圳市	广东省	(0755)25202051
Guangdong Shunde Foodstuffs Import & Export Company	Foshan	Guangdong	(0765)6383348
广东省顺德食品进出口公司	佛山市	广东省	(0765)6681345
Shandong Horizon International Transportation Co.,Ltd.	Qingdao	Shandong	(0532)2661591
山东华鑫国际货运代理有限公司	青岛市	山东省	(0532)2661586
Shenzhen Aquatic Products Company	Shenzhen	Guangdong	(0755)82223281
深圳市水产公司	深圳市	广东省	(0755)82222810
Xi'an Tonghai Aquatic Products & Non-staple Food Square	Xi'an	Shannxi	(029)7215718
西安通海水产副食品广场	西安市	陕西省	
Zhejiang Ocean Fishery Group Co.,Ltd.	Hangzhou	Zhejiang	(0571)87230058
浙江省远洋渔业集团股份有限公司	杭州市	浙江省	(0571)87227956
Shandong Shanhai Fishery Business Center	Jinan	Shandong	(0531)8556615
山东省山海水产贸易中心	济南市	山东省	(0531)8558288
Shandong Sanfod Trading Co.,ltd.	Qingdao	Shandong	(0532)5897888
山东山孚得贸易有限公司	青岛市	山东省	(0532)5895888
Shanwei Municipal Aquatic Products Wholesale Market Management Institute	Shanwei	Guangdong	(0660)3331240
汕尾市城区水产品批发市场管理所	汕尾市	广东省	(0660)3318660

1360: Salt 食用盐加工业

The industry accounts for 0.010% of the total revenue of China's industrial sector in 2002. The rate of return on assets is 1.68%. 73.91% of all firms in the industry made a profit while 26.09% had negative returns.The top province in terms of the industry's revenue is Henan, accounting for 26.58% of the total revenue.
2002年本行业收入占全行业的 0.010%，资产利润率为 1.68%。73.91%的企业赢利，26.09%的企业亏损。收入最高的省为河南省，占本行业的26.58%。

	Total number of firms 企业总数	Total number of employees 职工总数	Total revenue (Mil.RMB) 总销售收入（百万元）	Total profit (Mil.RMB) 总利润（百万元）	Return on assets 资产利润率（%）	Return on equity 权益利润率（%）	Labour productivity ('000 RMB/ worker) 劳动生产率（千元/人）	Debts/ assets 资产负债率（%）	Total assets (Mil.RMB) 总资产（百万元）
Industry Overall 行业总体	46	12,254	1,092	33	1.68	5.14	32.21	67.38	1,964

	Number of firms 企业个数	Average number of employees 平均职工人数	Average revenue ('000 RMB) 平均销售收入（千元）	Average profit ('000 RMB) 平均利润（千元）	Return on assets 资产利润率（%）	Return on equity 权益利润率（%）	Labour productivity ('000 RMB/ worker) 劳动生产率（千元/人）	Debts/ assets 资产负债率（%）	Average total assets ('000 RMB) 平均总资产（千元）
By ownership 产业所有权									
State-owned 国有	31	207	18,161	513	2.16	6.08	28.54	64.47	23,752
Collective-owned 集体	1	320		-1		-0.01		70.44	40,761
Foreign & Overseas Chinese Funded 三资	1	11	8,585	1,390	13.37	45.78	-659.82	70.80	10,397
By regional distribution 地区分布									
Central-North 华北	3	63	15,570	137	0.43	3.36	66.10	87.17	31,759
Beijing 北京	1	69	18,913	2,590	5.99	58.73	283.72	89.80	43,230
Tianjin 天津	1	11	8,585	1,390	13.37	45.78	-659.82	70.80	10,397
Hebei 河北	1	110	19,212	-3,569	-8.57	-74.73	2.18	88.53	41,651
Shanxi 山西									
Inner Mongolia 内蒙古									
Northeast 东北	8	64	6,007	122	1.64	4.04	34.16	59.39	7,460
Liaoning 辽宁	4	63	8,170	-35	-0.39	-1.21	49.71	67.83	9,027
Jilin 吉林	3	65	3,411	343	6.91	10.09	20.67	31.57	4,972
Heilongjiang 黑龙江	1	67	5,147	89	1.03	3.69	14.94	72.14	8,653
Central-East 华东	14	275	23,989	781	2.82	8.36	29.24	66.30	27,716
Shanghai 上海									
Jiangsu 江苏	6	275	22,998	1,045	3.22	6.53	30.96	50.72	32,441
Zhejiang 浙江	1	46	5,377	-135	-5.21		58.26	182.39	2,590
Anhui 安徽									
Fujian 福建	2	87	14,898	-34	-0.44	-0.58	44.87	23.80	7,602
Jiangxi 江西	1	433	50,444	1,229	2.60	9.98	27.00	73.97	47,315
Shandong 山东	4	387	28,062	911	2.84	27.85	25.41	89.80	32,067
Central-South 中南	9	711	64,627	1,922	1.37	4.12	32.91	66.86	140,636
Henan 河南	4	980	72,580	1,669	0.98	3.02	29.85	67.45	169,862
Hubei 湖北	3	771	91,120	3,150	1.66	4.90	37.16	66.04	189,402
Hunan 湖南									
Guangdong 广东	2	84	8,983	585	6.47	22.02	45.65	70.60	9,036
Guangxi 广西									
Hainan 海南									
Southwest 西南	6	147	9,069	325	2.10	5.41	31.97	61.20	15,497
Chongqing 重庆									
Sichuan 四川	3	139	12,485	1,391	5.99	13.18	51.32	54.55	23,223
Guizhou 贵州									
Yunnan 云南	2	213	5,084	-1,053	-17.69		8.93	139.95	5,951
Tibet 西藏	1	40	6,789	-117	-1.02	-1.28	75.55	19.68	11,415
Northwest 西北	6	70	4,284	225	2.16	7.52	31.76	71.23	10,401
Shaanxi 陕西									
Gansu 甘肃	1	225	9,738	78	0.20	0.88	34.73	77.35	38,974
Qinghai 青海									
Ningxia 宁夏									
Xinjiang 新疆	5	39	3,194	254	5.43	13.94	28.32	61.04	4,686

Year 年份	Number of firms 企业个数	Rate of change 变化率 (%)	Number of employees 职工人数 (人)	Rate of change 变化率 (%)	Total revenue (Mil. RMB) 总销售收入 (百万元)	Rate of change 变化率 (%)	Total profit (Mil RMB) 总利润 (百万元)	Rate of change 变化率 (%)
2000	43		13,234		892		22	
2001	48	11.63	13,013	-1.67	1,022	14.57	42	90.91
2002	46	-4.17	12,254	-5.83	1,092	6.85	33	-21.43

Major Products 主要产品	Output 产量	Unit 单位
Crude Salt 原盐	3,283	10,000 Tons 万吨

10 Main Firms with Maximal Revenue (year founded) 收入最大的十家主要企业（创办年份）	City 城市	Province 省	Telephone/ fax 电话/传真	Number of employees 职工人数	Ownership 产业所有权	Revenue ('000 RMB) 销售收入 (千元)	Profit('000 RMB) (rank) 利润(千元) (排名)	Total assets ('000 RMB) 总资产 (千元)	Major products 主要产品
Pingdingshan CNSIC Haolong Co., Ltd.	Pingdingshan	Henan	(0375)3632116		State Enterprises				Refined Salt
平顶山中盐皓龙有限责任公司(1994)	平顶山市	河南省	(0375)3632139	2,256	国有独资	222,435	8,745(1)	493,938	精制盐
CNSIC Hongbo Group Co., Ltd.	Xiaogan	Hubei	(0712)4325263		Limited-Liability				Common Salt
中盐宏博集团有限公司(1989)	孝感市	湖北省	(0712)4325510	1,503	有限公司	125,827	2,664(5)	442,183	食盐
Hubei Bluesky SaLt Chemical Plant	Xiaogan	Hubei	(0712)4650611		State-owned				Salt
湖北蓝天盐化厂(1971)	孝感市	湖北省	(0712)4650624	618	国有企业	74,184	6,782(2)	105,976	盐
Hubei Salt Industry General Company Repacking Factory	Xiaogan	Hubei	(0712)3249811		State-owned				Refined Salt
湖北省盐业总公司分装厂(2000)	孝感市	湖北省	(0712)3249810	191	国有企业	73,350	3(28)	20,047	精制盐
Jiangsu Huaihai Salt Industry Factory	Huaian	Jiangsu	(0517)3883332		State-owned				Refined Salt
江苏淮海盐化厂(1991)	淮安市	江苏省	(0517)3883310	874	国有企业	71,267	3,271(4)	119,099	精制盐
Tianhe Refined Salt Factory	Pingdingshan	Henan	(0375)8051569		State-owned				Refined Salt
平顶山天河盐业有限公司(1993)	平顶山市	河南省	(0375)8061798	928	国有企业	56,755	450(15)	102,516	精制盐
Jiangxi Xingan Refined Salt Factory	Ji'an	Jiangxi	(0796)2781260		State-owned				Refined Salt
江西省新干精制盐厂(1991)	吉安市	江西省	(0796)2781258	433	国有企业	50,444	1,229(11)	47,315	精制盐
Qingdao Guanhai Salt Chemical Co., Ltd.	Qingdao	Shandong	(0532)7811073		Limited-Liability				Refined Salt
青岛冠海盐化有限公司(1999)	青岛市	山东省	(0532)7811073	871	有限公司	39,529	305(19)	20,624	精制盐
Fujian Jinghui Refined Iodine Salt Factory	Quanzhou	Fujian	(0595)7487158		State-owned				Iodide Salt
福建省晶惠精制碘盐厂(1997)	泉州市	福建省	(0595)7489346	114	国有企业	25,561	-	13,321	碘盐
Hebei Yinshan Refined Iodine Salt Co., Ltd.	Cangzhou	Hebei	(0317)5268945		Limited-Liability				Iodide Salt
河北银山精制碘盐有限责任公司(1999)	沧州市	河北省	(0317)5268945	110	有限公司	19,212	-	41,651	碘盐

Top 10 Cities by Revenue 销售收入排名前10位城市	Province 省	Market share 市场份额 (%)	Number of firms 企业个数
Pingdingshan 平顶山市	Henan 河南省	26.58	4
Xiaogan 孝感市	Hubei 湖北省	25.02	3
Huaian 淮安市	Jiangsu 江苏省	7.86	2
Taian 泰安市	Shandong 山东省	4.64	1
Ji'an 吉安市	Jiangxi 江西省	4.62	1
Qingdao 青岛市	Shandong 山东省	3.62	1
Quanzhou 泉州市	Fujian 福建省	2.34	1
Anshan 鞍山市	Liaoning 辽宁省	2.30	2
Yancheng 盐城市	Jiangsu 江苏省	2.25	2
Cangzhou 沧州市	Hebei 河北省	1.76	1

10 Major Wholesalers 十家主要批发商	City 城市	Province 省	Telephone/Fax 电话/传真
Guangdong Foodstuffs Import & Export Group Corporation	Guangzhou	Guangdong	(020)83854888
广东省食品进出口集团公司	广州市	广东省	(020)83856823
Hubei Salt Industry General Company	Wuhan	Hubei	(027)82832190
湖北盐业总公司	武汉市	湖北省	(027)82816030
Henan Provincial Salt Business Administration Bureau (Henan Provincial Salt Industry General Company)	Zhengzhou	Henan	(0371)5907597
河南省盐务管理局(河南省盐业总公司)	郑州市	河南省	(0371)5906346
Sichuan Salt Industry General Company	Chengdu	Sichuan	(028)86652441
四川省盐业总公司	成都市	四川省	(028)86663440
China National Salt Tianjin Changlu Salt Industry Co.,Ltd.	Tianjin	Tianjin	(022)23022160
中盐天津市长芦盐业有限公司	天津市	天津市	(022)23022110
Zhejiang Salt Industry Company	Hangzhou	Zhejiang	(0571)87800292
浙江省盐业公司	杭州市	浙江省	(0571)87800082
Fujian Salt Industry Company	Fuzhou	Fujian	(0591)7534344
福建省盐业公司	福州市	福建省	(0591)7535047
Jiangxi Salt Industry General Company	Nanchang	Jiangxi	(0791)6816695
江西省盐业总公司	南昌市	江西省	(0791)6812316
Hubei Salt Transportation & Sale Company	Xiaogan	Hubei	(0712)3611320
湖北省盐业运销公司	孝感市	湖北省	(0712)3611244
Hunan Salt Industry Group Co.,Ltd.Jinshi Allocation & Transportation Company	Changde	Hunan	(0736)4223817
湖南省盐业集团有限责任公司津市调运公司	常德市	湖南省	(0736)4223817

1390: Other Food Processing 其他食品加工业

The industry accounts for 0.272% of the total revenue of China's industrial sector in 2002. The rate of return on assets is 4.14%. 81.99% of all firms in the industry made a profit while 18.01% had negative returns.The top province in terms of the industry's revenue is Shandong, accounting for 40.65% of the total revenue.
2002年本行业收入占全行业的0.272%，资产利润率为4.14%。81.99%的企业赢利，18.01%的企业亏损。收入最高的省为山东省，占本行业的40.65%。

	Total number of firms 企业总数	Total number of employees 职工总数	Total revenue (Mil.RMB) 总销售收入（百万元）	Total profit (Mil.RMB) 总利润（百万元）	Return on assets 资产利润率（%）	Return on equity 权益利润率（%）	Labour productivity ('000 RMB/worker) 劳动生产率（千元/人）	Debts/assets 资产负债率（%）	Total assets (Mil.RMB) 总资产（百万元）
Industry Overall 行业总体	1088	179,958	29,159	1,165	4.14	9.98	48.44	58.56	28,162

	Number of firms 企业个数	Average number of employees 平均职工人数	Average revenue ('000 RMB) 平均销售收入（千元）	Average profit ('000 RMB) 平均利润（千元）	Return on assets 资产利润率（%）	Return on equity 权益利润率（%）	Labour productivity ('000 RMB/worker) 劳动生产率（千元/人）	Debts/assets 资产负债率（%）	Average total assets ('000 RMB) 平均总资产（千元）
By ownership 产业所有权									
State-owned 国有	52	158	10,261	71	0.30	1.09	8.17	72.38	23,580
Collective-owned 集体	131	137	30,516	1,353	6.53	15.66	69.03	58.28	20,717
Foreign & Overseas Chinese Funded 三资	426	164	30,741	1,007	3.17	7.55	56.40	58.03	31,788
By regional distribution 地区分布									
Central-North 华北	117	147	22,397	681	2.85	6.59	50.91	56.73	23,893
Beijing 北京	20	258	46,112	2,448	4.08	7.64	92.68	46.59	60,025
Tianjin 天津	41	101	22,053	182	1.10	2.61	33.70	57.96	16,543
Hebei 河北	42	108	13,354	431	3.12	8.77	32.33	64.45	13,842
Shanxi 山西	6	216	10,957	-402	-2.87	-13.97	19.47	79.46	13,997
Inner Mongolia 内蒙古	8	251	20,933	947	3.01	12.76	41.40	76.39	31,420
Northeast 东北	76	88	12,128	417	3.18	6.34	43.57	49.89	13,108
Liaoning 辽宁	41	102	15,118	368	2.55	4.64	35.66	45.08	14,461
Jilin 吉林	16	59	6,839	238	2.20	3.68	63.48	40.27	10,800
Heilongjiang 黑龙江	19	84	10,129	672	5.54	18.14	52.41	69.45	12,130
Central-East 华东	646	185	30,877	1,150	4.10	10.08	48.15	59.34	28,082
Shanghai 上海	21	91	26,936	533	2.23	6.28	93.99	64.50	23,930
Jiangsu 江苏	85	167	27,167	492	2.62	5.66	48.74	53.74	18,781
Zhejiang 浙江	97	117	25,379	1,562	5.42	12.58	46.52	56.94	28,838
Anhui 安徽	33	135	11,633	402	3.15	9.04	26.57	65.14	12,774
Fujian 福建	101	162	23,209	-8	-0.03	-0.07	36.43	51.39	23,491
Jiangxi 江西	5	49	5,754	207	4.96	6.84	34.75	27.46	4,173
Shandong 山东	304	233	38,991	1,728	5.04	13.33	51.16	62.23	34,310
Central-South 中南	140	143	26,105	1,341	7.13	13.26	53.05	46.24	18,817
Henan 河南	40	97	17,282	1,294	13.59	19.57	59.25	30.57	9,525
Hubei 湖北	21	128	24,432	1,482	8.13	17.09	84.39	52.47	18,241
Hunan 湖南	31	198	36,958	2,525	16.17	26.89	52.23	39.86	15,609
Guangdong 广东	45	144	26,464	535	1.83	3.69	38.93	50.48	29,249
Guangxi 广西	2	115	3,893	-614	-3.11	-7.87	9.62	60.48	19,726
Hainan 海南	1	500	106,016	3,746	12.17	33.76	49.46	63.94	30,771
Southwest 西南	44	244	27,116	1,779	3.59	9.67	38.56	62.90	49,580
Chongqing 重庆	14	413	40,475	2,288	2.29	8.42	28.78	72.77	99,864
Sichuan 四川	21	193	20,261	2,105	7.65	14.18	48.27	46.06	27,511
Guizhou 贵州	4	88	11,218	273	1.25	1.96	42.41	36.30	21,847
Yunnan 云南	5	107	31,219	190	0.80	1.55	68.35	48.06	23,658
Tibet 西藏									
Northwest 西北	65	94	12,651	684	3.15	12.38	54.86	74.58	21,741
Shaanxi 陕西	5	149	14,173	43	0.17	0.40	28.01	57.03	25,193
Gansu 甘肃	55	73	12,949	779	3.67	17.99	76.16	79.60	21,216
Qinghai 青海	2	73	886	5	0.03	0.06	12.72	46.01	14,318
Ningxia 宁夏									
Xinjiang 新疆	3	414	12,485	475	1.55	2.76	7.44	43.67	30,568

1390: Other Food Processing 其他食品加工业

Year 年份	Number of firms 企业个数	Rate of change 变化率(%)	Number of employees 职工人数(人)	Rate of change 变化率(%)	Total revenue (Mil. RMB) 总销售收入(百万元)	Rate of change 变化率(%)	Total profit (Mil RMB) 总利润(百万元)	Rate of change 变化率(%)
2000	774		133,433		18,975		715	
2001	911	17.70	162,632	21.88	23,708	24.94	876	22.52
2002	1088	19.43	179,958	10.65	29,159	22.99	1,165	32.99

Major Products 主要产品	Output 产量	Unit 单位

10 Main Firms with Maximal Revenue (year founded) 收入最大的十家主要企业（创办年份）	City 城市	Province 省	Telephone/fax 电话/传真	Number of employees 职工人数	Ownership 产业所有权	Revenue ('000 RMB) 销售收入(千元)	Profit('000 RMB) (rank) 利润(千元)(排名)	Total assets ('000 RMB) 总资产(千元)	Major products 主要产品
Longda Foodstuff Group Co., Ltd.	Yantai	Shandong	(0535)7717369		Limited-Liability				Vegetable & Fruit
龙大食品集团有限公司(1993)	烟台市	山东省	(0535)7717880	14,924	有限公司	1,262,642	23,501(9)	1,311,196	蔬菜水果
Qingdao Wanfu Group Co.,Ltd.	Qingdao	Shandong	(0532)8438763		Joint Stock				Quick-frozen Vegetable
青岛万福集团股份有限公司(1986)	青岛市	山东省	(0532)8437666	4,200	股份制	830,100	24,653(8)	597,625	速冻菜
Shandong Jilong Industrial Co., Ltd.	Yantai	Shandong	(0535)7296129		Foreign Funded				Vegetable & Fruit
山东吉龙实业有限公司(1978)	烟台市	山东省	(0535)7296170	3,245	外商投资	418,740	26,200(6)	504,910	蔬菜水果
Ningbo Malting Co.,Ltd.	Ningbo	Zhejiang	(0574)86889888		Overseas Chinese-funded				Beer Malt啤
宁波麦芽有限公司(1994)	宁波市	浙江省	(0574)86883958	112	港澳台资	358,994	20,898(10)	543,925	酒用麦芽
Beijing Air Catering Co., Ltd.	Beijing	Beijing	(010)64562383		Overseas Chinese-funded				Aviation pantry
北京航空食品有限公司(1980)	北京市	北京市	(010)64562675	1,136	港澳台资	322,512	75,972(1)	273,555	航空配餐
Qidong Huanghua Group Co., Ltd.	Hengyang	Hunan	(0734)7860098		Collective-owned				Citron Day-lily
祁东县黄花集团有限公司(1994)	衡阳市	湖南省	(0734)7860090	372	集体企业	271,482	11,483(21)	158,013	黄花菜
Wendeng Dongxi Food Co., Ltd.	Weihai	Shandong	(0631)8898405		Foreign Funded				Peanut Products
文登东西食品有限公司(1995)	威海市	山东省	(0631)8898681	150	外商投资	253,280	13,700(14)	21,980	花生制品
Longkou Fook Huat Tong Kee Refrigeration Co., Ltd.	Yantai	Shandong	(0535)8857288		Foreign Funded				Apple
龙口复发中记冷藏有限公司(1993)	烟台市	山东省	(0535)8857847	603	外商投资	234,854	4,395(75)	763,915	苹果
Zhejiang Haitong Food Group Co., Ltd.	Ningbo	Zhejiang	(0574)63809988		Limited-Liability				Vegetables
浙江海通食品集团股份有限公司(1998)	宁波市	浙江省	(0574)63039898	731	有限公司	206,607	46,665(2)	540,141	蔬菜
Rushan Quanyuan Peanut Products Co., Ltd.	Weihai	Shandong	(0631)6466058		Overseas Chinese-funded				Toasted Fruit
乳山市泉源花生制品有限公司(1993)	威海市	山东省	(0631)6466558	256	港澳台资	198,047	7,268(39)	19,093	烤果

Top 10 Cities by Revenue 销售收入排名前10位城市	Province 省	Market share 市场份额 (%)	Number of firms 企业个数
Yantai 烟台市	Shandong 山东省	15.97	61
Qingdao 青岛市	Shandong 山东省	7.30	56
Linyi 临沂市	Shandong 山东省	4.32	50
Ningbo 宁波市	Zhejiang 浙江省	4.16	29
Zhangzhou 漳州市	Fujian 福建省	3.89	53
Weihai 威海市	Shandong 山东省	3.27	11
Weifang 潍坊市	Shandong 山东省	3.27	56
Beijing 北京市	Beijing 北京市	3.16	20
Tianjin 天津市	Tianjin 天津市	3.10	41
Yancheng 盐城市	Jiangsu 江苏省	2.74	19

10 Major Wholesalers 十家主要批发商	City 城市	Province 省	Telephone/Fax 电话/传真
Beijing Cigarette Sale Company	Beijing	Beijing	(010)64228158
北京市卷烟销售公司	北京市	北京市	(010)64228365
Anhui Technology Import & Export Co.,Ltd.	Hefei	Anhui	(0551)5101188
安徽省技术进出口股份有限公司	合肥市	安徽省	(0551)5101199
China Tobacco General Company Henan Province Filiale	Zhengzhou	Henan	(0371)5583070
中国烟草总公司河南省公司	郑州市	河南省	(0371)5957546
Shanghai Jieqiang Tobacco,Sugar & Wine Company Supplies & Sales Center	Shanghai	Shanghai	(021)62494080
上海捷强烟草糖酒公司配销中心	上海市	上海市	(021)62492584
Zhejiang Cigarette Sale Company	Hangzhou	Zhejiang	(0571)87073247
浙江省卷烟销售公司	杭州市	浙江省	(0571)87072474
Fujian Cereals, Oils & Foodstuffs Import Group Corp.	Fuzhou	Fujian	(0591)7506688
福建省粮油食品进口集团公司	福州市	福建省	(0591)7544543
Chongqing Hongta Cigarette Sale Co.,Ltd.	Chongqing	Chongqing	(023)67750222
重庆红塔卷烟销售有限责任公司	重庆市	重庆市	(023)67740477
China Buty Free (Group) General Company	Beijing	Beijing	(010)64649988
中国免税品（集团）总公司	北京市	北京市	(010)64635846
Shanghai Jieqiang Tobacco,Sugar & Wine (Group) Co.,Ltd.	Shanghai	Shanghai	(021)62522018
上海捷强烟草糖酒（集团）有限公司	上海市	上海市	(021)62522005
Shanghai Tobacco Group Chongming Tobacco, Sugar & Wine Co.,Ltd.	Shanghai	Shanghai	(021)59621368
上海烟草集团崇明烟草糖酒有限公司	上海市	上海市	(021)59621368

1411: Candy 糖果业

The industry accounts for 0.106% of the total revenue of China's industrial sector in 2002. The rate of return on assets is 5.63%. 77.27% of all firms in the industry made a profit while 22.73% had negative returns.The top province in terms of the industry's revenue is Guangdong, accounting for 40.31% of the total revenue.
2002年本行业收入占全行业的0.106%，资产利润率为5.63%。77.27%的企业赢利，22.73%的企业亏损。收入最高的省为广东省，占本行业的40.31%。

	Total number of firms 企业总数	Total number of employees 职工总数	Total revenue (Mil.RMB) 总销售收入(百万元)	Total profit (Mil.RMB) 总利润(百万元)	Return on assets 资产利润率(%)	Return on equity 权益利润率(%)	Labour productivity ('000 RMB/worker) 劳动生产率(千元/人)	Debts/assets 资产负债率(%)	Total assets (Mil.RMB) 总资产(百万元)
Industry Overall 行业总体	242	48,669	11,353	650	5.63	15.23	70.67	63.03	11,543

	Number of firms 企业个数	Average number of employees 平均职工人数	Average revenue ('000 RMB) 平均销售收入(千元)	Average profit ('000 RMB) 平均利润(千元)	Return on assets 资产利润率(%)	Return on equity 权益利润率(%)	Labour productivity ('000 RMB/worker) 劳动生产率(千元/人)	Debts/assets 资产负债率(%)	Average total assets ('000 RMB) 平均总资产(千元)
By ownership 产业所有权									
State-owned 国有	37	91	3,536	-156	-0.58	-7.05	7.44	91.81	26,967
Collective-owned 集体	27	148	13,582	384	2.54	6.10	22.61	58.36	15,145
Foreign & Overseas Chinese Funded 三资	72	354	118,543	7,673	7.31	18.59	103.70	60.66	104,932
By regional distribution 地区分布									
Central-North 华北	32	193	56,730	-4,190	-6.51		51.69	100.01	64,350
Beijing 北京	11	286	108,208	-21,356	-17.22		35.98	102.10	124,035
Tianjin 天津	11	156	46,171	7,869	15.44		81.60	103.08	50,966
Hebei 河北	6	139	14,868	2,294	14.63	50.48	63.68	71.02	15,681
Shanxi 山西	3	65	4,195	164	1.99	3.50	29.51	43.18	8,267
Inner Mongolia 内蒙古	1	281	15,388	7	0.05	0.16	24.09	72.07	15,297
Northeast 东北	6	125	9,114	-38	-0.14	-1.20	21.92	88.14	26,647
Liaoning 辽宁	1	45	7,950	-230	-4.72	-67.65	35.11	93.02	4,870
Jilin 吉林	1	169	332	-750	-11.05	-30.11	0.44	63.29	6,786
Heilongjiang 黑龙江	4	134	11,600	188	0.51	4.66	27.58	89.12	37,056
Central-East 华东	91	206	43,725	1,639	3.51	7.63	59.62	54.06	46,749
Shanghai 上海	30	223	51,735	-78	-0.10	-0.23	56.48	55.89	77,808
Jiangsu 江苏	16	338	79,971	3,073	4.96	12.82	59.21	61.34	62,016
Zhejiang 浙江	8	124	33,617	6,660	17.44	37.51	117.91	53.49	38,178
Anhui 安徽	5	112	8,925	-70	-0.60	-2.34	21.34	74.59	11,819
Fujian 福建	22	194	31,205	1,953	10.06	14.11	58.58	28.69	19,408
Jiangxi 江西	1	31	204				2.65	58.95	799
Shandong 山东	9	86	16,346	709	4.72	8.04	50.70	41.34	15,041
Central-South 中南	93	209	56,497	6,861	13.59	28.00	99.62	51.47	50,495
Henan 河南	10	317	42,293	3,940	11.12	23.31	45.25	52.31	35,434
Hubei 湖北	10	137	13,189	279	1.24	3.80	30.90	67.47	22,586
Hunan 湖南	10	118	9,894	276	3.30	5.55	33.13	40.45	8,364
Guangdong 广东	57	236	80,298	10,424	14.90	30.15	126.78	50.58	69,974
Guangxi 广西	4	55	1,308	-346	-3.76	-9.94	-6.86	62.15	9,189
Hainan 海南	2	43	9,128	151	4.37	16.22	141.84	73.03	3,452
Southwest 西南	12	206	12,828	-258	-1.74	-7.35	15.31	76.32	14,821
Chongqing 重庆	2	253	30,084	443	2.97	16.25	28.36	81.74	14,910
Sichuan 四川	8	234	11,718	-455	-2.92	-11.19	12.59	73.89	15,574
Guizhou 贵州	2	49	15	-170	-1.45	-8.20	-0.13	82.37	11,719
Yunnan 云南									
Tibet 西藏									
Northwest 西北	8	134	12,020	2	0.01		9.66	113.48	24,531
Shaanxi 陕西	2	286	43,246	210	1.02	1.48	9.16	31.10	20,536
Gansu 甘肃	4	88	1,088	-74	-0.83	-5.49	9.56	84.90	8,932
Qinghai 青海									
Ningxia 宁夏	1	140	5,317	42	0.27		12.38	107.85	15,648
Xinjiang 新疆	1	6		-149	-0.14			156.77	103,799

1411: Candy 糖果业

Year 年份	Number of firms 企业个数	Rate of change 变化率 (%)	Number of employees 职工人数 (人)	Rate of change 变化率 (%)	Total revenue (Mil. RMB) 总销售收入 (百万元)	Rate of change 变化率 (%)	Total profit (Mil RMB) 总利润 (百万元)	Rate of change 变化率 (%)
2000	231		54,103		8,776		630	
2001	228	-1.30	47,834	-11.59	9,935	13.21	825	30.95
2002	242	6.14	48,669	1.75	11,353	14.27	650	-21.21

Major Products 主要产品	Output 产量	Unit 单位
Candy 糖果	46	10,000 Tons 万吨

10 Main Firms with Maximal Revenue (year founded) 收入最大的十家主要企业（创办年份）	City 城市	Province 省	Telephone/fax 电话/传真	Number of employees 职工人数	Ownership 产业所有权	Revenue ('000 RMB) 销售收入 (千元)	Profit('000 RMB) (rank) 利润(千元) (排名)	Total assets ('000 RMB) 总资产 (千元)	Major products 主要产品
Wrigley Chewing Gum Co., ltd.	Guangzhou	Guangdong	(020)82218816		Foreign Funded				Chewing Gum
广州箭牌口香糖有限公司(1989)	广州市	广东省	(020)82215107	2,594	外商投资	1,701,336	411,728(1)	868,751	口香糖
Effem Foods (Beijing) Co.,Ltd.	Beijing	Beijing	(010)61667410		Foreign Funded				Chocolate
爱芬食品(北京)有限公司(1993)	北京市	北京市	(010)61667416	1,135	外商投资	970,596	-	709,335	巧克力
Dongguan Xsuchi Food Co.,Ltd .	Dongguan	Guangdong	(0769)2268957		Foreign Funded				Candy
东莞徐记食品有限公司(1997)	东莞市	广东省	(0769)2264864	700	外商投资	789,998	143,840(2)	859,703	糖果
Perfetti Van Melle Confectionary (China) Co., Ltd.	Shanghai	Shanghai	(021)64626300		Foreign Funded				Milk Candy
不凡帝（范梅勒）糖果（中国）有限公司(1994)	上海市	上海市	(021)64306398	1,120	外商投资	518,228	2,849(29)	259,642	奶糖
Nestle Tianjin Co., Ltd.	Tianjin	Tianjin	(022)25326313		Foreign Funded				Candy
天津雀巢有限公司(1996)	天津市	天津市	(022)25326314	633	外商投资	389,161	81,375(3)	394,547	糖果
Joyco Foodstuff (China) Co., Ltd.	Guangzhou	Guangdong	(020)84732801		Foreign Funded				Bubble Gum
佳口食品（中国）有限公司(1987)	广州市	广东省	(020)84740041	832	外商投资	377,605	50,851(4)	250,628	泡泡糖
Shanghai Guanshengyuan Food Co., Ltd.	Shanghai	Shanghai	(021)64367532		Limited-Liability				Candy
上海市冠生园食品有限公司(1999)	上海市	上海市	(021)64700604	1,269	有限公司	219,461	10,528(16)	510,742	糖果
Guangzhou Want & Want Foods Co.,Ltd.	Guangzhou	Guangdong	(020)82976666		Overseas Chinese-funded				QQ Sugar
广州旺旺食品有限公司(1995)	广州市	广东省	(020)82973453	290	港澳台资	173,048	41,569(6)	218,334	QQ糖
Warner-Lambert (Guangzhou) Co.,Ltd	Guangzhou	Guangdong	(020)82220771		Foreign Funded				Candy
华纳（广州）有限公司(1994)	广州市	广东省	(020)82214000	1,352	外商投资	172,036	-	432,282	糖果
Wuxi Jibao Candy Co., Ltd.	Wuxi	Jiangsu	(0510)5101102		Foreign Funded				Chewing Gum
无锡吉宝糖果有限公司(2000)	无锡市	江苏省	(0510)5100053	217	外商投资	162,524	12,574(14)	111,034	口香糖

Top 10 Cities by Revenue 销售收入排名前10位城市	Province 省	Market share 市场份额 (%)	Number of firms 企业个数
Guangzhou 广州市	Guangdong 广东省	24.00	13
Shanghai 上海市	Shanghai 上海市	13.67	30
Beijing 北京市	Beijing 北京市	10.48	11
Dongguan 东莞市	Guangdong 广东省	8.18	6
Nanjing 南京市	Jiangsu 江苏省	7.02	2
Quanzhou 泉州市	Fujian 福建省	5.77	18
Tianjin 天津市	Tianjin 天津市	4.47	11
Zhoukou 周口市	Henan 河南省	3.49	4
Shantou 汕头市	Guangdong 广东省	2.40	10
Hangzhou 杭州市	Zhejiang 浙江省	1.79	2

10 Major Wholesalers 十家主要批发商	City 城市	Province 省	Telephone/Fax 电话/传真
Beijing Chaoyang Non-Staple Foodstuffs General Company	Beijing	Beijing	(010)65016285
北京朝阳副食品总公司	北京市	北京市	(010)65016285
Beijing Sugar,Cigarette & Wine Company	Beijing	Beijing	(010)67210304
北京市糖业烟酒公司	北京市	北京市	(010)67210310
Shanghai Sugar Cigarette & Wine (Group) Co.,Ltd.	Shanghai	Shanghai	(021)63224190
上海市糖业烟酒(集团)有限公司	上海市	上海市	(021)63223169
Jiangsu Sutang Sugar & Wine Co.,Ltd.	Nanjing	Jiangsu	(025)6661088
江苏苏糖糖酒食品有限公司	南京市	江苏省	(025)6661088
Fujian Commerce (Group) Co.,Ltd.	Fuzhou	Fujian	(0591)7847148
福建省商业（集团）有限责任公司	福州市	福建省	(0591)7847145
Yantai Changyu Pioneer Winer Co., Ltd.	Yantai	Shandong	(0535)6602730
烟台张裕葡萄酿酒股份有限公司	烟台市	山东省	(0535)6214078
BlueRibbon Beer Sale Co.,Ltd.	Zhaoqing	Guangdong	(0758)2862322
蓝带啤酒销售有限公司	肇庆市	广东省	(0758)2862424
Fujian Shenlong Development Co.,Ltd.	Fuzhou	Fujian	(0591)7503218
福建省神龙发展股份有限公司	福州市	福建省	(0591)7503068
Guangdong Sugar, Cigarette & Wine Group Company	Guangzhou	Guangdong	(020)83566131
广东省糖烟酒集团公司	广州市	广东省	(020)83561421
Shunde Daliang Sugar, Cigarette & Wine Co.,Ltd.	Shunde	Guangdong	(0765)2231804
顺德市大良区糖烟酒有限公司	顺德市	广东省	(0765)2222300

1412: Pastry 糕点业

The industry accounts for 0.047% of the total revenue of China's industrial sector in 2002. The rate of return on assets is 1.07%. 69.63% of all firms in the industry made a profit while 30.37% had negative returns.The top province in terms of the industry's revenue is Shanghai, accounting for 22.77% of the total revenue.
2002年本行业收入占全行业的0.047%，资产利润率为1.07%。69.63%的企业赢利，30.37%的企业亏损。收入最高的省为上海市，占本行业的22.77%。

	Total number of firms 企业总数	Total number of employees 职工总数	Total revenue (Mil.RMB) 总销售收入（百万元）	Total profit (Mil.RMB) 总利润（百万元）	Return on assets 资产利润率（%）	Return on equity 权益利润率（%）	Labour productivity ('000 RMB/ worker) 劳动生产率（千元/人）	Debts/ assets 资产负债率（%）	Total assets (Mil.RMB) 总资产（百万元）
Industry Overall 行业总体	405	46,854	5,069	61	1.07	2.72	39.52	60.76	5,663

	Number of firms 企业个数	Average number of employees 平均职工人数	Average revenue ('000 RMB) 平均销售收入（千元）	Average profit ('000 RMB) 平均利润（千元）	Return on assets 资产利润率（%）	Return on equity 权益利润率（%）	Labour productivity ('000 RMB/ worker) 劳动生产率（千元/人）	Debts/ assets 资产负债率（%）	Average total assets ('000 RMB) 平均总资产（千元）
By ownership 产业所有权									
State-owned 国有	189	73	2,629	-75	-1.25	-8.52	13.13	85.29	5,963
Collective-owned 集体	29	105	16,300	1,589	18.15	44.20	44.55	58.94	8,754
Foreign & Overseas Chinese Funded 三资	86	198	33,797	71	0.19	0.40	67.13	51.89	37,317
By regional distribution 地区分布									
Central-North 华北	98	122	14,652	422	2.53	4.97	46.03	49.07	16,704
Beijing 北京	36	167	27,569	779	2.68	4.73	65.96	43.29	29,074
Tianjin 天津	14	134	5,769	413	4.92	15.40	19.94	68.08	8,391
Hebei 河北	25	104	12,503	355	2.63	5.24	29.97	49.89	13,534
Shanxi 山西	20	49	1,803	-138	-2.71	-19.07	28.01	85.80	5,085
Inner Mongolia 内蒙古	3	155	4,660	482	4.41	7.75	20.66	43.08	10,934
Northeast 东北	27	119	9,731	-1	-0.01	-0.06	27.52	76.35	8,470
Liaoning 辽宁	10	55	11,155	243	3.15	5.66	69.90	44.42	7,738
Jilin 吉林	7	199	9,927	-498	-3.98		15.04	122.29	12,494
Heilongjiang 黑龙江	10	128	8,171	102	1.60	3.33	23.03	52.12	6,386
Central-East 华东	109	155	19,625	186	0.90	2.44	48.14	63.09	20,603
Shanghai 上海	41	205	28,149	-4	-0.02	-0.04	58.65	65.45	26,966
Jiangsu 江苏	18	117	19,885	487	3.02	4.85	54.63	37.81	16,158
Zhejiang 浙江	13	193	21,149	623	3.77	8.81	40.29	57.17	16,513
Anhui 安徽									
Fujian 福建	9	104	10,011	327	1.73	2.79	33.87	37.86	18,879
Jiangxi 江西	9	97	3,888	-52	-0.86	-2.44	12.73	64.66	6,001
Shandong 山东	19	111	11,951	56	0.26	2.15	30.11	87.96	21,613
Central-South 中南	85	96	9,308	-34	-0.37	-0.97	28.30	62.32	9,202
Henan 河南	25	68	4,428	300	8.06	34.92	24.44	76.93	3,726
Hubei 湖北	11	110	4,456	-112	-1.75	-5.65	19.64	69.00	6,369
Hunan 湖南	12	84	5,189	156	3.87	10.31	10.30	62.43	4,029
Guangdong 广东	26	144	20,781	-414	-1.98	-4.66	39.27	57.57	20,924
Guangxi 广西	8	41	1,341	-86	-5.35		9.25	121.48	1,610
Hainan 海南	3	56	6,055	147	3.21	8.35	29.98	61.58	4,573
Southwest 西南	43	92	5,457	-158	-1.68	-5.54	20.30	69.78	9,413
Chongqing 重庆	6	133	10,562	637	5.64	10.08	30.25	43.99	11,282
Sichuan 四川	5	115	16,900	692	3.71	11.60	43.74	68.03	18,667
Guizhou 贵州	9	42	937	-52	-0.75	-3.13	4.75	76.11	6,912
Yunnan 云南	18	116	4,223	-736	-8.33	-44.18	13.33	81.14	8,837
Tibet 西藏	5	23	464	-69	-1.54	-3.56	11.62	56.80	4,487
Northwest 西北	43	62	4,780	199	2.35	9.67	32.96	75.72	8,477
Shaanxi 陕西	12	90	6,108	418	4.06	30.47	32.39	86.67	10,290
Gansu 甘肃	20	47	1,930	-83	-2.24	-6.22	20.06	64.02	3,727
Qinghai 青海	1	27	880	8	0.20	0.63	13.81	67.79	3,912
Ningxia 宁夏	2	84	7,959	477	3.20	11.17	50.36	71.36	14,890
Xinjiang 新疆	8	59	9,604	531	3.20	11.99	54.82	73.33	16,601

1412: Pastry 糕点业

Year 年份	Number of firms 企业个数	Rate of change 变化率 (%)	Number of employees 职工人数 (人)	Rate of change 变化率 (%)	Total revenue (Mil. RMB) 总销售收入 (百万元)	Rate of change 变化率 (%)	Total profit (Mil RMB) 总利润 (百万元)	Rate of change 变化率 (%)
2000	519		58,687		4,255		88	
2001	463	-10.79	50,689	-13.63	5,169	21.48	121	37.50
2002	405	-12.53	46,854	-7.57	5,069	-1.93	61	-49.59

Major Products 主要产品	Output 产量	Unit 单位
Pastry 糕点	21	10,000 Tons 万吨

10 Main Firms with Maximal Revenue (year founded) 收入最大的十家主要企业（创办年份）	City 城市	Province 省	Telephone/fax 电话/传真	Number of employees 职工人数	Ownership 产业所有权	Revenue ('000 RMB) 销售收入 (千元)	Profit('000 RMB) (rank) 利润(千元) (排名)	Total assets ('000 RMB) 总资产 (千元)	Major products 主要产品
Orion Food Co.,Ltd.	Langfang	Hebei	(0316)6077866		Foreign Funded				Food
好丽友食品有限公司(1996)	廊坊市	河北省	(0316)6088964	207	外商投资	211,289	6,750(7)	187,582	食品
Beijing Daoxiangcun Foodstuff Machining Factory	Beijing	Beijing	(010)84648186		Collective-owned				Cake
北京稻香村食品加工厂(1999)	北京市	北京市	(010)84649397	698	集体企业	209,816	37,047(1)	132,000	糕点
Lotte (China) Foods Co.,Ltd.	Beijing	Beijing	(010)67871417		Foreign Funded				Western Style Cake
乐天（中国）食品有限公司(1995)	北京市	北京市	(010)67882014	390	外商投资	192,389	-	418,824	西式糕点
Artal Food (Guangdong) Co., Ltd.	Jiangmen	Guangdong	(0750)8821028		Overseas Chinese-funded				Chocolate
鹤山市亚太食品(广东)有限公司(1994)	江门市	广东省	(0750)8820790	500	港澳台资	186,788	-	92,858	朱古力
Shanghai Fuwang Food Co., Ltd.	Shanghai	Shanghai	(021)64061257		Foreign Funded				Cake
上海福旺食品有限公司(1993)	上海市	上海市	(021)64017775	433	外商投资	150,387	-	156,901	糕点
Shanghai Yuanzu Food Co., Ltd.	Shanghai	Shanghai	(021)65411645		Foreign Funded				Cake
上海元祖食品有限公司(1993)	上海市	上海市	(021)65146137	620	外商投资	116,473	23,950(3)	55,300	糕点
Beijing Jingri Dongda Food Co., Ltd.	Beijing	Beijing	(010)63730450		Foreign Funded				Sweetened Bean Paste Products
北京京日东大食品有限公司(1994)	北京市	北京市	(010)63736529	365	外商投资	108,596	20,046(4)	91,818	豆沙类产品
Lianyungang Hongmei Food Co., Ltd.	Lianyungang	Jiangsu	(0518)6411588		Overseas Chinese-funded				Lie Fallow Food
连云港鸿美食品有限公司(2000)	连云港市	江苏省	(0518)6415205	118	港澳台资	107,140	1,320(39)	31,700	休闲米果
Shanghai Kelisiting Food Co., Ltd.	Shanghai	Shanghai	(021)64365555		Overseas Chinese-funded				Cake
上海克莉丝汀食品有限公司(1998)	上海市	上海市	(021)64365555	892	港澳台资	99,136	3,520(16)	73,910	糕点
Mankattan Food(Beijing) Co., Ltd.	Beijing	Beijing	(010)63818887		Foreign Funded				Cake
曼可顿食品(北京)有限公司(1994)	北京市	北京市	(010)63812545	477	外商投资	85,238	-	41,909	糕点

Top 10 Cities by Revenue 销售收入排名前10位城市	Province 省	Market share 市场份额 (%)	Number of firms 企业个数
Shanghai 上海市	Shanghai 上海市	22.77	41
Beijing 北京市	Beijing 北京市	19.58	36
Langfang 廊坊市	Hebei 河北省	4.85	3
Hangzhou 杭州市	Zhejiang 浙江省	4.67	8
Jiangmen 江门市	Guangdong 广东省	3.68	1
Lianyungang 连云港市	Jiangsu 江苏省	2.42	3
Shenyang 沈阳市	Liaoning 辽宁省	2.00	7
Guangzhou 广州市	Guangdong 广东省	1.99	6
Nanjing 南京市	Jiangsu 江苏省	1.98	5
Weihai 威海市	Shandong 山东省	1.68	1

10 Major Wholesalers 十家主要批发商	City 城市	Province 省	Telephone/Fax 电话/传真
Beijing Chaoyang Non-Staple Foodstuffs General Company	Beijing	Beijing	(010)65016285
北京朝阳副食品总公司	北京市	北京市	(010)65016285
Beijing Sugar,Cigarette & Wine Company	Beijing	Beijing	(010)67210304
北京市糖业烟酒公司	北京市	北京市	(010)67210310
Shanghai Sugar Cigarette & Wine (Group) Co.,Ltd.	Shanghai	Shanghai	(021)63224190
上海市糖业烟酒(集团)有限公司	上海市	上海市	(021)63223169
Jiangsu Sutang Sugar & Wine Co.,Ltd.	Nanjing	Jiangsu	(025)6661088
江苏苏糖糖酒食品有限公司	南京市	江苏省	(025)6661088
Fujian Commerce (Group) Co.,Ltd.	Fuzhou	Fujian	(0591)7847148
福建省商业（集团）有限责任公司	福州市	福建省	(0591)7847145
Yantai Changyu Pioneer Winer Co., Ltd.	Yantai	Shandong	(0535)6602730
烟台张裕葡萄酿酒股份有限公司	烟台市	山东省	(0535)6214078
BlueRibbon Beer Sale Co.,Ltd.	Zhaoqing	Guangdong	(0758)2862322
蓝带啤酒销售有限公司	肇庆市	广东省	(0758)2862424
Fujian Shenlong Development Co.,Ltd.	Fuzhou	Fujian	(0591)7503218
福建省神龙发展股份有限公司	福州市	福建省	(0591)7503068
Guangdong Sugar, Cigarette & Wine Group Company	Guangzhou	Guangdong	(020)83566131
广东省糖烟酒集团公司	广州市	广东省	(020)83561421
Shunde Daliang Sugar, Cigarette & Wine Co.,Ltd.	Shunde	Guangdong	(0765)2231804
顺德市大良区糖烟酒有限公司	顺德市	广东省	(0765)2222300

1413: Biscuits 饼干业

The industry accounts for 0.116% of the total revenue of China's industrial sector in 2002. The rate of return on assets is 2.70%. 84.25% of all firms in the industry made a profit while 15.75% had negative returns.The top province in terms of the industry's revenue is Shanghai, accounting for 19.35% of the total revenue.
2002年本行业收入占全行业的 0.116%，资产利润率为 2.70%。84.25%的企业赢利，15.75%的企业亏损。收入最高的省为上海市，占本行业的19.35%。

	Total number of firms 企业总数	Total number of employees 职工总数	Total revenue (Mil.RMB) 总销售收入(百万元)	Total profit (Mil.RMB) 总利润(百万元)	Return on assets 资产利润率(%)	Return on equity 权益利润率(%)	Labour productivity ('000 RMB/ worker) 劳动生产率(千元/人)	Debts/ assets 资产负债率(%)	Total assets (Mil.RMB) 总资产(百万元)
Industry Overall 行业总体	273	69,846	12,469	309	2.70	6.29	51.85	57.08	11,432

	Number of firms 企业个数	Average number of employees 平均职工人数	Average revenue ('000 RMB) 平均销售收入(千元)	Average profit ('000 RMB) 平均利润(千元)	Return on assets 资产利润率(%)	Return on equity 权益利润率(%)	Labour productivity ('000 RMB/ worker) 劳动生产率(千元/人)	Debts/ assets 资产负债率(%)	Average total assets ('000 RMB) 平均总资产(千元)
By ownership 产业所有权									
State-owned 国有	39	107	8,701	-44	-0.23	-0.89	22.40	74.36	19,052
Collective-owned 集体	25	458	60,372	1,766	4.47	10.11	37.08	55.77	39,509
Foreign & Overseas Chinese Funded 三资	91	381	82,696	1,390	1.61	3.82	63.06	57.97	86,475
By regional distribution 地区分布									
Central-North 华北	37	198	48,152	-460	-1.03	-2.76	64.81	62.85	44,807
Beijing 北京	7	334	81,995	-7,180	-7.54	-21.36	35.94	64.73	95,281
Tianjin 天津	7	416	72,574	-635	-0.59	-1.63	64.22	64.06	108,251
Hebei 河北	20	91	34,771	1,884	18.95	37.26	109.80	49.16	9,942
Shanxi 山西	3	85	1,406	3	0.03	0.12	15.04	78.76	11,438
Inner Mongolia 内蒙古									
Northeast 东北	10	210	35,547	6,055	16.00	27.46	51.19	41.74	37,845
Liaoning 辽宁	4	281	47,060	11,470	24.59	28.96	41.90	15.07	46,637
Jilin 吉林	2	187	5,653	968	5.16	14.09	15.27	63.40	18,767
Heilongjiang 黑龙江	4	151	38,982	3,185	8.25	26.36	90.65	68.70	38,594
Central-East 华东	92	332	66,591	922	1.88	4.89	53.98	61.53	48,965
Shanghai 上海	16	307	150,810	3,908	4.36	9.23	110.07	52.71	89,590
Jiangsu 江苏	11	301	79,348	-9,346	-12.14	-602.53	60.76	97.98	76,968
Zhejiang 浙江	15	293	52,848	3,178	5.69	13.05	65.26	56.41	55,888
Anhui 安徽	4	243	8,877	290	7.31	14.04	12.00	47.96	3,971
Fujian 福建	12	211	26,414	1,146	5.87	10.33	31.86	43.18	19,529
Jiangxi 江西	4	80	4,127	222	7.87	12.73	13.84	38.17	2,815
Shandong 山东	30	469	55,963	2,054	5.48	11.75	37.08	53.38	37,498
Central-South 中南	117	222	32,440	1,320	3.53	7.54	47.40	53.23	37,412
Henan 河南	42	144	25,021	944	7.19	11.86	48.13	39.35	13,122
Hubei 湖北	9	166	34,534	1,409	10.84	16.52	67.47	34.36	12,995
Hunan 湖南	6	716	42,197	1,174	1.19	2.85	26.29	58.31	98,753
Guangdong 广东	54	249	39,959	1,918	3.47	7.37	53.34	52.99	55,322
Guangxi 广西	6	106	3,813	-1,420	-6.59		9.94	111.86	21,531
Hainan 海南									
Southwest 西南	16	246	25,439	1,614	5.06	8.94	41.33	43.42	31,909
Chongqing 重庆									
Sichuan 四川	11	338	36,842	2,585	5.67	9.92	44.10	42.82	45,591
Guizhou 贵州	4	35	441	-652	-28.81	-125.82	-10.67	77.10	2,262
Yunnan 云南	1	76							
Tibet 西藏									
Northwest 西北	1	43	2,535	3	0.10	0.55	14.02	82.11	3,041
Shaanxi 陕西	1	43	2,535	3	0.10	0.55	14.02	82.11	3,041
Gansu 甘肃									
Qinghai 青海									
Ningxia 宁夏									
Xinjiang 新疆									

Year 年份	Number of firms 企业个数	Rate of change 变化率 (%)	Number of employees 职工人数 (人)	Rate of change 变化率 (%)	Total revenue (Mil. RMB) 总销售收入 (百万元)	Rate of change 变化率 (%)	Total profit (Mil RMB) 总利润 (百万元)	Rate of change 变化率 (%)
2000	235		52,363		9,180		386	
2001	243	3.40	57,453	9.72	10,020	9.15	518	34.20
2002	273	12.35	69,846	21.57	12,469	24.44	309	-40.35

Major Products 主要产品	Output 产量	Unit 单位
Biscuit 饼干	69	10,000 Tons 万吨

10 Main Firms with Maximal Revenue (year founded) 收入最大的十家主要企业（创办年份）	City 城市	Province 省	Telephone/fax 电话/传真	Number of employees 职工人数	Ownership 产业所有权	Revenue ('000 RMB) 销售收入 (千元)	Profit('000 RMB) (rank) 利润(千元)(排名)	Total assets ('000 RMB) 总资产 (千元)	Major products 主要产品
Li Way Way (China) Co.,Ltd. 上好佳（中国）有限公司(2000)	Shanghai 上海市	Shanghai 上海市	(021)59766770 (021)59766797	421	Foreign Funded 外商投资	824,469	-	178,538	Biscuit 饼干
Shandong Qingyuan Foodstuff (Group) Co.,Ltd. 山东青援食品有限公司(1998)	Linyi 临沂市	Shandong 山东省	(0539)2252837 (0539)2252837	5,979	Collective-owned 集体企业	688,022	15,188(9)	306,725	Biscuit 饼干
Shanghai Danone Biscuit Foods Co.,Ltd. 上海达能饼干食品有限公司(1992)	Shanghai 上海市	Shanghai 上海市	(021)34144588 (021)64752874	1,552	Foreign Funded 外商投资	658,959	65,112(1)	424,968	Biscuit 饼干
Nabisco Food (Suzhou)Co., Ltd. 纳贝斯克食品(苏州)有限公司(1996)	Suzhou 苏州市	Jiangsu 江苏省	(0512)67617540 (0512)67612021	750	Foreign Funded 外商投资	419,100	-	422,304	Biscuit 饼干
Shanghai PepsiCo Snack Co.,Ltd. 上海百事食品有限公司(1995)	Shanghai 上海市	Shanghai 上海市	(021)59155877 (021)59155077	325	Foreign Funded 外商投资	408,844	-	150,090	Lie Fallow Food 休闲食品
Tianjin Tingyuan International Food Co.,Ltd. 天津顶园国际食品有限公司(1995)	Tianjin 天津市	Tianjin 天津市	(022)25322478 (022)25321254	2,265	Overseas Chinese-funded 港澳台资	397,095	990(83)	596,746	Rice Biscuit 米饼
HuaJia Foods Co.,Ltd. 华嘉食品有限公司(1987)	Dongguan 东莞市	Guangdong 广东省	(0769)2467239 (0769)2481731	1,162	Overseas Chinese-funded 港澳台资	338,832	46,375(2)	384,297	Biscuit 饼干
Beijing Nabjsco Food Co., Ltd. 北京纳贝斯克食品有限公司(1995)	Beijing 北京市	Beijing 北京市	(010)63541188 (010)63546988	847	Foreign Funded 外商投资	311,845	-	277,796	Food 食品
HangZhou Tingyuan Food Co.,Ltd. 杭州顶园食品有限公司(1995)	Hangzhou 杭州市	Zhejiang 浙江省	(0571)86912966 (0571)86910100	1,508	Foreign Funded 外商投资	291,933	6,332(21)	330,524	Rice Biscuit 米饼
HangZhou Want Want Foods Co., Ltd. 杭州旺旺食品有限公司(1993)	Hangzhou 杭州市	Zhejiang 浙江省	(0571)86228917 (0571)86223981	1,013	Foreign Funded 外商投资	195,697	19,386(5)	289,356	Langweixian 浪味仙

Top 10 Cities by Revenue 销售收入排名前10位城市	Province 省	Market share 市场份额 (%)	Number of firms 企业个数
Shanghai 上海市	Shanghai 上海市	19.35	16
Luohe 漯河市	Henan 河南省	6.14	18
Linyi 临沂市	Shandong 山东省	6.12	7
Guangzhou 广州市	Guangdong 广东省	5.56	13
Beijing 北京市	Beijing 北京市	4.60	7
Hangzhou 杭州市	Zhejiang 浙江省	4.11	4
Dongguan 东莞市	Guangdong 广东省	4.11	6
Tianjin 天津市	Tianjin 天津市	4.07	7
Suzhou 苏州市	Jiangsu 江苏省	3.69	4
Qingdao 青岛市	Shandong 山东省	3.10	4

10 Major Wholesalers 十家主要批发商	City 城市	Province 省	Telephone/Fax 电话/传真
Beijing Chaoyang Non-Staple Foodstuffs General Company 北京朝阳副食品总公司	Beijing 北京市	Beijing 北京市	(010)65016285 (010)65016285
Beijing Sugar,Cigarette & Wine Company 北京市糖业烟酒公司	Beijing 北京市	Beijing 北京市	(010)67210304 (010)67210310
Shanghai Sugar Cigarette & Wine (Group) Co.,Ltd. 上海市糖业烟酒(集团)有限公司	Shanghai 上海市	Shanghai 上海市	(021)63224190 (021)63223169
Jiangsu Sutang Sugar & Wine Co.,Ltd. 江苏苏糖糖酒食品有限公司	Nanjing 南京市	Jiangsu 江苏省	(025)6661088 (025)6661088
Fujian Commerce (Group) Co.,Ltd. 福建省商业（集团）有限责任公司	Fuzhou 福州市	Fujian 福建省	(0591)7847148 (0591)7847145
Yantai Changyu Pioneer Winer Co., Ltd. 烟台张裕葡萄酿酒股份有限公司	Yantai 烟台市	Shandong 山东省	(0535)6602730 (0535)6214078
BlueRibbon Beer Sale Co.,Ltd. 蓝带啤酒销售有限公司	Zhaoqing 肇庆市	Guangdong 广东省	(0758)2862322 (0758)2862424
Fujian Shenlong Development Co.,Ltd. 福建省神龙发展股份有限公司	Fuzhou 福州市	Fujian 福建省	(0591)7503218 (0591)7503068
Guangdong Sugar, Cigarette & Wine Group Company 广东省糖烟酒集团公司	Guangzhou 广州市	Guangdong 广东省	(020)83566131 (020)83561421
Shunde Daliang Sugar, Cigarette & Wine Co.,Ltd. 顺德市大良区糖烟酒有限公司	Shunde 顺德市	Guangdong 广东省	(0765)2231804 (0765)2222300

1414: Convenient Principal Food 方便主食品业

The industry accounts for 0.210% of the total revenue of China's industrial sector in 2002. The rate of return on assets is 4.57%. 73.97% of all firms in the industry made a profit while 26.03% had negative returns.The top province in terms of the industry's revenue is Henan, accounting for 14.20% of the total revenue.
2002年本行业收入占全行业的0.210%，资产利润率为4.57%。73.97%的企业赢利，26.03%的企业亏损。收入最高的省为河南省，占本行业的14.20%。

	Total number of firms 企业总数	Total number of employees 职工总数	Total revenue (Mil.RMB) 总销售收入（百万元）	Total profit (Mil.RMB) 总利润（百万元）	Return on assets 资产利润率 (%)	Return on equity 权益利润率 (%)	Labour productivity ('000 RMB/ worker) 劳动生产率（千元/人）	Debts/ assets 资产负债率 (%)	Total assets (Mil.RMB) 总资产（百万元）
Industry Overall 行业总体	292	114,930	22,552	1,086	4.57	9.87	59.42	53.71	23,777

	Number of firms 企业个数	Average number of employees 平均职工人数	Average revenue ('000 RMB) 平均销售收入（千元）	Average profit ('000 RMB) 平均利润（千元）	Return on assets 资产利润率 (%)	Return on equity 权益利润率 (%)	Labour productivity ('000 RMB/ worker) 劳动生产率（千元/人）	Debts/ assets 资产负债率 (%)	Average total assets ('000 RMB) 平均总资产（千元）
By ownership 产业所有权									
State-owned 国有	38	171	19,584	872	1.98	4.87	37.60	59.34	44,025
Collective-owned 集体	28	794	95,064	2,656	2.62	6.96	35.86	62.36	101,427
Foreign & Overseas Chinese Funded 三资	97	477	145,572	8,721	5.70	10.94	90.90	47.91	153,013
By regional distribution 地区分布									
Central-North 华北	63	433	65,383	2,713	3.02	5.69	44.60	46.89	89,742
Beijing 北京	17	253	35,595	139	0.28	0.47	34.50	41.29	50,097
Tianjin 天津	11	512	147,256	10,711	4.17	6.62	58.13	36.97	256,820
Hebei 河北	24	647	75,559	1,993	2.62	7.25	45.64	63.87	76,099
Shanxi 山西	9	104	3,238	44	0.33	0.80	15.61	58.92	13,491
Inner Mongolia 内蒙古	2	439	25,807	1,269	8.67	20.99	19.54	58.69	14,634
Northeast 东北	24	309	92,416	5,109	4.62	10.37	92.96	55.44	110,591
Liaoning 辽宁	14	323	103,856	7,432	5.24	11.39	117.57	53.98	141,783
Jilin 吉林	6	183	33,015	270	0.90	3.85	44.46	76.53	29,839
Heilongjiang 黑龙江	4	451	141,475	4,237	3.46	7.46	60.63	53.67	122,550
Central-East 华东	94	283	69,660	3,277	4.84	10.63	74.67	54.52	67,764
Shanghai 上海	21	201	37,451	-1,702	-2.32	-6.18	54.59	62.37	73,198
Jiangsu 江苏	11	489	169,170	5,444	5.36	8.39	98.89	36.09	101,584
Zhejiang 浙江	11	410	149,097	17,131	13.95	33.10	104.40	57.87	122,836
Anhui 安徽	5	227	56,199	2,585	7.14	13.14	60.47	45.68	36,230
Fujian 福建	8	177	66,424	94	0.23	0.36	178.14	35.15	40,638
Jiangxi 江西	2	287	10,098	881	8.94	16.02	10.09	44.20	9,851
Shandong 山东	36	261	39,667	2,221	4.35	11.19	45.63	61.11	51,058
Central-South 中南	83	505	83,882	3,740	4.47	10.80	47.46	58.60	83,637
Henan 河南	39	672	82,127	2,015	2.51	7.14	35.02	64.86	80,301
Hubei 湖北	10	356	122,589	6,452	6.08	10.67	97.12	43.00	106,045
Hunan 湖南	5	146	13,622	1,373	19.02	44.90	20.73	57.64	7,217
Guangdong 广东	25	415	92,733	5,826	5.89	14.14	65.73	58.33	98,882
Guangxi 广西	3	282	36,206	2,490	5.11	10.34	15.30	50.57	48,728
Hainan 海南	1	201	38,309	7,327	7.68	14.23	80.82	46.02	95,406
Southwest 西南	15	494	132,480	8,890	10.86	20.94	95.27	48.12	81,851
Chongqing 重庆	1	1,631	645,244	66,938	14.04	24.38	116.10	42.41	476,707
Sichuan 四川	10	362	107,723	6,890	11.16	21.56	127.46	48.25	61,765
Guizhou 贵州	4	541	66,183	-620	-1.86	-5.80	25.73	67.94	33,355
Yunnan 云南									
Tibet 西藏									
Northwest 西北	13	330	55,212	3,123	4.37	9.80	56.04	55.44	71,511
Shaanxi 陕西	7	542	97,711	4,512	3.59	8.00	59.64	55.12	125,739
Gansu 甘肃	2	75	8,195	-1,920	-23.22		40.45	111.07	8,268
Qinghai 青海									
Ningxia 宁夏									
Xinjiang 新疆	4	87	4,348	3,213	39.03	61.14	23.42	36.17	8,233

1414: Convenient Principal Food 方便主食品业

Year 年份	Number of firms 企业个数	Rate of change 变化率 (%)	Number of employees 职工人数 (人)	Rate of change 变化率 (%)	Total revenue (Mil. RMB) 总销售收入 (百万元)	Rate of change 变化率 (%)	Total profit (Mil RMB) 总利润 (百万元)	Rate of change 变化率 (%)
2000	311		102,823		20,034		923	
2001	298	-4.18	106,388	3.47	21,545	7.54	835	-9.53
2002	292	-2.01	114,930	8.03	22,552	4.67	1,086	30.06

Major Products 主要产品	Output 产量	Unit 单位
Instant Staple Food 方便主食品	288	10,000 Tons 万吨
Instant Noodle 方便面	182	10,000 Tons 万吨

10 Main Firms with Maximal Revenue (year founded) 收入最大的十家主要企业（创办年份）	City 城市	Province 省	Telephone/ fax 电话/传真	Number of employees 职工人数	Ownership 产业所有权	Revenue ('000 RMB) 销售收入 (千元)	Profit('000 RMB) (rank) 利润(千元) (排名)	Total assets ('000 RMB) 总资产 (千元)	Major products 主要产品
Hangzhou Tingyi International Food Co.,Ltd.	Hangzhou	Zhejiang	(0571)86910122		Overseas Chinese-funded				Instant Noodle
杭州顶益食品有限公司(1995)	杭州市	浙江省	(0571)86910119	2,512	港澳台资	1,363,514	182,572(1)	1,030,646	方便面
Tianjin Tingyi Int'l Co., Ltd.	Tianjin	Tianjin	(022)25325954		Overseas Chinese-funded				Instant Noodle
天津顶益国际食品有限公司(1992)	天津市	天津市	(022)25321734	2,588	港澳台资	1,245,761	92,870(2)	2,513,954	方便面
Hebei Hualong Food Group Co., Ltd.	Xingtai	Hebei	(0319)6591908		Private Owned				Instant Noodle
河北华龙面业集团有限公司(1994)	邢台市	河北省	(0319)6591559	8,070	私营企业	1,134,995	30,861(15)	1,000,305	方便面
Chengdu Unification Enterprise Food Co., Ltd.	Chengdu	Sichuan	(028)87334320		Overseas Chinese-funded				Instant Noodle
成都统一企业食品有限公司(1993)	成都市	四川省	(028)87347633	1,382	港澳台资	788,679	61,028(4)	406,152	方便面
Wuhan President Enterprises Food Co.,Ltd.	Wuhan	Hubei	(027)83891886		Overseas Chinese-funded				Food
武汉统一企业食品有限公司(1993)	武汉市	湖北省	(027)83892507	1,400	港澳台资	728,297	43,300(13)	366,137	食品
Chongqing DingYi Food Co.,Ltd.	Chongqing	Chongqing	(023)62826999		Overseas Chinese-funded				Instant Noodle
重庆顶益食品有限公司(1995)	重庆市	重庆市	(023)62827124	1,631	港澳台资	645,244	66,938(3)	476,707	方便面
Guangzhou President Enterpise Co.,Ltd.	Guangzhou	Guangdong	(020)82240088		Overseas Chinese-funded				Instant Noodle
广州统一企业有限公司(1996)	广州市	广东省	(020)82235768	1,200	港澳台资	571,928	26,355(17)	358,226	方便面
Guangzhou Tingyi International Food Co., Ltd.	Guangzhou	Guangdong	(020)82268331		Overseas Chinese-funded				Instant Noodle
广州顶益国际食品有限公司(1994)	广州市	广东省	(020)82269306	1,200	港澳台资	560,278	50,998(8)	586,828	方便面
Shenyang TingYi International Food Co.,Ltd.	Shenyang	Liaoning	(024)25815240		Overseas Chinese-funded				Instant Noodle
沈阳顶益国际食品有限公司(1995)	沈阳市	辽宁省	(024)25815246	784	港澳台资	549,399	54,157(6)	449,782	方便面
Henan Keii Food Group Co., Ltd.	Shangqiu	Henan	(0370)4471305		Collective-owned				Can
科迪食品集团股份有限公司(1985)	商丘市	河南省	(0370)4471193	4,950	集体企业	495,565	39,905(14)	735,494	罐头

Top 10 Cities by Revenue 销售收入排名前10位城市	Province 省	Market share 市场份额 (%)	Number of firms 企业个数
Guangzhou 广州市	Guangdong 广东省	7.39	7
Tianjin 天津市	Tianjin 天津市	7.18	11
Xingtai 邢台市	Hebei 河北省	6.91	9
Luohe 漯河市	Henan 河南省	6.61	2
Hangzhou 杭州市	Zhejiang 浙江省	6.37	5
Suzhou 苏州市	Jiangsu 江苏省	6.24	2
Shenyang 沈阳市	Liaoning 辽宁省	5.74	7
Wuhan 武汉市	Hubei 湖北省	5.15	4
Chengdu 成都市	Sichuan 四川省	4.04	4
Shanghai 上海市	Shanghai 上海市	3.49	21

10 Major Wholesalers 十家主要批发商	City 城市	Province 省	Telephone/Fax 电话/传真
Beijing Chaoyang Non-Staple Foodstuffs General Company	Beijing	Beijing	(010)65016285
北京朝阳副食品总公司	北京市	北京市	(010)65016285
Beijing Sugar,Cigarette & Wine Company	Beijing	Beijing	(010)67210304
北京市糖业烟酒公司	北京市	北京市	(010)67210310
Shanghai Sugar Cigarette & Wine (Group) Co.,Ltd.	Shanghai	Shanghai	(021)63224190
上海市糖业烟酒(集团)有限公司	上海市	上海市	(021)63223169
Jiangsu Sutang Sugar & Wine Co.,Ltd.	Nanjing	Jiangsu	(025)6661088
江苏苏糖糖酒食品有限公司	南京市	江苏省	(025)6661088
Fujian Commerce (Group) Co.,Ltd.	Fuzhou	Fujian	(0591)7847148
福建省商业（集团）有限责任公司	福州市	福建省	(0591)7847145
Yantai Changyu Pioneer Winer Co., Ltd.	Yantai	Shandong	(0535)6602730
烟台张裕葡萄酿酒股份有限公司	烟台市	山东省	(0535)6214078
BlueRibbon Beer Sale Co.,Ltd.	Zhaoqing	Guangdong	(0758)2862322
蓝带啤酒销售有限公司	肇庆市	广东省	(0758)2862424
Fujian Shenlong Development Co.,Ltd.	Fuzhou	Fujian	(0591)7503218
福建省神龙发展股份有限公司	福州市	福建省	(0591)7503068
Guangdong Sugar, Cigarette & Wine Group Company	Guangzhou	Guangdong	(020)83566131
广东省糖烟酒集团公司	广州市	广东省	(020)83561421
Shunde Daliang Sugar, Cigarette & Wine Co.,Ltd.	Shunde	Guangdong	(0765)2231804
顺德市大良区糖烟酒有限公司	顺德市	广东省	(0765)2222300

1415: Preserved Fruits 蜜饯业

The industry accounts for 0.026% of the total revenue of China's industrial sector in 2002. The rate of return on assets is 3.32%. 86.79% of all firms in the industry made a profit while 13.21% had negative returns.The top province in terms of the industry's revenue is Guangdong, accounting for 35.91% of the total revenue.
2002年本行业收入占全行业的0.026%，资产利润率为3.32%。86.79%的企业赢利，13.21%的企业亏损。收入最高的省为广东省，占本行业的35.91%。

	Total number of firms 企业总数	Total number of employees 职工总数	Total revenue (Mil.RMB) 总销售收入（百万元）	Total profit (Mil.RMB) 总利润（百万元）	Return on assets 资产利润率（%）	Return on equity 权益利润率（%）	Labour productivity ('000 RMB/ worker) 劳动生产率（千元/人）	Debts/ assets 资产负债率（%）	Total assets (Mil.RMB) 总资产（百万元）
Industry Overall 行业总体	159	20,409	2,783	102	3.32	7.50	41.28	55.67	3,066

	Number of firms 企业个数	Average number of employees 平均职工人数	Average revenue ('000 RMB) 平均销售收入（千元）	Average profit ('000 RMB) 平均利润（千元）	Return on assets 资产利润率（%）	Return on equity 权益利润率（%）	Labour productivity ('000 RMB/ worker) 劳动生产率（千元/人）	Debts/ assets 资产负债率（%）	Average total assets ('000 RMB) 平均总资产（千元）
By ownership 产业所有权									
State-owned 国有	18	46	1,739	-309	-4.89		4.00	111.61	6,327
Collective-owned 集体	29	82	14,823	727	6.66	14.35	64.04	53.60	10,919
Foreign & Overseas Chinese Funded 三资	43	91	18,676	508	2.30	5.09	59.24	54.72	22,058
By regional distribution 地区分布									
Central-North 华北	17	250	22,716	1,152	7.02	15.96	33.30	55.98	16,395
Beijing 北京	4	56	10,708	481	6.00	10.61	76.68	43.40	8,015
Tianjin 天津	1	19					-1.00	83.61	5,990
Hebei 河北	7	468	37,626	1,866	9.15	19.65	29.23	53.44	20,388
Shanxi 山西	5	147	15,992	919	4.69	12.38	39.20	62.12	19,591
Inner Mongolia 内蒙古									
Northeast 东北	1	19	16,100	20	0.09	0.20	215.26	55.56	22,401
Liaoning 辽宁	1	19	16,100	20	0.09	0.20	215.26	55.56	22,401
Jilin 吉林									
Heilongjiang 黑龙江									
Central-East 华东	53	105	20,873	1,058	6.21	14.56	66.33	57.34	17,028
Shanghai 上海									
Jiangsu 江苏	1	50	6,278	113	1.18	12.26	28.58	90.33	9,538
Zhejiang 浙江	9	56	14,306	849	5.32	10.99	64.14	51.55	15,945
Anhui 安徽									
Fujian 福建	22	96	15,403	364	2.18	4.76	54.59	54.27	16,741
Jiangxi 江西	3	274	89,093	8,260	21.12	33.07	96.69	36.13	39,109
Shandong 山东	18	117	20,282	861	5.88	21.79	67.63	73.03	14,657
Central-South 中南	74	127	16,241	329	1.36	2.97	31.70	54.11	24,166
Henan 河南	8	207	9,621	-59	-0.53		14.70	105.86	11,012
Hubei 湖北	5	173	18,097	412	4.74	6.92	37.55	31.54	8,692
Hunan 湖南	2	40	14,888	1,399	25.14	37.06	108.45	32.17	5,564
Guangdong 广东	57	118	17,531	350	1.23	2.53	34.28	51.63	28,565
Guangxi 广西	2	49	2,654	16	0.18	2.98	27.44	93.84	8,720
Hainan 海南									
Southwest 西南	4	43	3,819	13	0.19	0.44	42.94	56.16	6,551
Chongqing 重庆									
Sichuan 四川									
Guizhou 贵州	2	8	165	-67	-5.79	-271.43	42.00	97.87	1,148
Yunnan 云南	2	78	7,473	92	0.77	1.61	43.03	52.15	11,953
Tibet 西藏									
Northwest 西北	10	97	5,703	183	3.85	20.29	21.57	81.01	4,755
Shaanxi 陕西	1	558	25,800	40	0.15	5.48	11.10	97.20	26,110
Gansu 甘肃	8	46	3,836	222	9.87	26.81	38.90	63.19	2,252
Qinghai 青海									
Ningxia 宁夏	1	40	540	14	0.41	0.84	8.58	51.29	3,420
Xinjiang 新疆									

Year 年份	Number of firms 企业个数	Rate of change 变化率(%)	Number of employees 职工人数(人)	Rate of change 变化率(%)	Total revenue (Mil. RMB) 总销售收入(百万元)	Rate of change 变化率(%)	Total profit (Mil RMB) 总利润(百万元)	Rate of change 变化率(%)
2000	138		17,056		2,214		83	
2001	139	0.72	17,973	5.38	2,312	4.43	75	-9.64
2002	159	14.39	20,409	13.55	2,783	20.37	102	36.00

Major Products 主要产品	Output 产量	Unit 单位

10 Main Firms with Maximal Revenue (year founded) 收入最大的十家主要企业（创办年份）	City 城市	Province 省	Telephone/fax 电话/传真	Number of employees 职工人数	Ownership 产业所有权	Revenue ('000 RMB) 销售收入(千元)	Profit('000 RMB) (rank) 利润(千元)(排名)	Total assets ('000 RMB) 总资产(千元)	Major products 主要产品
Jiangxi Wang's Bee Garden Co.,Ltd.	Nanchang	Jiangxi	(0791)3703810		Private Owned				Honey Products
江西汪氏蜜蜂有限公司(1998)	南昌市	江西省	(0791)3702819	650	私营企业	210,000	22,523(1)	96,351	蜂产品
Xinxing Dongbou Foodstuff Industrial Co.,Ltd.	Yunfu	Guangdong	(0766)2711003		Overseas Chinese-funded				Glazed Fruit
新兴县东宝食品工业有限公司(1993)	云浮市	广东省	(0766)2711201	380	港澳台资	95,000	4,745(4)	141,890	蜜饯果脯
Guangdong Yilong Industrial Group Co., Ltd.	Chaozhou	Guangdong	(0768)6732572		Private Owned				Salted Plums
广东翼龙实业集团有限公司(1996)	潮州市	广东省	(0768)6732570	112	私营企业	64,583	3,823(7)	85,369	盐梅
Gaoming Senheyuan Food Co., Ltd.	Foshan	Guangdong	(0757)8918888		Private Owned				Cotton Candy
高明市森和园食品有限公司(1994)	佛山市	广东省	(0757)8807789	435	私营企业	63,749	1,127(25)	10,112	棉花糖
Zhangzhou Longwen District Dongfang Food Co., Ltd.	Zhangzhou	Fujian	(0596)2101928		Private Owned				Glazed Candy
漳州市龙文区东方食品有限公司(1995)	漳州市	福建省	(0596)2102928	628	私营企业	61,388	4,319(6)	46,034	蜜饯糖果
Guangdong Fenhuang Food Industrial Co., Ltd.	Chaozhou	Guangdong	(0768)5819303		Private Owned				Jelly
庵埠汾煌食品工业有限公司(1986)	潮州市	广东省	(0768)5810183	916	私营企业	59,592	2,326(13)	547,988	凉果
Zhaoyuan Huayuan Fruit Products Co., Ltd.	Yantai	Shandong	(0535)8376287		Collective-owned				Dried Fruit Products
招远市华源果制品有限责任公司(1995)	烟台市	山东省	(0535)8376668	105	集体企业	49,680	5,610(2)	1,511	干果制品
Hebei Yida Food Group Co., Ltd.	Chengde	Hebei	(0314)5370001		Private Owned				Preserved Fruit
河北怡达食品集团有限公司(2000)	承德市	河北省	(0314)5370009	1,331	私营企业	48,578	3,615(8)	93,244	果脯
Guangdong Tongxiang Food Co., Ltd.	Jieyang	Guangdong	(0663)2281889		Private Enterprises				Fruit
广东同享食品有限公司(1992)	揭阳市	广东省	(0663)2283506	100	私营独资	48,200	15(108)	12,864	果子
Guangdong Jiabao Group Co., Ltd.	Chaozhou	Guangdong	(0768)6665480		Overseas Chinese-funded				Jelly Products
潮州市佳宝集团公司(1995)	潮州市	广东省	(0768)6665132	380	港澳台资	47,596	508(47)	58,451	凉果产品

Top 10 Cities by Revenue 销售收入排名前10位城市	Province 省	Market share 市场份额 (%)	Number of firms 企业个数
Jieyang 揭阳市	Guangdong 广东省	10.07	23
Chaozhou 潮州市	Guangdong 广东省	9.84	9
Zhangzhou 漳州市	Fujian 福建省	9.36	15
Nanchang 南昌市	Jiangxi 江西省	9.10	2
Binzhou 滨州市	Shandong 山东省	6.20	9
Chengde 承德市	Hebei 河北省	5.66	2
Yantai 烟台市	Shandong 山东省	5.61	4
Yunfu 云浮市	Guangdong 广东省	5.49	5
Hangzhou 杭州市	Zhejiang 浙江省	3.98	7
Shijiazhuang 石家庄市	Hebei 河北省	3.80	5

10 Major Wholesalers 十家主要批发商	City 城市	Province 省	Telephone/Fax 电话/传真
Beijing Chaoyang Non-Staple Foodstuffs General Company	Beijing	Beijing	(010)65016285
北京朝阳副食品总公司	北京市	北京市	(010)65016285
Beijing Sugar,Cigarette & Wine Company	Beijing	Beijing	(010)67210304
北京市糖业烟酒公司	北京市	北京市	(010)67210310
Shanghai Sugar Cigarette & Wine (Group) Co.,Ltd.	Shanghai	Shanghai	(021)63224190
上海市糖业烟酒(集团)有限公司	上海市	上海市	(021)63223169
Jiangsu Sutang Sugar & Wine Co.,Ltd.	Nanjing	Jiangsu	(025)6661088
江苏苏糖糖酒食品有限公司	南京市	江苏省	(025)6661088
Fujian Commerce (Group) Co.,Ltd.	Fuzhou	Fujian	(0591)7847148
福建省商业（集团）有限责任公司	福州市	福建省	(0591)7847145
Yantai Changyu Pioneer Winer Co., Ltd.	Yantai	Shandong	(0535)6602730
烟台张裕葡萄酿酒股份有限公司	烟台市	山东省	(0535)6214078
BlueRibbon Beer Sale Co.,Ltd.	Zhaoqing	Guangdong	(0758)2862322
蓝带啤酒销售有限公司	肇庆市	广东省	(0758)2862424
Fujian Shenlong Development Co.,Ltd.	Fuzhou	Fujian	(0591)7503218
福建省神龙发展股份有限公司	福州市	福建省	(0591)7503068
Guangdong Sugar, Cigarette & Wine Group Company	Guangzhou	Guangdong	(020)83566131
广东省糖烟酒集团公司	广州市	广东省	(020)83561421
Shunde Daliang Sugar, Cigarette & Wine Co.,Ltd.	Shunde	Guangdong	(0765)2231804
顺德市大良区糖烟酒有限公司	顺德市	广东省	(0765)2222300

1419: Other Pastry and Confectionery Manufacturing

其他糕点、糖果制造业

The industry accounts for 0.006% of the total revenue of China's industrial sector in 2002. The rate of return on assets is 1.80%. 74.14% of all firms in the industry made a profit while 25.86% had negative returns.The top province in terms of the industry's revenue is Shandong, accounting for 30.90% of the total revenue.
2002年本行业收入占全行业的 0.006%，资产利润率为 1.80%。74.14%的企业赢利，25.86%的企业亏损。收入最高的省为山东省，占本行业的30.90%。

	Total number of firms 企业总数	Total number of employees 职工总数	Total revenue (Mil.RMB) 总销售收入 (百万元)	Total profit (Mil.RMB) 总利润 (百万元)	Return on assets 资产利润率 (%)	Return on equity 权益利润率 (%)	Labour productivity ('000 RMB/ worker) 劳动生产率 (千元/人)	Debts/ assets 资产负债率 (%)	Total assets (Mil.RMB) 总资产 (百万元)
Industry Overall 行业总体	58	4,850	664	14	1.80	3.65	44.60	50.65	751

	Number of firms 企业个数	Average number of employees 平均职工人数	Average revenue ('000 RMB) 平均销售收入 (千元)	Average profit ('000 RMB) 平均利润 (千元)	Return on assets 资产利润率 (%)	Return on equity 权益利润率 (%)	Labour productivity ('000 RMB/ worker) 劳动生产率 (千元/人)	Debts/ assets 资产负债率 (%)	Average total assets ('000 RMB) 平均总资产 (千元)
By ownership 产业所有权									
State-owned 国有	15	88	3,834	-235	-2.68	-8.42	14.42	68.14	8,770
Collective-owned 集体	3	70	7,368	1,778	16.21	44.12	47.78	63.27	10,971
Foreign & Overseas Chinese Funded 三资	20	60	18,570	185	0.90	1.76	87.79	48.80	20,563
By regional distribution 地区分布									
Central-North 华北	8	90	8,851	-1,599	-9.13	-16.23	13.11	43.75	17,521
Beijing 北京	2	179	10,968	373	1.42	2.39	21.10	40.56	26,261
Tianjin 天津	4	62	9,492	-3,510	-17.50	-33.60	-3.13	47.91	20,052
Hebei 河北	2	57	5,450	250	6.72	8.55	23.38	21.37	3,720
Shanxi 山西									
Inner Mongolia 内蒙古									
Northeast 东北	1	20	171	-295	-1.65	-2.01	1.05	18.30	17,926
Liaoning 辽宁									
Jilin 吉林									
Heilongjiang 黑龙江	1	20	171	-295	-1.65	-2.01	1.05	18.30	17,926
Central-East 华东	16	122	18,181	1,501	9.31	27.67	51.59	66.35	16,119
Shanghai 上海	2	33	6,715	542	8.52	21.70	76.00	60.73	6,361
Jiangsu 江苏	4	95	6,013	-125	-1.22		14.83	142.11	10,266
Zhejiang 浙江									
Anhui 安徽	2	85	4,157	242	7.48	12.84	15.02	41.72	3,228
Fujian 福建	2	125	19,973	5,639	22.14	24.35	74.43	9.09	25,473
Jiangxi 江西									
Shandong 山东	6	181	34,192	1,945	7.95	23.81	63.52	66.59	24,454
Central-South 中南	22	68	11,676	107	0.97	1.67	60.91	42.02	11,045
Henan 河南	5	32	20,058	594	3.53	4.83	184.63	26.87	16,803
Hubei 湖北	3	102	7,572	347	3.66	4.07	23.50	10.11	9,475
Hunan 湖南	2	44	12,383	312	6.12	15.74	82.99	61.10	5,087
Guangdong 广东	7	57	13,392	-270	-1.87	-4.18	55.81	55.39	14,454
Guangxi 广西	1	70	600	-241	-5.21	-18.09	2.69	71.19	4,624
Hainan 海南	4	118	3,692	-39	-1.08	-4.53	52.59	76.22	3,645
Southwest 西南	5	80	7,617	75	0.72	1.12	24.61	35.49	10,321
Chongqing 重庆									
Sichuan 四川	4	101	9,521	93	0.72	1.12	24.61	35.49	12,902
Guizhou 贵州									
Yunnan 云南									
Tibet 西藏	1								
Northwest 西北	6	45	1,163	-23	-0.34	-0.86	20.31	60.16	6,666
Shaanxi 陕西	1	28	368	-103	-4.44		5.93	103.84	2,320
Gansu 甘肃	4	56	1,643	-9	-0.10	-0.24	23.36	58.73	8,754
Qinghai 青海									
Ningxia 宁夏									
Xinjiang 新疆	1	15	37	1	0.04	0.06	1.53	40.84	2,659

1419: Other Pastry and Confectionery Manufacturing

其他糕点、糖果制造业

Year 年份	Number of firms 企业个数	Rate of change 变化率 (%)	Number of employees 职工人数 (人)	Rate of change 变化率 (%)	Total revenue (Mil. RMB) 总销售收入 (百万元)	Rate of change 变化率 (%)	Total profit (Mil RMB) 总利润 (百万元)	Rate of change 变化率 (%)
2000	77		8,871		1,263		96	
2001	70	-9.09	7,164	-19.24	795	-37.05	19	-80.21
2002	58	-17.14	4,850	-32.30	664	-16.48	14	-26.32

Major Products 主要产品	Output 产量	Unit 单位
Candy 糖果	46	10,000 Tons 万吨
Pastry 糕点	21	10,000 Tons 万吨

10 Main Firms with Maximal Revenue (year founded) 收入最大的十家主要企业（创办年份）	City 城市	Province 省	Telephone/fax 电话/传真	Number of employees 职工人数	Ownership 产业所有权	Revenue ('000 RMB) 销售收入 (千元)	Profit('000 RMB) (rank) 利润(千元)(排名)	Total assets ('000 RMB) 总资产 (千元)	Major products 主要产品
Green Market Qingdao Giftmaker Co., Ltd.	Qingdao	Shandong	(0532)4810900		Foreign Funded				Condiment
青岛格林玛特礼品有限公司(1998)	青岛市	山东省	(0532)4821181	230	外商投资	91,728	6,201(2)	37,739	调味品
Dexiang Food Co., Ltd.	Luohe	Henan	(0395)8889649		Overseas Chinese-funded				Niuniu Food妞妞
德祥食品有限公司(2000)	漯河市	河南省	(0395)8890098	80	港澳台资	43,265	1,465(9)	31,456	膨化食品
Zibo Minyue Food Co., Ltd.	Zibo	Shandong	(0533)3242330		Private Enterprises				Preserved Fruit
淄博民悦食品有限公司(1987)	淄博市	山东省	(0533)3420301	420	私营独资	33,190	2,080(7)	27,290	果脯
Puning Shangpin Enterprise Food Co., Ltd.	Jieyang	Guangdong	(0663)2761198		Overseas Chinese-funded				Kazhi Food
普宁市尚品企业食品有限公司(1993)	揭阳市	广东省	(0663)2761208	20	港澳台资	32,900	-	23,850	咔吱食品
Qingdao CALLBEE Foods Co.,ltd.	Qingdao	Shandong	(0532)4825678		Foreign Funded				Shrimp Cracks
青岛卡乐比食品有限公司(1997)	青岛市	山东省	(0532)4825077	100	外商投资	32,282	3,503(5)	53,677	虾条
Fuzhou Want &Want Foods Co.,Ltd.	Fuzhou	Fujian	(0591)3509586		Foreign Funded				Small Steamed Bun
福州旺旺食品有限公司(1995)	福州市	福建省	(0591)3509603	209	外商投资	25,512	5,017(4)	39,565	小馒头
Weifang Huarong Food Co., Ltd.	Weifang	Shandong	(0536)8313457		Private Enterprises				Cake
潍坊华荣食品有限公司(1953)	潍坊市	山东省		210	私营独资	22,897	-	12,171	糕点
Xinhui Duruan Huachang Food Factory	Jiangmen	Guangdong	(0750)3676937		Private Enterprises				Dried Fruit
新会市杜阮华昌干果厂(1999)	江门市	广东省	(0750)3676937	17	私营独资	20,606	2,670(6)	13,970	干果
Qingdao Weimei Foods Co.,Ltd.	Qingdao	Shandong	(0532)5652145		Foreign Funded				Dried Vegetables
青岛味美食品有限公司(1990)	青岛市	山东省	(0532)5648285	45	外商投资	20,403	-	9,894	干燥蔬菜
Hunan Zhangjiajie Jiutian Food Co., Ltd.	Zhangjiajie	Hunan	(0744)6222648		Limited-Liability				Potherb
湖南张家界九天食品有限责任公司(1998)	张家界市	湖南省	(0744)6222646	58	有限公司	19,426	503(15)	8,081	野菜

Top 10 Cities by Revenue 销售收入排名前10位城市	Province 省	Market share 市场份额 (%)	Number of firms 企业个数
Qingdao 青岛市	Shandong 山东省	21.76	3
Luohe 漯河市	Henan 河南省	15.11	4
Tianjin 天津市	Tianjin 天津市	5.72	4
Zibo 淄博市	Shandong 山东省	5.00	1
Jieyang 揭阳市	Guangdong 广东省	4.96	1
Fuzhou 福州市	Fujian 福建省	3.84	1
Chengdu 成都市	Sichuan 四川省	3.83	3
Shantou 汕头市	Guangdong 广东省	3.50	2
Weifang 潍坊市	Shandong 山东省	3.45	1
Beijing 北京市	Beijing 北京市	3.30	2

10 Major Wholesalers 十家主要批发商	City 城市	Province 省	Telephone/Fax 电话/传真
Beijing Chaoyang Non-Staple Foodstuffs General Company	Beijing	Beijing	(010)65016285
北京朝阳副食品总公司	北京市	北京市	(010)65016285
Beijing Sugar,Cigarette & Wine Company	Beijing	Beijing	(010)67210304
北京市糖业烟酒公司	北京市	北京市	(010)67210310
Shanghai Sugar Cigarette & Wine (Group) Co.,Ltd.	Shanghai	Shanghai	(021)63224190
上海市糖业烟酒(集团)有限公司	上海市	上海市	(021)63223169
Jiangsu Sutang Sugar & Wine Co.,Ltd.	Nanjing	Jiangsu	(025)6661088
江苏苏糖糖酒食品有限公司	南京市	江苏省	(025)6661088
Fujian Commerce (Group) Co.,Ltd.	Fuzhou	Fujian	(0591)7847148
福建省商业（集团）有限责任公司	福州市	福建省	(0591)7847145
Yantai Changyu Pioneer Winer Co., Ltd.	Yantai	Shandong	(0535)6602730
烟台张裕葡萄酿酒股份有限公司	烟台市	山东省	(0535)6214078
BlueRibbon Beer Sale Co.,Ltd.	Zhaoqing	Guangdong	(0758)2862322
蓝带啤酒销售有限公司	肇庆市	广东省	(0758)2862424
Fujian Shenlong Development Co.,Ltd.	Fuzhou	Fujian	(0591)7503218
福建省神龙发展股份有限公司	福州市	福建省	(0591)7503068
Guangdong Sugar, Cigarette & Wine Group Company	Guangzhou	Guangdong	(020)83566131
广东省糖烟酒集团公司	广州市	广东省	(020)83561421
Shunde Daliang Sugar, Cigarette & Wine Co.,Ltd.	Shunde	Guangdong	(0765)2231804
顺德市大良区糖烟酒有限公司	顺德市	广东省	(0765)2222300

1420: Dairy Products 乳制品制造业

The industry accounts for 0.324% of the total revenue of China's industrial sector in 2002. The rate of return on assets is 7.18%. 75.75% of all firms in the industry made a profit while 24.25% had negative returns.The top province in terms of the industry's revenue is Heilong Jiang, accounting for 16.84% of the total revenue.
2002年本行业收入占全行业的0.324%，资产利润率为7.18%。75.75%的企业赢利，24.25%的企业亏损。收入最高的省为黑龙江省，占本行业的16.84%。

	Total number of firms 企业总数	Total number of employees 职工总数	Total revenue (Mil.RMB) 总销售收入（百万元）	Total profit (Mil.RMB) 总利润（百万元）	Return on assets 资产利润率（%）	Return on equity 权益利润率（%）	Labour productivity ('000 RMB/ worker) 劳动生产率（千元/人）	Debts/ assets 资产负债率（%）	Total assets (Mil.RMB) 总资产（百万元）
Industry Overall 行业总体	499	121,589	34,748	2,373	7.18	14.95	89.71	51.96	33,046

	Number of firms 企业个数	Average number of employees 平均职工人数	Average revenue ('000 RMB) 平均销售收入（千元）	Average profit ('000 RMB) 平均利润（千元）	Return on assets 资产利润率（%）	Return on equity 权益利润率（%）	Labour productivity ('000 RMB/ worker) 劳动生产率（千元/人）	Debts/ assets 资产负债率（%）	Average total assets ('000 RMB) 平均总资产（千元）
By ownership 产业所有权									
State-owned 国有	74	190	32,927	854	1.92	6.37	49.80	69.83	44,423
Collective-owned 集体	36	111	25,420	1,043	4.18	12.23	73.38	65.82	24,948
Foreign & Overseas Chinese Funded 三资	58	324	163,620	16,300	9.99	17.96	188.08	44.37	163,149
By regional distribution 地区分布									
Central-North 华北	128	303	97,485	6,275	7.62	14.37	100.27	47.01	82,391
Beijing 北京	21	274	72,957	4,073	4.44	11.74	97.67	62.20	91,757
Tianjin 天津	15	116	42,119	314	0.60	1.36	143.35	56.13	52,613
Hebei 河北	46	308	101,414	8,205	12.87	21.23	82.90	39.39	63,777
Shanxi 山西	16	142	23,649	1,609	4.72	11.98	61.60	60.61	34,096
Inner Mongolia 内蒙古	30	495	175,690	10,323	7.12	12.29	118.69	42.06	145,023
Northeast 东北	72	257	90,322	6,353	7.27	19.00	124.84	61.72	87,343
Liaoning 辽宁	12	182	49,804	3,127	3.98	8.89	66.68	55.25	78,639
Jilin 吉林	6	127	9,188	205	0.80	2.41	20.93	66.84	25,659
Heilongjiang 黑龙江	54	288	108,341	7,753	8.07	21.65	138.11	62.74	96,131
Central-East 华东	146	219	69,239	5,248	7.93	15.19	90.45	47.80	66,179
Shanghai 上海	15	508	263,968	26,504	10.01	16.40	149.27	38.96	264,717
Jiangsu 江苏	31	221	67,206	4,113	6.84	11.51	87.03	40.54	60,115
Zhejiang 浙江	37	173	28,533	1,613	5.08	12.48	37.84	59.33	31,780
Anhui 安徽	9	321	26,349	275	0.68	1.64	18.38	58.54	40,562
Fujian 福建	10	118	39,719	4,809	5.73	12.31	89.94	53.45	83,902
Jiangxi 江西	7	245	44,363	2,265	5.00	11.60	58.43	56.87	45,259
Shandong 山东	37	142	55,821	3,109	10.17	32.39	123.77	68.60	30,570
Central-South 中南	49	267	59,686	4,643	7.06	15.16	69.58	53.40	65,731
Henan 河南	14	170	20,611	511	2.21	4.67	30.06	52.75	23,130
Hubei 湖北	7	294	30,585	-158	-0.42	-1.13	26.80	62.75	37,628
Hunan 湖南	7	396	83,284	9,503	9.48	19.85	72.88	52.25	100,251
Guangdong 广东	15	302	116,262	11,223	9.40	19.82	120.10	52.60	119,450
Guangxi 广西	5	233	15,760	-630	-2.71	-6.01	29.43	54.96	23,286
Hainan 海南	1	180	16,217	-10,261	-43.36	-78.44	19.48	44.72	23,662
Southwest 西南	26	301	39,948	1,793	3.56	8.11	46.91	56.12	50,423
Chongqing 重庆	4	376	71,499	6,432	7.37	19.00	56.65	61.20	87,232
Sichuan 四川	14	179	27,662	735	1.98	4.09	71.70	51.61	37,141
Guizhou 贵州	2	1,120	47,482	1,225	1.68	4.03	9.77	58.20	72,763
Yunnan 云南	5	315	54,041	1,620	2.74	6.38	51.40	57.13	59,215
Tibet 西藏	1	15	216	62	12.40	12.40	8.47		500
Northwest 西北	78	147	21,723	924	3.58	9.51	47.36	62.41	25,859
Shaanxi 陕西	36	179	25,370	1,045	4.16	9.45	37.49	56.03	25,152
Gansu 甘肃	19	91	11,487	352	2.02	5.34	46.94	62.10	17,373
Qinghai 青海	3	66	4,871	-86	-0.56	-1.30	28.43	57.17	15,518
Ningxia 宁夏	11	148	34,886	1,887	4.54	19.23	106.74	76.39	41,552
Xinjiang 新疆	9	164	18,273	811	2.63	6.82	28.00	61.47	30,867

Year 年份	Number of firms 企业个数	Rate of change 变化率(%)	Number of employees 职工人数(人)	Rate of change 变化率(%)	Total revenue (Mil. RMB) 总销售收入(百万元)	Rate of change 变化率(%)	Total profit (Mil RMB) 总利润(百万元)	Rate of change 变化率(%)
2000	377		91,477		19,346		838	
2001	434	15.12	110,410	20.70	27,189	40.54	1,712	104.30
2002	499	14.98	121,589	10.12	34,748	27.80	2,373	38.61

Major Products 主要产品	Output 产量	Unit 单位
Dairy Products 乳制品	93	10,000 Tons 万吨

10 Main Firms with Maximal Revenue (year founded) 收入最大的十家主要企业（创办年份）	City 城市	Province 省	Telephone/fax 电话/传真	Number of employees 职工人数	Ownership 产业所有权	Revenue ('000 RMB) 销售收入(千元)	Profit('000 RMB) (rank) 利润(千元)(排名)	Total assets ('000 RMB) 总资产(千元)	Major products 主要产品
Shijiazhuang Sanlu Group Co.,Ltd.	Shijiazhuang	Hebei	(0311)7044184		Joint Stock				Dried Milk
石家庄三鹿集团股份有限公司(1956)	石家庄市	河北省	(0311)8615365	5,714	股份制	3,073,562	244,253(2)	1,667,777	奶粉
Shanghai Bright Dairy & Food Co.,Ltd.	Shanghai	Shanghai	(021)54584520		Overseas Chinese-funded				Liquid Milk
上海光明乳业股份有限公司(1997)	上海市	上海市	(021)64655033	3,025	港澳台资	2,125,026	185,527(3)	2,446,342	液体乳
Nestle Shuangcheng Co., Ltd.	Harbin	Heilongjiang	(0451)3123734		Foreign Funded				Dairy Products
双城雀巢有限公司(1990)	哈尔滨市	黑龙江省	(0451)3123712	557	外商投资	1,819,641	389,372(1)	1,077,410	乳制品
Wonder Sun Dairy Co., Ltd.	Harbin	Heilongjiang	(0451)82341887		Joint Stock				Dried Milk
黑龙江省完达山乳业股份有限公司(1996)	哈尔滨市	黑龙江省	(0451)82343776	3,866	股份制	1,064,670	51,350(9)	761,400	奶粉
Beijing Sanyuan Food Co.,Ltd.	Beijing	Beijing	(010)64031310		Foreign Funded				Milk Products
北京三元食品股份有限公司(1997)	北京市	北京市	(010)64005995	3,232	外商投资	972,809	78,307(8)	1,244,288	奶制品
International Nutrition Co.,Ltd.	Shanghai	Shanghai	(021)58990899		Foreign Funded				Dairy Products
英特儿营养乳品有限公司(1995)	上海市	上海市	(021)58995155	556	外商投资	687,460	122,748(6)	494,644	乳制品
Meadjohison(Guangzhou)Co.,Ltd.	Guangzhou	Guangdong	(020)82219180		Foreign Funded				Dairy Products
美赞臣（广州）有限公司(1993)	广州市	广东省	(020)82211277	147	外商投资	524,439	112,832(7)	459,296	乳制品
Wendeng Jinyang Milk Products (Group) Co., Ltd.	Weihai	Shandong	(0631)8681188		Joint Stock				Dairy Products
文登市金洋乳品（集团）有限公司(1995)	威海市	山东省	(0631)8681030	377	股份制	439,000	32,820(16)	74,710	乳制品
Heilongjiang Bright Pine Crane Milk Products Co., Ltd.	Qiqihar	Heilongjiang	(0452)3123888		State Enterprises				Dairy Products
黑龙江省光明松鹤乳品有限责任公司(1996)	齐齐哈尔市	黑龙江省	(0452)3136576	1,033	国有独资	383,992	8,102(50)	372,733	乳制品
Hunan Yahua Seed Enterprise Co., Ltd. Nanshan Green Food Company	Shaoyang	Hunan	(0739)7382138		Joint Stock				Dairy Products
湖南亚华种业股份有限公司南山绿色食品公司(1998)	邵阳市	湖南省	(0739)7380878	882	股份制	337,828	35,018(14)	302,841	乳制品

Top 10 Cities by Revenue 销售收入排名前10位城市	Province 省	Market share 市场份额(%)	Number of firms 企业个数
Huhhot 呼和浩特市	Inner Mongolia 内蒙古	13.72	7
Shanghai 上海市	Shanghai 上海市	11.40	15
Shijiazhuang 石家庄市	Hebei 河北省	10.55	10
Harbin 哈尔滨市	Heilongjiang 黑龙江省	10.33	10
Beijing 北京市	Beijing 北京市	4.41	21
Guangzhou 广州市	Guangdong 广东省	3.36	8
Qiqihar 齐齐哈尔市	Heilongjiang 黑龙江省	2.85	13
Suzhou 苏州市	Jiangsu 江苏省	2.49	5
Qingdao 青岛市	Shandong 山东省	2.44	7
Weihai 威海市	Shandong 山东省	1.97	4

10 Major Wholesalers 十家主要批发商	City 城市	Province 省	Telephone/Fax 电话/传真
Beijing Chaoyang Non-Staple Foodstuffs General Company	Beijing	Beijing	(010)65016285
北京朝阳副食品总公司	北京市	北京市	(010)65016285
Beijing Sugar,Cigarette & Wine Company	Beijing	Beijing	(010)67210304
北京市糖业烟酒公司	北京市	北京市	(010)67210310
Shanghai Sugar Cigarette & Wine (Group) Co.,Ltd.	Shanghai	Shanghai	(021)63224190
上海市糖业烟酒(集团)有限公司	上海市	上海市	(021)63223169
Jiangsu Sutang Sugar & Wine Co.,Ltd.	Nanjing	Jiangsu	(025)6661088
江苏苏糖糖酒食品有限公司	南京市	江苏省	(025)6661088
Fujian Commerce (Group) Co.,Ltd.	Fuzhou	Fujian	(0591)7847148
福建省商业（集团）有限责任公司	福州市	福建省	(0591)7847145
Yantai Changyu Pioneer Winer Co., Ltd.	Yantai	Shandong	(0535)6602730
烟台张裕葡萄酿酒股份有限公司	烟台市	山东省	(0535)6214078
BlueRibbon Beer Sale Co.,Ltd.	Zhaoqing	Guangdong	(0758)2862322
蓝带啤酒销售有限公司	肇庆市	广东省	(0758)2862424
Fujian Shenlong Development Co.,Ltd.	Fuzhou	Fujian	(0591)7503218
福建省神龙发展股份有限公司	福州市	福建省	(0591)7503068
Guangdong Sugar, Cigarette & Wine Group Company	Guangzhou	Guangdong	(020)83566131
广东省糖烟酒集团公司	广州市	广东省	(020)83561421
Shunde Daliang Sugar, Cigarette & Wine Co.,Ltd.	Shunde	Guangdong	(0765)2231804
顺德市大良区糖烟酒有限公司	顺德市	广东省	(0765)2222300

1431: Canned Meat 肉类罐头制造业

The industry accounts for 0.017% of the total revenue of China's industrial sector in 2002. The rate of return on assets is 0.38%. 77.59% of all firms in the industry made a profit while 22.41% had negative returns.The top province in terms of the industry's revenue is Sichuan, accounting for 25.56% of the total revenue.
2002年本行业收入占全行业的 0.017%，资产利润率为 0.38%。77.59%的企业赢利，22.41%的企业亏损。收入最高的省为四川省，占本行业的25.56%。

	Total number of firms 企业总数	Total number of employees 职工总数	Total revenue (Mil.RMB) 总销售收入 (百万元)	Total profit (Mil.RMB) 总利润 (百万元)	Return on assets 资产利润率 (%)	Return on equity 权益利润率 (%)	Labour productivity ('000 RMB/ worker) 劳动生产率 (千元/人)	Debts/ assets 资产负债率 (%)	Total assets (Mil.RMB) 总资产 (百万元)
Industry Overall 行业总体	58	13,707	1,784	11	0.38	0.92	27.90	59.21	2,966

	Number of firms 企业个数	Average number of employees 平均职工人数	Average revenue ('000 RMB) 平均销售收入 (千元)	Average profit ('000 RMB) 平均利润 (千元)	Return on assets 资产利润率 (%)	Return on equity 权益利润率 (%)	Labour productivity ('000 RMB/ worker) 劳动生产率 (千元/人)	Debts/ assets 资产负债率 (%)	Average total assets ('000 RMB) 平均总资产 (千元)
By ownership 产业所有权									
State-owned 国有	7	205	4,004	-3,899	-8.91		2.63	132.44	43,748
Collective-owned 集体	4	64	8,169	241	2.46	7.19	37.87	65.81	9,813
Foreign & Overseas Chinese Funded 三资	13	256	58,274	1,824	3.33	8.59	46.99	61.29	54,825
By regional distribution 地区分布									
Central-North 华北	7	301	23,399	-2,677	-5.57	-17.52	11.07	68.21	48,040
Beijing 北京	2	437	7,169	-3,183	-16.12	-20.09	7.99	19.73	19,743
Tianjin 天津	1	16						105.15	96,392
Hebei 河北	2	282	14,282	-4,886	-16.65	-80.81	-0.59	79.39	29,340
Shanxi 山西	1	34	650				7.35	217.06	10,152
Inner Mongolia 内蒙古	1	623	120,240	-2,599	-1.98	-3.25	26.40	39.21	131,574
Northeast 东北	3	459	21,531	-255	-0.86		19.19	206.50	29,749
Liaoning 辽宁									
Jilin 吉林	1	68	1,695	200	3.48	4.11	16.32	15.37	5,745
Heilongjiang 黑龙江	2	655	31,450	-482	-1.15		19.34	219.65	41,752
Central-East 华东	17	204	41,598	1,516	1.66	2.57	47.74	35.30	91,154
Shanghai 上海	3	404	150,462	8,376	1.94	2.85	78.30	32.00	431,455
Jiangsu 江苏	6	239	23,599	-301	-1.37	-3.83	20.51	64.32	22,038
Zhejiang 浙江	1	79	12,680	921	4.85	11.14	31.38	56.50	19,000
Anhui 安徽									
Fujian 福建	2	95	8,085	625	5.65	7.44	46.18	24.00	11,046
Jiangxi 江西									
Shandong 山东	5	109	17,067	55	0.34	0.55	54.31	38.68	16,385
Central-South 中南	13	244	17,863	-599	-1.43		16.97	103.07	41,829
Henan 河南	6	302	22,066	1,159	3.94	64.73	21.00	93.91	29,391
Hubei 湖北	2	91	2,932	4	0.19	0.25	29.12	23.78	2,063
Hunan 湖南	2	323	4,917	-26	-1.10	-4.76	4.14	76.94	2,370
Guangdong 广东	3	178	28,044	-4,901	-4.10		14.65	108.84	119,524
Guangxi 广西									
Hainan 海南									
Southwest 西南	16	218	38,035	780	2.86	6.06	32.23	52.88	27,286
Chongqing 重庆	4	209	34,379	1,295	5.47	14.86	19.54	63.21	23,691
Sichuan 四川	11	206	41,449	745	2.56	5.31	41.27	51.87	29,126
Guizhou 贵州									
Yunnan 云南	1	383	15,111	-897	-4.19	-5.39	6.51	22.30	21,421
Tibet 西藏									
Northwest 西北	2	52	3,720	104	2.01	3.26	13.67	38.55	5,185
Shaanxi 陕西									
Gansu 甘肃	2	52	3,720	104	2.01	3.26	13.67	38.55	5,185
Qinghai 青海									
Ningxia 宁夏									
Xinjiang 新疆									

1431: Canned Meat 肉类罐头制造业

Year 年份	Number of firms 企业个数	Rate of change 变化率 (%)	Number of employees 职工人数 (人)	Rate of change 变化率 (%)	Total revenue (Mil. RMB) 总销售收入 (百万元)	Rate of change 变化率 (%)	Total profit (Mil RMB) 总利润 (百万元)	Rate of change 变化率 (%)
2000	53		19,006		1,328		22	
2001	47	-11.32	12,280	-35.39	1,194	-10.09	40	81.82
2002	58	23.40	13,707	11.62	1,784	49.41	11	-72.50

Major Products 主要产品	Output 产量	Unit 单位
Can 罐头	223	10,000 Tons 万吨

10 Main Firms with Maximal Revenue (year founded) 收入最大的十家主要企业（创办年份）	City 城市	Province 省	Telephone/fax 电话/传真	Number of employees 职工人数	Ownership 产业所有权	Revenue ('000 RMB) 销售收入 (千元)	Profit('000 RMB) (rank) 利润(千元) (排名)	Total assets ('000 RMB) 总资产 (千元)	Major products 主要产品
Shanghai Maling Food Co.,Ltd.	Shanghai	Shanghai	(021)65667788		Overseas Chinese-funded				Can
上海梅林食品有限公司(1992)	上海市	上海市	(021)65663576	919	港澳台资	343,019	17,138(1)	225,761	罐头
Chengdu Xiwang Food Co., Ltd.	Chengdu	Sichuan	(028)82430118		Foreign Funded				Ham Sausage
成都希望食品有限公司(1993)	成都市	四川省	(028)82552688	338	外商投资	190,376	8,800(2)	91,426	火腿肠
Sichuan Meining Food Co., Ltd.	Suining	Sichuan	(0825)2637393		Private Owned				Food Can
四川省美宁食品有限公司(2001)	遂宁市	四川省	(0825)2635700	670	私营企业	124,060	3,505(4)	60,743	食品罐头
North-China Shuanghui Food Co.,Ltd.	Wulanchabu	InnerMongolia	(0474)8288899		Limited-Liability				Ham Sausage
华北双汇食品有限公司(1997)	乌兰察布	内蒙古	(0474)8284878	623	有限公司	120,240	-	131,574	火腿肠
Shanghai Plum Forest Zhengguanghe Stock Co., Ltd.	Shanghai	Shanghai	(021)65411993		Joint Stock				Can
上海梅林正广和股份有限公司(1997)	上海市	上海市	(021)65452699	223	股份制	84,343	7,045(3)	1,056,405	罐头
Chongqing Jinzhou Food Co.,Ltd.	Chongqing	Chongqing	(023)42732868		Private Owned				Canned Pork猪
重庆金州食品有限公司(1994)	重庆市	重庆市	(023)42731289	284	私营企业	58,402	1,233(9)	34,422	肉午餐肉
Haerbin Songjiang Can Factory	Harbin	Heilongjiang	(0451)2402430		Joint Owned				Canned Meat
哈尔滨松江罐头厂(1935)	哈尔滨市	黑龙江省	(0451)2430592	1,252	联营企业	55,419	-	79,244	肉类罐头
Jiangsu Rugao Changsheng Food Canned Co., Ltd.	Nantong	Jiangsu	(0513)7659965		Private Owned				Food Can
如皋市长生食品罐头有限公司(2001)	南通市	江苏省	(0513)7659965	794	私营企业	51,347	-	43,892	食品罐头
Qingzhou Gaoli Food Co.,Ltd.	Weifang	Shandong	(0536)3203780		Foreign Funded				Steak Can
青州高丽食品有限公司(1995)	潍坊市	山东省	(0536)3203780	84	外商投资	42,500	2,200(8)	13,743	牛排罐头
Chongqing Winsun Foodstuff Co.,Ltd.	Chongqing	Chongqing	(023)42889888		Private Owned				Canned Meat
重庆市永生食品有限公司(1984)	重庆市	重庆市	(023)42889888	300	私营企业	35,976	3,126(5)	38,446	肉类罐头

Top 10 Cities by Revenue 销售收入排名前10位城市	Province 省	Market share 市场份额 (%)	Number of firms 企业个数
Shanghai 上海市	Shanghai 上海市	25.31	3
Chengdu 成都市	Sichuan 四川省	12.42	2
Chongqing 重庆市	Chongqing 重庆市	7.71	4
Zhoukou 周口市	Henan 河南省	7.14	5
Suining 遂宁市	Sichuan 四川省	6.95	1
Wulanchabu 乌兰察布盟	Inner Mongolia 内蒙古	6.74	1
Nantong 南通市	Jiangsu 江苏省	5.55	3
Harbin 哈尔滨市	Heilongjiang 黑龙江省	3.11	1
Weifang 潍坊市	Shandong 山东省	2.99	2
Foshan 佛山市	Guangdong 广东省	2.49	1

10 Major Wholesalers 十家主要批发商	City 城市	Province 省	Telephone/Fax 电话/传真
Beijing Chaoyang Non-Staple Foodstuffs General Company	Beijing	Beijing	(010)65016285
北京朝阳副食品总公司	北京市	北京市	(010)65016285
Beijing Sugar,Cigarette & Wine Company	Beijing	Beijing	(010)67210304
北京市糖业烟酒公司	北京市	北京市	(010)67210310
Shanghai Sugar Cigarette & Wine (Group) Co.,Ltd.	Shanghai	Shanghai	(021)63224190
上海市糖业烟酒(集团)有限公司	上海市	上海市	(021)63223169
Jiangsu Sutang Sugar & Wine Co.,Ltd.	Nanjing	Jiangsu	(025)6661088
江苏苏糖糖酒食品有限公司	南京市	江苏省	(025)6661088
Fujian Commerce (Group) Co.,Ltd.	Fuzhou	Fujian	(0591)7847148
福建省商业（集团）有限责任公司	福州市	福建省	(0591)7847145
Yantai Changyu Pioneer Winer Co., Ltd.	Yantai	Shandong	(0535)6602730
烟台张裕葡萄酿酒股份有限公司	烟台市	山东省	(0535)6214078
BlueRibbon Beer Sale Co.,Ltd.	Zhaoqing	Guangdong	(0758)2862322
蓝带啤酒销售有限公司	肇庆市	广东省	(0758)2862424
Fujian Shenlong Development Co.,Ltd.	Fuzhou	Fujian	(0591)7503218
福建省神龙发展股份有限公司	福州市	福建省	(0591)7503068
Guangdong Sugar, Cigarette & Wine Group Company	Guangzhou	Guangdong	(020)83566131
广东省糖烟酒集团公司	广州市	广东省	(020)83561421
Shunde Daliang Sugar, Cigarette & Wine Co.,Ltd.	Shunde	Guangdong	(0765)2231804
顺德市大良区糖烟酒有限公司	顺德市	广东省	(0765)2222300

1433: Canned Seafood 水产罐头制造业

The industry accounts for 0.013% of the total revenue of China's industrial sector in 2002. The rate of return on assets is 0.55%. 74.19% of all firms in the industry made a profit while 25.81% had negative returns.The top province in terms of the industry's revenue is Guangdong, accounting for 85.00% of the total revenue.
2002年本行业收入占全行业的 0.013%，资产利润率为 0.55%。74.19%的企业赢利，25.81%的企业亏损。收入最高的省为广东省，占本行业的85.00%。

	Total number of firms 企业总数	Total number of employees 职工总数	Total revenue (Mil.RMB) 总销售收入 (百万元)	Total profit (Mil.RMB) 总利润 (百万元)	Return on assets 资产利润率 (%)	Return on equity 权益利润率 (%)	Labour productivity ('000 RMB/ worker) 劳动生产率 (千元/人)	Debts/ assets 资产负债率 (%)	Total assets (Mil.RMB) 总资产 (百万元)
Industry Overall 行业总体	31	10,066	1,442	10	0.55	1.32	34.64	58.74	1,849

	Number of firms 企业个数	Average number of employees 平均职工人数	Average revenue ('000 RMB) 平均销售收入 (千元)	Average profit ('000 RMB) 平均利润 (千元)	Return on assets 资产利润率 (%)	Return on equity 权益利润率 (%)	Labour productivity ('000 RMB/ worker) 劳动生产率 (千元/人)	Debts/ assets 资产负债率 (%)	Average total assets ('000 RMB) 平均总资产 (千元)
By ownership 产业所有权									
State-owned 国有	6	283	35,455	-5,020	-3.21	-7.95	17.43	59.58	156,303
Collective-owned 集体	1	62	18,109	4,266	111.85	169.69	59.47	34.08	3,814
Foreign & Overseas Chinese Funded 三资	13	382	60,439	749	1.71	4.16	42.95	58.89	43,813
By regional distribution 地区分布									
Central-North 华北	2	196	7,464	-65	-0.44	-1.36	-3.40	67.33	14,571
Beijing 北京									
Tianjin 天津	1	50	7,969	-129	-1.10	-5.92	-48.86	81.41	11,726
Hebei 河北									
Shanxi 山西									
Inner Mongolia 内蒙古	1	342	6,958				3.25	57.85	17,416
Northeast 东北	2	181	6,104	-55	-0.29	-0.65	45.33	55.96	19,295
Liaoning 辽宁	1	49	6,560	-140	-0.64	-0.83	90.00	22.73	21,855
Jilin 吉林									
Heilongjiang 黑龙江	1	313	5,647	30	0.18	28.57	38.34	99.37	16,734
Central-East 华东	8	174	22,886	44	0.20	0.80	52.72	75.24	22,139
Shanghai 上海	1	8	158	-38	-8.12		-5.00	1,898.93	468
Jiangsu 江苏	1	400	51,558	-1,973	-2.64	-4.28	101.81	38.22	74,617
Zhejiang 浙江	3	67	20,194	673	5.99	29.04	54.22	79.37	11,227
Anhui 安徽									
Fujian 福建									
Jiangxi 江西	1	330	5,800	180	5.99	10.78	5.35	44.46	3,005
Shandong 山东	2	225	32,496	82	0.25		44.18	103.75	32,670
Central-South 中南	19	417	64,820	526	0.62	1.44	32.86	56.83	84,455
Henan 河南									
Hubei 湖北	1	70	1,408				9.24	81.70	24,519
Hunan 湖南									
Guangdong 广东	17	456	72,093	594	0.64	1.48	33.39	56.47	92,289
Guangxi 广西	1	102	4,603	-93	-0.83	-1.74	8.77	52.29	11,206
Hainan 海南									
Southwest 西南									
Chongqing 重庆									
Sichuan 四川									
Guizhou 贵州									
Yunnan 云南									
Tibet 西藏									
Northwest 西北									
Shaanxi 陕西									
Gansu 甘肃									
Qinghai 青海									
Ningxia 宁夏									
Xinjiang 新疆									

1433: Canned Seafood 水产罐头制造业

Year 年份	Number of firms 企业个数	Rate of change 变化率 (%)	Number of employees 职工人数 (人)	Rate of change 变化率 (%)	Total revenue (Mil. RMB) 总销售收入 (百万元)	Rate of change 变化率 (%)	Total profit (Mil RMB) 总利润 (百万元)	Rate of change 变化率 (%)
2000	18		4,813		619		6	
2001	28	55.56	10,031	108.41	1,586	156.22	26	333.33
2002	31	10.71	10,066	0.35	1,442	-9.08	10	-61.54

Major Products 主要产品	Output 产量	Unit 单位
Can 罐头	223	10,000 Tons 万吨

10 Main Firms with Maximal Revenue (year founded) 收入最大的十家主要企业（创办年份）	City 城市	Province 省	Telephone/fax 电话/传真	Number of employees 职工人数	Ownership 产业所有权	Revenue ('000 RMB) 销售收入 (千元)	Profit('000 RMB) (rank) 利润(千元) (排名)	Total assets ('000 RMB) 总资产 (千元)	Major products 主要产品
Jingfa Food Industry (Jiedong) Co.,Ltd.	Jieyang	Guangdong	(0663)3268544		Overseas Chinese-funded				Food Can
进发食品工业(揭东)有限公司(2000)	揭阳市	广东省	(0663)3263388	980	港澳台资	211,172	4,581(4)	169,200	食品罐头
Jieyang Rex Food Co.,Ltd.	Jieyang	Guangdong	(0663)3267166		Foreign Funded				Tunny Can
揭阳市丽仕食品有限公司(1995)	揭阳市	广东省	(0663)3266998	1,648	外商投资	196,208	4,669(3)	85,786	金枪鱼罐头
Chaoyang Qiaofeng Group Co., Ltd.	Shantou	Guangdong	(0661)6680666		Limited-Liability				Aquatic Products
潮阳市侨丰集团有限公司(1995)	汕头市	广东省	(0661)6681666	1,200	有限公司	107,863	8,589(2)	62,179	水产品
Guangdong Ganzhu Can Co.,Ltd.	Foshan	Guangdong	(0765)7382205		Private Owned				Fish Can
广东甘竹罐头有限公司(1989)	佛山市	广东省	(0765)7681565	831	私营企业	87,958	4,140(6)	51,382	鱼类罐头
Shunde Pingroun Food Development Co., Ltd.	Foshan	Guangdong	(0765)5565205		Overseas Chinese-funded				Roasted Eel Food
顺德屏荣食品发展有限公司(1994)	佛山市	广东省	(0765)5568698	224	港澳台资	85,946	-	44,721	烤鳗鱼食品
Shunde Yuehua Canned Food Co., Ltd.	Foshan	Guangdong	(0765)8383623		Private Owned				Canned fish
顺德市粤花罐头食品有限公司(1995)	佛山市	广东省	(0765)8986460	210	私营企业	70,087	1,248(9)	50,303	罐头鱼
Shunde Longchang Roasted Eel Co.,Ltd.	Foshan	Guangdong	(0765)7776260		Overseas Chinese-funded				Roasted Eel
顺德龙昌烤鳗有限公司(1994)	佛山市	广东省	(0765)7776210	125	港澳台资	65,661	-	51,220	烤鳗
Zhenxiang Food Co., Ltd.	Suzhou	Jiangsu	(0512)67526675		Overseas Chinese-funded				Food
祯祥食品有限公司(1997)	苏州市	江苏省	(0512)67520271	400	港澳台资	51,558	-	74,617	食品
Shandong Juxian Shanfu Foodstuff Co., Ltd	Rizhao	Shandong	(0633)6222778		State-owned				Can
山东莒县山孚食品有限公司(1988)	日照市	山东省		260	国有企业	38,186	9(20)	38,495	罐头
Guangdong Flesh Food Co., Ltd.	Shanwei	Guangdong	(0660)8230811		Private Owned				Canned fish
广东福来喜食品有限公司(1995)	汕尾市	广东省	(0660)8238700	156	私营企业	36,698	-	87,162	罐头鱼

Top 10 Cities by Revenue 销售收入排名前10位城市	Province 省	Market share 市场份额 (%)	Number of firms 企业个数
Jieyang 揭阳市	Guangdong 广东省	30.40	3
Foshan 佛山市	Guangdong 广东省	21.48	4
Guangzhou 广州市	Guangdong 广东省	11.20	1
Shantou 汕头市	Guangdong 广东省	7.48	1
Zhongshan 中山市	Guangdong 广东省	4.23	2
Zhaoqing 肇庆市	Guangdong 广东省	3.81	2
Suzhou 苏州市	Jiangsu 江苏省	3.58	1
Ningbo 宁波市	Zhejiang 浙江省	2.84	1
Rizhao 日照市	Shandong 山东省	2.65	1
Yunfu 云浮市	Guangdong 广东省	2.57	1

10 Major Wholesalers 十家主要批发商	City 城市	Province 省	Telephone/Fax 电话/传真
Beijing Chaoyang Non-Staple Foodstuffs General Company	Beijing	Beijing	(010)65016285
北京朝阳副食品总公司	北京市	北京市	(010)65016285
Beijing Sugar,Cigarette & Wine Company	Beijing	Beijing	(010)67210304
北京市糖业烟酒公司	北京市	北京市	(010)67210310
Shanghai Sugar Cigarette & Wine (Group) Co.,Ltd.	Shanghai	Shanghai	(021)63224190
上海市糖业烟酒(集团)有限公司	上海市	上海市	(021)63223169
Jiangsu Sutang Sugar & Wine Co.,Ltd.	Nanjing	Jiangsu	(025)6661088
江苏苏糖糖酒食品有限公司	南京市	江苏省	(025)6661088
Fujian Commerce (Group) Co.,Ltd.	Fuzhou	Fujian	(0591)7847148
福建省商业（集团）有限责任公司	福州市	福建省	(0591)7847145
Yantai Changyu Pioneer Winer Co., Ltd.	Yantai	Shandong	(0535)6602730
烟台张裕葡萄酿酒股份有限公司	烟台市	山东省	(0535)6214078
BlueRibbon Beer Sale Co.,Ltd.	Zhaoqing	Guangdong	(0758)2862322
蓝带啤酒销售有限公司	肇庆市	广东省	(0758)2862424
Fujian Shenlong Development Co.,Ltd.	Fuzhou	Fujian	(0591)7503218
福建省神龙发展股份有限公司	福州市	福建省	(0591)7503068
Guangdong Sugar, Cigarette & Wine Group Company	Guangzhou	Guangdong	(020)83566131
广东省糖烟酒集团公司	广州市	广东省	(020)83561421
Shunde Daliang Sugar, Cigarette & Wine Co.,Ltd.	Shunde	Guangdong	(0765)2231804
顺德市大良区糖烟酒有限公司	顺德市	广东省	(0765)2222300

1434: Canned Fruits 水果罐头制造业

The industry accounts for 0.027% of the total revenue of China's industrial sector in 2002. The rate of return on assets is 3.59%. 75.18% of all firms in the industry made a profit while 24.82% had negative returns.The top province in terms of the industry's revenue is Zhejiang, accounting for 43.26% of the total revenue.
2002年本行业收入占全行业的0.027%，资产利润率为3.59%。75.18%的企业赢利，24.82%的企业亏损。收入最高的省为浙江省，占本行业的43.26%。

	Total number of firms 企业总数	Total number of employees 职工总数	Total revenue (Mil.RMB) 总销售收入（百万元）	Total profit (Mil.RMB) 总利润（百万元）	Return on assets 资产利润率（%）	Return on equity 权益利润率（%）	Labour productivity ('000 RMB/ worker) 劳动生产率（千元/人）	Debts/ assets 资产负债率（%）	Total assets (Mil.RMB) 总资产（百万元）
Industry Overall 行业总体	141	43,788	2,849	158	3.59	21.47	18.06	83.27	4,398

	Number of firms 企业个数	Average number of employees 平均职工人数	Average revenue ('000 RMB) 平均销售收入（千元）	Average profit ('000 RMB) 平均利润（千元）	Return on assets 资产利润率（%）	Return on equity 权益利润率（%）	Labour productivity ('000 RMB/ worker) 劳动生产率（千元/人）	Debts/ assets 资产负债率（%）	Average total assets ('000 RMB) 平均总资产（千元）
By ownership 产业所有权									
State-owned 国有	34	357	13,422	47	0.12		11.26	111.16	38,906
Collective-owned 集体	18	300	30,636	1,246	7.55	27.45	29.30	72.49	16,497
Foreign & Overseas Chinese Funded 三资	34	216	18,230	240	1.09	5.48	23.18	80.15	22,054
By regional distribution 地区分布									
Central-North 华北	13	213	15,853	191	0.55		14.21	116.41	34,575
Beijing 北京	1	50	8,293	-2,339	-10.41		-133.38	131.99	22,477
Tianjin 天津	3	51	2,100	117	0.42	4.37	-31.80	90.28	27,460
Hebei 河北	7	295	26,642	568	1.19		23.68	124.47	47,660
Shanxi 山西	2	250	2,500	250	4.55	7.08	3.86	35.82	5,500
Inner Mongolia 内蒙古									
Northeast 东北	7	157	15,666	463	2.52	6.17	32.99	59.21	18,389
Liaoning 辽宁	7	157	15,666	463	2.52	6.17	32.99	59.21	18,389
Jilin 吉林									
Heilongjiang 黑龙江									
Central-East 华东	59	430	30,349	2,267	4.86	23.71	18.66	79.49	46,607
Shanghai 上海									
Jiangsu 江苏	2	174	8,139	-235	-1.93	-8.79	44.82	78.07	12,166
Zhejiang 浙江	30	567	41,086	4,556	6.97	26.87	15.93	74.06	65,382
Anhui 安徽	4	286	8,420	-293	-1.28		21.91	124.47	22,845
Fujian 福建									
Jiangxi 江西	2	378	12,564	168	0.83	2.31	8.12	63.87	20,098
Shandong 山东	21	291	22,996	-79	-0.26	-2.86	25.45	90.88	30,116
Central-South 中南	53	262	13,664	359	1.85	10.09	16.68	81.69	19,450
Henan 河南	4	85	7,877	653	13.56	19.51	33.48	30.49	4,818
Hubei 湖北	9	415	20,946	338	3.29		14.66	139.11	10,279
Hunan 湖南	11	429	19,637	637	2.98	16.58	17.64	82.05	21,403
Guangdong 广东	7	111	8,395	354	8.30	17.13	16.96	51.56	4,268
Guangxi 广西	21	194	10,900	206	0.69	2.88	16.88	76.09	29,997
Hainan 海南	1	233	508	-433	-1.82	-10.30	0.78	82.37	23,850
Southwest 西南	2	27	2,248	3	0.10	0.36	31.36	72.75	2,536
Chongqing 重庆									
Sichuan 四川	1	53	4,496	5	0.18		31.36	113.00	2,793
Guizhou 贵州	1							23.43	2,279
Yunnan 云南									
Tibet 西藏									
Northwest 西北	7	88	2,019	-76	-1.56	-18.65	13.85	91.62	4,892
Shaanxi 陕西	1	467	7,493				7.54	163.68	8,358
Gansu 甘肃	4	19	661	-24	-3.17	-5.68	53.34	44.16	741
Qinghai 青海									
Ningxia 宁夏									
Xinjiang 新疆	2	38	1,998	-221	-1.92	-6.75	13.14	71.49	11,462

1434: Canned Fruits 水果罐头制造业

Year 年份	Number of firms 企业个数	Rate of change 变化率 (%)	Number of employees 职工人数 (人)	Rate of change 变化率 (%)	Total revenue (Mil. RMB) 总销售收入 (百万元)	Rate of change 变化率 (%)	Total profit (Mil RMB) 总利润 (百万元)	Rate of change 变化率 (%)
2000	157		46,305		2,559		54	
2001	146	-7.01	32,551	-29.70	2,396	-6.37	39	-27.78
2002	141	-3.42	43,788	34.52	2,849	18.91	158	305.13

Major Products 主要产品	Output 产量	Unit 单位
Can 罐头	223	10,000 Tons 万吨

10 Main Firms with Maximal Revenue (year founded) 收入最大的十家主要企业（创办年份）	City 城市	Province 省	Telephone/fax 电话/传真	Number of employees 职工人数	Ownership 产业所有权	Revenue ('000 RMB) 销售收入 (千元)	Profit('000 RMB) (rank) 利润(千元) (排名)	Total assets ('000 RMB) 总资产 (千元)	Major products 主要产品
Ningbo Wuzhouxing (Group) Co.,Ltd.	Ningbo	Zhejiang	(0574)88436827		Limited-Liability				Canned Fruit
宁波五洲星（集团）有限公司(1997)	宁波市	浙江省	(0574)88436777	1,244	有限公司	162,253	19,059(2)	382,232	水果罐头
Jinhua Iceman Food Co., Ltd.	Jinhua	Zhejiang	(0579)2342281		Private Owned				Can
金华爱斯曼食品有限公司(1997)	金华市	浙江省	(0579)2341718	1,417	私营企业	162,101	4,178(7)	121,960	罐头
Hongxin Food Co., Ltd.	Suizhou	Hubei	(0722)4811281		Collective-owned				Food
洪新食品有限公司(1998)	随州市	湖北省	(0722)4811281	1,406	集体企业	82,396	1,510(20)	15,375	食品
Yantai Dayuan Foodstuff Co., Ltd.	Yantai	Shandong	(0535)8472016		Collective-owned				Freezing Vegetables
烟台大远食品有限公司(1986)	烟台市	山东省	(0535)8472119	390	集体企业	71,910	3,753(8)	20,000	冷冻蔬菜
Hunan Lameizi Food Co.,Ltd.	Yiyang	Hunan	(0737)2721568		Limited-Liability				Lameizi Thick Chilli Paste辣
湖南洞庭食品有限责任公司(1997)	益阳市	湖南省	(0737)2721668	460	有限公司	71,160	6,468(3)	77,034	妹子辣酱
Lipu Canned Food Factory	Guilin	Guangxi	(0773)7235585		State-owned				Can
荔浦县罐头食品厂(1981)	桂林市	广西		396	国有企业	67,540	2,215(14)	95,580	罐头
Ninghai Dongda Food Co., Ltd.	Ningbo	Zhejiang	(0574)65116639		Private Owned				Sweet Water Orange
宁海县东达食品有限公司(1995)	宁波市	浙江省	(0574)65116658	800	私营企业	59,432	3,257(10)	43,673	糖水桔子
Zhejiang Yueqing Canned General Cannery	Wenzhou	Zhejiang	(0577)62313529		State-owned				Can
乐清市罐头总厂(1958)	温州市	浙江省	(0577)62312096	1,367	国有企业	57,445	1,518(19)	66,355	罐头
Zhejiang Xinchang Best Food Co., Ltd.	Shaoxing	Zhejiang	(0575)6120706		Foreign Funded				Can
浙江新昌百思得食品有限公司(1999)	绍兴市	浙江省	(0575)6120703	341	外商投资	46,190	4,626(5)	57,130	罐头
Ningbo Wuling Taihsin Foods Co.,Ltd.	Ningbo	Zhejiang	(0574)88850233		Overseas Chinese-funded				Canned Fruit
宁波武岭泰新食品有限公司(1991)	宁波市	浙江省	(0574)88850828	521	港澳台资	41,856	276(53)	38,343	水果罐头

Top 10 Cities by Revenue 销售收入排名前10位城市	Province 省	Market share 市场份额 (%)	Number of firms 企业个数
Ningbo 宁波市	Zhejiang 浙江省	19.26	16
Taizhou 台州市	Zhejiang 浙江省	13.57	8
Yantai 烟台市	Shandong 山东省	8.38	6
Jinhua 金华市	Zhejiang 浙江省	5.69	1
Baoding 保定市	Hebei 河北省	4.44	4
Guilin 桂林市	Guangxi 广西	4.02	8
Linyi 临沂市	Shandong 山东省	3.52	8
Yulin 玉林市	Guangxi 广西	2.97	5
Suizhou 随州市	Hubei 湖北省	2.89	1
Huanggang 黄冈市	Hubei 湖北省	2.87	3

10 Major Wholesalers 十家主要批发商	City 城市	Province 省	Telephone/Fax 电话/传真
Beijing Chaoyang Non-Staple Foodstuffs General Company	Beijing	Beijing	(010)65016285
北京朝阳副食品总公司	北京市	北京市	(010)65016285
Beijing Sugar,Cigarette & Wine Company	Beijing	Beijing	(010)67210304
北京市糖业烟酒公司	北京市	北京市	(010)67210310
Shanghai Sugar Cigarette & Wine (Group) Co.,Ltd.	Shanghai	Shanghai	(021)63224190
上海市糖业烟酒(集团)有限公司	上海市	上海市	(021)63223169
Jiangsu Sutang Sugar & Wine Co.,Ltd.	Nanjing	Jiangsu	(025)6661088
江苏苏糖糖酒食品有限公司	南京市	江苏省	(025)6661088
Fujian Commerce (Group) Co.,Ltd.	Fuzhou	Fujian	(0591)7847148
福建省商业（集团）有限责任公司	福州市	福建省	(0591)7847145
Yantai Changyu Pioneer Winer Co., Ltd.	Yantai	Shandong	(0535)6602730
烟台张裕葡萄酿酒股份有限公司	烟台市	山东省	(0535)6214078
BlueRibbon Beer Sale Co.,Ltd.	Zhaoqing	Guangdong	(0758)2862322
蓝带啤酒销售有限公司	肇庆市	广东省	(0758)2862424
Fujian Shenlong Development Co.,Ltd.	Fuzhou	Fujian	(0591)7503218
福建省神龙发展股份有限公司	福州市	福建省	(0591)7503068
Guangdong Sugar, Cigarette & Wine Group Company	Guangzhou	Guangdong	(020)83566131
广东省糖烟酒集团公司	广州市	广东省	(020)83561421
Shunde Daliang Sugar, Cigarette & Wine Co.,Ltd.	Shunde	Guangdong	(0765)2231804
顺德市大良区糖烟酒有限公司	顺德市	广东省	(0765)2222300

1435: Canned Vegetable 蔬菜罐头制造业

The industry accounts for 0.051% of the total revenue of China's industrial sector in 2002. The rate of return on assets is 2.24%. 78.34% of all firms in the industry made a profit while 21.66% had negative returns.The top province in terms of the industry's revenue is Fujian, accounting for 37.70% of the total revenue.
2002年本行业收入占全行业的0.051%，资产利润率为2.24%。78.34%的企业赢利，21.66%的企业亏损。收入最高的省为福建省，占本行业的37.70%。

	Total number of firms 企业总数	Total number of employees 职工总数	Total revenue (Mil.RMB) 总销售收入（百万元）	Total profit (Mil.RMB) 总利润（百万元）	Return on assets 资产利润率（%）	Return on equity 权益利润率（%）	Labour productivity ('000 RMB/ worker) 劳动生产率（千元/人）	Debts/ assets 资产负债率（%）	Total assets (Mil.RMB) 总资产（百万元）
Industry Overall 行业总体	217	39,582	5,462	151	2.24	8.00	35.59	71.94	6,724

	Number of firms 企业个数	Average number of employees 平均职工人数	Average revenue ('000 RMB) 平均销售收入（千元）	Average profit ('000 RMB) 平均利润（千元）	Return on assets 资产利润率（%）	Return on equity 权益利润率（%）	Labour productivity ('000 RMB/ worker) 劳动生产率（千元/人）	Debts/ assets 资产负债率（%）	Average total assets ('000 RMB) 平均总资产（千元）
By ownership 产业所有权									
State-owned 国有	27	161	21,990	51	0.13	0.42	47.30	69.13	39,445
Collective-owned 集体	17	118	13,014	504	4.61	14.33	37.80	67.79	10,917
Foreign & Overseas Chinese Funded 三资	67	211	23,961	358	1.64	4.40	26.36	62.80	21,834
By regional distribution 地区分布									
Central-North 华北	13	409	23,278	483	1.97	5.64	14.24	65.00	24,468
Beijing 北京									
Tianjin 天津	2	85	10,540	380	2.47	7.73	9.47	68.05	15,385
Hebei 河北	1	300	30,000	-790	-1.06	-2.76	24.42	61.45	74,264
Shanxi 山西	10	484	25,153	630	2.96	8.65	13.77	65.79	21,305
Inner Mongolia 内蒙古									
Northeast 东北	4	104	14,651	411	4.18	6.80	37.21	38.51	9,817
Liaoning 辽宁	3	104	17,424	547	4.38	7.15	46.80	38.80	12,510
Jilin 吉林									
Heilongjiang 黑龙江	1	104	6,332				8.45	32.22	1,738
Central-East 华东	143	169	23,033	391	1.89	5.76	32.83	67.24	20,726
Shanghai 上海									
Jiangsu 江苏	8	201	22,526	89	0.52	1.19	20.07	56.53	17,125
Zhejiang 浙江	39	73	14,705	558	4.30	11.26	39.16	61.85	12,997
Anhui 安徽	12	98	11,097	240	1.82	6.65	26.96	72.63	13,185
Fujian 福建	64	210	32,174	411	1.53	4.37	36.47	64.95	26,863
Jiangxi 江西	8	189	4,466	-776	-3.08	-99.39	13.01	96.90	25,150
Shandong 山东	12	299	26,003	875	4.35	15.91	30.18	72.65	20,112
Central-South 中南	22	154	10,696	229	1.50	2.68	24.50	44.19	15,320
Henan 河南	4	58	5,651	552	10.19	15.50	70.84	34.29	5,417
Hubei 湖北									
Hunan 湖南	9	130	4,376	173	2.41	6.08	9.73	60.27	7,156
Guangdong 广东	6	172	21,524	282	0.97	1.40	45.05	31.19	29,196
Guangxi 广西	2	414	17,622	-693	-2.12	-5.97	8.50	64.45	32,670
Hainan 海南	1	118	8,938	977	9.35	21.74	12.90	56.99	10,449
Southwest 西南	11	149	8,563	205	1.24	3.06	20.79	59.40	16,518
Chongqing 重庆	1	229	21,385	252	0.87	2.08	43.55	58.32	29,073
Sichuan 四川	5	193	10,966	365	4.62	13.93	13.70	66.80	7,893
Guizhou 贵州	3	42	1,758	-105	-1.02	-1.85	16.54	44.95	10,344
Yunnan 云南	2	162	6,350	248	0.60	1.58	27.47	61.70	41,067
Tibet 西藏									
Northwest 西北	24	194	61,570	3,321	2.76	15.38	87.53	82.03	120,152
Shaanxi 陕西									
Gansu 甘肃	1	50	4,160	200	5.70	11.05	22.46	48.43	3,510
Qinghai 青海									
Ningxia 宁夏	1	159						154.98	22,198
Xinjiang 新疆	22	202	66,979	3,613	2.78	15.04	91.40	81.51	129,907

1435: Canned Vegetable 蔬菜罐头制造业

Year 年份	Number of firms 企业个数	Rate of change 变化率 (%)	Number of employees 职工人数 (人)	Rate of change 变化率 (%)	Total revenue (Mil. RMB) 总销售收入 (百万元)	Rate of change 变化率 (%)	Total profit (Mil RMB) 总利润 (百万元)	Rate of change 变化率 (%)
2000	204		42,390		3,441		-85	
2001	219	7.35	38,184	-9.92	4,416	28.33	-74	12.94
2002	217	-0.91	39,582	3.66	5,462	23.69	151	-

Major Products 主要产品	Output 产量	Unit 单位
Can 罐头	223	10,000 Tons 万吨

10 Main Firms with Maximal Revenue (year founded) 收入最大的十家主要企业 (创办年份)	City 城市	Province 省	Telephone/fax 电话/传真	Number of employees 职工人数	Ownership 产业所有权	Revenue ('000 RMB) 销售收入 (千元)	Profit('000 RMB) (rank) 利润(千元) (排名)	Total assets ('000 RMB) 总资产 (千元)	Major products 主要产品
Xinjiang Tunhe Investment Co., Ltd Kaize Tomato Products Branch	Bayinguoleng	Xinjiang	(0996)6622371		Limited-Liability				Canned Food
新疆屯河投资股份有限公司凯泽番茄制品分公司(1990)	巴音郭楞州	新疆	(0996)6622022	269	有限公司	270,687	6,620(6)	267,022	罐头食品
Xinjiang Tunhe Investment Co.,Ltd.Changtong Tomato Products Branch	Changji	Xinjiang	(0994)2280946		Limited-Liability				Tomato Ketchup
新疆屯河投资股份有限公司昌通番茄制品分公司(1995)	昌吉州	新疆	(0994)2280946	235	有限公司	226,395	31,212(2)	252,525	番茄酱
Xiamen Canned Factory	Xiamen	Fujian	(0592)2220743		State-owned				Can
厦门罐头厂(1954)	厦门市	福建省	(0592)2205943	1,515	国有企业	214,054	11,158(4)	268,112	罐头
Fujian Jinfa Industrial Co.,Ltd.	Zhangzhou	Fujian	(0596)6766729		Overseas Chinese-funded				Mushroom Can
福建进发实业有限公司(2000)	漳州市	福建省	(0596)6766779	443	港澳台资	145,662	2,294(12)	132,698	蘑菇罐头
FuJian Zhangzhou Gangchang Canned Foods Co., Ltd.	Zhangzhou	Fujian	(0596)2122688		Overseas Chinese-funded				Can
福建漳州市港昌罐头食品有限公司(1996)	漳州市	福建省	(0596)2122701	750	港澳台资	119,199	1,503(29)	62,240	罐头
Fujian Yuxing Fruit & Vegetable Food Exploitation Co.,Ltd.	Zhangzhou	Fujian	(0596)2106438		Private Owned				Mushroom Can
福建裕兴果蔬食品开发有限公司(1992)	漳州市	福建省	(0596)2102688	839	私营企业	105,116	1,231(35)	81,982	蘑菇罐头
Jinfa Food Industry (Longhai)Co., Ltd.	Zhangzhou	Fujian	(0596)6766245		Overseas Chinese-funded				Mushroom Can
进发食品工业(龙海)有限公司(1995)	漳州市	福建省	(0596)6766294	310	港澳台资	104,764	1,855(19)	120,636	蘑菇罐头
Xinjiang Tunhe Investment Co.,Ltd. Kelin Tomato Products Branch	Shihezi	Xinjiang	(0993)2611721		Limited-Liability				Tomato Ketchup Can番
新疆中河投资股份有限公司科林番茄制品分公司(1995)	石河子市	新疆	(0993)2611058	175	有限公司	80,587	-	157,854	茄酱罐头
Xinjiang Tunhe Investment Co.,Ltd. Heshuo Tomato Products Branch	Bayinguoleng	Xinjiang	(0996)5621471		Limited-Liability				Canned Tomato
新疆屯河投资股份有限公司和硕番茄制品分公司(1998)	巴音郭楞州	新疆	(0996)5621471	67	有限公司	66,134	13,407(3)	43,337	蕃茄罐头
Xinjiang Tunhe Investment Co.,Ltd. Manas Tomato Products Branch	Changji	Xinjiang	(0994)6661215		Limited-Liability				Tomato Ketchup
新疆屯河投资股份有限公司玛纳斯番茄制品分公司(1987)	昌吉州	新疆	(0994)6661167	244	有限公司	65,953	-	146,442	番茄酱

Top 10 Cities by Revenue 销售收入排名前10位城市	Province 省	Market share 市场份额 (%)	Number of firms 企业个数
Zhangzhou 漳州市	Fujian 福建省	29.55	47
Bayinguoleng 巴音郭楞州	Xinjiang 新疆	9.34	9
Changji 昌吉州	Xinjiang 新疆	6.34	4
Hangzhou 杭州市	Zhojiang 浙江省	4.71	13
Xiamen 厦门市	Fujian 福建省	4.00	2
Yuncheng 运城市	Shanxi 山西省	3.49	8
Ningbo 宁波市	Zhejiang 浙江省	2.05	9
Heze 荷泽市	Shandong 山东省	2.01	4
Liaocheng 聊城市	Shandong 山东省	2.00	3

10 Major Wholesalers 十家主要批发商	City 城市	Province 省	Telephone/Fax 电话/传真
Beijing Chaoyang Non-Staple Foodstuffs General Company	Beijing	Beijing	(010)65016285
北京朝阳副食品总公司	北京市	北京市	(010)65016285
Beijing Sugar,Cigarette & Wine Company	Beijing	Beijing	(010)67210304
北京市糖业烟酒公司	北京市	北京市	(010)67210310
Shanghai Sugar Cigarette & Wine (Group) Co.,Ltd.	Shanghai	Shanghai	(021)63224190
上海市糖业烟酒(集团)有限公司	上海市	上海市	(021)63223169
Jiangsu Sutang Sugar & Wine Co.,Ltd.	Nanjing	Jiangsu	(025)6661088
江苏苏糖糖酒食品有限公司	南京市	江苏省	(025)6661088
Fujian Commerce (Group) Co.,Ltd.	Fuzhou	Fujian	(0591)7847148
福建省商业（集团）有限责任公司	福州市	福建省	(0591)7847145
Yantai Changyu Pioneer Winer Co., Ltd.	Yantai	Shandong	(0535)6602730
烟台张裕葡萄酿酒股份有限公司	烟台市	山东省	(0535)6214078
BlueRibbon Beer Sale Co.,Ltd.	Zhaoqing	Guangdong	(0758)2862322
蓝带啤酒销售有限公司	肇庆市	广东省	(0758)2862424
Fujian Shenlong Development Co.,Ltd.	Fuzhou	Fujian	(0591)7503218
福建省神龙发展股份有限公司	福州市	福建省	(0591)7503068
Guangdong Sugar, Cigarette & Wine Group Company	Guangzhou	Guangdong	(020)83566131
广东省糖烟酒集团公司	广州市	广东省	(020)83561421
Shunde Daliang Sugar, Cigarette & Wine Co.,Ltd.	Shunde	Guangdong	(0765)2231804
顺德市大良区糖烟酒有限公司	顺德市	广东省	(0765)2222300

1439: Other Canned Food 其他罐头食品制造业

The industry accounts for 0.034% of the total revenue of China's industrial sector in 2002. The rate of return on assets is 1.51%. 74.67% of all firms in the industry made a profit while 25.33% had negative returns.The top province in terms of the industry's revenue is Hebei, accounting for 31.94% of the total revenue.
2002年本行业收入占全行业的0.034%，资产利润率为1.51%。74.67%的企业赢利，25.33%的企业亏损。收入最高的省为河北省，占本行业的31.94%。

	Total number of firms 企业总数	Total number of employees 职工总数	Total revenue (Mil.RMB) 总销售收入（百万元）	Total profit (Mil.RMB) 总利润（百万元）	Return on assets 资产利润率 (%)	Return on equity 权益利润率 (%)	Labour productivity ('000 RMB/worker) 劳动生产率（千元/人）	Debts/assets 资产负债率 (%)	Total assets (Mil.RMB) 总资产（百万元）
Industry Overall 行业总体	75	32,992	3,594	73	1.51	3.66	21.19	58.81	4,868

	Number of firms 企业个数	Average number of employees 平均职工人数	Average revenue ('000 RMB) 平均销售收入（千元）	Average profit ('000 RMB) 平均利润（千元）	Return on assets 资产利润率 (%)	Return on equity 权益利润率 (%)	Labour productivity ('000 RMB/worker) 劳动生产率（千元/人）	Debts/assets 资产负债率 (%)	Average total assets ('000 RMB) 平均总资产（千元）
By ownership 产业所有权									
State-owned 国有	9	421	34,921	165	0.19	0.32	18.00	40.96	87,145
Collective-owned 集体	9	189	13,690	420	6.61	437.23	24.70	98.49	6,359
Foreign & Overseas Chinese Funded 三资	22	96	18,799	-919	-3.36	-11.20	56.89	70.02	27,371
By regional distribution 地区分布									
Central-North 华北	8	624	169,467	8,488	3.06	8.06	28.32	62.05	277,553
Beijing 北京									
Tianjin 天津	3	964	66,827	5,247	9.34	20.20	-16.42	53.75	56,156
Hebei 河北	3	660	382,683	17,386	2.55	6.84	93.88	62.69	680,824
Shanxi 山西	2	61	3,600	2	0.04	0.16	24.03	73.11	4,741
Inner Mongolia 内蒙古									
Northeast 东北	5	112	18,917	331	0.77	3.46	82.06	77.75	43,072
Liaoning 辽宁	2	198	39,297	461	0.56	2.34	96.16	76.04	82,316
Jilin 吉林	3	55	5,330	245	1.45	8.68	48.41	83.31	16,910
Heilongjiang 黑龙江									
Central-East 华东	34	132	17,180	-631	-3.10	-9.73	33.39	68.12	20,349
Shanghai 上海	5	128	21,553	-5,381	-17.42	-244.98	14.35	92.89	30,883
Jiangsu 江苏	4	123	24,508	-820	-2.71	-10.96	31.63	75.25	30,225
Zhejiang 浙江	3	119	13,143	673	4.90	6.83	25.06	28.21	13,715
Anhui 安徽	1	120	6,906	2	0.01	0.06	17.11	76.93	15,589
Fujian 福建	16	116	12,074	293	1.77	3.40	33.87	47.79	16,550
Jiangxi 江西	1	50	3,079	26	1.02	3.69	22.00	72.37	2,552
Shandong 山东	4	247	33,935	496	2.15	26.29	51.29	91.83	23,114
Central-South 中南	24	908	59,765	1,220	1.77	3.32	14.76	46.76	68,983
Henan 河南	2	58	7,760	550	20.86	30.75	30.92	32.15	2,636
Hubei 湖北	5	164	11,554	132	1.06	2.48	21.85	57.38	12,499
Hunan 湖南	2	121	14,709	268	4.87	10.28	55.79	52.66	5,498
Guangdong 广东	8	187	15,694	-92	-0.28	-0.98	16.35	71.83	33,389
Guangxi 广西	3	431	57,129	2,652	2.26	4.11	30.02	44.99	117,390
Hainan 海南	4	4,459	258,679	4,939	2.06	3.42	12.53	39.74	239,388
Southwest 西南	3	150	15,893	-1,422	-9.04	-50.35	30.32	82.04	15,724
Chongqing 重庆									
Sichuan 四川	2	169	13,505	626	4.87	6.53	25.79	25.36	12,839
Guizhou 贵州									
Yunnan 云南	1	112	20,670	-5,516	-25.66		43.97	149.76	21,494
Tibet 西藏									
Northwest 西北	1	688	77,809	269	0.72	6.27	37.66	88.55	37,490
Shaanxi 陕西	1	688	77,809	269	0.72	6.27	37.66	88.55	37,490
Gansu 甘肃									
Qinghai 青海									
Ningxia 宁夏									
Xinjiang 新疆									

1439: Other Canned Food 其他罐头食品制造业

Year 年份	Number of firms 企业个数	Rate of change 变化率 (%)	Number of employees 职工人数 (人)	Rate of change 变化率 (%)	Total revenue (Mil. RMB) 总销售收入 (百万元)	Rate of change 变化率 (%)	Total profit (Mil RMB) 总利润 (百万元)	Rate of change 变化率 (%)
2000	67		13,275		3,302		67	
2001	53	-20.90	11,302	-14.86	2,942	-10.90	57	-14.93
2002	75	41.51	32,992	191.91	3,594	22.16	73	28.07

Major Products 主要产品	Output 产量	Unit 单位
Can 罐头	223	10,000 Tons 万吨

10 Main Firms with Maximal Revenue (year founded) 收入最大的十家主要企业（创办年份）	City 城市	Province 省	Telephone/fax 电话/传真	Number of employees 职工人数	Ownership 产业所有权	Revenue ('000 RMB) 销售收入（千元）	Profit('000 RMB) (rank) 利润(千元)(排名)	Total assets ('000 RMB) 总资产（千元）	Major products 主要产品
LoLo Group Co.,Ltd.	Chengde	Hebei	(0314)2062808		State Enterprises				Almond Dew
露露集团有限责任公司(1950)	承德市	河北省	(0314)2062592	1,879	国有独资	1,125,232	51,690(1)	2,027,088	杏仁露
Coconut Palm Group(Nanhai Coconut Milk Drink) Co.,Ltd.	Haikou	Hainan	(0898)66516448		Joint Stock				Natural Coconut Milk
椰树集团（海南椰汁饮料）有限公司(1987)	海口市	海南省	(0898)66795357	16,029	股份制	816,558	20,764(2)	332,989	天然椰子汁
Coconut Palm Group Can-making Industry Co., Ltd.	Haikou	Hainan	(0898)66777124		State-owned				Canned Food
椰树制罐工业有限公司(1956)	海口市	海南省	(0898)66773891	1,610	国有企业	201,219	1,105(11)	613,607	罐头食品
Guangxi Havle Food Co., Ltd.	Yulin	Guangxi	(0775)5329888		Joint Stock				Black Sesame Paste
广西黑五类食品股份有限公司(1999)	玉林市	广西	(0775)5325055	1,030	股份制	157,334	8,026(4)	340,612	黑芝麻糊
Tianjin Food City Co., Ltd.	Tianjin	Tianjin	(022)23972429		Limited-Liability				Can
天津市食品城有限责任公司(1996)	天津市	天津市		2,215	有限公司	99,560	2,400(5)	106,740	罐头
Shandong Jiu Fa Fungus Co., Ltd. Qingzhou Branch	Weifang	Shandong	(0536)3814639		Limited-Liability				Can
山东九发食用菌有限公司青州分公司(1999)	潍坊市	山东省	(0536)3810003	400	有限公司	79,998	2,093(6)	69,314	罐头
Xi'an Taiyang Food Co., Ltd.	Xi'an	Shannxi	(029)5523228		State-owned				A'xiangpo Soy Sauce
西安太阳食品有限责任公司(1971)	西安市	陕西省	(029)5512797	688	国有企业	77,809	269(34)	37,490	阿香婆酱
Dalian Mishima Foods Co.,Ltd.	Dalian	Liaoning	(0411)7611161		Foreign Funded				Mild Can
大连三岛食品有限公司(1992)	大连市	辽宁省	(0411)7612034	246	外商投资	62,580	803(15)	150,031	软罐头
Guangdong Jialong Food Stock Co., Ltd.	Jieyang	Guangdong	(0663)2918011		Private Enterprises				Can
广东省佳隆食品股份有限公司(1993)	揭阳市	广东省	(0663)2918011	152	私营独资	41,252	132(40)	66,373	罐头
TianJin KaiFang Food Co., Ltd.	Tianjin	Tianjin	(022)29710236		Collective-owned				Peach Can
天津凯芳食品有限公司(1999)	天津市	天津市	(022)29710236	580	集体企业	37,350	1,490(8)	6,560	桃罐头

Top 10 Cities by Revenue 销售收入排名前10位城市	Province 省	Market share 市场份额 (%)	Number of firms 企业个数
Chengde 承德市	Hebei 河北省	31.58	2
Haikou 海口市	Hainan 海南省	28.79	4
Tianjin 天津市	Tianjin 天津市	5.58	3
Yulin 玉林市	Guangxi 广西	4.52	2
Shanghai 上海市	Shanghai 上海市	3.00	5
Nanping 南平市	Fujian 福建省	2.73	7
Weifang 潍坊市	Shandong 山东省	2.62	3
Jieyang 揭阳市	Guangdong 广东省	2.47	4
Xi'an 西安市	Shannxi 陕西省	2.16	1
Dalian 大连市	Liaoning 辽宁省	1.74	1

10 Major Wholesalers 十家主要批发商	City 城市	Province 省	Telephone/Fax 电话/传真
Beijing Chaoyang Non-Staple Foodstuffs General Company	Beijing	Beijing	(010)65016285
北京朝阳副食品总公司	北京市	北京市	(010)65016285
Beijing Sugar,Cigarette & Wine Company	Beijing	Beijing	(010)67210304
北京市糖业烟酒公司	北京市	北京市	(010)67210310
Shanghai Sugar Cigarette & Wine (Group) Co.,Ltd.	Shanghai	Shanghai	(021)63224190
上海市糖业烟酒(集团)有限公司	上海市	上海市	(021)63223169
Jiangsu Sutang Sugar & Wine Co.,Ltd.	Nanjing	Jiangsu	(025)6661088
江苏苏糖糖酒食品有限公司	南京市	江苏省	(025)6661088
Fujian Commerce (Group) Co.,Ltd.	Fuzhou	Fujian	(0591)7847148
福建省商业（集团）有限责任公司	福州市	福建省	(0591)7847145
Yantai Changyu Pioneer Winer Co., Ltd.	Yantai	Shandong	(0535)6602730
烟台张裕葡萄酿酒股份有限公司	烟台市	山东省	(0535)6214078
BlueRibbon Beer Sale Co.,Ltd.	Zhaoqing	Guangdong	(0758)2862322
蓝带啤酒销售有限公司	肇庆市	广东省	(0758)2862424
Fujian Shenlong Development Co.,Ltd.	Fuzhou	Fujian	(0591)7503218
福建省神龙发展股份有限公司	福州市	福建省	(0591)7503068
Guangdong Sugar, Cigarette & Wine Group Company	Guangzhou	Guangdong	(020)83566131
广东省糖烟酒集团公司	广州市	广东省	(020)83561421
Shunde Daliang Sugar, Cigarette & Wine Co.,Ltd.	Shunde	Guangdong	(0765)2231804
顺德市大良区糖烟酒有限公司	顺德市	广东省	(0765)2222300

1441: Amino Acid 氨基酸制造业

The industry accounts for 0.013% of the total revenue of China's industrial sector in 2002. The rate of return on assets is 10.06%. 89.66% of all firms in the industry made a profit while 10.34% had negative returns.The top province in terms of the industry's revenue is Shandong, accounting for 56.58% of the total revenue.
2002年本行业收入占全行业的0.013%，资产利润率为10.06%。89.66%的企业赢利，10.34%的企业亏损。收入最高的省为山东省，占本行业的56.58%。

	Total number of firms 企业总数	Total number of employees 职工总数	Total revenue (Mil.RMB) 总销售收入（百万元）	Total profit (Mil.RMB) 总利润（百万元）	Return on assets 资产利润率（%）	Return on equity 权益利润率（%）	Labour productivity ('000 RMB/ worker) 劳动生产率（千元/人）	Debts/ assets 资产负债率（%）	Total assets (Mil.RMB) 总资产（百万元）
Industry Overall 行业总体	29	4,912	1,352	102	10.06	18.25	107.83	44.85	1,017

	Number of firms 企业个数	Average number of employees 平均职工人数	Average revenue ('000 RMB) 平均销售收入（千元）	Average profit ('000 RMB) 平均利润（千元）	Return on assets 资产利润率（%）	Return on equity 权益利润率（%）	Labour productivity ('000 RMB/ worker) 劳动生产率（千元/人）	Debts/ assets 资产负债率（%）	Average total assets ('000 RMB) 平均总资产（千元）
By ownership 产业所有权									
State-owned 国有	3	18	694	8	0.20	0.79	8.62	74.97	3,865
Collective-owned 集体	2	31	11,811	806	12.87	19.18	125.61	32.87	6,261
Foreign & Overseas Chinese Funded 三资	4	83	46,692	1,911	4.89	9.00	209.65	45.69	39,091
By regional distribution 地区分布									
Central-North 华北	3	31	1,668	177	5.21	5.99	9.31	13.07	3,392
Beijing 北京									
Tianjin 天津									
Hebei 河北	2	31	2,500	265	8.55	9.81	13.94	12.90	3,100
Shanxi 山西	1	31	5				0.06	13.33	3,977
Inner Mongolia 内蒙古									
Northeast 东北	1	5	404				2.60	81.61	1,985
Liaoning 辽宁	1	5	404				2.60	81.61	1,985
Jilin 吉林									
Heilongjiang 黑龙江									
Central-East 华东	12	223	78,702	7,301	14.61	25.32	121.56	42.32	49,980
Shanghai 上海	2	50	25,515	2,649	6.63	10.06	163.08	34.10	39,953
Jiangsu 江苏	4	159	17,911	-1,397	-8.73	-78.75	16.72	88.91	15,997
Zhejiang 浙江	3	42	17,524	918	10.29	25.33	59.58	59.37	8,924
Anhui 安徽	1	80	4,474	250	2.43	17.22	25.31	85.89	10,288
Fujian 福建									
Jiangxi 江西									
Shandong 山东	2	866	382,350	42,448	20.27	31.00	166.59	34.61	209,403
Central-South 中南	12	150	26,031	815	3.00	5.51	93.21	45.63	27,193
Henan 河南	2	348	21,875	1			80.00	43.64	29,297
Hubei 湖北	8	122	20,543	1,017	3.97	6.88	62.33	42.29	25,592
Hunan 湖南									
Guangdong 广东	1	96	103,296	1,622	2.69	6.83	526.07	60.65	60,333
Guangxi 广西	1	25	978	23	0.87	0.92	6.40	6.40	2,658
Hainan 海南									
Southwest 西南									
Chongqing 重庆									
Sichuan 四川									
Guizhou 贵州									
Yunnan 云南									
Tibet 西藏									
Northwest 西北	1	346	89,365	4,417	5.61	15.61	105.48	64.06	78,706
Shaanxi 陕西									
Gansu 甘肃									
Qinghai 青海									
Ningxia 宁夏	1	346	89,365	4,417	5.61	15.61	105.48	64.06	78,706
Xinjiang 新疆									

1441: Amino Acid 氨基酸制造业

Year 年份	Number of firms 企业个数	Rate of change 变化率 (%)	Number of employees 职工人数 (人)	Rate of change 变化率 (%)	Total revenue (Mil. RMB) 总销售收入 (百万元)	Rate of change 变化率 (%)	Total profit (Mil RMB) 总利润 (百万元)	Rate of change 变化率 (%)
2000	25		5,197		676		28	
2001	23	-8.00	2,582	-50.32	557	-17.60	50	78.57
2002	29	26.09	4,912	90.24	1,352	142.73	102	104.00

Major Products 主要产品	Output 产量	Unit 单位

10 Main Firms with Maximal Revenue (year founded) 收入最大的十家主要企业（创办年份）	City 城市	Province 省	Telephone/fax 电话/传真	Number of employees 职工人数	Ownership 产业所有权	Revenue ('000 RMB) 销售收入 (千元)	Profit('000 RMB) (rank) 利润(千元)(排名)	Total assets ('000 RMB) 总资产 (千元)	Major products 主要产品
Shandong Snowflake Starch Co., Ltd.	Jining	Shandong	(0537)3866285		Limited-Liability				Glutamic Acid
山东雪花淀粉有限公司(2000)	济宁市	山东省	(0537)3866688	1,582	有限公司	740,909	81,794(1)	379,356	谷氨酸
Dari Refined Chemistry (Shenzhen) Co., Ltd.	Shenzhen	Guangdong	(0755)26454097		Overseas Chinese-funded				ABS Plastic Cement ABS
大日精化（深圳）有限公司(1993)	深圳市	广东省	(0755)27926133	96	港澳台资	103,296	1,622(8)	60,333	塑胶料
Ningxia Yipin Food Group Co., Ltd.	Yinchuan	Ningxia	(0951)8019348		Limited-Liability				Glutamic Acid
宁夏伊品食品集团有限公司(1992)	银川市	宁夏	(0951)8019332	346	有限公司	89,365	4,417(3)	78,706	谷氨酸
Shanghai Guanshengyuan Kyowa Amino-acid Co.,Ltd.	Shanghai	Shanghai	(021)52801270		Foreign Funded				Amono Acid
上海冠生园协和氨基酸有限公司(1998)	上海市	上海市	(021)52803162	70	外商投资	44,386	5,542(2)	75,078	氨基酸
Wuhan Zhoudong Lotus Monosodium Glutamate Co.,Ltd.	Wuhan	Hubei	(027)83092197		Limited-Liability				Glutamic Acid
武汉周东莲花味精有限责任公司(1995)	武汉市	湖北省	(027)83092536	405	有限公司	43,164	2,689(6)	68,212	谷氨酸
Ningbo Haide Amino-acids Industrial Co.,Ltd.	Ningbo	Zhejiang	(0574)86251555		Overseas Chinese-funded				Amono Acid
宁波海德氨基酸工业有限公司(1993)	宁波市	浙江省	(0574)86251777	72	港澳台资	33,984	1,629(7)	15,172	氨基酸
Wuxi Jinghai Amono-Acid Co., Ltd.	Wuxi	Jiangsu	(0510)8352898		Private Owned				Amono Acid Materials氨
无锡晶海氨基酸有限公司(1995)	无锡市	江苏省	(0510)8767518	138	私营企业	24,320	-	47,920	基酸原料
Zibo Regeneration Amino-acid Co., Ltd.	Zibo	Shandong	(0533)6010175		Limited-Liability				Amono Acid Liquid
淄博更生氨基酸有限责任公司(1999)	淄博市	山东省	(0533)6010175	150	有限公司	23,791	3,102(5)	39,450	氨基酸液
Wuhan Hufa Amono-Acid Co., Ltd.	Wuhan	Hubei	(027)85758802		Private Owned				Amono Acid
武汉沪发氨基酸有限公司(1995)	武汉市	湖北省	(027)85771585	220	私营企业	16,250	3,570(4)	72,940	氨基酸
Wuhan Joint Petrochemical Industry Co., Ltd.	Wuhan	Hubei	(027)86465188		Private Owned				Water-Reducing Admixture
武汉市联合石油化工有限责任公司(1978)	武汉市	湖北省	(027)86465128	68	私营企业	12,445	600(11)	15,950	减水剂

Top 10 Cities by Revenue 销售收入排名前10位城市	Province 省	Market share 市场份额 (%)	Number of firms 企业个数
Jining 济宁市	Shandong 山东省	54.82	1
Shenzhen 深圳市	Guangdong 广东省	7.64	1
Wuhan 武汉市	Hubei 湖北省	6.61	5
Yinchuan 银川市	Ningxia 宁夏	6.61	1
Shanghai 上海市	Shanghai 上海市	3.78	2
Ningbo 宁波市	Zhejiang 浙江省	2.98	2
Shangqiu 商丘市	Henan 河南省	2.77	1
Nantong 南通市	Jiangsu 江苏省	2.72	1
Wuxi 无锡市	Jiangsu 江苏省	2.18	2

10 Major Wholesalers 十家主要批发商	City 城市	Province 省	Telephone/Fax 电话/传真
Guangdong Foodstuffs Import & Export Group Corporation	Guangzhou	Guangdong	(020)83854888
广东省食品进出口集团公司	广州市	广东省	(020)83856823
Hubei Salt Industry General Company	Wuhan	Hubei	(027)82832190
湖北盐业总公司	武汉市	湖北省	(027)82816030
Henan Provincial Salt Business Administration Bureau (Henan Provincial Salt Industry General Company)	Zhengzhou	Henan	(0371)5907597
河南省盐务管理局(河南省盐业总公司)	郑州市	河南省	(0371)5906346
Sichuan Salt Industry General Company	Chengdu	Sichuan	(028)86652441
四川省盐业总公司	成都市	四川省	(028)86663440
China National Salt Tianjin Changlu Salt Industry Co.,Ltd.	Tianjin	Tianjin	(022)23022160
中盐天津市长芦盐业有限公司	天津市	天津市	(022)23022110
Zhejiang Salt Industry Company	Hangzhou	Zhejiang	(0571)87800292
浙江省盐业公司	杭州市	浙江省	(0571)87800082
Fujian Salt Industry Company	Fuzhou	Fujian	(0591)7534344
福建省盐业公司	福州市	福建省	(0591)7535047
Jiangxi Salt Industry General Company	Nanchang	Jiangxi	(0791)6816695
江西省盐业总公司	南昌市	江西省	(0791)6812316
Hubei Salt Transportation & Sale Company	Xiaogan	Hubei	(0712)3611320
湖北省盐业运销公司	孝感市	湖北省	(0712)3611244
Hunan Salt Industry Group Co.,Ltd.Jinshi Allocation & Transportation Company	Changde	Hunan	(0736)4223817
湖南省盐业集团有限责任公司津市调运公司	常德市	湖南省	(0736)4223817

1442: Gourmet Powder 味精制造业

The industry accounts for 0.101% of the total revenue of China's industrial sector in 2002. The rate of return on assets is 2.73%. 76.74% of all firms in the industry made a profit while 23.26% had negative returns.The top province in terms of the industry's revenue is Shandong, accounting for 21.06% of the total revenue.
2002年本行业收入占全行业的0.101%，资产利润率为2.73%。76.74%的企业赢利，23.26%的企业亏损。收入最高的省为山东省，占本行业的21.06%。

	Total number of firms 企业总数	Total number of employees 职工总数	Total revenue (Mil.RMB) 总销售收入(百万元)	Total profit (Mil.RMB) 总利润(百万元)	Return on assets 资产利润率(%)	Return on equity 权益利润率(%)	Labour productivity ('000 RMB/worker) 劳动生产率(千元/人)	Debts/assets 资产负债率(%)	Total assets (Mil.RMB) 总资产(百万元)
Industry Overall 行业总体	86	57,449	10,846	391	2.73	6.20	63.49	56.01	14,314

	Number of firms 企业个数	Average number of employees 平均职工人数	Average revenue ('000 RMB) 平均销售收入（千元）	Average profit ('000 RMB) 平均利润（千元）	Return on assets 资产利润率(%)	Return on equity 权益利润率(%)	Labour productivity ('000 RMB/worker) 劳动生产率(千元/人)	Debts/assets 资产负债率(%)	Average total assets ('000 RMB) 平均总资产(千元)
By ownership 产业所有权									
State-owned 国有	12	319	47,740	-1,948	-3.32	-15.33	33.80	78.35	58,687
Collective-owned 集体	11	876	126,240	5,910	5.13	10.73	41.89	52.19	115,201
Foreign & Overseas Chinese Funded 三资	14	669	178,133	7,339	3.60	7.12	70.67	49.41	203,655
By regional distribution 地区分布									
Central-North 华北	4	494	83,615	106	0.10	0.21	19.92	52.15	105,037
Beijing 北京									
Tianjin 天津	2	176	20,055	-1,749	-2.91	-4.84	9.47	39.96	60,158
Hebei 河北	1	1,350	238,587	3,887	1.85	5.34	20.13	65.39	210,206
Shanxi 山西									
Inner Mongolia 内蒙古	1	275	55,765	33	0.04	0.06	32.27	37.44	89,627
Northeast 东北	5	435	91,474	1,949	1.47	5.26	49.96	72.12	132,886
Liaoning 辽宁	3	548	130,811	3,643	1.69	5.90	47.68	71.40	216,031
Jilin 吉林	2	265	32,470	-592	-7.25		57.03	100.81	8,170
Heilongjiang 黑龙江									
Central-East 华东	47	565	133,606	5,844	5.04	11.08	63.14	54.54	116,002
Shanghai 上海	5	321	160,598	11,993	9.47	23.08	107.96	58.96	126,645
Jiangsu 江苏	14	257	100,121	968	1.45	3.36	100.89	56.77	66,718
Zhejiang 浙江	9	472	96,786	2,997	3.63	7.79	49.40	53.40	82,581
Anhui 安徽									
Fujian 福建	10	436	86,528	-484	-0.45	-0.86	54.82	48.15	108,015
Jiangxi 江西	3	140	17,949	214	1.03	2.67	18.59	61.20	20,695
Shandong 山东	6	2,056	380,768	29,730	8.92	20.17	55.50	55.77	333,229
Central-South 中南	19	1,235	173,042	5,837	1.53	3.41	71.22	55.06	380,565
Henan 河南	4	4,433	523,710	30,242	2.11	4.54	75.52	53.49	1,430,960
Hubei 湖北	1	701	166,524	5,305	3.01	4.90	86.78	38.58	176,430
Hunan 湖南	1	415	48,932	45	0.08	0.25	11.47	66.78	53,234
Guangdong 广东	10	339	82,573	-448	-0.45	-1.05	76.21	57.04	99,406
Guangxi 广西	3	407	50,593	-3,642	-3.86	-31.54	6.31	87.77	94,392
Hainan 海南									
Southwest 西南	8	297	48,652	3,883	8.36	16.78	57.27	50.18	46,439
Chongqing 重庆	2	508	83,093	3,446	4.85	11.74	44.27	58.72	71,077
Sichuan 四川	5	257	43,765	4,834	12.21	22.96	70.48	46.83	39,592
Guizhou 贵州									
Yunnan 云南	1	75	4,203	3	0.01	0.01	7.03	32.68	31,399
Tibet 西藏									
Northwest 西北	3	300	32,391	-12,084	-20.76		16.94	101.71	58,197
Shaanxi 陕西									
Gansu 甘肃									
Qinghai 青海									
Ningxia 宁夏	1	265	37,019	71	0.19	0.66	59.98	71.28	37,596
Xinjiang 新疆	2	318	30,077	-18,162	-26.51		-1.02	110.06	68,497

1442: Gourmet Powder 味精制造业

Year 年份	Number of firms 企业个数	Rate of change 变化率 (%)	Number of employees 职工人数 (人)	Rate of change 变化率 (%)	Total revenue (Mil. RMB) 总销售收入 (百万元)	Rate of change 变化率 (%)	Total profit (Mil RMB) 总利润 (百万元)	Rate of change 变化率 (%)
2000	86		53,411		9,431		516	
2001	91	5.81	56,379	5.56	9,038	-4.17	254	-50.78
2002	86	-5.49	57,449	1.90	10,846	20.00	391	53.94

Major Products 主要产品	Output 产量	Unit 单位
Monosodium Glutamate 味精	110	10,000 Tons 万吨

10 Main Firms with Maximal Revenue (year founded) 收入最大的十家主要企业（创办年份）	City 城市	Province 省	Telephone/fax 电话/传真	Number of employees 职工人数	Ownership 产业所有权	Revenue ('000 RMB) 销售收入(千元)	Profit('000 RMB) (rank) 利润(千元)(排名)	Total assets ('000 RMB) 总资产(千元)	Major products 主要产品
Henan Lotus Monosodium Glutamate Enterprise Group	Zhoukou	Henan	(0394)4298955		Joint Stock				Monosodium Glutamate
河南省莲花味精企业集团(1992)	周口市	河南省		16,752	股份制	2,039,298	120888(1)	5,508,952	味精
JiningLinghua Group Co.	Jining	Shandong	(0537)2080223		Collective-owned				Monosodium Glutamate
济宁市菱花集团公司(1979)	济宁市	山东省	(0537)2080658	7,380	集体企业	1,050,347	67655(3)	977,511	味精
Shanghai TotoLe Flavouring Food Co., Ltd.	Shanghai	Shanghai	(021)59134793		Foreign Funded				Condiment
上海太太乐调味食品有限公司(1997)	上海市	上海市	(021)59132674	905	外商投资	609,345	93,343(2)	413,096	调味食品
Jiangsu Chrysanthemum Monosodium Glutamate Group	Suzhou	Jiangsu	(0512)58481288		Joint Stock				Monosodium Glutamate
Company 江苏菊花味精集团公司(1978)	苏州市	江苏省	(0512)58481288	1,959	股份制	565,809	10,035(9)	372,989	味精
Shandong Sanjiu Monosodium Glutamate Co., Ltd.	Liaocheng	Shandong	(0635)4285419		Joint Stock				Monosodium Glutamate
山东三九味精有限公司(1999)	聊城市	山东省	(0635)4273999	2,298	股份制	506,168	51,877(4)	539,404	味精
Jiangsu Tianxiang group Co.,Ltd.	Changzhou	Jiangsu	(0519)6131027		Joint Stock				Monosodium Glutamate
江苏天香集团有限公司(1990)	常州市	江苏省	(0519)6134127	210	股份制	420,060	1,460(23)	285,150	味精
Guangdong Aoaang Monosodium Glutamate Food Co.,Ltd.	Guangzhou	Guangdong	(020)34336688		Foreign Funded				Monosodium Glutamate
广州奥桑味精食品有限公司(1995)	广州市	广东省	(020)34335974	831	外商投资	369,942	4,308(17)	394,561	味精
Shenyang Hongmei Enterprise group Co.,Ltd.	Shenyang	Liaoning	(024)25820821		State Enterprises				Monosodium Glutamate
沈阳红梅企业集团有限责任公司(1998)	沈阳市	辽宁省	(024)25820297	1,362	国有独资	363,043	10,632(8)	568,712	味精
Zhuhai Yili Group Company Doumen Yili Monosodium Glutamate	Zhuhai	Guangdong	(0756)5222452		Overseas Chinese-funded				Monosodium Glutamate
Co.,Ltd.益力集团公司珠海斗门益力味精有限公司(1989)	珠海市	广东省	(0756)5222498	1,239	港澳台资	261,512	-	471,882	味精
Quanzhou Farlim Group (China) Co., Ltd.	Quanzhou	Fujian	(0595)2183914		Foreign Funded				Monosodium Glutamate
泉州中侨(集团)股份有限公司(1992)	泉州市	福建省	(0595)2184258	2,332	外商投资	226,245	-	544,538	味精

Top 10 Cities by Revenue 销售收入排名前10位城市	Province 省	Market share 市场份额 (%)	Number of firms 企业个数
Zhoukou 周口市	Henan 河南省	18.80	1
Jining 济宁市	Shandong 山东省	9.68	1
Shanghai 上海市	Shanghai 上海市	7.40	5
Suzhou 苏州市	Jiangsu 江苏省	6.82	3
Liaocheng 聊城市	Shandong 山东省	4.67	1
Linyi 临沂市	Shandong 山东省	4.29	1
Changzhou 常州市	Jiangsu 江苏省	4.17	2
Guangzhou 广州市	Guangdong 广东省	3.52	2
Shenyang 沈阳市	Liaoning 辽宁省	3.40	2
Jinhua 金华市	Zhejiang 浙江省	3.23	2

10 Major Wholesalers 十家主要批发商	City 城市	Province 省	Telephone/Fax 电话/传真
Guangdong Foodstuffs Import & Export Group Corporation	Guangzhou	Guangdong	(020)83854888
广东省食品进出口集团公司	广州市	广东省	(020)83856823
Hubei Salt Industry General Company	Wuhan	Hubei	(027)82832190
湖北盐业总公司	武汉市	湖北省	(027)82816030
Henan Provincial Salt Business Administration Bureau (Henan Provincial Salt Industry General Company)	Zhengzhou	Henan	(0371)5907597
河南省盐务管理局(河南省盐业总公司)	郑州市	河南省	(0371)5906346
Sichuan Salt Industry General Company	Chengdu	Sichuan	(028)86652441
四川省盐业总公司	成都市	四川省	(028)86663440
China National Salt Tianjin Changlu Salt Industry Co.,Ltd.	Tianjin	Tianjin	(022)23022160
中盐天津市长芦盐业有限公司	天津市	天津市	(022)23022110
Zhejiang Salt Industry Company	Hangzhou	Zhejiang	(0571)87800292
浙江省盐业公司	杭州市	浙江省	(0571)87800082
Fujian Salt Industry Company	Fuzhou	Fujian	(0591)7534344
福建省盐业公司	福州市	福建省	(0591)7535047
Jiangxi Salt Industry General Company	Nanchang	Jiangxi	(0791)6816695
江西省盐业总公司	南昌市	江西省	(0791)6812316
Hubei Salt Transportation & Sale Company	Xiaogan	Hubei	(0712)3611320
湖北省盐业运销公司	孝感市	湖北省	(0712)3611244
Hunan Salt Industry Group Co.,Ltd.Jinshi Allocation & Transportation Company	Changde	Hunan	(0736)4223817
湖南省盐业集团有限责任公司津市调运公司	常德市	湖南省	(0736)4223817

1443: Citric Acid 柠檬酸制造业

The industry accounts for 0.027% of the total revenue of China's industrial sector in 2002. The rate of return on assets is 2.01%. 52.94% of all firms in the industry made a profit while 47.06% had negative returns.The top province in terms of the industry's revenue is Anhui, accounting for 66.34% of the total revenue.
2002年本行业收入占全行业的 0.027%，资产利润率为 2.01%。52.94%的企业赢利，47.06%的企业亏损。收入最高的省为安徽省，占本行业的66.34%。

	Total number of firms 企业总数	Total number of employees 职工总数	Total revenue (Mil.RMB) 总销售收入（百万元）	Total profit (Mil.RMB) 总利润（百万元）	Return on assets 资产利润率 (%)	Return on equity 权益利润率 (%)	Labour productivity ('000 RMB/ worker) 劳动生产率（千元/人）	Debts/ assets 资产负债率 (%)	Total assets (Mil.RMB) 总资产（百万元）
Industry Overall 行业总体	34	20,567	2,859	196	2.01	5.23	24.56	61.64	9,777

	Number of firms 企业个数	Average number of employees 平均职工人数	Average revenue ('000 RMB) 平均销售收入（千元）	Average profit ('000 RMB) 平均利润（千元）	Return on assets 资产利润率 (%)	Return on equity 权益利润率 (%)	Labour productivity ('000 RMB/ worker) 劳动生产率（千元/人）	Debts/ assets 资产负债率 (%)	Average total assets ('000 RMB) 平均总资产（千元）
By ownership 产业所有权									
State-owned 国有	1	70	9,211	-7,006	-2.96	-7.65	33.33	61.33	236,742
Collective-owned 集体	3	214	19,246	1,927	11.46	307.45	42.36	96.27	16,811
Foreign & Overseas Chinese Funded 三资	6	251	39,309	-838	-1.40	-4.95	27.29	71.67	59,798
By regional distribution 地区分布									
Central-North 华北	4	251	34,339	1,655	2.11	7.00	44.63	69.89	78,576
Beijing 北京									
Tianjin 天津	1	40							
Hebei 河北	1	200	48,440	8,300	47.13	86.34	122.90	45.41	17,610
Shanxi 山西	2	383	44,457	-840	-0.57	-1.98	26.50	71.35	148,348
Inner Mongolia 内蒙古									
Northeast 东北	2	118	9,244	-2,874	-2.18	-5.09	21.67	57.23	132,135
Liaoning 辽宁									
Jilin 吉林	2	118	9,244	-2,874	-2.18	-5.09	21.67	57.23	132,135
Heilongjiang 黑龙江									
Central-East 华东	17	935	139,432	12,318	2.43	6.18	24.05	60.66	506,600
Shanghai 上海									
Jiangsu 江苏	6	144	14,178	366	1.13	4.07	17.27	72.15	32,257
Zhejiang 浙江	1	286	2,697	-629	-2.82	-9.11	1.26	69.08	22,331
Anhui 安徽	2	5,665	948,510	107,394	2.78	6.88	23.06	59.63	3,866,038
Fujian 福建									
Jiangxi 江西									
Shandong 山东	8	428	48,195	-869	-1.05	-3.38	30.96	69.01	83,032
Central-South 中南	8	331	31,907	-1,105	-2.00	-6.53	22.42	69.35	55,268
Henan 河南									
Hubei 湖北	2	294	35,111	-800	-2.17		23.94	170.88	36,908
Hunan 湖南	3	536	42,050	113	0.12	0.23	21.51	47.62	93,615
Guangdong 广东	1	52	15,870	637	4.83	12.74	158.12	62.09	13,188
Guangxi 广西	2	200	21,506	-4,111	-11.07	-23.01	6.19	51.91	37,148
Hainan 海南									
Southwest 西南	2	210	11,582	-903	-4.42	-10.32	17.61	57.12	20,411
Chongqing 重庆									
Sichuan 四川	1	300	14,652	-885	-2.85	-5.33	15.98	46.55	31,066
Guizhou 贵州									
Yunnan 云南	1	120	8,512	-921	-9.44	-102.22	21.68	90.76	9,755
Tibet 西藏									
Northwest 西北	1	357	54,783	-3,584	-3.46	-210.70	16.49	98.36	103,684
Shaanxi 陕西									
Gansu 甘肃									
Qinghai 青海									
Ningxia 宁夏									
Xinjiang 新疆	1	357	54,783	-3,584	-3.46	-210.70	16.49	98.36	103,684

Year 年份	Number of firms 企业个数	Rate of change 变化率 (%)	Number of employees 职工人数 (人)	Rate of change 变化率 (%)	Total revenue (Mil. RMB) 总销售收入 (百万元)	Rate of change 变化率 (%)	Total profit (Mil RMB) 总利润 (百万元)	Rate of change 变化率 (%)
2000	33		15,934		2,342		123	
2001	32	-3.03	16,380	2.80	2,137	-8.75	151	22.76
2002	34	6.25	20,567	25.56	2,859	33.79	196	29.80

Major Products 主要产品	Output 产量	Unit 单位

10 Main Firms with Maximal Revenue (year founded) 收入最大的十家主要企业（创办年份）	City 城市	Province 省	Telephone/fax 电话/传真	Number of employees 职工人数	Ownership 产业所有权	Revenue ('000 RMB) 销售收入 (千元)	Profit('000 RMB) (rank) 利润(千元) (排名)	Total assets ('000 RMB) 总资产 (千元)	Major products 主要产品
Anhui Fengyuan Biochemistry Group Co.,Ltd. 安徽丰原生物化学集团有限公司(1998)	Bengbu 蚌埠市	Anhui 安徽省	(0555)3501260 (0555)4928487	10,470	Limited-Liability 有限公司	1,755,229	199,406(1)	7,355,820	Citric Acid 柠檬酸
Anhui Fengyuan Ma'anshan Biochemistry Co., Ltd. 安徽丰原马鞍山生物化学有限公司(2001)	Maanshan 马鞍山市	Anhui 安徽省	(0555)3500303 (0555)3501260	860	Limited-Liability 有限公司	141,791	15,381(2)	376,256	Citric Acid 柠檬酸
Shandong Mingmeng Biochemistry Co.,Ltd. 山东柠檬生化有限公司(1991)	Weifang 潍坊市	Shandong 山东省	(0536)4221818 (0536)4221500	279	Overseas Chinese-funded 港澳台资	120,717	2,150(5)	113,884	Citric Acid 柠檬酸
Hunan Yinhai Biochemistry Co., Ltd. 湖南银海石油化工有限公司(1998)	Changsha 长沙市	Hunan 湖南省	(0731)7881272 (0731)7882731	1,268	Joint Stock 股份制	99,239	596(12)	259,780	Citric Acid 柠檬酸
Xintai Taishan Biochemistry Group Co.,Ltd. 新泰泰山生化有限公司(1999)	Taian 泰安市	Shandong 山东省	(0538)7352491 (0538)7352491	365	Limited-Liability 有限公司	98,559	658(10)	35,560	Citric Acid Monohydrate一水柠檬酸
Yegan Group Yangtse River Chemical Co., Ltd. 冶钢集团扬子江化工有限公司(1997)	Huangshi 黄石市	Hubei 湖北省	(0714)6291456 (0714)6401356	399	Limited-Liability 有限公司	53,481	-	48,215	Citric Acid 柠檬酸
Shijiazhuang Yongxing Citric Acid Factory 石家庄市永兴柠檬酸厂(1987)	Shijiazhuang 石家庄市	Hebei 河北省	(0311)7772635 (0311)7765515	200	Collective-owned 集体企业	48,440	8,300(3)	17,610	Citric Acid 柠檬酸
Nanning Citric Acid Co., Ltd. 南宁柠檬酸有限公司(1988)	Nanning 南宁市	Guangxi 广西	(0771)3113658 (0771)3101323	220	Overseas Chinese-funded 港澳台资	37,184	-	48,455	Anhydrous Citric Acid无水柠檬酸
Rizhao Taishan Jiejing Biochemistry Co., Ltd. 日照泰山洁晶生化有限公司(2002)	Rizhao 日照市	Shandong 山东省	(0633)8282018 (0633)8282353	684	Limited-Liability 有限公司	25,843	18(15)	128,989	Citric Acid 柠檬酸
Zaozhuang Wanyuan Biochemistry Co., Ltd. 枣庄万源生化有限公司(2001)	Zaozhuang 枣庄市	Shandong 山东省	(0632)6619252 (0632)6619252	470	Limited-Liability 有限公司	20,680	91(14)	31,052	Citric Acid 柠檬酸

Top 10 Cities by Revenue 销售收入排名前10位城市	Province 省	Market share 市场份额 (%)	Number of firms 企业个数
Bengbu 蚌埠市	Anhui 安徽省	61.38	1
Maanshan 马鞍山市	Anhui 安徽省	4.96	1
Weifang 潍坊市	Shandong 山东省	4.22	1
Changsha 长沙市	Hunan 湖南省	3.94	2
Rizhao 日照市	Shandong 山东省	3.88	2
Taian 泰安市	Shandong 山东省	3.45	1
Yuncheng 运城市	Shanxi 山西省	2.98	1
Wuxi 无锡市	Jiangsu 江苏省	2.16	2
Huangshi 黄石市	Hubei 湖北省	1.87	1

10 Major Wholesalers 十家主要批发商	City 城市	Province 省	Telephone/Fax 电话/传真
Guangdong Foodstuffs Import & Export Group Corporation 广东省食品进出口集团公司	Guangzhou 广州市	Guangdong 广东省	(020)83854888 (020)83856823
Hubei Salt Industry General Company 湖北盐业总公司	Wuhan 武汉市	Hubei 湖北省	(027)82832190 (027)82816030
Henan Provincial Salt Business Administration Bureau (Henan Provincial Salt Industry General Company) 河南省盐务管理局(河南省盐业总公司)	Zhengzhou 郑州市	Henan 河南省	(0371)5907597 (0371)5906346
Sichuan Salt Industry General Company 四川省盐业总公司	Chengdu 成都市	Sichuan 四川省	(028)86652441 (028)86663440
China National Salt Tianjin Changlu Salt Industry Co.,Ltd. 中盐天津市长芦盐业有限公司	Tianjin 天津市	Tianjin 天津市	(022)23022160 (022)23022110
Zhejiang Salt Industry Company 浙江省盐业公司	Hangzhou 杭州市	Zhejiang 浙江省	(0571)87800292 (0571)87800082
Fujian Salt Industry Company 福建省盐业公司	Fuzhou 福州市	Fujian 福建省	(0591)7534344 (0591)7535047
Jiangxi Salt Industry General Company 江西省盐业总公司	Nanchang 南昌市	Jiangxi 江西省	(0791)6816695 (0791)6812316
Hubei Salt Transportation & Sale Company 湖北省盐业运销公司	Xiaogan 孝感市	Hubei 湖北省	(0712)3611320 (0712)3611244
Hunan Salt Industry Group Co.,Ltd.Jinshi Allocation & Transportation Company 湖南省盐业集团有限责任公司津市调运公司	Changde 常德市	Hunan 湖南省	(0736)4223817 (0736)4223817

1444: Yeast Products 酵母制造业

The industry accounts for 0.010% of the total revenue of China's industrial sector in 2002. The rate of return on assets is 5.14%. 75.86% of all firms in the industry made a profit while 24.14% had negative returns.The top province in terms of the industry's revenue is Hubei, accounting for 29.11% of the total revenue.
2002年本行业收入占全行业的 0.010%，资产利润率为 5.14%。75.86%的企业赢利，24.14%的企业亏损。收入最高的省为湖北省，占本行业的29.11%。

	Total number of firms 企业总数	Total number of employees 职工总数	Total revenue (Mil.RMB) 总销售收入 (百万元)	Total profit (Mil.RMB) 总利润 (百万元)	Return on assets 资产利润率 (%)	Return on equity 权益利润率 (%)	Labour productivity ('000 RMB/ worker) 劳动生产率 (千元/人)	Debts/ assets 资产负债率 (%)	Total assets (Mil.RMB) 总资产 (百万元)
Industry Overall 行业总体	29	4,709	1,072	118	5.14	8.55	99.11	39.92	2,298

	Number of firms 企业个数	Average number of employees 平均职工人数	Average revenue ('000 RMB) 平均销售收入 (千元)	Average profit ('000 RMB) 平均利润 (千元)	Return on assets 资产利润率 (%)	Return on equity 权益利润率 (%)	Labour productivity ('000 RMB/ worker) 劳动生产率 (千元/人)	Debts/ assets 资产负债率 (%)	Average total assets ('000 RMB) 平均总资产 (千元)
By ownership 产业所有权									
State-owned 国有	3	53	5,038	-176	-0.34	-1.40	34.79	75.82	51,816
Collective-owned 集体	5	93	21,714	409	2.69	47.56	68.85	94.34	15,186
Foreign & Overseas Chinese Funded 三资	7	146	58,186	12,395	11.86	16.70	173.78	28.99	104,517
By regional distribution 地区分布									
Central-North 华北	8	123	31,663	4,599	11.81	19.78	94.07	40.27	38,924
Beijing 北京	3	154	28,497	669	4.06		55.79	109.59	16,476
Tianjin 天津	1	40	5,360	640	30.48	40.76	29.00	25.24	2,100
Hebei 河北	3	123	48,914	9,574	13.53	19.14	150.85	29.31	70,781
Shanxi 山西									
Inner Mongolia 内蒙古	1	111	15,706	5,422	11.41	13.87	87.20	17.76	47,524
Northeast 东北	1	200	106,977	36,936	18.97	25.90	257.55	26.78	194,755
Liaoning 辽宁									
Jilin 吉林									
Heilongjiang 黑龙江	1	200	106,977	36,936	18.97	25.90	257.55	26.78	194,755
Central-East 华东	9	108	19,578	218	0.68	1.24	65.18	45.29	32,251
Shanghai 上海	1								
Jiangsu 江苏	2	98	19,384	946	7.49	26.62	45.82	71.85	12,620
Zhejiang 浙江	2	63	14,159	488	4.81	6.96	51.30	30.81	10,138
Anhui 安徽	1	155	52,155	-793	-0.60	-1.42	120.94	57.88	132,293
Fujian 福建	1	222	15,655	155	0.33	0.70	61.46	52.56	46,631
Jiangxi 江西									
Shandong 山东	2	137	20,655	-133	-0.40	-0.44	56.86	9.11	32,908
Central-South 中南	10	254	53,464	4,238	2.83	4.75	101.94	40.53	149,908
Henan 河南	2	105	17,067	810	2.89	54.99	54.47	94.74	27,996
Hubei 湖北	1	1,456	312,000	28,783	3.08	4.30	121.60	28.30	934,672
Hunan 湖南									
Guangdong 广东	5	145	36,457	2,543	3.56	7.04	94.14	49.34	71,342
Guangxi 广西	2	74	3,110	-371	-0.49	-1.97	14.03	75.11	75,853
Hainan 海南									
Southwest 西南									
Chongqing 重庆									
Sichuan 四川									
Guizhou 贵州									
Yunnan 云南									
Tibet 西藏									
Northwest 西北	1	15	800				36.87	32.73	2,200
Shaanxi 陕西									
Gansu 甘肃	1	15	800				36.87	32.73	2,200
Qinghai 青海									
Ningxia 宁夏									
Xinjiang 新疆									

1444: Yeast Products 酵母制造业

Year 年份	Number of firms 企业个数	Rate of change 变化率(%)	Number of employees 职工人数(人)	Rate of change 变化率(%)	Total revenue (Mil. RMB) 总销售收入(百万元)	Rate of change 变化率(%)	Total profit (Mil RMB) 总利润(百万元)	Rate of change 变化率(%)
2000	31		4,864		796		62	
2001	35	12.90	5,491	12.89	1,088	36.68	105	69.35
2002	29	-17.14	4,709	-14.24	1,072	-1.47	118	12.38

Major Products 主要产品	Output 产量	Unit 单位

10 Main Firms with Maximal Revenue (year founded) 收入最大的十家主要企业(创办年份)	City 城市	Province 省	Telephone/fax 电话/传真	Number of employees 职工人数	Ownership 产业所有权	Revenue ('000 RMB) 销售收入(千元)	Profit('000 RMB) (rank) 利润(千元)(排名)	Total assets ('000 RMB) 总资产(千元)	Major products 主要产品
Hubei Angel Yeast Group Co.,Ltd. 湖北安琪生物集团有限公司(1986)	Yichang 宜昌市	Hubei 湖北省	(0717)6351161 (0717)6355184	1,456	State Enterprises 国有独资	312,000	28,783(2)	934,672	Fermentum 酵母
Harbin Mavli Yeast Co.,Ltd. 哈尔滨马利酵母有限公司(1992)	Harbin 哈尔滨市	Heilongjiang 黑龙江省	(0451)3754938 (0451)3723106	200	Foreign Funded 外商投资	106,977	36,936(1)	194,755	High Active Compressed Fermentum 高活性压榨酵母
Pinggu Xinglong Village Malt Factory 平谷县兴隆庄大麦芽厂(1982)	Beijing 北京市	Beijing 北京市	(010)61906032 (010)61906032	300	Collective-owned 集体企业	65,664	574(12)	33,377	Barley Malt 大麦芽
Lesifu (Mingguan)Co., Ltd. 乐斯福(明光)有限公司(1999)	Chuzhou 滁州市	Anhui 安徽省	(0550)8099253 (0550)8099196	155	Foreign Funded 外商投资	52,155	-	132,293	Fresh Fermentum 干酵母
Guangdong Jiangmen Biological Technology Development Center 广东江门生物技术开发中心(1988)	Jiangmen 江门市	Guangdong 广东省	(0750)3793525 (0750)3793404	396	State Enterprises 国有独资	52,053	-	196,111	Medicinal Fermentum 药用酵母
Hebei Binyang Group Shanhaiguan Haiyi Malt Factory 河北斌杨集团山海关海亿麦芽厂(1996)	Qinhuangdao 秦皇岛市	Hebei 河北省	(0335)5054036 (0335)5063999	75	Collective-owned 集体企业	35,872	1,020(8)	30,280	Malt 麦芽
Hebei Malt Co., Ltd. 河北麦芽有限责任公司(1996)	Tangshan 唐山市	Hebei 河北省	(0315)2012347	170	Limited-Liability 有限公司	19,353	3(19)	21,677	Beer Barley Malt 啤酒大麦芽
Suixian Suizhou Yeast Co., Ltd. 睢县睢州酵母有限责任公司(1998)	Shangqiu 商丘市	Henan 河南省	(0370)8118858	135	Limited-Liability 有限公司	17,513	-	44,942	Active Fermentum 活性干酵母
Chifeng Guoguang Yeast Co., Ltd. 赤峰国光酵母有限公司(1998)	Chifeng 赤峰市	InnerMongolia 内蒙古	(0476)6328177 (0476)6330303	111	Overseas Chinese funded 港澳台资	15,706	5,422(5)	47,524	High Active Fresh Fermentum 高活性干酵母
Quzhou Qinglong Industry & Trade Co., Ltd. 衢州市青龙工贸有限公司(1994)	Quzhou 衢州市	Zhejiang 浙江省	(0570)8016888 (0570)8016789	26	Private Owned 私营企业	15,696	88(18)	8,464	Malt 麦芽

Top 10 Cities by Revenue 销售收入排名前10位城市	Province 省	Market share 市场份额(%)	Number of firms 企业个数
Yichang 宜昌市	Hubei 湖北省	29.11	1
Harbin 哈尔滨市	Heilongjiang 黑龙江省	9.98	1
Guangzhou 广州市	Guangdong 广东省	8.80	1
Zhangjiakou 张家口市	Hebei 河北省	8.54	1
Beijing 北京市	Beijing 北京市	7.98	3
Chuzhou 滁州市	Anhui 安徽省	4.87	1
Jiangmen 江门市	Guangdong 广东省	4.86	1
Qinhuangdao 秦皇岛市	Hebei 河北省	3.35	1
Yancheng 盐城市	Jiangsu 江苏省	3.04	1
Yantai 烟台市	Shandong 山东省	2.97	1

10 Major Wholesalers 十家主要批发商	City 城市	Province 省	Telephone/Fax 电话/传真
Guangdong Foodstuffs Import & Export Group Corporation 广东省食品进出口集团公司	Guangzhou 广州市	Guangdong 广东省	(020)83854888 (020)83856823
Hubei Salt Industry General Company 湖北盐业总公司	Wuhan 武汉市	Hubei 湖北省	(027)82832190 (027)82816030
Henan Provincial Salt Business Administration Bureau (Henan Provincial Salt Industry General Company) 河南省盐务管理局(河南省盐业总公司)	Zhengzhou 郑州市	Henan 河南省	(0371)5907597 (0371)5906346
Sichuan Salt Industry General Company 四川省盐业总公司	Chengdu 成都市	Sichuan 四川省	(028)86652441 (028)86663440
China National Salt Tianjin Changlu Salt Industry Co.,Ltd. 中盐天津市长芦盐业有限公司	Tianjin 天津市	Tianjin 天津市	(022)23022160 (022)23022110
Zhejiang Salt Industry Company 浙江省盐业公司	Hangzhou 杭州市	Zhejiang 浙江省	(0571)87800292 (0571)87800082
Fujian Salt Industry Company 福建省盐业公司	Fuzhou 福州市	Fujian 福建省	(0591)7534344 (0591)7535047
Jiangxi Salt Industry General Company 江西省盐业总公司	Nanchang 南昌市	Jiangxi 江西省	(0791)6816695 (0791)6812316
Hubei Salt Transportation & Sale Company 湖北省盐业运销公司	Xiaogan 孝感市	Hubei 湖北省	(0712)3611320 (0712)3611244
Hunan Salt Industry Group Co.,Ltd.Jinshi Allocation & Transportation Company 湖南省盐业集团有限责任公司津市调运公司	Changde 常德市	Hunan 湖南省	(0736)4223817 (0736)4223817

1445: Enzyme Preparations 酶制剂制造业

The industry accounts for 0.014% of the total revenue of China's industrial sector in 2002. The rate of return on assets is 7.88%. 67.50% of all firms in the industry made a profit while 32.50% had negative returns.The top province in terms of the industry's revenue is Shandong, accounting for 44.58% of the total revenue.
2002年本行业收入占全行业的 0.014%，资产利润率为 7.88%。67.50%的企业赢利，32.50%的企业亏损。收入最高的省为山东省，占本行业的44.58%。

	Total number of firms 企业总数	Total number of employees 职工总数	Total revenue (Mil.RMB) 总销售收入 (百万元)	Total profit (Mil.RMB) 总利润 (百万元)	Return on assets 资产利润率 (%)	Return on equity 权益利润率 (%)	Labour productivity ('000 RMB/ worker) 劳动生产率 (千元/人)	Debts/ assets 资产负债率 (%)	Total assets (Mil.RMB) 总资产 (百万元)
Industry Overall 行业总体	40	6,975	1,499	174	7.88	15.08	75.69	47.73	2,212

	Number of firms 企业个数	Average number of employees 平均职工人数	Average revenue ('000 RMB) 平均销售收入（千元）	Average profit ('000 RMB) 平均利润 (千元)	Return on assets 资产利润率 (%)	Return on equity 权益利润率 (%)	Labour productivity ('000 RMB/ worker) 劳动生产率 (千元/人)	Debts/ assets 资产负债率 (%)	Average total assets ('000 RMB) 平均总资产 (千元)
By ownership 产业所有权									
State-owned 国有	3	241	13,171	-328	-1.10	-11.58	19.72	90.52	29,887
Collective-owned 集体	7	150	12,923	479	3.04	14.18	24.97	78.53	15,718
Foreign & Overseas Chinese Funded 三资	8	181	118,766	19,662	11.30	17.62	250.96	35.85	173,992
By regional distribution 地区分布									
Central-North 华北	6	194	59,213	-1,926	-1.35	-2.19	75.36	38.16	142,368
Beijing 北京	2	84	7,562	-50	-0.59	-1.35	21.80	55.99	8,324
Tianjin 天津	1	239	312,387	-9,373	-1.22	-1.94	283.74	37.18	769,616
Hebei 河北	3	252	9,255	-694	-3.06	-5.55	21.45	44.85	22,648
Shanxi 山西									
Inner Mongolia 内蒙古									
Northeast 东北	4	158	5,912	-952	-3.47	-9.18	7.92	62.17	27,415
Liaoning 辽宁									
Jilin 吉林	3	126	2,495	-1,269	-6.14	-30.73	2.80	80.04	20,683
Heilongjiang 黑龙江	1	254	16,164				15.54	38.88	47,608
Central-East 华东	18	228	52,729	9,667	16.09	33.52	87.35	52.01	60,088
Shanghai 上海									
Jiangsu 江苏	6	108	28,730	-1,804	-4.86	-22.62	70.20	78.53	37,153
Zhejiang 浙江	3	63	19,578	217	0.81	5.86	43.08	86.17	26,713
Anhui 安徽									
Fujian 福建	1	120	45,228	2,066	3.27	9.47	98.16	65.49	63,251
Jiangxi 江西	1	52	4,660	6,333	15.44	36.42	-42.35	57.61	41,028
Shandong 山东	7	442	95,446	25,112	26.07	41.76	95.38	37.57	96,322
Central-South 中南	10	99	16,801	1,553	9.48	23.26	76.37	59.22	16,376
Henan 河南	3	118	8,124	132	0.94		17.34	150.73	14,055
Hubei 湖北	2	44	31,920	2,385	45.54	78.11	378.97	41.70	5,238
Hunan 湖南	3	82	6,341	146	1.32	1.53	26.19	13.45	11,060
Guangdong 广东	2	152	30,386	4,963	12.73	18.61	99.55	31.56	38,971
Guangxi 广西									
Hainan 海南									
Southwest 西南									
Chongqing 重庆									
Sichuan 四川									
Guizhou 贵州									
Yunnan 云南									
Tibet 西藏									
Northwest 西北	2	44	1,355	95	7.68	49.61	15.66	84.51	1,237
Shaanxi 陕西									
Gansu 甘肃	2	44	1,355	95	7.68	49.61	15.66	84.51	1,237
Qinghai 青海									
Ningxia 宁夏									
Xinjiang 新疆									

1445: Enzyme Preparations 酶制剂制造业

Year 年份	Number of firms 企业个数	Rate of change 变化率 (%)	Number of employees 职工人数 (人)	Rate of change 变化率 (%)	Total revenue (Mil. RMB) 总销售收入 (百万元)	Rate of change 变化率 (%)	Total profit (Mil RMB) 总利润 (百万元)	Rate of change 变化率 (%)
2000	33		4,139		387		-41	
2001	34	3.03	4,287	3.58	774	100.00	-38	7.32
2002	40	17.65	6,975	62.70	1,499	93.67	174	-

Major Products 主要产品	Output 产量	Unit 单位

10 Main Firms with Maximal Revenue (year founded) 收入最大的十家主要企业（创办年份）	City 城市	Province 省	Telephone/fax 电话/传真	Number of employees 职工人数	Ownership 产业所有权	Revenue ('000 RMB) 销售收入 (千元)	Profit('000 RMB) (rank) 利润(千元) (排名)	Total assets ('000 RMB) 总资产 (千元)	Major products 主要产品
Shandong Zhongxuan Co.,Ltd.	Zibo	Shandong	(0533)7211374		Foreign Funded				Grain Wine
山东中轩股份有限公司(1975)	淄博市	山东省	(0533)7216024	723	外商投资	461,137	174,363(1)	424,076	粮酒
Novogymes China Biological Technology Co.,Ltd.	Tianjin	Tianjin	(022)25322062		Foreign Funded				Ferment Pretaration
诺维信(中国)生物技术有限公司(1998)	天津市	天津市	(022)25322064	239	外商投资	312,387	-	769,616	酶制剂
ShanDong Duqing Co., Ltd.	Heze	Shandong	(0530)2793035		Joint Stock				Starch Sugar Dextrin淀
山东都庆股份有限公司(1988)	荷泽市	山东省	(0530)2791202	1,000	股份制	125,396	938(10)	178,930	粉糖糊精
Wuxi Genencor Bio-engineering Co.,Ltd.	Wuxi	Jiangsu	(0510)3709751		Foreign Funded				Ferment Pretaration
无锡杰能科生物工程有限公司(1998)	无锡市	江苏省	(0510)3709726	210	外商投资	85,407	-	138,969	酶制剂
Ezhou Huasheng Bio-engineering Co., Ltd.	Ezhou	Hubei	(0711)3812566		Overseas Chinese-funded				Cellulose Enzyme
鄂州华升生物工程有限公司(1999)	鄂州市	湖北省	(0711)3812566	67	港澳台资	56,940	3,810(4)	7,959	纤维素酶
Hui'an Jin Mai Beer Raw Stuff Company	Quanzhou	Fujian	(0595)7387299		Limited-Liability				Malt
惠安县金麦啤酒原料公司(1995)	泉州市	福建省	(0595)7387699	120	有限公司	45,228	2,066(7)	63,251	麦芽
Yixing Biochemical Company	Wuxi	Jiangsu	(0510)7281625		Collective-owned				Starch Acid
宜兴市生物工程公司(1992)	无锡市	江苏省	(0510)7281625	120	集体企业	45,116	3,404(5)	51,839	淀粉酸
Guangdong YiDuoLi Bioecomic Co., Ltd.	Zhuhai	Guangdong	(0756)8676888		Joint Owned				Compound Enzyme
广东溢多利生物科技股份有限公司(1991)	珠海市	广东省	(0756)8673989	197	联营企业	40,823	7,857(2)	53,699	复合酶
Pinghu Danghu Malt Co., Ltd.	Jiaxing	Zhejiang	(0573)5113998		Private Owned				Malt Beer Raw Materials麦芽
平湖市当湖麦芽有限责任公司(1986)	嘉兴市	浙江省	(0573)5117839	100	私营企业	27,890	210(20)	19,561	啤酒源料
Yishui LongDa Bio-engineering Co.,Ltd.	Linyi	Shandong	(0539)2257423		Limited-Liability				Saccharification Enzyme
沂水县隆达生物工程有限责任公司(1976)	临沂市	山东省	(0539)2268415	430	有限公司	25,734	-	7,493	糖化酶

Top 10 Cities by Revenue 销售收入排名前10位城市	Province 省	Market share 市场份额 (%)	Number of firms 企业个数
Zibo 淄博市	Shandong 山东省	30.77	1
Tianjin 天津市	Tianjin 天津市	20.84	1
Wuxi 无锡市	Jiangsu 江苏省	10.49	4
Heze 荷泽市	Shandong 山东省	8.37	1
Ezhou 鄂州市	Hubei 湖北省	4.26	2
Quanzhou 泉州市	Fujian 福建省	3.02	1
Zhuhai 珠海市	Guangdong 广东省	2.72	1
Jinan 济南市	Shandong 山东省	1.97	2
Jiaxing 嘉兴市	Zhejiang 浙江省	1.86	1
Linyi 临沂市	Shandong 山东省	1.72	1

10 Major Wholesalers 十家主要批发商	City 城市	Province 省	Telephone/Fax 电话/传真
Guangdong Foodstuffs Import & Export Group Corporation	Guangzhou	Guangdong	(020)83854888
广东省食品进出口集团公司	广州市	广东省	(020)83856823
Hubei Salt Industry General Company	Wuhan	Hubei	(027)82832190
湖北盐业总公司	武汉市	湖北省	(027)82816030
Henan Provincial Salt Business Administration Bureau (Henan Provincial Salt Industry General Company)	Zhengzhou	Henan	(0371)5907597
河南省盐务管理局(河南省盐业总公司)	郑州市	河南省	(0371)5906346
Sichuan Salt Industry General Company	Chengdu	Sichuan	(028)86652441
四川省盐业总公司	成都市	四川省	(028)86663440
China National Salt Tianjin Changlu Salt Industry Co.,Ltd.	Tianjin	Tianjin	(022)23022160
中盐天津市长芦盐业有限公司	天津市	天津市	(022)23022110
Zhejiang Salt Industry Company	Hangzhou	Zhejiang	(0571)87800292
浙江省盐业公司	杭州市	浙江省	(0571)87800082
Fujian Salt Industry Company	Fuzhou	Fujian	(0591)7534344
福建省盐业公司	福州市	福建省	(0591)7535047
Jiangxi Salt Industry General Company	Nanchang	Jiangxi	(0791)6816695
江西省盐业总公司	南昌市	江西省	(0791)6812316
Hubei Salt Transportation & Sale Company	Xiaogan	Hubei	(0712)3611320
湖北省盐业运销公司	孝感市	湖北省	(0712)3611244
Hunan Salt Industry Group Co.,Ltd.Jinshi Allocation & Transportation Company	Changde	Hunan	(0736)4223817
湖南省盐业集团有限责任公司津市调运公司	常德市	湖南省	(0736)4223817

1449: Other Fermented Products 其他发酵制品业

The industry accounts for 0.026% of the total revenue of China's industrial sector in 2002. The rate of return on assets is 2.56%. 93.18% of all firms in the industry made a profit while 6.82% had negative returns.The top province in terms of the industry's revenue is Shandong, accounting for 67.06% of the total revenue.
2002年本行业收入占全行业的0.026%，资产利润率为2.56%。93.18%的企业赢利，6.82%的企业亏损。收入最高的省为山东省，占本行业的67.06%。

	Total number of firms 企业总数	Total number of employees 职工总数	Total revenue (Mil.RMB) 总销售收入（百万元）	Total profit (Mil.RMB) 总利润（百万元）	Return on assets 资产利润率 (%)	Return on equity 权益利润率 (%)	Labour productivity ('000 RMB/ worker) 劳动生产率（千元/人）	Debts/ assets 资产负债率 (%)	Total assets (Mil.RMB) 总资产（百万元）
Industry Overall 行业总体	44	9,323	2,749	121	2.56	6.19	60.31	58.73	4,727

	Number of firms 企业个数	Average number of employees 平均职工人数	Average revenue ('000 RMB) 平均销售收入（千元）	Average profit ('000 RMB) 平均利润（千元）	Return on assets 资产利润率 (%)	Return on equity 权益利润率 (%)	Labour productivity ('000 RMB/ worker) 劳动生产率（千元/人）	Debts/ assets 资产负债率 (%)	Average total assets ('000 RMB) 平均总资产（千元）
By ownership 产业所有权									
State-owned 国有	5	247	39,981	1,779	3.21	13.91	43.63	76.95	55,519
Collective-owned 集体	10	139	39,915	1,245	2.64	10.82	-147.33	75.64	47,240
Foreign & Overseas Chinese Funded 三资	3	87	91,372	4,877	4.67	15.80	268.31	70.41	104,333
By regional distribution 地区分布									
Central-North 华北	5	206	55,648	3,675	3.40	10.20	-290.53	66.63	107,947
Beijing 北京	1	100	11,235	471	11.36	36.63	31.86	68.98	4,146
Tianjin 天津	1	260	41,080	-300	-0.36	-0.95	-1,402.69	61.57	82,290
Hebei 河北	3	223	75,309	6,068	4.02	12.37	94.08	67.53	151,100
Shanxi 山西									
Inner Mongolia 内蒙古									
Northeast 东北	2	261	34,465	2,716	2.89	6.63	32.17	56.44	94,052
Liaoning 辽宁									
Jilin 吉林									
Heilongjiang 黑龙江	2	261	34,465	2,716	2.89	6.63	32.17	56.44	94,052
Central-East 华东	18	280	107,060	4,211	2.32	5.06	137.07	54.23	181,784
Shanghai 上海									
Jiangsu 江苏	2	35	24,025	1,540	4.85	14.67	345.99	66.90	31,725
Zhejiang 浙江	1	96	16,720	500	5.21	40.00	46.77	86.98	9,600
Anhui 安徽	1	106	16,201	7	0.05	0.70	15.43	92.66	13,619
Fujian 福建	1	80	2,460	-130	-4.56	-128.71	5.70	96.46	2,850
Jiangxi 江西									
Shandong 山东	13	360	141,819	5,564	2.27	4.91	140.80	53.67	244,815
Central-South 中南	8	188	27,598	762	1.94	10.14	50.92	80.88	39,297
Henan 河南	4	245	34,353	1,137	1.99	17.38	40.19	88.55	57,118
Hubei 湖北	1	103	5,000	-240	-1.16	-5.04	43.23	76.97	20,665
Hunan 湖南									
Guangdong 广东	3	141	26,124	596	2.74	6.13	77.63	55.27	21,747
Guangxi 广西									
Hainan 海南									
Southwest 西南									
Chongqing 重庆									
Sichuan 四川									
Guizhou 贵州									
Yunnan 云南									
Tibet 西藏									
Northwest 西北	11	112	23,100	1,374	3.66	11.52	62.80	68.22	37,528
Shaanxi 陕西	1	138	60,014	2,892	2.27	9.82	116.68	76.88	127,380
Gansu 甘肃	7	93	18,150	1,157	4.60	12.95	70.35	64.51	25,176
Qinghai 青海									
Ningxia 宁夏	1	255	13,148	405	1.36		18.98	105.80	29,674
Xinjiang 新疆	2	97	26,941	1,856	4.67	9.07	56.77	48.55	39,761

1449: Other Fermented Products 其他发酵制品业

Year 年份	Number of firms 企业个数	Rate of change 变化率 (%)	Number of employees 职工人数 (人)	Rate of change 变化率 (%)	Total revenue (Mil. RMB) 总销售收入 (百万元)	Rate of change 变化率 (%)	Total profit (Mil RMB) 总利润 (百万元)	Rate of change 变化率 (%)
2000	45		6,475		944		14	
2001	49	8.89	6,640	2.55	1,067	13.03	35	150.00
2002	44	-10.20	9,323	40.41	2,749	157.64	121	245.71

Major Products 主要产品	Output 产量	Unit 单位

10 Main Firms with Maximal Revenue (year founded) 收入最大的十家主要企业（创办年份）	City 城市	Province 省	Telephone/fax 电话/传真	Number of employees 职工人数	Ownership 产业所有权	Revenue ('000 RMB) 销售收入 (千元)	Profit('000 RMB) (rank) 利润(千元) (排名)	Total assets ('000 RMB) 总资产 (千元)	Major products 主要产品
Ji'nan Agricultural-industrial-commercial Group Co., Ltd.	Jinan	Shandong	(0531)2977096		State Enterprises				Dairy Products
济南农工商集团有限公司(1950)	济南市	山东省	(0531)2742974	2,113	国有独资	678,242	41,217(1)	780,942	乳制品
King Nine Shangdong Co.,Ltd.	Jining	Shandong	(0537)2082799		Limited-Liability				Edible Alcohol
山东九九有限公司(1999)	济宁市	山东省	(0537)2367699	800	有限公司	392,227	-	1,782,908	食用酒精
Hebei Sihai Industrial Group Co., Ltd.	Chengde	Hebei	(0314)2262506		Limited-Liability				Barley Malt
河北四海实业集团有限公司(1985)	承德市	河北省	(0314)2122938	440	有限公司	207,212	17,861(2)	423,064	大麦芽
Yantai MDL Beer Raw Material Co.,Ltd.	Yantai	Shandong	(0535)6710908		Overseas Chinese-funded				Barley Malt
烟台麦多利啤酒原料有限公司(2000)	烟台市	山东省	(0535)6710262	95	港澳台资	198,221	9,900(3)	132,150	大麦芽
Yantai Malting Plant	Yantai	Shandong	(0535)6715033		Collective-owned				Barley Malt
烟台市麦芽厂(1981)	烟台市	山东省	(0535)6714277	290	集体企业	186,845	9,011(4)	154,614	大麦芽
Shandong Jianghai Malt Co., Ltd.	Weifang	Shandong	(0536)6761098		Limited-Liability				Beer Malt
山东江海麦芽有限公司(1997)	潍坊市	山东省	(0536)6761318	650	有限公司	178,234	8,626(5)	214,815	啤酒用麦芽
Luzhong Beer Co., Ltd.	Laiwu	Shandong	(0634)6095555		Collective-owned				Malt
鲁中啤酒有限公司(2000)	莱芜市	山东省	(0634)6097368	150	集体企业	100,200	351(26)	27,845	麦芽
Dancheng Jindan Lactic Acid Industrial Co.,Ltd.	Zhoukou	Henan	(0394)3195099		State-owned				Lactic Acid Products
郸城县金丹乳酸实业有限公司(1984)	周口市	河南省	(0394)3195329	469	国有企业	66,085	14(34)	95,185	乳酸制品
Heilongjiang Beidahuang Malt Group	Shuangyashan	Heilongjiang	(0469)5860114		State-owned				Barley Malt
黑龙江省北大荒麦芽有限公司(1997)	双鸭山市	黑龙江省	(0469)5860162	491	国有企业	63,630	5,350(6)	134,460	大麦芽
Henan Mengzhou Xinyuan Co.,Ltd.	Jiaozuo	Henan	(0391)8193625		State-owned				Malt Dextrin
河南省孟州市鑫源有限责任公司(1996)	焦作市	河南省	(0391)8193625	210	国有企业	54,168	2,304(10)	20,403	麦芽糊精

Top 10 Cities by Revenue 销售收入排名前10位城市	Province 省	Market share 市场份额 (%)	Number of firms 企业个数
Jinan 济南市	Shandong 山东省	24.67	1
Yantai 烟台市	Shandong 山东省	16.33	3
Jining 济宁市	Shandong 山东省	14.78	2
Chengde 承德市	Hebei 河北省	7.54	1
Weifang 潍坊市	Shandong 山东省	6.74	3
Laiwu 莱芜市	Shandong 山东省	3.64	1
Jiaozuo 焦作市	Henan 河南省	2.59	2
Zhoukou 周口市	Henan 河南省	2.40	1
Shuangyashan 双鸭山市	Heilongjiang 黑龙江省	2.31	1
Xianyang 咸阳市	Shannxi 陕西省	2.18	1

10 Major Wholesalers 十家主要批发商	City 城市	Province 省	Telephone/Fax 电话/传真
Guangdong Foodstuffs Import & Export Group Corporation	Guangzhou	Guangdong	(020)83854888
广东省食品进出口集团公司	广州市	广东省	(020)83856823
Hubei Salt Industry General Company	Wuhan	Hubei	(027)82832190
湖北盐业总公司	武汉市	湖北省	(027)82816030
Henan Provincial Salt Business Administration Bureau (Henan Provincial Salt Industry General Company)	Zhengzhou	Henan	(0371)5907597
河南省盐务管理局(河南省盐业总公司)	郑州市	河南省	(0371)5906346
Sichuan Salt Industry General Company	Chengdu	Sichuan	(028)86652441
四川省盐业总公司	成都市	四川省	(028)86663440
China National Salt Tianjin Changlu Salt Industry Co.,Ltd.	Tianjin	Tianjin	(022)23022160
中盐天津市长芦盐业有限公司	天津市	天津市	(022)23022110
Zhejiang Salt Industry Company	Hangzhou	Zhejiang	(0571)87800292
浙江省盐业公司	杭州市	浙江省	(0571)87800082
Fujian Salt Industry Company	Fuzhou	Fujian	(0591)7534344
福建省盐业公司	福州市	福建省	(0591)7535047
Jiangxi Salt Industry General Company	Nanchang	Jiangxi	(0791)6816695
江西省盐业总公司	南昌市	江西省	(0791)6812316
Hubei Salt Transportation & Sale Company	Xiaogan	Hubei	(0712)3611320
湖北省盐业运销公司	孝感市	湖北省	(0712)3611244
Hunan Salt Industry Group Co.,Ltd.Jinshi Allocation & Transportation Company	Changde	Hunan	(0736)4223817
湖南省盐业集团有限责任公司津市调运公司	常德市	湖南省	(0736)4223817

1451: Soy-sauce and Sauce 酱油、酱类制造业

The industry accounts for 0.069% of the total revenue of China's industrial sector in 2002. The rate of return on assets is 1.03%. 71.67% of all firms in the industry made a profit while 28.33% had negative returns.The top province in terms of the industry's revenue is Guangdong, accounting for 42.44% of the total revenue.
2002年本行业收入占全行业的0.069%，资产利润率为1.03%。71.67%的企业赢利，28.33%的企业亏损。收入最高的省为广东省，占本行业的42.44%。

	Total number of firms 企业总数	Total number of employees 职工总数	Total revenue (Mil.RMB) 总销售收入 (百万元)	Total profit (Mil.RMB) 总利润 (百万元)	Return on assets 资产利润率 (%)	Return on equity 权益利润率 (%)	Labour productivity ('000 RMB/ worker) 劳动生产率 (千元/人)	Debts/ assets 资产负债率 (%)	Total assets (Mil.RMB) 总资产 (百万元)
Industry Overall 行业总体	413	58,962	7,378	110	1.03	4.19	39.09	75.38	10,633

	Number of firms 企业个数	Average number of employees 平均职工人数	Average revenue ('000 RMB) 平均销售收入 (千元)	Average profit ('000 RMB) 平均利润 (千元)	Return on assets 资产利润率 (%)	Return on equity 权益利润率 (%)	Labour productivity ('000 RMB/ worker) 劳动生产率 (千元/人)	Debts/ assets 资产负债率 (%)	Average total assets ('000 RMB) 平均总资产 (千元)
By ownership 产业所有权									
State-owned 国有	195	109	4,560	-163	-1.38	-4.83	14.41	71.43	11,808
Collective-owned 集体	35	62	8,943	281	4.42	14.94	39.24	70.39	6,345
Foreign & Overseas Chinese Funded 三资	45	253	88,919	4,528	4.25	11.54	115.43	63.17	106,524
By regional distribution 地区分布									
Central-North 华北	51	145	11,375	348	1.76	4.31	28.49	59.25	19,823
Beijing 北京	6	187	15,809	431	1.83	3.56	37.71	48.73	23,571
Tianjin 天津	12	122	6,001	-280	-1.52	-4.50	7.56	66.21	18,439
Hebei 河北	25	163	15,597	802	3.49	8.07	36.36	56.72	22,951
Shanxi 山西	6	92	3,518	-219	-2.02	-12.06	14.42	83.26	10,827
Inner Mongolia 内蒙古	2	85	1,113	-103	-2.14	-3.75	4.30	42.85	4,783
Northeast 东北	46	175	10,271	457	1.98	4.29	19.08	53.88	23,082
Liaoning 辽宁	22	206	12,827	833	2.43	5.17	24.03	52.92	34,234
Jilin 吉林	11	138	7,110	37	0.32	0.69	7.69	53.86	11,764
Heilongjiang 黑龙江	13	153	8,619	174	1.26	3.00	16.46	57.91	13,784
Central-East 华东	128	147	16,174	-1,178	-4.81	-17.18	29.19	71.97	24,460
Shanghai 上海	7	277	91,610	-27,761	-17.10	-241.69	52.25	92.92	162,316
Jiangsu 江苏	32	120	10,637	508	2.76	5.75	24.49	52.03	18,400
Zhejiang 浙江	11	153	17,048	636	3.93	12.32	48.26	68.14	16,190
Anhui 安徽	11	133	6,413	-65	-0.68	-2.46	22.74	72.15	9,469
Fujian 福建	11	142	10,151	738	3.41	5.00	26.30	31.84	21,655
Jiangxi 江西	14	105	2,440	-158	-2.52	-8.04	8.43	68.64	6,269
Shandong 山东	42	163	16,303	361	1.90	6.33	27.09	70.03	18,993
Central-South 中南	122	147	31,359	2,106	5.57	42.22	68.22	86.81	37,814
Henan 河南	33	106	3,501	-86	-1.06	-72.77	11.56	98.54	8,083
Hubei 湖北	15	76	12,960	303	4.54	10.69	64.86	57.50	6,678
Hunan 湖南	16	82	20,647	801	7.47	10.51	59.71	28.90	10,719
Guangdong 广东	47	234	66,628	5,142	6.14	58.46	91.37	89.49	83,711
Guangxi 广西	11	83	4,909	63	0.49	2.59	22.89	80.96	12,769
Hainan 海南									
Southwest 西南	42	121	7,584	-279	-2.12	-6.10	26.58	65.19	13,121
Chongqing 重庆	4	203	6,553	-4,210	-19.47		4.99	111.51	21,627
Sichuan 四川	18	167	11,932	220	1.45	3.07	33.93	52.77	15,145
Guizhou 贵州	9	66	6,332	264	2.31	5.54	34.73	58.32	11,416
Yunnan 云南	9	70	2,283	-133	-1.34	-3.96	13.26	66.15	9,914
Tibet 西藏	2	19							
Northwest 西北	24	74	4,631	-979	-8.87	-61.20	20.56	85.50	11,033
Shaanxi 陕西	12	72	1,169	-1,374	-29.74	-145.76	6.34	79.60	4,620
Gansu 甘肃	9	76	9,946	-397	-2.04	-10.04	43.34	79.66	19,446
Qinghai 青海	1	12	204	-18	-2.22	-3.00	6.50	25.80	810
Ningxia 宁夏									
Xinjiang 新疆	2	104	3,705	-1,713	-10.22		4.79	127.17	16,765

Year 年份	Number of firms 企业个数	Rate of change 变化率 (%)	Number of employees 职工人数 (人)	Rate of change 变化率 (%)	Total revenue (Mil. RMB) 总销售收入 (百万元)	Rate of change 变化率 (%)	Total profit (Mil RMB) 总利润 (百万元)	Rate of change 变化率 (%)
2000	532		76,750		6,016		224	
2001	469	-11.84	65,828	-14.23	6,814	13.26	169	-24.55
2002	413	-11.94	58,962	-10.43	7,378	8.28	110	-34.91

Major Products 主要产品	Output 产量	Unit 单位
Soy Sauce 酱油	160	10,000 Tons 万吨

10 Main Firms with Maximal Revenue (year founded) 收入最大的十家主要企业（创办年份）	City 城市	Province 省	Telephone/fax 电话/传真	Number of employees 职工人数	Ownership 产业所有权	Revenue ('000 RMB) 销售收入 (千元)	Profit('000 RMB) (rank) 利润(千元) (排名)	Total assets ('000 RMB) 总资产 (千元)	Major products 主要产品
Foshan Haitian Flavouring Food Co.,Ltd. 佛山市海天调味食品有限公司(2000)	Foshan 佛山市	Guangdong 广东省	(0757)2832023 (0757)2832370	1,073	Overseas Chinese-funded 港澳台资	1,186,153	168,558(1)	1,284,930	Soy Sauce 酱油
Leekumkee(Guangzhou) Food Co.,Ltd. 李锦记（广州）有限公司(1994)	Guangzhou 广州市	Guangdong 广东省	(020)82216198 (020)82216194	565	Overseas Chinese-funded 港澳台资	326,231	82,229(2)	220,265	Thick Sauce 酱
Kaiping Master Flavouring Co.,Ltd. 开平市味事达调味品有限公司(1996)	Jiangmen 江门市	Guangdong 广东省	(0750)2393442 (0750)2299038	697	Foreign Funded 外商投资	231,314	41,600(3)	305,220	Soy Sauce 酱油
Shanghai Amoy Food Co.,Ltd. 上海淘大食品有限公司(1994)	Shanghai 上海市	Shanghai 上海市	(021)65313275 (021)65312144	657	Foreign Funded 外商投资	227,566	21,425(5)	179,303	Soy Sauce 酱油
Guangdong Meiweixian Flavoring Food Co.,Ltd. 中山市美味鲜食品有限公司(2000)	Zhongshan 中山市	Guangdong 广东省	(0760)8627990 (0760)8637834	650	Overseas Chinese-funded 港澳台资	225,734	24,971(4)	205,795	Soy Sauce 酱油
Unilever Food China Co.,Ltd. 联合利华食品(中国)有限公司(1998)	Shanghai 上海市	Shanghai 上海市	(021)57241777 (021)57241406	435	Foreign Funded 外商投资	219,128	-	618,711	Soy Sauce 酱油
Jiajia Sauce Changsha Co., Ltd. 加加酱业长沙有限公司(1997)	Changsha 长沙市	Hunan 湖南省	(0731)7801016 (0731)7801016	320	Overseas Chinese-funded 港澳台资	186,970	10,313(10)	40,014	Soy Sauce 酱油
Jammy Chai (Guangzhou) Foods Co., Ltd. 广州致美斋食品有限公司(1993)	Guangzhou 广州市	Guangdong 广东省	(020)86624314 (020)86625141	548	Overseas Chinese-funded 港澳台资	138,721	7,525(11)	165,048	Soy Sauce 酱油
Shenzhen Amoy Food Co., Ltd. 深圳淘化大同食品有限公司(1994)	Shenzhen 深圳市	Guangdong 广东省	(0755)84622481 (0755)84622837	1,820	Overseas Chinese-funded 港澳台资	127,403	3,606(19)	62,817	Thick Sauce Material 酱料
Leekumkee(Xinhui) Food Co., Ltd. 李锦记（新会）食品有限公司(1995)	Jiangmen 江门市	Guangdong 广东省	(0750)6499555 (0750)6499879	317	Overseas Chinese-funded 港澳台资	109,219	1,355(47)	197,339	Soy Sauce 酱油

Top 10 Cities by Revenue 销售收入排名前10位城市	Province 省	Market share 市场份额 (%)	Number of firms 企业个数
Foshan 佛山市	Guangdong 广东省	17.31	5
Guangzhou 广州市	Guangdong 广东省	10.83	13
Shanghai 上海市	Shanghai 上海市	8.69	7
Jiangmen 江门市	Guangdong 广东省	5.95	7
Zhongshan 中山市	Guangdong 广东省	4.60	3
Qingdao 青岛市	Shandong 山东省	2.55	4
Changsha 长沙市	Hunan 湖南省	2.53	1
Yueyang 岳阳市	Hunan 湖南省	1.82	7
Shenzhen 深圳市	Guangdong 广东省	1.80	2
Shijiazhuang 石家庄市	Hebei 河北省	1.72	3

10 Major Wholesalers 十家主要批发商	City 城市	Province 省	Telephone/Fax 电话/传真
Guangdong Foodstuffs Import & Export Group Corporation 广东省食品进出口集团公司	Guangzhou 广州市	Guangdong 广东省	(020)83854888 (020)83856823
Hubei Salt Industry General Company 湖北盐业总公司	Wuhan 武汉市	Hubei 湖北省	(027)82832190 (027)82816030
Henan Provincial Salt Business Administration Bureau (Henan Provincial Salt Industry General Company) 河南省盐务管理局(河南省盐业总公司)	Zhengzhou 郑州市	Henan 河南省	(0371)5907597 (0371)5906346
Sichuan Salt Industry General Company 四川省盐业总公司	Chengdu 成都市	Sichuan 四川省	(028)86652441 (028)86663440
China National Salt Tianjin Changlu Salt Industry Co.,Ltd. 中盐天津市长芦盐业有限公司	Tianjin 天津市	Tianjin 天津市	(022)23022160 (022)23022110
Zhejiang Salt Industry Company 浙江省盐业公司	Hangzhou 杭州市	Zhejiang 浙江省	(0571)87800292 (0571)87800082
Fujian Salt Industry Company 福建省盐业公司	Fuzhou 福州市	Fujian 福建省	(0591)7534344 (0591)7535047
Jiangxi Salt Industry General Company 江西省盐业总公司	Nanchang 南昌市	Jiangxi 江西省	(0791)6816695 (0791)6812316
Hubei Salt Transportation & Sale Company 湖北省盐业运销公司	Xiaogan 孝感市	Hubei 湖北省	(0712)3611320 (0712)3611244
Hunan Salt Industry Group Co.,Ltd.Jinshi Allocation & Transportation Company 湖南省盐业集团有限责任公司津市调运公司	Changde 常德市	Hunan 湖南省	(0736)4223817 (0736)4223817

1452: Vinegar 食醋制造业

The industry accounts for 0.008% of the total revenue of China's industrial sector in 2002. The rate of return on assets is 4.44%. 82.76% of all firms in the industry made a profit while 17.24% had negative returns.The top province in terms of the industry's revenue is Jiangsu, accounting for 52.68% of the total revenue.
2002年本行业收入占全行业的0.008%，资产利润率为4.44%。82.76%的企业赢利，17.24%的企业亏损。收入最高的省为江苏省，占本行业的52.68%。

	Total number of firms 企业总数	Total number of employees 职工总数	Total revenue (Mil.RMB) 总销售收入 (百万元)	Total profit (Mil.RMB) 总利润 (百万元)	Return on assets 资产利润率 (%)	Return on equity 权益利润率 (%)	Labour productivity ('000 RMB/ worker) 劳动生产率 (千元/人)	Debts/ assets 资产负债率 (%)	Total assets (Mil.RMB) 总资产 (百万元)
Industry Overall 行业总体	58	8,040	911	70	4.44	7.56	47.53	41.30	1,581

	Number of firms 企业个数	Average number of employees 平均职工人数	Average revenue ('000 RMB) 平均销售收入 (千元)	Average profit ('000 RMB) 平均利润 (千元)	Return on assets 资产利润率 (%)	Return on equity 权益利润率 (%)	Labour productivity ('000 RMB/ worker) 劳动生产率 (千元/人)	Debts/ assets 资产负债率 (%)	Average total assets ('000 RMB) 平均总资产 (千元)
By ownership 产业所有权									
State-owned 国有	22	125	14,556	2,192	6.34	9.36	61.65	32.26	34,574
Collective-owned 集体	6	62	5,505	575	13.89	35.26	50.05	60.62	4,138
Foreign & Overseas Chinese Funded 三资	2	179	19,275	1,552	6.32	7.33	58.07	13.67	24,541
By regional distribution 地区分布									
Central-North 华北	19	224	13,868	499	1.64	3.02	26.99	45.66	30,430
Beijing 北京	2	349	41,103	2,076	3.60	4.56	48.30	21.08	57,641
Tianjin 天津	3	175	15,824	1,027	3.75	7.09	39.09	47.10	27,388
Hebei 河北	5	131	2,604	10	0.11	0.18	6.35	39.40	9,141
Shanxi 山西	8	288	14,448	245	0.61	1.32	23.72	54.21	40,393
Inner Mongolia 内蒙古	1	72	5,203	240	2.02	5.90	24.75	65.73	11,872
Northeast 东北	1	206	5,871	4	0.02	0.04	1.01	52.56	22,098
Liaoning 辽宁	1	206	5,871	4	0.02	0.04	1.01	52.56	22,098
Jilin 吉林									
Heilongjiang 黑龙江									
Central-East 华东	15	165	35,863	3,555	6.01	9.44	91.99	36.34	59,153
Shanghai 上海	1	50	10,590	94	1.95	15.77	21.22	87.62	4,813
Jiangsu 江苏	7	243	68,552	7,478	6.64	10.23	123.57	35.08	112,634
Zhejiang 浙江									
Anhui 安徽									
Fujian 福建	1	76	5,323	253	2.53	4.86	46.32	47.86	9,982
Jiangxi 江西									
Shandong 山东	6	110	7,028	105	0.75	1.33	20.99	43.86	14,011
Central-South 中南	4	41	10,247	1,463	28.49	53.06	72.74	46.31	5,136
Henan 河南	3	50	13,567	1,965	29.37	54.76	79.29	46.36	6,689
Hubei 湖北									
Hunan 湖南									
Guangdong 广东	1	14	287	-41	-8.58	-15.30	2.64	43.93	478
Guangxi 广西									
Hainan 海南									
Southwest 西南	3	145	17,837	736	5.56	15.94	34.91	65.13	13,239
Chongqing 重庆									
Sichuan 四川	2	195	25,962	1,097	6.01	16.34	38.28	63.18	18,230
Guizhou 贵州	1	45	1,586	15	0.46	3.53	5.67	86.96	3,258
Yunnan 云南									
Tibet 西藏									
Northwest 西北	16	31	567	-43	-2.08	-5.06	23.52	58.95	2,085
Shaanxi 陕西	1	29	562	5	0.32	0.94	8.55	66.09	1,569
Gansu 甘肃	13	32	625	-28	-1.37	-3.71	27.21	63.15	2,079
Qinghai 青海									
Ningxia 宁夏	1	16	40	-56	-5.63	-6.05	2.94	7.04	995
Xinjiang 新疆	1	36	347	-273	-7.24	-11.97	1.56	39.54	3,773

1452: Vinegar 食醋制造业

Year 年份	Number of firms 企业个数	Rate of change 变化率 (%)	Number of employees 职工人数 (人)	Rate of change 变化率 (%)	Total revenue (Mil. RMB) 总销售收入 (百万元)	Rate of change 变化率 (%)	Total profit (Mil RMB) 总利润 (百万元)	Rate of change 变化率 (%)
2000	65		7,899		636		39	
2001	61	-6.15	7,874	-0.32	726	14.15	56	43.59
2002	58	-4.92	8,040	2.11	911	25.48	70	25.00

Major Products 主要产品	Output 产量	Unit 单位

10 Main Firms with Maximal Revenue (year founded) 收入最大的十家主要企业（创办年份）	City 城市	Province 省	Telephone/ fax 电话/传真	Number of employees 职工人数	Ownership 产业所有权	Revenue ('000 RMB) 销售收入 (千元)	Profit('000 RMB) (rank) 利润(千元) (排名)	Total assets ('000 RMB) 总资产 (千元)	Major products 主要产品
Jiangsu Hengshun Group Co., Ltd.	Zhenjiang	Jiangsu	(0511)5233758		State-owned				Vinegar
江苏恒顺集团有限公司(1988)	镇江市	江苏省	(0511)5230209	965	国有企业	271,449	49,376(1)	615,839	醋
Jiangsu Hengfeng Group Co.,Ltd.	Zhenjiang	Jiangsu	(0511)4561376		Limited-Liability				Table Vinegar
江苏恒丰集团有限公司(1996)	镇江市	江苏省	(0511)4561351	287	有限公司	182,246	3,210(3)	139,641	食醋
Shanxi Shuita Mature Vinegar Co., Ltd.	Taiyuan	Shanxi	(0351)5953034		Joint Stock				Table Vinegar
山西水塔老陈醋股份有限公司(1976)	太原市	山西省	(0351)5953143	857	股份制	66,108	2,032(6)	129,735	食醋
Tianjin Tianli Duliu Mature Vinegar Co.,Ltd.	Tianjin	Tianjin	(022)68815122		Limited-Liability				Table Vinegar
天津市天立独流老醋股份有限公司(1984)	天津市	天津市	(022)68816072	360	有限公司	34,843	1,472(7)	75,094	食醋
Beijing Longmen Wadakan Food Co.,Ltd.	Beijing	Beijing	(010)67912322		Foreign Funded				Table Vinegar
北京龙门和田宽食品有限公司(1992)	北京市	北京市	(010)67912322	247	外商投资	32,500	3,055(4)	41,624	食醋
Shanxi Mature Vinegar Group Co., Ltd.	Taiyuan	Shanxi	(0351)4420693		Limited-Liability				Vinegar
山西老陈醋集团有限公司	太原市	山西省	(0351)4425920	626	有限公司	31,472	105(19)	125,137	醋
Fangcheng Gongpu Duty Co., Ltd.	Nanyang	Henan	(0377)7232020		Private Enterprises				Table Vinegar
方城县公仆责任有限公司(1996)	南阳市	河南省	(0377)7232020	58	私营独资	24,270	4,081(2)	8,814	食醋
Xuyi Henghe Brewage Co., Ltd.	Huaian	Jiangsu	(0517)8511135		State-owned				Soy Sauce
盱眙恒河酿造有限公司(1986)	淮安市	江苏省	(0517)8511192	260	国有企业	12,095	-	19,341	酱油
Xuyi Luokou Brewage Co., Ltd.	Jinan	Shandong	(0531)5700947		Limited-Liability				Soy Sauce
济南泺口酿造总公司(1956)	济南市	山东省	(0531)5719373	256	有限公司	11,507	22(21)	27,423	酱油
Shandong Sincrown brewage Industry Co.,Ltd.	Zibo	Shandong	(0533)6680061		Limited-Liability				Table Vinegar
山东华王酿造有限公司(1997)	淄博市	山东省	(0533)6680061	66	有限公司	10,332	286(14)	14,849	食醋

Top 10 Cities by Revenue 销售收入排名前10位城市	Province 省	Market share 市场份额 (%)	Number of firms 企业个数
Zhenjiang 镇江市	Jiangsu 江苏省	50.46	4
Taiyuan 太原市	Shanxi 山西省	10.71	2
Beijing 北京市	Beijing 北京市	9.03	2
Tianjin 天津市	Tianjin 天津市	5.21	3
Nanchong 南充市	Sichuan 四川省	4.81	1
Nanyang 南阳市	Henan 河南省	2.66	1
Zibo 淄博市	Shandong 山东省	1.96	2
Jinan 济南市	Shandong 山东省	1.61	2
Huaian 淮安市	Jiangsu 江苏省	1.33	1
Jinzhong 晋中市	Shanxi 山西省	1.30	2

10 Major Wholesalers 十家主要批发商	City 城市	Province 省	Telephone/Fax 电话/传真
Guangdong Foodstuffs Import & Export Group Corporation	Guangzhou	Guangdong	(020)83854888
广东省食品进出口集团公司	广州市	广东省	(020)83856823
Hubei Salt Industry General Company	Wuhan	Hubei	(027)82832190
湖北盐业总公司	武汉市	湖北省	(027)82816030
Henan Provincial Salt Business Administration Bureau (Henan Provincial Salt Industry General Company)	Zhengzhou	Henan	(0371)5907597
河南省盐务管理局(河南省盐业总公司)	郑州市	河南省	(0371)5906346
Sichuan Salt Industry General Company	Chengdu	Sichuan	(028)86652441
四川省盐业总公司	成都市	四川省	(028)86663440
China National Salt Tianjin Changlu Salt Industry Co.,Ltd.	Tianjin	Tianjin	(022)23022160
中盐天津市长芦盐业有限公司	天津市	天津市	(022)23022110
Zhejiang Salt Industry Company	Hangzhou	Zhejiang	(0571)87800292
浙江省盐业公司	杭州市	浙江省	(0571)87800082
Fujian Salt Industry Company	Fuzhou	Fujian	(0591)7534344
福建省盐业公司	福州市	福建省	(0591)7535047
Jiangxi Salt Industry General Company	Nanchang	Jiangxi	(0791)6816695
江西省盐业总公司	南昌市	江西省	(0791)6812316
Hubei Salt Transportation & Sale Company	Xiaogan	Hubei	(0712)3611320
湖北省盐业运销公司	孝感市	湖北省	(0712)3611244
Hunan Salt Industry Group Co.,Ltd.Jinshi Allocation & Transportation Company	Changde	Hunan	(0736)4223817
湖南省盐业集团有限责任公司津市调运公司	常德市	湖南省	(0736)4223817

1453: Condiment 调味料制造业

The industry accounts for 0.031% of the total revenue of China's industrial sector in 2002. The rate of return on assets is 8.02%. 82.64% of all firms in the industry made a profit while 17.36% had negative returns.The top province in terms of the industry's revenue is Shandong, accounting for 20.08% of the total revenue.
2002年本行业收入占全行业的0.031%，资产利润率为8.02%。82.64%的企业赢利，17.36%的企业亏损。收入最高的省为山东省，占本行业的20.08%。

	Total number of firms 企业总数	Total number of employees 职工总数	Total revenue (Mil.RMB) 总销售收入（百万元）	Total profit (Mil.RMB) 总利润（百万元）	Return on assets 资产利润率（%）	Return on equity 权益利润率（%）	Labour productivity ('000 RMB/worker) 劳动生产率（千元/人）	Debts/assets 资产负债率（%）	Total assets (Mil.RMB) 总资产（百万元）
Industry Overall 行业总体	121	14,079	3,339	235	8.02	14.53	76.15	44.78	2,923

	Number of firms 企业个数	Average number of employees 平均职工人数	Average revenue ('000 RMB) 平均销售收入（千元）	Average profit ('000 RMB) 平均利润（千元）	Return on assets 资产利润率（%）	Return on equity 权益利润率（%）	Labour productivity ('000 RMB/worker) 劳动生产率（千元/人）	Debts/assets 资产负债率（%）	Average total assets ('000 RMB) 平均总资产（千元）
By ownership 产业所有权									
State-owned 国有	5	28	794	-49	-2.58	-16.49	11.57	84.35	1,891
Collective-owned 集体	7	79	13,745	927	9.92	15.55	50.12	36.21	9,349
Foreign & Overseas Chinese Funded 三资	37	127	49,320	3,932	8.60	15.22	133.23	43.48	45,718
By regional distribution 地区分布									
Central-North 华北	21	107	22,207	1,368	6.48	11.63	57.60	44.26	21,109
Beijing 北京	5	112	41,521	889	2.52	4.34	104.47	41.87	35,269
Tianjin 天津	7	181	26,716	2,979	10.30	16.78	38.07	38.60	28,905
Hebei 河北	9	47	7,970	382	5.32	16.91	54.13	68.52	7,180
Shanxi 山西									
Inner Mongolia 内蒙古									
Northeast 东北									
Liaoning 辽宁									
Jilin 吉林									
Heilongjiang 黑龙江									
Central-East 华东	47	115	31,686	2,195	8.33	14.26	73.60	41.61	26,360
Shanghai 上海	7	277	68,343	8,094	14.95	29.13	74.74	48.67	54,131
Jiangsu 江苏	5	80	29,615	-473	-1.30	-2.02	85.47	35.39	36,344
Zhejiang 浙江	4	40	40,784	-227	-0.72	-1.60	68.12	54.80	31,262
Anhui 安徽	1	75	2,407	-98	-2.88	-10.43	11.56	72.34	3,399
Fujian 福建	3	35	8,908	216	2.94	6.40	63.34	54.05	7,358
Jiangxi 江西									
Shandong 山东	27	101	24,834	1,823	9.33	14.31	73.47	34.84	19,547
Central-South 中南	35	142	35,376	2,731	9.00	17.06	97.89	47.22	30,327
Henan 河南	13	145	26,124	1,392	7.41	11.95	50.96	38.02	18,795
Hubei 湖北	5	127	38,170	1,536	8.20	20.80	112.53	60.60	18,737
Hunan 湖南	4	293	16,313	660	3.82	10.89	11.74	64.86	17,262
Guangdong 广东	11	84	55,777	6,115	10.91	19.69	319.82	44.57	56,021
Guangxi 广西	2	177	14,448	-56	-0.29	-1.84	26.51	84.19	19,069
Hainan 海南									
Southwest 西南	14	88	8,304	344	3.17	6.96	39.49	54.45	10,839
Chongqing 重庆	2	77	5,692	103	0.82	1.00	24.50	18.44	12,621
Sichuan 四川	6	136	13,217	256	1.48	4.33	44.63	65.96	17,342
Guizhou 贵州	5	51	5,032	608	14.29	24.75	36.98	42.24	4,255
Yunnan 云南									
Tibet 西藏	1	15	407	32	2.73	3.89	-43.07	29.78	1,172
Northwest 西北	4	58	7,370	561	8.14	15.79	44.45	48.47	6,893
Shaanxi 陕西	1	60	19,689	1,312	11.13	15.23	85.67	26.88	11,785
Gansu 甘肃	1	77	6	-22	-0.50	-5.45	8.87	90.76	4,370
Qinghai 青海	2	48	4,892	477	8.36	18.39	47.25	54.57	5,709
Ningxia 宁夏									
Xinjiang 新疆									

Year 年份	Number of firms 企业个数	Rate of change 变化率 (%)	Number of employees 职工人数 (人)	Rate of change 变化率 (%)	Total revenue (Mil. RMB) 总销售收入 (百万元)	Rate of change 变化率 (%)	Total profit (Mil RMB) 总利润 (百万元)	Rate of change 变化率 (%)
2000	90		10,882		3,259		302	
2001	108	20.00	12,938	18.89	3,230	-0.89	258	-14.57
2002	121	12.04	14,079	8.82	3,339	3.37	235	-8.91

Major Products 主要产品	Output 产量	Unit 单位
Monosodium Glutamate 味精	110	10,000 Tons 万吨

10 Main Firms with Maximal Revenue (year founded) 收入最大的十家主要企业（创办年份）	City 城市	Province 省	Telephone/fax 电话/传真	Number of employees 职工人数	Ownership 产业所有权	Revenue ('000 RMB) 销售收入 (千元)	Profit('000 RMB) (rank) 利润(千元)(排名)	Total assets ('000 RMB) 总资产 (千元)	Major products 主要产品
Shanghai Mccor Mick Foods Co.,Ltd. 上海味好美食品有限公司(1988)	Shanghai 上海市	Shanghai 上海市	(021)64760859 (021)64761620	1,000	Foreign Funded 外商投资	304,640	40,105(2)	120,481	Condiment 调味品
Mccor Mick(Guangzhou) Food Co.,Ltd. 味可美（广州）食品有限公司(1996)	Guangzhou 广州市	Guangdong 广东省	(020)82220832 (020)82213530	135	Foreign Funded 外商投资	237,861	24,222(3)	182,766	Compound Condiment 复合调味品
Henan Zhumadian Wang-Shou-Yi Shi-San Xiang Condiment Co. Ltd. 河南省驻马店市王首义十三香调味品有限公司(1984)	Zhumadian 驻马店市	Henan 河南省	(0396)2622111 (0396)2922101	1,048	Private Enterprises 私营独资	206,681	11,977(5)	181,368	Condiment 调味品
HangZhou Tingchun seasoning Co.,Ltd. 杭州顶醇调味料有限公司(1997)	Hangzhou 杭州市	Zhejiang 浙江省	(0571)86910122 (0571)8691009	56	Overseas Chinese-funded 港澳台资	129,810	-	85,765	Condiment 调味料
Shanghai Chuanqi Food Co., Ltd. 上海川崎食品有限公司(1991)	Shanghai 上海市	Shanghai 上海市	(021)38860188 (021)64367338	408	Private Owned 私营企业	85,812	9,030(8)	177,815	Flavoring 调料
Beijing CPC Foods Co.,Ltd. 北京喜临门食品有限公司(1995)	Beijing 北京市	Beijing 北京市	(010)67230010 (010)67238351	67	Foreign Funded 外商投资	81,529	-	20,595	Salad Soy Sauce 沙拉酱
Tianjin LiMin Seasoning Making Group Co.,Ltd. 天津市利民调料酿造集团有限公司(1998)	Tianjin 天津市	Tianjin 天津市	(022)26320743 (022)26330746	602	State Enterprises 国有独资	78,537	401(57)	90,924	Garlic Thick Chilli Sauce 蒜蓉辣酱
Luogaite Lianyungang Co., Ltd. 罗盖特连云港有限公司(1998)	Lianyungang 连云港市	Jiangsu 江苏省	(0518)2342816 (0518)2342577	171	Foreign Funded 外商投资	69,540	-	126,546	D-Sorbitol 山梨醇
Qingdao Aramk Foodstuff Co., Ltd. 青岛有明食品有限公司(1994)	Qingdao 青岛市	Shandong 山东省	(0532)8163152 (0532)8163151	134	Foreign Funded 外商投资	63,284	3,334(11)	83,916	
Beijing Q.P. Foods Co., Ltd. 北京丘比食品有限公司(1993)	Beijing 北京市	Beijing 北京市	(010)62984338 (010)62984340	220	Foreign Funded 外商投资	63,382	9,290(7)	70,201	Condiment 调味品

Top 10 Cities by Revenue 销售收入排名前10位城市	Province 省	Market share 市场份额 (%)	Number of firms 企业个数
Shanghai 上海市	Shanghai 上海市	14.33	7
Guangzhou 广州市	Guangdong 广东省	13.94	5
Dezhou 德州市	Shandong 山东省	8.98	10
Qingdao 青岛市	Shandong 山东省	8.81	12
Zhumadian 驻马店市	Henan 河南省	6.39	3
Beijing 北京市	Beijing 北京市	6.22	5
Tianjin 天津市	Tianjin 天津市	5.60	7
Hangzhou 杭州市	Zhejiang 浙江省	4.01	2
Wuhan 武汉市	Hubei 湖北省	2.41	2

10 Major Wholesalers 十家主要批发商	City 城市	Province 省	Telephone/Fax 电话/传真
Guangdong Foodstuffs Import & Export Group Corporation 广东省食品进出口集团公司	Guangzhou 广州市	Guangdong 广东省	(020)83854888 (020)83856823
Hubei Salt Industry General Company 湖北盐业总公司	Wuhan 武汉市	Hubei 湖北省	(027)82832190 (027)82816030
Henan Provincial Salt Business Administration Bureau (Henan Provincial Salt Industry General Company) 河南省盐务管理局(河南省盐业总公司)	Zhengzhou 郑州市	Henan 河南省	(0371)5907597 (0371)5906346
Sichuan Salt Industry General Company 四川省盐业总公司	Chengdu 成都市	Sichuan 四川省	(028)86652441 (028)86663440
China National Salt Tianjin Changlu Salt Industry Co.,Ltd. 中盐天津市长芦盐业有限公司	Tianjin 天津市	Tianjin 天津市	(022)23022160 (022)23022110
Zhejiang Salt Industry Company 浙江省盐业公司	Hangzhou 杭州市	Zhejiang 浙江省	(0571)87800292 (0571)87800082
Fujian Salt Industry Company 福建省盐业公司	Fuzhou 福州市	Fujian 福建省	(0591)7534344 (0591)7535047
Jiangxi Salt Industry General Company 江西省盐业总公司	Nanchang 南昌市	Jiangxi 江西省	(0791)6816695 (0791)6812316
Hubei Salt Transportation & Sale Company 湖北省盐业运销公司	Xiaogan 孝感市	Hubei 湖北省	(0712)3611320 (0712)3611244
Hunan Salt Industry Group Co.,Ltd.Jinshi Allocation & Transportation Company 湖南省盐业集团有限责任公司津市调运公司	Changde 常德市	Hunan 湖南省	(0736)4223817 (0736)4223817

1454: Seasoning Oil 调味油制造业

The industry accounts for 0.002% of the total revenue of China's industrial sector in 2002. The rate of return on assets is 5.83%. 90.00% of all firms in the industry made a profit while 10.00% had negative returns.The top province in terms of the industry's revenue is Guangdong, accounting for 23.72% of the total revenue.
2002年本行业收入占全行业的 0.002%，资产利润率为 5.83%。90.00%的企业赢利，10.00%的企业亏损。收入最高的省为广东省，占本行业的23.72%。

	Total number of firms 企业总数	Total number of employees 职工总数	Total revenue (Mil.RMB) 总销售收入（百万元）	Total profit (Mil.RMB) 总利润（百万元）	Return on assets 资产利润率（%）	Return on equity 权益利润率（%）	Labour productivity ('000 RMB/ worker) 劳动生产率（千元/人）	Debts/ assets 资产负债率（%）	Total assets (Mil.RMB) 总资产（百万元）
Industry Overall 行业总体	20	1,739	268	10	5.83	16.63	37.97	64.94	174

	Number of firms 企业个数	Average number of employees 平均职工人数	Average revenue ('000 RMB) 平均销售收入（千元）	Average profit ('000 RMB) 平均利润（千元）	Return on assets 资产利润率（%）	Return on equity 权益利润率（%）	Labour productivity ('000 RMB/ worker) 劳动生产率（千元/人）	Debts/ assets 资产负债率（%）	Average total assets ('000 RMB) 平均总资产（千元）
By ownership 产业所有权									
State-owned 国有	1								
Collective-owned 集体	2	172	15,280	285	4.38	11.30	25.82	61.20	6,500
Foreign & Overseas Chinese Funded 三资	3	70	11,804	378	3.11	9.65	37.75	67.74	12,159
By regional distribution 地区分布									
Central-North 华北	3	54	5,151	-31	-0.28	-10.36	23.37	97.32	11,150
Beijing 北京									
Tianjin 天津	1	8	6,953	-893	-5.43		170.38	102.75	16,450
Hebei 河北									
Shanxi 山西	2	77	4,250	400	4.71	59.26	15.69	92.06	8,500
Inner Mongolia 内蒙古									
Northeast 东北									
Liaoning 辽宁									
Jilin 吉林									
Heilongjiang 黑龙江									
Central-East 华东	5	91	17,206	471	4.14	10.83	41.65	61.76	11,385
Shanghai 上海	1	73	17,132	769	10.37	22.05	23.05	52.99	7,417
Jiangsu 江苏	1	31	23,755	244	6.98	11.46	214.52	39.06	3,495
Zhejiang 浙江	1	209	19,603	33	0.12	0.58	36.06	79.12	27,100
Anhui 安徽									
Fujian 福建	1	20	5,280	-105	-3.56	-3.75	-0.15	5.05	2,949
Jiangxi 江西									
Shandong 山东	1	120	20,261	1,416	8.87	18.40	25.00	51.81	15,966
Central-South 中南	7	90	12,638	657	11.66	32.78	40.73	64.42	5,630
Henan 河南	1	66	778				3.85	43.45	718
Hubei 湖北	1	60	24,190	3,563	59.38	356.30	136.20	83.33	6,000
Hunan 湖南									
Guangdong 广东	5	101	12,699	207	3.16	8.19	34.21	61.41	6,538
Guangxi 广西									
Hainan 海南									
Southwest 西南	5	99	15,552	661	7.43	13.53	35.85	45.11	8,893
Chongqing 重庆	1	132	5,357	45	0.39	0.57	5.33	32.32	11,595
Sichuan 四川	2	117	22,333	1,147	9.93	16.85	52.38	41.03	11,541
Guizhou 贵州	2	64	13,869	483	9.86	32.73	37.09	69.89	4,896
Yunnan 云南									
Tibet 西藏									
Northwest 西北									
Shaanxi 陕西									
Gansu 甘肃									
Qinghai 青海									
Ningxia 宁夏									
Xinjiang 新疆									

1454: Seasoning Oil 调味油制造业

Year 年份	Number of firms 企业个数	Rate of change 变化率(%)	Number of employees 职工人数(人)	Rate of change 变化率(%)	Total revenue (Mil. RMB) 总销售收入(百万元)	Rate of change 变化率(%)	Total profit (Mil RMB) 总利润(百万元)	Rate of change 变化率(%)
2000	19		1,562		195		-0.49	
2001	23	21.05	1,360	-12.93	186	-4.62	3	-
2002	20	-13.04	1,739	27.87	268	44.09	10	233.33

Major Products 主要产品	Output 产量	Unit 单位
Edible Vegetable Oil 食用植物油	943	10,000 Tons 万吨

10 Main Firms with Maximal Revenue (year founded) 收入最大的十家主要企业(创办年份)	City 城市	Province 省	Telephone/fax 电话/传真	Number of employees 职工人数	Ownership 产业所有权	Revenue ('000 RMB) 销售收入(千元)	Profit('000 RMB) (rank) 利润(千元)(排名)	Total assets ('000 RMB) 总资产(千元)	Major products 主要产品
Guizhou Jinshaguan Xiangfang Condiment Mill Co., Ltd. 贵州金沙冠香坊调味食品有限公司(1999)	bijie 毕杰地区	Guzhousheng 贵州省	(0857)8223537	100	Joint Stock 股份制	24,785	953(4)	6,645	Condiment 调味品
Wuhan Xinlan Food Co., Ltd. 武汉市新兰食品有限公司(2000)	Wuhan 武汉市	Hubei 湖北省	(027)84867233 (027)84866621	60	Private Owned 私营企业	24,190	3,563(1)	6,000	
Zhenjiang Hengshun New Type Condiment Co., Ltd. 镇江市恒顺新型调味品有限公司(1999)	Zhenjiang 镇江市	Jiangsu 江苏省	(0511)5721168 (0511)5721168	31	Joint Stock 股份制	23,755	244(9)	3,495	Condiment 调味品
Hanyuan Sanjiu Lihong Food Co., Ltd. 汉源县三九黎红食品有限公司(1999)	Yaan 雅安市	Sichuan 四川省	(0835)4385139 (0835)4382292	183	Overseas Chinese-funded 港澳台资	23,180	2,133(2)	17,078	Chinese Prickly Ash Oil 花椒油
Guangzhou Rufeng Fruit Condiment Mill Co., Ltd. 广州如丰果子调味食品有限公司(1986)	Guangzhou 广州市	Guangdong 广东省	(020)82922868 (020)82923878	64	Private Owned 私营企业	21,231	434(7)	10,168	Thick Sauce Material 酱料
Ruifu Oil & Condiment Co., Ltd. 潍坊瑞福油脂调料有限公司(1998)	Weifang 潍坊市	Shandong 山东省	(0536)8169568 (0536)8168117	120	Private Owned 私营企业	20,261	1,416(3)	15,966	Sesame Oil 香油
Ningbo Jinzhong Condiment Mill Co., Ltd. 宁波市金钟调味食品有限公司(1994)	Ningbo 宁波市	Zhejiang 浙江省	(0574)87832790 (0574)7833770	209	Private Owned 私营企业	19,603	33(13)	27,100	Vinegar 醋
Shanghai Wufu Condiment Mill Co., Ltd. 上海五福调味食品有限公司(1987)	Shanghai 上海市	Shanghai 上海市	(021)58737213 (021)58737213	73	Limited-Liability 有限公司	17,132	769(6)	7,417	Condiment 调味品
Deqing WuLong BaoJin Oil Of Cinnamon Factory 德庆县武垄宝金桂油厂(1990)	Zhaoqing 肇庆市	Guangdong 广东省	(0758)7521435	147	Collective-owned 集体企业	15,513	218(10)	5,071	Oil Of Cinnamon 桂油
Deqing Gaoliang Town HongYun Oil Of Cinnamon Factory 德庆县高良镇鸿运桂油厂(2001)	Zhaoqing 肇庆市	Guangdong 广东省	(0758)7393262 (0758)7393262	58	Private Enterprises 私营独资	8,865	19(14)	8,255	Oil Of Cinnamon 桂油

Top 10 Cities by Revenue 销售收入排名前10位城市	Province 省	Market share 市场份额(%)	Number of firms 企业个数
Zhaoqing 肇庆市	Guangdong 广东省	14.73	3
Bijie 毕节地区	Guizhou 贵州省	9.26	1
Wuhan 武汉市	Hubei 湖北省	9.04	1
Guangzhou 广州市	Guangdong 广东省	8.99	2
Zhenjiang 镇江市	Jiangsu 江苏省	8.87	1
Yaan 雅安市	Sichuan 四川省	8.66	1
Chengdu 成都市	Sichuan 四川省	8.03	1
Weifang 潍坊市	Shandong 山东省	7.57	1
Ningbo 宁波市	Zhejiang 浙江省	7.32	1
Shanghai 上海市	Shanghai 上海市	6.40	1

10 Major Wholesalers 十家主要批发商	City 城市	Province 省	Telephone/Fax 电话/传真
Guangdong Foodstuffs Import & Export Group Corporation 广东省食品进出口集团公司	Guangzhou 广州市	Guangdong 广东省	(020)83854888 (020)83856823
Hubei Salt Industry General Company 湖北盐业总公司	Wuhan 武汉市	Hubei 湖北省	(027)82832190 (027)82816030
Henan Provincial Salt Business Administration Bureau (Henan Provincial Salt Industry General Company) 河南省盐务管理局(河南省盐业总公司)	Zhengzhou 郑州市	Henan 河南省	(0371)5907597 (0371)5906346
Sichuan Salt Industry General Company 四川省盐业总公司	Chengdu 成都市	Sichuan 四川省	(028)86652441 (028)86663440
China National Salt Tianjin Changlu Salt Industry Co.,Ltd. 中盐天津市长芦盐业有限公司	Tianjin 天津市	Tianjin 天津市	(022)23022160 (022)23022110
Zhejiang Salt Industry Company 浙江省盐业公司	Hangzhou 杭州市	Zhejiang 浙江省	(0571)87800292 (0571)87800082
Fujian Salt Industry Company 福建省盐业公司	Fuzhou 福州市	Fujian 福建省	(0591)7534344 (0591)7535047
Jiangxi Salt Industry General Company 江西省盐业总公司	Nanchang 南昌市	Jiangxi 江西省	(0791)6816695 (0791)6812316
Hubei Salt Transportation & Sale Company 湖北省盐业运销公司	Xiaogan 孝感市	Hubei 湖北省	(0712)3611320 (0712)3611244
Hunan Salt Industry Group Co.,Ltd.Jinshi Allocation & Transportation Company 湖南省盐业集团有限责任公司津市调运公司	Changde 常德市	Hunan 湖南省	(0736)4223817 (0736)4223817

1459: Other Spices 其他调味品制造业

The industry accounts for 0.008% of the total revenue of China's industrial sector in 2002. The rate of return on assets is 4.84%. 78.00% of all firms in the industry made a profit while 22.00% had negative returns.The top province in terms of the industry's revenue is Guangdong, accounting for 23.41% of the total revenue.
2002年本行业收入占全行业的0.008%，资产利润率为4.84%。78.00%的企业赢利，22.00%的企业亏损。收入最高的省为广东省，占本行业的23.41%。

	Total number of firms 企业总数	Total number of employees 职工总数	Total revenue (Mil.RMB) 总销售收入 (百万元)	Total profit (Mil.RMB) 总利润 (百万元)	Return on assets 资产利润率 (%)	Return on equity 权益利润率 (%)	Labour productivity ('000 RMB/ worker) 劳动生产率 (千元/人)	Debts/ assets 资产负债率 (%)	Total assets (Mil.RMB) 总资产 (百万元)
Industry Overall 行业总体	50	3,952	889	33	4.84	10.03	70.24	51.70	686

	Number of firms 企业个数	Average number of employees 平均职工人数	Average revenue ('000 RMB) 平均销售收入（千元）	Average profit ('000 RMB) 平均利润 (千元)	Return on assets 资产利润率 (%)	Return on equity 权益利润率 (%)	Labour productivity ('000 RMB/ worker) 劳动生产率 (千元/人)	Debts/ assets 资产负债率 (%)	Average total assets ('000 RMB) 平均总资产 (千元)
By ownership 产业所有权									
State-owned 国有	7	54	2,235	-75	-2.45	-13.19	11.23	81.45	3,066
Collective-owned 集体	8	46	24,371	1,056	9.75	17.24	132.37	43.46	10,834
Foreign & Overseas Chinese Funded 三资	11	90	26,963	1,322	5.45	10.39	84.17	47.50	24,245
By regional distribution 地区分布									
Central-North 华北	5	50	22,333	1,690	9.52	26.14	137.24	63.58	17,755
Beijing 北京	1	120	38,659	14	0.05	1.12	38.63	95.31	26,651
Tianjin 天津	2	33	18,784	1,318	10.44	51.65	267.59	79.79	12,631
Hebei 河北	2	31	17,719	2,901	15.74	22.33	189.34	29.54	18,431
Shanxi 山西									
Inner Mongolia 内蒙古									
Northeast 东北	4	84	10,663	436	1.86	2.14	64.09	12.68	23,352
Liaoning 辽宁									
Jilin 吉林	2	125	18,755	1,246	3.12	3.32	83.64	5.95	39,905
Heilongjiang 黑龙江	2	42	2,571	-375	-5.52	-11.52	5.90	52.14	6,800
Central-East 华东	16	70	22,860	760	6.18	15.14	103.85	59.20	12,303
Shanghai 上海	3	59	32,758	1,738	17.21	25.63	50.58	32.86	10,099
Jiangsu 江苏	4	53	10,373	-178	-2.22	-28.29	63.17	92.14	7,983
Zhejiang 浙江									
Anhui 安徽	1	108	15,900	1,410	56.63	101.44	35.65	44.18	2,490
Fujian 福建	2	80	18,897	356	1.93	2.97	211.48	34.96	18,445
Jiangxi 江西	2	31	3,648	-38	-0.94	-2.76	31.44	65.97	4,050
Shandong 山东	4	99	41,252	1,402	6.44	19.13	135.86	66.36	21,787
Central-South 中南	19	84	15,898	536	3.95	8.33	57.31	52.58	13,577
Henan 河南	5	83	15,476	1,025	9.55	14.27	56.70	33.06	10,734
Hubei 湖北	2	77	8,236	185	2.47		33.57	113.99	7,483
Hunan 湖南									
Guangdong 广东	11	93	18,929	427	2.59	5.31	61.48	51.27	16,508
Guangxi 广西	1	6						100.00	7,727
Hainan 海南									
Southwest 西南	5	127	13,370	131	1.37	4.73	23.65	70.94	9,557
Chongqing 重庆									
Sichuan 四川	4	153	14,087	127	1.16	4.11	19.99	71.68	10,891
Guizhou 贵州	1	22	10,505	150	3.56	9.69	125.45	63.31	4,219
Yunnan 云南									
Tibet 西藏									
Northwest 西北	1	30	393	1	0.12	0.13	7.67	9.84	833
Shaanxi 陕西	1	30	393	1	0.12	0.13	7.67	9.84	833
Gansu 甘肃									
Qinghai 青海									
Ningxia 宁夏									
Xinjiang 新疆									

1459: Other Spices 其他调味品制造业

Year 年份	Number of firms 企业个数	Rate of change 变化率(%)	Number of employees 职工人数(人)	Rate of change 变化率(%)	Total revenue (Mil. RMB) 总销售收入(百万元)	Rate of change 变化率(%)	Total profit (Mil RMB) 总利润(百万元)	Rate of change 变化率(%)
2000	72		8,748		1,244		29	
2001	56	-22.22	7,570	-13.47	1,165	-6.35	39	34.48
2002	50	-10.71	3,952	-47.79	889	-23.69	33	-15.38

Major Products 主要产品	Output 产量	Unit 单位

10 Main Firms with Maximal Revenue (year founded) 收入最大的十家主要企业（创办年份）	City 城市	Province 省	Telephone/fax 电话/传真	Number of employees 职工人数	Ownership 产业所有权	Revenue ('000 RMB) 销售收入(千元)	Profit('000 RMB) (rank) 利润(千元)(排名)	Total assets ('000 RMB) 总资产(千元)	Major products 主要产品
Ji'nan Pingyin Xingzheng Chemical Industry Co., Ltd.	Jinan	Shandong	(0531)7700146		Limited-Liability				Chicken Extract
济南平阴兴正化工有限责任公司(1997)	济南市	山东省	(0531)7700228	260	有限公司	76,000	4,450(2)	26,300	鸡精
Shanghai Foshou Fengxian Condiment Factory	Shanghai	Shanghai	(021)57171307		Collective-owned				Chicken Extract
上海佛手奉贤调味品厂(1997)	上海市	上海市	(021)57171307	73	集体企业	75,620	1,265(10)	6,032	鸡精
Qingdao Hexing Food Co.,Ltd.	Qingdao	Shandong	(0532)3220053		Overseas Chinese-funded				Dry Chilli
青岛和兴食品有限公司(1994)	青岛市	山东省	(0532)3220201	62	港澳台资	59,567	1,217(11)	39,096	辣椒干
Beijing Meiquan Food Co., Ltd.	Beijing	Beijing	(010)63497979		Limited-Liability				Condiment
北京美全食品有限公司(1996)	北京市	北京市	(010)63441459	120	有限公司	38,659	14(30)	26,651	调味品
Jiangmen Ruiyile Sweet Life Factory Co., Ltd.	Jiangmen	Guangdong	(0750)3225133		Overseas Chinese-funded				Sweet Taste Condiment
江门瑞怡乐甜味剂厂有限公司(1997)	江门市	广东省	(0750)3225166	274	港澳台资	35,976	679(14)	43,065	甜味品
Sichuan Liji Preserved Vegetable Condiment Co., Ltd.	Meishan	Sichuan	(0833)8010666		Private Owned				Vegetable Pickled In Soy Sauce
四川李记酱菜调味品有限公司(1996)	眉山市	四川省	(0833)8010888	357	私营企业	35,568	-	28,964	酱菜
Changzhou Jiamei Flavor Essence Factory	Changzhou	Jiangsu	(0519)8781560		Joint Stock				Monosodium Glutamate
常州市佳美味精厂(1990)	常州市	江苏省	(0519)8782896	80	股份制	30,360	-	14,290	味精
Qingdao H & T Co., Ltd.	Qingdao	Shandong	(0532)3220053		Overseas Chinese-funded				Dry Chilli
青岛兴达食品有限公司(1994)	青岛市	山东省	(0532)3220201	40	港澳台资	23,345	258(24)	15,131	辣椒干
Fuzhou Tianshan Food Co., Ltd.	Fuzhou	Fujian	(0591)3622828		Foreign Funded				Food
福州天山食品有限公司(1999)	福州市	福建省		121	外商投资	21,834	356(20)	29,910	食品
Chao'an Shunda Chemical Industry Co., Ltd.	Chaozhou	Guangdong	(0768)6721777		Overseas Chinese-funded				Food Additive食
潮安县顺大化工有限公司(1995)	潮州市	广东省	(0768)6721778	20	港澳台资	21,645	598(16)	10,489	品添加剂

Top 10 Cities by Revenue 销售收入排名前10位城市	Province 省	Market share 市场份额(%)	Number of firms 企业个数
Shanghai 上海市	Shanghai 上海市	11.05	3
Qingdao 青岛市	Shandong 山东省	9.32	2
Jinan 济南市	Shandong 山东省	8.55	1
Luohe 漯河市	Henan 河南省	7.06	2
Shenzhen 深圳市	Guangdong 广东省	5.89	1
Chaozhou 潮州市	Guangdong 广东省	4.57	3
Changzhou 常州市	Jiangsu 江苏省	4.56	2
Beijing 北京市	Beijing 北京市	4.35	1
Tianjin 天津市	Tianjin 天津市	4.22	2
Baicheng 白城市	Jilin 吉林省	4.22	1

10 Major Wholesalers 十家主要批发商	City 城市	Province 省	Telephone/Fax 电话/传真
Guangdong Foodstuffs Import & Export Group Corporation	Guangzhou	Guangdong	(020)83854888
广东省食品进出口集团公司	广州市	广东省	(020)83856823
Hubei Salt Industry General Company	Wuhan	Hubei	(027)82832190
湖北盐业总公司	武汉市	湖北省	(027)82816030
Henan Provincial Salt Business Administration Bureau (Henan Provincial Salt Industry General Company)	Zhengzhou	Henan	(0371)5907597
河南省盐务管理局(河南省盐业总公司)	郑州市	河南省	(0371)5906346
Sichuan Salt Industry General Company	Chengdu	Sichuan	(028)86652441
四川省盐业总公司	成都市	四川省	(028)86663440
China National Salt Tianjin Changlu Salt Industry Co.,Ltd.	Tianjin	Tianjin	(022)23022160
中盐天津市长芦盐业有限公司	天津市	天津市	(022)23022110
Zhejiang Salt Industry Company	Hangzhou	Zhejiang	(0571)87800292
浙江省盐业公司	杭州市	浙江省	(0571)87800082
Fujian Salt Industry Company	Fuzhou	Fujian	(0591)7534344
福建省盐业公司	福州市	福建省	(0591)7535047
Jiangxi Salt Industry General Company	Nanchang	Jiangxi	(0791)6816695
江西省盐业总公司	南昌市	江西省	(0791)6812316
Hubei Salt Transportation & Sale Company	Xiaogan	Hubei	(0712)3611320
湖北省盐业运销公司	孝感市	湖北省	(0712)3611244
Hunan Salt Industry Group Co.,Ltd.Jinshi Allocation & Transportation Company	Changde	Hunan	(0736)4223817
湖南省盐业集团有限责任公司津市调运公司	常德市	湖南省	(0736)4223817

1491: Bean Products 豆制品制造业

The industry accounts for 0.029% of the total revenue of China's industrial sector in 2002. The rate of return on assets is 7.13%. 78.42% of all firms in the industry made a profit while 21.58% had negative returns.The top province in terms of the industry's revenue is Beijing, accounting for 15.55% of the total revenue.
2002年本行业收入占全行业的0.029%，资产利润率为7.13%。78.42%的企业赢利，21.58%的企业亏损。收入最高的省为北京市，占本行业的15.55%。

	Total number of firms 企业总数	Total number of employees 职工总数	Total revenue (Mil.RMB) 总销售收入（百万元）	Total profit (Mil.RMB) 总利润（百万元）	Return on assets 资产利润率（%）	Return on equity 权益利润率（%）	Labour productivity ('000 RMB/worker) 劳动生产率（千元/人）	Debts/assets 资产负债率（%）	Total assets (Mil.RMB) 总资产（百万元）
Industry Overall 行业总体	139	31,685	3,079	247	7.13	15.05	31.35	52.66	3,470

	Number of firms 企业个数	Average number of employees 平均职工人数	Average revenue ('000 RMB) 平均销售收入（千元）	Average profit ('000 RMB) 平均利润（千元）	Return on assets 资产利润率（%）	Return on equity 权益利润率（%）	Labour productivity ('000 RMB/worker) 劳动生产率（千元/人）	Debts/assets 资产负债率（%）	Average total assets ('000 RMB) 平均总资产（千元）
By ownership 产业所有权									
State-owned 国有	39	119	6,164	-60	-0.47	-2.32	18.21	79.86	12,909
Collective-owned 集体	13	292	24,516	2,816	20.87	40.22	30.07	48.11	13,491
Foreign & Overseas Chinese Funded 三资	26	174	23,771	1,213	3.76	6.49	43.36	42.09	32,267
By regional distribution 地区分布									
Central-North 华北	25	216	25,270	1,325	3.81	8.66	42.28	55.96	34,751
Beijing 北京	12	344	39,911	2,403	5.08	12.31	42.71	58.75	47,307
Tianjin 天津	5	86	16,036	607	1.58	2.76	62.26	42.81	38,432
Hebei 河北	3	88	15,271	878	8.94	13.87	59.51	35.54	9,828
Shanxi 山西	5	118	5,368	-275	-1.73	-7.03	16.92	75.39	15,889
Inner Mongolia 内蒙古									
Northeast 东北	19	157	15,473	1,493	3.68	7.27	32.86	49.36	40,563
Liaoning 辽宁	5	126	10,615	170	1.07	4.63	16.14	76.97	15,946
Jilin 吉林	5	137	9,997	196	0.82	1.92	32.87	57.04	23,814
Heilongjiang 黑龙江	9	186	21,214	2,948	4.64	8.27	39.12	43.91	63,543
Central-East 华东	47	147	20,201	1,037	5.86	14.03	41.57	58.20	17,681
Shanghai 上海	11	149	15,895	374	2.69	4.84	25.43	44.56	13,921
Jiangsu 江苏	12	117	16,316	402	2.46	6.10	44.56	59.72	16,355
Zhejiang 浙江	9	181	19,343	2,025	10.21	29.28	31.39	65.12	19,823
Anhui 安徽	3	251	32,156	1,514	7.52	13.94	21.49	46.06	20,130
Fujian 福建	3	36	6,667	62	0.87	1.29	94.54	33.07	7,167
Jiangxi 江西	1	20	623	18	2.07	3.14	9.35	33.99	868
Shandong 山东	8	167	35,953	2,103	7.63	22.84	78.30	66.58	27,555
Central-South 中南	33	432	24,023	933	4.79	10.64	16.80	55.01	19,483
Henan 河南	8	1,226	46,609	2,203	8.78	25.13	10.22	65.06	25,094
Hubei 湖北	4	104	21,951	-723	-2.39	-4.87	81.69	50.84	30,228
Hunan 湖南	5	50	6,650	322	8.62	14.19	39.13	39.23	3,732
Guangdong 广东	12	249	22,041	1,265	6.97	10.67	28.17	34.67	18,150
Guangxi 广西	4	203	8,589	-186	-0.88	-12.37	14.24	92.90	21,200
Hainan 海南									
Southwest 西南	10	189	37,430	10,558	33.70	46.03	66.14	26.78	31,330
Chongqing 重庆	2	155	7,130	215	1.20	2.62	2.23	54.01	17,857
Sichuan 四川	3	182	19,710	5,761	25.46	32.12	26.64	20.72	22,623
Guizhou 贵州	3	342	100,281	29,351	42.81	55.87	107.01	23.38	68,560
Yunnan 云南	2	5	34	-91	-4.51	-11.57	4.67	61.05	2,019
Tibet 西藏									
Northwest 西北	5	46	7,356	140	1.62	18.42	63.66	91.20	8,644
Shaanxi 陕西	3	48	12,171	235	2.22	10.57	90.45	78.99	10,564
Gansu 甘肃	2	44	133	-2	-0.03		19.83	124.75	5,765
Qinghai 青海									
Ningxia 宁夏									
Xinjiang 新疆									

Year 年份	Number of firms 企业个数	Rate of change 变化率 (%)	Number of employees 职工人数 (人)	Rate of change 变化率 (%)	Total revenue (Mil. RMB) 总销售收入 (百万元)	Rate of change 变化率 (%)	Total profit (Mil RMB) 总利润 (百万元)	Rate of change 变化率 (%)
2000	150		29,527		2,232		175	
2001	137	-8.67	31,337	6.13	2,826	26.61	196	12.00
2002	139	1.46	31,685	1.11	3,079	8.95	247	26.02

Major Products 主要产品	Output 产量	Unit 单位

10 Main Firms with Maximal Revenue (year founded) 收入最大的十家主要企业（创办年份）	City 城市	Province 省	Telephone/fax 电话/传真	Number of employees 职工人数	Ownership 产业所有权	Revenue ('000 RMB) 销售收入（千元）	Profit('000 RMB) (rank) 利润(千元)（排名）	Total assets ('000 RMB) 总资产（千元）	Major products 主要产品
Beijing Wanzhihe Food Group Co.,Ltd.	Beijing	Beijing	(010)63522160		Limited-Liability				Bean Products
北京王致和食品集团公司(1988)	北京市	北京市	(010)63520901	2,312	有限公司	302,399	9,305(7)	362,193	豆制品
Guiyang Nanming Lao-Gan-Ma Flavor Foods Co., Ltd.	Guiyang	Guizhou	(0851)5402220		Private Owned				Flavor Lobster Sauce
贵阳南明老干妈风味食品有限责任公司(1996)	贵阳市	贵州省	(0851)5406769	644	私营企业	270,535	84,945(1)	167,643	风味豆豉
Daqing Riyue Plant Protein Group Co., Ltd.	Daqing	Heilongjiang	(0459)3313118		Joint Stock				High Protein
大庆日月植物蛋白集团有限公司(1999)	大庆市	黑龙江省	(0459)3322489	580	股份制	114,120	29,600(2)	371,064	高蛋白
Ma'anshan Huangchi Food Co.,Ltd.	Maanshan	Anhui	(0555)6191238		Private Owned				Dried Bean Curd
马鞍山市黄池食品集团公司(1976)	马鞍山市	安徽省	(0555)6191245	518	私营企业	89,860	4,660(14)	50,800	茶干
Henan North Modern Agriculture Co., Ltd.	Zhengzhou	Henan	(0371)5630178		Limited-Liability				Bean oil
河南北方现代化农业有限公司(2001)	郑州市	河南省	(0371)5630156	134	有限公司	84,111	5(86)	31,305	豆油
Dupont Yunmeng Protein Co., Ltd.	Xiaogan	Hubei	(0712)4225255		Foreign Funded				High Protein
杜邦云梦蛋白有限公司(1990)	孝感市	湖北省	(0712)4220402	235	外商投资	70,084	-	114,514	高蛋白
Shandong Liyuan Co.,Ltd.	Yantai	Shandong	(0535)8477329		State-owned				Bean Powder
山东力源集团有限公司(1978)	烟台市	山东省	(0535)8476024	522	国有企业	53,205	650(43)	88,648	豆粉
Shandong Yishui Deli Food Co., Ltd.	Linyi	Shandong	(0539)2252173		Limited-Liability				Bean Milk Powder
山东沂水得力食品有限公司(1999)	临沂市	山东省	(0539)2252707	363	有限公司	52,821	293(57)	26,727	豆奶粉
Kaiping Guanghe Fermented Bean Curd Co.,Ltd.	Jiangmen	Guangdong	(0750)2715771		Foreign Funded				Fermented Bean Curd
开平广合腐乳有限公司(1996)	江门市	广东省	(0750)2725133	734	外商投资	52,025	1,250(30)	69,174	腐乳
Xuzhou Jinwei Food Co., Ltd.	Xuzhou	Jiangsu	(0516)7715427		Private Owned				Bean Products
徐州金维食品有限公司(1964)	徐州市	江苏省	(0516)7712004	110	私营企业	50,360	13(82)	14,305	豆制品

Top 10 Cities by Revenue 销售收入排名前10位城市	Province 省	Market share 市场份额 (%)	Number of firms 企业个数
Beijing 北京市	Beijing 北京市	15.55	12
Guiyang 贵阳市	Guizhou 贵州省	9.47	2
Shanghai 上海市	Shanghai 上海市	5.68	11
Anyang 安阳市	Henan 河南省	5.35	1
Daqing 大庆市	Heilongjiang 黑龙江省	3.71	1
Jiangmen 江门市	Guangdong 广东省	3.61	4
Maanshan 马鞍山市	Anhui 安徽省	3.09	2
Xuzhou 徐州市	Jiangsu 江苏省	3.06	3
Zhengzhou 郑州市	Henan 河南省	2.96	2
Tianjin 天津市	Tianjin 天津市	2.60	5

10 Major Wholesalers 十家主要批发商	City 城市	Province 省	Telephone/Fax 电话/传真
Beijing Cigarette Sale Company	Beijing	Beijing	(010)64228158
北京市卷烟销售公司	北京市	北京市	(010)64228365
Anhui Technology Import & Export Co.,Ltd.	Hefei	Anhui	(0551)5101188
安徽省技术进出口股份有限公司	合肥市	安徽省	(0551)5101199
China Tobacco General Company Henan Province Filiale	Zhengzhou	Henan	(0371)5583070
中国烟草总公司河南省公司	郑州市	河南省	(0371)5957546
Shanghai Jieqiang Tobacco,Sugar & Wine Company Supplies & Sales Center	Shanghai	Shanghai	(021)62494080
上海捷强烟草糖酒公司配销中心	上海市	上海市	(021)62492584
Zhejiang Cigarette Sale Company	Hangzhou	Zhejiang	(0571)87073247
浙江省卷烟销售公司	杭州市	浙江省	(0571)87072474
Fujian Cereals, Oils & Foodstuffs Import Group Corp.	Fuzhou	Fujian	(0591)7506688
福建省粮油食品进口集团公司	福州市	福建省	(0591)7544543
Chongqing Hongta Cigarette Sale Co.,Ltd.	Chongqing	Chongqing	(023)67750222
重庆红塔卷烟销售有限责任公司	重庆市	重庆市	(023)67740477
China Buty Free (Group) General Company	Beijing	Beijing	(010)64649988
中国免税品（集团）总公司	北京市	北京市	(010)64635846
Shanghai Jieqiang Tobacco,Sugar & Wine (Group) Co.,Ltd.	Shanghai	Shanghai	(021)62522018
上海捷强烟草糖酒（集团）有限公司	上海市	上海市	(021)62522005
Shanghai Tobacco Group Chongming Tobacco, Sugar & Wine Co.,Ltd.	Shanghai	Shanghai	(021)59621368
上海烟草集团崇明烟草糖酒有限公司	上海市	上海市	(021)59621368

1492: Starch and Starch Products 淀粉及淀粉制品业

The industry accounts for 0.175% of the total revenue of China's industrial sector in 2002. The rate of return on assets is 3.91%. 85.75% of all firms in the industry made a profit while 14.25% had negative returns.The top province in terms of the industry's revenue is Shandong, accounting for 29.77% of the total revenue.
2002年本行业收入占全行业的 0.175%，资产利润率为 3.91%。85.75%的企业赢利，14.25%的企业亏损。收入最高的省为山东省，占本行业的29.77%。

	Total number of firms 企业总数	Total number of employees 职工总数	Total revenue (Mil.RMB) 总销售收入 (百万元)	Total profit (Mil.RMB) 总利润 (百万元)	Return on assets 资产利润率 (%)	Return on equity 权益利润率 (%)	Labour productivity ('000 RMB/ worker) 劳动生产率 (千元/人)	Debts/ assets 资产负债率 (%)	Total assets (Mil.RMB) 总资产 (百万元)
Industry Overall 行业总体	414	74,162	18,814	582	3.91	13.76	79.09	71.58	14,883

	Number of firms 企业个数	Average number of employees 平均职工人数	Average revenue ('000 RMB) 平均销售收入 (千元)	Average profit ('000 RMB) 平均利润 (千元)	Return on assets 资产利润率 (%)	Return on equity 权益利润率 (%)	Labour productivity ('000 RMB/ worker) 劳动生产率 (千元/人)	Debts/ assets 资产负债率 (%)	Average total assets ('000 RMB) 平均总资产 (千元)
By ownership 产业所有权									
State-owned 国有	58	126	13,737	248	0.92	4.39	30.72	78.96	26,867
Collective-owned 集体	113	162	34,079	2,164	14.28	37.66	59.98	62.08	15,154
Foreign & Overseas Chinese Funded 三资	41	210	166,498	1,694	1.57	9.56	268.96	83.62	108,164
By regional distribution 地区分布									
Central-North 华北	100	163	37,383	2,078	7.29	18.54	66.79	60.68	28,496
Beijing 北京	1	190	24,210	-348	-0.75	-4.94	17.44	84.87	46,530
Tianjin 天津	7	115	14,913	863	10.76	21.14	17.77	49.11	8,022
Hebei 河北	74	174	42,364	2,695	10.02	25.53	68.84	60.76	26,895
Shanxi 山西	10	143	23,844	618	3.09	7.13	68.75	56.68	20,016
Inner Mongolia 内蒙古	8	125	29,541	-444	-0.64	-1.63	86.43	60.99	69,571
Northeast 东北	36	302	157,636	292	0.19	1.02	184.36	81.45	154,506
Liaoning 辽宁	10	143	21,513	33	0.13	0.39	37.96	67.12	25,331
Jilin 吉林	14	455	346,030	-928	-0.31	-2.44	276.42	87.38	302,004
Heilongjiang 黑龙江	12	257	51,277	1,930	2.14	5.58	61.80	61.61	90,070
Central-East 华东	107	214	60,036	3,037	11.87	32.17	75.30	63.10	25,582
Shanghai 上海	3	137	18,926	-145	-0.62	-1.80	6.46	65.57	23,439
Jiangsu 江苏	20	86	29,502	975	5.35	14.71	94.10	63.63	18,225
Zhejiang 浙江	2	17	9,683	43	0.69	2.72	61.21	74.62	6,157
Anhui 安徽	2	64	9,621	157	1.85	2.46	36.98	24.84	8,457
Fujian 福建	2	64	12,560	11	0.09	0.17	64.38	45.15	11,880
Jiangxi 江西	4	348	27,872	941	2.57	6.91	24.85	62.80	36,620
Shandong 山东	74	257	75,701	4,077	14.35	39.19	79.13	63.39	28,419
Central-South 中南	118	140	17,812	526	3.34	10.70	48.22	68.78	15,740
Henan 河南	51	180	20,210	856	7.37	21.36	47.37	65.52	11,619
Hubei 湖北	10	92	15,853	207	4.53	23.43	57.51	80.66	4,563
Hunan 湖南	10	76	20,218	867	14.06	34.61	108.61	59.37	6,162
Guangdong 广东	12	96	22,098	461	1.71	12.76	61.60	86.58	26,908
Guangxi 广西	30	134	12,559	-19	-0.08	-0.22	33.21	64.09	24,025
Hainan 海南	5	87	13,693	538	2.36	6.79	44.73	65.24	22,763
Southwest 西南	13	91	8,293	-831	-3.67	-25.31	32.04	85.52	22,667
Chongqing 重庆									
Sichuan 四川	8	95	9,165	-117	-0.67	-1.59	25.54	57.77	17,379
Guizhou 贵州	2	58	2,687	-405	-1.67	-33.35	9.08	94.99	24,198
Yunnan 云南	3	104	9,705	-3,020	-8.45		56.38	117.22	35,749
Tibet 西藏									
Northwest 西北	40	162	19,188	-310	-0.78	-2.79	33.76	71.88	39,546
Shaanxi 陕西	10	158	31,110	12	0.03	0.11	48.82	70.15	35,322
Gansu 甘肃	21	137	10,449	-518	-1.87	-11.13	30.40	83.18	27,692
Qinghai 青海	1	8						116.28	33,755
Ningxia 宁夏	6	303	32,913	-426	-0.45	-1.19	24.79	62.47	95,464
Xinjiang 新疆	2	110	19,747	459	2.26	2.86	44.86	20.81	20,278

1492: Starch and Starch Products 淀粉及淀粉制品业

Year 年份	Number of firms 企业个数	Rate of change 变化率 (%)	Number of employees 职工人数 (人)	Rate of change 变化率 (%)	Total revenue (Mil. RMB) 总销售收入 (百万元)	Rate of change 变化率 (%)	Total profit (Mil RMB) 总利润 (百万元)	Rate of change 变化率 (%)
2000	406		77,358		12,618		711	
2001	402	-0.99	72,292	-6.55	14,606	15.76	820	15.33
2002	414	2.99	74,162	2.59	18,814	28.81	582	-29.02

Major Products 主要产品	Output 产量	Unit 单位
Starch 淀粉	757	10,000 Tons 万吨

10 Main Firms with Maximal Revenue (year founded) 收入最大的十家主要企业（创办年份）	City 城市	Province 省	Telephone/fax 电话/传真	Number of employees 职工人数	Ownership 产业所有权	Revenue ('000 RMB) 销售收入(千元)	Profit('000 RMB) (rank) 利润(千元)(排名)	Total assets ('000 RMB) 总资产(千元)	Major products 主要产品
Changchun Dacheng Maize Developing Group Co., Ltd.	Changchun	Jilin	(0431)7879746		Overseas Chinese-funded				Corn Starch
长春大成玉米开发有限公司(1996)	长春市	吉林省	(0431)7873301	620	港澳台资	3,603,792	360,100(1)	1,031,290	玉米淀粉
Huanglong Food Industry Co., Ltd.	Siping	Jilin	(0434)6215466		Overseas Chinese-funded				
黄龙食品工业有限公司(1991)	四平市	吉林省	(0434)6213227	1,354	港澳台资	926,000	14,500(11)	746,255	
Binzhou Golden Link Maize Developing Co.,Ltd.	Binzhou	Shandong	(0543)3513128		Overseas Chinese-funded				Corn Starch
滨州金汇玉米开发有限公司(1997)	滨州市	山东省	(0543)3512126	1,226	港澳台资	695,472	25,416(4)	231,447	玉米淀粉
Qinhuangdao Lihua Starch Co.,Ltd.	Qinhuangdao	Hebei	(0335)6034302		Joint Stock				Corn Starch
秦皇岛市骊骅淀粉股份有限公司(1989)	秦皇岛市	河北省	(0335)6017779	1,194	股份制	609,023	37,194(2)	462,590	玉米淀粉
Yishui Dadi Maize Development Co., Ltd.	Linyi	Shandong	(0539)2711333		Limited-Liability				Corn Starch
沂水大地玉米开发有限公司(2000)	临沂市	山东省	(0539)2711244	950	有限公司	561,910	34,830(3)	161,546	玉米淀粉
Shandong Jincheng Co., Ltd.	Yantai	Shandong	(0535)8237161		Limited-Liability				Vermicelli
山东金城股份有限公司(2001)	烟台市	山东省	(0535)8212777	2,000	有限公司	353,515	22,574(6)	177,518	粉丝
Zhaoyuan Sanjia Vermicelli Protein Co., Ltd.	Yantai	Shandong	(0535)8332388		Collective-owned				Vermicelli
招远市三嘉粉丝蛋白有限公司(1987)	烟台市	山东省	(0535)8332999	618	集体企业	316,400	17,650(9)	13,730	粉丝
Heilongjiang Longfeng Maize Developing Co., Ltd.	Suihua	Heilongjiang	(0455)3233072		Limited-Liability				Corn Starch
黑龙江龙凤玉米开发有限公司(1999)	绥化市	黑龙江省	(0455)3233427	1,150	有限公司	279,463	3,061(51)	236,170	玉米淀粉
Zhaoyuan Jinxing Bean Products Co., Ltd.	Yantai	Shandong	(0535)83352388		Overseas Chinese-funded				Vermicelli
招远市金星豆制品有限公司(1998)	烟台市	山东省	(0535)83388801	420	港澳台资	256,800	10,550(17)	11,530	粉丝
Zhaoxian Limin Starch Group	Shijiazhuang	Hebei	(0311)4908666		Collective-owned				Starch
赵县利民淀粉集团(1992)	石家庄市	河北省	(0311)4908666	185	集体企业	236,970	23,260(5)	40,330	淀粉

Top 10 Cities by Revenue 销售收入排名前10位城市	Province 省	Market share 市场份额 (%)	Number of firms 企业个数
Changchun 长春市	Jilin 吉林省	19.49	4
Yantai 烟台市	Shandong 山东省	12.30	26
Shijiazhuang 石家庄市	Hebei 河北省	7.06	28
Siping 四平市	Jilin 吉林省	5.36	5
Qinhuangdao 秦皇岛市	Hebei 河北省	5.14	24
Binzhou 滨州市	Shandong 山东省	4.21	3
Zaozhuang 枣庄市	Shandong 山东省	3.53	14
Linyi 临沂市	Shandong 山东省	3.06	3
Xingtai 邢台市	Hebei 河北省	2.21	8
Suihua 绥化市	Heilongjiang 黑龙江省	2.16	3

10 Major Wholesalers 十家主要批发商	City 城市	Province 省	Telephone/Fax 电话/传真
Beijing Cigarette Sale Company	Beijing	Beijing	(010)64228158
北京市卷烟销售公司	北京市	北京市	(010)64228365
Anhui Technology Import & Export Co.,Ltd.	Hefei	Anhui	(0551)5101188
安徽省技术进出口股份有限公司	合肥市	安徽省	(0551)5101199
China Tobacco General Company Henan Province Filiale	Zhengzhou	Henan	(0371)5583070
中国烟草总公司河南省公司	郑州市	河南省	(0371)5957546
Shanghai Jieqiang Tobacco,Sugar & Wine Company Supplies & Sales Center	Shanghai	Shanghai	(021)62494080
上海捷强烟草糖酒公司配销中心	上海市	上海市	(021)62492584
Zhejiang Cigarette Sale Company	Hangzhou	Zhejiang	(0571)87073247
浙江省卷烟销售公司	杭州市	浙江省	(0571)87072474
Fujian Cereals, Oils & Foodstuffs Import Group Corp.	Fuzhou	Fujian	(0591)7506688
福建省粮油食品进口集团公司	福州市	福建省	(0591)7544543
Chongqing Hongta Cigarette Sale Co.,Ltd.	Chongqing	Chongqing	(023)67750222
重庆红塔卷烟销售有限责任公司	重庆市	重庆市	(023)67740477
China Buty Free (Group) General Company	Beijing	Beijing	(010)64649988
中国免税品（集团）总公司	北京市	北京市	(010)64635846
Shanghai Jieqiang Tobacco,Sugar & Wine (Group) Co.,Ltd.	Shanghai	Shanghai	(021)62522018
上海捷强烟草糖酒（集团）有限公司	上海市	上海市	(021)62522005
Shanghai Tobacco Group Chongming Tobacco, Sugar & Wine Co.,Ltd.	Shanghai	Shanghai	(021)59621368
上海烟草集团崇明烟草糖酒有限公司	上海市	上海市	(021)59621368

1493: Dairy Substitute 代乳品制造业

The industry accounts for 0.015% of the total revenue of China's industrial sector in 2002. The rate of return on assets is 6.81%. 75.76% of all firms in the industry made a profit while 24.24% had negative returns.The top province in terms of the industry's revenue is Shanghai, accounting for 20.94% of the total revenue.
2002年本行业收入占全行业的 0.015%，资产利润率为 6.81%。75.76%的企业赢利，24.24%的企业亏损。收入最高的省为上海市，占本行业的20.94%。

	Total number of firms 企业总数	Total number of employees 职工总数	Total revenue (Mil.RMB) 总销售收入(百万元)	Total profit (Mil.RMB) 总利润(百万元)	Return on assets 资产利润率(%)	Return on equity 权益利润率(%)	Labour productivity ('000 RMB/ worker) 劳动生产率(千元/人)	Debts/ assets 资产负债率(%)	Total assets (Mil.RMB) 总资产(百万元)
Industry Overall 行业总体	33	5,770	1,613	178	6.81	9.51	100.78	28.34	2,619

	Number of firms 企业个数	Average number of employees 平均职工人数	Average revenue ('000 RMB) 平均销售收入(千元)	Average profit ('000 RMB) 平均利润(千元)	Return on assets 资产利润率(%)	Return on equity 权益利润率(%)	Labour productivity ('000 RMB/ worker) 劳动生产率(千元/人)	Debts/ assets 资产负债率(%)	Average total assets ('000 RMB) 平均总资产(千元)
By ownership 产业所有权									
State-owned 国有	1	70	637	-410	-3.23	-4.65	-13.63	30.51	12,690
Collective-owned 集体	2	138	29,240	2,143	16.65	26.71	51.43	37.68	12,872
Foreign & Overseas Chinese Funded 三资	10	137	49,790	6,934	10.83	17.10	115.16	36.64	63,997
By regional distribution 地区分布									
Central-North 华北	2	308	137,063	4,927	2.75	4.25	107.66	35.34	179,346
Beijing 北京									
Tianjin 天津									
Hebei 河北	1	26	13,246	1,569	61.67	64.20	175.38	3.93	2,544
Shanxi 山西	1	589	260,880	8,285	2.33	3.61	104.67	35.56	356,148
Inner Mongolia 内蒙古									
Northeast 东北	3	130	45,777	18,107	21.07	38.71	223.17	45.57	85,952
Liaoning 辽宁	1	290	135,854	54,732	22.59	41.83	302.69	46.00	242,327
Jilin 吉林	2	50	739	-205	-2.64	-4.32	-7.42	38.90	7,765
Heilongjiang 黑龙江									
Central-East 华东	14	121	35,962	1,167	1.14	1.39	93.44	18.19	102,763
Shanghai 上海	9	131	37,527	2,903	2.24	2.64	129.20	15.08	129,432
Jiangsu 江苏	2	102	71,491	-3,962	-3.73	-4.96	-6.83	24.75	106,152
Zhejiang 浙江									
Anhui 安徽									
Fujian 福建	1	121	11,864	-2,131	-4.13	-10.55	36.21	60.83	51,580
Jiangxi 江西									
Shandong 山东	2	93	5,440	137	2.76	3.55	13.22	22.21	4,955
Central-South 中南	9	149	54,463	9,414	22.00	35.92	161.51	38.75	42,786
Henan 河南	5	108	33,268	1,076	8.98	15.01	97.96	40.17	11,979
Hubei 湖北	1	80	43,150				261.73	60.00	12,207
Hunan 湖南	1	240	62,823	28,941	71.75	80.47	153.95	10.83	40,334
Guangdong 广东	2	241	108,928	25,203	18.49	31.66	220.11	41.61	136,321
Guangxi 广西									
Hainan 海南									
Southwest 西南									
Chongqing 重庆									
Sichuan 四川									
Guizhou 贵州									
Yunnan 云南									
Tibet 西藏									
Northwest 西北	5	346	41,614	2,636	7.38	14.41	30.76	48.75	35,700
Shaanxi 陕西	3	550	64,412	4,294	8.11	15.89	28.20	48.98	52,961
Gansu 甘肃	1	20	8,100	-283	-9.41	-17.88	226.90	47.36	3,007
Qinghai 青海									
Ningxia 宁夏	1	60	6,732	579	3.49	6.56	35.90	46.83	16,610
Xinjiang 新疆									

Year 年份	Number of firms 企业个数	Rate of change 变化率 (%)	Number of employees 职工人数 (人)	Rate of change 变化率 (%)	Total revenue (Mil. RMB) 总销售收入 (百万元)	Rate of change 变化率 (%)	Total profit (Mil RMB) 总利润 (百万元)	Rate of change 变化率 (%)
2000	11		1,268		243		-9	
2001	17	54.55	1,961	54.65	378	55.56	-2	77.78
2002	33	94.12	5,770	194.24	1,613	326.72	178	-

Major Products 主要产品	Output 产量	Unit 单位
Liquid Milk 液体乳	354	10,000 Tons 万吨

10 Main Firms with Maximal Revenue (year founded) 收入最大的十家主要企业（创办年份）	City 城市	Province 省	Telephone/fax 电话/传真	Number of employees 职工人数	Ownership 产业所有权	Revenue ('000 RMB) 销售收入 (千元)	Profit('000 RMB) (rank) 利润(千元)(排名)	Total assets ('000 RMB) 总资产 (千元)	Major products 主要产品
Shanxi Hengkang Daily Co.,Ltd.	Taiyuan	Shanxi	(0351)7241168		Private Owned				Dairy Products
山西恒康乳业有限公司	太原市	山西省	(0351)7335430	589	私营企业	260,880	8,285(6)	356,148	乳制品
Zhongshan Perfect Co.,Ltd.	Zhongshan	Guangdong	(0760)8701828		Foreign Funded				Health Foods
中山市完美日用品有限公司(1995)	中山市	广东省	(0760)8711603	381	外商投资	209,524	50,280(2)	259,988	保健食品
ZhenAo Group Co.,Ltd.	Dalian	Liaoning	(0411)7406999		Joint Stock				Nucleic Acid Aapsule
珍奥集团股份有限公司(1996)	大连市	辽宁省	(0411)7406483	290	股份制	135,854	54,732(1)	242,327	核酸胶囊
Shannxi Hongda Industrial Co., Ltd.	Xianyang	Shannxi	(0910)2463189		Limited-Liability				Dairy Products
陕西宏达实业有限公司(1986)	咸阳市	陕西省	(0910)2463176	730	有限公司	86,000	389(16)	40,762	乳制品
Shannxi Shenguo Stock Co., Ltd.	Xianyang	Shannxi	(0910)7496067		Joint Stock				Dried Milk
陕西神果股份有限公司(1998)	咸阳市	陕西省	(0910)7496007	880	股份制	84,667	11,897(5)	112,635	奶粉
Changsha Wahaha Changrong Drink Co., Ltd.	Changsha	Hunan	(0731)4016062		Foreign Funded				AD Calcium Milk
长沙娃哈哈长荣饮料有限公司(1999)	长沙市	湖南省	(0731)4012563	240	外商投资	62,823	28,941(3)	40,334	AD钙奶
Ruzhou Julong Starch Factory	Pingdingshan	Henan	(0375)6971921		Joint Stock				Starch
汝州市巨龙淀粉厂(1997)	平顶山市	河南省	(0375)6971998	129	股份制	38,900	1,500(10)	14,033	淀粉
Mengzhou MaiTeLing Co.,Ltd.	Jiaozuo	Henan	(0391)8531148		Joint Stock				Malt Dextrin
孟州市麦特灵有限责任公司(1995)	焦作市	河南省	(0391)8531148	65	股份制	34,270	396(15)	9,300	麦芽糊精
Shanghai Dahan Glossy Ganoderma Health Products Co.,Ltd.	Shanghai	Shanghai	(021)64697805		Overseas Chinese-funded				Health Food
上海大汉灵芝保健品有限公司(1996)	上海市	上海市	(021)64288436	144	港澳台资	26,932	329(19)	7,339	保键品
Mengzhou Changxin Malt Dextrine Factory	Jiaozuo	Henan	(0391)8531377		Private Enterprises				Malt Dextrin
孟州市长鑫麦芽湖精厂(1995)	焦作市	河南省	(0391)8531351	50	私营独资	24,180	385(17)	7,500	麦芽糊精

Top 10 Cities by Revenue 销售收入排名前10位城市	Province 省	Market share 市场份额 (%)	Number of firms 企业个数
Shanghai 上海市	Shanghai 上海市	20.94	9
Taiyuan 太原市	Shanxi 山西省	16.17	1
Zhongshan 中山市	Guangdong 广东省	13.50	2
Xianyang 咸阳市	Shannxi 陕西省	11.98	3
Suzhou 苏州市	Jiangsu 江苏省	8.54	1
Dalian 大连市	Liaoning 辽宁省	8.42	1
Jiaozuo 焦作市	Henan 河南省	7.90	4
Changsha 长沙市	Hunan 湖南省	3.89	1
Wuhan 武汉市	Hubei 湖北省	2.67	1
Pingdingshan 平顶山市	Henan 河南省	2.41	1

10 Major Wholesalers 十家主要批发商	City 城市	Province 省	Telephone/Fax 电话/传真
Beijing Cigarette Sale Company	Beijing	Beijing	(010)64228158
北京市卷烟销售公司	北京市	北京市	(010)64228365
Anhui Technology Import & Export Co.,Ltd.	Hefei	Anhui	(0551)5101188
安徽省技术进出口股份有限公司	合肥市	安徽省	(0551)5101199
China Tobacco General Company Henan Province Filiale	Zhengzhou	Henan	(0371)5583070
中国烟草总公司河南省公司	郑州市	河南省	(0371)5957546
Shanghai Jieqiang Tobacco,Sugar & Wine Company Supplies & Sales Center	Shanghai	Shanghai	(021)62494080
上海捷强烟草糖酒公司配销中心	上海市	上海市	(021)62492584
Zhejiang Cigarette Sale Company	Hangzhou	Zhejiang	(0571)87073247
浙江省卷烟销售公司	杭州市	浙江省	(0571)87072474
Fujian Cereals, Oils & Foodstuffs Import Group Corp.	Fuzhou	Fujian	(0591)7506688
福建省粮油食品进口集团公司	福州市	福建省	(0591)7544543
Chongqing Hongta Cigarette Sale Co.,Ltd.	Chongqing	Chongqing	(023)67750222
重庆红塔卷烟销售有限责任公司	重庆市	重庆市	(023)67740477
China Buty Free (Group) General Company	Beijing	Beijing	(010)64649988
中国免税品（集团）总公司	北京市	北京市	(010)64635846
Shanghai Jieqiang Tobacco,Sugar & Wine (Group) Co.,Ltd.	Shanghai	Shanghai	(021)62522018
上海捷强烟草糖酒（集团）有限公司	上海市	上海市	(021)62522005
Shanghai Tobacco Group Chongming Tobacco, Sugar & Wine Co.,Ltd.	Shanghai	Shanghai	(021)59621368
上海烟草集团崇明烟草糖酒有限公司	上海市	上海市	(021)59621368

1495: Ice 制冰业

The industry accounts for 0.001% of the total revenue of China's industrial sector in 2002. The rate of return on assets is 0.96%. 60.87% of all firms in the industry made a profit while 39.13% had negative returns.The top province in terms of the industry's revenue is Guangdong, accounting for 54.88% of the total revenue.
2002年本行业收入占全行业的0.001%，资产利润率为0.96%。60.87%的企业赢利，39.13%的企业亏损。收入最高的省为广东省，占本行业的54.88%。

	Total number of firms 企业总数	Total number of employees 职工总数	Total revenue (Mil.RMB) 总销售收入 (百万元)	Total profit (Mil.RMB) 总利润 (百万元)	Return on assets 资产利润率 (%)	Return on equity 权益利润率 (%)	Labour productivity ('000 RMB/ worker) 劳动生产率 (千元/人)	Debts/ assets 资产负债率 (%)	Total assets (Mil.RMB) 总资产 (百万元)
Industry Overall 行业总体	23	1,730	107	2	0.96	2.34	20.62	59.22	232

	Number of firms 企业个数	Average number of employees 平均职工人数	Average revenue ('000 RMB) 平均销售收入 (千元)	Average profit ('000 RMB) 平均利润 (千元)	Return on assets 资产利润率 (%)	Return on equity 权益利润率 (%)	Labour productivity ('000 RMB/ worker) 劳动生产率 (千元/人)	Debts/ assets 资产负债率 (%)	Average total assets ('000 RMB) 平均总资产 (千元)
By ownership 产业所有权									
State-owned 国有	16	93	4,753	-19	-0.16	-0.49	14.88	68.14	11,957
Collective-owned 集体	1	20	2,697	262	6.07	22.37	40.65	72.89	4,319
Foreign & Overseas Chinese Funded 三资	1	5	5,000				1,055.20	121.45	867
By regional distribution 地区分布									
Central-North 华北	1	15	273	-406	-8.57		2.80	120.91	4,735
Beijing 北京									
Tianjin 天津	1	15	273	-406	-8.57		2.80	120.91	4,735
Hebei 河北									
Shanxi 山西									
Inner Mongolia 内蒙古									
Northeast 东北									
Liaoning 辽宁									
Jilin 吉林									
Heilongjiang 黑龙江									
Central-East 华东	8	70	4,909	155	0.98	2.23	29.38	55.94	15,780
Shanghai 上海	1	13	569	58	0.77	1.06	5.31	26.89	7,507
Jiangsu 江苏									
Zhejiang 浙江	4	118	5,623	238	0.89	2.37	20.19	62.34	26,566
Anhui 安徽									
Fujian 福建	3	23	5,403	77	1.85	2.28	95.94	18.81	4,155
Jiangxi 江西									
Shandong 山东									
Central-South 中南	12	63	5,026	116	1.57	4.06	21.31	61.32	7,374
Henan 河南									
Hubei 湖北									
Hunan 湖南									
Guangdong 广东	10	54	5,880	189	3.65	10.90	29.09	66.54	5,182
Guangxi 广西	1	183	769	-499	-1.49	-3.56	0.07	58.25	33,527
Hainan 海南	1	40	739	1	0.03	0.03	14.28	8.29	3,149
Southwest 西南	2	200	3,644	-1	-0.02	-0.03	7.78	54.23	6,449
Chongqing 重庆									
Sichuan 四川	1	319	4,588	-153	-1.71	-5.08	3.79	66.42	8,970
Guizhou 贵州									
Yunnan 云南	1	81	2,700	151	3.84	5.22	23.46	26.37	3,928
Tibet 西藏									
Northwest 西北									
Shaanxi 陕西									
Gansu 甘肃									
Qinghai 青海									
Ningxia 宁夏									
Xinjiang 新疆									

Year 年份	Number of firms 企业个数	Rate of change 变化率 (%)	Number of employees 职工人数 (人)	Rate of change 变化率 (%)	Total revenue (Mil. RMB) 总销售收入 (百万元)	Rate of change 变化率 (%)	Total profit (Mil RMB) 总利润 (百万元)	Rate of change 变化率 (%)
2000	31		2,389		206		10	
2001	23	-25.81	1,730	-27.58	225	9.22	11	10.00
2002	23	o	1,730	o	107	-52.44	2	-81.82

Major Products 主要产品	Output 产量	Unit 单位
Frozen Beverage 冷冻饮品	60	10,000 Tons 万吨

10 Main Firms with Maximal Revenue (year founded) 收入最大的十家主要企业（创办年份）	City 城市	Province 省	Telephone/fax 电话/传真	Number of employees 职工人数	Ownership 产业所有权	Revenue ('000 RMB) 销售收入 (千元)	Profit('000 RMB) (rank) 利润(千元)(排名)	Total assets ('000 RMB) 总资产 (千元)	Major products 主要产品
Nan'ao Village & Township Enterprise Development General	Shantou	Guangdong	(0754)6803407		State-owned				Ice
Company 南澳县乡镇企业发展总公司(1991)	汕头市	广东省	(0754)6802438	48	国有企业	42,330	196(5)	14,128	冰
Rui'an Yudu Ice-making General Factory	Wenzhou	Zhejiang	(0577)65602424		Joint Stock				Big Ice for Fishery
瑞安市渔都制冰总厂(1999)	温州市	浙江省	(0577)65602424	125	股份制	10,172	1,872(1)	21,566	渔用大冰
Zhejiang Aquatic Products Processing Cold Storage &	Ningbo	Zhejiang	(0574)87634591		State-owned				Machine-made Ice
Transport Corp 浙江省水产加工贮运公司(1979)	宁波市	浙江省	(0574)87633643	323	国有企业	9,458	-	80,304	机冰
Yong'an Ronggang Food Co., Ltd.	Sanming	Fujian	(0598)3617676		Private Enterprises				Ice
永安市融港食品有限公司(2000)	三明市	福建省	(0598)3658676	20	私营独资	6,120	116(8)	621	冰
Bazhong Feixia Industrial Co., Ltd.	Bazhong	Sichuan	(0827)5223103		State-owned				Ice Cream
巴中飞霞实业有限公司(1958)	巴中市	四川省	(0827)5223103	319	国有企业	4,588	-	8,970	冰淇淋
China Aquatic Products Zhanjiang Yinshan Freezing Factory	Zhanjiang	Guangdong	(0759)2203280		State-owned				Texture Freezing
中国水产湛江银山冷冻厂(1995)	湛江市	广东省		79	国有企业	4,581	880(3)	8,516	理冻
Guangdong Huazhou JianLian Freezing Factory	Maoming	Guangdong	(0668)7367883		Private Enterprises				Ice
广东省化州市鉴联冰冻厂(1981)	茂名市	广东省	(0668)7367883	30	私营独资	1,850	150(7)	2,630	冰
Lufeng Jiazi Freezing Factory	Shanwei	Guangdong	(0660)8851740		State-owned				Cold Storage
陆丰市甲子冷冻厂(1978)	汕尾市	广东省		176	国有企业	1,635	-	3,270	冷藏
Lianjiang Meats Joint Processing Factory	Zhanjiang	Guangdong	(0759)6622297		State-owned				Cold Storage
廉江市肉类联合加工厂(1905)	湛江市	广东省		22	国有企业	1,340	-	6,538	冷藏
Liuzhou Freezing General Factory	Liuzhou	Guangxi	(0772)3212139		State-owned				Cold Storage
柳州市冷冻总厂(1959)	柳州市	广西	(0772)3212139	183	国有企业	769	-	33,527	冷藏

Top 10 Cities by Revenue 销售收入排名前10位城市	Province 省	Market share 市场份额 (%)	Number of firms 企业个数
Shantou 汕头市	Guangdong 广东省	39.51	1
Zhanjiang 湛江市	Guangdong 广东省	11.62	5
Ningbo 宁波市	Zhejiang 浙江省	11.35	2
Wenzhou 温州市	Zhejiang 浙江省	9.65	2
Zhangzhou 漳州市	Fujian 福建省	9.42	2
Sanming 三明市	Fujian 福建省	5.71	1
Bazhong 巴中市	Sichuan 四川省	4.28	1
Kunming 昆明市	Yunnan 云南省	2.52	1
Maoming 茂名市	Guangdong 广东省	1.73	1
Shanwei 汕尾市	Guangdong 广东省	1.53	1

10 Major Wholesalers 十家主要批发商	City 城市	Province 省	Telephone/Fax 电话/传真
Beijing Cigarette Sale Company	Beijing	Beijing	(010)64228158
北京市卷烟销售公司	北京市	北京市	(010)64228365
Anhui Technology Import & Export Co.,Ltd.	Hefei	Anhui	(0551)5101188
安徽省技术进出口股份有限公司	合肥市	安徽省	(0551)5101199
China Tobacco General Company Henan Province Filiale	Zhengzhou	Henan	(0371)5583070
中国烟草总公司河南省公司	郑州市	河南省	(0371)5957546
Shanghai Jieqiang Tobacco,Sugar & Wine Company Supplies & Sales Center	Shanghai	Shanghai	(021)62494080
上海捷强烟草糖酒公司配销中心	上海市	上海市	(021)62492584
Zhejiang Cigarette Sale Company	Hangzhou	Zhejiang	(0571)87073247
浙江省卷烟销售公司	杭州市	浙江省	(0571)87072474
Fujian Cereals, Oils & Foodstuffs Import Group Corp.	Fuzhou	Fujian	(0591)7506688
福建省粮油食品进口集团公司	福州市	福建省	(0591)7544543
Chongqing Hongta Cigarette Sale Co.,Ltd.	Chongqing	Chongqing	(023)67750222
重庆红塔卷烟销售有限责任公司	重庆市	重庆市	(023)67740477
China Buty Free (Group) General Company	Beijing	Beijing	(010)64649988
中国免税品（集团）总公司	北京市	北京市	(010)64635846
Shanghai Jieqiang Tobacco,Sugar & Wine (Group) Co.,Ltd.	Shanghai	Shanghai	(021)62522018
上海捷强烟草糖酒（集团）有限公司	上海市	上海市	(021)62522005
Shanghai Tobacco Group Chongming Tobacco, Sugar & Wine Co.,Ltd.	Shanghai	Shanghai	(021)59621368
上海烟草集团崇明烟草糖酒有限公司	上海市	上海市	(021)59621368

1497: Starch Sugar 淀粉糖业

The industry accounts for 0.021% of the total revenue of China's industrial sector in 2002. The rate of return on assets is 9.48%. 73.68% of all firms in the industry made a profit while 26.32% had negative returns.The top province in terms of the industry's revenue is Shandong, accounting for 35.15% of the total revenue.
2002年本行业收入占全行业的0.021%，资产利润率为9.48%。73.68%的企业赢利，26.32%的企业亏损。收入最高的省为山东省，占本行业的35.15%。

	Total number of firms 企业总数	Total number of employees 职工总数	Total revenue (Mil.RMB) 总销售收入 (百万元)	Total profit (Mil.RMB) 总利润 (百万元)	Return on assets 资产利润率 (%)	Return on equity 权益利润率 (%)	Labour productivity ('000 RMB/worker) 劳动生产率 (千元/人)	Debts/assets 资产负债率 (%)	Total assets (Mil.RMB) 总资产 (百万元)
Industry Overall 行业总体	57	7,245	2,262	189	9.48	20.76	87.53	54.34	1,997

	Number of firms 企业个数	Average number of employees 平均职工人数	Average revenue ('000 RMB) 平均销售收入 (千元)	Average profit ('000 RMB) 平均利润 (千元)	Return on assets 资产利润率 (%)	Return on equity 权益利润率 (%)	Labour productivity ('000 RMB/worker) 劳动生产率 (千元/人)	Debts/assets 资产负债率 (%)	Average total assets ('000 RMB) 平均总资产 (千元)
By ownership 产业所有权									
State-owned 国有	12	96	4,077	-55	-0.30	-3.27	15.82	90.80	18,168
Collective-owned 集体	5	140	76,110	4,658	27.00	66.26	121.20	59.24	17,250
Foreign & Overseas Chinese Funded 三资	12	94	47,946	7,542	11.59	18.38	173.11	36.95	65,080
By regional distribution 地区分布									
Central-North 华北	12	107	54,617	7,952	20.86	32.77	164.36	36.34	38,114
Beijing 北京	6	121	45,312	11,806	21.56	31.35	165.61	31.21	54,750
Tianjin 天津	1	10		-100	-1.62	-12.47	-5.30	87.05	6,191
Hebei 河北	4	114	90,745	6,154	22.31	38.48	178.70	42.01	27,580
Shanxi 山西	1	87	20,549	74	0.60	16.86	98.40	96.45	12,362
Inner Mongolia 内蒙古									
Northeast 东北	2	108	74,716	4,125	20.64	38.13	142.13	45.86	19,983
Liaoning 辽宁	1	165	41,596	450	4.22	26.99	19.75	84.35	10,651
Jilin 吉林	1	50	107,835	7,800	26.61	39.06	546.00	31.87	29,314
Heilongjiang 黑龙江									
Central-East 华东	23	160	47,574	1,960	5.69	13.01	78.69	56.29	34,451
Shanghai 上海	4	83	53,383	2,576	5.53	14.19	92.00	61.05	46,607
Jiangsu 江苏									
Zhejiang 浙江	1	67	5,590	779	6.35	20.45	40.52	68.93	12,264
Anhui 安徽	1	350	8,098	15	0.14		6.72	100.26	10,708
Fujian 福建	4	66	15,070	-1,246	-2.35	-3.89	42.71	39.58	53,024
Jiangxi 江西	2	50	5,880	434	7.28	18.58	49.73	60.84	5,959
Shandong 山东	11	234	72,268	3,463	10.61	27.78	92.54	61.80	32,634
Central-South 中南	16	122	22,374	2,555	6.08	16.31	52.13	62.71	42,017
Henan 河南	6	158	5,518	-159	-0.59	-7.28	13.12	91.85	26,733
Hubei 湖北	1	128	11,337	1	0.01	0.03	46.59	56.66	7,822
Hunan 湖南									
Guangdong 广东	7	105	43,980	6,016	8.53	18.07	110.24	52.78	70,513
Guangxi 广西	2	68	2,837	-143	-2.73	-24.93	14.41	89.05	5,236
Hainan 海南									
Southwest 西南	1	79	3,100	120	0.86		9.68	113.52	14,013
Chongqing 重庆									
Sichuan 四川	1	79	3,100	120	0.86		9.68	113.52	14,013
Guizhou 贵州									
Yunnan 云南									
Tibet 西藏									
Northwest 西北	3	15	465	-157	-2.29	-12.96	31.61	82.34	6,857
Shaanxi 陕西	2	17	664	-236	-3.18	-18.11	15.15	82.45	7,411
Gansu 甘肃	1	10	67				87.60	82.05	5,749
Qinghai 青海									
Ningxia 宁夏									
Xinjiang 新疆									

1497: Starch Sugar 淀粉糖业

Year 年份	Number of firms 企业个数	Rate of change 变化率 (%)	Number of employees 职工人数 (人)	Rate of change 变化率 (%)	Total revenue (Mil. RMB) 总销售收入 (百万元)	Rate of change 变化率 (%)	Total profit (Mil RMB) 总利润 (百万元)	Rate of change 变化率 (%)
2000	65		9,279		1,855		115	
2001	66	1.54	9,900	6.69	2,385	28.57	217	88.70
2002	57	-13.64	7,245	-26.82	2,262	-5.16	189	-12.90

Major Products 主要产品	Output 产量	Unit 单位
Starch 淀粉	757	10,000 Tons 万吨

10 Main Firms with Maximal Revenue (year founded) 收入最大的十家主要企业（创办年份）	City 城市	Province 省	Telephone/fax 电话/传真	Number of employees 职工人数	Ownership 产业所有权	Revenue ('000 RMB) 销售收入 (千元)	Profit('000 RMB) (rank) 利润(千元) (排名)	Total assets ('000 RMB) 总资产 (千元)	Major products 主要产品
Shandong Luzhou Food Co.,Ltd.	Linyi	Shandong	(0539)2251686		Private Owned				High Malt Medicinal Syrup高
山东省鲁洲食品有限责任公司(1988)	临沂市	山东省	(0539)2321997	1,781	私营企业	668,415	35,863(2)	228,097	麦芽糖浆
Beijing Biwang Food Co., Ltd.	Beijing	Beijing	(010)69966789		Overseas Chinese-funded				Food
北京必旺食品有限公司(1996)	北京市	北京市	(010)69966699	292	港澳台资	166,049	64,332(1)	188,270	食品
Shanghai Rong-Shi Enterprise Co., Ltd.	Shanghai	Shanghai	(021)64325617		Limited-Liability				Maltose
上海融氏企业有限公司(1998)	上海市	上海市	(021)64326841	208	有限公司	113,172	3,822(9)	94,874	麦芽糖
Changchun Dihao Food Development Co., Ltd.	Changchun	Jilin	(0431)7868363		Foreign Funded				Glucose
长春市帝豪食品发展有限公司(1999)	长春市	吉林省	(0431)7874279	50	外商投资	107,835	7,800(6)	29,314	葡萄糖
Shanghai Haocheng Food Development Co., Ltd.	Shanghai	Shanghai	(021)54721702		Overseas Chinese-funded				Starch Syrup
上海好成食品发展有限公司(1998)	上海市	上海市	(021)54722288	68	港澳台资	54,105	5,113(8)	60,909	淀粉糖
Beijing Wang-Wang Food Co., Ltd.	Beijing	Beijing	(010)69966789		Foreign Funded				Recreation Food休
北京旺旺食品有限公司(1994)	北京市	北京市	(010)69966699	121	外商投资	45,389	7,789(7)	91,399	闲类食品
Fushun Luzhou Starch Sugar Products Co., Ltd.	Fushun	Liaoning	(0413)6102688		Private Owned				Starch Sugar
抚顺市鲁洲淀粉糖制品有限公司(1997)	抚顺市	辽宁省	(0413)6102688	165	私营企业	41,596	450(18)	10,651	淀粉糖
Quanzhou Sincere Food Development Co., Ltd.	Quanzhou	Fujian	(0595)2881999		Overseas Chinese-funded				Glucose Aqua
泉州新世纪食品开发有限公司(2001)	泉州市	福建省	(0595)2889799	100	港澳台资	38,390	872(13)	45,204	葡萄糖液
Ji'nan Licheng District Zhangyue Malt Factory	Jinan	Shandong	(0531)8734078		Private Enterprises				Malt
济南历城区张越麦芽厂 (1984)	济南市	山东省	(0531)8734078	81	私营独资	36,207	2,534(10)	9,722	麦芽
Beijing Tianrun Food Factory	Beijing	Beijing	(010)67474606		Private Enterprises				Glucose
北京天润食品厂(1998)	北京市	北京市	(010)67474606	111	私营独资	29,578	-	12,972	葡萄糖

Top 10 Cities by Revenue 销售收入排名前10位城市	Province 省	Market share 市场份额 (%)	Number of firms 企业个数
Linyi 临沂市	Shandong 山东省	30.64	4
Shijiazhuang 石家庄市	Hebei 河北省	14.95	2
Beijing 北京市	Beijing 北京市	12.02	6
Shanghai 上海市	Shanghai 上海市	9.44	4
Guangzhou 广州市	Guangdong 广东省	7.01	2
Zhaoqing 肇庆市	Guangdong 广东省	5.06	1
Changchun 长春市	Jilin 吉林省	4.77	1
Quanzhou 泉州市	Fujian 福建省	2.44	3
Fushun 抚顺市	Liaoning 辽宁省	1.84	1
Jinan 济南市	Shandong 山东省	1.82	2

10 Major Wholesalers 十家主要批发商	City 城市	Province 省	Telephone/Fax 电话/传真
Beijing Chaoyang Non-Staple Foodstuffs General Company	Beijing	Beijing	(010)65016285
北京朝阳副食品总公司	北京市	北京市	(010)65016285
Beijing Sugar,Cigarette & Wine Company	Beijing	Beijing	(010)67210304
北京市糖业烟酒公司	北京市	北京市	(010)67210310
Shanghai Sugar Cigarette & Wine (Group) Co.,Ltd.	Shanghai	Shanghai	(021)63224190
上海市糖业烟酒(集团)有限公司	上海市	上海市	(021)63223169
Jiangsu Sutang Sugar & Wine Co.,Ltd.	Nanjing	Jiangsu	(025)6661088
江苏苏糖糖酒食品有限公司	南京市	江苏省	(025)6661088
Fujian Commerce (Group) Co.,Ltd.	Fuzhou	Fujian	(0591)7847148
福建省商业（集团）有限责任公司	福州市	福建省	(0591)7847145
Yantai Changyu Pioneer Winer Co., Ltd.	Yantai	Shandong	(0535)6602730
烟台张裕葡萄酿酒股份有限公司	烟台市	山东省	(0535)6214078
BlueRibbon Beer Sale Co.,Ltd.	Zhaoqing	Guangdong	(0758)2862322
蓝带啤酒销售有限公司	肇庆市	广东省	(0758)2862424
Fujian Shenlong Development Co.,Ltd.	Fuzhou	Fujian	(0591)7503218
福建省神龙发展股份有限公司	福州市	福建省	(0591)7503068
Guangdong Sugar, Cigarette & Wine Group Company	Guangzhou	Guangdong	(020)83566131
广东省糖烟酒集团公司	广州市	广东省	(020)83561421
Shunde Daliang Sugar, Cigarette & Wine Co.,Ltd.	Shunde	Guangdong	(0765)2231804
顺德市大良区糖烟酒有限公司	顺德市	广东省	(0765)2222300

1498: Ice Cream and Frozen Desserts 冷饮品制造业

The industry accounts for 0.042% of the total revenue of China's industrial sector in 2002. The rate of return on assets is -4.35%. 68.85% of all firms in the industry made a profit while 31.15% had negative returns.The top province in terms of the industry's revenue is Zhejiang, accounting for 13.95% of the total revenue.
2002年本行业收入占全行业的 0.042%，资产利润率为 -4.35%。68.85%的企业赢利，31.15%的企业亏损。收入最高的省为浙江省，占本行业的13.95%。

	Total number of firms 企业总数	Total number of employees 职工总数	Total revenue (Mil.RMB) 总销售收入（百万元）	Total profit (Mil.RMB) 总利润（百万元）	Return on assets 资产利润率（%）	Return on equity 权益利润率（%）	Labour productivity ('000 RMB/ worker) 劳动生产率（千元/人）	Debts/ assets 资产负债率（%）	Total assets (Mil.RMB) 总资产（百万元）
Industry Overall 行业总体	183	33,950	4,558	-273	-4.35	-13.02	39.91	66.55	6,278

	Number of firms 企业个数	Average number of employees 平均职工人数	Average revenue ('000 RMB) 平均销售收入（千元）	Average profit ('000 RMB) 平均利润（千元）	Return on assets 资产利润率（%）	Return on equity 权益利润率（%）	Labour productivity ('000 RMB/ worker) 劳动生产率（千元/人）	Debts/ assets 资产负债率（%）	Average total assets ('000 RMB) 平均总资产（千元）
By ownership 产业所有权									
State-owned 国有	49	160	7,351	-215	-1.04	-5.07	16.81	79.58	20,750
Collective-owned 集体	15	121	17,093	334	2.03	7.49	44.60	72.90	16,462
Foreign & Overseas Chinese Funded 三资	32	229	50,772	-10,825	-13.53	-35.79	72.17	62.19	79,987
By regional distribution 地区分布									
Central-North 华北	31	160	38,512	-5,219	-11.06	-23.63	92.99	53.18	47,170
Beijing 北京	4	130	75,540	-51,226	-37.92	-44.87	396.11	15.49	135,100
Tianjin 天津	14	181	33,717	-89	-0.18	-0.84	38.40	77.95	48,343
Hebei 河北	7	53	10,134	193	2.67	8.13	62.91	67.16	7,232
Shanxi 山西	3	77	32	-418	-7.14		-0.74	157.64	5,858
Inner Mongolia 内蒙古	3	439	116,212	14,755	25.03	61.24	103.10	59.14	58,957
Northeast 东北	31	102	11,852	47	0.38	1.04	37.95	63.31	12,303
Liaoning 辽宁	15	115	13,118	21	0.14	0.36	43.59	62.70	15,533
Jilin 吉林	8	129	18,043	611	7.12	13.40	36.62	46.86	8,573
Heilongjiang 黑龙江	8	52	3,288	-467	-4.68	-22.51	17.91	79.20	9,976
Central-East 华东	49	225	35,991	-1,047	-1.99	-6.30	44.74	68.34	52,518
Shanghai 上海	11	264	41,963	-5,688	-11.33	-25.62	38.98	55.76	50,190
Jiangsu 江苏	11	198	25,170	-1,231	-1.65	-56.85	45.85	97.11	74,857
Zhejiang 浙江	10	265	63,580	1,748	2.69	5.20	56.84	48.29	64,973
Anhui 安徽	1	262	30,450	104	0.29	0.62	37.53	53.03	35,737
Fujian 福建	4	56	8,707	14	0.06	0.11	27.33	42.69	21,214
Jiangxi 江西	4	243	21,334	-37	-0.17	-0.47	39.95	64.45	22,014
Shandong 山东	8	226	29,834	915	2.16	6.43	40.70	66.45	42,437
Central-South 中南	48	253	20,969	-1,113	-3.82	-17.90	20.16	78.67	29,151
Henan 河南	20	346	25,732	532	1.98	11.12	21.63	82.18	26,862
Hubei 湖北	4	80	6,391	-299	-2.19	-7.80	19.36	71.96	13,680
Hunan 湖南	9	260	9,901	-847	-3.50		10.91	117.25	24,223
Guangdong 广东	13	167	26,257	-4,252	-10.35	-28.86	24.62	64.15	41,094
Guangxi 广西	2	186	17,939	11	0.04	0.06	25.80	39.21	27,540
Hainan 海南									
Southwest 西南	13	130	12,656	-12	-0.06	-0.20	8.33	70.20	20,955
Chongqing 重庆	2	101	9,942	64	0.36	0.69	27.10	47.84	17,742
Sichuan 四川	8	138	15,102	-79	-0.33	-1.11	-8.33	70.35	23,959
Guizhou 贵州	1	230	22,897	344	0.91	3.93	26.23	76.92	37,936
Yunnan 云南	2	73	466				80.46	139.73	3,664
Tibet 西藏									
Northwest 西北	11	90	5,620	-741	-4.30	-10.02	21.77	57.04	17,219
Shaanxi 陕西	4	158	6,616	-769	-12.10	-18.29	13.06	33.85	6,357
Gansu 甘肃	5	44	3,478	-590	-2.33	-5.74	44.06	59.41	25,326
Qinghai 青海									
Ningxia 宁夏									
Xinjiang 新疆	2	69	8,985	-1,063	-5.69	-16.16	26.36	64.79	18,675

1498: Ice Cream and Frozen Desserts 冷饮品制造业

Year 年份	Number of firms 企业个数	Rate of change 变化率 (%)	Number of employees 职工人数 (人)	Rate of change 变化率 (%)	Total revenue (Mil. RMB) 总销售收入 (百万元)	Rate of change 变化率 (%)	Total profit (Mil RMB) 总利润 (百万元)	Rate of change 变化率 (%)
2000	251		47,967		5,055		-151	
2001	194	-22.71	33,881	-29.37	3,784	-25.14	-286	-89.40
2002	183	-5.67	33,950	0.20	4,558	20.45	-273	4.55

Major Products 主要产品	Output 产量	Unit 单位
Frozen Beverage 冷冻饮品	60	10,000 Tons 万吨

10 Main Firms with Maximal Revenue (year founded) 收入最大的十家主要企业（创办年份）	City 城市	Province 省	Telephone/fax 电话/传真	Number of employees 职工人数	Ownership 产业所有权	Revenue ('000 RMB) 销售收入（千元）	Profit('000 RMB) (rank) 利润(千元)(排名)	Total assets ('000 RMB) 总资产（千元）	Major products 主要产品
You Can Food Group Co., Ltd.	Hangzhou	Zhejiang	(0571)85141777		Private Owned				Cold Drinks
佑康食品集团有限公司(1995)	杭州市	浙江省	(0571)85148327	1,271	私营企业	286,660	10,970(2)	301,720	冷饮
Hangzhou Wufeng Refrigerated Foods Co.,Ltd.	Hangzhou	Zhejiang	(0571)86804584		Overseas Chinese-funded				Cold Drinks
杭州五丰冷食有限公司(1992)	杭州市	浙江省	(0571)86064020	671	港澳台资	223,498	3,878(9)	138,403	冷饮
Walls (China) Co.,Ltd.	Beijing	Beijing	(010)67881068		Foreign Funded				Ice Cream
和路雪（中国）有限公司(1993)	北京市	北京市	(010)67881064	278	外商投资	222,511	-	439,875	冰淇淋
Shanghai Yi Li Ai Bei Food Co., Ltd.	Shanghai	Shanghai	(021)64306958		Overseas Chinese-funded				Frozen Food
上海伊利爱贝食品有限公司(1999)	上海市	上海市	(021)64306918	548	港澳台资	188,156	228(46)	106,077	冷冻食品
Tianjin Kangye Refigeated Foods Co., Ltd.	Tianjin	Tianjin	(022)28522222		Joint Stock				Frozen Food
天津市康业冷冻食品股份有限公司(1999)	天津市	天津市	(022)28522222	576	股份制	174,645	5,905(4)	188,662	冷冻食品
Shanghai Rin NO. 1 Food Co.,Ltd.	Shanghai	Shanghai	(021)65084949		Overseas Chinese-funded				Cold Drinks
上海益民食品一厂有限公司(1993)	上海市	上海市	(021)65080534	1,094	港澳台资	127,716	-	149,428	冷饮
Guangzhou Refigeated Foods Co.,Ltd.	Guangzhou	Guangdong	(020)83839883		Foreign Funded				Frozen Beverage
广州冷冻食品有限公司(1986)	广州市	广东省	(020)83824007	588	外商投资	83,278	-	61,965	冷冻饮品
Shandong Pengcheng Food Co., Ltd.	Weihai	Shandong	(0631)8571018		Joint Stock				Frozen Beverage
山东鹏程食品股份有限公司(1986)	威海市	山东省	(0631)8571035	442	股份制	72,884	63(69)	143,979	冷冻饮品
Shanghai Fuller Co.,Ltd.	Shanghai	Shanghai	(021)58995352		Foreign Funded				Ice Cream
上海福乐食品有限公司(1993)	上海市	上海市	(021)58992702	380	外商投资	64,407	-	93,133	冰淇淋
Tianjin Daqiaodao Refigeated Foods Factory	Tianjin	Tianjin	(022)24314336		Collective-owned				Cold Food
天津市大桥道冷食厂(1990)	天津市	天津市	(022)24314336	566	集体企业	63,605	410(36)	30,717	冷食

Top 10 Cities by Revenue 销售收入排名前10位城市	Province 省	Market share 市场份额 (%)	Number of firms 企业个数
Hangzhou 杭州市	Zhejiang 浙江省	11.48	4
Tianjin 天津市	Tianjin 天津市	10.36	14
Shanghai 上海市	Shanghai 上海市	10.13	11
Zhengzhou 郑州市	Henan 河南省	9.16	5
Baotou 包头市	Inner Mongolia 内蒙古	7.61	2
Beijing 北京市	Beijing 北京市	6.63	4
Suzhou 苏州市	Jiangsu 江苏省	4.91	1
Guangzhou 广州市	Guangdong 广东省	2.97	3
Shenyang 沈阳市	Liaoning 辽宁省	2.76	5
Jilin 吉林市	Jilin 吉林省	2.76	4

10 Major Wholesalers 十家主要批发商	City 城市	Province 省	Telephone/Fax 电话/传真
Beijing Cigarette Sale Company	Beijing	Beijing	(010)64228158
北京市卷烟销售公司	北京市	北京市	(010)64228365
Anhui Technology Import & Export Co.,Ltd.	Hefei	Anhui	(0551)5101188
安徽省技术进出口股份有限公司	合肥市	安徽省	(0551)5101199
China Tobacco General Company Henan Province Filiale	Zhengzhou	Henan	(0371)5583070
中国烟草总公司河南省公司	郑州市	河南省	(0371)5957546
Shanghai Jieqiang Tobacco,Sugar & Wine Company Supplies & Sales Center	Shanghai	Shanghai	(021)62494080
上海捷强烟草糖酒公司配销中心	上海市	上海市	(021)62492584
Zhejiang Cigarette Sale Company	Hangzhou	Zhejiang	(0571)87073247
浙江省卷烟销售公司	杭州市	浙江省	(0571)87072474
Fujian Cereals, Oils & Foodstuffs Import Group Corp.	Fuzhou	Fujian	(0591)7506688
福建省粮油食品进口集团公司	福州市	福建省	(0591)7544543
Chongqing Hongta Cigarette Sale Co.,Ltd.	Chongqing	Chongqing	(023)67750222
重庆红塔卷烟销售有限责任公司	重庆市	重庆市	(023)67740477
China Buty Free (Group) General Company	Beijing	Beijing	(010)64649988
中国免税品（集团）总公司	北京市	北京市	(010)64635846
Shanghai Jieqiang Tobacco,Sugar & Wine (Group) Co.,Ltd.	Shanghai	Shanghai	(021)62522018
上海捷强烟草糖酒（集团）有限公司	上海市	上海市	(021)62522005
Shanghai Tobacco Group Chongming Tobacco, Sugar & Wine Co.,Ltd.	Shanghai	Shanghai	(021)59621368
上海烟草集团崇明烟草糖酒有限公司	上海市	上海市	(021)59621368

1499: Other Food 其他类未包括的食品制造业

The industry accounts for 0.134% of the total revenue of China's industrial sector in 2002. The rate of return on assets is 4.23%. 81.70% of all firms in the industry made a profit while 18.30% had negative returns.The top province in terms of the industry's revenue is Shandong, accounting for 20.87% of the total revenue.
2002年本行业收入占全行业的 0.134%，资产利润率为 4.23%。81.70%的企业赢利，18.30%的企业亏损。收入最高的省为山东省，占本行业的20.87%。

	Total number of firms 企业总数	Total number of employees 职工总数	Total revenue (Mil.RMB) 总销售收入 (百万元)	Total profit (Mil.RMB) 总利润 (百万元)	Return on assets 资产利润率 (%)	Return on equity 权益利润率 (%)	Labour productivity ('000 RMB/ worker) 劳动生产率 (千元/人)	Debts/ assets 资产负债率 (%)	Total assets (Mil.RMB) 总资产 (百万元)
Industry Overall 行业总体	388	71,671	14,322	771	4.23	8.77	57.81	51.82	18,238

	Number of firms 企业个数	Average number of employees 平均职工人数	Average revenue ('000 RMB) 平均销售收入 (千元)	Average profit ('000 RMB) 平均利润 (千元)	Return on assets 资产利润率 (%)	Return on equity 权益利润率 (%)	Labour productivity ('000 RMB/ worker) 劳动生产率 (千元/人)	Debts/ assets 资产负债率 (%)	Average total assets ('000 RMB) 平均总资产 (千元)
By ownership 产业所有权									
State-owned 国有	33	199	39,408	2,651	4.12	12.79	51.04	67.74	64,269
Collective-owned 集体	51	176	31,534	685	2.38	4.68	24.49	49.25	28,852
Foreign & Overseas Chinese Funded 三资	127	162	44,139	2,563	4.47	9.83	85.32	54.53	57,362
By regional distribution 地区分布									
Central-North 华北	55	162	45,630	3,192	5.90	13.67	59.17	56.85	54,098
Beijing 北京	17	117	38,925	5,424	8.10	12.18	122.16	33.54	66,991
Tianjin 天津	17	171	56,856	2,002	2.99	13.64	0.07	78.11	67,052
Hebei 河北	18	217	48,277	2,732	7.31	18.06	72.20	59.52	37,374
Shanxi 山西	2	43	3,566	60	2.52	5.85	28.08	56.92	2,381
Inner Mongolia 内蒙古	1	28	5,229				3.54	84.63	19,157
Northeast 东北	39	105	26,360	-114	-0.30	-0.85	83.10	64.50	37,830
Liaoning 辽宁	11	186	62,048	-1,408	-1.33	-4.19	115.09	68.33	106,074
Jilin 吉林	17	73	12,656	48	0.52	1.06	54.65	51.45	9,362
Heilongjiang 黑龙江	11	73	11,851	929	6.84	13.27	45.42	48.47	13,581
Central-East 华东	161	217	42,986	2,523	5.63	11.77	55.84	52.17	44,821
Shanghai 上海	27	138	45,303	4,233	6.96	9.83	147.13	29.17	60,792
Jiangsu 江苏	36	136	27,463	900	2.50	7.17	46.36	65.11	35,985
Zhejiang 浙江	15	53	16,130	1,166	6.87	12.12	56.12	43.34	16,987
Anhui 安徽	16	442	72,184	1,885	4.38	20.00	24.45	78.11	43,056
Fujian 福建	10	165	23,385	1,283	7.10	10.95	38.82	35.16	18,067
Jiangxi 江西	8	67	11,238	67	1.00	4.57	54.78	78.13	6,734
Shandong 山东	49	333	60,986	4,052	6.40	14.05	53.21	54.44	63,288
Central-South 中南	99	213	34,746	1,976	3.52	6.03	55.75	41.64	56,121
Henan 河南	20	379	26,183	281	0.92	4.57	16.29	79.87	30,499
Hubei 湖北	24	160	18,441	977	5.93	15.32	44.52	61.32	16,494
Hunan 湖南	13	103	9,766	318	5.91	9.74	21.77	39.32	5,388
Guangdong 广东	37	187	55,643	3,998	3.43	5.20	111.85	34.04	116,502
Guangxi 广西	4	134	37,523	3,377	12.39	18.55	89.61	33.20	27,247
Hainan 海南	1	857	137,774	935	1.54	11.58	33.50	86.66	60,536
Southwest 西南	11	83	11,382	231	1.41	3.23	54.53	56.39	16,419
Chongqing 重庆	3	70	14,932	314	3.24	5.76	85.29	43.77	9,708
Sichuan 四川	3	170	19,744	584	4.26	5.55	60.11	23.23	13,709
Guizhou 贵州	1	86	9,453	1,541	9.79	16.50	30.19	40.66	15,744
Yunnan 云南	3	30	3,720	-633	-2.14	-10.87	-23.13	80.28	29,538
Tibet 西藏	1	13	565	204	3.40	5.10	31.23	33.33	6,000
Northwest 西北	23	75	12,977	-194	-0.53	-2.16	57.83	75.24	36,289
Shaanxi 陕西	4	223	32,724	445	0.94	36.83	38.76	97.44	47,156
Gansu 甘肃	15	42	8,579	42	0.43	1.60	84.49	73.27	9,901
Qinghai 青海	3	52	5,995	-436	-2.72	-5.31	36.85	48.78	16,033
Ningxia 宁夏									
Xinjiang 新疆	1	44	20,907	-5,568	-1.24	-4.05	134.43	69.40	449,409

Year 年份	Number of firms 企业个数	Rate of change 变化率 (%)	Number of employees 职工人数 (人)	Rate of change 变化率 (%)	Total revenue (Mil. RMB) 总销售收入 (百万元)	Rate of change 变化率 (%)	Total profit (Mil RMB) 总利润 (百万元)	Rate of change 变化率 (%)
2000	354		46,905		10,791		220	
2001	371	4.80	59,488	26.83	11,373	5.39	381	73.18
2002	388	4.58	71,671	20.48	14,322	25.93	771	102.36

Major Products 主要产品	Output 产量	Unit 单位

10 Main Firms with Maximal Revenue (year founded) 收入最大的十家主要企业（创办年份）	City 城市	Province 省	Telephone/fax 电话/传真	Number of employees 职工人数	Ownership 产业所有权	Revenue ('000 RMB) 销售收入 (千元)	Profit('000 RMB) (rank) 利润(千元) (排名)	Total assets ('000 RMB) 总资产 (千元)	Major products 主要产品
Hefei Huatai Food Co.,Ltd.	Hefei	Anhui	(0551)5572727		Limited-Liability				Qiaqia Melon Seeds
合肥华泰食品有限责任公司(1993)	合肥市	安徽省	(0551)3811310	4,918	有限公司	792,849	21,152(12)	473,466	洽洽瓜子
Shangdong Jiufa Group Company	Yantai	Shandong	(0535)4798203		State-owned				Double Sporule Mushroom
山东九发集团公司(1990)	烟台市	山东省	(0535)4798201	2,268	国有企业	600,427	79,198(3)	612,851	双胞菇
Guangzhou Malting Co.,Ltd.	Guangzhou	Guangdong	(020)82212497		Overseas Chinese-funded				Malt
广州麦芽有限公司(1987)	广州市	广东省	(020)82212988	134	港澳台资	451,074	25,956(10)	179,154	麦芽
Tangshan Dusheng Food Co.,Ltd.	Tangshan	Hebei	(0315)7447606		Private Owned				Pignut
唐山笃生食品有限公司(1993)	唐山市	河北省	(0315)7448035	160	私营企业	411,001	31,705(8)	52,002	花生米
Dalian Cofco Malt Co.,Ltd.	Dalian	Liaoning	(0411)3195588		Foreign Funded				Malt
大连中粮麦芽有限公司(1998)	大连市	辽宁省	(0411)3191435	185	外商投资	372,010	-	840,620	麦芽
Shandong Dongmeng Enterprise Group Co., Ltd.	Linyi	Shandong	(0539)4836618		Collective-owned				Malt
山东东蒙企业集团公司(1988)	临沂市	山东省	(0539)4271928	1,895	集体企业	362,685	29,886(9)	463,927	麦芽
Shenzhen Taitai Pharmaceutical Industry Co., Ltd.	Shenzhen	Guangdong	(0755)82463888		Joint Stock				Taitai Oral Liquids
深圳太太药业股份有限公司(1992)	深圳市	广东省	(0755)82461436	1,805	股份制	336,232	105,237(1)	2,150,947	太太口服液
Henan Sinian Quick Frozen Food Co., Ltd.	Zhengzhou	Henan	(0371)5697081		Private Owned				Quick-frozen food
河南思念速冻食品有限公司(1997)	郑州市	河南省	(0371)5697081	5,000	私营企业	297,844	3,096(52)	414,153	速冻食品
Haibawang (Shandou) Food Co., Ltd.	Shantou	Guangdong	(0754)8222011		Foreign Funded				Frozen Food
海霸王（汕头）食品有限公司(1994)	汕头市	广东省	(0754)8103431	600	外商投资	234,879	4,009(43)	615,278	冷冻食品
Rizhao Changhua Atic Foodstuff Co., Ltd.	Rizhao	Shandong	(0633)2611999		Private Owned				Imitated Crab Meat
日照市昌华食品集团有限公司(1997)	日照市	山东省	(0633)2611666	1,230	私营企业	197,375	10,391(17)	170,928	模拟蟹肉

Top 10 Cities by Revenue 销售收入排名前10位城市	Province 省	Market share 市场份额 (%)	Number of firms 企业个数
Shanghai 上海市	Shanghai 上海市	8.54	27
Yantai 烟台市	Shandong 山东省	7.56	11
Hefei 合肥市	Anhui 安徽省	6.94	6
Tianjin 天津市	Tianjin 天津市	6.75	17
Guangzhou 广州市	Guangdong 广东省	6.26	17
Beijing 北京市	Beijing 北京市	4.62	17
Tangshan 唐山市	Hebei 河北省	4.55	5
Dalian 大连市	Liaoning 辽宁省	3.77	4
Qingdao 青岛市	Shandong 山东省	3.69	8
Shenzhen 深圳市	Guangdong 广东省	3.18	6

10 Major Wholesalers 十家主要批发商	City 城市	Province 省	Telephone/Fax 电话/传真
Beijing Cigarette Sale Company	Beijing	Beijing	(010)64228158
北京市卷烟销售公司	北京市	北京市	(010)64228365
Anhui Technology Import & Export Co.,Ltd.	Hefei	Anhui	(0551)5101188
安徽省技术进出口股份有限公司	合肥市	安徽省	(0551)5101199
China Tobacco General Company Henan Province Filiale	Zhengzhou	Henan	(0371)5583070
中国烟草总公司河南省公司	郑州市	河南省	(0371)5957546
Shanghai Jieqiang Tobacco,Sugar & Wine Company Supplies & Sales Center	Shanghai	Shanghai	(021)62494080
上海捷强烟草糖酒公司配销中心	上海市	上海市	(021)62492584
Zhejiang Cigarette Sale Company	Hangzhou	Zhejiang	(0571)87073247
浙江省卷烟销售公司	杭州市	浙江省	(0571)87072474
Fujian Cereals, Oils & Foodstuffs Import Group Corp.	Fuzhou	Fujian	(0591)7506688
福建省粮油食品进口集团公司	福州市	福建省	(0591)7544543
Chongqing Hongta Cigarette Sale Co.,Ltd.	Chongqing	Chongqing	(023)67750222
重庆红塔卷烟销售有限责任公司	重庆市	重庆市	(023)67740477
China Buty Free (Group) General Company	Beijing	Beijing	(010)64649988
中国免税品（集团）总公司	北京市	北京市	(010)64635846
Shanghai Jieqiang Tobacco,Sugar & Wine (Group) Co.,Ltd.	Shanghai	Shanghai	(021)62522018
上海捷强烟草糖酒（集团）有限公司	上海市	上海市	(021)62522005
Shanghai Tobacco Group Chongming Tobacco, Sugar & Wine Co.,Ltd.	Shanghai	Shanghai	(021)59621368
上海烟草集团崇明烟草糖酒有限公司	上海市	上海市	(021)59621368

1511: Alcohol 酒精制造业

The industry accounts for 0.057% of the total revenue of China's industrial sector in 2002. The rate of return on assets is -0.09%. 67.88% of all firms in the industry made a profit while 32.12% had negative returns.The top province in terms of the industry's revenue is Henan, accounting for 18.20% of the total revenue.
2002年本行业收入占全行业的 0.057%，资产利润率为 -0.09%。67.88%的企业赢利，32.12%的企业亏损。收入最高的省为河南省，占本行业的18.20%。

	Total number of firms 企业总数	Total number of employees 职工总数	Total revenue (Mil.RMB) 总销售收入（百万元）	Total profit (Mil.RMB) 总利润（百万元）	Return on assets 资产利润率（%）	Return on equity 权益利润率（%）	Labour productivity ('000 RMB/worker) 劳动生产率（千元/人）	Debts/assets 资产负债率（%）	Total assets (Mil.RMB) 总资产（百万元）
Industry Overall 行业总体	137	36,300	6,089	-7	-0.09	-0.38	53.79	77.05	7,759

	Number of firms 企业个数	Average number of employees 平均职工人数	Average revenue ('000 RMB) 平均销售收入（千元）	Average profit ('000 RMB) 平均利润（千元）	Return on assets 资产利润率（%）	Return on equity 权益利润率（%）	Labour productivity ('000 RMB/worker) 劳动生产率（千元/人）	Debts/assets 资产负债率（%）	Average total assets ('000 RMB) 平均总资产（千元）
By ownership 产业所有权									
State-owned 国有	35	243	26,054	-1,128	-1.61	-15.04	20.73	89.31	70,237
Collective-owned 集体	14	154	45,059	1,293	6.53	34.43	82.14	81.03	19,799
Foreign & Overseas Chinese Funded 三资	7	521	175,863	4,365	2.72	7.24	135.35	62.38	160,336
By regional distribution 地区分布									
Central-North 华北	15	291	58,205	1,031	1.00	2.62	63.68	61.88	103,274
Beijing 北京	1	88	37,070	3,496	3.45	3.55	199.32	2.86	101,471
Tianjin 天津	6	551	124,552	1,165	0.57	1.52	52.17	62.46	203,961
Hebei 河北	6	92	9,858	343	1.10	12.71	141.00	91.31	31,008
Shanxi 山西	1	296	20,520	1,960	8.42	18.18	20.61	53.69	23,280
Inner Mongolia 内蒙古	1	126	9,033	962	6.61	17.16	32.12	61.48	14,552
Northeast 东北	16	400	88,106	-957	-0.79	-2.88	83.43	72.67	121,584
Liaoning 辽宁	4	103	8,624	-151	-1.04	-2.94	29.77	64.57	14,447
Jilin 吉林	8	408	52,770	-4,927	-3.69	-10.81	36.20	65.85	133,493
Heilongjiang 黑龙江	4	683	238,259	6,175	3.01	16.85	147.85	82.12	204,903
Central-East 华东	51	228	39,935	392	1.12	5.60	48.73	79.98	34,972
Shanghai 上海									
Jiangsu 江苏	23	148	35,736	491	2.01	9.81	57.59	79.53	24,449
Zhejiang 浙江	1	266	18,020	774	2.73	8.00	33.65	65.89	28,372
Anhui 安徽	9	287	34,427	-1,123	-1.57	-8.57	40.56	81.70	71,605
Fujian 福建	1	86	7,428	188	4.73	7.18	13.83	34.16	3,975
Jiangxi 江西									
Shandong 山东	17	312	51,732	1,051	3.28	15.98	48.37	79.46	32,028
Central-South 中南	40	210	32,620	-151	-0.36	-3.13	48.63	88.52	42,028
Henan 河南	15	414	73,901	1,495	1.88	12.92	55.53	85.43	79,430
Hubei 湖北	3	173	11,297	-448	-4.75	-11.89	23.69	60.02	9,429
Hunan 湖南	4	25	2,885	20	0.46		32.78	121.64	4,360
Guangdong 广东	7	90	12,053	-867	-4.04	-21.85	29.14	81.53	21,487
Guangxi 广西	10	88	4,980	-1,229	-6.01		23.71	132.45	20,453
Hainan 海南	1	80	16,668	-8,843	-9.94	-17.50	121.94	43.21	89,002
Southwest 西南	11	280	32,461	-96	-0.39	-1.22	46.01	68.19	24,597
Chongqing 重庆	2	196	26,486	111	0.83	4.92	31.36	83.22	13,377
Sichuan 四川	8	326	36,765	64	0.22	0.69	49.28	67.89	28,921
Guizhou 贵州									
Yunnan 云南	1	82	9,978	-1,787	-14.35	-24.45	11.87	41.29	12,452
Tibet 西藏									
Northwest 西北	4	600	26,982	-4,950	-3.74	-90.18	9.22	95.85	132,228
Shaanxi 陕西	2	695	31,169	-5,599	-3.34	-94.64	9.30	96.47	167,619
Gansu 甘肃	1	734	3,462	-5,971	-5.24		3.38	135.17	113,852
Qinghai 青海									
Ningxia 宁夏	1	277	42,127	-2,630	-3.29	-5.24	24.34	37.15	79,821
Xinjiang 新疆									

1511: Alcohol 酒精制造业

Year 年份	Number of firms 企业个数	Rate of change 变化率 (%)	Number of employees 职工人数 (人)	Rate of change 变化率 (%)	Total revenue (Mil. RMB) 总销售收入 (百万元)	Rate of change 变化率 (%)	Total profit (Mil RMB) 总利润 (百万元)	Rate of change 变化率 (%)
2000	147		45,480		5,454		-42	
2001	148	0.68	41,410	-8.95	5,760	5.61	-57	-35.71
2002	137	-7.43	36,300	-12.34	6,089	5.71	-7	87.72

Major Products 主要产品	Output 产量	Unit 单位
Ferment Alcohol 发酵酒精	213	10,000 Tons 万吨

10 Main Firms with Maximal Revenue (year founded) 收入最大的十家主要企业 (创办年份)	City 城市	Province 省	Telephone/fax 电话/传真	Number of employees 职工人数	Ownership 产业所有权	Revenue ('000 RMB) 销售收入 (千元)	Profit('000 RMB) (rank) 利润(千元) (排名)	Total assets ('000 RMB) 总资产 (千元)	Major products 主要产品
He'nan Tianguan Alcohol Chemical & Technology Group Co., Ltd 河南省天冠酒精化工集团有限公司(1939)	Nanyang 南阳市	Henan 河南省	(0377)3026688 (0377)3036688	2,272	State Enterprises 国有独资	354,120	5,512(6)	814,447	Alcohol 酒精
Mengzhou Alcohol General Factory 孟州市酒精总厂(1991)	Jiaozuo 焦作市	Henan 河南省	(0391)8571389 (0391)8571328	500	Collective-owned 集体企业	352,415	1,988(12)	63,090	Edible Alcohol 食用酒精
Tianjin Guanda Industrial General Company 天津市冠达实业总公司(1969)	Tianjin 天津市	Tianjin 天津市	(022)65592912 (022)69592912	581	State-owned 国有企业	310,827	104(49)	356,174	Alcohol 酒精
Longkou Zhenlong Alcohol Co.,Ltd. 龙口市振龙酒精有限公司(1989)	Yantai 烟台市	Shandong 山东省	(0535)8911450 (0535)8911078	220	Limited-Liability 有限公司	262,077	15,607(3)	73,241	Alcohol 酒精
Jiangsu Fangting Wine-making Industry Co., Ltd. 徐州房亭酒业有限责任公司(1958)	Xuzhou 徐州市	Jiangsu 江苏省	(0516)6739453 (0516)6739453	375	Limited-Liability 有限公司	195,204	1,520(15)	112,431	Alcohol 酒精
Tianjin Guayue Group Co.,Ltd. 天津市挂月集团有限公司(1995)	Tianjin 天津市	Tianjin 天津市	(022)29858164 (022)29858164	1,006	Limited-Liability 有限公司	174,581	776(24)	276,751	Alcohol 酒精
Bengbu Yingkesong Brewing Co., Ltd. 蚌埠迎客松酿造有限责任公司(2001)	Bengbu 蚌埠市	Anhui 安徽省	(0552)4081613 (0552)4081604	837	Limited-Liability 有限公司	172,603	47(55)	91,962	Alcohol 酒精
Taicang Xintai Alcohol Co., Ltd. 太仓新太酒精有限公司(1998)	Suzhou 苏州市	Jiangsu 江苏省	(0512)53515645 (0512)53515645	206	Foreign Funded 外商投资	155,960	7,710(4)	62,410	Alcohol 酒精
Harbin Wine-Making General Factory 哈尔滨酿酒总厂(1919)	Harbin 哈尔滨市	Heilongjiang 黑龙江省	(0451)4301950 (0451)4305624	388	State-owned 国有企业	152,785	2,401(10)	404,630	Alcohol 酒精
Tengzhou Jinghe Wine-making Industry Co., Ltd. 滕州市荆河酒业有限责任公司(1999)	Zaozhuang 枣庄市	Shandong 山东省	(0632)5583109 (0632)5583109	2,300	Limited-Liability 有限公司	150,520	2,390(11)	133,680	Alcohol 酒精

Top 10 Cities by Revenue 销售收入排名前10位城市	Province 省	Market share 市场份额 (%)	Number of firms 企业个数
Suihua 绥化市	Heilongjiang 黑龙江省	13.00	1
Tianjin 天津市	Tianjin 天津市	12.27	6
Nanyang 南阳市	Henan 河南省	7.89	3
Xuzhou 徐州市	Jiangsu 江苏省	6.42	6
Jiaozuo 焦作市	Henan 河南省	6.27	3
Bengbu 蚌埠市	Anhui 安徽省	4.43	6
Yantai 烟台市	Shandong 山东省	4.30	1
Neijiang 内江市	Sichuan 四川省	4.07	4
Siping 四平市	Jilin 吉林省	3.11	3
Sanmenxia 三门峡市	Henan 河南省	2.71	1

10 Major Wholesalers 十家主要批发商	City 城市	Province 省	Telephone/Fax 电话/传真
China Chemical Industry Supply & Sale (Group) General Company 中国化工供销(集团)总公司	Beijing 北京市	Beijing 北京市	(010)64238623 (010)64238623
China Chemical Industry Import & Export General Company 中国化工进出口总公司	Beijing 北京市	Beijing 北京市	(010)88078888 (010)88078890
Tianjin Bridge Group Welding Materials Supply & Sale Co., Ltd. 天津大桥集团电焊条供销有限公司	Tianjin 天津市	Tianjin 天津市	(022)83968861 (022)83968865
Taizhou Xingwei Chunlan Chain Stores Co., Ltd. 泰州星威春兰连锁店有限公司	Taizhou 泰州市	Jiangsu 江苏省	(0523)6611200 (0523)6224181
Taizhou Chunlan Sale Company 泰州春兰销售公司	Taizhou 泰州市	Jiangsu 江苏省	(0523)6611200 (0523)6224181
Shandong Tri-Union Co., Ltd. 山东三联有限责任公司	Jinan 济南市	Shandong 山东省	(0531)6086351 (0531)6093103
Haier Electrical Appliances Co.,Ltd. 海尔集团电器产业有限公司	Qingdao 青岛市	Shandong 山东省	(0532)8939175 (0532)8938086
Guangzhou Haier Industry & Trade Co.,Ltd. 广州海尔工贸有限公司	Guangzhou 广州市	Guangdong 广东省	(020)87397315 (020)87374302
Huizhou TCL Electrical Appliances Sales Co.,Ltd 惠州市TCL电器销售有限公司	Huizhou 惠州市	Guangdong 广东省	(0752)2289885 (0752)2280690
Guangdong Hardware Minerals Import & Export Group Company 广东省五金矿产进出口集团公司	Guangzhou 广州市	Guangdong 广东省	(020)87752204 (020)87752205

1512: Liquor 白酒制造业

The industry accounts for 0.468% of the total revenue of China's industrial sector in 2002. The rate of return on assets is 3.32%. 72.42% of all firms in the industry made a profit while 27.58% had negative returns.The top province in terms of the industry's revenue is Sichuan, accounting for 35.85% of the total revenue.
2002年本行业收入占全行业的0.468%，资产利润率为3.32%。72.42%的企业赢利，27.58%的企业亏损。收入最高的省为四川省，占本行业的35.85%。

	Total number of firms 企业总数	Total number of employees 职工总数	Total revenue (Mil.RMB) 总销售收入(百万元)	Total profit (Mil.RMB) 总利润(百万元)	Return on assets 资产利润率(%)	Return on equity 权益利润率(%)	Labour productivity ('000 RMB/worker) 劳动生产率(千元/人)	Debts/assets 资产负债率(%)	Total assets (Mil.RMB) 总资产(百万元)
Industry Overall 行业总体	1066	365,559	50,221	3,328	3.32	7.52	59.63	55.82	100,221

	Number of firms 企业个数	Average number of employees 平均职工人数	Average revenue ('000 RMB) 平均销售收入(千元)	Average profit ('000 RMB) 平均利润(千元)	Return on assets 资产利润率(%)	Return on equity 权益利润率(%)	Labour productivity ('000 RMB/worker) 劳动生产率(千元/人)	Debts/assets 资产负债率(%)	Average total assets ('000 RMB) 平均总资产(千元)
By ownership 产业所有权									
State-owned 国有	337	398	42,390	2,210	1.87	4.74	51.72	60.58	118,224
Collective-owned 集体	87	166	26,371	1,551	6.15	13.99	51.13	56.05	25,216
Foreign & Overseas Chinese Funded 三资	13	253	29,984	-71	-0.19	-0.55	39.50	65.91	37,768
By regional distribution 地区分布									
Central-North 华北	129	387	37,922	1,287	1.65	4.16	46.34	60.34	77,917
Beijing 北京	10	389	61,912	4,234	3.62	9.25	85.99	60.84	116,910
Tianjin 天津	11	177	26,347	1,335	4.58	10.50	47.36	56.42	29,162
Hebei 河北	52	357	29,499	305	0.49	1.63	38.45	69.96	62,105
Shanxi 山西	21	493	56,287	1,151	0.94	1.86	52.68	49.23	121,998
Inner Mongolia 内蒙古	35	434	36,202	1,969	2.49	6.16	41.38	59.63	79,142
Northeast 东北	115	189	16,179	-415	-1.95	-9.75	38.00	80.05	21,348
Liaoning 辽宁	32	169	18,414	-373	-1.46	-8.37	47.74	82.50	25,479
Jilin 吉林	43	184	9,747	-699	-4.25	-143.58	25.51	97.04	16,443
Heilongjiang 黑龙江	40	211	21,305	-144	-0.62	-1.76	43.50	65.04	23,315
Central-East 华东	304	433	45,230	472	0.53	1.54	37.63	65.64	89,020
Shanghai 上海	1	400	50,352	351	0.37	0.55	23.68	32.10	94,061
Jiangsu 江苏	67	413	38,950	-1,538	-2.85	-8.99	35.53	68.34	54,056
Zhejiang 浙江	9	75	16,542	57	0.18	0.32	73.06	44.62	32,278
Anhui 安徽	56	604	69,811	2,176	1.10	2.82	43.57	61.14	198,277
Fujian 福建	9	101	7,598	386	2.04	3.54	43.74	42.55	18,946
Jiangxi 江西	40	181	18,565	373	1.08	4.25	39.62	74.56	34,482
Shandong 山东	122	498	50,989	865	1.01	3.33	34.64	69.58	85,266
Central-South 中南	232	226	25,278	92	0.18	0.56	49.98	68.51	51,776
Henan 河南	87	337	23,844	341	0.62	2.48	33.77	74.87	54,663
Hubei 湖北	52	168	33,976	1,410	4.16	13.29	73.20	68.69	33,877
Hunan 湖南	31	249	30,057	-3,935	-3.11	-8.68	53.96	64.21	126,584
Guangdong 广东	42	118	23,063	814	3.11	7.33	96.37	57.56	26,154
Guangxi 广西	19	92	5,963	313	1.42	5.32	55.68	73.26	22,017
Hainan 海南	1	55	9,663	176	0.33	0.33	78.42		53,721
Southwest 西南	201	417	106,283	14,794	7.27	12.26	118.83	40.67	203,455
Chongqing 重庆	10	262	39,162	1,327	2.35	5.95	38.90	60.52	56,465
Sichuan 四川	113	550	159,338	20,407	7.48	12.13	125.44	38.35	272,957
Guizhou 贵州	60	307	49,147	10,944	6.99	13.16	111.41	46.91	156,637
Yunnan 云南	16	35	709	-187	-4.08	-14.45	18.26	71.79	4,583
Tibet 西藏	2	43	2,982	407	5.77	6.00	25.78	3.87	7,045
Northwest 西北	85	306	29,311	834	0.92	2.89	43.29	68.31	91,136
Shaanxi 陕西	19	316	29,222	-102	-0.18	-1.32	41.19	86.55	57,378
Gansu 甘肃	43	183	13,082	-467	-0.72	-2.48	40.29	71.20	65,319
Qinghai 青海	5	395	48,259	246	0.34	2.73	39.62	87.42	71,599
Ningxia 宁夏	5	286	27,125	1,783	4.19	25.74	31.98	83.71	42,526
Xinjiang 新疆	13	672	76,675	6,369	2.53	5.83	50.10	56.68	252,077

Year 年份	Number of firms 企业个数	Rate of change 变化率 (%)	Number of employees 职工人数 (人)	Rate of change 变化率 (%)	Total revenue (Mil. RMB) 总销售收入 (百万元)	Rate of change 变化率 (%)	Total profit (Mil RMB) 总利润 (百万元)	Rate of change 变化率 (%)
2000	1253		455,043		51,024		4,359	
2001	1151	-8.14	399,048	-12.31	49,302	-3.37	3,957	-9.22
2002	1066	-7.38	365,559	-8.39	50,221	1.86	3,328	-15.90

Major Products 主要产品	Output 产量	Unit 单位
Distilled Spirit 白酒	378	10,000 Tons 万吨
Ferment Alcohol 发酵酒精	213	10,000 Tons 万吨

10 Main Firms with Maximal Revenue (year founded) 收入最大的十家主要企业（创办年份）	City 城市	Province 省	Telephone/ fax 电话/ 传真	Number of employees 职工人数	Ownership 产业所有权	Revenue ('000 RMB) 销售收入 (千元)	Profit('000 RMB) (rank) 利润(千元) (排名)	Total assets ('000 RMB) 总资产 (千元)	Major products 主要产品
Sichuan Yibin Wuliangye Group Co.,Ltd.	Yibin	Sichuan	(0831)3553988		Limited-Liability				Distilled Spirit
四川省宜宾五粮液集团有限公司(1952)	宜宾市	四川省	(0831)3552624	19,253	有限公司	10,067,129	1,682,785(1)	14,216,562	白酒
China Kweichow Moutai Drstillery Co.,Ltd.	Zunyi	Guizhou	(0852)2386002		State-owned				Moutai
中国贵州茅台酒厂有限责任公司(1951)	遵义市	贵州省	(0852)2386005	6,594	国有企业	2,139,208	697,355(2)	6,707,440	茅台酒
Sichuan Jian-Nan-Chun Group Co., Ltd.	Deyang	Sichuan	(0838)6202206		State-owned				Distilled Spirit
四川剑南春集团有限责任公司(1996)	德阳市	四川省	(0838)6200643	7,275	国有企业	1,493,430	244,060(3)	2,904,300	白酒
Luzhou Laojiao Group Co.,Ltd.	Luzhou	Sichuan	(0830)2296262		State Enterprises				Distilled Spirit
泸州老窖集团有限责任公司(2000)	泸州市	四川省		2,242	国有独资	1,191,180	111,386(4)	2,517,612	白酒
Anhui Gujing Group Co., Ltd.	Bozhou	Anhui	(0558)5710760		State Enterprises				Distilled Spirit
安徽古井集团有限责任公司(1995)	亳州市	安徽省	(0558)5710006	9,328	国有独资	1,104,866	75,126(7)	3,657,012	白酒
Sichuan Tuopai Group Co., Ltd.	Suining	Sichuan	(0825)6766352		State Enterprises				Distilled Spirit
四川沱牌集团有限公司(1952)	遂宁市	四川省	(0825)6766868	10,898	国有独资	1,035,857	40,123(11)	2,702,995	白酒
Sichuan Quanxing Co., Ltd.	Chengdu	Sichuan	(028)87513999		State-owned				Distilled Spirit
四川全兴股份有限公司(1993)	成都市	四川省	(028)87513999	4,261	国有企业	1,008,074	80,718(6)	2,684,585	白酒
Shanxi Xinghuacun Fenjiu Group Conyany	Lvliang	Shanxi	(0358)7229026		State-owned				Distilled Spirit
山西省杏花村汾酒集团公司(1988)	吕梁	山西省	(0358)7229304	6,875	国有企业	975,610	28,331(15)	2,111,764	白酒
Shandong Tianfu Group Company	Yantai	Shandong	(0535)7541002		Collective-owned				Vino
山东天府集团公司(2000)	烟台市	山东省	(0535)7540183	1,800	集体企业	622,028	37,695(13)	383,032	酒
Anhui Kouzi Wine-making Co., Ltd.	Huaibei	Anhui	(0561)6899057		State-owned				Distilled Spirit
安徽口子酒业股份有限公司(1949)	淮北市	安徽省	(0561)6898222	2,847	国有企业	435,998	2,269(100)	992,077	白酒

Top 10 Cities by Revenue 销售收入排名前10位城市	Province 省	Market share 市场份额 (%)	Number of firms 企业个数
Yibin 宜宾市	Sichuan 四川省	20.71	13
Zunyi 遵义市	Guizhou 贵州省	5.30	25
Chengdu 成都市	Sichuan 四川省	3.82	46
Deyang 德阳市	Sichuan 四川省	3.56	6
Luzhou 泸州市	Sichuan 四川省	3.51	18
Bozhou 亳州市	Anhui 安徽省	3.02	6
Suqian 宿迁市	Jiangsu 江苏省	2.72	25
Suining 遂宁市	Sichuan 四川省	2.07	2
Lvliang 吕梁地区	Shanxi 山西省	2.01	7
Yichang 宜昌市	Hubei 湖北省	2.01	4

10 Major Wholesalers 十家主要批发商	City 城市	Province 省	Telephone/Fax 电话/传真
Beijing Chaoyang Non-Staple Foodstuffs General Company	Beijing	Beijing	(010)65016285
北京朝阳副食品总公司	北京市	北京市	(010)65016285
Beijing Sugar,Cigarette & Wine Company	Beijing	Beijing	(010)67210304
北京市糖业烟酒公司	北京市	北京市	(010)67210310
Shanghai Sugar Cigarette & Wine (Group) Co.,Ltd.	Shanghai	Shanghai	(021)63224190
上海市糖业烟酒(集团)有限公司	上海市	上海市	(021)63223169
Jiangsu Sutang Sugar & Wine Co.,Ltd.	Nanjing	Jiangsu	(025)6661088
江苏苏糖糖酒食品有限公司	南京市	江苏省	(025)6661088
Fujian Commerce (Group) Co.,Ltd.	Fuzhou	Fujian	(0591)7847148
福建省商业（集团）有限责任公司	福州市	福建省	(0591)7847145
Yantai Changyu Pioneer Winer Co., Ltd.	Yantai	Shandong	(0535)6602730
烟台张裕葡萄酿酒股份有限公司	烟台市	山东省	(0535)6214078
BlueRibbon Beer Sale Co.,Ltd.	Zhaoqing	Guangdong	(0758)2862322
蓝带啤酒销售有限公司	肇庆市	广东省	(0758)2862424
Fujian Shenlong Development Co.,Ltd.	Fuzhou	Fujian	(0591)7503218
福建省神龙发展股份有限公司	福州市	福建省	(0591)7503068
Guangdong Sugar, Cigarette & Wine Group Company	Guangzhou	Guangdong	(020)83566131
广东省糖烟酒集团公司	广州市	广东省	(020)83561421
Shunde Daliang Sugar, Cigarette & Wine Co.,Ltd.	Shunde	Guangdong	(0765)2231804
顺德市大良区糖烟酒有限公司	顺德市	广东省	(0765)2222300

1513: Beer 啤酒制造业

The industry accounts for 0.458% of the total revenue of China's industrial sector in 2002. The rate of return on assets is 2.19%. 62.28% of all firms in the industry made a profit while 37.72% had negative returns.The top province in terms of the industry's revenue is Shandong, accounting for 15.75% of the total revenue.
2002年本行业收入占全行业的 0.458%，资产利润率为 2.19%。62.28%的企业赢利，37.72%的企业亏损。收入最高的省为山东省，占本行业的15.75%。

	Total number of firms 企业总数	Total number of employees 职工总数	Total revenue (Mil.RMB) 总销售收入 (百万元)	Total profit (Mil.RMB) 总利润 (百万元)	Return on assets 资产利润率 (%)	Return on equity 权益利润率 (%)	Labour productivity ('000 RMB/ worker) 劳动生产率 (千元/人)	Debts/ assets 资产负债率 (%)	Total assets (Mil.RMB) 总资产 (百万元)
Industry Overall 行业总体	501	260,738	49,169	2,009	2.19	5.15	82.36	57.49	91,729

	Number of firms 企业个数	Average number of employees 平均职工人数	Average revenue ('000 RMB) 平均销售收入 (千元)	Average profit ('000 RMB) 平均利润 (千元)	Return on assets 资产利润率 (%)	Return on equity 权益利润率 (%)	Labour productivity ('000 RMB/ worker) 劳动生产率 (千元/人)	Debts/ assets 资产负债率 (%)	Average total assets ('000 RMB) 平均总资产 (千元)
By ownership 产业所有权									
State-owned 国有	68	615	120,010	7,905	3.14	6.74	80.25	53.38	251,427
Collective-owned 集体	39	407	64,854	3,655	4.34	17.70	61.78	75.48	84,244
Foreign & Overseas Chinese Funded 三资	108	728	162,924	3,643	1.15	2.53	102.04	54.64	318,041
By regional distribution 地区分布									
Central-North 华北	64	632	92,459	674	0.28	0.66	58.01	57.42	238,594
Beijing 北京	6	1,969	495,955	24,097	1.90	2.93	85.06	35.40	1,271,147
Tianjin 天津	2	554	102,545	-6,470	-2.79		82.61	104.95	231,715
Hebei 河北	31	548	55,055	-4,690	-2.66	-17.85	45.72	85.10	176,358
Shanxi 山西	9	351	35,649	95	0.16	0.51	37.50	68.21	58,886
Inner Mongolia 内蒙古	16	462	44,316	3,503	4.74	9.12	48.12	48.03	73,913
Northeast 东北	89	460	73,401	5,084	3.77	9.32	78.85	59.56	134,930
Liaoning 辽宁	26	632	104,469	10,905	5.33	10.57	86.68	49.63	204,715
Jilin 吉林	21	391	52,075	328	0.32	1.32	58.98	75.99	103,812
Heilongjiang 黑龙江	42	388	64,831	3,859	3.60	9.81	80.96	63.34	107,289
Central-East 华东	190	529	98,621	1,671	1.02	2.61	75.21	60.93	163,879
Shanghai 上海	5	405	168,717	-31,147	-8.09	-22.25	149.67	63.65	385,196
Jiangsu 江苏	34	420	78,616	-3,847	-2.79	-11.66	60.60	76.07	137,880
Zhejiang 浙江	43	369	68,545	1,855	1.48	4.10	85.10	63.82	125,197
Anhui 安徽	21	633	77,388	604	0.46	1.28	48.06	64.11	131,590
Fujian 福建	24	330	97,514	2,250	1.63	4.15	129.46	60.80	138,383
Jiangxi 江西	18	360	31,471	4		0.01	36.39	59.76	71,330
Shandong 山东	45	904	172,045	10,166	3.89	8.19	77.28	52.56	261,582
Central-South 中南	88	504	136,382	8,724	3.60	7.27	126.14	50.40	242,106
Henan 河南	27	546	55,136	-605	-0.62	-2.54	38.60	75.46	96,846
Hubei 湖北	19	582	161,012	15,534	7.21	12.80	118.76	43.62	215,328
Hunan 湖南	14	408	55,897	-237	-0.24	-0.46	53.79	46.56	97,119
Guangdong 广东	24	416	233,713	19,542	4.22	9.00	297.09	53.10	463,165
Guangxi 广西	3	843	290,607	15,389	3.32	6.27	148.63	47.00	462,861
Hainan 海南	1	363	190,202	-22,929	-3.12	-2.43	189.80	-28.25	735,044
Southwest 西南	43	425	85,699	7,509	4.34	9.83	95.89	55.87	173,187
Chongqing 重庆	8	500	91,784	7,944	3.71	8.80	105.28	57.89	214,262
Sichuan 四川	18	478	117,482	11,720	6.87	14.69	110.66	53.24	170,569
Guizhou 贵州	9	269	27,260	227	0.33	0.97	33.15	66.35	69,311
Yunnan 云南	7	383	64,099	759	0.38	0.99	78.56	61.04	197,132
Tibet 西藏	1	560	142,062	41,040	6.23	10.78	155.98	42.21	658,964
Northwest 西北	27	600	84,993	3,893	2.30	6.47	61.21	64.40	168,926
Shaanxi 陕西	6	768	217,848	14,833	7.67	16.69	99.89	54.04	193,395
Gansu 甘肃	9	667	52,207	-1,567	-0.71	-2.38	45.70	70.18	220,855
Qinghai 青海	1	178	4,535	-3,955	-6.00	-11.01	8.90	45.50	65,921
Ningxia 宁夏	2	910	47,029	840	0.53	1.07	26.18	50.35	157,837
Xinjiang 新疆	9	399	46,586	3,610	3.15	10.66	57.84	70.45	114,593

1513: Beer 啤酒制造业

Year 年份	Number of firms 企业个数	Rate of change 变化率 (%)	Number of employees 职工人数 (人)	Rate of change 变化率 (%)	Total revenue (Mil. RMB) 总销售收入 (百万元)	Rate of change 变化率 (%)	Total profit (Mil RMB) 总利润 (百万元)	Rate of change 变化率 (%)
2000	539		307,777		44,732		1,431	
2001	508	-5.75	264,800	-13.96	45,372	1.43	1,494	4.40
2002	501	-1.38	260,738	-1.53	49,169	8.37	2,009	34.47

Major Products 主要产品	Output 产量	Unit 单位
Beer 啤酒	2,387	10,000 Tons 万吨
Ferment Alcohol 发酵酒精	213	10,000 Tons 万吨

10 Main Firms with Maximal Revenue (year founded) 收入最大的十家主要企业（创办年份）	City 城市	Province 省	Telephone/fax 电话/传真	Number of employees 职工人数	Ownership 产业所有权	Revenue ('000 RMB) 销售收入 (千元)	Profit('000 RMB) (rank) 利润(千元) (排名)	Total assets ('000 RMB) 总资产 (千元)	Major products 主要产品
Beijing Yanjing Beer Group Company	Beijing	Beijing	(010)89492241		State-owned				Beer
北京燕京啤酒集团公司(1980)	北京市	北京市	(010)89495578	7,638	国有企业	2,449,538	250,716(4)	6,162,633	啤酒
Tsingdao Brewery Co.,Ltd.	Qingdao	Shandong	(0532)5711119		State Enterprises				Beer
青岛啤酒股份有限公司(1995)	青岛市	山东省	(0532)5714719	4,036	国有独资	2,239,564	290,027(1)	4,623,970	啤酒
Guangzhou Zhujiang Brewery Co., Ltd.	Guangzhou	Guangdong	(020)84206636		State-owned				Beer
广州珠江啤酒集团有限公司(1985)	广州市	广东省	(020)84202502	2,563	国有企业	1,979,217	257,711(2)	3,286,366	啤酒
Budweiser (Wuhan) International Brewing Co., Ltd.	Wuhan	Hubei	(027)84615574		Foreign Funded				Beer
百威（武汉）国际啤酒有限公司(1995)	武汉市	湖北省	(027)84615584	777	外商投资	1,773,624	255,245(3)	1,530,733	啤酒
Fujian Sedrin Brewery Co., Ltd.	Putian	Fujian	(0594)3597297		State-owned				Beer
福建雪津啤酒有限公司(1987)	莆田市	福建省	(0594)3597390	1,033	国有企业	909,969	52,132(17)	693,054	啤酒
Fujian Huiquan Brewage Group Inc.	Quanzhou	Fujian	(0595)7382369		Joint Stock				Beer
福建惠泉啤酒集团股份有限公司(1954)	泉州市	福建省	(0595)7384369	1,861	股份制	900,738	101,195(8)	1,116,411	啤酒
China Resources (ShenYan) Snowflake Brewery Co.,Ltd.	Shenyang	Liaoning	(024)25872059		Overseas Chinese-funded				Beer
沈阳华润雪花啤酒有限公司(1993)	沈阳市	辽宁省	(024)25852035	3,013	港澳台资	767,000	109,301(7)	1,292,118	啤酒
Yanjing Beer Guilin liquan Co.,Ltd.	Guilin	Guangxi	(0773)3832078		Joint Stock				Beer
燕京啤酒桂林漓泉股份有限公司(1993)	桂林市	广西	(0773)3832088	1,564	股份制	621,601	59,473(13)	548,919	啤酒
Shandong Wendeng Beer Factory	Weihai	Shandong	(0631)8361086		Collective-owned				Beer
山东省文登市啤酒厂(1984)	威海市	山东省	(0631)8561086	600	集体企业	564,530	92,700(9)	101,630	啤酒
Ji'nan Nobel Co., Ltd.	Jinan	Shandong	(0531)5596715		State-owned				Beer
济南啤酒集团总公司(1975)	济南市	山东省	(0531)5954658	2,707	国有企业	398,822	5,002(89)	1,118,861	啤酒

Top 10 Cities by Revenue 销售收入排名前10位城市	Province 省	Market share 市场份额 (%)	Number of firms 企业个数
Beijing 北京市	Beijing 北京市	6.05	6
Qingdao 青岛市	Shandong 山东省	5.37	5
Guangzhou 广州市	Guangdong 广东省	4.67	4
Wuhan 武汉市	Hubei 湖北省	4.33	2
Harbin 哈尔滨市	Heilongjiang 黑龙江省	3.71	13
Weihai 威海市	Shandong 山东省	2.23	6
Quanzhou 泉州市	Fujian 福建省	2.01	2
Shenzhen 深圳市	Guangdong 广东省	2.00	3
Putian 莆田市	Fujian 福建省	1.96	2
Deyang 德阳市	Sichuan 四川省	1.96	1

10 Major Wholesalers 十家主要批发商	City 城市	Province 省	Telephone/Fax 电话/传真
Beijing Chaoyang Non-Staple Foodstuffs General Company	Beijing	Beijing	(010)65016285
北京朝阳副食品总公司	北京市	北京市	(010)65016285
Beijing Sugar,Cigarette & Wine Company	Beijing	Beijing	(010)67210304
北京市糖业烟酒公司	北京市	北京市	(010)67210310
Shanghai Sugar Cigarette & Wine (Group) Co.,Ltd.	Shanghai	Shanghai	(021)63224190
上海市糖业烟酒(集团)有限公司	上海市	上海市	(021)63223169
Jiangsu Sutang Sugar & Wine Co.,Ltd.	Nanjing	Jiangsu	(025)6661088
江苏苏糖糖酒食品有限公司	南京市	江苏省	(025)6661088
Fujian Commerce (Group) Co.,Ltd.	Fuzhou	Fujian	(0591)7847148
福建省商业（集团）有限责任公司	福州市	福建省	(0591)7847145
Yantai Changyu Pioneer Winer Co., Ltd.	Yantai	Shandong	(0535)6602730
烟台张裕葡萄酿酒股份有限公司	烟台市	山东省	(0535)6214078
BlueRibbon Beer Sale Co.,Ltd.	Zhaoqing	Guangdong	(0758)2862322
蓝带啤酒销售有限公司	肇庆市	广东省	(0758)2862424
Fujian Shenlong Development Co.,Ltd.	Fuzhou	Fujian	(0591)7503218
福建省神龙发展股份有限公司	福州市	福建省	(0591)7503068
Guangdong Sugar, Cigarette & Wine Group Company	Guangzhou	Guangdong	(020)83566131
广东省糖烟酒集团公司	广州市	广东省	(020)83561421
Shunde Daliang Sugar, Cigarette & Wine Co.,Ltd.	Shunde	Guangdong	(0765)2231804
顺德市大良区糖烟酒有限公司	顺德市	广东省	(0765)2222300

1514: Cooking Wine 黄酒制造业

The industry accounts for 0.027% of the total revenue of China's industrial sector in 2002. The rate of return on assets is 3.83%. 82.61% of all firms in the industry made a profit while 17.39% had negative returns.The top province in terms of the industry's revenue is Zhejiang, accounting for 72.00% of the total revenue.
2002年本行业收入占全行业的 0.027%，资产利润率为 3.83%。82.61%的企业赢利，17.39%的企业亏损。收入最高的省为浙江省，占本行业的72.00%。

	Total number of firms 企业总数	Total number of employees 职工总数	Total revenue (Mil.RMB) 总销售收入（百万元）	Total profit (Mil.RMB) 总利润（百万元）	Return on assets 资产利润率（%）	Return on equity 权益利润率（%）	Labour productivity ('000 RMB/ worker) 劳动生产率（千元/人）	Debts/ assets 资产负债率（%）	Total assets (Mil.RMB) 总资产（百万元）
Industry Overall 行业总体	92	17,292	2,921	229	3.83	7.73	58.08	50.51	5,976

	Number of firms 企业个数	Average number of employees 平均职工人数	Average revenue ('000 RMB) 平均销售收入（千元）	Average profit ('000 RMB) 平均利润（千元）	Return on assets 资产利润率（%）	Return on equity 权益利润率（%）	Labour productivity ('000 RMB/ worker) 劳动生产率（千元/人）	Debts/ assets 资产负债率（%）	Average total assets ('000 RMB) 平均总资产（千元）
By ownership 产业所有权									
State-owned 国有	23	118	7,028	-190	-1.09	-7.56	22.80	85.53	17,402
Collective-owned 集体	7	69	8,222	140	1.48	5.57	45.95	73.52	9,471
Foreign & Overseas Chinese Funded 三资	6	241	37,133	4,093	3.63	7.29	78.20	50.29	112,899
By regional distribution 地区分布									
Central-North 华北	1	36	5,050	270	46.55	49.09	61.11	5.17	580
Beijing 北京									
Tianjin 天津									
Hebei 河北									
Shanxi 山西	1	36	5,050	270	46.55	49.09	61.11	5.17	580
Inner Mongolia 内蒙古									
Northeast 东北	2	55	3,725	1,469	11.58	32.72	38.99	64.62	12,686
Liaoning 辽宁	1	106	7,100	2,937	13.91	25.87	30.32	46.21	21,111
Jilin 吉林	1	3	350				345.33	155.87	4,260
Heilongjiang 黑龙江									
Central-East 华东	70	229	40,859	3,243	3.91	7.76	60.92	49.55	82,832
Shanghai 上海	6	283	74,203	4,474	5.11	9.91	110.85	48.45	87,572
Jiangsu 江苏	6	306	26,425	159	0.39	3.56	28.42	89.17	41,346
Zhejiang 浙江	42	242	50,077	4,737	4.47	8.20	67.49	45.47	105,952
Anhui 安徽	3	163	21,236	1,572	5.31	28.92	49.60	81.65	29,624
Fujian 福建	8	103	3,544	300	0.65	1.38	7.65	52.87	45,897
Jiangxi 江西	2	43	1,542	-69	-1.99	-1,254.55	11.61	99.84	3,475
Shandong 山东	3	314	19,318	-2,251	-6.04	-57.96	20.36	89.58	37,266
Central-South 中南	7	50	3,645	281	2.28	5.08	26.85	55.07	12,319
Henan 河南	4	29	1,586	143	1.19	2.31	22.92	48.69	12,017
Hubei 湖北									
Hunan 湖南	1	53	6,060	1,240	31.47	53.73	45.94	41.42	3,940
Guangdong 广东	1	169	13,032	193	1.08	3.55	24.91	69.67	17,923
Guangxi 广西									
Hainan 海南	1	11	83	-34	-0.21	-0.54	6.55	61.15	16,302
Southwest 西南	5	28	1,882	-255	-5.74		29.99	129.26	4,447
Chongqing 重庆									
Sichuan 四川	1	47	6,131	26	1.08	2.36	38.68	54.17	2,400
Guizhou 贵州	3	19	838	11	0.35	1.75	25.89	80.19	3,080
Yunnan 云南	1	39	767	-1,334	-12.59		25.38	189.09	10,594
Tibet 西藏									
Northwest 西北	7	89	1,928	-322	-5.25		12.34	122.41	6,120
Shaanxi 陕西	3	148	1,346	-871	-11.31		7.54	166.45	7,699
Gansu 甘肃	4	46	2,365	91	1.83	6.30	24.05	70.91	4,937
Qinghai 青海									
Ningxia 宁夏									
Xinjiang 新疆									

Year 年份	Number of firms 企业个数	Rate of change 变化率 (%)	Number of employees 职工人数 (人)	Rate of change 变化率 (%)	Total revenue (Mil. RMB) 总销售收入 (百万元)	Rate of change 变化率 (%)	Total profit (Mil RMB) 总利润 (百万元)	Rate of change 变化率 (%)
2000	97		20,233		2,281		197	
2001	91	-6.19	18,485	-8.64	2,558	12.14	185	-6.09
2002	92	1.10	17,292	-6.45	2,921	14.19	229	23.78

Major Products 主要产品	Output 产量	Unit 单位
Ferment Alcohol 发酵酒精	213	10,000 Tons 万吨

10 Main Firms with Maximal Revenue (year founded) 收入最大的十家主要企业（创办年份）	City 城市	Province 省	Telephone/fax 电话/传真	Number of employees 职工人数	Ownership 产业所有权	Revenue ('000 RMB) 销售收入(千元)	Profit('000 RMB) (rank) 利润(千元)(排名)	Total assets ('000 RMB) 总资产(千元)	Major products 主要产品
Dongfeng Shaoxing Winery Co., Ltd. 东风绍兴酒有限公司(1952)	Shaoxing 绍兴市	Zhejiang 浙江省	(0575)4292457 (0575)4293974	857	Overseas Chinese-funded 港澳台资	164,888	25,919(2)	420,317	Rice Wine 黄酒
Shanghai Jinfeng Brewery Co.,Ltd. 上海金枫酿酒公司(1939)	Shanghai 上海市	Shanghai 上海市	(021)57351203 (021)57353989	663	Joint Stock 股份制	158,619	14,012(4)	214,485	Rice Wine 黄酒
Zhejiang Jiashan Rice Wine Co., Ltd. 浙江嘉善黄酒股份有限公司(1999)	Jiaxing 嘉兴市	Zhejiang 浙江省	(0573)4564577 (0573)4564197	1,017	Joint Stock 股份制	158,111	18,824(3)	162,026	Rice Wine 黄酒
Zhejiang Xianheng Industry Group Co.,Ltd. 浙江咸亨实业集团公司(1994)	Shaoxing 绍兴市	Zhejiang 浙江省	(0575)4012323 (0575)4012268	355	Limited-Liability 有限公司	138,365	1,971(15)	279,754	Rice Wine 黄酒
Jiangsu Danyang Liquor Factory 江苏省丹阳酒厂(1958)	Zhenjiang 镇江市	Jiangsu 江苏省	(0511)6523211 (0511)6521918	771	State-owned 国有企业	79,928	541(31)	76,355	Alcoholic Drink 饮料酒
Shaoxing Nv-Er-Hong Wine Make Co., Ltd. 绍兴女儿红酿酒有限责任公司(1919)	Shaoxing 绍兴市	Zhejiang 浙江省	(0575)2051558 (0575)2053871	406	Limited-Liability 有限公司	77,527	2,013(14)	146,645	Rice Wine 黄酒
State-owned Rugao Wine-making Factory 国营如皋酒厂(1956)	Nantong 南通市	Jiangsu 江苏省	(0513)7514567 (0513)7512683	479	State-owned 国有企业	35,450	150(49)	48,102	Rice Wine 黄酒
Ningbo Yimin Wine-making Industry Co., Ltd. 宁波益民酒业有限公司(1838)	Ningbo 宁波市	Zhejiang 浙江省	(0574)7139119 (0574)7496702	170	Limited-Liability 有限公司	27,026	3,296(11)	29,340	Rice Wine 黄酒
T.C.C Ningbo Excellent Wine Co., Ltd. T.C.C宁波佳酿有限公司(1992)	Ningbo 宁波市	Zhejiang 浙江省	(0574)87116834 (0574)87142030	131	Foreign Funded 外商投资	27,009	1,060(21)	53,020	Rice Wine 黄酒
Huzhou Qianchang Wine-making Industry Co., Ltd. 湖州乾昌酒业有限责任公司(1956)	Huzhou 湖州市	Zhejiang 浙江省	(0572)2104227 (0572)2100246	107	Limited-Liability 有限公司	26,500	89(53)	19,867	Rice Wine 黄酒

Top 10 Cities by Revenue 销售收入排名前10位城市	Province 省	Market share 市场份额 (%)	Number of firms 企业个数
Shaoxing 绍兴市	Zhejiang 浙江省	56.02	17
Shanghai 上海市	Shanghai 上海市	15.24	6
Jiaxing 嘉兴市	Zhejiang 浙江省	6.13	3
Zhenjiang 镇江市	Jiangsu 江苏省	2.74	1
Xuancheng 宣城市	Anhui 安徽省	2.18	3
Huzhou 湖州市	Zhejiang 浙江省	2.08	4
Ningbo 宁波市	Zhejiang 浙江省	2.02	3
Qingdao 青岛市	Shandong 山东省	1.98	3
Nantong 南通市	Jiangsu 江苏省	1.85	2
Taizhou 台州市	Zhejiang 浙江省	1.78	4

10 Major Wholesalers 十家主要批发商	City 城市	Province 省	Telephone/Fax 电话/传真
Beijing Chaoyang Non-Staple Foodstuffs General Company 北京朝阳副食品总公司	Beijing 北京市	Beijing 北京市	(010)65016285 (010)65016285
Beijing Sugar,Cigarette & Wine Company 北京市糖业烟酒公司	Beijing 北京市	Beijing 北京市	(010)67210304 (010)67210310
Shanghai Sugar Cigarette & Wine (Group) Co.,Ltd. 上海市糖业烟酒(集团)有限公司	Shanghai 上海市	Shanghai 上海市	(021)63224190 (021)63223169
Jiangsu Sutang Sugar & Wine Co.,Ltd. 江苏苏糖糖酒食品有限公司	Nanjing 南京市	Jiangsu 江苏省	(025)6661088 (025)6661088
Fujian Commerce (Group) Co.,Ltd. 福建省商业（集团）有限责任公司	Fuzhou 福州市	Fujian 福建省	(0591)7847148 (0591)7847145
Yantai Changyu Pioneer Winer Co., Ltd. 烟台张裕葡萄酿酒股份有限公司	Yantai 烟台市	Shandong 山东省	(0535)6602730 (0535)6214078
BlueRibbon Beer Sale Co.,Ltd. 蓝带啤酒销售有限公司	Zhaoqing 肇庆市	Guangdong 广东省	(0758)2862322 (0758)2862424
Fujian Shenlong Development Co.,Ltd. 福建省神龙发展股份有限公司	Fuzhou 福州市	Fujian 福建省	(0591)7503218 (0591)7503068
Guangdong Sugar, Cigarette & Wine Group Company 广东省糖烟酒集团公司	Guangzhou 广州市	Guangdong 广东省	(020)83566131 (020)83561421
Shunde Daliang Sugar, Cigarette & Wine Co.,Ltd. 顺德市大良区糖烟酒有限公司	Shunde 顺德市	Guangdong 广东省	(0765)2231804 (0765)2222300

1515: Wine 葡萄酒制造业

The industry accounts for 0.053% of the total revenue of China's industrial sector in 2002. The rate of return on assets is 6.19%. 75.00% of all firms in the industry made a profit while 25.00% had negative returns.The top province in terms of the industry's revenue is Shandong, accounting for 46.28% of the total revenue.
2002年本行业收入占全行业的 0.053%，资产利润率为 6.19%。75.00%的企业赢利，25.00%的企业亏损。收入最高的省为山东省，占本行业的46.28%。

	Total number of firms 企业总数	Total number of employees 职工总数	Total revenue (Mil.RMB) 总销售收入 (百万元)	Total profit (Mil.RMB) 总利润 (百万元)	Return on assets 资产利润率 (%)	Return on equity 权益利润率 (%)	Labour productivity ('000 RMB/ worker) 劳动生产率 (千元/人)	Debts/ assets 资产负债率 (%)	Total assets (Mil.RMB) 总资产 (百万元)
Industry Overall 行业总体	104	16,091	5,656	635	6.19	11.91	133.06	48.00	10,261

	Number of firms 企业个数	Average number of employees 平均职工人数	Average revenue ('000 RMB) 平均销售收入 (千元)	Average profit ('000 RMB) 平均利润 (千元)	Return on assets 资产利润率 (%)	Return on equity 权益利润率 (%)	Labour productivity ('000 RMB/ worker) 劳动生产率 (千元/人)	Debts/ assets 资产负债率 (%)	Average total assets ('000 RMB) 平均总资产 (千元)
By ownership 产业所有权									
State-owned 国有	21	92	6,038	-213	-0.54	-1.40	16.66	61.07	39,079
Collective-owned 集体	3	83	51,188	2,496	16.69	63.84	190.14	73.86	14,958
Foreign & Overseas Chinese Funded 三资	26	135	83,113	11,458	9.20	21.42	284.26	57.03	124,507
By regional distribution 地区分布									
Central-North 华北	30	89	67,810	9,758	9.27	20.22	355.85	54.16	105,255
Beijing 北京	5	104	47,405	4,356	6.16	16.10	216.62	61.72	70,688
Tianjin 天津	6	125	138,084	31,939	18.47	32.76	524.10	43.61	172,924
Hebei 河北	18	74	52,746	4,386	4.53	11.02	329.49	58.87	96,796
Shanxi 山西	1	65	19,341	374	1.54	3.49	66.15	55.97	24,327
Inner Mongolia 内蒙古									
Northeast 东北	19	190	17,776	1,326	1.89	2.98	39.58	36.38	69,982
Liaoning 辽宁	3	201	10,398	493	0.56	1.40	26.23	60.05	88,135
Jilin 吉林	14	194	21,470	1,761	2.40	3.33	46.62	27.73	73,250
Heilongjiang 黑龙江	2	150	2,987	-473	-2.38		2.83	101.94	19,876
Central-East 华东	24	275	113,075	12,417	9.31	13.41	118.61	30.53	133,328
Shanghai 上海	3	84	19,640	-2,094	-5.17	-16.77	34.66	69.19	40,531
Jiangsu 江苏	2	32	5,440	-585	-2.60	-5.68	25.19	54.27	22,513
Zhejiang 浙江									
Anhui 安徽	2	236	13,125	-597	-1.37	-5.54	17.36	75.28	43,601
Fujian 福建									
Jiangxi 江西									
Shandong 山东	17	341	153,985	18,039	10.41	14.31	131.53	27.25	173,297
Central-South 中南	14	107	14,891	162	0.80	1.40	54.24	43.12	20,382
Henan 河南	8	123	18,657	-65	-0.31	-0.42	41.17	26.00	21,003
Hubei 湖北									
Hunan 湖南	1	13	2,273	51	2.15		47.77	146.45	2,368
Guangdong 广东									
Guangxi 广西	5	99	11,388	548	2.39	7.02	80.20	66.02	22,990
Hainan 海南									
Southwest 西南	3	141	34,966	4,141	8.09	40.09	144.32	79.82	51,184
Chongqing 重庆									
Sichuan 四川	1	110	266	14	0.13	0.34	2.28	62.59	11,081
Guizhou 贵州									
Yunnan 云南	2	156	52,317	6,204	8.71	46.22	194.40	81.16	71,235
Tibet 西藏									
Northwest 西北	14	94	18,356	337	0.22	0.75	95.90	70.69	152,522
Shaanxi 陕西	3	74	3,221	358	2.15	3.41	14.26	37.13	16,674
Gansu 甘肃	2	45	14,689	138	0.19	1.01	377.54	81.01	71,689
Qinghai 青海									
Ningxia 宁夏	2	109	21,138	-2,950	-1.81		78.65	100.44	162,923
Xinjiang 新疆	7	112	25,096	1,324	0.57	1.63	91.81	64.81	230,866

Year 年份	Number of firms 企业个数	Rate of change 变化率 (%)	Number of employees 职工人数 (人)	Rate of change 变化率 (%)	Total revenue (Mil. RMB) 总销售收入 (百万元)	Rate of change 变化率 (%)	Total profit (Mil RMB) 总利润 (百万元)	Rate of change 变化率 (%)
2000	79		15,912		4,439		473	
2001	93	17.72	15,999	0.55	4,977	12.12	567	19.87
2002	104	11.83	16,091	0.58	5,656	13.64	635	11.99

Major Products 主要产品	Output 产量	Unit 单位
Ferment Alcohol 发酵酒精	213	10,000 Tons 万吨
Grape Wine 葡萄酒	29	10,000 Tons 万吨

10 Main Firms with Maximal Revenue (year founded) 收入最大的十家主要企业（创办年份）	City 城市	Province 省	Telephone/fax 电话/传真	Number of employees 职工人数	Ownership 产业所有权	Revenue ('000 RMB) 销售收入 (千元)	Profit('000 RMB) (rank) 利润(千元) (排名)	Total assets ('000 RMB) 总资产 (千元)	Major products 主要产品
Yantai Zhangyu Group Co.,Ltd. 烟台张裕集团有限公司(1914)	Yantai 烟台市	Shandong 山东省	(0535)6691265 (0535)6691266	3,665	State Enterprises 国有独资	1,754,180	224,310(1)	2,093,414	Grape Wine 葡萄酒
Sino-Franch Joint-Venture Dynasty Co., Ltd. 中法合营王朝葡萄酿酒有限公司(1980)	Tianjin 天津市	Tianjin 天津市	(022)26998888 (022)26990996	231	Foreign Funded 外商投资	730,100	178,360(2)	707,757	Grape Wine 葡萄酒
China Great Wall Wine Co.,Ltd. 中国长城葡萄酒有限公司(1985)	Zhangjiakou 张家口市	Hebei 河北省	(0313)6232216 (0313)6253795	734	Overseas Chinese-funded 港澳台资	449,193	23,005(6)	666,425	Grape Wine 葡萄酒
Huaxia Winery Co.,Ltd. 华夏葡萄酿酒有限公司(1988)	Qinhuangdao 秦皇岛市	Hebei 河北省	(0335)2031837 (0335)2032836	54	Foreign Funded 外商投资	362,143	61,277(3)	295,111	Grape Wine 葡萄酒
Yantai Weilong Grape Wine Co.,Ltd. 烟台威龙葡萄酒股份有限公司(1982)	Yantai 烟台市	Shandong 山东省	(0535)8528103 (0535)8527948	478	Limited-Liability 有限公司	311,000	24,018(5)	309,006	Grape Wine 葡萄酒
Yantai Cofco Winery Co., Ltd. 烟台中粮葡萄酿酒有限公司(1999)	Yantai 烟台市	Shandong 山东省	(0535)5963688 (0535)5963777	85	Limited-Liability 有限公司	169,815	41,810(4)	218,993	Grape Wine 葡萄酒
Xintian International Grape Wine Co., Ltd. 新天国际葡萄酒业有限公司(1998)	Changji 昌吉州	Xinjiang 新疆	(0994)6633649 (0994)6633918	247	Limited-Liability 有限公司	134,866	14,195(9)	1,250,436	Grape Wine 葡萄酒
Yunnan Gaoyuan Grape Wine Co., Ltd. 云南高原葡萄酒有限公司(1997)	Honghe 红河州	Yunnan 云南省	(0873)6331094 (0873)6331973	184	Overseas Chinese-funded 港澳台资	100,874	15,665(7)	114,683	Grape Wine 葡萄酒
Yantai Baiyanghe Wine making Co., Ltd. 烟台白洋河酿酒有限责任公司(2001)	Yantai 烟台市	Shandong 山东省	(0535)5201502 (0535)5201208	320	Limited-Liability 有限公司	76,564	1,277(31)	68,755	Grape Wine 葡萄酒
Jilin Changbaishan Wine Industry Co., Ltd 吉林省长白山酒业集团有限公司(1999)	Jilin 吉林市	Jilin 吉林省	(0432)7533929 (0432)7531888	120	Private Enterprises 私营独资	66,194	290(46)	101,558	Grape Wine 葡萄酒

Top 10 Cities by Revenue 销售收入排名前10位城市	Province 省	Market share 市场份额 (%)	Number of firms 企业个数
Yantai 烟台市	Shandong 山东省	42.83	11
Tianjin 天津市	Tianjin 天津市	14.65	6
Qinhuangdao 秦皇岛市	Hebei 河北省	8.43	13
Zhangjiakou 张家口市	Hebei 河北省	8.22	3
Beijing 北京市	Beijing 北京市	4.19	5
Tonghua 通化市	Jilin 吉林省	3.38	8
Changji 昌吉州	Xinjiang 新疆	2.38	1
Jilin 吉林市	Jilin 吉林省	1.94	6
Honghe 红河州	Yunnan 云南省	1.85	2
Weihai 威海市	Shandong 山东省	1.79	1

10 Major Wholesalers 十家主要批发商	City 城市	Province 省	Telephone/Fax 电话/传真
Beijing Chaoyang Non-Staple Foodstuffs General Company 北京朝阳副食品总公司	Beijing 北京市	Beijing 北京市	(010)65016285 (010)65016285
Beijing Sugar,Cigarette & Wine Company 北京市糖业烟酒公司	Beijing 北京市	Beijing 北京市	(010)67210304 (010)67210310
Shanghai Sugar Cigarette & Wine (Group) Co.,Ltd. 上海市糖业烟酒(集团)有限公司	Shanghai 上海市	Shanghai 上海市	(021)63224190 (021)63223169
Jiangsu Sutang Sugar & Wine Co.,Ltd. 江苏苏糖糖酒食品有限公司	Nanjing 南京市	Jiangsu 江苏省	(025)6661088 (025)6661088
Fujian Commerce (Group) Co.,Ltd. 福建省商业（集团）有限责任公司	Fuzhou 福州市	Fujian 福建省	(0591)7847148 (0591)7847145
Yantai Changyu Pioneer Winer Co., Ltd. 烟台张裕葡萄酿酒股份有限公司	Yantai 烟台市	Shandong 山东省	(0535)6602730 (0535)6214078
BlueRibbon Beer Sale Co.,Ltd. 蓝带啤酒销售有限公司	Zhaoqing 肇庆市	Guangdong 广东省	(0758)2862322 (0758)2862424
Fujian Shenlong Development Co.,Ltd. 福建省神龙发展股份有限公司	Fuzhou 福州市	Fujian 福建省	(0591)7503218 (0591)7503068
Guangdong Sugar, Cigarette & Wine Group Company 广东省糖烟酒集团公司	Guangzhou 广州市	Guangdong 广东省	(020)83566131 (020)83561421
Shunde Daliang Sugar, Cigarette & Wine Co.,Ltd. 顺德市大良区糖烟酒有限公司	Shunde 顺德市	Guangdong 广东省	(0765)2231804 (0765)2222300

1516: Fruit Wine 果露酒制造业

The industry accounts for 0.013% of the total revenue of China's industrial sector in 2002. The rate of return on assets is 2.72%. 75.93% of all firms in the industry made a profit while 24.07% had negative returns.The top province in terms of the industry's revenue is Hainan, accounting for 38.69% of the total revenue.
2002年本行业收入占全行业的 0.013%，资产利润率为 2.72%。75.93%的企业赢利，24.07%的企业亏损。收入最高的省为海南省，占本行业的38.69%。

	Total number of firms 企业总数	Total number of employees 职工总数	Total revenue (Mil.RMB) 总销售收入 (百万元)	Total profit (Mil.RMB) 总利润 (百万元)	Return on assets 资产利润率 (%)	Return on equity 权益利润率 (%)	Labour productivity ('000 RMB/ worker) 劳动生产率 (千元/人)	Debts/ assets 资产负债率 (%)	Total assets (Mil.RMB) 总资产 (百万元)
Industry Overall 行业总体	54	7,955	1,407	73	2.72	5.43	70.01	49.88	2,677

	Number of firms 企业个数	Average number of employees 平均职工人数	Average revenue ('000 RMB) 平均销售收入 (千元)	Average profit ('000 RMB) 平均利润 (千元)	Return on assets 资产利润率 (%)	Return on equity 权益利润率 (%)	Labour productivity ('000 RMB/ worker) 劳动生产率 (千元/人)	Debts/ assets 资产负债率 (%)	Average total assets ('000 RMB) 平均总资产 (千元)
By ownership 产业所有权									
State-owned 国有	17	142	5,997	-1,251	-5.07	-36.03	27.23	85.94	24,700
Collective-owned 集体	3	69	16,320	972	17.12	21.84	71.59	21.61	5,678
Foreign & Overseas Chinese Funded 三资	8	67	11,336	-1,732	-5.68	-13.78	69.03	58.79	30,503
By regional distribution 地区分布									
Central-North 华北	6	93	13,689	2,286	6.84	12.73	59.36	46.29	33,433
Beijing 北京	1	35	9,500	760	7.68	11.71	108.71	34.44	9,900
Tianjin 天津	1	239	25,864	5,966	8.06	17.86	52.34	54.87	74,022
Hebei 河北	1	96	20,263	1,139	4.66	16.20	75.40	71.21	24,422
Shanxi 山西	2	50	9,337	2,916	21.43	28.89	44.02	25.83	13,608
Inner Mongolia 内蒙古	1	90	7,835	19	0.03	0.05	58.77	37.52	65,035
Northeast 东北	5	80	3,219	-355	-5.38		14.60	116.90	6,604
Liaoning 辽宁	1	107	5,015	-225	-11.49	-27.17	14.22	57.71	1,958
Jilin 吉林	2	127	2,941	-1,096	-7.82		9.98	131.99	14,002
Heilongjiang 黑龙江	2	20	2,600	320	20.92	25.10	44.75	16.67	1,530
Central-East 华东	10	50	8,590	-1,777	-10.95	-25.02	48.26	56.24	16,230
Shanghai 上海	2	33	7,224	-10,352	-26.59	-79.18	93.34	66.42	38,929
Jiangsu 江苏	2	86	9,055	135	2.15	52.94	18.43	95.94	6,285
Zhejiang 浙江	1	62	7,026	1,740	5.45	11.29	67.19	51.69	31,905
Anhui 安徽	1	52	4,201	104	1.91	3.89	18.85	50.87	5,439
Fujian 福建									
Jiangxi 江西	2	32	11,255	103	1.05	1.09	123.75	3.93	9,797
Shandong 山东	2	41	9,802	309	4.14	8.30	21.45	50.10	7,465
Central-South 中南	27	216	42,333	2,785	3.47	6.68	79.09	48.10	80,325
Henan 河南	4	232	19,108	824	4.82	31.55	30.50	84.72	17,085
Hubei 湖北	5	538	74,282	5,956	4.68	12.32	85.10	61.97	127,158
Hunan 湖南	5	58	9,914	108	0.80	1.78	78.74	55.06	13,503
Guangdong 广东	6	70	11,564	-168	-0.74		56.30	109.10	22,742
Guangxi 广西	2	401	15,857	-3,114	-5.32	-26.30	21.63	79.78	58,555
Hainan 海南	5	142	108,896	9,764	4.27	5.87	198.14	27.27	228,711
Southwest 西南	4	34	1,500	189	3.95	5.24	23.38	24.52	4,768
Chongqing 重庆									
Sichuan 四川	1	34	6,000	589	4.85	7.32	94.24	33.72	12,132
Guizhou 贵州	1	12		165	2.38	2.60	-4.00	8.44	6,941
Yunnan 云南	2	45							
Tibet 西藏									
Northwest 西北	2	264	37,166	1,355	2.90	9.46	55.29	69.35	46,747
Shaanxi 陕西									
Gansu 甘肃	1	42	4,842	300	3.23	5.39	38.93	39.98	9,277
Qinghai 青海									
Ningxia 宁夏	1	485	69,489	2,409	2.86	10.44	56.71	72.59	84,216
Xinjiang 新疆									

Year 年份	Number of firms 企业个数	Rate of change 变化率 (%)	Number of employees 职工人数 (人)	Rate of change 变化率 (%)	Total revenue (Mil. RMB) 总销售收入 (百万元)	Rate of change 变化率 (%)	Total profit (Mil RMB) 总利润 (百万元)	Rate of change 变化率 (%)
2000	64		10,349		1,070		56	
2001	54	-15.63	7,723	-25.37	1,257	17.48	40	-28.57
2002	54	o	7,955	3.00	1,407	11.93	73	82.50

Major Products 主要产品	Output 产量	Unit 单位
Alcoholic Drink 饮料酒	2,887	10,000 Tons 万吨
Ferment Alcohol 发酵酒精	213	10,000 Tons 万吨

10 Main Firms with Maximal Revenue (year founded) 收入最大的十家主要企业（创办年份）	City 城市	Province 省	Telephone/fax 电话/传真	Number of employees 职工人数	Ownership 产业所有权	Revenue ('000 RMB) 销售收入 (千元)	Profit('000 RMB) (rank) 利润(千元)(排名)	Total assets ('000 RMB) 总资产 (千元)	Major products 主要产品
Hainan Yedao Stock Co., Ltd.	Haikou	Hainan	(0898)68520911		Joint Stock				Rice Wine
海南椰岛股份有限公司(1954)	海口市	海南省	(0898)68520851	433	股份制	453,161	48,023(1)	879,230	黄酒
Jing Brand Co.,Ltd.	Huangshi	Hubei	(0714)8761818		Private Owned				Alcoholic Drink Mixed With Fruit Juice
劲牌有限公司(1997)	黄石市	湖北省	(0714)8761798	1,589	私营企业	299,332	39,802(2)	489,927	果露酒
Ningxia Xiangshan Zhongning Medlar Products Co.,Ltd.	Wuzhong	Ningxia	(0953)5792888		Private Owned				Medlar Wine
宁夏香山中宁枸杞制品有限公司(2000)	吴忠市	宁夏回族自治区	(0953)5792998	485	私营企业	69,489	2,409(5)	84,216	枸杞酒
Meizhou China-Franch Aquavit Co., Ltd.	Meizhou	Guangdong	(0753)2268722		Collective-owned				Alcoholic Drink Mixed With Fruit Juice
梅州市中法白兰地有限公司(1999)	梅州市	广东省	(0753)2268721	50	集体企业	32,400	90(26)	8,553	果露酒
Tianjin Huaren Wine & Drinks Co.,Ltd.	Tianjin	Tianjin	(022)69581854		Overseas Chinese-funded				Alcoholic Drink Mixed With Fruit Juice
天津华人酒饮有限公司(1994)	天津市	天津市	(022)69581854	239	港澳台资	25,864	5,966(3)	74,022	果露酒
Yongzhou Wine Brewery Co., Ltd.	Yongzhou	Hunan	(0746)3235888		Private Enterprises				Medicinal Liquor
永州市酿酒有限公司(1995)	永州市	湖南省	(0746)3218037	106	私营独资	24,060	1,400(9)	38,970	药酒
Jiangxi Chinese Goosebeery Wine Co., Ltd.	Yichun	Jiangxi	(0795)2905288		Private Owned				Chinese Goosebeery Wine
江西省猕猴桃酒业股份有限公司(1999)	宜春市	江西省	(0795)2905288	63	私营企业	22,510	205(22)	19,594	猕猴桃果酒
Wuzhou Longshan Animal & Plant Wine General Factory	Wuzhou	Guangxi	(0774)3827278		State-owned				Alcoholic Drink Mixed With Fruit Juice
梧州市龙山动植物酒总厂(1935)	梧州市	广西省		500	国有企业	20,720	-	54,798	露酒
Shanxi Linfen Qing'an China Deer & Tortoise Nectar Factory	Linfen	Shanxi	(0357)2210852		Private Partnership				China Deer & Tortoise Nectar
山西省临汾市情安鹿龟神酒厂(1997)	临汾市	山西省	(0357)2210852	60	私营合伙	18,494	5,832(4)	16,321	中华鹿龟神酒
Shandong Chaowei Medical Health Co.,Ltd.	Linyi	Shandong	(0539)5212052		Private Enterprises				Alcoholic Drink
山东超伟保健品有限公司(1998)	临沂市	山东省	(0539)5212052	42	私营独资	15,941	560(13)	3,582	饮料酒

Top 10 Cities by Revenue 销售收入排名前10位城市	Province 省	Market share 市场份额 (%)	Number of firms 企业个数
Haikou 海口市	Hainan 海南省	32.20	1
Huangshi 黄石市	Hubei 湖北省	22.16	2
Hainan 海南省	Hainan 海南省	6.49	4
Wuzhong 吴忠市	Ningxia 宁夏	4.94	1
Jiaozuo 焦作市	Henan 河南省	4.18	1
Xiangfan 襄樊市	Hubei 湖北省	3.52	1
Yongzhou 永州市	Hunan 湖南省	2.69	3
Meizhou 梅州市	Guangdong 广东省	2.30	1
Tianjin 天津市	Tianjin 天津市	1.84	1
Yichun 宜春市	Jiangxi 江西省	1.60	1

10 Major Wholesalers 十家主要批发商	City 城市	Province 省	Telephone/Fax 电话/传真
Beijing Chaoyang Non-Staple Foodstuffs General Company	Beijing	Beijing	(010)65016285
北京朝阳副食品总公司	北京市	北京市	(010)65016285
Beijing Sugar,Cigarette & Wine Company	Beijing	Beijing	(010)67210304
北京市糖业烟酒公司	北京市	北京市	(010)67210310
Shanghai Sugar Cigarette & Wine (Group) Co.,Ltd.	Shanghai	Shanghai	(021)63224190
上海市糖业烟酒(集团)有限公司	上海市	上海市	(021)63223169
Jiangsu Sutang Sugar & Wine Co.,Ltd.	Nanjing	Jiangsu	(025)6661088
江苏苏糖糖酒食品有限公司	南京市	江苏省	(025)6661088
Fujian Commerce (Group) Co.,Ltd.	Fuzhou	Fujian	(0591)7847148
福建省商业（集团）有限责任公司	福州市	福建省	(0591)7847145
Yantai Changyu Pioneer Winer Co., Ltd.	Yantai	Shandong	(0535)6602730
烟台张裕葡萄酿酒股份有限公司	烟台市	山东省	(0535)6214078
BlueRibbon Beer Sale Co.,Ltd.	Zhaoqing	Guangdong	(0758)2862322
蓝带啤酒销售有限公司	肇庆市	广东省	(0758)2862424
Fujian Shenlong Development Co.,Ltd.	Fuzhou	Fujian	(0591)7503218
福建省神龙发展股份有限公司	福州市	福建省	(0591)7503068
Guangdong Sugar, Cigarette & Wine Group Company	Guangzhou	Guangdong	(020)83566131
广东省糖烟酒集团公司	广州市	广东省	(020)83561421
Shunde Daliang Sugar, Cigarette & Wine Co.,Ltd.	Shunde	Guangdong	(0765)2231804
顺德市大良区糖烟酒有限公司	顺德市	广东省	(0765)2222300

1521: Carbonic-acid Beverage 碳酸饮料制造业

The industry accounts for 0.215% of the total revenue of China's industrial sector in 2002. The rate of return on assets is 9.48%. 74.62% of all firms in the industry made a profit while 25.38% had negative returns.The top province in terms of the industry's revenue is Guangdong, accounting for 20.17% of the total revenue.
2002年本行业收入占全行业的 0.215%，资产利润率为 9.48%。74.62%的企业赢利，25.38%的企业亏损。收入最高的省为广东省，占本行业的20.17%。

	Total number of firms 企业总数	Total number of employees 职工总数	Total revenue (Mil.RMB) 总销售收入 (百万元)	Total profit (Mil.RMB) 总利润 (百万元)	Return on assets 资产利润率 (%)	Return on equity 权益利润率 (%)	Labour productivity ('000 RMB/ worker) 劳动生产率 (千元/人)	Debts/ assets 资产负债率 (%)	Total assets (Mil.RMB) 总资产 (百万元)
Industry Overall 行业总体	197	47,807	23,076	1,860	9.48	18.33	141.10	48.29	19,622

	Number of firms 企业个数	Average number of employees 平均职工人数	Average revenue ('000 RMB) 平均销售收入 (千元)	Average profit ('000 RMB) 平均利润 (千元)	Return on assets 资产利润率 (%)	Return on equity 权益利润率 (%)	Labour productivity ('000 RMB/ worker) 劳动生产率 (千元/人)	Debts/ assets 资产负债率 (%)	Average total assets ('000 RMB) 平均总资产 (千元)
By ownership 产业所有权									
State-owned 国有	46	81	2,675	-542	-2.35	-18.51	-1.12	87.33	23,124
Collective-owned 集体	17	134	103,997	2,487	6.44	87.54	154.61	92.64	38,592
Foreign & Overseas Chinese Funded 三资	61	444	289,569	27,077	11.50	19.68	193.49	41.56	235,420
By regional distribution 地区分布									
Central-North 华北	42	188	107,889	3,587	4.03	10.32	104.83	60.94	89,031
Beijing 北京	11	164	61,546	1,314	2.84	4.88	99.90	41.72	46,217
Tianjin 天津	8	237	127,616	8,417	7.21	11.92	32.45	39.51	116,701
Hebei 河北	17	202	158,596	4,164	3.77	14.19	159.74	73.42	110,386
Shanxi 山西	5	139	27,315	-382	-0.46	-1.92	49.23	76.31	83,850
Inner Mongolia 内蒙古	1	42	726	-7	-0.47	-0.57	10.10	17.45	1,496
Northeast 东北	17	310	91,666	9,592	10.01	19.38	115.50	48.35	95,824
Liaoning 辽宁	8	317	91,858	14,217	12.41	20.72	124.07	40.10	114,517
Jilin 吉林	4	495	154,323	11,021	9.56	17.31	108.07	44.75	115,272
Heilongjiang 黑龙江	5	151	41,235	1,051	2.09	13.87	106.16	84.96	50,358
Central-East 华东	40	279	197,069	18,239	11.72	18.02	206.01	34.98	155,678
Shanghai 上海	3	816	1,413,611	164,674	15.26	22.81	467.89	33.07	1,078,858
Jiangsu 江苏	5	310	214,306	11,400	7.81	11.97	322.40	34.79	146,047
Zhejiang 浙江	4	366	218,306	22,109	14.87	26.96	120.53	44.86	148,715
Anhui 安徽	4	417	58,856	2,511	6.19	27.21	47.37	77.24	40,554
Fujian 福建	10	189	77,320	5,860	7.61	9.34	117.99	18.47	76,992
Jiangxi 江西	8	120	33,077	-490	-1.42	-3.11	39.99	54.46	34,529
Shandong 山东	6	195	70,658	4,227	5.55	8.81	114.80	37.00	76,178
Central-South 中南	61	253	118,495	11,294	11.94	22.68	159.23	47.34	94,553
Henan 河南	11	362	105,596	5,648	8.44	16.10	82.53	47.60	66,927
Hubei 湖北	14	234	68,850	7,899	12.95	22.90	161.12	43.44	60,980
Hunan 湖南	3	236	27,117	-1,916	-2.78	-9.24	19.78	69.85	68,800
Guangdong 广东	24	262	193,930	21,630	14.07	26.51	243.10	46.91	153,682
Guangxi 广西	8	116	19,955	-752	-3.15	-6.80	45.79	53.66	23,882
Hainan 海南	1	261	207,400	8,870	9.64	14.88	68.57	35.20	91,999
Southwest 西南	24	263	58,397	4,401	6.45	19.09	72.86	66.19	68,179
Chongqing 重庆	4	505	131,040	14,254	10.26	17.19	72.81	40.34	138,943
Sichuan 四川	14	260	51,801	3,177	5.27	26.28	80.74	79.96	60,325
Guizhou 贵州	4	63	3,127	9	0.14	0.36	14.20	61.41	6,102
Yunnan 云南	2	195	69,820	2,049	1.94	9.55	37.09	79.72	105,784
Tibet 西藏									
Northwest 西北	13	136	36,446	1,709	3.57	10.78	54.98	66.88	47,862
Shaanxi 陕西	6	250	71,867	1,398	1.68	4.89	53.51	65.71	83,373
Gansu 甘肃	7	39	6,085	1,976	11.34	40.07	63.12	71.71	17,423
Qinghai 青海									
Ningxia 宁夏									
Xinjiang 新疆									

Year 年份	Number of firms 企业个数	Rate of change 变化率 (%)	Number of employees 职工人数 (人)	Rate of change 变化率 (%)	Total revenue (Mil. RMB) 总销售收入 (百万元)	Rate of change 变化率 (%)	Total profit (Mil RMB) 总利润 (百万元)	Rate of change 变化率 (%)
2000	233		49,088		18,012		1,051	
2001	200	-14.16	45,485	-7.34	20,191	12.10	1,296	23.31
2002	197	-1.50	47,807	5.10	23,076	14.29	1,860	43.52

Major Products 主要产品	Output 产量	Unit 单位
Soft Drink 软饮料	2,025	10,000 Tons 万吨
Carbonated Drink 碳酸饮料	604	10,000 Tons 万吨

10 Main Firms with Maximal Revenue (year founded) 收入最大的十家主要企业（创办年份）	City 城市	Province 省	Telephone/fax 电话/传真	Number of employees 职工人数	Ownership 产业所有权	Revenue ('000 RMB) 销售收入 (千元)	Profit('000 RMB) (rank) 利润(千元) (排名)	Total assets ('000 RMB) 总资产 (千元)	Major products 主要产品
Coca-cola (China) Beverages Co., Ltd.	Shanghai	Shanghai	(021)38984656		Foreign Funded				Drink
可口可乐（中国）饮料有限公司(1995)	上海市	上海市	(021)50318848	400	外商投资	1,815,482	252,163(1)	1,190,405	饮料
Guangdong Jianlibao Beverage Co.,Ltd.	Foshan	Guangdong	(0757)7721102		Overseas Chinese-funded				Carbonated Drink
广东健力宝集团有限公司(1986)	佛山市	广东省	(0757)7731241	1,489	港澳台资	1,530,256	144,444(4)	936,747	碳酸饮料
Shanghai Shenmei Beverage & Food Co.,Ltd.	Shanghai	Shanghai	(021)50311688		Foreign Funded				Carbonated Drink
上海申美饮料食品有限公司(1987)	上海市	上海市	(021)50310258	870	外商投资	1,264,865	84,450(6)	1,053,632	碳酸饮料
Shanghai Pepsicola Beverage Co.,Ltd.	Shanghai	Shanghai	(021)64303280		Foreign Funded				Carbonated Drink
上海百事可乐饮料有限公司(1990)	上海市	上海市	(021)64301377	1,177	外商投资	1,160,485	157,408(3)	992,537	碳酸饮料
Swire Guangdong Coca-cola Co., Ltd.	Guangzhou	Guangdong	(020)82100933		Overseas Chinese-funded				Aerated Water
广东太古可口可乐有限公司(1995)	广州市	广东省	(020)82281551	1,069	港澳台资	1,023,941	80,255(7)	741,767	汽水
Tianjin Coca-cola Beverage Co.,Ltd.	Tianjin	Tianjin	(022)25328404		Foreign Funded				Carbonated Drink
天津可口可乐饮料有限公司(1993)	天津市	天津市	(022)25328408	1,451	外商投资	840,002	67,006(9)	462,080	碳酸饮料
Pepsiclo (China) Co.,Ltd.	Guangzhou	Guangdong	(020)82214888		Foreign Funded				Concentrated Liquid
百事（中国）有限公司(1988)	广州市	广东省	(020)82221351	70	外商投资	738,636	209,016(2)	570,349	浓缩液
Nanjing Zhongcui Food Co., Ltd.	Nanjing	Jiangsu	(025)8642131		Foreign Funded				Carbonated Drink
南京中萃食品有限公司(1989)	南京市	江苏省	(025)8649019	850	外商投资	723,870	42,340(15)	287,530	碳酸饮料
Hebei Xuri Health Protection Goods Co., Ltd.	Hengshui	Hebei	(0318)8612532		Limited-Liability				Drink
河北旭日保健制品有限公司(1994)	衡水市	河北省	(0318)8611220	102	有限公司	603,450	14,990(27)	556,900	饮料
Guangzhou Pepsicola Beverage Co., Ltd.	Guangzhou	Guangdong	(020)84223284		Foreign Funded				Carbonated Drink
广州百事可乐饮料有限公司(1995)	广州市	广东省	(020)84209430	606	外商投资	491,561	53,738(13)	376,198	碳酸饮料

Top 10 Cities by Revenue 销售收入排名前10位城市	Province 省	Market share 市场份额 (%)	Number of firms 企业个数
Shanghai 上海市	Shanghai 上海市	18.38	3
Hengshui 衡水市	Hebei 河北省	11.07	6
Guangzhou 广州市	Guangdong 广东省	10.08	7
Foshan 佛山市	Guangdong 广东省	6.67	3
Tianjin 天津市	Tianjin 天津市	4.42	8
Nanjing 南京市	Jiangsu 江苏省	3.80	2
Hangzhou 杭州市	Zhejiang 浙江省	3.66	2
Luohe 漯河市	Henan 河南省	3.12	2
Beijing 北京市	Beijing 北京市	2.93	11
Chengdu 成都市	Sichuan 四川省	2.35	2

10 Major Wholesalers 十家主要批发商	City 城市	Province 省	Telephone/Fax 电话/传真
Beijing Chaoyang Non-Staple Foodstuffs General Company	Beijing	Beijing	(010)65016285
北京朝阳副食品总公司	北京市	北京市	(010)65016285
Beijing Sugar,Cigarette & Wine Company	Beijing	Beijing	(010)67210304
北京市糖业烟酒公司	北京市	北京市	(010)67210310
Shanghai Sugar Cigarette & Wine (Group) Co.,Ltd.	Shanghai	Shanghai	(021)63224190
上海市糖业烟酒(集团)有限公司	上海市	上海市	(021)63223169
Jiangsu Sutang Sugar & Wine Co.,Ltd.	Nanjing	Jiangsu	(025)6661088
江苏苏糖糖酒食品有限公司	南京市	江苏省	(025)6661088
Fujian Commerce (Group) Co.,Ltd.	Fuzhou	Fujian	(0591)7847148
福建省商业（集团）有限责任公司	福州市	福建省	(0591)7847145
Yantai Changyu Pioneer Winer Co., Ltd.	Yantai	Shandong	(0535)6602730
烟台张裕葡萄酿酒股份有限公司	烟台市	山东省	(0535)6214078
BlueRibbon Beer Sale Co.,Ltd.	Zhaoqing	Guangdong	(0758)2862322
蓝带啤酒销售有限公司	肇庆市	广东省	(0758)2862424
Fujian Shenlong Development Co.,Ltd.	Fuzhou	Fujian	(0591)7503218
福建省神龙发展股份有限公司	福州市	福建省	(0591)7503068
Guangdong Sugar, Cigarette & Wine Group Company	Guangzhou	Guangdong	(020)83566131
广东省糖烟酒集团公司	广州市	广东省	(020)83561421
Shunde Daliang Sugar, Cigarette & Wine Co.,Ltd.	Shunde	Guangdong	(0765)2231804
顺德市大良区糖烟酒有限公司	顺德市	广东省	(0765)2222300

1522: Natural Mineral Water 天然矿泉水制造业

The industry accounts for 0.051% of the total revenue of China's industrial sector in 2002. The rate of return on assets is 2.50%. 70.00% of all firms in the industry made a profit while 30.00% had negative returns.The top province in terms of the industry's revenue is Guangdong, accounting for 17.71% of the total revenue.
2002年本行业收入占全行业的0.051%，资产利润率为2.50%。70.00%的企业赢利，30.00%的企业亏损。收入最高的省为广东省，占本行业的17.71%。

	Total number of firms 企业总数	Total number of employees 职工总数	Total revenue (Mil.RMB) 总销售收入(百万元)	Total profit (Mil.RMB) 总利润(百万元)	Return on assets 资产利润率(%)	Return on equity 权益利润率(%)	Labour productivity ('000 RMB/ worker) 劳动生产率(千元/人)	Debts/ assets 资产负债率(%)	Total assets (Mil.RMB) 总资产(百万元)
Industry Overall 行业总体	240	28,150	5,498	236	2.50	5.74	68.48	56.43	9,440

	Number of firms 企业个数	Average number of employees 平均职工人数	Average revenue ('000 RMB) 平均销售收入(千元)	Average profit ('000 RMB) 平均利润(千元)	Return on assets 资产利润率(%)	Return on equity 权益利润率(%)	Labour productivity ('000 RMB/ worker) 劳动生产率(千元/人)	Debts/ assets 资产负债率(%)	Average total assets ('000 RMB) 平均总资产(千元)
By ownership 产业所有权									
State-owned 国有	42	38	3,996	-249	-1.85	-6.31	30.43	70.75	13,493
Collective-owned 集体	20	122	14,429	1,016	6.91	22.49	44.94	69.26	14,698
Foreign & Overseas Chinese Funded 三资	60	185	47,595	1,698	2.32	6.00	93.52	61.23	73,029
By regional distribution 地区分布									
Central-North 华北	31	104	29,413	4,304	7.83	12.47	76.95	37.17	54,950
Beijing 北京	13	59	4,900	-215	-3.40		36.18	101.40	6,323
Tianjin 天津	11	170	62,946	12,050	9.20	13.99	97.73	34.23	130,951
Hebei 河北	6	68	24,947	651	2.30	3.19	84.94	27.76	28,259
Shanxi 山西									
Inner Mongolia 内蒙古	1	168	6,031	-236	-2.10	-14.70	11.26	85.73	11,245
Northeast 东北	28	78	15,568	1,226	3.55	6.93	91.64	48.72	34,510
Liaoning 辽宁	10	94	22,298	1,332	3.58	8.44	70.59	57.61	37,241
Jilin 吉林	12	76	15,971	1,915	4.88	8.40	138.94	41.91	39,271
Heilongjiang 黑龙江	6	54	3,546	-331	-1.62	-3.11	19.93	47.92	20,437
Central-East 华东	61	133	31,876	-1,775	-4.10	-16.92	72.57	75.78	43,320
Shanghai 上海	17	203	37,267	-8,805	-14.12	-413.00	60.31	96.58	62,338
Jiangsu 江苏	2	588	15,347	514	4.89	51.53	3.54	90.51	10,504
Zhejiang 浙江	14	80	55,272	1,030	1.29	3.76	171.17	65.81	80,136
Anhui 安徽	2	228	20,111	2,037	7.56	24.08	26.13	68.60	26,935
Fujian 福建	10	67	12,681	418	5.06	10.58	71.38	52.18	8,265
Jiangxi 江西	5	22	2,792	178	6.80	18.94	27.26	64.07	2,613
Shandong 山东	11	103	29,584	1,526	5.78	10.69	107.77	45.91	26,389
Central-South 中南	78	132	22,161	2,113	4.96	11.22	70.17	55.77	42,561
Henan 河南	12	125	8,207	1,255	12.33	14.82	28.10	16.80	10,174
Hubei 湖北	10	228	30,180	7,150	6.27	17.52	26.11	64.24	114,096
Hunan 湖南	9	97	27,918	4,584	11.20	15.64	104.16	28.37	40,914
Guangdong 广东	39	123	24,969	1,368	3.67	7.37	103.69	50.29	37,324
Guangxi 广西	3	69	4,576	186	1.84	4.05	31.46	54.60	10,110
Hainan 海南	5	127	17,892	-3,381	-8.35		39.48	120.84	40,507
Southwest 西南	31	126	11,007	45	0.28	0.55	30.31	49.39	16,231
Chongqing 重庆	3	165	20,957	591	1.40	2.51	45.05	44.23	42,189
Sichuan 四川	9	187	22,869	40	0.17	0.28	37.83	40.55	23,755
Guizhou 贵州	7	46	4,049	136	2.33	5.55	34.58	58.11	5,859
Yunnan 云南	6	204	6,332	-19	-0.13	-0.75	13.30	82.26	14,509
Tibet 西藏	6	28	1,033	-262	-4.53	-6.47	27.01	30.02	5,786
Northwest 西北	11	41	12,350	955	3.44	5.70	113.87	39.60	27,747
Shaanxi 陕西	2	73	12,637	914	1.85	6.15	101.22	69.87	49,313
Gansu 甘肃	5	35	18,030	1,876	7.46	8.17	167.28	8.68	25,128
Qinghai 青海	2	21	3,562	-1,154	-9.49	-15.65	78.17	39.33	12,155
Ningxia 宁夏									
Xinjiang 新疆	2	45	6,652	802	2.83	6.38	47.77	55.61	28,323

1522: Natural Mineral Water 天然矿泉水制造业

Year 年份	Number of firms 企业个数	Rate of change 变化率 (%)	Number of employees 职工人数 (人)	Rate of change 变化率 (%)	Total revenue (Mil. RMB) 总销售收入 (百万元)	Rate of change 变化率 (%)	Total profit (Mil RMB) 总利润 (百万元)	Rate of change 变化率 (%)
2000	159		15,314		2,351		94	
2001	212	33.33	22,935	49.76	4,753	102.17	199	111.70
2002	240	13.21	28,150	22.74	5,498	15.67	236	18.59

Major Products 主要产品	Output 产量	Unit 单位
Bottle (Tin) Filled Drinking Water 瓶(罐)装饮用水	810	10,000 Tons 万吨

10 Main Firms with Maximal Revenue (year founded) 收入最大的十家主要企业（创办年份）	City 城市	Province 省	Telephone/fax 电话/传真	Number of employees 职工人数	Ownership 产业所有权	Revenue ('000 RMB) 销售收入 (千元)	Profit('000 RMB) (rank) 利润(千元) (排名)	Total assets ('000 RMB) 总资产 (千元)	Major products 主要产品
Tianjin DingJin Food Co., Ltd.	Tianjin	Tianjin	(022)25329605		Overseas Chinese-funded				Mineral Water
天津顶津食品有限公司(1995)	天津市	天津市	(022)25320846	732	港澳台资	581,208	61,813(3)	542,742	矿泉水
Nongfu Spring Co., Ltd.	Hangzhou	Zhejiang	(0571)64711711		Joint Stock				Purified Water
农夫山泉股份有限公司(1996)	杭州市	浙江省	(0571)64711710	202	股份制	368,647	-	420,092	纯净水
C'estbon Food & Beverage (ShenZhen) Co.,Ltd.	Shenzhen	Guangdong	(0755)26983333		Foreign Funded				Purified Water
怡宝食品饮料（深圳）有限公司(1984)	深圳市	广东省	(0755)26980648	523	外商投资	210,656	7,735(15)	154,948	纯净水
Shanghai Zheng-Guang-He Drinking Water Co., Ltd.	Shanghai	Shanghai	(021)65121660		Foreign Funded				Drinking Water
上海正广和饮用水有限公司(1995)	上海市	上海市	(021)65350269	884	外商投资	159,332	11,473(11)	199,589	饮用水
Jilin Wahaha Food Co., Ltd.	Jilin	Jilin	(0432)3055168		Foreign Funded				Purified Water
吉林娃哈哈食品有限责任公司(2000)	吉林市	吉林省	(0432)3055199	83	外商投资	124,005	26,973(6)	122,555	纯净水
Lebaishi ChengDu Food & Beverage Co., Ltd.	Chengdu	Sichuan	(028)87988329		Foreign Funded				Mineral Water
乐百氏成都食品饮料有限公司(2000)	成都市	四川省	(028)87988411	1,000	外商投资	119,377	-	75,293	矿泉水
Shandong Wendeng Heibao Mineral Water Co., Ltd.	Weihai	Shandong	(0631)8832148		Limited-Liability				Mineral Water
山东文登黑豹矿泉水有限公司(1994)	威海市	山东省	(0631)8833388	132	有限公司	112,780	12,800(10)	13,540	矿泉水
Shenzhen Daneng Yili Beverage Co., Ltd.	Shenzhen	Guangdong	(0755)26788668		Overseas Chinese-funded				Mineral Water
深圳达能益力饮品有限公司(1995)	深圳市	广东省	(0755)26782738	361	港澳台资	103,436	11,085(12)	256,611	矿泉水
Changsha Wahaha Food Co., Ltd.	Changsha	Hunan	(0731)4016062		Foreign Funded				Purified Water
长沙娃哈哈食品有限公司(1998)	长沙市	湖南省	(0731)4012563	124	外商投资	96,836	14,911(9)	87,355	纯净水
Nestle Sources Shanghai Ltd.	Shanghai	Shanghai	(021)58549988		Foreign Funded				Drinking Water
上海雀巢饮用水有限公司(1996)	上海市	上海市	(021)58541188	496	外商投资	93,089	-	96,291	饮用水

Top 10 Cities by Revenue 销售收入排名前10位城市	Province 省	Market share 市场份额 (%)	Number of firms 企业个数
Tianjin 天津市	Tianjin 天津市	12.59	11
Hangzhou 杭州市	Zhejiang 浙江省	11.86	4
Shanghai 上海市	Shanghai 上海市	11.52	17
Shenzhen 深圳市	Guangdong 广东省	8.83	7
Wuhan 武汉市	Hubei 湖北省	4.60	2
Shenyang 沈阳市	Liaoning 辽宁省	3.57	5
Changsha 长沙市	Hunan 湖南省	3.30	2
Chengdu 成都市	Sichuan 四川省	3.27	7
Jilin 吉林市	Jilin 吉林省	2.57	3
Jiangmen 江门市	Guangdong 广东省	2.32	4

10 Major Wholesalers 十家主要批发商	City 城市	Province 省	Telephone/Fax 电话/传真
Beijing Chaoyang Non-Staple Foodstuffs General Company	Beijing	Beijing	(010)65016285
北京朝阳副食品总公司	北京市	北京市	(010)65016285
Beijing Sugar,Cigarette & Wine Company	Beijing	Beijing	(010)67210304
北京市糖业烟酒公司	北京市	北京市	(010)67210310
Shanghai Sugar Cigarette & Wine (Group) Co.,Ltd.	Shanghai	Shanghai	(021)63224190
上海市糖业烟酒(集团)有限公司	上海市	上海市	(021)63223169
Jiangsu Sutang Sugar & Wine Co.,Ltd.	Nanjing	Jiangsu	(025)6661088
江苏苏糖糖酒食品有限公司	南京市	江苏省	(025)6661088
Fujian Commerce (Group) Co.,Ltd.	Fuzhou	Fujian	(0591)7847148
福建省商业（集团）有限责任公司	福州市	福建省	(0591)7847145
Yantai Changyu Pioneer Winer Co., Ltd.	Yantai	Shandong	(0535)6602730
烟台张裕葡萄酿酒股份有限公司	烟台市	山东省	(0535)6214078
BlueRibbon Beer Sale Co.,Ltd.	Zhaoqing	Guangdong	(0758)2862322
蓝带啤酒销售有限公司	肇庆市	广东省	(0758)2862424
Fujian Shenlong Development Co.,Ltd.	Fuzhou	Fujian	(0591)7503218
福建省神龙发展股份有限公司	福州市	福建省	(0591)7503068
Guangdong Sugar, Cigarette & Wine Group Company	Guangzhou	Guangdong	(020)83566131
广东省糖烟酒集团公司	广州市	广东省	(020)83561421
Shunde Daliang Sugar, Cigarette & Wine Co.,Ltd.	Shunde	Guangdong	(0765)2231804
顺德市大良区糖烟酒有限公司	顺德市	广东省	(0765)2222300

1523: Fruit and Vegetable Juice Drinks 果菜汁饮料制造业

The industry accounts for 0.086% of the total revenue of China's industrial sector in 2002. The rate of return on assets is 2.83%. 77.64% of all firms in the industry made a profit while 22.36% had negative returns.The top province in terms of the industry's revenue is Guangdong, accounting for 15.86% of the total revenue.
2002年本行业收入占全行业的 0.086%，资产利润率为 2.83%。77.64%的企业赢利，22.36%的企业亏损。收入最高的省为广东省，占本行业的15.86%。

	Total number of firms 企业总数	Total number of employees 职工总数	Total revenue (Mil.RMB) 总销售收入(百万元)	Total profit (Mil.RMB) 总利润(百万元)	Return on assets 资产利润率 (%)	Return on equity 权益利润率 (%)	Labour productivity ('000 RMB/ worker) 劳动生产率 (千元/人)	Debts/ assets 资产负债率 (%)	Total assets (Mil.RMB) 总资产 (百万元)
Industry Overall 行业总体	246	35,572	9,244	463	2.83	7.13	82.39	60.26	16,336

	Number of firms 企业个数	Average number of employees 平均职工人数	Average revenue ('000 RMB) 平均销售收入（千元）	Average profit ('000 RMB) 平均利润（千元）	Return on assets 资产利润率 (%)	Return on equity 权益利润率 (%)	Labour productivity ('000 RMB/ worker) 劳动生产率 (千元/人)	Debts/ assets 资产负债率 (%)	Average total assets ('000 RMB) 平均总资产 (千元)
By ownership 产业所有权									
State-owned 国有	21	112	19,771	2,147	4.26	15.25	95.28	72.07	50,417
Collective-owned 集体	26	125	27,389	1,669	4.14	11.90	59.58	65.24	40,338
Foreign & Overseas Chinese Funded 三资	75	180	65,219	2,861	2.61	6.71	106.15	61.14	109,765
By regional distribution 地区分布									
Central-North 华北	54	150	41,966	2,039	3.17	10.68	82.45	70.30	64,245
Beijing 北京	11	265	117,981	6,592	3.32	10.96	147.30	69.67	198,320
Tianjin 天津	11	136	27,766	1,409	5.20	21.21	4.07	75.46	27,084
Hebei 河北	17	126	20,433	-224	-0.55	-2.02	53.52	72.90	40,816
Shanxi 山西	13	99	21,911	2,013	9.17	24.80	81.83	63.01	21,944
Inner Mongolia 内蒙古	2	128	15,369	-136	-2.55	-12.35	48.54	79.36	5,318
Northeast 东北	16	102	22,692	492	0.92	2.02	80.34	54.27	53,205
Liaoning 辽宁	6	104	17,309	569	0.88	2.57	50.88	65.59	64,462
Jilin 吉林	5	77	18,598	-166	-0.39	-0.82	89.72	52.76	42,780
Heilongjiang 黑龙江	5	123	33,246	1,057	2.11	3.41	104.33	38.10	50,122
Central-East 华东	72	141	45,386	2,530	4.08	8.96	101.29	54.45	62,008
Shanghai 上海	8	265	84,649	-966	-0.91	-2.94	83.94	69.02	106,058
Jiangsu 江苏	4	189	31,318	620	3.04	8.35	36.76	63.53	20,372
Zhejiang 浙江	9	92	11,709	275	1.83	3.83	20.39	52.15	14,976
Anhui 安徽	5	133	5,472	610	4.43	50.30	16.57	91.20	13,794
Fujian 福建	14	136	59,930	1,088	1.77	3.76	133.36	52.93	61,430
Jiangxi 江西	2	35	20,843	570	2.02	2.65	79.80	23.64	28,207
Shandong 山东	30	127	48,395	5,516	6.85	13.54	140.35	49.36	80,480
Central-South 中南	53	155	38,108	1,767	2.43	6.41	72.61	62.11	72,775
Henan 河南	20	150	21,904	464	0.91	4.59	33.02	80.18	51,031
Hubei 湖北	3	127	28,082	658	7.49	10.83	71.07	30.88	8,790
Hunan 湖南	3	41	796	-344	-0.64	-2.69	-1.87	76.29	53,927
Guangdong 广东	21	205	69,825	3,968	3.80	8.28	105.32	54.06	104,312
Guangxi 广西	1	166	8,203	118	2.03	4.30	17.61	52.91	5,823
Hainan 海南	5	54	4,092	-7	-0.01	-0.02	59.92	57.19	90,390
Southwest 西南	20	148	22,661	1,032	1.69	3.50	63.59	51.66	60,999
Chongqing 重庆	2	308	117,459	2,557	1.94	3.09	141.18	37.07	131,508
Sichuan 四川	6	108	24,306	4,049	4.72	10.08	130.31	53.19	85,797
Guizhou 贵州	7	192	5,871	-54	-0.12	-0.32	10.09	61.21	43,683
Yunnan 云南	5	70	6,274	-1,678	-6.15	-12.99	8.75	52.62	27,281
Tibet 西藏									
Northwest 西北	31	145	28,198	1,555	1.95	4.88	70.50	60.10	79,791
Shaanxi 陕西	18	166	34,305	1,311	1.30	3.37	72.67	61.35	100,712
Gansu 甘肃	6	39	3,568	137	1.27	1.81	71.69	29.66	10,711
Qinghai 青海	2	322	28,748	2,255	3.39	8.12	34.36	58.26	66,474
Ningxia 宁夏	1	122	15,641	-1,478	-4.11		30.34	108.67	36,000
Xinjiang 新疆	4	127	40,527	5,185	4.85	10.99	112.68	55.85	106,877

1523: Fruit and Vegetable Juice Drinks 果菜汁饮料制造业

Year 年份	Number of firms 企业个数	Rate of change 变化率 (%)	Number of employees 职工人数 (人)	Rate of change 变化率 (%)	Total revenue (Mil. RMB) 总销售收入 (百万元)	Rate of change 变化率 (%)	Total profit (Mil RMB) 总利润 (百万元)	Rate of change 变化率 (%)
2000	219		31,316		6,800		220	
2001	239	9.13	35,796	14.31	7,968	17.18	243	10.45
2002	246	2.93	35,572	-0.63	9,244	16.01	463	90.53

Major Products 主要产品	Output 产量	Unit 单位
Fruit Juice & Fruit Juice Drink 果汁及果汁饮料	2,129,947	Ton 吨
Soft Drink 软饮料	2,025	10,000 Tons 万吨

10 Main Firms with Maximal Revenue (year founded) 收入最大的十家主要企业（创办年份）	City 城市	Province 省	Telephone/ fax 电话/传真	Number of employees 职工人数	Ownership 产业所有权	Revenue ('000 RMB) 销售收入 (千元)	Profit('000 RMB) (rank) 利润(千元) (排名)	Total assets ('000 RMB) 总资产 (千元)	Major products 主要产品
Beijing Huiyuan Food & Beverage Group Co.,Ltd.	Beijing	Beijing	(010)60483366		Foreign Funded				Fruit & Vegetable Juice Drink
北京汇源食品饮料有限公司(1994)	北京市	北京市	(010)60483355	720	外商投资	556,695	81,758(1)	998,594	果蔬汁饮料
Guangzhou A.S.Watson Food & Beverage Co.,Ltd.	Guangzhou	Guangdong	(020)82222333		Overseas Chinese-funded				Soft Drink
广州屈臣氏食品饮料有限公司(1994)	广州市	广东省	(020)82213760	452	港澳台资	320,157	45,417(3)	439,223	软饮料
Xiamen Huierkang Food Co.,Ltd.	Xiamen	Fujian	(0592)7157504		Overseas Chinese-funded				Red Apple
厦门惠尔康食品有限公司(1992)	厦门市	福建省	(0592)7155765	327	港澳台资	284,915	3,450(39)	254,287	红苹果
Beibing Xinyuan Food & Beverage Co., Ltd.	Beijing	Beijing	(010)60691688		Collective-owned				Soft Drink
北京新源食品饮料有限公司(1998)	北京市	北京市	(010)60698328	168	集体企业	257,170	24,120(6)	383,954	软饮料
Xiamen Tongmao Canning Factory Co.,Ltd.	Xiamen	Fujian	(0592)7176588		Foreign Funded				Mixed Congee
厦门同茂食品罐头有限公司(1990)	厦门市	福建省	(0592)7176000	577	外商投资	217,299	4,114(36)	175,423	八宝粥
Shanghai Suntory-maling foods Co., Ltd.	Shanghai	Shanghai	(021)52340138		Foreign Funded				Soft Drink
上海三得利梅林食品有限公司(1995)	上海市	上海市	(021)52340375	706	外商投资	216,700	6,699(23)	230,050	软饮料
Yantai North Andre Juice Co.,Ltd.	Yantai	Shandong	(0535)4218988		Foreign Funded				Apple Juice
烟台北方安德利果汁有限公司(1996)	烟台市	山东省	(0535)4218858	100	外商投资	194,571	43,170(4)	380,895	苹果青汁
Shenhui Drink (Shandou) Ltd. Company	Shantou	Guangdong	(0754)7393389		Others				Soft Drink
深晖饮料(汕头)有限公司(1995)	汕头市	广东省	(0754)7391485	46	其他企业	189,959	1,353(69)	108,584	软饮料
Shantou H.N.Z Lolo Southern Co., Ltd.	Shantou	Guangdong	(0754)8268668		Overseas Chinese-funded				Almond Dew
汕头高新区露露南方有限公司(1996)	汕头市	广东省	(0754)8167663	190	港澳台资	133,419	1,422(67)	112,326	杏仁露
Dongshan LvYuan Food Co.,Ltd.	Zhangzhou	Fujian	(0596)5887960		Overseas Chinese-funded				Drink
东山绿沅食品有限公司(2000)	漳州市	福建省	(0596)5887055	85	港澳台资	124,143	7,982(20)	114,447	饮料

Top 10 Cities by Revenue 销售收入排名前10位城市	Province 省	Market share 市场份额 (%)	Number of firms 企业个数
Beijing 北京市	Beijing 北京市	14.04	11
Shanghai 上海市	Shanghai 上海市	7.33	8
Xiamen 厦门市	Fujian 福建省	6.39	5
Weihai 威海市	Shandong 山东省	5.39	5
Guangzhou 广州市	Guangdong 广东省	5.12	5
Yantai 烟台市	Shandong 山东省	4.71	7
Shantou 汕头市	Guangdong 广东省	3.52	2
Tianjin 天津市	Tianjin 天津市	3.30	11
Dezhou 德州市	Shandong 山东省	3.11	7
Shenzhen 深圳市	Guangdong 广东省	3.10	3

10 Major Wholesalers 十家主要批发商	City 城市	Province 省	Telephone/Fax 电话/传真
Beijing Chaoyang Non-Staple Foodstuffs General Company	Beijing	Beijing	(010)65016285
北京朝阳副食品总公司	北京市	北京市	(010)65016285
Beijing Sugar,Cigarette & Wine Company	Beijing	Beijing	(010)67210304
北京市糖业烟酒公司	北京市	北京市	(010)67210310
Shanghai Sugar Cigarette & Wine (Group) Co.,Ltd.	Shanghai	Shanghai	(021)63224190
上海市糖业烟酒(集团)有限公司	上海市	上海市	(021)63223169
Jiangsu Sutang Sugar & Wine Co.,Ltd.	Nanjing	Jiangsu	(025)6661088
江苏苏糖糖酒食品有限公司	南京市	江苏省	(025)6661088
Fujian Commerce (Group) Co.,Ltd.	Fuzhou	Fujian	(0591)7847148
福建省商业（集团）有限责任公司	福州市	福建省	(0591)7847145
Yantai Changyu Pioneer Winer Co., Ltd.	Yantai	Shandong	(0535)6602730
烟台张裕葡萄酿酒股份有限公司	烟台市	山东省	(0535)6214078
BlueRibbon Beer Sale Co.,Ltd.	Zhaoqing	Guangdong	(0758)2862322
蓝带啤酒销售有限公司	肇庆市	广东省	(0758)2862424
Fujian Shenlong Development Co.,Ltd.	Fuzhou	Fujian	(0591)7503218
福建省神龙发展股份有限公司	福州市	福建省	(0591)7503068
Guangdong Sugar, Cigarette & Wine Group Company	Guangzhou	Guangdong	(020)83566131
广东省糖烟酒集团公司	广州市	广东省	(020)83561421
Shunde Daliang Sugar, Cigarette & Wine Co.,Ltd.	Shunde	Guangdong	(0765)2231804
顺德市大良区糖烟酒有限公司	顺德市	广东省	(0765)2222300

1524: Instant Drinks 固体饮料制造业

The industry accounts for 0.105% of the total revenue of China's industrial sector in 2002. The rate of return on assets is 10.34%. 80.82% of all firms in the industry made a profit while 19.18% had negative returns.The top province in terms of the industry's revenue is Jiangsu, accounting for 58.14% of the total revenue.
2002年本行业收入占全行业的0.105%，资产利润率为10.34%。80.82%的企业赢利，19.18%的企业亏损。收入最高的省为江苏省，占本行业的58.14%。

	Total number of firms 企业总数	Total number of employees 职工总数	Total revenue (Mil.RMB) 总销售收入(百万元)	Total profit (Mil.RMB) 总利润(百万元)	Return on assets 资产利润率 (%)	Return on equity 权益利润率 (%)	Labour productivity ('000 RMB/ worker) 劳动生产率(千元/人)	Debts/ assets 资产负债率 (%)	Total assets (Mil.RMB) 总资产(百万元)
Industry Overall 行业总体	73	22,385	11,314	913	10.34	17.51	126.06	40.97	8,832

	Number of firms 企业个数	Average number of employees 平均职工人数	Average revenue ('000 RMB) 平均销售收入（千元）	Average profit ('000 RMB) 平均利润（千元）	Return on assets 资产利润率 (%)	Return on equity 权益利润率 (%)	Labour productivity ('000 RMB/ worker) 劳动生产率(千元/人)	Debts/ assets 资产负债率 (%)	Average total assets ('000 RMB) 平均总资产（千元）
By ownership 产业所有权									
State-owned 国有	10	223	66,589	390	1.70		61.08	123.83	23,000
Collective-owned 集体	10	91	17,686	701	10.88	50.44	59.99	78.43	6,446
Foreign & Overseas Chinese Funded 三资	17	261	179,331	15,441	8.12	14.86	152.92	45.36	190,135
By regional distribution 地区分布									
Central-North 华北	11	286	123,942	7,665	7.87	17.88	52.30	55.97	97,345
Beijing 北京	2	682	335,488	23,162	9.02	23.75	21.35	62.01	256,688
Tianjin 天津	3	228	149,730	5,125	3.14	6.17	165.15	49.12	163,261
Hebei 河北	5	157	44,309	4,294	36.29	98.55	90.49	63.18	11,833
Shanxi 山西									
Inner Mongolia 内蒙古	1	310	21,655	1,147	13.54	21.14	30.74	35.94	8,472
Northeast 东北	4	351	18,172	-26	-0.06	-0.22	13.04	74.71	46,877
Liaoning 辽宁	2	168	22,137	433	2.73	4.25	28.68	35.69	15,842
Jilin 吉林	1	98	3,653	-971	-15.52	-409.70	3.99	96.21	6,258
Heilongjiang 黑龙江	1	970	24,759				8.54	82.07	149,565
Central-East 华东	24	385	295,629	19,212	10.99	18.38	188.59	40.20	174,745
Shanghai 上海	3	139	99,403	-2,406	-2.35		112.85	103.84	102,507
Jiangsu 江苏	10	772	657,816	50,486	14.64	22.16	206.49	33.94	344,787
Zhejiang 浙江	5	87	20,213	868	5.86	9.62	81.11	39.17	14,821
Anhui 安徽									
Fujian 福建	3	167	33,641	-13,960	-18.89	-38.84	119.65	51.37	73,905
Jiangxi 江西	2	75	5,160	468	0.73	1.16	21.94	36.99	63,896
Shandong 山东	1	10	6,430	52	0.35	0.61	163.00	42.42	14,874
Central-South 中南	30	254	87,974	12,224	11.94	17.59	114.63	32.14	102,413
Henan 河南	4	47	8,263	1,520	88.12	189.97	52.33	53.62	1,725
Hubei 湖北	7	326	44,820	1,422	12.12	21.97	29.22	44.85	11,733
Hunan 湖南									
Guangdong 广东	9	339	211,625	37,439	12.72	17.88	223.66	28.86	294,356
Guangxi 广西	8	235	45,685	1,703	7.15	13.92	55.07	48.64	23,820
Hainan 海南	2	114	11,163	58	0.08	0.21	49.61	62.47	71,796
Southwest 西南	4	245	35,996	273	0.36	1.07	24.04	66.93	76,752
Chongqing 重庆									
Sichuan 四川	2	445	53,811	789	0.58	1.56	24.31	62.75	136,092
Guizhou 贵州									
Yunnan 云南	2	44	18,182	-243	-1.40	-328.38	21.34	99.57	17,412
Tibet 西藏									
Northwest 西北									
Shaanxi 陕西									
Gansu 甘肃									
Qinghai 青海									
Ningxia 宁夏									
Xinjiang 新疆									

Year 年份	Number of firms 企业个数	Rate of change 变化率 (%)	Number of employees 职工人数 (人)	Rate of change 变化率 (%)	Total revenue (Mil. RMB) 总销售收入 (百万元)	Rate of change 变化率 (%)	Total profit (Mil RMB) 总利润 (百万元)	Rate of change 变化率 (%)
2000	63		18,326		7,607		477	
2001	63	o	19,275	5.18	8,858	16.45	672	40.88
2002	73	15.87	22,385	16.13	11,314	27.73	913	35.86

Major Products 主要产品	Output 产量	Unit 单位

10 Main Firms with Maximal Revenue (year founded) 收入最大的十家主要企业（创办年份）	City 城市	Province 省	Telephone/fax 电话/传真	Number of employees 职工人数	Ownership 产业所有权	Revenue ('000 RMB) 销售收入(千元)	Profit('000 RMB) (rank) 利润(千元)(排名)	Total assets ('000 RMB) 总资产(千元)	Major products 主要产品
VeiVei Group	Xuzhou	Jiangsu	(0516)3299111		Joint Stock				Soft Drink
维维集团(1992)	徐州市	江苏省	(0516)2704888	6,812	股份制	6,016,724	491,024(1)	3,183,608	软饮料
Dongguan Nestle Co.,Ltd.	Dongguan	Guangdong	(0769)2404088		Foreign Funded				Solid Drink
东莞雀巢有限公司(1988)	东莞市	广东省	(0769)2402804	828	外商投资	1,023,198	222,718(2)	870,797	固体饮料
Beijing Coca-cola Beverage Co.,Ltd.	Beijing	Beijing	(010)67885588		Foreign Funded				Coca-cola
北京可口可乐饮料有限公司(1992)	北京市	北京市	(010)67880068	1,340	外商投资	650,084	46,289(5)	495,779	可口可乐
Guandong Strong Group Co.,Ltd.	Yangjiang	Guangdong	(0662)6617019		Private Owned				Fruit Jelly
阳东喜之郎实业有限公司(1999)	阳江市	广东省	(0662)6615078	1,500	私营企业	386,310	88,426(3)	981,505	果冻
Kraft Tianmei Food (Tianjin)Co.,Ltd.	Tianjin	Tianjin	(022)66204333		Foreign Funded				TANG Soft Powder Drink.TANG果珍
卡夫天美食品(天津)有限公司(1986)	天津市	天津市	(022)25323449	508	外商投资	379,750	58,705(4)	331,590	速溶饮品
Coca-cola Bottle Manufacturer (Dongguan) Co., Ltd.	Dongguan	Guangdong	(0769)2401678		Overseas Chinese-funded				Non Carbolic Acid Beverage非
可口可乐装瓶商生产（东莞）有限公司(1995)	东莞市	广东省	(0769)2402924	106	港澳台资	301,180	9,940(11)	270,490	碳酸饮料
Suizhou Food General Company	Suizhou	Hubei	(0722)3225528		State-owned				
随州市食品总公司(1984)	随州市	湖北省	(0722)3231441	1,369	国有企业	190,366	350(34)	53,163	
Guangxi Wuzhou Bingquan Industrial Stock Co., Ltd.	Wuzhou	Guangxi	(0774)5824028		Joint Stock				Solid Drink
广西梧州冰泉实业股份有限公司(1961)	梧州市	广西	(0774)5821545	1,007	股份制	163,521	4,460(16)	127,831	固体饮料
Nest Shanghai Co., Ltd.	Shanghai	Shanghai	(021)57741718		Foreign Funded				Solid Drink
上海雀巢有限公司(1994)	上海市	上海市	(021)57741706	170	外商投资	144,097	15,373(7)	125,796	固体饮料
Lipu Dafa Food & Beverage Co., Ltd.	Guilin	Guangxi	(0773)7212563		Private Owned				Solid Drink
荔浦县大发食品饮料有限公司(1992)	桂林市	广西		280	私营企业	100,967	5,962(13)	20,508	固体饮料

Top 10 Cities by Revenue 销售收入排名前10位城市	Province 省	Market share 市场份额 (%)	Number of firms 企业个数
Xuzhou 徐州市	Jiangsu 江苏省	57.06	3
Dongguan 东莞市	Guangdong 广东省	11.71	2
Beijing 北京市	Beijing 北京市	5.93	2
Tianjin 天津市	Tianjin 天津市	3.97	3
Yangjiang 阳江市	Guangdong 广东省	3.41	1
Shanghai 上海市	Shanghai 上海市	2.64	3
Shijiazhuang 石家庄市	Hebei 河北省	1.96	4
Suizhou 随州市	Hubei 湖北省	1.75	2
Guilin 桂林市	Guangxi 广西	1.71	6
Wuzhou 梧州市	Guangxi 广西	1.52	2

10 Major Wholesalers 十家主要批发商	City 城市	Province 省	Telephone/Fax 电话/传真
Beijing Chaoyang Non-Staple Foodstuffs General Company	Beijing	Beijing	(010)65016285
北京朝阳副食品总公司	北京市	北京市	(010)65016285
Beijing Sugar,Cigarette & Wine Company	Beijing	Beijing	(010)67210304
北京市糖业烟酒公司	北京市	北京市	(010)67210310
Shanghai Sugar Cigarette & Wine (Group) Co.,Ltd.	Shanghai	Shanghai	(021)63224190
上海市糖业烟酒(集团)有限公司	上海市	上海市	(021)63223169
Jiangsu Sutang Sugar & Wine Co.,Ltd.	Nanjing	Jiangsu	(025)6661088
江苏苏糖糖酒食品有限公司	南京市	江苏省	(025)6661088
Fujian Commerce (Group) Co.,Ltd.	Fuzhou	Fujian	(0591)7847148
福建省商业（集团）有限责任公司	福州市	福建省	(0591)7847145
Yantai Changyu Pioneer Winer Co., Ltd.	Yantai	Shandong	(0535)6602730
烟台张裕葡萄酿酒股份有限公司	烟台市	山东省	(0535)6214078
BlueRibbon Beer Sale Co.,Ltd.	Zhaoqing	Guangdong	(0758)2862322
蓝带啤酒销售有限公司	肇庆市	广东省	(0758)2862424
Fujian Shenlong Development Co.,Ltd.	Fuzhou	Fujian	(0591)7503218
福建省神龙发展股份有限公司	福州市	福建省	(0591)7503068
Guangdong Sugar, Cigarette & Wine Group Company	Guangzhou	Guangdong	(020)83566131
广东省糖烟酒集团公司	广州市	广东省	(020)83561421
Shunde Daliang Sugar, Cigarette & Wine Co.,Ltd.	Shunde	Guangdong	(0765)2231804
顺德市大良区糖烟酒有限公司	顺德市	广东省	(0765)2222300

1529: Other Soft Drinks 其他软饮料制造业

The industry accounts for 0.062% of the total revenue of China's industrial sector in 2002. The rate of return on assets is 8.74%. 85.29% of all firms in the industry made a profit while 14.71% had negative returns.The top province in terms of the industry's revenue is Guangdong, accounting for 36.20% of the total revenue.
2002年本行业收入占全行业的 0.062%，资产利润率为 8.74%。85.29%的企业赢利，14.71%的企业亏损。收入最高的省为广东省，占本行业的36.20%。

	Total number of firms 企业总数	Total number of employees 职工总数	Total revenue (Mil.RMB) 总销售收入 (百万元)	Total profit (Mil.RMB) 总利润 (百万元)	Return on assets 资产利润率 (%)	Return on equity 权益利润率 (%)	Labour productivity ('000 RMB/ worker) 劳动生产率 (千元/人)	Debts/ assets 资产负债率 (%)	Total assets (Mil.RMB) 总资产 (百万元)
Industry Overall 行业总体	102	20,172	6,666	659	8.74	19.59	130.98	55.39	7,536

	Number of firms 企业个数	Average number of employees 平均职工人数	Average revenue ('000 RMB) 平均销售收入 (千元)	Average profit ('000 RMB) 平均利润 (千元)	Return on assets 资产利润率 (%)	Return on equity 权益利润率 (%)	Labour productivity ('000 RMB/ worker) 劳动生产率 (千元/人)	Debts/ assets 资产负债率 (%)	Average total assets ('000 RMB) 平均总资产 (千元)
By ownership 产业所有权									
State-owned 国有	10	66	3,906	534	8.01		24.20	117.17	6,671
Collective-owned 集体	6	94	13,716	462	5.44	10.06	65.49	45.90	8,492
Foreign & Overseas Chinese Funded 三资	27	384	187,309	21,187	13.53	27.49	185.62	50.79	156,640
By regional distribution 地区分布									
Central-North 华北	20	114	42,747	4,155	10.37	17.73	200.25	41.52	40,068
Beijing 北京	1	390	455,891	26,353	8.10	10.99	756.48	26.26	325,188
Tianjin 天津	6	68	22,103	4,260	16.69	21.96	124.43	23.99	25,522
Hebei 河北	10	133	22,154	2,566	9.88	33.01	70.72	70.07	25,972
Shanxi 山西	2	49	20,382	2,736	9.49	17.78	139.98	46.63	28,824
Inner Mongolia 内蒙古	1	45	4,136	60	1.06	1.51	24.73	29.66	5,665
Northeast 东北	8	151	61,928	10,733	16.24	26.39	217.04	38.45	66,088
Liaoning 辽宁	3	202	134,658	24,798	21.34	32.89	351.47	35.13	116,218
Jilin 吉林	4	139	22,159	2,875	6.85	11.08	88.45	38.14	41,958
Heilongjiang 黑龙江	1	47	2,811	-35	-0.29		7.64	137.61	12,216
Central-East 华东	25	185	67,648	5,233	4.14	11.21	157.01	63.04	126,321
Shanghai 上海	2	151	7,027	2,770	0.36	1.02	-8.17	64.55	765,981
Jiangsu 江苏	5	103	101,941	11,090	10.40	32.84	228.85	68.32	106,580
Zhejiang 浙江	4	485	176,785	8,234	5.69	16.48	79.08	65.48	144,756
Anhui 安徽	2	235	64,825	14,392	27.90	29.50	116.07	5.43	51,579
Fujian 福建	7	121	34,830	513	0.95	2.50	449.15	61.89	53,818
Jiangxi 江西	2	20	175	7	0.45	1.32	-0.36	66.01	1,451
Shandong 山东	3	169	28,828	1,502	14.37	34.20	41.58	57.97	10,452
Central-South 中南	41	266	80,406	8,138	13.31	31.81	89.90	58.14	61,125
Henan 河南	8	73	6,487	645	6.74	56.07	22.40	87.97	9,558
Hubei 湖北	19	181	36,332	1,932	5.47	13.99	104.57	60.92	35,342
Hunan 湖南	3	300	10,604	308	1.59	2.00	12.84	20.49	19,397
Guangdong 广东	7	828	344,725	37,269	17.17	45.04	93.91	61.88	217,057
Guangxi 广西	2	58	43,720	9,073	13.89	15.33	360.54	9.40	65,327
Hainan 海南	2	34	11,050	5,925	23.74	35.41	142.61	32.96	24,959
Southwest 西南	6	179	52,347	4,398	5.05	7.61	198.78	33.64	87,121
Chongqing 重庆									
Sichuan 四川	4	180	63,760	5,144	5.23	7.96	172.30	34.33	98,350
Guizhou 贵州									
Yunnan 云南	2	177	29,521	2,907	4.50	6.57	252.50	31.55	64,663
Tibet 西藏									
Northwest 西北	2	50	6,765	-644	-6.64	-28.29	66.05	76.51	9,685
Shaanxi 陕西									
Gansu 甘肃	1	20	400	-483	-7.93	-87.50	25.45	90.94	6,090
Qinghai 青海									
Ningxia 宁夏									
Xinjiang 新疆	1	80	13,129	-804	-6.05	-20.11	76.20	69.89	13,280

1529: Other Soft Drinks 其他软饮料制造业

Year 年份	Number of firms 企业个数	Rate of change 变化率 (%)	Number of employees 职工人数 (人)	Rate of change 变化率 (%)	Total revenue (Mil. RMB) 总销售收入 (百万元)	Rate of change 变化率 (%)	Total profit (Mil RMB) 总利润 (百万元)	Rate of change 变化率 (%)
2000	116		22,450		6,375		282	
2001	102	-12.07	22,958	2.26	6,999	9.79	414	46.81
2002	102	o	20,172	-12.14	6,666	-4.76	659	59.18

Major Products 主要产品	Output 产量	Unit 单位
Soft Drink 软饮料	2,025	10,000 Tons 万吨

10 Main Firms with Maximal Revenue (year founded) 收入最大的十家主要企业（创办年份）	City 城市	Province 省	Telephone/fax 电话/传真	Number of employees 职工人数	Ownership 产业所有权	Revenue ('000 RMB) 销售收入 (千元)	Profit('000 RMB) (rank) 利润(千元) (排名)	Total assets ('000 RMB) 总资产 (千元)	Major products 主要产品
Robust (Guangdong) Food & Beverage Co.,Ltd.	Zhongshan	Guangdong	(0760)2101803		Foreign Funded				Lactic Acid Milk
乐百氏(广东)食品饮料有限公司(2000)	中山市	广东省		3,188	外商投资	1,165,187	108,207(2)	549,802	乳酸奶
Guangzhou Tingjin Food Co., Ltd.	Guangzhou	Guangdong	(020)82268125		Overseas Chinese-funded				Drink
广州市顶津食品有限公司(1995)	广州市	广东省	(020)82268251		港澳台资	967,552	126018(1)	693,314	饮料
Hangzhou Tingjin Food Co., Ltd.	Hangzhou	Zhejiang	(0571)86910856		Overseas Chinese-funded				Ice Black Tea Drink冰
杭州顶津食品有限公司(1996)	杭州市	浙江省	(0571)86910837	1,606	港澳台资	637,009	31,233(5)	437,642	红茶饮品
Nanjing Wang Wang Food Co., Ltd.	Nanjing	Jiangsu	(025)2101668		Foreign Funded				WangZai Milk
南京旺旺食品有限公司(1995)	南京市	江苏省	(025)2101732	110	外商投资	390,520	62,930(4)	330,740	旺仔牛奶
Shenyang Tingjin Food Co.,Ltd.	Shenyang	Liaoning	(024)23512242		Overseas Chinese-funded				Non-Alcohol Drink无
沈阳顶津食品有限公司(1995)	沈阳市	辽宁省	(024)23510165	525	港澳台资	388,133	71,994(3)	340,243	酒精饮料
Junyao Group Dairy Industry Co.,Ltd.	Yichang	Hubei	(0717)7826858		Joint Stock				Milk Products
均瑶集团乳业股份有限公司(1999)	宜昌市	湖北省	(0717)7833888	1,200	股份制	252,083	20,038(11)	268,378	乳品
Chengdu Jule Enterprise Group Co., Ltd.	Chengdu	Sichuan	(028)82687284		Joint Stock				Drink
成都菊乐企业集团股份有限公司(1993)	成都市	四川省	(028)85069113	450	股份制	139,807	5,269(21)	150,454	饮料
Wahaha Group Caohu Co., Ltd.	Chaohu	Anhui	(0565)2341000		Foreign Funded				Purified Water
娃哈哈集团巢湖市有限责任公司(1998)	巢湖市	安徽省	(0565)2341000	400	外商投资	122,710	28,611(6)	97,599	纯净水
Qujiang Wahaha Drink Co., Ltd	Shaoguan	Guangdong	(0751)6641855		Overseas Chinese-funded				Drink
曲江娃哈哈饮料有限公司(2000)	韶关市	广东省	(0751)6640420	468	港澳台资	116,291	24,158(10)	46,353	饮料
Wuhan GuangMing Milk Products Co., Ltd.	Wuhan	Hubei	(027)83892495		Limited-Liability				Dairy Products
武汉光明乳品有限公司(1998)	武汉市	湖北省		200	有限公司	98,332	1,741(30)	49,742	乳制品

Top 10 Cities by Revenue 销售收入排名前10位城市	Province 省	Market share 市场份额 (%)	Number of firms 企业个数
Zhongshan 中山市	Guangdong 广东省	17.57	2
Guangzhou 广州市	Guangdong 广东省	14.52	1
Hangzhou 杭州市	Zhejiang 浙江省	10.46	3
Beijing 北京市	Beijing 北京市	6.84	1
Nanjing 南京市	Jiangsu 江苏省	6.03	2
Shenyang 沈阳市	Liaoning 辽宁省	5.82	1
Yichang 宜昌市	Hubei 湖北省	3.93	2
Wuhan 武汉市	Hubei 湖北省	3.41	6
Fuzhou 福州市	Fujian 福建省	2.60	3
Chengdu 成都市	Sichuan 四川省	2.32	2

10 Major Wholesalers 十家主要批发商	City 城市	Province 省	Telephone/Fax 电话/传真
Beijing Chaoyang Non-Staple Foodstuffs General Company	Beijing	Beijing	(010)65016285
北京朝阳副食品总公司	北京市	北京市	(010)65016285
Beijing Sugar,Cigarette & Wine Company	Beijing	Beijing	(010)67210304
北京市糖业烟酒公司	北京市	北京市	(010)67210310
Shanghai Sugar Cigarette & Wine (Group) Co.,Ltd.	Shanghai	Shanghai	(021)63224190
上海市糖业烟酒(集团)有限公司	上海市	上海市	(021)63223169
Jiangsu Sutang Sugar & Wine Co.,Ltd.	Nanjing	Jiangsu	(025)6661088
江苏苏糖糖酒食品有限公司	南京市	江苏省	(025)6661088
Fujian Commerce (Group) Co.,Ltd.	Fuzhou	Fujian	(0591)7847148
福建省商业（集团）有限责任公司	福州市	福建省	(0591)7847145
Yantai Changyu Pioneer Winer Co., Ltd.	Yantai	Shandong	(0535)6602730
烟台张裕葡萄酿酒股份有限公司	烟台市	山东省	(0535)6214078
BlueRibbon Beer Sale Co.,Ltd.	Zhaoqing	Guangdong	(0758)2862322
蓝带啤酒销售有限公司	肇庆市	广东省	(0758)2862424
Fujian Shenlong Development Co.,Ltd.	Fuzhou	Fujian	(0591)7503218
福建省神龙发展股份有限公司	福州市	福建省	(0591)7503068
Guangdong Sugar, Cigarette & Wine Group Company	Guangzhou	Guangdong	(020)83566131
广东省糖烟酒集团公司	广州市	广东省	(020)83561421
Shunde Daliang Sugar, Cigarette & Wine Co.,Ltd.	Shunde	Guangdong	(0765)2231804
顺德市大良区糖烟酒有限公司	顺德市	广东省	(0765)2222300

1550: Tea 制茶业

The industry accounts for 0.051% of the total revenue of China's industrial sector in 2002. The rate of return on assets is 2.61%. 76.53% of all firms in the industry made a profit while 23.47% had negative returns.The top province in terms of the industry's revenue is Zhejiang, accounting for 29.47% of the total revenue.
2002年本行业收入占全行业的0.051%，资产利润率为2.61%。76.53%的企业赢利，23.47%的企业亏损。收入最高的省为浙江省，占本行业的29.47%。

	Total number of firms 企业总数	Total number of employees 职工总数	Total revenue (Mil.RMB) 总销售收入（百万元）	Total profit (Mil.RMB) 总利润（百万元）	Return on assets 资产利润率（%）	Return on equity 权益利润率（%）	Labour productivity ('000 RMB/ worker) 劳动生产率（千元/人）	Debts/ assets 资产负债率（%）	Total assets (Mil.RMB) 总资产（百万元）
Industry Overall 行业总体	375	37,855	5,444	173	2.61	7.01	38.42	62.82	6,653

	Number of firms 企业个数	Average number of employees 平均职工人数	Average revenue ('000 RMB) 平均销售收入（千元）	Average profit ('000 RMB) 平均利润（千元）	Return on assets 资产利润率（%）	Return on equity 权益利润率（%）	Labour productivity ('000 RMB/ worker) 劳动生产率（千元/人）	Debts/ assets 资产负债率（%）	Average total assets ('000 RMB) 平均总资产（千元）
By ownership 产业所有权									
State-owned 国有	96	105	5,356	-418	-3.63	-63.64	14.02	94.30	11,510
Collective-owned 集体	68	131	18,442	712	6.05	13.94	38.36	56.59	11,775
Foreign & Overseas Chinese Funded 三资	26	86	31,770	3,475	7.07	13.08	115.30	45.96	49,168
By regional distribution 地区分布									
Central-North 华北	5	57	10,364	1,126	14.64	33.44	82.89	56.23	7,694
Beijing 北京	3	65	14,961	1,428	12.77	31.58	107.91	59.55	11,181
Tianjin 天津	1	22	1,037	195	11.05	18.47	27.86	40.17	1,765
Hebei 河北	1	67	5,900	1,150	36.39	51.99	27.78	30.00	3,160
Shanxi 山西									
Inner Mongolia 内蒙古									
Northeast 东北	1	93	9,881	839	0.66	1.78	88.63	62.92	127,224
Liaoning 辽宁									
Jilin 吉林									
Heilongjiang 黑龙江	1	93	9,881	839	0.66	1.78	88.63	62.92	127,224
Central-East 华东	194	80	15,571	388	2.43	6.73	42.55	63.80	15,920
Shanghai 上海	2	80	16,589	-5,076	-21.02		-48.26	113.86	24,148
Jiangsu 江苏	17	103	18,374	720	12.72	30.96	40.89	58.89	5,656
Zhejiang 浙江	70	55	22,921	529	2.90	8.17	65.62	64.51	18,254
Anhui 安徽	18	107	9,038	21	0.17	0.50	25.71	66.01	12,445
Fujian 福建	68	86	9,793	322	2.79	5.53	35.27	49.59	11,554
Jiangxi 江西	15	92	3,459	-124	-0.74		18.68	117.89	16,687
Shandong 山东	4	152	47,552	3,913	3.85	7.66	101.62	49.73	101,574
Central-South 中南	107	139	14,492	308	1.91	4.37	31.67	56.23	16,120
Henan 河南	5	66	12,211	537	2.31	4.32	86.44	46.70	23,296
Hubei 湖北	31	165	13,727	555	3.59	6.43	33.12	44.11	15,437
Hunan 湖南	36	164	15,537	321	2.24	9.74	28.50	76.97	14,312
Guangdong 广东	22	104	18,148	344	1.83	3.69	36.62	50.31	18,780
Guangxi 广西	8	81	9,979	-69	-0.47	-1.45	29.31	67.32	14,669
Hainan 海南	5	125	5,134	-1,098	-6.53	-8.69	5.21	24.84	16,817
Southwest 西南	63	101	8,607	-127	-0.57	-2.11	28.34	73.06	22,293
Chongqing 重庆	8	52	8,784	112	0.60	2.90	53.05	79.42	18,690
Sichuan 四川	23	78	10,324	138	0.52	1.28	47.98	59.06	26,383
Guizhou 贵州	6	121	2,557	19	0.31	1.00	5.63	69.64	6,120
Yunnan 云南	26	131	8,429	-468	-1.99	-13.82	19.80	85.60	23,516
Tibet 西藏									
Northwest 西北	5	133	53,706	13,366	24.79	42.22	163.45	41.29	53,919
Shaanxi 陕西	3	204	88,342	22,267	24.99	42.63	172.26	41.39	89,108
Gansu 甘肃	2	26	1,753	15	1.28	1.83	59.60	30.25	1,136
Qinghai 青海									
Ningxia 宁夏									
Xinjiang 新疆									

Year 年份	Number of firms 企业个数	Rate of change 变化率(%)	Number of employees 职工人数(人)	Rate of change 变化率(%)	Total revenue (Mil. RMB) 总销售收入(百万元)	Rate of change 变化率(%)	Total profit (Mil RMB) 总利润(百万元)	Rate of change 变化率(%)
2000	315		43,281		4,396		12	
2001	332	5.40	38,994	-9.91	4,469	1.66	80	566.67
2002	375	12.95	37,855	-2.92	5,444	21.82	173	116.25

Major Products 主要产品	Output 产量	Unit 单位
Refined Tea 精制茶	33	10,000 Tons 万吨

10 Main Firms with Maximal Revenue (year founded) 收入最大的十家主要企业（创办年份）	City 城市	Province 省	Telephone/fax 电话/传真	Number of employees 职工人数	Ownership 产业所有权	Revenue ('000 RMB) 销售收入(千元)	Profit('000 RMB) (rank) 利润(千元)(排名)	Total assets ('000 RMB) 总资产(千元)	Major products 主要产品
Jiangsu Suyang Crude Medicines Group Company	Yancheng	Jiangsu	(0515)2632001		Collective-owned				Chrysanthemun Tea
江苏苏洋药材集团公司(1997)	盐城市	江苏省	(0515)2632001	320	集体企业	168,560	5,680(6)	32,240	菊花茶
Zhejiang Waha Export Tea Factory	Shaoxing	Zhejiang	(0575)3049788		Private Enterprises				Tea
浙江华发出口茶厂(1995)	绍兴市	浙江省	(0575)3346802	95	私营独资	156,837	1,476(29)	86,709	茶叶
Qingdao Dingyi Food Co., Ltd.	Qingdao	Shandong	(0532)8703908		Foreign Funded				Ice Black Tea Drink冰
青岛顶益食品有限公司(1997)	青岛市	山东省	(0532)8703908	384	外商投资	149,289	8,704(3)	334,188	红茶饮品
Guangdong Guobin Group Company	Chaozhou	Guangdong	(0768)7600958		Collective-owned				Tea
广东国宾集团公司(1993)	潮州市	广东省	(0768)7600022	480	集体企业	147,590	9,830(2)	80,570	茶叶
Shantou Great Inpression(Group) Co.,Ltd.	Shantou	Guangdong	(0661)2212063		Limited-Liability				Great Impression Reducing-weight Tea大印
潮阳市大印象（集团）有限公司(1996)	汕头市	广东省	(0661)2213389	298	有限公司	106,179	4,121(10)	185,574	象减肥茶
Ningbo RuiLong Tea Co., Ltd.	Ningbo	Zhejiang	(0574)62779494		Limited-Liability				Tea
宁波瑞龙茶业有限公司(1993)	宁波市	浙江省	(0574)62779045	104	有限公司	97,771	1,354(33)	74,813	茶叶
Xianyin Lanling Tea Factory	Yueyang	Hunan	(0730)2380268		Collective-owned				Tea
湘阴县兰岭茶厂(2000)	岳阳市	湖南省	(0730)2380258	158	集体企业	90,123	4,475(7)	47,290	茶叶
Guangdong Tea Import & Export Corp. NO. 1 Tea Factory	Guangzhou	Guangdong	(020)84331881		State-owned				Refined Tea
广东茶叶进出口公司一茶厂(1954)	广州市	广东省	(020)84367747	169	国有企业	66,668	-	29,471	精制茶
Hunan Changsha Tea Factory	Changsha	Hunan	(0731)4485017		State-owned				Refined Tea
湖南省长沙茶厂(1950)	长沙市	湖南省	(0731)4485690	439	国有企业	65,825	826(58)	91,683	精制茶
Hunan Linxiang Tea Group	Yueyang	Hunan	(0730)3722794		Collective-owned				
湖南临湘市茶叶集团(1999)	岳阳市	湖南省		795	集体企业	65,400	410(98)	4,698	

Top 10 Cities by Revenue 销售收入排名前10位城市	Province 省	Market share 市场份额(%)	Number of firms 企业个数
Shaoxing 绍兴市	Zhejiang 浙江省	14.84	28
Hangzhou 杭州市	Zhejiang 浙江省	4.85	12
Xi'an 西安市	Shannxi 陕西省	4.61	1
Yueyang 岳阳市	Hunan 湖南省	4.48	8
Ningbo 宁波市	Zhejiang 浙江省	3.66	8
Fuzhou 福州市	Fujian 福建省	3.35	19
Yancheng 盐城市	Jiangsu 江苏省	3.28	2
Qingdao 青岛市	Shandong 山东省	3.18	2
Huzhou 湖州市	Zhejiang 浙江省	3.07	11
Quanzhou 泉州市	Fujian 福建省	3.05	11

10 Major Wholesalers 十家主要批发商	City 城市	Province 省	Telephone/Fax 电话/传真
Shanghai Tea Import & Export Company	Shanghai	Shanghai	(021)65178888
上海茶叶进出口公司	上海市	上海市	(021)65161887
China Tuhsu Zhejiang Tea Imp. & Exp. Corp.	Hangzhou	Zhejiang	(0571)87069835
中国土产畜产浙江茶叶进出口公司	杭州市	浙江省	(0571)87075320
Shandong Suger,Wine & Tea Company	Jinan	Shandong	(0531)8559419
山东省糖酒茶叶公司	济南市	山东省	(0531)6559298
China Tuhsu Guangdong Tea Imp. & Exp. Corp.	Guangzhou	Guangdong	(020)38801465
中国土产畜产广东茶叶进出口公司	广州市	广东省	(020)38802270
China Tea Co.,Ltd.	Beijing	Beijing	(010)64248899
中国茶叶股份有限公司	北京市	北京市	(010)64204101
Fujian Tea Import & Export Co.,Ltd.	Fuzhou	Fujian	(0591)7853475
福建茶叶进出口有限责任公司	福州市	福建省	(0591)7853402
Ningbo Tea United Company	Ningbo	Zhejiang	(0574)87605142
宁波市茶叶联合公司	宁波市	浙江省	(0574)87605121
Xiamen Tea Import & Export Co.,Ltd.	Xiamen	Fujian	(0592)5111961
厦门茶叶进出口有限公司	厦门市	福建省	(0592)5077202
Chongqing Tobacco Company Wanzhou Branch	Chongqing	Chongqing	(023)58210695
重庆市烟草公司万州分公司	重庆市	重庆市	(023)58228695
China Tuhsu Yunnan Tea Imp. & Exp. Corp.	Kunming	Yunnan	(0871)7190065
中国土产畜产云南茶叶进出口公司	昆明市	云南省	(0871)7182658

1590: Other Beverages 其他饮料制造业

The industry accounts for 0.098% of the total revenue of China's industrial sector in 2002. The rate of return on assets is 13.89%. 82.00% of all firms in the industry made a profit while 18.00% had negative returns.The top province in terms of the industry's revenue is Zhejiang, accounting for 71.46% of the total revenue.
2002年本行业收入占全行业的 0.098%，资产利润率为 13.89%。82.00%的企业赢利，18.00%的企业亏损。收入最高的省为浙江省，占本行业的71.46%。

	Total number of firms 企业总数	Total number of employees 职工总数	Total revenue (Mil.RMB) 总销售收入（百万元）	Total profit (Mil.RMB) 总利润（百万元）	Return on assets 资产利润率（%）	Return on equity 权益利润率（%）	Labour productivity ('000 RMB/worker) 劳动生产率（千元/人）	Debts/assets 资产负债率（%）	Total assets (Mil.RMB) 总资产（百万元）
Industry Overall 行业总体	100	14,104	10,562	1,453	13.89	24.36	249.16	42.97	10,464

	Number of firms 企业个数	Average number of employees 平均职工人数	Average revenue ('000 RMB) 平均销售收入（千元）	Average profit ('000 RMB) 平均利润（千元）	Return on assets 资产利润率（%）	Return on equity 权益利润率（%）	Labour productivity ('000 RMB/worker) 劳动生产率（千元/人）	Debts/assets 资产负债率（%）	Average total assets ('000 RMB) 平均总资产（千元）
By ownership 产业所有权									
State-owned 国有	15	63	6,067	199	1.02	2.73	35.02	62.61	19,452
Collective-owned 集体	16	75	17,923	786	9.69	46.23	79.73	79.03	8,111
Foreign & Overseas Chinese Funded 三资	29	136	61,928	6,925	6.45	15.43	142.67	58.19	107,349
By regional distribution 地区分布									
Central-North 华北	9	102	63,162	12,699	7.39	21.83	222.97	66.12	171,748
Beijing 北京	4	72	121,039	26,168	7.19	21.33	623.02	66.31	364,095
Tianjin 天津	3	175	8,369	737	3.04	11.36	14.82	73.20	24,220
Hebei 河北	2	54	29,596	3,704	44.38	54.92	169.25	19.19	8,347
Shanxi 山西									
Inner Mongolia 内蒙古									
Northeast 东北	6	79	8,671	1,434	3.57	5.35	32.05	33.31	40,165
Liaoning 辽宁	5	75	10,336	1,721	3.76	5.56	40.42	32.25	45,711
Jilin 吉林	1	102	350				1.41	52.90	12,435
Heilongjiang 黑龙江									
Central-East 华东	28	261	293,953	43,827	18.34	28.10	371.30	34.72	238,954
Shanghai 上海	4	91	27,149	-2,501	-4.09	-5.46	70.96	25.13	61,212
Jiangsu 江苏	8	134	43,940	2,506	8.47	21.79	64.51	61.12	29,582
Zhejiang 浙江	5	925	1,509,605	241,874	20.22	30.43	549.17	33.57	1,196,501
Anhui 安徽	2	261	6,775	275	4.58	8.37	10.54	45.30	5,993
Fujian 福建	2	55	18,862	43	0.10	0.14	77.75	31.35	43,349
Jiangxi 江西	3	39	13,056	155	1.27	1.64	103.39	22.40	12,208
Shandong 山东	4	124	33,025	1,659	7.26	27.92	105.09	73.99	22,848
Central-South 中南	46	99	33,628	1,531	3.93	8.92	115.64	55.89	38,907
Henan 河南	10	47	8,529	661	9.05	21.63	65.80	58.13	7,305
Hubei 湖北	6	95	36,513	212	0.45	0.64	194.48	28.96	46,708
Hunan 湖南	3	227	172,101	13,029	7.03	15.81	183.19	55.56	185,413
Guangdong 广东	21	117	31,466	1,054	3.17	11.08	93.92	71.40	33,265
Guangxi 广西	5	61	12,118	220	0.65	1.07	89.22	38.83	33,662
Hainan 海南	1	67	4,850	217	1.63	2.21	33.12	26.43	13,317
Southwest 西南	4	99	24,068	7,955	59.11	82.50	78.93	28.36	13,457
Chongqing 重庆									
Sichuan 四川	1	302	77,244	32,760	82.84	94.29	81.00	12.14	39,546
Guizhou 贵州	2	22	8,535	-49	-0.98	-7.03	107.68	86.13	4,971
Yunnan 云南									
Tibet 西藏	1	50	1,957	-845	-19.46	-34.60	41.14	43.76	4,342
Northwest 西北	7	64	9,697	169	0.83	1.35	51.26	38.74	20,443
Shaanxi 陕西									
Gansu 甘肃	5	50	2,794	-1,074	-7.65	-12.96	22.59	40.96	14,040
Qinghai 青海									
Ningxia 宁夏	2	102	26,955	3,278	8.99	14.18	86.28	36.60	36,451
Xinjiang 新疆									

1590: Other Beverages 其他饮料制造业

Year 年份	Number of firms 企业个数	Rate of change 变化率 (%)	Number of employees 职工人数 (人)	Rate of change 变化率 (%)	Total revenue (Mil. RMB) 总销售收入 (百万元)	Rate of change 变化率 (%)	Total profit (Mil RMB) 总利润 (百万元)	Rate of change 变化率 (%)
2000	125		23,178		10,207		1,140	
2001	114	-8.80	16,900	-27.09	10,255	0.47	1,220	7.02
2002	100	-12.28	14,104	-16.54	10,562	2.99	1,453	19.10

Major Products 主要产品	Output 产量	Unit 单位

10 Main Firms with Maximal Revenue (year founded) 收入最大的十家主要企业（创办年份）	City 城市	Province 省	Telephone/fax 电话/传真	Number of employees 职工人数	Ownership 产业所有权	Revenue ('000 RMB) 销售收入 (千元)	Profit('000 RMB) (rank) 利润(千元) (排名)	Total assets ('000 RMB) 总资产 (千元)	Major products 主要产品
Hangzhou Wahaha Group Co.,Ltd.	Hangzhou	Zhejiang	(0571)86093933		Limited-Liability				Contained Milk Drink
杭州娃哈哈集团有限公司(1987)	杭州市	浙江省	(0571)86951532	4,369	有限公司	7,501,720	1,208,045(1)	5,937,413	含乳饮料
Redbull Vitamin Drink Co.,Ltd.	Beijing	Beijing	(010)61667094		Foreign Funded				Vitamin Drink维
红牛维他命饮料有限公司(1997)	北京市	北京市	(010)61667355	154	外商投资	407,410	102,026(2)	1,249,775	他命饮料
Changsha Want Want Food Co.,Ltd.	Changsha	Hunan	(0731)8063111		Overseas Chinese-funded				Drink
长沙旺旺食品有限公司(1995)	长沙市	湖南省	(0731)8063116	420	港澳台资	305,411	37,663(3)	410,627	饮料
Guangdong Shibabao medicine Health Products Co.,Ltd.	Maoming	Guangdong	(0668)6613618		Overseas Chinese-funded				Life NO.1
广东十八宝医药保健品有限公司(1995)	茂名市	广东省	(0668)6613782	350	港澳台资	303,123	213(46)	136,561	生命一号
Guangyuan Wahaha Guangfa Drink Co., Ltd.	Guangyuan	Sichuan	(0839)3604655		Foreign Funded				Calcium Milk
广元娃哈哈广发饮料有限公司(1999)	广元市	四川省	(0839)3422428	302	外商投资	77,244	32,760(4)	39,546	钙奶
Shanghai Nongle Biological Products Stock Co., Ltd.	Shanghai	Shanghai	(021)57744161		Joint Stock				Drink
上海农乐生物制品股份有限公司(1981)	上海市	上海市	(021)57744158	196	股份制	69,232	-	130,488	饮料
Guangzhou Zhujiang Meileduo Drink (Hongkong) Co.,Ltd.	Guangzhou	Guangdong	(020)84697583		Overseas Chinese-funded				Lactobacilus Milk多活性
广州珠江美乐多饮品(香港)有限公司(1992)	广州市	广东省		132	港澳台资	58,402	15,678(6)	109,052	乳酸菌奶
Beijing Hairun Biological Products Co., Ltd.	Beijing	Beijing	(010)61666088		Foreign Funded				Biotic Products
北京海润生物制品有限公司(1998)	北京市	北京市	(010)61668217	62	外商投资	54,350	2,350(18)	193,200	生物制品
Penglai Huatai Health Products Co., Ltd.	Yantai	Shandong	(0535)5630618		Limited-Liability				DHA
蓬莱华泰保健品有限公司(1998)	烟台市	山东省	(0535)5656890	99	有限公司	50,250	2,940(13)	37,840	DHA心脑灵
Zhongshan Renhe Health Products Co., Ltd.	Zhongshan	Guangdong	(0760)8508149		Limited-Liability				Nutrition Food营养
中山市仁和保健品有限公司(1996)	中山市	广东省	(0760)8508146	58	有限公司	49,677	2,579(15)	34,038	滋补食品

Top 10 Cities by Revenue 销售收入排名前10位城市	Province 省	Market share 市场份额 (%)	Number of firms 企业个数
Hangzhou 杭州市	Zhejiang 浙江省	71.02	1
Changsha 长沙市	Hunan 湖南省	4.84	2
Beijing 北京市	Beijing 北京市	4.58	4
Maoming 茂名市	Guangdong 广东省	3.11	2
Xuzhou 徐州市	Jiangsu 江苏省	1.81	1
Wuhan 武汉市	Hubei 湖北省	1.74	2
Nanjing 南京市	Jiangsu 江苏省	1.21	3
Yantai 烟台市	Shandong 山东省	1.20	3
Guangzhou 广州市	Guangdong 广东省	1.11	7
Shanghai 上海市	Shanghai 上海市	1.03	4

10 Major Wholesalers 十家主要批发商	City 城市	Province 省	Telephone/Fax 电话/传真
Beijing Chaoyang Non-Staple Foodstuffs General Company	Beijing	Beijing	(010)65016285
北京朝阳副食品总公司	北京市	北京市	(010)65016285
Beijing Sugar,Cigarette & Wine Company	Beijing	Beijing	(010)67210304
北京市糖业烟酒公司	北京市	北京市	(010)67210310
Shanghai Sugar Cigarette & Wine (Group) Co.,Ltd.	Shanghai	Shanghai	(021)63224190
上海市糖业烟酒(集团)有限公司	上海市	上海市	(021)63223169
Jiangsu Sutang Sugar & Wine Co.,Ltd.	Nanjing	Jiangsu	(025)6661088
江苏苏糖糖酒食品有限公司	南京市	江苏省	(025)6661088
Fujian Commerce (Group) Co.,Ltd.	Fuzhou	Fujian	(0591)7847148
福建省商业（集团）有限责任公司	福州市	福建省	(0591)7847145
Yantai Changyu Pioneer Winer Co., Ltd.	Yantai	Shandong	(0535)6602730
烟台张裕葡萄酿酒股份有限公司	烟台市	山东省	(0535)6214078
BlueRibbon Beer Sale Co.,Ltd.	Zhaoqing	Guangdong	(0758)2862322
蓝带啤酒销售有限公司	肇庆市	广东省	(0758)2862424
Fujian Shenlong Development Co.,Ltd.	Fuzhou	Fujian	(0591)7503218
福建省神龙发展股份有限公司	福州市	福建省	(0591)7503068
Guangdong Sugar, Cigarette & Wine Group Company	Guangzhou	Guangdong	(020)83566131
广东省糖烟酒集团公司	广州市	广东省	(020)83561421
Shunde Daliang Sugar, Cigarette & Wine Co.,Ltd.	Shunde	Guangdong	(0765)2231804
顺德市大良区糖烟酒有限公司	顺德市	广东省	(0765)2222300

1610: Tobacco Stemming and Redrying 烟叶复烤业

The industry accounts for 0.072% of the total revenue of China's industrial sector in 2002. The rate of return on assets is 4.07%. 85.90% of all firms in the industry made a profit while 14.10% had negative returns.The top province in terms of the industry's revenue is Yunnan, accounting for 30.37% of the total revenue.
2002年本行业收入占全行业的 0.072%，资产利润率为 4.07%。85.90%的企业赢利，14.10%的企业亏损。收入最高的省为云南省，占本行业的30.37%。

	Total number of firms 企业总数	Total number of employees 职工总数	Total revenue (Mil.RMB) 总销售收入（百万元）	Total profit (Mil.RMB) 总利润（百万元）	Return on assets 资产利润率 (%)	Return on equity 权益利润率 (%)	Labour productivity ('000 RMB/ worker) 劳动生产率（千元/人）	Debts/ assets 资产负债率 (%)	Total assets (Mil.RMB) 总资产（百万元）
Industry Overall 行业总体	78	26,786	7,727	470	4.07	13.20	143.78	69.17	11,555

	Number of firms 企业个数	Average number of employees 平均职工人数	Average revenue ('000 RMB) 平均销售收入（千元）	Average profit ('000 RMB) 平均利润（千元）	Return on assets 资产利润率 (%)	Return on equity 权益利润率 (%)	Labour productivity ('000 RMB/ worker) 劳动生产率（千元/人）	Debts/ assets 资产负债率 (%)	Average total assets ('000 RMB) 平均总资产（千元）
By ownership 产业所有权									
State-owned 国有	58	332	80,028	2,349	1.68	8.79	154.10	80.84	139,441
Collective-owned 集体	2	104	77,058	3,895	8.23		111.92	123.39	47,308
Foreign & Overseas Chinese Funded 三资	2	848	117,328	20,452	8.78	15.49	70.66	43.30	232,917
By regional distribution 地区分布									
Central-North 华北	1	236	19,504				30.97	70.79	31,302
Beijing 北京									
Tianjin 天津									
Hebei 河北									
Shanxi 山西	1	236	19,504				30.97	70.79	31,302
Inner Mongolia 内蒙古									
Northeast 东北	6	329	51,987	1,376	0.85	6.80	48.31	87.54	162,312
Liaoning 辽宁									
Jilin 吉林	3	187	21,811	278	0.56	3.21	42.90	82.47	49,470
Heilongjiang 黑龙江	3	471	82,163	2,473	0.90	7.78	50.46	88.45	275,153
Central-East 华东	13	298	157,044	20,543	14.56	32.64	117.14	55.38	141,063
Shanghai 上海									
Jiangsu 江苏									
Zhejiang 浙江									
Anhui 安徽	3	399	60,381	10,472	8.44	25.24	54.68	66.57	124,122
Fujian 福建	5	270	299,729	38,304	21.29	37.68	205.60	43.50	179,947
Jiangxi 江西	2	144	6,098	1,507	6.90	22.87	24.19	69.82	21,835
Shandong 山东	3	347	116,530	13,706	7.94	23.86	100.19	66.74	172,685
Central-South 中南	15	387	48,515	4,073	2.87	7.79	63.05	63.11	141,802
Henan 河南	7	415	32,595	4,137	3.23	9.53	48.95	66.05	127,921
Hubei 湖北	4	372	83,240	440	0.27	1.47	89.05	81.30	160,120
Hunan 湖南	2	305	42,310	7,213	4.44	10.45	74.63	57.54	162,524
Guangdong 广东	2	400	40,995	7,975	6.00	7.15	57.08	16.20	133,028
Guangxi 广西									
Hainan 海南									
Southwest 西南	34	411	131,452	3,943	2.18	7.58	207.06	71.28	181,195
Chongqing 重庆	2	419	64,347	5,437	2.93	9.04	47.28	67.58	185,549
Sichuan 四川	5	258	58,963	4,676	4.86	10.43	87.23	53.43	96,237
Guizhou 贵州	17	355	99,946	-4,167	-2.37	-12.89	162.28	81.64	176,047
Yunnan 云南	10	579	234,677	17,067	7.37	19.49	303.55	62.19	231,555
Tibet 西藏									
Northwest 西北	9	104	17,481	-19	-0.04	-0.29	40.65	86.17	47,627
Shaanxi 陕西	3	136	26,266	669	0.69	8.28	73.49	91.62	96,446
Gansu 甘肃	4	72	17,052	3	0.02	0.06	17.93	74.38	16,968
Qinghai 青海									
Ningxia 宁夏	1	33	3,428	-19	-0.12	-0.61	13.61	80.12	15,666
Xinjiang 新疆	1	210	6,898	-2,168	-3.89	-14.92	12.18	73.95	55,772

1610: Tobacco Stemming and Redrying 烟叶复烤业

Year 年份	Number of firms 企业个数	Rate of change 变化率 (%)	Number of employees 职工人数 (人)	Rate of change 变化率 (%)	Total revenue (Mil. RMB) 总销售收入 (百万元)	Rate of change 变化率 (%)	Total profit (Mil RMB) 总利润 (百万元)	Rate of change 变化率 (%)
2000	109		37,162		7,373		133	
2001	101	-7.34	30,855	-16.97	7,603	3.12	59	-55.64
2002	78	-22.77	26,786	-13.19	7,727	1.63	470	696.61

Major Products 主要产品	Output 产量	Unit 单位
Redried & Stemmed Tobacco Leaf 复烤烟叶	88	10,000 Tons 万吨

10 Main Firms with Maximal Revenue (year founded) 收入最大的十家主要企业（创办年份）	City 城市	Province 省	Telephone/ fax 电话/传真	Number of employees 职工人数	Ownership 产业所有权	Revenue ('000 RMB) 销售收入 (千元)	Profit('000 RMB) (rank) 利润(千元) (排名)	Total assets ('000 RMB) 总资产 (千元)	Major products 主要产品
Dali Tobacco Leaf Redried Factory	Dali	Yunnan	(0872)3121469		State-owned				Redried & Stemmed Tobacco Leaf
大理州复烤厂(1986)	大理州	云南省	(0872)3123039	208	国有企业	581,433	21,567(8)	324,451	复烤烟叶
Longyan Minte Tobacco Leaf Redried Co., Ltd.	Longyan	Fujian	(0597)2291807		Limited-Liability				Redried & Stemmed Tobacco Leaf
龙岩闽特烟叶复烤有限责任公司(2001)	龙岩市	福建省	(0597)2218345	45	有限公司	503,645	70,910(2)	214,243	复烤烟叶
Fujian Sanming Gold Leaf Redried Co., Ltd.	Sanming	Fujian	(0598)8311769		Limited-Liability				Tobacco Leaf
福建省三明金叶复烤有限公司(1998)	三明市	福建省	(0598)8310269	650	有限公司	476,788	92,390(1)	326,460	烟叶
Guizhou Bijie Tobacco Leaf Redried Factory	Bijie	Guizhou	(0857)8267449		State-owned				Tobacco Leaf
毕节地区烟叶复烤厂(1977)	毕节	贵州省	(0857)8267073	1,697	国有企业	452,576	23,097(7)	1,001,223	烟叶
Luxi Tobacco Leaf Redried Factory	Honghe	Yunnan	(0873)6621541		State-owned				Redried & Stemmed Tobacco Leaf
泸西烟叶复烤厂(1985)	红河州	云南省	(0873)6621541	120	国有企业	431,913	16,720(11)	333,672	复烤烟叶
Guizhou Zunyi Tobacco Co.,Ltd.	Zunyi	Guizhou	(0852)8642037		Joint Stock				Redried & Stemmed Tobacco Leaf
遵义烟叶有限责任公司(1999)	遵义市	贵州省	(0852)8642037	305	股份制	308,012	7,375(22)	200,912	复烤烟叶
Guizhou Nanming Tobacco Leaf Co., Ltd.	Guiyang	Guizhou	(0851)3929055		State-owned				Redried & Stemmed Tobacco Leaf
贵州南明烟叶有限责任公司(1998)	贵阳市	贵州省	(0851)3929055	816	国有企业	300,025	7,379(21)	350,743	复烤烟叶
Guizhou Shenyi Tobacco Leaf Redried Co., Ltd.	Zunyi	Guizhou	(0852)4251002		State-owned				Redried & Stemmed Tobacco Leaf
贵州申义烟叶复烤有限责任公司(1998)	遵义市	贵州省	(0852)4251245	448	国有企业	271,895	3,966(29)	172,814	复烤烟叶
Wenshan Tobacco Company	Wenshan	Yunnan	(0876)2184239		State-owned				Redried & Stemmed Tobacco Leaf
文山州烟草公司(1904)	文山州	云南省	(0876)2186870	619	国有企业	247,323	51,194(3)	266,301	复烤烟叶
Wenshan Tobacco Redrying Factory	Wenshan	Yunnan	(0876)2181902		State-owned				Redried & Stemmed Tobacco Leaf
云南烟草文山州复烤厂(1995)	文山州	云南省	(0876)2187771	456	国有企业	182,294	14,718(14)	266,228	复烤烟叶

Top 10 Cities by Revenue 销售收入排名前10位城市	Province 省	Market share 市场份额 (%)	Number of firms 企业个数
Zunyi 遵义市	Guizhou 贵州省	9.38	3
Sanming 三明市	Fujian 福建省	7.90	2
Kunming 昆明市	Yunnan 云南省	7.71	2
Dali 大理州	Yunnan 云南省	7.52	1
Longyan 龙岩市	Fujian 福建省	6.52	1
Bijie 毕节地区	Guizhou 贵州省	5.86	2
Honghe 红河州	Yunnan 云南省	5.59	1
Wenshan 文山州	Yunnan 云南省	5.56	2
Nanping 南平市	Fujian 福建省	4.98	2
Guiyang 贵阳市	Guizhou 贵州省	4.53	2

10 Major Wholesalers 十家主要批发商	City 城市	Province 省	Telephone/Fax 电话/传真
China Tobacco Leaf Production, Purchase & Sale Company	Beijing	Beijing	(010)63605152
中国烟叶生产购销公司	北京市	北京市	(010)63605913
China Tobacco Materials Corporation	Beijing	Beijing	(010)63601471
中国烟草物资公司	北京市	北京市	(010)63605214
Nanjing City Nanjing Cigarette Sale Co.,Ltd.	Nanjing	Jiangsu	(025)8187120
南京市南京烟销售有限公司	南京市	江苏省	(025)8888168
China Tobacco General Company Guangdong Branch	Guangzhou	Guangdong	(020)38803398
中国烟草总公司广东省公司	广州市	广东省	(020)38807898
Yunnan Tobacco Cigarette Sale Company	Kunming	Yunnan	(0871)5132194
云南省烟草卷烟销售公司	昆明市	云南省	(0871)5192187
Kunming Cigarette Factory	Kunming	Yunnan	(0871)5818118
昆明市卷烟厂	昆明市	云南省	(0871)5812822
Yunnan Tobacco Qujing Company	Qujing	Yunnan	(0874)3360801
云南省烟草曲靖市公司	曲靖市	云南省	(0874)3360801
Yuxi Hongta Tobacco (Group) Co.,Ltd.	Yuxi	Yunnan	(0877)2968165
玉溪红塔烟草集团有限责任公司	玉溪市	云南省	(0877)2968562
Yunnan Hongta(Group) Chuxiong Tobacco Company	Chuxiong	Yunnan	(0878)3012929
云南红塔集团楚雄州烟草公司	楚雄市	云南省	(0878)3012782
Gansu Provincial Tobacco Monopoly Bureau	Lanzhou	Gansu	(0931)8881311
甘肃省烟草专卖局	兰州市	甘肃省	(0931)8883114

1620: Cigarettes 卷烟制造业

The industry accounts for 1.777% of the total revenue of China's industrial sector in 2002. The rate of return on assets is 8.51%. 76.54% of all firms in the industry made a profit while 23.46% had negative returns.The top province in terms of the industry's revenue is Yunnan, accounting for 23.09% of the total revenue.
2002年本行业收入占全行业的 1.777%，资产利润率为 8.51%。76.54%的企业赢利，23.46%的企业亏损。收入最高的省为云南省，占本行业的23.09%。

	Total number of firms 企业总数	Total number of employees 职工总数	Total revenue (Mil.RMB) 总销售收入（百万元）	Total profit (Mil.RMB) 总利润（百万元）	Return on assets 资产利润率（%）	Return on equity 权益利润率（%）	Labour productivity ('000 RMB/ worker) 劳动生产率（千元/人）	Debts/ assets 资产负债率（%）	Total assets (Mil.RMB) 总资产（百万元）
Industry Overall 行业总体	179	199,822	190,569	20,705	8.51	15.61	659.50	45.51	243,388

	Number of firms 企业个数	Average number of employees 平均职工人数	Average revenue ('000 RMB) 平均销售收入（千元）	Average profit ('000 RMB) 平均利润（千元）	Return on assets 资产利润率（%）	Return on equity 权益利润率（%）	Labour productivity ('000 RMB/ worker) 劳动生产率（千元/人）	Debts/ assets 资产负债率（%）	Average total assets ('000 RMB) 平均总资产（千元）
By ownership 产业所有权									
State-owned 国有	139	1,225	1,240,889	141,997	9.08	16.00	716.06	43.25	1,564,424
Collective-owned 集体	17	533	100,045	112	0.06	0.44	76.56	86.71	192,145
Foreign & Overseas Chinese Funded 三资	3	255	233,163	17,499	5.54	9.16	578.78	39.53	315,957
By regional distribution 地区分布									
Central-North 华北	8	1,626	982,258	35,734	3.58	12.57	376.81	71.47	996,793
Beijing 北京	1	827	1,287,569	126,100	11.44	17.20	1,037.92	33.48	1,102,242
Tianjin 天津	1	1,844	776,660	8,998	0.75	4.27	261.51	82.42	1,198,954
Hebei 河北	3	2,211	1,345,292	35,686	2.93	15.62	371.66	81.25	1,218,649
Shanxi 山西	1	1,519	817,828	37,183	3.98	13.32	342.63	70.10	933,212
Inner Mongolia 内蒙古	2	1,095	470,067	3,268	0.60	1.78	263.46	66.21	541,994
Northeast 东北	13	958	438,120	8,997	1.49	6.17	253.49	75.85	603,795
Liaoning 辽宁	3	973	632,463	12,567	1.67	7.51	303.52	77.79	753,644
Jilin 吉林	4	1,103	514,186	6,259	0.92	6.75	282.15	86.30	676,924
Heilongjiang 黑龙江	6	853	290,237	9,038	1.88	5.31	200.23	64.52	480,117
Central-East 华东	43	1,128	1,452,248	226,770	14.65	21.11	955.16	30.61	1,548,150
Shanghai 上海	2	2,957	7,215,775	2,340,020	22.33	23.28	2,185.50	4.07	10,480,294
Jiangsu 江苏	4	1,651	2,503,085	417,562	20.83	33.24	1,095.19	37.33	2,004,319
Zhejiang 浙江	3	1,029	3,562,455	573,787	19.25	23.06	2,555.08	16.50	2,980,144
Anhui 安徽	11	999	751,048	31,468	5.30	11.67	483.78	54.57	593,559
Fujian 福建	3	1,209	2,180,545	246,409	11.51	20.33	1,572.64	43.38	2,140,528
Jiangxi 江西	6	1,183	681,547	59,933	10.66	29.36	363.72	63.68	562,041
Shandong 山东	14	799	601,639	16,749	1.90	4.06	419.10	53.18	880,657
Central-South 中南	67	988	704,197	54,938	6.54	15.65	459.85	58.19	839,551
Henan 河南	24	921	405,919	8,231	1.35	8.37	260.37	83.85	608,844
Hubei 湖北	14	1,148	572,876	9,228	1.12	3.95	240.65	71.56	822,020
Hunan 湖南	13	1,239	1,260,692	145,613	10.92	17.32	749.16	36.97	1,333,548
Guangdong 广东	9	802	1,089,484	141,040	15.52	23.20	935.40	33.09	908,753
Guangxi 广西	6	705	469,102	19,346	2.78	9.65	407.01	71.16	695,307
Hainan 海南	1	452	409,930	75,696	17.10	27.04	607.51	36.77	442,667
Southwest 西南	32	1,461	1,885,179	200,335	6.71	11.50	930.13	41.61	2,983,790
Chongqing 重庆	3	1,542	1,087,370	59,120	4.15	13.92	447.19	70.18	1,424,817
Sichuan 四川	7	856	965,601	77,214	6.38	20.80	665.70	69.34	1,210,610
Guizhou 贵州	10	1,407	630,048	15,008	1.40	31.84	188.34	95.59	1,068,794
Yunnan 云南	12	1,837	3,666,994	461,897	7.69	10.78	1,576.94	28.64	6,003,719
Tibet 西藏									
Northwest 西北	16	809	441,341	28,708	4.96	15.38	269.56	67.76	578,905
Shaanxi 陕西	10	1,016	427,737	16,194	2.30	10.18	210.77	77.37	702,811
Gansu 甘肃	4	458	570,019	75,741	19.98	29.00	605.34	31.10	379,052
Qinghai 青海									
Ningxia 宁夏	1	490	91,959	-1,738	-1.24	-1.92	88.35	35.43	139,959
Xinjiang 新疆	1	461	412,058	-3,842	-0.66	-1.48	423.54	54.95	578,198

Year 年份	Number of firms 企业个数	Rate of change 变化率(%)	Number of employees 职工人数(人)	Rate of change 变化率(%)	Total revenue (Mil. RMB) 总销售收入(百万元)	Rate of change 变化率(%)	Total profit (Mil RMB) 总利润(百万元)	Rate of change 变化率(%)
2000	202		238,759		134,961		14,077	
2001	191	-5.45	212,077	-11.18	167,464	24.08	17,608	25.08
2002	179	-6.28	199,822	-5.78	190,569	13.80	20,705	17.59

Major Products 主要产品	Output 产量	Unit 单位
Cigarette 卷烟	3,693	10,000 Boxes 万箱
No.3 Cigarette 三类卷烟	1,280	10,000 Boxes 万箱

10 Main Firms with Maximal Revenue (year founded) 收入最大的十家主要企业(创办年份)	City 城市	Province 省	Telephone/fax 电话/传真	Number of employees 职工人数	Ownership 产业所有权	Revenue ('000 RMB) 销售收入(千元)	Profit('000 RMB) (rank) 利润(千元)(排名)	Total assets ('000 RMB) 总资产(千元)	Major products 主要产品
Yuxi Hongta Tobacco(Group) Co.,Ltd.	Yuxi	Yunnan	(0877)2968872		State-owned				Cigarette
玉溪红塔烟草(集团)有限责任公司(1957)	玉溪市	云南省	(0877)2968872	4,018	国有企业	15,137,493	2,294,635(2)	36,108,426	卷烟
Shanghai Tobacco (Group) Corp.	Shanghai	Shanghai	(021)65418740		State-owned				Cigarette
上海烟草(集团)公司(1993)	上海市	上海市	(021)65129500	5,586	国有企业	14,188,637	4,652,291(1)	20,631,035	卷烟
Kunming Cigarette Factory	Kunming	Yunnan	(0871)5811713		State-owned				Cigarette
昆明卷烟厂(1942)	昆明市	云南省	(0871)5818588	4,891	国有企业	8,261,030	1,381,706(3)	11,199,963	卷烟
Changsha Cigarette Factory	Changsha	Hunan	(0731)5516888		State-owned				Cigarette
长沙卷烟厂(1947)	长沙市	湖南省	(0731)5559175	2,565	国有企业	7,879,698	1,206,969(4)	8,373,050	卷烟
Changde Cigarette Factory	Changde	Hunan	(0736)7299461		State-owned				Cigarette
常德卷烟厂(1951)	常德市	湖南省	(0736)7286888	5,156	国有企业	6,074,170	705,000(10)	5,044,000	卷烟
Honghe Cigarette Factory	Honghe	Yunnan	(0873)6196808		State-owned				Cigarette
红河卷烟厂(1988)	红河州	云南省	(0873)6196808	1,176	国有企业	6,029,918	792,931(8)	6,874,351	卷烟
Qujing Cigarette Factory	Qujing	Yunnan	(0874)3360106		State-owned				Cigarette
曲靖卷烟厂(1973)	曲靖市	云南省		3,259	国有企业	5,504,031	487,932(11)	6,384,912	卷烟
Ningbo Cigarette Factory	Ningbo	Zhejiang	(0574)87056868		State-owned				Cigarette
宁波卷烟厂(1955)	宁波市	浙江省	(0574)87056588	1,781	国有企业	5,006,008	717,492(9)	4,635,445	卷烟
Longyan Cigarette Factory	Longyan	Fujian	(0597)2776888		State-owned				Cigarette
龙岩卷烟厂(1951)	龙岩市	福建省	(0597)2779888	1,769	国有企业	3,478,960	429,890(13)	3,344,000	卷烟
Guangzhou Cigarette No.2 Factory	Guangzhou	Guangdong	(020)81812508		State-owned				Cigarette
广州卷烟二厂(1949)	广州市	广东省	(020)81816020	1,458	国有企业	3,431,600	800,521(7)	2,721,127	卷烟

Top 10 Cities by Revenue 销售收入排名前10位城市	Province 省	Market share 市场份额(%)	Number of firms 企业个数
Yuxi 玉溪市	Yunnan 云南省	8.06	2
Shanghai 上海市	Shanghai 上海市	7.57	2
Kunming 昆明市	Yunnan 云南省	4.74	2
Changsha 长沙市	Hunan 湖南省	4.13	1
Qujing 曲靖市	Yunnan 云南省	3.62	3
Changde 常德市	Hunan 湖南省	3.19	1
Honghe 红河州	Yunnan 云南省	3.16	1
Hangzhou 杭州市	Zhejiang 浙江省	2.97	1
Ningbo 宁波市	Zhejiang 浙江省	2.63	1
Guangzhou 广州市	Guangdong 广东省	2.58	2

10 Major Wholesalers 十家主要批发商	City 城市	Province 省	Telephone/Fax 电话/传真
China Tobacco Leaf Production, Purchase & Sale Company	Beijing	Beijing	(010)63605152
中国烟叶生产购销公司	北京市	北京市	(010)63605913
China Tobacco Materials Corporation	Beijing	Beijing	(010)63601471
中国烟草物资公司	北京市	北京市	(010)63605214
Nanjing City Nanjing Cigarette Sale Co.,Ltd.	Nanjing	Jiangsu	(025)8187120
南京市南京烟销售有限公司	南京市	江苏省	(025)8888168
China Tobacco General Company Guangdong Branch	Guangzhou	Guangdong	(020)38803398
中国烟草总公司广东省公司	广州市	广东省	(020)38807898
Yunnan Tobacco Cigarette Sale Company	Kunming	Yunnan	(0871)5132194
云南省烟草卷烟销售公司	昆明市	云南省	(0871)5192187
Kunming Cigarette Factory	Kunming	Yunnan	(0871)5818118
昆明市卷烟厂	昆明市	云南省	(0871)5812822
Yunnan Tobacco Qujing Company	Qujing	Yunnan	(0874)3360801
云南省烟草曲靖市公司	曲靖市	云南省	(0874)3360801
Yuxi Hongta Tobacco (Group) Co.,Ltd.	Yuxi	Yunnan	(0877)2968165
玉溪红塔烟草集团有限责任公司	玉溪市	云南省	(0877)2968562
Yunnan Hongta(Group) Chuxiong Tobacco Company	Chuxiong	Yunnan	(0878)3012929
云南红塔集团楚雄州烟草公司	楚雄市	云南省	(0878)3012782
Gansu Provincial Tobacco Monopoly Bureau	Lanzhou	Gansu	(0931)8881311
甘肃省烟草专卖局	兰州市	甘肃省	(0931)8883114

1690: Other Tobacco 其他烟草加工业

The industry accounts for 0.011% of the total revenue of China's industrial sector in 2002. The rate of return on assets is 5.42%. 66.67% of all firms in the industry made a profit while 33.33% had negative returns.The top province in terms of the industry's revenue is Hubei, accounting for 40.87% of the total revenue.
2002年本行业收入占全行业的0.011%，资产利润率为5.42%。66.67%的企业赢利，33.33%的企业亏损。收入最高的省为湖北省，占本行业的40.87%。

	Total number of firms 企业总数	Total number of employees 职工总数	Total revenue (Mil.RMB) 总销售收入（百万元）	Total profit (Mil.RMB) 总利润（百万元）	Return on assets 资产利润率（%）	Return on equity 权益利润率（%）	Labour productivity ('000 RMB/worker) 劳动生产率（千元/人）	Debts/assets 资产负债率（%）	Total assets (Mil.RMB) 总资产（百万元）
Industry Overall 行业总体	30	5,503	1,140	95	5.42	14.36	59.73	62.26	1,761

	Number of firms 企业个数	Average number of employees 平均职工人数	Average revenue ('000 RMB) 平均销售收入（千元）	Average profit ('000 RMB) 平均利润（千元）	Return on assets 资产利润率（%）	Return on equity 权益利润率（%）	Labour productivity ('000 RMB/worker) 劳动生产率（千元/人）	Debts/assets 资产负债率（%）	Average total assets ('000 RMB) 平均总资产（千元）
By ownership 产业所有权									
State-owned 国有	12	101	19,837	70	0.13	0.87	67.37	85.27	54,314
Collective-owned 集体	8	162	17,078	1,465	7.64	18.70	36.05	59.15	19,179
Foreign & Overseas Chinese Funded 三资									
By regional distribution 地区分布									
Central-North 华北									
Beijing 北京									
Tianjin 天津									
Hebei 河北									
Shanxi 山西									
Inner Mongolia 内蒙古									
Northeast 东北									
Liaoning 辽宁									
Jilin 吉林									
Heilongjiang 黑龙江									
Central-East 华东	9	192	36,701	3,730	8.59	18.99	67.87	54.76	43,415
Shanghai 上海	1	437	113,238	19,337	13.75	63.14	92.75	78.23	140,672
Jiangsu 江苏	2	223	69,571	5,347	7.66	11.72	103.75	34.68	69,832
Zhejiang 浙江	2	45	5,292	1,119	10.98	34.06	62.82	67.78	10,190
Anhui 安徽	2	341	33,062	881	2.06	3.98	35.29	48.17	42,705
Fujian 福建	2	37	613	-230	-9.95	-11.22	10.03	11.35	2,308
Jiangxi 江西									
Shandong 山东									
Central-South 中南	13	208	45,229	2,488	3.30	11.68	54.34	71.72	75,302
Henan 河南	2	301	30,556	1,030	2.99	6.78	15.27	55.99	34,488
Hubei 湖北	3	461	155,389	11,869	8.14	14.95	84.39	45.55	145,803
Hunan 湖南									
Guangdong 广东	7	82	7,754	-585	-0.94		32.48	103.79	62,400
Guangxi 广西	1	148	6,418	-1,224	-3.42	-4.92	17.11	30.43	35,747
Hainan 海南									
Southwest 西南	5	164	44,236	6,014	8.02	14.34	75.18	44.05	74,950
Chongqing 重庆									
Sichuan 四川	3	59	41,123	7,190	11.05	16.17	204.32	31.63	65,054
Guizhou 贵州									
Yunnan 云南	2	323	48,905	4,250	4.73	11.15	39.99	57.55	89,795
Tibet 西藏									
Northwest 西北	3	82	342	-180	-3.30	-44.77	10.33	92.63	5,444
Shaanxi 陕西									
Gansu 甘肃	3	82	342	-180	-3.30	-44.77	10.33	92.63	5,444
Qinghai 青海									
Ningxia 宁夏									
Xinjiang 新疆									

1690: Other Tobacco 其他烟草加工业

Year 年份	Number of firms 企业个数	Rate of change 变化率 (%)	Number of employees 职工人数 (人)	Rate of change 变化率 (%)	Total revenue (Mil. RMB) 总销售收入 (百万元)	Rate of change 变化率 (%)	Total profit (Mil RMB) 总利润 (百万元)	Rate of change 变化率 (%)
2000	32		5,529		741		49	
2001	28	-12.50	4,418	-20.09	630	-14.98	13	-73.47
2002	30	7.14	5,503	24.56	1,140	80.95	95	630.77

Major Products 主要产品	Output 产量	Unit 单位

10 Main Firms with Maximal Revenue (year founded) 收入最大的十家主要企业（创办年份）	City 城市	Province 省	Telephone/fax 电话/传真	Number of employees 职工人数	Ownership 产业所有权	Revenue ('000 RMB) 销售收入 (千元)	Profit('000 RMB) (rank) 利润(千元) (排名)	Total assets ('000 RMB) 总资产 (千元)	Major products 主要产品
Nantong Cigarette Filter Experimental Factory	Nantong	Jiangsu	(0513)5516813		State-owned				Tobacco Filter Tip
南通烟滤嘴实验工厂(1981)	南通市	江苏省	(0513)5511096	394	国有企业	128,811	5,424(4)	109,074	烟用滤咀
Shanghai White Yulan Tobacco Materials Co., Ltd.	Shanghai	Shanghai	(021)58953506		Limited-Liability				Tobacco Filter Tip烟
上海白玉兰烟草材料有限公司(1994)	上海市	上海市	(021)58559214	437	有限公司	113,238	19,337(2)	140,672	用过滤嘴
Yunnan Baoshan Perfume Tobacco Co.,Ltd.	Baoshan	Yunnan	(0875)2160906		Limited-Liability				Spicery Tobacco Leaf
云南烟草保山香料烟有限责任公司(1997)	保山市	云南省	(0875)2121089	584	有限公司	75,968	4,999(6)	162,921	香料烟叶
Hubei Tobacco Company Cigarette Materials Factory	Wuhan	Hubei	(027)84871813		State-owned				Tip Stick
湖北省烟草公司卷烟材料厂(1986)	武汉市	湖北省	(027)84871813	302	国有企业	60,590	-	100,990	咀棒
Chengdu Hongda Perfume Factory	Chengdu	Sichuan	(028)84630188		Collective-owned				Flavouring Essences
成都宏大香料厂(1994)	成都市	四川省	(028)84630188	30	集体企业	38,270	2,420(8)	45,837	香精
Lianjiang Lianjiang Cut Tobacco Factory	Zhanjiang	Guangdong	(0759)6256888		State-owned				Cut Tobacco
廉江市廉江烟丝厂(1956)	湛江市	广东省	(0759)6256838	71	国有企业	28,186	-	406,820	烟丝
Yunnan Dalitian New Packing Material Co., Ltd.	Dali	Yunnan	(0872)2318044		Joint Stock				Cigarette lining Aluminum Foil卷烟
云南大理天新包装材料有限公司(1996)	大理州	云南省	(0872)2323692	62	股份制	21,841	3,501(7)	16,668	内衬铝箔
Bengbu Gold Leaf Polypropylene Fibre Tow Co., Ltd.	Bengbu	Anhui	(0552)4080833		State Enterprises				Tobacco Polypropylene Fibre Tow烟用聚
蚌埠金叶丙纤丝束有限公司(1990)	蚌埠市	安徽省	(0552)4070161	149	国有独资	14,875	-	64,453	丙纤丝束
Chengdu Yadun Co., Ltd.	Chengdu	Sichuan	(028)87511798		Private Owned				Tobacco Auxiliary Materials
成都雅顿有限责任公司(2001)	成都市	四川省	(028)87512798	12	私营企业	11,014	587(12)	14,622	烟草辅料
Xinyi Cut Tobacco Factory	Maoming	Guangdong	(0668)8889182		Collective-owned				Cut Tobacco
信宜市烟丝厂(1994)	茂名市	广东省	(0668)8878128	175	集体企业	10,542	132(13)	5,767	烟丝

Top 10 Cities by Revenue 销售收入排名前10位城市	Province 省	Market share 市场份额 (%)	Number of firms 企业个数
Yichang 宜昌市	Hubei 湖北省	35.56	2
Nantong 南通市	Jiangsu 江苏省	11.29	1
Chengdu 成都市	Sichuan 四川省	10.82	3
Shanghai 上海市	Shanghai 上海市	9.93	1
Baoshan 保山市	Yunnan 云南省	6.66	1
Bengbu 蚌埠市	Anhui 安徽省	5.80	2
Wuhan 武汉市	Hubei 湖北省	5.31	1
Zhumadian 驻马店市	Henan 河南省	3.15	1
Zhanjiang 湛江市	Guangdong 广东省	2.47	1
Nanyang 南阳市	Henan 河南省	2.21	1

10 Major Wholesalers 十家主要批发商	City 城市	Province 省	Telephone/Fax 电话/传真
China Tobacco Leaf Production, Purchase & Sale Company	Beijing	Beijing	(010)63605152
中国烟叶生产购销公司	北京市	北京市	(010)63605913
China Tobacco Materials Corporation	Beijing	Beijing	(010)63601471
中国烟草物资公司	北京市	北京市	(010)63605214
Nanjing City Nanjing Cigarette Sale Co.,Ltd.	Nanjing	Jiangsu	(025)8187120
南京市南京烟销售有限公司	南京市	江苏省	(025)8888168
China Tobacco General Company Guangdong Branch	Guangzhou	Guangdong	(020)38803398
中国烟草总公司广东省公司	广州市	广东省	(020)38807898
Yunnan Tobacco Cigarette Sale Company	Kunming	Yunnan	(0871)5132194
云南省烟草卷烟销售公司	昆明市	云南省	(0871)5192187
Kunming Cigarette Factory	Kunming	Yunnan	(0871)5818118
昆明市卷烟厂	昆明市	云南省	(0871)5812822
Yunnan Tobacco Qujing Company	Qujing	Yunnan	(0874)3360801
云南省烟草曲靖市公司	曲靖市	云南省	(0874)3360801
Yuxi Hongta Tobacco (Group) Co.,Ltd.	Yuxi	Yunnan	(0877)2968165
玉溪红塔烟草集团有限责任公司	玉溪市	云南省	(0877)2968562
Yunnan Hongta(Group) Chuxiong Tobacco Company	Chuxiong	Yunnan	(0878)3012929
云南红塔集团楚雄州烟草公司	楚雄市	云南省	(0878)3012782
Gansu Provincial Tobacco Monopoly Bureau	Lanzhou	Gansu	(0931)8881311
甘肃省烟草专卖局	兰州市	甘肃省	(0931)8883114

1711: Cotton Ginning 轧花业

The industry accounts for 0.217% of the total revenue of China's industrial sector in 2002. The rate of return on assets is 1.27%. 81.18% of all firms in the industry made a profit while 18.82% had negative returns.The top province in terms of the industry's revenue is Shandong, accounting for 34.36% of the total revenue.
2002年本行业收入占全行业的 0.217%，资产利润率为 1.27%。81.18%的企业赢利，18.82%的企业亏损。收入最高的省为山东省，占本行业的34.36%。

	Total number of firms 企业总数	Total number of employees 职工总数	Total revenue (Mil.RMB) 总销售收入（百万元）	Total profit (Mil.RMB) 总利润（百万元）	Return on assets 资产利润率（%）	Return on equity 权益利润率（%）	Labour productivity ('000 RMB/ worker) 劳动生产率（千元/人）	Debts/ assets 资产负债率（%）	Total assets (Mil.RMB) 总资产（百万元）
Industry Overall 行业总体	797	161,867	23,292	392	1.27	14.88	35.30	91.47	30,908

	Number of firms 企业个数	Average number of employees 平均职工人数	Average revenue ('000 RMB) 平均销售收入（千元）	Average profit ('000 RMB) 平均利润（千元）	Return on assets 资产利润率（%）	Return on equity 权益利润率（%）	Labour productivity ('000 RMB/ worker) 劳动生产率（千元/人）	Debts/ assets 资产负债率（%）	Average total assets ('000 RMB) 平均总资产（千元）
By ownership 产业所有权									
State-owned 国有	86	202	28,223	631	2.27	18.33	31.75	87.62	27,799
Collective-owned 集体	480	214	30,078	315	0.66	16.29	33.55	95.92	47,389
Foreign & Overseas Chinese Funded 三资	8	223	43,519	-76	-0.09	-0.51	34.84	83.14	89,288
By regional distribution 地区分布									
Central-North 华北	66	106	23,317	720	1.84	11.95	68.63	84.58	39,088
Beijing 北京									
Tianjin 天津	2	22	90,017	1,362	0.83	2.06	450.70	59.75	163,872
Hebei 河北	55	116	22,217	814	2.11	18.33	65.62	88.46	38,494
Shanxi 山西	9	64	15,212	5	0.04	0.22	73.57	83.93	14,989
Inner Mongolia 内蒙古									
Northeast 东北									
Liaoning 辽宁									
Jilin 吉林									
Heilongjiang 黑龙江									
Central-East 华东	457	205	29,863	573	1.47	19.84	37.96	92.59	39,034
Shanghai 上海									
Jiangsu 江苏	120	207	29,698	147	0.50	5.54	32.30	90.98	29,398
Zhejiang 浙江	1	48	19,998	258	5.56	47.78	71.46	88.36	4,640
Anhui 安徽	115	212	17,318	-126	-0.34		21.50	111.68	36,941
Fujian 福建									
Jiangxi 江西	5	201	13,802	-160	-0.26		14.23	125.40	61,589
Shandong 山东	216	201	37,050	1,201	2.66	16.46	50.96	83.83	45,139
Central-South 中南	217	258	29,421	129	0.31	5.00	24.28	93.81	41,697
Henan 河南	139	238	25,946	384	1.01	55.08	11.91	98.16	37,887
Hubei 湖北	46	327	33,519	200	0.49	3.04	43.47	83.81	40,505
Hunan 湖南	32	249	38,629	-1,081	-1.80	-21.45	39.45	91.59	59,959
Guangdong 广东									
Guangxi 广西									
Hainan 海南									
Southwest 西南	2	308	29,322	101	0.32		11.83	160.81	31,333
Chongqing 重庆									
Sichuan 四川	2	308	29,322	101	0.32		11.83	160.81	31,333
Guizhou 贵州									
Yunnan 云南									
Tibet 西藏									
Northwest 西北	55	83	30,232	989	3.95	13.79	68.06	71.39	25,074
Shaanxi 陕西	1	985	371,000	610	0.24	1.33	32.98	81.69	250,995
Gansu 甘肃	36	50	15,170	545	3.84	11.39	96.94	66.27	14,188
Qinghai 青海									
Ningxia 宁夏									
Xinjiang 新疆	18	98	41,424	1,899	5.54	19.39	58.05	71.43	34,295

1711: Cotton Ginning 轧花业

Year 年份	Number of firms 企业个数	Rate of change 变化率 (%)	Number of employees 职工人数 (人)	Rate of change 变化率 (%)	Total revenue (Mil. RMB) 总销售收入 (百万元)	Rate of change 变化率 (%)	Total profit (Mil RMB) 总利润 (百万元)	Rate of change 变化率 (%)
2000	728		182,700		18,942		176	
2001	765	5.08	173,390	-5.10	20,431	7.86	208	18.18
2002	797	4.18	161,867	-6.65	23,292	14.00	392	88.46

Major Products 主要产品	Output 产量	Unit 单位
Cotton Lint 皮棉	200	10,000 Tons 万吨

10 Main Firms with Maximal Revenue (year founded) 收入最大的十家主要企业（创办年份）	City 城市	Province 省	Telephone/fax 电话/传真	Number of employees 职工人数	Ownership 产业所有权	Revenue ('000 RMB) 销售收入(千元)	Profit('000 RMB) (rank) 利润(千元)(排名)	Total assets ('000 RMB) 总资产(千元)	Major products 主要产品
Shannxi Dali Cotton Group Company 陕西省大荔县棉花集团公司(2001)	Weinan 渭南市	Shannxi 陕西省	(0913)3212230 (0913)3222092	985	Collective-owned 集体企业	371,000	610(148)	250,995	Cotton 棉花
Jiangsu New Jinhua Group Company 江苏新金花集团(1989)	Lianyungang 连云港市	Jiangsu 江苏省	(0518)3222159 (0518)3227020	2,620	Collective-owned 集体企业	300,730	5,300(17)	156,870	Cotton Lint 皮棉
Xihua Cotton & Linen Company Processing Factory 西华县棉麻公司综合加工厂(1996)	Zhoukou 周口市	Henan 河南省	(0394)2551533 (0394)2554596	4,211	Collective-owned 集体企业	297,087	299(208)	445,120	Cotton Lint 皮棉
Shandong Dezhou Yinxia Cotton & Linen Group Co.,Ltd. 山东省德州银夏棉麻集团有限公司(1999)	Dezhou 德州市	Shandong 山东省	(0534)3211672 (0534)3211525	803	Collective-owned 集体企业	272,737	27,210(1)	79,023	Cotton 棉花
Juye Jinyuan Cotton Processing Co., Ltd. 巨野县锦源棉花加工有限公司(2001)	Heze 荷泽市	Shandong 山东省	(0530)8531025 (0530)8534608	416	Limited-Liability 有限公司	260,387	7,116(12)	52,837	Cotton Lint 皮棉
Henan Yanling Cotton & Linen Company Cotton Processing General Factory 河南省鄢陵县棉麻公司棉花加工总厂(1958)	Xuchang 许昌市	Henan 河南省	(0374)7195102	1,332	Collective-owned 集体企业	244,497	-	129,832	Cotton 棉花
Hubei Qianjiang Cotton General Company 湖北省潜江市棉花总公司(1953)	Qianjian 潜江市	Hubei 湖北省	(0728)6241384 (0728)6299068	300	Collective-owned 集体企业	241,000	2,241(56)	7,930	Cotton 棉花
Anxiang Cotton & Linen General Company 安乡县棉麻总公司(1951)	Changde 常德市	Hunan 湖南省	(0736)4312274 (0736)4311216	1,008	Collective-owned 集体企业	206,439	-	655,001	Cotton & Linen 棉麻
Shandong Boxing NO.3 Oil & Cotton Factory 山东省博兴县第三油棉厂(1963)	Binzhou 滨州市	Shandong 山东省	(0543)2867034 (0543)2866027	270	Collective-owned 集体企业	194,817	-	130,630	Cotton Lint 皮棉
Dezhou Yinxia Cotton & Linen Group Co., Ltd. Trade Center 德州市银夏棉麻（集团）有限公司交易中心(1999)	Dezhou 德州市	Shandong 山东省	(0534)3882112 (0534)3884719	2,300	State-owned 国有企业	191,510	26,774(2)	61,215	Cotton 棉花

Top 10 Cities by Revenue 销售收入排名前10位城市	Province 省	Market share 市场份额 (%)	Number of firms 企业个数
Dezhou 德州市	Shandong 山东省	9.35	71
Binzhou 滨州市	Shandong 山东省	8.78	35
Yancheng 盐城市	Jiangsu 江苏省	7.08	43
Heze 荷泽市	Shandong 山东省	5.15	24
Lianyungang 连云港市	Jiangsu 江苏省	4.17	17
Kaifeng 开封市	Henan 河南省	3.25	39
Xuchang 许昌市	Henan 河南省	3.10	16
Zhoukou 周口市	Henan 河南省	2.94	9
Changde 常德市	Hunan 湖南省	2.79	18
Suzhou 宿州市	Anhui 安徽省	2.19	27

10 Major Wholesalers 十家主要批发商	City 城市	Province 省	Telephone/Fax 电话/传真
Shanghai Shenda Co.,Ltd. 上海申达股份有限公司	Shanghai 上海市	Shanghai 上海市	(021)62319898 (021)62317250
Orient International Holding Silk Group Corportion 东方国际集团丝绸进出口有限公司	Shanghai 上海市	Shanghai 上海市	(021)64662288 (021)64677788
Nanjing Textiles Import & Export Co.,Ltd. 南京纺织品进出口股份有限公司	Nanjing 南京市	Jiangsu 江苏省	(025)3306789 (025)3300518
Zhejiang Textiles Import & Export Group Co.,Ltd. 浙江省纺织品进出口集团有限公司	Hangzhou 杭州市	Zhejiang 浙江省	(0571)87075888 (0571)87079234
Zhejiang Orient Holdings Co.,Ltd. 浙江东方集团股份有限公司	Hangzhou 杭州市	Zhejiang 浙江省	(0571)87215678 (0571)87215000
Zhejiang Silk Holding Co.,ltd. 浙江省丝绸集团有限公司	Hangzhou 杭州市	Zhejiang 浙江省	(0571)85195588 (0571)85192540
Guangdong Silk (Group) Corporation 广东省丝绸（集团）公司	Guangzhou 广州市	Guangdong 广东省	(020)83337448 (020)83332995
Shanghai Costume Group Co.,Ltd. 上海服装（集团）有限公司	Shanghai 上海市	Shanghai 上海市	(021)62748598 (021)62414773
Orient International Holding Shanghai Textiles Import & Export Co.Ltd. 东方国际集团上海市针织品进出口有限公司	Shanghai 上海市	Shanghai 上海市	(021)63218855 (021)63299560
Jiangsu Textiles Import & Export Group Co.,Ltd. 江苏省纺织品进出口集团股份有限公司	Nanjing 南京市	Jiangsu 江苏省	(025)6895000 (025)4400800

1712: Wool Washing 洗毛业

The industry accounts for 0.003% of the total revenue of China's industrial sector in 2002. The rate of return on assets is -0.35%. 66.67% of all firms in the industry made a profit while 33.33% had negative returns.The top province in terms of the industry's revenue is Jiangsu, accounting for 39.19% of the total revenue.
2002年本行业收入占全行业的 0.003%，资产利润率为 -0.35%。66.67%的企业赢利，33.33%的企业亏损。收入最高的省为江苏省，占本行业的39.19%。

	Total number of firms 企业总数	Total number of employees 职工总数	Total revenue (Mil.RMB) 总销售收入 (百万元)	Total profit (Mil.RMB) 总利润 (百万元)	Return on assets 资产利润率 (%)	Return on equity 权益利润率 (%)	Labour productivity ('000 RMB/ worker) 劳动生产率 (千元/人)	Debts/ assets 资产负债率 (%)	Total assets (Mil.RMB) 总资产 (百万元)
Industry Overall 行业总体	24	5,206	309	-2	-0.35	-4.17	21.04	91.57	584

	Number of firms 企业个数	Average number of employees 平均职工人数	Average revenue ('000 RMB) 平均销售收入 (千元)	Average profit ('000 RMB) 平均利润 (千元)	Return on assets 资产利润率 (%)	Return on equity 权益利润率 (%)	Labour productivity ('000 RMB/ worker) 劳动生产率 (千元/人)	Debts/ assets 资产负债率 (%)	Average total assets ('000 RMB) 平均总资产 (千元)
By ownership 产业所有权									
State-owned 国有	3	821	32,409	-387	-0.40		16.23	115.13	96,297
Collective-owned 集体	4	190	12,403	-271	-1.32	-5.22	24.65	74.72	20,553
Foreign & Overseas Chinese Funded 三资	2	67	10,705	420	6.01	10.76	37.76	44.09	6,985
By regional distribution 地区分布									
Central-North 华北	5	384	21,553	53	0.13		27.56	108.19	41,513
Beijing 北京	1	10	9,909	449	10.93	34.62	623.90	68.43	4,108
Tianjin 天津	1	1,639	56,362	-18	-0.01		12.72	138.18	155,093
Hebei 河北	1	200	30,845	673	2.24	2.24	38.58		30,030
Shanxi 山西									
Inner Mongolia 内蒙古	2	36	5,324	-420	-4.58	-7.72	255.25	40.63	9,168
Northeast 东北	1	30	10,300				52.47	88.54	4,800
Liaoning 辽宁									
Jilin 吉林	1	30	10,300				52.47	88.54	4,800
Heilongjiang 黑龙江									
Central-East 华东	15	190	11,790	-179	-0.76	-4.57	17.72	83.33	23,477
Shanghai 上海									
Jiangsu 江苏	10	159	12,115	-35	-0.17	-0.99	17.46	82.72	20,375
Zhejiang 浙江	2	51	6,965	276	5.14	17.62	23.42	70.84	5,363
Anhui 安徽	3	388	13,927	-960	-2.09	-14.15	17.59	85.21	45,890
Fujian 福建									
Jiangxi 江西									
Shandong 山东									
Central-South 中南	2	123	6,523	171	3.24	7.03	14.16	53.89	5,275
Henan 河南									
Hubei 湖北	2	123	6,523	171	3.24	7.03	14.16	53.89	5,275
Hunan 湖南									
Guangdong 广东									
Guangxi 广西									
Hainan 海南									
Southwest 西南									
Chongqing 重庆									
Sichuan 四川									
Guizhou 贵州									
Yunnan 云南									
Tibet 西藏									
Northwest 西北	1	156	1,151	20	0.21	0.92	6.28	76.73	9,375
Shaanxi 陕西									
Gansu 甘肃	1	156	1,151	20	0.21	0.92	6.28	76.73	9,375
Qinghai 青海									
Ningxia 宁夏									
Xinjiang 新疆									

1712: Wool Washing 洗毛业

Year 年份	Number of firms 企业个数	Rate of change 变化率 (%)	Number of employees 职工人数 (人)	Rate of change 变化率 (%)	Total revenue (Mil. RMB) 总销售收入 (百万元)	Rate of change 变化率 (%)	Total profit (Mil RMB) 总利润 (百万元)	Rate of change 变化率 (%)
2000	26		5,119		357		0.10	
2001	25	-3.85	7,652	49.48	392	9.80	-4	-
2002	24	-4.00	5,206	-31.97	309	-21.17	-2	50.00

Major Products 主要产品	Output 产量	Unit 单位

10 Main Firms with Maximal Revenue (year founded) 收入最大的十家主要企业（创办年份）	City 城市	Province 省	Telephone/fax 电话/传真	Number of employees 职工人数	Ownership 产业所有权	Revenue ('000 RMB) 销售收入 (千元)	Profit('000 RMB) (rank) 利润(千元) (排名)	Total assets ('000 RMB) 总资产 (千元)	Major products 主要产品
Jixian Cotton Textile Mill	Tianjin	Tianjin	(022)82862463		State-owned				Cotton Goods
蓟县棉纺织厂(1980)	天津市	天津市	(022)82866266	1,639	国有企业	56,362	-	155,093	棉纺织品
Anhui Suzhou Weaving Printing & Dyeing General Factory	Suzhou	Anhui	(0557)3033003		State-owned				Coloured Woven Cloth
安徽省宿州色织印染总厂(1951)	宿州市	安徽省		539	国有企业	31,185	-	68,487	色织布
Dafeng Haihong Rabbit Hair Processing Factory	Yancheng	Jiangsu	(0515)3715688		Collective-owned				Rabbit Hair
大丰市海虹兔毛加工厂(1998)	盐城市	江苏省	(0515)3715688	60	集体企业	20,060	140(11)	4,720	兔毛绒
Shaoxing Wool Scouring Co., Ltd.	Shaoxing	Zhejiang	(0575)8010767		Private Owned				Wool Scouring
绍兴市洗毛有限公司(1999)	绍兴市	浙江省	(0575)8011375	50	私营企业	12,062	550(2)	9,009	洗毛
Nanjing Hualun Costume Washing Co., Ltd.	Nanjing	Jiangsu	(025)2703189		Foreign Funded				Costume Washing
南京华伦服装水洗有限公司(2000)	南京市	江苏省	(025)2703189	90	外商投资	10,980	350(6)	3,710	成衣水洗
Nanjing Dazhong Washing Co., Ltd.	Nanjing	Jiangsu	(025)2288347		Overseas Chinese-funded				Costume Washing
南京大众水洗有限公司(1993)	南京市	江苏省	(025)2287044	44	港澳台资	10,430	490(4)	10,260	成衣水洗
Wuxi NO.1 Carbonization Factory	Wuxi	Jiangsu	(0510)3391296		Private Owned				Wool Scouring
无锡市第一碳化厂(1992)	无锡市	江苏省	(0510)3397888	170	私营企业	10,230	-	14,380	洗毛
Beijing Changping Shahe Raw Wool Processing Factory	Beijing	Beijing	(010)69731575		llective-owned				Raw Wool
北京市昌平沙河原毛加工厂(1975)	北京市	北京市		10	集体企业	9,909	449(5)	4,108	原毛
Jiangsu Xuzhou Rabbit Hair Spinning Factory	Xuzhou	Jiangsu	(0516)4622216		State-owned				Rabbit Hair
江苏省徐州兔毛纺厂(1990)	徐州市	江苏省	(0516)4621541	286	国有企业	9,680	-	65,310	兔毛纱
Tianmen Hushi Cotton Weaving Co., Ltd.	Tianmen	Hubei	(0728)4841097		Collective-owned				Degrease Pledget
天门市胡市棉织有限责任公司(1986)	天门市	湖北省		125	集体企业	9,046	142(10)	5,550	脱脂纱布

Top 10 Cities by Revenue 销售收入排名前10位城市	Province 省	Market share 市场份额 (%)	Number of firms 企业个数
Tianjin 天津市	Tianjin 天津市	18.23	1
Wuxi 无锡市	Jiangsu 江苏省	11.24	4
Suzhou 宿州市	Anhui 安徽省	10.09	1
Baoding 保定市	Hebei 河北省	9.98	1
Nanjing 南京市	Jiangsu 江苏省	9.40	3
Suzhou 苏州市	Jiangsu 江苏省	8.93	1
Yancheng 盐城市	Jiangsu 江苏省	6.49	1
Shaoxing 绍兴市	Zhejiang 浙江省	3.90	1
Anqing 安庆市	Anhui 安徽省	3.43	1
Baicheng 白城市	Jilin 吉林省	3.33	1

10 Major Wholesalers 十家主要批发商	City 城市	Province 省	Telephone/Fax 电话/传真
Shanghai Shenda Co.,Ltd.	Shanghai	Shanghai	(021)62319898
上海申达股份有限公司	上海市	上海市	(021)62317250
Orient International Holding Silk Group Corportion	Shanghai	Shanghai	(021)64662288
东方国际集团丝绸进出口有限公司	上海市	上海市	(021)64677788
Nanjing Textiles Import & Export Co.,Ltd.	Nanjing	Jiangsu	(025)3306789
南京纺织品进出口股份有限公司	南京市	江苏省	(025)3300518
Zhejiang Textiles Import & Export Group Co.,Ltd.	Hangzhou	Zhejiang	(0571)87075888
浙江省纺织品进出口集团有限公司	杭州市	浙江省	(0571)87079234
Zhejiang Orient Holdings Co.,Ltd.	Hangzhou	Zhejiang	(0571)87215678
浙江东方集团股份有限公司	杭州市	浙江省	(0571)87215000
Zhejiang Silk Holding Co.,ltd.	Hangzhou	Zhejiang	(0571)85195588
浙江省丝绸集团有限公司	杭州市	浙江省	(0571)85192540
Guangdong Silk (Group) Corporation	Guangzhou	Guangdong	(020)83337448
广东省丝绸（集团）公司	广州市	广东省	(020)83332995
Shanghai Costume Group Co.,Ltd.	Shanghai	Shanghai	(021)62748598
上海服装（集团）有限公司	上海市	上海市	(021)62414773
Orient International Holding Shanghai Textiles Import & Export Co.Ltd.	Shanghai	Shanghai	(021)63218855
东方国际集团上海市针织品进出口有限公司	上海市	上海市	(021)63299560
Jiangsu Textiles Import & Export Group Co.,Ltd.	Nanjing	Jiangsu	(025)6895000
江苏省纺织品进出口集团股份有限公司	南京市	江苏省	(025)4400800

1713: Flax Fibre Primary 亚麻纤维初步加工业

The industry accounts for 0.004% of the total revenue of China's industrial sector in 2002. The rate of return on assets is 5.62%. 79.17% of all firms in the industry made a profit while 20.83% had negative returns.The top province in terms of the industry's revenue is Heilong Jiang, accounting for 51.72% of the total revenue.
2002年本行业收入占全行业的0.004%，资产利润率为5.62%。79.17%的企业赢利，20.83%的企业亏损。收入最高的省为黑龙江省，占本行业的51.72%。

	Total number of firms 企业总数	Total number of employees 职工总数	Total revenue (Mil.RMB) 总销售收入(百万元)	Total profit (Mil.RMB) 总利润(百万元)	Return on assets 资产利润率(%)	Return on equity 权益利润率(%)	Labour productivity ('000 RMB/ worker) 劳动生产率(千元/人)	Debts/ assets 资产负债率(%)	Total assets (Mil.RMB) 总资产(百万元)
Industry Overall 行业总体	24	9,113	457	59	5.62	21.71	19.33	74.13	1,059

	Number of firms 企业个数	Average number of employees 平均职工人数	Average revenue ('000 RMB) 平均销售收入(千元)	Average profit ('000 RMB) 平均利润(千元)	Return on assets 资产利润率(%)	Return on equity 权益利润率(%)	Labour productivity ('000 RMB/ worker) 劳动生产率(千元/人)	Debts/ assets 资产负债率(%)	Average total assets ('000 RMB) 平均总资产(千元)
By ownership 产业所有权									
State-owned 国有	5	540	10,259	-148	-0.14	-3.87	6.72	96.29	102,894
Collective-owned 集体	5	60	3,073	30	0.72	2.41	17.68	70.08	4,184
Foreign & Overseas Chinese Funded 三资	2	95	4,657	-67	-0.54	-1.06	45.44	48.83	12,331
By regional distribution 地区分布									
Central-North 华北	2	364	141	-505	-0.32		1.39	102.78	158,421
Beijing 北京									
Tianjin 天津	2	364	141	-505	-0.32		1.39	102.78	158,421
Hebei 河北									
Shanxi 山西									
Inner Mongolia 内蒙古									
Northeast 东北	12	476	19,711	2,433	5.81	16.13	16.44	63.94	41,833
Liaoning 辽宁									
Jilin 吉林									
Heilongjiang 黑龙江	12	476	19,711	2,433	5.81	16.13	16.44	63.94	41,833
Central-East 华东	2	72	41,055	990	5.51	60.49	107.41	90.90	17,977
Shanghai 上海									
Jiangsu 江苏	2	72	41,055	990	5.51	60.49	107.41	90.90	17,977
Zhejiang 浙江									
Anhui 安徽									
Fujian 福建									
Jiangxi 江西									
Shandong 山东									
Central-South 中南	1	179	9,031	-123	-0.82	-1.17	42.39	29.88	14,951
Henan 河南									
Hubei 湖北									
Hunan 湖南	1	179	9,031	-123	-0.82	-1.17	42.39	29.88	14,951
Guangdong 广东									
Guangxi 广西									
Hainan 海南									
Southwest 西南									
Chongqing 重庆									
Sichuan 四川									
Guizhou 贵州									
Yunnan 云南									
Tibet 西藏									
Northwest 西北	7	336	18,488	4,207	15.53	33.44	24.77	53.55	27,087
Shaanxi 陕西									
Gansu 甘肃	3	89	2,826	60	0.90	3.37	16.34	73.18	6,631
Qinghai 青海	1	15	836	-29	-5.80	-5.80	-55.13		500
Ningxia 宁夏									
Xinjiang 新疆	3	690	40,033	9,766	17.31	35.62	26.44	51.40	56,406

1713: Flax Fibre Primary 亚麻纤维初步加工业

Year 年份	Number of firms 企业个数	Rate of change 变化率(%)	Number of employees 职工人数(人)	Rate of change 变化率(%)	Total revenue (Mil. RMB) 总销售收入(百万元)	Rate of change 变化率(%)	Total profit (Mil RMB) 总利润(百万元)	Rate of change 变化率(%)
2000	25		10,444		384		10	
2001	29	16.00	10,394	-0.48	424	10.42	44	340.00
2002	24	-17.24	9,113	-12.32	457	7.78	59	34.09

Major Products 主要产品	Output 产量	Unit 单位
Ramie Cloth and Linen Cloth 苎麻布及亚麻布	10,424	10,000 Meters 万米

10 Main Firms with Maximal Revenue (year founded) 收入最大的十家主要企业(创办年份)	City 城市	Province 省	Telephone/fax 电话/传真	Number of employees 职工人数	Ownership 产业所有权	Revenue ('000 RMB) 销售收入(千元)	Profit('000 RMB) (rank) 利润(千元)(排名)	Total assets ('000 RMB) 总资产(千元)	Major products 主要产品
Yanshou Jijia Linen Textile Co., Ltd.	Harbin	Heilongjiang	(0451)3024376		Private Enterprises				Flax Yarn
延寿县继嘉亚麻纺织有限公司(1986)	哈尔滨市	黑龙江省	(0451)3024717	1,108	私营独资	78,921	26,363(1)	109,428	亚麻纱
Yixing Huayu Linen Textile Co., Ltd.	Wuxi	Jiangsu	(0510)7361859		Private Owned				Flax Cotton
宜兴市华裕亚麻纺织有限公司(2000)	无锡市	江苏省	(0510)7361498	93	私营企业	58,110	1,330(5)	25,080	亚麻棉
Xinjiang Yili Tianyi Industry Co.,Ltd. Xinyuan Branch	Yili	Xinjiang	(0999)5294154		Limited-Liability				Long Hemp
新疆伊犁天一实业有限责任公司新源分公司(1987)	伊犁州	新疆	(0999)5294126	860	有限公司	54,748	9,655(4)	79,169	长麻
Xinjiang Yili Tianyi Industry Co., Ltd. Yi'ning Branch	Yili	Xinjiang	(0999)4050468		Private Owned				Flax Fiber
新疆伊犁天一实业有限责任公司伊宁县分公司(2001)	伊犁州	新疆	(0999)4050005	510	私营企业	37,427	9,784(3)	36,687	亚麻纤维
Yixing Lingjin Linen Textile Factory	Wuxi	Jiangsu	(0510)7371058		Private Enterprises				Long Hemp
宜兴市凌津亚麻纺织厂(1997)	无锡市	江苏省	(0510)7371058	50	私营独资	24,000	650(9)	10,873	长麻
Yanshou Yanxing Linen Group Co., Ltd.	Harbin	Heilongjiang	(0451)53012369		State Enterprises				Flax Fiber
延寿县延兴亚麻集团有限公司(1993)	哈尔滨市	黑龙江省	(0451)53012369	500	国有独资	17,269	395(10)	42,801	亚麻纤维
Baiquan Wanda Flax Raw Material Factory	Qiqihar	Heilongjiang	(0452)7323706		State-owned				Flax Fiber
拜泉县万达亚麻原料厂(1935)	齐齐哈尔市	黑龙江省	(0452)7323138	537	国有企业	16,735	7(16)	33,058	亚麻纤维
Heilongjiang Bayan Flax Co., Ltd.	Harbin	Heilongjiang	(0451)57501234		Joint Stock				Flax Fiber
黑龙江省巴彦亚麻有限公司(1938)	哈尔滨市	黑龙江省	(0451)57501376	981	股份制	16,687	102(12)	65,492	亚麻纤维
Yueyang Spar Flax Hemp Textiles Mill Co.,Ltd.	Yueyang	Hunan	(0730)8783573		Foreign Funded				Flax Yarn
岳阳士达亚麻编织厂有限公司(1999)	岳阳市	湖南省	(0730)8781160	179	外商投资	9,031	-	14,951	亚麻纱
Heilongjiang Sunwu Flax Raw Material Factory	Heihe	Heilongjiang	(0456)8422716		State-owned				Flax Materials
黑龙江省孙吴县亚麻原料厂(1989)	黑河市	黑龙江省	(0456)8428694	327	国有企业	6,542	703(7)	19,872	亚麻原料

Top 10 Cities by Revenue 销售收入排名前10位城市	Province 省	Market share 市场份额(%)	Number of firms 企业个数
Harbin 哈尔滨市	Heilongjiang 黑龙江省	28.59	5
Yili 伊犁州	Xinjiang 新疆	26.26	3
Wuxi 无锡市	Jiangsu 江苏省	17.95	2
Qiqihar 齐齐哈尔市	Heilongjiang 黑龙江省	13.28	3
Suihua 绥化市	Heilongjiang 黑龙江省	6.13	2
Daqing 大庆市	Heilongjiang 黑龙江省	2.29	1
Yueyang 岳阳市	Hunan 湖南省	1.97	1
Heihe 黑河市	Heilongjiang 黑龙江省	1.43	1
Dingxi 定西地区	Gansu 甘肃省	1.08	1
Haidong 海东地区	Qinghai 青海省	0.18	1

10 Major Wholesalers 十家主要批发商	City 城市	Province 省	Telephone/Fax 电话/传真
Shanghai Shenda Co.,Ltd.	Shanghai	Shanghai	(021)62319898
上海申达股份有限公司	上海市	上海市	(021)62317250
Orient International Holding Silk Group Corportion	Shanghai	Shanghai	(021)64662288
东方国际集团丝绸进出口有限公司	上海市	上海市	(021)64677788
Nanjing Textiles Import & Export Co.,Ltd.	Nanjing	Jiangsu	(025)3306789
南京纺织品进出口股份有限公司	南京市	江苏省	(025)3300518
Zhejiang Textiles Import & Export Group Co.,Ltd.	Hangzhou	Zhejiang	(0571)87075888
浙江省纺织品进出口集团有限公司	杭州市	浙江省	(0571)87079234
Zhejiang Orient Holdings Co.,Ltd.	Hangzhou	Zhejiang	(0571)87215678
浙江东方集团股份有限公司	杭州市	浙江省	(0571)87215000
Zhejiang Silk Holding Co.,ltd.	Hangzhou	Zhejiang	(0571)85195588
浙江省丝绸集团有限公司	杭州市	浙江省	(0571)85192540
Guangdong Silk (Group) Corporation	Guangzhou	Guangdong	(020)83337448
广东省丝绸(集团)公司	广州市	广东省	(020)83332995
Shanghai Costume Group Co.,Ltd.	Shanghai	Shanghai	(021)62748598
上海服装(集团)有限公司	上海市	上海市	(021)62414773
Orient International Holding Shanghai Textiles Import & Export Co.Ltd.	Shanghai	Shanghai	(021)63218855
东方国际集团上海市针织品进出口有限公司	上海市	上海市	(021)63299560
Jiangsu Textiles Import & Export Group Co.,Ltd.	Nanjing	Jiangsu	(025)6895000
江苏省纺织品进出口集团股份有限公司	南京市	江苏省	(025)4400800

1714: Ramie Fibre Primary 苎麻纤维初步加工业

The industry accounts for 0.009% of the total revenue of China's industrial sector in 2002. The rate of return on assets is 4.51%. 90.00% of all firms in the industry made a profit while 10.00% had negative returns.The top province in terms of the industry's revenue is Jiangsu, accounting for 47.19% of the total revenue.
2002年本行业收入占全行业的 0.009%，资产利润率为 4.51%。90.00%的企业赢利，10.00%的企业亏损。收入最高的省为江苏省，占本行业的47.19%。

	Total number of firms 企业总数	Total number of employees 职工总数	Total revenue (Mil.RMB) 总销售收入 (百万元)	Total profit (Mil.RMB) 总利润 (百万元)	Return on assets 资产利润率 (%)	Return on equity 权益利润率 (%)	Labour productivity ('000 RMB/ worker) 劳动生产率 (千元/人)	Debts/ assets 资产负债率 (%)	Total assets (Mil.RMB) 总资产 (百万元)
Industry Overall 行业总体	30	6,046	982	28	4.51	9.65	38.16	53.21	613

	Number of firms 企业个数	Average number of employees 平均职工人数	Average revenue ('000 RMB) 平均销售收入 (千元)	Average profit ('000 RMB) 平均利润 (千元)	Return on assets 资产利润率 (%)	Return on equity 权益利润率 (%)	Labour productivity ('000 RMB/ worker) 劳动生产率 (千元/人)	Debts/ assets 资产负债率 (%)	Average total assets ('000 RMB) 平均总资产 (千元)
By ownership 产业所有权									
State-owned 国有									
Collective-owned 集体	7	135	18,436	724	7.91	24.32	30.73	67.48	9,154
Foreign & Overseas Chinese Funded 三资	1	64	47,954	2,409	17.28	20.41	223.66	15.34	13,940
By regional distribution 地区分布									
Central-North 华北									
Beijing 北京									
Tianjin 天津									
Hebei 河北									
Shanxi 山西									
Inner Mongolia 内蒙古									
Northeast 东北									
Liaoning 辽宁									
Jilin 吉林									
Heilongjiang 黑龙江									
Central-East 华东	8	183	68,513	1,895	3.55	7.64	88.26	53.46	53,308
Shanghai 上海									
Jiangsu 江苏	4	273	115,883	3,072	3.25	6.69	98.36	51.50	94,648
Zhejiang 浙江	1	163	23,072	67	0.35	1.73	18.92	79.45	18,888
Anhui 安徽	1	40	8,301	1	0.04	0.20	69.88	79.26	2,444
Fujian 福建									
Jiangxi 江西	1	102	5,250	390	3.10		13.24	110.71	12,600
Shandong 山东	1	64	47,954	2,409	17.28	20.41	223.66	15.34	13,940
Central-South 中南	21	205	20,124	623	7.53	16.38	23.25	54.01	8,262
Henan 河南									
Hubei 湖北	4	217	32,872	1,638	17.88	60.80	34.78	70.59	9,158
Hunan 湖南	16	211	17,412	376	4.63	9.02	19.84	48.62	8,112
Guangdong 广东	1	65	12,510	508	7.17	21.77	46.54	67.09	7,088
Guangxi 广西									
Hainan 海南									
Southwest 西南	1	275	11,488	-552	-4.21	-6.43	5.61	34.49	13,102
Chongqing 重庆	1	275	11,488	-552	-4.21	-6.43	5.61	34.49	13,102
Sichuan 四川									
Guizhou 贵州									
Yunnan 云南									
Tibet 西藏									
Northwest 西北									
Shaanxi 陕西									
Gansu 甘肃									
Qinghai 青海									
Ningxia 宁夏									
Xinjiang 新疆									

1714: Ramie Fibre Primary 苎麻纤维初步加工业

Year 年份	Number of firms 企业个数	Rate of change 变化率(%)	Number of employees 职工人数(人)	Rate of change 变化率(%)	Total revenue (Mil. RMB) 总销售收入(百万元)	Rate of change 变化率(%)	Total profit (Mil RMB) 总利润(百万元)	Rate of change 变化率(%)
2000	31		6,254		995		40	
2001	34	9.68	7,283	16.45	1,098	10.35	27	-32.50
2002	30	-11.76	6,046	-16.98	982	-10.56	28	3.70

Major Products 主要产品	Output 产量	Unit 单位

10 Main Firms with Maximal Revenue (year founded) 收入最大的十家主要企业(创办年份)	City 城市	Province 省	Telephone/fax 电话/传真	Number of employees 职工人数	Ownership 产业所有权	Revenue ('000 RMB) 销售收入(千元)	Profit('000 RMB) (rank) 利润(千元)(排名)	Total assets ('000 RMB) 总资产(千元)	Major products 主要产品
Jiangyin Kangyuan Printing & Dyeing Co., Ltd.	Wuxi	Jiangsu	(0510)6301968		Private Owned				Printing & Dyeing Processing
江阴市康源印染有限公司(1994)	无锡市	江苏省	(0510)6301955	880	私营企业	437,720	11,970(1)	340,760	印染加工
Chibi Xinfa Ramee Textile Co., Ltd.	Xianning	Hubei	(0715)5742232		Collective-owned				Textiles
赤壁市新发苎麻纺织厂(1982)	咸宁市	湖北省		440	集体企业	81,245	4,615(2)	15,004	纺织品
Ji'nan Julong Fiber Co., Ltd.	Jinan	Shandong	(0531)4561345		Overseas Chinese-funded				Composite Fibre
济南聚龙纤维有限公司(1999)	济南市	山东省	(0531)4561357	64	港澳台资	47,954	2,409(4)	13,940	复合纤维
Yangnan Tangxiang Ziyang Refined Flax Factory	Changde	Hunan	(0736)2041516		Private Enterprises				Refined Dry Flax
阳南塘乡紫阳精麻厂(1998)	常德市	湖南省	(0736)2041516	370	私营独资	30,900	1,510(5)	5,510	精干麻
Hunan Hanshou Zhulu Textile Co., Ltd.	Changde	Hunan	(0736)2872847		Private Owned				Refined Dry Flax
湖南汉寿县逐鹿纺织有限公司(1999)	常德市	湖南省	(0736)2870410	308	私营企业	27,010	70(17)	25,340	精干麻
Hunan Hanshou Yinxing Textile Co., Ltd.	Changde	Hunan	(0736)2872188		Private Owned				Refined Dry Flax
湖南省汉寿县银星纺织有限公司(2000)	常德市	湖南省	(0736)2872188	562	私营企业	26,494	261(12)	23,961	精干麻
Lishui Yuhai Refined Waste Flax Factory	Nanjing	Jiangsu	(025)7270032		Private Enterprises				Hemp
溧水县玉海精干麻厂(1982)	南京市	江苏省	(025)7270032	65	私营独资	17,720	260(13)	8,950	麻
Yangnan Tangxiang Supply & Marketing Refined Flax Factory	Changde	Hunan	(0736)2040917		Private Partnership				Refined Dry Flax
阳南塘乡供销精麻厂(1990)	常德市	湖南省		110	私营合伙	17,600	1,350(7)	2,570	精干麻
Hunan Yuanjiang Rongxin Textile Co., Ltd.	Yiyang	Hunan	(0737)2739308		Private Owned				Refined Dry Flax
湖南省沅江市荣信纺织有限公司(1998)	益阳市	湖南省	(0737)2739308	310	私营企业	17,263	-	8,282	精干麻
Hunan Liuyang Yujin Ramee Weaving Co., Ltd.	Changsha	Hunan	(0731)3680888		Joint Stock				Ramee Textiles
湖南省浏阳市禹进苎麻纺织有限公司(1999)	长沙市	湖南省	(0731)3655777	400	股份制	13,800	51(19)	9,194	苎麻纺织

Top 10 Cities by Revenue 销售收入排名前10位城市	Province 省	Market share 市场份额(%)	Number of firms 企业个数
Wuxi 无锡市	Jiangsu 江苏省	44.57	1
Changde 常德市	Hunan 湖南省	20.01	8
Xianning 咸宁市	Hubei 湖北省	9.66	2
Yiyang 益阳市	Hunan 湖南省	6.40	6
Jinan 济南市	Shandong 山东省	4.88	1
Huanggang 黄冈市	Hubei 湖北省	2.92	1
Taizhou 台州市	Zhejiang 浙江省	2.35	1
Nanjing 南京市	Jiangsu 江苏省	1.80	1
Changsha 长沙市	Hunan 湖南省	1.41	1
Jiangmen 江门市	Guangdong 广东省	1.27	1

10 Major Wholesalers 十家主要批发商	City 城市	Province 省	Telephone/Fax 电话/传真
Shanghai Shenda Co.,Ltd.	Shanghai	Shanghai	(021)62319898
上海申达股份有限公司	上海市	上海市	(021)62317250
Orient International Holding Silk Group Corportion	Shanghai	Shanghai	(021)64662288
东方国际集团丝绸进出口有限公司	上海市	上海市	(021)64677788
Nanjing Textiles Import & Export Co.,Ltd.	Nanjing	Jiangsu	(025)3306789
南京纺织品进出口股份有限公司	南京市	江苏省	(025)3300518
Zhejiang Textiles Import & Export Group Co.,Ltd.	Hangzhou	Zhejiang	(0571)87075888
浙江省纺织品进出口集团有限公司	杭州市	浙江省	(0571)87079234
Zhejiang Orient Holdings Co.,Ltd.	Hangzhou	Zhejiang	(0571)87215678
浙江东方集团股份有限公司	杭州市	浙江省	(0571)87215000
Zhejiang Silk Holding Co.,ltd.	Hangzhou	Zhejiang	(0571)85195588
浙江省丝绸集团有限公司	杭州市	浙江省	(0571)85192540
Guangdong Silk (Group) Corporation	Guangzhou	Guangdong	(020)83337448
广东省丝绸(集团)公司	广州市	广东省	(020)83332995
Shanghai Costume Group Co.,Ltd.	Shanghai	Shanghai	(021)62748598
上海服装(集团)有限公司	上海市	上海市	(021)62414773
Orient International Holding Shanghai Textiles Import & Export Co.Ltd.	Shanghai	Shanghai	(021)63218855
东方国际集团上海市针织品进出口有限公司	上海市	上海市	(021)63299560
Jiangsu Textiles Import & Export Group Co.,Ltd.	Nanjing	Jiangsu	(025)6895000
江苏省纺织品进出口集团股份有限公司	南京市	江苏省	(025)4400800

1719: Preliminary Processing Of Other Raw Fibre Materials

其他纤维原料初步加工业

The industry accounts for 0.064% of the total revenue of China's industrial sector in 2002. The rate of return on assets is 3.86%. 80.36% of all firms in the industry made a profit while 19.64% had negative returns.The top province in terms of the industry's revenue is Zhejiang, accounting for 72.50% of the total revenue.
2002年本行业收入占全行业的 0.064%，资产利润率为 3.86%。80.36%的企业赢利，19.64%的企业亏损。收入最高的省为浙江省，占本行业的72.50%。

	Total number of firms 企业总数	Total number of employees 职工总数	Total revenue (Mil.RMB) 总销售收入 (百万元)	Total profit (Mil.RMB) 总利润 (百万元)	Return on assets 资产利润率 (%)	Return on equity 权益利润率 (%)	Labour productivity ('000 RMB/ worker) 劳动生产率 (千元/人)	Debts/ assets 资产负债率 (%)	Total assets (Mil.RMB) 总资产 (百万元)
Industry Overall 行业总体	112	20,943	6,864	280	3.86	9.89	69.78	60.98	7,258

	Number of firms 企业个数	Average number of employees 平均职工人数	Average revenue ('000 RMB) 平均销售收入（千元）	Average profit ('000 RMB) 平均利润 (千元)	Return on assets 资产利润率 (%)	Return on equity 权益利润率 (%)	Labour productivity ('000 RMB/ worker) 劳动生产率 (千元/人)	Debts/ assets 资产负债率 (%)	Average total assets ('000 RMB) 平均总资产 (千元)
By ownership 产业所有权									
State-owned 国有	4	108	9,570	-561	-0.84	-2.70	31.74	68.80	66,558
Collective-owned 集体	10	209	18,636	524	3.19	24.40	20.65	86.94	16,438
Foreign & Overseas Chinese Funded 三资	25	197	40,117	630	1.07	2.64	94.01	59.57	59,099
By regional distribution 地区分布									
Central-North 华北	11	92	17,819	154	0.38	0.55	96.42	31.18	40,793
Beijing 北京	1	76	9,850	394	3.09	10.55	48.41	70.74	12,757
Tianjin 天津	6	89	22,215	-83	-0.17	-0.22	141.88	22.47	48,099
Hebei 河北	2	113	5,569	322	0.94	1.06	11.12	11.27	34,042
Shanxi 山西									
Inner Mongolia 内蒙古	2	87	20,865	578	1.46	5.52	88.44	73.61	39,648
Northeast 东北	5	92	13,289	526	5.70	8.41	39.63	32.19	9,224
Liaoning 辽宁	3	122	19,400	900	7.00	10.09	33.95	30.59	12,857
Jilin 吉林	2	48	4,124	-36	-0.94	-1.58	61.56	40.37	3,775
Heilongjiang 黑龙江									
Central-East 华东	78	207	79,823	3,516	4.37	11.44	76.38	61.84	80,538
Shanghai 上海	3	84	16,935	293	1.96	3.91	38.71	49.73	14,921
Jiangsu 江苏	21	121	23,633	793	6.35	25.31	51.99	74.92	12,493
Zhejiang 浙江	40	210	124,418	6,211	5.10	12.36	88.43	58.72	121,679
Anhui 安徽	3	280	7,949	260	2.29	6.90	14.29	66.87	11,393
Fujian 福建	2	335	62,738	124	0.39	0.79	162.99	50.93	31,896
Jiangxi 江西									
Shandong 山东	9	377	61,448	809	0.72	2.83	65.96	74.54	112,185
Central-South 中南	15	199	23,381	121	0.42	2.23	34.96	81.28	29,086
Henan 河南	7	147	21,293	791	7.71	80.31	35.71	90.40	10,259
Hubei 湖北	2	369	31,709	-400	-2.31	-19.61	45.06	88.20	17,261
Hunan 湖南									
Guangdong 广东	4	147	27,115	-793	-1.63	-10.56	43.88	84.57	48,683
Guangxi 广西	1	328	15,250	299	0.35	0.86	18.59	59.71	86,550
Hainan 海南	1	300	14,542	-44	-0.09	-0.76	7.99	88.15	48,673
Southwest 西南	1	265	18,677	827	2.65	8.42	28.28	68.48	31,175
Chongqing 重庆									
Sichuan 四川	1	265	18,677	827	2.65	8.42	28.28	68.48	31,175
Guizhou 贵州									
Yunnan 云南									
Tibet 西藏									
Northwest 西北	2	55	3,222	-546	-7.84	-33.55	28.42	76.62	6,961
Shaanxi 陕西	1	59	6,422	-1,093	-13.80		33.73	101.17	7,918
Gansu 甘肃	1	50	22	1	0.02	0.03	22.16	44.24	6,004
Qinghai 青海									
Ningxia 宁夏									
Xinjiang 新疆									

1719: Preliminary Processing Of Other Raw Fibre Materials

其他纤维原料初步加工业

Year 年份	Number of firms 企业个数	Rate of change 变化率 (%)	Number of employees 职工人数 (人)	Rate of change 变化率 (%)	Total revenue (Mil. RMB) 总销售收入 (百万元)	Rate of change 变化率 (%)	Total profit (Mil RMB) 总利润 (百万元)	Rate of change 变化率 (%)
2000	190		25,204		7,280		450	
2001	209	10.00	29,835	18.37	9,299	27.73	518	15.11
2002	112	-46.41	20,943	-29.80	6,864	-26.19	280	-45.95

Major Products 主要产品	Output 产量	Unit 单位
Synthetic Fibre 合成纤维	915	10,000 Tons 万吨
Polyester Fibre 涤纶纤维	772	10,000 Tons 万吨

10 Main Firms with Maximal Revenue (year founded) 收入最大的十家主要企业（创办年份）	City 城市	Province 省	Telephone/fax 电话/传真	Number of employees 职工人数	Ownership 产业所有权	Revenue ('000 RMB) 销售收入 (千元)	Profit('000 RMB) (rank) 利润(千元) (排名)	Total assets ('000 RMB) 总资产 (千元)	Major products 主要产品
Zhejiang King's Industry Co., Ltd.	Hangzhou	Zhejiang	(0571)82796520		Limited-Liability				Terylene Fiber
浙江开氏实业有限公司(1997)	杭州市	浙江省	(0571)82798132	1,279	有限公司	907,677	51,154(3)	937,251	涤纶丝
Zhejiang Yongli Industrial Group Co., Ltd.	Shaoxing	Zhejiang	(0575)4571511		Limited-Liability				Terylene Fibre
浙江永利实业集团有限公司(1993)	绍兴市	浙江省	(0575)4069654	1,206	有限公司	805,037	71,545(2)	804,927	涤丝
Qingdao Er-He Textile Co., Ltd.	Qingdao	Shandong	(0532)6461150		Foreign Funded				Chemical Fiber Cloth
青岛二和纤维有限公司(1993)	青岛市	山东省	(0532)6461147	850	外商投资	264,750	2,358(15)	659,042	化纤布
Hangzhou Xiaoshan Qingyun Textile Co., Ltd.	Hangzhou	Zhejiang	(0571)82795111		Private Owned				POY Silk
杭州萧山青云纺织有限公司(1999)	杭州市	浙江省	(0571)82795111	109	私营企业	146,737	5,485(5)	140,370	POY丝
Wuxi Huali Tyrd Cord Co.,Ltd.	Wuxi	Jiangsu	(0510)3231547		Private Owned				Cord Thread
无锡市华力帘子线有限公司(1998)	无锡市	江苏省	(0510)3231627	237	私营企业	130,560	1,810(19)	72,300	帘子线
Qingdao Cotton Textile Co.Ltd.	Qingdao	Shandong	(0532)6461160		Foreign Funded				Chemical Fiber Cloth
青岛棉花纤维有限公司(1994)	青岛市	山东省	(0532)6461158	750	外商投资	130,125	2,510(13)	133,850	化纤布
Quanzhou Sanhong Chemical Fibre Co., Ltd.	Quanzhou	Fujian	(0595)2499733		Overseas Chinese-funded				PP Yarn
泉州三宏化纤有限公司(1998)	泉州市	福建省	(0595)2462333	550	港澳台资	110,000	200(61)	62,800	PP纱
Tianjin Mujin Cashmere Co., Ltd.	Tianjin	Tianjin	(022)23286193		Overseas Chinese-funded				Non-Wool Velvet
天津牧津企业有限公司(1981)	天津市	天津市	(022)23286139	132	港澳台资	98,623	580(44)	144,887	无毛绒
Huzhou Shixi Livestock Products Processing Co., Ltd.	Huzhou	Zhejiang	(0572)3050338		Private Owned				Rabbit Hair Processing
湖州适溪畜产品加工有限公司(1994)	湖州市	浙江省	(0572)3050518	80	私营企业	81,798	627(41)	17,240	免毛加工
Hangzhou Xiaoshan Meibang Chemical Fibre Co., Ltd.	Hangzhou	Zhejiang	(0571)82585388		Private Owned				Polyurethane Package Silk
杭州萧山美邦化纤有限公司(1999)	杭州市	浙江省	(0571)82589616	150	私营企业	72,950	2,059(17)	16,579	氨纶包覆丝

Top 10 Cities by Revenue 销售收入排名前10位城市	Province 省	Market share 市场份额 (%)	Number of firms 企业个数
Hangzhou 杭州市	Zhejiang 浙江省	51.55	14
Shaoxing 绍兴市	Zhejiang 浙江省	13.46	9
Qingdao 青岛市	Shandong 山东省	6.19	3
Huzhou 湖州市	Zhejiang 浙江省	3.55	7
Wuxi 无锡市	Jiangsu 江苏省	2.41	5
Jiaxing 嘉兴市	Zhejiang 浙江省	2.38	3
Tianjin 天津市	Tianjin 天津市	1.94	6
Quanzhou 泉州市	Fujian 福建省	1.60	1
Jiangmen 江门市	Guangdong 广东省	1.58	4
Ningbo 宁波市	Zhejiang 浙江省	1.43	6

10 Major Wholesalers 十家主要批发商	City 城市	Province 省	Telephone/Fax 电话/传真
Shanghai Shenda Co.,Ltd.	Shanghai	Shanghai	(021)62319898
上海申达股份有限公司	上海市	上海市	(021)62317250
Orient International Holding Silk Group Corportion	Shanghai	Shanghai	(021)64662288
东方国际集团丝绸进出口有限公司	上海市	上海市	(021)64677788
Nanjing Textiles Import & Export Co.,Ltd.	Nanjing	Jiangsu	(025)3306789
南京纺织品进出口股份有限公司	南京市	江苏省	(025)3300518
Zhejiang Textiles Import & Export Group Co.,Ltd.	Hangzhou	Zhejiang	(0571)87075888
浙江省纺织品进出口集团有限公司	杭州市	浙江省	(0571)87079234
Zhejiang Orient Holdings Co.,Ltd.	Hangzhou	Zhejiang	(0571)87215678
浙江东方集团股份有限公司	杭州市	浙江省	(0571)87215000
Zhejiang Silk Holding Co.,ltd.	Hangzhou	Zhejiang	(0571)85195588
浙江省丝绸集团有限公司	杭州市	浙江省	(0571)85192540
Guangdong Silk (Group) Corporation	Guangzhou	Guangdong	(020)83337448
广东省丝绸（集团）公司	广州市	广东省	(020)83332995
Shanghai Costume Group Co.,Ltd.	Shanghai	Shanghai	(021)62748598
上海服装（集团）有限公司	上海市	上海市	(021)62414773
Orient International Holding Shanghai Textiles Import & Export Co.Ltd.	Shanghai	Shanghai	(021)63218855
东方国际集团上海市针织品进出口有限公司	上海市	上海市	(021)63299560
Jiangsu Textiles Import & Export Group Co.,Ltd.	Nanjing	Jiangsu	(025)6895000
江苏省纺织品进出口集团股份有限公司	南京市	江苏省	(025)4400800

1721: Cotton Spinning 棉纺业

The industry accounts for 1.333% of the total revenue of China's industrial sector in 2002. The rate of return on assets is 1.90%. 78.66% of all firms in the industry made a profit while 21.34% had negative returns.The top province in terms of the industry's revenue is Jiangsu, accounting for 24.09% of the total revenue.
2002年本行业收入占全行业的 1.333%，资产利润率为 1.90%。78.66%的企业赢利，21.34%的企业亏损。收入最高的省为江苏省，占本行业的24.09%。

	Total number of firms 企业总数	Total number of employees 职工总数	Total revenue (Mil.RMB) 总销售收入（百万元）	Total profit (Mil.RMB) 总利润（百万元）	Return on assets 资产利润率 (%)	Return on equity 权益利润率 (%)	Labour productivity ('000 RMB/ worker) 劳动生产率（千元/人）	Debts/ assets 资产负债率 (%)	Total assets (Mil.RMB) 总资产（百万元）
Industry Overall 行业总体	1729	1,610,700	142,934	3,326	1.90	6.09	24.73	68.89	175,446

	Number of firms 企业个数	Average number of employees 平均职工人数	Average revenue ('000 RMB) 平均销售收入（千元）	Average profit ('000 RMB) 平均利润（千元）	Return on assets 资产利润率 (%)	Return on equity 权益利润率 (%)	Labour productivity ('000 RMB/ worker) 劳动生产率（千元/人）	Debts/ assets 资产负债率 (%)	Average total assets ('000 RMB) 平均总资产（千元）
By ownership 产业所有权									
State-owned 国有	216	1,869	138,413	1,009	0.49	2.16	20.74	77.14	203,989
Collective-owned 集体	241	420	40,293	1,079	2.55	10.47	27.32	75.66	42,348
Foreign & Overseas Chinese Funded 三资	157	522	68,474	3,693	3.80	12.96	37.53	70.70	97,277
By regional distribution 地区分布									
Central-North 华北	163	1,278	76,139	957	0.83	2.50	17.21	66.88	115,414
Beijing 北京	8	1,458	100,248	3,735	2.14	4.97	17.61	56.88	174,163
Tianjin 天津	29	886	67,205	-561	-0.47	-1.84	19.66	74.77	120,474
Hebei 河北	100	1,238	80,017	1,776	1.62	5.00	18.91	67.52	109,369
Shanxi 山西	23	1,786	61,187	-1,426	-1.41	-4.11	11.55	65.68	101,055
Inner Mongolia 内蒙古	3	2,003	83,561	-811	-0.37	-0.61	9.50	39.91	221,426
Northeast 东北	69	1,258	60,083	-1,430	-1.04	-4.39	13.32	76.34	137,609
Liaoning 辽宁	43	1,201	57,858	-1,873	-1.46	-6.03	13.34	75.73	127,861
Jilin 吉林	10	2,005	110,851	-768	-0.28	-0.76	15.03	63.57	276,104
Heilongjiang 黑龙江	16	944	34,333	-655	-0.85		11.00	107.58	77,249
Central-East 华东	955	782	93,598	3,336	3.47	9.84	31.85	64.75	96,219
Shanghai 上海	58	583	105,888	3,925	4.03	7.18	29.15	43.90	97,389
Jiangsu 江苏	317	716	108,640	2,790	3.14	9.75	39.08	67.79	88,861
Zhejiang 浙江	139	376	61,526	2,905	4.76	14.30	36.48	66.71	61,021
Anhui 安徽	78	1,100	71,173	1,567	1.41	4.14	22.55	66.05	111,489
Fujian 福建	55	405	63,961	3,015	4.61	8.89	49.43	48.12	65,343
Jiangxi 江西	35	1,201	41,143	-126	-0.17	-0.47	12.14	64.42	75,953
Shandong 山东	273	1,039	108,954	5,079	4.00	11.99	29.89	66.62	126,891
Central-South 中南	405	867	66,404	1,131	1.32	5.89	23.43	77.65	85,891
Henan 河南	159	905	68,226	1,978	2.38	9.06	22.10	73.68	83,003
Hubei 湖北	128	911	65,897	683	0.86	2.70	23.80	68.15	79,543
Hunan 湖南	49	814	40,877	-783	-1.55	-6.68	15.74	76.84	50,610
Guangdong 广东	53	574	79,933	1,850	1.42		39.16	102.14	130,367
Guangxi 广西	16	1,284	85,732	-216	-0.17	-0.55	22.24	68.67	126,104
Hainan 海南									
Southwest 西南	56	1,598	61,872	-3,354	-2.75	-14.04	10.93	80.41	121,942
Chongqing 重庆	11	1,923	78,933	-4,993	-3.21		10.12	103.59	155,317
Sichuan 四川	30	1,465	70,320	-1,485	-1.30	-3.92	14.63	66.75	114,019
Guizhou 贵州	8	1,345	16,822	-4,287	-5.52	-28.86	2.85	80.86	77,620
Yunnan 云南	7	1,945	50,337	-7,718	-5.01	-37.78	6.61	86.74	154,109
Tibet 西藏									
Northwest 西北	81	1,585	81,884	-2,315	-1.38	-4.07	16.42	66.26	168,327
Shaanxi 陕西	31	2,115	95,341	1,348	0.78	1.70	15.18	54.25	173,756
Gansu 甘肃	8	600	18,120	-151	-0.47	-4.14	12.94	88.59	32,036
Qinghai 青海									
Ningxia 宁夏									
Xinjiang 新疆	42	1,380	84,098	-5,430	-2.85	-10.82	18.11	73.63	190,281

Year 年份	Number of firms 企业个数	Rate of change 变化率 (%)	Number of employees 职工人数 (人)	Rate of change 变化率 (%)	Total revenue (Mil. RMB) 总销售收入 (百万元)	Rate of change 变化率 (%)	Total profit (Mil RMB) 总利润 (百万元)	Rate of change 变化率 (%)
2000	1441		1,721,500		123,326		4,063	
2001	1546	7.29	1,635,100	-5.02	125,272	1.58	2,115	-47.94
2002	1729	11.84	1,610,700	-1.49	142,934	14.10	3,326	57.26

Major Products 主要产品	Output 产量	Unit 单位
Yarn 纱	802	10,000 Tons 万吨

10 Main Firms with Maximal Revenue (year founded) 收入最大的十家主要企业（创办年份）	City 城市	Province 省	Telephone/fax 电话/传真	Number of employees 职工人数	Ownership 产业所有权	Revenue ('000 RMB) 销售收入 (千元)	Profit('000 RMB) (rank) 利润(千元) (排名)	Total assets ('000 RMB) 总资产 (千元)	Major products 主要产品
Shandong Weiqiao Textile Group Co., Ltd.	Binzhou	Shandong	(0543)4721194		State-owned				Cotton Yarn
山东魏桥纺织集团有限责任公司(1951)	滨州市	山东省	(0543)4721200	23,852	国有企业	4,897,568	450,120(1)	5,945,485	棉纱
Zhangjiagang Huafang Group Co., Ltd.	Suzhou	Jiangsu	(0512)58441711		Joint Stock				Cotton Yarn
张家港华芳集团有限公司(1976)	苏州市	江苏省	(0512)58441073	15,600	股份制	4,579,520	133,130(5)	3,516,730	棉纺纱
Shanghai Shenda Co. Ltd.	Shanghai	Shanghai	(021)62317257		Joint Stock				Yarn
上海申达股份有限公司(1986)	上海市	上海市	(021)62317250	4,108	股份制	3,203,695	157,443(2)	2,267,041	纱
Shandong Demian Group Co., Ltd.	Dezhou	Shandong	(0534)2413001		State Enterprises				Cotton Yarn
山东德棉集团有限公司(1997)	德州市	山东省	(0534)2413002	14,401	国有独资	2,149,809	58,813(11)	2,389,280	棉纱
Shijiazhuang Changshan Textile Co., Ltd.	Shijiazhuang	Hebei	(0311)6674239		Joint Stock				Cotton Yarn
石家庄常山纺织股份有限公司(1998)	石家庄市	河北省	(0311)6673929	28,199	股份制	1,897,433	135,293(4)	2,090,632	棉纱
Wuxi Qingfeng Group Co., Ltd.	Wuxi	Jiangsu	(0510)2355496		State Enterprises				Cotton Yarn
无锡庆丰集团有限公司(1998)	无锡市	江苏省	(0510)2357620	4,388	国有独资	1,171,667	77,078(9)	1,842,753	棉纱
Wuxi NO.1 Cotton Mill	Wuxi	Jiangsu	(0510)2851567		State-owned				Cotton Yarn
无锡市第一棉纺织厂(1919)	无锡市	江苏省	(0510)2852374	3,221	国有企业	1,101,610	99,600(7)	836,851	棉纱
Henan Xinye Textile (Group)Co., Ltd.	Nanyang	Henan	(0377)6221701		Joint Stock				Cotton Yarn
河南新野纺织(集团)股份有限公司(1969)	南阳市	河南省	(0377)6221731	9,035	股份制	1,098,378	42,406(17)	1,236,822	棉纱
Hangzhou Daoyuan Chemical Fibre Co., Ltd.	Hangzhou	Zhejiang	(0571)82852008		Private Owned				Terylene Fibre
杭州道远化纤有限公司(1999)	杭州市	浙江省	(0571)82856073	1,060	私营企业	1,032,870	33,377(12)	811,330	涤丝
Lutai Textile Co., Ltd.	Zibo	Shandong	(0533)5280809		Foreign Funded				Coloured Woven Cloth
鲁泰纺织股份有限公司(1990)	淄博市	山东省	(0533)5282188	4,476	外商投资	925,660	150,781(3)	1,659,441	色织布

Top 10 Cities by Revenue 销售收入排名前10位城市	Province 省	Market share 市场份额 (%)	Number of firms 企业个数
Suzhou 苏州市	Jiangsu 江苏省	5.36	54
Yancheng 盐城市	Jiangsu 江苏省	4.75	52
Binzhou 滨州市	Shandong 山东省	4.74	22
Shanghai 上海市	Shanghai 上海市	4.30	58
Wuxi 无锡市	Jiangsu 江苏省	3.99	38
Dezhou 德州市	Shandong 山东省	2.83	45
Nantong 南通市	Jiangsu 江苏省	2.59	55
Hangzhou 杭州市	Zhejiang 浙江省	2.18	34
Shijiazhuang 石家庄市	Hebei 河北省	2.05	24
Xuzhou 徐州市	Jiangsu 江苏省	2.00	23

10 Major Wholesalers 十家主要批发商	City 城市	Province 省	Telephone/Fax 电话/传真
Shanghai Shenda Co.,Ltd.	Shanghai	Shanghai	(021)62319898
上海申达股份有限公司	上海市	上海市	(021)62317250
Orient International Holding Silk Group Corportion	Shanghai	Shanghai	(021)64662288
东方国际集团丝绸进出口有限公司	上海市	上海市	(021)64677788
Nanjing Textiles Import & Export Co.,Ltd.	Nanjing	Jiangsu	(025)3306789
南京纺织品进出口股份有限公司	南京市	江苏省	(025)3300518
Zhejiang Textiles Import & Export Group Co.,Ltd.	Hangzhou	Zhejiang	(0571)87075888
浙江省纺织品进出口集团有限公司	杭州市	浙江省	(0571)87079234
Zhejiang Orient Holdings Co.,Ltd.	Hangzhou	Zhejiang	(0571)87215678
浙江东方集团股份有限公司	杭州市	浙江省	(0571)87215000
Zhejiang Silk Holding Co.,ltd.	Hangzhou	Zhejiang	(0571)85195588
浙江省丝绸集团有限公司	杭州市	浙江省	(0571)85192540
Guangdong Silk (Group) Corporation	Guangzhou	Guangdong	(020)83337448
广东省丝绸（集团）公司	广州市	广东省	(020)83332995
Shanghai Costume Group Co.,Ltd.	Shanghai	Shanghai	(021)62748598
上海服装（集团）有限公司	上海市	上海市	(021)62414773
Orient International Holding Shanghai Textiles Import & Export Co.Ltd.	Shanghai	Shanghai	(021)63218833
东方国际集团上海市针织品进出口有限公司	上海市	上海市	(021)63299560
Jiangsu Textiles Import & Export Group Co.,Ltd.	Nanjing	Jiangsu	(025)6895000
江苏省纺织品进出口集团股份有限公司	南京市	江苏省	(025)4400800

1722: Cotton Weaving 棉织业

The industry accounts for 0.562% of the total revenue of China's industrial sector in 2002. The rate of return on assets is 3.42%. 80.94% of all firms in the industry made a profit while 19.06% had negative returns.The top province in terms of the industry's revenue is Jiangsu, accounting for 35.89% of the total revenue.
2002年本行业收入占全行业的0.562%，资产利润率为3.42%。80.94%的企业赢利，19.06%的企业亏损。收入最高的省为江苏省，占本行业的35.89%。

	Total number of firms 企业总数	Total number of employees 职工总数	Total revenue (Mil.RMB) 总销售收入 (百万元)	Total profit (Mil.RMB) 总利润 (百万元)	Return on assets 资产利润率 (%)	Return on equity 权益利润率 (%)	Labour productivity ('000 RMB/ worker) 劳动生产率 (千元/人)	Debts/ assets 资产负债率 (%)	Total assets (Mil.RMB) 总资产 (百万元)
Industry Overall 行业总体	1537	491,954	60,229	1,975	3.42	9.70	32.75	64.74	57,717

	Number of firms 企业个数	Average number of employees 平均职工人数	Average revenue ('000 RMB) 平均销售收入 (千元)	Average profit ('000 RMB) 平均利润 (千元)	Return on assets 资产利润率 (%)	Return on equity 权益利润率 (%)	Labour productivity ('000 RMB/ worker) 劳动生产率 (千元/人)	Debts/ assets 资产负债率 (%)	Average total assets ('000 RMB) 平均总资产 (千元)
By ownership 产业所有权									
State-owned 国有	138	654	38,353	-634	-0.92	-6.97	16.86	86.77	68,746
Collective-owned 集体	235	252	27,601	792	3.59	13.19	32.19	72.79	22,071
Foreign & Overseas Chinese Funded 三资	178	319	61,954	2,889	3.68	7.62	54.99	51.72	78,478
By regional distribution 地区分布									
Central-North 华北	132	266	26,096	352	1.02	8.84	27.39	88.51	34,658
Beijing 北京	8	441	35,945	406	0.54	1.36	23.60	60.58	75,726
Tianjin 天津	39	166	20,198	230	0.52	16.23	19.92	96.79	44,192
Hebei 河北	78	280	28,339	440	1.77	16.65	31.22	89.40	24,920
Shanxi 山西	5	131	10,063	132	0.49	3.58	22.39	86.17	26,670
Inner Mongolia 内蒙古	2	1,334	54,301	-370	-0.44	-10.80	20.36	95.93	84,255
Northeast 东北	40	381	16,819	-287	-0.84		10.64	101.64	34,146
Liaoning 辽宁	25	351	20,245	-94	-0.25		14.14	104.61	37,336
Jilin 吉林	10	174	10,571	-694	-2.66	-114.27	13.90	97.67	26,123
Heilongjiang 黑龙江	5	942	12,182	-435	-1.27	-14.92	2.92	91.49	34,244
Central-East 华东	975	282	43,344	1,753	4.92	12.24	38.41	59.79	35,627
Shanghai 上海	40	209	17,706	128	0.68	2.15	20.39	68.39	18,861
Jiangsu 江苏	434	296	49,803	1,697	4.71	12.43	41.35	62.07	36,003
Zhejiang 浙江	256	168	43,472	2,396	6.69	15.43	51.89	56.66	35,820
Anhui 安徽	26	316	15,937	53	0.38	1.39	15.60	72.51	13,842
Fujian 福建	42	246	46,836	2,159	3.20	5.82	75.12	45.09	67,491
Jiangxi 江西	12	211	12,436	67	0.42	0.83	13.85	49.70	16,115
Shandong 山东	165	447	38,051	1,580	4.50	12.57	25.71	64.24	35,144
Central-South 中南	323	398	37,676	801	1.82	5.26	30.34	65.37	44,004
Henan 河南	84	518	27,451	200	0.59	1.92	16.57	69.04	33,723
Hubei 湖北	120	446	35,485	775	2.21	10.64	28.64	79.19	34,976
Hunan 湖南	14	204	12,207	140	1.32	8.71	21.64	84.79	10,562
Guangdong 广东	99	269	53,841	1,561	2.24	4.85	58.22	53.75	69,610
Guangxi 广西	6	334	17,373	-1,258	-5.24		16.61	126.02	24,015
Hainan 海南									
Southwest 西南	50	445	21,690	139	0.50	1.48	14.47	66.28	27,762
Chongqing 重庆	11	195	15,583	-115	-0.96	-2.65	17.95	63.80	11,969
Sichuan 四川	34	572	25,942	267	0.84	2.19	14.31	61.87	32,004
Guizhou 贵州	3	151	8,029	-188	-0.47	-3.50	5.13	86.54	39,854
Yunnan 云南	2	87	3,473	-165	-0.67		13.60	121.73	24,372
Tibet 西藏									
Northwest 西北	17	957	35,107	-2,039	-2.41	-7.02	13.69	65.68	84,627
Shaanxi 陕西	11	1,256	48,010	-1,407	-1.21	-3.08	14.18	60.88	116,626
Gansu 甘肃	3	72	7,772	307	6.38	8.98	43.43	28.92	4,805
Qinghai 青海									
Ningxia 宁夏									
Xinjiang 新疆	3	746	15,132	-6,698	-14.21		7.79	113.01	47,119

1722: Cotton Weaving 棉织业

Year 年份	Number of firms 企业个数	Rate of change 变化率 (%)	Number of employees 职工人数 (人)	Rate of change 变化率 (%)	Total revenue (Mil. RMB) 总销售收入 (百万元)	Rate of change 变化率 (%)	Total profit (Mil RMB) 总利润 (百万元)	Rate of change 变化率 (%)
2000	1320		514,354		46,892		1,214	
2001	1378	4.39	489,712	-4.79	48,956	4.40	965	-20.51
2002	1537	11.54	491,954	0.46	60,229	23.03	1,975	104.66

Major Products 主要产品	Output 产量	Unit 单位
Cloth 布	227	100,000,000 Meters 亿米
Cotton Cloth 棉布	116	100,000,000 Meters 亿米

10 Main Firms with Maximal Revenue (year founded) 收入最大的十家主要企业（创办年份）	City 城市	Province 省	Telephone/fax 电话/传真	Number of employees 职工人数	Ownership 产业所有权	Revenue ('000 RMB) 销售收入(千元)	Profit('000 RMB) (rank) 利润(千元)(排名)	Total assets ('000 RMB) 总资产(千元)	Major products 主要产品
Black Peony (Group)Co., Ltd.	Changzhou	Jiangsu	(0519)8111238		Joint Stock				Jean
黑牡丹(集团)股份有限公司(1940)	常州市	江苏省	(0519)8108817	2,890	股份制	1,411,100	240,360(1)	1,388,660	牛仔布
Jiangsu Menglan (Group) Co., Ltd.	Suzhou	Jiangsu	(0512)52831881		Limited-Liability				Bedclothes
江苏梦兰集团有限公司(1994)	苏州市	江苏省	(0512)52837196	997	有限公司	809,730	58,930(2)	766,730	床上用品
Jiangyin Red Star Group Co., Ltd.	Wuxi	Jiangsu	(0510)6884964		State-owned				Coloured Woven Cloth
江阴市红星集团有限责任公司(1946)	无锡市	江苏省	(0510)6882059	3,032	国有企业	712,319	697(397)	665,726	色织布
Dinghu Yongsheng PPY Co., Ltd	Zhaoqing	Guangdong	(0758)2611688		Foreign Funded				Cotton Fabric
鼎湖永盛化纤纺织印染厂有限公司(1995)	肇庆市	广东省	(0758)2611775	3,097	外商投资	627,851	46,609(6)	1,390,590	棉织品
Jiangsu Taiqing Group Co., Ltd.	Wuxi	Jiangsu	(0510)6201622		Limited-Liability				Weaving Cloth
江苏泰清集团有限公司(1995)	无锡市	江苏省	(0510)6201412	1,669	有限公司	607,240	13,220(33)	437,700	织布
Wuhan NO.1 Textile Group Co., Ltd.	Wuhan	Hubei	(027)84712911		State-owned				Cotton Yarn
武汉一棉集团有限公司(1952)	武汉市	湖北省	(027)84711560	5,302	国有企业	548,109	11,995(39)	611,257	棉纱
Zhejiang Jianpei Textiles Co. Ltd.	Shaoxing	Zhejiang	(0575)7695868		Private Owned				Cotton Fabric
浙江建培纺织有限公司(1998)	绍兴市	浙江省	(0575)7694181	428	私营企业	523,370	51,310(5)	115,580	棉织品
Wuxi Pacific Group Co., Ltd.	Wuxi	Jiangsu	(0510)2854741		State Enterprises				Coloured Woven Cloth
无锡太平洋集团有限公司(1997)	无锡市	江苏省	(0510)2853246	3,442	国有独资	502,070	10,230(42)	562,702	色织布
Hangzhou Deli Textile Co., Ltd.	Hangzhou	Zhejiang	(0571)86912428		Foreign Funded				Dyeing Terylene Cloth染色
杭州得力纺织有限公司(1998)	杭州市	浙江省	(0571)86911418	721	外商投资	474,483	39,296(8)	595,794	涤纶面料
Changzhou Canvas Mill	Changzhou	Jiangsu	(0519)8811491		Joint Stock				Weaving Cloth
常州市帆布厂(1982)	常州市	江苏省	(0519)8811491	1,548	股份制	468,490	6,670(66)	162,720	织布

Top 10 Cities by Revenue 销售收入排名前10位城市	Province 省	Market share 市场份额 (%)	Number of firms 企业个数
Changzhou 常州市	Jiangsu 江苏省	10.20	107
Shaoxing 绍兴市	Zhejiang 浙江省	9.25	106
Wuxi 无锡市	Jiangsu 江苏省	8.10	79
Nantong 南通市	Jiangsu 江苏省	6.43	108
Hangzhou 杭州市	Zhejiang 浙江省	5.69	71
Weifang 潍坊市	Shandong 山东省	3.68	57
Suzhou 苏州市	Jiangsu 江苏省	3.23	34
Foshan 佛山市	Guangdong 广东省	2.95	27
Wuhan 武汉市	Hubei 湖北省	2.70	19
Yancheng 盐城市	Jiangsu 江苏省	2.13	39

10 Major Wholesalers 十家主要批发商	City 城市	Province 省	Telephone/Fax 电话/传真
Shanghai Shenda Co.,Ltd.	Shanghai	Shanghai	(021)62319898
上海申达股份有限公司	上海市	上海市	(021)62317250
Orient International Holding Silk Group Corportion	Shanghai	Shanghai	(021)64662288
东方国际集团丝绸进出口有限公司	上海市	上海市	(021)64677788
Nanjing Textiles Import & Export Co.,Ltd.	Nanjing	Jiangsu	(025)3306789
南京纺织品进出口股份有限公司	南京市	江苏省	(025)3300518
Zhejiang Textiles Import & Export Group Co.,Ltd.	Hangzhou	Zhejiang	(0571)87075888
浙江省纺织品进出口集团有限公司	杭州市	浙江省	(0571)87079234
Zhejiang Orient Holdings Co.,Ltd.	Hangzhou	Zhejiang	(0571)87215678
浙江东方集团股份有限公司	杭州市	浙江省	(0571)87215000
Zhejiang Silk Holding Co.,ltd.	Hangzhou	Zhejiang	(0571)85195588
浙江省丝绸集团有限公司	杭州市	浙江省	(0571)85192540
Guangdong Silk (Group) Corporation	Guangzhou	Guangdong	(020)83337448
广东省丝绸（集团）公司	广州市	广东省	(020)83332995
Shanghai Costume Group Co.,Ltd.	Shanghai	Shanghai	(021)62748598
上海服装（集团）有限公司	上海市	上海市	(021)62414773
Orient International Holding Shanghai Textiles Import & Export Co.Ltd.	Shanghai	Shanghai	(021)63218855
东方国际集团上海市针织品进出口有限公司	上海市	上海市	(021)63299560
Jiangsu Textiles Import & Export Group Co.,Ltd.	Nanjing	Jiangsu	(025)6895000
江苏省纺织品进出口集团股份有限公司	南京市	江苏省	(025)4400800

1723: Cotton Printing and Dyeing 印染业

The industry accounts for 0.648% of the total revenue of China's industrial sector in 2002. The rate of return on assets is 2.86%. 80.13% of all firms in the industry made a profit while 19.87% had negative returns.The top province in terms of the industry's revenue is Guangdong, accounting for 27.67% of the total revenue.
2002年本行业收入占全行业的0.648%，资产利润率为2.86%。80.13%的企业赢利，19.87%的企业亏损。收入最高的省为广东省，占本行业的27.67%。

	Total number of firms 企业总数	Total number of employees 职工总数	Total revenue (Mil.RMB) 总销售收入（百万元）	Total profit (Mil.RMB) 总利润（百万元）	Return on assets 资产利润率（%）	Return on equity 权益利润率（%）	Labour productivity ('000 RMB/ worker) 劳动生产率（千元/人）	Debts/ assets 资产负债率（%）	Total assets (Mil.RMB) 总资产（百万元）
Industry Overall 行业总体	1067	297,263	69,450	1,852	2.86	7.57	55.04	62.27	64,863

	Number of firms 企业个数	Average number of employees 平均职工人数	Average revenue ('000 RMB) 平均销售收入（千元）	Average profit ('000 RMB) 平均利润（千元）	Return on assets 资产利润率（%）	Return on equity 权益利润率（%）	Labour productivity ('000 RMB/ worker) 劳动生产率（千元/人）	Debts/ assets 资产负债率（%）	Average total assets ('000 RMB) 平均总资产（千元）
By ownership 产业所有权									
State-owned 国有	56	495	47,385	-2,422	-1.68	-59.91	21.77	97.20	144,611
Collective-owned 集体	136	174	31,333	1,121	5.71	16.72	49.65	65.82	19,616
Foreign & Overseas Chinese Funded 三资	276	318	96,402	2,138	2.38	5.01	73.24	52.53	89,947
By regional distribution 地区分布									
Central-North 华北	95	305	37,320	932	1.64	19.13	30.59	91.41	56,722
Beijing 北京	9	393	60,437	698	0.55	1.75	34.45	68.46	126,510
Tianjin 天津	36	116	17,950	699	1.74		42.71	110.09	40,198
Hebei 河北	45	415	49,857	1,366	2.78	50.79	27.56	94.52	49,052
Shanxi 山西	5	514	22,347	-870	-0.73	-3.38	27.60	78.38	119,107
Inner Mongolia 内蒙古									
Northeast 东北	19	374	90,935	3,331	3.70	25.96	46.36	85.76	90,111
Liaoning 辽宁	16	404	106,164	3,996	3.96	26.08	48.68	84.81	100,871
Jilin 吉林	2	289	14,568	72	0.37	9.28	24.57	96.05	19,624
Heilongjiang 黑龙江	1	52		-794	-1.35		0.08	104.93	58,937
Central-East 华东	637	278	65,952	2,391	4.00	9.62	55.29	58.38	59,737
Shanghai 上海	44	147	42,506	647	1.73	3.97	57.58	56.43	37,460
Jiangsu 江苏	229	252	65,104	1,128	2.16	6.14	56.38	64.81	52,232
Zhejiang 浙江	212	302	67,759	3,337	5.40	13.74	47.66	60.69	61,787
Anhui 安徽	9	597	102,709	659	0.44	1.15	49.28	61.93	150,559
Fujian 福建	68	220	44,381	3,433	5.80	9.55	63.97	39.28	59,227
Jiangxi 江西	7	468	35,551	-812	-1.18	-4.28	24.21	72.51	69,070
Shandong 山东	68	373	98,180	4,343	5.39	11.07	71.56	51.30	80,563
Central-South 中南	291	257	72,530	748	1.20	2.79	67.64	57.02	62,393
Henan 河南	29	224	29,445	144	0.46	2.73	24.10	83.12	31,197
Hubei 湖北	13	326	35,937	-965	-2.50		50.21	121.06	38,604
Hunan 湖南	9	330	47,057	-363	-0.82	-2.52	25.87	67.48	44,313
Guangdong 广东	238	255	80,755	906	1.33	2.85	75.64	53.47	68,176
Guangxi 广西	1	130	9,333	-1,466	-36.11		0.15	132.96	4,060
Hainan 海南	1	385	132,524	15,286	12.64	19.51	79.83	35.19	120,886
Southwest 西南	19	277	37,920	-298	-0.70	-3.17	41.93	77.89	42,600
Chongqing 重庆	4	294	52,689	2,159	4.83	12.88	39.68	62.51	44,700
Sichuan 四川	11	298	44,090	-913	-2.09	-202.21	50.75	98.97	43,708
Guizhou 贵州									
Yunnan 云南	4	201	6,184	-1,065	-2.84	-3.98	9.20	28.61	37,456
Tibet 西藏									
Northwest 西北	6	654	56,548	-5,875	-4.73		17.38	107.38	124,096
Shaanxi 陕西	6	654	56,548	-5,875	-4.73		17.38	107.38	124,096
Gansu 甘肃									
Qinghai 青海									
Ningxia 宁夏									
Xinjiang 新疆									

1723: Cotton Printing and Dyeing 印染业

Year 年份	Number of firms 企业个数	Rate of change 变化率(%)	Number of employees 职工人数(人)	Rate of change 变化率(%)	Total revenue (Mil. RMB) 总销售收入(百万元)	Rate of change 变化率(%)	Total profit (Mil RMB) 总利润(百万元)	Rate of change 变化率(%)
2000	858		268,654		51,330		1,153	
2001	962	12.12	284,620	5.94	58,761	14.48	1,503	30.36
2002	1067	10.91	297,263	4.44	69,450	18.19	1,852	23.22

Major Products 主要产品	Output 产量	Unit 单位
Printing & Dyeing Cloth 印染布	211	100,000,000 Meters 亿米

10 Main Firms with Maximal Revenue (year founded) 收入最大的十家主要企业（创办年份）	City 城市	Province 省	Telephone/fax 电话/传真	Number of employees 职工人数	Ownership 产业所有权	Revenue ('000 RMB) 销售收入(千元)	Profit('000 RMB) (rank) 利润(千元)(排名)	Total assets ('000 RMB) 总资产(千元)	Major products 主要产品
Dongguan FI Textiles Co., Ltd.	Dongguan	Guangdong	(0769)5532318		Overseas Chinese-funded				Knitting Grey Cloth
东莞福安纺织印染有限公司(1988)	东莞市	广东省	(0769)5532005	5,651	港澳台资	3,399,400	150,242(1)	2,283,791	针织坯布
Dongguan Winca Textile Co., Ltd.	Dongguan	Guangdong	(0769)8821738		Overseas Chinese-funded				Cotton Knitting Dyeing Finished Cloth
东莞市永佳纺织制衣有限公司(1992)	东莞市	广东省	(0769)8822084	3,866	港澳台资	2,276,407	13,882(34)	1,994,184	织染整布
Shandong Longxi Group Company	Yantai	Shandong	(0535)8565858		Limited-Liability				Printing & Dyeing Cloth
山东龙喜集团公司(1992)	烟台市	山东省	(0535)8565777	2,732	有限公司	1,703,200	109,308(3)	1,031,779	印染布
Zhejiang Hangmin Industrial Group Co., Ltd.	Hangzhou	Zhejiang	(0571)82551588		Limited-Liability				Printing & Dyeing Cloth
浙江航民实业集团有限公司(1997)	杭州市	浙江省	(0571)82553288	8,240	有限公司	1,655,015	139,401(2)	1,605,226	印染布
Binzhou Huafang Co., Ltd.	Binzhou	Shandong	(0543)3288608		Joint Stock				Pure Cotton Printing & Dyeing
滨州华纺股份有限公司(1999)	滨州市	山东省	(0543)3288519	1,340	股份制	807,491	-	935,000	纯棉印染
Shunde Jinfeng Bleaching & Dyeing Co., Ltd.	Foshan	Guangdong	(0765)7772909		Overseas Chinese-funded				Tubular Yarn Bleaching & Dyeing筒
顺德金丰漂染有限公司(1990)	佛山市	广东省	(0765)7772865	1,980	港澳台资	783,469	937(339)	681,292	子纱漂染
Zhejiang Wanhengsheng Printing & Dyeing Co., Ltd.	Shaoxing	Zhejiang	(0575)5654899		Overseas Chinese-funded				Dyeing Processing
浙江万亨盛印染有限公司(1993)	绍兴市	浙江省	(0575)5654363	1,818	港澳台资	744,952	35,926(7)	402,290	染色加工
Zhuhai Qianshan Yuxin Weaving & Dyeing Works Co., Ltd.	Zhuhai	Guangdong	(0756)8630794		Overseas Chinese-funded				Dyeing Cotton Yarn
珠海市前山裕新织染厂有限公司(1988)	珠海市	广东省	(0756)8611847	2,050	港澳台资	726,096	41,383(5)	207,022	染色棉纱
Yixing Lucky Textile Printing & Dyeing Co., Ltd.	Wuxi	Jiangsu	(0510)7933516		Joint Stock				Printing & Dyeing Textile印
宜兴市乐祺纺织印染有限公司(1993)	无锡市	江苏省	(0510)7932400	840	股份制	680,686	7,103(88)	428,686	染纺织品
Zhejiang Sintyear Group Co., Ltd.	Hangzhou	Zhejiang	(0571)82110370		Private Owned				Printing & Dyeing Textile印
浙江三元集团有限公司(2000)	杭州市	浙江省	(0571)82111137	2,701	私营企业	651,600	42,080(4)	732,040	染纺织品

Top 10 Cities by Revenue 销售收入排名前10位城市	Province 省	Market share 市场份额(%)	Number of firms 企业个数
Dongguan 东莞市	Guangdong 广东省	9.43	20
Shaoxing 绍兴市	Zhejiang 浙江省	7.30	63
Wuxi 无锡市	Jiangsu 江苏省	7.23	78
Hangzhou 杭州市	Zhejiang 浙江省	6.91	56
Suzhou 苏州市	Jiangsu 江苏省	5.15	59
Changzhou 常州市	Jiangsu 江苏省	4.79	38
Foshan 佛山市	Guangdong 广东省	4.47	47
Guangzhou 广州市	Guangdong 广东省	3.82	51
Yantai 烟台市	Shandong 山东省	2.90	8
Shanghai 上海市	Shanghai 上海市	2.69	44

10 Major Wholesalers 十家主要批发商	City 城市	Province 省	Telephone/Fax 电话/传真
Shanghai Shenda Co.,Ltd.	Shanghai	Shanghai	(021)62319898
上海申达股份有限公司	上海市	上海市	(021)62317250
Orient International Holding Silk Group Corportion	Shanghai	Shanghai	(021)64662288
东方国际集团丝绸进出口有限公司	上海市	上海市	(021)64677788
Nanjing Textiles Import & Export Co.,Ltd.	Nanjing	Jiangsu	(025)3306789
南京纺织品进出口股份有限公司	南京市	江苏省	(025)3300518
Zhejiang Textiles Import & Export Group Co.,Ltd.	Hangzhou	Zhejiang	(0571)87075888
浙江省纺织品进出口集团有限公司	杭州市	浙江省	(0571)87079234
Zhejiang Orient Holdings Co.,Ltd.	Hangzhou	Zhejiang	(0571)87215678
浙江东方集团股份有限公司	杭州市	浙江省	(0571)87215000
Zhejiang Silk Holding Co.,ltd.	Hangzhou	Zhejiang	(0571)85195588
浙江省丝绸集团有限公司	杭州市	浙江省	(0571)85192540
Guangdong Silk (Group) Corporation	Guangzhou	Guangdong	(020)83337448
广东省丝绸（集团）公司	广州市	广东省	(020)83332995
Shanghai Costume Group Co.,Ltd.	Shanghai	Shanghai	(021)62748598
上海服装（集团）有限公司	上海市	上海市	(021)62414773
Orient International Holding Shanghai Textiles Import & Export Co.Ltd.	Shanghai	Shanghai	(021)63218855
东方国际集团上海市针织品进出口有限公司	上海市	上海市	(021)63299560
Jiangsu Textiles Import & Export Group Co.,Ltd.	Nanjing	Jiangsu	(025)6895000
江苏省纺织品进出口集团股份有限公司	南京市	江苏省	(025)4400800

1724: Cotton Products 棉制品业

The industry accounts for 0.281% of the total revenue of China's industrial sector in 2002. The rate of return on assets is 4.86%. 80.30% of all firms in the industry made a profit while 19.70% had negative returns.The top province in terms of the industry's revenue is Shandong, accounting for 39.12% of the total revenue.
2002年本行业收入占全行业的0.281%，资产利润率为4.86%。80.30%的企业赢利，19.70%的企业亏损。收入最高的省为山东省，占本行业的39.12%。

	Total number of firms 企业总数	Total number of employees 职工总数	Total revenue (Mil.RMB) 总销售收入(百万元)	Total profit (Mil.RMB) 总利润(百万元)	Return on assets 资产利润率(%)	Return on equity 权益利润率(%)	Labour productivity ('000 RMB/worker) 劳动生产率(千元/人)	Debts/assets 资产负债率(%)	Total assets (Mil.RMB) 总资产(百万元)
Industry Overall 行业总体	878	246,749	30,128	1,477	4.86	12.15	30.18	59.99	30,376

	Number of firms 企业个数	Average number of employees 平均职工人数	Average revenue ('000 RMB) 平均销售收入(千元)	Average profit ('000 RMB) 平均利润(千元)	Return on assets 资产利润率(%)	Return on equity 权益利润率(%)	Labour productivity ('000 RMB/worker) 劳动生产率(千元/人)	Debts/assets 资产负债率(%)	Average total assets ('000 RMB) 平均总资产(千元)
By ownership 产业所有权									
State-owned 国有	86	320	22,499	59	0.14	1.25	18.51	88.75	41,703
Collective-owned 集体	124	412	70,653	5,732	7.40	13.07	49.31	43.37	77,428
Foreign & Overseas Chinese Funded 三资	198	249	35,800	1,616	4.81	10.57	23.52	54.45	33,566
By regional distribution 地区分布									
Central-North 华北	73	132	10,097	241	1.36	7.21	24.60	81.08	17,638
Beijing 北京	11	85	10,110	-133	-0.83	-4.45	35.04	81.30	15,961
Tianjin 天津	34	124	8,923	138	0.55	2.79	22.44	80.20	24,874
Hebei 河北	27	156	11,698	532	5.54	34.17	25.69	83.80	9,602
Shanxi 山西	1	276	6,671				5.63	81.34	6,995
Inner Mongolia 内蒙古									
Northeast 东北	27	309	23,034	832	2.60	5.74	20.78	54.70	31,978
Liaoning 辽宁	21	330	24,702	1,085	3.19	6.53	21.41	51.13	34,031
Jilin 吉林	3	149	11,216	1	0.01	0.05	22.62	89.59	13,111
Heilongjiang 黑龙江	3	329	23,177	-110	-0.30	-0.87	15.46	65.44	36,477
Central-East 华东	559	306	43,856	2,400	5.70	13.01	33.53	56.20	42,104
Shanghai 上海	88	190	27,740	364	1.15	3.28	37.60	64.97	31,747
Jiangsu 江苏	151	230	32,459	985	4.69	13.42	13.19	65.03	20,985
Zhejiang 浙江	144	158	31,674	1,727	6.40	17.50	38.81	63.45	26,990
Anhui 安徽	19	411	19,970	-139	-0.60	-2.06	16.00	70.95	23,196
Fujian 福建	15	196	24,974	467	1.34	2.08	26.05	35.77	34,966
Jiangxi 江西	10	185	7,209	168	1.14	3.73	16.44	69.53	14,745
Shandong 山东	132	639	89,286	6,864	7.21	14.40	41.93	49.96	95,259
Central-South 中南	194	263	20,254	508	2.36	8.32	23.13	71.65	21,534
Henan 河南	50	324	17,190	534	3.17	28.14	20.14	88.72	16,822
Hubei 湖北	42	328	17,569	47	0.18	0.88	21.41	79.24	25,531
Hunan 湖南	31	192	22,088	432	2.37	10.11	27.02	76.54	18,220
Guangdong 广东	58	178	24,064	1,082	4.62	9.16	31.51	49.60	23,447
Guangxi 广西	13	370	19,338	-482	-1.85	-12.74	15.31	85.52	26,110
Hainan 海南									
Southwest 西南	15	242	11,833	-168	-0.94	-7.73	15.84	87.79	17,809
Chongqing 重庆	1	157	3,958	6	0.12	0.22	6.94	45.60	4,978
Sichuan 四川	10	292	17,018	30	0.14	0.87	16.94	84.32	22,169
Guizhou 贵州	2	200	85	-149	-1.35		-0.26	101.87	11,072
Yunnan 云南	1	110	2,930	-2,541	-14.60		-0.17	130.87	17,401
Tibet 西藏	1	43	262	9	0.97	0.97	164.81		929
Northwest 西北	10	282	14,636	-34	-0.14		19.60	102.95	24,393
Shaanxi 陕西	5	521	27,900				20.23	102.33	45,818
Gansu 甘肃	2	60	250	-75	-3.72	-8.31	10.03	55.31	2,019
Qinghai 青海									
Ningxia 宁夏									
Xinjiang 新疆	3	32	2,121	-61	-1.70		14.47	133.72	3,601

Year 年份	Number of firms 企业个数	Rate of change 变化率 (%)	Number of employees 职工人数 (人)	Rate of change 变化率 (%)	Total revenue (Mil. RMB) 总销售收入 (百万元)	Rate of change 变化率 (%)	Total profit (Mil RMB) 总利润 (百万元)	Rate of change 变化率 (%)
2000	650		247,073		21,486		773	
2001	728	12.00	236,256	-4.38	24,404	13.58	1,145	48.12
2002	878	20.60	246,749	4.44	30,128	23.46	1,477	29.00

Major Products 主要产品	Output 产量	Unit 单位

10 Main Firms with Maximal Revenue (year founded) 收入最大的十家主要企业（创办年份）	City 城市	Province 省	Telephone/fax 电话/传真	Number of employees 职工人数	Ownership 产业所有权	Revenue ('000 RMB) 销售收入 (千元)	Profit('000 RMB) (rank) 利润(千元) (排名)	Total assets ('000 RMB) 总资产 (千元)	Major products 主要产品
Nanshan Group Company 南山集团公司(1996)	Yantai 烟台市	Shandong 山东省	(0535)8616003 (0535)8616056	24,036	Collective-owned 集体企业	5,030,030	600,410(1)	6,860,128	Cotton Towel-ling Coverlet 毛巾被
Shandong Yaguang Textile Group 山东亚光纺织集团(2000)	Binzhou 滨州市	Shandong 山东省	(0543)3512928 (0543)3512688	3,076	State-owned 国有企业	807,824	33,634(6)	942,064	Towel 毛巾
Longkou Zhuyou Towel Factory 龙口市诸由毛巾厂(1984)	Yantai 烟台市	Shandong 山东省	(0535)8562700 (0535)8561129	1,012	Collective-owned 集体企业	655,620	4,300(47)	206,620	Jacquard Pattern Towel 提花毛巾
Zhejiang Longbai Group Company 浙江龙柏集团公司(1994)	Shaoxing 绍兴市	Zhejiang 浙江省	(0575)2150784 (0575)2159083	1,100	Collective-owned 集体企业	578,960	40,813(5)	271,736	Towel 毛巾
Beyond Textile Co., Ltd. 宁波博洋纺织有限公司(1995)	Ningbo 宁波市	Zhejiang 浙江省	(0574)87495606 (0574)87471552	349	Limited-Liability 有限公司	572,335	10,907(18)	367,525	Family Spinning Products 家纺产品
Jiangsu Hongliu Bedsheet Group Co. 江苏红柳床单集团公司(1967)	Wuxi 无锡市	Jiangsu 江苏省	(0510)6282341 (0510)6281023	2,430	Collective-owned 集体企业	493,284	15,581(13)	365,198	Bedsheet 床单
Shanghai Vchino Towel Co., Ltd. 上海市内野毛巾有限公司(1993)	Shanghai 上海市	Shanghai 上海市	(021)59544627 (021)59544232	1,819	Foreign Funded 外商投资	314,709	-	462,578	Cotton Yarn 棉纱
Longkou Huangheying Textile Co., Ltd. 龙口市黄河营纺织有限公司(1991)	Yantai 烟台市	Shandong 山东省	(0535)8588815	254	Private Enterprises 私营独资	256,890	15,630(12)	4,030	Pillow Cover 枕巾
Ningbo Weike Group Co., Ltd. 宁波维科集团股份有限公司(1998)	Ningbo 宁波市	Zhejiang 浙江省	(0574)87233690 (0574)87253691	811	Joint Stock 股份制	228,092	60,704(3)	693,788	Knitting Sweater & Trousers 针织衫裤
Nantong Shengtang Textiles Co., Ltd. 南通盛唐纺织品有限公司(2000)	Nantong 南通市	Jiangsu 江苏省	(0513)6110512 (0513)6110520	751	Overseas Chinese-funded 港澳台资	218,999	50,766(4)	225,696	Bedclothes 床上用品

Top 10 Cities by Revenue 销售收入排名前10位城市	Province 省	Market share 市场份额 (%)	Number of firms 企业个数
Yantai 烟台市	Shandong 山东省	20.38	8
Shanghai 上海市	Shanghai 上海市	8.10	88
Ningbo 宁波市	Zhejiang 浙江省	5.89	33
Nantong 南通市	Jiangsu 江苏省	5.20	42
Weifang 潍坊市	Shandong 山东省	5.03	26
Binzhou 滨州市	Shandong 山东省	3.10	8
Wuxi 无锡市	Jiangsu 江苏省	2.84	17
Shaoxing 绍兴市	Zhejiang 浙江省	2.35	9
Qingdao 青岛市	Shandong 山东省	2.31	22
Zibo 淄博市	Shandong 山东省	2.28	22

10 Major Wholesalers 十家主要批发商	City 城市	Province 省	Telephone/Fax 电话/传真
Shanghai Shenda Co.,Ltd. 上海申达股份有限公司	Shanghai 上海市	Shanghai 上海市	(021)62319898 (021)62317250
Orient International Holding Silk Group Corportion 东方国际集团丝绸进出口有限公司	Shanghai 上海市	Shanghai 上海市	(021)64662288 (021)64677788
Nanjing Textiles Import & Export Co.,Ltd. 南京纺织品进出口股份有限公司	Nanjing 南京市	Jiangsu 江苏省	(025)3306789 (025)3300518
Zhejiang Textiles Import & Export Group Co.,Ltd. 浙江省纺织品进出口集团有限公司	Hangzhou 杭州市	Zhejiang 浙江省	(0571)87075888 (0571)87079234
Zhejiang Orient Holdings Co.,Ltd. 浙江东方集团股份有限公司	Hangzhou 杭州市	Zhejiang 浙江省	(0571)87215678 (0571)87215000
Zhejiang Silk Holding Co.,ltd. 浙江省丝绸集团有限公司	Hangzhou 杭州市	Zhejiang 浙江省	(0571)85195588 (0571)85192540
Guangdong Silk (Group) Corporation 广东省丝绸（集团）公司	Guangzhou 广州市	Guangdong 广东省	(020)83337448 (020)83332995
Shanghai Costume Group Co.,Ltd. 上海服装（集团）有限公司	Shanghai 上海市	Shanghai 上海市	(021)62748598 (021)62414773
Orient International Holding Shanghai Textiles Import & Export Co.Ltd. 东方国际集团上海市针织品进出口有限公司	Shanghai 上海市	Shanghai 上海市	(021)63218855 (021)63299560
Jiangsu Textiles Import & Export Group Co.,Ltd. 江苏省纺织品进出口集团股份有限公司	Nanjing 南京市	Jiangsu 江苏省	(025)6895000 (025)4400800

1725: Cotton Thread 棉线带制造业

The industry accounts for 0.050% of the total revenue of China's industrial sector in 2002. The rate of return on assets is 4.11%. 81.58% of all firms in the industry made a profit while 18.42% had negative returns.The top province in terms of the industry's revenue is Zhejiang, accounting for 33.51% of the total revenue.
2002年本行业收入占全行业的0.050%，资产利润率为4.11%。81.58%的企业赢利，18.42%的企业亏损。收入最高的省为浙江省，占本行业的33.51%。

	Total number of firms 企业总数	Total number of employees 职工总数	Total revenue (Mil.RMB) 总销售收入 (百万元)	Total profit (Mil.RMB) 总利润 (百万元)	Return on assets 资产利润率 (%)	Return on equity 权益利润率 (%)	Labour productivity ('000 RMB/ worker) 劳动生产率 (千元/人)	Debts/ assets 资产负债率 (%)	Total assets (Mil.RMB) 总资产 (百万元)
Industry Overall 行业总体	190	35,389	5,380	208	4.11	8.35	36.53	50.83	5,056

	Number of firms 企业个数	Average number of employees 平均职工人数	Average revenue ('000 RMB) 平均销售收入（千元）	Average profit ('000 RMB) 平均利润 (千元)	Return on assets 资产利润率 (%)	Return on equity 权益利润率 (%)	Labour productivity ('000 RMB/ worker) 劳动生产率 (千元/人)	Debts/ assets 资产负债率 (%)	Average total assets ('000 RMB) 平均总资产 (千元)
By ownership 产业所有权									
State-owned 国有	13	135	6,267	-320	-1.33		11.19	104.84	24,060
Collective-owned 集体	30	174	22,293	67	0.57	1.84	35.90	68.89	11,639
Foreign & Overseas Chinese Funded 三资	50	281	44,326	1,969	4.26	7.07	40.34	39.66	46,190
By regional distribution 地区分布									
Central-North 华北	8	95	5,892	30	0.11	1.28	10.27	91.74	28,216
Beijing 北京									
Tianjin 天津	7	74	6,132	37	0.12	1.54	13.62	92.11	30,600
Hebei 河北	1	241	4,213	-21	-0.18	-1.20	3.09	84.88	11,531
Shanxi 山西									
Inner Mongolia 内蒙古									
Northeast 东北	7	175	9,870	-432	-3.08		13.29	111.05	14,030
Liaoning 辽宁	2	30	2,531	111	7.15	78.93	14.05	90.94	1,545
Jilin 吉林	3	252	21,181	7	0.04	0.28	18.36	86.23	18,072
Heilongjiang 黑龙江	2	203	243	-1,633	-7.98		3.74	145.45	20,453
Central-East 华东	105	196	32,367	1,472	4.65	8.71	38.62	46.58	31,631
Shanghai 上海	21	113	19,808	1,072	5.21	9.91	51.08	47.44	20,568
Jiangsu 江苏	32	119	18,136	222	2.02	5.94	40.58	65.99	10,997
Zhejiang 浙江	41	195	43,977	2,198	5.31	9.69	37.64	45.14	41,358
Anhui 安徽									
Fujian 福建	5	551	91,814	6,717	4.93	7.32	62.03	32.68	136,390
Jiangxi 江西	1	380	17,800	908	2.32	4.23	16.78	45.19	39,132
Shandong 山东	5	663	24,462	64	0.27	1.90	12.89	86.01	24,123
Central-South 中南	69	182	27,024	814	4.03	7.97	37.61	49.45	20,206
Henan 河南	7	109	6,953	122	1.77	29.84	16.62	94.08	6,888
Hubei 湖北	5	170	4,451	-390	-3.67		11.69	126.19	10,647
Hunan 湖南	4	263	14,987	-18	-0.26	-3.09	16.42	91.49	6,659
Guangdong 广东	53	186	32,713	1,082	4.53	8.03	43.71	43.64	23,889
Guangxi 广西									
Hainan 海南									
Southwest 西南									
Chongqing 重庆									
Sichuan 四川									
Guizhou 贵州									
Yunnan 云南									
Tibet 西藏									
Northwest 西北	1	280	1,024	-286	-1.76		7.17	106.30	16,287
Shaanxi 陕西	1	280	1,024	-286	-1.76		7.17	106.30	16,287
Gansu 甘肃									
Qinghai 青海									
Ningxia 宁夏									
Xinjiang 新疆									

1725: Cotton Thread 棉线带制造业

Year 年份	Number of firms 企业个数	Rate of change 变化率 (%)	Number of employees 职工人数 (人)	Rate of change 变化率 (%)	Total revenue (Mil. RMB) 总销售收入 (百万元)	Rate of change 变化率 (%)	Total profit (Mil RMB) 总利润 (百万元)	Rate of change 变化率 (%)
2000	156		25,543		3,980		132	
2001	167	7.05	28,187	10.35	4,049	1.73	146	10.61
2002	190	13.77	35,389	25.55	5,380	32.87	208	42.47

Major Products 主要产品	Output 产量	Unit 单位

10 Main Firms with Maximal Revenue (year founded) 收入最大的十家主要企业（创办年份）	City 城市	Province 省	Telephone/fax 电话/传真	Number of employees 职工人数	Ownership 产业所有权	Revenue ('000 RMB) 销售收入 (千元)	Profit('000 RMB) (rank) 利润(千元) (排名)	Total assets ('000 RMB) 总资产 (千元)	Major products 主要产品
Taishan Joris Elastic Fabric Mill 台山宝捷弹性织物厂(1995)	Jiangmen 江门市	Guangdong 广东省	(0750)5612328 (0750)5611828	360	Overseas Chinese-funded 港澳台资	200,856	1,687(18)	84,179	Elastic Fabric Strip 弹性织物带
Ningbo Weike Group Co., Ltd. 宁波维科集团股份有限公司(1993)	Ningbo 宁波市	Zhejiang 浙江省	(0574)87253690 (0574)81253691	3,658	Joint Stock 股份制	1,178,009	65,988(1)	1,098,409	Yarn 纱
Jinjiang Baihong Elasticity Weaving Co., Ltd. 晋江市百宏弹性织造有限公司(1997)	Quanzhou 泉州市	Fujian 福建省	(0595)5228888 (0595)5229999	2,300	Overseas Chinese-funded 港澳台资	416,735	32,133(3)	648,812	Woven Strip 织带
Coats Guangzhou Co.,Ltd. 广州高士线业有限公司(1991)	Guangzhou 广州市	Guangdong 广东省	(020)84212898 (020)84205279	948	Overseas Chinese-funded 港澳台资	323,659	36,779(2)	300,064	Sewing Thread 缝纫线
Doumen Chenghui Clothing Making Auxiliary Material Co., Ltd. 斗门区成辉制衣辅料有限公司(1993)	Zhuhai 珠海市	Guangdong 广东省	(0756)5587575 (0756)5589993	48	Overseas Chinese-funded 港澳台资	80,266	347(65)	3,814	Rope & Strip 绳带
Wilson Dyeing & Weaving Huadu Co., Ltd. 广州市花都威扬织造有限公司(1994)	Guangzhou 广州市	Guangdong 广东省	(020)86848711 (020)86848855	80	Overseas Chinese-funded 港澳台资	77,984	2,795(13)	18,361	Cotton Strip 棉带
Guangzhou Xinhua Thread Co., Ltd. 广州新华线业有限公司(1993)	Guangzhou 广州市	Guangdong 广东省	(020)81415777 (020)81415048	250	Overseas Chinese-funded 港澳台资	75,368	6,160(5)	66,856	Sewing Thread 缝纫线
Youji Woven Belt Mill 有记织带厂(1999)	Guangzhou 广州市	Guangdong 广东省	(020)86841247 (020)86717238	358	Collective-owned 集体企业	62,954	128(99)	14,271	Pure Chemical Fabric Cloth 纯化纤布
FUJIK(Shanghai) Thread Co., Ltd. 上海富士克制线有限公司(1993)	Shanghai 上海市	Shanghai 上海市	(021)59201110 (021)59203507	116	Foreign Funded 外商投资	60,807	2,191(15)	77,140	Sewing Thread 缝纫线
Shanghai No.3 Thread-making Mill 上海第三制线厂(1998)	Shanghai 上海市	Shanghai 上海市	(021)58566283 (021)63778215	293	Joint Owned 联营企业	60,448	2,237(14)	80,032	Embroidery Thread 绣花线

Top 10 Cities by Revenue 销售收入排名前10位城市	Province 省	Market share 市场份额 (%)	Number of firms 企业个数
Ningbo 宁波市	Zhejiang 浙江省	24.43	9
Guangzhou 广州市	Guangdong 广东省	14.14	21
Quanzhou 泉州市	Fujian 福建省	7.86	2
Shanghai 上海市	Shanghai 上海市	7.73	21
Jinhua 金华市	Zhejiang 浙江省	5.08	17
Dongguan 东莞市	Guangdong 广东省	4.55	8
Jiangmen 江门市	Guangdong 广东省	3.73	1
Changzhou 常州市	Jiangsu 江苏省	3.26	6
Zhongshan 中山市	Guangdong 广东省	2.87	8
Foshan 佛山市	Guangdong 广东省	2.51	6

10 Major Wholesalers 十家主要批发商	City 城市	Province 省	Telephone/Fax 电话/传真
Shanghai Shenda Co.,Ltd. 上海申达股份有限公司	Shanghai 上海市	Shanghai 上海市	(021)62319898 (021)62317250
Orient International Holding Silk Group Corportion 东方国际集团丝绸进出口有限公司	Shanghai 上海市	Shanghai 上海市	(021)64662288 (021)64677788
Nanjing Textiles Import & Export Co.,Ltd. 南京纺织品进出口股份有限公司	Nanjing 南京市	Jiangsu 江苏省	(025)3306789 (025)3300518
Zhejiang Textiles Import & Export Group Co.,Ltd. 浙江省纺织品进出口集团有限公司	Hangzhou 杭州市	Zhejiang 浙江省	(0571)87075888 (0571)87079234
Zhejiang Orient Holdings Co.,Ltd. 浙江东方集团股份有限公司	Hangzhou 杭州市	Zhejiang 浙江省	(0571)87215678 (0571)87215000
Zhejiang Silk Holding Co.,ltd. 浙江省丝绸集团有限公司	Hangzhou 杭州市	Zhejiang 浙江省	(0571)85195588 (0571)85192540
Guangdong Silk (Group) Corporation 广东省丝绸（集团）公司	Guangzhou 广州市	Guangdong 广东省	(020)83337448 (020)83332995
Shanghai Costume Group Co.,Ltd. 上海服装（集团）有限公司	Shanghai 上海市	Shanghai 上海市	(021)62748598 (021)62414773
Orient International Holding Shanghai Textiles Import & Export Co.Ltd. 东方国际集团上海市针织品进出口有限公司	Shanghai 上海市	Shanghai 上海市	(021)63218855 (021)63299560
Jiangsu Textiles Import & Export Group Co.,Ltd. 江苏省纺织品进出口集团股份有限公司	Nanjing 南京市	Jiangsu 江苏省	(025)6895000 (025)4400800

1726: Cotton Cord Fabric 帘子布制造业

The industry accounts for 0.049% of the total revenue of China's industrial sector in 2002. The rate of return on assets is 2.82%. 85.48% of all firms in the industry made a profit while 14.52% had negative returns.The top province in terms of the industry's revenue is Jiangsu, accounting for 51.28% of the total revenue.
2002年本行业收入占全行业的0.049%，资产利润率为2.82%。85.48%的企业赢利，14.52%的企业亏损。收入最高的省为江苏省，占本行业的51.28%。

	Total number of firms 企业总数	Total number of employees 职工总数	Total revenue (Mil.RMB) 总销售收入（百万元）	Total profit (Mil.RMB) 总利润（百万元）	Return on assets 资产利润率（%）	Return on equity 权益利润率（%）	Labour productivity ('000 RMB/ worker) 劳动生产率（千元/人）	Debts/ assets 资产负债率（%）	Total assets (Mil.RMB) 总资产（百万元）
Industry Overall 行业总体	62	28,907	5,208	193	2.82	7.69	49.65	63.33	6,859

	Number of firms 企业个数	Average number of employees 平均职工人数	Average revenue ('000 RMB) 平均销售收入（千元）	Average profit ('000 RMB) 平均利润（千元）	Return on assets 资产利润率（%）	Return on equity 权益利润率（%）	Labour productivity ('000 RMB/ worker) 劳动生产率（千元/人）	Debts/ assets 资产负债率（%）	Average total assets ('000 RMB) 平均总资产（千元）
By ownership 产业所有权									
State-owned 国有	3	909	118,068	-779	-0.79	-3.62	17.86	78.23	98,756
Collective-owned 集体	8	236	40,009	1,785	3.57	12.43	40.30	71.29	50,008
Foreign & Overseas Chinese Funded 三资	8	185	80,800	373	0.26	0.54	172.94	51.99	143,590
By regional distribution 地区分布									
Central-North 华北	4	103	16,788	1,081	7.06	19.48	44.42	63.74	15,308
Beijing 北京	1	36	16,456	18	0.14	0.39	360.08	64.79	13,018
Tianjin 天津	2	87	20,077	1,928	9.53	22.42	13.63	57.50	20,230
Hebei 河北	1	202	10,543	451	5.82	107.13	14.69	94.57	7,755
Shanxi 山西									
Inner Mongolia 内蒙古									
Northeast 东北	2	85	72,148	2,760	13.28	58.07	259.96	77.13	20,777
Liaoning 辽宁	1	119	95,000	5,000	90.74	490.20	247.48	81.49	5,510
Jilin 吉林	1	50	49,296	520	1.44	6.13	289.66	76.46	36,043
Heilongjiang 黑龙江									
Central-East 华东	47	560	102,661	3,869	2.74	7.33	50.42	62.61	141,139
Shanghai 上海	5	211	25,921	-897	-1.47	-17.17	35.87	91.45	61,090
Jiangsu 江苏	23	454	116,122	4,966	5.07	16.21	60.51	68.72	97,913
Zhejiang 浙江	8	1,347	151,413	10,630	3.72	9.40	35.87	60.38	285,444
Anhui 安徽	1	398	271,356	720	0.10	0.16	343.60	34.38	704,267
Fujian 福建	3	74	12,029	561	3.98	5.23	36.66	24.01	14,114
Jiangxi 江西									
Shandong 山东	7	488	72,270	-2,188	-1.46	-4.37	36.68	66.50	149,415
Central-South 中南	5	158	27,596	653	5.40	15.36	44.42	64.84	12,088
Henan 河南									
Hubei 湖北	1	124	24,110				64.76	79.67	10,380
Hunan 湖南	1	352	20,100	260	2.28	12.32	18.09	81.46	11,380
Guangdong 广东	3	105	31,257	1,001	7.77	17.64	65.83	55.97	12,893
Guangxi 广西									
Hainan 海南									
Southwest 西南	1	178	17,053	724	16.24	28.73	22.93	43.47	4,458
Chongqing 重庆									
Sichuan 四川									
Guizhou 贵州									
Yunnan 云南	1	178	17,053	724	16.24	28.73	22.93	43.47	4,458
Tibet 西藏									
Northwest 西北	3	348	5,609	-741	-3.82		6.79	134.86	19,384
Shaanxi 陕西	1	884	5,033	-2,896	-10.06		3.44	191.02	28,779
Gansu 甘肃	2	81	5,898	337	2.29	11.36	25.18	79.83	14,687
Qinghai 青海									
Ningxia 宁夏									
Xinjiang 新疆									

1726: Cotton Cord Fabric 帘子布制造业

Year 年份	Number of firms 企业个数	Rate of change 变化率 (%)	Number of employees 职工人数 (人)	Rate of change 变化率 (%)	Total revenue (Mil. RMB) 总销售收入 (百万元)	Rate of change 变化率 (%)	Total profit (Mil RMB) 总利润 (百万元)	Rate of change 变化率 (%)
2000	60		31,200		4,705		84	
2001	59	-1.67	29,049	-6.89	4,623	-1.74	120	42.86
2002	62	5.08	28,907	-0.49	5,208	12.65	193	60.83

Major Products 主要产品	Output 产量	Unit 单位
Cord Fabric 帘子布	266,248	Ton 吨
Polymide Fibre 锦纶纤维	47	10,000 Tons 万吨

10 Main Firms with Maximal Revenue (year founded) 收入最大的十家主要企业（创办年份）	City 城市	Province 省	Telephone/fax 电话/传真	Number of employees 职工人数	Ownership 产业所有权	Revenue ('000 RMB) 销售收入 (千元)	Profit('000 RMB) (rank) 利润(千元) (排名)	Total assets ('000 RMB) 总资产 (千元)	Major products 主要产品
Kingring Co., Ltd.	Ningbo	Zhejiang	(0574)63205943		Joint Stock				Cord Fabric
金轮集团股份有限公司(2000)	宁波市	浙江省	(0574)63205943	9,495	股份制	1,061,798	79,516(2)	2,181,260	帘子布
Jiangsu Junma Group Co., Ltd.	Suzhou	Jiangsu	(0512)58291688		Joint Stock				Polyamide Fibre Cord Fabric锦
张家港江苏骏马集团有限责任公司(1994)	苏州市	江苏省	(0512)58292308	1,873	股份制	1,025,230	83,410(1)	711,460	纶帘子线
Jiangsu Qunfa Chemical Group Co.,Ltd.	Yangzhou	Jiangsu	(0514)7230690		Limited-Liability				Polyamide Fibre -6 Dip Glue Cord Fabric锦纶-6浸
江苏群发化工有限公司(1964)	扬州市	江苏省	(0514)7232380	2,338	有限公司	490,398	11,204(3)	544,384	胶帘子布
Xuzhou Cord Fabric Factory	Xuzhou	Jiangsu	(0516)5759901		State-owned				Polyamide Fibre Cord Fabric锦
徐州市帘子布厂(1964)	徐州市	江苏省	(0516)5765754	1,490	国有企业	329,070	300(34)	256,109	纶帘子线
Anhui Jiayuan Industry Fiber Co., Ltd.	Hefei	Anhui	(0551)3811515		Foreign Funded				Cord Fabric
安徽佳元工业纤维有限公司(1995)	合肥市	安徽省	(0551)3811616	398	外商投资	271,356	720(22)	704,267	帘子布
Nanhua Group Taizhou Chemical Fibres Company	Taizhou	Jiangsu	(0523)6559771		Collective-owned				Kapron Cord Fabric锦
南化集团泰州化纤公司(1970)	泰州市	江苏省	(0523)6558656	1,083	集体企业	190,646	6,288(5)	269,410	纶帘子布
Qingdao Lian-Chuang Industry & Commerce Co., Ltd.	Qingdao	Shandong	(0532)3717402		Limited-Liability				Kapron Cord Fabric锦
青岛联创实业有限公司(1917)	青岛市	山东省	(0532)3710893	2,329	有限公司	173,771	-	629,632	纶帘子布
Weifang Dalong Chemical Fibre Co., Ltd.	Weifang	Shandong	(0536)4381158		Foreign Funded				Cord Fabric
潍坊大龙化纤有限公司(1994)	潍坊市	山东省	(0536)4381187	515	外商投资	165,896	1,263(15)	270,001	帘子布
Wuxi Wonder Industry Cloth Co., Ltd.	Wuxi	Jiangsu	(0510)3203518		Private Owned				Kapron Cord Fabric锦
无锡市威利达工业布有限公司(1991)	无锡市	江苏省	(0510)3232130	549	私营企业	110,920	560(26)	108,830	纶帘子布
Wuxi Shuangyi Textile Co., Ltd.	Wuxi	Jiangsu	(0510)8711733		Limited-Liability				Cord Fabric
无锡市双益纺织有限公司(1984)	无锡市	江苏省	(0510)8711180	290	有限公司	66,120	850(18)	51,500	帘子布

Top 10 Cities by Revenue 销售收入排名前10位城市	Province 省	Market share 市场份额 (%)	Number of firms 企业个数
Ningbo 宁波市	Zhejiang 浙江省	20.39	1
Suzhou 苏州市	Jiangsu 江苏省	19.78	2
Yangzhou 扬州市	Jiangsu 江苏省	9.65	2
Xuzhou 徐州市	Jiangsu 江苏省	6.32	1
Qingdao 青岛市	Shandong 山东省	5.27	2
Hefei 合肥市	Anhui 安徽省	5.21	1
Wuxi 无锡市	Jiangsu 江苏省	5.03	8
Taizhou 泰州市	Jiangsu 江苏省	4.82	3
Weifang 潍坊市	Shandong 山东省	3.34	2
Changzhou 常州市	Jiangsu 江苏省	2.97	2

10 Major Wholesalers 十家主要批发商	City 城市	Province 省	Telephone/Fax 电话/传真
Shanghai Shenda Co.,Ltd.	Shanghai	Shanghai	(021)62319898
上海申达股份有限公司	上海市	上海市	(021)62317250
Orient International Holding Silk Group Corportion	Shanghai	Shanghai	(021)64662288
东方国际集团丝绸进出口有限公司	上海市	上海市	(021)64677788
Nanjing Textiles Import & Export Co.,Ltd.	Nanjing	Jiangsu	(025)3306789
南京纺织品进出口股份有限公司	南京市	江苏省	(025)3300518
Zhejiang Textiles Import & Export Group Co.,Ltd.	Hangzhou	Zhejiang	(0571)87075888
浙江省纺织品进出口集团有限公司	杭州市	浙江省	(0571)87079234
Zhejiang Orient Holdings Co.,Ltd.	Hangzhou	Zhejiang	(0571)87215678
浙江东方集团股份有限公司	杭州市	浙江省	(0571)87215000
Zhejiang Silk Holding Co.,ltd.	Hangzhou	Zhejiang	(0571)85195588
浙江省丝绸集团有限公司	杭州市	浙江省	(0571)85192540
Guangdong Silk (Group) Corporation	Guangzhou	Guangdong	(020)83337448
广东省丝绸（集团）公司	广州市	广东省	(020)83332995
Shanghai Costume Group Co.,Ltd.	Shanghai	Shanghai	(021)62748598
上海服装（集团）有限公司	上海市	上海市	(021)62414773
Orient International Holding Shanghai Textiles Import & Export Co.Ltd.	Shanghai	Shanghai	(021)63218855
东方国际集团上海市针织品进出口有限公司	上海市	上海市	(021)63299560
Jiangsu Textiles Import & Export Group Co.,Ltd.	Nanjing	Jiangsu	(025)6895000
江苏省纺织品进出口集团股份有限公司	南京市	江苏省	(025)4400800

1729: Other Cotton Goods 其他棉纺织业

The industry accounts for 0.067% of the total revenue of China's industrial sector in 2002. The rate of return on assets is 2.56%. 75.96% of all firms in the industry made a profit while 24.04% had negative returns.The top province in terms of the industry's revenue is Jiangsu, accounting for 24.83% of the total revenue.
2002年本行业收入占全行业的0.067%，资产利润率为2.56%。75.96%的企业赢利，24.04%的企业亏损。收入最高的省为江苏省，占本行业的24.83%。

	Total number of firms 企业总数	Total number of employees 职工总数	Total revenue (Mil.RMB) 总销售收入 (百万元)	Total profit (Mil.RMB) 总利润 (百万元)	Return on assets 资产利润率 (%)	Return on equity 权益利润率 (%)	Labour productivity ('000 RMB/ worker) 劳动生产率 (千元/人)	Debts/ assets 资产负债率 (%)	Total assets (Mil.RMB) 总资产 (百万元)
Industry Overall 行业总体	183	59,016	7,133	196	2.56	7.15	33.70	64.13	7,642

	Number of firms 企业个数	Average number of employees 平均职工人数	Average revenue ('000 RMB) 平均销售收入（千元）	Average profit ('000 RMB) 平均利润 (千元)	Return on assets 资产利润率 (%)	Return on equity 权益利润率 (%)	Labour productivity ('000 RMB/ worker) 劳动生产率 (千元/人)	Debts/ assets 资产负债率 (%)	Average total assets ('000 RMB) 平均总资产 (千元)
By ownership 产业所有权									
State-owned 国有	15	1,258	79,727	-1,103	-0.72	-3.20	30.85	77.58	153,909
Collective-owned 集体	23	154	43,310	4,210	13.26	28.95	89.28	54.19	31,744
Foreign & Overseas Chinese Funded 三资	35	274	46,425	704	1.05	2.07	27.69	49.15	67,006
By regional distribution 地区分布									
Central-North 华北	15	311	25,199	870	1.24	4.24	21.36	70.86	70,344
Beijing 北京	3	140	17,332	225	1.60	2.32	40.10	30.98	14,069
Tianjin 天津	3	213	14,107	973	4.91		11.97	106.71	19,843
Hebei 河北	8	447	35,361	1,182	0.99	3.35	20.92	70.40	119,125
Shanxi 山西	1	28	784	-6	-1.40	-2.99	10.00	53.04	428
Inner Mongolia 内蒙古									
Northeast 东北	11	693	15,221	81	0.38	1.07	7.43	64.68	21,479
Liaoning 辽宁	6	128	7,285	115	1.40	2.89	21.10	51.45	8,215
Jilin 吉林	2	46						100.91	6,226
Heilongjiang 黑龙江	3	2,256	41,240	66	0.11	0.33	5.99	65.84	58,177
Central-East 华东	115	221	44,334	1,698	4.36	11.22	47.74	61.18	38,971
Shanghai 上海	13	230	36,889	895	4.32	16.00	45.40	73.02	20,735
Jiangsu 江苏	51	129	34,729	1,741	6.05	13.78	59.86	56.11	28,783
Zhejiang 浙江	25	201	35,527	1,604	5.09	12.93	54.30	60.63	31,503
Anhui 安徽	5	241	33,598	272	0.83	2.78	42.20	70.28	32,861
Fujian 福建	10	188	54,138	908	0.99	2.26	40.45	56.36	91,905
Jiangxi 江西	2	189	50,713	418	0.96	2.74	147.09	64.77	43,358
Shandong 山东	9	817	127,635	4,824	5.52	18.69	31.08	70.46	87,390
Central-South 中南	37	544	38,787	-180	-0.37	-1.15	30.18	67.70	48,355
Henan 河南	5	509	9,796	-680	-2.86	-11.56	6.05	75.28	23,813
Hubei 湖北	10	1,400	99,784	-817	-0.75	-3.47	36.00	78.36	108,699
Hunan 湖南	3	226	12,115	267	1.83	3.35	14.71	45.47	14,577
Guangdong 广东	18	160	19,552	229	0.77	1.43	27.00	46.43	29,901
Guangxi 广西	1	11	36				3.64		1,125
Hainan 海南									
Southwest 西南	3	131	7,349	-2,354	-19.99	-41.96	10.71	52.35	11,772
Chongqing 重庆									
Sichuan 四川	3	131	7,349	-2,354	-19.99	-41.96	10.71	52.35	11,772
Guizhou 贵州									
Yunnan 云南									
Tibet 西藏									
Northwest 西北	2	415	16,149	223	1.00	2.84	11.11	64.70	22,219
Shaanxi 陕西	1	780	26,932	160	0.37	1.06	9.56	64.96	43,087
Gansu 甘肃	1	50	5,365	285	21.11	48.31	35.28	56.30	1,350
Qinghai 青海									
Ningxia 宁夏									
Xinjiang 新疆									

1729: Other Cotton Goods 其他棉纺织业

Year 年份	Number of firms 企业个数	Rate of change 变化率 (%)	Number of employees 职工人数 (人)	Rate of change 变化率 (%)	Total revenue (Mil. RMB) 总销售收入 (百万元)	Rate of change 变化率 (%)	Total profit (Mil RMB) 总利润 (百万元)	Rate of change 变化率 (%)
2000	166		72,036		6,829		132	
2001	157	-5.42	61,444	-14.70	6,206	-9.12	112	-15.15
2002	183	16.56	59,016	-3.95	7,133	14.94	196	75.00

Major Products 主要产品	Output 产量	Unit 单位

10 Main Firms with Maximal Revenue (year founded) 收入最大的十家主要企业（创办年份）	City 城市	Province 省	Telephone/fax 电话/传真	Number of employees 职工人数	Ownership 产业所有权	Revenue ('000 RMB) 销售收入 (千元)	Profit('000 RMB) (rank) 利润(千元) (排名)	Total assets ('000 RMB) 总资产 (千元)	Major products 主要产品
Shandong Daiyin Textile Group Stock Co., Ltd.	Taian	Shandong	(0538)6117569		Joint Stock				Cotton Yarn
山东岱银纺织集团股份有限公司(1994)	泰安市	山东省	(0538)6115373	3,380	股份制	709,525	23,852(2)	465,788	棉纱
Hubei Xiangfan No.1 Cotton Group Company	Xiangfan	Hubei	(0710)3224457		State-owned				Cotton Yarn
湖北襄樊一棉集团公司(1975)	襄樊市	湖北省	(0710)3223169	4,474	国有企业	395,754	14,132(4)	392,109	棉纱
Changshu Automobile Inner Decorations Materials Factory	Suzhou	Jiangsu	(0520)52810560		Collective-owned				Automobile Inner Decorations
常熟市汽车内饰件材料厂(1996)	苏州市	江苏省	(0520)52810234	180	集体企业	366,490	76,070(1)	328,170	汽车内饰件
Hubei Xiangfan Cotton Texitile Group Corp.	Xiangfan	Hubei	(0710)3224247		State-owned				Yarn
湖北襄棉集团总公司(1969)	襄樊市	湖北省	(0710)3223169	6,371	国有企业	345,178	-	557,823	纱
Xiamen Huacheng Industrial Co., Ltd.	Xiamen	Fujian	(0592)7107598		Overseas Chinese-funded				Terylene Fiber
厦门华诚实业有限公司(1995)	厦门市	福建省	(0592)7107568	546	港澳台资	264,756	9,298(7)	382,585	涤纶丝
Xiamen Donglun Weaving Co., Ltd.	Xiamen	Fujian	(0592)7013945		Overseas Chinese-funded				Polyamide Fibre
厦门东纶织造有限公司(1998)	厦门市	福建省	(0592)7015222	590	港澳台资	195,805	7,530(9)	312,110	锦纶
Nantong Hymo Co., Ltd.	Nantong	Jiangsu	(0513)5508100		Foreign Funded				Lining Cloth
南通海盟股份有限公司(1984)	南通市	江苏省	(0513)5128203	406	外商投资	188,109	11,355(6)	134,602	衬布
Shanghai Botai Industrial Co.,Ltd.	Shanghai	Shanghai	(021)58668652		Collective-owned				Cotton Yarn
上海博泰实业有限公司(1991)	上海市	上海市	(021)37290066	180	集体企业	182,910	9,194(8)	52,220	棉纱
Huimin Huarun Textile Co., Ltd.	Binzhou	Shandong	(0543)5330201		Overseas Chinese-funded				
惠民县华润纺织有限公司(1999)	滨州市	山东省	(0543)5332848	2,104	港澳台资	176,208	12,131(5)	175,325	
Yuyao Yuling Chemical Fibre Co., Ltd.	Ningbo	Zhejiang	(0574)62181868		Limited-Liability				Polyamide Fibre Thread
余姚市宇岭化纤有限公司(1996)	宁波市	浙江省	(0574)62181257	121	有限公司	123,507	2,896(19)	73,395	锦纶丝线

Top 10 Cities by Revenue 销售收入排名前10位城市	Province 省	Market share 市场份额 (%)	Number of firms 企业个数
Xiangfan 襄樊市	Hubei 湖北省	13.24	4
Taian 泰安市	Shandong 山东省	9.95	1
Suzhou 苏州市	Jiangsu 江苏省	9.80	17
Nantong 南通市	Jiangsu 江苏省	7.11	8
Xiamen 厦门市	Fujian 福建省	6.99	5
Shanghai 上海市	Shanghai 上海市	6.72	13
Ningbo 宁波市	Zhejiang 浙江省	4.69	5
Changzhou 常州市	Jiangsu 江苏省	3.78	11
Shaoxing 绍兴市	Zhejiang 浙江省	2.52	4
Binzhou 滨州市	Shandong 山东省	2.47	1

10 Major Wholesalers 十家主要批发商	City 城市	Province 省	Telephone/Fax 电话/传真
Shanghai Shenda Co.,Ltd.	Shanghai	Shanghai	(021)62319898
上海申达股份有限公司	上海市	上海市	(021)62317250
Orient International Holding Silk Group Corportion	Shanghai	Shanghai	(021)64662288
东方国际集团丝绸进出口有限公司	上海市	上海市	(021)64677788
Nanjing Textiles Import & Export Co.,Ltd.	Nanjing	Jiangsu	(025)3306789
南京纺织品进出口股份有限公司	南京市	江苏省	(025)3300518
Zhejiang Textiles Import & Export Group Co.,Ltd.	Hangzhou	Zhejiang	(0571)87075888
浙江省纺织品进出口集团有限公司	杭州市	浙江省	(0571)87079234
Zhejiang Orient Holdings Co.,Ltd.	Hangzhou	Zhejiang	(0571)87215678
浙江东方集团股份有限公司	杭州市	浙江省	(0571)87215000
Zhejiang Silk Holding Co.,ltd.	Hangzhou	Zhejiang	(0571)85195588
浙江省丝绸集团有限公司	杭州市	浙江省	(0571)85192540
Guangdong Silk (Group) Corporation	Guangzhou	Guangdong	(020)83337448
广东省丝绸（集团）公司	广州市	广东省	(020)83332995
Shanghai Costume Group Co.,Ltd.	Shanghai	Shanghai	(021)62748598
上海服装（集团）有限公司	上海市	上海市	(021)62414773
Orient International Holding Shanghai Textiles Import & Export Co.Ltd.	Shanghai	Shanghai	(021)63218855
东方国际集团上海市针织品进出口有限公司	上海市	上海市	(021)63299560
Jiangsu Textiles Import & Export Group Co.,Ltd.	Nanjing	Jiangsu	(025)6895000
江苏省纺织品进出口集团股份有限公司	南京市	江苏省	(025)4400800

1741: Wool Tops 毛条加工业

The industry accounts for 0.041% of the total revenue of China's industrial sector in 2002. The rate of return on assets is 1.10%. 73.68% of all firms in the industry made a profit while 26.32% had negative returns.The top province in terms of the industry's revenue is Jiangsu, accounting for 47.12% of the total revenue.
2002年本行业收入占全行业的0.041%，资产利润率为1.10%。73.68%的企业赢利，26.32%的企业亏损。收入最高的省为江苏省，占本行业的47.12%。

	Total number of firms 企业总数	Total number of employees 职工总数	Total revenue (Mil.RMB) 总销售收入（百万元）	Total profit (Mil.RMB) 总利润（百万元）	Return on assets 资产利润率（%）	Return on equity 权益利润率（%）	Labour productivity ('000 RMB/ worker) 劳动生产率（千元/人）	Debts/ assets 资产负债率（%）	Total assets (Mil.RMB) 总资产（百万元）
Industry Overall 行业总体	76	19,843	4,437	51	1.10	2.91	40.53	62.20	4,622

	Number of firms 企业个数	Average number of employees 平均职工人数	Average revenue ('000 RMB) 平均销售收入（千元）	Average profit ('000 RMB) 平均利润（千元）	Return on assets 资产利润率（%）	Return on equity 权益利润率（%）	Labour productivity ('000 RMB/ worker) 劳动生产率（千元/人）	Debts/ assets 资产负债率（%）	Average total assets ('000 RMB) 平均总资产（千元）
By ownership 产业所有权									
State-owned 国有	9	81	5,756	-672	-1.72	-4.45	23.47	61.46	39,127
Collective-owned 集体	11	122	45,137	562	3.83	13.74	49.91	72.12	14,665
Foreign & Overseas Chinese Funded 三资	11	311	80,528	1,422	1.21	2.69	51.75	55.04	117,395
By regional distribution 地区分布									
Central-North 华北	16	174	20,322	-580	-1.66	-4.81	35.86	65.60	35,023
Beijing 北京									
Tianjin 天津	3	241	25,185	411	0.59	1.66	21.40	64.74	70,137
Hebei 河北	4	133	21,091	1,436	7.59	27.23	62.76	72.13	18,919
Shanxi 山西	2	272	17,345	-7,005	-10.65	-34.63	15.31	69.25	65,785
Inner Mongolia 内蒙古	7	141	18,651	-321	-1.57	-3.94	43.31	60.04	20,388
Northeast 东北	2	16	5,129				42.55	85.18	9,030
Liaoning 辽宁	1	19	10,257				69.42	91.88	5,890
Jilin 吉林	1	12						81.94	12,170
Heilongjiang 黑龙江									
Central-East 华东	41	322	84,502	1,447	1.88	4.81	40.90	60.99	77,084
Shanghai 上海	6	304	104,101	558	1.00	2.17	36.70	53.81	55,680
Jiangsu 江苏	28	322	74,661	1,275	1.80	6.17	42.16	70.78	70,685
Zhejiang 浙江	3	266	216,669	6,238	2.79	4.99	84.37	44.23	223,978
Anhui 安徽	2	698	17,398	-222	-0.28	-0.38	8.70	27.00	79,652
Fujian 福建									
Jiangxi 江西									
Shandong 山东	2	83	32,340	1,015	12.74	21.66	79.96	41.20	7,968
Central-South 中南	7	386	66,848	109	0.12	0.45	39.53	73.45	91,614
Henan 河南									
Hubei 湖北	1	14	35,310	408	8.75	74.18	854.57	88.20	4,661
Hunan 湖南									
Guangdong 广东	5	458	81,008	286	0.23	0.86	40.02	73.13	124,211
Guangxi 广西	1	400	27,584	-1,073	-6.89	-37.68	8.14	81.72	15,582
Hainan 海南									
Southwest 西南	3	82	1,817	-456	-1.39	-1.51	8.00	8.17	32,898
Chongqing 重庆									
Sichuan 四川	1	116	3,300	1	0.02	0.02	4.31	12.90	4,650
Guizhou 贵州									
Yunnan 云南									
Tibet 西藏	2	66	1,076	-685	-1.46	-1.58	11.27	7.94	47,022
Northwest 西北	7	126	23,342	208	1.02	2.53	61.95	59.80	20,425
Shaanxi 陕西	1	183	3,421	191	0.84	1.15	9.19	27.52	22,834
Gansu 甘肃	5	89	30,340	693	4.03	9.24	116.02	56.42	17,203
Qinghai 青海									
Ningxia 宁夏									
Xinjiang 新疆	1	257	8,270	-2,201	-6.45	-63.80	5.92	89.89	34,125

1741: Wool Tops 毛条加工业

Year 年份	Number of firms 企业个数	Rate of change 变化率（%）	Number of employees 职工人数（人）	Rate of change 变化率（%）	Total revenue (Mil. RMB) 总销售收入（百万元）	Rate of change 变化率（%）	Total profit (Mil RMB) 总利润（百万元）	Rate of change 变化率（%）
2000	83		23,373		3,343		50	
2001	79	-4.82	19,519	-16.49	3,622	8.35	37	-26.00
2002	76	-3.80	19,843	1.66	4,437	22.50	51	37.84

Major Products 主要产品	Output 产量	Unit 单位

10 Main Firms with Maximal Revenue (year founded) 收入最大的十家主要企业（创办年份）	City 城市	Province 省	Telephone/fax 电话/传真	Number of employees 职工人数	Ownership 产业所有权	Revenue ('000 RMB) 销售收入（千元）	Profit('000 RMB) (rank) 利润（千元）（排名）	Total assets ('000 RMB) 总资产（千元）	Major products 主要产品
Jiangsu Chengda Group Co., Ltd.	Suzhou	Jiangsu	(0512)52691033		Private Owned				Wool Yarn
江苏澄达集团有限公司(1997)	苏州市	江苏省	(0512)52691356	1,942	私营企业	561,289	9,501(2)	482,152	毛纱
Reward(Ningbo) Wool Industry Co., Ltd.	Ningbo	Zhejiang	(0574)86177765		Overseas Chinese-funded				Wool Bar
利华(宁波)羊毛工业股份有限公司(1994)	宁波市	浙江省	(0574)86177551	551	港澳台资	398,883	14,122(1)	631,391	羊毛条
Shanghai Petrochemistry Yali Industrial Development Co.,Ltd.	Shanghai	Shanghai	(021)57941699		Joint Stock				Acrylic Wool Top
上海石化桠力实业发展有限公司(1996)	上海市	上海市	(021)57946508	973	股份制	332,047	374(28)	132,345	腈纶毛条
Nanhai Wool Textile Enterprise (Group) Co., Ltd.	Foshan	Guangdong	(0757)6779888		Joint Stock				Wool Bar
南海毛纺织企业（集团）股份有限公司(1956)	佛山市	广东省	(0757)6778728	1,525	股份制	330,085	2,300(9)	583,334	毛条
Changzhou Wollen Thread Co., Ltd.	Changzhou	Jiangsu	(0519)8814752		Limited-Liability				Wool Bar
常州市毛条厂有限公司(1952)	常州市	江苏省	(0519)8826136	753	有限公司	272,140	3,730(7)	197,210	毛条
Jiangsu Lingfeng Textile Group Co., Ltd.	Suzhou	Jiangsu	(0512)52541565		Private Enterprises				Wool Fabric
江苏灵丰纺织集团有限公司(1993)	苏州市	江苏省	(0512)52541423	1,867	私营独资	269,194	6,529(4)	436,586	呢绒
Shanghai Shenyi Wollen Thread Co., Ltd.	Shanghai	Shanghai	(021)55213093		Limited-Liability				Wool Bar
上海申一毛条有限公司(2000)	上海市	上海市	(021)55213552	536	有限公司	240,078	2,007(11)	127,706	毛条
Changshu Suhua Wollen Thread Co., Ltd.	Suzhou	Jiangsu	(0512)52851784		Overseas Chinese-funded				Acrylic Wool Top
常熟苏华毛条有限公司(1989)	苏州市	江苏省	(0512)52851784	252	港澳台资	137,634	7,369(3)	209,243	腈纶毛条
Zhangjiagang Longma Fine Yarn Co., Ltd.	Suzhou	Jiangsu	(0512)58763108		Overseas Chinese-funded				Xueni'er Yarn
张家港龙马特种纱线有限公司(1990)	苏州市	江苏省	(0512)58763338	872	港澳台资	108,577	1,257(16)	129,455	雪尼尔纱
Kunshan Hengyi Wollen Thread Factory	Suzhou	Jiangsu	(0520)57682666		Collective-owned				Wool Washing
昆山市恒一毛条厂(2000)	苏州市	江苏省	(0520)57687333	108	集体企业	66,935	375(27)	18,009	洗毛

Top 10 Cities by Revenue 销售收入排名前10位城市	Province 省	Market share 市场份额（%）	Number of firms 企业个数
Suzhou 苏州市	Jiangsu 江苏省	32.97	14
Ningbo 宁波市	Zhejiang 浙江省	14.13	2
Shanghai 上海市	Shanghai 上海市	14.08	6
Foshan 佛山市	Guangdong 广东省	7.44	1
Changzhou 常州市	Jiangsu 江苏省	6.13	1
Wuxi 无锡市	Jiangsu 江苏省	4.14	9
Taizhou 泰州市	Jiangsu 江苏省	3.09	2
Lanzhou 兰州市	Gansu 甘肃省	3.02	3
Tianjin 天津市	Tianjin 天津市	1.70	3
Zibo 淄博市	Shandong 山东省	1.23	1

10 Major Wholesalers 十家主要批发商	City 城市	Province 省	Telephone/Fax 电话/传真
Shanghai Shenda Co.,Ltd.	Shanghai	Shanghai	(021)62319898
上海申达股份有限公司	上海市	上海市	(021)62317250
Orient International Holding Silk Group Corportion	Shanghai	Shanghai	(021)64662288
东方国际集团丝绸进出口有限公司	上海市	上海市	(021)64677788
Nanjing Textiles Import & Export Co.,Ltd.	Nanjing	Jiangsu	(025)3306789
南京纺织品进出口股份有限公司	南京市	江苏省	(025)3300518
Zhejiang Textiles Import & Export Group Co.,Ltd.	Hangzhou	Zhejiang	(0571)87075888
浙江省纺织品进出口集团有限公司	杭州市	浙江省	(0571)87079234
Zhejiang Orient Holdings Co.,Ltd.	Hangzhou	Zhejiang	(0571)87215678
浙江东方集团股份有限公司	杭州市	浙江省	(0571)87215000
Zhejiang Silk Holding Co.,ltd.	Hangzhou	Zhejiang	(0571)85195588
浙江省丝绸集团有限公司	杭州市	浙江省	(0571)85192540
Guangdong Silk (Group) Corporation	Guangzhou	Guangdong	(020)83337448
广东省丝绸（集团）公司	广州市	广东省	(020)83332995
Shanghai Costume Group Co.,Ltd.	Shanghai	Shanghai	(021)62748598
上海服装（集团）有限公司	上海市	上海市	(021)62414773
Orient International Holding Shanghai Textiles Import & Export Co.Ltd.	Shanghai	Shanghai	(021)63218855
东方国际集团上海市针织品进出口有限公司	上海市	上海市	(021)63299560
Jiangsu Textiles Import & Export Group Co.,Ltd.	Nanjing	Jiangsu	(025)6895000
江苏省纺织品进出口集团股份有限公司	南京市	江苏省	(025)4400800

1742: Wool Spinning 毛纺业

The industry accounts for 0.369% of the total revenue of China's industrial sector in 2002. The rate of return on assets is 2.55%. 75.61% of all firms in the industry made a profit while 24.39% had negative returns.The top province in terms of the industry's revenue is Jiangsu, accounting for 45.93% of the total revenue.
2002年本行业收入占全行业的0.369%，资产利润率为2.55%。75.61%的企业赢利，24.39%的企业亏损。收入最高的省为江苏省，占本行业的45.93%。

	Total number of firms 企业总数	Total number of employees 职工总数	Total revenue (Mil.RMB) 总销售收入(百万元)	Total profit (Mil.RMB) 总利润(百万元)	Return on assets 资产利润率(%)	Return on equity 权益利润率(%)	Labour productivity ('000 RMB/worker) 劳动生产率(千元/人)	Debts/assets 资产负债率(%)	Total assets (Mil.RMB) 总资产(百万元)
Industry Overall 行业总体	652	254,768	39,605	1,381	2.55	7.18	40.75	64.43	54,086

	Number of firms 企业个数	Average number of employees 平均职工人数	Average revenue ('000 RMB) 平均销售收入(千元)	Average profit ('000 RMB) 平均利润(千元)	Return on assets 资产利润率(%)	Return on equity 权益利润率(%)	Labour productivity ('000 RMB/worker) 劳动生产率(千元/人)	Debts/assets 资产负债率(%)	Average total assets ('000 RMB) 平均总资产(千元)
By ownership 产业所有权									
State-owned 国有	69	546	19,965	-3,015	-3.01		10.45	101.85	100,299
Collective-owned 集体	67	438	104,673	7,947	6.68	17.92	65.16	62.73	119,003
Foreign & Overseas Chinese Funded 三资	115	355	67,402	1,027	1.28	3.46	52.16	62.98	80,124
By regional distribution 地区分布									
Central-North 华北	178	234	37,171	1,804	5.29	20.46	41.44	74.16	34,129
Beijing 北京	10	493	28,280	-4,759	-5.71	-28.59	16.06	80.03	83,375
Tianjin 天津	20	243	12,779	-696	-1.17		2.32	109.73	59,715
Hebei 河北	133	187	42,431	2,930	13.94	29.71	60.12	53.07	21,011
Shanxi 山西	5	510	21,635	-691	-0.76		20.64	108.51	90,598
Inner Mongolia 内蒙古	10	457	32,668	-361	-0.45	-1.46	20.41	69.15	79,934
Northeast 东北	18	381	17,140	-689	-0.78	-2.80	11.16	72.22	88,590
Liaoning 辽宁	9	275	21,760	-1,229	-2.31	-6.67	15.97	65.33	53,158
Jilin 吉林	7	476	11,060	-196	-0.16	-0.60	6.84	72.92	120,385
Heilongjiang 黑龙江	2	523	17,635	21	0.01	0.08	13.55	82.14	136,750
Central-East 华东	346	430	82,082	3,857	3.83	9.24	49.77	58.52	100,654
Shanghai 上海	37	329	50,408	-1,314	-1.41	-2.91	31.54	51.45	92,897
Jiangsu 江苏	156	495	116,611	6,950	5.12	11.35	63.78	54.86	135,621
Zhejiang 浙江	93	245	48,497	2,433	5.22	11.90	43.74	56.11	46,607
Anhui 安徽	5	180	7,464	-379	-2.42		8.50	480.22	15,692
Fujian 福建	6	410	72,163	-227	-0.44	-1.55	24.47	71.32	51,147
Jiangxi 江西	3	168	8,307	-6,173	-8.05		26.46	109.38	76,697
Shandong 山东	46	717	72,576	2,053	1.79	6.07	31.26	70.58	114,832
Central-South 中南	64	564	53,639	-1,041	-1.07	-3.45	24.08	68.94	97,105
Henan 河南	19	829	12,844	205	0.50	3.32	5.18	84.95	41,103
Hubei 湖北	6	88	10,011	-830	-4.45		37.55	104.71	18,668
Hunan 湖南	4	566	14,896	-3,861	-7.05		4.97	101.51	54,803
Guangdong 广东	33	487	89,488	-1,550	-1.09	-2.85	45.58	61.80	142,202
Guangxi 广西	1	570	46,838	971	6.66	11.18	23.71	40.42	14,576
Hainan 海南	1	897	69,293	107	0.03	0.53	11.32	94.92	395,342
Southwest 西南	10	270	12,226	-948	-2.87		10.40	125.25	32,968
Chongqing 重庆	3	206	28,993	-2,026	-3.16		28.27	159.16	64,104
Sichuan 四川	4	479	7,494	-891	-2.83	-15.35	3.73	81.55	31,472
Guizhou 贵州	2	38	231	-109	-5.35	-31.59	1.84	83.06	2,028
Yunnan 云南									
Tibet 西藏	1	91	4,850	384	5.17	5.79	36.22	10.77	7,431
Northwest 西北	36	513	20,111	-5,176	-3.69	-19.96	14.45	81.50	140,159
Shaanxi 陕西	5	606	3,647	-22,736	-10.63		0.56	156.95	213,909
Gansu 甘肃	23	459	24,566	-1,115	-1.30	-2.51	21.15	48.18	85,889
Qinghai 青海	1	257	4,169	-11	-0.24	-0.94	4.47	74.54	4,575
Ningxia 宁夏									
Xinjiang 新疆	7	661	19,509	-6,716	-2.36	-9.08	8.82	74.06	285,165

1742: Wool Spinning 毛纺业

Year 年份	Number of firms 企业个数	Rate of change 变化率 (%)	Number of employees 职工人数 (人)	Rate of change 变化率 (%)	Total revenue (Mil. RMB) 总销售收入 (百万元)	Rate of change 变化率 (%)	Total profit (Mil RMB) 总利润 (百万元)	Rate of change 变化率 (%)
2000	577		317,939		33,253		913	
2001	571	-1.04	264,719	-16.74	32,919	-1.00	792	-13.25
2002	652	14.19	254,768	-3.76	39,605	20.31	1,381	74.37

Major Products 主要产品	Output 产量	Unit 单位
Wool 绒线（毛线）	44	10,000 Tons 万吨

10 Main Firms with Maximal Revenue (year founded) 收入最大的十家主要企业（创办年份）	City 城市	Province 省	Telephone/fax 电话/传真	Number of employees 职工人数	Ownership 产业所有权	Revenue ('000 RMB) 销售收入 (千元)	Profit('000 RMB) (rank) 利润(千元) (排名)	Total assets ('000 RMB) 总资产 (千元)	Major products 主要产品
Jiangsu Sunshine Group	Wuxi	Jiangsu	(0510)6121888		Joint Stock				Spinning Wool Fabric
江苏阳光集团(1993)	无锡市	江苏省	(0510)6121188	9,140	股份制	3,863,550	285,768(2)	5,576,093	精纺呢绒
Heilan Group Corporation	Wuxi	Jiangsu	(0510)6121478		Collective-owned				Spinning Wool Fabric
海澜集团公司(1989)	无锡市	江苏省	(0510)6121377	5,800	集体企业	2,033,323	292,083(1)	3,928,999	精纺呢绒
Jiangsu Aoyang Induatrial (Group) Co., Ltd.	Suzhou	Jiangsu	(0520)58591800		Limited-Liability				Machine-Woven Yarn
江苏澳洋实业(集团)有限公司(1980)	苏州市	江苏省	(0520)58598688	3,493	有限公司	1,404,480	78,010(4)	1,496,010	机织纱
Jiangsu Nijiaxiang Group Co., ltd.	Wuxi	Jiangsu	(0510)6221568		Private Enterprises				Spinning Wool Fabric
江苏倪家巷集团公司(1994)	无锡市	江苏省	(0510)6221161	2,538	私营独资	925,810	81,170(3)	795,200	精纺呢绒
Guangdong Meiya Group Stock Co., Ltd.	Jiangmen	Guangdong	(0750)8888888		Joint Stock				Acrylic Fibre Wool Top
广东美雅集团股份有限公司(1992)	江门市	广东省	(0750)8889673	4,478	股份制	858,502	-	2,366,962	晴纶毛条
Dinghu Yongsheng PPY Co., Ltd	Wuxi	Jiangsu	(0510)6209763		Collective-owned				Acrylic Fibre Yarn
江苏华士集团公司(1992)	无锡市	江苏省	(0510)6201235	2,756	集体企业	802,010	67,610(5)	286,440	腈纶纱
Wuxi Xiexin Group Co., Ltd.	Wuxi	Jiangsu	(0510)2629999		State Enterprises				Spinning Wool Fabric
无锡协新集团有限公司(1935)	无锡市	江苏省	(0510)2621378	2,318	国有独资	643,180	10,600(35)	1,062,137	精纺呢绒
Shandong Ruyi Woollen Textile Group Co., Ltd.	Jining	Shandong	(0537)2933032		State Enterprises				Spinning Wool Fabric
山东如意毛纺集团有限责任公司(1996)	济宁市	山东省	(0537)2316688	6,197	国有独资	571,280	41,044(7)	1,325,049	精纺呢绒
Nanjing New Century Woolen Textile Co., Ltd.	Nanjing	Jiangsu	(025)2453217		Limited-Liability				Acrylic Fibre Yarn
南京新世纪毛纺织有限公司(2000)	南京市	江苏省	(025)2453217	1,196	有限公司	472,110	31,310(9)	111,240	晴纶纱
Lianyungang Xingyun Wool & Velvet Co., Ltd.	Lianyungang	Jiangsu	(0518)8812332		Overseas Chinese-funded				Cutting Rill Fine Hair
连云港市星云毛绒有限公司(1992)	连云港市	江苏省	(0518)8812851	715	港澳台资	461,890	8,200(42)	69,850	割圈绒

Top 10 Cities by Revenue 销售收入排名前10位城市	Province 省	Market share 市场份额 (%)	Number of firms 企业个数
Wuxi 无锡市	Jiangsu 江苏省	26.78	55
Suzhou 苏州市	Jiangsu 江苏省	10.96	56
Xingtai 邢台市	Hebei 河北省	7.25	71
Baoding 保定市	Hebei 河北省	6.40	54
Shanghai 上海市	Shanghai 上海市	4.71	37
Jiaxing 嘉兴市	Zhejiang 浙江省	3.55	18
Qingdao 青岛市	Shandong 山东省	3.53	11
Huzhou 湖州市	Zhejiang 浙江省	2.90	11
Jiangmen 江门市	Guangdong 广东省	2.83	4
Ningbo 宁波市	Zhejiang 浙江省	2.14	18

10 Major Wholesalers 十家主要批发商	City 城市	Province 省	Telephone/Fax 电话/传真
Shanghai Shenda Co.,Ltd.	Shanghai	Shanghai	(021)62319898
上海申达股份有限公司	上海市	上海市	(021)62317250
Orient International Holding Silk Group Corportion	Shanghai	Shanghai	(021)64662288
东方国际集团丝绸进出口有限公司	上海市	上海市	(021)64677788
Nanjing Textiles Import & Export Co.,Ltd.	Nanjing	Jiangsu	(025)3306789
南京纺织品进出口股份有限公司	南京市	江苏省	(025)3300518
Zhejiang Textiles Import & Export Group Co.,Ltd.	Hangzhou	Zhejiang	(0571)87075888
浙江省纺织品进出口集团有限公司	杭州市	浙江省	(0571)87079234
Zhejiang Orient Holdings Co.,Ltd.	Hangzhou	Zhejiang	(0571)87215678
浙江东方集团股份有限公司	杭州市	浙江省	(0571)87215000
Zhejiang Silk Holding Co.,ltd.	Hangzhou	Zhejiang	(0571)85195588
浙江省丝绸集团有限公司	杭州市	浙江省	(0571)85192540
Guangdong Silk (Group) Corporation	Guangzhou	Guangdong	(020)83337448
广东省丝绸（集团）公司	广州市	广东省	(020)83332995
Shanghai Costume Group Co.,Ltd.	Shanghai	Shanghai	(021)62748598
上海服装（集团）有限公司	上海市	上海市	(021)62414773
Orient International Holding Shanghai Textiles Import & Export Co.Ltd.	Shanghai	Shanghai	(021)63218833
东方国际集团上海市针织品进出口有限公司	上海市	上海市	(021)63299560
Jiangsu Textiles Import & Export Group Co.,Ltd.	Nanjing	Jiangsu	(025)6895000
江苏省纺织品进出口集团股份有限公司	南京市	江苏省	(025)4400800

1743: Wool Weaving 毛织业

The industry accounts for 0.077% of the total revenue of China's industrial sector in 2002. The rate of return on assets is 3.20%. 78.13% of all firms in the industry made a profit while 21.88% had negative returns.The top province in terms of the industry's revenue is Jiangsu, accounting for 35.83% of the total revenue.
2002年本行业收入占全行业的 0.077%，资产利润率为 3.20%。78.13%的企业赢利，21.88%的企业亏损。收入最高的省为江苏省，占本行业的35.83%。

	Total number of firms 企业总数	Total number of employees 职工总数	Total revenue (Mil.RMB) 总销售收入 (百万元)	Total profit (Mil.RMB) 总利润 (百万元)	Return on assets 资产利润率 (%)	Return on equity 权益利润率 (%)	Labour productivity ('000 RMB/ worker) 劳动生产率 (千元/人)	Debts/ assets 资产负债率 (%)	Total assets (Mil.RMB) 总资产 (百万元)
Industry Overall 行业总体	192	101,820	8,292	474	3.20	7.40	22.69	56.75	14,806

	Number of firms 企业个数	Average number of employees 平均职工人数	Average revenue ('000 RMB) 平均销售收入（千元）	Average profit ('000 RMB) 平均利润 (千元)	Return on assets 资产利润率 (%)	Return on equity 权益利润率 (%)	Labour productivity ('000 RMB/ worker) 劳动生产率 (千元/人)	Debts/ assets 资产负债率 (%)	Average total assets ('000 RMB) 平均总资产 (千元)
By ownership 产业所有权									
State-owned 国有	16	458	17,274	-2,548	-2.80	-28.24	14.62	90.09	91,061
Collective-owned 集体	25	199	18,606	426	3.59	9.86	27.78	63.59	11,874
Foreign & Overseas Chinese Funded 三资	50	371	44,780	4,175	4.54	7.57	27.81	39.99	91,955
By regional distribution 地区分布									
Central-North 华北	41	428	40,131	2,244	2.85	5.91	35.46	51.72	78,671
Beijing 北京	5	178	10,538	439	10.43	47.09	17.77	77.85	4,212
Tianjin 天津	8	359	47,042	844	0.54	0.87	5.95	37.92	156,477
Hebei 河北	17	277	26,604	1,209	4.14	12.22	24.29	66.17	29,233
Shanxi 山西									
Inner Mongolia 内蒙古	11	826	69,462	5,682	4.29	10.29	52.30	58.28	132,332
Northeast 东北	6	354	10,357	-637	-0.72		9.10	113.23	89,051
Liaoning 辽宁	2	392	3,291	-4,076	-1.72		4.58	120.76	237,570
Jilin 吉林	4	335	13,890	1,083	7.32	15.51	11.75	52.82	14,791
Heilongjiang 黑龙江									
Central-East 华东	97	674	53,820	3,488	3.88	8.49	17.67	54.26	89,809
Shanghai 上海	8	390	82,272	30,665	8.25	11.27	62.65	26.80	371,610
Jiangsu 江苏	43	380	69,098	2,459	3.15	8.19	34.41	61.47	77,969
Zhejiang 浙江	26	287	41,927	-408	-0.72	-2.83	31.11	74.45	56,389
Anhui 安徽									
Fujian 福建	3	185	6,597	18	0.16	0.18	9.93	7.70	11,327
Jiangxi 江西	2	115	7,750	585	1.95		30.87	103.98	29,995
Shandong 山东	15	2,508	31,050	-227	-0.41	-3.02	4.03	86.35	55,058
Central-South 中南	38	411	35,627	1,334	2.30	5.51	32.45	58.27	58,045
Henan 河南	1								
Hubei 湖北	2	1,204	157,291	20,402	3.24	7.18	75.66	54.85	629,400
Hunan 湖南									
Guangdong 广东	35	378	29,693	283	1.05	2.81	24.58	62.82	27,055
Guangxi 广西									
Hainan 海南									
Southwest 西南	5	153	889	-75	-0.46	-2.49	2.15	81.41	16,162
Chongqing 重庆									
Sichuan 四川									
Guizhou 贵州	1	629	4,000	-499	-0.63	-3.72	2.19	83.01	79,060
Yunnan 云南									
Tibet 西藏	4	34	112	31	7.14	7.87	1.98	9.25	438
Northwest 西北	5	80	1,077	-531	-5.56		11.86	106.29	9,551
Shaanxi 陕西									
Gansu 甘肃	5	80	1,077	-531	-5.56		11.86	106.29	9,551
Qinghai 青海									
Ningxia 宁夏									
Xinjiang 新疆									

1743: Wool Weaving 毛织业

Year 年份	Number of firms 企业个数	Rate of change 变化率 (%)	Number of employees 职工人数 (人)	Rate of change 变化率 (%)	Total revenue (Mil. RMB) 总销售收入 (百万元)	Rate of change 变化率 (%)	Total profit (Mil RMB) 总利润 (百万元)	Rate of change 变化率 (%)
2000	231		89,194		7,381		372	
2001	209	-9.52	80,756	-9.46	7,704	4.38	435	16.94
2002	192	-8.13	101,820	26.08	8,292	7.63	474	8.97

Major Products 主要产品	Output 产量	Unit 单位
Woolen Cloth 呢绒	27,096	10,000 Meters 万米

10 Main Firms with Maximal Revenue (year founded) 收入最大的十家主要企业（创办年份）	City 城市	Province 省	Telephone/fax 电话/传真	Number of employees 职工人数	Ownership 产业所有权	Revenue ('000 RMB) 销售收入(千元)	Profit('000 RMB) (rank) 利润(千元)(排名)	Total assets ('000 RMB) 总资产(千元)	Major products 主要产品
Jiangsu Xinwu Group	Wuxi	Jiangsu	(0510)6151260		Joint Stock				Spinning Wool Fabric
江苏新伍集团(1986)	无锡市	江苏省	(0510)6151666	2,200	股份制	964,751	45,499(4)	792,360	精纺呢绒
Inner Mongolia Mongolia King Group	Eerduosi	InnerMongolia	(0477)5295166		Limited-Liability				Cashmere Products
内蒙古蒙古王集团(1996)	鄂尔多斯市	内蒙古	(0477)5295394	3,992	有限公司	406,570	61,044(2)	850,640	羊绒制品
Zhangjiagang Pukun Textile Industrial Co., Ltd.	Suzhou	Jiangsu	(0512)58442888		Limited-Liability				Spinning Wool Fabric
张家港普坤纺织实业有限公司(1992)	苏州市	江苏省	(0512)58444792	1,200	有限公司	371,710	8,760(12)	401,120	精纺呢绒
Jiangsu Kuangda Group Co.,ltd.	Changzhou	Jiangsu	(0519)6543081		Limited-Liability				Pure Chemical Fibre Textiles纯
江苏旷达集团有限公司(1989)	常州市	江苏省	(0519)6543841	586	有限公司	288,400	31,680(6)	447,550	化纤织物
Shaoxing Kunlong Wool & Velvet Products Co., Ltd.	Shaoxing	Zhejiang	(0575)2033668		Overseas Chinese-funded				Blanket
绍兴昆隆毛绒制品有限公司(1998)	绍兴市	浙江省	(0575)2031168	865	港澳台资	273,205	17,245(8)	65,296	毛毯
Shanghai Haixin Group Stock Co., Ltd.	Shanghai	Shanghai	(021)57698009		Overseas Chinese-funded				Fur
上海海欣集团股份有限公司(1986)	上海市	上海市	(021)57698200	596	港澳台资	255,191	172,376(1)	2,167,760	毛皮
Hubei Xiantao Woolen Textile Group Co.Ltd.	Xiantao	Hubei	(0728)3222150		Joint Stock				Blanket
湖北仙桃毛纺集团有限公司(1992)	仙桃市	湖北省	(0728)3223426	1,899	股份制	251,247	39,817(5)	1,232,502	毛毯
Tianjin Sanxing Wool Textile .Co., Ltd.	Tianjin	Tianjin	(022)28514771		Foreign Funded				Spinning Wool Fabric
天津三星毛纺织有限公司(1995)	天津市	天津市	(022)28514779	806	外商投资	231,386	4,997(18)	374,739	精纺呢绒
Koyo Zhedong (Ningbo) Blanket Co., Ltd.	Ningbo	Zhejiang	(0574)86177998		Foreign Funded				Blanket
兴洋浙东（宁波）毛毯有限公司(1996)	宁波市	浙江省	(0374)86177088	471	外商投资	151,280	-	287,125	毛毯
Yangzhou Guangrui Wool & Velvet Co., Ltd.	Yangzhou	Jiangsu	(0514)7863238		Joint Stock				Plush
扬州广瑞毛绒有限责任公司(1999)	扬州市	江苏省	(0514)7888141	1,317	股份制	139,484	-	288,250	长毛绒

Top 10 Cities by Revenue 销售收入排名前10位城市	Province 省	Market share 市场份额 (%)	Number of firms 企业个数
Wuxi 无锡市	Jiangsu 江苏省	14.65	14
Suzhou 苏州市	Jiangsu 江苏省	9.24	12
Shanghai 上海市	Shanghai 上海市	7.94	8
Eerduosi 鄂尔多斯市	Inner Mongolia 内蒙古	6.82	5
Changzhou 常州市	Jiangsu 江苏省	6.11	10
Baoding 保定市	Hebei 河北省	4.81	10
Tianjin 天津市	Tianjin 天津市	4.54	8
Shaoxing 绍兴市	Zhejiang 浙江省	4.38	4
Ningbo 宁波市	Zhejiang 浙江省	3.41	12

10 Major Wholesalers 十家主要批发商	City 城市	Province 省	Telephone/Fax 电话/传真
Shanghai Shenda Co.,Ltd.	Shanghai	Shanghai	(021)62319898
上海申达股份有限公司	上海市	上海市	(021)62317250
Orient International Holding Silk Group Corportion	Shanghai	Shanghai	(021)64662288
东方国际集团丝绸进出口有限公司	上海市	上海市	(021)64677788
Nanjing Textiles Import & Export Co.,Ltd.	Nanjing	Jiangsu	(025)3306789
南京纺织品进出口股份有限公司	南京市	江苏省	(025)3300518
Zhejiang Textiles Import & Export Group Co.,Ltd.	Hangzhou	Zhejiang	(0571)87075888
浙江省纺织品进出口集团有限公司	杭州市	浙江省	(0571)87079234
Zhejiang Orient Holdings Co.,Ltd.	Hangzhou	Zhejiang	(0571)87215678
浙江东方集团股份有限公司	杭州市	浙江省	(0571)87215000
Zhejiang Silk Holding Co.,ltd.	Hangzhou	Zhejiang	(0571)85195588
浙江省丝绸集团有限公司	杭州市	浙江省	(0571)85192540
Guangdong Silk (Group) Corporation	Guangzhou	Guangdong	(020)83337448
广东省丝绸（集团）公司	广州市	广东省	(020)83332995
Shanghai Costume Group Co.,Ltd.	Shanghai	Shanghai	(021)62748598
上海服装（集团）有限公司	上海市	上海市	(021)62414773
Orient International Holding Shanghai Textiles Import & Export Co.Ltd.	Shanghai	Shanghai	(021)63218833
东方国际集团上海市针织品进出口有限公司	上海市	上海市	(021)63299560
Jiangsu Textiles Import & Export Group Co.,Ltd.	Nanjing	Jiangsu	(025)6895000
江苏省纺织品进出口集团股份有限公司	南京市	江苏省	(025)4400800

1744: Wool Printing and Dyeing 毛染整业

The industry accounts for 0.027% of the total revenue of China's industrial sector in 2002. The rate of return on assets is 2.49%. 84.54% of all firms in the industry made a profit while 15.46% had negative returns.The top province in terms of the industry's revenue is Jiangsu, accounting for 24.73% of the total revenue.
2002年本行业收入占全行业的 0.027%，资产利润率为 2.49%。84.54%的企业赢利，15.46%的企业亏损。收入最高的省为江苏省，占本行业的24.73%。

	Total number of firms 企业总数	Total number of employees 职工总数	Total revenue (Mil.RMB) 总销售收入（百万元）	Total profit (Mil.RMB) 总利润（百万元）	Return on assets 资产利润率（%）	Return on equity 权益利润率（%）	Labour productivity ('000 RMB/ worker) 劳动生产率（千元/人）	Debts/ assets 资产负债率（%）	Total assets (Mil.RMB) 总资产（百万元）
Industry Overall 行业总体	97	17,482	2,892	79	2.49	7.52	43.63	66.88	3,187

	Number of firms 企业个数	Average number of employees 平均职工人数	Average revenue ('000 RMB) 平均销售收入（千元）	Average profit ('000 RMB) 平均利润（千元）	Return on assets 资产利润率（%）	Return on equity 权益利润率（%）	Labour productivity ('000 RMB/ worker) 劳动生产率（千元/人）	Debts/ assets 资产负债率（%）	Average total assets ('000 RMB) 平均总资产（千元）
By ownership 产业所有权									
State-owned 国有	2	1,008	45,775	-9,057	-4.97		11.01	107.69	182,327
Collective-owned 集体	12	165	41,219	3,182	11.46	33.16	81.13	65.44	27,774
Foreign & Overseas Chinese Funded 三资	31	181	35,656	1,048	2.18	4.62	44.90	52.77	48,053
By regional distribution 地区分布									
Central-North 华北	11	344	53,829	-780	-0.73	-3.90	36.50	81.31	106,944
Beijing 北京	2	1,156	53,442	-9,673	-5.19		14.03	106.87	186,528
Tianjin 天津	1	118	20,260	430	3.72	11.17	11.19	66.72	11,570
Hebei 河北									
Shanxi 山西									
Inner Mongolia 内蒙古	8	169	58,122	1,292	1.31	4.28	77.17	69.48	98,970
Northeast 东北	1	86	78,000	4,760	19.10	56.60	156.51	66.25	24,920
Liaoning 辽宁	1	86	78,000	4,760	19.10	56.60	156.51	66.25	24,920
Jilin 吉林									
Heilongjiang 黑龙江									
Central-East 华东	65	151	25,285	1,089	4.46	10.89	47.86	59.00	24,389
Shanghai 上海	21	130	24,936	1,292	5.12	12.11	63.94	57.70	25,222
Jiangsu 江苏	24	189	29,798	838	3.97	14.67	37.85	72.95	21,124
Zhejiang 浙江	14	144	21,472	1,427	6.54	18.28	46.89	64.22	21,827
Anhui 安徽									
Fujian 福建	4	107	16,490	415	0.78	0.97	43.19	20.09	53,577
Jiangxi 江西									
Shandong 山东	2	64	19,077	943	6.55	22.94	90.13	71.45	14,392
Central-South 中南	20	189	28,921	618	3.09	6.98	37.16	55.75	20,021
Henan 河南	2	88	5,280	22	0.57	1.06	47.27	46.57	3,803
Hubei 湖北									
Hunan 湖南	1	129	5,000	100	1.50	116.28	8.63	98.71	6,683
Guangdong 广东	17	204	33,110	719	3.16	7.06	37.71	55.19	22,713
Guangxi 广西									
Hainan 海南									
Southwest 西南									
Chongqing 重庆									
Sichuan 四川									
Guizhou 贵州									
Yunnan 云南									
Tibet 西藏									
Northwest 西北									
Shaanxi 陕西									
Gansu 甘肃									
Qinghai 青海									
Ningxia 宁夏									
Xinjiang 新疆									

1744: Wool Printing and Dyeing 毛染整业

Year 年份	Number of firms 企业个数	Rate of change 变化率 (%)	Number of employees 职工人数 (人)	Rate of change 变化率 (%)	Total revenue (Mil. RMB) 总销售收入 (百万元)	Rate of change 变化率 (%)	Total profit (Mil RMB) 总利润 (百万元)	Rate of change 变化率 (%)
2000	76		18,629		2,746		28	
2001	71	-6.58	16,033	-13.94	2,388	-13.04	2	-92.86
2002	97	36.62	17,482	9.04	2,892	21.11	79	3,850.00

Major Products 主要产品	Output 产量	Unit 单位
Woolen Cloth 呢绒	27,096	10,000 Meters 万米
Wool 绒线（毛线）	44	10,000 Tons 万吨

10 Main Firms with Maximal Revenue (year founded) 收入最大的十家主要企业（创办年份）	City 城市	Province 省	Telephone/ fax 电话/传真	Number of employees 职工人数	Ownership 产业所有权	Revenue ('000 RMB) 销售收入 (千元)	Profit('000 RMB) (rank) 利润(千元) (排名)	Total assets ('000 RMB) 总资产 (千元)	Major products 主要产品
Changzhou Qinyi Dyeing & Weaving Co., Ltd.	Changzhou	Jiangsu	(0519)8781374		Joint Stock				Coloured Woven Cloth
常州勤益染织有限公司(2001)	常州市	江苏省	(0519)8781374	829	股份制	165,050	8,550(3)	135,740	色织布
Weixin (Linhe) Cashmere Industrial Co., Ltd.	Bayannaoer	Inner Mongolia	(0478)8235123		Overseas Chinese-funded				Non-Wool Velvet
维信（临河）羊绒实业有限公司(1993)	巴彦淖尔	内蒙古	(0478)8216938	292	港澳台资	154,835	9,002(2)	554,125	无毛绒
Inner Mongolia Linhe Daxing Cashmere Products Co.,Ltd.	Bayannaoer	Inner Mongolia	(0478)8610985		Private Owned				Non-Wool Velvet
内蒙古临河市大兴羊绒制品有限公司(1996)	巴彦淖尔	内蒙古	(0478)8236523	403	私营企业	143,662	256(60)	99,445	无毛绒
Shaoxing Wool Manufacturing General Mill	Shaoxing	Zhejiang	(0575)8010138		Collective-owned				Textiles Printing & Dyeing纺织品
绍兴市毛纺织总厂(1979)	绍兴市	浙江省	(0575)8010839	441	集体企业	122,382	6,021(4)	127,538	印花染色
Shanghai Xinyuan Red Dyeing Yarn Co., Ltd.	Shanghai	Shanghai	(021)59830202		Foreign Funded				Yarn Dyeing
上海欣原红染纱有限公司(1994)	上海市	上海市	(021)59838394	174	外商投资	99,278	2,433(10)	62,211	纱线染色
Dongguan Yifang Bleaching & Dyeing Co., Ltd.	Dongguan	Guangdong	(0769)8814795		Overseas Chinese-funded				Knitting Wool Bleaching & Dyeing
东莞溢纺漂染有限公司(1993)	东莞市	广东省	(0769)8811307	300	港澳台资	92,448	978(30)	26,920	毛线漂染
Wuxi Tongzhou Printing & Dyeing Co., Ltd.	Wuxi	Jiangsu	(0510)3399141		Overseas Chinese-funded				Printing Cloth
无锡通洲印染有限公司(1992)	无锡市	江苏省	(0510)3396797	418	港澳台资	92,130	3,980(7)	23,310	印花布
Haicheng Yixin Printing & Dyeing Factory	Anshan	Liaoning	(0412)3192619		Collective-owned				Wool Acrylic Fibre Printing & Dyeing毛
海城市艺新印染厂(1992)	鞍山市	辽宁省	(0412)3191469	86	集体企业	78,000	4,760(5)	24,920	腈纱印染
Dongguan Fudong Bleaching & Dyeing Works Co., Ltd.	Dongguan	Guangdong	(0769)8852717		Overseas Chinese-funded				Bleaching & Dyeing Blended Thread漂
东莞富东漂染厂有限公司(1992)	东莞市	广东省	(0769)8852914	534	港澳台资	71,199	-	68,831	染混纺线
Linhe Shunxiang Fission Plush Co., Ltd.	Bayannaoer	Inner Mongolia	(0478)8236626		Private Owned				Non-Wool Velvet
临河市顺祥分梳绒毛有限公司(1993)	巴彦淖尔	内蒙古	(0478)8236626	260	私营企业	60,979	236(61)	72,744	无毛绒

Top 10 Cities by Revenue 销售收入排名前10位城市	Province 省	Market share 市场份额 (%)	Number of firms 企业个数
Shanghai 上海市	Shanghai 上海市	18.11	21
Bayannaoer 巴彦淖尔盟	Inner Mongolia 内蒙古	16.08	8
Wuxi 无锡市	Jiangsu 江苏省	10.04	10
Changzhou 常州市	Jiangsu 江苏省	7.98	3
Dongguan 东莞市	Guangdong 广东省	7.01	5
Guangzhou 广州市	Guangdong 广东省	6.05	6
Suzhou 苏州市	Jiangsu 江苏省	5.80	10
Shaoxing 绍兴市	Zhejiang 浙江省	4.23	1
Beijing 北京市	Beijing 北京市	3.70	2
Zhaoqing 肇庆市	Guangdong 广东省	2.81	2

10 Major Wholesalers 十家主要批发商	City 城市	Province 省	Telephone/Fax 电话/传真
Shanghai Shenda Co.,Ltd.	Shanghai	Shanghai	(021)62319898
上海申达股份有限公司	上海市	上海市	(021)62317250
Orient International Holding Silk Group Corportion	Shanghai	Shanghai	(021)64662288
东方国际集团丝绸进出口有限公司	上海市	上海市	(021)64677788
Nanjing Textiles Import & Export Co.,Ltd.	Nanjing	Jiangsu	(025)3306789
南京纺织品进出口股份有限公司	南京市	江苏省	(025)3300518
Zhejiang Textiles Import & Export Group Co.,Ltd.	Hangzhou	Zhejiang	(0571)87075888
浙江省纺织品进出口集团有限公司	杭州市	浙江省	(0571)87079234
Zhejiang Orient Holdings Co.,Ltd.	Hangzhou	Zhejiang	(0571)87215678
浙江东方集团股份有限公司	杭州市	浙江省	(0571)87215000
Zhejiang Silk Holding Co.,ltd.	Hangzhou	Zhejiang	(0571)85195588
浙江省丝绸集团有限公司	杭州市	浙江省	(0571)85192540
Guangdong Silk (Group) Corporation	Guangzhou	Guangdong	(020)83337448
广东省丝绸（集团）公司	广州市	广东省	(020)83332995
Shanghai Costume Group Co.,Ltd.	Shanghai	Shanghai	(021)62748598
上海服装（集团）有限公司	上海市	上海市	(021)62414773
Orient International Holding Shanghai Textiles Import & Export Co.Ltd.	Shanghai	Shanghai	(021)63218855
东方国际集团上海市针织品进出口有限公司	上海市	上海市	(021)63299560
Jiangsu Textiles Import & Export Group Co.,Ltd.	Nanjing	Jiangsu	(025)6895000
江苏省纺织品进出口集团股份有限公司	南京市	江苏省	(025)4400800

1745: Industrial Woolen and Felt Products 工业用呢、工业用毡制造业

The industry accounts for 0.008% of the total revenue of China's industrial sector in 2002. The rate of return on assets is 0.94%. 73.47% of all firms in the industry made a profit while 26.53% had negative returns.The top province in terms of the industry's revenue is Shanghai, accounting for 31.34% of the total revenue.
2002年本行业收入占全行业的0.008%，资产利润率为0.94%。73.47%的企业赢利，26.53%的企业亏损。收入最高的省为上海市，占本行业的31.34%。

	Total number of firms 企业总数	Total number of employees 职工总数	Total revenue (Mil.RMB) 总销售收入（百万元）	Total profit (Mil.RMB) 总利润（百万元）	Return on assets 资产利润率（%）	Return on equity 权益利润率（%）	Labour productivity ('000 RMB/worker) 劳动生产率（千元/人）	Debts/assets 资产负债率（%）	Total assets (Mil.RMB) 总资产（百万元）
Industry Overall 行业总体	49	10,515	860	16	0.94	3.91	24.56	76.06	1,687

	Number of firms 企业个数	Average number of employees 平均职工人数	Average revenue ('000 RMB) 平均销售收入（千元）	Average profit ('000 RMB) 平均利润（千元）	Return on assets 资产利润率（%）	Return on equity 权益利润率（%）	Labour productivity ('000 RMB/worker) 劳动生产率（千元/人）	Debts/assets 资产负债率（%）	Average total assets ('000 RMB) 平均总资产（千元）
By ownership 产业所有权									
State-owned 国有	8	327	18,865	-208	-0.20	-1.53	19.07	86.80	102,703
Collective-owned 集体	10	108	12,873	545	7.57	21.92	25.46	65.47	7,199
Foreign & Overseas Chinese Funded 三资	2	241	42,565	-2,725	-2.19	-7.58	45.97	71.11	124,354
By regional distribution 地区分布									
Central-North 华北	12	248	15,003	706	2.01	26.49	19.19	92.42	35,140
Beijing 北京									
Tianjin 天津	6	258	17,181	310	0.51	10.42	16.93	95.14	61,270
Hebei 河北	5	277	15,274	1,501	15.53	41.21	22.14	62.32	9,663
Shanxi 山西									
Inner Mongolia 内蒙古	1	44	579	-898	-15.61		5.84	171.44	5,752
Northeast 东北	1	950	47,885	-250	-0.53	-2.57	4.81	79.39	47,241
Liaoning 辽宁									
Jilin 吉林									
Heilongjiang 黑龙江	1	950	47,885	-250	-0.53	-2.57	4.81	79.39	47,241
Central-East 华东	24	224	22,689	181	0.38	1.34	30.27	71.37	47,140
Shanghai 上海	11	236	24,493	-286	-0.41	-1.64	29.21	74.68	69,036
Jiangsu 江苏	8	230	29,949	1,041	3.00	7.30	43.20	58.91	34,719
Zhejiang 浙江									
Anhui 安徽	1	73	2,148	-21	-0.92	-2.68	10.89	65.66	2,283
Fujian 福建									
Jiangxi 江西									
Shandong 山东	4	217	8,342	-203	-0.88	-4.84	7.62	81.78	22,984
Central-South 中南	7	132	10,015	421	5.08	11.64	22.42	56.36	8,287
Henan 河南	4	130	7,012	514	5.44	11.86	14.75	54.11	9,442
Hubei 湖北	1	300	28,400	850	19.08	85.51	30.37	77.68	4,454
Hunan 湖南									
Guangdong 广东	2	53	6,827	21	0.27	0.60	37.66	55.71	7,895
Guangxi 广西									
Hainan 海南									
Southwest 西南	2	84	4,715	7	0.05	0.12	33.43	53.84	12,117
Chongqing 重庆	1	21	936	-50	-4.37	-5.20	13.62	15.84	1,143
Sichuan 四川	1	146	8,493	63	0.27	0.62	36.27	55.72	23,090
Guizhou 贵州									
Yunnan 云南									
Tibet 西藏									
Northwest 西北	3	37	2,582	91	5.84	15.48	65.46	62.28	1,553
Shaanxi 陕西									
Gansu 甘肃	3	37	2,582	91	5.84	15.48	65.46	62.28	1,553
Qinghai 青海									
Ningxia 宁夏									
Xinjiang 新疆									

1745: Industrial Woolen and Felt Products 工业用呢、工业用毡制造业

Year 年份	Number of firms 企业个数	Rate of change 变化率 (%)	Number of employees 职工人数 (人)	Rate of change 变化率 (%)	Total revenue (Mil. RMB) 总销售收入 (百万元)	Rate of change 变化率 (%)	Total profit (Mil RMB) 总利润 (百万元)	Rate of change 变化率 (%)
2000	39		5,777		446		10	
2001	44	12.82	7,030	21.69	572	28.25	28	180.00
2002	49	11.36	10,515	49.57	860	50.35	16	-42.86

Major Products 主要产品	Output 产量	Unit 单位

10 Main Firms with Maximal Revenue (year founded) 收入最大的十家主要企业（创办年份）	City 城市	Province 省	Telephone/fax 电话/传真	Number of employees 职工人数	Ownership 产业所有权	Revenue ('000 RMB) 销售收入 (千元)	Profit('000 RMB) (rank) 利润(千元) (排名)	Total assets ('000 RMB) 总资产 (千元)	Major products 主要产品
Shanghai Great Success Artificial Fur Co., Ltd.	Shanghai	Shanghai	(021)62960958		Overseas Chinese-funded				Plush
上海大顺人造毛皮有限公司(1989)	上海市	上海市	(021)62960333	445	港澳台资	71,809	-	222,813	长毛绒
Jiangsu Jinni Group	Nantong	Jiangsu	(0513)2662300		Joint Stock				Papermaking Blanket
江苏金呢集团(1996)	南通市	江苏省	(0513)2663668	439	股份制	54,560	2,380(5)	81,820	造纸毛毯
Heilongjiang Sino-austrian Joint Venture Carpet Industry	Mudanjiang	Heilongjiang	(0453)6384358		Joint Stock				Blanket
Co., Ltd. 黑龙江中澳毯业股份有限公司(2002)	牡丹江市	黑龙江省	(0453)6383188	950	股份制	47,885	-	47,241	毛毯
Shanghai Industry Woollen Cloth Factory	Shanghai	Shanghai	(021)62396500		State-owned				Industrial Fabrics
上海工业用呢厂(1937)	上海市	上海市	(021)62398270	637	国有企业	38,928	2(33)	152,756	工业用呢
Shanghai Phoenix Blanket Factory	Shanghai	Shanghai	(021)62507663		State-owned				Blanket
上海凤凰厂业有限公司(1922)	上海市	上海市	(021)62509636	408	国有企业	33,418	-	169,130	毛毯
Shanghai Gaofeng Textiles Co., Ltd.	Shanghai	Shanghai	(021)57238877		Private Partnership				Blanket
上海高峰纺织品有限公司(1999)	上海市	上海市	(021)57238877	210	私营合伙	30,111	1,140(10)	19,877	毛毯
Yingcheng Yihe Industrial Development Co., Ltd.	Xiaogan	Hubei	(0712)3239605		Private Owned				Industrial Fabrics
应城市怡禾实业发展有限公司(2001)	孝感市	湖北省	(0712)3230712	300	私营企业	28,400	850(13)	4,454	工业用呢
Baoding Xuri Blanket Textile Co., Ltd.	Baoding	Hebei	(0312)5275108		Joint Stock				Blanket
保定旭日毛毯纺织有限公司(1999)	保定市	河北省	(0312)5275793	1,100	股份制	23,000	242(20)	2,250	毛毯
Tangshan Longhai Industrial Woollen Cloth Co.,Ltd.	Tangshan	Hebei	(0315)8711669		Joint Stock				Industrial Fabrics
唐山市龙海工业用呢有限公司(2001)	唐山市	河北省	(0315)8711669	110	股份制	21,326	3,585(1)	17,658	工业用呢
Zhenjiang Lida Fiber Industry Co., Ltd.	Zhenjiang	Jiangsu	(0511)8827465		Limited-Liability				Woollen Felt
镇江立达纤维工业有限责任公司(1996)	镇江市	江苏省	(0511)8823392	113	有限公司	19,414	123(23)	25,048	毛毡

Top 10 Cities by Revenue 销售收入排名前10位城市	Province 省	Market share 市场份额 (%)	Number of firms 企业个数
Shanghai 上海市	Shanghai 上海市	31.34	11
Tianjin 天津市	Tianjin 天津市	11.99	6
Nantong 南通市	Jiangsu 江苏省	6.98	2
Xuzhou 徐州市	Jiangsu 江苏省	6.28	1
Mudanjiang 牡丹江市	Heilongjiang 黑龙江省	5.57	1
Yancheng 盐城市	Jiangsu 江苏省	5.39	1
Baoding 保定市	Hebei 河北省	3.60	2
Wuxi 无锡市	Jiangsu 江苏省	3.30	1
Xiaogan 孝感市	Hubei 湖北省	3.30	1
Weifang 潍坊市	Shandong 山东省	2.60	3

10 Major Wholesalers 十家主要批发商	City 城市	Province 省	Telephone/Fax 电话/传真
Shanghai Shenda Co.,Ltd.	Shanghai	Shanghai	(021)62319898
上海申达股份有限公司	上海市	上海市	(021)62317250
Orient International Holding Silk Group Corportion	Shanghai	Shanghai	(021)64662288
东方国际集团丝绸进出口有限公司	上海市	上海市	(021)64677788
Nanjing Textiles Import & Export Co.,Ltd.	Nanjing	Jiangsu	(025)3306789
南京纺织品进出口股份有限公司	南京市	江苏省	(025)3300518
Zhejiang Textiles Import & Export Group Co.,Ltd.	Hangzhou	Zhejiang	(0571)87075888
浙江省纺织品进出口集团有限公司	杭州市	浙江省	(0571)87079234
Zhejiang Orient Holdings Co.,Ltd.	Hangzhou	Zhejiang	(0571)87215678
浙江东方集团股份有限公司	杭州市	浙江省	(0571)87215000
Zhejiang Silk Holding Co.,ltd.	Hangzhou	Zhejiang	(0571)85195588
浙江省丝绸集团有限公司	杭州市	浙江省	(0571)85192540
Guangdong Silk (Group) Corporation	Guangzhou	Guangdong	(020)83337448
广东省丝绸（集团）公司	广州市	广东省	(020)83332995
Shanghai Costume Group Co.,Ltd.	Shanghai	Shanghai	(021)62748598
上海服装（集团）有限公司	上海市	上海市	(021)62414773
Orient International Holding Shanghai Textiles Import & Export Co.Ltd.	Shanghai	Shanghai	(021)63218833
东方国际集团上海市针织品进出口有限公司	上海市	上海市	(021)63299560
Jiangsu Textiles Import & Export Group Co.,Ltd.	Nanjing	Jiangsu	(025)6895000
江苏省纺织品进出口集团股份有限公司	南京市	江苏省	(025)4400800

1749: Other Wool Spinning and Weaving 其他毛纺织业

The industry accounts for 0.095% of the total revenue of China's industrial sector in 2002. The rate of return on assets is 3.57%. 79.72% of all firms in the industry made a profit while 20.28% had negative returns.The top province in terms of the industry's revenue is Inner mongolia, accounting for 45.47% of the total revenue.
2002年本行业收入占全行业的0.095%，资产利润率为3.57%。79.72%的企业赢利，20.28%的企业亏损。收入最高的省为内蒙古，占本行业的45.47%。

	Total number of firms 企业总数	Total number of employees 职工总数	Total revenue (Mil.RMB) 总销售收入（百万元）	Total profit (Mil.RMB) 总利润（百万元）	Return on assets 资产利润率（%）	Return on equity 权益利润率（%）	Labour productivity ('000 RMB/ worker) 劳动生产率（千元/人）	Debts/ assets 资产负债率（%）	Total assets (Mil.RMB) 总资产（百万元）
Industry Overall 行业总体	143	49,886	10,197	510	3.57	8.43	52.73	57.61	14,269

	Number of firms 企业个数	Average number of employees 平均职工人数	Average revenue ('000 RMB) 平均销售收入（千元）	Average profit ('000 RMB) 平均利润（千元）	Return on assets 资产利润率（%）	Return on equity 权益利润率（%）	Labour productivity ('000 RMB/ worker) 劳动生产率（千元/人）	Debts/ assets 资产负债率（%）	Average total assets ('000 RMB) 平均总资产（千元）
By ownership 产业所有权									
State-owned 国有	9	239	16,514	-1,114	-0.96	-3.22	18.33	70.28	116,346
Collective-owned 集体	14	72	16,066	387	3.20	17.48	52.27	81.71	12,114
Foreign & Overseas Chinese Funded 三资	49	539	135,840	8,620	4.41	8.76	65.16	49.71	195,612
By regional distribution 地区分布									
Central-North 华北	43	566	109,991	6,681	3.20	6.48	53.47	50.55	208,588
Beijing 北京	1	43	12,512	-372	-4.46	-20.84	49.28	78.61	8,345
Tianjin 天津	4	91	6,451	59	1.73	2.74	43.29	36.85	3,408
Hebei 河北	5	257	10,202	-444	-3.33	-7.70	16.17	56.80	13,358
Shanxi 山西	1	280	3,573	-1,359	-2.42	-7.69	1.67	68.53	56,122
Inner Mongolia 内蒙古	32	699	144,898	9,094	3.30	6.65	56.43	50.39	275,762
Northeast 东北	1								
Liaoning 辽宁	1								
Jilin 吉林									
Heilongjiang 黑龙江									
Central-East 华东	68	257	46,909	1,200	2.68	8.04	41.12	66.62	44,742
Shanghai 上海	7	279	64,815	-780	-1.25	-3.52	27.33	64.54	62,467
Jiangsu 江苏	32	235	33,784	678	2.67	11.03	36.97	75.74	25,353
Zhejiang 浙江	13	228	60,114	3,311	4.60	17.66	49.70	73.97	72,017
Anhui 安徽	1	50	10,650	117	1.81	2.29	103.86	21.12	6,469
Fujian 福建	4	160	23,197	-2,191	-6.88	-16.66	65.15	58.69	31,827
Jiangxi 江西									
Shandong 山东	11	393	70,011	2,817	4.28	8.55	44.40	49.95	65,809
Central-South 中南	18	352	102,948	6,748	6.41	24.45	66.14	73.79	105,302
Henan 河南	5	149	9,105	37	0.58	2.73	21.01	78.88	6,460
Hubei 湖北	2	481	30,349	-38	-0.06	-0.72	36.32	91.28	60,168
Hunan 湖南									
Guangdong 广东	11	421	158,803	11,032	6.96	25.31	79.60	72.49	158,436
Guangxi 广西									
Hainan 海南									
Southwest 西南	2	163	429	100	1.25	1.75	1.37	28.68	7,986
Chongqing 重庆									
Sichuan 四川									
Guizhou 贵州									
Yunnan 云南									
Tibet 西藏	2	163	429	100	1.25	1.75	1.37	28.68	7,986
Northwest 西北	11	131	38,519	1,752	5.57	21.38	133.37	73.95	31,463
Shaanxi 陕西									
Gansu 甘肃	3	114	311	-309	-1.72		6.89	148.67	18,009
Qinghai 青海									
Ningxia 宁夏	8	138	52,847	2,525	6.92	17.35	172.56	60.13	36,508
Xinjiang 新疆									

1749: Other Wool Spinning and Weaving 其他毛纺织业

Year 年份	Number of firms 企业个数	Rate of change 变化率 (%)	Number of employees 职工人数 (人)	Rate of change 变化率 (%)	Total revenue (Mil. RMB) 总销售收入 (百万元)	Rate of change 变化率 (%)	Total profit (Mil RMB) 总利润 (百万元)	Rate of change 变化率 (%)
2000	111		43,020		5,803		362	
2001	130	17.12	49,573	15.23	8,852	52.54	493	36.19
2002	143	10.00	49,886	0.63	10,197	15.19	510	3.45

Major Products 主要产品	Output 产量	Unit 单位

10 Main Firms with Maximal Revenue (year founded) 收入最大的十家主要企业（创办年份）	City 城市	Province 省	Telephone/fax 电话/传真	Number of employees 职工人数	Ownership 产业所有权	Revenue ('000 RMB) 销售收入 (千元)	Profit('000 RMB) (rank) 利润(千元) (排名)	Total assets ('000 RMB) 总资产 (千元)	Major products 主要产品
Inner Mongolia Erdos Cashmere Products Co., Ltd.	Eerduosi	Inner Mongolia	(0477)8525834		Foreign Funded				Cashmere Sweater
鄂尔多斯羊绒制品股份有限公司(1990)	鄂尔多斯市	内蒙古	(0477)8523812	3,861	外商投资	1,391,381	199,007(1)	3,938,856	羊绒衫
Dongguan Shatian Lihai Textile Printing & Dyeing Co.,Ltd.	Dongguan	Guangdong	(0769)8866583		Foreign Funded				Tiffany
东莞沙田丽海纺织印染有限公司(1996)	东莞市	广东省	(0769)8866584	2,231	外商投资	1,259,961	121,076(2)	772,688	丝绢
Inner Mongolia Kingdeer Cashmere Group Company	Baotou	Inner Mongolia	(0472)4171155		Overseas Chinese-funded				Cashmere Sweater
内蒙古鹿王羊绒集团公司(1995)	包头市	内蒙古	(0472)4172523	4,560	港澳台资	801,670	30,208(3)	1,137,581	羊绒衫
Inner Mongolia Erdos Cashmere Products Co.,Ltd.Raw Stuff Branch	Eerduosi	Inner Mongolia	(0477)8543667		Foreign Funded				Velvet Washing
内蒙古鄂尔多斯羊绒制品股份有限公司原料分公司(2002)	鄂尔多斯市	内蒙古	(0477)8543676	506	外商投资	707,066	1,602(37)	492,609	洗绒
Shandong Zibo Knitting Wool Works	Zibo	Shandong	(0533)5686605		Joint Stock				Acrylic Fibre Yarn
山东淄博绒线厂(1987)	淄博市	山东省	(0533)5687349	1,514	股份制	315,920	22,752(5)	102,540	晴纶纱
Zibo Huayang Group Wool & Velvet Co., ltd.	Zibo	Shandong	(0533)5162400		Overseas Chinese-funded				Cashmere Cloth
淄博华洋集团毛绒有限公司(1992)	淄博市	山东省	(0533)5181203	1,316	港澳台资	176,322	2,080(32)	296,930	毛绒布料
Inner Mongolia Donghao Cashmere Products Co., Ltd.	Eerduosi	Inner Mongolia	(0477)8536800		Foreign Funded				Cashmere Scarf
内蒙古东昊羊绒制品有限公司(1995)	鄂尔多斯市	内蒙古	(0477)8527044	740	外商投资	140,255	24,647(4)	270,672	羊绒围巾
Shanghai Weide Textiles Co., Ltd.	Shanghai	Shanghai	(021)64931800		Overseas Chinese-funded				Grain Cloth
上海威德纺织品有限公司(1998)	上海市	上海市	(021)64346682	398	港澳台资	132,227	1,279(41)	86,571	摇粒布
Nanjing Ri Sheng Textile Group Co., Ltd	Nanjing	Jiangsu	(025)7212319		Limited-Liability				Acrylic Fibre Thread
南京日升纺织集团有限公司(1989)	南京市	江苏省	(025)7212292	1,590	有限公司	131,750	2,200(31)	138,040	晴纶线
Otog Qi Cashmere Factory	Eerduosi	Inner Mongolia	(0470)6221233		Private Owned				Non-Wool Velvet
鄂托克旗绒毛厂(1996)	鄂尔多斯市	内蒙古	(0470)6218972	180	私营企业	130,940	68(95)	32,280	无毛绒

Top 10 Cities by Revenue 销售收入排名前10位城市	Province 省	Market share 市场份额 (%)	Number of firms 企业个数
Eerduosi 鄂尔多斯市	Inner Mongolia 内蒙古	29.95	25
Baotou 包头市	Inner Mongolia 内蒙古	15.09	6
Dongguan 东莞市	Guangdong 广东省	12.36	1
Zibo 淄博市	Shandong 山东省	4.95	3
Hangzhou 杭州市	Zhejiang 浙江省	4.76	5
Suzhou 苏州市	Jiangsu 江苏省	4.46	13
Shanghai 上海市	Shanghai 上海市	4.45	7
Wuzhong 吴忠市	Ningxia 宁夏	4.15	8
Yunfu 云浮市	Guangdong 广东省	2.70	4
Shaoxing 绍兴市	Zhejiang 浙江省	2.24	3

10 Major Wholesalers 十家主要批发商	City 城市	Province 省	Telephone/Fax 电话/传真
Shanghai Shenda Co.,Ltd.	Shanghai	Shanghai	(021)62319898
上海申达股份有限公司	上海市	上海市	(021)62317250
Orient International Holding Silk Group Corportion	Shanghai	Shanghai	(021)64662288
东方国际集团丝绸进出口有限公司	上海市	上海市	(021)64677788
Nanjing Textiles Import & Export Co.,Ltd.	Nanjing	Jiangsu	(025)3306789
南京纺织品进出口股份有限公司	南京市	江苏省	(025)3300518
Zhejiang Textiles Import & Export Group Co.,Ltd.	Hangzhou	Zhejiang	(0571)87075888
浙江省纺织品进出口集团有限公司	杭州市	浙江省	(0571)87079234
Zhejiang Orient Holdings Co.,Ltd.	Hangzhou	Zhejiang	(0571)87215678
浙江东方集团股份有限公司	杭州市	浙江省	(0571)87215000
Zhejiang Silk Holding Co.,ltd.	Hangzhou	Zhejiang	(0571)85195588
浙江省丝绸集团有限公司	杭州市	浙江省	(0571)85192540
Guangdong Silk (Group) Corporation	Guangzhou	Guangdong	(020)83337448
广东省丝绸（集团）公司	广州市	广东省	(020)83332995
Shanghai Costume Group Co.,Ltd.	Shanghai	Shanghai	(021)62748598
上海服装（集团）有限公司	上海市	上海市	(021)62414773
Orient International Holding Shanghai Textiles Import & Export Co.Ltd.	Shanghai	Shanghai	(021)63218855
东方国际集团上海市针织品进出口有限公司	上海市	上海市	(021)63299560
Jiangsu Textiles Import & Export Group Co.,Ltd.	Nanjing	Jiangsu	(025)6895000
江苏省纺织品进出口集团股份有限公司	南京市	江苏省	(025)4400800

1761: Ramie Spinning and Weaving 苎麻纺织业

The industry accounts for 0.032% of the total revenue of China's industrial sector in 2002. The rate of return on assets is 1.10%. 83.95% of all firms in the industry made a profit while 16.05% had negative returns.The top province in terms of the industry's revenue is Hubei, accounting for 25.25% of the total revenue.
2002年本行业收入占全行业的0.032%，资产利润率为1.10%。83.95%的企业赢利，16.05%的企业亏损。收入最高的省为湖北省，占本行业的25.25%。

	Total number of firms 企业总数	Total number of employees 职工总数	Total revenue (Mil.RMB) 总销售收入（百万元）	Total profit (Mil.RMB) 总利润（百万元）	Return on assets 资产利润率（%）	Return on equity 权益利润率（%）	Labour productivity ('000 RMB/ worker) 劳动生产率（千元/人）	Debts/ assets 资产负债率（%）	Total assets (Mil.RMB) 总资产（百万元）
Industry Overall 行业总体	81	57,519	3,394	50	1.10	4.12	17.15	73.21	4,548

	Number of firms 企业个数	Average number of employees 平均职工人数	Average revenue ('000 RMB) 平均销售收入（千元）	Average profit ('000 RMB) 平均利润（千元）	Return on assets 资产利润率（%）	Return on equity 权益利润率（%）	Labour productivity ('000 RMB/ worker) 劳动生产率（千元/人）	Debts/ assets 资产负债率（%）	Average total assets ('000 RMB) 平均总资产（千元）
By ownership 产业所有权									
State-owned 国有	16	662	32,024	-897	-1.22	-9.03	11.76	86.53	73,730
Collective-owned 集体	14	268	18,234	266	1.53		16.38	113.21	17,378
Foreign & Overseas Chinese Funded 三资	8	879	39,845	1,044	1.80	4.46	14.24	59.59	57,961
By regional distribution 地区分布									
Central-North 华北									
Beijing 北京									
Tianjin 天津									
Hebei 河北									
Shanxi 山西									
Inner Mongolia 内蒙古									
Northeast 东北									
Liaoning 辽宁									
Jilin 吉林									
Heilongjiang 黑龙江									
Central-East 华东	36	497	33,834	1,005	2.30	5.92	21.38	61.13	43,629
Shanghai 上海									
Jiangsu 江苏	8	212	26,128	897	3.32	7.84	44.67	57.67	27,027
Zhejiang 浙江	1	51	5,215	157	5.58	22.05	31.98	74.70	2,814
Anhui 安徽	8	1,050	90,257	3,723	4.27	13.93	24.39	69.34	87,195
Fujian 福建	1	527	12,027	-830	-1.33		16.07	132.09	62,230
Jiangxi 江西	16	433	16,182	-15	-0.04	-0.07	12.70	44.16	36,073
Shandong 山东	2	157	5,392	56	0.76	5.22	13.61	85.50	7,335
Central-South 中南	30	918	56,243	391	0.54	3.29	16.12	83.66	72,827
Henan 河南									
Hubei 湖北	13	807	65,940	1,914	4.26	23.32	23.97	81.73	44,937
Hunan 湖南	14	1,048	50,556	-707	-0.74	-4.42	11.13	83.21	95,343
Guangdong 广东	2	1,082	47,651	-140	-0.16	-0.57	10.54	72.67	89,367
Guangxi 广西	1	222	26,986	-2,968	-3.41		30.00	125.96	87,089
Hainan 海南									
Southwest 西南	15	804	32,601	154	0.29	0.92	13.21	68.33	52,840
Chongqing 重庆	4	1,356	59,031	599	0.50	1.16	16.19	57.05	120,186
Sichuan 四川	10	564	24,942	244	0.79	4.92	12.30	83.92	30,892
Guizhou 贵州	1	1,000	3,477	-2,525	-86.12		2.13	274.39	2,932
Yunnan 云南									
Tibet 西藏									
Northwest 西北									
Shaanxi 陕西									
Gansu 甘肃									
Qinghai 青海									
Ningxia 宁夏									
Xinjiang 新疆									

Year 年份	Number of firms 企业个数	Rate of change 变化率(%)	Number of employees 职工人数(人)	Rate of change 变化率(%)	Total revenue (Mil. RMB) 总销售收入(百万元)	Rate of change 变化率(%)	Total profit (Mil RMB) 总利润(百万元)	Rate of change 变化率(%)
2000	78		61,270		3,262		70	
2001	68	-12.82	54,728	-10.68	2,475	-24.13	55	-21.43
2002	81	19.12	57,519	5.10	3,394	37.13	50	-9.09

Major Products 主要产品	Output 产量	Unit 单位
Ramie Cloth and Linen Cloth 苎麻布及亚麻布	10,424	10,000 Meters 万米

10 Main Firms with Maximal Revenue (year founded) 收入最大的十家主要企业（创办年份）	City 城市	Province 省	Telephone/fax 电话/传真	Number of employees 职工人数	Ownership 产业所有权	Revenue ('000 RMB) 销售收入(千元)	Profit('000 RMB) (rank) 利润(千元)(排名)	Total assets ('000 RMB) 总资产(千元)	Major products 主要产品
TongLing Huayuan Hemp Co., Ltd. 铜陵市华源麻业有限公司(1997)	Tongling 铜陵市	Anhui 安徽省	(0562)5818401 (0562)2824340	6,560	Limited-Liability 有限公司	536,687	24,521(1)	555,615	Yarn 纱
Hunan Dongting Ramie Textile Printing & Dyeing Factory 湖南洞庭苎麻纺织印染厂(1986)	Yueyang 岳阳市	Hunan 湖南省	(0730)8782411 (0730)8781241	4,750	State-owned 国有企业	283,077	2,032(11)	376,553	Ramee Textile 苎麻纺织品
Hubei Yinquan Textile Stock Co.,Ltd. 湖北银泉纺织股份有限公司(1986)	Xianning 咸宁市	Hubei 湖北省	(0715)8313208 (0715)8322726	2,804	Joint Stock 股份制	262,348	4,152(5)	166,289	Yarn 纱
Isunte Textile Printing & Dyeing Co., Ltd. 益鑫泰纺织印染股份有限公司(1982)	Yiyang 益阳市	Hunan 湖南省	(0737)4428818 (0737)4431114	4,164	State Enterprises 国有独资	219,993	2,817(9)	488,081	Ramee Textile 苎麻纺织品
Chongqing Fuling Jindi Industry Group Co., Ltd. 重庆市涪陵金帝工业集团有限公司(1982)	Chongqing 重庆市	Chongqing 重庆市	(023)72380008 (023)72380028	4,950	Limited-Liability 有限公司	167,418	1,879(12)	396,263	Ramie Yarn 苎麻纱线
Hubei Tianhua Hemp Co., Ltd. 湖北天化麻业股份有限公司(2002)	Xianning 咸宁市	Hubei 湖北省	(0715)8256875 (0715)8251525	1,901	Joint Stock 股份制	136,587	4,377(4)	103,563	Line & Cotton Blended Thread 麻棉混纺纱线
Xinnyi Shuanglin Enda Textile Printing & Dyeing Co.,Ltd. 新宜市双林恩达纺织印染有限公司(1997)	Xinyu 新余市	Jiangxi 江西省	(0790)5771023 (0790)5773309	2,524	Foreign Funded 外商投资	75,600	2,970(8)	59,500	Ramie Cloth 夏布
Dazhu Jinqiao Hemp Co., Ltd. 大竹县金桥麻业有限责任公司(1998)	Dazhou 达州市	Sichuan 四川省	(0818)6236182 (0818)6236180	1,100	Limited-Liability 有限公司	64,006	1,800(13)	23,580	Pure Gunny 纯麻布
Haimen Ramie Weaving Factory 海门市苎麻纺织厂(1985)	Nantong 南通市	Jiangsu 江苏省	(0513)2608088 (0513)2608088	386	Private Enterprises 私营独资	63,310	990(16)	30,500	Refined Dry Flax 精干麻
Zhuzhou Xuesong Hemp Co., Ltd. 株洲雪松麻业有限责任公司(1958)	Zhuzhou 株洲市	Hunan 湖南省	(0733)2205355 (0733)2205249	2,351	State-owned 国有企业	58,385	-	246,517	Ramie Yarn 苎麻纱线

Top 10 Cities by Revenue 销售收入排名前10位城市	Province 省	Market share 市场份额(%)	Number of firms 企业个数
Xianning 咸宁市	Hubei 湖北省	20.27	4
Tongling 铜陵市	Anhui 安徽省	17.74	3
Yiyang 益阳市	Hunan 湖南省	10.11	10
Yueyang 岳阳市	Hunan 湖南省	8.34	1
Chongqing 重庆市	Chongqing 重庆市	6.96	4
Dazhou 达州市	Sichuan 四川省	5.88	7
Xinyu 新余市	Jiangxi 江西省	2.60	3
Shaoguan 韶关市	Guangdong 广东省	2.53	1
Nantong 南通市	Jiangsu 江苏省	2.30	2
Yichun 宜春市	Jiangxi 江西省	2.00	3

10 Major Wholesalers 十家主要批发商	City 城市	Province 省	Telephone/Fax 电话/传真
Shanghai Shenda Co.,Ltd. 上海申达股份有限公司	Shanghai 上海市	Shanghai 上海市	(021)62319898 (021)62317250
Orient International Holding Silk Group Corportion 东方国际集团丝绸进出口有限公司	Shanghai 上海市	Shanghai 上海市	(021)64662288 (021)64677788
Nanjing Textiles Import & Export Co.,Ltd. 南京纺织品进出口股份有限公司	Nanjing 南京市	Jiangsu 江苏省	(025)3306789 (025)3300518
Zhejiang Textiles Import & Export Group Co.,Ltd. 浙江省纺织品进出口集团有限公司	Hangzhou 杭州市	Zhejiang 浙江省	(0571)87075888 (0571)87079234
Zhejiang Orient Holdings Co.,Ltd. 浙江东方集团股份有限公司	Hangzhou 杭州市	Zhejiang 浙江省	(0571)87215678 (0571)87215000
Zhejiang Silk Holding Co.,ltd. 浙江省丝绸集团有限公司	Hangzhou 杭州市	Zhejiang 浙江省	(0571)85195588 (0571)85192540
Guangdong Silk (Group) Corporation 广东省丝绸（集团）公司	Guangzhou 广州市	Guangdong 广东省	(020)83337448 (020)83332995
Shanghai Costume Group Co.,Ltd. 上海服装（集团）有限公司	Shanghai 上海市	Shanghai 上海市	(021)62748598 (021)62414773
Orient International Holding Shanghai Textiles Import & Export Co.Ltd. 东方国际集团上海市针织品进出口有限公司	Shanghai 上海市	Shanghai 上海市	(021)63218855 (021)63299560
Jiangsu Textiles Import & Export Group Co.,Ltd. 江苏省纺织品进出口集团股份有限公司	Nanjing 南京市	Jiangsu 江苏省	(025)6895000 (025)4400800

1762: Flax Spinning and Weaving 亚麻纺织业

The industry accounts for 0.026% of the total revenue of China's industrial sector in 2002. The rate of return on assets is -0.37%. 69.23% of all firms in the industry made a profit while 30.77% had negative returns.The top province in terms of the industry's revenue is Heilong Jiang, accounting for 47.55% of the total revenue.
2002年本行业收入占全行业的0.026%，资产利润率为 -0.37%。69.23%的企业赢利，30.77%的企业亏损。收入最高的省为黑龙江省，占本行业的47.55%。

	Total number of firms 企业总数	Total number of employees 职工总数	Total revenue (Mil.RMB) 总销售收入 (百万元)	Total profit (Mil.RMB) 总利润 (百万元)	Return on assets 资产利润率 (%)	Return on equity 权益利润率 (%)	Labour productivity ('000 RMB/ worker) 劳动生产率 (千元/人)	Debts/ assets 资产负债率 (%)	Total assets (Mil.RMB) 总资产 (百万元)
Industry Overall 行业总体	65	40,116	2,740	-21	-0.37	-1.59	20.15	76.82	5,607

	Number of firms 企业个数	Average number of employees 平均职工人数	Average revenue ('000 RMB) 平均销售收入 (千元)	Average profit ('000 RMB) 平均利润 (千元)	Return on assets 资产利润率 (%)	Return on equity 权益利润率 (%)	Labour productivity ('000 RMB/ worker) 劳动生产率 (千元/人)	Debts/ assets 资产负债率 (%)	Average total assets ('000 RMB) 平均总资产 (千元)
By ownership 产业所有权									
State-owned 国有	10	664	26,180	-535	-0.65	-47.24	15.74	98.63	82,972
Collective-owned 集体	3	152	4,886	-34	-0.26		11.28	144.00	12,836
Foreign & Overseas Chinese Funded 三资	19	611	46,071	30	0.04	0.11	18.03	64.09	75,849
By regional distribution 地区分布									
Central-North 华北	3	805	79,163	-443	-0.30	-0.71	33.57	57.34	145,930
Beijing 北京									
Tianjin 天津	1	290	120,820	2,570	5.00	11.63	79.90	57.00	51,400
Hebei 河北									
Shanxi 山西	1	674	60,215	-1,423	-0.99	-1.28	30.95	23.01	144,342
Inner Mongolia 内蒙古	1	1,452	56,455	-2,477	-1.02	-4.63	25.54	77.88	242,049
Northeast 东北	37	816	46,394	-1,468	-1.38	-8.93	16.14	84.50	106,024
Liaoning 辽宁	4	1,210	49,601	734	1.41	4.15	4.56	66.13	52,203
Jilin 吉林	5	630	43,095	893	1.13	3.41	23.11	66.95	79,183
Heilongjiang 黑龙江	28	793	46,525	-2,204	-1.86	-15.18	17.68	87.74	118,506
Central-East 华东	15	290	47,166	3,725	5.37	10.54	46.88	49.09	69,398
Shanghai 上海									
Jiangsu 江苏	7	319	53,676	927	1.81	9.17	45.28	80.26	51,175
Zhejiang 浙江	4	175	29,246	2,203	6.43	11.65	49.39	44.77	34,247
Anhui 安徽	1	193	7,260	350	3.82	7.84	14.22	51.34	9,174
Fujian 福建	1	529	6,887	689	9.01	13.57	6.16	33.59	7,646
Jiangxi 江西									
Shandong 山东	2	353	100,316	19,769	7.48	10.57	88.90	29.28	264,467
Central-South 中南	6	201	7,699	81	0.85	6.03	23.82	85.86	9,507
Henan 河南	2	24	5,082	277	12.23	22.43	154.02	45.47	2,265
Hubei 湖北	1	150	2,330	3	0.11	100.00	2.18	99.89	2,766
Hunan 湖南	1	155	9,557	-102	-1.30	-5.30	18.57	75.42	7,833
Guangdong 广东	2	425	12,072	16	0.07	0.85	21.24	91.25	20,958
Guangxi 广西									
Hainan 海南									
Southwest 西南	1	287	14,136	-1,420	-3.77	-3.92	9.12	4.01	37,694
Chongqing 重庆									
Sichuan 四川	1	287	14,136	-1,420	-3.77	-3.92	9.12	4.01	37,694
Guizhou 贵州									
Yunnan 云南									
Tibet 西藏									
Northwest 西北	3	551	5,974	-6,634	-17.96		2.47	162.64	36,931
Shaanxi 陕西									
Gansu 甘肃	1	1					875.00	2.16	185
Qinghai 青海									
Ningxia 宁夏	1	999	2,367	-2,327	-4.62		0.16	247.16	50,388
Xinjiang 新疆	1	653	15,556	-17,574	-29.18	-384.64	4.66	92.41	60,221

1762: Flax Spinning and Weaving 亚麻纺织业

Year 年份	Number of firms 企业个数	Rate of change 变化率(%)	Number of employees 职工人数(人)	Rate of change 变化率(%)	Total revenue (Mil. RMB) 总销售收入(百万元)	Rate of change 变化率(%)	Total profit (Mil RMB) 总利润(百万元)	Rate of change 变化率(%)
2000	48		39,311		2,481		88	
2001	54	12.50	36,660	-6.74	2,110	-14.95	-22	-
2002	65	20.37	40,116	9.43	2,740	29.86	-21	4.55

Major Products 主要产品	Output 产量	Unit 单位
Ramie Cloth and Linen Cloth 苎麻布及亚麻布	10,424	10,000 Meters 万米

10 Main Firms with Maximal Revenue (year founded) 收入最大的十家主要企业（创办年份）	City 城市	Province 省	Telephone/fax 电话/传真	Number of employees 职工人数	Ownership 产业所有权	Revenue ('000 RMB) 销售收入(千元)	Profit('000 RMB) (rank) 利润(千元)(排名)	Total assets ('000 RMB) 总资产(千元)	Major products 主要产品
Heilongjiang Yuanbao Textile Holding Co., ltd.	Harbin	Heilongjiang	(0451)53322719		Joint Stock				Flax & Cotton Blended Yarn亚麻
黑龙江圆宝纺织股份有限公司(1990)	哈尔滨市	黑龙江省	(0451)53324307	2,800	股份制	190,729	5,088(4)	220,154	棉混纺纱
Yantai Xinchao Industrial Co.,Ltd. Foundry Branch Company	Yantai	Shandong	(0535)4259857		Joint Stock				Wool Yarn
烟台新潮实业股份有限公司铸造分公司(1989)	烟台市	山东省	(0535)4259856	475	股份制	189,751	39,078(1)	513,033	毛纱
Qiqihar Linen Textile Mill	Qiqihar	Heilongjiang	(0452)2347211		State-owned				Flax Yarn
齐齐哈尔亚麻纺织厂(1989)	齐齐哈尔市	黑龙江省	(0452)2347047	2,044	国有企业	141,290	913(18)	347,487	亚麻纱
Jiamusi Jiapeng Flax Co., Ltd.	Jiamusi	Heilongjiang	(0454)8555241		Limited-Liability				Flax Yarn
佳木斯佳鹏亚麻有限责任公司(2000)	佳木斯市	黑龙江省	(0454)8355839	2,497	有限公司	135,485	500(22)	227,360	亚麻纱
Zhaorong Flax Textile Co., Ltd.	Daqing	Heilongjiang	(0459)8541510		Overseas Chinese-funded				Flax Yarn
肇融亚麻纺织有限公司(1990)	大庆市	黑龙江省	(0459)8522266	1,400	港澳台资	132,686	4,570(5)	152,682	亚麻纱
Kaiyuan Jixing Linen Textile Co., Ltd.	Tieling	Liaoning	(0410)3714479		Overseas Chinese-funded				Flax Yarn
开原吉星亚麻纺织有限公司(1993)	铁岭市	辽宁省		4,267	港澳台资	122,968	-	121,538	亚麻纱
Da Fan Textile Industry (Tianjin)Co., Ltd.	Tianjin	Tianjin	(022)28580147		Foreign Funded				Knitting Wool
天津市大风纺织有限公司(1995)	天津市	天津市	(022)28589337	290	外商投资	120,820	2,570(8)	51,400	绒线
Keshan Linen Textile Co.Ltd.	Qiqihar	Heilongjiang	(0452)4538384		Private Owned				Flax Yarn
克山金鼎亚麻纺织有限责任公司(1998)	齐齐哈尔市	黑龙江省	(0452)4525072	1,897	私营企业	110,000	8,564(2)	166,856	亚麻纱
Yanbian Jinlong Linen Textile Co., Ltd.	Yanbian	Jilin	(0433)3222696		Joint Stock				
延边金龙亚麻纺织股份有限公司(1996)	延边州	吉林省	(0433)3222837	1,786	股份制	104,390	3,160(7)	157,740	
Harbin Jijia Textile Co., Ltd.	Harbin	Heilongjiang	(0451)2333991		Overseas Chinese-funded				
哈尔滨继佳纺织有限公司(1993)	哈尔滨市	黑龙江省	(0451)2322245	250	港澳台资	76,934	1,007(14)	89,328	

Top 10 Cities by Revenue 销售收入排名前10位城市	Province 省	Market share 市场份额 (%)	Number of firms 企业个数
Harbin 哈尔滨市	Heilongjiang 黑龙江省	21.51	11
Qiqihar 齐齐哈尔市	Heilongjiang 黑龙江省	9.17	2
Yantai 烟台市	Shandong 山东省	7.32	2
Suihua 绥化市	Heilongjiang 黑龙江省	6.58	11
Wuxi 无锡市	Jiangsu 江苏省	5.59	1
Suzhou 苏州市	Jiangsu 江苏省	5.13	2
Daqing 大庆市	Heilongjiang 黑龙江省	5.05	2
Jiamusi 佳木斯市	Heilongjiang 黑龙江省	4.95	1
Tieling 铁岭市	Liaoning 辽宁省	4.49	1
Tianjin 天津市	Tianjin 天津市	4.41	1

10 Major Wholesalers 十家主要批发商	City 城市	Province 省	Telephone/Fax 电话/传真
Shanghai Shenda Co.,Ltd.	Shanghai	Shanghai	(021)62319898
上海申达股份有限公司	上海市	上海市	(021)62317250
Orient International Holding Silk Group Corportion	Shanghai	Shanghai	(021)64662288
东方国际集团丝绸进出口有限公司	上海市	上海市	(021)64677788
Nanjing Textiles Import & Export Co.,Ltd.	Nanjing	Jiangsu	(025)3306789
南京纺织品进出口股份有限公司	南京市	江苏省	(025)3300518
Zhejiang Textiles Import & Export Group Co.,Ltd.	Hangzhou	Zhejiang	(0571)87075888
浙江省纺织品进出口集团有限公司	杭州市	浙江省	(0571)87079234
Zhejiang Orient Holdings Co.,Ltd.	Hangzhou	Zhejiang	(0571)87215678
浙江东方集团股份有限公司	杭州市	浙江省	(0571)87215000
Zhejiang Silk Holding Co.,ltd.	Hangzhou	Zhejiang	(0571)85195588
浙江省丝绸集团有限公司	杭州市	浙江省	(0571)85192540
Guangdong Silk (Group) Corporation	Guangzhou	Guangdong	(020)83337448
广东省丝绸（集团）公司	广州市	广东省	(020)83332995
Shanghai Costume Group Co.,Ltd.	Shanghai	Shanghai	(021)62748598
上海服装（集团）有限公司	上海市	上海市	(021)62414773
Orient International Holding Shanghai Textiles Import & Export Co.Ltd.	Shanghai	Shanghai	(021)63218855
东方国际集团上海市针织品进出口有限公司	上海市	上海市	(021)63299560
Jiangsu Textiles Import & Export Group Co.,Ltd.	Nanjing	Jiangsu	(025)6895000
江苏省纺织品进出口集团股份有限公司	南京市	江苏省	(025)4400800

1763: Jute Spinning and Weaving 黄、洋、青麻纺织业

The industry accounts for 0.010% of the total revenue of China's industrial sector in 2002. The rate of return on assets is 0.15%. 75.44% of all firms in the industry made a profit while 24.56% had negative returns.The top province in terms of the industry's revenue is Jiangsu, accounting for 38.63% of the total revenue.
2002年本行业收入占全行业的 0.010%，资产利润率为 0.15%。75.44%的企业赢利，24.56%的企业亏损。收入最高的省为江苏省，占本行业的38.63%。

	Total number of firms 企业总数	Total number of employees 职工总数	Total revenue (Mil.RMB) 总销售收入(百万元)	Total profit (Mil.RMB) 总利润(百万元)	Return on assets 资产利润率(%)	Return on equity 权益利润率(%)	Labour productivity ('000 RMB/worker) 劳动生产率(千元/人)	Debts/assets 资产负债率(%)	Total assets (Mil.RMB) 总资产(百万元)
Industry Overall 行业总体	57	17,124	1,030	3	0.15	1.50	18.17	89.65	1,952

	Number of firms 企业个数	Average number of employees 平均职工人数	Average revenue ('000 RMB) 平均销售收入(千元)	Average profit ('000 RMB) 平均利润(千元)	Return on assets 资产利润率(%)	Return on equity 权益利润率(%)	Labour productivity ('000 RMB/worker) 劳动生产率(千元/人)	Debts/assets 资产负债率(%)	Average total assets ('000 RMB) 平均总资产(千元)
By ownership 产业所有权									
State-owned 国有	23	262	3,841	-373	-0.89	-26.59	10.96	96.67	42,068
Collective-owned 集体	12	209	14,348	154	1.53		25.10	103.04	10,042
Foreign & Overseas Chinese Funded 三资	2	216	13,124	12	0.09	0.23	17.60	62.73	13,358
By regional distribution 地区分布									
Central-North 华北	3	54	2,049	5	0.08	0.69	20.06	88.59	5,920
Beijing 北京	1	4	31	-11	-2.46	-2.82	5.75	12.95	448
Tianjin 天津									
Hebei 河北									
Shanxi 山西	2	79	3,058	13	0.14	1.53	20.43	90.55	8,656
Inner Mongolia 内蒙古									
Northeast 东北	4	397	13,305	14	0.03	0.19	1.78	82.54	42,364
Liaoning 辽宁	1								
Jilin 吉林	3	529	17,740	19	0.03	0.19	1.78	82.54	56,485
Heilongjiang 黑龙江									
Central-East 华东	14	361	39,638	506	0.85	11.73	26.02	92.79	59,858
Shanghai 上海									
Jiangsu 江苏	2	1,210	198,897	1,293	0.94	4.60	28.77	79.56	137,456
Zhejiang 浙江	2	107	19,179	851	6.71	14.66	50.18	54.23	12,677
Anhui 安徽	6	240	8,230	-22	-0.06	-1.01	14.07	93.55	34,443
Fujian 福建									
Jiangxi 江西	2	230	2,023	-141	-0.12	-9.84	8.90	98.77	116,611
Shandong 山东	2	260	32,680	1,607	3.28		51.54	124.10	48,931
Central-South 中南	31	284	11,973	-164	-0.60	-5.00	17.81	88.02	27,378
Henan 河南	14	266	9,356	220	0.94	6.71	19.67	85.95	23,303
Hubei 湖北	7	178	16,454	-285	-1.30	-12.00	43.37	89.16	21,944
Hunan 湖南	2	585	23,627	299	0.68	1.36	13.51	49.71	43,756
Guangdong 广东	3	166	23,631	62	0.27	1.66	25.54	83.61	22,824
Guangxi 广西	5	435	1,372	-1,389	-3.26		0.56	107.52	42,574
Hainan 海南									
Southwest 西南	3	399	10,884	11	0.07	0.61	10.23	88.84	16,242
Chongqing 重庆									
Sichuan 四川	1	276	5,051	5	0.11	0.50	8.04	79.14	4,761
Guizhou 贵州	1	512	18,045	1		20.00	13.11	99.98	25,451
Yunnan 云南	1	408	9,555	27	0.15	0.61	8.11	76.02	18,513
Tibet 西藏									
Northwest 西北	2	163	5,783	458	3.12	31.86	14.15	90.19	14,657
Shaanxi 陕西	1	275	2,802	9	0.04		5.40	105.21	21,058
Gansu 甘肃	1	50	8,763	907	10.99	22.83	62.26	51.88	8,255
Qinghai 青海									
Ningxia 宁夏									
Xinjiang 新疆									

1763: Jute Spinning and Weaving 黄、洋、青麻纺织业

Year 年份	Number of firms 企业个数	Rate of change 变化率(%)	Number of employees 职工人数(人)	Rate of change 变化率(%)	Total revenue (Mil. RMB) 总销售收入(百万元)	Rate of change 变化率(%)	Total profit (Mil RMB) 总利润(百万元)	Rate of change 变化率(%)
2000	72		47,209		1,263		-7	
2001	69	-4.17	24,128	-48.89	1,017	-19.48	-20	-185.71
2002	57	-17.39	17,124	-29.03	1,030	1.28	3	-

Major Products 主要产品	Output 产量	Unit 单位
Gunny Bag 麻袋（混合数）	5,392	10,000 Pieces 万条

10 Main Firms with Maximal Revenue (year founded) 收入最大的十家主要企业（创办年份）	City 城市	Province 省	Telephone/fax 电话/传真	Number of employees 职工人数	Ownership 产业所有权	Revenue ('000 RMB) 销售收入(千元)	Profit('000 RMB) (rank) 利润(千元)(排名)	Total assets ('000 RMB) 总资产(千元)	Major products 主要产品
Wuxi Tianyuan Industrial Co.,Ltd. 无锡天元实业有限公司(1999)	Wuxi 无锡市	Jiangsu 江苏省	(0510)2852071 (0510)2855898	2,223	Limited-Liability 有限公司	389,514	3,135(1)	262,252	Yarn 纱
Guangdong Xinhui Linen Textile Mill Co., Ltd. 江门市新会区麻纺织厂有限公司(2000)	Jiangmen 江门市	Guangdong 广东省	(0750)6311288 (0750)6653757	464	Limited-Liability 有限公司	63,264	-	65,781	Silk Cloth 纱罗布
Jilin Baicheng Linen Textile Stock Co., ltd. 吉林省白城麻纺织股份有限公司(1998)	Baicheng 白城市	Jilin 吉林省	(0436)3224512 (0436)3236291	888	Joint Stock 股份制	50,682	57(19)	87,895	
Shanxian Linen (Group) Co., Ltd. 山东单县麻纺（集团）有限公司(1976)	Heze 荷泽市	Shandong 山东省	(0530)4682625 (0530)4686091	510	Private Owned 私营企业	49,789	2,411(2)	93,865	Gunnybag 麻袋
Jianli Jute Textile Factory 监利县黄麻经纺厂(1954)	Jingzhou 荆州市	Hubei 湖北省	(0716)3574232	10	Collective-owned 集体企业	40,000	240(17)	7,220	Jute Thread 缝口线
Hubei State-owned Xidayuan Farm Linen Textile Works 湖北省国营西大垸农场麻纺织厂(1988)	Qianjiang 潜江市	Hubei 湖北省	(0728)6831222	265	State-owned 国有企业	32,626	800(10)	25,823	Gunnybag 麻袋
Hunan Chenzhou Linen Products Factory 湖南省郴州麻制品厂(1997)	Chenzhou 郴州市	Hunan 湖南省	(0735)2823126 (0735)2823130	934	Joint Stock 股份制	29,286	24(25)	73,457	Gunnybag 麻袋
Henan Shangcheng Jingwei Linen Textile Co., Ltd. 河南省商城县经纬麻纺织有限公司(1978)	Xinyang 信阳市	Henan 河南省	(0376)7921792	280	Collective-owned 集体企业	21,600	900(7)	7,714	Gunnybag 麻袋
Henan Xixian Jinda Linen Textile Group Co., Ltd. 河南省息县金达麻纺集团有限责任公司(1996)	Xinyang 信阳市	Henan 河南省	(0376)5951126	300	Limited-Liability 有限公司	21,470	23(26)	40,822	Ramie Yarn 麻纱线
Xiangcheng Linen Textile Factory 襄城县麻纺织厂(1975)	Xuchang 许昌市	Henan 河南省	(0374)3582348	306	Collective-owned 集体企业	18,950	280(16)	4,965	Flax 麻布

Top 10 Cities by Revenue 销售收入排名前10位城市	Province 省	Market share 市场份额(%)	Number of firms 企业个数
Wuxi 无锡市	Jiangsu 江苏省	37.83	1
Xinyang 信阳市	Henan 河南省	6.99	7
Jiangmen 江门市	Guangdong 广东省	6.14	1
Baicheng 白城市	Jilin 吉林省	5.17	2
Heze 荷泽市	Shandong 山东省	4.84	1
Jingzhou 荆州市	Hubei 湖北省	4.49	2
Xuchang 许昌市	Henan 河南省	3.44	2
Lu'an 六安市	Anhui 安徽省	3.27	3
Chenzhou 郴州市	Hunan 湖南省	2.84	1

10 Major Wholesalers 十家主要批发商	City 城市	Province 省	Telephone/Fax 电话/传真
Shanghai Shenda Co.,Ltd. 上海申达股份有限公司	Shanghai 上海市	Shanghai 上海市	(021)62319898 (021)62317250
Orient International Holding Silk Group Corportion 东方国际集团丝绸进出口有限公司	Shanghai 上海市	Shanghai 上海市	(021)64662288 (021)64677788
Nanjing Textiles Import & Export Co.,Ltd. 南京纺织品进出口股份有限公司	Nanjing 南京市	Jiangsu 江苏省	(025)3306789 (025)3300518
Zhejiang Textiles Import & Export Group Co.,Ltd. 浙江省纺织品进出口集团有限公司	Hangzhou 杭州市	Zhejiang 浙江省	(0571)87075888 (0571)87079234
Zhejiang Orient Holdings Co.,Ltd. 浙江东方集团股份有限公司	Hangzhou 杭州市	Zhejiang 浙江省	(0571)87215678 (0571)87215000
Zhejiang Silk Holding Co.,ltd. 浙江省丝绸集团有限公司	Hangzhou 杭州市	Zhejiang 浙江省	(0571)85195588 (0571)85192540
Guangdong Silk (Group) Corporation 广东省丝绸（集团）公司	Guangzhou 广州市	Guangdong 广东省	(020)83337448 (020)83332995
Shanghai Costume Group Co.,Ltd. 上海服装（集团）有限公司	Shanghai 上海市	Shanghai 上海市	(021)62748598 (021)62414773
Orient International Holding Shanghai Textiles Import & Export Co.Ltd. 东方国际集团上海市针织品进出口有限公司	Shanghai 上海市	Shanghai 上海市	(021)63218855 (021)63299560
Jiangsu Textiles Import & Export Group Co.,Ltd. 江苏省纺织品进出口集团股份有限公司	Nanjing 南京市	Jiangsu 江苏省	(025)6895000 (025)4400800

1769: Other Flax,Ramie and Jute Spinning and Weaving

其他麻纺织业

The industry accounts for 0.004% of the total revenue of China's industrial sector in 2002. The rate of return on assets is 3.24%. 78.57% of all firms in the industry made a profit while 21.43% had negative returns.The top province in terms of the industry's revenue is Shandong, accounting for 50.06% of the total revenue.
2002年本行业收入占全行业的 0.004%，资产利润率为 3.24%。78.57%的企业赢利，21.43%的企业亏损。收入最高的省为山东省，占本行业的50.06%。

	Total number of firms 企业总数	Total number of employees 职工总数	Total revenue (Mil.RMB) 总销售收入 (百万元)	Total profit (Mil.RMB) 总利润 (百万元)	Return on assets 资产利润率 (%)	Return on equity 权益利润率 (%)	Labour productivity ('000 RMB/ worker) 劳动生产率 (千元/人)	Debts/ assets 资产负债率 (%)	Total assets (Mil.RMB) 总资产 (百万元)
Industry Overall 行业总体	28	5,889	478	13	3.24	16.64	21.07	80.55	397

	Number of firms 企业个数	Average number of employees 平均职工人数	Average revenue ('000 RMB) 平均销售收入 (千元)	Average profit ('000 RMB) 平均利润 (千元)	Return on assets 资产利润率 (%)	Return on equity 权益利润率 (%)	Labour productivity ('000 RMB/ worker) 劳动生产率 (千元/人)	Debts/ assets 资产负债率 (%)	Average total assets ('000 RMB) 平均总资产 (千元)
By ownership 产业所有权									
State-owned 国有	7	441	19,250	651	2.48		14.06	104.14	26,264
Collective-owned 集体	4	133	8,406	85	1.24	2.37	18.43	47.80	6,856
Foreign & Overseas Chinese Funded 三资	2	210	24,617	-1,965	-8.00	-38.11	16.29	79.01	24,561
By regional distribution 地区分布									
Central-North 华北	1	145	6,800	213	7.02	21.01	12.10	66.59	3,035
Beijing 北京									
Tianjin 天津									
Hebei 河北	1	145	6,800	213	7.02	21.01	12.10	66.59	3,035
Shanxi 山西									
Inner Mongolia 内蒙古									
Northeast 东北	2	33	5,140	695	16.39	55.60	48.32	70.52	4,240
Liaoning 辽宁									
Jilin 吉林	1	5						91.23	4,560
Heilongjiang 黑龙江	1	60	10,280	1,390	35.46	66.19	52.35	46.43	3,920
Central-East 华东	13	338	26,267	1,060	5.48	36.97	21.98	85.18	19,343
Shanghai 上海									
Jiangsu 江苏	2	130	12,105	103	2.16	6.31	25.44	65.79	4,751
Zhejiang 浙江	3	146	11,002	176	2.15	7.88	16.54	72.66	8,153
Anhui 安徽	1	270	7,020	74	1.46	2.90	5.75	49.75	5,075
Fujian 福建	2	180	19,059	424	5.78	12.39	35.85	53.36	7,328
Jiangxi 江西									
Shandong 山东	5	613	47,824	2,426	6.13	67.56	22.26	90.92	39,554
Central-South 中南	9	107	11,769	-284	-2.21	-8.84	19.36	75.03	12,871
Henan 河南	1	15						176.11	13,469
Hubei 湖北									
Hunan 湖南									
Guangdong 广东	5	131	17,913	-664	-3.86	-9.31	18.20	58.59	17,221
Guangxi 广西	3	98	5,451	255	4.70	21.70	22.92	78.32	5,420
Hainan 海南									
Southwest 西南	3	108	4,386	5	0.08	0.20	12.48	58.47	5,981
Chongqing 重庆									
Sichuan 四川	1	268	12,203	4	0.03	0.08	16.38	58.93	12,187
Guizhou 贵州									
Yunnan 云南	1	45	654	-48	-0.93	-2.57	-8.40	63.93	5,176
Tibet 西藏	1	12	301	59	10.15	10.15	3.75		581
Northwest 西北									
Shaanxi 陕西									
Gansu 甘肃									
Qinghai 青海									
Ningxia 宁夏									
Xinjiang 新疆									

1769: Other Flax,Ramie and Jute Spinning and Weaving

其他麻纺织业

Year 年份	Number of firms 企业个数	Rate of change 变化率(%)	Number of employees 职工人数(人)	Rate of change 变化率(%)	Total revenue (Mil. RMB) 总销售收入(百万元)	Rate of change 变化率(%)	Total profit (Mil RMB) 总利润(百万元)	Rate of change 变化率(%)
2000	27		6,333		261		0.11	
2001	31	14.81	6,482	2.35	432	65.52	10	89.91
2002	28	-9.68	5,889	-9.15	478	10.65	13	30.00

Major Products 主要产品	Output 产量	Unit 单位

10 Main Firms with Maximal Revenue (year founded) 收入最大的十家主要企业（创办年份）	City 城市	Province 省	Telephone/fax 电话/传真	Number of employees 职工人数	Ownership 产业所有权	Revenue ('000 RMB) 销售收入(千元)	Profit('000 RMB) (rank) 利润(千元)(排名)	Total assets ('000 RMB) 总资产(千元)	Major products 主要产品
Zhouji Taiya Flax Textile Co., Ltd.	Taian	Shandong	(0538)2822625		State-owned				Flax
洲际泰亚麻纺织有限公司(1976)	泰安市	山东省	(0538)2821834	2,730	国有企业	117,742	3,841(2)	144,381	麻布
Zaozhuang Taierzhuang Jiantouji Town Hemp Textile Factory	Zaozhuang	Shandong	(0632)6751188		Private Partnership				Gunny Mat
枣庄市台儿庄区涧头集镇大麻纺织厂(1979)	枣庄市	山东省		140	私营合伙	78,220	5,649(1)	28,290	大麻席
Boluo Rongtai Textile Co., Ltd.	Huizhou	Guangdong	(0752)6915896		Overseas Chinese-funded				Wool Flannelette
博罗县荣泰纺织有限公司(2001)	惠州市	广东省	(0752)6988451	190	港澳台资	30,000	45(17)	26,842	毛绒布
Nanhai Jibei Textile Co., Ltd.	Foshan	Guangdong	(0757)6833119		Private Enterprises				Textile Cloth
南海吉贝纺织有限公司(2002)	佛山市	广东省	(0757)6892399	110	私营独资	21,159	635(8)	18,752	纺织布
Fujian Changle Jinfeng Canvas Cloth Works	Fuzhou	Fujian	(0591)8672070		Collective-owned				Canvas
福建省长乐市金峰帆布厂(1987)	福州市	福建省	(0591)8674363	150	集体企业	19,528	230(12)	10,056	帆布
Guangzhou Panyu Jinbao Printing & Dyeing Co., Ltd.	Guangzhou	Guangdong	(020)84892925		Overseas Chinese-funded				Flax Brocade Dyeing Cloth亚麻
广州市番禺锦宝印染有限公司(2000)	广州市	广东省	(020)84895757	230	港澳台资	19,233	-	22,280	锦染色布
Fuzhou Fengxiang Camping Produets Co., Ltd.	Fuzhou	Fujian	(0591)2252949		Private Owned				Sleeping Bag
福州丰祥野营用品有限公司(1988)	福州市	福建省	(0591)2254582	210	私营企业	18,590	617(9)	4,599	睡袋
Zhongshan Sanma Shoes Material Co.,Ltd.	Zhongshan	Guangdong	(0760)5702691		Private Owned				Non-woven Fabric
中山市三马鞋材有限公司(2000)	中山市	广东省	(0760)5702901	24	私营企业	12,400	-	6,520	无纺布
Guangxi Pubei Dongjian Co., Ltd.	Qinzhou	Guangxi	(0777)8638307		State-owned				Sisal Cloth
广西浦北县东剑有限责任公司(1999)	钦州市	广西壮族自治区	(0777)8639656	185	国有企业	12,351	800(6)	9,836	剑麻布
Bayan Huatai Linen Co., Ltd.	Harbin	Heilongjiang	(0451)7561060		Private Enterprises				Linen & Cotton
巴彦县华泰麻业有限公司(2000)	哈尔滨市	黑龙江省		60	私营独资	10,280	1,390(3)	3,920	麻棉

Top 10 Cities by Revenue 销售收入排名前10位城市	Province 省	Market share 市场份额(%)	Number of firms 企业个数
Taian 泰安市	Shandong 山东省	26.63	2
Zaozhuang 枣庄市	Shandong 山东省	16.38	1
Fuzhou 福州市	Fujian 福建省	7.98	2
Huizhou 惠州市	Guangdong 广东省	6.28	1
Suzhou 苏州市	Jiangsu 江苏省	5.07	2
Foshan 佛山市	Guangdong 广东省	4.43	1
Dezhou 德州市	Shandong 山东省	4.40	1
Guangzhou 广州市	Guangdong 广东省	4.03	1
Huzhou 湖州市	Zhejiang 浙江省	3.94	1
Qingdao 青岛市	Shandong 山东省	2.66	1

10 Major Wholesalers 十家主要批发商	City 城市	Province 省	Telephone/Fax 电话/传真
Shanghai Shenda Co.,Ltd.	Shanghai	Shanghai	(021)62319898
上海申达股份有限公司	上海市	上海市	(021)62317250
Orient International Holding Silk Group Corportion	Shanghai	Shanghai	(021)64662288
东方国际集团丝绸进出口有限公司	上海市	上海市	(021)64677788
Nanjing Textiles Import & Export Co.,Ltd.	Nanjing	Jiangsu	(025)3306789
南京纺织品进出口股份有限公司	南京市	江苏省	(025)3300518
Zhejiang Textiles Import & Export Group Co.,Ltd.	Hangzhou	Zhejiang	(0571)87075888
浙江省纺织品进出口集团有限公司	杭州市	浙江省	(0571)87079234
Zhejiang Orient Holdings Co.,Ltd.	Hangzhou	Zhejiang	(0571)87215678
浙江东方集团股份有限公司	杭州市	浙江省	(0571)87215000
Zhejiang Silk Holding Co.,ltd.	Hangzhou	Zhejiang	(0571)85195588
浙江省丝绸集团有限公司	杭州市	浙江省	(0571)85192540
Guangdong Silk (Group) Corporation	Guangzhou	Guangdong	(020)83337448
广东省丝绸（集团）公司	广州市	广东省	(020)83332995
Shanghai Costume Group Co.,Ltd.	Shanghai	Shanghai	(021)62748598
上海服装（集团）有限公司	上海市	上海市	(021)62414773
Orient International Holding Shanghai Textiles Import & Export Co.Ltd.	Shanghai	Shanghai	(021)63218855
东方国际集团上海市针织品进出口有限公司	上海市	上海市	(021)63299560
Jiangsu Textiles Import & Export Group Co.,Ltd.	Nanjing	Jiangsu	(025)6895000
江苏省纺织品进出口集团股份有限公司	南京市	江苏省	(025)4400800

1771: Silk Reeling 缫丝业

The industry accounts for 0.103% of the total revenue of China's industrial sector in 2002. The rate of return on assets is -0.86%. 62.22% of all firms in the industry made a profit while 37.78% had negative returns.The top province in terms of the industry's revenue is Jiangsu, accounting for 30.50% of the total revenue.
2002年本行业收入占全行业的 0.103%，资产利润率为 -0.86%。62.22%的企业赢利，37.78%的企业亏损。收入最高的省为江苏省，占本行业的30.50%。

	Total number of firms 企业总数	Total number of employees 职工总数	Total revenue (Mil.RMB) 总销售收入 (百万元)	Total profit (Mil.RMB) 总利润 (百万元)	Return on assets 资产利润率 (%)	Return on equity 权益利润率 (%)	Labour productivity ('000 RMB/ worker) 劳动生产率 (千元/人)	Debts/ assets 资产负债率 (%)	Total assets (Mil.RMB) 总资产 (百万元)
Industry Overall 行业总体	487	163,650	11,030	-93	-0.86	-3.91	17.68	78.03	10,850

	Number of firms 企业个数	Average number of employees 平均职工人数	Average revenue ('000 RMB) 平均销售收入（千元）	Average profit ('000 RMB) 平均利润 (千元)	Return on assets 资产利润率 (%)	Return on equity 权益利润率 (%)	Labour productivity ('000 RMB/ worker) 劳动生产率 (千元/人)	Debts/ assets 资产负债率 (%)	Average total assets ('000 RMB) 平均总资产 (千元)
By ownership 产业所有权									
State-owned 国有	44	668	28,041	-2,174	-4.46	-109.32	11.93	95.92	48,689
Collective-owned 集体	83	284	23,636	727	3.36	13.61	21.42	75.29	21,599
Foreign & Overseas Chinese Funded 三资	3	440	27,410	23	0.18	1.69	15.09	89.41	13,004
By regional distribution 地区分布									
Central-North 华北	3	1,905	36,620	1,191	1.36	3.60	8.18	62.13	87,465
Beijing 北京									
Tianjin 天津									
Hebei 河北									
Shanxi 山西	3	1,905	36,620	1,191	1.36	3.60	8.18	62.13	87,465
Inner Mongolia 内蒙古									
Northeast 东北	28	187	8,414	200	1.57	2.63	9.37	40.46	12,790
Liaoning 辽宁	28	187	8,414	200	1.57	2.63	9.37	40.46	12,790
Jilin 吉林									
Heilongjiang 黑龙江									
Central-East 华东	296	291	25,913	169	0.81	3.90	22.78	79.32	20,938
Shanghai 上海									
Jiangsu 江苏	129	272	26,078	284	1.91	11.00	25.12	82.67	14,897
Zhejiang 浙江	92	233	29,110	306	1.28	4.50	26.28	71.49	23,856
Anhui 安徽	28	306	15,445	-129	-0.54	-3.91	16.22	86.17	23,832
Fujian 福建									
Jiangxi 江西	15	281	10,800	24	0.12	1.22	12.94	89.96	19,870
Shandong 山东	32	528	32,303	-363	-1.04	-5.79	19.26	82.00	34,872
Central-South 中南	38	294	17,672	271	1.89	10.48	23.07	81.99	14,358
Henan 河南	6	131	6,148	271	4.03	26.77	17.24	84.93	6,721
Hubei 湖北	10	364	24,532	904	5.83	18.13	32.94	67.83	15,490
Hunan 湖南									
Guangdong 广东	6	368	21,612	221	1.12	4.91	17.06	77.18	19,753
Guangxi 广西	16	284	16,228	-106	-0.73	-11.09	19.11	93.41	14,490
Hainan 海南									
Southwest 西南	108	467	20,021	-1,121	-3.99	-15.33	10.64	73.99	28,106
Chongqing 重庆	30	491	19,119	-655	-2.70	-9.67	11.51	72.11	24,286
Sichuan 四川	75	413	20,016	-892	-3.22	-10.50	11.64	69.35	27,710
Guizhou 贵州	1	209	7,161	-212	-2.17	-2.29	13.55	5.39	9,792
Yunnan 云南	2	2,228	40,161	-17,130	-15.65		0.66	127.41	109,431
Tibet 西藏									
Northwest 西北	14	358	12,920	-2,966	-9.22		8.29	121.76	32,187
Shaanxi 陕西	11	401	15,011	-3,504	-9.61		8.63	114.59	36,471
Gansu 甘肃	1	70	3,707	330	7.68	106.80	8.93	92.81	4,299
Qinghai 青海									
Ningxia 宁夏									
Xinjiang 新疆	2	265	6,025	-1,656	-7.33		5.37	188.28	22,572

Year 年份	Number of firms 企业个数	Rate of change 变化率(%)	Number of employees 职工人数(人)	Rate of change 变化率(%)	Total revenue (Mil. RMB) 总销售收入(百万元)	Rate of change 变化率(%)	Total profit (Mil RMB) 总利润(百万元)	Rate of change 变化率(%)
2000	433		213,472		11,130		65	
2001	464	7.16	176,947	-17.11	11,445	2.83	19	-70.77
2002	487	4.96	163,650	-7.51	11,030	-3.63	-93	-

Major Products 主要产品	Output 产量	Unit 单位
Silk 丝	83,329	Ton 吨

10 Main Firms with Maximal Revenue (year founded) 收入最大的十家主要企业(创办年份)	City 城市	Province 省	Telephone/fax 电话/传真	Number of employees 职工人数	Ownership 产业所有权	Revenue ('000 RMB) 销售收入(千元)	Profit('000 RMB) (rank) 利润(千元)(排名)	Total assets ('000 RMB) 总资产(千元)	Major products 主要产品
Shaoxing Fuling Industrial Group Co., Ltd. 绍兴富陵实业集团有限公司(1997)	Shaoxing 绍兴市	Zhejiang 浙江省	(0575)8038009	874	Collective-owned 集体企业	582,186	55,761(1)	457,317	Textile 纺织品
Zhejiang Sanhua Silk Co.,Ltd. 浙江三环丝绸股份有限公司(2000)	Jiaxing 嘉兴市	Zhejiang 浙江省	(0573)6023358 (0573)6021678	1,337	Joint Stock 股份制	202,974	3,336(12)	146,949	Cocoon Silk 茧丝
Sichuan Nanchong Liuhe (Group) Co.Ltd. 四川南充六合（集团）有限责任公司(1998)	Nanchong 南充市	Sichuan 四川省	(0817)3300076 (0817)3300111	2,076	State-owned 国有企业	200,122	4,478(5)	156,140	Mulberry Silk 桑蚕丝
Yancheng Danfeng Silk Fabric Co., Ltd. 盐城丹凤丝品有限公司(1984)	Yancheng 盐城市	Jiangsu 江苏省	(0515)8701515 (0515)8701188	270	Joint Owned 联营企业	185,080	4,020(8)	16,460	White Filature Silk 白厂丝
Zhejiang Huashen Silk Group 浙江花神丝绸集团(1935)	Jiaxing 嘉兴市	Zhejiang 浙江省	(0573)8027577 (0573)8033266	1,389	Limited-Liability 有限公司	155,907	-	133,665	White Filature Silk 白厂丝
Zhejiang Huazhi Silk Co., Ltd. 浙江华芝丝绸有限责任公司(1996)	Jiaxing 嘉兴市	Zhejiang 浙江省	(0573)8451363 (0573)8451102	599	Limited-Liability 有限公司	120,630	2,186(15)	75,119	White Filature Silk 白厂丝
Dafeng Hongda Silk Co., Ltd. 大丰市虹达丝绸有限责任公司(1983)	Yancheng 盐城市	Jiangsu 江苏省	(0515)3412088 (0515)3412088	963	Joint Stock 股份制	118,870	1,520(25)	36,350	White Filature Silk 白厂丝
Sichuan Neijiang Songlin Silk Weaving Mill 四川省内江市松林丝织总厂(1980)	Neijiang 内江市	Sichuan 四川省	(0832)2945175 (0832)2945316	1,766	Joint Stock 股份制	115,807	-	132,161	White Filature Silk 白厂丝
Hechuan Taihe Filature General Factory 合川市太和缫丝总厂(1980)	Chongqing 重庆市	Chongqing 重庆市	(023)42668242 (023)42669498	2,368	Collective-owned 集体企业	98,559	5,539(4)	80,184	Filature 缫丝
Dongtai Tianhua Pongee Co., Ltd. 东台市天华茧丝绸有限公司(1993)	Yancheng 盐城市	Jiangsu 江苏省	(0515)5651210 (0515)5651207	390	Private Owned 私营企业	95,350	600(77)	24,840	White Filature Silk 白厂丝

Top 10 Cities by Revenue 销售收入排名前10位城市	Province 省	Market share 市场份额(%)	Number of firms 企业个数
Yancheng 盐城市	Jiangsu 江苏省	12.23	28
Jiaxing 嘉兴市	Zhejiang 浙江省	10.48	35
Huzhou 湖州市	Zhejiang 浙江省	6.09	37
Shaoxing 绍兴市	Zhejiang 浙江省	5.64	4
Chongqing 重庆市	Chongqing 重庆市	5.20	30
Suqian 宿迁市	Jiangsu 江苏省	4.59	16
Nanchong 南充市	Sichuan 四川省	4.22	22
Nantong 南通市	Jiangsu 江苏省	3.77	26
Huaian 淮安市	Jiangsu 江苏省	3.19	18
Suzhou 苏州市	Jiangsu 江苏省	2.20	14

10 Major Wholesalers 十家主要批发商	City 城市	Province 省	Telephone/Fax 电话/传真
Shanghai Shenda Co.,Ltd. 上海申达股份有限公司	Shanghai 上海市	Shanghai 上海市	(021)62319898 (021)62317250
Orient International Holding Silk Group Corportion 东方国际集团丝绸进出口有限公司	Shanghai 上海市	Shanghai 上海市	(021)64662288 (021)64677788
Nanjing Textiles Import & Export Co.,Ltd. 南京纺织品进出口股份有限公司	Nanjing 南京市	Jiangsu 江苏省	(025)3306789 (025)3300518
Zhejiang Textiles Import & Export Group Co.,Ltd. 浙江省纺织品进出口集团有限公司	Hangzhou 杭州市	Zhejiang 浙江省	(0571)87075888 (0571)87079234
Zhejiang Orient Holdings Co.,Ltd. 浙江东方集团股份有限公司	Hangzhou 杭州市	Zhejiang 浙江省	(0571)87215678 (0571)87215000
Zhejiang Silk Holding Co.,ltd. 浙江省丝绸集团有限公司	Hangzhou 杭州市	Zhejiang 浙江省	(0571)85195588 (0571)85192540
Guangdong Silk (Group) Corporation 广东省丝绸（集团）公司	Guangzhou 广州市	Guangdong 广东省	(020)83337448 (020)83332995
Shanghai Costume Group Co.,Ltd. 上海服装（集团）有限公司	Shanghai 上海市	Shanghai 上海市	(021)62748598 (021)62414773
Orient International Holding Shanghai Textiles Import & Export Co.Ltd. 东方国际集团上海市针织品进出口有限公司	Shanghai 上海市	Shanghai 上海市	(021)63218855 (021)63299560
Jiangsu Textiles Import & Export Group Co.,Ltd. 江苏省纺织品进出口集团股份有限公司	Nanjing 南京市	Jiangsu 江苏省	(025)6895000 (025)4400800

1772: Silk Spinning 绢纺业

The industry accounts for 0.055% of the total revenue of China's industrial sector in 2002. The rate of return on assets is 2.80%. 81.65% of all firms in the industry made a profit while 18.35% had negative returns.The top province in terms of the industry's revenue is Zhejiang, accounting for 57.81% of the total revenue.
2002年本行业收入占全行业的0.055%，资产利润率为2.80%。81.65%的企业赢利，18.35%的企业亏损。收入最高的省为浙江省，占本行业的57.81%。

	Total number of firms 企业总数	Total number of employees 职工总数	Total revenue (Mil.RMB) 总销售收入 (百万元)	Total profit (Mil.RMB) 总利润 (百万元)	Return on assets 资产利润率 (%)	Return on equity 权益利润率 (%)	Labour productivity ('000 RMB/ worker) 劳动生产率 (千元/人)	Debts/ assets 资产负债率 (%)	Total assets (Mil.RMB) 总资产 (百万元)
Industry Overall 行业总体	109	48,092	5,913	150	2.80	8.15	27.69	65.62	5,359

	Number of firms 企业个数	Average number of employees 平均职工人数	Average revenue ('000 RMB) 平均销售收入 (千元)	Average profit ('000 RMB) 平均利润 (千元)	Return on assets 资产利润率 (%)	Return on equity 权益利润率 (%)	Labour productivity ('000 RMB/ worker) 劳动生产率 (千元/人)	Debts/ assets 资产负债率 (%)	Average total assets ('000 RMB) 平均总资产 (千元)
By ownership 产业所有权									
State-owned 国有	6	1,057	90,988	2,735	1.30	3.96	24.86	67.10	209,921
Collective-owned 集体	16	370	60,923	515	1.26	26.54	38.34	95.24	40,795
Foreign & Overseas Chinese Funded 三资	10	430	58,598	410	0.73	1.45	30.64	49.94	56,404
By regional distribution 地区分布									
Central-North 华北									
Beijing 北京									
Tianjin 天津									
Hebei 河北									
Shanxi 山西									
Inner Mongolia 内蒙古									
Northeast 东北	14	382	34,234	728	3.21	6.26	19.57	48.66	22,670
Liaoning 辽宁	12	309	28,703	277	1.18	2.46	19.20	52.18	23,493
Jilin 吉林									
Heilongjiang 黑龙江	2	826	67,422	3,435	19.37	24.44	20.39	20.74	17,731
Central-East 华东	84	467	62,348	1,669	3.01	8.42	30.01	64.28	55,528
Shanghai 上海	2	249	31,302	-186	-0.50	-0.94	33.03	47.32	37,324
Jiangsu 江苏	29	435	58,426	924	1.99	7.21	32.19	72.45	46,526
Zhejiang 浙江	49	503	69,761	2,308	3.60	9.22	29.64	60.96	64,122
Anhui 安徽	1	98	3,200	370	3.85	3.85	17.76		9,610
Fujian 福建									
Jiangxi 江西	1	128	10,998	-388	-9.29		25.93	115.83	4,175
Shandong 山东	2	602	23,913	353	0.83	3.63	15.01	77.04	42,345
Central-South 中南	3	416	23,873	-1,440	-4.39		13.87	106.78	32,782
Henan 河南	1	891	48,500				9.52	85.50	47,034
Hubei 湖北									
Hunan 湖南									
Guangdong 广东	1	130	20,790	100	1.00	1.00	63.88		10,000
Guangxi 广西	1	228	2,330	-4,420	-10.70		2.38	156.85	41,312
Hainan 海南									
Southwest 西南	6	351	18,817	853	3.91		13.14	122.94	21,815
Chongqing 重庆	1	170	10,354	-4,826	-29.12		23.19	144.69	16,575
Sichuan 四川	4	464	24,240	2,481	9.28		11.75	122.12	26,741
Guizhou 贵州	1	79	5,586	24	0.33	2.29	24.19	85.73	7,353
Yunnan 云南									
Tibet 西藏									
Northwest 西北	2	84	6,042	-531	-0.72	-2.10	29.46	65.99	74,168
Shaanxi 陕西	2	84	6,042	-531	-0.72	-2.10	29.46	65.99	74,168
Gansu 甘肃									
Qinghai 青海									
Ningxia 宁夏									
Xinjiang 新疆									

Year 年份	Number of firms 企业个数	Rate of change 变化率 (%)	Number of employees 职工人数 (人)	Rate of change 变化率 (%)	Total revenue (Mil. RMB) 总销售收入 (百万元)	Rate of change 变化率 (%)	Total profit (Mil RMB) 总利润 (百万元)	Rate of change 变化率 (%)
2000	109		56,190		4,743		62	
2001	113	3.67	59,468	5.83	5,346	12.71	122	96.77
2002	109	-3.54	48,092	-19.13	5,913	10.61	150	22.95

Major Products 主要产品	Output 产量	Unit 单位
Silk Fabric 丝织品	534,145	10,000 Meters 万米

10 Main Firms with Maximal Revenue (year founded) 收入最大的十家主要企业（创办年份）	City 城市	Province 省	Telephone/fax 电话/传真	Number of employees 职工人数	Ownership 产业所有权	Revenue ('000 RMB) 销售收入 (千元)	Profit('000 RMB) (rank) 利润(千元)(排名)	Total assets ('000 RMB) 总资产 (千元)	Major products 主要产品
Furun Textile Group Co., Ltd.	Shaoxing	Zhejiang	(0575)7223016		State-owned				Spun Silk
富润纺织集团有限公司(1982)	绍兴市	浙江省	(0575)7223018	3,806	国有企业	435,142	25,952(1)	990,375	绢丝
Zhejiang Hongjuan Textile Co., Ltd.	Shaoxing	Zhejiang	(0575)7669229		Limited-Liability				Spun Silk
浙江虹绢纺织有限公司(1996)	绍兴市	浙江省	(0575)7669229	1,031	有限公司	333,451	9,004(5)	169,817	绢丝
jiaxing Longyuan Spun Silk & Hemp Textile Co.Ltd.	Jiaxing	Zhejiang	(0573)3322039		Overseas Chinese-funded				Spun Silk
嘉兴龙源绢麻纺织有限公司(1994)	嘉兴市	浙江省	(0573)3322754	1,823	港澳台资	256,383	2,870(18)	346,080	绢丝
Changzhou Wanshun Textile Group Co., Ltd.	Changzhou	Jiangsu	(0519)8824976		Limited-Liability				Coloured Woven Cloth
常州市万顺纺织集团有限公司(1998)	常州市	江苏省	(0519)8814976	713	有限公司	226,100	19,340(2)	242,950	色织布
Jiangsu Danqi Spun Silk Textile Co., Ltd.	Zhenjiang	Jiangsu	(0511)6525411		Overseas Chinese-funded				Mixing Fiber Silk
江苏丹祈绢丝纺织有限公司(1990)	镇江市	江苏省	(0511)6528032	1,210	港澳台资	195,001	-	85,227	合纤绸
Yixing Dinding New Dingqiu Spum Silk Textile Co., Ltd.	Wuxi	Jiangsu	(0510)7383888		Joint Stock				Printing Silk
宜兴市新鼎球绢纺织有限公司(1986)	无锡市	江苏省	(0510)7381652	850	股份制	185,553	1,500(28)	150,567	印花绸
Zhejiang Hengyue Spun Silk Textile Co., Ltd.	Jiaxing	Zhejiang	(0573)6455568		Limited-Liability				Spun Silk
浙江恒越绢纺有限公司(1993)	嘉兴市	浙江省	(0573)6458202	2,324	有限公司	171,288	50(71)	88,817	绢丝
Baysalt Feilong Spum Silk Products Co., Ltd.	Jiaxing	Zhejiang	(0573)6811717		Limited-Liability				Tiffany
海盐飞龙丝绢制品有限公司(1997)	嘉兴市	浙江省	(0573)6811387	750	有限公司	135,190	2,310(23)	103,370	丝绢
Tongxiang Heshan Weiye Textile Co., Ltd.	Jiaxing	Zhejiang	(0573)8677118		Private Owned				Spun Silk
桐乡市河山伟业纺织有限责任公司(1999)	嘉兴市	浙江省	(0573)8677091	1,098	私营企业	111,330	4,350(13)	113,790	绢丝
Jiaxing Huayi Spun Silk Co., Ltd.	Jiaxing	Zhejiang	(0573)8021965		Private Owned				Spun Silk
嘉兴市华益丝绢有限公司(2001)	嘉兴市	浙江省	(0573)8020347	1,118	私营企业	109,562	3,594(16)	69,729	绢丝

Top 10 Cities by Revenue 销售收入排名前10位城市	Province 省	Market share 市场份额 (%)	Number of firms 企业个数
Jiaxing 嘉兴市	Zhejiang 浙江省	28.46	28
Huzhou 湖州市	Zhejiang 浙江省	15.00	15
Shaoxing 绍兴市	Zhejiang 浙江省	13.42	4
Wuxi 无锡市	Jiangsu 江苏省	10.01	13
Zhenjiang 镇江市	Jiangsu 江苏省	7.26	3
Yingkou 营口市	Liaoning 辽宁省	4.81	9
Changzhou 常州市	Jiangsu 江苏省	4.54	2
Suzhou 苏州市	Jiangsu 江苏省	4.33	6
Harbin 哈尔滨市	Heilongjiang 黑龙江省	2.28	2
Suqian 宿迁市	Jiangsu 江苏省	1.90	2

10 Major Wholesalers 十家主要批发商	City 城市	Province 省	Telephone/Fax 电话/传真
Shanghai Shenda Co.,Ltd.	Shanghai	Shanghai	(021)62319898
上海申达股份有限公司	上海市	上海市	(021)62317250
Orient International Holding Silk Group Corportion	Shanghai	Shanghai	(021)64662288
东方国际集团丝绸进出口有限公司	上海市	上海市	(021)64677788
Nanjing Textiles Import & Export Co.,Ltd.	Nanjing	Jiangsu	(025)3306789
南京纺织品进出口股份有限公司	南京市	江苏省	(025)3300518
Zhejiang Textiles Import & Export Group Co.,Ltd.	Hangzhou	Zhejiang	(0571)87075888
浙江省纺织品进出口集团有限公司	杭州市	浙江省	(0571)87079234
Zhejiang Orient Holdings Co.,Ltd.	Hangzhou	Zhejiang	(0571)87215678
浙江东方集团股份有限公司	杭州市	浙江省	(0571)87215000
Zhejiang Silk Holding Co.,ltd.	Hangzhou	Zhejiang	(0571)85195588
浙江省丝绸集团有限公司	杭州市	浙江省	(0571)85192540
Guangdong Silk (Group) Corporation	Guangzhou	Guangdong	(020)83337448
广东省丝绸（集团）公司	广州市	广东省	(020)83332995
Shanghai Costume Group Co.,Ltd.	Shanghai	Shanghai	(021)62748598
上海服装（集团）有限公司	上海市	上海市	(021)62414773
Orient International Holding Shanghai Textiles Import & Export Co.Ltd.	Shanghai	Shanghai	(021)63218855
东方国际集团上海市针织品进出口有限公司	上海市	上海市	(021)63299560
Jiangsu Textiles Import & Export Group Co.,Ltd.	Nanjing	Jiangsu	(025)6895000
江苏省纺织品进出口集团股份有限公司	南京市	江苏省	(025)4400800

1773: Silk Weaving 丝织业

The industry accounts for 0.444% of the total revenue of China's industrial sector in 2002. The rate of return on assets is 3.93%. 86.82% of all firms in the industry made a profit while 13.18% had negative returns.The top province in terms of the industry's revenue is Zhejiang, accounting for 79.03% of the total revenue.
2002年本行业收入占全行业的 0.444%，资产利润率为 3.93%。86.82%的企业赢利，13.18%的企业亏损。收入最高的省为浙江省，占本行业的79.03%。

	Total number of firms 企业总数	Total number of employees 职工总数	Total revenue (Mil.RMB) 总销售收入（百万元）	Total profit (Mil.RMB) 总利润（百万元）	Return on assets 资产利润率 (%)	Return on equity 权益利润率 (%)	Labour productivity ('000 RMB/ worker) 劳动生产率（千元/人）	Debts/ assets 资产负债率 (%)	Total assets (Mil.RMB) 总资产（百万元）
Industry Overall 行业总体	888	211,609	47,618	1,728	3.93	11.02	45.61	64.35	43,989

	Number of firms 企业个数	Average number of employees 平均职工人数	Average revenue ('000 RMB) 平均销售收入（千元）	Average profit ('000 RMB) 平均利润（千元）	Return on assets 资产利润率 (%)	Return on equity 权益利润率 (%)	Labour productivity ('000 RMB/ worker) 劳动生产率（千元/人）	Debts/ assets 资产负债率 (%)	Average total assets ('000 RMB) 平均总资产（千元）
By ownership 产业所有权									
State-owned 国有	43	556	76,136	2,348	1.62	10.01	41.62	83.86	145,333
Collective-owned 集体	69	372	82,591	3,126	3.57	10.19	48.86	64.96	87,553
Foreign & Overseas Chinese Funded 三资	65	341	64,738	2,290	2.96	7.83	44.58	62.18	77,314
By regional distribution 地区分布									
Central-North 华北	21	85	6,658	-180	-0.43	-3.62	17.38	88.16	41,933
Beijing 北京	1	100	5,758	-265	-5.04	-26.88	-13.68	81.24	5,255
Tianjin 天津	13	80	6,425	254	0.46	8.13	19.87	94.34	55,171
Hebei 河北	6	107	8,422	-1,135	-4.32	-10.89	18.23	60.30	26,253
Shanxi 山西	1	1						70.00	600
Inner Mongolia 内蒙古									
Northeast 东北	6	152	6,348	-172	-0.33		6.82	116.99	52,331
Liaoning 辽宁	5	176	7,449	-205	-0.33		6.43	117.56	62,038
Jilin 吉林	1	32	844	-3	-0.08	-0.27	17.44	70.55	3,796
Heilongjiang 黑龙江									
Central-East 华东	811	233	56,861	2,143	4.30	11.49	48.72	62.61	49,886
Shanghai 上海	8	129	18,310	1,503	6.51	14.92	46.73	56.38	23,092
Jiangsu 江苏	115	343	64,181	1,397	1.83	6.77	49.76	72.92	76,256
Zhejiang 浙江	652	210	57,717	2,394	5.20	12.71	51.04	59.09	46,018
Anhui 安徽	12	246	18,567	-93	-0.35	-0.63	15.69	44.27	26,675
Fujian 福建	5	88	14,709	-514	-1.59	-6.17	45.44	74.33	32,433
Jiangxi 江西	2	289	5,220	300	2.37	13.37	10.42	82.27	12,650
Shandong 山东	17	470	38,151	477	0.82	4.70	19.20	82.61	58,361
Central-South 中南	27	314	27,338	-28	-0.06	-0.79	26.83	91.82	43,091
Henan 河南	8	377	20,238	74	0.20	1.36	16.85	85.59	37,850
Hubei 湖北	4	359	20,476	146	0.46		40.03	117.04	32,024
Hunan 湖南									
Guangdong 广东	12	300	37,815	-16	-0.04	-0.26	31.42	86.14	44,843
Guangxi 广西	2	189	15,513	-923	-0.97		9.32	102.19	95,202
Hainan 海南	1	59	9,507	107	2.64	3.64	48.73	27.37	4,052
Southwest 西南	21	455	27,181	132	0.30	0.77	16.89	61.15	44,032
Chongqing 重庆	4	287	14,954	-826	-3.43	-8.17	13.40	58.03	24,103
Sichuan 四川	17	495	30,058	358	0.73	1.91	17.36	61.51	48,721
Guizhou 贵州									
Yunnan 云南									
Tibet 西藏									
Northwest 西北	2	847	8,297	-3,879	-3.12	-15.46	5.83	79.83	124,380
Shaanxi 陕西	1	648	5,813	-3,783	-2.07	-27.58	8.40	92.51	183,103
Gansu 甘肃									
Qinghai 青海									
Ningxia 宁夏									
Xinjiang 新疆	1	1,045	10,781	-3,975	-6.05	-10.91	4.24	44.48	65,656

Year 年份	Number of firms 企业个数	Rate of change 变化率 (%)	Number of employees 职工人数 (人)	Rate of change 变化率 (%)	Total revenue (Mil. RMB) 总销售收入 (百万元)	Rate of change 变化率 (%)	Total profit (Mil RMB) 总利润 (百万元)	Rate of change 变化率 (%)
2000	759		252,758		35,568		858	
2001	934	23.06	239,879	-5.10	41,568	16.87	1,245	45.10
2002	888	-4.93	211,609	-11.79	47,618	14.55	1,728	38.80

Major Products 主要产品	Output 产量	Unit 单位
Silk Fabric 丝织品	534,145	10,000 Meters 万米

10 Main Firms with Maximal Revenue (year founded) 收入最大的十家主要企业（创办年份）	City 城市	Province 省	Telephone/fax 电话/传真	Number of employees 职工人数	Ownership 产业所有权	Revenue ('000 RMB) 销售收入 (千元)	Profit('000 RMB) (rank) 利润(千元) (排名)	Total assets ('000 RMB) 总资产 (千元)	Major products 主要产品
Zhejiang Yongtong Dyeing & Weaving Group Co., Ltd. 浙江永通染织集团有限公司(1996)	Shaoxing 绍兴市	Zhejiang 浙江省	(0575)4056122 (0575)4055098	5,849	Limited-Liability 有限公司	3,019,951	28,516(11)	1,001,659	Chemical Fiber Cloth 化纤布
Zhejiang Nanfang Group 浙江南方集团(1993)	Shaoxing 绍兴市	Zhejiang 浙江省	(0575)5182188 (0575)5187666	3,906	Private Owned 私营企业	2,006,558	123,407(2)	1,145,985	Chemical Fiber Cloth 化纤布
Shaoxing Rongmao Textile Co., Ltd. 绍兴荣贸纺织有限公司(1999)	Shaoxing 绍兴市	Zhejiang 浙江省	(0575)4094549 (0575)4883223	2,746	Private Owned 私营企业	1,003,048	40,016(7)	1,179,824	Silk Fabric 丝织品
Zhejiang Huzhou Xiaolong Textile Group Co., Ltd. 浙江湖州小龙纺织集团有限公司(1992)	Huzhou 湖州市	Zhejiang 浙江省	(0572)3331120 (0572)3330752	1,438	Overseas Chinese-funded 港澳台资	831,296	45,902(5)	620,768	Silk Fabric 丝织品
Hangzhou Xiangsheng Textile Co., Ltd. 杭州翔盛纺织有限公司(1997)	Hangzhou 杭州市	Zhejiang 浙江省	(0571)82537787 (0571)82523888	1,002	Limited-Liability 有限公司	655,990	33,201(9)	531,111	Chemical Fiber Cloth 化纤布
Zhejiang Xinghui Chemical Fibre Group Co., Ltd. 浙江兴惠化纤集团有限公司(1996)	Hangzhou 杭州市	Zhejiang 浙江省	(0571)82784328 (0571)82784288	995	Limited-Liability 有限公司	516,476	9,623(32)	423,053	Chemical Fiber Cloth 化纤布
Zhejiang Shaoxing Huatian Industrial Group Co., Ltd. 浙江绍兴县华天实业集团公司(2000)	Shaoxing 绍兴市	Zhejiang 浙江省	(0575)4074577 (0575)4081258	1,275	Private Owned 私营企业	458,899	16,603(17)	396,191	Silk Fabric 丝织品
Zhejiang Qingsheng Textile Group Co., Ltd. 浙江庆盛纺织集团有限公司(1995)	Shaoxing 绍兴市	Zhejiang 浙江省	(0575)4509837 (0575)4509715	921	Limited-Liability 有限公司	416,995	36,923(8)	392,627	Chemical Fiber Cloth 化纤布
Jiangsu Wujin Silk Weaving Factory 江苏省武进丝织厂(1984)	Changzhou 常州市	Jiangsu 江苏省	(0519)6701154 (0519)6701152	410	Joint Owned 联营企业	408,950	-	165,980	Silk Fabric 丝织品
Shaoxing Xinghui Textile Co., Ltd. 绍兴兴惠纺织有限公司(1996)	Shaoxing 绍兴市	Zhejiang 浙江省	(0575)4075105 (0575)4881995	1,900	Overseas Chinese-funded 港澳台资	401,017	32,993(10)	585,890	Zou Hemp 邹麻

Top 10 Cities by Revenue 销售收入排名前10位城市	Province 省	Market share 市场份额 (%)	Number of firms 企业个数
Shaoxing 绍兴市	Zhejiang 浙江省	50.45	244
Hangzhou 杭州市	Zhejiang 浙江省	19.44	254
Suzhou 苏州市	Jiangsu 江苏省	11.01	62
Huzhou 湖州市	Zhejiang 浙江省	6.94	120
Jiaxing 嘉兴市	Zhejiang 浙江省	2.10	28
Changzhou 常州市	Jiangsu 江苏省	1.39	5
Yancheng 盐城市	Jiangsu 江苏省	0.83	7
Wuxi 无锡市	Jiangsu 江苏省	0.73	9
Foshan 佛山市	Guangdong 广东省	0.56	11
Nantong 南通市	Jiangsu 江苏省	0.51	12

10 Major Wholesalers 十家主要批发商	City 城市	Province 省	Telephone/Fax 电话/传真
Shanghai Shenda Co.,Ltd. 上海申达股份有限公司	Shanghai 上海市	Shanghai 上海市	(021)62319898 (021)62317250
Orient International Holding Silk Group Corportion 东方国际集团丝绸进出口有限公司	Shanghai 上海市	Shanghai 上海市	(021)64662288 (021)64677788
Nanjing Textiles Import & Export Co.,Ltd. 南京纺织品进出口股份有限公司	Nanjing 南京市	Jiangsu 江苏省	(025)3306789 (025)3300518
Zhejiang Textiles Import & Export Group Co.,Ltd. 浙江省纺织品进出口集团有限公司	Hangzhou 杭州市	Zhejiang 浙江省	(0571)87075888 (0571)87079234
Zhejiang Orient Holdings Co.,Ltd. 浙江东方集团股份有限公司	Hangzhou 杭州市	Zhejiang 浙江省	(0571)87215678 (0571)87215000
Zhejiang Silk Holding Co.,ltd. 浙江省丝绸集团有限公司	Hangzhou 杭州市	Zhejiang 浙江省	(0571)85195588 (0571)85192540
Guangdong Silk (Group) Corporation 广东省丝绸（集团）公司	Guangzhou 广州市	Guangdong 广东省	(020)83337448 (020)83332995
Shanghai Costume Group Co.,Ltd. 上海服装（集团）有限公司	Shanghai 上海市	Shanghai 上海市	(021)62748598 (021)62414773
Orient International Holding Shanghai Textiles Import & Export Co.Ltd. 东方国际集团上海市针织品进出口有限公司	Shanghai 上海市	Shanghai 上海市	(021)63218855 (021)63299560
Jiangsu Textiles Import & Export Group Co.,Ltd. 江苏省纺织品进出口集团股份有限公司	Nanjing 南京市	Jiangsu 江苏省	(025)6895000 (025)4400800

1774: Silk Printing and Dyeing 丝印染业

The industry accounts for 0.107% of the total revenue of China's industrial sector in 2002. The rate of return on assets is 5.22%. 86.01% of all firms in the industry made a profit while 13.99% had negative returns.The top province in terms of the industry's revenue is Zhejiang, accounting for 72.29% of the total revenue.
2002年本行业收入占全行业的 0.107%，资产利润率为 5.22%。86.01%的企业赢利，13.99%的企业亏损。收入最高的省为浙江省，占本行业的72.29%。

	Total number of firms 企业总数	Total number of employees 职工总数	Total revenue (Mil.RMB) 总销售收入 (百万元)	Total profit (Mil.RMB) 总利润 (百万元)	Return on assets 资产利润率 (%)	Return on equity 权益利润率 (%)	Labour productivity ('000 RMB/ worker) 劳动生产率 (千元/人)	Debts/ assets 资产负债率 (%)	Total assets (Mil.RMB) 总资产 (百万元)
Industry Overall 行业总体	193	55,201	11,485	579	5.22	13.60	46.49	61.57	11,081

	Number of firms 企业个数	Average number of employees 平均职工人数	Average revenue ('000 RMB) 平均销售收入（千元）	Average profit ('000 RMB) 平均利润 (千元)	Return on assets 资产利润率 (%)	Return on equity 权益利润率 (%)	Labour productivity ('000 RMB/ worker) 劳动生产率 (千元/人)	Debts/ assets 资产负债率 (%)	Average total assets ('000 RMB) 平均总资产 (千元)
By ownership 产业所有权									
State-owned 国有	11	178	23,974	-2,716	-3.53	-26.55	22.87	86.71	76,956
Collective-owned 集体	19	156	42,005	2,405	7.56	21.35	65.47	64.60	31,828
Foreign & Overseas Chinese Funded 三资	35	304	51,581	2,196	4.27	7.74	40.95	44.87	51,455
By regional distribution 地区分布									
Central-North 华北	8	89	6,221	442	1.95	17.11	22.37	88.57	22,595
Beijing 北京	1	96	6,458	1,170	23.55	34.40	42.20	31.54	4,968
Tianjin 天津	5	93	4,964	86	0.25	3.59	8.10	92.90	33,820
Hebei 河北	2	74	9,244	966	28.88	36.84	54.44	21.61	3,345
Shanxi 山西									
Inner Mongolia 内蒙古									
Northeast 东北	1	200	48,840	250	1.19	1.19	62.40		21,000
Liaoning 辽宁	1	200	48,840	250	1.19	1.19	62.40		21,000
Jilin 吉林									
Heilongjiang 黑龙江									
Central-East 华东	166	311	66,294	3,346	5.51	14.66	47.52	62.41	60,741
Shanghai 上海	12	233	40,426	6,168	10.17	23.94	52.91	57.53	60,667
Jiangsu 江苏	46	297	46,428	148	0.31	1.66	38.47	81.27	47,654
Zhejiang 浙江	105	328	79,077	4,463	6.59	15.42	50.76	57.25	67,697
Anhui 安徽	1	65	4,312	-2	-0.02	-0.03	20.37	20.67	8,316
Fujian 福建									
Jiangxi 江西	1	70	11,800	950	15.82	25.85	50.14	38.81	6,006
Shandong 山东	1	506	64,776	5,157	12.73	24.00	45.01	46.95	40,512
Central-South 中南	16	154	19,934	1,219	2.59	4.80	33.77	46.07	47,147
Henan 河南	3	219	10,246	183	0.41	0.81	13.56	49.00	44,298
Hubei 湖北									
Hunan 湖南									
Guangdong 广东	13	139	22,169	1,458	3.05	5.59	41.13	45.44	47,804
Guangxi 广西									
Hainan 海南									
Southwest 西南	2	140	31,583	46	0.22	0.48	17.90	53.87	20,719
Chongqing 重庆									
Sichuan 四川	2	140	31,583	46	0.22	0.48	17.90	53.87	20,719
Guizhou 贵州									
Yunnan 云南									
Tibet 西藏									
Northwest 西北									
Shaanxi 陕西									
Gansu 甘肃									
Qinghai 青海									
Ningxia 宁夏									
Xinjiang 新疆									

Year 年份	Number of firms 企业个数	Rate of change 变化率 (%)	Number of employees 职工人数 (人)	Rate of change 变化率 (%)	Total revenue (Mil. RMB) 总销售收入 (百万元)	Rate of change 变化率 (%)	Total profit (Mil RMB) 总利润 (百万元)	Rate of change 变化率 (%)
2000	179		57,500		8,855		354	
2001	185	3.35	50,208	-12.68	9,089	2.64	467	31.92
2002	193	4.32	55,201	9.94	11,485	26.36	579	23.98

Major Products 主要产品	Output 产量	Unit 单位
Printed and Dyed Silk Fabric 印染丝织品	272,202	10,000 Meters 万米

10 Main Firms with Maximal Revenue (year founded) 收入最大的十家主要企业（创办年份）	City 城市	Province 省	Telephone/ fax 电话/ 传真	Number of employees 职工人数	Ownership 产业所有权	Revenue ('000 RMB) 销售收入 (千元)	Profit('000 RMB) (rank) 利润(千元) (排名)	Total assets ('000 RMB) 总资产 (千元)	Major products 主要产品
Zhejiang Yatai High Technology Co., Ltd.	Shaoxing	Zhejiang	(0575)5652689		Joint Stock				Printing & Dyeing Chemical Fiber Cloth
浙江亚太高科股份有限公司(1999)	绍兴市	浙江省	(0575)5654274	1,280	股份制	800,720	50,517(3)	769,098	印染化纤布
Shaoxing Huayu Printing & Dyeing Textile Co., Ltd.	Shaoxing	Zhejiang	(0575)4880777		Limited-Liability				Printing & Dyeing Cloth
绍兴华宇印染纺织有限公司(1996)	绍兴市	浙江省	(0575)4882198	1,587	有限公司	518,050	90,840(1)	550,630	印染布
Yingxiang Chemical Fibre Group Co., Ltd.	Suzhou	Jiangsu	(0512)63555588		Limited-Liability				Chemical Fibre
鹰翔化纤有限责任公司(1999)	苏州市	江苏省	(0512)63554265	2,790	有限公司	504,016	2,266(44)	574,332	化学纤维
Zhejiang Huagang Dyeing & Weaving Co., Ltd.	Shaoxing	Zhejiang	(0575)4881552		Limited-Liability				Printing & Dyeing Silk
浙江华港染织有限公司(1965)	绍兴市	浙江省	(0575)4881156	1,200	有限公司	500,462	40,830(5)	233,260	印染丝
Zhejiang Jishan Enterprise Group Co., Ltd.	Shaoxing	Zhejiang	(0575)4022668		Limited-Liability				Silk
浙江稽山企业集团公司(1994)	绍兴市	浙江省	(0575)4021130	1,219	有限公司	490,564	45,071(4)	217,425	丝绸
Zhejiang Fuqiang Industrial Group Co., Ltd.	Shaoxing	Zhejiang	(0575)4021111		Limited-Liability				Printing & Dyeing Cloth
浙江富强实业集团有限公司(1995)	绍兴市	浙江省	(0575)4021178	1,287	有限公司	480,516	23,658(7)	246,332	印染布
Zhejiang Tianma Printing & Dyeing Co., Ltd.	Shaoxing	Zhejiang	(0575)5629825		Overseas Chinese-funded				Printing & Dyeing Cloth
浙江天马印染有限公司(1993)	绍兴市	浙江省	(0575)5101074	2,221	港澳台资	449,824	29,811(6)	477,720	印染布
Shanghai Tiqiao Weaving & Yarn Dyeing Co., Ltd.	Shanghai	Shanghai	(021)64292434		Private Owned				Printing & Dyeing Cloth
上海题桥纺织染纱有限公司(1997)	上海市	上海市	(021)64291058	718	私营企业	257,778	72,507(2)	362,568	印染布
Shaoxing Hongfu Industrial Co.,Ltd.	Shaoxing	Zhejiang	(0575)4021426		Limited-Liability				Printing & Dyeing Silk Fabric
绍兴县宏福实业有限公司(1994)	绍兴市	浙江省	(0575)4027656	480	有限公司	175,381	8,158(17)	89,294	印染丝织品
Jiangwu Shenghong Printing & Dyeing Co., Ltd.	Suzhou	Jiangsu	(0512)63562523		Private Owned				Printing & Dyeing Silk Fabric
吴江市盛虹印染有限公司(1992)	苏州市	江苏省	(0512)63505823	1,000	私营企业	152,890	5,842(23)	171,700	印染丝织品

Top 10 Cities by Revenue 销售收入排名前10位城市	Province 省	Market share 市场份额 (%)	Number of firms 企业个数
Shaoxing 绍兴市	Zhejiang 浙江省	58.04	55
Suzhou 苏州市	Jiangsu 江苏省	15.87	37
Hangzhou 杭州市	Zhejiang 浙江省	6.35	26
Shanghai 上海市	Shanghai 上海市	4.22	12
Huzhou 湖州市	Zhejiang 浙江省	4.09	14
Jiaxing 嘉兴市	Zhejiang 浙江省	2.73	8
Wuxi 无锡市	Jiangsu 江苏省	1.39	2
Guangzhou 广州市	Guangdong 广东省	0.99	5
Ningbo 宁波市	Zhejiang 浙江省	0.79	1
Changzhou 常州市	Jiangsu 江苏省	0.58	3

10 Major Wholesalers 十家主要批发商	City 城市	Province 省	Telephone/Fax 电话/传真
Shanghai Shenda Co.,Ltd.	Shanghai	Shanghai	(021)62319898
上海申达股份有限公司	上海市	上海市	(021)62317250
Orient International Holding Silk Group Corportion	Shanghai	Shanghai	(021)64662288
东方国际集团丝绸进出口有限公司	上海市	上海市	(021)64677788
Nanjing Textiles Import & Export Co.,Ltd.	Nanjing	Jiangsu	(025)3306789
南京纺织品进出口股份有限公司	南京市	江苏省	(025)3300518
Zhejiang Textiles Import & Export Group Co.,Ltd.	Hangzhou	Zhejiang	(0571)87075888
浙江省纺织品进出口集团有限公司	杭州市	浙江省	(0571)87079234
Zhejiang Orient Holdings Co.,Ltd.	Hangzhou	Zhejiang	(0571)87215678
浙江东方集团股份有限公司	杭州市	浙江省	(0571)87215000
Zhejiang Silk Holding Co.,ltd.	Hangzhou	Zhejiang	(0571)85195588
浙江省丝绸集团有限公司	杭州市	浙江省	(0571)85192540
Guangdong Silk (Group) Corporation	Guangzhou	Guangdong	(020)83337448
广东省丝绸（集团）公司	广州市	广东省	(020)83332995
Shanghai Costume Group Co.,Ltd.	Shanghai	Shanghai	(021)62748598
上海服装（集团）有限公司	上海市	上海市	(021)62414773
Orient International Holding Shanghai Textiles Import & Export Co.Ltd.	Shanghai	Shanghai	(021)63218855
东方国际集团上海市针织品进出口有限公司	上海市	上海市	(021)63299560
Jiangsu Textiles Import & Export Group Co.,Ltd.	Nanjing	Jiangsu	(025)6895000
江苏省纺织品进出口集团股份有限公司	南京市	江苏省	(025)4400800

1775: Silk Products 丝制品业

The industry accounts for 0.030% of the total revenue of China's industrial sector in 2002. The rate of return on assets is 6.16%. 81.13% of all firms in the industry made a profit while 18.87% had negative returns.The top province in terms of the industry's revenue is Zhejiang, accounting for 42.85% of the total revenue.
2002年本行业收入占全行业的 0.030%，资产利润率为 6.16%。81.13%的企业赢利，18.87%的企业亏损。收入最高的省为浙江省，占本行业的42.85%。

	Total number of firms 企业总数	Total number of employees 职工总数	Total revenue (Mil.RMB) 总销售收入（百万元）	Total profit (Mil.RMB) 总利润（百万元）	Return on assets 资产利润率 (%)	Return on equity 权益利润率 (%)	Labour productivity ('000 RMB/ worker) 劳动生产率（千元/人）	Debts/ assets 资产负债率 (%)	Total assets (Mil.RMB) 总资产（百万元）
Industry Overall 行业总体	106	19,881	3,239	179	6.16	15.50	40.69	60.26	2,898

	Number of firms 企业个数	Average number of employees 平均职工人数	Average revenue ('000 RMB) 平均销售收入（千元）	Average profit ('000 RMB) 平均利润（千元）	Return on assets 资产利润率 (%)	Return on equity 权益利润率 (%)	Labour productivity ('000 RMB/ worker) 劳动生产率（千元/人）	Debts/ assets 资产负债率 (%)	Average total assets ('000 RMB) 平均总资产（千元）
By ownership 产业所有权									
State-owned 国有	4	113	553	-260	-2.10	-12.35	17.25	83.01	12,392
Collective-owned 集体	8	171	20,719	1,081	10.85	43.57	43.96	75.09	9,959
Foreign & Overseas Chinese Funded 三资	41	170	38,556	2,690	7.73	20.39	54.83	62.09	34,801
By regional distribution 地区分布									
Central-North 华北	6	56	6,571	477	4.79	16.33	49.70	70.64	9,941
Beijing 北京	1	27	13,809	2,658	25.41	45.30	110.63	43.90	10,460
Tianjin 天津	3	43	6,102	264	2.04	11.10	81.62	81.60	12,909
Hebei 河北	2	89	3,656	-295	-5.64	-13.06	17.32	56.80	5,229
Shanxi 山西									
Inner Mongolia 内蒙古									
Northeast 东北	1	200	6,790	-110	-0.48	-18.64	14.98	97.42	22,860
Liaoning 辽宁	1	200	6,790	-110	-0.48	-18.64	14.98	97.42	22,860
Jilin 吉林									
Heilongjiang 黑龙江									
Central-East 华东	81	155	27,116	1,589	7.43	17.36	42.23	57.19	21,381
Shanghai 上海	3	101	23,703	1,383	12.70	22.74	67.83	44.14	10,888
Jiangsu 江苏	17	236	30,163	2,382	10.40	23.05	30.67	54.90	22,908
Zhejiang 浙江	48	134	28,911	1,865	8.47	19.84	47.97	57.29	22,014
Anhui 安徽	3	95	9,566	15	0.11	0.15	66.70	24.01	13,419
Fujian 福建	2	92	23,149	-381	-7.07	-8.94	58.17	20.95	5,389
Jiangxi 江西	2	32	3,019	248	27.68	44.09	52.05	37.22	896
Shandong 山东	6	212	23,956	-873	-2.62	-9.35	35.36	72.03	33,384
Central-South 中南	10	173	22,339	-1,174	-6.13		31.95	139.75	19,132
Henan 河南	2	63	2,247	-8	-0.05	-0.08	10.70	38.25	14,989
Hubei 湖北	2	234	38,203	963	23.09	91.54	64.01	74.78	4,169
Hunan 湖南	1	20	568	-415	-17.13	-74.11	4.60	76.88	2,422
Guangdong 广东	4	226	33,182	-3,327	-9.10		24.45	168.34	36,542
Guangxi 广西	1	210	9,191	77	1.74	2.89	8.01	39.61	4,418
Hainan 海南									
Southwest 西南	8	637	96,611	7,350	6.59	12.56	40.28	47.54	111,594
Chongqing 重庆	2	376	1,593	-142	-0.59	-1.78	1.18	66.67	23,841
Sichuan 四川	6	725	128,284	9,848	6.99	13.06	47.04	46.46	140,845
Guizhou 贵州									
Yunnan 云南									
Tibet 西藏									
Northwest 西北									
Shaanxi 陕西									
Gansu 甘肃									
Qinghai 青海									
Ningxia 宁夏									
Xinjiang 新疆									

1775: Silk Products 丝制品业

Year 年份	Number of firms 企业个数	Rate of change 变化率 (%)	Number of employees 职工人数 (人)	Rate of change 变化率 (%)	Total revenue (Mil. RMB) 总销售收入 (百万元)	Rate of change 变化率 (%)	Total profit (Mil RMB) 总利润 (百万元)	Rate of change 变化率 (%)
2000	108		18,262		2,625		94	
2001	118	9.26	20,028	9.67	3,346	27.47	-44	-
2002	106	-10.17	19,881	-0.73	3,239	-3.20	179	-

Major Products 主要产品	Output 产量	Unit 单位
Silk Fabric 丝织品	534,145	10,000 Meters 万米

10 Main Firms with Maximal Revenue (year founded) 收入最大的十家主要企业 (创办年份)	City 城市	Province 省	Telephone/fax 电话/传真	Number of employees 职工人数	Ownership 产业所有权	Revenue ('000 RMB) 销售收入 (千元)	Profit('000 RMB) (rank) 利润(千元) (排名)	Total assets ('000 RMB) 总资产 (千元)	Major products 主要产品
Chengdu Tianyou Development Co., Ltd.	Chengdu	Sichuan	(028)85066666		Private Owned				Silk
成都天友发展有限公司(1992)	成都市	四川省	(028)85065555	2,200	私营企业	555,580	53,067(1)	497,651	丝
Zhejiang Jintianlai Necktie & Garment Co., Ltd.	Shaoxing	Zhejiang	(0575)3047161		Foreign Funded				Necktie
浙江金天来领带服饰有限公司(1993)	绍兴市	浙江省	(0575)3047160	458	外商投资	139,933	25,565(2)	124,978	领带
Hangzhou Gang'an Thread Making Co., Ltd.	Hangzhou	Zhejiang	(0571)63872802		Overseas Chinese-funded				Computer Embroidery Thread
杭州港安制线有限公司(1993)	杭州市	浙江省	(0571)63872422	368	港澳台资	138,401	11,815(5)	79,637	电脑绣花线
Shaoxing Jili Necktie Weaving Co., ltd.	Shaoxing	Zhejiang	(0575)3046666		Foreign Funded				Necktie
绍兴吉利领带织造有限公司(1999)	绍兴市	浙江省	(0575)3349621	320	外商投资	134,570	15,900(4)	81,790	领带
Jiaxing Idea Silk Co., Ltd.	Jiaxing	Zhejiang	(0573)2200422		Foreign Funded				Twisting Silk
嘉兴埃迪尔丝绸有限公司(1994)	嘉兴市	浙江省	(0573)2201324	332	外商投资	115,533	4,384(11)	184,573	捻线丝
Sichuan Yibin Huimei Thread Co., Ltd.	Yibin	Sichuan	(0831)2332981		Overseas Chinese-funded				Grey Thread
四川省宜宾惠美线业有限责任公司(2001)	宜宾市	四川省	(0831)2400410	923	港澳台资	91,284	5,181(7)	170,908	白坯线
Sichuan EW Textiles Co.,ltd.	Nanchong	Sichuan	(0817)3661914		Foreign Funded				Silk Fabric
四川依格尔纺织品有限公司(1993)	南充市	四川省	(0817)3661553	700	外商投资	78,300	230(48)	108,000	丝织品
Deqing Zili Thin Silk Spinning Co., Ltd.	Huzhou	Zhejiang	(0572)8475163		Limited-Liability				Silk Fabric
德清县自立绢纺织造有限公司(1997)	湖州市	浙江省	(0572)8475231	154	有限公司	56,193	585(33)	49,118	丝织品
Shengzhou Xinlida Costume & Necktie Co., Ltd.	Shaoxing	Zhejiang	(0575)3041686		Foreign Funded				Necktie
嵊州市鑫利达服装领带有限公司(1993)	绍兴市	浙江省	(0575)3041766	140	外商投资	55,316	4,732(9)	32,890	领带
Wuxi New Xinjinmao Chemical Fibre Co., Ltd.	Wuxi	Jiangsu	(0510)5219698		Foreign Funded				Imitated Chemical Fibre
无锡新金贸化纤有限公司(1999)	无锡市	江苏省	(0510)5211698	200	外商投资	54,200	6,690(6)	22,050	仿真化学纤维

Top 10 Cities by Revenue 销售收入排名前10位城市	Province 省	Market share 市场份额 (%)	Number of firms 企业个数
Shaoxing 绍兴市	Zhejiang 浙江省	20.79	22
Chengdu 成都市	Sichuan 四川省	17.15	1
Hangzhou 杭州市	Zhejiang 浙江省	8.06	7
Jiaxing 嘉兴市	Zhejiang 浙江省	6.50	8
Suzhou 苏州市	Jiangsu 江苏省	6.50	8
Nantong 南通市	Jiangsu 江苏省	4.91	4
Ningbo 宁波市	Zhejiang 浙江省	3.88	4
Shenzhen 深圳市	Guangdong 广东省	3.65	2
Nanchong 南充市	Sichuan 四川省	3.20	2
Huzhou 湖州市	Zhejiang 浙江省	3.12	4

10 Major Wholesalers 十家主要批发商	City 城市	Province 省	Telephone/Fax 电话/传真
Shanghai Shenda Co.,Ltd.	Shanghai	Shanghai	(021)62319898
上海申达股份有限公司	上海市	上海市	(021)62317250
Orient International Holding Silk Group Corportion	Shanghai	Shanghai	(021)64662288
东方国际集团丝绸进出口有限公司	上海市	上海市	(021)64677788
Nanjing Textiles Import & Export Co.,Ltd.	Nanjing	Jiangsu	(025)3306789
南京纺织品进出口股份有限公司	南京市	江苏省	(025)3300518
Zhejiang Textiles Import & Export Group Co.,Ltd.	Hangzhou	Zhejiang	(0571)87075888
浙江省纺织品进出口集团有限公司	杭州市	浙江省	(0571)87079234
Zhejiang Orient Holdings Co.,Ltd.	Hangzhou	Zhejiang	(0571)87215678
浙江东方集团股份有限公司	杭州市	浙江省	(0571)87215000
Zhejiang Silk Holding Co.,ltd.	Hangzhou	Zhejiang	(0571)85195588
浙江省丝绸集团有限公司	杭州市	浙江省	(0571)85192540
Guangdong Silk (Group) Corporation	Guangzhou	Guangdong	(020)83337448
广东省丝绸(集团)公司	广州市	广东省	(020)83332995
Shanghai Costume Group Co.,Ltd.	Shanghai	Shanghai	(021)62748598
上海服装(集团)有限公司	上海市	上海市	(021)62414773
Orient International Holding Shanghai Textiles Import & Export Co.Ltd.	Shanghai	Shanghai	(021)63218855
东方国际集团上海市针织品进出口有限公司	上海市	上海市	(021)63299560
Jiangsu Textiles Import & Export Group Co.,Ltd.	Nanjing	Jiangsu	(025)6895000
江苏省纺织品进出口集团股份有限公司	南京市	江苏省	(025)4400800

1779: Other Silk Fabrics 其他丝绢纺织业

The industry accounts for 0.014% of the total revenue of China's industrial sector in 2002. The rate of return on assets is 0.83%. 71.43% of all firms in the industry made a profit while 28.57% had negative returns.The top province in terms of the industry's revenue is Zhejiang, accounting for 52.21% of the total revenue.
2002年本行业收入占全行业的 0.014%，资产利润率为 0.83%。71.43%的企业赢利，28.57%的企业亏损。收入最高的省为浙江省，占本行业的52.21%。

	Total number of firms 企业总数	Total number of employees 职工总数	Total revenue (Mil.RMB) 总销售收入 (百万元)	Total profit (Mil.RMB) 总利润 (百万元)	Return on assets 资产利润率 (%)	Return on equity 权益利润率 (%)	Labour productivity ('000 RMB/ worker) 劳动生产率 (千元/人)	Debts/ assets 资产负债率 (%)	Total assets (Mil.RMB) 总资产 (百万元)
Industry Overall 行业总体	49	6,718	1,473	10	0.83	2.12	50.96	60.98	1,251

	Number of firms 企业个数	Average number of employees 平均职工人数	Average revenue ('000 RMB) 平均销售收入 (千元)	Average profit ('000 RMB) 平均利润 (千元)	Return on assets 资产利润率 (%)	Return on equity 权益利润率 (%)	Labour productivity ('000 RMB/ worker) 劳动生产率 (千元/人)	Debts/ assets 资产负债率 (%)	Average total assets ('000 RMB) 平均总资产 (千元)
By ownership 产业所有权									
State-owned 国有	2	7	228	-10	-9.18	-15.20	12.64	39.61	104
Collective-owned 集体	2	97	24,125	2,575	43.68	91.17	84.69	52.09	5,895
Foreign & Overseas Chinese Funded 三资	13	138	23,192	-1,326	-3.06	-6.33	39.62	51.60	43,279
By regional distribution 地区分布									
Central-North 华北	1	36	6,330	380	24.68	27.34	40.83	9.74	1,540
Beijing 北京									
Tianjin 天津	1	36	6,330	380	24.68	27.34	40.83	9.74	1,540
Hebei 河北									
Shanxi 山西									
Inner Mongolia 内蒙古									
Northeast 东北	1	180	27,228	194	0.31	0.36	16.09	15.63	63,160
Liaoning 辽宁									
Jilin 吉林									
Heilongjiang 黑龙江	1	180	27,228	194	0.31	0.36	16.09	15.63	63,160
Central-East 华东	36	145	35,026	880	3.89	10.97	56.83	64.51	22,603
Shanghai 上海									
Jiangsu 江苏	14	76	11,717	-162	-1.63	-6.05	47.05	73.09	9,952
Zhejiang 浙江	16	160	48,069	594	1.93	7.11	53.52	72.91	30,815
Anhui 安徽									
Fujian 福建									
Jiangxi 江西									
Shandong 山东	6	266	54,635	4,077	13.49	20.78	68.66	35.10	30,225
Central-South 中南	11	116	16,241	-1,991	-5.88	-15.15	32.10	61.16	33,846
Henan 河南	2	38	4,195	461	12.12	12.12	34.49		3,800
Hubei 湖北									
Hunan 湖南	1	14	456	-19	-9.18	-15.20	12.64	39.61	207
Guangdong 广东	8	148	21,226	-2,850	-6.26	-16.66	32.18	62.45	45,562
Guangxi 广西									
Hainan 海南									
Southwest 西南									
Chongqing 重庆									
Sichuan 四川									
Guizhou 贵州									
Yunnan 云南									
Tibet 西藏									
Northwest 西北									
Shaanxi 陕西									
Gansu 甘肃									
Qinghai 青海									
Ningxia 宁夏									
Xinjiang 新疆									

1779: Other Silk Fabrics 其他丝绸纺织业

Year 年份	Number of firms 企业个数	Rate of change 变化率 (%)	Number of employees 职工人数 (人)	Rate of change 变化率 (%)	Total revenue (Mil. RMB) 总销售收入 (百万元)	Rate of change 变化率 (%)	Total profit (Mil RMB) 总利润 (百万元)	Rate of change 变化率 (%)
2000	41		9,070		1,248		7	
2001	47	14.63	8,412	-7.25	1,517	21.55	-34	-
2002	49	4.26	6,718	-20.14	1,473	-2.90	10	-

Major Products 主要产品	Output 产量	Unit 单位

10 Main Firms with Maximal Revenue (year founded) 收入最大的十家主要企业（创办年份）	City 城市	Province 省	Telephone/fax 电话/传真	Number of employees 职工人数	Ownership 产业所有权	Revenue ('000 RMB) 销售收入 (千元)	Profit('000 RMB) (rank) 利润(千元) (排名)	Total assets ('000 RMB) 总资产 (千元)	Major products 主要产品
Hangzhou Xiaoshan Daodao Chemical Fibre Co., Ltd.	Hangzhou	Zhejiang	(0571)82162264		Private Owned				Terylene Fiber
杭州萧山道道化纤有限公司(1998)	杭州市	浙江省	(0571)82162264	383	私营企业	336,551	6,499(2)	94,846	涤纶丝
Hangzhou Dongnan Wool Spinning & Dyeing Co., Ltd.	Hangzhou	Zhejiang	(0571)82161526		Private Owned				POY Silk
杭州东南毛纺织染整有限公司(1995)	杭州市	浙江省	(0571)82161526	140	私营企业	123,121	2,215(4)	161,154	POY丝
Zhejiang Kenking Industrial Co., Ltd.	Shaoxing	Zhejiang	(0575)6024902		Limited-Liability				Pure Terylene Sewing Thread
浙江耿基实业有限公司(1980)	绍兴市	浙江省	(0575)6022155	480	有限公司	78,955	-	71,080	纯涤纶缝纫线
Qingdao Zhongtai Synthetic Fabric Co.,ltd.	Qingdao	Shandong	(0532)6898363		Limited-Liability				Chemical Fibre Embryo Silk
青岛中泰化纤丝绸有限责仁公司(1998)	青岛市	山东省	(0532)6895654	380	有限公司	71,373	75(23)	80,088	化纤胚绸
Shandou F.T.Z. Zhongwang Synthetic Fibre Co., Ltd.	Shantou	Guangdong	(0754)7590109		Overseas Chinese-funded				Chemical Fibre
汕头保税区中旺化纤有限公司(1997)	汕头市	广东省	(0754)7593054	100	港澳台资	57,733	-	254,340	化纤
Hangzhou Haodi Plastic Textile Co., Ltd.	Hangzhou	Zhejiang	(0571)86182017		Overseas Chinese-funded				Cases & Bags Cloth
杭州豪迪塑胶纺织有限公司(1996)	杭州市	浙江省	(0571)86182216	150	港澳台资	42,730	660(9)	29,650	箱包布
Jiaxing Tongjiang Quilt Co., Ltd.	Jiaxing	Zhejiang	(0573)8332139		Overseas Chinese-funded				Bedclothes
嘉兴桐江被服有限公司(1993)	嘉兴市	浙江省	(0573)8332203	263	港澳台资	38,310	720(8)	12,970	床上用品
Nanhai Shishan Gaodali Textiles Co., Ltd.	Foshan	Guangdong	(0757)6688638		Limited-Liability				
南海市狮山高达利纺织品有限公司(2001)	佛山市	广东省	(0757)6688611	370	有限公司	27,934	-	35,989	
Deqing Jingzhe Moganshan Acrilan Factory	Huzhou	Zhejiang	(0572)8081128		Joint Owned				Polypropylene Fibre Filament
德清县京浙莫干山丙纶厂(1991)	湖州市	浙江省	(0572)8080902	119	联营企业	20,677	49(26)	18,589	丙纶丝
Weihai Hengli Fabric Co., Ltd.	Weihai	Shandong	(0631)5321268		Foreign Funded				Silk
威海恒利织物有限公司(1996)	威海市	山东省	(0631)5221268	180	外商投资	20,571	-	27,223	真丝绸

Top 10 Cities by Revenue 销售收入排名前10位城市	Province 省	Market share 市场份额 (%)	Number of firms 企业个数
Hangzhou 杭州市	Zhejiang 浙江省	36.27	6
Weihai 威海市	Shandong 山东省	14.10	3
Suzhou 苏州市	Jiangsu 江苏省	7.55	8
Huzhou 湖州市	Zhejiang 浙江省	6.19	5
Shaoxing 绍兴市	Zhejiang 浙江省	5.36	1
Qingdao 青岛市	Shandong 山东省	4.84	1
Jiaxing 嘉兴市	Zhejiang 浙江省	4.38	4
Shantou 汕头市	Guangdong 广东省	3.92	1
Guangzhou 广州市	Guangdong 广东省	2.92	3
Jinan 济南市	Shandong 山东省	2.60	1

10 Major Wholesalers 十家主要批发商	City 城市	Province 省	Telephone/Fax 电话/传真
Shanghai Shenda Co.,Ltd.	Shanghai	Shanghai	(021)62319898
上海申达股份有限公司	上海市	上海市	(021)62317250
Orient International Holding Silk Group Corportion	Shanghai	Shanghai	(021)64662288
东方国际集团丝绸进出口有限公司	上海市	上海市	(021)64677788
Nanjing Textiles Import & Export Co.,Ltd.	Nanjing	Jiangsu	(025)3306789
南京纺织品进出口股份有限公司	南京市	江苏省	(025)3300518
Zhejiang Textiles Import & Export Group Co.,Ltd.	Hangzhou	Zhejiang	(0571)87075888
浙江省纺织品进出口集团有限公司	杭州市	浙江省	(0571)87079234
Zhejiang Orient Holdings Co.,Ltd.	Hangzhou	Zhejiang	(0571)87215678
浙江东方集团股份有限公司	杭州市	浙江省	(0571)87215000
Zhejiang Silk Holding Co.,ltd.	Hangzhou	Zhejiang	(0571)85195588
浙江省丝绸集团有限公司	杭州市	浙江省	(0571)85192540
Guangdong Silk (Group) Corporation	Guangzhou	Guangdong	(020)83337448
广东省丝绸（集团）公司	广州市	广东省	(020)83332995
Shanghai Costume Group Co.,Ltd.	Shanghai	Shanghai	(021)62748598
上海服装（集团）有限公司	上海市	上海市	(021)62414773
Orient International Holding Shanghai Textiles Import & Export Co.Ltd.	Shanghai	Shanghai	(021)63218855
东方国际集团上海市针织品进出口有限公司	上海市	上海市	(021)63299560
Jiangsu Textiles Import & Export Group Co.,Ltd.	Nanjing	Jiangsu	(025)6895000
江苏省纺织品进出口集团股份有限公司	南京市	江苏省	(025)4400800

1781: Cotton Knitwear 棉针织品业

The industry accounts for 0.350% of the total revenue of China's industrial sector in 2002. The rate of return on assets is 3.16%. 79.90% of all firms in the industry made a profit while 20.10% had negative returns.The top province in terms of the industry's revenue is Guangdong, accounting for 24.60% of the total revenue.
2002年本行业收入占全行业的0.350%，资产利润率为3.16%。79.90%的企业赢利，20.10%的企业亏损。收入最高的省为广东省，占本行业的24.60%。

	Total number of firms 企业总数	Total number of employees 职工总数	Total revenue (Mil.RMB) 总销售收入(百万元)	Total profit (Mil.RMB) 总利润(百万元)	Return on assets 资产利润率(%)	Return on equity 权益利润率(%)	Labour productivity ('000 RMB/ worker) 劳动生产率(千元/人)	Debts/ assets 资产负债率(%)	Total assets (Mil.RMB) 总资产(百万元)
Industry Overall 行业总体	1204	291,143	37,571	1,194	3.16	8.60	35.53	63.26	37,815

	Number of firms 企业个数	Average number of employees 平均职工人数	Average revenue ('000 RMB) 平均销售收入（千元）	Average profit ('000 RMB) 平均利润(千元)	Return on assets 资产利润率(%)	Return on equity 权益利润率(%)	Labour productivity ('000 RMB/ worker) 劳动生产率(千元/人)	Debts/ assets 资产负债率(%)	Average total assets ('000 RMB) 平均总资产(千元)
By ownership 产业所有权									
State-owned 国有	98	283	14,905	-288	-0.67	-28.03	13.09	97.63	43,293
Collective-owned 集体	104	227	29,327	1,479	6.50	21.37	33.64	69.57	22,740
Foreign & Overseas Chinese Funded 三资	408	260	39,679	958	2.48	5.35	44.24	53.63	38,648
By regional distribution 地区分布									
Central-North 华北	83	232	18,360	752	1.76	7.47	30.41	76.44	42,751
Beijing 北京	16	227	33,925	1,075	1.70	3.35	85.17	49.17	63,092
Tianjin 天津	34	236	18,333	1,487	4.17	24.64	19.80	83.07	35,644
Hebei 河北	26	186	11,624	-78	-0.32	-2.97	20.31	89.30	24,592
Shanxi 山西	6	305	4,318	-282	-0.29	-42.64	5.08	99.31	96,420
Inner Mongolia 内蒙古	1	944	29,598	-1,619	-1.48	-3.58	10.31	58.49	109,065
Northeast 东北	46	306	20,649	-477	-1.19	-3.92	30.33	69.76	40,175
Liaoning 辽宁	32	287	19,288	-38	-0.11	-0.25	20.25	56.93	35,501
Jilin 吉林	11	414	28,487	-1,713	-2.80	-46.72	51.94	94.01	61,263
Heilongjiang 黑龙江	3	119	6,435	-623	-4.91	-6.41	13.68	23.44	12,698
Central-East 华东	755	236	32,478	1,340	4.59	11.68	36.52	60.67	29,154
Shanghai 上海	100	244	35,640	1,524	3.57	8.70	35.27	58.95	42,685
Jiangsu 江苏	193	230	32,179	790	3.73	11.45	36.82	67.44	21,182
Zhejiang 浙江	251	190	28,418	1,823	7.15	16.18	35.68	55.80	25,484
Anhui 安徽	15	299	13,901	180	1.00	2.93	12.66	66.00	18,054
Fujian 福建	62	179	16,259	206	0.92	1.50	31.99	38.91	22,406
Jiangxi 江西	36	275	20,393	491	2.85	11.35	20.08	74.86	17,214
Shandong 山东	98	370	57,781	2,204	4.34	13.09	46.91	66.84	50,801
Central-South 中南	289	236	35,560	506	1.54	4.06	39.53	61.93	32,740
Henan 河南	36	227	16,786	389	2.42	22.07	16.15	89.01	16,033
Hubei 湖北	19	168	9,891	-395	-2.65	-12.27	28.11	78.36	14,895
Hunan 湖南	13	308	16,973	227	1.95	129.67	17.79	98.50	11,623
Guangdong 广东	217	242	42,585	634	1.64	3.96	45.57	58.65	38,705
Guangxi 广西	3	97	4,097	-218	-2.12		35.74	119.83	10,255
Hainan 海南	1	100	10,688	-193	-0.93	-2.25	26.30	58.87	20,858
Southwest 西南	12	178	9,796	43	0.19	0.51	26.88	62.46	22,521
Chongqing 重庆	2	120	3,411	-717	-3.79		5.21	127.75	18,890
Sichuan 四川	6	137	14,902	242	1.08	2.66	58.69	59.31	22,387
Guizhou 贵州	3	24		-299	-6.32		-2.81	151.24	4,736
Yunnan 云南	1	1,006	21,316	1,391	1.66	2.15	8.32	23.09	83,947
Tibet 西藏									
Northwest 西北	19	488	9,574	-231	-0.65	-3.20	7.68	79.70	35,506
Shaanxi 陕西	8	301	5,746	-406	-1.60	-16.69	7.00	90.41	25,382
Gansu 甘肃	8	594	7,957	15	0.07	0.11	5.19	36.18	21,514
Qinghai 青海									
Ningxia 宁夏									
Xinjiang 新疆	3	702	24,094	-419	-0.42	-16.47	14.07	97.45	99,817

Year 年份	Number of firms 企业个数	Rate of change 变化率(%)	Number of employees 职工人数(人)	Rate of change 变化率(%)	Total revenue (Mil. RMB) 总销售收入(百万元)	Rate of change 变化率(%)	Total profit (Mil RMB) 总利润(百万元)	Rate of change 变化率(%)
2000	863		236,065		25,816		566	
2001	998	15.64	263,056	11.43	31,433	21.76	1,046	84.81
2002	1204	20.64	291,143	10.68	37,571	19.53	1,194	14.15

Major Products 主要产品	Output 产量	Unit 单位
Knitted Clothing 针织服装	409,076	10,000 Pieces 万件

10 Main Firms with Maximal Revenue (year founded) 收入最大的十家主要企业（创办年份）	City 城市	Province 省	Telephone/fax 电话/传真	Number of employees 职工人数	Ownership 产业所有权	Revenue ('000 RMB) 销售收入(千元)	Profit('000 RMB) (rank) 利润(千元)(排名)	Total assets ('000 RMB) 总资产(千元)	Major products 主要产品
Qingdao Jifa Group Co., Ltd.	Qingdao	Shandong	(0532)8513493		Joint Stock				Knitting Underwear
青岛即发集团股份有限公司(1997)	青岛市	山东省	(0532)8514298	3,646	股份制	1,778,101	107,804(1)	1,198,385	针织内衣
Hutai (Panyu) Textile Printing & Dyeing Co.,Ltd.	Guangzhou	Guangdong	(020)84948868		Overseas Chinese-funded				Knitting Cloth
互太(番禺)纺织印染有限公司(1997)	广州市	广东省	(020)84946959	2,500	港澳台资	853,994	7,789(33)	663,871	针织布
Guangdong Exquel Knitters Co., Ltd.	Foshan	Guangdong	(0757)8682222		Overseas Chinese-funded				Textiles
广东溢达针织有限公司(1994)	佛山市	广东省	(0757)8681510	1,652	港澳台资	617,560	10,294(25)	368,254	纺织品
Shanghai NO.9 Knitting Factory	Shanghai	Shanghai	(021)63737888		Joint Stock				Knitting Cotton Textile
上海针织九厂(1958)	上海市	上海市	(021)63852936	4,279	股份制	616,547	52,062(3)	1,328,850	针棉织品
Zhejiang Gabriel Industrial Textile Co.,ltd.	Shaoxing	Zhejiang	(0575)4571788		Private Owned				Knitting & Spinning Products
浙江加佰利纺织实业有限公司(2001)	绍兴市	浙江省	(0575)4571787	1,680	私营企业	605,291	66,381(2)	841,158	针纺织品
Guangdong Guanhua Knitting Works Co., Ltd.	Jiangmen	Guangdong	(0750)6462168		Overseas Chinese-funded				Knitting Cloth
广东省新会冠华针织厂有限公司(1992)	江门市	广东省	(0750)6462398	1,554	港澳台资	593,688	743(328)	364,749	针织布
Dongguan Minghai Dyeing Works Co., Ltd.	Dongguan	Guangdong	(0769)8835171		Overseas Chinese-funded				Colored Cloth
东莞明海整染厂有限公司(1995)	东莞市	广东省	(0769)8833388	1,118	港澳台资	417,612	6,540(43)	168,276	色布
Zhaoyuan Knitting Works Co., Ltd.	Yantai	Shandong	(0535)8216238		Collective-owned				Knitting Cotton Textile
招远市针织厂有限公司(1986)	烟台市	山东省	(0535)8211884	1,631	集体企业	309,980	4,010(92)	479,522	针棉织品
Qingdao Huajin Group Co., Ltd.	Qingdao	Shandong	(0532)3833085		Joint Stock				Knitting Sweater & Trousers
青岛华金集团股份有限公司(1997)	青岛市	山东省	(0532)3833085	1,101	股份制	266,835	6,870(39)	355,779	针织衫裤
Jiangsu Aoxing Knitted Dress Factory	Nantong	Jiangsu	(0513)3688186		Private Owned				Costume
江苏澳兴针织服装厂(1979)	南通市	江苏省	(0513)3688925	900	私营企业	237,978	6,250(47)	80,751	服装

Top 10 Cities by Revenue 销售收入排名前10位城市	Province 省	Market share 市场份额 (%)	Number of firms 企业个数
Shanghai 上海市	Shanghai 上海市	9.49	100
Qingdao 青岛市	Shandong 山东省	8.96	41
Guangzhou 广州市	Guangdong 广东省	7.88	51
Shaoxing 绍兴市	Zhejiang 浙江省	6.74	50
Foshan 佛山市	Guangdong 广东省	6.38	57
Ningbo 宁波市	Zhejiang 浙江省	5.38	63
Suzhou 苏州市	Jiangsu 江苏省	4.82	60
Jinhua 金华市	Zhejiang 浙江省	3.54	68
Nantong 南通市	Jiangsu 江苏省	3.26	29
Jiangmen 江门市	Guangdong 广东省	2.91	13

10 Major Wholesalers 十家主要批发商	City 城市	Province 省	Telephone/Fax 电话/传真
Shanghai Shenda Co.,Ltd.	Shanghai	Shanghai	(021)62319898
上海申达股份有限公司	上海市	上海市	(021)62317250
Orient International Holding Silk Group Corportion	Shanghai	Shanghai	(021)64662288
东方国际集团丝绸进出口有限公司	上海市	上海市	(021)64677788
Nanjing Textiles Import & Export Co.,Ltd.	Nanjing	Jiangsu	(025)3306789
南京纺织品进出口股份有限公司	南京市	江苏省	(025)3300518
Zhejiang Textiles Import & Export Group Co.,Ltd.	Hangzhou	Zhejiang	(0571)87075888
浙江省纺织品进出口集团有限公司	杭州市	浙江省	(0571)87079234
Zhejiang Orient Holdings Co.,Ltd.	Hangzhou	Zhejiang	(0571)87215678
浙江东方集团股份有限公司	杭州市	浙江省	(0571)87215000
Zhejiang Silk Holding Co.,ltd.	Hangzhou	Zhejiang	(0571)85195588
浙江省丝绸集团有限公司	杭州市	浙江省	(0571)85192540
Guangdong Silk (Group) Corporation	Guangzhou	Guangdong	(020)83337448
广东省丝绸（集团）公司	广州市	广东省	(020)83332995
Shanghai Costume Group Co.,Ltd.	Shanghai	Shanghai	(021)62748598
上海服装（集团）有限公司	上海市	上海市	(021)62414773
Orient International Holding Shanghai Textiles Import & Export Co.Ltd.	Shanghai	Shanghai	(021)63218855
东方国际集团上海市针织品进出口有限公司	上海市	上海市	(021)63299560
Jiangsu Textiles Import & Export Group Co.,Ltd.	Nanjing	Jiangsu	(025)6895000
江苏省纺织品进出口集团股份有限公司	南京市	江苏省	(025)4400800

1782: Wool Knitwear 毛针织品业

The industry accounts for 0.223% of the total revenue of China's industrial sector in 2002. The rate of return on assets is 3.51%. 81.95% of all firms in the industry made a profit while 18.05% had negative returns.The top province in terms of the industry's revenue is Guangdong, accounting for 23.37% of the total revenue.
2002年本行业收入占全行业的0.223%，资产利润率为3.51%。81.95%的企业赢利，18.05%的企业亏损。收入最高的省为广东省，占本行业的23.37%。

	Total number of firms 企业总数	Total number of employees 职工总数	Total revenue (Mil.RMB) 总销售收入（百万元）	Total profit (Mil.RMB) 总利润（百万元）	Return on assets 资产利润率（%）	Return on equity 权益利润率（%）	Labour productivity ('000 RMB/ worker) 劳动生产率（千元/人）	Debts/ assets 资产负债率（%）	Total assets (Mil.RMB) 总资产（百万元）
Industry Overall 行业总体	931	251,097	23,925	751	3.51	8.64	28.25	59.36	21,391

	Number of firms 企业个数	Average number of employees 平均职工人数	Average revenue ('000 RMB) 平均销售收入（千元）	Average profit ('000 RMB) 平均利润（千元）	Return on assets 资产利润率（%）	Return on equity 权益利润率（%）	Labour productivity ('000 RMB/ worker) 劳动生产率（千元/人）	Debts/ assets 资产负债率（%）	Average total assets ('000 RMB) 平均总资产（千元）
By ownership 产业所有权									
State-owned 国有	29	399	47,995	2,014	3.04	11.25	39.12	72.94	66,150
Collective-owned 集体	106	237	21,664	671	4.73	10.33	32.82	54.24	14,195
Foreign & Overseas Chinese Funded 三资	366	328	28,870	763	2.99	6.56	25.39	54.45	25,550
By regional distribution 地区分布									
Central-North 华北	134	287	28,852	971	2.79	7.88	31.31	64.61	34,837
Beijing 北京	47	245	28,817	847	2.34	7.78	36.96	69.87	36,126
Tianjin 天津	27	305	17,119	513	1.58	4.57	10.23	65.48	32,554
Hebei 河北	34	243	27,753	1,734	8.86	20.17	32.72	56.08	19,573
Shanxi 山西	1								
Inner Mongolia 内蒙古	25	417	44,241	703	1.23	3.23	40.61	61.81	57,030
Northeast 东北	22	173	9,774	1	0.01	0.02	13.64	69.87	9,669
Liaoning 辽宁	16	128	11,477	8	0.07	0.25	19.18	72.00	11,746
Jilin 吉林	6	294	5,235	-20	-0.47	-1.02	7.21	53.73	4,131
Heilongjiang 黑龙江									
Central-East 华东	544	235	25,043	1,100	5.85	15.08	31.83	61.23	18,814
Shanghai 上海	122	177	23,921	1,582	8.55	24.06	39.57	64.48	18,510
Jiangsu 江苏	147	255	29,486	980	4.59	12.42	35.65	63.07	21,355
Zhejiang 浙江	172	201	20,363	962	5.43	14.56	27.91	62.69	17,703
Anhui 安徽	3	132	4,257	-8	-0.35	-0.85	8.86	59.06	2,192
Fujian 福建	39	387	30,695	517	2.98	4.09	23.20	27.28	17,381
Jiangxi 江西	3	540	5,573	3	0.06	0.09	5.00	36.10	5,998
Shandong 山东	58	291	28,306	1,308	6.96	20.85	32.30	66.61	18,793
Central-South 中南	218	350	26,287	186	0.90	1.75	21.65	48.37	20,682
Henan 河南	10	208	9,681	550	6.35	43.82	21.51	85.50	8,654
Hubei 湖北	1	164	11,050	460	3.25	8.06	24.26	59.68	14,160
Hunan 湖南	4	203	3,911	90	1.60	8.52	4.70	81.22	5,641
Guangdong 广东	202	352	27,684	183	0.85	1.61	22.44	47.43	21,679
Guangxi 广西	1	2,200	14,912	-2,671	-42.32	-82.57	2.39	48.74	6,311
Hainan 海南									
Southwest 西南	1	153	27	-1,745	-1.98		-3.71	112.53	87,997
Chongqing 重庆									
Sichuan 四川									
Guizhou 贵州	1	153	27	-1,745	-1.98		-3.71	112.53	87,997
Yunnan 云南									
Tibet 西藏									
Northwest 西北	12	387	40,793	-1,380	-0.99	-2.39	25.94	58.81	139,896
Shaanxi 陕西	2	198	2,931	-8,223	-14.87		3.25	148.24	55,279
Gansu 甘肃	4	74	231	-365	-10.36		9.20	126.74	3,518
Qinghai 青海	1	860	78,490	5,950	5.15	17.69	36.90	70.92	115,630
Ningxia 宁夏	1								
Xinjiang 新疆	4	774	101,060	-1,151	-0.32	-0.64	27.39	50.30	359,624

Year 年份	Number of firms 企业个数	Rate of change 变化率 (%)	Number of employees 职工人数 (人)	Rate of change 变化率 (%)	Total revenue (Mil. RMB) 总销售收入 (百万元)	Rate of change 变化率 (%)	Total profit (Mil RMB) 总利润 (百万元)	Rate of change 变化率 (%)
2000	620		173,161		15,904		444	
2001	802	29.35	213,225	23.14	18,533	16.53	412	-7.21
2002	931	16.08	251,097	17.76	23,925	29.09	751	82.28

Major Products 主要产品	Output 产量	Unit 单位
Knitted Clothing 针织服装	409,076	10,000 Pieces 万件

10 Main Firms with Maximal Revenue (year founded) 收入最大的十家主要企业（创办年份）	City 城市	Province 省	Telephone/fax 电话/传真	Number of employees 职工人数	Ownership 产业所有权	Revenue ('000 RMB) 销售收入 (千元)	Profit('000 RMB) (rank) 利润(千元) (排名)	Total assets ('000 RMB) 总资产 (千元)	Major products 主要产品
Jiangsu Hongda Group	Yancheng	Jiangsu	(0515)8594188		State-owned				Plush
江苏宏大集团(1995)	盐城市	江苏省	(0515)8593637	2,950	国有企业	801,270	60,870(1)	685,260	长毛绒
Beijing Snow Lotus Cashmere CO., Ltd.	Beijing	Beijing	(010)64664480		Joint Stock				Cashmere Sweater
北京雪莲羊绒股份有限公司(1988)	北京市	北京市	(010)64668812	1,184	股份制	429,086	12,047(8)	560,932	羊绒衫
Xinjiang Tianshan Wool Textile Co., Ltd.	Urumqi	Xinjiang	(0991)4311866		Joint Stock				Cashmere Sweater
新疆天山毛纺织股份有限公司(1981)	乌鲁木齐市	新疆	(0991)4310472	2,045	股份制	346,082	90(463)	1,173,796	羊绒衫
Wendeng Eikang Treading Co.,ltd.	Weihai	Shandong	(0631)8873806		Foreign Funded				Textile Sweater
文登伊康纤维有限公司(1992)	威海市	山东省	(0631)8871668	550	外商投资	289,351	29,840(3)	32,540	纺织衫
Zhejiang Zhenbei Cashmere Co.,ltd.	Huzhou	Zhejiang	(0572)3187878		Private Owned				Woollen Sweater
湖州珍贝有限公司(1995)	湖州市	浙江省	(0572)3927888	1,206	私营企业	260,537	14,892(6)	266,573	羊毛衫
Linhe Viction Shenxi Wool Textile (Group) Co., ltd.	Bayannaoer	Inner Mongolia	(0478)8235123		Foreign Funded				Cashmere Sweater
临河市维信深喜绒毛纺织有限公司(1995)	巴彦淖尔	内蒙古	(0478)8226611	1,080	外商投资	178,237	7,480(18)	307,607	羊绒衫
Nantong Rongxiang Clothing Making Co., Ltd.	Nantong	Jiangsu	(0513)2271118		Foreign Funded				Woollen Sweater
南通荣祥制衣有限公司(1995)	南通市	江苏省	(0513)2271328	1,000	外商投资	162,920	4,500(46)	75,430	羊毛衫
Zhaoqing Zhuli-Detai Clothing Making Factory Co., Ltd.	Zhaoqing	Guangdong	(0758)8362729		Overseas Chinese-funded				Knitting Wool Pullover针织绒
肇庆市珠利德泰制衣厂有限公司(1998)	肇庆市	广东省	(0758)8361925	728	港澳台资	158,970	4,640(44)	35,171	毛套头衫
Press Freld Knitting (Haifeng)Co., ltd.	Shanwei	Guangdong	(0660)6451888		Overseas Chinese-funded				Wool Knitted Dress
敏兴毛织(海丰)有限公司(1996)	汕尾市	广东省	(0660)6452222	1,813	港澳台资	157,507	-	116,828	毛针织品
Wuxi Fushi Fashion Wear Co., Ltd.	Wuxi	Jiangsu	(0510)5556513		Foreign Funded				Knitting Dress
无锡富士时装有限公司(1992)	无锡市	江苏省	(0510)5555052	700	外商投资	148,665	19,758(4)	79,348	针织服装

Top 10 Cities by Revenue 销售收入排名前10位城市	Province 省	Market share 市场份额 (%)	Number of firms 企业个数
Shanghai 上海市	Shanghai 上海市	12.20	122
Suzhou 苏州市	Jiangsu 江苏省	7.01	67
Beijing 北京市	Beijing 北京市	5.66	47
Yancheng 盐城市	Jiangsu 江苏省	4.47	10
Jiaxing 嘉兴市	Zhejiang 浙江省	3.79	47
Quanzhou 泉州市	Fujian 福建省	3.30	25
Nantong 南通市	Jiangsu 江苏省	3.09	34
Ningbo 宁波市	Zhejiang 浙江省	2.92	37
Dongguan 东莞市	Guangdong 广东省	2.77	21
Yantai 烟台市	Shandong 山东省	2.67	36

10 Major Wholesalers 十家主要批发商	City 城市	Province 省	Telephone/Fax 电话/传真
Shanghai Shenda Co.,Ltd.	Shanghai	Shanghai	(021)62319898
上海申达股份有限公司	上海市	上海市	(021)62317250
Orient International Holding Silk Group Corportion	Shanghai	Shanghai	(021)64662288
东方国际集团丝绸进出口有限公司	上海市	上海市	(021)64677788
Nanjing Textiles Import & Export Co.,Ltd.	Nanjing	Jiangsu	(025)3306789
南京纺织品进出口股份有限公司	南京市	江苏省	(025)3300518
Zhejiang Textiles Import & Export Group Co.,Ltd.	Hangzhou	Zhejiang	(0571)87075888
浙江省纺织品进出口集团有限公司	杭州市	浙江省	(0571)87079234
Zhejiang Orient Holdings Co.,Ltd.	Hangzhou	Zhejiang	(0571)87215678
浙江东方集团股份有限公司	杭州市	浙江省	(0571)87215000
Zhejiang Silk Holding Co.,ltd.	Hangzhou	Zhejiang	(0571)85195588
浙江省丝绸集团有限公司	杭州市	浙江省	(0571)85192540
Guangdong Silk (Group) Corporation	Guangzhou	Guangdong	(020)83337448
广东省丝绸（集团）公司	广州市	广东省	(020)83332995
Shanghai Costume Group Co.,Ltd.	Shanghai	Shanghai	(021)62748598
上海服装（集团）有限公司	上海市	上海市	(021)62414773
Orient International Holding Shanghai Textiles Import & Export Co.Ltd.	Shanghai	Shanghai	(021)63218855
东方国际集团上海市针织品进出口有限公司	上海市	上海市	(021)63299560
Jiangsu Textiles Import & Export Group Co.,Ltd.	Nanjing	Jiangsu	(025)6895000
江苏省纺织品进出口集团股份有限公司	南京市	江苏省	(025)4400800

1783: Silk Knitwear 丝针织品业

The industry accounts for 0.068% of the total revenue of China's industrial sector in 2002. The rate of return on assets is 4.10%. 84.16% of all firms in the industry made a profit while 15.84% had negative returns.The top province in terms of the industry's revenue is Zhejiang, accounting for 49.46% of the total revenue.
2002年本行业收入占全行业的 0.068%，资产利润率为 4.10%。84.16%的企业赢利，15.84%的企业亏损。收入最高的省为浙江省，占本行业的49.46%。

	Total number of firms 企业总数	Total number of employees 职工总数	Total revenue (Mil.RMB) 总销售收入(百万元)	Total profit (Mil.RMB) 总利润(百万元)	Return on assets 资产利润率(%)	Return on equity 权益利润率(%)	Labour productivity ('000 RMB/ worker) 劳动生产率(千元/人)	Debts/ assets 资产负债率(%)	Total assets (Mil.RMB) 总资产(百万元)
Industry Overall 行业总体	202	42,770	7,294	314	4.10	9.70	57.12	57.72	7,651

	Number of firms 企业个数	Average number of employees 平均职工人数	Average revenue ('000 RMB) 平均销售收入（千元）	Average profit ('000 RMB) 平均利润(千元)	Return on assets 资产利润率(%)	Return on equity 权益利润率(%)	Labour productivity ('000 RMB/ worker) 劳动生产率(千元/人)	Debts/ assets 资产负债率(%)	Average total assets ('000 RMB) 平均总资产(千元)
By ownership 产业所有权									
State-owned 国有	10	118	5,019	-642	-2.06		22.62	107.47	31,167
Collective-owned 集体	12	170	31,253	1,127	5.23	13.39	39.14	60.92	21,545
Foreign & Overseas Chinese Funded 三资	68	290	51,412	999	1.60	3.52	69.44	54.54	62,398
By regional distribution 地区分布									
Central-North 华北	7	166	6,863	37	0.10	0.62	28.35	83.49	36,077
Beijing 北京									
Tianjin 天津	4	160	8,950	198	0.61	3.12	31.98	80.57	32,665
Hebei 河北	2	125	5,760	-100	-0.18	-1.73	47.58	89.69	56,176
Shanxi 山西	1	273	720	-331	-3.47	-7.01	2.24	50.44	9,532
Inner Mongolia 内蒙古									
Northeast 东北	8	146	10,482	-7	-0.05	-0.23	34.44	76.41	13,724
Liaoning 辽宁	6	121	13,336	105	0.95	1.94	48.98	51.15	11,030
Jilin 吉林									
Heilongjiang 黑龙江	2	223	1,918	-343	-1.57		10.79	114.74	21,806
Central-East 华东	165	213	37,057	2,170	5.88	13.39	54.77	56.09	36,908
Shanghai 上海	12	204	17,461	138	0.45	0.90	28.27	49.60	30,517
Jiangsu 江苏	24	183	42,193	671	2.21	7.29	46.67	69.73	30,419
Zhejiang 浙江	99	235	36,440	2,938	8.90	20.37	44.19	56.31	33,012
Anhui 安徽									
Fujian 福建	20	122	36,670	2,238	6.39	8.33	87.32	23.30	35,016
Jiangxi 江西									
Shandong 山东	10	266	55,122	473	0.46	1.56	155.40	70.36	102,513
Central-South 中南	21	244	49,908	-1,983	-3.60	-8.91	86.11	59.60	55,092
Henan 河南	1	15	10,600				773.33	406.73	5,690
Hubei 湖北	2	82	3,250	-314	-2.12		14.53	179.07	14,801
Hunan 湖南	1	61	51,170	80	2.18	2.88	337.26	24.25	3,670
Guangdong 广东	17	287	57,635	-2,418	-3.68	-8.13	83.25	54.79	65,762
Guangxi 广西									
Hainan 海南									
Southwest 西南	1	108		-2,800	-6.74	-11.05	2.15	38.96	41,527
Chongqing 重庆									
Sichuan 四川									
Guizhou 贵州	1	108		-2,800	-6.74	-11.05	2.15	38.96	41,527
Yunnan 云南									
Tibet 西藏									
Northwest 西北									
Shaanxi 陕西									
Gansu 甘肃									
Qinghai 青海									
Ningxia 宁夏									
Xinjiang 新疆									

1783: Silk Knitwear 丝针织品业

Year 年份	Number of firms 企业个数	Rate of change 变化率 (%)	Number of employees 职工人数 (人)	Rate of change 变化率 (%)	Total revenue (Mil. RMB) 总销售收入 (百万元)	Rate of change 变化率 (%)	Total profit (Mil RMB) 总利润 (百万元)	Rate of change 变化率 (%)
2000	196		42,891		6,991		243	
2001	203	3.57	48,079	12.10	7,915	13.22	288	18.52
2002	202	-0.49	42,770	-11.04	7,294	-7.85	314	9.03

Major Products 主要产品	Output 产量	Unit 单位
Knitted Clothing 针织服装	409,076	10,000 Pieces 万件

10 Main Firms with Maximal Revenue (year founded) 收入最大的十家主要企业（创办年份）	City 城市	Province 省	Telephone/fax 电话/传真	Number of employees 职工人数	Ownership 产业所有权	Revenue ('000 RMB) 销售收入 (千元)	Profit('000 RMB) (rank) 利润(千元) (排名)	Total assets ('000 RMB) 总资产 (千元)	Major products 主要产品
Puning Qiye Clothing Making Co., Ltd.	Jieyang	Guangdong	(0663)2347939		Overseas Chinese-funded				Costume
普宁市启业制衣有限公司(1993)	揭阳市	广东省	(0663)2348781	307	港澳台资	268,909	1,035(65)	52,634	服装
Qingdao E-hwa Textile Co., Ltd.	Qingdao	Shandong	(0532)5181842		Foreign Funded				Chemical Fiber Cloth
青岛二和纤维有限公司(胶南)(1993)	青岛市	山东省	(0532)5181847	900	外商投资	249,796	6,601(13)	659,042	化纤布
Shenzhen Huasi Enterprise Stock Co., Ltd.	Shenzhen	Guangdong	(0755)26691710		Overseas Chinese-funded				Silk Costume
深圳华丝企业股份有限公司(1985)	深圳市	广东省	(0755)26692704	1,780	港澳台资	222,805	19,171(7)	310,201	真丝服装
Jiangsu Golden Morning Knitting Co., ltd.	Suzhou	Jiangsu	(0512)52528206		Private Owned				Polar Flace
江苏金辰针纺织有限公司(2001)	苏州市	江苏省	(0512)52528866	372	私营企业	206,301	1,077(63)	64,577	摇粒绒
Rui'an Guangyu Knitting Co., Ltd.	Wenzhou	Zhejiang	(0577)65475206		Foreign Funded				silk Stockings
瑞安光裕针织有限公司(1992)	温州市	浙江省	(0577)65477688	1,132	外商投资	200,410	1,408(54)	133,460	丝袜
Zhejiang Hongda Warp Knitting Co., Ltd.	Jiaxing	Zhejiang	(0573)7566079		Joint Stock				303 Rill Fine Hair
浙江宏达经编股份有限公司(2001)	嘉兴市	浙江省	(0573)7566616	443	股份制	160,778	33,171(1)	292,093	303圈绒
Luoding Xiangfa Elasticity Knitting Cloth Factory	Yunfu	Guangdong	(0766)3826268		Overseas Chinese-funded				Elasticity Knitting Cloth
罗定祥发弹力针织布厂(1988)	云浮市	广东省	(0766)3821394	258	港澳台资	147,389	612(80)	100,764	力针织布
Shaoxing County Huaxin Knitting Co., Ltd.	Shaoxing	Zhejiang	(0575)4573536		Private Owned				Tricot
绍兴县华欣针织有限公司(2000)	绍兴市	浙江省	(0575)4571988	404	私营企业	129,677	29,337(2)	90,247	经编织品
Changle Tiansuo Textile Industrial Co., Ltd.	Fuzhou	Fujian	(0591)8116888		Private Owned				Terylene Yarn
长乐市天梭纺织实业有限公司(2001)	福州市	福建省	(0591)8116111	235	私营企业	115,050	-	26,016	涤纶纱
Zhejiang Jinda New Materials Co., Ltd.	Jiaxing	Zhejiang	(0573)7024130		Joint Stock				Compound New Materials合
浙江锦达新材料股份有限公司(1998)	嘉兴市	浙江省	(0573)7766320	472	股份制	113,867	20,184(6)	146,391	成新材料

Top 10 Cities by Revenue 销售收入排名前10位城市	Province 省	Market share 市场份额 (%)	Number of firms 企业个数
Jiaxing 嘉兴市	Zhejiang 浙江省	17.76	32
Shaoxing 绍兴市	Zhejiang 浙江省	16.95	34
Suzhou 苏州市	Jiangsu 江苏省	11.12	14
Fuzhou 福州市	Fujian 福建省	9.32	18
Hangzhou 杭州市	Zhejiang 浙江省	7.95	19
Qingdao 青岛市	Shandong 山东省	6.80	8
Jieyang 揭阳市	Guangdong 广东省	4.82	2
Shenzhen 深圳市	Guangdong 广东省	3.05	1
Shanghai 上海市	Shanghai 上海市	2.87	12
Wenzhou 温州市	Zhejiang 浙江省	2.87	2

10 Major Wholesalers 十家主要批发商	City 城市	Province 省	Telephone/Fax 电话/传真
Shanghai Shenda Co.,Ltd.	Shanghai	Shanghai	(021)62319898
上海申达股份有限公司	上海市	上海市	(021)62317250
Orient International Holding Silk Group Corportion	Shanghai	Shanghai	(021)64662288
东方国际集团丝绸进出口有限公司	上海市	上海市	(021)64677788
Nanjing Textiles Import & Export Co.,Ltd.	Nanjing	Jiangsu	(025)3306789
南京纺织品进出口股份有限公司	南京市	江苏省	(025)3300518
Zhejiang Textiles Import & Export Group Co.,Ltd.	Hangzhou	Zhejiang	(0571)87075888
浙江省纺织品进出口集团有限公司	杭州市	浙江省	(0571)87079234
Zhejiang Orient Holdings Co.,Ltd.	Hangzhou	Zhejiang	(0571)87215678
浙江东方集团股份有限公司	杭州市	浙江省	(0571)87215000
Zhejiang Silk Holding Co.,ltd.	Hangzhou	Zhejiang	(0571)85195588
浙江省丝绸集团有限公司	杭州市	浙江省	(0571)85192540
Guangdong Silk (Group) Corporation	Guangzhou	Guangdong	(020)83337448
广东省丝绸（集团）公司	广州市	广东省	(020)83332995
Shanghai Costume Group Co.,Ltd.	Shanghai	Shanghai	(021)62748598
上海服装（集团）有限公司	上海市	上海市	(021)62414773
Orient International Holding Shanghai Textiles Import & Export Co.Ltd.	Shanghai	Shanghai	(021)63218855
东方国际集团上海市针织品进出口有限公司	上海市	上海市	(021)63299560
Jiangsu Textiles Import & Export Group Co.,Ltd.	Nanjing	Jiangsu	(025)6895000
江苏省纺织品进出口集团股份有限公司	南京市	江苏省	(025)4400800

1789: Other Knitwear 其他针织品业

The industry accounts for 0.068% of the total revenue of China's industrial sector in 2002. The rate of return on assets is 3.88%. 83.52% of all firms in the industry made a profit while 16.48% had negative returns.The top province in terms of the industry's revenue is Zhejiang, accounting for 25.68% of the total revenue.
2002年本行业收入占全行业的 0.068%，资产利润率为 3.88%。83.52%的企业赢利，16.48%的企业亏损。收入最高的省为浙江省，占本行业的25.68%。

	Total number of firms 企业总数	Total number of employees 职工总数	Total revenue (Mil.RMB) 总销售收入 (百万元)	Total profit (Mil.RMB) 总利润 (百万元)	Return on assets 资产利润率 (%)	Return on equity 权益利润率 (%)	Labour productivity ('000 RMB/ worker) 劳动生产率 (千元/人)	Debts/ assets 资产负债率 (%)	Total assets (Mil.RMB) 总资产 (百万元)
Industry Overall 行业总体	273	50,589	7,322	245	3.88	9.20	39.24	57.88	6,318

	Number of firms 企业个数	Average number of employees 平均职工人数	Average revenue ('000 RMB) 平均销售收入 (千元)	Average profit ('000 RMB) 平均利润 (千元)	Return on assets 资产利润率 (%)	Return on equity 权益利润率 (%)	Labour productivity ('000 RMB/ worker) 劳动生产率 (千元/人)	Debts/ assets 资产负债率 (%)	Average total assets ('000 RMB) 平均总资产 (千元)
By ownership 产业所有权									
State-owned 国有	7	208	5,506	-419	-1.14	-5.73	19.39	80.09	36,743
Collective-owned 集体	31	191	25,264	1,418	8.57	31.29	39.54	72.61	16,550
Foreign & Overseas Chinese Funded 三资	107	182	27,817	754	2.20	4.74	40.98	53.63	34,297
By regional distribution 地区分布									
Central-North 华北	13	147	15,304	1,087	5.15	29.16	32.83	82.32	21,081
Beijing 北京	1	36	5,802	33	2.58	3.12	12.25	17.41	1,281
Tianjin 天津	5	99	14,112	376	4.82	9.97	56.91	51.67	7,797
Hebei 河北	6	161	20,432	2,036	5.33	45.10	35.53	88.17	38,167
Shanxi 山西	1	420						69.32	4,781
Inner Mongolia 内蒙古									
Northeast 东北	7	338	25,345	1,311	7.66	12.86	41.29	40.43	17,121
Liaoning 辽宁	4	469	40,105	2,240	12.00	21.81	47.65	44.96	18,663
Jilin 吉林	2	70	6,033	109	0.87	1.12	41.24	22.89	12,535
Heilongjiang 黑龙江	1	352	4,927				7.43	45.49	20,130
Central-East 华东	192	176	26,624	1,087	4.83	10.87	38.02	55.60	22,534
Shanghai 上海	22	169	29,166	1,015	4.64	9.54	47.66	51.37	21,879
Jiangsu 江苏	68	161	21,339	394	1.74	4.35	31.83	60.08	22,658
Zhejiang 浙江	66	179	28,484	1,301	7.02	16.21	36.39	56.66	18,518
Anhui 安徽	2	126	16,962	-115	-0.54	-5.29	48.68	89.84	21,311
Fujian 福建	23	126	28,684	2,587	7.50	12.72	67.26	41.04	34,497
Jiangxi 江西	2	230	5,619	137	0.76	0.92	4.89	17.04	17,955
Shandong 山东	9	414	48,241	1,588	6.79	35.55	32.30	80.89	23,374
Central-South 中南	59	207	30,853	250	0.95	2.47	43.99	61.56	26,237
Henan 河南	5	207	15,366	681	6.34	16.11	54.35	60.65	10,743
Hubei 湖北	5	118	10,767	-31	-0.12	-0.40	63.83	68.81	24,999
Hunan 湖南	2	60	10,965	2,058	13.37	28.77	58.80	53.52	15,388
Guangdong 广东	47	222	35,484	156	0.55	1.41	41.68	61.11	28,479
Guangxi 广西									
Hainan 海南									
Southwest 西南	2	164	6,728	-960	-3.85	-7.46	10.16	48.39	24,920
Chongqing 重庆									
Sichuan 四川	1	156	2,688	-2,509	-7.05	-14.32	5.75	50.73	35,575
Guizhou 贵州	1	171	10,767	590	4.14	7.20	14.19	42.54	14,264
Yunnan 云南									
Tibet 西藏									
Northwest 西北									
Shaanxi 陕西									
Gansu 甘肃									
Qinghai 青海									
Ningxia 宁夏									
Xinjiang 新疆									

1789: Other Knitwear 其他针织品业

Year 年份	Number of firms 企业个数	Rate of change 变化率 (%)	Number of employees 职工人数 (人)	Rate of change 变化率 (%)	Total revenue (Mil. RMB) 总销售收入 (百万元)	Rate of change 变化率 (%)	Total profit (Mil RMB) 总利润 (百万元)	Rate of change 变化率 (%)
2000	238		41,861		5,907		151	
2001	247	3.78	47,690	13.92	6,836	15.73	180	19.21
2002	273	10.53	50,589	6.08	7,322	7.11	245	36.11

Major Products 主要产品	Output 产量	Unit 单位
Knitted Clothing 针织服装	409,076	10,000 Pieces 万件

10 Main Firms with Maximal Revenue (year founded) 收入最大的十家主要企业（创办年份）	City 城市	Province 省	Telephone/fax 电话/传真	Number of employees 职工人数	Ownership 产业所有权	Revenue ('000 RMB) 销售收入(千元)	Profit('000 RMB) (rank) 利润(千元)(排名)	Total assets ('000 RMB) 总资产(千元)	Major products 主要产品
Guangzhou Meiye Knitting Printing & Dyeing Factory	Guangzhou	Guangdong	(020)81415888		Overseas Chinese-funded				Knitgoods
Co., Ltd. 广州美业针织印染厂有限公司(1990)	广州市	广东省	(020)81414746	560	港澳台资	263,705	4,109(16)	192,087	针织品
Fujian Fengzhu Textile Science & Technology Co.,ltd.	Quanzhou	Fujian	(0595)5656506		Overseas Chinese-funded				Bleaching & Dyeing Light Grey Cloth漂
福建凤竹纺织科技股份有限公司(1991)	泉州市	福建省	(0595)5688093	736	港澳台资	246,801	37,921(1)	315,068	染光坯布
Tonglu Yali Import & Export Trade Co., Ltd.	Hangzhou	Zhejiang	(0571)64213387		Private Owned				Other Knitgoods其
桐庐雅丽进出口贸易有限公司(2000)	杭州市	浙江省	(0571)64213380	1,195	私营企业	162,894	5,124(13)	86,908	他针织品
Guangdong Deqing Warp knitting Mill Co.Ltd.	Zhaoqing	Guangdong	(0758)7783683		Overseas Chinese-funded				Warp Knitting Elasticity Underwear Cloth经编弹力
德庆经编针织厂有限公司(1996)	肇庆市	广东省	(0758)7783683	442	港澳台资	136,540	3,549(20)	166,881	内衣布料
Dongguan Lijin Clothing Making Co., Ltd.	Dongguan	Guangdong	(0769)5822228		Overseas Chinese-funded				Knitted Dress
东莞励进制衣有限公司(1997)	东莞市	广东省	(0769)5828288	1,500	港澳台资	130,814	2,033(45)	62,412	针织服装
Quanzhou Dongyuan Non-woven Co., Ltd.	Quanzhou	Fujian	(0595)2487812		Overseas Chinese-funded				Woven Belt
泉州东源电脑织唛有限公司(1996)	泉州市	福建省	(0595)2487810	345	港澳台资	119,154	10,009(3)	106,318	织带
Shanghai Tahui Knitting Factory	Shanghai	Shanghai	(021)57846145		Joint Stock				Knitting Shirt
上海塔汇针织厂(1978)	上海市	上海市	(021)57841018	295	股份制	114,721	1,725(50)	23,317	针织衫
Yingkou Lunan High-tech Industrial Devolopment Zone Devolopment	Yingkou	Liaoning	(0417)3842007		Collective-owned				Magical Glove
General Corp.营口市路南高新技术产业开发区开发总公司(1997)	营口市	辽宁省		850	集体企业	114,170	7,840(4)	28,940	魔术手套
Shandong Penglai Tianshan Dyeing Co., Ltd.	Yantai	Shandong	(0535)5921833		Joint Stock				Dyed Thread
山东蓬莱大山染业有限公司(1988)	烟台市	山东省	(0535)5915606	1,200	股份制	106,220	3,310(21)	45,440	染线
Shaoxingxian Jinfeng Yinxi Co., Ltd.	Shaoxing	Zhejiang	(0575)4017688		Private Owned				Knitting & Spinning Products
绍兴县金峰银锡有限公司(2000)	绍兴市	浙江省	(0575)4019028	90	私营企业	101,087	5,033(14)	47,704	针纺织品

Top 10 Cities by Revenue 销售收入排名前10位城市	Province 省	Market share 市场份额 (%)	Number of firms 企业个数
Suzhou 苏州市	Jiangsu 江苏省	10.70	35
Hangzhou 杭州市	Zhejiang 浙江省	10.42	25
Shanghai 上海市	Shanghai 上海市	8.76	22
Shaoxing 绍兴市	Zhejiang 浙江省	8.03	13
Quanzhou 泉州市	Fujian 福建省	7.08	13
Shantou 汕头市	Guangdong 广东省	6.62	11
Guangzhou 广州市	Guangdong 广东省	4.74	5
Ningbo 宁波市	Zhejiang 浙江省	4.34	16
Dongguan 东莞市	Guangdong 广东省	3.52	8
Linyi 临沂市	Shandong 山东省	3.06	1

10 Major Wholesalers 十家主要批发商	City 城市	Province 省	Telephone/Fax 电话/传真
Shanghai Shenda Co.,Ltd.	Shanghai	Shanghai	(021)62319898
上海申达股份有限公司	上海市	上海市	(021)62317250
Orient International Holding Silk Group Corportion	Shanghai	Shanghai	(021)64662288
东方国际集团丝绸进出口有限公司	上海市	上海市	(021)64677788
Nanjing Textiles Import & Export Co.,Ltd.	Nanjing	Jiangsu	(025)3306789
南京纺织品进出口股份有限公司	南京市	江苏省	(025)3300518
Zhejiang Textiles Import & Export Group Co.,Ltd.	Hangzhou	Zhejiang	(0571)87075888
浙江省纺织品进出口集团有限公司	杭州市	浙江省	(0571)87079234
Zhejiang Orient Holdings Co.,Ltd.	Hangzhou	Zhejiang	(0571)87215678
浙江东方集团股份有限公司	杭州市	浙江省	(0571)87215000
Zhejiang Silk Holding Co.,ltd.	Hangzhou	Zhejiang	(0571)85195588
浙江省丝绸集团有限公司	杭州市	浙江省	(0571)85192540
Guangdong Silk (Group) Corporation	Guangzhou	Guangdong	(020)83337448
广东省丝绸（集团）公司	广州市	广东省	(020)83332995
Shanghai Costume Group Co.,Ltd.	Shanghai	Shanghai	(021)62748598
上海服装（集团）有限公司	上海市	上海市	(021)62414773
Orient International Holding Shanghai Textiles Import & Export Co.Ltd.	Shanghai	Shanghai	(021)63218855
东方国际集团上海市针织品进出口有限公司	上海市	上海市	(021)63299560
Jiangsu Textiles Import & Export Group Co.,Ltd.	Nanjing	Jiangsu	(025)6895000
江苏省纺织品进出口集团股份有限公司	南京市	江苏省	(025)4400800

1790: Other Textiles 其他纺织业

The industry accounts for 0.193% of the total revenue of China's industrial sector in 2002. The rate of return on assets is 3.38%. 82.13% of all firms in the industry made a profit while 17.87% had negative returns.The top province in terms of the industry's revenue is Jiangsu, accounting for 32.06% of the total revenue.
2002年本行业收入占全行业的 0.193%，资产利润率为 3.38%。82.13%的企业赢利，17.87%的企业亏损。收入最高的省为江苏省，占本行业的32.06%。

	Total number of firms 企业总数	Total number of employees 职工总数	Total revenue (Mil.RMB) 总销售收入 (百万元)	Total profit (Mil.RMB) 总利润 (百万元)	Return on assets 资产利润率 (%)	Return on equity 权益利润率 (%)	Labour productivity ('000 RMB/ worker) 劳动生产率 (千元/人)	Debts/ assets 资产负债率 (%)	Total assets (Mil.RMB) 总资产 (百万元)
Industry Overall 行业总体	733	102,593	20,697	874	3.38	7.53	57.63	55.17	25,902

	Number of firms 企业个数	Average number of employees 平均职工人数	Average revenue ('000 RMB) 平均销售收入 (千元)	Average profit ('000 RMB) 平均利润 (千元)	Return on assets 资产利润率 (%)	Return on equity 权益利润率 (%)	Labour productivity ('000 RMB/ worker) 劳动生产率 (千元/人)	Debts/ assets 资产负债率 (%)	Average total assets ('000 RMB) 平均总资产 (千元)
By ownership 产业所有权									
State-owned 国有	28	466	38,925	669	0.72	4.40	24.08	83.68	93,037
Collective-owned 集体	57	200	32,153	1,484	6.38	19.46	50.09	67.21	23,258
Foreign & Overseas Chinese Funded 三资	234	154	32,443	1,330	3.11	5.96	67.28	47.77	42,760
By regional distribution 地区分布									
Central-North 华北	57	205	24,642	592	1.32	3.13	39.07	57.79	44,861
Beijing 北京	12	115	14,086	-523	-1.82	-3.15	32.87	42.34	28,744
Tianjin 天津	20	109	23,438	960	1.94	8.36	66.67	76.82	49,529
Hebei 河北	23	332	32,823	1,588	3.43	6.63	35.08	48.33	46,338
Shanxi 山西	1	73	5,450	273	1.61	3.87	32.47	58.28	16,928
Inner Mongolia 内蒙古	1	400	6,445	-15,961	-11.49	-17.15	-13.26	33.00	138,881
Northeast 东北	24	94	14,869	134	0.54	1.90	41.83	71.70	24,876
Liaoning 辽宁	18	92	17,685	620	2.39	5.63	47.85	57.58	25,951
Jilin 吉林	3	116	11,808	-1,766	-5.34		36.28	140.05	33,097
Heilongjiang 黑龙江	3	87	1,039	-883	-8.65	-25.02	10.99	65.42	10,205
Central-East 华东	518	121	30,159	1,519	4.37	9.36	70.82	53.32	34,743
Shanghai 上海	44	96	28,702	1,526	3.70	6.60	74.28	43.96	41,278
Jiangsu 江苏	241	106	27,535	978	3.65	8.25	75.05	55.67	26,770
Zhejiang 浙江	143	132	35,550	2,542	5.07	11.22	62.08	54.84	50,172
Anhui 安徽	8	228	21,316	467	1.35	4.71	28.95	71.29	34,512
Fujian 福建	29	134	27,513	965	2.96	4.29	110.88	31.03	32,654
Jiangxi 江西	3	161	10,773	29	0.36	0.78	37.78	53.34	7,954
Shandong 山东	50	152	32,780	1,771	6.77	16.38	68.06	58.66	26,152
Central-South 中南	126	203	25,584	395	1.09	2.69	35.26	59.52	36,310
Henan 河南	8	197	12,020	-12	-0.04	-0.20	21.04	79.24	29,100
Hubei 湖北	26	355	27,583	429	2.57	5.88	31.42	56.29	16,680
Hunan 湖南	8	263	21,522	-69	-0.21	-1.08	22.16	80.32	32,548
Guangdong 广东	81	143	25,174	330	0.96	2.65	39.19	63.65	34,269
Guangxi 广西	1	537	7,416	-2,580	-7.30	-34.94	2.23	79.11	35,353
Hainan 海南	2	253	95,741	7,594	1.81	2.78	148.93	34.71	418,535
Southwest 西南	4	73	5,878	-573	-2.03	-4.04	27.96	49.59	28,169
Chongqing 重庆	2	62	5,680	-664	-1.85	-4.02	18.35	54.04	35,878
Sichuan 四川	1	142	12,153	29	0.11	0.13	43.42	13.29	26,677
Guizhou 贵州	1	24		-994	-6.98	-144.27	-13.96	95.16	14,242
Yunnan 云南									
Tibet 西藏									
Northwest 西北	4	71	16,542	717	4.57	5.43	84.51	15.94	15,694
Shaanxi 陕西									
Gansu 甘肃	4	71	16,542	717	4.57	5.43	84.51	15.94	15,694
Qinghai 青海									
Ningxia 宁夏									
Xinjiang 新疆									

1790: Other Textiles 其他纺织业

Year 年份	Number of firms 企业个数	Rate of change 变化率 (%)	Number of employees 职工人数 (人)	Rate of change 变化率 (%)	Total revenue (Mil. RMB) 总销售收入 (百万元)	Rate of change 变化率 (%)	Total profit (Mil RMB) 总利润 (百万元)	Rate of change 变化率 (%)
2000	429		78,319		15,515		730	
2001	569	32.63	95,528	21.97	17,877	15.22	785	7.53
2002	733	28.82	102,593	7.40	20,697	15.77	874	11.34

Major Products 主要产品	Output 产量	Unit 单位
Union Cloth 混纺交织布	58	100,000,000 Meters 亿米
Pure Chemical Fabric 纯化纤布	52	100,000,000 Meters 亿米

10 Main Firms with Maximal Revenue (year founded) 收入最大的十家主要企业（创办年份）	City 城市	Province 省	Telephone/fax 电话/传真	Number of employees 职工人数	Ownership 产业所有权	Revenue ('000 RMB) 销售收入 (千元)	Profit('000 RMB) (rank) 利润(千元) (排名)	Total assets ('000 RMB) 总资产 (千元)	Major products 主要产品
Hangzhou Lin'an Jinjiang Group Co., ltd.	Hangzhou	Zhejiang	(0571)88389111		Private Owned				Textiles
杭州临安锦江集团有限公司(1993)	杭州市	浙江省	(0571)88388848	2,967	私营企业	993,956	77,441(1)	3,253,568	纺织品
Jiangsu Sanxing Embroideries Group Co., Ltd.	Nantong	Jiangsu	(0513)2352308		Joint Stock				Bedclothes
江苏三星绣品集团有限公司(1997)	南通市	江苏省	(0513)2352308	293	股份制	528,400	6,560(30)	53,010	床上用品
Zhejiang Hexing Industrial Co., Ltd.	Jiaxing	Zhejiang	(0573)2313700		Limited-Liability				Humid PU Artificial Leather湿法
浙江禾欣实业股份有限公司(1988)	嘉兴市	浙江省	(0573)2311600	627	有限公司	464,645	48,127(3)	461,670	PU人造革
Zhejiang Huzhou Jinsanjiao Costume Auxiliary Material Group	Huzhou	Zhejiang	(0572)6230888		Collective-owned				Adhesive Line
Co., Ltd.浙江湖州金三发服装辅料集团有限公司(1996)	湖州市	浙江省	(0572)6203999	501	集体企业	300,970	21,290(8)	146,900	粘合衬
Kunshan Insung Artificial Fur Co., ltd.	Suzhou	Jiangsu	(0512)57405931		Foreign Funded				Plush
昆山仁成人造毛皮有限公司(2000)	苏州市	江苏省	(0512)57406935	231	外商投资	235,008	60,410(2)	188,167	长毛绒
Nantong Teigin Co., Ltd.	Nantong	Jiangsu	(0513)3599838		Foreign Funded				Chemical Fibre Printing & Dyeing Cloth化
南通帝人有限公司(1995)	南通市	江苏省	(0513)3597819	794	外商投资	216,955	-	649,037	纤印染布
Shijiazhuang Textile Factory	Shijiazhuang	Hebei	(0311)6828941		State-owned				Cloth
石家庄纺织厂(1999)	石家庄市	河北省	(0311)6824795	3,588	国有企业	184,246	59(389)	286,558	布
Kangnaxiang Enterprise (Shanghai)Co., Ltd.	Shanghai	Shanghai	(021)69211200		Foreign Funded				Non-woven Cloth
康那香企业(上海)有限公司(1998)	上海市	上海市	(021)39202003	389	外商投资	176,759	3,269(62)	299,418	无纺布
China Dragon Textile (Huizhou) Co., Ltd.	Huizhou	Guangdong	(0752)6862888		Overseas Chinese-funded				Nylon Cloth
盛龙纺织（惠州）有限公司(1998)	惠州市	广东省	(0752)6898999	138	港澳台资	175,472	1,742(96)	164,509	尼龙布
BCA (china) Airlaid Co., ltd.	Tianjin	Tianjin	(022)25329333		Foreign Funded				Non-woven Cloth
博爱(中国)膨化芯材有限公司(1999)	天津市	天津市	(022)25329338	167	外商投资	174,605	10,915(21)	503,994	无纺布

Top 10 Cities by Revenue 销售收入排名前10位城市	Province 省	Market share 市场份额 (%)	Number of firms 企业个数
Suzhou 苏州市	Jiangsu 江苏省	13.24	156
Hangzhou 杭州市	Zhejiang 浙江省	8.07	33
Shanghai 上海市	Shanghai 上海市	6.10	44
Jiaxing 嘉兴市	Zhejiang 浙江省	6.01	31
Nantong 南通市	Jiangsu 江苏省	5.82	12
Yancheng 盐城市	Jiangsu 江苏省	3.34	4
Wuxi 无锡市	Jiangsu 江苏省	3.30	25
Yangzhou 扬州市	Jiangsu 江苏省	3.15	10
Huzhou 湖州市	Zhejiang 浙江省	2.84	10
Qingdao 青岛市	Shandong 山东省	2.52	13

10 Major Wholesalers 十家主要批发商	City 城市	Province 省	Telephone/Fax 电话/传真
Shanghai Shenda Co.,Ltd.	Shanghai	Shanghai	(021)62319898
上海申达股份有限公司	上海市	上海市	(021)62317250
Orient International Holding Silk Group Corportion	Shanghai	Shanghai	(021)64662288
东方国际集团丝绸进出口有限公司	上海市	上海市	(021)64677788
Nanjing Textiles Import & Export Co.,Ltd.	Nanjing	Jiangsu	(025)3306789
南京纺织品进出口股份有限公司	南京市	江苏省	(025)3300518
Zhejiang Textiles Import & Export Group Co.,Ltd.	Hangzhou	Zhejiang	(0571)87075888
浙江省纺织品进出口集团有限公司	杭州市	浙江省	(0571)87079234
Zhejiang Orient Holdings Co.,Ltd.	Hangzhou	Zhejiang	(0571)87215678
浙江东方集团股份有限公司	杭州市	浙江省	(0571)87215000
Zhejiang Silk Holding Co.,ltd.	Hangzhou	Zhejiang	(0571)85195588
浙江省丝绸集团有限公司	杭州市	浙江省	(0571)85192540
Guangdong Silk (Group) Corporation	Guangzhou	Guangdong	(020)83337448
广东省丝绸（集团）公司	广州市	广东省	(020)83332995
Shanghai Costume Group Co.,Ltd.	Shanghai	Shanghai	(021)62748598
上海服装（集团）有限公司	上海市	上海市	(021)62414773
Orient International Holding Shanghai Textiles Import & Export Co.Ltd.	Shanghai	Shanghai	(021)63218855
东方国际集团上海市针织品进出口有限公司	上海市	上海市	(021)63299560
Jiangsu Textiles Import & Export Group Co.,Ltd.	Nanjing	Jiangsu	(025)6895000
江苏省纺织品进出口集团股份有限公司	南京市	江苏省	(025)4400800

1810: Apparel 服装制造业

The industry accounts for 2.247% of the total revenue of China's industrial sector in 2002. The rate of return on assets is 5.40%. 80.81% of all firms in the industry made a profit while 19.19% had negative returns.The top province in terms of the industry's revenue is Guangdong, accounting for 22.59% of the total revenue.
2002年本行业收入占全行业的2.247%，资产利润率为5.40%。80.81%的企业赢利，19.19%的企业亏损。收入最高的省为广东省，占本行业的22.59%。

	Total number of firms 企业总数	Total number of employees 职工总数	Total revenue (Mil.RMB) 总销售收入 (百万元)	Total profit (Mil.RMB) 总利润 (百万元)	Return on assets 资产利润率 (%)	Return on equity 权益利润率 (%)	Labour productivity ('000 RMB/ worker) 劳动生产率 (千元/人)	Debts/ assets 资产负债率 (%)	Total assets (Mil.RMB) 总资产 (百万元)
Industry Overall 行业总体	7938	2,316,376	241,003	10,051	5.40	12.40	28.56	56.47	186,199

	Number of firms 企业个数	Average number of employees 平均职工人数	Average revenue ('000 RMB) 平均销售收入（千元）	Average profit ('000 RMB) 平均利润 (千元)	Return on assets 资产利润率 (%)	Return on equity 权益利润率 (%)	Labour productivity ('000 RMB/ worker) 劳动生产率 (千元/人)	Debts/ assets 资产负债率 (%)	Average total assets ('000 RMB) 平均总资产 (千元)
By ownership 产业所有权									
State-owned 国有	232	376	17,934	-240	-0.90	-3.78	13.40	76.15	26,684
Collective-owned 集体	829	311	29,693	1,038	4.74	14.09	26.65	66.35	21,904
Foreign & Overseas Chinese Funded 三资	3,274	330	33,030	1,262	5.15	11.14	27.83	53.79	24,515
By regional distribution 地区分布									
Central-North 华北	689	341	23,244	963	4.17	9.86	20.67	57.70	23,106
Beijing 北京	211	321	20,864	67	0.28	0.82	22.06	66.49	24,213
Tianjin 天津	270	301	23,273	1,215	8.00	21.08	18.73	62.04	15,186
Hebei 河北	175	412	26,621	1,788	6.41	13.77	22.00	53.44	27,874
Shanxi 山西	13	385	15,747	593	1.65	3.26	10.54	49.46	35,960
Inner Mongolia 内蒙古	20	433	23,270	57	0.08	0.12	22.71	29.77	68,271
Northeast 东北	278	311	19,488	574	2.94	6.86	21.04	57.19	19,550
Liaoning 辽宁	227	316	21,543	732	3.68	8.13	22.40	54.70	19,870
Jilin 吉林	41	300	10,454	-12	-0.07	-0.22	12.84	69.59	18,231
Heilongjiang 黑龙江	10	233	9,880	-595	-3.36	-10.60	22.57	68.26	17,701
Central-East 华东	4,702	271	32,060	1,706	7.25	16.41	31.84	55.82	23,528
Shanghai 上海	818	213	27,288	1,400	6.71	14.82	35.74	54.74	20,881
Jiangsu 江苏	1,235	289	38,276	1,780	7.72	18.46	33.90	58.16	23,055
Zhejiang 浙江	1,634	254	32,329	2,033	7.66	17.12	32.67	55.24	26,533
Anhui 安徽	107	237	12,014	169	1.47	4.43	16.46	66.91	11,537
Fujian 福建	467	309	27,519	1,565	8.06	14.34	25.49	43.79	19,415
Jiangxi 江西	56	241	12,205	-127	-0.71	-2.13	16.99	66.45	17,852
Shandong 山东	385	369	35,084	1,595	5.89	15.41	30.04	61.76	27,068
Central-South 中南	2,126	322	31,066	543	2.36	5.44	26.65	56.60	22,998
Henan 河南	83	183	10,121	312	2.84	11.26	19.91	74.81	11,014
Hubei 湖北	197	449	47,786	1,456	3.49	8.19	34.48	57.38	41,684
Hunan 湖南	57	210	14,851	462	3.24	8.04	21.03	59.71	14,260
Guangdong 广东	1,767	317	30,817	454	2.08	4.74	25.76	56.03	21,793
Guangxi 广西	16	218	9,696	4	0.04	0.09	12.47	52.62	9,924
Hainan 海南	6	772	56,202	2,232	4.67	8.57	31.80	45.52	47,807
Southwest 西南	70	309	20,130	179	0.50	0.99	15.55	48.95	35,557
Chongqing 重庆	10	243	23,521	726	2.97	6.87	12.50	56.80	24,463
Sichuan 四川	25	523	36,509	193	0.27	0.49	17.84	44.41	71,005
Guizhou 贵州	8	427	20,082	68	0.26	0.63	13.31	58.66	26,227
Yunnan 云南	13	176	7,479	-22	-0.12	-0.36	11.10	65.84	18,341
Tibet 西藏	14	29	235	14	0.96	2.03	3.77	52.54	1,501
Northwest 西北	73	243	18,774	521	1.34	6.12	24.12	78.04	38,781
Shaanxi 陕西	21	436	18,583	-582	-1.99		15.14	117.99	29,231
Gansu 甘肃	36	92	6,489	275	4.52	9.46	28.80	52.21	6,074
Qinghai 青海	2	567	143,802	12,375	2.94	6.81	22.18	56.88	421,197
Ningxia 宁夏	4	681	101,687	5,711	2.18	9.66	57.43	77.41	261,664
Xinjiang 新疆	10	143	5,234	-724	-6.61	-25.84	8.84	74.43	10,948

1810: Apparel 服装制造业

Year 年份	Number of firms 企业个数	Rate of change 变化率 (%)	Number of employees 职工人数 (人)	Rate of change 变化率 (%)	Total revenue (Mil. RMB) 总销售收入 (百万元)	Rate of change 变化率 (%)	Total profit (Mil RMB) 总利润 (百万元)	Rate of change 变化率 (%)
2000	6130		1,708,607		185,733		7,723	
2001	6908	12.69	2,031,450	18.90	210,602	13.39	9,011	16.68
2002	7938	14.91	2,316,376	14.03	241,003	14.44	10,051	11.54

Major Products 主要产品	Output 产量	Unit 单位
Clothing 服装	877,249	10,000 Pieces 万件
Woven Clothing 梭织服装	459,073	10,000 Pieces 万件

10 Main Firms with Maximal Revenue (year founded) 收入最大的十家主要企业（创办年份）	City 城市	Province 省	Telephone/fax 电话/传真	Number of employees 职工人数	Ownership 产业所有权	Revenue ('000 RMB) 销售收入 (千元)	Profit('000 RMB) (rank) 利润(千元) (排名)	Total assets ('000 RMB) 总资产 (千元)	Major products 主要产品
Hongdou Group Company	Wuxi	Jiangsu	(0510)8761888		Joint Stock				Costume
红豆集团公司(1992)	无锡市	江苏省	(0510)8761777	8,828	股份制	3,015,720	118,150(7)	2,008,890	服装
Jiangsu Zongyi Co., Ltd.	Nantong	Jiangsu	(0513)6563931		Joint Stock				Costume
江苏综艺股份有限公司(1992)	南通市	江苏省	(0513)6563502	3,296	股份制	3,007,320	445,860(1)	1,782,410	服装
Jiangsu Boston Stock Co., Ltd.	Suzhou	Jiangsu	(0512)52532888		Joint Stock				Down Costume
江苏波司登股份有限公司(1994)	苏州市	江苏省	(0512)52538039	9,667	股份制	2,901,593	261,554(3)	2,104,278	羽绒服
Singbo Shenzhou Weaving Group Co., Ltd.	Ningbo	Zhejiang	(0574)86885510		Overseas Chinese-funded				Knitting Dress
宁波申洲织造集团有限公司(1990)	宁波市	浙江省	(0574)86884375	12,479	港澳台资	1,855,484	216,413(4)	1,239,822	针织服装
Youngor Group Co., Ltd.	Ningbo	Zhejiang	(0574)88262530		Joint Stock				Shirt & Western-style Clothes
雅戈尔集团股份有限公司(1993)	宁波市	浙江省	(0574)87425390	13,142	股份制	1,743,061	335,263(2)	4,261,641	衬衫西服
Wuhan Economic & Technology Development Zone Dunkou	Wuhan	Hubei	(027)84891608		Collective-owned				Costume
Industrial General Corp武汉经济技术开发区沌口实业总公司(1994)	武汉市	湖北省	(027)84891608	2,651	集体企业	1,570,487	87,598(13)	331,257	服装
Guangdong Esquel Textiles Co., Ltd.	Foshan	Guangdong	(0757)8826112		Overseas Chinese-funded				Ready-made Clothes
广东溢达纺织有限公司(1988)	佛山市	广东省	(0757)8881510	11,749	港澳台资	1,241,823	72,376(19)	1,064,836	成衣
Zhejiang Jiaxin Silk Co., Ltd.	Jiaxing	Zhejiang	(0573)2085227		Joint Stock				Silk Knitting Dress
浙江嘉欣丝绸股份有限公司(1983)	嘉兴市	浙江省	(0573)2084568	2,533	股份制	1,216,635	32,889(41)	762,795	针织服装
Chengde Dixian Knitting & Spinning Co., Ltd.	Chengde	Hebei	(0314)3115014		Joint Stock				Knitting Dress
承德帝贤针纺股份有限公司(1999)	承德市	河北省	(0314)3011988	12,000	股份制	1,096,580	130,910(5)	1,810,988	针织服装
Jiangsu Chenfeng Group Co., Ltd.	Changzhou	Jiangsu	(0519)2399999		Joint Stock				Silk Costume
江苏晨风集团股份有限公司(1992)	常州市	江苏省	(0519)2390000	8,688	股份制	817,440	76,060(17)	658,240	丝绸服装

Top 10 Cities by Revenue 销售收入排名前10位城市	Province 省	Market share 市场份额 (%)	Number of firms 企业个数
Shanghai 上海市	Shanghai 上海市	9.26	818
Ningbo 宁波市	Zhejiang 浙江省	6.26	409
Guangzhou 广州市	Guangdong 广东省	5.08	453
Suzhou 苏州市	Jiangsu 江苏省	4.70	296
Jiaxing 嘉兴市	Zhejiang 浙江省	3.82	248
Quanzhou 泉州市	Fujian 福建省	3.79	303
Wuxi 无锡市	Jiangsu 江苏省	3.79	155
Nantong 南通市	Jiangsu 江苏省	3.59	214
Shaoxing 绍兴市	Zhejiang 浙江省	3.52	243
Hangzhou 杭州市	Zhejiang 浙江省	2.81	241

10 Major Wholesalers 十家主要批发商	City 城市	Province 省	Telephone/Fax 电话/传真
Jiangsu Sainty Co.,Ltd.	Nanjing	Jiangsu	(025)4208688
江苏舜天股份有限公司	南京市	江苏省	(025)4200397
Zhejiang Zhongda Group Co.,Ltd.	Hangzhou	Zhejiang	(0571)85155000
浙江中大集团股份有限公司	杭州市	浙江省	(0571)85777050
Guangdong Textiles Import & Export (Group) Company	Guangzhou	Guangdong	(020)83558988
广东省纺织品进出口（集团）公司	广州市	广东省	(020)83553900
Zhejiang Shindri Group Co., ltd.	Hangzhou	Zhejiang	(0571)87795067
浙江新大集团有限公司	杭州市	浙江省	(0571)87031999
China-Base Ningbo Foreign Trade Co.,Ltd.	Ningbo	Zhejiang	(0574)87425510
中基宁波对外贸易股份有限公司	宁波市	浙江省	(0574)87425666
Jiaxing Import & Export Corporation	Jiaxing	Zhejiang	(0573)2062785
嘉兴市进出口公司	嘉兴市	浙江省	(0573)2084488
Liaoning Times Costume Import & Export Co.,Ltd.	Dalian	Liaoning	(0411)2798320
辽宁时代服装进出口股份有限公司	大连市	辽宁省	(0411)2798000
China Drawnwork Shanghai Import & Export Company	Shanghai	Shanghai	(021)63258888
中国抽纱上海进出口公司	上海市	上海市	(021)63246020
China (Fujian) Foreign Trade Center (Holdings)	Fuzhou	Fujian	(0591)7553065
中国（福建）对外贸易中心集团	福州市	福建省	(0591)7537173
Xiamen Xinde Co., Ltd.	Xiamen	Fujian	(0592)6027854
厦门信达股份有限公司	厦门市	福建省	(0592)6021391

1820: Hats 制帽业

The industry accounts for 0.034% of the total revenue of China's industrial sector in 2002. The rate of return on assets is 4.47%. 82.74% of all firms in the industry made a profit while 17.26% had negative returns.The top province in terms of the industry's revenue is Jiangsu, accounting for 32.89% of the total revenue.
2002年本行业收入占全行业的0.034%，资产利润率为4.47%。82.74%的企业赢利，17.26%的企业亏损。收入最高的省为江苏省，占本行业的32.89%。

	Total number of firms 企业总数	Total number of employees 职工总数	Total revenue (Mil.RMB) 总销售收入 (百万元)	Total profit (Mil.RMB) 总利润 (百万元)	Return on assets 资产利润率 (%)	Return on equity 权益利润率 (%)	Labour productivity ('000 RMB/ worker) 劳动生产率 (千元/人)	Debts/ assets 资产负债率 (%)	Total assets (Mil.RMB) 总资产 (百万元)
Industry Overall 行业总体	168	40,781	3,690	120	4.47	10.25	25.41	56.35	2,684

	Number of firms 企业个数	Average number of employees 平均职工人数	Average revenue ('000 RMB) 平均销售收入 (千元)	Average profit ('000 RMB) 平均利润 (千元)	Return on assets 资产利润率 (%)	Return on equity 权益利润率 (%)	Labour productivity ('000 RMB/ worker) 劳动生产率 (千元/人)	Debts/ assets 资产负债率 (%)	Average total assets ('000 RMB) 平均总资产 (千元)
By ownership 产业所有权									
State-owned 国有	3	221	991	-657	-6.28	-27.27	0.91	76.98	10,471
Collective-owned 集体	21	222	21,707	956	8.84	21.23	29.03	58.36	10,811
Foreign & Overseas Chinese Funded 三资	76	264	27,145	844	4.06	8.22	26.34	50.65	20,799
By regional distribution 地区分布									
Central-North 华北	15	266	15,891	1,389	8.34	19.23	16.04	56.65	16,659
Beijing 北京	3	290	9,525	45	0.25	0.57	10.81	55.30	17,944
Tianjin 天津	6	107	12,888	2,072	31.52	67.69	21.22	53.43	6,572
Hebei 河北	6	414	22,077	1,378	5.28	12.54	16.53	57.92	26,105
Shanxi 山西									
Inner Mongolia 内蒙古									
Northeast 东北	3	248	12,012	192	1.34	2.67	17.31	49.91	14,337
Liaoning 辽宁	2	288	14,758	247	1.51	4.07	13.12	62.88	16,361
Jilin 吉林	1	170	6,520	81	0.79	0.86	31.48	8.65	10,290
Heilongjiang 黑龙江									
Central-East 华东	95	245	25,450	793	4.74	13.59	28.50	65.16	16,744
Shanghai 上海	19	183	29,855	1,057	4.49	15.68	31.78	71.37	23,549
Jiangsu 江苏	48	249	25,285	837	5.41	14.93	32.28	63.77	15,464
Zhejiang 浙江	14	183	17,084	994	10.99	31.38	21.81	64.99	9,050
Anhui 安徽									
Fujian 福建	3	207	39,026	-385	-1.77	-3.89	49.44	54.50	21,744
Jiangxi 江西									
Shandong 山东	11	422	25,505	211	1.11	2.79	17.20	60.22	19,002
Central-South 中南	53	232	18,282	393	2.66	4.36	23.31	39.07	14,768
Henan 河南	2	140	6,574	2	0.02	0.05	13.58	61.37	8,334
Hubei 湖北	3	204	11,437	280	6.64	18.67	20.84	64.44	4,222
Hunan 湖南									
Guangdong 广东	48	238	19,197	416	2.65	4.28	23.68	38.16	15,696
Guangxi 广西									
Hainan 海南									
Southwest 西南									
Chongqing 重庆									
Sichuan 四川									
Guizhou 贵州									
Yunnan 云南									
Tibet 西藏									
Northwest 西北	2	236	14,619	1,258	14.16	23.62	19.81	40.04	8,882
Shaanxi 陕西									
Gansu 甘肃	1	51	4,127	106	3.67	4.80	32.59	23.49	2,886
Qinghai 青海	1	420	25,110	2,410	16.20	28.54	18.26	43.25	14,878
Ningxia 宁夏									
Xinjiang 新疆									

Year 年份	Number of firms 企业个数	Rate of change 变化率 (%)	Number of employees 职工人数 (人)	Rate of change 变化率 (%)	Total revenue (Mil. RMB) 总销售收入 (百万元)	Rate of change 变化率 (%)	Total profit (Mil RMB) 总利润 (百万元)	Rate of change 变化率 (%)
2000	147		35,475		3,018		75	
2001	158	7.48	39,769	12.10	3,554	17.76	119	58.67
2002	168	6.33	40,781	2.54	3,690	3.83	120	0.84

Major Products 主要产品	Output 产量	Unit 单位
Sutured Cap 缝制帽	47,026	10,000 Pieces 万顶

10 Main Firms with Maximal Revenue (year founded) 收入最大的十家主要企业（创办年份）	City 城市	Province 省	Telephone/fax 电话/传真	Number of employees 职工人数	Ownership 产业所有权	Revenue ('000 RMB) 销售收入(千元)	Profit('000 RMB) (rank) 利润(千元)(排名)	Total assets ('000 RMB) 总资产(千元)	Major products 主要产品
Asian Scourcing Headwear MFG Co., Ltd.	Shanghai	Shanghai	(021)54950011		Foreign Funded				Hat
上海亚源制帽有限公司(1996)	上海市	上海市	(021)64952032	532	外商投资	167,211	9,810(3)	100,760	帽子
Zhongshan Weili Textiles Co., Ltd.	Zhongshan	Guangdong	(0760)6682368		Overseas Chinese-funded				Sports Cap
中山伟立纺织品有限公司(1995)	中山市	广东省	(0760)6686524	1,140	港澳台资	150,827	2,698(14)	146,901	运动帽
Qingdao Dachang Caps Co., Ltd.	Qingdao	Shandong	(0532)8288970		Overseas Chinese-funded				Sports Cap
青岛大昌制帽有限公司(1998)	青岛市	山东省	(0532)8283251	1,800	港澳台资	115,532	823(40)	101,670	运动帽
Shanghai Fantai Cap Making Co., Ltd.	Shanghai	Shanghai	(021)54950011		Foreign Funded				Hat
上海泛太制帽有限公司(2000)	上海市	上海市	(021)64952032	300	外商投资	114,190	2,690(15)	41,534	帽子
Zhangpu Cailan Caps Co., Ltd.	Zhangzhou	Fujian	(0596)3225371		Foreign Funded				Cloth Hat
漳浦彩蓝制帽有限公司(1995)	漳州市	福建省	(0596)3225373	400	外商投资	70,084	315(72)	30,214	布帽
Changshu Hats Factory	Suzhou	Jiangsu	(0520)52770414		Limited-Liability				Artistic Hat
常熟市帽厂(1997)	苏州市	江苏省	(0520)52774034	763	有限公司	66,508	1,203(27)	76,165	工艺帽
Dongguan Lucky Zone Hat Products Co., Ltd.	Dongguan	Guangdong	(0769)6655951		Foreign Funded				Sunbonnet
东莞好事域制帽有限公司(1994)	东莞市	广东省	(0769)6653193	505	外商投资	60,178	400(63)	21,837	太阳帽
Hebei Lihua Cap Making Group Co., Ltd.	Baoding	Hebei	(0312)6922075		Limited-Liability				Hat
河北丽华制帽集团有限公司(1985)	保定市	河北省	(0312)6922886	1,594	有限公司	50,540	225(83)	111,258	礼帽
Jurong Kitting Caps Factory	Zhenjiang	Jiangsu	(0511)7671097		Private Enterprises				Kitting Hat
句容市针织制帽厂(1982)	镇江市	江苏省	(0511)7671028	505	私营独资	48,028	827(38)	22,578	针织帽
Jinzhou Hat Industry Co., Ltd.	Shijiazhuang	Hebei	(0311)4358506		Collective-owned				Hat
晋州市帽业有限公司(1997)	石家庄市	河北省	(0311)4359892	280	集体企业	44,225	4,720(7)	8,109	帽子

Top 10 Cities by Revenue 销售收入排名前10位城市	Province 省	Market share 市场份额 (%)	Number of firms 企业个数
Shanghai 上海市	Shanghai 上海市	15.37	19
Yangzhou 扬州市	Jiangsu 江苏省	7.94	17
Suzhou 苏州市	Jiangsu 江苏省	7.63	3
Qingdao 青岛市	Shandong 山东省	6.69	9
Guangzhou 广州市	Guangdong 广东省	6.55	14
Nantong 南通市	Jiangsu 江苏省	6.50	14
Dongguan 东莞市	Guangdong 广东省	5.01	6
Zhongshan 中山市	Guangdong 广东省	4.47	3
Yangjiang 阳江市	Guangdong 广东省	4.02	12
Wuxi 无锡市	Jiangsu 江苏省	3.77	2

10 Major Wholesalers 十家主要批发商	City 城市	Province 省	Telephone/Fax 电话/传真
Wenzhou M & C Foreign Trade Corp	Wenzhou	Zhejiang	(0577)88862999
温州市五机化医外贸有限公司	温州市	浙江省	(0577)88862901
Light Industrial Products Arts and Crafts Import & Export (Group) Corporation	Quanzhou	Fujian	(0595)2552255
轻工工艺进出口集团公司	泉州市	福建省	(0595)2552233
Shanghai Handicrafts Gloves & Hat Industry Import & Export Co.,Ltd.	Shanghai	Shanghai	(021)58990180
上海市工艺品手套帽业进出口有限公司	上海市	上海市	(021)58991146
Shanghai Shen'an Foreign Economic & Trade Corporation	Shanghai	Shanghai	(021)62871088
上海申安对外经济贸易公司	上海市	上海市	(021)62871108
Wenzhou Cereals ,Oils & Foodstuffs Foreign Trade Corp.	Wenzhou	Zhejiang	(0577)88862756
温州市粮油食品对外贸易公司	温州市	浙江省	(0577)88826303
Wenzhou Foreign Trade Industial Products Co., Ltd.	Wenzhou	Zhejiang	(0577)88862788
温州外贸工业品有限公司	温州市	浙江省	(0577)88862799
Zhejiang Ouhai International Trade Corp.	Wenzhou	Zhejiang	(0577)88820092
浙江省瓯海对外贸易公司	温州市	浙江省	(0577)88829093
Shenzhen Light Industry Prodacts Import & Export Company	Shenzhen	Guangdong	(0755)82379000
深圳轻工业品进出口公司	深圳市	广东省	(0755)82379466
Zhejiang Chinabase Impex Co.,Ltd.	Hangzhou	Zhejiang	(0571)87819435
浙江中基进出口有限公司	杭州市	浙江省	(0571)87819437
Zhejiang Qingtian Foreign Trade Co.,ltd.	Lishui	Zhejiang	(0578)6833651
浙江省青田县对外贸易有限公司	丽水市	浙江省	(0578)6822963

1830: Shoes 制鞋业

The industry accounts for 0.158% of the total revenue of China's industrial sector in 2002. The rate of return on assets is 4.36%. 85.45% of all firms in the industry made a profit while 14.55% had negative returns.The top province in terms of the industry's revenue is Guangdong, accounting for 24.60% of the total revenue.
2002年本行业收入占全行业的 0.158%，资产利润率为 4.36%。85.45%的企业赢利，14.55%的企业亏损。收入最高的省为广东省，占本行业的24.60%。

	Total number of firms 企业总数	Total number of employees 职工总数	Total revenue (Mil.RMB) 总销售收入 (百万元)	Total profit (Mil.RMB) 总利润 (百万元)	Return on assets 资产利润率 (%)	Return on equity 权益利润率 (%)	Labour productivity ('000 RMB/ worker) 劳动生产率 (千元/人)	Debts/ assets 资产负债率 (%)	Total assets (Mil.RMB) 总资产 (百万元)
Industry Overall 行业总体	605	223,337	16,967	492	4.36	10.39	21.90	58.06	11,301

	Number of firms 企业个数	Average number of employees 平均职工人数	Average revenue ('000 RMB) 平均销售收入 (千元)	Average profit ('000 RMB) 平均利润 (千元)	Return on assets 资产利润率 (%)	Return on equity 权益利润率 (%)	Labour productivity ('000 RMB/ worker) 劳动生产率 (千元/人)	Debts/ assets 资产负债率 (%)	Average total assets ('000 RMB) 平均总资产 (千元)
By ownership 产业所有权									
State-owned 国有	11	160	11,365	-786	-3.98	-24.31	17.82	83.62	19,742
Collective-owned 集体	66	362	33,986	1,676	12.40	40.29	30.52	69.22	13,518
Foreign & Overseas Chinese Funded 三资	185	657	43,945	835	2.46	5.63	20.38	56.38	34,001
By regional distribution 地区分布									
Central-North 华北	23	328	65,489	4,554	23.77	58.22	60.44	59.17	19,158
Beijing 北京	6	262	17,299	244	1.81	4.68	17.70	61.38	13,518
Tianjin 天津	8	258	31,743	2,483	17.87	57.60	38.81	68.97	13,896
Hebei 河北	9	435	127,613	9,267	33.58	73.10	89.02	54.06	27,596
Shanxi 山西									
Inner Mongolia 内蒙古									
Northeast 东北	7	219	12,957	-223	-0.86	-1.75	16.97	50.90	26,049
Liaoning 辽宁	2	410	4,320	-1,756	-3.51	-4.53	1.42	22.47	50,036
Jilin 吉林	2	208	18,836				24.15	93.62	21,471
Heilongjiang 黑龙江	3	100	14,795	649	4.95	21.14	49.52	76.58	13,111
Central-East 华东	415	288	23,461	643	4.37	10.33	23.91	57.66	14,695
Shanghai 上海	28	163	19,690	1,176	13.39	39.54	26.02	66.14	8,787
Jiangsu 江苏	73	298	30,036	617	4.36	18.42	27.57	76.33	14,144
Zhejiang 浙江	190	181	15,784	498	4.93	9.81	21.25	49.70	10,097
Anhui 安徽	6	268	12,435	949	9.67	16.33	14.99	40.76	9,804
Fujian 福建	77	522	34,294	838	3.19	6.23	24.35	48.83	26,293
Jiangxi 江西	2	125	6,750	135	0.83		80.78	101.68	16,240
Shandong 山东	39	437	32,432	608	3.02	10.81	23.00	72.09	20,138
Central-South 中南	146	614	35,600	626	2.19	5.37	16.23	59.12	28,519
Henan 河南	34	307	23,690	1,131	7.02	18.80	23.75	62.67	16,113
Hubei 湖北	6	464	22,235	1,289	12.86	24.39	17.08	47.27	10,023
Hunan 湖南	6	268	14,225	175	0.99	1.35	18.50	26.68	17,687
Guangdong 广东	100	748	41,734	442	1.28	3.18	15.11	59.77	34,496
Guangxi 广西									
Hainan 海南									
Southwest 西南	9	521	47,161	3,376	7.57	17.43	18.61	56.56	44,579
Chongqing 重庆	4	289	12,701	796	5.60	17.56	7.24	68.13	14,221
Sichuan 四川	1	2,470	363,320	28,538	10.18	17.65	30.83	42.31	280,358
Guizhou 贵州	1	563	6,232	-189	-0.93	-20.88	1.93	95.53	20,258
Yunnan 云南	1	451	3,663	-1,215	-2.88		3.70	118.21	42,188
Tibet 西藏	2	28	216	32	4.14	5.21	1.20	20.50	761
Northwest 西北	5	58	2,258	121	4.07	5.16	19.52	21.20	2,970
Shaanxi 陕西									
Gansu 甘肃	5	58	2,258	121	4.07	5.16	19.52	21.20	2,970
Qinghai 青海									
Ningxia 宁夏									
Xinjiang 新疆									

Year 年份	Number of firms 企业个数	Rate of change 变化率(%)	Number of employees 职工人数(人)	Rate of change 变化率(%)	Total revenue (Mil. RMB) 总销售收入(百万元)	Rate of change 变化率(%)	Total profit (Mil RMB) 总利润(百万元)	Rate of change 变化率(%)
2000	443		227,296		14,461		431	
2001	598	34.99	220,976	-2.78	16,366	13.17	433	0.46
2002	605	1.17	223,337	1.07	16,967	3.67	492	13.63

Major Products 主要产品	Output 产量	Unit 单位
Shoe Leather 皮鞋	152,282	10,000 Pairs 万双
Cloth Shoes 布鞋	53,251	10,000 Pairs 万双

10 Main Firms with Maximal Revenue (year founded) 收入最大的十家主要企业（创办年份）	City 城市	Province 省	Telephone/fax 电话/传真	Number of employees 职工人数	Ownership 产业所有权	Revenue ('000 RMB) 销售收入(千元)	Profit('000 RMB) (rank) 利润(千元)(排名)	Total assets ('000 RMB) 总资产(千元)	Major products 主要产品
Sihui Jinbaoli Rubber Shoes Factory Co., Ltd.	Zhaoqing	Guangdong	(0758)3367112		Overseas Chinese-funded				Shoes
四会金宝利橡胶鞋厂有限公司(1988)	肇庆市	广东省	(0758)3321818	3,928	港澳台资	551,930	3,012(37)	439,688	鞋
NiKe (Suzhou) Sports Products Co.Ltd.	Suzhou	Jiangsu	(0512)53589898		Foreign Funded				Nike Gym Shoes耐
耐克(苏州)体育用品有限公司(1996)	苏州市	江苏省	(0512)53589958	3,723	外商投资	403,720	13,170(7)	145,210	克运动鞋
Zhongshan Jingmei Shoes Wear Co.Ltd.	Zhongshan	Guangdong	(0760)5314511		Foreign Funded				Finished Shoes
中山精美鞋业有限公司(2000)	中山市	广东省	(0760)5315439	2,000	外商投资	372,500	-	256,873	成品鞋
Neijiang Santai Shoes Co., Ltd.	Neijiang	Sichuan	(0832)2101432		Limited-Liability				Liberation shoes
内江市三泰鞋服有限公司(1998)	内江市	四川省	(0832)2115079	2,470	有限公司	363,320	28,538(2)	280,358	解放鞋
Shijiazhuang Jizhong Industrial Company	Shijiazhuang	Hebei	(0311)7754957		Collective-owned				Shoes
石家庄市冀中实业公司(1993)	石家庄市	河北省	(0311)7754965	1,180	集体企业	335,710	26,580(3)	29,073	鞋
Rongguang Group Co., Ltd.	Wenzhou	Zhejiang	(0577)65600898		Limited-Liability				Rubber Shoes With Cloth Cover
荣光集团有限公司(1999)	温州市	浙江省	(0577)65600898	4,020	有限公司	306,071	6,058(18)	385,500	布面胶鞋
Putian Synco Shoes Wear Co., Ltd.	Putian	Fujian	(0594)3991178		Foreign Funded				Man and Woman's Portable Shoes男
莆田新果鞋业有限公司(1988)	莆田市	福建省	(0594)3991279	3,000	外商投资	247,561	6,807(16)	150,147	女轻便鞋
Xuchang Hongde Shoes Industry Co., Ltd.	Xuchang	Henan	(0374)5651591		Overseas Chinese-funded				Cloth Shoes
许昌宏德鞋业有限公司(1996)	许昌市	河南省	(0374)5651590	2,600	港澳台资	214,134	11,452(11)	216,733	布鞋
Putian Huafeng Shoes Industry Co., Ltd.	Putian	Fujian	(0594)5365888		Private Owned				Gym Shoes
莆田市华丰鞋业有限公司(1993)	莆田市	福建省	(0594)5367842	1,450	私营企业	184,662	5,893(20)	32,374	运动鞋
Yongfeng Shoes Industry (Bao'an) Co., Ltd.	Shenzhen	Guangdong	(0755)27098888		Overseas Chinese-funded				Shoes
永丰鞋业（宝安）有限公司(1989)	深圳市	广东省	(0755)27098152	3,500	港澳台资	179,871	639(173)	119,128	鞋

Top 10 Cities by Revenue 销售收入排名前10位城市	Province 省	Market share 市场份额(%)	Number of firms 企业个数
Wenzhou 温州市	Zhejiang 浙江省	11.35	116
Putian 莆田市	Fujian 福建省	7.38	30
Quanzhou 泉州市	Fujian 福建省	5.90	33
Dongguan 东莞市	Guangdong 广东省	5.79	19
Suzhou 苏州市	Jiangsu 江苏省	5.41	12
Zhongshan 中山市	Guangdong 广东省	4.82	14
Hengshui 衡水市	Hebei 河北省	4.37	2
Zhaoqing 肇庆市	Guangdong 广东省	4.15	10
Qingdao 青岛市	Shandong 山东省	3.69	11
Guangzhou 广州市	Guangdong 广东省	3.30	20

10 Major Wholesalers 十家主要批发商	City 城市	Province 省	Telephone/Fax 电话/传真
Wenzhou M & C Foreign Trade Corp	Wenzhou	Zhejiang	(0577)88862999
温州市五机化医外贸有限公司	温州市	浙江省	(0577)88862901
Light Industrial Products Arts and Crafts Import & Export (Group) Corporation	Quanzhou	Fujian	(0595)2552255
轻工工艺进出口集团公司	泉州市	福建省	(0595)2552233
Shanghai Handicrafts Gloves & Hat Industry Import & Export Co.,Ltd.	Shanghai	Shanghai	(021)58990180
上海市工艺品手套帽业进出口有限公司	上海市	上海市	(021)58991146
Shanghai Shen'an Foreign Economic & Trade Corporation	Shanghai	Shanghai	(021)62871088
上海申安对外经济贸易公司	上海市	上海市	(021)62871108
Wenzhou Cereals ,Oils & Foodstuffs Foreign Trade Corp.	Wenzhou	Zhejiang	(0577)88862756
温州市粮油食品对外贸易公司	温州市	浙江省	(0577)88826303
Wenzhou Foreign Trade Industial Products Co., Ltd.	Wenzhou	Zhejiang	(0577)88862788
温州外贸工业品有限公司	温州市	浙江省	(0577)88862799
Zhejiang Ouhai International Trade Corp.	Wenzhou	Zhejiang	(0577)88820092
浙江省瓯海对外贸易公司	温州市	浙江省	(0577)88829093
Shenzhen Light Industry Prodacts Import & Export Company	Shenzhen	Guangdong	(0755)82379000
深圳轻工业品进出口公司	深圳市	广东省	(0755)82379466
Zhejiang Chinabase Impex Co.,Ltd.	Hangzhou	Zhejiang	(0571)87819435
浙江中基进出口有限公司	杭州市	浙江省	(0571)87819437
Zhejiang Qingtian Foreign Trade Co.,ltd.	Lishui	Zhejiang	(0578)6833651
浙江省青田县对外贸易有限公司	丽水市	浙江省	(0578)6822963

1890: Other Apparel 其他纤维制品制造业

The industry accounts for 0.102% of the total revenue of China's industrial sector in 2002. The rate of return on assets is 5.94%. 86.86% of all firms in the industry made a profit while 13.14% had negative returns.The top province in terms of the industry's revenue is Jiangsu, accounting for 29.45% of the total revenue.
2002年本行业收入占全行业的 0.102%，资产利润率为 5.94%。86.86%的企业赢利，13.14%的企业亏损。收入最高的省为江苏省，占本行业的29.45%。

	Total number of firms 企业总数	Total number of employees 职工总数	Total revenue (Mil.RMB) 总销售收入（百万元）	Total profit (Mil.RMB) 总利润（百万元）	Return on assets 资产利润率（%）	Return on equity 权益利润率（%）	Labour productivity ('000 RMB/worker) 劳动生产率（千元/人）	Debts/assets 资产负债率（%）	Total assets (Mil.RMB) 总资产（百万元）
Industry Overall 行业总体	350	76,968	10,890	456	5.94	13.87	32.78	57.20	7,673

	Number of firms 企业个数	Average number of employees 平均职工人数	Average revenue ('000 RMB) 平均销售收入（千元）	Average profit ('000 RMB) 平均利润（千元）	Return on assets 资产利润率（%）	Return on equity 权益利润率（%）	Labour productivity ('000 RMB/worker) 劳动生产率（千元/人）	Debts/assets 资产负债率（%）	Average total assets ('000 RMB) 平均总资产（千元）
By ownership 产业所有权									
State-owned 国有	13	277	15,223	257	0.76	4.11	14.09	81.55	33,933
Collective-owned 集体	40	178	20,943	804	5.90	12.25	34.10	51.81	13,621
Foreign & Overseas Chinese Funded 三资	155	238	36,317	1,651	5.80	12.40	27.94	53.27	28,496
By regional distribution 地区分布									
Central-North 华北	24	194	13,884	1,097	7.41	34.19	20.95	78.33	14,803
Beijing 北京	7	116	10,589	-103	-1.49	-3.10	21.80	52.12	6,942
Tianjin 天津	13	151	18,660	2,013	14.06	28.30	37.42	50.33	14,325
Hebei 河北	4	473	4,129	217	0.72		3.47	132.19	30,113
Shanxi 山西									
Inner Mongolia 内蒙古									
Northeast 东北	10	246	41,549	3,541	15.35	26.21	36.46	41.44	23,074
Liaoning 辽宁	7	285	55,429	4,904	17.19	28.00	35.14	38.59	28,524
Jilin 吉林	2	183	13,645	542	3.83	9.02	52.12	57.55	14,136
Heilongjiang 黑龙江	1	100	200				5.60	82.14	2,800
Central-East 华东	223	213	36,387	1,638	6.72	15.82	36.54	57.54	24,382
Shanghai 上海	25	114	35,630	2,248	10.76	17.53	101.67	38.59	20,879
Jiangsu 江苏	62	224	51,738	2,109	5.89	15.62	56.34	62.28	35,811
Zhejiang 浙江	38	137	22,053	1,525	10.40	20.95	38.20	50.37	14,668
Anhui 安徽	3	227	20,015	468	0.91	15.40	24.42	94.09	51,421
Fujian 福建	71	241	33,562	1,183	5.69	13.64	12.90	58.29	20,792
Jiangxi 江西	1	400	4,197	527	7.31	10.15	6.69	27.99	7,213
Shandong 山东	23	319	31,767	1,492	6.87	14.07	30.59	51.20	21,731
Central-South 中南	87	247	22,936	324	1.77	3.81	27.12	53.49	18,259
Henan 河南	5	108	11,214	-20	-0.24	-3.25	21.86	92.70	8,435
Hubei 湖北	32	376	24,519	814	7.49	18.93	25.55	60.41	10,869
Hunan 湖南	2	147	7,561	1		0.02	18.98	73.43	21,209
Guangdong 广东	44	187	25,438	66	0.28	0.52	30.49	46.79	23,871
Guangxi 广西	3	89	3,221	39	0.76	2.45	10.24	68.81	5,148
Hainan 海南	1	78	10,656	-827	-0.92	-3.58	38.63	74.42	90,333
Southwest 西南	3	214	5,614	110	0.73	1.26	18.01	41.65	15,039
Chongqing 重庆	3	214	5,614	110	0.73	1.26	18.01	41.65	15,039
Sichuan 四川									
Guizhou 贵州									
Yunnan 云南									
Tibet 西藏									
Northwest 西北	3	84	5,033	62	1.16		27.21	112.34	5,382
Shaanxi 陕西									
Gansu 甘肃	3	84	5,033	62	1.16		27.21	112.34	5,382
Qinghai 青海									
Ningxia 宁夏									
Xinjiang 新疆									

1890: Other Apparel 其他纤维制品制造业

Year 年份	Number of firms 企业个数	Rate of change 变化率 (%)	Number of employees 职工人数 (人)	Rate of change 变化率 (%)	Total revenue (Mil. RMB) 总销售收入 (百万元)	Rate of change 变化率 (%)	Total profit (Mil RMB) 总利润 (百万元)	Rate of change 变化率 (%)
2000	344		69,191		10,089		414	
2001	373	8.43	78,509	13.47	11,075	9.77	506	22.22
2002	350	-6.17	76,968	-1.96	10,890	-1.67	456	-9.88

Major Products 主要产品	Output 产量	Unit 单位

10 Main Firms with Maximal Revenue (year founded) 收入最大的十家主要企业（创办年份）	City 城市	Province 省	Telephone/fax 电话/传真	Number of employees 职工人数	Ownership 产业所有权	Revenue ('000 RMB) 销售收入 (千元)	Profit('000 RMB) (rank) 利润(千元) (排名)	Total assets ('000 RMB) 总资产 (千元)	Major products 主要产品
Xiamen Jinxiong Enterprise Co., Ltd.	Xiamen	Fujian	(0592)6022106		Overseas Chinese-funded				Tent
厦门进雄企业有限公司(1988)	厦门市	福建省	(0592)6022108	2,380	港澳台资	1,285,587	56,435(1)	1,028,646	帐篷
Jiangsu Jiangnan High Polyner Fiber Co., Ltd.	Suzhou	Jiangsu	(0512)65481181		Limited-Liability				Terylene Staple Yarn
江苏江南化纤集团有限公司(1970)	苏州市	江苏省	(0512)65481181	674	有限公司	1,111,520	45,670(2)	657,440	涤纶短丝
Qingdao Nannan Co., Ltd.	Qingdao	Shandong	(0532)4835888		Foreign Funded				Woman Underwear
青岛南南有限公司(1993)	青岛市	山东省	(0532)4835688	2,115	外商投资	271,003	20,253(4)	228,912	女用内衣
Huzhou Huanqiu Light Industry Textile Group Co.,Ltd.	Huzhou	Zhejiang	(0572)2262528		Limited-Liability				Gloves
浙江环球轻纺集团有限公司(1989)	湖州市	浙江省	(0572)2260939	485	有限公司	191,708	16,776(6)	92,655	手套
Shanghai Guangming Knitting Head Factory	Shanghai	Shanghai	(021)65132223		Collective-owned				Knitting Dress
上海光明针织总厂(1979)	上海市	上海市	(021)35011110	374	集体企业	180,841	1,025(74)	19,091	针织服装
No.3521 Factory	Nanjing	Jiangsu	(025)4593521		State-owned				Costume
第三五二一工厂(1941)	南京市	江苏省	(025)4583521	1,262	国有企业	160,000	3,000(32)	237,040	服装
Suzhou Eusedio Sporting Co., Ltd.	Suzhou	Jiangsu	(0512)53445368		Overseas Chinese-funded				Sleeping Bag
苏州锦园旅游用品有限公司(1995)	苏州市	江苏省	(0512)53447857	351	港澳台资	145,000	10,100(9)	82,660	睡袋
Xinhui Tioneer Elastic Fabric Co., Ltd.	Jiangmen	Guangdong	(0750)6890680		Overseas Chinese-funded				Other Fibre Products
新会弹性织物有限公司(1993)	江门市	广东省	(0750)6890188	450	港澳台资	108,701	786(90)	187,753	其他纤维制品
Yingkou MS Sewing Products Co., Ltd.	Yingkou	Liaoning	(0417)6239419		Foreign Funded				Ski Glove
营口刚进缝制品有限公司(1989)	营口市	辽宁省	(0417)6239753	536	外商投资	102,820	23,450(3)	41,022	滑雪手套
Qidong Honghai Non-woven Fabric Co., Ltd.	Nantong	Jiangsu	(0513)3799098		Private Owned				Chemical Fabric Cloth
启东鸿海无纺织物有限公司(1996)	南通市	江苏省	(0513)3799088	72	私营企业	98,855	2,818(33)	4,853	化纤布

Top 10 Cities by Revenue 销售收入排名前10位城市	Province 省	Market share 市场份额 (%)	Number of firms 企业个数
Suzhou 苏州市	Jiangsu 江苏省	13.32	8
Xiamen 厦门市	Fujian 福建省	12.53	7
Shanghai 上海市	Shanghai 上海市	8.18	25
Quanzhou 泉州市	Fujian 福建省	7.68	57
Qingdao 青岛市	Shandong 山东省	4.36	10
Zhenjiang 镇江市	Jiangsu 江苏省	3.99	14
Nantong 南通市	Jiangsu 江苏省	2.86	10
Yangzhou 扬州市	Jiangsu 江苏省	2.57	8
Nanjing 南京市	Jiangsu 江苏省	2.48	4

10 Major Wholesalers 十家主要批发商	City 城市	Province 省	Telephone/Fax 电话/传真
Shanghai Shenda Co.,Ltd.	Shanghai	Shanghai	(021)62319898
上海申达股份有限公司	上海市	上海市	(021)62317250
Orient International Holding Silk Group Corportion	Shanghai	Shanghai	(021)64662288
东方国际集团丝绸进出口有限公司	上海市	上海市	(021)64677788
Nanjing Textiles Import & Export Co.,Ltd.	Nanjing	Jiangsu	(025)3306789
南京纺织品进出口股份有限公司	南京市	江苏省	(025)3300518
Zhejiang Textiles Import & Export Group Co.,Ltd.	Hangzhou	Zhejiang	(0571)87075888
浙江省纺织品进出口集团有限公司	杭州市	浙江省	(0571)87079234
Zhejiang Orient Holdings Co.,Ltd.	Hangzhou	Zhejiang	(0571)87215678
浙江东方集团股份有限公司	杭州市	浙江省	(0571)87215000
Zhejiang Silk Holding Co.,ltd.	Hangzhou	Zhejiang	(0571)85195588
浙江省丝绸集团有限公司	杭州市	浙江省	(0571)85192540
Guangdong Silk (Group) Corporation	Guangzhou	Guangdong	(020)83337448
广东省丝绸（集团）公司	广州市	广东省	(020)83332995
Shanghai Costume Group Co.,Ltd.	Shanghai	Shanghai	(021)62748598
上海服装（集团）有限公司	上海市	上海市	(021)62414773
Orient International Holding Shanghai Textiles Import & Export Co.Ltd.	Shanghai	Shanghai	(021)63218855
东方国际集团上海市针织品进出口有限公司	上海市	上海市	(021)63299560
Jiangsu Textiles Import & Export Group Co.,Ltd.	Nanjing	Jiangsu	(025)6895000
江苏省纺织品进出口集团股份有限公司	南京市	江苏省	(025)4400800

1911: Light Leather 轻革业

The industry accounts for 0.255% of the total revenue of China's industrial sector in 2002. The rate of return on assets is 7.02%. 83.65% of all firms in the industry made a profit while 16.35% had negative returns.The top province in terms of the industry's revenue is Zhejiang, accounting for 27.95% of the total revenue.
2002年本行业收入占全行业的 0.255%，资产利润率为 7.02%。83.65%的企业赢利，16.35%的企业亏损。收入最高的省为浙江省，占本行业的27.95%。

	Total number of firms 企业总数	Total number of employees 职工总数	Total revenue (Mil.RMB) 总销售收入（百万元）	Total profit (Mil.RMB) 总利润（百万元）	Return on assets 资产利润率（%）	Return on equity 权益利润率（%）	Labour productivity ('000 RMB/ worker) 劳动生产率（千元/人）	Debts/ assets 资产负债率（%）	Total assets (Mil.RMB) 总资产（百万元）
Industry Overall 行业总体	477	88,488	27,389	1,269	7.02	19.19	77.31	63.40	18,073

	Number of firms 企业个数	Average number of employees 平均职工人数	Average revenue ('000 RMB) 平均销售收入（千元）	Average profit ('000 RMB) 平均利润（千元）	Return on assets 资产利润率（%）	Return on equity 权益利润率（%）	Labour productivity ('000 RMB/ worker) 劳动生产率（千元/人）	Debts/ assets 资产负债率（%）	Average total assets ('000 RMB) 平均总资产（千元）
By ownership 产业所有权									
State-owned 国有	16	81	17,749	-307	-0.78	-31.34	68.25	97.52	39,392
Collective-owned 集体	82	171	43,106	2,608	11.21	31.25	72.46	64.11	23,258
Foreign & Overseas Chinese Funded 三资	127	231	80,384	2,358	3.70	10.04	77.82	63.14	63,693
By regional distribution 地区分布									
Central-North 华北	41	381	108,785	7,971	18.99	47.79	81.44	60.26	41,964
Beijing 北京	1	212	2,942	21	0.02		0.47	100.08	111,202
Tianjin 天津	7	165	55,403	3,424	10.44	32.50	0.61	67.86	32,786
Hebei 河北	32	445	127,170	9,463	22.16	50.07	89.20	55.73	42,695
Shanxi 山西									
Inner Mongolia 内蒙古	1	2						61.25	13,586
Northeast 东北	10	177	12,901	-360	-0.79	-2.65	28.00	70.13	45,432
Liaoning 辽宁	6	196	16,440	-53	-0.11	-0.63	31.58	82.41	48,019
Jilin 吉林	2	98	5,890	-650	-2.11	-2.29	23.95	7.79	30,846
Heilongjiang 黑龙江	2	202	9,294	-990	-1.89	-7.03	19.52	73.08	52,257
Central-East 华东	225	175	65,422	2,937	7.21	20.70	78.81	65.16	40,738
Shanghai 上海	8	297	164,907	4,210	5.67	48.82	94.10	88.38	74,241
Jiangsu 江苏	24	184	81,985	4,434	6.51	26.33	101.28	75.28	68,104
Zhejiang 浙江	123	148	62,245	2,807	8.50	21.51	77.56	60.45	33,005
Anhui 安徽	5	104	20,549	161	0.62	2.88	55.21	78.63	26,109
Fujian 福建	30	147	26,725	1,468	5.76	9.03	40.67	36.26	25,503
Jiangxi 江西	2	66	13,051	41	0.30	0.50	59.39	40.99	13,769
Shandong 山东	33	282	86,250	3,957	6.68	22.41	86.45	70.19	59,233
Central-South 中南	174	164	42,423	1,570	4.45	11.01	75.86	59.57	35,273
Henan 河南	61	172	47,298	3,138	7.94	19.35	110.60	58.97	39,525
Hubei 湖北	6	130	33,687	428	1.85	3.82	57.80	51.65	23,200
Hunan 湖南	26	111	31,382	802	4.71	29.01	92.25	83.75	17,020
Guangdong 广东	71	174	45,716	726	1.78	4.11	52.42	56.75	40,846
Guangxi 广西	10	211	23,249	673	2.75	6.83	24.24	59.74	24,481
Hainan 海南									
Southwest 西南	13	114	27,207	-85	-0.50	-24.22	77.83	97.96	17,194
Chongqing 重庆	1	66	6,339	-1,563	-24.14		33.67	261.58	6,476
Sichuan 四川	11	128	31,578	41	0.21	3.03	79.90	93.07	19,731
Guizhou 贵州	1								
Yunnan 云南									
Tibet 西藏									
Northwest 西北	14	122	24,643	931	3.51	11.17	80.13	68.57	26,544
Shaanxi 陕西	1	120	89,973	619	0.27	0.90	311.52	70.37	231,364
Gansu 甘肃	12	121	20,571	991	8.87	25.20	66.76	64.82	11,174
Qinghai 青海	1	132	8,178	533	8.66	50.05	16.69	82.69	6,153
Ningxia 宁夏									
Xinjiang 新疆									

Year 年份	Number of firms 企业个数	Rate of change 变化率 (%)	Number of employees 职工人数 (人)	Rate of change 变化率 (%)	Total revenue (Mil. RMB) 总销售收入 (百万元)	Rate of change 变化率 (%)	Total profit (Mil RMB) 总利润 (百万元)	Rate of change 变化率 (%)
2000	427		76,581		19,897		561	
2001	440	3.04	79,773	4.17	23,707	19.15	889	58.47
2002	477	8.41	88,488	10.92	27,389	15.53	1,269	42.74

Major Products 主要产品	Output 产量	Unit 单位
Light Leather 轻革	47,870	10,000 Sq.M. 万平方米

10 Main Firms with Maximal Revenue (year founded) 收入最大的十家主要企业（创办年份）	City 城市	Province 省	Telephone/fax 电话/传真	Number of employees 职工人数	Ownership 产业所有权	Revenue ('000 RMB) 销售收入 (千元)	Profit('000 RMB) (rank) 利润(千元) (排名)	Total assets ('000 RMB) 总资产 (千元)	Major products 主要产品
Zhejiang Kasen Industrial Group Co., Ltd.	Jiaxing	Zhejiang	(0573)7781111		Joint Stock				Hogskin
浙江卡森实业股份有限公司(1988)	嘉兴市	浙江省	(0573)7788157	3,255	股份制	2,097,516	194,724(1)	1,286,033	猪皮革
Hebei Xinji Leather Industrial Zone Board Of Trustee	Shijiazhuang	Hebei	(0311)3206122		Private Enterprises				Leather
辛集制革工业区管理委员会(1997)	石家庄市	河北省	(0311)3206669	2,000	私营独资	1,430,070	130,020(2)	232,395	皮革
Hebei Xinji Shipaoying Leather Industry Zone	Shijiazhuang	Hebei	(0311)3328097		Private Enterprises				Light Leather
辛集市试炮营皮革工业区(1997)	石家庄市	河北省	(0311)3329376	3,046	私营独资	666,350	47,677(4)	244,580	轻革
Shanghai Fuguo Leather Co., Ltd.	Shanghai	Shanghai	(021)62503354		Foreign Funded				Light Leather
上海富国皮革有限公司(1995)	上海市	上海市	(021)62504455	1,647	外商投资	627,835	38,150(6)	224,133	轻革
Zhongshan Nanyi Leather Factory Co., Ltd.	Zhongshan	Guangdong	(0760)3115878		Foreign Funded				Leather
中山市南艺制革厂有限公司(1988)	中山市	广东省	(0760)3116132	524	外商投资	428,049	16,800(16)	176,799	皮革
Wenzhou Fareast Leather Co., Ltd.	Wenzhou	Zhejiang	(0577)63859888		Overseas Chinese-funded				Hogskin
温州远东皮革有限公司(1999)	温州市	浙江省	(0577)63852558	518	港澳台资	387,581	18,727(14)	99,165	猪皮革
Pingyang Jinxi Leather General Factory	Wenzhou	Zhejiang	(0577)63857672		Collective-owned				Hogskin
平阳县金溪制革总厂(1994)	温州市	浙江省		995	集体企业	355,670	445(210)	36,823	猪皮革
Wendeng Leather Factory	Weihai	Shandong	(0631)8251667		Collective-owned				Hogskin
文登市制革厂(1953)	威海市	山东省	(0631)8251667	1,430	集体企业	341,100	40,690(5)	377,220	猪皮革
Qingdao Xinwu Leather Co., Ltd	Qingdao	Shandong	(0532)2279360		Foreign Funded				Cow Leather
青岛信五皮革有限公司(1995)	青岛市	山东省	(0532)2279367	418	外商投资	334,910	1,257(139)	118,159	牛皮革
Pingyang Jinfeng Leather General Factory	Wenzhou	Zhejiang	(0577)63851141		Joint Stock				Hogskin
平阳县金凤制革总厂(1991)	温州市	浙江省		640	股份制	328,300	6,526(45)	23,811	猪皮革

Top 10 Cities by Revenue 销售收入排名前10位城市	Province 省	Market share 市场份额 (%)	Number of firms 企业个数
Shijiazhuang 石家庄市	Hebei 河北省	13.39	13
Wenzhou 温州市	Zhejiang 浙江省	13.07	74
Jiaxing 嘉兴市	Zhejiang 浙江省	9.20	7
Zhoukou 周口市	Henan 河南省	7.27	26
Shanghai 上海市	Shanghai 上海市	4.82	8
Jiangmen 江门市	Guangdong 广东省	2.76	16
Weihai 威海市	Shandong 山东省	2.60	3
Xiangtan 湘潭市	Hunan 湖南省	2.44	15
Suzhou 苏州市	Jiangsu 江苏省	2.42	6
Quanzhou 泉州市	Fujian 福建省	2.26	20

10 Major Wholesalers 十家主要批发商	City 城市	Province 省	Telephone/Fax 电话/传真
Jiangsu Animal By-products Imp And Exp ,Group Corp.	Nanjing	Jiangsu	(025)2306185
江苏开元国际集团畜产进出口股份有限公司	南京市	江苏省	(025)2306282
Zhejiang Native Produce & By-products I/E Group Corp.	Hangzhou	Zhejiang	(0571)85773807
浙江省土产畜产进出口集团公司	杭州市	浙江省	(0571)85773780
Zhejiang G & B Foreign Trading Co.,Ltd.	Hangzhou	Zhejiang	(0571)85773807
浙江惠元对外贸易有限责任公司	杭州市	浙江省	(0571)85773866
Zhejiang G & F Foreign Trading Co.,Ltd.	Hangzhou	Zhejiang	(0571)85773807
浙江惠隆对外贸易有限责任公司	杭州市	浙江省	(0571)85773925
Zhejiang Willing Foreign Trading Co.,Ltd.	Hangzhou	Zhejiang	(0571)85773807
浙江惠灵对外贸易有限责任公司	杭州市	浙江省	(0571)85773720
Guangzhou Livestock Products Import & Export Company	Guangzhou	Guangdong	(020)83852888
广州畜产进出口公司	广州市	广东省	(020)83824187
China Grain & Oil Feedstuff Co.,Ltd.	Beijing	Beijing	(010)64248899
中国粮油饲料有限公司	北京市	北京市	(010)64205100
Zhejing Huashen Silk Group Company	Jiaxing	Zhejiang	(0573)8021696
浙江花神丝绸集团公司	嘉兴市	浙江省	(0573)8038299
Guangdong Dongguan Local Products Import & Export Company	Dongguan	Guangdong	(0769)2221910
广东省东莞土产进出口公司	东莞市	广东省	(0769)2226400
Yunnan Native Produce Import And Export Corp.	Kunming	Yunnan	(0871)3136461
云南省土产进出口公司	昆明市	云南省	(0871)3136378

1912: Heavy Leather 重革业

The industry accounts for 0.015% of the total revenue of China's industrial sector in 2002. The rate of return on assets is 1.14%. 93.55% of all firms in the industry made a profit while 6.45% had negative returns.The top province in terms of the industry's revenue is Zhejiang, accounting for 85.52% of the total revenue.
2002年本行业收入占全行业的0.015%，资产利润率为1.14%。93.55%的企业赢利，6.45%的企业亏损。收入最高的省为浙江省，占本行业的85.52%。

	Total number of firms 企业总数	Total number of employees 职工总数	Total revenue (Mil.RMB) 总销售收入（百万元）	Total profit (Mil.RMB) 总利润（百万元）	Return on assets 资产利润率（%）	Return on equity 权益利润率（%）	Labour productivity ('000 RMB/ worker) 劳动生产率（千元/人）	Debts/ assets 资产负债率（%）	Total assets (Mil.RMB) 总资产（百万元）
Industry Overall 行业总体	31	6,207	1,638	16	1.14	3.55	74.75	67.94	1,430

	Number of firms 企业个数	Average number of employees 平均职工人数	Average revenue ('000 RMB) 平均销售收入（千元）	Average profit ('000 RMB) 平均利润（千元）	Return on assets 资产利润率（%）	Return on equity 权益利润率（%）	Labour productivity ('000 RMB/ worker) 劳动生产率（千元/人）	Debts/ assets 资产负债率（%）	Average total assets ('000 RMB) 平均总资产（千元）
By ownership 产业所有权									
State-owned 国有	2	194	2,616	-7,494	-9.19		6.27	119.20	81,558
Collective-owned 集体	2	69	31,239	415	4.62	17.50	71.32	73.60	8,980
Foreign & Overseas Chinese Funded 三资	8	604	165,918	2,800	2.08	5.87	80.71	64.50	134,417
By regional distribution 地区分布									
Central-North 华北									
Beijing 北京									
Tianjin 天津									
Hebei 河北									
Shanxi 山西									
Inner Mongolia 内蒙古									
Northeast 东北	1	95	3,638	-485	-0.59	-1.63	19.12	63.89	82,620
Liaoning 辽宁	1	95	3,638	-485	-0.59	-1.63	19.12	63.89	82,620
Jilin 吉林									
Heilongjiang 黑龙江									
Central-East 华东	24	241	66,307	658	1.22	3.74	77.74	67.37	53,968
Shanghai 上海									
Jiangsu 江苏	2	1,476	95,484	-2,363	-1.00	-10.49	19.78	90.47	236,563
Zhejiang 浙江	22	129	63,654	932	2.49	5.43	138.01	54.08	37,368
Anhui 安徽									
Fujian 福建									
Jiangxi 江西									
Shandong 山东									
Central-South 中南	6	54	7,097	161	1.86	16.40	37.13	88.65	8,663
Henan 河南	5	60	4,782	82	0.86	11.61	22.62	92.59	9,532
Hubei 湖北									
Hunan 湖南									
Guangdong 广东	1	20	18,674	558	12.93	23.52	255.50	45.05	4,317
Guangxi 广西									
Hainan 海南									
Southwest 西南									
Chongqing 重庆									
Sichuan 四川									
Guizhou 贵州									
Yunnan 云南									
Tibet 西藏									
Northwest 西北									
Shaanxi 陕西									
Gansu 甘肃									
Qinghai 青海									
Ningxia 宁夏									
Xinjiang 新疆									

Year 年份	Number of firms 企业个数	Rate of change 变化率(%)	Number of employees 职工人数(人)	Rate of change 变化率(%)	Total revenue (Mil. RMB) 总销售收入(百万元)	Rate of change 变化率(%)	Total profit (Mil RMB) 总利润(百万元)	Rate of change 变化率(%)
2000	20		5,124		509		2	
2001	15	-25.00	2,955	-42.33	378	-25.74	-10	-
2002	31	106.67	6,207	110.05	1,638	333.33	16	-

Major Products 主要产品	Output 产量	Unit 单位
Shoe Leather 皮鞋	152,282	10,000 Pairs 万双

10 Main Firms with Maximal Revenue (year founded) 收入最大的十家主要企业（创办年份）	City 城市	Province 省	Telephone/fax 电话/传真	Number of employees 职工人数	Ownership 产业所有权	Revenue ('000 RMB) 销售收入(千元)	Profit('000 RMB) (rank) 利润(千元)(排名)	Total assets ('000 RMB) 总资产(千元)	Major products 主要产品
Tyche Leather Co., Ltd.	Wenzhou	Zhejiang	(0577)86636645		Overseas Chinese-funded				Cow Leather
泰庆皮革有限公司(1997)	温州市	浙江省	(0577)86636480	820	港澳台资	696,259	2,680(3)	405,932	牛皮革
Kunshan Zhenxing Shoe Co., Ltd.	Suzhou	Jiangsu	(0512)57971118		Overseas Chinese-funded				Shoe Leather
昆山珍兴鞋业有限公司(1997)	苏州市	江苏省	(0512)57601734	2,660	港澳台资	189,375	9,777(1)	392,629	皮鞋
Wenzhou Yatai Leather Co., Ltd.	Wenzhou	Zhejiang	(0577)86362885		Overseas Chinese-funded				Cowskin
温州亚泰皮革有限公司(1994)	温州市	浙江省	(0577)86362883	312	港澳台资	178,348	4,291(2)	104,959	牛皮
Wenzhou Yellow River Leather Co., Ltd.	Wenzhou	Zhejiang	(0577)86783589		Foreign Funded				Cow Leather
温州黄河皮革有限公司(1995)	温州市	浙江省	(0577)86362338	490	外商投资	118,978	2,658(4)	84,099	牛皮革
Huzhou Dongfang Leather Co., Ltd.	Huzhou	Zhejiang	(0572)3601633		Foreign Funded				Hogskin
湖州东方皮革有限公司(1999)	湖州市	浙江省	(0572)3601961	85	外商投资	52,820	2,127(5)	12,500	猪皮革
Wenzhou Mengdehao Group Co., Ltd.	Wenzhou	Zhejiang	(0577)88793788		Limited-Liability				Cowskin
温州市梦德豪集团有限公司(1998)	温州市	浙江省	(0577)88792588	224	有限公司	49,737	1,705(6)	48,725	牛皮
Wenzhou Heryi Leather Industry Co., Ltd.	Wenzhou	Zhejiang	(0577)86262893		Foreign Funded				Cowskin
温州市荷尔意皮业有限公司(1994)	温州市	浙江省	(0577)86268608	65	外商投资	31,926	340(14)	20,499	牛皮
Wenzhou Ouhai Guoxi Leather Factory	Wenzhou	Zhejiang	(0577)86130115		Joint Stock				Cow Leather
温州市瓯海郭溪制革厂(2000)	温州市	浙江省	(0577)86130508	20	股份制	26,600	1,705(6)	18,275	牛面革
Guangzhou Huadu Huashan Xianhua Leather & Fur Processing	Guangzhou	Guangdong	(020)86854836		Private Enterprises				Cowskin
Factory 广州市花都区花山显华皮毛加工厂(1993)	广州市	广东省		20	私营独资	10,674	558(10)	4,317	牛皮
Wenzhou Liyuan Leather Co., Ltd.	Wenzhou	Zhejiang	(0577)88796318		Private Owned				Cowskin
温州市利园皮革有限公司(2001)	温州市	浙江省	(0577)88796378	49	私营企业	18,233	157(20)	3,686	牛皮

Top 10 Cities by Revenue 销售收入排名前10位城市	Province 省	Market share 市场份额(%)	Number of firms 企业个数
Wenzhou 温州市	Zhejiang 浙江省	78.65	20
Suzhou 苏州市	Jiangsu 江苏省	11.56	1
Huzhou 湖州市	Zhejiang 浙江省	6.87	2
Pingdingshan 平顶山市	Henan 河南省	1.46	3
Guangzhou 广州市	Guangdong 广东省	1.14	1
Shenyang 沈阳市	Liaoning 辽宁省	0.22	1
Xuzhou 徐州市	Jiangsu 江苏省	0.10	1

10 Major Wholesalers 十家主要批发商	City 城市	Province 省	Telephone/Fax 电话/传真
Jiangsu Animal By-products Imp And Exp ,Group Corp.	Nanjing	Jiangsu	(025)2306185
江苏开元国际集团畜产进出口股份有限公司	南京市	江苏省	(025)2306282
Zhejiang Native Produce & By-products I/E Group Corp.	Hangzhou	Zhejiang	(0571)85773807
浙江省土产畜产进出口集团公司	杭州市	浙江省	(0571)85773780
Zhejiang G & B Foreign Trading Co.,Ltd.	Hangzhou	Zhejiang	(0571)85773807
浙江惠元对外贸易有限责任公司	杭州市	浙江省	(0571)85773866
Zhejiang G & F Foreign Trading Co.,Ltd.	Hangzhou	Zhejiang	(0571)85773807
浙江惠隆对外贸易有限责任公司	杭州市	浙江省	(0571)85773925
Zhejiang Willing Foreign Trading Co.,Ltd.	Hangzhou	Zhejiang	(0571)85773807
浙江惠灵对外贸易有限责任公司	杭州市	浙江省	(0571)85773720
Guangzhou Livestock Products Import & Export Company	Guangzhou	Guangdong	(020)83852888
广州畜产进出口公司	广州市	广东省	(020)83824187
China Grain & Oil Feedstuff Co.,Ltd.	Beijing	Beijing	(010)64248899
中国粮油饲料有限公司	北京市	北京市	(010)64205100
Zhejing Huashen Silk Group Company	Jiaxing	Zhejiang	(0573)8021696
浙江花神丝绸集团公司	嘉兴市	浙江省	(0573)8038299
Guangdong Dongguan Local Products Import & Export Company	Dongguan	Guangdong	(0769)2221910
广东省东莞土产进出口公司	东莞市	广东省	(0769)2226400
Yunnan Native Produce Import And Export Corp.	Kunming	Yunnan	(0871)3136461
云南省土产进出口公司	昆明市	云南省	(0871)3136378

1919: Other Leather 其他制革业

The industry accounts for 0.020% of the total revenue of China's industrial sector in 2002. The rate of return on assets is 3.04%. 86.42% of all firms in the industry made a profit while 13.58% had negative returns.The top province in terms of the industry's revenue is Guangdong, accounting for 30.83% of the total revenue.
2002年本行业收入占全行业的0.020%，资产利润率为3.04%。86.42%的企业赢利，13.58%的企业亏损。收入最高的省为广东省，占本行业的30.83%。

	Total number of firms 企业总数	Total number of employees 职工总数	Total revenue (Mil.RMB) 总销售收入(百万元)	Total profit (Mil.RMB) 总利润(百万元)	Return on assets 资产利润率(%)	Return on equity 权益利润率(%)	Labour productivity ('000 RMB/ worker) 劳动生产率(千元/人)	Debts/ assets 资产负债率(%)	Total assets (Mil.RMB) 总资产(百万元)
Industry Overall 行业总体	81	10,412	2,133	59	3.04	8.03	57.59	62.15	1,930

	Number of firms 企业个数	Average number of employees 平均职工人数	Average revenue ('000 RMB) 平均销售收入（千元)	Average profit ('000 RMB) 平均利润(千元)	Return on assets 资产利润率(%)	Return on equity 权益利润率(%)	Labour productivity ('000 RMB/ worker) 劳动生产率(千元/人)	Debts/ assets 资产负债率(%)	Average total assets ('000 RMB) 平均总资产(千元)
By ownership 产业所有权									
State-owned 国有	2	41	2,790	-42	-1.83	-7.59	14.93	75.93	2,297
Collective-owned 集体	12	197	43,697	3,818	11.30	25.51	63.96	55.69	33,778
Foreign & Overseas Chinese Funded 三资	33	149	30,664	-443	-1.33	-4.00	60.26	66.69	33,266
By regional distribution 地区分布									
Central-North 华北	5	112	10,721	555	3.74	7.36	23.82	49.16	14,829
Beijing 北京	3	106	10,703	698	3.60	6.09	24.20	40.84	19,388
Tianjin 天津	1	90	13,690	680	23.78	69.39	35.56	65.73	2,860
Hebei 河北	1	150	7,809				15.96	82.42	13,121
Shanxi 山西									
Inner Mongolia 内蒙古									
Northeast 东北	1	106	3,846	51	0.93		10.59	108.30	5,468
Liaoning 辽宁	1	106	3,846	51	0.93		10.59	108.30	5,468
Jilin 吉林									
Heilongjiang 黑龙江									
Central-East 华东	22	156	38,790	107	0.28	0.99	82.10	71.33	37,718
Shanghai 上海	1	14	11,027	-821	-11.93		406.43	147.55	6,881
Jiangsu 江苏	2	64	13,206	129	2.34	10.09	25.04	76.82	5,516
Zhejiang 浙江	13	114	14,943	581	5.16	16.73	40.96	69.14	11,260
Anhui 安徽									
Fujian 福建	4	167	41,100	3,007	7.14	10.34	68.02	30.91	42,098
Jiangxi 江西									
Shandong 山东	2	573	228,640	-8,334	-3.35	-21.61	145.83	84.49	248,556
Central-South 中南	49	121	24,253	1,068	5.52	13.22	49.01	58.25	19,351
Henan 河南	14	105	34,726	3,103	14.42	42.57	89.59	66.13	21,526
Hubei 湖北	2	59	22,282	-133	-1.53	-1.59	135.38	3.34	8,665
Hunan 湖南									
Guangdong 广东	33	131	19,929	278	1.46	3.31	32.97	55.99	19,076
Guangxi 广西									
Hainan 海南									
Southwest 西南									
Chongqing 重庆									
Sichuan 四川									
Guizhou 贵州									
Yunnan 云南									
Tibet 西藏									
Northwest 西北	4	99	8,548	273	1.51	1.84	33.76	17.90	18,088
Shaanxi 陕西									
Gansu 甘肃	4	99	8,548	273	1.51	1.84	33.76	17.90	18,088
Qinghai 青海									
Ningxia 宁夏									
Xinjiang 新疆									

1919: Other Leather 其他制革业

Year 年份	Number of firms 企业个数	Rate of change 变化率 (%)	Number of employees 职工人数 (人)	Rate of change 变化率 (%)	Total revenue (Mil. RMB) 总销售收入 (百万元)	Rate of change 变化率 (%)	Total profit (Mil RMB) 总利润 (百万元)	Rate of change 变化率 (%)
2000	79		15,823		3,718		239	
2001	96	21.52	13,922	-12.01	2,979	-19.88	98	-59.00
2002	81	-15.63	10,412	-25.21	2,133	-28.40	59	-39.80

Major Products 主要产品	Output 产量	Unit 单位

10 Main Firms with Maximal Revenue (year founded) 收入最大的十家主要企业（创办年份）	City 城市	Province 省	Telephone/fax 电话/传真	Number of employees 职工人数	Ownership 产业所有权	Revenue ('000 RMB) 销售收入 (千元)	Profit('000 RMB) (rank) 利润(千元) (排名)	Total assets ('000 RMB) 总资产 (千元)	Major products 主要产品
Qingdao Daemyung Leather Co., Ltd.	Qingdao	Shandong	(0532)7273623		Foreign Funded				Leather Products
青岛大明皮革有限公司(1997)	青岛市	山东省	(0532)7273641	943	外商投资	444,230	-	493,368	皮革制品
Henan Great Wall Group Co.Ltd.	Jiaozuo	Henan	(0391)5693475		Collective-owned				Cow Leather
河南长城集团公司(1987)	焦作市	河南省	(0391)5695006	980	集体企业	219,471	30,315(1)	191,772	牛皮革
Fujian Jinjiang Anhai Xingye Leather Products Factory	Quanzhou	Fujian	(0595)5799962		Collective-owned				Cowskin
福建省晋江市安海兴业皮制品厂(1992)	泉州市	福建省	(0595)5799969	341	集体企业	83,521	11,088(2)	91,599	牛皮
Boluo Longxi Town Hongfu Shoe Village Manufacturing Factory 博罗县龙溪镇宏福鞋村制造厂(2000)	Huizhou	Guangdong	(0752)6872968		Others				
	惠州市	广东省	(0752)6871389	180	其他企业	55,835	156(47)	59,434	二榔皮
Guangzhou Shunyang Shoes Material Co., Ltd.	Guangzhou	Guangdong	(020)86796958		Overseas Chinese-funded				Shoes material
广州顺阳鞋材有限公司(2000)	广州市	广东省	(020)86855843	70	港澳台资	52,974	1,282(13)	14,047	鞋材
Chenghai Huadafu Leather Co., Ltd.	Shantou	Guangdong	(0754)5754547		Overseas Chinese-funded				PVC Emulsification Leather
澄海市华达富皮革有限公司(1993)	汕头市	广东省	(0754)5754546	102	港澳台资	49,425	-	38,630	PVC乳化皮
Hangzhou New Fumei Garments Co., ltd.	Hangzhou	Zhejiang	(0571)63464672		Overseas Chinese-funded				Leather Sofa Cover
杭州新富美时装有限公司(1995)	杭州市	浙江省	(0571)63464162	360	港澳台资	44,670	1,040(18)	37,110	皮沙发套
Fujian Putian Dongtai Leather Co., Ltd.	Putian	Fujian	(0594)3504369		Collective-owned				Hogskin
福建省莆田市东泰皮革有限公司(1993)	莆田市	福建省		71	集体企业	40,401	648(24)	17,344	猪皮革
Gaoming Mingzhao Plastic Leather Co., Ltd	Foshan	Guangdong	(0757)8628997		Limited-Liability				PU Synthetic Leather
高明市明兆塑胶皮革有限公司(1999)	佛山市	广东省	(0757)8628991	152	有限公司	36,886	1,118(15)	14,459	PU合成革
Zhaoqing Huangcheng Leather Ornaments Co., Ltd.	Zhaoqing	Guangdong	(0758)3623510		Foreign Funded				Leather
肇庆市皇城皮饰有限公司(1999)	肇庆市	广东省	(0758)3623513	86	外商投资	34,929	1,079(17)	28,542	皮革

Top 10 Cities by Revenue 销售收入排名前10位城市	Province 省	Market share 市场份额 (%)	Number of firms 企业个数
Qingdao 青岛市	Shandong 山东省	21.43	2
Jiaozuo 焦作市	Henan 河南省	10.29	1
Luohe 漯河市	Henan 河南省	9.42	8
Guangzhou 广州市	Guangdong 广东省	8.50	10
Quanzhou 泉州市	Fujian 福建省	5.81	3
Foshan 佛山市	Guangdong 广东省	4.96	4
Wenzhou 温州市	Zhejiang 浙江省	3.62	7
Chaozhou 潮州市	Guangdong 广东省	3.02	3
Ningbo 宁波市	Zhejiang 浙江省	2.92	3
Shenzhen 深圳市	Guangdong 广东省	2.71	5

10 Major Wholesalers 十家主要批发商	City 城市	Province 省	Telephone/Fax 电话/传真
Jiangsu Animal By-products Imp And Exp ,Group Corp.	Nanjing	Jiangsu	(025)2306185
江苏开元国际集团畜产进出口股份有限公司	南京市	江苏省	(025)2306282
Zhejiang Native Produce & By-products I/E Group Corp.	Hangzhou	Zhejiang	(0571)85773807
浙江省土产畜产进出口集团公司	杭州市	浙江省	(0571)85773780
Zhejiang G & B Foreign Trading Co.,Ltd.	Hangzhou	Zhejiang	(0571)85773807
浙江惠元对外贸易有限责任公司	杭州市	浙江省	(0571)85773866
Zhejiang G & F Foreign Trading Co.,Ltd.	Hangzhou	Zhejiang	(0571)85773807
浙江惠隆对外贸易有限责任公司	杭州市	浙江省	(0571)85773925
Zhejiang Willing Foreign Trading Co.,Ltd.	Hangzhou	Zhejiang	(0571)85773807
浙江惠灵对外贸易有限责任公司	杭州市	浙江省	(0571)85773720
Guangzhou Livestock Products Import & Export Company	Guangzhou	Guangdong	(020)83852888
广州畜产进出口公司	广州市	广东省	(020)83824187
China Grain & Oil Feedstuff Co.,Ltd.	Beijing	Beijing	(010)64248899
中国粮油饲料有限公司	北京市	北京市	(010)64205100
Zhejing Huashen Silk Group Company	Jiaxing	Zhejiang	(0573)8021696
浙江花神丝绸集团公司	嘉兴市	浙江省	(0573)8038299
Guangdong Dongguan Local Products Import & Export Company	Dongguan	Guangdong	(0769)2221910
广东省东莞土产进出口公司	东莞市	广东省	(0769)2226400
Yunnan Native Produce Import And Export Corp.	Kunming	Yunnan	(0871)3136461
云南省土产进出口公司	昆明市	云南省	(0871)3136378

1921: Leather Shoes 皮鞋制造业

The industry accounts for 0.609% of the total revenue of China's industrial sector in 2002. The rate of return on assets is 4.49%. 84.05% of all firms in the industry made a profit while 15.95% had negative returns.The top province in terms of the industry's revenue is Guangdong, accounting for 32.87% of the total revenue.
2002年本行业收入占全行业的 0.609%，资产利润率为 4.49%。84.05%的企业赢利，15.95%的企业亏损。收入最高的省为广东省，占本行业的32.87%。

	Total number of firms 企业总数	Total number of employees 职工总数	Total revenue (Mil.RMB) 总销售收入（百万元）	Total profit (Mil.RMB) 总利润（百万元）	Return on assets 资产利润率（%）	Return on equity 权益利润率（%）	Labour productivity ('000 RMB/ worker) 劳动生产率（千元/人）	Debts/ assets 资产负债率（%）	Total assets (Mil.RMB) 总资产（百万元）
Industry Overall 行业总体	1304	769,873	65,327	2,078	4.49	11.32	26.37	60.32	46,281

	Number of firms 企业个数	Average number of employees 平均职工人数	Average revenue ('000 RMB) 平均销售收入（千元）	Average profit ('000 RMB) 平均利润（千元）	Return on assets 资产利润率（%）	Return on equity 权益利润率（%）	Labour productivity ('000 RMB/ worker) 劳动生产率（千元/人）	Debts/ assets 资产负债率（%）	Average total assets ('000 RMB) 平均总资产（千元）
By ownership 产业所有权									
State-owned 国有	54	332	15,018	-1,788	-4.61	-31.07	15.75	85.15	38,757
Collective-owned 集体	87	337	31,234	1,182	8.91	25.62	29.38	65.21	13,261
Foreign & Overseas Chinese Funded 三资	609	924	71,189	1,899	3.78	9.63	24.24	60.79	50,310
By regional distribution 地区分布									
Central-North 华北	50	336	40,989	684	2.09	6.76	11.91	69.02	32,669
Beijing 北京	7	173	6,881	-368	-1.45	-15.81	13.40	90.79	25,313
Tianjin 天津	30	397	51,236	945	3.06	9.80	7.40	68.78	30,901
Hebei 河北	10	255	38,968	87	0.22	0.63	24.11	65.87	40,293
Shanxi 山西	2	382	501	-792	-3.38	-27.49	0.51	87.71	23,443
Inner Mongolia 内蒙古	1	348	73,504	9,124	11.49	16.00	96.81	28.20	79,440
Northeast 东北	20	643	47,694	-144	-0.40	-2.51	20.09	84.29	36,378
Liaoning 辽宁	16	732	57,115	131	0.34	1.17	21.06	71.13	38,607
Jilin 吉林	1	447	20,554	243	2.06	4.79	14.82	56.95	11,792
Heilongjiang 黑龙江	3	230	6,493	-1,736	-5.31		7.05	170.47	32,688
Central-East 华东	825	494	48,000	2,140	7.39	15.89	33.56	53.49	28,954
Shanghai 上海	52	442	36,922	-872	-2.10	-8.40	28.28	75.05	41,590
Jiangsu 江苏	81	372	58,491	2,640	7.32	22.70	43.60	67.74	36,053
Zhejiang 浙江	404	303	35,632	2,082	11.62	21.20	31.64	45.18	17,922
Anhui 安徽	7	389	10,594	-279	-0.86	-9.13	8.85	90.55	32,303
Fujian 福建	220	813	60,971	2,713	7.43	13.52	33.61	45.04	36,513
Jiangxi 江西	4	190	6,549	341	7.28	17.22	7.49	57.75	4,680
Shandong 山东	57	866	88,303	2,796	4.85	13.11	36.21	63.00	57,648
Central-South 中南	376	867	59,271	832	1.63	4.88	18.62	66.67	51,153
Henan 河南	17	435	22,177	-485	-1.52	-7.01	16.88	78.37	31,965
Hubei 湖北	13	254	20,075	645	4.82	25.44	31.52	81.07	13,384
Hunan 湖南	10	336	15,243	250	1.71		12.94	133.52	14,653
Guangdong 广东	332	938	64,683	936	1.70	4.94	18.61	65.62	55,167
Guangxi 广西	4	156	5,160	-164	-1.21	-5.44	6.13	77.74	13,507
Hainan 海南									
Southwest 西南	22	230	16,303	413	1.51	4.71	16.78	68.02	27,406
Chongqing 重庆	8	273	21,932	1,237	6.95	15.49	22.80	55.15	17,795
Sichuan 四川	6	169	11,766	153	1.39	4.64	13.78	70.00	11,006
Guizhou 贵州	2	50	289	-116	-0.89		-9.36	161.30	13,006
Yunnan 云南	5	331	21,480	-339	-0.53	-1.88	11.25	71.81	64,035
Tibet 西藏	1	104	4,633	196	0.41	0.56	32.41	27.89	48,343
Northwest 西北	11	161	7,181	-3,685	-20.56	-129.61	10.51	84.13	17,921
Shaanxi 陕西	2	756	37,525	-20,062	-22.14	-171.21	7.81	87.07	90,613
Gansu 甘肃	9	29	438	-46	-2.61	-5.29	26.04	50.71	1,768
Qinghai 青海									
Ningxia 宁夏									
Xinjiang 新疆									

Year 年份	Number of firms 企业个数	Rate of change 变化率 (%)	Number of employees 职工人数 (人)	Rate of change 变化率 (%)	Total revenue (Mil. RMB) 总销售收入 (百万元)	Rate of change 变化率 (%)	Total profit (Mil RMB) 总利润 (百万元)	Rate of change 变化率 (%)
2000	988		628,814		49,202		1,154	
2001	1122	13.56	682,728	8.57	55,519	12.84	1,198	3.81
2002	1304	16.22	769,873	12.76	65,327	17.67	2,078	73.46

Major Products 主要产品	Output 产量	Unit 单位
Shoe Leather 皮鞋	152,282	10,000 Pairs 万双

10 Main Firms with Maximal Revenue (year founded) 收入最大的十家主要企业（创办年份）	City 城市	Province 省	Telephone/fax 电话/传真	Number of employees 职工人数	Ownership 产业所有权	Revenue ('000 RMB) 销售收入 (千元)	Profit('000 RMB) (rank) 利润(千元) (排名)	Total assets ('000 RMB) 总资产 (千元)	Major products 主要产品
Jiangsu Senda Group Co., Ltd. 江苏森达集团公司(1976)	Yancheng 盐城市	Jiangsu 江苏省	(0515)6290088 (0515)6291900	8,607	Limited-Liability 有限公司	2,190,190	133,860(1)	1,551,790	Shoe Leather 皮鞋
Fujian Shunda Sports Products Co., Ltd. 福建顺大运动品有限公司(1991)	Fuzhou 福州市	Fujian 福建省	(0591)3628888 (0591)3621051	11,378	Foreign Funded 外商投资	1,105,478	9,086(57)	334,742	Gym Shoes 运动鞋
Qingdao Taekuang Shoes Co., Ltd. 青岛泰光制鞋有限公司(1996)	Qingdao 青岛市	Shandong 山东省	(0532)6491140 (0532)6491340	8,933	Foreign Funded 外商投资	1,064,792	23,806(18)	448,179	Traveling Shoes 旅游鞋
China Aolang Group Co., Ltd. 中国奥康集团有限公司(1995)	Wenzhou 温州市	Zhejiang 浙江省	(0577)67284444 (0577)67284444	2,635	Limited-Liability 有限公司	911,610	107,729(2)	289,412	Shoe Leather 皮鞋
Guangzhou Apache Footwear Co., Ltd. 广州万邦鞋业有限公司(1991)	Guangzhou 广州市	Guangdong 广东省	(020)86029591 (020)86029961	8,032	Foreign Funded 外商投资	814,921	31,524(11)	294,333	Adidas Gym Shoes. Adidas 运动鞋
Fujian Lifeng Footwear Development Co., Ltd. 福建荔丰鞋业开发有限公司(1988)	Putian 莆田市	Fujian 福建省	(0594)3991998 (0594)3991113	6,949	Foreign Funded 外商投资	806,730	66,021(3)	339,514	Gym Shoes 运动鞋
Fujian Sanfeng Footwear Co., Ltd. 福建三丰鞋业有限公司(1992)	Fuzhou 福州市	Fujian 福建省	(0591)3497668 (0591)3497978	6,962	Overseas Chinese-funded 港澳台资	702,319	43,441(8)	283,685	Gym Shoes 运动鞋
Fujian Xiefeng Shoes Industry Co., Ltd. 福建协丰鞋业有限公司(1989)	Putian 莆田市	Fujian 福建省	(0594)2894210 (0594)2893130	5,828	Foreign Funded 外商投资	657,722	64,213(4)	268,306	Finished Shoes 成品鞋
Qingdao Shiyuan Footwear Co., Ltd. 青岛世原鞋业有限公司(1993)	Qingdao 青岛市	Shandong 山东省	(0532)6239241 (0532)6239401	6,399	Foreign Funded 外商投资	621,609	12,110(42)	250,543	Shoes 鞋
Zhongshan Xinchang Shoes Industry Co., Ltd. 中山欣昌鞋业有限公司(1997)	Zhongshan 中山市	Guangdong 广东省	(0760)6217200 (0760)6217231	6,000	Overseas Chinese-funded 港澳台资	545,539	3,044(159)	539,092	Cow Leather Footware 牛皮工作鞋

Top 10 Cities by Revenue 销售收入排名前10位城市	Province 省	Market share 市场份额 (%)	Number of firms 企业个数
Wenzhou 温州市	Zhejiang 浙江省	16.43	265
Guangzhou 广州市	Guangdong 广东省	12.84	91
Quanzhou 泉州市	Fujian 福建省	7.68	141
Putian 莆田市	Fujian 福建省	6.11	40
Qingdao 青岛市	Shandong 山东省	5.17	28
Fuzhou 福州市	Fujian 福建省	5.07	17
Foshan 佛山市	Guangdong 广东省	4.50	64
Zhongshan 中山市	Guangdong 广东省	4.41	31
Yancheng 盐城市	Jiangsu 江苏省	3.50	2
Taizhou 台州市	Zhejiang 浙江省	3.38	107

10 Major Wholesalers 十家主要批发商	City 城市	Province 省	Telephone/Fax 电话/传真
Wenzhou M & C Foreign Trade Corp 温州市五机化医外贸有限公司	Wenzhou 温州市	Zhejiang 浙江省	(0577)88862999 (0577)88862901
Light Industrial Products Arts and Crafts Import & Export (Group) Corporation 轻工工艺进出口集团公司	Quanzhou 泉州市	Fujian 福建省	(0595)2552255 (0595)2552233
Shanghai Handicrafts Gloves & Hat Industry Import & Export Co.,Ltd. 上海市工艺品手套帽业进出口有限公司	Shanghai 上海市	Shanghai 上海市	(021)58990180 (021)58991146
Shanghai Shen'an Foreign Economic & Trade Corporation 上海申安对外经济贸易公司	Shanghai 上海市	Shanghai 上海市	(021)62871088 (021)62871108
Wenzhou Cereals ,Oils & Foodstuffs Foreign Trade Corp. 温州市粮油食品对外贸易公司	Wenzhou 温州市	Zhejiang 浙江省	(0577)88862756 (0577)88826303
Wenzhou Foreign Trade Industial Products Co., Ltd. 温州外贸工业品有限公司	Wenzhou 温州市	Zhejiang 浙江省	(0577)88862788 (0577)88862799
Zhejiang Ouhai International Trade Corp. 浙江省瓯海对外贸易公司	Wenzhou 温州市	Zhejiang 浙江省	(0577)88820092 (0577)88829093
Shenzhen Light Industry Prodacts Import & Export Company 深圳轻工业品进出口公司	Shenzhen 深圳市	Guangdong 广东省	(0755)82379000 (0755)82379466
Zhejiang Chinabase Impex Co.,Ltd. 浙江中基进出口有限公司	Hangzhou 杭州市	Zhejiang 浙江省	(0571)87819435 (0571)87819437
Zhejiang Qingtian Foreign Trade Co.,ltd. 浙江省青田县对外贸易有限公司	Lishui 丽水市	Zhejiang 浙江省	(0578)6833651 (0578)6822963

1923: Leather Apparel 革皮服装制造业

The industry accounts for 0.172% of the total revenue of China's industrial sector in 2002. The rate of return on assets is 8.76%. 83.82% of all firms in the industry made a profit while 16.18% had negative returns.The top province in terms of the industry's revenue is Zhejiang, accounting for 41.80% of the total revenue.
2002年本行业收入占全行业的 0.172%，资产利润率为 8.76%。83.82%的企业赢利，16.18%的企业亏损。收入最高的省为浙江省，占本行业的41.80%。

	Total number of firms 企业总数	Total number of employees 职工总数	Total revenue (Mil.RMB) 总销售收入 (百万元)	Total profit (Mil.RMB) 总利润 (百万元)	Return on assets 资产利润率 (%)	Return on equity 权益利润率 (%)	Labour productivity ('000 RMB/ worker) 劳动生产率 (千元/人)	Debts/ assets 资产负债率 (%)	Total assets (Mil.RMB) 总资产 (百万元)
Industry Overall 行业总体	377	111,133	18,400	852	8.76	24.09	39.80	63.63	9,726

	Number of firms 企业个数	Average number of employees 平均职工人数	Average revenue ('000 RMB) 平均销售收入（千元）	Average profit ('000 RMB) 平均利润 (千元)	Return on assets 资产利润率 (%)	Return on equity 权益利润率 (%)	Labour productivity ('000 RMB/ worker) 劳动生产率 (千元/人)	Debts/ assets 资产负债率 (%)	Average total assets ('000 RMB) 平均总资产 (千元)
By ownership 产业所有权									
State-owned 国有	8	164	4,630	-780	-2.05	-14.05	7.11	85.40	38,036
Collective-owned 集体	36	207	37,651	1,709	6.10	18.80	39.72	67.56	28,023
Foreign & Overseas Chinese Funded 三资	129	345	35,224	723	2.92	7.44	17.07	60.71	24,715
By regional distribution 地区分布									
Central-North 华北	33	389	116,781	12,938	31.44	68.16	60.59	53.87	41,149
Beijing 北京	9	132	18,096	567	1.86	6.11	33.14	69.61	30,560
Tianjin 天津	10	191	17,500	820	5.31	15.13	8.32	64.91	15,442
Hebei 河北	13	737	270,051	31,819	50.60	87.29	75.08	42.03	62,886
Shanxi 山西									
Inner Mongolia 内蒙古	1	136	5,242	2		0.01	14.10	86.66	110,952
Northeast 东北	9	193	25,688	1,017	6.78	15.37	29.42	55.90	15,007
Liaoning 辽宁	8	206	22,111	221	2.26	5.38	20.81	58.03	9,788
Jilin 吉林									
Heilongjiang 黑龙江	1	91	54,307	7,388	13.02	27.67	185.08	52.96	56,757
Central-East 华东	251	302	46,101	1,476	5.74	17.15	37.91	66.54	25,728
Shanghai 上海	9	128	17,476	81	0.43	1.10	29.65	60.58	18,671
Jiangsu 江苏	43	220	22,412	550	6.70	19.95	26.27	66.42	8,210
Zhejiang 浙江	131	294	58,715	1,968	5.87	17.64	43.43	66.74	33,550
Anhui 安徽	4	374	10,174	277	2.82		5.69	156.61	9,830
Fujian 福建	6	248	26,575	2,216	9.86	12.18	36.36	19.00	22,465
Jiangxi 江西	2	258	24,481	-946	-2.60	-11.43	31.44	77.23	36,358
Shandong 山东	56	414	44,816	1,354	5.86	18.45	36.23	68.26	23,120
Central-South 中南	69	215	30,140	584	3.03	6.83	37.67	55.63	19,269
Henan 河南	14	88	27,282	803	4.05	18.08	78.57	77.60	19,822
Hubei 湖北	2	95	3,884	65	1.25	12.62	19.48	90.08	5,190
Hunan 湖南	12	241	27,208	914	4.93	12.78	31.28	61.40	18,527
Guangdong 广东	39	255	34,143	498	2.50	4.55	36.66	45.00	19,909
Guangxi 广西	2	277	15,935	-753	-3.51	-10.79	4.19	67.47	21,438
Hainan 海南									
Southwest 西南	9	549	70,530	736	1.98	7.45	31.45	73.46	37,198
Chongqing 重庆									
Sichuan 四川	9	549	70,530	736	1.98	7.45	31.45	73.46	37,198
Guizhou 贵州									
Yunnan 云南									
Tibet 西藏									
Northwest 西北	6	177	4,838	-268	-1.45	-14.36	9.67	89.89	18,429
Shaanxi 陕西	2	413	7,803	-140	-0.30	-1.75	6.43	82.56	45,985
Gansu 甘肃	3	71	4,367	388	20.95	24.97	23.28	16.09	1,852
Qinghai 青海									
Ningxia 宁夏									
Xinjiang 新疆	1	26	322	-2,489	-19.08		0.85	173.01	13,047

Year 年份	Number of firms 企业个数	Rate of change 变化率 (%)	Number of employees 职工人数 (人)	Rate of change 变化率 (%)	Total revenue (Mil. RMB) 总销售收入 (百万元)	Rate of change 变化率 (%)	Total profit (Mil RMB) 总利润 (百万元)	Rate of change 变化率 (%)
2000	320		86,024		11,096		524	
2001	353	10.31	104,956	22.01	15,443	39.18	759	44.85
2002	377	6.80	111,133	5.89	18,400	19.15	852	12.25

Major Products 主要产品	Output 产量	Unit 单位
Leather Costume 革皮服装	7,013	10,000 Pieces 万件

10 Main Firms with Maximal Revenue (year founded) 收入最大的十家主要企业（创办年份）	City 城市	Province 省	Telephone/fax 电话/传真	Number of employees 职工人数	Ownership 产业所有权	Revenue ('000 RMB) 销售收入 (千元)	Profit('000 RMB) (rank) 利润(千元)(排名)	Total assets ('000 RMB) 总资产 (千元)	Major products 主要产品
Zhejiang Fukoda Leather Group Co., Ltd.	Hangzhou	Zhejiang	(0571)82407858		Joint Stock				Leather Costume
浙江富可达皮业集团股份有限公司(1986)	杭州市	浙江省	(0571)82406748	1,550	股份制	1,532,412	25,159(4)	288,156	皮革服装
Xuebao Group Company	Jiaxing	Zhejiang	(0573)7411025		Collective-owned				Leather Costume
雪豹集团公司(1984)	嘉兴市	浙江省	(0573)7411089	1,299	集体企业	631,561	42,317(3)	421,279	革皮服装
Rongcheng Huayu Costume Co., Ltd.	Weihai	Shandong	(0631)7559985		Limited-Liability				Down Costume
荣成市华羽服装有限责任公司(2001)	威海市	山东省	(0631)7559985	280	有限公司	504,600	45,180(2)	46,080	羽绒服
Pinghu Costume Group Co., Ltd.	Jiaxing	Zhejiang	(0573)5523957		Private Owned				Imitated Leather Costume
平湖服装集团有限公司(1997)	嘉兴市	浙江省	(0573)5523458	1,450	私营企业	394,790	21,260(7)	461,320	仿皮服装
Gaomi Sanzhen Leather Clothing Co., Ltd.	Weifang	Shandong	(0536)2576196		Foreign Funded				Leather Costume
高密三真皮革服装有限公司(1994)	潍坊市	山东省	(0536)2576057	910	外商投资	276,287	13,765(9)	175,529	皮革服装
Qingdao Xinyuan Garment Co., ltd.	Qingdao	Shandong	(0532)8456791		Foreign Funded				Leather Costume
青岛信元服装有限公司(1993)	青岛市	山东省	(0532)8456797	1,676	外商投资	264,710	937(84)	63,081	皮革服装
Qingdao Shuanglong Apparel Co., Ltd.	Qingdao	Shandong	(0532)8505141		Foreign Funded				Leather Clothes
青岛双龙服装有限公司(1993)	青岛市	山东省	(0532)8505140	1,037	外商投资	240,744	5(243)	162,072	皮衣
Longjin Costume (Shenzhen) Co., Ltd.	Shenzhen	Guangdong	(0755)28135592		Overseas Chinese-funded				Mink
龙津服装（深圳）有限公司(1992)	深圳市	广东省	(0755)28135309	850	港澳台资	237,672	4,313(23)	160,852	水貂衣
Ningling Tianhe Leather Industry Group Company	Shangqiu	Henan	(0370)7010120		Collective-owned				Leather Products
宁陵县天河皮业集团公司(1990)	商丘市	河南省	(0370)7836812	90	集体企业	211,382	-	127,654	皮件
Qingdao Wande Group Stock Co., Ltd.	Qingdao	Shandong	(0532)4121087		Joint Stock				Costume
青岛万德集团股份有限公司(1994)	青岛市	山东省	(0532)4121685	2,000	股份制	195,997	2,463(45)	107,970	服装

Top 10 Cities by Revenue 销售收入排名前10位城市	Province 省	Market share 市场份额 (%)	Number of firms 企业个数
Jiaxing 嘉兴市	Zhejiang 浙江省	20.45	70
Hangzhou 杭州市	Zhejiang 浙江省	18.98	45
Shijiazhuang 石家庄市	Hebei 河北省	18.22	6
Qingdao 青岛市	Shandong 山东省	5.60	25
Weihai 威海市	Shandong 山东省	3.15	2
Yangzhou 扬州市	Jiangsu 江苏省	2.06	12
Weifang 潍坊市	Shandong 山东省	1.89	7
Foshan 佛山市	Guangdong 广东省	1.84	10
Chengdu 成都市	Sichuan 四川省	1.79	6
Huzhou 湖州市	Zhejiang 浙江省	1.55	8

10 Major Wholesalers 十家主要批发商	City 城市	Province 省	Telephone/Fax 电话/传真
Jiangsu Sainty Co.,Ltd.	Nanjing	Jiangsu	(025)4208688
江苏舜天股份有限公司	南京市	江苏省	(025)4200397
Zhejiang Zhongda Group Co.,Ltd.	Hangzhou	Zhejiang	(0571)85155000
浙江中大集团股份有限公司	杭州市	浙江省	(0571)85777050
Guangdong Textiles Import & Export (Group) Company	Guangzhou	Guangdong	(020)83558988
广东省纺织品进出口（集团）公司	广州市	广东省	(020)83553900
Zhejiang Shindri Group Co., ltd.	Hangzhou	Zhejiang	(0571)87795067
浙江新大集团有限公司	杭州市	浙江省	(0571)87031999
China-Base Ningbo Foreign Trade Co.,Ltd.	Ningbo	Zhejiang	(0574)87425510
中基宁波对外贸易股份有限公司	宁波市	浙江省	(0574)87425666
Jiaxing Import & Export Corporation	Jiaxing	Zhejiang	(0573)2062785
嘉兴市进出口公司	嘉兴市	浙江省	(0573)2084488
Liaoning Times Costume Import & Export Co.,Ltd.	Dalian	Liaoning	(0411)2798320
辽宁时代服装进出口股份有限公司	大连市	辽宁省	(0411)2798000
China Drawnwork Shanghai Import & Export Company	Shanghai	Shanghai	(021)63258888
中国抽纱上海进出口公司	上海市	上海市	(021)63246020
China (Fujian) Foreign Trade Center (Holdings)	Fuzhou	Fujian	(0591)7553065
中国（福建）对外贸易中心集团	福州市	福建省	(0591)7537173
Xiamen Xinde Co., Ltd.	Xiamen	Fujian	(0592)6027854
厦门信达股份有限公司	厦门市	福建省	(0592)6021391

1924: Leather Luggage and Handbags 皮箱制造业

The industry accounts for 0.051% of the total revenue of China's industrial sector in 2002. The rate of return on assets is 3.26%. 85.52% of all firms in the industry made a profit while 14.48% had negative returns.The top province in terms of the industry's revenue is Zhejiang, accounting for 37.72% of the total revenue.
2002年本行业收入占全行业的0.051%，资产利润率为3.26%。85.52%的企业赢利，14.48%的企业亏损。收入最高的省为浙江省，占本行业的37.72%。

	Total number of firms 企业总数	Total number of employees 职工总数	Total revenue (Mil.RMB) 总销售收入（百万元）	Total profit (Mil.RMB) 总利润（百万元）	Return on assets 资产利润率（%）	Return on equity 权益利润率（%）	Labour productivity ('000 RMB/worker) 劳动生产率（千元/人）	Debts/assets 资产负债率（%）	Total assets (Mil.RMB) 总资产（百万元）
Industry Overall 行业总体	221	52,991	5,490	118	3.26	10.61	25.32	69.28	3,614

	Number of firms 企业个数	Average number of employees 平均职工人数	Average revenue ('000 RMB) 平均销售收入（千元）	Average profit ('000 RMB) 平均利润（千元）	Return on assets 资产利润率（%）	Return on equity 权益利润率（%）	Labour productivity ('000 RMB/worker) 劳动生产率（千元/人）	Debts/assets 资产负债率（%）	Average total assets ('000 RMB) 平均总资产（千元）
By ownership 产业所有权									
State-owned 国有	1	90	2,044	-237	-16.20	-30.46	6.02	46.82	1,463
Collective-owned 集体	13	272	30,014	587	2.29	9.95	26.03	77.03	25,662
Foreign & Overseas Chinese Funded 三资	69	315	31,723	387	1.45	3.95	23.67	63.22	26,625
By regional distribution 地区分布									
Central-North 华北	7	158	6,452	-29	-0.11	-0.35	16.19	67.91	25,155
Beijing 北京	3	262	5,875	-11	-0.02	-0.06	11.51	63.31	49,365
Tianjin 天津	3	103	8,821	-16	-0.33		30.08	122.74	4,979
Hebei 河北	1	11	1,077	-117	-0.90	-2.10	-40.45	57.41	13,056
Shanxi 山西									
Inner Mongolia 内蒙古									
Northeast 东北	2	160	2,585	226	6.67	10.13	3.75	34.12	3,379
Liaoning 辽宁	1	296	4,720	450	7.72	10.34	3.41	25.39	5,830
Jilin 吉林	1	23	449	1	0.11	0.98	8.13	89.01	928
Heilongjiang 黑龙江									
Central-East 华东	172	235	24,687	611	4.68	16.61	26.72	71.83	13,059
Shanghai 上海	33	229	23,685	697	4.94	15.60	25.22	68.31	14,100
Jiangsu 江苏	27	237	31,126	429	3.83	13.19	33.62	70.93	11,178
Zhejiang 浙江	93	216	22,266	621	4.96	18.09	25.33	72.56	12,504
Anhui 安徽	2	280	27,745	1,161	6.87	63.68	34.92	89.21	16,896
Fujian 福建	5	213	22,684	513	3.08	4.88	18.74	36.98	16,673
Jiangxi 江西	1	32	5,100	2	0.11	0.37	45.78	69.32	1,760
Shandong 山东	11	430	34,500	723	4.03	36.43	26.39	88.93	17,939
Central-South 中南	40	278	29,828	310	1.05	2.98	21.77	64.86	29,614
Henan 河南	2	120	1,857	-115	-2.56	-5.91	19.62	56.74	4,479
Hubei 湖北	2	184	16,852	301	0.91	22.55	22.36	95.99	33,191
Hunan 湖南	3	165	14,070	-120	-1.63	-4.93	42.84	66.86	7,370
Guangdong 广东	33	304	33,743	375	1.14	3.08	20.76	62.98	32,943
Guangxi 广西									
Hainan 海南									
Southwest 西南									
Chongqing 重庆									
Sichuan 四川									
Guizhou 贵州									
Yunnan 云南									
Tibet 西藏									
Northwest 西北									
Shaanxi 陕西									
Gansu 甘肃									
Qinghai 青海									
Ningxia 宁夏									
Xinjiang 新疆									

1924: Leather Luggage and Handbags 皮箱制造业

Year 年份	Number of firms 企业个数	Rate of change 变化率 (%)	Number of employees 职工人数 (人)	Rate of change 变化率 (%)	Total revenue (Mil. RMB) 总销售收入 (百万元)	Rate of change 变化率 (%)	Total profit (Mil RMB) 总利润 (百万元)	Rate of change 变化率 (%)
2000	129		31,294		3,419		53	
2001	158	22.48	39,124	25.02	3,769	10.24	65	22.64
2002	221	39.87	52,991	35.44	5,490	45.66	118	81.54

Major Products 主要产品	Output 产量	Unit 单位

10 Main Firms with Maximal Revenue (year founded) 收入最大的十家主要企业（创办年份）	City 城市	Province 省	Telephone/ fax 电话/传真	Number of employees 职工人数	Ownership 产业所有权	Revenue ('000 RMB) 销售收入 (千元)	Profit('000 RMB) (rank) 利润(千元) (排名)	Total assets ('000 RMB) 总资产 (千元)	Major products 主要产品
Haiyang Hongyuan Cases & Bags Co., Ltd.	Yantai	Shandong	(0535)3255876		Collective-owned				Cases & Bags
海阳市鸿源箱包有限责任公司(1993)	烟台市	山东省	(0535)3255998	1,010	集体企业	235,880	6,860(3)	100,788	箱包
Qidong Hehe Changjiang Cases & Bags Factory	Nantong	Jiangsu	(0513)3713000		Private Enterprises				Cases & Bags
启东市和合长江箱包厂(1996)	南通市	江苏省	(0513)3733478	680	私营独资	183,007	4,722(6)	50,538	箱包
Dongguan Sanhe Plastic Products Co., Ltd.	Dongguan	Guangdong	(0769)3392589		Overseas Chinese-funded				Portable Case
东莞三和塑胶制品有限公司(1993)	东莞市	广东省	(0769)3392314	1,275	港澳台资	149,292	2,461(13)	107,660	手提箱
Zhongshan Huangguan Leather Articles Co., Ltd.	Zhongshan	Guangdong	(0760)6683756		Overseas Chinese-funded				Portable Case
中山皇冠皮件有限公司(1992)	中山市	广东省	(0760)6683758	769	港澳台资	112,739	1,544(21)	136,122	手提箱
Pinghu Zhongcun Cases & Bags Co., Ltd.	Jiaxing	Zhejiang	(0573)5645188		Private Owned				Cases & Bags
平湖市中村箱包有限公司(2000)	嘉兴市	浙江省	(0573)5644207	833	私营企业	95,940	360(75)	35,514	箱包
Wenzhou Fantai Cases & Bags Co., Ltd.	Wenzhou	Zhejiang	(0577)86875300		Overseas Chinese-funded				Cases & Bags
温州泛太箱包有限公司(1994)	温州市	浙江省	(0577)86873441	628	港澳台资	88,244	1,550(20)	41,420	箱包
Guangzhou Panyu Chongguang Leather Articles Co.,Ltd.	Guangzhou	Guangdong	(020)84583399		Overseas Chinese-funded				leatheroid Portable Attache Case人造革手
广州市番禺区崇光皮件有限公司(1995)	广州市	广东省	(020)84586192	500	港澳台资	78,696	380(72)	11,251	提公文箱
Jiangsu Yangzhou Guanghua Leather Products Co.,Ltd.	Yangzhou	Jiangsu	(0514)4222599		Limited-Liability				EVA Leather Suitcase
扬州市光华皮件制品有限公司(1980)	扬州市	江苏省	(0514)4222110	980	有限公司	73,520	600(58)	27,930	EVA皮箱
Hangzhou Yuhang Yuanda Industrial Co., Ltd	Hangzhou	Zhejiang	(0571)86210560		Private Owned				Cases & Bags
杭州余杭远大实业有限公司(1999)	杭州市	浙江省	(0571)86210222	200	私营企业	67,000	-	61,150	箱包
Pinghu Nanqiao Luggage Co., Ltd.	Jiaxing	Zhejiang	(0573)5644645		Private Owned				Leather Suitcase
平湖市南桥箱包有限公司(1987)	嘉兴市	浙江省	(0573)5644000	668	私营企业	65,690	2,650(12)	37,027	皮箱

Top 10 Cities by Revenue 销售收入排名前10位城市	Province 省	Market share 市场份额 (%)	Number of firms 企业个数
Jiaxing 嘉兴市	Zhejiang 浙江省	20.97	45
Shanghai 上海市	Shanghai 上海市	14.24	33
Wenzhou 温州市	Zhejiang 浙江省	9.18	26
Hangzhou 杭州市	Zhejiang 浙江省	5.57	15
Dongguan 东莞市	Guangdong 广东省	5.36	7
Nantong 南通市	Jiangsu 江苏省	4.80	5
Yantai 烟台市	Shandong 山东省	4.40	2
Shenzhen 深圳市	Guangdong 广东省	4.40	5
Guangzhou 广州市	Guangdong 广东省	3.39	6
Zhongshan 中山市	Guangdong 广东省	3.12	3

10 Major Wholesalers 十家主要批发商	City 城市	Province 省	Telephone/Fax 电话/传真
Kunming Department Store Group Co.,Ltd.	Kunming	Yunnan	(0871)3313618
昆明百货集团股份有限公司	昆明市	云南省	(0871)3314961
Jiangsu Skyrun International Group	Nanjing	Jiangsu	(025)4468888
江苏开元国际集团	南京市	江苏省	(025)4209409
Guangdong Light Industry Products Imp.& Exp.(Group) Corporation	Guangzhou	Guangdong	(020)83344557
广东省轻工业品进出口（集团）公司	广州市	广东省	(020)83330181
Shanghai Cheer (Group) Co.,Ltd.	Shanghai	Shanghai	(021)63069764
上海七百（集团）有限公司	上海市	上海市	(021)63069537
Fujian Tiancheng Group Co.,Ltd.	Fuzhou	Fujian	(0591)7503388
福建天成集团有限公司	福州市	福建省	(0591)7609279
Shanghai Century Lianhua Supermaket Development Co.,ltd.	Shanghai	Shanghai	(021)53544600
上海世纪联华超市发展有限公司	上海市	上海市	(021)62252610
Suzhou General Merchandise General Company	Suzhou	Jiangsu	(0512)65222247
苏州百货总公司	苏州市	江苏省	(0512)65222247
Zhejiang Light Industry Products Import & Export Corporation	Hangzhou	Zhejiang	(0571)88391888
浙江省轻工业品进出口公司	杭州市	浙江省	(0571)88391666
Zhejiang Winsun Import & Export Co., Ltd.	Jiaxing	Zhejiang	(0573)2117091
浙江汇信进出口有限公司	嘉兴市	浙江省	(0573)2117020
Shenzhen CATIC Trade Company	Shenzhen	Guangdong	(0755)83790111
深圳中航商贸公司	深圳市	广东省	(0755)83790462

1925: Leather Bags 皮包制造业

The industry accounts for 0.129% of the total revenue of China's industrial sector in 2002. The rate of return on assets is 4.55%. 80.93% of all firms in the industry made a profit while 19.07% had negative returns.The top province in terms of the industry's revenue is Guangdong, accounting for 46.31% of the total revenue.
2002年本行业收入占全行业的0.129%，资产利润率为4.55%。80.93%的企业赢利，19.07%的企业亏损。收入最高的省为广东省，占本行业的46.31%。

	Total number of firms 企业总数	Total number of employees 职工总数	Total revenue (Mil.RMB) 总销售收入(百万元)	Total profit (Mil.RMB) 总利润(百万元)	Return on assets 资产利润率(%)	Return on equity 权益利润率(%)	Labour productivity ('000 RMB/worker) 劳动生产率(千元/人)	Debts/assets 资产负债率(%)	Total assets (Mil.RMB) 总资产(百万元)
Industry Overall 行业总体	493	153,217	13,883	389	4.55	10.22	23.75	55.46	8,550

	Number of firms 企业个数	Average number of employees 平均职工人数	Average revenue ('000 RMB) 平均销售收入(千元)	Average profit ('000 RMB) 平均利润(千元)	Return on assets 资产利润率(%)	Return on equity 权益利润率(%)	Labour productivity ('000 RMB/worker) 劳动生产率(千元/人)	Debts/assets 资产负债率(%)	Average total assets ('000 RMB) 平均总资产(千元)
By ownership 产业所有权									
State-owned 国有	5	273	17,002	439	1.78	5.17	16.40	65.49	24,599
Collective-owned 集体	46	356	18,458	421	4.23	12.25	18.77	65.48	9,945
Foreign & Overseas Chinese Funded 三资	249	406	36,220	776	3.29	8.07	22.82	59.30	23,620
By regional distribution 地区分布									
Central-North 华北	18	143	27,460	2,973	8.27	10.40	47.99	20.44	35,927
Beijing 北京	3	88	11,078	166	1.20		48.55	118.92	13,908
Tianjin 天津	6	119	17,680	519	4.63	12.15	26.17	61.85	11,205
Hebei 河北	9	179	39,441	5,544	9.28	10.04	57.55	7.62	59,747
Shanxi 山西									
Inner Mongolia 内蒙古									
Northeast 东北	3	1,624	133,718	-3,232	-6.00	-23.92	15.98	74.92	53,878
Liaoning 辽宁	3	1,624	133,718	-3,232	-6.00	-23.92	15.98	74.92	53,878
Jilin 吉林									
Heilongjiang 黑龙江									
Central-East 华东	220	283	29,397	1,042	6.83	15.39	27.73	55.62	15,255
Shanghai 上海	28	214	31,095	1,338	5.37	9.68	39.04	44.56	24,946
Jiangsu 江苏	33	262	31,845	784	5.47	14.61	30.54	62.55	14,318
Zhejiang 浙江	68	193	18,376	488	4.85	15.06	23.26	67.78	10,054
Anhui 安徽	4	199	9,537	189	5.21	11.99	12.77	56.55	3,629
Fujian 福建	55	348	30,582	811	5.18	10.88	22.32	52.40	15,661
Jiangxi 江西	1	325	5,665	56	3.01	3.11	3.33	3.44	1,862
Shandong 山东	31	462	50,657	2,815	13.99	30.42	34.02	54.02	20,122
Central-South 中南	251	332	25,974	463	2.65	6.58	20.49	59.76	17,465
Henan 河南	2	149	8,131	1,119	31.93	75.63	18.51	57.79	3,505
Hubei 湖北	1	113	29,120				93.46	14.21	12,106
Hunan 湖南	2	69	13,179	238	7.28	209.69	64.34	96.53	3,269
Guangdong 广东	244	338	26,349	465	2.61	6.52	20.34	59.87	17,789
Guangxi 广西	1	200	7,170	-322	-9.13	-16.04	5.02	43.06	3,525
Hainan 海南	1	159	11,289	234	1.69	3.57	30.14	52.78	13,880
Southwest 西南									
Chongqing 重庆									
Sichuan 四川									
Guizhou 贵州									
Yunnan 云南									
Tibet 西藏									
Northwest 西北	1	36	613	-58	-3.60	-28.43	4.69	87.35	1,613
Shaanxi 陕西									
Gansu 甘肃									
Qinghai 青海									
Ningxia 宁夏									
Xinjiang 新疆	1	36	613	-58	-3.60	-28.43	4.69	87.35	1,613

1925: Leather Bags 皮包制造业

Year 年份	Number of firms 企业个数	Rate of change 变化率(%)	Number of employees 职工人数(人)	Rate of change 变化率(%)	Total revenue (Mil. RMB) 总销售收入(百万元)	Rate of change 变化率(%)	Total profit (Mil RMB) 总利润(百万元)	Rate of change 变化率(%)
2000	411		130,236		11,221		429	
2001	469	14.11	141,755	8.84	12,400	10.51	432	0.70
2002	493	5.12	153,217	8.09	13,883	11.96	389	-9.95

Major Products 主要产品	Output 产量	Unit 单位
Leather Bag 皮包、袋	82,123	10,000 Units 万个

10 Main Firms with Maximal Revenue (year founded) 收入最大的十家主要企业（创办年份）	City 城市	Province 省	Telephone/fax 电话/传真	Number of employees 职工人数	Ownership 产业所有权	Revenue ('000 RMB) 销售收入(千元)	Profit('000 RMB) (rank) 利润(千元)(排名)	Total assets ('000 RMB) 总资产(千元)	Major products 主要产品
Panyu Simone Handbag Co., Ltd. 番禺世门手袋有限公司(1992)	Guangzhou 广州市	Guangdong 广东省	(020)84754777 (020)84755459	3,264	Foreign Funded 外商投资	560,455	1,597(73)	203,455	Handbag 手袋
Huaxia Yamani Industrial Co.,Ltd. 华夏山二实业有限公司(1925)	Xiamen 厦门市	Fujian 福建省	(0592)7131234 (0592)7131200	2,669	Foreign Funded 外商投资	405,430	3,705(27)	322,470	Wallet 皮夹
Yingkou IL Shim Bag Co.,Ltd. 营口一心箱包有限公司(1993)	Yingkou 营口市	Liaoning 辽宁省	(0417)6272650 (0417)6270211	3,897	Foreign Funded 外商投资	336,353	-	114,144	Cases & Bags 箱包
Wendeng Tianma Portfolio Co., Ltd. 文登天马皮包有限公司(1995)	Weihai 威海市	Shandong 山东省	(0631)8898397 (0631)8898444	415	Foreign Funded 外商投资	282,230	29,030(2)	45,020	Portfolio 皮包
Hebei Gaobeidian Baigou Town Cases & Bags Group Co.,Ltd. 河北省高碑店市白沟镇箱包集团有限公司(1997)	Baoding 保定市	Hebei 河北省	(0312)2883177 (0312)2892220	860	Limited-Liability 有限公司	280,429	38,327(1)	504,408	Portfolio 皮包
Weihai Yongbai Leather Products Corp 威海永柏革制品有限公司(1994)	Weihai 威海市	Shandong 山东省	(0631)8545414 (0631)8545177	400	Foreign Funded 外商投资	275,000	27,500(3)	36,240	Leather Bags 皮革包
Zhaoqing Haide Handbags Co., Ltd. 肇庆海德有限公司(1991)	Zhaoqing 肇庆市	Guangdong 广东省	(0758)8471539 (0758)8417354	1,880	Overseas Chinese-funded 港澳台资	214,563	7,296(7)	47,512	Handbag 手袋
Shanghai Aisi Travelling Articles Co., Ltd. 上海爱思旅行用品有限公司(1988)	Shanghai 上海市	Shanghai 上海市	(021)65422410 (021)65442717	962	Foreign Funded 外商投资	168,646	18,645(4)	161,860	Cases & Bags 箱包
Kaiping Shagang Meilin Products Factory 开平沙冈美林制品厂(1994)	Jiangmen 江门市	Guangdong 广东省	(0750)2298056 (0750)2289185	850	Collective-owned 集体企业	167,800	2,906(37)	49,130	Leather Products 皮革制品
Quanzhou Fangyuan Travelling Articles Co., Ltd. 泉州芳源游用品有限公司(1985)	Quanzhou 泉州市	Fujian 福建省	(0595)7580100 (0595)7581100	1,000	Overseas Chinese-funded 港澳台资	149,003	3,165(34)	35,256	Travel Bags 旅游包袋

Top 10 Cities by Revenue 销售收入排名前10位城市	Province 省	Market share 市场份额(%)	Number of firms 企业个数
Guangzhou 广州市	Guangdong 广东省	18.51	96
Quanzhou 泉州市	Fujian 福建省	7.03	42
Shanghai 上海市	Shanghai 上海市	6.27	28
Dongguan 东莞市	Guangdong 广东省	6.06	32
Weihai 威海市	Shandong 山东省	5.97	4
Qingdao 青岛市	Shandong 山东省	4.52	21
Shenzhen 深圳市	Guangdong 广东省	4.44	23
Xiamen 厦门市	Fujian 福建省	3.90	6
Zhongshan 中山市	Guangdong 广东省	3.86	26
Zhaoqing 肇庆市	Guangdong 广东省	3.55	8

10 Major Wholesalers 十家主要批发商	City 城市	Province 省	Telephone/Fax 电话/传真
Kunming Department Store Group Co.,Ltd. 昆明百货集团股份有限公司	Kunming 昆明市	Yunnan 云南省	(0871)3313618 (0871)3314961
Jiangsu Skyrun International Group 江苏开元国际集团	Nanjing 南京市	Jiangsu 江苏省	(025)4468888 (025)4209409
Guangdong Light Industry Products Imp.& Exp.(Group) Corporation 广东省轻工业品进出口（集团）公司	Guangzhou 广州市	Guangdong 广东省	(020)83344557 (020)83330181
Shanghai Cheer (Group) Co.,Ltd. 上海七百（集团）有限公司	Shanghai 上海市	Shanghai 上海市	(021)63069764 (021)63069537
Fujian Tiancheng Group Co.,Ltd. 福建天成集团有限公司	Fuzhou 福州市	Fujian 福建省	(0591)7503388 (0591)7609279
Shanghai Century Lianhua Supermaket Development Co.,ltd. 上海世纪联华超市发展有限公司	Shanghai 上海市	Shanghai 上海市	(021)53544600 (021)62252610
Suzhou General Merchandise General Company 苏州百货总公司	Suzhou 苏州市	Jiangsu 江苏省	(0512)65222247 (0512)65222247
Zhejiang Light Industry Products Import & Export Corporation 浙江省轻工业品进出口公司	Hangzhou 杭州市	Zhejiang 浙江省	(0571)88391888 (0571)88391666
Zhejiang Winsun Import & Export Co., Ltd. 浙江汇信进出口有限公司	Jiaxing 嘉兴市	Zhejiang 浙江省	(0573)2117091 (0573)2117020
Shenzhen CATIC Trade Company 深圳中航商贸公司	Shenzhen 深圳市	Guangdong 广东省	(0755)83790111 (0755)83790462

1929: Other Leather Products 其他类未包括的皮革制品业

The industry accounts for 0.090% of the total revenue of China's industrial sector in 2002. The rate of return on assets is 4.55%. 84.96% of all firms in the industry made a profit while 15.04% had negative returns.The top province in terms of the industry's revenue is Guangdong, accounting for 46.78% of the total revenue.
2002年本行业收入占全行业的0.090%，资产利润率为4.55%。84.96%的企业赢利，15.04%的企业亏损。收入最高的省为广东省，占本行业的46.78%。

	Total number of firms 企业总数	Total number of employees 职工总数	Total revenue (Mil.RMB) 总销售收入(百万元)	Total profit (Mil.RMB) 总利润(百万元)	Return on assets 资产利润率(%)	Return on equity 权益利润率(%)	Labour productivity ('000 RMB/ worker) 劳动生产率(千元/人)	Debts/ assets 资产负债率(%)	Total assets (Mil.RMB) 总资产(百万元)
Industry Overall 行业总体	339	91,633	9,625	259	4.55	11.59	29.13	60.75	5,687

	Number of firms 企业个数	Average number of employees 平均职工人数	Average revenue ('000 RMB) 平均销售收入(千元)	Average profit ('000 RMB) 平均利润(千元)	Return on assets 资产利润率(%)	Return on equity 权益利润率(%)	Labour productivity ('000 RMB/ worker) 劳动生产率(千元/人)	Debts/ assets 资产负债率(%)	Average total assets ('000 RMB) 平均总资产(千元)
By ownership 产业所有权									
State-owned 国有	3	58	1,378	-429	-9.08		1.86	157.52	4,727
Collective-owned 集体	33	261	15,570	202	1.84	8.40	18.11	78.03	10,939
Foreign & Overseas Chinese Funded 三资	199	318	35,104	846	4.09	10.05	30.28	59.34	20,698
By regional distribution 地区分布									
Central-North 华北	12	113	8,390	766	10.63	24.65	24.26	56.87	7,204
Beijing 北京	4	85	7,540	629	10.96	17.00	38.33	35.52	5,740
Tianjin 天津	3	77	7,187	594	30.64	78.81	21.60	61.11	1,937
Hebei 河北	5	158	9,791	978	8.48	24.20	19.00	64.95	11,535
Shanxi 山西									
Inner Mongolia 内蒙古									
Northeast 东北	7	212	20,827	235	2.44	5.72	26.20	57.38	9,655
Liaoning 辽宁	5	269	25,414	315	3.12	7.07	24.89	55.80	10,087
Jilin 吉林									
Heilongjiang 黑龙江	2	70	9,359	36	0.41	1.09	38.79	62.03	8,575
Central-East 华东	162	254	28,310	1,103	5.74	15.95	28.97	64.01	19,212
Shanghai 上海	24	129	17,061	452	4.17	12.03	35.05	65.37	10,846
Jiangsu 江苏	51	284	36,247	1,324	4.71	13.83	29.16	65.96	28,113
Zhejiang 浙江	49	195	24,065	1,208	8.62	18.63	31.98	53.77	14,021
Anhui 安徽	2	121	5,934	-27	-0.81		7.55	102.64	3,334
Fujian 福建	21	342	31,586	424	2.38	7.19	31.11	66.90	17,820
Jiangxi 江西	6	420	11,546	111	1.36	3.25	8.28	58.31	8,195
Shandong 山东	9	456	44,945	3,513	10.49	39.49	26.91	73.43	33,476
Central-South 中南	155	304	30,735	440	2.85	6.49	29.57	56.06	15,443
Henan 河南	5	132	9,210	794	11.74	26.07	22.02	54.97	6,764
Hubei 湖北	6	203	13,052	281	2.23	6.54	26.03	65.93	12,586
Hunan 湖南	3	139	9,719	30	1.25	3.35	16.76	62.56	2,420
Guangdong 广东	136	321	33,103	457	2.80	6.16	30.09	54.56	16,324
Guangxi 广西	5	237	21,674	78	0.69		22.89	101.27	11,396
Hainan 海南									
Southwest 西南	2	98	11,666	477	4.08		11.82	112.77	11,684
Chongqing 重庆	2	98	11,666	477	4.08		11.82	112.77	11,684
Sichuan 四川									
Guizhou 贵州									
Yunnan 云南									
Tibet 西藏									
Northwest 西北	1	230	4,627	40	1.29		29.34	190.58	3,089
Shaanxi 陕西									
Gansu 甘肃	1	230	4,627	40	1.29		29.34	190.58	3,089
Qinghai 青海									
Ningxia 宁夏									
Xinjiang 新疆									

1929: Other Leather Products 其他类未包括的皮革制品业

Year 年份	Number of firms 企业个数	Rate of change 变化率(%)	Number of employees 职工人数(人)	Rate of change 变化率(%)	Total revenue (Mil. RMB) 总销售收入(百万元)	Rate of change 变化率(%)	Total profit (Mil RMB) 总利润(百万元)	Rate of change 变化率(%)
2000	259		73,079		6,526		128	
2001	297	14.67	84,660	15.85	7,808	19.64	191	49.22
2002	339	14.14	91,633	8.24	9,625	23.27	259	35.60

Major Products 主要产品	Output 产量	Unit 单位

10 Main Firms with Maximal Revenue (year founded) 收入最大的十家主要企业（创办年份）	City 城市	Province 省	Telephone/fax 电话/传真	Number of employees 职工人数	Ownership 产业所有权	Revenue ('000 RMB) 销售收入(千元)	Profit('000 RMB) (rank) 利润(千元)(排名)	Total assets ('000 RMB) 总资产(千元)	Major products 主要产品
Jiangshu Maydiang Leather Goods Co., ltd. 江苏美迪洋集团(1989)	Suzhou 苏州市	Jiangsu 江苏省	(0512)52381854 (0512)52381567	1,774	Foreign Funded 外商投资	490,372	26,772(1)	458,437	Ticket Wallet 票夹
Asian American (Xiamen) Leather Co., Ltd. 亚美（厦门）皮件有限公司(1997)	Xiamen 厦门市	Fujian 福建省	(0592)7125216 (0592)7125214	788	Overseas Chinese-funded 港澳台资	232,829	2,421(23)	103,790	Leather Belt 皮带
Nanjing Jiadan Label Co., Ltd. 南京嘉丹标牌有限公司(1993)	Nanjing 南京市	Jiangsu 江苏省	(025)6802554 (025)6802024	398	Overseas Chinese-funded 港澳台资	197,580	4,040(11)	12,700	Costume Label 服装标牌
Zhongshan Yongmeng Leather Articles Co.,Ltd. 中山泳盟皮件有限公司(1990)	Zhongshan 中山市	Guangdong 广东省	(0760)6502015 (0760)6502525	3,662	Overseas Chinese-funded 港澳台资	177,626	-	98,198	Leather Articles 皮件
Sihui Meinper Leather Ornaments Co., Ltd. 四会美斯特皮饰有限公司(1990)	Zhaoqing 肇庆市	Guangdong 广东省	(0758)3323257 (0758)3333507	403	Overseas Chinese-funded 港澳台资	124,190	778(75)	30,713	strap 皮带
Zhejiang Pinghu Huashen Leather(Group) Co.,Ltd. 浙江省平湖市华神皮革(集团)有限公司(2000)	Jiaxing 嘉兴市	Zhejiang 浙江省	(0573)5090220 (0573)5090872	413	Joint Stock 股份制	110,960	8,430(6)	86,678	Leather Glove 革皮手套
Gaozhou Yixing Leather Products Co., Ltd. 高州怡兴皮革制品有限公司(2000)	Maoming 茂名市	Guangdong 广东省	(0668)6616773	510	Overseas Chinese-funded 港澳台资	99,417	176(172)	12,487	Leather Glove 皮革手套
Gaozhou Yifeng Leather Products Co., Ltd. 高州怡丰皮革制品有限公司(2000)	Maoming 茂名市	Guangdong 广东省	(0668)6681905 (0668)6665217	598	Overseas Chinese-funded 港澳台资	98,448	518(110)	37,005	Leather Glove 皮革手套
Sihui Maishiduo Leather Products Co., Ltd. 四会迈士多皮制品有限公司(1995)	Zhaoqing 肇庆市	Guangdong 广东省	(0758)3333531 (0758)3333536	250	Overseas Chinese-funded 港澳台资	93,000	567(102)	19,394	strap 皮带
Zhejiang Jinsake Trappings & Leather Utensil Co.,Ltd. 浙江金萨克服饰皮具有限公司(1996)	Wenzhou 温州市	Zhejiang 浙江省	(0577)63720888 (0577)63738999	160	Private Owned 私营企业	92,583	3,703(14)	39,338	strap 皮带

Top 10 Cities by Revenue 销售收入排名前10位城市	Province 省	Market share 市场份额(%)	Number of firms 企业个数
Maoming 茂名市	Guangdong 广东省	27.54	63
Suzhou 苏州市	Jiangsu 江苏省	11.12	23
Wenzhou 温州市	Zhejiang 浙江省	5.87	26
Shanghai 上海市	Shanghai 上海市	4.25	24
Guangzhou 广州市	Guangdong 广东省	4.00	24
Nanjing 南京市	Jiangsu 江苏省	3.67	7
Jiaxing 嘉兴市	Zhejiang 浙江省	3.35	8
Xiamen 厦门市	Fujian 福建省	3.21	3
Zhongshan 中山市	Guangdong 广东省	3.02	8
Jiangmen 江门市	Guangdong 广东省	2.84	10

10 Major Wholesalers 十家主要批发商	City 城市	Province 省	Telephone/Fax 电话/传真
Kunming Department Store Group Co.,Ltd. 昆明百货集团股份有限公司	Kunming 昆明市	Yunnan 云南省	(0871)3313618 (0871)3314961
Jiangsu Skyrun International Group 江苏开元国际集团	Nanjing 南京市	Jiangsu 江苏省	(025)4468888 (025)4209409
Guangdong Light Industry Products Imp.& Exp.(Group) Corporation 广东省轻工业品进出口（集团）公司	Guangzhou 广州市	Guangdong 广东省	(020)83344557 (020)83330181
Shanghai Cheer (Group) Co.,Ltd. 上海七百（集团）有限公司	Shanghai 上海市	Shanghai 上海市	(021)63069764 (021)63069537
Fujian Tiancheng Group Co.,Ltd. 福建天成集团有限公司	Fuzhou 福州市	Fujian 福建省	(0591)7503388 (0591)7609279
Shanghai Century Lianhua Supermaket Development Co.,ltd. 上海世纪联华超市发展有限公司	Shanghai 上海市	Shanghai 上海市	(021)53544600 (021)62252610
Suzhou General Merchandise General Company 苏州百货总公司	Suzhou 苏州市	Jiangsu 江苏省	(0512)65222247 (0512)65222247
Zhejiang Light Industry Products Import & Export Corporation 浙江省轻工业品进出口公司	Hangzhou 杭州市	Zhejiang 浙江省	(0571)88391888 (0571)88391666
Zhejiang Winsun Import & Export Co., Ltd. 浙江汇信进出口有限公司	Jiaxing 嘉兴市	Zhejiang 浙江省	(0573)2117091 (0573)2117020
Shenzhen CATIC Trade Company 深圳中航商贸公司	Shenzhen 深圳市	Guangdong 广东省	(0755)83790111 (0755)83790462

1931: Fur Tanning 毛皮鞣制业

The industry accounts for 0.023% of the total revenue of China's industrial sector in 2002. The rate of return on assets is 4.35%. 93.67% of all firms in the industry made a profit while 6.33% had negative returns.The top province in terms of the industry's revenue is Henan, accounting for 16.60% of the total revenue.
2002年本行业收入占全行业的 0.023%，资产利润率为 4.35%。93.67%的企业赢利，6.33%的企业亏损。收入最高的省为河南省，占本行业的16.60%。

	Total number of firms 企业总数	Total number of employees 职工总数	Total revenue (Mil.RMB) 总销售收入（百万元）	Total profit (Mil.RMB) 总利润（百万元）	Return on assets 资产利润率（%）	Return on equity 权益利润率（%）	Labour productivity ('000 RMB/ worker) 劳动生产率（千元/人）	Debts/ assets 资产负债率（%）	Total assets (Mil.RMB) 总资产（百万元）
Industry Overall 行业总体	79	12,179	2,444	77	4.35	12.12	56.84	64.10	1,773

	Number of firms 企业个数	Average number of employees 平均职工人数	Average revenue ('000 RMB) 平均销售收入（千元）	Average profit ('000 RMB) 平均利润（千元）	Return on assets 资产利润率（%）	Return on equity 权益利润率（%）	Labour productivity ('000 RMB/ worker) 劳动生产率（千元/人）	Debts/ assets 资产负债率（%）	Average total assets ('000 RMB) 平均总资产（千元）
By ownership 产业所有权									
State-owned 国有	5	409	15,572	-1,597	-4.27		11.19	107.99	37,438
Collective-owned 集体	30	88	14,906	917	12.35	33.80	54.36	63.47	7,422
Foreign & Overseas Chinese Funded 三资	15	170	59,651	1,492	4.38	9.90	99.42	55.71	34,037
By regional distribution 地区分布									
Central-North 华北	16	88	15,608	651	6.09		51.36	120.66	10,698
Beijing 北京	1	49	19,984	319	4.87	5.80	37.06	16.15	6,556
Tianjin 天津									
Hebei 河北	13	96	15,705	745	6.56		48.52	133.55	11,360
Shanxi 山西									
Inner Mongolia 内蒙古	2	54	12,790	208	2.45	4.78	91.19	48.72	8,467
Northeast 东北	1	261	173,105	10,565	17.00		110.39	108.50	62,130
Liaoning 辽宁	1	261	173,105	10,565	17.00		110.39	108.50	62,130
Jilin 吉林									
Heilongjiang 黑龙江									
Central-East 华东	18	176	38,362	1,132	5.63	10.82	67.20	48.00	20,123
Shanghai 上海									
Jiangsu 江苏	1	160	6,530				13.13	79.87	9,290
Zhejiang 浙江	3	82	36,867	475	2.73	20.85	64.58	86.90	17,375
Anhui 安徽	2	95	9,450	784	28.10		34.58	107.53	2,790
Fujian 福建	5	244	34,941	1,460	4.74	5.47	48.67	13.32	30,809
Jiangxi 江西									
Shandong 山东	7	193	54,254	1,442	7.15	21.68	95.48	67.02	20,169
Central-South 中南	37	103	26,203	846	6.26	15.90	73.80	60.62	13,511
Henan 河南	31	92	13,085	790	9.78	23.81	44.35	58.90	8,079
Hubei 湖北									
Hunan 湖南									
Guangdong 广东	5	148	50,087	1,358	3.34	9.03	84.59	63.01	40,647
Guangxi 广西	1	210	313,445				436.68	59.44	46,227
Hainan 海南									
Southwest 西南	4	401	57,120	665	0.53	1.37	32.22	61.16	125,151
Chongqing 重庆	1	300	11,252	297	1.87	4.74	14.01	60.47	15,855
Sichuan 四川	3	434	72,409	788	0.49	1.26	36.42	61.18	161,583
Guizhou 贵州									
Yunnan 云南									
Tibet 西藏									
Northwest 西北	3	644	44,318	613	1.04	1.88	23.64	44.94	59,068
Shaanxi 陕西									
Gansu 甘肃	1	1,708	77,828	10	0.01	0.01	13.39	49.03	142,150
Qinghai 青海									
Ningxia 宁夏	2	113	27,563	915	5.22	7.28	101.48	28.34	17,527
Xinjiang 新疆									

Year 年份	Number of firms 企业个数	Rate of change 变化率 (%)	Number of employees 职工人数 (人)	Rate of change 变化率 (%)	Total revenue (Mil. RMB) 总销售收入 (百万元)	Rate of change 变化率 (%)	Total profit (Mil RMB) 总利润 (百万元)	Rate of change 变化率 (%)
2000	76		12,901		1,626		33	
2001	77	1.32	12,640	-2.02	1,734	6.64	41	24.24
2002	79	2.60	12,179	-3.65	2,444	40.95	77	87.80

Major Products 主要产品	Output 产量	Unit 单位
Fur (Convert into Woolfell) 毛皮(折羊毛皮)	401	10,000 Pieces 万张

10 Main Firms with Maximal Revenue (year founded) 收入最大的十家主要企业（创办年份）	City 城市	Province 省	Telephone/fax 电话/传真	Number of employees 职工人数	Ownership 产业所有权	Revenue ('000 RMB) 销售收入 (千元)	Profit('000 RMB) (rank) 利润(千元) (排名)	Total assets ('000 RMB) 总资产 (千元)	Major products 主要产品
Kehong Leather Co., ltd.	Beihai	Guangxi	(0779)7285511		Overseas Chinese-funded				PU Raw leather
北海科红制革有限公司(1991)	北海市	广西	(0779)7292855	210	港澳台资	313,445	-	46,227	PU胚皮
Yingkou Luoxing Leather Co., Ltd.	Yingkou	Liaoning	(0417)6272664		Foreign Funded				Cow Leather
营口罗星皮革有限公司(1993)	营口市	辽宁省	(0417)6272340	261	外商投资	173,105	10,565(1)	62,130	牛皮革
Sichuan Leshan Zhenjing Leather Products Co.,Ltd. Xinhua Leather	Leshan	Sichuan	(0833)3340655		Joint Stock				Cow Leather
Factory 四川省乐山振静皮革制品有限公司新华制革厂(2000)	乐山市	四川省	(0833)3340971	950	股份制	147,772	1,735(16)	457,988	牛皮革
Boluo Longhua Binhua Leather Co., Ltd.	Huizhou	Guangdong	(0752)6862999		Overseas Chinese-funded				Fur & Leather Products
博罗龙华宾华皮革有限公司(1994)	惠州市	广东省	(0752)6862996	210	港澳台资	125,260	2,627(11)	169,920	毛皮制品
Hebei Suning Leather Factory	Cangzhou	Hebei	(0317)5090458		Collective-owned				Leather
河北省肃宁县制革厂(1990)	沧州市	河北省	(0317)5099223	180	集体企业	64,800	5,580(2)	16,730	皮革
Ji'nan Anqiao Leather Industry Co., Ltd.	Jinan	Shandong	(0531)7651065		Private Enterprises				Leather
济南市安侨皮业有限公司(1995)	济南市	山东省	(0531)7651365	128	私营独资	62,280	3,830(5)	15,290	皮革
Xinhui Duruan Zhujiang Leather Factory	Jiangmen	Guangdong	(0750)3672022		Private Owned				Cowskin
新会市杜阮珠江皮革厂(2001)	江门市	广东省	(0750)3672795	143	私营企业	55,638	3,478(6)	9,829	牛皮
Deqing Shengda Leather Factroy	Huzhou	Zhejiang	(0572)8444365		Private Enterprises				Hogskin
德清县升大皮革厂(2000)	湖州市	浙江省	(0572)8442616	150	私营独资	54,560	843(31)	13,840	猪皮革
Jinjiang Feng'an Leather Enterprise Co.,Ltd.	Quanzhou	Fujian	(0595)5690491		Overseas Chinese-funded				Cowskin
晋江峰安皮业有限公司(1992)	泉州市	福建省	(0595)5687565	248	港澳台资	52,230	3,095(7)	51,915	牛皮
Hangzhou Tianyuan Animal Products Factory	Hangzhou	Zhejiang	(0571)86060780		Limited-Liability				Leather
杭州天元畜产品厂(1993)	杭州市	浙江省	(0571)86809412	71	有限公司	47,906	507(44)	33,556	皮革

Top 10 Cities by Revenue 销售收入排名前10位城市	Province 省	Market share 市场份额 (%)	Number of firms 企业个数
Beihai 北海市	Guangxi 广西	12.82	1
Yingkou 营口市	Liaoning 辽宁省	7.08	1
Heze 荷泽市	Shandong 山东省	6.89	1
Leshan 乐山市	Sichuan 四川省	6.05	1
Cangzhou 沧州市	Hebei 河北省	5.41	4
Quanzhou 泉州市	Fujian 福建省	5.32	3
Liaocheng 聊城市	Shandong 山东省	5.21	2
Huizhou 惠州市	Guangdong 广东省	5.12	1
Zhumadian 驻马店市	Henan 河南省	4.79	10
Shangqiu 商丘市	Henan 河南省	4.06	4

10 Major Wholesalers 十家主要批发商	City 城市	Province 省	Telephone/Fax 电话/传真
Jiangsu Animal By-products Imp And Exp ,Group Corp.	Nanjing	Jiangsu	(025)2306185
江苏开元国际集团畜产进出口股份有限公司	南京市	江苏省	(025)2306282
Zhejiang Native Produce & By-products I/E Group Corp.	Hangzhou	Zhejiang	(0571)85773807
浙江省土产畜产进出口集团公司	杭州市	浙江省	(0571)85773780
Zhejiang G & B Foreign Trading Co.,Ltd.	Hangzhou	Zhejiang	(0571)85773807
浙江惠元对外贸易有限责任公司	杭州市	浙江省	(0571)85773866
Zhejiang G & F Foreign Trading Co.,Ltd.	Hangzhou	Zhejiang	(0571)85773807
浙江惠隆对外贸易有限责任公司	杭州市	浙江省	(0571)85773925
Zhejiang Willing Foreign Trading Co.,Ltd.	Hangzhou	Zhejiang	(0571)85773807
浙江惠灵对外贸易有限责任公司	杭州市	浙江省	(0571)85773720
Guangzhou Livestock Products Import & Export Company	Guangzhou	Guangdong	(020)83852888
广州畜产进出口公司	广州市	广东省	(020)83824187
China Grain & Oil Feedstuff Co.,Ltd.	Beijing	Beijing	(010)64248899
中国粮油饲料有限公司	北京市	北京市	(010)64205100
Zhejing Huashen Silk Group Company	Jiaxing	Zhejiang	(0573)8021696
浙江花神丝绸集团公司	嘉兴市	浙江省	(0573)8038299
Guangdong Dongguan Local Products Import & Export Company	Dongguan	Guangdong	(0769)2221910
广东省东莞土产进出口公司	东莞市	广东省	(0769)2226400
Yunnan Native Produce Import And Export Corp.	Kunming	Yunnan	(0871)3136461
云南省土产进出口公司	昆明市	云南省	(0871)3136378

1932: Fur Clothes 毛皮服装业

The industry accounts for 0.014% of the total revenue of China's industrial sector in 2002. The rate of return on assets is 3.55%. 81.97% of all firms in the industry made a profit while 18.03% had negative returns.The top province in terms of the industry's revenue is Guangdong, accounting for 19.00% of the total revenue.
2002年本行业收入占全行业的0.014%，资产利润率为3.55%。81.97%的企业赢利，18.03%的企业亏损。收入最高的省为广东省，占本行业的19.00%。

	Total number of firms 企业总数	Total number of employees 职工总数	Total revenue (Mil.RMB) 总销售收入（百万元）	Total profit (Mil.RMB) 总利润（百万元）	Return on assets 资产利润率（%）	Return on equity 权益利润率（%）	Labour productivity ('000 RMB/ worker) 劳动生产率（千元/人）	Debts/ assets 资产负债率（%）	Total assets (Mil.RMB) 总资产（百万元）
Industry Overall 行业总体	61	10,449	1,499	46	3.55	10.37	43.87	65.73	1,308

	Number of firms 企业个数	Average number of employees 平均职工人数	Average revenue ('000 RMB) 平均销售收入（千元）	Average profit ('000 RMB) 平均利润（千元）	Return on assets 资产利润率（%）	Return on equity 权益利润率（%）	Labour productivity ('000 RMB/ worker) 劳动生产率（千元/人）	Debts/ assets 资产负债率（%）	Average total assets ('000 RMB) 平均总资产（千元）
By ownership 产业所有权									
State-owned 国有	3	326	20,185	1,402	5.85	11.68	14.78	49.97	23,987
Collective-owned 集体	11	121	14,180	488	3.47	16.48	33.17	78.94	14,055
Foreign & Overseas Chinese Funded 三资	22	167	30,774	515	1.86	4.56	66.99	59.21	27,670
By regional distribution 地区分布									
Central-North 华北	14	155	18,227	1,336	9.73	20.52	30.42	52.56	13,719
Beijing 北京	1	8	16,776	142	2.23	5.86	270.38	61.97	6,372
Tianjin 天津	4	60	7,595	623	11.81	32.68	17.88	63.87	5,273
Hebei 河北	8	147	18,451	1,423	10.92	32.31	38.62	66.19	13,026
Shanxi 山西									
Inner Mongolia 内蒙古	1	756	60,421	4,681	7.75	10.21	19.15	24.09	60,397
Northeast 东北	6	246	20,361	610	2.23	5.39	12.47	58.69	27,389
Liaoning 辽宁	6	246	20,361	610	2.23	5.39	12.47	58.69	27,389
Jilin 吉林									
Heilongjiang 黑龙江									
Central-East 华东	18	175	32,232	1,705	6.52	19.37	61.82	66.35	26,149
Shanghai 上海	2	388	76,469	9,325	16.96	35.07	48.60	51.64	54,973
Jiangsu 江苏	7	149	18,622	317	3.59	11.53	31.22	68.86	8,843
Zhejiang 浙江	2	110	36,225	279	1.31	4.87	86.33	73.17	21,340
Anhui 安徽									
Fujian 福建									
Jiangxi 江西									
Shandong 山东	7	159	32,062	1,323	3.62	12.43	94.87	70.92	36,593
Central-South 中南	19	151	27,380	325	2.04	4.24	60.25	51.85	15,919
Henan 河南	13	133	18,109	538	5.09	18.37	48.21	72.28	10,561
Hubei 湖北									
Hunan 湖南									
Guangdong 广东	6	189	47,468	-136	-0.49	-0.76	78.65	34.87	27,529
Guangxi 广西									
Hainan 海南									
Southwest 西南	1	174	10,373	-438	-1.84	-4.11	37.38	55.13	23,755
Chongqing 重庆									
Sichuan 四川	1	174	10,373	-438	-1.84	-4.11	37.38	55.13	23,755
Guizhou 贵州									
Yunnan 云南									
Tibet 西藏									
Northwest 西北	3	203	3,598	-4,112	-7.99		0.29	116.54	51,490
Shaanxi 陕西									
Gansu 甘肃	2	22	153	1	0.03	2.15	35.84	98.76	3,750
Qinghai 青海									
Ningxia 宁夏									
Xinjiang 新疆	1	567	10,488	-12,338	-8.39		-2.41	117.45	146,971

1932: Fur Clothes 毛皮服装业

Year 年份	Number of firms 企业个数	Rate of change 变化率 (%)	Number of employees 职工人数 (人)	Rate of change 变化率 (%)	Total revenue (Mil. RMB) 总销售收入 (百万元)	Rate of change 变化率 (%)	Total profit (Mil RMB) 总利润 (百万元)	Rate of change 变化率 (%)
2000	58		11,991		1,731		42	
2001	58	o	9,482	-20.92	1,375	-20.57	1	-97.62
2002	61	5.17	10,449	10.20	1,499	9.02	46	4,500.00

Major Products 主要产品	Output 产量	Unit 单位
Fur Clothes 毛皮服装	93	10,000 Pieces 万件

10 Main Firms with Maximal Revenue (year founded) 收入最大的十家主要企业 (创办年份)	City 城市	Province 省	Telephone/fax 电话/传真	Number of employees 职工人数	Ownership 产业所有权	Revenue ('000 RMB) 销售收入 (千元)	Profit('000 RMB) (rank) 利润(千元) (排名)	Total assets ('000 RMB) 总资产 (千元)	Major products 主要产品
Huilai Kuikeng Leather and Furs Co.,Ltd.	Jieyang	Guangdong	(0663)6682578		Overseas Chinese-funded				Leather & Fur Costume
惠来县葵铿皮草厂有限公司(1991)	揭阳市	广东省	(0663)6682558	326	港澳台资	212,140	160(34)	77,721	皮草服装
Qingdao Donglin Fur Co., Ltd.	Qingdao	Shandong	(0532)5173111		Foreign Funded				Plush
青岛东林毛皮有限公司(1996)	青岛市	山东省	(0532)5173110	380	外商投资	114,363	7,630(2)	157,373	长毛绒
Qingdao Sanyi Costume Co., Ltd.	Qingdao	Shandong	(0532)6200159		Joint Stock				Down Costume
青岛三易服装有限公司(1996)	青岛市	山东省	(0532)6200059	260	股份制	73,092	-	14,297	羽绒服
Hebei Suning Sushen Leather Factory	Cangzhou	Hebei	(0317)5099110		Private Partnership				Leather Clothing
河北省肃宁县肃沈制革厂(1991)	沧州市	河北省	(0317)5099025	500	私营合伙	66,700	5,600(3)	15,580	皮衣
No.1 Branch Of 5303 Factory	Bayannaoer	Inner Mongolia	(0478)8321008		State-owned				Police Costume
5303工厂一分厂(1989)	巴彦淖尔	内蒙古	(0478)8321000	756	国有企业	60,421	4,681(4)	60,397	武警服装
Zhejiang Chengxiang Furs And Leather Costume Co., Ltd.	Huzhou	Zhejiang	(0572)3578386		Private Owned				Furs And Leather Costume
浙江呈祥裘皮服装有限公司(1997)	湖州市	浙江省	(0572)3578298	110	私营企业	45,000	357(27)	36,949	裘皮服装
Jiaozuo Aiyilan Co., ltd.	Jiaozuo	Henan	(0391)8190589		Foreign Funded				Shoes Inner Leather
焦作市爱伊兰有限公司(1994)	焦作市	河南省	(0391)8593616	110	外商投资	36,791	75(37)	9,814	鞋里皮
Henan Suixian NO.2 Leather & Fur Factory	Shangqiu	Henan	(0370)8113620		Collective-owned				Cashmere
睢县城关镇第二皮毛厂(1994)	商丘市	河南省	(0370)8111260	365	集体企业	36,138	1,392(11)	12,950	羊剪绒
Dongguan Jiaming Fashionable Dress Co., Ltd	Dongguan	Guangdong	(0769)7721508		Overseas Chinese-funded				Fur Costume
东莞加明时装有限公司(1993)	东莞市	广东省	(0769)7721307	300	港澳台资	33,475	-	36,628	毛皮服装
Shanghai Yixing Artificial Plush Costume Co., Ltd.	Shanghai	Shanghai	(021)39770194		Overseas Chinese-funded				Artificial Plush Cloth人造
上海亿兴人造毛绒服装有限公司(2001)	上海市	上海市	(021)59770478	175	港澳台资	31,989	-	29,682	毛绒服装

Top 10 Cities by Revenue 销售收入排名前10位城市	Province 省	Market share 市场份额 (%)	Number of firms 企业个数
Jieyang 揭阳市	Guangdong 广东省	14.15	1
Qingdao 青岛市	Shandong 山东省	12.51	2
Shanghai 上海市	Shanghai 上海市	10.20	2
Jiaozuo 焦作市	Henan 河南省	7.01	6
Shangqiu 商丘市	Henan 河南省	5.91	2
Cangzhou 沧州市	Hebei 河北省	4.45	1
Bayannaoer 巴彦淖尔盟	Inner Mongolia 内蒙古	4.03	1
Nanjing 南京市	Jiangsu 江苏省	3.90	2
Huludao 葫芦岛市	Liaoning 辽宁省	3.71	2
Zhenjiang 镇江市	Jiangsu 江苏省	3.47	3

10 Major Wholesalers 十家主要批发商	City 城市	Province 省	Telephone/Fax 电话/传真
Jiangsu Sainty Co.,Ltd.	Nanjing	Jiangsu	(025)4208688
江苏舜天股份有限公司	南京市	江苏省	(025)4200397
Zhejiang Zhongda Group Co.,Ltd.	Hangzhou	Zhejiang	(0571)85155000
浙江中大集团股份有限公司	杭州市	浙江省	(0571)85777050
Guangdong Textiles Import & Export (Group) Company	Guangzhou	Guangdong	(020)83558988
广东省纺织品进出口（集团）公司	广州市	广东省	(020)83553900
Zhejiang Shindri Group Co., ltd.	Hangzhou	Zhejiang	(0571)87795067
浙江新大集团有限公司	杭州市	浙江省	(0571)87031999
China-Base Ningbo Foreign Trade Co.,Ltd.	Ningbo	Zhejiang	(0574)87425510
中基宁波对外贸易股份有限公司	宁波市	浙江省	(0574)87425666
Jiaxing Import & Export Corporation	Jiaxing	Zhejiang	(0573)2062785
嘉兴市进出口公司	嘉兴市	浙江省	(0573)2084488
Liaoning Times Costume Import & Export Co.,Ltd.	Dalian	Liaoning	(0411)2798320
辽宁时代服装进出口股份有限公司	大连市	辽宁省	(0411)2798000
China Drawnwork Shanghai Import & Export Company	Shanghai	Shanghai	(021)63258888
中国抽纱上海进出口公司	上海市	上海市	(021)63246020
China (Fujian) Foreign Trade Center (Holdings)	Fuzhou	Fujian	(0591)7553065
中国（福建）对外贸易中心集团	福州市	福建省	(0591)7537173
Xiamen Xinde Co., Ltd.	Xiamen	Fujian	(0592)6027854
厦门信达股份有限公司	厦门市	福建省	(0592)6021391

1939: Other Fur Products Manufacturing 其他毛皮制品业

The industry accounts for 0.025% of the total revenue of China's industrial sector in 2002. The rate of return on assets is 6.16%. 87.18% of all firms in the industry made a profit while 12.82% had negative returns.The top province in terms of the industry's revenue is Jiangsu, accounting for 43.78% of the total revenue.
2002年本行业收入占全行业的0.025%，资产利润率为6.16%。87.18%的企业赢利，12.82%的企业亏损。收入最高的省为江苏省，占本行业的43.78%。

	Total number of firms 企业总数	Total number of employees 职工总数	Total revenue (Mil.RMB) 总销售收入 (百万元)	Total profit (Mil.RMB) 总利润 (百万元)	Return on assets 资产利润率 (%)	Return on equity 权益利润率 (%)	Labour productivity ('000 RMB/ worker) 劳动生产率 (千元/人)	Debts/ assets 资产负债率 (%)	Total assets (Mil.RMB) 总资产 (百万元)
Industry Overall 行业总体	78	13,874	2,678	119	6.16	18.37	37.02	66.49	1,934

	Number of firms 企业个数	Average number of employees 平均职工人数	Average revenue ('000 RMB) 平均销售收入 (千元)	Average profit ('000 RMB) 平均利润 (千元)	Return on assets 资产利润率 (%)	Return on equity 权益利润率 (%)	Labour productivity ('000 RMB/ worker) 劳动生产率 (千元/人)	Debts/ assets 资产负债率 (%)	Average total assets ('000 RMB) 平均总资产 (千元)
By ownership 产业所有权									
State-owned 国有	9	51	2,645	-7	-0.03	-0.24	22.69	87.27	23,270
Collective-owned 集体	12	95	16,431	1,343	15.34	32.64	42.13	53.02	8,755
Foreign & Overseas Chinese Funded 三资	31	216	52,427	2,698	9.25	30.73	49.51	69.89	29,163
By regional distribution 地区分布									
Central-North 华北	26	157	21,520	1,111	5.61	19.10	29.97	70.65	19,820
Beijing 北京	1	5	6,760	50	1.79	4.23	342.60	57.73	2,796
Tianjin 天津	7	68	18,116	-21	-0.07	-0.34	10.87	80.84	31,833
Hebei 河北	13	231	30,506	2,217	11.70	29.71	34.53	60.63	18,951
Shanxi 山西	3	113	3,548	4	0.04	0.26	16.93	83.40	9,857
Inner Mongolia 内蒙古	2	135	9,358	77	1.12	2.82	23.74	60.31	6,872
Northeast 东北	6	71	2,751	-82	-0.87		11.90	131.35	9,433
Liaoning 辽宁	4	75	3,845	-109	-1.20		15.48	151.68	9,105
Jilin 吉林	1	85	1,126	64	0.48	0.81	4.95	41.01	13,439
Heilongjiang 黑龙江	1	41		-117	-1.74			201.68	6,736
Central-East 华东	20	305	78,543	2,855	5.88	15.57	38.68	62.26	48,586
Shanghai 上海	1								
Jiangsu 江苏	10	376	117,238	4,585	6.32	18.43	42.16	65.70	72,507
Zhejiang 浙江	6	262	28,219	600	2.63	7.34	21.35	64.24	22,839
Anhui 安徽									
Fujian 福建	3	260	76,389	2,547	6.97	11.07	56.89	37.05	36,540
Jiangxi 江西									
Shandong 山东									
Central-South 中南	22	138	23,029	1,507	9.37	24.40	47.46	61.60	16,074
Henan 河南	20	133	21,874	1,182	7.35	19.72	43.13	62.71	16,067
Hubei 湖北									
Hunan 湖南									
Guangdong 广东	2	190	34,581	4,757	29.47	59.60	77.69	50.56	16,142
Guangxi 广西									
Hainan 海南									
Southwest 西南	1	10	47				1.20	55.03	6,120
Chongqing 重庆									
Sichuan 四川									
Guizhou 贵州	1	10	47				1.20	55.03	6,120
Yunnan 云南									
Tibet 西藏									
Northwest 西北	3	68	8,119	133	1.32	4.38	27.84	69.85	10,054
Shaanxi 陕西	1	75	6,720	501	4.78	16.70	32.00	71.37	10,480
Gansu 甘肃									
Qinghai 青海									
Ningxia 宁夏	2	65	8,818	-52	-0.52	-1.69	25.42	69.03	9,842
Xinjiang 新疆									

1939: Other Fur Products Manufacturing 其他毛皮制品业

Year 年份	Number of firms 企业个数	Rate of change 变化率 (%)	Number of employees 职工人数 (人)	Rate of change 变化率 (%)	Total revenue (Mil. RMB) 总销售收入 (百万元)	Rate of change 变化率 (%)	Total profit (Mil RMB) 总利润 (百万元)	Rate of change 变化率 (%)
2000	75		11,180		1,441		34	
2001	82	9.33	13,614	21.77	2,158	49.76	82	141.18
2002	78	-4.88	13,874	1.91	2,678	24.10	119	45.12

Major Products 主要产品	Output 产量	Unit 单位

10 Main Firms with Maximal Revenue (year founded) 收入最大的十家主要企业（创办年份）	City 城市	Province 省	Telephone/fax 电话/传真	Number of employees 职工人数	Ownership 产业所有权	Revenue ('000 RMB) 销售收入 (千元)	Profit('000 RMB) (rank) 利润(千元)(排名)	Total assets ('000 RMB) 总资产 (千元)	Major products 主要产品
HTL International Furniture (China) Co., Ltd.	Suzhou	Jiangsu	(0512)57635130		Foreign Funded				
华达利家具(中国)有限公司(1994)	苏州市	江苏省	(0512)57636232	1,800	外商投资	738,224	36,975(1)	314,647	
Jiangsu Qinhu Group Co., Ltd.	Suzhou	Jiangsu	(0512)52730005		Joint Stock				Leather Articles
江苏琴湖集团有限公司(2001)	苏州市	江苏省	(0512)52730372	913	股份制	293,449	2,731(10)	323,984	皮件
Suning Huasi Fur & Leather Products Co., Ltd.	Cangzhou	Hebei	(0317)5099808		Foreign Funded				Furs And Leather Tick
肃宁华斯裘革制品有限公司(1994)	沧州市	河北省	(0317)5099109	1,200	外商投资	224,000	18,370(2)	65,460	裘皮褥子
Fujian Changle Jinhe Wool & Velvet Co., Ltd.	Fuzhou	Fujian	(0591)8957101		Private Owned				Blanket
福建省长乐市金鹤毛绒有限公司(1996)	福州市	福建省	(0591)8955666	420	私营企业	210,203	7,736(4)	100,381	毛毯
Tongxiang Xiongying Leather Co., Ltd.	Jiaxing	Zhejiang	(0573)8382531		Private Owned				Furs And Leather Scarf
桐乡市雄鹰皮革有限公司(2000)	嘉兴市	浙江省		712	私营企业	55,281	966(21)	62,236	裘皮围巾
Tianjin Jinghai Hualong Leather & Fur Craftworks Factory	Tianjin	Tianjin	(022)68865629		Collective-owned				Cashmere Blanket
天津市静海县华隆皮毛工艺品厂(1994)	天津市	天津市	(022)68865629	72	集体企业	55,020	5,430(6)	17,370	羊剪绒毯
Lixian Haixing Leather & Fur Products Co., Ltd.	Baoding	Hebei	(0312)6339279		Foreign Funded				Furs And Leather
蠡县海星皮毛制品有限公司(1993)	保定市	河北省	(0312)6335141	136	外商投资	51,600	684(25)	52,000	裘皮
Tongxiang Zhonghui Fur & Leather Co., Ltd.	Jiaxing	Zhejiang	(0573)8355052		Private Owned				Furs And Leather
桐乡市中辉皮革有限责任公司(1999)	嘉兴市	浙江省	(0573)8353688	380	私营企业	47,101	527(28)	42,111	裘皮
Qinyang Jinhui Leather Industry Co., Ltd.	Jiaozuo	Henan	(0391)5055015		Overseas Chinese-funded				Cashmere
沁阳市金辉皮业有限公司(1993)	焦作市	河南省	(0391)5050888	140	港澳台资	40,375	4,037(8)	6,870	羊剪绒
Yangyuan Beiyuan Fur Co., Ltd.	Zhangjiakou	Hebei	(0313)7512124		Foreign Funded				Furs And Leather Costume
阳原县北元毛皮有限公司(1996)	张家口市	河北省	(0313)7511378	200	外商投资	36,120	6,415(5)	36,900	裘皮服装

Top 10 Cities by Revenue 销售收入排名前10位城市	Province 省	Market share 市场份额 (%)	Number of firms 企业个数
Suzhou 苏州市	Jiangsu 江苏省	39.45	4
Jiaozuo 焦作市	Henan 河南省	12.70	14
Cangzhou 沧州市	Hebei 河北省	8.36	1
Fuzhou 福州市	Fujian 福建省	7.85	1
Tianjin 天津市	Tianjin 天津市	4.74	7
Jiaxing 嘉兴市	Zhejiang 浙江省	3.82	2
Zhangjiakou 张家口市	Hebei 河北省	2.52	4
Baoding 保定市	Hebei 河北省	2.21	2
Huizhou 惠州市	Guangdong 广东省	2.02	1
Wuxi 无锡市	Jiangsu 江苏省	1.82	3

10 Major Wholesalers 十家主要批发商	City 城市	Province 省	Telephone/Fax 电话/传真
Jiangsu Animal By-products Imp And Exp ,Group Corp.	Nanjing	Jiangsu	(025)2306185
江苏开元国际集团畜产进出口股份有限公司	南京市	江苏省	(025)2306282
Zhejiang Native Produce & By-products I/E Group Corp.	Hangzhou	Zhejiang	(0571)85773807
浙江省土产畜产进出口集团公司	杭州市	浙江省	(0571)85773780
Zhejiang G & B Foreign Trading Co.,Ltd.	Hangzhou	Zhejiang	(0571)85773807
浙江惠元对外贸易有限责任公司	杭州市	浙江省	(0571)85773866
Zhejiang G & F Foreign Trading Co.,Ltd.	Hangzhou	Zhejiang	(0571)85773807
浙江惠隆对外贸易有限责任公司	杭州市	浙江省	(0571)85773925
Zhejiang Willing Foreign Trading Co.,Ltd.	Hangzhou	Zhejiang	(0571)85773807
浙江惠灵对外贸易有限责任公司	杭州市	浙江省	(0571)85773720
Guangzhou Livestock Products Import & Export Company	Guangzhou	Guangdong	(020)83852888
广州畜产进出口公司	广州市	广东省	(020)83824187
China Grain & Oil Feedstuff Co.,Ltd.	Beijing	Beijing	(010)64248899
中国粮油饲料有限公司	北京市	北京市	(010)64205100
Zhejing Huashen Silk Group Company	Jiaxing	Zhejiang	(0573)8021696
浙江花神丝绸集团公司	嘉兴市	浙江省	(0573)8038299
Guangdong Dongguan Local Products Import & Export Company	Dongguan	Guangdong	(0769)2221910
广东省东莞土产进出口公司	东莞市	广东省	(0769)2226400
Yunnan Native Produce Import And Export Corp.	Kunming	Yunnan	(0871)3136461
云南省土产进出口公司	昆明市	云南省	(0871)3136378

1951: Feather (Down) Processing 羽毛(绒)加工业

The industry accounts for 0.051% of the total revenue of China's industrial sector in 2002. The rate of return on assets is 5.29%. 85.07% of all firms in the industry made a profit while 14.93% had negative returns.The top province in terms of the industry's revenue is Zhejiang, accounting for 32.29% of the total revenue.
2002年本行业收入占全行业的0.051%，资产利润率为5.29%。85.07%的企业赢利，14.93%的企业亏损。收入最高的省为浙江省，占本行业的32.29%。

	Total number of firms 企业总数	Total number of employees 职工总数	Total revenue (Mil.RMB) 总销售收入（百万元）	Total profit (Mil.RMB) 总利润（百万元）	Return on assets 资产利润率（%）	Return on equity 权益利润率（%）	Labour productivity ('000 RMB/ worker) 劳动生产率（千元/人）	Debts/ assets 资产负债率（%）	Total assets (Mil.RMB) 总资产（百万元）
Industry Overall 行业总体	134	19,139	5,467	185	5.29	13.61	66.49	61.12	3,496

	Number of firms 企业个数	Average number of employees 平均职工人数	Average revenue ('000 RMB) 平均销售收入（千元）	Average profit ('000 RMB) 平均利润（千元）	Return on assets 资产利润率（%）	Return on equity 权益利润率（%）	Labour productivity ('000 RMB/ worker) 劳动生产率（千元/人）	Debts/ assets 资产负债率（%）	Average total assets ('000 RMB) 平均总资产（千元）
By ownership 产业所有权									
State-owned 国有	6	174	2,169	-1,399	-4.70		-2.45	104.84	29,763
Collective-owned 集体	18	90	28,560	820	7.33	17.57	85.03	58.26	11,181
Foreign & Overseas Chinese Funded 三资	24	293	80,369	4,116	5.90	15.89	62.45	62.83	69,715
By regional distribution 地区分布									
Central-North 华北	12	173	17,530	192	0.72	1.63	26.35	55.76	26,596
Beijing 北京									
Tianjin 天津	2	472	20,570	-1,326	-1.89	-6.14	4.61	69.23	70,189
Hebei 河北	9	125	18,801	551	2.84	5.14	44.75	44.72	19,405
Shanxi 山西	1	7	5				0.57	64.70	4,136
Inner Mongolia 内蒙古									
Northeast 东北	3	37	21,521	605	6.94	20.00	128.24	65.30	8,722
Liaoning 辽宁	2	30	17,685	123	1.07	3.31	71.98	67.72	11,508
Jilin 吉林									
Heilongjiang 黑龙江	1	50	29,192	1,570	49.84	95.15	195.74	47.62	3,150
Central-East 华东	66	187	51,930	1,855	6.28	16.79	63.63	62.58	29,531
Shanghai 上海	1	61	35,210	537	3.93	47.52	294.39	91.73	13,672
Jiangsu 江苏	11	101	30,966	780	5.52	13.42	51.01	58.88	14,139
Zhejiang 浙江	19	118	92,907	2,826	5.78	22.71	147.84	74.54	48,883
Anhui 安徽	19	274	28,234	1,920	10.64	15.99	33.01	33.45	18,039
Fujian 福建	8	28	48,281	-46	-0.18	-0.50	435.29	63.47	25,387
Jiangxi 江西	2	230	9,168	137	3.69	6.33	9.18	41.65	3,696
Shandong 山东	6	505	57,552	3,878	7.81	19.19	34.70	59.30	49,643
Central-South 中南	34	83	33,862	1,331	6.31	15.09	97.57	58.21	21,108
Henan 河南	5	89	12,865	1,310	30.35	34.64	40.66	12.39	4,317
Hubei 湖北									
Hunan 湖南	1	181	3,070	-1,173	-4.26		3.14	189.00	27,508
Guangdong 广东	20	93	48,775	2,110	6.98	13.31	126.05	47.53	30,216
Guangxi 广西	8	41	13,551	-291	-3.62		65.30	118.02	8,033
Hainan 海南									
Southwest 西南	17	83	29,577	351	1.91	5.19	86.52	63.26	18,406
Chongqing 重庆	7	32	21,472	367	3.89	9.29	78.10	58.16	9,448
Sichuan 四川	10	118	35,251	340	1.38	3.90	88.11	64.63	24,676
Guizhou 贵州									
Yunnan 云南									
Tibet 西藏									
Northwest 西北	2	199	55,120	3,571	4.18	11.04	56.49	62.18	85,506
Shaanxi 陕西									
Gansu 甘肃	1	46					17.54	48.11	4,120
Qinghai 青海									
Ningxia 宁夏	1	351	110,240	7,141	4.28	11.42	61.60	62.53	166,892
Xinjiang 新疆									

1951: Feather (Down) Processing 羽毛(绒)加工业

Year 年份	Number of firms 企业个数	Rate of change 变化率 (%)	Number of employees 职工人数 (人)	Rate of change 变化率 (%)	Total revenue (Mil. RMB) 总销售收入 (百万元)	Rate of change 变化率 (%)	Total profit (Mil RMB) 总利润 (百万元)	Rate of change 变化率 (%)
2000	106		15,805		4,620		128	
2001	132	24.53	18,793	18.91	5,537	19.85	141	10.16
2002	134	1.52	19,139	1.84	5,467	-1.26	185	31.21

Major Products 主要产品	Output 产量	Unit 单位

10 Main Firms with Maximal Revenue (year founded) 收入最大的十家主要企业（创办年份）	City 城市	Province 省	Telephone/fax 电话/传真	Number of employees 职工人数	Ownership 产业所有权	Revenue ('000 RMB) 销售收入 (千元)	Profit('000 RMB) (rank) 利润(千元) (排名)	Total assets ('000 RMB) 总资产 (千元)	Major products 主要产品
Zhejiang Multi Glory International Feather Co., Ltd.	Hangzhou	Zhejiang	(0571)82475666		Overseas Chinese-funded				Down
浙江三弘国际羽毛有限公司(1994)	杭州市	浙江省	(0571)82475679	361	港澳台资	499,370	20,879(3)	313,229	羽绒
Guangdong Shanhe Group Co., Ltd.	Zhanjiang	Guangdong	(0759)3381688		Limited-Liability				Washing Down & Its Products
广东山河集团有限公司(1997)	湛江市	广东省	(0759)3380338	280	有限公司	294,180	1,125(33)	158,435	水洗羽绒及制品
Mikeda (Qingdao) Sports Commodities Co., Ltd.	Qingdao	Shandong	(0532)4826667		Foreign Funded				Gym Shoes
迈可达（青岛）运动用品有限公司(1998)	青岛市	山东省	(0532)4819816	1,501	外商投资	207,428	16,302(4)	145,461	运动鞋
Zhanjiang Zijing Down Products Co.,Ltd.	Zhanjiang	Guangdong	(0759)5906736		Limited-Liability				Down
湛江紫荆羽绒制品有限公司(1993)	湛江市	广东省	(0759)5909577	120	有限公司	151,825	1,498(27)	58,409	羽绒
Hangzhou Wanxiang Down Products Co., Ltd.	Hangzhou	Zhejiang	(0571)82716329		Overseas Chinese-funded				Down
杭州万翔羽绒制品有限公司(1997)	杭州市	浙江省	(0571)82786416	261	港澳台资	137,239	1,225(31)	86,241	羽绒
China Light Industry Textile City Down Market Co., Ltd.	Shaoxing	Zhejiang	(0575)5185588		Limited-Liability				Feather
绍兴县中国轻纺城羽绒市场有限公司(1999)	绍兴市	浙江省	(0575)5185588	130	有限公司	119,071	1,619(22)	38,322	羽毛
Nanhai Haixin Plush Co.,Ltd.	Foshan	Guangdong	(0757)5100332		Overseas Chinese-funded				Plush
南海海欣长毛绒有限公司(2001)	佛山市	广东省	(0757)5100665	480	港澳台资	117,052	22,727(2)	187,009	长毛绒
Ningxia Masite Cashmere Group CO.,Ltd.	Yinchuan	Ningxia	(0951)5012688		Overseas Chinese-funded				Cashmere
宁夏马斯特羊绒集团有限公司(1993)	银川市	宁夏	(0951)5011688	351	港澳台资	110,240	7,141(7)	166,892	羊绒
Zhejiang Shaoxing Maolong Down Products Co., Ltd.	Shaoxing	Zhejiang	(0575)5381837		Overseas Chinese funded				Down
浙江绍兴茂龙羽绒制品有限公司(1993)	绍兴市	浙江省	(0575)5382402	200	港澳台资	104,272	8,132(6)	130,714	羽绒
Changle Lubei Down Washing Factory	Fuzhou	Fujian	(0591)8954551		Collective-owned				Down Washing
长乐市路北羽绒水洗厂(1993)	福州市	福建省		30	集体企业	95,100	292(67)	35,442	羽绒水洗

Top 10 Cities by Revenue 销售收入排名前10位城市	Province 省	Market share 市场份额 (%)	Number of firms 企业个数
Hangzhou 杭州市	Zhejiang 浙江省	16.92	8
Shaoxing 绍兴市	Zhejiang 浙江省	14.98	10
Zhanjiang 湛江市	Guangdong 广东省	10.76	9
Lu'an 六安市	Anhui 安徽省	8.90	15
Fuzhou 福州市	Fujian 福建省	7.07	8
Qingdao 青岛市	Shandong 山东省	4.51	2
Maoming 茂名市	Guangdong 广东省	3.66	4
Nanjing 南京市	Jiangsu 江苏省	3.43	5
Neijiang 内江市	Sichuan 四川省	3.14	4
Chongqing 重庆市	Chongqing 重庆市	2.75	7

10 Major Wholesalers 十家主要批发商	City 城市	Province 省	Telephone/Fax 电话/传真
Jiangsu Animal By-products Imp And Exp ,Group Corp.	Nanjing	Jiangsu	(025)2306185
江苏开元国际集团畜产进出口股份有限公司	南京市	江苏省	(025)2306282
Zhejiang Native Produce & By-products I/E Group Corp.	Hangzhou	Zhejiang	(0571)85773807
浙江省土产畜产进出口集团公司	杭州市	浙江省	(0571)85773780
Zhejiang G & B Foreign Trading Co.,Ltd.	Hangzhou	Zhejiang	(0571)85773807
浙江惠元对外贸易有限责任公司	杭州市	浙江省	(0571)85773866
Zhejiang G & F Foreign Trading Co.,Ltd.	Hangzhou	Zhejiang	(0571)85773807
浙江惠隆对外贸易有限责任公司	杭州市	浙江省	(0571)85773925
Zhejiang Willing Foreign Trading Co.,Ltd.	Hangzhou	Zhejiang	(0571)85773807
浙江惠灵对外贸易有限责任公司	杭州市	浙江省	(0571)85773720
Guangzhou Livestock Products Import & Export Company	Guangzhou	Guangdong	(020)83852888
广州畜产进出口公司	广州市	广东省	(020)83824187
China Grain & Oil Feedstuff Co.,Ltd.	Beijing	Beijing	(010)64248899
中国粮油饲料有限公司	北京市	北京市	(010)64205100
Zhejing Huashen Silk Group Company	Jiaxing	Zhejiang	(0573)8021696
浙江花神丝绸集团公司	嘉兴市	浙江省	(0573)8038299
Guangdong Dongguan Local Products Import & Export Company	Dongguan	Guangdong	(0769)2221910
广东省东莞土产进出口公司	东莞市	广东省	(0769)2226400
Yunnan Native Produce Import And Export Corp.	Kunming	Yunnan	(0871)3136461
云南省土产进出口公司	昆明市	云南省	(0871)3136378

1952: Feather (Down) Products 羽毛(绒)制品业

The industry accounts for 0.109% of the total revenue of China's industrial sector in 2002. The rate of return on assets is 2.88%. 76.26% of all firms in the industry made a profit while 23.74% had negative returns.The top province in terms of the industry's revenue is Zhejiang, accounting for 41.58% of the total revenue.
2002年本行业收入占全行业的 0.109%，资产利润率为 2.88%。76.26%的企业赢利，23.74%的企业亏损。收入最高的省为浙江省，占本行业的41.58%。

	Total number of firms 企业总数	Total number of employees 职工总数	Total revenue (Mil.RMB) 总销售收入 (百万元)	Total profit (Mil.RMB) 总利润 (百万元)	Return on assets 资产利润率 (%)	Return on equity 权益利润率 (%)	Labour productivity ('000 RMB/ worker) 劳动生产率 (千元/人)	Debts/ assets 资产负债率 (%)	Total assets (Mil.RMB) 总资产 (百万元)
Industry Overall 行业总体	257	73,304	11,741	283	2.88	9.95	35.19	71.03	9,815

	Number of firms 企业个数	Average number of employees 平均职工人数	Average revenue ('000 RMB) 平均销售收入 (千元)	Average profit ('000 RMB) 平均利润 (千元)	Return on assets 资产利润率 (%)	Return on equity 权益利润率 (%)	Labour productivity ('000 RMB/ worker) 劳动生产率 (千元/人)	Debts/ assets 资产负债率 (%)	Average total assets ('000 RMB) 平均总资产 (千元)
By ownership 产业所有权									
State-owned 国有	24	412	22,474	-1,112	-2.22	-126.21	15.39	98.24	50,004
Collective-owned 集体	24	284	46,158	1,383	4.87	16.77	39.56	70.97	28,404
Foreign & Overseas Chinese Funded 三资	82	295	65,826	1,824	4.10	12.67	41.98	67.60	44,437
By regional distribution 地区分布									
Central-North 华北	14	357	23,319	1,038	2.82	7.61	13.37	62.96	36,806
Beijing 北京	3	165	13,922	-2,691	-8.89	-21.10	19.60	57.89	30,285
Tianjin 天津	5	567	17,201	1,769	10.16	38.49	9.28	73.60	17,409
Hebei 河北	6	277	33,116	2,293	4.08	10.61	18.48	61.57	56,230
Shanxi 山西									
Inner Mongolia 内蒙古									
Northeast 东北	13	158	13,926	287	2.13	5.71	36.46	62.66	13,482
Liaoning 辽宁	8	172	9,112	296	2.25	6.21	19.34	63.80	13,186
Jilin 吉林	3	149	29,139	352	2.35	5.92	77.74	60.31	14,991
Heilongjiang 黑龙江	2	116	10,365	154	1.24	3.27	58.77	62.06	12,406
Central-East 华东	181	297	54,811	1,363	3.40	11.85	37.63	71.32	40,104
Shanghai 上海	6	270	91,567	7,754	21.98	40.49	85.96	45.71	35,275
Jiangsu 江苏	46	303	61,725	1,172	2.66	6.77	44.67	60.66	44,006
Zhejiang 浙江	86	213	56,764	1,461	3.94	14.68	44.17	73.14	37,062
Anhui 安徽	12	429	70,490	3,182	9.02	22.55	28.04	59.98	35,261
Fujian 福建	9	175	15,286	173	1.06	2.13	23.47	50.12	16,240
Jiangxi 江西	9	961	43,547	-2,052	-2.16	-429.56	15.54	99.50	95,087
Shandong 山东	13	345	21,150	-43	-0.14	-0.82	30.32	83.37	31,580
Central-South 中南	42	257	26,042	181	0.51	2.09	34.20	75.48	35,329
Henan 河南	3	254	6,915	367	0.54	4.89	84.62	88.86	67,396
Hubei 湖北	6	400	30,569	222	0.25	1.33	34.35	81.46	90,057
Hunan 湖南	2	12	2,580	1		0.55	63.78	99.24	11,842
Guangdong 广东	29	260	29,451	194	0.82	2.50	28.86	67.36	23,709
Guangxi 广西	1	52	15,776	3	0.03	0.19	15.12	83.46	9,431
Hainan 海南	1	32	14,588	-428	-2.08	-2.87	89.84	27.73	20,602
Southwest 西南	5	302	40,333	1,938	3.04	7.68	28.05	60.42	63,745
Chongqing 重庆	3	99	51,255	3,248	6.99	16.66	129.87	58.02	46,444
Sichuan 四川	1	1,119	46,376	265	0.15	0.40	2.88	61.32	172,844
Guizhou 贵州	1	94	1,523	-319	-4.87	-39.33	6.01	87.61	6,548
Yunnan 云南									
Tibet 西藏									
Northwest 西北	2	128	8,660	226	0.71	2.96	21.12	75.95	31,647
Shaanxi 陕西	1	220	10,399	-49	-0.27	-0.68	15.47	60.95	18,402
Gansu 甘肃									
Qinghai 青海	1	35	6,920	500	1.11	6.22	56.63	82.10	44,891
Ningxia 宁夏									
Xinjiang 新疆									

1952: Feather (Down) Products 羽毛(绒)制品业

Year 年份	Number of firms 企业个数	Rate of change 变化率(%)	Number of employees 职工人数(人)	Rate of change 变化率(%)	Total revenue (Mil. RMB) 总销售收入(百万元)	Rate of change 变化率(%)	Total profit (Mil RMB) 总利润(百万元)	Rate of change 变化率(%)
2000	216		55,156		8,814		159	
2001	240	11.11	65,957	19.58	9,982	13.25	234	47.17
2002	257	7.08	73,304	11.14	11,741	17.62	283	20.94

Major Products 主要产品	Output 产量	Unit 单位
Down Costume 羽绒服装	8,968	10,000 Pieces 万件

10 Main Firms with Maximal Revenue (year founded) 收入最大的十家主要企业（创办年份）	City 城市	Province 省	Telephone/fax 电话/传真	Number of employees 职工人数	Ownership 产业所有权	Revenue ('000 RMB) 销售收入(千元)	Profit('000 RMB) (rank) 利润(千元)(排名)	Total assets ('000 RMB) 总资产(千元)	Major products 主要产品
Zhejiang Liuqiao Feather Co., Ltd.	Hangzhou	Zhejiang	(0571)82721751		Overseas Chinese-funded				Feather & Down Costume羽毛
浙江柳桥羽毛有限公司(1995)	杭州市	浙江省	(0571)82714861	620	港澳台资	831,977	9,136(9)	384,975	羽绒服装
Jiangsu Guangfeng Feather Co., Ltd.	Nanjing	Jiangsu	(025)8183935		Overseas Chinese-funded				Down Products
江苏广丰羽毛有限公司(1997)	南京市	江苏省	(025)8183898	236	港澳台资	386,640	16,330(4)	114,680	羽绒制品
Zhejiang Jiaxing Banyu Group Co., ltd.	Jiaxing	Zhejiang	(0573)5800008		Private Owned				Down Costume
浙江嘉兴伴宇服饰有限公司(1980)	嘉兴市	浙江省	(0573)5800086	2,200	私营企业	295,030	8,431(11)	114,450	羽绒服装
Tongcheng Hongrun Group Company	Anqing	Anhui	(0556)6204424		Collective-owned				
桐城市鸿润集团公司(1991)	安庆市	安徽省	(0556)6203401	1,476	集体企业	290,988	28,095(2)	113,241	
Zhejiang Xinghe Down Products Co., Ltd.	Hangzhou	Zhejiang	(0571)86049952		Overseas Chinese-funded				Down Products羽绒
浙江兴合羽绒制品有限公司(1993)	杭州市	浙江省	(0571)86042897	890	港澳台资	248,863	15,037(5)	134,033	及其制品
CNGG Zhejiang North Swan Dress Holdings Co.,Ltd.	Hangzhou	Zhejiang	(0571)82626750		Joint Stock				Down Products
中服浙江北天鹅服饰股份有限公司(1998)	杭州市	浙江省	(0571)82700061	285	股份制	221,065	4,195(23)	111,027	羽绒制品
Hangzhou Jinjiang Down Products Factory	Hangzhou	Zhejiang	(0571)86072162		Collective-owned				Down Products
杭州近江羽绒制品厂(1993)	杭州市	浙江省	(0571)86057805	146	集体企业	219,959	1,774(37)	144,181	羽绒制品
Hangzhou Weimei Home Textiles Co., Ltd.	Hangzhou	Zhejiang	(0571)82711188		Foreign Funded				Down Products
杭州维美家用纺织品有限公司(1998)	杭州市	浙江省	(0571)82711166	386	外商投资	198,056	8,452(10)	153,719	羽绒制品
Nanjing Dafeng Down Ltd. Company	Nanjing	Jiangsu	(025)2738888		Foreign Funded				Down Costume
南京达丰羽绒制品有限公司(1990)	南京市	江苏省	(025)2736899	500	外商投资	190,380	6,130(14)	62,270	羽绒服装
Hangzhou Jinhong Sanniao Down Products Co., Ltd.	Hangzhou	Zhejiang	(0571)82733887		Overseas Chinese-funded				Down
杭州金弘三鸟羽绒制品有限公司(1998)	杭州市	浙江省	(0571)82716321	250	港澳台资	173,355	727(72)	110,418	羽绒

Top 10 Cities by Revenue 销售收入排名前10位城市	Province 省	Market share 市场份额 (%)	Number of firms 企业个数
Hangzhou 杭州市	Zhejiang 浙江省	29.34	45
Suzhou 苏州市	Jiangsu 江苏省	8.42	15
Nanjing 南京市	Jiangsu 江苏省	6.67	6
Shaoxing 绍兴市	Zhejiang 浙江省	6.31	17
Shanghai 上海市	Shanghai 上海市	4.68	6
Yangzhou 扬州市	Jiangsu 江苏省	4.15	8
Jiaxing 嘉兴市	Zhejiang 浙江省	4.11	12
Anqing 安庆市	Anhui 安徽省	3.55	2
Jiujiang 九江市	Jiangxi 江西省	2.69	5
Jiangmen 江门市	Guangdong 广东省	2.46	10

10 Major Wholesalers 十家主要批发商	City 城市	Province 省	Telephone/Fax 电话/传真
Jiangsu Animal By-products Imp And Exp ,Group Corp.	Nanjing	Jiangsu	(025)2306185
江苏开元国际集团畜产进出口股份有限公司	南京市	江苏省	(025)2306282
Zhejiang Native Produce & By-products I/E Group Corp.	Hangzhou	Zhejiang	(0571)85773807
浙江省土产畜产进出口集团公司	杭州市	浙江省	(0571)85773780
Zhejiang G & B Foreign Trading Co.,Ltd.	Hangzhou	Zhejiang	(0571)85773807
浙江惠元对外贸易有限责任公司	杭州市	浙江省	(0571)85773866
Zhejiang G & F Foreign Trading Co.,Ltd.	Hangzhou	Zhejiang	(0571)85773807
浙江惠隆对外贸易有限责任公司	杭州市	浙江省	(0571)85773925
Zhejiang Willing Foreign Trading Co.,Ltd.	Hangzhou	Zhejiang	(0571)85773807
浙江惠灵对外贸易有限责任公司	杭州市	浙江省	(0571)85773720
Guangzhou Livestock Products Import & Export Company	Guangzhou	Guangdong	(020)83852888
广州畜产进出口公司	广州市	广东省	(020)83824187
China Grain & Oil Feedstuff Co.,Ltd.	Beijing	Beijing	(010)64248899
中国粮油饲料有限公司	北京市	北京市	(010)64205100
Zhejing Huashen Silk Group Company	Jiaxing	Zhejiang	(0573)8021696
浙江花神丝绸集团公司	嘉兴市	浙江省	(0573)8038299
Guangdong Dongguan Local Products Import & Export Company	Dongguan	Guangdong	(0769)2221910
广东省东莞土产进出口公司	东莞市	广东省	(0769)2226400
Yunnan Native Produce Import And Export Corp.	Kunming	Yunnan	(0871)3136461
云南省土产进出口公司	昆明市	云南省	(0871)3136378

2011: Sawing Lumber Processing 锯材加工业

The industry accounts for 0.033% of the total revenue of China's industrial sector in 2002. The rate of return on assets is 0.79%. 81.86% of all firms in the industry made a profit while 18.14% had negative returns.The top province in terms of the industry's revenue is Henan, accounting for 17.52% of the total revenue.
2002年本行业收入占全行业的0.033%，资产利润率为0.79%。81.86%的企业赢利，18.14%的企业亏损。收入最高的省为河南省，占本行业的17.52%。

	Total number of firms 企业总数	Total number of employees 职工总数	Total revenue (Mil.RMB) 总销售收入(百万元)	Total profit (Mil.RMB) 总利润(百万元)	Return on assets 资产利润率(%)	Return on equity 权益利润率(%)	Labour productivity ('000 RMB/worker) 劳动生产率(千元/人)	Debts/assets 资产负债率(%)	Total assets (Mil.RMB) 总资产(百万元)
Industry Overall 行业总体	237	32,290	3,503	33	0.79	2.31	29.35	65.86	4,235

	Number of firms 企业个数	Average number of employees 平均职工人数	Average revenue ('000 RMB) 平均销售收入(千元)	Average profit ('000 RMB) 平均利润(千元)	Return on assets 资产利润率(%)	Return on equity 权益利润率(%)	Labour productivity ('000 RMB/worker) 劳动生产率(千元/人)	Debts/assets 资产负债率(%)	Average total assets ('000 RMB) 平均总资产(千元)
By ownership 产业所有权									
State-owned 国有	67	199	11,591	-912	-2.59	-10.42	11.82	75.12	35,178
Collective-owned 集体	48	129	18,353	1,094	17.33	28.31	38.45	38.77	6,312
Foreign & Overseas Chinese Funded 三资	24	121	14,743	-750	-2.67	-6.03	26.25	55.76	28,082
By regional distribution 地区分布									
Central-North 华北	16	195	14,242	-2,207	-6.33	-12.96	-3.65	51.18	34,882
Beijing 北京	3	43	3,434	117	9.06	24.44	22.62	62.93	1,288
Tianjin 天津	10	146	14,247	-4,024	-7.60	-15.40	-29.65	50.67	52,958
Hebei 河北	2	670	34,869	2,260	25.40	44.24	19.89	42.59	8,899
Shanxi 山西									
Inner Mongolia 内蒙古	1	192	5,362	61	0.89		11.83	106.31	6,863
Northeast 东北	34	270	23,443	-702	-2.16	-10.00	28.66	78.41	32,545
Liaoning 辽宁	13	193	33,131	503	1.91	4.81	48.76	60.35	26,402
Jilin 吉林	11	403	18,177	-2,765	-7.97	-102.51	16.51	92.23	34,700
Heilongjiang 黑龙江	10	222	16,642	-1		-0.01	30.21	80.85	38,162
Central-East 华东	82	92	12,327	332	2.82	9.39	35.42	69.97	11,777
Shanghai 上海	8	59	19,954	334	2.34	8.12	51.37	71.19	14,271
Jiangsu 江苏	25	87	11,020	398	7.06	21.62	33.71	67.32	5,632
Zhejiang 浙江	5	162	20,418	807	2.27	8.26	30.42	72.55	35,592
Anhui 安徽	16	87	6,941	215	4.65		27.03	102.66	4,623
Fujian 福建	8	83	12,875	345	1.08	3.77	29.61	71.32	31,869
Jiangxi 江西	5	158	11,393	-774	-4.01	-7.49	9.99	46.43	19,292
Shandong 山东	15	82	13,506	550	7.67	20.91	64.57	63.31	7,162
Central-South 中南	64	125	19,886	1,089	7.61	15.21	46.61	49.94	14,308
Henan 河南	27	135	22,736	1,980	24.91	35.20	43.32	29.23	7,948
Hubei 湖北	5	227	27,706	2,776	8.39	14.21	36.20	40.94	33,066
Hunan 湖南	2	143	9,695	168	2.06	2.56	18.81	19.30	8,148
Guangdong 广东	18	71	19,242	96	1.13	2.46	83.80	53.82	8,458
Guangxi 广西	4	150	27,956	201	0.36	0.87	32.01	58.61	55,825
Hainan 海南	8	130	5,342	-59	-0.33	-1.44	39.91	77.07	17,992
Southwest 西南	33	112	5,407	14	0.08	0.31	12.56	72.76	16,269
Chongqing 重庆	1	92	25,903	64	1.07	1.70	17.66	37.42	6,000
Sichuan 四川	8	51	6,681	135	2.25	7.27	49.16	69.02	5,977
Guizhou 贵州	6	122	2,392	-253	-1.91	-16.11	6.93	88.16	13,263
Yunnan 云南	5	218	3,632	-1,396	-3.51	-25.12	3.14	86.01	39,737
Tibet 西藏	13	106	5,119	601	3.81	8.64	11.80	55.83	15,754
Northwest 西北	8	95	2,041	-608	-3.20	-12.16	12.90	73.65	18,988
Shaanxi 陕西	3	196	4,724	-382	-0.98	-1.89	10.21	47.90	38,847
Gansu 甘肃	5	35	431	-744	-10.52		21.97	158.51	7,072
Qinghai 青海									
Ningxia 宁夏									
Xinjiang 新疆									

2011: Sawing Lumber Processing 锯材加工业

Year 年份	Number of firms 企业个数	Rate of change 变化率 (%)	Number of employees 职工人数 (人)	Rate of change 变化率 (%)	Total revenue (Mil. RMB) 总销售收入 (百万元)	Rate of change 变化率 (%)	Total profit (Mil RMB) 总利润 (百万元)	Rate of change 变化率 (%)
2000	261		40,535		3,730		-4	
2001	233	-10.73	35,939	-11.34	3,360	-9.92	69	-
2002	237	1.72	32,290	-10.15	3,503	4.26	33	-52.17

Major Products 主要产品	Output 产量	Unit 单位
Sawmilling 锯材	270	10,000 Stere 万立方米

10 Main Firms with Maximal Revenue (year founded) 收入最大的十家主要企业（创办年份）	City 城市	Province 省	Telephone/fax 电话/传真	Number of employees 职工人数	Ownership 产业所有权	Revenue ('000 RMB) 销售收入 (千元)	Profit('000 RMB) (rank) 利润(千元) (排名)	Total assets ('000 RMB) 总资产 (千元)	Major products 主要产品
Xinbin Manchu Autonomous County Nanzamu Town Wooden	Fushun	Liaoning	(0413)5261538		Private Enterprises				Sawmilling
Products Group新宾满族自治县南杂木镇木制品集团(1998)	抚顺市	辽宁省	(0413)5264555	1,500	私营独资	234,791	4,659(6)	66,330	锯材
Liu Zhou Wood Antisepsis Factory	Liuzhou	Guangxi	(0772)3619242		State-owned				Antiseptic Sleeper
柳州木材防腐厂(1957)	柳州市	广西	(0772)3616642	330	国有企业	81,156	638(58)	209,522	防腐枕木
Xiamen Yongquan Science & Technology Development	Xiamen	Fujian	(0592)6381672		Joint Stock				Sawmilling
Holding Co.,Ltd.厦门涌泉科技发展股份有限公司(1998)	厦门市	福建省	(0592)6093468	252	股份制	75,860	6,102(4)	186,952	锯材
Railway Department Wuhan Wood Antisepsis Factory	Wuhan	Hubei	(027)85324551		State-owned				Antiseptic Timber
铁道部武汉木材防腐厂(1954)	武汉市	湖北省	(027)84844827	352	国有企业	73,229	11,016(1)	136,494	防腐木材
Qingdao Lianyi Woods Co., Ltd.	Qingdao	Shandong	(0532)8283733		Joint Stock				Floorboard
青岛联谊木业有限公司(1995)	青岛市	山东省	(0532)8288618	360	股份制	70,590	1,950(24)	23,160	地板
Tainjin American Style Furniture Co., Ltd	Tianjin	Tianjin	(022)25324746		Overseas Chinese-funded				Sawmilling
天津美式家具有限公司(1993)	天津市	天津市	(022)25324744	808	港澳台资	64,148	-	221,561	锯材
Song Lang Wooden Articles Factory	Jiangmen	Guangdong	(0750)2512828		Private Enterprises				Packing Box Board包
松朗木器厂(1995)	江门市	广东省	(0750)2513188	180	私营独资	58,920	-	15,233	装箱木板
Guozhuang Wooden Articles Industry Co., Ltd.	Shijiazhuang	Hebei	(0311)5749069		Collective-owned				Wooden Thread
郭庄木器工业有限公司(1997)	石家庄市	河北省	(0311)5749069	1,300	集体企业	57,530	4,580(7)	6,870	木线
Hangzhou Timber General Factory	Hangzhou	Zhejiang	(0571)86051344		State-owned				Sawmilling
杭州木材总厂(1951)	杭州市	浙江省	(0571)86051806	539	国有企业	54,153	2,003(23)	147,769	锯材
Railway Department Harbin Timber Antiseptic Factory	Harbin	Heilongjiang	(0451)2400018		State-owned				Sleeper
铁道部哈尔滨木材防腐厂(1934)	哈尔滨市	黑龙江省	(0451)2421173	602	国有企业	52,799	5,013(5)	141,793	枕木

Top 10 Cities by Revenue 销售收入排名前10位城市	Province 省	Market share 市场份额 (%)	Number of firms 企业个数
Kaifeng 开封市	Henan 河南省	8.18	10
Fushun 抚顺市	Liaoning 辽宁省	6.70	1
Zhaoqing 肇庆市	Guangdong 广东省	5.49	11
Suqian 宿迁市	Jiangsu 江苏省	5.42	19
Shanghai 上海市	Shanghai 上海市	4.56	8
Tianjin 天津市	Tianjin 天津市	4.07	10
Qingdao 青岛市	Shandong 山东省	3.47	7
Jiangmen 江门市	Guangdong 广东省	2.82	3
Shangqiu 商丘市	Henan 河南省	2.60	5
Liuzhou 柳州市	Guangxi 广西	2.32	1

10 Major Wholesalers 十家主要批发商	City 城市	Province 省	Telephone/Fax 电话/传真
Shanghai Xinmei (Group) Co.,Ltd.	Shanghai	Shanghai	(021)58120888
上海新美（集团）有限公司	上海市	上海市	(021)67559188
Guangdong Native Products Import & Export (Group) Corporation	Guangzhou	Guangdong	(020)84244025
广东省土产进出口（集团）公司	广州市	广东省	(020)84423070
China Timber Import & Export Co.,Ltd.	Beijing	Beijing	(010)64203414
中国木材进出口股份有限公司	北京市	北京市	(010)64208900
Xiamen Yongquan Group Co.,Ltd.	Xiamen	Fujian	(0592)5161286
厦门涌泉集团有限公司	厦门市	福建省	(0592)5162966
China National Forest Products Marketing Co.	Beijing	Beijing	(010)64228370
中国林产品经销公司	北京市	北京市	(010)64216443
Liaoning Huiming International Trade Co.,Ltd.	Dalian	Liaoning	(0411)3620626
大连市辽宁汇明国际贸易有限公司	大连市	辽宁省	(0411)3636995
Shanghai Senda Wood Industry Co.,Ltd.	Shanghai	Shanghai	(021)54367592
上海森大木业有限公司	上海市	上海市	(021)54360331
Shanghai Timber General Corp.	Shanghai	Shanghai	(021)63230138
上海市木材总公司	上海市	上海市	(021)63236079
Guangdong Nanyou Economic Development Corp.	Guangzhou	Guangdong	(020)87304129
广东南油经济发展公司	广州市	广东省	(020)87756069
Zhuhai S.E.Z.Materials Company	Zhuhai	Guangdong	(0756)2116092
珠海经济特区物资公司	珠海市	广东省	(0756)2116718

2012: Wood Chip Processing 木片加工业

The industry accounts for 0.017% of the total revenue of China's industrial sector in 2002. The rate of return on assets is 4.41%. 88.00% of all firms in the industry made a profit while 12.00% had negative returns.The top province in terms of the industry's revenue is Jiangsu, accounting for 18.52% of the total revenue.
2002年本行业收入占全行业的 0.017%，资产利润率为 4.41%。88.00%的企业赢利，12.00%的企业亏损。收入最高的省为江苏省，占本行业的18.52%。

	Total number of firms 企业总数	Total number of employees 职工总数	Total revenue (Mil.RMB) 总销售收入(百万元)	Total profit (Mil.RMB) 总利润(百万元)	Return on assets 资产利润率(%)	Return on equity 权益利润率(%)	Labour productivity ('000 RMB/worker) 劳动生产率(千元/人)	Debts/assets 资产负债率(%)	Total assets (Mil.RMB) 总资产(百万元)
Industry Overall 行业总体	125	14,216	1,849	84	4.41	8.34	37.49	47.12	1,903

	Number of firms 企业个数	Average number of employees 平均职工人数	Average revenue ('000 RMB) 平均销售收入(千元)	Average profit ('000 RMB) 平均利润(千元)	Return on assets 资产利润率(%)	Return on equity 权益利润率(%)	Labour productivity ('000 RMB/worker) 劳动生产率(千元/人)	Debts/assets 资产负债率(%)	Average total assets ('000 RMB) 平均总资产(千元)
By ownership 产业所有权									
State-owned 国有	10	108	4,248	112	1.12	3.09	48.74	63.63	10,018
Collective-owned 集体	16	72	14,886	605	8.35	19.60	55.75	57.43	7,252
Foreign & Overseas Chinese Funded 三资	21	134	29,011	1,825	3.32	5.60	44.67	40.73	54,948
By regional distribution 地区分布									
Central-North 华北	6	145	62,149	3,297	2.67	3.88	71.58	31.21	123,663
Beijing 北京	3	95	101,056	10,646	6.79	8.49	249.76	19.98	156,767
Tianjin 天津	3	195	23,242	-4,052	-4.47	-9.07	-15.67	50.67	90,558
Hebei 河北									
Shanxi 山西									
Inner Mongolia 内蒙古									
Northeast 东北	12	83	18,712	277	1.47	3.56	60.31	58.79	18,860
Liaoning 辽宁	7	42	18,871	407	2.63	4.74	99.15	44.51	15,476
Jilin 吉林	4	130	12,391	484	3.05	14.08	23.38	78.34	15,867
Heilongjiang 黑龙江	1	180	42,880	-1,463	-2.68	-7.54	102.89	64.40	54,520
Central-East 华东	50	141	13,558	839	10.51	18.20	29.39	42.27	7,985
Shanghai 上海	3	67	25,119	4,194	9.19	16.37	135.20	43.87	45,646
Jiangsu 江苏	29	91	11,808	551	12.29	21.30	33.33	42.31	4,485
Zhejiang 浙江									
Anhui 安徽	4	171	3,156	252	1.85	2.78	5.61	33.46	13,633
Fujian 福建	2	33	6,360	240	12.21		62.46	114.50	1,965
Jiangxi 江西	2	35	2,565				23.00	47.62	525
Shandong 山东	10	339	22,963	1,189	16.35	28.10	24.29	41.84	7,272
Central-South 中南	54	96	10,583	347	3.68	11.08	38.97	66.84	9,434
Henan 河南	21	89	8,815	642	16.13	41.10	28.13	60.76	3,979
Hubei 湖北	2	152	14,034	-663	-2.58	-10.62	41.00	75.71	25,710
Hunan 湖南	2	78	13,925	705	20.68	40.31	47.99	48.70	3,410
Guangdong 广东	22	102	12,981	122	0.80	2.58	34.56	68.91	15,218
Guangxi 广西	5	112	3,556	479	8.46	18.68	10.85	54.71	5,658
Hainan 海南	2	32	13,535	43	1.88	2.62	735.57	28.32	2,260
Southwest 西南	2	19	1,189	83	0.70	6.37	28.63	89.03	11,800
Chongqing 重庆									
Sichuan 四川	1	20						95.24	21,000
Guizhou 贵州	1	18	2,378	165	6.35	10.38	60.44	38.85	2,600
Yunnan 云南									
Tibet 西藏									
Northwest 西北	1	68	180				0.93	69.20	2,760
Shaanxi 陕西	1	68	180				0.93	69.20	2,760
Gansu 甘肃									
Qinghai 青海									
Ningxia 宁夏									
Xinjiang 新疆									

2012: Wood Chip Processing 木片加工业

Year 年份	Number of firms 企业个数	Rate of change 变化率 (%)	Number of employees 职工人数 (人)	Rate of change 变化率 (%)	Total revenue (Mil. RMB) 总销售收入 (百万元)	Rate of change 变化率 (%)	Total profit (Mil RMB) 总利润 (百万元)	Rate of change 变化率 (%)
2000	84		7,761		1,368		44	
2001	123	46.43	14,081	81.43	2,014	47.22	82	86.36
2002	125	1.63	14,216	0.96	1,849	-8.19	84	2.44

Major Products 主要产品	Output 产量	Unit 单位
Man-made Board 人造板	2,532	10,000 Stere 万立方米

10 Main Firms with Maximal Revenue (year founded) 收入最大的十家主要企业（创办年份）	City 城市	Province 省	Telephone/fax 电话/传真	Number of employees 职工人数	Ownership 产业所有权	Revenue ('000 RMB) 销售收入 (千元)	Profit('000 RMB) (rank) 利润(千元) (排名)	Total assets ('000 RMB) 总资产 (千元)	Major products 主要产品
Beijing Kronosen Hua Flooring Co., Ltd.	Beijing	Beijing	(010)67272266		Foreign Funded				Manmade Board
北京森华人造板有限公司(2000)	北京市	北京市	(010)67238325	188	外商投资	234,362	30,392(1)	433,005	人造板
Jinxiang Yalong Wood Industry Group	Jining	Shandong	(0537)8851969		Private Owned				Timber
金乡县亚龙木业集团(2000)	济宁市	山东省		2,379	私营企业	119,230	5,280(3)	24,700	木材
Juken Shanghai Co., Ltd.	Shanghai	Shanghai	(021)56872060		Foreign Funded				Timber
住建<上海>有限公司(1996)	上海市	上海市	(021)56872613	195	外商投资	67,802	11,826(2)	131,498	木材
Tianjin Kasite Wood Processing Co., Ltd.	Tianjin	Tianjin	(022)24960580		Foreign Funded				Pencil
天津卡斯特木业品有限公司(1996)	天津市	天津市	(022)24960581	539	外商投资	58,993	-	231,204	铅笔
Beijing Sanyou Jingnan Decorative Materials Factory	Beijing	Beijing	(010)87602523		Collective-owned				Ornaments Paper
北京三优京南装饰材料厂(1994)	北京市	北京市	(010)87603312	48	集体企业	44,569	1,314(14)	18,199	装饰纸
Harbin Xinghua Wood Working Co.,Ltd.	Harbin	Heilongjiang	(0451)86519807		Private Owned				Hub
哈尔滨兴华木业有限责任公司(1999)	哈尔滨市	黑龙江省	(0451)86519854	180	私营企业	42,880	-	54,520	木片
Suzhou Hongren Window Decorations CO., Ltd.	Suzhou	Jiangsu	(0520)53553378		Overseas Chinese-funded				Wooden Window
苏州鸿仁窗饰有限公司(1994)	苏州市	江苏省	(0520)53554477	350	港澳台资	39,450	4,960(4)	35,260	木制窗
Yingkou Economic & Technology Devolopment Zone Leichi Industry &	Yingkou	Liaoning	(0417)6149409		Private Owned				Hub
Trade Co., Ltd.营口经济技术开发区雷驰工贸有限公司(1997)	营口市	辽宁省	(0417)6149409	82	私营企业	31,400	150(79)	9,336	木片
Dandong MaoLin Timber Industry Co., Ltd.	Dandong	Liaoning	(0415)7142327		Overseas Chinese-funded				Hub
丹东懋林木业有限公司(2000)	丹东市	辽宁省	(0415)7142004	40	港澳台资	26,967	2,056(9)	4,903	木片
Donggang Changhua Forest Products Co., Ltd.	Dandong	Liaoning	(0415)7144379		Foreign Funded				Wooden Scrapes
东港昌华林产有限公司(1998)	丹东市	辽宁省	(0415)7147466	48	外商投资	24,282	-	16,193	木屑片

Top 10 Cities by Revenue 销售收入排名前10位城市	Province 省	Market share 市场份额 (%)	Number of firms 企业个数
Beijing 北京市	Beijing 北京市	16.39	3
Suqian 宿迁市	Jiangsu 江苏省	12.15	19
Zhanjiang 湛江市	Guangdong 广东省	7.05	9
Jining 济宁市	Shandong 山东省	6.45	1
Shanghai 上海市	Shanghai 上海市	4.07	3
Tianjin 天津市	Tianjin 天津市	3.77	3
Kaifeng 开封市	Henan 河南省	3.18	3
Dandong 丹东市	Liaoning 辽宁省	2.77	2
Zaozhuang 枣庄市	Shandong 山东省	2.42	1
Guangzhou 广州市	Guangdong 广东省	2.41	4

10 Major Wholesalers 十家主要批发商	City 城市	Province 省	Telephone/Fax 电话/传真
Shanghai Xinmei (Group) Co.,Ltd.	Shanghai	Shanghai	(021)58120888
上海新美（集团）有限公司	上海市	上海市	(021)67559188
Guangdong Native Products Import & Export (Group) Corporation	Guangzhou	Guangdong	(020)84244025
广东省土产进出口（集团）公司	广州市	广东省	(020)84423070
China Timber Import & Export Co.,Ltd.	Beijing	Beijing	(010)64203414
中国木材进出口股份有限公司	北京市	北京市	(010)64208900
Xiamen Yongquan Group Co.,Ltd.	Xiamen	Fujian	(0592)5161286
厦门涌泉集团有限公司	厦门市	福建省	(0592)5162966
China National Forest Products Marketing Co.	Beijing	Beijing	(010)64228370
中国林产品经销公司	北京市	北京市	(010)64216443
Liaoning Huiming International Trade Co.,Ltd.	Dalian	Liaoning	(0411)3620626
大连市辽宁汇明国际贸易有限公司	大连市	辽宁省	(0411)3636995
Shanghai Senda Wood Industry Co.,Ltd.	Shanghai	Shanghai	(021)54367592
上海森大木业有限公司	上海市	上海市	(021)54360331
Shanghai Timber General Corp.	Shanghai	Shanghai	(021)63230138
上海市木材总公司	上海市	上海市	(021)63236079
Guangdong Nanyou Economic Development Corp	Guangzhou	Guangdong	(020)87304129
广东南油经济发展公司	广州市	广东省	(020)87756069
Zhuhai S.E.Z.Materials Company	Zhuhai	Guangdong	(0756)2116092
珠海经济特区物资公司	珠海市	广东省	(0756)2116718

2021: Plywood 胶合板制造业

The industry accounts for 0.224% of the total revenue of China's industrial sector in 2002. The rate of return on assets is 2.41%. 84.83% of all firms in the industry made a profit while 15.17% had negative returns.The top province in terms of the industry's revenue is Jiangsu, accounting for 26.62% of the total revenue.
2002年本行业收入占全行业的0.224%，资产利润率为2.41%。84.83%的企业赢利，15.17%的企业亏损。收入最高的省为江苏省，占本行业的26.62%。

	Total number of firms 企业总数	Total number of employees 职工总数	Total revenue (Mil.RMB) 总销售收入(百万元)	Total profit (Mil.RMB) 总利润(百万元)	Return on assets 资产利润率(%)	Return on equity 权益利润率(%)	Labour productivity ('000 RMB/ worker) 劳动生产率(千元/人)	Debts/ assets 资产负债率(%)	Total assets (Mil.RMB) 总资产(百万元)
Industry Overall 行业总体	837	159,344	24,001	496	2.41	6.30	39.71	61.82	20,614

	Number of firms 企业个数	Average number of employees 平均职工人数	Average revenue ('000 RMB) 平均销售收入（千元）	Average profit ('000 RMB) 平均利润(千元)	Return on assets 资产利润率(%)	Return on equity 权益利润率(%)	Labour productivity ('000 RMB/ worker) 劳动生产率(千元/人)	Debts/ assets 资产负债率(%)	Average total assets ('000 RMB) 平均总资产(千元)
By ownership 产业所有权									
State-owned 国有	50	175	9,703	-1,275	-3.82	-12.23	18.60	68.77	33,399
Collective-owned 集体	79	258	27,438	758	3.46	11.07	32.27	68.73	21,899
Foreign & Overseas Chinese Funded 三资	86	265	42,798	-644	-1.00	-2.91	33.91	65.52	64,248
By regional distribution 地区分布									
Central-North 华北	51	192	25,285	1,787	13.15	28.28	40.67	53.49	13,585
Beijing 北京	2	90	24,782	1,044	13.43	20.21	33.91	33.58	7,775
Tianjin 天津	5	148	17,576	1,157	3.01	6.15	21.47	50.97	38,386
Hebei 河北	42	206	27,015	2,013	20.53	50.14	43.20	59.06	9,805
Shanxi 山西	1								
Inner Mongolia 内蒙古	1	192	17,451	-1,258	-1.71	-2.56	6.98	33.08	73,557
Northeast 东北	36	300	13,803	-1,030	-2.60	-7.16	15.67	63.65	39,587
Liaoning 辽宁	6	137	21,000	-1,718	-4.05	-9.12	60.30	55.55	42,373
Jilin 吉林	24	314	12,405	-777	-2.69	-6.61	12.41	59.26	28,837
Heilongjiang 黑龙江	6	404	12,197	-1,352	-1.69	-6.59	10.68	74.29	79,801
Central-East 华东	525	193	31,903	884	3.53	8.61	38.72	59.01	25,022
Shanghai 上海	25	361	115,271	716	0.59	1.59	34.34	62.90	121,257
Jiangsu 江苏	146	258	43,767	1,363	5.44	12.89	36.41	57.78	25,056
Zhejiang 浙江	93	150	35,647	1,610	5.80	14.95	53.14	61.22	27,778
Anhui 安徽	62	133	16,528	283	4.08	9.36	36.74	56.43	6,946
Fujian 福建	80	128	12,224	253	1.60	3.32	46.51	51.78	15,817
Jiangxi 江西	64	132	9,591	279	2.94	7.14	25.28	58.80	9,500
Shandong 山东	55	255	28,106	755	2.66	6.24	36.84	57.33	28,356
Central-South 中南	209	159	24,957	-139	-0.59	-1.88	51.98	68.75	23,638
Henan 河南	38	84	10,104	760	6.26	15.93	37.71	60.70	12,144
Hubei 湖北	22	123	14,564	458	5.37	10.21	39.02	47.40	8,527
Hunan 湖南	91	112	11,313	169	1.80	4.01	33.32	54.99	9,382
Guangdong 广东	46	323	72,233	-401	-0.60	-1.73	76.68	65.29	66,555
Guangxi 广西	10	138	6,098	-5,016	-33.13		3.86	141.93	15,139
Hainan 海南	2	473	49,216	-7,431	-6.62		19.56	153.25	112,292
Southwest 西南	15	259	16,561	464	1.67	7.04	25.46	76.33	27,854
Chongqing 重庆	1	134	6,857	52	0.25	1.81	8.82	85.94	20,447
Sichuan 四川	7	129	9,571	380	4.52	6.82	27.05	33.80	8,418
Guizhou 贵州	2	151	9,180	20	0.53	0.98	24.88	45.67	3,656
Yunnan 云南	5	510	31,242	842	1.27	7.94	25.83	83.99	66,225
Tibet 西藏									
Northwest 西北	1	70	577	49	3.18	3.22	6.14	1.23	1,540
Shaanxi 陕西									-
Gansu 甘肃	1	70	577	49	3.18	3.22	6.14	1.23	1,540
Qinghai 青海									
Ningxia 宁夏									
Xinjiang 新疆									

Year 年份	Number of firms 企业个数	Rate of change 变化率 (%)	Number of employees 职工人数 (人)	Rate of change 变化率 (%)	Total revenue (Mil. RMB) 总销售收入 (百万元)	Rate of change 变化率 (%)	Total profit (Mil RMB) 总利润 (百万元)	Rate of change 变化率 (%)
2000	614		150,835		21,864		487	
2001	750	22.15	168,515	11.72	22,078	0.98	379	-22.18
2002	837	11.60	159,344	-5.44	24,001	8.71	496	30.87

Major Products 主要产品	Output 产量	Unit 单位
Veneer 胶合板	1,252	10,000 Stere 万立方米

10 Main Firms with Maximal Revenue (year founded) 收入最大的十家主要企业（创办年份）	City 城市	Province 省	Telephone/fax 电话/传真	Number of employees 职工人数	Ownership 产业所有权	Revenue ('000 RMB) 销售收入 (千元)	Profit('000 RMB) (rank) 利润(千元) (排名)	Total assets ('000 RMB) 总资产 (千元)	Major products 主要产品
Nanhai Huaguang Decorative Board Co., Ltd.	Foshan	Guangdong	(0757)6918266		Limited-Liability				Veneer
南海市华光板材实业有限公司(2001)	佛山市	广东省	(0757)6915020	5,680	有限公司	1,731,000	568(215)	903,416	胶合板
Jiangsu Shengyang Timber Industry Group Co., Ltd.	Xuzhou	Jiangsu	(0516)2730699		Private Owned				Veneer
江苏胜阳木业集团有限公司(1995)	徐州市	江苏省	(0516)2730632	5,008	私营企业	1,476,680	62,060(1)	502,743	胶合板
Zhejiang Deren Group Co., Ltd.	Taizhou	Zhejiang	(0576)5125626		Private Owned				Three Plywood
德仁集团有限公司(1996)	台州市	浙江省	(0576)5123499	2,136	私营企业	805,050	45,118(2)	585,843	三夹板
Xinmei Group Co., Ltd.	Shanghai	Shanghai	(021)57582270		Private Owned				Veneer
新美集团公司(2000)	上海市	上海市	(021)58121788	1,500	私营企业	636,608	30,874(4)	860,564	胶合板
Vicwood (Suzhou) Industry Co., Ltd.	Suzhou	Jiangsu	(0512)65393117		Overseas Chinese-funded				Veneer
维德木业(苏州)有限公司(1993)	苏州市	江苏省	(0512)66711444	2,313	港澳台资	362,919	-	884,819	胶合板
Global Timber Industry Co., Ltd.	Yantai	Shandong	(0535)5600308		Overseas Chinese-funded				Veneer
环球木业有限公司(2000)	烟台市	山东省	(0535)5645404	3,869	港澳台资	355,055	-	697,278	胶合板
Yong'an Forestry Group Co., Ltd.	Sanming	Fujian	(0598)3606285		Joint Stock				Timber
永安林业集团股份有限公司(1994)	三明市	福建省	(0598)3633415	2,304	股份制	331,235	12,808(7)	776,602	木材
Luli Group Co., Ltd.	Weifang	Shandong	(0536)5361300		Collective-owned				Veneer
鲁丽集团有限公司(1980)	潍坊市	山东省	(0536)5361300	3,400	集体企业	331,078	22,135(5)	354,958	胶合板
Yang Zhou Happy Group	Yangzhou	Jiangsu	(0514)6716031		Collective-owned				Veneer
扬州市快乐集团公司(1973)	扬州市	江苏省	(0514)6716217	3,600	集体企业	310,000	3,650(41)	132,382	胶合板
Dongtai Zhongyang Timber Industry Co., Ltd.	Yancheng	Jiangsu	(0515)5420298		Foreign Funded				Veneer
东台市中阳木业有限公司(1994)	盐城市	江苏省	(0515)5421199	998	外商投资	283,330	15,560(6)	111,380	胶合板

Top 10 Cities by Revenue 销售收入排名前10位城市	Province 省	Market share 市场份额 (%)	Number of firms 企业个数
Shanghai 上海市	Shanghai 上海市	12.01	25
Xuzhou 徐州市	Jiangsu 江苏省	11.72	52
Foshan 佛山市	Guangdong 广东省	9.42	12
Suzhou 苏州市	Jiangsu 江苏省	4.26	9
Hangzhou 杭州市	Zhejiang 浙江省	3.62	29
Jiaxing 嘉兴市	Zhejiang 浙江省	3.39	21
Taizhou 台州市	Zhejiang 浙江省	3.38	4
Sanming 三明市	Fujian 福建省	2.75	41
Shijiazhuang 石家庄市	Hebei 河北省	2.67	17
Huzhou 湖州市	Zhejiang 浙江省	2.50	27

10 Major Wholesalers 十家主要批发商	City 城市	Province 省	Telephone/Fax 电话/传真
Shanghai Xinmei (Group) Co.,Ltd.	Shanghai	Shanghai	(021)58120888
上海新美（集团）有限公司	上海市	上海市	(021)67559188
Guangdong Native Products Import & Export (Group) Corporation	Guangzhou	Guangdong	(020)84244025
广东省土产进出口（集团）公司	广州市	广东省	(020)84423070
China Timber Import & Export Co.,Ltd.	Beijing	Beijing	(010)64203414
中国木材进出口股份有限公司	北京市	北京市	(010)64208900
Xiamen Yongquan Group Co.,Ltd.	Xiamen	Fujian	(0592)5161286
厦门涌泉集团有限公司	厦门市	福建省	(0592)5162966
China National Forest Products Marketing Co.	Beijing	Beijing	(010)64228370
中国林产品经销公司	北京市	北京市	(010)64216443
Liaoning Huiming International Trade Co.,Ltd.	Dalian	Liaoning	(0411)3620626
大连市辽宁汇明国际贸易有限公司	大连市	辽宁省	(0411)3636995
Shanghai Senda Wood Industry Co.,Ltd.	Shanghai	Shanghai	(021)54367592
上海森大木业有限公司	上海市	上海市	(021)54360331
Shanghai Timber General Corp.	Shanghai	Shanghai	(021)63230138
上海市木材总公司	上海市	上海市	(021)63236079
Guangdong Nanyou Economic Development Corp.	Guangzhou	Guangdong	(020)87304129
广东南油经济发展公司	广州市	广东省	(020)87756069
Zhuhai S.E.Z.Materials Company	Zhuhai	Guangdong	(0756)2116092
珠海经济特区物资公司	珠海市	广东省	(0756)2116718

2022: Fibreboard 纤维板制造业

The industry accounts for 0.090% of the total revenue of China's industrial sector in 2002. The rate of return on assets is 4.06%. 74.77% of all firms in the industry made a profit while 25.23% had negative returns.The top province in terms of the industry's revenue is Guangdong, accounting for 20.26% of the total revenue.
2002年本行业收入占全行业的 0.090%，资产利润率为 4.06%。74.77%的企业赢利，25.23%的企业亏损。收入最高的省为广东省，占本行业的20.26%。

	Total number of firms 企业总数	Total number of employees 职工总数	Total revenue (Mil.RMB) 总销售收入(百万元)	Total profit (Mil.RMB) 总利润(百万元)	Return on assets 资产利润率(%)	Return on equity 权益利润率(%)	Labour productivity ('000 RMB/ worker) 劳动生产率(千元/人)	Debts/ assets 资产负债率(%)	Total assets (Mil.RMB) 总资产(百万元)
Industry Overall 行业总体	222	48,284	9,665	657	4.06	10.60	72.56	61.67	16,185

	Number of firms 企业个数	Average number of employees 平均职工人数	Average revenue ('000 RMB) 平均销售收入（千元）	Average profit ('000 RMB) 平均利润（千元）	Return on assets 资产利润率(%)	Return on equity 权益利润率(%)	Labour productivity ('000 RMB/ worker) 劳动生产率(千元/人)	Debts/ assets 资产负债率(%)	Average total assets ('000 RMB) 平均总资产(千元)
By ownership 产业所有权									
State-owned 国有	44	269	36,734	257	0.31	1.49	39.75	79.49	83,884
Collective-owned 集体	27	329	66,379	3,201	4.96	13.29	59.21	62.70	64,597
Foreign & Overseas Chinese Funded 三资	35	187	69,121	6,458	4.61	11.72	140.19	60.63	140,011
By regional distribution 地区分布									
Central-North 华北	18	220	44,372	1,568	3.15	8.38	60.07	62.47	49,844
Beijing 北京	1	103	78,311	-19,094	-15.94	-19.04	89.06	16.27	119,786
Tianjin 天津									
Hebei 河北	11	250	59,126	4,316	8.31	27.34	71.09	69.60	51,932
Shanxi 山西	2	64	668	-101	-5.66	-111.60	4.95	94.93	1,785
Inner Mongolia 内蒙古	4	244	17,165	9	0.02	0.06	33.26	69.12	50,648
Northeast 东北	16	321	24,700	-195	-0.24	-0.84	32.37	71.54	81,883
Liaoning 辽宁	9	156	19,717	611	1.50	2.99	38.60	50.00	40,859
Jilin 吉林	2	252	14,598	52	0.10	0.20	30.75	49.86	50,215
Heilongjiang 黑龙江	5	646	37,710	-1,744	-1.04	-6.29	29.91	83.53	168,394
Central-East 华东	92	193	39,712	3,885	7.31	17.33	74.54	57.85	53,182
Shanghai 上海	3	129	61,461	-304	-0.25	-0.79	148.43	68.02	120,537
Jiangsu 江苏	6	143	45,826	5,585	18.22	37.54	79.46	51.45	30,647
Zhejiang 浙江	12	213	47,440	9,901	13.20	24.23	113.77	45.53	75,034
Anhui 安徽	11	228	27,010	3,090	6.20	14.00	45.27	55.75	49,873
Fujian 福建	17	179	46,469	5,384	8.33	15.08	103.65	44.78	64,654
Jiangxi 江西	10	233	43,792	3,510	6.01	12.07	61.76	50.24	58,420
Shandong 山东	33	183	33,331	1,376	3.74	20.04	54.99	81.35	36,815
Central-South 中南	73	202	52,600	3,064	3.25	8.42	102.48	61.46	94,390
Henan 河南	22	202	19,106	671	2.40	7.64	29.83	68.64	27,986
Hubei 湖北	10	267	57,130	7,254	6.56	16.58	175.53	60.44	110,603
Hunan 湖南	9	119	13,660	890	2.65	8.34	55.15	68.26	33,627
Guangdong 广东	17	213	115,183	4,459	2.53	5.34	168.96	52.59	176,231
Guangxi 广西	15	198	51,140	3,506	2.81	10.34	81.39	72.82	124,681
Hainan 海南									
Southwest 西南	19	256	44,175	2,653	2.71	6.93	46.78	60.92	97,889
Chongqing 重庆	1	165	23,577	117	0.32	0.80	29.82	59.61	36,368
Sichuan 四川	6	279	67,576	8,137	6.38	12.31	61.23	48.16	127,461
Guizhou 贵州	3	144	10,458	-1,111	-8.75		10.64	107.45	12,697
Yunnan 云南	9	288	42,103	533	0.47	1.51	44.54	68.79	113,406
Tibet 西藏									
Northwest 西北	4	462	34,598	174	0.21	1.40	20.70	85.09	83,637
Shaanxi 陕西	2	603	58,993	1,466	1.29	3.74	25.54	65.62	113,989
Gansu 甘肃	2	321	10,203	-1,118	-2.10		11.60	126.72	53,286
Qinghai 青海									
Ningxia 宁夏									
Xinjiang 新疆									

Year 年份	Number of firms 企业个数	Rate of change 变化率 (%)	Number of employees 职工人数 (人)	Rate of change 变化率 (%)	Total revenue (Mil. RMB) 总销售收入 (百万元)	Rate of change 变化率 (%)	Total profit (Mil RMB) 总利润 (百万元)	Rate of change 变化率 (%)
2000	165		49,005		6,758		356	
2001	189	14.55	47,243	-3.60	7,753	14.72	446	25.28
2002	222	17.46	48,284	2.20	9,665	24.66	657	47.31

Major Products 主要产品	Output 产量	Unit 单位
Fibreboard 纤维板	727	10,000 Stere 万立方米

10 Main Firms with Maximal Revenue (year founded) 收入最大的十家主要企业（创办年份）	City 城市	Province 省	Telephone/fax 电话/传真	Number of employees 职工人数	Ownership 产业所有权	Revenue ('000 RMB) 销售收入 (千元)	Profit('000 RMB) (rank) 利润(千元) (排名)	Total assets ('000 RMB) 总资产 (千元)	Major products 主要产品
Zhaoqing Hongzhan Industrial Delvolopment Co.,Ltd. Deqing Filiale 肇庆市宏展实业发展有限公司德庆分公司(1993)	Zhaoqing 肇庆市	Guangdong 广东省	(0758)7788388 (0758)7787310	376	Collective-owned 集体企业	865,475	6,472(34)	437,658	Medium-density Fibre Board 中密度纤维板
Guangxi Sanwei Forest Products Industry Co., Ltd. 广西三威林产工业有限公司(1954)	Wuzhou 梧州市	Guangxi 广西	(0774)3817180 (0774)3814168	640	State-owned 国有企业	336,395	9,983(23)	923,901	Chipboard 刨花板
Hubei Jixiang Plantation Products Co., Ltd. 湖北吉象人造林制品有限公司(1996)	Jingzhou 荆州市	Hubei 湖北省	(0716)7295888 (0716)7295780	435	Foreign Funded 外商投资	314,350	74,794(1)	559,894	Medium-density Fibre Board 中密度纤维板
Fengkai Fenghua MBF Board Co., Ltd 封开枫华中纤板有限公司(2001)	Zhaoqing 肇庆市	Guangdong 广东省	(0758)6713311 (0758)6713315	360	Limited-Liability 有限公司	287,838	8,810(27)	184,323	Medium-density Fibre Board 中纤板
Fujian Furen Timber Industry Co., Ltd. 福建福人木业有限公司(1979)	Fuzhou 福州市	Fujian 福建省	(0591)3662395 (0591)3662464	817	Limited-Liability 有限公司	254,108	31,807(6)	564,755	Medium-density Fibre Board 中密度纤维板
Shandong Heyou Group Company 山东禹城市贺友集团公司(1980)	Dezhou 德州市	Shandong 山东省	(0534)7421205 (0534)7421318	720	State-owned 国有企业	218,610	8,210(29)	232,001	Medium-density Fibre Board 中纤板
Nanning Medium-density Fibre Borad Factory 南宁市中密度纤维板厂(1996)	Nanning 南宁市	Guangxi 广西	(0771)4018477 (0771)4018315	316	Foreign Funded 外商投资	175,790	45,950(4)	274,907	Fibre Board 纤维板
Hubei Juning Forest Industry Co., Ltd. 湖北巨宁森工股份有限公司(1996)	Xianning 咸宁市	Hubei 湖北省	(0715)8331688 (0715)8324915	568	Joint Stock 股份制	171,206	6,281(36)	211,276	High-density Fibre Board 高密板
Yuehai(Zhanjiang)MBF Board Limited 粤海(湛江)中纤板有限公司(1994)	Zhanjiang 湛江市	Guangdong 广东省	(0759)2358040 (0759)2244830	175	Overseas Chinese-funded 港澳台资	154,707	20,729(11)	326,877	Medium-density Fibre Board 中密度纤维板
Zhejiang Liren Artificial Board Co., Ltd. 丽水市人造板有限责任公司(1995)	Lishui 丽水市	Zhejiang 浙江省	(0578)2133397 (0578)2282339	300	Limited-Liability 有限公司	142,706	21,627(10)	211,300	Medium-density Fibre Board 中密度纤维板

Top 10 Cities by Revenue 销售收入排名前10位城市	Province 省	Market share 市场份额 (%)	Number of firms 企业个数
Zhaoqing 肇庆市	Guangdong 广东省	12.54	4
Shijiazhuang 石家庄市	Hebei 河北省	4.42	6
Lishui 丽水市	Zhejiang 浙江省	4.39	5
Nanping 南平市	Fujian 福建省	3.94	8
Wuzhou 梧州市	Guangxi 广西	3.49	2
Jingzhou 荆州市	Hubei 湖北省	3.41	4
Leshan 乐山市	Sichuan 四川省	3.29	1
Nanning 南宁市	Guangxi 广西	3.23	3
Guangzhou 广州市	Guangdong 广东省	2.68	4
Fuzhou 福州市	Fujian 福建省	2.63	1

10 Major Wholesalers 十家主要批发商	City 城市	Province 省	Telephone/Fax 电话/传真
Shanghai Xinmei (Group) Co.,Ltd. 上海新美（集团）有限公司	Shanghai 上海市	Shanghai 上海市	(021)58120888 (021)67559188
Guangdong Native Products Import & Export (Group) Corporation 广东省土产进出口（集团）公司	Guangzhou 广州市	Guangdong 广东省	(020)84244025 (020)84423070
China Timber Import & Export Co.,Ltd. 中国木材进出口股份有限公司	Beijing 北京市	Beijing 北京市	(010)64203414 (010)64208900
Xiamen Yongquan Group Co.,Ltd. 厦门涌泉集团有限公司	Xiamen 厦门市	Fujian 福建省	(0592)5161286 (0592)5162966
China National Forest Products Marketing Co. 中国林产品经销公司	Beijing 北京市	Beijing 北京市	(010)64228370 (010)64216443
Liaoning Huiming International Trade Co.,Ltd. 大连市辽宁汇明国际贸易有限公司	Dalian 大连市	Liaoning 辽宁省	(0411)3620626 (0411)3636995
Shanghai Senda Wood Industry Co.,Ltd. 上海森大木业有限公司	Shanghai 上海市	Shanghai 上海市	(021)54367592 (021)54360331
Shanghai Timber General Corp. 上海市木材总公司	Shanghai 上海市	Shanghai 上海市	(021)63230138 (021)63236079
Guangdong Nanyou Economic Development Corp. 广东南油经济发展公司	Guangzhou 广州市	Guangdong 广东省	(020)87304129 (020)87756069
Zhuhai S.E.Z.Materials Company 珠海经济特区物资公司	Zhuhai 珠海市	Guangdong 广东省	(0756)2116092 (0756)2116718

2023: Shipboard 刨花板制造业

The industry accounts for 0.026% of the total revenue of China's industrial sector in 2002. The rate of return on assets is 1.04%. 73.33% of all firms in the industry made a profit while 26.67% had negative returns.The top province in terms of the industry's revenue is Jilin, accounting for 27.99% of the total revenue.
2002年本行业收入占全行业的 0.026%，资产利润率为 1.04%。73.33%的企业赢利，26.67%的企业亏损。收入最高的省为吉林省，占本行业的27.99%。

	Total number of firms 企业总数	Total number of employees 职工总数	Total revenue (Mil.RMB) 总销售收入 (百万元)	Total profit (Mil.RMB) 总利润 (百万元)	Return on assets 资产利润率 (%)	Return on equity 权益利润率 (%)	Labour productivity ('000 RMB/ worker) 劳动生产率 (千元/人)	Debts/ assets 资产负债率 (%)	Total assets (Mil.RMB) 总资产 (百万元)
Industry Overall 行业总体	105	23,439	2,740	67	1.04	2.91	36.90	64.31	6,464

	Number of firms 企业个数	Average number of employees 平均职工人数	Average revenue ('000 RMB) 平均销售收入 (千元)	Average profit ('000 RMB) 平均利润 (千元)	Return on assets 资产利润率 (%)	Return on equity 权益利润率 (%)	Labour productivity ('000 RMB/ worker) 劳动生产率 (千元/人)	Debts/ assets 资产负债率 (%)	Average total assets ('000 RMB) 平均总资产 (千元)
By ownership 产业所有权									
State-owned 国有	29	255	19,189	-1,514	-1.75	-10.13	20.28	82.71	86,425
Collective-owned 集体	18	96	9,934	628	6.75	13.19	25.34	48.77	9,295
Foreign & Overseas Chinese Funded 三资	14	250	42,536	1,329	1.82	4.02	67.83	54.70	73,008
By regional distribution 地区分布									
Central-North 华北	13	143	29,937	1,455	3.62	8.24	68.49	56.08	40,234
Beijing 北京									
Tianjin 天津	2	125	12,645	370	1.62	4.23	2.52	61.78	22,870
Hebei 河北	7	180	48,389	2,576	4.98	11.28	90.50	55.82	51,686
Shanxi 山西									
Inner Mongolia 内蒙古	4	89	6,292	38	0.13	0.29	36.85	54.63	28,876
Northeast 东北	14	459	69,814	2,826	1.84	4.59	52.30	59.96	153,776
Liaoning 辽宁	2	86	4,966	116	3.38	3.78	12.25	10.41	3,415
Jilin 吉林	6	656	127,814	6,650	2.74	5.40	63.28	49.35	243,126
Heilongjiang 黑龙江	6	386	33,430	-96	-0.08	-0.49	36.63	82.97	114,545
Central-East 华东	33	166	15,848	711	1.72	8.69	25.15	80.17	41,277
Shanghai 上海									
Jiangsu 江苏	4	88	11,080	440	9.54	17.70	30.26	46.11	4,614
Zhejiang 浙江	3	155	27,020	897	5.33	15.22	44.33	64.96	16,823
Anhui 安徽	5	204	30,644	2,118	5.40	9.80	31.88	44.85	39,202
Fujian 福建	9	120	6,837	-129	-0.65	-3.70	20.63	82.43	19,936
Jiangxi 江西	5	120	5,697	-395	-0.93	-2.27	13.40	58.85	42,255
Shandong 山东	7	279	22,054	1,653	1.64	72.79	22.27	97.75	100,932
Central-South 中南	32	222	20,500	-228	-0.37	-0.81	29.39	53.76	60,771
Henan 河南	13	178	12,655	627	3.80	7.86	18.75	51.71	16,526
Hubei 湖北	2	119	17,932	982	1.68	9.34	149.92	82.04	58,538
Hunan 湖南	5	427	34,335	287	0.17	0.30	24.84	41.45	165,135
Guangdong 广东	10	156	17,029	-1,961	-4.47	-17.78	29.52	74.88	43,928
Guangxi 广西	1	276	12,897	-738	-0.75		8.18	133.73	98,223
Hainan 海南	1	577	100,767	1,518	0.61	0.71	49.29	14.33	249,577
Southwest 西南	8	273	17,925	-1,731	-3.58	-32.12	16.78	88.84	48,302
Chongqing 重庆	1	963	46,603	4,128	9.20	27.20	16.67	66.18	44,877
Sichuan 四川	1	15	561	100	2.10	2.41	24.73	13.04	4,771
Guizhou 贵州	3	182	14,047	-5,450	-10.64		14.42	127.02	51,212
Yunnan 云南	3	221	18,032	-576	-0.94	-2.64	18.71	64.35	61,043
Tibet 西藏									
Northwest 西北	5	80	10,131	1,274	6.75	226.00	46.59	97.01	18,886
Shaanxi 陕西									
Gansu 甘肃	3	78	5,892	507	8.74	51.49	32.96	83.02	5,804
Qinghai 青海									
Ningxia 宁夏									
Xinjiang 新疆	2	82	16,491	2,425	6.30		66.04	100.18	38,508

Year 年份	Number of firms 企业个数	Rate of change 变化率 (%)	Number of employees 职工人数 (人)	Rate of change 变化率 (%)	Total revenue (Mil. RMB) 总销售收入 (百万元)	Rate of change 变化率 (%)	Total profit (Mil RMB) 总利润 (百万元)	Rate of change 变化率 (%)
2000	115		27,879		2,612		78	
2001	111	-3.48	27,261	-2.22	2,768	5.97	63	-19.23
2002	105	-5.41	23,439	-14.02	2,740	-1.01	67	6.35

Major Products 主要产品	Output 产量	Unit 单位
Flakeboard 刨花板	243	10,000 Stere 万立方米

10 Main Firms with Maximal Revenue (year founded) 收入最大的十家主要企业（创办年份）	City 城市	Province 省	Telephone/fax 电话/传真	Number of employees 职工人数	Ownership 产业所有权	Revenue ('000 RMB) 销售收入(千元)	Profit('000 RMB) (rank) 利润(千元)(排名)	Total assets ('000 RMB) 总资产(千元)	Major products 主要产品
Hebei Yin'gang Artificial Board Company	Shijiazhuang	Hebei	(0311)8711594		Overseas Chinese-funded				Flakeboard
河北银港人造板公司(1993)	石家庄市	河北省	(0311)8711302	450	港澳台资	250,004	14,300(3)	120,000	刨花板
Jilin Forest Industry Co., Ltd Lushuihe Flakeboard Factory	Baishan	Jilin	(0439)6369764		Joint Stock				Flakeboard
吉林森林工业股份有限公司露水河刨花板分公司(1990)	白山市	吉林省	(0439)6369314	713	股份制	164,883	20,186(1)	254,567	刨花板
Chuzhou Huaneng Artificial Board Co.,Ltd.	Chuzhou	Anhui	(0550)3073010		Limited-Liability				Flakeboard
安徽省滁州华能人造板有限责任公司(1989)	滁州市	安徽省	(0550)3055935	617	有限公司	105,302	10,201(4)	147,650	刨花板
Jilin Forest Industry Co., Ltd. Sanchazi Flakeboard Branch	Baishan	Jilin	(0439)3748969		Joint Stock				
吉林森林工业股份有限公司三岔子刨花板分公司(2001)	白山市	吉林省	(0439)3749905	461	股份制	75,034	16,616(2)	127,765	
Shandong Lindun Timber Industry Co.,Ltd.	Heze	Shandong	(0530)2150004		Limited-Liability				Flakeboard
山东林盾木业有限责任公司(1998)	荷泽市	山东省	(0530)2150007	501	有限公司	69,233	8,878(5)	56,426	刨花板
Yichun Fuwang Timber Industry Co., Ltd.	Yichun	Heilongjiang	(0458)3535754		Foreign Funded				Flakeboard
伊春福旺木业有限公司(2000)	伊春市	黑龙江省	(0458)3532762	610	外商投资	55,052	7,402(6)	83,463	刨花板
Muling Senfu Timber Industry Co., Ltd.	Mudanjiang	Heilongjiang	(0453)3096165		Limited-Liability				Flakeboard
穆棱市森福木业有限责任公司(2000)	牡丹江市	黑龙江省	(0453)3097748	180	有限公司	51,710	3,590(10)	55,040	刨花板
Mudanjiang Comprehensive Wood Processing Plant	Mudanjiang	Heilongjiang	(0453)6683388		State-owned				Flakeboard
国营牡丹江木材综合加工厂(1949)	牡丹江市	黑龙江省	(0453)6684614	901	国有企业	51,307	-	315,208	刨花板
Kunming Xinfeilin Artificial Board Co., Ltd.	Kunming	Yunnan	(0871)5319586		Limited-Liability				Wooden Flakeboard木
昆明新飞林人造板有限公司(1952)	昆明市	云南省	(0871)5326392	436	有限公司	46,615	-	177,649	质刨花板
Chongqing Kaixian Xingxing Building Materials Co., Ltd.	Chongqing	Chongqing	(023)52412022		Limited-Liability				Hollow Board
重庆市开县星星建材有限责任公司(1962)	重庆市	重庆市	(023)52412022	963	有限公司	46,603	4,128(9)	44,877	空心板

Top 10 Cities by Revenue 销售收入排名前10位城市	Province 省	Market share 市场份额 (%)	Number of firms 企业个数
Baishan 白山市	Jilin 吉林省	23.21	4
Shijiazhuang 石家庄市	Hebei 河北省	9.13	1
Changsha 长沙市	Hunan 湖南省	4.95	2
Yanbian 延边州	Jilin 吉林省	4.78	2
Mudanjiang 牡丹江市	Heilongjiang 黑龙江省	4.38	3
Chuzhou 滁州市	Anhui 安徽省	3.84	1
Heze 荷泽市	Shandong 山东省	2.53	1
Zhaoqing 肇庆市	Guangdong 广东省	2.39	2
Yichun 伊春市	Heilongjiang 黑龙江省	2.23	2
Nanping 南平市	Fujian 福建省	2.07	8

10 Major Wholesalers 十家主要批发商	City 城市	Province 省	Telephone/Fax 电话/传真
Shanghai Xinmei (Group) Co.,Ltd.	Shanghai	Shanghai	(021)58120888
上海新美（集团）有限公司	上海市	上海市	(021)67559188
Guangdong Native Products Import & Export (Group) Corporation	Guangzhou	Guangdong	(020)84244025
广东省土产进出口（集团）公司	广州市	广东省	(020)84423070
China Timber Import & Export Co.,Ltd.	Beijing	Beijing	(010)64203414
中国木材进出口股份有限公司	北京市	北京市	(010)64208900
Xiamen Yongquan Group Co.,Ltd.	Xiamen	Fujian	(0592)5161286
厦门涌泉集团有限公司	厦门市	福建省	(0592)5162966
China National Forest Products Marketing Co.	Beijing	Beijing	(010)64228370
中国林产品经销公司	北京市	北京市	(010)64216443
Liaoning Huiming International Trade Co.,Ltd.	Dalian	Liaoning	(0411)3620626
大连市辽宁汇明国际贸易有限公司	大连市	辽宁省	(0411)3636995
Shanghai Senda Wood Industry Co.,Ltd.	Shanghai	Shanghai	(021)54367592
上海森大木业有限公司	上海市	上海市	(021)54360331
Shanghai Timber General Corp.	Shanghai	Shanghai	(021)63230138
上海市木材总公司	上海市	上海市	(021)63236079
Guangdong Nanyou Economic Development Corp.	Guangzhou	Guangdong	(020)87304129
广东南油经济发展公司	广州市	广东省	(020)87756069
Zhuhai S.E.Z.Materials Company	Zhuhai	Guangdong	(0756)2116092
珠海经济特区物资公司	珠海市	广东省	(0756)2116718

2029: Other Artificial Boards 其他人造板制造业

The industry accounts for 0.114% of the total revenue of China's industrial sector in 2002. The rate of return on assets is 3.90%. 84.01% of all firms in the industry made a profit while 15.99% had negative returns.The top province in terms of the industry's revenue is Jiangsu, accounting for 28.11% of the total revenue.
2002年本行业收入占全行业的 0.114%，资产利润率为 3.90%。84.01%的企业赢利，15.99%的企业亏损。收入最高的省为江苏省，占本行业的28.11%。

	Total number of firms 企业总数	Total number of employees 职工总数	Total revenue (Mil.RMB) 总销售收入 (百万元)	Total profit (Mil.RMB) 总利润 (百万元)	Return on assets 资产利润率 (%)	Return on equity 权益利润率 (%)	Labour productivity ('000 RMB/ worker) 劳动生产率 (千元/人)	Debts/ assets 资产负债率 (%)	Total assets (Mil.RMB) 总资产 (百万元)
Industry Overall 行业总体	369	67,251	12,242	484	3.90	9.41	41.78	58.60	12,420

	Number of firms 企业个数	Average number of employees 平均职工人数	Average revenue ('000 RMB) 平均销售收入 (千元)	Average profit ('000 RMB) 平均利润 (千元)	Return on assets 资产利润率 (%)	Return on equity 权益利润率 (%)	Labour productivity ('000 RMB/ worker) 劳动生产率 (千元/人)	Debts/ assets 资产负债率 (%)	Average total assets ('000 RMB) 平均总资产 (千元)
By ownership 产业所有权									
State-owned 国有	20	273	45,853	2,272	2.01	7.81	41.69	74.20	112,785
Collective-owned 集体	22	150	22,543	2,691	9.81	20.92	13.30	53.11	27,429
Foreign & Overseas Chinese Funded 三资	76	226	52,623	2,493	3.86	8.82	56.40	56.18	64,512
By regional distribution 地区分布									
Central-North 华北	22	121	17,402	241	1.25	1.85	34.59	32.23	19,180
Beijing 北京	3	161	68,109	1,077	1.46	1.66	59.16	12.17	74,016
Tianjin 天津	6	121	11,401	11	0.10	0.21	29.13	50.59	10,239
Hebei 河北	12	117	8,758	148	1.48	3.58	28.58	58.68	10,016
Shanxi 山西									
Inner Mongolia 内蒙古	1	43	5,012	217	1.19	1.99	46.74	40.33	18,278
Northeast 东北	48	210	26,544	268	0.45	1.22	35.51	63.14	59,539
Liaoning 辽宁	21	138	30,295	1,203	2.20	4.02	43.79	45.31	54,777
Jilin 吉林	13	274	23,043	261	0.77	2.03	31.54	62.10	33,944
Heilongjiang 黑龙江	14	258	24,168	-1,128	-1.25	-6.15	32.76	79.70	90,448
Central-East 华东	237	187	35,264	1,475	5.28	12.46	43.49	57.64	27,941
Shanghai 上海	21	282	109,838	5,221	5.12	10.10	64.66	49.37	102,050
Jiangsu 江苏	132	150	26,074	1,195	6.95	16.01	45.93	56.58	17,197
Zhejiang 浙江	30	409	65,174	2,600	5.26	13.49	37.11	61.05	49,478
Anhui 安徽	6	87	10,285	151	2.68	16.81	31.05	84.04	5,616
Fujian 福建	19	75	7,685	106	1.25	3.09	25.97	59.55	8,459
Jiangxi 江西	2	250	20,556	-18	-0.13	-0.47	39.71	73.57	14,350
Shandong 山东	27	144	15,007	50	0.27	1.72	27.54	84.39	18,575
Central-South 中南	55	162	36,291	2,023	5.56	14.39	40.98	61.38	36,415
Henan 河南	9	129	15,788	1,095	12.59	22.64	47.60	44.38	8,695
Hubei 湖北	9	210	39,982	623	0.92	2.42	62.03	62.21	68,130
Hunan 湖南	7	76	11,684	690	11.02	46.52	57.53	76.32	6,261
Guangdong 广东	30	178	47,076	3,032	7.18	18.65	30.47	61.52	42,252
Guangxi 广西									
Hainan 海南									
Southwest 西南	4	274	57,332	1,385	1.11	2.52	59.83	55.93	124,709
Chongqing 重庆									
Sichuan 四川	2	393	106,054	3,090	1.32	3.03	75.62	56.45	233,996
Guizhou 贵州									
Yunnan 云南	2	154	8,610	-320	-2.07	-3.98	19.54	47.99	15,422
Tibet 西藏									
Northwest 西北	3	68	784	-230	-4.27	-19.22	12.18	77.79	5,396
Shaanxi 陕西									
Gansu 甘肃	3	68	784	-230	-4.27	-19.22	12.18	77.79	5,396
Qinghai 青海									
Ningxia 宁夏									
Xinjiang 新疆									

2029: Other Artificial Boards 其他人造板制造业

Year 年份	Number of firms 企业个数	Rate of change 变化率(%)	Number of employees 职工人数(人)	Rate of change 变化率(%)	Total revenue (Mil. RMB) 总销售收入(百万元)	Rate of change 变化率(%)	Total profit (Mil RMB) 总利润(百万元)	Rate of change 变化率(%)
	270		44,898		8,428		211	
2001	328	21.48	55,651	23.95	9,847	16.84	304	44.08
2002	369	12.50	67,251	20.84	12,242	24.32	484	59.21

Major Products 主要产品	Output 产量	Unit 单位
Man-made Second Processing Plaque 人造板二次加工装饰板	14,308	10,000 Sq.M. 万平方米

10 Main Firms with Maximal Revenue (year founded) 收入最大的十家主要企业（创办年份）	City 城市	Province 省	Telephone/fax 电话/传真	Number of employees 职工人数	Ownership 产业所有权	Revenue ('000 RMB) 销售收入(千元)	Profit('000 RMB) (rank) 利润(千元)(排名)	Total assets ('000 RMB) 总资产(千元)	Major products 主要产品
Zhejiang Dehua Wooden Stock Co., Ltd.	Huzhou	Zhejiang	(0572)8405810		Joint Stock				Crossbanding
浙江德华木业股份有限公司(1998)	湖州市	浙江省	(0572)8405326	4,979	股份制	824,000	54,200(1)	512,590	装饰面板
Shanghai Xinjia Timber Industry Company	Shanghai	Shanghai	(021)58120888		Private Owned				Crossbanding
上海新加木业公司(1996)	上海市	上海市	(021)58121788	1,000	私营企业	504,683	4,220(19)	539,098	装饰板
Shunde Likai Packing Co., Ltd.	Foshan	Guangdong	(0765)2277634		Private Owned				Aluminum Moulding Composite Coating铝
顺德市力凯包装有限公司(1976)	佛山市	广东省	(0765)2201561	975	私营企业	441,390	38,305(6)	37,080	塑复合膜
Shanghai Senda Factory Wood Co., ltd	Shanghai	Shanghai	(021)54367592		Overseas Chinese-funded				Timber Slices
上海森大木业有限公司(1990)	上海市	上海市	(021)54360311	800	港澳台资	297,852	21,698(8)	130,959	木材切片
DaLian Global Wood Products Co.,Ltd.	Dalian	Liaoning	(0411)6428310		Foreign Funded				Subereous Products
大连环球木业有限公司(1995)	大连市	辽宁省	(0411)6429076	1,117	外商投资	267,865	20(203)	324,824	软木制品
Taizhou Jili Decorative Materials Co.,Ltd.	Taizhou	Zhejiang	(0576)2520381		Limited-Liability				Integrated Wood
台州吉利装璜材料有限公司(1998)	台州市	浙江省	(0576)2451301	1,001	有限公司	245,120	11,280(9)	157,640	集成材
Xinhui CIMC Container Flooring Co., ltd.	Jiangmen	Guangdong	(0750)6248888		Overseas Chinese-funded				Aluminum Bend Board
新会中集集装箱木地板有限公司(2000)	江门市	广东省	(0750)6248666	550	港澳台资	213,600	2,320(35)	164,272	美铝曲板
Shanghai Fumeijia Decorative Material Co.,Ltd.	Shanghai	Shanghai	(021)59201143		Foreign Funded				Wooden Floor
上海富美家装饰材料有限公司(1994)	上海市	上海市	(021)63523158	200	外商投资	204,197	38,840(5)	164,950	木地板
Zhejiang Desheng Timber Industry Co., Ltd.	Huzhou	Zhejiang	(0572)8435205		Overseas Chinese-funded				Fireproof Board
浙江德升木业有限公司(1999)	湖州市	浙江省	(0572)8433777	1,415	港澳台资	203,304	6,112(14)	229,600	防火板
Hubei Fu Jiang Timber Industry Co., Ltd.	Jingzhou	Hubei	(0716)3325188		Overseas Chinese-funded				Three-plywood
湖北福江木业有限公司(1993)	荆州市	湖北省	(0716)3325555	533	港澳台资	192,367	7,695(12)	135,723	三夹板

Top 10 Cities by Revenue 销售收入排名前10位城市	Province 省	Market share 市场份额 (%)	Number of firms 企业个数
Shanghai 上海市	Shanghai 上海市	18.84	21
Suqian 宿迁市	Jiangsu 江苏省	13.23	91
Huzhou 湖州市	Zhejiang 浙江省	10.44	8
Suzhou 苏州市	Jiangsu 江苏省	6.80	8
Foshan 佛山市	Guangdong 广东省	4.18	5
Zhenjiang 镇江市	Jiangsu 江苏省	3.36	2
Dalian 大连市	Liaoning 辽宁省	2.88	7
Jiangmen 江门市	Guangdong 广东省	2.37	3
Taizhou 台州市	Zhejiang 浙江省	2.17	3
Huaian 淮安市	Jiangsu 江苏省	1.84	12

10 Major Wholesalers 十家主要批发商	City 城市	Province 省	Telephone/Fax 电话/传真
Shanghai Xinmei (Group) Co.,Ltd.	Shanghai	Shanghai	(021)58120888
上海新美（集团）有限公司	上海市	上海市	(021)67559188
Guangdong Native Products Import & Export (Group) Corporation	Guangzhou	Guangdong	(020)84244025
广东省土产进出口（集团）公司	广州市	广东省	(020)84423070
China Timber Import & Export Co.,Ltd.	Beijing	Beijing	(010)64203414
中国木材进出口股份有限公司	北京市	北京市	(010)64208900
Xiamen Yongquan Group Co.,Ltd.	Xiamen	Fujian	(0592)5161286
厦门涌泉集团有限公司	厦门市	福建省	(0592)5162966
China National Forest Products Marketing Co.	Beijing	Beijing	(010)64228370
中国林产品经销公司	北京市	北京市	(010)64216443
Liaoning Huiming International Trade Co.,Ltd.	Dalian	Liaoning	(0411)3620626
大连市辽宁汇明国际贸易有限公司	大连市	辽宁省	(0411)3636995
Shanghai Senda Wood Industry Co.,Ltd.	Shanghai	Shanghai	(021)54367592
上海森大木业有限公司	上海市	上海市	(021)54360331
Shanghai Timber General Corp.	Shanghai	Shanghai	(021)63230138
上海市木材总公司	上海市	上海市	(021)63236079
Guangdong Nanyou Economic Development Corp.	Guangzhou	Guangdong	(020)87304129
广东南油经济发展公司	广州市	广东省	(020)87756069
Zhuhai S.E.Z.Materials Company	Zhuhai	Guangdong	(0756)2116092
珠海经济特区物资公司	珠海市	广东省	(0756)2116718

2031: Industrial Wood Products 生产用木制品业

The industry accounts for 0.098% of the total revenue of China's industrial sector in 2002. The rate of return on assets is 1.31%. 80.00% of all firms in the industry made a profit while 20.00% had negative returns.The top province in terms of the industry's revenue is Liaoning, accounting for 15.63% of the total revenue.
2002年本行业收入占全行业的 0.098%，资产利润率为 1.31%。80.00%的企业赢利，20.00%的企业亏损。收入最高的省为辽宁省，占本行业的15.63%。

	Total number of firms 企业总数	Total number of employees 职工总数	Total revenue (Mil.RMB) 总销售收入 (百万元)	Total profit (Mil.RMB) 总利润 (百万元)	Return on assets 资产利润率 (%)	Return on equity 权益利润率 (%)	Labour productivity ('000 RMB/ worker) 劳动生产率 (千元/人)	Debts/ assets 资产负债率 (%)	Total assets (Mil.RMB) 总资产 (百万元)
Industry Overall 行业总体	500	70,859	10,531	136	1.31	3.69	44.71	64.55	10,413

	Number of firms 企业个数	Average number of employees 平均职工人数	Average revenue ('000 RMB) 平均销售收入 (千元)	Average profit ('000 RMB) 平均利润 (千元)	Return on assets 资产利润率 (%)	Return on equity 权益利润率 (%)	Labour productivity ('000 RMB/ worker) 劳动生产率 (千元/人)	Debts/ assets 资产负债率 (%)	Average total assets ('000 RMB) 平均总资产 (千元)
By ownership 产业所有权									
State-owned 国有	53	71	2,998	17	0.14	0.54	31.03	74.14	12,456
Collective-owned 集体	91	140	21,028	926	6.03	16.32	50.82	63.08	15,360
Foreign & Overseas Chinese Funded 三资	131	154	24,556	-1,422	-4.05	-14.05	39.42	71.20	35,152
By regional distribution 地区分布									
Central-North 华北	58	104	19,406	131	0.56	2.74	51.57	79.70	23,608
Beijing 北京	18	126	29,956	-628	-1.84	-19.71	59.01	90.65	34,057
Tianjin 天津	26	74	11,377	611	4.18	11.55	48.14	63.82	14,625
Hebei 河北	14	130	20,752	215	0.80	3.62	45.89	77.92	26,856
Shanxi 山西									
Inner Mongolia 内蒙古									
Northeast 东北	94	258	32,254	277	0.77	1.93	44.22	60.11	35,897
Liaoning 辽宁	27	284	60,977	-1,015	-1.88	-4.42	55.36	57.43	53,966
Jilin 吉林	31	237	18,746	230	0.85	2.22	40.29	61.81	27,143
Heilongjiang 黑龙江	36	255	22,344	1,286	4.30	11.45	38.07	62.42	29,884
Central-East 华东	191	115	17,999	526	3.74	9.10	39.16	58.89	14,061
Shanghai 上海	51	81	18,053	186	1.15	3.28	54.16	64.83	16,107
Jiangsu 江苏	46	88	15,433	591	5.54	13.10	45.75	57.69	10,672
Zhejiang 浙江	19	117	23,476	718	4.32	9.26	31.92	53.36	16,624
Anhui 安徽	19	101	11,019	304	5.68	20.87	33.36	72.79	5,348
Fujian 福建	18	130	17,078	441	1.74	3.02	31.45	42.47	25,439
Jiangxi 江西	12	308	12,695	419	4.60	8.21	15.29	43.97	9,092
Shandong 山东	26	141	26,616	1,207	8.08	29.09	51.48	72.24	14,951
Central-South 中南	111	108	20,469	330	2.10	5.61	59.54	62.54	15,723
Henan 河南	20	106	18,866	1,452	14.78	28.00	64.78	47.21	9,818
Hubei 湖北	8	62	15,203	983	12.80	20.76	95.27	38.34	7,678
Hunan 湖南	13	62	9,228	166	1.59	4.72	48.85	66.39	10,473
Guangdong 广东	64	127	25,173	66	0.37	0.96	57.02	61.39	17,932
Guangxi 广西	3	39	9,732	780	49.48	114.15	123.00	56.65	1,576
Hainan 海南	3	101	4,309	-3,001	-4.53	-42.25	36.00	89.29	66,306
Southwest 西南	35	154	17,196	-926	-2.94	-11.78	35.43	75.01	31,479
Chongqing 重庆	4	217	21,183	168	0.75	1.73	30.03	56.80	22,552
Sichuan 四川	9	150	27,839	1,047	4.70	10.88	67.03	56.80	22,274
Guizhou 贵州	4	24	1,944	4	0.05	0.13	18.17	60.92	7,151
Yunnan 云南	14	195	18,137	-3,105	-6.52	-42.28	15.96	84.57	47,602
Tibet 西藏	4	84	1,217	235	0.81	2.63	84.92	69.19	29,013
Northwest 西北	11	115	5,604	-175	-1.40	-5.49	16.79	74.41	12,438
Shaanxi 陕西	2	109	3,302	-2,518	-6.17	-25.56	10.56	75.85	40,780
Gansu 甘肃	6	41	5,548	620	16.12	54.94	56.61	70.65	3,846
Qinghai 青海									
Ningxia 宁夏	1	150	3,973	499	7.12	12.22	8.89	41.72	7,004
Xinjiang 新疆	2	324	8,889	-553	-4.39	-24.79	5.59	82.30	12,591

Year 年份	Number of firms 企业个数	Rate of change 变化率 (%)	Number of employees 职工人数 (人)	Rate of change 变化率 (%)	Total revenue (Mil. RMB) 总销售收入 (百万元)	Rate of change 变化率 (%)	Total profit (Mil RMB) 总利润 (百万元)	Rate of change 变化率 (%)
2000	494		68,599		8,000		265	
2001	480	-2.83	65,732	-4.18	8,284	3.55	263	-0.75
2002	500	4.17	70,859	7.80	10,531	27.12	136	-48.29

Major Products 主要产品	Output 产量	Unit 单位
Wood Articles For Production 生产用木制品	48	100,000,000 Yuan 亿元

10 Main Firms with Maximal Revenue (year founded) 收入最大的十家主要企业（创办年份）	City 城市	Province 省	Telephone/fax 电话/传真	Number of employees 职工人数	Ownership 产业所有权	Revenue ('000 RMB) 销售收入 (千元)	Profit('000 RMB) (rank) 利润(千元) (排名)	Total assets ('000 RMB) 总资产 (千元)	Major products 主要产品
Jinhua Floor Board Group	Fushun	Liaoning	(0413)4180271		Private Partnership				Floor
金花地板集团(1998)	抚顺市	辽宁省		1,152	私营合伙	389,130	6,626(9)	34,520	地板
Heilongjiang Fubang Group Co., ltd.	Mudanjiang	Heilongjiang	(0453)3061227		Overseas Chinese-funded				Wood Floor
黑龙江富邦集团公司(1996)	牡丹江市	黑龙江省	(0453)3061217	965	港澳台资	239,290	20,050(3)	69,190	实木地板
Rushan Machine-Room Equipment Factory	Weihai	Shandong	(0631)6723123		Collective-owned				Antistatic Floor
乳山市机房设备厂(1992)	威海市	山东省	(0631)6723123	128	集体企业	232,068	11,486(5)	16,535	静电地板
Shanghai Anxin Floor Board Co.,Ltd.	Shanghai	Shanghai	(021)64279988		Private Owned				Wooden Floor
上海安信地板有限公司(1998)	上海市	上海市	(021)62198686	61	私营企业	160,433	12,949(4)	41,049	木地板
Jilin Xinyuan Timber Industrial Stock Co.,Ltd.	Yanbian	Jilin	(0433)6368332		Joint Stock				Wooden Floor
吉林新元木业股份有限公司(1987)	延边州	吉林省	(0433)6369668	1,641	股份制	136,451	3,522(21)	293,744	木地板
Nefa Paking Engineer (Wuxi) Co.,Ltd.	Wuxi	Jiangsu	(0510)5200310		Foreign Funded				Wooden Container
耐帆包装工程（无锡）有限公司(1997)	无锡市	江苏省	(0510)5200402	114	外商投资	136,000	24,430(2)	81,600	木容器
Zhanjiang Sunwin Handicraftst Co., ltd.	Zhanjiang	Guangdong	(0759)2173037		Overseas Chinese-funded				Wooden Furniture
湛江信威工艺品有限公司(1997)	湛江市	广东省	(0759)2194505	556	港澳台资	120,498	-	68,228	木家具
Guangzhou Fulin Floor Board Timber Industry Co.,Ltd.	Guangzhou	Guangdong	(020)82288288		Overseas Chinese-funded				Wooden Floor
广州富林地板木业有限公司(1998)	广州市	广东省	(020)82278310	400	港澳台资	114,447	1,442(74)	125,191	木地板
Velux (China) Co.,Ltd.	Langfang	Hebei	(0316)6072728		Foreign Funded				Lucarne
威卢克斯（中国）有限公司(1993)	廊坊市	河北省	(0316)6089710	204	外商投资	89,503	-	83,127	屋顶窗
Tostem Housing Products (Dalian)Co,. Ltd.	Dalian	Liaoning	(0411)7629998		Foreign Funded				Wooden Door & window
大连通世泰建材有限公司(2001)	大连市	辽宁省	(0411)7633377	752	外商投资	85,405	-	688,756	木制门窗

Top 10 Cities by Revenue 销售收入排名前10位城市	Province 省	Market share 市场份额 (%)	Number of firms 企业个数
Fushun 抚顺市	Liaoning 辽宁省	12.86	7
Shanghai 上海市	Shanghai 上海市	8.74	51
Beijing 北京市	Beijing 北京市	5.12	18
Mudanjiang 牡丹江市	Heilongjiang 黑龙江省	3.44	7
Yanbian 延边州	Jilin 吉林省	3.38	17
Yichun 伊春市	Heilongjiang 黑龙江省	3.24	19
Zhaoqing 肇庆市	Guangdong 广东省	3.16	14
Tianjin 天津市	Tianjin 天津市	2.81	26
Jiangmen 江门市	Guangdong 广东省	2.64	10
Weihai 威海市	Shandong 山东省	2.27	2

10 Major Wholesalers 十家主要批发商	City 城市	Province 省	Telephone/Fax 电话/传真
Shanghai Xinmei (Group) Co.,Ltd.	Shanghai	Shanghai	(021)58120888
上海新美（集团）有限公司	上海市	上海市	(021)67559188
Guangdong Native Products Import & Export (Group) Corporation	Guangzhou	Guangdong	(020)84244025
广东省土产进出口（集团）公司	广州市	广东省	(020)84423070
China Timber Import & Export Co.,Ltd.	Beijing	Beijing	(010)64203414
中国木材进出口股份有限公司	北京市	北京市	(010)64208900
Xiamen Yongquan Group Co.,Ltd.	Xiamen	Fujian	(0592)5161286
厦门涌泉集团有限公司	厦门市	福建省	(0592)5162966
China National Forest Products Marketing Co.	Beijing	Beijing	(010)64228370
中国林产品经销公司	北京市	北京市	(010)64216443
Liaoning Huiming International Trade Co.,Ltd.	Dalian	Liaoning	(0411)3620626
大连市辽宁汇明国际贸易有限公司	大连市	辽宁省	(0411)3636995
Shanghai Senda Wood Industry Co.,Ltd.	Shanghai	Shanghai	(021)54367592
上海森大木业有限公司	上海市	上海市	(021)54360331
Shanghai Timber General Corp.	Shanghai	Shanghai	(021)63230138
上海市木材总公司	上海市	上海市	(021)63236079
Guangdong Nanyou Economic Development Corp.	Guangzhou	Guangdong	(020)87304129
广东南油经济发展公司	广州市	广东省	(020)87756069
Zhuhai S.E.Z.Materials Company	Zhuhai	Guangdong	(0756)2116092
珠海经济特区物资公司	珠海市	广东省	(0756)2116718

2033: Domestic Wood Products 生活用木制品业

The industry accounts for 0.074% of the total revenue of China's industrial sector in 2002. The rate of return on assets is 4.39%. 80.12% of all firms in the industry made a profit while 19.88% had negative returns.The top province in terms of the industry's revenue is Guangdong, accounting for 37.55% of the total revenue.
2002年本行业收入占全行业的 0.074%，资产利润率为 4.39%。80.12%的企业赢利，19.88%的企业亏损。收入最高的省为广东省，占本行业的37.55%。

	Total number of firms 企业总数	Total number of employees 职工总数	Total revenue (Mil.RMB) 总销售收入（百万元）	Total profit (Mil.RMB) 总利润（百万元）	Return on assets 资产利润率 (%)	Return on equity 权益利润率 (%)	Labour productivity ('000 RMB/ worker) 劳动生产率（千元/人）	Debts/ assets 资产负债率 (%)	Total assets (Mil.RMB) 总资产（百万元）
Industry Overall 行业总体	332	53,409	7,903	269	4.39	10.41	36.26	57.86	6,144

	Number of firms 企业个数	Average number of employees 平均职工人数	Average revenue ('000 RMB) 平均销售收入（千元）	Average profit ('000 RMB) 平均利润（千元）	Return on assets 资产利润率 (%)	Return on equity 权益利润率 (%)	Labour productivity ('000 RMB/ worker) 劳动生产率（千元/人）	Debts/ assets 资产负债率 (%)	Average total assets ('000 RMB) 平均总资产（千元）
By ownership 产业所有权									
State-owned 国有	23	58	3,404	-189	-1.69	-29.29	20.12	94.24	11,222
Collective-owned 集体	29	156	16,177	479	5.02	15.35	29.23	67.27	9,529
Foreign & Overseas Chinese Funded 三资	148	176	23,766	593	2.54	6.30	32.32	59.69	23,334
By regional distribution 地区分布									
Central-North 华北	22	156	27,796	1,807	9.29	19.71	31.40	52.86	19,446
Beijing 北京	4	52	3,947	-5	-0.15	-0.59	27.04	75.07	3,390
Tianjin 天津	12	144	42,701	2,971	10.30	21.39	48.34	51.84	28,836
Hebei 河北	4	293	19,236	823	5.58	12.28	13.30	54.58	14,751
Shanxi 山西	1	20	502				11.10	92.19	4,753
Inner Mongolia 内蒙古	1	305	5,856	827	18.55	18.55	9.52		4,459
Northeast 东北	83	140	14,129	674	3.98	9.99	30.23	60.20	16,962
Liaoning 辽宁	42	116	19,283	1,074	6.91	13.72	39.87	49.67	15,547
Jilin 吉林	19	100	5,445	-153	-0.97	-5.68	21.86	83.00	15,901
Heilongjiang 黑龙江	22	219	11,790	628	3.05	7.66	23.82	60.19	20,579
Central-East 华东	127	160	19,299	326	2.45	5.73	32.66	57.33	13,314
Shanghai 上海	16	130	20,461	1,176	5.90	11.31	36.28	47.82	19,936
Jiangsu 江苏	17	141	29,242	357	3.13	9.65	48.08	67.54	11,386
Zhejiang 浙江	34	145	16,176	632	7.22	17.95	26.41	59.78	8,752
Anhui 安徽	3	90	9,593	98	2.68	7.54	32.68	64.45	3,667
Fujian 福建	29	237	22,285	-377	-1.83	-4.58	29.67	60.09	20,634
Jiangxi 江西	4	75	2,437	128	4.85	43.18	11.47	88.77	2,628
Shandong 山东	24	142	16,318	215	1.97	4.00	36.57	50.68	10,871
Central-South 中南	87	190	40,255	1,599	6.34	14.30	46.85	55.66	25,226
Henan 河南	7	107	12,206	930	16.26	24.06	22.26	32.43	5,717
Hubei 湖北	4	144	18,254	495	7.02	22.51	46.31	68.83	7,051
Hunan 湖南	7	78	8,013	512	8.84	15.16	34.89	41.70	5,795
Guangdong 广东	51	211	58,184	2,274	6.18	13.84	55.40	55.37	36,819
Guangxi 广西	11	301	19,730	760	11.26	24.89	20.45	54.75	6,744
Hainan 海南	7	81	14,744	395	2.06	6.59	83.99	68.67	19,126
Southwest 西南	6	192	21,108	-1,469	-2.93	-9.61	26.43	69.48	50,090
Chongqing 重庆									
Sichuan 四川	3	311	40,371	648	0.84	1.60	39.89	47.67	77,463
Guizhou 贵州									
Yunnan 云南	3	73	1,845	-3,587	-15.79		-31.25	143.85	22,717
Tibet 西藏									
Northwest 西北	7	66	5,646	285	1.63	4.89	28.24	66.67	17,512
Shaanxi 陕西	2	123	13,098	772	1.49	4.31	29.45	65.33	51,632
Gansu 甘肃	4	29	90	-92	-5.05	-31.09	24.04	83.76	1,827
Qinghai 青海									
Ningxia 宁夏									
Xinjiang 新疆	1	100	12,967	823	6.85	21.25	30.17	67.75	12,010

2033: Domestic Wood Products 生活用木制品业

Year 年份	Number of firms 企业个数	Rate of change 变化率 (%)	Number of employees 职工人数 (人)	Rate of change 变化率 (%)	Total revenue (Mil. RMB) 总销售收入 (百万元)	Rate of change 变化率 (%)	Total profit (Mil RMB) 总利润 (百万元)	Rate of change 变化率 (%)
2000	326		46,314		6,209		198	
2001	333	2.15	55,827	20.54	7,492	20.66	253	27.78
2002	332	-0.30	53,409	-4.33	7,903	5.49	269	6.32

Major Products 主要产品	Output 产量	Unit 单位
Wood Articles For Life 生活用木制品	77	100,000,000 Yuan 亿元

10 Main Firms with Maximal Revenue (year founded) 收入最大的十家主要企业（创办年份）	City 城市	Province 省	Telephone/fax 电话/传真	Number of employees 职工人数	Ownership 产业所有权	Revenue ('000 RMB) 销售收入（千元）	Profit('000 RMB) (rank) 利润(千元)(排名)	Total assets ('000 RMB) 总资产（千元）	Major products 主要产品
Guangdong Yihua Timber Industry Co.,Ltd.	Shantou	Guangdong	(0754)5100989		Private Owned				Floor
广东省宜华企业（集团）有限公司(1995)	汕头市	广东省	(0754)5745583	2,782	私营企业	1,680,000	96,028(1)	916,944	地板
Tianjin Jiawen Industrial Co., Ltd.	Tianjin	Tianjin	(022)26950683		Overseas Chinese-funded				Wooden Persian Blinds
天津嘉文实业有限公司(1994)	天津市	天津市	(022)26950681	350	港澳台资	247,710	21,880(2)	77,240	木百叶窗帘
Shanghai Xiehe Timber Industry Co., Ltd.	Shanghai	Shanghai	(021)59100911		Foreign Funded				Wooden Products
上海协和木业有限公司(1994)	上海市	上海市	(021)59101340	210	外商投资	111,995	12,756(3)	80,018	木制品
Lisen (Boluo) Wooden Articles Co.,Ltd.	Huizhou	Guangdong	(0752)6657228		Overseas Chinese-funded				Wooden Persian Blinds
立森（博罗）木器有限公司(1992)	惠州市	广东省	(0752)6657237	538	港澳台资	108,754	8,222(6)	149,168	木百叶窗帘
Xiamen Shangmao Decoration Industry Co.,Ltd.	Xiamen	Fujian	(0592)6025725		Foreign Funded				Curtain Suspended Utensils
厦门尚贸家饰工业有限公司(1992)	厦门市	福建省	(0592)6025726	916	外商投资	108,350	1,012(58)	77,185	窗帘吊具
Sichuan Haoyun Group Co.,Ltd.	Guangyuan	Sichuan	(0839)3370349		Limited-Liability				Wooden Floor
四川豪运集团有限公司(1983)	广元市	四川省	(0839)3370841	745	有限公司	98,123	1,526(40)	213,871	实木地板
Tianjin Foya Industrial Co.,Ltd.	Tianjin	Tianjin	(022)26785010		Overseas Chinese-funded				Floor
天津福亚实业有限公司(1995)	天津市	天津市	(022)26321396	312	港澳台资	90,655	1,551(38)	159,132	地板
Heiling Xida Timber Industry Co., ltd.	Mudanjiang	Heilongjiang	(0453)3199081		Private Owned				Wood Sticker
穆棱市悉达木业有限公司(1999)	牡丹江市	黑龙江省	(0453)3199081	120	私营企业	72,190	4,160(10)	21,290	木签
Xiamen Quanyu Wood Products Co.,Ltd.	Xiamen	Fujian	(0592)5217051		Overseas Chinese-funded				Wooden Products
厦门权昱木材制品有限公司(1999)	厦门市	福建省	(0592)5217052	1,130	港澳台资	67,824	-	61,042	木材制品
Fuzhou Jinshan Wood Products Co.,Ltd.	Fuzhou	Fujian	(0591)3747168		Foreign Funded				Wooden Floor
福州金山木材制品有限公司(1993)	福州市	福建省	(0591)3747188	277	外商投资	67,139	-	49,050	木地板

Top 10 Cities by Revenue 销售收入排名前10位城市	Province 省	Market share 市场份额 (%)	Number of firms 企业个数
Shantou 汕头市	Guangdong 广东省	21.26	1
Dalian 大连市	Liaoning 辽宁省	6.57	25
Tianjin 天津市	Tianjin 天津市	6.48	12
Zhaoqing 肇庆市	Guangdong 广东省	4.43	20
Shanghai 上海市	Shanghai 上海市	4.14	16
Guangzhou 广州市	Guangdong 广东省	4.04	10
Nanjing 南京市	Jiangsu 江苏省	3.07	4
Xiamen 厦门市	Fujian 福建省	2.85	6
Guilin 桂林市	Guangxi 广西	2.24	5
Dandong 丹东市	Liaoning 辽宁省	2.17	6

10 Major Wholesalers 十家主要批发商	City 城市	Province 省	Telephone/Fax 电话/传真
Shanghai Xinmei (Group) Co.,Ltd.	Shanghai	Shanghai	(021)58120888
上海新美（集团）有限公司	上海市	上海市	(021)67559188
Guangdong Native Products Import & Export (Group) Corporation	Guangzhou	Guangdong	(020)84244025
广东省土产进出口（集团）公司	广州市	广东省	(020)84423070
China Timber Import & Export Co.,Ltd.	Beijing	Beijing	(010)64203414
中国木材进出口股份有限公司	北京市	北京市	(010)64208900
Xiamen Yongquan Group Co.,Ltd.	Xiamen	Fujian	(0592)5161286
厦门涌泉集团有限公司	厦门市	福建省	(0592)5162966
China National Forest Products Marketing Co.	Beijing	Beijing	(010)64228370
中国林产品经销公司	北京市	北京市	(010)64216443
Liaoning Huiming International Trade Co.,Ltd.	Dalian	Liaoning	(0411)3620626
大连市辽宁汇明国际贸易有限公司	大连市	辽宁省	(0411)3636995
Shanghai Senda Wood Industry Co.,Ltd.	Shanghai	Shanghai	(021)54367592
上海森大木业有限公司	上海市	上海市	(021)54360331
Shanghai Timber General Corp.	Shanghai	Shanghai	(021)63230138
上海市木材总公司	上海市	上海市	(021)63236079
Guangdong Nanyou Economic Development Corp.	Guangzhou	Guangdong	(020)87304129
广东南油经济发展公司	广州市	广东省	(020)87756069
Zhuhai S.E.Z.Materials Company	Zhuhai	Guangdong	(0756)2116092
珠海经济特区物资公司	珠海市	广东省	(0756)2116718

2040: Bamboo, Rattan, Palm and Straw Products 竹、藤、棕、草制品业

The industry accounts for 0.044% of the total revenue of China's industrial sector in 2002. The rate of return on assets is 7.13%. 84.64% of all firms in the industry made a profit while 15.36% had negative returns.The top province in terms of the industry's revenue is Zhejiang, accounting for 26.11% of the total revenue.
2002年本行业收入占全行业的 0.044%，资产利润率为 7.13%。84.64%的企业赢利，15.36%的企业亏损。收入最高的省为浙江省，占本行业的26.11%。

	Total number of firms 企业总数	Total number of employees 职工总数	Total revenue (Mil.RMB) 总销售收入 (百万元)	Total profit (Mil.RMB) 总利润 (百万元)	Return on assets 资产利润率 (%)	Return on equity 权益利润率 (%)	Labour productivity ('000 RMB/ worker) 劳动生产率 (千元/人)	Debts/ assets 资产负债率 (%)	Total assets (Mil.RMB) 总资产 (百万元)
Industry Overall 行业总体	306	48,053	4,675	181	7.13	14.34	27.09	50.26	2,537

	Number of firms 企业个数	Average number of employees 平均职工人数	Average revenue ('000 RMB) 平均销售收入（千元）	Average profit ('000 RMB) 平均利润 (千元)	Return on assets 资产利润率 (%)	Return on equity 权益利润率 (%)	Labour productivity ('000 RMB/ worker) 劳动生产率 (千元/人)	Debts/ assets 资产负债率 (%)	Average total assets ('000 RMB) 平均总资产 (千元)
By ownership 产业所有权									
State-owned 国有	8	44	3,121	25	0.71	1.25	26.70	43.47	3,547
Collective-owned 集体	39	215	15,049	869	16.94	31.56	20.81	46.34	5,133
Foreign & Overseas Chinese Funded 三资	96	148	15,928	497	4.52	9.21	27.14	50.97	10,992
By regional distribution 地区分布									
Central-North 华北	10	77	19,122	983	19.86	48.24	69.92	58.84	4,951
Beijing 北京	1	160	35,270	845	12.77	24.14	45.27	47.08	6,616
Tianjin 天津	7	68	18,629	1,057	25.26	71.84	82.27	64.84	4,185
Hebei 河北	2	69	12,770	793	11.66	24.10	55.99	51.62	6,796
Shanxi 山西									
Inner Mongolia 内蒙古									
Northeast 东北	4	125	6,765	347	5.16	14.83	21.99	65.21	6,716
Liaoning 辽宁	3	153	6,153	309	4.01	13.77	16.48	70.89	7,702
Jilin 吉林									
Heilongjiang 黑龙江	1	43	8,600	460	12.23	17.56	80.70	30.32	3,760
Central-East 华东	186	150	13,931	721	8.55	17.07	24.03	49.94	8,431
Shanghai 上海	8	91	16,223	112	0.91	1.85	30.88	50.96	12,389
Jiangsu 江苏	13	107	18,171	412	5.46	13.94	58.30	60.83	7,552
Zhejiang 浙江	96	81	12,715	553	7.17	14.29	35.48	49.80	7,708
Anhui 安徽	20	582	20,264	2,182	21.65	51.30	10.02	57.80	10,079
Fujian 福建	30	134	12,337	543	7.14	12.54	26.39	43.04	7,599
Jiangxi 江西	9	138	7,260	267	6.49	9.63	18.14	32.59	4,111
Shandong 山东	10	120	16,386	1,238	7.52	14.28	40.33	47.31	16,448
Central-South 中南	97	179	18,566	380	4.41	8.51	31.24	48.19	8,626
Henan 河南	9	159	11,875	772	8.62	17.78	22.12	51.50	8,955
Hubei 湖北	7	82	13,474	752	10.09	14.39	53.22	29.84	7,448
Hunan 湖南	25	325	27,775	227	1.85	3.77	28.74	50.99	12,287
Guangdong 广东	44	129	18,596	403	5.05	9.34	40.13	45.95	7,974
Guangxi 广西	12	133	7,259	108	2.81	7.32	12.68	61.62	3,833
Hainan 海南									
Southwest 西南	8	176	8,117	-154	-2.22	-9.27	14.28	76.01	6,905
Chongqing 重庆	1	205	4,943	-19	-1.20	-3.95	6.39	69.71	1,588
Sichuan 四川	4	105	8,029	105	1.59	5.35	15.80	70.19	6,554
Guizhou 贵州	3	261	9,292	-542	-5.93	-32.84	15.52	81.94	9,146
Yunnan 云南									
Tibet 西藏									
Northwest 西北	1	13	5	2	0.54	0.56	75.92	3.52	369
Shaanxi 陕西									
Gansu 甘肃	1	13	5	2	0.54	0.56	75.92	3.52	369
Qinghai 青海									
Ningxia 宁夏									
Xinjiang 新疆									

2040: Bamboo, Rattan, Palm and Straw Products 竹、藤、棕、草制品业

Year 年份	Number of firms 企业个数	Rate of change 变化率 (%)	Number of employees 职工人数 (人)	Rate of change 变化率 (%)	Total revenue (Mil. RMB) 总销售收入 (百万元)	Rate of change 变化率 (%)	Total profit (Mil RMB) 总利润 (百万元)	Rate of change 变化率 (%)
2000	223		38,488		3,130		139	
2001	261	17.04	42,648	10.81	4,076	30.22	150	7.91
2002	306	17.24	48,053	12.67	4,675	14.70	181	20.67

Major Products 主要产品	Output 产量	Unit 单位

10 Main Firms with Maximal Revenue (year founded) 收入最大的十家主要企业（创办年份）	City 城市	Province 省	Telephone/fax 电话/传真	Number of employees 职工人数	Ownership 产业所有权	Revenue ('000 RMB) 销售收入 (千元)	Profit('000 RMB) (rank) 利润(千元) (排名)	Total assets ('000 RMB) 总资产 (千元)	Major products 主要产品
Qidong Jinqiao Straw Mat Group Co.,Ltd.	Hengyang	Hunan	(0734)6320378		Private Owned				Straw Mat
祁东县金桥草席集团有限公司(2000)	衡阳市	湖南省		4,350	私营企业	373,600	3,940(5)	69,600	草席
Shouxian Banqiao Straw Mat Group Company	Lu'an	Anhui	(0564)4599118		Joint Stock				Straw Mat
寿县板桥草席集团公司(1993)	六安市	安徽省		3,000	股份制	165,600	18,900(2)	47,070	草席
Hengshan Straw Mat Group Company	Hengyang	Hunan	(0734)5951123		Joint Stock				Straw Mat
衡山县草席集团公司(1996)	衡阳市	湖南省		1,000	股份制	117,130	1,054(48)	12,540	草席
Xiangtan Hengdun (Group) Kitchenware General Factory	Xiangtan	Hunan	(0732)8289777		Joint Stock				Bamboo Chopping Block
湘潭市恒盾(集团)厨房用具制品总厂(1999)	湘潭市	湖南省	(0732)8289555	280	股份制	57,428	105(163)	12,067	竹砧板
Sino Basket(Tianjin) Arts Co., Ltd.	Tianjin	Tianjin	(022)23928264		Overseas Chinese-funded				Woven Products
塞纳篮(天津)工艺品有限公司(1993)	天津市	天津市	(022)23928263	52	港澳台资	43,276	476(97)	10,264	编制品
Guangdong Sihui Wanli Rattan Products Co., Ltd.	Zhaoqing	Guangdong	(0758)3866404		Overseas Chinese-funded				Rattan Woven Products
四会万利藤业制品有限公司(1995)	肇庆市	广东省	(0758)3866474	85	港澳台资	42,822	1,564(35)	12,408	藤制品
Guangning Dayu Bamboo Products Co., Ltd.	Zhaoqing	Guangdong	(0758)8628480		Collective-owned				Round Bamboo Bone
广宁县大宇竹制品有限公司(1998)	肇庆市	广东省		172	集体企业	39,807	1,194(41)	7,480	圆型竹骨
Guangzhou Guanghong Fibre Products Co.,Ltd.	Guangzhou	Guangdong	(020)82611511		Overseas Chinese-funded				Coconut Fibre Mat椰
广州广鸿纤维制品有限公司(1992)	广州市	广东省	(020)82614511	100	港澳台资	39,249	-	20,499	子纤维垫
Nibo Kaseen Arts & Crafts Co.,Ltd	Ningbo	Zhejiang	(0574)88016321		Foreign Funded				Tatami
宁波开诚工艺品有限公司(2000)	宁波市	浙江省	(0574)88110209	114	外商投资	38,815	1,574(32)	18,346	榻榻米
Yixing Xingli Bamboo & Wood Products Co.,Ltd.	Wuxi	Jiangsu	(0510)7341124		Overseas Chinese-funded				Bamboo Floor
宜兴兴立竹木制品有限公司(1989)	无锡市	江苏省	(0510)7342226	368	港澳台资	36,172	580(85)	27,783	竹地板

Top 10 Cities by Revenue 销售收入排名前10位城市	Province 省	Market share 市场份额 (%)	Number of firms 企业个数
Huzhou 湖州市	Zhejiang 浙江省	12.63	44
Hengyang 衡阳市	Hunan 湖南省	10.56	3
Zhaoqing 肇庆市	Guangdong 广东省	8.58	18
Ningbo 宁波市	Zhejiang 浙江省	8.18	28
Lu'an 六安市	Anhui 安徽省	6.10	4
Tianjin 天津市	Tianjin 天津市	2.79	7
Shanghai 上海市	Shanghai 上海市	2.78	8
Jiangmen 江门市	Guangdong 广东省	2.65	2
Fuzhou 福州市	Fujian 福建省	2.56	12
Sanming 三明市	Fujian 福建省	2.18	4

10 Major Wholesalers 十家主要批发商	City 城市	Province 省	Telephone/Fax 电话/传真
Harbin ChinaSun Group Co., Ltd.	Harbin	Heilongjiang	(0451)84885100
哈尔滨中央红集团股份有限公司	哈尔滨市	黑龙江省	(0451)84885111
Guangzhou Yuexiu Enterprise (Group) Company	Guangzhou	Guangdong	(020)85597130
广州越秀企业（集团）公司	广州市	广东省	(020)85599018
China Reed Screen Imp. & Exp. Corp.Ltd.	Beijing	Beijing	(010)65521133
中艺苇帘进出口有限责任公司	北京市	北京市	(010)65513995
Hebei Xintai Foreign Trade Corp.ltd.	Shijiazhuang	Hebei	(0311)7767908
河北信泰对外贸易有限公司	石家庄市	河北省	(0311)7755347
Hebei Arts & Crafts Imp. & Exp. Corp.	Shijiazhuang	Hebei	(0311)7764345
河北省工艺品进出口公司	石家庄市	河北省	(0311)7755347
Shanghai Hengda Ceramic Building Materials Trade Market	Shanghai	Shanghai	(021)58425842
上海恒大陶瓷建材交易市场	上海市	上海市	(021)58427389
Hangzhou Local Product General Corporation	Hangzhou	Zhejiang	(0571)87026301
杭州市土特产总公司	杭州市	浙江省	(0571)87026323
Ningbo Zhonglin Foreign Trade Co.,Ltd.	Ningbo	Zhejiang	(0574)87871797
宁波中蔺对外贸易有限公司	宁波市	浙江省	(0574)87871790
Wuyi Local Products Daily Groceries Co.,Ltd.	Jinhua	Zhejiang	(0579)7623401
武义县土产日用杂品有限责任公司	金华市	浙江省	(0579)7623401
Guangdong Shunde Local Products Import & Export Company	Foshan	Guangdong	(0765)6682839
广东省顺德土产进出口公司	佛山市	广东省	(0765)6681441

2110: Wood Furniture 木制家具制造业

The industry accounts for 0.281% of the total revenue of China's industrial sector in 2002. The rate of return on assets is 4.38%. 82.63% of all firms in the industry made a profit while 17.37% had negative returns.The top province in terms of the industry's revenue is Guangdong, accounting for 25.85% of the total revenue.
2002年本行业收入占全行业的 0.281%，资产利润率为 4.38%。82.63%的企业赢利，17.37%的企业亏损。收入最高的省为广东省，占本行业的25.85%。

	Total number of firms 企业总数	Total number of employees 职工总数	Total revenue (Mil.RMB) 总销售收入 (百万元)	Total profit (Mil.RMB) 总利润 (百万元)	Return on assets 资产利润率 (%)	Return on equity 权益利润率 (%)	Labour productivity ('000 RMB/ worker) 劳动生产率 (千元/人)	Debts/ assets 资产负债率 (%)	Total assets (Mil.RMB) 总资产 (百万元)
Industry Overall 行业总体	1186	223,607	30,158	1,236	4.38	9.57	38.24	54.29	28,246

	Number of firms 企业个数	Average number of employees 平均职工人数	Average revenue ('000 RMB) 平均销售收入 (千元)	Average profit ('000 RMB) 平均利润 (千元)	Return on assets 资产利润率 (%)	Return on equity 权益利润率 (%)	Labour productivity ('000 RMB/ worker) 劳动生产率 (千元/人)	Debts/ assets 资产负债率 (%)	Average total assets ('000 RMB) 平均总资产 (千元)
By ownership 产业所有权									
State-owned 国有	93	89	5,829	-316	-2.90	-12.14	14.41	76.14	10,902
Collective-owned 集体	149	164	27,074	1,099	7.54	17.12	43.37	55.92	14,570
Foreign & Overseas Chinese Funded 三资	356	274	37,963	1,574	4.14	9.54	39.34	56.66	38,068
By regional distribution 地区分布									
Central-North 华北	150	184	28,504	2,014	7.26	16.56	44.00	56.15	27,731
Beijing 北京	56	138	14,943	282	1.78	4.30	27.46	58.58	15,847
Tianjin 天津	37	243	55,865	5,162	11.64	26.28	65.63	55.72	44,354
Hebei 河北	47	200	28,423	1,976	6.14	13.91	42.78	55.86	32,196
Shanxi 山西	5	208	4,910	464	3.75	7.10	8.64	47.15	12,372
Inner Mongolia 内蒙古	5	103	2,275	8	0.07	0.13	7.81	48.30	11,210
Northeast 东北	83	301	30,139	1,758	3.14	6.07	33.53	48.30	55,980
Liaoning 辽宁	41	207	32,687	2,836	4.99	7.69	52.60	35.11	56,845
Jilin 吉林	11	222	11,290	-806	-2.19	-13.60	13.28	83.93	36,881
Heilongjiang 黑龙江	31	453	33,457	1,242	2.02	4.67	25.50	56.83	61,613
Central-East 华东	449	177	27,107	1,012	4.39	10.74	41.57	59.10	23,039
Shanghai 上海	86	144	24,532	634	2.40	6.14	37.43	61.00	26,474
Jiangsu 江苏	78	156	26,902	845	3.11	8.76	48.63	64.48	27,147
Zhejiang 浙江	75	138	29,106	1,069	5.17	11.63	41.52	55.58	20,685
Anhui 安徽	13	222	24,589	2,211	5.81	9.60	32.85	39.52	38,068
Fujian 福建	43	266	31,240	-265	-1.04	-2.32	36.21	55.14	25,533
Jiangxi 江西	21	127	5,417	102	1.59	4.77	15.13	66.61	6,405
Shandong 山东	133	207	30,099	1,760	8.76	21.98	46.01	60.14	20,087
Central-South 中南	406	189	24,818	653	3.67	8.29	36.76	55.74	17,797
Henan 河南	48	141	13,960	747	9.18	22.30	33.40	58.85	8,144
Hubei 湖北	44	106	17,041	892	8.65	16.38	67.62	47.17	10,309
Hunan 湖南	26	76	23,092	798	10.78	17.46	96.46	38.25	7,401
Guangdong 广东	276	220	28,244	593	2.78	6.42	33.48	56.65	21,300
Guangxi 广西	4	71	5,170	334	9.48	50.76	22.28	81.31	3,522
Hainan 海南	8	297	29,957	525	1.42	3.29	22.06	56.74	36,942
Southwest 西南	38	198	12,048	147	0.92	1.69	20.27	45.20	15,945
Chongqing 重庆	12	143	13,256	390	3.14	6.18	26.98	49.20	12,410
Sichuan 四川	14	298	19,385	533	3.11	6.35	24.46	51.05	17,135
Guizhou 贵州	4	76	2,700	-126	-2.20	-4.25	8.09	48.25	5,703
Yunnan 云南	1	343	10,152	-8,939	-11.00	-34.22	2.74	67.84	81,237
Tibet 西藏	7	143	916	415	2.57	2.87	0.93	10.65	16,153
Northwest 西北	60	123	11,270	1,052	4.99	6.82	30.36	26.80	21,065
Shaanxi 陕西	14	193	5,538	47	0.32	0.60	9.89	46.82	14,703
Gansu 甘肃	30	82	2,752	-135	-2.69	-8.85	20.64	69.57	5,014
Qinghai 青海	3	35	470	-104	-4.44	-6.50	7.34	31.62	2,333
Ningxia 宁夏	1	129	9,141	119	1.49	2.13	18.79	30.21	7,998
Xinjiang 新疆	12	165	42,128	5,559	7.47	8.78	72.31	14.91	74,385

2110: Wood Furniture 木制家具制造业

Year 年份	Number of firms 企业个数	Rate of change 变化率 (%)	Number of employees 职工人数 (人)	Rate of change 变化率 (%)	Total revenue (Mil. RMB) 总销售收入 (百万元)	Rate of change 变化率 (%)	Total profit (Mil RMB) 总利润 (百万元)	Rate of change 变化率 (%)
2000	1061		178,528		21,898		938	
2001	1095	3.20	194,806	9.12	24,092	10.02	1,076	14.71
2002	1186	8.31	223,607	14.78	30,158	25.18	1,236	14.87

Major Products 主要产品	Output 产量	Unit 单位
Furniture 家具	13,376	10,000 Pieces 万件
Wooden Furniture 木制家具	5,495	10,000 Pieces 万件

10 Main Firms with Maximal Revenue (year founded) 收入最大的十家主要企业（创办年份）	City 城市	Province 省	Telephone/fax 电话/传真	Number of employees 职工人数	Ownership 产业所有权	Revenue ('000 RMB) 销售收入 (千元)	Profit('000 RMB) (rank) 利润(千元) (排名)	Total assets ('000 RMB) 总资产 (千元)	Major products 主要产品
Markor Furniture(Tianjin) International Co.,Ltd.	Tianjin	Tianjin	(022)66201276		Overseas Chinese-funded				Wooden Furniture
美克国际家私(天津)制造有限公司(1997)	天津市	天津市	(022)25320858	1,522	港澳台资	530,475	62,943(2)	607,549	木制家具
Dalian Huafeng Furniture Co.,Ltd.	Dalian	Liaoning	(0411)8702688		Foreign Funded				Wooden Furniture
大连华丰家俱有限公司(1988)	大连市	辽宁省	(0411)8613307	1,750	外商投资	470,270	88,510(1)	808,080	木制家具
Zhaoqing Yuemei Furniture Co.,Ltd.	Zhaoqing	Guangdong	(0758)8495888		Overseas Chinese-funded				Furniture
肇庆粤美家私有限公司(1993)	肇庆市	广东省	(0758)8495017	1,453	港澳台资	240,064	7,995(33)	75,128	家具
Shandong Wanjiayuan Group Co., Ltd.	Zibo	Shandong	(0533)8555876		Limited-Liability				Office Work Furniture
山东万家园集团股份有限公司(2001)	淄博市	山东省		689	有限公司	237,966	17,102(13)	110,009	办公家具
Tsingtao Liangmu Stock Co.,Ltd.	Qingdao	Shandong	(0532)4903641		Collective-owned				Wooden Furniture
青岛良木股份有限公司(2000)	青岛市	山东省	(0532)4907872	1,480	集体企业	237,692	8,687(30)	90,310	实木家具
Guangming Group Furniture Co.,Ltd.	Yichun	Heilongjiang	(0458)3667170		Joint Stock				Jointed Board of Tung Wood
光明集团家具股份有限公司(1992)	伊春市	黑龙江省	(0458)3666097	2,827	股份制	230,750	1,800(173)	900,000	桐木拼板
Qingdao Wooden Articles No.11 Factory	Qingdao	Shandong	(0532)8183211		Joint Stock				Wooden Furniture
青岛木器十一厂(1976)	青岛市	山东省	(0532)8185111	750	股份制	230,000	5,056(55)	164,670	木制家具
Shenyang Hongfa Furniture Co., Ltd.	Shenyang	Liaoning	(024)89361253		Limited-Liability				Wooden Furniture
沈阳宏发家具有限公司(1998)	沈阳市	辽宁省	(024)89361730	1,200	有限公司	215,969	14,310(20)	292,037	木制家具
Wenden Xingdu Technology Furniture Company	Weihai	Shandong	(0631)8545027		Foreign Funded				Office Work Furniture
文登星都工艺家具有限公司(1993)	威海市	山东省	(0631)8545173	160	外商投资	215,000	21,500(8)	24,920	办公家具
Tianjin Longqing Co.,Ltd.	Tianjin	Tianjin	(022)27471587		Joint Stock				Furniture
天津市隆庆股份有限公司(1999)	天津市	天津市	(022)27374219	1,472	股份制	214,880	23,284(7)	426,482	家具

Top 10 Cities by Revenue 销售收入排名前10位城市	Province 省	Market share 市场份额 (%)	Number of firms 企业个数
Shanghai 上海市	Shanghai 上海市	7.00	86
Tianjin 天津市	Tianjin 天津市	6.85	37
Guangzhou 广州市	Guangdong 广东省	5.05	54
Dongguan 东莞市	Guangdong 广东省	3.05	26
Huzhou 湖州市	Zhejiang 浙江省	2.99	7
Qingdao 青岛市	Shandong 山东省	2.96	21
Foshan 佛山市	Guangdong 广东省	2.91	34
Dalian 大连市	Liaoning 辽宁省	2.80	15
Beijing 北京市	Beijing 北京市	2.77	56
Shenzhen 深圳市	Guangdong 广东省	2.69	21

10 Major Wholesalers 十家主要批发商	City 城市	Province 省	Telephone/Fax 电话/传真
Kunming Department Store Group Co.,Ltd.	Kunming	Yunnan	(0871)3313618
昆明百货集团股份有限公司	昆明市	云南省	(0871)3314961
Jiangsu Skyrun International Group	Nanjing	Jiangsu	(025)4468888
江苏开元国际集团	南京市	江苏省	(025)4209409
Guangdong Light Industry Products Imp.& Exp.(Group) Corporation	Guangzhou	Guangdong	(020)83344557
广东省轻工业品进出口（集团）公司	广州市	广东省	(020)83330181
Shanghai Cheer (Group) Co.,Ltd.	Shanghai	Shanghai	(021)63069764
上海七百（集团）有限公司	上海市	上海市	(021)63069537
Fujian Tiancheng Group Co.,Ltd.	Fuzhou	Fujian	(0591)7503388
福建天成集团有限公司	福州市	福建省	(0591)7609279
Shanghai Century Lianhua Supermaket Development Co.,ltd.	Shanghai	Shanghai	(021)53544600
上海世纪联华超市发展有限公司	上海市	上海市	(021)62252610
Suzhou General Merchandise General Company	Suzhou	Jiangsu	(0512)65222247
苏州百货总公司	苏州市	江苏省	(0512)65222247
Zhejiang Light Industry Products Import & Export Corporation	Hangzhou	Zhejiang	(0571)88391888
浙江省轻工业品进出口公司	杭州市	浙江省	(0571)88391666
Zhejiang Winsun Import & Export Co., Ltd.	Jiaxing	Zhejiang	(0573)2117091
浙江汇信进出口有限公司	嘉兴市	浙江省	(0573)2117020
Shenzhen CATIC Trade Company	Shenzhen	Guangdong	(0755)83790111
深圳中航商贸公司	深圳市	广东省	(0755)83790462

2130: Metal Furniture 金属家具制造业

The industry accounts for 0.108% of the total revenue of China's industrial sector in 2002. The rate of return on assets is 4.37%. 84.83% of all firms in the industry made a profit while 15.17% had negative returns.The top province in terms of the industry's revenue is Guangdong, accounting for 27.63% of the total revenue.
2002年本行业收入占全行业的 0.108%，资产利润率为 4.37%。84.83%的企业赢利，15.17%的企业亏损。收入最高的省为广东省，占本行业的27.63%。

	Total number of firms 企业总数	Total number of employees 职工总数	Total revenue (Mil.RMB) 总销售收入 (百万元)	Total profit (Mil.RMB) 总利润 (百万元)	Return on assets 资产利润率 (%)	Return on equity 权益利润率 (%)	Labour productivity ('000 RMB/worker) 劳动生产率 (千元/人)	Debts/assets 资产负债率 (%)	Total assets (Mil.RMB) 总资产 (百万元)
Industry Overall 行业总体	356	72,515	11,546	430	4.37	10.26	47.90	57.43	9,849

	Number of firms 企业个数	Average number of employees 平均职工人数	Average revenue ('000 RMB) 平均销售收入 (千元)	Average profit ('000 RMB) 平均利润 (千元)	Return on assets 资产利润率 (%)	Return on equity 权益利润率 (%)	Labour productivity ('000 RMB/worker) 劳动生产率 (千元/人)	Debts/assets 资产负债率 (%)	Average total assets ('000 RMB) 平均总资产 (千元)
By ownership 产业所有权									
State-owned 国有	21	68	2,891	-197	-1.52	-5.88	18.54	74.21	13,017
Collective-owned 集体	46	115	13,761	115	1.08	4.00	32.98	72.91	10,571
Foreign & Overseas Chinese Funded 三资	99	390	64,465	2,114	3.81	9.04	50.67	57.85	55,469
By regional distribution 地区分布									
Central-North 华北	47	222	34,470	1,342	2.87	6.15	55.36	53.26	46,687
Beijing 北京	15	245	47,797	2,819	6.22	13.35	42.64	53.45	45,350
Tianjin 天津	16	287	42,282	980	1.18	2.58	74.92	54.16	83,015
Hebei 河北	11	133	15,539	567	4.59	7.18	35.35	36.12	12,362
Shanxi 山西	5	144	11,139	-226	-2.26	-8.47	36.17	73.27	9,966
Inner Mongolia 内蒙古									
Northeast 东北	6	253	34,479	3,615	14.65	21.67	41.19	32.40	24,681
Liaoning 辽宁	1	11	128				4.27	93.04	158
Jilin 吉林	1	160	5,740				9.86	102.09	6,210
Heilongjiang 黑龙江	4	336	50,251	5,422	15.30	21.64	45.21	29.28	35,429
Central-East 华东	145	215	39,352	1,650	5.84	13.11	48.25	55.43	28,237
Shanghai 上海	19	136	38,620	4,969	19.73	36.94	84.55	46.59	25,182
Jiangsu 江苏	25	171	39,178	843	2.17	4.35	96.78	50.03	38,776
Zhejiang 浙江	67	208	38,274	1,326	4.98	12.05	36.20	58.66	26,620
Anhui 安徽									
Fujian 福建	28	340	48,798	1,354	4.77	10.73	36.87	55.58	28,408
Jiangxi 江西									
Shandong 山东	6	140	10,356	-495	-4.39		18.12	108.67	11,260
Central-South 中南	137	203	28,261	753	3.27	8.97	45.52	63.55	23,029
Henan 河南	20	137	20,315	2,777	36.51	43.83	48.72	16.69	7,606
Hubei 湖北	9	191	28,361	1,323	7.11	47.34	51.34	84.99	18,618
Hunan 湖南	1	157	13,650	110	7.95		24.34	156.72	1,384
Guangdong 广东	106	217	30,098	335	1.26	3.56	45.08	64.69	26,621
Guangxi 广西	1	137	6,156	48	0.40	1.97	8.28	79.77	12,047
Hainan 海南									
Southwest 西南	9	75	5,223	-189	-2.29	-4.26	23.68	46.10	8,231
Chongqing 重庆	2	40	3,183	407	28.98	30.38	34.48	4.60	1,403
Sichuan 四川	4	108	8,931	-693	-4.24	-8.10	26.70	47.65	16,346
Guizhou 贵州	1	94	3,889	1	0.03	0.09	14.41	63.16	2,934
Yunnan 云南									
Tibet 西藏	2	35	517	130	8.74	13.32	5.01	34.33	1,481
Northwest 西北	12	78	7,847	401	2.62	9.18	51.89	71.47	15,297
Shaanxi 陕西	3	70	7,479	372	3.95	9.21	26.14	57.05	9,414
Gansu 甘肃	7	57	4,800	375	14.62	26.21	39.92	44.22	2,562
Qinghai 青海									
Ningxia 宁夏									
Xinjiang 新疆	2	161	19,065	535	0.78	3.54	83.67	78.00	68,690

2130: Metal Furniture 金属家具制造业

Year 年份	Number of firms 企业个数	Rate of change 变化率 (%)	Number of employees 职工人数 (人)	Rate of change 变化率 (%)	Total revenue (Mil. RMB) 总销售收入 (百万元)	Rate of change 变化率 (%)	Total profit (Mil RMB) 总利润 (百万元)	Rate of change 变化率 (%)
2000	260		45,297		7,051		330	
2001	317	21.92	62,857	38.77	9,752	38.31	353	6.97
2002	356	12.30	72,515	15.37	11,546	18.40	430	21.81

Major Products 主要产品	Output 产量	Unit 单位
Metal Furniture 金属家具	6,118	10,000 Pieces 万件

10 Main Firms with Maximal Revenue (year founded) 收入最大的十家主要企业（创办年份）	City 城市	Province 省	Telephone/fax 电话/传真	Number of employees 职工人数	Ownership 产业所有权	Revenue ('000 RMB) 销售收入 (千元)	Profit('000 RMB) (rank) 利润(千元) (排名)	Total assets ('000 RMB) 总资产 (千元)	Major products 主要产品
Zhejiang Huayue Furniture Industry Co.,Ltd.	Hangzhou	Zhejiang	(0571)82836086		Foreign Funded				Steel Moulding Furniture
浙江华越家具工业有限公司(1998)	杭州市	浙江省	(0571)82835856	2,897	外商投资	539,536	20,012(6)	385,094	钢塑家具
Beijing Tiantan Co.,Ltd.	Beijing	Beijing	(010)84287502		Joint Stock				Furniture
北京天坛股份有限公司(1999)	北京市	北京市	(010)84285848	1,699	股份制	439,542	28,078(4)	429,275	家具
Xiamen Newtec Integration Co.,Ltd.	Xiamen	Fujian	(0592)5774869		Foreign Funded				Desk & Chair
厦门新技术集成有限公司(1993)	厦门市	福建省	(0592)5771055	1,519	外商投资	335,643	16,178(7)	166,029	桌椅
Zhejiang Himax Furniture Industry Co.,Ltd.	Hangzhou	Zhejiang	(0571)82618240		Foreign Funded				Steel Moulding Wood Furniture
浙江华邦家俱工业有限公司(1993)	杭州市	浙江省	(0571)82616689	658	外商投资	255,530	7,026(14)	92,750	钢塑木家俱
Feili Group (Fujian) Co., Ltd.	Quanzhou	Fujian	(0595)5983573		Overseas Chinese-funded				Furniture
菲莉集团（福建）有限公司(1996)	泉州市	福建省	(0595)5984487	800	港澳台资	209,966	13,060(10)	128,850	家具
Hangzhou Hongyue Furniture Ind Co.,Ltd.	Hangzhou	Zhejiang	(0571)82835223		Overseas Chinese-funded				Steel Moulding Wood Furniture
杭州宏越家具工业有限公司(2000)	杭州市	浙江省	(0571)82831495	450	港澳台资	196,903	1,467(70)	76,726	钢塑木家俱
Harbin Feiyun Industrial Co., Ltd.	Harbin	Heilongjiang	(0451)82630160		Limited-Liability				Iron Cabinet
哈尔滨飞云实业有限公司(1999)	哈尔滨市	黑龙江省	(0451)82805226	932	有限公司	185,218	21,488(5)	116,746	铁柜
Jiaxing Hero Metal Furniture Co., Ltd.	Jiaxing	Zhejiang	(0573)3544776		Private Owned				Aluminous Products
嘉兴市豪杰金属家具有限公司(1996)	嘉兴市	浙江省	(0573)3544116	1,500	私营企业	177,115	3,513(34)	89,787	铝制品
Quanzhou Feili Furniture Development Co., Ltd.	Quanzhou	Fujian	(0595)2480999		Overseas Chinese-funded				Steel-made Furniture
泉州市菲莉家俱发展有限公司(1999)	泉州市	福建省	(0595)2481999	850	港澳台资	145,375	8,978(11)	77,905	钢家俱
Xinhui Tianjian Steel Furniture factory	Jiangmen	Guangdong	(0750)6100755		Private Partnership				Steel-made Furniture
新会天健钢家具厂(1980)	江门市	广东省	(0750)6577368	1,368	私营合伙	139,748	229(169)	172,223	钢家具

Top 10 Cities by Revenue 销售收入排名前10位城市	Province 省	Market share 市场份额 (%)	Number of firms 企业个数
Hangzhou 杭州市	Zhejiang 浙江省	12.17	13
Shanghai 上海市	Shanghai 上海市	6.36	19
Beijing 北京市	Beijing 北京市	6.21	15
Tianjin 天津市	Tianjin 天津市	5.86	16
Shenzhen 深圳市	Guangdong 广东省	5.68	8
Xiamen 厦门市	Fujian 福建省	5.23	5
Suzhou 苏州市	Jiangsu 江苏省	5.09	10
Foshan 佛山市	Guangdong 广东省	5.04	20
Jiangmen 江门市	Guangdong 广东省	4.86	20
Huzhou 湖州市	Zhejiang 浙江省	4.12	24

10 Major Wholesalers 十家主要批发商	City 城市	Province 省	Telephone/Fax 电话/传真
Kunming Department Store Group Co.,Ltd.	Kunming	Yunnan	(0871)3313618
昆明百货集团股份有限公司	昆明市	云南省	(0871)3314961
Jiangsu Skyrun International Group	Nanjing	Jiangsu	(025)4468888
江苏开元国际集团	南京市	江苏省	(025)4209409
Guangdong Light Industry Products Imp.& Exp.(Group) Corporation	Guangzhou	Guangdong	(020)83344557
广东省轻工业品进出口（集团）公司	广州市	广东省	(020)83330181
Shanghai Cheer (Group) Co.,Ltd.	Shanghai	Shanghai	(021)63069764
上海七百（集团）有限公司	上海市	上海市	(021)63069537
Fujian Tiancheng Group Co.,Ltd.	Fuzhou	Fujian	(0591)7503388
福建天成集团有限公司	福州市	福建省	(0591)7609279
Shanghai Century Lianhua Supermaket Development Co.,ltd.	Shanghai	Shanghai	(021)53544600
上海世纪联华超市发展有限公司	上海市	上海市	(021)62252610
Suzhou General Merchandise General Company	Suzhou	Jiangsu	(0512)65222247
苏州百货总公司	苏州市	江苏省	(0512)65222247
Zhejiang Light Industry Products Import & Export Corporation	Hangzhou	Zhejiang	(0571)88391888
浙江省轻工业品进出口公司	杭州市	浙江省	(0571)88391666
Zhejiang Winsun Import & Export Co., Ltd	Jiaxing	Zhejiang	(0573)2117091
浙江汇信进出口有限公司	嘉兴市	浙江省	(0573)2117020
Shenzhen CATIC Trade Company	Shenzhen	Guangdong	(0755)83790111
深圳中航商贸公司	深圳市	广东省	(0755)83790462

2190: Other Furniture 其他家具制造业

The industry accounts for 0.061% of the total revenue of China's industrial sector in 2002. The rate of return on assets is 4.39%. 81.03% of all firms in the industry made a profit while 18.97% had negative returns.The top province in terms of the industry's revenue is Guangdong, accounting for 25.56% of the total revenue.
2002年本行业收入占全行业的0.061%，资产利润率为4.39%。81.03%的企业赢利，18.97%的企业亏损。收入最高的省为广东省，占本行业的25.56%。

	Total number of firms 企业总数	Total number of employees 职工总数	Total revenue (Mil.RMB) 总销售收入 (百万元)	Total profit (Mil.RMB) 总利润 (百万元)	Return on assets 资产利润率 (%)	Return on equity 权益利润率 (%)	Labour productivity ('000 RMB/ worker) 劳动生产率 (千元/人)	Debts/ assets 资产负债率 (%)	Total assets (Mil.RMB) 总资产 (百万元)
Industry Overall 行业总体	195	37,138	6,568	265	4.39	9.91	43.42	55.65	6,035

	Number of firms 企业个数	Average number of employees 平均职工人数	Average revenue ('000 RMB) 平均销售收入 (千元)	Average profit ('000 RMB) 平均利润 (千元)	Return on assets 资产利润率 (%)	Return on equity 权益利润率 (%)	Labour productivity ('000 RMB/ worker) 劳动生产率 (千元/人)	Debts/ assets 资产负债率 (%)	Average total assets ('000 RMB) 平均总资产 (千元)
By ownership 产业所有权									
State-owned 国有	8	166	14,890	-759	-2.01		21.81	107.21	37,714
Collective-owned 集体	22	205	43,055	1,717	4.06	11.78	56.39	65.54	42,317
Foreign & Overseas Chinese Funded 三资	71	233	40,110	1,717	5.23	10.44	47.46	49.85	32,810
By regional distribution 地区分布									
Central-North 华北	21	134	18,398	681	3.83	9.72	34.48	60.57	17,778
Beijing 北京	13	126	18,153	-210	-0.99	-2.74	34.46	63.99	21,259
Tianjin 天津	4	146	31,154	4,040	27.28	46.22	59.81	40.98	14,808
Hebei 河北	4	147	6,437	219	2.32	6.90	9.44	66.29	9,432
Shanxi 山西									
Inner Mongolia 内蒙古									
Northeast 东北	7	294	49,296	6,539	8.63	11.43	47.91	24.45	75,747
Liaoning 辽宁	4	150	23,579	1,532	7.53	9.69	38.54	22.31	20,344
Jilin 吉林	1	111	11,421	-2,753	-26.51	-137.31	14.59	80.69	10,384
Heilongjiang 黑龙江	2	674	119,667	21,199	9.67	12.64	54.81	23.51	219,235
Central-East 华东	82	159	36,313	1,329	3.89	8.86	53.43	56.10	34,153
Shanghai 上海	26	120	23,931	918	4.66	9.41	38.57	50.45	19,683
Jiangsu 江苏	11	162	36,388	668	1.04	2.90	45.42	64.25	64,484
Zhejiang 浙江	20	160	51,442	2,785	6.61	15.55	56.45	57.48	42,140
Anhui 安徽	2	148	10,942	48	0.60	1.67	33.61	64.17	8,038
Fujian 福建	11	211	59,739	1,004	4.26	9.36	89.73	54.54	23,597
Jiangxi 江西	2	88	9,475	404	2.18	4.03	36.88	46.01	18,536
Shandong 山东	10	210	22,841	1,010	2.38	4.58	41.67	48.05	42,395
Central-South 中南	74	235	36,055	1,192	5.01	13.38	38.48	62.58	23,798
Henan 河南	10	62	8,669	493	9.36	21.45	42.87	56.35	5,265
Hubei 湖北	5	270	34,061	1,301	7.28	12.45	43.54	41.53	17,863
Hunan 湖南	4	536	172,766	8,477	18.32	44.76	81.69	59.08	46,276
Guangdong 广东	51	249	32,919	924	3.47	10.49	30.92	66.90	26,614
Guangxi 广西	3	153	11,566	-61	-0.84	-1.32	25.88	36.73	7,344
Hainan 海南	1	86	6,446	-4,124	-7.55	-9.21	33.40	18.03	54,634
Southwest 西南	8	196	20,049	879	1.39	3.40	29.13	59.12	63,274
Chongqing 重庆	2	83	8,990	682	6.10	13.77	52.53	55.72	11,176
Sichuan 四川	3	336	35,900	2,032	1.40	3.24	28.62	56.63	144,690
Guizhou 贵州									
Yunnan 云南	3	133	11,571	-142	-0.86	-4.87	20.69	82.38	16,589
Tibet 西藏									
Northwest 西北	3	111	10,212	322	1.51	2.88	25.30	47.55	21,333
Shaanxi 陕西	2	153	14,670	443	1.55	2.87	25.16	45.90	28,506
Gansu 甘肃	1	28	1,298	81	1.16	2.97	26.89	61.02	6,988
Qinghai 青海									
Ningxia 宁夏									
Xinjiang 新疆									

2190: Other Furniture 其他家具制造业

Year 年份	Number of firms 企业个数	Rate of change 变化率 (%)	Number of employees 职工人数 (人)	Rate of change 变化率 (%)	Total revenue (Mil. RMB) 总销售收入 (百万元)	Rate of change 变化率 (%)	Total profit (Mil RMB) 总利润 (百万元)	Rate of change 变化率 (%)
2000	145		25,359		4,649		267	
2001	180	24.14	35,375	39.50	6,259	34.63	294	10.11
2002	195	8.33	37,138	4.98	6,568	4.94	265	-9.86

Major Products 主要产品	Output 产量	Unit 单位
Soft Ware Furniture (Inclding Mattress, Sofa) 软体家具（包括床垫、沙发）	880	10,000 Pieces 万件

10 Main Firms with Maximal Revenue (year founded) 收入最大的十家主要企业（创办年份）	City 城市	Province 省	Telephone/ fax 电话/传真	Number of employees 职工人数	Ownership 产业所有权	Revenue ('000 RMB) 销售收入 (千元)	Profit('000 RMB) (rank) 利润(千元) (排名)	Total assets ('000 RMB) 总资产 (千元)	Major products 主要产品
Fujian Zhengsheng Consumer Products Co.,Ltd.	Fuzhou	Fujian	(0591)3410195		Foreign Funded				Sand Beach Chairs
福建正盛日用品有限公司(1996)	福州市	福建省	(0591)3466369	1,372	外商投资	444,753	4,663(17)	169,773	沙滩椅
Decrco Shuhua Furniture (Shenzhen) Co., Ltd.	Shenzhen	Guangdong	(0755)84207514		Overseas Chinese-funded				Leather Sofa
迪高乐梳化家私(深圳)有限公司(1993)	深圳市	广东省	(0755)84891110	1,367	港澳台资	404,720	6,273(11)	157,656	真皮沙发
Zhejiang Huaweimei GroupCo.,Ltd.	Shaoxing	Zhejiang	(0575)4026666		Private Owned				Soft Cushion Mattresses软
浙江花为媒集团有限公司(1998)	绍兴市	浙江省	(0575)4021687	672	私营企业	366,969	13,169(5)	280,898	垫席梦思
Xilinmen Group Co..Ltd.	Shaoxing	Zhejiang	(0575)5160844		Private Owned				Furniture
喜临门集团有限公司(1984)	绍兴市	浙江省	(0575)5160798	509	私营企业	280,427	12,519(6)	258,706	家俱
Ebest (Shanghai) Co., Ltd.	Shanghai	Shanghai	(021)54386363		Overseas Chinese-funded				sofa
意特尔（上海）有限公司(2001)	上海市	上海市	(021)54385718	579	港澳台资	219,090	13,276(4)	246,363	沙发
Changzhou Hongxing Furniture Group Company	Changzhou	Jiangsu	(0519)5318888		Collective-owned				Furniture
常州红星家具集团公司(1998)	常州市	江苏省	(0519)5319088	652	集体企业	155,620	3,010(26)	531,440	家具
Shunde Jinbaoma Furniture Making Co., Ltd.	Foshan	Guangdong	(0765)3883180		Overseas Chinese-funded				Mattress
顺德金宝马家私制造有限公司(1996)	佛山市	广东省	(0765)3364095	856	港澳台资	118,000	2,170(36)	35,998	床垫
Fuzhou Dongfa Steel & Wood Products Co., Ltd.	Fuzhou	Fujian	(0591)3563088		Limited-Liability				Sand Beach Folding Chair沙
福州东发钢木制品有限公司(1996)	福州市	福建省	(0591)3562666	170	有限公司	87,200	1,580(42)	9,327	滩折叠椅
Conghua No.2 Light Industry Furniture Factory	Guangzhou	Guangdong	(020)87910144		Private Enterprises				Furniture
从化二轻家具厂(1996)	广州市	广东省	(020)87910144	180	私营独资	82,635	4,132(22)	29,250	家具
Shaoxing Mengxing Group Co., Ltd.	Shaoxing	Zhejiang	(0575)8019985		Private Owned				Mattress
绍兴市梦星集团有限公司(1992)	绍兴市	浙江省	(0575)8019985	180	私营企业	80,251	5,853(12)	54,003	床垫

Top 10 Cities by Revenue 销售收入排名前10位城市	Province 省	Market share 市场份额 (%)	Number of firms 企业个数
Shaoxing 绍兴市	Zhejiang 浙江省	12.00	5
Shanghai 上海市	Shanghai 上海市	9.47	26
Shenzhen 深圳市	Guangdong 广东省	9.22	10
Fuzhou 福州市	Fujian 福建省	9.14	7
Yueyang 岳阳市	Hunan 湖南省	7.99	1
Guangzhou 广州市	Guangdong 广东省	7.21	15
Foshan 佛山市	Guangdong 广东省	4.40	7
Harbin 哈尔滨市	Heilongjiang 黑龙江省	3.64	2
Beijing 北京市	Beijing 北京市	3.59	13
Changzhou 常州市	Jiangsu 江苏省	2.59	3

10 Major Wholesalers 十家主要批发商	City 城市	Province 省	Telephone/Fax 电话/传真
Kunming Department Store Group Co.,Ltd.	Kunming	Yunnan	(0871)3313618
昆明百货集团股份有限公司	昆明市	云南省	(0871)3314961
Jiangsu Skyrun International Group	Nanjing	Jiangsu	(025)4468888
江苏开元国际集团	南京市	江苏省	(025)4209409
Guangdong Light Industry Products Imp.& Exp.(Group) Corporation	Guangzhou	Guangdong	(020)83344557
广东省轻工业品进出口（集团）公司	广州市	广东省	(020)83330181
Shanghai Cheer (Group) Co.,Ltd.	Shanghai	Shanghai	(021)63069764
上海七百（集团）有限公司	上海市	上海市	(021)63069537
Fujian Tiancheng Group Co.,Ltd.	Fuzhou	Fujian	(0591)7503388
福建天成集团有限公司	福州市	福建省	(0591)7609279
Shanghai Century Lianhua Supermaket Development Co.,ltd.	Shanghai	Shanghai	(021)53544600
上海世纪联华超市发展有限公司	上海市	上海市	(021)62252610
Suzhou General Merchandise General Company	Suzhou	Jiangsu	(0512)65222247
苏州百货总公司	苏州市	江苏省	(0512)65222247
Zhejiang Light Industry Products Import & Export Corporation	Hangzhou	Zhejiang	(0571)88391888
浙江省轻工业品进出口公司	杭州市	浙江省	(0571)88391666
Zhejiang Winsun Import & Export Co., Ltd.	Jiaxing	Zhejiang	(0573)2117091
浙江汇信进出口有限公司	嘉兴市	浙江省	(0573)2117020
Shenzhen CATIC Trade Company	Shenzhen	Guangdong	(0755)83790111
深圳中航商贸公司	深圳市	广东省	(0755)83790462

2210: Paper Pulp 纸浆制造业

The industry accounts for 0.035% of the total revenue of China's industrial sector in 2002. The rate of return on assets is -3.58%. 80.26% of all firms in the industry made a profit while 19.74% had negative returns.The top province in terms of the industry's revenue is Guangxi, accounting for 13.22% of the total revenue.
2002年本行业收入占全行业的 0.035%，资产利润率为 -3.58%。80.26%的企业赢利，19.74%的企业亏损。收入最高的省为广西，占本行业的13.22%。

	Total number of firms 企业总数	Total number of employees 职工总数	Total revenue (Mil.RMB) 总销售收入 (百万元)	Total profit (Mil.RMB) 总利润 (百万元)	Return on assets 资产利润率 (%)	Return on equity 权益利润率 (%)	Labour productivity ('000 RMB/ worker) 劳动生产率 (千元/人)	Debts/ assets 资产负债率 (%)	Total assets (Mil.RMB) 总资产 (百万元)
Industry Overall 行业总体	76	26,599	3,715	-382	-3.58	-10.03	41.22	64.32	10,665

	Number of firms 企业个数	Average number of employees 平均职工人数	Average revenue ('000 RMB) 平均销售收入 (千元)	Average profit ('000 RMB) 平均利润 (千元)	Return on assets 资产利润率 (%)	Return on equity 权益利润率 (%)	Labour productivity ('000 RMB/ worker) 劳动生产率 (千元/人)	Debts/ assets 资产负债率 (%)	Average total assets ('000 RMB) 平均总资产 (千元)
By ownership 产业所有权									
State-owned 国有	9	299	30,884	-14,737	-6.80	-17.58	60.27	61.31	216,693
Collective-owned 集体	19	120	20,452	582	5.04	12.90	51.74	60.91	11,550
Foreign & Overseas Chinese Funded 三资	6	498	106,272	10,905	7.97	18.57	76.09	57.09	136,837
By regional distribution 地区分布									
Central-North 华北	4	895	90,509	1,024	0.78	2.39	39.07	67.13	130,438
Beijing 北京	1	246	21,517	-612	-7.94	-10.90	25.46	27.21	7,711
Tianjin 天津									
Hebei 河北	1	61	13,500	1,098	11.56	20.72	70.79	44.21	9,500
Shanxi 山西									
Inner Mongolia 内蒙古	2	1,636	163,510	1,805	0.72	2.25	39.50	68.17	252,271
Northeast 东北	5	306	18,785	-352	-0.94	-1.25	16.62	25.25	37,611
Liaoning 辽宁	2	142	16,783	452	6.45	7.76	30.91	16.87	7,003
Jilin 吉林	1	504	2,964	1	0.01		1.77	100.00	19,349
Heilongjiang 黑龙江	2	370	28,699	-1,333	-1.72	-2.07	21.25	16.66	77,351
Central-East 华东	14	434	77,347	-8,761	-4.41	-14.33	52.61	69.23	198,638
Shanghai 上海									
Jiangsu 江苏	2	923	143,158	6,274	4.25	17.02	51.34	75.06	147,776
Zhejiang 浙江	1	99	8,650	41	0.77	1.81	21.91	57.63	5,339
Anhui 安徽									
Fujian 福建	3	682	141,768	-49,332	-6.87	-20.21	47.30	66.03	718,385
Jiangxi 江西									
Shandong 山东	8	261	45,323	1,595	3.93	26.83	60.39	85.37	40,611
Central-South 中南	38	276	42,473	-3,499	-2.92	-9.29	35.75	68.57	119,878
Henan 河南	16	224	24,852	1,197	2.87	10.40	34.11	72.44	41,764
Hubei 湖北	9	318	35,499	473	1.81	3.68	36.95	50.77	26,114
Hunan 湖南	7	184	22,546	415	1.84	2.82	37.49	34.63	22,517
Guangdong 广东	3	218	82,616	17,027	11.28	21.20	125.54	46.79	150,980
Guangxi 广西	3	705	163,720	-70,120	-6.92	-26.70	8.04	74.09	1,013,851
Hainan 海南									
Southwest 西南	6	308	52,614	-21,180	-6.71	-14.97	80.81	55.15	315,543
Chongqing 重庆									
Sichuan 四川	3	309	39,235	2,878	3.45	4.26	31.23	19.07	83,541
Guizhou 贵州	2	34	6,225	150	1.38	7.91	36.21	82.53	10,863
Yunnan 云南	1	852	185,527	-136,012	-8.39	-21.17	138.27	60.37	1,620,911
Tibet 西藏									
Northwest 西北	9	341	27,382	-130	-0.16	-0.33	28.31	50.91	80,661
Shaanxi 陕西	3	131	3,773	235	2.04	4.51	10.24	54.74	11,511
Gansu 甘肃	4	175	7,575	217	1.51	3.45	19.70	56.32	14,366
Qinghai 青海									
Ningxia 宁夏									
Xinjiang 新疆	2	987	102,408	-1,370	-0.43	-0.87	34.96	50.21	316,976

2210: Paper Pulp 纸浆制造业

Year 年份	Number of firms 企业个数	Rate of change 变化率 (%)	Number of employees 职工人数 (人)	Rate of change 变化率 (%)	Total revenue (Mil. RMB) 总销售收入 (百万元)	Rate of change 变化率 (%)	Total profit (Mil RMB) 总利润 (百万元)	Rate of change 变化率 (%)
2000	67		18,019		2,549		-29	
2001	74	10.45	24,530	36.13	3,155	23.77	-424	-1,362.07
2002	76	2.70	26,599	8.43	3,715	17.75	-382	9.91

Major Products 主要产品	Output 产量	Unit 单位
Paper Pulp 纸浆	1,132	10,000 Tons 万吨

10 Main Firms with Maximal Revenue (year founded) 收入最大的十家主要企业（创办年份）	City 城市	Province 省	Telephone/fax 电话/传真	Number of employees 职工人数	Ownership 产业所有权	Revenue ('000 RMB) 销售收入（千元）	Profit('000 RMB) (rank) 利润(千元)（排名）	Total assets ('000 RMB) 总资产（千元）	Major products 主要产品
Fujian Qingzhou Paper Making Co.,Ltd.	Sanming	Fujian	(0598)5656888		Limited-Liability				Original Color Pulp Board
福建省青州造纸有限责任公司(1994)	三明市	福建省	(0598)5653336	1,116	有限公司	306,295	-	1,508,022	本色浆板
Chinese-foreign Joint Venture Zhenjiang Golden River Pulp &	Zhenjiang	Jiangsu	(0511)3362295		Foreign Funded				Bleaching Pulp Board
Paper Co.,Ltd.中外合资镇江金河纸业有限公司(1992)	镇江市	江苏省	(0511)3361362	1,766	外商投资	272,685	12,488(2)	282,332	漂白浆板
Guangxi Nanning Phenix Paper Industry Co.,Ltd.	Nanning	Guangxi	(0771)4590270		State Enterprises				Paper Pulp
广西南宁凤凰纸业有限公司(1999)	南宁市	广西	(0771)4516683	808	国有独资	271,876	-	1,962,946	纸浆
Guangdong Dingfeng Paper Industry Co.,Ltd.	Zhaoqing	Guangdong	(0758)8656548		Overseas Chinese-funded				Bleaching Pulp Board
广东鼎丰纸业有限公司(2000)	肇庆市	广东省	(0758)8656450	500	港澳台资	218,613	51,241(1)	433,208	漂白浆板
Guangxi Hoda Pulp & Paper Co.,Ltd.	Hezhou	Guangxi	(0774)5100081		Limited-Liability				Bleaching Sulphate Deal Pulp漂白硫酸
广西贺达纸业有限责任公司(1996)	贺州市	广西	(0774)5125154	896	有限公司	213,861	-	1,070,708	盐松木浆
Yunnan Yunjing Paper Co.,Ltd.	Simao	Yunnan	(0879)5410006		State-owned				Paper Pulp
云南云景林纸股份有限公司(2000)	思茅	云南省	(0879)5410193	852	国有企业	185,527	-	1,620,911	纸浆
Xinjiang Bositeng Lake Reed Industry (Group) Co.,Ltd.	Bayinguoleng	Xinjiang	(0996)2153997		State Enterprises				Paper Pulp
新疆博斯腾湖苇业（集团）有限责任公司(1999)	巴音郭楞州	新疆	(0996)2152730	1,435	国有独资	171,189	2,235(13)	577,345	纸浆
Inner mongolia Forest Industry Group Fulun Paper Industry	Hulunbeir	Inner Mongolia	(0470)3303820		State Enterprises				Wood Pulp
Co.,Ltd.内蒙古自治区森工集团富伦纸业有限公司(1975)	呼伦贝尔市	内蒙古	(0470)3303820	1,672	国有独资	157,183	79(37)	324,412	木浆
Fujian Shaowu Zhongzhu Paper Industry Co., Ltd.	Nanping	Fujian	(0599)6541026		State Enterprises				Paper Pulp
邵武中竹纸业有限责任公司(2002)	南平市	福建省	(0599)6541090	723	国有独资	103,027	-	499,382	纸浆
Ya'an Zhongzhu Paper Industry Co., Ltd.	Ya'an	Sichuan	(0835)2850862		Limited-Liability				Bamboo Pulp Board
雅安中竹纸业有限责任公司(2000)	雅安市	四川省	(0835)2850092	779	有限公司	96,042	8,162(3)	194,663	竹浆板

Top 10 Cities by Revenue 销售收入排名前10位城市	Province 省	Market share 市场份额 (%)	Number of firms 企业个数
Sanming 三明市	Fujian 福建省	8.62	2
Zhenjiang 镇江市	Jiangsu 江苏省	7.34	1
Nanning 南宁市	Guangxi 广西	7.32	1
Hezhou 贺州市	Guangxi 广西	5.90	2
Jingzhou 荆州市	Hubei 湖北省	5.90	5
Zhaoqing 肇庆市	Guangdong 广东省	5.88	1
Simao 思茅地区	Yunnan 云南省	4.99	1
Bayinguoleng 巴音郭楞州	Xinjiang 新疆	4.61	1
Bayannaoer 巴彦淖尔盟	Inner Mongolia 内蒙古	4.57	1
Hulunbeir 呼伦贝尔市	Inner Mongolia 内蒙古	4.23	1

10 Major Wholesalers 十家主要批发商	City 城市	Province 省	Telephone/Fax 电话/传真
Yihua Kangqi Chemical Fibre Co.,Ltd.	Yangzhou	Jiangsu	(0514)3235499
仪化康祺化纤有限责任公司	扬州市	江苏省	(0514)3233847
Sinochem Guangdong Import & Export Company	Guangzhou	Guangdong	(020)86672288
中化广东进出口公司	广州市	广东省	(020)86507512
Sinochem Shanghai Import & Export Company	Shanghai	Shanghai	(021)63289888
中化上海进出口公司	上海市	上海市	(021)63283968
Sinochem Tianjin Import & Export Company	Tianjin	Tianjin	(022)23146216
中化天津进出口公司	天津市	天津市	(022)23146215
China Chemical Sales & Supply (North China) Corporation	Tianjin	Tianjin	(022)23011031
中国化工供销华北公司	天津市	天津市	(022)23011032
China Chemical Sales & Supply (North China) Corporation	Shanghai	Shanghai	(021)62103300
中国化工供销华东公司	上海市	上海市	(021)62515799
Nantong Chemical Light Industry Co.,Ltd.	Nantong	Jiangsu	(0513)5518397
南通化工轻工股份有限公司	南通市	江苏省	(0513)5512735
Taizhou Heshun Plastics Co.,Ltd.	Taizhou	Zhejiang	(0576)2510220
台州市和顺塑料有限公司	台州市	浙江省	(0576)2510160
China Petroleum Technology Development Corporation	Beijing	Beijing	(010)84080722
中国石油技术开发公司	北京市	北京市	(010)84080800
China National Chemical Fiber Corporation	Beijing	Beijing	(010)65816699
中国化纤总公司	北京市	北京市	(010)65813483

2221: Machine-made Paper and Paperboard 机制纸及纸板制造业

The industry accounts for 1.112% of the total revenue of China's industrial sector in 2002. The rate of return on assets is 3.17%. 79.88% of all firms in the industry made a profit while 20.12% had negative returns.The top province in terms of the industry's revenue is Shandong, accounting for 23.17% of the total revenue.
2002年本行业收入占全行业的 1.112%，资产利润率为 3.17%。79.88%的企业赢利，20.12%的企业亏损。收入最高的省为山东省，占本行业的23.17%。

	Total number of firms 企业总数	Total number of employees 职工总数	Total revenue (Mil.RMB) 总销售收入（百万元）	Total profit (Mil.RMB) 总利润（百万元）	Return on assets 资产利润率（%）	Return on equity 权益利润率（%）	Labour productivity ('000 RMB/ worker) 劳动生产率（千元/人）	Debts/ assets 资产负债率（%）	Total assets (Mil.RMB) 总资产（百万元）
Industry Overall 行业总体	2316	730,968	119,292	6,552	3.17	9.12	48.88	65.18	206,403

	Number of firms 企业个数	Average number of employees 平均职工人数	Average revenue ('000 RMB) 平均销售收入（千元）	Average profit ('000 RMB) 平均利润（千元）	Return on assets 资产利润率（%）	Return on equity 权益利润率（%）	Labour productivity ('000 RMB/ worker) 劳动生产率（千元/人）	Debts/ assets 资产负债率（%）	Average total assets ('000 RMB) 平均总资产（千元）
By ownership 产业所有权									
State-owned 国有	262	418	48,909	1,625	1.37	4.45	36.58	69.20	118,491
Collective-owned 集体	680	220	27,480	1,547	6.35	15.80	38.48	59.82	24,361
Foreign & Overseas Chinese Funded 三资	161	458	212,425	17,066	4.24	11.75	138.60	63.93	402,589
By regional distribution 地区分布									
Central-North 华北	293	273	32,582	1,747	4.13	13.02	34.30	68.28	42,311
Beijing 北京	16	173	28,457	1,085	3.73	11.13	50.00	66.52	29,093
Tianjin 天津	57	140	15,947	-166	-0.36	-1.29	14.80	72.21	46,548
Hebei 河北	189	317	39,292	2,506	5.89	18.18	36.83	67.60	42,543
Shanxi 山西	22	205	15,865	833	2.73	7.64	27.38	64.22	30,491
Inner Mongolia 内蒙古	9	537	45,230	1,359	2.16	6.30	32.66	65.78	62,996
Northeast 东北	122	604	49,560	-107	-0.05	-0.16	22.55	69.21	220,631
Liaoning 辽宁	51	451	33,138	-180	-0.13	-0.42	18.75	69.74	140,806
Jilin 吉林	33	629	31,330	-6,007	-2.68	-8.44	17.57	68.23	224,062
Heilongjiang 黑龙江	38	788	87,430	5,115	1.57	5.16	28.91	69.49	324,786
Central-East 华东	829	354	78,282	5,067	3.84	10.97	64.75	65.01	131,998
Shanghai 上海	33	181	69,356	1,454	1.35	3.03	79.46	55.46	107,658
Jiangsu 江苏	112	342	151,609	9,344	3.28	11.46	130.64	71.38	284,798
Zhejiang 浙江	261	172	38,467	2,173	4.81	13.20	54.55	63.61	45,232
Anhui 安徽	55	245	33,067	1,773	3.78	11.22	39.57	66.31	46,911
Fujian 福建	118	184	42,049	1,490	1.86	3.46	70.70	46.16	79,921
Jiangxi 江西	42	309	27,827	-1,971	-2.21	-19.04	29.08	88.41	89,301
Shandong 山东	208	752	132,874	11,290	5.06	13.90	55.26	63.59	223,121
Central-South 中南	810	244	39,111	2,070	3.97	9.89	49.63	59.85	52,134
Henan 河南	336	272	26,135	1,706	6.56	17.05	33.01	61.54	26,030
Hubei 湖北	91	223	42,197	2,978	6.26	16.28	67.36	61.52	47,552
Hunan 湖南	121	254	35,495	1,734	2.68	5.71	39.88	53.04	64,650
Guangdong 广东	213	181	60,933	2,854	3.46	8.70	94.89	60.26	82,557
Guangxi 广西	46	350	38,024	424	0.53	1.55	31.96	65.82	79,808
Hainan 海南	3	118	12,010	-1,642	-6.45	-48.09	33.55	86.58	25,433
Southwest 西南	154	287	29,836	1,060	1.92	6.84	36.96	71.90	55,200
Chongqing 重庆	21	184	21,821	167	0.70	2.09	28.72	66.67	23,988
Sichuan 四川	91	330	34,908	681	1.13	4.28	36.58	73.51	60,063
Guizhou 贵州	16	200	10,028	-715	-3.07	-56.08	12.30	94.53	23,300
Yunnan 云南	26	275	30,748	4,204	5.06	14.53	54.05	65.16	83,022
Tibet 西藏									
Northwest 西北	108	387	23,417	113	0.18	0.60	20.79	70.73	64,200
Shaanxi 陕西	58	319	14,783	-264	-0.72	-2.49	14.34	71.01	36,696
Gansu 甘肃	26	208	8,251	-297	-1.70	-10.56	16.43	83.93	17,533
Qinghai 青海	2	275	7,086	-2,430	-5.43	-25.98	18.54	79.08	44,714
Ningxia 宁夏	13	1,011	84,272	4,098	1.80	6.27	29.57	71.24	227,127
Xinjiang 新疆	9	471	38,596	-1,461	-1.01	-2.79	27.56	63.93	145,254

2221: Machine-made Paper and Paperboard 机制纸及纸板制造业

Year 年份	Number of firms 企业个数	Rate of change 变化率 (%)	Number of employees 职工人数 (人)	Rate of change 变化率 (%)	Total revenue (Mil. RMB) 总销售收入 (百万元)	Rate of change 变化率 (%)	Total profit (Mil RMB) 总利润 (百万元)	Rate of change 变化率 (%)
2000	2297		792,587		95,013		4,153	
2001	2386	3.87	751,552	-5.18	106,714	12.32	4,445	7.03
2002	2316	-2.93	730,968	-2.74	119,292	11.79	6,552	47.40

Major Products 主要产品	Output 产量	Unit 单位
Machine-made Paper 机制纸	2,054	10,000 Tons 万吨
Machine-made Paperboard 机制纸板	1,448	10,000 Tons 万吨

10 Main Firms with Maximal Revenue (year founded) 收入最大的十家主要企业（创办年份）	City 城市	Province 省	Telephone/fax 电话/传真	Number of employees 职工人数	Ownership 产业所有权	Revenue ('000 RMB) 销售收入 (千元)	Profit('000 RMB) (rank) 利润(千元) (排名)	Total assets ('000 RMB) 总资产 (千元)	Major products 主要产品
Jindong Paper Industry (Jiangsu) Co.,Ltd.	Zhenjiang	Jiangsu	(0511)3375800		Foreign Funded				Machine-made Paper
金东纸业(江苏)有限公司(1997)	镇江市	江苏省	(0511)3375799	3,798	外商投资	6,085,194	618,850(2)	13,378,496	机制纸
Shandong Chenming Paper Group Co.,Ltd.	Weifang	Shandong	(0536)5280000		Foreign Funded				Machine-made Paper
山东晨鸣纸业集团股份有限公司(1958)	潍坊市	山东省	(0536)5221843	13,858	外商投资	4,546,446	731,759(1)	9,784,624	机制纸
Huatai Group Co., Ltd.	Dongying	Shandong	(0546)6888839		Limited-Liability				Machine-made Paper
华泰集团有限公司(1997)	东营市	山东省	(0546)6888018	4,350	有限公司	2,363,102	352,660(3)	4,051,626	机制纸
Shandong Sun Paper Industry Co.,Ltd.	Jining	Shandong	(0537)3658649		Joint Stock				Reprography Paper
山东太阳纸业股份有限公司(2000)	济宁市	山东省	(0537)3633489	5,691	股份制	2,303,406	282,681(4)	2,387,790	复印纸
Dongguan Nine Dragons Paper Industries Co.,Ltd.	Dongguan	Guangdong	(0769)8826888		Overseas Chinese-funded				Machine-made Paper
东莞玖龙纸业有限公司(1995)	东莞市	广东省	(0769)8824198	1,504	港澳台资	1,913,692	164,840(8)	2,821,638	机制纸
Zhuhai Hongta Renheng Paper Co., Ltd.	Zhuhai	Guangdong	(0756)8610208		Overseas Chinese-funded				White Paper Board
珠海经济特区红塔仁恒纸业有限公司(1991)	珠海市	广东省	(0756)8615037	874	港澳台资	1,476,568	184,808(7)	2,848,539	白卡纸
Wuhan Chenming Hanyang Paper Industry Co., Ltd.	Wuhan	Hubei	(027)84894245		Joint Stock				Paper Products
武汉晨鸣汉阳纸业股份有限公司(1998)	武汉市	湖北省	(027)84894586	2,925	股份制	1,263,202	201,107(6)	2,095,832	纸制品
Heilongjiang Heilong Co., Ltd.	Qiqihar	Heilongjiang	(0452)2712175		Joint Stock				Newsprint
黑龙江黑龙股份有限公司(1993)	齐齐哈尔市	黑龙江省		11,944	股份制	1,245,350	19,204(60)	3,535,978	新闻纸
Fujian Nanzhi Co., Ltd.	Nanping	Fujian	(0599)8808888		Joint Stock				Newsprint
福建南纸股份有限公司(1958)	南平市	福建省	(0599)8801260	3,146	股份制	1,174,893	94,940(13)	2,389,144	新闻纸
Shandong Quanlin Paper Industry Co., Ltd.	Liaocheng	Shandong	(0635)3961824		Limited-Liability				Machine-made Paper
山东泉林纸业有限责任公司(1978)	聊城市	山东省	(0635)3961597	5,917	有限公司	1,054,719	91,772(16)	3,077,234	机制纸

Top 10 Cities by Revenue 销售收入排名前10位城市	Province 省	Market share 市场份额 (%)	Number of firms 企业个数
Zhenjiang 镇江市	Jiangsu 江苏省	5.49	4
Weifang 潍坊市	Shandong 山东省	5.44	30
Suzhou 苏州市	Jiangsu 江苏省	5.09	17
Hangzhou 杭州市	Zhejiang 浙江省	3.60	135
Dongguan 东莞市	Guangdong 广东省	3.21	55
Jining 济宁市	Shandong 山东省	2.85	12
Zhengzhou 郑州市	Henan 河南省	2.31	100
Dongying 东营市	Shandong 山东省	2.15	4
Tangshan 唐山市	Hebei 河北省	2.00	46
Jiaxing 嘉兴市	Zhejiang 浙江省	1.95	21

10 Major Wholesalers 十家主要批发商	City 城市	Province 省	Telephone/Fax 电话/传真
Yihua Kangqi Chemical Fibre Co.,Ltd.	Yangzhou	Jiangsu	(0514)3235499
仪化康祺化纤有限责任公司	扬州市	江苏省	(0514)3233847
Sinochem Guangdong Import & Export Company	Guangzhou	Guangdong	(020)86672288
中化广东进出口公司	广州市	广东省	(020)86507512
Sinochem Shanghai Import & Export Company	Shanghai	Shanghai	(021)63289888
中化上海进出口公司	上海市	上海市	(021)63283968
Sinochem Tianjin Import & Export Company	Tianjin	Tianjin	(022)23146216
中化天津进出口公司	天津市	天津市	(022)23146215
China Chemical Sales & Supply (North China) Corporation	Tianjin	Tianjin	(022)23011031
中国化工供销华北公司	天津市	天津市	(022)23011032
China Chemical Sales & Supply (North China) Corporation	Shanghai	Shanghai	(021)62103300
中国化工供销华东公司	上海市	上海市	(021)62515799
Nantong Chemical Light Industry Co.,Ltd.	Nantong	Jiangsu	(0513)5518397
南通化工轻工股份有限公司	南通市	江苏省	(0513)5512735
Taizhou Heshun Plastics Co.,Ltd.	Taizhou	Zhejiang	(0576)2510220
台州市和顺塑料有限公司	台州市	浙江省	(0576)2510160
China Petroleum Technology Development Corporation	Beijing	Beijing	(010)84080722
中国石油技术开发公司	北京市	北京市	(010)84080800
China National Chemical Fiber Corporation	Beijing	Beijing	(010)65816699
中国化纤总公司	北京市	北京市	(010)65813483

2224: Processed Paper 加工纸制造业

The industry accounts for 0.115% of the total revenue of China's industrial sector in 2002. The rate of return on assets is 5.47%. 88.36% of all firms in the industry made a profit while 11.64% had negative returns.The top province in terms of the industry's revenue is Zhejiang, accounting for 48.18% of the total revenue.
2002年本行业收入占全行业的0.115%，资产利润率为5.47%。88.36%的企业赢利，11.64%的企业亏损。收入最高的省为浙江省，占本行业的48.18%。

	Total number of firms 企业总数	Total number of employees 职工总数	Total revenue (Mil.RMB) 总销售收入 (百万元)	Total profit (Mil.RMB) 总利润 (百万元)	Return on assets 资产利润率 (%)	Return on equity 权益利润率 (%)	Labour productivity ('000 RMB/ worker) 劳动生产率 (千元/人)	Debts/ assets 资产负债率 (%)	Total assets (Mil.RMB) 总资产 (百万元)
Industry Overall 行业总体	275	41,601	12,315	855	5.47	13.93	78.09	60.71	15,621

	Number of firms 企业个数	Average number of employees 平均职工人数	Average revenue ('000 RMB) 平均销售收入（千元)	Average profit ('000 RMB) 平均利润 (千元)	Return on assets 资产利润率 (%)	Return on equity 权益利润率 (%)	Labour productivity ('000 RMB/ worker) 劳动生产率 (千元/人)	Debts/ assets 资产负债率 (%)	Average total assets ('000 RMB) 平均总资产 (千元)
By ownership 产业所有权									
State-owned 国有	8	237	22,420	-422	-0.48	-3.06	17.00	84.17	87,093
Collective-owned 集体	41	172	23,123	1,681	9.89	23.96	34.89	58.70	16,987
Foreign & Overseas Chinese Funded 三资	44	221	139,836	13,382	6.52	16.02	177.86	59.32	205,265
By regional distribution 地区分布									
Central-North 华北	15	104	66,254	18,122	32.80	84.81	218.55	61.32	55,250
Beijing 北京	5	112	149,077	53,711	41.86	81.72	564.32	48.78	128,313
Tianjin 天津	9	61	25,460	486	3.16		25.27	100.43	15,400
Hebei 河北	1	452	19,278	-1,094	-2.25		25.44	115.41	48,582
Shanxi 山西									
Inner Mongolia 内蒙古									
Northeast 东北	3	80	8,877	61	0.44	0.82	23.66	46.98	13,945
Liaoning 辽宁	3	80	8,877	61	0.44	0.82	23.66	46.98	13,945
Jilin 吉林									
Heilongjiang 黑龙江									
Central-East 华东	176	155	48,421	2,422	3.65	8.79	74.68	58.42	66,297
Shanghai 上海	15	169	46,569	1,604	2.76	6.69	48.25	58.76	58,151
Jiangsu 江苏	14	137	76,581	3,914	7.36	24.01	89.08	69.35	53,168
Zhejiang 浙江	122	149	48,635	2,567	3.64	8.65	84.79	57.91	70,472
Anhui 安徽	4	50	17,454	788	13.21	35.85	147.87	63.15	5,961
Fujian 福建	6	103	20,326	1,237	5.69	8.27	24.11	31.18	21,727
Jiangxi 江西	2	197	16,959	829	6.03	12.00	27.50	49.75	13,753
Shandong 山东	13	263	45,555	1,694	1.73	4.13	42.83	58.14	97,872
Central-South 中南	63	165	32,538	1,199	3.25	12.02	63.91	73.00	36,937
Henan 河南	16	341	27,567	1,364	9.56	21.83	28.73	56.19	14,261
Hubei 湖北	7	71	7,310	54	1.27	2.33	58.97	45.29	4,274
Hunan 湖南	3	79	6,783	10	0.21	0.64	18.88	67.33	4,588
Guangdong 广东	37	114	41,548	1,441	2.59	10.50	112.35	75.30	55,546
Guangxi 广西									
Hainan 海南									
Southwest 西南	15	127	45,329	5,169	11.19	26.31	98.97	57.47	46,190
Chongqing 重庆									
Sichuan 四川	3	145	10,218	8	0.05	0.09	11.33	42.71	15,302
Guizhou 贵州	3	36	6,161	19	0.46	0.66	27.49	30.44	4,185
Yunnan 云南	9	151	70,088	8,606	12.21	29.83	132.92	59.07	70,488
Tibet 西藏									
Northwest 西北	3	87	14,274	1,233	5.96	18.86	55.78	68.41	20,691
Shaanxi 陕西	2	30	18,066	1,741	5.77	19.25	207.08	70.03	30,177
Gansu 甘肃	1	200	6,692	218	12.69	14.32	10.39	11.41	1,718
Qinghai 青海									
Ningxia 宁夏									
Xinjiang 新疆									

2224: Processed Paper 加工纸制造业

Year 年份	Number of firms 企业个数	Rate of change 变化率(%)	Number of employees 职工人数(人)	Rate of change 变化率(%)	Total revenue (Mil. RMB) 总销售收入(百万元)	Rate of change 变化率(%)	Total profit (Mil RMB) 总利润(百万元)	Rate of change 变化率(%)
2000	175		26,136		5,875		227	
2001	174	-0.57	29,064	11.20	5,580	-5.02	201	-11.45
2002	275	58.05	41,601	43.14	12,315	120.70	855	325.37

Major Products 主要产品	Output 产量	Unit 单位
Newsprint 新闻纸	183	10,000 Tons 万吨
Typographic Paper 凸版纸	82	10,000 Tons 万吨

10 Main Firms with Maximal Revenue (year founded) 收入最大的十家主要企业（创办年份）	City 城市	Province 省	Telephone/fax 电话/传真	Number of employees 职工人数	Ownership 产业所有权	Revenue ('000 RMB) 销售收入(千元)	Profit('000 RMB) (rank) 利润(千元)(排名)	Total assets ('000 RMB) 总资产(千元)	Major products 主要产品
Ningbo Zhonghua Paper Co.,Ltd.	Ningbo	Zhejiang	(0574)87464811		Foreign Funded				Grey Background White Paperboard涂布灰
宁波中华纸业有限公司(1992)	宁波市	浙江省	(0574)87493450	1,644	外商投资	2,239,032	189,928(2)	5,029,736	底白纸板
Beijing Tetra Pak Packaging Co.,ltd.	Beijing	Beijing	(010)67739355		Foreign Funded				Lile Packing Materials利乐包
北京利乐包包装有限公司(1995)	北京市	北京市	(010)67748806	160	外商投资	718,659	268,010(1)	415,524	包装材料
Guangdong Guanhao High-Tech Co.,ltd.	Zhanjiang	Guangdong	(0759)3399898		Joint Stock				Carbonless Manifold Paper无
广东冠豪高新技术股份有限公司(1993)	湛江市	广东省	(0759)3382109	414	股份制	326,057	28,585(5)	368,126	碳复写纸
Guangdong Guanlong Paper Industry Co.,Ltd.	Zhanjiang	Guangdong	(0759)2738002		Overseas Chinese-funded				Carbonless Manifold Paper无
广东冠龙纸业有限公司(2000)	湛江市	广东省	(0759)2738009	316	港澳台资	288,413	13,002(10)	847,708	碳复写纸
Jinan Hanzhang Printing Co., Ltd.	Jinan	Shandong	(0531)8023125		Private Enterprises				Paper Products
济南含章印务有限公司(1995)	济南市	山东省	(0531)8012000	933	私营独资	189,623	6,516(16)	645,329	纸制品
Henan New Asia Industrial Company	Xinxiang	Henan	(0373)5680286		Collective-owned				Paper
河南省新亚实业总公司(1986)	新乡市	河南省	(0373)5680390	3,942	集体企业	187,100	11,600(12)	96,000	纸
Yuxi Hongta Printing Co.,Ltd.	Yuxi	Yunnan	(0877)2770815		Overseas Chinese-funded				Yew Paper
玉溪红塔印刷有限公司(1993)	玉溪市	云南省	(0877)2771528	409	港澳台资	181,120	24,380(7)	189,860	水松纸
Xinnan (Tianjin) Paper Co.,Ltd.	Tianjin	Tianjin	(022)25797770		Foreign Funded				Paper
新南（天津）纸业有限公司(1996)	天津市	天津市	(022)84758893	40	外商投资	179,000	810(76)	46,330	纸
Yunnan Yuxi Yew Paper Factory	Yuxi	Yunnan	(0877)2770815		Collective-owned				Yew Paper
云南省玉溪水松纸厂(1989)	玉溪市	云南省	(0877)2771528	136	集体企业	166,139	31,990(4)	108,296	水松纸
Hangzhou Banqiao Paper Industry Co., Ltd.	Hangzhou	Zhejiang	(0571)63585660		Foreign Funded				White Paperboard
杭州板桥纸业有限公司(1997)	杭州市	浙江省	(0571)63585660	493	外商投资	156,891	12,444(11)	115,361	白板纸

Top 10 Cities by Revenue 销售收入排名前10位城市	Province 省	Market share 市场份额(%)	Number of firms 企业个数
Hangzhou 杭州市	Zhejiang 浙江省	26.15	94
Ningbo 宁波市	Zhejiang 浙江省	18.92	4
Suzhou 苏州市	Jiangsu 江苏省	6.15	3
Beijing 北京市	Beijing 北京市	6.05	5
Shanghai 上海市	Shanghai 上海市	5.67	15
Zhanjiang 湛江市	Guangdong 广东省	5.22	3
Yuxi 玉溪市	Yunnan 云南省	4.43	5
Jinan 济南市	Shandong 山东省	2.75	3
Xinxiang 新乡市	Henan 河南省	1.98	5
Tianjin 天津市	Tianjin 天津市	1.86	9

10 Major Wholesalers 十家主要批发商	City 城市	Province 省	Telephone/Fax 电话/传真
King Paper Source Trade (shanghai) Co.,Ltd.	Shanghai	Shanghai	(021)62720808
金纸源贸易（上海）有限公司	上海市	上海市	(021)62720909
China National Paper & Pulp Corpration	Beijing	Beijing	(010)67780346
中国纸张纸浆进出口公司	北京市	北京市	(010)67747294
Sinar Mas Linjiang Paper Industry Trade (Beijing) Co.,Ltd.	Beijing	Beijing	(010)65666688
金光林浆纸业贸易(北京)有限公司	北京市	北京市	(010)65669599
Sinar Mas Paper Industry (Xishan) Co.,Ltd.	Wuxi	Jiangsu	(0510)8251188
金光纸业(锡山)有限公司	无锡市	江苏省	(0510)8250906
China Printing Materials General Company	Beijing	Beijing	(010)63442905
中国印刷物资总公司	北京市	北京市	(010)63442900
TSS Eortune Co., ltd.	Tianjin	Tianjin	(022)28131350
天津同鑫进出口有限公司	天津市	天津市	(022)28131353
Wenzhou Import & Export Corpration	Wenzhou	Zhejiang	(0577)88862681
温州市进出口公司	温州市	浙江省	(0577)88844557
Sinar Mas Paper Industry (Xiamen) Co.,Ltd.	Xiamen	Fujian	(0592)2962018
金光纸业（厦门）有限公司	厦门市	福建省	(0592)2962010
Sinar Mas Paper Industry (Shenzhen) Co.,Ltd.	Shenzhen	Guangdong	(0755)83516701
金光纸业（深圳）有限公司	深圳市	广东省	(0755)83516773
Jieyang Ocean Shipping Supply Group Co.,Ltd.	Jieyang	Guangdong	(0663)8239634
揭阳市外轮供应集团有限公司	揭阳市	广东省	(0663)8236186

2230: Paper Products 纸制品业

The industry accounts for 0.572% of the total revenue of China's industrial sector in 2002. The rate of return on assets is 4.59%. 82.49% of all firms in the industry made a profit while 17.51% had negative returns.The top province in terms of the industry's revenue is Guangdong, accounting for 27.22% of the total revenue.
2002年本行业收入占全行业的0.572%，资产利润率为4.59%。82.49%的企业赢利，17.51%的企业亏损。收入最高的省为广东省，占本行业的27.22%。

	Total number of firms 企业总数	Total number of employees 职工总数	Total revenue (Mil.RMB) 总销售收入 (百万元)	Total profit (Mil.RMB) 总利润 (百万元)	Return on assets 资产利润率 (%)	Return on equity 权益利润率 (%)	Labour productivity ('000 RMB/ worker) 劳动生产率 (千元/人)	Debts/ assets 资产负债率 (%)	Total assets (Mil.RMB) 总资产 (百万元)
Industry Overall 行业总体	2604	347,598	61,355	2,796	4.59	11.34	48.75	59.55	60,941

	Number of firms 企业个数	Average number of employees 平均职工人数	Average revenue ('000 RMB) 平均销售收入（千元）	Average profit ('000 RMB) 平均利润 (千元)	Return on assets 资产利润率 (%)	Return on equity 权益利润率 (%)	Labour productivity ('000 RMB/ worker) 劳动生产率 (千元/人)	Debts/ assets 资产负债率 (%)	Average total assets ('000 RMB) 平均总资产 (千元)
By ownership 产业所有权									
State-owned 国有	191	96	7,252	3	0.02	0.07	24.87	71.95	15,963
Collective-owned 集体	572	135	17,071	857	5.78	15.48	36.14	62.66	14,821
Foreign & Overseas Chinese Funded 三资	546	173	43,034	2,203	4.39	9.78	71.62	55.10	50,182
By regional distribution 地区分布									
Central-North 华北	277	126	18,622	1,036	5.06	11.04	39.14	54.19	20,492
Beijing 北京	68	109	17,759	16	0.05	0.11	50.87	55.17	31,477
Tianjin 天津	99	116	20,374	1,461	8.85	16.39	35.32	45.99	16,502
Hebei 河北	95	147	18,911	1,455	8.20	20.00	36.08	58.98	17,739
Shanxi 山西	9	109	6,819	35	0.22	0.98	24.82	77.12	15,800
Inner Mongolia 内蒙古	6	151	12,635	464	3.72	8.03	53.78	53.68	12,470
Northeast 东北	121	130	16,661	839	3.94	9.61	38.62	59.04	21,309
Liaoning 辽宁	61	139	19,364	1,251	4.82	10.00	38.81	51.84	25,967
Jilin 吉林	22	83	10,341	313	2.61	7.02	61.20	62.81	11,977
Heilongjiang 黑龙江	38	142	15,981	483	2.51	9.40	30.69	73.27	19,235
Central-East 华东	1,141	126	25,942	1,395	5.58	13.67	56.51	59.16	24,984
Shanghai 上海	159	107	29,137	2,015	6.98	14.53	68.93	52.00	28,889
Jiangsu 江苏	246	140	29,689	814	2.91	10.05	53.23	71.03	27,962
Zhejiang 浙江	301	116	26,838	1,534	6.22	14.79	57.56	57.91	24,646
Anhui 安徽	34	113	10,130	168	1.96	4.85	30.35	59.67	8,608
Fujian 福建	178	117	23,477	1,800	6.20	12.70	62.41	51.15	29,023
Jiangxi 江西	27	96	6,788	104	1.17	2.80	24.01	58.17	8,904
Shandong 山东	196	155	24,892	1,431	7.16	17.73	54.05	59.61	19,983
Central-South 中南	849	144	25,291	850	3.64	9.06	48.19	59.82	23,336
Henan 河南	84	130	14,954	788	6.32	15.52	38.73	59.30	12,467
Hubei 湖北	110	130	17,597	547	3.28	6.58	43.51	50.19	16,706
Hunan 湖南	62	114	15,744	789	6.55	15.21	40.59	56.92	12,039
Guangdong 广东	552	151	30,260	958	3.40	8.72	51.80	61.05	28,220
Guangxi 广西	30	190	17,141	498	2.81	7.66	30.98	63.35	17,735
Hainan 海南	11	45	7,844	211	3.23	6.66	91.54	51.46	6,531
Southwest 西南	133	161	18,542	569	2.28	6.60	34.34	65.43	24,933
Chongqing 重庆	23	125	19,927	715	2.30	5.34	38.32	56.91	31,060
Sichuan 四川	73	173	19,614	513	2.33	6.53	35.35	64.36	22,053
Guizhou 贵州	16	128	9,627	88	0.38	1.70	21.66	77.36	22,826
Yunnan 云南	21	186	20,090	969	3.25	11.17	34.79	70.93	29,840
Tibet 西藏									
Northwest 西北	83	118	7,745	226	1.79	7.68	23.39	76.72	12,664
Shaanxi 陕西	20	206	16,124	485	1.78	9.31	28.65	80.87	27,225
Gansu 甘肃	49	79	4,247	175	2.63	9.17	20.01	71.31	6,654
Qinghai 青海	1	124	3,296	-1,101	-16.57	-110.65	11.25	85.02	6,644
Ningxia 宁夏	2	117	8,355	259	2.40	4.38	40.66	45.32	10,788
Xinjiang 新疆	11	129	8,386	100	0.72	3.22	15.51	77.58	13,851

Year 年份	Number of firms 企业个数	Rate of change 变化率 (%)	Number of employees 职工人数 (人)	Rate of change 变化率 (%)	Total revenue (Mil. RMB) 总销售收入 (百万元)	Rate of change 变化率 (%)	Total profit (Mil RMB) 总利润 (百万元)	Rate of change 变化率 (%)
2000	2118		300,152		46,692		1,587	
2001	2383	12.51	329,989	9.94	52,979	13.46	1,981	24.83
2002	2604	9.27	347,598	5.34	61,355	15.81	2,796	41.14

Major Products 主要产品	Output 产量	Unit 单位
Paper Products 纸制品	860	10,000 Tons 万吨
Paper Box 纸箱	405	10,000 Tons 万吨

10 Main Firms with Maximal Revenue (year founded) 收入最大的十家主要企业（创办年份）	City 城市	Province 省	Telephone/fax 电话/传真	Number of employees 职工人数	Ownership 产业所有权	Revenue ('000 RMB) 销售收入 (千元)	Profit('000 RMB) (rank) 利润(千元) (排名)	Total assets ('000 RMB) 总资产 (千元)	Major products 主要产品
Tetra Pak Huaxin (Foshan) Packaging Co., Ltd.	Foshan	Guangdong	(0757)3831626		Foreign Funded				Lile Packing Materials
利乐华新(佛山)包装有限公司(1995)	佛山市	广东省	(0757)3832872	177	外商投资	872,129	260,038(1)	920,400	利乐包材
Tetra Pak (Kunshan) Packaging Co.,Ltd.	Suzhou	Jiangsu	(0512)57703148		Foreign Funded				Printing Machine
利乐包装(昆山)有限公司(1997)	苏州市	江苏省	(0512)57717729	170	外商投资	723,877	-	864,663	印刷机
Procter & Gamble (Guangzhou) Co., Ltd.	Guangzhou	Guangdong	(020)86698828		Overseas Chinese-funded				Paper Diaper
广州宝洁有限公司(1990)	广州市	广东省	(020)86693339	206	港澳台资	702,783	-	895,542	卫生巾
Shanghai Gold Leaf Packing Materials Co.,Ltd.	Shanghai	Shanghai	(021)66958521		Limited-Liability				Aluminium Foil Paper
上海金叶包装材料有限公司(1997)	上海市	上海市	(021)66959709	196	有限公司	307,883	55,029(4)	179,822	铝箔卡
Meifu Watong Paper Products (Shenzhen)Co.,Ltd.	Shenzhen	Guangdong	(0755)83591447		Overseas Chinese-funded				Packing Products
美福瓦通纸品(深圳)有限公司(1995)	深圳市	广东省	(0755)83592002	978	港澳台资	283,804	5,718(118)	496,182	包装产品
Jinhai Paper Products (Kunshan) Co.,Ltd.	Suzhou	Jiangsu	(0512)57538688		Foreign Funded				Paper Products
金海纸制品(昆山)有限公司(1998)	苏州市	江苏省	(0512)57511726	618	外商投资	276,348	5,330(127)	466,401	纸制品
Yongfengyu Paper(KunShan) Co.,Ltd.	Suzhou	Jiangsu	(0512)57791088		Overseas Chinese-funded				Paper Board Box
永丰余纸业(昆山)有限公司(1996)	苏州市	江苏省	(0512)57791699	642	港澳台资	276,146	11,000(47)	429,627	纸箱
Jinxin (Qingyuan) Paper Industry Co., Ltd.	Qingyuan	Guangdong	(0763)3483520		Foreign Funded				Reprography Paper
金鑫（清远）纸业有限公司(1995)	清远市	广东省	(0763)3483510	343	外商投资	272,405	6,768(95)	236,993	复印纸
Lijia Packing (Shenzhen) Co., Ltd.	Shenzhen	Guangdong	(0755)28868161		Overseas Chinese-funded				Paperboard
力嘉包装（深圳）有限公司(1993)	深圳市	广东省	(0755)28863216	2,785	港澳台资	258,386	4,333(156)	223,432	纸板
JiNan Tungkang Printing Co.,Ltd.	Jinan	Shandong	(0531)8904590		Foreign Funded				Paper Products
东港安全印刷有限公司(1996)	济南市	山东省	(0531)8906868	387	外商投资	230,220	32,281(11)	173,478	纸制品

Top 10 Cities by Revenue 销售收入排名前10位城市	Province 省	Market share 市场份额 (%)	Number of firms 企业个数
Shanghai 上海市	Shanghai 上海市	7.55	159
Guangzhou 广州市	Guangdong 广东省	6.16	124
Foshan 佛山市	Guangdong 广东省	4.65	78
Suzhou 苏州市	Jiangsu 江苏省	4.23	49
Shenzhen 深圳市	Guangdong 广东省	3.76	44
Zhongshan 中山市	Guangdong 广东省	3.67	79
Hangzhou 杭州市	Zhejiang 浙江省	3.32	83
Tianjin 天津市	Tianjin 天津市	3.29	99
Quanzhou 泉州市	Fujian 福建省	3.16	54
Dongguan 东莞市	Guangdong 广东省	2.70	47

10 Major Wholesalers 十家主要批发商	City 城市	Province 省	Telephone/Fax 电话/传真
King Paper Source Trade (shanghai) Co.,Ltd.	Shanghai	Shanghai	(021)62720808
金纸源贸易（上海）有限公司	上海市	上海市	(021)62720909
China National Paper & Pulp Corpration	Beijing	Beijing	(010)67780346
中国纸张纸浆进出口公司	北京市	北京市	(010)67747294
Sinar Mas Linjiang Paper Industry Trade (Beijing) Co.,Ltd.	Beijing	Beijing	(010)65666688
金光林浆纸业贸易(北京)有限公司	北京市	北京市	(010)65669599
Sinar Mas Paper Industry (Xishan) Co.,Ltd.	Wuxi	Jiangsu	(0510)8251188
金光纸业(锡山)有限公司	无锡市	江苏省	(0510)8250906
China Printing Materials General Company	Beijing	Beijing	(010)63442905
中国印刷物资总公司	北京市	北京市	(010)63442900
TSS Eortune Co., ltd.	Tianjin	Tianjin	(022)28131350
天津同鑫进出口有限公司	天津市	天津市	(022)28131353
Wenzhou Import & Export Corpration	Wenzhou	Zhejiang	(0577)88862681
温州市进出口公司	温州市	浙江省	(0577)88844557
Sinar Mas Paper Industry (Xiamen) Co.,Ltd.	Xiamen	Fujian	(0592)2962018
金光纸业（厦门）有限公司	厦门市	福建省	(0592)2962010
Sinar Mas Paper Industry (Shenzhen) Co.,Ltd.	Shenzhen	Guangdong	(0755)83516701
金光纸业（深圳）有限公司	深圳市	广东省	(0755)83516773
Jieyang Ocean Shipping Supply Group Co.,Ltd.	Jieyang	Guangdong	(0663)8239634
揭阳市外轮供应集团有限公司	揭阳市	广东省	(0663)8236186

2311: Book, Newspaper, and Magazine Printing 书、报、刊印刷业

The industry accounts for 0.181% of the total revenue of China's industrial sector in 2002. The rate of return on assets is 2.07%. 67.76% of all firms in the industry made a profit while 32.24% had negative returns.The top province in terms of the industry's revenue is Guangdong, accounting for 20.50% of the total revenue.
2002年本行业收入占全行业的 0.181%，资产利润率为 2.07%。67.76%的企业赢利，32.24%的企业亏损。收入最高的省为广东省，占本行业的20.50%。

	Total number of firms 企业总数	Total number of employees 职工总数	Total revenue (Mil.RMB) 总销售收入 (百万元)	Total profit (Mil.RMB) 总利润 (百万元)	Return on assets 资产利润率 (%)	Return on equity 权益利润率 (%)	Labour productivity ('000 RMB/ worker) 劳动生产率 (千元/人)	Debts/ assets 资产负债率 (%)	Total assets (Mil.RMB) 总资产 (百万元)
Industry Overall 行业总体	1498	244,252	19,421	707	2.07	4.56	32.15	54.60	34,156

	Number of firms 企业个数	Average number of employees 平均职工人数	Average revenue ('000 RMB) 平均销售收入 (千元)	Average profit ('000 RMB) 平均利润 (千元)	Return on assets 资产利润率 (%)	Return on equity 权益利润率 (%)	Labour productivity ('000 RMB/ worker) 劳动生产率 (千元/人)	Debts/ assets 资产负债率 (%)	Average total assets ('000 RMB) 平均总资产 (千元)
By ownership 产业所有权									
State-owned 国有	901	156	8,820	93	0.46	1.05	26.93	56.42	20,238
Collective-owned 集体	133	114	11,103	505	5.20	13.42	32.34	61.27	9,708
Foreign & Overseas Chinese Funded 三资	83	346	49,023	3,589	4.28	7.60	51.72	43.68	83,832
By regional distribution 地区分布									
Central-North 华北	335	163	11,491	322	1.31	2.74	33.20	52.12	24,570
Beijing 北京	200	154	13,035	468	1.63	3.27	34.63	50.15	28,752
Tianjin 天津	31	113	7,534	352	3.48	5.50	86.30	36.65	10,104
Hebei 河北	55	236	13,576	139	0.49	1.13	23.77	56.59	28,148
Shanxi 山西	32	146	6,053	-32	-0.24	-0.73	22.61	67.07	13,508
Inner Mongolia 内蒙古	17	159	4,034	-194	-1.76	-5.35	11.82	67.01	11,003
Northeast 东北	117	135	6,779	126	0.72	1.81	20.67	60.33	17,511
Liaoning 辽宁	54	141	8,248	102	0.43	1.02	22.70	57.95	23,733
Jilin 吉林	30	127	5,735	276	2.14	7.02	22.17	69.48	12,897
Heilongjiang 黑龙江	33	133	5,325	28	0.24	0.59	15.82	59.07	11,522
Central-East 华东	390	173	16,101	684	2.86	6.86	34.90	58.33	23,943
Shanghai 上海	55	123	20,452	1,293	3.52	6.80	55.25	48.26	36,773
Jiangsu 江苏	82	201	15,232	396	2.04	6.11	27.42	66.70	19,453
Zhejiang 浙江	61	110	13,583	847	5.45	10.10	46.87	45.98	15,540
Anhui 安徽	37	179	9,451	19	0.10	0.26	25.45	59.98	18,414
Fujian 福建	47	127	14,871	1,445	7.98	17.85	47.50	55.33	18,116
Jiangxi 江西	33	247	21,120	792	3.07	8.33	35.88	63.11	25,773
Shandong 山东	75	223	17,750	225	0.71	2.02	27.99	65.05	31,854
Central-South 中南	415	180	15,675	654	2.62	5.33	32.86	50.87	24,989
Henan 河南	79	168	7,776	219	1.30	3.28	23.44	60.35	16,810
Hubei 湖北	61	182	11,782	728	3.45	7.89	29.77	56.27	21,088
Hunan 湖南	53	144	13,095	16	0.11	0.27	29.56	56.99	13,922
Guangdong 广东	146	232	27,268	1,269	3.11	5.83	39.71	46.76	40,879
Guangxi 广西	54	121	6,038	-119	-1.06	-3.07	23.53	65.39	11,141
Hainan 海南	22	97	7,767	1,361	6.68	9.89	39.36	32.47	20,379
Southwest 西南	118	125	7,369	378	2.48	7.19	31.71	65.50	15,264
Chongqing 重庆	10	262	10,317	-611	-2.61	-7.51	19.14	65.24	23,379
Sichuan 四川	37	151	11,095	1,215	6.31	26.51	35.30	76.21	19,262
Guizhou 贵州	28	80	4,801	98	1.03	4.74	19.04	78.17	9,520
Yunnan 云南	33	97	5,314	118	0.90	1.92	48.44	53.12	13,085
Tibet 西藏	10	112	4,604	-83	-0.53	-0.76	20.90	29.63	15,623
Northwest 西北	123	139	9,140	15	0.08	0.16	25.81	51.62	19,245
Shaanxi 陕西	35	190	19,036	181	0.47	1.03	34.59	53.84	38,252
Gansu 甘肃	37	149	5,892	-152	-1.01	-1.96	19.89	48.23	15,013
Qinghai 青海	4	185	8,200	-212	-1.46	-3.90	22.70	62.60	14,559
Ningxia 宁夏	2	26	3,393	738	25.07	56.73	63.02	55.81	2,944
Xinjiang 新疆	45	93	4,454	11	0.13	0.24	19.72	47.32	9,082

2311: Book, Newspaper, and Magazine Printing 书、报、刊印刷业

Year 年份	Number of firms 企业个数	Rate of change 变化率 (%)	Number of employees 职工人数 (人)	Rate of change 变化率 (%)	Total revenue (Mil. RMB) 总销售收入 (百万元)	Rate of change 变化率 (%)	Total profit (Mil RMB) 总利润 (百万元)	Rate of change 变化率 (%)
2000	1437		266,889		14,794		478	
2001	1472	2.44	255,504	-4.27	16,579	12.07	438	-8.37
2002	1498	1.77	244,252	-4.40	19,421	17.14	707	61.42

Major Products 主要产品	Output 产量	Unit 单位
Multichrome Printed Products 多色印刷品	42,207	10,000 Reams 万对开色令
Monochrome Printed Products 单色印刷品	11,856	10,000 Reams 万令

10 Main Firms with Maximal Revenue (year founded) 收入最大的十家主要企业（创办年份）	City 城市	Province 省	Telephone/ fax 电话/传真	Number of employees 职工人数	Ownership 产业所有权	Revenue ('000 RMB) 销售收入（千元）	Profit('000 RMB) (rank) 利润(千元)(排名)	Total assets ('000 RMB) 总资产（千元）	Major products 主要产品
Heshan Artori Printing Co.,Ltd.	Jiangmen	Guangdong	(0750)8766115		Overseas Chinese-funded				Printing Articles
鹤山市雅图仕印刷有限公司(1991)	江门市	广东省	(0750)8766369	8,000	港澳台资	660,077	19,642(11)	900,759	印刷品
Hunan Xinhua Printing Group Co.., Ltd.	Changsha	Hunan	(0731)5584119		State Enterprises				Monochrome Printed Proodducts单
湖南新华印刷集团有限责任公司(1970)	长沙市	湖南省	(0731)5581309	1,663	国有独资	409,963	6,935(32)	302,295	色印刷品
Shenzhen Donnelley Printing Co., Ltd.	Shenzhen	Guangdong	(0755)84190499		Foreign Funded				Printing Articles
深圳市当纳旭日印刷有限公司(1993)	深圳市	广东省	(0755)84190014	858	外商投资	335,999	56,453(1)	497,187	印刷品
C & C Joint Printing (Guangdong)Co.,Ltd.	Shenzhen	Guangdong	(0755)83307607		Overseas Chinese-funded				Printing Articles
中华商务联合印刷（广东）有限公司(1997)	深圳市	广东省	(0755)28459911	773	港澳台资	198,855	6,706(34)	383,740	印刷品
Tianshi Printing(ShenZhen) Co.,Ltd.	Shenzhen	Guangdong	(0755)28883302		Overseas Chinese-funded				Printing Articles
天时印刷（深圳）有限公司(1990)	深圳市	广东省	(0755)28883223	1,300	港澳台资	192,459	23,687(6)	436,735	印刷品
Fuji Film Star-light Co., ltd.	Langfang	Hebei	(0316)3316342		Foreign Funded				PS Board
富士星光有限公司(1995)	廊坊市	河北省	(0316)3316342	305	外商投资	151,696	18,727(12)	281,412	PS板
Beijing Nitpo Printing Co.,Ltd.	Beijing	Beijing	(010)67881680		Foreign Funded				Color Printing Articles彩
北京日邦印刷有限公司(1993)	北京市	北京市	(010)67881747	219	外商投资	145,163	17,063(14)	269,196	色印刷品
Dongguan Xinyang Printing Co., Ltd.	Dongguan	Guangdong	(0769)2260640		Overseas Chinese-funded				Printing Articles
东莞新扬印刷有限公司(1989)	东莞市	广东省	(0769)2263943	700	港澳台资	134,800	1,738(114)	100,981	印刷品
Xiamen Wufu Printing Co.,Ltd.	Xiamen	Fujian	(0592)5082168		Overseas Chinese-funded				Multichrome Printed Product多
厦门五福印务有限公司(1994)	厦门市	福建省	(0592)5080168	297	港澳台资	126,193	37,620(3)	86,045	色印刷品
Shanghai Zhonghua Printing Co., Ltd.	Shanghai	Shanghai	(021)62662100		Limited-Liability				Book & Newspapers Printing书
上海中华印刷有限公司(1912)	上海市	上海市	(021)62669809	410	有限公司	121,017	7,044(31)	183,226	报刊印刷

Top 10 Cities by Revenue 销售收入排名前10位城市	Province 省	Market share 市场份额 (%)	Number of firms 企业个数
Beijing 北京市	Beijing 北京市	13.42	200
Shenzhen 深圳市	Guangdong 广东省	6.26	20
Shanghai 上海市	Shanghai 上海市	5.79	55
Guangzhou 广州市	Guangdong 广东省	4.28	51
Jiangmen 江门市	Guangdong 广东省	4.23	9
Xi'an 西安市	Shannxi 陕西省	2.99	17
Changsha 长沙市	Hunan 湖南省	2.86	15
Hangzhou 杭州市	Zhejiang 浙江省	2.74	24
Zhengzhou 郑州市	Henan 河南省	2.40	27
Shangrao 上饶市	Jiangxi 江西省	1.89	3

10 Major Wholesalers 十家主要批发商	City 城市	Province 省	Telephone/Fax 电话/传真
Jiangsu Xinhua Bookstore Group Co.,Ltd.	Nanjing	Jiangsu	(025)3600009
江苏省新华书店集团有限公司	南京市	江苏省	(025)7713941
Zhejiang Book Plaza	Hangzhou	Zhejiang	(0571)88831111
浙江图书大厦	杭州市	浙江省	(0571)88062641
Shandong Books Audiovisual Issue General Company.Shandong Xinhua Bookstore	Jinan	Shandong	(0531)2776547
山东省图书音像发行总公司山东省新华书店	济南市	山东省	(0531)2772748
Hunan Xinhua Bookstore	Changsha	Hunan	(0731)4308527
湖南省新华书店	长沙市	湖南省	(0731)4308500
Xinhua Bookstore Head Office	Beijing	Beijing	(010)88374693
新华书店总店	北京市	北京市	(010)68348424
Fujian Xinhua BookStore	Fuzhou	Fujian	(0591)7559410
福建省新华书店	福州市	福建省	(0591)7559404
Jiangxi Xinhua Bookstore	Nanchang	Jiangxi	(0791)6219204
江西省新华书店	南昌市	江西省	(0791)6219204
Henan Xinhua Bookstore	Zhengzhou	Henan	(0371)6223385
河南省新华书店	郑州市	河南省	(0371)6230424
Guangdong Xinhua Bookstore Teaching Material Bookstore	Guangzhou	Guangdong	(020)83373394
广东省新华书店教材书店	广州市	广东省	(020)83370232
Chongqing Xinhua Bookstore (Group) Co.,Ltd.	Chongqing	Chongqing	(023)63814724
重庆新华书店（集团）有限责任公司	重庆市	重庆市	(023)63814724

2312: Packaging Printing 包装装潢印刷业

The industry accounts for 0.370% of the total revenue of China's industrial sector in 2002. The rate of return on assets is 5.44%. 81.62% of all firms in the industry made a profit while 18.38% had negative returns.The top province in terms of the industry's revenue is Guangdong, accounting for 26.59% of the total revenue.
2002年本行业收入占全行业的 0.370%，资产利润率为 5.44%。81.62%的企业赢利，18.38%的企业亏损。收入最高的省为广东省，占本行业的26.59%。

	Total number of firms 企业总数	Total number of employees 职工总数	Total revenue (Mil.RMB) 总销售收入 (百万元)	Total profit (Mil.RMB) 总利润 (百万元)	Return on assets 资产利润率 (%)	Return on equity 权益利润率 (%)	Labour productivity ('000 RMB/ worker) 劳动生产率 (千元/人)	Debts/ assets 资产负债率 (%)	Total assets (Mil.RMB) 总资产 (百万元)
Industry Overall 行业总体	1420	214,807	39,646	3,106	5.44	11.64	60.73	53.32	57,151

	Number of firms 企业个数	Average number of employees 平均职工人数	Average revenue ('000 RMB) 平均销售收入（千元）	Average profit ('000 RMB) 平均利润 (千元)	Return on assets 资产利润率 (%)	Return on equity 权益利润率 (%)	Labour productivity ('000 RMB/ worker) 劳动生产率 (千元/人)	Debts/ assets 资产负债率 (%)	Average total assets ('000 RMB) 平均总资产 (千元)
By ownership 产业所有权									
State-owned 国有	156	162	17,908	40	0.08	0.17	31.53	52.91	49,180
Collective-owned 集体	165	148	28,546	2,210	7.57	16.49	64.66	54.08	29,195
Foreign & Overseas Chinese Funded 三资	313	239	51,598	5,383	7.81	14.99	79.15	47.88	68,908
By regional distribution 地区分布									
Central-North 华北	99	173	29,755	2,184	2.77	5.33	55.83	48.07	78,914
Beijing 北京	43	130	16,276	1,271	4.52	8.11	44.19	44.20	28,103
Tianjin 天津	25	158	56,315	6,468	3.00	5.46	123.44	45.08	215,665
Hebei 河北	23	237	29,603	263	0.62	1.60	33.16	61.47	42,589
Shanxi 山西	8	267	19,636	-772	-2.65	-14.01	19.36	81.07	29,107
Inner Mongolia 内蒙古									
Northeast 东北	40	146	22,994	339	0.52	1.60	49.28	67.27	64,524
Liaoning 辽宁	17	204	43,537	482	0.37	1.09	65.52	65.61	129,050
Jilin 吉林	10	82	7,891	600	4.04	15.13	32.30	73.31	14,852
Heilongjiang 黑龙江	13	121	7,748	-49	-0.27	-1.27	22.29	78.85	18,352
Central-East 华东	669	115	23,384	2,060	6.92	14.65	63.18	52.77	29,757
Shanghai 上海	96	127	35,378	3,682	7.81	13.06	87.11	40.17	47,130
Jiangsu 江苏	142	120	21,716	1,283	4.50	10.76	63.86	58.20	28,540
Zhejiang 浙江	286	89	20,466	2,136	9.02	20.07	63.16	55.08	23,694
Anhui 安徽	21	174	39,800	3,706	9.37	21.03	68.64	55.44	39,550
Fujian 福建	51	119	16,880	1,174	5.06	9.53	52.04	46.96	23,213
Jiangxi 江西	10	79	9,514	186	1.34	5.31	38.63	74.88	13,955
Shandong 山东	63	182	24,108	1,454	3.82	9.91	42.60	61.48	38,089
Central-South 中南	479	184	31,671	2,049	5.12	10.86	60.96	52.82	39,996
Henan 河南	63	192	22,495	2,120	8.83	19.61	40.06	54.98	24,005
Hubei 湖北	46	184	37,368	1,780	3.52	7.50	94.58	53.04	50,526
Hunan 湖南	46	109	28,156	6,205	20.08	41.67	133.00	51.81	30,904
Guangdong 广东	311	195	33,899	1,589	3.66	7.61	55.46	51.89	43,404
Guangxi 广西	10	157	14,260	-1,457	-5.02	-14.05	27.02	64.29	29,045
Hainan 海南	3	70	17,878	253	0.69		43.40	114.79	36,922
Southwest 西南	110	210	41,957	4,438	7.68	17.60	63.81	56.38	57,802
Chongqing 重庆	21	119	21,410	2,172	8.73	35.90	57.75	75.69	24,895
Sichuan 四川	34	187	26,399	2,125	5.37	11.26	50.78	52.31	39,586
Guizhou 贵州	21	236	18,296	1,091	3.21	8.60	23.31	62.66	33,987
Yunnan 云南	33	282	87,388	10,527	9.20	20.00	95.98	53.98	114,403
Tibet 西藏	1	16	38	14	2.80	3.11	14.06	10.00	500
Northwest 西北	23	168	15,274	1,269	2.19	5.16	27.10	57.63	58,009
Shaanxi 陕西	13	225	21,589	1,503	1.63	4.09	25.98	60.23	92,291
Gansu 甘肃	4	32	1,030	-42	-2.28	-20.64	17.39	88.97	1,844
Qinghai 青海	1	160	8,318	233	1.54	2.16	17.56	28.48	15,102
Ningxia 宁夏	1	137	5,607	69	0.72	1.31	14.21	45.06	9,554
Xinjiang 新疆	4	128	13,152	2,378	9.29	13.34	42.39	30.36	25,594

2312: Packaging Printing 包装装潢印刷业

Year 年份	Number of firms 企业个数	Rate of change 变化率 (%)	Number of employees 职工人数 (人)	Rate of change 变化率 (%)	Total revenue (Mil. RMB) 总销售收入 (百万元)	Rate of change 变化率 (%)	Total profit (Mil RMB) 总利润 (百万元)	Rate of change 变化率 (%)
2000	1043		179,549		28,402		2,521	
2001	1249	19.75	192,031	6.95	34,532	21.58	2,846	12.89
2002	1420	13.69	214,807	11.86	39,646	14.81	3,106	9.14

Major Products 主要产品	Output 产量	Unit 单位
Multichrome Printed Products 多色印刷品	42,207	10,000 Reams 万对开色令
Monochrome Printed Products 单色印刷品	11,856	10,000 Reams 万令

10 Main Firms with Maximal Revenue (year founded) 收入最大的十家主要企业（创办年份）	City 城市	Province 省	Telephone/fax 电话/传真	Number of employees 职工人数	Ownership 产业所有权	Revenue ('000 RMB) 销售收入 (千元)	Profit('000 RMB) (rank) 利润(千元) (排名)	Total assets ('000 RMB) 总资产 (千元)	Major products 主要产品
Hongxing Printing(ShenZhen) Co.,Ltd.	Shenzhen	Guangdong	(0755)27392288		Overseas Chinese-funded				Color Box
鸿兴印刷（深圳）有限公司(1992)	深圳市	广东省	(0755)27382961	7,500	港澳台资	567,219	105,518(4)	943,104	彩盒
Shanghai Tobacco Industry Printing Factory	Shanghai	Shanghai	(021)65459091		State-owned				Multichrome Printed Product多
上海烟草工业印刷厂(1929)	上海市	上海市	(021)65122604	772	国有企业	505,608	59,879(10)	507,847	色印刷品
Hunan Jinshali Color Printing Co.,Ltd.	Changsha	Hunan	(0731)4060188		Overseas Chinese-funded				Printing Articles
湖南金沙利彩色印刷有限公司(1995)	长沙市	湖南省	(0731)4060280	303	港澳台资	456,479	153,042(1)	367,265	印刷品
Yunnan Qiaotong Packing & Printing Co.,Ltd.	Zhaotong	Yunnan	(0870)2232445		Overseas Chinese-funded				Tobacco Trademark
云南侨通包装印刷有限公司(1994)	昭通市	云南省	(0870)2223868	617	港澳台资	432,115	95,729(6)	475,459	烟标
Dongguan Hucais Printing Co., Ltd.	Dongguan	Guangdong	(0769)5113189		Overseas Chinese-funded				Printing Articles
东莞市虎彩印刷有限公司(1989)	东莞市	广东省	(0769)5114119	772	港澳台资	390,276	50,559(14)	441,361	印刷品
Changde Goldroc Rotogravure Printing Co.,Ltd.	Changde	Hunan	(0736)7170538		Overseas Chinese-funded				Packaging Printing Products包
常德金鹏凹版印刷有限公司(1995)	常德市	湖南省	(0736)7280198	530	港澳台资	384,926	110,989(3)	359,878	装印刷品
Hangzhou Dingzheng Paking Materials Co., Ltd.	Hangzhou	Zhejiang	(0571)86912329		Foreign Funded				Packaging Materials
杭州顶正包材有限公司(1996)	杭州市	浙江省	(0571)86912337	505	外商投资	381,980	59,534(11)	450,145	包装材料
Yunnan Jiujiu Colour Printing Co.,Ltd.	Kunming	Yunnan	(0871)5813564		Overseas Chinese-funded				Cigarette Paper
云南九九彩印有限公司(1998)	昆明市	云南省	(0871)5812310	612	港澳台资	376,947	35,851(19)	303,047	卷烟盘纸
Tianjin Global Magnetic Card Co.,Ltd.	Tianjin	Tianjin	(022)23262878		Joint Stock				Offset Printing
天津环球磁卡股份有限公司(1930)	天津市	天津市	(022)23269333	1,358	股份制	366,822	42,132(17)	2,897,875	胶印印刷
Tianjin People Printing Factory	Tianjin	Tianjin	(022)23262878		State-owned				Printing Articles
天津市人民印刷厂(1998)	天津市	天津市	(022)23269333	280	国有企业	323,390	-	1,641,643	印刷品

Top 10 Cities by Revenue 销售收入排名前10位城市	Province 省	Market share 市场份额 (%)	Number of firms 企业个数
Shanghai 上海市	Shanghai 上海市	8.57	96
Wenzhou 温州市	Zhejiang 浙江省	5.06	142
Hangzhou 杭州市	Zhejiang 浙江省	4.41	50
Shantou 汕头市	Guangdong 广东省	4.36	42
Dongguan 东莞市	Guangdong 广东省	3.88	37
Wuxi 无锡市	Jiangsu 江苏省	3.80	58
Tianjin 天津市	Tianjin 天津市	3.55	25
Zhongshan 中山市	Guangdong 广东省	3.31	42
Shenzhen 深圳市	Guangdong 广东省	3.05	27
Foshan 佛山市	Guangdong 广东省	3.02	43

10 Major Wholesalers 十家主要批发商	City 城市	Province 省	Telephone/Fax 电话/传真
Jiangsu Xinhua Bookstore Group Co.,Ltd.	Nanjing	Jiangsu	(025)3600009
江苏省新华书店集团有限公司	南京市	江苏省	(025)7713941
Zhejiang Book Plaza	Hangzhou	Zhejiang	(0571)88831111
浙江图书大厦	杭州市	浙江省	(0571)88062641
Shandong Books Audiovisual Issue General Company.Shandong Xinhua Bookstore	Jinan	Shandong	(0531)2776547
山东省图书音像发行总公司山东省新华书店	济南市	山东省	(0531)2772748
Hunan Xinhua Bookstore	Changsha	Hunan	(0731)4308527
湖南省新华书店	长沙市	湖南省	(0731)4308500
Xinhua Bookstore Head Office	Beijing	Beijing	(010)88374693
新华书店总店	北京市	北京市	(010)68348424
Fujian Xinhua BookStore	Fuzhou	Fujian	(0591)7559410
福建省新华书店	福州市	福建省	(0591)7559404
Jiangxi Xinhua Bookstore	Nanchang	Jiangxi	(0791)6219204
江西省新华书店	南昌市	江西省	(0791)6219204
Henan Xinhua Bookstore	Zhengzhou	Henan	(0371)6223385
河南省新华书店	郑州市	河南省	(0371)6230424
Guangdong Xinhua Bookstore Teaching Material Bookstore	Guangzhou	Guangdong	(020)83373394
广东省新华书店教材书店	广州市	广东省	(020)83370232
Chongqing Xinhua Bookstore (Group) Co.,Ltd.	Chongqing	Chongqing	(023)63814724
重庆新华书店（集团）有限责任公司	重庆市	重庆市	(023)63814724

2319: Other Printing Industries 其他印刷业

The industry accounts for 0.142% of the total revenue of China's industrial sector in 2002. The rate of return on assets is 10.08%. 75.76% of all firms in the industry made a profit while 24.24% had negative returns.The top province in terms of the industry's revenue is Shanghai, accounting for 18.12% of the total revenue.
2002年本行业收入占全行业的0.142%，资产利润率为10.08%。75.76%的企业赢利，24.24%的企业亏损。收入最高的省为上海市，占本行业的18.12%。

	Total number of firms 企业总数	Total number of employees 职工总数	Total revenue (Mil.RMB) 总销售收入（百万元）	Total profit (Mil.RMB) 总利润（百万元）	Return on assets 资产利润率（%）	Return on equity 权益利润率（%）	Labour productivity ('000 RMB/ worker) 劳动生产率（千元/人）	Debts/ assets 资产负债率（%）	Total assets (Mil.RMB) 总资产（百万元）
Industry Overall 行业总体	821	85,856	15,178	1,906	10.08	17.99	69.73	43.98	18,916

	Number of firms 企业个数	Average number of employees 平均职工人数	Average revenue ('000 RMB) 平均销售收入（千元）	Average profit ('000 RMB) 平均利润（千元）	Return on assets 资产利润率（%）	Return on equity 权益利润率（%）	Labour productivity ('000 RMB/ worker) 劳动生产率（千元/人）	Debts/ assets 资产负债率（%）	Average total assets ('000 RMB) 平均总资产（千元）
By ownership 产业所有权									
State-owned 国有	369	86	16,024	2,825	13.11	20.97	97.56	37.51	21,552
Collective-owned 集体	102	106	14,422	1,380	8.57	17.55	52.06	51.17	16,101
Foreign & Overseas Chinese Funded 三资	118	154	35,582	4,286	8.90	16.35	60.88	45.57	48,179
By regional distribution 地区分布									
Central-North 华北	152	99	19,420	2,958	12.07	21.17	61.77	42.96	24.502
Beijing 北京	76	92	22,048	3,329	10.65	18.07	45.72	41.07	31,260
Tianjin 天津	36	39	3,080	338	17.40	36.23	18.13	51.98	1,943
Hebei 河北	23	230	45,109	8,051	17.96	35.16	96.35	48.92	44,828
Shanxi 山西	13	64	5,755	-659	-4.73	-7.30	41.63	35.14	13,922
Inner Mongolia 内蒙古	4	123	13,247	1,970	11.84	16.82	77.05	29.59	16,630
Northeast 东北	70	65	4,016	203	2.77	8.41	29.60	67.10	7,337
Liaoning 辽宁	30	75	4,212	176	2.02	5.94	26.32	65.93	8,697
Jilin 吉林	25	67	3,458	360	6.71	16.58	19.65	59.53	5,358
Heilongjiang 黑龙江	15	43	4,551	-4	-0.04	-0.20	66.77	78.20	7,916
Central-East 华东	266	111	24,100	3,287	11.79	20.20	85.62	41.60	27,872
Shanghai 上海	97	118	28,346	3,888	11.32	17.77	99.38	36.31	34,344
Jiangsu 江苏	36	129	31,352	4,829	13.91	28.87	91.42	51.80	34,708
Zhejiang 浙江	39	75	15,882	1,852	8.24	14.28	66.42	42.32	22,484
Anhui 安徽	14	138	16,036	1,703	8.63	18.45	52.61	53.20	19,724
Fujian 福建	34	101	17,465	1,421	8.93	15.66	61.29	42.98	15,921
Jiangxi 江西	18	115	32,830	8,560	21.26	31.04	149.14	31.52	40,268
Shandong 山东	28	114	17,984	894	6.05	15.08	50.42	59.91	14,779
Central-South 中南	201	104	14,135	792	4.46	9.13	52.59	51.09	17,743
Henan 河南	38	93	8,262	285	2.22	5.72	27.73	61.12	12,839
Hubei 湖北	27	94	11,864	75	0.70	1.60	58.47	56.12	10,661
Hunan 湖南	22	90	7,058	961	9.72	19.30	38.59	49.63	9,887
Guangdong 广东	78	145	24,897	1,499	4.94	9.72	63.98	49.13	30,326
Guangxi 广西	29	37	1,971	3	0.07	0.26	37.01	72.77	3,742
Hainan 海南	7	76	7,484	1,167	8.24	9.53	31.65	13.58	14,165
Southwest 西南	71	131	23,341	2,964	9.06	15.22	79.55	40.49	32,732
Chongqing 重庆	15	114	20,136	694	3.18	7.70	64.03	58.67	21,814
Sichuan 四川	16	309	70,037	11,255	11.94	16.51	108.85	27.67	94,250
Guizhou 贵州	14	33	3,119	214	6.86	14.77	21.54	53.53	3,110
Yunnan 云南	24	90	7,894	707	3.82	12.47	37.63	69.39	18,512
Tibet 西藏	2	14	727	7	1.38	1.95	15.41	29.18	470
Northwest 西北	61	105	16,992	3,252	14.44	23.46	85.28	38.45	22,521
Shaanxi 陕西	21	239	47,040	9,392	15.70	24.98	103.21	37.17	59,841
Gansu 甘肃	32	35	1,241	38	1.23	2.46	23.22	50.03	3,066
Qinghai 青海	3	28	309	-69	-7.50	-15.16	4.86	50.49	915
Ningxia 宁夏	1	96	5,797	10	0.09	0.33	18.55	73.13	11,312
Xinjiang 新疆	4	24	563	24	1.94	3.74	9.96	48.10	1,237

2319: Other Printing Industries 其他印刷业

Year 年份	Number of firms 企业个数	Rate of change 变化率 (%)	Number of employees 职工人数 (人)	Rate of change 变化率 (%)	Total revenue (Mil. RMB) 总销售收入 (百万元)	Rate of change 变化率 (%)	Total profit (Mil RMB) 总利润 (百万元)	Rate of change 变化率 (%)
2000	1165		108,782		13,932		1,630	
2001	911	-21.80	88,313	-18.82	14,072	1.00	1,910	17.18
2002	821	-9.88	85,856	-2.78	15,178	7.86	1,906	-0.21

Major Products 主要产品	Output 产量	Unit 单位
Multichrome Printed Products 多色印刷品	42,207	10,000 Reams 万对开色令
Monochrome Printed Products 单色印刷品	11,856	10,000 Reams 万令

10 Main Firms with Maximal Revenue (year founded) 收入最大的十家主要企业（创办年份）	City 城市	Province 省	Telephone/fax 电话/传真	Number of employees 职工人数	Ownership 产业所有权	Revenue ('000 RMB) 销售收入 (千元)	Profit('000 RMB) (rank) 利润(千元) (排名)	Total assets ('000 RMB) 总资产 (千元)	Major products 主要产品
Chengdu Banknote Printing Complexy	Chengdu	Sichuan	(028)82995934		State-owned				Paper Money
成都印钞公司(1989)	成都市	四川省	(028)82995168	3,714	国有企业	935,405	156,801(4)	1,248,107	钞票
Shanghai Banknote Printing Factory	Shanghai	Shanghai	(021)52931111		State-owned				Paper Money
上海印钞厂(1941)	上海市	上海市	(021)52931038	2,287	国有企业	851,896	188,173(2)	939,546	钞票
Xi'an Banknote Printing Plant	Xi'an	Shannxi	(029)4262320		State-owned				Paper Money
西安印钞厂(1952)	西安市	陕西省	(029)4262066	2,012	国有企业	693,021	162,382(3)	720,163	钞票
Shijiazhuang Banknote Printing Factory	Shijiazhuang	Hebei	(0311)5051875		State-owned				Paper Money
石家庄印钞厂(1989)	石家庄市	河北省	(0311)5052872	1,184	国有企业	554,905	144,215(6)	582,963	钞票
Nanchang Banknote Printing Factory	Nanchang	Jiangxi	(0791)5273244		State-owned				Paper Money
南昌印钞厂(1990)	南昌市	江西省	(0791)5276461	1,155	国有企业	528,897	151,196(5)	636,792	钞票
Shenzhen Jinjia Color Printing Co.,Ltd.	Shenzhen	Guangdong	(0755)27300555		Overseas Chinese-funded				Fireworks Packing
深圳劲嘉彩印有限公司(1996)	深圳市	广东省	(0755)27301000	857	港澳台资	307,985	62,261(8)	611,612	烟火包
Baoding Geology Picture Printing Factory	Baoding	Hebei	(0312)3135971		State-owned				Multichrome Printed Products多
保定地质图制印厂(1939)	保定市	河北省	(0312)3137480	920	国有企业	272,301	25,755(13)	248,892	色印刷品
Shanghai SML Labels Co.,Ltd.	Shanghai	Shanghai	(021)52271688		Overseas Chinese-funded				Computer Trademark Products电脑
上海西文电脑商标服饰有限公司(1998)	上海市	上海市	(021)62209037	389	港澳台资	198,040	8,450(33)	69,633	商标制品
Kunshan Zhangpu Color Printing Factory	Suzhou	Jiangsu	(0512)57441723		Collective-owned				Composite Film
昆山市张浦彩印厂(1984)	苏州市	江苏省	(0512)57441009	259	集体企业	194,378	40,883(9)	292,860	复合膜
Shanghai Zihua Colour Printing &Packing Co., Ltd.	Shanghai	Shanghai	(021)64901517		Overseas Chinese-funded				Plastic Colour Printed Products塑料
上海紫华彩印包装有限公司(1994)	上海市	上海市	(021)64901799	563	港澳台资	180,702	10,549(23)	227,354	彩印制品

Top 10 Cities by Revenue 销售收入排名前10位城市	Province 省	Market share 市场份额 (%)	Number of firms 企业个数
Shanghai 上海市	Shanghai 上海市	18.12	97
Beijing 北京市	Beijing 北京市	11.04	76
Chengdu 成都市	Sichuan 四川省	6.55	10
Xi'an 西安市	Shannxi 陕西省	5.49	7
Guangzhou 广州市	Guangdong 广东省	4.28	22
Shijiazhuang 石家庄市	Hebei 河北省	4.20	3
Nanchang 南昌市	Jiangxi 江西省	3.83	7
Shenzhen 深圳市	Guangdong 广东省	2.89	9
Xiamen 厦门市	Fujian 福建省	2.89	16
Nanjing 南京市	Jiangsu 江苏省	2.76	8

10 Major Wholesalers 十家主要批发商	City 城市	Province 省	Telephone/Fax 电话/传真
Jiangsu Xinhua Bookstore Group Co.,Ltd.	Nanjing	Jiangsu	(025)3600009
江苏省新华书店集团有限公司	南京市	江苏省	(025)7713941
Zhejiang Book Plaza	Hangzhou	Zhejiang	(0571)88831111
浙江图书大厦	杭州市	浙江省	(0571)88062641
Shandong Books Audiovisual Issue General Company.Shandong Xinhua Bookstore	Jinan	Shandong	(0531)2776547
山东省图书音像发行总公司山东省新华书店	济南市	山东省	(0531)2772748
Hunan Xinhua Bookstore	Changsha	Hunan	(0731)4308527
湖南省新华书店	长沙市	湖南省	(0731)4308500
Xinhua Bookstore Head Office	Beijing	Beijing	(010)88374693
新华书店总店	北京市	北京市	(010)68348424
Fujian Xinhua BookStore	Fuzhou	Fujian	(0591)7559410
福建省新华书店	福州市	福建省	(0591)7559404
Jiangxi Xinhua Bookstore	Nanchang	Jiangxi	(0791)6219204
江西省新华书店	南昌市	江西省	(0791)6219204
Henan Xinhua Bookstore	Zhengzhou	Henan	(0371)6223385
河南省新华书店	郑州市	河南省	(0371)6230424
Guangdong Xinhua Bookstore Teaching Material Bookstore	Guangzhou	Guangdong	(020)83373394
广东省新华书店教材书店	广州市	广东省	(020)83370232
Chongqing Xinhua Bookstore (Group) Co.,Ltd.	Chongqing	Chongqing	(023)63814724
重庆新华书店（集团）有限责任公司	重庆市	重庆市	(023)63814724

2320: Recording Media Duplicating 记录媒介的复制

The industry accounts for 0.027% of the total revenue of China's industrial sector in 2002. The rate of return on assets is 2.91%. 70.15% of all firms in the industry made a profit while 29.85% had negative returns.The top province in terms of the industry's revenue is Guangdong, accounting for 26.18% of the total revenue.
2002年本行业收入占全行业的0.027%，资产利润率为2.91%。70.15%的企业赢利，29.85%的企业亏损。收入最高的省为广东省，占本行业的26.18%。

	Total number of firms 企业总数	Total number of employees 职工总数	Total revenue (Mil.RMB) 总销售收入 (百万元)	Total profit (Mil.RMB) 总利润 (百万元)	Return on assets 资产利润率 (%)	Return on equity 权益利润率 (%)	Labour productivity ('000 RMB/ worker) 劳动生产率 (千元/人)	Debts/ assets 资产负债率 (%)	Total assets (Mil.RMB) 总资产 (百万元)
Industry Overall 行业总体	67	9,724	2,916	175	2.91	5.95	109.92	51.03	6,012

	Number of firms 企业个数	Average number of employees 平均职工人数	Average revenue ('000 RMB) 平均销售收入 (千元)	Average profit ('000 RMB) 平均利润 (千元)	Return on assets 资产利润率 (%)	Return on equity 权益利润率 (%)	Labour productivity ('000 RMB/ worker) 劳动生产率 (千元/人)	Debts/ assets 资产负债率 (%)	Average total assets ('000 RMB) 平均总资产 (千元)
By ownership 产业所有权									
State-owned 国有	18	124	12,675	182	0.46	0.95	24.51	51.63	39,461
Collective-owned 集体	2	43	9,151	333	3.94	11.58	89.62	66.01	8,449
Foreign & Overseas Chinese Funded 三资	25	192	65,227	2,656	2.35	5.24	116.27	55.17	113,040
By regional distribution 地区分布									
Central-North 华北	24	107	44,074	3,250	4.53	11.54	90.84	60.76	71,772
Beijing 北京	20	101	18,821	1,008	2.41	5.45	44.06	55.82	41,862
Tianjin 天津	2	203	326,001	25,453	6.65	18.72	325.91	64.48	382,666
Hebei 河北	1	93	29,078	6,934	5.96	22.23	120.60	73.21	116,435
Shanxi 山西									
Inner Mongolia 内蒙古	1	46	279	5	0.14	0.17	4.48	16.01	3,516
Northeast 东北	2	133	20,383	1,592	2.63	10.42	40.05	74.76	60,531
Liaoning 辽宁	1	101	29,264	3,036	2.87	10.05	93.52	71.45	105,824
Jilin 吉林	1	164	11,501	147	0.96	43.11	7.12	97.76	15,238
Heilongjiang 黑龙江									
Central-East 华东	9	171	69,675	4,813	4.54	8.81	213.94	48.49	105,984
Shanghai 上海	2	195	46,179	2,713	3.23	4.25	51.74	24.01	83,964
Jiangsu 江苏	2	145	57,067	11,222	14.97	22.56	177.31	33.65	74,972
Zhejiang 浙江	2	217	44,294	3,693	3.32	6.70	96.17	50.38	111,127
Anhui 安徽									
Fujian 福建	2	166	156,149	3,609	2.19	5.78	630.50	62.08	164,691
Jiangxi 江西									
Shandong 山东	1	96	19,702	842	1.00	2.89	73.74	65.50	84,354
Central-South 中南	29	175	40,872	1,773	1.63	2.98	98.00	45.43	108,995
Henan 河南	2	157	37,953	3,145	3.80	15.86	103.54	76.05	82,805
Hubei 湖北	3	153	110,515	15,266	5.13	7.78	358.75	34.02	297,413
Hunan 湖南									
Guangdong 广东	23	184	33,191	-87	-0.10	-0.19	68.80	48.81	89,195
Guangxi 广西									
Hainan 海南	1	60	14,444	1,329	2.58	2.87	128.95	10.16	51,504
Southwest 西南	3	99	1,704	-297	-1.67	-4.24	-0.17	60.55	17,759
Chongqing 重庆									
Sichuan 四川	1	203	2,590	-393	-1.22	-2.85	-3.08	57.37	32,315
Guizhou 贵州	1	79	2,278	-495	-2.44	-7.29	5.91	66.47	20,255
Yunnan 云南	1	14	243	-4	-0.57	-0.89	7.64	36.12	706
Tibet 西藏									
Northwest 西北									
Shaanxi 陕西									
Gansu 甘肃									
Qinghai 青海									
Ningxia 宁夏									
Xinjiang 新疆									

2320: Recording Media Duplicating 记录媒介的复制

Year 年份	Number of firms 企业个数	Rate of change 变化率(%)	Number of employees 职工人数(人)	Rate of change 变化率(%)	Total revenue (Mil. RMB) 总销售收入(百万元)	Rate of change 变化率(%)	Total profit (Mil RMB) 总利润(百万元)	Rate of change 变化率(%)
2000	58		9,624		1,672		102	
2001	59	1.72	10,809	12.31	2,742	64.00	150	47.06
2002	67	13.56	9,724	-10.04	2,916	6.35	175	16.67

Major Products 主要产品	Output 产量	Unit 单位
Laser Disk 激光盘	94,261	10,000 Pieces 万片
Video Tape 录像带	10,282	10,000 Boxes 万盒

10 Main Firms with Maximal Revenue (year founded) 收入最大的十家主要企业(创办年份)	City 城市	Province 省	Telephone/fax 电话/传真	Number of employees 职工人数	Ownership 产业所有权	Revenue ('000 RMB) 销售收入(千元)	Profit('000 RMB) (rank) 利润(千元)(排名)	Total assets ('000 RMB) 总资产(千元)	Major products 主要产品
Tianjin Gemplus Smart Card Co.,Ltd.	Tianjin	Tianjin	(022)83710322		Foreign Funded				IC Telephone Card
天津杰普智能卡有限公司(1997)	天津市	天津市	(022)83710325	246	外商投资	597,197	48,340(1)	627,516	IC电话卡
Indesen(Fujian) Tape Co.,Ltd.	Fuzhou	Fujian	(0591)5380195		Overseas Chinese-funded				Blank Video Tap空
永德信(福建)磁带有限公司(1991)	福州市	福建省	(0591)5380176	265	港澳台资	289,480	6,446(8)	231,396	白录像带
Jiangsu Xinguanglian Laser Disc Co.,Ltd.	Wuxi	Jiangsu	(0510)8701888		Private Owned				CD
江苏新广联光盘有限公司(1999)	无锡市	江苏省	(0510)8700742	220	私营企业	100,064	22,694(3)	145,833	CD类光盘
Sihui MingHua Aohan Technology Co.,Ltd.	Zhaoqing	Guangdong	(0758)3619003		Private Owned				Intelligence Cards
四会市明华澳汉科技有限公司(1997)	肇庆市	广东省	(0758)3619013	355	私营企业	83,983	2,785(18)	88,812	智能卡
Zhejiang Huahong Photoelectricity Co., Ltd.	Hangzhou	Zhejiang	(0571)86911000		Limited-Liability				Laser Disc Duplicating
浙江华虹光电有限公司(1998)	杭州市	浙江省	(0571)86911302	222	有限公司	80,979	6,808(6)	220,138	光盘复制
HuiZhou TCL Audio & Video Products Co.,Ltd.	Huizhou	Guangdong	(0752)2612801		Overseas Chinese-funded				Audio Tap
惠州TCL音像制品有限公司(1989)	惠州市	广东省	(0752)2612800	117	港澳台资	63,343	2,666(19)	42,335	录音带
TianJin Tianbao Laser Disc Co.,Ltd.	Tianjin	Tianjin	(022)82123274		Overseas Chinese-funded				Laser Disc
天津天宝光碟有限公司(1992)	天津市	天津市	(022)82116120	160	港澳台资	54,804	2,565(21)	137,816	光盘
Shanghai United Laser Disc Co.,Ltd.	Shanghai	Shanghai	(021)64856655		Foreign Funded				Laser Disc
上海联合光盘有限公司(1991)	上海市	上海市	(021)64954235	96	外商投资	52,549	4,365(12)	87,264	光盘
Henan Xianda Laser Disc Co., Ltd.	Zhengzhou	Henan	(0371)6782846		Limited-Liability				Multimedia Laser Disc多
河南先达光碟有限公司(1999)	郑州市	河南省	(0371)6782400	108	有限公司	46,793	6,098(9)	131,030	媒体光盘
Beijing Polystar Digidisc Co.,ltd.	Beijing	Beijing	(010)84566052		Overseas Chinese-funded				Laser Disc Duplicating
北京保利星数据光盘有限公司(1999)	北京市	北京市	(010)64321619	105	港澳台资	44,161	7,303(4)	97,312	光盘复制

Top 10 Cities by Revenue 销售收入排名前10位城市	Province 省	Market share 市场份额(%)	Number of firms 企业个数
Tianjin 天津市	Tianjin 天津市	22.36	2
Beijing 北京市	Beijing 北京市	12.91	20
Wuhan 武汉市	Hubei 湖北省	11.37	3
Fuzhou 福州市	Fujian 福建省	9.93	1
Shenzhen 深圳市	Guangdong 广东省	7.70	2
Foshan 佛山市	Guangdong 广东省	5.41	5
Wuxi 无锡市	Jiangsu 江苏省	3.43	1
Zhaoqing 肇庆市	Guangdong 广东省	3.17	2
Shanghai 上海市	Shanghai 上海市	3.17	2
Hangzhou 杭州市	Zhejiang 浙江省	3.04	2

10 Major Wholesalers 十家主要批发商	City 城市	Province 省	Telephone/Fax 电话/传真
Jiangsu Xinhua Bookstore Group Co.,Ltd.	Nanjing	Jiangsu	(025)3600009
江苏省新华书店集团有限公司	南京市	江苏省	(025)7713941
Zhejiang Book Plaza	Hangzhou	Zhejiang	(0571)88831111
浙江图书大厦	杭州市	浙江省	(0571)88062641
Shandong Books Audiovisual Issue General Company.Shandong Xinhua Bookstore	Jinan	Shandong	(0531)2776547
山东省图书音像发行总公司山东省新华书店	济南市	山东省	(0531)2772748
Hunan Xinhua Bookstore	Changsha	Hunan	(0731)4308527
湖南省新华书店	长沙市	湖南省	(0731)4308500
Xinhua Bookstore Head Office	Beijing	Beijing	(010)88374693
新华书店总店	北京市	北京市	(010)68348424
Fujian Xinhua BookStore	Fuzhou	Fujian	(0591)7559410
福建省新华书店	福州市	福建省	(0591)7559404
Jiangxi Xinhua Bookstore	Nanchang	Jiangxi	(0791)6219204
江西省新华书店	南昌市	江西省	(0791)6219204
Henan Xinhua Bookstore	Zhengzhou	Henan	(0371)6223385
河南省新华书店	郑州市	河南省	(0371)6230424
Guangdong Xinhua Bookstore Teaching Material Bookstore	Guangzhou	Guangdong	(020)83373391
广东省新华书店教材书店	广州市	广东省	(020)83370232
Chongqing Xinhua Bookstore (Group) Co.,Ltd.	Chongqing	Chongqing	(023)63814724
重庆新华书店（集团）有限责任公司	重庆市	重庆市	(023)63814724

2411: Stationery Products 文具制造业

The industry accounts for 0.057% of the total revenue of China's industrial sector in 2002. The rate of return on assets is 5.54%. 84.65% of all firms in the industry made a profit while 15.35% had negative returns.The top province in terms of the industry's revenue is Zhejiang, accounting for 48.20% of the total revenue.
2002年本行业收入占全行业的0.057%，资产利润率为5.54%。84.65%的企业赢利，15.35%的企业亏损。收入最高的省为浙江省，占本行业的48.20%。

	Total number of firms 企业总数	Total number of employees 职工总数	Total revenue (Mil.RMB) 总销售收入（百万元）	Total profit (Mil.RMB) 总利润（百万元）	Return on assets 资产利润率 (%)	Return on equity 权益利润率 (%)	Labour productivity ('000 RMB/ worker) 劳动生产率（千元/人）	Debts/ assets 资产负债率 (%)	Total assets (Mil.RMB) 总资产（百万元）
Industry Overall 行业总体	215	41,630	6,118	306	5.54	9.84	36.03	43.71	5,531

	Number of firms 企业个数	Average number of employees 平均职工人数	Average revenue ('000 RMB) 平均销售收入（千元）	Average profit ('000 RMB) 平均利润（千元）	Return on assets 资产利润率 (%)	Return on equity 权益利润率 (%)	Labour productivity ('000 RMB/ worker) 劳动生产率（千元/人）	Debts/ assets 资产负债率 (%)	Average total assets ('000 RMB) 平均总资产（千元）
By ownership 产业所有权									
State-owned 国有	14	84	2,820	-2,500	-12.65	-73.17	8.34	82.71	19,758
Collective-owned 集体	21	96	7,816	222	3.22	7.74	19.39	58.42	6,894
Foreign & Overseas Chinese Funded 三资	99	253	29,820	1,146	3.86	7.42	29.68	48.04	29,707
By regional distribution 地区分布									
Central-North 华北	13	165	15,366	490	2.76	6.03	16.01	54.32	17,760
Beijing 北京	5	94	6,958	243	3.85	14.47	25.90	73.37	6,316
Tianjin 天津	7	216	23,295	781	2.85	5.86	13.85	51.41	27,434
Hebei 河北									
Shanxi 山西	1	159	1,908	-316	-4.35	-8.44	7.40	48.49	7,270
Inner Mongolia 内蒙古									
Northeast 东北	2	105	7,412	-153	-1.66	-6.88	18.20	75.95	9,210
Liaoning 辽宁	1	184	14,728	-312	-1.77	-8.46	20.65	79.02	17,578
Jilin 吉林									
Heilongjiang 黑龙江	1	26	96	7	0.83	0.94	0.88	11.88	842
Central-East 华东	142	185	33,304	1,959	6.54	10.93	46.20	40.23	29,968
Shanghai 上海	36	140	26,462	547	1.94	3.78	49.20	48.79	28,252
Jiangsu 江苏	12	227	32,713	1,206	3.01	6.11	51.89	50.83	40,133
Zhejiang 浙江	70	205	42,125	3,247	10.46	15.50	46.81	32.51	31,037
Anhui 安徽	2	89	11,520	1,617	7.42	15.41	47.56	51.86	21,797
Fujian 福建	18	182	18,922	775	3.27	6.12	36.44	46.65	23,717
Jiangxi 江西	1	178	11,404	96	0.27	0.35	19.79	25.08	36,132
Shandong 山东	3	156	20,074	-196	-0.76	-1.34	40.23	43.38	25,846
Central-South 中南	50	252	22,739	376	1.89	4.21	18.44	55.13	19,889
Henan 河南	2	33	14,431	396	3.32	3.94	132.06	15.87	11,933
Hubei 湖北									
Hunan 湖南	3	87	8,599	290	6.23	21.22	31.22	70.63	4,649
Guangdong 广东	44	277	24,483	390	1.81	4.12	17.56	56.08	21,542
Guangxi 广西	1	75	5,039	-20	-0.23	-0.35	17.32	34.16	8,798
Hainan 海南									
Southwest 西南	5	78	7,325	646	10.57	24.20	38.78	56.33	6,111
Chongqing 重庆	1	119	11,516	2,313	14.66	23.54	54.15	37.72	15,778
Sichuan 四川	2	65	9,129	419	13.84	49.12	47.62	71.82	3,028
Guizhou 贵州	2	72	3,427	39	0.89	4.31	17.95	79.25	4,362
Yunnan 云南									
Tibet 西藏									
Northwest 西北	3	15	263	13	2.59	6.63	48.04	61.02	516
Shaanxi 陕西									
Gansu 甘肃	3	15	263	13	2.59	6.63	48.04	61.02	516
Qinghai 青海									
Ningxia 宁夏									
Xinjiang 新疆									

2411: Stationery Products 文具制造业

Year 年份	Number of firms 企业个数	Rate of change 变化率 (%)	Number of employees 职工人数 (人)	Rate of change 变化率 (%)	Total revenue (Mil. RMB) 总销售收入 (百万元)	Rate of change 变化率 (%)	Total profit (Mil RMB) 总利润 (百万元)	Rate of change 变化率 (%)
2000	175		27,833		3,905		123	
2001	193	10.29	37,366	34.25	5,713	46.30	322	161.79
2002	215	11.40	41,630	11.41	6,118	7.09	306	-4.97

Major Products 主要产品	Output 产量	Unit 单位
Pencil Case 文具盒	3,519	10,000 Units 万个

10 Main Firms with Maximal Revenue (year founded) 收入最大的十家主要企业（创办年份）	City 城市	Province 省	Telephone/fax 电话/传真	Number of employees 职工人数	Ownership 产业所有权	Revenue ('000 RMB) 销售收入 (千元)	Profit('000 RMB) (rank) 利润(千元)(排名)	Total assets ('000 RMB) 总资产 (千元)	Major products 主要产品
Huamao Group Co.,Ltd.	Ningbo	Zhejiang	(0574)88449510		Joint Stock				Education Necessary Accessories
华茂集团股份有限公司(1985)	宁波市	浙江省	(0574)88440232	1,497	股份制	1,408,394	135,639(1)	1,093,801	教育配套材料
Ningbo Deli Group Co.,Ltd.	Ningbo	Zhejiang	(0574)65278079		Private Owned				Pensil Cutting Machine
宁波得力集团有限公司(1997)	宁波市	浙江省	(0574)65273660	2,006	私营企业	252,707	25,898(2)	221,455	削笔器
Ningbo Binbin Stationery Co.,Ltd.	Ningbo	Zhejiang	(0574)65195988		Private Owned				Stapler
宁波彬彬文具有限公司(1996)	宁波市	浙江省	(0574)65195062	594	私营企业	189,650	8,730(7)	86,640	订书机
Colart Tianjin Art Materials Co.,Ltd.	Tianjin	Tianjin	(022)27367907		Foreign Funded				Art Materials
天津柯雅美术材料有限公司(1997)	天津市	天津市	(022)27362015	481	外商投资	125,910	7,874(10)	83,902	美术材料
Gaoming New Times Stationery Co.,Ltd.	Foshan	Guangdong	(0757)8229393		Overseas Chinese-funded				Stationery Articles
高明市新时代文具有限公司(1997)	佛山市	广东省	(0757)8227841	625	港澳台资	120,390	3,655(20)	47,261	文具用品
Panyu All-purpose Stationery Products Co., Ltd.	Guangzhou	Guangdong	(020)84766778		Overseas Chinese-funded				Stapler
番禺通用文具制品厂有限公司(1991)	广州市	广东省	(020)84769399	1,098	港澳台资	109,056	775(62)	96,304	订书机
Chaoyang qixin Stationery Products Factory Co.,Ltd.	Shantou	Guangdong	(0661)7595888		Overseas Chinese-funded				Various Stationeries
潮阳市齐心文具制品有限公司(1997)	汕头市	广东省	(0661)7597888	441	港澳台资	102,743	8,826(6)	9,803	各式文具
SDI (jiangsu) Corporation	Suzhou	Jiangsu	(0512)58320292		Overseas Chinese-funded				Stationery
顺德工业(江苏)有限公司(1999)	苏州市	江苏省	(0512)58320293	606	港澳台资	102,556	-	259,038	文具
Dongguan Worldwild Mfg. Co., Ltd.	Dongguan	Guangdong	(0769)5561686		Overseas Chinese-funded				Stationery Nip
东莞南侧国际文具制造有限公司(1992)	东莞市	广东省	(0769)5561549	1,308	港澳台资	95,753	570(74)	123,337	文具夹
Shanghai Qingpu Ace Luggage & Bags Co.,Ltd.	Shanghai	Shanghai	(021)59770016		Foreign Funded				Sports Bags
上海青浦爱思箱包有限公司(1995)	上海市	上海市	(021)59770968	670	外商投资	94,146	11,187(4)	64,643	运动包

Top 10 Cities by Revenue 销售收入排名前10位城市	Province 省	Market share 市场份额 (%)	Number of firms 企业个数
Ningbo 宁波市	Zhejiang 浙江省	41.09	35
Shanghai 上海市	Shanghai 上海市	15.57	36
Guangzhou 广州市	Guangdong 广东省	6.06	14
Shantou 汕头市	Guangdong 广东省	3.72	10
Suzhou 苏州市	Jiangsu 江苏省	3.32	3
Foshan 佛山市	Guangdong 广东省	2.79	4
Tianjin 天津市	Tianjin 天津市	2.67	7
Wenzhou 温州市	Zhejiang 浙江省	2.63	10
Dongguan 东莞市	Guangdong 广东省	2.47	5
Quanzhou 泉州市	Fujian 福建省	2.25	9

10 Major Wholesalers 十家主要批发商	City 城市	Province 省	Telephone/Fax 电话/传真
King Paper Source Trade (shanghai) Co.,Ltd.	Shanghai	Shanghai	(021)62720808
金纸源贸易（上海）有限公司	上海市	上海市	(021)62720909
China National Paper & Pulp Corpration	Beijing	Beijing	(010)67780346
中国纸张纸浆进出口公司	北京市	北京市	(010)67747294
Sinar Mas Linjiang Paper Industry Trade (Beijing) Co.,Ltd.	Beijing	Beijing	(010)65666688
金光林浆纸业贸易(北京)有限公司	北京市	北京市	(010)65669599
Sinar Mas Paper Industry (Xishan) Co.,Ltd.	Wuxi	Jiangsu	(0510)8251188
金光纸业(锡山)有限公司	无锡市	江苏省	(0510)8250906
China Printing Materials General Company	Beijing	Beijing	(010)63442905
中国印刷物资总公司	北京市	北京市	(010)63442900
TSS Eortune Co., ltd.	Tianjin	Tianjin	(022)28131350
天津同鑫进出口有限公司	天津市	天津市	(022)28131353
Wenzhou Import & Export Corpration	Wenzhou	Zhejiang	(0577)88862681
温州市进出口公司	温州市	浙江省	(0577)88844557
Sinar Mas Paper Industry (Xiamen) Co.,Ltd.	Xiamen	Fujian	(0592)2962018
金光纸业（厦门）有限公司	厦门市	福建省	(0592)2962010
Sinar Mas Paper Industry (Shenzhen) Co.,Ltd.	Shenzhen	Guangdong	(0755)83516701
金光纸业（深圳）有限公司	深圳市	广东省	(0755)83516773
Jieyang Ocean Shipping Supply Group Co.,Ltd.	Jieyang	Guangdong	(0663)8239634
揭阳市外轮供应集团有限公司	揭阳市	广东省	(0663)8236186

2413: Notebooks 本册制造业

The industry accounts for 0.023% of the total revenue of China's industrial sector in 2002. The rate of return on assets is 4.32%. 76.98% of all firms in the industry made a profit while 23.02% had negative returns.The top province in terms of the industry's revenue is Zhejiang, accounting for 25.67% of the total revenue.
2002年本行业收入占全行业的 0.023%，资产利润率为 4.32%。76.98%的企业赢利，23.02%的企业亏损。收入最高的省为浙江省，占本行业的25.67%。

	Total number of firms 企业总数	Total number of employees 职工总数	Total revenue (Mil.RMB) 总销售收入 (百万元)	Total profit (Mil.RMB) 总利润 (百万元)	Return on assets 资产利润率 (%)	Return on equity 权益利润率 (%)	Labour productivity ('000 RMB/ worker) 劳动生产率 (千元/人)	Debts/ assets 资产负债率 (%)	Total assets (Mil.RMB) 总资产 (百万元)
Industry Overall 行业总体	126	18,173	2,474	126	4.32	8.86	37.00	51.30	2,916

	Number of firms 企业个数	Average number of employees 平均职工人数	Average revenue ('000 RMB) 平均销售收入 (千元)	Average profit ('000 RMB) 平均利润 (千元)	Return on assets 资产利润率 (%)	Return on equity 权益利润率 (%)	Labour productivity ('000 RMB/ worker) 劳动生产率 (千元/人)	Debts/ assets 资产负债率 (%)	Average total assets ('000 RMB) 平均总资产 (千元)
By ownership 产业所有权									
State-owned 国有	37	35	3,464	339	4.32	14.17	39.01	69.52	7,856
Collective-owned 集体	20	76	4,620	13	0.34	1.67	17.49	79.93	3,953
Foreign & Overseas Chinese Funded 三资	25	278	34,640	434	0.95	1.70	29.88	44.46	45,877
By regional distribution 地区分布									
Central-North 华北	17	95	9,385	591	3.01	6.87	46.44	56.10	19,594
Beijing 北京	5	52	11,241	1,466	6.91	10.36	130.13	33.30	21,218
Tianjin 天津	5	65	5,006	122	0.66	4.36	5.78	84.81	18,461
Hebei 河北	6	166	12,941	360	1.67	3.64	39.30	54.16	21,584
Shanxi 山西	1	41	671	-64	-1.23	-3.09	5.34	60.16	5,206
Inner Mongolia 内蒙古									
Northeast 东北	1	51	1,046	2	0.05	0.71	6.04	92.51	3,740
Liaoning 辽宁									
Jilin 吉林									
Heilongjiang 黑龙江	1	51	1,046	2	0.05	0.71	6.04	92.51	3,740
Central-East 华东	51	173	31,433	1,933	5.77	12.07	48.17	52.22	33,517
Shanghai 上海	16	101	19,685	1,630	5.22	10.46	57.65	50.14	31,237
Jiangsu 江苏	4	104	35,019	-1,241	-1.72	-2.57	82.86	33.11	72,088
Zhejiang 浙江	16	270	39,691	2,460	7.33	18.47	31.03	60.32	33,563
Anhui 安徽	1	110	4,120	180	4.17	9.89	7.78	57.87	4,320
Fujian 福建	1	632	153,577	20,134	82.21	83.14	111.37	1.12	24,492
Jiangxi 江西	6	15	1,325	11	1.40	2.67	31.84	47.38	760
Shandong 山东	7	234	49,617	2,531	5.05	13.31	54.42	62.05	50,123
Central-South 中南	33	214	21,023	509	2.00	3.76	22.66	46.89	25,445
Henan 河南	2	29	3,721	294	41.54	163.51	34.74	74.59	707
Hubei 湖北	3	389	96,810	6,973	11.11	14.79	62.44	24.90	62,782
Hunan 湖南	6	80	2,112	32	0.47	1.75	14.05	72.89	6,725
Guangdong 广东	20	254	17,985	-241	-0.92	-1.91	13.75	52.05	26,340
Guangxi 广西	1	91	5,183	-188	-1.01	-6.65	18.68	84.86	18,677
Hainan 海南	1	212	18,327	102	0.16	0.27	34.77	41.10	64,088
Southwest 西南	10	27	812	17	0.99	3.79	15.61	73.84	1,707
Chongqing 重庆									
Sichuan 四川	5	23	1,032	28	1.69	4.31	14.50	60.81	1,682
Guizhou 贵州	1	48	796	-89	-5.73		7.10	130.71	1,553
Yunnan 云南	3	26	309	-31	-4.27		3.45	146.87	718
Tibet 西藏	1	26	1,231	208	4.20	7.83	72.31	46.33	4,949
Northwest 西北	14	23	580	19	2.10	4.18	21.09	49.80	905
Shaanxi 陕西	3	25	861	17	1.17	3.42	10.54	65.68	1,422
Gansu 甘肃	10	23	525	22	3.28	5.63	26.31	41.86	656
Qinghai 青海	1	23	291	1	0.05	0.09	4.30	41.33	1,846
Ningxia 宁夏									
Xinjiang 新疆									

2413: Notebooks 本册制造业

Year 年份	Number of firms 企业个数	Rate of change 变化率(%)	Number of employees 职工人数(人)	Rate of change 变化率(%)	Total revenue (Mil. RMB) 总销售收入(百万元)	Rate of change 变化率(%)	Total profit (Mil RMB) 总利润(百万元)	Rate of change 变化率(%)
2000	119		15,753		1,286		9	
2001	112	-5.88	15,188	-3.59	1,816	41.21	79	777.78
2002	126	12.50	18,173	19.65	2,474	36.23	126	59.49

Major Products 主要产品	Output 产量	Unit 单位
Monochrome Printed Products 单色印刷品	11,856	10,000 Reams 万令
Notebook 本册	5	100,000,000 Pieces 亿本

10 Main Firms with Maximal Revenue (year founded) 收入最大的十家主要企业（创办年份）	City 城市	Province 省	Telephone/fax 电话/传真	Number of employees 职工人数	Ownership 产业所有权	Revenue ('000 RMB) 销售收入(千元)	Profit('000 RMB) (rank) 利润(千元)(排名)	Total assets ('000 RMB) 总资产(千元)	Major products 主要产品
Wuhan Dafeng Co.,Ltd.	Wuhan	Hubei	(027)83226146		Joint Stock				Paper Products
武汉大枫股份有限公司(1997)	武汉市	湖北省	(027)83223133	990	股份制	253,525	20,485(2)	180,868	纸张制品
Suzhou Industrial Park Sip Asia Pacific Paper Converting	Suzhou	Jiangsu	(0512)62743888		Foreign Funded				Pat Cardboard
Co.,Ltd 苏州工业园区亚太纸品加工有限公司(1996)	苏州市	江苏省	(0512)62742888	293	外商投资	112,515	-	270,969	拍纸板
Star-light Print (ShenZhen) Co.,Ltd.	Shenzhen	Guangdong	(0755)27496111		Overseas Chinese-funded				Color Presswork彩
星光印刷（深圳）有限公司(1992)	深圳市	广东省	(0755)27494978	1,000	港澳台资	109,614	3,366(9)	219,442	色印刷品
Shanghai Hongshuangxi (Group) Co., Ltd.	Shanghai	Shanghai	(021)63774068		Limited-Liability				Culture & Education Products
上海红双喜(集团)有限公司(2000)	上海市	上海市	(021)63774060	162	有限公司	53,551	4,456(8)	172,457	文教产品
Shanghai Pudong Xinqu Printing Facotry	Shanghai	Shanghai	(021)58997999		State-owned				Presswork
上海浦东新区印刷厂(1952)	上海市	上海市	(021)58997126	200	国有企业	49,874	11,216(5)	127,679	印刷制品
Huabei Delta Print &Packing Co., Ltd.	Tangshan	Hebei	(0315)7681519		Foreign Funded				Color Presswork彩
华北戴尔特印刷包装有限公司(2001)	唐山市	河北省	(0315)7681538	587	外商投资	48,927	890(19)	100,719	色印刷品
Qingdao Boyuan Arts & Crafts Co., Ltd.	Qingdao	Shandong	(0532)8280304		Foreign Funded				Photoframe
青岛宝原工艺品有限公司(1993)	青岛市	山东省	(0532)8280301	327	外商投资	46,665	2,263(11)	38,316	像框
Shanghai Bei Printing Factory Co.,Ltd.	Shanghai	Shanghai	(021)56550779		Limited-Liability				Printing
上海市北印刷厂有限公司(1979)	上海市	上海市	(021)56552030	156	有限公司	46,577	7,396(6)	59,887	印刷
Qingdao Baoyuan Alunminiun Products Co.,Ltd.	Qingdao	Shandong	(0532)3280187		Foreign Funded				Photoframe
青岛宝原铝制品有限公司(1994)	青岛市	山东省	(0532)3280557	300	外商投资	41,818	-	29,535	像框
Guangzhou Atop Stationery Company	Guangzhou	Guangdong	(020)82394933		Overseas Chinese-funded				Notepad
广州巧登文化用品有限公司(1998)	广州市	广东省	(020)82394936	910	港澳台资	37,901	-	39,553	记事本

Top 10 Cities by Revenue 销售收入排名前10位城市	Province 省	Market share 市场份额 (%)	Number of firms 企业个数
Ningbo 宁波市	Zhejiang 浙江省	18.13	2
Shanghai 上海市	Shanghai 上海市	12.73	16
Wuhan 武汉市	Hubei 湖北省	11.58	2
Liaocheng 聊城市	Shandong 山东省	8.10	1
Quanzhou 泉州市	Fujian 福建省	6.21	1
Shenzhen 深圳市	Guangdong 广东省	5.47	2
Suzhou 苏州市	Jiangsu 江苏省	4.55	1
Guangzhou 广州市	Guangdong 广东省	3.78	3
Qingdao 青岛市	Shandong 山东省	3.58	2
Dongguan 东莞市	Guangdong 广东省	2.55	5

10 Major Wholesalers 十家主要批发商	City 城市	Province 省	Telephone/Fax 电话/传真
King Paper Source Trade (shanghai) Co.,Ltd.	Shanghai	Shanghai	(021)62720808
金纸源贸易（上海）有限公司	上海市	上海市	(021)62720909
China National Paper & Pulp Corpration	Beijing	Beijing	(010)67780346
中国纸张纸浆进出口公司	北京市	北京市	(010)67747294
Sinar Mas Linjiang Paper Industry Trade (Beijing) Co.,Ltd.	Beijing	Beijing	(010)65666688
金光林浆纸业贸易(北京)有限公司	北京市	北京市	(010)65669599
Sinar Mas Paper Industry (Xishan) Co.,Ltd.	Wuxi	Jiangsu	(0510)8251188
金光纸业(锡山)有限公司	无锡市	江苏省	(0510)8250906
China Printing Materials General Company	Beijing	Beijing	(010)63442905
中国印刷物资总公司	北京市	北京市	(010)63442900
TSS Eortune Co., ltd.	Tianjin	Tianjin	(022)28131350
天津同鑫进出口有限公司	天津市	天津市	(022)28131353
Wenzhou Import & Export Corpration	Wenzhou	Zhejiang	(0577)88862681
温州市进出口公司	温州市	浙江省	(0577)88844557
Sinar Mas Paper Industry (Xiamen) Co.,Ltd.	Xiamen	Fujian	(0592)2962018
金光纸业（厦门）有限公司	厦门市	福建省	(0592)2962010
Sinar Mas Paper Industry (Shenzhen) Co.,Ltd.	Shenzhen	Guangdong	(0755)83516701
金光纸业（深圳）有限公司	深圳市	广东省	(0755)83516773
Jieyang Ocean Shipping Supply Group Co.,Ltd.	Jieyang	Guangdong	(0663)8239634
揭阳市外轮供应集团有限公司	揭阳市	广东省	(0663)8236186

2415: Pens 笔制造业

The industry accounts for 0.045% of the total revenue of China's industrial sector in 2002. The rate of return on assets is 4.09%. 87.89% of all firms in the industry made a profit while 12.11% had negative returns.The top province in terms of the industry's revenue is Zhejiang, accounting for 39.81% of the total revenue.
2002年本行业收入占全行业的0.045%，资产利润率为4.09%。87.89%的企业赢利，12.11%的企业亏损。收入最高的省为浙江省，占本行业的39.81%。

	Total number of firms 企业总数	Total number of employees 职工总数	Total revenue (Mil.RMB) 总销售收入（百万元）	Total profit (Mil.RMB) 总利润（百万元）	Return on assets 资产利润率（%）	Return on equity 权益利润率（%）	Labour productivity ('000 RMB/ worker) 劳动生产率（千元/人）	Debts/ assets 资产负债率（%）	Total assets (Mil.RMB) 总资产（百万元）
Industry Overall 行业总体	223	39,122	4,855	227	4.09	9.87	31.79	58.60	5,550

	Number of firms 企业个数	Average number of employees 平均职工人数	Average revenue ('000 RMB) 平均销售收入（千元）	Average profit ('000 RMB) 平均利润（千元）	Return on assets 资产利润率（%）	Return on equity 权益利润率（%）	Labour productivity ('000 RMB/ worker) 劳动生产率（千元/人）	Debts/ assets 资产负债率（%）	Average total assets ('000 RMB) 平均总资产（千元）
By ownership 产业所有权									
State-owned 国有	15	175	12,912	-1,256	-3.16	-94.93	14.51	96.67	39,772
Collective-owned 集体	28	101	16,796	898	12.11	28.34	47.15	57.28	7,422
Foreign & Overseas Chinese Funded 三资	47	296	46,069	3,611	6.67	13.42	34.10	50.29	54,124
By regional distribution 地区分布									
Central-North 华北	12	112	11,861	-674	-2.75	-10.91	27.58	74.82	24,519
Beijing 北京	2	125	16,000	-6,527	-9.77		76.80	113.42	66,785
Tianjin 天津	9	111	11,350	498	3.05	5.21	16.12	41.44	16,304
Hebei 河北	1	102	8,182	493	3.54	8.10	18.81	56.26	13,922
Shanxi 山西									
Inner Mongolia 内蒙古									
Northeast 东北	7	175	9,267	450	1.31		18.62	103.05	34,440
Liaoning 辽宁	2	90	3,054	-2,177	-3.08		22.19	134.98	70,721
Jilin 吉林									
Heilongjiang 黑龙江	5	209	11,752	1,501	7.53	17.81	18.01	57.72	19,928
Central-East 华东	193	175	23,223	1,206	4.85	10.95	33.67	55.65	24,842
Shanghai 上海	33	170	35,776	2,191	3.46	6.46	41.09	46.38	63,243
Jiangsu 江苏	23	145	15,427	390	3.08	9.01	31.39	65.77	12,629
Zhejiang 浙江	102	163	18,949	784	5.00	12.45	27.78	59.83	15,668
Anhui 安徽	6	222	8,103	1,063	10.90	21.03	15.68	48.14	9,746
Fujian 福建	2	108	11,146	1,127	11.55	20.88	55.73	44.69	9,760
Jiangxi 江西	13	66	8,785	449	8.92	17.02	63.27	47.62	5,039
Shandong 山东	14	412	59,191	4,076	8.45	29.99	43.72	71.82	48,243
Central-South 中南	8	330	19,270	-137	-0.54	-1.23	16.74	55.79	25,236
Henan 河南									
Hubei 湖北									
Hunan 湖南	2	66	10,304	-197	-1.99	-7.68	36.89	74.11	9,901
Guangdong 广东	5	439	25,707	-74	-0.22	-0.48	16.66	53.57	33,125
Guangxi 广西	1	309	5,020	-329	-2.00	-4.55	8.80	56.11	16,458
Hainan 海南									
Southwest 西南	1	79	2,240	-404	-2.88	-3.39	7.22	14.88	14,007
Chongqing 重庆									
Sichuan 四川									
Guizhou 贵州	1	79	2,240	-404	-2.88	-3.39	7.22	14.88	14,007
Yunnan 云南									
Tibet 西藏									
Northwest 西北	2	52	4,763	278	11.88	14.51	32.38	18.15	2,341
Shaanxi 陕西									
Gansu 甘肃	2	52	4,763	278	11.88	14.51	32.38	18.15	2,341
Qinghai 青海									
Ningxia 宁夏									
Xinjiang 新疆									

2415: Pens 笔制造业

Year 年份	Number of firms 企业个数	Rate of change 变化率 (%)	Number of employees 职工人数 (人)	Rate of change 变化率 (%)	Total revenue (Mil. RMB) 总销售收入 (百万元)	Rate of change 变化率 (%)	Total profit (Mil RMB) 总利润 (百万元)	Rate of change 变化率 (%)
2000	158		36,385		3,825		202	
2001	185	17.09	34,690	-4.66	3,989	4.29	222	9.90
2002	223	20.54	39,122	12.78	4,855	21.71	227	2.25

Major Products 主要产品	Output 产量	Unit 单位
Fountain Pen 自来水笔	6,128	10,000 Units 万支
Pencil 铅笔	77	100,000,000 Units 亿支

10 Main Firms with Maximal Revenue (year founded) 收入最大的十家主要企业（创办年份）	City 城市	Province 省	Telephone/fax 电话/传真	Number of employees 职工人数	Ownership 产业所有权	Revenue ('000 RMB) 销售收入 (千元)	Profit('000 RMB) (rank) 利润(千元) (排名)	Total assets ('000 RMB) 总资产 (千元)	Major products 主要产品
Ningbo Beifa Group Co.,Ltd. 宁波贝发集团有限公司(1996)	Ningbo 宁波市	Zhejiang 浙江省	(0574)86186888 (0574)86155295	3,054	Foreign Funded 外商投资	522,163	24,470(1)	428,968	Pen 笔
Qingdao Changlong Stationery Co., Ltd. 青岛昌隆文具有限公司(1988)	Qingdao 青岛市	Shandong 山东省	(0532)3716789 (0532)3716987	854	Foreign Funded 外商投资	155,541	19,160(2)	167,184	Writing Pens 书写用笔
Shandong Tianxiang Group Company 山东天象集团公司(1990)	Qingdao 青岛市	Shandong 山东省	(0532)7388078 (0532)7388127	700	Private Enterprises 私营独资	121,504	9,152(10)	213,244	Pencil & Lead Core 笔、铅芯
Wenzhou Aihao Pen Industry Co., Ltd. 温州市爱好笔业有限公司(1995)	Wenzhou 温州市	Zhejiang 浙江省	(0577)86558866 (0577)86558768	936	Private Owned 私营企业	113,029	3,899(23)	90,824	Pen 笔
ShangHai Hero Pen Factory Lishui Co,.Ltd. . 上海英雄金笔厂丽水有限公司(1970)	Lishui 丽水市	Zhejiang 浙江省	(0578)2133127 (0578)2131498	363	Joint Stock 股份制	96,726	7,058(14)	152,799	Fountain Pen 自来水笔
Shanghai Sanxing Culture & Education Industrial Company 上海三星文教实业公司(1931)	Shanghai 上海市	Shanghai 上海市	(021)68463726 (021)68462485	520	State-owned 国有企业	94,302	2,525(25)	89,827	Pen 笔
Shanghai Parker Pen Co., Ltd. 上海派克笔有限公司(2001)	Shanghai 上海市	Shanghai 上海市	(021)62719900 (021)62726967	37	Foreign Funded 外商投资	91,397	2,026(29)	56,052	Ball Pen 宝珠笔
Shanghai Heraeus Industrial Technology Materials Co.,Ltd. 上海贺利氏工业技术材料有限公司(1994)	Shanghai 上海市	Shanghai 上海市	(021)64890060 (021)64890022	142	Foreign Funded 外商投资	86,395	17,152(3)	83,089	Hard Alloy Bead硬质合金珠
Shanghai Foster Pen Industry Co., Ltd. 上海幅斯特笔业有限公司(1994)	Shanghai 上海市	Shanghai 上海市	(021)58549624 (021)50992997	164	Overseas Chinese-funded 港澳台资	86,288	11,337(5)	117,270	Pen 笔
Shanghai Lotus Stationery Co., Ltd. 上海乐美文具有限公司(1999)	Shanghai 上海市	Shanghai 上海市	(021)59759788 (021)59759608	410	Overseas Chinese-funded 港澳台资	86,212	2,406(26)	52,107	Ball Pen 圆珠笔

Top 10 Cities by Revenue 销售收入排名前10位城市	Province 省	Market share 市场份额 (%)	Number of firms 企业个数
Shanghai 上海市	Shanghai 上海市	24.32	33
Ningbo 宁波市	Zhejiang 浙江省	16.92	25
Wenzhou 温州市	Zhejiang 浙江省	13.16	36
Qingdao 青岛市	Shandong 山东省	5.99	3
Yantai 烟台市	Shandong 山东省	5.77	4
Lishui 丽水市	Zhejiang 浙江省	4.09	13
Yangzhou 扬州市	Jiangsu 江苏省	2.99	14
Suzhou 苏州市	Jiangsu 江苏省	2.63	5
Weihai 威海市	Shandong 山东省	2.58	3
Jinan 济南市	Shandong 山东省	2.58	3

10 Major Wholesalers 十家主要批发商	City 城市	Province 省	Telephone/Fax 电话/传真
King Paper Source Trade (shanghai) Co.,Ltd. 金纸源贸易（上海）有限公司	Shanghai 上海市	Shanghai 上海市	(021)62720808 (021)62720909
China National Paper & Pulp Corpration 中国纸张纸浆进出口公司	Beijing 北京市	Beijing 北京市	(010)67780346 (010)67747294
Sinar Mas Linjiang Paper Industry Trade (Beijing) Co.,Ltd. 金光林浆纸业贸易(北京)有限公司	Beijing 北京市	Beijing 北京市	(010)65666688 (010)65669599
Sinar Mas Paper Industry (Xishan) Co.,Ltd. 金光纸业(锡山)有限公司	Wuxi 无锡市	Jiangsu 江苏省	(0510)8251188 (0510)8250906
China Printing Materials General Company 中国印刷物资总公司	Beijing 北京市	Beijing 北京市	(010)63442905 (010)63442900
TSS Eortune Co., ltd. 天津同鑫进出口有限公司	Tianjin 天津市	Tianjin 天津市	(022)28131350 (022)28131353
Wenzhou Import & Export Corpration 温州市进出口公司	Wenzhou 温州市	Zhejiang 浙江省	(0577)88862681 (0577)88844557
Sinar Mas Paper Industry (Xiamen) Co.,Ltd. 金光纸业（厦门）有限公司	Xiamen 厦门市	Fujian 福建省	(0592)2962018 (0592)2962010
Sinar Mas Paper Industry (Shenzhen) Co.,Ltd. 金光纸业（深圳）有限公司	Shenzhen 深圳市	Guangdong 广东省	(0755)83516701 (0755)83516773
Jieyang Ocean Shipping Supply Group Co.,Ltd. 揭阳市外轮供应集团有限公司	Jieyang 揭阳市	Guangdong 广东省	(0663)8239634 (0663)8236186

2417: Teaching Samples and Models 教学标本、模型制造业

The industry accounts for 0.009% of the total revenue of China's industrial sector in 2002. The rate of return on assets is 9.75%. 81.58% of all firms in the industry made a profit while 18.42% had negative returns.The top province in terms of the industry's revenue is Jiangsu, accounting for 73.37% of the total revenue.
2002年本行业收入占全行业的 0.009%，资产利润率为 9.75%。81.58%的企业赢利，18.42%的企业亏损。收入最高的省为江苏省，占本行业的73.37%。

	Total number of firms 企业总数	Total number of employees 职工总数	Total revenue (Mil.RMB) 总销售收入 (百万元)	Total profit (Mil.RMB) 总利润 (百万元)	Return on assets 资产利润率 (%)	Return on equity 权益利润率 (%)	Labour productivity ('000 RMB/ worker) 劳动生产率 (千元/人)	Debts/ assets 资产负债率 (%)	Total assets (Mil.RMB) 总资产 (百万元)
Industry Overall 行业总体	38	7,075	915	62	9.75	18.60	39.23	47.55	636

	Number of firms 企业个数	Average number of employees 平均职工人数	Average revenue ('000 RMB) 平均销售收入 (千元)	Average profit ('000 RMB) 平均利润 (千元)	Return on assets 资产利润率 (%)	Return on equity 权益利润率 (%)	Labour productivity ('000 RMB/ worker) 劳动生产率 (千元/人)	Debts/ assets 资产负债率 (%)	Average total assets ('000 RMB) 平均总资产 (千元)
By ownership 产业所有权									
State-owned 国有	10	70	2,645	182	3.15	4.89	10.58	35.60	5,794
Collective-owned 集体	10	79	10,377	1,135	10.82	18.01	26.59	39.92	10,482
Foreign & Overseas Chinese Funded 三资	4	102	8,940	-728	-7.13	-11.68	24.62	38.94	10,198
By regional distribution 地区分布									
Central-North 华北	2	53	10,097	-828	-7.06	-17.71	46.39	60.16	11,725
Beijing 北京	2	53	10,097	-828	-7.06	-17.71	46.39	60.16	11,725
Tianjin 天津									
Hebei 河北									
Shanxi 山西									
Inner Mongolia 内蒙古									
Northeast 东北	1	37	1,872	-260	-10.67	-16.84	16.68	36.64	2,437
Liaoning 辽宁									
Jilin 吉林									
Heilongjiang 黑龙江	1	37	1,872	-260	-10.67	-16.84	16.68	36.64	2,437
Central-East 华东	22	234	35,326	2,329	10.36	20.82	46.71	50.21	22,475
Shanghai 上海	7	71	10,787	1,581	13.15	20.87	53.62	36.97	12,022
Jiangsu 江苏	8	537	83,928	4,825	10.22	21.99	48.12	53.52	47,198
Zhejiang 浙江	2	46	4,617	334	4.14	5.92	38.52	30.10	8,061
Anhui 安徽									
Fujian 福建	2	86	9,088	427	7.41	15.89	14.91	53.36	5,760
Jiangxi 江西	2	14	345	24	2.07	4.08	7.50	49.16	1,158
Shandong 山东	1	66	2,128	12	0.43		13.67	106.68	2,769
Central-South 中南	10	166	9,651	1,101	10.99	15.59	18.56	29.54	10,021
Henan 河南									
Hubei 湖北	2	255	5,737	-367	-2.78	-3.85	5.08	27.76	13,178
Hunan 湖南	4	58	5,493	131	5.02	5.64	29.93	10.91	2,607
Guangdong 广东	4	230	15,766	2,805	17.69	26.54	23.18	33.34	15,857
Guangxi 广西									
Hainan 海南									
Southwest 西南	3	41	6,474	565	10.91	28.56	5.52	61.82	5,181
Chongqing 重庆	2	24	1,478	480	35.63	55.27	25.32	35.52	1,347
Sichuan 四川	1	77	16,466	735	5.72	17.51	-6.56	67.33	12,849
Guizhou 贵州									
Yunnan 云南									
Tibet 西藏									
Northwest 西北									
Shaanxi 陕西									
Gansu 甘肃									
Qinghai 青海									
Ningxia 宁夏									
Xinjiang 新疆									

2417: Teaching Samples and Models 教学标本、模型制造业

Year 年份	Number of firms 企业个数	Rate of change 变化率 (%)	Number of employees 职工人数 (人)	Rate of change 变化率 (%)	Total revenue (Mil. RMB) 总销售收入 (百万元)	Rate of change 变化率 (%)	Total profit (Mil RMB) 总利润 (百万元)	Rate of change 变化率 (%)
2000	29		7,981		2,036		179	
2001	36	24.14	5,955	-25.39	643	-68.42	40	-77.65
2002	38	5.56	7,075	18.81	915	42.30	62	55.00

Major Products 主要产品	Output 产量	Unit 单位

10 Main Firms with Maximal Revenue (year founded) 收入最大的十家主要企业（创办年份）	City 城市	Province 省	Telephone/fax 电话/传真	Number of employees 职工人数	Ownership 产业所有权	Revenue ('000 RMB) 销售收入 (千元)	Profit('000 RMB) (rank) 利润(千元) (排名)	Total assets ('000 RMB) 总资产 (千元)	Major products 主要产品
Family Health Equipment(ShangHai) Co.,Ltd.	Nanjing	Jiangsu	(025)2428132		Private Owned				Teaching Instrument
南京金陵教具集团有限公司(2000)	南京市	江苏省	(025)2418602	824	私营企业	313,840	22,590(1)	142,090	教学仪器
Nantong Haiyi Label Factory	Nantong	Jiangsu	(0513)2216758		Joint Stock				Learning Tool
南通海易标牌有限公司(1986)	南通市	江苏省	(0513)2216758	235	股份制	97,590	6,820(4)	45,320	学具
Zhujiang Xingyu Model Industrial Co., ltd.	Zhuhai	Guangdong	(0756)5225888		Private Owned				Aviation Model
珠海星宇模型实业有限公司(1993)	珠海市	广东省	(0756)5225600	480	私营企业	31,480	9,002(3)	24,361	航空模型
Qingbaijiang Teaching Instrument Factory	Chengdu	Sichuan	(028)83650022		Collective-owned				Daily Tool Of Laboratory实验室
青白江区教学仪器厂(1983)	成都市	四川省	(028)83650382	77	集体企业	16,466	735(13)	12,849	常用工具
Fujian Quanzhou No.5 Radio Factory	Quanzhou	Fujian	(0595)2455381		Joint Stock				AACV-2000 Language Learning Series.AACV-2000语
福建省泉州市无线电五厂(1973)	泉州市	福建省	(0595)2456989	115	股份制	15,410	762(12)	8,742	言学习系列
Shanghai Fengpu Education Products Co.,Ltd.	Shanghai	Shanghai	(021)57432101		Joint Stock				Teaching Desk & Chairs教
上海奉浦教育用品有限公司(1997)	上海市	上海市	(021)37184078	90	股份制	15,080	1,989(7)	5,633	育课桌椅
Zhuhai Sanchao Model Co., Ltd.	Zhuhai	Guangdong	(0756)3326285		Overseas Chinese-funded				Airplane Model
珠海市三超模型有限公司(2000)	珠海市	广东省	(0756)3326130	260	港澳台资	14,583	-	10,232	飞机模型
Jiangdu Yangzi Industry Equipment Manufacturing Factory	Yangzhou	Jiangsu	(0514)6974192		Collective-owned				Teaching Apparatus
江都市扬子工业设备制造厂(1976)	扬州市	江苏省		106	集体企业	13,800	330(18)	12,230	教学器材
Beijing Yuxin Teaching Equipment Co., Ltd.	Beijing	Beijing	(010)66178217		Overseas Chinese-funded				Teaching Tool
北京裕鑫教学设备有限公司(1991)	北京市	北京市		18	港澳台资	12,097	-	13,744	教具
Guangzhou Teaching Instrument Factory	Guangzhou	Guangdong	(020)86500107		State-owned				School Specimen
广州市广州教学仪器厂(1981)	广州市	广东省	(020)86510263	60	国有企业	11,980	1,836(8)	13,177	教学标本

Top 10 Cities by Revenue 销售收入排名前10位城市	Province 省	Market share 市场份额 (%)	Number of firms 企业个数
Nanjing 南京市	Jiangsu 江苏省	34.29	1
Huaian 淮安市	Jiangsu 江苏省	25.41	1
Nantong 南通市	Jiangsu 江苏省	10.89	2
Shanghai 上海市	Shanghai 上海市	8.25	7
Zhuhai 珠海市	Guangdong 广东省	5.03	2
Beijing 北京市	Beijing 北京市	2.21	2
Quanzhou 泉州市	Fujian 福建省	1.99	2
Guangzhou 广州市	Guangdong 广东省	1.86	2
Chengdu 成都市	Sichuan 四川省	1.80	1
Yiyang 益阳市	Hunan 湖南省	1.64	3

10 Major Wholesalers 十家主要批发商	City 城市	Province 省	Telephone/Fax 电话/传真
King Paper Source Trade (shanghai) Co.,Ltd.	Shanghai	Shanghai	(021)62720808
金纸源贸易（上海）有限公司	上海市	上海市	(021)62720909
China National Paper & Pulp Corpration	Beijing	Beijing	(010)67780346
中国纸张纸浆进出口公司	北京市	北京市	(010)67747294
Sinar Mas Linjiang Paper Industry Trade (Beijing) Co.,Ltd.	Beijing	Beijing	(010)65666688
金光林浆纸业贸易(北京)有限公司	北京市	北京市	(010)65669599
Sinar Mas Paper Industry (Xishan) Co.,Ltd.	Wuxi	Jiangsu	(0510)8251188
金光纸业(锡山)有限公司	无锡市	江苏省	(0510)8250906
China Printing Materials General Company	Beijing	Beijing	(010)63442905
中国印刷物资总公司	北京市	北京市	(010)63442900
TSS Eortune Co., ltd.	Tianjin	Tianjin	(022)28131350
天津同鑫进出口有限公司	天津市	天津市	(022)28131353
Wenzhou Import & Export Corpration	Wenzhou	Zhejiang	(0577)88862681
温州市进出口公司	温州市	浙江省	(0577)88844557
Sinar Mas Paper Industry (Xiamen) Co.,Ltd.	Xiamen	Fujian	(0592)2962018
金光纸业（厦门）有限公司	厦门市	福建省	(0592)2962010
Sinar Mas Paper Industry (Shenzhen) Co.,Ltd.	Shenzhen	Guangdong	(0755)83516701
金光纸业（深圳）有限公司	深圳市	广东省	(0755)83516773
Jieyang Ocean Shipping Supply Group Co.,Ltd.	Jieyang	Guangdong	(0663)8239634
揭阳市外轮供应集团有限公司	揭阳市	广东省	(0663)8236186

2419: Other Cultural and Educational Products 其他文化用品制造业

The industry accounts for 0.009% of the total revenue of China's industrial sector in 2002. The rate of return on assets is 2.95%. 76.19% of all firms in the industry made a profit while 23.81% had negative returns.The top province in terms of the industry's revenue is Shanghai, accounting for 30.71% of the total revenue.
2002年本行业收入占全行业的 0.009%，资产利润率为 2.95%。76.19%的企业赢利，23.81%的企业亏损。收入最高的省为上海市，占本行业的30.71%。

	Total number of firms 企业总数	Total number of employees 职工总数	Total revenue (Mil.RMB) 总销售收入 (百万元)	Total profit (Mil.RMB) 总利润 (百万元)	Return on assets 资产利润率 (%)	Return on equity 权益利润率 (%)	Labour productivity ('000 RMB/ worker) 劳动生产率 (千元/人)	Debts/ assets 资产负债率 (%)	Total assets (Mil.RMB) 总资产 (百万元)
Industry Overall 行业总体	63	10,004	1,009	28	2.95	6.92	28.51	57.32	954

	Number of firms 企业个数	Average number of employees 平均职工人数	Average revenue ('000 RMB) 平均销售收入 (千元)	Average profit ('000 RMB) 平均利润 (千元)	Return on assets 资产利润率 (%)	Return on equity 权益利润率 (%)	Labour productivity ('000 RMB/ worker) 劳动生产率 (千元/人)	Debts/ assets 资产负债率 (%)	Average total assets ('000 RMB) 平均总资产 (千元)
By ownership 产业所有权									
State-owned 国有	12	47	2,088	-281	-3.63	-11.24	13.46	67.74	7,748
Collective-owned 集体	10	135	15,715	312	4.60	11.70	23.81	60.64	6,770
Foreign & Overseas Chinese Funded 三资	14	167	13,088	826	5.89	10.27	28.24	42.61	14,021
By regional distribution 地区分布									
Central-North 华北	5	97	6,692	71	0.81	2.23	19.25	63.59	8,755
Beijing 北京									
Tianjin 天津	5	97	6,692	71	0.81	2.23	19.25	63.59	8,755
Hebei 河北									
Shanxi 山西									
Inner Mongolia 内蒙古									
Northeast 东北	4	340	16,104	-628	-2.35	-8.74	11.99	73.08	26,690
Liaoning 辽宁									
Jilin 吉林	1	16	101				0.38	7.73	15,635
Heilongjiang 黑龙江	3	448	21,438	-837	-2.76	-17.55	12.12	84.29	30,374
Central-East 华东	42	144	17,674	670	4.11	9.30	33.86	55.80	16,298
Shanghai 上海	14	162	22,132	1,100	5.93	12.78	36.85	53.61	18,539
Jiangsu 江苏	5	196	17,821	181	2.26	13.93	20.60	83.78	8,024
Zhejiang 浙江	14	117	20,343	865	3.85	8.53	49.55	54.83	22,444
Anhui 安徽	1	49	366	10	0.60	1.97	3.55	69.60	1,671
Fujian 福建	4	183	5,708	-253	-1.90	-4.31	15.68	55.99	13,331
Jiangxi 江西	2	43	4,355	15	1.06	1.62	34.28	34.59	1,371
Shandong 山东	2	153	13,313	357	5.54	9.02	18.46	38.60	6,444
Central-South 中南	10	207	16,751	211	1.81	3.61	26.06	49.91	11,640
Henan 河南	2	70	12,888	832	21.40	40.80	53.01	47.55	3,886
Hubei 湖北	1	550	67,740	3,300	39.76	113.79	45.75	65.06	8,300
Hunan 湖南									
Guangdong 广东	7	197	10,571	-408	-2.85	-5.57	15.46	48.84	14,332
Guangxi 广西									
Hainan 海南									
Southwest 西南	1	12	259	151	37.75	42.54	13.50	11.25	400
Chongqing 重庆	1	12	259	151	37.75	42.54	13.50	11.25	400
Sichuan 四川									
Guizhou 贵州									
Yunnan 云南									
Tibet 西藏									
Northwest 西北	1	22	871	-92	-5.00	-7.84	19.91	36.28	1,841
Shaanxi 陕西									
Gansu 甘肃	1	22	871	-92	-5.00	-7.84	19.91	36.28	1,841
Qinghai 青海									
Ningxia 宁夏									
Xinjiang 新疆									

2419: Other Cultural and Educational Products 其他文化用品制造业

Year 年份	Number of firms 企业个数	Rate of change 变化率 (%)	Number of employees 职工人数 (人)	Rate of change 变化率 (%)	Total revenue (Mil. RMB) 总销售收入 (百万元)	Rate of change 变化率 (%)	Total profit (Mil RMB) 总利润 (百万元)	Rate of change 变化率 (%)
2000	69		12,349		858		21	
2001	63	-8.70	9,485	-23.19	872	1.63	29	38.10
2002	63	o	10,004	5.47	1,009	15.71	28	-3.45

Major Products 主要产品	Output 产量	Unit 单位

10 Main Firms with Maximal Revenue (year founded) 收入最大的十家主要企业（创办年份）	City 城市	Province 省	Telephone/ fax 电话/传真	Number of employees 职工人数	Ownership 产业所有权	Revenue ('000 RMB) 销售收入 (千元)	Profit('000 RMB) (rank) 利润(千元) (排名)	Total assets ('000 RMB) 总资产 (千元)	Major products 主要产品
Ningbo 3A (Group) Co.,Ltd.	Ningbo	Zhejiang	(0574)63302301		Private Owned				Playing Card
宁波三A集团有限公司(1995)	宁波市	浙江省	(0574)63301888	425	私营企业	153,971	9,229(2)	213,171	扑克牌
Shanghai Yuchen Playing Cards Co.,ltd.	Shanghai	Shanghai	(021)69565552		Private Owned				Playing Card
上海宇琛扑克实业有限公司(1994)	上海市	上海市	(021)69591767	510	私营企业	78,222	2,834(4)	99,332	扑克牌
Yingcheng Huangtan Chalk Co.,Ltd.	Xiaogan	Hubei	(0712)3712158		Private Partnership				Chalk
应城市黄滩镇粉笔厂(1980)	孝感市	湖北省	(0712)3712103	550	私营合伙	67,740	3,300(3)	8,300	粉笔
Jiamusi Golden Dragon Group Co., Ltd.	Jiamusi	Heilongjiang	(0454)8559338		Limited-Liability				Playing Card
佳木斯金龙集团有限公司(1996)	佳木斯市	黑龙江省	(0454)8559498	1,174	有限公司	55,193	-	81,844	扑克牌
Wuxi Phoenix Artist Materials Co., Ltd.	Wuxi	Jiangsu	(0510)5600278		Private Partnership				Canvas Frame
无锡凤凰画材有限公司(1988)	无锡市	江苏省	(0510)5600165	650	私营合伙	53,320	800(12)	20,970	油画框
Shanghai Pudong Wenbao Paper Products Factory	Shanghai	Shanghai	(021)58672975		Joint Stock				Notebook with Rigid Cover
上海浦东文宝纸品厂(1995)	上海市	上海市	(021)58674564	205	股份制	37,899	285(20)	17,099	硬面钞
Shanghai Fangzhi Electronic Co., Ltd.	Shanghai	Shanghai	(021)59512188		Overseas Chinese-funded				Two-sided Glue
上海方志电子配件有限公司(1999)	上海市	上海市	(021)59512168	218	港澳台资	29,771	13,416(1)	22,875	双面胶
Shanghai Changkong Typewriter Factory	Shanghai	Shanghai	(021)66957537		Joint Owned				Foreign Language Typewriter外
上海长空打字机厂(1994)	上海市	上海市	(021)66957537	350	联营企业	26,624	668(13)	17,706	文打字机
Ningbo Yaning Printing Co., Ltd.	Ningbo	Zhejiang	(0574)87363828		Foreign Funded				Playing Card
宁波雅宁印刷有限公司(1992)	宁波市	浙江省	(0574)87344502	147	外商投资	25,259	-	18,630	扑克
Qingdao Daxing Stationery Co.,Ltd.	Qingdao	Shandong	(0532)8200804		Foreign Funded				Album
青岛大星文化用品有限公司(1995)	青岛市	山东省	(0532)8200803	260	外商投资	23,202	278(21)	9,483	相册

Top 10 Cities by Revenue 销售收入排名前10位城市	Province 省	Market share 市场份额 (%)	Number of firms 企业个数
Shanghai 上海市	Shanghai 上海市	30.71	14
Ningbo 宁波市	Zhejiang 浙江省	19.17	3
Xiaogan 孝感市	Hubei 湖北省	6.71	1
Wuxi 无锡市	Jiangsu 江苏省	6.40	3
Jiamusi 佳木斯市	Heilongjiang 黑龙江省	6.36	2
Guangzhou 广州市	Guangdong 广东省	4.76	4
Tianjin 天津市	Tianjin 天津市	3.32	5
Shaoxing 绍兴市	Zhejiang 浙江省	2.57	2
Qingdao 青岛市	Shandong 山东省	2.30	1
Jinhua 金华市	Zhejiang 浙江省	1.99	2

10 Major Wholesalers 十家主要批发商	City 城市	Province 省	Telephone/Fax 电话/传真
King Paper Source Trade (shanghai) Co.,Ltd.	Shanghai	Shanghai	(021)62720808
金纸源贸易（上海）有限公司	上海市	上海市	(021)62720909
China National Paper & Pulp Corpration	Beijing	Beijing	(010)67780346
中国纸张纸浆进出口公司	北京市	北京市	(010)67747294
Sinar Mas Linjiang Paper Industry Trade (Beijing) Co.,Ltd.	Beijing	Beijing	(010)65666688
金光林浆纸业贸易(北京)有限公司	北京市	北京市	(010)65669599
Sinar Mas Paper Industry (Xishan) Co.,Ltd.	Wuxi	Jiangsu	(0510)8251188
金光纸业(锡山)有限公司	无锡市	江苏省	(0510)8250906
China Printing Materials General Company	Beijing	Beijing	(010)63442905
中国印刷物资总公司	北京市	北京市	(010)63442900
TSS Eortune Co., ltd.	Tianjin	Tianjin	(022)28131350
天津同鑫进出口有限公司	天津市	天津市	(022)28131353
Wenzhou Import & Export Corpration	Wenzhou	Zhejiang	(0577)88862681
温州市进出口公司	温州市	浙江省	(0577)88844557
Sinar Mas Paper Industry (Xiamen) Co.,Ltd.	Xiamen	Fujian	(0592)2962018
金光纸业（厦门）有限公司	厦门市	福建省	(0592)2962010
Sinar Mas Paper Industry (Shenzhen) Co.,Ltd.	Shenzhen	Guangdong	(0755)83516701
金光纸业（深圳）有限公司	深圳市	广东省	(0755)83516773
Jieyang Ocean Shipping Supply Group Co.,Ltd.	Jieyang	Guangdong	(0663)8239634
揭阳市外轮供应集团有限公司	揭阳市	广东省	(0663)8236186

2421: Balls 各种球类制造业

The industry accounts for 0.022% of the total revenue of China's industrial sector in 2002. The rate of return on assets is 3.73%. 79.59% of all firms in the industry made a profit while 20.41% had negative returns.The top province in terms of the industry's revenue is Guangdong, accounting for 31.61% of the total revenue.
2002年本行业收入占全行业的0.022%，资产利润率为3.73%。79.59%的企业赢利，20.41%的企业亏损。收入最高的省为广东省，占本行业的31.61%。

	Total number of firms 企业总数	Total number of employees 职工总数	Total revenue (Mil.RMB) 总销售收入 (百万元)	Total profit (Mil.RMB) 总利润 (百万元)	Return on assets 资产利润率 (%)	Return on equity 权益利润率 (%)	Labour productivity ('000 RMB/ worker) 劳动生产率 (千元/人)	Debts/ assets 资产负债率 (%)	Total assets (Mil.RMB) 总资产 (百万元)
Industry Overall 行业总体	98	29,399	2,349	79	3.73	8.33	21.91	55.24	2,127

	Number of firms 企业个数	Average number of employees 平均职工人数	Average revenue ('000 RMB) 平均销售收入（千元）	Average profit ('000 RMB) 平均利润 (千元)	Return on assets 资产利润率 (%)	Return on equity 权益利润率 (%)	Labour productivity ('000 RMB/ worker) 劳动生产率 (千元/人)	Debts/ assets 资产负债率 (%)	Average total assets ('000 RMB) 平均总资产 (千元)
By ownership 产业所有权									
State-owned 国有	5	381	10,682	150	0.29	1.24	10.26	76.33	51,145
Collective-owned 集体	12	170	17,798	442	3.39	7.02	24.99	51.75	13,043
Foreign & Overseas Chinese Funded 三资	51	377	29,261	1,003	3.80	7.45	21.57	48.99	26,395
By regional distribution 地区分布									
Central-North 华北	10	195	13,525	837	3.74	14.85	15.61	74.78	22,339
Beijing 北京	1	1,004	10,310				1.02	82.43	158,604
Tianjin 天津	5	143	13,842	1,047	13.14	23.17	18.12	43.31	7,972
Hebei 河北	4	57	13,934	782	12.55	53.28	72.21	76.44	6,231
Shanxi 山西									
Inner Mongolia 内蒙古									
Northeast 东北	1	320	11,220	21	0.26	0.40	8.78	33.55	7,956
Liaoning 辽宁	1	320	11,220	21	0.26	0.40	8.78	33.55	7,956
Jilin 吉林									
Heilongjiang 黑龙江									
Central-East 华东	63	276	22,763	719	3.40	7.91	23.63	57.04	21,173
Shanghai 上海	14	269	26,351	654	2.11	4.96	32.60	57.43	30,965
Jiangsu 江苏	14	238	19,523	476	2.45	8.37	22.46	70.68	19,392
Zhejiang 浙江	15	197	15,673	534	4.17	9.61	16.38	56.61	12,814
Anhui 安徽	4	318	8,472	385	5.94	17.91	9.60	66.84	6,472
Fujian 福建	12	398	27,646	1,519	6.26	10.51	22.73	40.44	24,259
Jiangxi 江西									
Shandong 山东	4	320	47,775	426	1.42	3.90	34.24	63.56	29,919
Central-South 中南	23	416	33,040	1,119	4.66	8.22	20.53	43.30	23,992
Henan 河南									
Hubei 湖北									
Hunan 湖南	1	138	3,617	-51	-4.33	-11.36	7.01	61.85	1,177
Guangdong 广东	21	443	35,365	1,177	4.54	7.94	20.77	42.83	25,940
Guangxi 广西									
Hainan 海南	1	135	13,650	1,050	17.77	104.79	17.85	83.04	5,909
Southwest 西南									
Chongqing 重庆									
Sichuan 四川									
Guizhou 贵州									
Yunnan 云南									
Tibet 西藏									
Northwest 西北	1	191	8,952	-96	-0.97	-2.14	21.46	54.68	9,891
Shaanxi 陕西									
Gansu 甘肃	1	191	8,952	-96	-0.97	-2.14	21.46	54.68	9,891
Qinghai 青海									
Ningxia 宁夏									
Xinjiang 新疆									

2421: Balls 各种球类制造业

Year 年份	Number of firms 企业个数	Rate of change 变化率（%）	Number of employees 职工人数（人）	Rate of change 变化率（%）	Total revenue (Mil. RMB) 总销售收入（百万元）	Rate of change 变化率（%）	Total profit (Mil RMB) 总利润（百万元）	Rate of change 变化率（%）
2000	82		24,742		1,948		41	
2001	93	13.41	25,227	1.96	2,108	8.21	41	o
2002	98	5.38	29,399	16.54	2,349	11.43	79	92.68

Major Products 主要产品	Output 产量	Unit 单位
Sports Products & Appliance 体育用品及用具	74	100,000,000 Yuan 亿元

10 Main Firms with Maximal Revenue (year founded) 收入最大的十家主要企业（创办年份）	City 城市	Province 省	Telephone/fax 电话/传真	Number of employees 职工人数	Ownership 产业所有权	Revenue ('000 RMB) 销售收入（千元）	Profit('000 RMB) (rank) 利润（千元）（排名）	Total assets ('000 RMB) 总资产（千元）	Major products 主要产品
Dongguan Guanhe Sporting Goods Co.,Ltd.	Dongguan	Guangdong	(0769)5551210		Foreign Funded				Balls Products
东莞冠贺运动器材有限公司(1996)	东莞市	广东省	(0769)5551953	2,800	外商投资	203,233	1,707(14)	106,120	球类产品
Shanghai Hongshuangxi Guandu Sports Products Co.,Ltd.	Shanghai	Shanghai	(021)63789977		Overseas Chinese-funded				Sports Products
上海红双喜冠都体育用品有限公司(1996)	上海市	上海市	(021)63787863	803	港澳台资	135,009	7,000(3)	192,514	体育用品
Dongguan Dayang Sports Equipment Co., Ltd.	Dongguan	Guangdong	(0769)5594466		Overseas Chinese-funded				Softball
东莞大扬运动器材有限公司(1993)	东莞市	广东省	(0769)5597209	1,336	港澳台资	102,653	1,641(16)	29,253	棒垒球
Qingdao Synsheen Sporting Goods Co.,Ltd.	Qingdao	Shandong	(0532)8703554		Foreign Funded				Basketball
青岛新新体育用品有限公司(1991)	青岛市	山东省	(0532)8701824	882	外商投资	98,561	-	100,313	篮球
Xiamen Youlaisi Ball Industry Co., Ltd.	Xiamen	Fujian	(0592)7029600		Overseas Chinese-funded				Rubber Ball
厦门悠来斯球业有限公司(1989)	厦门市	福建省	(0592)7127392	950	港澳台资	85,231	10,492(2)	43,130	橡胶球
Guangzhou Health Balls Manufacturing Co.,Ltd.	Guangzhou	Guangdong	(020)86849168		Limited-Liability				Rubber Ball
广州海乐斯球业制造有限公司(2000)	广州市	广东省	(020)86761489	212	有限公司	79,517	2,825(6)	10,086	橡胶球类
Xiamen Yuan Bao Sports Equipment Co., Ltd.	Xiamen	Fujian	(0592)6228072		Overseas Chinese-funded				B7 Basketball
厦门元保运动器材有限公司(1992)	厦门市	福建省	(0592)6075097	876	港澳台资	73,161	1,326(20)	61,364	B7篮球
Qingdao Gold Star Sports Goods Co., ltd.	Qingdao	Shandong	(0532)7657575		Foreign Funded				Golf Cue Bag高
青岛金星体育用品有限公司(1992)	青岛市	山东省	(0532)7657577	180	外商投资	53,602	86(58)	11,115	尔夫球包
Shaoxing Xue Feng Group Co., Ltd.	Shaoxing	Zhejiang	(0575)5137746		Collective-owned				Badminton
绍兴雪峰集团有限公司(1997)	绍兴市	浙江省	(0575)5133474	577	集体企业	50,704	507(35)	55,681	羽毛球
Nanjing Shengli Sports Products Industrial Co., Ltd.	Nanjing	Jiangsu	(025)8289480		Overseas Chinese-funded				Badminton
南京胜利体育用品实业有限公司(1994)	南京市	江苏省	(025)8289482	418	港澳台资	41,300	780(28)	49,440	羽毛球

Top 10 Cities by Revenue 销售收入排名前10位城市	Province 省	Market share 市场份额（%）	Number of firms 企业个数
Shanghai 上海市	Shanghai 上海市	15.70	14
Dongguan 东莞市	Guangdong 广东省	15.08	5
Guangzhou 广州市	Guangdong 广东省	9.05	8
Xiamen 厦门市	Fujian 福建省	8.02	4
Qingdao 青岛市	Shandong 山东省	6.48	2
Nanjing 南京市	Jiangsu 江苏省	5.14	5
Shenzhen 深圳市	Guangdong 广东省	5.07	3
Wuxi 无锡市	Jiangsu 江苏省	4.83	4
Zhangzhou 漳州市	Fujian 福建省	4.72	5
Shaoxing 绍兴市	Zhejiang 浙江省	3.47	4

10 Major Wholesalers 十家主要批发商	City 城市	Province 省	Telephone/Fax 电话/传真
King Paper Source Trade (shanghai) Co.,Ltd.	Shanghai	Shanghai	(021)62720808
金纸源贸易（上海）有限公司	上海市	上海市	(021)62720909
China National Paper & Pulp Corpration	Beijing	Beijing	(010)67780346
中国纸张纸浆进出口公司	北京市	北京市	(010)67747294
Sinar Mas Linjiang Paper Industry Trade (Beijing) Co.,Ltd.	Beijing	Beijing	(010)65666688
金光林浆纸业贸易(北京)有限公司	北京市	北京市	(010)65669599
Sinar Mas Paper Industry (Xishan) Co.,Ltd.	Wuxi	Jiangsu	(0510)8251188
金光纸业(锡山)有限公司	无锡市	江苏省	(0510)8250906
China Printing Materials General Company	Beijing	Beijing	(010)63442905
中国印刷物资总公司	北京市	北京市	(010)63442900
TSS Eortune Co., ltd.	Tianjin	Tianjin	(022)28131350
天津同鑫进出口有限公司	天津市	天津市	(022)28131353
Wenzhou Import & Export Corpration	Wenzhou	Zhejiang	(0577)88862681
温州市进出口公司	温州市	浙江省	(0577)88844557
Sinar Mas Paper Industry (Xiamen) Co.,Ltd.	Xiamen	Fujian	(0592)2962018
金光纸业（厦门）有限公司	厦门市	福建省	(0592)2962010
Sinar Mas Paper Industry (Shenzhen) Co.,Ltd.	Shenzhen	Guangdong	(0755)83516701
金光纸业（深圳）有限公司	深圳市	广东省	(0755)83516773
Jieyang Ocean Shipping Supply Group Co.,Ltd.	Jieyang	Guangdong	(0663)8239634
揭阳市外轮供应集团有限公司	揭阳市	广东省	(0663)8236186

2423: Sports Equipment 各种体育器材制造业

The industry accounts for 0.053% of the total revenue of China's industrial sector in 2002. The rate of return on assets is 4.07%. 79.56% of all firms in the industry made a profit while 20.44% had negative returns.The top province in terms of the industry's revenue is Guangdong, accounting for 28.55% of the total revenue.
2002年本行业收入占全行业的 0.053%，资产利润率为 4.07%。79.56%的企业赢利，20.44%的企业亏损。收入最高的省为广东省，占本行业的28.55%。

	Total number of firms 企业总数	Total number of employees 职工总数	Total revenue (Mil.RMB) 总销售收入 (百万元)	Total profit (Mil.RMB) 总利润 (百万元)	Return on assets 资产利润率 (%)	Return on equity 权益利润率 (%)	Labour productivity ('000 RMB/ worker) 劳动生产率 (千元/人)	Debts/ assets 资产负债率 (%)	Total assets (Mil.RMB) 总资产 (百万元)
Industry Overall 行业总体	137	40,813	5,688	193	4.07	9.36	37.87	56.57	4,741

	Number of firms 企业个数	Average number of employees 平均职工人数	Average revenue ('000 RMB) 平均销售收入 (千元)	Average profit ('000 RMB) 平均利润 (千元)	Return on assets 资产利润率 (%)	Return on equity 权益利润率 (%)	Labour productivity ('000 RMB/ worker) 劳动生产率 (千元/人)	Debts/ assets 资产负债率 (%)	Average total assets ('000 RMB) 平均总资产 (千元)
By ownership 产业所有权									
State-owned 国有	2	36	3,629	-54	-0.66	-18.98	20.63	96.52	8,165
Collective-owned 集体	5	151	13,293	614	7.86	13.31	36.69	40.96	7,815
Foreign & Overseas Chinese Funded 三资	82	387	52,264	1,646	3.47	7.87	34.24	55.89	47,415
By regional distribution 地区分布									
Central-North 华北	11	215	23,773	473	2.40	8.39	46.98	71.40	19,711
Beijing 北京	2	119	33,488	1,311	3.69	24.36	139.03	84.87	35,565
Tianjin 天津	5	125	11,905	297	1.95	7.13	28.45	72.70	15,235
Hebei 河北									
Shanxi 山西	4	375	33,750	274	1.58	3.60	40.15	56.19	17,379
Inner Mongolia 内蒙古									
Northeast 东北	1	115	53,600	4,800	6.01	11.70	123.95	48.63	79,890
Liaoning 辽宁	1	115	53,600	4,800	6.01	11.70	123.95	48.63	79,890
Jilin 吉林									
Heilongjiang 黑龙江									
Central-East 华东	86	304	42,997	1,867	5.53	12.62	40.10	56.15	33,735
Shanghai 上海	10	577	107,069	5,757	6.89	18.56	33.49	62.87	83,553
Jiangsu 江苏	18	145	23,893	488	3.24	9.38	43.71	65.44	15,044
Zhejiang 浙江	20	240	40,202	2,660	9.20	20.52	44.76	55.18	28,916
Anhui 安徽	1	248	7,695	-118	-2.25		8.63	109.81	5,239
Fujian 福建	29	383	33,199	156	0.45	0.93	31.94	51.31	34,560
Jiangxi 江西									
Shandong 山东	8	198	52,810	4,571	17.48	30.06	106.44	41.83	26,141
Central-South 中南	36	329	45,502	624	1.49	3.30	29.40	54.87	41,856
Henan 河南									
Hubei 湖北	1	20	14,147				137.75	75.03	63,732
Hunan 湖南									
Guangdong 广东	35	338	46,398	642	1.56	3.38	29.22	53.98	41,231
Guangxi 广西									
Hainan 海南									
Southwest 西南	1	170	5,829	-2,445	-9.67		75.18	116.05	25,285
Chongqing 重庆									
Sichuan 四川	1	170	5,829	-2,445	-9.67		75.18	116.05	25,285
Guizhou 贵州									
Yunnan 云南									
Tibet 西藏									
Northwest 西北	2	90	15,500	1,100	20.51	27.91	62.39	26.52	5,364
Shaanxi 陕西									
Gansu 甘肃	2	90	15,500	1,100	20.51	27.91	62.39	26.52	5,364
Qinghai 青海									
Ningxia 宁夏									
Xinjiang 新疆									

2423: Sports Equipment 各种体育器材制造业

Year 年份	Number of firms 企业个数	Rate of change 变化率(%)	Number of employees 职工人数(人)	Rate of change 变化率(%)	Total revenue (Mil. RMB) 总销售收入(百万元)	Rate of change 变化率(%)	Total profit (Mil RMB) 总利润(百万元)	Rate of change 变化率(%)
2000	110		27,405		2,879		42	
2001	113	2.73	32,840	19.83	4,341	50.78	74	76.19
2002	137	21.24	40,813	24.28	5,688	31.03	193	160.81

Major Products 主要产品	Output 产量	Unit 单位
Sports Products & Appliance 体育用品及用具	74	100,000,000 Yuan 亿元

10 Main Firms with Maximal Revenue (year founded) 收入最大的十家主要企业（创办年份）	City 城市	Province 省	Telephone/fax 电话/传真	Number of employees 职工人数	Ownership 产业所有权	Revenue ('000 RMB) 销售收入(千元)	Profit('000 RMB) (rank) 利润(千元)(排名)	Total assets ('000 RMB) 总资产(千元)	Major products 主要产品
Shanghai Keysheen Leisure Products Co., Ltd. 上海基舜休闲制品有限公司(1995)	Shanghai 上海市	Shanghai 上海市	(021)59758888 (021)59758666	3,516	Foreign Funded 外商投资	780,441	52,241(1)	490,726	Indoor & Outdoor Lie Fallow Articles室内外休闲用品
Zhongshan Worldmark Sporting Goods Co.,Ltd. 中山广盛运动器材有限公司(1992)	Zhongshan 中山市	Guangdong 广东省	(0760)5596821 (0760)5596825	3,000	Overseas Chinese-funded 港澳台资	564,916	26,987(3)	368,488	Golf Cue Caput高尔夫球杆头
Zhejiang Tianlong Group Co.,Ltd. 浙江天龙集团有限公司(1998)	Wenzhou 温州市	Zhejiang 浙江省	(0577)86356616 (0577)86351838	1,202	Limited-Liability 有限公司	279,322	9,356(8)	110,602	Recreation & Sports Articles 文体用品
Tianqi Sports Goods (Ningbo) Co.,Ltd. 天旗运动用品(宁波)有限公司(1999)	Ningbo 宁波市	Zhejiang 浙江省	(0574)86874199 (0574)86802188	1,204	Overseas Chinese-funded 港澳台资	264,438	27,279(2)	284,775	Sports Equipment 运动器材
China Tai'an Sports Equipment Co.,ltd. 泰山体育器材集团有限公司(1998)	Dezhou 德州市	Shandong 山东省	(0534)6602013 (0534)6326999	254	Private Owned 私营企业	226,830	16,077(4)	27,282	Sports Equipment 体育器材
Xiamen Keentech Composite Tech Co.,Ltd. 厦门新凯复材科技有限公司(1993)	Xiamen 厦门市	Fujian 福建省	(0592)6210452 (0592)6211450	2,188	Overseas Chinese-funded 港澳台资	203,232	7,170(10)	169,087	Tennis Racket 网球拍
Xiamen Qiaoxing Industrial Co., Ltd. 厦门侨兴工业有限公司(1988)	Xiamen 厦门市	Fujian 福建省	(0592)6022020 (0592)6022038	1,643	Overseas Chinese-funded 港澳台资	180,982	10,422(6)	102,978	Tennis Racket 网球拍
Donghui Plastic Products (shanghai) Co., ltd. 东辉塑胶(上海)有限公司(1999)	Shanghai 上海市	Shanghai 上海市	(021)57402084 (021)57401306	960	Overseas Chinese-funded 港澳台资	154,475	7,513(9)	73,492	Sports Equipment 运动器材
Guangzhou Shuangyu Sports Products Group Co., Ltd. 广州双鱼体育用品集团有限公司(1998)	Guangzhou 广州市	Guangdong 广东省	(020)84350225 (020)84350225	560	Limited-Liability 有限公司	108,387	815(33)	176,814	Table Tennis Table 乒乓球台
Yangzhou Jiuyi Handware Machinery Co.,Ltd. 扬州久毅五金机械有限公司(1997)	Yangzhou 扬州市	Jiangsu 江苏省	(0514)7301306 (0514)7301336	500	Overseas Chinese-funded 港澳台资	97,240	500(47)	54,790	Gymnasium Machine 健身机

Top 10 Cities by Revenue 销售收入排名前10位城市	Province 省	Market share 市场份额(%)	Number of firms 企业个数
Shanghai 上海市	Shanghai 上海市	18.82	10
Xiamen 厦门市	Fujian 福建省	11.26	12
Zhongshan 中山市	Guangdong 广东省	10.34	4
Guangzhou 广州市	Guangdong 广东省	6.36	7
Wenzhou 温州市	Zhejiang 浙江省	4.91	1
Ningbo 宁波市	Zhejiang 浙江省	4.82	2
Dongguan 东莞市	Guangdong 广东省	4.38	11
Dezhou 德州市	Shandong 山东省	4.24	2
Jiangmen 江门市	Guangdong 广东省	2.67	4
Yangzhou 扬州市	Jiangsu 江苏省	2.54	6

10 Major Wholesalers 十家主要批发商	City 城市	Province 省	Telephone/Fax 电话/传真
King Paper Source Trade (shanghai) Co.,Ltd. 金纸源贸易（上海）有限公司	Shanghai 上海市	Shanghai 上海市	(021)62720808 (021)62720909
China National Paper & Pulp Corpration 中国纸张纸浆进出口公司	Beijing 北京市	Beijing 北京市	(010)67780346 (010)67747294
Sinar Mas Linjiang Paper Industry Trade (Beijing) Co.,Ltd. 金光林浆纸业贸易(北京)有限公司	Beijing 北京市	Beijing 北京市	(010)65666688 (010)65669599
Sinar Mas Paper Industry (Xishan) Co.,Ltd. 金光纸业(锡山)有限公司	Wuxi 无锡市	Jiangsu 江苏省	(0510)8251188 (0510)8250906
China Printing Materials General Company 中国印刷物资总公司	Beijing 北京市	Beijing 北京市	(010)63442905 (010)63442900
TSS Eortune Co., ltd. 天津同鑫进出口有限公司	Tianjin 天津市	Tianjin 天津市	(022)28131350 (022)28131353
Wenzhou Import & Export Corpration 温州市进出口公司	Wenzhou 温州市	Zhejiang 浙江省	(0577)88862681 (0577)88844557
Sinar Mas Paper Industry (Xiamen) Co.,Ltd. 金光纸业（厦门）有限公司	Xiamen 厦门市	Fujian 福建省	(0592)2962018 (0592)2962010
Sinar Mas Paper Industry (Shenzhen) Co.,Ltd 金光纸业（深圳）有限公司	Shenzhen 深圳市	Guangdong 广东省	(0755)83516701 (0755)83516773
Jieyang Ocean Shipping Supply Group Co.,Ltd. 揭阳市外轮供应集团有限公司	Jieyang 揭阳市	Guangdong 广东省	(0663)8239634 (0663)8236186

2429: Other Sports Products 其他体育用品制造业

The industry accounts for 0.060% of the total revenue of China's industrial sector in 2002. The rate of return on assets is 4.79%. 86.32% of all firms in the industry made a profit while 13.68% had negative returns.The top province in terms of the industry's revenue is Shanghai, accounting for 24.32% of the total revenue.
2002年本行业收入占全行业的 0.060%，资产利润率为 4.79%。86.32%的企业赢利，13.68%的企业亏损。收入最高的省为上海市，占本行业的24.32%。

	Total number of firms 企业总数	Total number of employees 职工总数	Total revenue (Mil.RMB) 总销售收入（百万元）	Total profit (Mil.RMB) 总利润（百万元）	Return on assets 资产利润率（%）	Return on equity 权益利润率（%）	Labour productivity ('000 RMB/ worker) 劳动生产率（千元/人）	Debts/ assets 资产负债率（%）	Total assets (Mil.RMB) 总资产（百万元）
Industry Overall 行业总体	190	42,240	6,391	226	4.79	11.60	42.08	58.73	4,714

	Number of firms 企业个数	Average number of employees 平均职工人数	Average revenue ('000 RMB) 平均销售收入（千元）	Average profit ('000 RMB) 平均利润（千元）	Return on assets 资产利润率（%）	Return on equity 权益利润率（%）	Labour productivity ('000 RMB/ worker) 劳动生产率（千元/人）	Debts/ assets 资产负债率（%）	Average total assets ('000 RMB) 平均总资产（千元）
By ownership 产业所有权									
State-owned 国有	6	124	4,224	-546	-2.42	-19.40	7.07	87.51	22,537
Collective-owned 集体	15	107	13,849	580	4.85	10.67	34.32	54.60	11,969
Foreign & Overseas Chinese Funded 三资	103	260	44,483	1,509	4.60	10.10	47.41	54.48	32,817
By regional distribution 地区分布									
Central-North 华北	23	388	22,758	451	1.94	5.96	19.89	67.43	23,218
Beijing 北京	4	251	23,317	525	1.57	2.77	30.33	43.53	33,540
Tianjin 天津	6	112	13,642	705	9.40	16.86	32.57	44.22	7,502
Hebei 河北	6	154	15,219	437	5.36	14.47	33.55	62.93	8,145
Shanxi 山西	7	905	36,715	202	0.46	2.57	14.90	82.04	43,711
Inner Mongolia 内蒙古									
Northeast 东北	4	85	3,713	82	0.36	0.42	10.51	15.77	23,093
Liaoning 辽宁	3	97	3,407	109	0.43	0.51	8.72	14.27	25,193
Jilin 吉林	1	50	4,630				20.92	22.56	16,792
Heilongjiang 黑龙江									
Central-East 华东	131	159	33,894	1,460	6.37	15.51	55.26	58.94	22,930
Shanghai 上海	34	219	45,715	1,692	5.21	11.12	63.53	53.10	32,460
Jiangsu 江苏	40	116	26,166	1,423	9.21	23.34	54.28	60.55	15,450
Zhejiang 浙江	40	114	25,336	1,738	12.09	28.78	48.29	57.99	14,376
Anhui 安徽	3	176	51,065	2,660	4.84	61.56	69.27	92.15	55,004
Fujian 福建	7	309	51,797	-1,904	-5.67	-12.93	35.29	56.16	33,592
Jiangxi 江西									
Shandong 山东	7	212	44,286	1,803	4.11	11.04	62.26	62.77	43,859
Central-South 中南	32	380	44,136	741	2.19	5.15	36.73	57.53	33,870
Henan 河南	1	21	7,285	331	5.85	15.40	115.48	62.03	5,662
Hubei 湖北									
Hunan 湖南	2	38	5,091	590	10.67	28.50	58.99	62.56	5,530
Guangdong 广东	28	428	49,657	792	2.09	4.88	36.52	57.14	37,915
Guangxi 广西	1	67	4,492	13	0.24		23.22	117.85	5,485
Hainan 海南									
Southwest 西南									
Chongqing 重庆									
Sichuan 四川									
Guizhou 贵州									
Yunnan 云南									
Tibet 西藏									
Northwest 西北									
Shaanxi 陕西									
Gansu 甘肃									
Qinghai 青海									
Ningxia 宁夏									
Xinjiang 新疆									

2429: Other Sports Products 其他体育用品制造业

Year 年份	Number of firms 企业个数	Rate of change 变化率 (%)	Number of employees 职工人数 (人)	Rate of change 变化率 (%)	Total revenue (Mil. RMB) 总销售收入 (百万元)	Rate of change 变化率 (%)	Total profit (Mil RMB) 总利润 (百万元)	Rate of change 变化率 (%)
2000	112		25,152		4,092		217	
2001	139	24.11	30,602	21.67	5,128	25.32	233	7.37
2002	190	36.69	42,240	38.03	6,391	24.63	226	-3.00

Major Products 主要产品	Output 产量	Unit 单位
Sports Products & Appliance 体育用品及用具	74	100,000,000 Yuan 亿元

10 Main Firms with Maximal Revenue (year founded) 收入最大的十家主要企业（创办年份）	City 城市	Province 省	Telephone/fax 电话/传真	Number of employees 职工人数	Ownership 产业所有权	Revenue ('000 RMB) 销售收入 (千元)	Profit('000 RMB) (rank) 利润(千元) (排名)	Total assets ('000 RMB) 总资产 (千元)	Major products 主要产品
Huiyang Goodway Sporting Co,.Ltd.	Huizhou	Guangdong	(0752)3869888		Overseas Chinese-funded				Physical Trainning Bicycle
惠阳国威运动器材有限公司(1992)	惠州市	广东省	(0752)3869369	1,200	港澳台资	378,525	8,255(10)	299,983	健身单车
Family Health Equipment(ShangHai) Co.,Ltd.	Shanghai	Shanghai	(021)54421789		Foreign Funded				Massage Chair
发美利健康器械(上海)有限公司(1998)	上海市	上海市	(021)54421165	1,059	外商投资	312,360	15,106(5)	75,260	按摩椅
DAITO-OSIM Health Care Appliances (Suzhou) Co.,Ltd.	Suzhou	Jiangsu	(0512)67611238		Foreign Funded				Health Protection Equipment
大东傲胜保健器(苏州)有限公司(1996)	苏州市	江苏省	(0512)67615068	118	外商投资	213,820	22,346(2)	112,334	保健器材
Xiamen Weijia Sports Co., Ltd.	Xiamen	Fujian	(0592)6221233		Foreign Funded				Body-building Equipment
厦门纬嘉运动器材有限公司(1992)	厦门市	福建省	(0592)6281270	712	外商投资	174,665	6,692(15)	53,407	健身器材
Johnson Sports Goods (Shanghai) Co., Ltd.	Shanghai	Shanghai	(021)59101515		Overseas Chinese-funded				Body-building Equipment
乔山健身器材（上海）有限公司(2000)	上海市	上海市	(021)59103474	749	港澳台资	160,341	-	177,492	健身器材
Zhongshan Tengfei Industrial Co.,Ltd.	Zhongshan	Guangdong	(0760)2310686		Private Owned				Folding Slide Board Bicycle折叠
中山市腾飞实业有限公司(1995)	中山市	广东省	(0760)2319333	188	私营企业	149,147	6,819(14)	45,692	式滑板车
Hefei Andi Body-building Articles Company	Hefei	Anhui	(0551)3412222		Private Enterprises				Body-building Equipment
合肥安迪健身用品公司(1991)	合肥市	安徽省	(0551)2650333	318	私营独资	136,537	7,591(12)	154,761	健身器材
Taigu Xinhe Machinery Equipment Co., Ltd.	Jinzhong	Shanxi	(0354)6322039		Private Enterprises				Body-building Equipment
太谷县新和机械设备有限公司(1999)	晋中市	山西省	(0354)6323039	1,000	私营独资	123,634	464(80)	34,059	健身器材
Shanghai Donggeng Metal Products Co., Ltd.	Shanghai	Shanghai	(021)59100663		Overseas Chinese-funded				Sports Equipment
上海东庚金属制品有限公司(2001)	上海市	上海市	(021)59101569	300	港澳台资	103,873	487(79)	64,289	运动器材
Shanghai Qihong Sports Articles Co., Ltd.	Shanghai	Shanghai	(021)59703330		Overseas Chinese-funded				Other Sports Articles其他
上海骐鸿运动用品有限公司(1998)	上海市	上海市	(021)59700880	325	港澳台资	101,167	5,491(18)	42,903	体育用品

Top 10 Cities by Revenue 销售收入排名前10位城市	Province 省	Market share 市场份额 (%)	Number of firms 企业个数
Shanghai 上海市	Shanghai 上海市	24.32	34
Huizhou 惠州市	Guangdong 广东省	6.24	2
Nantong 南通市	Jiangsu 江苏省	5.93	21
Suzhou 苏州市	Jiangsu 江苏省	5.52	5
Hangzhou 杭州市	Zhejiang 浙江省	5.44	12
Xiamen 厦门市	Fujian 福建省	5.33	4
Ningbo 宁波市	Zhejiang 浙江省	5.20	6
Qingdao 青岛市	Shandong 山东省	4.58	5
Zhuhai 珠海市	Guangdong 广东省	4.10	1
Zhongshan 中山市	Guangdong 广东省	3.92	5

10 Major Wholesalers 十家主要批发商	City 城市	Province 省	Telephone/Fax 电话/传真
King Paper Source Trade (shanghai) Co.,Ltd.	Shanghai	Shanghai	(021)62720808
金纸源贸易（上海）有限公司	上海市	上海市	(021)62720909
China National Paper & Pulp Corpration	Beijing	Beijing	(010)67780346
中国纸张纸浆进出口公司	北京市	北京市	(010)67747294
Sinar Mas Linjiang Paper Industry Trade (Beijing) Co.,Ltd.	Beijing	Beijing	(010)65666688
金光林浆纸业贸易(北京)有限公司	北京市	北京市	(010)65669599
Sinar Mas Paper Industry (Xishan) Co.,Ltd.	Wuxi	Jiangsu	(0510)8251188
金光纸业(锡山)有限公司	无锡市	江苏省	(0510)8250906
China Printing Materials General Company	Beijing	Beijing	(010)63442905
中国印刷物资总公司	北京市	北京市	(010)63442900
TSS Eortune Co., ltd.	Tianjin	Tianjin	(022)28131350
天津同鑫进出口有限公司	天津市	天津市	(022)28131353
Wenzhou Import & Export Corpration	Wenzhou	Zhejiang	(0577)88862681
温州市进出口公司	温州市	浙江省	(0577)88844557
Sinar Mas Paper Industry (Xiamen) Co.,Ltd.	Xiamen	Fujian	(0592)2962018
金光纸业（厦门）有限公司	厦门市	福建省	(0592)2962010
Sinar Mas Paper Industry (Shenzhen) Co.,Ltd.	Shenzhen	Guangdong	(0755)83516701
金光纸业（深圳）有限公司	深圳市	广东省	(0755)83516773
Jieyang Ocean Shipping Supply Group Co.,Ltd.	Jieyang	Guangdong	(0663)8239634
揭阳市外轮供应集团有限公司	揭阳市	广东省	(0663)8236186

2431: Chinese Musical Instruments 中乐器制造业

The industry accounts for 0.003% of the total revenue of China's industrial sector in 2002. The rate of return on assets is 6.80%. 90.00% of all firms in the industry made a profit while 10.00% had negative returns.The top province in terms of the industry's revenue is Shanghai, accounting for 27.72% of the total revenue.
2002年本行业收入占全行业的 0.003%，资产利润率为 6.80%。90.00%的企业赢利，10.00%的企业亏损。收入最高的省为上海市，占本行业的27.72%。

	Total number of firms 企业总数	Total number of employees 职工总数	Total revenue (Mil.RMB) 总销售收入 (百万元)	Total profit (Mil.RMB) 总利润 (百万元)	Return on assets 资产利润率 (%)	Return on equity 权益利润率 (%)	Labour productivity ('000 RMB/ worker) 劳动生产率 (千元/人)	Debts/ assets 资产负债率 (%)	Total assets (Mil.RMB) 总资产 (百万元)
Industry Overall 行业总体	20	5,488	318	17	6.80	14.77	22.63	53.94	245

	Number of firms 企业个数	Average number of employees 平均职工人数	Average revenue ('000 RMB) 平均销售收入 (千元)	Average profit ('000 RMB) 平均利润 (千元)	Return on assets 资产利润率 (%)	Return on equity 权益利润率 (%)	Labour productivity ('000 RMB/ worker) 劳动生产率 (千元/人)	Debts/ assets 资产负债率 (%)	Average total assets ('000 RMB) 平均总资产 (千元)
By ownership 产业所有权									
State-owned 国有	2	48	1,451	281	5.74	7.17	12.92	19.98	4,898
Collective-owned 集体	5	233	19,958	1,135	6.50	12.18	33.25	46.64	17,473
Foreign & Overseas Chinese Funded 三资	6	198	22,328	862	5.09	13.10	27.61	61.11	16,917
By regional distribution 地区分布									
Central-North 华北	3	197	8,113	563	7.40	11.72	22.38	36.86	7,607
Beijing 北京									
Tianjin 天津									
Hebei 河北	2	288	12,070	873	8.36	13.30	22.82	37.17	10,441
Shanxi 山西	1	15	200	-56	-2.89	-4.35	5.20	33.54	1,938
Inner Mongolia 内蒙古									
Northeast 东北									
Liaoning 辽宁									
Jilin 吉林									
Heilongjiang 黑龙江									
Central-East 华东	10	174	15,970	787	5.49	14.35	44.25	61.72	14,332
Shanghai 上海	3	191	29,346	1,852	9.28	26.35	51.69	64.76	19,948
Jiangsu 江苏	4	136	10,532	130	1.53	14.30	37.09	89.30	8,462
Zhejiang 浙江									
Anhui 安徽									
Fujian 福建	1	120	8,110	442	5.81	10.95	180.82	46.97	7,612
Jiangxi 江西									
Shandong 山东	2	250	10,714	678	3.23	5.19	10.71	37.84	21,007
Central-South 中南	6	514	21,806	1,082	9.14	17.53	10.72	47.88	11,845
Henan 河南	4	102	10,308	974	21.08	32.28	27.92	34.70	4,620
Hubei 湖北	1	2,250	12,337	618	13.29	19.62	2.32	32.26	4,650
Hunan 湖南									
Guangdong 广东	1	425	77,266	1,980	4.13	9.07	38.69	54.47	47,939
Guangxi 广西									
Hainan 海南									
Southwest 西南									
Chongqing 重庆									
Sichuan 四川									
Guizhou 贵州									
Yunnan 云南									
Tibet 西藏									
Northwest 西北	1	80	2,702	618	7.86	9.43	14.36	16.63	7,858
Shaanxi 陕西	1	80	2,702	618	7.86	9.43	14.36	16.63	7,858
Gansu 甘肃									
Qinghai 青海									
Ningxia 宁夏									
Xinjiang 新疆									

2431: Chinese Musical Instruments 中乐器制造业

Year 年份	Number of firms 企业个数	Rate of change 变化率 (%)	Number of employees 职工人数 (人)	Rate of change 变化率 (%)	Total revenue (Mil. RMB) 总销售收入 (百万元)	Rate of change 变化率 (%)	Total profit (Mil RMB) 总利润 (百万元)	Rate of change 变化率 (%)
2000	16		2,174		218		7	
2001	17	6.25	3,136	44.25	298	36.70	23	228.57
2002	20	17.65	5,488	75.00	318	6.71	17	-26.09

Major Products 主要产品	Output 产量	Unit 单位
National Musical Instrument 民族乐器	1	100,000,000 Yuan 亿元

10 Main Firms with Maximal Revenue (year founded) 收入最大的十家主要企业（创办年份）	City 城市	Province 省	Telephone/fax 电话/传真	Number of employees 职工人数	Ownership 产业所有权	Revenue ('000 RMB) 销售收入 (千元)	Profit('000 RMB) (rank) 利润(千元) (排名)	Total assets ('000 RMB) 总资产 (千元)	Major products 主要产品
Shanghai No.1 National Musical Instruments Factory	Shanghai	Shanghai	(021)64885377		Collective-owned				Chinese Musical Instrument
上海民族乐器一厂(1958)	上海市	上海市	(021)64880351	315	集体企业	61,996	4,050(1)	38,532	中乐器
Jiangyin Mingde Sports Products Co., Ltd.	Wuxi	Jiangsu	(0510)6511880		Overseas Chinese-funded				Balls
江阴明德体育用品有限公司(1993)	无锡市	江苏省	(0510)6502225	200	港澳台资	16,800	172(14)	10,455	球类
WeiHai Jeong Sam Musical Instrument Co.,Ltd.	Weihai	Shandong	(0631)5764473		Foreign Funded				San Wei Ban Qin
威海正三乐器有限公司(1991)	威海市	山东省	(0631)5764061	270	外商投资	16,300	2,340(3)	19,330	三味伴琴
Suzhou No.1 National Musical Instrument Factory Co.,Ltd.	Suzhou	Jiangsu	(0512)65223456		Private Owned				Bow Instrument
苏州民族乐器一厂有限公司(1999)	苏州市	江苏省	(0512)65224238	206	私营企业	16,236	127(15)	16,258	弓弦乐器
Raoyang Musical Instrument Company	Hengshui	Hebei	(0318)7319730		Collective-owned				Yang Qin
河北省饶阳县乐器公司(1998)	衡水市	河北省	(0318)7319850	386	集体企业	15,840	1,225(5)	14,600	扬琴
Shanghai Dunhuang Musical Instrument Co.,Ltd.	Shanghai	Shanghai	(021)57412662		Overseas Chinese-funded				Chinese Musical Instrument
上海敦煌乐器有限公司(1993)	上海市	上海市	(021)54530900	92	港澳台资	14,582	453(10)	13,408	中乐器
Shanghai Guibao Musical Instrument Co.,Ltd.	Shanghai	Shanghai	(021)58082182		Collective Owned				Chinese Musical Instrument
上海瑰宝乐器有限公司(1985)	上海市	上海市	(021)58082182	166	集体企业	11,460	1,053(6)	7,903	中乐器
Xianghe Tianyin Musical Instrument Co., ltd.	Langfang	Hebei	(0316)8217340		Collective-owned				Accordion
香河县天音乐器有限公司(1976)	廊坊市	河北省	(0316)8219333	190	集体企业	8,300	520(9)	6,282	手风琴
Quanzhou Yida Electric Appliance for Vehicle Co., Ltd.	Quanzhou	Fujian	(0595)2463598		Private Owned				Horn
泉州艺达车用电器有限公司(1994)	泉州市	福建省	(0595)2463587	120	私营企业	8,110	442(11)	7,612	喇叭
Lankao Shanghai Peony Nation Musical Instrument Co.,Ltd.	Kaifeng	Henan	(0378)6263547		Private Owned				Gu Zheng
兰考县上海牡丹民族乐器有限公司(2000)	开封市	河南省	(0378)6263547	97	私营企业	5,984	107(16)	4,195	古筝

Top 10 Cities by Revenue 销售收入排名前10位城市	Province 省	Market share 市场份额 (%)	Number of firms 企业个数
Shanghai 上海市	Shanghai 上海市	27.72	3
Shenzhen 深圳市	Guangdong 广东省	24.33	1
Xuchang 许昌市	Henan 河南省	7.26	1
Kaifeng 开封市	Henan 河南省	5.72	3
Wuxi 无锡市	Jiangsu 江苏省	5.29	1
Weihai 威海市	Shandong 山东省	5.13	1
Suzhou 苏州市	Jiangsu 江苏省	5.11	1
Hengshui 衡水市	Hebei 河北省	4.99	1
Wuhan 武汉市	Hubei 湖北省	3.88	1
Langfang 廊坊市	Hebei 河北省	2.61	1

10 Major Wholesalers 十家主要批发商	City 城市	Province 省	Telephone/Fax 电话/传真
King Paper Source Trade (shanghai) Co.,Ltd.	Shanghai	Shanghai	(021)62720808
金纸源贸易（上海）有限公司	上海市	上海市	(021)62720909
China National Paper & Pulp Corpration	Beijing	Beijing	(010)67780346
中国纸张纸浆进出口公司	北京市	北京市	(010)67747294
Sinar Mas Linjiang Paper Industry Trade (Beijing) Co.,Ltd.	Beijing	Beijing	(010)65666688
金光林浆纸业贸易(北京)有限公司	北京市	北京市	(010)65669599
Sinar Mas Paper Industry (Xishan) Co.,Ltd.	Wuxi	Jiangsu	(0510)8251188
金光纸业(锡山)有限公司	无锡市	江苏省	(0510)8250906
China Printing Materials General Company	Beijing	Beijing	(010)63442905
中国印刷物资总公司	北京市	北京市	(010)63442900
TSS Eortune Co., ltd.	Tianjin	Tianjin	(022)28131350
天津同鑫进出口有限公司	天津市	天津市	(022)28131353
Wenzhou Import & Export Corpration	Wenzhou	Zhejiang	(0577)88862681
温州市进出口公司	温州市	浙江省	(0577)88844557
Sinar Mas Paper Industry (Xiamen) Co.,Ltd.	Xiamen	Fujian	(0592)2962018
金光纸业（厦门）有限公司	厦门市	福建省	(0592)2962010
Sinar Mas Paper Industry (Shenzhen) Co.,Ltd.	Shenzhen	Guangdong	(0755)83516701
金光纸业（深圳）有限公司	深圳市	广东省	(0755)83516773
Jieyang Ocean Shipping Supply Group Co.,Ltd.	Jieyang	Guangdong	(0663)8239634
揭阳市外轮供应集团有限公司	揭阳市	广东省	(0663)8236186

2433: Western Musical Instruments 西乐器制造业

The industry accounts for 0.035% of the total revenue of China's industrial sector in 2002. The rate of return on assets is 7.42%. 90.36% of all firms in the industry made a profit while 9.64% had negative returns.The top province in terms of the industry's revenue is Guangdong, accounting for 30.21% of the total revenue.
2002年本行业收入占全行业的 0.035%，资产利润率为 7.42%。90.36%的企业赢利，9.64%的企业亏损。收入最高的省为广东省，占本行业的30.21%。

	Total number of firms 企业总数	Total number of employees 职工总数	Total revenue (Mil.RMB) 总销售收入 (百万元)	Total profit (Mil.RMB) 总利润 (百万元)	Return on assets 资产利润率 (%)	Return on equity 权益利润率 (%)	Labour productivity ('000 RMB/ worker) 劳动生产率 (千元/人)	Debts/ assets 资产负债率 (%)	Total assets (Mil.RMB) 总资产 (百万元)
Industry Overall 行业总体	83	30,835	3,713	378	7.42	14.68	41.13	49.44	5,089

	Number of firms 企业个数	Average number of employees 平均职工人数	Average revenue ('000 RMB) 平均销售收入 (千元)	Average profit ('000 RMB) 平均利润 (千元)	Return on assets 资产利润率 (%)	Return on equity 权益利润率 (%)	Labour productivity ('000 RMB/ worker) 劳动生产率 (千元/人)	Debts/ assets 资产负债率 (%)	Average total assets ('000 RMB) 平均总资产 (千元)
By ownership 产业所有权									
State-owned 国有	8	432	38,052	415	0.59	8.82	32.60	93.32	70,481
Collective-owned 集体	4	235	12,811	875	10.29	52.53	18.04	80.42	8,501
Foreign & Overseas Chinese Funded 三资	41	335	40,776	3,271	6.70	10.36	38.64	35.35	48,851
By regional distribution 地区分布									
Central-North 华北	34	410	39,582	3,014	5.88	11.30	30.65	47.92	51,240
Beijing 北京	11	406	47,946	2,033	3.29	10.48	42.12	68.61	61,813
Tianjin 天津	14	490	50,395	4,657	6.86	10.55	29.94	34.98	67,858
Hebei 河北	9	290	12,538	1,658	13.30	19.60	12.89	32.14	12,469
Shanxi 山西									
Inner Mongolia 内蒙古									
Northeast 东北	2	970	125,590	4,078	1.86	23.60	43.66	92.11	219,070
Liaoning 辽宁	2	970	125,590	4,078	1.86	23.60	43.66	92.11	219,070
Jilin 吉林									
Heilongjiang 黑龙江									
Central-East 华东	32	288	31,065	4,165	10.48	21.39	34.27	51.00	39,736
Shanghai 上海	10	304	29,080	8,597	14.92	36.98	31.75	59.66	57,626
Jiangsu 江苏	11	252	21,112	827	5.17	13.70	29.44	62.28	15,992
Zhejiang 浙江	5	249	48,670	3,951	6.92	9.77	49.97	29.14	57,068
Anhui 安徽									
Fujian 福建	3	222	29,222	2,092	9.01	13.57	31.48	33.59	23,214
Jiangxi 江西									
Shandong 山东	3	493	46,676	4,065	7.42	16.08	36.55	53.86	54,804
Central-South 中南	15	384	74,785	8,927	8.18	13.28	76.59	38.42	109,146
Henan 河南									
Hubei 湖北									
Hunan 湖南									
Guangdong 广东	15	384	74,785	8,927	8.18	13.28	76.59	38.42	109,146
Guangxi 广西									
Hainan 海南									
Southwest 西南									
Chongqing 重庆									
Sichuan 四川									
Guizhou 贵州									
Yunnan 云南									
Tibet 西藏									
Northwest 西北									
Shaanxi 陕西									
Gansu 甘肃									
Qinghai 青海									
Ningxia 宁夏									
Xinjiang 新疆									

2433: Western Musical Instruments 西乐器制造业

Year 年份	Number of firms 企业个数	Rate of change 变化率 (%)	Number of employees 职工人数 (人)	Rate of change 变化率 (%)	Total revenue (Mil. RMB) 总销售收入 (百万元)	Rate of change 变化率 (%)	Total profit (Mil RMB) 总利润 (百万元)	Rate of change 变化率 (%)
2000	68		26,720		2,812		230	
2001	80	17.65	27,993	4.76	3,519	25.14	275	19.57
2002	83	3.75	30,835	10.15	3,713	5.51	378	37.45

Major Products 主要产品	Output 产量	Unit 单位
Western Musical Instrument 西乐器	24	100,000,000 Yuan 亿元

10 Main Firms with Maximal Revenue (year founded) 收入最大的十家主要企业（创办年份）	City 城市	Province 省	Telephone/fax 电话/传真	Number of employees 职工人数	Ownership 产业所有权	Revenue ('000 RMB) 销售收入（千元）	Profit('000 RMB) (rank) 利润(千元)(排名)	Total assets ('000 RMB) 总资产（千元）	Major products 主要产品
Guangzhou Zhujiang Piano Group Co., Ltd.	Guangzhou	Guangdong	(020)81502729		State Enterprises				Piano
广州珠江钢琴集团有限公司(1956)	广州市	广东省	(020)81509247	2,369	国有独资	732,223	120,003(1)	1,300,546	钢琴
Tianjin Jimaiduo Musical Instrument Co., Ltd.	Tianjin	Tianjin	(022)82122742		Overseas Chinese-funded				Musical Instrument
天津杰麦多乐器有限公司(1992)	天津市	天津市	(022)82115974	1,656	港澳台资	257,143	21,298(4)	319,608	乐器
Yingkou Northeast China Piano (Group) Co.,Ltd.	Yingkou	Liaoning	(0417)4838500		State-owned				Vertical Piano
营口东北钢琴集团公司(1980)	营口市	辽宁省	(0417)4839057	1,813	国有企业	245,799	9,464(9)	427,786	立式钢琴
Youngchang Piano Co., Ltd.	Tianjin	Tianjin	(022)24956664		Foreign Funded				Piano
天津英昌乐器有限公司(1993)	天津市	天津市	(022)24395492	1,237	外商投资	231,180	24,370(3)	391,820	钢琴
Xiaoshan Yamaha Musical Instrument Co.,Ltd.	Hangzhou	Zhejiang	(0571)82833018		Foreign Funded				Musical Instrument belong to Piano钢
萧山雅马哈乐器有限公司(1997)	杭州市	浙江省	(0571)82833016	430	外商投资	126,260	13,431(7)	188,382	琴类乐器
Shanghai Zhongya Piano Co.,Ltd.	Shanghai	Shanghai	(021)59213710		Overseas Chinese-funded				Piano
上海中雅钢琴有限公司(1994)	上海市	上海市	(021)59212351	861	港澳台资	117,639	19,635(5)	187,386	钢琴
Ningbo Orient Piano Industries Inc.	Ningbo	Zhejiang	(0574)63544646		Joint Stock				Piano Parts
宁波东方琴业总公司(1993)	宁波市	浙江省	(0574)63549381	690	股份制	101,288	5,804(11)	85,122	钢琴部件
Guangzhou Bourjade Musical Instrument Factory Co.,Ltd.	Guangzhou	Guangdong	(020)34042338		Overseas Chinese-funded				Guitar Box
广州保嘉乐器制造厂有限公司(1997)	广州市	广东省	(020)34042338	1,130	港澳台资	99,217	697(35)	23,094	吉它盒
Guangzhou Yamaha Zhujiang Piano Co.,Ltd.	Guangzhou	Guangdong	(020)82269478		Foreign Funded				Piano
广州雅马哈珠江钢琴有限公司(1996)	广州市	广东省	(020)82268008	185	外商投资	98,370	3,293(18)	105,647	钢琴
Tianjin Jinbao Musical Instrument Co., Ltd.	Tianjin	Tianjin	(022)29241326		Joint Stock				Copper Tube Musical Instrument
天津市津宝乐器有限公司(1998)	天津市	天津市	(022)29245361	1,300	股份制	73,230	11,250(8)	37,030	铜管乐器

Top 10 Cities by Revenue 销售收入排名前10位城市	Province 省	Market share 市场份额 (%)	Number of firms 企业个数
Guangzhou 广州市	Guangdong 广东省	27.69	9
Tianjin 天津市	Tianjin 天津市	19.00	14
Beijing 北京市	Beijing 北京市	14.21	11
Shanghai 上海市	Shanghai 上海市	7.03	10
Yingkou 营口市	Liaoning 辽宁省	6.62	1
Hangzhou 杭州市	Zhejiang 浙江省	3.40	1
Yantai 烟台市	Shandong 山东省	2.81	2
Ningbo 宁波市	Zhejiang 浙江省	2.73	1
Taizhou 泰州市	Jiangsu 江苏省	2.63	3
Hengshui 衡水市	Hebei 河北省	1.75	6

10 Major Wholesalers 十家主要批发商	City 城市	Province 省	Telephone/Fax 电话/传真
King Paper Source Trade (shanghai) Co.,Ltd.	Shanghai	Shanghai	(021)62720808
金纸源贸易（上海）有限公司	上海市	上海市	(021)62720909
China National Paper & Pulp Corpration	Beijing	Beijing	(010)67780346
中国纸张纸浆进出口公司	北京市	北京市	(010)67747294
Sinar Mas Linjiang Paper Industry Trade (Beijing) Co.,Ltd.	Beijing	Beijing	(010)65666688
金光林浆纸业贸易(北京)有限公司	北京市	北京市	(010)65669599
Sinar Mas Paper Industry (Xishan) Co.,Ltd.	Wuxi	Jiangsu	(0510)8251188
金光纸业(锡山)有限公司	无锡市	江苏省	(0510)8250906
China Printing Materials General Company	Beijing	Beijing	(010)63442905
中国印刷物资总公司	北京市	北京市	(010)63442900
TSS Eortune Co., ltd.	Tianjin	Tianjin	(022)28131350
天津同鑫进出口有限公司	天津市	天津市	(022)28131353
Wenzhou Import & Export Corpration	Wenzhou	Zhejiang	(0577)88862681
温州市进出口公司	温州市	浙江省	(0577)88844557
Sinar Mas Paper Industry (Xiamen) Co.,Ltd.	Xiamen	Fujian	(0592)2962018
金光纸业（厦门）有限公司	厦门市	福建省	(0592)2962010
Sinar Mas Paper Industry (Shenzhen) Co.,Ltd.	Shenzhen	Guangdong	(0755)83516701
金光纸业（深圳）有限公司	深圳市	广东省	(0755)83516773
Jieyang Ocean Shipping Supply Group Co.,Ltd.	Jieyang	Guangdong	(0663)8239634
揭阳市外轮供应集团有限公司	揭阳市	广东省	(0663)8236186

2435: Electrical Musical Instruments 电子乐器制造业

The industry accounts for 0.016% of the total revenue of China's industrial sector in 2002. The rate of return on assets is 13.45%. 76.00% of all firms in the industry made a profit while 24.00% had negative returns.The top province in terms of the industry's revenue is Tianjin, accounting for 54.95% of the total revenue.
2002年本行业收入占全行业的 0.016%，资产利润率为 13.45%。76.00%的企业赢利，24.00%的企业亏损。收入最高的省为天津市，占本行业的54.95%。

	Total number of firms 企业总数	Total number of employees 职工总数	Total revenue (Mil.RMB) 总销售收入 (百万元)	Total profit (Mil.RMB) 总利润 (百万元)	Return on assets 资产利润率 (%)	Return on equity 权益利润率 (%)	Labour productivity ('000 RMB/ worker) 劳动生产率 (千元/人)	Debts/ assets 资产负债率 (%)	Total assets (Mil.RMB) 总资产 (百万元)
Industry Overall 行业总体	25	6,105	1,686	107	13.45	21.21	69.40	36.59	796

	Number of firms 企业个数	Average number of employees 平均职工人数	Average revenue ('000 RMB) 平均销售收入（千元)	Average profit ('000 RMB) 平均利润 (千元)	Return on assets 资产利润率 (%)	Return on equity 权益利润率 (%)	Labour productivity ('000 RMB/ worker) 劳动生产率 (千元/人)	Debts/ assets 资产负债率 (%)	Average total assets ('000 RMB) 平均总资产 (千元)
By ownership 产业所有权									
State-owned 国有									
Collective-owned 集体									
Foreign & Overseas Chinese Funded 三资	15	220	93,287	6,970	14.83	21.73	104.72	31.73	46,991
By regional distribution 地区分布									
Central-North 华北	4	274	234,596	22,025	25.74	34.90	239.53	26.25	85,577
Beijing 北京	1	50	12,118	341	7.38	14.34	42.32	48.56	4,623
Tianjin 天津	3	348	308,756	29,253	25.99	35.09	248.96	25.95	112,562
Hebei 河北									
Shanxi 山西									
Inner Mongolia 内蒙古									
Northeast 东北	3	187	19,532	210	1.01	2.21	17.04	54.30	20,833
Liaoning 辽宁	2	258	26,856	485	1.98	3.91	16.21	49.46	24,554
Jilin 吉林									
Heilongjiang 黑龙江	1	45	4,885	-340	-2.54	-9.08	26.51	72.04	13,393
Central-East 华东	12	136	17,916	702	3.78	6.37	39.48	40.74	18,574
Shanghai 上海	3	202	22,357	67	0.16	0.29	18.44	46.23	42,658
Jiangsu 江苏	1	30	18,880	210	1.93	8.17	161.00	76.38	10,880
Zhejiang 浙江	2	145	15,114	2,589	23.42	32.54	40.80	28.02	11,055
Anhui 安徽									
Fujian 福建	1	145	72,223	1,960	4.14	4.89	200.97	15.33	47,365
Jiangxi 江西									
Shandong 山东	5	113	5,317	174	5.98	18.63	13.50	67.91	2,911
Central-South 中南	6	469	78,969	1,661	5.90	10.84	31.01	45.53	28,129
Henan 河南									
Hubei 湖北									
Hunan 湖南									
Guangdong 广东	6	469	78,969	1,661	5.90	10.84	31.01	45.53	28,129
Guangxi 广西									
Hainan 海南									
Southwest 西南									
Chongqing 重庆									
Sichuan 四川									
Guizhou 贵州									
Yunnan 云南									
Tibet 西藏									
Northwest 西北									
Shaanxi 陕西									
Gansu 甘肃									
Qinghai 青海									
Ningxia 宁夏									
Xinjiang 新疆									

2435: Electrical Musical Instruments 电子乐器制造业

Year 年份	Number of firms 企业个数	Rate of change 变化率 (%)	Number of employees 职工人数 (人)	Rate of change 变化率 (%)	Total revenue (Mil. RMB) 总销售收入 (百万元)	Rate of change 变化率 (%)	Total profit (Mil RMB) 总利润 (百万元)	Rate of change 变化率 (%)
2000	10		2,947		1,463		112	
2001	16	60.00	4,779	62.16	1,550	5.95	116	3.57
2002	25	56.25	6,105	27.75	1,686	8.77	107	-7.76

Major Products 主要产品	Output 产量	Unit 单位
Western Musical Instrument 西乐器	24	100,000,000 Yuan 亿元

10 Main Firms with Maximal Revenue (year founded) 收入最大的十家主要企业（创办年份）	City 城市	Province 省	Telephone/fax 电话/传真	Number of employees 职工人数	Ownership 产业所有权	Revenue ('000 RMB) 销售收入(千元)	Profit('000 RMB) (rank) 利润(千元)(排名)	Total assets ('000 RMB) 总资产(千元)	Major products 主要产品
Tianjin Yamaha Electronic Musical Instrument Inc	Tianjin	Tianjin	(022)25329379		Foreign Funded				Electronic Organ
天津雅马哈电子乐器有限公司(1990)	天津市	天津市	(022)25329143	800	外商投资	908,584	88,746(1)	329,074	电子琴
Guangdong Sihui Huasheng Musical Instrument Factory	Zhaoqing	Guangdong	(0758)3619108		Private Enterprises				Violin
广东省四会市华声乐器厂(1993)	肇庆市	广东省	(0758)3619102	1,953	私营独资	197,850	-	33,844	提琴
Casio Electronics (Zhuhai) Co.,Ltd.	Zhuhai	Guangdong	(0756)8670888		Foreign Funded				Electronic Organ
卡西欧电子（珠海）有限公司(1995)	珠海市	广东省	(0756)8670588	305	外商投资	180,491	7,213(2)	66,588	电子琴
Yako Musical Instrument(ZhangZhou) Co.,Ltd.	Zhangzhou	Fujian	(0596)2569186		Overseas Chinese-funded				Electric Guitar
雅歌乐器(漳州)有限公司(1995)	漳州市	福建省	(0596)2569018	145	港澳台资	72,223	1,960(5)	47,365	电吉他
Medeli Electronics (ShenZhen) Co.,Ltd.	Shenzhen	Guangdong	(0755)26613371		Overseas Chinese-funded				Electronic Organ
美得理电子（深圳）有限公司(1993)	深圳市	广东省	(0755)26611846	241	港澳台资	53,265	2,905(4)	29,387	电子琴
Shanghai Huaxin Electronic Equipment General Factory	Shanghai	Shanghai	(021)58820000		Overseas Chinese-funded				Electronic Organ
上海华新电子电器总厂(1995)	上海市	上海市	(021)58783113	486	港澳台资	53,139	392(13)	113,262	电子琴
Dalian Orient Musical Instrument Co.,Ltd.	Dalian	Liaoning	(0411)6271562		Foreign Funded				Electric Guitar
大连东方乐器有限公司(1997)	大连市	辽宁省	(0411)6270973	285	外商投资	44,530	1,190(6)	35,980	电吉他
Guangzhou Guzhi Musical Instrument Manufacturing Co.,Ltd.	Guangzhou	Guangdong	(020)82394926		Private Owned				Guitar
广州市故知乐器制造有限公司(1998)	广州市	广东省	(020)82394926	117	私营企业	21,626	316(15)	2,668	吉他
Ningbo Shunshen Musical Instrument Co.,Ltd.	Ningbo	Zhejiang	(0574)62380508		Overseas Chinese funded				Musical Instrument Fittings
宁波舜申乐器有限公司(1994)	宁波市	浙江省	(0574)62382887	150	港澳台资	18,838	4,545(3)	16,910	乐器配件
Wild Wood Musical Instrument Co.,Ltd.	Tianjin	Tianjin	(022)84365672		Foreign Funded				Guitar
瓦尔德乐器（天津）有限公司(2000)	天津市	天津市	(022)84366543	98	外商投资	11,543	-	7,012	吉他

Top 10 Cities by Revenue 销售收入排名前10位城市	Province 省	Market share 市场份额 (%)	Number of firms 企业个数
Tianjin 天津市	Tianjin 天津市	54.95	3
Zhaoqing 肇庆市	Guangdong 广东省	11.74	1
Zhuhai 珠海市	Guangdong 广东省	10.71	1
Shenzhen 深圳市	Guangdong 广东省	4.38	3
Zhangzhou 漳州市	Fujian 福建省	4.28	1
Shanghai 上海市	Shanghai 上海市	3.98	3
Dalian 大连市	Liaoning 辽宁省	3.19	2
Weifang 潍坊市	Shandong 山东省	1.29	4
Guangzhou 广州市	Guangdong 广东省	1.28	1
Changzhou 常州市	Jiangsu 江苏省	1.12	1

10 Major Wholesalers 十家主要批发商	City 城市	Province 省	Telephone/Fax 电话/传真
King Paper Source Trade (shanghai) Co.,Ltd.	Shanghai	Shanghai	(021)62720808
金纸源贸易（上海）有限公司	上海市	上海市	(021)62720909
China National Paper & Pulp Corpration	Beijing	Beijing	(010)67780346
中国纸张纸浆进出口公司	北京市	北京市	(010)67747294
Sinar Mas Linjiang Paper Industry Trade (Beijing) Co.,Ltd.	Beijing	Beijing	(010)65666688
金光林浆纸业贸易(北京)有限公司	北京市	北京市	(010)65669599
Sinar Mas Paper Industry (Xishan) Co.,Ltd.	Wuxi	Jiangsu	(0510)8251188
金光纸业(锡山)有限公司	无锡市	江苏省	(0510)8250906
China Printing Materials General Company	Beijing	Beijing	(010)63442905
中国印刷物资总公司	北京市	北京市	(010)63442900
TSS Eortune Co., ltd.	Tianjin	Tianjin	(022)28131350
天津同鑫进出口有限公司	天津市	天津市	(022)28131353
Wenzhou Import & Export Corpration	Wenzhou	Zhejiang	(0577)88862681
温州市进出口公司	温州市	浙江省	(0577)88844557
Sinar Mas Paper Industry (Xiamen) Co.,Ltd.	Xiamen	Fujian	(0592)2962018
金光纸业（厦门）有限公司	厦门市	福建省	(0592)2962010
Sinar Mas Paper Industry (Shenzhen) Co.,Ltd.	Shenzhen	Guangdong	(0755)83516701
金光纸业（深圳）有限公司	深圳市	广东省	(0755)83516773
Jieyang Ocean Shipping Supply Group Co.,Ltd.	Jieyang	Guangdong	(0663)8239634
揭阳市外轮供应集团有限公司	揭阳市	广东省	(0663)8236186

2439: Other Musical Instruments 其他乐器及文娱用品制造业

The industry accounts for 0.003% of the total revenue of China's industrial sector in 2002. The rate of return on assets is 6.61%. 86.96% of all firms in the industry made a profit while 13.04% had negative returns.The top province in terms of the industry's revenue is Guangdong, accounting for 27.54% of the total revenue.
2002年本行业收入占全行业的0.003%，资产利润率为6.61%。86.96%的企业赢利，13.04%的企业亏损。收入最高的省为广东省，占本行业的27.54%。

	Total number of firms 企业总数	Total number of employees 职工总数	Total revenue (Mil.RMB) 总销售收入 (百万元)	Total profit (Mil.RMB) 总利润 (百万元)	Return on assets 资产利润率 (%)	Return on equity 权益利润率 (%)	Labour productivity ('000 RMB/ worker) 劳动生产率 (千元/人)	Debts/ assets 资产负债率 (%)	Total assets (Mil.RMB) 总资产 (百万元)
Industry Overall 行业总体	23	3,261	329	20	6.61	12.87	33.08	48.60	307

	Number of firms 企业个数	Average number of employees 平均职工人数	Average revenue ('000 RMB) 平均销售收入 (千元)	Average profit ('000 RMB) 平均利润 (千元)	Return on assets 资产利润率 (%)	Return on equity 权益利润率 (%)	Labour productivity ('000 RMB/ worker) 劳动生产率 (千元/人)	Debts/ assets 资产负债率 (%)	Average total assets ('000 RMB) 平均总资产 (千元)
By ownership 产业所有权									
State-owned 国有	1	189	23,583	2,258	8.56	15.55	34.89	44.93	26,370
Collective-owned 集体	5	160	16,252	783	6.70	12.56	42.29	46.66	11,682
Foreign & Overseas Chinese Funded 三资	7	150	15,623	1,025	6.32	12.89	24.68	51.00	16,227
By regional distribution 地区分布									
Central-North 华北	7	118	9,313	587	7.55	12.09	30.60	37.58	7,782
Beijing 北京									
Tianjin 天津	2	71	9,944	1,345	20.67	23.56	-0.64	12.27	6,508
Hebei 河北	5	137	9,061	284	3.43	6.30	37.06	45.52	8,291
Shanxi 山西									
Inner Mongolia 内蒙古									
Northeast 东北	2	155	25,067	1,648	6.30	16.41	40.91	61.58	26,139
Liaoning 辽宁									
Jilin 吉林	1	90	8,698	45	1.49	27.44	46.53	94.56	3,017
Heilongjiang 黑龙江	1	219	41,436	3,250	6.60	16.32	38.60	59.56	49,260
Central-East 华东	6	159	16,555	1,809	9.17	14.61	40.97	37.27	19,733
Shanghai 上海	3	159	14,198	1,243	5.17	8.36	28.38	38.11	24,020
Jiangsu 江苏									
Zhejiang 浙江	3	159	18,912	2,375	15.38	24.01	53.49	35.96	15,447
Anhui 安徽									
Fujian 福建									
Jiangxi 江西									
Shandong 山东									
Central-South 中南	7	140	12,935	-33	-0.42	-1.58	24.68	73.26	7,881
Henan 河南									
Hubei 湖北									
Hunan 湖南									
Guangdong 广东	7	140	12,935	-33	-0.42	-1.58	24.68	73.26	7,881
Guangxi 广西									
Hainan 海南									
Southwest 西南									
Chongqing 重庆									
Sichuan 四川									
Guizhou 贵州									
Yunnan 云南									
Tibet 西藏									
Northwest 西北	1	189	23,583	2,258	8.56	15.55	34.89	44.93	26,370
Shaanxi 陕西									
Gansu 甘肃	1	189	23,583	2,258	8.56	15.55	34.89	44.93	26,370
Qinghai 青海									
Ningxia 宁夏									
Xinjiang 新疆									

2439: Other Musical Instruments 其他乐器及文娱用品制造业

Year 年份	Number of firms 企业个数	Rate of change 变化率 (%)	Number of employees 职工人数 (人)	Rate of change 变化率 (%)	Total revenue (Mil. RMB) 总销售收入 (百万元)	Rate of change 变化率 (%)	Total profit (Mil RMB) 总利润 (百万元)	Rate of change 变化率 (%)
2000	18		2,375		368		-6	
2001	20	11.11	2,412	1.56	231	-37.23	11	-
2002	23	15.00	3,261	35.20	329	42.42	20	81.82

Major Products 主要产品	Output 产量	Unit 单位

10 Main Firms with Maximal Revenue (year founded) 收入最大的十家主要企业（创办年份）	City 城市	Province 省	Telephone/fax 电话/传真	Number of employees 职工人数	Ownership 产业所有权	Revenue ('000 RMB) 销售收入 (千元)	Profit('000 RMB) (rank) 利润(千元) (排名)	Total assets ('000 RMB) 总资产 (千元)	Major products 主要产品
Harbin Sanyi Musical Instrument Co., Ltd.	Harbin	Heilongjiang	(0451)3721555		Foreign Funded				Musical Instrument
哈市三益乐器有限公司(1989)	哈尔滨市	黑龙江省		219	外商投资	41,436	3250(2)	49,260	乐器
Guangzhou Pearl River Musical Instrument Industrial Company	Guangzhou	Guangdong	(020)81544331		Collective-owned				Musical Instrument Chair
广州珠江乐器实业公司(1993)	广州市	广东省	(020)81562319	330	集体企业	28,845	747(9)	11,354	琴凳
Gansu University of Technology Machinery Factory	Lanzhou	Gansu	(0931)2755807		State-owned				Stage Equipment
甘肃工业大学机械工厂(1958)	兰州市	甘肃省	(0931)2755807	189	国有企业	23,583	2,258(4)	26,370	舞台设备
Langfang Risheng Sport Stationery & Musical Instrument Co.,ltd.	Langfang	Hebei	(0316)2860223		Collective-owned				Musical Instrument Packaging
廊坊市日升文体乐器有限公司(1989)	廊坊市	河北省	(0316)2860655	200	集体企业	21,800	1,000(7)	18,600	乐器包装
Nanhai Pingzhou Huisheng Piano Casting Co.,Ltd.	Foshan	Guangdong	(0757)6781240		Private Owned				Piano Fittings
南海市平洲汇声钢琴铸件有限公司(1996)	佛山市	广东省		96	私营企业	18,636	-	15,851	钢琴配件
Shanghai Aikeshen Piano Components Factory	Shanghai	Shanghai	(021)56043112		Collective-owned				Piano & Its Fittings
上海爱克申钢琴部件厂(1992)	上海市	上海市	(021)56043112	170	集体企业	18,134	1,587(6)	21,657	钢琴及配件
Hangzhou Hongyi Metal Products Co.,Ltd.	Hangzhou	Zhejiang	(0571)87643383		Private Owned				Musical Instrument Rack
杭州宏亿金属制品有限公司(1999)	杭州市	浙江省	(0571)87648510	112	私营企业	17,980	526(10)	7,115	乐器架
Shanghai Huayue Piano Parts Co.,Ltd.	Shanghai	Shanghai	(021)58378980		Overseas Chinese-funded				Musical Instrument
上海华粤琴业有限公司(1992)	上海市	上海市	(021)58377958	202	港澳台资	15,040	1,802(5)	22,178	乐器
Hangzhou Taiying Metal Products Co.,Ltd.	Hangzhou	Zhejiang	(0571)87643043		Foreign Funded				Musical Instrument Rack
杭州泰盈金属制品有限公司(1999)	杭州市	浙江省	(0571)87645289	92	外商投资	13,442	770(8)	11,579	乐器架
Binwei Metal(ShenZhen) Co.,Ltd.	Shenzhen	Guangdong	(0755)28985387		Overseas Chinese-funded				Musical Instrument Fittings
宾玮五金(深圳)有限公司(1995)	深圳市	广东省	(0755)28985317	290	港澳台资	10,529	383(11)	6,533	乐器配件

Top 10 Cities by Revenue 销售收入排名前10位城市	Province 省	Market share 市场份额 (%)	Number of firms 企业个数
Guangzhou 广州市	Guangdong 广东省	15.58	4
Shanghai 上海市	Shanghai 上海市	12.96	3
Harbin 哈尔滨市	Heilongjiang 黑龙江省	12.60	1
Hangzhou 杭州市	Zhejiang 浙江省	9.56	2
Langfang 廊坊市	Hebei 河北省	8.23	2
Ningbo 宁波市	Zhejiang 浙江省	7.70	1
Lanzhou 兰州市	Gansu 甘肃省	7.17	1
Tianjin 天津市	Tianjin 天津市	6.05	2
Foshan 佛山市	Guangdong 广东省	5.67	1
Chengde 承德市	Hebei 河北省	3.89	2

10 Major Wholesalers 十家主要批发商	City 城市	Province 省	Telephone/Fax 电话/传真
King Paper Source Trade (shanghai) Co.,Ltd.	Shanghai	Shanghai	(021)62720808
金纸源贸易（上海）有限公司	上海市	上海市	(021)62720909
China National Paper & Pulp Corpration	Beijing	Beijing	(010)67780346
中国纸张纸浆进出口公司	北京市	北京市	(010)67747294
Sinar Mas Linjiang Paper Industry Trade (Beijing) Co.,Ltd.	Beijing	Beijing	(010)65666688
金光林浆纸业贸易(北京)有限公司	北京市	北京市	(010)65669599
Sinar Mas Paper Industry (Xishan) Co.,Ltd.	Wuxi	Jiangsu	(0510)8251188
金光纸业(锡山)有限公司	无锡市	江苏省	(0510)8250906
China Printing Materials General Company	Beijing	Beijing	(010)63442905
中国印刷物资总公司	北京市	北京市	(010)63442900
TSS Eortune Co., ltd.	Tianjin	Tianjin	(022)28131350
天津同鑫进出口有限公司	天津市	天津市	(022)28131353
Wenzhou Import & Export Corpration	Wenzhou	Zhejiang	(0577)88862681
温州市进出口公司	温州市	浙江省	(0577)88844557
Sinar Mas Paper Industry (Xiamen) Co.,Ltd.	Xiamen	Fujian	(0592)2962018
金光纸业（厦门）有限公司	厦门市	福建省	(0592)2962010
Sinar Mas Paper Industry (Shenzhen) Co.,Ltd	Shenzhen	Guangdong	(0755)83516701
金光纸业（深圳）有限公司	深圳市	广东省	(0755)83516773
Jieyang Ocean Shipping Supply Group Co.,Ltd.	Jieyang	Guangdong	(0663)8239634
揭阳市外轮供应集团有限公司	揭阳市	广东省	(0663)8236186

2440: Toys 玩具制造业

The industry accounts for 0.333% of the total revenue of China's industrial sector in 2002. The rate of return on assets is 4.79%. 80.39% of all firms in the industry made a profit while 19.61% had negative returns.The top province in terms of the industry's revenue is Guangdong, accounting for 48.60% of the total revenue.
2002年本行业收入占全行业的0.333%，资产利润率为4.79%。80.39%的企业赢利，19.61%的企业亏损。收入最高的省为广东省，占本行业的48.60%。

	Total number of firms 企业总数	Total number of employees 职工总数	Total revenue (Mil.RMB) 总销售收入（百万元）	Total profit (Mil.RMB) 总利润（百万元）	Return on assets 资产利润率（%）	Return on equity 权益利润率（%）	Labour productivity ('000 RMB/ worker) 劳动生产率（千元/人）	Debts/ assets 资产负债率（%）	Total assets (Mil.RMB) 总资产（百万元）
Industry Overall 行业总体	1015	468,115	35,691	1,288	4.79	10.79	21.59	55.61	26,887

	Number of firms 企业个数	Average number of employees 平均职工人数	Average revenue ('000 RMB) 平均销售收入（千元）	Average profit ('000 RMB) 平均利润（千元）	Return on assets 资产利润率（%）	Return on equity 权益利润率（%）	Labour productivity ('000 RMB/ worker) 劳动生产率（千元/人）	Debts/ assets 资产负债率（%）	Average total assets ('000 RMB) 平均总资产（千元）
By ownership 产业所有权									
State-owned 国有	16	321	7,040	65	0.82	7.89	7.75	89.58	7,881
Collective-owned 集体	89	614	37,345	1,557	5.84	12.73	17.27	54.15	26,679
Foreign & Overseas Chinese Funded 三资	550	577	42,406	1,499	4.35	9.53	21.17	54.34	34,454
By regional distribution 地区分布									
Central-North 华北	19	278	16,878	-428	-2.65	-10.45	13.50	74.65	16,164
Beijing 北京	12	135	11,432	-1,045	-7.60	-53.46	16.72	85.79	13,754
Tianjin 天津	6	443	27,227	535	3.12	17.50	14.03	82.15	17,108
Hebei 河北	1	1,000	20,144	1,189	3.02	3.29	6.89	8.43	39,411
Shanxi 山西									
Inner Mongolia 内蒙古									
Northeast 东北	2	210	22,593	3,049	19.45	35.25	34.17	44.82	15,673
Liaoning 辽宁	2	210	22,593	3,049	19.45	35.25	34.17	44.82	15,673
Jilin 吉林									
Heilongjiang 黑龙江									
Central-East 华东	625	296	28,405	1,175	6.89	17.46	25.73	60.55	17,057
Shanghai 上海	97	298	35,615	2,216	9.02	23.20	27.24	61.11	24,565
Jiangsu 江苏	253	276	31,908	1,074	6.54	16.99	30.96	61.52	16,427
Zhejiang 浙江	142	206	21,076	988	6.66	17.44	24.81	61.80	14,831
Anhui 安徽	27	499	16,212	166	1.34	3.60	12.52	62.69	12,356
Fujian 福建	36	276	20,608	882	4.41	8.30	21.62	46.83	19,992
Jiangxi 江西	4	173	14,341	38	0.29	0.37	21.04	21.48	12,984
Shandong 山东	66	492	30,244	1,076	7.80	21.71	20.79	64.07	13,794
Central-South 中南	369	753	47,620	1,506	3.50	7.28	18.97	51.95	43,057
Henan 河南	4	262	14,419	276	2.65	8.05	19.47	67.10	10,398
Hubei 湖北	9	198	17,600	789	7.02	32.82	33.08	78.62	11,242
Hunan 湖南	2	178	5,205	721	14.46	24.15	11.42	40.15	4,988
Guangdong 广东	354	775	48,998	1,543	3.47	7.19	18.89	51.74	44,450
Guangxi 广西									
Hainan 海南									
Southwest 西南									
Chongqing 重庆									
Sichuan 四川									
Guizhou 贵州									
Yunnan 云南									
Tibet 西藏									
Northwest 西北									
Shaanxi 陕西									
Gansu 甘肃									
Qinghai 青海									
Ningxia 宁夏									
Xinjiang 新疆									

Year 年份	Number of firms 企业个数	Rate of change 变化率（%）	Number of employees 职工人数（人）	Rate of change 变化率（%）	Total revenue (Mil. RMB) 总销售收入（百万元）	Rate of change 变化率（%）	Total profit (Mil RMB) 总利润（百万元）	Rate of change 变化率（%）
2000	850		426,208		31,844		1,002	
2001	881	3.65	425,283	-0.22	31,737	-0.34	929	-7.29
2002	1015	15.21	468,115	10.07	35,691	12.46	1,288	38.64

Major Products 主要产品	Output 产量	Unit 单位
Toy 玩具	294	100,000,000 Yuan 亿元

10 Main Firms with Maximal Revenue (year founded) 收入最大的十家主要企业（创办年份）	City 城市	Province 省	Telephone/fax 电话/传真	Number of employees 职工人数	Ownership 产业所有权	Revenue ('000 RMB) 销售收入（千元）	Profit('000 RMB) (rank) 利润（千元）（排名）	Total assets ('000 RMB) 总资产（千元）	Major products 主要产品
Good Baby Group Co., Ltd.	Suzhou	Jiangsu	(0512)57678200		Private Owned				Childern's Car
好孩子集团有限公司(1975)	苏州市	江苏省	(0512)67671515	4,368	私营企业	1,017,990	79,152(1)	1,108,467	童车
Nanhai Sino-U.S.A Toy Factory	Foshan	Guangdong	(0757)5881238		Collective-owned				Toy
南海市中美玩具厂(1985)	佛山市	广东省	(0757)5887627	3,136	集体企业	855,430	29,500(7)	382,240	玩具
Nanhai Huaxuan Toy Factoly	Foshan	Guangdong	(0757)5889203		Limited-Liability				Alloy Plastic Toy Car
南海市华轩玩具厂(1998)	佛山市	广东省	(0757)5889063	899	有限公司	505,310	4,300(70)	132,310	合金塑料玩具车
Zhongshan Lerdo Daily Articles Co., Ltd.	Zhongshan	Guangdong	(0760)3372800		Overseas Chinese-funded				Childern's Car
中山市隆成日用制品有限公司(1988)	中山市	广东省	(0760)3372577	2,808	港澳台资	402,914	10,949(30)	132,003	童车
Zhongshan International Toys Co.,Ltd.	Zhongshan	Guangdong	(0760)5596778		Overseas Chinese-funded				Plastic Toy
中山国际玩具有限公司(1989)	中山市	广东省	(0760)5596716	4,900	港澳台资	399,597	4,143(76)	286,069	塑料玩具
Dongguan Radica Manufacture Co., ltd.	Dongguan	Guangdong	(0769)5551775		Foreign Funded				Toy Playing Machine
东莞乐迪卡游戏机制造厂有限公司(1996)	东莞市	广东省	(0769)5551226	1,650	外商投资	363,350	8,980(33)	518,910	玩具游戏机
Zhongshan Chonggao Toys Factory Co., Ltd.	Zhongshan	Guangdong	(0760)8402969		Overseas Chinese-funded				Plastic Toy
中山崇高玩具制品厂有限公司(1991)	中山市	广东省	(0760)8411724	6,004	港澳台资	351,607	4,184(75)	117,749	塑胶玩具
Zepta (China) Industrial Co.,Ltd.	Guangzhou	Guangdong	(020)84926666		Overseas Chinese-funded				Plastic Toy
镇泰（中国）工业有限公司(1995)	广州市	广东省	(020)84926868	5,800	港澳台资	330,973	-	249,252	塑料玩具
Suzhou Taiyuan Toy Co., Ltd.	Suzhou	Jiangsu	(0512)65010660		Foreign Funded				Toy
苏州泰渊玩具有限公司(1993)	苏州市	江苏省	(0512)65015880	1,950	外商投资	305,320	14,888(19)	101,440	玩具
Zhongshan Taiping Toy Co., Ltd.	Zhongshan	Guangdong	(0760)6506972		Overseas Chinese-funded				Toy
中山太平玩具有限公司(1995)	中山市	广东省	(0760)6506363	2,924	港澳台资	277,320	7,667(35)	178,327	玩具

Top 10 Cities by Revenue 销售收入排名前10位城市	Province 省	Market share 市场份额（%）	Number of firms 企业个数
Dongguan 东莞市	Guangdong 广东省	10.37	82
Shanghai 上海市	Shanghai 上海市	9.68	97
Zhongshan 中山市	Guangdong 广东省	8.01	39
Guangzhou 广州市	Guangdong 广东省	7.96	65
Shenzhen 深圳市	Guangdong 广东省	7.48	49
Foshan 佛山市	Guangdong 广东省	7.07	29
Suzhou 苏州市	Jiangsu 江苏省	5.61	26
Yangzhou 扬州市	Jiangsu 江苏省	5.31	80
Nanjing 南京市	Jiangsu 江苏省	4.09	40
Zhenjiang 镇江市	Jiangsu 江苏省	3.62	34

10 Major Wholesalers 十家主要批发商	City 城市	Province 省	Telephone/Fax 电话/传真
Jiangsu Holly Corporation	Nanjing	Jiangsu	(025)2301288
江苏弘业股份有限公司	南京市	江苏省	(025)2308351
Wujin Commerce (Group) Company	Changzhou	Jiangsu	(0519)8110048
武进商业（集团）公司	常州市	江苏省	(0519)8104604
Wenzhou N & A Foreign Trade Corp.	Wenzhou	Zhejiang	(0577)88862582
温州市土产畜产品对外贸易公司	温州市	浙江省	(0577)88862588
Guangzhou Economic Developing Zone Construction Import & Export Trade Co.,Ltd.	Guangzhou	Guangdong	(020)38870988
广州经济开发区建设进出口贸易有限公司	广州市	广东省	(020)38870902
Guangzhou Cascade Trade Co.,Ltd.	Guangzhou	Guangdong	(020)86667016
广州浩霖贸易有限公司	广州市	广东省	(020)86668051
Guangdong Dongguan Light Industrial Products Import & Export Co.,ltd.	Dongguan	Guangdong	(0769)2212413
广东省东莞轻工业品进出口有限公司	东莞市	广东省	(0769)2222784
Shanghai Zijiang International Trading Co.Ltd.	Shanghai	Shanghai	(021)64676900
上海紫江国际贸易有限公司	上海市	上海市	(021)64676901
Suzhou Jinmilan Furniture Co.,Ltd.	Suzhou	Jiangsu	(0512)65458833
苏州市金米兰家具有限公司	苏州市	江苏省	(0512)65755838
China MEHECO Oriental Trade Company	Beijing	Beijing	(010)67116688
美康东方贸易公司	北京市	北京市	(010)67121579
Wenzhou Longwan Foreign Trade Co.,ltd.	Wenzhou	Zhejiang	(0577)88918990
温州市龙湾区对外贸易有限公司	温州市	浙江省	(0577)88918991

2450: Game Machines 游艺器材制造业

The industry accounts for 0.004% of the total revenue of China's industrial sector in 2002. The rate of return on assets is 1.33%. 75.00% of all firms in the industry made a profit while 25.00% had negative returns.The top province in terms of the industry's revenue is Guangdong, accounting for 48.24% of the total revenue.
2002年本行业收入占全行业的0.004%，资产利润率为1.33%。75.00%的企业赢利，25.00%的企业亏损。收入最高的省为广东省，占本行业的48.24%。

	Total number of firms 企业总数	Total number of employees 职工总数	Total revenue (Mil.RMB) 总销售收入(百万元)	Total profit (Mil.RMB) 总利润(百万元)	Return on assets 资产利润率(%)	Return on equity 权益利润率(%)	Labour productivity ('000 RMB/worker) 劳动生产率(千元/人)	Debts/assets 资产负债率(%)	Total assets (Mil.RMB) 总资产(百万元)
Industry Overall 行业总体	24	4,087	482	14	1.33	2.78	32.41	52.14	1,066

	Number of firms 企业个数	Average number of employees 平均职工人数	Average revenue ('000 RMB) 平均销售收入(千元)	Average profit ('000 RMB) 平均利润(千元)	Return on assets 资产利润率(%)	Return on equity 权益利润率(%)	Labour productivity ('000 RMB/worker) 劳动生产率(千元/人)	Debts/assets 资产负债率(%)	Average total assets ('000 RMB) 平均总资产(千元)
By ownership 产业所有权									
State-owned 国有	2	93	5,791	262	2.94		39.58	111.16	8,901
Collective-owned 集体	2	60	4,034	264	12.35	24.46	17.06	49.51	2,138
Foreign & Overseas Chinese Funded 三资	11	255	32,533	729	0.93	1.77	32.64	47.46	78,199
By regional distribution 地区分布									
Central-North 华北	5	147	21,264	1,401	3.04	10.37	64.20	70.66	46,018
Beijing 北京	4	175	25,722	1,576	2.79	9.85	65.20	71.71	56,561
Tianjin 天津									
Hebei 河北	1	35	3,433	698	18.14	19.85	44.06	8.60	3,847
Shanxi 山西									
Inner Mongolia 内蒙古									
Northeast 东北									
Liaoning 辽宁									
Jilin 吉林									
Heilongjiang 黑龙江									
Central-East 华东	6	227	19,233	1,453	7.84	14.67	25.09	46.57	18,531
Shanghai 上海	1	185	11,581	524	2.94		39.79	111.16	17,800
Jiangsu 江苏									
Zhejiang 浙江	5	235	20,763	1,639	8.77	13.34	22.78	34.26	18,677
Anhui 安徽									
Fujian 福建									
Jiangxi 江西									
Shandong 山东									
Central-South 中南	11	170	22,973	-190	-0.29	-0.55	26.22	47.11	65,516
Henan 河南	2	59	9,972	-35	-0.32	-1.28	22.15	75.40	11,086
Hubei 湖北									
Hunan 湖南									
Guangdong 广东	9	195	25,862	-224	-0.29	-0.54	26.49	46.21	77,611
Guangxi 广西									
Hainan 海南									
Southwest 西南									
Chongqing 重庆									
Sichuan 四川									
Guizhou 贵州									
Yunnan 云南									
Tibet 西藏									
Northwest 西北	2	60	4,034	264	12.35	24.46	17.06	49.51	2,138
Shaanxi 陕西	1,	70	7,840	528	20.47	31.43	21.14	34.88	2,580
Gansu 甘肃	1	49	227				11.22	71.76	1,696
Qinghai 青海									
Ningxia 宁夏									
Xinjiang 新疆									

Year 年份	Number of firms 企业个数	Rate of change 变化率 (%)	Number of employees 职工人数 (人)	Rate of change 变化率 (%)	Total revenue (Mil. RMB) 总销售收入 (百万元)	Rate of change 变化率 (%)	Total profit (Mil RMB) 总利润 (百万元)	Rate of change 变化率 (%)
2000	17		1,787		188		-5	
2001	22	29.41	4,367	144.38	579	207.98	-12	-140.00
2002	24	9.09	4,087	-6.41	482	-16.75	14	-

Major Products 主要产品	Output 产量	Unit 单位

10 Main Firms with Maximal Revenue (year founded) 收入最大的十家主要企业（创办年份）	City 城市	Province 省	Telephone/fax 电话/传真	Number of employees 职工人数	Ownership 产业所有权	Revenue ('000 RMB) 销售收入 (千元)	Profit('000 RMB) (rank) 利润(千元) (排名)	Total assets ('000 RMB) 总资产 (千元)	Major products 主要产品
Jiangmen Apolo Electronics Co., Ltd.	Jiangmen	Guangdong	(0750)6103538		Overseas Chinese-funded				Playing Machine
江门市阿波罗电子有限公司(1992)	江门市	广东省	(0750)6127702	81	港澳台资	64,331	-	39,271	游戏机
Superior Sporting Goods (Zhejiang) Co., ltd.	Jiaxing	Zhejiang	(0573)4753386		Overseas Chinese-funded				Playing Table
加胜运动器材（浙江）有限公司(2001)	嘉兴市	浙江省	(0573)4753395	808	港澳台资	59,673	5,877(1)	59,080	游戏桌
Beijing Xingwei Sports Goods Co.,Ltd.	Beijing	Beijing	(010)61258493		Overseas Chinese-funded				Billiard Table
北京星伟体育用品有限公司(1991)	北京市	北京市	(010)61251333	243	港澳台资	29,140	3,010(4)	78,770	台球桌
Henan Jiabaohua Sport Equipment & Entertainment Co.,Ltd.	Xuchang	Henan	(0374)6216728		Overseas Chinese-funded				Dart
河南嘉宝华运动器材娱乐有限公司(1997)	许昌市	河南省	(0374)6216778	117	港澳台资	19,943	-	22,170	飞镖
Dongguan Hongxiang Electronics Co., Ltd.	Dongguan	Guangdong	(0769)5540725		Overseas Chinese-funded				Game Machine Rocker游
东莞弘祥电子有限公司(1996)	东莞市	广东省	(0769)5540727	110	港澳台资	18,090	4,599(2)	21,748	戏机摇杆
Zhongshan Golden Horse Amusement Equipment Co.,Ltd.	Zhongshan	Guangdong	(0760)8784183		Limited-Liability				Recreation Apparatus
中山市金马游艺机有限公司(1999)	中山市	广东省	(0760)8701368	176	有限公司	14,262	179(13)	19,136	游艺器材
Ninghai Tengda Machinery Co.,Ltd.	Ningbo	Zhejiang	(0574)65566400		Private Owned				Travel Products
宁海县腾达机械有限公司(1998)	宁波市	浙江省	(0574)65573330	136	私营企业	13,429	686(7)	5,889	旅游产品
Shanghai Xidu Neihe Engineering Ship Repair & Manufacturing	Shanghai	Shanghai	(021)57158393		State-owned				Recreation Machine
Factory上海西渡内河工程船舶修造厂(1962)	上海市	上海市		185	国有企业	11,581	524(9)	17,800	游艺机
Dongguan Baohong Electronics Co., Ltd.	Dongguan	Guangdong	(0769)5553295		Overseas Chinese-funded				TV Game Machine电
东莞堡宏电子有限公司(1994)	东莞市	广东省	(0769)5553350	300	港澳台资	11,200	50(15)	19,311	视游戏机
Wenzhou South Amusement Equipment General Factory	Wenzhou	Zhejiang	(0577)88722168		Joint Stock				Recreation Equipment
温州市南方游乐设备总厂(1982)	温州市	浙江省	(0577)88717441	97	股份制	8,086	251(12)	10,330	游乐设备

Top 10 Cities by Revenue 销售收入排名前10位城市	Province 省	Market share 市场份额 (%)	Number of firms 企业个数
Shenzhen 深圳市	Guangdong 广东省	24.27	2
Beijing 北京市	Beijing 北京市	21.32	4
Jiangmen 江门市	Guangdong 广东省	13.55	2
Jiaxing 嘉兴市	Zhejiang 浙江省	12.37	1
Dongguan 东莞市	Guangdong 广东省	6.07	2
Hangzhou 杭州市	Zhejiang 浙江省	4.69	2
Xuchang 许昌市	Henan 河南省	4.13	1
Zhongshan 中山市	Guangdong 广东省	3.35	2
Ningbo 宁波市	Zhejiang 浙江省	2.78	1
Shanghai 上海市	Shanghai 上海市	2.40	1

10 Major Wholesalers 十家主要批发商	City 城市	Province 省	Telephone/Fax 电话/传真
Jiangsu Holly Corporation	Nanjing	Jiangsu	(025)2301288
江苏弘业股份有限公司	南京市	江苏省	(025)2308351
Wujin Commerce (Group) Company	Changzhou	Jiangsu	(0519)8110048
武进商业（集团）公司	常州市	江苏省	(0519)8104604
Wenzhou N & A Foreign Trade Corp.	Wenzhou	Zhejiang	(0577)88862582
温州市土产畜产品对外贸易公司	温州市	浙江省	(0577)88862588
Guangzhou Economic Developing Zone Construction Import & Export Trade Co.,Ltd.	Guangzhou	Guangdong	(020)38870988
广州经济开发区建设进出口贸易有限公司	广州市	广东省	(020)38870902
Guangzhou Cascade Trade Co.,Ltd.	Guangzhou	Guangdong	(020)86667016
广州浩霖贸易有限公司	广州市	广东省	(020)86668051
Guangdong Dongguan Light Industrial Products Import & Export Co.,ltd.	Dongguan	Guangdong	(0769)2212413
广东省东莞轻工业品进出口有限公司	东莞市	广东省	(0769)2222784
Shanghai Zijiang International Trading Co.Ltd.	Shanghai	Shanghai	(021)64676900
上海紫江国际贸易有限公司	上海市	上海市	(021)64676901
Suzhou Jinmilan Furniture Co.,Ltd.	Suzhou	Jiangsu	(0512)65458833
苏州市金米兰家具有限公司	苏州市	江苏省	(0512)65755838
China MEHECO Oriental Trade Company	Beijing	Beijing	(010)67116688
美康东方贸易公司	北京市	北京市	(010)67121579
Wenzhou Longwan Foreign Trade Co.,ltd.	Wenzhou	Zhejiang	(0577)88918990
温州市龙湾区对外贸易有限公司	温州市	浙江省	(0577)88918991

2490: Other Cultural, Educational and Sports Products

其他类未包括的文教体育用品制造业

The industry accounts for 0.013% of the total revenue of China's industrial sector in 2002. The rate of return on assets is 4.42%. 80.85% of all firms in the industry made a profit while 19.15% had negative returns.The top province in terms of the industry's revenue is Zhejiang, accounting for 32.66% of the total revenue.
2002年本行业收入占全行业的 0.013%，资产利润率为 4.42%。80.85%的企业赢利，19.15%的企业亏损。收入最高的省为浙江省，占本行业的32.66%。

	Total number of firms 企业总数	Total number of employees 职工总数	Total revenue (Mil.RMB) 总销售收入 (百万元)	Total profit (Mil.RMB) 总利润 (百万元)	Return on assets 资产利润率 (%)	Return on equity 权益利润率 (%)	Labour productivity ('000 RMB/ worker) 劳动生产率 (千元/人)	Debts/ assets 资产负债率 (%)	Total assets (Mil.RMB) 总资产 (百万元)
Industry Overall 行业总体	47	9,293	1,348	63	4.42	10.51	36.83	57.95	1,431

	Number of firms 企业个数	Average number of employees 平均职工人数	Average revenue ('000 RMB) 平均销售收入（千元）	Average profit ('000 RMB) 平均利润 (千元)	Return on assets 资产利润率 (%)	Return on equity 权益利润率 (%)	Labour productivity ('000 RMB/ worker) 劳动生产率 (千元/人)	Debts/ assets 资产负债率 (%)	Average total assets ('000 RMB) 平均总资产 (千元)
By ownership 产业所有权									
State-owned 国有	3	32	1,876	289	7.23	11.12	22.68	34.99	4,000
Collective-owned 集体	3	55	6,401	94	3.12	4.16	44.18	25.12	3,005
Foreign & Overseas Chinese Funded 三资	15	244	30,165	700	2.14	4.94	31.11	56.77	32,753
By regional distribution 地区分布									
Central-North 华北	5	145	22,523	1,009	3.56	26.81	55.34	86.73	28,359
Beijing 北京	3	46	7,466	718	5.06	22.85	67.29	77.88	14,197
Tianjin 天津	2	293	45,109	1,446	2.91	30.78	52.50	90.53	49,601
Hebei 河北									
Shanxi 山西									
Inner Mongolia 内蒙古									
Northeast 东北									
Liaoning 辽宁									
Jilin 吉林									
Heilongjiang 黑龙江									
Central-East 华东	30	210	29,791	1,689	4.58	9.90	38.49	53.76	36,892
Shanghai 上海	3	279	53,111	1,997	1.27	2.47	33.80	48.46	156,802
Jiangsu 江苏	4	100	17,103	730	10.36	34.52	55.96	69.99	7,048
Zhejiang 浙江	13	263	33,867	2,661	8.31	18.54	31.31	55.21	32,036
Anhui 安徽									
Fujian 福建	3	209	8,529	-37	-0.50	-0.91	14.58	44.99	7,439
Jiangxi 江西	1	50	3,589	666	12.72	14.71	24.40	13.49	5,234
Shandong 山东	6	161	32,754	1,101	4.02	11.48	77.13	64.96	27,358
Central-South 中南	9	226	36,622	798	4.18	10.92	27.78	61.73	19,111
Henan 河南									
Hubei 湖北									
Hunan 湖南	2	60	32,410	3,079	18.34	33.64	116.13	45.48	16,790
Guangdong 广东	7	273	37,826	147	0.74	2.16	22.24	65.68	19,775
Guangxi 广西									
Hainan 海南									
Southwest 西南	2	109	6,100	175	3.69	7.13	11.08	48.18	4,737
Chongqing 重庆	1	186	10,356	154	4.47	8.08	8.17	44.69	3,448
Sichuan 四川									
Guizhou 贵州									
Yunnan 云南	1	32	1,844	196	3.25	6.53	28.03	50.17	6,025
Tibet 西藏									
Northwest 西北	1	16	1				44.75	57.61	736
Shaanxi 陕西									
Gansu 甘肃	1	16	1				44.75	57.61	736
Qinghai 青海									
Ningxia 宁夏									
Xinjiang 新疆									

2490: Other Cultural, Educational and Sports Products

其他类未包括的文教体育用品制造业

Year 年份	Number of firms 企业个数	Rate of change 变化率 (%)	Number of employees 职工人数 (人)	Rate of change 变化率 (%)	Total revenue (Mil. RMB) 总销售收入 (百万元)	Rate of change 变化率 (%)	Total profit (Mil RMB) 总利润 (百万元)	Rate of change 变化率 (%)
2000	46		6,957		1,087		104	
2001	54	17.39	9,775	40.51	1,901	74.89	184	76.92
2002	47	-12.96	9,293	-4.93	1,348	-29.09	63	-65.76

Major Products 主要产品	Output 产量	Unit 单位

10 Main Firms with Maximal Revenue (year founded) 收入最大的十家主要企业（创办年份）	City 城市	Province 省	Telephone/fax 电话/传真	Number of employees 职工人数	Ownership 产业所有权	Revenue ('000 RMB) 销售收入 (千元)	Profit('000 RMB) (rank) 利润(千元) (排名)	Total assets ('000 RMB) 总资产 (千元)	Major products 主要产品
Shanghai ZhongLu Industrial Co.,Ltd. 上海中路实业有限公司(1995)	Shanghai 上海市	Shanghai 上海市	(021)58033099 (021)58037623	760	Private Owned 私营企业	141,576	6,487(2)	387,339	Bowling Equipment保龄球设备
Ningbo Haibo Precise Machinery Co., ltd. 宁波市海伯精密机械制造有限公司(1994)	Ningbo 宁波市	Zhejiang 浙江省	(0574)86887290 (0574)86882132	502	Limited-Liability 有限公司	103,378	15,261(1)	123,770	Wave Wheel 摇轮
BHL Bags Manufacturing(HuiZhou) Co.,Ltd. 幸运体育袋制造厂（惠州）有限公司(1994)	Huizhou 惠州市	Guangdong 广东省	(0752)2383680 (0752)2264267	350	Overseas Chinese-funded 港澳台资	100,583	213(27)	23,781	Sports Bags体育运动袋
Zhuhai Liming Industrial Co., Ltd. 珠海市利明实业有限公司(1999)	Zhuhai 珠海市	Guangdong 广东省	(0756)8682818 (0756)8682838	559	Limited-Liability 有限公司	99,806	1,949(12)	43,313	Electronic Game Machine电子游戏机
Ningbo Chenglu Group Co.,Ltd. 宁波成路集团有限公司(1997)	Ningbo 宁波市	Zhejiang 浙江省	(0574)86175539 (0574)86178086	1,041	Overseas Chinese-funded 港澳台资	96,050	4,330(5)	132,370	Recreation & Sports Daily Use Articles文体日用品
Tengzhou Sports Equipment Co.,Ltd. 滕州市运动设施有限公司(1985)	Zaozhuang 枣庄市	Shandong 山东省	(0632)2656198 (0632)2656198	260	Private Enterprises 私营独资	69,000	5,460(3)	19,320	Teaching Equipment 教学设备
Changsha Xicheng Electron Co.,Ltd. 长沙西城电子有限公司(1996)	Changsha 长沙市	Hunan 湖南省	(0731)8865880 (0731)8864980	72	Private Owned 私营企业	54,870	5,250(4)	25,969	CMS Multimedia Teaching Network.CMS多媒体教学网络
Qingdao Sunwoo Sporting Goods Co.,Ltd. 青岛鲜宇体育用品有限公司(1994)	Qingdao 青岛市	Shandong 山东省	(0532)8597651 (0532)8597403	325	Foreign Funded 外商投资	53,459	1,542(13)	29,637	Golf Cue高尔夫球杆
Zhejiang Shaoxing Yuanfa Recreation & Sports Articles Co., Ltd. 浙江绍兴源发文体用品有限公司(1996)	Shaoxing 绍兴市	Zhejiang 浙江省	(0575)8734253 (0575)8734141	230	Overseas Chinese-funded 港澳台资	34,930	2,714(8)	18,073	Recreation & Teaching Articles 文教用品
Hongzheng Photoelectricity Media Co., Ltd. 宏正光电传媒有限公司(1999)	Yantai 烟台市	Shandong 山东省	(0535)6718288 (0535)6718288	100	Limited-Liability 有限公司	31,123	-	91,378	Laser Disc 光盘

Top 10 Cities by Revenue 销售收入排名前10位城市	Province 省	Market share 市场份额 (%)	Number of firms 企业个数
Ningbo 宁波市	Zhejiang 浙江省	25.50	8
Shanghai 上海市	Shanghai 上海市	11.82	3
Huizhou 惠州市	Guangdong 广东省	8.93	2
Zhuhai 珠海市	Guangdong 广东省	7.40	1
Tianjin 天津市	Tianjin 天津市	6.69	2
Zaozhuang 枣庄市	Shandong 山东省	5.12	1
Qingdao 青岛市	Shandong 山东省	4.27	2
Jinhua 金华市	Zhejiang 浙江省	4.07	3
Changsha 长沙市	Hunan 湖南省	4.07	1
Jinan 济南市	Shandong 山东省	2.89	2

10 Major Wholesalers 十家主要批发商	City 城市	Province 省	Telephone/Fax 电话/传真
King Paper Source Trade (shanghai) Co.,Ltd. 金纸源贸易（上海）有限公司	Shanghai 上海市	Shanghai 上海市	(021)62720808 (021)62720909
China National Paper & Pulp Corpration 中国纸张纸浆进出口公司	Beijing 北京市	Beijing 北京市	(010)67780346 (010)67747294
Sinar Mas Linjiang Paper Industry Trade (Beijing) Co.,Ltd. 金光林浆纸业贸易(北京)有限公司	Beijing 北京市	Beijing 北京市	(010)65666688 (010)65669599
Sinar Mas Paper Industry (Xishan) Co.,Ltd. 金光纸业(锡山)有限公司	Wuxi 无锡市	Jiangsu 江苏省	(0510)8251188 (0510)8250906
China Printing Materials General Company 中国印刷物资总公司	Beijing 北京市	Beijing 北京市	(010)63442905 (010)63442900
TSS Eortune Co., ltd. 天津同鑫进出口有限公司	Tianjin 天津市	Tianjin 天津市	(022)28131350 (022)28131353
Wenzhou Import & Export Corpration 温州市进出口公司	Wenzhou 温州市	Zhejiang 浙江省	(0577)88862681 (0577)88844557
Sinar Mas Paper Industry (Xiamen) Co.,Ltd. 金光纸业（厦门）有限公司	Xiamen 厦门市	Fujian 福建省	(0592)2962018 (0592)2962010
Sinar Mas Paper Industry (Shenzhen) Co.,Ltd. 金光纸业（深圳）有限公司	Shenzhen 深圳市	Guangdong 广东省	(0755)83516701 (0755)83516773
Jieyang Ocean Shipping Supply Group Co.,Ltd. 揭阳市外轮供应集团有限公司	Jieyang 揭阳市	Guangdong 广东省	(0663)8239634 (0663)8236186

2520: Processing of Crude Oil 原油加工业

The industry accounts for 3.872% of the total revenue of China's industrial sector in 2002. The rate of return on assets is 1.16%. 77.35% of all firms in the industry made a profit while 22.65% had negative returns.The top province in terms of the industry's revenue is Liaoning, accounting for 17.03% of the total revenue.
2002年本行业收入占全行业的3.872%，资产利润率为1.16%。77.35%的企业赢利，22.65%的企业亏损。收入最高的省为辽宁省，占本行业的17.03%。

	Total number of firms 企业总数	Total number of employees 职工总数	Total revenue (Mil.RMB) 总销售收入（百万元）	Total profit (Mil.RMB) 总利润（百万元）	Return on assets 资产利润率（%）	Return on equity 权益利润率（%）	Labour productivity ('000 RMB/ worker) 劳动生产率（千元/人）	Debts/ assets 资产负债率（%）	Total assets (Mil.RMB) 总资产（百万元）
Industry Overall 行业总体	309	295,174	415,289	3,432	1.16	2.64	278.71	56.30	296,967

	Number of firms 企业个数	Average number of employees 平均职工人数	Average revenue ('000 RMB) 平均销售收入（千元）	Average profit ('000 RMB) 平均利润（千元）	Return on assets 资产利润率（%）	Return on equity 权益利润率（%）	Labour productivity ('000 RMB/ worker) 劳动生产率（千元/人）	Debts/ assets 资产负债率（%）	Average total assets ('000 RMB) 平均总资产（千元）
By ownership 产业所有权									
State-owned 国有	50	2,147	2,924,363	17,287	0.84	2.11	264.77	60.20	2,054,781
Collective-owned 集体	67	261	56,330	1,947	4.10	10.77	60.67	61.96	47,550
Foreign & Overseas Chinese Funded 三资	30	742	1,302,977	52,262	4.25	8.27	385.11	48.54	1,228,260
By regional distribution 地区分布									
Central-North 华北	54	879	1,069,032	4,122	0.50	1.13	243.83	56.31	832,050
Beijing 北京	22	1,188	1,278,103	23,132	2.22	4.42	166.10	49.68	1,039,806
Tianjin 天津	8	962	1,675,174	1,606	0.17	0.44	226.93	62.70	971,140
Hebei 河北	17	621	811,151	-18,635	-2.47	-6.71	488.36	63.17	753,955
Shanxi 山西	5	257	55,412	3,525	7.11	18.05	70.06	60.60	49,578
Inner Mongolia 内蒙古	2	910	1,070,729	10			136.54	66.78	610,354
Northeast 东北	56	1,389	1,915,695	-7,978	-0.60	-1.32	247.58	54.24	1,325,088
Liaoning 辽宁	38	1,105	1,861,036	-630	-0.05	-0.11	279.70	55.12	1,229,702
Jilin 吉林	7	848	637,659	-4,187	-1.26	-2.04	188.14	38.33	332,569
Heilongjiang 黑龙江	11	2,712	2,917,815	-35,774	-1.56	-3.41	214.19	54.08	2,286,203
Central-East 华东	104	766	1,223,126	32,432	3.96	7.95	331.47	50.18	818,393
Shanghai 上海	2	11,883	17,299,403	588,825	3.65	6.83	313.00	46.52	16,125,097
Jiangsu 江苏	42	296	395,492	9,477	5.58	14.79	225.65	62.28	169,924
Zhejiang 浙江	5	2,287	4,728,060	273,955	10.76	15.23	437.51	29.34	2,546,524
Anhui 安徽	4	1,286	1,676,442	-33,277	-2.93	-13.04	221.76	77.49	1,133,883
Fujian 福建	1	2,842	6,648,250	290,090	8.49	11.89	358.63	28.59	3,415,580
Jiangxi 江西	3	941	2,080,865	-55,678	-4.32	-14.47	390.26	70.12	1,288,006
Shandong 山东	47	451	696,993	9,309	2.07	4.94	372.15	58.19	450,598
Central-South 中南	40	1,065	1,928,278	20,186	1.69	4.37	334.14	61.18	1,191,027
Henan 河南	11	638	1,063,725	21,163	2.15	8.38	202.30	74.29	982,610
Hubei 湖北	9	878	1,453,017	11,170	1.24	2.29	266.66	45.82	900,063
Hunan 湖南	3	4,663	4,257,130	-60,097	-1.50	-5.41	244.55	72.34	4,019,465
Guangdong 广东	12	999	3,167,086	47,208	3.55	7.32	570.21	51.52	1,329,644
Guangxi 广西	5	342	315,310	17,580	12.25	34.66	264.94	64.66	143,533
Hainan 海南									
Southwest 西南	9	454	66,173	1,811	1.41	3.25	35.00	56.69	128,678
Chongqing 重庆	2	37	4,934	41	1.18	1.66	21.85	29.02	3,470
Sichuan 四川	7	574	83,670	2,317	1.41	3.27	35.24	56.86	164,451
Guizhou 贵州									
Yunnan 云南									
Tibet 西藏									
Northwest 西北	46	948	985,891	-11,750	-1.23	-3.66	244.58	66.35	954,763
Shaanxi 陕西	8	813	923,180	44,216	6.86	25.10	261.89	72.67	644,579
Gansu 甘肃	22	868	696,973	-26,937	-4.18	-13.30	232.34	68.59	644,694
Qinghai 青海									
Ningxia 宁夏	3	1,056	558,474	-12,955	-2.54	-11.30	94.38	77.54	510,602
Xinjiang 新疆	13	1,141	1,612,056	-20,210	-1.14	-3.07	284.83	62.81	1,772,876

2520: Processing of Crude Oil 原油加工业

Year 年份	Number of firms 企业个数	Rate of change 变化率 (%)	Number of employees 职工人数 (人)	Rate of change 变化率 (%)	Total revenue (Mil. RMB) 总销售收入 (百万元)	Rate of change 变化率 (%)	Total profit (Mil RMB) 总利润 (百万元)	Rate of change 变化率 (%)
2000	322		600,563		398,069		-698	
2001	286	-11.18	334,029	-44.38	394,182	-0.98	-1,702	-143.84
2002	309	8.04	295,174	-11.63	415,289	5.35	3,432	-

Major Products 主要产品	Output 产量	Unit 单位
Crude Oil Processing Volume 原油加工量	21,955	10,000 Tons 万吨
Diesel Oil 柴油	7,699	10,000 Tons 万吨

10 Main Firms with Maximal Revenue (year founded) 收入最大的十家主要企业（创办年份）	City 城市	Province 省	Telephone/fax 电话/传真	Number of employees 职工人数	Ownership 产业所有权	Revenue ('000 RMB) 销售收入 (千元)	Profit('000 RMB) (rank) 利润(千元) (排名)	Total assets ('000 RMB) 总资产 (千元)	Major products 主要产品
Shanghai Petrochemical Co., Ltd. 上海石油化工股份有限公司(1993)	Shanghai 上海市	Shanghai 上海市	(021)57941941 (021)57942267	18,323	Overseas Chinese-funded 港澳台资	19,971,716	944,042(2)	24,508,423	Crude Oil 原油
Sinopec Maoming Oil Refining Chemical Industry Co.,Ltd 中国石化茂名炼油化工股份有限公司(1965)	Maoming 茂名市	Guangdong 广东省	(0668)2242241 (0668)2269317	5,536	State-owned 国有企业	19,662,011	421,565(4)	5,065,033	Crude Oil 原油
Petrochina Fushun Petrochemical Filiale 中国石油天然气股份有限公司抚顺石化分公司(1999)	Fushun 抚顺市	Liaoning 辽宁省	(0413)2433351 (0413)2420988	9,940	Joint Stock 股份制	18,055,800	224,400(9)	13,736,360	Crude Oil 原油
Sinopec Qilu Branch 中国石化股份有限公司齐鲁分公司(2000)	Zibo 淄博市	Shandong 山东省	(0533)7180777 (0533)7180406		Joint Stock 股份制	14,856,724	-	9,429,443	Crude Oil 原油
Sinopec Shanghai Gaoqiao Filiale 中国石化股份有限公司上海高桥分公司(2000)	Shanghai 上海市	Shanghai 上海市	(021)58711001 (021)58712207	5,442	State-owned 国有企业	14,627,090	233,607(8)	7,741,770	Crude Oil 原油
Petrochina Daqing Petrochemistry Filiale 中国石油大庆石化分公司(1999)	Daqing 大庆市	Heilongjiang 黑龙江省	(0459)6742440 (0459)6763838	13,255	Joint Stock 股份制	14,285,030	-	9,931,620	Crude Oil 原油
Petrochina Lanzhou Filiale 中国石油天然气股份公司兰州石化公司(1958)	Lanzhou 兰州市	Gansu 甘肃省	(0931)7579816 (0931)7561499	13,189	State-owned 国有企业	14,000,580	-	12,851,300	Gasoline 汽油
Petrochina Dalian Filiale 中国石油天然气股份有限公司大连石化分公司(1935)	Dalian 大连市	Liaoning 辽宁省	(0411)6773114 (0411)6672517	4,665	Joint Stock 股份制	13,190,310	-	8,832,030	Crude Oil 原油
Sinopec Jinling Filiale 中国石油化工股份有限公司金陵分公司(1965)	Nanjing 南京市	Jiangsu 江苏省	(025)5509555 (025)5392004	6,092	Joint Stock 股份制	13,158,750	300,200(6)	5,425,790	Crude Oil 原油
Sinopec Guangzhou Filiale 中国石油化工股份有限公司广州分公司(2000)	Guangzhou 广州市	Guangdong 广东省	(020)82121181	5,043	Joint Stock 股份制	12,981,000	138,900(14)	7,811,200	Crude Oil 原油

Top 10 Cities by Revenue 销售收入排名前10位城市	Province 省	Market share 市场份额 (%)	Number of firms 企业个数
Shanghai 上海市	Shanghai 上海市	8.33	2
Beijing 北京市	Beijing 北京市	6.77	22
Dalian 大连市	Liaoning 辽宁省	6.38	4
Daqing 大庆市	Heilongjiang 黑龙江省	6.29	4
Ningbo 宁波市	Zhejiang 浙江省	5.41	1
Maoming 茂名市	Guangdong 广东省	4.73	1
Fushun 抚顺市	Liaoning 辽宁省	4.35	2
Zibo 淄博市	Shandong 山东省	3.77	10
Lanzhou 兰州市	Gansu 甘肃省	3.48	16
Tianjin 天津市	Tianjin 天津市	3.23	8

10 Major Wholesalers 十家主要批发商	City 城市	Province 省	Telephone/Fax 电话/传真
HLJ Petroleumchemical Marketing Corp. 黑龙江省石油化工销售总公司	Harbin 哈尔滨市	Heilongjiang 黑龙江省	(0451)84612530 (0451)84610195
PetroChina Northeast Sale Company Daqing Filiale 石油天然气股份有限公司东北销售大庆分公司	Daqing 大庆市	Heilongjiang 黑龙江省	(0459)6215380 (0459)6215361
China Railway Goods & Materials Shanghai Company 中国铁路物资上海公司	Shanghai 上海市	Shanghai 上海市	(021)56309366 (021)56632150
SINOPEC Hubei Petroleum General Company 中国石化集团湖北石油总公司	Wuhan 武汉市	Hubei 湖北省	(027)83601087 (027)83601075
South China Bluesky Aviation Oilseed Co.,Ltd. 华南蓝天航空油料有限公司	Guangzhou 广州市	Guangdong 广东省	(020)86120888 (020)86650789
Guangdong Petroleum Enterprise Group Company 广东省石油企业集团公司	Guangzhou 广州市	Guangdong 广东省	(020)81298040 (020)81298098
Shenzhen Huaan Liuefied Petroleum Gas Co.,Ltd. 深圳华安液化石油气有限公司	Shenzhen 深圳市	Guangdong 广东省	(0755)84231898 (0755)82461896
SINOPEC Sale Southwest Company 中国石化销售西南公司	Maoming 茂名市	Guangdong 广东省	(0668)2868292 (0668)2868278
Guangdong Dongguan Petroleum Company 广东省东莞市石油公司	Dongguan 东莞市	Guangdong 广东省	(0769)2258741 (0769)2506290
PetroChina Sichuan Sale Company 中国石油天然气股份有限公司四川销售公司	Chengdu 成都市	Sichuan 四川省	(028)86520001 (028)86520001

2530: Petroleum Products 石油制品业

The industry accounts for 0.444% of the total revenue of China's industrial sector in 2002. The rate of return on assets is 3.25%. 81.03% of all firms in the industry made a profit while 18.97% had negative returns.The top province in terms of the industry's revenue is Shandong, accounting for 26.46% of the total revenue.
2002年本行业收入占全行业的 0.444%，资产利润率为 3.25%。81.03%的企业赢利，18.97%的企业亏损。收入最高的省为山东省，占本行业的26.46%。

	Total number of firms 企业总数	Total number of employees 职工总数	Total revenue (Mil.RMB) 总销售收入 (百万元)	Total profit (Mil.RMB) 总利润 (百万元)	Return on assets 资产利润率 (%)	Return on equity 权益利润率 (%)	Labour productivity ('000 RMB/ worker) 劳动生产率 (千元/人)	Debts/ assets 资产负债率 (%)	Total assets (Mil.RMB) 总资产 (百万元)
Industry Overall 行业总体	406	81,808	47,584	1,202	3.25	6.48	132.46	49.90	37,023

	Number of firms 企业个数	Average number of employees 平均职工人数	Average revenue ('000 RMB) 平均销售收入 (千元)	Average profit ('000 RMB) 平均利润 (千元)	Return on assets 资产利润率 (%)	Return on equity 权益利润率 (%)	Labour productivity ('000 RMB/ worker) 劳动生产率 (千元/人)	Debts/ assets 资产负债率 (%)	Average total assets ('000 RMB) 平均总资产 (千元)
By ownership 产业所有权									
State-owned 国有	42	515	272,017	2,484	0.88	1.64	76.39	46.33	282,342
Collective-owned 集体	84	299	79,748	1,530	2.93	6.89	79.32	57.51	52,286
Foreign & Overseas Chinese Funded 三资	63	76	125,426	7,978	7.39	15.37	347.45	51.92	107,965
By regional distribution 地区分布									
Central-North 华北	61	127	75,187	4,650	7.66	15.45	69.33	50.40	60,667
Beijing 北京	18	139	125,240	3,275	3.84	9.90	113.88	61.17	85,203
Tianjin 天津	21	86	72,433	1,277	1.72	2.74	69.55	37.28	74,439
Hebei 河北	18	169	43,259	10,977	37.83	88.62	37.54	57.31	29,012
Shanxi 山西	4	94	8,084	74	0.36	0.81	29.09	54.98	20,397
Inner Mongolia 内蒙古									
Northeast 东北	74	380	130,820	-1,720	-1.05	-1.58	67.66	33.52	163,889
Liaoning 辽宁	42	468	153,953	-2,689	-1.35	-2.00	67.43	32.39	198,876
Jilin 吉林	7	405	26,097	-1,851	-2.31	-2.71	11.44	14.68	80,045
Heilongjiang 黑龙江	25	225	121,278	-55	-0.04	-0.07	96.80	39.74	128,586
Central-East 华东	151	120	138,729	5,110	6.63	15.58	280.61	57.46	77,092
Shanghai 上海	32	65	34,581	1,872	6.91	15.39	101.76	55.08	27,074
Jiangsu 江苏	46	81	112,104	8,511	11.85	22.22	398.65	46.68	71,842
Zhejiang 浙江	18	44	92,374	-1,352	-1.21	-4.24	179.77	71.45	111,664
Anhui 安徽	3	21	23,293	2,121	5.37	10.96	358.61	50.97	39,474
Fujian 福建	6	52	37,690	1,480	8.10	15.82	96.35	48.80	18,270
Jiangxi 江西	5	214	27,512	-112	-0.65	-1.64	36.07	60.49	17,353
Shandong 山东	41	246	307,034	8,045	6.41	15.87	312.46	59.60	125,490
Central-South 中南	82	189	105,826	1,187	1.60	5.94	151.53	73.00	74,003
Henan 河南	28	127	21,239	898	3.87	7.53	48.36	48.59	23,194
Hubei 湖北	9	262	171,610	-9,020	-21.75	-48.93	338.81	55.54	41,464
Hunan 湖南	7	112	131,055	5,469	5.61	8.99	295.90	37.58	97,467
Guangdong 广东	33	257	157,267	1,221	1.00	7.60	117.54	86.91	122,683
Guangxi 广西	4	33	9,384	-112	-0.36	-0.74	23.04	51.28	31,034
Hainan 海南	1	155	393,787	75,202	39.43	61.49	906.89	35.88	190,732
Southwest 西南	17	200	23,532	-19	-0.06	-0.11	32.57	42.29	29,790
Chongqing 重庆	5	292	54,193	718	1.36	1.86	48.31	26.71	52,750
Sichuan 四川	7	202	12,582	256	1.27	2.46	27.44	48.42	20,203
Guizhou 贵州	2	118	3,164	-126	-1.10	-1.98	8.97	44.48	11,415
Yunnan 云南	3	95	11,559	-1,819	-6.96	-40.91	-3.15	82.99	26,141
Tibet 西藏									
Northwest 西北	21	427	156,697	8,442	5.95	10.03	95.28	40.66	141,861
Shaanxi 陕西	3	33	8,494	35	0.56	2.03	63.98	72.40	6,188
Gansu 甘肃	8	589	241,341	11,260	6.95	9.90	112.80	29.82	162,105
Qinghai 青海									
Ningxia 宁夏									
Xinjiang 新疆	10	417	133,444	8,709	5.23	10.22	76.19	48.76	166,368

2530: Petroleum Products 石油制品业

Year 年份	Number of firms 企业个数	Rate of change 变化率 (%)	Number of employees 职工人数 (人)	Rate of change 变化率 (%)	Total revenue (Mil. RMB) 总销售收入 (百万元)	Rate of change 变化率 (%)	Total profit (Mil RMB) 总利润 (百万元)	Rate of change 变化率 (%)
2000	336		86,960		43,481		850	
2001	378	12.50	95,334	9.63	49,423	13.67	206	-75.76
2002	406	7.41	81,808	-14.19	47,584	-3.72	1,202	483.50

Major Products 主要产品	Output 产量	Unit 单位
Fuel Oil 燃料油	1,848	10,000 Tons 万吨
Petroluem Asphalt 石油沥青	723	10,000 Tons 万吨

10 Main Firms with Maximal Revenue (year founded) 收入最大的十家主要企业（创办年份）	City 城市	Province 省	Telephone/fax 电话/传真	Number of employees 职工人数	Ownership 产业所有权	Revenue ('000 RMB) 销售收入 (千元)	Profit('000 RMB) (rank) 利润(千元) (排名)	Total assets ('000 RMB) 总资产 (千元)	Major products 主要产品
Shandong Binhua Group Co., Ltd.	Binzhou	Shandong	(0543)3308000		State-owned				Caustic Soda
山东滨化集团有限公司(1970)	滨州市	山东省	(0543)3308888	2,569	国有企业	5,383,358	107,115(4)	1,399,939	烧碱
Tsingtao Guangyuanfa (Group) Company	Qingdao	Shandong	(0532)7785168		Collective-owned				Asphalt
青岛广源发集团有限公司(1994)	青岛市	山东省	(0532)7785168	2,891	集体企业	3,101,267	53,627(9)	1,647,186	沥青
Petrochina Fushun Petrochemical Company	Fushun	Liaoning	(0413)2636292		State-owned				First Second Ketone
中国石油抚顺石油化工公司(1928)	抚顺市	辽宁省	(0413)2629892	8,506	国有企业	2,002,220	-	5,791,417	甲乙酮
Sinopec Lubricating Oil Group Filiale	Beijing	Beijing	(010)62949864		Limited-Liability				Lubricating Oil
中国石化润滑油集团分公司(1958)	北京市	北京市	(010)62928148	1,018	有限公司	1,209,683	20,622(19)	931,800	润滑油
Mobil (Taicang) Petroleum Co., Ltd.	Suzhou	Jiangsu	(0512)53643000		Foreign Funded				Petroleum Produsts
美孚(太仓)石油有限公司(2002)	苏州市	江苏省	(0512)53646245	145	外商投资	1,055,908	214,310(1)	550,901	石油制品
Shandong Huaxing Petrochemical Group Co., Ltd.	Dongying	Shandong	(0546)6872758		Limited-Liability				Diesel Oil
山东华星石油化工集团有限公司(2000)	东营市	山东省		637	有限公司	986,995	12,299(32)	499,808	柴油
Panjin Northern Asphalt Co., Ltd.	Panjin	Liaoning	(0427)2851925		Joint Stock				Asphalt
盘锦北方沥青股份有限公司(1994)	盘锦市	辽宁省	(0427)2851995	1,217	股份制	981,756	-	575,652	沥青
Petrochina Lanzhou Lubricating Oil Factory	Lanzhou	Gansu	(0931)7541773		Joint Stock				Lubricating Oil
中国石油天然气股份公司兰州润滑油厂(2001)	兰州市	甘肃省	(0931)7572597	318	股份制	966,660	47,613(10)	390,420	润滑油
Jintong Petrochemical Co.,Ltd.	Nanjing	Jiangsu	(025)5563140		Overseas Chinese-funded				Straight Chain Alkyl Benzene
金桐石油化工有限公司(1993)	南京市	江苏省	(025)5563340	266	港澳台资	895,610	109,000(3)	560,760	直链烷基苯
Zhangjiagang Oriental Unocal Energy Co.,Ltd.	Suzhou	Jiangsu	(0512)58721888		Foreign Funded				Liquefied Gas
张家港东华优尼科能源有限公司(2000)	苏州市	江苏省	(0512)58322500	110	外商投资	818,865	28,143(14)	387,400	液化气

Top 10 Cities by Revenue 销售收入排名前10位城市	Province 省	Market share 市场份额 (%)	Number of firms 企业个数
Binzhou 滨州市	Shandong 山东省	11.33	2
Maoming 茂名市	Guangdong 广东省	6.94	17
Qingdao 青岛市	Shandong 山东省	6.94	5
Daqing 大庆市	Heilongjiang 黑龙江省	6.33	21
Panjin 盘锦市	Liaoning 辽宁省	5.12	15
Suzhou 苏州市	Jiangsu 江苏省	4.82	7
Beijing 北京市	Beijing 北京市	4.74	18
Fushun 抚顺市	Liaoning 辽宁省	4.31	5
Lanzhou 兰州市	Gansu 甘肃省	3.61	7
Tianjin 天津市	Tianjin 天津市	3.20	21

10 Major Wholesalers 十家主要批发商	City 城市	Province 省	Telephone/Fax 电话/传真
HLJ Petroleumchemical Marketing Corp.	Harbin	Heilongjiang	(0451)84612530
黑龙江省石油化工销售总公司	哈尔滨市	黑龙江省	(0451)84610195
PetroChina Northeast Sale Company Daqing Filiale	Daqing	Heilongjiang	(0459)6215380
石油天然气股份有限公司东北销售大庆分公司	大庆市	黑龙江省	(0459)6215361
China Railway Goods & Materials Shanghai Company	Shanghai	Shanghai	(021)56309366
中国铁路物资上海公司	上海市	上海市	(021)56632150
SINOPEC Hubei Petroleum General Company	Wuhan	Hubei	(027)83601087
中国石化集团湖北石油总公司	武汉市	湖北省	(027)83601075
South China Bluesky Aviation Oilseed Co.,Ltd.	Guangzhou	Guangdong	(020)86120888
华南蓝天航空油料有限公司	广州市	广东省	(020)86650789
Guangdong Petroleum Enterprise Group Company	Guangzhou	Guangdong	(020)81298040
广东省石油企业集团公司	广州市	广东省	(020)81298098
Shenzhen Huaan Liuefied Petroleum Gas Co.,Ltd.	Shenzhen	Guangdong	(0755)84231898
深圳华安液化石油气有限公司	深圳市	广东省	(0755)82461896
SINOPEC Sale Southwest Company	Maoming	Guangdong	(0668)2868292
中国石化销售西南公司	茂名市	广东省	(0668)2868278
Guangdong Dongguan Petroleum Company	Dongguan	Guangdong	(0769)2258741
广东省东莞市石油公司	东莞市	广东省	(0769)2506290
PetroChina Sichuan Sale Company	Chengdu	Sichuan	(028)86520001
中国石油天然气股份有限公司四川销售公司	成都市	四川省	(028)86520001

2570: Coking 炼焦业

The industry accounts for 0.245% of the total revenue of China's industrial sector in 2002. The rate of return on assets is 0.84%. 79.85% of all firms in the industry made a profit while 20.15% had negative returns.The top province in terms of the industry's revenue is Shanxi, accounting for 49.17% of the total revenue.
2002年本行业收入占全行业的 0.245%，资产利润率为 0.84%。79.85%的企业赢利，20.15%的企业亏损。收入最高的省为山西省，占本行业的49.17%。

	Total number of firms 企业总数	Total number of employees 职工总数	Total revenue (Mil.RMB) 总销售收入（百万元）	Total profit (Mil.RMB) 总利润（百万元）	Return on assets 资产利润率（%）	Return on equity 权益利润率（%）	Labour productivity ('000 RMB/worker) 劳动生产率（千元/人）	Debts/assets 资产负债率（%）	Total assets (Mil.RMB) 总资产（百万元）
Industry Overall 行业总体	412	180,294	26,246	445	0.84	2.20	40.07	61.90	53,076

	Number of firms 企业个数	Average number of employees 平均职工人数	Average revenue ('000 RMB) 平均销售收入（千元）	Average profit ('000 RMB) 平均利润（千元）	Return on assets 资产利润率（%）	Return on equity 权益利润率（%）	Labour productivity ('000 RMB/worker) 劳动生产率（千元/人）	Debts/assets 资产负债率（%）	Average total assets ('000 RMB) 平均总资产（千元）
By ownership 产业所有权									
State-owned 国有	51	677	101,309	544	0.25	0.86	32.96	70.41	214,108
Collective-owned 集体	66	262	29,498	941	2.67	8.09	38.73	66.98	35,253
Foreign & Overseas Chinese Funded 三资	14	626	94,116	2,165	1.44	3.77	57.35	61.68	149,829
By regional distribution 地区分布									
Central-North 华北	280	403	59,078	1,360	1.17	3.29	44.64	64.43	116,216
Beijing 北京	2	2,539	745,100	1,501	0.13	0.29	17.96	53.96	1,138,824
Tianjin 天津	1	87	52,650	-740	-1.55	-11.82	5.63	86.90	47,790
Hebei 河北	26	378	73,744	2,616	1.91	6.51	51.83	70.64	136,941
Shanxi 山西	245	393	52,670	1,244	1.16	3.25	45.22	64.35	107,266
Inner Mongolia 内蒙古	6	259	29,594	957	1.53	5.51	52.17	72.17	62,387
Northeast 东北	18	619	59,579	-638	-0.26	-1.37	20.70	81.31	249,569
Liaoning 辽宁	5	112	44,362	440	0.91	24.79	81.03	96.32	48,226
Jilin 吉林									
Heilongjiang 黑龙江	13	814	65,432	-1,053	-0.32	-1.65	17.50	80.46	327,008
Central-East 华东	28	1,223	214,576	724	0.17	0.30	31.90	42.37	417,548
Shanghai 上海	2	2,529	1,179,245	-3,320	-0.13	-0.15	71.17	16.72	2,652,871
Jiangsu 江苏	7	1,357	252,978	1,922	0.54	1.38	23.35	60.49	353,477
Zhejiang 浙江									
Anhui 安徽	2	1,368	165,840	-3,407	-1.35	-13.13	22.15	89.75	253,134
Fujian 福建	2	152	24,477	2,035	8.26	10.97	66.41	24.71	24,622
Jiangxi 江西	2	1,882	300,820	19,844	3.06	7.47	55.93	59.11	649,530
Shandong 山东	13	991	68,963	-1,807	-1.14	-3.26	17.02	64.95	158,207
Central-South 中南	31	251	37,932	506	1.08	4.23	50.32	74.50	46,861
Henan 河南	21	200	39,241	805	2.47	5.40	71.73	54.28	32,624
Hubei 湖北	3	773	38,485	-2,761	-1.65		10.88	107.20	167,347
Hunan 湖南	4	259	42,515	165	0.38	1.31	27.64	70.78	43,020
Guangdong 广东	2	65	22,911	3,000	6.84	15.44	256.34	55.70	43,864
Guangxi 广西	1	92	20,488	389	6.77	9.39	30.36	27.83	5,742
Hainan 海南									
Southwest 西南	20	168	24,555	2,844	7.49	19.71	51.55	61.99	37,975
Chongqing 重庆									
Sichuan 四川	7	224	42,445	6,190	11.26	25.29	56.67	55.48	54,969
Guizhou 贵州	5	74	7,357	392	4.71	12.45	35.24	62.16	8,314
Yunnan 云南	8	177	19,650	1,450	3.48	11.41	50.11	69.49	41,644
Tibet 西藏									
Northwest 西北	35	310	27,339	-499	-0.82	-4.22	27.25	80.63	61,135
Shaanxi 陕西	25	283	27,953	-759	-1.46	-8.36	30.72	82.55	52,032
Gansu 甘肃	5	235	8,204	-1,114	-2.05	-15.95	14.57	87.17	54,442
Qinghai 青海	1	8	5,131	58	4.33	4.60	72.00	5.82	1,340
Ningxia 宁夏	3	697	51,648	835	0.94	3.91	19.49	76.08	89,195
Xinjiang 新疆	1	483	56,941	4,513	1.52	5.17	40.08	70.68	297,795

Year 年份	Number of firms 企业个数	Rate of change 变化率(%)	Number of employees 职工人数(人)	Rate of change 变化率(%)	Total revenue (Mil. RMB) 总销售收入(百万元)	Rate of change 变化率(%)	Total profit (Mil RMB) 总利润(百万元)	Rate of change 变化率(%)
2000	323		142,785		14,887		76	
2001	347	7.43	161,825	13.33	18,735	25.85	257	238.16
2002	412	18.73	180,294	11.41	26,246	40.09	445	73.15

Major Products 主要产品	Output 产量	Unit 单位
Coke 焦炭	11,237	10,000 Tons 万吨

10 Main Firms with Maximal Revenue (year founded) 收入最大的十家主要企业（创办年份）	City 城市	Province 省	Telephone/fax 电话/传真	Number of employees 职工人数	Ownership 产业所有权	Revenue ('000 RMB) 销售收入(千元)	Profit('000 RMB) (rank) 利润(千元)(排名)	Total assets ('000 RMB) 总资产(千元)	Major products 主要产品
Shanghai Coking Chemistry Co.,Ltd.	Shanghai	Shanghai	(021)64343649		Limited-Liability				Coke
上海焦化有限公司(1959)	上海市	上海市	(021)64345267	5,018	有限公司	2,332,137	-	5,251,396	焦炭
Beijing Coking Chemistry Works	Beijing	Beijing	(010)67364218		State-owned				Coke
北京炼焦化学厂(1959)	北京市	北京市	(010)67364147	5,054	国有企业	1,487,800	2,662(58)	2,277,277	焦炭
Shanxi Coking Chemistry (Group) Co.,Ltd.	Linfen	Shanxi	(0357)6626292		State Enterprises				Synthetic Ammonia
山西焦化集团有限公司(1979)	临汾市	山西省	(0357)6625444	5,913	国有独资	1,022,677	-	2,466,479	合成氨
Shanghai Meishan Enterprise Development Co., Ltd.	Nanjing	Jiangsu	(025)6714206		State Enterprises				Nitrobenzene
上海梅山企业发展有限公司(2000)	南京市	江苏省	(025)6714206	4,724	国有独资	834,530	20,600(8)	693,190	硝化用苯
Shijiazhuang Coking Chemistry(Group) Co.,Ltd.	Shijiazhuang	Hebei	(0311)5051996		State-owned				Coke
石家庄焦化集团有限责任公司(1925)	石家庄市	河北省	(0311)5053276	3,021	国有企业	817,410	28,713(6)	1,475,559	焦炭
Shanxi Antai (Group) Co.,Ltd.	Jinzhong	Shanxi	(0354)7531002		Joint Stock				Coke
山西安泰集团股份有限公司(1984)	晋中市	山西省	(0354)7536557	4,000	股份制	779,560	60,400(2)	1,302,026	焦炭
Jingdezhen Coking Gas General Factory	Jingdezhen	Jiangxi	(0798)8399166		State-owned				Coke
景德镇市焦化煤气总厂(1986)	景德镇市	江西省	(0798)8391618	3,622	国有企业	583,640	39,681(3)	1,286,315	焦炭
Zhenjiang Coking Gas (Group) Co., Ltd.	Zhenjiang	Jiangsu	(0511)8825060		Limited-Liability				Metallurgy Coke
镇江焦化煤气集团有限公司(1970)	镇江市	江苏省	(0511)8822811	1,869	有限公司	462,162	2,135(66)	1,030,749	冶金焦
Taiyuan Dongsheng Coking Gas Co., Ltd	Taiyuan	Shanxi	(0351)5733225		Private Enterprises				
太原市东盛焦化煤气有限公司(2000)	太原市	山西省	(0351)5727483	830	私营独资	369,213	-	453,225	
Shanxi Sanjia Coal Chemistry Co., Ltd.	Jinzhong	Shanxi	(0354)7398069		Foreign Funded				Coke
山西三佳煤化有限公司(1984)	晋中市	山西省	(0354)7398169	4,500	外商投资	358,560	850(125)	530,000	焦炭

Top 10 Cities by Revenue 销售收入排名前10位城市	Province 省	Market share 市场份额(%)	Number of firms 企业个数
Linfen 临汾市	Shanxi 山西省	10.77	48
Yuncheng 运城市	Shanxi 山西省	10.35	46
Taiyuan 太原市	Shanxi 山西省	9.84	25
Jinzhong 晋中市	Shanxi 山西省	9.56	47
Shanghai 上海市	Shanghai 上海市	8.99	2
Beijing 北京市	Beijing 北京市	5.68	2
Lvliang 吕梁地区	Shanxi 山西省	5.01	41
Shijiazhuang 石家庄市	Hebei 河北省	3.71	6
Nanjing 南京市	Jiangsu 江苏省	3.23	3
Changzhi 长治市	Shanxi 山西省	2.84	27

10 Major Wholesalers 十家主要批发商	City 城市	Province 省	Telephone/Fax 电话/传真
HLJ Petroleumchemical Marketing Corp.	Harbin	Heilongjiang	(0451)84612530
黑龙江省石油化工销售总公司	哈尔滨市	黑龙江省	(0451)84610195
PetroChina Northeast Sale Company Daqing Filiale	Daqing	Heilongjiang	(0459)6215380
石油天然气股份有限公司东北销售大庆分公司	大庆市	黑龙江省	(0459)6215361
China Railway Goods & Materials Shanghai Company	Shanghai	Shanghai	(021)56309366
中国铁路物资上海公司	上海市	上海市	(021)56632150
SINOPEC Hubei Petroleum General Company	Wuhan	Hubei	(027)83601087
中国石化集团湖北石油总公司	武汉市	湖北省	(027)83601075
South China Bluesky Aviation Oilseed Co.,Ltd.	Guangzhou	Guangdong	(020)86120888
华南蓝天航空油料有限公司	广州市	广东省	(020)86650789
Guangdong Petroleum Enterprise Group Company	Guangzhou	Guangdong	(020)81298040
广东省石油企业集团公司	广州市	广东省	(020)81298098
Shenzhen Huaan Liuefied Petroleum Gas Co.,Ltd.	Shenzhen	Guangdong	(0755)84231898
深圳华安液化石油气有限公司	深圳市	广东省	(0755)82461896
SINOPEC Sale Southwest Company	Maoming	Guangdong	(0668)2868292
中国石化销售西南公司	茂名市	广东省	(0668)2868278
Guangdong Dongguan Petroleum Company	Dongguan	Guangdong	(0769)2258741
广东省东莞市石油公司	东莞市	广东省	(0769)2506290
PetroChina Sichuan Sale Company	Chengdu	Sichuan	(028)86520001
中国石油天然气股份有限公司四川销售公司	成都市	四川省	(028)86520001

2611: Inorganic Acids 无机酸制造业

The industry accounts for 0.108% of the total revenue of China's industrial sector in 2002. The rate of return on assets is 1.93%. 76.52% of all firms in the industry made a profit while 23.48% had negative returns.The top province in terms of the industry's revenue is Jiangsu, accounting for 15.01% of the total revenue.
2002年本行业收入占全行业的 0.108%，资产利润率为 1.93%。76.52%的企业赢利，23.48%的企业亏损。收入最高的省为江苏省，占本行业的15.01%。

	Total number of firms 企业总数	Total number of employees 职工总数	Total revenue (Mil.RMB) 总销售收入(百万元)	Total profit (Mil.RMB) 总利润(百万元)	Return on assets 资产利润率(%)	Return on equity 权益利润率(%)	Labour productivity ('000 RMB/ worker) 劳动生产率(千元/人)	Debts/ assets 资产负债率(%)	Total assets (Mil.RMB) 总资产(百万元)
Industry Overall 行业总体	362	84,355	11,538	340	1.93	5.01	37.73	61.42	17,577

	Number of firms 企业个数	Average number of employees 平均职工人数	Average revenue ('000 RMB) 平均销售收入(千元)	Average profit ('000 RMB) 平均利润(千元)	Return on assets 资产利润率(%)	Return on equity 权益利润率(%)	Labour productivity ('000 RMB/ worker) 劳动生产率(千元/人)	Debts/ assets 资产负债率(%)	Average total assets ('000 RMB) 平均总资产(千元)
By ownership 产业所有权									
State-owned 国有	41	220	23,277	245	0.57	2.51	27.93	77.18	42,810
Collective-owned 集体	68	127	25,306	1,307	8.72	27.65	49.06	68.45	14,982
Foreign & Overseas Chinese Funded 三资	37	108	44,991	2,206	4.82	10.78	132.95	55.31	45,796
By regional distribution 地区分布									
Central-North 华北	58	576	55,704	2,107	1.34	3.08	22.48	56.33	156,835
Beijing 北京	4	132	17,585	646	3.49	5.99	67.55	41.78	18,537
Tianjin 天津	9	226	76,315	9,185	15.23	45.20	-1.78	66.30	60,302
Hebei 河北	26	124	27,803	1,285	6.90	22.82	71.43	69.76	18,624
Shanxi 山西	13	1,755	78,835	-5,364	-1.28	-3.98	13.19	67.88	419,263
Inner Mongolia 内蒙古	6	807	120,990	12,211	2.88	3.96	39.05	27.34	424,153
Northeast 东北	27	179	24,606	100	0.45	1.40	46.69	68.16	22,488
Liaoning 辽宁	21	146	18,678	-210	-1.38	-5.20	34.52	73.49	15,244
Jilin 吉林	4	353	58,477	1,785	2.77	6.04	77.41	54.21	64,518
Heilongjiang 黑龙江	2	172	19,112	-7	-0.05		29.24	133.50	14,489
Central-East 华东	135	151	33,106	1,328	4.40	13.68	64.99	67.80	30,162
Shanghai 上海	11	80	22,012	390	1.58	3.03	66.86	47.68	24,582
Jiangsu 江苏	61	133	28,399	439	1.82	6.26	55.52	70.94	24,124
Zhejiang 浙江	14	128	41,017	3,076	10.18	24.10	65.84	57.77	30,222
Anhui 安徽	4	397	49,950	825	0.82	2.62	46.51	68.83	101,155
Fujian 福建	6	55	19,014	219	1.66	5.04	58.66	67.01	13,176
Jiangxi 江西	3	287	43,370	2,758	11.59	17.12	53.56	32.30	23,803
Shandong 山东	36	188	41,017	2,563	6.83	25.45	81.98	73.17	37,549
Central-South 中南	84	180	24,981	586	2.31	7.60	40.13	69.61	25,390
Henan 河南	23	299	36,853	1,481	3.98	24.90	34.61	84.02	37,206
Hubei 湖北	9	111	16,068	527	3.10	5.70	85.65	45.66	17,004
Hunan 湖南	24	190	17,614	421	2.88	5.64	29.58	48.97	14,651
Guangdong 广东	19	76	21,652	-62	-0.25	-0.89	53.48	71.63	24,761
Guangxi 广西	9	136	30,223	168	0.50	1.31	57.54	61.83	33,548
Hainan 海南									
Southwest 西南	35	125	23,380	258	1.06	3.47	39.55	69.49	24,360
Chongqing 重庆	4	66	15,750	1,588	15.09	25.10	60.99	39.89	10,528
Sichuan 四川	20	154	30,280	599	2.05	6.93	39.27	70.43	29,243
Guizhou 贵州	7	91	9,159	-428	-2.72	-9.20	18.30	70.45	15,756
Yunnan 云南	4	97	21,402	-1,576	-5.47	-21.56	62.05	74.65	28,836
Tibet 西藏									
Northwest 西北	23	273	11,169	-976	-2.75	-5.68	16.64	51.49	35,463
Shaanxi 陕西	5	151	6,311	-289	-3.07	-16.27	13.05	81.13	9,406
Gansu 甘肃	8	162	4,742	-617	-3.37	-7.97	10.52	57.68	18,311
Qinghai 青海	5	596	24,404	-2,085	-2.23	-4.02	15.79	44.67	93,642
Ningxia 宁夏	2	306	12,802	-4,456	-30.27	-160.20	22.75	81.11	14,722
Xinjiang 新疆	3	210	13,261	1,088	2.62	5.42	31.64	51.66	41,489

Year 年份	Number of firms 企业个数	Rate of change 变化率 (%)	Number of employees 职工人数 (人)	Rate of change 变化率 (%)	Total revenue (Mil. RMB) 总销售收入 (百万元)	Rate of change 变化率 (%)	Total profit (Mil RMB) 总利润 (百万元)	Rate of change 变化率 (%)
2000	310		90,408		10,003		329	
2001	333	7.42	84,297	-6.76	11,477	14.74	240	-27.05
2002	362	8.71	84,355	0.07	11,538	0.53	340	41.67

Major Products 主要产品	Output 产量	Unit 单位
Sulfuric Acid(Converting into 100%) 硫酸（折１００％）	2,967	10,000 Tons 万吨
Thick Nitric Acid(Converting into 100%) 浓硝酸（折１００％）	99	10,000 Tons 万吨

10 Main Firms with Maximal Revenue (year founded) 收入最大的十家主要企业（创办年份）	City 城市	Province 省	Telephone/fax 电话/传真	Number of employees 职工人数	Ownership 产业所有权	Revenue ('000 RMB) 销售收入 (千元)	Profit('000 RMB) (rank) 利润(千元) (排名)	Total assets ('000 RMB) 总资产 (千元)	Major products 主要产品
Taiyuan Chemical Industry (Group) Corporation	Taiyuan	Shanxi	(0351)6071267		State Enterprises				Ammonium Nitrate
太原化学工业公司（1992）	太原市	山西省	(0351)6070565	19,966	国有独资	820,721	-	5,097,456	硝酸铵
Baotou Tomorrow Technology Co.,Ltd.	Baotou	ıner Mongol	(0472)5980883	Joint Stock					Polyvinyl Chloride Resin聚氯
包头市明天科技股份有限公司(1997)	包头市	内蒙古	(0472)5980883	3,090	股份制	458,195	66,600(1)	2,362,004	乙稀树脂
Tianjin Great Wall Chemical Factory	Tianjin	Tianjin	(022)87985971		Collective-owned				2 Amino Naphthalene Sulfonic Acid
天津市长城化工厂(1989)	天津市	天津市	(022)87983835	759	集体企业	424,000	60,150(2)	148,830	吐氏酸
Zhejiang Yingpeng Chemical Industry Co., Ltd.	Jinhua	Zhejiang	(0579)7264107	oreign Funded					Anhydrous Hydrogen Fluoride无
浙江鹰鹏化工有限公司(1996)	金华市	浙江省	(0579)7264101	456	外商投资	269,393	21,841(4)	209,366	水氟化氢
Shandong Qifeng Chemical Light Industry Group Company	Zibo	Shandong	(0533)7780677	Joint Stock					Maleic Anhydride顺丁
山东齐峰化轻集团公司(1996)	淄博市	山东省	(0533)7788998	480	股份制	207,570	26,114(3)	198,332	烯二酸酐
Inner Mongolia Baiyanhu Chemical Industry Co., Ltd.	Wulanchabu	ıner Mongol	(0474)6202046	Joint Stock					Inorganic Acid
内蒙古白雁湖化工股份有限公司(2001)	乌兰察布	内蒙古	(0474)6206874	1,365	股份制	195,307	6,128(13)	112,463	无机酸
Cangzhou Jianxin Chemical Factory	Cangzhou	Hebei	(0317)4046089	vate Enterprises					Meta-Aminobenzenesulfonic Acid间氨
沧州市建新化工厂(1984)	沧州市	河北省	(0317)4046170	260	私营独资	194,974	7,677(10)	54,232	基苯磺酸
Jilin Inviting Outside Investment Group Co., Ltd.	Jilin	Jilin	(0432)4641844	mited-Liability					
吉林市招商集团有限责任公司(1992)	吉林市	吉林省	(0432)4641833	436	有限公司	156,220	5,320(17)	158,962	
Kaimei Keruiya (Jiangsu) Chemical Industry Co., Ltd.	Zhenjiang	Jiangsu	(0511)7781750	oreign Funded					Chemical Industrial Products化
凯美科瑞亚(江苏)化工有限公司(1997)	镇江市	江苏省	(0511)7781749	280	外商投资	130,575	2,152(48)	39,045	学工业品
Guangxi Lily Chemical Industry Co., Ltd.	Baise	Guangxi	(0776)5806356	vate Partnership					Tilanium Dioxide
广西百合化工股份有限公司(1996)	百色市	广西		520	私营合伙	127,283	4,705(21)	148,432	钛白粉

Top 10 Cities by Revenue 销售收入排名前10位城市	Province 省	Market share 市场份额 (%)	Number of firms 企业个数
Taiyuan 太原市	Shanxi 山西省	7.11	1
Tianjin 天津市	Tianjin 天津市	5.95	9
Baotou 包头市	Inner Mongolia 内蒙古	3.97	1
Zibo 淄博市	Shandong 山东省	3.32	11
Jinhua 金华市	Zhejiang 浙江省	2.97	3
Zhenjiang 镇江市	Jiangsu 江苏省	2.91	8
Yantai 烟台市	Shandong 山东省	2.39	3
Cangzhou 沧州市	Hebei 河北省	2.30	3
Yancheng 盐城市	Jiangsu 江苏省	2.29	8
Yingkou 营口市	Liaoning 辽宁省	2.28	13

10 Major Wholesalers 十家主要批发商	City 城市	Province 省	Telephone/Fax 电话/传真
China Chemical Industry Supply & Sale (Group) General Company	Beijing	Beijing	(010)64238623
中国化工供销(集团)总公司	北京市	北京市	(010)64238623
China Chemical Industry Import & Export General Company	Beijing	Beijing	(010)88078888
中国化工进出口总公司	北京市	北京市	(010)88078890
Tianjin Bridge Group Welding Materials Supply & Sale Co., Ltd.	Tianjin	Tianjin	(022)83968861
天津大桥集团电焊条供销有限公司	天津市	天津市	(022)83968865
Taizhou Xingwei Chunlan Chain Stores Co., Ltd.	Taizhou	Jiangsu	(0523)6611200
泰州星威春兰连锁店有限公司	泰州市	江苏省	(0523)6224181
Taizhou Chunlan Sale Company	Taizhou	Jiangsu	(0523)6611200
泰州春兰销售公司	泰州市	江苏省	(0523)6224181
Shandong Tri-Union Co., Ltd.	Jinan	Shandong	(0531)6086351
山东三联有限责任公司	济南市	山东省	(0531)6093103
Haier Electrical Appliances Co.,Ltd.	Qingdao	Shandong	(0532)8939175
海尔集团电器产业有限公司	青岛市	山东省	(0532)8938086
Guangzhou Haier Industry & Trade Co.,Ltd.	Guangzhou	Guangdong	(020)87397315
广州海尔工贸有限公司	广州市	广东省	(020)87374302
Huizhou TCL Electrical Appliances Sales Co.,Ltd.	Huizhou	Guangdong	(0752)2289885
惠州市TCL电器销售有限公司	惠州市	广东省	(0752)2280690
Guangdong Hardware Minerals Import & Export Group Company	Guangzhou	Guangdong	(020)87752204
广东省五金矿产进出口集团公司	广州市	广东省	(020)87752205

2613: Caustic Soda 烧碱制造业

The industry accounts for 0.231% of the total revenue of China's industrial sector in 2002. The rate of return on assets is 1.15%. 76.97% of all firms in the industry made a profit while 23.03% had negative returns.The top province in terms of the industry's revenue is Tianjin, accounting for 13.94% of the total revenue.
2002年本行业收入占全行业的 0.231%，资产利润率为 1.15%。76.97%的企业赢利，23.03%的企业亏损。收入最高的省为天津市，占本行业的13.94%。

	Total number of firms 企业总数	Total number of employees 职工总数	Total revenue (Mil.RMB) 总销售收入 (百万元)	Total profit (Mil.RMB) 总利润 (百万元)	Return on assets 资产利润率 (%)	Return on equity 权益利润率 (%)	Labour productivity ('000 RMB/ worker) 劳动生产率 (千元/人)	Debts/ assets 资产负债率 (%)	Total assets (Mil.RMB) 总资产 (百万元)
Industry Overall 行业总体	165	145,003	24,826	511	1.15	3.34	39.48	65.57	44,488

	Number of firms 企业个数	Average number of employees 平均职工人数	Average revenue ('000 RMB) 平均销售收入 (千元)	Average profit ('000 RMB) 平均利润 (千元)	Return on assets 资产利润率 (%)	Return on equity 权益利润率 (%)	Labour productivity ('000 RMB/ worker) 劳动生产率 (千元/人)	Debts/ assets 资产负债率 (%)	Average total assets ('000 RMB) 平均总资产 (千元)
By ownership 产业所有权									
State-owned 国有	41	880	104,161	166	0.08	0.35	31.54	77.97	218,392
Collective-owned 集体	20	247	33,084	35	0.10	0.55	34.93	81.81	34,599
Foreign & Overseas Chinese Funded 三资	9	367	125,098	8,703	4.26	8.37	91.83	49.09	204,262
By regional distribution 地区分布									
Central-North 华北	34	628	137,571	1,111	0.49	2.36	42.29	79.35	228,381
Beijing 北京									
Tianjin 天津	20	593	173,074	-591	-0.22	-1.60	35.88	86.10	265,688
Hebei 河北	5	587	73,557	126	0.11	4.49	29.44	97.60	116,789
Shanxi 山西	2	395	30,137	-382	-0.42	-4.96	15.61	91.51	90,741
Inner Mongolia 内蒙古	7	823	112,551	7,106	2.95	5.96	65.69	50.47	240,824
Northeast 东北	8	2,838	319,532	-14,706	-1.40	-3.60	17.17	61.04	1,049,039
Liaoning 辽宁	3	5,327	694,587	-38,465	-1.62	-4.04	20.50	60.00	2,378,804
Jilin 吉林	2	1,605	88,050	1,010	0.31	1.43	1.77	78.13	323,001
Heilongjiang 黑龙江	3	1,172	98,799	-1,424	-0.70	-1.56	16.07	55.17	203,298
Central-East 华东	52	780	164,856	5,724	2.39	8.05	53.14	70.27	239,087
Shanghai 上海									
Jiangsu 江苏	12	756	247,041	12,215	4.84	13.87	80.08	65.08	252,182
Zhejiang 浙江	7	713	212,568	14,485	6.03	18.42	77.96	67.27	240,222
Anhui 安徽	3	1,532	143,787	2,373	0.79	1.58	26.51	50.35	301,585
Fujian 福建	5	760	181,280	3,638	1.45	4.43	51.49	67.25	250,539
Jiangxi 江西	6	1,063	108,416	-3,053	-0.72	-7.22	30.75	90.03	423,734
Shandong 山东	19	617	112,198	2,247	1.41	4.37	44.90	67.72	159,208
Central-South 中南	32	948	134,397	1,568	0.66	1.44	31.19	54.07	237,214
Henan 河南	8	639	46,040	780	0.66	4.03	25.59	83.73	118,962
Hubei 湖北	8	1,089	161,689	-5,189	-1.91	-3.71	17.12	48.65	272,161
Hunan 湖南	7	1,269	169,026	4,867	1.46	3.05	38.52	52.11	333,271
Guangdong 广东	5	700	159,513	4,396	2.22	4.45	56.12	50.17	198,387
Guangxi 广西	4	1,036	164,531	7,346	2.58	4.88	30.92	47.05	284,255
Hainan 海南									
Southwest 西南	33	665	104,789	6,925	3.67	9.60	46.26	61.75	188,589
Chongqing 重庆	3	1,081	86,572	451	0.19	0.65	23.09	71.06	240,316
Sichuan 四川	24	600	110,186	9,905	5.09	12.19	51.82	58.23	194,565
Guizhou 贵州	3	677	123,710	1,928	1.57	6.22	72.99	74.83	123,088
Yunnan 云南	3	763	60,906	-5,439	-3.52	-12.68	20.40	72.25	154,554
Tibet 西藏									
Northwest 西北	6	1,350	210,116	2,471	0.71	1.68	38.92	57.63	347,373
Shaanxi 陕西	3	1,763	155,839	-13,941	-3.05	-5.96	19.68	48.94	457,746
Gansu 甘肃	1	96	4,000	50	0.23		26.56	111.44	21,674
Qinghai 青海									
Ningxia 宁夏	1	1,794	437,283	25,450	7.11	28.62	67.15	75.14	357,767
Xinjiang 新疆	1	918	351,896	31,147	9.39	32.64	95.87	71.22	331,559

2613: Caustic Soda 烧碱制造业

Year 年份	Number of firms 企业个数	Rate of change 变化率 (%)	Number of employees 职工人数 (人)	Rate of change 变化率 (%)	Total revenue (Mil. RMB) 总销售收入 (百万元)	Rate of change 变化率 (%)	Total profit (Mil RMB) 总利润 (百万元)	Rate of change 变化率 (%)
2000	133		168,084		22,710		932	
2001	151	13.53	156,419	-6.94	23,995	5.66	464	-50.21
2002	165	9.27	145,003	-7.30	24,826	3.46	511	10.13

Major Products 主要产品	Output 产量	Unit 单位
Caustic Soda(Converting into 100%) 氢氧化钠（烧碱）（折１００％）	823	10,000 Tons 万吨
Ion Film Caustic Soda 离子膜法烧碱	189	10,000 Tons 万吨

10 Main Firms with Maximal Revenue (year founded) 收入最大的十家主要企业（创办年份）	City 城市	Province 省	Telephone/fax 电话/传真	Number of employees 职工人数	Ownership 产业所有权	Revenue ('000 RMB) 销售收入 (千元)	Profit('000 RMB) (rank) 利润(千元) (排名)	Total assets ('000 RMB) 总资产 (千元)	Major products 主要产品
Tianjin Dagu Chemical Industry Co., ltd.	Tianjin	Tianjin	(022)25391450		State Enterprises				100% Caustic Soda
天津大沽化工有限责任公司(1942)	天津市	天津市	(022)25387908	5,157	国有独资	1,873,629	30,665(11)	2,766,409	100%烧碱
Jinhua Chemical Industry (Group) Co.,Ltd.	Huludao	Liaoning	(0429)2709164		State Enterprises				Caustic Soda
锦化化工（集团）有限责任公司(1949)	葫芦岛市	辽宁省	(0429)2902606	12,043	国有独资	1,415,237	-	4,911,749	烧碱
Tianjin Bohai Chemical Industry Group Co.,Ltd.	Tianjin	Tianjin	(022)23390288		State Enterprises				Caustic Soda
天津渤海化工集团有限责任公司(1938)	天津市	天津市		5,024	国有独资	1,244,680	-	2,301,828	烧碱
Wuhan Gehua Group Co.,Ltd.	Wuhan	Hubei	(027)82834540		State Enterprises				Caustic Soda
武汉葛化集团有限公司(1959)	武汉市	湖北省	(027)87600357	7,004	国有独资	1,123,286	-	1,968,662	烧碱
Yibin Tianyuan Co., Ltd.	Yibin	Sichuan	(0831)3602960		Joint Stock				Caustic Soda
宜宾天原股份有限公司(1946)	宜宾市	四川省	(0831)3601446	3,656	股份制	918,109	85,540(2)	1,637,411	氢氧化钠
Jiangsu Yangnong Chemical Industry Co.,Ltd.	Yangzhou	Jiangsu	(0514)7813243		State Enterprises				Pesticide
江苏扬农化工集团(1958)	扬州市	江苏省	(0514)7814008	2,431	国有独资	835,230	48,560(3)	1,169,559	农药
Jiangsu Jiangdong Chemical Industry Co., Ltd.	Changzhou	Jiangsu	(0519)8811413		Joint Stock				Caustic Soda
江苏江东化工股份有限公司(2001)	常州市	江苏省	(0519)8820786	943	股份制	811,150	46,000(4)	481,580	烧碱
ShenYang Chemical Industry Co.,Ltd.	Shenyang	Liaoning	(024)25820516		Joint Stock				Caustic Soda
沈阳化工股份有限公司(1938)	沈阳市	辽宁省	(024)25827733	3,362	股份制	625,034	7,906(22)	2,044,856	烧碱
Qingdao Haijing Chemical Industry Group Co., Ltd.	Qingdao	Shandong	(0532)4851022		State Enterprises				Caustic Soda
青岛海晶化工集团有限公司(1947)	青岛市	山东省	(0532)4857329	2,462	国有独资	545,576	9,615(21)	996,661	烧碱
Nanning Chemical Industry Co., Ltd.	Nanning	Guangxi	(0771)2104331		Joint Stock				Caustic Soda
南宁化工股份有限公司(1998)	南宁市	广西	(0771)2106434	2,139	股份制	501,316	38,141(7)	778,836	烧碱

Top 10 Cities by Revenue 销售收入排名前10位城市	Province 省	Market share 市场份额 (%)	Number of firms 企业个数
Tianjin 天津市	Tianjin 天津市	13.94	20
Deyang 德阳市	Sichuan 四川省	5.77	13
Huludao 葫芦岛市	Liaoning 辽宁省	5.70	1
Wuhan 武汉市	Hubei 湖北省	4.57	4
Yibin 宜宾市	Sichuan 四川省	3.70	1
Zhuzhou 株洲市	Hunan 湖南省	3.52	2
Yangzhou 扬州市	Jiangsu 江苏省	3.39	2
Changzhou 常州市	Jiangsu 江苏省	3.27	1
Qingdao 青岛市	Shandong 山东省	3.17	2
Taizhou 泰州市	Jiangsu 江苏省	2.65	2

10 Major Wholesalers 十家主要批发商	City 城市	Province 省	Telephone/Fax 电话/传真
China Chemical Industry Supply & Sale (Group) General Company	Beijing	Beijing	(010)64238623
中国化工供销(集团)总公司	北京市	北京市	(010)64238623
China Chemical Industry Import & Export General Company	Beijing	Beijing	(010)88078888
中国化工进出口总公司	北京市	北京市	(010)88078890
Tianjin Bridge Group Welding Materials Supply & Sale Co., Ltd.	Tianjin	Tianjin	(022)83968861
天津大桥集团电焊条供销有限公司	天津市	天津市	(022)83968865
Taizhou Xingwei Chunlan Chain Stores Co., Ltd.	Taizhou	Jiangsu	(0523)6611200
泰州星威春兰连锁店有限公司	泰州市	江苏省	(0523)6224181
Taizhou Chunlan Sale Company	Taizhou	Jiangsu	(0523)6611200
泰州春兰销售公司	泰州市	江苏省	(0523)6224181
Shandong Tri-Union Co., Ltd.	Jinan	Shandong	(0531)6086351
山东三联有限责任公司	济南市	山东省	(0531)6093103
Haier Electrical Appliances Co.,Ltd.	Qingdao	Shandong	(0532)8939175
海尔集团电器产业有限公司	青岛市	山东省	(0532)8938086
Guangzhou Haier Industry & Trade Co.,Ltd.	Guangzhou	Guangdong	(020)87397315
广州海尔工贸有限公司	广州市	广东省	(020)87374302
Huizhou TCL Electrical Appliances Sales Co.,Ltd.	Huizhou	Guangdong	(0752)2289885
惠州市TCL电器销售有限公司	惠州市	广东省	(0752)2280690
Guangdong Hardware Minerals Import & Export Group Company	Guangzhou	Guangdong	(020)87752204
广东省五金矿产进出口集团公司	广州市	广东省	(020)87752205

2615: Soda Ash 纯碱制造业

The industry accounts for 0.127% of the total revenue of China's industrial sector in 2002. The rate of return on assets is 1.62%. 77.65% of all firms in the industry made a profit while 22.35% had negative returns.The top province in terms of the industry's revenue is Liaoning, accounting for 20.53% of the total revenue.
2002年本行业收入占全行业的0.127%，资产利润率为1.62%。77.65%的企业赢利，22.35%的企业亏损。收入最高的省为辽宁省，占本行业的20.53%。

	Total number of firms 企业总数	Total number of employees 职工总数	Total revenue (Mil.RMB) 总销售收入(百万元)	Total profit (Mil.RMB) 总利润(百万元)	Return on assets 资产利润率(%)	Return on equity 权益利润率(%)	Labour productivity ('000 RMB/ worker) 劳动生产率(千元/人)	Debts/ assets 资产负债率(%)	Total assets (Mil.RMB) 总资产(百万元)
Industry Overall 行业总体	85	80,785	13,574	527	1.62	3.52	46.76	53.90	32,476

	Number of firms 企业个数	Average number of employees 平均职工人数	Average revenue ('000 RMB) 平均销售收入(千元)	Average profit ('000 RMB) 平均利润(千元)	Return on assets 资产利润率(%)	Return on equity 权益利润率(%)	Labour productivity ('000 RMB/ worker) 劳动生产率(千元/人)	Debts/ assets 资产负债率(%)	Average total assets ('000 RMB) 平均总资产(千元)
By ownership 产业所有权									
State-owned 国有	15	1,602	287,518	10,730	1.38	2.97	43.71	53.60	778,679
Collective-owned 集体	18	271	38,481	1,259	3.26	8.51	42.09	61.63	38,570
Foreign & Overseas Chinese Funded 三资	5	279	119,004	1,494	0.39	0.85	79.82	53.91	379,461
By regional distribution 地区分布									
Central-North 华北	23	685	109,570	3,188	1.11	2.61	51.61	57.50	286,886
Beijing 北京	2	153	17,081	-1,822	-4.08	-127.24	13.10	96.80	44,683
Tianjin 天津	8	622	113,123	847	0.30	0.98	37.47	68.94	277,945
Hebei 河北	5	1,036	205,898	13,993	2.68	4.00	63.00	33.06	522,852
Shanxi 山西	2								
Inner Mongolia 内蒙古	6	882	91,913	40	0.01	0.07	55.98	78.41	278,534
Northeast 东北	7	2,520	401,813	1,111	0.09	0.20	27.43	55.35	1,223,664
Liaoning 辽宁	3	5,808	929,000	2,594	0.09	0.20	27.30	55.18	2,839,643
Jilin 吉林	3	60	6,880	-3	-0.02	-0.16	40.57	86.44	13,738
Heilongjiang 黑龙江	1	33	5,051	7	0.13	1.46	24.30	91.30	5,504
Central-East 华东	28	649	149,783	14,220	5.14	8.80	68.51	41.58	276,590
Shanghai 上海	5	111	14,007	1,099	7.80	20.90	45.55	62.67	14,081
Jiangsu 江苏	7	442	154,043	13,360	4.29	6.52	95.69	34.15	311,263
Zhejiang 浙江	4	360	63,516	2,990	4.05	13.31	52.02	69.55	73,770
Anhui 安徽	4	70	3,976	-265	-6.76	-37.07	25.21	81.75	3,910
Fujian 福建	2	45	2,752	-44	-0.96	-1.68	17.29	42.86	4,581
Jiangxi 江西	1	218	36,303				14.40	99.48	22,418
Shandong 山东	5	2,497	546,763	57,668	5.60	9.72	66.97	42.46	1,030,594
Central-South 中南	16	1,071	155,363	4,071	1.09	2.63	42.83	58.39	372,544
Henan 河南	6	1,266	132,333	-1,038	-0.38	-2.20	27.85	82.88	275,645
Hubei 湖北	2	3,294	565,688	8,591	0.60	1.07	50.60	43.93	1,431,528
Hunan 湖南	4	493	44,793	201	0.46	2.01	29.19	77.24	43,974
Guangdong 广东	3	330	127,085	17,794	4.21	9.68	133.17	56.50	422,629
Guangxi 广西	1								
Hainan 海南									
Southwest 西南	8	1,009	140,026	4,559	1.88	5.33	45.33	64.66	242,088
Chongqing 重庆	2	194	8,521	-88	-0.74	-4.51	17.45	83.49	11,748
Sichuan 四川	6	1,281	183,862	6,107	1.92	5.38	46.74	64.43	318,868
Guizhou 贵州									
Yunnan 云南									
Tibet 西藏									
Northwest 西北	3	1,340	147,147	-17,823	-3.20	-8.18	33.91	60.84	556,661
Shaanxi 陕西									
Gansu 甘肃	1	2,990	320,049	-62,550	-4.25	-11.22	31.00	62.16	1,473,069
Qinghai 青海	1	417	45,853	7,208	7.84	15.13	44.94	48.13	91,881
Ningxia 宁夏									
Xinjiang 新疆	1	612	75,538	1,874	1.78	3.84	40.63	53.55	105,033

Year 年份	Number of firms 企业个数	Rate of change 变化率(%)	Number of employees 职工人数(人)	Rate of change 变化率(%)	Total revenue (Mil. RMB) 总销售收入(百万元)	Rate of change 变化率(%)	Total profit (Mil RMB) 总利润(百万元)	Rate of change 变化率(%)
2000	75		112,470		13,077		345	
2001	85	13.33	98,193	-12.69	13,870	6.06	584	69.28
2002	85	o	80,785	-17.73	13,574	-2.13	527	-9.76

Major Products 主要产品	Output 产量	Unit 单位
Sodium Carbonate 碳酸钠（纯碱）	1,019	10,000 Tons 万吨
Active Precipitated Calcium Carbonate 轻质碳酸钙	249	10,000 Tons 万吨

10 Main Firms with Maximal Revenue (year founded) 收入最大的十家主要企业（创办年份）	City 城市	Province 省	Telephone/fax 电话/传真	Number of employees 职工人数	Ownership 产业所有权	Revenue ('000 RMB) 销售收入(千元)	Profit('000 RMB) (rank) 利润(千元)(排名)	Total assets ('000 RMB) 总资产(千元)	Major products 主要产品
Dahua Group Co.,Ltd.	Dalian	Liaoning	(0411)6672229		State-owned				Synthetic Ammonia
大化集团有限责任公司(1933)	大连市	辽宁省	(0411)6671199	15,307	国有企业	2,672,535	10,639(10)	8,392,164	合成氨
Shandong Haiua Co.,Ltd.	Weifang	Shandong	(0536)5329428		Joint Stock				Sodium Carbonate
山东海化股份有限公司(1972)	潍坊市	山东省	(0536)5329703	3,483	股份制	1,136,549	200,591(1)	2,340,697	纯碱
Tangshan Sanyou Alkali (Group) Co.,Ltd.	Tangshan	Hebei	(0315)8517680		State Enterprises				Sodium Carbonate
唐山三友碱业（集团）有限公司(1989)	唐山市	河北省		4,886	国有独资	1,000,799	69,656(3)	2,561,113	纯碱
Hubei Shuanghuan Chemical Industry Group Co.,Ltd.	Xiaogan	Hubei	(0712)3591003		State Enterprises				Sodium Carbonate
湖北双环化工集团有限公司(1980)	孝感市	湖北省	(0712)3591003	5,433	国有独资	994,335	17,090(7)	2,617,229	纯碱
Sinopec Nanjing Chemical Industry Co.,Ltd. Lianyungang Alkali Plant	Lianyungang	Jiangsu	(0518)2310301		State-owned				Sodium Carbonate
中国石化南京化学工业有限公司连云港碱厂(1989)	连云港市	江苏省	(0518)2311440	2,815	国有企业	868,121	140,160(2)	1,597,555	纯碱
Bohai Chemical Industry Co.,Ltd. Tianjin Alkali Plant	Tianjin	Tianjin	(022)25893951		State Enterprises				Sodium Carbonate
天津渤海化工有限责任公司天津碱厂(1924)	天津市	天津市	(022)25895881	4,613	国有独资	847,680	4,912(15)	2,146,166	纯碱
Shandong Shuguang Group Company	Zibo	Shandong	(0533)7171388		Collective-owned				Sodium Carbonate
山东曙光集团公司(1993)	淄博市	山东省	(0533)7171366	935	集体企业	332,740	14,615(8)	261,790	纯碱
Jinchang Chemical Industry (Group) Co.,Ltd.	Jinchang	Gansu	(0935)7351605		Joint Stock				Sodium Carbonate
金昌化工(集团)有限公司(1967)	金昌市	甘肃省	(0935)7322525	2,990	股份制	320,049	-	1,473,069	纯碱
Guangdong Nanfang Alkali Making Co., Ltd.	Guangzhou	Guangdong	(020)87428039		Overseas Chinese-funded				Sodium Carbonate
广东南方制碱有限公司(1989)	广州市	广东省	(020)82233027	922	港澳台资	319,713	33,131(5)	1,247,263	纯碱
Jiaozuo Xin'an Group Co.,Ltd.	Jiaozuo	Henan	(0391)2925951		State Enterprises				Sodium Carbonate
焦作鑫安集团有限责任公司(1958)	焦作市	河南省		3,818	国有独资	318,630	-	938,674	纯碱

Top 10 Cities by Revenue 销售收入排名前10位城市	Province 省	Market share 市场份额（%）	Number of firms 企业个数
Dalian 大连市	Liaoning 辽宁省	19.69	1
Weifang 潍坊市	Shandong 山东省	8.37	1
Qingdao 青岛市	Shandong 山东省	8.01	1
Zigong 自贡市	Sichuan 四川省	7.56	3
Tangshan 唐山市	Hebei 河北省	7.42	2
Xiaogan 孝感市	Hubei 湖北省	7.33	1
Tianjin 天津市	Tianjin 天津市	6.67	8
Lianyungang 连云港市	Jiangsu 江苏省	6.40	1
Jiaozuo 焦作市	Henan 河南省	4.05	2
Zibo 淄博市	Shandong 山东省	2.45	1

10 Major Wholesalers 十家主要批发商	City 城市	Province 省	Telephone/Fax 电话/传真
China Chemical Industry Supply & Sale (Group) General Company	Beijing	Beijing	(010)64238623
中国化工供销(集团)总公司	北京市	北京市	(010)64238623
China Chemical Industry Import & Export General Company	Beijing	Beijing	(010)88078888
中国化工进出口总公司	北京市	北京市	(010)88078890
Tianjin Bridge Group Welding Materials Supply & Sale Co., Ltd.	Tianjin	Tianjin	(022)83968861
天津大桥集团电焊条供销有限公司	天津市	天津市	(022)83968865
Taizhou Xingwei Chunlan Chain Stores Co., Ltd.	Taizhou	Jiangsu	(0523)6611200
泰州星威春兰连锁店有限公司	泰州市	江苏省	(0523)6224181
Taizhou Chunlan Sale Company	Taizhou	Jiangsu	(0523)6611200
泰州春兰销售公司	泰州市	江苏省	(0523)6224181
Shandong Tri-Union Co., Ltd.	Jinan	Shandong	(0531)6086351
山东三联有限责任公司	济南市	山东省	(0531)6093103
Haier Electrical Appliances Co.,Ltd.	Qingdao	Shandong	(0532)8939175
海尔集团电器产业有限公司	青岛市	山东省	(0532)8938086
Guangzhou Haier Industry & Trade Co.,Ltd.	Guangzhou	Guangdong	(020)87397315
广州海尔工贸有限公司	广州市	广东省	(020)87374302
Huizhou TCL Electrical Appliances Sales Co.,Ltd.	Huizhou	Guangdong	(0752)2289885
惠州市TCL电器销售有限公司	惠州市	广东省	(0752)2280690
Guangdong Hardware Minerals Import & Export Group Company	Guangzhou	Guangdong	(020)87752204
广东省五金矿产进出口集团公司	广州市	广东省	(020)87752205

2617: Inorganic Salts 无机盐制造业

The industry accounts for 0.277% of the total revenue of China's industrial sector in 2002. The rate of return on assets is 2.67%. 77.23% of all firms in the industry made a profit while 22.77% had negative returns.The top province in terms of the industry's revenue is Jiangsu, accounting for 28.45% of the total revenue.
2002年本行业收入占全行业的0.277%，资产利润率为2.67%。77.23%的企业赢利，22.77%的企业亏损。收入最高的省为江苏省，占本行业的28.45%。

	Total number of firms 企业总数	Total number of employees 职工总数	Total revenue (Mil.RMB) 总销售收入 (百万元)	Total profit (Mil.RMB) 总利润 (百万元)	Return on assets 资产利润率 (%)	Return on equity 权益利润率 (%)	Labour productivity ('000 RMB/ worker) 劳动生产率 (千元/人)	Debts/ assets 资产负债率 (%)	Total assets (Mil.RMB) 总资产 (百万元)
Industry Overall 行业总体	751	166,422	29,732	1,045	2.67	6.59	49.20	59.58	39,220

	Number of firms 企业个数	Average number of employees 平均职工人数	Average revenue ('000 RMB) 平均销售收入（千元）	Average profit ('000 RMB) 平均利润 (千元)	Return on assets 资产利润率 (%)	Return on equity 权益利润率 (%)	Labour productivity ('000 RMB/ worker) 劳动生产率 (千元/人)	Debts/ assets 资产负债率 (%)	Average total assets ('000 RMB) 平均总资产 (千元)
By ownership 产业所有权									
State-owned 国有	94	311	25,223	-1,095	-1.53	-5.94	23.95	74.30	71,666
Collective-owned 集体	168	152	22,808	744	5.36	14.50	40.21	63.02	13,872
Foreign & Overseas Chinese Funded 三资	65	195	75,106	6,262	6.38	10.75	105.23	40.61	98,088
By regional distribution 地区分布									
Central-North 华北	134	274	30,774	1,143	2.10	5.17	35.22	59.37	54,444
Beijing 北京	3	159	18,589	-2	-0.01	-0.10	22.43	90.26	20,254
Tianjin 天津	34	84	13,904	882	3.11	9.87	19.50	68.49	28,373
Hebei 河北	48	307	31,544	1,659	4.41	13.46	29.87	67.23	37,616
Shanxi 山西	27	390	48,493	1,686	1.48	2.79	45.46	46.86	113,827
Inner Mongolia 内蒙古	22	368	35,082	-90	-0.14	-0.46	37.98	69.12	63,237
Northeast 东北	55	192	18,792	-138	-0.35	-1.27	21.01	72.65	39,757
Liaoning 辽宁	28	278	22,136	-571	-1.02	-3.45	17.19	70.46	56,017
Jilin 吉林	10	81	6,551	-211	-1.25		22.72	106.43	16,954
Heilongjiang 黑龙江	17	115	20,484	618	2.34	7.21	35.57	67.52	26,389
Central-East 华东	252	178	58,394	2,401	4.29	9.89	81.27	56.63	55,961
Shanghai 上海	21	141	28,621	336	0.93		42.72	119.75	35,981
Jiangsu 江苏	103	139	82,120	3,148	6.76	14.30	138.91	52.69	46,544
Zhejiang 浙江	35	109	18,087	682	3.62	8.20	39.11	55.90	18,852
Anhui 安徽	14	242	61,625	4,669	8.46	15.57	70.26	45.63	55,159
Fujian 福建	7	256	40,300	716	0.37	1.39	47.72	73.37	194,178
Jiangxi 江西	13	222	19,837	381	1.05	2.51	43.96	58.05	36,164
Shandong 山东	59	266	61,359	2,960	3.30	6.40	59.47	48.45	89,680
Central-South 中南	175	180	30,099	1,382	3.28	8.12	46.15	59.58	42,113
Henan 河南	41	118	18,666	633	3.57	10.06	49.09	64.51	17,741
Hubei 湖北	33	312	47,921	1,781	1.80	3.96	44.03	54.46	98,821
Hunan 湖南	60	161	21,731	109	0.43	1.30	39.23	67.05	25,430
Guangdong 广东	29	152	46,189	5,090	9.27	22.49	71.39	58.78	54,923
Guangxi 广西	12	191	23,112	250	1.14	3.93	30.05	70.96	21,895
Hainan 海南									
Southwest 西南	90	329	39,607	1,972	3.21	7.29	41.85	55.89	61,349
Chongqing 重庆	18	284	37,479	3,045	4.83	10.78	47.20	55.21	63,060
Sichuan 四川	45	328	35,206	1,093	2.07	5.37	41.59	61.53	52,872
Guizhou 贵州	12	347	75,277	7,521	6.76	10.97	65.88	38.42	111,317
Yunnan 云南	15	373	26,827	-1,118	-2.50	-8.86	19.81	71.81	44,754
Tibet 西藏									
Northwest 西北	45	294	22,842	-2,770	-4.54	-16.41	25.45	72.32	60,984
Shaanxi 陕西	9	294	19,505	-1,661	-4.43	-20.86	24.22	78.78	37,537
Gansu 甘肃	16	154	13,631	-755	-3.73	-78.32	35.10	95.23	20,211
Qinghai 青海	4	187	16,801	39	0.08	0.20	69.11	59.60	48,370
Ningxia 宁夏	6	520	44,552	-16,920	-9.05	-100.44	3.83	90.99	187,068
Xinjiang 新疆	10	423	29,972	375	0.49	0.76	28.86	35.72	76,719

Year 年份	Number of firms 企业个数	Rate of change 变化率 (%)	Number of employees 职工人数 (人)	Rate of change 变化率 (%)	Total revenue (Mil. RMB) 总销售收入 (百万元)	Rate of change 变化率 (%)	Total profit (Mil RMB) 总利润 (百万元)	Rate of change 变化率 (%)
2000	687		193,626		22,411		791	
2001	757	10.19	176,140	-9.03	25,391	13.30	822	3.92
2002	751	-0.79	166,422	-5.52	29,732	17.10	1,045	27.13

Major Products 主要产品	Output 产量	Unit 单位
Sodium Bichromate 红矾钠	161,197	Ton 吨
Sodium Tripolyphosphate 三聚磷酸钠	94	10,000 Tons 万吨

10 Main Firms with Maximal Revenue (year founded) 收入最大的十家主要企业（创办年份）	City 城市	Province 省	Telephone/fax 电话/传真	Number of employees 职工人数	Ownership 产业所有权	Revenue ('000 RMB) 销售收入 (千元)	Profit('000 RMB) (rank) 利润(千元) (排名)	Total assets ('000 RMB) 总资产 (千元)	Major products 主要产品
Jiangsu ChengXing Phosphor-Chemicals Co.,Ltd.	Wuxi	Jiangsu	(0510)6281316		Joint Stock				Phosphoric Acid
江苏澄星磷化工股份有限公司(1984)	无锡市	江苏省	(0510)6281884	1,475	股份制	3,583,523	173,032(1)	1,958,082	磷酸
Nanfeng Chemical Industry (Group) Co.,Ltd.	Yuncheng	Shanxi	(0359)8967022		Joint Stock				Sodium Hydrosulfite
南风化工集团股份有限公司(1996)	运城市	山西省	(0359)2023302	5,349	股份制	811,589	42,000(9)	2,294,645	保险粉
Chevron Phillips Chemical(China) Co.,Ltd.	Suzhou	Jiangsu	(0512)58386688		Foreign Funded				Polystyrene
雪佛龙飞蒲利普丝化工(中国)有限公司(1999)	苏州市	江苏省	(0512)58386605	110	外商投资	666,610	-	845,005	聚苯乙烯
Weifang Yaxing Chemistry Co., Ltd.	Weifang	Shandong	(0536)8667941		Overseas Chinese-funded				Inorganic Salts
潍坊亚星化学股份有限公司(1923)	潍坊市	山东省	(0536)8666877	1,601	港澳台资	606,290	55,260(7)	1,377,390	无机盐
Hunan Xiangl û Co.,Ltd.	Xiangtan	Hunan	(0732)6808683		Limited-Liability				Barium Carbonate
湖南湘铝有限责任公司(1960)	湘潭市	湖南省	(0732)6808013	2,977	有限公司	492,939	5,255(41)	654,679	碳酸钡
Anhui Hongsifang Chemical Co.,Ltd.	Hefei	Anhui	(0551)3515025		Limited-Liability				Fluoride
安徽红四方股份有限公司(1958)	合肥市	安徽省	(0551)3525570	2,280	有限公司	455,049	1,243(136)	350,002	氟化盐
Ji'nan Yuxing Chemical Industry General Factory	Jinan	Shandong	(0531)5952322		State-owned				Sodium Tripolyphosphate三
济南裕兴化工总厂(1919)	济南市	山东省	(0531)5951148	2,495	国有企业	379,181	308(290)	1,222,545	聚磷酸钠
Hebei Chengxin Co., Ltd.	Shijiazhuang	Hebei	(0311)4623437		Limited-Liability				Sodium Bichromade
河北诚信有限责任公司(1990)	石家庄市	河北省	(0311)4623697	345	有限公司	351,963	68,864(4)	173,625	红矾钠
Sichuan Shifang Yingfeng Industrial General Company	Deyang	Sichuan	(0838)8230010		Joint Stock				Liquid Sodium Cyanide液
四川省什邡蓥峰实业总公司(1975)	德阳市	四川省	(0838)8231636	1,677	股份制	348,300	31,224(11)	666,598	体氰化钠
Hebei Xinji Chemical Industry Group Co., Ltd.	Shijiazhuang	Hebei	(0311)3290020		State Enterprises				Mono-ammonium Phosphate
河北辛集化工集团有限责任公司(1947)	石家庄市	河北省		2,975	国有独资	310,829	672(215)	480,338	磷酸一铵

Top 10 Cities by Revenue 销售收入排名前10位城市	Province 省	Market share 市场份额 (%)	Number of firms 企业个数
Wuxi 无锡市	Jiangsu 江苏省	12.55	8
Nanjing 南京市	Jiangsu 江苏省	4.18	22
Weifang 潍坊市	Shandong 山东省	4.00	14
Suzhou 苏州市	Jiangsu 江苏省	3.94	13
Shijiazhuang 石家庄市	Hebei 河北省	3.57	30
Dongguan 东莞市	Guangdong 广东省	2.78	1
Yuncheng 运城市	Shanxi 山西省	2.78	2
Yichang 宜昌市	Hubei 湖北省	2.64	7
Qingdao 青岛市	Shandong 山东省	2.43	2
Zibo 淄博市	Shandong 山东省	2.40	22

10 Major Wholesalers 十家主要批发商	City 城市	Province 省	Telephone/Fax 电话/传真
China Chemical Industry Supply & Sale (Group) General Company	Beijing	Beijing	(010)64238623
中国化工供销(集团)总公司	北京市	北京市	(010)64238623
China Chemical Industry Import & Export General Company	Beijing	Beijing	(010)88078888
中国化工进出口总公司	北京市	北京市	(010)88078890
Tianjin Bridge Group Welding Materials Supply & Sale Co., Ltd.	Tianjin	Tianjin	(022)83968861
天津大桥集团电焊条供销有限公司	天津市	天津市	(022)83968865
Taizhou Xingwei Chunlan Chain Stores Co., Ltd.	Taizhou	Jiangsu	(0523)6611200
泰州星威春兰连锁店有限公司	泰州市	江苏省	(0523)6224181
Taizhou Chunlan Sale Company	Taizhou	Jiangsu	(0523)6611200
泰州春兰销售公司	泰州市	江苏省	(0523)6224181
Shandong Tri-Union Co., Ltd.	Jinan	Shandong	(0531)6086351
山东三联有限责任公司	济南市	山东省	(0531)6093103
Haier Electrical Appliances Co.,Ltd.	Qingdao	Shandong	(0532)8939175
海尔集团电器产业有限公司	青岛市	山东省	(0532)8938086
Guangzhou Haier Industry & Trade Co.,Ltd.	Guangzhou	Guangdong	(020)87397315
广州海尔工贸有限公司	广州市	广东省	(020)87374302
Huizhou TCL Electrical Appliances Sales Co.,Ltd.	Huizhou	Guangdong	(0752)2289885
惠州市TCL电器销售有限公司	惠州市	广东省	(0752)2280690
Guangdong Hardware Minerals Import & Export Group Company	Guangzhou	Guangdong	(020)87752204
广东省五金矿产进出口集团公司	广州市	广东省	(020)87752205

2619: Other Basic Chemical Raw Materials 其他基本化学原料制造业

The industry accounts for 0.273% of the total revenue of China's industrial sector in 2002. The rate of return on assets is 2.68%. 74.64% of all firms in the industry made a profit while 25.36% had negative returns.The top province in terms of the industry's revenue is Jiangsu, accounting for 25.81% of the total revenue.
2002年本行业收入占全行业的0.273%，资产利润率为2.68%。74.64%的企业赢利，25.36%的企业亏损。收入最高的省为江苏省，占本行业的25.81%。

	Total number of firms 企业总数	Total number of employees 职工总数	Total revenue (Mil.RMB) 总销售收入（百万元）	Total profit (Mil.RMB) 总利润（百万元）	Return on assets 资产利润率（%）	Return on equity 权益利润率（%）	Labour productivity ('000 RMB/ worker) 劳动生产率（千元/人）	Debts/ assets 资产负债率（%）	Total assets (Mil.RMB) 总资产（百万元）
Industry Overall 行业总体	895	148,913	29,297	1,114	2.68	6.25	56.29	57.05	41,497

	Number of firms 企业个数	Average number of employees 平均职工人数	Average revenue ('000 RMB) 平均销售收入（千元）	Average profit ('000 RMB) 平均利润（千元）	Return on assets 资产利润率（%）	Return on equity 权益利润率（%）	Labour productivity ('000 RMB/ worker) 劳动生产率（千元/人）	Debts/ assets 资产负债率（%）	Average total assets ('000 RMB) 平均总资产（千元）
By ownership 产业所有权									
State-owned 国有	124	172	37,723				39.97	69.90	43,071
Collective-owned 集体	182	173	24,124	1,118	6.33	16.64	42.96	61.96	17,669
Foreign & Overseas Chinese Funded 三资	108	117	55,865	5,039	5.57	9.30	161.17	40.06	90,438
By regional distribution 地区分布									
Central-North 华北	153	167	25,092	1,353	4.31	8.60	43.36	49.90	31,410
Beijing 北京	24	136	22,651	2,120	5.21	8.46	64.94	38.42	40,712
Tianjin 天津	27	122	26,042	2,502	5.84	8.66	33.69	32.65	42,878
Hebei 河北	36	108	25,859	1,440	6.89	18.54	50.60	62.83	20,901
Shanxi 山西	56	235	23,147	488	1.71	4.39	31.97	61.00	28,484
Inner Mongolia 内蒙古	10	197	36,514	941	2.91	7.55	85.42	61.49	32,339
Northeast 东北	51	203	14,240	7	0.02	0.04	31.41	49.30	32,294
Liaoning 辽宁	30	168	16,525	6	0.02	0.03	45.87	43.41	40,278
Jilin 吉林	11	206	14,709	-149	-0.49	-1.34	27.36	63.40	30,250
Heilongjiang 黑龙江	10	304	6,872	182	1.72	6.16	10.42	72.15	10,590
Central-East 华东	317	165	44,982	2,126	3.54	7.71	72.99	54.08	60,021
Shanghai 上海	73	155	45,110	2,579	4.23	7.34	75.87	42.42	60,975
Jiangsu 江苏	114	186	66,321	3,323	3.44	7.37	90.22	53.27	96,479
Zhejiang 浙江	40	104	18,435	1,142	4.95	14.30	48.78	65.40	23,087
Anhui 安徽	14	71	11,534	154	1.60	5.06	43.43	68.33	9,613
Fujian 福建	10	168	34,306	2,927	4.90	10.16	62.80	51.78	59,765
Jiangxi 江西	12	83	16,948	732	4.52	10.66	60.65	57.57	16,176
Shandong 山东	54	219	36,303	389	1.22	6.95	52.77	82.51	31,981
Central-South 中南	191	139	27,386	1,351	3.93	9.48	57.50	58.57	34,414
Henan 河南	47	187	29,370	1,191	3.37	12.24	41.93	72.42	35,299
Hubei 湖北	35	163	14,555	-316	-1.85	-11.43	35.53	83.79	17,042
Hunan 湖南	36	133	21,789	1,502	5.20	10.74	58.93	51.58	28,867
Guangdong 广东	55	91	37,650	2,252	5.04	9.10	104.54	44.54	44,648
Guangxi 广西	16	133	29,979	2,220	4.47	12.32	69.04	63.70	49,626
Hainan 海南	2	50	3,046	-139	-0.97	-1.73	8.51	44.14	14,391
Southwest 西南	133	203	34,184	-141	-0.22	-0.65	51.78	66.00	64,481
Chongqing 重庆	10	134	20,276	2,921	6.98	13.73	99.28	49.14	41,824
Sichuan 四川	43	246	30,008	-895	-1.24	-5.07	42.16	75.53	72,225
Guizhou 贵州	34	176	29,718	-798	-1.63	-5.43	45.67	70.07	49,105
Yunnan 云南	45	202	45,394	391	0.52	1.22	60.02	57.33	75,151
Tibet 西藏	1	7	199	6	0.84	0.93	39.43	9.82	713
Northwest 西北	50	146	13,907	-136	-0.78	-3.33	29.69	76.48	17,376
Shaanxi 陕西	16	190	19,851	-564	-3.15	-31.94	32.83	90.15	17,932
Gansu 甘肃	24	88	6,460	-133	-1.85	-6.01	29.35	69.25	7,168
Qinghai 青海									
Ningxia 宁夏	8	176	21,757	-661	-2.29	-9.21	26.40	75.18	28,930
Xinjiang 新疆	2	358	24,328	5,346	5.99	16.26	23.88	63.14	89,221

2619: Other Basic Chemical Raw Materials 其他基本化学原料制造业

Year 年份	Number of firms 企业个数	Rate of change 变化率 (%)	Number of employees 职工人数 (人)	Rate of change 变化率 (%)	Total revenue (Mil. RMB) 总销售收入 (百万元)	Rate of change 变化率 (%)	Total profit (Mil RMB) 总利润 (百万元)	Rate of change 变化率 (%)
2000	815		161,588		20,719		664	
2001	818	0.37	146,433	-9.38	24,285	17.21	906	36.45
2002	895	9.41	148,913	1.69	29,297	20.64	1,114	22.96

Major Products 主要产品	Output 产量	Unit 单位
Calcium Carbide(Converting into 300 Litres/kg) 碳化钙（电石）（折 300升 / 千克）	426	10,000 Tons 万吨
Yellow Phosphorus 黄磷	69	10,000 Tons 万吨

10 Main Firms with Maximal Revenue (year founded) 收入最大的十家主要企业（创办年份）	City 城市	Province 省	Telephone/fax 电话/传真	Number of employees 职工人数	Ownership 产业所有权	Revenue ('000 RMB) 销售收入 (千元)	Profit('000 RMB) (rank) 利润(千元) (排名)	Total assets ('000 RMB) 总资产 (千元)	Major products 主要产品
Jiangsu Lingguang Group 江苏陵光集团(1970)	Taizhou 泰州市	Jiangsu 江苏省	(0523)6558888 (0523)6558088	1,698	State-owned 国有企业	2,209,301	35,200(6)	849,535	Chemical Industry Products 化工产品
Jiangsu Huachang Group Co.,Ltd. 江苏华昌集团有限公司(1972)	Suzhou 苏州市	Jiangsu 江苏省	(0512)58683240 (0512)58684850	2,774	State Enterprises 国有独资	903,602	159,971(1)	1,120,015	Compound Fertilizer 复合肥
Jiaozuo Chemical Electric Group Co., Ltd. 焦作化电集团有限责任公司(1969)	Jiaozuo 焦作市	Henan 河南省	(0391)3970000 (0391)3933276	2,668	State Enterprises 国有独资	488,939	13,616(28)	698,587	Caustic Soda 烧碱
Nanjing Steel Group Co., Ltd. 南京钢铁集团有限公司(1993)	Nanjing 南京市	Jiangsu 江苏省	(025)7792100 (025)7792159	4,044	State Enterprises 国有独资	430,330	38,490(2)	6,321,440	Industry Gas 工业气体
LongKou Hengxin Economic & Trade Co.,Ltd. 龙口市恒鑫经贸有限公司(1993)	Yantai 烟台市	Shandong 山东省	(0535)8591457 (0535)8591081	1,210	Collective-owned 集体企业	425,432	32,637(9)	188,732	Hydrogen Peroxide Solution 双氧水
Sichuan Chuantou Electro Metallurgy Co.,Ltd. 四川川投电冶有限公司(1998)	Panzhihua 攀枝花市	Sichuan 四川省	(0812)8120091 (0812)8120091	375	Overseas Chinese-funded 港澳台资	388,113	28,358(11)	603,380	Yellow Phosphorus 黄磷
Guizhou Qianneng Tianhe Phosphorus Industry Co., Ltd. 贵州黔能天和磷业有限公司(2000)	Guiyang 贵阳市	Guizhou 贵州省	(0851)7552262 (0851)7552262	980	Limited-Liability 有限公司	305,050	221(365)	324,957	Yellow Phosphorus 黄磷
Zhongshan Nanrong Chemical Industry Co., Ltd. 中山市南荣化工有限公司(1997)	Zhongshan 中山市	Guangdong 广东省	(0760)3113908 (0760)3113912	120	Foreign Funded 外商投资	291,037	-	232,730	Polystyrene 聚苯乙烯
Shanghai Zhongyuan Chemical Industry Co.,Ltd. 上海中远化工有限公司(1989)	Shanghai 上海市	Shanghai 上海市	(021)56993888 (021)56754337	2,442	State Enterprises 国有独资	264,927	4,324(80)	1,049,824	Synthetic Ammonia 合成氨
Hunan Xiangtan Electro Chemical Group Company 湖南湘潭电化集团公司(1958)	Xiangtan 湘潭市	Hunan 湖南省	(0732)5544099 (0732)5542370	1,092	State-owned 国有企业	256,557	36,027(3)	366,888	Manganese Dioxide 二氧化锰

Top 10 Cities by Revenue 销售收入排名前10位城市	Province 省	Market share 市场份额 (%)	Number of firms 企业个数
Shanghai 上海市	Shanghai 上海市	11.24	73
Taizhou 泰州市	Jiangsu 江苏省	7.98	9
Suzhou 苏州市	Jiangsu 江苏省	6.84	27
Nanjing 南京市	Jiangsu 江苏省	3.46	12
Guangzhou 广州市	Guangdong 广东省	2.91	18
Yuxi 玉溪市	Yunnan 云南省	2.79	14
Tianjin 天津市	Tianjin 天津市	2.40	27
Wuxi 无锡市	Jiangsu 江苏省	2.31	16
Yantai 烟台市	Shandong 山东省	2.18	6
Guiyang 贵阳市	Guizhou 贵州省	1.98	13

10 Major Wholesalers 十家主要批发商	City 城市	Province 省	Telephone/Fax 电话/传真
China Chemical Industry Supply & Sale (Group) General Company 中国化工供销(集团)总公司	Beijing 北京市	Beijing 北京市	(010)64238623 (010)64238623
China Chemical Industry Import & Export General Company 中国化工进出口总公司	Beijing 北京市	Beijing 北京市	(010)88078888 (010)88078890
Tianjin Bridge Group Welding Materials Supply & Sale Co., Ltd. 天津大桥集团电焊条供销有限公司	Tianjin 天津市	Tianjin 天津市	(022)83968861 (022)83968865
Taizhou Xingwei Chunlan Chain Stores Co., Ltd. 泰州星威春兰连锁店有限公司	Taizhou 泰州市	Jiangsu 江苏省	(0523)6611200 (0523)6224181
Taizhou Chunlan Sale Company 泰州春兰销售公司	Taizhou 泰州市	Jiangsu 江苏省	(0523)6611200 (0523)6224181
Shandong Tri-Union Co., Ltd. 山东三联有限责任公司	Jinan 济南市	Shandong 山东省	(0531)6086351 (0531)6093103
Haier Electrical Appliances Co.,Ltd. 海尔集团电器产业有限公司	Qingdao 青岛市	Shandong 山东省	(0532)8939175 (0532)8938086
Guangzhou Haier Industry & Trade Co.,Ltd. 广州海尔工贸有限公司	Guangzhou 广州市	Guangdong 广东省	(020)87397315 (020)87374302
Huizhou TCL Electrical Appliances Sales Co.,Ltd. 惠州市TCL电器销售有限公司	Huizhou 惠州市	Guangdong 广东省	(0752)2289885 (0752)2280690
Guangdong Hardware Minerals Import & Export Group Company 广东省五金矿产进出口集团公司	Guangzhou 广州市	Guangdong 广东省	(020)87752204 (020)87752205

2621: Nitrogenous Fertilizer 氮肥制造业

The industry accounts for 0.591% of the total revenue of China's industrial sector in 2002. The rate of return on assets is 1.03%. 67.58% of all firms in the industry made a profit while 32.42% had negative returns. The top province in terms of the industry's revenue is Shandong, accounting for 17.13% of the total revenue.
2002年本行业收入占全行业的0.591%，资产利润率为1.03%。67.58%的企业赢利，32.42%的企业亏损。收入最高的省为山东省，占本行业的17.13%。

	Total number of firms 企业总数	Total number of employees 职工总数	Total revenue (Mil.RMB) 总销售收入（百万元）	Total profit (Mil.RMB) 总利润（百万元）	Return on assets 资产利润率（%）	Return on equity 权益利润率（%）	Labour productivity ('000 RMB/ worker) 劳动生产率（千元/人）	Debts/ assets 资产负债率（%）	Total assets (Mil.RMB) 总资产（百万元）
Industry Overall 行业总体	586	513,527	63,420	1,287	1.03	3.00	34.98	65.74	125,148

	Number of firms 企业个数	Average number of employees 平均职工人数	Average revenue ('000 RMB) 平均销售收入（千元）	Average profit ('000 RMB) 平均利润（千元）	Return on assets 资产利润率（%）	Return on equity 权益利润率（%）	Labour productivity ('000 RMB/ worker) 劳动生产率（千元/人）	Debts/ assets 资产负债率（%）	Average total assets ('000 RMB) 平均总资产（千元）
By ownership 产业所有权									
State-owned 国有	254	852	90,329	951	0.49	1.60	29.15	69.46	194,854
Collective-owned 集体	10	331	37,594	108	0.25	1.25	26.80	80.04	43,141
Foreign & Overseas Chinese Funded 三资	5	474	79,923	11,320	14.08	35.70	56.57	60.56	80,392
By regional distribution 地区分布									
Central-North 华北	110	818	76,707	368	0.20	0.67	27.81	70.62	186,817
Beijing 北京	2	473	5,008	-1,314	-0.70	-2.38	3.14	70.54	187,590
Tianjin 天津	2	1,253	118,784	850	0.25	6.13	25.22	95.89	337,009
Hebei 河北	52	807	82,286	58	0.03	0.12	27.22	72.49	171,510
Shanxi 山西	47	837	62,621	1,769	1.27	5.51	24.57	77.03	139,837
Inner Mongolia 内蒙古	7	748	138,311	-6,397	-1.12	-2.31	62.53	51.74	572,832
Northeast 东北	11	2,108	385,198	-5,920	-0.55	-1.56	26.00	64.54	1,072,567
Liaoning 辽宁	6	2,675	626,038	-6,667	-0.39	-1.06	29.75	62.96	1,692,634
Jilin 吉林	3	1,747	108,297	-6,954	-1.37	-5.14	20.81	73.34	508,052
Heilongjiang 黑龙江	2	946	78,034	-2,127	-3.60	-26.22	8.54	86.28	59,138
Central-East 华东	162	952	129,933	3,546	1.91	5.86	39.83	67.46	186,111
Shanghai 上海	5	381	37,515	-1,990	-5.56	-19.77	13.40	71.87	35,785
Jiangsu 江苏	31	943	110,759	3,711	2.93	10.29	29.94	71.52	126,598
Zhejiang 浙江	12	551	82,283	7,313	7.97	16.94	48.16	52.95	91,758
Anhui 安徽	28	925	108,726	382	0.24	0.74	29.64	68.35	162,215
Fujian 福建	22	807	96,865	1,188	0.95	2.39	33.74	60.03	124,546
Jiangxi 江西	4	1,071	100,355	-9,258	-3.33	-42.36	16.13	92.13	277,873
Shandong 山东	60	1,142	181,063	6,364	2.31	6.94	50.88	66.74	275,864
Central-South 中南	178	762	79,104	946	0.63	2.08	29.39	69.61	149,494
Henan 河南	71	978	92,649	1,161	0.64	2.57	24.32	75.02	180,797
Hubei 湖北	36	606	76,638	-3,099	-2.61	-9.04	42.08	71.13	118,758
Hunan 湖南	50	590	51,361	-248	-0.25	-0.76	22.04	66.72	97,966
Guangdong 广东	4	543	60,600	168	0.24	0.75	28.20	68.04	70,269
Guangxi 广西	16	757	82,911	2,619	1.51	4.04	25.46	62.55	173,075
Hainan 海南	1	528	606,356	167,415	10.81	18.80	678.82	42.52	1,549,421
Southwest 西南	94	809	117,234	6,917	2.61	5.35	45.32	51.20	265,011
Chongqing 重庆	14	657	66,499	2,205	2.50	10.93	23.72	77.12	88,174
Sichuan 四川	45	736	118,307	7,486	2.82	4.96	54.45	43.10	265,127
Guizhou 贵州	14	862	100,742	6,893	2.64	4.79	33.46	44.91	261,176
Yunnan 云南	21	1,031	159,750	8,855	2.30	6.05	47.16	62.03	385,210
Tibet 西藏									
Northwest 西北	31	1,115	148,235	-2,616	-0.73	-3.13	37.17	76.70	359,011
Shaanxi 陕西	18	1,304	133,174	-3,745	-0.97	-8.14	27.41	88.12	387,276
Gansu 甘肃	4	955	115,570	-7,689	-4.84	-28.79	25.24	83.19	158,872
Qinghai 青海									
Ningxia 宁夏	8	618	185,429	1,504	0.42	0.90	92.83	53.57	358,465
Xinjiang 新疆	1	2,327	252,438	5,055	0.77	1.54	37.03	50.05	655,162

2621: Nitrogenous Fertilizer 氮肥制造业

Year 年份	Number of firms 企业个数	Rate of change 变化率 (%)	Number of employees 职工人数 (人)	Rate of change 变化率 (%)	Total revenue (Mil. RMB) 总销售收入 (百万元)	Rate of change 变化率 (%)	Total profit (Mil RMB) 总利润 (百万元)	Rate of change 变化率 (%)
2000	673		717,831		62,371		-128	
2001	619	-8.02	572,643	-20.23	56,200	-9.89	305	-
2002	586	-5.33	513,527	-10.32	63,420	12.85	1,287	321.97

Major Products 主要产品	Output 产量	Unit 单位
Synthetic Ammonia 合成氨	3,654	10,000 Tons 万吨
Nitrogenous Fertilizer(Converting into containing N 100%) 氮肥（折含N 100%）	2,743	10,000 Tons 万吨

10 Main Firms with Maximal Revenue (year founded) 收入最大的十家主要企业（创办年份）	City 城市	Province 省	Telephone/fax 电话/传真	Number of employees 职工人数	Ownership 产业所有权	Revenue ('000 RMB) 销售收入 (千元)	Profit('000 RMB) (rank) 利润(千元)(排名)	Total assets ('000 RMB) 总资产 (千元)	Major products 主要产品
Liaoning Huajin Chemical Industry (Group)Co.,Ltd.	Panjin	Liaoning	(0427)5855960		Limited-Liability				Carbamide
辽宁华锦化工(集团)有限责任公司(1976)	盘锦市	辽宁省	(0427)5856199	11,263	有限公司	2,821,307	-	7,896,283	尿素
PetroChina Natural Gas Co.,Ltd.Ningxia Petrochemical Branch	Yinchuan	Ningxia	(0951)2972701		Joint Stock				Synthetic Ammonia
中国石油天然气股份有限公司宁夏石化分公司(2000)	银川市	宁夏	(0951)2021379	1,211	股份制	1,130,480	42,050(13)	2,277,140	合成氨
Sichuan Chemical Industrial (Group)Co.,Ltd.	Chengdu	Sichuan	(028)83302896		State-owned				Carbamide
川化集团有限责任公司(1959)	成都市	四川省	(028)83301649	7,541	国有企业	1,083,280	10,630(46)	2,683,932	尿素
Lutianhua Group Co.,Ltd.	Luzhou	Sichuan	(0830)4122222		Limited-Liability				Synthetic Ammonia
泸天化集团有限责任公司(1959)	泸州市	四川省	(0830)4122513	3,963	有限公司	1,001,826	85,060(6)	3,199,716	合成氨
Anhui Huainan Chemical Group Co.,Ltd.	Huainan	Anhui	(0554)6414556		Limited-Liability				Synthetic Ammonia
安徽淮化集团有限公司(1958)	淮南市	安徽省	(0554)6413347	7,127	有限公司	870,313	24,200(29)	2,280,708	合成氨
Jiangsu Xinyuan Group Company	Wuxi	Jiangsu	(0510)3311460		State-owned				Carbamide
江苏新苑集团公司(1965)	无锡市	江苏省	(0510)3311237	3,163	国有企业	823,460	9(280)	1,047,600	尿素
Yunnan Yuntianhua Co.,Ltd.	Zhaotong	Yunnan	(0870)8663402		Joint Stock				Synthetic Ammonia
云南云天化股份有限公司(1997)	昭通市	云南省	(0870)8636337	1,758	股份制	819,645	177,544(1)	1,925,881	合成氨
Shandong Lianmeng Chemical Industry Group Co.,Ltd.	Weifang	Shandong	(0536)5202237		State-owned				Carbamide
山东联盟化工集团有限公司(1970)	潍坊市	山东省	(0536)5200380	2,732	国有企业	812,766	56,192(10)	631,307	尿素
Fujian Petrochemcal Group Sanming Chemical Industry	Sanming	Fujian	(0598)8222801		State Enterprises				Carbamide
Co.,Ltd. 福建石化集团三明化工有限责任公司(1958)	三明市	福建省	(0598)8241905	6,653	国有独资	784,362	3,849(91)	1,272,687	尿素
Shanxi Fengxi Fertilizer Industry (Group) Co., Ltd.	Yuncheng	Shanxi	(0359)2064005		Joint Stock				Synthetic Ammonia
山西丰喜肥业（集团）股份有限公司(1998)	运城市	山西省	(0359)2064003	7,991	股份制	783,462	24,537(28)	1,969,736	合成氨

Top 10 Cities by Revenue 销售收入排名前10位城市	Province 省	Market share 市场份额 (%)	Number of firms 企业个数
Panjin 盘锦市	Liaoning 辽宁省	4.74	2
Luzhou 泸州市	Sichuan 四川省	2.64	8
Yichang 宜昌市	Hubei 湖北省	2.36	6
Chengdu 成都市	Sichuan 四川省	2.35	6
Shijiazhuang 石家庄市	Hebei 河北省	2.22	9
Dezhou 德州市	Shandong 山东省	2.13	6
Yinchuan 银川市	Ningxia 宁夏	2.10	3
Qujing 曲靖市	Yunnan 云南省	2.09	6
Taian 泰安市	Shandong 山东省	1.98	5
Liaocheng 聊城市	Shandong 山东省	1.89	3

10 Major Wholesalers 十家主要批发商	City 城市	Province 省	Telephone/Fax 电话/传真
Ningbo Haitian Group General Company	Ningbo	Zhejiang	(0574)87195360
宁波海田集团总公司	宁波市	浙江省	(0574)87195821
Heilongjiang Agriculture Means Of Production Company	Harbin	Heilongjiang	(0451)88383752
黑龙江省农业生产资料公司	哈尔滨市	黑龙江省	(0451)88382367
Yantai Agriculture Means Of Production General Company	Yantai	Shandong	(0535)6216374
烟台市农业生产资料总公司	烟台市	山东省	(0535)6211348
Guangdong Agriculture Means Of Production General Company	Guangzhou	Guangdong	(020)87773051
广东省农业生产资料总公司	广州市	广东省	(020)87754117
Inner Mongolia Autonomous Region Agriculture & Animal Husbandry Means Of Production Co.,Ltd.	Huhhot	Inner Mongolia	(0471)6963132
内蒙古自治区农牧业生产资料股份有限公司	呼和浩特市	内蒙古	(0471)6964434
Shanghai Agriculture Means Of Production Company	Shanghai	Shanghai	(021)63807100
上海市农业生产资料公司	上海市	上海市	(021)63806807
Ningbo Haitian International Trade Co.,Ltd.	Ningbo	Zhejiang	(0574)87345251
宁波海田国际贸易有限公司	宁波市	浙江省	(0574)87345620
Fujian AMP Incorpration	Fuzhou	Fujian	(0591)7508666
福建省农资集团公司	福州市	福建省	(0591)7614839
Shandong Agricultural Machinery Group General Company	Jinan	Shandong	(0531)8951240
山东省农业机械集团总公司	济南市	山东省	(0531)8951240
Shandong Yantai Agriculture Means Of Production Purchasing Supply Station	Yantai	Shandong	(0535)6222126
山东省烟台市农业生产资料采购供应站	烟台市	山东省	(0535)6216440

2622: Phosphate Fertilizer 磷肥制造业

The industry accounts for 0.142% of the total revenue of China's industrial sector in 2002. The rate of return on assets is -1.59%. 70.66% of all firms in the industry made a profit while 29.34% had negative returns.The top province in terms of the industry's revenue is Jiangsu, accounting for 18.46% of the total revenue.
2002年本行业收入占全行业的 0.142%，资产利润率为 -1.59%。70.66%的企业赢利，29.34%的企业亏损。收入最高的省为江苏省，占本行业的18.46%。

	Total number of firms 企业总数	Total number of employees 职工总数	Total revenue (Mil.RMB) 总销售收入 (百万元)	Total profit (Mil.RMB) 总利润 (百万元)	Return on assets 资产利润率 (%)	Return on equity 权益利润率 (%)	Labour productivity ('000 RMB/ worker) 劳动生产率 (千元/人)	Debts/ assets 资产负债率 (%)	Total assets (Mil.RMB) 总资产 (百万元)
Industry Overall 行业总体	484	154,467	15,205	-523	-1.59	-6.16	23.08	74.27	32,963

	Number of firms 企业个数	Average number of employees 平均职工人数	Average revenue ('000 RMB) 平均销售收入 (千元)	Average profit ('000 RMB) 平均利润 (千元)	Return on assets 资产利润率 (%)	Return on equity 权益利润率 (%)	Labour productivity ('000 RMB/ worker) 劳动生产率 (千元/人)	Debts/ assets 资产负债率 (%)	Average total assets ('000 RMB) 平均总资产 (千元)
By ownership 产业所有权									
State-owned 国有	145	434	40,002	-4,132	-3.15	-16.35	16.92	80.72	131,040
Collective-owned 集体	72	138	11,950	192	1.74	5.32	21.50	67.23	11,002
Foreign & Overseas Chinese Funded 三资	3	122	48,064	344	2.02	5.17	49.07	60.87	16,993
By regional distribution 地区分布									
Central-North 华北	43	179	17,967	494	2.03	8.42	21.71	75.86	24,298
Beijing 北京									
Tianjin 天津	2	305	53,820	4,697	10.08	15.92	36.02	36.69	46,596
Hebei 河北	26	184	20,383	651	2.49	13.27	24.69	81.27	26,198
Shanxi 山西	15	156	8,998	-339	-1.88	-7.75	11.87	75.74	18,030
Inner Mongolia 内蒙古									
Northeast 东北	9	113	5,569	-792	-2.15	-25.65	3.39	91.63	36,904
Liaoning 辽宁	6	84	5,711	-822	-2.34	-37.02	-3.20	93.68	35,122
Jilin 吉林	1	72	2,532				38.06	86.46	1,890
Heilongjiang 黑龙江	2	219	6,663	-1,099	-1.84	-15.46	5.26	88.11	59,760
Central-East 华东	115	406	48,165	328	0.31	0.93	26.01	66.54	105,243
Shanghai 上海	1	180	31,572	206	1.43	4.28	14.18	66.61	14,398
Jiangsu 江苏	37	631	75,858	581	0.30	0.92	22.66	67.72	196,573
Zhejiang 浙江	12	83	14,984	231	1.66	7.15	33.14	76.83	13,929
Anhui 安徽	27	502	56,451	389	0.32	0.93	28.94	65.35	121,113
Fujian 福建	11	292	28,906	-1,227	-1.85	-3.99	16.12	53.61	66,305
Jiangxi 江西	8	128	7,479	293	2.19	9.84	19.90	77.70	13,347
Shandong 山东	19	233	32,572	730	2.56	8.49	42.16	69.85	28,528
Central-South 中南	146	322	26,657	-1,545	-2.77	-8.56	25.40	67.67	55,837
Henan 河南	37	225	12,551	-2	-0.01	-0.07	21.41	85.79	22,961
Hubei 湖北	44	414	39,977	275	0.46	1.10	37.23	58.04	59,590
Hunan 湖南	32	242	16,164	-78	-0.27	-0.83	19.21	67.76	29,053
Guangdong 广东	13	318	35,263	540	1.02	2.96	22.96	65.50	52,858
Guangxi 广西	19	434	35,829	-12,607	-7.89	-27.45	11.14	71.25	159,745
Hainan 海南	1	312	12,134	-2,618	-9.12	-47.70	5.86	80.88	28,702
Southwest 西南	113	373	39,526	-3,015	-3.32	-30.61	19.27	89.15	90,758
Chongqing 重庆	9	388	27,830	-585	-1.14	-3.38	18.14	66.32	51,461
Sichuan 四川	39	294	21,199	-408	-1.26	-5.55	14.33	77.37	32,466
Guizhou 贵州	32	281	24,100	198	0.45	1.77	15.25	74.32	43,504
Yunnan 云南	33	554	79,333	-9,873	-4.57	-104.10	24.57	95.61	216,187
Tibet 西藏									
Northwest 西北	58	169	8,365	-141	-0.76	-2.03	17.55	62.44	18,538
Shaanxi 陕西	11	505	17,137	-985	-1.87	-7.57	14.60	75.30	52,655
Gansu 甘肃	40	71	4,284	84	1.31	2.74	27.55	52.18	6,411
Qinghai 青海									
Ningxia 宁夏	5	234	20,042	-466	-1.15	-1.83	5.83	37.08	40,543
Xinjiang 新疆	2	134	12,557	796	4.32	14.94	24.20	71.10	18,427

2622: Phosphate Fertilizer 磷肥制造业

Year 年份	Number of firms 企业个数	Rate of change 变化率 (%)	Number of employees 职工人数 (人)	Rate of change 变化率 (%)	Total revenue (Mil. RMB) 总销售收入 (百万元)	Rate of change 变化率 (%)	Total profit (Mil RMB) 总利润 (百万元)	Rate of change 变化率 (%)
2000	554		222,351		13,830		-366	
2001	513	-7.40	180,214	-18.95	13,777	-0.38	-124	66.12
2002	484	-5.65	154,467	-14.29	15,205	10.37	-523	-321.77

Major Products 主要产品	Output 产量	Unit 单位
Sulfuric Acid(Converting into 100%) 硫酸（折１００％）	2,967	10,000 Tons 万吨
Phosphate Fertilizer(Converting into Containing P2O5 100%) 磷肥（折合P2O5 100%）	776	10,000 Tons 万吨

10 Main Firms with Maximal Revenue (year founded) 收入最大的十家主要企业（创办年份）	City 城市	Province 省	Telephone/fax 电话/传真	Number of employees 职工人数	Ownership 产业所有权	Revenue ('000 RMB) 销售收入（千元）	Profit('000 RMB) (rank) 利润(千元)(排名)	Total assets ('000 RMB) 总资产（千元）	Major products 主要产品
Sinopec Nanjing Chemical Industry Co.,Ltd.	Nanjing	Jiangsu	(025)7765017		State-owned				Calcium Superphosphate
中国石化集团南京化学工业有限公司(1934)	南京市	江苏省	(025)7792812	12,511	国有企业	1,542,790	16,490(2)	6,381,840	过磷酸钙
Tongling Chemical Industry Group Co.,Ltd.	Tongling	Anhui	(0562)3801769		State Enterprises				Sulfurous Iron Ore
铜陵市化学工业集团有限公司(1962)	铜陵市	安徽省	(0562)3801961	7,880	国有独资	1,111,714	8,770(9)	2,740,555	硫铁矿
Yunnan Three Circles Chemical Industry Co.,Ltd.	Kunming	Yunnan	(0871)8596600		Limited-Liability				Triple Superphosphate重
云南三环化工有限公司(1982)	昆明市	云南省	(0871)8596611	2,263	有限公司	523,770	25,069(1)	1,521,250	过磷酸钙
Yunnan Phosphate Fertilizer Industry Co.,Ltd.	Kunming	Yunnan	(0871)8750285		State-owned				Triple Superphosphate
云南磷肥工业有限公司(1991)	昆明市	云南省	(0871)8750281	2,000	国有企业	428,621	-	2,632,825	重钙
Hubei Huangmailing Phosphor Chemical Industry Group Co.	Xiaogan	Hubei	(0712)7422014		State-owned				Phosphoreted Ore
湖北省黄麦岭磷化工集团公司(1973)	孝感市	湖北省	(0712)7422010	3,401	国有企业	352,762	10,847(5)	392,290	磷矿石
Guiyang Zhonghua Kaiming Chemical Group Company	Guiyang	Guizhou	(0851)7714003		State-owned				Phosphate Fertilizer
贵阳中化开明化学有限公司(1994)	贵阳市	贵州省	(0851)7714006	1,123	国有企业	323,181	15,210(3)	646,045	磷肥
Hubei Xiangyun Group Chemical Industry Co.,Ltd.	Huanggang	Hubei	(0713)6542467		Joint Stock				Mono-ammonium Phosphate
湖北祥云集团化工股份有限公司(1970)	黄冈市	湖北省	(0713)6542455	1,551	股份制	271,041	12,842(4)	313,383	磷酸一铵
Guangxi Luzhai Chemical Fertilizer Co., Ltd.	Liuzhou	Guangxi	(0772)6821571		State-owned				Twain-ammonium Phosphate
广西鹿寨化肥有限责任公司(2001)	柳州市	广西	(0772)6819206	1,603	国有企业	221,681	-	2,117,590	磷酸二铵
Yunnan Kunyang Phosphate Fertilizer Factory	Kunming	Yunnan	(0871)7891118		State-owned				Calcium Magnesium Phosphate Fertilizer
云南昆阳磷肥厂(1954)	昆明市	云南省	(0871)7891597	2,098	国有企业	198,002	-	265,201	钙镁磷肥
Sichuan Yinshan Chemical Industry (Group) Co.,Ltd.	Neijiang	Sichuan	(0832)5452219		Joint Stock				Calcium Superphosphate
四川银山化工（集团）股份有限公司(1963)	内江市	四川省	(0832)5452216	4,011	股份制	194,119	-	610,988	过磷酸钙

Top 10 Cities by Revenue 销售收入排名前10位城市	Province 省	Market share 市场份额 (%)	Number of firms 企业个数
Kunming 昆明市	Yunnan 云南省	10.97	19
Nanjing 南京市	Jiangsu 江苏省	10.71	4
Tongling 铜陵市	Anhui 安徽省	7.56	3
Honghe 红河州	Yunnan 云南省	4.89	4
Liuzhou 柳州市	Guangxi 广西	2.76	4
Xiaogan 孝感市	Hubei 湖北省	2.51	2
Huanggang 黄冈市	Hubei 湖北省	2.46	2
Guiyang 贵阳市	Guizhou 贵州省	2.39	4
Neijiang 内江市	Sichuan 四川省	2.11	2
Yancheng 盐城市	Jiangsu 江苏省	2.05	5

10 Major Wholesalers 十家主要批发商	City 城市	Province 省	Telephone/Fax 电话/传真
Ningbo Haitian Group General Company	Ningbo	Zhejiang	(0574)87195360
宁波海田集团总公司	宁波市	浙江省	(0574)87195821
Heilongjiang Agriculture Means Of Production Company	Harbin	Heilongjiang	(0451)88383752
黑龙江省农业生产资料公司	哈尔滨市	黑龙江省	(0451)88382367
Yantai Agriculture Means Of Production General Company	Yantai	Shandong	(0535)6216374
烟台市农业生产资料总公司	烟台市	山东省	(0535)6211348
Guangdong Agriculture Means Of Production General Company	Guangzhou	Guangdong	(020)87773051
广东省农业生产资料总公司	广州市	广东省	(020)87754117
Inner Mongolia Autonomous Region Agriculture & Animal Husbandry Means Of Production Co.,Ltd.	Huhhot	Inner Mongolia	(0471)6963132
内蒙古自治区农牧业生产资料股份有限公司	呼和浩特市	内蒙古	(0471)6964434
Shanghai Agriculture Means Of Production Company	Shanghai	Shanghai	(021)63807100
上海市农业生产资料公司	上海市	上海市	(021)63806807
Ningbo Haitian International Trade Co.,Ltd.	Ningbo	Zhejiang	(0574)87345251
宁波海田国际贸易有限公司	宁波市	浙江省	(0574)87345620
Fujian AMP Incorpration	Fuzhou	Fujian	(0591)7508666
福建省农资集团公司	福州市	福建省	(0591)7614839
Shandong Agricultural Machinery Group General Company	Jinan	Shandong	(0531)8951240
山东省农业机械集团总公司	济南市	山东省	(0531)8951240
Shandong Yantai Agriculture Means Of Production Purchasing Supply Station	Yantai	Shandong	(0535)6222126
山东省烟台市农业生产资料采购供应站	烟台市	山东省	(0535)6216440

2623: Potash Fertilizer 钾肥制造业

The industry accounts for 0.014% of the total revenue of China's industrial sector in 2002. The rate of return on assets is 2.95%. 77.14% of all firms in the industry made a profit while 22.86% had negative returns.The top province in terms of the industry's revenue is Qinghai, accounting for 55.60% of the total revenue.
2002年本行业收入占全行业的0.014%，资产利润率为2.95%。77.14%的企业赢利，22.86%的企业亏损。收入最高的省为青海省，占本行业的55.60%。

	Total number of firms 企业总数	Total number of employees 职工总数	Total revenue (Mil.RMB) 总销售收入（百万元）	Total profit (Mil.RMB) 总利润（百万元）	Return on assets 资产利润率（%）	Return on equity 权益利润率（%）	Labour productivity ('000 RMB/ worker) 劳动生产率（千元/人）	Debts/ assets 资产负债率（%）	Total assets (Mil.RMB) 总资产（百万元）
Industry Overall 行业总体	35	9,256	1,497	172	2.95	5.93	57.24	50.26	5,846

	Number of firms 企业个数	Average number of employees 平均职工人数	Average revenue ('000 RMB) 平均销售收入（千元）	Average profit ('000 RMB) 平均利润（千元）	Return on assets 资产利润率（%）	Return on equity 权益利润率（%）	Labour productivity ('000 RMB/ worker) 劳动生产率（千元/人）	Debts/ assets 资产负债率（%）	Average total assets ('000 RMB) 平均总资产（千元）
By ownership 产业所有权									
State-owned 国有	9	203	30,119	2,898	5.11	15.92	92.79	67.89	56,708
Collective-owned 集体	3	228	27,037	1,095	3.06	7.13	78.32	57.13	35,803
Foreign & Overseas Chinese Funded 三资	5	43	38,137	1,768	2.47	3.23	94.72	23.66	71,721
By regional distribution 地区分布									
Central-North 华北	7	264	38,538	977	1.08	2.24	20.54	52.06	90,898
Beijing 北京									
Tianjin 天津	2	125	43,728	985	1.61	2.20	22.41	26.57	61,078
Hebei 河北	2	111	11,386	609	1.54	3.08	33.27	50.01	39,598
Shanxi 山西	3	460	53,179	1,218	0.84	2.08	18.16	59.60	144,978
Inner Mongolia 内蒙古									
Northeast 东北	1	50	5,162	4	0.11	0.11	37.74	1.94	3,608
Liaoning 辽宁	1	50	5,162	4	0.11	0.11	37.74	1.94	3,608
Jilin 吉林									
Heilongjiang 黑龙江									
Central-East 华东	3	58	24,159	596	1.37	2.62	66.89	47.89	43,573
Shanghai 上海									
Jiangsu 江苏									
Zhejiang 浙江									
Anhui 安徽	1	38	3,500	198	2.17	3.40	39.47	36.15	9,120
Fujian 福建	1	50	50,772	1,560	1.57	2.93	107.80	46.34	99,217
Jiangxi 江西									
Shandong 山东	1	86	18,205	30	0.13	0.33	55.21	59.55	22,383
Central-South 中南	8	99	31,084	2,840	7.44	10.59	110.66	29.75	38,191
Henan 河南	2	248	51,746	4,145	9.47	23.71	53.98	60.08	43,787
Hubei 湖北	1	42	28,722	-2,284	-4.27	-5.10	233.45	16.40	53,519
Hunan 湖南	2	53	4,166	704	13.88	17.90	93.88	22.45	5,068
Guangdong 广东	2	43	39,052	4,793	7.39	8.52	368.42	13.25	64,846
Guangxi 广西	1	65	30,021	5,724	23.26	39.33	149.28	40.87	24,611
Hainan 海南									
Southwest 西南	1	45	5,700	29	0.90	1.77	17.29	49.35	3,236
Chongqing 重庆									
Sichuan 四川	1	45	5,700	29	0.90	1.77	17.29	49.35	3,236
Guizhou 贵州									
Yunnan 云南									
Tibet 西藏									
Northwest 西北	15	423	59,709	9,402	2.96	6.09	61.43	51.43	317,785
Shaanxi 陕西	1	103	63,142	12,439	9.30	16.27	178.36	42.88	133,813
Gansu 甘肃									
Qinghai 青海	14	446	59,464	9,186	2.78	5.74	59.50	51.68	330,926
Ningxia 宁夏									
Xinjiang 新疆									

2623: Potash Fertilizer 钾肥制造业

Year 年份	Number of firms 企业个数	Rate of change 变化率 (%)	Number of employees 职工人数 (人)	Rate of change 变化率 (%)	Total revenue (Mil. RMB) 总销售收入 (百万元)	Rate of change 变化率 (%)	Total profit (Mil RMB) 总利润 (百万元)	Rate of change 变化率 (%)
2000	45		9,686		1,432		131	
2001	34	-24.44	8,802	-9.13	1,348	-5.87	181	38.17
2002	35	2.94	9,256	5.16	1,497	11.05	172	-4.97

Major Products 主要产品	Output 产量	Unit 单位
Hydrochloric Acid(Content over 31%) 盐酸（含量３１％以上）	493	10,000 Tons 万吨
Potassic Fertilizer(Converting into containing K2O 100%) 钾肥（折含K2O 100%）	147	10,000 Tons 万吨

10 Main Firms with Maximal Revenue (year founded) 收入最大的十家主要企业（创办年份）	City 城市	Province 省	Telephone/fax 电话/传真	Number of employees 职工人数	Ownership 产业所有权	Revenue ('000 RMB) 销售收入 (千元)	Profit('000 RMB) (rank) 利润(千元) (排名)	Total assets ('000 RMB) 总资产 (千元)	Major products 主要产品
Qinghai Salt Lake Industry Group Co.,Ltd.	Haixi	Qinghai	(0979)8448448		State Enterprises				Potassium Chloride
青海盐湖集团工业有限责任公司(1996)	海西州	青海省	(0979)8448000	3,887	国有独资	505,889	92,431(1)	3,799,839	氯化钾
Shanxi Potassium Fertilizer Co.,Ltd.	Yuncheng	Shanxi	(0359)8962103		Limited-Liability				Potassium Sulfate
山西省钾肥责任有限公司(2000)	运城市	山西省	(0359)8962121	492	有限公司	101,600	-	331,933	硫酸钾
Puyang Organic Chemical Plant	Puyang	Henan	(0393)7222021		State-owned				Methylamine
濮阳市有机化工厂(1993)	濮阳市	河南省	(0393)7225966	410	国有企业	92,954	5,398(7)	74,153	甲胺
Haohai Enterprise Group Co.,Ltd.	Haixi	Qinghai	(0979)8463536		State-owned				Potassium Fertilizer
瀚海企业（集团）有限责任公司(1987)	海西州	青海省	(0979)8463216	679	国有企业	92,942	17,017(3)	204,927	钾肥
Germu Sanyuan Potassic Fertilizer Co.,Ltd.	Haixi	Qinghai	(0979)8448170		Joint Stock				Potassium Chloride
格尔木三元钾肥公司(1995)	海西州	青海省	(0979)8448173	158	股份制	76,901	17,749(2)	268,860	氯化钾
Wenshui Jintai Chemical Industry Co., Ltd.	Lvliang	Shanxi	(0358)3060005		Private Enterprises				Potassium Carbonate
文水县金泰化工有限公司(1996)	吕梁	山西省	(0358)3060004	658	私营独资	52,438	3,000(10)	80,000	碳酸钾
Qingshang Chemical Industry (Xiamen) Co.,Ltd.	Xiamen	Fujian	(0592)6512317		Overseas Chinese-funded				Potassium Sulfate
青上化工（厦门）有限公司(1996)	厦门市	福建省	(0592)6512312	50	港澳台资	50,772	1,560(14)	99,217	硫酸钾
Qingshang Chemical Industry (Guangzhou) Co., Ltd.	Guangzhou	Guangdong	(020)82701146		Overseas Chinese-funded				Potassium Sulfate Fertilizer
青上化工（广州）有限公司(1995)	广州市	广东省	(020)82701145	35	港澳台资	31,771	1,604(13)	64,511	硫酸钾肥
Liuzhou Dali Lemery Salt Factory	Liuzhou	Guangxi	(0772)2533187		Joint Stock				Potassium Sulfate
柳州市大力硫酸钾厂(1998)	柳州市	广西	(0772)2333187	63	股份制	30,021	3,724(8)	24,611	硫酸钾
Hubei Xiangqing Chemical Fertilizer Co., Ltd.	Yichang	Hubei	(0717)4219088		Overseas Chinese-funded				Potassium Sulfate
湖北香青化肥有限公司(1995)	宜昌市	湖北省	(0717)4219088	42	港澳台资	28,722	-	53,519	硫酸钾

Top 10 Cities by Revenue 销售收入排名前10位城市	Province 省	Market share 市场份额 (%)	Number of firms 企业个数
Haixi 海西州	Qinghai 青海省	55.60	14
Yuncheng 运城市	Shanxi 山西省	6.79	1
Puyang 濮阳市	Henan 河南省	6.21	1
Tianjin 天津市	Tianjin 天津市	5.84	2
Guangzhou 广州市	Guangdong 广东省	5.22	2
Xianyang 咸阳市	Shannxi 陕西省	4.22	1
Lvliang 吕梁地区	Shanxi 山西省	3.87	2
Xiamen 厦门市	Fujian 福建省	3.39	1
Liuzhou 柳州市	Guangxi 广西	2.00	1
Yichang 宜昌市	Hubei 湖北省	1.92	1

10 Major Wholesalers 十家主要批发商	City 城市	Province 省	Telephone/Fax 电话/传真
Ningbo Haitian Group General Company	Ningbo	Zhejiang	(0574)87195360
宁波海田集团总公司	宁波市	浙江省	(0574)87195821
Heilongjiang Agriculture Means Of Production Company	Harbin	Heilongjiang	(0451)88383752
黑龙江省农业生产资料公司	哈尔滨市	黑龙江省	(0451)88382367
Yantai Agriculture Means Of Production General Company	Yantai	Shandong	(0535)6216374
烟台市农业生产资料总公司	烟台市	山东省	(0535)6211348
Guangdong Agriculture Means Of Production General Company	Guangzhou	Guangdong	(020)87773051
广东省农业生产资料总公司	广州市	广东省	(020)87754117
Inner Mongolia Autonomous Region Agriculture & Animal Husbandry Means Of Production Co.,Ltd.	Huhhot	Inner Mongolia	(0471)6963132
内蒙古自治区农牧业生产资料股份有限公司	呼和浩特市	内蒙古	(0471)6964434
Shanghai Agriculture Means Of Production Company	Shanghai	Shanghai	(021)63807100
上海市农业生产资料公司	上海市	上海市	(021)63806807
Ningbo Haitian International Trade Co.,Ltd.	Ningbo	Zhejiang	(0574)87345251
宁波海田国际贸易有限公司	宁波市	浙江省	(0574)87345620
Fujian AMP Incorpration	Fuzhou	Fujian	(0591)7508666
福建省农资集团公司	福州市	福建省	(0591)7614839
Shandong Agricultural Machinery Group General Company	Jinan	Shandong	(0531)8951240
山东省农业机械集团总公司	济南市	山东省	(0531)8951240
Shandong Yantai Agriculture Means Of Production Purchasing Supply Station	Yantai	Shandong	(0535)6222126
山东省烟台市农业生产资料采购供应站	烟台市	山东省	(0535)6216440

2624: Compound Fertilizer 复合肥料制造业

The industry accounts for 0.197% of the total revenue of China's industrial sector in 2002. The rate of return on assets is 3.85%. 81.05% of all firms in the industry made a profit while 18.95% had negative returns.The top province in terms of the industry's revenue is Shandong, accounting for 26.88% of the total revenue.
2002年本行业收入占全行业的 0.197%，资产利润率为 3.85%。81.05%的企业赢利，18.95%的企业亏损。收入最高的省为山东省，占本行业的26.88%。

	Total number of firms 企业总数	Total number of employees 职工总数	Total revenue (Mil.RMB) 总销售收入(百万元)	Total profit (Mil.RMB) 总利润(百万元)	Return on assets 资产利润率(%)	Return on equity 权益利润率(%)	Labour productivity ('000 RMB/worker) 劳动生产率(千元/人)	Debts/assets 资产负债率(%)	Total assets (Mil.RMB) 总资产(百万元)
Industry Overall 行业总体	475	84,031	21,090	1,117	3.85	8.84	67.37	56.39	28,985

	Number of firms 企业个数	Average number of employees 平均职工人数	Average revenue ('000 RMB) 平均销售收入(千元)	Average profit ('000 RMB) 平均利润(千元)	Return on assets 资产利润率(%)	Return on equity 权益利润率(%)	Labour productivity ('000 RMB/worker) 劳动生产率(千元/人)	Debts/assets 资产负债率(%)	Average total assets ('000 RMB) 平均总资产(千元)
By ownership 产业所有权									
State-owned 国有	60	252	32,099	1,949	2.55	9.52	46.92	73.17	76,307
Collective-owned 集体	104	100	23,691	700	4.06	17.49	61.33	76.76	17,231
Foreign & Overseas Chinese Funded 三资	38	138	72,688	1,692	2.10	6.02	101.92	65.08	80,465
By regional distribution 地区分布									
Central-North 华北	38	291	71,630	2,885	2.21	3.91	77.45	43.43	130,309
Beijing 北京	5	97	36,867	599	2.90	42.46	142.81	93.18	20,674
Tianjin 天津	11	106	28,965	1,495	8.22	30.04	92.91	72.65	18,197
Hebei 河北	15	202	86,747	4,427	3.74	15.38	76.76	75.69	118,371
Shanxi 山西	3	2,050	288,568	7,586	0.80	0.99	69.28	19.26	946,664
Inner Mongolia 内蒙古	4	60	13,018	262	3.21	7.14	88.24	55.03	8,162
Northeast 东北	41	137	38,878	1,986	3.29	11.27	72.46	70.78	60,321
Liaoning 辽宁	15	195	46,846	3,849	4.40	16.93	45.91	73.98	87,381
Jilin 吉林	9	90	16,973	-209	-0.47	-1.01	69.62	53.66	44,649
Heilongjiang 黑龙江	17	112	43,445	1,504	3.36	13.08	114.45	74.31	44,743
Central-East 华东	152	219	64,877	4,115	4.81	10.51	73.52	54.22	85,500
Shanghai 上海	4	120	78,562	2,213	3.47	7.07	66.00	50.98	63,850
Jiangsu 江苏	63	124	34,894	351	1.45	4.85	52.29	70.08	24,208
Zhejiang 浙江	8	116	50,073	6,452	16.40	31.83	98.82	48.46	39,329
Anhui 安徽	18	164	36,384	368	1.19	4.76	29.47	75.00	30,909
Fujian 福建	8	99	19,038	71	0.71	1.44	24.47	51.00	9,995
Jiangxi 江西	5	454	94,569	-1,410	-0.52	-0.77	27.29	32.22	271,773
Shandong 山东	46	393	123,221	11,798	6.09	13.22	96.70	53.89	193,603
Central-South 中南	132	98	23,798	497	2.22	7.09	65.35	68.73	22,399
Henan 河南	29	94	13,537	733	5.17	26.16	46.80	80.24	14,189
Hubei 湖北	29	171	48,126	1,543	4.42	15.82	80.76	72.06	34,892
Hunan 湖南	19	98	21,312	-33	-0.16	-0.41	63.15	61.51	20,473
Guangdong 广东	46	66	18,515	-124	-0.55	-1.62	56.41	66.23	22,577
Guangxi 广西	2	68	6,552	44	0.42	0.98	12.65	57.19	10,326
Hainan 海南	7	40	11,904	830	6.83	11.34	110.21	39.82	12,161
Southwest 西南	78	222	43,093	2,888	4.61	12.35	56.61	62.63	62,590
Chongqing 重庆	8	945	139,641	15,233	6.42	20.59	55.73	68.80	237,165
Sichuan 四川	30	121	20,617	329	2.21	6.33	34.58	65.08	14,864
Guizhou 贵州	28	148	31,964	3,051	6.12	17.21	76.69	64.43	49,840
Yunnan 云南	12	164	60,883	677	0.71	1.40	58.35	49.23	95,273
Tibet 西藏									
Northwest 西北	34	111	12,072	290	1.36	2.36	32.14	42.43	21,341
Shaanxi 陕西	3	80	13,473	-126	-0.32	-0.98	47.90	67.14	39,089
Gansu 甘肃	22	34	5,897	163	4.08	6.83	73.03	40.30	4,008
Qinghai 青海									
Ningxia 宁夏	4	525	40,133	1,592	1.75	2.27	16.55	22.89	90,914
Xinjiang 新疆	5	137	15,953	57	0.18	0.61	29.79	70.51	31,301

2624: Compound Fertilizer 复合肥料制造业

Year 年份	Number of firms 企业个数	Rate of change 变化率 (%)	Number of employees 职工人数 (人)	Rate of change 变化率 (%)	Total revenue (Mil. RMB) 总销售收入 (百万元)	Rate of change 变化率 (%)	Total profit (Mil RMB) 总利润 (百万元)	Rate of change 变化率 (%)
2000	466		83,381		15,214		840	
2001	462	-0.86	87,676	5.15	18,588	22.18	1,018	21.19
2002	475	2.81	84,031	-4.16	21,090	13.46	1,117	9.72

Major Products 主要产品	Output 产量	Unit 单位
Phosphatic Ammonium Fertilizer 磷酸铵肥	257	10,000 Tons 万吨
Aqua Fortis Phosphate Fertilizer 硝酸磷肥	85	10,000 Tons 万吨

10 Main Firms with Maximal Revenue (year founded) 收入最大的十家主要企业（创办年份）	City 城市	Province 省	Telephone/fax 电话/传真	Number of employees 职工人数	Ownership 产业所有权	Revenue ('000 RMB) 销售收入 (千元)	Profit('000 RMB) (rank) 利润(千元) (排名)	Total assets ('000 RMB) 总资产 (千元)	Major products 主要产品
Shandong Lubei Enterprise Group General Company	Binzhou	Shandong	(0543)6451057		Joint Stock				Compound Fertilizer
山东鲁北企业集团总公司(1977)	滨州市	山东省	(0543)6451057	3,193	股份制	2,117,952	364,502(1)	5,062,321	磷铵
Sino-Arab Chemical Fertilizers Co.,Ltd.	Qinhuangdao	Hebei	(0335)3013245		Foreign Funded				NPK High Concentration Compound Fertilizer.NPK高
中国-阿拉伯化肥有限公司(1985)	秦皇岛市	河北省	(0335)7911301	545	外商投资	916,195	34,238(8)	1,218,277	浓度复合肥
Tianji Coal Chemical Industry Group Co.,Ltd.	Changzhi	Shanxi	(0355)6891243		Limited-Liability				Synthetic Ammonia
天脊煤化工集团有限公司(1987)	长治市	山西省	(0355)6763015	6,106	有限公司	836,677	15,931(13)	2,794,063	合成氨
Hubei Yangfeng Group	Jingmen	Hubei	(0724)8661388		Collective-owned				Compound Fertilizer硫基
湖北洋丰集团(1982)	荆门市	湖北省	(0724)8661389	1,200	集体企业	562,387	20,956(11)	348,838	氮磷钾肥
Liaoning Occident Special Fertilizer Co.,Ltd.	Jinzhou	Liaoning	(0416)5568061		Private Owned				Compound Fertilizer
辽宁西洋特肥股份有限公司(1998)	锦州市	辽宁省	(0416)5568126	1,200	私营企业	521,150	70,500(4)	540,009	复合肥
Shandong Xianglong Industrial Group Co., Ltd.	Linyi	Shandong	(0539)8328689		Foreign Funded				Compound Fertilizer
山东翔龙实业集团有限公司(2001)	临沂市	山东省	(0539)8313136	1,375	外商投资	516,699	15,877(14)	233,535	复合肥
Jiangxi Fertilizer Co.,Ltd.	Yingtan	Jiangxi	(0701)3358888		Limited-Liability				Compound Fertilizer
江西化肥有限责任公司(1991)	鹰潭市	江西省	(0701)3353851	2,084	有限公司	450,832	-	1,341,897	复合肥料
Fuling Chemical Industry Co., Ltd.	Chongqing	Chongqing	(023)72884093		Joint Stock				Mono-ammonium Phosphate
涪陵化工股份有限公司(1968)	重庆市	重庆市	(023)72884100	1,283	股份制	386,028	31,068(9)	473,623	磷酸一铵
Jiangsu Zhongdong Group Co., Ltd.	Changzhou	Jiangsu	(0519)3801103		Joint Stock				Compound Fertilizer
江苏中东集团有限公司(1998)	常州市	江苏省	(0519)3801182	658	股份制	343,650	7,280(22)	162,810	复合肥
Heilongjiang Dalong Ecological Fertilizer Co., Ltd.	Qiqihar	Heilongjiang	(0452)2936912		Private Owned				Compound Fertilizer
黑龙江省大龙生态肥股份有限公司(1994)	齐齐哈尔市	黑龙江省	(0452)8913777	260	私营企业	308,000	20,700(12)	257,040	复合肥

Top 10 Cities by Revenue 销售收入排名前10位城市	Province 省	Market share 市场份额 (%)	Number of firms 企业个数
Binzhou 滨州市	Shandong 山东省	10.04	1
Linyi 临沂市	Shandong 山东省	7.01	4
Chongqing 重庆市	Chongqing 重庆市	5.30	8
Qinhuangdao 秦皇岛市	Hebei 河北省	5.07	2
Changzhi 长治市	Shanxi 山西省	3.97	2
Guiyang 贵阳市	Guizhou 贵州省	2.91	8
Jingmen 荆门市	Hubei 湖北省	2.67	1
Wuxi 无锡市	Jiangsu 江苏省	2.54	4
Jinzhou 锦州市	Liaoning 辽宁省	2.50	2
Dezhou 德州市	Shandong 山东省	2.43	5

10 Major Wholesalers 十家主要批发商	City 城市	Province 省	Telephone/Fax 电话/传真
Ningbo Haitian Group General Company	Ningbo	Zhejiang	(0574)87195360
宁波海田集团总公司	宁波市	浙江省	(0574)87195821
Heilongjiang Agriculture Means Of Production Company	Harbin	Heilongjiang	(0451)88383752
黑龙江省农业生产资料公司	哈尔滨市	黑龙江省	(0451)88382367
Yantai Agriculture Means Of Production General Company	Yantai	Shandong	(0535)6216374
烟台市农业生产资料总公司	烟台市	山东省	(0535)6211348
Guangdong Agriculture Means Of Production General Company	Guangzhou	Guangdong	(020)87773051
广东省农业生产资料总公司	广州市	广东省	(020)87754117
Inner Mongolia Autonomous Region Agriculture & Animal Husbandry Means Of Production Co.,Ltd.	Huhhot	Inner Mongolia	(0471)6963132
内蒙古自治区农牧业生产资料股份有限公司	呼和浩特市	内蒙古	(0471)6964434
Shanghai Agriculture Means Of Production Company	Shanghai	Shanghai	(021)63807100
上海市农业生产资料公司	上海市	上海市	(021)63806807
Ningbo Haitian International Trade Co.,Ltd.	Ningbo	Zhejiang	(0574)87345251
宁波海田国际贸易有限公司	宁波市	浙江省	(0574)87345620
Fujian AMP Incorpration	Fuzhou	Fujian	(0591)7508666
福建省农资集团公司	福州市	福建省	(0591)7614839
Shandong Agricultural Machinery Group General Company	Jinan	Shandong	(0531)8951240
山东省农业机械集团总公司	济南市	山东省	(0531)8951240
Shandong Yantai Agriculture Means Of Production Purchasing Supply Station	Yantai	Shandong	(0535)6222126
山东省烟台市农业生产资料采购供应站	烟台市	山东省	(0535)6216440

2625: Trace Element Fertilizer 微量元素肥料制造业

The industry accounts for 0.003% of the total revenue of China's industrial sector in 2002. The rate of return on assets is 2.40%. 76.92% of all firms in the industry made a profit while 23.08% had negative returns.The top province in terms of the industry's revenue is Jilin, accounting for 13.92% of the total revenue.
2002年本行业收入占全行业的0.003%，资产利润率为2.40%。76.92%的企业赢利，23.08%的企业亏损。收入最高的省为吉林省，占本行业的13.92%。

	Total number of firms 企业总数	Total number of employees 职工总数	Total revenue (Mil.RMB) 总销售收入 (百万元)	Total profit (Mil.RMB) 总利润 (百万元)	Return on assets 资产利润率 (%)	Return on equity 权益利润率 (%)	Labour productivity ('000 RMB/ worker) 劳动生产率 (千元/人)	Debts/ assets 资产负债率 (%)	Total assets (Mil.RMB) 总资产 (百万元)
Industry Overall 行业总体	26	2,494	362	15	2.40	5.36	46.74	55.27	646

	Number of firms 企业个数	Average number of employees 平均职工人数	Average revenue ('000 RMB) 平均销售收入（千元）	Average profit ('000 RMB) 平均利润 (千元)	Return on assets 资产利润率 (%)	Return on equity 权益利润率 (%)	Labour productivity ('000 RMB/ worker) 劳动生产率 (千元/人)	Debts/ assets 资产负债率 (%)	Average total assets ('000 RMB) 平均总资产 (千元)
By ownership 产业所有权									
State-owned 国有	2	21	389	3	0.45	0.66	5.57	31.87	672
Collective-owned 集体	3	83	11,079	-90	-0.61	-4.07	29.15	85.12	14,786
Foreign & Overseas Chinese Funded 三资	5	114	22,648	742	1.07	2.47	56.10	56.77	69,611
By regional distribution 地区分布									
Central-North 华北	2	210	19,403	-283	-0.31	-0.66	33.54	52.55	89,945
Beijing 北京	1	240	18,233	145	0.68	0.80	18.73	15.48	21,466
Tianjin 天津									
Hebei 河北									
Shanxi 山西									
Inner Mongolia 内蒙古	1	180	20,573	-710	-0.45	-1.06	53.28	57.58	158,423
Northeast 东北	3	112	20,208	235	4.28	9.31	59.89	54.06	5,493
Liaoning 辽宁	1	92	9,024	177	6.38	7.65	20.66	16.52	2,773
Jilin 吉林	1	210	50,400	452	4.75	42.80	86.58	88.89	9,506
Heilongjiang 黑龙江	1	34	1,200	76	1.81	1.81	1.21		4,200
Central-East 华东	7	133	18,175	979	4.67	9.39	50.04	50.30	20,968
Shanghai 上海									
Jiangsu 江苏	1	120	14,970	660	3.95	46.15	28.38	91.45	16,730
Zhejiang 浙江	1	106	17,671	-204	-1.06	-2.90	24.65	63.34	19,164
Anhui 安徽	2	260	22,538	1,752	4.19	7.12	46.09	41.14	41,783
Fujian 福建									
Jiangxi 江西									
Shandong 山东	3	61	16,502	965	10.60	18.91	90.42	43.97	9,105
Central-South 中南	9	60	12,013	588	2.62	8.08	54.85	67.61	22,474
Henan 河南	4	30	6,730	240	3.67		68.44	169.78	6,529
Hubei 湖北									
Hunan 湖南	1	106	2,720	569	29.84	57.24	19.02	47.88	1,907
Guangdong 广东	3	65	15,990	-569	-3.26	-540.51	71.96	99.40	17,457
Guangxi 广西	1	115	30,506	5,473	4.49	6.64	44.56	32.37	121,874
Hainan 海南									
Southwest 西南	1	5	1,274	-312	-12.15		50.60	198.29	2,567
Chongqing 重庆									
Sichuan 四川									
Guizhou 贵州	1	5	1,274	-312	-12.15		50.60	198.29	2,567
Yunnan 云南									
Tibet 西藏									
Northwest 西北	4	67	6,484	878	3.59	5.85	23.18	38.60	24,414
Shaanxi 陕西	2	61	4,421	1,666	4.25	6.61	27.49	35.66	39,198
Gansu 甘肃	1	30	8,000	180	8.37	45.00	80.97	81.40	2,150
Qinghai 青海									
Ningxia 宁夏									
Xinjiang 新疆	1	117	9,096	-2	-0.01	-0.02	3.91	46.70	17,111

2625: Trace Element Fertilizer 微量元素肥料制造业

Year 年份	Number of firms 企业个数	Rate of change 变化率 (%)	Number of employees 职工人数 (人)	Rate of change 变化率 (%)	Total revenue (Mil. RMB) 总销售收入 (百万元)	Rate of change 变化率 (%)	Total profit (Mil RMB) 总利润 (百万元)	Rate of change 变化率 (%)
2000	25		2,317		283		14	
2001	32	28.00	3,276	41.39	567	100.35	16	14.29
2002	26	-18.75	2,494	-23.87	362	-36.16	15	-6.25

Major Products 主要产品	Output 产量	Unit 单位

10 Main Firms with Maximal Revenue (year founded) 收入最大的十家主要企业（创办年份）	City 城市	Province 省	Telephone/fax 电话/传真	Number of employees 职工人数	Ownership 产业所有权	Revenue ('000 RMB) 销售收入 (千元)	Profit('000 RMB) (rank) 利润(千元) (排名)	Total assets ('000 RMB) 总资产 (千元)	Major products 主要产品
Ji'nan Zhuangjiashen Green Fertilizer Co.,Ltd. 济南庄稼神绿色肥料有限公司(1996)	Jinan 济南市	Shandong 山东省	(0531)4551209 (0531)4551209	80	Private Owned 私营企业	31,500	2,694(2)	13,110	Zhongwei Double Effects Fertilizer双效中微肥王
Guangxi Beihai Penshibao Co.,Ltd. 广西北海喷施宝有限责任公司(1995)	Beihai 北海市	Guangxi 广西	(0779)2050998 (0779)2050999	115	Foreign Funded 外商投资	30,506	5,473(1)	121,874	Pen Shi Bao 喷施宝
Gaoming Jinkuizi Science & Technology Co.,Ltd. 高明金葵子科技有限公司(1998)	Foshan 佛山市	Guangdong 广东省	(0757)8832662 (0757)8832762	37	Overseas Chinese-funded 港澳台资	26,691	766(8)	13,027	Active Organic Fertilizer活性有机肥
Anhui Fengbao Chemical Industry Co., Ltd. 安徽丰宝化工股份有限公司(1998)	Hefei 合肥市	Anhui 安徽省	(0551)6511558 (0551)6511558	260	Joint Stock 股份制	24,977	2,173(4)	59,102	Compound Fertilizer 复合肥
Inner Mongolia Sanbao Kaolin Co., Ltd. 内蒙古三保高岭土有限公司(1994)	Huhhot 呼和浩特市	Inner Mongolia 内蒙古	(0471)3601034 (0471)3601169	180	Overseas Chinese-funded 港澳台资	20,573	-	158,423	Kaoline Fertilizer高岭土肥料
Shunde Kruppchen Plastics Technology Co.,Ltd. 顺德市克虏伯震雄塑料科技有限公司(1994)	Foshan 佛山市	Guangdong 广东省	(0765)2339100 (0765)2620366	117	Foreign Funded 外商投资	20,502	-	38,001	Hollow Shaping Machine中空成型机
Yuexi Zhuangzhong Chemical Fertilizer Co.,Ltd. 岳西县撞钟化肥公司(1985)	Anqing 安庆市	Anhui 安徽省	(0556)2478091 (0556)2478080	260	Limited-Liability 有限公司	20,098	1,330(5)	24,464	Microelement Fertilizer Compound Crystal微肥复合晶
Beijing Ciyuan Science & Technology Co.,Ltd. 北京磁源科技有限公司(2000)	Beijing 北京市	Beijing 北京市	(010)87704465 (010)87704473	240	Joint Stock 股份制	18,233	145(15)	21,466	Rare Earth Material 稀土材料
Hangzhou Yongdeli Industry & Trade General Company 杭州永得利工贸总公司(1993)	Hangzhou 杭州市	Zhejiang 浙江省	(0571)86013213 (0571)86012412	106	Collective-owned 集体企业	17,671	-	19,164	Acetic Acid Benzene DBED醋酸苯星DBED
Jiangsu Yuan Bioengineering Co., Ltd. 江苏原生物工程有限公司(2000)	Xuzhou 徐州市	Jiangsu 江苏省	(0516)7181552 (0516)7181551	120	Overseas Chinese-funded 港澳台资	14,970	660(9)	16,730	High Zoology Fertilizer 高生态肥

Top 10 Cities by Revenue 销售收入排名前10位城市	Province 省	Market share 市场份额 (%)	Number of firms 企业个数
Changchun 长春市	Jilin 吉林省	13.92	1
Foshan 佛山市	Guangdong 广东省	13.04	2
Jinan 济南市	Shandong 山东省	8.70	1
Beihai 北海市	Guangxi 广西	8.43	1
Hefei 合肥市	Anhui 安徽省	6.90	1
Huhhot 呼和浩特市	Inner Mongolia 内蒙古	5.68	1
Anqing 安庆市	Anhui 安徽省	5.55	1
Beijing 北京市	Beijing 北京市	5.04	1
Hangzhou 杭州市	Zhejiang 浙江省	4.88	1
Xuzhou 徐州市	Jiangsu 江苏省	4.14	1

10 Major Wholesalers 十家主要批发商	City 城市	Province 省	Telephone/Fax 电话/传真
Ningbo Haitian Group General Company 宁波海田集团总公司	Ningbo 宁波市	Zhejiang 浙江省	(0574)87195360 (0574)87195821
Heilongjiang Agriculture Means Of Production Company 黑龙江省农业生产资料公司	Harbin 哈尔滨市	Heilongjiang 黑龙江省	(0451)88383752 (0451)88382367
Yantai Agriculture Means Of Production General Company 烟台市农业生产资料总公司	Yantai 烟台市	Shandong 山东省	(0535)6216374 (0535)6211348
Guangdong Agriculture Means Of Production General Company 广东省农业生产资料总公司	Guangzhou 广州市	Guangdong 广东省	(020)87773051 (020)87754117
Inner Mongolia Autonomous Region Agriculture & Animal Husbandry Means Of Production Co.,Ltd. 内蒙古自治区农牧业生产资料股份有限公司	Huhhot 呼和浩特市	Inner Mongolia 内蒙古	(0471)6963132 (0471)6964434
Shanghai Agriculture Means Of Production Company 上海市农业生产资料公司	Shanghai 上海市	Shanghai 上海市	(021)63807100 (021)63806807
Ningbo Haitian International Trade Co.,Ltd. 宁波海田国际贸易有限公司	Ningbo 宁波市	Zhejiang 浙江省	(0574)87345251 (0574)87345620
Fujian AMP Incorpration 福建省农资集团公司	Fuzhou 福州市	Fujian 福建省	(0591)7508666 (0591)7614839
Shandong Agricultural Machinery Group General Company 山东省农业机械集团总公司	Jinan 济南市	Shandong 山东省	(0531)8951240 (0531)8951240
Shandong Yantai Agriculture Means Of Production Purchasing Supply Station 山东省烟台市农业生产资料采购供应站	Yantai 烟台市	Shandong 山东省	(0535)6222126 (0535)6216440

2629: Other Chemical Fertilizer 其他化学肥料制造业

The industry accounts for 0.058% of the total revenue of China's industrial sector in 2002. The rate of return on assets is -2.32%. 78.43% of all firms in the industry made a profit while 21.57% had negative returns.The top province in terms of the industry's revenue is Hunan, accounting for 25.58% of the total revenue.
2002年本行业收入占全行业的 0.058%，资产利润率为 -2.32%。78.43%的企业赢利，21.57%的企业亏损。收入最高的省为湖南省，占本行业的25.58%。

	Total number of firms 企业总数	Total number of employees 职工总数	Total revenue (Mil.RMB) 总销售收入(百万元)	Total profit (Mil.RMB) 总利润(百万元)	Return on assets 资产利润率(%)	Return on equity 权益利润率(%)	Labour productivity ('000 RMB/worker) 劳动生产率(千元/人)	Debts/assets 资产负债率(%)	Total assets (Mil.RMB) 总资产(百万元)
Industry Overall 行业总体	204	29,622	6,202	-205	-2.32	-6.67	54.44	65.18	8,836

	Number of firms 企业个数	Average number of employees 平均职工人数	Average revenue ('000 RMB) 平均销售收入(千元)	Average profit ('000 RMB) 平均利润(千元)	Return on assets 资产利润率(%)	Return on equity 权益利润率(%)	Labour productivity ('000 RMB/worker) 劳动生产率(千元/人)	Debts/assets 资产负债率(%)	Average total assets ('000 RMB) 平均总资产(千元)
By ownership 产业所有权									
State-owned 国有	36	91	11,925	199	1.04	4.72	40.91	77.94	19,087
Collective-owned 集体	45	170	33,845	1,456	5.32	21.95	45.44	75.74	27,353
Foreign & Overseas Chinese Funded 三资	24	80	24,041	1,604	4.76	7.64	78.74	37.68	33,681
By regional distribution 地区分布									
Central-North 华北	22	63	23,100	1,735	9.13	14.98	81.89	39.04	19,001
Beijing 北京	9	31	13,533	714	5.96	12.45	95.76	52.14	11,983
Tianjin 天津	3	102	40,380	2,580	18.05	72.07	46.21	74.95	14,293
Hebei 河北	5	64	26,276	2,562	6.58	7.71	149.41	14.59	38,934
Shanxi 山西	3	137	38,080	1,815	12.43	41.32	25.12	69.92	14,607
Inner Mongolia 内蒙古	2	37	9,820	2,871	19.93	44.07	201.78	54.77	14,401
Northeast 东北	18	132	17,193	1,512	3.48	6.92	62.32	49.68	43,394
Liaoning 辽宁	5	162	30,548	911	1.66	6.43	81.79	74.11	54,768
Jilin 吉林	6	86	12,338	213	1.31	3.00	97.92	56.49	16,338
Heilongjiang 黑龙江	7	151	11,815	3,053	5.22	7.65	30.01	31.69	58,461
Central-East 华东	73	181	34,913	1,289	4.91	20.12	50.30	75.58	26,235
Shanghai 上海	5	79	8,598	77	1.22	2.59	21.84	53.04	6,370
Jiangsu 江苏	20	164	37,980	1,154	7.47	29.46	55.96	74.64	15,451
Zhejiang 浙江	3	322	43,498	2,214	5.04	18.52	47.84	72.78	43,911
Anhui 安徽	3	61	5,420	200	4.46	9.65	21.73	53.78	4,490
Fujian 福建	8	64	13,900	703	3.87	7.92	23.89	51.12	18,152
Jiangxi 江西	7	116	16,608	334	2.55	10.79	28.07	76.35	13,076
Shandong 山东	27	262	50,809	2,053	4.65	23.13	54.79	79.90	44,160
Central-South 中南	61	151	39,955	-5,759	-7.66	-25.22	68.28	69.61	75,146
Henan 河南	7	67	7,533	288	3.10	21.10	25.64	85.32	9,296
Hubei 湖北	10	128	11,721	647	8.34	23.19	44.72	64.04	7,756
Hunan 湖南	6	733	264,382	-62,784	-9.83	-33.72	95.89	70.84	638,491
Guangdong 广东	13	53	21,000	1,384	10.93	21.73	86.66	49.69	12,661
Guangxi 广西	24	95	16,791	85	0.48	1.38	33.15	65.39	17,818
Hainan 海南	1	60	5,042	-3,115	-17.25	-41.89	9.67	58.81	18,056
Southwest 西南	13	72	8,867	44	0.51	1.46	26.88	64.97	8,497
Chongqing 重庆	2	59	22,429	79	1.16	2.97	7.34	61.14	6,795
Sichuan 四川	3	48	11,135	595	6.24	12.10	94.03	48.44	9,538
Guizhou 贵州	8	85	4,626	-172	-2.02	-7.37	16.11	72.66	8,532
Yunnan 云南									
Tibet 西藏									
Northwest 西北	17	148	16,682	-814	-1.35	-2.61	13.30	48.48	60,440
Shaanxi 陕西	7	252	22,103	-4,798	-4.00	-7.17	-9.96	44.16	119,809
Gansu 甘肃	3	33	4,325	193	11.87	20.63	57.16	42.48	1,626
Qinghai 青海									
Ningxia 宁夏	1	186	6,217	-2,206	-9.68	-140.33	-1.42	93.10	22,790
Xinjiang 新疆	6	79	18,280	3,562	13.26	37.71	96.87	64.83	26,858

2629: Other Chemical Fertilizer 其他化学肥料制造业

Year 年份	Number of firms 企业个数	Rate of change 变化率(%)	Number of employees 职工人数(人)	Rate of change 变化率(%)	Total revenue (Mil. RMB) 总销售收入(百万元)	Rate of change 变化率(%)	Total profit (Mil RMB) 总利润(百万元)	Rate of change 变化率(%)
2000	158		25,628		3,016		66	
2001	203	28.48	25,642	0.05	4,177	38.49	138	109.09
2002	204	0.49	29,622	15.52	6,202	48.48	-205	

Major Products 主要产品	Output 产量	Unit 单位
Fertilizer 农用氮、磷、钾化学肥料总计（折纯）	3,666	10,000 Tons 万吨

10 Main Firms with Maximal Revenue (year founded) 收入最大的十家主要企业（创办年份）	City 城市	Province 省	Telephone/fax 电话/传真	Number of employees 职工人数	Ownership 产业所有权	Revenue ('000 RMB) 销售收入(千元)	Profit('000 RMB) (rank) 利润(千元)(排名)	Total assets ('000 RMB) 总资产(千元)	Major products 主要产品
PetroChina Co.,Ltd. Baling Filiale	Yueyang	Hunan	(0730)8501988		Joint Stock				Carbamide
中国石油化工股份公司巴陵分公司(1979)	岳阳市	湖南省	(0730)8501303	3,451	股份制	1,316,590	-	3,412,298	尿素
Hunan Yueyang Chemical Industry Co.,Ltd.	Yueyang	Hunan	(0730)8320311		Joint Stock				Carbamide
湖南岳阳化工有限公司(1967)	岳阳市	湖南省	(0730)8320311	683	股份制	210,716	20,465(2)	396,633	尿素
Nanjing Chemistry Industry Co.,Ltd. Collective Enterprise Management	Nanjing	Jiangsu	(025)7766438		Collective-owned				Compound Fertilizer
Department南京化学工业有限公司集体企业管理处(1978)	南京市	江苏省	(025)7792933	2,307	集体企业	163,410	2,570(27)	95,340	复合肥
Linyi Jindadi Compound Fertilizer Co.,Ltd.	Linyi	Shandong	(0539)6218888		Limited-Liability				Compound Fertilizer
临沂市金大地复合肥有限公司(1998)	临沂市	山东省	(0539)6212637	219	有限公司	162,211	10,222(7)	114,632	复混肥
Linyi Huafeng Chemical Fertilizer Co.,Ltd.	Linyi	Shandong	(0539)6216666		Limited-Liability				Compound Fertilizer
临沂市华丰化肥有限公司(1998)	临沂市	山东省	(0539)6201077	800	有限公司	144,587	5,021(13)	43,878	复混肥
Taicang Huifeng Chemical Fertilizer Ltd. Company	Suzhou	Jiangsu	(0512)53100517		Overseas Chinese-funded				Other Fertilizer
太仓汇丰化学肥料有限公司(1998)	苏州市	江苏省	(0512)53103476	63	港澳台资	139,400	2,320(29)	80,480	其他肥料
Linshu Fengshou Chemical Fertilizer Factory	Linyi	Shandong	(0539)6212292		Collective-owned				Compound Fertilizer
临沭县丰收化肥厂(1996)	临沂市	山东省	(0539)6212167	586	集体企业	130,170	3,094(22)	57,713	复混肥
Yantai Xinhai Chemical Fertilizer Industry Co.,Ltd.	Yantai	Shandong	(0535)3862059		State-owned				Ammonium Hydrogen Carbonate
烟台鑫海化肥工业有限公司(1973)	烟台市	山东省	(0535)3861333	614	国有企业	110,110	1,789(38)	159,819	碳酸氢铵
Tianjin Jinqu Chemical Industry Factory	Tianjin	Tianjin	(022)26823295		Collective-owned				α-Naphthol
天津市进取化工厂(1997)	天津市	天津市	(022)26398513	270	集体企业	103,640	7,430(8)	39,010	α-萘酚
Pilot Plant Of Shenyang Research Institute Of Chemical	Shenyang	Liaoning	(024)25641402		State-owned				Chlorin Quinoline Acid
Industry 沈阳化工研究院试验厂(1989)	沈阳市	辽宁省	(024)85869043	430	国有企业	84,744	-	116,850	氯喹啉酸

Top 10 Cities by Revenue 销售收入排名前10位城市	Province 省	Market share 市场份额(%)	Number of firms 企业个数
Yueyang 岳阳市	Hunan 湖南省	24.62	2
Linyi 临沂市	Shandong 山东省	12.74	12
Yantai 烟台市	Shandong 山东省	6.05	4
Lianyungang 连云港市	Jiangsu 江苏省	5.47	12
Guangzhou 广州市	Guangdong 广东省	3.06	6
Nanjing 南京市	Jiangsu 江苏省	2.63	1
Suzhou 苏州市	Jiangsu 江苏省	2.25	1
Beijing 北京市	Beijing 北京市	1.96	9
Xianyang 咸阳市	Shannxi 陕西省	1.96	2
Tianjin 天津市	Tianjin 天津市	1.95	3

10 Major Wholesalers 十家主要批发商	City 城市	Province 省	Telephone/Fax 电话/传真
Ningbo Haitian Group General Company	Ningbo	Zhejiang	(0574)87195360
宁波海田集团总公司	宁波市	浙江省	(0574)87195821
Heilongjiang Agriculture Means Of Production Company	Harbin	Heilongjiang	(0451)88383752
黑龙江省农业生产资料公司	哈尔滨市	黑龙江省	(0451)88382367
Yantai Agriculture Means Of Production General Company	Yantai	Shandong	(0535)6216374
烟台市农业生产资料总公司	烟台市	山东省	(0535)6211348
Guangdong Agriculture Means Of Production General Company	Guangzhou	Guangdong	(020)87773051
广东省农业生产资料总公司	广州市	广东省	(020)87754117
Inner Mongolia Autonomous Region Agriculture & Animal Husbandry Means Of Production Co.,Ltd.	Huhhot	Inner Mongolia	(0471)6963132
内蒙古自治区农牧业生产资料股份有限公司	呼和浩特市	内蒙古	(0471)6964434
Shanghai Agriculture Means Of Production Company	Shanghai	Shanghai	(021)63807100
上海市农业生产资料公司	上海市	上海市	(021)63806807
Ningbo Haitian International Trade Co.,Ltd.	Ningbo	Zhejiang	(0574)87345251
宁波海田国际贸易有限公司	宁波市	浙江省	(0574)87345620
Fujian AMP Incorpration	Fuzhou	Fujian	(0591)7508666
福建省农资集团公司	福州市	福建省	(0591)7614839
Shandong Agricultural Machinery Group General Company	Jinan	Shandong	(0531)8951240
山东省农业机械集团总公司	济南市	山东省	(0531)8951240
Shandong Yantai Agriculture Means Of Production Purchasing Supply Station	Yantai	Shandong	(0535)6222126
山东省烟台市农业生产资料采购供应站	烟台市	山东省	(0535)6216440

2631: Agricultural Chemical Materials 农药原药制造业

The industry accounts for 0.182% of the total revenue of China's industrial sector in 2002. The rate of return on assets is 2.53%. 80.16% of all firms in the industry made a profit while 19.84% had negative returns.The top province in terms of the industry's revenue is Jiangsu, accounting for 42.99% of the total revenue.
2002年本行业收入占全行业的 0.182%，资产利润率为 2.53%。80.16%的企业赢利，19.84%的企业亏损。收入最高的省为江苏省，占本行业的42.99%。

	Total number of firms 企业总数	Total number of employees 职工总数	Total revenue (Mil.RMB) 总销售收入 (百万元)	Total profit (Mil.RMB) 总利润 (百万元)	Return on assets 资产利润率 (%)	Return on equity 权益利润率 (%)	Labour productivity ('000 RMB/ worker) 劳动生产率 (千元/人)	Debts/ assets 资产负债率 (%)	Total assets (Mil.RMB) 总资产 (百万元)
Industry Overall 行业总体	247	90,753	19,489	736	2.53	6.54	55.46	61.27	29,049

	Number of firms 企业个数	Average number of employees 平均职工人数	Average revenue ('000 RMB) 平均销售收入（千元）	Average profit ('000 RMB) 平均利润 (千元)	Return on assets 资产利润率 (%)	Return on equity 权益利润率 (%)	Labour productivity ('000 RMB/ worker) 劳动生产率 (千元/人)	Debts/ assets 资产负债率 (%)	Average total assets ('000 RMB) 平均总资产 (千元)
By ownership 产业所有权									
State-owned 国有	38	285	40,890	13	0.02	0.11	36.81	85.85	81,928
Collective-owned 集体	30	146	34,623	2,323	9.14	24.38	52.69	62.49	25,407
Foreign & Overseas Chinese Funded 三资	25	196	103,039	8,995	9.86	25.37	165.30	61.15	91,248
By regional distribution 地区分布									
Central-North 华北	32	346	49,203	872	0.77	3.18	27.27	75.74	113,026
Beijing 北京									
Tianjin 天津	12	170	49,265	2,352	3.94	8.38	35.06	52.99	59,708
Hebei 河北	17	513	54,058	-154	-0.10	-0.44	24.58	77.47	155,782
Shanxi 山西	3	97	21,437	767	0.91		53.36	122.27	84,015
Inner Mongolia 内蒙古									
Northeast 东北	17	188	24,423	-441	-0.63	-3.52	44.60	82.12	69,931
Liaoning 辽宁	11	205	33,531	-432	-0.47	-3.23	62.62	85.53	92,419
Jilin 吉林	4	89	6,033	306	1.65	3.55	6.01	53.61	18,554
Heilongjiang 黑龙江	2	291	11,110	-1,981	-4.04	-12.78	-1.93	68.39	49,000
Central-East 华东	137	408	100,255	5,141	4.47	10.76	65.78	58.40	114,878
Shanghai 上海	12	164	72,577	3,350	6.11	15.78	186.02	61.28	54,814
Jiangsu 江苏	61	484	137,345	7,535	5.53	14.72	76.25	62.41	136,202
Zhejiang 浙江	23	399	103,604	5,326	4.59	9.71	54.59	52.75	116,042
Anhui 安徽	8	186	38,652	4,403	11.83	26.23	68.50	54.90	37,223
Fujian 福建	5	444	73,731	1,567	0.64	1.42	22.73	54.84	243,742
Jiangxi 江西	8	184	23,351	-118	-0.41	-0.72	29.65	42.69	28,530
Shandong 山东	20	502	61,917	1,990	1.69	3.64	36.15	53.65	117,924
Central-South 中南	46	353	67,276	635	0.55	1.42	47.85	61.40	116,125
Henan 河南	15	83	17,956	1,115	10.48	36.35	69.99	71.18	10,637
Hubei 湖北	13	673	135,262	-2,082	-0.99	-2.16	50.65	54.22	211,062
Hunan 湖南	8	488	78,528	4,331	1.99	5.23	40.79	61.98	217,715
Guangdong 广东	6	207	53,007	1,192	1.31	11.91	46.79	88.97	90,759
Guangxi 广西	4	279	30,177	-565	-1.49	-6.03	26.93	75.37	38,028
Hainan 海南									
Southwest 西南	13	320	49,240	-1,295	-0.55	-1.11	30.97	50.98	237,626
Chongqing 重庆	3	850	121,379	-19,731	-6.07	-15.92	25.31	61.90	325,202
Sichuan 四川	5	167	27,544	1,689	3.69	7.40	40.43	50.20	45,822
Guizhou 贵州	3	58	12,834	-805	-5.75	-19.10	8.09	69.89	13,996
Yunnan 云南	2	305	49,883	18,163	1.97	3.58	48.25	44.87	921,214
Tibet 西藏									
Northwest 西北	2	94	14,689	-384	-1.03	-2.08	30.03	50.36	37,066
Shaanxi 陕西	1	76	19,925	-891	-6.07	-10.57	17.45	42.54	14,673
Gansu 甘肃									
Qinghai 青海									
Ningxia 宁夏									
Xinjiang 新疆	1	111	9,452	124	0.21	0.44	38.65	52.29	59,458

Year 年份	Number of firms 企业个数	Rate of change 变化率 (%)	Number of employees 职工人数 (人)	Rate of change 变化率 (%)	Total revenue (Mil. RMB) 总销售收入 (百万元)	Rate of change 变化率 (%)	Total profit (Mil RMB) 总利润 (百万元)	Rate of change 变化率 (%)
2000	247		112,833		17,577		671	
2001	229	-7.29	98,353	-12.83	17,851	1.56	663	-1.19
2002	247	7.86	90,753	-7.73	19,489	9.18	736	11.01

Major Products 主要产品	Output 产量	Unit 单位
Pesticide Emulsion 农药乳剂	272,134	Ton 吨
Farm Chemical 化学农药	82	10,000 Tons 万吨

10 Main Firms with Maximal Revenue (year founded) 收入最大的十家主要企业（创办年份）	City 城市	Province 省	Telephone/ fax 电话/ 传真	Number of employees 职工人数	Ownership 产业所有权	Revenue ('000 RMB) 销售收入 (千元)	Profit('000 RMB) (rank) 利润(千元) (排名)	Total assets ('000 RMB) 总资产 (千元)	Major products 主要产品
Jiangsu Chemical Pesticide Group Co., Ltd.	Suzhou	Jiangsu	(0512)65251605		State Enterprises				Methamidophos
江苏化工农药集团有限公司(1990)	苏州市	江苏省	(0512)65251980	3,076	国有独资	1,628,041	66,661(2)	1,884,984	甲胺磷
Zhejiang Xin'an Chemical Industry Group Co.,Ltd.	Hangzhou	Zhejiang	(0571)64723891		Joint Stock				Glyphosate
浙江新安化工集团股份有限公司(1965)	杭州市	浙江省	(0571)64721344	1,926	股份制	714,504	38,169(7)	790,087	草甘膦
Nantong Jiangshan Pesticide Chemical Industry Co.,Ltd.	Nantong	Jiangsu	(0513)3517081		Joint Stock				Caustic Soda
南通江山农药化工股份有限公司(1958)	南通市	江苏省	(0513)3510690	1,622	股份制	625,547	51,200(3)	902,331	烧碱
Jiangsu Changlong Chemical Industry Co.,Ltd.	Changzhou	Jiangsu	(0519)5481542		Limited-Liability				Pesticide
江苏常隆化工有限公司(1958)	常州市	江苏省	(0519)5210023	1,192	有限公司	552,990	45,060(5)	485,550	农药
Changzhou Kangmei Chemical Industry Ltd. Company	Changzhou	Jiangsu	(0519)2882229		Foreign Funded				Japothrin
常州康美化工有限公司(1995)	常州市	江苏省	(0519)2561216	410	外商投资	469,360	49,020(4)	233,760	喃烯菊酯
Shandong Dacheng Pesticide Co.,Ltd.	Zibo	Shandong	(0533)2111999		Joint Stock				Caustic Soda
山东大成农药股份有限公司(1949)	淄博市	山东省	(0533)2113511	3,504	股份制	442,294	6,414(35)	1,013,696	烧碱
Hangzhou Qingfeng Agricultural Chemistry Co.,Ltd.	Hangzhou	Zhejiang	(0571)86408951		Limited-Liability				Pesticide Raw Medicine
杭州庆丰农化有限公司(2000)	杭州市	浙江省	(0571)86406335	1,514	有限公司	428,793	13,371(17)	377,671	农药原药
Jiangsu Kesheng Group Company	Yancheng	Jiangsu	(0515)6267666		Joint Stock				Sao Man Jing
江苏克胜集团公司(1992)	盐城市	江苏省	(0515)6264301	2,495	股份制	420,800	12,160(19)	142,660	扫螨净
Kunshan Kunhua Group (Industrial)Company	Suzhou	Jiangsu	(0512)57302401		State-owned				Acetochlor
昆山昆化集团(实业)公司(江苏绿利来)(1958)	苏州市	江苏省	(0512)57353741	2,098	国有企业	348,280	2,540(64)	493,400	乙草胺
Chongqing Minfeng Agricultural Chemistry Co.,Ltd.	Chongqing	Chongqing	(023)65180520		Joint Stock				Cygon
重庆民丰农化股份有限公司(1999)	重庆市	重庆市	(023)65180655	2,230	股份制	342,880	-	955,868	乐果

Top 10 Cities by Revenue 销售收入排名前10位城市	Province 省	Market share 市场份额 (%)	Number of firms 企业个数
Suzhou 苏州市	Jiangsu 江苏省	11.56	5
Nantong 南通市	Jiangsu 江苏省	8.23	9
Hangzhou 杭州市	Zhejiang 浙江省	7.52	9
Yancheng 盐城市	Jiangsu 江苏省	7.47	10
Jingzhou 荆州市	Hubei 湖北省	7.41	4
Changzhou 常州市	Jiangsu 江苏省	6.08	6
Shanghai 上海市	Shanghai 上海市	4.47	12
Nanjing 南京市	Jiangsu 江苏省	4.12	7
Tianjin 天津市	Tianjin 天津市	3.03	12
Zibo 淄博市	Shandong 山东省	2.40	3

10 Major Wholesalers 十家主要批发商	City 城市	Province 省	Telephone/Fax 电话/传真
Ningbo Haitian Group General Company	Ningbo	Zhejiang	(0574)87195360
宁波海田集团总公司	宁波市	浙江省	(0574)87195821
Heilongjiang Agriculture Means Of Production Company	Harbin	Heilongjiang	(0451)88383752
黑龙江省农业生产资料公司	哈尔滨市	黑龙江省	(0451)88382367
Yantai Agriculture Means Of Production General Company	Yantai	Shandong	(0535)6216374
烟台市农业生产资料总公司	烟台市	山东省	(0535)6211348
Guangdong Agriculture Means Of Production General Company	Guangzhou	Guangdong	(020)87773051
广东省农业生产资料总公司	广州市	广东省	(020)87754117
Inner Mongolia Autonomous Region Agriculture & Animal Husbandry Means Of Production Co.,Ltd.	Huhhot	Inner Mongolia	(0471)6963132
内蒙古自治区农牧业生产资料股份有限公司	呼和浩特市	内蒙古	(0471)6964434
Shanghai Agriculture Means Of Production Company	Shanghai	Shanghai	(021)63807100
上海市农业生产资料公司	上海市	上海市	(021)63806807
Ningbo Haitian International Trade Co.,Ltd.	Ningbo	Zhejiang	(0574)87345251
宁波海田国际贸易有限公司	宁波市	浙江省	(0574)87345620
Fujian AMP Incorpration	Fuzhou	Fujian	(0591)7508666
福建省农资集团公司	福州市	福建省	(0591)7614839
Shandong Agricultural Machinery Group General Company	Jinan	Shandong	(0531)8951240
山东省农业机械集团总公司	济南市	山东省	(0531)8951240
Shandong Yantai Agriculture Means Of Production Purchasing Supply Station	Yantai	Shandong	(0535)6222126
山东省烟台市农业生产资料采购供应站	烟台市	山东省	(0535)6216440

2633: Agricultural Chemical Products 农药制剂制造业

The industry accounts for 0.107% of the total revenue of China's industrial sector in 2002. The rate of return on assets is 2.88%. 77.03% of all firms in the industry made a profit while 22.97% had negative returns.The top province in terms of the industry's revenue is Jiangsu, accounting for 28.01% of the total revenue.
2002年本行业收入占全行业的0.107%，资产利润率为2.88%。77.03%的企业赢利，22.97%的企业亏损。收入最高的省为江苏省，占本行业的28.01%。

	Total number of firms 企业总数	Total number of employees 职工总数	Total revenue (Mil.RMB) 总销售收入 (百万元)	Total profit (Mil.RMB) 总利润 (百万元)	Return on assets 资产利润率 (%)	Return on equity 权益利润率 (%)	Labour productivity ('000 RMB/ worker) 劳动生产率 (千元/人)	Debts/ assets 资产负债率 (%)	Total assets (Mil.RMB) 总资产 (百万元)
Industry Overall 行业总体	370	57,587	11,430	384	2.88	9.57	50.10	69.91	13,325

	Number of firms 企业个数	Average number of employees 平均职工人数	Average revenue ('000 RMB) 平均销售收入 (千元)	Average profit ('000 RMB) 平均利润 (千元)	Return on assets 资产利润率 (%)	Return on equity 权益利润率 (%)	Labour productivity ('000 RMB/ worker) 劳动生产率 (千元/人)	Debts/ assets 资产负债率 (%)	Average total assets ('000 RMB) 平均总资产 (千元)
By ownership 产业所有权									
State-owned 国有	63	180	23,486	-23	-0.06	-0.53	28.03	87.70	34,962
Collective-owned 集体	61	96	21,693	1,374	12.30	40.10	64.38	69.32	11,172
Foreign & Overseas Chinese Funded 三资	25	123	41,048	1,788	4.62	13.64	100.40	66.13	38,701
By regional distribution 地区分布									
Central-North 华北	44	170	32,349	2,642	7.56	22.96	64.32	67.08	34,943
Beijing 北京	7	65	6,946	-375	-2.53	-9.68	24.93	73.87	14,847
Tianjin 天津	9	96	26,377	1,880	12.09	18.48	68.25	34.59	15,555
Hebei 河北	22	255	48,596	4,219	8.58	31.89	67.05	73.10	49,197
Shanxi 山西	5	97	6,891	181	1.01	10.70	31.02	90.58	17,998
Inner Mongolia 内蒙古	1	62	33,786	8,205	6.77	9.34	312.00	27.55	121,247
Northeast 东北	17	165	30,157	1,246	2.46	10.51	57.25	76.57	50,599
Liaoning 辽宁	6	207	60,879	4,280	4.09	10.95	85.85	62.67	104,728
Jilin 吉林	4	77	12,629	33	0.14	0.84	74.91	82.74	22,980
Heilongjiang 黑龙江	7	179	13,839	-662	-3.31		24.63	134.96	19,986
Central-East 华东	179	156	37,776	1,153	3.16	11.97	50.43	73.60	36,466
Shanghai 上海	4	441	108,332	-18,778	-5.70	-112.55	12.40	94.94	329,704
Jiangsu 江苏	70	162	45,734	1,705	4.79	17.77	44.49	73.04	35,600
Zhejiang 浙江	35	153	36,234	2,010	5.34	13.18	55.50	59.49	37,658
Anhui 安徽	14	96	6,813	137	0.84	2.67	25.79	68.31	16,210
Fujian 福建	3	42	7,479	1,284	10.81	16.59	92.29	34.83	11,870
Jiangxi 江西	12	144	13,399	-94	-0.39	-1.21	34.10	68.02	24,362
Shandong 山东	41	155	38,546	2,124	10.32	33.20	76.15	68.91	20,577
Central-South 中南	101	149	23,110	328	0.89	2.68	47.84	66.81	36,833
Henan 河南	36	144	20,298	362	1.03	4.54	53.65	77.35	35,181
Hubei 湖北	17	104	12,714	-25	-0.22	-0.92	32.25	75.81	11,479
Hunan 湖南	18	222	22,875	-531	-1.14	-4.44	28.73	74.28	46,473
Guangdong 广东	14	153	47,204	1,134	1.55	3.34	60.41	53.41	72,968
Guangxi 广西	14	126	19,899	621	2.79	6.62	71.15	57.79	22,247
Hainan 海南	2	86	18,025	2,762	6.21	7.10	81.62	12.56	44,468
Southwest 西南	23	169	16,594	414	1.75	4.07	27.33	56.93	23,606
Chongqing 重庆	3	160	11,206	643	6.77	7.95	21.88	14.94	9,508
Sichuan 四川	14	216	23,225	584	1.74	4.23	30.53	58.89	33,601
Guizhou 贵州	3	42	3,911	119	1.62	3.08	18.74	47.40	7,344
Yunnan 云南	3	87	3,720	-314	-4.29	-20.46	4.42	79.02	7,322
Tibet 西藏									
Northwest 西北	6	66	2,775	-434	-1.91	-2.38	16.62	19.78	22,783
Shaanxi 陕西	3	96	3,907	-1,019	-2.58	-2.96	10.72	13.04	39,523
Gansu 甘肃	3	36	1,642	150	2.49	6.88	32.49	63.85	6,043
Qinghai 青海									
Ningxia 宁夏									
Xinjiang 新疆									

2633: Agricultural Chemical Products 农药制剂制造业

Year 年份	Number of firms 企业个数	Rate of change 变化率 (%)	Number of employees 职工人数 (人)	Rate of change 变化率 (%)	Total revenue (Mil. RMB) 总销售收入 (百万元)	Rate of change 变化率 (%)	Total profit (Mil RMB) 总利润 (百万元)	Rate of change 变化率 (%)
2000	364		57,562		8,410		247	
2001	379	4.12	59,793	3.88	9,689	15.21	334	35.22
2002	370	-2.37	57,587	-3.69	11,430	17.97	384	14.97

Major Products 主要产品	Output 产量	Unit 单位
Herbicide 除草剂	202,350	Ton 吨
Bactericide 杀菌剂	74,731	Ton 吨

10 Main Firms with Maximal Revenue (year founded) 收入最大的十家主要企业（创办年份）	City 城市	Province 省	Telephone/fax 电话/传真	Number of employees 职工人数	Ownership 产业所有权	Revenue ('000 RMB) 销售收入(千元)	Profit('000 RMB) (rank) 利润(千元)(排名)	Total assets ('000 RMB) 总资产(千元)	Major products 主要产品
Zhongshan Aestar Fine Chemical Inc.Ltd.	Zhongshan	Guangdong	(0760)8700113		Joint Stock				Aerosol
中山市凯达精细化工股份有限公司(1965)	中山市	广东省	(0760)8700139	1,353	股份制	529,659	7,691(22)	800,156	气雾剂
Zhenjiang Jiangnan Chemical Industry Factory	Zhenjiang	Jiangsu	(0511)5515247		State-owned				Solid Glyphosate固
镇江江南化工厂(1976)	镇江市	江苏省	(0511)5511726	556	国有企业	389,857	766(111)	299,002	体草甘膦
Dalian Razer Pesticides Co.,Ltd.	Dalian	Liaoning	(0411)7687594		Joint Stock				Acetochor
大连瑞泽农药股份有限公司(1985)	大连市	辽宁省	(0411)7686646	498	股份制	274,380	25,450(3)	500,950	乙草胺
Binzhou Qiaochang Co., Ltd.	Binzhou	Shandong	(0543)3325826		Overseas Chinese-funded				Pesticide
滨州侨昌有限公司(1993)	滨州市	山东省	(0543)3221861	854	港澳台资	255,384	12,857(6)	93,112	农药
Weihai Pesticide Factory	Weihai	Shandong	(0631)6842174		Collective-owned				Pesticide
威海市农药厂(1984)	威海市	山东省	(0631)6842098	125	集体企业	226,077	10,003(13)	24,900	农药
Jiangsu Shennong Chemistry Industry Group Co., Ltd.	Xuzhou	Jiangsu	(0516)2730323		Limited-Liability				Pesticide
江苏神农化工集团有限责任公司(1998)	徐州市	江苏省	(0516)2730332	450	有限公司	188,351	8,737(17)	208,818	农药
Hebei Xuanhua Pesticide Co., Ltd.	Zhangjiakou	Hebei	(0313)3018832		Limited-Liability				Atrazine莠去
河北宣化农药有限责任公司(1970)	张家口市	河北省	(0313)3018590	919	有限公司	187,891	11,500(9)	268,553	津胶悬剂
Jiangsu Changqing Agricultural Chemistry Co., Ltd.	Yangzhou	Jiangsu	(0514)6435868		Joint Stock				Tricyclazole三
江苏长青农化股份有限公司(2001)	扬州市	江苏省	(0514)6421039	409	股份制	154,735	9,105(15)	98,376	环唑粉剂
Cangxian Dongdai Chemical Industry Co., Ltd.	Cangzhou	Hebei	(0317)4728062		Limited-Liability				Chlorine Ethane
沧县东代化工有限公司(1987)	沧州市	河北省	(0317)4728062	112	有限公司	148,200	1,735(72)	11,458	氯乙烷
Fengcheng Changli Boron Magnesium Fertilizer Factory	Dandong	Liaoning	(0415)8518099		Collective-owned				Boracic Acid
凤城市昌利硼镁肥厂(2001)	丹东市	辽宁省		92	集体企业	9,024	177(181)	2,773	硼酸

Top 10 Cities by Revenue 销售收入排名前10位城市	Province 省	Market share 市场份额 (%)	Number of firms 企业个数
Changzhou 常州市	Jiangsu 江苏省	5.40	8
Yancheng 盐城市	Jiangsu 江苏省	4.91	14
Zhongshan 中山市	Guangdong 广东省	4.63	1
Zhenjiang 镇江市	Jiangsu 江苏省	4.37	5
Weihai 威海市	Shandong 山东省	4.23	5
Suzhou 苏州市	Jiangsu 江苏省	4.05	7
Shanghai 上海市	Shanghai 上海市	3.79	4
Wenzhou 温州市	Zhejiang 浙江省	3.74	10
Baoding 保定市	Hebei 河北省	3.00	5
Dalian 大连市	Liaoning 辽宁省	2.98	3

10 Major Wholesalers 十家主要批发商	City 城市	Province 省	Telephone/Fax 电话/传真
Ningbo Haitian Group General Company	Ningbo	Zhejiang	(0574)87195360
宁波海田集团总公司	宁波市	浙江省	(0574)87195821
Heilongjiang Agriculture Means Of Production Company	Harbin	Heilongjiang	(0451)88383752
黑龙江省农业生产资料公司	哈尔滨市	黑龙江省	(0451)88382367
Yantai Agriculture Means Of Production General Company	Yantai	Shandong	(0535)6216374
烟台市农业生产资料总公司	烟台市	山东省	(0535)6211348
Guangdong Agriculture Means Of Production General Company	Guangzhou	Guangdong	(020)87773051
广东省农业生产资料总公司	广州市	广东省	(020)87754117
Inner Mongolia Autonomous Region Agriculture & Animal Husbandry Means Of Production Co.,Ltd.	Huhhot	Inner Mongolia	(0471)6963132
内蒙古自治区农牧业生产资料股份有限公司	呼和浩特市	内蒙古	(0471)6964434
Shanghai Agriculture Means Of Production Company	Shanghai	Shanghai	(021)63807100
上海市农业生产资料公司	上海市	上海市	(021)63806807
Ningbo Haitian International Trade Co.,Ltd.	Ningbo	Zhejiang	(0574)87345251
宁波海田国际贸易有限公司	宁波市	浙江省	(0574)87345620
Fujian AMP Incorpration	Fuzhou	Fujian	(0591)7508666
福建省农资集团公司	福州市	福建省	(0591)7614839
Shandong Agricultural Machinery Group General Company	Jinan	Shandong	(0531)8951240
山东省农业机械集团总公司	济南市	山东省	(0531)8951240
Shandong Yantai Agriculture Means Of Production Purchasing Supply Station	Yantai	Shandong	(0535)6222126
山东省烟台市农业生产资料采购供应站	烟台市	山东省	(0535)6216440

2651: Industrial Organic Chemical 有机化工原料制造业

The industry accounts for 0.798% of the total revenue of China's industrial sector in 2002. The rate of return on assets is 1.47%. 81.02% of all firms in the industry made a profit while 18.98% had negative returns.The top province in terms of the industry's revenue is Jiangsu, accounting for 36.63% of the total revenue.
2002年本行业收入占全行业的0.798%，资产利润率为1.47%。81.02%的企业赢利，18.98%的企业亏损。收入最高的省为江苏省，占本行业的36.63%。

	Total number of firms 企业总数	Total number of employees 职工总数	Total revenue (Mil.RMB) 总销售收入 (百万元)	Total profit (Mil.RMB) 总利润 (百万元)	Return on assets 资产利润率 (%)	Return on equity 权益利润率 (%)	Labour productivity ('000 RMB/ worker) 劳动生产率 (千元/人)	Debts/ assets 资产负债率 (%)	Total assets (Mil.RMB) 总资产 (百万元)
Industry Overall 行业总体	906	256,201	85,616	1,864	1.47	4.05	77.02	63.72	126,893

	Number of firms 企业个数	Average number of employees 平均职工人数	Average revenue ('000 RMB) 平均销售收入 (千元)	Average profit ('000 RMB) 平均利润 (千元)	Return on assets 资产利润率 (%)	Return on equity 权益利润率 (%)	Labour productivity ('000 RMB/ worker) 劳动生产率 (千元/人)	Debts/ assets 资产负债率 (%)	Average total assets ('000 RMB) 平均总资产 (千元)
By ownership 产业所有权									
State-owned 国有	91	605	92,811	179	0.07	0.14	37.88	51.30	263,841
Collective-owned 集体	153	132	28,972	1,154	5.02	12.63	56.97	60.23	22,987
Foreign & Overseas Chinese Funded 三资	96	137	74,246	5,747	7.57	15.03	164.72	49.63	75,892
By regional distribution 地区分布									
Central-North 华北	132	325	85,517	361	0.20	1.05	58.22	81.37	184,477
Beijing 北京	12	820	360,732	-20,002	-1.75	-19.55	94.94	91.03	1,141,296
Tianjin 天津	30	200	49,851	4,922	7.50	23.98	50.73	68.74	65,657
Hebei 河北	63	321	73,560	1,799	1.74	7.55	46.81	76.93	103,332
Shanxi 山西	23	238	29,889	1,074	1.43	2.70	39.02	47.15	75,319
Inner Mongolia 内蒙古	4	335	35,551	501	0.45	0.73	72.69	38.13	110,861
Northeast 东北	98	672	217,185	-2,464	-0.55	-1.56	82.26	64.83	448,752
Liaoning 辽宁	44	137	35,023	1,193	2.29	9.94	59.71	76.95	52,086
Jilin 吉林	32	1,651	535,291	-10,253	-0.85	-2.39	84.38	64.41	1,204,057
Heilongjiang 黑龙江	22	316	118,812	1,554	1.08	2.79	85.74	61.17	143,459
Central-East 华东	518	204	91,080	3,637	4.17	9.25	93.83	54.90	87,132
Shanghai 上海	48	233	109,569	7,431	4.80	8.34	131.91	42.41	154,777
Jiangsu 江苏	244	228	128,513	4,059	3.46	8.04	101.79	56.98	117,406
Zhejiang 浙江	96	101	37,430	2,860	8.64	18.26	87.44	52.70	33,112
Anhui 安徽	12	450	51,875	3,490	3.16	7.87	24.89	59.91	110,612
Fujian 福建	3	58	17,515	559	3.72	8.51	43.59	56.29	15,037
Jiangxi 江西	10	237	41,450	-1,047	-2.61	-11.12	46.99	76.55	40,168
Shandong 山东	105	202	56,001	2,181	5.58	14.29	79.00	60.96	39,095
Central-South 中南	97	200	23,583	-333	-0.84	-2.59	39.91	67.57	39,581
Henan 河南	45	243	21,759	-667	-1.68	-13.39	27.98	87.46	39,726
Hubei 湖北	19	112	22,266	619	6.62	10.62	87.12	37.65	9,351
Hunan 湖南	18	204	24,295	667	1.18	2.52	36.53	53.25	56,634
Guangdong 广东	9	111	41,228	-1,781	-4.55	-8.61	110.29	47.12	39,129
Guangxi 广西	6	277	12,834	-1,667	-1.99	-4.05	23.08	50.80	83,744
Hainan 海南									
Southwest 西南	38	392	69,707	5,111	2.39	4.66	52.77	48.69	213,837
Chongqing 重庆	12	479	124,602	12,186	4.73	10.69	81.53	55.79	257,752
Sichuan 四川	16	131	32,730	2,177	5.03	10.27	69.55	51.08	43,318
Guizhou 贵州	4	1,163	100,010	1,176	0.57	1.57	28.01	63.66	206,120
Yunnan 云南	6	402	38,322	1,407	0.24	0.39	17.38	38.46	585,869
Tibet 西藏									
Northwest 西北	23	324	40,352	516	0.81	4.39	45.40	81.52	63,696
Shaanxi 陕西	11	265	33,694	-389	-0.67	-27.68	56.90	97.58	58,032
Gansu 甘肃	7	157	18,534	301	1.22	4.09	44.83	70.12	24,650
Qinghai 青海									
Ningxia 宁夏	4	855	106,931	3,533	2.23	6.62	35.84	66.28	158,216
Xinjiang 新疆	1	6		-87	-0.41			145.59	21,244

Year 年份	Number of firms 企业个数	Rate of change 变化率 (%)	Number of employees 职工人数 (人)	Rate of change 变化率 (%)	Total revenue (Mil. RMB) 总销售收入 (百万元)	Rate of change 变化率 (%)	Total profit (Mil RMB) 总利润 (百万元)	Rate of change 变化率 (%)
2000	776		277,065		69,955		2,106	
2001	872	12.37	249,867	-9.82	67,287	-3.81	-247	-
2002	906	3.90	256,201	2.53	85,616	27.24	1,864	-

Major Products 主要产品	Output 产量	Unit 单位
Ethene 乙烯	541	10,000 Tons 万吨
Ethylene Glycol 乙二醇	91	10,000 Tons 万吨

10 Main Firms with Maximal Revenue (year founded) 收入最大的十家主要企业（创办年份）	City 城市	Province 省	Telephone/fax 电话/传真	Number of employees 职工人数	Ownership 产业所有权	Revenue ('000 RMB) 销售收入 (千元)	Profit('000 RMB) (rank) 利润(千元) (排名)	Total assets ('000 RMB) 总资产 (千元)	Major products 主要产品
Yangzi Petrochemical Industry Co.,Ltd.	Nanjing	Jiangsu	(025)7782954		Joint Stock				Refined Terephthalic Acid
扬子石油化工股份有限公司(1998)	南京市	江苏省	(025)7782318	9,294	股份制	15,137,290	735,910(1)	13,523,830	精对苯二甲酸
PetroChina Jilin Petrochemistry Branch	Jilin	Jilin	(0432)3903623		Joint Stock				
中油吉林石化分公司(2000)	吉林市	吉林省	(0432)3068982	25,028	股份制	13,376,470	-	22,927,030	
Sinopec Jinling Petrochemical Industry Co., Ltd.	Nanjing	Jiangsu	(025)5097755		State Enterprises				Alkyl Benzene
中国石化集团金陵石油化工有限责任公司(1982)	南京市	江苏省	(025)5410220	11,000	国有独资	6,950,020	38,820(9)	5,363,950	烷基苯
Beijing Chemistry Industry Group Co.,Ltd.	Beijing	Beijing	(010)63022806		State Enterprises				Ethene & Propylene
北京化学工业集团有限责任公司(1991)	北京市	北京市	(010)63012342	6,875	国有独资	3,417,614	-	11,286,731	乙烯丙烯
Shanghai Baoshan Iron & Steel Chemical Industry Co.,Ltd.	Shanghai	Shanghai	(021)26648409		Limited-Liability				Pure Benzene
上海宝钢化工有限公司(1997)	上海市	上海市	(021)56196149	805	有限公司	1,642,647	255,818(2)	2,448,934	纯苯
Shanghai Gaoqiao Petrochemistry Crylic Acid Factory	Shanghai	Shanghai	(021)58611739		State-owned				Crylic Acid
上海高桥石化丙烯酸厂(1993)	上海市	上海市	(021)58612283	538	国有企业	959,733	26,247(13)	1,258,266	丙烯酸
Shijiazhuang Duplex Chemical Industry Group Co.,Ltd.	Shijiazhuang	Hebei	(0311)3028643		State Enterprises				Phthalate Anhydride
石家庄双联工集团有限公司(1998)	石家庄市	河北省	(0311)3999923	4,845	国有独资	838,466	18,886(22)	1,029,455	邻苯二甲酸酐
Jiangsu Sopo. (Group) Co.,Ltd.	Zhenjiang	Jiangsu	(0511)3366136		State Enterprises				Acetic Acid
江苏索普(集团)有限公司(1966)	镇江市	江苏省	(0511)3362036	3,637	国有独资	807,748	-	2,817,179	醋酸
Shanghai Wujing Chemical Industry Co., Ltd.	Shanghai	Shanghai	(021)64343040		State Enterprises				Acetic Acid
上海吴泾化工有限公司(1963)	上海市	上海市	(021)64345529	2,337	国有独资	788,728	281(391)	2,019,337	醋酸
Peony River Petrochemical Industry Factory	Mudanjiang	Heilongjiang	(0453)6823756		State-owned				Modified Polypropylene
牡丹江石油化工厂(1977)	牡丹江市	黑龙江省	(0453)6820513	1,020	国有企业	612,970	7,000(62)	410,370	改性聚丙烯

Top 10 Cities by Revenue 销售收入排名前10位城市	Province 省	Market share 市场份额 (%)	Number of firms 企业个数
Nanjing 南京市	Jiangsu 江苏省	27.50	35
Jilin 吉林市	Jilin 吉林省	19.80	14
Shanghai 上海市	Shanghai 上海市	6.14	48
Beijing 北京市	Beijing 北京市	3.06	12
Zibo 淄博市	Shandong 山东省	3.00	23
Shijiazhuang 石家庄市	Hebei 河北省	2.08	19
Cangzhou 沧州市	Hebei 河北省	1.91	9
Tianjin 天津市	Tianjin 天津市	1.75	30
Chongqing 重庆市	Chongqing 重庆市	1.75	12
Changzhou 常州市	Jiangsu 江苏省	1.65	38

10 Major Wholesalers 十家主要批发商	City 城市	Province 省	Telephone/Fax 电话/传真
China Chemical Industry Supply & Sale (Group) General Company	Beijing	Beijing	(010)64238623
中国化工供销(集团)总公司	北京市	北京市	(010)64238623
China Chemical Industry Import & Export General Company	Beijing	Beijing	(010)88078888
中国化工进出口总公司	北京市	北京市	(010)88078890
Tianjin Bridge Group Welding Materials Supply & Sale Co., Ltd.	Tianjin	Tianjin	(022)83968861
天津大桥集团电焊条供销有限公司	天津市	天津市	(022)83968865
Taizhou Xingwei Chunlan Chain Stores Co., Ltd.	Taizhou	Jiangsu	(0523)6611200
泰州星威春兰连锁店有限公司	泰州市	江苏省	(0523)6224181
Taizhou Chunlan Sale Company	Taizhou	Jiangsu	(0523)6611200
泰州春兰销售公司	泰州市	江苏省	(0523)6224181
Shandong Tri-Union Co., Ltd.	Jinan	Shandong	(0531)6086351
山东三联有限责任公司	济南市	山东省	(0531)6093103
Haier Electrical Appliances Co.,Ltd.	Qingdao	Shandong	(0532)8939175
海尔集团电器产业有限公司	青岛市	山东省	(0532)8938086
Guangzhou Haier Industry & Trade Co.,Ltd.	Guangzhou	Guangdong	(020)87397315
广州海尔工贸有限公司	广州市	广东省	(020)87374302
Huizhou TCL Electrical Appliances Sales Co.,Ltd.	Huizhou	Guangdong	(0752)2289885
惠州市TCL电器销售有限公司	惠州市	广东省	(0752)2280690
Guangdong Hardware Minerals Import & Export Group Company	Guangzhou	Guangdong	(020)87752204
广东省五金矿产进出口集团公司	广州市	广东省	(020)87752205

2652: Paint 涂料制造业

The industry accounts for 0.321% of the total revenue of China's industrial sector in 2002. The rate of return on assets is 7.82%. 86.50% of all firms in the industry made a profit while 13.50% had negative returns.The top province in terms of the industry's revenue is Guangdong, accounting for 24.68% of the total revenue.
2002年本行业收入占全行业的 0.321%，资产利润率为 7.82%。86.50%的企业赢利，13.50%的企业亏损。收入最高的省为广东省，占本行业的24.68%。

	Total number of firms 企业总数	Total number of employees 职工总数	Total revenue (Mil.RMB) 总销售收入 (百万元)	Total profit (Mil.RMB) 总利润 (百万元)	Return on assets 资产利润率 (%)	Return on equity 权益利润率 (%)	Labour productivity ('000 RMB/ worker) 劳动生产率 (千元/人)	Debts/ assets 资产负债率 (%)	Total assets (Mil.RMB) 总资产 (百万元)
Industry Overall 行业总体	1030	120,037	34,402	2,857	7.82	14.89	80.19	47.47	36,529

	Number of firms 企业个数	Average number of employees 平均职工人数	Average revenue ('000 RMB) 平均销售收入 (千元)	Average profit ('000 RMB) 平均利润 (千元)	Return on assets 资产利润率 (%)	Return on equity 权益利润率 (%)	Labour productivity ('000 RMB/ worker) 劳动生产率 (千元/人)	Debts/ assets 资产负债率 (%)	Average total assets ('000 RMB) 平均总资产 (千元)
By ownership 产业所有权									
State-owned 国有	77	128	14,723			0.01	36.08	66.82	25,631
Collective-owned 集体	155	98	20,861	1,044	6.53	16.67	69.31	60.80	15,983
Foreign & Overseas Chinese Funded 三资	229	105	63,722	7,740	12.28	21.03	163.58	41.59	63,008
By regional distribution 地区分布									
Central-North 华北	125	132	32,607	3,077	8.50	17.44	84.35	51.26	36,205
Beijing 北京	35	96	23,117	1,798	7.83	14.38	81.48	45.52	22,951
Tianjin 天津	52	115	32,538	3,784	9.41	17.80	77.00	47.12	40,193
Hebei 河北	30	211	50,259	4,153	8.36	19.50	99.73	57.12	49,680
Shanxi 山西	6	71	9,059	124	0.67	4.72	35.86	85.87	18,635
Inner Mongolia 内蒙古	2	176	6,325	-186	-1.23	-4.77	19.33	74.21	15,067
Northeast 东北	47	141	24,089	1,421	3.51	9.79	65.18	64.14	40,479
Liaoning 辽宁	19	89	20,763	2,141	3.89	9.83	82.56	60.46	55,071
Jilin 吉林	16	195	29,896	1,358	4.20	15.50	74.11	72.94	32,370
Heilongjiang 黑龙江	12	152	21,614	365	1.29	3.41	33.81	62.03	28,186
Central-East 华东	489	103	34,971	3,231	9.06	17.23	93.86	47.46	35,684
Shanghai 上海	112	110	54,896	6,909	10.06	16.08	138.81	37.46	68,695
Jiangsu 江苏	171	95	32,935	2,496	9.65	21.26	91.70	54.61	25,861
Zhejiang 浙江	77	102	29,042	2,711	8.90	19.94	73.44	55.38	30,468
Anhui 安徽	25	79	22,500	1,912	8.84	17.83	94.49	50.41	21,624
Fujian 福建	37	63	12,707	326	2.12	4.33	51.85	51.04	15,366
Jiangxi 江西	8	117	7,976	579	3.98	6.78	29.05	41.21	14,529
Shandong 山东	59	146	33,697	1,803	6.04	15.45	70.42	60.92	29,864
Central-South 中南	307	111	34,375	2,492	7.37	12.95	78.10	43.06	33,801
Henan 河南	26	130	15,767	-51	-0.42	-1.02	46.35	58.51	12,145
Hubei 湖北	28	109	23,241	1,097	4.46	7.06	72.24	36.82	24,599
Hunan 湖南	18	161	32,730	4,914	12.55	20.91	74.92	39.99	39,154
Guangdong 广东	219	102	38,777	2,928	7.75	13.40	86.64	42.15	37,775
Guangxi 广西	13	162	26,702	431	1.68	4.87	51.25	65.49	25,649
Hainan 海南	3	78	21,292	107	0.52	1.74	76.55	69.89	20,473
Southwest 西南	31	253	34,655	1,356	3.66	6.46	38.25	43.38	37,057
Chongqing 重庆	11	314	43,577	2,598	4.09	6.08	36.90	32.77	63,529
Sichuan 四川	12	282	42,256	1,148	4.95	10.55	45.97	53.04	23,171
Guizhou 贵州	4	119	6,911	-157	-1.11	-2.23	15.51	50.26	14,161
Yunnan 云南	4	131	15,063	74	0.26	1.35	17.95	81.06	28,811
Tibet 西藏									
Northwest 西北	31	153	15,034	583	1.60	3.14	26.15	48.95	36,328
Shaanxi 陕西	10	205	25,796	1,019	3.18	8.48	28.92	62.54	32,093
Gansu 甘肃	17	121	7,859	436	1.08	1.81	25.49	40.28	40,243
Qinghai 青海									
Ningxia 宁夏									
Xinjiang 新疆	4	156	18,623	118	0.39	1.02	19.23	61.93	30,275

Year 年份	Number of firms 企业个数	Rate of change 变化率 (%)	Number of employees 职工人数 (人)	Rate of change 变化率 (%)	Total revenue (Mil. RMB) 总销售收入 (百万元)	Rate of change 变化率 (%)	Total profit (Mil RMB) 总利润 (百万元)	Rate of change 变化率 (%)
2000	880		133,156		27,234		1,645	
2001	927	5.34	121,218	-8.97	29,245	7.38	1,941	17.99
2002	1030	11.11	120,037	-0.97	34,402	17.63	2,857	47.19

Major Products 主要产品	Output 产量	Unit 单位
Oil Paint 油漆	136	10,000 Tons 万吨
Architectural Coating 建筑涂料	65	10,000 Tons 万吨

10 Main Firms with Maximal Revenue (year founded) 收入最大的十家主要企业（创办年份）	City 城市	Province 省	Telephone/fax 电话/传真	Number of employees 职工人数	Ownership 产业所有权	Revenue ('000 RMB) 销售收入（千元）	Profit('000 RMB) (rank) 利润(千元)(排名)	Total assets ('000 RMB) 总资产（千元）	Major products 主要产品
Nippon Paint (China) Co.,Ltd.	Shanghai	Shanghai	(021)58384799		Foreign Funded				Building Paints
立邦涂料(中国)有限公司(1995)	上海市	上海市	(021)58384882	1,193	外商投资	1,026,313	137,443(3)	738,005	建筑涂料
DuPont China Holding Co., ltd.	Shenzhen	Guangdong	(0755)83307848		Foreign Funded				Resistance Silk
杜邦中国集团有限公司(1989)	深圳市	广东省	(0755)83307047	500	外商投资	690,304	151,584(1)	1,679,003	耐力丝
Guangzhou Zhujiang Chemical Industry Group Co.,Ltd.	Guangzhou	Guangdong	(020)81037491		State Enterprises				Oil Paint
广州珠江化工集团有限公司(2000)	广州市	广东省	(020)81037210	1,725	国有独资	655,774	8,188(71)	648,550	油漆
Langfang Nippon Paints Co., Ltd.	Langfang	Hebei	(0316)6088535		Overseas Chinese-funded				Paints
廊坊立邦涂料有限公司(1996)	廊坊市	河北省	(0316)6082582	510	港澳台资	590,232	102,966(5)	384,994	涂料
Shanghai International Oil Paint Co.,Ltd.	Shanghai	Shanghai	(021)58993845		Foreign Funded				Paints
上海国际油漆有限公司(1989)	上海市	上海市	(021)58990872	294	外商投资	475,117	95,394(6)	400,270	涂料
PPG Dope (Tianjin)Co., Ltd.	Tianjin	Tianjin	(022)25321261		Foreign Funded				Oil Paint
PPG涂料(天津)有限公司(1994)	天津市	天津市	(022)25325183	193	外商投资	430,724	151,028(2)	476,338	油漆
Guangdong Huarun Dope Plant Co.,Ltd.	Foshan	Guangdong	(0765)8376688		Overseas Chinese-funded				Watermanship Paints
顺德市华润涂料厂有限公司(1994)	佛山市	广东省	(0765)8376666	504	港澳台资	420,408	24,910(27)	216,038	水性涂料
Shanghai Dope Co.,Ltd.	Shanghai	Shanghai	(021)64314588		State Enterprises				Paints
上海涂料有限公司(1996)	上海市	上海市	(021)64318172	1,859	国有独资	382,732	50,629(13)	622,606	涂料
Haihong Lao Ren Dope (Kunshan) Co., Ltd.	Suzhou	Jiangsu	(0512)57440886		Overseas Chinese-funded				Oil Paint
海虹老人牌涂料(昆山)有限公司(1996)	苏州市	江苏省	(0512)57440389	237	港澳台资	382,615	71,303(8)	226,877	油漆
China Paints Chemical Industry Shanghai Co.,ltd.	Shanghai	Shanghai	(021)59572123		Overseas Chinese-funded				Oil Paint
中涂化工(上海)有限公司(1994)	上海市	上海市	(021)59579678	200	港澳台资	366,171	39,445(17)	370,654	油漆

Top 10 Cities by Revenue 销售收入排名前10位城市	Province 省	Market share 市场份额 (%)	Number of firms 企业个数
Shanghai 上海市	Shanghai 上海市	17.87	112
Guangzhou 广州市	Guangdong 广东省	7.77	72
Suzhou 苏州市	Jiangsu 江苏省	6.66	42
Shenzhen 深圳市	Guangdong 广东省	5.56	23
Tianjin 天津市	Tianjin 天津市	4.92	52
Foshan 佛山市	Guangdong 广东省	4.36	40
Wuxi 无锡市	Jiangsu 江苏省	2.58	33
Changzhou 常州市	Jiangsu 江苏省	2.49	37
Hangzhou 杭州市	Zhejiang 浙江省	2.48	17
Beijing 北京市	Beijing 北京市	2.35	35

10 Major Wholesalers 十家主要批发商	City 城市	Province 省	Telephone/Fax 电话/传真
Yihua Kangqi Chemical Fibre Co.,Ltd.	Yangzhou	Jiangsu	(0514)3235499
仪化康祺化纤有限责任公司	扬州市	江苏省	(0514)3233847
Sinochem Guangdong Import & Export Company	Guangzhou	Guangdong	(020)86672288
中化广东进出口公司	广州市	广东省	(020)86507512
Sinochem Shanghai Import & Export Company	Shanghai	Shanghai	(021)63289888
中化上海进出口公司	上海市	上海市	(021)63283968
Sinochem Tianjin Import & Export Company	Tianjin	Tianjin	(022)23146216
中化天津进出口公司	天津市	天津市	(022)23146215
China Chemical Sales & Supply (North China) Corporation	Tianjin	Tianjin	(022)23011031
中国化工供销华北公司	天津市	天津市	(022)23011032
China Chemical Sales & Supply (North China) Corporation	Shanghai	Shanghai	(021)62103300
中国化工供销华东公司	上海市	上海市	(021)62515799
Nantong Chemical Light Industry Co.,Ltd.	Nantong	Jiangsu	(0513)5518397
南通化工轻工股份有限公司	南通市	江苏省	(0513)5512735
Taizhou Heshun Plastics Co.,Ltd.	Taizhou	Zhejiang	(0576)2510220
台州市和顺塑料有限公司	台州市	浙江省	(0576)2510160
China Petroleum Technology Development Corporation	Beijing	Beijing	(010)84080722
中国石油技术开发公司	北京市	北京市	(010)84080800
China National Chemical Fiber Corporation	Beijing	Beijing	(010)65816699
中国化纤总公司	北京市	北京市	(010)65813483

2653: Printing Ink 油墨制造业

The industry accounts for 0.051% of the total revenue of China's industrial sector in 2002. The rate of return on assets is 7.41%. 86.59% of all firms in the industry made a profit while 13.41% had negative returns.The top province in terms of the industry's revenue is Guangdong, accounting for 30.32% of the total revenue.
2002年本行业收入占全行业的 0.051%，资产利润率为 7.41%。86.59%的企业赢利，13.41%的企业亏损。收入最高的省为广东省，占本行业的30.32%。

	Total number of firms 企业总数	Total number of employees 职工总数	Total revenue (Mil.RMB) 总销售收入(百万元)	Total profit (Mil.RMB) 总利润(百万元)	Return on assets 资产利润率(%)	Return on equity 权益利润率(%)	Labour productivity ('000 RMB/ worker) 劳动生产率(千元/人)	Debts/ assets 资产负债率(%)	Total assets (Mil.RMB) 总资产(百万元)
Industry Overall 行业总体	164	16,443	5,493	435	7.41	14.23	95.21	47.96	5,866

	Number of firms 企业个数	Average number of employees 平均职工人数	Average revenue ('000 RMB) 平均销售收入(千元)	Average profit ('000 RMB) 平均利润(千元)	Return on assets 资产利润率(%)	Return on equity 权益利润率(%)	Labour productivity ('000 RMB/ worker) 劳动生产率(千元/人)	Debts/ assets 资产负债率(%)	Average total assets ('000 RMB) 平均总资产(千元)
By ownership 产业所有权									
State-owned 国有	8	112	19,213	415	1.37	3.55	51.97	61.45	30,349
Collective-owned 集体	17	137	36,524	2,465	7.61	16.95	59.93	55.10	32,389
Foreign & Overseas Chinese Funded 三资	60	109	46,878	4,236	7.82	14.59	124.39	46.44	54,199
By regional distribution 地区分布									
Central-North 华北	21	149	54,345	5,054	7.33	9.99	93.05	26.69	68,974
Beijing 北京	5	55	41,462	3,972	16.20	25.07	166.17	35.39	24,520
Tianjin 天津	8	281	79,972	4,985	3.74	4.81	48.00	22.13	133,127
Hebei 河北	4	36	13,858	1,222	13.30	33.04	79.02	59.77	9,189
Shanxi 山西	4	116	59,680	10,377	18.52	29.95	272.26	38.15	56,022
Inner Mongolia 内蒙古									
Northeast 东北	5	44	7,838	492	4.45	9.57	37.53	53.51	11,063
Liaoning 辽宁	4	32	9,229	614	4.56	9.75	56.75	53.23	13,473
Jilin 吉林	1	92	2,274	4	0.28	0.79	10.99	64.42	1,422
Heilongjiang 黑龙江									
Central-East 华东	73	99	34,359	3,195	9.01	18.54	100.35	51.41	35,471
Shanghai 上海	26	120	51,724	5,085	9.53	20.83	135.57	54.23	53,345
Jiangsu 江苏	17	61	17,410	1,360	9.16	21.74	60.54	57.87	14,849
Zhejiang 浙江	11	96	46,213	5,622	14.74	22.06	136.13	33.18	38,135
Anhui 安徽	2	50	19,273	2,674	26.73	62.00	133.57	56.89	10,006
Fujian 福建	6	86	24,355	460	1.35	2.91	59.23	53.72	34,131
Jiangxi 江西	1	50	3,440	516	6.97	9.96	17.98	30.04	7,403
Shandong 山东	10	136	17,094	744	2.49	5.80	37.60	57.03	29,832
Central-South 中南	59	83	28,565	1,485	5.83	14.97	104.29	61.07	25,485
Henan 河南	2	58	4,923	388	6.50	15.64	33.96	58.41	5,957
Hubei 湖北	1	17	3,516	370	14.96	41.11	188.41	63.61	2,473
Hunan 湖南	1	17	800	1	0.20	0.46	15.24	57.09	508
Guangdong 广东	54	87	30,843	1,596	5.82	14.94	105.73	61.02	27,416
Guangxi 广西	1	30	5,663	299	3.60	13.18	151.90	72.66	8,299
Hainan 海南									
Southwest 西南	6	164	19,830	848	1.89	4.18	32.28	54.83	44,882
Chongqing 重庆									
Sichuan 四川	1	384	10,856	587	12.50	18.74	7.79	33.30	4,696
Guizhou 贵州	2	95	4,559	-147	-1.36	-10.19	6.07	86.67	10,822
Yunnan 云南	3	137	33,002	1,597	1.97	4.14	67.12	52.41	80,984
Tibet 西藏									
Northwest 西北									
Shaanxi 陕西									
Gansu 甘肃									
Qinghai 青海									
Ningxia 宁夏									
Xinjiang 新疆									

2653: Printing Ink 油墨制造业

Year 年份	Number of firms 企业个数	Rate of change 变化率 (%)	Number of employees 职工人数 (人)	Rate of change 变化率 (%)	Total revenue (Mil. RMB) 总销售收入 (百万元)	Rate of change 变化率 (%)	Total profit (Mil RMB) 总利润 (百万元)	Rate of change 变化率 (%)
2000	121		12,961		3,909		288	
2001	141	16.53	14,689	13.33	4,551	16.42	379	31.60
2002	164	16.31	16,443	11.94	5,493	20.70	435	14.78

Major Products 主要产品	Output 产量	Unit 单位
Printing Ink 油墨	17	10,000 Tons 万吨

10 Main Firms with Maximal Revenue (year founded) 收入最大的十家主要企业（创办年份）	City 城市	Province 省	Telephone/fax 电话/传真	Number of employees 职工人数	Ownership 产业所有权	Revenue ('000 RMB) 销售收入 (千元)	Profit('000 RMB) (rank) 利润(千元) (排名)	Total assets ('000 RMB) 总资产 (千元)	Major products 主要产品
Shanghai Silian Industrial General Company 上海泗联实业总公司(1994)	Shanghai 上海市	Shanghai 上海市	(021)57611258	830	Collective-owned 集体企业	292,605	18,478(6)	291,230	Printing Ink 油墨
Shanghai DIC Printing Ink Co.,Ltd. 上海DIC油墨有限公司(1993)	Shanghai 上海市	Shanghai 上海市	(021)64890888 (021)64890688	140	Foreign Funded 外商投资	209,340	44,079(1)	218,811	Printing Ink 油墨
Tianjin Angel Chemical Group Co., ltd. 天津天女化工集团股份有限责任贫(1949)	Tianjin 天津市	Tianjin 天津市	(022)84783830 (022)84783658	504	Joint Stock 股份制	208,671	2,688(33)	375,138	Printing Ink 油墨
Taiyuan Coates Lorilleux Printing Ink Chemical Ltd. 太原高氏劳瑞油墨化学有限公司	Taiyuan 太原市	Shanxi 山西省	(0351)4292147 (0351)4294539	317	Foreign Funded 外商投资	174,885	34,635(3)	158,839	Printing Ink 油墨
China Banknot SACPA Security Ink Co.,Ltd. 北京中钞锡克拜安全油墨有限公司(1999)	Beijing 北京市	Beijing 北京市	(010)67871566 (010)67889446	24	Foreign Funded 外商投资	167,964	17,779(7)	86,264	Printing Ink 油墨
Jiangmen Printing Ink Chemical Industry Co.,Ltd. 江门市油墨化工有限公司(1995)	Jiangmen 江门市	Guangdong 广东省	(0750)3532618 (0750)3558265	224	Limited-Liability 有限公司	167,165	14,884(10)	216,238	Printing Ink 油墨
Shenzhen Shenri Printing Ink Co., Ltd. 深圳深日油墨有限公司(1987)	Shenzhen 深圳市	Guangdong 广东省	(0755)26432333 (0755)26640133	189	Foreign Funded 外商投资	146,888	26,253(5)	143,943	Surface Printing Ink 平版油墨
Zhongshan Youcheng Petrochemical Industry Co.,Ltd. 中山友成石油化工有限公司(1992)	Zhongshan 中山市	Guangdong 广东省	(0760)6502232 (0760)6500848	207	Overseas Chinese-funded 港澳台资	107,416	1,865(45)	95,979	Printing Ink 油墨
Coates (Guangzhou) PRC Co., Ltd. 高氏（广州）涂料有限公司(1994)	Guangzhou 广州市	Guangdong 广东省	(020)82975200 (020)82975201	105	Overseas Chinese-funded 港澳台资	106,441	3,088(31)	77,392	Printing Ink 油墨
Zhejiang Xindongfang Printing Ink Group Co., Ltd. 浙江新东方油墨集团有限公司(1984)	Taizhou 台州市	Zhejiang 浙江省	(0576)4275520 (0576)4275666	282	Limited-Liability 有限公司	100,990	16,370(8)	85,091	Printing Ink 油墨

Top 10 Cities by Revenue 销售收入排名前10位城市	Province 省	Market share 市场份额 (%)	Number of firms 企业个数
Shanghai 上海市	Shanghai 上海市	24.48	26
Tianjin 天津市	Tianjin 天津市	11.65	8
Hangzhou 杭州市	Zhejiang 浙江省	6.40	3
Jiangmen 江门市	Guangdong 广东省	5.90	8
Guangzhou 广州市	Guangdong 广东省	5.68	12
Zhongshan 中山市	Guangdong 广东省	4.88	10
Taiyuan 太原市	Shanxi 山西省	4.35	4
Beijing 北京市	Beijing 北京市	3.77	5
Shenzhen 深圳市	Guangdong 广东省	3.56	4
Zhaoqing 肇庆市	Guangdong 广东省	3.05	3

10 Major Wholesalers 十家主要批发商	City 城市	Province 省	Telephone/Fax 电话/传真
Yihua Kangqi Chemical Fibre Co.,Ltd. 仪化康祺化纤有限责任公司	Yangzhou 扬州市	Jiangsu 江苏省	(0514)3235499 (0514)3233847
Sinochem Guangdong Import & Export Company 中化广东进出口公司	Guangzhou 广州市	Guangdong 广东省	(020)86672288 (020)86507512
Sinochem Shanghai Import & Export Company 中化上海进出口公司	Shanghai 上海市	Shanghai 上海市	(021)63289888 (021)63283968
Sinochem Tianjin Import & Export Company 中化天津进出口公司	Tianjin 天津市	Tianjin 天津市	(022)23146216 (022)23146215
China Chemical Sales & Supply (North China) Corporation 中国化工供销华北公司	Tianjin 天津市	Tianjin 天津市	(022)23011031 (022)23011032
China Chemical Sales & Supply (North China) Corporation 中国化工供销华东公司	Shanghai 上海市	Shanghai 上海市	(021)62103300 (021)62515799
Nantong Chemical Light Industry Co.,Ltd. 南通化工轻工股份有限公司	Nantong 南通市	Jiangsu 江苏省	(0513)5518397 (0513)5512735
Taizhou Heshun Plastics Co.,Ltd. 台州市和顺塑料有限公司	Taizhou 台州市	Zhejiang 浙江省	(0576)2510220 (0576)2510160
China Petroleum Technology Development Corporation 中国石油技术开发公司	Beijing 北京市	Beijing 北京市	(010)84080722 (010)84080800
China National Chemical Fiber Corporation 中国化纤总公司	Beijing 北京市	Beijing 北京市	(010)65816699 (010)65813483

2654: Pigment 颜料制造业

The industry accounts for 0.093% of the total revenue of China's industrial sector in 2002. The rate of return on assets is 6.11%. 89.36% of all firms in the industry made a profit while 10.64% had negative returns.The top province in terms of the industry's revenue is Jiangsu, accounting for 24.40% of the total revenue.
2002年本行业收入占全行业的0.093%，资产利润率为6.11%。89.36%的企业赢利，10.64%的企业亏损。收入最高的省为江苏省，占本行业的24.40%。

	Total number of firms 企业总数	Total number of employees 职工总数	Total revenue (Mil.RMB) 总销售收入 (百万元)	Total profit (Mil.RMB) 总利润 (百万元)	Return on assets 资产利润率 (%)	Return on equity 权益利润率 (%)	Labour productivity ('000 RMB/ worker) 劳动生产率 (千元/人)	Debts/ assets 资产负债率 (%)	Total assets (Mil.RMB) 总资产 (百万元)
Industry Overall 行业总体	282	39,742	10,022	564	6.11	12.99	72.09	52.97	9,236

	Number of firms 企业个数	Average number of employees 平均职工人数	Average revenue ('000 RMB) 平均销售收入 (千元)	Average profit ('000 RMB) 平均利润 (千元)	Return on assets 资产利润率 (%)	Return on equity 权益利润率 (%)	Labour productivity ('000 RMB/ worker) 劳动生产率 (千元/人)	Debts/ assets 资产负债率 (%)	Average total assets ('000 RMB) 平均总资产 (千元)
By ownership 产业所有权									
State-owned 国有	18	232	39,314	1,844	5.13	15.63	48.31	67.15	35,924
Collective-owned 集体	53	124	25,764	1,041	5.98	14.92	67.25	59.89	17,404
Foreign & Overseas Chinese Funded 三资	74	151	50,394	3,505	6.19	11.34	96.48	45.36	56,596
By regional distribution 地区分布									
Central-North 华北	38	122	22,489	1,550	7.28	20.59	48.14	64.63	21,272
Beijing 北京	2	50	19,380	1,210	17.36	28.31	101.84	38.67	6,969
Tianjin 天津	13	129	27,606	2,138	7.97	25.93	36.19	69.26	26,825
Hebei 河北	20	120	21,484	1,399	7.78	18.42	60.51	57.77	17,985
Shanxi 山西	3	161	9,085	233	0.81	3.82	17.25	78.70	28,651
Inner Mongolia 内蒙古									
Northeast 东北	8	194	69,041	9,217	9.81	15.79	107.28	37.85	93,947
Liaoning 辽宁	8	194	69,041	9,217	9.81	15.79	107.28	37.85	93,947
Jilin 吉林									
Heilongjiang 黑龙江									
Central-East 华东	156	131	40,154	2,136	6.64	15.21	86.15	56.33	32,169
Shanghai 上海	22	114	40,746	3,365	10.14	17.26	90.69	41.25	33,178
Jiangsu 江苏	49	172	49,894	1,859	4.66	13.77	81.09	66.17	39,896
Zhejiang 浙江	46	104	35,717	2,004	6.28	16.08	77.18	60.94	31,904
Anhui 安徽	7	65	9,403	305	3.97	8.75	50.29	54.63	7,677
Fujian 福建	4	113	29,353	502	2.28	3.08	112.31	25.82	22,001
Jiangxi 江西	1	40	1,875	108	0.65	1.04	58.95	37.32	16,568
Shandong 山东	27	139	40,546	2,656	10.13	16.75	107.33	39.51	26,209
Central-South 中南	72	165	30,781	1,334	3.95	7.29	57.37	45.84	33,809
Henan 河南	9	132	23,218	1,585	6.70	14.26	47.47	53.02	23,659
Hubei 湖北	7	99	6,906	63	0.50	3.17	27.17	84.23	12,533
Hunan 湖南	11	289	38,924	1,012	3.35	9.82	43.25	65.90	30,230
Guangdong 广东	36	137	33,755	1,680	3.85	5.99	75.07	35.79	43,661
Guangxi 广西	9	211	35,070	1,084	4.25	11.91	52.27	64.29	25,472
Hainan 海南									
Southwest 西南	5	197	24,899	336	0.80	2.35	30.34	65.82	41,758
Chongqing 重庆	3	230	32,739	696	1.15	3.32	37.49	65.41	60,515
Sichuan 四川	1	160	15,203	363	4.03	31.21	19.08	87.09	9,009
Guizhou 贵州									
Yunnan 云南	1	136	11,074	-772	-4.23	-10.40	7.31	59.30	18,238
Tibet 西藏									
Northwest 西北	3	93	3,369	193	3.91	6.44	22.62	39.36	4,942
Shaanxi 陕西	1	110	8,728	480	6.76	16.72	43.04	59.58	7,103
Gansu 甘肃	2	85	690	50	1.28	1.62	9.41	20.76	3,862
Qinghai 青海									
Ningxia 宁夏									
Xinjiang 新疆									

Year 年份	Number of firms 企业个数	Rate of change 变化率 (%)	Number of employees 职工人数 (人)	Rate of change 变化率 (%)	Total revenue (Mil. RMB) 总销售收入 (百万元)	Rate of change 变化率 (%)	Total profit (Mil RMB) 总利润 (百万元)	Rate of change 变化率 (%)
2000	226		34,376		6,798		461	
2001	258	14.16	37,791	9.93	7,196	5.85	335	-27.33
2002	282	9.30	39,742	5.16	10,022	39.27	564	68.36

Major Products 主要产品	Output 产量	Unit 单位
Pigment 颜料	108	10,000 Tons 万吨

10 Main Firms with Maximal Revenue (year founded) 收入最大的十家主要企业（创办年份）	City 城市	Province 省	Telephone/fax 电话/传真	Number of employees 职工人数	Ownership 产业所有权	Revenue ('000 RMB) 销售收入 (千元)	Profit('000 RMB) (rank) 利润(千元) (排名)	Total assets ('000 RMB) 总资产 (千元)	Major products 主要产品
Dalian Lu Ming Science & Technology Co., Ltd. 大连路明科技集团有限公司(1992)	Dalian 大连市	Liaoning 辽宁省	(0411)4791334 (0411)4791339	434	Private Owned 私营企业	420,000	72,122(1)	319,470	luminescence Pigment 发光颜料
Changzhou Bei Mei Pigment Chemistry Co., Ltd. 常州北美颜料化学有限公司(1997)	Changzhou 常州市	Jiangsu 江苏省	(0519)6263188 (0519)6261200	768	Foreign Funded 外商投资	393,920	17,420(6)	858,010	Pigment 颜料
Jiangsu Taibai Group Company 江苏太白集团公司(1979)	Zhenjiang 镇江市	Jiangsu 江苏省	(0511)5271180 (0511)5290302	1,551	State-owned 国有企业	342,779	20,892(4)	241,966	Tilanium Dioxide 钛白粉
Guangdong Sanshui Dahong Glaze Co., Ltd. 广东三水大鸿制釉有限公司(1993)	Foshan 佛山市	Guangdong 广东省	(0757)7293010 (0757)7293862	326	Overseas Chinese-funded 港澳台资	285,634	1,934(65)	346,540	Frit Glaze 熔块釉
Hanghou Baihe Chemical Industry Co.,Ltd. 杭州百合化工有限公司(1989)	Hangzhou 杭州市	Zhejiang 浙江省	(0571)82961888 (0571)82961000	492	Private Owned 私营企业	245,076	16,332(8)	174,852	Organic Pigment 有机颜料
Clariant Pigment (Tianjin) Co., Ltd. 科莱恩颜料（天津）有限公司(1996)	Tianjin 天津市	Tianjin 天津市	(022)24722778 (022)24729834	279	Foreign Funded 外商投资	185,512	16,490(7)	209,090	Organic Pigment 有机颜料
Jiangsu Shuangle Chemical Industry Pigment Co., Ltd. 江苏双乐化工颜料有限公司(1994)	Taizhou 泰州市	Jiangsu 江苏省	(0523)3764206 (0523)3761630	420	Limited-Liability 有限公司	165,520	6,910(20)	77,719	Phthalocyanine 酞菁系列
Song Bai Chemical Industry Group 松柏化工集团(1995)	Hengyang 衡阳市	Hunan 湖南省	(0734)8080018	925	Collective-owned 集体企业	155,000	3,600(45)	46,006	Zinc Oxide 氧化锌
Hangzhou Pigment Chemical Plant 杭州颜料化工厂(1987)	Hangzhou 杭州市	Zhejiang 浙江省	(0571)82131323 (0571)82131576	128	Collective owned 集体企业	140,209	13,057(9)	121,392	Pigment 颜料
Henan Xinxiang Dyestuff Chemical General Factory 河南新乡染化总厂(1976)	Xinxiang 新乡市	Henan 河南省	(0373)5030006 (0373)5036170	560	Collective-owned 集体企业	131,570	6,123(25)	152,616	Ferric Oxide Pigment 氧化铁红

Top 10 Cities by Revenue 销售收入排名前10位城市	Province 省	Market share 市场份额 (%)	Number of firms 企业个数
Hangzhou 杭州市	Zhejiang 浙江省	9.56	21
Shanghai 上海市	Shanghai 上海市	8.94	22
Changzhou 常州市	Jiangsu 江苏省	7.31	4
Zhenjiang 镇江市	Jiangsu 江苏省	4.59	8
Dalian 大连市	Liaoning 辽宁省	4.45	3
Foshan 佛山市	Guangdong 广东省	4.12	6
Tianjin 天津市	Tianjin 天津市	3.58	13
Zibo 淄博市	Shandong 山东省	3.52	10
Jinan 济南市	Shandong 山东省	3.09	6
Guangzhou 广州市	Guangdong 广东省	3.00	7

10 Major Wholesalers 十家主要批发商	City 城市	Province 省	Telephone/Fax 电话/传真
Yihua Kangqi Chemical Fibre Co.,Ltd. 仪化康祺化纤有限责任公司	Yangzhou 扬州市	Jiangsu 江苏省	(0514)3235499 (0514)3233847
Sinochem Guangdong Import & Export Company 中化广东进出口公司	Guangzhou 广州市	Guangdong 广东省	(020)86672288 (020)86507512
Sinochem Shanghai Import & Export Company 中化上海进出口公司	Shanghai 上海市	Shanghai 上海市	(021)63289888 (021)63283968
Sinochem Tianjin Import & Export Company 中化天津进出口公司	Tianjin 天津市	Tianjin 天津市	(022)23146216 (022)23146215
China Chemical Sales & Supply (North China) Corporation 中国化工供销华北公司	Tianjin 天津市	Tianjin 天津市	(022)23011031 (022)23011032
China Chemical Sales & Supply (North China) Corporation 中国化工供销华东公司	Shanghai 上海市	Shanghai 上海市	(021)62103300 (021)62515799
Nantong Chemical Light Industry Co.,Ltd. 南通化工轻工股份有限公司	Nantong 南通市	Jiangsu 江苏省	(0513)5518397 (0513)5512735
Taizhou Heshun Plastics Co.,Ltd. 台州市和顺塑料有限公司	Taizhou 台州市	Zhejiang 浙江省	(0576)2510220 (0576)2510160
China Petroleum Technology Development Corporation 中国石油技术开发公司	Beijing 北京市	Beijing 北京市	(010)84080722 (010)84080800
China National Chemical Fiber Corporation 中国化纤总公司	Beijing 北京市	Beijing 北京市	(010)65816699 (010)65813483

2655: Dyestuff 染料制造业

The industry accounts for 0.193% of the total revenue of China's industrial sector in 2002. The rate of return on assets is 7.96%. 83.52% of all firms in the industry made a profit while 16.48% had negative returns.The top province in terms of the industry's revenue is Zhejiang, accounting for 34.06% of the total revenue.
2002年本行业收入占全行业的0.193%，资产利润率为7.96%。83.52%的企业赢利，16.48%的企业亏损。收入最高的省为浙江省，占本行业的34.06%。

	Total number of firms 企业总数	Total number of employees 职工总数	Total revenue (Mil.RMB) 总销售收入（百万元）	Total profit (Mil.RMB) 总利润（百万元）	Return on assets 资产利润率 (%)	Return on equity 权益利润率 (%)	Labour productivity ('000 RMB/ worker) 劳动生产率（千元/人）	Debts/ assets 资产负债率 (%)	Total assets (Mil.RMB) 总资产（百万元）
Industry Overall 行业总体	352	69,535	20,703	1,550	7.96	19.28	77.46	58.70	19,466

	Number of firms 企业个数	Average number of employees 平均职工人数	Average revenue ('000 RMB) 平均销售收入（千元）	Average profit ('000 RMB) 平均利润（千元）	Return on assets 资产利润率 (%)	Return on equity 权益利润率 (%)	Labour productivity ('000 RMB/ worker) 劳动生产率（千元/人）	Debts/ assets 资产负债率 (%)	Average total assets ('000 RMB) 平均总资产（千元）
By ownership 产业所有权									
State-owned 国有	29	397	31,547	-319	-0.37	-1.75	29.53	79.12	87,263
Collective-owned 集体	89	154	45,637	3,753	12.02	34.33	72.44	65.00	31,233
Foreign & Overseas Chinese Funded 三资	57	166	78,888	8,274	9.18	18.37	137.76	50.01	90,106
By regional distribution 地区分布									
Central-North 华北	104	178	38,772	2,641	6.51	17.18	60.86	62.13	40,588
Beijing 北京	3	455	54,041	-2,261	-2.14	-8.77	16.28	75.61	105,664
Tianjin 天津	62	171	37,555	2,978	7.27	17.93	52.94	59.46	40,979
Hebei 河北	37	144	35,134	2,263	7.81	21.37	84.16	63.44	28,959
Shanxi 山西	1	1,071	152,072	3,746	2.01	8.04	37.86	74.96	185,975
Inner Mongolia 内蒙古	1	170	89,709	9,318	8.79	17.52	326.54	49.87	106,062
Northeast 东北	11	363	38,051	389	0.40	2.55	21.00	84.49	98,347
Liaoning 辽宁	9	350	45,687	931	0.97	4.22	25.42	76.98	95,955
Jilin 吉林	2	422	3,693	-2,050	-1.88		4.50	114.21	109,109
Heilongjiang 黑龙江									
Central-East 华东	207	203	75,056	5,991	9.45	20.78	93.33	54.53	63,403
Shanghai 上海	33	182	81,271	7,970	7.11	12.85	127.89	44.68	112,113
Jiangsu 江苏	87	184	50,093	2,972	7.36	22.30	74.41	66.97	40,363
Zhejiang 浙江	55	240	128,212	11,771	14.93	35.06	110.67	57.40	78,819
Anhui 安徽	9	182	17,480	-61	-0.23	-0.66	37.42	65.55	26,829
Fujian 福建	1	50	46,415	1,845	36.10	60.51	587.20	40.34	5,111
Jiangxi 江西	2	16	299				11.78	100.00	3,727
Shandong 山东	20	254	62,035	3,490	5.27	8.43	80.69	37.48	66,198
Central-South 中南	27	156	24,345	1,207	3.79	17.51	53.87	78.34	31,829
Henan 河南	12	202	24,634	708	3.54	15.64	33.96	77.35	19,989
Hubei 湖北	5	130	15,632	-1,497	-5.16		70.43	141.81	29,036
Hunan 湖南	3	177	19,129	-625	-0.86	-8.97	23.42	90.40	72,653
Guangdong 广东	7	88	32,307	4,780	13.05	19.50	140.45	33.09	36,625
Guangxi 广西									
Hainan 海南									
Southwest 西南	2	233	23,500	945	4.09	18.25	30.17	77.57	23,088
Chongqing 重庆	2	233	23,500	945	4.09	18.25	30.17	77.57	23,088
Sichuan 四川									
Guizhou 贵州									
Yunnan 云南									
Tibet 西藏									
Northwest 西北	1	221	11,270	-3,507	-2.64	-3.21	19.27	17.94	133,084
Shaanxi 陕西									
Gansu 甘肃	1	221	11,270	-3,507	-2.64	-3.21	19.27	17.94	133,084
Qinghai 青海									
Ningxia 宁夏									
Xinjiang 新疆									

2655: Dyestuff 染料制造业

Year 年份	Number of firms 企业个数	Rate of change 变化率（%）	Number of employees 职工人数（人）	Rate of change 变化率（%）	Total revenue (Mil. RMB) 总销售收入（百万元）	Rate of change 变化率（%）	Total profit (Mil RMB) 总利润（百万元）	Rate of change 变化率（%）
2000	338		73,718		15,467		616	
2001	344	1.78	71,213	-3.40	16,892	9.21	990	60.71
2002	352	2.33	69,535	-2.36	20,703	22.56	1,550	56.57

Major Products 主要产品	Output 产量	Unit 单位
Dyestuff 染料	72	10,000 Tons 万吨

10 Main Firms with Maximal Revenue (year founded) 收入最大的十家主要企业（创办年份）	City 城市	Province 省	Telephone/ fax 电话/传真	Number of employees 职工人数	Ownership 产业所有权	Revenue ('000 RMB) 销售收入（千元）	Profit('000 RMB) (rank) 利润（千元）（排名）	Total assets ('000 RMB) 总资产（千元）	Major products 主要产品
Zhejiang Longsheng Group Co.,Ltd.	Shaoxing	Zhejiang	(0575)2046589		Joint Stock				Dyestuff
浙江龙盛集团股份有限公司(1970)	绍兴市	浙江省	(0575)2042878	1,749	股份制	1,506,462	200,226(1)	696,570	染料
Bass Colorants And Chemical Co.,Ltd.	Shanghai	Shanghai	(021)58611828		Foreign Funded				Organic Pigment
巴斯夫染料化工有限公司(1994)	上海市	上海市	(021)58613752	981	外商投资	1,057,170	158,696(2)	1,528,496	有机颜料
Zhejiang Runtu Chemical Industry Group Co.,Ltd.	Shaoxing	Zhejiang	(0575)2042875		Limited-Liability				Dyestuff
浙江闰土化工集团有限公司(1986)	绍兴市	浙江省	(0575)2041282	1,683	有限公司	966,636	121,670(3)	499,749	染料
Jiangsu Zhongdan Chemical Industry Group Company	Taizhou	Jiangsu	(0523)7483096		Collective-owned				Phenyl Anisidine对氮
江苏中丹化工集团公司(1979)	泰州市	江苏省	(0523)7484262	2,315	集体企业	737,117	61,029(5)	604,631	基苯甲醚
Hangzhou Di Kai Chemical Industry Co., Ltd.	Hangzhou	Zhejiang	(0571)82989002		Foreign Funded				C.I.Disperse Blue 56.分
杭州帝凯化工有限公司(1994)	杭州市	浙江省	(0571)82989001	428	外商投资	359,258	15,580(20)	160,741	散兰56#
Shandong Longkou Shuanglong Chemical Industry Co., Ltd.	Yantai	Shandong	(0535)8812637		Limited-Liability				Dyeing Intermediates染
山东龙口双龙化工有限公司(1976)	烟台市	山东省	(0535)8811694	576	有限公司	332,200	18,020(17)	96,490	料中间体
Zhejiang Lianhe Chemical Technology Co., Ltd.	Taizhou	Zhejiang	(0576)4275121		Joint Stock				C.I.Disperse Blue 79.分
浙江联化科技股份有限公司(1986)	台州市	浙江省	(0576)4275170	608	股份制	324,390	14,520(22)	191,640	散兰79号
Dalian Dye & Chemical Co.,Ltd.	Dalian	Liaoning	(0411)6861000		Limited-Liability				Dyestuff & Dyeing Intermediates染料
大连染料化工集团有限公司(1999)	大连市	辽宁省	(0411)6861018	2,292	有限公司	301,899	5,081(58)	668,640	及中间体
Shanghai Huanyuan Industry General Company	Shanghai	Shanghai	(021)63557859		State Enterprises				Dyestuff
上海华元实业总公司(1992)	上海市	上海市	(021)63844027	1,740	国有独资	296,273	922(141)	994,024	染料
Shanghai Matex Chemical Co.,Ltd.	Shanghai	Shanghai	(021)58964553		Foreign Funded				Dyestuff
上海万得化工有限公司(1993)	上海市	上海市	(021)58961541	288	外商投资	219,534	55,335(7)	229,599	染料

Top 10 Cities by Revenue 销售收入排名前10位城市	Province 省	Market share 市场份额（%）	Number of firms 企业个数
Shaoxing 绍兴市	Zhejiang 浙江省	14.70	11
Shanghai 上海市	Shanghai 上海市	12.95	33
Tianjin 天津市	Tianjin 天津市	11.25	62
Hangzhou 杭州市	Zhejiang 浙江省	7.86	11
Taizhou 台州市	Zhejiang 浙江省	7.73	10
Suzhou 苏州市	Jiangsu 江苏省	5.73	29
Taizhou 泰州市	Jiangsu 江苏省	4.40	6
Zhenjiang 镇江市	Jiangsu 江苏省	3.31	8
Wuxi 无锡市	Jiangsu 江苏省	2.82	14
Hengshui 衡水市	Hebei 河北省	2.76	11

10 Major Wholesalers 十家主要批发商	City 城市	Province 省	Telephone/Fax 电话/传真
Yihua Kangqi Chemical Fibre Co.,Ltd.	Yangzhou	Jiangsu	(0514)3235499
仪化康祺化纤有限责任公司	扬州市	江苏省	(0514)3233847
Sinochem Guangdong Import & Export Company	Guangzhou	Guangdong	(020)86672288
中化广东进出口公司	广州市	广东省	(020)86507512
Sinochem Shanghai Import & Export Company	Shanghai	Shanghai	(021)63289888
中化上海进出口公司	上海市	上海市	(021)63283968
Sinochem Tianjin Import & Export Company	Tianjin	Tianjin	(022)23146216
中化天津进出口公司	天津市	天津市	(022)23146215
China Chemical Sales & Supply (North China) Corporation	Tianjin	Tianjin	(022)23011031
中国化工供销华北公司	天津市	天津市	(022)23011032
China Chemical Sales & Supply (North China) Corporation	Shanghai	Shanghai	(021)62103300
中国化工供销华东公司	上海市	上海市	(021)62515799
Nantong Chemical Light Industry Co.,Ltd.	Nantong	Jiangsu	(0513)5518397
南通化工轻工股份有限公司	南通市	江苏省	(0513)5512735
Taizhou Heshun Plastics Co.,Ltd.	Taizhou	Zhejiang	(0576)2510220
台州市和顺塑料有限公司	台州市	浙江省	(0576)2510160
China Petroleum Technology Development Corporation	Beijing	Beijing	(010)84080722
中国石油技术开发公司	北京市	北京市	(010)84080800
China National Chemical Fiber Corporation	Beijing	Beijing	(010)65816699
中国化纤总公司	北京市	北京市	(010)65813483

2659: Other Organic Chemical Products 其他有机化学产品制造业

The industry accounts for 0.116% of the total revenue of China's industrial sector in 2002. The rate of return on assets is 6.01%. 83.56% of all firms in the industry made a profit while 16.44% had negative returns. The top province in terms of the industry's revenue is Jiangsu, accounting for 20.32% of the total revenue.
2002年本行业收入占全行业的 0.116%，资产利润率为 6.01%。83.56%的企业赢利，16.44%的企业亏损。收入最高的省为江苏省，占本行业的20.32%。

	Total number of firms 企业总数	Total number of employees 职工总数	Total revenue (Mil.RMB) 总销售收入 (百万元)	Total profit (Mil.RMB) 总利润 (百万元)	Return on assets 资产利润率 (%)	Return on equity 权益利润率 (%)	Labour productivity ('000 RMB/ worker) 劳动生产率 (千元/人)	Debts/ assets 资产负债率 (%)	Total assets (Mil.RMB) 总资产 (百万元)
Industry Overall 行业总体	432	51,693	12,489	762	6.01	12.19	62.39	50.72	12,688

	Number of firms 企业个数	Average number of employees 平均职工人数	Average revenue ('000 RMB) 平均销售收入 (千元)	Average profit ('000 RMB) 平均利润 (千元)	Return on assets 资产利润率 (%)	Return on equity 权益利润率 (%)	Labour productivity ('000 RMB/ worker) 劳动生产率 (千元/人)	Debts/ assets 资产负债率 (%)	Average total assets ('000 RMB) 平均总资产 (千元)
By ownership 产业所有权									
State-owned 国有	32	244	27,810	-331	-0.77	-2.43	17.82	68.13	42,714
Collective-owned 集体	95	168	25,103	1,087	4.27	7.13	38.28	40.20	25,492
Foreign & Overseas Chinese Funded 三资	77	100	49,087	4,115	7.53	12.92	135.14	41.73	54,687
By regional distribution 地区分布									
Central-North 华北	66	73	26,288	1,839	7.36	18.19	92.50	59.55	24,997
Beijing 北京	22	51	34,193	3,018	9.27	18.11	131.64	48.84	32,572
Tianjin 天津	18	66	20,295	1,291	7.00	15.20	90.22	53.97	18,453
Hebei 河北	17	84	26,262	1,628	9.12	37.54	99.41	75.70	17,853
Shanxi 山西	7	107	20,857	349	1.07	4.75	43.90	77.55	32,725
Inner Mongolia 内蒙古	2	160	12,509	802	2.34	7.08	46.51	66.91	34,231
Northeast 东北	28	392	36,473	607	1.05	1.72	24.04	38.99	57,797
Liaoning 辽宁	22	480	41,996	559	0.79	1.27	20.74	38.22	71,136
Jilin 吉林	6	71	16,220	786	8.85	23.05	106.20	61.62	8,886
Heilongjiang 黑龙江									
Central-East 华东	214	113	29,858	2,062	7.12	14.04	71.86	49.29	28,965
Shanghai 上海	17	84	38,990	2,227	4.40	7.98	106.47	44.93	50,641
Jiangsu 江苏	98	97	25,892	1,212	5.07	11.18	67.35	54.69	23,937
Zhejiang 浙江	49	85	31,045	2,841	9.59	18.30	93.94	47.61	29,636
Anhui 安徽	5	640	30,751	-2,104	-3.56	-47.97	10.00	92.57	59,012
Fujian 福建	8	237	66,499	4,709	6.61	8.10	102.95	18.33	71,204
Jiangxi 江西	4	171	12,623	-365	-1.89	-5.35	25.09	64.56	19,253
Shandong 山东	33	99	28,239	3,627	20.02	36.19	93.80	44.68	18,116
Central-South 中南	104	98	30,347	1,683	5.80	12.65	70.87	54.16	29,010
Henan 河南	20	107	21,533	680	6.39	20.01	55.19	68.07	10,640
Hubei 湖北	12	52	12,830	583	5.27	7.42	76.09	29.00	11,064
Hunan 湖南	7	266	17,328	-484	-1.21	-3.76	7.50	67.81	39,967
Guangdong 广东	63	87	38,736	2,494	6.60	13.98	97.19	52.78	37,773
Guangxi 广西	1	40	5,716	619	12.92	17.67	185.28	26.87	4,790
Hainan 海南	1	17	4,151	67	0.92	1.85	22.94	50.13	7,265
Southwest 西南	10	48	9,238	741	10.88	20.86	58.20	47.84	6,812
Chongqing 重庆	1	94	8,176	733	6.47	21.55	38.69	69.97	11,327
Sichuan 四川	7	40	10,471	837	11.96	22.31	78.72	46.39	6,994
Guizhou 贵州	2	53	5,456	411	10.49	13.96	21.70	24.89	3,915
Yunnan 云南									
Tibet 西藏									
Northwest 西北	10	108	9,422	-3	-0.02	-0.09	28.69	73.18	13,678
Shaanxi 陕西	2	221	7,510	-863	-6.26	-59.18	18.74	89.43	13,785
Gansu 甘肃	5	41	1,250	8	0.11	0.32	27.54	65.94	7,824
Qinghai 青海									
Ningxia 宁夏	2	181	29,210	471	1.64	9.32	36.61	82.44	28,774
Xinjiang 新疆	1	72	14,528	708	5.65	6.85	53.39	17.55	12,542

2659: Other Organic Chemical Products 其他有机化学产品制造业

Year 年份	Number of firms 企业个数	Rate of change 变化率 (%)	Number of employees 职工人数 (人)	Rate of change 变化率 (%)	Total revenue (Mil. RMB) 总销售收入 (百万元)	Rate of change 变化率 (%)	Total profit (Mil RMB) 总利润 (百万元)	Rate of change 变化率 (%)
2000	399		64,362		11,863		447	
2001	464	16.29	59,882	-6.96	12,090	1.91	514	14.99
2002	432	-6.90	51,693	-13.68	12,489	3.30	762	48.25

Major Products 主要产品	Output 产量	Unit 单位
Formaldehyde 甲醛	256	10,000 Tons 万吨
Extractive Carbinol 精甲醇	211	10,000 Tons 万吨

10 Main Firms with Maximal Revenue (year founded) 收入最大的十家主要企业（创办年份）	City 城市	Province 省	Telephone/fax 电话/传真	Number of employees 职工人数	Ownership 产业所有权	Revenue ('000 RMB) 销售收入 (千元)	Profit('000 RMB) (rank) 利润(千元) (排名)	Total assets ('000 RMB) 总资产 (千元)	Major products 主要产品
Nanhai Nanguang Chemical Industry Packing Co., Ltd.	Foshan	Guangdong	(0757)5992888		Overseas Chinese-funded				Plastics Can
南海南光化工包装有限公司(1991)	佛山市	广东省	(0757)5992096	269	港澳台资	298,180	22,720(6)	319,950	塑料罐
China Chemical Fibre General Corporation	Beijing	Beijing	(010)65816699		State-owned				Polymer Fire-retardant Terylene聚合物型
中国化纤总公司(1987)	北京市	北京市	(010)65813483	70	国有企业	290,769	9,686(24)	364,166	阻燃涤纶
Fujian Shishi Huabao Group Company	Quanzhou	Fujian	(0595)8900495		Collective-owned				N-Dextrose of Acetamide N-乙酰
石狮市华宝集团公司(1990)	泉州市	福建省	(0595)8930501	1,435	集体企业	278,497	30,278(4)	377,235	氨葡萄糖
Jiangmen Qianxin Chemical Industry Development Co., Ltd.	Jiangmen	Guangdong	(0750)3795839		Overseas Chinese-funded				Ethyl Acetate
江门谦信化工发展有限公司(1993)	江门市	广东省	(0750)3795819	90	港澳台资	267,312	3,030(53)	104,978	醋酸乙酯
Zhejiang Fluorescencen Chemical Co., Ltd.	Jinhua	Zhejiang	(0579)6686203		Foreign Funded				Anhydrous Sodium
浙江莹光化工有限公司(1965)	金华市	浙江省	(0579)6686197	406	外商投资	218,630	21,416(10)	252,290	无水酸
Nippon Carbide Industries(Hang Zhou) Co.,Ltd.	Hangzhou	Zhejiang	(0571)82696666		Foreign Funded				Reflect Membrane
恩希爱杭州化工有限公司(1994)	杭州市	浙江省	(0571)82696473	373	外商投资	212,912	10,016(23)	316,781	反光膜
Kao Chemical Corporation Shanghai	Shanghai	Shanghai	(021)64092880		Foreign Funded				Surface Active Reagent表
上海花王化学有限公司(1995)	上海市	上海市	(021)64092881	117	外商投资	211,574	5,159(37)	255,056	面活性剂
Fenghua Nanhai Pharmaceutical Chemistry Group Co., Ltd.	Ningbo	Zhejiang	(0574)88765159		Limited-Liability				solvent leveling Reagent
奉化市南海药化集团有限公司(1986)	宁波市	浙江省	(0574)88765701	149	有限公司	186,456	13,026(17)	191,993	流平剂
Liaoning Tian He Fine Chemicals Co., Ltd.	Jinzhou	Liaoning	(0416)4147247		Joint Stock				Fine Chemical Industry
辽宁天合精细化工股份有限公司(1998)	锦州市	辽宁省	(0416)4140975	860	股份制	175,600	7,500(30)	338,849	精细化工
Arnugell (Guangzhou) Co.,ltd	Guangzhou	Guangdong	(020)83634518		Foreign Funded				Rubber Thermal Insulating Material橡胶
阿乐斯绝热材料（广州）有限公司(1994)	广州市	广东省	(020)84865692	125	外商投资	142,944	23,232(5)	130,000	保温材料

Top 10 Cities by Revenue 销售收入排名前10位城市	Province 省	Market share 市场份额 (%)	Number of firms 企业个数
Jiangmen 江门市	Guangdong 广东省	6.54	11
Beijing 北京市	Beijing 北京市	6.02	22
Shanghai 上海市	Shanghai 上海市	5.31	17
Wuxi 无锡市	Jiangsu 江苏省	4.94	22
Guangzhou 广州市	Guangdong 广东省	4.55	17
Suzhou 苏州市	Jiangsu 江苏省	4.49	13
Foshan 佛山市	Guangdong 广东省	3.61	9
Taizhou 泰州市	Jiangsu 江苏省	3.00	16
Jinhua 金华市	Zhejiang 浙江省	3.00	5
Tianjin 天津市	Tianjin 天津市	2.93	18

10 Major Wholesalers 十家主要批发商	City 城市	Province 省	Telephone/Fax 电话/传真
Yihua Kangqi Chemical Fibre Co.,Ltd.	Yangzhou	Jiangsu	(0514)3235499
仪化康祺化纤有限责任公司	扬州市	江苏省	(0514)3233847
Sinochem Guangdong Import & Export Company	Guangzhou	Guangdong	(020)86672288
中化广东进出口公司	广州市	广东省	(020)86507512
Sinochem Shanghai Import & Export Company	Shanghai	Shanghai	(021)63289888
中化上海进出口公司	上海市	上海市	(021)63283968
Sinochem Tianjin Import & Export Company	Tianjin	Tianjin	(022)23146216
中化天津进出口公司	天津市	天津市	(022)23146215
China Chemical Sales & Supply (North China) Corporation	Tianjin	Tianjin	(022)23011031
中国化工供销华北公司	天津市	天津市	(022)23011032
China Chemical Sales & Supply (North China) Corporation	Shanghai	Shanghai	(021)62103300
中国化工供销华东公司	上海市	上海市	(021)62515799
Nantong Chemical Light Industry Co.,Ltd.	Nantong	Jiangsu	(0513)5518397
南通化工轻工股份有限公司	南通市	江苏省	(0513)5512735
Taizhou Heshun Plastics Co.,Ltd.	Taizhou	Zhejiang	(0576)2510220
台州市和顺塑料有限公司	台州市	浙江省	(0576)2510160
China Petroleum Technology Development Corporation	Beijing	Beijing	(010)84080722
中国石油技术开发公司	北京市	北京市	(010)84080800
China National Chemical Fiber Corporation	Beijing	Beijing	(010)65816699
中国化纤总公司	北京市	北京市	(010)65813483

2661: Polyolefin Plastic 聚烯烃塑料制造业

The industry accounts for 0.306% of the total revenue of China's industrial sector in 2002. The rate of return on assets is 0.77%. 76.23% of all firms in the industry made a profit while 23.77% had negative returns.The top province in terms of the industry's revenue is Guangdong, accounting for 31.35% of the total revenue.
2002年本行业收入占全行业的0.306%，资产利润率为0.77%。76.23%的企业赢利，23.77%的企业亏损。收入最高的省为广东省，占本行业的31.35%。

	Total number of firms 企业总数	Total number of employees 职工总数	Total revenue (Mil.RMB) 总销售收入（百万元）	Total profit (Mil.RMB) 总利润（百万元）	Return on assets 资产利润率（%）	Return on equity 权益利润率（%）	Labour productivity ('000 RMB/worker) 劳动生产率（千元/人）	Debts/assets 资产负债率（%）	Total assets (Mil.RMB) 总资产（百万元）
Industry Overall 行业总体	122	88,355	32,873	361	0.77	1.25	89.71	38.90	47,111

	Number of firms 企业个数	Average number of employees 平均职工人数	Average revenue ('000 RMB) 平均销售收入（千元）	Average profit ('000 RMB) 平均利润（千元）	Return on assets 资产利润率（%）	Return on equity 权益利润率（%）	Labour productivity ('000 RMB/worker) 劳动生产率（千元/人）	Debts/assets 资产负债率（%）	Average total assets ('000 RMB) 平均总资产（千元）
By ownership 产业所有权									
State-owned 国有	13	1,509	838,424	-16,042	-0.77	-1.19	106.79	35.24	2,075,285
Collective-owned 集体	19	1,464	52,602	3,216	8.84	24.00	11.03	63.17	36,389
Foreign & Overseas Chinese Funded 三资	37	111	226,900	11,922	6.00	10.65	465.14	43.71	198,851
By regional distribution 地区分布									
Central-North 华北	17	313	142,525	1,118	0.59	1.26	83.07	52.80	187,967
Beijing 北京	7	489	163,376	711	0.25	0.46	91.79	44.79	278,890
Tianjin 天津	3	92	362,873	4,164	1.22	3.67	284.32	66.82	342,040
Hebei 河北	7	232	27,239	218	0.70	1.70	30.44	58.58	31,013
Shanxi 山西									
Inner Mongolia 内蒙古									
Northeast 东北	9	224	138,717	-9,403	-3.63	-7.20	71.21	49.60	259,055
Liaoning 辽宁	6	141	43,019	2,295	9.51	20.77	48.33	54.19	24,126
Jilin 吉林	1	62	5,000	320	7.80	106.67	19.35	92.68	4,100
Heilongjiang 黑龙江	2	555	492,670	-49,358	-4.52	-8.91	91.57	49.21	1,091,321
Central-East 华东	62	543	247,854	5,995	2.57	4.60	130.89	44.13	233,089
Shanghai 上海	5	88	181,830	30,151	14.23	21.90	718.62	35.04	211,942
Jiangsu 江苏	21	306	278,296	9,952	3.77	8.17	222.98	53.80	263,647
Zhejiang 浙江	10	92	63,773	3,245	8.80	26.05	90.09	66.22	36,877
Anhui 安徽	2	43	7,163	103	1.48	6.02	34.79	75.41	6,923
Fujian 福建	2	97	45,176	570	1.78	5.23	10.21	65.95	31,990
Jiangxi 江西	4	468	46,738	-3,219	-3.41	-46.84	28.65	92.71	94,309
Shandong 山东	18	1,319	426,900	-497	-0.13	-0.19	106.06	33.86	390,633
Central-South 中南	32	1,463	421,469	1,338	0.16	0.24	60.76	33.55	835,812
Henan 河南	7	681	313,197	-20,902	-3.20	-7.70	56.00	58.40	652,722
Hubei 湖北	6	3,992	31,068	-2,864	-6.05	-15.80	1.65	61.68	47,311
Hunan 湖南	3	308	267,082	3,209	5.98	9.18	451.84	34.83	53,646
Guangdong 广东	16	1,073	644,185	12,292	0.91	1.26	123.47	27.95	1,358,257
Guangxi 广西									
Hainan 海南									
Southwest 西南									
Chongqing 重庆									
Sichuan 四川									
Guizhou 贵州									
Yunnan 云南									
Tibet 西藏									
Northwest 西北	2	269	173,695	6,168	3.19	4.82	166.19	33.94	193,506
Shaanxi 陕西	1	360	56,633	4,101	10.93	33.13	40.17	67.00	37,510
Gansu 甘肃	1	178	290,756	8,234	2.36	3.38	421.07	30.40	349,501
Qinghai 青海									
Ningxia 宁夏									
Xinjiang 新疆									

Year 年份	Number of firms 企业个数	Rate of change 变化率(%)	Number of employees 职工人数(人)	Rate of change 变化率(%)	Total revenue (Mil. RMB) 总销售收入(百万元)	Rate of change 变化率(%)	Total profit (Mil RMB) 总利润(百万元)	Rate of change 变化率(%)
2000	97		36,965		18,203		557	
2001	109	12.37	29,367	-20.55	15,100	-17.05	-194	-
2002	122	11.93	88,355	200.86	32,873	117.70	361	-

Major Products 主要产品	Output 产量	Unit 单位
Polypropylene Resin 聚丙烯树脂	374	10,000 Tons 万吨
Polyethylene Resin 聚乙烯树脂	355	10,000 Tons 万吨

10 Main Firms with Maximal Revenue (year founded) 收入最大的十家主要企业（创办年份）	City 城市	Province 省	Telephone/fax 电话/传真	Number of employees 职工人数	Ownership 产业所有权	Revenue ('000 RMB) 销售收入(千元)	Profit('000 RMB) (rank) 利润(千元)(排名)	Total assets ('000 RMB) 总资产(千元)	Major products 主要产品
Sinopec Maoming Petrochemical Corporation	Maoming	Guangdong	(0668)2242241		State-owned				Enthene
中国石化集团茂名石油化工公司(1965)	茂名市	广东省	(0668)2269317	14,194	国有企业	8,013,311	85,169(4)	20,007,452	乙烯
Sinopec Qilu Co.,Ltd.	Zibo	Shandong	(0533)3583728		Joint Stock				Polythene
中国石化齐鲁股份有限公司(1998)	淄博市	山东省	(0533)3583718	22,146	股份制	7,149,280	-	6,728,315	聚乙烯
Zhongyuan Petrochemical Co.,Ltd.	Puyang	Henan	(0393)4471212		State-owned				Polyolefine
中原石油化工有限责任公司(1996)	濮阳市	河南省	(0393)4416227	1,410	国有企业	1,743,400	-	4,156,701	聚烯烃
Maoming Petrochemical Shihua Stock Co., Ltd.	Maoming	Guangdong	(0668)2883198		Joint Stock				Polypropylene
茂名石化实华股份有限公司(1988)	茂名市	广东省	(0668)2281965	744	股份制	1,434,931	93,281(3)	695,051	聚丙烯
Zhenjiang Qimei Chemical Co.,Ltd	Zhenjiang	Jiangsu	(0511)3121300		Foreign Funded				Polystyrene Resin聚苯
镇江奇美化工有限公司(1996)	镇江市	江苏省	(0511)3121787	216	外商投资	1,103,974	37,749(6)	624,046	乙烯树脂
Tianjin Lejin Dagu Chemical Co., Ltd.	Tianjin	Tianjin	(022)25386666		Foreign Funded				Polyvinyl Chloride
天津乐金大沽化学有限公司(1995)	天津市	天津市	(022)25388311	225	外商投资	1,073,497	11,970(11)	992,319	聚氯乙烯
Beijing No.2 Chemical Co.,Ltd.	Beijing	Beijing	(010)67712277		Joint Stock				Plastic Products
北京化二股份有限公司(1997)	北京市	北京市	(010)67781459	2,164	股份制	830,908	2,053(30)	1,546,302	塑料制品
Zhenjiang JPPC Chemical Co.,Ltd.	Zhenjiang	Jiangsu	(0511)3121155		Foreign Funded				ABS Resin
镇江国亨化学有限公司(1999)	镇江市	江苏省	(0511)3121224	133	外商投资	706,158	5,225(21)	414,441	ABS树脂
Jiangsu Bei Fang Chlorine Alkali Group Co., Ltd.	Xuzhou	Jiangsu	(0516)7767897		State Enterprises				Polyvinyl Chloride
江苏北方氯碱集团有限公司(1958)	徐州市	江苏省	(0516)7767151	3,486	国有独资	542,980	-	1,187,700	聚氯已烯
Yueyang Tonghai Industry Park	Yueyang	Hunan	(0730)8711446		Others				
岳阳通海工业园(1993)	岳阳市	湖南省	(0730)8711446	780	其他企业	497,520	-	107,008	

Top 10 Cities by Revenue 销售收入排名前10位城市	Province 省	Market share 市场份额(%)	Number of firms 企业个数
Maoming 茂名市	Guangdong 广东省	28.74	2
Zibo 淄博市	Shandong 山东省	21.94	4
Zhenjiang 镇江市	Jiangsu 江苏省	8.14	4
Puyang 濮阳市	Henan 河南省	5.30	2
Nanjing 南京市	Jiangsu 江苏省	3.79	1
Beijing 北京市	Beijing 北京市	3.48	7
Tianjin 天津市	Tianjin 天津市	3.31	3
Shanghai 上海市	Shanghai 上海市	2.77	5
Wuxi 无锡市	Jiangsu 江苏省	2.75	7
Daqing 大庆市	Heilongjiang 黑龙江省	2.49	1

10 Major Wholesalers 十家主要批发商	City 城市	Province 省	Telephone/Fax 电话/传真
Yihua Kangqi Chemical Fibre Co.,Ltd.	Yangzhou	Jiangsu	(0514)3235499
仪化康祺化纤有限责任公司	扬州市	江苏省	(0514)3233847
Sinochem Guangdong Import & Export Company	Guangzhou	Guangdong	(020)86672288
中化广东进出口公司	广州市	广东省	(020)86507512
Sinochem Shanghai Import & Export Company	Shanghai	Shanghai	(021)63289888
中化上海进出口公司	上海市	上海市	(021)63283968
Sinochem Tianjin Import & Export Company	Tianjin	Tianjin	(022)23146216
中化天津进出口公司	天津市	天津市	(022)23146215
China Chemical Sales & Supply (North China) Corporation	Tianjin	Tianjin	(022)23011031
中国化工供销华北公司	天津市	天津市	(022)23011032
China Chemical Sales & Supply (North China) Corporation	Shanghai	Shanghai	(021)62103300
中国化工供销华东公司	上海市	上海市	(021)62515799
Nantong Chemical Light Industry Co.,Ltd.	Nantong	Jiangsu	(0513)5518397
南通化工轻工股份有限公司	南通市	江苏省	(0513)5512735
Taizhou Heshun Plastics Co.,Ltd.	Taizhou	Zhejiang	(0576)2510220
台州市和顺塑料有限公司	台州市	浙江省	(0576)2510160
China Petroleum Technology Development Corporation	Beijing	Beijing	(010)84080722
中国石油技术开发公司	北京市	北京市	(010)84080800
China National Chemical Fiber Corporation	Beijing	Beijing	(010)65816699
中国化纤总公司	北京市	北京市	(010)65813483

2662: Resinoid and Plastic 热固性树脂及塑料制造业

The industry accounts for 0.106% of the total revenue of China's industrial sector in 2002. The rate of return on assets is 1.99%. 84.82% of all firms in the industry made a profit while 15.18% had negative returns.The top province in terms of the industry's revenue is Shanghai, accounting for 39.10% of the total revenue.
2002年本行业收入占全行业的 0.106%，资产利润率为 1.99%。84.82%的企业赢利，15.18%的企业亏损。收入最高的省为上海市，占本行业的39.10%。

	Total number of firms 企业总数	Total number of employees 职工总数	Total revenue (Mil.RMB) 总销售收入 (百万元)	Total profit (Mil.RMB) 总利润 (百万元)	Return on assets 资产利润率 (%)	Return on equity 权益利润率 (%)	Labour productivity ('000 RMB/ worker) 劳动生产率 (千元/人)	Debts/ assets 资产负债率 (%)	Total assets (Mil.RMB) 总资产 (百万元)
Industry Overall 行业总体	191	32,410	11,395	285	1.99	3.29	86.41	39.42	14,320

	Number of firms 企业个数	Average number of employees 平均职工人数	Average revenue ('000 RMB) 平均销售收入 (千元)	Average profit ('000 RMB) 平均利润 (千元)	Return on assets 资产利润率 (%)	Return on equity 权益利润率 (%)	Labour productivity ('000 RMB/ worker) 劳动生产率 (千元/人)	Debts/ assets 资产负债率 (%)	Average total assets ('000 RMB) 平均总资产 (千元)
By ownership 产业所有权									
State-owned 国有	11	399	154,610	2,513	0.65	0.76	65.40	13.64	384,029
Collective-owned 集体	28	152	33,427	949	3.46	12.82	59.15	72.99	27,404
Foreign & Overseas Chinese Funded 三资	43	253	116,881	2,772	1.83	3.12	122.44	41.32	151,466
By regional distribution 地区分布									
Central-North 华北	19	80	17,152	499	3.60	9.93	55.40	63.74	13,876
Beijing 北京	4	21	5,714	222	6.34	26.05	70.84	75.67	3,503
Tianjin 天津	5	34	15,766	698	4.02	11.16	92.75	63.94	17,362
Hebei 河北	7	70	17,188	600	5.35	16.77	69.17	68.10	11,216
Shanxi 山西	2	353	45,234	96	0.27	0.71	31.79	62.08	35,289
Inner Mongolia 内蒙古	1	70	13,432	717	5.22	7.90	87.17	33.84	13,725
Northeast 东北	11	129	19,882	-11	-0.04	-0.17	31.81	74.12	24,898
Liaoning 辽宁	6	127	16,990	-242	-0.77	-2.35	26.20	67.18	31,393
Jilin 吉林	3	24	4,671	968	9.34	38.79	119.04	75.91	10,364
Heilongjiang 黑龙江	2	294	51,373	-788	-2.89	-99.62	28.52	97.09	27,211
Central-East 华东	112	209	80,156	1,864	1.76	2.69	95.37	34.50	105,704
Shanghai 上海	14	774	318,251	4,091	0.64	0.86	92.35	25.35	635,671
Jiangsu 江苏	36	159	51,533	1,418	3.86	11.25	101.24	65.72	36,767
Zhejiang 浙江	25	74	40,939	1,429	6.04	14.99	97.29	59.68	23,641
Anhui 安徽	14	131	24,390	312	2.47	8.03	55.82	69.20	12,605
Fujian 福建	7	85	48,675	1,870	4.99	8.44	165.78	40.89	37,480
Jiangxi 江西	2	229	18,690	-453	-2.00	-3.32	4.91	39.78	22,627
Shandong 山东	14	155	65,982	3,445	8.92	26.43	126.70	66.25	38,623
Central-South 中南	42	104	39,859	1,353	3.73	9.89	83.89	62.34	36,326
Henan 河南	5	114	20,504	1,473	7.18	33.57	33.66	78.62	20,531
Hubei 湖北	3	57	17,910	1,782	18.55	30.09	143.18	38.35	9,604
Hunan 湖南	1	71	3,200				5.63	125.54	11,533
Guangdong 广东	32	110	47,165	1,376	3.19	8.24	91.13	61.27	43,092
Guangxi 广西	1	32	5,360	90	2.42	2.42	43.47		3,720
Hainan 海南									
Southwest 西南	6	236	25,500	931	1.45	3.43	34.22	57.66	64,042
Chongqing 重庆	1	649	47,864	-2,793	-1.42	-4.00	13.54	64.60	197,073
Sichuan 四川	5	154	21,028	1,676	4.48	9.02	51.70	50.34	37,436
Guizhou 贵州									
Yunnan 云南									
Tibet 西藏									
Northwest 西北	1	252	45,676	4,688	14.04	27.45	83.86	48.88	33,401
Shaanxi 陕西									
Gansu 甘肃	1	252	45,676	4,688	14.04	27.45	83.86	48.88	33,401
Qinghai 青海									
Ningxia 宁夏									
Xinjiang 新疆									

2662: Resinoid and Plastic 热固性树脂及塑料制造业

Year 年份	Number of firms 企业个数	Rate of change 变化率(%)	Number of employees 职工人数(人)	Rate of change 变化率(%)	Total revenue (Mil. RMB) 总销售收入(百万元)	Rate of change 变化率(%)	Total profit (Mil RMB) 总利润(百万元)	Rate of change 变化率(%)
2000	153		36,112		9,635		321	
2001	166	8.50	30,916	-14.39	11,289	17.17	171	-46.73
2002	191	15.06	32,410	4.83	11,395	0.94	285	66.67

Major Products 主要产品	Output 产量	Unit 单位
Plastic Resin & Copolymer 塑料树脂及共聚物	1,366	10,000 Tons 万吨
Polyester 聚脂	314	10,000 Tons 万吨

10 Main Firms with Maximal Revenue (year founded) 收入最大的十家主要企业（创办年份）	City 城市	Province 省	Telephone/fax 电话/传真	Number of employees 职工人数	Ownership 产业所有权	Revenue ('000 RMB) 销售收入(千元)	Profit('000 RMB) (rank) 利润(千元)(排名)	Total assets ('000 RMB) 总资产(千元)	Major products 主要产品
Sinopec Shanghai Gaoqiao Petrochemical Company 中国石化上海高桥石化公司(1981)	Shanghai 上海市	Shanghai 上海市	(021)58711001 (021)58712207	2,976	State-owned 国有企业	1,589,299	27,213(2)	3,945,660	Polyether 聚醚
Eternal Chemical (China) Co., Ltd 长兴化学工业(中国)有限公司(1995)	Suzhou 苏州市	Jiangsu 江苏省	(0512)57622168 (0512)57621859	210	Foreign Funded 外商投资	321,600	15,660(4)	266,103	Vinylite 合成树脂
Zhejiang Tianhe Resin Co.,Ltd. 浙江天和树脂有限公司(1996)	Taizhou 台州市	Zhejiang 浙江省	(0576)5178365 (0576)5178258	267	Limited-Liability 有限公司	308,725	4,557(24)	154,104	Unsaturaled Polyester Resin不饱和聚酯树脂
Dangyang Hua Mei Plastics Co., Ltd. 丹阳华美塑料有限公司(1992)	Zhenjiang 镇江市	Jiangsu 江苏省	(0511)6388777 (0511)6388787	189	Overseas Chinese-funded 港澳台资	226,005	1,106(57)	74,261	Dye Plastic Pellet染色塑料粒子
Eternal Chemical (Guangzhou) Co.,Ltd. 长兴（广州）化学工业有限公司(1995)	Guangzhou 广州市	Guangdong 广东省	(020)82222990 (020)82221884	60	Overseas Chinese-funded 港澳台资	209,064	8,593(12)	59,606	Dry Anti-erode Film光致抗蚀干膜
Dongguan Yi Xing Plastic Material Co., Ltd. 东莞毅兴塑胶原料有限公司(1993)	Dongguan 东莞市	Guangdong 广东省	(0769)5588755 (0769)5581756	400	Overseas Chinese-funded 港澳台资	178,879	29,558(1)	153,058	Toner 色粉
Jiangsu Jinyi Group Company 江苏金益集团公司(1992)	Zhenjiang 镇江市	Jiangsu 江苏省	(0511)3361470 (0511)3361969	1,451	Collective-owned 集体企业	155,628	-	287,471	Polyvinyl Chloride Resin聚氯乙烯树脂
Zhongshan Ju He Chemistry Co., Ltd. 中山市聚和化学有限公司(1986)	Zhongshan 中山市	Guangdong 广东省	(0760)8895274 (0760)8892200	132	Limited-Liability 有限公司	151,629	-	54,684	Unsaturaled Polyester Resin不饱和聚酯树脂
Jiangsu Su Qing Water Treatment Group Co., Ltd. 江苏苏青水处理工种集团有限公司(1996)	Wuxi 无锡市	Jiangsu 江苏省	(0510)6331801 (0510)6331672	364	Collective-owned 集体企业	150,358	9,797(6)	133,094	Resin 树脂
Jinling DSM Resins Co., Ltd 金陵蒂斯曼树脂有限公司(1992)	Nanjing 南京市	Jiangsu 江苏省	(025)5570570 (025)5564848	92	Foreign Funded 外商投资	144,540	7,790(14)	73,360	Unsaturaled Polyester Resin不饱和聚酯树脂

Top 10 Cities by Revenue 销售收入排名前10位城市	Province 省	Market share 市场份额 (%)	Number of firms 企业个数
Shanghai 上海市	Shanghai 上海市	39.10	14
Suzhou 苏州市	Jiangsu 江苏省	5.06	8
Zhenjiang 镇江市	Jiangsu 江苏省	4.63	8
Dongguan 东莞市	Guangdong 广东省	4.10	9
Taizhou 台州市	Zhejiang 浙江省	3.78	3
Wenzhou 温州市	Zhejiang 浙江省	3.09	8
Foshan 佛山市	Guangdong 广东省	3.02	6
Guangzhou 广州市	Guangdong 广东省	2.61	4
Zibo 淄博市	Shandong 山东省	2.59	5
Qingdao 青岛市	Shandong 山东省	2.56	3

10 Major Wholesalers 十家主要批发商	City 城市	Province 省	Telephone/Fax 电话/传真
Yihua Kangqi Chemical Fibre Co.,Ltd. 仪化康祺化纤有限责任公司	Yangzhou 扬州市	Jiangsu 江苏省	(0514)3235499 (0514)3233847
Sinochem Guangdong Import & Export Company 中化广东进出口公司	Guangzhou 广州市	Guangdong 广东省	(020)86672288 (020)86507512
Sinochem Shanghai Import & Export Company 中化上海进出口公司	Shanghai 上海市	Shanghai 上海市	(021)63289888 (021)63283968
Sinochem Tianjin Import & Export Company 中化天津进出口公司	Tianjin 天津市	Tianjin 天津市	(022)23146216 (022)23146215
China Chemical Sales & Supply (North China) Corporation 中国化工供销华北公司	Tianjin 天津市	Tianjin 天津市	(022)23011031 (022)23011032
China Chemical Sales & Supply (North China) Corporation 中国化工供销华东公司	Shanghai 上海市	Shanghai 上海市	(021)62103300 (021)62515799
Nantong Chemical Light Industry Co.,Ltd. 南通化工轻工股份有限公司	Nantong 南通市	Jiangsu 江苏省	(0513)5518397 (0513)5512735
Taizhou Heshun Plastics Co.,Ltd. 台州市和顺塑料有限公司	Taizhou 台州市	Zhejiang 浙江省	(0576)2510220 (0576)2510160
China Petroleum Technology Development Corporation 中国石油技术开发公司	Beijing 北京市	Beijing 北京市	(010)84080722 (010)84080800
China National Chemical Fiber Corporation 中国化纤总公司	Beijing 北京市	Beijing 北京市	(010)65816699 (010)65813483

2663: Engineering Plastic 工程塑料制造业

The industry accounts for 0.074% of the total revenue of China's industrial sector in 2002. The rate of return on assets is 5.28%. 76.92% of all firms in the industry made a profit while 23.08% had negative returns.The top province in terms of the industry's revenue is Zhejiang, accounting for 31.24% of the total revenue.
2002年本行业收入占全行业的 0.074%，资产利润率为 5.28%。76.92%的企业赢利，23.08%的企业亏损。收入最高的省为浙江省，占本行业的31.24%。

	Total number of firms 企业总数	Total number of employees 职工总数	Total revenue (Mil.RMB) 总销售收入(百万元)	Total profit (Mil.RMB) 总利润(百万元)	Return on assets 资产利润率(%)	Return on equity 权益利润率(%)	Labour productivity ('000 RMB/worker) 劳动生产率(千元/人)	Debts/assets 资产负债率(%)	Total assets (Mil.RMB) 总资产(百万元)
Industry Overall 行业总体	117	14,350	7,938	459	5.28	13.36	136.85	60.49	8,696

	Number of firms 企业个数	Average number of employees 平均职工人数	Average revenue ('000 RMB) 平均销售收入(千元)	Average profit ('000 RMB) 平均利润(千元)	Return on assets 资产利润率(%)	Return on equity 权益利润率(%)	Labour productivity ('000 RMB/worker) 劳动生产率(千元/人)	Debts/assets 资产负债率(%)	Average total assets ('000 RMB) 平均总资产(千元)
By ownership 产业所有权									
State-owned 国有	10	352	47,022	-926	-1.05	-8.57	29.84	87.70	87,893
Collective-owned 集体	13	93	17,276	1,011	6.27	12.24	67.07	48.80	16,142
Foreign & Overseas Chinese Funded 三资	35	128	151,258	10,289	6.36	14.62	294.07	56.48	161,694
By regional distribution 地区分布									
Central-North 华北	12	118	36,825	-2,651	-5.41	-34.37	89.01	84.25	48,968
Beijing 北京	5	99	39,811	-5,565	-9.32	-284.39	210.04	96.72	59,717
Tianjin 天津	2	97	67,194	-3,618	-4.56	-26.68	-6.90	82.92	79,393
Hebei 河北	4	149	22,778	819	3.37	6.28	25.55	46.28	24,287
Shanxi 山西	1	126	17,346	-26	-0.08	-0.75	59.67	89.53	33,095
Inner Mongolia 内蒙古									
Northeast 东北	5	119	18,630	4,972	17.81	29.36	63.11	39.33	27,915
Liaoning 辽宁	3	78	21,859	3,288	12.96	16.89	121.06	23.29	25,380
Jilin 吉林									
Heilongjiang 黑龙江	2	181	13,787	7,498	23.64	57.07	25.55	58.58	31,719
Central-East 华东	63	106	72,150	4,843	6.63	14.92	129.13	55.57	73,066
Shanghai 上海	13	176	63,232	4,462	4.52	10.10	68.21	55.22	98,671
Jiangsu 江苏	20	83	45,220	3,260	8.42	20.65	139.61	59.22	38,719
Zhejiang 浙江	16	91	154,996	11,122	8.22	17.64	237.33	53.40	135,286
Anhui 安徽									
Fujian 福建	7	107	27,612	-234	-0.67	-1.57	88.09	57.61	35,230
Jiangxi 江西	3	44	8,668	265	1.63	4.49	79.55	63.64	16,229
Shandong 山东	4	95	29,954	1,200	5.57	20.14	131.04	72.35	21,543
Central-South 中南	34	110	78,178	4,445	5.33	13.79	223.28	61.32	83,323
Henan 河南	3	139	33,297	1,276	8.65	33.92	27.13	74.49	14,749
Hubei 湖北	2	139	30,939	1,248	7.27	9.57	74.42	24.06	17,167
Hunan 湖南	1	80	7,045	135	2.41	3.93	20.99	38.78	5,604
Guangdong 广东	23	110	104,882	6,253	5.33	13.85	306.46	61.49	117,225
Guangxi 广西	5	89	15,392	171	1.62	5.09	62.38	68.18	10,523
Hainan 海南									
Southwest 西南	3	641	66,569	3,207	1.81	8.16	53.03	77.86	177,445
Chongqing 重庆									
Sichuan 四川	2	948	94,548	4,798	1.83	8.51	53.31	78.49	262,007
Guizhou 贵州									
Yunnan 云南	1	28	10,610	24	0.29	0.46	34.07	37.86	8,320
Tibet 西藏									
Northwest 西北									
Shaanxi 陕西									
Gansu 甘肃									
Qinghai 青海									
Ningxia 宁夏									
Xinjiang 新疆									

Year 年份	Number of firms 企业个数	Rate of change 变化率 (%)	Number of employees 职工人数 (人)	Rate of change 变化率 (%)	Total revenue (Mil. RMB) 总销售收入 (百万元)	Rate of change 变化率 (%)	Total profit (Mil RMB) 总利润 (百万元)	Rate of change 变化率 (%)
2000	83		10,236		4,318		615	
2001	113	36.14	13,607	32.93	7,247	67.83	559	-9.11
2002	117	3.54	14,350	5.46	7,938	9.53	459	-17.89

Major Products 主要产品	Output 产量	Unit 单位
Plastic Resin & Copolymer 塑料树脂及共聚物	1,366	10,000 Tons 万吨
Adhesive 粘合剂	77	10,000 Tons 万吨

10 Main Firms with Maximal Revenue (year founded) 收入最大的十家主要企业（创办年份）	City 城市	Province 省	Telephone/fax 电话/传真	Number of employees 职工人数	Ownership 产业所有权	Revenue ('000 RMB) 销售收入 (千元)	Profit('000 RMB) (rank) 利润(千元) (排名)	Total assets ('000 RMB) 总资产 (千元)	Major products 主要产品
Ningbo Xin Qiao Chemical Industral Co., Ltd.	Ningbo	Zhejiang	(0574)86228270		Overseas Chinese-funded				Polystyrene
宁波新桥化工有限公司(1996)	宁波市	浙江省	(0574)86221715	64	港澳台资	650,878	51,928(3)	311,249	聚苯乙烯
Dongguan Dainichiseia Chemical Co., Ltd.	Dongguan	Guangdong	(0769)5556675		Overseas Chinese-funded				Plastics Pellet
东莞大日化工有限公司(1997)	东莞市	广东省	(0769)5556695	138	港澳台资	226,353	8,824(14)	317,958	塑料粒
Wuxi Tian Lian Chemical Industry Co., Ltd.	Wuxi	Jiangsu	(0510)3302377		Private Owned				Polyester Slices
无锡市天联化工有限公司(1999)	无锡市	江苏省	(0510)3302377	60	私营企业	207,400	-	85,560	聚酯切片
Liao Yuan Radio Factory Of China Aerospace Science & Technology	Chengdu	Sichuan	(028)84807105		State-owned				Engineering Plastic Pressured Parts工
Group Corp中国航天科技集团公司燎原无线电厂(1975)	成都市	四川省	(028)84802939	1,833	国有企业	172,367	10,178(10)	433,799	程塑压件
Perlos (Guangzhou) Engineering Plastics Co., Ltd.	Guangzhou	Guangdong	(020)82266000		Foreign Funded				Plastics Mobile Telephone Shell
贝尔罗斯（广州）工程塑料有限公司(1999)	广州市	广东省	(020)82266001	542	外商投资	162,948	18,943(5)	246,549	手机外壳
DSM Engineering Plastics (Jiangsu) Co.,ltd	Wuxi	Jiangsu	(0510)6224507		Foreign Funded				EP Engineering Plastic
帝斯曼工程塑料(江苏)有限公司(1995)	无锡市	江苏省	(0510)6223519	94	外商投资	158,350	9,340(12)	120,110	EP工程塑料
KB (Panyu) Chemical Co., Ltd.	Guangzhou	Guangdong	(020)84976933		Overseas Chinese-funded				Formaldehyde
建滔(番禺)化工有限公司(1997)	广州市	广东省	(020)84975242	230	港澳台资	150,960	5,962(17)	376,119	甲醛
Wenzhou Deng Da Chemical Industry Co., Ltd.	Wenzhou	Zhejiang	(0577)88774701		Private Owned				Polyurethane
温州市登达化工有限公司(2000)	温州市	浙江省	(0577)88788883	120	私营企业	137,572		39,701	聚氨酯
Bayer Guangyi Plates Co., Ltd	Beijing	Beijing	(010)67883331		Foreign Funded				Polyurethane Board
拜耳光塑板材有限责任公司(1997)	北京市	北京市	(010)67882663	96	外商投资	129,959	-	107,649	碳酸酯板
Wenwei Plastic (Shenzhen) Co.,Ltd.	Shenzhen	Guangdong	(0755)27929188		Overseas Chinese-funded				Polyvinyl Chloride Products聚氯
文威塑胶（深圳）有限公司(1993)	深圳市	广东省	(0755)27929033	197	港澳台资	116,598	2,815(23)	74,511	乙烯制品

Top 10 Cities by Revenue 销售收入排名前10位城市	Province 省	Market share 市场份额 (%)	Number of firms 企业个数
Ningbo 宁波市	Zhejiang 浙江省	26.65	6
Guangzhou 广州市	Guangdong 广东省	23.61	10
Shanghai 上海市	Shanghai 上海市	10.36	13
Wuxi 无锡市	Jiangsu 江苏省	5.51	8
Changzhou 常州市	Jiangsu 江苏省	3.47	1
Dongguan 东莞市	Guangdong 广东省	2.96	2
Wenzhou 温州市	Zhejiang 浙江省	2.86	3
Shenzhen 深圳市	Guangdong 广东省	2.55	5
Beijing 北京市	Beijing 北京市	2.51	5
Chengdu 成都市	Sichuan 四川省	2.17	1

10 Major Wholesalers 十家主要批发商	City 城市	Province 省	Telephone/Fax 电话/传真
Yihua Kangqi Chemical Fibre Co.,Ltd.	Yangzhou	Jiangsu	(0514)3235499
仪化康祺化纤有限责任公司	扬州市	江苏省	(0514)3233847
Sinochem Guangdong Import & Export Company	Guangzhou	Guangdong	(020)86672288
中化广东进出口公司	广州市	广东省	(020)86507512
Sinochem Shanghai Import & Export Company	Shanghai	Shanghai	(021)63289888
中化上海进出口公司	上海市	上海市	(021)63283968
Sinochem Tianjin Import & Export Company	Tianjin	Tianjin	(022)23146216
中化天津进出口公司	天津市	天津市	(022)23146215
China Chemical Sales & Supply (North China) Corporation	Tianjin	Tianjin	(022)23011031
中国化工供销华北公司	天津市	天津市	(022)23011032
China Chemical Sales & Supply (North China) Corporation	Shanghai	Shanghai	(021)62103300
中国化工供销华东公司	上海市	上海市	(021)62515799
Nantong Chemical Light Industry Co.,Ltd.	Nantong	Jiangsu	(0513)5518397
南通化工轻工股份有限公司	南通市	江苏省	(0513)5512735
Taizhou Heshun Plastics Co.,Ltd.	Taizhou	Zhejiang	(0576)2510220
台州市和顺塑料有限公司	台州市	浙江省	(0576)2510160
China Petroleum Technology Development Corporation	Beijing	Beijing	(010)84080722
中国石油技术开发公司	北京市	北京市	(010)84080800
China National Chemical Fiber Corporation	Beijing	Beijing	(010)65816699
中国化纤总公司	北京市	北京市	(010)65813483

2664: Functional Polymer 功能高分子制造业

The industry accounts for 0.086% of the total revenue of China's industrial sector in 2002. The rate of return on assets is 7.45%. 80.69% of all firms in the industry made a profit while 19.31% had negative returns.The top province in terms of the industry's revenue is Jiangsu, accounting for 34.23% of the total revenue.
2002年本行业收入占全行业的 0.086%，资产利润率为 7.45%。80.69%的企业赢利，19.31%的企业亏损。收入最高的省为江苏省，占本行业的34.23%。

	Total number of firms 企业总数	Total number of employees 职工总数	Total revenue (Mil.RMB) 总销售收入 (百万元)	Total profit (Mil.RMB) 总利润 (百万元)	Return on assets 资产利润率 (%)	Return on equity 权益利润率 (%)	Labour productivity ('000 RMB/ worker) 劳动生产率 (千元/人)	Debts/ assets 资产负债率 (%)	Total assets (Mil.RMB) 总资产 (百万元)
Industry Overall 行业总体	145	21,457	9,255	633	7.45	16.54	107.53	54.95	8,491

	Number of firms 企业个数	Average number of employees 平均职工人数	Average revenue ('000 RMB) 平均销售收入 (千元)	Average profit ('000 RMB) 平均利润 (千元)	Return on assets 资产利润率 (%)	Return on equity 权益利润率 (%)	Labour productivity ('000 RMB/ worker) 劳动生产率 (千元/人)	Debts/ assets 资产负债率 (%)	Average total assets ('000 RMB) 平均总资产 (千元)
By ownership 产业所有权									
State-owned 国有	13	304	48,886	3,555	3.61	9.08	54.09	60.18	98,364
Collective-owned 集体	18	91	23,518	1,813	9.92	22.51	73.86	55.91	18,274
Foreign & Overseas Chinese Funded 三资	38	101	56,681	2,164	3.85	10.17	150.51	62.13	56,170
By regional distribution 地区分布									
Central-North 华北	16	80	30,646	1,905	7.69	17.35	-9.98	55.71	24,781
Beijing 北京	4	95	89,208	9,983	19.32	35.29	-135.23	45.24	51,657
Tianjin 天津	5	35	9,894	654	19.29	62.40	38.06	69.09	3,390
Hebei 河北	6	90	11,932	-613	-3.55	-7.96	47.39	55.44	17,282
Shanxi 山西									
Inner Mongolia 内蒙古	1	181	12,438	-9,046	-13.07	-82.09	34.65	84.08	69,223
Northeast 东北	11	149	18,700	3,403	3.36	5.11	37.81	34.40	101,418
Liaoning 辽宁	5	165	11,853	-863	-2.30	-7.51	15.63	69.42	37,613
Jilin 吉林	2	250	29,348	8,989	2.40	3.02	49.66	20.80	375,285
Heilongjiang 黑龙江	4	80	21,934	5,943	13.43	29.77	76.23	54.87	44,242
Central-East 华东	75	151	80,170	5,256	8.22	18.76	137.91	56.17	63,909
Shanghai 上海	12	81	38,580	-33	-0.06	-0.17	141.07	62.51	52,589
Jiangsu 江苏	35	172	90,528	4,497	6.58	14.46	135.28	54.50	68,344
Zhejiang 浙江	14	173	120,476	12,112	14.76	33.03	144.58	55.32	82,060
Anhui 安徽	1	259	9,233	-369	-0.84		14.25	121.45	43,995
Fujian 福建	3	43	17,029	126	0.42	0.67	3.77	37.36	30,052
Jiangxi 江西	1	35	4,185	54	2.29	5.75	23.46	60.13	2,355
Shandong 山东	9	164	70,012	7,512	13.95	31.50	171.72	55.72	53,858
Central-South 中南	36	185	68,292	4,528	7.83	21.16	101.32	63.02	57,866
Henan 河南	4	96	18,282	330	0.58	10.24	47.71	94.31	56,643
Hubei 湖北	5	248	18,337	450	0.73	2.16	32.77	66.17	61,628
Hunan 湖南	3	165	63,033	6,607	14.73	31.14	92.58	52.71	44,859
Guangdong 广东	23	196	91,167	6,056	9.88	23.61	125.89	58.14	61,278
Guangxi 广西	1	24	7,752	350	7.78		66.50	107.85	4,497
Hainan 海南									
Southwest 西南	6	77	13,061	769	5.54	13.23	50.24	58.13	13,882
Chongqing 重庆	1	43	10,194	185	4.48	112.80	-12.81	96.03	4,128
Sichuan 四川	5	84	13,635	886	5.60	12.76	56.71	56.16	15,833
Guizhou 贵州									
Yunnan 云南									
Tibet 西藏									
Northwest 西北	1	140	9,856	2,903	14.85	25.08	26.05	40.78	19,550
Shaanxi 陕西									
Gansu 甘肃									
Qinghai 青海									
Ningxia 宁夏	1	140	9,856	2,903	14.85	25.08	26.05	40.78	19,550
Xinjiang 新疆									

2664: Functional Polymer 功能高分子制造业

Year 年份	Number of firms 企业个数	Rate of change 变化率 (%)	Number of employees 职工人数 (人)	Rate of change 变化率 (%)	Total revenue (Mil. RMB) 总销售收入 (百万元)	Rate of change 变化率 (%)	Total profit (Mil RMB) 总利润 (百万元)	Rate of change 变化率 (%)
2000	117		17,678		6,221		367	
2001	131	11.97	29,251	65.47	6,367	2.35	358	-2.45
2002	145	10.69	21,457	-26.65	9,255	45.36	633	76.82

Major Products 主要产品	Output 产量	Unit 单位
Plastic Resin & Copolymer 塑料树脂及共聚物	1,366	10,000 Tons 万吨

10 Main Firms with Maximal Revenue (year founded) 收入最大的十家主要企业（创办年份）	City 城市	Province 省	Telephone/fax 电话/传真	Number of employees 职工人数	Ownership 产业所有权	Revenue ('000 RMB) 销售收入 (千元)	Profit('000 RMB) (rank) 利润(千元) (排名)	Total assets ('000 RMB) 总资产 (千元)	Major products 主要产品
Guangzhou Kingfa Science & Technology Development	Guangzhou	Guangdong	(020)87037818		Private Owned				Gaochong H2P5
Co.,Ltd. 广州金发科技发展有限公司(1993)	广州市	广东省	(020)87037827	870	私营企业	1,136,472	85,132(2)	572,229	高冲H2P5
Tianma Group Company	Changzhou	Jiangsu	(0519)5212676		State-owned				Unsaturaled Polyester Resin
天马集团公司(1993)	常州市	江苏省	(0519)5210145	1,750	国有企业	369,380	19,840(6)	479,250	不饱和聚酯树脂
Dongguan Hongde Chemical Industry Co.,Ltd.	Dongguan	Guangdong	(0769)5533620		Overseas Chinese-funded				Organic Chemistry Products
东莞宏德化学工业有限公司(1993)	东莞市	广东省	(0769)5533635	320	港澳台资	326,086	16,058(14)	152,678	有机化学产品
Beijing Eastern Acrylic Chemical Technology Co.,Ltd.	Beijing	Beijing	(010)61567430		Limited-Liability				Acrylic Copolymer
北京东方亚科力化工科技有限公司(2000)	北京市	北京市	(010)61567410	186	有限公司	287,554	19,806(7)	79,768	丙烯酸树脂
Shengquan Group Stock Co., Ltd.	Jinan	Shandong	(0531)3511076		Joint Stock				Xylitol
章丘市圣泉集团股份有限公司(1981)	济南市	山东省	(0531)3511356	738	股份制	254,880	32,000(4)	247,700	糖醇
Jiangsu Full Mark Chemical Group Co.,Ltd	Wuxi	Jiangsu	(0510)6651029		Joint Stock				Resin
江苏富丽化工集团公司(1994)	无锡市	江苏省	(0510)6651333	248	股份制	186,170	4,312(29)	173,308	树脂
Hunan Yada New Materials Co., Ltd.	Changsha	Hunan	(0731)4632998		Joint Stock				Ultraviolet Ray Cure Aluminium
湖南省亚大新材料股份有限公司(1998)	长沙市	湖南省	(0731)4610165	268	股份制	182,460	19,505(8)	132,505	紫外光固化树脂
Hanjiang Jia Mei Macromolecule Materials Co., Ltd.	Yangzhou	Jiangsu	(0514)7730766		Private Owned				Engineering Plastics
邗江县佳美高分子材料有限公司(1999)	扬州市	江苏省	(0514)7730766	180	私营企业	162,390	1,710(47)	27,440	工程塑料
Nanjing Yangzi Eastman Chemical Ltd.	Nanjing	Jiangsu	(025)8646271		Foreign Funded				C5
南京扬子伊士曼化工有限公司(1998)	南京市	江苏省	(025)8646288	87	外商投资	161,310	-	300,290	C5
Shanghai You Xi Bi Special Chemical Co.,Ltd.	Shanghai	Shanghai	(021)57466587		Foreign Funded				Polyester Agent
上海优西比特种化工有限公司(1999)	上海市	上海市	(021)57465056	105	外商投资	137,887	-	292,629	聚脂添加剂

Top 10 Cities by Revenue 销售收入排名前10位城市	Province 省	Market share 市场份额 (%)	Number of firms 企业个数
Wuxi 无锡市	Jiangsu 江苏省	17.41	14
Guangzhou 广州市	Guangdong 广东省	15.47	9
Wenzhou 温州市	Zhejiang 浙江省	14.04	4
Changzhou 常州市	Jiangsu 江苏省	5.56	5
Shanghai 上海市	Shanghai 上海市	5.00	12
Beijing 北京市	Beijing 北京市	3.86	4
Nanjing 南京市	Jiangsu 江苏省	3.77	6
Dongguan 东莞市	Guangdong 广东省	3.52	1
Yancheng 盐城市	Jiangsu 江苏省	2.76	2
Jinan 济南市	Shandong 山东省	2.75	1

10 Major Wholesalers 十家主要批发商	City 城市	Province 省	Telephone/Fax 电话/传真
Yihua Kangqi Chemical Fibre Co.,Ltd.	Yangzhou	Jiangsu	(0514)3235499
仪化康祺化纤有限责任公司	扬州市	江苏省	(0514)3233847
Sinochem Guangdong Import & Export Company	Guangzhou	Guangdong	(020)86672288
中化广东进出口公司	广州市	广东省	(020)86507512
Sinochem Shanghai Import & Export Company	Shanghai	Shanghai	(021)63289888
中化上海进出口公司	上海市	上海市	(021)63283968
Sinochem Tianjin Import & Export Company	Tianjin	Tianjin	(022)23146216
中化天津进出口公司	天津市	天津市	(022)23146215
China Chemical Sales & Supply (North China) Corporation	Tianjin	Tianjin	(022)23011031
中国化工供销华北公司	天津市	天津市	(022)23011032
China Chemical Sales & Supply (North China) Corporation	Shanghai	Shanghai	(021)62103300
中国化工供销华东公司	上海市	上海市	(021)62515799
Nantong Chemical Light Industry Co.,Ltd.	Nantong	Jiangsu	(0513)5518397
南通化工轻工股份有限公司	南通市	江苏省	(0513)5512735
Taizhou Heshun Plastics Co.,Ltd.	Taizhou	Zhejiang	(0576)2510220
台州市和顺塑料有限公司	台州市	浙江省	(0576)2510160
China Petroleum Technology Development Corporation	Beijing	Beijing	(010)84080722
中国石油技术开发公司	北京市	北京市	(010)84080800
China National Chemical Fiber Corporation	Beijing	Beijing	(010)65816699
中国化纤总公司	北京市	北京市	(010)65813483

2665: Organic Silicofluoride Material 有机硅氟材料制造业

The industry accounts for 0.060% of the total revenue of China's industrial sector in 2002. The rate of return on assets is 2.18%. 82.28% of all firms in the industry made a profit while 17.72% had negative returns.The top province in terms of the industry's revenue is Zhejiang, accounting for 51.30% of the total revenue.
2002年本行业收入占全行业的 0.060%，资产利润率为 2.18%。82.28%的企业赢利，17.72%的企业亏损。收入最高的省为浙江省，占本行业的51.30%。

	Total number of firms 企业总数	Total number of employees 职工总数	Total revenue (Mil.RMB) 总销售收入 (百万元)	Total profit (Mil.RMB) 总利润 (百万元)	Return on assets 资产利润率 (%)	Return on equity 权益利润率 (%)	Labour productivity ('000 RMB/worker) 劳动生产率 (千元/人)	Debts/assets 资产负债率 (%)	Total assets (Mil.RMB) 总资产 (百万元)
Industry Overall 行业总体	79	38,364	6,467	277	2.18	6.74	54.75	67.62	12,717

	Number of firms 企业个数	Average number of employees 平均职工人数	Average revenue ('000 RMB) 平均销售收入 (千元)	Average profit ('000 RMB) 平均利润 (千元)	Return on assets 资产利润率 (%)	Return on equity 权益利润率 (%)	Labour productivity ('000 RMB/worker) 劳动生产率 (千元/人)	Debts/assets 资产负债率 (%)	Average total assets ('000 RMB) 平均总资产 (千元)
By ownership 产业所有权									
State-owned 国有	11	881	135,070	8,956	3.58	17.31	52.31	79.34	250,356
Collective-owned 集体	8	48	13,629	136	1.68	4.33	108.58	61.10	8,085
Foreign & Overseas Chinese Funded 三资	14	112	36,199	-4	-0.01	-0.02	92.92	55.20	59,055
By regional distribution 地区分布									
Central-North 华北	7	120	14,594	1,184	2.40	3.53	50.24	32.00	49,351
Beijing 北京	1	51	25,060	3,218	1.27	1.75	31.18	27.58	253,731
Tianjin 天津	3	26	874	13	0.85	0.99	32.97	14.02	1,491
Hebei 河北	2	242	36,448	2,510	6.67	11.33	64.88	41.17	37,650
Shanxi 山西									
Inner Mongolia 内蒙古	1	225	1,579	12	0.10	0.40	29.06	74.84	11,955
Northeast 东北	5	271	31,780	-1,562	-1.75	-39.21	37.90	95.53	89,210
Liaoning 辽宁	4	292	22,467	-2,165	-1.99	-46.96	29.13	95.76	108,801
Jilin 吉林	1	191	69,033	848	7.82	57.10	91.45	86.31	10,844
Heilongjiang 黑龙江									
Central-East 华东	43	734	127,169	5,339	2.05	6.48	54.07	68.34	260,098
Shanghai 上海	4	293	100,529	4,637	2.14	3.51	96.34	39.07	216,981
Jiangsu 江苏	11	224	85,849	5,736	9.47	23.28	92.71	59.31	60,560
Zhejiang 浙江	16	1,388	207,346	7,599	1.53	4.80	49.87	68.09	496,430
Anhui 安徽	1	85	27,586	828	5.69	29.79	181.22	80.91	14,555
Fujian 福建	3	44	36,234	257	1.15	3.22	114.82	64.47	22,469
Jiangxi 江西	2	1,409	225,131	10,836	1.91		43.45	102.00	568,604
Shandong 山东	6	446	36,285	512	0.63	1.52	39.03	58.65	81,350
Central-South 中南	20	68	22,599	846	8.05	18.42	109.22	56.28	10,501
Henan 河南	1	7	553	9	0.23		180.71	236.41	3,971
Hubei 湖北	12	57	21,369	790	9.68	18.90	128.50	48.80	8,158
Hunan 湖南	3	134	26,976	1,078	6.96	14.89	70.09	53.28	15,493
Guangdong 广东	4	67	28,519	1,050	6.81	16.53	117.30	58.81	15,417
Guangxi 广西									
Hainan 海南									
Southwest 西南	2	1,510	122,037	16,007	6.88	14.78	45.43	53.44	232,660
Chongqing 重庆	1	94	15,044	13	0.26	0.34	17.45	24.08	4,970
Sichuan 四川	1	2,925	229,029	32,000	6.95	15.03	46.33	53.76	460,350
Guizhou 贵州									
Yunnan 云南									
Tibet 西藏									
Northwest 西北	2	120	20,700	-810	-2.45	-12.02	65.39	79.63	33,090
Shaanxi 陕西	1	190	30,400	-2,070	-4.40	-41.40	55.12	89.36	47,010
Gansu 甘肃	1	50	11,000	450	2.35	5.31	104.42	55.76	19,170
Qinghai 青海									
Ningxia 宁夏									
Xinjiang 新疆									

2665: Organic Silicofluoride Material 有机硅氟材料制造业

Year 年份	Number of firms 企业个数	Rate of change 变化率 (%)	Number of employees 职工人数 (人)	Rate of change 变化率 (%)	Total revenue (Mil. RMB) 总销售收入 (百万元)	Rate of change 变化率 (%)	Total profit (Mil RMB) 总利润 (百万元)	Rate of change 变化率 (%)
2000	57		12,100		1,821		99	
2001	70	22.81	43,097	256.17	5,377	195.28	269	171.72
2002	79	12.86	38,364	-10.98	6,467	20.27	277	2.97

Major Products 主要产品	Output 产量	Unit 单位

10 Main Firms with Maximal Revenue (year founded) 收入最大的十家主要企业（创办年份）	City 城市	Province 省	Telephone/fax 电话/传真	Number of employees 职工人数	Ownership 产业所有权	Revenue ('000 RMB) 销售收入 (千元)	Profit('000 RMB) (rank) 利润(千元) (排名)	Total assets ('000 RMB) 总资产 (千元)	Major products 主要产品
Juhua Group Company 巨化集团公司(1958)	Quzhou 衢州市	Zhejiang 浙江省	(0570)3096668 (0570)3091678	20,155	State Enterprises 国有独资	2,510,415	75,118(1)	7,231,461	Polytef聚四氟乙烯
Jiangsu Meilan Electrochemical Factory (Group) 江苏梅兰电化厂(集团)(1958)	Taizhou 泰州市	Jiangsu 江苏省	(0523)6552276 (0523)6552323	1,643	State-owned 国有企业	644,629	46,583(2)	539,766	Polytef聚四氟乙烯
Blue Star Fire Chemical Industry Factory 蓝星星火化工厂(1968)	Jiujiang 九江市	Jiangxi 江西省	(0792)3170002 (0792)3170009	2,776	State-owned 国有企业	445,178	21,520(6)	1,135,443	Organic Silicon Raw Monocase有机硅粗单体
Zhejiang Blue Sky Environmental Protection High-tech Co.,Ltd. 浙江蓝天环保高科技股份有限公司(2000)	Hangzhou 杭州市	Zhejiang 浙江省	(0571)88190594 (0571)88904005	602	Joint Stock 股份制	337,264	33,035(4)	295,287	Chemical Industry Products 化工产品
Shanghai 3F New Materials Co., Ltd. 上海三爱富新材料股份有限公司(1959)	Shanghai 上海市	Shanghai 上海市	(021)64340154 (021)64345915	1,015	Joint Stock 股份制	263,463	42,961(3)	585,509	Polytef聚四氟乙烯
Zhonghao Chenguang Research Institute Of Chemical Industry 中昊晨光化工研究院(1965)	Zigong 自贡市	Sichuan 四川省	(0813)7202180 (0813)7201124	2,925	State-owned 国有企业	229,029	32,000(5)	460,350	Polyvinyl Chloride 聚氯乙烯
Nan'an San Jing Silicon Refining Co., Ltd. 南安市三晶硅品精制有限公司(1996)	Quanzhou 泉州市	Fujian 福建省	(0595)6373387 (0595)6396887	65	Joint Stock 股份制	98,996	930(26)	56,886	Silicon Products 硅制品
Zhejiang Kaihua Synthetic Material Co., Ltd. 浙江新安集团开化合成材料有限公司(1978)	Quzhou 衢州市	Zhejiang 浙江省	(0570)6181105 (0570)6181190	389	Limited-Liability 有限公司	92,150	-	146,378	Organic Silicon Monocase有机硅单体
Guangzhou Tian Ci Advanced New Materials Science & Technology Co., Ltd.广州市天赐高新材料科技有限公司(2000)	Guangzhou 广州市	Guangdong 广东省	(020)87360557 (020)87365725	99	Private Owned 私营企业	82,863	1,658(18)	38,891	Organic Silicon Products有机硅产品
Hangzhou Zhi Jiang Organic Silicon Chemical Industry Co., Ltd. 杭州之江有机硅化工有限公司(1996)	Hangzhou 杭州市	Zhejiang 浙江省	(0571)82369673 (0571)82363371	171	Limited-Liability 有限公司	78,967	2,747(15)	71,597	Organic Silicon Products有机硅产品

Top 10 Cities by Revenue 销售收入排名前10位城市	Province 省	Market share 市场份额 (%)	Number of firms 企业个数
Quzhou 衢州市	Zhejiang 浙江省	40.25	2
Taizhou 泰州市	Jiangsu 江苏省	9.97	1
Hangzhou 杭州市	Zhejiang 浙江省	7.31	6
Jiujiang 九江市	Jiangxi 江西省	6.88	1
Shanghai 上海市	Shanghai 上海市	6.22	4
Zigong 自贡市	Sichuan 四川省	3.54	1
Nanjing 南京市	Jiangsu 江苏省	3.26	3
Xiaogan 孝感市	Hubei 湖北省	2.93	8
Taizhou 台州市	Zhejiang 浙江省	2.39	2
Jinan 济南市	Shandong 山东省	1.94	2

10 Major Wholesalers 十家主要批发商	City 城市	Province 省	Telephone/Fax 电话/传真
Yihua Kangqi Chemical Fibre Co.,Ltd. 仪化康祺化纤有限责任公司	Yangzhou 扬州市	Jiangsu 江苏省	(0514)3235499 (0514)3233847
Sinochem Guangdong Import & Export Company 中化广东进出口公司	Guangzhou 广州市	Guangdong 广东省	(020)86672288 (020)86507512
Sinochem Shanghai Import & Export Company 中化上海进出口公司	Shanghai 上海市	Shanghai 上海市	(021)63289888 (021)63283968
Sinochem Tianjin Import & Export Company 中化天津进出口公司	Tianjin 天津市	Tianjin 天津市	(022)23146216 (022)23146215
China Chemical Sales & Supply (North China) Corporation 中国化工供销华北公司	Tianjin 天津市	Tianjin 天津市	(022)23011031 (022)23011032
China Chemical Sales & Supply (North China) Corporation 中国化工供销华东公司	Shanghai 上海市	Shanghai 上海市	(021)62103300 (021)62515799
Nantong Chemical Light Industry Co.,Ltd. 南通化工轻工股份有限公司	Nantong 南通市	Jiangsu 江苏省	(0513)5518397 (0513)5512735
Taizhou Heshun Plastics Co.,Ltd. 台州市和顺塑料有限公司	Taizhou 台州市	Zhejiang 浙江省	(0576)2510220 (0576)2510160
China Petroleum Technology Development Corporation 中国石油技术开发公司	Beijing 北京市	Beijing 北京市	(010)84080722 (010)84080800
China National Chemical Fiber Corporation 中国化纤总公司	Beijing 北京市	Beijing 北京市	(010)65816699 (010)65813483

2666: Synthetic Rubber 合成橡胶制造业

The industry accounts for 0.040% of the total revenue of China's industrial sector in 2002. The rate of return on assets is 6.19%. 87.78% of all firms in the industry made a profit while 12.22% had negative returns.The top province in terms of the industry's revenue is Jiangsu, accounting for 21.93% of the total revenue.
2002年本行业收入占全行业的 0.040%，资产利润率为 6.19%。87.78%的企业赢利，12.22%的企业亏损。收入最高的省为江苏省，占本行业的21.93%。

	Total number of firms 企业总数	Total number of employees 职工总数	Total revenue (Mil.RMB) 总销售收入（百万元）	Total profit (Mil.RMB) 总利润（百万元）	Return on assets 资产利润率 (%)	Return on equity 权益利润率 (%)	Labour productivity ('000 RMB/ worker) 劳动生产率（千元/人）	Debts/ assets 资产负债率 (%)	Total assets (Mil.RMB) 总资产（百万元）
Industry Overall 行业总体	90	20,065	4,311	277	6.19	15.69	52.75	60.53	4,468

	Number of firms 企业个数	Average number of employees 平均职工人数	Average revenue ('000 RMB) 平均销售收入（千元）	Average profit ('000 RMB) 平均利润（千元）	Return on assets 资产利润率 (%)	Return on equity 权益利润率 (%)	Labour productivity ('000 RMB/ worker) 劳动生产率（千元/人）	Debts/ assets 资产负债率 (%)	Average total assets ('000 RMB) 平均总资产（千元）
By ownership 产业所有权									
State-owned 国有	3	433	28,926	-4,401	-1.98	-12.80	-5.57	84.54	222,341
Collective-owned 集体	15	131	35,571	2,170	15.32	40.35	85.29	62.03	14,166
Foreign & Overseas Chinese Funded 三资	26	186	72,920	8,333	11.84	24.08	75.01	50.81	70,357
By regional distribution 地区分布									
Central-North 华北	18	450	52,797	1,711	2.67	7.33	31.81	63.59	64,111
Beijing 北京	5	215	30,642	996	4.19	14.04	25.33	70.15	23,759
Tianjin 天津	4	72	17,727	2,313	12.95	24.43	45.02	46.98	17,855
Hebei 河北	7	370	41,860	1,681	5.88	20.61	29.43	71.49	28,603
Shanxi 山西	2	2,078	216,608	2,397	0.63	1.65	34.05	62.05	381,775
Inner Mongolia 内蒙古									
Northeast 东北	2	318	25,672	3,246	10.32	14.71	15.84	29.87	31,455
Liaoning 辽宁	1	499	32,689	6,491	12.48	15.54	9.08	19.67	52,003
Jilin 吉林	1	136	18,654				40.63	78.49	10,906
Heilongjiang 黑龙江									
Central-East 华东	43	80	49,058	5,037	13.47	27.61	155.25	51.23	37,401
Shanghai 上海	14	58	55,785	6,895	15.66	22.55	229.20	30.57	44,040
Jiangsu 江苏	15	99	63,035	6,752	11.91	33.25	133.05	64.20	56,716
Zhejiang 浙江	3	34	8,054	112	3.35	15.19	49.87	77.94	3,352
Anhui 安徽	1	38	7,022	-19	-0.40	-2.86	52.63	85.95	4,734
Fujian 福建	2	47	14,218	545	9.08	15.13	114.04	39.97	6,002
Jiangxi 江西									
Shandong 山东	8	114	40,419	2,171	15.21	41.79	145.82	63.60	14,272
Central-South 中南	22	149	30,877	1,594	6.76	11.54	54.18	41.38	23,566
Henan 河南	5	124	31,025	2,169	20.48	35.18	82.39	41.78	10,589
Hubei 湖北	4	285	30,875	1,379	17.45	23.83	51.78	26.80	7,901
Hunan 湖南	1	238	11,050	-730	-1.28	-1.99	17.63	35.93	57,118
Guangdong 广东	12	106	32,468	1,619	5.16	9.11	49.48	43.38	31,398
Guangxi 广西									
Hainan 海南									
Southwest 西南	5	923	104,168	-2,433	-1.08	-5.77	17.25	81.24	224,813
Chongqing 重庆	3	1,491	167,584	-3,464	-0.98	-4.96	15.81	80.18	352,500
Sichuan 四川	1	34	11,012	552	10.54	29.93	137.53	64.78	5,236
Guizhou 贵州									
Yunnan 云南	1	108	7,077	-2,324	-3.79		38.95	100.93	61,331
Tibet 西藏									
Northwest 西北									
Shaanxi 陕西									
Gansu 甘肃									
Qinghai 青海									
Ningxia 宁夏									
Xinjiang 新疆									

Year 年份	Number of firms 企业个数	Rate of change 变化率 (%)	Number of employees 职工人数 (人)	Rate of change 变化率 (%)	Total revenue (Mil. RMB) 总销售收入 (百万元)	Rate of change 变化率 (%)	Total profit (Mil RMB) 总利润 (百万元)	Rate of change 变化率 (%)
2000	61		14,888		3,071		77	
2001	73	19.67	28,191	89.35	10,860	253.63	356	362.34
2002	90	23.29	20,065	-28.82	4,311	-60.30	277	-22.19

Major Products 主要产品	Output 产量	Unit 单位
Synthetic Rubber 合成橡胶	117	10,000 Tons 万吨

10 Main Firms with Maximal Revenue (year founded) 收入最大的十家主要企业（创办年份）	City 城市	Province 省	Telephone/fax 电话/传真	Number of employees 职工人数	Ownership 产业所有权	Revenue ('000 RMB) 销售收入 (千元)	Profit('000 RMB) (rank) 利润(千元) (排名)	Total assets ('000 RMB) 总资产 (千元)	Major products 主要产品
Shen Hua Chemical Industry Co.,Ltd.	Nantong	Jiangsu	(0513)3592662		Foreign Funded				Butadiene Styrene Rubber
申华化学工业有限公司(1996)	南通市	江苏省	(0513)3595050	285	外商投资	529,185	89,647(1)	686,432	丁苯橡胶
Shanghai Gao Qiao Basf Dispersoid Co.,Ltd.	Shanghai	Shanghai	(021)58670303		Foreign Funded				Carboxyl SBR Latex羧基
上海高桥巴斯夫分散体有限公司(1993)	上海市	上海市	(021)58675050	143	外商投资	489,375	78,982(2)	395,143	丁苯胶乳
Chongqing Changshou Chemical Industry Co., Ltd.	Chongqing	Chongqing	(023)40262656		Limited-Liability				Neoprene
重庆长寿化工有限责任公司(2001)	重庆市	重庆市	(023)40510596	3,720	有限公司	435,450	9,052(5)	441,992	氯丁橡胶
Union Carbide (Zhongshan) Co.,Ltd.	Zhongshan	Guangdong	(0760)2101288		Foreign Funded				Synthetic Latex
联合碳化(广东中山)有限公司(1991)	中山市	广东省	(0760)2100823	68	外商投资	149,952	19,049(3)	84,733	合成胶乳
Zhaoyuan Wuyun Mountain Auxiliary Reagent Factory	Yantai	Shandong	(0535)8379017		Collective-owned				Rubber Auxiliary
招远市雾云山助剂厂(1996)	烟台市	山东省	(0535)8379017	73	集体企业	97,880	9,950(4)	2,187	橡胶助剂
Qingdao Protective Tariff Zone Guo Gren International Trade	Qingdao	Shandong	(0532)6767558		Limited-Liability				Compound Rubber
Co., Ltd.青岛保税区国人国际贸易有限公司(1997)	青岛市	山东省	(0532)6767558	85	有限公司	73,903	507(52)	35,892	复合橡胶
Beijing Huateng Rubber Plastic & Latex Product Co., Ltd.	Beijing	Beijing	(010)65921892		Collective-owned				Latex Products
北京华腾橡塑乳胶制品有限公司(1961)	北京市	北京市	(010)81501449	620	集体企业	69,367	758(38)	75,118	乳胶制品
Yancheng De Bao Chemical Industry Co., Ltd.	Yancheng	Jiangsu	(0515)2352500		Overseas Chinese-funded				Acrylic Rubber
盐城德宝化工有限公司(1998)	盐城市	江苏省	(0515)2351066	24	港澳台资	59,900	6,290(8)	21,860	雪珀胶
Shanghai Nytex Composite Material Products Co., Ltd.	Shanghai	Shanghai	(021)59573168		Overseas Chinese funded				PA
上海耐特复合材料制品有限公司(1996)	上海市	上海市	(021)59573707	85	港澳台资	56,025	3,855(14)	69,244	PA
Yixing Guang Hui Adhesive Chemical Industry Factory	Wuxi	Jiangsu	(0510)7551166		Joint Stock				Latex
宜兴市光辉胶粘剂化工厂(1992)	无锡市	江苏省	(0510)7551347	135	股份制	54,800	850(35)	31,103	乳胶

Top 10 Cities by Revenue 销售收入排名前10位城市	Province 省	Market share 市场份额 (%)	Number of firms 企业个数
Shanghai 上海市	Shanghai 上海市	18.12	14
Nantong 南通市	Jiangsu 江苏省	12.27	1
Chongqing 重庆市	Chongqing 重庆市	11.66	3
Datong 大同市	Shanxi 山西省	10.05	2
Shijiazhuang 石家庄市	Hebei 河北省	4.85	3
Zhenjiang 镇江市	Jiangsu 江苏省	4.72	6
Qingdao 青岛市	Shandong 山东省	4.19	6
Zhongshan 中山市	Guangdong 广东省	3.89	2
Beijing 北京市	Beijing 北京市	3.55	5
Jiaozuo 焦作市	Henan 河南省	2.49	1

10 Major Wholesalers 十家主要批发商	City 城市	Province 省	Telephone/Fax 电话/传真
Yihua Kangqi Chemical Fibre Co.,Ltd.	Yangzhou	Jiangsu	(0514)3235499
仪化康祺化纤有限责任公司	扬州市	江苏省	(0514)3233847
Sinochem Guangdong Import & Export Company	Guangzhou	Guangdong	(020)86672288
中化广东进出口公司	广州市	广东省	(020)86507512
Sinochem Shanghai Import & Export Company	Shanghai	Shanghai	(021)63289888
中化上海进出口公司	上海市	上海市	(021)63283968
Sinochem Tianjin Import & Export Company	Tianjin	Tianjin	(022)23146216
中化天津进出口公司	天津市	天津市	(022)23146215
China Chemical Sales & Supply (North China) Corporation	Tianjin	Tianjin	(022)23011031
中国化工供销华北公司	天津市	天津市	(022)23011032
China Chemical Sales & Supply (North China) Corporation	Shanghai	Shanghai	(021)62103300
中国化工供销华东公司	上海市	上海市	(021)62515799
Nantong Chemical Light Industry Co.,Ltd.	Nantong	Jiangsu	(0513)5518397
南通化工轻工股份有限公司	南通市	江苏省	(0513)5512735
Taizhou Heshun Plastics Co.,Ltd.	Taizhou	Zhejiang	(0576)2510220
台州市和顺塑料有限公司	台州市	浙江省	(0576)2510160
China Petroleum Technology Development Corporation	Beijing	Beijing	(010)84080722
中国石油技术开发公司	北京市	北京市	(010)84080800
China National Chemical Fiber Corporation	Beijing	Beijing	(010)65816699
中国化纤总公司	北京市	北京市	(010)65813483

2667: Synthetic Fibre 合成纤维单(聚合)体制造业

The industry accounts for 0.275% of the total revenue of China's industrial sector in 2002. The rate of return on assets is -0.32%. 70.00% of all firms in the industry made a profit while 30.00% had negative returns.The top province in terms of the industry's revenue is Liaoning, accounting for 28.65% of the total revenue.
2002年本行业收入占全行业的 0.275%，资产利润率为 -0.32%。70.00%的企业赢利，30.00%的企业亏损。收入最高的省为辽宁省，占本行业的28.65%。

	Total number of firms 企业总数	Total number of employees 职工总数	Total revenue (Mil.RMB) 总销售收入（百万元）	Total profit (Mil.RMB) 总利润（百万元）	Return on assets 资产利润率（%）	Return on equity 权益利润率（%）	Labour productivity ('000 RMB/ worker) 劳动生产率（千元/人）	Debts/ assets 资产负债率（%）	Total assets (Mil.RMB) 总资产（百万元）
Industry Overall 行业总体	70	53,347	29,484	-164	-0.32	-0.86	94.60	63.04	51,658

	Number of firms 企业个数	Average number of employees 平均职工人数	Average revenue ('000 RMB) 平均销售收入（千元）	Average profit ('000 RMB) 平均利润（千元）	Return on assets 资产利润率（%）	Return on equity 权益利润率（%）	Labour productivity ('000 RMB/ worker) 劳动生产率（千元/人）	Debts/ assets 资产负债率（%）	Average total assets ('000 RMB) 平均总资产（千元）
By ownership 产业所有权									
State-owned 国有	5	3,134	1,903,152	4,943	0.12	0.37	78.69	68.77	4,277,503
Collective-owned 集体	10	83	36,917	548	3.76	8.79	112.98	57.24	14,597
Foreign & Overseas Chinese Funded 三资	17	319	210,782	-7,168	-2.14	-7.87	50.20	72.77	334,475
By regional distribution 地区分布									
Central-North 华北	6	2,115	1,062,483	-329	-0.01	-0.03	40.98	62.22	2,598,630
Beijing 北京	2	32	7,930	1,037	11.52	97.28	53.56	88.16	8,999
Tianjin 天津	2	5,052	2,882,577	-45,616	-0.65	-1.83	31.40	64.38	6,984,564
Hebei 河北	1	120	8,145	102	2.10	5.54	6.83	62.16	4,862
Shanxi 山西	1	2,405	585,741	87,085	5.44	9.56	82.61	43.08	1,599,793
Inner Mongolia 内蒙古									
Northeast 东北	6	1,934	1,412,302	-51,727	-2.72	-6.42	150.59	57.61	1,901,013
Liaoning 辽宁	4	2,892	2,112,113	-77,412	-2.72	-6.40	150.57	57.59	2,850,189
Jilin 吉林	2	18	12,680	-358	-13.44	-280.39	157.44	95.21	2,660
Heilongjiang 黑龙江									
Central-East 华东	40	454	181,778	1,393	0.49	1.11	70.63	55.81	283,037
Shanghai 上海	6	412	145,313	32	0.02	0.03	70.42	49.43	184,282
Jiangsu 江苏	19	242	113,999	-4,424	-2.41	-7.89	44.88	69.45	183,607
Zhejiang 浙江	10	243	201,770	5,658	2.61	5.44	148.84	52.05	217,019
Anhui 安徽									
Fujian 福建	2	160	144,698	-4,760	-1.69		-22.68	111.78	281,442
Jiangxi 江西	1	2,948	307,498	-15,790	-2.44	-6.91	23.64	64.71	647,618
Shandong 山东	2	2,691	809,334	54,153	3.24	4.98	88.73	35.00	1,673,280
Central-South 中南	15	522	429,902	3,278	0.44	1.83	159.67	76.06	747,896
Henan 河南	1								
Hubei 湖北	1	120	6,208	113	3.90	6.57	19.08	40.67	2,899
Hunan 湖南	1	430	64,212	3,514	1.19	2.02	44.87	41.06	295,029
Guangdong 广东	10	459	571,710	-1,374	-0.14	-0.72	237.29	80.31	967,573
Guangxi 广西	1	2,465	345,598	57,265	13.13	33.85	40.87	61.22	436,259
Hainan 海南	1	229	315,412	2,018	0.25	0.46	171.18	46.02	808,522
Southwest 西南	1	2,362	290,510	17,074	2.03	4.00	33.03	49.22	841,485
Chongqing 重庆									
Sichuan 四川									
Guizhou 贵州									
Yunnan 云南	1	2,362	290,510	17,074	2.03	4.00	33.03	49.22	841,485
Tibet 西藏									
Northwest 西北	2	353	312,402	13,206	2.07	10.39	238.50	80.11	639,354
Shaanxi 陕西									
Gansu 甘肃									
Qinghai 青海									
Ningxia 宁夏									
Xinjiang 新疆	2	353	312,402	13,206	2.07	10.39	238.50	80.11	639,354

2667: Synthetic Fibre 合成纤维单(聚合)体制造业

Year 年份	Number of firms 企业个数	Rate of change 变化率 (%)	Number of employees 职工人数 (人)	Rate of change 变化率 (%)	Total revenue (Mil. RMB) 总销售收入 (百万元)	Rate of change 变化率 (%)	Total profit (Mil RMB) 总利润 (百万元)	Rate of change 变化率 (%)
2000	50		37,612		19,034		-257	
2001	57	14.00	55,580	47.77	35,496	86.49	-2,289	-790.66
2002	70	22.81	53,347	-4.02	29,484	-16.94	-164	92.84

Major Products 主要产品	Output 产量	Unit 单位
Synthetic Fibre Polymer 合成纤维聚合物	493	10,000 Tons 万吨
Synthetic Fibre Monomer 合成纤维单体	351	10,000 Tons 万吨

10 Main Firms with Maximal Revenue (year founded) 收入最大的十家主要企业(创办年份)	City 城市	Province 省	Telephone/fax 电话/传真	Number of employees 职工人数	Ownership 产业所有权	Revenue ('000 RMB) 销售收入(千元)	Profit('000 RMB) (rank) 利润(千元)(排名)	Total assets ('000 RMB) 总资产(千元)	Major products 主要产品
Liaoyang Petrochemical Branch Company	Liaoyang	Liaoning	(0419)5154458		Joint Stock				Synthon Monomer合成
辽阳石化分公司(1999)	辽阳市	辽宁省	(0419)5154916	11,150	股份制	7,967,960	-	10,833,670	纤维单体
SINOPEC Tianjin Co.,Ltd.	Tianjin	Tianjin	(022)63804634		State-owned				Polyester
中国石化集团总公司天津石化公司(2000)	天津市	天津市	(022)63804718	10,079	国有企业	5,759,633	-	13,963,688	聚脂
Yantai Wanhua Synthetic Leather Group Co., Ltd.	Yantai	Shandong	(0535)6837888		State Enterprises				Synthetic Leather
烟台万华合成革集团有限公司(1985)	烟台市	山东省	(0535)6837594	4,837	国有独资	1,520,000	85,600(3)	3,171,437	合成革
Zhejiang United Chemical Fibre Group Co.,Ltd.	Shaoxing	Zhejiang	(0575)8064167		Limited-Liability				Polyester Slices
浙江化纤联合集团有限公司(1984)	绍兴市	浙江省	(0575)8067783	1,726	有限公司	1,184,330	5,689(13)	1,694,340	聚酯切片
Zhuhai Yu Hua Polyester Co., Ltd.	Zhuhai	Guangdong	(0756)3311868		Joint Stock				Polyester Slices
珠海裕华聚酯有限公司(1988)	珠海市	广东省	(0756)3311483	575	股份制	897,763	-	1,701,999	聚酯切片
Shanghai Lian Ji Synthetic Fibre Co.,Ltd.	Shanghai	Shanghai	(021)57502753		Foreign Funded				Polyester Slices
上海联吉合纤有限公司(1994)	上海市	上海市	(021)57502644	407	外商投资	721,313	10,038(12)	846,028	聚酯切片
Yihua Foshan Polyester Co.,Ltd.	Foshan	Guangdong	(0757)3983901		Foreign Funded				Polyester
仪化佛山聚脂有限公司(1986)	佛山市	广东省	(0757)2812522	1,218	外商投资	687,043	15,356(9)	774,284	聚脂
Shanxi Sanwei Group Co.,Ltd.	Linfen	Shanxi	(0357)6568699		Joint Stock				Polyvinyl Alcohol
山西三维集团股份有限公司(1984)	临汾市	山西省	(0357)6568699	2,405	股份制	585,741	87,085(2)	1,599,793	聚乙烯醇
Hangzhou Longda Distinction Polyester Co., Ltd.	Hangzhou	Zhejiang	(0571)82617798		Limited-Liability				Polyester
杭州龙达差别化聚脂有限公司(1999)	杭州市	浙江省	(0571)82617798	86	有限公司	495,440	38,940(6)	336,790	聚脂
Guangzhou Asian American Polyester Co., Ltd.	Guangzhou	Guangdong	(020)82098863		Foreign Funded				Polyester Slices
广州亚美聚酯有限公司(1991)	广州市	广东省	(020)82099021	185	外商投资	402,613	-	360,689	聚酯切片

Top 10 Cities by Revenue 销售收入排名前10位城市	Province 省	Market share 市场份额 (%)	Number of firms 企业个数
Liaoyang 辽阳市	Liaoning 辽宁省	27.28	2
Tianjin 天津市	Tianjin 天津市	19.55	2
Jiangmen 江门市	Guangdong 广东省	11.29	2
Yantai 烟台市	Shandong 山东省	5.16	1
Zhuhai 珠海市	Guangdong 广东省	4.25	2
Shaoxing 绍兴市	Zhejiang 浙江省	4.02	1
Shanghai 上海市	Shanghai 上海市	2.96	6
Nanjing 南京市	Jiangsu 江苏省	2.42	2
Changzhou 常州市	Jiangsu 江苏省	2.42	2
Foshan 佛山市	Guangdong 广东省	2.33	1

10 Major Wholesalers 十家主要批发商	City 城市	Province 省	Telephone/Fax 电话/传真
Yihua Kangqi Chemical Fibre Co.,Ltd.	Yangzhou	Jiangsu	(0514)3235499
仪化康祺化纤有限责任公司	扬州市	江苏省	(0514)3233847
Sinochem Guangdong Import & Export Company	Guangzhou	Guangdong	(020)86672288
中化广东进出口公司	广州市	广东省	(020)86507512
Sinochem Shanghai Import & Export Company	Shanghai	Shanghai	(021)63289888
中化上海进出口公司	上海市	上海市	(021)63283968
Sinochem Tianjin Import & Export Company	Tianjin	Tianjin	(022)23146216
中化天津进出口公司	天津市	天津市	(022)23146215
China Chemical Sales & Supply (North China) Corporation	Tianjin	Tianjin	(022)23011031
中国化工供销华北公司	天津市	天津市	(022)23011032
China Chemical Sales & Supply (North China) Corporation	Shanghai	Shanghai	(021)62103300
中国化工供销华东公司	上海市	上海市	(021)62515799
Nantong Chemical Light Industry Co.,Ltd.	Nantong	Jiangsu	(0513)5518397
南通化工轻工股份有限公司	南通市	江苏省	(0513)5512735
Taizhou Heshun Plastics Co.,Ltd.	Taizhou	Zhejiang	(0576)2510220
台州市和顺塑料有限公司	台州市	浙江省	(0576)2510160
China Petroleum Technology Development Corporation	Beijing	Beijing	(010)84080722
中国石油技术开发公司	北京市	北京市	(010)84080800
China National Chemical Fiber Corporation	Beijing	Beijing	(010)65816699
中国化纤总公司	北京市	北京市	(010)65813483

2669: Other Synthetic Materials 其他合成材料制造业

The industry accounts for 0.066% of the total revenue of China's industrial sector in 2002. The rate of return on assets is 1.67%. 82.19% of all firms in the industry made a profit while 17.81% had negative returns.The top province in terms of the industry's revenue is Jiangsu, accounting for 36.08% of the total revenue.
2002年本行业收入占全行业的0.066%，资产利润率为1.67%。82.19%的企业赢利，17.81%的企业亏损。收入最高的省为江苏省，占本行业的36.08%。

	Total number of firms 企业总数	Total number of employees 职工总数	Total revenue (Mil.RMB) 总销售收入(百万元)	Total profit (Mil.RMB) 总利润(百万元)	Return on assets 资产利润率(%)	Return on equity 权益利润率(%)	Labour productivity ('000 RMB/ worker) 劳动生产率(千元/人)	Debts/ assets 资产负债率(%)	Total assets (Mil.RMB) 总资产(百万元)
Industry Overall 行业总体	146	19,636	7,051	157	1.67	4.49	72.76	62.84	9,388

	Number of firms 企业个数	Average number of employees 平均职工人数	Average revenue ('000 RMB) 平均销售收入(千元)	Average profit ('000 RMB) 平均利润(千元)	Return on assets 资产利润率(%)	Return on equity 权益利润率(%)	Labour productivity ('000 RMB/ worker) 劳动生产率(千元/人)	Debts/ assets 资产负债率(%)	Average total assets ('000 RMB) 平均总资产(千元)
By ownership 产业所有权									
State-owned 国有	12	361	62,137	2,392	1.76	7.37	40.23	76.16	136,115
Collective-owned 集体	22	138	30,064	1,668	5.93	16.48	80.25	64.03	28,135
Foreign & Overseas Chinese Funded 三资	37	111	74,952	1,062	1.02	2.90	111.42	64.68	103,788
By regional distribution 地区分布									
Central-North 华北	13	104	23,895	-1,768	-1.87	-2.46	46.40	23.83	94,475
Beijing 北京	2	216	37,125	-17,354	-4.24	-5.25	51.59	19.27	409,517
Tianjin 天津	7	89	26,497	314	0.73	1.05	23.21	30.92	43,229
Hebei 河北	4	75	12,728	2,382	8.94	14.61	87.39	38.79	26,635
Shanxi 山西									
Inner Mongolia 内蒙古									
Northeast 东北	12	95	19,455	35	0.18	0.69	60.03	73.78	19,413
Liaoning 辽宁	5	126	28,386	-1,805	-6.49	-24.36	53.66	73.35	27,809
Jilin 吉林	4	63	16,058	2,486	17.98	40.64	115.13	55.76	13,823
Heilongjiang 黑龙江	3	85	9,100	-165	-1.28		21.57	101.13	12,872
Central-East 华东	82	157	53,033	1,449	2.55	8.14	73.99	68.70	56,876
Shanghai 上海	17	122	30,662	-1,577	-3.43	-14.27	73.33	75.99	46,010
Jiangsu 江苏	29	186	87,716	2,398	2.73	11.21	74.88	75.64	87,818
Zhejiang 浙江	9	43	18,416	1,094	3.20	6.55	80.34	51.17	34,190
Anhui 安徽	6	112	34,669	1,028	4.80	14.43	58.76	66.71	21,408
Fujian 福建	7	44	13,940	667	7.61	14.36	88.08	47.02	8,770
Jiangxi 江西									
Shandong 山东	14	289	58,027	3,955	6.61	13.00	73.99	49.14	59,814
Central-South 中南	31	105	61,524	558	0.63	1.99	86.95	68.21	88,223
Henan 河南	2	11	1,407	39	2.99	2.99	148.38		1,286
Hubei 湖北	5	70	9,150	559	8.19	43.69	46.19	81.25	6,823
Hunan 湖南	2	104	10,918	528	2.21	5.00	25.22	55.85	23,896
Guangdong 广东	22	122	83,493	608	0.50	1.59	96.58	68.33	120,474
Guangxi 广西									
Hainan 海南									
Southwest 西南	4	95	55,121	10,811	13.45	37.10	131.61	63.74	80,359
Chongqing 重庆									
Sichuan 四川	3	119	72,628	14,411	13.78	38.46	136.67	64.18	104,602
Guizhou 贵州	1	20	2,600	9	0.12	0.22	41.00	45.87	7,630
Yunnan 云南									
Tibet 西藏									
Northwest 西北	4	160	7,635	3	0.01	0.03	19.24	77.71	51,722
Shaanxi 陕西	4	160	7,635	3	0.01	0.03	19.24	77.71	51,722
Gansu 甘肃									
Qinghai 青海									
Ningxia 宁夏									
Xinjiang 新疆									

2669: Other Synthetic Materials 其他合成材料制造业

Year 年份	Number of firms 企业个数	Rate of change 变化率 (%)	Number of employees 职工人数 (人)	Rate of change 变化率 (%)	Total revenue (Mil. RMB) 总销售收入 (百万元)	Rate of change 变化率 (%)	Total profit (Mil RMB) 总利润 (百万元)	Rate of change 变化率 (%)
2000	137		21,658		6,976		230	
2001	129	-5.84	19,013	-12.21	7,801	11.83	258	12.17
2002	146	13.18	19,636	3.28	7,051	-9.61	157	-39.15

Major Products 主要产品	Output 产量	Unit 单位
Plastic Resin & Copolymer 塑料树脂及共聚物	1,366	10,000 Tons 万吨

10 Main Firms with Maximal Revenue (year founded) 收入最大的十家主要企业（创办年份）	City 城市	Province 省	Telephone/fax 电话/传真	Number of employees 职工人数	Ownership 产业所有权	Revenue ('000 RMB) 销售收入（千元）	Profit('000 RMB) (rank) 利润(千元)(排名)	Total assets ('000 RMB) 总资产（千元）	Major products 主要产品
Jiangsu Ya Bang Group Company	Changzhou	Jiangsu	(0519)6395881		Joint Stock				C.I.Disperse Red
江苏亚邦集团公司(1993)	常州市	江苏省	(0519)6395888	2,036	股份制	1,337,490	33,150(3)	1,140,720	分散红
Wuxi Petrochemical General Factory	Wuxi	Jiangsu	(0510)2401334		State-owned				Epoxide Resin
无锡市石油化工总厂(1958)	无锡市	江苏省	(0510)2401228	1,554	国有企业	486,778	21,510(5)	911,862	环氧树脂
Dow Chemical (Guangzhou) Co., Ltd.	Guangzhou	Guangdong	(020)82223223		Foreign Funded				Polyurethane Material聚胺
陶氏化学（广州）有限公司(1996)	广州市	广东省	(020)83224143	31	外商投资	181,401	-	125,683	脂组合料
Chengdu Zhong Fu Bottle Embryo Co., Ltd.	Chengdu	Sichuan	(028)83933405		Foreign Funded				Plastics Bottle Embryo
成都中富瓶胚有限公司(2000)	成都市	四川省	(028)83934762	43	外商投资	163,197	42,969(2)	242,253	塑料瓶胚
Basf Zhanyu (China) Co., Ltd.	Guangzhou	Guangdong	(020)84982560		Foreign Funded				Polyurethane Material聚胺
巴斯夫展宇聚胺酯(中国)有限公司(1998)	广州市	广东省	(020)84982561	175	外商投资	161,438	5,255(11)	93,984	脂组合料
Dongguan Inoac Metal & Elastomer Co.,Ltd.	Dongguan	Guangdong	(0769)8863344		Foreign Funded				Duplicator Parts复
东莞井上五金橡塑有限公司(1997)	东莞市	广东省	(0769)8866544	656	外商投资	155,507	-	320,882	印机零件
Tianjing Four Dimension Enperprise Co.,Ltd.	Tianjin	Tianjin	(022)25292929		Foreign Funded				Adhesive Tape
天津四维企业有限公司(1992)	天津市	天津市	(022)66200246	221	外商投资	142,928	820(46)	273,328	胶纸带
Zhongshan Ai Mei Gao Special Type Chemical Industry	Zhongshan	Guangdong	(0760)2101288		Foreign Funded				Polyquaternary Ammonium Compounds聚季铵
Co., Ltd.广东中山爱美高特种化工有限公司(1995)	中山市	广东省	(0760)2100823	14	外商投资	105,781	50,427(1)	130,682	盐化合物
Shanghai Jin Sen Petroleum Resin Co., Ltd.	Shanghai	Shanghai	(021)57962323		Foreign Funded				Synthetic Materials
上海金森石油树脂有限公司(1998)	上海市	上海市	(021)67242266	98	外商投资	103,340	86(90)	245,309	合成材料
Fushun Ji Te Chemical Industry Co., Ltd.	Fushun	Liaoning	(0413)6880917		Limited-Liability				Methacrylic Acid甲
抚顺吉特化工有限公司(2001)	抚顺市	辽宁省	(0413)6657707	230	有限公司	84,972	95(87)	30,206	基丙烯酸

Top 10 Cities by Revenue 销售收入排名前10位城市	Province 省	Market share 市场份额 (%)	Number of firms 企业个数
Changzhou 常州市	Jiangsu 江苏省	19.99	6
Shantou 汕头市	Guangdong 广东省	11.61	4
Wuxi 无锡市	Jiangsu 江苏省	8.96	11
Shanghai 上海市	Shanghai 上海市	7.39	17
Guangzhou 广州市	Guangdong 广东省	6.55	7
Taian 泰安市	Shandong 山东省	4.77	1
Suzhou 苏州市	Jiangsu 江苏省	3.01	5
Nanjing 南京市	Jiangsu 江苏省	2.87	2
Tianjin 天津市	Tianjin 天津市	2.63	7
Chengdu 成都市	Sichuan 四川省	2.56	2

10 Major Wholesalers 十家主要批发商	City 城市	Province 省	Telephone/Fax 电话/传真
Yihua Kangqi Chemical Fibre Co.,Ltd.	Yangzhou	Jiangsu	(0514)3235499
仪化康祺化纤有限责任公司	扬州市	江苏省	(0514)3233847
Sinochem Guangdong Import & Export Company	Guangzhou	Guangdong	(020)86672288
中化广东进出口公司	广州市	广东省	(020)86507512
Sinochem Shanghai Import & Export Company	Shanghai	Shanghai	(021)63289888
中化上海进出口公司	上海市	上海市	(021)63283968
Sinochem Tianjin Import & Export Company	Tianjin	Tianjin	(022)23146216
中化天津进出口公司	天津市	天津市	(022)23146215
China Chemical Sales & Supply (North China) Corporation	Tianjin	Tianjin	(022)23011031
中国化工供销华北公司	天津市	天津市	(022)23011032
China Chemical Sales & Supply (North China) Corporation	Shanghai	Shanghai	(021)62103300
中国化工供销华东公司	上海市	上海市	(021)62515799
Nantong Chemical Light Industry Co.,Ltd.	Nantong	Jiangsu	(0513)5518397
南通化工轻工股份有限公司	南通市	江苏省	(0513)5512735
Taizhou Heshun Plastics Co.,Ltd.	Taizhou	Zhejiang	(0576)2510220
台州市和顺塑料有限公司	台州市	浙江省	(0576)2510160
China Petroleum Technology Development Corporation	Beijing	Beijing	(010)84080722
中国石油技术开发公司	北京市	北京市	(010)84080800
China National Chemical Fiber Corporation	Beijing	Beijing	(010)65816699
中国化纤总公司	北京市	北京市	(010)65813483

2671: Chemical Reagent and Auxiliaries 化学试剂、助剂制造业

The industry accounts for 0.350% of the total revenue of China's industrial sector in 2002. The rate of return on assets is 4.97%. 85.84% of all firms in the industry made a profit while 14.16% had negative returns.The top province in terms of the industry's revenue is Jiangsu, accounting for 26.82% of the total revenue.
2002年本行业收入占全行业的 0.350%，资产利润率为 4.97%。85.84%的企业赢利，14.16%的企业亏损。收入最高的省为江苏省，占本行业的26.82%。

	Total number of firms 企业总数	Total number of employees 职工总数	Total revenue (Mil.RMB) 总销售收入 (百万元)	Total profit (Mil.RMB) 总利润 (百万元)	Return on assets 资产利润率 (%)	Return on equity 权益利润率 (%)	Labour productivity ('000 RMB/ worker) 劳动生产率 (千元/人)	Debts/ assets 资产负债率 (%)	Total assets (Mil.RMB) 总资产 (百万元)
Industry Overall 行业总体	1116	152,438	37,543	1,920	4.97	11.32	70.40	56.12	38,639

	Number of firms 企业个数	Average number of employees 平均职工人数	Average revenue ('000 RMB) 平均销售收入（千元）	Average profit ('000 RMB) 平均利润 (千元)	Return on assets 资产利润率 (%)	Return on equity 权益利润率 (%)	Labour productivity ('000 RMB/ worker) 劳动生产率 (千元/人)	Debts/ assets 资产负债率 (%)	Average total assets ('000 RMB) 平均总资产 (千元)
By ownership 产业所有权									
State-owned 国有	105	251	24,603	42	0.08	0.24	30.44	65.95	51,778
Collective-owned 集体	239	115	29,489	1,524	8.06	21.77	80.31	62.99	18,917
Foreign & Overseas Chinese Funded 三资	132	96	45,361	3,040	5.73	9.53	155.24	39.89	53,060
By regional distribution 地区分布									
Central-North 华北	172	118	23,383	1,311	4.50	9.28	57.49	51.46	29,108
Beijing 北京	38	100	29,975	1,373	3.52	6.52	73.99	46.03	39,040
Tianjin 天津	64	108	22,473	1,244	4.11	7.80	52.46	47.33	30,291
Hebei 河北	45	122	20,824	1,422	6.65	15.85	61.60	58.06	21,399
Shanxi 山西	19	135	20,543	937	3.95	11.82	48.65	66.58	23,740
Inner Mongolia 内蒙古	6	268	19,521	1,986	6.99	22.05	40.14	68.30	28,413
Northeast 东北	105	137	21,995	1,360	4.01	10.28	50.80	61.01	33,924
Liaoning 辽宁	71	142	23,160	1,304	3.66	9.26	46.52	60.52	35,656
Jilin 吉林	12	204	26,535	1,366	3.14	7.55	67.91	58.43	43,508
Heilongjiang 黑龙江	22	87	15,758	1,537	6.65	19.60	51.41	66.07	23,108
Central-East 华东	595	121	39,490	2,255	7.19	16.18	85.70	55.57	31,381
Shanghai 上海	89	97	36,387	3,342	9.85	17.51	99.40	43.71	33,918
Jiangsu 江苏	241	125	41,781	1,883	6.57	14.92	91.57	55.97	28,655
Zhejiang 浙江	128	92	34,590	2,187	7.03	17.31	83.71	59.36	31,091
Anhui 安徽	9	52	20,717	1,204	3.12	7.99	110.95	60.95	38,597
Fujian 福建	15	57	18,920	677	4.26	8.70	105.80	51.03	15,875
Jiangxi 江西	12	122	13,274	-253	-0.63	-2.32	49.88	72.66	39,859
Shandong 山东	101	185	50,809	2,900	7.91	18.83	72.42	58.01	36,667
Central-South 中南	179	150	36,015	1,058	2.43	5.81	81.08	58.22	43,561
Henan 河南	61	144	27,023	1,060	4.56	12.14	62.27	62.43	23,235
Hubei 湖北	31	102	40,858	2,017	8.16	21.48	162.43	62.01	24,716
Hunan 湖南	20	451	65,907	780	0.53	1.29	48.22	59.16	147,887
Guangdong 广东	62	91	34,004	616	1.50	3.25	118.51	53.72	40,951
Guangxi 广西	5	65	21,069	1,672	7.14	16.39	69.07	56.43	23,415
Hainan 海南									
Southwest 西南	36	130	15,658	442	1.59	3.54	47.66	55.13	27,802
Chongqing 重庆	10	164	13,710	282	1.14	3.90	25.36	70.85	24,787
Sichuan 四川	17	140	20,539	1,152	3.65	7.20	62.66	49.31	31,573
Guizhou 贵州	4	49	3,398	96	1.83	5.93	27.56	69.21	5,268
Yunnan 云南	5	91	12,766	-1,378	-3.53	-7.01	58.01	49.65	39,039
Tibet 西藏									
Northwest 西北	29	484	24,295	149	0.17	0.38	17.87	56.48	89,671
Shaanxi 陕西	10	154	29,334	2,746	5.18	13.07	81.96	60.38	53,015
Gansu 甘肃	5	2,352	44,147	-3,730	-1.06	-2.30	7.05	54.00	351,948
Qinghai 青海									
Ningxia 宁夏	1	14	637	97	5.55	7.95	13.57	30.17	1,747
Xinjiang 新疆	13	56	14,603	-352	-1.48	-4.12	56.90	64.06	23,756

2671: Chemical Reagent and Auxiliaries 化学试剂、助剂制造业

Year 年份	Number of firms 企业个数	Rate of change 变化率 (%)	Number of employees 职工人数 (人)	Rate of change 变化率 (%)	Total revenue (Mil. RMB) 总销售收入 (百万元)	Rate of change 变化率 (%)	Total profit (Mil RMB) 总利润 (百万元)	Rate of change 变化率 (%)
2000	909		163,272		27,852		1,119	
2001	1040	14.41	155,876	-4.53	31,468	12.98	1,570	40.30
2002	1116	7.31	152,438	-2.21	37,543	19.31	1,920	22.29

Major Products 主要产品	Output 产量	Unit 单位
Chemical Reagent 化学试剂	230,471	Ton 吨
Catalyst 催化剂	135,846	Ton 吨

10 Main Firms with Maximal Revenue (year founded) 收入最大的十家主要企业（创办年份）	City 城市	Province 省	Telephone/fax 电话/传真	Number of employees 职工人数	Ownership 产业所有权	Revenue ('000 RMB) 销售收入 (千元)	Profit('000 RMB) (rank) 利润(千元) (排名)	Total assets ('000 RMB) 总资产 (千元)	Major products 主要产品
Wuxi GRAP Chemical Industry Stock Co., Ltd. 无锡格林艾普化工股份有限公司(1958)	Wuxi 无锡市	Jiangsu 江苏省	(0510)3101601 (0510)3101678	2,598	Joint Stock 股份制	1,202,698	56,768(2)	619,992	Surface Active Reagent表面活性剂
Changling Refining Chemical Co., Ltd. 长岭炼化有限责任公司(1970)	Yueyang 岳阳市	Hunan 湖南省	(0730)8451000 (0730)8451010	6,363	State Enterprises 国有独资	1,056,008	5,087(98)	2,412,498	Oil Refining Chemical Industry 炼油化工
Shandong Qi Lu Plasticizers Co.,Ltd. 山东齐鲁增塑剂股份有限公司(1989)	Zibo 淄博市	Shandong 山东省	(0533)7180593 (0533)7324666	367	Joint Stock 股份制	949,355	20,940(15)	366,461	Di-n-octyl Phthalate邻苯二甲酸二辛酯
SINOPEC Nanjing Chemical Plant 中国石化集团南京化工厂(1947)	Nanjing 南京市	Jiangsu 江苏省	(025)5315414 (025)5302204	2,605	State-owned 国有企业	871,690	15,360(23)	710,550	Rubber Aging Inhibiter橡胶防老剂
Zhejiang Transfer Chemical Group Co.,Ltd. 浙江传化化学集团有限公司(1995)	Hangzhou 杭州市	Zhejiang 浙江省	(0571)82602866 (0571)82602700	1,539	Private Owned 私营企业	818,499	40,325(6)	1,200,815	Printing-dyeing Auxiliary 印染助剂
Hubei Chuyuan Fine Chemical Industry Group Co.,Ltd. 湖北楚源精细化工集团股份有限公司(1994)	Jingzhou 荆州市	Hubei 湖北省	(0716)7295753 (0716)7296097	436	Joint Stock 股份制	606,550	45,000(3)	462,550	P-phentidine对氨基苯乙醚
Suzhou Fine Chemicals Co., Ltd. 苏州精细化工集团有限公司(1923)	Suzhou 苏州市	Jiangsu 江苏省	(0512)67243601 (0512)67248490	1,893	Limited-Liability 有限公司	591,712	40,846(5)	622,502	Formaldehyde 甲醛
Weihai Jinhong Chemical Industry (Group) Co.,Ltd. 威海市金泓化工集团有限公司(1997)	Weihai 威海市	Shandong 山东省	(0631)5584120 (0631)5584217	1,200	Collective-owned 集体企业	527,593	42,109(4)	148,940	Chlorizate Polythene氯化聚乙烯
Shanghai Cognis Oil Chemical Co., Ltd. 上海科宁油脂化学品有限公司(1994)	Shanghai 上海市	Shanghai 上海市	(021)37260710 (021)57260783	411	Foreign Funded 外商投资	428,435	-	529,459	Active Agent 活性剂
Shanghai Cabot Chemical Industry Co., Ltd. 上海市卡博特化工有限公司(1988)	Shanghai 上海市	Shanghai 上海市	(021)64345809 (021)64345532	101	Foreign Funded 外商投资	403,822	85,995(1)	480,361	Carbon Black 碳黑

Top 10 Cities by Revenue 销售收入排名前10位城市	Province 省	Market share 市场份额 (%)	Number of firms 企业个数
Wuxi 无锡市	Jiangsu 江苏省	9.22	67
Shanghai 上海市	Shanghai 上海市	8.63	89
Suzhou 苏州市	Jiangsu 江苏省	5.82	45
Hangzhou 杭州市	Zhejiang 浙江省	5.73	32
Zibo 淄博市	Shandong 山东省	4.79	16
Nanjing 南京市	Jiangsu 江苏省	4.03	22
Tianjin 天津市	Tianjin 天津市	3.83	64
Changzhou 常州市	Jiangsu 江苏省	3.50	50
Beijing 北京市	Beijing 北京市	3.03	38
Yueyang 岳阳市	Hunan 湖南省	2.86	3

10 Major Wholesalers 十家主要批发商	City 城市	Province 省	Telephone/Fax 电话/传真
Yihua Kangqi Chemical Fibre Co.,Ltd. 仪化康祺化纤有限责任公司	Yangzhou 扬州市	Jiangsu 江苏省	(0514)3235499 (0514)3233847
Sinochem Guangdong Import & Export Company 中化广东进出口公司	Guangzhou 广州市	Guangdong 广东省	(020)86672288 (020)86507512
Sinochem Shanghai Import & Export Company 中化上海进出口公司	Shanghai 上海市	Shanghai 上海市	(021)63289888 (021)63283968
Sinochem Tianjin Import & Export Company 中化天津进出口公司	Tianjin 天津市	Tianjin 天津市	(022)23146216 (022)23146215
China Chemical Sales & Supply (North China) Corporation 中国化工供销华北公司	Tianjin 天津市	Tianjin 天津市	(022)23011031 (022)23011032
China Chemical Sales & Supply (North China) Corporation 中国化工供销华东公司	Shanghai 上海市	Shanghai 上海市	(021)62103300 (021)62515799
Nantong Chemical Light Industry Co.,Ltd. 南通化工轻工股份有限公司	Nantong 南通市	Jiangsu 江苏省	(0513)5518397 (0513)5512735
Taizhou Heshun Plastics Co.,Ltd. 台州市和顺塑料有限公司	Taizhou 台州市	Zhejiang 浙江省	(0576)2510220 (0576)2510160
China Petroleum Technology Development Corporation 中国石油技术开发公司	Beijing 北京市	Beijing 北京市	(010)84080722 (010)84080800
China National Chemical Fiber Corporation 中国化纤总公司	Beijing 北京市	Beijing 北京市	(010)65816699 (010)65813483

2672: Special Chemistry Articles 专项化学用品制造业

The industry accounts for 0.192% of the total revenue of China's industrial sector in 2002. The rate of return on assets is 8.25%. 86.88% of all firms in the industry made a profit while 13.12% had negative returns.The top province in terms of the industry's revenue is Shandong, accounting for 25.70% of the total revenue.
2002年本行业收入占全行业的 0.192%，资产利润率为 8.25%。86.88%的企业赢利，13.12%的企业亏损。收入最高的省为山东省，占本行业的25.70%。

	Total number of firms 企业总数	Total number of employees 职工总数	Total revenue (Mil.RMB) 总销售收入（百万元）	Total profit (Mil.RMB) 总利润（百万元）	Return on assets 资产利润率（%）	Return on equity 权益利润率（%）	Labour productivity ('000 RMB/ worker) 劳动生产率（千元/人）	Debts/ assets 资产负债率（%）	Total assets (Mil.RMB) 总资产（百万元）
Industry Overall 行业总体	602	72,100	20,640	1,636	8.25	16.43	89.15	49.78	19,826

	Number of firms 企业个数	Average number of employees 平均职工人数	Average revenue ('000 RMB) 平均销售收入（千元）	Average profit ('000 RMB) 平均利润（千元）	Return on assets 资产利润率（%）	Return on equity 权益利润率（%）	Labour productivity ('000 RMB/ worker) 劳动生产率（千元/人）	Debts/ assets 资产负债率（%）	Average total assets ('000 RMB) 平均总资产（千元）
By ownership 产业所有权									
State-owned 国有	43	172	33,947	2,066	5.02	12.75	71.77	60.65	41,196
Collective-owned 集体	109	141	30,233	2,374	8.87	17.83	67.04	50.28	26,770
Foreign & Overseas Chinese Funded 三资	107	103	58,283	5,017	8.72	16.18	168.25	46.13	57,543
By regional distribution 地区分布									
Central-North 华北	88	96	22,759	1,747	5.53	11.39	75.11	51.44	31,600
Beijing 北京	31	81	22,946	1,481	3.32	5.80	106.89	42.75	44,593
Tianjin 天津	23	98	24,986	2,111	9.57	20.22	39.49	52.67	22,061
Hebei 河北	28	109	20,871	1,985	7.18	19.12	74.72	62.46	27,660
Shanxi 山西	3	115	18,373	455	2.27	10.17	43.43	77.66	20,006
Inner Mongolia 内蒙古	3	91	25,773	775	4.11	15.98	122.46	74.25	18,839
Northeast 东北	59	74	17,495	1,422	6.73	14.49	66.46	53.58	21,136
Liaoning 辽宁	34	78	20,775	1,291	5.80	12.70	70.75	54.32	22,257
Jilin 吉林	13	68	12,456	1,329	6.67	14.73	45.66	54.72	19,932
Heilongjiang 黑龙江	12	66	13,658	1,891	9.81	19.58	75.18	49.88	19,265
Central-East 华东	285	136	44,153	3,450	9.16	17.52	101.08	47.69	37,648
Shanghai 上海	23	98	55,615	5,654	9.73	12.90	104.46	24.63	58,125
Jiangsu 江苏	108	96	37,015	3,146	9.24	17.27	115.33	46.52	34,051
Zhejiang 浙江	51	94	30,576	2,171	7.46	15.23	86.97	51.04	29,111
Anhui 安徽	9	101	7,997	-132	-1.15	-3.13	28.71	63.27	11,501
Fujian 福建	9	52	14,722	933	6.10	10.20	78.99	40.19	15,291
Jiangxi 江西	11	102	21,610	952	4.38	11.02	78.06	60.31	21,760
Shandong 山东	74	256	71,691	5,204	10.27	22.70	101.90	54.76	50,676
Central-South 中南	123	115	33,312	2,731	9.29	21.12	91.39	56.00	29,391
Henan 河南	34	170	21,037	1,971	9.14	23.50	59.80	61.08	21,550
Hubei 湖北	20	145	20,439	1,068	6.14	18.95	53.24	67.59	17,395
Hunan 湖南	3	37	26,891	350	2.06	6.09	72.59	66.13	16,947
Guangdong 广东	61	85	45,935	3,354	8.93	18.22	146.85	50.97	37,549
Guangxi 广西	2	50	4,486	-1,907	-9.74		42.65	101.25	19,565
Hainan 海南	3	36	27,223	15,231	29.65	86.19	202.65	65.60	51,365
Southwest 西南	18	148	18,626	2,151	7.33	14.31	32.88	48.79	29,355
Chongqing 重庆	3	49	12,437	704	4.39	6.24	74.93	29.64	16,026
Sichuan 四川	12	155	20,771	2,653	7.45	13.98	34.30	46.71	35,618
Guizhou 贵州	1	541	16,114	1,743	18.94	132.95	5.95	85.76	9,205
Yunnan 云南	2	53	16,295	1,510	6.91	39.26	87.14	82.39	21,846
Tibet 西藏									
Northwest 西北	29	125	20,295	1,408	4.41	7.38	53.67	40.20	31,905
Shaanxi 陕西	4	106	20,029	1,626	10.77	19.27	72.84	44.13	15,106
Gansu 甘肃	20	89	13,187	885	3.10	4.84	51.18	36.06	28,601
Qinghai 青海									
Ningxia 宁夏									
Xinjiang 新疆	5	285	48,940	3,323	5.68	10.80	51.07	47.45	58,560

2672: Special Chemistry Articles 专项化学用品制造业

Year 年份	Number of firms 企业个数	Rate of change 变化率 (%)	Number of employees 职工人数 (人)	Rate of change 变化率 (%)	Total revenue (Mil. RMB) 总销售收入 (百万元)	Rate of change 变化率 (%)	Total profit (Mil RMB) 总利润 (百万元)	Rate of change 变化率 (%)
2000	497		48,322		11,093		579	
2001	516	3.82	56,925	17.80	13,547	22.12	862	48.88
2002	602	16.67	72,100	26.66	20,640	52.36	1,636	89.79

Major Products 主要产品	Output 产量	Unit 单位
Surface-active Reagent 表面活性剂	294,214	Ton 吨
Adhesive 粘合剂	77	10,000 Tons 万吨

10 Main Firms with Maximal Revenue (year founded) 收入最大的十家主要企业 (创办年份)	City 城市	Province 省	Telephone/fax 电话/传真	Number of employees 职工人数	Ownership 产业所有权	Revenue ('000 RMB) 销售收入 (千元)	Profit('000 RMB) (rank) 利润(千元) (排名)	Total assets ('000 RMB) 总资产 (千元)	Major products 主要产品
Shandong Jin Yi Meng Group Co., Ltd.	Linyi	Shandong	(0539)6213888		State-owned				Polyvinyl Chloride Resin聚氯
山东省金沂蒙集团有限公司(1975)	临沂市	山东省	(0539)6212918	1,980	国有企业	555,679	30,800(11)	360,796	乙烯树脂
Changshu Refrigeration Reagent Factory	Suzhou	Jiangsu	(0512)52621243		Collective-owned				F11,F12,F113
常熟市致冷剂厂(1976)	苏州市	江苏省		940	集体企业	501,488	87,378(1)	394,060	F11F12F113
Shandong Dong Yue Chemical Industry Co.,Ltd.	Zibo	Shandong	(0533)8510072		Foreign Funded				Anhydrous Hydrogen Fluoride无
山东东岳化工有限公司(1987)	淄博市	山东省	(0533)8510071	840	外商投资	403,210	10,872(38)	307,204	水氟化氢
Avery Dennison(China) Co.,Ltd.	Suzhou	Jiangsu	(0512)57702174		Foreign Funded				Pressure-sensitive Adhesive Label Materials不干胶
艾利(中国)有限公司(1994)	苏州市	江苏省	(0512)57707448	250	外商投资	351,277	52,925(4)	290,960	标签材料
Guangzhou Hongchang Adhesive Tape Factory	Guangzhou	Guangdong	(020)86867028		Overseas Chinese-funded				Adhesive Tape
广州宏昌胶粘带厂(1992)	广州市	广东省	(020)86868080	410	港澳台资	322,415	8,547(50)	180,232	胶粘带
Jinling Group Co.Shandong China	Dongying	Shandong	(0546)6884582		Collective-owned				Guar Gum
山东金岭集团公司(1994)	东营市	山东省	(0546)6881718	411	集体企业	289,572	29,982(12)	292,670	瓜尔胶粉
Shunde De Mei Chemical Industry Co., Ltd.	Foshan	Guangdong	(0765)8399088		Private Owned				Adhesive
顺德市德美化工实业有限公司(1998)	佛山市	广东省	(0765)8396930	509	私营企业	275,951	49,164(6)	296,449	粘合剂
Zhejiang Huang Ma Chemical Industry Group Co., Ltd.	Shaoxing	Zhejiang	(0575)2097088		Collective-owned				Oil Pharmaceutical Of Chemical Fibre
浙江皇马化工集团有限公司(1997)	绍兴市	浙江省	(0575)2096153	420	集体企业	244,427	17,154(25)	168,062	化纤油剂
Nanjing Petrochemical Industry Co., Ltd	Nanjing	Jiangsu	(025)8855999		Joint Stock				Oil Refining Auxiliary
南京石油化工有限公司(1992)	南京市	江苏省	(025)8833000	247	股份制	223,000	38,200(9)	437,780	炼油助剂
Beijing Luo Di Ya Dongfang Chemical Industry Co., Ltd.	Beijing	Beijing	(010)61561321		Foreign Funded				Surface Active Reagent表
北京罗地亚东方化工有限公司(1997)	北京市	北京市	(010)61561325	122	外商投资	216,598	4,357(76)	282,573	面活性剂

Top 10 Cities by Revenue 销售收入排名前10位城市	Province 省	Market share 市场份额 (%)	Number of firms 企业个数
Dongying 东营市	Shandong 山东省	7.32	9
Suzhou 苏州市	Jiangsu 江苏省	6.86	15
Guangzhou 广州市	Guangdong 广东省	6.78	19
Shanghai 上海市	Shanghai 上海市	6.20	23
Linyi 临沂市	Shandong 山东省	5.13	10
Zibo 淄博市	Shandong 山东省	5.02	11
Changzhou 常州市	Jiangsu 江苏省	3.74	32
Beijing 北京市	Beijing 北京市	3.45	31
Wuxi 无锡市	Jiangsu 江苏省	3.20	25
Nanjing 南京市	Jiangsu 江苏省	3.02	9

10 Major Wholesalers 十家主要批发商	City 城市	Province 省	Telephone/Fax 电话/传真
Yihua Kangqi Chemical Fibre Co.,Ltd.	Yangzhou	Jiangsu	(0514)3235499
仪化康祺化纤有限责任公司	扬州市	江苏省	(0514)3233847
Sinochem Guangdong Import & Export Company	Guangzhou	Guangdong	(020)86672288
中化广东进出口公司	广州市	广东省	(020)86507512
Sinochem Shanghai Import & Export Company	Shanghai	Shanghai	(021)63289888
中化上海进出口公司	上海市	上海市	(021)63283968
Sinochem Tianjin Import & Export Company	Tianjin	Tianjin	(022)23146216
中化天津进出口公司	天津市	天津市	(022)23146215
China Chemical Sales & Supply (North China) Corporation	Tianjin	Tianjin	(022)23011031
中国化工供销华北公司	天津市	天津市	(022)23011032
China Chemical Sales & Supply (North China) Corporation	Shanghai	Shanghai	(021)62103300
中国化工供销华东公司	上海市	上海市	(021)62515799
Nantong Chemical Light Industry Co.,Ltd.	Nantong	Jiangsu	(0513)5518397
南通化工轻工股份有限公司	南通市	江苏省	(0513)5512735
Taizhou Heshun Plastics Co.,Ltd.	Taizhou	Zhejiang	(0576)2510220
台州市和顺塑料有限公司	台州市	浙江省	(0576)2510160
China Petroleum Technology Development Corporation	Beijing	Beijing	(010)84080722
中国石油技术开发公司	北京市	北京市	(010)84080800
China National Chemical Fiber Corporation	Beijing	Beijing	(010)65816699
中国化纤总公司	北京市	北京市	(010)65813483

2673: Forest Chemical Products 林产化学产品制造业

The industry accounts for 0.039% of the total revenue of China's industrial sector in 2002. The rate of return on assets is 2.68%. 73.91% of all firms in the industry made a profit while 26.09% had negative returns.The top province in terms of the industry's revenue is Guangdong, accounting for 33.45% of the total revenue.
2002年本行业收入占全行业的 0.039%，资产利润率为 2.68%。73.91%的企业赢利，26.09%的企业亏损。收入最高的省为广东省，占本行业的33.45%。

	Total number of firms 企业总数	Total number of employees 职工总数	Total revenue (Mil.RMB) 总销售收入(百万元)	Total profit (Mil.RMB) 总利润(百万元)	Return on assets 资产利润率(%)	Return on equity 权益利润率(%)	Labour productivity ('000 RMB/ worker) 劳动生产率(千元/人)	Debts/ assets 资产负债率(%)	Total assets (Mil.RMB) 总资产(百万元)
Industry Overall 行业总体	253	24,908	4,186	123	2.68	6.64	52.73	59.62	4,599

	Number of firms 企业个数	Average number of employees 平均职工人数	Average revenue ('000 RMB) 平均销售收入(千元)	Average profit ('000 RMB) 平均利润(千元)	Return on assets 资产利润率(%)	Return on equity 权益利润率(%)	Labour productivity ('000 RMB/ worker) 劳动生产率(千元/人)	Debts/ assets 资产负债率(%)	Average total assets ('000 RMB) 平均总资产(千元)
By ownership 产业所有权									
State-owned 国有	62	94	5,360	-102	-0.85	-4.62	15.89	81.53	11,909
Collective-owned 集体	53	73	12,969	314	3.92	8.30	50.61	52.77	8,007
Foreign & Overseas Chinese Funded 三资	21	90	34,100	1,728	5.42	9.88	103.70	45.09	31,846
By regional distribution 地区分布									
Central-North 华北	12	208	13,477	-1,559	-6.29	-29.78	13.97	78.88	24,800
Beijing 北京									
Tianjin 天津									
Hebei 河北	4	117	9,329	-440	-3.41	-16.40	26.74	79.23	12,918
Shanxi 山西	6	123	16,554	598	2.49	8.78	26.34	71.64	24,010
Inner Mongolia 内蒙古	2	647	12,541	-10,270	-20.16	-182.59	2.30	88.96	50,931
Northeast 东北	4	115	7,454	314	0.99	3.04	76.81	67.24	31,548
Liaoning 辽宁	1								
Jilin 吉林	3	153	9,938	418	0.99	3.04	76.81	67.24	42,064
Heilongjiang 黑龙江									
Central-East 华东	83	71	11,612	357	3.50	8.49	48.41	58.73	10,198
Shanghai 上海	7	31	17,933	868	8.72	15.82	213.39	44.90	9,956
Jiangsu 江苏	6	80	17,105	612	6.19	13.27	58.93	53.36	9,885
Zhejiang 浙江	13	66	11,081	197	2.17	5.79	43.85	62.54	9,055
Anhui 安徽	1	120	8,176	1,070	14.22	90.68	18.13	84.31	7,522
Fujian 福建	29	65	11,618	325	2.41	5.13	52.05	53.10	13,520
Jiangxi 江西	25	92	7,635	268	3.82	14.17	25.91	73.02	7,014
Shandong 山东	2	25	27,810	79	0.64	2.33	270.90	72.72	12,357
Central-South 中南	133	92	20,126	598	3.27	8.03	63.69	59.26	18,270
Henan 河南	12	172	14,046	1,183	9.18	13.05	34.82	29.69	12,890
Hubei 湖北	5	47	11,413	234	4.97	8.04	67.82	38.11	4,712
Hunan 湖南	8	64	7,616	829	22.18	36.89	42.06	39.89	3,737
Guangdong 广东	51	74	27,456	695	3.09	7.75	113.41	60.12	22,502
Guangxi 广西	48	83	17,210	441	2.59	7.51	49.87	65.56	17,053
Hainan 海南	9	189	18,206	94	0.33	0.78	26.06	57.38	28,397
Southwest 西南	17	192	19,602	1,935	4.09	8.51	50.72	51.87	47,262
Chongqing 重庆									
Sichuan 四川	3	75	6,355	234	2.96	22.42	16.10	86.78	7,897
Guizhou 贵州	2	58	5,545	-105	-1.12	-2.83	37.65	60.34	9,306
Yunnan 云南	11	266	27,553	2,945	4.26	8.61	53.91	50.57	69,195
Tibet 西藏	1								
Northwest 西北	4	119	5,189	-325	-1.36	-4.82	17.93	71.80	23,948
Shaanxi 陕西	3	150	6,918	-426	-1.34	-4.79	17.30	72.01	31,751
Gansu 甘肃	1	24	1	-23	-4.29	-6.63	29.83	35.26	536
Qinghai 青海									
Ningxia 宁夏									
Xinjiang 新疆									

2673: Forest Chemical Products 林产化学产品制造业

Year 年份	Number of firms 企业个数	Rate of change 变化率 (%)	Number of employees 职工人数 (人)	Rate of change 变化率 (%)	Total revenue (Mil. RMB) 总销售收入 (百万元)	Rate of change 变化率 (%)	Total profit (Mil RMB) 总利润 (百万元)	Rate of change 变化率 (%)
2000	237		30,122		3,472		52	
2001	235	-0.84	26,367	-12.47	3,865	11.32	75	44.23
2002	253	7.66	24,908	-5.53	4,186	8.31	123	64.00

Major Products 主要产品	Output 产量	Unit 单位
Rosin 松香	38	10,000 Tons 万吨

10 Main Firms with Maximal Revenue (year founded) 收入最大的十家主要企业（创办年份）	City 城市	Province 省	Telephone/fax 电话/传真	Number of employees 职工人数	Ownership 产业所有权	Revenue ('000 RMB) 销售收入 (千元)	Profit('000 RMB) (rank) 利润(千元) (排名)	Total assets ('000 RMB) 总资产 (千元)	Major products 主要产品
Guangdong Hua Lin Chemical CTD Co., Ltd. 封开县华林化工有限公司(1989)	Zhaoqing 肇庆市	Guangdong 广东省	(0758)6711427 (0758)6711858	452	State Owned 国有企业	211,627	5,530(6)	153,066	Gum Rosin 脂松香
Guang Dong De Qing Forestry Chemical Industry Co.,Ltd. 广东省德庆林产化工(集团)股分有限公司(1969)	Zhaoqing 肇庆市	Guangdong 广东省	(0758)7762326 (0758)7765461	564	Joint Stock 股份制	199,391	3,198(12)	428,026	Rosin 松香
Jinggu Forestry Co.,Ltd. 景谷县林业股份有限公司(1998)	Simao 思茅	Yunnan 云南省	(0879)5225312 (0879)5223881	1,697	Joint Stock 股份制	158,166	23,151(1)	558,370	Rosin 松香
Guangxi Wuzhou Turpentine Factory 广西壮族自治区梧州松脂厂(1950)	Wuzhou 梧州市	Guangxi 广西	(0774)3811538 (0774)3811538	450	Joint Stock 股份制	147,230	18,191(2)	245,569	Rosin 松香
Wuzhou Richeng Forestry Chemical Industry Co.,Ltd. 梧州日成林产化工有限公司(1985)	Wuzhou 梧州市	Guangxi 广西	(0774)2693397 (0774)2683737	268	Overseas Chinese-funded 港澳台资	119,103	5,338(7)	103,379	Gum Rosin 脂松香
Gaoyao Sen Yuan Forest Products Chemical Industry Co., Ltd. 高要市森源林产化工有限公司(2002)	Zhaoqing 肇庆市	Guangdong 广东省	(0758)8219628 (0758)8219638	79	Private Owned 私营企业	77,090	220(99)	15,661	Rosin 松香
Hainan Mei Lian Rubber Co., Ltd. 海南美联橡胶有限公司(2001)	Hainan 海口市	Hainan 海南省	(0898)23501282 (0898)23501088	129	Foreign Funded 外商投资	58,220	219(100)	40,599	Concentrated latex 浓缩乳胶
Jingdong Forest Products Group Co., Ltd. 景东南国莹银林产集团有限责任公司(1975)	Simao 思茅	Yunnan 云南省	(0879)6221611 (0879)6221611	629	Limited-Liability 有限公司	53,203	3,066(13)	100,482	Rosin 松香
Xinxing Huashi Rosin Production Base Co.,Ltd. 新兴县华实松香生产基地有限公司(1999)	Yunfu 云浮市	Guangdong 广东省	(0766)2712818 (0766)2711832	53	Private Owned 私营企业	48,885	-	38,247	Rosin 松香
Guangdong Huajun High-tech Chemical Industry Co.,Ltd. 郁南县高科化工有限公司广东华骏(1999)	Yunfu 云浮市	Guangdong 广东省	(0766)7269089 (0766)7269341	60	Private Owned 私营企业	48,676	3,472(10)	3,900	Rosin 松香

Top 10 Cities by Revenue 销售收入排名前10位城市	Province 省	Market share 市场份额 (%)	Number of firms 企业个数
Zhaoqing 肇庆市	Guangdong 广东省	24.94	28
Wuzhou 梧州市	Guangxi 广西	7.65	6
Simao 思茅地区	Yunnan 云南省	6.06	7
Hainan 海南省	Hainan 海南省	3.91	9
Maoming 茂名市	Guangdong 广东省	3.56	3
Sanming 三明市	Fujian 福建省	3.42	13
Yunfu 云浮市	Guangdong 广东省	3.40	6
Shanghai 上海市	Shanghai 上海市	3.00	7
Yulin 玉林市	Guangxi 广西	2.84	8
Guilin 桂林市	Guangxi 广西	2.83	8

10 Major Wholesalers 十家主要批发商	City 城市	Province 省	Telephone/Fax 电话/传真
Yihua Kangqi Chemical Fibre Co.,Ltd. 仪化康祺化纤有限责任公司	Yangzhou 扬州市	Jiangsu 江苏省	(0514)3235499 (0514)3233847
Sinochem Guangdong Import & Export Company 中化广东进出口公司	Guangzhou 广州市	Guangdong 广东省	(020)86672288 (020)86507512
Sinochem Shanghai Import & Export Company 中化上海进出口公司	Shanghai 上海市	Shanghai 上海市	(021)63289888 (021)63283968
Sinochem Tianjin Import & Export Company 中化天津进出口公司	Tianjin 天津市	Tianjin 天津市	(022)23146216 (022)23146215
China Chemical Sales & Supply (North China) Corporation 中国化工供销华北公司	Tianjin 天津市	Tianjin 天津市	(022)23011031 (022)23011032
China Chemical Sales & Supply (North China) Corporation 中国化工供销华东公司	Shanghai 上海市	Shanghai 上海市	(021)62103300 (021)62515799
Nantong Chemical Light Industry Co.,Ltd. 南通化工轻工股份有限公司	Nantong 南通市	Jiangsu 江苏省	(0513)5518397 (0513)5512735
Taizhou Heshun Plastics Co.,Ltd. 台州市和顺塑料有限公司	Taizhou 台州市	Zhejiang 浙江省	(0576)2510220 (0576)2510160
China Petroleum Technology Development Corporation 中国石油技术开发公司	Beijing 北京市	Beijing 北京市	(010)84080722 (010)84080800
China National Chemical Fiber Corporation 中国化纤总公司	Beijing 北京市	Beijing 北京市	(010)65816699 (010)65813483

2675: Information Chemical Products 信息化学品制造业

The industry accounts for 0.121% of the total revenue of China's industrial sector in 2002. The rate of return on assets is 2.63%. 78.67% of all firms in the industry made a profit while 21.33% had negative returns.The top province in terms of the industry's revenue is Fujian, accounting for 27.33% of the total revenue.
2002年本行业收入占全行业的 0.121%，资产利润率为 2.63%。78.67%的企业赢利，21.33%的企业亏损。收入最高的省为福建省，占本行业的27.33%。

	Total number of firms 企业总数	Total number of employees 职工总数	Total revenue (Mil.RMB) 总销售收入(百万元)	Total profit (Mil.RMB) 总利润(百万元)	Return on assets 资产利润率(%)	Return on equity 权益利润率(%)	Labour productivity ('000 RMB/worker) 劳动生产率(千元/人)	Debts/assets 资产负债率(%)	Total assets (Mil.RMB) 总资产(百万元)
Industry Overall 行业总体	150	37,782	13,028	574	2.63	7.51	123.36	64.90	21,796

	Number of firms 企业个数	Average number of employees 平均职工人数	Average revenue ('000 RMB) 平均销售收入（千元）	Average profit ('000 RMB) 平均利润(千元)	Return on assets 资产利润率(%)	Return on equity 权益利润率(%)	Labour productivity ('000 RMB/worker) 劳动生产率(千元/人)	Debts/assets 资产负债率(%)	Average total assets ('000 RMB) 平均总资产(千元)
By ownership 产业所有权									
State-owned 国有	25	514	94,866	7,795	3.31	6.44	62.30	48.69	235,710
Collective-owned 集体	9	169	42,622	10,625	37.89	75.07	109.00	49.52	28,038
Foreign & Overseas Chinese Funded 三资	67	245	131,538	2,832	1.41	5.25	195.36	73.07	200,335
By regional distribution 地区分布									
Central-North 华北	18	378	64,471	6,916	3.54	5.83	68.97	39.27	195,443
Beijing 北京	6	92	15,513	-2,045	-7.32	-13.72	86.28	46.65	27,941
Tianjin 天津	3	338	23,994	-24	-0.02		26.19	102.88	145,176
Hebei 河北	7	747	142,203	19,894	4.79	6.76	75.65	29.13	415,111
Shanxi 山西	1	1							
Inner Mongolia 内蒙古	1	15		-2,430	-26.93	-968.13		97.22	9,024
Northeast 东北	5	172	32,910	1,026	2.44	11.99	71.39	79.64	42,050
Liaoning 辽宁	3	111	41,632	-1,642	-3.82	-29.45	147.91	87.01	42,935
Jilin 吉林	2	263	19,827	5,029	12.35	38.55	22.70	67.97	40,723
Heilongjiang 黑龙江									
Central-East 华东	64	171	126,813	3,350	1.61	7.59	267.21	78.83	208,561
Shanghai 上海	19	86	28,415	1,503	3.37	5.80	90.43	41.85	44,545
Jiangsu 江苏	18	207	164,053	7,453	3.58	17.97	162.13	80.09	208,311
Zhejiang 浙江	9	267	71,761	4,620	2.77	9.25	74.13	70.06	166,913
Anhui 安徽	3	55	12,571	3,439	32.45	75.58	127.29	57.07	10,600
Fujian 福建	8	212	445,037	-2,656	-0.30	-2.11	1,093.54	85.57	871,309
Jiangxi 江西	1	56	18,222	519	1.21	1.26	166.55	4.50	43,000
Shandong 山东	6	214	60,185	3,421	10.04	26.81	89.88	62.56	34,075
Central-South 中南	52	332	58,606	3,385	4.37	7.64	59.54	42.81	77,434
Henan 河南	4	846	198,618	29,022	13.94	23.81	87.56	41.46	208,246
Hubei 湖北	9	192	21,023	-547	-1.36	-22.55	52.52	93.99	40,348
Hunan 湖南	4	417	69,146	6,856	6.78	16.83	47.97	59.71	101,094
Guangdong 广东	31	324	54,123	1,042	1.44	2.11	50.52	31.90	72,549
Guangxi 广西	4	107	27,364	1,284	2.90	5.20	123.59	44.27	44,261
Hainan 海南									
Southwest 西南	10	149	41,708	2,507	4.79	11.38	82.99	57.96	52,394
Chongqing 重庆	2	87	40,331	5,652	8.31	11.50	231.03	27.75	68,029
Sichuan 四川	6	212	53,522	2,305	3.72	12.29	58.02	69.70	61,932
Guizhou 贵州	1	25	14,415	28	0.20	0.28	355.20	29.68	14,247
Yunnan 云南	1	14	870	-90	-4.41		27.00	132.11	2,043
Tibet 西藏									
Northwest 西北	1	401	122,693	29,143	17.16	23.68	118.04	27.53	169,825
Shaanxi 陕西	1	401	122,693	29,143	17.16	23.68	118.04	27.53	169,825
Gansu 甘肃									
Qinghai 青海									
Ningxia 宁夏									
Xinjiang 新疆									

2675: Information Chemical Products 信息化学品制造业

Year 年份	Number of firms 企业个数	Rate of change 变化率 (%)	Number of employees 职工人数 (人)	Rate of change 变化率 (%)	Total revenue (Mil. RMB) 总销售收入 (百万元)	Rate of change 变化率 (%)	Total profit (Mil RMB) 总利润 (百万元)	Rate of change 变化率 (%)
2000	152		39,469		11,275		-337	
2001	150	-1.32	38,327	-2.89	11,276	0.01	-331	1.78
2002	150	0	37,782	-1.42	13,028	15.54	574	-

Major Products 主要产品	Output 产量	Unit 单位
Diskette 软磁盘	71,715	10,000 Pieces 万片
Magnetic Tape(convert into 6.30mm) 磁带 （折6.30毫米）	255	100,000,000 Meters 亿米

10 Main Firms with Maximal Revenue (year founded) 收入最大的十家主要企业（创办年份）	City 城市	Province 省	Telephone/fax 电话/传真	Number of employees 职工人数	Ownership 产业所有权	Revenue ('000 RMB) 销售收入 (千元)	Profit('000 RMB) (rank) 利润(千元) (排名)	Total assets ('000 RMB) 总资产 (千元)	Major products 主要产品
Kodak(China) Co.,Ltd. Xiamen branch 柯达（中国）股份有限公司厦门分公司(1998)	Xiamen 厦门市	Fujian 福建省	(0592)6801749 (0592)6801694	1,253	Foreign Funded 外商投资	3,426,735	-	6,793,886	Colour Printing Paper 彩色相纸
Wuxi Sharp Electronics Co.,Ltd. 无锡夏普电子元器件有限公司(1994)	Wuxi 无锡市	Jiangsu 江苏省	(0510)5212490 (0510)5216585	782	Foreign Funded 外商投资	1,602,868	30,176(5)	739,606	Liquid Crystal Display液晶显示器
China Lucky Film Group Corporation 中国乐凯胶片公司(1960)	Baoding 保定市	Hebei 河北省	(0312)7922826 (0312)7923000	4,274	State-owned 国有企业	760,995	47,149(4)	2,686,378	Sensitization Materials 感光材料
The Second Film Factory of Lucky Group 中国乐凯胶片公司第二胶片厂(1977)	Nanyang 南阳市	Henan 河南省	(0377)3132128 (0377)3132092	3,142	State-owned 国有企业	742,099	113,530(1)	798,174	Printing Film 印刷胶片
Kunshan Hu Tek Photoelectricity Science & Technology Co., Ltd. 昆山沪铼光电科技有限公司(1999)	Suzhou 苏州市	Jiangsu 江苏省	(0512)57358989 (0512)57359090	774	Foreign Funded 外商投资	569,985	-	1,580,452	Information Chemical信息化学品
Changsha Liyuan New Materials Co., Ltd. 长沙力元新材料股份有限公司(1998)	Changsha 长沙市	Hunan 湖南省	(0731)4016961 (0731)4016101	790	Joint Stock 股份制	242,889	26,722(7)	332,426	Cobalt Coated Nickel Foam连续化带状泡沫镍
Kodak(Wuxi) Co., Ltd. 柯达（无锡）股份有限公司(1998)	Wuxi 无锡市	Jiangsu 江苏省	(0510)5213333 (0510)5213399	139	Foreign Funded 外商投资	238,537	61,220(3)	337,267	Kodak Reversal Reagent柯达冲印药水
Sichuan Juguang Printing Equipment Co., Ltd. 四川炬光印刷器材有限公司(1994)	Chengdu 成都市	Sichuan 四川省	(028)83012051 (028)83974613	300	Limited-Liability 有限公司	238,232	8,439(22)	127,014	ps Edition ps版
Weicheng Cassettes Factory(Shenzhen) Co., Ltd. 伟成盒带厂（深圳）有限公司(1989)	Shenzhen 深圳市	Guangdong 广东省	(0755)27946902 (0755)27495341	1,160	Overseas Chinese-funded 港澳台资	222,747	1,983(50)	138,155	Blank Video Tap空白录像带
Chuangfu Video Tap (Shenzhen) Co., Ltd. 创富录像带（深圳）有限公司(1991)	Shenzhen 深圳市	Guangdong 广东省	(0755)27948816 (0755)27948313	1,600	Overseas Chinese-funded 港澳台资	210,891	2,409(44)	59,121	Blank Video Tap空白录像带

Top 10 Cities by Revenue 销售收入排名前10位城市	Province 省	Market share 市场份额 (%)	Number of firms 企业个数
Xiamen 厦门市	Fujian 福建省	26.55	2
Wuxi 无锡市	Jiangsu 江苏省	15.62	7
Shenzhen 深圳市	Guangdong 广东省	6.25	7
Baoding 保定市	Hebei 河北省	6.05	3
Nanyang 南阳市	Henan 河南省	5.70	1
Suzhou 苏州市	Jiangsu 江苏省	4.91	4
Shanghai 上海市	Shanghai 上海市	4.14	19
Hangzhou 杭州市	Zhejiang 浙江省	4.03	4
Chengdu 成都市	Sichuan 四川省	2.07	3
Changsha 长沙市	Hunan 湖南省	2.04	3

10 Major Wholesalers 十家主要批发商	City 城市	Province 省	Telephone/Fax 电话/传真
Yihua Kangqi Chemical Fibre Co.,Ltd. 仪化康祺化纤有限责任公司	Yangzhou 扬州市	Jiangsu 江苏省	(0514)3235499 (0514)3233847
Sinochem Guangdong Import & Export Company 中化广东进出口公司	Guangzhou 广州市	Guangdong 广东省	(020)86672288 (020)86507512
Sinochem Shanghai Import & Export Company 中化上海进出口公司	Shanghai 上海市	Shanghai 上海市	(021)63289888 (021)63283968
Sinochem Tianjin Import & Export Company 中化天津进出口公司	Tianjin 天津市	Tianjin 天津市	(022)23146216 (022)23146215
China Chemical Sales & Supply (North China) Corporation 中国化工供销华北公司	Tianjin 天津市	Tianjin 天津市	(022)23011031 (022)23011032
China Chemical Sales & Supply (North China) Corporation 中国化工供销华东公司	Shanghai 上海市	Shanghai 上海市	(021)62103300 (021)62515799
Nantong Chemical Light Industry Co.,Ltd. 南通化工轻工股份有限公司	Nantong 南通市	Jiangsu 江苏省	(0513)5518397 (0513)5512735
Taizhou Heshun Plastics Co.,Ltd. 台州市和顺塑料有限公司	Taizhou 台州市	Zhejiang 浙江省	(0576)2510220 (0576)2510160
China Petroleum Technology Development Corporation 中国石油技术开发公司	Beijing 北京市	Beijing 北京市	(010)84080722 (010)84080800
China National Chemical Fiber Corporation 中国化纤总公司	Beijing 北京市	Beijing 北京市	(010)65816699 (010)65813483

2677: Chemical Additive 添加剂制造业

The industry accounts for 0.076% of the total revenue of China's industrial sector in 2002. The rate of return on assets is 6.02%. 85.29% of all firms in the industry made a profit while 14.71% had negative returns.The top province in terms of the industry's revenue is Guangdong, accounting for 17.82% of the total revenue.
2002年本行业收入占全行业的0.076%，资产利润率为6.02%。85.29%的企业赢利，14.71%的企业亏损。收入最高的省为广东省，占本行业的17.82%。

	Total number of firms 企业总数	Total number of employees 职工总数	Total revenue (Mil.RMB) 总销售收入（百万元）	Total profit (Mil.RMB) 总利润（百万元）	Return on assets 资产利润率（%）	Return on equity 权益利润率（%）	Labour productivity ('000 RMB/ worker) 劳动生产率（千元/人）	Debts/ assets 资产负债率（%）	Total assets (Mil.RMB) 总资产（百万元）
Industry Overall 行业总体	238	33,839	8,192	499	6.02	13.76	66.41	56.25	8,291

	Number of firms 企业个数	Average number of employees 平均职工人数	Average revenue ('000 RMB) 平均销售收入（千元）	Average profit ('000 RMB) 平均利润（千元）	Return on assets 资产利润率（%）	Return on equity 权益利润率（%）	Labour productivity ('000 RMB/ worker) 劳动生产率（千元/人）	Debts/ assets 资产负债率（%）	Average total assets ('000 RMB) 平均总资产（千元）
By ownership 产业所有权									
State-owned 国有	32	137	9,324	-234	-1.03	-2.84	18.97	63.59	22,683
Collective-owned 集体	29	118	37,452	2,836	9.24	23.45	95.72	60.60	30,692
Foreign & Overseas Chinese Funded 三资	53	195	58,294	4,236	6.79	13.48	71.35	49.63	62,395
By regional distribution 地区分布									
Central-North 华北	31	190	38,904	1,519	2.97	7.69	61.07	61.43	51,223
Beijing 北京	8	275	42,532	3,665	6.44	17.45	43.47	63.12	56,948
Tianjin 天津	11	73	20,821	509	3.90	9.72	63.44	59.85	13,049
Hebei 河北	8	166	16,681	-1,316	-3.37	-7.28	28.02	53.68	39,051
Shanxi 山西	3	105	1,376	17	0.25	0.72	9.08	64.58	6,552
Inner Mongolia 内蒙古	1	1,253	499,180	22,648	3.45	9.63	138.43	64.20	656,738
Northeast 东北	14	108	11,190	580	1.81	4.95	23.47	63.46	32,077
Liaoning 辽宁	5	34	3,513	3	0.04	0.11	15.57	67.78	8,119
Jilin 吉林	3	105	17,496	1,576	4.70	9.74	52.85	51.72	33,506
Heilongjiang 黑龙江	6	171	14,435	563	1.10	3.29	15.76	66.72	51,328
Central-East 华东	108	176	36,547	2,681	8.58	20.54	58.61	58.20	31,230
Shanghai 上海	14	74	22,191	1,838	7.36	14.99	96.17	50.90	24,968
Jiangsu 江苏	35	118	37,057	1,389	6.52	21.71	76.25	69.98	21,308
Zhejiang 浙江	19	150	45,965	4,457	13.02	24.95	78.37	47.82	34,238
Anhui 安徽	7	267	23,237	1,598	3.21	9.31	46.15	65.53	49,791
Fujian 福建	5	131	61,479	11,240	24.37	43.50	150.75	43.98	46,128
Jiangxi 江西	7	226	23,273	-59	-0.17	-0.39	19.02	56.48	34,522
Shandong 山东	21	328	39,670	3,026	7.88	19.83	37.90	60.26	38,390
Central-South 中南	67	85	32,384	1,959	6.20	12.26	96.75	49.48	31,622
Henan 河南	18	98	17,735	647	4.18	11.03	38.70	62.08	15,461
Hubei 湖北	6	74	21,644	903	6.21	11.04	132.95	43.78	14,536
Hunan 湖南	3	122	39,259	-16	-0.24	-0.69	63.17	65.10	6,532
Guangdong 广东	32	73	45,610	4,305	9.93	17.23	141.61	42.36	43,357
Guangxi 广西	8	100	17,921	-2,938	-6.79	-21.49	89.04	68.41	43,262
Hainan 海南									
Southwest 西南	8	153	82,519	3,341	4.37	8.25	141.79	47.01	76,395
Chongqing 重庆	1	36	5,860	-817	-10.65	-15.45	27.58	31.04	7,668
Sichuan 四川	6	108	91,023	4,858	6.62	9.97	229.69	33.60	73,419
Guizhou 贵州	1	536	108,157	-1,605	-0.98	-6.15	43.20	83.98	162,976
Yunnan 云南									
Tibet 西藏									
Northwest 西北	10	50	5,280	-340	-2.24	-7.26	26.49	69.07	15,154
Shaanxi 陕西	3	69	5,628	-930	-3.23	-11.08	21.94	70.89	28,821
Gansu 甘肃	3	23	3,072	131	7.90	15.04	75.26	47.45	1,653
Qinghai 青海									
Ningxia 宁夏									
Xinjiang 新疆	4	57	6,674	-251	-1.67	-5.26	15.83	68.22	15,031

Year 年份	Number of firms 企业个数	Rate of change 变化率(%)	Number of employees 职工人数(人)	Rate of change 变化率(%)	Total revenue (Mil. RMB) 总销售收入(百万元)	Rate of change 变化率(%)	Total profit (Mil RMB) 总利润(百万元)	Rate of change 变化率(%)
2000	167		20,139		3,885		90	
2001	200	19.76	24,851	23.40	6,000	54.44	296	228.89
2002	238	19.00	33,839	36.17	8,192	36.53	499	68.58

Major Products 主要产品	Output 产量	Unit 单位
Food Additive 食品添加剂	485,091	Ton 吨
Feedstuff Additive 饲料添加剂	44	10,000 Tons 万吨

10 Main Firms with Maximal Revenue (year founded) 收入最大的十家主要企业(创办年份)	City 城市	Province 省	Telephone/fax 电话/传真	Number of employees 职工人数	Ownership 产业所有权	Revenue ('000 RMB) 销售收入(千元)	Profit('000 RMB) (rank) 利润(千元)(排名)	Total assets ('000 RMB) 总资产(千元)	Major products 主要产品
Zhongshan Unicizers Induserial Co.,Ltd.	Zhongshan	Guangdong	(0760)3382456		Overseas Chinese-funded				DOP Plasticizing Neat
中山联成化学工业有限公司(1997)	中山市	广东省	(0760)5310400	247	港澳台资	519,958	59,881(1)	378,853	DOP增塑齐
Inner Mongolia Jinhe Industrial Company	Huhhot	Inner Mongolia	(0471)8514595		Limited-Liability				Aureomycin
内蒙古金河实业集团有限公司(1988)	呼和浩特市	内蒙古	(0471)8513618	1,253	有限公司	499,180	22648(6)	656,738	金霉素
Guangdong Vantico Polymers Co.,Ltd.	Guangzhou	Guangdong	(020)84865123		Foreign Funded				Epoxide Resin
广东泛达化工有限公司(1995)	广州市	广东省	(020)84865122	297	外商投资	293,456	37,948(3)	272,795	环氧树脂
Shuang Lui Zheng Da Co.,Ltd.	Chengdu	Sichuan	(028)85869111		Overseas Chinese-funded				Feedstuff
双流正大有限公司(1995)	成都市	四川省	(028)85868312	182	港澳台资	291,036	13,520(10)	86,037	饲料
Pucheng Chiatai Biochemistry Co.,Ltd.	Nanping	Fujian	(0599)2827005		Overseas Chinese-funded				Feedstuff Aureomycin饲
浦城县正大生化有限公司(1995)	南平市	福建省	(0599)2823294	389	港澳台资	229,899	49,830(2)	192,075	料金霉素
Jianhu Meichang Chemical Industry Co., Ltd.	Yancheng	Jiangsu	(0515)6435388		Private Owned				Sorbic Acid
建湖县美昌化工有限责任公司(1998)	盐城市	江苏省	(0515)6435548	400	私营企业	224,950	15,900(8)	36,710	山梨酸
Chang Zhou Niutang Chemical Plants	Changzhou	Jiangsu	(0519)6391136		Joint Stock				Folic Acid
常州市武进牛塘化工厂(1969)	常州市	江苏省	(0519)6391145	680	股份制	200,850	3,810(31)	135,130	叶酸
Sichuan Chuanhua Wei Zhi Su Co., Ltd.	Chengdu	Sichuan	(028)83604174		Foreign Funded				L-Lysine
四川川化味之素有限公司(1994)	成都市	四川省	(028)83604053	187	外商投资	196,076	13,281(11)	288,207	赖氨酸
Ningbo Wanglong Group Co., Ltd.	Ningbo	Zhejiang	(0574)62092570		Private Owned				Potassium Sorbic Acid
宁波王龙集团有限公司(1992)	宁波市	浙江省	(0574)62092570	346	私营企业	168,252	16,551(7)	84,330	山梨酸钾
Zhejiang Jindadi Bioengineering Co.,Ltd. Zhuji branch	Shaoxing	Zhejiang	(0575)7379168		Joint Stock				Feedstuff Additive饲
浙江金大地生物工程股份有限公司诸暨分公司(1996)	绍兴市	浙江省	(0575)7379578	187	股份制	131,789	11,992(13)	64,436	料添加剂

Top 10 Cities by Revenue 销售收入排名前10位城市	Province 省	Market share 市场份额(%)	Number of firms 企业个数
Guangzhou 广州市	Guangdong 广东省	7.83	19
Zhongshan 中山市	Guangdong 广东省	6.69	2
Huhhot 呼和浩特市	Inner Mongolia 内蒙古	6.09	1
Chengdu 成都市	Sichuan 四川省	6.05	3
Dezhou 德州市	Shandong 山东省	4.70	3
Beijing 北京市	Beijing 北京市	4.15	8
Shanghai 上海市	Shanghai 上海市	3.79	14
Hangzhou 杭州市	Zhejiang 浙江省	3.76	9
Changzhou 常州市	Jiangsu 江苏省	3.52	7
Yancheng 盐城市	Jiangsu 江苏省	3.06	2

10 Major Wholesalers 十家主要批发商	City 城市	Province 省	Telephone/Fax 电话/传真
COFCO International (Beijing) Ltd.	Beijing	Beijing	(010)65268888
中粮国际(北京)有限公司	北京市	北京市	(010)65223623
China National Cereals, Oils & Foodstuffs Imp. & Exp. Corp.	Beijing	Beijing	(010)65268888
中国粮油食品进出口(集团)有限公司	北京市	北京市	(010)62578612
China Grains and Oils Group Corp.	Beijing	Beijing	(010)88518866
中谷粮油集团公司	北京市	北京市	(010)68476847
China Tobacco General Company Beijing Company	Beijing	Beijing	(010)64434106
中国烟草总公司北京市公司	北京市	北京市	(010)64418742
Jilin Grain Group Import & Export Ltd.	Changchun	Jilin	(0431)5598115
吉林粮食集团进出口有限公司	长春市	吉林省	(0431)5598118
Zhejiang Cereals, Oils & Foodstuffs Import & Export Co.,Ltd.	Hangzhou	Zhejiang	(0571)85779999
浙江省粮油食品进出口股份有限公司	杭州市	浙江省	(0571)85152514
China Tobacco General Company Shenzhen Company	Shenzhen	Guangdong	(0755)82230333
中国烟草总公司深圳市公司	深圳市	广东省	(0755)82206815
China National Vegetable Oil Corporation	Beijing	Beijing	(010)68083380
中国植物油公司	北京市	北京市	(010)68081127
Beijing Yangu Grain & Oil Purchase & Sale Company	Beijing	Beijing	(010)63041782
北京市燕谷粮油购销公司	北京市	北京市	(010)63034914
Shanghai Good Companion Sea Lion Industrial Co., Ltd Sale Filiale	Shanghai	Shanghai	(021)63321662
上海良友海狮油脂实业有限公司销售分公司	上海市	上海市	(021)54095735

2681: Soap, Washing Powder and Synthetic Detergent

肥皂及皂粉、合成洗涤剂制造业

The industry accounts for 0.320% of the total revenue of China's industrial sector in 2002. The rate of return on assets is 9.46%. 72.53% of all firms in the industry made a profit while 27.47% had negative returns.The top province in terms of the industry's revenue is Guangdong, accounting for 43.13% of the total revenue.
2002年本行业收入占全行业的 0.320%，资产利润率为 9.46%。72.53%的企业赢利，27.47%的企业亏损。收入最高的省为广东省，占本行业的43.13%。

	Total number of firms 企业总数	Total number of employees 职工总数	Total revenue (Mil.RMB) 总销售收入（百万元）	Total profit (Mil.RMB) 总利润（百万元）	Return on assets 资产利润率（%）	Return on equity 权益利润率（%）	Labour productivity ('000 RMB/ worker) 劳动生产率（千元/人）	Debts/ assets 资产负债率（%）	Total assets (Mil.RMB) 总资产（百万元）
Industry Overall 行业总体	324	78,953	34,354	2,828	9.46	22.03	121.96	57.05	29,883

	Number of firms 企业个数	Average number of employees 平均职工人数	Average revenue ('000 RMB) 平均销售收入（千元）	Average profit ('000 RMB) 平均利润（千元）	Return on assets 资产利润率（%）	Return on equity 权益利润率（%）	Labour productivity ('000 RMB/ worker) 劳动生产率（千元/人）	Debts/ assets 资产负债率（%）	Average total assets ('000 RMB) 平均总资产（千元）
By ownership 产业所有权									
State-owned 国有	52	192	13,144	-1,729	-3.15	-11.01	7.43	71.39	54,904
Collective-owned 集体	41	110	38,968	2,393	13.05	30.21	121.46	56.80	18,336
Foreign & Overseas Chinese Funded 三资	61	318	313,303	36,834	14.24	31.95	318.36	55.43	258,695
By regional distribution 地区分布									
Central-North 华北	56	119	21,668	98	0.28	0.60	92.05	53.54	35,305
Beijing 北京	18	61	18,966	999	3.14	4.68	169.70	33.02	31,846
Tianjin 天津	10	81	27,086	-2,739	-5.96	-17.78	252.76	66.50	45,978
Hebei 河北	18	156	27,064	514	2.17	5.72	63.80	62.07	23,680
Shanxi 山西	8	191	14,115	760	1.28	2.57	27.97	50.09	59,374
Inner Mongolia 内蒙古	2	220	541	-201	-0.94		3.82	142.47	21,406
Northeast 东北	14	190	35,063	-3,065	-6.01	-17.75	30.12	66.15	51,032
Liaoning 辽宁	7	290	43,106	-2,912	-3.58	-13.28	26.56	73.06	81,404
Jilin 吉林	1	313	106,057	-25,420	-28.00	-33.52	36.45	16.45	90,774
Heilongjiang 黑龙江	6	53	13,848	482	5.37	23.17	46.55	76.83	8,975
Central-East 华东	110	274	122,728	3,097	3.97	9.66	86.92	58.91	77,988
Shanghai 上海	27	204	130,391	-6,263	-7.84	-28.34	126.58	72.35	79,902
Jiangsu 江苏	31	159	44,242	514	1.66	2.92	65.61	43.22	31,013
Zhejiang 浙江	8	660	681,466	57,968	18.23	35.16	142.24	48.15	317,928
Anhui 安徽	12	511	132,385	2,456	2.17	7.39	68.66	70.64	113,136
Fujian 福建	6	96	49,280	777	3.48	8.42	70.59	58.73	22,345
Jiangxi 江西	4	182	19,151	979	1.28	4.07	21.29	68.61	76,661
Shandong 山东	22	318	54,333	-362	-0.71	-1.55	53.26	54.05	50,824
Central-South 中南	100	261	167,470	25,679	16.71	36.65	221.36	54.41	153,678
Henan 河南	17	231	36,102	676	1.54	5.00	41.69	69.11	43,777
Hubei 湖北	13	235	31,241	-15,867	-19.68		31.91	100.15	80,609
Hunan 湖南	8	330	36,898	213	0.28	0.57	33.40	51.23	77,007
Guangdong 广东	53	259	279,575	51,751	22.14	43.83	381.01	49.49	233,712
Guangxi 广西	7	332	86,498	2,650	3.53	8.74	88.81	59.64	75,132
Hainan 海南	2	236	4,486	-164	-0.70	-4.21	5.03	83.40	23,443
Southwest 西南	31	304	56,065	-1,378	-1.89	-5.15	38.61	63.31	72,931
Chongqing 重庆	10	202	40,343	123	0.35	1.37	36.15	74.43	35,228
Sichuan 四川	12	327	76,191	173	0.22	0.37	73.90	40.15	77,649
Guizhou 贵州	3	374	61,992	-442	-0.60	-1.24	29.97	51.88	73,992
Yunnan 云南	5	470	46,821	-8,931	-5.92	-60.10	-13.94	90.14	150,770
Tibet 西藏	1	12	220	-34	-3.45	-6.42	8.33	46.25	986
Northwest 西北	13	299	51,106	-74	-0.10	-0.31	42.28	68.11	75,710
Shaanxi 陕西	3	741	159,342	1,802	0.80	2.31	53.00	65.46	225,378
Gansu 甘肃	6	115	19,441	-445	-1.59	-4.86	54.73	67.26	27,940
Qinghai 青海									
Ningxia 宁夏	1	370	52,471	2		0.01	14.41	52.77	56,471
Xinjiang 新疆	3	203	5,747	-1,234	-4.41		5.94	101.49	27,995

2681: Soap, Washing Powder and Synthetic Detergent

肥皂及皂粉、合成洗涤剂制造业

Year 年份	Number of firms 企业个数	Rate of change 变化率 (%)	Number of employees 职工人数 (人)	Rate of change 变化率 (%)	Total revenue (Mil. RMB) 总销售收入 (百万元)	Rate of change 变化率 (%)	Total profit (Mil RMB) 总利润 (百万元)	Rate of change 变化率 (%)
2000	320		92,463		26,398		1,158	
2001	329	2.81	84,092	-9.05	30,961	17.29	1,406	21.42
2002	324	-1.52	78,953	-6.11	34,354	10.96	2,828	101.14

Major Products 主要产品	Output 产量	Unit 单位
Synthetic Detergent 合成洗涤剂	328	10,000 Tons 万吨
Synthetic Washing Powder 合成洗衣粉	207	10,000 Tons 万吨

10 Main Firms with Maximal Revenue (year founded) 收入最大的十家主要企业（创办年份）	City 城市	Province 省	Telephone/fax 电话/传真	Number of employees 职工人数	Ownership 产业所有权	Revenue ('000 RMB) 销售收入 (千元)	Profit('000 RMB) (rank) 利润(千元) (排名)	Total assets ('000 RMB) 总资产 (千元)	Major products 主要产品
Zhejiang Nice Chemical Industry Co.,Ltd.	Lishui	Zhejiang	(0578)2179954		Joint Stock				Washing Soap
浙江纳爱斯化工股份有限公司(1968)	丽水市	浙江省	(0578)2135514	3,483	股份制	5,211,439	459,653(3)	2,242,799	洗涤皂
Am Way (China) Co.,Ltd.	Guangzhou	Guangdong	(020)38911368		Foreign Funded				Detergent
安利（中国）日用品有限公司(1995)	广州市	广东省	(020)38912801	1,974	外商投资	4,809,096	1,653,895(1)	3,900,463	洗涤剂
Unilever Stock Co., Ltd.	Shanghai	Shanghai	(021)62370788		Foreign Funded				Synthetic Detergent合
联合利华股份有限公司(1999)	上海市	上海市	(021)62372188	934	外商投资	1,506,868	-	609,602	成洗涤剂
Shang Hai White Cat Co, Ltd.	Shanghai	Shanghai	(021)54098000		Overseas Chinese-funded				Synthetic Detergent合
上海白猫有限公司(1993)	上海市	上海市	(021)54096025	1,210	港澳台资	1,058,622	4,669(32)	606,088	成洗涤剂
Anhui Quanli Group	Anqing	Anhui	(0556)8925018		Joint Stock				Washing Powder
安徽全力集团(1992)	安庆市	安徽省	(0556)8933801	2,182	股份制	505,711	14,974(6)	560,932	洗衣粉
Shanghai Soap Co., Ltd.	Shanghai	Shanghai	(021)65431130		Overseas Chinese-funded				Soap
上海制皂有限公司(1995)	上海市	上海市	(021)65431254	1,224	港澳台资	353,398	665(106)	426,901	肥皂
Hunan Lichen Industrial Co., Ltd.	Changsha	Hunan	(0731)4223211		State Enterprises				Synthetic Detergent合
湖南丽臣实业有限责任公司(1946)	长沙市	湖南省	(0731)4223602	1,479	国有独资	275,532	3,032(44)	226,745	成洗涤剂
Jiangsu Ai Te Fu Aerosol Co., Ltd.	Huaian	Jiangsu	(0517)6405284		Overseas Chinese-funded				disinfect Liquid
江苏爱特福气雾剂有限公司(1972)	淮安市	江苏省	(0517)6407484	400	港澳台资	261,516	10,986(9)	85,201	消毒液
Shandong Li Bo Daily Chemistry Co., Ltd.	Weifang	Shandong	(0536)8667921		Joint Stock				Synthetic Detergent合
山东丽波日化股份有限公司(1969)	潍坊市	山东省	(0536)8666149	804	股份制	239,027	5,007(26)	274,963	成洗涤剂
Guangxi Softto Co., Ltd.	Wuzhou	Guangxi	(0774)3844469		Foreign Funded				fancy soap
广西索芙特股份有限公司(1992)	梧州市	广西	(0774)3859278	365	外商投资	228,912	13,064(7)	197,823	香皂

Top 10 Cities by Revenue 销售收入排名前10位城市	Province 省	Market share 市场份额 (%)	Number of firms 企业个数
Guangzhou 广州市	Guangdong 广东省	40.17	24
Lishui 丽水市	Zhejiang 浙江省	15.18	2
Shanghai 上海市	Shanghai 上海市	10.25	27
Anqing 安庆市	Anhui 安徽省	2.33	4
Hefei 合肥市	Anhui 安徽省	1.52	2
Huaian 淮安市	Jiangsu 江苏省	1.45	7
Yantai 烟台市	Shandong 山东省	1.40	2
Xi'an 西安市	Shannxi 陕西省	1.33	2
Shijiazhuang 石家庄市	Hebei 河北省	1.22	12
Chengdu 成都市	Sichuan 四川省	1.19	5

10 Major Wholesalers 十家主要批发商	City 城市	Province 省	Telephone/Fax 电话/传真
Kunming Department Store Group Co.,Ltd.	Kunming	Yunnan	(0871)3313618
昆明百货集团股份有限公司	昆明市	云南省	(0871)3314961
Jiangsu Skyrun International Group	Nanjing	Jiangsu	(025)4468888
江苏开元国际集团	南京市	江苏省	(025)4209409
Guangdong Light Industry Products Imp.& Exp.(Group) Corporation	Guangzhou	Guangdong	(020)83344557
广东省轻工业品进出口（集团）公司	广州市	广东省	(020)83330181
Shanghai Cheer (Group) Co.,Ltd.	Shanghai	Shanghai	(021)63069764
上海七百（集团）有限公司	上海市	上海市	(021)63069537
Fujian Tiancheng Group Co.,Ltd.	Fuzhou	Fujian	(0591)7503388
福建天成集团有限公司	福州市	福建省	(0591)7609279
Shanghai Century Lianhua Supermaket Development Co.,ltd.	Shanghai	Shanghai	(021)53544600
上海世纪联华超市发展有限公司	上海市	上海市	(021)62252610
Suzhou General Merchandise General Company	Suzhou	Jiangsu	(0512)65222247
苏州百货总公司	苏州市	江苏省	(0512)65222247
Zhejiang Light Industry Products Import & Export Corporation	Hangzhou	Zhejiang	(0571)88391888
浙江省轻工业品进出口公司	杭州市	浙江省	(0571)88391666
Zhejiang Winsun Import & Export Co.,Ltd.	Jiaxing	Zhejiang	(0573)2117091
浙江汇信进出口有限公司	嘉兴市	浙江省	(0573)2117020
Shenzhen CATIC Trade Company	Shenzhen	Guangdong	(0755)83790111
深圳中航商贸公司	深圳市	广东省	(0755)83790462

2682: Synthetic Fatty Acid 合成脂肪酸制造业

The industry accounts for 0.004% of the total revenue of China's industrial sector in 2002. The rate of return on assets is 3.95%. 86.36% of all firms in the industry made a profit while 13.64% had negative returns.The top province in terms of the industry's revenue is Henan, accounting for 25.26% of the total revenue.
2002年本行业收入占全行业的0.004%，资产利润率为3.95%。86.36%的企业赢利，13.64%的企业亏损。收入最高的省为河南省，占本行业的25.26%。

	Total number of firms 企业总数	Total number of employees 职工总数	Total revenue (Mil.RMB) 总销售收入（百万元）	Total profit (Mil.RMB) 总利润（百万元）	Return on assets 资产利润率 (%)	Return on equity 权益利润率 (%)	Labour productivity ('000 RMB/ worker) 劳动生产率（千元/人）	Debts/ assets 资产负债率 (%)	Total assets (Mil.RMB) 总资产（百万元）
Industry Overall 行业总体	22	2,743	436	18	3.95	12.05	49.79	67.26	468

	Number of firms 企业个数	Average number of employees 平均职工人数	Average revenue ('000 RMB) 平均销售收入（千元）	Average profit ('000 RMB) 平均利润（千元）	Return on assets 资产利润率 (%)	Return on equity 权益利润率 (%)	Labour productivity ('000 RMB/ worker) 劳动生产率（千元/人）	Debts/ assets 资产负债率 (%)	Average total assets ('000 RMB) 平均总资产（千元）
By ownership 产业所有权									
State-owned 国有	3	196	8,578	79	0.26	6.40	16.74	95.99	30,753
Collective-owned 集体	3	153	33,060	2,860	10.05	19.45	71.50	48.31	28,445
Foreign & Overseas Chinese Funded 三资	2	53	4,390	-390	-3.26	-9.95	10.47	67.28	11,980
By regional distribution 地区分布									
Central-North 华北	2	61	12,027	639	13.14	28.84	60.33	54.45	4,861
Beijing 北京									
Tianjin 天津									
Hebei 河北	1	60	12,969	620	14.45	23.05	62.33	37.30	4,290
Shanxi 山西	1	62	11,085	657	12.09	37.80	58.39	68.00	5,432
Inner Mongolia 内蒙古									
Northeast 东北	2	42	7,241	34	0.24	0.83	20.61	71.76	14,433
Liaoning 辽宁	1	40	1,700	-10	-0.07	-0.28	7.50	73.85	13,690
Jilin 吉林									
Heilongjiang 黑龙江	1	44	12,781	78	0.51	1.71	32.52	69.87	15,175
Central-East 华东	12	116	19,719	476	2.47	6.77	59.46	63.52	19,257
Shanghai 上海	1	22	13,904	300	3.23	4.61	72.68	29.85	9,284
Jiangsu 江苏	7	97	13,734	335	3.62	10.39	35.87	65.12	9,258
Zhejiang 浙江	1	128	17,221	72	0.93	2.44	23.53	61.84	7,725
Anhui 安徽									
Fujian 福建									
Jiangxi 江西									
Shandong 山东	3	188	36,456	996	2.00	5.72	95.52	65.00	49,756
Central-South 中南	5	201	23,533	1,654	4.81	19.53	41.24	75.39	34,402
Henan 河南	4	237	27,561	2,052	5.14	19.76	40.82	73.97	39,903
Hubei 湖北									
Hunan 湖南									
Guangdong 广东	1	57	7,420	61	0.49	7.64	48.28	93.56	12,396
Guangxi 广西									
Hainan 海南									
Southwest 西南									
Chongqing 重庆									
Sichuan 四川									
Guizhou 贵州									
Yunnan 云南									
Tibet 西藏									
Northwest 西北	1	136	43,627	3,126	12.06	22.52	22.21	46.43	25,918
Shaanxi 陕西	1	136	43,627	3,126	12.06	22.52	22.21	46.43	25,918
Gansu 甘肃									
Qinghai 青海									
Ningxia 宁夏									
Xinjiang 新疆									

2682: Synthetic Fatty Acid 合成脂肪酸制造业

Year 年份	Number of firms 企业个数	Rate of change 变化率 (%)	Number of employees 职工人数 (人)	Rate of change 变化率 (%)	Total revenue (Mil. RMB) 总销售收入 (百万元)	Rate of change 变化率 (%)	Total profit (Mil RMB) 总利润 (百万元)	Rate of change 变化率 (%)
2000	22		2,345		324		17	
2001	22	o	2,620	11.73	407	25.62	15	-11.76
2002	22	o	2,743	4.69	436	7.13	18	20.00

Major Products 主要产品	Output 产量	Unit 单位

10 Main Firms with Maximal Revenue (year founded) 收入最大的十家主要企业（创办年份）	City 城市	Province 省	Telephone/fax 电话/传真	Number of employees 职工人数	Ownership 产业所有权	Revenue ('000 RMB) 销售收入 (千元)	Profit('000 RMB) (rank) 利润(千元)(排名)	Total assets ('000 RMB) 总资产 (千元)	Major products 主要产品
Shenxian Siqiang Chemical Industry Co., Ltd.	Liaocheng	Shandong	(0635)7889919		Joint Stock				Sebacic Acid
莘县四强化工有限公司(2000)	聊城市	山东省	(0635)7889919	260	股份制	56,925	1,996(3)	62,625	癸二酸
Weinan Grease Chemical Industry Co., Ltd.	Weinan	Shannxi	(0913)2117173		Joint Stock				Fatty Acid
渭南市油脂化工有限公司(1995)	渭南市	陕西省	(0913)2113888	136	股份制	43,627	3,126(2)	25,918	脂肪酸
Shenxian Zhongke Grease Chemical Industry Co., Ltd.	Liaocheng	Shandong	(0635)7361513		Limited-Liability				Stearic Acid
莘县中科油脂化工有限公司(2001)	聊城市	山东省	(0635)7361288	243	有限公司	42,838	614(8)	81,333	硬脂酸
Lianyungang Wanda Chemical Industry Company	Lianyungang	Jiangsu	(0518)5370054		Joint Stock				Synthetic Fat & Oil
连云港市万达化工公司(1987)	连云港市	江苏省	(0518)5370108	23	股份制	30,540	1,612(4)	6,659	合脂油
Quzhou Hengshun Chemical Industry Co., Ltd.	Quzhou	Zhejiang	(0570)2931242		Private Enterprises				Low Carbon fatty Acid低
衢州恒顺化工有限公司(1997)	衢州市	浙江省	(0570)2933242	128	私营独资	17,221	72(17)	7,725	碳脂肪酸
Shengxian No.2 Grease Chemical Industry Factory	Hengshui	Hebei	(0318)3620018		Collective-owned				Fatty Acid
深州市第二油脂化工厂(1993)	衡水市	河北省	(0318)2020878	60	集体企业	12,969	620(7)	4,290	脂肪酸
Daqing Oilfield Ludi Chemical Industry Co., Ltd.	Daqing	Heilongjiang	(0459)5797682		Limited-Liability				Antifreeze
大庆油田路迪化工有限公司(1999)	大庆市	黑龙江省	(0459)5691294	44	有限公司	12,781	78(16)	15,175	防冻液
Changzhi Shuangle Grease Chemical Industry Co., Ltd.	Changzhi	Shanxi	(0355)5058623		Limited-Liability				Fatty Alcohol
长治市双乐油脂化工有限公司(2001)	长治市	山西省	(0355)5058623	62	有限公司	11,085	657(6)	5,432	脂肪醇
Wuxian Shi Lianhai Grease Chemical Industry Factory	Suzhou	Jiangsu	(0512)66911072		Private Enterprises				Lipidic Acid
吴县市连海油脂化工厂(1995)	苏州市	江苏省	(0512)66911231	45	私营独资	10,130	688(5)	6,690	油脂酸
Huixian Grease Chemical Industry Factory	Xinxiang	Henan	(0373)6283773		Collective-owned				Stearic Acid
辉县市油脂化工厂(1974)	新乡市	河南省	(0373)6283773	80	集体企业	9,810	110(14)	5,484	硬脂酸

Top 10 Cities by Revenue 销售收入排名前10位城市	Province 省	Market share 市场份额 (%)	Number of firms 企业个数
Liaocheng 聊城市	Shandong 山东省	22.86	2
Shangqiu 商丘市	Henan 河南省	22.33	2
Weinan 渭南市	Shannxi 陕西省	10.00	1
Lianyungang 连云港市	Jiangsu 江苏省	7.00	1
Suqian 宿迁市	Jiangsu 江苏省	6.85	1
Suzhou 苏州市	Jiangsu 江苏省	6.43	3
Quzhou 衢州市	Zhejiang 浙江省	3.95	1
Shanghai 上海市	Shanghai 上海市	3.19	1
Hengshui 衡水市	Hebei 河北省	2.97	1
Daqing 大庆市	Heilongjiang 黑龙江省	2.93	1

10 Major Wholesalers 十家主要批发商	City 城市	Province 省	Telephone/Fax 电话/传真
Kunming Department Store Group Co.,Ltd.	Kunming	Yunnan	(0871)3313618
昆明百货集团股份有限公司	昆明市	云南省	(0871)3314961
Jiangsu Skyrun International Group	Nanjing	Jiangsu	(025)4468888
江苏开元国际集团	南京市	江苏省	(025)4209409
Guangdong Light Industry Products Imp.& Exp.(Group) Corporation	Guangzhou	Guangdong	(020)83344557
广东省轻工业品进出口（集团）公司	广州市	广东省	(020)83330181
Shanghai Cheer (Group) Co.,Ltd.	Shanghai	Shanghai	(021)63069764
上海七百（集团）有限公司	上海市	上海市	(021)63069537
Fujian Tiancheng Group Co.,Ltd.	Fuzhou	Fujian	(0591)7503388
福建天成集团有限公司	福州市	福建省	(0591)7609279
Shanghai Century Lianhua Supermaket Development Co.,ltd.	Shanghai	Shanghai	(021)53544600
上海世纪联华超市发展有限公司	上海市	上海市	(021)62252610
Suzhou General Merchandise General Company	Suzhou	Jiangsu	(0512)65222247
苏州百货总公司	苏州市	江苏省	(0512)65222247
Zhejiang Light Industry Products Import & Export Corporation	Hangzhou	Zhejiang	(0571)88391888
浙江省轻工业品进出口公司	杭州市	浙江省	(0571)88391666
Zhejiang Winsun Import & Export Co., Ltd.	Jiaxing	Zhejiang	(0573)2117091
浙江汇信进出口有限公司	嘉兴市	浙江省	(0573)2117020
Shenzhen CATIC Trade Company	Shenzhen	Guangdong	(0755)83790111
深圳中航商贸公司	深圳市	广东省	(0755)83790462

2683: Stearic Acid and Stearin Oil 硬脂酸、硬化油制造业

The industry accounts for 0.012% of the total revenue of China's industrial sector in 2002. The rate of return on assets is 3.86%. 77.27% of all firms in the industry made a profit while 22.73% had negative returns.The top province in terms of the industry's revenue is Jiangsu, accounting for 41.68% of the total revenue.
2002年本行业收入占全行业的 0.012%，资产利润率为 3.86%。77.27%的企业赢利，22.73%的企业亏损。收入最高的省为江苏省，占本行业的41.68%。

	Total number of firms 企业总数	Total number of employees 职工总数	Total revenue (Mil.RMB) 总销售收入（百万元）	Total profit (Mil.RMB) 总利润（百万元）	Return on assets 资产利润率 (%)	Return on equity 权益利润率 (%)	Labour productivity ('000 RMB/ worker) 劳动生产率（千元/人）	Debts/ assets 资产负债率 (%)	Total assets (Mil.RMB) 总资产（百万元）
Industry Overall 行业总体	44	4,807	1,244	33	3.86	11.93	58.57	67.67	859

	Number of firms 企业个数	Average number of employees 平均职工人数	Average revenue ('000 RMB) 平均销售收入（千元）	Average profit ('000 RMB) 平均利润（千元）	Return on assets 资产利润率 (%)	Return on equity 权益利润率 (%)	Labour productivity ('000 RMB/ worker) 劳动生产率（千元/人）	Debts/ assets 资产负债率 (%)	Average total assets ('000 RMB) 平均总资产（千元）
By ownership 产业所有权									
State-owned 国有	2	60	8,602	-12	-0.39	-1.73	9.94	77.24	2,924
Collective-owned 集体	6	34	8,869	441	11.57	30.27	65.35	61.79	3,816
Foreign & Overseas Chinese Funded 三资	4	40	20,275	-563	-2.03	-4.50	68.18	54.97	27,762
By regional distribution 地区分布									
Central-North 华北	3	65	8,095	272	4.22	16.27	22.10	74.05	6,450
Beijing 北京									
Tianjin 天津									
Hebei 河北	1	31	6,868	56	1.41		13.35	122.89	3,972
Shanxi 山西	2	82	8,709	381	4.95	12.83	23.76	61.43	7,689
Inner Mongolia 内蒙古									
Northeast 东北	1	229	8,818	-31	-0.52	-1.59	-3.93	67.23	5,953
Liaoning 辽宁	1	229	8,818	-31	-0.52	-1.59	-3.93	67.23	5,953
Jilin 吉林									
Heilongjiang 黑龙江									
Central-East 华东	31	118	33,939	814	3.32	10.49	64.83	68.39	24,527
Shanghai 上海	2	108	35,795	813	3.44	10.73	46.94	67.95	23,622
Jiangsu 江苏	12	131	43,202	339	1.31	3.30	79.10	60.25	25,874
Zhejiang 浙江	7	168	45,868	2,087	5.30	27.84	43.96	80.96	39,367
Anhui 安徽	3	67	6,205	-33	-0.61	-6.00	25.26	89.90	5,501
Fujian 福建	2	44	12,821	-1,492	-4.62	-7.64	74.00	39.49	32,269
Jiangxi 江西	1	30	4,075	40	3.62	20.00	64.10	81.90	1,105
Shandong 山东	4	93	23,174	1,990	17.74	95.05	99.93	81.34	11,220
Central-South 中南	6	46	11,172	427	6.03	17.69	67.92	65.95	7,089
Henan 河南	1	22	3,150	44	4.07	5.49	40.77	25.88	1,082
Hubei 湖北	1	68	6,837	22	0.24	0.77	107.10	68.47	9,046
Hunan 湖南	2	60	8,602	-12	-0.39	-1.73	9.94	77.24	2,924
Guangdong 广东	2	34	19,920	1,260	9.49	26.53	139.85	64.23	13,280
Guangxi 广西									
Hainan 海南									
Southwest 西南	2	190	32,552	1,289	12.92	22.74	36.54	43.17	9,974
Chongqing 重庆	2	190	32,552	1,289	12.92	22.74	36.54	43.17	9,974
Sichuan 四川									
Guizhou 贵州									
Yunnan 云南									
Tibet 西藏									
Northwest 西北	1	70	26,366	1,974	18.06	43.03	118.96	58.04	10,931
Shaanxi 陕西									
Gansu 甘肃	1	70	26,366	1,974	18.06	43.03	118.96	58.04	10,931
Qinghai 青海									
Ningxia 宁夏									
Xinjiang 新疆									

Year 年份	Number of firms 企业个数	Rate of change 变化率 (%)	Number of employees 职工人数 (人)	Rate of change 变化率 (%)	Total revenue (Mil. RMB) 总销售收入 (百万元)	Rate of change 变化率 (%)	Total profit (Mil RMB) 总利润 (百万元)	Rate of change 变化率 (%)
2000	52		5,321		1,036		31	
2001	47	-9.62	8,425	58.33	1,194	15.25	47	51.61
2002	44	-6.38	4,807	-42.94	1,244	4.19	33	-29.79

Major Products 主要产品	Output 产量	Unit 单位
Lubricating Oil 润滑油	363	10,000 Tons 万吨

10 Main Firms with Maximal Revenue (year founded) 收入最大的十家主要企业（创办年份）	City 城市	Province 省	Telephone/fax 电话/传真	Number of employees 职工人数	Ownership 产业所有权	Revenue ('000 RMB) 销售收入 (千元)	Profit('000 RMB) (rank) 利润(千元) (排名)	Total assets ('000 RMB) 总资产 (千元)	Major products 主要产品
Jiangsu Zhongding Chemistry Co., Ltd. 江苏中鼎化学有限公司(1976)	Suzhou 苏州市	Jiangsu 江苏省	(0512)58450193 (0512)58451273	406	Joint Stock 股份制	135,120	3,474(5)	68,249	Stearic Acid 硬脂酸
Zhangjiagang Jinguan Chemical Industry Co., Ltd. 张家港金冠化工有限公司(1993)	Suzhou 苏州市	Jiangsu 江苏省	(0512)58450202 (0512)58450340	206	Joint Stock 股份制	112,168	-	110,937	Polyurethane Resin聚氨脂树脂
Hangzhou Grease Chemical Industry Co., Ltd. 杭州油脂化工有限公司(2001)	Hangzhou 杭州市	Zhejiang 浙江省	(0571)86617528 (0571)86617540	361	Limited-Liability 有限公司	109,674	6,516(1)	100,755	Stearic Acid Hardening Oil硬脂酸硬化油
Shanghai Huayuan Zhejiang Fenghuang Chemical Industry Branch 上海华源浙江凤凰化工分公司(2001)	Jinhua 金华市	Zhejiang 浙江省	(0579)8230910 (0579)8230909	514	Joint Stock 股份制	102,790	253(22)	110,651	Stearic Acid 硬脂酸
Jiangsu Kunbao Group Co.,Ltd. 江苏昆宝集团有限责任公司(1970)	Suzhou 苏州市	Jiangsu 江苏省	(0512)57891304 (0512)57891312	310	Private Owned 私营企业	94,636	3,589(4)	50,988	Stearic Acid 硬脂酸
Chongqing Changjiang Yangfan Chemical Industry Co., Ltd. 重庆长江扬帆化工有限公司(2001)	Chongqing 重庆市	Chongqing 重庆市	(023)62836615 (023)62802395	351	Limited-Liability 有限公司	56,634	2,291(9)	17,059	Stearic Acid 硬酯酸
Zhejiang Henghua Grease Chemical Industry Co., Ltd. 浙江恒华油脂化工有限公司(1995)	Huzhou 湖州市	Zhejiang 浙江省	(0572)3770256 (0572)3771889	119	Private Owned 私营企业	50,050	2,864(6)	21,669	Polyamide Resin聚酰胺树脂
Shanghai Coking General Factory Yan'an Grease Chemical Plant Jiading Branch上海焦化总厂延安油脂化工厂嘉定分厂(1993)	Shanghai 上海市	Shanghai 上海市	(021)59950446 (021)59950759	180	Joint Owned 联营企业	37,412	813(12)	19,062	Stearic Acid 硬脂酸
Haiyan Chengcheng Daily Chemistry Science & Technology Co., Ltd海盐成成日化科技有限公司(1998)	Jiaxing 嘉兴市	Zhejiang 浙江省	(0573)6123081 (0573)6122773	52	Limited-Liability 有限公司	36,662	3,634(3)	27,354	Stearic Acid 硬脂酸
Liyang Jinyang Chemical Plant 溧阳市金阳化工厂(1998)	Changzhou 常州市	Jiangsu 江苏省	(0519)7670481 (0519)7670298	62	Private Enterprises 私营独资	28,470	30(32)	3,580	Stearic Acid 硬脂酸

Top 10 Cities by Revenue 销售收入排名前10位城市	Province 省	Market share 市场份额 (%)	Number of firms 企业个数
Suzhou 苏州市	Jiangsu 江苏省	29.14	6
Hangzhou 杭州市	Zhejiang 浙江省	8.82	1
Jinhua 金华市	Zhejiang 浙江省	8.26	1
Zibo 淄博市	Shandong 山东省	5.86	2
Nantong 南通市	Jiangsu 江苏省	5.80	2
Shanghai 上海市	Shanghai 上海市	5.76	2
Chongqing 重庆市	Chongqing 重庆市	5.23	2
Jiaxing 嘉兴市	Zhejiang 浙江省	4.16	3
Huzhou 湖州市	Zhejiang 浙江省	4.02	1
Changzhou 常州市	Jiangsu 江苏省	3.27	2

10 Major Wholesalers 十家主要批发商	City 城市	Province 省	Telephone/Fax 电话/传真
Kunming Department Store Group Co.,Ltd. 昆明百货集团股份有限公司	Kunming 昆明市	Yunnan 云南省	(0871)3313618 (0871)3314961
Jiangsu Skyrun International Group 江苏开元国际集团	Nanjing 南京市	Jiangsu 江苏省	(025)4468888 (025)4209409
Guangdong Light Industry Products Imp.& Exp.(Group) Corporation 广东省轻工业品进出口（集团）公司	Guangzhou 广州市	Guangdong 广东省	(020)83344557 (020)83330181
Shanghai Cheer (Group) Co.,Ltd. 上海七百（集团）有限公司	Shanghai 上海市	Shanghai 上海市	(021)63069764 (021)63069537
Fujian Tiancheng Group Co.,Ltd. 福建天成集团有限公司	Fuzhou 福州市	Fujian 福建省	(0591)7503388 (0591)7609279
Shanghai Century Lianhua Supermaket Development Co.,ltd. 上海世纪联华超市发展有限公司	Shanghai 上海市	Shanghai 上海市	(021)53544600 (021)62252610
Suzhou General Merchandise General Company 苏州百货总公司	Suzhou 苏州市	Jiangsu 江苏省	(0512)65222247 (0512)65222247
Zhejiang Light Industry Products Import & Export Corporation 浙江省轻工业品进出口公司	Hangzhou 杭州市	Zhejiang 浙江省	(0571)88391888 (0571)88391666
Zhejiang Winsun Import & Export Co., Ltd. 浙江汇信进出口有限公司	Jiaxing 嘉兴市	Zhejiang 浙江省	(0573)2117091 (0573)2117020
Shenzhen CATIC Trade Company 深圳中航商贸公司	Shenzhen 深圳市	Guangdong 广东省	(0755)83790111 (0755)83790462

2684: Perfumes and Essences 香料、香精制造业

The industry accounts for 0.078% of the total revenue of China's industrial sector in 2002. The rate of return on assets is 9.99%. 81.98% of all firms in the industry made a profit while 18.02% had negative returns.The top province in terms of the industry's revenue is Shanghai, accounting for 26.82% of the total revenue.
2002•••••••••• 0.078%•••••• 9.99%•81.98%•••••18.02%•••••••••••••••••••••26.82%•

	Total number of firms 企业总数	Total number of employees 职工总数	Total revenue (Mil.RMB) 总销售收入 (百万元)	Total profit (Mil.RMB) 总利润 (百万元)	Return on assets 资产利润率 (%)	Return on equity 权益利润率 (%)	Labour productivity ('000 RMB/ worker) 劳动生产率 (千元/人)	Debts/ assets 资产负债率 (%)	Total assets (Mil.RMB) 总资产 (百万元)
Industry Overall 行业总体	222	19,060	8,347	765	9.99	21.59	131.73	53.72	7,657

	Number of firms 企业个数	Average number of employees 平均职工人数	Average revenue ('000 RMB) 平均销售收入 (千元)	Average profit ('000 RMB) 平均利润 (千元)	Return on assets 资产利润率 (%)	Return on equity 权益利润率 (%)	Labour productivity ('000 RMB/ worker) 劳动生产率 (千元/人)	Debts/ assets 资产负债率 (%)	Average total assets ('000 RMB) 平均总资产 (千元)
By ownership 产业所有权									
State-owned 国有	20	79	7,890	-357	-2.35	-22.01	17.35	89.32	15,201
Collective-owned 集体	37	90	31,687	3,024	15.69	33.84	105.20	53.64	19,270
Foreign & Overseas Chinese Funded 三资	47	104	80,188	8,569	10.94	23.27	238.75	53.00	78,329
By regional distribution 地区分布									
Central-North 华北	15	106	19,400	820	4.52	12.44	53.82	63.65	18,135
Beijing 北京	1	245	131,025	5,207	5.04	9.05	157.55	44.34	103,352
Tianjin 天津	11	110	8,611	374	2.82	16.60	23.35	83.00	13,260
Hebei 河北	2	28	21,364	1,456	36.30	45.35	232.45	19.95	4,011
Shanxi 山西	1	79	22,530	66	0.45	0.65	73.35	31.41	14,793
Inner Mongolia 内蒙古									
Northeast 东北	4	105	8,575	315	1.62	73.77	37.42	97.81	19,501
Liaoning 辽宁	1	261	11,147	-291	-0.54	-3.13	18.30	82.68	53,724
Jilin 吉林	1	38	2,763	34	0.97		23.42	100.00	3,512
Heilongjiang 黑龙江	2	61	10,195	759	7.30		82.66	136.58	10,384
Central-East 华东	94	107	46,412	5,230	11.26	25.44	135.82	55.73	46,449
Shanghai 上海	27	115	82,904	14,491	16.18	35.52	261.93	54.44	89,553
Jiangsu 江苏	24	91	26,684	77	0.32	1.30	62.51	75.56	24,185
Zhejiang 浙江	15	213	71,066	5,690	8.21	16.02	93.73	48.78	69,349
Anhui 安徽	7	43	11,563	-438	-2.93	-6.71	73.51	56.38	14,972
Fujian 福建	5	103	10,492	47	0.35	0.98	13.84	63.93	13,314
Jiangxi 江西	8	31	18,709	649	6.82	14.71	203.03	53.66	9,526
Shandong 山东	8	63	16,853	1,353	13.52	21.00	72.76	35.61	10,005
Central-South 中南	80	66	36,691	3,020	12.20	23.58	177.97	48.25	24,743
Henan 河南	18	71	28,088	2,151	15.27	32.57	118.40	53.12	14,086
Hubei 湖北	3	45	13,512	238	4.02	19.03	92.25	78.86	5,915
Hunan 湖南	7	44	8,617	23	0.20	0.43	31.89	54.10	11,609
Guangdong 广东	41	77	51,233	3,641	10.14	19.23	214.12	47.27	35,898
Guangxi 广西	7	46	9,358	-2	-0.02	-0.05	22.56	61.55	11,084
Hainan 海南	4	20	40,694	13,182	68.03	90.03	1,024.94	24.44	19,376
Southwest 西南	27	62	26,758	671	1.89	3.74	61.38	49.46	35,461
Chongqing 重庆	3	95	13,957	-2,373	-3.47	-6.14	45.60	43.43	68,346
Sichuan 四川	4	83	14,943	-349	-2.95	-74.56	33.15	96.04	11,810
Guizhou 贵州	7	43	6,237	-134	-0.97	-2.46	42.13	60.68	13,854
Yunnan 云南	13	59	44,397	2,120	4.53	8.40	86.71	46.08	46,783
Tibet 西藏									
Northwest 西北	2	13	508	15	0.81	1.84	18.54	56.11	1,861
Shaanxi 陕西									
Gansu 甘肃	1	21	1,015	30	3.03	4.27	22.95	29.06	991
Qinghai 青海									
Ningxia 宁夏									
Xinjiang 新疆	1	5						65.93	2,730

2684: Perfumes and Essences 香料、香精制造业

Year 年份	Number of firms 企业个数	Rate of change 变化率 (%)	Number of employees 职工人数 (人)	Rate of change 变化率 (%)	Total revenue (Mil. RMB) 总销售收入 (百万元)	Rate of change 变化率 (%)	Total profit (Mil RMB) 总利润 (百万元)	Rate of change 变化率 (%)
2000	186		17,071		5,824		380	
2001	210	12.90	19,386	13.56	7,207	23.75	600	57.89
2002	222	5.71	19,060	-1.68	8,347	15.82	765	27.50

Major Products 主要产品	Output 产量	Unit 单位
Essences 香精	5	10,000 Tons 万吨

10 Main Firms with Maximal Revenue (year founded) 收入最大的十家主要企业（创办年份）	City 城市	Province 省	Telephone/fax 电话/传真	Number of employees 职工人数	Ownership 产业所有权	Revenue ('000 RMB) 销售收入 (千元)	Profit('000 RMB) (rank) 利润(千元) (排名)	Total assets ('000 RMB) 总资产 (千元)	Major products 主要产品
International Flavors & Fragrances (China) Co., Ltd.	Guangzhou	Guangdong	(020)82219838		Foreign Funded				Essences
国际香料（广州）有限公司(1990)	广州市	广东省	(020)82219828	200	外商投资	675,946	65,730(3)	334,544	香精
Zhejiang Jiaxing Zhonghua Chemical Industry Group Co., Ltd.	Jiaxing	Zhejiang	(0573)3016781		Collective-owned				
浙江嘉兴中华化工集团有限责任公司(1995)	嘉兴市	浙江省	(0573)2088200	1,515	集体企业	525,550	36,190(9)	367,410	
Huabao Food Flavour & Fragrance(Shanghai) Co., Ltd.	Shanghai	Shanghai	(021)59166888		Overseas Chinese-funded				Flavors & Fragrances
华宝食用香精香料(上海)有限公司(1996)	上海市	上海市	(021)59161999	90	港澳台资	469,918	80,752(2)	495,110	香精香料
Shanghai Givaudan Co., Ltd.	Shanghai	Shanghai	(021)50801288		Foreign Funded				Flavors & Fragrances
上海奇华顿有限公司(1995)	上海市	上海市	(021)50801100	162	外商投资	383,537	89,257(1)	327,301	香精香料
Kunming Firmenich Aromatics Co.,Ltd.	Kunming	Yunnan	(0871)3808123		Foreign Funded				Nature Spicery
昆明芬美意香料有限公司(1959)	昆明市	云南省	(0871)3812076	209	外商投资	160,036	16,334(12)	198,846	天然香料
International Flavors & Fragrances (Hangzhou) Co.,Ltd.	Hangzhou	Zhejiang	(0571)64797342		Foreign Funded				Cedarwood
国际香料香精（杭州）有限公司(1994)	杭州市	浙江省	(0571)64743092	186	外商投资	159,398	33,662(10)	277,551	柏木油
Yunnan Tianhong Flavors & Fragrances Co., Ltd.	Yuxi	Yunnan	(0877)2073535		Foreign Funded				Essences
云南天宏香精香料有限公司(2000)	玉溪市	云南省	(0877)2073358	90	外商投资	151,196	7,653(19)	147,317	香精
Shanghai Wanxiang Daily Chemistry Co., Ltd.	Shanghai	Shanghai	(021)38110452		Limited-Liability				Corn Mint Product
上海万香日化有限公司(1995)	上海市	上海市	(021)58116511	110	有限公司	147,557	1,357(64)	70,114	薄荷产品
Beijing Peking University Zoteq Co., Ltd.	Beijing	Beijing	(010)62753973		Limited-Liability				Chemical Industry Products
北京北大正元科技有限公司(2000)	北京市	北京市	(010)62758924	245	有限公司	131,025	5,207(28)	103,352	化工产品
Shanghai Apple Flavor & Fragrance Co., Ltd.	Shanghai	Shanghai	(021)56868966		Private Owned				Spicery
上海爱普香料有限公司(1995)	上海市	上海市	(021)56869075	293	私营企业	129,116	52,139(4)	177,150	香料

Top 10 Cities by Revenue 销售收入排名前10位城市	Province 省	Market share 市场份额 (%)	Number of firms 企业个数
Shanghai 上海市	Shanghai 上海市	26.82	27
Guangzhou 广州市	Guangdong 广东省	12.54	11
Jiaxing 嘉兴市	Zhejiang 浙江省	8.29	4
Maoming 茂名市	Guangdong 广东省	6.81	14
Kunming 昆明市	Yunnan 云南省	4.64	9
Suzhou 苏州市	Jiangsu 江苏省	4.34	11
Hangzhou 杭州市	Zhejiang 浙江省	4.27	8
Zhengzhou 郑州市	Henan 河南省	2.98	7
Kaifeng 开封市	Henan 河南省	2.35	7
Yuxi 玉溪市	Yunnan 云南省	2.20	3

10 Major Wholesalers 十家主要批发商	City 城市	Province 省	Telephone/Fax 电话/传真
Kunming Department Store Group Co.,Ltd.	Kunming	Yunnan	(0871)3313618
昆明百货集团股份有限公司	昆明市	云南省	(0871)3314961
Jiangsu Skyrun International Group	Nanjing	Jiangsu	(025)4468888
江苏开元国际集团	南京市	江苏省	(025)4209409
Guangdong Light Industry Products Imp.& Exp.(Group) Corporation	Guangzhou	Guangdong	(020)83344557
广东省轻工业品进出口（集团）公司	广州市	广东省	(020)83330181
Shanghai Cheer (Group) Co.,Ltd.	Shanghai	Shanghai	(021)63069764
上海七百（集团）有限公司	上海市	上海市	(021)63069537
Fujian Tiancheng Group Co.,Ltd.	Fuzhou	Fujian	(0591)7503388
福建天成集团有限公司	福州市	福建省	(0591)7609279
Shanghai Century Lianhua Supermaket Development Co.,ltd.	Shanghai	Shanghai	(021)53544600
上海世纪联华超市发展有限公司	上海市	上海市	(021)62252610
Suzhou General Merchandise General Company	Suzhou	Jiangsu	(0512)65222247
苏州百货总公司	苏州市	江苏省	(0512)65222247
Zhejiang Light Industry Products Import & Export Corporation	Hangzhou	Zhejiang	(0571)88391888
浙江省轻工业品进出口公司	杭州市	浙江省	(0571)88391666
Zhejiang Winsun Import & Export Co., Ltd.	Jiaxing	Zhejiang	(0573)2117091
浙江汇信进出口有限公司	嘉兴市	浙江省	(0573)2117020
Shenzhen CATIC Trade Company	Shenzhen	Guangdong	(0755)83790111
深圳中航商贸公司	深圳市	广东省	(0755)83790462

2685: Cosmetics 化妆品制造业

The industry accounts for 0.195% of the total revenue of China's industrial sector in 2002. The rate of return on assets is 6.68%. 75.49% of all firms in the industry made a profit while 24.51% had negative returns.The top province in terms of the industry's revenue is Guangdong, accounting for 23.86% of the total revenue.
2002年本行业收入占全行业的 0.195%，资产利润率为 6.68%。75.49%的企业赢利，24.51%的企业亏损。收入最高的省为广东省，占本行业的23.86%。

	Total number of firms 企业总数	Total number of employees 职工总数	Total revenue (Mil.RMB) 总销售收入（百万元）	Total profit (Mil.RMB) 总利润（百万元）	Return on assets 资产利润率 (%)	Return on equity 权益利润率 (%)	Labour productivity ('000 RMB/ worker) 劳动生产率（千元/人）	Debts/ assets 资产负债率 (%)	Total assets (Mil.RMB) 总资产（百万元）
Industry Overall 行业总体	257	51,489	20,936	1,415	6.68	13.25	132.20	49.58	21,172

	Number of firms 企业个数	Average number of employees 平均职工人数	Average revenue ('000 RMB) 平均销售收入（千元）	Average profit ('000 RMB) 平均利润（千元）	Return on assets 资产利润率 (%)	Return on equity 权益利润率 (%)	Labour productivity ('000 RMB/ worker) 劳动生产率（千元/人）	Debts/ assets 资产负债率 (%)	Average total assets ('000 RMB) 平均总资产（千元）
By ownership 产业所有权									
State-owned 国有	22	65	12,640	2,084	2.72	4.06	489.04	32.92	76,519
Collective-owned 集体	32	174	59,614	3,406	7.15	21.59	89.13	66.88	47,639
Foreign & Overseas Chinese Funded 三资	94	265	140,052	8,481	6.61	13.43	152.44	50.76	128,297
By regional distribution 地区分布									
Central-North 华北	32	221	72,645	14,482	9.74	15.35	250.45	36.54	148,645
Beijing 北京	17	280	100,479	22,114	11.99	17.95	330.52	33.18	184,433
Tianjin 天津	12	157	42,153	6,620	5.28	9.17	92.31	42.42	125,308
Hebei 河北	1	120	100,133	6,600	23.22	36.03	109.28	35.56	28,428
Shanxi 山西									
Inner Mongolia 内蒙古	2	154	5,265	724	1.62	3.68	32.18	55.91	44,576
Northeast 东北	4	121	22,066	1,050	2.60	6.24	50.77	58.28	40,339
Liaoning 辽宁	4	121	22,066	1,050	2.60	6.24	50.77	58.28	40,339
Jilin 吉林									
Heilongjiang 黑龙江									
Central-East 华东	121	215	86,295	3,570	4.12	8.43	91.01	51.07	86,572
Shanghai 上海	39	249	124,885	-1,061	-0.76	-1.52	93.03	49.88	139,752
Jiangsu 江苏	40	242	78,966	4,950	6.44	14.52	89.26	55.69	76,924
Zhejiang 浙江	26	174	81,893	9,644	16.06	32.33	111.11	50.34	60,059
Anhui 安徽	1								
Fujian 福建	9	176	20,070	685	2.81	3.80	34.74	26.05	24,397
Jiangxi 江西	3	80	7,336	185	0.85	1.30	33.20	34.35	21,698
Shandong 山东	3	97	26,912	5,969	17.60	35.74	123.50	50.77	33,916
Central-South 中南	92	173	83,232	5,652	10.33	25.24	150.11	59.07	54,707
Henan 河南	4	39	9,740	846	27.84	39.35	69.02	29.26	3,039
Hubei 湖北	6	779	398,692	12,296	5.49	23.18	169.58	76.34	224,171
Hunan 湖南	1	47	9,126	-129	-1.65	-7.05	39.47	76.63	7,829
Guangdong 广东	73	141	68,421	5,393	11.32	24.46	146.47	53.73	47,642
Guangxi 广西	3	111	19,406	1,178	6.78	9.54	46.07	28.86	17,359
Hainan 海南	5	94	32,840	9,144	33.09	53.50	147.35	38.15	27,631
Southwest 西南	7	276	60,322	-713	-0.67	-1.24	127.44	46.01	106,370
Chongqing 重庆	3	474	93,577	-7,179	-4.16	-8.48	45.71	50.98	172,625
Sichuan 四川	3	164	46,790	5,516	7.38	11.22	366.75	34.24	74,761
Guizhou 贵州									
Yunnan 云南	1	15	1,152				10.87	72.42	2,429
Tibet 西藏									
Northwest 西北	1	26	1,860	199	26.89	36.85	32.54	27.03	740
Shaanxi 陕西									
Gansu 甘肃	1	26	1,860	199	26.89	36.85	32.54	27.03	740
Qinghai 青海									
Ningxia 宁夏									
Xinjiang 新疆									

Year 年份	Number of firms 企业个数	Rate of change 变化率（%）	Number of employees 职工人数（人）	Rate of change 变化率（%）	Total revenue (Mil. RMB) 总销售收入（百万元）	Rate of change 变化率（%）	Total profit (Mil RMB) 总利润（百万元）	Rate of change 变化率（%）
2000	238		44,274		13,793		810	
2001	221	-7.14	43,094	-2.67	17,233	24.94	1,172	44.69
2002	257	16.29	51,489	19.48	20,936	21.49	1,415	20.73

Major Products 主要产品	Output 产量	Unit 单位
Synthetic Detergent 合成洗涤剂	328	10,000 Tons 万吨
Cosmetics 化妆品	185	100,000,000 Yuan 亿元

10 Main Firms with Maximal Revenue (year founded) 收入最大的十家主要企业（创办年份）	City 城市	Province 省	Telephone/fax 电话/传真	Number of employees 职工人数	Ownership 产业所有权	Revenue ('000 RMB) 销售收入（千元）	Profit('000 RMB) (rank) 利润(千元)(排名)	Total assets ('000 RMB) 总资产（千元）	Major products 主要产品
Hubei C-Bons Co., Ltd.	Xiantao	Hubei	(0728)3269666		Overseas Chinese-funded				Cosmetics
湖北丝宝股份有限公司(1990)	仙桃市	湖北省	(0728)3270128	2,850	港澳台资	1,439,935	44,286(11)	399,835	化妆品
Shanghai Jahwa United Co., Ltd.	Shanghai	Shanghai	(021)65456400		Foreign Funded				Cosmetics
上海家化联合股份有限公司(1995)	上海市	上海市	(021)65458990	1,154	外商投资	1,331,970	84,552(8)	1,645,351	化妆品
Johnson & Johnson(China) Co.,Ltd.	Shanghai	Shanghai	(021)64302010		Foreign Funded				Cosmetics
强生(中国)有限公司(1992)	上海市	上海市	(021)64304220	642	外商投资	1,209,223	97,932(6)	486,701	化妆品
Kao Corp. Shanghai	Shanghai	Shanghai	(021)62199999		Foreign Funded				Skin Care & Shampoo护
上海花王有限公司(1993)	上海市	上海市	(021)64094930	1,350	外商投资	818,258	-	689,931	肤洗发品
Beijing Da Bao Cosmetics Co., Ltd.	Beijing	Beijing	(010)67871843		Limited-Liability				Cosmetics
北京大宝化妆品有限公司(1999)	北京市	北京市	(010)67879665	1,066	有限公司	678,565	97,174(7)	828,926	化妆品
Guangzhou Si Bao Fine Chemical Industry Co., Ltd.	Guangzhou	Guangdong	(020)87811139		Overseas Chinese-funded				Cosmetics
广州丝宝精细化工有限公司(1992)	广州市	广东省	(020)87813882	235	港澳台资	556,690	40,770(13)	183,468	化妆品
Shiseido Liyuan Cosmetics Co.,Ltd.	Beijing	Beijing	(010)67883330		Foreign Funded				Cosmetics
资生堂丽源化妆品有限公司(1991)	北京市	北京市	(010)67881140	1,676	外商投资	547,789	160,812(1)	528,120	化妆品
Shanghai Huasheng Enterprise (Group) Co., Ltd.	Shanghai	Shanghai	(021)59791658		Limited-Liability				Aerosol
上海华盛企业(集团)有限公司(1997)	上海市	上海市	(021)59791337	1,892	有限公司	380,029	17,584(24)	628,319	气雾剂
Mentholatum (Zhongshan) Pharmacy Industry Co.,Ltd.	Zhongshan	Guangdong	(0760)6685596		Overseas Chinese-funded				Lipstick
曼秀雷敦（中山）药业有限公司(1990)	中山市	广东省	(0760)6685433	320	港澳台资	341,310	34,536(15)	217,474	润唇膏
Guangzhou Anway Co., Ltd.	Guangzhou	Guangdong	(020)82211633		Foreign Funded				Cosmetics
广州安利日用品制造有限公司(1999)	广州市	广东省	(020)82219475	450	外商投资	293,785	4,147(41)	116,875	化妆品

Top 10 Cities by Revenue 销售收入排名前10位城市	Province 省	Market share 市场份额（%）	Number of firms 企业个数
Shanghai 上海市	Shanghai 上海市	23.26	39
Guangzhou 广州市	Guangdong 广东省	13.19	27
Suzhou 苏州市	Jiangsu 江苏省	10.98	21
Beijing 北京市	Beijing 北京市	8.16	17
Shengzhixiaxingzhengdanwei 省直辖行政单位	Hubei 湖北省	6.88	1
Hangzhou 杭州市	Zhejiang 浙江省	4.46	4
Shaoxing 绍兴市	Zhejiang 浙江省	4.01	2
Shantou 汕头市	Guangdong 广东省	3.51	19
Wuhan 武汉市	Hubei 湖北省	2.84	1
Tianjin 天津市	Tianjin 天津市	2.42	12

10 Major Wholesalers 十家主要批发商	City 城市	Province 省	Telephone/Fax 电话/传真
Kunming Department Store Group Co.,Ltd.	Kunming	Yunnan	(0871)3313618
昆明百货集团股份有限公司	昆明市	云南省	(0871)3314961
Jiangsu Skyrun International Group	Nanjing	Jiangsu	(025)4468888
江苏开元国际集团	南京市	江苏省	(025)4209409
Guangdong Light Industry Products Imp.& Exp.(Group) Corporation	Guangzhou	Guangdong	(020)83344557
广东省轻工业品进出口（集团）公司	广州市	广东省	(020)83330181
Shanghai Cheer (Group) Co.,Ltd.	Shanghai	Shanghai	(021)63069764
上海七百（集团）有限公司	上海市	上海市	(021)63069537
Fujian Tiancheng Group Co.,Ltd.	Fuzhou	Fujian	(0591)7503388
福建天成集团有限公司	福州市	福建省	(0591)7609279
Shanghai Century Lianhua Supermaket Development Co.,ltd.	Shanghai	Shanghai	(021)53544600
上海世纪联华超市发展有限公司	上海市	上海市	(021)62252610
Suzhou General Merchandise General Company	Suzhou	Jiangsu	(0512)65222247
苏州百货总公司	苏州市	江苏省	(0512)65222247
Zhejiang Light Industry Products Import & Export Corporation	Hangzhou	Zhejiang	(0571)88391888
浙江省轻工业品进出口公司	杭州市	浙江省	(0571)88391666
Zhejiang Winsun Import & Export Co., Ltd.	Jiaxing	Zhejiang	(0573)2117091
浙江汇信进出口有限公司	嘉兴市	浙江省	(0573)2117020
Shenzhen CATIC Trade Company	Shenzhen	Guangdong	(0755)83790111
深圳中航商贸公司	深圳市	广东省	(0755)83790462

2686: Toothpaste 牙膏制造业

The industry accounts for 0.052% of the total revenue of China's industrial sector in 2002. The rate of return on assets is 8.43%. 70.27% of all firms in the industry made a profit while 29.73% had negative returns.The top province in terms of the industry's revenue is Guangdong, accounting for 55.77% of the total revenue.
2002年本行业收入占全行业的 0.052%，资产利润率为 8.43%。70.27%的企业赢利，29.73%的企业亏损。收入最高的省为广东省，占本行业的55.77%。

	Total number of firms 企业总数	Total number of employees 职工总数	Total revenue (Mil.RMB) 总销售收入 (百万元)	Total profit (Mil.RMB) 总利润 (百万元)	Return on assets 资产利润率 (%)	Return on equity 权益利润率 (%)	Labour productivity ('000 RMB/ worker) 劳动生产率 (千元/人)	Debts/ assets 资产负债率 (%)	Total assets (Mil.RMB) 总资产 (百万元)
Industry Overall 行业总体	37	12,988	5,555	487	8.43	18.79	161.16	55.15	5,782

	Number of firms 企业个数	Average number of employees 平均职工人数	Average revenue ('000 RMB) 平均销售收入 (千元)	Average profit ('000 RMB) 平均利润 (千元)	Return on assets 资产利润率 (%)	Return on equity 权益利润率 (%)	Labour productivity ('000 RMB/ worker) 劳动生产率 (千元/人)	Debts/ assets 资产负债率 (%)	Average total assets ('000 RMB) 平均总资产 (千元)
By ownership 产业所有权									
State-owned 国有	3	271	9,356	-99	-0.34	-1.98	10.08	82.61	28,658
Collective-owned 集体	2	100	11,166	627	4.70	44.22	28.12	89.37	13,334
Foreign & Overseas Chinese Funded 三资	8	330	363,347	32,252	11.50	35.22	437.46	67.35	280,426
By regional distribution 地区分布									
Central-North 华北	1	1,234	231,345	54,729	24.89	38.30	93.81	35.03	219,906
Beijing 北京									
Tianjin 天津	1	1,234	231,345	54,729	24.89	38.30	93.81	35.03	219,906
Hebei 河北									
Shanxi 山西									
Inner Mongolia 内蒙古									
Northeast 东北									
Liaoning 辽宁									
Jilin 吉林									
Heilongjiang 黑龙江									
Central-East 华东	19	339	81,527	588	0.46	0.87	72.14	47.79	128,762
Shanghai 上海	7	178	60,495	5,493	7.94	12.89	63.17	38.40	69,189
Jiangsu 江苏	6	248	19,323	-99	-0.28	-1.24	14.26	77.31	35,131
Zhejiang 浙江	1	646	79,455	3,420	5.83	18.42	38.52	68.35	58,653
Anhui 安徽	1	757	60,195	-9,054	-3.53	-8.33	121.27	57.67	256,770
Fujian 福建	1	86	7,423	-85,622	-79.40	-90.71	33.67	12.47	107,830
Jiangxi 江西	2	1,032	388,101	31,759	5.07	9.47	103.57	46.48	626,425
Shandong 山东	1	156	86,343	1,050	1.40	2.70	200.71	48.25	75,263
Central-South 中南	11	352	308,960	34,456	13.66	39.42	349.49	65.34	252,160
Henan 河南	1								
Hubei 湖北									
Hunan 湖南									
Guangdong 广东	7	495	442,614	51,471	14.37	48.42	326.51	70.33	358,247
Guangxi 广西	2	165	145,054	9,235	7.92	9.54	670.56	16.96	116,576
Hainan 海南	1	81	10,160	251	0.76	1.06	28.60	27.96	32,876
Southwest 西南	5	250	72,264	8,449	13.44	20.91	123.76	35.73	62,863
Chongqing 重庆	1	714	341,175	42,234	16.79	22.68	186.37	26.00	251,603
Sichuan 四川	1	281						96.77	32,111
Guizhou 贵州	1	50	898	-76	-2.09	-4.80	14.86	56.45	3,633
Yunnan 云南	2	102	9,625	44	0.33	0.67	101.72	51.01	13,485
Tibet 西藏									
Northwest 西北	1	191	15,240	122	0.44	1.25	18.66	64.70	27,552
Shaanxi 陕西	1	191	15,240	122	0.44	1.25	18.66	64.70	27,552
Gansu 甘肃									
Qinghai 青海									
Ningxia 宁夏									
Xinjiang 新疆									

2686: Toothpaste 牙膏制造业

Year 年份	Number of firms 企业个数	Rate of change 变化率 (%)	Number of employees 职工人数 (人)	Rate of change 变化率 (%)	Total revenue (Mil. RMB) 总销售收入 (百万元)	Rate of change 变化率 (%)	Total profit (Mil RMB) 总利润 (百万元)	Rate of change 变化率 (%)
2000	37		14,450		6,238		465	
2001	35	-5.41	14,659	1.45	5,570	-10.71	684	47.10
2002	37	5.71	12,988	-11.40	5,555	-0.27	487	-28.80

Major Products 主要产品	Output 产量	Unit 单位
Toothpaste 牙膏（自然支）	38	100,000,000 Pieces 亿支

10 Main Firms with Maximal Revenue (year founded) 收入最大的十家主要企业（创办年份）	City 城市	Province 省	Telephone/fax 电话/传真	Number of employees 职工人数	Ownership 产业所有权	Revenue ('000 RMB) 销售收入(千元)	Profit('000 RMB) (rank) 利润(千元)(排名)	Total assets ('000 RMB) 总资产(千元)	Major products 主要产品
Guangzhou Colgate Palmolive Co.,Ltd.	Guangzhou	Guangdong	(020)87551991		Foreign Funded				Toothpaste
广州高露洁棕榄有限公司(1995)	广州市	广东省	(020)82216091	505	外商投资	1,228,038	106,216(2)	741,872	牙膏
Chengzhi Co., Ltd.	Nanchang	Jiangxi	(0791)6304758		Joint Stock				Toothpaste
诚志股份有限公司(1998)	南昌市	江西省	(0791)6304524	1,744	股份制	752,322	59,747(3)	1,231,260	牙膏
Guangzhou P&G Mouth Health-care Articles Co., Ltd.	Guangzhou	Guangdong	(020)86698828		Overseas Chinese-funded				Toothpaste
广州宝洁口腔保健用品有限公司(1996)	广州市	广东省	(020)86693339	97	港澳台资	555,275	40,409(6)	400,642	牙膏
Hawley&Hazel Chemistry (Zhongshan) Co., Ltd.	Zhongshan	Guangdong	(0760)8551339		Foreign Funded				Darlie Toothpaste
好来化工（中山）有限公司(1995)	中山市	广东省	(0760)8551360	529	外商投资	508,160	143,745(1)	351,288	黑人牙膏
Masson Group Co.,Ltd.	Guangzhou	Guangdong	(020)86626470		Joint Stock				Toothpaste
美晨集团股份有限公司(1896)	广州市	广东省	(020)86626484	1,074	股份制	500,042	40,196(7)	631,628	牙膏
Chongqing Dengkang Mouth Care Articles Co., Ltd.	Chongqing	Chongqing	(023)67012997		Joint Stock				Toothpaste
重庆登康口腔护理用品股份有限公司(2001)	重庆市	重庆市	(023)67012679	714	股份制	341,175	42,234(5)	251,603	牙膏
Shanghai White Cat Co., Ltd.	Shanghai	Shanghai	(021)52700559		Joint Stock				Toothpaste
上海白猫股份有限公司(2001)	上海市	上海市	(021)52700505	529	股份制	320,937	31,392(9)	351,052	牙膏
Guangzhou Colgate Co., Ltd.	Guangzhou	Guangdong	(020)82214468		Foreign Funded				Toothpaste
广州高露洁有限公司(1992)	广州市	广东省	(020)82216091	922	外商投资	240,382	32,844(8)	325,185	牙膏
Hangzhou Toothpaste Factory	Hangzhou	Zhejiang	(0571)86064368		Joint Stock				Toothpaste
杭州牙膏厂(1999)	杭州市	浙江省	(0571)86064175	646	股份制	79,455	3,420(12)	58,653	牙膏
Anhui Fangcao Daily Chemistry Co., Ltd	Hefei	Anhui	(0551)5561657		Joint Stock				Toothpaste
安徽芳草日化股份有限公司(1957)	合肥市	安徽省	(0551)5578600	757	股份制	60,195	-	256,770	牙膏

Top 10 Cities by Revenue 销售收入排名前10位城市	Province 省	Market share 市场份额 (%)	Number of firms 企业个数
Guangzhou 广州市	Guangdong 广东省	46.62	6
Nanchang 南昌市	Jiangxi 江西省	13.54	1
Zhongshan 中山市	Guangdong 广东省	9.15	1
Shanghai 上海市	Shanghai 上海市	7.62	7
Chongqing 重庆市	Chongqing 重庆市	6.14	1
Liuzhou 柳州市	Guangxi 广西	4.89	1
Tianjin 天津市	Tianjin 天津市	4.16	1
Qingdao 青岛市	Shandong 山东省	1.55	1
Hangzhou 杭州市	Zhejiang 浙江省	1.43	1
Nanjing 南京市	Jiangsu 江苏省	1.23	2

10 Major Wholesalers 十家主要批发商	City 城市	Province 省	Telephone/Fax 电话/传真
Kunming Department Store Group Co.,Ltd.	Kunming	Yunnan	(0871)3313618
昆明百货集团股份有限公司	昆明市	云南省	(0871)3314961
Jiangsu Skyrun International Group	Nanjing	Jiangsu	(025)4468888
江苏开元国际集团	南京市	江苏省	(025)4209409
Guangdong Light Industry Products Imp.& Exp.(Group) Corporation	Guangzhou	Guangdong	(020)83344557
广东省轻工业品进出口（集团）公司	广州市	广东省	(020)83330181
Shanghai Cheer (Group) Co.,Ltd.	Shanghai	Shanghai	(021)63069764
上海七百（集团）有限公司	上海市	上海市	(021)63069537
Fujian Tiancheng Group Co.,Ltd.	Fuzhou	Fujian	(0591)7503388
福建天成集团有限公司	福州市	福建省	(0591)7609279
Shanghai Century Lianhua Supermaket Development Co.,ltd.	Shanghai	Shanghai	(021)53544600
上海世纪联华超市发展有限公司	上海市	上海市	(021)62252610
Suzhou General Merchandise General Company	Suzhou	Jiangsu	(0512)65222247
苏州百货总公司	苏州市	江苏省	(0512)65222247
Zhejiang Light Industry Products Import & Export Corporation	Hangzhou	Zhejiang	(0571)88391888
浙江省轻工业品进出口公司	杭州市	浙江省	(0571)88391666
Zhejiang Winsun Import & Export Co., Ltd.	Jiaxing	Zhejiang	(0573)2117091
浙江汇信进出口有限公司	嘉兴市	浙江省	(0573)2117020
Shenzhen CATIC Trade Company	Shenzhen	Guangdong	(0755)83790111
深圳中航商贸公司	深圳市	广东省	(0755)83790462

2687: Matches 火柴制造业

The industry accounts for 0.005% of the total revenue of China's industrial sector in 2002. The rate of return on assets is -0.57%. 62.00% of all firms in the industry made a profit while 38.00% had negative returns.The top province in terms of the industry's revenue is Hebei, accounting for 27.38% of the total revenue.
2002年本行业收入占全行业的0.005%，资产利润率为-0.57%。62.00%的企业赢利，38.00%的企业亏损。收入最高的省为河北省，占本行业的27.38%。

	Total number of firms 企业总数	Total number of employees 职工总数	Total revenue (Mil.RMB) 总销售收入（百万元）	Total profit (Mil.RMB) 总利润（百万元）	Return on assets 资产利润率（%）	Return on equity 权益利润率（%）	Labour productivity ('000 RMB/worker) 劳动生产率（千元/人）	Debts/assets 资产负债率（%）	Total assets (Mil.RMB) 总资产（百万元）
Industry Overall 行业总体	50	12,902	560	-5	-0.57	-1.47	12.18	61.26	805

	Number of firms 企业个数	Average number of employees 平均职工人数	Average revenue ('000 RMB) 平均销售收入（千元）	Average profit ('000 RMB) 平均利润（千元）	Return on assets 资产利润率（%）	Return on equity 权益利润率（%）	Labour productivity ('000 RMB/worker) 劳动生产率（千元/人）	Debts/assets 资产负债率（%）	Average total assets ('000 RMB) 平均总资产（千元）
By ownership 产业所有权									
State-owned 国有	18	258	6,623	-814	-3.81	-23.85	5.75	84.05	21,387
Collective-owned 集体	5	129	27,886	1,597	25.80	49.80	62.15	48.20	6,192
Foreign & Overseas Chinese Funded 三资									
By regional distribution 地区分布									
Central-North 华北	5	393	30,648	903	3.57	4.52	20.58	20.99	25,273
Beijing 北京									
Tianjin 天津	1	99						6.10	33,471
Hebei 河北	4	467	38,310	1,129	4.86	6.60	21.67	26.35	23,223
Shanxi 山西									
Inner Mongolia 内蒙古									
Northeast 东北	8	330	12,691	-10	-0.05	-0.37	11.00	87.23	20,144
Liaoning 辽宁	2	167	25,175	170	0.36	1.11	32.19	67.51	47,160
Jilin 吉林	2	306	6,727	-264	-3.50	-4.96	11.18	29.34	7,521
Heilongjiang 黑龙江	4	423	9,431	28	0.21	0.28	6.77	139.96	12,947
Central-East 华东	10	222	10,690	733	6.38	14.79	15.96	56.88	11,494
Shanghai 上海									
Jiangsu 江苏	1	183	7,040	150	8.06	11.11	9.23	27.42	1,860
Zhejiang 浙江	1	197	13,060	978	1.80	3.74	21.64	51.84	54,253
Anhui 安徽	2	355	8,184	73	1.28	19.92	7.68	93.58	5,669
Fujian 福建	2	35	164	3	0.03	0.21	2.96	85.13	7,868
Jiangxi 江西	1	327	1,401	8	0.12		1.57	100.00	6,913
Shandong 山东	3	243	22,902	2,014	24.32	31.77	31.87	23.43	8,282
Central-South 中南	18	222	7,527	-669	-4.76	-19.31	8.94	75.35	14,054
Henan 河南	3	433	13,347	-1,290	-2.86	-12.35	3.88	76.81	45,044
Hubei 湖北	3	71	16,943	279	5.17	9.55	63.80	45.92	5,395
Hunan 湖南	5	266	3,926	-568	-8.37		5.82	131.96	6,790
Guangdong 广东	2	119	4,914	-1,613	-45.96	-177.45	17.93	74.10	3,510
Guangxi 广西	5	182	3,030	-589	-4.85	-9.40	5.60	48.41	12,139
Hainan 海南									
Southwest 西南	4	170	3,925	-1,200	-11.26	-33.89	5.22	66.78	10,655
Chongqing 重庆									
Sichuan 四川	2	168	5,045	-2,155	-17.85	-60.48	8.22	70.49	12,075
Guizhou 贵州	1							43.26	5,642
Yunnan 云南	1	343	5,612	-488	-3.80	-12.74	2.29	70.14	12,829
Tibet 西藏									
Northwest 西北	5	283	9,383	99	0.46	0.76	9.26	38.86	21,321
Shaanxi 陕西	1	480	14,463	1,083	6.78	10.00	5.83	32.22	15,983
Gansu 甘肃	3	175	2,179	-143	-0.67	-0.87	7.47	22.97	21,468
Qinghai 青海									
Ningxia 宁夏									
Xinjiang 新疆	1	412	25,915	-159	-0.61	-3.35	15.52	81.91	26,220

Year 年份	Number of firms 企业个数	Rate of change 变化率 (%)	Number of employees 职工人数 (人)	Rate of change 变化率 (%)	Total revenue (Mil. RMB) 总销售收入 (百万元)	Rate of change 变化率 (%)	Total profit (Mil RMB) 总利润 (百万元)	Rate of change 变化率 (%)
2000	66		23,178		588		-12	
2001	61	-7.58	16,539	-28.64	603	2.55	10	-
2002	50	-18.03	12,902	-21.99	560	-7.13	-5	-

Major Products 主要产品	Output 产量	Unit 单位
Match 火柴	1,305	10,000 Pieces 万件

10 Main Firms with Maximal Revenue (year founded) 收入最大的十家主要企业（创办年份）	City 城市	Province 省	Telephone/fax 电话/传真	Number of employees 职工人数	Ownership 产业所有权	Revenue ('000 RMB) 销售收入 (千元)	Profit('000 RMB) (rank) 利润(千元) (排名)	Total assets ('000 RMB) 总资产 (千元)	Major products 主要产品
Ningjin Julong Match Co., Ltd. 宁津县炬龙火柴有限公司(1990)	Dezhou 德州市	Shandong 山东省	(0534)5681249 (0534)5683777	516	Private Enterprises 私营独资	38,970	2,960(2)	12,828	Match 火柴
Potou Match Co., Ltd 泊头市火柴有限责任公司(1912)	Cangzhou 沧州市	Hebei 河北省	(0317)8287055 (0317)8287043	1,366	Joint Stock 股份制	28,100	-	68,783	Match 火柴
Henan Anyang Match Factory 河南省安阳火柴厂(1946)	Anyang 安阳市	Henan 河南省	(0372)3932348 (0372)3934283	730	State-owned 国有企业	27,070	-	100,797	Match 火柴
Benxi Match Factory 本溪火柴厂(1970)	Benxi 本溪市	Liaoning 辽宁省	(0414)6821479 (0414)6821479	123	State-owned 国有企业	26,750	-	69,900	Match 火柴
Jingzhou Dadi Match Factory 荆州市大地火柴厂(1958)	Jingzhou 荆州市	Hubei 湖北省	(0716)4738745 (0716)4738745	110	Private Enterprises 私营独资	26,550	250(13)	8,700	Match 火柴
Xinjiang Xinmei Wood Industry Co., Ltd. 新疆新美木业有限公司(1959)	Urumqi 乌鲁木齐市	Xinjiang 新疆	(0991)3712040 (0991)3729602	412	Private Owned 私营企业	25,915	-	26,220	Match 火柴
Taian Huangsha Town Match Factory 台安县黄沙火柴厂(1988)	Anshan 鞍山市	Liaoning 辽宁省	(0412)4611095 (0412)4614501	210	Private Enterprises 私营独资	23,600	2,120(4)	24,420	Match 火柴
Meibao Antipoisoning Pharmacy Industry Group Company 美宝消毒药业集团公司(1987)	Baoji 宝鸡市	Shannxi 陕西省	(0917)6664416 (0917)6664396	480	Private Owned 私营企业	14,463	1,083(5)	15,983	Match 火柴
Bengbu Hutou Match Co., Ltd 蚌埠虎头火柴有限责任公司(2000)	Bengbu 蚌埠市	Anhui 安徽省	(0552)4081596 (0552)4081596	687	Limited-Liability 有限公司	14,379	145(15)	9,018	Match 火柴
Hangzhou Guanghua Industrial Co., Ltd. 杭州光华实业股份合作公司(1999)	Hangzhou 杭州市	Zhejiang 浙江省	(0571)86081200 (0571)86081200	197	Joint Stock 股份制	13,060	978(6)	54,253	Match 火柴

Top 10 Cities by Revenue 销售收入排名前10位城市	Province 省	Market share 市场份额 (%)	Number of firms 企业个数
Hengshui 衡水市	Hebei 河北省	21.41	2
Dezhou 德州市	Shandong 山东省	12.27	3
Anyang 安阳市	Henan 河南省	7.06	2
Cangzhou 沧州市	Hebei 河北省	5.97	2
Benxi 本溪市	Liaoning 辽宁省	4.78	1
Jingzhou 荆州市	Hubei 湖北省	4.74	1
Urumqi 乌鲁木齐市	Xinjiang 新疆	4.63	1
Anshan 鞍山市	Liaoning 辽宁省	4.22	1
Baoji 宝鸡市	Shannxi 陕西省	2.58	1
Bengbu 蚌埠市	Anhui 安徽省	2.57	1

10 Major Wholesalers 十家主要批发商	City 城市	Province 省	Telephone/Fax 电话/传真
Kunming Department Store Group Co.,Ltd. 昆明百货集团股份有限公司	Kunming 昆明市	Yunnan 云南省	(0871)3313618 (0871)3314961
Jiangsu Skyrun International Group 江苏开元国际集团	Nanjing 南京市	Jiangsu 江苏省	(025)4468888 (025)4209409
Guangdong Light Industry Products Imp.& Exp.(Group) Corporation 广东省轻工业品进出口（集团）公司	Guangzhou 广州市	Guangdong 广东省	(020)83344557 (020)83330181
Shanghai Cheer (Group) Co.,Ltd. 上海七百（集团）有限公司	Shanghai 上海市	Shanghai 上海市	(021)63069764 (021)63069537
Fujian Tiancheng Group Co.,Ltd. 福建天成集团有限公司	Fuzhou 福州市	Fujian 福建省	(0591)7503388 (0591)7609279
Shanghai Century Lianhua Supermaket Development Co.,ltd. 上海世纪联华超市发展有限公司	Shanghai 上海市	Shanghai 上海市	(021)53544600 (021)62252610
Suzhou General Merchandise General Company 苏州百货总公司	Suzhou 苏州市	Jiangsu 江苏省	(0512)65222247 (0512)65222247
Zhejiang Light Industry Products Import & Export Corporation 浙江省轻工业品进出口公司	Hangzhou 杭州市	Zhejiang 浙江省	(0571)88391888 (0571)88391666
Zhejiang Winsun Import & Export Co., Ltd. 浙江汇信进出口有限公司	Jiaxing 嘉兴市	Zhejiang 浙江省	(0573)2117091 (0573)2117020
Shenzhen CATIC Trade Company 深圳中航商贸公司	Shenzhen 深圳市	Guangdong 广东省	(0755)83790111 (0755)83790462

2688: Animal Jelly 动物胶制造业

The industry accounts for 0.013% of the total revenue of China's industrial sector in 2002. The rate of return on assets is 4.25%. 86.89% of all firms in the industry made a profit while 13.11% had negative returns.The top province in terms of the industry's revenue is Guangdong, accounting for 12.50% of the total revenue.
2002年本行业收入占全行业的 0.013%，资产利润率为 4.25%。86.89%的企业赢利，13.11%的企业亏损。收入最高的省为广东省，占本行业的12.50%。

	Total number of firms 企业总数	Total number of employees 职工总数	Total revenue (Mil.RMB) 总销售收入（百万元）	Total profit (Mil.RMB) 总利润（百万元）	Return on assets 资产利润率（%）	Return on equity 权益利润率（%）	Labour productivity ('000 RMB/ worker) 劳动生产率（千元/人）	Debts/ assets 资产负债率（%）	Total assets (Mil.RMB) 总资产（百万元）
Industry Overall 行业总体	61	9,047	1,389	89	4.25	9.17	45.12	53.60	2,083

	Number of firms 企业个数	Average number of employees 平均职工人数	Average revenue ('000 RMB) 平均销售收入（千元）	Average profit ('000 RMB) 平均利润（千元）	Return on assets 资产利润率（%）	Return on equity 权益利润率（%）	Labour productivity ('000 RMB/ worker) 劳动生产率（千元/人）	Debts/ assets 资产负债率（%）	Average total assets ('000 RMB) 平均总资产（千元）
By ownership 产业所有权									
State-owned 国有	7	185	14,168	554	1.48	6.76	15.05	78.19	37,577
Collective-owned 集体	8	103	11,717	646	5.40	14.82	27.60	63.57	11,967
Foreign & Overseas Chinese Funded 三资	3	273	96,195	12,003	13.08	20.74	93.22	36.94	91,763
By regional distribution 地区分布									
Central-North 华北	7	146	14,339	1,066	3.53	5.57	40.10	36.50	30,170
Beijing 北京									
Tianjin 天津									
Hebei 河北	3	89	12,075	547	2.03	2.91	65.63	30.21	26,887
Shanxi 山西	2	96	10,260	-39	-0.24	-0.99	25.84	75.84	16,069
Inner Mongolia 内蒙古	2	283	21,814	2,950	6.00	8.42	32.90	28.82	49,198
Northeast 东北	4	121	10,290	74	0.28	1.55	27.26	81.70	26,130
Liaoning 辽宁									
Jilin 吉林	4	121	10,290	74	0.28	1.55	27.26	81.70	26,130
Heilongjiang 黑龙江									
Central-East 华东	27	130	24,882	930	4.38	10.46	49.52	58.14	21,240
Shanghai 上海	3	27	45,919	2,476	6.06	13.39	170.28	54.72	40,832
Jiangsu 江苏	3	96	33,371	1,112	7.90	43.27	82.98	81.74	14,075
Zhejiang 浙江	7	143	24,772	787	3.56	9.56	38.71	62.81	22,138
Anhui 安徽	3	48	10,359	714	11.54	18.53	32.92	37.72	6,185
Fujian 福建									
Jiangxi 江西	4	207	22,621	799	3.35	5.70	46.81	41.30	23,875
Shandong 山东	7	167	19,852	501	2.51	6.80	46.11	63.04	19,963
Central-South 中南	12	177	32,716	3,421	8.58	18.65	50.60	54.01	39,874
Henan 河南	9	154	18,539	932	4.51	13.33	28.00	66.14	20,661
Hubei 湖北	1	139	46,014	502	0.68	1.74	46.68	60.77	73,579
Hunan 湖南	1	34	6,000	-578	-1.28		278.82	125.06	45,066
Guangdong 广东	1	564	173,721	32,739	18.83	23.46	93.39	19.75	173,893
Guangxi 广西									
Hainan 海南									
Southwest 西南	3	134	9,853	-109	-0.76	-1.19	19.79	36.52	14,474
Chongqing 重庆									
Sichuan 四川									
Guizhou 贵州	1	76	11,869	-532	-2.93	-3.70	22.17	20.76	18,144
Yunnan 云南	2	164	8,846	102	0.81	1.55	19.24	47.84	12,639
Tibet 西藏									
Northwest 西北	8	189	19,216	1,873	2.23	4.60	43.07	51.53	83,959
Shaanxi 陕西	1	26	467	1	0.08	0.11	7.65	24.02	1,203
Gansu 甘肃	5	175	7,996	149	0.63	2.39	17.20	73.49	23,445
Qinghai 青海	1	588	112,246	14,600	2.66	4.97	84.58	46.51	548,673
Ningxia 宁夏	1	27	1,035	-361	-7.89	-445.68	9.33	98.23	4,575
Xinjiang 新疆									

2688: Animal Jelly 动物胶制造业

Year 年份	Number of firms 企业个数	Rate of change 变化率 (%)	Number of employees 职工人数 (人)	Rate of change 变化率 (%)	Total revenue (Mil. RMB) 总销售收入 (百万元)	Rate of change 变化率 (%)	Total profit (Mil RMB) 总利润 (百万元)	Rate of change 变化率 (%)
2000	64		10,142		856		37	
2001	52	-18.75	8,552	-15.68	999	16.71	43	16.22
2002	61	17.31	9,047	5.79	1,389	39.04	89	106.98

Major Products 主要产品	Output 产量	Unit 单位

10 Main Firms with Maximal Revenue (year founded) 收入最大的十家主要企业（创办年份）	City 城市	Province 省	Telephone/fax 电话/传真	Number of employees 职工人数	Ownership 产业所有权	Revenue ('000 RMB) 销售收入(千元)	Profit('000 RMB) (rank) 利润(千元)(排名)	Total assets ('000 RMB) 总资产(千元)	Major products 主要产品
Rousselog (Guangdong) Jelatin Co.,Ltd.	Jiangmen	Guangdong	(0750)2212323		Foreign Funded				Glutin
罗赛洛（广东）明珠有限公司(1995)	江门市	广东省	(0750)2292119	564	外商投资	173,721	32,739(1)	173,893	明胶
Qinghai Glutin Co., Ltd.	Xining	Qinghai	(0971)8012703		Joint Stock				Glutin
青海明胶股份有限公司(1956)	西宁市	青海省	(0971)8012106	588	股份制	112,246	14,600(2)	548,673	明胶
Shanghai Shuangfeng Bone Glutin Co., Ltd.	Shanghai	Shanghai	(021)58493939		Private Owned				Bone Glutin
上海双凤骨明胶有限公司(2001)	上海市	上海市	(021)58490025	51	私营企业	85,369	5,139(4)	76,165	骨明胶
Asian Technology (kunshan) Co., Ltd.	Suzhou	Jiangsu	(0512)57799399		Foreign Funded				Adhesive Tape
亚化科技粘胶制品(昆山)有限公司(2000)	苏州市	江苏省	(0512)57791559	115	外商投资	68,851	2,767(7)	27,818	胶带
Henan Jiaozuo Jinjian Industrial General Company	Jiaozuo	Henan	(0391)3593043		State-owned				Adhesive Tape
河南省焦作金箭实业总公司(1966)	焦作市	河南省	(0391)3593009	636	国有企业	51,294	4,019(5)	129,929	胶带
Pingyang Sanming Food Additive Factory	Wenzhou	Zhejiang	(0577)63681057		Joint Stock				Bone Glue
平阳县三明食品添加剂厂(1996)	温州市	浙江省	(0577)63681551	216	股份制	50,820	1,050(15)	31,220	骨胶
Yantai Jiyuan Health Products Co., Ltd.	Yantai	Shandong	(0535)7182698		Private Owned				Vitriol Cartilage
烟台技源保健品有限公司(2001)	烟台市	山东省		80	私营企业	44,563	-	31,636	硫酸软骨
Wenzhou Meilin Zhengguanghe Glutin Co., Ltd.	Wenzhou	Zhejiang	(0577)63668922		Limited-Liability				Glutin
温州梅林正广和明胶有限公司(2000)	温州市	浙江省	(0577)63681999	150	有限公司	40,412	452(26)	41,000	明胶
Baotou Dongbao Lucky Color Film Glutin Co,.Ltd.	Baotou	Inner Mongolia	(0472)4358389		Private Owned				Glutin
包头东宝乐凯彩感明胶股份有限公司(1997)	包头市	内蒙古	(0472)4351423	435	私营企业	38,770	5,900(3)	76,696	明胶
Ningbo Ansheng Capsule Factory	Ningbo	Zhejiang	(0574)88428626		Private Enterprises				Bone Glutin
宁波安生胶囊厂(1968)	宁波市	浙江省	(0574)88428083	217	私营独资	33,498	3,772(6)	19,937	骨明胶

Top 10 Cities by Revenue 销售收入排名前10位城市	Province 省	Market share 市场份额 (%)	Number of firms 企业个数
Jiangmen 江门市	Guangdong 广东省	12.50	1
Shanghai 上海市	Shanghai 上海市	9.92	3
Wenzhou 温州市	Zhejiang 浙江省	8.61	5
Xining 西宁市	Qinghai 青海省	8.08	1
Suzhou 苏州市	Jiangsu 江苏省	4.96	1
Luohe 漯河市	Henan 河南省	4.78	4
Fuzhou 抚州市	Jiangxi 江西省	4.18	1
Jiaozuo 焦作市	Henan 河南省	3.69	1
xiantao 仙桃市	Hubei 湖北省	3.31	1
Yantai 烟台市	Shandong 山东省	3.21	1

10 Major Wholesalers 十家主要批发商	City 城市	Province 省	Telephone/Fax 电话/传真
Kunming Department Store Group Co.,Ltd.	Kunming	Yunnan	(0871)3313618
昆明百货集团股份有限公司	昆明市	云南省	(0871)3314961
Jiangsu Skyrun International Group	Nanjing	Jiangsu	(025)4468888
江苏开元国际集团	南京市	江苏省	(025)4209409
Guangdong Light Industry Products Imp.& Exp.(Group) Corporation	Guangzhou	Guangdong	(020)83344557
广东省轻工业品进出口（集团）公司	广州市	广东省	(020)83330181
Shanghai Cheer (Group) Co.,Ltd.	Shanghai	Shanghai	(021)63069764
上海七百（集团）有限公司	上海市	上海市	(021)63069537
Fujian Tiancheng Group Co.,Ltd.	Fuzhou	Fujian	(0591)7503388
福建天成集团有限公司	福州市	福建省	(0591)7609279
Shanghai Century Lianhua Supermaket Development Co.,ltd.	Shanghai	Shanghai	(021)53544600
上海世纪联华超市发展有限公司	上海市	上海市	(021)62252610
Suzhou General Merchandise General Company	Suzhou	Jiangsu	(0512)65222247
苏州市百货总公司	苏州市	江苏省	(0512)65222247
Zhejiang Light Industry Products Import & Export Corporation	Hangzhou	Zhejiang	(0571)88391888
浙江省轻工业品进出口公司	杭州市	浙江省	(0571)88391666
Zhejiang Winsun Import & Export Co., Ltd.	Jiaxing	Zhejiang	(0573)2117091
浙江汇信进出口有限公司	嘉兴市	浙江省	(0573)2117020
Shenzhen CATIC Trade Company	Shenzhen	Guangdong	(0755)83790111
深圳中航商贸公司	深圳市	广东省	(0755)83790462

2689: Other Household Chemical Products 其他日用化学产品制造业

The industry accounts for 0.057% of the total revenue of China's industrial sector in 2002. The rate of return on assets is 7.09%. 77.89% of all firms in the industry made a profit while 22.11% had negative returns.The top province in terms of the industry's revenue is Guangdong, accounting for 23.20% of the total revenue.
2002年本行业收入占全行业的 0.057%，资产利润率为 7.09%。77.89%的企业赢利，22.11%的企业亏损。收入最高的省为广东省，占本行业的23.20%。

	Total number of firms 企业总数	Total number of employees 职工总数	Total revenue (Mil.RMB) 总销售收入 (百万元)	Total profit (Mil.RMB) 总利润 (百万元)	Return on assets 资产利润率 (%)	Return on equity 权益利润率 (%)	Labour productivity ('000 RMB/worker) 劳动生产率 (千元/人)	Debts/assets 资产负债率 (%)	Total assets (Mil.RMB) 总资产 (百万元)
Industry Overall 行业总体	190	30,069	6,164	354	7.09	15.82	60.80	55.15	4,987

	Number of firms 企业个数	Average number of employees 平均职工人数	Average revenue ('000 RMB) 平均销售收入 (千元)	Average profit ('000 RMB) 平均利润 (千元)	Return on assets 资产利润率 (%)	Return on equity 权益利润率 (%)	Labour productivity ('000 RMB/worker) 劳动生产率 (千元/人)	Debts/assets 资产负债率 (%)	Average total assets ('000 RMB) 平均总资产 (千元)
By ownership 产业所有权									
State-owned 国有	8	150	18,839	237	0.95	3.19	44.26	70.37	25,016
Collective-owned 集体	39	112	23,971	1,364	10.64	27.64	65.09	61.50	12,822
Foreign & Overseas Chinese Funded 三资	48	169	44,616	2,603	5.71	13.40	78.81	57.41	45,607
By regional distribution 地区分布									
Central-North 华北	24	237	34,619	1,952	7.67	17.37	48.76	55.87	25,461
Beijing 北京	3	159	80,495	2,023	5.57	8.11	162.93	31.35	36,350
Tianjin 天津	14	150	24,300	958	6.53	15.10	51.60	56.76	14,676
Hebei 河北	7	445	35,596	3,910	9.23	25.83	29.33	64.28	42,365
Shanxi 山西									
Inner Mongolia 内蒙古									
Northeast 东北	7	105	8,670	-221	-1.96	-6.20	18.55	68.36	11,254
Liaoning 辽宁	5	81	8,260	-64	-0.91	-9.85	23.25	90.75	6,978
Jilin 吉林	1	32	9,850	101	0.78	1.14	62.81	31.90	12,980
Heilongjiang 黑龙江	1	299	9,538	-1,328	-4.30	-10.33	7.47	58.41	30,909
Central-East 华东	91	149	36,118	1,667	7.03	13.58	69.88	48.24	23,715
Shanghai 上海	14	105	54,953	-1,616	-3.77	-6.14	135.41	38.64	42,878
Jiangsu 江苏	22	79	19,439	1,147	8.92	29.99	67.31	70.24	12,850
Zhejiang 浙江	22	248	63,393	5,500	18.81	32.78	69.28	42.62	29,243
Anhui 安徽	1	145	2,306	1	0.01	0.13	6.09	89.27	6,953
Fujian 福建	15	149	17,146	504	2.30	4.54	48.19	49.32	21,914
Jiangxi 江西	4	60	8,683	480	14.72	38.20	47.21	61.46	3,257
Shandong 山东	13	174	30,836	1,429	6.56	15.09	58.51	56.50	21,773
Central-South 中南	59	151	32,683	2,663	7.65	19.92	64.00	61.62	34,829
Henan 河南	5	101	14,387	347	7.94	13.01	60.05	38.97	4,374
Hubei 湖北	10	201	30,933	2,795	13.44	70.06	38.11	80.82	20,795
Hunan 湖南	4	144	8,994	-1,233	-4.40	-13.12	29.76	66.48	28,034
Guangdong 广东	37	147	38,646	3,492	8.02	20.56	77.71	61.01	43,548
Guangxi 广西	3	121	27,050	1,055	3.11	4.56	62.06	31.63	33,884
Hainan 海南									
Southwest 西南	7	163	8,169	-51	-0.43	-1.01	16.78	57.38	11,824
Chongqing 重庆	4	127	7,059	-12	-0.17	-0.47	8.67	63.92	7,199
Sichuan 四川	3	211	9,649	-102	-0.57	-1.23	23.29	53.88	17,991
Guizhou 贵州									
Yunnan 云南									
Tibet 西藏									
Northwest 西北	2	23	170	16	3.17	3.49	26.28	9.20	489
Shaanxi 陕西									
Gansu 甘肃	2	23	170	16	3.17	3.49	26.28	9.20	489
Qinghai 青海									
Ningxia 宁夏									
Xinjiang 新疆									

2689: Other Household Chemical Products 其他日用化学产品制造业

Year 年份	Number of firms 企业个数	Rate of change 变化率 (%)	Number of employees 职工人数 (人)	Rate of change 变化率 (%)	Total revenue (Mil. RMB) 总销售收入 (百万元)	Rate of change 变化率 (%)	Total profit (Mil RMB) 总利润 (百万元)	Rate of change 变化率 (%)
2000	186		28,926		5,917		363	
2001	187	0.54	31,688	9.55	6,396	8.10	299	-17.63
2002	190	1.60	30,069	-5.11	6,164	-3.63	354	18.39

Major Products 主要产品	Output 产量	Unit 单位
Insecticide 杀虫剂	46	10,000 Tons 万吨

10 Main Firms with Maximal Revenue (year founded) 收入最大的十家主要企业（创办年份）	City 城市	Province 省	Telephone/fax 电话/传真	Number of employees 职工人数	Ownership 产业所有权	Revenue ('000 RMB) 销售收入 (千元)	Profit('000 RMB) (rank) 利润(千元) (排名)	Total assets ('000 RMB) 总资产 (千元)	Major products 主要产品
Shanghai Johnson Family Company 上海庄臣有限公司(1991)	Shanghai 上海市	Shanghai 上海市	(021)58994833 (021)58990288	459	Foreign Funded 外商投资	516,265	-	391,859	Insecticide 杀虫剂
Sunrider(GuangZhou) Co.,Ltd. 仙妮蕾德（广州）有限公司(1993)	Guangzhou 广州市	Guangdong 广东省	(020)82208288 (020)82209053	195	Foreign Funded 外商投资	327,771	114,617(1)	465,934	Washing Things 洗涤用品
Zhejiang Heimaoshen Mosquito-repellent Incense Group Co., Ltd.浙江黑猫神蚊香集团有限公司(1996)	Shaoxing 绍兴市	Zhejiang 浙江省	(0575)7861055 (0575)7861868	850	Limited-Liability 有限公司	209,088	27,607(3)	138,091	Mosquito-repellent Incense 蚊香
Beijing Yanhua Dongfang Industry & Trade Co., Ltd. 北京燕化东方工贸有限公司(2000)	Beijing 北京市	Beijing 北京市	(010)69342548 (010)69342548	252	Collective-owned 集体企业	203,679	5,442(10)	71,233	Parffin 石蜡
Wendeng Gejia Chemical Plant 文登市葛家化工厂(1989)	Weihai 威海市	Shandong 山东省	(0631)8881191 (0631)8881191	124	Collective-owned 集体企业	108,920	7,480(8)	7,509	Bleaching Powder 漂白粉
Zhongshan Lanju Daily Use Products Co., Ltd. 中山榄菊日用制品有限公司(1999)	Zhongshan 中山市	Guangdong 广东省	(0760)2129535 (0760)2123331	182	Private Owned 私营企业	102,575	2,617(19)	70,055	Mosquito-repellent Incense 蚊香
Fujian Jinlu Daily Chemistry Co., Ltd. 福建省金鹿日化股份有限公司(1981)	Quanzhou 泉州市	Fujian 福建省	(0595)6696828 (0595)6696688	700	Joint Stock 股份制	95,563	1,874(28)	142,701	Mosquito-repellent Incense 蚊香
Shanghai Johnson Professional Chemical Products Ltd. 上海庄臣专业化学品有限公司(1998)	Shanghai 上海市	Shanghai 上海市	(021)64180000 (021)64030636	109	Foreign Funded 外商投资	91,983	4,680(11)	68,869	Cleanser for Commercial商用清洁剂
Market Group Chemistry Co.,Ltd. 麦科特集团化学有限公司(1992)	Huizhou 惠州市	Guangdong 广东省	(0752)2311688 (0752)2311000	64	Limited-Liability 有限公司	91,194	6,763(9)	83,487	Spraying Leather Shoeshine喷雾皮鞋油
Dongguan Quanwei Candle Co., Ltd. 东莞铨威烛业有限公司(1999)	Dongguan 东莞市	Guangdong 广东省	(0769)8283468 (0769)8280756	717	Foreign Funded 外商投资	90,320	1,062(45)	37,546	Candle Handicrafts 工艺蜡烛

Top 10 Cities by Revenue 销售收入排名前10位城市	Province 省	Market share 市场份额 (%)	Number of firms 企业个数
Shaoxing 绍兴市	Zhejiang 浙江省	18.59	6
Shanghai 上海市	Shanghai 上海市	12.48	14
Guangzhou 广州市	Guangdong 广东省	8.61	9
Tianjin 天津市	Tianjin 天津市	5.52	14
Beijing 北京市	Beijing 北京市	3.92	3
Baoding 保定市	Hebei 河北省	3.64	5
Weihai 威海市	Shandong 山东省	3.12	3
Foshan 佛山市	Guangdong 广东省	2.87	4
Suizhou 随州市	Hubei 湖北省	2.61	1
Quanzhou 泉州市	Fujian 福建省	2.44	5

10 Major Wholesalers 十家主要批发商	City 城市	Province 省	Telephone/Fax 电话/传真
Kunming Department Store Group Co.,Ltd. 昆明百货集团股份有限公司	Kunming 昆明市	Yunnan 云南省	(0871)3313618 (0871)3314961
Jiangsu Skyrun International Group 江苏开元国际集团	Nanjing 南京市	Jiangsu 江苏省	(025)4468888 (025)4209409
Guangdong Light Industry Products Imp.& Exp.(Group) Corporation 广东省轻工业品进出口（集团）公司	Guangzhou 广州市	Guangdong 广东省	(020)83344557 (020)83330181
Shanghai Cheer (Group) Co.,Ltd. 上海七百（集团）有限公司	Shanghai 上海市	Shanghai 上海市	(021)63069764 (021)63069537
Fujian Tiancheng Group Co.,Ltd. 福建天成集团有限公司	Fuzhou 福州市	Fujian 福建省	(0591)7503388 (0591)7609279
Shanghai Century Lianhua Supermaket Development Co.,ltd. 上海世纪联华超市发展有限公司	Shanghai 上海市	Shanghai 上海市	(021)53544600 (021)62252610
Suzhou General Merchandise General Company 苏州百货总公司	Suzhou 苏州市	Jiangsu 江苏省	(0512)65222247 (0512)65222247
Zhejiang Light Industry Products Import & Export Corporation 浙江省轻工业品进出口公司	Hangzhou 杭州市	Zhejiang 浙江省	(0571)88391888 (0571)88391666
Zhejiang Winsun Import & Export Co., Ltd. 浙江汇信进出口有限公司	Jiaxing 嘉兴市	Zhejiang 浙江省	(0573)2117091 (0573)2117020
Shenzhen CATIC Trade Company 深圳中航商贸公司	Shenzhen 深圳市	Guangdong 广东省	(0755)83790111 (0755)83790462

2710: Medicines and Chemical Reagents 化学药品原药制造业

The industry accounts for 0.614% of the total revenue of China's industrial sector in 2002. The rate of return on assets is 3.29%. 75.69% of all firms in the industry made a profit while 24.31% had negative returns.The top province in terms of the industry's revenue is Hebei, accounting for 21.73% of the total revenue.
2002年本行业收入占全行业的0.614%，资产利润率为3.29%。75.69%的企业赢利，24.31%的企业亏损。收入最高的省为河北省，占本行业的21.73%。

	Total number of firms 企业总数	Total number of employees 职工总数	Total revenue (Mil.RMB) 总销售收入（百万元）	Total profit (Mil.RMB) 总利润（百万元）	Return on assets 资产利润率（%）	Return on equity 权益利润率（%）	Labour productivity ('000 RMB/worker) 劳动生产率（千元/人）	Debts/assets 资产负债率（%）	Total assets (Mil.RMB) 总资产（百万元）
Industry Overall 行业总体	728	315,267	65,880	3,665	3.29	8.45	56.90	61.07	111,401

	Number of firms 企业个数	Average number of employees 平均职工人数	Average revenue ('000 RMB) 平均销售收入（千元）	Average profit ('000 RMB) 平均利润（千元）	Return on assets 资产利润率（%）	Return on equity 权益利润率（%）	Labour productivity ('000 RMB/worker) 劳动生产率（千元/人）	Debts/assets 资产负债率（%）	Average total assets ('000 RMB) 平均总资产（千元）
By ownership 产业所有权									
State-owned 国有	100	579	67,746	2,747	1.49	4.73	28.24	68.54	184,606
Collective-owned 集体	81	241	46,416	3,678	7.31	21.18	51.84	65.48	50,305
Foreign & Overseas Chinese Funded 三资	100	204	66,541	2,407	2.64	7.09	91.35	62.83	91,307
By regional distribution 地区分布									
Central-North 华北	111	653	168,539	11,985	3.51	9.24	62.97	62.06	341,810
Beijing 北京	9	199	30,515	1,859	3.76	6.92	77.26	45.62	49,400
Tianjin 天津	29	398	119,891	10,341	4.10	8.15	57.83	49.76	252,492
Hebei 河北	48	1,041	298,200	21,263	3.59	10.39	69.85	65.48	592,600
Shanxi 山西	15	207	12,374	-1,016	-2.34	-7.59	28.74	69.20	43,464
Inner Mongolia 内蒙古	10	612	45,712	836	0.78	1.84	29.70	57.79	107,726
Northeast 东北	37	1,050	265,468	12,134	3.00	7.92	60.07	62.11	404,485
Liaoning 辽宁	23	573	110,867	1,719	0.57	1.72	46.09	66.89	301,805
Jilin 吉林	7	447	43,766	2,564	1.87	4.28	44.99	56.41	137,289
Heilongjiang 黑龙江	7	3,223	995,148	55,927	5.54	13.26	70.32	58.19	1,009,060
Central-East 华东	333	358	77,432	4,220	3.94	10.23	58.46	61.50	107,134
Shanghai 上海	37	324	86,523	-714	-0.60	-2.26	40.65	73.36	118,788
Jiangsu 江苏	103	310	47,597	1,420	2.54	7.30	42.88	65.26	55,984
Zhejiang 浙江	115	258	75,133	7,535	7.01	16.77	74.69	58.20	107,469
Anhui 安徽	10	452	58,746	1,044	0.79	1.76	26.24	55.21	132,664
Fujian 福建	9	207	48,152	3,911	4.05	11.58	166.64	65.01	96,546
Jiangxi 江西	10	520	51,911	1,982	2.49	6.41	40.66	61.19	79,628
Shandong 山东	49	693	153,079	7,210	3.48	8.44	66.26	58.80	207,419
Central-South 中南	150	377	53,551	3,129	3.05	6.64	52.92	54.16	102,736
Henan 河南	45	407	44,748	3,072	3.52	8.34	47.96	57.76	87,164
Hubei 湖北	54	430	58,740	2,332	2.27	4.84	47.84	53.02	102,680
Hunan 湖南	16	319	25,955	-2,111	-2.61	-14.64	25.33	82.17	80,844
Guangdong 广东	25	233	77,196	9,036	7.90	14.95	113.77	47.16	114,399
Guangxi 广西	8	446	55,260	995	0.47	0.80	48.23	41.44	211,625
Hainan 海南	2	194	29,867	2,564	5.30	7.38	82.07	28.23	48,402
Southwest 西南	53	384	46,265	-757	-0.76	-2.31	32.07	67.12	99,674
Chongqing 重庆	17	501	48,395	-6,842	-4.72	-21.74	3.46	78.30	145,022
Sichuan 四川	27	382	55,182	2,619	2.82	6.78	53.76	58.45	92,999
Guizhou 贵州	5	181	17,171	970	3.27	5.46	43.68	40.06	29,644
Yunnan 云南	4	159	13,384	150	0.38	0.86	46.93	55.89	39,533
Tibet 西藏									
Northwest 西北	44	179	24,558	1,156	2.39	6.60	54.53	63.74	48,313
Shaanxi 陕西	34	152	20,332	60	0.15	0.40	50.28	62.02	39,362
Gansu 甘肃	2	254	19,694	3,242	8.41	24.35	32.86	65.47	38,554
Qinghai 青海									
Ningxia 宁夏	2	685	152,061	24,584	9.50	25.79	96.25	63.17	258,787
Xinjiang 新疆	6	134	7,628	-1,142	-3.55	-15.12	24.55	76.49	32,133

2710: Medicines and Chemical Reagents 化学药品原药制造业

Year 年份	Number of firms 企业个数	Rate of change 变化率 (%)	Number of employees 职工人数 (人)	Rate of change 变化率 (%)	Total revenue (Mil. RMB) 总销售收入 (百万元)	Rate of change 变化率 (%)	Total profit (Mil RMB) 总利润 (百万元)	Rate of change 变化率 (%)
2000	685		329,498		49,518		2,533	
2001	731	6.72	334,027	1.37	59,238	19.63	3,337	31.74
2002	728	-0.41	315,267	-5.62	65,880	11.21	3,665	9.83

Major Products 主要产品	Output 产量	Unit 单位
Chemical Raw Material Medicine 化学原料药	56	10,000 Tons 万吨

10 Main Firms with Maximal Revenue (year founded) 收入最大的十家主要企业（创办年份）	City 城市	Province 省	Telephone/fax 电话/传真	Number of employees 职工人数	Ownership 产业所有权	Revenue ('000 RMB) 销售收入 (千元)	Profit('000 RMB) (rank) 利润(千元) (排名)	Total assets ('000 RMB) 总资产 (千元)	Major products 主要产品
Harbin Pharmaceutical Group Holding Co.,Ltd. 哈药集团有限公司(1989)	Harbin 哈尔滨市	Heilongjiang 黑龙江省	(0451)84851994 (0451)84856783	20,556	State Enterprises 国有独资	6,870,764	398,267(2)	6,552,369	Chemical Raw Material Medicine 化学原料药
North China Pharmaceutical Group Corp. 华北制药集团有限责任公司(1996)	Shijiazhuang 石家庄市	Hebei 河北省	(0311)5051133 (0311)6672430	17,895	State Enterprises 国有独资	6,290,000	340,000(3)	15,538,260	Antibiotic Raw Material 抗生素原料
Shijiazhuang Pharmaceutical Group Co.,Ltd. 石家庄制药集团有限公司(1997)	Shijiazhuang 石家庄市	Hebei 河北省	(0311)7029285 (0311)7039608	12,787	State Enterprises 国有独资	4,247,204	405,830(1)	6,400,359	Vitamin 维生素
Shandong Xinhua Medicine Group Co., Ltd. 山东新华医药集团有限责任公司(1995)	Zibo 淄博市	Shandong 山东省	(0533)2184223 (0533)2184991	8,902	State Enterprises 国有独资	3,070,694	124,784(7)	2,808,760	Analgen 安乃近
Tianjin Jinyao Group Co., Ltd. 天津金耀集团有限公司(2001)	Tianjin 天津市	Tianjin 天津市	(022)24160853 (022)24160869	4,129	State Enterprises 国有独资	2,314,900	263,260(4)	5,710,169	Chemical Raw Material Medicine 化学原料药
Shandong Lukang Pharmaceutical Group Co.,Ltd. 山东鲁抗医药集团有限公司(1966)	Jining 济宁市	Shandong 山东省	(0537)2213961 (0537)2218814	7,191	Limited-Liability 有限公司	1,554,893	118,045(8)	3,248,150	Chemistry Medicine 化学医药
Northeast Pharmaceutical General Factory 东北制药总厂(1946)	Shenyang 沈阳市	Liaoning 辽宁省	(024)25806110 (024)25806888	5,492	State-owned 国有企业	1,317,732	34,752(21)	3,723,168	Vitamin C 维生素C
Hangzhou East-China Pharmaceutical Group Co.,Ltd. 杭州华东医药集团有限公司(1992)	Hangzhou 杭州市	Zhejiang 浙江省	(0571)88173388 (0571)88174336	3,915	State-owned 国有企业	1,220,541	209,389(5)	2,694,854	Chemical Raw Material Medicine 化学原料药
Zhejiang Haizheng Group Co., Ltd. 浙江海正集团有限公司(1956)	Taizhou 台州市	Zhejiang 浙江省	(0576)8827890 (0576)8827887	2,772	Joint Stock 股份制	939,992	82,066(12)	2,309,464	Chemical Raw Material Medicine 化学原料药
Zhejiang Xinhecheng Co., Ltd. 浙江新和成股份有限公司(1988)	Shaoxing 绍兴市	Zhejiang 浙江省	(0575)6128692 (0575)6124975	1,766	Joint Stock 股份制	743,840	99,276(9)	862,055	Vitamin E Raw Product 维生素E粗品

Top 10 Cities by Revenue 销售收入排名前10位城市	Province 省	Market share 市场份额 (%)	Number of firms 企业个数
Shijiazhuang 石家庄市	Hebei 河北省	19.97	21
Harbin 哈尔滨市	Heilongjiang 黑龙江省	10.43	2
Taizhou 台州市	Zhejiang 浙江省	5.93	54
Zibo 淄博市	Shandong 山东省	5.40	7
Tianjin 天津市	Tianjin 天津市	5.28	29
Shanghai 上海市	Shanghai 上海市	4.86	37
Shenyang 沈阳市	Liaoning 辽宁省	2.83	8
Jining 济宁市	Shandong 山东省	2.41	2
Hangzhou 杭州市	Zhejiang 浙江省	2.30	11
Shaoxing 绍兴市	Zhejiang 浙江省	1.94	16

10 Major Wholesalers 十家主要批发商	City 城市	Province 省	Telephone/Fax 电话/传真
China National Medicine (Group) Shanghai Corporation 中国医药集团上海公司	Shanghai 上海市	Shanghai 上海市	(021)63211750 (021)63294805
Beijing Medicine Co.,Ltd. 北京医药股份有限公司	Beijing 北京市	Beijing 北京市	(010)84031166 (010)84043500
North China Pharmaceutical Group Sale Co., Ltd. 华药销售有限公司	Shijiazhuang 石家庄市	Hebei 河北省	(0311)6671042 (0311)5051133
Zhejiang Medicines & Health Products Imp & Exp Co.,Ltd. 浙江省医药保健品进出口有限责任公司	Hangzhou 杭州市	Zhejiang 浙江省	(0571)87013288 (0571)87016777
Eastchina Medicine Co.,Ltd. 华东医药股份有限公司	Hangzhou 杭州市	Zhejiang 浙江省	(0571)85159647 (0571)85178578
Ningbo Pharmcutical Co.,Ltd. 宁波医药股份有限公司	Ningbo 宁波市	Zhejiang 浙江省	(0574)87267909 (0574)87267909
Chongqing Medicine Co.,Ltd. 重庆医药股份有限公司	Chongqing 重庆市	Chongqing 重庆市	(023)63842684 (023)63841227
Shanghai Medicines & Health Products Import & Export Corp. 上海市医药保健品进出口公司	Shanghai 上海市	Shanghai 上海市	(021)63290161 (021)63291609
Nanjing Medicine Co.,Ltd. 南京医药股份有限公司	Nanjing 南京市	Jiangsu 江苏省	(025)4520707 (025)4523033
Zhejiang Int'l Medicine Co.,Ltd. 浙江英特药业有限责任公司	Hangzhou 杭州市	Zhejiang 浙江省	(0571)87038653 (0571)87038653

2720: Pharmaceutical Preparations 化学药品制剂制造业

The industry accounts for 0.660% of the total revenue of China's industrial sector in 2002. The rate of return on assets is 6.46%. 75.78% of all firms in the industry made a profit while 24.22% had negative returns.The top province in terms of the industry's revenue is Jiangsu, accounting for 12.96% of the total revenue.
2002年本行业收入占全行业的 0.660%，资产利润率为 6.46%。75.78%的企业赢利，24.22%的企业亏损。收入最高的省为江苏省，占本行业的12.96%。

	Total number of firms 企业总数	Total number of employees 职工总数	Total revenue (Mil.RMB) 总销售收入（百万元）	Total profit (Mil.RMB) 总利润（百万元）	Return on assets 资产利润率 (%)	Return on equity 权益利润率 (%)	Labour productivity ('000 RMB/ worker) 劳动生产率（千元/人）	Debts/ assets 资产负债率 (%)	Total assets (Mil.RMB) 总资产（百万元）
Industry Overall 行业总体	1028	306,940	70,801	6,707	6.46	14.18	89.91	54.41	103,762

	Number of firms 企业个数	Average number of employees 平均职工人数	Average revenue ('000 RMB) 平均销售收入（千元）	Average profit ('000 RMB) 平均利润（千元）	Return on assets 资产利润率 (%)	Return on equity 权益利润率 (%)	Labour productivity ('000 RMB/ worker) 劳动生产率（千元/人）	Debts/ assets 资产负债率 (%)	Average total assets ('000 RMB) 平均总资产（千元）
By ownership 产业所有权									
State-owned 国有	179	285	37,324	2,132	2.98	10.02	44.71	70.27	71,589
Collective-owned 集体	72	270	38,394	2,768	4.89	10.92	48.59	55.23	56,626
Foreign & Overseas Chinese Funded 三资	225	249	121,501	13,240	9.28	18.15	203.01	48.90	142,744
By regional distribution 地区分布									
Central-North 华北	160	282	75,337	7,334	6.09	10.67	102.77	42.93	120,430
Beijing 北京	45	294	109,760	15,152	8.90	14.28	182.40	37.71	170,316
Tianjin 天津	26	340	153,175	12,504	5.06	7.60	97.24	33.47	247,275
Hebei 河北	42	191	32,400	1,119	2.28	7.15	45.88	68.04	48,965
Shanxi 山西	36	362	43,561	3,190	4.14	10.00	66.18	58.61	77,029
Inner Mongolia 内蒙古	11	179	18,471	425	1.35	3.32	68.10	59.36	31,449
Northeast 东北	120	214	31,602	1,461	2.27	5.22	68.69	56.48	64,284
Liaoning 辽宁	51	228	39,184	1,824	2.62	6.31	65.09	58.56	69,705
Jilin 吉林	43	179	23,793	1,490	2.50	5.06	84.53	50.58	59,544
Heilongjiang 黑龙江	26	246	29,643	701	1.14	2.94	56.18	61.29	61,489
Central-East 华东	357	326	81,321	7,573	7.25	17.16	83.43	57.79	104,515
Shanghai 上海	59	314	134,720	8,443	5.07	12.37	120.95	59.06	166,688
Jiangsu 江苏	100	317	91,732	12,740	11.64	24.46	108.94	52.40	109,422
Zhejiang 浙江	72	271	80,458	6,560	6.99	18.26	77.41	61.70	93,797
Anhui 安徽	29	394	42,693	3,214	4.05	8.38	38.29	51.72	79,454
Fujian 福建	24	355	45,620	2,926	3.71	8.03	54.97	53.82	78,915
Jiangxi 江西	20	435	33,502	1,088	1.33	5.20	31.81	74.48	81,957
Shandong 山东	53	341	58,753	5,167	6.94	17.97	73.62	61.37	74,423
Central-South 中南	248	291	63,388	4,854	4.51	10.89	87.61	58.54	107,529
Henan 河南	59	384	38,695	1,108	1.46	4.15	24.62	64.80	75,814
Hubei 湖北	35	306	49,669	4,231	4.11	7.59	59.64	45.88	103,037
Hunan 湖南	35	168	20,679	2,039	5.32	14.00	63.80	61.97	38,301
Guangdong 广东	73	334	120,906	7,720	4.02	10.24	158.52	60.71	191,835
Guangxi 广西	17	250	24,932	1,471	2.96	8.73	54.22	66.06	49,681
Hainan 海南	29	147	59,485	11,393	13.77	26.86	153.06	48.72	82,713
Southwest 西南	91	304	57,383	6,338	7.70	15.78	83.74	51.21	82,337
Chongqing 重庆	14	393	81,136	7,634	6.90	14.82	76.05	53.41	110,583
Sichuan 四川	38	344	59,879	6,207	7.52	17.82	88.09	57.82	82,593
Guizhou 贵州	16	243	24,323	2,892	5.67	13.23	52.61	57.10	50,956
Yunnan 云南	23	225	61,797	8,164	9.43	14.89	104.30	36.65	86,550
Tibet 西藏									
Northwest 西北	52	384	95,802	16,807	16.47	35.16	142.85	53.16	102,066
Shaanxi 陕西	42	365	109,220	19,998	18.46	37.80	176.78	51.15	108,302
Gansu 甘肃	6	410	29,199	405	0.62	2.61	24.54	76.24	65,347
Qinghai 青海	2	729	85,734	15,298	11.96	25.11	45.36	52.37	127,896
Ningxia 宁夏									
Xinjiang 新疆	2	357	23,891	531	0.96	2.17	20.70	55.88	55,444

2720: Pharmaceutical Preparations 化学药品制剂制造业

Year 年份	Number of firms 企业个数	Rate of change 变化率 (%)	Number of employees 职工人数 (人)	Rate of change 变化率 (%)	Total revenue (Mil. RMB) 总销售收入 (百万元)	Rate of change 变化率 (%)	Total profit (Mil RMB) 总利润 (百万元)	Rate of change 变化率 (%)
2000	934		293,845		50,549		4,187	
2001	961	2.89	294,958	0.38	58,200	15.14	4,972	18.75
2002	1028	6.97	306,940	4.06	70,801	21.65	6,707	34.90

Major Products 主要产品	Output 产量	Unit 单位

10 Main Firms with Maximal Revenue (year founded) 收入最大的十家主要企业（创办年份）	City 城市	Province 省	Telephone/fax 电话/传真	Number of employees 职工人数	Ownership 产业所有权	Revenue ('000 RMB) 销售收入 (千元)	Profit('000 RMB) (rank) 利润(千元) (排名)	Total assets ('000 RMB) 总资产 (千元)	Major products 主要产品
Xi'an Janssen Pharmaceutical Ltd. 西安扬森制药有限公司(1985)	Xi'an 西安市	Shannxi 陕西省	(029)3234455 (029)3235161	1,146	Foreign Funded 外商投资	2,485,470	618,362(1)	1,391,583	Motilium Tablet 吗丁啉片
Tianjin Pacific Holdings Ltd. 天津太平（集团）有限公司(1994)	Tianjin 天津市	Tianjin 天津市	(022)23392317 (022)23392317	991	Foreign Funded 外商投资	1,631,813	27,206(63)	856,959	Western Medicine Preparations 西药制剂
Livzon Pharmaceutical Group Inc. 丽珠医药集团服份有限公司(1985)	Zhuhai 珠海市	Guangdong 广东省	(0756)8135902 (0756)8886002	2,355	Overseas Chinese-funded 港澳台资	1,578,600	118,814(11)	1,875,259	Tablet 片剂
Rejoy Group Ltd. Company 利君集团有限责任公司(1938)	Xi'an 西安市	Shannxi 陕西省	(029)4243841 (029)4261550	4,577	Limited-Liability 有限公司	1,154,798	190,018(3)	1,487,102	Erythromycin Alkali 红霉素碱
Beijing Double-Crane Pharmaceutical Co., Ltd. 北京双鹤药业经营有限责任公司(1988)	Beijing 北京市	Beijing 北京市	(010)65060077 (010)65864208	835	Limited-Liability 有限公司	933,999	21,449(85)	346,603	Cefalexin Tablet头孢氨苄片
Zhejiang Medicine Co.,Ltd.-Xinchang Pharmaceutical Factory 浙江医药股份有限公司-新昌制药厂(1954)	Shaoxing 绍兴市	Zhejiang 浙江省	(0575)6022860 (0575)6022746	2,530	Joint Stock 股份制	925,997	112,379(12)	1,078,631	Vitamin E 维生素E
Sino-American Shanghai Squibb Pharmaceutical Co., Ltd. 中美上海施贵宝制药有限公司(1985)	Shanghai 上海市	Shanghai 上海市	(021)64302740 (021)64301498	861	Foreign Funded 外商投资	882,243	52,456(31)	627,113	Chemical Medicine Preparation化学药品制剂
Shanghai Roche Pharmaceutical Ltd. 上海罗氏制药有限公司(1994)	Shanghai 上海市	Shanghai 上海市	(021)50801888 (021)50801800	850	Foreign Funded 外商投资	856,667	59,437(27)	591,423	Chemical Medicine Preparation化学药品制剂
Shanghai New Asiatic Pharmaceutical Co.,Ltd. 上海新亚药业有限公司(1926)	Shanghai 上海市	Shanghai 上海市	(021)58563780 (021)58563797	1,055	Limited-Liability 有限公司	828,876	98,000(15)	969,887	Chemical Medicine Preparation化学药品制剂
Shanghai Xin Xian Feng Pharmaceutical Co., Ltd. 上海新先锋药业有限公司(1950)	Shanghai 上海市	Shanghai 上海市	(021)58552452 (021)58558449	1,587	State-owned 国有企业	805,919	14,936(122)	1,108,404	Chemical Medicine Preparation化学药品制剂

Top 10 Cities by Revenue 销售收入排名前10位城市	Province 省	Market share 市场份额 (%)	Number of firms 企业个数
Shanghai 上海市	Shanghai 上海市	11.23	59
Beijing 北京市	Beijing 北京市	6.98	45
Xi'an 西安市	Shannxi 陕西省	5.89	23
Tianjin 天津市	Tianjin 天津市	5.62	26
Guangzhou 广州市	Guangdong 广东省	4.34	25
Suzhou 苏州市	Jiangsu 江苏省	3.92	26
Zhuhai 珠海市	Guangdong 广东省	3.58	5
Wuxi 无锡市	Jiangsu 江苏省	2.88	8
Shaoxing 绍兴市	Zhejiang 浙江省	2.44	6
Chengdu 成都市	Sichuan 四川省	2.17	20

10 Major Wholesalers 十家主要批发商	City 城市	Province 省	Telephone/Fax 电话/传真
China National Medicine (Group) Shanghai Corporation 中国医药集团上海公司	Shanghai 上海市	Shanghai 上海市	(021)63211750 (021)63294805
Beijing Medicine Co.,Ltd. 北京医药股份有限公司	Beijing 北京市	Beijing 北京市	(010)84031166 (010)84043500
North China Pharmaceutical Group Sale Co., Ltd. 华药销售有限公司	Shijiazhuang 石家庄市	Hebei 河北省	(0311)6671042 (0311)5051133
Zhejiang Medicines & Health Products Imp & Exp Co.,Ltd. 浙江省医药保健品进出口有限责任公司	Hangzhou 杭州市	Zhejiang 浙江省	(0571)87013288 (0571)87016777
Eastchina Medicine Co.,Ltd. 华东医药股份有限公司	Hangzhou 杭州市	Zhejiang 浙江省	(0571)85159647 (0571)85178578
Ningbo Pharmcutical Co.,Ltd. 宁波医药股份有限公司	Ningbo 宁波市	Zhejiang 浙江省	(0574)87267909 (0574)87267909
Chongqing Medicine Co.,Ltd. 重庆医药股份有限公司	Chongqing 重庆市	Chongqing 重庆市	(023)63842684 (023)63841227
Shanghai Medicines & Health Products Import & Export Corp. 上海市医药保健品进出口公司	Shanghai 上海市	Shanghai 上海市	(021)63290161 (021)63291609
Nanjing Medicine Co.,Ltd. 南京医药股份有限公司	Nanjing 南京市	Jiangsu 江苏省	(025)4520707 (025)4523033
Zhejiang Int'l Medicine Co.,Ltd. 浙江英特药业有限责任公司	Hangzhou 杭州市	Zhejiang 浙江省	(0571)87038653 (0571)87038653

2730: Chinese Medicines 中药材及中成药加工业

The industry accounts for 0.641% of the total revenue of China's industrial sector in 2002. The rate of return on assets is 6.54%. 77.50% of all firms in the industry made a profit while 22.50% had negative returns.The top province in terms of the industry's revenue is Jiangsu, accounting for 11.34% of the total revenue.
2002年本行业收入占全行业的0.641%，资产利润率为6.54%。77.50%的企业赢利，22.50%的企业亏损。收入最高的省为江苏省，占本行业的11.34%。

	Total number of firms 企业总数	Total number of employees 职工总数	Total revenue (Mil.RMB) 总销售收入（百万元）	Total profit (Mil.RMB) 总利润（百万元）	Return on assets 资产利润率（%）	Return on equity 权益利润率（%）	Labour productivity ('000 RMB/ worker) 劳动生产率（千元/人）	Debts/ assets 资产负债率（%）	Total assets (Mil.RMB) 总资产（百万元）
Industry Overall 行业总体	1329	325,510	68,769	7,427	6.54	12.57	88.81	48.02	113,651

	Number of firms 企业个数	Average number of employees 平均职工人数	Average revenue ('000 RMB) 平均销售收入（千元）	Average profit ('000 RMB) 平均利润（千元）	Return on assets 资产利润率（%）	Return on equity 权益利润率（%）	Labour productivity ('000 RMB/ worker) 劳动生产率（千元/人）	Debts/ assets 资产负债率（%）	Average total assets ('000 RMB) 平均总资产（千元）
By ownership 产业所有权									
State-owned 国有	260	178	18,027	1,457	3.87	9.43	51.42	58.99	37,673
Collective-owned 集体	108	148	66,093	6,278	10.10	17.54	160.88	42.42	62,142
Foreign & Overseas Chinese Funded 三资	181	224	52,712	4,423	5.63	11.94	100.31	52.86	78,618
By regional distribution 地区分布									
Central-North 华北	175	274	62,713	7,169	7.14	13.28	73.82	46.24	100,427
Beijing 北京	51	270	59,298	9,906	8.41	13.87	77.35	39.38	117,795
Tianjin 天津	23	613	204,914	17,502	5.81	9.87	67.65	41.16	301,393
Hebei 河北	59	217	40,568	4,696	8.99	23.79	79.96	62.21	52,229
Shanxi 山西	24	183	16,730	-92	-0.27	-1.26	50.90	78.28	33,759
Inner Mongolia 内蒙古	18	164	24,584	4,002	9.69	18.55	94.37	47.76	41,302
Northeast 东北	195	218	38,824	6,575	6.73	11.92	111.76	43.55	97,696
Liaoning 辽宁	31	157	19,662	900	2.31	7.76	93.26	70.28	39,007
Jilin 吉林	122	219	45,143	8,495	6.87	11.32	127.83	39.32	123,689
Heilongjiang 黑龙江	42	259	34,609	5,188	7.92	17.59	80.48	54.98	65,512
Central-East 华东	278	298	81,819	8,400	8.62	16.49	97.96	47.75	97,479
Shanghai 上海	36	238	83,808	2,756	2.48	6.14	50.35	59.55	110,941
Jiangsu 江苏	32	481	243,761	27,667	12.72	19.98	161.56	36.31	217,444
Zhejiang 浙江	52	220	62,938	10,739	12.29	24.33	118.11	49.50	87,397
Anhui 安徽	37	187	18,007	862	2.24	4.98	44.80	55.01	38,462
Fujian 福建	21	182	42,084	7,290	12.88	21.76	151.62	40.83	56,622
Jiangxi 江西	54	304	62,146	4,016	6.80	14.24	81.32	52.26	59,091
Shandong 山东	46	442	81,514	8,484	6.73	13.24	80.00	49.16	126,073
Central-South 中南	354	233	39,974	3,382	4.72	9.50	79.98	50.35	71,698
Henan 河南	56	274	27,102	1,975	3.48	8.04	43.70	56.79	56,803
Hubei 湖北	65	207	34,986	3,123	6.69	13.74	71.76	51.31	46,684
Hunan 湖南	52	222	34,682	4,059	5.87	12.47	59.98	52.92	69,147
Guangdong 广东	104	237	52,494	2,875	2.57	4.86	115.61	47.11	111,914
Guangxi 广西	68	237	41,407	5,430	10.87	23.87	82.95	54.45	49,948
Hainan 海南	9	142	31,146	487	0.82	1.24	59.72	33.67	59,394
Southwest 西南	216	227	50,221	5,448	6.08	12.47	95.86	51.24	89,596
Chongqing 重庆	17	457	90,287	11,230	5.40	13.31	93.99	59.45	208,074
Sichuan 四川	75	283	56,006	6,477	5.89	10.20	82.47	42.25	109,979
Guizhou 贵州	63	169	44,885	3,839	6.32	18.78	91.04	66.35	60,750
Yunnan 云南	44	179	46,545	4,517	6.87	13.93	133.75	50.69	65,766
Tibet 西藏	17	90	13,921	3,492	7.02	11.34	129.29	38.11	49,774
Northwest 西北	111	186	22,338	1,636	3.50	6.78	58.27	48.41	46,775
Shaanxi 陕西	57	187	23,144	1,827	4.21	7.22	59.45	41.70	43,383
Gansu 甘肃	29	222	23,459	2,533	5.52	11.00	50.08	49.84	45,910
Qinghai 青海	8	155	18,491	-1,779	-2.08	-4.08	82.32	49.11	85,590
Ningxia 宁夏	4	122	11,210	-104	-0.23	-1.18	66.91	80.54	45,276
Xinjiang 新疆	13	143	22,102	1,431	3.56	10.04	61.60	64.49	40,157

2730: Chinese Medicines 中药材及中成药加工业

Year 年份	Number of firms 企业个数	Rate of change 变化率 (%)	Number of employees 职工人数 (人)	Rate of change 变化率 (%)	Total revenue (Mil. RMB) 总销售收入 (百万元)	Rate of change 变化率 (%)	Total profit (Mil RMB) 总利润 (百万元)	Rate of change 变化率 (%)
2000	1180		300,559		48,252		5,371	
2001	1260	6.78	304,295	1.24	56,330	16.74	6,324	17.74
2002	1329	5.48	325,510	6.97	68,769	22.08	7,427	17.44

Major Products 主要产品	Output 产量	Unit 单位
Chinese Patent Medicine 中成药	60	10,000 Tons 万吨

10 Main Firms with Maximal Revenue (year founded) 收入最大的十家主要企业（创办年份）	City 城市	Province 省	Telephone/fax 电话/传真	Number of employees 职工人数	Ownership 产业所有权	Revenue ('000 RMB) 销售收入(千元)	Profit('000 RMB) (rank) 利润(千元)(排名)	Total assets ('000 RMB) 总资产(千元)	Major products 主要产品
Jiangsu Yangtse River Pharmacy Industry Group Company 江苏扬子江药业集团公司(1971)	Taizhou 泰州市	Jiangsu 江苏省	(0523)6961999 (0523)6914769	1,209	Collective-owned 集体企业	4,054,204	429,012(1)	2,198,931	Fluconazole Tablet 氟康唑片
Jiangxi Hui Ren Group Co., Ltd. 汇仁集团有限公司(1996)	Nanchang 南昌市	Jiangxi 江西省	(0791)5761666 (0791)5761696	4,582	Limited-Liability 有限公司	1,538,464	79,295(20)	664,202	Kidney Treasure 肾宝
Shanghai Leiyun Shang Pharmacy Industry Co., Ltd. 上海雷允上药业有限公司(1998)	Shanghai 上海市	Shanghai 上海市	(021)63503535 (021)63502061	2,754	Limited-Liability 有限公司	1,363,630	43,763(39)	1,142,524	Chinese Patent Medicine 中成药
Beijing Tongrentang Co.,Ltd. 北京同仁堂股份有限公司(1997)	Beijing 北京市	Beijing 北京市	(010)67171775 (010)67171775	2,316	Joint Stock 股份制	1,236,794	262,233(4)	1,913,465	Traditional Chinese Medicine 中药
Nanjing Medicine Industry (Group) Co., Ltd 南京医药产业(集团)有限责任公司(2000)	Nanjing 南京市	Jiangsu 江苏省	(025)4415515 (025)4524848	4,206	State-owned 国有企业	1,028,750	191,960(7)	2,319,130	Chemical Raw Material Medicine 化学原料药
Chiatai Qingchun Bao Pharmaceutical Co.,Ltd. 正大青春宝药业有限公司(1992)	Hangzhou 杭州市	Zhejiang 浙江省	(0571)85121024 (0571)85152635	1,437	Overseas Chinese-funded 港澳台资	890,539	245,074(5)	704,310	Traditional Chinese Medicine Injection 中药针剂
Taiji Group Co., Ltd. 太极集团有限公司(1972)	Chongqing 重庆市	Chongqing 重庆市	(023)72800237 (023)72800513	3,007	Joint Stock 股份制	872,258	83,678(19)	2,336,627	Qumei Reducing Weight Capsule 曲美胶囊
Chengdu Di'ao Pharmaceutical Group Co.,Ltd. 成都地奥集团(1989)	Chengdu 成都市	Sichuan 四川省	(028)85195043 (028)85181150	2,442	Limited-Liability 有限公司	846,002	159,155(8)	1,735,133	Di'ao Xinxiekang Capsule 地奥心血康胶囊
Lu Nan Pharmacy Co., Ltd. 鲁南制药股份有限公司(1995)	Linyi 临沂市	Shandong 山东省	(0539)8225067 (0539)8225390	2,486	Foreign Funded 外商投资	813,398	63,630(28)	1,188,179	Chinese Patent Medicine 中成药
Beijing Tongrentang Science & Technology Development Co., Ltd. 北京同仁堂科技发展股份有限公司(2000)	Beijing 北京市	Beijing 北京市	(010)67621166 (010)67615182	1,460	Joint Stock 股份制	656,853	146,242(11)	739,077	Traditional Chinese Medicine 中药

Top 10 Cities by Revenue 销售收入排名前10位城市	Province 省	Market share 市场份额 (%)	Number of firms 企业个数
Tianjin 天津市	Tianjin 天津市	6.85	23
Taizhou 泰州市	Jiangsu 江苏省	5.91	2
Tonghua 通化市	Jilin 吉林省	4.98	53
Beijing 北京市	Beijing 北京市	4.40	51
Shanghai 上海市	Shanghai 上海市	4.39	36
Chengdu 成都市	Sichuan 四川省	3.91	27
Nanchang 南昌市	Jiangxi 江西省	3.84	7
Guangzhou 广州市	Guangdong 广东省	2.78	23
Hangzhou 杭州市	Zhejiang 浙江省	2.74	19
Guiyang 贵阳市	Guizhou 贵州省	2.70	43

10 Major Wholesalers 十家主要批发商	City 城市	Province 省	Telephone/Fax 电话/传真
China National Medicines & Health Products Import & Export Corporation 中国医药保健品进出口公司	Beijing 北京市	Beijing 北京市	(010)67116688 (010)67121579
Shenzhen Sanjiu Medical & Pharmaceutical Trade Co.,Ltd. 深圳市三九医药贸易有限公司	Shenzhen 深圳市	Guangdong 广东省	(0755)83360999 (0755)83350338
China National Medical Beijing Company 中国医药北京采购供应站	Beijing 北京市	Beijing 北京市	(010)67241347 (010)67241347
Jiangxi Huiren Marketing Co.,Ltd. 江西汇仁营销有限公司	Nanchang 南昌市	Jiangxi 江西省	(0791)5761666 (0791)5761696
Guangdong Medicine Materials Co. 广东省药材公司	Guangzhou 广州市	Guangdong 广东省	(020)87304691 (020)87693175
Shenzhen Medicine Company 深圳市医药公司	Shenzhen 深圳市	Guangdong 广东省	(0755)82489518 (0755)82489632
China Medicine Company 中国医药公司	Beijing 北京市	Beijing 北京市	(010)64952211 (010)64956712
Jiangxi Huiren Group Medicine Scientific Research & Marketing Co.,Ltd. 江西汇仁集团医药科研营销有限公司	Nanchang 南昌市	Jiangxi 江西省	(0791)8108926 (0791)8109466
Ji'nan Pharmacy Industry Group Co.,Ltd. 济南药业集团有限责任公司	Jinan 济南市	Shandong 山东省	(0531)6011745 (0531)6920196
Guangdong Medical & Health Products Imp & Exp Corp. 广东省医药保健品进出口公司	Guangzhou 广州市	Guangdong 广东省	(020)87750820 (020)87750806

2740: Veterinary Medicines 动物药品制造业

The industry accounts for 0.051% of the total revenue of China's industrial sector in 2002. The rate of return on assets is 6.72%. 79.31% of all firms in the industry made a profit while 20.69% had negative returns. The top province in terms of the industry's revenue is Shandong, accounting for 21.65% of the total revenue.
2002年本行业收入占全行业的0.051%，资产利润率为6.72%。79.31%的企业赢利，20.69%的企业亏损。收入最高的省为山东省，占本行业的21.65%。

	Total number of firms 企业总数	Total number of employees 职工总数	Total revenue (Mil.RMB) 总销售收入 (百万元)	Total profit (Mil.RMB) 总利润 (百万元)	Return on assets 资产利润率 (%)	Return on equity 权益利润率 (%)	Labour productivity ('000 RMB/ worker) 劳动生产率 (千元/人)	Debts/ assets 资产负债率 (%)	Total assets (Mil.RMB) 总资产 (百万元)
Industry Overall 行业总体	261	31,740	5,490	413	6.72	14.24	63.97	52.85	6,146

	Number of firms 企业个数	Average number of employees 平均职工人数	Average revenue ('000 RMB) 平均销售收入（千元）	Average profit ('000 RMB) 平均利润 (千元)	Return on assets 资产利润率 (%)	Return on equity 权益利润率 (%)	Labour productivity ('000 RMB/ worker) 劳动生产率 (千元/人)	Debts/ assets 资产负债率 (%)	Average total assets ('000 RMB) 平均总资产 (千元)
By ownership 产业所有权									
State-owned 国有	57	65	5,915	-96	-0.80	-2.17	38.13	63.10	12,028
Collective-owned 集体	40	138	21,576	1,034	7.75	17.73	52.68	56.30	13,349
Foreign & Overseas Chinese Funded 三资	19	131	58,147	6,643	9.56	24.68	156.73	61.27	69,482
By regional distribution 地区分布									
Central-North 华北	43	106	16,696	2,123	12.32	30.75	67.74	59.92	17,231
Beijing 北京	14	80	6,851	305	2.57	5.23	38.49	50.88	11,871
Tianjin 天津	6	166	21,425	1,685	7.13	13.33	37.92	46.52	23,624
Hebei 河北	17	72	18,553	1,206	13.38	48.31	77.63	72.31	9,018
Shanxi 山西	5	106	6,343	231	1.47	3.56	20.79	58.65	15,692
Inner Mongolia 内蒙古	1	670	146,344	55,275	27.47	85.53	180.13	67.89	201,247
Northeast 东北	10	90	7,174	46	0.44	0.97	22.80	54.37	10,257
Liaoning 辽宁	5	136	10,688	45	0.36	1.27	18.82	72.01	12,588
Jilin 吉林	3	32	3,200	42	0.56	0.71	31.80	21.33	7,475
Heilongjiang 黑龙江	2	61	4,347	54	0.62	0.93	37.80	32.91	8,600
Central-East 华东	103	137	30,571	2,699	8.48	17.07	80.90	50.29	31,808
Shanghai 上海	10	103	35,929	9,635	22.44	31.88	132.81	29.61	42,939
Jiangsu 江苏	21	183	41,785	1,509	3.48	5.42	83.07	35.73	43,338
Zhejiang 浙江	14	84	25,713	2,318	8.94	22.28	78.89	59.89	25,944
Anhui 安徽	9	123	7,315	298	3.41	8.80	12.31	61.27	8,744
Fujian 福建	3	175	43,545	6,250	12.54	26.19	144.99	52.12	49,832
Jiangxi 江西	9	118	18,551	654	5.64	10.05	63.41	43.92	11,599
Shandong 山东	37	144	32,126	2,436	7.26	20.71	81.14	64.93	33,539
Central-South 中南	78	93	12,550	371	2.52	4.98	48.08	49.42	14,717
Henan 河南	24	104	13,765	797	5.89	13.52	42.29	56.41	13,517
Hubei 湖北	14	90	19,838	962	4.92	8.20	86.37	40.04	19,575
Hunan 湖南	10	67	6,770	42	0.86	2.26	35.23	61.80	4,908
Guangdong 广东	16	68	14,198	-509	-2.21	-4.45	72.83	50.33	23,009
Guangxi 广西	14	124	5,427	288	3.05	5.50	18.15	44.57	9,444
Hainan 海南									
Southwest 西南	20	212	27,059	679	1.76	4.37	46.64	59.79	38,684
Chongqing 重庆	1	868	250,116	18,278	5.65	10.74	101.85	47.38	323,507
Sichuan 四川	12	217	22,316	-203	-0.64	-1.64	37.71	61.01	31,720
Guizhou 贵州	4	116	2,428	-66	-0.84		6.48	117.14	7,815
Yunnan 云南	3	102	4,519	-668	-5.24		27.02	105.79	12,755
Tibet 西藏									
Northwest 西北	7	103	4,533	71	0.48	1.48	22.96	67.80	14,889
Shaanxi 陕西	4	93	5,002	313	2.34	4.88	32.16	52.14	13,396
Gansu 甘肃	2	172	4,933	-400	-1.64	-10.46	12.71	84.37	24,462
Qinghai 青海									
Ningxia 宁夏									
Xinjiang 新疆	1	11	1,857	46	2.67	17.23	33.18	84.48	1,720

2740: Veterinary Medicines 动物药品制造业

Year 年份	Number of firms 企业个数	Rate of change 变化率 (%)	Number of employees 职工人数 (人)	Rate of change 变化率 (%)	Total revenue (Mil. RMB) 总销售收入 (百万元)	Rate of change 变化率 (%)	Total profit (Mil RMB) 总利润 (百万元)	Rate of change 变化率 (%)
2000	231		28,241		3,201		152	
2001	231	o	27,329	-3.23	3,851	20.31	254	67.11
2002	261	12.99	31,740	16.14	5,490	42.56	413	62.60

Major Products 主要产品	Output 产量	Unit 单位

10 Main Firms with Maximal Revenue (year founded) 收入最大的十家主要企业（创办年份）	City 城市	Province 省	Telephone/fax 电话/传真	Number of employees 职工人数	Ownership 产业所有权	Revenue ('000 RMB) 销售收入 (千元)	Profit('000 RMB) (rank) 利润(千元) (排名)	Total assets ('000 RMB) 总资产 (千元)	Major products 主要产品
Qilu Antibioticos Pharmaceutical Co.,Ltd. 齐鲁安替比奥制药有限公司(1998)	Jinan 济南市	Shandong 山东省	(0531)8202743 (0531)8202744	210	Foreign Funded 外商投资	341,424	31,986(4)	409,833	Cephalosporins Products头孢类原料药
Jiangsu Kanion Pharmaceutical Co., Ltd. 江苏康缘药业股份有限公司(1975)	Lianyungang 连云港市	Jiangsu 江苏省	(0518)5521940 (0518)5521983	822	Joint Stock 股份制	237,580	29,960(5)	426,580	Troche 片剂
Ji'nan Guta Veterinary Pharmacy Co., Ltd. 济南古塔兽药有限责任公司(1992)	Jinan 济南市	Shandong 山东省	(0531)2843079 (0531)2843170	55	Collective-owned 集体企业	150,170	9,560(10)	15,562	Animal's Injection 兽用针剂
Inner Mongolia Biological Pharmaceutical Factory 内蒙古生物药品厂(1958)	Huhhot 呼和浩特市	Inner Mongolia 内蒙古	(0471)3964070 (0471)3964070	670	Joint Stock 股份制	146,344	55,275(1)	201,247	Biological Pharmaceutical For Animals 生物药品
Shanghai Novartis Animal Health Co., Ltd. 上海诺华动物保健有限公司(1990)	Shanghai 上海市	Shanghai 上海市	(021)57160873 (021)57162047	180	Foreign Funded 外商投资	144,821	45,065(2)	195,398	Animal's Medicine 兽药
Hengdian Group Tospo Pharmaceutical (Vet.) Co., Ltd. 横店集团得邦药业（兽药）有限公司(2000)	Jinhua 金华市	Zhejiang 浙江省	(0579)6557197 (0579)6557848	180	Limited-Liability 有限公司	122,381	18,013(8)	181,846	Animal's Medicine 兽药
Xiamen Kingdomway Vitamin Incorporation 厦门金达威维生素股份有限公司(1997)	Xiamen 厦门市	Fujian 福建省	(0592)6511111 (0592)6513636	470	Joint Stock 股份制	118,395	18,429(6)	144,011	Vitamin A 维生素A
Nantong Tian Cheng Health Products Co., Ltd. 南通天成保健品有限公司(1998)	Nantong 南通市	Jiangsu 江苏省	(0513)8802159 (0513)8802389	110	Joint Stock 股份制	108,864	8,024(12)	48,682	Medicine For Poultry 禽药
Zhumadian Hua Zhong Chiatai Co.,Ltd. 驻马店华中正大有限公司(1997)	Zhumadian 驻马店市	Henan 河南省	(0396)2127529 (0396)2623049	261	Foreign Funded 外商投资	106,736	5,603(17)	107,745	Feedstuff Additive饲料添加剂
Shanghai Bao Da Veterinary Pharmaceutical Co., Ltd. 上海宝达兽药制造有限公司(1992)	Shanghai 上海市	Shanghai 上海市	(021)56861616 (021)56860619	175	Foreign Funded 外商投资	88,078	42,786(3)	73,560	Fenbendazole 苯硫咪唑

Top 10 Cities by Revenue 销售收入排名前10位城市	Province 省	Market share 市场份额 (%)	Number of firms 企业个数
Jinan 济南市	Shandong 山东省	14.48	13
Shanghai 上海市	Shanghai 上海市	6.54	10
Chongqing 重庆市	Chongqing 重庆市	4.56	1
Lianyungang 连云港市	Jiangsu 江苏省	4.33	1
Shijiazhuang 石家庄市	Hebei 河北省	3.73	5
Jinhua 金华市	Zhejiang 浙江省	3.71	4
Yancheng 盐城市	Jiangsu 江苏省	3.51	4
Chengdu 成都市	Sichuan 四川省	3.45	5
Guangzhou 广州市	Guangdong 广东省	2.68	7
Huhhot 呼和浩特市	Inner Mongolia 内蒙古	2.67	1

10 Major Wholesalers 十家主要批发商	City 城市	Province 省	Telephone/Fax 电话/传真
China National Medicine (Group) Shanghai Corporation 中国医药集团上海公司	Shanghai 上海市	Shanghai 上海市	(021)63211750 (021)63294805
Beijing Medicine Co.,Ltd. 北京医药股份有限公司	Beijing 北京市	Beijing 北京市	(010)84031166 (010)84043500
North China Pharmaceutical Group Sale Co., Ltd. 华药销售有限公司	Shijiazhuang 石家庄市	Hebei 河北省	(0311)6671042 (0311)5051133
Zhejiang Medicines & Health Products Imp & Exp Co.,Ltd. 浙江省医药保健品进出口有限责任公司	Hangzhou 杭州市	Zhejiang 浙江省	(0571)87013288 (0571)87016777
Eastchina Medicine Co.,Ltd. 华东医药股份有限公司	Hangzhou 杭州市	Zhejiang 浙江省	(0571)85159647 (0571)85178578
Ningbo Pharmcutical Co.,Ltd. 宁波医药股份有限公司	Ningbo 宁波市	Zhejiang 浙江省	(0574)87267909 (0574)87267909
Chongqing Medicine Co.,Ltd. 重庆医药股份有限公司	Chongqing 重庆市	Chongqing 重庆市	(023)63842684 (023)63841227
Shanghai Medicines & Health Products Import & Export Corp. 上海市医药保健品进出口公司	Shanghai 上海市	Shanghai 上海市	(021)63290161 (021)63291609
Nanjing Medicine Co.,Ltd. 南京医药股份有限公司	Nanjing 南京市	Jiangsu 江苏省	(025)4520707 (025)4523033
Zhejiang Int'l Medicine Co.,Ltd. 浙江英特药业有限责任公司	Hangzhou 杭州市	Zhejiang 浙江省	(0571)87038653 (0571)87038653

2750: Biological Products 生物制造业

The industry accounts for 0.159% of the total revenue of China's industrial sector in 2002. The rate of return on assets is 5.61%. 79.10% of all firms in the industry made a profit while 20.90% had negative returns.The top province in terms of the industry's revenue is Hubei, accounting for 19.45% of the total revenue.
2002年本行业收入占全行业的 0.159%，资产利润率为 5.61%。79.10%的企业赢利，20.90%的企业亏损。收入最高的省为湖北省，占本行业的19.45%。

	Total number of firms 企业总数	Total number of employees 职工总数	Total revenue (Mil.RMB) 总销售收入 (百万元)	Total profit (Mil.RMB) 总利润 (百万元)	Return on assets 资产利润率 (%)	Return on equity 权益利润率 (%)	Labour productivity ('000 RMB/ worker) 劳动生产率 (千元/人)	Debts/ assets 资产负债率 (%)	Total assets (Mil.RMB) 总资产 (百万元)
Industry Overall 行业总体	335	75,581	17,057	1,930	5.61	10.95	92.49	48.76	34,401
	Number of firms 企业个数	**Average number of employees 平均职工人数**	**Average revenue ('000 RMB) 平均销售收入 (千元)**	**Average profit ('000 RMB) 平均利润 (千元)**	**Return on assets 资产利润率 (%)**	**Return on equity 权益利润率 (%)**	**Labour productivity ('000 RMB/ worker) 劳动生产率 (千元/人)**	**Debts/ assets 资产负债率 (%)**	**Average total assets ('000 RMB) 平均总资产 (千元)**
By ownership 产业所有权									
State-owned 国有	49	360	28,856	1,040	0.75	1.71	41.00	56.36	139,395
Collective-owned 集体	13	89	22,649	4,186	8.44	11.49	134.48	26.56	49,616
Foreign & Overseas Chinese Funded 三资	79	164	61,661	5,951	5.65	10.59	170.45	46.71	105,414
By regional distribution 地区分布									
Central-North 华北	45	191	42,544	3,571	2.82	5.72	109.60	50.74	126,649
Beijing 北京	28	201	34,172	2,407	1.60	3.32	84.17	51.83	150,353
Tianjin 天津	8	106	80,343	11,104	12.81	23.35	361.07	45.13	86,674
Hebei 河北	7	126	14,309	892	2.29	4.14	81.60	44.63	38,868
Shanxi 山西	2	630	107,370	-895	-0.34	-0.72	72.84	52.52	261,919
Inner Mongolia 内蒙古									
Northeast 东北	31	220	35,303	6,060	5.48	10.99	84.60	50.09	110,506
Liaoning 辽宁	11	162	42,113	9,958	9.67	17.18	150.79	43.69	102,948
Jilin 吉林	16	288	32,248	4,140	3.24	6.82	56.69	52.41	127,613
Heilongjiang 黑龙江	4	103	28,794	3,022	4.81	12.04	110.27	60.09	62,864
Central-East 华东	129	170	45,143	4,375	5.72	11.14	100.50	48.69	76,527
Shanghai 上海	28	173	49,949	5,834	4.68	8.03	133.69	41.72	124,651
Jiangsu 江苏	26	136	36,519	3,206	9.55	19.43	71.72	50.83	33,563
Zhejiang 浙江	21	332	92,983	10,340	7.54	15.05	99.33	49.91	137,201
Anhui 安徽	9	123	23,655	3,387	5.82	16.79	117.53	65.35	58,218
Fujian 福建	10	113	22,000	554	0.78	2.00	88.86	61.26	71,439
Jiangxi 江西	8	109	14,525	1,185	2.71	4.63	93.19	41.32	43,667
Shandong 山东	27	127	36,063	2,038	5.29	11.10	85.86	52.36	38,528
Central-South 中南	88	317	75,323	9,503	7.77	14.73	92.60	47.28	122,348
Henan 河南	13	140	29,147	3,665	6.18	17.35	169.10	64.38	59,295
Hubei 湖北	28	620	118,503	14,236	9.58	17.03	67.14	43.75	148,591
Hunan 湖南	4	88	27,396	7,411	8.16	13.00	81.56	37.26	90,847
Guangdong 广东	34	201	71,077	7,588	6.95	13.93	130.97	50.09	109,130
Guangxi 广西	6	202	38,304	5,842	2.49	5.08	95.71	50.99	234,449
Hainan 海南	3	114	58,463	22,441	18.98	23.10	210.70	17.85	118,238
Southwest 西南	29	204	31,768	3,658	5.26	10.87	69.55	51.56	69,485
Chongqing 重庆	1	106	5,833	-8,343	-14.29	-220.60		93.52	58,390
Sichuan 四川	21	213	36,964	5,775	10.32	23.80	70.40	56.64	55,956
Guizhou 贵州	3	154	18,680	124	0.21	0.47	59.30	55.07	58,153
Yunnan 云南	4	216	20,783	-1,806	-1.19	-1.88	79.23	36.68	151,784
Tibet 西藏									
Northwest 西北	13	343	51,885	5,764	2.86	5.39	61.79	46.95	201,739
Shaanxi 陕西	7	227	64,350	7,075	2.77	4.99	78.67	44.39	255,095
Gansu 甘肃	4	699	48,935	4,487	2.54	5.75	45.83	55.84	176,767
Qinghai 青海	1	50	25,410	7,129	31.94	41.35	440.80	22.74	22,317
Ningxia 宁夏									
Xinjiang 新疆	1	26	2,904	324	0.30	0.47	18.50	36.06	107,559

2750: Biological Products 生物制造业

Year 年份	Number of firms 企业个数	Rate of change 变化率 (%)	Number of employees 职工人数 (人)	Rate of change 变化率 (%)	Total revenue (Mil. RMB) 总销售收入 (百万元)	Rate of change 变化率 (%)	Total profit (Mil RMB) 总利润 (百万元)	Rate of change 变化率 (%)
2000	271		53,072		11,228		1,414	
2001	305	12.55	69,307	30.59	14,820	31.99	1,918	35.64
2002	335	9.84	75,581	9.05	17,057	15.09	1,930	0.63

Major Products 主要产品	Output 产量	Unit 单位

10 Main Firms with Maximal Revenue (year founded) 收入最大的十家主要企业（创办年份）	City 城市	Province 省	Telephone/fax 电话/传真	Number of employees 职工人数	Ownership 产业所有权	Revenue ('000 RMB) 销售收入 (千元)	Profit('000 RMB) (rank) 利润(千元) (排名)	Total assets ('000 RMB) 总资产 (千元)	Major products 主要产品
Wanji Pharmacy Industry Co., Ltd.	Shenzhen	Guangdong	(0755)25505322		Overseas Chinese-funded				American Ginseng Products
万基药业有限公司(1991)	深圳市	广东省	(0755)25505265	3,600	港澳台资	1,450,119	173,976(1)	1,444,836	洋参制品
Sheng Hua Group Stock Co., Ltd.	Huzhou	Zhejiang	(0572)8401888		Limited-Liability				Biological Pesticide
升华集团控股有限公司(2001)	湖州市	浙江省	(0572)8401828	4,753	有限公司	1,355,105	132,827(3)	1,928,655	生物农药
Hong Tao K Group Co., Ltd.	Wuhan	Hubei	(027)67128632		Joint Stock				Haematic Tonic红桃
红桃开集团股份有限公司(1994)	武汉市	湖北省	(027)67128559	8,538	股份制	757,408	94,889(4)	1,403,653	K生血剂
Wuhan Spring Biological Engineering Stock Co.,Ltd.	Wuhan	Hubei	(027)87889790		Joint Stock				Cough and Asthma Tablet
武汉春天生物工程股份有限公司(1995)	武汉市	湖北省	(027)87640797	385	股份制	487,807	133,946(2)	340,156	咳喘片
Shanghai Institute Of Biological Products	Shanghai	Shanghai	(021)62803189		State-owned				Blood Products
上海生物制品研究所(1949)	上海市	上海市	(021)62801807	1,463	国有企业	332,414	39,088(12)	659,134	血液制品
Shandong Green Leaves Pharmacy Co., Ltd.	Yantai	Shandong	(0535)6717618		Joint Stock				Medicine injection
山东绿叶制药股份有限公司(1994)	烟台市	山东省	(0535)6717718	866	股份制	259,028	37,053(15)	360,430	针剂
Shanghai Xinxing Medicine Co., Ltd.	Shanghai	Shanghai	(021)68560091		Joint Stock				Biological Pharmaceutical
上海新兴医药股份有限公司(1989)	上海市	上海市	(021)68568490	371	股份制	254,121	17,415(37)	423,923	生物制品
Chengdu Rong Sheng Pharmaceutical Co., Ltd.	Chengdu	Sichuan	(028)84418893		Limited-Liability				Blood Products
成都蓉生药业有限责任公司(1997)	成都市	四川省	(028)84418893	630	有限公司	245,490	59,885(7)	308,558	血液制品
Shanghai RAAS Blood Products Co.,Ltd.	Shanghai	Shanghai	(021)64303911		Foreign Funded				Human Serum Albumin人
上海莱士血制品有限公司(1992)	上海市	上海市	(021)64301713	756	外商投资	213,139	33,118(16)	422,437	血白蛋白
Guangxi Beisheng Pharmaceutical Ltd.	Beihai	Guangxi	(0779)3226335		Joint Stock				Biological Pharmaceutical
广西北生药业股份有限公司(1993)	北海市	广西	(0779)3226336	669	股份制	199,118	34,831(17)	1,156,378	生物制药

Top 10 Cities by Revenue 销售收入排名前10位城市	Province 省	Market share 市场份额 (%)	Number of firms 企业个数
Wuhan 武汉市	Hubei 湖北省	18.52	20
Shenzhen 深圳市	Guangdong 广东省	11.15	12
Huzhou 湖州市	Zhejiang 浙江省	8.80	4
Shanghai 上海市	Shanghai 上海市	8.20	28
Beijing 北京市	Beijing 北京市	5.61	28
Chengdu 成都市	Sichuan 四川省	4.20	11
Tianjin 天津市	Tianjin 天津市	3.77	8
Yantai 烟台市	Shandong 山东省	3.01	5
Changchun 长春市	Jilin 吉林省	2.87	12
Xi'an 西安市	Shannxi 陕西省	2.52	3

10 Major Wholesalers 十家主要批发商	City 城市	Province 省	Telephone/Fax 电话/传真
China National Medicine (Group) Shanghai Corporation	Shanghai	Shanghai	(021)63211750
中国医药集团上海公司	上海市	上海市	(021)63294805
Beijing Medicine Co.,Ltd.	Beijing	Beijing	(010)84031166
北京医药股份有限公司	北京市	北京市	(010)84043500
North China Pharmaceutical Group Sale Co., Ltd.	Shijiazhuang	Hebei	(0311)6671042
华药销售有限公司	石家庄市	河北省	(0311)5051133
Zhejiang Medicines & Health Products Imp & Exp Co.,Ltd.	Hangzhou	Zhejiang	(0571)87013288
浙江省医药保健品进出口有限责任公司	杭州市	浙江省	(0571)87016777
Eastchina Medicine Co.,Ltd.	Hangzhou	Zhejiang	(0571)85159647
华东医药股份有限公司	杭州市	浙江省	(0571)85178578
Ningbo Pharmceutical Co.,Ltd.	Ningbo	Zhejiang	(0574)87267909
宁波医药股份有限公司	宁波市	浙江省	(0574)87267909
Chongqing Medicine Co.,Ltd.	Chongqing	Chongqing	(023)63842684
重庆医药股份有限公司	重庆市	重庆市	(023)63841227
Shanghai Medicines & Health Products Import & Export Corp.	Shanghai	Shanghai	(021)63290161
上海市医药保健品进出口公司	上海市	上海市	(021)63291609
Nanjing Medicine Co.,Ltd.	Nanjing	Jiangsu	(025)4520707
南京医药股份有限公司	南京市	江苏省	(025)4523033
Zhejiang Int'l Medicine Co.,Ltd.	Hangzhou	Zhejiang	(0571)87038653
浙江英特药业有限责任公司	杭州市	浙江省	(0571)87038653

2811: Synthetic Fibre Pulp 化纤浆粕制造业

The industry accounts for 0.022% of the total revenue of China's industrial sector in 2002. The rate of return on assets is 1.21%. 83.33% of all firms in the industry made a profit while 16.67% had negative returns.The top province in terms of the industry's revenue is Shandong, accounting for 29.90% of the total revenue.
2002年本行业收入占全行业的0.022%，资产利润率为1.21%。83.33%的企业赢利，16.67%的企业亏损。收入最高的省为山东省，占本行业的29.90%。

	Total number of firms 企业总数	Total number of employees 职工总数	Total revenue (Mil.RMB) 总销售收入（百万元）	Total profit (Mil.RMB) 总利润（百万元）	Return on assets 资产利润率（%）	Return on equity 权益利润率（%）	Labour productivity ('000 RMB/ worker) 劳动生产率（千元/人）	Debts/ assets 资产负债率（%）	Total assets (Mil.RMB) 总资产（百万元）
Industry Overall 行业总体	30	15,836	2,319	50	1.21	5.04	59.13	76.07	4,181

	Number of firms 企业个数	Average number of employees 平均职工人数	Average revenue ('000 RMB) 平均销售收入（千元）	Average profit ('000 RMB) 平均利润（千元）	Return on assets 资产利润率（%）	Return on equity 权益利润率（%）	Labour productivity ('000 RMB/ worker) 劳动生产率（千元/人）	Debts/ assets 资产负债率（%）	Average total assets ('000 RMB) 平均总资产（千元）
By ownership 产业所有权									
State-owned 国有	5	1,474	208,109	2,886	0.70	3.74	37.39	81.38	414,194
Collective-owned 集体	6	146	18,628	-12	-0.04	-0.15	22.21	71.90	27,636
Foreign & Overseas Chinese Funded 三资	5	239	51,004	3,096	4.10	15.70	41.29	73.88	75,505
By regional distribution 地区分布									
Central-North 华北	3	834	123,887	15,223	7.42	23.74	176.85	68.74	205,172
Beijing 北京									
Tianjin 天津	1	300	28,000	3,300	3.38	8.41	23.40	59.80	97,660
Hebei 河北	2	1,102	171,831	21,185	8.18	27.67	197.75	70.43	258,929
Shanxi 山西									
Inner Mongolia 内蒙古									
Northeast 东北	3	681	79,945	-9,204	-3.81	-14.34	23.82	73.43	241,540
Liaoning 辽宁	1	12	18,456	20	1.85	3.54	131.58	47.64	1,079
Jilin 吉林	2	1,016	110,690	-13,817	-3.82	-14.40	23.18	73.47	361,770
Heilongjiang 黑龙江									
Central-East 华东	14	364	85,263	496	0.57	2.65	58.29	78.32	86,238
Shanghai 上海	2	212	49,379	-3,290	-3.40	-24.58	25.70	86.16	96,744
Jiangsu 江苏	4	278	56,545	1,423	2.35	33.94	38.88	93.09	60,648
Zhejiang 浙江	1	294	65,064	2,553	5.80	33.73	44.71	82.81	44,035
Anhui 安徽	4	253	27,544	542	1.90	11.28	39.10	83.20	28,566
Fujian 福建									
Jiangxi 江西									
Shandong 山东	3	752	231,166	1,037	0.51	1.62	84.37	68.77	204,319
Central-South 中南	7	808	59,756	3,331	1.54	7.58	22.55	79.65	215,981
Henan 河南	4	1,316	86,148	5,018	1.40	7.61	20.74	81.62	358,818
Hubei 湖北									
Hunan 湖南									
Guangdong 广东	3	132	24,568	1,083	4.24	7.41	46.59	42.74	25,533
Guangxi 广西									
Hainan 海南									
Southwest 西南									
Chongqing 重庆									
Sichuan 四川									
Guizhou 贵州									
Yunnan 云南									
Tibet 西藏									
Northwest 西北	3	178	31,884	711	1.75	4.63	38.14	62.13	40,555
Shaanxi 陕西									
Gansu 甘肃	1	53	5,620	210	2.70	9.21	64.51	70.69	7,780
Qinghai 青海									
Ningxia 宁夏									
Xinjiang 新疆	2	241	45,017	962	1.69	4.39	35.23	61.55	56,942

2811: Synthetic Fibre Pulp 化纤浆粕制造业

Year 年份	Number of firms 企业个数	Rate of change 变化率 (%)	Number of employees 职工人数 (人)	Rate of change 变化率 (%)	Total revenue (Mil. RMB) 总销售收入 (百万元)	Rate of change 变化率 (%)	Total profit (Mil RMB) 总利润 (百万元)	Rate of change 变化率 (%)
2000	30		17,512		2,680		78	
2001	30	o	16,933	-3.31	2,411	-10.04	-30	-
2002	30	o	15,836	-6.48	2,319	-3.82	50	-

Major Products 主要产品	Output 产量	Unit 单位
Chemical Fibre 化学纤维	991	10,000 Tons 万吨
Chemical Fibre Pulp Dreg 化纤用浆泊	37	10,000 Tons 万吨

10 Main Firms with Maximal Revenue (year founded) 收入最大的十家主要企业（创办年份）	City 城市	Province 省	Telephone/fax 电话/传真	Number of employees 职工人数	Ownership 产业所有权	Revenue ('000 RMB) 销售收入 (千元)	Profit('000 RMB) (rank) 利润(千元) (排名)	Total assets ('000 RMB) 总资产 (千元)	Major products 主要产品
Shandong Gaomi Chemical Fibre Group Co., Ltd. 山东高密化纤股份有限公司(1971)	Weifang 潍坊市	Shandong 山东省	(0536)2323121 (0536)2323187	2,029	State-owned 国有企业	624,837	234(16)	526,905	Cotton Pulp 棉浆粕
Hebei Jigao Chemical Fibre Co., Ltd. 河北吉藁化纤有限责任公司(1989)	Shihjiazhuang 石家庄市	Hebei 河北省	(0311)8158029 (0311)8048224	1,783	Limited-Liability 有限公司	282,879	42350(1)	450,649	Cotton Pulp 棉浆粕
Henan Shen Li Group Co.,Ltd. 河南神力集团有限公司(1994)	Sanmenxia 三门峡市	Henan 河南省	(0398)3833573 (0398)3832214	4,576	State-owned 国有企业	250,481	16,589(2)	1,297,131	Cotton Pulp 棉浆粕
Jilin Chen Ming Paper Co., Ltd. 吉林晨鸣纸业有限公司(2001)	Yanbian 延边州	Jilin 吉林省	(0433)3406624 (0433)3419200	1,286	Joint Stock 股份制	164,980	6,717(4)	209,400	
Kabool (Lianyungang) Royoa Co.,Ltd. 甲乙(连云港)粘胶有限公司(1995)	Lianyungang 连云港市	Jiangsu 江苏省	(0518)5150851 (0518)5150014	328	Foreign Funded 外商投资	120,818	7,246(3)	167,736	Viscose Fibre Cotton Pulp 粘胶纤维棉浆粕
Luoyang High-Tecnology Development Zone Naneng Polyester Co.,Ltd. 洛阳市高新技术开发区南峰聚酯有限公司(1997)	Luoyang 洛阳市	Henan 河南省	(0379)4759391 (0379)4759783	216	Limited-Liability 有限公司	84,481	4,568(5)	67,391	Polyester Slices 聚酯切片
Anhui Xue Long Chemical Fibre Co., Ltd. 安徽雪龙化纤有限公司(2000)	Suzhou 宿州市	Anhui 安徽省	(0557)3903355 (0557)3900500	526	Limited-Liability 有限公司	82,641	440(14)	76,658	Cotton Pulp 棉浆粕
Shanghai Chemical Fibre Pulp Dreg General Factory 上海化纤浆粕总厂(1996)	Shanghai 上海市	Shanghai 上海市	(021)57503231 (021)57503231	389	State-owned 国有企业	79,336	-	185,744	Cotton Pulp 棉浆粕
Manas Chemical Fibre & Cotton Pulp Dreg Factory 玛纳斯县化纤棉浆粕厂(1995)	Changji 昌吉州	Xinjiang 新疆	(0994)6620040 (0994)6620095	331	Collective-owned 集体企业	72,801	590(13)	84,220	Cotton Pulp 棉浆粕
Shangyu Chemical Fibre Co., Ltd. 上虞化纤有限责任公司(1970)	Shaoxing 绍兴市	Zhejiang 浙江省	(0575)2164161 (0575)2163116	294	Limited-Liability 有限公司	65,064	2,553(9)	44,035	Cotton Pulp 棉浆粕

Top 10 Cities by Revenue 销售收入排名前10位城市	Province 省	Market share 市场份额 (%)	Number of firms 企业个数
Weifang 潍坊市	Shandong 山东省	26.94	1
Shijiazhuang 石家庄市	Hebei 河北省	12.20	1
Sanmenxia 三门峡市	Henan 河南省	10.80	1
Yanbian 延边州	Jilin 吉林省	9.55	2
Lianyungang 连云港市	Jiangsu 江苏省	5.21	1
Shanghai 上海市	Shanghai 上海市	4.26	2
Luoyang 洛阳市	Henan 河南省	3.64	1
Suzhou 宿州市	Anhui 安徽省	3.56	1
Changji 昌吉州	Xinjiang 新疆	3.14	1
Jining 济宁市	Shandong 山东省	2.96	1

10 Major Wholesalers 十家主要批发商	City 城市	Province 省	Telephone/Fax 电话/传真
Shanghai Shenda Co.,Ltd. 上海申达股份有限公司	Shanghai 上海市	Shanghai 上海市	(021)62319898 (021)62317250
Orient International Holding Silk Group Corportion 东方国际集团丝绸进出口有限公司	Shanghai 上海市	Shanghai 上海市	(021)64662288 (021)64677788
Nanjing Textiles Import & Export Co.,Ltd. 南京纺织品进出口股份有限公司	Nanjing 南京市	Jiangsu 江苏省	(025)3306789 (025)3300518
Zhejiang Textiles Import & Export Group Co.,Ltd. 浙江省纺织品进出口集团有限公司	Hangzhou 杭州市	Zhejiang 浙江省	(0571)87075888 (0571)87079234
Zhejiang Orient Holdings Co.,Ltd. 浙江东方集团股份有限公司	Hangzhou 杭州市	Zhejiang 浙江省	(0571)87215678 (0571)87215000
Zhejiang Silk Holding Co.,ltd. 浙江省丝绸集团有限公司	Hangzhou 杭州市	Zhejiang 浙江省	(0571)85195588 (0571)85192540
Guangdong Silk (Group) Corporation 广东省丝绸（集团）公司	Guangzhou 广州市	Guangdong 广东省	(020)83337448 (020)83332995
Shanghai Costume Group Co.,Ltd. 上海服装（集团）有限公司	Shanghai 上海市	Shanghai 上海市	(021)62748598 (021)62414773
Orient International Holding Shanghai Textiles Import & Export Co.Ltd. 东方国际集团上海市针织品进出口有限公司	Shanghai 上海市	Shanghai 上海市	(021)63218855 (021)63299560
Jiangsu Textiles Import & Export Group Co.,Ltd. 江苏省纺织品进出口集团股份有限公司	Nanjing 南京市	Jiangsu 江苏省	(025)6895000 (025)4400800

2812: Rayon Fibre 粘胶纤维制造业

The industry accounts for 0.091% of the total revenue of China's industrial sector in 2002. The rate of return on assets is 0.94%. 80.95% of all firms in the industry made a profit while 19.05% had negative returns.The top province in terms of the industry's revenue is Jilin, accounting for 19.53% of the total revenue.
2002年本行业收入占全行业的 0.091%，资产利润率为 0.94%。80.95%的企业赢利，19.05%的企业亏损。收入最高的省为吉林省，占本行业的19.53%。

	Total number of firms 企业总数	Total number of employees 职工总数	Total revenue (Mil.RMB) 总销售收入 (百万元)	Total profit (Mil.RMB) 总利润 (百万元)	Return on assets 资产利润率 (%)	Return on equity 权益利润率 (%)	Labour productivity ('000 RMB/ worker) 劳动生产率 (千元/人)	Debts/ assets 资产负债率 (%)	Total assets (Mil.RMB) 总资产 (百万元)
Industry Overall 行业总体	63	66,673	9,745	194	0.94	2.68	37.61	65.06	20,687

	Number of firms 企业个数	Average number of employees 平均职工人数	Average revenue ('000 RMB) 平均销售收入 (千元)	Average profit ('000 RMB) 平均利润 (千元)	Return on assets 资产利润率 (%)	Return on equity 权益利润率 (%)	Labour productivity ('000 RMB/ worker) 劳动生产率 (千元/人)	Debts/ assets 资产负债率 (%)	Average total assets ('000 RMB) 平均总资产 (千元)
By ownership 产业所有权									
State-owned 国有	4	340	75,608	-7,831	-2.84	-7.95	32.04	64.33	276,123
Collective-owned 集体	7	139	26,185	910	9.01	22.55	16.73	60.04	10,092
Foreign & Overseas Chinese Funded 三资	13	345	76,627	1,231	1.42	3.12	58.74	54.63	86,928
By regional distribution 地区分布									
Central-North 华北	6	1,619	182,466	-7,905	-1.49	-3.34	28.09	55.26	528,818
Beijing 北京	1	85	6,682	56	0.97	1.77	24.73	45.54	5,793
Tianjin 天津	1	541	86,058	-1,611	-4.63	-27.36	-13.84	83.06	34,767
Hebei 河北	3	2,666	280,108	-16,522	-1.60	-3.57	30.38	55.28	1,034,331
Shanxi 山西	1	1,093	161,733	3,692	12.58	16.14	32.33	22.07	29,352
Inner Mongolia 内蒙古									
Northeast 东北	4	4,386	662,198	11,320	0.71	2.07	35.24	65.60	1,587,872
Liaoning 辽宁	3	2,348	248,414	-16,433	-1.79	-8.93	9.67	79.94	917,289
Jilin 吉林	1	10,497	1,903,550	94,578	2.63	5.79	52.40	54.63	3,599,623
Heilongjiang 黑龙江									
Central-East 华东	35	599	103,008	1,893	1.04	3.86	44.43	72.95	181,580
Shanghai 上海	8	195	39,699	1,111	4.98	11.77	37.41	57.65	22,286
Jiangsu 江苏	8	533	132,484	7,198	4.58	9.28	72.48	50.60	157,049
Zhejiang 浙江	10	384	69,067	1,685	1.77	3.44	42.41	48.48	94,940
Anhui 安徽									
Fujian 福建	3	139	119,220	2,087	3.24	3.91	268.25	17.10	64,446
Jiangxi 江西	2	2,042	187,056	-16,416	-2.23	-5.45	20.13	59.07	736,444
Shandong 山东	4	1,703	201,346	2,383	0.41		30.44	109.95	576,252
Central-South 中南	15	797	86,675	3,477	1.78	3.82	32.46	53.42	195,229
Henan 河南	5	1,768	197,732	12,240	2.44	4.75	36.62	48.63	502,039
Hubei 湖北	3	93	27,174	320	3.06	11.59	90.04	73.56	10,433
Hunan 湖南	1	2,375	146,259	-11,692	-3.76	-41.78	10.53	91.00	311,031
Guangdong 广东	6	76	13,947	280	2.22	4.40	30.83	49.62	12,651
Guangxi 广西									
Hainan 海南									
Southwest 西南	3	2,164	365,414	25,833	4.13	14.32	45.73	71.19	626,122
Chongqing 重庆									
Sichuan 四川	3	2,164	365,414	25,833	4.13	14.32	45.73	71.19	626,122
Guizhou 贵州									
Yunnan 云南									
Tibet 西藏									
Northwest 西北									
Shaanxi 陕西									
Gansu 甘肃									
Qinghai 青海									
Ningxia 宁夏									
Xinjiang 新疆									

Year 年份	Number of firms 企业个数	Rate of change 变化率 (%)	Number of employees 职工人数 (人)	Rate of change 变化率 (%)	Total revenue (Mil. RMB) 总销售收入 (百万元)	Rate of change 变化率 (%)	Total profit (Mil RMB) 总利润 (百万元)	Rate of change 变化率 (%)
2000	74		73,777		10,199		225	
2001	64	-13.51	72,296	-2.01	9,521	-6.65	-255	-
2002	63	-1.56	66,673	-7.78	9,745	2.35	194	-

Major Products 主要产品	Output 产量	Unit 单位
Viscose Fibre 粘胶纤维	68	10,000 Tons 万吨

10 Main Firms with Maximal Revenue (year founded) 收入最大的十家主要企业（创办年份）	City 城市	Province 省	Telephone/fax 电话/传真	Number of employees 职工人数	Ownership 产业所有权	Revenue ('000 RMB) 销售收入(千元)	Profit('000 RMB) (rank) 利润(千元)(排名)	Total assets ('000 RMB) 总资产(千元)	Major products 主要产品
Jilin Chemical Fibre Group Co.,Ltd.	Jilin	Jilin	(0432)3502420		State Enterprises				Viscose staple Fiber粘
吉林化纤集团有限责任公司(1964)	吉林市	吉林省	(0432)3058453	10,497	国有独资	1,903,550	94578(1)	3,599,623	胶短纤维
Dandong Chemical Fibre (Group) Co.,Ltd.	Dandong	Liaoning	(0415)6192379		State Enterprises				Viscose staple Fiber粘
丹东化学纤维集团股份有限公司(1957)	丹东市	辽宁省	(0415)6160297	6,927	国有独资	736,883	-	2,740,217	胶短纤维
Shandong Weifang Hai Long Co., Ltd.	Weifang	Shandong	(0536)7275000		Joint Stock				Viscose staple Fiber粘
山东潍坊海龙股份有限公司(1989)	潍坊市	山东省	(0536)7252479	4,328	股份制	681,451	34,616(5)	1,270,365	胶短纤维
Nanjing Chemical Fibre Co., Ltd.	Nanjing	Jiangsu	(025)5561011		Joint Stock				Viscose Filament
南京化纤股份有限公司(1992)	南京市	江苏省	(025)5562252	2,426	股份制	500,730	50,060(4)	779,050	粘胶长丝
Hangzhou B.P.Chemical Fibre Co.,Ltd.	Hangzhou	Zhejiang	(0571)88091888		Overseas Chinese-funded				Viscose Filament
杭州蓝孔雀化学纤维〈股份〉有限公司(1993)	杭州市	浙江省	(0571)88095538	2,763	港澳台资	358,559	2,034(19)	596,245	粘胶长丝
Chengdu Huaming Cellophane Co.,Ltd.	Chengdu	Sichuan	(028)83302560		Joint Stock				Viscose staple Fiber粘
成都华明玻璃纸股份有限公司(1993)	成都市	四川省	(028)83302625	1,484	股份制	309,988	6,612(8)	281,465	胶短纤维
Sanyou Group Chemical Fibre Co., Ltd	Tangshan	Hebei	(0315)8333851		State-owned				Viscose staple Fiber粘
唐山三友集团化纤有限公司(1999)	唐山市	河北省	(0315)8333990	951	国有企业	254,390	-	949,007	胶短纤维
Yuyao Shuang Xiang Chemical Fibre Co., Ltd.	Ningbo	Zhejiang	(0574)62625400		Limited-Liability				Viscose staple Fiber粘
余姚双象化纤有限责任公司(1963)	宁波市	浙江省	(0574)62625172	621	有限公司	235,858	5,596(9)	283,913	胶短纤维
Jiujiang Chemical Fibre Co., Ltd.	Jiujiang	Jiangxi	(0792)8316114		Joint Stock				Viscose Filament
九江化纤股份有限公司(1996)	九江市	江西省	(0792)8316565	3,318	股份制	219,624	8,840(7)	759,665	粘胶长丝
Fujian Qiao Cheng Chemical Fibre Co., Ltd.	Quanzhou	Fujian	(0595)8093663		Overseas Chinese-funded				Chemical Fibre
福建侨成化纤有限公司(2001)	泉州市	福建省	(0595)8091663	168	港澳台资	181,700	2,285(17)	113,160	化纤

Top 10 Cities by Revenue 销售收入排名前10位城市	Province 省	Market share 市场份额 (%)	Number of firms 企业个数
Jilin 吉林市	Jilin 吉林省	19.53	1
Xinxiang 新乡市	Henan 河南省	9.44	2
Dandong 丹东市	Liaoning 辽宁省	7.56	1
Weifang 潍坊市	Shandong 山东省	7.55	2
Yibin 宜宾市	Sichuan 四川省	7.42	1
Baoding 保定市	Hebei 河北省	5.94	1
Nanjing 南京市	Jiangsu 江苏省	5.36	2
Suzhou 苏州市	Jiangsu 江苏省	3.95	2
Jiujiang 九江市	Jiangxi 江西省	3.84	2
Hangzhou 杭州市	Zhejiang 浙江省	3.84	2

10 Major Wholesalers 十家主要批发商	City 城市	Province 省	Telephone/Fax 电话/传真
Shanghai Shenda Co.,Ltd.	Shanghai	Shanghai	(021)62319898
上海申达股份有限公司	上海市	上海市	(021)62317250
Orient International Holding Silk Group Corportion	Shanghai	Shanghai	(021)64662288
东方国际集团丝绸进出口有限公司	上海市	上海市	(021)64677788
Nanjing Textiles Import & Export Co.,Ltd.	Nanjing	Jiangsu	(025)3306789
南京纺织品进出口股份有限公司	南京市	江苏省	(025)3300518
Zhejiang Textiles Import & Export Group Co.,Ltd.	Hangzhou	Zhejiang	(0571)87075888
浙江省纺织品进出口集团有限公司	杭州市	浙江省	(0571)87079234
Zhejiang Orient Holdings Co.,Ltd.	Hangzhou	Zhejiang	(0571)87215678
浙江东方集团股份有限公司	杭州市	浙江省	(0571)87215000
Zhejiang Silk Holding Co.,ltd.	Hangzhou	Zhejiang	(0571)85195588
浙江省丝绸集团有限公司	杭州市	浙江省	(0571)85192540
Guangdong Silk (Group) Corporation	Guangzhou	Guangdong	(020)83337448
广东省丝绸（集团）公司	广州市	广东省	(020)83332995
Shanghai Costume Group Co.,Ltd.	Shanghai	Shanghai	(021)62748598
上海服装（集团）有限公司	上海市	上海市	(021)62414773
Orient International Holding Shanghai Textiles Import & Export Co.Ltd.	Shanghai	Shanghai	(021)63218855
东方国际集团上海市针织品进出口有限公司	上海市	上海市	(021)63299560
Jiangsu Textiles Import & Export Group Co.,Ltd.	Nanjing	Jiangsu	(025)6895000
江苏省纺织品进出口集团股份有限公司	南京市	江苏省	(025)4400800

2819: Cellulose Fibre 其他纤维素纤维制造业

The industry accounts for 0.047% of the total revenue of China's industrial sector in 2002. The rate of return on assets is 13.82%. 79.41% of all firms in the industry made a profit while 20.59% had negative returns.The top province in terms of the industry's revenue is Hubei, accounting for 42.53% of the total revenue.
2002年本行业收入占全行业的0.047%，资产利润率为13.82%。79.41%的企业赢利，20.59%的企业亏损。收入最高的省为湖北省，占本行业的42.53%。

	Total number of firms 企业总数	Total number of employees 职工总数	Total revenue (Mil.RMB) 总销售收入（百万元）	Total profit (Mil.RMB) 总利润（百万元）	Return on assets 资产利润率 (%)	Return on equity 权益利润率 (%)	Labour productivity ('000 RMB/ worker) 劳动生产率（千元/人）	Debts/ assets 资产负债率 (%)	Total assets (Mil.RMB) 总资产（百万元）
Industry Overall 行业总体	34	12,206	4,998	691	13.82	21.21	123.84	34.84	5,003

	Number of firms 企业个数	Average number of employees 平均职工人数	Average revenue ('000 RMB) 平均销售收入（千元）	Average profit ('000 RMB) 平均利润（千元）	Return on assets 资产利润率 (%)	Return on equity 权益利润率 (%)	Labour productivity ('000 RMB/ worker) 劳动生产率（千元/人）	Debts/ assets 资产负债率 (%)	Average total assets ('000 RMB) 平均总资产（千元）
By ownership 产业所有权									
State-owned 国有	1	85	4,500				9.84	68.35	1,580
Collective-owned 集体	2	84	17,858	1,285	17.84	32.93	97.05	45.84	7,205
Foreign & Overseas Chinese Funded 三资	12	215	204,673	51,526	22.96	25.89	492.70	11.32	224,418
By regional distribution 地区分布									
Central-North 华北	4	102	14,199	631	9.85	21.40	49.61	53.95	6,404
Beijing 北京									
Tianjin 天津									
Hebei 河北	3	64	11,791	829	11.55	25.49	87.89	54.71	7,182
Shanxi 山西									
Inner Mongolia 内蒙古	1	216	21,422	36	0.88	1.77	15.58	49.95	4,070
Northeast 东北									
Liaoning 辽宁									
Jilin 吉林									
Heilongjiang 黑龙江									
Central-East 华东	19	145	85,371	23,534	29.11	34.82	334.26	16.42	80,857
Shanghai 上海									
Jiangsu 江苏	9	229	158,936	48,777	32.28	38.16	423.92	15.41	151,119
Zhejiang 浙江	3	84	19,697	1,542	8.78	15.55	50.06	43.53	17,553
Anhui 安徽									
Fujian 福建	2	76	17,351	728	3.77	3.89	45.10	2.93	19,288
Jiangxi 江西									
Shandong 山东	5	58	19,568	413	2.43	3.11	97.43	21.85	16,995
Central-South 中南	6	1,342	434,052	20,126	4.81	9.91	35.85	51.45	418,189
Henan 河南									
Hubei 湖北	2	3,603	1,062,673	31,833	3.24	8.01	19.25	59.53	982,145
Hunan 湖南									
Guangdong 广东	4	211	119,741	14,273	10.48	13.49	177.63	22.34	136,212
Guangxi 广西									
Hainan 海南									
Southwest 西南	3	239	147,966	21,501	11.17	14.37	240.04	22.24	192,443
Chongqing 重庆	2	187	27,966	48	0.09	6.93	33.47	98.73	54,106
Sichuan 四川									
Guizhou 贵州									
Yunnan 云南	1	344	387,965	64,407	13.73	14.39	464.02	4.60	469,117
Tibet 西藏									
Northwest 西北	2	137	135,378	28,243	15.94	19.03	397.99	16.21	177,131
Shaanxi 陕西	2	137	135,378	28,243	15.94	19.03	397.99	16.21	177,131
Gansu 甘肃									
Qinghai 青海									
Ningxia 宁夏									
Xinjiang 新疆									

2819: Cellulose Fibre 其他纤维素纤维制造业

Year 年份	Number of firms 企业个数	Rate of change 变化率 (%)	Number of employees 职工人数 (人)	Rate of change 变化率 (%)	Total revenue (Mil. RMB) 总销售收入 (百万元)	Rate of change 变化率 (%)	Total profit (Mil RMB) 总利润 (百万元)	Rate of change 变化率 (%)
2000	34		12,800		2,594		411	
2001	39	14.71	12,257	-4.24	2,496	-3.78	183	-55.47
2002	34	-12.82	12,206	-0.42	4,998	100.24	691	277.60

Major Products 主要产品	Output 产量	Unit 单位

10 Main Firms with Maximal Revenue (year founded) 收入最大的十家主要企业（创办年份）	City 城市	Province 省	Telephone/fax 电话/传真	Number of employees 职工人数	Ownership 产业所有权	Revenue ('000 RMB) 销售收入 (千元)	Profit('000 RMB) (rank) 利润(千元) (排名)	Total assets ('000 RMB) 总资产 (千元)	Major products 主要产品
Hubei Chemical Fibre Group Co.,Ltd. 湖北化纤集团有限公司(1972)	Xiangfan 襄樊市	Hubei 湖北省	(0710)2108340 (0710)21079988	7,149	State Enterprises 国有独资	2,111,435	63341(3)	1,947,226	Viscose staple Fiber粘胶短纤维
Jiangsu Acetate Fibers Co.,Ltd. 江苏南通醋酸纤维有限公司(1987)	Nantong 南通市	Jiangsu 江苏省	(0513)3560512 (0513)3560794	800	Foreign Funded 外商投资	1,222,913	435,173(1)	1,201,725	Di-acetate Silk Sheaves二醋酸纤维丝束
Kunming Acetate Fibers Co., Ltd. 昆明醋酸纤维有限公司(1993)	Kunming 昆明市	Yunnan 云南省	(0871)5631028 (0871)5627158	344	Foreign Funded 外商投资	387,965	64,407(2)	469,117	Di-acetate Silk Sheaves二醋酸纤维丝束
Zhuhai Acetate Fibers Co.,Ltd. 珠海醋酸纤维有限公司(1996)	Zhuhai 珠海市	Guangdong 广东省	(0756)8619933 (0756)8618654	346	Foreign Funded 外商投资	379,279	59,570(4)	425,916	Di-acetate Silk Sheaves二醋酸纤维丝束
Xi'an Hui Da Chemical Industry Co.,Ltd. 西安惠大化学工业有限公司(1992)	Xi'an 西安市	Shannxi 陕西省	(029)4969040 (029)4969901	184	Foreign Funded 外商投资	267,812	56,604(5)	334,634	Di-acetate Silk Sheaves二醋酸纤维丝束
Donghai Wanyuan Granule-making Factory 东海县万源造粒厂(1999)	Lianyungang 连云港市	Jiangsu 江苏省	(0518)7453553 (0518)7453553	130	Private Enterprises 私营独资	53,788	1,135(13)	8,980	≥mical Fibre Regeneration Granule化学纤维再生造粒
Sheyang Guang Yang Cellulose Factory 射阳县广阳纤维素厂(1998)	Yancheng 盐城市	Jiangsu 江苏省	(0515)2235568 (0515)2235187	75	Private Partnership 私营合伙	49,690	1,150(12)	12,310	CMC.羟甲基纤维素钠
Chongqing Qiaofeng Chemical Industry Factory 重庆市侨丰化工厂(1987)	Chongqing 重庆市	Chongqing 重庆市	(023)62753589 (023)62751375	283	Joint Stock 股份制	47,815	-	106,495	CMC.羟甲基纤维素钠
Tongxiang Jia Long Chemical Industry Co., Ltd. 桐乡佳龙化工有限公司(1995)	Jiaxing 嘉兴市	Zhejiang 浙江省	(0573)8591165 (0573)8591165	108	Foreign Funded 外商投资	33,705	2,348(6)	33,544	Nitration Cotton硝化棉
Xuzhou Huafang Chemical Fibre Co.,Ltd. 徐州华纺化纤有限责任公司(1989)	Xuzhou 徐州市	Jiangsu 江苏省	(0516)4629014 (0516)4629014	462	Limited-Liability 有限公司	33,520	35(25)	56,178	Polypropylene Short Fibre丙纶短丝

Top 10 Cities by Revenue 销售收入排名前10位城市	Province 省	Market share 市场份额 (%)	Number of firms 企业个数
Xiangfan 襄樊市	Hubei 湖北省	42.25	1
Nantong 南通市	Jiangsu 江苏省	24.47	1
Kunming 昆明市	Yunnan 云南省	7.76	1
Zhuhai 珠海市	Guangdong 广东省	7.59	1
Xi'an 西安市	Shannxi 陕西省	5.42	2
Foshan 佛山市	Guangdong 广东省	1.62	1
Yancheng 盐城市	Jiangsu 江苏省	1.50	2
Lianyungang 连云港市	Jiangsu 江苏省	1.12	2
Chongqing 重庆市	Chongqing 重庆市	1.12	2
Binzhou 滨州市	Shandong 山东省	1.11	1

10 Major Wholesalers 十家主要批发商	City 城市	Province 省	Telephone/Fax 电话/传真
Shanghai Shenda Co.,Ltd. 上海申达股份有限公司	Shanghai 上海市	Shanghai 上海市	(021)62319898 (021)62317250
Orient International Holding Silk Group Corportion 东方国际集团丝绸进出口有限公司	Shanghai 上海市	Shanghai 上海市	(021)64662288 (021)64677788
Nanjing Textiles Import & Export Co.,Ltd. 南京纺织品进出口股份有限公司	Nanjing 南京市	Jiangsu 江苏省	(025)3306789 (025)3300518
Zhejiang Textiles Import & Export Group Co.,Ltd. 浙江省纺织品进出口集团有限公司	Hangzhou 杭州市	Zhejiang 浙江省	(0571)87075888 (0571)87079234
Zhejiang Orient Holdings Co.,Ltd. 浙江东方集团股份有限公司	Hangzhou 杭州市	Zhejiang 浙江省	(0571)87215678 (0571)87215000
Zhejiang Silk Holding Co.,ltd. 浙江省丝绸集团有限公司	Hangzhou 杭州市	Zhejiang 浙江省	(0571)85195588 (0571)85192540
Guangdong Silk (Group) Corporation 广东省丝绸（集团）公司	Guangzhou 广州市	Guangdong 广东省	(020)83337448 (020)83332995
Shanghai Costume Group Co.,Ltd. 上海服装（集团）有限公司	Shanghai 上海市	Shanghai 上海市	(021)62748598 (021)62414773
Orient International Holding Shanghai Textiles Import & Export Co.Ltd. 东方国际集团上海市针织品进出口有限公司	Shanghai 上海市	Shanghai 上海市	(021)63218855 (021)63299560
Jiangsu Textiles Import & Export Group Co.,Ltd. 江苏省纺织品进出口集团股份有限公司	Nanjing 南京市	Jiangsu 江苏省	(025)6895000 (025)4400800

2821: Polyamide Fibre 锦纶纤维制造业

The industry accounts for 0.083% of the total revenue of China's industrial sector in 2002. The rate of return on assets is -1.58%. 67.90% of all firms in the industry made a profit while 32.10% had negative returns.The top province in terms of the industry's revenue is Henan, accounting for 25.29% of the total revenue.
2002年本行业收入占全行业的 0.083%，资产利润率为 -1.58%。67.90%的企业赢利，32.10%的企业亏损。收入最高的省为河南省，占本行业的25.29%。

	Total number of firms 企业总数	Total number of employees 职工总数	Total revenue (Mil.RMB) 总销售收入 (百万元)	Total profit (Mil.RMB) 总利润 (百万元)	Return on assets 资产利润率 (%)	Return on equity 权益利润率 (%)	Labour productivity ('000 RMB/ worker) 劳动生产率 (千元/人)	Debts/ assets 资产负债率 (%)	Total assets (Mil.RMB) 总资产 (百万元)
Industry Overall 行业总体	81	34,994	8,857	-267	-1.58	-6.99	58.28	77.41	16,895

	Number of firms 企业个数	Average number of employees 平均职工人数	Average revenue ('000 RMB) 平均销售收入（千元）	Average profit ('000 RMB) 平均利润 (千元)	Return on assets 资产利润率 (%)	Return on equity 权益利润率 (%)	Labour productivity ('000 RMB/ worker) 劳动生产率 (千元/人)	Debts/ assets 资产负债率 (%)	Average total assets ('000 RMB) 平均总资产 (千元)
By ownership 产业所有权									
State-owned 国有	13	532	62,464	-3,786	-2.00	-59.70	19.74	96.65	189,124
Collective-owned 集体	5	78	8,468	295	4.49	12.12	28.71	62.95	6,563
Foreign & Overseas Chinese Funded 三资	19	207	95,056	-4,095	-2.74	-7.79	128.33	64.87	149,623
By regional distribution 地区分布									
Central-North 华北	7	453	29,735	-12,445	-7.09	-751.82	-0.94	99.06	175,552
Beijing 北京	2	327	10,206	-31,874	-17.27		-59.31	129.69	184,534
Tianjin 天津	2	223	34,313	-455	-0.27	-1.96	31.03	86.29	169,359
Hebei 河北	2	356	24,099	-4,138	-3.61		17.17	120.70	114,743
Shanxi 山西	1	1,359	70,913	-14,179	-4.86	-11.60	7.16	58.09	291,593
Inner Mongolia 内蒙古									
Northeast 东北	2	969	110,409	-12,542	-2.71	-7.72	14.80	64.93	463,121
Liaoning 辽宁	2	969	110,409	-12,542	-2.71	-7.72	14.80	64.93	463,121
Jilin 吉林									
Heilongjiang 黑龙江									
Central-East 华东	55	215	72,780	1,326	2.13	6.85	80.40	68.93	62,272
Shanghai 上海	6	182	27,604	689	1.30	2.74	63.48	52.39	52,852
Jiangsu 江苏	26	232	85,845	129	0.26	2.52	75.76	89.64	49,385
Zhejiang 浙江	8	137	36,483	729	1.51	5.33	47.28	71.64	48,263
Anhui 安徽	4	288	24,958	1,896	9.03	21.92	26.86	58.82	21,001
Fujian 福建	3	145	77,352	8,798	8.58	15.43	298.97	44.39	102,512
Jiangxi 江西									
Shandong 山东	8	256	122,692	3,201	2.45	5.51	104.37	55.55	130,777
Central-South 中南	15	1,177	291,470	-15,440	-2.07	-9.44	59.31	78.11	747,014
Henan 河南	2	5,356	1,120,179	-54,050	-1.63	-7.60	48.66	78.49	3,306,306
Hubei 湖北	2	507	82,704	-12,395	-3.98		29.68	134.15	311,062
Hunan 湖南	4	552	56,207	607	0.71	3.33	52.18	78.70	85,485
Guangdong 广东	5	540	319,086	-16,389	-2.79	-7.41	132.85	62.39	587,794
Guangxi 广西	2	514	73,011	-9,594	-2.78	-29.62	21.76	90.61	344,779
Hainan 海南									
Southwest 西南	2	195	26,789	2,007	3.66		37.15	134.16	54,848
Chongqing 重庆	1	209	7,197	-1,603	-2.42		8.51	196.45	66,171
Sichuan 四川	1	180	46,380	5,617	12.91	21.32	70.41	39.46	43,525
Guizhou 贵州									
Yunnan 云南									
Tibet 西藏									
Northwest 西北									
Shaanxi 陕西									
Gansu 甘肃									
Qinghai 青海									
Ningxia 宁夏									
Xinjiang 新疆									

2821: Polyamide Fibre 锦纶纤维制造业

Year 年份	Number of firms 企业个数	Rate of change 变化率 (%)	Number of employees 职工人数 (人)	Rate of change 变化率 (%)	Total revenue (Mil. RMB) 总销售收入 (百万元)	Rate of change 变化率 (%)	Total profit (Mil RMB) 总利润 (百万元)	Rate of change 变化率 (%)
2000	75		32,705		8,011		91	
2001	69	-8.00	37,603	14.98	7,088	-11.52	-266	-
2002	81	17.39	34,994	-6.94	8,857	24.96	-267	-0.38

Major Products 主要产品	Output 产量	Unit 单位
Polymide Fibre 锦纶纤维	47	10,000 Tons 万吨

10 Main Firms with Maximal Revenue (year founded) 收入最大的十家主要企业（创办年份）	City 城市	Province 省	Telephone/fax 电话/传真	Number of employees 职工人数	Ownership 产业所有权	Revenue ('000 RMB) 销售收入 (千元)	Profit('000 RMB) (rank) 利润(千元) (排名)	Total assets ('000 RMB) 总资产 (千元)	Major products 主要产品
China Shen Ma Group Co.,Ltd.	Pingdingshan	Henan	(0375)3921901		Joint Stock				Polyamide Filament
中国神马集团有限责任公司(1999)	平顶山市	河南省	(0375)3921100	10,648	股份制	2,234,557	-	6,609,611	锦纶长丝
Guangdong Xinhui Mei Da Nylon Co.,Ltd.	Jiangmen	Guangdong	(0750)6103333		Joint Stock				Polyamide Fiber
广东新会美达锦纶股份有限公司(1992)	江门市	广东省	(0750)6107975	1,634	股份制	1,175,298	53,287(1)	1,815,688	锦纶丝
Wuxi Chang'an Macromolecule Materials Factory	Wuxi	Jiangsu	(0510)3761302		Private Partnership				Polyamide Fibre 6 Slices锦
无锡市长安高分子材料厂(1982)	无锡市	江苏省	(0510)3761631	200	私营合伙	349,360	610(25)	149,800	纶6切片
China Resources Yantai Nylon Co.,Ltd.	Yantai	Shandong	(0535)6371688		Overseas Chinese-funded				Polyamide Elastic Yarn锦
烟台华润锦纶有限公司(1988)	烟台市	山东省	(0535)6372777	664	港澳台资	336,060	28,377(2)	259,341	纶弹力丝
Wuxi Ming Te Chemical Fibre Co., Ltd.	Wuxi	Jiangsu	(0510)3789725		Private Owned				Polyamide Fibre Slices锦
无锡明特化纤有限公司(2000)	无锡市	江苏省	(0510)3789710	131	私营企业	239,970	-	48,510	纶丝切片
Qingdao Zhong Da Chemical Fibre Co.,Ltd.	Qingdao	Shandong	(0532)6898043		Foreign Funded				Polyamide Filament
青岛中达化纤有限公司(1991)	青岛市	山东省	(0532)6897751	499	外商投资	224,916	1,430(18)	394,124	锦纶长丝
Liaoning Yinzhu (Group) Co., Ltd.	Yingkou	Liaoning	(0417)3810522		Limited-Liability				Polyamide Fibre
辽宁银珠（集团）有限责任公司(1997)	营口市	辽宁省	(0417)3842382	1,808	有限公司	197,409	-	916,210	锦纶纤维
Shandong Da Cheng Chemical Industry Group Co.,Ltd.Nylon	Zibo	Shandong	(0533)3980056		Overseas Chinese-funded				Polyamide Chemical Filament
Branch山东大成化工集团有限公司锦纶分公司(1977)	淄博市	山东省	(0533)3980299	190	港澳台资	165,970	1,311(19)	50,536	锦纶化纤
Wuxi Xin Xin Chemical Fibre Materials Co., Ltd.	Wuxi	Jiangsu	(0510)3767425		Private Owned				Polyamide Fibre 6 Slices锦
无锡欣欣化纤材料有限责任公司(1997)	无锡市	江苏省	(0510)3761092	165	私营企业	159,760	1,080(21)	101,620	纶6切片
Ji'nan Ju Da Fiber Co., Ltd.	Jinan	Shandong	(0531)8919342		Overseas Chinese-funded				Polyamide Filament
济南聚大纤维有限公司(1994)	济南市	山东省	(0531)8916047	202	港澳台资	150,592	-	246,704	锦纶长丝

Top 10 Cities by Revenue 销售收入排名前10位城市	Province 省	Market share 市场份额 (%)	Number of firms 企业个数
Pingdingshan 平顶山市	Henan 河南省	25.23	1
Wuxi 无锡市	Jiangsu 江苏省	16.20	8
Jiangmen 江门市	Guangdong 广东省	13.27	1
Zhaoqing 肇庆市	Guangdong 广东省	4.15	1
Yantai 烟台市	Shandong 山东省	3.79	1
Suzhou 苏州市	Jiangsu 江苏省	2.78	4
Qingdao 青岛市	Shandong 山东省	2.62	2
Quanzhou 泉州市	Fujian 福建省	2.59	2
Nantong 南通市	Jiangsu 江苏省	2.53	6
Jinan 济南市	Shandong 山东省	2.41	3

10 Major Wholesalers 十家主要批发商	City 城市	Province 省	Telephone/Fax 电话/传真
Shanghai Shenda Co.,Ltd.	Shanghai	Shanghai	(021)62319898
上海申达股份有限公司	上海市	上海市	(021)62317250
Orient International Holding Silk Group Corportion	Shanghai	Shanghai	(021)64662288
东方国际集团丝绸进出口有限公司	上海市	上海市	(021)64677788
Nanjing Textiles Import & Export Co.,Ltd.	Nanjing	Jiangsu	(025)3306789
南京纺织品进出口股份有限公司	南京市	江苏省	(025)3300518
Zhejiang Textiles Import & Export Group Co.,Ltd.	Hangzhou	Zhejiang	(0571)87075888
浙江省纺织品进出口集团有限公司	杭州市	浙江省	(0571)87079234
Zhejiang Orient Holdings Co.,Ltd.	Hangzhou	Zhejiang	(0571)87215678
浙江东方集团股份有限公司	杭州市	浙江省	(0571)87215000
Zhejiang Silk Holding Co.,ltd.	Hangzhou	Zhejiang	(0571)85195588
浙江省丝绸集团有限公司	杭州市	浙江省	(0571)85192540
Guangdong Silk (Group) Corporation	Guangzhou	Guangdong	(020)83337448
广东省丝绸（集团）公司	广州市	广东省	(020)83332995
Shanghai Costume Group Co.,Ltd.	Shanghai	Shanghai	(021)62748598
上海服装（集团）有限公司	上海市	上海市	(021)62414773
Orient International Holding Shanghai Textiles Import & Export Co.Ltd.	Shanghai	Shanghai	(021)63218855
东方国际集团上海市针织品进出口有限公司	上海市	上海市	(021)63299560
Jiangsu Textiles Import & Export Group Co.,Ltd.	Nanjing	Jiangsu	(025)6895000
江苏省纺织品进出口集团股份有限公司	南京市	江苏省	(025)4400800

2822: Polyester Fibre 涤纶纤维制造业

The industry accounts for 0.593% of the total revenue of China's industrial sector in 2002. The rate of return on assets is 1.38%. 68.80% of all firms in the industry made a profit while 31.20% had negative returns.The top province in terms of the industry's revenue is Zhejiang, accounting for 31.72% of the total revenue.
2002年本行业收入占全行业的 0.593%，资产利润率为 1.38%。68.80%的企业赢利，31.20%的企业亏损。收入最高的省为浙江省，占本行业的31.72%。

	Total number of firms 企业总数	Total number of employees 职工总数	Total revenue (Mil.RMB) 总销售收入 (百万元)	Total profit (Mil.RMB) 总利润 (百万元)	Return on assets 资产利润率 (%)	Return on equity 权益利润率 (%)	Labour productivity ('000 RMB/ worker) 劳动生产率 (千元/人)	Debts/ assets 资产负债率 (%)	Total assets (Mil.RMB) 总资产 (百万元)
Industry Overall 行业总体	359	160,558	63,630	1,154	1.38	3.24	78.24	57.33	83,576

	Number of firms 企业个数	Average number of employees 平均职工人数	Average revenue ('000 RMB) 平均销售收入（千元）	Average profit ('000 RMB) 平均利润 (千元)	Return on assets 资产利润率 (%)	Return on equity 权益利润率 (%)	Labour productivity ('000 RMB/ worker) 劳动生产率 (千元/人)	Debts/ assets 资产负债率 (%)	Average total assets ('000 RMB) 平均总资产 (千元)
By ownership 产业所有权									
State-owned 国有	28	563	84,862	-3,226	-1.28	-14.59	23.35	91.26	252,957
Collective-owned 集体	35	458	154,360	5,209	4.24	13.83	75.67	69.34	122,848
Foreign & Overseas Chinese Funded 三资	76	376	234,637	1,528	0.48	1.10	114.78	56.71	320,890
By regional distribution 地区分布									
Central-North 华北	20	307	24,190	-398	-0.57	-3.34	20.91	82.93	69,913
Beijing 北京	3	155	19,490	648	1.07	2.57	18.48	58.28	60,368
Tianjin 天津	5	238	17,885	915	6.22	50.27	8.85	87.63	14,714
Hebei 河北	9	457	32,865	-1,551	-1.37	-11.64	23.32	88.22	113,139
Shanxi 山西	3	126	13,373	-177	-0.42	-1.55	35.56	72.78	41,778
Inner Mongolia 内蒙古									
Northeast 东北	12	564	210,324	180	0.03	0.11	45.75	67.03	516,763
Liaoning 辽宁	8	214	60,076	-4,273	-2.01	-7.02	27.96	71.39	212,622
Jilin 吉林	3	475	97,688	8,679	2.36	6.06	65.49	60.99	367,021
Heilongjiang 黑龙江	1	3,635	1,750,224	10,306	0.30	0.91	46.36	66.80	3,399,121
Central-East 华东	257	482	216,699	4,814	1.89	4.03	91.63	53.07	254,554
Shanghai 上海	25	266	142,645	1,733	0.99	1.81	141.02	45.13	174,761
Jiangsu 江苏	100	510	201,718	-511	-0.20	-0.40	86.29	50.72	260,767
Zhejiang 浙江	81	413	249,186	10,531	5.63	13.77	84.13	59.14	187,146
Anhui 安徽	1	94	37,123	127	2.31	83.55	119.66	97.23	5,487
Fujian 福建	21	520	248,120	6,465	1.60	3.09	109.90	48.06	403,017
Jiangxi 江西	5	631	117,837	2,382	0.89	2.37	31.06	62.59	268,978
Shandong 山东	24	773	247,202	10,169	2.44	5.60	101.52	56.39	416,751
Central-South 中南	61	326	70,220	-784	-0.59	-2.94	36.33	80.07	133,721
Henan 河南	10	314	14,087	-1,389	-1.60	-10.26	19.17	84.44	87,054
Hubei 湖北	9	512	96,203	-1,833	-0.95	-6.32	26.75	84.90	191,990
Hunan 湖南	5	608	220,215	-1,561	-0.45	-1.40	54.40	67.63	344,533
Guangdong 广东	29	199	52,626	-719	-1.01	-12.12	35.41	91.69	71,462
Guangxi 广西	3	475	59,384	-175	-0.16	-1.30	14.10	87.82	110,839
Hainan 海南	5	381	94,269	2,352	0.82	2.56	78.43	67.94	286,191
Southwest 西南	7	502	86,324	-1,380	-0.50	-1.08	16.19	53.34	274,511
Chongqing 重庆									
Sichuan 四川	6	541	94,345	-1,538	-0.48	-1.03	17.01	53.26	319,555
Guizhou 贵州	1	268	38,203	-432	-10.17	-102.13	6.25	90.04	4,248
Yunnan 云南									
Tibet 西藏									
Northwest 西北	2	229	21,420	-10,055	-4.21	-13.36	2.73	68.47	238,688
Shaanxi 陕西									
Gansu 甘肃									
Qinghai 青海									
Ningxia 宁夏	1	256	32,738	-7,986	-4.13		0.48	131.39	193,494
Xinjiang 新疆	1	202	10,102	-12,124	-4.27	-5.74	5.58	25.58	283,881

Year 年份	Number of firms 企业个数	Rate of change 变化率 (%)	Number of employees 职工人数 (人)	Rate of change 变化率 (%)	Total revenue (Mil. RMB) 总销售收入 (百万元)	Rate of change 变化率 (%)	Total profit (Mil RMB) 总利润 (百万元)	Rate of change 变化率 (%)
2000	326		191,163		78,796		4,531	
2001	350	7.36	170,776	-10.66	55,343	-29.76	1,064	-76.52
2002	359	2.57	160,558	-5.98	63,630	14.97	1,154	8.46

Major Products 主要产品	Output 产量	Unit 单位
Polyester Fibre 涤纶纤维	772	10,000 Tons 万吨

10 Main Firms with Maximal Revenue (year founded) 收入最大的十家主要企业（创办年份）	City 城市	Province 省	Telephone/fax 电话/传真	Number of employees 职工人数	Ownership 产业所有权	Revenue ('000 RMB) 销售收入 (千元)	Profit('000 RMB) (rank) 利润(千元) (排名)	Total assets ('000 RMB) 总资产 (千元)	Major products 主要产品
Zhejiang Tongkun Chemical Fiber Group Stock Co.Ltd.	Jiaxing	Zhejiang	(0573)8510006		Joint Stock				Terylene Fiber
浙江桐昆化纤集团股份有限公司(1999)	嘉兴市	浙江省	(0573)8511867	4,605	股份制	3,511,738	191,766(2)	1,669,577	涤纶丝
Zhejiang Yuan Dong Chemical Fibre Group Co., Ltd	Shaoxing	Zhejiang	(0575)5101079		Overseas Chinese-funded				Chemical Fibre Raw Stuff
浙江远东化纤集团有限公司(1994)	绍兴市	浙江省	(0575)5101468	1,693	港澳台资	3,215,385	164,237(3)	2,685,288	化纤原料
Wan Jie Group Company	Zibo	Shandong	(0533)4650660		Joint Stock				Chemical Filament Textiles化纤长
万杰集团公司(1992)	淄博市	山东省	(0533)4657567	4,850	股份制	2,660,182	233,214(1)	3,005,489	丝机织物
Xiang Lu Terylene Fibers (xiamen) Co., ltd	Xiamen	Fujian	(0592)6051111		Overseas Chinese-funded				Polyester Filament
翔鹭涤纶纺纤（厦门）有限公司(1989)	厦门市	福建省	(0592)6051281	2,290	港澳台资	2,452,273	42,084(12)	4,152,201	涤纶长丝
Far Estern Industries (Shanghai) Ltd.	Shanghai	Shanghai	(021)57501888		Overseas Chinese-funded				Chemical Fibre
远纺工业（上海）有限公司(1999)	上海市	上海市	(021)37500002	1,550	港澳台资	2,010,360	109,953(5)	2,253,212	化学纤维
Rongsheng Chemical Fibre Group Co.,Ltd.	Hangzhou	Zhejiang	(0571)82526378		Limited-Liability				Chemical Fibre Textiles化
荣盛化纤集团有限公司(1995)	杭州市	浙江省	(0571)82527208	1,370	有限公司	1,938,739	85,003(6)	1,210,212	纤纺织品
Heilongjiang Longdi Group Co., Ltd.	Harbin	Heilongjiang	(0451)53715337		State Enterprises				Terylene Filament
黑龙江省龙涤集团有限公司(1980)	哈尔滨市	黑龙江省	(0451)53717949	3,635	国有独资	1,750,224	10,306(35)	3,399,121	涤纶长丝
Jiaxing Chaotong Chemical Fibre Co., Ltd.	Jiaxing	Zhejiang	(0573)6776949		Limited-Liability				Terylene Filament
加兴超同化纤有限责任公司(1999)	嘉兴市	浙江省	(0573)6776877	2,025	有限公司	1,054,897	44,421(11)	445,809	涤纶长丝
Qingdao KOHAP Co.,Ltd.	Qingdao	Shandong	(0532)6768215		Foreign Funded				Polyester Slices
青岛高合有限公司(1996)	青岛市	山东省	(0532)6768206	569	外商投资	901,213		1,156,583	聚脂切片
Jiangyin Jin Da Lai Group	Wuxi	Jiangsu	(0510)6531838		Collective-owned				Terylener Staple Fiber涤
江阴市金达来集团(1985)	无锡市	江苏省	(0510)6531833	2,012	集体企业	851,527	32,971(16)	332,833	纶短纤维

Top 10 Cities by Revenue 销售收入排名前10位城市	Province 省	Market share 市场份额 (%)	Number of firms 企业个数
Shaoxing 绍兴市	Zhejiang 浙江省	12.23	17
Jiaxing 嘉兴市	Zhejiang 浙江省	12.03	20
Yangzhou 扬州市	Jiangsu 江苏省	11.97	3
Wuxi 无锡市	Jiangsu 江苏省	8.02	34
Suzhou 苏州市	Jiangsu 江苏省	7.47	39
Shanghai 上海市	Shanghai 上海市	5.60	25
Hangzhou 杭州市	Zhejiang 浙江省	5.31	16
Zibo 淄博市	Shandong 山东省	4.91	5
Xiamen 厦门市	Fujian 福建省	4.26	4
Harbin 哈尔滨市	Heilongjiang 黑龙江省	2.75	1

10 Major Wholesalers 十家主要批发商	City 城市	Province 省	Telephone/Fax 电话/传真
Shanghai Shenda Co.,Ltd.	Shanghai	Shanghai	(021)62319898
上海申达股份有限公司	上海市	上海市	(021)62317250
Orient International Holding Silk Group Corportion	Shanghai	Shanghai	(021)64662288
东方国际集团丝绸进出口有限公司	上海市	上海市	(021)64677788
Nanjing Textiles Import & Export Co.,Ltd.	Nanjing	Jiangsu	(025)3306789
南京纺织品进出口股份有限公司	南京市	江苏省	(025)3300518
Zhejiang Textiles Import & Export Group Co.,Ltd.	Hangzhou	Zhejiang	(0571)87075888
浙江省纺织品进出口集团有限公司	杭州市	浙江省	(0571)87079234
Zhejiang Orient Holdings Co.,Ltd.	Hangzhou	Zhejiang	(0571)87215678
浙江东方集团股份有限公司	杭州市	浙江省	(0571)87215000
Zhejiang Silk Holding Co.,ltd.	Hangzhou	Zhejiang	(0571)85195588
浙江省丝绸集团有限公司	杭州市	浙江省	(0571)85192540
Guangdong Silk (Group) Corporation	Guangzhou	Guangdong	(020)83337448
广东省丝绸（集团）公司	广州市	广东省	(020)83332995
Shanghai Costume Group Co.,Ltd.	Shanghai	Shanghai	(021)62748598
上海服装（集团）有限公司	上海市	上海市	(021)62414773
Orient International Holding Shanghai Textiles Import & Export Co.Ltd.	Shanghai	Shanghai	(021)63218855
东方国际集团上海市针织品进出口有限公司	上海市	上海市	(021)63299560
Jiangsu Textiles Import & Export Group Co.,Ltd.	Nanjing	Jiangsu	(025)6895000
江苏省纺织品进出口集团股份有限公司	南京市	江苏省	(025)4400800

2823: Acrylic Fibre 腈纶纤维制造业

The industry accounts for 0.049% of the total revenue of China's industrial sector in 2002. The rate of return on assets is 2.51%. 75.00% of all firms in the industry made a profit while 25.00% had negative returns.The top province in terms of the industry's revenue is Jiangsu, accounting for 76.28% of the total revenue.
2002年本行业收入占全行业的0.049%，资产利润率为2.51%。75.00%的企业赢利，25.00%的企业亏损。收入最高的省为江苏省，占本行业的76.28%。

	Total number of firms 企业总数	Total number of employees 职工总数	Total revenue (Mil.RMB) 总销售收入 (百万元)	Total profit (Mil.RMB) 总利润 (百万元)	Return on assets 资产利润率 (%)	Return on equity 权益利润率 (%)	Labour productivity ('000 RMB/ worker) 劳动生产率 (千元/人)	Debts/ assets 资产负债率 (%)	Total assets (Mil.RMB) 总资产 (百万元)
Industry Overall 行业总体	24	12,068	5,268	142	2.51	6.58	91.97	61.90	5,669

	Number of firms 企业个数	Average number of employees 平均职工人数	Average revenue ('000 RMB) 平均销售收入（千元）	Average profit ('000 RMB) 平均利润 (千元)	Return on assets 资产利润率 (%)	Return on equity 权益利润率 (%)	Labour productivity ('000 RMB/ worker) 劳动生产率 (千元/人)	Debts/ assets 资产负债率 (%)	Average total assets ('000 RMB) 平均总资产 (千元)
By ownership 产业所有权									
State-owned 国有	2	879	257,000	-8,963	-1.03	-2.09	42.46	50.61	867,064
Collective-owned 集体	1	137	26,178	305	1.09	4.68	44.49	76.58	27,856
Foreign & Overseas Chinese Funded 三资	7	164	27,474	479	2.27	4.37	44.43	48.08	21,149
By regional distribution 地区分布									
Central-North 华北	2	429	165,174	450	0.07	0.12	64.68	43.25	644,643
Beijing 北京									
Tianjin 天津									
Hebei 河北	2	429	165,174	450	0.07	0.12	64.68	43.25	644,643
Shanxi 山西									
Inner Mongolia 内蒙古									
Northeast 东北	1	150	9,120	80	0.69	1.26	6.47	45.17	11,600
Liaoning 辽宁	1	150	9,120	80	0.69	1.26	6.47	45.17	11,600
Jilin 吉林									
Heilongjiang 黑龙江									
Central-East 华东	20	551	245,758	7,061	3.24	9.94	95.47	67.43	218,154
Shanghai 上海	2	661	105,301	-10,307	-4.34	-16.11	17.44	73.03	237,222
Jiangsu 江苏	11	546	365,302	18,588	8.45	15.65	150.31	46.02	220,048
Zhejiang 浙江	4	371	132,778	-7,016	-2.56	-18.06	62.03	85.82	273,993
Anhui 安徽									
Fujian 福建									
Jiangxi 江西									
Shandong 山东	3	737	51,708	-4,857	-3.92		15.49	145.40	124,043
Central-South 中南	1	39	13,330	2	0.04	0.26	31.15	84.59	4,900
Henan 河南									
Hubei 湖北	1	39	13,330	2	0.04	0.26	31.15	84.59	4,900
Hunan 湖南									
Guangdong 广东									
Guangxi 广西									
Hainan 海南									
Southwest 西南									
Chongqing 重庆									
Sichuan 四川									
Guizhou 贵州									
Yunnan 云南									
Tibet 西藏									
Northwest 西北									
Shaanxi 陕西									
Gansu 甘肃									
Qinghai 青海									
Ningxia 宁夏									
Xinjiang 新疆									

2823: Acrylic Fibre 腈纶纤维制造业

Year 年份	Number of firms 企业个数	Rate of change 变化率 (%)	Number of employees 职工人数 (人)	Rate of change 变化率 (%)	Total revenue (Mil. RMB) 总销售收入 (百万元)	Rate of change 变化率 (%)	Total profit (Mil RMB) 总利润 (百万元)	Rate of change 变化率 (%)
2000	23		15,143		5,614		81	
2001	23	o	12,220	-19.30	4,807	-14.37	102	25.93
2002	24	4.35	12,068	-1.24	5,268	9.59	142	39.22

Major Products 主要产品	Output 产量	Unit 单位
Acrylic Fibre 腈纶纤维	59	10,000 Tons 万吨

10 Main Firms with Maximal Revenue (year founded) 收入最大的十家主要企业（创办年份）	City 城市	Province 省	Telephone/fax 电话/传真	Number of employees 职工人数	Ownership 产业所有权	Revenue ('000 RMB) 销售收入 (千元)	Profit('000 RMB) (rank) 利润(千元) (排名)	Total assets ('000 RMB) 总资产 (千元)	Major products 主要产品
Jiangsu San Fang Xiang Industrial Group General Company 江苏三房巷实业集团总公司(1993)	Wuxi 无锡市	Jiangsu 江苏省	(0510)6229898 (0510)6229800	4,077	Private Enterprises 私营独资	3,712,990	199,410(1)	2,160,729	Terylene Fibre 涤纶纤维
Zhejiang Jin Yong Acrylic Fibre Co., Ltd. 浙江金甬腈纶有限公司(1997)	Ningbo 宁波市	Zhejiang 浙江省	(0574)86300000 (0574)86302903	1,017	Limited-Liability 有限公司	483,502	-	1,071,443	Acrytic Fibre 腈纶纤维
Hebei Qinhuangdao Acrylic Fibre Factory 河北省秦皇岛腈纶厂(1991)	Qinhuangdao 秦皇岛市	Hebei 河北省	(0335)3010079 (0335)3011549	817	State-owned 国有企业	322,935	1,026(5)	1,283,954	Acrytic Fibre 腈纶纤维
Shanghai Jinyang Acrylic Fibre Factory 上海金阳腈纶厂(1991)	Shanghai 上海市	Shanghai 上海市	(021)57940940 (021)57942450	941	State-owned 国有企业	191,065	-	450,174	Acrytic Fibre 腈纶纤维
Shandong Xueyin Chemical Fibre Group Stock Co., Ltd. 山东雪银化纤集团股份有限公司(1977)	Zibo 淄博市	Shandong 山东省	(0533)3980131 (0533)3980001	1,936	Joint Stock 股份制	128,212	-	343,318	Acrytic Fibre 腈纶纤维
Yangzhou Huade Travel & Sport Articles Co., Ltd. 扬州华德旅游用品有限公司(1992)	Yangzhou 扬州市	Jiangsu 江苏省	(0514)7303222 (0514)7301634	382	Foreign Funded 外商投资	70,060	1,510(2)	18,010	Nylon Bags 尼龙包
Huai'an Tian Yi Textile Co., Ltd. 淮安市天意纺织有限公司(2002)	Huaian 淮安市	Jiangsu 江苏省	(0517)3963912 (0517)3963027	300	Joint Stock 股份制	38,606	490(9)	63,166	Acrylic Fibre 晴纶丝
Funing Knitting Velvet Co., Ltd. 阜宁县针织绒有限公司(1998)	Yancheng 盐城市	Jiangsu 江苏省	(0515)7214443 (0515)7214443	264	Limited-Liability 有限公司	31,860	520(7)	6,210	Acrylic Fibre 腈纶线
Zibo Pan Yang Wool Co., Ltd. 淄博磐羊绒线有限责仕公司(1999)	Zibo 淄博市	Shandong 山東省	(0533)5310138 (0533)2263310	205	Limited-Liability 有限公司	21,320	1,170(4)	5,360	Plush 毛绒
Shanghai Dong Lin Woolen Co., Ltd. 上海东林毛纺有限公司(2000)	Shanghai 上海市	Shanghai 上海市	(021)57891441 (021)57893492	380	Private Owned 私营企业	19,536	-	24,269	Acrylic Fibre 晴纶丝

Top 10 Cities by Revenue 销售收入排名前10位城市	Province 省	Market share 市场份额 (%)	Number of firms 企业个数
Wuxi 无锡市	Jiangsu 江苏省	71.12	3
Ningbo 宁波市	Zhejiang 浙江省	9.18	1
Qinhuangdao 秦皇岛市	Hebei 河北省	6.13	1
Shanghai 上海市	Shanghai 上海市	4.00	2
Zibo 淄博市	Shandong 山东省	2.84	2
Yangzhou 扬州市	Jiangsu 江苏省	1.33	1
Huaian 淮安市	Jiangsu 江苏省	1.18	2
Nantong 南通市	Jiangsu 江苏省	1.13	1
Shaoxing 绍兴市	Zhejiang 浙江省	0.74	1
Suzhou 苏州市	Jiangsu 江苏省	0.62	2

10 Major Wholesalers 十家主要批发商	City 城市	Province 省	Telephone/Fax 电话/传真
Shanghai Shenda Co.,Ltd. 上海申达股份有限公司	Shanghai 上海市	Shanghai 上海市	(021)62319898 (021)62317250
Orient International Holding Silk Group Corportion 东方国际集团丝绸进出口有限公司	Shanghai 上海市	Shanghai 上海市	(021)64662288 (021)64677788
Nanjing Textiles Import & Export Co.,Ltd. 南京纺织品进出口股份有限公司	Nanjing 南京市	Jiangsu 江苏省	(025)3306789 (025)3300518
Zhejiang Textiles Import & Export Group Co.,Ltd. 浙江省纺织品进出口集团有限公司	Hangzhou 杭州市	Zhejiang 浙江省	(0571)87075888 (0571)87079234
Zhejiang Orient Holdings Co.,Ltd. 浙江东方集团股份有限公司	Hangzhou 杭州市	Zhejiang 浙江省	(0571)87215678 (0571)87215000
Zhejiang Silk Holding Co.,ltd. 浙江省丝绸集团有限公司	Hangzhou 杭州市	Zhejiang 浙江省	(0571)85195588 (0571)85192540
Guangdong Silk (Group) Corporation 广东省丝绸（集团）公司	Guangzhou 广州市	Guangdong 广东省	(020)83337448 (020)83332995
Shanghai Costume Group Co.,Ltd. 上海服装（集团）有限公司	Shanghai 上海市	Shanghai 上海市	(021)62748598 (021)62414773
Orient International Holding Shanghai Textiles Import & Export Co.Ltd. 东方国际集团上海市针织品进出口有限公司	Shanghai 上海市	Shanghai 上海市	(021)63218855 (021)63299560
Jiangsu Textiles Import & Export Group Co.,Ltd. 江苏省纺织品进出口集团股份有限公司	Nanjing 南京市	Jiangsu 江苏省	(025)6895000 (025)4400800

2829: Other Synthetic Fibre 其他合成纤维制造业

The industry accounts for 0.070% of the total revenue of China's industrial sector in 2002. The rate of return on assets is 5.13%. 76.92% of all firms in the industry made a profit while 23.08% had negative returns.The top province in terms of the industry's revenue is Jiangsu, accounting for 33.81% of the total revenue.
2002年本行业收入占全行业的 0.070%，资产利润率为 5.13%。76.92%的企业赢利，23.08%的企业亏损。收入最高的省为江苏省，占本行业的33.81%。

	Total number of firms 企业总数	Total number of employees 职工总数	Total revenue (Mil.RMB) 总销售收入（百万元）	Total profit (Mil.RMB) 总利润（百万元）	Return on assets 资产利润率（%）	Return on equity 权益利润率（%）	Labour productivity ('000 RMB/ worker) 劳动生产率（千元/人）	Debts/ assets 资产负债率（%）	Total assets (Mil.RMB) 总资产（百万元）
Industry Overall 行业总体	169	30,754	7,539	614	5.13	11.39	70.52	54.93	11,968

	Number of firms 企业个数	Average number of employees 平均职工人数	Average revenue ('000 RMB) 平均销售收入（千元）	Average profit ('000 RMB) 平均利润（千元）	Return on assets 资产利润率（%）	Return on equity 权益利润率（%）	Labour productivity ('000 RMB/ worker) 劳动生产率（千元/人）	Debts/ assets 资产负债率（%）	Average total assets ('000 RMB) 平均总资产（千元）
By ownership 产业所有权									
State-owned 国有	10	217	10,678	-715	-1.44	-16.90	13.60	91.50	49,796
Collective-owned 集体	18	107	21,310	706	3.30	10.08	52.11	67.23	21,388
Foreign & Overseas Chinese Funded 三资	43	150	57,255	4,322	4.39	9.91	137.33	55.72	98,470
By regional distribution 地区分布									
Central-North 华北	13	198	34,107	8,729	4.49	8.16	-17.81	44.91	194,224
Beijing 北京	4	77	7,375	-212	-1.18	-2.55	29.19	53.51	17,871
Tianjin 天津	5	162	68,283	23,264	5.30	8.34	-86.34	36.48	439,158
Hebei 河北	4	365	18,118	-499	-0.77		10.28	114.41	64,408
Shanxi 山西									
Inner Mongolia 内蒙古									
Northeast 东北	7	167	12,702	228	0.70	2.32	25.02	69.63	32,350
Liaoning 辽宁	5	98	7,837	-145	-0.71	-1.76	35.60	59.77	20,577
Jilin 吉林	1	260	3,703				4.31	80.08	94,867
Heilongjiang 黑龙江	1	422	46,030	2,320	8.08	27.34	25.50	70.43	28,700
Central-East 华东	117	190	50,347	3,995	6.20	14.37	81.52	56.87	64,469
Shanghai 上海	13	110	68,958	5,434	4.36	10.50	231.27	58.50	124,686
Jiangsu 江苏	41	263	62,161	3,956	5.68	13.68	69.07	58.49	69,666
Zhejiang 浙江	29	120	37,367	2,713	9.53	21.48	61.54	55.65	28,479
Anhui 安徽	3	81	31,438	1,769	2.14	5.64	89.32	62.07	82,716
Fujian 福建	1	185	67,506	4,285	15.00	22.14	80.22	32.26	28,565
Jiangxi 江西	1	98	63,280	1,780	15.48	36.33	255.82	57.39	11,500
Shandong 山东	29	207	39,201	4,985	7.41	15.88	76.73	53.36	67,297
Central-South 中南	30	155	37,093	1,061	1.91	4.66	79.97	59.13	55,692
Henan 河南	7	245	36,308	237	0.37	1.11	36.17	66.83	64,335
Hubei 湖北	4	133	18,563	-146	-0.47	-0.79	46.22	39.57	30,649
Hunan 湖南	2	84	15,136	2,224	6.89	9.44	92.34	27.01	32,260
Guangdong 广东	17	132	44,360	1,548	2.55	6.38	120.48	60.10	60,783
Guangxi 广西									
Hainan 海南									
Southwest 西南									
Chongqing 重庆									
Sichuan 四川									
Guizhou 贵州									
Yunnan 云南									
Tibet 西藏									
Northwest 西北	2	63	1,539	-85	-6.37		7.16	161.07	1,335
Shaanxi 陕西									
Gansu 甘肃	2	63	1,539	-85	-6.37		7.16	161.07	1,335
Qinghai 青海									
Ningxia 宁夏									
Xinjiang 新疆									

2829: Other Synthetic Fibre 其他合成纤维制造业

Year 年份	Number of firms 企业个数	Rate of change 变化率(%)	Number of employees 职工人数(人)	Rate of change 变化率(%)	Total revenue (Mil. RMB) 总销售收入(百万元)	Rate of change 变化率(%)	Total profit (Mil RMB) 总利润(百万元)	Rate of change 变化率(%)
2000	130		26,130		6,505		737	
2001	164	26.15	30,538	16.87	8,281	27.30	918	24.56
2002	169	3.05	30,754	0.71	7,539	-8.96	614	-33.12

Major Products 主要产品	Output 产量	Unit 单位
Vinylon Fibre 维纶纤维	32,450	Ton 吨
Polypropylene Fibre 丙纶纤维	30	10,000 Tons 万吨

10 Main Firms with Maximal Revenue (year founded) 收入最大的十家主要企业（创办年份）	City 城市	Province 省	Telephone/fax 电话/传真	Number of employees 职工人数	Ownership 产业所有权	Revenue ('000 RMB) 销售收入(千元)	Profit('000 RMB) (rank) 利润(千元)(排名)	Total assets ('000 RMB) 总资产(千元)	Major products 主要产品
Yantai Polyurethane Fibre Group Co., Ltd. 烟台氨纶集团有限公司(1989)	Yantai 烟台市	Shandong 山东省	(0535)6379333 (0535)6371234	598	Joint Stock 股份制	546,490	134,596(1)	1,059,803	Polyurethane Fibre 氨纶丝
Tianjin TEDA.Co.,Ltd. 天津泰达股份有限公司(1956)	Tianjin 天津市	Tianjin 天津市	(022)26391700 (022)26392950	679	Joint Stock 股份制	324,795	115,248(2)	2,177,972	Air Filtering Material空气 过滤材料
Shaoxing County Guqiandao Chemical Fibre Co., Ltd. 绍兴县古纤道化纤有限公司(1999)	Shaoxing 绍兴市	Zhejiang 浙江省	(0575)4058053 (0575)4056608	1,062	Limited-Liability 有限公司	287,410	44,207(5)	332,000	Special Type Chemical Fibre 特种化纤
Basf -Hua Yuan Nylon Co., Ltd. 巴斯夫-华源尼龙有限公司(1997)	Shanghai 上海市	Shanghai 上海市	(021)69716060 (021)69716262	223	Foreign Funded 外商投资	227,392	-	548,466	Nylon Carpet Fiber BCF6尼龙地 毯丝BCF6
Jiangsu Lv Yu Chemical Fibre Industrial Co., Ltd. 江苏绿玉化纤实业有限公司(1984)	Suzhou 苏州市	Jiangsu 江苏省	(0512)52691034 (0512)52698092	522	Private Owned 私营企业	201,442	-	180,330	Terylene Fiber 涤纶丝
Jiangsu Nan Huanghai Industrial Stock Co., Ltd. 江苏南黄海实业股份有限公司(1981)	Nantong 南通市	Jiangsu 江苏省	(0513)4410080 (0513)4541728	1,702	Joint Stock 股份制	199,774	27,758(6)	393,330	Tobacco Polypropylene Fibre Tow 丙纤丝束
Shaoxing County Zhongyi Polyurethane Fibre Co., Ltd. 绍兴县中意氨纶有限公司(1992)	Shaoxing 绍兴市	Zhejiang 浙江省	(0575)4293506 (0575)4293114	102	Limited-Liability 有限公司	198,006	8,052(12)	68,682	Polyurethane Fibre Make & Replies Yarn 氨 纶包复纱
Nanhai Nan Xin Non-woven Cloth Co.,Ltd. 南海南新无纺布有限公司(1994)	Foshan 佛山市	Guangdong 广东省	(0757)6265152 (0757)6265180	155	Foreign Funded 外商投资	176,130	15,233(10)	318,347	Wool Spinning Cloth 毛纺布
Zhangjiagang Hua Fu Polyurethane Fibre Yarn Knitting Textile Co., Ltd.张家港市华福氨纶纱线编纺织有限公司(1996)	Suzhou 苏州市	Jiangsu 江苏省	(0512)58722188 (0512)58750431	920	Private Partnership 私营合伙	155,830	23,455(9)	84,112	Polyurethane Replies Yarn氨 纶包蕊纱
Henan Zhong Zhou Burang Tai Ke Si Chemical Fibre Industry Co., Ltd.河南省中州普兰太克斯化纤工业有限公司(1984)	Zhengzhou 郑州市	Henan 河南省	(0371)4136875 (0371)4134444	820	Foreign Funded 外商投资	144,500	2,420(29)	216,622	Tobacco Polypropylene Fibre Tow 丙烯丝束

Top 10 Cities by Revenue 销售收入排名前10位城市	Province 省	Market share 市场份额(%)	Number of firms 企业个数
Suzhou 苏州市	Jiangsu 江苏省	12.77	14
Shanghai 上海市	Shanghai 上海市	11.89	13
Shaoxing 绍兴市	Zhejiang 浙江省	10.66	10
Nantong 南通市	Jiangsu 江苏省	7.38	10
Yantai 烟台市	Shandong 山东省	7.25	1
Tianjin 天津市	Tianjin 天津市	4.53	5
Lianyungang 连云港市	Jiangsu 江苏省	4.08	1
Changzhou 常州市	Jiangsu 江苏省	3.88	6
Foshan 佛山市	Guangdong 广东省	3.58	3
Zhengzhou 郑州市	Henan 河南省	2.53	4

10 Major Wholesalers 十家主要批发商	City 城市	Province 省	Telephone/Fax 电话/传真
Shanghai Shenda Co.,Ltd. 上海申达股份有限公司	Shanghai 上海市	Shanghai 上海市	(021)62319898 (021)62317250
Orient International Holding Silk Group Corportion 东方国际集团丝绸进出口有限公司	Shanghai 上海市	Shanghai 上海市	(021)64662288 (021)64677788
Nanjing Textiles Import & Export Co.,Ltd. 南京纺织品进出口股份有限公司	Nanjing 南京市	Jiangsu 江苏省	(025)3306789 (025)3300518
Zhejiang Textiles Import & Export Group Co.,Ltd. 浙江省纺织品进出口集团有限公司	Hangzhou 杭州市	Zhejiang 浙江省	(0571)87075888 (0571)87079234
Zhejiang Orient Holdings Co.,Ltd. 浙江东方集团股份有限公司	Hangzhou 杭州市	Zhejiang 浙江省	(0571)87215678 (0571)87215000
Zhejiang Silk Holding Co.,ltd. 浙江省丝绸集团有限公司	Hangzhou 杭州市	Zhejiang 浙江省	(0571)85195588 (0571)85192540
Guangdong Silk (Group) Corporation 广东省丝绸（集团）公司	Guangzhou 广州市	Guangdong 广东省	(020)83337448 (020)83332995
Shanghai Costume Group Co.,Ltd. 上海服装（集团）有限公司	Shanghai 上海市	Shanghai 上海市	(021)62748598 (021)62414773
Orient International Holding Shanghai Textiles Import & Export Co.Ltd 东方国际集团上海市针织品进出口有限公司	Shanghai 上海市	Shanghai 上海市	(021)63218855 (021)63299560
Jiangsu Textiles Import & Export Group Co.,Ltd. 江苏省纺织品进出口集团股份有限公司	Nanjing 南京市	Jiangsu 江苏省	(025)6895000 (025)4400800

2854: Fishing Net 渔网制造业

The industry accounts for 0.015% of the total revenue of China's industrial sector in 2002. The rate of return on assets is 3.27%. 79.03% of all firms in the industry made a profit while 20.97% had negative returns.The top province in terms of the industry's revenue is Jiangsu, accounting for 32.20% of the total revenue.
2002年本行业收入占全行业的 0.015%，资产利润率为 3.27%。79.03%的企业赢利，20.97%的企业亏损。收入最高的省为江苏省，占本行业的32.20%。

	Total number of firms 企业总数	Total number of employees 职工总数	Total revenue (Mil.RMB) 总销售收入(百万元)	Total profit (Mil.RMB) 总利润(百万元)	Return on assets 资产利润率(%)	Return on equity 权益利润率(%)	Labour productivity ('000 RMB/ worker) 劳动生产率(千元/人)	Debts/ assets 资产负债率(%)	Total assets (Mil.RMB) 总资产(百万元)
Industry Overall 行业总体	62	15,943	1,619	47	3.27	8.20	37.38	60.13	1,448

	Number of firms 企业个数	Average number of employees 平均职工人数	Average revenue ('000 RMB) 平均销售收入（千元）	Average profit ('000 RMB) 平均利润(千元)	Return on assets 资产利润率(%)	Return on equity 权益利润率(%)	Labour productivity ('000 RMB/ worker) 劳动生产率(千元/人)	Debts/ assets 资产负债率(%)	Average total assets ('000 RMB) 平均总资产(千元)
By ownership 产业所有权									
State-owned 国有	6	343	8,746	-5	-0.02	-0.31	7.66	94.28	25,168
Collective-owned 集体	12	318	43,465	742	2.62	7.08	76.31	63.08	28,368
Foreign & Overseas Chinese Funded 三资	13	239	33,960	1,749	4.70	8.95	40.11	47.52	37,221
By regional distribution 地区分布									
Central-North 华北	4	348	51,471	810	2.86	10.25	148.86	72.06	28,294
Beijing 北京									
Tianjin 天津	2	674	102,680	2,057	4.26	11.15	153.85	61.80	48,290
Hebei 河北	2	23	262	-437	-5.26		-0.64	131.76	8,299
Shanxi 山西									
Inner Mongolia 内蒙古									
Northeast 东北	2	135	5,463	210	0.52	6.76	5.18	92.35	40,587
Liaoning 辽宁	2	135	5,463	210	0.52	6.76	5.18	92.35	40,587
Jilin 吉林									
Heilongjiang 黑龙江									
Central-East 华东	37	254	26,968	1,158	5.90	14.77	28.53	60.02	19,609
Shanghai 上海	1	52	26,230	569	3.62	41.59	94.52	91.30	15,723
Jiangsu 江苏	17	168	30,660	683	3.37	8.72	45.67	61.40	20,273
Zhejiang 浙江	6	242	14,865	1		0.01	16.10	68.91	34,162
Anhui 安徽	5	673	9,139	771	6.48	7.38	4.20	12.18	11,899
Fujian 福建	1	80	5,260	149	2.43	3.77	30.63	35.53	6,138
Jiangxi 江西									
Shandong 山东	7	229	44,315	3,808	28.18	74.54	58.06	62.19	13,510
Central-South 中南	18	259	22,051	34	0.12	0.25	24.82	53.06	29,028
Henan 河南									
Hubei 湖北	1	60	5,170	15	0.68	2.14	35.38	68.18	2,200
Hunan 湖南	4	228	24,444	242	1.73	9.54	27.96	81.86	13,976
Guangdong 广东	12	304	24,444	-31	-0.08	-0.16	24.20	49.26	38,504
Guangxi 广西									
Hainan 海南	1	50	651	-6	-0.26		0.82	100.00	2,350
Southwest 西南	1	212	7,216	230	4.13	5.57	15.09	25.91	5,574
Chongqing 重庆	1	212	7,216	230	4.13	5.57	15.09	25.91	5,574
Sichuan 四川									
Guizhou 贵州									
Yunnan 云南									
Tibet 西藏									
Northwest 西北									
Shaanxi 陕西									
Gansu 甘肃									
Qinghai 青海									
Ningxia 宁夏									
Xinjiang 新疆									

2854: Fishing Net 渔网制造业

Year 年份	Number of firms 企业个数	Rate of change 变化率 (%)	Number of employees 职工人数 (人)	Rate of change 变化率 (%)	Total revenue (Mil. RMB) 总销售收入 (百万元)	Rate of change 变化率 (%)	Total profit (Mil RMB) 总利润 (百万元)	Rate of change 变化率 (%)
2000	70		13,692		1,640		19	
2001	60	-14.29	14,582	6.50	1,534	-6.46	44	131.58
2002	62	3.33	15,943	9.33	1,619	5.54	47	6.82

Major Products 主要产品	Output 产量	Unit 单位
Plastic Silk & Knitting Products 塑料丝及编织制品	161	10,000 Tons 万吨

10 Main Firms with Maximal Revenue (year founded) 收入最大的十家主要企业（创办年份）	City 城市	Province 省	Telephone/fax 电话/传真	Number of employees 职工人数	Ownership 产业所有权	Revenue ('000 RMB) 销售收入 (千元)	Profit('000 RMB) (rank) 利润(千元) (排名)	Total assets ('000 RMB) 总资产 (千元)	Major products 主要产品
Tianjin Fishing Net (Group) Co.,Ltd.	Tianjin	Tianjin	(022)67296687		Collective-owned				Fishnet
天津渔网集团公司(1980)	天津市	天津市	(022)67296261	1,260	集体企业	194,000	3,610(5)	92,460	渔网
Kunshan Kingthou Net MFG. Co., Ltd.	Suzhou	Jiangsu	(0512)57301219		Overseas Chinese-funded				Fishnet
昆山金洲制网有限公司(1994)	苏州市	江苏省	(0512)57312566	500	港澳台资	114,932	4,312(3)	129,497	渔网
Jinhu Fishing Net Factory	Huaian	Jiangsu	(0517)6551800		Joint Stock				knitting Net
金湖县渔网厂(1982)	淮安市	江苏省	(0517)6551135	399	股份制	104,240	1,310(10)	17,820	编织网
Sheyang Zheng Xin Fishing Tackle Co., Ltd.	Yancheng	Jiangsu	(0515)2321737		Private Enterprises				Fishnet
射阳县正信渔具有限公司(1995)	盐城市	江苏省	(0515)2311617	240	私营独资	89,330	1,890(6)	21,910	渔网
Longkou liangjia Aquaculture Breeding Equipment Factory	Yantai	Shandong	(0535)8627149		Collective-owned				Breeding Net
龙口市亮甲水产养殖器材厂(1989)	烟台市	山东省		153	集体企业	64,240	3,850(4)	5,350	养殖网
Sheyang Haixinda Fishing Tackle Co., Ltd.	Yancheng	Jiangsu	(0515)2321727		Private Owned				Plastics Netting Twine
射阳县海信达渔具有限公司(1998)	盐城市	江苏省	(0515)2321727	115	私营企业	53,410	1,100(12)	9,300	塑料网线
Wenzhou Fishing Net Plant	Wenzhou	Zhejiang	(0577)88133746		Collective-owned				Fishnet
温州渔网厂(1954)	温州市	浙江省	(0577)88132748	692	集体企业	44,416	128(34)	68,756	渔网
Shandong Huichang Fishing Gears Company	Yantai	Shandong	(0535)7690888		Joint Stock				Fishnet
山东会昌网线集团公司(1972)	烟台市	山东省	(0535)7690078	350	股份制	42,900	4,620(2)	25,930	渔网
Wuchuan Fuqiang Net Industry Co., Ltd.	Zhanjiang	Guangdong	(0759)5908319		Private Enterprises				Fishnet
广东吴川富强网业有限公司(1989)	湛江市	广东省	(0759)5908319	60	私营独资	32,500	1,700(7)	13,967	渔网
Chenghai North Ocean Fishing Gears Co., Ltd.	Shantou	Guangdong	(0754)5727028		Foreign Funded				Nylon Fishnet
澄海市北洋渔具有限公司(1989)	汕头市	广东省	(0754)5725511	449	外商投资	31,919	652(13)	61,435	尼龙渔网

Top 10 Cities by Revenue 销售收入排名前10位城市	Province 省	Market share 市场份额 (%)	Number of firms 企业个数
Yantai 烟台市	Shandong 山东省	17.56	4
Tianjin 天津市	Tianjin 天津市	12.69	2
Yancheng 盐城市	Jiangsu 江苏省	9.75	3
Suzhou 苏州市	Jiangsu 江苏省	7.10	1
Huaian 淮安市	Jiangsu 江苏省	6.83	2
Zhanjiang 湛江市	Guangdong 广东省	6.47	6
Jieyang 揭阳市	Guangdong 广东省	5.98	1
Shantou 汕头市	Guangdong 广东省	5.67	5
Lianyungang 连云港市	Jiangsu 江苏省	4.44	5
Yiyang 益阳市	Hunan 湖南省	3.82	3

10 Major Wholesalers 十家主要批发商	City 城市	Province 省	Telephone/Fax 电话/传真
Ningbo Haitian Group General Company	Ningbo	Zhejiang	(0574)87195360
宁波海田集团总公司	宁波市	浙江省	(0574)87195821
Heilongjiang Agriculture Means Of Production Company	Harbin	Heilongjiang	(0451)88383752
黑龙江省农业生产资料公司	哈尔滨市	黑龙江省	(0451)88382367
Yantai Agriculture Means Of Production General Company	Yantai	Shandong	(0535)6216374
烟台市农业生产资料总公司	烟台市	山东省	(0535)6211348
Guangdong Agriculture Means Of Production General Company	Guangzhou	Guangdong	(020)87773051
广东省农业生产资料总公司	广州市	广东省	(020)87754117
Inner Mongolia Autonomous Region Agriculture & Animal Husbandry Means Of Production Co.,Ltd.	Huhhot	Inner Mongolia	(0471)6963132
内蒙古自治区农牧业生产资料股份有限公司	呼和浩特市	内蒙古	(0471)6964434
Shanghai Agriculture Means Of Production Company	Shanghai	Shanghai	(021)63807100
上海市农业生产资料公司	上海市	上海市	(021)63806807
Ningbo Haitian International Trade Co.,Ltd.	Ningbo	Zhejiang	(0574)87345251
宁波海田国际贸易有限公司	宁波市	浙江省	(0574)87345620
Fujian AMP Incorpration	Fuzhou	Fujian	(0591)7508666
福建省农资集团公司	福州市	福建省	(0591)7614839
Shandong Agricultural Machinery Group General Company	Jinan	Shandong	(0531)8951240
山东省农业机械集团总公司	济南市	山东省	(0531)8951240
Shandong Yantai Agriculture Means Of Production Purchasing Supply Station	Yantai	Shandong	(0535)6222126
山东省烟台市农业生产资料采购供应站	烟台市	山东省	(0535)6216440

2859: Other Fishing Tackle Products 其他渔具制造业

The industry accounts for 0.014% of the total revenue of China's industrial sector in 2002. The rate of return on assets is 8.93%. 88.00% of all firms in the industry made a profit while 12.00% had negative returns.The top province in terms of the industry's revenue is Shandong, accounting for 58.21% of the total revenue.
2002年本行业收入占全行业的 0.014%，资产利润率为 8.93%。88.00%的企业赢利，12.00%的企业亏损。收入最高的省为山东省，占本行业的58.21%。

	Total number of firms 企业总数	Total number of employees 职工总数	Total revenue (Mil.RMB) 总销售收入 (百万元)	Total profit (Mil.RMB) 总利润 (百万元)	Return on assets 资产利润率 (%)	Return on equity 权益利润率 (%)	Labour productivity ('000 RMB/ worker) 劳动生产率 (千元/人)	Debts/ assets 资产负债率 (%)	Total assets (Mil.RMB) 总资产 (百万元)
Industry Overall 行业总体	50	9,944	1,452	79	8.93	23.44	40.27	61.91	880

	Number of firms 企业个数	Average number of employees 平均职工人数	Average revenue ('000 RMB) 平均销售收入 (千元)	Average profit ('000 RMB) 平均利润 (千元)	Return on assets 资产利润率 (%)	Return on equity 权益利润率 (%)	Labour productivity ('000 RMB/ worker) 劳动生产率 (千元/人)	Debts/ assets 资产负债率 (%)	Average total assets ('000 RMB) 平均总资产 (千元)
By ownership 产业所有权									
State-owned 国有	1	211	5,517				13.89	43.35	11,902
Collective-owned 集体	4	239	29,166	844	9.88	28.00	46.62	64.72	8,538
Foreign & Overseas Chinese Funded 三资	27	222	33,656	1,930	8.22	20.93	36.90	60.73	23,479
By regional distribution 地区分布									
Central-North 华北	2	114	8,230	-378	-2.81	-6.60	12.71	57.43	13,447
Beijing 北京									
Tianjin 天津	2	114	8,230	-378	-2.81	-6.60	12.71	57.43	13,447
Hebei 河北									
Shanxi 山西									
Inner Mongolia 内蒙古									
Northeast 东北	3	108	8,853	123	1.51	2.63	23.11	42.62	8,140
Liaoning 辽宁	3	108	8,853	123	1.51	2.63	23.11	42.62	8,140
Jilin 吉林									
Heilongjiang 黑龙江									
Central-East 华东	39	207	33,226	1,877	9.93	27.82	44.22	64.32	18,914
Shanghai 上海	1	276	9,205	-467	-7.66	-32.30	7.52	76.28	6,097
Jiangsu 江苏	4	235	45,234	1,493	4.26	10.94	39.68	61.01	35,007
Zhejiang 浙江	7	323	26,443	1,346	5.64	25.14	19.96	77.58	23,874
Anhui 安徽	1	132	4,643	446	31.19	39.47	9.97	20.98	1,430
Fujian 福建	4	94	16,313	156	1.18	4.80	45.77	75.35	13,202
Jiangxi 江西	1	104	5,719	100	1.57	2.14	56.38	26.89	6,385
Shandong 山东	21	191	40,236	2,720	15.70	37.86	62.19	58.53	17,322
Central-South 中南	6	218	18,790	959	6.29	12.32	24.81	48.99	15,246
Henan 河南									
Hubei 湖北									
Hunan 湖南	1	156	4,026	-398	-5.64		9.01	109.65	7,060
Guangdong 广东	5	230	21,743	1,230	7.28	12.99	26.95	43.91	16,883
Guangxi 广西									
Hainan 海南									
Southwest 西南									
Chongqing 重庆									
Sichuan 四川									
Guizhou 贵州									
Yunnan 云南									
Tibet 西藏									
Northwest 西北									
Shaanxi 陕西									
Gansu 甘肃									
Qinghai 青海									
Ningxia 宁夏									
Xinjiang 新疆									

2859: Other Fishing Tackle Products 其他渔具制造业

Year 年份	Number of firms 企业个数	Rate of change 变化率 (%)	Number of employees 职工人数 (人)	Rate of change 变化率 (%)	Total revenue (Mil. RMB) 总销售收入 (百万元)	Rate of change 变化率 (%)	Total profit (Mil RMB) 总利润 (百万元)	Rate of change 变化率 (%)
2000	43		7,862		955		48	
2001	56	30.23	12,288	56.30	1,760	84.29	99	106.25
2002	50	-10.71	9,944	-19.08	1,452	-17.50	79	-20.20

Major Products 主要产品	Output 产量	Unit 单位

10 Main Firms with Maximal Revenue (year founded) 收入最大的十家主要企业（创办年份）	City 城市	Province 省	Telephone/fax 电话/传真	Number of employees 职工人数	Ownership 产业所有权	Revenue ('000 RMB) 销售收入 (千元)	Profit('000 RMB) (rank) 利润(千元) (排名)	Total assets ('000 RMB) 总资产 (千元)	Major products 主要产品
Rushan Guo Xing Fishing Tackle Co., Ltd.	Weihai	Shandong	(0631)6466052		Private Owned				Fishing Pole & Tackle
乳山市国兴钓具有限公司(1998)	威海市	山东省	(0631)6466952	143	私营企业	129,922	7,268(3)	18,560	渔杆钓具
Yangzhou Jiu Yang Fishing Tackle Co.,Ltd.	Yangzhou	Jiangsu	(0514)7307888		Overseas Chinese-funded				Fishing Tackle & Fittings
扬州久扬渔具有限公司(1992)	扬州市	江苏省	(0514)7301458	450	港澳台资	122,845	5,432(5)	98,333	渔具及配件
Rainbow Fishing Tackle Co., Ltd.	Ningbo	Zhejiang	(0574)63203651		Foreign Funded				Fishing Tackle
宁波瑞宝渔具有限公司(2000)	宁波市	浙江省	(0574)63204572	902	外商投资	74,033	4,695(6)	60,982	渔具
Weihai Wei Jian Industrial Co., Ltd.	Weihai	Shandong	(0631)5757011		Private Owned				Fishing Pole
威海伟建实业有限公司(1998)	威海市	山东省	(0631)5752800	260	私营企业	71,720	2,070(13)	17,990	渔杆
Ningbo Ever Winner Fishing Tackle Co., Ltd.	Ningbo	Zhejiang	(0574)86881232		Foreign Funded				Fishing Tackle
宁波达金兴业渔具有限公司(1995)	宁波市	浙江省	(0574)86881235	675	外商投资	64,210	2,699(9)	69,310	渔具
Qingdao Dayang Fish Hook Co.,Ltd.	Qingdao	Shandong	(0532)8598171		Foreign Funded				Fishing Tackle
青岛大洋钓针有限公司(1994)	青岛市	山东省	(0532)8598172	200	外商投资	53,200	1,131(16)	21,495	渔具
Gamakatsu Shantou Sports Co., Ltd.	Shantou	Guangdong	(0754)8362806		Foreign Funded				Fishing Tackle
汕头伽玛卡兹体育用品有限公司(1990)	汕头市	广东省	(0754)8362099	150	外商投资	45,428	4,170(7)	48,923	渔具
Wendeng Sun Finish Machining Fishing Trackle co., Ltd.	Weihai	Shandong	(0631)8355573		Foreign Funded				Fishing Thread Wheel
文登太阳精工钓具有限公司(1995)	威海市	山东省	(0631)8355575	276	外商投资	44,051	9,184(2)	39,911	渔线轮
Panyu Zi Qiang Plastic & Hardware Factory	Guangzhou	Guangdong	(020)84909682		Overseas Chinese-funded				Fishing Tackle Fittings
番禺自强塑胶五金制品厂(1999)	广州市	广东省	(020)84909683	199	港澳台资	40,381	1,541(15)	19,029	渔具配件
Qingdao Xianyu Fishing Trackle Co., Ltd.	Qingdao	Shandong	(0532)7527992		Foreign Funded				Fishing Tackle
青岛鲜宇渔具有限公司(1993)	青岛市	山东省	(0532)7527966	66	外商投资	35,824	3,500(8)	35,844	渔具

Top 10 Cities by Revenue 销售收入排名前10位城市	Province 省	Market share 市场份额 (%)	Number of firms 企业个数
Weihai 威海市	Shandong 山东省	45.59	14
Ningbo 宁波市	Zhejiang 浙江省	12.20	6
Yangzhou 扬州市	Jiangsu 江苏省	10.58	2
Qingdao 青岛市	Shandong 山东省	9.02	5
Guangzhou 广州市	Guangdong 广东省	3.82	3
Shantou 汕头市	Guangdong 广东省	3.67	2
Fuzhou 福州市	Fujian 福建省	3.18	3
Yantai 烟台市	Shandong 山东省	2.41	1
Suzhou 苏州市	Jiangsu 江苏省	1.39	1
Xiamen 厦门市	Fujian 福建省	1.32	1

10 Major Wholesalers 十家主要批发商	City 城市	Province 省	Telephone/Fax 电话/传真
Ningbo Haitian Group General Company	Ningbo	Zhejiang	(0574)87195360
宁波海田集团总公司	宁波市	浙江省	(0574)87195821
Heilongjiang Agriculture Means Of Production Company	Harbin	Heilongjiang	(0451)88383752
黑龙江省农业生产资料公司	哈尔滨市	黑龙江省	(0451)88382367
Yantai Agriculture Means Of Production General Company	Yantai	Shandong	(0535)6216374
烟台市农业生产资料总公司	烟台市	山东省	(0535)6211348
Guangdong Agriculture Means Of Production General Company	Guangzhou	Guangdong	(020)87773051
广东省农业生产资料总公司	广州市	广东省	(020)87754117
Inner Mongolia Autonomous Region Agriculture & Animal Husbandry Means Of Production Co.,Ltd.	Huhhot	Inner Mongolia	(0471)6963132
内蒙古自治区农牧业生产资料股份有限公司	呼和浩特市	内蒙古	(0471)6964434
Shanghai Agriculture Means Of Production Company	Shanghai	Shanghai	(021)63807100
上海市农业生产资料公司	上海市	上海市	(021)63806807
Ningbo Haitian International Trade Co.,Ltd.	Ningbo	Zhejiang	(0574)87345251
宁波海田国际贸易有限公司	宁波市	浙江省	(0574)87345620
Fujian AMP Incorpration	Fuzhou	Fujian	(0591)7508666
福建省农资集团公司	福州市	福建省	(0591)7614839
Shandong Agricultural Machinery Group General Company	Jinan	Shandong	(0531)8951240
山东省农业机械集团总公司	济南市	山东省	(0531)8951240
Shandong Yantai Agriculture Means Of Production Purchasing Supply Station	Yantai	Shandong	(0535)6222126
山东省烟台市农业生产资料采购供应站	烟台市	山东省	(0535)6216440

2910: Tires 轮胎制造业

The industry accounts for 0.452% of the total revenue of China's industrial sector in 2002. The rate of return on assets is 2.63%. 80.80% of all firms in the industry made a profit while 19.20% had negative returns.The top province in terms of the industry's revenue is Shandong, accounting for 33.96% of the total revenue.
2002年本行业收入占全行业的0.452%，资产利润率为2.63%。80.80%的企业赢利，19.20%的企业亏损。收入最高的省为山东省，占本行业的33.96%。

	Total number of firms 企业总数	Total number of employees 职工总数	Total revenue (Mil.RMB) 总销售收入 (百万元)	Total profit (Mil.RMB) 总利润 (百万元)	Return on assets 资产利润率 (%)	Return on equity 权益利润率 (%)	Labour productivity ('000 RMB/ worker) 劳动生产率 (千元/人)	Debts/ assets 资产负债率 (%)	Total assets (Mil.RMB) 总资产 (百万元)
Industry Overall 行业总体	224	196,655	48,533	1,849	2.63	7.10	75.29	63.02	70,406

	Number of firms 企业个数	Average number of employees 平均职工人数	Average revenue ('000 RMB) 平均销售收入 (千元)	Average profit ('000 RMB) 平均利润 (千元)	Return on assets 资产利润率 (%)	Return on equity 权益利润率 (%)	Labour productivity ('000 RMB/ worker) 劳动生产率 (千元/人)	Debts/ assets 资产负债率 (%)	Average total assets ('000 RMB) 平均总资产 (千元)
By ownership 产业所有权									
State-owned 国有	15	1,132	101,983	-1,092	-0.47	-1.26	30.97	63.11	234,287
Collective-owned 集体	21	538	103,216	3,479	4.63	22.86	66.22	79.74	75,108
Foreign & Overseas Chinese Funded 三资	38	1,543	601,456	41,035	4.66	11.15	122.30	58.26	881,498
By regional distribution 地区分布									
Central-North 华北	23	701	119,460	2,131	1.09	4.57	52.43	76.13	195,539
Beijing 北京	1	2,028	373,367	927	0.09	0.68	47.19	86.54	1,016,846
Tianjin 天津	10	444	122,924	5,673	2.75	13.93	67.13	80.26	206,376
Hebei 河北	9	705	51,387	1,463	2.70	8.45	25.20	68.03	54,149
Shanxi 山西	2	1,210	298,777	506	0.12	0.29	103.37	57.30	407,600
Inner Mongolia 内蒙古	1	885	84,950	-22,816	-19.97	-89.28	46.77	77.63	114,240
Northeast 东北	19	1,357	217,593	5,842	1.20	3.84	42.98	68.64	485,026
Liaoning 辽宁	15	1,175	214,454	21,941	5.26	14.72	59.17	64.26	417,064
Jilin 吉林	3	885	116,441	-3,350	-0.87	-4.65	51.49	81.35	386,303
Heilongjiang 黑龙江	1	5,499	568,142	-208,073	-11.56	-47.48	-13.03	75.66	1,800,621
Central-East 华东	132	768	250,771	12,475	4.11	10.05	101.19	59.15	303,735
Shanghai 上海	10	1,052	329,888	-16,210	-2.71	-8.55	68.34	68.28	598,059
Jiangsu 江苏	8	1,086	430,449	45,694	7.33	16.69	125.75	56.10	623,522
Zhejiang 浙江	9	1,089	423,215	25,698	6.00	15.76	113.90	61.93	428,338
Anhui 安徽	2	2,539	1,562,278	95,105	5.04	13.29	146.07	62.08	1,887,194
Fujian 福建	5	1,583	536,702	73,627	9.90	17.32	139.80	42.88	744,036
Jiangxi 江西	3	378	86,430	208	0.21	0.51	102.10	58.08	96,729
Shandong 山东	95	613	173,506	6,873	3.73	9.14	92.15	59.13	184,047
Central-South 中南	33	1,056	158,608	-125	-0.04	-0.12	43.73	66.63	318,810
Henan 河南	13	1,016	153,067	2,714	1.05	3.99	45.89	73.62	257,559
Hubei 湖北	4	1,236	187,555	71	0.02	0.14	51.63	89.42	466,315
Hunan 湖南	3	198	12,662	-157	-1.19	-5.80	13.92	79.43	13,139
Guangdong 广东	10	890	193,168	3,680	0.93	1.72	59.36	45.65	394,563
Guangxi 广西	2	2,969	254,052	-11,718	-2.03	-5.70	19.89	64.31	576,376
Hainan 海南	1	1,275	16,201	-52,582	-31.04		6.54	178.74	169,409
Southwest 西南	11	1,033	177,413	4,836	1.62	4.67	42.17	65.22	297,727
Chongqing 重庆	3	609	25,186	-2,527	-4.40	-421.93	12.69	98.96	57,460
Sichuan 四川	3	813	94,214	872	0.74	2.13	38.08	65.29	118,101
Guizhou 贵州	3	2,084	517,776	19,760	2.24	6.08	57.06	63.13	881,725
Yunnan 云南	2	423	20,009	-558	-1.08	-2.85	7.67	62.13	51,571
Tibet 西藏									
Northwest 西北	6	1,188	227,265	-1,143	-0.24	-0.66	82.54	62.71	467,390
Shaanxi 陕西	1	400	14,462	-4,040	-11.94	-74.11	14.98	83.89	33,830
Gansu 甘肃	1	160					6.36	51.06	317,775
Qinghai 青海									
Ningxia 宁夏	2	1,961	470,981	-2,843	-0.32	-0.86	102.22	62.58	884,222
Xinjiang 新疆	2	1,323	203,582	1,433	0.42	1.28	68.20	67.40	342,146

2910: Tires 轮胎制造业

Year 年份	Number of firms 企业个数	Rate of change 变化率 (%)	Number of employees 职工人数 (人)	Rate of change 变化率 (%)	Total revenue (Mil. RMB) 总销售收入 (百万元)	Rate of change 变化率 (%)	Total profit (Mil RMB) 总利润 (百万元)	Rate of change 变化率 (%)
2000	200		194,742		34,771		-33	
2001	218	9.00	198,422	1.89	39,302	13.03	1,150	-
2002	224	2.75	196,655	-0.89	48,533	23.49	1,849	60.78

Major Products 主要产品	Output 产量	Unit 单位
Outer Tyre 轮胎外胎	16,046	10,000 Pieces 万条
Meridian Tire Cover 子午线轮胎外胎	4,882	10,000 Pieces 万条

10 Main Firms with Maximal Revenue (year founded) 收入最大的十家主要企业（创办年份）	City 城市	Province 省	Telephone/fax 电话/传真	Number of employees 职工人数	Ownership 产业所有权	Revenue ('000 RMB) 销售收入 (千元)	Profit('000 RMB) (rank) 利润(千元) (排名)	Total assets ('000 RMB) 总资产 (千元)	Major products 主要产品
Anhui Grantour Tyre Co.,Ltd.	Hefei	Anhui	(0551)3811555		Foreign Funded				Tyre Cover
安徽佳通轮胎有限公司(1993)	合肥市	安徽省	(0551)3811666	4,868	外商投资	3,106,987	193,306(3)	3,668,435	轮胎外胎
Hangzhou Zhong Ce Rubber Co., Ltd.	Hangzhou	Zhejiang	(0571)86053939		Foreign Funded				Tyre
杭州中策橡胶有限公司(1992)	杭州市	浙江省	(0571)86062011	6,155	外商投资	2,537,280	130,662(6)	1,915,276	轮胎
Triangle Group Co.,Ltd.	Weihai	Shandong	(0631)5305391		State Enterprises				Tyre
三角集团有限公司(1978)	威海市	山东省	(0631)5321246	5,241	国有独资	2,291,457	129,176(7)	2,217,649	轮胎
Rongcheng Rubber Factory	Weihai	Shandong	(0631)7523205		Joint Stock				Tyre
荣成市橡胶厂(1994)	威海市	山东省	(0631)7523888	5,630	股份制	2,071,293	50,439(14)	3,000,240	轮胎
Shandong Rongcheng Ya Tou Industrial Group Co., Ltd.	Weihai	Shandong	(0631)7571556		Limited-Liability				Rubber Products
山东荣成崖头实业集团有限公司(2000)	威海市	山东省	(0631)7571031	1,580	有限公司	1,890,500	78,700(12)	145,330	橡胶制品
Chengshin Rubber (Xiamen) Ind. Ltd.	Xiamen	Fujian	(0592)6211606		Overseas Chinese-funded				Bicycle Inner & Outer Tyre
厦门正新橡胶工业有限公司(1991)	厦门市	福建省	(0592)6210420	4,261	港澳台资	1,715,442	311,222(1)	1,588,536	自行车内外胎
Guizhou Tyre Co., Ltd.	Guiyang	Guizhou	(0851)4767316		Joint Stock				Tyre
贵州轮胎股份有限公司(1966)	贵阳市	贵州省	(0851)4764248	5,238	股份制	1,550,983	45,032(16)	2,416,253	轮胎
Shandong Ling Long Rubber Co., Ltd.	Yantai	Shandong	(0535)8242670		Limited-Liability				Tyre Cover
山东玲珑橡胶有限公司(1993)	烟台市	山东省	(0535)8213349	2,167	有限公司	1,108,655	35,259(18)	1,212,121	轮胎外胎
CHENG SHIN-TOYO Tire & Rubber (China) Co.,Ltd.	Suzhou	Jiangsu	(0512)57673888		Foreign Funded				Tyre
正新橡胶(中国)有限公司(1997)	苏州市	江苏省	(0512)57672342	2,231	外商投资	1,077,661	226,405(2)	1,945,702	轮胎
Fujian Jia Tong Tyre Co., Ltd.	Putian	Fujian	(0594)5898385		Foreign Funded				Meridian Tyre
福建佳通轮胎有限公司(1995)	莆田市	福建省	(0594)5898688	1,950	外商投资	907,645	94,732(11)	1,986,383	子午线轮胎

Top 10 Cities by Revenue 销售收入排名前10位城市	Province 省	Market share 市场份额 (%)	Number of firms 企业个数
Weihai 威海市	Shandong 山东省	14.56	9
Qingdao 青岛市	Shandong 山东省	7.05	32
Shanghai 上海市	Shanghai 上海市	6.80	10
Hefei 合肥市	Anhui 安徽省	6.44	2
Hangzhou 杭州市	Zhejiang 浙江省	5.61	5
Weifang 潍坊市	Shandong 山东省	4.36	25
Xiamen 厦门市	Fujian 福建省	3.63	2
Yantai 烟台市	Shandong 山东省	3.61	5
Guangzhou 广州市	Guangdong 广东省	3.60	4
Jiaozuo 焦作市	Henan 河南省	3.57	4

10 Major Wholesalers 十家主要批发商	City 城市	Province 省	Telephone/Fax 电话/传真
Faw Trade General Company	Changchun	Jilin	(0431)5904147
一汽贸易总公司	长春市	吉林省	(0431)5909761
Shanghai Automobile Import & Export Company	Shanghai	Shanghai	(021)22011717
上海汽车进出口公司	上海市	上海市	(021)22011789
Shiyan Ronghua Dongfeng Automobile Monopoly Co.,Ltd.	Shiyan	Hubei	(0719)8669242
十堰荣华东风汽车专营有限公司	十堰市	湖北省	(0719)8689666
Shenzhen Automobile Industry & Trade General Company	Shenzhen	Guangdong	(0755)83617079
深圳市汽车工业贸易总公司	深圳市	广东省	(0755)83346186
Shanghai Volkswagen Automobile (Tianjin) Co.,Ltd.	Tianjin	Tianjin	(022)25320000
上海大众汽车（天津）有限公司	天津市	天津市	(022)25320532
Shanghai Dongfang Automobile Fittings City Co.,Ltd.	Shanghai	Shanghai	(021)59185910
上海东方汽配城有限公司	上海市	上海市	(021)59184868
Zhejiang Aotong Automobile Co.,Ltd.	Hangzhou	Zhejiang	(0571)85368000
浙江奥通汽车有限公司	杭州市	浙江省	(0571)85365099
Runhua Group Co.,Ltd.	Jinan	Shandong	(0531)7519704
润华集团股份有限公司	济南市	山东省	(0531)7983746
Shenzhen Motors Ind.Import & Export Co.	Shenzhen	Guangdong	(0755)83626234
深圳市汽车工业进出口公司	深圳市	广东省	(0755)26711560
Shenzhen Dongfeng Real Estate Co.,Ltd.	Shenzhen	Guangdong	(0755)83210279
深圳东风置业有限公司	深圳市	广东省	(0755)83257208

2920: Inner Tubes 力车胎制造业

The industry accounts for 0.037% of the total revenue of China's industrial sector in 2002. The rate of return on assets is 2.57%. 71.95% of all firms in the industry made a profit while 28.05% had negative returns.The top province in terms of the industry's revenue is Jiangsu, accounting for 37.84% of the total revenue.
2002年本行业收入占全行业的 0.037%，资产利润率为 2.57%。71.95%的企业赢利，28.05%的企业亏损。收入最高的省为江苏省，占本行业的37.84%。

	Total number of firms 企业总数	Total number of employees 职工总数	Total revenue (Mil.RMB) 总销售收入 (百万元)	Total profit (Mil.RMB) 总利润 (百万元)	Return on assets 资产利润率 (%)	Return on equity 权益利润率 (%)	Labour productivity ('000 RMB/ worker) 劳动生产率 (千元/人)	Debts/ assets 资产负债率 (%)	Total assets (Mil.RMB) 总资产 (百万元)
Industry Overall 行业总体	82	27,805	3,947	133	2.57	7.11	31.29	63.77	5,162

	Number of firms 企业个数	Average number of employees 平均职工人数	Average revenue ('000 RMB) 平均销售收入 (千元)	Average profit ('000 RMB) 平均利润 (千元)	Return on assets 资产利润率 (%)	Return on equity 权益利润率 (%)	Labour productivity ('000 RMB/ worker) 劳动生产率 (千元/人)	Debts/ assets 资产负债率 (%)	Average total assets ('000 RMB) 平均总资产 (千元)
By ownership 产业所有权									
State-owned 国有	4	27	148	-2,655	-6.27		140.95	126.82	42,379
Collective-owned 集体	21	366	50,201	3,172	6.22	14.75	5.68	57.84	51,005
Foreign & Overseas Chinese Funded 三资	15	413	92,463	3,322	2.77	7.45	58.87	62.83	119,979
By regional distribution 地区分布									
Central-North 华北	17	369	56,992	3,452	3.61	11.12	4.95	67.51	95,500
Beijing 北京									
Tianjin 天津	13	384	68,830	4,241	3.72	11.56	1.15	67.81	113,995
Hebei 河北	4	323	18,519	888	2.51	7.04	19.64	64.37	35,392
Shanxi 山西									
Inner Mongolia 内蒙古									
Northeast 东北	2	61	8,209	-152	-0.62	-1.05	37.72	41.44	24,577
Liaoning 辽宁	1	60	9,916	196	0.61	0.87	50.95	30.62	32,330
Jilin 吉林									
Heilongjiang 黑龙江	1	61	6,502	-499	-2.97	-7.85	24.70	62.23	16,823
Central-East 华东	45	397	58,417	1,773	2.68	6.78	41.41	60.40	66,075
Shanghai 上海	11	223	24,630	76	0.24	0.77	38.59	68.77	31,308
Jiangsu 江苏	16	451	93,326	3,843	3.35	8.78	56.43	61.79	114,598
Zhejiang 浙江	6	491	67,687	2,507	4.43	8.68	29.31	48.92	56,546
Anhui 安徽	3	396	29,897	-266	-0.47	-1.51	24.78	68.61	56,295
Fujian 福建									
Jiangxi 江西	1	70	9,355	32	0.51	0.56	45.83	7.80	6,218
Shandong 山东	8	502	44,934	401	1.14	2.34	29.85	51.17	35,129
Central-South 中南	16	161	15,045	-402	-1.60	-5.24	32.49	69.54	25,176
Henan 河南	3	64	7,803	411	3.77	10.91	50.09	65.48	10,906
Hubei 湖北	4	201	5,507	-1,576	-5.19	-27.80	9.70	81.32	30,356
Hunan 湖南	4	61	5,897	-571	-4.53		38.75	101.73	12,615
Guangdong 广东	5	269	34,339	185	0.47	1.03	42.48	54.80	39,643
Guangxi 广西									
Hainan 海南									
Southwest 西南	2	468	45,918	565	1.00	8.26	10.53	87.89	56,489
Chongqing 重庆									
Sichuan 四川									
Guizhou 贵州									
Yunnan 云南	2	468	45,918	565	1.00	8.26	10.53	87.89	56,489
Tibet 西藏									
Northwest 西北									
Shaanxi 陕西									
Gansu 甘肃									
Qinghai 青海									
Ningxia 宁夏									
Xinjiang 新疆									

2920: Inner Tubes 力车胎制造业

Year 年份	Number of firms 企业个数	Rate of change 变化率 (%)	Number of employees 职工人数 (人)	Rate of change 变化率 (%)	Total revenue (Mil. RMB) 总销售收入 (百万元)	Rate of change 变化率 (%)	Total profit (Mil RMB) 总利润 (百万元)	Rate of change 变化率 (%)
2000	79		36,673		4,254		178	
2001	78	-1.27	26,241	-28.45	3,122	-26.61	67	-62.36
2002	82	5.13	27,805	5.96	3,947	26.43	133	98.51

Major Products 主要产品	Output 产量	Unit 单位
Rickshaw Cover 力车胎外胎	35,186	10,000 Pieces 万条

10 Main Firms with Maximal Revenue (year founded) 收入最大的十家主要企业(创办年份)	City 城市	Province 省	Telephone/fax 电话/传真	Number of employees 职工人数	Ownership 产业所有权	Revenue ('000 RMB) 销售收入(千元)	Profit('000 RMB) (rank) 利润(千元)(排名)	Total assets ('000 RMB) 总资产(千元)	Major products 主要产品
Kenda Rubber (China) Co., Ltd. 建大橡胶(中国)有限公司(1994)	Suzhou 苏州市	Jiangsu 江苏省	(0512)57614172 (0512)57614171	1,800	Overseas Chinese-funded 港澳台资	531,014	42,474(2)	715,526	Bicycle Inner & Outer Tyre 自行车内外胎
Hua Feng Rubber (China) Co.,Ltd. 华丰橡胶(中国)有限公司(1996)	Suzhou 苏州市	Jiangsu 江苏省	(0512)52811788 (0512)52813323	1,002	Foreign Funded 外商投资	347,860	5,730(8)	412,640	Bicycle Tyre 自行车胎
Jiangsu Fei Chi Co., Ltd. 江苏飞驰股份有限公司(1965)	Yancheng 盐城市	Jiangsu 江苏省	(0515)8551088 (0515)8555318	1,570	Joint Stock 股份制	236,220	7,020(5)	376,710	Bicycle Inner & Outer Tyre 自行车内外胎
Shandong Jinlun Stock Co., Ltd. 山东锦轮股份有限公司(1970)	Taian 泰安市	Shandong 山东省	(0538)2821032 (0538)2821132	1,822	Joint Stock 股份制	174,165	377(27)	131,764	Bicycle Inner & Outer Tyre 自行车内外胎
Xuzhou Suquan Rubber Co., Ltd. 徐州苏泉橡胶有限公司(1996)	Xuzhou 徐州市	Jiangsu 江苏省	(0516)6768135 (0516)6768135	400	Private Owned 私营企业	129,500	6,700(6)	18,400	Pedicab Inner Tyre 力车内胎
Innova Rubber (Pinghu) Co., Ltd. 伊诺华橡胶(平湖)有限公司(2001)	Jiaxing 嘉兴市	Zhejiang 浙江省	(0573)5025419 (0573)5025423	607	Overseas Chinese-funded 港澳台资	111,646	-	116,743	Bicycle Tyre 自行车车胎
Shanghai Wanhong Rubber Products Co.,Ltd. 上海万虹胶制品有限公司(1989)	Shanghai 上海市	Shanghai 上海市	(021)64065885 (021)64701067	840	Overseas Chinese-funded 港澳台资	87,630	322(31)	121,467	Bicycle Tyre 自行车轮胎
Lixin Rubber (Taicang) Co.,Ltd. 立新橡胶(太仓)有限公司(1999)	Suzhou 苏州市	Jiangsu 江苏省	(0512)53459818 (0512)53459817	638	Overseas Chinese-funded 港澳台资	86,690	150(35)	144,330	Bicycle Inner & Outer Tyre 自行车内外胎
Rizhao Donggang Ju Feng Welfare Rubber Factory 日照市东港区巨峰福利橡胶厂(1998)	Rizhao 日照市	Shandong 山东省	(0633)8631298 (0633)8641158	790	Private Enterprises 私营独资	71,210	1,160(15)	29,610	Tyre 轮胎
Anhui Tian Di Ren Group Co., Ltd. 安徽天地人集团股份有限公司(1995)	Huaibei 淮北市	Anhui 安徽省	(0561)3111211 (0561)3111567	560	Joint Stock 股份制	66,692	2,080(12)	137,074	Rubber Products 橡胶制品

Top 10 Cities by Revenue 销售收入排名前10位城市	Province 省	Market share 市场份额 (%)	Number of firms 企业个数
Suzhou 苏州市	Jiangsu 江苏省	24.65	4
Tianjin 天津市	Tianjin 天津市	22.67	13
Shanghai 上海市	Shanghai 上海市	6.86	11
Yancheng 盐城市	Jiangsu 江苏省	5.99	1
Shaoxing 绍兴市	Zhejiang 浙江省	4.81	1
Taian 泰安市	Shandong 山东省	4.76	2
Guangzhou 广州市	Guangdong 广东省	3.97	3
Xuzhou 徐州市	Jiangsu 江苏省	3.28	1
Jiaxing 嘉兴市	Zhejiang 浙江省	2.83	1
Wuxi 无锡市	Jiangsu 江苏省	2.51	7

10 Major Wholesalers 十家主要批发商	City 城市	Province 省	Telephone/Fax 电话/传真
China Chemical Industry Supply & Sale (Group) General Company 中国化工供销(集团)总公司	Beijing 北京市	Beijing 北京市	(010)64238623 (010)64238623
China Chemical Industry Import & Export General Company 中国化工进出口总公司	Beijing 北京市	Beijing 北京市	(010)88078888 (010)88078890
Tianjin Bridge Group Welding Materials Supply & Sale Co., Ltd. 天津大桥集团电焊条供销有限公司	Tianjin 天津市	Tianjin 天津市	(022)83968861 (022)83968865
Taizhou Xingwei Chunlan Chain Stores Co., Ltd. 泰州星威春兰连锁店有限公司	Taizhou 泰州市	Jiangsu 江苏省	(0523)6611200 (0523)6224181
Taizhou Chunlan Sale Company 泰州春兰销售公司	Taizhou 泰州市	Jiangsu 江苏省	(0523)6611200 (0523)6224181
Shandong Tri-Union Co., Ltd. 山东三联有限责任公司	Jinan 济南市	Shandong 山东省	(0531)6086351 (0531)6093103
Haier Electrical Appliances Co.,Ltd. 海尔集团电器产业有限公司	Qingdao 青岛市	Shandong 山东省	(0532)8939175 (0532)8938086
Guangzhou Haier Industry & Trade Co.,Ltd. 广州海尔工贸有限公司	Guangzhou 广州市	Guangdong 广东省	(020)87397315 (020)87374302
Huizhou TCL Electrical Appliances Sales Co.,Ltd. 惠州市TCL电器销售有限公司	Huizhou 惠州市	Guangdong 广东省	(0752)2289885 (0752)2280690
Guangdong Hardware Minerals Import & Export Group Company 广东省五金矿产进出口集团公司	Guangzhou 广州市	Guangdong 广东省	(020)87752204 (020)87752205

2930: Rubber Sheet ,Tube and Belt Products 橡胶板、管、带制造业

The industry accounts for 0.089% of the total revenue of China's industrial sector in 2002. The rate of return on assets is 3.12%. 80.54% of all firms in the industry made a profit while 19.46% had negative returns.The top province in terms of the industry's revenue is Jiangsu, accounting for 14.78% of the total revenue.
2002年本行业收入占全行业的0.089%，资产利润率为3.12%。80.54%的企业赢利，19.46%的企业亏损。收入最高的省为江苏省，占本行业的14.78%。

	Total number of firms 企业总数	Total number of employees 职工总数	Total revenue (Mil.RMB) 总销售收入(百万元)	Total profit (Mil.RMB) 总利润(百万元)	Return on assets 资产利润率(%)	Return on equity 权益利润率(%)	Labour productivity ('000 RMB/ worker) 劳动生产率(千元/人)	Debts/ assets 资产负债率(%)	Total assets (Mil.RMB) 总资产(百万元)
Industry Overall 行业总体	370	87,976	9,589	450	3.12	8.76	33.35	64.39	14,427

	Number of firms 企业个数	Average number of employees 平均职工人数	Average revenue ('000 RMB) 平均销售收入(千元)	Average profit ('000 RMB) 平均利润(千元)	Return on assets 资产利润率(%)	Return on equity 权益利润率(%)	Labour productivity ('000 RMB/ worker) 劳动生产率(千元/人)	Debts/ assets 资产负债率(%)	Average total assets ('000 RMB) 平均总资产(千元)
By ownership 产业所有权									
State-owned 国有	40	341	16,643	-605	-1.29	-6.45	17.62	80.02	46,934
Collective-owned 集体	82	214	19,762	865	3.33	12.80	29.56	73.98	25,984
Foreign & Overseas Chinese Funded 三资	41	195	45,998	4,557	6.95	12.96	67.41	46.38	65,581
By regional distribution 地区分布									
Central-North 华北	81	157	17,202	1,115	6.09	13.49	34.04	54.84	18,301
Beijing 北京	2	204	20,067	182	1.45	4.50	30.97	67.73	12,510
Tianjin 天津	23	116	17,664	1,019	5.19	12.88	50.33	59.74	19,642
Hebei 河北	48	114	15,185	1,236	8.50	16.24	44.21	47.65	14,546
Shanxi 山西	8	528	27,264	895	2.33	6.29	10.88	62.94	38,424
Inner Mongolia 内蒙古									
Northeast 东北	29	403	30,501	877	1.03	4.58	26.38	77.51	85,089
Liaoning 辽宁	16	551	44,544	1,774	1.72	4.41	23.19	61.00	103,126
Jilin 吉林	6	143	7,211	264	2.24	34.92	34.17	93.58	11,775
Heilongjiang 黑龙江	7	289	18,366	-647	-0.61		36.96	112.47	106,701
Central-East 华东	164	224	32,052	2,131	5.05	12.78	41.32	60.52	42,231
Shanghai 上海	26	185	30,176	2,041	3.44	8.97	42.99	61.68	59,366
Jiangsu 江苏	46	177	30,806	1,539	5.02	11.23	46.13	55.24	30,641
Zhejiang 浙江	34	244	38,916	2,873	7.97	20.16	40.00	60.48	36,051
Anhui 安徽	14	271	19,047	313	1.10	5.01	32.99	78.03	28,412
Fujian 福建	4	71	10,851	981	7.08	10.69	73.54	33.76	13,843
Jiangxi 江西	4	177	7,739	-122	-0.85	-12.29	12.14	93.08	14,379
Shandong 山东	36	296	38,630	3,337	5.37	13.35	41.96	59.77	62,123
Central-South 中南	71	261	23,336	-143	-0.39	-1.10	27.85	64.79	36,959
Henan 河南	28	328	20,113	519	1.86	9.00	17.66	79.28	27,828
Hubei 湖北	11	234	24,641	-2,269	-2.66	-5.73	34.56	53.60	85,350
Hunan 湖南	6	278	19,533	-612	-2.86	-8.38	19.69	65.85	21,359
Guangdong 广东	19	207	34,281	283	0.83	1.91	53.07	56.53	34,100
Guangxi 广西	5	201	8,622	-160	-0.75		18.31	101.34	21,389
Hainan 海南	2	102	5,517	-318	-2.76	-21.33	28.24	87.07	11,512
Southwest 西南	7	339	20,454	-42	-0.11	-0.28	21.34	61.18	38,379
Chongqing 重庆	3	358	28,947	490	1.03	2.44	23.96	57.92	47,641
Sichuan 四川	3	291	15,308	1,714	6.18	17.68	23.38	65.05	27,741
Guizhou 贵州									
Yunnan 云南	1	425	10,412	-6,907	-16.25	-45.83	10.53	64.54	42,504
Tibet 西藏									
Northwest 西北	18	328	14,113	-261	-0.71	-3.13	18.27	77.24	36,597
Shaanxi 陕西	9	391	18,149	427	0.86	3.18	21.50	72.86	49,476
Gansu 甘肃	6	199	3,429	35	0.19	1.29	9.23	84.96	17,974
Qinghai 青海									
Ningxia 宁夏	2	501	22,059	-4,401	-10.58	-76.96	13.01	86.25	41,598
Xinjiang 新疆	1	190	26,010	59	0.26	4.14	43.03	93.65	22,424

2930: Rubber Sheet ,Tube and Belt Products 橡胶板、管、带制造业

Year 年份	Number of firms 企业个数	Rate of change 变化率 (%)	Number of employees 职工人数 (人)	Rate of change 变化率 (%)	Total revenue (Mil. RMB) 总销售收入 (百万元)	Rate of change 变化率 (%)	Total profit (Mil RMB) 总利润 (百万元)	Rate of change 变化率 (%)
2000	357		108,741		8,898		259	
2001	379	6.16	101,794	-6.39	8,819	-0.89	243	-6.18
2002	370	-2.37	87,976	-13.57	9,589	8.73	450	85.19

Major Products 主要产品	Output 产量	Unit 单位
Rubber Pipe 橡胶胶管	76,733	10,000 Standard Meters 万标米
Triangle Belt 三角带	69,263	10,000 A Meters 万A米

10 Main Firms with Maximal Revenue (year founded) 收入最大的十家主要企业（创办年份）	City 城市	Province 省	Telephone/fax 电话/传真	Number of employees 职工人数	Ownership 产业所有权	Revenue ('000 RMB) 销售收入 (千元)	Profit('000 RMB) (rank) 利润(千元) (排名)	Total assets ('000 RMB) 总资产 (千元)	Major products 主要产品
Yin He Depreux Rubber Co.,Ltd.	Jining	Shandong	(0537)3653319		Foreign Funded				Conveyer Belt
山东银河德普胶带有限公司(1998)	济宁市	山东省	(0537)3653316	516	外商投资	339,000	82,007(1)	449,372	输送带
Qingdao Rubber Six Group Co.,Ltd.	Qingdao	Shandong	(0532)3834184		State Enterprises				Rubber Conveyer Belt
青岛橡六集团有限公司(1852)	青岛市	山东省	(0532)3808791	2,410	国有独资	268,508	1,678(77)	785,480	胶输送带
Shaoxing SanLux Rubber Co.,Ltd.	Shaoxing	Zhejiang	(0575)4361766		Private Owned				V Band
绍兴三力士橡胶有限公司(1998)	绍兴市	浙江省	(0575)4363282	755	私营企业	200,512	21,243(3)	174,847	三角带
Lanxi Fuchuen Indder Co., Ltd.	Jinhua	Zhejiang	(0579)8766589		Joint Stock				Convey Belt
兰西富春橡胶有限公司(1966)	金华市	浙江省	(0579)8766555	1,047	股份制	183,989	2,780(51)	251,836	输送带
Longkou Plastic and Rubber Pipe Group Company	Yantai	Shandong	(0535)8581231		Limited-Liability				Rubber & Plastic Pipe
龙口市橡塑胶管有限公司(1998)	烟台市	山东省	(0535)8581231	345	有限公司	172,680	7,500(13)	9,610	橡塑胶管
Fuxin Rubber Group Co., Ltd.	Fuxin	Liaoning	(0418)2901745		Limited-Liability				Convey Belt
阜新橡胶集团有限责任公司(1955)	阜新市	辽宁省	(0418)2900927	2,040	有限公司	145,725	4,160(34)	549,008	输送带
Shanxi Hua Yi Industrial Company	Changzhi	Shanxi	(0355)5932382		Collective-owned				Rubber Pipe
山西省华亿实业有限公司(1983)	长治市	山西省	(0355)5933491	3,027	集体企业	128,193	433(151)	144,622	胶管
Zhejiang Shuang Jian Rubber Co., Ltd.	Jiaxing	Zhejiang	(0573)8532333		Joint Stock				Rubber Board & Pipe & Belt橡胶
浙江双箭橡胶股份有限公司(1986)	嘉兴市	浙江省	(0573)8531023	518	股份制	123,907	18,342(4)	122,364	板.管.带
Shenyang No.4 Rubber Plant	Shenyang	Liaoning	(024)23804673		State owned				Rubber Dam
沈阳第四橡胶厂(1938)	沈阳市	辽宁省	(024)25850327	1,903	国有企业	114,296	-	380,683	橡胶水坝
Wuxi Rubber & Plastic Products Co., Ltd.	Wuxi	Jiangsu	(0510)2417003		Overseas Chinese-funded				Seal Strip For Ship船
无锡橡塑制品有限公司(1987)	无锡市	江苏省	(0510)2406712	589	港澳台资	109,750	11,900(8)	115,940	用密封条

Top 10 Cities by Revenue 销售收入排名前10位城市	Province 省	Market share 市场份额 (%)	Number of firms 企业个数
Shanghai 上海市	Shanghai 上海市	8.18	26
Shenyang 沈阳市	Liaoning 辽宁省	5.14	9
Taizhou 台州市	Zhejiang 浙江省	4.40	18
Tianjin 天津市	Tianjin 天津市	4.24	23
Jining 济宁市	Shandong 山东省	4.09	4
Wuxi 无锡市	Jiangsu 江苏省	4.05	9
Hengshui 衡水市	Hebei 河北省	3.54	14
Qingdao 青岛市	Shandong 山东省	3.17	3
Kaifeng 开封市	Henan 河南省	2.82	5
Suzhou 苏州市	Jiangsu 江苏省	2.66	8

10 Major Wholesalers 十家主要批发商	City 城市	Province 省	Telephone/Fax 电话/传真
Yihua Kangqi Chemical Fibre Co.,Ltd.	Yangzhou	Jiangsu	(0514)3235499
仪化康祺化纤有限责任公司	扬州市	江苏省	(0514)3233847
Sinochem Guangdong Import & Export Company	Guangzhou	Guangdong	(020)86672288
中化广东进出口公司	广州市	广东省	(020)86507512
Sinochem Shanghai Import & Export Company	Shanghai	Shanghai	(021)63289888
中化上海进出口公司	上海市	上海市	(021)63283968
Sinochem Tianjin Import & Export Company	Tianjin	Tianjin	(022)23146216
中化天津进出口公司	天津市	天津市	(022)23146215
China Chemical Sales & Supply (North China) Corporation	Tianjin	Tianjin	(022)23011031
中国化工供销华北公司	天津市	天津市	(022)23011032
China Chemical Sales & Supply (North China) Corporation	Shanghai	Shanghai	(021)62103300
中国化工供销华东公司	上海市	上海市	(021)62515799
Nantong Chemical Light Industry Co.,Ltd.	Nantong	Jiangsu	(0513)5518397
南通化工轻工股份有限公司	南通市	江苏省	(0513)5512735
Taizhou Heshun Plastics Co.,Ltd.	Taizhou	Zhejiang	(0576)2510220
台州市和顺塑料有限公司	台州市	浙江省	(0576)2510160
China Petroleum Technology Development Corporation	Beijing	Beijing	(010)84080722
中国石油技术开发公司	北京市	北京市	(010)84080800
China National Chemical Fiber Corporation	Beijing	Beijing	(010)65816699
中国化纤总公司	北京市	北京市	(010)65813483

2940: Rubber Parts 橡胶零件制品业

The industry accounts for 0.074% of the total revenue of China's industrial sector in 2002. The rate of return on assets is 6.12%. 83.54% of all firms in the industry made a profit while 16.46% had negative returns.The top province in terms of the industry's revenue is Shandong, accounting for 17.51% of the total revenue.
2002年本行业收入占全行业的 0.074%，资产利润率为 6.12%。83.54%的企业赢利，16.46%的企业亏损。收入最高的省为山东省，占本行业的17.51%。

	Total number of firms 企业总数	Total number of employees 职工总数	Total revenue (Mil.RMB) 总销售收入（百万元）	Total profit (Mil.RMB) 总利润（百万元）	Return on assets 资产利润率（%）	Return on equity 权益利润率（%）	Labour productivity ('000 RMB/ worker) 劳动生产率（千元/人）	Debts/ assets 资产负债率（%）	Total assets (Mil.RMB) 总资产（百万元）
Industry Overall 行业总体	322	67,108	7,893	609	6.12	12.65	39.07	51.61	9,958

	Number of firms 企业个数	Average number of employees 平均职工人数	Average revenue ('000 RMB) 平均销售收入（千元）	Average profit ('000 RMB) 平均利润（千元）	Return on assets 资产利润率（%）	Return on equity 权益利润率（%）	Labour productivity ('000 RMB/ worker) 劳动生产率（千元/人）	Debts/ assets 资产负债率（%）	Average total assets ('000 RMB) 平均总资产（千元）
By ownership 产业所有权									
State-owned 国有	27	318	17,152	159	0.32	0.79	20.86	59.10	49,557
Collective-owned 集体	62	122	13,881	1,002	6.98	13.93	35.64	49.86	14,357
Foreign & Overseas Chinese Funded 三资	72	280	36,935	2,839	5.89	11.27	40.63	47.75	48,202
By regional distribution 地区分布									
Central-North 华北	45	175	17,488	1,859	6.03	11.45	36.57	47.37	30,836
Beijing 北京	9	189	16,034	584	1.75	3.24	18.28	45.90	33,272
Tianjin 天津	17	165	15,757	1,703	5.69	10.44	38.85	45.50	29,928
Hebei 河北	16	184	21,840	3,047	8.70	17.26	46.86	49.61	35,023
Shanxi 山西	3	138	8,444	233	3.68	8.13	22.91	54.73	6,344
Inner Mongolia 内蒙古									
Northeast 东北	21	191	9,318	546	3.48	6.51	17.49	46.62	15,720
Liaoning 辽宁	14	164	9,007	465	3.06	5.90	18.56	48.12	15,191
Jilin 吉林	3	44	7,333	426	11.60	46.39	39.25	74.99	3,675
Heilongjiang 黑龙江	4	395	11,896	921	3.46	5.83	14.13	40.69	26,608
Central-East 华东	171	220	29,224	2,369	7.35	15.42	45.06	52.32	32,226
Shanghai 上海	34	114	15,618	1,612	8.14	14.55	45.44	44.10	19,819
Jiangsu 江苏	53	187	24,650	2,048	7.30	16.12	45.65	54.75	28,069
Zhejiang 浙江	41	143	15,565	1,564	8.01	17.16	38.33	53.34	19,531
Anhui 安徽	11	755	59,978	9,023	10.27	19.12	31.90	46.28	87,825
Fujian 福建	11	358	42,892	2,221	5.40	8.88	33.23	39.10	41,101
Jiangxi 江西	2	148	3,974	81	1.38	2.79	5.16	50.70	5,850
Shandong 山东	19	287	72,742	2,832	4.81	13.32	81.74	63.88	58,866
Central-South 中南	58	176	26,372	1,884	6.07	11.94	38.87	49.18	31,041
Henan 河南	7	85	21,238	1,104	7.54	19.33	53.72	61.00	14,640
Hubei 湖北	12	238	23,944	1,446	4.68	14.24	48.07	67.11	30,869
Hunan 湖南	7	156	26,705	4,652	7.89	9.52	47.27	17.09	58,929
Guangdong 广东	27	195	31,170	1,806	5.48	12.15	30.98	54.87	32,919
Guangxi 广西	5	83	13,011	577	11.04	28.84	32.33	61.73	5,226
Hainan 海南									
Southwest 西南	20	338	17,736	-48	-0.11	-0.28	22.16	59.87	43,664
Chongqing 重庆	2	159	6,145	-412	-9.30	-35.61	9.85	73.88	4,429
Sichuan 四川	11	220	10,089	-166	-0.60	-1.41	21.45	57.52	27,575
Guizhou 贵州	4	950	56,417	1,295	0.99	2.63	24.55	62.31	130,563
Yunnan 云南	3	74	1,923	-1,167	-9.02	-15.58	6.58	42.13	12,948
Tibet 西藏									
Northwest 西北	7	82	4,073	107	1.36	4.04	32.98	66.47	7,928
Shaanxi 陕西	3	151	7,928	206	1.37	4.06	34.67	66.28	15,065
Gansu 甘肃	4	31	1,183	34	1.30	3.98	26.74	67.28	2,576
Qinghai 青海									
Ningxia 宁夏									
Xinjiang 新疆									

2940: Rubber Parts 橡胶零件制品业

Year 年份	Number of firms 企业个数	Rate of change 变化率 (%)	Number of employees 职工人数 (人)	Rate of change 变化率 (%)	Total revenue (Mil. RMB) 总销售收入 (百万元)	Rate of change 变化率 (%)	Total profit (Mil RMB) 总利润 (百万元)	Rate of change 变化率 (%)
2000	254		55,560		4,743		251	
2001	274	7.87	58,064	4.51	6,250	31.77	342	36.25
2002	322	17.52	67,108	15.58	7,893	26.29	609	78.07

Major Products 主要产品	Output 产量	Unit 单位
Seal Part 密封件	138,552	10,000 Pieces 万件

10 Main Firms with Maximal Revenue (year founded) 收入最大的十家主要企业（创办年份）	City 城市	Province 省	Telephone/fax 电话/传真	Number of employees 职工人数	Ownership 产业所有权	Revenue ('000 RMB) 销售收入 (千元)	Profit('000 RMB) (rank) 利润(千元) (排名)	Total assets ('000 RMB) 总资产 (千元)	Major products 主要产品
Shandong Guangrao Petrochemistry Group Stock Co., Ltd.	Dongying	Shandong	(0546)6261074		Joint Stock				Rubber Article
山东广饶石化集团股份有限公司(1994)	东营市	山东省	(0546)6261072	1,472	股份制	1,062,577	45,627(2)	584,650	橡胶件
Guizhou Yongli Rubber Group Co., Ltd.	Guiyang	Guizhou	(0851)6871523		State-owned				Rubber Pipes & Hoses橡胶
贵州永力橡胶集团有限公司(1997)	贵阳市	贵州省	(0851)6819316	3,094	国有企业	196,580	4,869(35)	497,137	本件管带
Asinco Components Co.,Ltd.(Anhui)	Xuancheng	Anhui	(0563)4674806		Foreign Funded				Rubber Seal Part橡
亚新科零部件(安徽)有限公司(1994)	宣城市	安徽省	(0563)4674880	3,144	外商投资	175,643	13,341(7)	306,817	胶密封件
Wuxi No.2 Rubber Co., Ltd.	Wuxi	Jiangsu	(0510)2803862		Joint Stock				Rubber Roller
无锡二橡胶股份有限公司(1971)	无锡市	江苏省	(0510)2800675	1,060	股份制	135,601	28,743(5)	113,682	胶辊
Xiamen Xia Hui Rubber & Metal Industrial Co.,Ltd.	Xiamen	Fujian	(0592)6210902		Overseas Chinese-funded				Cycle Valve
厦门厦晖橡胶金属工业有限公司(1990)	厦门市	福建省	(0592)6210901	486	港澳台资	134,884	12,311(9)	108,315	气门咀
Zhuzhou Times New Materials Technology Co., Ltd.	Zhuzhou	Hunan	(0733)2884798		Joint Stock				Rubber & Plastics Rubber Mat
株洲时代新材料科技股份有限公司(1994)	株洲市	湖南省	(0733)2884788	248	股份制	127,276	31,623(4)	362,956	橡塑垫
Xiamen Ontop Rubber Plastics & Hurdware Industrial INC.	Xiamen	Fujian	(0592)6079122		Overseas Chinese-funded				Rubber Footplate橡
厦门永大橡塑五金工业有限公司(1991)	厦门市	福建省	(0592)6076580	823	港澳台资	97,828	2,201(58)	85,553	胶脚踏板
Hutchinson-DFEDC Automotive Seals Co., Ltd.	Shiyan	Hubei	(0719)8236182		Foreign Funded				Automobile Sealing Part汽
十堰东森汽车密封件有限公司(1995)	十堰市	湖北省	(0719)8782330	450	外商投资	96,968	12,495(8)	125,732	车密封件
BeJing Chemical Industry Group Rrbber&Plastic Products	Beijing	Beijing	(010)81501306		State owned				Regenerated Rubber
Factory北京化学工业集团橡胶塑料制品厂(1956)	北京市	北京市	(010)81501509	1,328	国有企业	90,014	-	238,555	橡胶制品
Tang Xin Rubber & Plastic Products Co., Ltd.	Shanghai	Shanghai	(021)57605808		Foreign Funded				Rubber Products
唐心橡塑制品（上海）有限公司(2001)	上海市	上海市	(021)57605538	160	外商投资	88,020	7,157(25)	42,046	橡胶制品

Top 10 Cities by Revenue 销售收入排名前10位城市	Province 省	Market share 市场份额 (%)	Number of firms 企业个数
Dongying 东营市	Shandong 山东省	13.46	1
Xuancheng 宣城市	Anhui 安徽省	6.91	4
Shanghai 上海市	Shanghai 上海市	6.73	34
Xiamen 厦门市	Fujian 福建省	5.39	7
Zhongshan 中山市	Guangdong 广东省	5.10	5
Suzhou 苏州市	Jiangsu 江苏省	4.90	12
Wuxi 无锡市	Jiangsu 江苏省	4.90	9
Taizhou 台州市	Zhejiang 浙江省	4.20	24
Tianjin 天津市	Tianjin 天津市	3.39	17
Guiyang 贵阳市	Guizhou 贵州省	2.86	4

10 Major Wholesalers 十家主要批发商	City 城市	Province 省	Telephone/Fax 电话/传真
Yihua Kangqi Chemical Fibre Co.,Ltd.	Yangzhou	Jiangsu	(0514)3235499
仪化康祺化纤有限责任公司	扬州市	江苏省	(0514)3233847
Sinochem Guangdong Import & Export Company	Guangzhou	Guangdong	(020)86672288
中化广东进出口公司	广州市	广东省	(020)86507512
Sinochem Shanghai Import & Export Company	Shanghai	Shanghai	(021)63289888
中化上海进出口公司	上海市	上海市	(021)63283968
Sinochem Tianjin Import & Export Company	Tianjin	Tianjin	(022)23146216
中化天津进出口公司	天津市	天津市	(022)23146215
China Chemical Sales & Supply (North China) Corporation	Tianjin	Tianjin	(022)23011031
中国化工供销华北公司	天津市	天津市	(022)23011032
China Chemical Sales & Supply (North China) Corporation	Shanghai	Shanghai	(021)62103300
中国化工供销华东公司	上海市	上海市	(021)62515799
Nantong Chemical Light Industry Co.,Ltd.	Nantong	Jiangsu	(0513)5518397
南通化工轻工股份有限公司	南通市	江苏省	(0513)5512735
Taizhou Heshun Plastics Co.,Ltd.	Taizhou	Zhejiang	(0576)2510220
台州市和顺塑料有限公司	台州市	浙江省	(0576)2510160
China Petroleum Technology Development Corporation	Beijing	Beijing	(010)84080722
中国石油技术开发公司	北京市	北京市	(010)84080800
China National Chemical Fiber Corporation	Beijing	Beijing	(010)65816699
中国化纤总公司	北京市	北京市	(010)65813483

2950: Recycled Rubber 再生橡胶制品业

The industry accounts for 0.015% of the total revenue of China's industrial sector in 2002. The rate of return on assets is 7.39%. 89.89% of all firms in the industry made a profit while 10.11% had negative returns.The top province in terms of the industry's revenue is Fujian, accounting for 19.29% of the total revenue.
2002年本行业收入占全行业的0.015%，资产利润率为7.39%。89.89%的企业赢利，10.11%的企业亏损。收入最高的省为福建省，占本行业的19.29%。

	Total number of firms 企业总数	Total number of employees 职工总数	Total revenue (Mil.RMB) 总销售收入（百万元）	Total profit (Mil.RMB) 总利润（百万元）	Return on assets 资产利润率（%）	Return on equity 权益利润率（%）	Labour productivity ('000 RMB/ worker) 劳动生产率（千元/人）	Debts/ assets 资产负债率（%）	Total assets (Mil.RMB) 总资产（百万元）
Industry Overall 行业总体	89	12,300	1,573	106	7.39	16.58	41.88	55.44	1,432

	Number of firms 企业个数	Average number of employees 平均职工人数	Average revenue ('000 RMB) 平均销售收入（千元）	Average profit ('000 RMB) 平均利润（千元）	Return on assets 资产利润率（%）	Return on equity 权益利润率（%）	Labour productivity ('000 RMB/ worker) 劳动生产率（千元/人）	Debts/ assets 资产负债率（%）	Average total assets ('000 RMB) 平均总资产（千元）
By ownership 产业所有权									
State-owned 国有	4	34	1,614	13	0.29	0.53	14.36	45.34	4,479
Collective-owned 集体	25	105	12,917	598	9.22	19.77	40.09	53.38	6,487
Foreign & Overseas Chinese Funded 三资	2	263	58,125	5,139	12.56	21.43	65.38	41.38	40,901
By regional distribution 地区分布									
Central-North 华北	20	139	16,294	952	5.43	16.46	39.61	66.99	17,524
Beijing 北京									
Tianjin 天津	3	92	5,312	-101	-1.70	-7.40	4.40	77.08	5,939
Hebei 河北	13	152	21,016	1,535	6.49	19.40	50.89	66.53	23,639
Shanxi 山西	4	134	9,184	-152	-2.40	-6.94	16.26	65.39	6,340
Inner Mongolia 内蒙古									
Northeast 东北	3	219	6,609	1,123	3.56	9.58	10.19	62.88	31,567
Liaoning 辽宁	2	289	9,914	1,684	3.65	9.61	11.60	62.04	46,149
Jilin 吉林	1	80						95.05	2,403
Heilongjiang 黑龙江									
Central-East 华东	37	136	23,693	1,662	9.97	18.79	54.38	46.96	16,679
Shanghai 上海	4	97	15,497	1,936	11.75	19.08	27.19	38.42	16,478
Jiangsu 江苏	9	146	22,439	742	6.77	19.64	42.59	65.53	10,968
Zhejiang 浙江	10	98	13,465	507	4.49	10.83	32.32	58.52	11,280
Anhui 安徽									
Fujian 福建	3	293	101,168	11,373	19.54	20.34	124.86	3.93	58,202
Jiangxi 江西	3	192	23,376	90	0.38	1.63	46.81	76.91	23,756
Shandong 山东	8	115	13,051	954	8.13	35.13	43.54	76.85	11,728
Central-South 中南	25	131	11,505	780	6.13	14.28	31.29	57.10	12,725
Henan 河南	6	88	9,301	455	7.76	15.24	28.79	49.10	5,863
Hubei 湖北	4	306	28,492	1,007	5.83	13.50	36.99	56.83	17,265
Hunan 湖南	6	117	5,366	10	0.22	0.84	19.71	73.48	4,556
Guangdong 广东	9	91	9,518	1,408	6.79	15.54	34.28	56.30	20,729
Guangxi 广西									
Hainan 海南									
Southwest 西南	3	141	10,894	145	1.04	2.98	27.92	65.09	13,950
Chongqing 重庆									
Sichuan 四川	2	141	12,610	207	1.74	4.76	29.15	63.43	11,858
Guizhou 贵州									
Yunnan 云南	1	142	7,463	23	0.13	0.39	25.46	67.26	18,133
Tibet 西藏									
Northwest 西北	1	115	30,500	1,982	20.48	22.41	82.17	8.61	9,678
Shaanxi 陕西									
Gansu 甘肃	1	115	30,500	1,982	20.48	22.41	82.17	8.61	9,678
Qinghai 青海									
Ningxia 宁夏									
Xinjiang 新疆									

2950: Recycled Rubber 再生橡胶制品业

Year 年份	Number of firms 企业个数	Rate of change 变化率 (%)	Number of employees 职工人数 (人)	Rate of change 变化率 (%)	Total revenue (Mil. RMB) 总销售收入 (百万元)	Rate of change 变化率 (%)	Total profit (Mil RMB) 总利润 (百万元)	Rate of change 变化率 (%)
2000	83		12,833		979		39	
2001	88	6.02	14,017	9.23	1,416	44.64	98	151.28
2002	89	1.14	12,300	-12.25	1,573	11.09	106	8.16

Major Products 主要产品	Output 产量	Unit 单位

10 Main Firms with Maximal Revenue (year founded) 收入最大的十家主要企业（创办年份）	City 城市	Province 省	Telephone/fax 电话/传真	Number of employees 职工人数	Ownership 产业所有权	Revenue ('000 RMB) 销售收入 (千元)	Profit('000 RMB) (rank) 利润(千元) (排名)	Total assets ('000 RMB) 总资产 (千元)	Major products 主要产品
Nantong Huili Rubber Group Co., Ltd.	Nantong	Jiangsu	(0513)2671668		Joint Stock				Regenerated Rubber
南通回力橡胶集团有限公司(1975)	南通市	江苏省	(0513)2671708	594	股份制	100,047	5,381(3)	51,630	再生胶
Hengshui Rubber Co., Ltd.	Hengshui	Hebei	(0318)2024574		Limited-Liability				Rubber Products
衡水橡胶股份有限公司(1995)	衡水市	河北省	(0318)2033847	550	有限公司	75,859	4,864(4)	146,148	橡胶制品
Egang Sanhe Rubber Co., Ltd.	Xiantao	Hubei	(0728)2892064		Overseas Chinese-funded				Regenerated Rubber
鄂港三合橡胶股份有限公司(1999)	仙桃市	湖北省	(0728)2892061	455	港澳台资	73,571	3,201(12)	36,745	再生胶
Renqiu Jing Dong Rubber Industrial Company	Cangzhou	Hebei	(0317)2258908		Private Owned				Rubber
任丘市京东橡胶实业公司(1985)	沧州市	河北省		400	私营企业	51,000	4,500(5)	52,200	橡胶
Shanghai Tobu Rubber Center Co., Ltd.	Shanghai	Shanghai	(021)57742505		Foreign Funded				Synthetic Rubber
上海东武橡胶中心有限公司(1995)	上海市	上海市	(021)57742473	70	外商投资	42,678	7,076(2)	45,056	合成橡胶
Ningbo Hua Xing Regenerative Rubber Co., Ltd.	Ningbo	Zhejiang	(0574)63738238		Private Owned				Regenerated Rubber
宁波华星再生橡胶有限公司(2000)	宁波市	浙江省		260	私营企业	38,282	977(21)	23,681	再生橡胶
Jiangxi Guoyan Rubber Co.,Ltd.	Nanchang	Jiangxi	(0791)8302018		Collective-owned				Rubber
江西国燕橡胶有限公司(1997)	南昌市	江西省	(0791)8301161	130	集体企业	30,540	260(43)	5,000	橡胶
Tangshan Bei Fang Rubber Co., Ltd.	Tangshan	Hebei	(0315)6113689		Private Owned				Rubber Products
唐山北方橡胶有限责任公司(2000)	唐山市	河北省		261	私营企业	25,857	-	21,871	橡胶制品
Haimen Jiang Hai Rubber Co., Ltd.	Nantong	Jiangsu	(0513)2632131		Limited-Liability				Regenerated Rubber
海门市江海橡胶有限公司(1987)	南通市	江苏省	(0513)2781936	86	有限公司	20,720	10(67)	7,900	再生胶
Sichuan Longchang Petrel Rubber Co., Ltd.	Neijiang	Sichuan	(0832)3954850		Limited-Liability				Regenerated Rubber
四川省隆昌海橡胶有限公司(1956)	内江市	四川省	(0832)3956052	186	有限公司	19,097	400(38)	18,903	再生橡胶

Top 10 Cities by Revenue 销售收入排名前10位城市	Province 省	Market share 市场份额 (%)	Number of firms 企业个数
Quanzhou 泉州市	Fujian 福建省	19.29	2
Nantong 南通市	Jiangsu 江苏省	8.68	4
Tangshan 唐山市	Hebei 河北省	5.36	6
Hengshui 衡水市	Hebei 河北省	5.33	2
Ningbo 宁波市	Zhejiang 浙江省	4.19	4
Shanghai 上海市	Shanghai 上海市	3.94	4
Nanchang 南昌市	Jiangxi 江西省	3.59	2
Cangzhou 沧州市	Hebei 河北省	3.52	2
Qingdao 青岛市	Shandong 山东省	2.86	1

10 Major Wholesalers 十家主要批发商	City 城市	Province 省	Telephone/Fax 电话/传真
Yihua Kangqi Chemical Fibre Co.,Ltd.	Yangzhou	Jiangsu	(0514)3235499
仪化康祺化纤有限责任公司	扬州市	江苏省	(0514)3233847
Sinochem Guangdong Import & Export Company	Guangzhou	Guangdong	(020)86672288
中化广东进出口公司	广州市	广东省	(020)86507512
Sinochem Shanghai Import & Export Company	Shanghai	Shanghai	(021)63289888
中化上海进出口公司	上海市	上海市	(021)63283968
Sinochem Tianjin Import & Export Company	Tianjin	Tianjin	(022)23146216
中化天津进出口公司	天津市	天津市	(022)23146215
China Chemical Sales & Supply (North China) Corporation	Tianjin	Tianjin	(022)23011031
中国化工供销华北公司	天津市	天津市	(022)23011032
China Chemical Sales & Supply (North China) Corporation	Shanghai	Shanghai	(021)62103300
中国化工供销华东公司	上海市	上海市	(021)62515799
Nantong Chemical Light Industry Co.,Ltd.	Nantong	Jiangsu	(0513)5518397
南通化工轻工股份有限公司	南通市	江苏省	(0513)5512735
Taizhou Heshun Plastics Co.,Ltd.	Taizhou	Zhejiang	(0576)2510220
台州市和顺塑料有限公司	台州市	浙江省	(0576)2510160
China Petroleum Technology Development Corporation	Beijing	Beijing	(010)84080722
中国石油技术开发公司	北京市	北京市	(010)84080800
China National Chemical Fiber Corporation	Beijing	Beijing	(010)65816699
中国化纤总公司	北京市	北京市	(010)65813483

2960: Rubber Shoes 橡胶靴鞋制造业

The industry accounts for 0.123% of the total revenue of China's industrial sector in 2002. The rate of return on assets is 1.88%. 70.28% of all firms in the industry made a profit while 29.72% had negative returns.The top province in terms of the industry's revenue is Shandong, accounting for 39.16% of the total revenue.
2002年本行业收入占全行业的 0.123%，资产利润率为 1.88%。70.28%的企业赢利，29.72%的企业亏损。收入最高的省为山东省，占本行业的39.16%。

	Total number of firms 企业总数	Total number of employees 职工总数	Total revenue (Mil.RMB) 总销售收入（百万元）	Total profit (Mil.RMB) 总利润（百万元）	Return on assets 资产利润率（%）	Return on equity 权益利润率（%）	Labour productivity ('000 RMB/ worker) 劳动生产率（千元/人）	Debts/ assets 资产负债率（%）	Total assets (Mil.RMB) 总资产（百万元）
Industry Overall 行业总体	286	144,786	13,142	237	1.88	6.09	27.86	69.07	12,584

	Number of firms 企业个数	Average number of employees 平均职工人数	Average revenue ('000 RMB) 平均销售收入（千元）	Average profit ('000 RMB) 平均利润（千元）	Return on assets 资产利润率（%）	Return on equity 权益利润率（%）	Labour productivity ('000 RMB/ worker) 劳动生产率（千元/人）	Debts/ assets 资产负债率（%）	Average total assets ('000 RMB) 平均总资产（千元）
By ownership 产业所有权									
State-owned 国有	28	720	43,330	-1,503	-1.75	-10.67	27.33	83.64	86,053
Collective-owned 集体	47	358	27,625	1,195	4.65	12.54	17.25	62.93	25,721
Foreign & Overseas Chinese Funded 三资	80	593	52,927	920	2.55	6.90	27.33	63.01	36,062
By regional distribution 地区分布									
Central-North 华北	43	397	26,952	56	0.17	0.63	19.99	73.53	33,086
Beijing 北京	1	361	25,567	-49	-0.57	-1.80	14.32	68.41	8,625
Tianjin 天津	26	345	28,648	1,228	4.39	13.08	24.94	66.41	27,949
Hebei 河北	14	458	21,801	-1,438	-3.99	-22.62	12.26	82.38	36,079
Shanxi 山西	2	670	41,666	-4,676	-5.13	-22.93	25.44	77.63	91,150
Inner Mongolia 内蒙古									
Northeast 东北	15	502	24,616	-279	-0.53	-2.54	13.84	79.22	52,961
Liaoning 辽宁	11	512	31,176	568	1.00	5.07	18.09	80.18	56,540
Jilin 吉林	1	530	6,628	-4,118	-8.03	-38.68	-0.30	79.23	51,263
Heilongjiang 黑龙江	3	457	6,557	-2,106	-5.21	-20.28	1.86	74.30	40,402
Central-East 华东	144	537	56,602	1,466	2.93	8.50	31.61	65.50	49,985
Shanghai 上海	22	350	27,559	269	1.27	3.27	20.78	61.29	21,206
Jiangsu 江苏	31	447	29,947	974	3.97	11.56	19.99	65.67	24,560
Zhejiang 浙江	39	306	22,667	931	3.58	9.25	21.92	61.35	26,047
Anhui 安徽	5	536	20,126	262	0.81	1.69	11.04	51.87	32,275
Fujian 福建	22	305	21,659	-220	-1.30	-4.25	23.04	69.29	16,876
Jiangxi 江西	1	139	8,284	248	9.63	18.34	19.73	47.52	2,576
Shandong 山东	24	1,429	214,439	5,917	3.21	9.75	45.44	67.06	184,120
Central-South 中南	55	539	45,401	577	1.53	4.49	23.94	65.91	37,732
Henan 河南	12	423	27,756	681	2.46	10.83	17.85	77.32	27,731
Hubei 湖北	4	391	18,668	-32	-0.12		12.89	106.00	27,596
Hunan 湖南	9	720	60,725	1,799	3.42	6.36	24.47	46.18	52,534
Guangdong 广东	28	533	53,355	657	1.79	4.95	28.28	63.79	36,631
Guangxi 广西	2	821	24,431	-5,441	-8.14	-84.82	11.73	90.40	66,821
Hainan 海南									
Southwest 西南	25	453	37,776	-100	-0.27	-0.83	37.74	67.60	37,294
Chongqing 重庆	10	465	27,163	689	2.78	6.62	14.92	58.02	24,786
Sichuan 四川	7	342	48,599	-101	-0.29	-1.70	46.05	82.74	34,564
Guizhou 贵州	5	579	48,544	1,629	2.57	4.56	78.28	43.58	63,302
Yunnan 云南	3	459	29,951	-5,606	-13.34		14.97	117.67	42,011
Tibet 西藏									
Northwest 西北	4	472	5,514	-365	-0.90		3.68	188.52	40,346
Shaanxi 陕西	2	581	8,378	-930	-1.55		3.84	220.61	59,807
Gansu 甘肃	2	364	2,650	200	0.96	28.29	3.43	96.61	20,886
Qinghai 青海									
Ningxia 宁夏									
Xinjiang 新疆									

2960: Rubber Shoes 橡胶靴鞋制造业

Year 年份	Number of firms 企业个数	Rate of change 变化率 (%)	Number of employees 职工人数 (人)	Rate of change 变化率 (%)	Total revenue (Mil. RMB) 总销售收入 (百万元)	Rate of change 变化率 (%)	Total profit (Mil RMB) 总利润 (百万元)	Rate of change 变化率 (%)
2000	390		180,663		10,908		7	
2001	279	-28.46	138,747	-23.20	11,257	3.20	148	2,014.29
2002	286	2.51	144,786	4.35	13,142	16.75	237	60.14

Major Products 主要产品	Output 产量	Unit 单位
Rubber Pipe 胶鞋	95,863	10,000 Pairs 万双
Cloth Shoes 布鞋	53,251	10,000 Pairs 万双

10 Main Firms with Maximal Revenue (year founded) 收入最大的十家主要企业（创办年份）	City 城市	Province 省	Telephone/fax 电话/传真	Number of employees 职工人数	Ownership 产业所有权	Revenue ('000 RMB) 销售收入 (千元)	Profit('000 RMB) (rank) 利润(千元) (排名)	Total assets ('000 RMB) 总资产 (千元)	Major products 主要产品
Double Star Group Company	Qingdao	Shandong	(0532)2680528		State Enterprises				Rubber Shoes
双星集团有限责任公司(1921)	青岛市	山东省	(0532)2689796	13,579	国有独资	3,411,558	106,939(1)	3,345,299	胶鞋
Guangzhou Panyu Daxing Shoes-making Industry Co., Ltd.	Guangzhou	Guangdong	(020)84937909		Overseas Chinese-funded				Sports Shoes
广州番禺大兴制鞋实业有限公司(1988)	广州市	广东省	(020)87933389	2,650	港澳台资	394,101	4,990(19)	159,960	运动鞋
Sichuan Ziyang Zhengfeng Shoes Industry Ltd. Company	Ziyang	Sichuan	(0832)6180388		Limited-Liability				Rubber Shoes
四川省资阳市征峰鞋业有限责任公司(1954)	资阳市	四川省	(0832)6182290	320	有限公司	251,860	3,400(28)	117,543	胶鞋
Heshan Ya Yao Zengzhao Shoes Factory	Jiangmen	Guangdong	(0750)8283183		Overseas Chinese-funded				Cold Sticking Sneaker
鹤山市雅瑶增兆鞋厂(1999)	江门市	广东省	(0750)8283212	2,200	港澳台资	238,320	2,501(36)	101,432	冷粘运动鞋
China People's Liberation Army No.3537 Factory	Qiannan	Guizhou	(0854)5739000		State-owned				Rubber Shoes
第三五三七工厂(1966)	黔南州	贵州省	(0854)5739001	1,650	国有企业	211,034	10,731(6)	271,604	橡胶鞋
Zhejiang Zhonghua Shoes Group Co., Ltd.	Hangzhou	Zhejiang	(0571)88111251		Collective-owned				Rubber Shoes
浙江中华鞋业集团有限公司(1984)	杭州市	浙江省	(0571)88111531	2,221	集体企业	190,283	6,518(11)	360,340	胶鞋
Heshan Gang Rong Shoes Sole Factory	Jiangmen	Guangdong	(0750)8283002		Overseas Chinese-funded				Sole
鹤山市冈荣鞋底厂(1992)	江门市	广东省	(0750)8283001	1,040	港澳台资	167,584	405(104)	91,521	鞋底
Shandong Wendeng Welfare Leather & Rubber Factory	Weihai	Shandong	(0631)8735698		Collective-owned				Rubber Shoes Sole
山东省文登市福利皮革橡胶厂(1988)	威海市	山东省	(0631)8731048	212	集体企业	142,780	11,710(4)	25,370	橡胶鞋底
Qingdao Double Star Group Lu Zhong Co., Ltd	Zibo	Shandong	(0533)3311343		Limited-Liability				Rubber Shoes
青岛双星集团鲁中有限公司(1992)	淄博市	山东省	(0533)3310069	2,400	有限公司	131,320	116(141)	54,367	胶鞋
Shanghai Da Bo Wen Shoes Industry Co., Ltd.	Shanghai	Shanghai	(021)58412322		Overseas Chinese-funded				Rubber Shoes
上海大博文鞋业有限公司(1993)	上海市	上海市	(021)58411702	903	港澳台资	126,477	554(84)	72,930	胶鞋

Top 10 Cities by Revenue 销售收入排名前10位城市	Province 省	Market share 市场份额 (%)	Number of firms 企业个数
Qingdao 青岛市	Shandong 山东省	34.84	12
Guangzhou 广州市	Guangdong 广东省	6.02	11
Tianjin 天津市	Tianjin 天津市	5.67	26
Shanghai 上海市	Shanghai 上海市	4.61	22
Hangzhou 杭州市	Zhejiang 浙江省	3.23	8
Jiangmen 江门市	Guangdong 广东省	3.15	3
Suzhou 苏州市	Jiangsu 江苏省	2.53	12
Yueyang 岳阳市	Hunan 湖南省	2.43	2
Chongqing 重庆市	Chongqing 重庆市	2.07	10
Changzhou 常州市	Jiangsu 江苏省	1.93	4

10 Major Wholesalers 十家主要批发商	City 城市	Province 省	Telephone/Fax 电话/传真
Yihua Kangqi Chemical Fibre Co.,Ltd.	Yangzhou	Jiangsu	(0514)3235499
仪化康祺化纤有限责任公司	扬州市	江苏省	(0514)3233847
Sinochem Guangdong Import & Export Company	Guangzhou	Guangdong	(020)86672288
中化广东进出口公司	广州市	广东省	(020)86507512
Sinochem Shanghai Import & Export Company	Shanghai	Shanghai	(021)63289888
中化上海进出口公司	上海市	上海市	(021)63283968
Sinochem Tianjin Import & Export Company	Tianjin	Tianjin	(022)23146216
中化天津进出口公司	天津市	天津市	(022)23146215
China Chemical Sales & Supply (North China) Corporation	Tianjin	Tianjin	(022)23011031
中国化工供销华北公司	天津市	天津市	(022)23011032
China Chemical Sales & Supply (North China) Corporation	Shanghai	Shanghai	(021)62103300
中国化工供销华东公司	上海市	上海市	(021)62515799
Nantong Chemical Light Industry Co.,Ltd.	Nantong	Jiangsu	(0513)5518397
南通化工轻工股份有限公司	南通市	江苏省	(0513)5512735
Taizhou Heshun Plastics Co.,Ltd.	Taizhou	Zhejiang	(0576)2510220
台州市和顺塑料有限公司	台州市	浙江省	(0576)2510160
China Petroleum Technology Development Corporation	Beijing	Beijing	(010)84080722
中国石油技术开发公司	北京市	北京市	(010)84080800
China National Chemical Fiber Corporation	Beijing	Beijing	(010)65816699
中国化纤总公司	北京市	北京市	(010)65813483

2970: Household Rubber Products 日用橡胶制品业

The industry accounts for 0.042% of the total revenue of China's industrial sector in 2002. The rate of return on assets is 5.33%. 87.59% of all firms in the industry made a profit while 12.41% had negative returns.The top province in terms of the industry's revenue is Guangdong, accounting for 29.79% of the total revenue.
2002年本行业收入占全行业的0.042%，资产利润率为5.33%。87.59%的企业赢利，12.41%的企业亏损。收入最高的省为广东省，占本行业的29.79%。

	Total number of firms 企业总数	Total number of employees 职工总数	Total revenue (Mil.RMB) 总销售收入(百万元)	Total profit (Mil.RMB) 总利润(百万元)	Return on assets 资产利润率(%)	Return on equity 权益利润率(%)	Labour productivity ('000 RMB/ worker) 劳动生产率(千元/人)	Debts/ assets 资产负债率(%)	Total assets (Mil.RMB) 总资产(百万元)
Industry Overall 行业总体	145	30,346	4,454	203	5.33	14.00	50.16	61.93	3,806

	Number of firms 企业个数	Average number of employees 平均职工人数	Average revenue ('000 RMB) 平均销售收入(千元)	Average profit ('000 RMB) 平均利润(千元)	Return on assets 资产利润率(%)	Return on equity 权益利润率(%)	Labour productivity ('000 RMB/ worker) 劳动生产率(千元/人)	Debts/ assets 资产负债率(%)	Average total assets ('000 RMB) 平均总资产(千元)
By ownership 产业所有权									
State-owned 国有	12	336	22,027	-637	-1.72	-7.64	18.76	77.49	37,045
Collective-owned 集体	24	191	34,606	2,722	12.89	32.36	116.73	60.16	21,115
Foreign & Overseas Chinese Funded 三资	55	233	39,763	1,379	4.50	10.72	42.51	58.06	30,670
By regional distribution 地区分布									
Central-North 华北	20	350	35,132	1,515	4.22	15.67	29.15	73.06	35,902
Beijing 北京	1	285	35,556	333	2.19	4.95	39.68	55.79	15,233
Tianjin 天津	13	317	22,888	609	1.91	7.68	15.77	75.19	31,969
Hebei 河北	5	457	72,289	4,414	9.42	29.53	53.95	68.10	46,850
Shanxi 山西									
Inner Mongolia 内蒙古	1	314	8,099	-23	-0.04	-0.26	15.18	83.36	52,959
Northeast 东北	5	213	15,173	411	2.00	10.19	22.36	80.35	20,539
Liaoning 辽宁	4	257	18,098	514	2.18	14.74	20.17	85.22	23,593
Jilin 吉林	1	40	3,473				78.65	25.12	8,321
Heilongjiang 黑龙江									
Central-East 华东	69	213	31,242	2,039	7.14	16.86	62.51	57.68	28,572
Shanghai 上海	12	227	35,920	1,742	4.46	9.48	34.55	52.98	39,058
Jiangsu 江苏	19	246	27,972	1,146	5.78	17.14	33.93	66.28	19,833
Zhejiang 浙江	15	139	20,869	1,569	6.85	17.50	36.74	60.83	22,889
Anhui 安徽	4	287	21,590	1,085	3.60	14.67	20.81	75.48	30,155
Fujian 福建	6	124	9,970	395	8.89	19.37	21.80	54.13	4,447
Jiangxi 江西									
Shandong 山东	13	254	56,462	5,213	10.67	21.83	165.67	51.13	48,869
Central-South 中南	48	155	31,188	612	2.94	7.43	50.13	60.49	20,842
Henan 河南	2	93	7,043	385	10.66	16.28	17.88	34.56	3,613
Hubei 湖北	3	229	46,008	647	2.82	13.48	77.52	79.04	22,907
Hunan 湖南	1	124	2,224	-319	-4.91	-138.10	7.98	96.45	6,498
Guangdong 广东	41	145	32,366	890	4.23	9.46	53.22	55.31	21,049
Guangxi 广西									
Hainan 海南	1	512	15,658	-9,503	-17.30		-0.65	117.75	54,944
Southwest 西南	3	49	7,534	158	3.43	7.74	21.88	55.69	4,619
Chongqing 重庆	1	84	9,213	402	4.94	9.31	26.44	46.91	8,136
Sichuan 四川	1	35	12,350	29	0.71	5.89	22.26	88.01	4,104
Guizhou 贵州	1	28	1,039	44	2.72	3.31	7.71	17.86	1,618
Yunnan 云南									
Tibet 西藏									
Northwest 西北									
Shaanxi 陕西									
Gansu 甘肃									
Qinghai 青海									
Ningxia 宁夏									
Xinjiang 新疆									

2970: Household Rubber Products 日用橡胶制品业

Year 年份	Number of firms 企业个数	Rate of change 变化率 (%)	Number of employees 职工人数 (人)	Rate of change 变化率 (%)	Total revenue (Mil. RMB) 总销售收入 (百万元)	Rate of change 变化率 (%)	Total profit (Mil RMB) 总利润 (百万元)	Rate of change 变化率 (%)
2000	113		25,004		3,727		138	
2001	121	7.08	24,721	-1.13	3,952	6.04	169	22.46
2002	145	19.83	30,346	22.75	4,454	12.70	203	20.12

Major Products 主要产品	Output 产量	Unit 单位

10 Main Firms with Maximal Revenue (year founded) 收入最大的十家主要企业（创办年份）	City 城市	Province 省	Telephone/fax 电话/传真	Number of employees 职工人数	Ownership 产业所有权	Revenue ('000 RMB) 销售收入 (千元)	Profit('000 RMB) (rank) 利润(千元) (排名)	Total assets ('000 RMB) 总资产 (千元)	Major products 主要产品
Kaiping Changsha Science & Technology Woven Belt Factory	Jiangmen	Guangdong	(0750)2211128		Overseas Chinese-funded				Rubber Strip
开平市长沙科技织带厂(1990)	江门市	广东省	(0750)2272004	300	港澳台资	288,700	24(106)	33,213	橡根带
Qingdao Shuangdie Group Co., Ltd.	Qingdao	Shandong	(0532)3619205		Joint Stock				Daily Use Rubber Products日用
青岛双蝶集团股份有限公司(1956)	青岛市	山东省	(0532)3617653	1,055	股份制	186,996	12,293(5)	202,386	橡胶制品
Tangshan Zhonghong Pulin Food Co., Ltd.	Tangshan	Hebei	(0315)4167653		Foreign Funded				Pvc Gloves
唐山中红普林食品有限公司(2000)	唐山市	河北省	(0315)4167664	1,200	外商投资	178,381	5,200(12)	146,983	pvc手套
Zhangjiagang Dayu Rubber Products Co.,Ltd.	Suzhou	Jiangsu	(0512)58450023		Foreign Funded				Emulsion Gloves
张家港大裕橡胶制品有限公司(1994)	苏州市	江苏省	(0512)58422800	1,420	外商投资	117,836	-	79,279	乳胶手套
Guangzhou Wanwei Rubber Industry Co., Ltd.	Guangzhou	Guangdong	(020)82391742		Overseas Chinese-funded				Rubber Shoes Sole
广州万威胶业有限公司(1990)	广州市	广东省	(020)82393344	500	港澳台资	101,726	288(75)	67,180	橡胶鞋底
Shandong Ke Yi Da Group Co.,Ltd.	Yantai	Shandong	(0535)8918178		Collective-owned				Waterproof Ventilated Cloth防
山东科亿达集团有限公司(1989)	烟台市	山东省	(0535)8918201	147	集体企业	98,500	6,010(10)	39,050	雨透气布
Shanghai Latex Factory	Shanghai	Shanghai	(021)55090975		State-owned				Rubber Gloves for Doctor橡胶
上海乳胶厂(1959)	上海市	上海市	(021)55061248	819	国有企业	97,718	766(46)	113,824	医用手套
Zhongshan Fuzhou Paper Plastic Products Co., Ltd.	Zhongshan	Guangdong	(0760)5592838		Overseas Chinese-funded				Affixing Film and Paper粘贴
中山市富洲纸塑料制品有限公司(1995)	中山市	广东省	(0760)5597023	408	港澳台资	92,422	2,355(26)	27,641	膜粘贴纸
Haining Haixiang Group Co., Ltd.	Jiaxing	Zhejiang	(0573)7274632		Limited-Liability				Rubber Products
海宁海橡集团有限公司(1976)	嘉兴市	浙江省	(0573)7279999	279	有限公司	83,737	13,422(3)	117,222	橡胶制品
Zhejiang Yong Xin Rong Latex Products Co., Ltd.	Shaoxing	Zhejiang	(0575)7382161		Overseas Chinese-funded				Emulsion Gloves
浙江永鑫荣乳胶制品有限公司(1997)	绍兴市	浙江省	(0575)7381762	270	港澳台资	78,134	3,001(21)	78,787	胶手指套

Top 10 Cities by Revenue 销售收入排名前10位城市	Province 省	Market share 市场份额 (%)	Number of firms 企业个数
Shanghai 上海市	Shanghai 上海市	9.68	12
Jiangmen 江门市	Guangdong 广东省	9.61	7
Yantai 烟台市	Shandong 山东省	8.59	4
Tianjin 天津市	Tianjin 天津市	6.68	13
Guangzhou 广州市	Guangdong 广东省	6.44	9
Qingdao 青岛市	Shandong 山东省	5.99	5
Suzhou 苏州市	Jiangsu 江苏省	4.54	5
Tangshan 唐山市	Hebei 河北省	4.18	2
Zhenjiang 镇江市	Jiangsu 江苏省	3.16	2
Shijiazhuang 石家庄市	Hebei 河北省	3.04	1

10 Major Wholesalers 十家主要批发商	City 城市	Province 省	Telephone/Fax 电话/传真
Yihua Kangqi Chemical Fibre Co.,Ltd.	Yangzhou	Jiangsu	(0514)3235499
仪化康祺化纤有限责任公司	扬州市	江苏省	(0514)3233847
Sinochem Guangdong Import & Export Company	Guangzhou	Guangdong	(020)86672288
中化广东进出口公司	广州市	广东省	(020)86507512
Sinochem Shanghai Import & Export Company	Shanghai	Shanghai	(021)63289888
中化上海进出口公司	上海市	上海市	(021)63283968
Sinochem Tianjin Import & Export Company	Tianjin	Tianjin	(022)23146216
中化天津进出口公司	天津市	天津市	(022)23146215
China Chemical Sales & Supply (North China) Corporation	Tianjin	Tianjin	(022)23011031
中国化工供销华北公司	天津市	天津市	(022)23011032
China Chemical Sales & Supply (North China) Corporation	Shanghai	Shanghai	(021)62103300
中国化工供销华东公司	上海市	上海市	(021)62515799
Nantong Chemical Light Industry Co.,Ltd.	Nantong	Jiangsu	(0513)5518397
南通化工轻工股份有限公司	南通市	江苏省	(0513)5512735
Taizhou Heshun Plastics Co.,Ltd.	Taizhou	Zhejiang	(0576)2510220
台州市和顺塑料有限公司	台州市	浙江省	(0576)2510160
China Petroleum Technology Development Corporation	Beijing	Beijing	(010)84080722
中国石油技术开发公司	北京市	北京市	(010)84080800
China National Chemical Fiber Corporation	Beijing	Beijing	(010)65816699
中国化纤总公司	北京市	北京市	(010)65813483

2981: Tire Repairing 轮胎翻新业

The industry accounts for 0.004% of the total revenue of China's industrial sector in 2002. The rate of return on assets is 4.30%. 87.10% of all firms in the industry made a profit while 12.90% had negative returns.The top province in terms of the industry's revenue is Shandong, accounting for 21.89% of the total revenue.
2002年本行业收入占全行业的 0.004%，资产利润率为 4.30%。87.10%的企业赢利，12.90%的企业亏损。收入最高的省为山东省，占本行业的21.89%。

	Total number of firms 企业总数	Total number of employees 职工总数	Total revenue (Mil.RMB) 总销售收入（百万元）	Total profit (Mil.RMB) 总利润（百万元）	Return on assets 资产利润率（%）	Return on equity 权益利润率（%）	Labour productivity ('000 RMB/ worker) 劳动生产率（千元/人）	Debts/ assets 资产负债率（%）	Total assets (Mil.RMB) 总资产（百万元）
Industry Overall 行业总体	31	3,059	428	16	4.30	9.22	38.21	53.39	367

	Number of firms 企业个数	Average number of employees 平均职工人数	Average revenue ('000 RMB) 平均销售收入（千元）	Average profit ('000 RMB) 平均利润（千元）	Return on assets 资产利润率（%）	Return on equity 权益利润率（%）	Labour productivity ('000 RMB/ worker) 劳动生产率（千元/人）	Debts/ assets 资产负债率（%）	Average total assets ('000 RMB) 平均总资产（千元）
By ownership 产业所有权									
State-owned 国有	11	95	5,554	-89	-0.80	-1.56	13.29	48.33	11,003
Collective-owned 集体	8	84	10,679	411	7.15	17.48	40.39	59.07	5,747
Foreign & Overseas Chinese Funded 三资	2	138	35,304	1,945	7.56	16.27	60.91	53.55	25,731
By regional distribution 地区分布									
Central-North 华北	5	123	21,913	686	3.92	6.18	39.85	36.65	17,517
Beijing 北京	1	72	35,511	82	0.15	0.20	29.50	25.94	55,109
Tianjin 天津	2	83	6,969	375	7.15	9.20	22.51	22.31	5,241
Hebei 河北	2	188	30,058	1,300	11.82	39.83	49.44	70.32	10,996
Shanxi 山西									
Inner Mongolia 内蒙古									
Northeast 东北	4	49	4,430	-193	-4.94	-20.46	20.81	75.86	3,913
Liaoning 辽宁	3	49	5,494	-232	-5.09	-30.11	25.63	83.11	4,568
Jilin 吉林									
Heilongjiang 黑龙江	1	48	1,236	-76	-3.90	-5.19	6.17	24.81	1,947
Central-East 华东	7	97	23,109	1,129	8.53	23.51	76.67	63.70	13,231
Shanghai 上海									
Jiangsu 江苏	1	136	21,720	830	5.30	8.07	53.90	34.25	15,650
Zhejiang 浙江	2	103	19,394	1,127	6.46		38.68	101.30	17,432
Anhui 安徽									
Fujian 福建	1	66	2,517	25	0.68	1.45	27.33	52.91	3,674
Jiangxi 江西	1	31	5,130	886	30.47	32.23	57.87	5.47	2,908
Shandong 山东	2	120	46,805	1,955	11.01	20.26	138.18	45.66	17,760
Central-South 中南	7	89	14,544	455	2.74	7.54	42.54	63.65	16,595
Henan 河南	1	70	904				21.00	83.28	29,952
Hubei 湖北	1	72	10,187	62	0.54	1.24	28.10	56.76	11,544
Hunan 湖南	1	33	410	-187	-11.91		14.91	127.64	1,570
Guangdong 广东	4	112	22,577	827	4.53	10.13	50.26	55.33	18,275
Guangxi 广西									
Hainan 海南									
Southwest 西南	4	172	9,056	501	4.09	6.10	10.15	32.99	12,251
Chongqing 重庆	1	188	21,029	2,297	6.81	8.80	15.13	22.63	33,750
Sichuan 四川	1	100	9,514	187	4.75	6.02	22.35	21.16	3,937
Guizhou 贵州	2	200	2,841	-240	-4.24	-13.25	4.75	67.98	5,659
Yunnan 云南									
Tibet 西藏									
Northwest 西北	4	66	122	3	0.17	0.34	10.93	47.84	1,431
Shaanxi 陕西									
Gansu 甘肃	4	66	122	3	0.17	0.34	10.93	47.84	1,431
Qinghai 青海									
Ningxia 宁夏									
Xinjiang 新疆									

2981: Tire Repairing 轮胎翻新业

Year 年份	Number of firms 企业个数	Rate of change 变化率(%)	Number of employees 职工人数(人)	Rate of change 变化率(%)	Total revenue (Mil. RMB) 总销售收入(百万元)	Rate of change 变化率(%)	Total profit (Mil RMB) 总利润(百万元)	Rate of change 变化率(%)
2000	41		5,151		289		7	
2001	40	-2.44	4,319	-16.15	369	27.68	9	28.57
2002	31	-22.50	3,059	-29.17	428	15.99	16	77.78

Major Products 主要产品	Output 产量	Unit 单位
Triangle Belt 三角带	69,263	10,000 A Meters 万A米
Outer Tyre 轮胎外胎	16,046	10,000 Pieces 万条

10 Main Firms with Maximal Revenue (year founded) 收入最大的十家主要企业（创办年份）	City 城市	Province 省	Telephone/fax 电话/传真	Number of employees 职工人数	Ownership 产业所有权	Revenue ('000 RMB) 销售收入(千元)	Profit('000 RMB) (rank) 利润(千元)(排名)	Total assets ('000 RMB) 总资产(千元)	Major products 主要产品
Qingdao Xinying Rubber Factory	Qingdao	Shandong	(0532)8532798		Private Enterprises				V Band
青岛新颖橡胶厂(1986)	青岛市	山东省	(0532)7553178	180	私营独资	56,060	1,450(6)	32,390	V Band
Qingdao Shuangfeng Rubber Factory	Qingdao	Shandong	(0532)8521670		Private Enterprises				Tyre
青岛双丰橡胶厂(1994)	青岛市	山东省	(0532)8521670	60	私营独资	37,550	2,460(3)	3,130	Tyre
Beijing Jinyuntong Large-type Ac Motor Tyre Renovating	Beijing	Beijing	(010)61667010		State-owned				Renovated Tyre
Factory 北京金运通大型轮胎翻修厂(1992)	北京市	北京市	(010)61668484	72	国有企业	35,511	82(15)	55,109	翻新轮胎
Changzhou Yisheng Rubber Products Co., Ltd.	Changzhou	Jiangsu	(0519)6543281		Limited-Liability				Renovated Tyre
常州市逸盛橡胶制品有限公司(1988)	常州市	江苏省	(0519)6547021	136	有限公司	21,720	830(8)	15,650	翻新轮胎
Chongqing Chaoke Industrial Co., Ltd.	Chongqing	Chongqing	(023)62801338		Limited-Liability				Renovated Tyre
重庆超科实业有限公司(1944)	重庆市	重庆市	(023)62803361	188	有限公司	21,029	2,297(4)	33,750	翻新轮胎
Haida Tyre Retreaded co., Ltd.	Foshan	Guangdong	(0757)7676036		Private Owned				Tyre
海达轮胎有限公司(2001)	佛山市	广东省	(0757)7676037	85	私营企业	19,000	100(13)	17,194	轮胎
Benxi Steel Company Nanfen Tyre Renovating Factory	Benxi	Liaoning	(0414)7832111		Collective-owned				Renovated Tyre
本溪钢铁公司南芬轮胎翻新厂(1996)	本溪市	辽宁省	(0414)7832111	88	集体企业	15,338	38(18)	10,894	翻新轮胎
Wenzhou Autoways Tyre Co., Ltd.	Wenzhou	Zhejiang	(0577)63651698		Foreign Funded				Tyre
温州阿多威轮胎有限公司(1994)	温州市	浙江省	(0577)63653070	19	外商投资	10,647	740(9)	8,653	轮胎
Yichang Sanxia Tyre Renovating Factory	Yichang	Hubei	(0717)6312388		Collective Owned				Automobile Renovated Tyre
宜昌市三峡轮胎翻新厂(1994)	宜昌市	湖北省	(0717)6312388	72	集体企业	10,187	62(16)	11,544	翻新轮胎
Sichuan Xindu San Yi Tyre Retreading Ltd. Company	Chengdu	Sichuan	(028)83961729		Limited-Liability				Renovated Tyre
四川省新都三益翻胎有限公司(1970)	成都市	四川省	(028)83951752	100	有限公司	9,514	187(11)	3,937	翻新轮胎

Top 10 Cities by Revenue 销售收入排名前10位城市	Province 省	Market share 市场份额(%)	Number of firms 企业个数
Qingdao 青岛市	Shandong 山东省	21.89	2
Guangzhou 广州市	Guangdong 广东省	15.56	2
Tangshan 唐山市	Hebei 河北省	12.95	1
Beijing 北京市	Beijing 北京市	8.31	1
Shaoxing 绍兴市	Zhejiang 浙江省	6.58	1
Changzhou 常州市	Jiangsu 江苏省	5.08	1
Chongqing 重庆市	Chongqing 重庆市	4.92	1
Foshan 佛山市	Guangdong 广东省	4.44	1
Benxi 本溪市	Liaoning 辽宁省	3.59	1
Tianjin 天津市	Tianjin 天津市	3.26	2

10 Major Wholesalers 十家主要批发商	City 城市	Province 省	Telephone/Fax 电话/传真
Yihua Kangqi Chemical Fibre Co.,Ltd.	Yangzhou	Jiangsu	(0514)3235499
仪化康祺化纤有限责任公司	扬州市	江苏省	(0514)3233847
Sinochem Guangdong Import & Export Company	Guangzhou	Guangdong	(020)86672288
中化广东进出口公司	广州市	广东省	(020)86507512
Sinochem Shanghai Import & Export Company	Shanghai	Shanghai	(021)63289888
中化上海进出口公司	上海市	上海市	(021)63283968
Sinochem Tianjin Import & Export Company	Tianjin	Tianjin	(022)23146216
中化天津进出口公司	天津市	天津市	(022)23146215
China Chemical Sales & Supply (North China) Corporation	Tianjin	Tianjin	(022)23011031
中国化工供销华北公司	天津市	天津市	(022)23011032
China Chemical Sales & Supply (North China) Corporation	Shanghai	Shanghai	(021)62103300
中国化工供销华东公司	上海市	上海市	(021)62515799
Nantong Chemical Light Industry Co.,Ltd.	Nantong	Jiangsu	(0513)5518397
南通化工轻工股份有限公司	南通市	江苏省	(0513)5512735
Taizhou Heshun Plastics Co.,Ltd.	Taizhou	Zhejiang	(0576)2510220
台州市和顺塑料有限公司	台州市	浙江省	(0576)2510160
China Petroleum Technology Development Corporation	Beijing	Beijing	(010)84080722
中国石油技术开发公司	北京市	北京市	(010)84080800
China National Chemical Fiber Corporation	Beijing	Beijing	(010)65816699
中国化纤总公司	北京市	北京市	(010)65813483

2990: Other Rubber Products 其他橡胶制品业

The industry accounts for 0.061% of the total revenue of China's industrial sector in 2002. The rate of return on assets is 6.34%. 86.52% of all firms in the industry made a profit while 13.48% had negative returns.The top province in terms of the industry's revenue is Guangdong, accounting for 15.68% of the total revenue.
2002年本行业收入占全行业的0.061%，资产利润率为6.34%。86.52%的企业赢利，13.48%的企业亏损。收入最高的省为广东省，占本行业的15.68%。

	Total number of firms 企业总数	Total number of employees 职工总数	Total revenue (Mil.RMB) 总销售收入（百万元）	Total profit (Mil.RMB) 总利润（百万元）	Return on assets 资产利润率（%）	Return on equity 权益利润率（%）	Labour productivity ('000 RMB/worker) 劳动生产率（千元/人）	Debts/assets 资产负债率（%）	Total assets (Mil.RMB) 总资产（百万元）
Industry Overall 行业总体	267	50,428	6,518	432	6.34	14.69	35.93	56.87	6,821

	Number of firms 企业个数	Average number of employees 平均职工人数	Average revenue ('000 RMB) 平均销售收入（千元）	Average profit ('000 RMB) 平均利润（千元）	Return on assets 资产利润率（%）	Return on equity 权益利润率（%）	Labour productivity ('000 RMB/worker) 劳动生产率（千元/人）	Debts/assets 资产负债率（%）	Average total assets ('000 RMB) 平均总资产（千元）
By ownership 产业所有权									
State-owned 国有	22	203	19,354	144	0.36	1.21	29.84	69.90	39,557
Collective-owned 集体	54	129	27,677	1,766	10.09	25.30	63.72	60.11	17,496
Foreign & Overseas Chinese Funded 三资	68	289	30,984	2,545	6.58	13.40	25.36	50.88	38,646
By regional distribution 地区分布									
Central-North 华北	46	207	24,561	2,146	8.83	16.14	35.89	45.26	24,302
Beijing 北京	8	150	26,047	3,951	11.04	17.63	65.45	37.35	35,774
Tianjin 天津	12	157	20,602	3,399	21.36	38.62	37.47	44.70	15,917
Hebei 河北	25	251	26,731	1,051	4.14	8.07	30.35	48.75	25,416
Shanxi 山西	1	150	5,957	67	1.26	5.00	10.63	74.78	5,309
Inner Mongolia 内蒙古									
Northeast 东北	12	126	17,581	540	2.89	8.31	23.40	65.18	18,681
Liaoning 辽宁	6	182	22,263	200	0.62	1.78	10.04	65.16	32,176
Jilin 吉林	6	69	12,899	881	16.99	48.95	58.51	65.29	5,185
Heilongjiang 黑龙江									
Central-East 华东	132	192	26,428	2,207	8.57	19.87	38.90	56.88	25,760
Shanghai 上海	34	99	21,322	2,815	11.79	20.51	68.94	42.52	23,883
Jiangsu 江苏	33	170	28,758	2,355	7.99	24.24	50.90	67.03	29,464
Zhejiang 浙江	18	139	22,452	2,269	9.28	18.18	46.79	48.96	24,454
Anhui 安徽	4	88	8,372	866	10.84	29.22	24.40	62.89	7,984
Fujian 福建	10	293	35,428	1,208	3.65	6.96	-6.09	47.55	33,126
Jiangxi 江西	2	1,702	4,750	100	1.03	221.11	1.09	99.53	9,624
Shandong 山东	31	230	32,683	1,980	7.74	22.86	49.80	66.16	25,594
Central-South 中南	70	194	23,549	611	2.14	5.58	32.16	61.59	28,529
Henan 河南	9	107	24,633	992	5.12	20.62	67.75	75.20	19,388
Hubei 湖北	3	808	121,195	5,642	2.69	7.88	40.77	65.91	209,875
Hunan 湖南	4	236	9,166	-1,119	-3.01	-74.37	12.12	95.96	37,229
Guangdong 广东	52	176	19,653	432	2.18	4.49	28.44	51.39	19,794
Guangxi 广西									
Hainan 海南	2	37	2,249	-547	-7.45	-39.84	3.93	81.31	7,346
Southwest 西南	5	99	5,859	-1,544	-10.75	-48.42	18.59	77.81	14,365
Chongqing 重庆	2	102	5,804	98	2.20	23.67	19.19	90.69	4,425
Sichuan 四川	2	72	4,890	-3,975	-22.59		28.19	101.16	17,596
Guizhou 贵州	1	149	7,910	37	0.13	0.24	8.49	44.14	27,785
Yunnan 云南									
Tibet 西藏									
Northwest 西北	2	29	5,475	301	6.21	23.58	106.40	73.66	4,838
Shaanxi 陕西	2	29	5,475	301	6.21	23.58	106.40	73.66	4,838
Gansu 甘肃									
Qinghai 青海									
Ningxia 宁夏									
Xinjiang 新疆									

2990: Other Rubber Products 其他橡胶制品业

Year 年份	Number of firms 企业个数	Rate of change 变化率 (%)	Number of employees 职工人数 (人)	Rate of change 变化率 (%)	Total revenue (Mil. RMB) 总销售收入 (百万元)	Rate of change 变化率 (%)	Total profit (Mil RMB) 总利润 (百万元)	Rate of change 变化率 (%)
2000	259		37,098		4,530		188	
2001	293	13.13	49,320	32.95	6,085	34.33	398	111.70
2002	267	-8.87	50,428	2.25	6,518	7.12	432	8.54

Major Products 主要产品	Output 产量	Unit 单位

10 Main Firms with Maximal Revenue (year founded) 收入最大的十家主要企业 (创办年份)	City 城市	Province 省	Telephone/fax 电话/传真	Number of employees 职工人数	Ownership 产业所有权	Revenue ('000 RMB) 销售收入 (千元)	Profit('000 RMB) (rank) 利润(千元) (排名)	Total assets ('000 RMB) 总资产 (千元)	Major products 主要产品
ITT Electronic Industry Corp.Ltd.	Nantong	Jiangsu	(0513)3596388		Foreign Funded				Silica Gel Depressed Key
埃梯梯科能(南通)电子工业有限公司(1991)	南通市	江苏省	(0513)3596678	2,106	外商投资	198,908	30,170(3)	195,997	硅胶按键
Wendeng Kaitai Rubber Factory	Weihai	Shandong	(0631)8631049		Collective-owned				Rubber Products
文登市开泰橡塑有限公司(1993)	威海市	山东省	(0631)8631035	220	集体企业	162,220	17,870(6)	36,430	橡胶制品
BeiJing Wanyuan GDX Automotive Sealing Products Co.Ltd.	Beijing	Beijing	(010)68383467		Foreign Funded				Automobile Sealing Joint Strip汽
北京万源金德汽车密封制品有限公司(1996)	北京市	北京市	(010)68383491	269	外商投资	130,447	24,818(4)	175,850	车密封条
Shengzhen Gong Tai Rubber Auxiliary Reagent Factory	Hengshui	Hebei	(0318)3420432		Collective-owned				Rubber Auxiliary Reagent
深州市贡台橡胶助剂厂(1995)	衡水市	河北省	(0318)3420432	60	集体企业	120,000	500(121)	1,920	橡胶助剂
Hubei Hua Qiang Science & Technology Co., Ltd.	Yichang	Hubei	(0717)6331426		Limited-Liability				Butyl Rubber Bottle Plug丁基
湖北华强科技有限责任公司(2001)	宜昌市	湖北省	(0717)6331556	974	有限公司	112,438	4,334(31)	324,011	橡胶瓶塞
Luohe Rubber Glass Products Co., Ltd.	Luohe	Henan	(0395)6811030		Collective-owned				Rubber Glass Products橡胶
漯河市橡胶玻璃制品厂(1993)	漯河市	河南省	(0395)6813396	360	集体企业	104,293	3,560(35)	49,673	玻璃制品
Shanghai Pengpu Rubber Products General Factory	Shanghai	Shanghai	(021)56687700		Joint Stock				Others Rubber Products
上海彭浦橡胶制品总厂(1964)	上海市	上海市	(021)56689222	458	股份制	102,507	7,976(11)	173,404	橡胶制品
Xiamen Ge Xin Plastic Cement Products Co., Ltd.	Xiamen	Fujian	(0592)6282862		Foreign Funded				Plastic Cement fittings for Beach Chair沙滩椅
厦门革新塑胶制品有限公司(2000)	厦门市	福建省	(0592)6662556	1,091	外商投资	102,301	14,066(8)	58,626	塑胶配件
Shanghai O.P.T.Rubber & Plastics Co., Ltd.	Shanghai	Shanghai	(021)67648952		Foreign Funded				Others Rubber Products
上海大冢橡塑实业有限公司(1996)	上海市	上海市	(021)67648000	101	外商投资	92,748	42,993(1)	120,392	橡胶制品
Weihai Beihai Welfare Rubber Products Factory	Weihai	Shandong	(0631)5704092		Collective-owned				Single Rubber Strip
威海市北海福利橡胶制品厂(1992)	威海市	山东省		130	集体企业	91,654	14,974(7)	21,906	单胶带

Top 10 Cities by Revenue 销售收入排名前10位城市	Province 省	Market share 市场份额 (%)	Number of firms 企业个数
Shanghai 上海市	Shanghai 上海市	11.12	34
Hengshui 衡水市	Hebei 河北省	6.24	8
Weihai 威海市	Shandong 山东省	5.11	4
Qingdao 青岛市	Shandong 山东省	4.17	12
Guangzhou 广州市	Guangdong 广东省	3.93	10
Tianjin 天津市	Tianjin 天津市	3.79	12
Nantong 南通市	Jiangsu 江苏省	3.57	3
Beijing 北京市	Beijing 北京市	3.20	8
Xiaogan 孝感市	Hubei 湖北省	3.19	1
Zhenjiang 镇江市	Jiangsu 江苏省	3.12	1

10 Major Wholesalers 十家主要批发商	City 城市	Province 省	Telephone/Fax 电话/传真
Yihua Kangqi Chemical Fibre Co.,Ltd.	Yangzhou	Jiangsu	(0514)3235499
仪化康祺化纤有限责任公司	扬州市	江苏省	(0514)3233847
Sinochem Guangdong Import & Export Company	Guangzhou	Guangdong	(020)86672288
中化广东进出口公司	广州市	广东省	(020)86507512
Sinochem Shanghai Import & Export Company	Shanghai	Shanghai	(021)63289888
中化上海进出口公司	上海市	上海市	(021)63283968
Sinochem Tianjin Import & Export Company	Tianjin	Tianjin	(022)23146216
中化天津进出口公司	天津市	天津市	(022)23146215
China Chemical Sales & Supply (North China) Corporation	Tianjin	Tianjin	(022)23011031
中国化工供销华北公司	天津市	天津市	(022)23011032
China Chemical Sales & Supply (North China) Corporation	Shanghai	Shanghai	(021)62103300
中国化工供销华东公司	上海市	上海市	(021)62515799
Nantong Chemical Light Industry Co.,Ltd.	Nantong	Jiangsu	(0513)5518397
南通化工轻工股份有限公司	南通市	江苏省	(0513)5512735
Taizhou Heshun Plastics Co.,Ltd.	Taizhou	Zhejiang	(0576)2510220
台州市和顺塑料有限公司	台州市	浙江省	(0576)2510160
China Petroleum Technology Development Corporation	Beijing	Beijing	(010)84080722
中国石油技术开发公司	北京市	北京市	(010)84080800
China National Chemical Fiber Corporation	Beijing	Beijing	(010)65816699
中国化纤总公司	北京市	北京市	(010)65813483

3010: Plastic Films 塑料薄膜制造业

The industry accounts for 0.376% of the total revenue of China's industrial sector in 2002. The rate of return on assets is 4.06%. 76.82% of all firms in the industry made a profit while 23.18% had negative returns.The top province in terms of the industry's revenue is Guangdong, accounting for 27.80% of the total revenue.
2002年本行业收入占全行业的 0.376%，资产利润率为 4.06%。76.82%的企业赢利，23.18%的企业亏损。收入最高的省为广东省，占本行业的27.80%。

	Total number of firms 企业总数	Total number of employees 职工总数	Total revenue (Mil.RMB) 总销售收入 (百万元)	Total profit (Mil.RMB) 总利润 (百万元)	Return on assets 资产利润率 (%)	Return on equity 权益利润率 (%)	Labour productivity ('000 RMB/ worker) 劳动生产率 (千元/人)	Debts/ assets 资产负债率 (%)	Total assets (Mil.RMB) 总资产 (百万元)
Industry Overall 行业总体	785	163,041	40,300	2,038	4.06	9.95	60.72	59.22	50,258

	Number of firms 企业个数	Average number of employees 平均职工人数	Average revenue ('000 RMB) 平均销售收入（千元）	Average profit ('000 RMB) 平均利润 (千元)	Return on assets 资产利润率 (%)	Return on equity 权益利润率 (%)	Labour productivity ('000 RMB/ worker) 劳动生产率 (千元/人)	Debts/ assets 资产负债率 (%)	Average total assets ('000 RMB) 平均总资产 (千元)
By ownership 产业所有权									
State-owned 国有	74	146	18,426	-795	-1.83	-10.31	31.94	82.26	43,475
Collective-owned 集体	140	203	58,244	2,739	6.20	19.03	66.51	67.41	44,171
Foreign & Overseas Chinese Funded 三资	192	206	67,459	4,287	4.87	10.00	83.27	51.24	87,970
By regional distribution 地区分布									
Central-North 华北	94	210	38,982	1,688	1.77	4.84	44.10	63.39	95,209
Beijing 北京	21	156	19,856	652	0.86	1.57	28.14	45.52	76,116
Tianjin 天津	24	155	32,641	1,538	1.94	4.52	51.91	57.04	79,180
Hebei 河北	34	319	66,365	3,207	2.13	7.24	50.57	70.55	150,352
Shanxi 山西	11	144	16,710	-97	-0.36	-1.56	16.67	77.13	27,293
Inner Mongolia 内蒙古	4	79	5,928	40	0.42	1.08	32.79	61.39	9,676
Northeast 东北	46	201	33,751				44.80	77.89	65,364
Liaoning 辽宁	17	219	30,433	-1,677	-2.12	-11.51	23.95	81.55	79,002
Jilin 吉林	13	260	43,407	167	0.25	1.31	49.52	80.87	66,690
Heilongjiang 黑龙江	16	135	29,430	1,648	3.31	10.49	73.45	68.46	49,797
Central-East 华东	329	174	54,135	3,157	6.42	14.98	72.01	57.13	49,153
Shanghai 上海	64	121	34,902	2,344	5.41	10.49	69.33	48.40	43,290
Jiangsu 江苏	68	201	72,996	4,420	6.11	14.31	83.87	57.28	72,308
Zhejiang 浙江	77	98	56,470	4,999	13.66	33.01	132.93	58.61	36,584
Anhui 安徽	18	195	29,995	1,055	2.84	6.78	30.39	58.16	37,164
Fujian 福建	26	344	82,169	2,134	2.98	6.36	40.72	53.15	71,564
Jiangxi 江西	8	166	5,736	130	0.54	2.63	21.95	79.42	23,959
Shandong 山东	68	216	52,096	1,877	4.33	12.21	64.81	64.51	43,317
Central-South 中南	205	264	69,385	3,617	4.53	10.25	65.98	55.79	79,824
Henan 河南	36	425	47,003	1,933	5.15	9.99	25.12	48.49	37,555
Hubei 湖北	15	149	49,017	3,182	3.54	8.84	135.41	59.97	89,962
Hunan 湖南	10	97	30,692	3,294	5.79	11.98	104.89	51.64	56,868
Guangdong 广东	135	257	82,986	4,364	4.69	10.45	77.06	55.11	93,041
Guangxi 广西	8	90	21,431	67	0.20	1.30	134.48	84.39	32,978
Hainan 海南	1	236	114,926	1,523	0.57	3.52	64.22	83.96	269,480
Southwest 西南	52	110	23,941	1,134	3.05	7.49	55.80	59.26	37,145
Chongqing 重庆	2	141	8,552				21.38	86.19	7,796
Sichuan 四川	24	114	22,000	80	0.31	0.59	37.51	47.76	25,976
Guizhou 贵州	4	92	7,783	-49	-0.48	-i.21	17.74	60.48	10,179
Yunnan 云南	22	105	30,396	2,601	4.57	12.92	87.85	64.61	56,901
Tibet 西藏									
Northwest 西北	59	285	30,570	690	1.06	2.54	35.19	58.29	64,992
Shaanxi 陕西	10	139	6,230	-322	-1.79		26.11	101.98	18,011
Gansu 甘肃	26	514	56,301	2,926	2.39	5.07	36.37	52.84	122,434
Qinghai 青海									
Ningxia 宁夏	1	138	12,607	221	0.91	2.81	39.89	67.66	24,308
Xinjiang 新疆	22	88	12,041	-1,472	-7.25	-34.43	33.22	78.96	20,310

3010: Plastic Films 塑料薄膜制造业

Year 年份	Number of firms 企业个数	Rate of change 变化率 (%)	Number of employees 职工人数 (人)	Rate of change 变化率 (%)	Total revenue (Mil. RMB) 总销售收入 (百万元)	Rate of change 变化率 (%)	Total profit (Mil RMB) 总利润 (百万元)	Rate of change 变化率 (%)
2000	714		154,618		33,760		1,088	
2001	741	3.78	164,717	6.53	34,927	3.46	1,718	57.90
2002	785	5.94	163,041	-1.02	40,300	15.38	2,038	18.63

Major Products 主要产品	Output 产量	Unit 单位
Plastic Film 塑料薄膜	280	10,000 Tons 万吨
Agricultural Membrane 农用薄膜	81	10,000 Tons 万吨

10 Main Firms with Maximal Revenue (year founded) 收入最大的十家主要企业（创办年份）	City 城市	Province 省	Telephone/fax 电话/传真	Number of employees 职工人数	Ownership 产业所有权	Revenue ('000 RMB) 销售收入 (千元)	Profit('000 RMB) (rank) 利润(千元)(排名)	Total assets ('000 RMB) 总资产 (千元)	Major products 主要产品
Foshan Plastics Group Co., Ltd. 佛山塑料集团股份有限公司(1988)	Foshan 佛山市	Guangdong 广东省	(0757)3988188 (0757)3985216	4,298	Joint Stock 股份制	2,803,888	202,094(1)	3,444,788	Shoes Glue Products 鞋类粘胶制品
Zhejiang Great Southeast Plastic Co., Ltd 浙江大东南塑胶集团有限公司(1993)	Shaoxing 绍兴市	Zhejiang 浙江省	(0575)7092218 (0575)7091595	1,220	Collective-owned 集体企业	2,058,218	178,524(2)	572,434	Plastic Products 塑料制品
Shenda Group Company 申达集团公司(1985)	Wuxi 无锡市	Jiangsu 江苏省	(0510)6621666 (0510)6621021	1,592	Collective-owned 集体企业	1,817,979	166,511(3)	1,332,341	Plastic Products 塑料制品
China BS Group Co.,Ltd. 河北宝硕集团有限公司(1957)	Baoding 保定市	Hebei 河北省	(0312)3209683 (0312)3209655	6,050	State Enterprises 国有独资	1,320,478	63,731(7)	3,400,903	Plastic Film 塑料薄膜
Mingda Plastics (Xiamen) Co., Ltd. 明达塑胶（厦门）有限公司(1995)	Xiamen 厦门市	Fujian 福建省	(0592)6512222 (0592)6518879	3,687	Foreign Funded 外商投资	1,038,103	40,231(11)	838,543	PVCRubberized Fabric PVC胶布
Suzhou Huasu Plastics Co., Ltd. 苏州华苏塑料有限公司(1992)	Suzhou 苏州市	Jiangsu 江苏省	(0512)53645183 (0512)53645857	523	Foreign Funded 外商投资	760,351	20,280(29)	891,204	PVCMembrane PVC树脂
Luohe Huaqiang Plastic Cement Co., Ltd. 漯河华强塑胶有限公司(1999)	Luohe 漯河市	Henan 河南省	(0395)2167026 (0395)2167730	10,500	Private Owned 私营企业	690,301	22,243(27)	169,178	Plastic Pakage 塑料包装
Nanya Plastic Cement Industry (Guangzhou) Co., Ltd. 南亚塑胶工业(广州)有限公司(1994)	Guangzhou 广州市	Guangdong 广东省	(020)86407900 (020)86407627	639	Foreign Funded 外商投资	513,796	36,901(12)	637,864	Rubberized Fabric and Rubber 胶布胶皮
Pacific PVC (Fujian) Co., Ltd. 太平洋塑胶(福建)有限公司(1988)	Fuzhou 福州市	Fujian 福建省	(0591)5376032 (0591)5380109	566	Foreign Funded 外商投资	434,746	11,352(36)	261,050	Polyvinyl Chloride (pvc) Membrane 聚氯乙稀薄膜
Guangzhou Plastics Industry Stock Co., Ltd. 广州市塑料工业股份有限公司(1993)	Guangzhou 广州市	Guangdong 广东省	(020)83312936 (020)83337311	836	Joint Stock 股份制	380,181	5,294(74)	274,372	Plastic Film 塑料薄膜

Top 10 Cities by Revenue 销售收入排名前10位城市	Province 省	Market share 市场份额 (%)	Number of firms 企业个数
Foshan 佛山市	Guangdong 广东省	9.82	20
Guangzhou 广州市	Guangdong 广东省	5.88	24
Shaoxing 绍兴市	Zhejiang 浙江省	5.73	6
Wuxi 无锡市	Jiangsu 江苏省	5.65	13
Shanghai 上海市	Shanghai 上海市	5.54	64
Baoding 保定市	Hebei 河北省	4.09	10
Xiamen 厦门市	Fujian 福建省	2.93	7
Suzhou 苏州市	Jiangsu 江苏省	2.60	14
Wenzhou 温州市	Zhejiang 浙江省	2.56	22
Zhongshan 中山市	Guangdong 广东省	2.56	24

10 Major Wholesalers 十家主要批发商	City 城市	Province 省	Telephone/Fax 电话/传真
Yihua Kangqi Chemical Fibre Co.,Ltd. 仪化康祺化纤有限责任公司	Yangzhou 扬州市	Jiangsu 江苏省	(0514)3235499 (0514)3233847
Sinochem Guangdong Import & Export Company 中化广东进出口公司	Guangzhou 广州市	Guangdong 广东省	(020)86672288 (020)86507512
Sinochem Shanghai Import & Export Company 中化上海进出口公司	Shanghai 上海市	Shanghai 上海市	(021)63289888 (021)63283968
Sinochem Tianjin Import & Export Company 中化天津进出口公司	Tianjin 天津市	Tianjin 天津市	(022)23146216 (022)23146215
China Chemical Sales & Supply (North China) Corporation 中国化工供销华北公司	Tianjin 天津市	Tianjin 天津市	(022)23011031 (022)23011032
China Chemical Sales & Supply (North China) Corporation 中国化工供销华东公司	Shanghai 上海市	Shanghai 上海市	(021)62103300 (021)62515799
Nantong Chemical Light Industry Co.,Ltd. 南通化工轻工股份有限公司	Nantong 南通市	Jiangsu 江苏省	(0513)5518397 (0513)5512735
Taizhou Heshun Plastics Co.,Ltd. 台州市和顺塑料有限公司	Taizhou 台州市	Zhejiang 浙江省	(0576)2510220 (0576)2510160
China Petroleum Technology Development Corporation 中国石油技术开发公司	Beijing 北京市	Beijing 北京市	(010)84080722 (010)84080800
China National Chemical Fiber Corporation 中国化纤总公司	Beijing 北京市	Beijing 北京市	(010)65816699 (010)65813483

3020: Plastic Sheet, Pipe and Rods 塑料板、管、棒材制造业

The industry accounts for 0.377% of the total revenue of China's industrial sector in 2002. The rate of return on assets is 3.97%. 79.69% of all firms in the industry made a profit while 20.31% had negative returns.The top province in terms of the industry's revenue is Jiangsu, accounting for 19.35% of the total revenue.
2002年本行业收入占全行业的 0.377%，资产利润率为 3.97%。79.69%的企业赢利，20.31%的企业亏损。收入最高的省为江苏省，占本行业的19.35%。

	Total number of firms 企业总数	Total number of employees 职工总数	Total revenue (Mil.RMB) 总销售收入 (百万元)	Total profit (Mil.RMB) 总利润 (百万元)	Return on assets 资产利润率 (%)	Return on equity 权益利润率 (%)	Labour productivity ('000 RMB/ worker) 劳动生产率 (千元/人)	Debts/ assets 资产负债率 (%)	Total assets (Mil.RMB) 总资产 (百万元)
Industry Overall 行业总体	1108	155,530	40,415	1,997	3.97	9.13	73.80	56.50	50,265

	Number of firms 企业个数	Average number of employees 平均职工人数	Average revenue ('000 RMB) 平均销售收入 (千元)	Average profit ('000 RMB) 平均利润 (千元)	Return on assets 资产利润率 (%)	Return on equity 权益利润率 (%)	Labour productivity ('000 RMB/ worker) 劳动生产率 (千元/人)	Debts/ assets 资产负债率 (%)	Average total assets ('000 RMB) 平均总资产 (千元)
By ownership 产业所有权									
State-owned 国有	72	190	28,518	-461	-0.55	-1.67	44.42	67.10	83,854
Collective-owned 集体	138	137	27,087	1,077	4.07	12.83	57.67	68.26	26,435
Foreign & Overseas Chinese Funded 三资	270	156	52,437	2,873	4.31	9.67	92.91	55.46	66,739
By regional distribution 地区分布									
Central-North 华北	112	122	18,618	485	1.25	4.08	59.93	69.24	38,719
Beijing 北京	13	63	15,970	758	2.34	5.17	85.27	54.87	32,447
Tianjin 天津	25	114	14,964	-9	-0.02	-0.14	68.35	82.72	34,330
Hebei 河北	62	140	22,769	714	1.61	4.83	58.88	66.68	44,356
Shanxi 山西	7	76	9,432	310	1.06	4.37	50.55	75.65	29,117
Inner Mongolia 内蒙古	5	156	5,163	-339	-1.65	-5.78	20.86	71.48	20,530
Northeast 东北	100	126	36,743	639	1.12	3.28	76.80	65.78	56,905
Liaoning 辽宁	57	124	53,072	822	1.08	3.56	104.06	69.66	76,011
Jilin 吉林	18	134	14,949	222	1.30	3.02	41.67	57.09	17,150
Heilongjiang 黑龙江	25	127	15,204	524	1.25	2.62	42.87	52.34	41,967
Central-East 华东	558	140	40,369	2,506	5.70	12.30	81.60	53.67	43,999
Shanghai 上海	103	102	25,907	1,291	3.80	8.06	59.41	52.89	33,995
Jiangsu 江苏	156	156	50,140	2,364	5.60	12.35	84.90	54.65	42,200
Zhejiang 浙江	131	130	33,779	2,779	7.33	17.41	68.91	57.88	37,890
Anhui 安徽	23	237	123,380	14,711	7.04	12.40	162.71	43.25	209,003
Fujian 福建	33	130	49,516	2,361	4.59	9.50	129.22	51.68	51,454
Jiangxi 江西	9	90	7,788	557	4.13	10.71	22.91	61.40	13,488
Shandong 山东	103	152	29,793	1,082	3.88	10.59	66.84	63.41	27,931
Central-South 中南	242	144	35,854	1,542	3.89	8.03	70.26	51.49	39,599
Henan 河南	38	103	14,756	599	4.36	15.32	42.25	71.52	13,736
Hubei 湖北	39	142	31,298	3,128	6.82	10.69	91.30	36.15	45,841
Hunan 湖南	27	111	14,246	-93	-0.32	-0.61	38.15	47.32	29,134
Guangdong 广东	134	160	47,678	1,685	3.55	7.86	75.69	54.78	47,410
Guangxi 广西	4	250	30,446	1,287	3.85	7.23	43.22	46.78	33,410
Hainan 海南									
Southwest 西南	64	170	26,332	573	1.48	3.26	53.95	54.44	38,592
Chongqing 重庆	14	124	23,024	-601	-1.41	-2.65	54.93	46.81	42,640
Sichuan 四川	42	198	30,053	1,416	3.95	8.26	56.17	52.24	35,891
Guizhou 贵州	5	117	9,325	-637	-4.18	-10.53	25.59	60.27	15,221
Yunnan 云南	3	89	18,025	-3,745	-3.88	-19.53	40.46	80.13	96,466
Tibet 西藏									
Northwest 西北	32	171	55,236	2,188	1.93	4.87	52.32	60.42	113,549
Shaanxi 陕西	8	211	8,690	-1,110	-3.85	-44.57	14.29	91.36	28,852
Gansu 甘肃	9	21	524	2	0.08	0.11	98.12	26.32	2,856
Qinghai 青海	1	188	2,987	-1,336	-3.05	-10.23	3.79	70.14	43,747
Ningxia 宁夏	1	101	5,400	23	0.08	0.12	19.95	36.30	29,604
Xinjiang 新疆	13	254	129,610	6,167	2.43	5.86	72.94	58.61	254,131

3020: Plastic Sheet, Pipe and Rods 塑料板、管、棒材制造业

Year 年份	Number of firms 企业个数	Rate of change 变化率 (%)	Number of employees 职工人数 (人)	Rate of change 变化率 (%)	Total revenue (Mil. RMB) 总销售收入 (百万元)	Rate of change 变化率 (%)	Total profit (Mil RMB) 总利润 (百万元)	Rate of change 变化率 (%)
2000	813		123,484		24,691		1,121	
2001	934	14.88	136,166	10.27	34,148	38.30	1,790	59.68
2002	1108	18.63	155,530	14.22	40,415	18.35	1,997	11.56

Major Products 主要产品	Output 产量	Unit 单位
Plastic Stick & Pipe Material 塑料棒管材	137	10,000 Tons 万吨
Plastic Plate & Piece Material 塑料板片材	85	10,000 Tons 万吨

10 Main Firms with Maximal Revenue (year founded) 收入最大的十家主要企业（创办年份）	City 城市	Province 省	Telephone/fax 电话/传真	Number of employees 职工人数	Ownership 产业所有权	Revenue ('000 RMB) 销售收入 (千元)	Profit('000 RMB) (rank) 利润(千元) (排名)	Total assets ('000 RMB) 总资产 (千元)	Major products 主要产品
Jiangyin Moulding Group Co., Ltd.	Wuxi	Jiangsu	(0510)6221226		Limited-Liability				Santana Insurance Bar桑塔
江阴市模塑集团有限公司(1994)	无锡市	江苏省	(0510)6401459	2,159	有限公司	1,318,813	116,640(2)	1,233,138	纳保险杠
Dalian Shide Plastic Cement Industry Co., Ltd.	Dalian	Liaoning	(0411)7609888		Foreign Funded				Plastic Door & Window Section Steel塑料
大连实德塑胶工业有限公司(1994)	大连市	辽宁省	(0411)7602517	337	外商投资	1,106,260	-	1,494,990	门窗型材
Anhui Guo Feng Group CO., Ltd.	Hefei	Anhui	(0551)2885333		State-owned				Plastic Building Materials
安徽国风集团有限公司(1979)	合肥市	安徽省	(0551)2888835	2,640	国有企业	1,095,834	75,361(5)	3,043,502	塑胶建材
Jiangsu Qionghua High-Tch. Co., Ltd.	Yangzhou	Jiangsu	(0514)7271301		Private Owned				PVCBoard
江苏琼花高科技股份有限公司(1984)	扬州市	江苏省	(0514)7273004	600	私营企业	691,182	51,808(9)	648,277	PVC板
Jiangsu Yinshan Industrial Group Co., Ltd.	Nanjing	Jiangsu	(025)4128743		Private Owned				Plastic Section Steel
江苏省银杉实业集团有限公司(1991)	南京市	江苏省	(025)4128823	988	私营企业	636,160	15,120(30)	272,840	塑料型材
Dalian Shide Plastics Building Materials Co., Ltd.	Dalian	Liaoning	(0411)7609888		Foreign Funded				Plastics & Steel Shapes
大连实德塑料建材有限公司(1999)	大连市	辽宁省	(0411)7602517	201	外商投资	597,960	63,600(7)	1,038,330	塑钢型材
Fujian Aton Advanced Materials Science & Technology	Fuzhou	Fujian	(0591)5315909		Foreign Funded				Plastic Pipe
Co., Ltd. 福建亚通新材料科技股份有限公司(1994)	福州市	福建省	(0591)5311542	400	外商投资	576,549	29,553(15)	275,115	塑料管材
Hubei Kaile New Materials Science & Technology Holding	Jingzhou	Hubei	(0716)5209604		Joint Stock				PVCPlaque
Co.,Ltd.湖北凯乐集团新材料科技股份有限公司(1982)	荆州市	湖北省	(0716)5209379	1,595	股份制	510,379	102,307(3)	1,023,859	PVC平管
Changzhou Ju Li Plastics Group Co., Ltd.	Changzhou	Jiangsu	(0519)6974949		Joint Owned				Plastic Board Sheet塑
常州巨力塑料集团有限公司(1993)	常州市	江苏省	(0519)6968554	509	联营企业	429,730	27,880(16)	507,010	料板片材
Shunde Lian Su Science & Technology Industrial Co., Ltd.	Foshan	Guangdong	(0765)3888333		Overseas Chinese-funded				Metal Plastic Tubular Product金属
顺德市联塑科技实业有限公司(1999)	佛山市	广东省	(0765)3888555	1,128	港澳台资	398,060	2,200(185)	125,000	塑料管材

Top 10 Cities by Revenue 销售收入排名前10位城市	Province 省	Market share 市场份额 (%)	Number of firms 企业个数
Shanghai 上海市	Shanghai 上海市	6.60	103
Wuxi 无锡市	Jiangsu 江苏省	5.30	35
Dalian 大连市	Liaoning 辽宁省	4.71	11
Guangzhou 广州市	Guangdong 广东省	4.32	33
Wuhu 芜湖市	Anhui 安徽省	3.99	4
Foshan 佛山市	Guangdong 广东省	3.53	28
Hangzhou 杭州市	Zhejiang 浙江省	3.52	44
Yangzhou 扬州市	Jiangsu 江苏省	3.40	16
Taizhou 台州市	Zhejiang 浙江省	3.00	23

10 Major Wholesalers 十家主要批发商	City 城市	Province 省	Telephone/Fax 电话/传真
Yihua Kangqi Chemical Fibre Co.,Ltd.	Yangzhou	Jiangsu	(0514)3235499
仪化康祺化纤有限责任公司	扬州市	江苏省	(0514)3233847
Sinochem Guangdong Import & Export Company	Guangzhou	Guangdong	(020)86672288
中化广东进出口公司	广州市	广东省	(020)86507512
Sinochem Shanghai Import & Export Company	Shanghai	Shanghai	(021)63289888
中化上海进出口公司	上海市	上海市	(021)63283968
Sinochem Tianjin Import & Export Company	Tianjin	Tianjin	(022)23146216
中化天津进出口公司	天津市	天津市	(022)23146215
China Chemical Sales & Supply (North China) Corporation	Tianjin	Tianjin	(022)23011031
中国化工供销华北公司	天津市	天津市	(022)23011032
China Chemical Sales & Supply (North China) Corporation	Shanghai	Shanghai	(021)62103300
中国化工供销华东公司	上海市	上海市	(021)62515799
Nantong Chemical Light Industry Co.,Ltd.	Nantong	Jiangsu	(0513)5518397
南通化工轻工股份有限公司	南通市	江苏省	(0513)5512735
Taizhou Heshun Plastics Co.,Ltd.	Taizhou	Zhejiang	(0576)2510220
台州市和顺塑料有限公司	台州市	浙江省	(0576)2510160
China Petroleum Technology Development Corporation	Beijing	Beijing	(010)84080722
中国石油技术开发公司	北京市	北京市	(010)84080800
China National Chemical Fiber Corporation	Beijing	Beijing	(010)65816699
中国化纤总公司	北京市	北京市	(010)65813483

3030: Plastic Thread, Rope and Products 塑料丝、绳及编织品制造业

The industry accounts for 0.195% of the total revenue of China's industrial sector in 2002. The rate of return on assets is 2.97%. 82.10% of all firms in the industry made a profit while 17.90% had negative returns.The top province in terms of the industry's revenue is Shandong, accounting for 20.69% of the total revenue.
2002年本行业收入占全行业的 0.195%，资产利润率为 2.97%。82.10%的企业赢利，17.90%的企业亏损。收入最高的省为山东省，占本行业的20.69%。

	Total number of firms 企业总数	Total number of employees 职工总数	Total revenue (Mil.RMB) 总销售收入（百万元）	Total profit (Mil.RMB) 总利润（百万元）	Return on assets 资产利润率（%）	Return on equity 权益利润率（%）	Labour productivity ('000 RMB/ worker) 劳动生产率（千元/人）	Debts/ assets 资产负债率（%）	Total assets (Mil.RMB) 总资产（百万元）
Industry Overall 行业总体	1106	191,788	20,955	569	2.97	7.65	30.43	61.15	19,144

	Number of firms 企业个数	Average number of employees 平均职工人数	Average revenue ('000 RMB) 平均销售收入（千元）	Average profit ('000 RMB) 平均利润（千元）	Return on assets 资产利润率（%）	Return on equity 权益利润率（%）	Labour productivity ('000 RMB/ worker) 劳动生产率（千元/人）	Debts/ assets 资产负债率（%）	Average total assets ('000 RMB) 平均总资产（千元）
By ownership 产业所有权									
State-owned 国有	95	190	7,006	-841	-2.95	-6.51	13.98	54.64	28,488
Collective-owned 集体	240	183	21,831	529	2.85	8.38	28.95	65.99	18,578
Foreign & Overseas Chinese Funded 三资	134	200	28,614	823	2.58	9.96	41.75	74.11	31,904
By regional distribution 地区分布									
Central-North 华北	98	169	19,026	886	5.72	14.53	30.83	60.61	15,488
Beijing 北京	13	125	14,565	-212	-1.29	-3.18	27.29	59.35	16,423
Tianjin 天津	31	137	11,077	415	3.79	12.96	27.38	70.76	10,936
Hebei 河北	40	174	29,967	1,841	9.43	23.33	43.93	59.57	19,515
Shanxi 山西	10	349	12,166	320	2.05	3.99	11.55	48.51	15,554
Inner Mongolia 内蒙古	4	56	2,865	-18	-0.24	-0.43	16.17	44.55	7,293
Northeast 东北	71	206	13,712	170	0.82	2.32	21.06	64.52	20,689
Liaoning 辽宁	45	190	13,425	79	0.42	1.14	21.96	62.84	18,666
Jilin 吉林	13	197	8,392	-65	-0.45	-0.98	14.30	53.48	14,387
Heilongjiang 黑龙江	13	267	20,028	723	2.13	7.69	23.82	72.37	33,996
Central-East 华东	504	180	22,601	719	3.84	11.26	32.03	65.90	18,707
Shanghai 上海	26	126	20,946	1,346	7.04	13.05	54.34	46.04	19,115
Jiangsu 江苏	90	152	23,717	894	4.64	10.69	42.26	56.61	19,268
Zhejiang 浙江	165	171	19,121	510	4.13	8.18	26.58	49.47	12,357
Anhui 安徽	59	158	12,101	246	1.80	4.58	24.69	60.75	13,706
Fujian 福建	24	146	14,605	908	5.47	10.08	38.42	45.77	16,600
Jiangxi 江西	14	213	11,261	91	0.71	1.20	16.16	41.27	12,815
Shandong 山东	126	237	34,402	992	3.31	23.78	33.13	86.07	29,936
Central-South 中南	308	145	17,624	515	4.00	9.78	37.61	59.05	12,871
Henan 河南	119	134	10,540	625	7.86	14.74	29.03	46.66	7,946
Hubei 湖北	55	163	19,986	610	5.77	12.02	39.34	51.97	10,563
Hunan 湖南	20	159	11,910	-36	-0.25	-1.47	23.88	83.15	14,347
Guangdong 广东	78	151	30,596	384	1.91	5.28	51.68	63.90	20,143
Guangxi 广西	32	138	12,675	678	4.89	12.14	39.03	59.72	13,857
Hainan 海南	4	124	11,098	-21	-0.06	-0.18	24.65	66.39	34,056
Southwest 西南	72	164	10,191	122	1.00	2.14	17.47	53.10	12,121
Chongqing 重庆	5	138	8,572	135	2.94	10.17	-3.45	71.13	4,610
Sichuan 四川	28	218	11,605	201	1.73	3.25	20.63	46.86	11,630
Guizhou 贵州	12	162	11,693	71	0.33	0.55	14.74	39.02	21,258
Yunnan 云南	26	115	8,632	71	0.69	2.54	17.73	72.72	10,188
Tibet 西藏	1	45	1,250	-225	-5.56	-12.82	9.58	56.61	4,045
Northwest 西北	53	253	10,650	-1,133	-3.17	-5.61	16.66	43.43	35,700
Shaanxi 陕西	13	147	6,512	280	3.00	11.96	15.35	74.94	9,345
Gansu 甘肃	28	108	7,846	116	1.24	2.85	28.68	56.56	9,406
Qinghai 青海	2	104	3,739	-257	-3.08	-39.22	9.49	92.15	8,336
Ningxia 宁夏	4	373	17,610	953	4.71	15.11	18.55	68.83	20,243
Xinjiang 新疆	6	1,126	30,367	-11,707	-4.98	-7.81	11.45	36.23	234,933

3030: Plastic Thread, Rope and Products 塑料丝、绳及编织品制造业

Year 年份	Number of firms 企业个数	Rate of change 变化率 (%)	Number of employees 职工人数 (人)	Rate of change 变化率 (%)	Total revenue (Mil. RMB) 总销售收入 (百万元)	Rate of change 变化率 (%)	Total profit (Mil RMB) 总利润 (百万元)	Rate of change 变化率 (%)
2000	1031		182,412		17,079		479	
2001	1045	1.36	183,545	0.62	18,925	10.81	367	-23.38
2002	1106	5.84	191,788	4.49	20,955	10.73	569	55.04

Major Products 主要产品	Output 产量	Unit 单位
Plastic Silk & Knitting Products 塑料丝及编织制品	161	10,000 Tons 万吨

10 Main Firms with Maximal Revenue (year founded) 收入最大的十家主要企业（创办年份）	City 城市	Province 省	Telephone/fax 电话/传真	Number of employees 职工人数	Ownership 产业所有权	Revenue ('000 RMB) 销售收入 (千元)	Profit('000 RMB) (rank) 利润(千元) (排名)	Total assets ('000 RMB) 总资产 (千元)	Major products 主要产品
Kaiping Changsha Overseas Chinese Nylon Technology Factory 开平市长沙华侨尼龙工艺厂(1990)	Jiangmen 江门市	Guangdong 广东省	(0750)2218789	272	Collective-owned 集体企业	283,751	-	71,404	Nylon Rubber Strip尼龙橡胶织带
Zhenhai Smelting Industry Trade General Company 镇海炼化工业贸易总公司(1979)	Ningbo 宁波市	Zhejiang 浙江省	(0574)86444951	707	Collective-owned 集体企业	240,453	4,544(31)	147,310	Plastics Knitting 塑料编织
QingDao Chengjin Plastics CO., Ltd. 青岛成进塑料有限公司(1997)	Qingdao 青岛市	Shandong 山东省	(0532)8435242 (0532)8435344	420	Foreign Funded 外商投资	226,980	9,863(12)	32,600	Plastics Tarpaulin 塑料蓬布
Langfang Xinxing Package Products Co., Ltd. 廊坊新兴包装制品有限公司(1984)	Langfang 廊坊市	Hebei 河北省	(0316)5070098	300	Private Owned 私营企业	210,000	1,692(109)	9,709	Packer Strip 打包带
Wenzhou Chen'guang Group Co., Ltd. 温州晨光集团有限公司(1998)	Wenzhou 温州市	Zhejiang 浙江省	(0577)63568886 (0577)63569398	1,650	Limited-Liability 有限公司	171,521	10,290(10)	92,068	Woven Bag 编织袋
Zhengding Changshan Plastic Products Co., Ltd. 正定县常山塑料制品厂(1979)	Shijiazhuang 石家庄市	Hebei 河北省	(0311)8711572 (0311)8711572	270	Private Partnership 私营合伙	161,020	8,800(13)	29,420	Plastic Bags 塑料袋
Zhejiang Huaqing Group Co., Ltd. 浙江华庆集团有限公司(1998)	Wenzhou 温州市	Zhejiang 浙江省	(0577)63563885 (0577)63563883	1,980	Private Owned 私营企业	160,125	12,108(6)	104,944	Plastics Woven Bag塑料编织袋
Dongguan Cai Yang Plastic Products Co., Ltd. 东莞彩扬塑胶制品有限公司(1995)	Dongguan 东莞市	Guangdong 广东省	(0769)3354117 (0769)3355440	141	Foreign Funded 外商投资	135,435	4,420(32)	96,037	PVCRubberized Fabric PVC胶布
PetroChina Urumqi Petrochemical General Factory 中国石油乌鲁木齐石油化工总厂(1975)	Urumqi 乌鲁木齐市	Xinjiang 新疆	(0991)6902601 (0991)6906666	5,921	State-owned 国有企业	124,757	-	1,347,621	Plastics Woven Bag塑料编织袋
Shanghai Lian Bin Plastic Cement Industry Co., Ltd. 上海联宾塑胶工业有限公司(1992)	Shanghai 上海市	Shanghai 上海市	(021)64061772 (021)64496588	637	Overseas Chinese-funded 港澳台资	123,419	13,379(5)	145,916	Plastics Woven Bag塑料编织袋

Top 10 Cities by Revenue 销售收入排名前10位城市	Province 省	Market share 市场份额 (%)	Number of firms 企业个数
Wenzhou 温州市	Zhejiang 浙江省	11.61	125
Zibo 淄博市	Shandong 山东省	7.84	13
Wuxi 无锡市	Jiangsu 江苏省	2.75	9
Jiangmen 江门市	Guangdong 广东省	2.62	11
Shanghai 上海市	Shanghai 上海市	2.60	26
Yantai 烟台市	Shandong 山东省	2.26	18
Shijiazhuang 石家庄市	Hebei 河北省	2.17	14
Qingdao 青岛市	Shandong 山东省	2.13	16
Zaozhuang 枣庄市	Shandong 山东省	2.03	10
Weihai 威海市	Shandong 山东省	2.01	10

10 Major Wholesalers 十家主要批发商	City 城市	Province 省	Telephone/Fax 电话/传真
Yihua Kangqi Chemical Fibre Co.,Ltd. 仪化康祺化纤有限责任公司	Yangzhou 扬州市	Jiangsu 江苏省	(0514)3235499 (0514)3233847
Sinochem Guangdong Import & Export Company 中化广东进出口公司	Guangzhou 广州市	Guangdong 广东省	(020)86672288 (020)86507512
Sinochem Shanghai Import & Export Company 中化上海进出口公司	Shanghai 上海市	Shanghai 上海市	(021)63289888 (021)63283968
Sinochem Tianjin Import & Export Company 中化天津进出口公司	Tianjin 天津市	Tianjin 天津市	(022)23146216 (022)23146215
China Chemical Sales & Supply (North China) Corporation 中国化工供销华北公司	Tianjin 天津市	Tianjin 天津市	(022)23011031 (022)23011032
China Chemical Sales & Supply (North China) Corporation 中国化工供销华东公司	Shanghai 上海市	Shanghai 上海市	(021)62103300 (021)62515799
Nantong Chemical Light Industry Co.,Ltd. 南通化工轻工股份有限公司	Nantong 南通市	Jiangsu 江苏省	(0513)5518397 (0513)5512735
Taizhou Heshun Plastics Co.,Ltd. 台州市和顺塑料有限公司	Taizhou 台州市	Zhejiang 浙江省	(0576)2510220 (0576)2510160
China Petroleum Technology Development Corporation 中国石油技术开发公司	Beijing 北京市	Beijing 北京市	(010)84080722 (010)84080800
China National Chemical Fiber Corporation 中国化纤总公司	Beijing 北京市	Beijing 北京市	(010)65816699 (010)65813483

3040: Aerated Plastics, Imitation Leather, and Synthetic Leather

泡沫塑料及人造革、合成革制造业

The industry accounts for 0.268% of the total revenue of China's industrial sector in 2002. The rate of return on assets is 4.54%. 82.98% of all firms in the industry made a profit while 17.02% had negative returns.The top province in terms of the industry's revenue is Zhejiang, accounting for 24.52% of the total revenue.
2002年本行业收入占全行业的0.268%，资产利润率为4.54%。82.98%的企业赢利，17.02%的企业亏损。收入最高的省为浙江省，占本行业的24.52%。

	Total number of firms 企业总数	Total number of employees 职工总数	Total revenue (Mil.RMB) 总销售收入（百万元）	Total profit (Mil.RMB) 总利润（百万元）	Return on assets 资产利润率（%）	Return on equity 权益利润率（%）	Labour productivity ('000 RMB/ worker) 劳动生产率（千元/人）	Debts/ assets 资产负债率（%）	Total assets (Mil.RMB) 总资产（百万元）
Industry Overall 行业总体	840	107,129	28,751	1,243	4.54	10.84	66.15	58.13	27,398

	Number of firms 企业个数	Average number of employees 平均职工人数	Average revenue ('000 RMB) 平均销售收入（千元）	Average profit ('000 RMB) 平均利润（千元）	Return on assets 资产利润率（%）	Return on equity 权益利润率（%）	Labour productivity ('000 RMB/ worker) 劳动生产率（千元/人）	Debts/ assets 资产负债率（%）	Average total assets ('000 RMB) 平均总资产（千元）
By ownership 产业所有权									
State-owned 国有	36	166	13,464	387	1.04	3.15	27.21	66.90	37,205
Collective-owned 集体	117	107	18,029	787	3.74	12.85	45.59	70.85	21,015
Foreign & Overseas Chinese Funded 三资	241	144	45,505	1,940	3.69	8.08	79.00	54.36	52,615
By regional distribution 地区分布									
Central-North 华北	77	135	21,017	895	3.07	8.35	35.75	63.20	29,147
Beijing 北京	28	150	23,143	635	1.63	5.37	21.38	69.61	38,915
Tianjin 天津	13	126	20,545	1,120	6.75	17.64	55.73	61.71	16,575
Hebei 河北	33	65	15,817	878	5.54	12.80	59.57	56.75	15,852
Shanxi 山西	2	156	14,342	423	1.00	6.61	3.78	84.91	42,390
Inner Mongolia 内蒙古	1	2,106	152,528	6,801	2.05	3.93	29.48	47.74	331,367
Northeast 东北	35	141	28,864	1,734	4.96	12.07	55.56	58.90	34,974
Liaoning 辽宁	18	100	34,172	2,741	7.51	16.74	87.26	55.15	36,497
Jilin 吉林	10	134	19,554	-174	-0.66	-2.44	36.05	73.12	26,575
Heilongjiang 黑龙江	7	254	28,517	1,873	4.35	9.57	38.13	54.55	43,057
Central-East 华东	511	126	36,771	1,605	5.22	12.53	69.11	58.39	30,781
Shanghai 上海	73	97	21,421	498	1.82	3.63	44.46	49.79	27,268
Jiangsu 江苏	139	138	47,380	1,968	5.56	15.01	82.60	62.97	35,396
Zhejiang 浙江	173	138	40,746	1,927	5.79	13.73	65.74	57.80	33,262
Anhui 安徽	20	103	24,429	1,364	5.20	16.12	64.16	67.74	26,228
Fujian 福建	49	125	31,729	1,307	5.11	9.25	56.94	44.80	25,594
Jiangxi 江西	3	104	8,274	494	0.92	6.49	55.68	85.83	53,730
Shandong 山东	54	106	28,211	1,563	7.50	20.55	83.70	63.48	20,822
Central-South 中南	195	129	35,864	1,486	3.74	8.58	74.60	56.43	39,734
Henan 河南	14	119	26,910	1,659	3.74	7.16	48.93	47.80	44,377
Hubei 湖北	15	204	26,421	411	1.05	2.89	39.67	63.50	39,026
Hunan 湖南	11	116	13,370	853	5.66	16.03	33.16	64.71	15,067
Guangdong 广东	151	124	39,839	1,672	4.01	9.15	86.51	56.18	41,707
Guangxi 广西	3	133	16,907	-531	-2.25	-8.34	24.63	73.08	23,646
Hainan 海南	1	20	6,977	119	1.68	10.74	14.20	84.34	7,075
Southwest 西南	14	120	21,128	129	0.46	0.91	59.26	49.85	28,256
Chongqing 重庆	7	98	14,133	94	0.98	2.18	36.85	55.03	9,561
Sichuan 四川	2	68	17,149	-651	-3.11	-6.47	147.84	51.95	20,937
Guizhou 贵州	3	183	31,418	317	0.52	0.75	67.51	30.12	60,782
Yunnan 云南	2	159	34,154	753	1.44	7.26	55.37	80.14	52,220
Tibet 西藏									
Northwest 西北	8	72	5,443	217	3.07	7.17	25.74	57.21	7,081
Shaanxi 陕西									
Gansu 甘肃	4	77	4,100	92	2.84	3.56	29.10	20.31	3,239
Qinghai 青海									
Ningxia 宁夏	1	60	6,710	96	0.74	4.48	43.30	83.51	12,999
Xinjiang 新疆	3	70	6,811	425	4.15	10.82	15.75	61.65	10,231

3040: Aerated Plastics, Imitation Leather, and Synthetic Leather

泡沫塑料及人造革、合成革制造业

Year 年份	Number of firms 企业个数	Rate of change 变化率 (%)	Number of employees 职工人数 (人)	Rate of change 变化率 (%)	Total revenue (Mil. RMB) 总销售收入 (百万元)	Rate of change 变化率 (%)	Total profit (Mil RMB) 总利润 (百万元)	Rate of change 变化率 (%)
2000	706		100,963		21,839		432	
2001	765	8.36	106,691	5.67	23,907	9.47	787	82.18
2002	840	9.80	107,129	0.41	28,751	20.26	1,243	57.94

Major Products 主要产品	Output 产量	Unit 单位
Plastic Synthetic Leather 塑料合成革	280,434	Ton 吨
Foam 泡沫塑料	67	10,000 Tons 万吨

10 Main Firms with Maximal Revenue (year founded) 收入最大的十家主要企业（创办年份）	City 城市	Province 省	Telephone/fax 电话/传真	Number of employees 职工人数	Ownership 产业所有权	Revenue ('000 RMB) 销售收入(千元)	Profit('000 RMB) (rank) 利润(千元)(排名)	Total assets ('000 RMB) 总资产(千元)	Major products 主要产品
Zhejiang Wuming Leather & Plastics Group Co., Ltd. 浙江无名皮塑集团有限责任公司(1995)	Shaoxing 绍兴市	Zhejiang 浙江省	(0575)4021346 (0575)4021978	935	Joint Stock 股份制	632,288	50,119(3)	467,798	Artificial Leather 人造革
Guangzhou Hongming Plastic Cement Industry Co., Ltd. 广州宏铭塑胶工业有限公司(1995)	Guangzhou 广州市	Guangdong 广东省	(020)82266687 (020)82266657	340	Overseas Chinese-funded 港澳台资	558,371	195,143(1)	943,510	Polyacrylonitrile 聚丙烯腈
Yi De Plastic Cement (Fujian) Co., Ltd. 镒得塑胶(福建)有限公司(1990)	Fuzhou 福州市	Fujian 福建省	(0591)3651495 (0591)3651494	1,684	Foreign Funded 外商投资	452,797	18,659(9)	146,528	Plastic Products 塑料制品
Nanya Plastics (Nantong) Co., ltd. 南亚塑胶工业（南通）有限公司(1998)	Nantong 南通市	Jiangsu 江苏省	(0513)5291811 (0513)5291646	647	Overseas Chinese-funded 港澳台资	375,878	45,303(4)	583,377	PVCRubberized Fabric PVC胶布
Tai Da Chemical Industry (Zhongshan)CO., Ltd. 台达化工(中山)有限公司(1999)	Zhongshan 中山市	Guangdong 广东省	(0760)5316689 (0760)3382484	92	Overseas Chinese-funded 港澳台资	361,610	18,307(10)	160,161	Polystyrene 聚苯乙烯
Huaxia Plastics (Zhongshan) Co., Ltd. 华夏塑料(中山)有限公司(1997)	Zhongshan 中山市	Guangdong 广东省	(0760)5316689 (0760)5318569	694	Overseas Chinese-funded 港澳台资	307,442	17,623(12)	357,198	PVCRubberized Fabric PVC胶布
Anhui An Li Artificial Leather Co., Ltd. 安徽安利合成革有限公司(1995)	Hefei 合肥市	Anhui 安徽省	(0551)8991557 (0551)8991640	360	Overseas Chinese-funded 港澳台资	293,253	15,216(14)	205,661	Plastic Synthetic Leather 塑料合成革
Guangzhou Hongqing Plastic Industry Co., Ltd 广州宏庆塑胶工业有限公司(1996)	Guangzhou 广州市	Guangdong 广东省	(020)82266188 (020)82266478	428	Foreign Funded 外商投资	285,605	-	314,376	pu Synthetic Leather pu合成皮
Wuxi Civil Administration Chemical Industry Factory 无锡市民政化工厂(1997)	Wuxi 无锡市	Jiangsu 江苏省	(0510)8705491 (0510)8700124	70	Joint Stock 股份制	270,600	15,450(13)	51,350	Anti-burning EPS Grain 阻燃型EPS珠粒
Zibo Bao Feng Leather & Plastic Chemical Industry Co.,Ltd. 淄博宝沣皮塑化工有限公司(1992)	Zibo 淄博市	Shandong 山东省	(0533)2081437 (0533)2081584	114	Foreign Funded 外商投资	249,680	9,680(26)	44,572	pu Synthetic Leather PU革

Top 10 Cities by Revenue 销售收入排名前10位城市	Province 省	Market share 市场份额 (%)	Number of firms 企业个数
Wenzhou 温州市	Zhejiang 浙江省	13.64	94
Wuxi 无锡市	Jiangsu 江苏省	9.60	19
Guangzhou 广州市	Guangdong 广东省	6.85	28
Shanghai 上海市	Shanghai 上海市	5.44	73
Foshan 佛山市	Guangdong 广东省	4.19	35
Suzhou 苏州市	Jiangsu 江苏省	4.09	37
Nantong 南通市	Jiangsu 江苏省	3.58	17
Zhongshan 中山市	Guangdong 广东省	3.43	20
Shaoxing 绍兴市	Zhejiang 浙江省	3.14	12
Fuzhou 福州市	Fujian 福建省	2.44	10

10 Major Wholesalers 十家主要批发商	City 城市	Province 省	Telephone/Fax 电话/传真
Yihua Kangqi Chemical Fibre Co.,Ltd. 仪化康祺化纤有限责任公司	Yangzhou 扬州市	Jiangsu 江苏省	(0514)3235499 (0514)3233847
Sinochem Guangdong Import & Export Company 中化广东进出口公司	Guangzhou 广州市	Guangdong 广东省	(020)86672288 (020)86507512
Sinochem Shanghai Import & Export Company 中化上海进出口公司	Shanghai 上海市	Shanghai 上海市	(021)63289888 (021)63283968
Sinochem Tianjin Import & Export Company 中化天津进出口公司	Tianjin 天津市	Tianjin 天津市	(022)23146216 (022)23146215
China Chemical Sales & Supply (North China) Corporation 中国化工供销华北公司	Tianjin 天津市	Tianjin 天津市	(022)23011031 (022)23011032
China Chemical Sales & Supply (North China) Corporation 中国化工供销华东公司	Shanghai 上海市	Shanghai 上海市	(021)62103300 (021)62515799
Nantong Chemical Light Industry Co.,Ltd. 南通化工轻工股份有限公司	Nantong 南通市	Jiangsu 江苏省	(0513)5518397 (0513)5512735
Taizhou Heshun Plastics Co.,Ltd. 台州市和顺塑料有限公司	Taizhou 台州市	Zhejiang 浙江省	(0576)2510220 (0576)2510160
China Petroleum Technology Development Corporation 中国石油技术开发公司	Beijing 北京市	Beijing 北京市	(010)84080722 (010)84080800
China National Chemical Fiber Corporation 中国化纤总公司	Beijing 北京市	Beijing 北京市	(010)65816699 (010)65813483

3050: Plastic Containers 塑料包装箱及容器制造业

The industry accounts for 0.142% of the total revenue of China's industrial sector in 2002. The rate of return on assets is 4.37%. 81.83% of all firms in the industry made a profit while 18.17% had negative returns.The top province in terms of the industry's revenue is Guangdong, accounting for 22.69% of the total revenue.
2002年本行业收入占全行业的0.142%，资产利润率为4.37%。81.83%的企业赢利，18.17%的企业亏损。收入最高的省为广东省，占本行业的22.69%。

	Total number of firms 企业总数	Total number of employees 职工总数	Total revenue (Mil.RMB) 总销售收入（百万元）	Total profit (Mil.RMB) 总利润（百万元）	Return on assets 资产利润率（%）	Return on equity 权益利润率（%）	Labour productivity ('000 RMB/ worker) 劳动生产率（千元/人）	Debts/ assets 资产负债率（%）	Total assets (Mil.RMB) 总资产（百万元）
Industry Overall 行业总体	622	79,075	15,213	1,046	4.37	8.44	63.18	48.24	23,940

	Number of firms 企业个数	Average number of employees 平均职工人数	Average revenue ('000 RMB) 平均销售收入（千元）	Average profit ('000 RMB) 平均利润（千元）	Return on assets 资产利润率（%）	Return on equity 权益利润率（%）	Labour productivity ('000 RMB/ worker) 劳动生产率（千元/人）	Debts/ assets 资产负债率（%）	Average total assets ('000 RMB) 平均总资产（千元）
By ownership 产业所有权									
State-owned 国有	36	115	5,813	145	0.45	1.05	9.32	56.88	31,932
Collective-owned 集体	83	121	15,349	609	3.77	10.95	42.71	65.59	16,161
Foreign & Overseas Chinese Funded 三资	203	151	40,126	3,538	5.03	8.97	100.27	43.90	70,309
By regional distribution 地区分布									
Central-North 华北	69	149	21,915	1,208	2.70	5.11	52.01	47.19	44,749
Beijing 北京	26	81	18,656	-986	-2.36	-3.34	76.07	29.26	41,742
Tianjin 天津	25	133	22,202	2,696	5.95	13.52	61.36	56.03	45,349
Hebei 河北	15	286	27,772	2,371	4.49	10.25	34.10	56.24	52,858
Shanxi 山西	1	305	6,911	-789	-3.82	-324.69	0.29	98.82	20,673
Inner Mongolia 内蒙古	2	146	24,266	3,398	12.32	39.33	89.54	68.68	27,578
Northeast 东北	30	171	24,364	2,346	5.61	12.18	101.94	53.94	41,812
Liaoning 辽宁	22	199	17,752	1,167	3.14	8.13	97.25	61.38	37,158
Jilin 吉林	5	58	45,073	5,912	12.05	17.30	218.87	30.33	49,057
Heilongjiang 黑龙江	3	158	38,335	5,055	7.91	16.63	73.47	52.41	63,866
Central-East 华东	316	120	25,069	2,091	6.20	11.59	61.55	46.47	33,697
Shanghai 上海	91	138	35,068	3,438	5.42	9.69	74.92	44.08	63,441
Jiangsu 江苏	71	117	23,986	574	2.39	4.84	55.64	50.55	23,980
Zhejiang 浙江	92	101	20,053	2,948	14.12	26.10	62.31	45.92	20,879
Anhui 安徽	14	139	12,413	-293	-1.47	-3.27	20.69	54.92	19,888
Fujian 福建	18	79	13,456	856	4.80	9.37	55.91	48.81	17,852
Jiangxi 江西	4	63	5,560	163	4.96	6.78	27.78	26.86	3,276
Shandong 山东	26	153	28,634	915	3.73	8.17	53.90	54.38	24,570
Central-South 中南	171	126	25,951	1,220	2.59	5.05	62.83	48.63	47,063
Henan 河南	16	98	12,584	587	4.35	11.71	32.00	62.87	13,505
Hubei 湖北	24	120	22,120	1,553	6.19	13.08	68.43	52.63	25,074
Hunan 湖南	15	120	11,233	-145	-1.05	-3.01	24.51	65.19	13,822
Guangdong 广东	110	133	31,376	1,444	2.30	4.39	70.09	47.53	62,697
Guangxi 广西	4	88	9,947	469	5.07	7.26	53.93	30.07	9,238
Hainan 海南	2	100	22,896	1,715	3.85	6.53	52.48	40.94	44,487
Southwest 西南	27	141	19,169	682	2.37	6.25	61.79	62.02	28,758
Chongqing 重庆	6	148	16,706	234	0.69	1.95	33.66	64.62	33,937
Sichuan 四川	13	155	24,394	1,310	4.95	13.77	89.69	64.09	26,481
Guizhou 贵州	3	126	18,801	185	0.59	1.26	29.94	53.42	31,360
Yunnan 云南	4	99	10,548	-161	-0.56	-1.58	21.00	64.84	28,859
Tibet 西藏	1	138	1,619	86	0.45	0.58	39.13	22.21	19,092
Northwest 西北	9	61	10,296	459	3.30	7.66	46.04	56.97	13,920
Shaanxi 陕西	4	74	13,638	307	1.59	3.34	35.44	52.49	19,365
Gansu 甘肃	4	23	7,124	645	8.94	19.86	144.33	54.97	7,213
Qinghai 青海	1	164	9,620	320	1.69	7.77	9.90	78.29	18,970
Ningxia 宁夏									
Xinjiang 新疆									

3050: Plastic Containers 塑料包装箱及容器制造业

Year 年份	Number of firms 企业个数	Rate of change 变化率 (%)	Number of employees 职工人数 (人)	Rate of change 变化率 (%)	Total revenue (Mil. RMB) 总销售收入 (百万元)	Rate of change 变化率 (%)	Total profit (Mil RMB) 总利润 (百万元)	Rate of change 变化率 (%)
2000	471		60,152		11,449		758	
2001	548	16.35	64,892	7.88	12,877	12.47	855	12.80
2002	622	13.50	79,075	21.86	15,213	18.14	1,046	22.34

Major Products 主要产品	Output 产量	Unit 单位
Plastic Packing Box & Container 塑料包装箱及容器	63	10,000 Tons 万吨

10 Main Firms with Maximal Revenue (year founded) 收入最大的十家主要企业（创办年份）	City 城市	Province 省	Telephone/fax 电话/传真	Number of employees 职工人数	Ownership 产业所有权	Revenue ('000 RMB) 销售收入 (千元)	Profit('000 RMB) (rank) 利润(千元) (排名)	Total assets ('000 RMB) 总资产 (千元)	Major products 主要产品
Shanghai Zi Jiang Enterprise Group Stock Co., Ltd.	Shanghai	Shanghai	(021)54421100		Overseas Chinese-funded				Plastic Packing Box塑
上海紫江企业集团股份有限公司(1989)	上海市	上海市	(021)54422900	963	港澳台资	712,031	153,233(1)	2,740,852	料包装箱
Lei Sheng De Kui Enterprise (Shanghai) Co., Ltd.	Shanghai	Shanghai	(021)57578066		Overseas Chinese-funded				Plastic Products
雷盛德奎企业(上海)有限公司(1993)	上海市	上海市	(021)57576617	1,452	港澳台资	305,518	23,763(8)	424,441	塑料制品
ZhuHai Zhong Fu Enterprise Co., Ltd.	Zhuhai	Guangdong	(0756)8821449		Joint Stock				PETPlastic Products.PET
珠海中富实业股份有限公司(1992)	珠海市	广东省	(0756)8821103	620	股份制	299,246	836(185)	2,197,012	塑料制品
Nanhai Nan Fang Packing Co., Ltd.	Foshan	Guangdong	(0757)6788388		Overseas Chinese-funded				Plastic Pakage Bottle塑
南海市南方包装有限公司(1991)	佛山市	广东省	(0757)6772333	625	港澳台资	235,953	24,835(7)	369,810	料包装瓶
Sanshui Jian Li Bao Plastic Products Co., Ltd.	Foshan	Guangdong	(0757)7737668		Overseas Chinese-funded				PET Drink Bottle.PET
三水市健力宝塑料制品有限公司(1994)	佛山市	广东省	(0757)7728212	459	港澳台资	206,652	22,460(9)	288,983	饮料瓶
Shanghai Ming Xin Plastic Co., Ltd.	Shanghai	Shanghai	(021)64780209		Overseas Chinese-funded				Plastics Compose Tools Cases塑料组
上海明欣塑胶有限公司(1994)	上海市	上海市	(021)64193370	210	港澳台资	197,672	1,468(132)	118,171	合工具箱
Wendeng Jin Guang Plastic Products Co., Ltd.	Weihai	Shandong	(0631)8545144		Foreign Funded				Plastic Products
文登金光塑料制品有限公司(1997)	威海市	山东省	(0631)8546640	110	外商投资	185,000	4,658(56)	4,670	塑料制品
Hebei Hui Er Xin New Materials Co., Ltd.	Xingtai	Hebei	(0319)5850299		Joint Stock				Calcium and Plastics Corrugated Box钙
河北省邢台市宁晋县惠尔信新材料有限公司(1990)	邢台市	河北省	(0319)5850081	387	股份制	162,179	6,837(39)	118,136	塑瓦楞箱
WuHan Zi Jiang Packing Co., Ltd	Wuhan	Hubei	(027)84892322		Overseas Chinese-funded				Plastic Container Products塑料
武汉紫江包装有限公司(1995)	武汉市	湖北省	(027)84891809	220	港澳台资	144,926	32,929(5)	184,595	容器制品
Tianjin Shifa -Zijiang Packing Co., Ltd.	Tianjin	Tianjin	(022)25292751		Overseas Chinese-funded				Plastic Bottle
天津实发-紫江包装有限公司(1996)	天津市	天津市	(022)25327248	242	港澳台资	137,950	21,680(10)	222,756	塑料瓶

Top 10 Cities by Revenue 销售收入排名前10位城市	Province 省	Market share 市场份额 (%)	Number of firms 企业个数
Shanghai 上海市	Shanghai 上海市	20.98	91
Guangzhou 广州市	Guangdong 广东省	6.09	24
Suzhou 苏州市	Jiangsu 江苏省	5.28	21
Foshan 佛山市	Guangdong 广东省	5.06	17
Hangzhou 杭州市	Zhejiang 浙江省	4.71	23
Zhuhai 珠海市	Guangdong 广东省	4.65	12
Tianjin 天津市	Tianjin 天津市	3.65	25
Beijing 北京市	Beijing 北京市	3.19	26
Wuxi 无锡市	Jiangsu 江苏省	2.11	14
Ningbo 宁波市	Zhejiang 浙江省	2.08	19

10 Major Wholesalers 十家主要批发商	City 城市	Province 省	Telephone/Fax 电话/传真
Yihua Kangqi Chemical Fibre Co.,Ltd.	Yangzhou	Jiangsu	(0514)3235499
仪化康祺化纤有限责任公司	扬州市	江苏省	(0514)3233847
Sinochem Guangdong Import & Export Company	Guangzhou	Guangdong	(020)86672288
中化广东进出口公司	广州市	广东省	(020)86507512
Sinochem Shanghai Import & Export Company	Shanghai	Shanghai	(021)63289888
中化上海进出口公司	上海市	上海市	(021)63283968
Sinochem Tianjin Import & Export Company	Tianjin	Tianjin	(022)23146216
中化天津进出口公司	天津市	天津市	(022)23146215
China Chemical Sales & Supply (North China) Corporation	Tianjin	Tianjin	(022)23011031
中国化工供销华北公司	天津市	天津市	(022)23011032
China Chemical Sales & Supply (North China) Corporation	Shanghai	Shanghai	(021)62103300
中国化工供销华东公司	上海市	上海市	(021)62515799
Nantong Chemical Light Industry Co.,Ltd.	Nantong	Jiangsu	(0513)5518397
南通化工轻工股份有限公司	南通市	江苏省	(0513)5512735
Taizhou Heshun Plastics Co.,Ltd.	Taizhou	Zhejiang	(0576)2510220
台州市和顺塑料有限公司	台州市	浙江省	(0576)2510160
China Petroleum Technology Development Corporation	Beijing	Beijing	(010)84080722
中国石油技术开发公司	北京市	北京市	(010)84080800
China National Chemical Fiber Corporation	Beijing	Beijing	(010)65816699
中国化纤总公司	北京市	北京市	(010)65813483

3060: Plastic Shoes 塑料鞋制造业

The industry accounts for 0.082% of the total revenue of China's industrial sector in 2002. The rate of return on assets is 4.14%. 84.17% of all firms in the industry made a profit while 15.83% had negative returns.The top province in terms of the industry's revenue is Fujian, accounting for 39.62% of the total revenue.
2002年本行业收入占全行业的0.082%，资产利润率为4.14%。84.17%的企业赢利，15.83%的企业亏损。收入最高的省为福建省，占本行业的39.62%。

	Total number of firms 企业总数	Total number of employees 职工总数	Total revenue (Mil.RMB) 总销售收入（百万元）	Total profit (Mil.RMB) 总利润（百万元）	Return on assets 资产利润率 (%)	Return on equity 权益利润率 (%)	Labour productivity ('000 RMB/ worker) 劳动生产率（千元/人）	Debts/ assets 资产负债率 (%)	Total assets (Mil.RMB) 总资产（百万元）
Industry Overall 行业总体	417	83,986	8,750	260	4.14	8.29	29.72	50.01	6,272

	Number of firms 企业个数	Average number of employees 平均职工人数	Average revenue ('000 RMB) 平均销售收入（千元）	Average profit ('000 RMB) 平均利润（千元）	Return on assets 资产利润率 (%)	Return on equity 权益利润率 (%)	Labour productivity ('000 RMB/ worker) 劳动生产率（千元/人）	Debts/ assets 资产负债率 (%)	Average total assets ('000 RMB) 平均总资产（千元）
By ownership 产业所有权									
State-owned 国有	6	213	8,067	-435	-2.91	-5.75	20.94	49.34	14,947
Collective-owned 集体	55	133	17,117	373	5.19	13.55	48.79	61.67	7,191
Foreign & Overseas Chinese Funded 三资	144	308	30,436	740	2.68	4.99	27.41	46.26	27,596
By regional distribution 地区分布									
Central-North 华北	3	252	18,791	2	0.01	0.02	7.13	32.63	19,303
Beijing 北京									
Tianjin 天津	2	334	15,721	-1,022	-3.86	-5.52	-1.81	30.05	26,470
Hebei 河北	1	90	24,930	2,050	41.25	103.54	73.44	60.16	4,970
Shanxi 山西									
Inner Mongolia 内蒙古									
Northeast 东北	1	188	8,943	1,379	11.56	19.26	10.10	39.95	11,925
Liaoning 辽宁									
Jilin 吉林									
Heilongjiang 黑龙江	1	188	8,943	1,379	11.56	19.26	10.10	39.95	11,925
Central-East 华东	268	188	21,116	780	6.27	11.90	33.57	47.27	12,428
Shanghai 上海	7	121	21,817	1,998	16.90	51.08	45.47	66.91	11,821
Jiangsu 江苏	16	106	14,504	-47	-0.38	-2.13	45.52	81.94	12,250
Zhejiang 浙江	92	147	13,948	752	11.23	23.40	24.04	52.01	6,693
Anhui 安徽	6	175	6,956	-118	-2.28	-14.48	11.41	84.23	5,182
Fujian 福建	136	216	25,489	770	5.01	8.52	37.36	41.17	15,362
Jiangxi 江西	1	650	87,406	795	1.34	2.64	30.92	49.17	59,242
Shandong 山东	10	319	39,553	2,178	8.49	16.27	37.44	47.84	25,664
Central-South 中南	142	225	21,022	351	1.77	3.82	24.84	53.61	19,814
Henan 河南	13	63	8,659	574	16.89	22.11	34.86	23.59	3,401
Hubei 湖北	7	327	31,094	2,284	9.13	27.49	36.14	66.78	25,016
Hunan 湖南	3	146	6,451	41	0.82	1.28	19.08	36.37	5,016
Guangdong 广东	114	244	22,861	252	1.13	2.43	23.80	53.36	22,228
Guangxi 广西	5	101	5,873	-491	-5.42	-11.16	19.49	51.40	9,057
Hainan 海南									
Southwest 西南	3	273	13,414	-85	-0.44	-0.92	8.98	52.37	19,424
Chongqing 重庆	2	364	12,429	-196	-0.96	-1.68	4.10	42.86	20,396
Sichuan 四川									
Guizhou 贵州									
Yunnan 云南	1	92	15,385	137	0.78	3.08	47.63	74.57	17,482
Tibet 西藏									
Northwest 西北									
Shaanxi 陕西									
Gansu 甘肃									
Qinghai 青海									
Ningxia 宁夏									
Xinjiang 新疆									

Year 年份	Number of firms 企业个数	Rate of change 变化率 (%)	Number of employees 职工人数 (人)	Rate of change 变化率 (%)	Total revenue (Mil. RMB) 总销售收入 (百万元)	Rate of change 变化率 (%)	Total profit (Mil RMB) 总利润 (百万元)	Rate of change 变化率 (%)
2000	289		70,131		6,079		95	
2001	335	15.92	71,646	2.16	6,884	13.24	120	26.32
2002	417	24.48	83,986	17.22	8,750	27.11	260	116.67

Major Products 主要产品	Output 产量	Unit 单位
Plastic Shoes 塑料鞋	189,397	Ton 吨

10 Main Firms with Maximal Revenue (year founded) 收入最大的十家主要企业（创办年份）	City 城市	Province 省	Telephone/fax 电话/传真	Number of employees 职工人数	Ownership 产业所有权	Revenue ('000 RMB) 销售收入 (千元)	Profit('000 RMB) (rank) 利润(千元)(排名)	Total assets ('000 RMB) 总资产 (千元)	Major products 主要产品
Fujian Hong Wei Shoes Plastic Co., Ltd.	Quanzhou	Fujian	(0595)5123456		Foreign Funded				Shoes Sole
福建宏玮鞋塑有限公司(2001)	泉州市	福建省	(0595)5199488	1,100	外商投资	190,504	6,244(9)	187,896	鞋底
Fuzhou Yexia Plastic & Leather Co., Ltd.	Fuzhou	Fujian	(0591)3440308		Private Owned				Plastics Slippers
福州叶下塑革有限公司(1984)	福州市	福建省	(0591)3430333	642	私营企业	167,113	1,943(38)	25,083	塑料拖鞋
Jinjiang Yi Tai Shoe-making Material Co., Ltd.	Quanzhou	Fujian	(0595)5192995		Overseas Chinese-funded				ECA Shoes Sole
晋江市亿泰鞋用材料有限公司(1995)	泉州市	福建省	(0595)5197995	1,000	港澳台资	150,779	14,936(1)	83,082	ECA鞋底
Quan Yu Industrial Co., Ltd.	Quanzhou	Fujian	(0595)7788168		Overseas Chinese-funded				TPR shoes Sole
泉州泉昱实业有限公司(1998)	泉州市	福建省	(0595)7788158	1,150	港澳台资	133,447	3,215(13)	168,734	TPR鞋底
Guangdong Jin Han Group Co., Ltd.	Chaozhou	Guangdong	(0768)2296277		Private Owned				Plastic Shoes
广东金汉集团有限公司(1997)	潮州市	广东省	(0768)2291006	482	私营企业	129,323	2,041(33)	51,326	塑料鞋
Qingdao Han Rui Rubber Co., Ltd.	Qingdao	Shandong	(0532)7790363		Foreign Funded				Shoes Sole
青岛韩瑞橡胶有限公司(1994)	青岛市	山东省	(0532)7790464	1,000	外商投资	103,670	9,684(5)	74,278	鞋底
Fulian (Fujian) Shoes Plastic Co., Ltd.	Quanzhou	Fujian	(0595)5199899		Overseas Chinese-funded				Traveling Shoes
福联(福建)鞋塑有限公司(1999)	泉州市	福建省	(0595)5199799	1,528	港澳台资	102,520	5,166(10)	50,484	旅游鞋
Feixian Xinqiao Xinxing Shoes Industry Co., Ltd.	Linyi	Shandong	(0539)5778300		Private Enterprises				shoes
费县新桥鑫星鞋业有限公司(1996)	临沂市	山东省	(0539)5778300	120	私营独资	98,813	10,988(4)	26,000	鞋
Jieyang Guan Yi Plastic Industrial Co., Ltd.	Jieyang	Guangdong	(0663)8686638		Overseas Chinese-funded				Plastic Shoes
揭阳市冠义塑胶实业有限公司(1992)	揭阳市	广东省	(0663)8678497	1,101	港澳台资	93,646	1,140(67)	48,301	塑料鞋
Nanhai Rui Jie Shoes Industry Co., Ltd.	Foshan	Guangdong	(0757)5227869		Overseas Chinese-funded				Plastic Materials for Shoes
南海瑞杰鞋业有限公司(1992)	佛山市	广东省	(0757)5228869	385	港澳台资	93,084	3,018(18)	59,439	塑料鞋材

Top 10 Cities by Revenue 销售收入排名前10位城市	Province 省	Market share 市场份额 (%)	Number of firms 企业个数
Quanzhou 泉州市	Fujian 福建省	16.96	34
Fuzhou 福州市	Fujian 福建省	15.21	76
Chaozhou 潮州市	Guangdong 广东省	7.24	19
Wenzhou 温州市	Zhejiang 浙江省	6.93	33
Putian 莆田市	Fujian 福建省	6.73	21
Taizhou 台州市	Zhejiang 浙江省	6.54	50
Dongguan 东莞市	Guangdong 广东省	6.11	21
Guangzhou 广州市	Guangdong 广东省	4.88	21
Foshan 佛山市	Guangdong 广东省	4.35	15
Jieyang 揭阳市	Guangdong 广东省	3.32	13

10 Major Wholesalers 十家主要批发商	City 城市	Province 省	Telephone/Fax 电话/传真
Wenzhou M & C Foreign Trade Corp	Wenzhou	Zhejiang	(0577)88862999
温州市五机化医外贸有限公司	温州市	浙江省	(0577)88862901
Light Industrial Products Arts and Crafts Import & Export (Group) Corporation	Quanzhou	Fujian	(0595)2552255
轻工工艺进出口集团公司	泉州市	福建省	(0595)2552233
Shanghai Handicrafts Gloves & Hat Industry Import & Export Co.,Ltd.	Shanghai	Shanghai	(021)58990180
上海市工艺品手套帽业进出口有限公司	上海市	上海市	(021)58991146
Shanghai Shen'an Foreign Economic & Trade Corporation	Shanghai	Shanghai	(021)62871088
上海申安对外经济贸易公司	上海市	上海市	(021)62871108
Wenzhou Cereals ,Oils & Foodstuffs Foreign Trade Corp.	Wenzhou	Zhejiang	(0577)88862756
温州市粮油食品对外贸易公司	温州市	浙江省	(0577)88826303
Wenzhou Foreign Trade Industial Products Co., Ltd.	Wenzhou	Zhejiang	(0577)88862788
温州外贸工业品有限公司	温州市	浙江省	(0577)88862799
Zhejiang Ouhai International Trade Corp.	Wenzhou	Zhejiang	(0577)88820092
浙江省瓯海对外贸易公司	温州市	浙江省	(0577)88829093
Shenzhen Light Industry Prodacts Import & Export Company	Shenzhen	Guangdong	(0755)82379000
深圳轻工业品进出口公司	深圳市	广东省	(0755)82379466
Zhejiang Chinabase Impex Co.,Ltd.	Hangzhou	Zhejiang	(0571)87819435
浙江中基进出口有限公司	杭州市	浙江省	(0571)87819437
Zhejiang Qingtian Foreign Trade Co.,ltd.	Lishui	Zhejiang	(0578)6833651
浙江省青田县对外贸易有限公司	丽水市	浙江省	(0578)6822963

3070: Household Plastic Goods 日用塑料杂品制造业

The industry accounts for 0.199% of the total revenue of China's industrial sector in 2002. The rate of return on assets is 4.99%. 84.90% of all firms in the industry made a profit while 15.10% had negative returns.The top province in terms of the industry's revenue is Guangdong, accounting for 36.12% of the total revenue.
2002年本行业收入占全行业的 0.199%，资产利润率为 4.99%。84.90%的企业赢利，15.10%的企业亏损。收入最高的省为广东省，占本行业的36.12%。

	Total number of firms 企业总数	Total number of employees 职工总数	Total revenue (Mil.RMB) 总销售收入 (百万元)	Total profit (Mil.RMB) 总利润 (百万元)	Return on assets 资产利润率 (%)	Return on equity 权益利润率 (%)	Labour productivity ('000 RMB/ worker) 劳动生产率 (千元/人)	Debts/ assets 资产负债率 (%)	Total assets (Mil.RMB) 总资产 (百万元)
Industry Overall 行业总体	722	124,217	21,320	815	4.99	10.09	43.99	50.51	16,316

	Number of firms 企业个数	Average number of employees 平均职工人数	Average revenue ('000 RMB) 平均销售收入 (千元)	Average profit ('000 RMB) 平均利润 (千元)	Return on assets 资产利润率 (%)	Return on equity 权益利润率 (%)	Labour productivity ('000 RMB/ worker) 劳动生产率 (千元/人)	Debts/ assets 资产负债率 (%)	Average total assets ('000 RMB) 平均总资产 (千元)
By ownership 产业所有权									
State-owned 国有	31	88	3,904	49	0.36	1.67	19.56	78.49	13,629
Collective-owned 集体	80	134	24,276	585	3.75	10.54	41.62	64.45	15,612
Foreign & Overseas Chinese Funded 三资	254	247	37,951	1,253	3.27	6.26	42.35	47.76	38,279
By regional distribution 地区分布									
Central-North 华北	48	96	16,765	1,111	4.79	9.03	54.13	46.96	23,209
Beijing 北京	25	77	16,534	908	5.15	9.57	74.79	46.21	17,642
Tianjin 天津	16	110	20,762	1,618	4.10	7.57	49.59	45.86	39,480
Hebei 河北	6	114	9,024	804	13.73	43.75	24.01	68.62	5,853
Shanxi 山西	1	242	5,023	-63	-1.02	-9.89	7.02	89.71	6,189
Inner Mongolia 内蒙古									
Northeast 东北	16	165	16,458	1,845	6.91	18.18	33.39	61.99	26,695
Liaoning 辽宁	11	199	19,928	1,631	7.37	15.59	25.26	52.69	22,125
Jilin 吉林	4	111	9,917	2,838	6.27	24.75	67.45	74.64	45,226
Heilongjiang 黑龙江	1	10	4,459	225	7.93	16.80	296.10	52.84	2,839
Central-East 华东	367	150	31,178	1,501	6.83	14.66	51.54	53.39	21,973
Shanghai 上海	39	124	42,943	2,228	4.82	10.40	82.65	53.68	46,241
Jiangsu 江苏	58	220	49,202	965	3.45	7.00	58.39	50.77	27,984
Zhejiang 浙江	169	134	27,581	1,951	12.67	28.00	41.59	54.73	15,397
Anhui 安徽	10	55	7,328	620	8.82	15.74	33.67	43.97	7,023
Fujian 福建	49	185	22,826	855	3.40	6.55	43.95	48.08	25,114
Jiangxi 江西	3	30	8,940	76	1.72	4.49	69.32	61.66	4,436
Shandong 山东	39	131	26,511	770	4.16	11.41	64.16	63.54	18,501
Central-South 中南	272	222	32,021	672	2.81	5.26	37.42	46.66	23,938
Henan 河南	11	83	7,411	259	3.19	13.61	35.28	76.58	8,125
Hubei 湖北	21	206	28,891	902	4.91	7.51	48.00	34.67	18,391
Hunan 湖南	5	253	47,257	1,242	16.55	21.26	38.35	22.15	7,507
Guangdong 广东	228	229	33,777	657	2.53	4.77	37.12	46.97	25,985
Guangxi 广西	5	295	14,531	336	2.73	7.42	16.68	63.24	12,333
Hainan 海南	2	48	5,752	1,591	27.39	57.18	51.39	52.10	5,809
Southwest 西南	13	73	6,347	-19	-0.17	-0.35	19.81	51.95	11,056
Chongqing 重庆	5	80	7,804	-353	-2.63	-4.10	20.01	35.80	13,426
Sichuan 四川	4	77	8,003	525	3.75	21.84	29.07	82.85	14,023
Guizhou 贵州	2	54	2,609	-531	-12.35	-14.88	-4.06	17.01	4,297
Yunnan 云南	1	72	6,000	898	13.85	19.33	22.24	28.34	6,482
Tibet 西藏	1	60	263	-414	-7.62	-9.06	10.92	15.89	5,436
Northwest 西北	6	86	2,965	-286	-3.07	-7.93	14.02	61.29	9,326
Shaanxi 陕西									
Gansu 甘肃	5	93	2,451	-106	-1.05	-2.83	13.72	62.87	10,057
Qinghai 青海									
Ningxia 宁夏									
Xinjiang 新疆	1	50	5,534	-1,189	-20.98	-39.82	16.80	47.32	5,668

3070: Household Plastic Goods 日用塑料杂品制造业

Year 年份	Number of firms 企业个数	Rate of change 变化率 (%)	Number of employees 职工人数 (人)	Rate of change 变化率 (%)	Total revenue (Mil. RMB) 总销售收入 (百万元)	Rate of change 变化率 (%)	Total profit (Mil RMB) 总利润 (百万元)	Rate of change 变化率 (%)
2000	408		74,219		12,019		368	
2001	585	43.38	96,278	29.72	16,336	35.92	600	63.04
2002	722	23.42	124,217	29.02	21,320	30.51	815	35.83

Major Products 主要产品	Output 产量	Unit 单位
Daily Use Plastic Products 日用塑料制品	142	10,000 Tons 万吨

10 Main Firms with Maximal Revenue (year founded) 收入最大的十家主要企业（创办年份）	City 城市	Province 省	Telephone/ fax 电话/传真	Number of employees 职工人数	Ownership 产业所有权	Revenue ('000 RMB) 销售收入(千元)	Profit('000 RMB) (rank) 利润(千元)(排名)	Total assets ('000 RMB) 总资产(千元)	Major products 主要产品
NingBo Lishi Plastic Co., Ltd.	Ningbo	Zhejiang	(0574)88021888		Overseas Chinese-funded				Plastic Products
宁波利时塑胶有限公司(1993)	宁波市	浙江省	(0574)88021466	1,332	港澳台资	492,386	51,207(2)	274,285	塑料制品
Shanghai Jing Xuan Plastic Products Co., ltd	Shanghai	Shanghai	(021)69153443		Foreign Funded				Plastic Products
上海敬炫塑胶制品有限公司(1993)	上海市	上海市	(021)69154756	817	外商投资	378,835	9,549(15)	283,624	塑料制品
ShangHai Zi Jiang Color Printing And Packing Co., Ltd.	Shanghai	Shanghai	(021)64426888		Overseas Chinese-funded				Plastic Pakage Products塑料
上海紫江彩印包装有限公司(1991)	上海市	上海市	(021)64426080	703	港澳台资	314,188	16,154(7)	566,789	包装制品
Jiangsu Bat Plastic Group Co., Ltd.	Wuxi	Jiangsu	(0510)6203118		Collective-owned				Artificial Leather
江苏蝙蝠塑料集团有限公司(1958)	无锡市	江苏省	(0510)6203118	560	集体企业	303,330	-	224,780	人造革
Jieyang Rong Tai Industrial Co., Ltd.	Jieyang	Guangdong	(0663)3276282		Private Owned				Amido Multiple-unit Material 氨基
广东榕泰实业股份有限公司(2001)	揭阳市	广东省	(0663)3273960	888	私营企业	294,144	4,892(42)	138,464	复合材料
Penglai Fu Xin Rubber & Plastics Co., Ltd.	Yantai	Shandong	(0535)5961407		Others				pvc Coated Cloth
蓬莱市福鑫橡塑有限公司(2000)	烟台市	山东省	(0535)5961408	498	其他企业	245,988	4,988(41)	47,324	pvc涂层布
Dongguan Run Feng Metal Plastic Cement Co., Ltd.	Dongguan	Guangdong	(0769)3320898		Overseas Chinese-funded				Placed Etagere
东莞润丰金属塑胶有限公司(1998)	东莞市	广东省	(0769)3320898	750	港澳台资	222,884	3,299(55)	269,896	置物架
Miluo Dongfang Zhiye Co.,ltd	Yueyang	Hunan	(0730)5228073		Collective-owned				Plastic
汨罗市东方置业有限公司(1999)	岳阳市	湖南省	(0730)5222460	921	集体企业	200,000	5,610(35)	20,000	塑料
Whole wide Home Creation Co., Ltd.	Shenzhen	Guangdong	(0755)27706666		Overseas Chinese-funded				Plastic Cement Commodity塑
厚宏日用制品（深圳）有限公司(1991)	深圳市	广东省	(0755)27701243	1,317	港澳台资	168,091	10,800(14)	161,015	胶日用品
Dongtao Machine Shanghai Co., Ltd.	Shanghai	Shanghai	(021)57741193		Foreign Funded				toilet-pot
东陶机器上海有限公司(1997)	上海市	上海市		201	外商投资	159,536	22,419(6)	149,173	卫生洁具

Top 10 Cities by Revenue 销售收入排名前10位城市	Province 省	Market share 市场份额 (%)	Number of firms 企业个数
Taizhou 台州市	Zhejiang 浙江省	11.68	67
Guangzhou 广州市	Guangdong 广东省	8.25	41
Shanghai 上海市	Shanghai 上海市	7.86	39
Yangzhou 扬州市	Jiangsu 江苏省	7.36	14
Shenzhen 深圳市	Guangdong 广东省	6.43	30
Ningbo 宁波市	Zhejiang 浙江省	5.06	38
Dongguan 东莞市	Guangdong 广东省	3.99	22
Jiangmen 江门市	Guangdong 广东省	2.71	23
Wuxi 无锡市	Jiangsu 江苏省	2.58	11
Zhongshan 中山市	Guangdong 广东省	2.25	23

10 Major Wholesalers 十家主要批发商	City 城市	Province 省	Telephone/Fax 电话/传真
Harbin ChinaSun Group Co., Ltd.	Harbin	Heilongjiang	(0451)84885100
哈尔滨中央红集团股份有限公司	哈尔滨市	黑龙江省	(0451)84885111
Guangzhou Yuexiu Enterprise (Group) Company	Guangzhou	Guangdong	(020)85597130
广州越秀企业（集团）公司	广州市	广东省	(020)85599018
China Reed Screen Imp. & Exp. Corp.Ltd.	Beijing	Beijing	(010)65521133
中艺苇帘进出口有限责任公司	北京市	北京市	(010)65513995
Hebei Xintai Foreign Trade Corp.ltd.	Shijiazhuang	Hebei	(0311)7767908
河北信泰对外贸易有限公司	石家庄市	河北省	(0311)7755347
Hebei Arts & Crafts Imp. & Exp. Corp.	Shijiazhuang	Hebei	(0311)7764345
河北省工艺品进出口公司	石家庄市	河北省	(0311)7755347
Shanghai Hengda Ceramic Building Materials Trade Market	Shanghai	Shanghai	(021)58425842
上海恒大陶瓷建材交易市场	上海市	上海市	(021)58427389
Hangzhou Local Product General Corporation	Hangzhou	Zhejiang	(0571)87026301
杭州市土特产总公司	杭州市	浙江省	(0571)87026323
Ningbo Zhonglin Foreign Trade Co.,Ltd.	Ningbo	Zhejiang	(0574)87871797
宁波中蔺对外贸易有限公司	宁波市	浙江省	(0574)87871790
Wuyi Local Products Daily Groceries Co.,Ltd.	Jinhua	Zhejiang	(0579)7623401
武义县土产日用杂品有限责任公司	金华市	浙江省	(0579)7623401
Guangdong Shunde Local Products Import & Export Company	Foshan	Guangdong	(0765)6682839
广东省顺德土产进出口公司	佛山市	广东省	(0765)6681441

3080: Plastic Parts 塑料零件制造业

The industry accounts for 0.180% of the total revenue of China's industrial sector in 2002. The rate of return on assets is 7.18%. 86.36% of all firms in the industry made a profit while 13.64% had negative returns.The top province in terms of the industry's revenue is Guangdong, accounting for 32.97% of the total revenue.
2002年本行业收入占全行业的 0.180%，资产利润率为 7.18%。86.36%的企业赢利，13.64%的企业亏损。收入最高的省为广东省，占本行业的32.97%。

	Total number of firms 企业总数	Total number of employees 职工总数	Total revenue (Mil.RMB) 总销售收入（百万元）	Total profit (Mil.RMB) 总利润（百万元）	Return on assets 资产利润率（%）	Return on equity 权益利润率（%）	Labour productivity ('000 RMB/ worker) 劳动生产率（千元/人）	Debts/ assets 资产负债率（%）	Total assets (Mil.RMB) 总资产（百万元）
Industry Overall 行业总体	550	109,234	19,300	1,374	7.18	14.47	53.21	50.36	19,128

	Number of firms 企业个数	Average number of employees 平均职工人数	Average revenue ('000 RMB) 平均销售收入（千元）	Average profit ('000 RMB) 平均利润（千元）	Return on assets 资产利润率（%）	Return on equity 权益利润率（%）	Labour productivity ('000 RMB/ worker) 劳动生产率（千元/人）	Debts/ assets 资产负债率（%）	Average total assets ('000 RMB) 平均总资产（千元）
By ownership 产业所有权									
State-owned 国有	16	360	12,254	147	0.65	1.78	9.66	63.40	22,632
Collective-owned 集体	60	196	38,466	1,912	7.10	14.07	56.68	49.54	26,922
Foreign & Overseas Chinese Funded 三资	206	289	56,290	4,279	7.42	13.93	59.63	46.76	57,687
By regional distribution 地区分布									
Central-North 华北	48	196	47,013	6,198	14.78	30.37	101.26	51.32	41,922
Beijing 北京	9	171	19,450	-507	-1.33	-3.60	47.86	63.07	38,083
Tianjin 天津	35	210	57,721	8,340	18.22	35.60	115.88	48.81	45,769
Hebei 河北	4	129	15,336	2,545	15.05	30.80	52.10	51.14	16,908
Shanxi 山西									
Inner Mongolia 内蒙古									
Northeast 东北	12	173	21,676	2,537	6.15	11.24	46.73	45.31	41,279
Liaoning 辽宁	8	186	29,309	3,304	7.62	13.51	60.52	43.55	43,329
Jilin 吉林	3	84	6,879	1,335	5.47	45.38	21.87	87.96	24,434
Heilongjiang 黑龙江	1	332	5,010	10	0.01	0.02	3.84	11.93	75,413
Central-East 华东	333	150	30,016	2,145	7.12	15.03	55.43	52.64	30,126
Shanghai 上海	63	177	38,243	4,218	9.30	18.80	59.98	50.54	45,352
Jiangsu 江苏	68	148	28,485	1,663	5.62	11.48	52.13	50.99	29,581
Zhejiang 浙江	150	117	21,554	1,371	6.40	14.08	44.46	54.56	21,435
Anhui 安徽	10	395	117,138	4,708	5.55	10.69	69.16	48.07	84,806
Fujian 福建	14	204	30,126	2,434	10.40	25.59	87.24	59.36	23,407
Jiangxi 江西									
Shandong 山东	28	152	29,390	1,731	6.28	15.24	62.37	58.82	27,585
Central-South 中南	144	321	46,247	2,266	5.21	9.85	42.18	47.07	43,460
Henan 河南	5	270	22,315	201	0.78	1.75	31.82	55.53	25,951
Hubei 湖北	9	130	17,306	1,062	5.04	15.01	52.71	66.44	21,076
Hunan 湖南	3	143	7,490	111	1.13	4.41	23.44	74.45	9,828
Guangdong 广东	125	346	50,912	2,523	5.35	9.92	42.40	46.11	47,187
Guangxi 广西	1	75	5,200	164	1.73	3.40	52.68	49.25	9,496
Hainan 海南	1	15	526	-186	-12.05	-31.47	6.53	61.70	1,543
Southwest 西南	12	114	10,676	526	2.10	3.72	34.68	43.53	25,029
Chongqing 重庆	6	109	9,253	592	3.40	7.02	30.18	51.54	17,400
Sichuan 四川	5	94	6,993	421	4.78	10.15	32.26	52.88	8,797
Guizhou 贵州	1	248	37,627	657	0.43	0.67	51.07	35.31	151,960
Yunnan 云南									
Tibet 西藏									
Northwest 西北	1	288	703	-457	-1.53	-3.97	3.19	61.40	29,797
Shaanxi 陕西									
Gansu 甘肃	1	288	703	-457	-1.53	-3.97	3.19	61.40	29,797
Qinghai 青海									
Ningxia 宁夏									
Xinjiang 新疆									

3080: Plastic Parts 塑料零件制造业

Year 年份	Number of firms 企业个数	Rate of change 变化率 (%)	Number of employees 职工人数 (人)	Rate of change 变化率 (%)	Total revenue (Mil. RMB) 总销售收入 (百万元)	Rate of change 变化率 (%)	Total profit (Mil RMB) 总利润 (百万元)	Rate of change 变化率 (%)
2000	390		66,449		15,159		906	
2001	457	17.18	85,791	29.11	17,225	13.63	1,075	18.65
2002	550	20.35	109,234	27.33	19,300	12.05	1,374	27.81

Major Products 主要产品	Output 产量	Unit 单位

10 Main Firms with Maximal Revenue (year founded) 收入最大的十家主要企业（创办年份）	City 城市	Province 省	Telephone/fax 电话/传真	Number of employees 职工人数	Ownership 产业所有权	Revenue ('000 RMB) 销售收入 (千元)	Profit('000 RMB) (rank) 利润(千元) (排名)	Total assets ('000 RMB) 总资产 (千元)	Major products 主要产品
Anhui Tian Da Enterprise (Group)Company 安徽天大企业(集团)公司(1972)	Chuzhou 滁州市	Anhui 安徽省	(0550)7518500 (0550)7511023	2,400	Collective-owned 集体企业	984,040	44,481(6)	598,079	Engineering Plastics 工程塑料
PEMSTAR (Tainjin) Co.,Ltd. 鹏思特(天津)实业有限公司(1998)	Tianjin 天津市	Tianjin 天津市	(022)82110485 (022)82110486	1,708	Foreign Funded 外商投资	598,035	75,114(2)	416,030	Plastics Parts 塑料零件
Yaguang Nypro Precision Moulding (Tianjin) Co., Ltd. 亚光耐普罗精密注塑（天津）有限公司(1995)	Tianjin 天津市	Tianjin 天津市	(022)88241960 (022)88240675	1,080	Foreign Funded 外商投资	492,741	111,320(1)	257,209	Plastic Components 塑料件
Shenzhen Mei Yang Moulding Co., Ltd. 深圳美阳注塑有限公司(1992)	Shenzhen 深圳市	Guangdong 广东省	(0755)83308459 (0755)83305500	1,150	Overseas Chinese-funded 港澳台资	433,229	31,295(9)	231,063	Plastic Moulding Fittings 塑料注塑件
Desay Precision Parts Ltd. 惠州市德赛精密部件有限公司(1997)	Huizhou 惠州市	Guangdong 广东省	(0752)2619673 (0752)2619666	830	Overseas Chinese-funded 港澳台资	402,073	2,664(103)	66,121	Plastic Moulding Products 注塑产品
Taishan Ji Lian Wire & Cable Co., ltd. 台山市吉联电线电缆有限公司(1997)	Jiangmen 江门市	Guangdong 广东省	(0750)5578789 (0750)5578559	420	Overseas Chinese-funded 港澳台资	295,787	180(318)	109,644	Plastic Cover Electric Wire 塑皮电线
Shanghai Ying Ji Electronic Plastic Cement Co., Ltd. 上海英济电子塑胶有限公司(1993)	Shanghai 上海市	Shanghai 上海市	(021)69211111	1,863	Foreign Funded 外商投资	271,180	45,294(5)	268,223	Moulding Fittings 注塑件
Jinxiang Ci Xun (Shenzhen) co., Ltd. 金像磁讯（深圳）有限公司(1993)	Shenzhen 深圳市	Guangdong 广东省	(0755)28772283 (0755)28891452	850	Overseas Chinese-funded 港澳台资	247,884	1,138(165)	159,147	Plastic Shell 塑胶外壳
V.S. Technology Industry Park (zhuhai)Co., Ltd 威士茂科技工业园（珠海）有限公司(2000)	Zhuhai 珠海市	Guangdong 广东省	(0756)3392338 (0756)3385691	1,245	Overseas Chinese-funded 港澳台资	239,222	38,570(8)	455,785	Plastic Components 塑胶件
H.I.P (Shanhai) Co.,Ltd 赫比（上海）家用电器产品有限公司(2002)	Shanghai 上海市	Shanghai 上海市	(021)50313636 (021)50312266	491	Foreign Funded 外商投资	234,181	8,463(46)	187,991	Moulding Fittings 注塑件

Top 10 Cities by Revenue 销售收入排名前10位城市	Province 省	Market share 市场份额 (%)	Number of firms 企业个数
Shanghai 上海市	Shanghai 上海市	12.48	63
Tianjin 天津市	Tianjin 天津市	10.47	35
Ningbo 宁波市	Zhejiang 浙江省	9.67	86
Shenzhen 深圳市	Guangdong 广东省	9.31	23
Zhuhai 珠海市	Guangdong 广东省	6.78	23
Chuzhou 滁州市	Anhui 安徽省	5.18	2
Huizhou 惠州市	Guangdong 广东省	3.78	10
Dongguan 东莞市	Guangdong 广东省	3.38	12
Suzhou 苏州市	Jiangsu 江苏省	3.24	22
Taizhou 台州市	Zhejiang 浙江省	2.64	18

10 Major Wholesalers 十家主要批发商	City 城市	Province 省	Telephone/Fax 电话/传真
Yihua Kangqi Chemical Fibre Co.,Ltd. 仪化康祺化纤有限责任公司	Yangzhou 扬州市	Jiangsu 江苏省	(0514)3235499 (0514)3233847
Sinochem Guangdong Import & Export Company 中化广东进出口公司	Guangzhou 广州市	Guangdong 广东省	(020)86672288 (020)86507512
Sinochem Shanghai Import & Export Company 中化上海进出口公司	Shanghai 上海市	Shanghai 上海市	(021)63289888 (021)63283968
Sinochem Tianjin Import & Export Company 中化天津进出口公司	Tianjin 天津市	Tianjin 天津市	(022)23146216 (022)23146215
China Chemical Sales & Supply (North China) Corporation 中国化工供销华北公司	Tianjin 天津市	Tianjin 天津市	(022)23011031 (022)23011032
China Chemical Sales & Supply (North China) Corporation 中国化工供销华东公司	Shanghai 上海市	Shanghai 上海市	(021)62103300 (021)62515799
Nantong Chemical Light Industry Co.,Ltd. 南通化工轻工股份有限公司	Nantong 南通市	Jiangsu 江苏省	(0513)5518397 (0513)5512735
Taizhou Heshun Plastics Co.,Ltd. 台州市和顺塑料有限公司	Taizhou 台州市	Zhejiang 浙江省	(0576)2510220 (0576)2510160
China Petroleum Technology Development Corporation 中国石油技术开发公司	Beijing 北京市	Beijing 北京市	(010)84080722 (010)84080800
China National Chemical Fiber Corporation 中国化纤总公司	Beijing 北京市	Beijing 北京市	(010)65816699 (010)65813483

3090: Other Plastic Products 其他塑料制品业

The industry accounts for 0.393% of the total revenue of China's industrial sector in 2002. The rate of return on assets is 4.61%. 82.71% of all firms in the industry made a profit while 17.29% had negative returns.The top province in terms of the industry's revenue is Guangdong, accounting for 39.02% of the total revenue.
2002年本行业收入占全行业的 0.393%，资产利润率为 4.61%。82.71%的企业赢利，17.29%的企业亏损。收入最高的省为广东省，占本行业的39.02%。

	Total number of firms 企业总数	Total number of employees 职工总数	Total revenue (Mil.RMB) 总销售收入(百万元)	Total profit (Mil.RMB) 总利润(百万元)	Return on assets 资产利润率(%)	Return on equity 权益利润率(%)	Labour productivity ('000 RMB/worker) 劳动生产率(千元/人)	Debts/assets 资产负债率(%)	Total assets (Mil.RMB) 总资产(百万元)
Industry Overall 行业总体	1515	281,604	42,148	1,895	4.61	9.74	41.25	52.61	41,079

	Number of firms 企业个数	Average number of employees 平均职工人数	Average revenue ('000 RMB) 平均销售收入(千元)	Average profit ('000 RMB) 平均利润(千元)	Return on assets 资产利润率(%)	Return on equity 权益利润率(%)	Labour productivity ('000 RMB/worker) 劳动生产率(千元/人)	Debts/assets 资产负债率(%)	Average total assets ('000 RMB) 平均总资产(千元)
By ownership 产业所有权									
State-owned 国有	63	91	4,970	-76	-0.73	-2.33	14.30	68.78	10,406
Collective-owned 集体	172	139	17,889	770	4.34	11.95	39.95	63.66	17,722
Foreign & Overseas Chinese Funded 三资	601	284	39,915	1,628	3.93	7.68	39.14	48.80	41,425
By regional distribution 地区分布									
Central-North 华北	104	158	18,380	1,156	4.48	9.06	29.62	50.51	25,773
Beijing 北京	37	125	11,741	494	2.87	5.39	29.99	46.73	17,216
Tianjin 天津	36	137	27,351	2,750	8.60	14.76	39.72	41.71	31,960
Hebei 河北	26	257	18,523	191	0.59	1.66	22.65	64.19	32,265
Shanxi 山西	3	39	2,109	-17	-0.24	-1.24	6.24	80.35	6,981
Inner Mongolia 内蒙古	2	58	2,280	-1,007	-6.10	-16.94	12.28	64.01	16,505
Northeast 东北	48	242	38,447	1,883	3.61	6.31	42.28	42.84	52,213
Liaoning 辽宁	27	327	60,084	2,713	3.82	6.30	47.24	39.34	70,957
Jilin 吉林	9	116	10,856	248	1.00	1.88	29.47	47.03	24,874
Heilongjiang 黑龙江	12	146	10,456	1,242	4.07	9.81	24.94	58.53	30,545
Central-East 华东	774	138	25,412	1,380	5.68	12.79	50.69	55.59	24,291
Shanghai 上海	145	140	31,639	1,693	4.87	10.28	52.33	52.66	34,774
Jiangsu 江苏	194	114	26,185	1,220	4.98	11.41	61.60	56.32	24,475
Zhejiang 浙江	243	116	18,191	1,029	6.03	14.46	37.71	58.30	17,065
Anhui 安徽	22	153	21,472	1,559	7.36	20.46	44.36	64.03	21,186
Fujian 福建	93	199	26,368	1,240	5.19	10.00	43.09	48.09	23,898
Jiangxi 江西	4	133	36,104	6,026	12.79	31.97	95.86	59.99	47,106
Shandong 山东	73	193	34,410	2,220	8.16	21.26	67.06	61.64	27,213
Central-South 中南	541	261	33,680	1,056	3.54	7.17	35.62	50.69	29,848
Henan 河南	31	263	29,705	1,644	8.65	16.08	30.27	46.22	19,008
Hubei 湖北	34	138	18,920	443	4.29	9.95	47.48	56.88	10,337
Hunan 湖南	9	172	11,986	1,431	3.05	5.20	29.57	41.30	46,900
Guangdong 广东	460	274	35,750	1,060	3.33	6.82	35.60	51.16	31,834
Guangxi 广西	5	175	13,706	-192	-1.10	-1.36	28.98	18.92	17,401
Hainan 海南	2	75	17,772	2,925	10.71	23.89	76.29	55.16	27,306
Southwest 西南	25	129	11,778	818	3.07	8.02	30.66	61.69	26,628
Chongqing 重庆	7	101	5,983	67	0.28	2.32	18.31	87.82	23,563
Sichuan 四川	14	154	11,476	66	0.25	0.61	28.44	59.58	26,640
Guizhou 贵州	2	71	5,892	224	3.75	24.35	12.26	84.60	5,975
Yunnan 云南	2	104	40,059	9,308	16.07	22.59	108.38	28.88	57,925
Tibet 西藏									
Northwest 西北	23	87	8,985	1,092	9.05	17.66	41.38	48.77	12,064
Shaanxi 陕西	6	107	9,072	-163	-1.07	-1.97	27.63	45.66	15,229
Gansu 甘肃	11	55	3,192	155	5.76	10.18	32.22	43.44	2,683
Qinghai 青海									
Ningxia 宁夏	2	161	13,382	1,342	10.20	38.10	36.16	73.23	13,151
Xinjiang 新疆	4	108	22,586	5,426	16.66	31.57	78.41	47.23	32,570

3090: Other Plastic Products 其他塑料制品业

Year 年份	Number of firms 企业个数	Rate of change 变化率 (%)	Number of employees 职工人数 (人)	Rate of change 变化率 (%)	Total revenue (Mil. RMB) 总销售收入 (百万元)	Rate of change 变化率 (%)	Total profit (Mil RMB) 总利润 (百万元)	Rate of change 变化率 (%)
2000	1408		259,997		37,898		1,834	
2001	1474	4.69	261,702	0.66	38,830	2.46	1,850	0.87
2002	1515	2.78	281,604	7.60	42,148	8.54	1,895	2.43

Major Products 主要产品	Output 产量	Unit 单位
Other Plastic Products 其它塑料制品	375	10,000 Tons 万吨

10 Main Firms with Maximal Revenue (year founded) 收入最大的十家主要企业（创办年份）	City 城市	Province 省	Telephone/fax 电话/传真	Number of employees 职工人数	Ownership 产业所有权	Revenue ('000 RMB) 销售收入 (千元)	Profit('000 RMB) (rank) 利润(千元) (排名)	Total assets ('000 RMB) 总资产 (千元)	Major products 主要产品
Weihai Guang Wei Fishing Tackle Co., Ltd. 威海光威渔具有限公司(1989)	Weihai 威海市	Shandong 山东省	(0631)5298619 (0631)5251990	2,025	Limited-Liability 有限公司	744,112	81,227(1)	443,601	Fishing pole 渔竿
GE Plastics ShangHai Co., Ltd. GE塑料上海有限公司(1999)	Shanghai 上海市	Shanghai 上海市	(021)50460000 (021)50460100	141	Foreign Funded 外商投资	721,699	45,794(3)	825,486	Polymer Carbonic Acid Grease 聚碳酸脂
Mingda Plastic (Fujian)Co., Ltd. 明达塑胶(福建)有限公司(1990)	Fuzhou 福州市	Fujian 福建省	(0591)5381890 (0591)5380101	2,392	Foreign Funded 外商投资	564,000	9,620(51)	240,069	PVC Plastic Products.PVC 塑胶制品
Shunde Daliang North District Resident Commission 顺德大良北区居委会(1969)	Foshan 佛山市	Guangdong 广东省	(0765)2277838	1,184	Private Owned 私营企业	552,140	75,658(2)	51,490	Plastic Products 塑料制品
Yong Hua International (Huizhou) Electronics Co., Ltd. 雍华国际(惠州)电子有限公司(1993)	Huizhou 惠州市	Guangdong 广东省	(0752)6910000 (0752)6910066	317	Overseas Chinese-funded 港澳台资	521,812	5,200(95)	54,808	Plastic Products 塑胶制品
Dalian Aris Oyama Industry & Trade Co., Ltd. 大连爱丽思欧雅玛工贸有限公司(1997)	Dalian 大连市	Liaoning 辽宁省	(0411)7303804 (0411)7301418	2,232	Foreign Funded 外商投资	460,802	42,505(5)	461,210	Plastic Products 塑料制品
Guangdong Gao Le Toys Manufacturing Co., Ltd. 广东高乐玩具制造股份有限公司(1986)	Jieyang 揭阳市	Guangdong 广东省	(0663)2348472 (0663)2348055	1,309	Overseas Chinese-funded 港澳台资	367,060	5,486(92)	144,450	Plastic Toy 塑料玩具
Yong Da Adhesive Products Factory Co., Ltd. 中山市永大胶粘制品厂有限公司(1985)	Zhongshan 中山市	Guangdong 广东省	(0760)2253110 (0760)2250186	830	Overseas Chinese-funded 港澳台资	344,540	7,983(63)	287,988	Sealing Case Adhesive Tape封箱胶粘带
Rixin (Tianjin) Plastic Co., Ltd. 日新(天津)塑胶有限公司(1995)	Tianjin 天津市	Tianjin 天津市	(022)23972357 (022)23972359	1,086	Foreign Funded 外商投资	338,830	41,820(6)	337,850	Plastic Products 塑胶制品
Suiping Hua Qiang Plastic Cement Co., Ltd. 遂平县华强塑胶有限公司(1995)	Zhumadian 驻马店市	Henan 河南省	(0396)4925612 (0396)4803868	4,549	Private Owned 私营企业	317,061	23,998(10)	203,401	Plastic Bags 塑料袋

Top 10 Cities by Revenue 销售收入排名前10位城市	Province 省	Market share 市场份额 (%)	Number of firms 企业个数
Shanghai 上海市	Shanghai 上海市	10.88	145
Shenzhen 深圳市	Guangdong 广东省	8.78	81
Foshan 佛山市	Guangdong 广东省	6.44	62
Ningbo 宁波市	Zhejiang 浙江省	5.79	117
Guangzhou 广州市	Guangdong 广东省	5.53	87
Suzhou 苏州市	Jiangsu 江苏省	5.28	76
Dongguan 东莞市	Guangdong 广东省	4.28	60
Zhongshan 中山市	Guangdong 广东省	4.12	40
Fuzhou 福州市	Fujian 福建省	3.65	35
Weihai 威海市	Shandong 山东省	3.06	15

10 Major Wholesalers 十家主要批发商	City 城市	Province 省	Telephone/Fax 电话/传真
Yihua Kangqi Chemical Fibre Co.,Ltd. 仪化康祺化纤有限责任公司	Yangzhou 扬州市	Jiangsu 江苏省	(0514)3235499 (0514)3233847
Sinochem Guangdong Import & Export Company 中化广东进出口公司	Guangzhou 广州市	Guangdong 广东省	(020)86672288 (020)86507512
Sinochem Shanghai Import & Export Company 中化上海进出口公司	Shanghai 上海市	Shanghai 上海市	(021)63289888 (021)63283968
Sinochem Tianjin Import & Export Company 中化天津进出口公司	Tianjin 天津市	Tianjin 天津市	(022)23146216 (022)23146215
China Chemical Sales & Supply (North China) Corporation 中国化工供销华北公司	Tianjin 天津市	Tianjin 天津市	(022)23011031 (022)23011032
China Chemical Sales & Supply (North China) Corporation 中国化工供销华东公司	Shanghai 上海市	Shanghai 上海市	(021)62103300 (021)62515799
Nantong Chemical Light Industry Co.,Ltd. 南通化工轻工股份有限公司	Nantong 南通市	Jiangsu 江苏省	(0513)5518397 (0513)5512735
Taizhou Heshun Plastics Co.,Ltd. 台州市和顺塑料有限公司	Taizhou 台州市	Zhejiang 浙江省	(0576)2510220 (0576)2510160
China Petroleum Technology Development Corporation 中国石油技术开发公司	Beijing 北京市	Beijing 北京市	(010)84080722 (010)84080800
China National Chemical Fiber Corporation 中国化纤总公司	Beijing 北京市	Beijing 北京市	(010)65816699 (010)65813483

3110: Cement 水泥制造业

The industry accounts for 1.379% of the total revenue of China's industrial sector in 2002. The rate of return on assets is 1.63%. 68.64% of all firms in the industry made a profit while 31.36% had negative returns.The top province in terms of the industry's revenue is Shandong, accounting for 12.66% of the total revenue.
2002年本行业收入占全行业的 1.379%，资产利润率为 1.63%。68.64%的企业赢利，31.36%的企业亏损。收入最高的省为山东省，占本行业的12.66%。

	Total number of firms 企业总数	Total number of employees 职工总数	Total revenue (Mil.RMB) 总销售收入 (百万元)	Total profit (Mil.RMB) 总利润 (百万元)	Return on assets 资产利润率 (%)	Return on equity 权益利润率 (%)	Labour productivity ('000 RMB/ worker) 劳动生产率 (千元/人)	Debts/ assets 资产负债率 (%)	Total assets (Mil.RMB) 总资产 (百万元)
Industry Overall 行业总体	4754	1,502,151	147,871	4,653	1.63	4.56	32.61	64.19	284,796

	Number of firms 企业个数	Average number of employees 平均职工人数	Average revenue ('000 RMB) 平均销售收入 (千元)	Average profit ('000 RMB) 平均利润 (千元)	Return on assets 资产利润率 (%)	Return on equity 权益利润率 (%)	Labour productivity ('000 RMB/ worker) 劳动生产率 (千元/人)	Debts/ assets 资产负债率 (%)	Average total assets ('000 RMB) 平均总资产 (千元)
By ownership 产业所有权									
State-owned 国有	744	383	28,346	-276	-0.40	-1.41	24.94	71.71	69,074
Collective-owned 集体	1,112	241	22,187	573	1.98	7.80	29.34	74.68	29,013
Foreign & Overseas Chinese Funded 三资	175	344	71,842	3,715	1.90	4.21	67.04	54.74	195,194
By regional distribution 地区分布									
Central-North 华北	607	310	28,854	1,404	1.96	4.88	34.42	59.84	71,596
Beijing 北京	42	455	62,639	3,293	1.62	3.64	49.62	55.58	203,882
Tianjin 天津	19	302	61,172	1,457	0.96	1.88	20.03	48.91	151,710
Hebei 河北	343	295	28,477	1,735	3.27	8.12	37.55	59.72	53,032
Shanxi 山西	142	308	16,372	-216	-0.34	-1.02	19.69	66.93	63,745
Inner Mongolia 内蒙古	61	302	26,701	1,996	2.55	6.55	40.94	61.04	78,227
Northeast 东北	275	405	32,840	1,036	1.31	3.59	27.77	63.46	78,844
Liaoning 辽宁	152	364	25,617	-76	-0.11	-0.31	21.54	65.49	71,777
Jilin 吉林	54	405	44,720	3,751	4.17	11.09	41.12	62.39	89,975
Heilongjiang 黑龙江	69	498	39,454	1,359	1.59	4.02	29.28	60.59	85,699
Central-East 华东	1,306	334	45,783	1,979	2.75	7.15	41.74	61.51	71,867
Shanghai 上海	20	263	89,081	5,675	4.38	9.81	67.12	55.39	129,716
Jiangsu 江苏	249	363	52,350	1,688	2.19	5.60	39.40	60.95	77,143
Zhejiang 浙江	253	297	54,671	3,472	4.59	11.31	53.42	59.41	75,611
Anhui 安徽	152	328	38,477	3,717	3.89	9.08	43.45	57.14	95,502
Fujian 福建	182	164	18,972	-714	-1.83	-5.21	38.64	64.81	38,934
Jiangxi 江西	144	262	21,699	19	0.04	0.11	30.42	64.48	51,054
Shandong 山东	306	484	61,169	2,399	3.06	8.76	39.27	65.04	78,341
Central-South 中南	1,440	289	25,472	27	0.05	0.18	28.36	69.12	49,792
Henan 河南	282	369	24,414	824	1.62	5.02	25.75	67.74	50,837
Hubei 湖北	195	313	32,312	722	1.37	3.66	39.32	62.67	52,783
Hunan 湖南	310	277	16,579	-254	-0.85	-3.17	19.65	73.12	29,747
Guangdong 广东	432	236	31,832	-163	-0.27	-0.90	36.28	69.95	60,603
Guangxi 广西	202	288	19,249	-692	-1.44	-6.04	20.56	76.13	48,026
Hainan 海南	19	252	37,636	-2,388	-2.30	-4.49	27.33	48.62	103,590
Southwest 西南	765	298	20,752	334	0.81	2.42	26.07	66.36	40,980
Chongqing 重庆	132	307	23,302	117	0.27	1.17	28.67	76.78	43,060
Sichuan 四川	286	341	24,968	527	1.27	3.49	26.56	63.54	41,349
Guizhou 贵州	168	244	11,634	484	1.86	4.31	16.29	56.91	26,043
Yunnan 云南	166	272	20,166	-269	-0.51	-1.67	28.34	69.61	52,860
Tibet 西藏	13	312	27,444	4,047	7.63	14.45	61.77	47.22	53,051
Northwest 西北	361	338	24,870	1,766	2.80	8.19	28.24	65.76	63,011
Shaanxi 陕西	146	320	19,445	197	0.41	1.62	23.71	74.50	47,705
Gansu 甘肃	115	307	20,453	1,066	2.09	5.24	23.65	60.20	51,115
Qinghai 青海	20	344	29,158	2,134	4.38	12.33	33.80	64.48	48,726
Ningxia 宁夏	24	396	34,617	3,961	4.58	13.91	33.96	67.06	86,421
Xinjiang 新疆	56	418	42,373	6,224	5.08	13.18	40.28	61.43	122,415

3110: Cement 水泥制造业

Year 年份	Number of firms 企业个数	Rate of change 变化率(%)	Number of employees 职工人数(人)	Rate of change 变化率(%)	Total revenue (Mil. RMB) 总销售收入(百万元)	Rate of change 变化率(%)	Total profit (Mil RMB) 总利润(百万元)	Rate of change 变化率(%)
2000	4602		1,690,001		116,808		633	
2001	4621	0.41	1,560,164	-7.68	129,603	10.95	2,964	368.25
2002	4754	2.88	1,502,151	-3.72	147,871	14.10	4,653	56.98

Major Products 主要产品	Output 产量	Unit 单位
Cement 水泥	70,472	10,000 Tons 万吨

10 Main Firms with Maximal Revenue (year founded) 收入最大的十家主要企业(创办年份)	City 城市	Province 省	Telephone/fax 电话/传真	Number of employees 职工人数	Ownership 产业所有权	Revenue ('000 RMB) 销售收入(千元)	Profit('000 RMB) (rank) 利润(千元)(排名)	Total assets ('000 RMB) 总资产(千元)	Major products 主要产品
Ji'nan Shanshui Group Co., Ltd	Jinan	Shandong	(0531)8360186		State Enterprises				Cement
济南市山水集团有限公司(1997)	济南市	山东省	(0531)7800741	7,069	国有独资	1,546,020	98,940(6)	2,203,879	水泥
Tangshan Ji Dong Cement Co., Ltd.	Tangshan	Hebei	(0315)3241351		Joint Stock				Cement
唐山冀东水泥股份有限公司(1985)	唐山市	河北省	(0315)3245466	4,169	股份制	1,097,517	151,986(1)	3,345,416	水泥
Beijing Kingyu Group Co., Ltd.	Beijing	Beijing	(010)66416688		State Enterprises				Cement
北京金隅集团有限责任公司(1992)	北京市	北京市	(010)66412028	6,882	国有独资	1,060,773	53,467(14)	4,253,233	水泥
Zhejiang Jian Feng Group Co., Ltd.	Jinhua	Zhejiang	(0579)2326868		Joint Stock				Sillcate Cement
浙江尖峰集团股份有限公司(1958)	金华市	浙江省	(0579)2324666	3,760	股份制	1,057,912	48,741(18)	1,750,000	普硅水泥
Hua Xin Cement Co., Ltd.	Huangshi	Hubei	(0714)6328359		Joint Stock				Cement
华新水泥股份有限公司(1993)	黄石市	湖北省	(0714)6223053	3,246	股份制	815,707	34,776(33)	2,306,379	水泥
Shandong Yizhou Cement Group Co., Ltd.	Linyi	Shandong	(0539)8928017		State-owned				Sillcate Cement
山东沂州水泥集团总公司(1958)	临沂市	山东省	(0539)8928888	1,871	国有企业	716,776	33,032(35)	504,095	普硅水泥
Anhui Chaodong Cement Co., Ltd.	Chaohu	Anhui	(0565)2391918		Joint Stock				Cement
安徽巢东水泥股份有限公司(1999)	巢湖市	安徽省	(0565)2391918	3,176	股份制	694,506	27,413(45)	1,395,478	水泥
Jiangsu ShuangLong Group Co., Ltd.	Nanjing	Jiangsu	(025)3759259		State-owned				Cement
江苏双龙集团有限公司(1991)	南京市	江苏省	(025)3759200	587	国有企业	676,270	14,050(96)	1,155,650	水泥
Mudanjiang Cement Group Co., Ltd.	Mudanjiang	Heilongjiang	(0453)6497517		Limited-Liability				Cement
牡丹江水泥集团有限责任公司(1953)	牡丹江市	黑龙江省	(0453)6497515	6,686	有限公司	620,152	2,169(550)	1,400,589	水泥
Anhui Ningguo Cement Factory	Xuancheng	Anhui	(0563)4888405		State-owned				Cement
安徽省宁国水泥厂(1985)	宣城市	安徽省	(0563)4888588	1,574	国有企业	603,892	140,434(3)	1,569,324	水泥

Top 10 Cities by Revenue 销售收入排名前10位城市	Province 省	Market share 市场份额(%)	Number of firms 企业个数
Tangshan 唐山市	Hebei 河北省	2.78	105
Zaozhuang 枣庄市	Shandong 山东省	2.21	71
Guangzhou 广州市	Guangdong 广东省	2.14	93
Chongqing 重庆市	Chongqing 重庆市	2.08	132
Zibo 淄博市	Shandong 山东省	2.08	37
Huzhou 湖州市	Zhejiang 浙江省	1.89	53
Yantai 烟台市	Shandong 山东省	1.89	39
Beijing 北京市	Beijing 北京市	1.78	42
Jinan 济南市	Shandong 山东省	1.76	23
Nanjing 南京市	Jiangsu 江苏省	1.74	26

10 Major Wholesalers 十家主要批发商	City 城市	Province 省	Telephone/Fax 电话/传真
Xuzhou New Century Building Materials Decorative City	Xuzhou	Jiangsu	(0516)83666780
徐州市新世纪建材装饰城	徐州市	江苏省	(0516)63804485
Orienthome Co.,Ltd.	Beijing	Beijing	(010)63808294
东方家园有限公司	北京市	北京市	
Shanghai Jinkai Goods & Materials Co.,Ltd.	Shanghai	Shanghai	(021)52193967
上海金凯物资有限公司	上海市	上海市	
Guangzhou Building Materials Development Co.,Ltd.	Guangzhou	Guangdong	(020)83335062
广州市建材发展有限公司	广州市	广东省	(020)83341110
Guangxi Qiaofeng Goods & Materials Trade Co.,Ltd.	Nanning	Guangxi	(0771)2631539
广西侨丰物资贸易有限责任公司	南宁市	广西	(0771)2631539
Gansu Building Materials State-owned Assets Marketing Co.,Ltd.	Lanzhou	Gansu	(0931)8821359
甘肃建材国有资产经营有限责任公司	兰州市	甘肃省	(0931)8960243
Shanghai East Asia United Building Materials Co.,Ltd.	Shanghai	Shanghai	(021)33134520
上海东亚联合建材有限公司	上海市	上海市	(021)63216165
Shanghai Zhuzong Materials General Company	Shanghai	Shanghai	(021)32240030
上海住总物资总公司	上海市	上海市	(021)32240024
Guangdong Building Materials Company	Guangzhou	Guangdong	(020)83802713
广东省建材公司	广州市	广东省	(020)83817640
Guangdong Dongguan Hardware Minerals Import & Export Co.,Ltd	Dongguan	Guangdong	(0769)2227090
广东省东莞五金矿产进出口公司	东莞市	广东省	(0769)2221045

3121: Cement Products 水泥制品业

The industry accounts for 0.280% of the total revenue of China's industrial sector in 2002. The rate of return on assets is 3.56%. 80.11% of all firms in the industry made a profit while 19.89% had negative returns.The top province in terms of the industry's revenue is Guangdong, accounting for 14.70% of the total revenue.
2002年本行业收入占全行业的 0.280%，资产利润率为 3.56%。80.11%的企业赢利，19.89%的企业亏损。收入最高的省为广东省，占本行业的14.70%。

	Total number of firms 企业总数	Total number of employees 职工总数	Total revenue (Mil.RMB) 总销售收入（百万元）	Total profit (Mil.RMB) 总利润（百万元）	Return on assets 资产利润率（%）	Return on equity 权益利润率（%）	Labour productivity ('000 RMB/ worker) 劳动生产率（千元/人）	Debts/ assets 资产负债率（%）	Total assets (Mil.RMB) 总资产（百万元）
Industry Overall 行业总体	1242	185,932	30,009	1,407	3.56	9.33	51.46	61.83	39,513

	Number of firms 企业个数	Average number of employees 平均职工人数	Average revenue ('000 RMB) 平均销售收入（千元）	Average profit ('000 RMB) 平均利润（千元）	Return on assets 资产利润率（%）	Return on equity 权益利润率（%）	Labour productivity ('000 RMB/ worker) 劳动生产率（千元/人）	Debts/ assets 资产负债率（%）	Average total assets ('000 RMB) 平均总资产（千元）
By ownership 产业所有权									
State-owned 国有	273	180	14,084	-72	-0.25	-0.90	29.18	72.41	29,146
Collective-owned 集体	235	135	16,658	843	5.61	14.14	41.29	60.36	15,041
Foreign & Overseas Chinese Funded 三资	168	112	44,807	2,664	4.37	9.25	122.66	52.73	60,918
By regional distribution 地区分布									
Central-North 华北	193	176	25,279	1,139	2.89	7.38	57.50	60.82	39,418
Beijing 北京	71	210	39,946	2,120	3.50	9.30	70.15	62.33	60,506
Tianjin 天津	27	129	25,883	1,013	2.24	4.68	113.12	52.06	45,170
Hebei 河北	57	154	15,466	523	2.54	7.37	37.74	65.51	20,578
Shanxi 山西	25	196	13,268	347	1.21	2.65	23.63	54.18	28,620
Inner Mongolia 内蒙古	13	140	10,044	266	1.70	7.71	33.52	77.96	15,671
Northeast 东北	87	151	13,862	268	0.89	2.47	31.21	63.78	29,983
Liaoning 辽宁	45	135	17,504	808	2.43	5.62	42.96	56.80	33,244
Jilin 吉林	21	153	8,449	-188	-0.67	-3.19	17.43	79.11	28,182
Heilongjiang 黑龙江	21	183	11,471	-433	-1.75	-5.20	24.19	66.41	24,798
Central-East 华东	451	135	29,624	1,677	5.09	13.00	65.34	60.86	32,966
Shanghai 上海	73	105	47,390	3,110	5.15	14.06	131.86	63.36	60,372
Jiangsu 江苏	111	126	25,981	1,274	5.69	13.71	54.77	58.49	22,393
Zhejiang 浙江	86	150	38,102	2,842	7.00	19.46	71.90	64.03	40,597
Anhui 安徽	36	138	14,781	251	1.38	3.51	32.43	60.62	18,124
Fujian 福建	41	117	24,603	1,066	4.28	8.27	72.11	48.24	24,899
Jiangxi 江西	25	99	6,666	-129	-1.15	-3.07	29.25	62.41	11,138
Shandong 山东	79	180	25,733	1,190	3.71	9.16	49.43	59.46	32,045
Central-South 中南	316	135	22,502	690	2.37	6.50	45.98	63.52	29,120
Henan 河南	65	137	13,673	700	4.08	9.54	32.57	57.25	17,155
Hubei 湖北	66	153	15,168	698	4.04	8.98	41.11	55.04	17,288
Hunan 湖南	25	221	15,015	-236	-0.90	-2.60	21.20	65.32	26,151
Guangdong 广东	132	114	33,429	926	2.16	6.46	66.10	66.49	42,794
Guangxi 广西	22	128	15,517	1,098	5.22	12.26	46.40	57.41	21,036
Hainan 海南	6	59	15,263	-2,349	-7.81	-27.95	54.92	72.07	30,085
Southwest 西南	86	213	21,798	762	2.47	6.21	34.64	60.24	30,851
Chongqing 重庆	13	175	29,404	1,525	6.75	12.71	55.77	46.87	22,585
Sichuan 四川	37	284	29,079	1,363	3.64	8.59	32.98	57.64	37,462
Guizhou 贵州	14	215	14,381	-685	-2.80	-8.43	13.79	66.84	24,501
Yunnan 云南	15	153	13,776	347	0.89	2.95	49.37	69.93	39,146
Tibet 西藏	7	36	1,207	-50	-0.81	-1.63	27.77	50.45	6,191
Northwest 西北	109	155	14,485	1,138	4.82	13.41	36.98	64.06	23,615
Shaanxi 陕西	29	214	15,137	611	2.06	8.59	26.52	75.97	29,592
Gansu 甘肃	54	111	6,734	353	3.62	8.89	38.97	59.26	9,752
Qinghai 青海	5	166	11,302	256	1.27	5.28	27.43	75.88	20,098
Ningxia 宁夏	6	184	20,730	1,042	3.24	8.31	47.06	61.00	32,160
Xinjiang 新疆	15	184	39,689	5,315	8.90	19.69	55.06	54.80	59,723

Year 年份	Number of firms 企业个数	Rate of change 变化率 (%)	Number of employees 职工人数 (人)	Rate of change 变化率 (%)	Total revenue (Mil. RMB) 总销售收入 (百万元)	Rate of change 变化率 (%)	Total profit (Mil RMB) 总利润 (百万元)	Rate of change 变化率 (%)
2000	1165		196,856		22,862		913	
2001	1209	3.78	183,045	-7.02	25,249	10.44	1,085	18.84
2002	1242	2.73	185,932	1.58	30,009	18.85	1,407	29.68

Major Products 主要产品	Output 产量	Unit 单位
Cement Telegraph Pole 水泥电杆	465	10,000 Tons 万吨
Cement DrainPipe 水泥排水管	274	10,000 Tons 万吨

10 Main Firms with Maximal Revenue (year founded) 收入最大的十家主要企业（创办年份）	City 城市	Province 省	Telephone/fax 电话/传真	Number of employees 职工人数	Ownership 产业所有权	Revenue ('000 RMB) 销售收入 (千元)	Profit('000 RMB) (rank) 利润(千元) (排名)	Total assets ('000 RMB) 总资产 (千元)	Major products 主要产品
Ningbo Zhedong Building Materials Group Co., Ltd.	Ningbo	Zhejiang	(0574)88355026		Limited-Liability				Cement Waterpipe水
宁波浙东建材集团有限公司(1999)	宁波市	浙江省	(0574)88412229	1,682	有限公司	759,680	92,618(1)	497,920	泥输水管
Xinjiang West Construction Co., Ltd.	Urumqi	Xinjiang	(0991)8853229		Limited-Liability				Cement Products
新疆西部建设股份有限公司(2000)	乌鲁木齐市	新疆	(0991)8856806	421	有限公司	320,472	59,733(2)	294,298	水泥制品
Zhongshan Jianhua Pipe Pile Co., Ltd.	Zhongshan	Guangdong	(0760)2108661		Overseas Chinese-funded				Pipe Pile
中山建华管桩有限公司(1993)	中山市	广东省	(0760)2102325	585	港澳台资	317,179	3,348(133)	172,076	管桩
Rinker Materials (Tianjin) Concrete Industry Co., ltd.	Tianjin	Tianjin	(022)23119048		Foreign Funded				Prefabricated Mixing Concrete预
瑞科尔建筑材料（天津）混凝土工业有限公司(1994)	天津市	天津市	(022)23119885	443	外商投资	232,251	11,655(23)	318,931	拌混凝土
Jiangsu Shuanglong Group Co.Ltd.Shuanghou Concrete Brancl	Nanjing	Jiangsu	(025)6808827		Collective Owned				Concrete
江苏双龙集团有限公司双猴混凝土分公司(1997)	南京市	江苏省	(025)6808948	300	集体企业	219,130	7,990(39)	39,900	混凝土
China Railway Chengdu Bridge Factory	Chengdu	Sichuan	(028)82953030		State-owned				Concrete Bridge混
中铁成都桥梁工厂(1966)	成都市	四川省	(028)83601714	1,092	国有企业	200,690	350(470)	289,200	凝土桥梁
Shenzhen Hua Li Sheng Concrete Co., Ltd.	Shenzhen	Guangdong	(0755)26792886		Overseas Chinese-funded				Concrete
深圳华丽生混凝土有限公司(1999)	深圳市	广东省	(0755)26780614	230	港澳台资	185,694	7,402(48)	163,205	混凝土
San Hu Concrete Group Co., Ltd.	Wenzhou	Zhejiang	(0577)86554642		Private Owned				Concrete
三虎混凝土集团有限公司(1996)	温州市	浙江省	(0577)86554643	436	私营企业	174,155	18,516(8)	229,406	混凝土
Nanjing Hong Tian Concrete Co., Ltd.	Nanjing	Jiangsu	(025)5692973		Foreign Funded				Concrete
南京宏田混凝土有限公司(1996)	南京市	江苏省	(025)5692973	227	外商投资	168,760	22,390(4)	211,590	混凝土
Fengtai Bridge Factory	Beijing	Beijing	(010)63717563		State-owned				Sleeper
丰台桥梁工厂(1940)	北京市	北京市	(010)63726290	1,946	国有企业	165,563	-	318,958	轨枕

Top 10 Cities by Revenue 销售收入排名前10位城市	Province 省	Market share 市场份额 (%)	Number of firms 企业个数
Shanghai 上海市	Shanghai 上海市	11.53	73
Beijing 北京市	Beijing 北京市	9.45	71
Hangzhou 杭州市	Zhejiang 浙江省	4.22	38
Guangzhou 广州市	Guangdong 广东省	3.57	30
Ningbo 宁波市	Zhejiang 浙江省	3.42	10
Shenzhen 深圳市	Guangdong 广东省	3.04	15
Nanjing 南京市	Jiangsu 江苏省	2.93	14
Zhongshan 中山市	Guangdong 广东省	2.48	12
Tianjin 天津市	Tianjin 天津市	2.33	27
Foshan 佛山市	Guangdong 广东省	2.08	18

10 Major Wholesalers 十家主要批发商	City 城市	Province 省	Telephone/Fax 电话/传真
Xuzhou New Century Building Materials Decorative City	Xuzhou	Jiangsu	(0516)83666780
徐州市新世纪建材装饰城	徐州市	江苏省	(0516)63804485
Orienthome Co.,Ltd.	Beijing	Beijing	(010)63808294
东方家园有限公司	北京市	北京市	
Shanghai Jinkai Goods & Materials Co.,Ltd.	Shanghai	Shanghai	(021)52193967
上海金凯物资有限公司	上海市	上海市	
Guangzhou Building Materials Development Co.,Ltd.	Guangzhou	Guangdong	(020)83335062
广州市建材发展有限公司	广州市	广东省	(020)83341110
Guangxi Qiaofeng Goods & Materials Trade Co.,Ltd.	Nanning	Guangxi	(0771)2631539
广西侨丰物资贸易有限责任公司	南宁市	广西	(0771)2631539
Gansu Building Materials State-owned Assets Marketing Co.,Ltd.	Lanzhou	Gansu	(0931)8821359
甘肃建材国有资产经营有限责任公司	兰州市	甘肃省	(0931)8960243
Shanghai East Asia United Building Materials Co.,Ltd.	Shanghai	Shanghai	(021)33134520
上海东亚联合建材有限公司	上海市	上海市	(021)63216165
Shanghai Zhuzong Materials General Company	Shanghai	Shanghai	(021)32240030
上海住总物资总公司	上海市	上海市	(021)32240024
Guangdong Building Materials Company	Guangzhou	Guangdong	(020)83802713
广东省建材公司	广州市	广东省	(020)83817640
Guangdong Dongguan Hardware Minerals Import & Export Co.,Ltd	Dongguan	Guangdong	(0769)2227090
广东省东莞五金矿产进出口公司	东莞市	广东省	(0769)2221045

3123: Concrete Construction Member 混凝土结构构件制造业

The industry accounts for 0.089% of the total revenue of China's industrial sector in 2002. The rate of return on assets is 3.31%. 85.11% of all firms in the industry made a profit while 14.89% had negative returns.The top province in terms of the industry's revenue is Shanghai, accounting for 19.91% of the total revenue.
2002年本行业收入占全行业的0.089%，资产利润率为3.31%。85.11%的企业赢利，14.89%的企业亏损。收入最高的省为上海市，占本行业的19.91%。

	Total number of firms 企业总数	Total number of employees 职工总数	Total revenue (Mil.RMB) 总销售收入（百万元）	Total profit (Mil.RMB) 总利润（百万元）	Return on assets 资产利润率（%）	Return on equity 权益利润率（%）	Labour productivity ('000 RMB/ worker) 劳动生产率（千元/人）	Debts/ assets 资产负债率（%）	Total assets (Mil.RMB) 总资产（百万元）
Industry Overall 行业总体	423	61,564	9,530	407	3.31	9.47	48.34	65.02	12,296

	Number of firms 企业个数	Average number of employees 平均职工人数	Average revenue ('000 RMB) 平均销售收入（千元）	Average profit ('000 RMB) 平均利润（千元）	Return on assets 资产利润率（%）	Return on equity 权益利润率（%）	Labour productivity ('000 RMB/ worker) 劳动生产率（千元/人）	Debts/ assets 资产负债率（%）	Average total assets ('000 RMB) 平均总资产（千元）
By ownership 产业所有权									
State-owned 国有	73	149	19,464	-443	-0.96	-3.46	41.55	72.19	46,136
Collective-owned 集体	147	130	17,153	820	5.64	12.66	41.46	55.43	14,538
Foreign & Overseas Chinese Funded 三资	25	195	40,918	1,929	3.33	8.01	63.60	58.45	57,960
By regional distribution 地区分布									
Central-North 华北	62	174	19,595	682	1.60	4.11	32.75	61.07	42,576
Beijing 北京	24	258	32,421	1,369	2.23	7.70	37.54	71.05	61,393
Tianjin 天津	9	122	24,838	835	2.46	5.79	32.44	57.54	33,939
Hebei 河北	18	96	6,838	89	0.32	0.54	24.08	39.69	27,430
Shanxi 山西	6	196	7,620	-826	-2.46	-7.04	16.09	64.98	33,501
Inner Mongolia 内蒙古	5	114	8,891	1,050	3.16	5.10	41.79	37.93	33,210
Northeast 东北	37	112	8,401	-94	-0.49	-1.12	27.68	56.77	19,336
Liaoning 辽宁	19	112	7,316	-344	-1.73	-4.56	22.34	62.08	19,930
Jilin 吉林	9	122	12,478	283	1.76	4.23	38.06	58.46	16,101
Heilongjiang 黑龙江	9	100	6,616	57	0.27	0.49	27.65	45.00	21,317
Central-East 华东	143	172	35,885	1,871	4.35	13.76	62.10	68.42	43,047
Shanghai 上海	40	185	47,443	1,418	2.48	9.93	60.98	75.05	57,189
Jiangsu 江苏	39	148	24,239	537	2.32	8.01	47.71	71.04	23,140
Zhejiang 浙江	27	174	48,111	5,335	7.08	19.83	100.96	64.28	75,333
Anhui 安徽	5	142	14,098	1,219	12.03	21.09	29.96	42.93	10,131
Fujian 福建	4	129	29,914	1,202	2.74	13.87	84.42	80.22	43,800
Jiangxi 江西	4	101	5,478	47	0.17	0.28	17.15	40.76	28,011
Shandong 山东	24	209	32,397	1,449	5.86	13.61	49.72	56.97	24,742
Central-South 中南	118	147	21,123	769	4.56	12.89	48.31	64.65	16,862
Henan 河南	45	97	12,683	664	10.26	16.34	39.26	37.18	6,466
Hubei 湖北	40	157	16,784	680	9.11	20.12	48.04	54.73	7,466
Hunan 湖南	10	228	33,501	1,279	9.00	14.47	47.11	37.77	14,207
Guangdong 广东	21	192	38,560	420	0.77	3.43	55.02	77.63	54,703
Guangxi 广西	1	184	28,348	1,375	6.11	10.95	42.84	44.19	22,492
Hainan 海南	1	180	77,360	10,620	12.24	38.82	148.26	68.46	86,739
Southwest 西南	15	126	12,219	367	2.24	6.70	30.52	66.51	16,347
Chongqing 重庆	5	98	9,327	1,111	11.29	28.20	14.89	59.97	9,845
Sichuan 四川	4	161	27,487	672	1.85	4.28	37.30	56.73	36,307
Guizhou 贵州	3	191	6,871	-920	-5.88		11.11	102.09	15,636
Yunnan 云南	2	92	3,048	6	0.31	2.20	109.36	85.82	1,925
Tibet 西藏	1								
Northwest 西北	48	61	4,093	97	0.85	1.98	31.23	57.25	11,468
Shaanxi 陕西	4	140	14,622	172	0.39	1.34	30.84	71.13	44,615
Gansu 甘肃	37	53	2,489	-87	-1.58	-2.97	26.92	46.58	5,479
Qinghai 青海									
Ningxia 宁夏	4	49	1,723	-178	-1.47	-4.33	11.58	66.07	12,107
Xinjiang 新疆	3	70	13,005	2,630	6.53	13.36	90.82	51.14	40,292

3123: Concrete Construction Member 混凝土结构构件制造业

Year 年份	Number of firms 企业个数	Rate of change 变化率 (%)	Number of employees 职工人数 (人)	Rate of change 变化率 (%)	Total revenue (Mil. RMB) 总销售收入 (百万元)	Rate of change 变化率 (%)	Total profit (Mil RMB) 总利润 (百万元)	Rate of change 变化率 (%)
2000	477		69,324		7,612		257	
2001	437	-8.39	65,741	-5.17	8,763	15.12	428	66.54
2002	423	-3.20	61,564	-6.35	9,530	8.75	407	-4.91

Major Products 主要产品	Output 产量	Unit 单位
Cement Prefabricated Components 水泥预制构件	1,813	10,000 Stere 万立方米
Cement DrainPipe 水泥排水管	274	10,000 Tons 万吨

10 Main Firms with Maximal Revenue (year founded) 收入最大的十家主要企业（创办年份）	City 城市	Province 省	Telephone/fax 电话/传真	Number of employees 职工人数	Ownership 产业所有权	Revenue ('000 RMB) 销售收入 (千元)	Profit('000 RMB) (rank) 利润(千元) (排名)	Total assets ('000 RMB) 总资产 (千元)	Major products 主要产品
Shanghai Building Components Products Co. 上海市建筑构件制品有限公司(1993)	Shanghai 上海市	Shanghai 上海市	(021)65681817 (021)65671870	1,886	State-owned 国有企业	486,538	6,534(12)	727,990	Concrete Components混凝土构件
Baoye Group Co., Ltd. 宝业集团股份有限公司(1975)	Shaoxing 绍兴市	Zhejiang 浙江省	(0575)4069418 (0575)4069415	582	Limited-Liability 有限公司	467,524	111,787(1)	864,493	Drain Pipe 排水管
Beijing Fengtai Yushu Village Components Factory 北京市丰台区榆树庄构件厂(1980)	Beijing 北京市	Beijing 北京市	(010)83601669 (010)83601526	939	Collective-owned 集体企业	186,877	13,850(2)	243,049	Concrete Components混凝土构件
Shanghai Pudong New District Concrete Components Factory 上海浦东新区混凝土构件厂(1960)	Shanghai 上海市	Shanghai 上海市	(021)58551220 (021)58575298	118	Joint Stock 股份制	151,621	2,207(50)	79,205	Cement Prefabricated Member水泥预制构件
Hangzhou Building Components Company 杭州建筑构件有限公司(1982)	Hangzhou 杭州市	Zhejiang 浙江省	(0571)87076455 (0571)87076455	521	State-owned 国有企业	136,101	6,206(13)	171,535	Concrete Prefabricated Components混凝土预制构件
Tianjin Building Components Engineering Company 天津市建筑构件工程公司(1964)	Tianjin 天津市	Tianjin 天津市	(022)23382652 (022)23380298	456	State-owned 国有企业	112,127	1,001(105)	172,093	Cement Prefabricated Member水泥预制构件
Xishan No.3 Construction And Installation Project Co., Ltd. 无锡市锡山三建实业有限公司(1985)	Wuxi 无锡市	Jiangsu 江苏省	(0510)3791637 (0510)3792860	217	Private Owned 私营企业	108,900	1,350(87)	181,550	Concrete Structure Components砼结构构件
Jiangying Building Group Co., Ltd 江阳建设集团有限公司(1964)	Wuxi 无锡市	Jiangsu 江苏省	(0510)6287215 (0510)6286034	793	Joint Stock 股份制	107,491	11,065(5)	191,452	Prefabricated Components 预制构件
Shanghai Hongda Concrete Co., Ltd. 上海宏达混凝土有限公司(1997)	Shanghai 上海市	Shanghai 上海市	(021)64530968 (021)64530968	146	Limited-Liability 有限公司	105,101	5,244(16)	62,873	Commercial Concrete 商品砼
Nanjing Bo Ding Decorative Materials Co., Ltd. 南京博鼎装饰材料有限公司(1999)	Nanjing 南京市	Jiangsu 江苏省	(025)6801679	118	Private Owned 私营企业	100,610	3,740(26)	6,090	Rome-Style Pillar 罗马柱

Top 10 Cities by Revenue 销售收入排名前10位城市	Province 省	Market share 市场份额 (%)	Number of firms 企业个数
Shanghai 上海市	Shanghai 上海市	19.91	40
Beijing 北京市	Beijing 北京市	8.16	24
Shaoxing 绍兴市	Zhejiang 浙江省	5.34	3
Suizhou 随州市	Hubei 湖北省	4.42	20
Hangzhou 杭州市	Zhejiang 浙江省	4.26	8
Weihai 威海市	Shandong 山东省	3.94	5
Jiangmen 江门市	Guangdong 广东省	3.14	7
Hengyang 衡阳市	Hunan 湖南省	2.96	3
Guangzhou 广州市	Guangdong 广东省	2.86	8
Wuxi 无锡市	Jiangsu 江苏省	2.82	4

10 Major Wholesalers 十家主要批发商	City 城市	Province 省	Telephone/Fax 电话/传真
Xuzhou New Century Building Materials Decorative City 徐州市新世纪建材装饰城	Xuzhou 徐州市	Jiangsu 江苏省	(0516)83666780 (0516)63804485
Orienthome Co.,Ltd. 东方家园有限公司	Beijing 北京市	Beijing 北京市	(010)63808294
Shanghai Jinkai Goods & Materials Co.,Ltd. 上海金凯物资有限公司	Shanghai 上海市	Shanghai 上海市	(021)52193967
Guangzhou Building Materials Development Co.,Ltd. 广州市建材发展有限公司	Guangzhou 广州市	Guangdong 广东省	(020)83335062 (020)83341110
Guangxi Qiaofeng Goods & Materials Trade Co.,Ltd. 广西侨丰物资贸易有限责任公司	Nanning 南宁市	Guangxi 广西	(0771)2631539 (0771)2631539
Gansu Building Materials State-owned Assets Marketing Co.,Ltd. 甘肃建材国有资产经营有限责任公司	Lanzhou 兰州市	Gansu 甘肃省	(0931)8821359 (0931)8960243
Shanghai East Asia United Building Materials Co.,Ltd. 上海东亚联合建材有限公司	Shanghai 上海市	Shanghai 上海市	(021)33134520 (021)63216165
Shanghai Zhuzong Materials General Company 上海住总物资总公司	Shanghai 上海市	Shanghai 上海市	(021)32240030 (021)32240024
Guangdong Building Materials Company 广东省建材公司	Guangzhou 广州市	Guangdong 广东省	(020)83802713 (020)83817640
Guangdong Dongguan Hardware Minerals Import & Export Co.,Ltd 广东省东莞五金矿产进出口公司	Dongguan 东莞市	Guangdong 广东省	(0769)2227090 (0769)2221045

3124: Asbestos Cement Products 石棉水泥制品业

The industry accounts for 0.018% of the total revenue of China's industrial sector in 2002. The rate of return on assets is 6.05%. 75.86% of all firms in the industry made a profit while 24.14% had negative returns.The top province in terms of the industry's revenue is Henan, accounting for 45.85% of the total revenue.
2002年本行业收入占全行业的 0.018%，资产利润率为 6.05%。75.86%的企业赢利，24.14%的企业亏损。收入最高的省为河南省，占本行业的45.85%。

	Total number of firms 企业总数	Total number of employees 职工总数	Total revenue (Mil.RMB) 总销售收入（百万元）	Total profit (Mil.RMB) 总利润（百万元）	Return on assets 资产利润率（%）	Return on equity 权益利润率（%）	Labour productivity ('000 RMB/ worker) 劳动生产率（千元/人）	Debts/ assets 资产负债率（%）	Total assets (Mil.RMB) 总资产（百万元）
Industry Overall 行业总体	87	18,892	1,936	101	6.05	15.08	31.39	59.90	1,671

	Number of firms 企业个数	Average number of employees 平均职工人数	Average revenue ('000 RMB) 平均销售收入（千元）	Average profit ('000 RMB) 平均利润（千元）	Return on assets 资产利润率（%）	Return on equity 权益利润率（%）	Labour productivity ('000 RMB/ worker) 劳动生产率（千元/人）	Debts/ assets 资产负债率（%）	Average total assets ('000 RMB) 平均总资产（千元）
By ownership 产业所有权									
State-owned 国有	13	139	7,923	-950	-3.26	-37.61	12.33	91.33	29,139
Collective-owned 集体	26	237	34,239	2,765	21.78	46.53	45.33	53.19	12,693
Foreign & Overseas Chinese Funded 三资	3	225	32,464	462	0.89	1.57	48.61	43.39	52,090
By regional distribution 地区分布									
Central-North 华北	18	89	8,004	309	3.38	7.23	28.90	53.23	9,137
Beijing 北京	4	143	10,802	-354	-1.40	-3.23	28.81	56.75	25,301
Tianjin 天津	4	59	5,473	507	9.26	36.66	13.05	74.74	5,478
Hebei 河北	10	79	7,897	495	11.97	17.93	33.72	33.21	4,135
Shanxi 山西									
Inner Mongolia 内蒙古									
Northeast 东北	12	205	10,003	-206	-0.69	-4.05	15.87	82.87	29,675
Liaoning 辽宁	5	120	6,346	-944	-2.00	-89.97	22.40	97.78	47,185
Jilin 吉林	3	328	16,258	501	1.98	3.88	15.20	48.95	25,267
Heilongjiang 黑龙江	4	219	9,883	186	1.67	4.35	12.15	61.52	11,096
Central-East 华东	24	193	18,492	899	3.83	12.12	27.68	68.42	23,472
Shanghai 上海	4	43	21,439	879	3.62	6.54	108.94	44.64	24,280
Jiangsu 江苏	6	184	27,765	970	5.92	23.87	40.39	75.20	16,381
Zhejiang 浙江									
Anhui 安徽	4	149	3,421	127	1.62	4.15	6.41	60.88	7,820
Fujian 福建	1	336	29,767	-346	-0.46	-2.17	9.11	78.82	75,422
Jiangxi 江西	3	77	3,602	-134	-2.01		19.49	113.62	6,700
Shandong 山东	6	366	22,868	2,079	5.17	16.79	24.48	69.19	40,187
Central-South 中南	23	351	51,313	3,596	18.44	28.76	45.26	35.88	19,500
Henan 河南	13	383	68,270	6,139	57.34	103.24	56.38	44.46	10,707
Hubei 湖北	7	338	33,667	992	3.23	4.35	28.40	25.69	30,702
Hunan 湖南	1	401	28,114	37	0.10	0.19	23.66	49.09	37,807
Guangdong 广东	1	248	23,402	-4,121	-7.56	-13.49	28.38	43.94	54,499
Guangxi 广西	1	80	5,507	30	1.44	3.90	11.99	62.98	2,077
Hainan 海南									
Southwest 西南	4	376	7,430	-1,382	-7.13	-14.63	3.60	51.28	19,385
Chongqing 重庆									
Sichuan 四川									
Guizhou 贵州	1	110		-591	-5.46	-17.71	2.64	69.14	10,818
Yunnan 云南	3	465	9,907	-1,646	-7.40	-14.34	3.68	48.39	22,241
Tibet 西藏									
Northwest 西北	6	104	2,991	-123	-1.20	-2.54	14.08	52.68	10,208
Shaanxi 陕西	2	119	3,519	-147	-2.36	-7.22	10.42	67.29	6,200
Gansu 甘肃	3	42	348	-167	-3.31	-7.79	16.94	57.49	5,041
Qinghai 青海									
Ningxia 宁夏	1	263	9,865	57	0.17	0.31	16.02	45.16	33,727
Xinjiang 新疆									

3124: Asbestos Cement Products 石棉水泥制品业

Year 年份	Number of firms 企业个数	Rate of change 变化率 (%)	Number of employees 职工人数 (人)	Rate of change 变化率 (%)	Total revenue (Mil. RMB) 总销售收入 (百万元)	Rate of change 变化率 (%)	Total profit (Mil RMB) 总利润 (百万元)	Rate of change 变化率 (%)
2000	84		16,666		1,247		44	
2001	74	-11.90	17,142	2.86	1,402	12.43	63	43.18
2002	87	17.57	18,892	10.21	1,936	38.09	101	60.32

Major Products 主要产品	Output 产量	Unit 单位
Asbestos Cement Tile 石棉水泥瓦	17,936	10,000 Sq.M. 万平方米
Cement Prefabricated Components 水泥预制构件	1,813	10,000 Stere 万立方米

10 Main Firms with Maximal Revenue (year founded) 收入最大的十家主要企业（创办年份）	City 城市	Province 省	Telephone/fax 电话/传真	Number of employees 职工人数	Ownership 产业所有权	Revenue ('000 RMB) 销售收入 (千元)	Profit('000 RMB) (rank) 利润(千元) (排名)	Total assets ('000 RMB) 总资产 (千元)	Major products 主要产品
Henan Jianxi Building Materials Co.,Ltd 河南建喜建筑材料有限公司(1994)	Zhengzhou 郑州市	Henan 河南省	(0371)2522045 (0371)2521860	2,000	Collective-owned 集体企业	356,817	35,515(1)	34,710	Machine-made Tile 机制瓦
Dangyang Qunfeng Group Industrial Company 当阳市群丰集团实业公司(1979)	Yichang 宜昌市	Hubei 湖北省	(0717)3380251	1,600	Joint Stock 股份制	132,380	5200(6)	41,760	Asbestos Tile 石棉瓦
Xinzheng Shuanglong Machine-made Tile Factory 新郑市双龙机制瓦厂(1996)	Zhengzhou 郑州市	Henan 河南省	(0371)2522064 (0371)2521752	580	Collective-owned 集体企业	132,461	13,609(2)	13,848	Machine-made Tile 机制瓦
Hubei Xishui Shiyue Mount Paper Industry Group Co., Ltd. 湖北浠水十月装帧纸业集团股份有限公司(1987)	Huanggang 黄冈市	Hubei 湖北省	(0713)4225543 (0713)4232828	269	Joint Stock 股份制	66,193	984(22)	124,638	PVC Bind Paper.PVC 装帧纸
Qingdao Yuanding Non-metal Products Co., Ltd. 青岛元鼎非金属制品有限责任公司(1980)	Qingdao 青岛市	Shandong 山东省	(0532)5622568 (0532)5622568	701	Limited-Liability 有限公司	59,893	8,186(3)	136,240	Vinylon Cement Cable Pipe维纶水泥电缆管
Nanjing Yuli Asbestos Products Factory 南京宇力石棉制品厂(1993)	Nanjing 南京市	Jiangsu 江苏省	(025)7443001 (025)7443001	277	Private Partnership 私营合伙	58,970	1,590(16)	14,560	Asbestos Tile 石棉瓦
Henan Xinzheng Jinxing Cement Machine-made Tile Factory 河南省新郑市金星水泥机制瓦厂(2000)	Zhengzhou 郑州市	Henan 河南省	(0371)2663399 (0371)2663369	150	Private Enterprises 私营独资	55,710	1,058(20)	2,990	Cement Machine-made Tile水泥机制瓦
Xinzheng Guifa Building Materials Factory 新郑市贵发建材厂(1996)	Zhengzhou 郑州市	Henan 河南省	(0371)2522196 (0371)2523888	185	Collective-owned 集体企业	47,987	5,276(5)	6,978	Asbestos Tile 石棉瓦
Yantai Shichuan Sealing Chair Plate Co., Ltd. 烟台石川密封垫板有限公司(1991)	Yantai 烟台市	Shandong 山东省	(0535)6531648 (0535)6536245	545	Foreign Funded 外商投资	45,536	684(25)	67,648	Asbestos Products 石棉制品
Jiaozuo Fuxing Building Materials Factory 焦作市福星建筑材料厂(1993)	Jiaozuo 焦作市	Henan 河南省	(0391)8810982	144	Collective-owned 集体企业	38,490	2,840(10)	5,950	Cement Tile水泥小波瓦

Top 10 Cities by Revenue 销售收入排名前10位城市	Province 省	Market share 市场份额 (%)	Number of firms 企业个数
Zhengzhou 郑州市	Henan 河南省	40.15	10
Yichang 宜昌市	Hubei 湖北省	6.84	1
Shanghai 上海市	Shanghai 上海市	4.43	4
Tangshan 唐山市	Hebei 河北省	3.90	9
Qingdao 青岛市	Shandong 山东省	3.60	2
Huanggang 黄冈市	Hubei 湖北省	3.42	1
Nanjing 南京市	Jiangsu 江苏省	3.40	2
Luohe 漯河市	Henan 河南省	3.23	1
Taizhou 泰州市	Jiangsu 江苏省	2.89	2
Yantai 烟台市	Shandong 山东省	2.69	2

10 Major Wholesalers 十家主要批发商	City 城市	Province 省	Telephone/Fax 电话/传真
Xuzhou New Century Building Materials Decorative City 徐州市新世纪建材装饰城	Xuzhou 徐州市	Jiangsu 江苏省	(0516)83666780 (0516)63804485
Orienthome Co.,Ltd. 东方家园有限公司	Beijing 北京市	Beijing 北京市	(010)63808294
Shanghai Jinkai Goods & Materials Co.,Ltd. 上海金凯物资有限公司	Shanghai 上海市	Shanghai 上海市	(021)52193967
Guangzhou Building Materials Development Co.,Ltd. 广州市建材发展有限公司	Guangzhou 广州市	Guangdong 广东省	(020)83335062 (020)83341110
Guangxi Qiaofeng Goods & Materials Trade Co.,Ltd. 广西侨丰物资贸易有限责任公司	Nanning 南宁市	Guangxi 广西	(0771)2631539 (0771)2631539
Gansu Building Materials State-owned Assets Marketing Co.,Ltd. 甘肃建材国有资产经营有限责任公司	Lanzhou 兰州市	Gansu 甘肃省	(0931)8821359 (0931)8960243
Shanghai East Asia United Building Materials Co.,Ltd. 上海东亚联合建材有限公司	Shanghai 上海市	Shanghai 上海市	(021)33134520 (021)63216165
Shanghai Zhuzong Materials General Company 上海住总物资总公司	Shanghai 上海市	Shanghai 上海市	(021)32240030 (021)32240024
Guangdong Building Materials Company 广东省建材公司	Guangzhou 广州市	Guangdong 广东省	(020)83802713 (020)83817640
Guangdong Dongguan Hardware Minerals Import & Export Co.,Ltd 广东省东莞五金矿产进出口公司	Dongguan 东莞市	Guangdong 广东省	(0769)2227090 (0769)2221045

3129: Other Cement and Asbestos Products 其他水泥制品业

The industry accounts for 0.008% of the total revenue of China's industrial sector in 2002. The rate of return on assets is 3.66%. 80.00% of all firms in the industry made a profit while 20.00% had negative returns.The top province in terms of the industry's revenue is Guangdong, accounting for 38.42% of the total revenue.
2002年本行业收入占全行业的 0.008%，资产利润率为 3.66%。80.00%的企业赢利，20.00%的企业亏损。收入最高的省为广东省，占本行业的38.42%。

	Total number of firms 企业总数	Total number of employees 职工总数	Total revenue (Mil.RMB) 总销售收入（百万元）	Total profit (Mil.RMB) 总利润（百万元）	Return on assets 资产利润率 (%)	Return on equity 权益利润率 (%)	Labour productivity ('000 RMB/ worker) 劳动生产率（千元/人）	Debts/ assets 资产负债率 (%)	Total assets (Mil.RMB) 总资产（百万元）
Industry Overall 行业总体	35	4,757	852	25	3.66	7.67	57.20	52.29	685

	Number of firms 企业个数	Average number of employees 平均职工人数	Average revenue ('000 RMB) 平均销售收入（千元）	Average profit ('000 RMB) 平均利润（千元）	Return on assets 资产利润率 (%)	Return on equity 权益利润率 (%)	Labour productivity ('000 RMB/ worker) 劳动生产率（千元/人）	Debts/ assets 资产负债率 (%)	Average total assets ('000 RMB) 平均总资产（千元）
By ownership 产业所有权									
State-owned 国有	2	49	11,451	-316	-2.94	-9.83	138.91	70.14	10,744
Collective-owned 集体	11	200	30,391	1,261	6.88	15.36	43.50	55.20	18,325
Foreign & Overseas Chinese Funded 三资	7	135	33,933	772	2.60	4.10	82.05	36.61	29,661
By regional distribution 地区分布									
Central-North 华北	8	107	13,894	267	3.01	8.45	59.98	64.35	8,877
Beijing 北京	4	84	18,266	517	3.96	15.77	120.12	74.89	13,044
Tianjin 天津	2	65	6,487	-131	-16.27	-19.26	7.95	15.53	805
Hebei 河北	1	106	5,827	203	2.41	2.43	29.88	0.95	8,440
Shanxi 山西	1	286	19,287	131	1.49	5.25	24.55	71.63	8,790
Inner Mongolia 内蒙古									
Northeast 东北									
Liaoning 辽宁									
Jilin 吉林									
Heilongjiang 黑龙江									
Central-East 华东	12	123	25,473	614	2.74	5.49	56.01	50.08	22,407
Shanghai 上海	6	47	12,219	-120	-0.66	-1.11	78.00	40.49	18,145
Jiangsu 江苏	2	196	83,340	3,515	10.16	18.64	103.75	45.49	34,600
Zhejiang 浙江									
Anhui 安徽									
Fujian 福建									
Jiangxi 江西									
Shandong 山东	4	199	16,420	266	1.17	3.35	24.70	65.07	22,703
Central-South 中南	11	180	37,703	1,366	4.94	9.63	66.44	48.67	27,643
Henan 河南	1	670	61,100	5,180	128.57	179.92	26.07	28.54	4,029
Hubei 湖北	2	129	13,208	225	2.26	7.85	37.63	71.25	9,972
Hunan 湖南									
Guangdong 广东	8	132	40,902	1,175	3.36	6.37	99.18	47.35	35,013
Guangxi 广西									
Hainan 海南									
Southwest 西南	3	111	6,325	41	0.35	1.50	16.52	76.67	11,822
Chongqing 重庆	1	163	6,207	-10	-0.09	-0.18	17.38	51.13	11,259
Sichuan 四川									
Guizhou 贵州									
Yunnan 云南	1	170	12,768	134	0.55	4.83	15.69	88.54	24,206
Tibet 西藏	1								
Northwest 西北	1	114	1,135	386	7.47	14.30	10.06	47.76	5,167
Shaanxi 陕西									
Gansu 甘肃	1	114	1,135	386	7.47	14.30	10.06	47.76	5,167
Qinghai 青海									
Ningxia 宁夏									
Xinjiang 新疆									

3129: Other Cement and Asbestos Products 其他水泥制品业

Year 年份	Number of firms 企业个数	Rate of change 变化率(%)	Number of employees 职工人数(人)	Rate of change 变化率(%)	Total revenue (Mil. RMB) 总销售收入(百万元)	Rate of change 变化率(%)	Total profit (Mil RMB) 总利润(百万元)	Rate of change 变化率(%)
2000	31		3,848		480		26	
2001	31	0	4,678	21.57	523	8.96	18	-30.77
2002	35	12.90	4,757	1.69	852	62.91	25	38.89

Major Products 主要产品	Output 产量	Unit 单位
Air Entraining Concrete 加气混凝土	932	10,000 Stere 万立方米

10 Main Firms with Maximal Revenue (year founded) 收入最大的十家主要企业（创办年份）	City 城市	Province 省	Telephone/fax 电话/传真	Number of employees 职工人数	Ownership 产业所有权	Revenue ('000 RMB) 销售收入(千元)	Profit('000 RMB) (rank) 利润(千元)(排名)	Total assets ('000 RMB) 总资产(千元)	Major products 主要产品
Jiangning Roads Construction Materials Factory 江宁县道路建设材料厂(1995)	Nanjing 南京市	Jiangsu 江苏省	(025)2183901 (025)6630885	270	Collective-owned 集体企业	144,310	6,580(1)	66,930	Road Mending Materials路面修补材料
Zhongshan Xin Jian Hua Pipe Pile Co., Ltd. 中山市新建华管桩有限公司(2000)	Zhongshan 中山市	Guangdong 广东省	(0760)5578860 (0760)5578860	320	Overseas Chinese-funded 港澳台资	110,918	950(8)	61,381	Pipe Pile 管桩
Guangzhou Eternit Co., Ltd. 广州埃特尼特有限公司(1987)	Guangzhou 广州市	Guangdong 广东省	(020)81587551 (020)81803536	273	Foreign Funded 外商投资	74,508	4,926(3)	60,812	Fiber Cement Tile纤维水泥瓦
Shandong Pingyuan Building Materials General Factory 山东省平原县建筑材料总厂(1970)	Dezhou 德州市	Shandong 山东省	(0534)4211260 (0534)4211260	450	Collective-owned 集体企业	45,737	257(14)	46,579	Cement 水泥
Shanghai San Yi Concrete Co., Ltd. 上海三依混凝土有限公司(1994)	Shanghai 上海市	Shanghai 上海市	(021)57637171 (021)57637285	69	Limited-Liability 有限公司	30,833	661(11)	33,978	Coment Products 水泥制品
Guangzhou Economic & Technology Development Zone Nanwei Building Materials Co.,Ltd.广州经济技术开发区南围建材有限公司(2000)	Guangzhou 广州市	Guangdong 广东省	(020)82098084 (020)82098186	47	Overseas Chinese-funded 港澳台资	29,732	1,109(7)	25,216	Concrete 混凝土
Guangzhou Tianhe Dong Pu Mixing Station 广州市天河区东圃搅拌站(1988)	Guangzhou 广州市	Guangdong 广东省	(020)82590292 (020)82591197	68	Collective-owned 集体企业	27,780	171(20)	26,010	Cement Concrete Processing水泥混凝加工
Beijing Xinzhuang Hui Qiang Additive Co., Ltd. 北京辛庄汇强外加剂有限责任公司(1985)	Beijing 北京市	Beijing 北京市	(010)83873545 (010)83873545	167	Limited-Liability 有限公司	25,806	1,346(6)	15,658	Cement Additive水泥外加剂
Beijing Joint Rong Da Engineering Material Co., Ltd. 北京联合荣大工程材料有限责任公司(1996)	Beijing 北京市	Beijing 北京市	(010)61681444 (010)61683157	70	Private Owned 私营企业	20,322	-	8,487	Wash Annotate Material 洗注料
Beijing Zhong Yan Special Engineering Materials Corp. 北京中岩特种工程材料公司(1993)	Beijing 北京市	Beijing 北京市	(010)51167788 (010)65721721	54	State-owned 国有企业	15,662	-	14,675	Cement Additive水泥外加剂

Top 10 Cities by Revenue 销售收入排名前10位城市	Province 省	Market share 市场份额(%)	Number of firms 企业个数
Guangzhou 广州市	Guangdong 广东省	25.40	7
Nanjing 南京市	Jiangsu 江苏省	19.57	2
Zhongshan 中山市	Guangdong 广东省	13.02	1
Shanghai 上海市	Shanghai 上海市	8.61	6
Beijing 北京市	Beijing 北京市	8.58	4
Kaifeng 开封市	Henan 河南省	7.17	1
Dezhou 德州市	Shandong 山东省	5.37	1
Linfen 临汾市	Shanxi 山西省	2.26	1
Suizhou 随州市	Hubei 湖北省	1.62	1
Tianjin 天津市	Tianjin 天津市	1.52	2

10 Major Wholesalers 十家主要批发商	City 城市	Province 省	Telephone/Fax 电话/传真
Xuzhou New Century Building Materials Decorative City 徐州市新世纪建材装饰城	Xuzhou 徐州市	Jiangsu 江苏省	(0516)83666780 (0516)63804485
Orienthome Co.,Ltd. 东方家园有限公司	Beijing 北京市	Beijing 北京市	(010)63808294
Shanghai Jinkai Goods & Materials Co.,Ltd. 上海金凯物资有限公司	Shanghai 上海市	Shanghai 上海市	(021)52193967
Guangzhou Building Materials Development Co.,Ltd. 广州市建材发展有限公司	Guangzhou 广州市	Guangdong 广东省	(020)83335062 (020)83341110
Guangxi Qiaofeng Goods & Materials Trade Co.,Ltd. 广西侨丰物资贸易有限责任公司	Nanning 南宁市	Guangxi 广西	(0771)2631539 (0771)2631539
Gansu Building Materials State-owned Assets Marketing Co.,Ltd. 甘肃建材国有资产经营有限责任公司	Lanzhou 兰州市	Gansu 甘肃省	(0931)8821359 (0931)8960243
Shanghai East Asia United Building Materials Co.,Ltd. 上海东亚联合建材有限公司	Shanghai 上海市	Shanghai 上海市	(021)33134520 (021)63216165
Shanghai Zhuzong Materials General Company 上海住总物资总公司	Shanghai 上海市	Shanghai 上海市	(021)32240030 (021)32240024
Guangdong Building Materials Company 广东省建材公司	Guangzhou 广州市	Guangdong 广东省	(020)83802713 (020)83817640
Guangdong Dongguan Hardware Minerals Import & Export Co.,Ltd 广东省东莞五金矿产进出口公司	Dongguan 东莞市	Guangdong 广东省	(0769)2227090 (0769)2221045

3131: Brick and Tile 砖瓦制造业

The industry accounts for 0.127% of the total revenue of China's industrial sector in 2002. The rate of return on assets is 4.41%. 85.91% of all firms in the industry made a profit while 14.09% had negative returns.The top province in terms of the industry's revenue is Hubei, accounting for 13.44% of the total revenue.
2002年本行业收入占全行业的0.127%，资产利润率为4.41%。85.91%的企业赢利，14.09%的企业亏损。收入最高的省为湖北省，占本行业的13.44%。

	Total number of firms 企业总数	Total number of employees 职工总数	Total revenue (Mil.RMB) 总销售收入(百万元)	Total profit (Mil.RMB) 总利润(百万元)	Return on assets 资产利润率(%)	Return on equity 权益利润率(%)	Labour productivity ('000 RMB/worker) 劳动生产率(千元/人)	Debts/assets 资产负债率(%)	Total assets (Mil.RMB) 总资产(百万元)
Industry Overall 行业总体	1384	277,688	13,636	598	4.41	10.42	17.45	57.68	13,562

	Number of firms 企业个数	Average number of employees 平均职工人数	Average revenue ('000 RMB) 平均销售收入(千元)	Average profit ('000 RMB) 平均利润(千元)	Return on assets 资产利润率(%)	Return on equity 权益利润率(%)	Labour productivity ('000 RMB/worker) 劳动生产率(千元/人)	Debts/assets 资产负债率(%)	Average total assets ('000 RMB) 平均总资产(千元)
By ownership 产业所有权									
State-owned 国有	345	179	3,638	-82	-0.57	-1.44	7.83	60.09	14,230
Collective-owned 集体	530	197	11,702	618	10.76	22.48	20.35	52.14	5,739
Foreign & Overseas Chinese Funded 三资	19	94	15,108	-62	-0.13	-0.74	46.30	82.31	47,376
By regional distribution 地区分布									
Central-North 华北	171	226	9,494	590	4.06	8.32	16.59	51.21	14,553
Beijing 北京	34	183	9,275	678	4.83	10.59	22.04	54.41	14,047
Tianjin 天津	35	160	7,877	738	3.51	5.49	18.26	36.01	21,010
Hebei 河北	71	277	11,413	630	6.38	15.76	15.58	59.50	9,866
Shanxi 山西	17	272	8,366	316	1.53	4.66	13.70	67.17	20,662
Inner Mongolia 内蒙古	14	177	5,707	145	0.91	1.60	12.62	43.36	15,992
Northeast 东北	116	179	8,574	137	1.04	3.77	17.08	72.44	13,198
Liaoning 辽宁	32	114	9,493	40	0.26	6.19	9.32	95.85	15,408
Jilin 吉林	46	177	8,111	170	1.82	3.79	22.90	51.91	9,322
Heilongjiang 黑龙江	38	236	8,361	179	1.12	3.49	14.98	67.95	16,031
Central-East 华东	356	202	12,148	638	6.21	14.99	19.27	58.61	10,283
Shanghai 上海	5	60	12,475	-932	-4.21		40.13	105.27	22,148
Jiangsu 江苏	138	207	12,848	354	3.29	8.54	16.75	61.47	10,753
Zhejiang 浙江	80	219	11,065	1,142	14.01	39.09	20.72	64.16	8,152
Anhui 安徽	39	266	8,417	115	0.85	1.80	12.30	52.62	13,449
Fujian 福建	10	61	6,306	151	3.63	10.24	32.08	64.58	4,155
Jiangxi 江西	26	119	5,074	174	2.82	8.08	12.20	65.09	6,158
Shandong 山东	58	196	18,637	1,399	11.80	20.47	30.45	42.36	11,856
Central-South 中南	424	227	13,091	523	6.34	14.02	20.56	54.73	8,241
Henan 河南	111	382	16,445	1,022	11.73	22.00	14.33	46.70	8,717
Hubei 湖北	156	204	11,748	394	4.66	12.77	25.85	63.53	8,449
Hunan 湖南	55	214	16,684	371	6.67	15.87	21.57	57.96	5,564
Guangdong 广东	74	95	12,253	414	5.84	11.81	38.51	50.55	7,090
Guangxi 广西	23	113	2,333	-92	-0.84	-1.80	6.00	53.24	10,921
Hainan 海南	5	146	2,886	-418	-1.65	-2.62	14.51	36.91	25,327
Southwest 西南	82	243	7,290	155	0.98	2.29	9.93	57.15	15,797
Chongqing 重庆	24	218	7,056	290	1.37	2.57	11.61	46.59	21,132
Sichuan 四川	26	412	13,469	273	1.15	3.28	10.88	64.84	23,636
Guizhou 贵州	20	170	3,540	36	0.54	1.28	5.39	57.59	6,736
Yunnan 云南	10	53	660	-214	-5.87	-23.12	4.01	74.59	3,643
Tibet 西藏	2	26	440	36	2.89	4.25	0.92	32.06	1,248
Northwest 西北	235	129	2,320	82	1.77	4.28	9.49	58.70	4,648
Shaanxi 陕西	14	194	2,321	-117	-0.91	-8.83	5.07	89.73	12,893
Gansu 甘肃	203	122	2,178	92	2.70	5.59	9.85	51.76	3,398
Qinghai 青海	10	211	4,452	174	1.24	3.18	8.85	61.04	14,019
Ningxia 宁夏	2	70	2,871	177	4.17	8.69	12.26	52.00	4,233
Xinjiang 新疆	6	106	3,388	38	0.31	0.55	15.76	43.93	12,233

3131: Brick and Tile 砖瓦制造业

Year 年份	Number of firms 企业个数	Rate of change 变化率 (%)	Number of employees 职工人数 (人)	Rate of change 变化率 (%)	Total revenue (Mil. RMB) 总销售收入 (百万元)	Rate of change 变化率 (%)	Total profit (Mil RMB) 总利润 (百万元)	Rate of change 变化率 (%)
2000	1620		322,969		14,137		457	
2001	1449	-10.56	280,029	-13.30	12,981	-8.18	508	11.16
2002	1384	-4.49	277,688	-0.84	13,636	5.05	598	17.72

Major Products 主要产品	Output 产量	Unit 单位
Brick 砖（折标准砖）	1,159	100,000,000 Blocks 亿块
Tile 瓦	84	100,000,000 Pieces 亿片

10 Main Firms with Maximal Revenue (year founded) 收入最大的十家主要企业（创办年份）	City 城市	Province 省	Telephone/fax 电话/传真	Number of employees 职工人数	Ownership 产业所有权	Revenue ('000 RMB) 销售收入 (千元)	Profit('000 RMB) (rank) 利润(千元) (排名)	Total assets ('000 RMB) 总资产 (千元)	Major products 主要产品
Baiyin Xingchuan Co., Ltd. 白银兴川有限责任公司	Baiyin 白银市	Gansu 甘肃省	(0943)6622252		Collective-owned 集体企业	110,030	5680(14)	107,037	Brick 砖
Miluo Brick & Tile Building Materials Group Company 汨罗市汨罗砖瓦建材集团公司(1999)	Yueyang 岳阳市	Hunan 湖南省	(0730)5130085	1,200	Collective-owned 集体企业	200,000	4,370(22)	10,530	Red Brick 红砖
Wendeng Kou Zi Building Materials Factory 文登市口子建材厂(1994)	Weihai 威海市	Shandong 山东省	(0631)8631038	160	Collective-owned 集体企业	159,230	17,400(1)	24,710	Brick 砖
Huarong County Tashiyi Town Building Materials Factory 华容县塔市驿镇建材厂(1978)	Yueyang 岳阳市	Hunan 湖南省	(0730)4420026	620	Collective-owned 集体企业	121,380	1,020(166)	8,360	Brick & Tile 砖瓦
Ningbo Blue Sky Color Steel Plate Co., Ltd. 宁波蓝天彩钢板有限公司(2000)	Ningbo 宁波市	Zhejiang 浙江省	(0574)65186999 (0574)65186999	117	Private Owned 私营企业	118,871	4,003(24)	46,751	Building Steel Tile 建筑钢瓦
Linying Wa Dian Building Materials Group Company 临颍县瓦店建材集团公司(2001)	Luohe 漯河市	Henan 河南省	(0395)8438285 (0395)8882486	33	Private Partnership 私营合伙	80,245	2,045(68)	72,156	Building Materials 建筑材料
Shangcai Wolonggang Building Materials General Company 上蔡县卧龙岗建材总公司(2001)	Zhumadian 驻马店市	Henan 河南省	(0396)6920364	2,546	Private Owned 私营企业	79,792	7,810(8)	18,000	Red Brick 红砖
Hubei Baoshan (Group) Industrial Co., Ltd 湖北宝山（集团）实业有限公司	Jingmen 荆门市	Hubei 湖北省	(0724)2211804 (0724)2211117	429	Collective-owned 集体企业	75,161	4,460(20)	19,183	Floor Brick 地面砖
Shuangyashan Oriental Industrial Company 双鸭山东方工业公司(1994)	Shuangyashan 双鸭山市	Heilongjiang 黑龙江省	(0469)4224163 (0469)4226504	763	Joint Stock 股份制	70,811	8,335(7)	221,210	Brick Machine 制砖机
Jinxiang Chemical and Construction Group Co., Ltd 通州市金翔化建集团有限公司(1975)	Nantong 南通市	Jiangsu 江苏省	(0513)2591165 (0513)2591165	418	Limited-Liability 有限公司	67,200	1,550(101)	28,010	Standard Brick 标准砖

Top 10 Cities by Revenue 销售收入排名前10位城市	Province 省	Market share 市场份额 (%)	Number of firms 企业个数
Zhumadian 驻马店市	Henan 河南省	5.17	30
Yueyang 岳阳市	Hunan 湖南省	4.98	25
Yancheng 盐城市	Jiangsu 江苏省	4.45	39
Jiaxing 嘉兴市	Zhejiang 浙江省	4.17	58
Suizhou 随州市	Hubei 湖北省	3.64	27
Luohe 漯河市	Henan 河南省	2.93	10
Huanggang 黄冈市	Hubei 湖北省	2.65	32
Zhaoqing 肇庆市	Guangdong 广东省	2.64	29
Langfang 廊坊市	Hebei 河北省	2.45	14
Beijing 北京市	Beijing 北京市	2.31	34

10 Major Wholesalers 十家主要批发商	City 城市	Province 省	Telephone/Fax 电话/传真
Xuzhou New Century Building Materials Decorative City 徐州市新世纪建材装饰城	Xuzhou 徐州市	Jiangsu 江苏省	(0516)83666780 (0516)63804485
Orienthome Co.,Ltd. 东方家园有限公司	Beijing 北京市	Beijing 北京市	(010)63808294
Shanghai Jinkai Goods & Materials Co.,Ltd. 上海金凯物资有限公司	Shanghai 上海市	Shanghai 上海市	(021)52193967
Guangzhou Building Materials Development Co.,Ltd. 广州市建材发展有限公司	Guangzhou 广州市	Guangdong 广东省	(020)83335062 (020)83341110
Guangxi Qiaofeng Goods & Materials Trade Co.,Ltd. 广西侨丰物资贸易有限责任公司	Nanning 南宁市	Guangxi 广西	(0771)2631539 (0771)2631539
Gansu Building Materials State-owned Assets Marketing Co.,Ltd. 甘肃建材国有资产经营有限责任公司	Lanzhou 兰州市	Gansu 甘肃省	(0931)8821359 (0931)8960243
Shanghai East Asia United Building Materials Co.,Ltd. 上海东亚联合建材有限公司	Shanghai 上海市	Shanghai 上海市	(021)33134520 (021)63216165
Shanghai Zhuzong Materials General Company 上海住总物资总公司	Shanghai 上海市	Shanghai 上海市	(021)32240030 (021)32240024
Guangdong Building Materials Company 广东省建材公司	Guangzhou 广州市	Guangdong 广东省	(020)83802713 (020)83817640
Guangdong Dongguan Hardware Minerals Import & Export Co.,Ltd 广东省东莞五金矿产进出口公司	Dongguan 东莞市	Guangdong 广东省	(0769)2227090 (0769)2221045

3132: Lime 石灰制造业

The industry accounts for 0.026% of the total revenue of China's industrial sector in 2002. The rate of return on assets is 1.04%. 85.03% of all firms in the industry made a profit while 14.97% had negative returns.The top province in terms of the industry's revenue is Shandong, accounting for 21.63% of the total revenue.
2002年本行业收入占全行业的 0.026%，资产利润率为 1.04%。85.03%的企业赢利，14.97%的企业亏损。收入最高的省为山东省，占本行业的21.63%。

	Total number of firms 企业总数	Total number of employees 职工总数	Total revenue (Mil.RMB) 总销售收入 (百万元)	Total profit (Mil.RMB) 总利润 (百万元)	Return on assets 资产利润率 (%)	Return on equity 权益利润率 (%)	Labour productivity ('000 RMB/ worker) 劳动生产率 (千元/人)	Debts/ assets 资产负债率 (%)	Total assets (Mil.RMB) 总资产 (百万元)
Industry Overall 行业总体	147	26,196	2,792	47	1.04	3.90	33.85	73.47	4,501

	Number of firms 企业个数	Average number of employees 平均职工人数	Average revenue ('000 RMB) 平均销售收入（千元）	Average profit ('000 RMB) 平均利润 (千元)	Return on assets 资产利润率 (%)	Return on equity 权益利润率 (%)	Labour productivity ('000 RMB/ worker) 劳动生产率 (千元/人)	Debts/ assets 资产负债率 (%)	Average total assets ('000 RMB) 平均总资产 (千元)
By ownership 产业所有权									
State-owned 国有	26	285	15,437	-1,339	-2.75		17.17	130.87	48,716
Collective-owned 集体	49	171	17,842	908	11.42	24.36	33.44	53.13	7,954
Foreign & Overseas Chinese Funded 三资	3	144	75,844	-5,676	-1.01	-1.93	221.85	47.59	560,844
By regional distribution 地区分布									
Central-North 华北	29	193	15,464	830	9.23	21.41	27.81	56.91	8,997
Beijing 北京	1	108	5,986	309	3.61	9.07	23.34	60.18	8,555
Tianjin 天津	4	148	6,464	135	2.71	5.59	29.66	51.49	4,974
Hebei 河北	22	216	18,937	1,057	10.67	23.92	28.32	55.37	9,900
Shanxi 山西	2	68		-15	-0.20	-1.39	5.19	85.23	7,328
Inner Mongolia 内蒙古									
Northeast 东北	10	158	7,294	-397	-2.39	-6.71	9.86	64.38	16,617
Liaoning 辽宁	4	122	9,108	-1,209	-4.96	-13.31	13.94	62.73	24,375
Jilin 吉林	3	119	4,477	74	0.73	8.13	12.88	90.99	10,053
Heilongjiang 黑龙江	3	245	7,691	215	1.67	3.20	5.67	47.72	12,837
Central-East 华东	50	214	23,630	236	0.68		32.04	111.23	34,580
Shanghai 上海	3	84	16,726	2,147	8.73	15.62	79.60	44.10	24,599
Jiangsu 江苏	16	148	19,445	976	9.97	22.20	36.36	55.11	9,792
Zhejiang 浙江	6	207	18,612	615	2.52	20.88	23.99	87.95	24,453
Anhui 安徽	3	88	11,731	1,002	13.47	32.53	47.01	58.58	7,438
Fujian 福建	2	216	27,059	1,852	6.15	8.86	25.59	30.62	30,134
Jiangxi 江西	6	60	2,534	31	0.90	1.94	14.01	53.61	3,432
Shandong 山东	14	412	43,145	-1,489	-1.67		30.84	130.75	89,190
Central-South 中南	42	151	17,391	607	6.18	11.03	38.76	44.01	9,827
Henan 河南	12	133	17,441	767	16.34	21.05	38.22	22.40	4,692
Hubei 湖北	14	136	19,662	848	5.45	9.04	56.45	39.69	15,559
Hunan 湖南	6	298	21,848	407	3.62	8.25	25.09	56.11	11,237
Guangdong 广东	10	106	11,479	198	2.78	7.50	30.96	62.85	7,117
Guangxi 广西									
Hainan 海南									
Southwest 西南	9	174	35,222	-2,071	-1.00	-1.93	66.64	48.42	207,650
Chongqing 重庆	2	155	55,519	3,220	5.02	9.99	58.31	49.73	64,131
Sichuan 四川	7	180	29,423	-3,582	-1.44	-2.79	68.69	48.32	248,656
Guizhou 贵州									
Yunnan 云南									
Tibet 西藏									
Northwest 西北	7	61	5,980	1,119	12.40	36.41	53.95	65.95	9,021
Shaanxi 陕西									
Gansu 甘肃	5	20	203	6	0.56	1.13	35.59	50.64	1,039
Qinghai 青海									
Ningxia 宁夏	1	231	16,980	4,124	24.93	109.65	35.10	77.26	16,542
Xinjiang 新疆	1	91	23,864	3,677	8.88	24.22	122.38	63.34	41,412

3132: Lime 石灰制造业

Year 年份	Number of firms 企业个数	Rate of change 变化率 (%)	Number of employees 职工人数 (人)	Rate of change 变化率 (%)	Total revenue (Mil. RMB) 总销售收入 (百万元)	Rate of change 变化率 (%)	Total profit (Mil RMB) 总利润 (百万元)	Rate of change 变化率 (%)
2000	140		22,533		1,544		70	
2001	149	6.43	20,148	-10.58	1,839	19.11	62	-11.43
2002	147	-1.34	26,196	30.02	2,792	51.82	47	-24.19

Major Products 主要产品	Output 产量	Unit 单位

10 Main Firms with Maximal Revenue (year founded) 收入最大的十家主要企业（创办年份）	City 城市	Province 省	Telephone/fax 电话/传真	Number of employees 职工人数	Ownership 产业所有权	Revenue ('000 RMB) 销售收入 (千元)	Profit('000 RMB) (rank) 利润(千元) (排名)	Total assets ('000 RMB) 总资产 (千元)	Major products 主要产品
China Aluminium Industry Co., Ltd. Shandong Branch	Zibo	Shandong	(0533)2930114		State-owned				limestone
中国铝业股份有限公司山东分公司(1954)	淄博市	山东省	(0533)2981427	4,654	国有企业	260,887	-	1,101,604	石灰石
Dujiangyan La Fa Ji Cement Co., Ltd.	Chengdu	Sichuan	(028)87196888		Foreign Funded				Cement Products
都江堰市拉法基水泥有限公司(1999)	成都市	四川省	(028)87196999	348	外商投资	115,518	-	1,655,138	水泥制品
Wuhan Qing Yuan Electric Power Group Co., Ltd.	Wuhan	Hubei	(027)86592222		Limited-Liability				Powder Coal
武汉青源电力集团有限公司(1999)	武汉市	湖北省	(027)86516409	168	有限公司	88,760	5,929(2)	131,954	粉煤炭
Handan Fuxing Metallurgy Building Materials General Factory	Handan	Hebei	(0310)4042216		Collective-owned				Lime
邯郸市复兴冶金建材总厂(1994)	邯郸市	河北省	(0310)4042216	489	集体企业	85,971	2,661(14)	37,148	白灰
Chongqing Yujiang Construction Engineering Ltd. Company	Chongqing	Chongqing	(023)67731798		Joint Stock				Concrete
重庆市渝江建筑工程有限公司(1998)	重庆市	重庆市	(023)67731798	165	股份制	82,874	6,429(1)	89,440	混凝土
Zhejiang Genglou Chemical Industry Ltd. Company	Hangzhou	Zhejiang	(0571)64738270		Limited-Liability				Calcium Carbonate
浙江更楼化工有限公司(1963)	杭州市	浙江省	(0571)64738186	626	有限公司	41,165	-	77,636	碳酸钙
Yixing Shanjuan Xinhe Lime Factory	Wuxi	Jiangsu	(0510)7391796		Private Enterprises				Lime
宜兴市善卷镇新河石灰厂(1995)	无锡市	江苏省	(0510)7395698	30	私营独资	40,000	1,090(34)	7,050	石灰
Sanming San Gang Mine Development Ltd. Company	Sanming	Fujian	(0598)8205842		State-owned				Lime
三明三钢矿山开发有限公司(2000)	三明市	福建省	(0598)8205846	271	国有企业	38,680	2,952(11)	56,944	石灰
Xi Liu Lime Smelting Plant	Nanjing	Jiangsu	(025)4128639		Joint Stock				Lime
江宁区麒麟镇西流炼灰厂(1985)	南京市	江苏省		215	股份制	32,550	1,440(30)	4,690	石灰
Shenyang Sifang Commodity Concrete Ltd. Company	Shenyang	Liaoning	(024)23730065		Private Owned				Concrete
沈阳四方商品混凝土有限责任公司(2001)	沈阳市	辽宁省	(024)23736333	172	私营企业	32,334	-	93,801	混凝土

Top 10 Cities by Revenue 销售收入排名前10位城市	Province 省	Market share 市场份额 (%)	Number of firms 企业个数
Zibo 淄博市	Shandong 山东省	9.77	2
Shijiazhuang 石家庄市	Hebei 河北省	5.59	9
Wuhan 武汉市	Hubei 湖北省	4.61	3
Chengdu 成都市	Sichuan 四川省	4.47	2
Nanjing 南京市	Jiangsu 江苏省	4.25	7
Xingtai 邢台市	Hebei 河北省	4.02	4
Chongqing 重庆市	Chongqing 重庆市	3.98	2
Handan 邯郸市	Hebei 河北省	3.72	3
Hangzhou 杭州市	Zhejiang 浙江省	3.62	5
Changzhou 常州市	Jiangsu 江苏省	3.57	3

10 Major Wholesalers 十家主要批发商	City 城市	Province 省	Telephone/Fax 电话/传真
Xuzhou New Century Building Materials Decorative City	Xuzhou	Jiangsu	(0516)83666780
徐州市新世纪建材装饰城	徐州市	江苏省	(0516)63804485
Orienthome Co.,Ltd.	Beijing	Beijing	(010)63808294
东方家园有限公司	北京市	北京市	
Shanghai Jinkai Goods & Materials Co.,Ltd.	Shanghai	Shanghai	(021)52193967
上海金凯物资有限公司	上海市	上海市	
Guangzhou Building Materials Development Co.,Ltd.	Guangzhou	Guangdong	(020)83335062
广州市建材发展有限公司	广州市	广东省	(020)83341110
Guangxi Qiaofeng Goods & Materials Trade Co.,Ltd.	Nanning	Guangxi	(0771)2631539
广西侨丰物资贸易有限责任公司	南宁市	广西	(0771)2631539
Gansu Building Materials State-owned Assets Marketing Co.,Ltd.	Lanzhou	Gansu	(0931)8821359
甘肃建材国有资产经营有限责任公司	兰州市	甘肃省	(0931)8960243
Shanghai East Asia United Building Materials Co.,Ltd.	Shanghai	Shanghai	(021)33134520
上海东亚联合建材有限公司	上海市	上海市	(021)63216165
Shanghai Zhuzong Materials General Company	Shanghai	Shanghai	(021)32240030
上海住总物资总公司	上海市	上海市	(021)32240024
Guangdong Building Materials Company	Guangzhou	Guangdong	(020)83802713
广东省建材公司	广州市	广东省	(020)83817640
Guangdong Dongguan Hardware Minerals Import & Export Co.,Ltd	Dongguan	Guangdong	(0769)2227090
广东省东莞五金矿产进出口公司	东莞市	广东省	(0769)2221045

3133: Construction Stone 建筑用石加工业

The industry accounts for 0.146% of the total revenue of China's industrial sector in 2002. The rate of return on assets is 7.99%. 87.98% of all firms in the industry made a profit while 12.02% had negative returns.The top province in terms of the industry's revenue is Fujian, accounting for 29.91% of the total revenue.
2002年本行业收入占全行业的0.146%，资产利润率为7.99%。87.98%的企业赢利，12.02%的企业亏损。收入最高的省为福建省，占本行业的29.91%。

	Total number of firms 企业总数	Total number of employees 职工总数	Total revenue (Mil.RMB) 总销售收入(百万元)	Total profit (Mil.RMB) 总利润(百万元)	Return on assets 资产利润率(%)	Return on equity 权益利润率(%)	Labour productivity ('000 RMB/ worker) 劳动生产率(千元/人)	Debts/ assets 资产负债率(%)	Total assets (Mil.RMB) 总资产(百万元)
Industry Overall 行业总体	774	98,042	15,648	1,077	7.99	15.01	50.57	46.79	13,491

	Number of firms 企业个数	Average number of employees 平均职工人数	Average revenue ('000 RMB) 平均销售收入（千元）	Average profit ('000 RMB) 平均利润(千元)	Return on assets 资产利润率(%)	Return on equity 权益利润率(%)	Labour productivity ('000 RMB/ worker) 劳动生产率(千元/人)	Debts/ assets 资产负债率(%)	Average total assets ('000 RMB) 平均总资产(千元)
By ownership 产业所有权									
State-owned 国有	55	76	6,047	209	1.43	4.78	45.67	70.14	14,667
Collective-owned 集体	174	208	29,326	1,572	15.42	30.06	44.04	48.70	10,195
Foreign & Overseas Chinese Funded 三资	208	105	22,784	823	3.04	6.30	62.52	51.74	27,052
By regional distribution 地区分布									
Central-North 华北	62	99	12,867	955	10.71	24.27	47.68	55.87	8,911
Beijing 北京	13	57	10,354	286	2.59	5.78	55.92	55.25	11,055
Tianjin 天津	6	39	1,555	-19	-0.12	-0.20	-5.89	38.16	15,259
Hebei 河北	27	154	20,813	1,861	23.48	73.67	47.55	68.12	7,924
Shanxi 山西	9	38	2,440	73	1.24	3.00	27.82	58.74	5,924
Inner Mongolia 内蒙古	7	96	9,990	667	9.35	14.28	68.31	34.56	7,133
Northeast 东北	32	172	11,513	497	3.10	7.48	19.15	58.62	16,053
Liaoning 辽宁	12	249	9,250	477	2.82	9.00	-3.05	68.68	16,917
Jilin 吉林	12	153	8,077	512	3.74	6.51	17.15	42.59	13,708
Heilongjiang 黑龙江	8	86	20,063	504	2.76	7.39	121.20	62.67	18,273
Central-East 华东	471	115	22,376	1,138	6.69	12.18	58.20	45.04	16,999
Shanghai 上海	43	60	24,891	560	1.73	4.02	87.08	56.94	32,298
Jiangsu 江苏	42	139	17,271	412	4.42	9.06	35.70	51.22	9,325
Zhejiang 浙江	23	60	12,524	819	10.22	18.22	48.40	43.91	8,014
Anhui 安徽	3	46	10,044	1,024	32.76	111.03	87.87	70.50	3,125
Fujian 福建	266	100	17,593	991	6.63	10.26	52.11	35.42	14,958
Jiangxi 江西	6	66	5,983	241	2.99	5.55	30.56	46.16	8,072
Shandong 山东	88	194	42,152	2,356	10.34	22.81	72.14	54.65	22,784
Central-South 中南	175	160	20,529	785	6.04	13.49	44.43	55.24	12,995
Henan 河南	72	156	15,767	906	13.53	32.83	44.37	58.77	6,696
Hubei 湖北	23	147	15,922	590	4.77	10.53	45.15	54.76	12,386
Hunan 湖南	13	343	40,918	993	13.06	25.50	32.65	48.78	7,606
Guangdong 广东	61	99	19,916	513	2.36	5.25	60.60	55.02	21,756
Guangxi 广西	6	470	57,374	2,381	17.61	33.48	27.81	47.40	13,519
Hainan 海南									
Southwest 西南	21	127	5,135	256	1.91	3.82	18.08	50.09	13,423
Chongqing 重庆	2	150	4,050	361	15.78	16.40	12.10	3.80	2,288
Sichuan 四川	9	178	8,008	578	2.72	4.56	25.71	40.36	21,259
Guizhou 贵州	3	37		-145	-1.22			104.92	11,960
Yunnan 云南	2	294	13,493	-66	-0.29	-0.63	4.37	54.38	23,094
Tibet 西藏	5	12	137	5	0.64	0.87	11.39	26.79	784
Northwest 西北	13	138	18,638	24,912	17.39	27.85	70.69	37.55	143,267
Shaanxi 陕西	4	106	3,203	5	0.07	1.21	8.07	93.85	6,400
Gansu 甘肃	5	60	2,964	59	0.36	2.28	25.15	84.16	16,305
Qinghai 青海									
Ningxia 宁夏									
Xinjiang 新疆	4	270	53,665	80,886	18.43	28.17	107.76	34.57	438,836

3133: Construction Stone 建筑用石加工业

Year 年份	Number of firms 企业个数	Rate of change 变化率 (%)	Number of employees 职工人数 (人)	Rate of change 变化率 (%)	Total revenue (Mil. RMB) 总销售收入 (百万元)	Rate of change 变化率 (%)	Total profit (Mil RMB) 总利润 (百万元)	Rate of change 变化率 (%)
2000	673		91,001		11,489		703	
2001	688	2.23	92,199	1.32	12,546	9.20	902	28.31
2002	774	12.50	98,042	6.34	15,648	24.73	1,077	19.40

Major Products 主要产品	Output 产量	Unit 单位
Granite Slab 花岗石板材	5,688	10,000 Sq.M. 万平方米
Marble Slab 大理石板材	1,407	10,000 Sq.M. 万平方米

10 Main Firms with Maximal Revenue (year founded) 收入最大的十家主要企业（创办年份）	City 城市	Province 省	Telephone/fax 电话/传真	Number of employees 职工人数	Ownership 产业所有权	Revenue ('000 RMB) 销售收入 (千元)	Profit('000 RMB) (rank) 利润(千元) (排名)	Total assets ('000 RMB) 总资产 (千元)	Major products 主要产品
Wendeng Dong Yi Stone Materials Co., Ltd. 文登东意石材有限公司(1993)	Weihai 威海市	Shandong 山东省	(0631)8881196 (0631)8882868	128	Foreign Funded 外商投资	278,580	20,070(6)	22,564	Granite Board Materials 花岗石板
Miluo Gaojiafang Granite Development Group Company 汨罗市高家坊花岗岩开发集团公司(2000)	Yueyang 岳阳市	Hunan 湖南省	(0730)5870398	3,600	Collective-owned 集体企业	265,000	6,000(28)	27,000	Rough Stone 麻石
Fujian Hong Fa Group Company 福建宏发集团公司(1989)	Quanzhou 泉州市	Fujian 福建省	(0595)6355868 (0595)6355288	750	Collective-owned 集体企业	249,800	20,238(5)	133,102	Stone Materials 石材
Rushan Jia Xin Stone Material Ltd. Company 乳山市佳鑫石材有限公司(1994)	Weihai 威海市	Shandong 山东省	(0631)6726240 (0631)6726240	285	Foreign Funded 外商投资	231,582	9,400(22)	19,161	Stone Products 石制品
Wendeng Stone Material Company 文登市石材公司(1979)	Weihai 威海市	Shandong 山东省	(0631)8535558	100	Collective-owned 集体企业	229,360	18,020(7)	21,090	Granite 花岗岩
Liubu Red Granite Processing Factory 济南历城区柳埠红花岗石加工厂(1984)	Jinan 济南市	Shandong 山东省	(0531)2843032	370	Collective-owned 集体企业	221,400	16,800(8)	20,439	Rough Granite Material花岗石荒料
Xinle Zhengmo Marble Technology Group 新乐市正莫大理石工艺集团(1984)	Shijiazhuang 石家庄市	Hebei 河北省	(0311)8511219 (0311)8511219	1,350	Collective-owned 集体企业	220,590	25,760(2)	34,050	Marble Slab大理石板材
Fujian Xishi Group Co., Ltd. 福建溪石集团有限公司(1990)	Quanzhou 泉州市	Fujian 福建省	(0595)6352948 (0595)6355068	710	Joint Stock 股份制	214,230	21,556(4)	164,792	Special-shaped Stone Material 异形石材
Xinjiang Guanghui Stone Material Stock Co., Ltd. 新疆广汇实业股份有限责任公司(2000)	Urumqi 乌鲁木齐市	Xinjiang 新疆	(0991)3742733 (0991)3718130	854	Joint Stock 股份制	195,951	325,544(1)	1,664,159	Granite Slab花岗岩板材
Xinyi Dacheng Town Southeast Stone Material Co., Ltd. 信宜市大成镇东南石料有限公司(1993)	Maoming 茂名市	Guangdong 广东省	(0668)8288358	450	Collective-owned 集体企业	146,100	10,330(17)	36,870	Granite Slab花岗岩板材

Top 10 Cities by Revenue 销售收入排名前10位城市	Province 省	Market share 市场份额 (%)	Number of firms 企业个数
Quanzhou 泉州市	Fujian 福建省	15.27	102
Weihai 威海市	Shandong 山东省	9.34	18
Yantai 烟台市	Shandong 山东省	6.88	34
Shanghai 上海市	Shanghai 上海市	6.84	43
Nanyang 南阳市	Henan 河南省	4.95	35
Ningde 宁德市	Fujian 福建省	4.53	47
Jinan 济南市	Shandong 山东省	4.51	6
Fuzhou 福州市	Fujian 福建省	4.23	71
Xiamen 厦门市	Fujian 福建省	3.40	17
Yueyang 岳阳市	Hunan 湖南省	3.04	7

10 Major Wholesalers 十家主要批发商	City 城市	Province 省	Telephone/Fax 电话/传真
Xuzhou New Century Building Materials Decorative City 徐州市新世纪建材装饰城	Xuzhou 徐州市	Jiangsu 江苏省	(0516)83666780 (0516)63804485
Orienthome Co.,Ltd. 东方家园有限公司	Beijing 北京市	Beijing 北京市	(010)63808294
Shanghai Jinkai Goods & Materials Co.,Ltd. 上海金凯物资有限公司	Shanghai 上海市	Shanghai 上海市	(021)52193967
Guangzhou Building Materials Development Co.,Ltd. 广州市建材发展有限公司	Guangzhou 广州市	Guangdong 广东省	(020)83335062 (020)83341110
Guangxi Qiaofeng Goods & Materials Trade Co.,Ltd. 广西侨丰物资贸易有限责任公司	Nanning 南宁市	Guangxi 广西	(0771)2631539 (0771)2631539
Gansu Building Materials State-owned Assets Marketing Co.,Ltd. 甘肃建材国有资产经营有限责任公司	Lanzhou 兰州市	Gansu 甘肃省	(0931)8821359 (0931)8960243
Shanghai East Asia United Building Materials Co.,Ltd. 上海东亚联合建材有限公司	Shanghai 上海市	Shanghai 上海市	(021)33134520 (021)63216165
Shanghai Zhuzong Materials General Company 上海住总物资总公司	Shanghai 上海市	Shanghai 上海市	(021)32240030 (021)32240024
Guangdong Building Materials Company 广东省建材公司	Guangzhou 广州市	Guangdong 广东省	(020)83802713 (020)83817640
Guangdong Dongguan Hardware Minerals Import & Export Co.,Ltd 广东省东莞五金矿产进出口公司	Dongguan 东莞市	Guangdong 广东省	(0769)2227090 (0769)2221045

3134: Light Construction Materials 轻质建筑材料制造业

The industry accounts for 0.072% of the total revenue of China's industrial sector in 2002. The rate of return on assets is 1.22%. 84.76% of all firms in the industry made a profit while 15.24% had negative returns.The top province in terms of the industry's revenue is Shandong, accounting for 19.87% of the total revenue.
2002年本行业收入占全行业的0.072%，资产利润率为1.22%。84.76%的企业赢利，15.24%的企业亏损。收入最高的省为山东省，占本行业的19.87%。

	Total number of firms 企业总数	Total number of employees 职工总数	Total revenue (Mil.RMB) 总销售收入 (百万元)	Total profit (Mil.RMB) 总利润 (百万元)	Return on assets 资产利润率 (%)	Return on equity 权益利润率 (%)	Labour productivity ('000 RMB/ worker) 劳动生产率 (千元/人)	Debts/ assets 资产负债率 (%)	Total assets (Mil.RMB) 总资产 (百万元)
Industry Overall 行业总体	269	44,207	7,761	135	1.22	2.09	58.03	41.55	11,015

	Number of firms 企业个数	Average number of employees 平均职工人数	Average revenue ('000 RMB) 平均销售收入 (千元)	Average profit ('000 RMB) 平均利润 (千元)	Return on assets 资产利润率 (%)	Return on equity 权益利润率 (%)	Labour productivity ('000 RMB/ worker) 劳动生产率 (千元/人)	Debts/ assets 资产负债率 (%)	Average total assets ('000 RMB) 平均总资产 (千元)
By ownership 产业所有权									
State-owned 国有	28	137	14,738	297	0.63	1.46	32.97	56.67	46,838
Collective-owned 集体	53	214	37,625	1,991	9.18	20.10	49.60	54.33	21,691
Foreign & Overseas Chinese Funded 三资	40	188	41,249	-5,834	-6.14	-10.03	90.05	38.80	95,068
By regional distribution 地区分布									
Central-North 华北	46	184	34,813	2,724	3.78	5.17	62.56	26.87	72,060
Beijing 北京	17	204	70,762	6,308	3.94	4.78	126.94	17.45	160,025
Tianjin 天津	13	118	19,510	1,083	5.43	25.40	20.35	78.64	19,950
Hebei 河北	11	259	11,173	380	1.89	9.71	17.75	80.54	20,094
Shanxi 山西	3	133	6,327	81	0.23	0.28	15.59	18.67	34,806
Inner Mongolia 内蒙古	2	105	1,469	-213	-4.46		3.46	152.44	4,762
Northeast 东北	16	249	19,962	743	2.42	6.03	26.15	59.82	30,656
Liaoning 辽宁	12	280	20,898	946	2.54	6.08	26.41	58.30	37,320
Jilin 吉林	2	88	18,551	113	1.26	3.49	46.33	63.78	8,903
Heilongjiang 黑龙江	2	219	15,760	150	1.21	7.70	16.10	84.33	12,424
Central-East 华东	78	167	44,049	1,035	2.27	4.47	70.35	49.16	45,592
Shanghai 上海	17	67	35,365	-547	-1.02	-1.76	99.30	41.91	53,460
Jiangsu 江苏	15	207	50,383	54	0.10	0.25	59.53	58.05	52,414
Zhejiang 浙江	6	153	17,344	2,568	7.76	15.24	42.88	49.11	33,097
Anhui 安徽	3	556	126,589	-5,744	-3.39	-5.39	72.71	37.00	169,248
Fujian 福建	2	65	10,659	160	0.84	1.52	139.44	44.96	19,077
Jiangxi 江西	4	90	7,913	225	0.77	1.74	44.84	55.91	29,412
Shandong 山东	31	184	49,744	2,898	8.99	19.68	74.19	54.30	32,226
Central-South 中南	93	150	23,254	-926	-2.71	-4.60	66.98	41.03	34,146
Henan 河南	7	131	29,475	2,010	16.45	72.78	80.09	77.40	12,224
Hubei 湖北	36	142	18,581	752	6.66	13.06	44.38	49.02	11,288
Hunan 湖南	11	120	7,045	1,027	9.95	15.25	23.06	34.75	10,316
Guangdong 广东	37	172	31,536	-3,716	-5.51	-9.07	92.29	39.21	67,424
Guangxi 广西	2	132	21,551	-551	-1.46	-1.98	72.05	26.20	37,747
Hainan 海南									
Southwest 西南	7	232	8,705	109	0.71	1.68	14.96	58.02	15,462
Chongqing 重庆	2	427	16,893	-299	-0.99	-4.06	19.34	75.60	30,133
Sichuan 四川	4	174	5,485	234	2.50	4.20	11.09	40.55	9,373
Guizhou 贵州									
Yunnan 云南									
Tibet 西藏	1	80	5,212	424	4.05	5.02	1.83	19.46	10,479
Northwest 西北	29	107	6,226	70	0.55	2.23	16.97	75.39	12,759
Shaanxi 陕西	5	185	11,696	149	0.92	3.03	14.28	69.66	16,230
Gansu 甘肃	15	46	2,579	147	4.77	12.37	25.94	61.42	3,088
Qinghai 青海									
Ningxia 宁夏	4	221	7,440	-592	-1.87	-39.55	10.67	95.28	31,708
Xinjiang 新疆	5	122	10,724	289	1.25	3.39	20.08	63.19	23,144

3134: Light Construction Materials 轻质建筑材料制造业

Year 年份	Number of firms 企业个数	Rate of change 变化率 (%)	Number of employees 职工人数 (人)	Rate of change 变化率 (%)	Total revenue (Mil. RMB) 总销售收入 (百万元)	Rate of change 变化率 (%)	Total profit (Mil RMB) 总利润 (百万元)	Rate of change 变化率 (%)
2000	221		32,676		4,923		167	
2001	247	11.76	37,750	15.53	5,171	5.04	186	11.38
2002	269	8.91	44,207	17.10	7,761	50.09	135	-27.42

Major Products 主要产品	Output 产量	Unit 单位
Gypsum Slab 石膏板	17,332	10,000 Sq.M. 万平方米
Air Entraining Concrete 加气混凝土	932	10,000 Stere 万立方米

10 Main Firms with Maximal Revenue (year founded) 收入最大的十家主要企业 (创办年份)	City 城市	Province 省	Telephone/fax 电话/传真	Number of employees 职工人数	Ownership 产业所有权	Revenue ('000 RMB) 销售收入 (千元)	Profit('000 RMB) (rank) 利润(千元) (排名)	Total assets ('000 RMB) 总资产 (千元)	Major products 主要产品
BNBM Building Materials Co., Ltd.	Beijing	Beijing	(010)82913831		Joint Stock				Paper-faced Gypsum Board纸
北新集团建材股份有限公司(1984)	北京市	北京市	(010)82915566	1,186	股份制	617,960	78,818(1)	1,796,260	面石膏板
Rongcheng Xinzhuang Joint Enterprise General Company	Weihai	Shandong	(0631)7551121		Collective-owned				Waterproof Materials
荣成市新庄联合企业总公司(1988)	威海市	山东省	(0631)7551121	500	集体企业	563,000	28,220(4)	91,610	防水材料
Jiangsu Changsheng Group Co., Ltd.	Suzhou	Jiangsu	(0520)52581109		Collective-owned				Steel Structural Parts
江苏常盛集团有限公司(1995)	苏州市	江苏省	(0520)52581238	380	集体企业	388,081	20,953(5)	299,328	钢结构件
Fangda Group Co., Ltd.	Shenzhen	Guangdong	(0755)26788571		Overseas Chinese-funded				New Type Building Materials新型
方大集团股份有限公司(1994)	深圳市	广东省	(0755)26788357	2,430	港澳台资	302,116	-	1,325,848	建筑材料
Caohu Fu Huang Light Building Materials Co., Ltd.	Chaohu	Anhui	(0565)8562917		Joint Stock				Color Steel Plate
巢湖市富煌轻型建材有限责任公司(1987)	巢湖市	安徽省	(0565)8562915	1,479	股份制	281,657	32,729(3)	211,971	彩钢板
Beijing Star Building Materials Co., Ltd.	Beijing	Beijing	(010)85765544		State-owned				Sound Absorption Board
北京星牌建材有限责任公司(2000)	北京市	北京市	(010)85765027	751	国有企业	271,380	9,815(9)	605,327	吸声板
Shanghai Jinjiang Concrete Mixed In Advance Co., Ltd.	Shanghai	Shanghai	(021)64773898		Limited-Liability				Concrete
上海锦江城预拌混凝土有限公司(1995)	上海市	上海市	(021)64773898	86	有限公司	115,126	-	117,972	混凝土
Knauf Plasterboard Co., ltd.	Wuhu	Anhui	(0553)5842053		Foreign Funded				Paper-faced Gypsum Board纸
可耐福石膏板(芜湖)有限公司(1998)	芜湖市	安徽省	(0553)5841416	150	外商投资	92,281	-	282,817	面石膏板
Guangdong Knauf New Building Material Co., ltd.	Dongguan	Guangdong	(0769)8222708		Foreign Funded				Gypsum Slab
广东可耐福新型建筑材料有限公司(1998)	东莞市	广东省	(0769)8222709	164	外商投资	84,569	-	254,235	石膏板
Shanghai Di Kong Nei Shan Concrete Co.,Ltd.	Shanghai	Shanghai	(021)66522942		Foreign Funded				Concrete
上海地空内山混凝土有限公司(1995)	上海市	上海市	(021)56653509	102	外商投资	84,323	3,874(19)	85,724	混凝土

Top 10 Cities by Revenue 销售收入排名前10位城市	Province 省	Market share 市场份额 (%)	Number of firms 企业个数
Beijing 北京市	Beijing 北京市	15.50	17
Shanghai 上海市	Shanghai 上海市	7.75	17
Weihai 威海市	Shandong 山东省	7.25	1
Suzhou 苏州市	Jiangsu 江苏省	5.19	2
Shenzhen 深圳市	Guangdong 广东省	4.99	4
Xiaogan 孝感市	Hubei 湖北省	4.55	19
Guangzhou 广州市	Guangdong 广东省	4.44	18
Taian 泰安市	Shandong 山东省	4.00	2
Chaohu 巢湖市	Anhui 安徽省	3.63	1
Yantai 烟台市	Shandong 山东省	3.28	6

10 Major Wholesalers 十家主要批发商	City 城市	Province 省	Telephone/Fax 电话/传真
Xuzhou New Century Building Materials Decorative City	Xuzhou	Jiangsu	(0516)83666780
徐州市新世纪建材装饰城	徐州市	江苏省	(0516)63804485
Orienthome Co.,Ltd.	Beijing	Beijing	(010)63808294
东方家园有限公司	北京市	北京市	
Shanghai Jinkai Goods & Materials Co.,Ltd.	Shanghai	Shanghai	(021)52193967
上海金凯物资有限公司	上海市	上海市	
Guangzhou Building Materials Development Co.,Ltd.	Guangzhou	Guangdong	(020)83335062
广州市建材发展有限公司	广州市	广东省	(020)83341110
Guangxi Qiaofeng Goods & Materials Trade Co.,Ltd.	Nanning	Guangxi	(0771)2631539
广西侨丰物资贸易有限责任公司	南宁市	广西	(0771)2631539
Gansu Building Materials State-owned Assets Marketing Co.,Ltd.	Lanzhou	Gansu	(0931)8821359
甘肃建材国有资产经营有限责任公司	兰州市	甘肃省	(0931)8960243
Shanghai East Asia United Building Materials Co.,Ltd.	Shanghai	Shanghai	(021)33134520
上海东亚联合建材有限公司	上海市	上海市	(021)63216165
Shanghai Zhuzong Materials General Company	Shanghai	Shanghai	(021)32240030
上海仕总物资总公司	上海市	上海市	(021)32240024
Guangdong Building Materials Company	Guangzhou	Guangdong	(020)83802713
广东省建材公司	广州市	广东省	(020)83817640
Guangdong Dongguan Hardware Minerals Import & Export Co.,Ltd	Dongguan	Guangdong	(0769)2227090
广东省东莞五金矿产进出口公司	东莞市	广东省	(0769)2221045

3135: Water-proof Construction Materials 防水密封建筑材料制造业

The industry accounts for 0.027% of the total revenue of China's industrial sector in 2002. The rate of return on assets is 3.34%. 84.39% of all firms in the industry made a profit while 15.61% had negative returns.The top province in terms of the industry's revenue is Shandong, accounting for 29.83% of the total revenue.
2002年本行业收入占全行业的0.027%，资产利润率为3.34%。84.39%的企业赢利，15.61%的企业亏损。收入最高的省为山东省，占本行业的29.83%。

	Total number of firms 企业总数	Total number of employees 职工总数	Total revenue (Mil.RMB) 总销售收入(百万元)	Total profit (Mil.RMB) 总利润(百万元)	Return on assets 资产利润率(%)	Return on equity 权益利润率(%)	Labour productivity ('000 RMB/worker) 劳动生产率(千元/人)	Debts/assets 资产负债率(%)	Total assets (Mil.RMB) 总资产(百万元)
Industry Overall 行业总体	173	20,469	2,878	112	3.34	9.09	46.37	63.29	3,363

	Number of firms 企业个数	Average number of employees 平均职工人数	Average revenue ('000 RMB) 平均销售收入(千元)	Average profit ('000 RMB) 平均利润(千元)	Return on assets 资产利润率(%)	Return on equity 权益利润率(%)	Labour productivity ('000 RMB/worker) 劳动生产率(千元/人)	Debts/assets 资产负债率(%)	Average total assets ('000 RMB) 平均总资产(千元)
By ownership 产业所有权									
State-owned 国有	17	235	10,691	-448	-0.68	-1.34	8.47	49.09	65,570
Collective-owned 集体	28	101	12,153	698	6.83	15.46	40.28	55.82	10,225
Foreign & Overseas Chinese Funded 三资	13	155	24,094	718	2.49	6.30	58.05	60.51	28,882
By regional distribution 地区分布									
Central-North 华北	30	106	11,992	280	0.76	1.40	37.46	45.43	36,750
Beijing 北京	13	117	16,591	498	1.93	3.58	49.76	46.10	25,822
Tianjin 天津	3	52	5,989	-11	-0.03	-0.11	89.45	73.23	36,030
Hebei 河北	8	147	10,480	127	0.17	0.28	13.18	39.27	75,427
Shanxi 山西	5	66	8,452	189	1.74	3.58	42.83	51.44	10,855
Inner Mongolia 内蒙古	1	3						199.71	1,049
Northeast 东北	18	126	13,841	-146	-0.60	-32.01	40.97	98.11	24,152
Liaoning 辽宁	10	115	19,157	-429	-1.34		56.20	107.85	32,139
Jilin 吉林	4	177	9,726	493	3.03	9.85	32.31	69.21	16,255
Heilongjiang 黑龙江	4	104	4,667	-76	-0.63	-2.28	13.59	72.28	12,081
Central-East 华东	78	106	20,267	975	6.85	21.19	57.99	67.65	14,233
Shanghai 上海	9	85	17,369	439	1.49	3.65	38.09	59.11	29,413
Jiangsu 江苏	13	134	27,700	936	6.46		55.69	103.23	14,493
Zhejiang 浙江	7	92	21,430	1,856	10.81	26.58	60.76	59.35	17,175
Anhui 安徽	4	136	12,526	104	0.93	2.18	42.42	57.15	11,130
Fujian 福建	1	42	5,840	180	45.11	600.00	43.07	92.48	399
Jiangxi 江西									
Shandong 山东	44	102	19,511	1,054	9.43	24.54	63.85	61.58	11,179
Central-South 中南	29	122	17,187	708	6.94	31.79	44.19	78.17	10,200
Henan 河南	10	126	16,183	1,312	23.00	42.51	39.98	45.90	5,707
Hubei 湖北	9	179	19,135	103	0.71		32.09	111.20	14,671
Hunan 湖南	5	84	7,633	222	5.29	26.19	34.24	79.80	4,199
Guangdong 广东	4	58	30,468	1,291	7.68	18.33	165.71	58.09	16,803
Guangxi 广西									
Hainan 海南	1	15	4,346	204	1.10	1.27	90.87	13.03	18,482
Southwest 西南	8	162	17,500	1,527	6.64	13.51	59.39	50.88	23,011
Chongqing 重庆	3	272	11,395	681	1.93	5.50	21.89	64.86	35,231
Sichuan 四川	3	101	27,859	2,505	13.11	19.53	166.81	32.84	19,100
Guizhou 贵州	1	41	1,063	32	0.58	4.86	23.10	88.15	5,560
Yunnan 云南	1	133	21,173	2,628	16.92	18.58	55.93	8.94	15,532
Tibet 西藏									
Northwest 西北	10	193	4,972	-235	-1.00	-2.13	13.11	53.10	23,552
Shaanxi 陕西	3	386	5,292	15	0.03	0.05	5.97	42.10	55,973
Gansu 甘肃	6	71	2,575	-185	-3.74	-8.48	22.55	55.90	4,953
Qinghai 青海									
Ningxia 宁夏									
Xinjiang 新疆	1	344	18,400	-1,284	-3.39	-917.14	25.44	99.63	37,880

3135: Water-proof Construction Materials 防水密封建筑材料制造业

Year 年份	Number of firms 企业个数	Rate of change 变化率 (%)	Number of employees 职工人数 (人)	Rate of change 变化率 (%)	Total revenue (Mil. RMB) 总销售收入 (百万元)	Rate of change 变化率 (%)	Total profit (Mil RMB) 总利润 (百万元)	Rate of change 变化率 (%)
2000	176		25,585		3,078		31	
2001	179	1.70	23,436	-8.40	3,309	7.50	95	206.45
2002	173	-3.35	20,469	-12.66	2,878	-13.03	112	17.89

Major Products 主要产品	Output 产量	Unit 单位
Asphalt Felt & Oilpaper 油毡油纸	1,502	10,000 Rolls 万卷
Petroleum Asphalt 石油沥青	723	10,000 Tons 万吨

10 Main Firms with Maximal Revenue (year founded) 收入最大的十家主要企业（创办年份）	City 城市	Province 省	Telephone/fax 电话/传真	Number of employees 职工人数	Ownership 产业所有权	Revenue ('000 RMB) 销售收入 (千元)	Profit('000 RMB) (rank) 利润(千元)(排名)	Total assets ('000 RMB) 总资产 (千元)	Major products 主要产品
Nanjing Yu Wang Building Materials Co., Ltd. 南京禹王建材有限公司(1998)	Nanjing 南京市	Jiangsu 江苏省	(025)4100111 (025)4108666	89	Private Enterprises 私营独资	172,500	5,910(4)	22,200	Waterproof Materials 防水材料
Hubei Yong Yang Water-proofer Material Co., Ltd. 湖北永阳防水材料股份有限公司(1972)	Suizhou 随州市	Hubei 湖北省	(0712)6261874 (0712)6261276	254	Joint Stock 股份制	96,315	2,541(15)	41,492	PVC Water-proof Materials.PVC 防水材料
Shandong Weifang Bohai New Type Water-proofer Material Company 山东省潍坊市渤海新型防水材料公司(1994)	Weifang 潍坊市	Shandong 山东省	(0536)5511038 (0536)5511666	163	Private Enterprises 私营独资	58,200	2,684(12)	19,334	Asphalt Felt 油毡
Panjin Yu Wang Waterproof Building Materials Group Co.,Ltd.盘锦禹王防水建材集团有限公司(1987)	Panjin 盘锦市	Liaoning 辽宁省	(0427)2856916 (0427)2856995	684	Private Owned 私营企业	55,736	-	181,836	Modified Pitch Water-proofer 防水材料
BeiJing Carlisle Waterproof Materials Co., Ltd. 北京卡莱尔防水材料有限公司(2000)	Beijing 北京市	Beijing 北京市	(010)67964998 (010)67965004	225	Foreign Funded 外商投资	51,851	-	67,800	Waterproof Equipment 防水器材
Changshu San Heng Building Materials Co., Ltd. 常熟市三恒建材有限责任公司(1975)	Suzhou 苏州市	Jiangsu 江苏省	(0520)52774949 (0520)52798840	275	Limited-Liability 有限公司	45,713	8,176(3)	56,692	Waterproofer 防水材料
Lin'an Chemical Industry Preparation Factory 林业部林产工业设计院临安化工制剂厂(1992)	Hangzhou 杭州市	Zhejiang 浙江省	(0571)63722247 (0571)63714640	80	Collective Owned 集体企业	41,291	5,862(6)	38,192	Waterproof Seal Materials 建筑材料
Beijing Dongfang Yu Hong Waterproof Technology Co., Ltd. 北京东方雨虹防水技术有限责任公司(1998)	Beijing 北京市	Beijing 北京市	(010)85757844 (010)85785519	175	Joint Stock 股份制	40,533	2,211(21)	94,168	Waterproof Roll Materials 防水卷材
Shenyang Rustproof Packaging Material Co., ltd. 沈阳防锈包装材料公司(1989)	Shenyang 沈阳市	Liaoning 辽宁省	(024)86617041 (024)86617354	180	Collective-owned 集体企业	40,233	2,645(13)	39,628	Antirust Paper 防锈纸
Jurong Tian Xin Waterproof Material Factory 句容市天信防水材料厂(2002)	Zhenjiang 镇江市	Jiangsu 江苏省	(0511)7757247 (0511)7757247	118	Private Enterprises 私营独资	39,650	690(59)	17,660	Asphalt Felt 油毡

Top 10 Cities by Revenue 销售收入排名前10位城市	Province 省	Market share 市场份额 (%)	Number of firms 企业个数
Weifang 潍坊市	Shandong 山东省	17.77	33
Beijing 北京市	Beijing 北京市	7.49	13
Nanjing 南京市	Jiangsu 江苏省	7.28	4
Weihai 威海市	Shandong 山东省	6.06	2
Shanghai 上海市	Shanghai 上海市	5.43	9
Suizhou 随州市	Hubei 湖北省	3.35	1
Guangzhou 广州市	Guangdong 广东省	3.30	2
Chengdu 成都市	Sichuan 四川省	2.72	2
Panjin 盘锦市	Liaoning 辽宁省	2.63	2
Ningbo 宁波市	Zhejiang 浙江省	2.22	3

10 Major Wholesalers 十家主要批发商	City 城市	Province 省	Telephone/Fax 电话/传真
Xuzhou New Century Building Materials Decorative City 徐州市新世纪建材装饰城	Xuzhou 徐州市	Jiangsu 江苏省	(0516)83666780 (0516)63804485
Orienthome Co.,Ltd. 东方家园有限公司	Beijing 北京市	Beijing 北京市	(010)63808294
Shanghai Jinkai Goods & Materials Co.,Ltd. 上海金凯物资有限公司	Shanghai 上海市	Shanghai 上海市	(021)52193967
Guangzhou Building Materials Development Co.,Ltd. 广州市建材发展有限公司	Guangzhou 广州市	Guangdong 广东省	(020)83335062 (020)83341110
Guangxi Qiaofeng Goods & Materials Trade Co.,Ltd. 广西侨丰物资贸易有限责任公司	Nanning 南宁市	Guangxi 广西	(0771)2631539 (0771)2631539
Gansu Building Materials State-owned Assets Marketing Co.,Ltd. 甘肃建材国有资产经营有限责任公司	Lanzhou 兰州市	Gansu 甘肃省	(0931)8821359 (0931)8960243
Shanghai East Asia United Building Materials Co.,Ltd. 上海东亚联合建材有限公司	Shanghai 上海市	Shanghai 上海市	(021)33134520 (021)63216165
Shanghai Zhuzong Materials General Company 上海住总物资总公司	Shanghai 上海市	Shanghai 上海市	(021)32240030 (021)32240024
Guangdong Building Materials Company 广东省建材公司	Guangzhou 广州市	Guangdong 广东省	(020)83802713 (020)83817640
Guangdong Dongguan Hardware Minerals Import & Export Co.,Ltd 广东省东莞五金矿产进出口公司	Dongguan 东莞市	Guangdong 广东省	(0769)2227090 (0769)2221045

3136: Heat-barrier Material 隔热保温材料制造业

The industry accounts for 0.028% of the total revenue of China's industrial sector in 2002. The rate of return on assets is 4.80%. 85.62% of all firms in the industry made a profit while 14.38% had negative returns.The top province in terms of the industry's revenue is Jiangsu, accounting for 20.53% of the total revenue.
2002年本行业收入占全行业的0.028%，资产利润率为4.80%。85.62%的企业赢利，14.38%的企业亏损。收入最高的省为江苏省，占本行业的20.53%。

	Total number of firms 企业总数	Total number of employees 职工总数	Total revenue (Mil.RMB) 总销售收入 (百万元)	Total profit (Mil.RMB) 总利润 (百万元)	Return on assets 资产利润率 (%)	Return on equity 权益利润率 (%)	Labour productivity ('000 RMB/ worker) 劳动生产率 (千元/人)	Debts/ assets 资产负债率 (%)	Total assets (Mil.RMB) 总资产 (百万元)
Industry Overall 行业总体	153	16,404	2,966	168	4.80	9.61	49.94	50.08	3,494

	Number of firms 企业个数	Average number of employees 平均职工人数	Average revenue ('000 RMB) 平均销售收入（千元）	Average profit ('000 RMB) 平均利润 (千元)	Return on assets 资产利润率 (%)	Return on equity 权益利润率 (%)	Labour productivity ('000 RMB/ worker) 劳动生产率 (千元/人)	Debts/ assets 资产负债率 (%)	Average total assets ('000 RMB) 平均总资产 (千元)
By ownership 产业所有权									
State-owned 国有	19	102	3,482	115	0.80	2.55	15.58	68.57	14,433
Collective-owned 集体	32	133	16,730	1,317	8.62	21.28	35.30	59.50	15,290
Foreign & Overseas Chinese Funded 三资	20	99	40,601	1,823	2.85	4.28	88.72	33.37	63,974
By regional distribution 地区分布									
Central-North 华北	43	99	19,552	1,696	7.70	18.53	25.39	58.45	22,027
Beijing 北京	11	97	28,755	1,880	4.61	9.26	12.91	50.24	40,803
Tianjin 天津	11	50	16,263	665	5.75	36.18	-22.23	84.11	11,563
Hebei 河北	15	148	20,943	2,686	12.41	32.57	48.72	61.88	21,639
Shanxi 山西	4	65	503	102	1.98	3.45	14.93	42.66	5,176
Inner Mongolia 内蒙古	2	76	14,689	2,113	16.36	29.26	-37.60	44.08	12,914
Northeast 东北	14	99	8,711	432	2.12	4.23	27.99	49.78	20,312
Liaoning 辽宁	4	73	12,353	1,623	7.89	14.00	38.17	43.67	20,569
Jilin 吉林	4	34	4,064	-746	-5.30	-24.43	68.43	78.31	14,081
Heilongjiang 黑龙江	6	160	9,382	423	1.74	3.01	19.15	42.20	24,295
Central-East 华东	57	117	25,771	1,558	5.85	11.82	72.06	50.48	26,611
Shanghai 上海	13	99	32,011	3,685	6.85	11.37	147.28	39.78	53,825
Jiangsu 江苏	21	99	29,007	586	2.72	7.57	71.18	64.02	21,514
Zhejiang 浙江	6	115	13,827	470	2.81	5.50	27.60	48.85	16,718
Anhui 安徽	1	170	8,500	-110	-0.52		25.47	104.85	21,240
Fujian 福建									
Jiangxi 江西	1	20	10,910	565	15.45	18.42	168.30	16.11	3,656
Shandong 山东	15	162	22,751	1,687	10.54	22.21	48.02	52.55	16,007
Central-South 中南	27	119	15,723	-137	-0.62	-1.02	46.33	39.30	22,101
Henan 河南	13	124	10,088	583	3.74	8.62	26.33	56.56	15,559
Hubei 湖北	8	103	10,968	462	6.78	16.11	48.00	57.89	6,811
Hunan 湖南	1	40	10,180	1,180	9.56	55.95	43.80	82.91	12,337
Guangdong 广东	5	151	39,092	-3,231	-4.93	-6.48	87.08	23.91	65,526
Guangxi 广西									
Hainan 海南									
Southwest 西南	4	82	10,738	667	4.90	6.86	56.15	28.53	13,614
Chongqing 重庆	2	95	6,336	514	3.83	4.77	45.33	19.80	13,424
Sichuan 四川	2	68	15,140	821	5.95	9.44	71.27	37.03	13,804
Guizhou 贵州									
Yunnan 云南									
Tibet 西藏									
Northwest 西北	8	67	8,417	101	0.86	1.46	43.83	41.11	11,755
Shaanxi 陕西	2	93	6,485	-83	-0.46	-0.73	50.53	36.47	17,783
Gansu 甘肃	3	30	4,485	119	3.64	6.46	50.08	43.66	3,258
Qinghai 青海									
Ningxia 宁夏	1	160	20,210	100	0.37	0.46	19.74	19.57	26,954
Xinjiang 新疆	2	49	10,352	259	2.38	9.24	64.80	74.23	10,875

Year 年份	Number of firms 企业个数	Rate of change 变化率 (%)	Number of employees 职工人数 (人)	Rate of change 变化率 (%)	Total revenue (Mil. RMB) 总销售收入 (百万元)	Rate of change 变化率 (%)	Total profit (Mil RMB) 总利润 (百万元)	Rate of change 变化率 (%)
2000	166		20,864		2,612		169	
2001	154	-7.23	17,310	-17.03	2,715	3.94	134	-20.71
2002	153	-0.65	16,404	-5.23	2,966	9.24	168	25.37

Major Products 主要产品	Output 产量	Unit 单位
Fire-Resistant Materials Product 耐火材料制品	1,177	10,000 Tons 万吨

10 Main Firms with Maximal Revenue (year founded) 收入最大的十家主要企业（创办年份）	City 城市	Province 省	Telephone/fax 电话/传真	Number of employees 职工人数	Ownership 产业所有权	Revenue ('000 RMB) 销售收入 (千元)	Profit('000 RMB) (rank) 利润(千元) (排名)	Total assets ('000 RMB) 总资产 (千元)	Major products 主要产品
Nantong Jinyang Xingwang Group Co.,Ltd.	Nantong	Jiangsu	(0513)3777016		Private Enterprises				Centrifugal Glass
南通金洋兴旺集团有限公司(1995)	南通市	江苏省	(0513)3776388	187	私营独资	210,710	2,062(23)	89,081	离心玻璃
Beijing HTN District Heat Equipment Co.,Ltd.	Beijing	Beijing	(010)67882588		Overseas Chinese-funded				Prefabricated Upright Embedding Attemperator预制直埋
北京豪特耐集中供热设备有限公司(1995)	北京市	北京市	(010)67882369	163	港澳台资	193,058	15,051(2)	219,033	保温设备
Jiangyin Tian Bao Industrial Co., Ltd.	Wuxi	Jiangsu	(0510)6406522		Joint Stock				Centrifugal Glass Wool离
江阴市天宝实业有限公司(1993)	无锡市	江苏省	(0510)6406533	183	股份制	89,328	-	79,474	心玻璃棉
Xisr Glass Wool(Guangdong) Co., Ltd.	Zhuhai	Guangdong	(0756)5511448		Foreign Funded				Glass Wool
西斯尔（广东）玻璃制品有限公司(1995)	珠海市	广东省	(0756)5511447	187	外商投资	65,103	-	168,200	玻璃棉
Shenxian Yi He Cheng Industrial Co.,Ltd.	Liaocheng	Shandong	(0635)7889057		Private Owned				Exceed The Thin Glass Wool超
莘县义和诚实业有限公司(1991)	聊城市	山东省	(0635)7889777	580	私营企业	62,883	4,052(11)	29,290	细玻璃棉
Shanghai Building Materials Group New Materials Co.,Ltd.	Shanghai	Shanghai	(021)63600808		Limited-Liability				Mineral Cotton Products
上海建筑材料集团新材料有限公司(2000)	上海市	上海市	(021)63507954	425	有限公司	62,590	1,859(25)	102,485	矿棉制品
Guangzhou Conghua Yao Hua New Type Building Materials	Guangzhou	Guangdong	(020)87832369		Limited-Liability				Stone Cotton Board
Co.,Ltd.广州从化耀华新型建材有限公司(1996)	广州市	广东省	(020)87832000	265	有限公司	60,800	3,040(15)	26,727	岩棉板
Rongcheng Yong Heng Thermal Insulating Material Factory	Weihai	Shandong	(0631)7681169		Collective-owned				Thermal Insulating Material
荣成永恒保温材料厂(1999)	威海市	山东省		80	集体企业	59,000	5,500(7)	7,660	保温材料
Tianjin Sino-czech Colour Painting Press Plates Co.,Ltd.	Tianjin	Tianjin	(022)27514174		Private Owned				New Type Building Materials新型
天津市中捷彩涂压型板材有限公司(1997)	天津市	天津市	(022)27514174	10	私营企业	57,371	1,222(33)	17,874	建筑材料
Saint-Gobain Isover Beijing Glass Wool Co.,Ltd.	Beijing	Beijing	(010)64301116		Foreign Funded				Glass Products
北京圣戈班依索维尔玻璃棉有限公司(1996)	北京市	北京市	(010)64301100	152	外商投资	52,096	1,013(41)	115,031	玻璃制品

Top 10 Cities by Revenue 销售收入排名前10位城市	Province 省	Market share 市场份额 (%)	Number of firms 企业个数
Shanghai 上海市	Shanghai 上海市	14.03	13
Beijing 北京市	Beijing 北京市	10.66	11
Nantong 南通市	Jiangsu 江苏省	7.86	4
Tianjin 天津市	Tianjin 天津市	6.03	11
Wuxi 无锡市	Jiangsu 江苏省	5.23	4
Cangzhou 沧州市	Hebei 河北省	4.03	2
Weihai 威海市	Shandong 山东省	3.61	2
Langfang 廊坊市	Hebei 河北省	3.41	4
Nanjing 南京市	Jiangsu 江苏省	3.20	4
Liaocheng 聊城市	Shandong 山东省	2.94	3

10 Major Wholesalers 十家主要批发商	City 城市	Province 省	Telephone/Fax 电话/传真
Xuzhou New Century Building Materials Decorative City	Xuzhou	Jiangsu	(0516)83666780
徐州市新世纪建材装饰城	徐州市	江苏省	(0516)63804485
Orienthome Co.,Ltd.	Beijing	Beijing	(010)63808294
东方家园有限公司	北京市	北京市	
Shanghai Jinkai Goods & Materials Co.,Ltd.	Shanghai	Shanghai	(021)52193967
上海金凯物资有限公司	上海市	上海市	
Guangzhou Building Materials Development Co.,Ltd.	Guangzhou	Guangdong	(020)83335062
广州市建材发展有限公司	广州市	广东省	(020)83341110
Guangxi Qiaofeng Goods & Materials Trade Co.,Ltd.	Nanning	Guangxi	(0771)2631539
广西侨丰物资贸易有限责任公司	南宁市	广西	(0771)2631539
Gansu Building Materials State-owned Assets Marketing Co.,Ltd.	Lanzhou	Gansu	(0931)8821359
甘肃建材国有资产经营有限责任公司	兰州市	甘肃省	(0931)8960243
Shanghai East Asia United Building Materials Co.,Ltd.	Shanghai	Shanghai	(021)33134520
上海东亚联合建材有限公司	上海市	上海市	(021)63216165
Shanghai Zhuzong Materials General Company	Shanghai	Shanghai	(021)32240030
上海住总物资总公司	上海市	上海市	(021)32240024
Guangdong Building Materials Company	Guangzhou	Guangdong	(020)83802713
广东省建材公司	广州市	广东省	(020)83817640
Guangdong Dongguan Hardware Minerals Import & Export Co.,Ltd	Dongguan	Guangdong	(0769)2227090
广东省东莞五金矿产进出口公司	东莞市	广东省	(0769)2221045

3139:Other Bricks and Tiles, Lime and Light Construction Materials

其他砖瓦、石灰和轻质建筑材料制造业

The industry accounts for 0.021% of the total revenue of China's industrial sector in 2002. The rate of return on assets is 4.55%. 83.78% of all firms in the industry made a profit while 16.22% had negative returns.The top province in terms of the industry's revenue is Guangdong, accounting for 16.54% of the total revenue.
2002年本行业收入占全行业的0.021%，资产利润率为4.55%。83.78%的企业赢利，16.22%的企业亏损。收入最高的省为广东省，占本行业的16.54%。

	Total number of firms 企业总数	Total number of employees 职工总数	Total revenue (Mil.RMB) 总销售收入(百万元)	Total profit (Mil.RMB) 总利润(百万元)	Return on assets 资产利润率(%)	Return on equity 权益利润率(%)	Labour productivity ('000 RMB/ worker) 劳动生产率(千元/人)	Debts/ assets 资产负债率(%)	Total assets (Mil.RMB) 总资产(百万元)
Industry Overall 行业总体	148	16,198	2,268	120	4.55	12.35	35.66	63.11	2,627

	Number of firms 企业个数	Average number of employees 平均职工人数	Average revenue ('000 RMB) 平均销售收入（千元）	Average profit ('000 RMB) 平均利润(千元)	Return on assets 资产利润率(%)	Return on equity 权益利润率(%)	Labour productivity ('000 RMB/ worker) 劳动生产率(千元/人)	Debts/ assets 资产负债率(%)	Average total assets ('000 RMB) 平均总资产(千元)
By ownership 产业所有权									
State-owned 国有	23	119	11,985	124	0.81	2.06	20.35	60.63	15,315
Collective-owned 集体	24	120	16,274	703	5.79	12.28	47.21	52.81	12,126
Foreign & Overseas Chinese Funded 三资	23	143	27,981	1,904	4.91	16.99	60.72	71.09	38,762
By regional distribution 地区分布									
Central-North 华北	26	153	14,688	1,816	4.86	12.37	13.64	60.73	37,394
Beijing 北京	6	148	27,706	3,113	4.07	11.89	54.36	65.79	76,528
Tianjin 天津	9	112	16,651	2,993	9.38	24.60	-29.90	61.89	31,918
Hebei 河北	7	87	2,781	58	1.20	4.43	14.31	73.03	4,862
Shanxi 山西	2	373	12,635	-359	-0.54	-1.02	24.50	47.32	66,615
Inner Mongolia 内蒙古	2	360	10,529	959	3.28	5.35	12.58	38.80	29,266
Northeast 东北	8	169	32,442	452	2.46	7.68	37.55	68.00	18,388
Liaoning 辽宁	5	232	50,637	737	2.62	8.27	41.47	68.28	28,073
Jilin 吉林	3	64	2,116	-23	-1.04	-2.75	13.88	62.25	2,246
Heilongjiang 黑龙江									
Central-East 华东	56	77	13,637	515	4.31	11.41	52.35	62.25	11,949
Shanghai 上海	19	44	13,114	537	4.02	10.90	93.14	63.13	13,373
Jiangsu 江苏	11	68	21,068	582	8.36	15.70	72.00	46.74	6,962
Zhejiang 浙江	7	90	9,214	237	3.32	8.56	23.70	61.14	7,141
Anhui 安徽	6	77	3,784	29	0.59	1.80	18.03	67.35	4,870
Fujian 福建	3	136	20,988	857	5.81	9.28	32.36	37.40	14,753
Jiangxi 江西	1	65	1,723	-208	-18.79	-34.49	9.54	45.53	1,107
Shandong 山东	9	127	14,544	890	3.74	13.15	48.71	71.55	23,767
Central-South 中南	46	111	16,818	762	5.01	16.30	41.34	69.24	15,194
Henan 河南	9	144	27,766	731	2.69	20.03	46.60	86.56	27,163
Hubei 湖北	13	60	8,552	423	6.70	10.91	57.22	38.63	6,314
Hunan 湖南	6	84	4,910	64	0.89	1.97	19.68	54.55	7,114
Guangdong 广东	15	159	25,004	1,504	7.24	22.19	38.38	67.37	20,778
Guangxi 广西	3	35	2,683	6	0.11	0.18	28.68	40.85	6,010
Hainan 海南									
Southwest 西南	6	105	7,941	350	2.65	5.06	29.83	47.61	13,182
Chongqing 重庆	2	157	4,904	749	7.78	12.62	5.21	38.35	9,622
Sichuan 四川	1	72	5,362	1,123	9.28	13.24	24.97	29.96	12,107
Guizhou 贵州	2	64	10,289	-166	-2.04	-26.02	34.20	92.16	8,115
Yunnan 云南	1	113	11,898	-192	-0.61	-0.97	96.37	37.09	31,514
Tibet 西藏									
Northwest 西北	6	145	6,960	478	4.74	9.16	21.88	48.29	10,091
Shaanxi 陕西	3	237	10,587	839	4.51	9.27	19.97	51.31	18,584
Gansu 甘肃	3	52	3,333	117	7.30	8.41	30.53	13.17	1,597
Qinghai 青海									
Ningxia 宁夏									
Xinjiang 新疆									

3139:Other Bricks and Tiles, Lime and Light Construction Materials

其他砖瓦、石灰和轻质建筑材料制造业

Year 年份	Number of firms 企业个数	Rate of change 变化率 (%)	Number of employees 职工人数 (人)	Rate of change 变化率 (%)	Total revenue (Mil. RMB) 总销售收入 (百万元)	Rate of change 变化率 (%)	Total profit (Mil RMB) 总利润 (百万元)	Rate of change 变化率 (%)
2000	145		18,587		1,992		80	
2001	151	4.14	18,919	1.79	1,941	-2.56	97	21.25
2002	148	-1.99	16,198	-14.38	2,268	16.85	120	23.71

Major Products 主要产品	Output 产量	Unit 单位
Glazed Brick 釉面砖	65,191	10,000 Sq.M. 万平方米
Active Precipitated Calcium Carbonate 轻质碳酸钙	249	10,000 Tons 万吨

10 Main Firms with Maximal Revenue (year founded) 收入最大的十家主要企业（创办年份）	City 城市	Province 省	Telephone/fax 电话/传真	Number of employees 职工人数	Ownership 产业所有权	Revenue ('000 RMB) 销售收入 (千元)	Profit('000 RMB) (rank) 利润(千元) (排名)	Total assets ('000 RMB) 总资产 (千元)	Major products 主要产品
Xinmei Ceramics Industrial Co., Ltd.Zhengzhou Branch	Zhengzhou	Henan	(0371)2684222		Foreign Funded				Floor
新美陶瓷工业有限公司郑州分公司(1995)	郑州市	河南省	(0371)2573347	570	外商投资	178,437	3,251(7)	199,861	地坂
Shenyang Urban Construction Pitch and Concrete Factory	Shenyang	Liaoning	(024)88090643		State-owned				Pitch Earth
沈阳市城建沥青混泥土厂(1964)	沈阳市	辽宁省	(024)88093247	301	国有企业	177,574	1,395(22)	87,495	沥青土
Beijing LuXin Pitch & Concrete Co.,Ltd.	Beijing	Beijing	(010)61759708		Limited-Liability				Pitch Concrete沥
北京路新沥青混凝土有限公司(1953)	北京市	北京市	(010)84851882	242	有限公司	132,860	18,670(2)	370,498	青混凝土
Jiatai Ceramics (Guangzhou) Co., Ltd.	Guangzhou	Guangdong	(020)82972827		Foreign Funded				Western Style Glazed Tile西
嘉泰陶瓷（广州）有限公司(1993)	广州市	广东省	(020)82971468	150	外商投资	71,557	9,346(3)	109,007	式琉璃瓦
Guangzhou Huadong New Materials Co.,Ltd	Guangzhou	Guangdong	(020)82708042		Overseas Chinese-funded				Decorative Materials
广州华东新型材料有限公司(1994)	广州市	广东省	(020)82705551	180	港澳台资	41,510	1,421(20)	11,068	装饰材料
Zhenjiang Mei Lun Road Asphalt Co.,Ltd.	Zhenjiang	Jiangsu	(0511)4514611		Joint Stock				Pitch
镇江美仑道路沥青有限公司(2000)	镇江市	江苏省	(0511)4514611	22	股份制	40,199	1,243(25)	12,581	沥青
Quanzhou Jinshan Stone Material Industry & Trade Company	Quanzhou	Fujian	(0595)2595470		Collective-owned				Stone Materials
泉州金山石材工贸公司(1993)	泉州市	福建省	(0595)2590960	221	集体企业	39,930	1,903(13)	19,489	石材
Nanjing Wan Li New Type Building Materials Co., Ltd.	Nanjing	Jiangsu	(025)2187514		Foreign Funded				NBS Multiple-unit Board Materials.NBS
南京万力新型建材有限公司(1993)	南京市	江苏省	(025)2187514	51	外商投资	39,510	2,030(12)	16,730	复合板材
Shanghai Sima Expo Co., Ltd.	Shanghai	Shanghai	(021)62388811		Overseas Chinese-funded				Aluminium Fabrics
上海司马展览建造有限公司(1994)	上海市	上海市	(021)62093166	40	港澳台资	37,989	767(36)	12,910	铝型材
Air Building Materials (Tianjin) Co., Ltd.	Tianjin	Tianjin	(022)83969988		Overseas Chinese-funded				Colour Ground Brick
爱尔建材（天津）有限公司(2000)	天津市	天津市	(022)83966565	100	港澳台资	37,055	19,018(1)	123,166	彩色地砖

Top 10 Cities by Revenue 销售收入排名前10位城市	Province 省	Market share 市场份额 (%)	Number of firms 企业个数
Shanghai 上海市	Shanghai 上海市	10.99	19
Zhengzhou 郑州市	Henan 河南省	8.86	2
Shenyang 沈阳市	Liaoning 辽宁省	8.57	2
Guangzhou 广州市	Guangdong 广东省	7.51	6
Beijing 北京市	Beijing 北京市	7.33	6
Tianjin 天津市	Tianjin 天津市	6.61	9
Foshan 佛山市	Guangdong 广东省	4.34	3
Wuxi 无锡市	Jiangsu 江苏省	3.91	6
Nanjing 南京市	Jiangsu 江苏省	3.50	2
Wuhan 武汉市	Hubei 湖北省	2.88	4

10 Major Wholesalers 十家主要批发商	City 城市	Province 省	Telephone/Fax 电话/传真
Xuzhou New Century Building Materials Decorative City	Xuzhou	Jiangsu	(0516)83666780
徐州市新世纪建材装饰城	徐州市	江苏省	(0516)63804485
Orienthome Co.,Ltd.	Beijing	Beijing	(010)63808294
东方家园有限公司	北京市	北京市	
Shanghai Jinkai Goods & Materials Co.,Ltd.	Shanghai	Shanghai	(021)52193967
上海金凯物资有限公司	上海市	上海市	
Guangzhou Building Materials Development Co.,Ltd.	Guangzhou	Guangdong	(020)83335062
广州市建材发展有限公司	广州市	广东省	(020)83341110
Guangxi Qiaofeng Goods & Materials Trade Co.,Ltd.	Nanning	Guangxi	(0771)2631539
广西侨丰物资贸易有限责任公司	南宁市	广西	(0771)2631539
Gansu Building Materials State-owned Assets Marketing Co.,Ltd.	Lanzhou	Gansu	(0931)8821359
甘肃建材国有资产经营有限责任公司	兰州市	甘肃省	(0931)8960243
Shanghai East Asia United Building Materials Co.,Ltd.	Shanghai	Shanghai	(021)33134520
上海东亚联合建材有限公司	上海市	上海市	(021)63216165
Shanghai Zhuzong Materials General Company	Shanghai	Shanghai	(021)32240030
上海住总物资总公司	上海市	上海市	(021)32240024
Guangdong Building Materials Company	Guangzhou	Guangdong	(020)83802713
广东省建材公司	广州市	广东省	(020)83817640
Guangdong Dongguan Hardware Minerals Import & Export Co.,Ltd	Dongguan	Guangdong	(0769)2227090
广东省东莞五金矿产进出口公司	东莞市	广东省	(0769)2221045

3141: Construction Glass 建筑用玻璃制品业

The industry accounts for 0.170% of the total revenue of China's industrial sector in 2002. The rate of return on assets is -0.15%. 67.84% of all firms in the industry made a profit while 32.16% had negative returns.The top province in terms of the industry's revenue is Hebei, accounting for 12.12% of the total revenue.
2002年本行业收入占全行业的 0.170%，资产利润率为 -0.15%。67.84%的企业赢利，32.16%的企业亏损。收入最高的省为河北省，占本行业的12.12%。

	Total number of firms 企业总数	Total number of employees 职工总数	Total revenue (Mil.RMB) 总销售收入（百万元）	Total profit (Mil.RMB) 总利润（百万元）	Return on assets 资产利润率 (%)	Return on equity 权益利润率 (%)	Labour productivity ('000 RMB/ worker) 劳动生产率（千元/人）	Debts/ assets 资产负债率 (%)	Total assets (Mil.RMB) 总资产（百万元）
Industry Overall 行业总体	227	134,101	18,280	-73	-0.15	-0.38	36.68	60.83	49,268

	Number of firms 企业个数	Average number of employees 平均职工人数	Average revenue ('000 RMB) 平均销售收入（千元）	Average profit ('000 RMB) 平均利润（千元）	Return on assets 资产利润率 (%)	Return on equity 权益利润率 (%)	Labour productivity ('000 RMB/ worker) 劳动生产率（千元/人）	Debts/ assets 资产负债率 (%)	Average totai assets ('000 RMB) 平均总资产（千元）
By ownership 产业所有权									
State-owned 国有	23	493	67,943	-3,741	-1.77	-10.31	24.07	82.82	211,296
Collective-owned 集体	44	361	27,751	782	1.34	4.37	22.24	69.31	58,386
Foreign & Overseas Chinese Funded 三资	49	383	93,809	105	0.04	0.10	87.21	55.97	236,676
By regional distribution 地区分布									
Central-North 华北	55	597	60,365	-5,085	-2.91	-7.48	17.62	61.05	174,639
Beijing 北京	10	441	25,816	-167	-0.13	-0.42	28.22	68.22	123,929
Tianjin 天津	4	472	86,901	-14,688	-4.42	-35.50	-5.64	87.55	332,444
Hebei 河北	37	574	59,878	-2,252	-1.51	-2.81	20.09	46.01	148,622
Shanxi 山西	1	2,071	164,410	-119,446	-18.81	-807.45	-11.67	97.67	635,151
Inner Mongolia 内蒙古	3	1,073	111,479	-5,502	-1.83	-8.32	19.35	78.00	300,646
Northeast 东北	18	596	64,588	-12,057	-4.34	-24.98	22.23	82.63	277,870
Liaoning 辽宁	9	648	86,932	-15,445	-3.81	-27.50	27.40	86.14	405,144
Jilin 吉林	3	428	47,566	35	0.02		18.95	101.69	208,719
Heilongjiang 黑龙江	6	602	39,582	-13,022	-10.71	-20.89	15.04	48.72	121,535
Central-East 华东	51	694	134,747	10,838	3.49	7.23	64.66	51.76	310,842
Shanghai 上海	6	507	179,802	20,264	4.81	5.68	157.70	15.36	421,620
Jiangsu 江苏	15	622	121,775	4,118	1.63	6.41	52.22	74.66	253,406
Zhejiang 浙江	6	645	234,736	26,714	5.21	9.12	93.22	42.86	512,580
Anhui 安徽	4	608	60,224	5,383	1.86	3.83	34.12	51.52	289,811
Fujian 福建	4	459	122,026	27,032	9.63	10.36	100.74	7.03	280,716
Jiangxi 江西	2	275	18,046	266	1.46	3.54	23.80	58.77	18,188
Shandong 山东	14	1,024	128,084	5,637	1.91	6.77	47.44	71.76	294,872
Central-South 中南	76	501	71,570	-1,764	-0.93	-2.69	34.64	65.38	189,469
Henan 河南	19	951	102,927	-4,311	-1.25	-3.03	18.83	58.75	345,370
Hubei 湖北	13	446	66,211	1,873	1.29	2.73	38.97	52.72	144,889
Hunan 湖南	7	680	64,321	-14,153	-7.26	-56.71	23.56	87.20	194,964
Guangdong 广东	33	252	62,360	681	0.53	1.99	73.70	73.59	129,405
Guangxi 广西	3	361	38,205	92	0.09	0.32	24.02	72.46	105,890
Hainan 海南	1	12	227	-137	-10.69		-0.25	220.44	1,282
Southwest 西南	13	679	96,466	7,084	3.10	5.07	48.74	38.94	228,855
Chongqing 重庆	3	366	17,256	-258	-1.22	-3.83	12.03	68.08	21,057
Sichuan 四川	7	839	142,772	18,517	5.81	8.04	67.92	27.67	318,455
Guizhou 贵州	1	701	5,080	-2,416	-1.40	-17.72	1.07	92.09	172,393
Yunnan 云南	2	580	98,902	-17,167	-6.73	-20.14	15.21	66.60	255,188
Tibet 西藏									
Northwest 西北	14	591	16,563	-6,220	-6.07	-36.85	7.72	83.52	102,411
Shaanxi 陕西	5	574	18,180	-10,217	-10.83		3.85	119.01	94,334
Gansu 甘肃	6	646	18,768	-5,387	-4.41	-8.59	11.29	48.65	122,134
Qinghai 青海	1	590						128.53	120,532
Ningxia 宁夏	1	556	16,390	-1,718	-2.04		9.15	117.41	84,036
Xinjiang 新疆	1	385	11,989	-1,960	-7.93		10.33	105.22	24,717

Year 年份	Number of firms 企业个数	Rate of change 变化率 (%)	Number of employees 职工人数 (人)	Rate of change 变化率 (%)	Total revenue (Mil. RMB) 总销售收入 (百万元)	Rate of change 变化率 (%)	Total profit (Mil RMB) 总利润 (百万元)	Rate of change 变化率 (%)
2000	233		158,589		18,184		1,670	
2001	225	-3.43	136,451	-13.96	17,712	-2.60	499	-70.12
2002	227	0.89	134,101	-1.72	18,280	3.21	-73	-

Major Products 主要产品	Output 产量	Unit 单位
Plate Glass 平板玻璃	22,801	10,000 Weight Boxes 万重量箱

10 Main Firms with Maximal Revenue (year founded) 收入最大的十家主要企业（创办年份）	City 城市	Province 省	Telephone/fax 电话/传真	Number of employees 职工人数	Ownership 产业所有权	Revenue ('000 RMB) 销售收入 (千元)	Profit('000 RMB) (rank) 利润(千元) (排名)	Total assets ('000 RMB) 总资产 (千元)	Major products 主要产品
Jiangsu Huarun Group Company	Suzhou	Jiangsu	(0512)58550102		Joint Stock				Float Glass
江苏华润集团公司(1973)	苏州市	江苏省	(0512)58550252	4,072	股份制	1,138,456	90,205(5)	2,808,378	浮法玻璃
Shaoxing County Guang Yu Group Co., Ltd.	Shaoxing	Zhejiang	(0575)4509556		Limited-Liability				Float Glass
绍兴县光宇集团公司(1994)	绍兴市	浙江省	(0575)4509580	1,315	有限公司	1,015,022	103,005(4)	2,072,679	浮法玻璃
Shanghai Yao Hua Pilkington Glass Co., Ltd.	Shanghai	Shanghai	(021)58839305		Foreign Funded				Plate Glass
上海耀华皮尔金顿玻璃股份有限公司(1983)	上海市	上海市	(021)58801554	1,527	外商投资	823,435	126,642(1)	1,891,151	平板玻璃
China Guo Dong Construction Co., Ltd.	Chengdu	Sichuan	(028)86154162		Joint Stock				Coated Centrifugal Glass镀膜
四川国栋建设股份有限公司(1993)	成都市	四川省	(028)85804146	2,813	股份制	512,332	119,240(2)	1,165,439	中空玻璃
Shandong Blue Star Glass Group Co., Ltd.	Weihai	Shandong	(0631)5223241		Limited-Liability				Plate Glass
山东蓝星玻璃集团有限公司(1964)	威海市	山东省	(0631)5226676	2,107	有限公司	444,565	48,188(7)	751,372	平板玻璃
Hangzhou Glass Group Co., Ltd.	Hangzhou	Zhejiang	(0571)88144501		Limited-Liability				Glass Fibre Yarn玻
杭州玻璃集团有限公司(1957)	杭州市	浙江省	(0571)88145649	2,233	有限公司	346,880	54,074(6)	896,550	璃纤维纱
Dezhou Jing Hua Group Co., Ltd.	Dezhou	Shandong	(0534)2612213		Limited-Liability				Plate Glass
德州晶华集团有限公司(1998)	德州市	山东省	(0534)2348984	6,287	有限公司	341,026	17,695(14)	1,344,532	平板玻璃
Qinhuangdao Bei Fang Glass Group Co., Ltd.	Qinhuangdao	Hebei	(0335)3867488		State Enterprises				Float Glass
秦皇岛北方玻璃集团有限公司(1996)	秦皇岛市	河北省	(0335)3861668	2,831	国有独资	330,174	640(64)	779,282	浮法玻璃
Shangqiu Zhen Hua Glass Factory	Shangqiu	Henan	(0370)2599607		State-owned				Plate Glass
商丘市振华玻璃厂(1952)	商丘市	河南省	(0370)2599619	966	国有企业	315,881	280(90)	935,506	平板玻璃
Zhongshan Sheng Xing Curtain Wall Co., Ltd.	Zhongshan	Guangdong	(0760)8508068		Private Owned				Glass Products
中山市盛兴幕墙有限公司(1995)	中山市	广东省	(0760)8508979	902	私营企业	315,300	26,010(8)	679,584	玻璃制品

Top 10 Cities by Revenue 销售收入排名前10位城市	Province 省	Market share 市场份额 (%)	Number of firms 企业个数
Qinhuangdao 秦皇岛市	Hebei 河北省	7.85	10
Suzhou 苏州市	Jiangsu 江苏省	7.05	4
Luoyang 洛阳市	Henan 河南省	5.99	4
Shanghai 上海市	Shanghai 上海市	5.90	6
Shaoxing 绍兴市	Zhejiang 浙江省	5.55	1
Chengdu 成都市	Sichuan 四川省	4.48	2
Qingdao 青岛市	Shandong 山东省	3.79	5
Zhongshan 中山市	Guangdong 广东省	3.74	6
Weihai 威海市	Shandong 山东省	3.52	2
Xingtai 邢台市	Hebei 河北省	3.51	22

10 Major Wholesalers 十家主要批发商	City 城市	Province 省	Telephone/Fax 电话/传真
Xuzhou New Century Building Materials Decorative City	Xuzhou	Jiangsu	(0516)83666780
徐州市新世纪建材装饰城	徐州市	江苏省	(0516)63804485
Orienthome Co.,Ltd.	Beijing	Beijing	(010)63808294
东方家园有限公司	北京市	北京市	
Shanghai Jinkai Goods & Materials Co.,Ltd.	Shanghai	Shanghai	(021)52193967
上海金凯物资有限公司	上海市	上海市	
Guangzhou Building Materials Development Co.,Ltd.	Guangzhou	Guangdong	(020)83335062
广州市建材发展有限公司	广州市	广东省	(020)83341110
Guangxi Qiaofeng Goods & Materials Trade Co.,Ltd.	Nanning	Guangxi	(0771)2631539
广西侨丰物资贸易有限责任公司	南宁市	广西	(0771)2631539
Gansu Building Materials State-owned Assets Marketing Co.,Ltd.	Lanzhou	Gansu	(0931)8821359
甘肃建材国有资产经营有限责任公司	兰州市	甘肃省	(0931)8960243
Shanghai East Asia United Building Materials Co.,Ltd.	Shanghai	Shanghai	(021)33134520
上海东亚联合建材有限公司	上海市	上海市	(021)63216165
Shanghai Zhuzong Materials General Company	Shanghai	Shanghai	(021)32240030
上海住总物资总公司	上海市	上海市	(021)32240024
Guangdong Building Materials Company	Guangzhou	Guangdong	(020)83802713
广东省建材公司	广州市	广东省	(020)83817640
Guangdong Dongguan Hardware Minerals Import & Export Co.,Ltd	Dongguan	Guangdong	(0769)2227090
广东省东莞五金矿产进出口公司	东莞市	广东省	(0769)2221045

3142: Industrial Glass 工业技术用玻璃制造业

The industry accounts for 0.061% of the total revenue of China's industrial sector in 2002. The rate of return on assets is 5.40%. 82.58% of all firms in the industry made a profit while 17.42% had negative returns.The top province in terms of the industry's revenue is Fujian, accounting for 21.55% of the total revenue.
2002年本行业收入占全行业的0.061%，资产利润率为5.40%。82.58%的企业赢利，17.42%的企业亏损。收入最高的省为福建省，占本行业的21.55%。

	Total number of firms 企业总数	Total number of employees 职工总数	Total revenue (Mil.RMB) 总销售收入（百万元）	Total profit (Mil.RMB) 总利润（百万元）	Return on assets 资产利润率（%）	Return on equity 权益利润率（%）	Labour productivity ('000 RMB/ worker) 劳动生产率（千元/人）	Debts/ assets 资产负债率（%）	Total assets (Mil.RMB) 总资产（百万元）
Industry Overall 行业总体	155	28,791	6,558	655	5.40	12.58	74.99	57.08	12,132

	Number of firms 企业个数	Average number of employees 平均职工人数	Average revenue ('000 RMB) 平均销售收入（千元）	Average profit ('000 RMB) 平均利润（千元）	Return on assets 资产利润率（%）	Return on equity 权益利润率（%）	Labour productivity ('000 RMB/ worker) 劳动生产率（千元/人）	Debts/ assets 资产负债率（%）	Average total assets ('000 RMB) 平均总资产（千元）
By ownership 产业所有权									
State-owned 国有	11	139	14,021	265	0.79		29.55	111.68	33,754
Collective-owned 集体	15	170	22,049	934	4.39	15.84	35.69	72.31	21,282
Foreign & Overseas Chinese Funded 三资	53	235	75,563	9,421	6.48	13.57	116.48	52.23	145,353
By regional distribution 地区分布									
Central-North 华北	30	149	22,781	932	1.97	5.42	58.00	63.62	47,256
Beijing 北京	10	129	15,061	741	2.45		35.63	101.71	30,297
Tianjin 天津	2	99	18,538	1,391	3.62	8.21	59.78	55.95	38,460
Hebei 河北	16	137	25,819	749	1.30	2.79	77.01	53.44	57,710
Shanxi 山西	1	738	51,632	1,578	1.54	2.93	39.93	47.34	102,225
Inner Mongolia 内蒙古	1	68	31,000	4,200	34.43	127.27	59.81	72.95	12,200
Northeast 东北	13	114	21,794	-163	-0.39	-0.68	51.24	43.18	41,850
Liaoning 辽宁	10	87	18,218	-774	-2.04	-4.46	29.71	54.26	37,922
Jilin 吉林	3	206	33,716	1,875	3.41	4.14	81.59	17.68	54,942
Heilongjiang 黑龙江									
Central-East 华东	64	234	63,515	7,190	6.09	13.98	73.92	56.43	118,043
Shanghai 上海	15	139	45,585	2,545	4.24	8.38	100.37	49.44	60,070
Jiangsu 江苏	18	193	47,542	3,261	3.56	7.66	74.65	53.50	91,571
Zhejiang 浙江	10	193	18,729	1,045	5.19	10.93	30.70	52.48	20,113
Anhui 安徽	1	101	20,080	1,380	8.84	12.78	40.23	30.81	15,610
Fujian 福建	5	517	282,695	58,136	10.90	22.84	148.51	52.28	533,247
Jiangxi 江西									
Shandong 山东	15	319	60,305	4,050	2.86	8.80	39.63	67.47	141,497
Central-South 中南	42	146	31,921	3,614	6.81	15.78	106.34	56.84	53,079
Henan 河南	11	146	24,094	2,048	7.50	10.20	64.14	26.51	27,315
Hubei 湖北	7	104	6,060	78	0.60	2.31	40.97	74.09	12,948
Hunan 湖南	8	58	14,594	633	8.59	45.86	71.57	81.26	7,360
Guangdong 广东	14	207	59,444	8,467	7.40	20.55	160.98	64.00	114,437
Guangxi 广西	2	218	42,131	2,567	2.90	3.95	44.32	26.61	88,604
Hainan 海南									
Southwest 西南	5	330	37,137	3,437	4.52	13.93	39.67	67.55	76,044
Chongqing 重庆	2	268	40,692	7,378	6.98	14.51	45.33	51.92	105,746
Sichuan 四川	2	438	42,787	782	1.18	15.55	38.67	92.44	66,474
Guizhou 贵州									
Yunnan 云南	1	240	18,730	864	2.41	7.41	30.68	67.42	35,780
Tibet 西藏									
Northwest 西北	1	95					7.82	18.40	5,604
Shaanxi 陕西									
Gansu 甘肃	1	95					7.82	18.40	5,604
Qinghai 青海									
Ningxia 宁夏									
Xinjiang 新疆									

3142: Industrial Glass 工业技术用玻璃制造业

Year 年份	Number of firms 企业个数	Rate of change 变化率 (%)	Number of employees 职工人数 (人)	Rate of change 变化率 (%)	Total revenue (Mil. RMB) 总销售收入 (百万元)	Rate of change 变化率 (%)	Total profit (Mil RMB) 总利润 (百万元)	Rate of change 变化率 (%)
2000	109		20,103		4,953		495	
2001	136	24.77	27,754	38.06	5,417	9.37	548	10.71
2002	155	13.97	28,791	3.74	6,558	21.06	655	19.53

Major Products 主要产品	Output 产量	Unit 单位

10 Main Firms with Maximal Revenue (year founded) 收入最大的十家主要企业（创办年份）	City 城市	Province 省	Telephone/fax 电话/传真	Number of employees 职工人数	Ownership 产业所有权	Revenue ('000 RMB) 销售收入 (千元)	Profit('000 RMB) (rank) 利润(千元) (排名)	Total assets ('000 RMB) 总资产 (千元)	Major products 主要产品
Fujian Fuyao Glass Industries Group Co., Ltd.	Fuzhou	Fujian	(0591)5383777		Overseas Chinese-funded				Laminated Glass
福建省福耀玻璃工业股份有限公司(1987)	福州市	福建省	(0591)5383666	956	港澳台资	794,080	143,925(1)	1,707,253	夹层玻璃
Shandong Glass General Company	Zibo	Shandong	(0533)4166055		Joint Owned				Plate Glass
山东玻璃总公司（山东玻璃集团）(1959)	淄博市	山东省	(0533)4183666	1,867	联营企业	550,126	41,001(6)	1,922,083	平板玻璃
Fujian Wan Da Auto Glass Industry Group Co., Ltd.	Fuzhou	Fujian	(0591)5383777		Overseas Chinese-funded				Automobile Laminated Glass汽车
福建省万达汽车玻璃工业有限公司(1996)	福州市	福建省	(0591)5383666	916	港澳台资	381,146	90,513(2)	574,432	夹层玻璃
ChangJiang Float Glass Co., Ltd.	Suzhou	Jiangsu	(0512)57440001		Overseas Chinese-funded				Glass
长江浮法玻璃有限公司(1994)	苏州市	江苏省	(0512)57440666	1,022	港澳台资	309,084	14,726(10)	1,063,085	玻璃
Xinyi Automobile Glass (Shenzhen)Co., Ltd.	Shenzhen	Guangdong	(0755)28631333		Overseas Chinese-funded				Laminated Glass
信义汽车玻璃（深圳）有限公司(1988)	深圳市	广东省	(0755)28630993	500	港澳台资	255,112	41,203(5)	596,262	夹层玻璃
Fuzhou Lvrong Glass Industry Group Co., Ltd.	Fuzhou	Fujian	(0591)5383777		Overseas Chinese-funded				Glass Products
福州绿榕玻璃有限公司(2000)	福州市	福建省	(0591)5383666	393	港澳台资	223,782	56,390(3)	337,093	玻璃制品
Qinhuangdao Hai Yan Safety Glass Co., Ltd.	Qinhuangdao	Hebei	(0335)3627254		Foreign Funded				Toughened Glass
秦皇岛海燕安全玻璃有限公司(1992)	秦皇岛市	河北省	(0335)3066239	358	外商投资	153,289	13,625(12)	243,530	钢化玻璃
Shanghai Meite Curtain Wall Co., Ltd.	Shanghai	Shanghai	(021)58863323		Foreign Funded				Construction Curtain Wall
上海美特幕墙有限公司(1993)	上海市	上海市	(021)58742165	137	外商投资	139,155	2,608(32)	224,546	建筑幕墙
Yi De Glass (Shenzhen) Development Co., Ltd.	Shenzhen	Guangdong	(0755)28631333		Overseas Chinese-funded				Automobile Glass
义德玻璃（深圳）发展有限公司(1994)	深圳市	广东省		400	港澳台资	126,269	46,716(4)	249,297	汽车玻璃
Guangzhou Hua Bao Glass Industrial Ltd. Company	Guangzhou	Guangdong	(020)84857241		Overseas Chinese-funded				Glass Products
广州华宝玻璃实业有限公司(1991)	广州市	广东省	(020)84858007	635	港澳台资	99,770	1,850(42)	133,380	玻璃制品

Top 10 Cities by Revenue 销售收入排名前10位城市	Province 省	Market share 市场份额 (%)	Number of firms 企业个数
Fuzhou 福州市	Fujian 福建省	21.53	4
Shanghai 上海市	Shanghai 上海市	10.43	15
Shenzhen 深圳市	Guangdong 广东省	8.83	7
Zibo 淄博市	Shandong 山东省	8.39	1
Suzhou 苏州市	Jiangsu 江苏省	6.27	4
Qinhuangdao 秦皇岛市	Hebei 河北省	3.92	7
Changzhou 常州市	Jiangsu 江苏省	3.48	5
Puyang 濮阳市	Henan 河南省	2.30	2
Beijing 北京市	Beijing 北京市	2.30	10
Shenyang 沈阳市	Liaoning 辽宁省	2.20	6

10 Major Wholesalers 十家主要批发商	City 城市	Province 省	Telephone/Fax 电话/传真
Xuzhou New Century Building Materials Decorative City	Xuzhou	Jiangsu	(0516)83666780
徐州市新世纪建材装饰城	徐州市	江苏省	(0516)63804485
Orienthome Co.,Ltd.	Beijing	Beijing	(010)63808294
东方家园有限公司	北京市	北京市	
Shanghai Jinkai Goods & Materials Co.,Ltd.	Shanghai	Shanghai	(021)52193967
上海金凯物资有限公司	上海市	上海市	
Guangzhou Building Materials Development Co.,Ltd.	Guangzhou	Guangdong	(020)83335062
广州市建材发展有限公司	广州市	广东省	(020)83341110
Guangxi Qiaofeng Goods & Materials Trade Co.,Ltd.	Nanning	Guangxi	(0771)2631539
广西侨丰物资贸易有限责任公司	南宁市	广西	(0771)2631539
Gansu Building Materials State-owned Assets Marketing Co.,Ltd.	Lanzhou	Gansu	(0931)8821359
甘肃建材国有资产经营有限责任公司	兰州市	甘肃省	(0931)8960243
Shanghai East Asia United Building Materials Co.,Ltd.	Shanghai	Shanghai	(021)33134520
上海东亚联合建材有限公司	上海市	上海市	(021)63216165
Shanghai Zhuzong Materials General Company	Shanghai	Shanghai	(021)32240030
上海住总物资总公司	上海市	上海市	(021)32240024
Guangdong Building Materials Company	Guangzhou	Guangdong	(020)83802713
广东省建材公司	广州市	广东省	(020)83817640
Guangdong Dongguan Hardware Minerals Import & Export Co.,Ltd	Dongguan	Guangdong	(0769)2227090
广东省东莞五金矿产进出口公司	东莞市	广东省	(0769)2221045

3143: Optical Glass 光学玻璃制造业

The industry accounts for 0.020% of the total revenue of China's industrial sector in 2002. The rate of return on assets is 2.56%. 73.02% of all firms in the industry made a profit while 26.98% had negative returns.The top province in terms of the industry's revenue is Jiangsu, accounting for 27.31% of the total revenue.
2002年本行业收入占全行业的0.020%，资产利润率为2.56%。73.02%的企业赢利，26.98%的企业亏损。收入最高的省为江苏省，占本行业的27.31%。

	Total number of firms 企业总数	Total number of employees 职工总数	Total revenue (Mil.RMB) 总销售收入（百万元）	Total profit (Mil.RMB) 总利润（百万元）	Return on assets 资产利润率 (%)	Return on equity 权益利润率 (%)	Labour productivity ('000 RMB/ worker) 劳动生产率（千元/人）	Debts/ assets 资产负债率 (%)	Total assets (Mil.RMB) 总资产（百万元）
Industry Overall 行业总体	63	20,294	2,132	78	2.56	5.34	31.46	52.13	3,068

	Number of firms 企业个数	Average number of employees 平均职工人数	Average revenue ('000 RMB) 平均销售收入（千元）	Average profit ('000 RMB) 平均利润（千元）	Return on assets 资产利润率 (%)	Return on equity 权益利润率 (%)	Labour productivity ('000 RMB/ worker) 劳动生产率（千元/人）	Debts/ assets 资产负债率 (%)	Average total assets ('000 RMB) 平均总资产（千元）
By ownership 产业所有权									
State-owned 国有	6	441	61,630	899	0.75	1.35	33.86	44.21	119,574
Collective-owned 集体	9	204	38,128	1,161	7.75	14.91	59.29	48.05	14,982
Foreign & Overseas Chinese Funded 三资	25	281	35,669	2,168	4.80	8.83	34.50	45.67	45,177
By regional distribution 地区分布									
Central-North 华北	5	165	12,050	890	4.52	7.70	17.55	41.28	19,688
Beijing 北京	3	180	8,178	-30	-0.12	-0.20	15.02	37.45	24,247
Tianjin 天津	2	144	17,858	2,271	17.67	36.90	22.28	52.11	12,851
Hebei 河北									
Shanxi 山西									
Inner Mongolia 内蒙古									
Northeast 东北	1	199	45,458	-1,513	-6.31	-31.08	54.10	79.71	23,995
Liaoning 辽宁	1	199	45,458	-1,513	-6.31	-31.08	54.10	79.71	23,995
Jilin 吉林									
Heilongjiang 黑龙江									
Central-East 华东	32	267	36,780	2,049	5.64	11.89	35.44	52.54	36,306
Shanghai 上海	8	300	48,530	2,880	4.23	8.98	28.05	52.91	68,106
Jiangsu 江苏	14	240	41,602	1,190	5.94	12.43	50.35	52.25	20,050
Zhejiang 浙江	2	214	8,239	703	4.47	23.13	19.18	80.67	15,727
Anhui 安徽	2	208	19,302	1,712	7.77	14.25	32.43	45.49	22,034
Fujian 福建	5	362	29,097	4,190	8.20	16.38	23.31	49.92	51,080
Jiangxi 江西	1	120	5,740	100	1.88	3.57	16.34	47.37	5,320
Shandong 山东									
Central-South 中南	15	411	28,718	-89	-0.14	-0.40	26.65	63.60	61,755
Henan 河南	7	473	23,324	-1,176	-3.52	-9.93	24.10	64.54	33,424
Hubei 湖北	3	805	72,337	2,413	1.13	2.95	28.40	61.68	213,105
Hunan 湖南	2	52	6,075	280	11.88	38.03	30.58	68.76	2,353
Guangdong 广东	3	109	12,779	-298	-1.85	-11.61	38.41	84.05	16,114
Guangxi 广西									
Hainan 海南									
Southwest 西南	9	494	45,775	1,234	1.30	2.17	32.49	39.78	94,655
Chongqing 重庆									
Sichuan 四川	9	494	45,775	1,234	1.30	2.17	32.49	39.78	94,655
Guizhou 贵州									
Yunnan 云南									
Tibet 西藏									
Northwest 西北	1	127	7,065	195	3.33	4.14	16.45	19.55	5,856
Shaanxi 陕西	1	127	7,065	195	3.33	4.14	16.45	19.55	5,856
Gansu 甘肃									
Qinghai 青海									
Ningxia 宁夏									
Xinjiang 新疆									

3143: Optical Glass 光学玻璃制造业

Year 年份	Number of firms 企业个数	Rate of change 变化率 (%)	Number of employees 职工人数 (人)	Rate of change 变化率 (%)	Total revenue (Mil. RMB) 总销售收入 (百万元)	Rate of change 变化率 (%)	Total profit (Mil RMB) 总利润 (百万元)	Rate of change 变化率 (%)
2000	59		21,916		2,219		106	
2001	59	o	19,533	-10.87	2,066	-6.90	86	-18.87
2002	63	6.78	20,294	3.90	2,132	3.19	78	-9.30

Major Products 主要产品	Output 产量	Unit 单位

10 Main Firms with Maximal Revenue (year founded) 收入最大的十家主要企业（创办年份）	City 城市	Province 省	Telephone/fax 电话/传真	Number of employees 职工人数	Ownership 产业所有权	Revenue ('000 RMB) 销售收入 (千元)	Profit('000 RMB) (rank) 利润(千元) (排名)	Total assets ('000 RMB) 总资产 (千元)	Major products 主要产品
Jiangsu Zhongcheng Optical Co.,Ltd.	Zhenjiang	Jiangsu	(0511)6525373		Collective-owned				Telescope
丹阳市中诚集团公司(1981)	镇江市	江苏省	(0511)6525907	852	集体企业	265,484	3,312(12)	65,726	望远镜
Chengdu Guang Ming Optoelectronic Information Material Co	Chengdu	Sichuan	(028)84331612		State-owned				Optics Glass Products光学
成都光明光电信息材料有限公司(1959)	成都市	四川省	(028)84332218	1,476	国有企业	257,610	6,790(5)	573,490	玻璃制品
Shanghai Essilor Optics Co., Ltd.	Shanghai	Shanghai	(021)57742888		Foreign Funded				Optics Lens
上海依视路光学有限公司(1998)	上海市	上海市	(021)57741295	668	外商投资	180,815	11,953(1)	314,012	光学镜片
Hubei Huaguang New Materials Co., ltd.	Xiangfan	Hubei	(0710)3349810		State Enterprises				Optical Instrument光学
湖北华光新材料有限公司(2000)	襄樊市	湖北省	(0710)3340494	2,130	国有独资	177,080	5,180(8)	586,640	玻璃材料
Nanjing Weining Optics Co., Ltd.	Nanjing	Jiangsu	(025)2161104		Overseas Chinese-funded				Optics Glass
南京伟宁光学有限公司(1995)	南京市	江苏省	(025)2160142	170	港澳台资	128,970	6,710(6)	30,650	光学玻璃
Shanghai Xinhu Glass Factory	Shanghai	Shanghai	(021)59923272		State-owned				Optics Glass
上海新沪玻璃厂(1960)	上海市	上海市	(021)59925160	709	国有企业	90,866	114(36)	82,071	光学玻璃
Nanyang lida Optical & Electronic Co., ltd.	Nanyang	Henan	(0377)3152375		Foreign Funded				Optics Glass
南阳利达光电有限公司(1995)	南阳市	河南省	(0377)3865100	970	外商投资	85,753	-	96,946	光学玻璃
Shanghai Kangnaite Optics Co., Ltd.	Shanghai	Shanghai	(021)58370299		Foreign Funded				lens
上海康耐特光学有限公司(1996)	上海市	上海市	(021)58376066	398	外商投资	34,721	5,195(7)	60,382	眼镜片
Tianjin Dacheng Optics Co., Ltd	Tianjin	Tianjin	(022)26721827		Foreign Funded				lens
天津大成光学有限公司(2000)	天津市	天津市	(022)26721827	216	外商投资	32,510	4,800(9)	15,560	镜片
Nantong Yudi Optical Instrument Co., Ltd.	Nantong	Jiangsu	(0513)4614703		Private Owned				Magnifier
南通宇迪光学仪器有限公司(1993)	南通市	江苏省	(0513)4611063	619	私营企业	31,761	7,119(4)	31,253	放大镜

Top 10 Cities by Revenue 销售收入排名前10位城市	Province 省	Market share 市场份额 (%)	Number of firms 企业个数
Shanghai 上海市	Shanghai 上海市	18.21	8
Chengdu 成都市	Sichuan 四川省	17.40	8
Zhenjiang 镇江市	Jiangsu 江苏省	12.72	2
Nanjing 南京市	Jiangsu 江苏省	9.67	6
Xiangfan 襄樊市	Hubei 湖北省	8.30	1
Nanyang 南阳市	Henan 河南省	7.30	6
Xiamen 厦门市	Fujian 福建省	6.26	2
Nantong 南通市	Jiangsu 江苏省	2.91	3
Dalian 大连市	Liaoning 辽宁省	2.13	1
Meishan 眉山市	Sichuan 四川省	1.92	1

10 Major Wholesalers 十家主要批发商	City 城市	Province 省	Telephone/Fax 电话/传真
Xuzhou New Century Building Materials Decorative City	Xuzhou	Jiangsu	(0516)83666780
徐州市新世纪建材装饰城	徐州市	江苏省	(0516)63804485
Orienthome Co.,Ltd.	Beijing	Beijing	(010)63808294
东方家园有限公司	北京市	北京市	
Shanghai Jinkai Goods & Materials Co.,Ltd.	Shanghai	Shanghai	(021)52193967
上海金凯物资有限公司	上海市	上海市	
Guangzhou Building Materials Development Co.,Ltd.	Guangzhou	Guangdong	(020)83335062
广州市建材发展有限公司	广州市	广东省	(020)83341110
Guangxi Qiaofeng Goods & Materials Trade Co.,Ltd.	Nanning	Guangxi	(0771)2631539
广西侨丰物资贸易有限责任公司	南宁市	广西	(0771)2631539
Gansu Building Materials State-owned Assets Marketing Co.,Ltd.	Lanzhou	Gansu	(0931)8821359
甘肃建材国有资产经营有限责任公司	兰州市	甘肃省	(0931)8960243
Shanghai East Asia United Building Materials Co.,Ltd.	Shanghai	Shanghai	(021)33134520
上海东亚联合建材有限公司	上海市	上海市	(021)63216165
Shanghai Zhuzong Materials General Company	Shanghai	Shanghai	(021)32240030
上海住总物资总公司	上海市	上海市	(021)32240024
Guangdong Building Materials Company	Guangzhou	Guangdong	(020)83802713
广东省建材公司	广州市	广东省	(020)83817640
Guangdong Dongguan Hardware Minerals Import & Export Co.,Ltd	Dongguan	Guangdong	(0769)2227090
广东省东莞五金矿产进出口公司	东莞市	广东省	(0769)2221045

3145: Glass Instruments 玻璃仪器制造业

The industry accounts for 0.016% of the total revenue of China's industrial sector in 2002. The rate of return on assets is 6.24%. 74.00% of all firms in the industry made a profit while 26.00% had negative returns.The top province in terms of the industry's revenue is Shandong, accounting for 31.59% of the total revenue.
2002年本行业收入占全行业的 0.016%，资产利润率为 6.24%。74.00%的企业赢利，26.00%的企业亏损。收入最高的省为山东省，占本行业的31.59%。

	Total number of firms 企业总数	Total number of employees 职工总数	Total revenue (Mil.RMB) 总销售收入 (百万元)	Total profit (Mil.RMB) 总利润 (百万元)	Return on assets 资产利润率 (%)	Return on equity 权益利润率 (%)	Labour productivity ('000 RMB/ worker) 劳动生产率 (千元/人)	Debts/ assets 资产负债率 (%)	Total assets (Mil.RMB) 总资产 (百万元)
Industry Overall 行业总体	50	11,487	1,669	124	6.24	25.74	56.65	75.76	1,994

	Number of firms 企业个数	Average number of employees 平均职工人数	Average revenue ('000 RMB) 平均销售收入 (千元)	Average profit ('000 RMB) 平均利润 (千元)	Return on assets 资产利润率 (%)	Return on equity 权益利润率 (%)	Labour productivity ('000 RMB/ worker) 劳动生产率 (千元/人)	Debts/ assets 资产负债率 (%)	Average total assets ('000 RMB) 平均总资产 (千元)
By ownership 产业所有权									
State-owned 国有	5	289	6,823	-716	-0.63		-3.79	108.15	113,915
Collective-owned 集体	11	256	49,967	4,923	10.93	146.68	72.20	92.55	45,024
Foreign & Overseas Chinese Funded 三资	4	157	22,503	2,033	4.94	7.24	79.36	31.73	41,113
By regional distribution 地区分布									
Central-North 华北	9	99	6,148	-180	-0.84	-10.25	19.22	91.84	21,492
Beijing 北京	2	49	8,342	264	2.56	5.30	53.24	51.76	10,304
Tianjin 天津	1	143	1,837	-3,104	-2.10	-301.95	0.75	99.30	147,599
Hebei 河北	5	91	6,323	146	5.64		22.86	107.54	2,585
Shanxi 山西	1	200	5,200	230	1.87	3.97	7.50	52.85	12,300
Inner Mongolia 内蒙古									
Northeast 东北									
Liaoning 辽宁									
Jilin 吉林									
Heilongjiang 黑龙江									
Central-East 华东	16	338	54,122	4,094	5.59	93.76	52.40	94.04	73,283
Shanghai 上海	3	361	16,745	-44	-0.03		-6.15	106.99	144,198
Jiangsu 江苏	9	276	31,023	799	6.31	75.87	33.72	91.69	12,672
Zhejiang 浙江	1	42	5,644	4	0.15	0.80	22.90	81.04	2,653
Anhui 安徽									
Fujian 福建									
Jiangxi 江西	1	59	3,603				50.31	60.31	1,625
Shandong 山东	2	871	263,632	29,219	9.40	65.31	116.16	85.60	310,802
Central-South 中南	10	259	57,647	5,686	14.39	16.56	104.69	13.11	39,513
Henan 河南	5	374	103,093	9,694	16.96	17.93	129.60	5.41	57,146
Hubei 湖北									
Hunan 湖南	2	213	5,282	55	0.55		8.08	103.10	10,026
Guangdong 广东	2	45	22,696	4,098	9.77	11.79	268.54	17.11	41,926
Guangxi 广西	1	210	5,050	80	1.45	1.92	8.90	24.18	5,500
Hainan 海南									
Southwest 西南	13	182	12,792	282	1.66	7.43	31.75	77.72	17,032
Chongqing 重庆	1	228	13,693	-494	-3.24	-28.55	22.14	88.67	15,269
Sichuan 四川	12	179	12,717	347	2.02	8.74	32.78	76.91	17,179
Guizhou 贵州									
Yunnan 云南									
Tibet 西藏									
Northwest 西北	2	110	2,621	14	0.25	0.55	15.10	55.47	5,696
Shaanxi 陕西	2	110	2,621	14	0.25	0.55	15.10	55.47	5,696
Gansu 甘肃									
Qinghai 青海									
Ningxia 宁夏									
Xinjiang 新疆									

3145: Glass Instruments 玻璃仪器制造业

Year 年份	Number of firms 企业个数	Rate of change 变化率 (%)	Number of employees 职工人数 (人)	Rate of change 变化率 (%)	Total revenue (Mil. RMB) 总销售收入 (百万元)	Rate of change 变化率 (%)	Total profit (Mil RMB) 总利润 (百万元)	Rate of change 变化率 (%)
2000	22		7,687		905		49	
2001	31	40.91	8,563	11.40	1,181	30.50	82	67.35
2002	50	61.29	11,487	34.15	1,669	41.32	124	51.22

Major Products 主要产品	Output 产量	Unit 单位

10 Main Firms with Maximal Revenue (year founded) 收入最大的十家主要企业（创办年份）	City 城市	Province 省	Telephone/fax 电话/传真	Number of employees 职工人数	Ownership 产业所有权	Revenue ('000 RMB) 销售收入 (千元)	Profit('000 RMB) (rank) 利润(千元) (排名)	Total assets ('000 RMB) 总资产 (千元)	Major products 主要产品
Ji'nan Linuo Glass Ware Co., ltd.	Jinan	Shandong	(0531)4759599		Collective-owned				Vacuum Glass Pipe
山东力诺集团有限责任公司济南分公司(1995)	济南市	山东省	(0531)4759099	1,090	集体企业	438,668	52,128(1)	360,169	真空玻璃管
Yancheng Hua'ou Industrial Co., Ltd.	Yancheng	Jiangsu	(0515)8701666		Joint Stock				Glass Apparatus
盐城市华鸥实业有限公司(1967)	盐城市	江苏省	(0515)8701486	570	股份制	185,260	6,720(5)	36,340	玻璃仪器
Shandong Linuo New Materials Co., Ltd.	Jinan	Shandong	(0531)4883497		Private Enterprises				Coated Tube
山东力诺新材料有限公司(1998)	济南市	山东省	(0531)4880663	652	私营独资	88,596	6,310(6)	261,435	镀膜管
Shenzhen Wellight Conductive Coating Co., Ltd.	Shenzhen	Guangdong	(0755)26680788		Overseas Chinese-funded				ITO Electric Conduction Glass.ITO
深圳伟光导电膜有限公司(1993)	深圳市	广东省	(0755)26893268	40	港澳台资	39,350	8,010(4)	80,322	导电玻璃
Kaifeng Juli Glass Products Co., Ltd.	Kaifeng	Henan	(0378)38544075		Collective-owned				Glass Products
开封巨力玻璃制品有限公司(1999)	开封市	河南省	(0378)38544075	290	集体企业	31,870	165(26)	10,410	玻璃制品
Chengdu Xiang Feng Package Container Co., Ltd.	Chengdu	Sichuan	(028)85178822		Overseas Chinese-funded				PET Bottle
成都翔峰包装容器有限公司(1999)	成都市	四川省	(028)85189962	92	港澳台资	30,310	-	46,284	PET瓶
Shanghai Glass Factory	Shanghai	Shanghai	(021)56383988		State-owned				Glass Apparatus
上海玻璃厂(1953)	上海市	上海市	(021)56384129	771	国有企业	19,651	108(28)	371,586	玻璃仪器
Shanghai Haichang Glass Factory	Shanghai	Shanghai	(021)57853771		Collective-owned				Glass Products
上海海昌玻璃厂(1993)	上海市	上海市	(021)57853772	219	集体企业	18,857	-	48,014	玻璃制品
Funing Shuoji Shuaiqi Company	Yancheng	Jiangsu	(0515)7551276		Private Enterprises				Temperature Meter
阜宁县硕集帅旗公司(1999)	盐城市	江苏省	(0515)7552166	85	私营独资	18,000	300(16)	2,300	温度仪表
Taizhou Glass Apparatus Manufacturing Co., Ltd.	Taizhou	Jiangsu	(0523)6921143		Private Partnership				Glass Apparatus
北京玻璃集团泰州玻璃仪器厂(1987)	泰州市	江苏省	(0523)6921502	200	私营合伙	15,519	406(18)	7,529	玻璃仪器

Top 10 Cities by Revenue 销售收入排名前10位城市	Province 省	Market share 市场份额 (%)	Number of firms 企业个数
Jinan 济南市	Shandong 山东省	31.59	2
Puyang 濮阳市	Henan 河南省	28.18	2
Yancheng 盐城市	Jiangsu 江苏省	12.18	2
Deyang 德阳市	Sichuan 四川省	6.51	9
Shanghai 上海市	Shanghai 上海市	3.01	3
Shenzhen 深圳市	Guangdong 广东省	2.36	1
Chengdu 成都市	Sichuan 四川省	2.13	2
Kaifeng 开封市	Henan 河南省	1.91	1
Taizhou 泰州市	Jiangsu 江苏省	1.85	3
Hengshui 衡水市	Hebei 河北省	1.30	3

10 Major Wholesalers 十家主要批发商	City 城市	Province 省	Telephone/Fax 电话/传真
Xuzhou New Century Building Materials Decorative City	Xuzhou	Jiangsu	(0516)83666780
徐州市新世纪建材装饰城	徐州市	江苏省	(0516)63804485
Orienthome Co.,Ltd.	Beijing	Beijing	(010)63808294
东方家园有限公司	北京市	北京市	
Shanghai Jinkai Goods & Materials Co.,Ltd.	Shanghai	Shanghai	(021)52193967
上海金凯物资有限公司	上海市	上海市	
Guangzhou Building Materials Development Co.,Ltd.	Guangzhou	Guangdong	(020)83335062
广州市建材发展有限公司	广州市	广东省	(020)83341110
Guangxi Qiaofeng Goods & Materials Trade Co.,Ltd.	Nanning	Guangxi	(0771)2631539
广西侨丰物资贸易有限责任公司	南宁市	广西	(0771)2631539
Gansu Building Materials State-owned Assets Marketing Co.,Ltd.	Lanzhou	Gansu	(0931)8821359
甘肃建材国有资产经营有限责任公司	兰州市	甘肃省	(0931)8960243
Shanghai East Asia United Building Materials Co.,Ltd.	Shanghai	Shanghai	(021)33134520
上海东亚联合建材有限公司	上海市	上海市	(021)63216165
Shanghai Zhuzong Materials General Company	Shanghai	Shanghai	(021)32240030
上海住总物资总公司	上海市	上海市	(021)32240024
Guangdong Building Materials Company	Guangzhou	Guangdong	(020)83802713
广东省建材公司	广州市	广东省	(020)83817640
Guangdong Dongguan Hardware Minerals Import & Export Co.,Ltd	Dongguan	Guangdong	(0769)2227090
广东省东莞五金矿产进出口公司	东莞市	广东省	(0769)2221045

3147: Household Glass Products 日用玻璃制品业

The industry accounts for 0.148% of the total revenue of China's industrial sector in 2002. The rate of return on assets is 1.41%. 81.18% of all firms in the industry made a profit while 18.82% had negative returns.The top province in terms of the industry's revenue is Shandong, accounting for 19.96% of the total revenue.
2002年本行业收入占全行业的 0.148%，资产利润率为 1.41%。81.18%的企业赢利，18.82%的企业亏损。收入最高的省为山东省，占本行业的19.96%。

	Total number of firms 企业总数	Total number of employees 职工总数	Total revenue (Mil.RMB) 总销售收入(百万元)	Total profit (Mil.RMB) 总利润(百万元)	Return on assets 资产利润率(%)	Return on equity 权益利润率(%)	Labour productivity ('000 RMB/worker) 劳动生产率(千元/人)	Debts/assets 资产负债率(%)	Total assets (Mil.RMB) 总资产(百万元)
Industry Overall 行业总体	558	187,636	15,873	318	1.41	3.84	26.57	63.36	22,661

	Number of firms 企业个数	Average number of employees 平均职工人数	Average revenue ('000 RMB) 平均销售收入(千元)	Average profit ('000 RMB) 平均利润(千元)	Return on assets 资产利润率(%)	Return on equity 权益利润率(%)	Labour productivity ('000 RMB/worker) 劳动生产率(千元/人)	Debts/assets 资产负债率(%)	Average total assets ('000 RMB) 平均总资产(千元)
By ownership 产业所有权									
State-owned 国有	45	497	27,608	-1,341	-1.22	-7.22	19.46	83.10	109,908
Collective-owned 集体	82	259	19,008	424	2.20	7.49	22.20	70.63	19,287
Foreign & Overseas Chinese Funded 三资	79	322	45,147	-81	-0.11	-0.21	40.15	48.46	75,049
By regional distribution 地区分布									
Central-North 华北	80	461	23,115	-172	-0.30	-1.46	18.33	79.10	56,321
Beijing 北京	3	1,323	78,929	-1,155	-0.22	-0.78	24.78	71.79	525,602
Tianjin 天津	10	117	11,083	-3,766	-5.34		1.48	103.25	70,536
Hebei 河北	37	402	26,790	243	0.63	2.70	23.34	76.67	38,457
Shanxi 山西	22	649	17,562	803	3.01	12.39	10.93	75.72	26,693
Inner Mongolia 内蒙古	8	322	15,497	93	0.35	1.64	28.11	78.78	26,667
Northeast 东北	14	288	17,121	-174	-0.36	-1.51	17.13	75.90	47,736
Liaoning 辽宁	9	226	15,214	-446	-0.96	-3.82	14.26	74.92	46,563
Jilin 吉林	4	445	22,318	345	0.60	2.69	19.91	77.62	57,309
Heilongjiang 黑龙江	1	209	13,491	199	0.99	4.29	21.57	76.82	20,001
Central-East 华东	221	323	35,359	1,088	2.57	6.21	33.65	58.62	42,345
Shanghai 上海	27	192	30,358	1,557	3.85	5.47	48.12	29.57	40,393
Jiangsu 江苏	76	284	30,189	430	1.43	3.66	32.16	60.89	30,058
Zhejiang 浙江	29	154	20,314	97	0.37	1.22	29.24	69.58	26,174
Anhui 安徽	18	529	35,854	212	0.40	2.50	23.58	84.04	53,344
Fujian 福建	5	193	43,096	-1,524	-1.25	-2.74	79.77	54.20	121,438
Jiangxi 江西	6	178	13,697	434	3.72	12.63	24.41	70.53	11,661
Shandong 山东	60	474	52,803	2,737	4.58	10.75	34.99	57.39	59,779
Central-South 中南	162	225	24,710	379	1.19	2.76	32.22	56.73	31,756
Henan 河南	40	180	13,002	502	2.78	9.76	25.19	71.58	18,098
Hubei 湖北	16	211	21,224	1,471	6.06	12.60	33.54	51.92	24,297
Hunan 湖南	19	158	7,992	144	1.57	5.54	17.37	71.56	9,151
Guangdong 广东	79	230	34,909	486	1.15	2.23	41.48	48.33	42,110
Guangxi 广西	8	577	29,210	-2,910	-4.38	-35.90	15.51	87.79	66,402
Hainan 海南									
Southwest 西南	65	537	27,977	512	1.24	3.15	17.50	60.43	41,102
Chongqing 重庆	15	456	28,165	-250	-0.59	-2.49	15.23	76.16	42,055
Sichuan 四川	44	600	29,835	788	1.84	4.06	18.04	54.78	42,909
Guizhou 贵州	5	226	12,099	445	1.93	8.05	15.72	76.03	23,034
Yunnan 云南	1	529	22,777	95	0.25	0.37	23.69	31.87	37,632
Tibet 西藏									
Northwest 西北	16	263	9,250	-40	-0.20	-1.41	14.21	85.59	19,541
Shaanxi 陕西	7	328	12,607	-446	-1.71	-52.16	12.97	96.73	26,138
Gansu 甘肃	5	150	3,212	77	0.79	1.75	11.85	55.20	9,751
Qinghai 青海	1	334	4,023	-1,431	-4.87		7.80	100.73	29,370
Ningxia 宁夏									
Xinjiang 新疆	3	277	13,220	1,178	6.85	20.25	22.36	66.16	17,188

3147: Household Glass Products 日用玻璃制品业

Year 年份	Number of firms 企业个数	Rate of change 变化率 (%)	Number of employees 职工人数 (人)	Rate of change 变化率 (%)	Total revenue (Mil. RMB) 总销售收入 (百万元)	Rate of change 变化率 (%)	Total profit (Mil RMB) 总利润 (百万元)	Rate of change 变化率 (%)
2000	510		194,939		13,054		245	
2001	530	3.92	188,580	-3.26	13,878	6.31	206	-15.92
2002	558	5.28	187,636	-0.50	15,873	14.38	318	54.37

Major Products 主要产品	Output 产量	Unit 单位
Vacuum Glass Container 玻璃保温容器	30,295	10,000 Units 万个
Daily Glass Products 日用玻璃制品	644	10,000 Tons 万吨

10 Main Firms with Maximal Revenue (year founded) 收入最大的十家主要企业（创办年份）	City 城市	Province 省	Telephone/fax 电话/传真	Number of employees 职工人数	Ownership 产业所有权	Revenue ('000 RMB) 销售收入 (千元)	Profit('000 RMB) (rank) 利润(千元)(排名)	Total assets ('000 RMB) 总资产 (千元)	Major products 主要产品
Shandong Pharmaceutical Glass Co., Ltd.	Zibo	Shandong	(0533)3242312		Joint Stock				Daily Glass Products
山东药用玻璃股份有限公司(1970)	淄博市	山东省	(0533)3243376	2,980	股份制	406,658	70,655(1)	871,218	玻璃制品
ACI Guangdong Glass Co., Ltd.	Guangzhou	Guangdong	(020)85525021		Overseas Chinese-funded				Daily Glass Products
广东澳联玻璃有限公司(1994)	广州市	广东省	(020)85524207	756	港澳台资	406,015	20,637(3)	743,564	玻璃制品
ACI Shanghai Glass Co., Ltd.	Shanghai	Shanghai	(021)64775068		Overseas Chinese-funded				Daily Glass Products
上海澳联玻璃有限公司(1993)	上海市	上海市	(021)64760470	596	港澳台资	232,580	14,937(7)	481,331	玻璃制品
Kind light Manufactory Co., Ltd.	Huizhou	Guangdong	(0752)6863888		Overseas Chinese-funded				Painted Glass Light Decorations彩色
惠州市商亮灯饰有限公司(1995)	惠州市	广东省	(0752)6863969	1,000	港澳台资	227,407	5,132(20)	60,913	玻璃灯饰
Nanhai Huaxing Glass Co., Ltd.	Foshan	Guangdong	(0757)6443541		Private Owned				Daily Glass Products
南海华兴玻璃有限公司(1987)	佛山市	广东省	(0757)6431661	856	私营企业	203,884	2,528(55)	164,521	玻璃制品
Qingdao Jinghua Glass Factory	Qingdao	Shandong	(0532)3761302		State-owned				Daily Glass
国营青岛晶华玻璃厂(1932)	青岛市	山东省	(0532)3717234	1,533	国有企业	189,489	101(276)	527,837	日用玻璃
Shandong Zaozhuang Lianxing Glass Co., Ltd.	Zaozhuang	Shandong	(0632)4682469		Joint Stock				Daily Glass Products
山东省枣庄市联兴玻璃有限公司(1980)	枣庄市	山东省	(0632)4682717	682	股份制	163,941	12,704(9)	68,375	玻璃制品
Jiangsu Kaihua Group	Taizhou	Jiangsu	(0523)3761194		Limited-Liability				Glass Medicine Bottle
江苏凯华集团(1961)	泰州市	江苏省	(0523)3762549	1,236	有限公司	163,190	6,650(16)	185,160	玻璃药瓶
Wuxi Huazhong Glass Co., Ltd	Wuxi	Jiangsu	(0510)2357179		Foreign Funded				Daily Glass Products
无锡华众玻璃有限公司(1993)	无锡市	江苏省	(0510)2352496	1,061	外商投资	160,452	7,646(13)	383,000	玻璃制品
Shaoxing Jingxing Mirror Glasses Co.,ltd	Shaoxing	Zhejiang	(0575)2032016		Private Owned				Ornaments Glass
绍兴晶兴镜业有限公司(1997)	绍兴市	浙江省	(0575)2031717	180	私营企业	148,540	9,358(12)	46,603	装饰玻璃

Top 10 Cities by Revenue 销售收入排名前10位城市	Province 省	Market share 市场份额 (%)	Number of firms 企业个数
Zibo 淄博市	Shandong 山东省	6.13	21
Shanghai 上海市	Shanghai 上海市	5.16	27
Guangzhou 广州市	Guangdong 广东省	4.33	11
Foshan 佛山市	Guangdong 广东省	3.50	18
Nantong 南通市	Jiangsu 江苏省	3.39	16
Qingdao 青岛市	Shandong 山东省	2.78	5
Chongqing 重庆市	Chongqing 重庆市	2.66	15
Taizhou 泰州市	Jiangsu 江苏省	2.47	6
Weifang 潍坊市	Shandong 山东省	2.31	4
Chengdu 成都市	Sichuan 四川省	2.18	9

10 Major Wholesalers 十家主要批发商	City 城市	Province 省	Telephone/Fax 电话/传真
Xuzhou New Century Building Materials Decorative City	Xuzhou	Jiangsu	(0516)83666780
徐州市新世纪建材装饰城	徐州市	江苏省	(0516)63804485
Orienthome Co.,Ltd.	Beijing	Beijing	(010)63808294
东方家园有限公司	北京市	北京市	
Shanghai Jinkai Goods & Materials Co.,Ltd.	Shanghai	Shanghai	(021)52193967
上海金凯物资有限公司	上海市	上海市	
Guangzhou Building Materials Development Co.,Ltd.	Guangzhou	Guangdong	(020)83335062
广州市建材发展有限公司	广州市	广东省	(020)83341110
Guangxi Qiaofeng Goods & Materials Trade Co.,Ltd.	Nanning	Guangxi	(0771)2631539
广西侨丰物资贸易有限责任公司	南宁市	广西	(0771)2631539
Gansu Building Materials State-owned Assets Marketing Co.,Ltd.	Lanzhou	Gansu	(0931)8821359
甘肃建材国有资产经营有限责任公司	兰州市	甘肃省	(0931)8960243
Shanghai East Asia United Building Materials Co.,Ltd.	Shanghai	Shanghai	(021)33134520
上海东亚联合建材有限公司	上海市	上海市	(021)63216165
Shanghai Zhuzong Materials General Company	Shanghai	Shanghai	(021)32240030
上海住总物资总公司	上海市	上海市	(021)32240024
Guangdong Building Materials Company	Guangzhou	Guangdong	(020)83802713
广东省建材公司	广州市	广东省	(020)83817640
Guangdong Dongguan Hardware Minerals Import & Export Co.,Ltd	Dongguan	Guangdong	(0769)2227090
广东省东莞五金矿产进出口公司	东莞市	广东省	(0769)2221045

3148: Glass Thermal Containers 玻璃保温容器制造业

The industry accounts for 0.014% of the total revenue of China's industrial sector in 2002. The rate of return on assets is -1.09%. 65.52% of all firms in the industry made a profit while 34.48% had negative returns.The top province in terms of the industry's revenue is Shanghai, accounting for 17.13% of the total revenue.
2002年本行业收入占全行业的0.014%，资产利润率为 -1.09%。65.52%的企业赢利，34.48%的企业亏损。收入最高的省为上海市，占本行业的17.13%。

	Total number of firms 企业总数	Total number of employees 职工总数	Total revenue (Mil.RMB) 总销售收入（百万元）	Total profit (Mil.RMB) 总利润（百万元）	Return on assets 资产利润率（%）	Return on equity 权益利润率（%）	Labour productivity ('000 RMB/ worker) 劳动生产率（千元/人）	Debts/ assets 资产负债率（%）	Total assets (Mil.RMB) 总资产（百万元）
Industry Overall 行业总体	58	21,884	1,465	-22	-1.09	-3.38	21.35	67.81	2,031

	Number of firms 企业个数	Average number of employees 平均职工人数	Average revenue ('000 RMB) 平均销售收入（千元）	Average profit ('000 RMB) 平均利润（千元）	Return on assets 资产利润率（%）	Return on equity 权益利润率（%）	Labour productivity ('000 RMB/ worker) 劳动生产率（千元/人）	Debts/ assets 资产负债率（%）	Average total assets ('000 RMB) 平均总资产（千元）
By ownership 产业所有权									
State-owned 国有	7	730	25,903	-5,285	-8.29		11.86	112.60	63,727
Collective-owned 集体	8	366	20,372	616	1.42	30.77	19.12	95.39	43,421
Foreign & Overseas Chinese Funded 三资	9	192	35,529	752	1.79	2.64	50.73	32.26	42,078
By regional distribution 地区分布									
Central-North 华北	6	571	37,328	-4,355	-6.69		26.87	105.11	65,143
Beijing 北京	1	2,091	196,459	2,694	2.12	4.59	41.93	53.93	127,277
Tianjin 天津	2	60		-11,006	-12.67			113.04	86,882
Hebei 河北	3	404	9,169	-2,272	-7.59		3.58	162.31	29,939
Shanxi 山西									
Inner Mongolia 内蒙古									
Northeast 东北									
Liaoning 辽宁									
Jilin 吉林									
Heilongjiang 黑龙江									
Central-East 华东	33	332	22,268	197	0.58	1.43	19.09	59.14	33,819
Shanghai 上海	9	193	27,885	632	1.72	2.35	38.68	26.90	36,734
Jiangsu 江苏	3	380	33,338	-374	-1.38	-9.82	22.94	85.99	27,150
Zhejiang 浙江	10	88	11,700	416	4.29	9.64	27.64	55.51	9,708
Anhui 安徽	8	661	27,766	-714	-1.55	-4.01	11.76	61.24	45,946
Fujian 福建									
Jiangxi 江西	1	574	17,377	-345	-10.98	-13.95	12.04	21.27	3,141
Shandong 山东	2	678	13,681	1,921	1.63	25.91	16.78	93.72	118,096
Central-South 中南	17	381	29,491	-147	-0.60	-2.04	25.21	70.55	24,435
Henan 河南	2	1,189	40,977	413	0.81	2.12	13.13	61.79	50,951
Hubei 湖北	4	603	49,143	-1,766	-4.24	-15.17	30.45	72.08	41,687
Hunan 湖南	1	1,108	36,096	-2,904	-5.56		12.77	104.02	52,271
Guangdong 广东	10	58	18,673	665	7.03	17.08	76.81	58.81	9,447
Guangxi 广西									
Hainan 海南									
Southwest 西南	1	182							58,438
Chongqing 重庆									
Sichuan 四川	1	182							58,438
Guizhou 贵州									
Yunnan 云南									
Tibet 西藏									
Northwest 西北	1	831	5,120	-2		-0.01	3.06	26.70	50,361
Shaanxi 陕西									
Gansu 甘肃									
Qinghai 青海									
Ningxia 宁夏									
Xinjiang 新疆	1	831	5,120	-2		-0.01	3.06	26.70	50,361

3148: Glass Thermal Containers 玻璃保温容器制造业

Year 年份	Number of firms 企业个数	Rate of change 变化率(%)	Number of employees 职工人数(人)	Rate of change 变化率(%)	Total revenue (Mil. RMB) 总销售收入(百万元)	Rate of change 变化率(%)	Total profit (Mil RMB) 总利润(百万元)	Rate of change 变化率(%)
2000	64		36,523		1,841		20	
2001	58	-9.38	27,245	-25.40	1,536	-16.57	-50	-
2002	58	o	21,884	-19.68	1,465	-4.62	-22	56.00

Major Products 主要产品	Output 产量	Unit 单位
Vacuum Glass Container 玻璃保温容器	30,295	10,000 Units 万个

10 Main Firms with Maximal Revenue (year founded) 收入最大的十家主要企业(创办年份)	City 城市	Province 省	Telephone/fax 电话/传真	Number of employees 职工人数	Ownership 产业所有权	Revenue ('000 RMB) 销售收入(千元)	Profit('000 RMB) (rank) 利润(千元)(排名)	Total assets ('000 RMB) 总资产(千元)	Major products 主要产品
Beijing Deer Urban Daily Articles Co., Ltd.	Beijing	Beijing	(010)69771061		Limited-Liability				Vacuum Glass Container玻璃
北京鹿牌都市生活用品有限公司(2000)	北京市	北京市	(010)69771239	2,091	有限公司	196,459	2,694(6)	127,277	保温容器
Wuhan Fanghua Glass Wool Products Co.,Ltd.	Wuhan	Hubei	(027)86550100		Limited-Liability				Glass Wool
武汉芳华玻璃棉制品有限责任公司(1995)	武汉市	湖北省	(027)86550229	80	有限公司	114,105	3,888(3)	4,400	玻璃棉
Shanghai Wansheng Vacuum Flask & Vessel Co., Ltd.	Shanghai	Shanghai	(021)64785002		Foreign Funded				Vacuum Glass Container玻璃
上海万盛保温容器有限公司(1997)	上海市	上海市	(021)64193408	220	外商投资	95,351	8,838(1)	55,369	保温容器
Wuhu Guanghua Group Co., Ltd.	Wuhu	Anhui	(0553)5846056		Limited-Liability				Vacuum Flask
芜湖光华集团有限公司(1997)	芜湖市	安徽省	(0553)5846036	1,215	有限公司	56,513	-	186,052	保温瓶
Heshan Jia Hui Vacuum Flask Factory	Jiangmen	Guangdong	(0750)8991333		Overseas Chinese-funded				Vacuum Flask
鹤山市嘉辉保温瓶厂(1998)	江门市	广东省	(0750)8984289	90	港澳台资	50,049	2,530(7)	27,510	保温瓶
Shanghai Nissho Vacuum Flask Refill Co., Ltd.	Shanghai	Shanghai	(021)56811531		Foreign Funded				Vacuum Glass Container玻璃
上海日硝保温瓶胆有限公司(1997)	上海市	上海市	(021)56811652	640	外商投资	46,933	-	194,659	保温容器
Jiangyin Yaoyao Vacuum Flask Container Manufacturing	Wuxi	Jiangsu	(0510)6321275		Private Owned				Vacuum Container
Co., Ltd.江阴瑶瑶保温瓶容器制造有限公司(1990)	无锡市	江苏省	(0510)6324900	677	私营企业	42,712	-	29,362	保温容器
Wuhan Vacuum Flask Factory	Wuhan	Hubei	(027)87801471		State-owned				Vacuum Flask
武汉保温瓶厂(1970)	武汉市	湖北省	(027)87802418	898	国有企业	36,494	-	47,848	保温瓶
Suzhou Shunfan Vacuum Flask Co., Ltd	Suzhou	Jiangsu	(0520)57671172		Overseas Chinese-funded				Vacuum Flask
苏州顺帆保温瓶有限公司(1992)	苏州市	江苏省	(0520)57671172	334	港澳台资	31,934	1,932(8)	23,182	保温瓶
Taishan Yongguang Plastic Products Factory	Jiangmen	Guangdong	(0750)5611789		Collective-owned				Magnetization Cup
台山市永光塑料制品厂(1990)	江门市	广东省		66	集体企业	31,072	205(26)	7,875	磁水杯

Top 10 Cities by Revenue 销售收入排名前10位城市	Province 省	Market share 市场份额(%)	Number of firms 企业个数
Shanghai 上海市	Shanghai 上海市	17.13	9
Beijing 北京市	Beijing 北京市	13.41	1
Wuhan 武汉市	Hubei 湖北省	10.28	2
Taizhou 台州市	Zhejiang 浙江省	6.70	8
Bengbu 蚌埠市	Anhui 安徽省	5.82	5
Xinxiang 新乡市	Henan 河南省	5.59	1
Jiangmen 江门市	Guangdong 广东省	5.54	2
Chuzhou 滁州市	Anhui 安徽省	5.48	2
Suzhou 苏州市	Jiangsu 江苏省	3.91	2
Wuhu 芜湖市	Anhui 安徽省	3.86	1

10 Major Wholesalers 十家主要批发商	City 城市	Province 省	Telephone/Fax 电话/传真
Kunming Department Store Group Co.,Ltd.	Kunming	Yunnan	(0871)3313618
昆明百货集团股份有限公司	昆明市	云南省	(0871)3314961
Jiangsu Skyrun International Group	Nanjing	Jiangsu	(025)4468888
江苏开元国际集团	南京市	江苏省	(025)4209409
Guangdong Light Industry Products Imp.& Exp.(Group) Corporation	Guangzhou	Guangdong	(020)83344557
广东省轻工业品进出口(集团)公司	广州市	广东省	(020)83330181
Shanghai Cheer (Group) Co.,Ltd.	Shanghai	Shanghai	(021)63069764
上海七百(集团)有限公司	上海市	上海市	(021)63069537
Fujian Tiancheng Group Co.,Ltd.	Fuzhou	Fujian	(0591)7503388
福建天成集团有限公司	福州市	福建省	(0591)7609279
Shanghai Century Lianhua Supermaket Development Co.,ltd.	Shanghai	Shanghai	(021)53544600
上海世纪联华超市发展有限公司	上海市	上海市	(021)62252610
Suzhou General Merchandise General Company	Suzhou	Jiangsu	(0512)65222247
苏州百货总公司	苏州市	江苏省	(0512)65222247
Zhejiang Light Industry Products Import & Export Corporation	Hangzhou	Zhejiang	(0571)88391888
浙江省轻工业品进出口公司	杭州市	浙江省	(0571)88391666
Zhejiang Winsun Import & Export Co., Ltd.	Jiaxing	Zhejiang	(0573)2117091
浙江汇信进出口有限公司	嘉兴市	浙江省	(0573)2117020
Shenzhen CATIC Trade Company	Shenzhen	Guangdong	(0755)83790111
深圳中航商贸公司	深圳市	广东省	(0755)83790462

3149: Other Glass and Glass Products 其他玻璃及玻璃制品业

The industry accounts for 0.032% of the total revenue of China's industrial sector in 2002. The rate of return on assets is 2.40%. 80.00% of all firms in the industry made a profit while 20.00% had negative returns.The top province in terms of the industry's revenue is Guangdong, accounting for 25.50% of the total revenue.
2002年本行业收入占全行业的0.032%，资产利润率为2.40%。80.00%的企业赢利，20.00%的企业亏损。收入最高的省为广东省，占本行业的25.50%。

	Total number of firms 企业总数	Total number of employees 职工总数	Total revenue (Mil.RMB) 总销售收入（百万元）	Total profit (Mil.RMB) 总利润（百万元）	Return on assets 资产利润率（%）	Return on equity 权益利润率（%）	Labour productivity ('000 RMB/ worker) 劳动生产率（千元/人）	Debts/ assets 资产负债率（%）	Total assets (Mil.RMB) 总资产（百万元）
Industry Overall 行业总体	175	28,279	3,389	125	2.40	5.75	46.34	58.30	5,218

	Number of firms 企业个数	Average number of employees 平均职工人数	Average revenue ('000 RMB) 平均销售收入（千元）	Average profit ('000 RMB) 平均利润（千元）	Return on assets 资产利润率（%）	Return on equity 权益利润率（%）	Labour productivity ('000 RMB/ worker) 劳动生产率（千元/人）	Debts/ assets 资产负债率（%）	Average total assets ('000 RMB) 平均总资产（千元）
By ownership 产业所有权									
State-owned 国有	13	86	2,028	-96	-0.48		7.96	105.17	19,980
Collective-owned 集体	28	233	29,637	787	3.18	9.34	39.63	65.96	24,760
Foreign & Overseas Chinese Funded 三资	26	155	26,222	371	0.39	0.87	121.46	55.34	94,972
By regional distribution 地区分布									
Central-North 华北	32	140	12,439	1,530	4.79	9.30	40.79	48.46	31,919
Beijing 北京	7	211	23,834	6,774	8.25	11.29	70.44	26.94	82,116
Tianjin 天津	5	137	13,195	-202	-0.98	-3.80	32.22	74.06	20,548
Hebei 河北	17	123	9,381	149	0.79	3.43	24.48	76.96	18,865
Shanxi 山西	2	43	247				0.60	93.42	5,973
Inner Mongolia 内蒙古	1	120	5,254	12	0.11	0.23	39.32	54.18	11,208
Northeast 东北	11	197	13,580	227	1.13		21.04	108.11	20,164
Liaoning 辽宁	6	138	6,712	41	0.23		10.98	122.56	17,480
Jilin 吉林	4	228	17,684	51	0.38	3.54	15.53	89.23	13,236
Heilongjiang 黑龙江	1	433	38,370	2,050	3.20		51.80	100.03	63,980
Central-East 华东	72	175	18,688	416	2.42	6.36	31.20	61.95	17,204
Shanghai 上海	5	126	18,436	738	4.21	8.57	33.57	50.88	17,544
Jiangsu 江苏	28	171	17,387	204	1.66	10.36	24.72	84.03	12,327
Zhejiang 浙江	14	80	12,374	210	1.10	2.12	36.65	48.33	19,143
Anhui 安徽	6	332	22,083	456	1.23	2.55	30.23	51.66	36,921
Fujian 福建	2	279	18,113	206	0.72	1.79	25.11	59.96	28,796
Jiangxi 江西	3	79	6,203	140	3.61	37.19	21.06	90.29	3,884
Shandong 山东	14	235	28,999	1,004	5.69	13.59	40.65	58.16	17,645
Central-South 中南	52	161	27,035	655	1.29	2.94	78.66	56.25	50,881
Henan 河南	16	178	18,348	1,033	9.37	23.75	30.29	60.54	11,021
Hubei 湖北	6	324	38,107	927	2.13	5.08	41.15	57.99	43,472
Hunan 湖南	3	151	6,428	155	1.83	4.56	13.31	59.94	8,479
Guangdong 广东	27	116	32,013	426	0.53	1.19	155.34	55.65	80,860
Guangxi 广西									
Hainan 海南									
Southwest 西南	5	71	14,418	2,235	25.46	80.29	59.21	68.29	8,776
Chongqing 重庆									
Sichuan 四川	5	71	14,418	2,235	25.46	80.29	59.21	68.29	8,776
Guizhou 贵州									
Yunnan 云南									
Tibet 西藏									
Northwest 西北	3	97	6,058	-476	-3.11	-5.80	30.56	46.34	15,294
Shaanxi 陕西	1	40	8,614	-860	-2.54	-4.01	61.58	36.61	33,823
Gansu 甘肃	1	13	5	2	0.54	0.56	75.92	3.52	369
Qinghai 青海									
Ningxia 宁夏									
Xinjiang 新疆	1	238	9,554	-570	-4.88	-20.17	22.87	75.83	11,690

3149: Other Glass and Glass Products 其他玻璃及玻璃制品业

Year 年份	Number of firms 企业个数	Rate of change 变化率 (%)	Number of employees 职工人数 (人)	Rate of change 变化率 (%)	Total revenue (Mil. RMB) 总销售收入 (百万元)	Rate of change 变化率 (%)	Total profit (Mil RMB) 总利润 (百万元)	Rate of change 变化率 (%)
2000	150		25,255		2,584		66	
2001	156	4.00	26,489	4.89	2,943	13.89	80	21.21
2002	175	12.18	28,279	6.76	3,389	15.15	125	56.25

Major Products 主要产品	Output 产量	Unit 单位

10 Main Firms with Maximal Revenue (year founded) 收入最大的十家主要企业（创办年份）	City 城市	Province 省	Telephone/fax 电话/传真	Number of employees 职工人数	Ownership 产业所有权	Revenue ('000 RMB) 销售收入 (千元)	Profit('000 RMB) (rank) 利润(千元) (排名)	Total assets ('000 RMB) 总资产 (千元)	Major products 主要产品
Taishan Daheng Glass Technology Co., Ltd.	Jiangmen	Guangdong	(0750)5456889		Limited-Liability				Hardware Glass
台山市大亨玻璃工艺有限公司(1998)	江门市	广东省	(0750)5457077	260	有限公司	166,542	812(35)	76,801	五金玻璃
Hanchuan Medicinal Glass General Factory	Xiaogan	Hubei	(0712)8663479		Collective-owned				Medicinal Glass Products药用
汉川药用玻璃总厂(1979)	孝感市	湖北省		950	集体企业	110,200	124(92)	49,872	玻璃制品
Ji'nan Meili Lakr Tourism Economic Development Zone Industrial	Jinan	Shandong	(0531)5970845		Collective-owned				Solar Energy Water Heater太阳
General Co.济南美里湖旅游经济开发区实业总公司(2001)	济南市	山东省	(0531)5970843	486	集体企业	105,965	1,235(26)	42,819	能热水器
Dongguan Yin Tong Glass Co., Ltd.	Dongguan	Guangdong	(0769)8864883		Private Owned				Glass Products
东莞银通玻璃有限公司(2000)	东莞市	广东省	(0769)8864882	216	私营企业	92,153	206(81)	38,603	玻璃制品
China South Glass Co., Ltd.	Shenzhen	Guangdong	(0755)27377688		Overseas Chinese-funded				Glass
深圳南方超薄浮法玻璃有限公司(1993)	深圳市	广东省	(0755)27376389	440	港澳台资	85,478	5,797(5)	1,519,611	玻璃
Hubei Golden Dragon King Investment Stock Co., Ltd.	Jingmen	Hubei	(0724)2299965		Private Owned				Beer Bottle
湖北金龙王投资股份有限公司(2000)	荆门市	湖北省	(0724)2333398	653	私营企业	83,871	4,625(7)	191,686	啤酒瓶
Jinhu Glass Apparatus Factory	Huaian	Jiangsu	(0517)6986031		Collective-owned				Medical Bottle
金湖县玻璃仪器厂(1971)	淮安市	江苏省	(0517)6986031	140	集体企业	65,190	1,360(25)	29,934	曲颈安瓶
Taishan Shun Bao Toughened Glass Ornaments Co., Ltd.	Jiangmen	Guangdong	(0750)5455552		Overseas Chinese-funded				Toughened Glass
台山顺宝钢化玻璃装饰有限公司(1997)	江门市	广东省	(0750)5455552	89	港澳台资	64,631	-	124,630	钢化玻璃
Zhangqiu Zhen Da Glass Products Co., Ltd.	Jinan	Shandong	(0531)3471537		Joint Stock				Glass Products
章丘市振达玻璃制品有限公司(1999)	济南市	山东省	(0531)3473900	240	股份制	60,300	4,200(8)	8,088	玻璃制品
Shanghai Coloured Glaze Gong Fang Coloured Glaze Craft	Shanghai	Shanghai	(021)64790238		Overseas Chinese-funded				Glass Ceramics Articles琉璃
Co., ltd.上海琉璃工房琉璃艺术品有限公司(1996)	上海市	上海市	(021)64793208	366	港澳台资	49,836	2,622(15)	57,521	陶瓷用品

Top 10 Cities by Revenue 销售收入排名前10位城市	Province 省	Market share 市场份额 (%)	Number of firms 企业个数
Jiangmen 江门市	Guangdong 广东省	7.98	4
Jinan 济南市	Shandong 山东省	5.68	4
Beijing 北京市	Beijing 北京市	4.92	7
Weifang 潍坊市	Shandong 山东省	3.77	2
Xiaogan 孝感市	Hubei 湖北省	3.48	2
Guangzhou 广州市	Guangdong 广东省	3.28	4
Luohe 漯河市	Henan 河南省	3.21	2
Yancheng 盐城市	Jiangsu 江苏省	3.07	4
Shenzhen 深圳市	Guangdong 广东省	2.98	2
Foshan 佛山市	Guangdong 广东省	2.87	6

10 Major Wholesalers 十家主要批发商	City 城市	Province 省	Telephone/Fax 电话/传真
Xuzhou New Century Building Materials Decorative City	Xuzhou	Jiangsu	(0516)83666780
徐州市新世纪建材装饰城	徐州市	江苏省	(0516)63804485
Orienthome Co.,Ltd.	Beijing	Beijing	(010)63808294
东方家园有限公司	北京市	北京市	
Shanghai Jinkai Goods & Materials Co.,Ltd.	Shanghai	Shanghai	(021)52193967
上海金凯物资有限公司	上海市	上海市	
Guangzhou Building Materials Development Co.,Ltd.	Guangzhou	Guangdong	(020)83335062
广州市建材发展有限公司	广州市	广东省	(020)83341110
Guangxi Qiaofeng Goods & Materials Trade Co.,Ltd.	Nanning	Guangxi	(0771)2631539
广西侨丰物资贸易有限责任公司	南宁市	广西	(0771)2631539
Gansu Building Materials State-owned Assets Marketing Co.,Ltd.	Lanzhou	Gansu	(0931)8821359
甘肃建材国有资产经营有限责任公司	兰州市	甘肃省	(0931)8960243
Shanghai East Asia United Building Materials Co.,Ltd.	Shanghai	Shanghai	(021)33134520
上海东亚联合建材有限公司	上海市	上海市	(021)63216165
Shanghai Zhuzong Materials General Company	Shanghai	Shanghai	(021)32240030
上海住总物资总公司	上海市	上海市	(021)32240024
Guangdong Building Materials Company	Guangzhou	Guangdong	(020)83802713
广东省建材公司	广州市	广东省	(020)83817640
Guangdong Dongguan Hardware Minerals Import & Export Co.,Ltd	Dongguan	Guangdong	(0769)2227090
广东省东莞五金矿产进出口公司	东莞市	广东省	(0769)2221045

3151: Construction and Hygienic Ceramics 建筑、卫生陶瓷制造业

The industry accounts for 0.382% of the total revenue of China's industrial sector in 2002. The rate of return on assets is 3.65%. 80.49% of all firms in the industry made a profit while 19.51% had negative returns.The top province in terms of the industry's revenue is Guangdong, accounting for 40.83% of the total revenue.
2002年本行业收入占全行业的 0.382%，资产利润率为 3.65%。80.49%的企业赢利，19.51%的企业亏损。收入最高的省为广东省，占本行业的40.83%。

	Total number of firms 企业总数	Total number of employees 职工总数	Total revenue (Mil.RMB) 总销售收入(百万元)	Total profit (Mil.RMB) 总利润(百万元)	Return on assets 资产利润率(%)	Return on equity 权益利润率(%)	Labour productivity ('000 RMB/worker) 劳动生产率(千元/人)	Debts/assets 资产负债率(%)	Total assets (Mil.RMB) 总资产(百万元)
Industry Overall 行业总体	1061	274,630	40,945	1,968	3.65	8.93	49.24	59.11	53,879

	Number of firms 企业个数	Average number of employees 平均职工人数	Average revenue ('000 RMB) 平均销售收入(千元)	Average profit ('000 RMB) 平均利润(千元)	Return on assets 资产利润率(%)	Return on equity 权益利润率(%)	Labour productivity ('000 RMB/worker) 劳动生产率(千元/人)	Debts/assets 资产负债率(%)	Average total assets ('000 RMB) 平均总资产(千元)
By ownership 产业所有权									
State-owned 国有	59	272	11,873	-85	-0.17	-1.48	16.40	88.73	51,091
Collective-owned 集体	147	311	48,064	2,541	4.85	12.37	51.10	60.80	52,400
Foreign & Overseas Chinese Funded 三资	193	331	77,036	4,403	3.47	7.53	80.54	53.98	127,052
By regional distribution 地区分布									
Central-North 华北	72	386	34,312	3,795	6.61	14.62	44.62	54.79	57,413
Beijing 北京	4	475	104,468	14,850	6.97	13.86	151.84	49.71	213,009
Tianjin 天津	5	116	22,531	2,660	6.24	7.71	148.82	19.06	42,630
Hebei 河北	47	398	33,128	4,029	9.27	19.49	38.41	52.44	43,466
Shanxi 山西	11	426	27,751	2,197	3.77	12.14	22.83	68.97	58,316
Inner Mongolia 内蒙古	5	389	15,530	-2,601	-3.38	-13.38	20.93	74.70	76,834
Northeast 东北	12	154	7,889	-926	-3.73	-9.11	17.27	59.04	24,819
Liaoning 辽宁	6	185	8,590	-2,540	-5.84	-15.55	15.79	62.45	43,492
Jilin 吉林	1	2						40.19	8,410
Heilongjiang 黑龙江	5	149	8,625	826	14.50	21.77	19.52	33.38	5,693
Central-East 华东	420	216	40,635	2,917	5.68	12.22	64.72	53.52	51,367
Shanghai 上海	16	356	109,459	12,142	5.91	9.74	110.69	39.35	205,594
Jiangsu 江苏	23	361	62,829	3,877	2.71	5.73	55.57	52.79	143,270
Zhejiang 浙江	59	125	26,530	1,018	2.25	5.96	61.20	62.25	45,295
Anhui 安徽	6	201	4,891	-1,208	-2.46	-5.97	11.40	58.83	49,116
Fujian 福建	167	123	20,189	1,689	6.39	9.31	58.97	31.36	26,434
Jiangxi 江西	15	318	16,594	-775	-1.46	-13.96	16.77	89.51	52,934
Shandong 山东	134	319	64,590	4,615	9.08	27.69	70.61	67.22	50,850
Central-South 中南	401	279	45,562	1,058	1.95	5.41	47.38	63.91	54,218
Henan 河南	44	343	18,954	499	1.23	12.07	17.63	89.80	40,536
Hubei 湖北	20	179	16,015	-34	-0.12	-0.64	28.27	81.61	29,098
Hunan 湖南	22	185	13,246	324	1.35	3.55	20.88	61.89	23,896
Guangdong 广东	304	286	54,992	1,411	2.34	5.81	55.64	59.77	60,316
Guangxi 广西	10	216	9,592	-1,024	-2.84	-29.61	10.39	90.40	36,041
Hainan 海南	1	127	11,195	-22,753	-14.78		-53.65	134.42	153,951
Southwest 西南	146	276	20,436	427	1.10	2.95	26.16	62.65	38,705
Chongqing 重庆	13	403	53,995	3,253	1.99	4.94	47.32	59.63	163,272
Sichuan 四川	128	268	17,252	173	0.65	1.79	23.02	63.80	26,686
Guizhou 贵州	3	97	2,994	-843	-4.21	-24.93	9.51	83.10	20,000
Yunnan 云南	2	275	32,261	233	0.89	6.47	28.94	86.29	26,282
Tibet 西藏									
Northwest 西北	10	200	5,893	-596	-1.24	-10.40	11.25	88.09	48,082
Shaanxi 陕西	4	269	9,726	-1,399	-1.40	-15.11	11.62	90.76	100,130
Gansu 甘肃	3	74	900	12	0.27	0.59	10.52	54.13	4,558
Qinghai 青海									
Ningxia 宁夏	1	330	6,081	-629	-1.69		6.70	113.97	37,192
Xinjiang 新疆	2	187	5,621	115	0.78	1.20	14.67	34.83	14,718

3151: Construction and Hygienic Ceramics 建筑、卫生陶瓷制造业

Year 年份	Number of firms 企业个数	Rate of change 变化率 (%)	Number of employees 职工人数 (人)	Rate of change 变化率 (%)	Total revenue (Mil. RMB) 总销售收入 (百万元)	Rate of change 变化率 (%)	Total profit (Mil RMB) 总利润 (百万元)	Rate of change 变化率 (%)
2000	933		295,964		30,886		1,113	
2001	967	3.64	275,387	-6.95	33,332	7.92	1,363	22.46
2002	1061	9.72	274,630	-0.27	40,945	22.84	1,968	44.39

Major Products 主要产品	Output 产量	Unit 单位
Wall Brick & Terra Brick 墙地砖	121,662	10,000 Sq.M. 万平方米
Glazed Brick 釉面砖	65,191	10,000 Sq.M. 万平方米

10 Main Firms with Maximal Revenue (year founded) 收入最大的十家主要企业（创办年份）	City 城市	Province 省	Telephone/fax 电话/传真	Number of employees 职工人数	Ownership 产业所有权	Revenue ('000 RMB) 销售收入 (千元)	Profit('000 RMB) (rank) 利润(千元) (排名)	Total assets ('000 RMB) 总资产 (千元)	Major products 主要产品
Sanshui Xinzhongyuan Ceramics Co., Ltd.	Foshan	Guangdong	(0757)7567838		Overseas Chinese-funded				Wear-resisting Ornaments Brick耐
三水市新中源陶瓷有限公司(2001)	佛山市	广东省	(0757)7567988	2,900	港澳台资	671,410	12,510(42)	425,779	磨装饰砖
Shenzhen Chenglin Cleaning Utensil Co., Ltd.	Shenzhen	Guangdong	(0755)28011493		Overseas Chinese-funded				Tap
深圳成霖洁具有限公司(1993)	深圳市	广东省		2,000	港澳台资	581,084	44,520(8)	358,473	水龙头
Foshan Ying Pai Ceramics Co., Ltd.	Foshan	Guangdong	(0757)3963605		Overseas Chinese-funded				Wall Brick & Ground Brick
佛山市鹰牌陶瓷有限公司(1993)	佛山市	广东省	(0757)2271664	837	港澳台资	574,704	-	799,121	墙地砖
Shanghai Cimic Building Ceramics Co., Ltd.	Shanghai	Shanghai	(021)64110567		Foreign Funded				Construction Ceramic建筑
上海斯米克建筑陶瓷有限公司(1995)	上海市	上海市	(021)64110553	988	外商投资	552,358	72,161(3)	774,648	陶瓷制品
Hangzhou Concord Chian Co., Ltd.	Hangzhou	Zhejiang	(0571)88686818		Overseas Chinese-funded				Construction Ceramic建筑
杭州协和陶瓷有限公司(1992)	杭州市	浙江省	(0571)88681789	1,331	港澳台资	518,858	47,783(7)	637,945	陶瓷制品
Shanghai Fortune Ceramics Co., Ltd.	Shanghai	Shanghai	(021)64975555		Foreign Funded				Glazed Brick
上海福祥陶瓷有限公司(1993)	上海市	上海市	(021)64975987	1,354	外商投资	456,970	36,440(12)	519,520	釉面砖
Imperial Ware Co., Ltd.	Zhongshan	Guangdong	(0760)3370688		Overseas Chinese-funded				Ceramics Sanitary陶瓷
英陶洁具有限公司(1993)	中山市	广东省	(0760)7728073	553	港澳台资	429,970	-	341,235	卫生洁具
Wordful Ceramics Co., Ltd.	Dongguan	Guangdong	(0769)2469008		Collective-owned				Ceramic Products
东莞市唯美陶瓷工业公司(1992)	东莞市	广东省	(0769)2469008	758	集体企业	420,808	7,218(79)	354,629	陶瓷制品
Guangdong Fo Tao Group Diamond Ceramics Co., Ltd.	Foshan	Guangdong	(0757)2272268		Joint Stock				Wall Brick & Ground Brick
广东佛陶集团钻石陶瓷有限公司(1996)	佛山市	广东省	(0757)2271215	3,477	股份制	386,220	10,338(32)	349,601	墙地砖
Shandong Crown Ceramics Co., ltd.	Zibo	Shandong	(0533)5480501		Joint Stock				Floor Brick
山东皇冠陶瓷股份有限公司(1996)	淄博市	山东省	(0533)5490098	920	股份制	349,383	25,000(18)	184,620	地板砖

Top 10 Cities by Revenue 销售收入排名前10位城市	Province 省	Market share 市场份额 (%)	Number of firms 企业个数
Foshan 佛山市	Guangdong 广东省	33.32	248
Zibo 淄博市	Shandong 山东省	18.52	92
Quanzhou 泉州市	Fujian 福建省	5.05	107
Shanghai 上海市	Shanghai 上海市	4.28	16
Leshan 乐山市	Sichuan 四川省	3.34	95
Suzhou 苏州市	Jiangsu 江苏省	2.61	11
Tangshan 唐山市	Hebei 河北省	2.35	19
Fuzhou 福州市	Fujian 福建省	1.86	44
Chongqing 重庆市	Chongqing 重庆市	1.71	13
Hangzhou 杭州市	Zhejiang 浙江省	1.59	3

10 Major Wholesalers 十家主要批发商	City 城市	Province 省	Telephone/Fax 电话/传真
Xuzhou New Century Building Materials Decorative City	Xuzhou	Jiangsu	(0516)83666780
徐州市新世纪建材装饰城	徐州市	江苏省	(0516)63804485
Orienthome Co.,Ltd.	Beijing	Beijing	(010)63808294
东方家园有限公司	北京市	北京市	
Shanghai Jinkai Goods & Materials Co.,Ltd.	Shanghai	Shanghai	(021)52193967
上海金凯物资有限公司	上海市	上海市	
Guangzhou Building Materials Development Co.,Ltd.	Guangzhou	Guangdong	(020)83335062
广州市建材发展有限公司	广州市	广东省	(020)83341110
Guangxi Qiaofeng Goods & Materials Trade Co.,Ltd.	Nanning	Guangxi	(0771)2631539
广西侨丰物资贸易有限责任公司	南宁市	广西	(0771)2631539
Gansu Building Materials State-owned Assets Marketing Co.,Ltd.	Lanzhou	Gansu	(0931)8821359
甘肃建材国有资产经营有限责任公司	兰州市	甘肃省	(0931)8960243
Shanghai East Asia United Building Materials Co.,Ltd.	Shanghai	Shanghai	(021)33134520
上海东亚联合建材有限公司	上海市	上海市	(021)63216165
Shanghai Zhuzong Materials General Company	Shanghai	Shanghai	(021)32240030
上海住总物资总公司	上海市	上海市	(021)32240024
Guangdong Building Materials Company	Guangzhou	Guangdong	(020)83802713
广东省建材公司	广州市	广东省	(020)83817640
Guangdong Dongguan Hardware Minerals Import & Export Co.,Ltd	Dongguan	Guangdong	(0769)2227090
广东省东莞五金矿产进出口公司	东莞市	广东省	(0769)2221045

3153: Industrial Ceramics 工业用陶瓷制造业

The industry accounts for 0.046% of the total revenue of China's industrial sector in 2002. The rate of return on assets is 1.85%. 80.28% of all firms in the industry made a profit while 19.72% had negative returns.The top province in terms of the industry's revenue is Henan, accounting for 24.20% of the total revenue.
2002年本行业收入占全行业的0.046%，资产利润率为1.85%。80.28%的企业赢利，19.72%的企业亏损。收入最高的省为河南省，占本行业的24.20%。

	Total number of firms 企业总数	Total number of employees 职工总数	Total revenue (Mil.RMB) 总销售收入（百万元）	Total profit (Mil.RMB) 总利润（百万元）	Return on assets 资产利润率 (%)	Return on equity 权益利润率 (%)	Labour productivity ('000 RMB/worker) 劳动生产率（千元/人）	Debts/assets 资产负债率 (%)	Total assets (Mil.RMB) 总资产（百万元）
Industry Overall 行业总体	213	52,077	4,967	158	1.85	4.61	35.15	59.98	8,569

	Number of firms 企业个数	Average number of employees 平均职工人数	Average revenue ('000 RMB) 平均销售收入（千元）	Average profit ('000 RMB) 平均利润（千元）	Return on assets 资产利润率 (%)	Return on equity 权益利润率 (%)	Labour productivity ('000 RMB/worker) 劳动生产率（千元/人）	Debts/assets 资产负债率 (%)	Average total assets ('000 RMB) 平均总资产（千元）
By ownership 产业所有权									
State-owned 国有	32	316	18,588	-667	-0.76	-3.78	26.72	79.76	87,225
Collective-owned 集体	26	394	46,688	3,459	8.84	13.74	39.71	35.64	39,118
Foreign & Overseas Chinese Funded 三资	38	183	34,868	1,330	2.63	5.23	71.11	49.66	50,543
By regional distribution 地区分布									
Central-North 华北	24	228	17,058	-50	-0.11	-0.35	31.41	70.17	46,824
Beijing 北京	3	119	8,811	244	1.87	4.26	17.36	56.21	13,068
Tianjin 天津	2	71	2,294	-832	-6.64	-139.60	6.27	95.25	12,539
Hebei 河北	12	265	24,624	-106	-0.16	-0.53	37.08	68.86	64,931
Shanxi 山西	5	275	12,125	310	0.85	4.55	18.12	81.34	36,559
Inner Mongolia 内蒙古	2	213	11,134	-267	-0.55	-1.33	51.97	58.88	48,760
Northeast 东北	12	478	30,381	-830	-0.51	-1.21	21.23	58.23	163,687
Liaoning 辽宁	9	570	36,928	-1,032	-0.50	-1.15	22.12	56.83	207,827
Jilin 吉林	1	149	9,636				19.07	90.41	56,333
Heilongjiang 黑龙江	2	229	11,292	-337	-1.80	-8.84	11.95	79.65	18,734
Central-East 华东	96	213	19,310	568	1.68	4.48	35.83	62.54	33,786
Shanghai 上海	8	59	24,231	74	0.22	0.38	236.01	42.59	34,196
Jiangsu 江苏	18	288	28,650	-140	-0.21	-0.51	33.12	59.60	67,683
Zhejiang 浙江	10	143	12,651	628	2.99	5.80	30.21	48.33	20,966
Anhui 安徽	2	248	12,467	-56	-0.29	-4.03	22.12	92.76	19,028
Fujian 福建	12	204	15,311	-43	-0.32	-2.05	43.21	84.46	13,494
Jiangxi 江西	32	213	10,257	139	0.95	6.45	14.39	85.22	14,603
Shandong 山东	14	258	34,345	3,308	5.30	12.85	52.97	58.78	62,480
Central-South 中南	68	267	32,955	1,761	6.09	11.47	41.60	46.92	28,926
Henan 河南	13	606	92,451	7,582	8.82	14.19	48.16	37.80	85,927
Hubei 湖北	3	62	4,792	366	10.58	33.43	32.45	68.34	3,461
Hunan 湖南	31	195	8,630	247	1.89	4.52	22.56	58.04	13,012
Guangdong 广东	21	192	36,055	593	2.86	7.05	57.80	59.46	20,769
Guangxi 广西									
Hainan 海南									
Southwest 西南	10	159	7,849	-500	-2.90	-45.90	21.21	93.68	17,224
Chongqing 重庆	1	42	13,000	500	1.69	2.07	129.52	18.52	29,596
Sichuan 四川	6	120	7,657	87	1.11	6.74	26.10	83.61	7,903
Guizhou 贵州	2	151	3,945	-175	-1.27	-2.61	14.06	51.42	13,829
Yunnan 云南	1	528	11,656	-5,669	-8.39		10.01	150.97	67,565
Tibet 西藏									
Northwest 西北	3	223	6,740	3	0.01	0.23	22.85	96.44	32,744
Shaanxi 陕西	1	320	7,929	1			25.49	120.45	50,853
Gansu 甘肃	1	249	8,432				12.39	78.96	30,254
Qinghai 青海	1	100	3,860	7	0.04	0.09	40.44	56.03	17,124
Ningxia 宁夏									
Xinjiang 新疆									

3153: Industrial Ceramics 工业用陶瓷制造业

Year 年份	Number of firms 企业个数	Rate of change 变化率 (%)	Number of employees 职工人数 (人)	Rate of change 变化率 (%)	Total revenue (Mil. RMB) 总销售收入 (百万元)	Rate of change 变化率 (%)	Total profit (Mil RMB) 总利润 (百万元)	Rate of change 变化率 (%)
2000	161		47,140		3,461		46	
2001	192	19.25	49,346	4.68	4,161	20.23	83	80.43
2002	213	10.94	52,077	5.53	4,967	19.37	158	90.36

Major Products 主要产品	Output 产量	Unit 单位
Industrial Ceramics 工业陶瓷	38	10,000 Tons 万吨

10 Main Firms with Maximal Revenue (year founded) 收入最大的十家主要企业（创办年份）	City 城市	Province 省	Telephone/fax 电话/传真	Number of employees 职工人数	Ownership 产业所有权	Revenue ('000 RMB) 销售收入(千元)	Profit('000 RMB) (rank) 利润(千元)(排名)	Total assets ('000 RMB) 总资产(千元)	Major products 主要产品
Henan Ge Tian Group Co., Ltd.	Xuchang	Henan	(0374)6611088		Collective-owned				High-Voltage Electro-Porcelain
河南省葛天集团有限责任公司(1993)	许昌市	河南省	(0374)6612228	5,980	集体企业	949,186	84,793(1)	763,659	高压电瓷
Zibo Industrial Ceramics Refractory Co.,Ltd.	Zibo	Shandong	(0533)4280462		Foreign Funded				Fire-resistant Materials
淄博工陶耐火材料有限公司(2001)	淄博市	山东省	(0533)4282498	1,535	外商投资	251,576	35,853(2)	472,817	耐火材料
Amperor(Shenzhen) INC Ltd.	Shenzhen	Guangdong	(0755)27475570		Foreign Funded				Power Source Supply Equipment电源供应器
皇源电子（深圳）有限公司(1995)	深圳市	广东省	(0755)27475804	1,050	外商投资	216,555	1,425(24)	101,083	
Nanhai Hongtao Ceramics Co., Ltd.	Foshan	Guangdong	(0757)5889068		Private Owned				Ceramic Tile
南海市宏陶陶瓷有限公司(1999)	佛山市	广东省	(0757)5889888	406	私营企业	161,718	619(56)	30,518	瓷砖
Dalian Electric Ceramics Factory	Dalian	Liaoning	(0411)3635229		State-owned				High-Voltage Circuit Electroceramics高压线路电瓷
大连电瓷厂(1915)	大连市	辽宁省	(0411)3635229	1,708	国有企业	161,606	1,092(32)	308,136	
Shanghai Dahong Glaze-making Co., Ltd.	Shanghai	Shanghai	(021)64975566		Overseas Chinese-funded				Glaze Frit
上海大鸿制釉有限公司(1996)	上海市	上海市	(021)64973535	130	港澳台资	146,537	2,370(15)	153,697	熔块
Nanjing Electric Group Co., Ltd.	Nanjing	Jiangsu	(025)5316636		Limited-Liability				High-Voltage Electro-Porcelain
南京电气(集团)有限责任公司(1997)	南京市	江苏省	(025)5311634	2,287	有限公司	146,390	-	745,730	高压电瓷
NGK Insulation Ltd. Cd	Tangshan	Hebei	(0315)3208313		Foreign Funded				Hanging Insulation悬式瓷绝缘子
NGK唐山电瓷有限公司(1996)	唐山市	河北省	(0315)3208315	353	外商投资	133,338	6,578(3)	319,437	
Fushun Hua Tai Electro-Porcelain Electrical Appliance Manufacturing	Fushun	Liaoning	(0413)2424053		State Enterprises				High Voltage Electro Porcelain
Co. Ltd 抚顺华泰电瓷电器制造有限公司(2001)	抚顺市	辽宁省	(0413)2434923	2,349	国有独资	102,570	8(136)	362,490	高压电瓷
Tangshan High Voltage Electro-Porcelain Factory	Tangshan	Hebei	(0315)3271261		State-owned				High-Voltage Electro-Porcelain
唐山市高压电瓷厂(1952)	唐山市	河北省	(0315)3271472	1,149	国有企业	64,825	3,470(9)	160,442	高压电瓷

Top 10 Cities by Revenue 销售收入排名前10位城市	Province 省	Market share 市场份额 (%)	Number of firms 企业个数
Xuchang 许昌市	Henan 河南省	21.12	4
Zibo 淄博市	Shandong 山东省	7.70	7
Foshan 佛山市	Guangdong 广东省	6.10	11
Pingxiang 萍乡市	Jiangxi 江西省	6.08	30
Zhuzhou 株洲市	Hunan 湖南省	4.97	25
Tangshan 唐山市	Hebei 河北省	4.63	4
Shenzhen 深圳市	Guangdong 广东省	4.53	2
Guangzhou 广州市	Guangdong 广东省	4.01	3
Shanghai 上海市	Shanghai 上海市	3.90	8
Nanjing 南京市	Jiangsu 江苏省	3.47	3

10 Major Wholesalers 十家主要批发商	City 城市	Province 省	Telephone/Fax 电话/传真
Xuzhou New Century Building Materials Decorative City	Xuzhou	Jiangsu	(0516)83666780
徐州市新世纪建材装饰城	徐州市	江苏省	(0516)63804485
Orienthome Co.,Ltd.	Beijing	Beijing	(010)63808294
东方家园有限公司	北京市	北京市	
Shanghai Jinkai Goods & Materials Co.,Ltd.	Shanghai	Shanghai	(021)52193967
上海金凯物资有限公司	上海市	上海市	
Guangzhou Building Materials Development Co.,Ltd.	Guangzhou	Guangdong	(020)83335062
广州市建材发展有限公司	广州市	广东省	(020)83341110
Guangxi Qiaofeng Goods & Materials Trade Co.,Ltd.	Nanning	Guangxi	(0771)2631539
广西侨丰物资贸易有限责任公司	南宁市	广西	(0771)2631539
Gansu Building Materials State-owned Assets Marketing Co.,Ltd.	Lanzhou	Gansu	(0931)8821359
甘肃建材国有资产经营有限责任公司	兰州市	甘肃省	(0931)8960243
Shanghai East Asia United Building Materials Co.,Ltd.	Shanghai	Shanghai	(021)33134520
上海东亚联合建材有限公司	上海市	上海市	(021)63216165
Shanghai Zhuzong Materials General Company	Shanghai	Shanghai	(021)32240030
上海住总物资总公司	上海市	上海市	(021)32240024
Guangdong Building Materials Company	Guangzhou	Guangdong	(020)83802713
广东省建材公司	广州市	广东省	(020)83817640
Guangdong Dongguan Hardware Minerals Import & Export Co.,Ltd	Dongguan	Guangdong	(0769)2227090
广东省东莞五金矿产进出口公司	东莞市	广东省	(0769)2221045

3155: Household Ceramics 日用陶瓷制造业

The industry accounts for 0.140% of the total revenue of China's industrial sector in 2002. The rate of return on assets is 1.20%. 77.20% of all firms in the industry made a profit while 22.80% had negative returns.The top province in terms of the industry's revenue is Guangdong, accounting for 29.34% of the total revenue.
2002年本行业收入占全行业的 0.140%，资产利润率为 1.20%。77.20%的企业赢利，22.80%的企业亏损。收入最高的省为广东省，占本行业的29.34%。

	Total number of firms 企业总数	Total number of employees 职工总数	Total revenue (Mil.RMB) 总销售收入（百万元）	Total profit (Mil.RMB) 总利润（百万元）	Return on assets 资产利润率（%）	Return on equity 权益利润率（%）	Labour productivity ('000 RMB/ worker) 劳动生产率（千元/人）	Debts/ assets 资产负债率（%）	Total assets (Mil.RMB) 总资产（百万元）
Industry Overall 行业总体	706	346,995	15,009	285	1.20	4.50	14.82	73.30	23,734

	Number of firms 企业个数	Average number of employees 平均职工人数	Average revenue ('000 RMB) 平均销售收入（千元）	Average profit ('000 RMB) 平均利润（千元）	Return on assets 资产利润率（%）	Return on equity 权益利润率（%）	Labour productivity ('000 RMB/ worker) 劳动生产率（千元/人）	Debts/ assets 资产负债率（%）	Average total assets ('000 RMB) 平均总资产（千元）
By ownership 产业所有权									
State-owned 国有	100	531	14,463	-354	-1.00	-12.66	10.36	92.11	35,489
Collective-owned 集体	133	409	16,239	370	2.09	9.63	13.86	78.34	17,710
Foreign & Overseas Chinese Funded 三资	190	381	22,595	569	2.76	6.43	17.49	57.08	20,613
By regional distribution 地区分布									
Central-North 华北	54	961	29,604	-1,952	-1.74	-23.49	12.58	92.58	112,042
Beijing 北京	1	40	7,000	360	24.13		58.88	218.03	1,492
Tianjin 天津	3	83	8,444	529	13.99	82.56	21.34	83.05	3,778
Hebei 河北	27	1,443	48,343	-4,215	-2.10	-36.93	12.73	94.31	200,591
Shanxi 山西	22	562	11,613	288	1.07	4.72	11.80	77.27	26,841
Inner Mongolia 内蒙古	1	302	5,572	126	0.41	2.01	11.83	79.79	30,946
Northeast 东北	9	275	3,778	-266	-1.51	-4.24	6.04	64.39	17,591
Liaoning 辽宁	3	130	5,052	17	0.11	0.30	16.03	64.73	15,845
Jilin 吉林	3	476	2,949	-773	-2.73	-7.99	2.43	65.86	28,313
Heilongjiang 黑龙江	3	218	3,334	-41	-0.48	-1.17	7.94	58.95	8,614
Central-East 华东	256	484	21,615	1,014	2.86	8.88	16.68	67.76	35,402
Shanghai 上海	1	81	13,020	139	1.00	1.21	47.68	16.97	13,840
Jiangsu 江苏	30	462	33,093	2,338	5.70	15.75	27.56	63.79	41,015
Zhejiang 浙江	6	207	27,216	1,818	10.22	24.30	43.15	57.95	17,790
Anhui 安徽	5	832	22,302	207	0.52	5.86	12.34	91.21	40,072
Fujian 福建	124	358	13,998	757	6.19	10.77	17.13	42.50	12,230
Jiangxi 江西	33	597	12,636	-327	-0.57	-3.71	8.71	84.74	57,777
Shandong 山东	57	712	36,844	1,653	2.30	7.60	15.92	69.69	71,725
Central-South 中南	358	437	20,937	424	2.07	5.72	14.30	63.84	20,482
Henan 河南	24	860	24,722	760	2.50	10.69	11.20	76.62	30,403
Hubei 湖北	4	73	4,328	43	0.93		28.74	100.58	4,560
Hunan 湖南	86	498	15,290	394	1.64	6.42	12.55	74.42	23,985
Guangdong 广东	207	303	21,274	424	2.47	4.89	17.67	49.48	17,171
Guangxi 广西	35	854	33,048	322	1.18	7.26	11.70	83.71	27,241
Hainan 海南	2	67	4,587	186	2.65	14.40	19.99	81.59	7,019
Southwest 西南	20	489	16,339	-609	-1.30	-4.94	16.35	73.80	47,002
Chongqing 重庆	6	772	28,246	-1,799	-1.61	-5.77	17.77	72.15	112,031
Sichuan 四川	6	221	9,727	-134	-0.73	-2.62	22.27	72.35	18,423
Guizhou 贵州									
Yunnan 云南	8	478	12,368	-72	-0.37	-2.02	12.57	81.84	19,665
Tibet 西藏									
Northwest 西北	9	260	2,351	-692	-3.28	-47.01	3.66	93.03	21,116
Shaanxi 陕西	5	179	596	-259	-1.27	-220.99	2.25	99.43	20,443
Gansu 甘肃	3	262	2,532	-634	-3.28	-15.15	3.86	78.33	19,321
Qinghai 青海									
Ningxia 宁夏	1	659	10,579	-3,027	-10.14	-3,120.62	5.35	99.68	29,866
Xinjiang 新疆									

3155: Household Ceramics 日用陶瓷制造业

Year 年份	Number of firms 企业个数	Rate of change 变化率 (%)	Number of employees 职工人数 (人)	Rate of change 变化率 (%)	Total revenue (Mil. RMB) 总销售收入 (百万元)	Rate of change 变化率 (%)	Total profit (Mil RMB) 总利润 (百万元)	Rate of change 变化率 (%)
2000	601		351,701		11,971		-64	
2001	668	11.15	333,094	-5.29	13,051	9.02	109	-
2002	706	5.69	346,995	4.17	15,009	15.00	285	161.47

Major Products 主要产品	Output 产量	Unit 单位
Household Ceramics 日用陶瓷	92	100,000,000 Pieces 亿件

10 Main Firms with Maximal Revenue (year founded) 收入最大的十家主要企业（创办年份）	City 城市	Province 省	Telephone/fax 电话/传真	Number of employees 职工人数	Ownership 产业所有权	Revenue ('000 RMB) 销售收入 (千元)	Profit('000 RMB) (rank) 利润(千元) (排名)	Total assets ('000 RMB) 总资产 (千元)	Major products 主要产品
Guangxi Sanhuan Enterprise Group Co., Ltd. 广西三环企业集团股份有限公司(1998)	Yulin 玉林市	Guangxi 广西	(0775)6222859 (0775)6222851	5,218	Joint Stock 股份制	558,628	16,966(7)	354,785	Household Ceramics 日用陶瓷
Jiangsu Yixing Ceramics Co. 江苏省宜兴陶瓷公司(1956)	Wuxi 无锡市	Jiangsu 江苏省	(0510)7401532 (0510)7402786	5,293	State-owned 国有企业	425,563	15,000(9)	654,158	Household Ceramics 日用陶瓷
Huaguang Ceramics Group Co., Ltd. 华光陶瓷集团有限公司(1995)	Zibo 淄博市	Shandong 山东省	(0533)2064346 (0533)2888702	5,085	State Enterprises 国有独资	380,427	2,970(32)	1,917,001	Household Ceramics 日用陶瓷
Fujian Dehua Jiamei Ceramics Plant 福建省德化佳美瓷厂(1992)	Quanzhou 泉州市	Fujian 福建省	(0595)3523888 (0595)3522690	7,315	Joint Stock 股份制	227,185	15,029(8)	77,235	Ceramic Products 陶瓷制品
Shandong Meihua Group Co., Ltd 山东美华瓷业集团股份有限公司(1995)	Linyi 临沂市	Shandong 山东省	(0539)8241171 (0539)8249615	6,355	Joint Stock 股份制	224,624	28,400(3)	310,052	Household Ceramics 日用白瓷
Guangdong Great Wall Group Co., Ltd. 广东长城集团有限公司(1996)	Chaozhou 潮州市	Guangdong 广东省	(0768)6881518 (0768)6871661	750	Limited-Liability 有限公司	166,332	1,440(63)	60,000	Craft Ceramics 工艺陶瓷
Hunan Guo Guang Ceramics Group Co., Ltd. 湖南国光瓷业集团股份有限公司(1958)	Zhuzhou 株洲市	Hunan 湖南省	(0733)3221614 (0733)3225111	4,689	Joint Stock 股份制	151,566	24,744(4)	746,459	Household Ceramics 日用陶瓷
Zibo Zhulin Group Co., Ltd. 淄博竹林集团有限公司(1995)	Zibo 淄博市	Shandong 山东省	(0533)4418510 (0533)4408843	1,944	Collective-owned 集体企业	137,382	2,199(41)	235,400	Ceramics 陶瓷
Shandong Linyi Ceramics Enterprise Group General Company 山东临沂陶瓷企业集团总公司(1993)	Linyi 临沂市	Shandong 山东省	(0539)8251291 (0539)8241840	3,003	State Enterprises 国有独资	125,773	9,288(12)	198,978	Household Ceramics 日用陶瓷
Chaozhou Zhong Xia Ceramics Producing Factory Co.,Ltd. 潮州市中厦陶瓷制作厂有限公司(1996)	Chaozhou 潮州市	Guangdong 广东省	(0768)6888235 (0768)2972489	250	Overseas Chinese-funded 港澳台资	125,614	448(184)	55,238	Household Ceramics 日用陶瓷

Top 10 Cities by Revenue 销售收入排名前10位城市	Province 省	Market share 市场份额 (%)	Number of firms 企业个数
Chaozhou 潮州市	Guangdong 广东省	18.82	140
Quanzhou 泉州市	Fujian 福建省	10.22	110
Zibo 淄博市	Shandong 山东省	8.55	30
Yulin 玉林市	Guangxi 广西	6.99	27
Zhuzhou 株洲市	Hunan 湖南省	5.54	50
Tangshan 唐山市	Hebei 河北省	5.36	13
Wuxi 无锡市	Jiangsu 江苏省	4.97	20
Linyi 临沂市	Shandong 山东省	3.80	13
Handan 邯郸市	Hebei 河北省	2.33	2
Zhaoqing 肇庆市	Guangdong 广东省	2.27	5

10 Major Wholesalers 十家主要批发商	City 城市	Province 省	Telephone/Fax 电话/传真
Harbin ChinaSun Group Co., Ltd. 哈尔滨中央红集团股份有限公司	Harbin 哈尔滨市	Heilongjiang 黑龙江省	(0451)84885100 (0451)84885111
Guangzhou Yuexiu Enterprise (Group) Company 广州越秀企业（集团）公司	Guangzhou 广州市	Guangdong 广东省	(020)85597130 (020)85599018
China Reed Screen Imp. & Exp. Corp.Ltd. 中艺苇帘进出口有限责任公司	Beijing 北京市	Beijing 北京市	(010)65521133 (010)65513995
Hebei Xintai Foreign Trade Corp.ltd. 河北信泰对外贸易有限公司	Shijiazhuang 石家庄市	Hebei 河北省	(0311)7767908 (0311)7755347
Hebei Arts & Crafts Imp. & Exp. Corp. 河北省工艺品进出口公司	Shijiazhuang 石家庄市	Hebei 河北省	(0311)7764345 (0311)7755347
Shanghai Hengda Ceramic Building Materials Trade Market 上海恒大陶瓷建材交易市场	Shanghai 上海市	Shanghai 上海市	(021)58425842 (021)58427389
Hangzhou Local Product General Corporation 杭州市土特产总公司	Hangzhou 杭州市	Zhejiang 浙江省	(0571)87026301 (0571)87026323
Ningbo Zhonglin Foreign Trade Co.,Ltd. 宁波中蔺对外贸易有限公司	Ningbo 宁波市	Zhejiang 浙江省	(0574)87871797 (0574)87871790
Wuyi Local Products Daily Groceries Co.,Ltd. 武义县土产日用杂品有限责任公司	Jinhua 金华市	Zhejiang 浙江省	(0579)7623401 (0579)7623401
Guangdong Shunde Local Products Import & Export Company 广东省顺德土产进出口公司	Foshan 佛山市	Guangdong 广东省	(0765)6682839 (0765)6681441

3159: Other Ceramics 其他陶瓷制造业

The industry accounts for 0.011% of the total revenue of China's industrial sector in 2002. The rate of return on assets is 3.00%. 72.58% of all firms in the industry made a profit while 27.42% had negative returns.The top province in terms of the industry's revenue is Guangdong, accounting for 40.44% of the total revenue.
2002年本行业收入占全行业的0.011%，资产利润率为 3.00%。72.58%的企业赢利，27.42%的企业亏损。收入最高的省为广东省，占本行业的40.44%。

	Total number of firms 企业总数	Total number of employees 职工总数	Total revenue (Mil.RMB) 总销售收入（百万元）	Total profit (Mil.RMB) 总利润（百万元）	Return on assets 资产利润率（%）	Return on equity 权益利润率（%）	Labour productivity ('000 RMB/ worker) 劳动生产率（千元/人）	Debts/ assets 资产负债率（%）	Total assets (Mil.RMB) 总资产（百万元）
Industry Overall 行业总体	62	13,783	1,177	40	3.00	6.85	22.61	56.16	1,344

	Number of firms 企业个数	Average number of employees 平均职工人数	Average revenue ('000 RMB) 平均销售收入（千元）	Average profit ('000 RMB) 平均利润（千元）	Return on assets 资产利润率（%）	Return on equity 权益利润率（%）	Labour productivity ('000 RMB/ worker) 劳动生产率（千元/人）	Debts/ assets 资产负债率（%）	Average total assets ('000 RMB) 平均总资产（千元）
By ownership 产业所有权									
State-owned 国有	4	227	4,262	-135	-0.91	-4.32	6.77	78.86	14,823
Collective-owned 集体	6	136	11,981	635	7.38	29.49	23.89	74.98	8,601
Foreign & Overseas Chinese Funded 三资	25	310	24,477	736	2.41	4.61	20.27	47.69	30,539
By regional distribution 地区分布									
Central-North 华北	4	434	48,543	3,783	9.84	26.14	35.22	62.35	38,430
Beijing 北京	2	205	20,870	573	2.62	7.22	48.78	63.64	21,840
Tianjin 天津	1	127	35,120	4,220	25.07	63.17	46.46	60.31	16,830
Hebei 河北	1	1,200	117,310	9,766	10.48	27.65	29.39	62.11	93,211
Shanxi 山西									
Inner Mongolia 内蒙古									
Northeast 东北	3	71	14,933	1,562	12.81	20.94	62.96	38.84	12,191
Liaoning 辽宁	3	71	14,933	1,562	12.81	20.94	62.96	38.84	12,191
Jilin 吉林									
Heilongjiang 黑龙江									
Central-East 华东	15	276	23,035	597	1.66	2.85	25.22	41.91	35,983
Shanghai 上海	2	521	28,606	700	2.78	5.33	19.48	47.81	25,134
Jiangsu 江苏	5	345	43,817	1,209	1.59	2.58	33.58	38.49	76,082
Zhejiang 浙江	1	32	6,121	129	6.43	11.71	57.50	45.04	2,005
Anhui 安徽									
Fujian 福建									
Jiangxi 江西									
Shandong 山东	7	193	9,015	197	1.29	2.64	18.22	51.25	15,294
Central-South 中南	33	209	15,222	330	2.19	6.41	16.16	65.78	15,045
Henan 河南	4	226	4,408	-22	-0.21	-0.76	5.77	72.79	10,404
Hubei 湖北	1	255	8,576	70	0.27	0.53	12.16	48.92	25,935
Hunan 湖南									
Guangdong 广东	28	205	17,004	390	2.54	7.51	17.98	66.12	15,319
Guangxi 广西									
Hainan 海南									
Southwest 西南	4	162	17,826	49	0.21	1.90	18.75	89.02	23,386
Chongqing 重庆									
Sichuan 四川	4	162	17,826	49	0.21	1.90	18.75	89.02	23,386
Guizhou 贵州									
Yunnan 云南									
Tibet 西藏									
Northwest 西北	3	48	6,447	179	2.22	3.50	60.99	36.61	8,073
Shaanxi 陕西	2	52	9,179	219	1.91	3.04	81.07	37.14	11,475
Gansu 甘肃	1	40	983	100	7.87	10.79	8.80	27.01	1,270
Qinghai 青海									
Ningxia 宁夏									
Xinjiang 新疆									

3159: Other Ceramics 其他陶瓷制造业

Year 年份	Number of firms 企业个数	Rate of change 变化率 (%)	Number of employees 职工人数 (人)	Rate of change 变化率 (%)	Total revenue (Mil. RMB) 总销售收入 (百万元)	Rate of change 变化率 (%)	Total profit (Mil RMB) 总利润 (百万元)	Rate of change 变化率 (%)
2000	60		11,736		892		25	
2001	59	-1.67	15,153	29.12	1,019	14.24	43	72.00
2002	62	5.08	13,783	-9.04	1,177	15.51	40	-6.98

Major Products 主要产品	Output 产量	Unit 单位

10 Main Firms with Maximal Revenue (year founded) 收入最大的十家主要企业（创办年份）	City 城市	Province 省	Telephone/fax 电话/传真	Number of employees 职工人数	Ownership 产业所有权	Revenue ('000 RMB) 销售收入 (千元)	Profit('000 RMB) (rank) 利润(千元) (排名)	Total assets ('000 RMB) 总资产 (千元)	Major products 主要产品
Tangshan Yali Ceramics Co., Ltd. 唐山亚利陶瓷有限公司(1995)	Tangshan 唐山市	Hebei 河北省	(0315)8158059 (0315)8169356	1,200	Foreign Funded 外商投资	117,310	9,766(1)	93,211	Ceramics Handicrafts陶瓷工艺品
HCT Puckaing Co., ltd. 藤兴工业有限公司(1992)	Suzhou 苏州市	Jiangsu 江苏省	(0512)65010670 (0512)65010672	1,203	Foreign Funded 外商投资	69,010	4,914(2)	182,020	Cosmetics Outer Package Container化妆品外包装容器
Guangzhou Panyu Rongxiang Water Supply & Heating Equipment Co., ltd.广州市番禺区荣祥水暖器材有限公司(2000)	Guangzhou 广州市	Guangdong 广东省	(020)84559766 (020)84559876	400	Private Owned 私营企业	45,225	31(42)	71,401	Ceramic Valve 陶瓷阀芯
Suzhou kyoritsu electronics industry Co., Ltd. 苏州共立电子工业有限公司(1995)	Suzhou 苏州市	Jiangsu 江苏省	(0512)68253916 (0512)68250536	296	Foreign Funded 外商投资	45,122	-	116,061	Aluminium Oxide Ceramics Base Plate氧化铝陶瓷基板
Bhnson Matthey Ceramics (Jiangsu) Co., ltd. 庄信万丰(江苏)陶瓷有限公司(1994)	Changzhou 常州市	Jiangsu 江苏省	(0519)3581167 (0519)3581201	27	Foreign Funded 外商投资	45,010	1,840(9)	63,220	Zircon Sand and Products锆英砂及制品
Sichuan Deyang Hualong Pottery Co., Ltd. 四川德阳华龙陶业有限公司(1998)	Deyang 德阳市	Sichuan 四川省	(0838)3900053 (0838)3900048	193	Limited-Liability 有限公司	44,256	1,058(13)	28,179	Ceramic Glaze Frit陶瓷釉熔块
Zhuhai Mingshi Pottery and Porcelain Valve Co., Ltd. 珠海市名实陶瓷阀有限公司(1994)	Zhuhai 珠海市	Guangdong 广东省	(0756)8515368 (0756)8515166	500	Private Owned 私营企业	42,630	2,006(8)	15,870	Hardware Building materials 五金建材
Venus Guangzhou Ceramics Development Co., Ltd. 广州维纳斯陶瓷发展有限公司(1999)	Guangzhou 广州市	Guangdong 广东省	(020)82631838 (020)82633055	60	Joint Owned 联营企业	37,227	156(34)	10,992	Ceramics 陶瓷
Shanghai Dongai Ceramics Co., Ltd. 上海东爱陶瓷有限公司(1994)	Shanghai 上海市	Shanghai 上海市	(021)57642886 (021)57642988	975	Overseas Chinese-funded 港澳台资	36,867		21,310	Ceramics Products 陶瓷制品
Tianjin Focus Arts and Craft Co., Ltd. 天津福克思工艺品有限公司(1997)	Tianjin 天津市	Tianjin 天津市	(022)28580697 (022)28587296	127	Overseas Chinese-funded 港澳台资	35,120	4,220(4)	16,830	Ceramics Mural 陶瓷壁画

Top 10 Cities by Revenue 销售收入排名前10位城市	Province 省	Market share 市场份额 (%)	Number of firms 企业个数
Guangzhou 广州市	Guangdong 广东省	14.51	7
Zhuhai 珠海市	Guangdong 广东省	10.85	5
Tangshan 唐山市	Hebei 河北省	9.96	1
Suzhou 苏州市	Jiangsu 江苏省	9.69	2
Shanghai 上海市	Shanghai 上海市	4.86	2
Foshan 佛山市	Guangdong 广东省	4.53	5
Chaozhou 潮州市	Guangdong 广东省	4.41	5
Yancheng 盐城市	Jiangsu 江苏省	4.25	1
Changzhou 常州市	Jiangsu 江苏省	3.82	1
Deyang 德阳市	Sichuan 四川省	3.76	1

10 Major Wholesalers 十家主要批发商	City 城市	Province 省	Telephone/Fax 电话/传真
Xuzhou New Century Building Materials Decorative City 徐州市新世纪建材装饰城	Xuzhou 徐州市	Jiangsu 江苏省	(0516)83666780 (0516)63804485
Orienthome Co.,Ltd. 东方家园有限公司	Beijing 北京市	Beijing 北京市	(010)63808294
Shanghai Jinkai Goods & Materials Co.,Ltd. 上海金凯物资有限公司	Shanghai 上海市	Shanghai 上海市	(021)52193967
Guangzhou Building Materials Development Co.,Ltd. 广州市建材发展有限公司	Guangzhou 广州市	Guangdong 广东省	(020)83335062 (020)83341110
Guangxi Qiaofeng Goods & Materials Trade Co.,Ltd. 广西侨丰物资贸易有限责任公司	Nanning 南宁市	Guangxi 广西	(0771)2631539 (0771)2631539
Gansu Building Materials State-owned Assets Marketing Co.,Ltd. 甘肃建材国有资产经营有限责任公司	Lanzhou 兰州市	Gansu 甘肃省	(0931)8821359 (0931)8960243
Shanghai East Asia United Building Materials Co.,Ltd. 上海东亚联合建材有限公司	Shanghai 上海市	Shanghai 上海市	(021)33134520 (021)63216165
Shanghai Zhuzong Materials General Company 上海住总物资总公司	Shanghai 上海市	Shanghai 上海市	(021)32240030 (021)32240024
Guangdong Building Materials Company 广东省建材公司	Guangzhou 广州市	Guangdong 广东省	(020)83802713 (020)83817640
Guangdong Dongguan Hardware Minerals Import & Export Co.,Ltd 广东省东莞五金矿产进出口公司	Dongguan 东莞市	Guangdong 广东省	(0769)2227090 (0769)2221045

3161: Asbestos Products 石棉制品业

The industry accounts for 0.015% of the total revenue of China's industrial sector in 2002. The rate of return on assets is 4.38%. 82.95% of all firms in the industry made a profit while 17.05% had negative returns.The top province in terms of the industry's revenue is Hebei, accounting for 28.52% of the total revenue.
2002年本行业收入占全行业的0.015%，资产利润率为4.38%。82.95%的企业赢利，17.05%的企业亏损。收入最高的省为河北省，占本行业的28.52%。

	Total number of firms 企业总数	Total number of employees 职工总数	Total revenue (Mil.RMB) 总销售收入 (百万元)	Total profit (Mil.RMB) 总利润 (百万元)	Return on assets 资产利润率 (%)	Return on equity 权益利润率 (%)	Labour productivity ('000 RMB/ worker) 劳动生产率 (千元/人)	Debts/ assets 资产负债率 (%)	Total assets (Mil.RMB) 总资产 (百万元)
Industry Overall 行业总体	88	15,057	1,604	89	4.38	12.47	30.92	64.88	2,032

	Number of firms 企业个数	Average number of employees 平均职工人数	Average revenue ('000 RMB) 平均销售收入 (千元)	Average profit ('000 RMB) 平均利润 (千元)	Return on assets 资产利润率 (%)	Return on equity 权益利润率 (%)	Labour productivity ('000 RMB/ worker) 劳动生产率 (千元/人)	Debts/ assets 资产负债率 (%)	Average total assets ('000 RMB) 平均总资产 (千元)
By ownership 产业所有权									
State-owned 国有	17	314	6,231	-650	-1.77	-11.75	8.09	84.98	36,837
Collective-owned 集体	16	157	24,521	1,403	7.07	19.64	41.55	63.99	19,835
Foreign & Overseas Chinese Funded 三资	3	104	15,782	846	6.34	15.05	51.15	57.90	13,347
By regional distribution 地区分布									
Central-North 华北	23	86	21,069	1,601	9.41	20.43	55.51	53.96	17,015
Beijing 北京	2	85	4,436	-627	-1.83	-3.87	26.56	52.64	34,252
Tianjin 天津	2	45	8,250	-172	-1.06	-4.13	26.16	74.34	16,167
Hebei 河北	17	92	26,906	2,300	16.56	32.92	64.80	49.70	13,893
Shanxi 山西	2	73	901	-346	-1.27	-3.34	6.86	61.97	27,170
Inner Mongolia 内蒙古									
Northeast 东北	8	264	9,597	-99	-0.27		14.79	106.38	35,856
Liaoning 辽宁	2	207	5,045	7	0.01		10.92	157.74	54,752
Jilin 吉林	4	369	13,834	-190	-0.50	-2.01	15.25	74.93	37,557
Heilongjiang 黑龙江	2	111	5,677	-22	-0.16	-0.61	18.98	73.26	13,557
Central-East 华东	37	140	19,541	1,032	3.99	9.21	38.70	56.71	25,900
Shanghai 上海	3	127	11,410	634	2.92	12.97	24.66	77.49	21,707
Jiangsu 江苏	8	179	40,504	1,811	5.12	13.56	53.55	62.27	35,404
Zhejiang 浙江	16	125	17,898	1,235	4.10	7.39	42.14	44.53	30,113
Anhui 安徽									
Fujian 福建	1	55	5,644	1,975	70.51	160.57	24.64	56.09	2,801
Jiangxi 江西	1	70	450	-170	-2.80	-6.52	3.16	57.00	6,061
Shandong 山东	8	157	9,034	31	0.21	1.12	23.12	81.41	14,909
Central-South 中南	12	241	20,932	1,609	9.80	24.64	34.12	60.22	16,417
Henan 河南	7	158	20,962	2,289	29.05	64.16	44.00	54.73	7,882
Hubei 湖北	4	409	25,416	860	2.55	7.13	29.83	64.26	33,772
Hunan 湖南									
Guangdong 广东									
Guangxi 广西	1	146	2,781	-162	-2.40	-3.18	6.99	24.27	6,736
Hainan 海南									
Southwest 西南	2	414	16,447	78	0.25	5.14	10.56	95.11	30,812
Chongqing 重庆	1	729	13,537	82	0.15	1.90	7.99	91.92	53,473
Sichuan 四川	1	98	19,356	73	0.90		29.69	116.07	8,150
Guizhou 贵州									
Yunnan 云南									
Tibet 西藏									
Northwest 西北	6	344	5,860	-783	-3.44	-8.47	8.01	59.40	22,755
Shaanxi 陕西	1	934	8,626	-648	-0.98	-1.20	5.33	17.80	65,952
Gansu 甘肃	4	267	6,391	-1,012	-6.03		10.65	101.92	16,785
Qinghai 青海									
Ningxia 宁夏									
Xinjiang 新疆	1	64	968				3.23	27.01	3,440

3161: Asbestos Products 石棉制品业

Year 年份	Number of firms 企业个数	Rate of change 变化率 (%)	Number of employees 职工人数 (人)	Rate of change 变化率 (%)	Total revenue (Mil. RMB) 总销售收入 (百万元)	Rate of change 变化率 (%)	Total profit (Mil RMB) 总利润 (百万元)	Rate of change 变化率 (%)
2000	95		19,913		1,404		55	
2001	91	-4.21	16,690	-16.19	1,240	-11.68	180	227.27
2002	88	-3.30	15,057	-9.78	1,604	29.35	89	-50.56

Major Products 主要产品	Output 产量	Unit 单位
Asbestos Cement Tile 石棉水泥瓦	17,936	10,000 Sq.M. 万平方米
Asbestos Products 石棉制品	16	10,000 Tons 万吨

10 Main Firms with Maximal Revenue (year founded) 收入最大的十家主要企业（创办年份）	City 城市	Province 省	Telephone/fax 电话/传真	Number of employees 职工人数	Ownership 产业所有权	Revenue ('000 RMB) 销售收入 (千元)	Profit('000 RMB) (rank) 利润(千元) (排名)	Total assets ('000 RMB) 总资产 (千元)	Major products 主要产品
Jiangsu Veectory Internation Co., Ltd . 江苏威特集团公司(1994)	Yancheng 盐城市	Jiangsu 江苏省	(0515)8334004 (0515)8335644	523	Collective-owned 集体企业	121,660	6,050(1)	166,600	Clutch Facing Blade离合器面片
Jiangyan Jin Ji Airproof Insulating Products Group Co. 姜堰市金鸡密封保温制品集团公司(1978)	Taizhou 泰州市	Jiangsu 江苏省	(0523)8324321 (0523)8324020	300	Collective-owned 集体企业	105,000	4,800(5)	44,000	Asbestos Products 石棉制品
Hangzhou HangCheng Friction Material Co., Ltd. 杭州杭城摩擦材料有限公司(2001)	Hangzhou 杭州市	Zhejiang 浙江省	(0571)85460190 (0571)85457319	791	Limited-Liability 有限公司	93,431	5,072(4)	275,046	Friction Products 摩擦制品
Qinyang Huamei Co., Ltd. 沁阳市华美有限公司(1996)	Jiaozuo 焦作市	Henan 河南省	(0391)5697968 (0391)5697628	300	Private Owned 私营企业	67,410	5,770(2)	13,345	Anticorrosion Thermal Insulation Materials防腐保温材料
Jinzhou Xinghua Mineral Cotton Plank Co., Ltd. 晋州兴华矿棉板厂(1997)	Shijiazhuang 石家庄市	Hebei 河北省	(0311)4430123 (0311)4433200	70	Private Enterprises 私营独资	60,812	4,414(9)	9,960	Mineral Cotton Board 矿棉板
Hebei Bo Ling Friction Materials Co.,Ltd. 河北博陵磨擦材料有限公司(1995)	Hengshui 衡水市	Hebei 河北省	(0318)3465720 (0318)3460966	95	Private Owned 私营企业	53,599	4,545(6)	13,091	Brake Blade 刹车片
Sutai Friction Material Factory 姜堰市苏泰摩擦材料厂(1985)	Taizhou 泰州市	Jiangsu 江苏省	(0523)8321157 (0523)8321003	95	Joint Stock 股份制	46,060	1,700(23)	10,593	Friction Materials 摩擦材料
Hubei Fei Long Friction Materials Co., Ltd. 湖北飞龙摩擦材料股份有限公司(1998)	Xiangfan 襄樊市	Hubei 湖北省	(0710)6329671 (0710)6321825	776	Joint Stock 股份制	40,117	61(62)	55,517	Brake Blade 刹车片
Cixi Mingshi Automobile Fittings Factory 慈溪市鸣石汽车配件厂(1997)	Ningbo 宁波市	Zhejiang 浙江省	(0574)63672142 (0574)63672059	96	Private Enterprises 私营独资	36,409	1,007(27)	23,590	Asbestos Clutch Blade石棉离合器片
Jinzhou Decorative Materials Factory 晋州装饰材料厂(1995)	Shijiazhuang 石家庄市	Hebei 河北省	(0311)4430088 (0311)4430735	154	Private Enterprises 私营独资	34,544	4,472(7)	15,370	Gypsum Board 石膏板

Top 10 Cities by Revenue 销售收入排名前10位城市	Province 省	Market share 市场份额 (%)	Number of firms 企业个数
Shijiazhuang 石家庄市	Hebei 河北省	20.57	9
Taizhou 泰州市	Jiangsu 江苏省	10.04	3
Yancheng 盐城市	Jiangsu 江苏省	7.59	1
Hangzhou 杭州市	Zhejiang 浙江省	6.72	3
Xiangfan 襄樊市	Hubei 湖北省	5.26	3
Jiaozuo 焦作市	Henan 河南省	4.80	2
Ningbo 宁波市	Zhejiang 浙江省	4.18	5
Hengshui 衡水市	Hebei 河北省	3.73	2
Cangzhou 沧州市	Hebei 河北省	3.42	5
Huzhou 湖州市	Zhejiang 浙江省	3.39	4

10 Major Wholesalers 十家主要批发商	City 城市	Province 省	Telephone/Fax 电话/传真
Xuzhou New Century Building Materials Decorative City 徐州市新世纪建材装饰城	Xuzhou 徐州市	Jiangsu 江苏省	(0516)83666780 (0516)63804485
Orienthome Co.,Ltd. 东方家园有限公司	Beijing 北京市	Beijing 北京市	(010)63808294
Shanghai Jinkai Goods & Materials Co.,Ltd. 上海金凯物资有限公司	Shanghai 上海市	Shanghai 上海市	(021)52193967
Guangzhou Building Materials Development Co.,Ltd. 广州市建材发展有限公司	Guangzhou 广州市	Guangdong 广东省	(020)83335062 (020)83341110
Guangxi Qiaofeng Goods & Materials Trade Co.,Ltd. 广西侨丰物资贸易有限责任公司	Nanning 南宁市	Guangxi 广西	(0771)2631539 (0771)2631539
Gansu Building Materials State-owned Assets Marketing Co.,Ltd. 甘肃建材国有资产经营有限责任公司	Lanzhou 兰州市	Gansu 甘肃省	(0931)8821359 (0931)8960243
Shanghai East Asia United Building Materials Co.,Ltd. 上海东亚联合建材有限公司	Shanghai 上海市	Shanghai 上海市	(021)33134520 (021)63216165
Shanghai Zhuzong Materials General Company 上海住总物资总公司	Shanghai 上海市	Shanghai 上海市	(021)32240030 (021)32240024
Guangdong Building Materials Company 广东省建材公司	Guangzhou 广州市	Guangdong 广东省	(020)83802713 (020)83817640
Guangdong Dongguan Hardware Minerals Import & Export Co.,Ltd 广东省东莞五金矿产进出口公司	Dongguan 东莞市	Guangdong 广东省	(0769)2227090 (0769)2221045

3163: Mica Products 云母制品业

The industry accounts for 0.005% of the total revenue of China's industrial sector in 2002. The rate of return on assets is 6.79%. 87.10% of all firms in the industry made a profit while 12.90% had negative returns.The top province in terms of the industry's revenue is Hebei, accounting for 44.09% of the total revenue.
2002年本行业收入占全行业的 0.005%，资产利润率为 6.79%。87.10%的企业赢利，12.90%的企业亏损。收入最高的省为河北省，占本行业的44.09%。

	Total number of firms 企业总数	Total number of employees 职工总数	Total revenue (Mil.RMB) 总销售收入 (百万元)	Total profit (Mil.RMB) 总利润 (百万元)	Return on assets 资产利润率 (%)	Return on equity 权益利润率 (%)	Labour productivity ('000 RMB/ worker) 劳动生产率 (千元/人)	Debts/ assets 资产负债率 (%)	Total assets (Mil.RMB) 总资产 (百万元)
Industry Overall 行业总体	31	4,684	511	32	6.79	15.51	37.27	56.21	473

	Number of firms 企业个数	Average number of employees 平均职工人数	Average revenue ('000 RMB) 平均销售收入 (千元)	Average profit ('000 RMB) 平均利润 (千元)	Return on assets 资产利润率 (%)	Return on equity 权益利润率 (%)	Labour productivity ('000 RMB/ worker) 劳动生产率 (千元/人)	Debts/ assets 资产负债率 (%)	Average total assets ('000 RMB) 平均总资产 (千元)
By ownership 产业所有权									
State-owned 国有	5	122	11,563	166	0.70	2.31	32.00	69.63	23,629
Collective-owned 集体	5	134	10,004	1,087	17.40	48.92	31.04	64.44	6,246
Foreign & Overseas Chinese Funded 三资	4	161	16,319	2,770	15.98	24.44	52.65	34.63	17,338
By regional distribution 地区分布									
Central-North 华北	11	151	20,464	1,969	15.10	36.56	46.16	58.71	13,040
Beijing 北京									
Tianjin 天津									
Hebei 河北	11	151	20,464	1,969	15.10	36.56	46.16	58.71	13,040
Shanxi 山西									
Inner Mongolia 内蒙古									
Northeast 东北									
Liaoning 辽宁									
Jilin 吉林									
Heilongjiang 黑龙江									
Central-East 华东	6	130	26,956	-257	-1.05	-2.48	47.96	57.59	24,450
Shanghai 上海	1	122	8,219	-3,730	-8.38	-19.58	-8.18	57.19	44,490
Jiangsu 江苏	4	131	38,180	568	2.91	6.34	72.76	54.12	19,523
Zhejiang 浙江	1	133	798	-81	-0.34	-1.10	1.95	69.58	24,114
Anhui 安徽									
Fujian 福建									
Jiangxi 江西									
Shandong 山东									
Central-South 中南	9	163	10,438	1,340	9.40	18.32	31.90	48.69	14,249
Henan 河南	1	50	340	1	0.01	0.08	-0.30	89.93	12,510
Hubei 湖北	3	215	11,054	824	5.27	11.36	19.06	53.58	15,622
Hunan 湖南	3	119	3,138	63	1.30	4.36	16.77	70.29	4,860
Guangdong 广东	2	208	25,513	4,698	17.31	24.44	68.70	29.17	27,140
Guangxi 广西									
Hainan 海南									
Southwest 西南	4	175	7,255	-11	-0.09	-0.24	17.68	64.04	13,123
Chongqing 重庆									
Sichuan 四川	4	175	7,255	-11	-0.09	-0.24	17.68	64.04	13,123
Guizhou 贵州									
Yunnan 云南									
Tibet 西藏									
Northwest 西北	1	74	748	22	0.87	1.85	17.34	52.86	2,516
Shaanxi 陕西									
Gansu 甘肃									
Qinghai 青海									
Ningxia 宁夏									
Xinjiang 新疆	1	74	748	22	0.87	1.85	17.34	52.86	2,516

3163: Mica Products 云母制品业

Year 年份	Number of firms 企业个数	Rate of change 变化率 (%)	Number of employees 职工人数 (人)	Rate of change 变化率 (%)	Total revenue (Mil. RMB) 总销售收入 (百万元)	Rate of change 变化率 (%)	Total profit (Mil RMB) 总利润 (百万元)	Rate of change 变化率 (%)
2000	30		4,705		477		37	
2001	32	6.67	4,732	0.57	531	11.32	40	8.11
2002	31	-3.13	4,684	-1.01	511	-3.77	32	-20.00

Major Products 主要产品	Output 产量	Unit 单位

10 Main Firms with Maximal Revenue (year founded) 收入最大的十家主要企业（创办年份）	City 城市	Province 省	Telephone/fax 电话/传真	Number of employees 职工人数	Ownership 产业所有权	Revenue ('000 RMB) 销售收入 (千元)	Profit('000 RMB) (rank) 利润(千元) (排名)	Total assets ('000 RMB) 总资产 (千元)	Major products 主要产品
Jiangsu Bingshen Group Co., Ltd.	Zhenjiang	Jiangsu	(0511)6387451		Private Enterprises				Mica Products
江苏省冰神集团有限公司(1975)	镇江市	江苏省	(0511)6389553	365	私营独资	118,689	1,470(7)	61,333	云母制品
Lingshou Zhong Fei Mica General Factory	Shijiazhuang	Hebei	(0311)2630281		Collective-owned				Mica Powder
灵寿县中非云母总厂(1969)	石家庄市	河北省	(0311)2630241	40	集体企业	29,313	4,173(4)	5,780	云母粉
HeEei Lingshou Yida Mica Factory	Shijiazhuang	Hebei	(0311)2580005		State-owned				Mica Powder
河北灵寿亿达云母厂(1971)	石家庄市	河北省	(0311)2580005	56	国有企业	29,000	4,500(3)	6,100	云母粉
Mai Ka Electric Material Co., Ltd.	Shanwei	Guangdong	(0660)5525123		Overseas Chinese-funded				Mica Board
麦卡电工器材（陆河）有限公司(2000)	汕尾市	广东省	(0660)5525333	246	港澳台资	26,041	6,041(2)	28,588	云母板
Tongcheng Yun Qi Mica Products Co., Ltd.	Xianning	Hubei	(0715)4646228		Joint Stock				Mica Paper
通城县云奇云母制品有限公司(1992)	咸宁市	湖北省	(0715)4646226	375	股份制	23,475	636(11)	25,435	云母纸
Hebei XingTai Shahe Paper Making China Clay Factory	Xingtai	Hebei	(0319)8804585		State-owned				Papermaking China Clay
河北省邢台市沙河市造纸瓷土厂(1988)	邢台市	河北省	(0319)8803080	325	国有企业	18,919	38(23)	57,390	造纸瓷土
Suzhou Kangdawei Fiber Particle Factory	Suzhou	Jiangsu	(0512)65441749		Private Enterprises				Terylene Particle
苏州市康达纤维母粒厂(1996)	苏州市	江苏省	(0512)65447592	53	私营独资	18,166	458(14)	5,525	涤沦母粒
Hebei Xingtai Shahe Mineral Products Processing Factory	Xingtai	Hebei	(0319)8802504		Private Enterprises				Porcelain Clay
河北省邢台市沙河市矿产品加工厂(1995)	邢台市	河北省	(0319)8811321	110	私营独资	11,620	750(8)	6,175	瓷土
Sichuan Meifeng Mica Industry Co., Ltd.	Yaan	Sichuan	(0835)2221153		Limited-Liability				Mica Paper
四川美丰云母工业有限责任公司(2000)	雅安市	四川省	(0835)2224228	295	有限公司	10,296	687(10)	18,755	云母纸
Guannan Fuda Insulation Material Co., Ltd.	Lianyungang	Jiangsu	(0518)3221074		Private Owned				Mica Products
灌南县福达绝缘材料有限公司(1976)	连云港市	江苏省	(0518)3238201	65	私营企业	9,578	206(17)	6,489	云母制品

Top 10 Cities by Revenue 销售收入排名前10位城市	Province 省	Market share 市场份额 (%)	Number of firms 企业个数
Xingtai 邢台市	Hebei 河北省	30.88	7
Zhenjiang 镇江市	Jiangsu 江苏省	23.25	1
Shijiazhuang 石家庄市	Hebei 河北省	13.21	4
Xianning 咸宁市	Hubei 湖北省	6.50	3
Shanwei 汕尾市	Guangdong 广东省	5.10	1
Shenzhen 深圳市	Guangdong 广东省	4.89	1
Yaan 雅安市	Sichuan 四川省	3.68	2
Suzhou 苏州市	Jiangsu 江苏省	3.56	1
Lianyungang 连云港市	Jiangsu 江苏省	3.11	2
Yueyang 岳阳市	Hunan 湖南省	1.84	3

10 Major Wholesalers 十家主要批发商	City 城市	Province 省	Telephone/Fax 电话/传真
Xuzhou New Century Building Materials Decorative City	Xuzhou	Jiangsu	(0516)83666780
徐州市新世纪建材装饰城	徐州市	江苏省	(0516)63804485
Orienthome Co.,Ltd.	Beijing	Beijing	(010)63808294
东方家园有限公司	北京市	北京市	
Shanghai Jinkai Goods & Materials Co.,Ltd.	Shanghai	Shanghai	(021)52193967
上海金凯物资有限公司	上海市	上海市	
Guangzhou Building Materials Development Co.,Ltd.	Guangzhou	Guangdong	(020)83335062
广州市建材发展有限公司	广州市	广东省	(020)83341110
Guangxi Qiaofeng Goods & Materials Trade Co.,Ltd.	Nanning	Guangxi	(0771)2631539
广西侨丰物资贸易有限责任公司	南宁市	广西	(0771)2631539
Gansu Building Materials State-owned Assets Marketing Co.,Ltd.	Lanzhou	Gansu	(0931)8821359
甘肃建材国有资产经营有限责任公司	兰州市	甘肃省	(0931)8960243
Shanghai East Asia United Building Materials Co.,Ltd.	Shanghai	Shanghai	(021)33134520
上海东亚联合建材有限公司	上海市	上海市	(021)63216165
Shanghai Zhuzong Materials General Company	Shanghai	Shanghai	(021)32240030
上海住总物资总公司	上海市	上海市	(021)32240024
Guangdong Building Materials Company	Guangzhou	Guangdong	(020)83802713
广东省建材公司	广州市	广东省	(020)83817640
Guangdong Dongguan Hardware Minerals Import & Export Co.,Ltd	Dongguan	Guangdong	(0769)2227090
广东省东莞五金矿产进出口公司	东莞市	广东省	(0769)2221045

3169: Other Fireproof Material 其他耐火材料制品业

The industry accounts for 0.227% of the total revenue of China's industrial sector in 2002. The rate of return on assets is 4.89%. 83.16% of all firms in the industry made a profit while 16.84% had negative returns.The top province in terms of the industry's revenue is Liaoning, accounting for 36.18% of the total revenue.
2002年本行业收入占全行业的 0.227%，资产利润率为 4.89%。83.16%的企业赢利，16.84%的企业亏损。收入最高的省为辽宁省，占本行业的36.18%。

	Total number of firms 企业总数	Total number of employees 职工总数	Total revenue (Mil.RMB) 总销售收入 (百万元)	Total profit (Mil.RMB) 总利润 (百万元)	Return on assets 资产利润率 (%)	Return on equity 权益利润率 (%)	Labour productivity ('000 RMB/ worker) 劳动生产率 (千元/人)	Debts/ assets 资产负债率 (%)	Total assets (Mil.RMB) 总资产 (百万元)
Industry Overall 行业总体	772	166,900	24,307	1,389	4.89	13.02	47.57	62.41	28,377

	Number of firms 企业个数	Average number of employees 平均职工人数	Average revenue ('000 RMB) 平均销售收入 (千元)	Average profit ('000 RMB) 平均利润 (千元)	Return on assets 资产利润率 (%)	Return on equity 权益利润率 (%)	Labour productivity ('000 RMB/ worker) 劳动生产率 (千元/人)	Debts/ assets 资产负债率 (%)	Average total assets ('000 RMB) 平均总资产 (千元)
By ownership 产业所有权									
State-owned 国有	67	296	17,027	-211	-0.39	-2.29	20.36	82.94	54,075
Collective-owned 集体	249	225	35,540	2,394	7.23	19.01	56.07	61.97	33,113
Foreign & Overseas Chinese Funded 三资	47	146	52,628	3,615	6.21	10.04	83.13	38.08	58,168
By regional distribution 地区分布									
Central-North 华北	85	221	19,957	1,200	3.74	8.49	30.04	55.94	32,080
Beijing 北京	12	115	26,331	2,955	7.38	12.66	75.88	41.69	40,023
Tianjin 天津	6	73	40,022	4,265	10.37	17.70	27.25	41.42	41,132
Hebei 河北	32	186	13,736	427	2.02	4.79	24.49	57.81	21,094
Shanxi 山西	28	292	14,241	70	0.24	0.72	22.07	66.65	29,007
Inner Mongolia 内蒙古	7	401	43,138	3,624	4.95	11.47	42.94	56.86	73,221
Northeast 东北	168	298	53,383	3,103	4.87	11.96	56.01	59.24	63,662
Liaoning 辽宁	158	304	55,666	3,278	4.95	12.01	57.25	58.77	66,236
Jilin 吉林	6	213	26,604	1,015	3.49	12.87	35.68	72.85	29,067
Heilongjiang 黑龙江	4	180	3,355	-705	-5.07		9.31	104.49	13,901
Central-East 华东	204	175	28,985	1,441	4.68	11.45	49.63	59.11	30,773
Shanghai 上海	23	194	27,725	866	1.74	3.86	29.32	54.87	49,744
Jiangsu 江苏	64	127	25,478	660	2.25	5.63	45.18	60.05	29,380
Zhejiang 浙江	36	130	26,234	1,693	6.06	13.49	62.99	55.11	27,956
Anhui 安徽	13	145	6,673	62	0.77	1.99	15.86	61.37	8,115
Fujian 福建									
Jiangxi 江西	4	176	6,464	-1,637	-4.71	-82.19	-0.14	94.27	34,783
Shandong 山东	64	247	40,432	2,758	8.82	22.09	59.92	60.09	31,286
Central-South 中南	267	195	26,724	1,786	6.53	19.87	49.49	67.16	27,358
Henan 河南	211	207	29,628	2,063	6.94	20.93	52.41	66.85	29,728
Hubei 湖北	23	115	13,235	1,057	10.06	20.65	42.93	51.30	10,514
Hunan 湖南	18	219	11,546	-14	-0.06	-0.37	22.02	85.02	25,772
Guangdong 广东	13	124	27,929	1,370	6.41	15.79	56.06	59.38	21,360
Guangxi 广西	1	278	6,873	-550	-1.49	-2.48	12.11	39.77	36,860
Hainan 海南	1	45	1,478	89	0.75		11.00	122.54	11,858
Southwest 西南	35	242	14,370	261	0.84	5.62	23.20	85.07	31,170
Chongqing 重庆	7	331	24,412	668	1.42	10.19	29.48	86.02	46,867
Sichuan 四川	21	175	11,327	398	2.12	5.40	23.46	60.69	18,765
Guizhou 贵州	5	375	14,607	-702	-1.12		13.42	121.01	62,748
Yunnan 云南	2	299	10,583	-187	-0.68	-1.33	27.98	49.12	27,547
Tibet 西藏									
Northwest 西北	13	144	7,035	-1,120	-5.17		15.95	108.42	21,644
Shaanxi 陕西	4	241	7,694	-3,475	-7.67		9.08	122.08	45,310
Gansu 甘肃	4	54	1,792				25.87	79.19	3,859
Qinghai 青海	3	99	13,769	76	0.74	4.04	31.88	81.69	10,215
Ningxia 宁夏									
Xinjiang 新疆	2	203	6,101	-444	-1.64	-11.81	15.36	86.11	27,028

3169: Other Fireproof Material 其他耐火材料制品业

Year 年份	Number of firms 企业个数	Rate of change 变化率 (%)	Number of employees 职工人数 (人)	Rate of change 变化率 (%)	Total revenue (Mil. RMB) 总销售收入 (百万元)	Rate of change 变化率 (%)	Total profit (Mil RMB) 总利润 (百万元)	Rate of change 变化率 (%)
2000	684		169,364		18,213		933	
2001	719	5.12	162,434	-4.09	20,907	14.79	1,230	31.83
2002	772	7.37	166,900	2.75	24,307	16.26	1,389	12.93

Major Products 主要产品	Output 产量	Unit 单位
Fire-Resistant Materials Product 耐火材料制品	1,177	10,000 Tons 万吨

10 Main Firms with Maximal Revenue (year founded) 收入最大的十家主要企业（创办年份）	City 城市	Province 省	Telephone/fax 电话/传真	Number of employees 职工人数	Ownership 产业所有权	Revenue ('000 RMB) 销售收入（千元）	Profit('000 RMB) (rank) 利润（千元）（排名）	Total assets ('000 RMB) 总资产（千元）	Major products 主要产品
Yingkou Qinghua GroupCo., Ltd.	Yingkou	Liaoning	(0417)5631810		Limited-Liability				Magnesia Brick
营口青花集团有限公司(2000)	营口市	辽宁省	(0417)5631810	2,630	有限公司	1,056,000	88,600(1)	647,017	镁砖
HaiCheng XiYang Fireproof Material Co., ltd.	Anshan	Liaoning	(0412)3276666		Collective-owned				Refractory Material Products耐火
海城市西洋耐火材料有限公司(1999)	鞍山市	辽宁省	(0412)3277060	3,335	集体企业	804,790	35,650(5)	1,140,460	材料制品
Jiangsu Su Jia Investment Group Co., Ltd.	Wuxi	Jiangsu	(0510)3231624		Joint Stock				Magnesia & Carbon Brick
江苏苏嘉投资集团有限公司(1983)	无锡市	江苏省	(0510)3231514	1,726	股份制	557,450	13,950(17)	761,760	镁碳砖
Haicheng Hua Yu Refractory Group Company	Anshan	Liaoning	(0412)3243648		Limited-Liability				Refractory Material
海城华宇耐火材料集团公司(1999)	鞍山市	辽宁省	(0412)3243300	3,200	有限公司	432,770	15,080(15)	711,070	耐火材料
Haicheng Fengchi Refractory General Company	Anshan	Liaoning	(0412)3264064		Collective-owned				Magnesia & Carbon Brick Tile
海城市峰驰耐火材料总公司(1985)	鞍山市	辽宁省	(0412)3264209	2,400	集体企业	394,970	52,460(3)	420,330	镁碳砖瓦
Haicheng Pai Lou Magnesium Mine Company	Anshan	Liaoning	(0412)3772582		Private Enterprises				Magnesite Clinker
海城市牌楼镁矿公司(1982)	鞍山市	辽宁省	(0412)3772360	2,548	私营独资	359,900	33,180(6)	280,800	镁砂
Jinan Magnesia & Carbon Brick plant	Jinan	Shandong	(0531)8991172		Foreign Funded				Magnesia & Carbon Brick
济南市镁碳砖厂(1986)	济南市	山东省	(0531)8991327	561	外商投资	355,000	28,500(7)	178,300	镁碳砖
Luoyang Fireproof Material Group Co., Ltd.	Luoyang	Henan	(0379)4208817		State Enterprises				Refractory Material Products耐火
洛阳耐火材料集团有限责任公司(1959)	洛阳市	河南省	(0379)4208817	4,222	国有独资	302,584	2,002(179)	954,492	材料制品
Henan Geng Sheng Fireproof Co., Ltd.	Zhengzhou	Henan	(0371)4059858		Joint Stock				Refractory Material
河南省耕生耐火股份有限公司(1986)	郑州市	河南省	(0371)4059837	387	股份制	267,648	19,735(12)	95,034	耐火材料
Inner Mongolia Baotou Iron & Steel Company New Type Refractory	Baotou	Inner Mongol	(0472)2184340		State-owned				Refractory Material
Co.,Ltd.内蒙古包钢新型耐火材料股份有限公司(1999)	包头市	内蒙古	(0472)2185351	1,779	国有企业	263,995	15,321(13)	441,958	耐火材料

Top 10 Cities by Revenue 销售收入排名前10位城市	Province 省	Market share 市场份额 (%)	Number of firms 企业个数
Zhengzhou 郑州市	Henan 河南省	19.76	151
Anshan 鞍山市	Liaoning 辽宁省	19.59	56
Yingkou 营口市	Liaoning 辽宁省	14.94	77
Zibo 淄博市	Shandong 山东省	5.94	40
Wuxi 无锡市	Jiangsu 江苏省	4.97	42
Jinan 济南市	Shandong 山东省	3.40	11
Huzhou 湖州市	Zhejiang 浙江省	2.82	24
Shanghai 上海市	Shanghai 上海市	2.62	23
Luoyang 洛阳市	Henan 河南省	2.46	17
Guangzhou 广州市	Guangdong 广东省	1.43	9

10 Major Wholesalers 十家主要批发商	City 城市	Province 省	Telephone/Fax 电话/传真
Xuzhou New Century Building Materials Decorative City	Xuzhou	Jiangsu	(0516)83666780
徐州市新世纪建材装饰城	徐州市	江苏省	(0516)63804485
Orienthome Co.,Ltd.	Beijing	Beijing	(010)63808294
东方家园有限公司	北京市	北京市	
Shanghai Jinkai Goods & Materials Co.,Ltd.	Shanghai	Shanghai	(021)52193967
上海金凯物资有限公司	上海市	上海市	
Guangzhou Building Materials Development Co.,Ltd.	Guangzhou	Guangdong	(020)83335062
广州市建材发展有限公司	广州市	广东省	(020)83341110
Guangxi Qiaofeng Goods & Materials Trade Co.,Ltd.	Nanning	Guangxi	(0771)2631539
广西侨丰物资贸易有限责任公司	南宁市	广西	(0771)2631539
Gansu Building Materials State-owned Assets Marketing Co.,Ltd.	Lanzhou	Gansu	(0931)8821359
甘肃建材国有资产经营有限责任公司	兰州市	甘肃省	(0931)8960243
Shanghai East Asia United Building Materials Co.,Ltd.	Shanghai	Shanghai	(021)33134520
上海东亚联合建材有限公司	上海市	上海市	(021)63216165
Shanghai Zhuzong Materials General Company	Shanghai	Shanghai	(021)32240030
上海住总物资总公司	上海市	上海市	(021)32240024
Guangdong Building Materials Company	Guangzhou	Guangdong	(020)83802713
广东省建材公司	广州市	广东省	(020)83817640
Guangdong Dongguan Hardware Minerals Import & Export Co.,Ltd	Dongguan	Guangdong	(0769)2227090
广东省东莞五金矿产进出口公司	东莞市	广东省	(0769)2221045

3171: Metallurgical Coke 冶金用碳素制品业

The industry accounts for 0.069% of the total revenue of China's industrial sector in 2002. The rate of return on assets is 1.64%. 78.41% of all firms in the industry made a profit while 21.59% had negative returns.The top province in terms of the industry's revenue is Henan, accounting for 20.59% of the total revenue.
2002年本行业收入占全行业的 0.069%，资产利润率为 1.64%。78.41%的企业赢利，21.59%的企业亏损。收入最高的省为河南省，占本行业的20.59%。

	Total number of firms 企业总数	Total number of employees 职工总数	Total revenue (Mil.RMB) 总销售收入（百万元）	Total profit (Mil.RMB) 总利润（百万元）	Return on assets 资产利润率（%）	Return on equity 权益利润率（%）	Labour productivity ('000 RMB/ worker) 劳动生产率（千元/人）	Debts/ assets 资产负债率（%）	Total assets (Mil.RMB) 总资产（百万元）
Industry Overall 行业总体	227	63,043	7,424	254	1.64	4.60	35.28	64.39	15,511

	Number of firms 企业个数	Average number of employees 平均职工人数	Average revenue ('000 RMB) 平均销售收入（千元）	Average profit ('000 RMB) 平均利润（千元）	Return on assets 资产利润率（%）	Return on equity 权益利润率（%）	Labour productivity ('000 RMB/ worker) 劳动生产率（千元/人）	Debts/ assets 资产负债率（%）	Average total assets ('000 RMB) 平均总资产（千元）
By ownership 产业所有权									
State-owned 国有	34	396	27,096	-2		-0.01	21.24	62.78	91,339
Collective-owned 集体	55	202	32,785	2,514	8.17	24.51	55.91	66.65	30,762
Foreign & Overseas Chinese Funded 三资	16	100	18,403	222	0.63	1.66	54.27	61.71	34,974
By regional distribution 地区分布									
Central-North 华北	49	268	28,819	1,564	2.47	6.35	39.68	61.08	63,272
Beijing 北京	1	12	638	12	0.74	0.74	37.83	0.25	1,630
Tianjin 天津	4	192	21,644	801	2.04	6.44	68.56	68.28	39,199
Hebei 河北	11	213	31,810	1,251	2.86	13.02	53.44	78.05	43,764
Shanxi 山西	29	311	28,410	1,690	2.17	5.06	30.81	57.19	77,994
Inner Mongolia 内蒙古	4	252	37,778	2,666	5.37	13.11	65.14	59.05	49,663
Northeast 东北	27	481	50,143	-1,481	-0.83	-2.67	17.13	68.95	178,518
Liaoning 辽宁	19	214	22,286	259	0.53	1.48	14.61	64.00	48,671
Jilin 吉林	6	1,458	152,972	-7,467	-1.16	-3.91	18.29	70.26	642,222
Heilongjiang 黑龙江	2	79	6,294	-49	-0.23	-0.56	18.08	58.42	20,957
Central-East 华东	42	278	42,056	2,573	4.27	13.42	45.31	68.20	60,289
Shanghai 上海	2	726	54,107	6,018	2.64	6.16	19.13	57.13	227,835
Jiangsu 江苏	21	208	34,805	1,335	3.81	15.12	53.63	74.82	35,082
Zhejiang 浙江	2	30	7,981	440	10.37	21.85	50.65	52.54	4,237
Anhui 安徽	2	375	36,070	278	0.29	0.64	33.29	54.17	95,281
Fujian 福建	3	27	13,888	156	1.50	4.57	290.12	67.09	10,396
Jiangxi 江西	1	77	6,889	572	7.24	12.06	30.45	39.94	7,899
Shandong 山东	11	444	71,870	5,955	5.95	20.59	43.55	71.13	100,147
Central-South 中南	65	202	28,471	1,720	5.15	16.37	47.94	68.57	33,423
Henan 河南	46	199	33,225	2,312	6.51	19.60	55.18	66.77	35,511
Hubei 湖北	5	308	11,405	-218	-0.57	-2.32	20.66	75.59	38,474
Hunan 湖南	9	157	18,545	246	1.94	7.34	41.05	73.52	12,653
Guangdong 广东	4	196	18,803	279	0.62	3.64	33.32	82.86	44,737
Guangxi 广西	1	207	23,164	3,163	5.88	9.80	33.10	39.98	53,773
Hainan 海南									
Southwest 西南	17	130	16,949	258	1.06	2.31	37.19	54.06	24,252
Chongqing 重庆	1	280	7,217	3	0.04	0.11	7.29	68.84	8,439
Sichuan 四川	8	110	21,320	2		0.01	50.62	48.11	31,405
Guizhou 贵州	6	145	14,388	523	2.37	5.86	32.04	59.56	22,078
Yunnan 云南	2	90	12,019	613	6.08	42.97	42.82	85.84	10,069
Tibet 西藏									
Northwest 西北	27	368	27,877	-257	-0.28	-0.61	24.25	53.83	91,632
Shaanxi 陕西	6	275	25,412	-166	-0.38		29.74	108.91	43,543
Gansu 甘肃	16	479	33,628	-660	-0.54	-1.02	21.44	46.63	121,816
Qinghai 青海									
Ningxia 宁夏	5	125	12,432	924	1.75	3.69	44.26	52.51	52,752
Xinjiang 新疆									

Year 年份	Number of firms 企业个数	Rate of change 变化率 (%)	Number of employees 职工人数 (人)	Rate of change 变化率 (%)	Total revenue (Mil. RMB) 总销售收入 (百万元)	Rate of change 变化率 (%)	Total profit (Mil RMB) 总利润 (百万元)	Rate of change 变化率 (%)
2000	176		55,155		5,184		36	
2001	190	7.95	74,933	35.86	6,435	24.13	231	541.67
2002	227	19.47	63,043	-15.87	7,424	15.37	254	9.96

Major Products 主要产品	Output 产量	Unit 单位
Graphite & Carbon Products 石墨及碳素制品	303	10,000 Tons 万吨

10 Main Firms with Maximal Revenue (year founded) 收入最大的十家主要企业（创办年份）	City 城市	Province 省	Telephone/fax 电话/传真	Number of employees 职工人数	Ownership 产业所有权	Revenue ('000 RMB) 销售收入 (千元)	Profit('000 RMB) (rank) 利润(千元) (排名)	Total assets ('000 RMB) 总资产 (千元)	Major products 主要产品
Jilin Carbon Group Co., Ltd.	Jilin	Jilin	(0432)2749000		State Enterprises				Graphite Electrode
吉林炭素集团有限责任公司(1955)	吉林市	吉林省	(0432)2749999	8,430	国有独资	906,740	-	3,806,688	石墨电极
Hailong New Material Science and Technology Co., Ltd.	Lanzhou	Gansu	(0931)6231511		Joint Stock				Graphite Electrode
海龙新材料科技股份有限公司(1966)	兰州市	甘肃省	(0931)6233833	6,222	股份制	449,321	-	1,812,681	石墨电极
Jining Carbon Industry General Company	Jining	Shandong	(0537)2319123		Joint Stock				Carbon Block
济宁碳素工业总公司(1987)	济宁市	山东省	(0537)2333506	1,339	股份制	312,881	26,122(2)	306,662	碳块
Henan Xixia Protective Materials Group Co., Ltd.	Nanyang	Henan	(0377)4662366		Collective-owned				Composite Residue
河南省西峡县保护材料集团有限公司(1969)	南阳市	河南省	(0377)4686018	1,192	集体企业	260,745	17,753(4)	198,094	复合渣
Nantong Carbon Co., Ltd.	Nantong	Jiangsu	(0513)5559289		State-owned				Graphite Anode
南通碳素厂(1967)	南通市	江苏省	(0513)5559268	1,395	国有企业	190,742	6,600(19)	318,752	石墨电极
Shanxi Jinneng Group Datong Energy Development Co.,Ltd Carbon Branch	Datong	Shanxi	(0352)6019098		State-owned				Graphite Electrode
山西晋能集团大同能源发展有限公司碳素分公司(1940)	大同市	山西省	(0352)6019228	1,725	国有企业	184,621	10,447(9)	738,530	石墨电极
Shanxi Jinda Carbon Stock Co.,Ltd.	Yangquan	Shanxi	(0353)6120267		Collective-owned				Carbon Products
山西晋达碳素股份有限公司(1986)	阳泉市	山西省	(0353)6121220	1,650	集体企业	152,974	20,871(3)	151,171	碳素制品
Liaoyang Carbon Co., ltd.	Liaoyang	Liaoning	(0419)2122635		Limited-Liability				Graphite Electrode
辽阳炭素有限公司(1934)	辽阳市	辽宁省	(0419)2122636	501	有限公司	111,806	1,528(47)	155,553	石墨电极
Gongyi Carbon Factory	Zhengzhou	Henan	(0371)4312214		Collective-owned				Anode Paste
巩义市碳素厂(1986)	郑州市	河南省	(0371)4312214	410	集体企业	97,028	3,978(29)	53,959	阳极糊
Laishui Great Wall Electrode Co., Ltd.	Baoding	Hebei	(0312)4699130		Limited-Liability				Carbon Electrode
涞水县长城电极有限公司(1987)	保定市	河北省	(0312)4699736	240	有限公司	94,665	3,431(30)	122,200	碳电极

Top 10 Cities by Revenue 销售收入排名前10位城市	Province 省	Market share 市场份额 (%)	Number of firms 企业个数
Jilin 吉林市	Jilin 吉林省	12.33	4
Zhengzhou 郑州市	Henan 河南省	8.69	21
Lanzhou 兰州市	Gansu 甘肃省	7.25	16
Zhenjiang 镇江市	Jiangsu 江苏省	5.86	10
Jiaozuo 焦作市	Henan 河南省	4.95	9
Jinzhong 晋中市	Shanxi 山西省	4.81	17
Jining 济宁市	Shandong 山东省	4.21	1
Nanyang 南阳市	Henan 河南省	4.01	5
Nantong 南通市	Jiangsu 江苏省	3.06	5
Jinan 济南市	Shandong 山东省	3.02	4

10 Major Wholesalers 十家主要批发商	City 城市	Province 省	Telephone/Fax 电话/传真
Xuzhou New Century Building Materials Decorative City	Xuzhou	Jiangsu	(0516)83666780
徐州市新世纪建材装饰城	徐州市	江苏省	(0516)63804485
Orienthome Co.,Ltd.	Beijing	Beijing	(010)63808294
东方家园有限公司	北京市	北京市	
Shanghai Jinkai Goods & Materials Co.,Ltd.	Shanghai	Shanghai	(021)52193967
上海金凯物资有限公司	上海市	上海市	
Guangzhou Building Materials Development Co.,Ltd.	Guangzhou	Guangdong	(020)83335062
广州市建材发展有限公司	广州市	广东省	(020)83341110
Guangxi Qiaofeng Goods & Materials Trade Co.,Ltd.	Nanning	Guangxi	(0771)2631539
广西侨丰物资贸易有限责任公司	南宁市	广西	(0771)2631539
Gansu Building Materials State-owned Assets Marketing Co.,Ltd.	Lanzhou	Gansu	(0931)8821359
甘肃建材国有资产经营有限责任公司	兰州市	甘肃省	(0931)8960243
Shanghai East Asia United Building Materials Co.,Ltd.	Shanghai	Shanghai	(021)33134520
上海东亚联合建材有限公司	上海市	上海市	(021)63216165
Shanghai Zhuzong Materials General Company	Shanghai	Shanghai	(021)32240030
上海住总物资总公司	上海市	上海市	(021)32240024
Guangdong Building Materials Company	Guangzhou	Guangdong	(020)83802713
广东省建材公司	广州市	广东省	(020)83817640
Guangdong Dongguan Hardware Minerals Import & Export Co.,Ltd	Dongguan	Guangdong	(0769)2227090
广东省东莞五金矿产进出口公司	东莞市	广东省	(0769)2221045

3172: Graphite Products 电工用碳素制品业

The industry accounts for 0.012% of the total revenue of China's industrial sector in 2002. The rate of return on assets is 2.40%. 84.00% of all firms in the industry made a profit while 16.00% had negative returns.The top province in terms of the industry's revenue is Shanghai, accounting for 16.87% of the total revenue.
2002年本行业收入占全行业的 0.012%，资产利润率为 2.40%。84.00%的企业赢利，16.00%的企业亏损。收入最高的省为上海市，占本行业的16.87%。

	Total number of firms 企业总数	Total number of employees 职工总数	Total revenue (Mil.RMB) 总销售收入（百万元）	Total profit (Mil.RMB) 总利润（百万元）	Return on assets 资产利润率（%）	Return on equity 权益利润率（%）	Labour productivity ('000 RMB/ worker) 劳动生产率（千元/人）	Debts/ assets 资产负债率（%）	Total assets (Mil.RMB) 总资产（百万元）
Industry Overall 行业总体	50	10,037	1,273	47	2.40	6.09	45.43	60.61	1,975

	Number of firms 企业个数	Average number of employees 平均职工人数	Average revenue ('000 RMB) 平均销售收入（千元）	Average profit ('000 RMB) 平均利润（千元）	Return on assets 资产利润率（%）	Return on equity 权益利润率（%）	Labour productivity ('000 RMB/ worker) 劳动生产率（千元/人）	Debts/ assets 资产负债率（%）	Average total assets ('000 RMB) 平均总资产（千元）
By ownership 产业所有权									
State-owned 国有	2	656	20,908	-2,377	-1.69	-7.25	7.03	76.62	140,252
Collective-owned 集体	8	138	26,044	1,667	8.96	24.71	82.80	63.75	18,613
Foreign & Overseas Chinese Funded 三资	11	184	41,470	1,511	3.00	6.08	84.78	50.64	50,339
By regional distribution 地区分布									
Central-North 华北	4	122	22,103	332	1.16	1.70	81.56	31.90	28,629
Beijing 北京									
Tianjin 天津	1	38	914	77	5.74	15.34	11.87	62.59	1,342
Hebei 河北	3	150	29,166	416	1.10	1.61	87.46	31.54	37,725
Shanxi 山西									
Inner Mongolia 内蒙古									
Northeast 东北	4	432	37,948	1,478	1.76	5.52	21.13	68.05	83,753
Liaoning 辽宁	2	209	53,395	5,371	19.67	25.84	64.53	23.85	27,301
Jilin 吉林	1	36	4,100				22.56	68.80	1,250
Heilongjiang 黑龙江	1	1,274	40,901	-4,830	-1.73	-7.42	6.89	76.69	279,162
Central-East 华东	20	101	23,914	1,380	4.50	9.05	96.21	50.27	30,689
Shanghai 上海	6	122	35,778	446	0.67	1.22	147.73	45.36	66,869
Jiangsu 江苏	3	41	5,860	140	3.16	8.68	39.84	63.58	4,430
Zhejiang 浙江	5	117	14,065	827	6.94	14.29	29.17	51.39	11,913
Anhui 安徽									
Fujian 福建	1	72	18,844	827	25.05	28.00	68.88	10.54	3,302
Jiangxi 江西	1	46	15,685	6,654	55.57	179.55	110.11	69.05	11,974
Shandong 山东	4	114	35,292	3,223	10.36	28.32	117.37	63.41	31,108
Central-South 中南	16	204	23,517	708	3.75	15.01	41.55	75.05	18,897
Henan 河南	7	226	28,771	1,052	4.65	32.07	52.70	85.50	22,618
Hubei 湖北	3	149	9,288	460	3.07	7.57	22.96	59.38	14,970
Hunan 湖南	4	192	28,922	499	3.23	7.35	52.05	56.08	15,444
Guangdong 广东	2	230	15,664	296	1.59	8.32	3.57	80.93	18,668
Guangxi 广西									
Hainan 海南									
Southwest 西南	4	618	39,444	165	0.11	0.32	17.94	64.73	147,501
Chongqing 重庆	1	448	58,620	8,627	4.67	21.83	41.45	78.59	184,544
Sichuan 四川	3	674	33,052	-2,656	-1.97	-4.73	12.73	58.42	135,153
Guizhou 贵州									
Yunnan 云南									
Tibet 西藏									
Northwest 西北	2	39	10,122	272	2.83	12.95	78.45	78.15	9,617
Shaanxi 陕西	2	39	10,122	272	2.83	12.95	78.45	78.15	9,617
Gansu 甘肃									
Qinghai 青海									
Ningxia 宁夏									
Xinjiang 新疆									

Year 年份	Number of firms 企业个数	Rate of change 变化率 (%)	Number of employees 职工人数 (人)	Rate of change 变化率 (%)	Total revenue (Mil. RMB) 总销售收入 (百万元)	Rate of change 变化率 (%)	Total profit (Mil RMB) 总利润 (百万元)	Rate of change 变化率 (%)
2000	33		9,111		663		28	
2001	38	15.15	9,865	8.28	954	43.89	51	82.14
2002	50	31.58	10,037	1.74	1,273	33.44	47	-7.84

Major Products 主要产品	Output 产量	Unit 单位
Graphite & Carbon Products 石墨及碳素制品	303	10,000 Tons 万吨

10 Main Firms with Maximal Revenue (year founded) 收入最大的十家主要企业（创办年份）	City 城市	Province 省	Telephone/fax 电话/传真	Number of employees 职工人数	Ownership 产业所有权	Revenue ('000 RMB) 销售收入 (千元)	Profit('000 RMB) (rank) 利润(千元) (排名)	Total assets ('000 RMB) 总资产 (千元)	Major products 主要产品
Shanghai Morgan Carbon Co.,ltd 上海摩根碳制品有限公司(1992)	Shanghai 上海市	Shanghai 上海市	(021)64343350 (021)64342850	343	Foreign Funded 外商投资	99,771	16,654(1)	150,919	Electrican & Carbon Products石墨及碳素制品
Hebi Graphite Products Factory 鹤壁市石墨制品厂(1988)	Hebi 鹤壁市	Henan 河南省	(0392)2623888 (0392)2623888	300	Collective-owned 集体企业	77,210	1,068(17)	8,991	Battery Carbon Stick 电池碳棒
Shanghai Dongyang Carbon Co., Ltd. 上海东洋炭素有限公司(1996)	Shanghai 上海市	Shanghai 上海市	(021)57741529 (021)57741762	137	Foreign Funded 外商投资	73,873	11,168(2)	73,573	Carbon Brush 碳刷
HuNan Chenbei Mining Industry Co., Ltd. 湖南郴北矿业有限公司(2000)	Chenzhou 郴州市	Hunan 湖南省	(0735)2884177 (0735)2893288	204	Foreign Funded 外商投资	61,260	1,260(16)	14,008	Graphite Grit 石墨砂
Chongqing Tuoyuan Huaguan Carbon Co., Ltd. 重庆拓源华冠碳素有限公司(1997)	Chongqing 重庆市	Chongqing 重庆市	(023)62984081 (023)62984032	448	Joint Stock 股份制	58,620	8,627(4)	184,544	Electrican & Carbon Products石墨及碳素制品
Shiling Carbon Products Co., Ltd. 石灵碳素制品有限公司(1997)	Shijiazhuang 石家庄市	Hebei 河北省	(0311)2510364 (0311)2511258	249	Limited-Liability 有限公司	56,240	591(22)	94,723	Calcination Coke 煅烧焦
Anyang Matsushita Carbon Co., Ltd. 安阳松下炭素有限公司(1995)	Anyang 安阳市	Henan 河南省	(0372)2911493 (0372)2928034	616	Foreign Funded 外商投资	50,532	2,588(9)	65,821	Carbon Stick Of Dry Battery干电池用炭棒
Zibo Huantai Social Welfare Carbon Factory 淄博桓台社会福利炭素厂(1995)	Zibo 淄博市	Shandong 山东省	(0533)8510155 (0533)8510155	183	Collective-owned 集体企业	50,505	8,156(5)	63,390	Pre-baked Anode 预焙阳极
ChengDu Rong Guang Carbon Stock Co.,Ltd 成都蓉光炭素股份有限公司(1992)	Chengdu 成都市	Sichuan 四川省	(028)84852796 (028)84861154	526	Joint Stock 股份制	45,726	-	161,660	Graphite Electric Board 石墨电板
Harbin Electric Carbon Factory 哈尔滨电碳厂(1958)	Harbin 哈尔滨市	Heilongjiang 黑龙江省	(0451)55101961 (0451)55103394	1,274	State-owned 国有企业	40,901	-	279,162	Machinery Carbon Products 碳素制品

Top 10 Cities by Revenue 销售收入排名前10位城市	Province 省	Market share 市场份额 (%)	Number of firms 企业个数
Shanghai 上海市	Shanghai 上海市	16.87	6
Zibo 淄博市	Shandong 山东省	10.23	3
Hebi 鹤壁市	Henan 河南省	7.75	3
Chenzhou 郴州市	Hunan 湖南省	6.63	2
Dalian 大连市	Liaoning 辽宁省	6.40	1
Shijiazhuang 石家庄市	Hebei 河北省	6.24	2
Chongqing 重庆市	Chongqing 重庆市	4.61	1
Anyang 安阳市	Henan 河南省	4.47	2
Zigong 自贡市	Sichuan 四川省	4.20	2
Chengdu 成都市	Sichuan 四川省	3.59	1

10 Major Wholesalers 十家主要批发商	City 城市	Province 省	Telephone/Fax 电话/传真
Xuzhou New Century Building Materials Decorative City 徐州市新世纪建材装饰城	Xuzhou 徐州市	Jiangsu 江苏省	(0516)83666780 (0516)63804485
Orienthome Co.,Ltd. 东方家园有限公司	Beijing 北京市	Beijing 北京市	(010)63808294
Shanghai Jinkai Goods & Materials Co.,Ltd. 上海金凯物资有限公司	Shanghai 上海市	Shanghai 上海市	(021)52193967
Guangzhou Building Materials Development Co.,Ltd. 广州市建材发展有限公司	Guangzhou 广州市	Guangdong 广东省	(020)83335062 (020)83341110
Guangxi Qiaofeng Goods & Materials Trade Co.,Ltd. 广西侨丰物资贸易有限责任公司	Nanning 南宁市	Guangxi 广西	(0771)2631539 (0771)2631539
Gansu Building Materials State-owned Assets Marketing Co.,Ltd. 甘肃建材国有资产经营有限责任公司	Lanzhou 兰州市	Gansu 甘肃省	(0931)8821359 (0931)8960243
Shanghai East Asia United Building Materials Co.,Ltd. 上海东亚联合建材有限公司	Shanghai 上海市	Shanghai 上海市	(021)33134520 (021)63216165
Shanghai Zhuzong Materials General Company 上海住总物资总公司	Shanghai 上海市	Shanghai 上海市	(021)32240030 (021)32240024
Guangdong Building Materials Company 广东省建材公司	Guangzhou 广州市	Guangdong 广东省	(020)83802713 (020)83817640
Guangdong Dongguan Hardware Minerals Import & Export Co.,Ltd 广东省东莞五金矿产进出口公司	Dongguan 东莞市	Guangdong 广东省	(0769)2227090 (0769)2221045

3179: Other Graphite and Carbon Products 其他石墨及碳素制品业

The industry accounts for 0.024% of the total revenue of China's industrial sector in 2002. The rate of return on assets is 5.61%. 90.76% of all firms in the industry made a profit while 9.24% had negative returns.The top province in terms of the industry's revenue is Shandong, accounting for 29.73% of the total revenue.
2002年本行业收入占全行业的0.024%，资产利润率为5.61%。90.76%的企业赢利，9.24%的企业亏损。收入最高的省为山东省，占本行业的29.73%。

	Total number of firms 企业总数	Total number of employees 职工总数	Total revenue (Mil.RMB) 总销售收入(百万元)	Total profit (Mil.RMB) 总利润(百万元)	Return on assets 资产利润率(%)	Return on equity 权益利润率(%)	Labour productivity ('000 RMB/ worker) 劳动生产率(千元/人)	Debts/ assets 资产负债率(%)	Total assets (Mil.RMB) 总资产(百万元)
Industry Overall 行业总体	119	15,521	2,597	104	5.61	14.29	50.50	60.74	1,850

	Number of firms 企业个数	Average number of employees 平均职工人数	Average revenue ('000 RMB) 平均销售收入(千元)	Average profit ('000 RMB) 平均利润(千元)	Return on assets 资产利润率(%)	Return on equity 权益利润率(%)	Labour productivity ('000 RMB/ worker) 劳动生产率(千元/人)	Debts/ assets 资产负债率(%)	Average total assets ('000 RMB) 平均总资产(千元)
By ownership 产业所有权									
State-owned 国有	11	79	3,969	-140	-1.38	-4.32	25.41	68.07	10,112
Collective-owned 集体	24	139	17,550	1,066	9.03	22.49	43.58	59.84	11,802
Foreign & Overseas Chinese Funded 三资	14	79	39,292	1,572	6.24	15.11	91.55	58.69	25,184
By regional distribution 地区分布									
Central-North 华北	20	92	25,149	972	6.96	19.11	61.09	63.60	13,974
Beijing 北京	1	20	9,483	2,128	25.89	72.48	144.40	64.28	8,220
Tianjin 天津	4	106	87,293	2,347	6.63	28.99	120.45	77.13	35,400
Hebei 河北	5	75	17,818	1,210	13.32	23.33	69.65	42.89	9,084
Shanxi 山西	9	108	5,180	201	2.60	4.85	29.98	46.32	7,738
Inner Mongolia 内蒙古	1	50	8,607	61	0.42	1.98	67.20	78.91	14,603
Northeast 东北	5	42	8,072	293	7.67	15.28	74.88	49.78	3,824
Liaoning 辽宁	3	43	11,181	417	14.28	23.96	103.64	40.38	2,917
Jilin 吉林	2	40	3,408	109	2.09	4.95	28.85	57.71	5,184
Heilongjiang 黑龙江									
Central-East 华东	56	136	23,336	815	5.85	14.87	49.89	60.69	13,931
Shanghai 上海	2	26	8,108	2,030	28.24	45.50	121.52	37.92	7,186
Jiangsu 江苏	14	39	17,581	68	1.00	7.88	123.15	87.29	6,781
Zhejiang 浙江	6	96	12,836	711	4.77	10.92	39.22	56.32	14,898
Anhui 安徽	6	389	26,315	-77	-0.27	-0.62	15.61	56.04	28,196
Fujian 福建	3	139	9,410	1,638	15.18	44.09	23.81	65.58	10,793
Jiangxi 江西	2	48	4,580	120	0.85	2.26	48.54	62.40	14,152
Shandong 山东	23	156	33,573	1,376	9.00	21.03	64.87	57.20	15,287
Central-South 中南	26	172	21,663	1,256	6.10	15.83	49.11	61.49	20,604
Henan 河南	13	154	19,420	1,889	12.09	26.60	45.00	54.54	15,626
Hubei 湖北	2	471	55,905	270	0.31	1.07	83.43	70.64	86,165
Hunan 湖南	10	132	11,777	363	5.89	10.56	29.01	44.21	6,153
Guangdong 广东	1	210	81,203	3,924	3.98	13.52	60.70	70.61	98,710
Guangxi 广西									
Hainan 海南									
Southwest 西南	6	113	10,714	523	4.09	13.87	36.37	70.53	12,806
Chongqing 重庆									
Sichuan 四川	5	115	10,838	606	4.74	13.43	28.39	64.71	12,781
Guizhou 贵州									
Yunnan 云南	1	105	10,095	111	0.86	123.33	79.87	99.30	12,934
Tibet 西藏									
Northwest 西北	6	120	19,903	240	0.91	1.82	44.74	49.99	26,453
Shaanxi 陕西									
Gansu 甘肃	1	45	8,026	667	14.35	40.50	87.80	64.56	4,647
Qinghai 青海	1	210	62,691	268	0.27	0.45	71.45	38.80	97,908
Ningxia 宁夏	3	133	15,169	135	0.78	2.33	30.92	66.45	17,285
Xinjiang 新疆	1	63	3,195	102	2.37	25.31	12.76	90.64	4,307

3179: Other Graphite and Carbon Products 其他石墨及碳素制品业

Year 年份	Number of firms 企业个数	Rate of change 变化率 (%)	Number of employees 职工人数 (人)	Rate of change 变化率 (%)	Total revenue (Mil. RMB) 总销售收入 (百万元)	Rate of change 变化率 (%)	Total profit (Mil RMB) 总利润 (百万元)	Rate of change 变化率 (%)
2000	103		12,891		1,493		61	
2001	120	16.50	18,431	42.98	2,495	67.11	87	42.62
2002	119	-0.83	15,521	-15.79	2,597	4.09	104	19.54

Major Products 主要产品	Output 产量	Unit 单位

10 Main Firms with Maximal Revenue (year founded) 收入最大的十家主要企业（创办年份）	City 城市	Province 省	Telephone/fax 电话/传真	Number of employees 职工人数	Ownership 产业所有权	Revenue ('000 RMB) 销售收入(千元)	Profit('000 RMB) (rank) 利润(千元)(排名)	Total assets ('000 RMB) 总资产(千元)	Major products 主要产品
TianJin Litong Carbon Products Co., Ltd.	Tianjin	Tianjin	(022)25323616		Foreign Funded				Carbon Products
天津丽通炭素制品有限公司	天津市	天津市	(022)25329401	87	外商投资	322,211	10,886(2)	109,411	炭素制品
Qingdao Black Dragon Graphite Co., Ltd.	Qingdao	Shandong	(0532)6376666		Private Enterprises				Medium,High-carbon Graphite中
青岛黑龙石墨有限公司(1992)	青岛市	山东省	(0532)6371398	600	私营独资	120,502	5,603(4)	34,372	高碳石墨
Qingdao Hai Da Graphite Co., Ltd.	Qingdao	Shandong	(0532)7388065		Private Enterprises				Graphite
青岛海达石墨有限公司(1993)	青岛市	山东省	(0532)7389018	410	私营独资	115,503	5,203(6)	51,203	石墨
HuBei Yichang Hengda Graphite(Group)Co., Ltd.	Yichang	Hubei	(0717)7829999		Limited-Liability				Graphite
湖北省宜昌恒达石墨有限责任公司(1989)	宜昌市	湖北省	(0717)7828466	917	有限公司	111,810	540(40)	170,308	石墨
Anhui Ya Zhu Diamond Stock Co., Ltd.	Bozhou	Anhui	(0558)5559624		Joint Stock				Artificial Diamond人
安徽亚珠金刚石股份有限公司(1985)	亳州市	安徽省	(0558)5559661	860	股份制	106,102	980(27)	69,729	造金刚石
Weihai Hua Xing Graphite Products Co., Ltd.	Weihai	Shandong	(0631)5704017		Private Owned				Graphite Carbon Stick石
威海华兴石墨制品有限公司(1982)	威海市	山东省	(0631)5704558	164	私营企业	91,376	8,507(3)	11,815	墨化碳棒
ALDILA Graphite Products (Zhuhai)Co., Ltd	Zhuhai	Guangdong	(0756)8637217		Foreign Funded				Golf Pole高
艾德拉石墨产品（珠海）有限公司(1995)	珠海市	广东省	(0756)8637617	210	外商投资	81,203	3,924(9)	98,710	尔夫球杆
Qinghai Dongsheng Chemical Industry Co., Ltd.	Xining	Qinghai	(0971)8016515		Limited-Liability				Basic Chemical Materials基本
青海东胜化工有限公司(2000)	西宁市	青海省	(0971)8016521	210	有限公司	62,691	268(56)	97,908	化学原料
Ji'nan Changqing Magnetic Materials Factory	Jinan	Shandong	(0531)7382946		Joint Stock				Graphite Powder
济南市长清县磁性材料厂(1994)	济南市	山东省	(0531)7382946	271	股份制	58,610	3,270(11)	31,290	石墨粉
Pingdu Guang Yi Graphite Mills Co., Ltd.	Qingdao	Shandong	(0532)7310879		Private Owned				Graphite
平度市广益石墨有限公司(1990)	青岛市	山东省	(0532)7312684	378	私营企业	47,240	340(51)	15,600	石墨

Top 10 Cities by Revenue 销售收入排名前10位城市	Province 省	Market share 市场份额 (%)	Number of firms 企业个数
Qingdao 青岛市	Shandong 山东省	15.34	9
Tianjin 天津市	Tianjin 天津市	13.44	4
Bozhou 亳州市	Anhui 安徽省	4.80	3
Nanyang 南阳市	Henan 河南省	4.61	2
Yichang 宜昌市	Hubei 湖北省	4.31	2
Weihai 威海市	Shandong 山东省	3.52	1
Dezhou 德州市	Shandong 山东省	3.33	2
Hengshui 衡水市	Hebei 河北省	3.24	2
Zhuhai 珠海市	Guangdong 广东省	3.13	1
Binzhou 滨州市	Shandong 山东省	2.97	4

10 Major Wholesalers 十家主要批发商	City 城市	Province 省	Telephone/Fax 电话/传真
Xuzhou New Century Building Materials Decorative City	Xuzhou	Jiangsu	(0516)83666780
徐州市新世纪建材装饰城	徐州市	江苏省	(0516)63804485
Orienthome Co.,Ltd.	Beijing	Beijing	(010)63808294
东方家园有限公司	北京市	北京市	
Shanghai Jinkai Goods & Materials Co.,Ltd.	Shanghai	Shanghai	(021)52193967
上海金凯物资有限公司	上海市	上海市	
Guangzhou Building Materials Development Co.,Ltd.	Guangzhou	Guangdong	(020)83335062
广州市建材发展有限公司	广州市	广东省	(020)83341110
Guangxi Qiaofeng Goods & Materials Trade Co.,Ltd.	Nanning	Guangxi	(0771)2631539
广西侨丰物资贸易有限责任公司	南宁市	广西	(0771)2631539
Gansu Building Materials State-owned Assets Marketing Co.,Ltd.	Lanzhou	Gansu	(0931)8821359
甘肃建材国有资产经营有限责任公司	兰州市	甘肃省	(0931)8960243
Shanghai East Asia United Building Materials Co.,Ltd.	Shanghai	Shanghai	(021)33134520
上海东亚联合建材有限公司	上海市	上海市	(021)63216165
Shanghai Zhuzong Materials General Company	Shanghai	Shanghai	(021)32240030
上海住总物资总公司	上海市	上海市	(021)32240024
Guangdong Building Materials Company	Guangzhou	Guangdong	(020)83802713
广东省建材公司	广州市	广东省	(020)83817640
Guangdong Dongguan Hardware Minerals Import & Export Co.,Ltd	Dongguan	Guangdong	(0769)2227090
广东省东莞五金矿产进出口公司	东莞市	广东省	(0769)2221045

3181: Fibreglass Products 玻璃纤维及其制品业

The industry accounts for 0.054% of the total revenue of China's industrial sector in 2002. The rate of return on assets is 1.34%. 82.39% of all firms in the industry made a profit while 17.61% had negative returns.The top province in terms of the industry's revenue is Jiangsu, accounting for 22.47% of the total revenue.
2002年本行业收入占全行业的 0.054%，资产利润率为 1.34%。82.39%的企业赢利，17.61%的企业亏损。收入最高的省为江苏省，占本行业的22.47%。

	Total number of firms 企业总数	Total number of employees 职工总数	Total revenue (Mil.RMB) 总销售收入 (百万元)	Total profit (Mil.RMB) 总利润 (百万元)	Return on assets 资产利润率 (%)	Return on equity 权益利润率 (%)	Labour productivity ('000 RMB/ worker) 劳动生产率 (千元/人)	Debts/ assets 资产负债率 (%)	Total assets (Mil.RMB) 总资产 (百万元)
Industry Overall 行业总体	176	53,935	5,809	128	1.34	4.50	34.26	70.32	9,594

	Number of firms 企业个数	Average number of employees 平均职工人数	Average revenue ('000 RMB) 平均销售收入（千元）	Average profit ('000 RMB) 平均利润（千元）	Return on assets 资产利润率 (%)	Return on equity 权益利润率 (%)	Labour productivity ('000 RMB/ worker) 劳动生产率 (千元/人)	Debts/ assets 资产负债率 (%)	Average total assets ('000 RMB) 平均总资产 (千元)
By ownership 产业所有权									
State-owned 国有	20	694	29,602	-4,553	-5.40	-38.24	14.88	85.88	84,316
Collective-owned 集体	25	274	23,791	1,167	6.15	17.99	30.69	65.84	18,989
Foreign & Overseas Chinese Funded 三资	28	261	66,317	1,048	0.77	3.28	66.20	76.52	135,903
By regional distribution 地区分布									
Central-North 华北	27	282	17,146	-2,401	-6.10	-22.21	17.62	72.53	39,364
Beijing 北京	4	135	28,224	-5,749	-9.58	-23.43	79.32	59.11	60,020
Tianjin 天津	4	258	18,119	128	0.13	0.34	13.01	60.94	96,151
Hebei 河北	17	318	15,942	-2,489	-10.02	-93.10	13.92	89.24	24,837
Shanxi 山西	2	320	3,285	-19	-0.23		4.36	111.90	7,949
Inner Mongolia 内蒙古									
Northeast 东北	4	332	17,845	194	0.70	1.29	26.56	45.74	27,695
Liaoning 辽宁	4	332	17,845	194	0.70	1.29	26.56	45.74	27,695
Jilin 吉林									
Heilongjiang 黑龙江									
Central-East 华东	100	292	39,870	1,766	3.04	8.82	40.79	65.57	58,122
Shanghai 上海	9	342	56,604	-4,002	-3.08	-12.46	28.35	75.29	129,953
Jiangsu 江苏	37	222	35,272	1,830	6.49	16.91	42.29	61.64	28,207
Zhejiang 浙江	13	321	62,539	4,711	4.85	16.03	52.63	69.74	97,100
Anhui 安徽	12	238	16,887	645	3.45	5.47	28.72	36.96	18,682
Fujian 福建	1	31	9,913	-6	-0.13	-0.83	119.68	83.85	4,477
Jiangxi 江西	9	526	23,666	661	1.63	5.62	20.54	70.94	40,532
Shandong 山东	19	320	49,153	3,682	4.01	10.26	57.92	60.90	91,747
Central-South 中南	23	198	20,948	-1,196	-2.60	-11.22	34.76	76.79	45,933
Henan 河南	11	202	11,624	441	4.20	9.07	19.77	53.71	10,510
Hubei 湖北	2	171	42,029	876	5.35	11.66	78.77	54.12	16,362
Hunan 湖南	4	165	5,607	-783	-7.32		9.70	123.10	10,700
Guangdong 广东	5	193	46,390	-4,785	-2.87	-11.96	77.39	76.01	166,805
Guangxi 广西	1	366	15,497	-7,047	-22.50		17.30	143.20	31,316
Hainan 海南									
Southwest 西南	16	428	34,300	2,407	3.48	15.66	29.81	77.77	69,134
Chongqing 重庆	2	504	104,897	12,364	3.89	24.05	67.99	83.82	317,786
Sichuan 四川	12	483	28,112	1,152	2.97	9.65	23.22	69.22	38,773
Guizhou 贵州	1	50	1,655	-45	-0.85		24.64	102.34	5,295
Yunnan 云南	1	1							
Tibet 西藏									
Northwest 西北	6	734	42,830	772	1.04	133.47	28.52	99.22	74,202
Shaanxi 陕西	2	2,140	123,559	2,083	0.96	133.37	27.95	99.28	216,301
Gansu 甘肃	4	31	2,466	117	3.72	134.38	48.50	97.23	3,153
Qinghai 青海									
Ningxia 宁夏									
Xinjiang 新疆									

3181: Fibreglass Products 玻璃纤维及其制品业

Year 年份	Number of firms 企业个数	Rate of change 变化率(%)	Number of employees 职工人数(人)	Rate of change 变化率(%)	Total revenue (Mil. RMB) 总销售收入(百万元)	Rate of change 变化率(%)	Total profit (Mil RMB) 总利润(百万元)	Rate of change 变化率(%)
2000	145		55,225		4,759		126	
2001	167	15.17	56,731	2.73	5,674	19.23	177	40.48
2002	176	5.39	53,935	-4.93	5,809	2.38	128	-27.68

Major Products 主要产品	Output 产量	Unit 单位
Glass Fibre Yarn 玻璃纤维纱	39	10,000 Tons 万吨

10 Main Firms with Maximal Revenue (year founded) 收入最大的十家主要企业（创办年份）	City 城市	Province 省	Telephone/fax 电话/传真	Number of employees 职工人数	Ownership 产业所有权	Revenue ('000 RMB) 销售收入(千元)	Profit('000 RMB) (rank) 利润(千元)(排名)	Total assets ('000 RMB) 总资产(千元)	Major products 主要产品
Jushi Group Co., Ltd.	Jiaxing	Zhejiang	(0573)8181039		Foreign Funded				Glass Fibre Yarn玻
巨石集团有限公司(1994)	嘉兴市	浙江省	(0573)8181001	2,613	外商投资	605,066	49,139(1)	1,085,420	璃纤维纱
Jiangsu Jiuding Group Stock Co., Ltd.	Nantong	Jiangsu	(0513)7514543		Joint Stock				Glass Fiber Cloth玻
江苏九鼎集团股份有限公司(1972)	南通市	江苏省	(0513)7513082	1,075	股份制	398,504	16,876(4)	244,564	璃纤维布
Fiber Glass TaiShan Co., Ltd	Taian	Shandong	(0538)6622008		Joint Stock				Glass Fibre Yarn玻
泰山玻璃纤维股份有限公司(1999)	泰安市	山东省	(0538)6622009	989	股份制	394,235	46,043(2)	1,145,230	璃纤维纱
Shanghai Pocher Industry Co., Ltd.	Shanghai	Shanghai	(021)59720102		Foreign Funded				Glass Fiber Cloth玻
上海博舍工业有限公司(1995)	上海市	上海市	(021)59720110	304	外商投资	217,128	-	405,977	璃纤维布
Shaanxi Coking Factory	Weinan	Shannxi	(0913)8677234		State-owned				Glass Fibre Ball玻
陕西省焦化厂(1970)	渭南市	陕西省	(0913)8677338	1,251	国有企业	147,044	29(120)	330,367	璃纤维球
Jushi Group Jiujiang Co., Ltd	Jiujiang	Jiangxi	(0792)8252016		Limited-Liability				Glass Fibre & Products玻璃
巨石集团九江有限公司(2001)	九江市	江西省	(0792)8252011	2,389	有限公司	115,409	2,275(24)	210,998	维及制品
Sichuan Glass Fiber Co., Ltd.	Deyang	Sichuan	(0838)3121481		Limited-Liability				Glass Fibre Yarn玻
四川玻纤有限责任公司(1970)	德阳市	四川省	(0838)3121455	2,980	有限公司	113,885	8,080(8)	198,677	璃纤维纱
Owens- Kening(Shanhai) Fiber Glass Co., Ltd.	Shanghai	Shanghai	(021)58141818		Foreign Funded				Glass Wool Products玻
上海欧文斯一科宁玻璃纤维有限公司(1995)	上海市	上海市	(021)58140202	144	外商投资	109,419	12,739(6)	246,528	璃棉制品
Zoucheng Dongsheng Industry and Trade Group Co., Ltd.	Jining	Shandong	(0537)5213929		Collective-owned				Plastics Woven Bag塑
邹城市东升工贸集团有限公司(1998)	济宁市	山东省		364	集体企业	109,031	11,035(7)	42,039	料编织袋
Huate Glass Fiber Co.,ltd	Xianyang	Shannxi	(0910)8822901		State-owned				Glass Fibre
华特玻璃纤维有限公司(1966)	咸阳市	陕西省	(0910)8822946	3,029	国有企业	100,074	4,136(15)	102,234	玻璃纤维

Top 10 Cities by Revenue 销售收入排名前10位城市	Province 省	Market share 市场份额(%)	Number of firms 企业个数
Jiaxing 嘉兴市	Zhejiang 浙江省	11.18	3
Taian 泰安市	Shandong 山东省	10.39	7
Shanghai 上海市	Shanghai 上海市	8.77	9
Nantong 南通市	Jiangsu 江苏省	7.08	3
Changzhou 常州市	Jiangsu 江苏省	4.66	6
Nanjing 南京市	Jiangsu 江苏省	4.20	6
Chongqing 重庆市	Chongqing 重庆市	3.61	2
Weinan 渭南市	Shannxi 陕西省	2.53	1
Jining 济宁市	Shandong 山东省	2.51	3
Jiujiang 九江市	Jiangxi 江西省	2.42	3

10 Major Wholesalers 十家主要批发商	City 城市	Province 省	Telephone/Fax 电话/传真
Xuzhou New Century Building Materials Decorative City	Xuzhou	Jiangsu	(0516)83666780
徐州市新世纪建材装饰城	徐州市	江苏省	(0516)63804485
Orienthome Co.,Ltd.	Beijing	Beijing	(010)63808294
东方家园有限公司	北京市	北京市	
Shanghai Jinkai Goods & Materials Co.,Ltd.	Shanghai	Shanghai	(021)52193967
上海金凯物资有限公司	上海市	上海市	
Guangzhou Building Materials Development Co.,Ltd.	Guangzhou	Guangdong	(020)83335062
广州市建材发展有限公司	广州市	广东省	(020)83341110
Guangxi Qiaofeng Goods & Materials Trade Co.,Ltd.	Nanning	Guangxi	(0771)2631539
广西侨丰物资贸易有限责任公司	南宁市	广西	(0771)2631539
Gansu Building Materials State-owned Assets Marketing Co.,Ltd.	Lanzhou	Gansu	(0931)8821359
甘肃建材国有资产经营有限责任公司	兰州市	甘肃省	(0931)8960243
Shanghai East Asia United Building Materials Co.,Ltd.	Shanghai	Shanghai	(021)33134520
上海东亚联合建材有限公司	上海市	上海市	(021)63216165
Shanghai Zhuzong Materials General Company	Shanghai	Shanghai	(021)32240030
上海住总物资总公司	上海市	上海市	(021)32240024
Guangdong Building Materials Company	Guangzhou	Guangdong	(020)83802713
广东省建材公司	广州市	广东省	(020)83817640
Guangdong Dongguan Hardware Minerals Import & Export Co.,Ltd	Dongguan	Guangdong	(0769)2227090
广东省东莞五金矿产进出口公司	东莞市	广东省	(0769)2221045

3182: Glass Fibre Reinforced Plastic 玻璃钢制品业

The industry accounts for 0.084% of the total revenue of China's industrial sector in 2002. The rate of return on assets is 5.48%. 85.04% of all firms in the industry made a profit while 14.96% had negative returns.The top province in terms of the industry's revenue is Zhejiang, accounting for 23.91% of the total revenue.
2002年本行业收入占全行业的 0.084%，资产利润率为 5.48%。85.04%的企业赢利，14.96%的企业亏损。收入最高的省为浙江省，占本行业的23.91%。

	Total number of firms 企业总数	Total number of employees 职工总数	Total revenue (Mil.RMB) 总销售收入（百万元）	Total profit (Mil.RMB) 总利润（百万元）	Return on assets 资产利润率（%）	Return on equity 权益利润率（%）	Labour productivity ('000 RMB/ worker) 劳动生产率（千元/人）	Debts/ assets 资产负债率（%）	Total assets (Mil.RMB) 总资产（百万元）
Industry Overall 行业总体	254	38,605	9,029	472	5.48	13.20	82.21	58.50	8,609

	Number of firms 企业个数	Average number of employees 平均职工人数	Average revenue ('000 RMB) 平均销售收入（千元）	Average profit ('000 RMB) 平均利润（千元）	Return on assets 资产利润率（%）	Return on equity 权益利润率（%）	Labour productivity ('000 RMB/ worker) 劳动生产率（千元/人）	Debts/ assets 资产负债率（%）	Average total assets ('000 RMB) 平均总资产（千元）
By ownership 产业所有权									
State-owned 国有	23	251	108,610	2,314	2.74	5.98	142.01	54.25	84,548
Collective-owned 集体	60	133	24,121	1,925	15.02	34.93	81.82	57.01	12,823
Foreign & Overseas Chinese Funded 三资	41	164	34,404	2,657	4.19	11.66	71.36	64.05	63,356
By regional distribution 地区分布									
Central-North 华北	30	165	30,525	2,048	3.93	12.78	84.70	69.27	52,133
Beijing 北京	10	211	22,725	1,432	5.06	11.68	44.86	56.72	28,326
Tianjin 天津	3	99	16,767	652	2.51	5.83	101.24	57.00	25,984
Hebei 河北	16	157	39,459	2,804	3.80	14.09	116.56	73.01	73,714
Shanxi 山西	1	42	6,870	290	1.24	4.72	59.36	73.68	23,343
Inner Mongolia 内蒙古									
Northeast 东北	16	90	12,849	795	3.24	8.98	54.04	63.89	24,522
Liaoning 辽宁	10	86	11,043	629	3.05	8.25	54.07	63.06	20,649
Jilin 吉林	2	67	5,485	410	4.12	5.47	33.28	24.63	9,952
Heilongjiang 黑龙江	4	112	21,046	1,402	3.38	11.12	60.23	69.63	41,489
Central-East 华东	111	170	52,291	2,445	6.60	13.19	91.49	49.95	37,043
Shanghai 上海	8	135	29,420	3,860	9.75	28.13	75.09	65.32	39,574
Jiangsu 江苏	52	136	35,259	1,757	6.61	14.67	68.07	54.97	26,596
Zhejiang 浙江	12	233	179,909	1,281	0.97	1.57	200.13	38.21	131,836
Anhui 安徽	3	93	4,854	78	2.36	3.68	19.28	35.88	3,288
Fujian 福建	2	119	17,330	5,542	38.73	54.95	99.81	29.52	14,310
Jiangxi 江西	1	1,480	73,081	281	0.15	0.39	17.08	60.80	182,192
Shandong 山东	33	178	44,068	3,701	20.04	48.85	92.75	58.97	18,467
Central-South 中南	80	131	20,836	1,325	6.21	17.89	71.10	65.31	21,356
Henan 河南	47	134	23,994	2,377	21.43	48.78	75.08	56.07	11,091
Hubei 湖北	7	125	19,925	397	3.10	10.22	70.80	69.67	12,814
Hunan 湖南	7	119	11,641	-247	-1.02	-2.13	28.24	52.29	24,266
Guangdong 广东	18	138	17,424	-375	-0.74	-2.77	76.07	73.39	50,888
Guangxi 广西									
Hainan 海南	1	12	4,611				-37.67	0.26	11,645
Southwest 西南	12	198	24,022	36	0.08	0.23	56.45	63.91	44,005
Chongqing 重庆	3	293	15,299	-2,364	-6.23	-105.71	19.12	94.10	37,916
Sichuan 四川	8	175	28,852	1,025	2.09	4.86	81.68	57.02	49,026
Guizhou 贵州									
Yunnan 云南	1	101	11,548	-672	-3.04	-4.40	32.11	30.96	22,103
Tibet 西藏									
Northwest 西北	5	105	29,690	3,946	6.49	18.11	141.99	64.15	60,789
Shaanxi 陕西	1	50	17,389	108	1.21	2.33	141.20	47.97	8,910
Gansu 甘肃	2	39	1,205	40	1.78	2.40	74.03	26.06	2,251
Qinghai 青海									
Ningxia 宁夏									
Xinjiang 新疆	2	198	64,327	9,772	6.73	19.35	155.47	65.23	145,268

3182: Glass Fibre Reinforced Plastic 玻璃钢制品业

Year 年份	Number of firms 企业个数	Rate of change 变化率 (%)	Number of employees 职工人数 (人)	Rate of change 变化率 (%)	Total revenue (Mil. RMB) 总销售收入 (百万元)	Rate of change 变化率 (%)	Total profit (Mil RMB) 总利润 (百万元)	Rate of change 变化率 (%)
2000	240		36,827		7,600		377	
2001	241	0.42	36,641	-0.51	8,089	6.43	371	-1.59
2002	254	5.39	38,605	5.36	9,029	11.62	472	27.22

Major Products 主要产品	Output 产量	Unit 单位

10 Main Firms with Maximal Revenue (year founded) 收入最大的十家主要企业（创办年份）	City 城市	Province 省	Telephone/fax 电话/传真	Number of employees 职工人数	Ownership 产业所有权	Revenue ('000 RMB) 销售收入 (千元)	Profit('000 RMB) (rank) 利润(千元) (排名)	Total assets ('000 RMB) 总资产 (千元)	Major products 主要产品
Jiangsu Shenhai Corp.Group p.r China 江苏申海集团股份有限公司(1974)	Nantong 南通市	Jiangsu 江苏省	(0513)2673038 (0513)2673028	544	Joint Stock 股份制	502,390	14,200(5)	220,400	Blower 风机
Hebei Jizhou Sino-italy Glass Fiber Reinforced Plastic Factory河北冀州市中意玻璃钢厂(1987)	Hengshui 衡水市	Hebei 河北省	(0318)8613754 (0318)8612721	252	State-owned 国有企业	210,000	16,010(4)	371,719	Glass Steel Products玻璃钢制品
Wendeng Banax Fishing Tackle Co., ltd. 文登半岛渔具有限公司(1999)	Weihai 威海市	Shandong 山东省	(0631)8546107 (0631)8546127	120	Foreign Funded 外商投资	195,000	19,500(1)	20,300	Fishing Pole 渔杆
Yancheng Fangxing Environmental Proctection Engineering Co., Ltd.盐城方行环保工程有限公司(1977)	Yancheng 盐城市	Jiangsu 江苏省	(0515)6312568 (0515)6314017	202	Joint Stock 股份制	125,530	1,460(93)	11,730	Glass Steel Products玻璃钢制品
Xinjiang Yongchang Composites Materials Stock Co., Ltd. 新疆永昌复合材料股份有限公司(1993)	Changji 昌吉州	Xinjiang 新疆	(0994)5318888 (0994)5318666	350	Foreign Funded 外商投资	123,353	18,900(2)	273,988	Glass Steel Products玻璃钢制品
Shandong Zhong Nan Group Ltd. Company 山东中南集团有限公司(1994)	Dezhou 德州市	Shandong 山东省	(0534)6651111 (0534)6653333	217	Private Owned 私营企业	111,736	11,321(9)	59,363	SMC Aassembled Water Tank.SMC组合水箱
Wucheng Hua Neng Glass Fiber Reinforced Plastic Group Co., Ltd.武城华能玻璃钢集团有限公司(1993)	Dezhou 德州市	Shandong 山东省	(0534)6352412 (0534)6351014	410	Foreign Funded 外商投资	110,759	5,268(25)	18,957	Glass Steel Ventilated Pipeline玻璃钢通风管道
Henan Yong Wei Fire Fighting Equipment Co., Ltd. 河南永威消防器材有限公司(1992)	Jiaozuo 焦作市	Henan 河南省	(0391)5099145 (0391)5099226	540	Private Owned 私营企业	109,300	12,350(7)	49,300	Glass Steel 玻璃钢
Sichuan Jin Wei Group Co., Ltd. 四川金炜集团有限公司(1979)	Chengdu 成都市	Sichuan 四川省	(028)87513776 (028)87507681	566	Limited-Liability 有限公司	99,931	2,988(54)	163,508	Glass Steel Products玻璃钢制品
Beijing Glass Fiber Reinforced Plastic Research & Designing Institute 北京玻璃钢研究设计院(1958)	Beijing 北京市	Beijing 北京市	(010)61161236 (010)61162500	1,211	State-owned 国有企业	96,785	11,615(8)	131,289	Water Tank Board 水箱板

Top 10 Cities by Revenue 销售收入排名前10位城市	Province 省	Market share 市场份额 (%)	Number of firms 企业个数
Wenzhou 温州市	Zhejiang 浙江省	22.32	3
Jiaozuo 焦作市	Henan 河南省	12.25	42
Dezhou 德州市	Shandong 山东省	10.41	17
Nantong 南通市	Jiangsu 江苏省	6.72	7
Hengshui 衡水市	Hebei 河北省	6.46	14
Wuxi 无锡市	Jiangsu 江苏省	3.99	12
Weihai 威海市	Shandong 山东省	3.76	6
Shanghai 上海市	Shanghai 上海市	2.61	8
Beijing 北京市	Beijing 北京市	2.52	10
Yancheng 盐城市	Jiangsu 江苏省	2.51	4

10 Major Wholesalers 十家主要批发商	City 城市	Province 省	Telephone/Fax 电话/传真
Xuzhou New Century Building Materials Decorative City 徐州市新世纪建材装饰城	Xuzhou 徐州市	Jiangsu 江苏省	(0516)83666780 (0516)63804485
Orienthome Co.,Ltd. 东方家园有限公司	Beijing 北京市	Beijing 北京市	(010)63808294
Shanghai Jinkai Goods & Materials Co.,Ltd. 上海金凯物资有限公司	Shanghai 上海市	Shanghai 上海市	(021)52193967
Guangzhou Building Materials Development Co.,Ltd. 广州市建材发展有限公司	Guangzhou 广州市	Guangdong 广东省	(020)83335062 (020)83341110
Guangxi Qiaofeng Goods & Materials Trade Co.,Ltd. 广西侨丰物资贸易有限责任公司	Nanning 南宁市	Guangxi 广西	(0771)2631539 (0771)2631539
Gansu Building Materials State-owned Assets Marketing Co.,Ltd. 甘肃建材国有资产经营有限责任公司	Lanzhou 兰州市	Gansu 甘肃省	(0931)8821359 (0931)8960243
Shanghai East Asia United Building Materials Co.,Ltd. 上海东亚联合建材有限公司	Shanghai 上海市	Shanghai 上海市	(021)33134520 (021)63216165
Shanghai Zhuzong Materials General Company 上海住总物资总公司	Shanghai 上海市	Shanghai 上海市	(021)32240030 (021)32240024
Guangdong Building Materials Company 广东省建材公司	Guangzhou 广州市	Guangdong 广东省	(020)83802713 (020)83817640
Guangdong Dongguan Hardware Minerals Import & Export Co.,Ltd 广东省东莞五金矿产进出口公司	Dongguan 东莞市	Guangdong 广东省	(0769)2227090 (0769)2221045

3190: Other Non-metal Mineral Products 其他类未包括的非金属矿物制品业

The industry accounts for 0.188% of the total revenue of China's industrial sector in 2002. The rate of return on assets is 1.89%. 76.38% of all firms in the industry made a profit while 23.62% had negative returns.The top province in terms of the industry's revenue is Jiangsu, accounting for 41.79% of the total revenue.
2002年本行业收入占全行业的 0.188%，资产利润率为 1.89%。76.38%的企业赢利，23.62%的企业亏损。收入最高的省为江苏省，占本行业的41.79%。

	Total number of firms 企业总数	Total number of employees 职工总数	Total revenue (Mil.RMB) 总销售收入（百万元）	Total profit (Mil.RMB) 总利润（百万元）	Return on assets 资产利润率 (%)	Return on equity 权益利润率 (%)	Labour productivity ('000 RMB/ worker) 劳动生产率（千元/人）	Debts/ assets 资产负债率 (%)	Total assets (Mil.RMB) 总资产（百万元）
Industry Overall 行业总体	652	119,972	20,134	458	1.89	4.44	45.22	57.46	24,293

	Number of firms 企业个数	Average number of employees 平均职工人数	Average revenue ('000 RMB) 平均销售收入（千元）	Average profit ('000 RMB) 平均利润（千元）	Return on assets 资产利润率 (%)	Return on equity 权益利润率 (%)	Labour productivity ('000 RMB/ worker) 劳动生产率（千元/人）	Debts/ assets 资产负债率 (%)	Average total assets ('000 RMB) 平均总资产（千元）
By ownership 产业所有权									
State-owned 国有	94	214	13,576	-493	-1.05	-3.12	18.29	66.43	47,128
Collective-owned 集体	154	152	24,309	1,374	7.09	15.13	38.66	53.15	19,388
Foreign & Overseas Chinese Funded 三资	88	234	95,650	2,315	3.27	7.15	105.25	54.30	70,876
By regional distribution 地区分布									
Central-North 华北	57	169	19,579	-517	-0.96	-2.54	33.48	62.20	53,869
Beijing 北京	11	111	11,635	561	2.76	4.73	35.32	41.71	20,364
Tianjin 天津	14	115	15,264	534	2.38	5.96	34.40	60.14	22,496
Hebei 河北	22	98	15,625	1,273	7.02	11.40	57.19	38.44	18,135
Shanxi 山西	8	561	52,784	-8,893	-3.35	-10.90	21.90	69.22	265,174
Inner Mongolia 内蒙古	2	93	4,146	13	0.23	0.44	17.02	47.72	5,625
Northeast 东北	50	172	13,894	488	1.79	5.56	31.61	67.82	27,276
Liaoning 辽宁	39	180	14,837	587	1.98	5.97	24.98	66.81	29,664
Jilin 吉林	6	197	10,399	200	0.78	3.46	66.33	77.39	25,552
Heilongjiang 黑龙江	5	73	10,735	62	0.58	1.52	47.02	62.09	10,720
Central-East 华东	209	188	53,637	1,474	3.41	7.80	75.62	56.34	43,272
Shanghai 上海	9	156	34,039	337	0.53	1.73	47.88	69.33	63,312
Jiangsu 江苏	80	244	105,174	2,376	3.47	8.03	110.52	56.75	68,384
Zhejiang 浙江	21	147	18,059	592	1.75	5.64	27.42	69.00	33,862
Anhui 安徽	14	195	14,086	764	3.37	6.29	20.44	46.48	22,698
Fujian 福建	21	76	12,986	1,467	9.32	24.07	57.44	61.26	15,732
Jiangxi 江西	14	138	5,225	-180	-1.04	-2.61	8.39	59.94	17,191
Shandong 山东	50	181	31,353	1,272	4.53	8.02	55.12	43.50	28,068
Central-South 中南	240	204	25,532	1,055	3.22	7.02	33.25	54.11	32,758
Henan 河南	126	181	29,145	1,251	3.44	8.40	37.82	59.02	36,325
Hubei 湖北	25	395	28,223	1,347	4.18	8.97	23.99	53.44	32,236
Hunan 湖南	30	332	25,050	1,145	2.46	3.68	20.84	33.04	46,538
Guangdong 广东	42	100	19,283	658	4.20	10.71	66.76	60.83	15,682
Guangxi 广西	15	134	11,850	-23	-0.09	-0.22	19.58	61.07	27,203
Hainan 海南	2	79	5,411	132	1.63	5.26	18.61	69.01	8,097
Southwest 西南	67	171	11,920	-1,420	-3.73	-9.09	16.32	58.95	38,033
Chongqing 重庆	2	265	19,918	255	0.24	0.31	52.63	22.76	105,203
Sichuan 四川	27	136	14,370	527	1.79	4.58	39.41	60.89	29,415
Guizhou 贵州	34	202	10,292	-3,238	-7.37	-19.60	-0.47	62.41	43,950
Yunnan 云南	4	96	5,225	51	0.41	1.82	45.87	77.22	12,329
Tibet 西藏									
Northwest 西北	29	71	6,445	-97	-0.69	-2.12	22.24	67.42	13,949
Shaanxi 陕西	6	122	5,116	-563	-2.65	-20.03	5.88	86.79	21,258
Gansu 甘肃	7	55	5,685	-181	-4.01	-13.68	31.92	70.66	4,507
Qinghai 青海	11	46	6,123	363	2.39	4.83	46.12	50.51	15,199
Ningxia 宁夏	4	77	9,790	-81	-0.53	-1.64	15.25	67.57	15,252
Xinjiang 新疆	1	131	9,918	-1,829	-10.62	-57.92	10.06	81.67	17,227

3190: Other Non-metal Mineral Products 其他类未包括的非金属矿物制品业

Year 年份	Number of firms 企业个数	Rate of change 变化率 (%)	Number of employees 职工人数 (人)	Rate of change 变化率 (%)	Total revenue (Mil. RMB) 总销售收入 (百万元)	Rate of change 变化率 (%)	Total profit (Mil RMB) 总利润 (百万元)	Rate of change 变化率 (%)
2000	620		120,563		16,767		770	
2001	622	0.32	115,069	-4.56	18,205	8.58	612	-20.52
2002	652	4.82	119,972	4.26	20,134	10.60	458	-25.16

Major Products 主要产品	Output 产量	Unit 单位
Polysilicon 多晶硅	101	10,000 Kg 万千克
Abrasive Tool 磨具	20	10,000 Tons 万吨

10 Main Firms with Maximal Revenue (year founded) 收入最大的十家主要企业（创办年份）	City 城市	Province 省	Telephone/fax 电话/传真	Number of employees 职工人数	Ownership 产业所有权	Revenue ('000 RMB) 销售收入 (千元)	Profit('000 RMB) (rank) 利润(千元) (排名)	Total assets ('000 RMB) 总资产 (千元)	Major products 主要产品
Suzhou Epson Co., Ltd. 苏州爱普生有限公司(1997)	Suzhou 苏州市	Jiangsu 江苏省	(0512)68257002 (0512)68251978	7,410	Foreign Funded 外商投资	5,800,585	89,956(2)	3,577,420	Liquid Crystal Display液晶显示器
Henan Yellow River Industrial (Group)Company 河南黄河实业(集团)公司(1994)	Xuchang 许昌市	Henan 河南省	(0374)6123706 (0374)6128688	3,891	Collective-owned 集体企业	1,011,401	93,220(1)	1,405,217	Diamond Saw Blade金金石锯片
Foreign Exclusive Investment Zhenjiang Ke Shi Pitch Products Co.,Ltd.外商独资镇江科氏沥青产品有限公司(2002)	Zhenjiang 镇江市	Jiangsu 江苏省	(0511)3370802 (0511)3370801	39	Foreign Funded 外商投资	271,245	21,671(5)	164,884	Asphalt 沥青
White Pigeon Group Co.,Ltd. 白鸽集团股份有限责任公司(1998)	Zhengzhou 郑州市	Henan 河南省	(0371)7635588 (0371)7611702	5,820	State-owned 国有企业	231,570	-	1,590,854	Abrasive 磨料
Hubei Yuli Abrasive Belts Co., Ltd. 湖北玉立砂带股份有限公司(1978)	Xianning 咸宁市	Hubei 湖北省	(0715)4323562 (0715)4322718	1,600	Joint Stock 股份制	202,603	15,146(8)	204,925	Grit Strip 砂带
Qichun Jiukesong Man-made Board Co.,Ltd 蕲春县九棵松人造板有限责任公司(1981)	Huanggang 黄冈市	Hubei 湖北省	(0713)7644032 (0713)7644024	2,787	Overseas Chinese-funded 港澳台资	193,000	10,600(11)	266,946	Man-made Board 人造板
Shanghai Grinding Wheel Works 上海砂轮厂(1952)	Shanghai 上海市	Shanghai 上海市	(021)58890015 (021)58811181	794	State-owned 国有企业	181,024	1,210(138)	403,981	Abrasive 磨料
Wendeng Modern Grinding Materials Co., Ltd. 文登现代研磨材料有限公司(1997)	Weihai 威海市	Shandong 山东省	(0631)8872072 (0631)8872074	180	Foreign Funded 外商投资	165,252	15,310(7)	26,410	Abrasive 研磨材料
Henan Fei Meng Company 河南省飞孟公司(1994)	Jiaozuo 焦作市	Henan 河南省	(0391)8551092 (0391)8551155	490	Limited-Liability 有限公司	146,600	6,325(22)	36,915	Artificial Diamond人造金刚石
Si Sha Co., Ltd. 四砂股份有限公司(1950)	Zibo 淄博市	Shandong 山东省	(0533)2980151 (0533)2980888	2,019	Joint Stock 股份制	130,000	-	553,000	Abrasive 磨料

Top 10 Cities by Revenue 销售收入排名前10位城市	Province 省	Market share 市场份额 (%)	Number of firms 企业个数
Suzhou 苏州市	Jiangsu 江苏省	32.75	13
Zhengzhou 郑州市	Henan 河南省	6.58	66
Xuchang 许昌市	Henan 河南省	5.76	5
Lianyungang 连云港市	Jiangsu 江苏省	4.29	31
Jiaozuo 焦作市	Henan 河南省	2.82	8
Zibo 淄博市	Shandong 山东省	2.57	13
Zhenjiang 镇江市	Jiangsu 江苏省	2.28	9
Changsha 长沙市	Hunan 湖南省	2.17	9
Taiyuan 太原市	Shanxi 山西省	1.58	1
Shanghai 上海市	Shanghai 上海市	1.52	9

10 Major Wholesalers 十家主要批发商	City 城市	Province 省	Telephone/Fax 电话/传真
Xuzhou New Century Building Materials Decorative City 徐州市新世纪建材装饰城	Xuzhou 徐州市	Jiangsu 江苏省	(0516)83666780 (0516)63804485
Orienthome Co.,Ltd. 东方家园有限公司	Beijing 北京市	Beijing 北京市	(010)63808294
Shanghai Jinkai Goods & Materials Co.,Ltd. 上海金凯物资有限公司	Shanghai 上海市	Shanghai 上海市	(021)52193967
Guangzhou Building Materials Development Co.,Ltd. 广州市建材发展有限公司	Guangzhou 广州市	Guangdong 广东省	(020)83335062 (020)83341110
Guangxi Qiaofeng Goods & Materials Trade Co.,Ltd. 广西侨丰物资贸易有限责任公司	Nanning 南宁市	Guangxi 广西	(0771)2631539 (0771)2631539
Gansu Building Materials State-owned Assets Marketing Co.,Ltd. 甘肃建材国有资产经营有限责任公司	Lanzhou 兰州市	Gansu 甘肃省	(0931)8821359 (0931)8960243
Shanghai East Asia United Building Materials Co.,Ltd. 上海东亚联合建材有限公司	Shanghai 上海市	Shanghai 上海市	(021)33134520 (021)63216165
Shanghai Zhuzong Materials General Company 上海住总物资总公司	Shanghai 上海市	Shanghai 上海市	(021)32240030 (021)32240024
Guangdong Building Materials Company 广东省建材公司	Guangzhou 广州市	Guangdong 广东省	(020)83802713 (020)83817640
Guangdong Dongguan Hardware Minerals Import & Export Co.,Ltd 广东省东莞五金矿产进出口公司	Dongguan 东莞市	Guangdong 广东省	(0769)2227090 (0769)2221045

3210: Iron Smelting 炼铁业

The industry accounts for 0.316% of the total revenue of China's industrial sector in 2002. The rate of return on assets is 2.42%. 79.25% of all firms in the industry made a profit while 20.75% had negative returns.The top province in terms of the industry's revenue is Shanxi, accounting for 27.73% of the total revenue.
2002年本行业收入占全行业的0.316%，资产利润率为2.42%。79.25%的企业赢利，20.75%的企业亏损。收入最高的省为山西省，占本行业的27.73%。

	Total number of firms 企业总数	Total number of employees 职工总数	Total revenue (Mil.RMB) 总销售收入 (百万元)	Total profit (Mil.RMB) 总利润 (百万元)	Return on assets 资产利润率 (%)	Return on equity 权益利润率 (%)	Labour productivity ('000 RMB/ worker) 劳动生产率 (千元/人)	Debts/ assets 资产负债率 (%)	Total assets (Mil.RMB) 总资产 (百万元)
Industry Overall 行业总体	617	215,680	33,910	844	2.42	7.06	43.64	65.71	34,855

	Number of firms 企业个数	Average number of employees 平均职工人数	Average revenue ('000 RMB) 平均销售收入 (千元)	Average profit ('000 RMB) 平均利润 (千元)	Return on assets 资产利润率 (%)	Return on equity 权益利润率 (%)	Labour productivity ('000 RMB/ worker) 劳动生产率 (千元/人)	Debts/ assets 资产负债率 (%)	Average total assets ('000 RMB) 平均总资产 (千元)
By ownership 产业所有权									
State-owned 国有	84	583	66,868	-47	-0.04	-0.16	28.61	74.03	113,812
Collective-owned 集体	117	213	37,553	1,045	4.04	11.69	50.54	65.40	25,851
Foreign & Overseas Chinese Funded 三资	22	398	153,912	4,088	2.59	12.03	80.41	78.45	157,701
By regional distribution 地区分布									
Central-North 华北	363	293	45,477	1,214	2.76	7.68	47.06	64.07	43,971
Beijing 北京	1	47	28,904	122	0.58	3.90	198.87	85.20	21,155
Tianjin 天津	8	60	39,938	1,428	2.64	3.20	146.52	17.50	54,123
Hebei 河北	71	412	90,713	3,759	4.56	16.03	58.81	71.57	82,473
Shanxi 山西	274	266	34,316	558	1.71	4.31	41.85	60.31	32,627
Inner Mongolia 内蒙古	9	409	35,153	1,044	1.32	5.82	42.07	77.33	79,086
Northeast 东北	26	495	48,779	1,554	1.78	4.92	25.31	63.87	87,374
Liaoning 辽宁	15	182	19,351	-416	-1.50	-5.13	26.50	70.76	27,685
Jilin 吉林	3	1,188	163,719	17,944	4.29	10.43	39.47	58.86	418,241
Heilongjiang 黑龙江	8	822	60,856	-901	-1.20	-3.93	17.15	69.55	75,216
Central-East 华东	78	524	105,979	2,493	2.43	6.86	53.10	64.50	102,398
Shanghai 上海	4	47	26,412	2,079	4.84	7.69	146.12	37.05	42,942
Jiangsu 江苏	26	547	121,667	1,909	1.81	5.46	59.15	66.77	105,223
Zhejiang 浙江	1	46	8,613	-50	-1.22	-2.53	38.50	51.81	4,109
Anhui 安徽	7	660	107,671	1,431	1.16	2.79	30.02	58.25	122,940
Fujian 福建	10	361	44,058	-1,534	-2.06	-5.02	14.71	58.91	74,323
Jiangxi 江西	3	168	40,043	479	2.33	7.50	77.92	68.96	20,574
Shandong 山东	27	655	136,088	5,202	4.12	12.40	60.44	66.78	126,289
Central-South 中南	79	396	62,545	1,738	2.86	11.13	39.65	74.26	60,697
Henan 河南	37	530	89,157	3,986	4.74	14.90	42.33	68.20	84,133
Hubei 湖北	12	125	26,219	972	7.10	16.42	74.04	56.74	13,684
Hunan 湖南	13	357	39,644	-45	-0.09	-5.03	26.25	98.17	48,613
Guangdong 广东	9	233	51,599	130	0.41	2.50	59.11	83.77	32,013
Guangxi 广西	8	429	43,482	-2,801	-3.75	-19.44	15.49	80.72	74,733
Hainan 海南									
Southwest 西南	59	304	40,507	1,550	3.23	7.17	31.23	54.89	47,905
Chongqing 重庆	3	515	60,830	394	0.61	1.11	23.27	44.92	64,554
Sichuan 四川	17	235	24,232	-336	-1.16	-4.68	12.99	75.28	29,037
Guizhou 贵州	18	201	14,907	290	1.56	3.14	20.97	50.25	18,569
Yunnan 云南	21	419	72,723	4,321	5.03	10.31	45.12	51.25	85,947
Tibet 西藏									
Northwest 西北	12	519	44,683	-5,018	-5.94	-119.55	16.82	95.03	84,473
Shaanxi 陕西	8	533	46,955	-7,521	-8.50		12.13	118.43	88,533
Gansu 甘肃	2	791	74,697	144	0.18	0.37	31.60	51.95	81,813
Qinghai 青海									
Ningxia 宁夏	1	132	11,164	-331	-3.01		23.22	103.24	11,006
Xinjiang 新疆	1	248						21.54	130,787

Year 年份	Number of firms 企业个数	Rate of change 变化率 (%)	Number of employees 职工人数 (人)	Rate of change 变化率 (%)	Total revenue (Mil. RMB) 总销售收入 (百万元)	Rate of change 变化率 (%)	Total profit (Mil RMB) 总利润 (百万元)	Rate of change 变化率 (%)
2000	589		281,664		29,432		281	
2001	620	5.26	249,674	-11.36	30,921	5.06	568	102.14
2002	617	-0.48	215,680	-13.62	33,910	9.67	844	48.59

Major Products 主要产品	Output 产量	Unit 单位
Pig Iron 生铁	17,075	10,000 Tons 万吨

10 Main Firms with Maximal Revenue (year founded) 收入最大的十家主要企业（创办年份）	City 城市	Province 省	Telephone/fax 电话/传真	Number of employees 职工人数	Ownership 产业所有权	Revenue ('000 RMB) 销售收入(千元)	Profit('000 RMB) (rank) 利润(千元)(排名)	Total assets ('000 RMB) 总资产(千元)	Major products 主要产品
Anyang Yongxing Iron & Steel Ltd. Company	Anyang	Henan	(0372)5862905		Private Owned				Pig Iron
安阳永兴钢铁有限责任公司(1994)	安阳市	河南省	(0372)5862219	3,060	私营企业	967,657	127,110(1)	681,091	生 铁
Xuzhou Iron & Steel General Factory	Xuzhou	Jiangsu	(0516)7773981		State-owned				Pig Iron
徐州钢铁总厂(1958)	徐州市	江苏省	(0516)7773817	5,664	国有企业	926,110	18,390(10)	1,500,510	生铁
Zhangdian Iron & Steel Works	Zibo	Shandong	(0533)3152603		State-owned				Pig Iron
张店钢铁总厂(1958)	淄博市	山东省	(0533)3183728	3,404	国有企业	811,805	1,250(121)	1,015,011	生铁
Sichuan Desheng Group Chuxiong Iron & Steel Co., Ltd.	Chuxiong	Yunnan	(0878)4127495		Private Owned				Billet
四川德胜集团楚雄钢铁有限公司(2000)	楚雄州	云南省	(0878)4122483	1,978	私营企业	650,716	80,143(2)	901,960	钢坯
Shanxi Changping Group Co., Ltd.	Changzhi	Shanxi	(0355)8778215		Limited-Liability				Pig Iron
山西常平集团有限公司(1993)	长治市	山西省	(0355)8778215	3,900	有限公司	500,677	20,767(9)	751,646	生铁
Handan Fuchuan Iron-smelting Co., Ltd.	Handan	Hebei	(0310)6072101		Foreign Funded				Pig Iron
邯郸富川炼铁有限公司(1996)	邯郸市	河北省	(0310)3292152	102	外商投资	400,699	15,806(17)	210,376	生铁
Hebei Dongshan Metallurgy Industry Co., Ltd.	Handan	Hebei	(0310)5569988		Limited-Liability				Pig Iron
河北东山冶金工业有限公司(1988)	邯郸市	河北省	(0310)5569981	1,213	有限公司	393,263	5,539(43)	141,255	生铁
Ji'nan Geng Chen Iron And Steel Co., Ltd.	Jinan	Shandong	(0531)8991506		Limited-Liability				Steel-making
济南庚辰钢铁有限公司(1972)	济南市	山东省	(0531)8991363	1,951	有限公司	388,836	530(189)	290,819	炼铁
Wuhu Xinxing Cast Pipe Co., Ltd.	Wuhu	Anhui	(0553)4113457		State-owned				Pig Iron
芜湖新兴铸管有限责任公司(1958)	芜湖市	安徽省	(0553)4114050	2,261	国有企业	381,135	3,768(55)	581,533	生铁
Xuzhou Huanyu Special Type Alloy Co., Ltd.	Xuzhou	Jiangsu	(0516)5770216		Foreign Funded				Molybdenum Iron
徐州市环宇特种合金有限公司(1995)	徐州市	江苏省	(0516)5777958	350	外商投资	380,840	8,390(30)	99,030	钼铁

Top 10 Cities by Revenue 销售收入排名前10位城市	Province 省	Market share 市场份额 (%)	Number of firms 企业个数
Linfen 临汾市	Shanxi 山西省	12.53	126
Anyang 安阳市	Henan 河南省	7.10	20
Handan 邯郸市	Hebei 河北省	6.82	17
Tangshan 唐山市	Hebei 河北省	6.34	27
Xuzhou 徐州市	Jiangsu 江苏省	4.96	6
Lvliang 吕梁地区	Shanxi 山西省	4.46	58
Zibo 淄博市	Shandong 山东省	3.75	9
Changzhi 长治市	Shanxi 山西省	3.69	20
Jinan 济南市	Shandong 山东省	2.89	5
Datong 大同市	Shanxi 山西省	2.13	3

10 Major Wholesalers 十家主要批发商	City 城市	Province 省	Telephone/Fax 电话/传真
China Ordins Corporation	Beijing	Beijing	(010)68962929
中国兵工物资总公司	北京市	北京市	(010)68962922
China Shougang International Trade & Engineering Corp.	Beijing	Beijing	(010)88297572
中国首钢国际贸易工程公司	北京市	北京市	(010)88297500
Tianjin Baosteel North Trade Co.,Ltd.	Tianjin	Tianjin	(022)28236341
天津宝钢北方贸易有限公司	天津市	天津市	(022)28267197
China Railway Goods & Materials Shenyang Company	Shenyang	Liaoning	(024)23506794
中国铁路物资沈阳公司	沈阳市	辽宁省	(024)23506622
Shanghai Hardware Minerals Import & Export Company	Shanghai	Shanghai	(021)63815858
上海市五金矿产进出口公司	上海市	上海市	(021)63806600
Baosteel Iron & Steel Trade Co.,Ltd. Shanghai Filiale	Shanghai	Shanghai	(021)68404611
上海宝钢钢材贸易有限公司分公司	上海市	上海市	(021)68404618
Jiangsu Foreign Trade Corpration	Nanjing	Jiangsu	(025)3190088
江苏省对外经贸股份有限公司	南京市	江苏省	(025)3190001
Nanjing Goods & Materials Industrial Group General Company	Nanjing	Jiangsu	(025)4549090
南京物资实业集团总公司	南京市	江苏省	(025)4408957
Zhejiang Metal Material Company	Hangzhou	Zhejiang	(0571)85271168
浙江省金属材料公司	杭州市	浙江省	(0571)85271111
Ma Steel International Trade & Economic Corp.	Maanshan	Anhui	(0555)2882092
马钢国际经济贸易总公司	马鞍山市	安徽省	(0555)2321079

3220: Steel Smelting 炼钢业

The industry accounts for 2.231% of the total revenue of China's industrial sector in 2002. The rate of return on assets is 2.69%. 78.72% of all firms in the industry made a profit while 21.28% had negative returns.The top province in terms of the industry's revenue is Liaoning, accounting for 12.07% of the total revenue.
2002年本行业收入占全行业的 2.231%，资产利润率为 2.69%。78.72%的企业赢利，21.28%的企业亏损。收入最高的省为辽宁省，占本行业的12.07%。

	Total number of firms 企业总数	Total number of employees 职工总数	Total revenue (Mil.RMB) 总销售收入 (百万元)	Total profit (Mil.RMB) 总利润 (百万元)	Return on assets 资产利润率 (%)	Return on equity 权益利润率 (%)	Labour productivity ('000 RMB/ worker) 劳动生产率 (千元/人)	Debts/ assets 资产负债率 (%)	Total assets (Mil.RMB) 总资产 (百万元)
Industry Overall 行业总体	235	915,777	239,345	11,160	2.69	5.56	80.35	51.62	414,794

	Number of firms 企业个数	Average number of employees 平均职工人数	Average revenue ('000 RMB) 平均销售收入 (千元)	Average profit ('000 RMB) 平均利润 (千元)	Return on assets 资产利润率 (%)	Return on equity 权益利润率 (%)	Labour productivity ('000 RMB/ worker) 劳动生产率 (千元/人)	Debts/ assets 资产负债率 (%)	Average total assets ('000 RMB) 平均总资产 (千元)
By ownership 产业所有权									
State-owned 国有	37	12,342	2,617,701	141,633	2.47	4.94	73.07	49.98	5,736,713
Collective-owned 集体	42	380	104,279	4,263	4.54	14.55	70.80	68.77	93,819
Foreign & Overseas Chinese Funded 三资	19	780	652,000	24,417	2.95	6.71	161.26	56.08	828,290
By regional distribution 地区分布									
Central-North 华北	49	2,849	839,014	48,564	3.78	9.76	83.42	61.30	1,285,239
Beijing 北京									
Tianjin 天津	7	4,309	1,158,051	33,808	1.96	5.87	44.45	66.61	1,723,513
Hebei 河北	29	3,101	896,024	54,951	3.61	9.42	93.18	61.68	1,522,500
Shanxi 山西	8	2,343	871,038	68,728	8.23	16.17	101.34	49.13	835,373
Inner Mongolia 内蒙古	5	157	10,472	-86	-0.56	-1.90	35.28	70.56	15,331
Northeast 东北	21	8,806	1,681,934	56,055	1.30	2.42	63.52	46.15	4,296,600
Liaoning 辽宁	17	9,355	1,699,429	64,122	1.31	2.36	62.52	44.63	4,912,937
Jilin 吉林	1	15,890	5,102,606	76,337	1.78	4.20	87.42	57.48	4,278,217
Heilongjiang 黑龙江	3	3,330	442,572	3,578	0.44	2.08	41.45	78.74	810,154
Central-East 华东	63	3,213	1,259,808	53,536	3.17	6.11	107.61	48.12	1,688,159
Shanghai 上海	11	2,125	1,422,059	3,118	0.13	0.24	118.38	46.80	2,443,540
Jiangsu 江苏	12	2,171	1,363,314	67,493	4.89	10.66	110.69	54.14	1,380,124
Zhejiang 浙江	14	1,091	400,722	33,656	5.80	9.04	108.90	35.86	580,338
Anhui 安徽	6	7,716	1,908,624	74,687	2.60	3.70	90.43	29.78	2,874,504
Fujian 福建	9	1,373	481,109	48,947	9.01	18.17	133.89	50.40	543,233
Jiangxi 江西	6	7,898	1,848,429	66,518	3.05	7.42	63.67	58.94	2,183,436
Shandong 山东	5	6,335	2,976,623	153,925	3.94	9.43	177.10	58.26	3,910,426
Central-South 中南	61	3,546	871,990	53,294	3.50	7.01	80.37	50.10	1,524,729
Henan 河南	21	2,982	600,726	27,406	3.52	5.73	64.69	38.60	778,979
Hubei 湖北	12	8,757	1,975,701	140,797	3.31	6.25	82.38	46.95	4,247,765
Hunan 湖南	9	2,846	653,158	34,486	4.33	12.47	76.70	65.27	796,460
Guangdong 广东	15	1,461	720,250	44,906	3.66	9.95	121.73	63.22	1,227,154
Guangxi 广西	3	309	56,186	556	1.76	2.82	45.73	37.67	31,688
Hainan 海南	1	180	17,016	189	3.02	6.24	29.12	51.50	6,248
Southwest 西南	29	5,008	818,674	21,041	1.19	2.92	59.33	59.15	1,765,607
Chongqing 重庆	5	1,702	102,432	-16,693	-2.15	-9.75	8.07	77.92	775,108
Sichuan 四川	15	6,714	1,243,149	46,862	2.10	4.76	66.48	56.02	2,236,253
Guizhou 贵州	4	2,314	105,042	-39,176	-7.22	-28.75	4.96	74.89	542,692
Yunnan 云南	5	5,354	832,396	29,481	1.27	3.09	67.51	58.98	2,322,499
Tibet 西藏									
Northwest 西北	12	2,271	551,003	30,778	3.35	7.07	88.31	52.61	918,660
Shaanxi 陕西	6	1,612	135,676	-6,117	-1.59	-5.60	22.68	71.67	385,743
Gansu 甘肃	1	35	7,970	200	7.33	7.91	143.89	7.33	2,730
Qinghai 青海	1	7,875	1,421,654	3,293	0.09	0.28	48.13	68.01	3,661,051
Ningxia 宁夏	1	108	9,500	534	2.57	3.64	70.92	29.19	20,744
Xinjiang 新疆	3	3,189	1,452,952	134,001	8.00	11.89	187.68	32.73	1,674,979

3220: Steel Smelting 炼钢业

Year 年份	Number of firms 企业个数	Rate of change 变化率 (%)	Number of employees 职工人数 (人)	Rate of change 变化率 (%)	Total revenue (Mil. RMB) 总销售收入 (百万元)	Rate of change 变化率 (%)	Total profit (Mil RMB) 总利润 (百万元)	Rate of change 变化率 (%)
2000	273		1,169,727		191,161		7,027	
2001	251	-8.06	1,037,561	-11.30	219,843	15.00	9,853	40.22
2002	235	-6.37	915,777	-11.74	239,345	8.87	11,160	13.27

Major Products 主要产品	Output 产量	Unit 单位
Steel 钢	18,155	10,000 Tons 万吨
Plain Carbon Steel 普通碳素钢	8,186	10,000 Tons 万吨

10 Main Firms with Maximal Revenue (year founded) 收入最大的十家主要企业 (创办年份)	City 城市	Province 省	Telephone/fax 电话/传真	Number of employees 职工人数	Ownership 产业所有权	Revenue ('000 RMB) 销售收入 (千元)	Profit('000 RMB) (rank) 利润(千元) (排名)	Total assets ('000 RMB) 总资产 (千元)	Major products 主要产品
China Anshan Iron & Steel Group Corporation	Anshan	Liaoning	(0412)6724292		State-owned				Rolled Steel
鞍山钢铁集团公司(1916)	鞍山市	辽宁省	(0412)6723080	137,962	国有企业	24,555,350	1,158,930(2)	68,185,050	钢材
Wuhan Iron & Steel(group) Corporation	Wuhan	Hubei	(027)86863718		State-owned				Iron
武汉钢铁（集团）公司(1958)	武汉市	湖北省	(027)86862325	85,378	国有企业	19,756,495	1,505,016(1)	47,017,585	铁
Maanshan Iron & Steel Co., Ltd.	Maanshan	Anhui	(0555)2883492		Joint Stock				Rolled Steel
马鞍山钢铁股份有限公司(1993)	马鞍山市	安徽省	(0555)2884350	45,794	股份制	11,307,030	448,699(9)	17,172,939	钢材
Tangshan Iron & Steel Group Co., Ltd.	Tangshan	Hebei	(0315)2702409		State Enterprises				Rolled Steel
唐山钢铁集团有限责任公司(1944)	唐山市	河北省	(0315)2702449	40,551	国有独资	9,565,491	629,353(3)	16,486,287	钢材
Handan Iron & Steel Group Co.,Ltd.	Handan	Hebei	(0310)6072141		State-owned				Pig Iron
邯郸钢铁集团有限责任公司(1958)	邯郸市	河北省	(0310)6071970	26,547	国有企业	9,112,776	514,025(5)	22,594,057	生铁
Jinan Iron & Steel Group General Company	Jinan	Shandong	(0531)8869748		State Owned				Pig Iron
济南钢铁集团总公司(1958)	济南市	山东省	(0531)8982126	16,829	国有企业	8,188,095	510,320(6)	13,281,758	生铁
Anyang Iron & Steel Group Co., Ltd.	Anyang	Henan	(0372)3122219		State Enterprises				Rolled Steel
安阳钢铁集团有限责任公司(1958)	安阳市	河南省	(0372)3931892	35,176	国有独资	7,094,926	404,010(11)	9,368,964	钢材
Qingdao Iron And Steel Holding Group Co., Ltd.	Qingdao	Shandong	(0532)4816857		State Enterprises				Iron
青岛钢铁控股集团有限责任公司(1958)	青岛市	山东省	(0532)4816057	12,760	国有独资	6,166,640	290,910(14)	5,855,970	铁
Guangdong Shaoguan Iron & Steel Group Co., Ltd.	Shaoguan	Guangdong	(0751)8786140		State-owned				steel making
广东省韶关钢铁集团有限公司(1966)	韶关市	广东省	(0751)8485701	13,601	国有企业	5,582,584	564,662(4)	8,716,062	炼钢
Shanghai San Gang Co., Ltd.	Shanghai	Shanghai	(021)58839180		Limited-Liability				Steel Plate
上海三钢有限责任公司(2001)	上海市	上海市	(021)63201284	4,860	有限公司	5,251,519	5,135(66)	8,157,717	钢板

Top 10 Cities by Revenue 销售收入排名前10位城市	Province 省	Market share 市场份额 (%)	Number of firms 企业个数
Anshan 鞍山市	Liaoning 辽宁省	10.31	5
Wuhan 武汉市	Hubei 湖北省	8.27	2
Shanghai 上海市	Shanghai 上海市	6.54	11
Tangshan 唐山市	Hebei 河北省	5.60	14
Handan 邯郸市	Hebei 河北省	4.78	8
Maanshan 马鞍山市	Anhui 安徽省	4.75	3
Panzhihua 攀枝花市	Sichuan 四川省	4.30	1
Jinan 济南市	Shandong 山东省	3.42	1
Tianjin 天津市	Tianjin 天津市	3.39	7
Wuxi 无锡市	Jiangsu 江苏省	3.08	5

10 Major Wholesalers 十家主要批发商	City 城市	Province 省	Telephone/Fax 电话/传真
China Ordins Corporation	Beijing	Beijing	(010)68962929
中国兵工物资总公司	北京市	北京市	(010)68962922
China Shougang International Trade & Engineering Corp.	Beijing	Beijing	(010)88297572
中国首钢国际贸易工程公司	北京市	北京市	(010)88297500
Tianjin Baosteel North Trade Co.,Ltd.	Tianjin	Tianjin	(022)28236341
天津宝钢北方贸易有限公司	天津市	天津市	(022)28267197
China Railway Goods & Materials Shenyang Company	Shenyang	Liaoning	(024)23506794
中国铁路物资沈阳公司	沈阳市	辽宁省	(024)23506622
Shanghai Hardware Minerals Import & Export Company	Shanghai	Shanghai	(021)63815858
上海市五金矿产进出口公司	上海市	上海市	(021)63806600
Baosteel Iron & Steel Trade Co.,Ltd. Shanghai Filiale	Shanghai	Shanghai	(021)68404611
上海宝钢钢材贸易有限公司分公司	上海市	上海市	(021)68404618
Jiangsu Foreign Trade Corpration	Nanjing	Jiangsu	(025)3190088
江苏省对外经贸股份有限公司	南京市	江苏省	(025)3190001
Nanjing Goods & Materials Industrial Group General Company	Nanjing	Jiangsu	(025)4549090
南京物资实业集团总公司	南京市	江苏省	(025)4408957
Zhejiang Metal Material Company	Hangzhou	Zhejiang	(0571)85271168
浙江省金属材料公司	杭州市	浙江省	(0571)85271111
Ma Steel International Trade & Economic Corp.	Maanshan	Anhui	(0555)2882092
马钢国际经济贸易总公司	马鞍山市	安徽省	(0555)2321079

3240: Steel Rolling 钢压延加工业

The industry accounts for 3.271% of the total revenue of China's industrial sector in 2002. The rate of return on assets is 3.72%. 83.09% of all firms in the industry made a profit while 16.91% had negative returns.The top province in terms of the industry's revenue is Jiangsu, accounting for 15.84% of the total revenue.
2002年本行业收入占全行业的3.271%，资产利润率为3.72%。83.09%的企业赢利，16.91%的企业亏损。收入最高的省为江苏省，占本行业的15.84%。

	Total number of firms 企业总数	Total number of employees 职工总数	Total revenue (Mil.RMB) 总销售收入 (百万元)	Total profit (Mil.RMB) 总利润 (百万元)	Return on assets 资产利润率 (%)	Return on equity 权益利润率 (%)	Labour productivity ('000 RMB/ worker) 劳动生产率 (千元/人)	Debts/ assets 资产负债率 (%)	Total assets (Mil.RMB) 总资产 (百万元)
Industry Overall 行业总体	1833	1,108,370	350,830	17,725	3.72	8.60	82.56	56.81	477,109

	Number of firms 企业个数	Average number of employees 平均职工人数	Average revenue ('000 RMB) 平均销售收入 (千元)	Average profit ('000 RMB) 平均利润 (千元)	Return on assets 资产利润率 (%)	Return on equity 权益利润率 (%)	Labour productivity ('000 RMB/ worker) 劳动生产率 (千元/人)	Debts/ assets 资产负债率 (%)	Average total assets ('000 RMB) 平均总资产 (千元)
By ownership 产业所有权									
State-owned 国有	105	960	200,338	8,812	2.65	8.35	49.91	68.30	333,011
Collective-owned 集体	393	409	97,640	2,927	4.39	13.74	50.24	68.02	66,616
Foreign & Overseas Chinese Funded 三资	145	335	213,505	11,367	5.16	12.27	157.17	57.96	220,407
By regional distribution 地区分布									
Central-North 华北	345	1,227	342,577	16,255	3.34	7.29	73.62	54.17	486,696
Beijing 北京	12	7,079	1,844,296	38,951	1.14	1.94	73.25	41.05	3,407,529
Tianjin 天津	117	396	170,397	7,448	4.37	13.05	54.91	66.54	170,519
Hebei 河北	186	752	245,122	17,656	7.09	19.52	93.23	63.68	249,048
Shanxi 山西	12	6,382	1,219,868	44,148	1.95	3.84	56.60	49.12	2,258,727
Inner Mongolia 内蒙古	18	4,206	882,776	25,299	1.35	2.93	66.43	53.74	1,868,968
Northeast 东北	183	988	222,168	5,343	1.49	3.75	50.63	60.32	358,897
Liaoning 辽宁	151	970	241,367	7,170	1.84	4.51	55.55	59.07	388,770
Jilin 吉林	25	828	120,725	1,425	1.05	2.93	35.98	64.16	135,658
Heilongjiang 黑龙江	7	1,957	170,304	-20,084	-3.92	-17.28	20.12	77.29	511,758
Central-East 华东	788	305	176,365	11,776	5.51	12.26	147.40	55.02	213,557
Shanghai 上海	96	356	463,868	64,282	8.33	16.48	460.46	49.44	771,352
Jiangsu 江苏	337	263	164,919	5,465	3.35	8.08	125.97	58.54	163,161
Zhejiang 浙江	176	134	56,453	2,483	4.93	9.99	77.75	50.68	50,382
Anhui 安徽	36	585	88,218	2,013	1.60	3.55	32.92	55.02	125,856
Fujian 福建	39	194	133,332	1,591	1.52	3.74	176.18	59.39	104,902
Jiangxi 江西	28	235	41,589	494	1.85	5.53	35.60	66.46	26,676
Shandong 山东	76	775	255,135	8,968	3.24	9.55	75.50	66.03	276,474
Central-South 中南	331	325	87,237	3,572	3.27	9.22	84.51	64.53	109,190
Henan 河南	47	320	65,917	1,203	2.52	7.59	57.30	66.80	47,715
Hubei 湖北	46	449	109,274	3,760	2.05	9.03	102.86	77.28	183,173
Hunan 湖南	47	749	137,037	7,383	3.53	9.82	62.46	64.02	208,907
Guangdong 广东	171	108	57,186	1,063	2.13	5.81	128.01	63.38	49,976
Guangxi 广西	16	1,098	265,504	27,197	6.56	11.40	84.93	42.44	414,380
Hainan 海南	4	162	70,790	-2,805	-2.34		80.28	166.57	119,639
Southwest 西南	128	831	136,554	3,492	2.14	7.33	41.69	70.83	163,430
Chongqing 重庆	38	554	146,747	6,637	4.56	9.49	63.74	51.93	145,472
Sichuan 四川	63	791	109,163	1,996	1.32	6.41	30.00	79.42	151,210
Guizhou 贵州	7	4,165	504,105	7,422	1.08	5.63	42.89	80.86	688,359
Yunnan 云南	19	329	78,749	885	1.63	3.01	55.35	45.84	54,236
Tibet 西藏	1	50	226	287	1.80	8.68	-0.80	79.23	15,929
Northwest 西北	58	853	114,738	3,981	1.27	2.74	44.09	53.70	313,386
Shaanxi 陕西	15	555	113,153	1,634	0.70	2.17	54.16	67.85	234,444
Gansu 甘肃	24	1,574	180,794	8,762	1.50	2.99	42.57	49.73	583,633
Qinghai 青海									
Ningxia 宁夏	1	243	5,432	19	0.34		9.05	109.14	5,545
Xinjiang 新疆	18	175	34,058	-217	-0.60	-1.59	38.48	62.10	35,943

Year 年份	Number of firms 企业个数	Rate of change 变化率 (%)	Number of employees 职工人数 (人)	Rate of change 变化率 (%)	Total revenue (Mil. RMB) 总销售收入 (百万元)	Rate of change 变化率 (%)	Total profit (Mil RMB) 总利润 (百万元)	Rate of change 变化率 (%)
2000	1575		1,062,864		251,090		8,744	
2001	1697	7.75	1,044,484	-1.73	290,669	15.76	10,016	14.55
2002	1833	8.01	1,108,370	6.12	350,830	20.70	17,725	76.97

Major Products 主要产品	Output 产量	Unit 单位
Thin Steel Plate 薄钢板	2,245	10,000 Tons 万吨
Steel Strip 钢带	1,505	10,000 Tons 万吨

10 Main Firms with Maximal Revenue (year founded) 收入最大的十家主要企业（创办年份）	City 城市	Province 省	Telephone/fax 电话/传真	Number of employees 职工人数	Ownership 产业所有权	Revenue ('000 RMB) 销售收入 (千元)	Profit('000 RMB) (rank) 利润(千元) (排名)	Total assets ('000 RMB) 总资产 (千元)	Major products 主要产品
Baoshan Iron And Steel Co., ltd. 宝山钢铁股份有限公司(1982)	Shanghai 上海市	Shanghai 上海市	(021)26648040 (021)26648046	16,229	Joint Stock 股份制	33,770,108	5,922,638(1)	61,507,474	Steel Plate 钢板
Capital Iron & Steel Coporation General Co. 首钢总公司(1919)	Beijing 北京市	Beijing 北京市	(010)88293002 (010)88295578	82,698	State Enterprises 国有独资	21,660,424	492,177(6)	39,859,507	Steel 钢
Jiangsu Shagang Group Co., Ltd. 江苏沙钢集团有限公司(1975)	Suzhou 苏州市	Jiangsu 江苏省	(0520)58550801 (0520)58550818	8,579	Limited-Liability 有限公司	14,511,965	798,879(2)	14,470,532	Electric Steel 电炉钢
Beitai Iron & Steel (Group) Co., ltd 北台钢铁(集团)有限责任公司(1971)	Benxi 本溪市	Liaoning 辽宁省	(0414)4868858 (0414)4843613	23,467	State Enterprises 国有独资	11,786,115	67,762(33)	9,804,124	Pig Iron 生铁
Benxi Iron and steel (Group) Co., Ltd. 本钢钢铁（集团）有限责任公司(1905)	Benxi 本溪市	Liaoning 辽宁省	(0414)2843889 (0414)2842074	60,303	State Enterprises 国有独资	11,637,288	561,549(4)	30,210,051	Pig Iron 生铁
Taiyuan Iron & Steel (group)Co., Ltd. 太原钢铁(集团)有限公司	Taiyuan 太原市	Shanxi 山西省	(0351)3012615 (0351)3134170	50,138	State Enterprises 国有独资	10,951,710	392,080(10)	22,735,420	Pig Iron 生铁
Baotou Iron And Steel (Group) Co., Ltd. 包头钢铁（集团）有限责任公司(1998)	Baotou 包头市	ıner Mongol 内蒙古	(0472)2183163 (0472)5155484	58,364	State Enterprises 国有独资	7,900,000	8,000(162)	24,180,000	Iron And Steel Works 钢铁
Jiangsu Huaxi Group Company 江苏华西集团公司(1993)	Wuxi 无锡市	Jiangsu 江苏省	(0510)6201349 (0510)6216296	8,263	Collective-owned 集体企业	6,278,970	370,240(11)	3,849,360	Wire 线材
Shanghai Meishan Iron And Steel Co., Ltd 上海梅山钢铁股份有限公司(1970)	Nanjing 南京市	Jiangsu 江苏省	(025)6703644 (025)6701886	7,579	Joint Stock 股份制	4,211,760	84,380(27)	11,406,560	Pig Iron 生铁
Lianyuan Iron And Steel Group Co., Ltd. 涟源钢铁集团有限公司(1958)	Loudi 娄底市	Hunan 湖南省	(0738)8661234 (0738)8663103	19,452	State-owned 国有企业	3,915,254	246,895(16)	5,795,008	Rolled Steel 钢材

Top 10 Cities by Revenue 销售收入排名前10位城市	Province 省	Market share 市场份额 (%)	Number of firms 企业个数
Shanghai 上海市	Shanghai 上海市	12.69	96
Benxi 本溪市	Liaoning 辽宁省	6.73	14
Beijing 北京市	Beijing 北京市	6.31	12
Suzhou 苏州市	Jiangsu 江苏省	6.11	51
Tianjin 天津市	Tianjin 天津市	5.68	117
Tangshan 唐山市	Hebei 河北省	5.61	101
Wuxi 无锡市	Jiangsu 江苏省	4.85	134
Baotou 包头市	Inner Mongolia 内蒙古	4.38	16
Taiyuan 太原市	Shanxi 山西省	3.16	5
Laiwu 莱芜市	Shandong 山东省	2.49	11

10 Major Wholesalers 十家主要批发商	City 城市	Province 省	Telephone/Fax 电话/传真
China Ordins Corporation 中国兵工物资总公司	Beijing 北京市	Beijing 北京市	(010)68962929 (010)68962922
China Shougang International Trade & Engineering Corp. 中国首钢国际贸易工程公司	Beijing 北京市	Beijing 北京市	(010)88297572 (010)88297500
Tianjin Baosteel North Trade Co.,Ltd. 天津宝钢北方贸易有限公司	Tianjin 天津市	Tianjin 天津市	(022)28236341 (022)28267197
China Railway Goods & Materials Shenyang Company 中国铁路物资沈阳公司	Shenyang 沈阳市	Liaoning 辽宁省	(024)23506794 (024)23506622
Shanghai Hardware Minerals Import & Export Company 上海市五金矿产进出口公司	Shanghai 上海市	Shanghai 上海市	(021)63815858 (021)63806600
Baosteel Iron & Steel Trade Co.,Ltd. Shanghai Filiale 上海宝钢钢材贸易有限公司分公司	Shanghai 上海市	Shanghai 上海市	(021)68404611 (021)68404618
Jiangsu Foreign Trade Corpration 江苏省对外经贸股份有限公司	Nanjing 南京市	Jiangsu 江苏省	(025)3190088 (025)3190001
Nanjing Goods & Materials Industrial Group General Company 南京物资实业集团总公司	Nanjing 南京市	Jiangsu 江苏省	(025)4549090 (025)4408957
Zhejiang Metal Material Company 浙江省金属材料公司	Hangzhou 杭州市	Zhejiang 浙江省	(0571)85271168 (0571)85271111
Ma Steel International Trade & Economic Corp. 马钢国际经济贸易总公司	Maanshan 马鞍山市	Anhui 安徽省	(0555)2882092 (0555)2321079

3260: Ferroalloy Smelting and Refining 铁合金冶炼业

The industry accounts for 0.215% of the total revenue of China's industrial sector in 2002. The rate of return on assets is -0.77%. 57.41% of all firms in the industry made a profit while 42.59% had negative returns.The top province in terms of the industry's revenue is Guizhou, accounting for 11.33% of the total revenue.
2002年本行业收入占全行业的0.215%，资产利润率为-0.77%。57.41%的企业赢利，42.59%的企业亏损。收入最高的省为贵州省，占本行业的11.33%。

	Total number of firms 企业总数	Total number of employees 职工总数	Total revenue (Mil.RMB) 总销售收入（百万元）	Total profit (Mil.RMB) 总利润（百万元）	Return on assets 资产利润率（%）	Return on equity 权益利润率（%）	Labour productivity ('000 RMB/worker) 劳动生产率（千元/人）	Debts/assets 资产负债率（%）	Total assets (Mil.RMB) 总资产（百万元）
Industry Overall 行业总体	648	153,039	23,065	-253	-0.77	-2.59	35.56	70.40	32,997

	Number of firms 企业个数	Average number of employees 平均职工人数	Average revenue ('000 RMB) 平均销售收入（千元）	Average profit ('000 RMB) 平均利润（千元）	Return on assets 资产利润率（%）	Return on equity 权益利润率（%）	Labour productivity ('000 RMB/worker) 劳动生产率（千元/人）	Debts/assets 资产负债率（%）	Average total assets ('000 RMB) 平均总资产（千元）
By ownership 产业所有权									
State-owned 国有	105	268	31,615	-1,176	-2.40	-13.48	23.54	82.23	49,071
Collective-owned 集体	146	148	20,661	127	0.60	2.12	34.74	71.93	21,274
Foreign & Overseas Chinese Funded 三资	31	328	68,754	2,374	2.87	8.63	51.96	66.76	82,804
By regional distribution 地区分布									
Central-North 华北	62	238	39,318	939	2.51	6.75	48.94	62.86	37,427
Beijing 北京									
Tianjin 天津	1	389		-3,600	-4.76	-15.33	-51.78	68.94	75,590
Hebei 河北	10	171	44,700	144	0.37	1.39	37.87	73.27	38,830
Shanxi 山西	23	364	55,181	1,395	2.61	7.04	48.12	62.97	53,485
Inner Mongolia 内蒙古	28	154	25,769	1,010	4.51	10.14	64.01	55.48	22,373
Northeast 东北	51	331	52,977	-2,931	-2.29	-10.92	23.50	79.08	128,260
Liaoning 辽宁	38	254	52,010	-3,483	-4.15	-23.31	31.21	82.22	84,014
Jilin 吉林	11	639	62,686	-1,549	-0.52	-2.19	12.27	76.33	299,117
Heilongjiang 黑龙江	2	110	17,945	-50	-0.17	-0.46	44.33	62.79	29,216
Central-East 华东	72	245	53,979	1,492	2.36	5.15	50.94	54.14	63,193
Shanghai 上海	12	598	101,426	1,957	1.29	2.67	29.46	51.67	151,837
Jiangsu 江苏	16	276	101,393	7,044	7.83	15.99	94.76	51.03	89,969
Zhejiang 浙江	9	248	53,181	-4,688	-5.45	-15.75	32.90	65.39	86,014
Anhui 安徽	1	93	32,117	656	4.76	20.64	93.66	76.93	13,775
Fujian 福建	32	87	10,875	-22	-0.23	-0.50	45.45	53.37	9,562
Jiangxi 江西									
Shandong 山东	2	470	94,175	6,739	6.93	15.47	63.72	55.22	97,242
Central-South 中南	163	229	33,669	-33	-0.08	-0.21	30.33	64.39	43,031
Henan 河南	36	204	45,374	1,156	2.65	12.20	44.91	78.31	43,667
Hubei 湖北	12	254	43,307	140	0.34	1.47	38.13	76.85	41,070
Hunan 湖南	68	209	20,229	-1,021	-3.17	-8.72	21.97	63.62	32,198
Guangdong 广东	3	143	64,100	6,968	12.10	37.96	314.86	68.13	57,604
Guangxi 广西	44	280	40,160	-3	-0.01	-0.01	19.46	53.95	58,792
Hainan 海南									
Southwest 西南	198	212	27,437	-1,181	-2.93	-12.03	36.05	75.65	40,331
Chongqing 重庆	11	319	29,537	-1,545	-3.08	-24.24	23.60	87.31	50,223
Sichuan 四川	71	208	30,771	499	1.06	3.27	42.17	67.63	47,161
Guizhou 贵州	101	217	25,870	-2,523	-6.62	-34.45	31.57	80.80	38,130
Yunnan 云南	15	114	20,660	163	1.05	4.77	66.01	78.05	15,567
Tibet 西藏									
Northwest 西北	102	239	30,575	-288	-0.64	-2.92	31.85	78.02	44,961
Shaanxi 陕西	11	149	19,150	274	1.69	8.55	1.67	80.25	16,200
Gansu 甘肃	46	197	22,255	-418	-0.93	-8.09	34.89	88.51	44,988
Qinghai 青海	22	220	36,988	358	0.64	1.41	41.09	54.30	55,662
Ningxia 宁夏	17	479	57,942	-317	-0.54	-2.99	29.10	82.08	59,168
Xinjiang 新疆	6	122	14,248	-2,610	-14.51		31.12	104.53	17,984

3260: Ferroalloy Smelting and Refining 铁合金冶炼业

Year 年份	Number of firms 企业个数	Rate of change 变化率 (%)	Number of employees 职工人数 (人)	Rate of change 变化率 (%)	Total revenue (Mil. RMB) 总销售收入 (百万元)	Rate of change 变化率 (%)	Total profit (Mil RMB) 总利润 (百万元)	Rate of change 变化率 (%)
2000	560		159,744		17,022		-243	
2001	608	8.57	161,722	1.24	18,631	9.45	-265	-9.05
2002	648	6.58	153,039	-5.37	23,065	23.80	-253	4.53

Major Products 主要产品	Output 产量	Unit 单位
Ferro Alloy 铁合金	484	10,000 Tons 万吨

10 Main Firms with Maximal Revenue (year founded) 收入最大的十家主要企业（创办年份）	City 城市	Province 省	Telephone/fax 电话/传真	Number of employees 职工人数	Ownership 产业所有权	Revenue ('000 RMB) 销售收入(千元)	Profit('000 RMB) (rank) 利润(千元)(排名)	Total assets ('000 RMB) 总资产(千元)	Major products 主要产品
Jiangsu Jiangnan Industrial Group	Changzhou	Jiangsu	(0519)8601794		Joint Stock				Aluminium Alloy
江苏江南实业集团(1994)	常州市	江苏省	(0519)8601549	2,735	股份制	1,010,190	97,200(1)	1,049,230	铝合金
Guangxi Ba Yi Ferro Alloy (Group) Co., Ltd.	Laibin	Guangxi	(0772)6689426		State Enterprises				Ferroalloy
广西八一铁合金(集团)有限责任公司(1959)	来宾市	广西		3,032	国有独资	654,190	7,453(18)	1,354,151	铁合金
Sichuan Chuantou E Mei Ferroalloy (Group) Co., Ltd.	Leshan	Sichuan	(0833)5576237		State Enterprises				Ferroalloy
四川川投峨眉铁合金(集团)有限责任公司(1994)	乐山市	四川省	(0833)5576490	3,281	国有独资	613,852	10,079(16)	1,449,313	铁合金
Henan Dancheng Cai Xin Group Co., Ltd.	Zhoukou	Henan	(0394)3196056		State-owned				Ferroalloy
河南省郸城财鑫集团有限责任公司(2001)	周口市	河南省	(0394)3196960	2,230	国有企业	587,651	21,695(3)	352,701	铁合金
Jilin Ferroalloy Co., Ltd.	Jilin	Jilin	(0432)2707197		Joint Stock				Ferroalloy
吉林铁合金有限责任公司(1999)	吉林市	吉林省	(0432)2734458	3,680	股份制	530,000	1,500(64)	1,600,000	铁合金
Shanghai Silicon Steel Co., Ltd.	Shanghai	Shanghai	(021)65661333		State Enterprises				Silico-steel slice
上海矽钢有限公司(1958)	上海市	上海市		1,045	国有独资	400,497	37(235)	356,522	硅钢片
Hunan Ferroalloy (group)Co., Ltd.	Xiangtan	Hunan	(0732)6806089		Limited-Liability				Ferroalloy
湖南铁合金有限责任公司(2001)	湘潭市	湖南省	(0732)6806425	2,615	有限公司	350,994	-	586,612	铁合金
Shanghai Shenjia Ferroalloy Co., Ltd.	Shanghai	Shanghai	(021)56823456		Overseas Chinese-funded				Ferroalloy
上海申佳铁合金有限公司(1993)	上海市	上海市	(021)56820073	2,316	港澳台资	350,940	1,258(77)	753,910	铁合金
Jinzhou Singhorn Enterprise Co.Ltd.	Jinzhou	Liaoning	(0416)5171649		Joint Stock				Molybdenum Iron
锦州市沈宏实业股份有限公司(1990)	锦州市	辽宁省	(0416)5171920	1,000	股份制	322,190	14,680(11)	187,670	钼铁
Henan Xichuan Aluminium Industry Group	Nanyang	Henan	(0377)4260914		State-owned				Silica Iron
河南省淅川县铝业集团(1975)	南阳市	河南省	(0377)4260901	1,245	国有企业	301,373	15,387(10)	287,963	硅铁

Top 10 Cities by Revenue 销售收入排名前10位城市	Province 省	Market share 市场份额 (%)	Number of firms 企业个数
Jinzhou 锦州市	Liaoning 辽宁省	5.36	17
Shanghai 上海市	Shanghai 上海市	5.28	12
Changzhou 常州市	Jiangsu 江苏省	4.75	4
Leshan 乐山市	Sichuan 四川省	4.13	14
Laibin 来宾市	Guangxi 广西	3.84	5
Lanzhou 兰州市	Gansu 甘肃省	3.50	28
Qiannan 黔南州	Guizhou 贵州省	3.49	20
Jilin 吉林市	Jilin 吉林省	2.65	6
Zhoukou 周口市	Henan 河南省	2.57	3
Xiangxi 湘西州	Hunan 湖南省	2.52	26

10 Major Wholesalers 十家主要批发商	City 城市	Province 省	Telephone/Fax 电话/传真
China Ordins Corporation	Beijing	Beijing	(010)68962929
中国兵工物资总公司	北京市	北京市	(010)68962922
China Shougang International Trade & Engineering Corp.	Beijing	Beijing	(010)88297572
中国首钢国际贸易工程公司	北京市	北京市	(010)88297500
Tianjin Baosteel North Trade Co.,Ltd.	Tianjin	Tianjin	(022)28236341
天津宝钢北方贸易有限公司	天津市	天津市	(022)28267197
China Railway Goods & Materials Shenyang Company	Shenyang	Liaoning	(024)23506794
中国铁路物资沈阳公司	沈阳市	辽宁省	(024)23506622
Shanghai Hardware Minerals Import & Export Company	Shanghai	Shanghai	(021)63815858
上海市五金矿产进出口公司	上海市	上海市	(021)63806600
Baosteel Iron & Steel Trade Co.,Ltd. Shanghai Filiale	Shanghai	Shanghai	(021)68404611
上海宝钢钢材贸易有限公司分公司	上海市	上海市	(021)68404618
Jiangsu Foreign Trade Corpration	Nanjing	Jiangsu	(025)3190088
江苏省对外经贸股份有限公司	南京市	江苏省	(025)3190001
Nanjing Goods & Materials Industrial Group General Company	Nanjing	Jiangsu	(025)4549090
南京物资实业集团总公司	南京市	江苏省	(025)4408957
Zhejiang Metal Material Company	Hangzhou	Zhejiang	(0571)85271168
浙江省金属材料公司	杭州市	浙江省	(0571)85271111
Ma Steel International Trade & Economic Corp.	Maanshan	Anhui	(0555)2882092
马钢国际经济贸易总公司	马鞍山市	安徽省	(0555)2321079

3410: Metal Structures 金属结构制造业

The industry accounts for 0.297% of the total revenue of China's industrial sector in 2002. The rate of return on assets is 4.06%. 84.17% of all firms in the industry made a profit while 15.83% had negative returns.The top province in terms of the industry's revenue is Shanghai, accounting for 16.45% of the total revenue.
2002年本行业收入占全行业的 0.297%，资产利润率为 4.06%。84.17%的企业赢利，15.83%的企业亏损。收入最高的省为上海市，占本行业的16.45%。

	Total number of firms 企业总数	Total number of employees 职工总数	Total revenue (Mil.RMB) 总销售收入(百万元)	Total profit (Mil.RMB) 总利润(百万元)	Return on assets 资产利润率(%)	Return on equity 权益利润率(%)	Labour productivity ('000 RMB/worker) 劳动生产率(千元/人)	Debts/assets 资产负债率(%)	Total assets (Mil.RMB) 总资产(百万元)
Industry Overall 行业总体	1099	169,802	31,866	1,363	4.06	10.39	54.53	60.95	33,610

	Number of firms 企业个数	Average number of employees 平均职工人数	Average revenue ('000 RMB) 平均销售收入(千元)	Average profit ('000 RMB) 平均利润(千元)	Return on assets 资产利润率(%)	Return on equity 权益利润率(%)	Labour productivity ('000 RMB/worker) 劳动生产率(千元/人)	Debts/assets 资产负债率(%)	Average total assets ('000 RMB) 平均总资产(千元)
By ownership 产业所有权									
State-owned 国有	90	289	27,427	-590	-1.07	-4.30	38.12	75.22	55,360
Collective-owned 集体	215	168	22,640	1,095	5.99	18.56	39.63	67.75	18,288
Foreign & Overseas Chinese Funded 三资	174	148	45,413	2,253	4.50	9.38	78.95	52.08	50,106
By regional distribution 地区分布									
Central-North 华北	186	144	23,482	773	2.95	9.59	41.86	69.21	26,174
Beijing 北京	65	134	19,401	589	2.62	7.36	41.51	64.38	22,470
Tianjin 天津	47	83	20,626	1,150	4.07	12.35	29.10	67.06	28,260
Hebei 河北	60	163	31,508	719	2.77	11.54	57.19	75.96	25,921
Shanxi 山西	10	394	21,543	521	1.08	3.69	17.77	70.82	48,316
Inner Mongolia 内蒙古	4	104	7,823	760	7.37	11.59	37.56	36.40	10,300
Northeast 东北	49	228	31,170	946	2.85	8.74	36.76	67.40	33,203
Liaoning 辽宁	35	173	22,133	478	2.43	7.95	28.98	69.39	19,636
Jilin 吉林	7	394	46,652	267	0.37	1.03	54.13	63.98	71,665
Heilongjiang 黑龙江	7	336	60,873	3,970	6.34	19.95	36.47	68.20	62,578
Central-East 华东	552	139	32,995	1,739	5.44	13.72	65.88	60.34	31,960
Shanghai 上海	159	102	32,966	1,749	4.89	9.79	92.73	50.05	35,742
Jiangsu 江苏	178	152	29,229	1,178	3.86	12.38	50.26	68.82	30,512
Zhejiang 浙江	95	118	40,793	2,946	8.44	23.95	93.52	64.76	34,905
Anhui 安徽	20	154	21,031	1,550	7.89	25.11	43.85	68.57	19,651
Fujian 福建	23	127	39,507	1,913	4.78	9.87	72.29	51.58	40,022
Jiangxi 江西	16	197	16,737	564	2.47	4.28	24.47	42.30	22,866
Shandong 山东	61	220	37,649	1,781	7.09	21.05	55.19	66.33	25,119
Central-South 中南	237	172	25,417	694	2.29	5.08	47.59	55.02	30,349
Henan 河南	22	158	17,600	348	1.65	7.27	25.95	77.30	21,096
Hubei 湖北	60	231	22,766	543	2.08	7.09	38.38	70.62	26,078
Hunan 湖南	15	148	15,845	-84	-0.17	-0.45	21.20	61.79	48,949
Guangdong 广东	130	150	30,230	982	3.04	5.56	63.08	45.31	32,305
Guangxi 广西	9	171	10,341	-272	-1.11	-2.78	22.92	60.12	24,569
Hainan 海南	1	108	10,187	381	4.26	7.89	32.37	46.03	8,946
Southwest 西南	43	228	30,104	879	2.34	6.77	58.54	65.36	37,513
Chongqing 重庆	6	71	15,503	1,449	5.81	14.39	85.36	59.67	24,966
Sichuan 四川	21	277	29,377	519	1.41	3.99	62.52	64.81	36,943
Guizhou 贵州	5	312	65,631	3,761	5.12	21.26	52.14	75.90	73,398
Yunnan 云南	10	196	25,638	-60	-0.19	-0.44	46.66	57.31	32,048
Tibet 西藏	1	26					9.54		
Northwest 西北	32	141	13,722	326	1.57	3.45	34.35	54.62	20,844
Shaanxi 陕西	7	219	25,523	96	0.27	0.58	40.74	53.98	35,957
Gansu 甘肃	18	86	5,215	219	2.32	6.36	37.06	63.46	9,417
Qinghai 青海	2	110	14,609	321	1.71	9.83	14.87	82.62	18,798
Ningxia 宁夏	1	582	4,376	-4,715	-5.51	-14.35	2.24	61.60	85,576
Xinjiang 新疆	4	159	33,243	2,477	8.08	11.59	48.49	30.28	30,654

3410: Metal Structures 金属结构制造业

Year 年份	Number of firms 企业个数	Rate of change 变化率 (%)	Number of employees 职工人数 (人)	Rate of change 变化率 (%)	Total revenue (Mil. RMB) 总销售收入 (百万元)	Rate of change 变化率 (%)	Total profit (Mil RMB) 总利润 (百万元)	Rate of change 变化率 (%)
2000	777		137,061		20,725		747	
2001	946	21.75	153,043	11.66	26,820	29.41	994	33.07
2002	1099	16.17	169,802	10.95	31,866	18.81	1,363	37.12

Major Products 主要产品	Output 产量	Unit 单位
Metal Structure Products 金属结构制品	252	10,000 Tons 万吨

10 Main Firms with Maximal Revenue (year founded) 收入最大的十家主要企业（创办年份）	City 城市	Province 省	Telephone/fax 电话/传真	Number of employees 职工人数	Ownership 产业所有权	Revenue ('000 RMB) 销售收入 (千元)	Profit('000 RMB) (rank) 利润(千元) (排名)	Total assets ('000 RMB) 总资产 (千元)	Major products 主要产品
Butler (Shanghai) Inc 巴特勒上海有限公司(1995)	Shanghai 上海市	Shanghai 上海市	(021)57741717 (021)57741813	379	Foreign Funded 外商投资	819,780	72,216(2)	606,047	Metal Steel Structure 钢结构
Hangzhou Dongnan Net Frame Group 浙江东南网架集团(1997)	Hangzhou 杭州市	Zhejiang 浙江省	(0571)82783318 (0571)82783470	1,255	Limited-Liability 有限公司	805,864	101,579(1)	774,064	Metal Net Frame 金属网架
Shanghai ABC Steel Structure Co., Ltd. 上海美建钢结构有限公司(1994)	Shanghai 上海市	Shanghai 上海市	(021)69154733 (021)62783000	128	Foreign Funded 外商投资	527,797	12,134(21)	139,291	Steel Structure Components 钢结构件
Jiangnan Heavy Industry Co., Ltd. 江南重工股份有限公司(1997)	Shanghai 上海市	Shanghai 上海市	(021)53023456 (021)63141103	991	Joint Stock 股份制	467,736	35,673(5)	1,102,847	Large-type Steel Structure大型钢结构
Heilongjiang Shengli Real Estate Development Group Co., Ltd. 黑龙江生力房地产开发集团有限责任公司(1997)	Qiqihar 齐齐哈尔市	Heilongjiang 黑龙江省	(0452)6867728 (0452)6851617	218	Limited-Liability 有限公司	300,383	27,624(7)	198,700	Construction Metal Products建筑金属制品
Hebei Xingtai Longhai Iron And Steel Products Co., Ltd. 河北省邢台市龙海钢铁制品有限公司(2000)	Xingtai 邢台市	Hebei 河北省	(0319)3976927 (0319)3976180	399	Limited-Liability 有限公司	291,513	1,890(187)	221,261	Coil Strip 盘条
Zhejiang Qiang Huang Building Materials Co., Ltd. 浙江墙煌建材有限公司(1996)	Shaoxing 绍兴市	Zhejiang 浙江省	(0575)4881477	193	Foreign Funded 外商投资	265,023	7,947(35)	169,958	Aluminium And Plastic Mulriple Board铝塑复合板
Sihui Aluminium Alloy Shapes Factory 四会市铝合金型材厂(1996)	Zhaoqing 肇庆市	Guangdong 广东省	(0758)3662988 (0758)3662507	179	Private Enterprises 私营独资	251,739	2,150(162)	78,912	Aluminium Alloy Shapes铝合金型材
Guizhou Electric Circuit Equipment Factory 贵州电力线路器材厂(1958)	Guiyang 贵阳市	Guizhou 贵州省	(0851)3833075 (0851)3833073	901	State-owned 国有企业	251,510	10,437(24)	294,167	Galvanized Iron Tower 镀锌铁塔
Shanghai Wei Meng Te Special Steel Tube Co., Ltd. 上海维蒙特异型钢管有限公司(1994)	Shanghai 上海市	Shanghai 上海市	(021)57609200 (021)57609222	210	Foreign Funded 外商投资	244,254	38,682(4)	236,915	lampstandard 路灯杆

Top 10 Cities by Revenue 销售收入排名前10位城市	Province 省	Market share 市场份额 (%)	Number of firms 企业个数
Shanghai 上海市	Shanghai 上海市	16.45	159
Hangzhou 杭州市	Zhejiang 浙江省	7.61	47
Beijing 北京市	Beijing 北京市	3.96	65
Suzhou 苏州市	Jiangsu 江苏省	3.28	30
Guangzhou 广州市	Guangdong 广东省	3.15	32
Tianjin 天津市	Tianjin 天津市	3.04	47
Wuxi 无锡市	Jiangsu 江苏省	2.88	37
Nanjing 南京市	Jiangsu 江苏省	2.63	22
Hengshui 衡水市	Hebei 河北省	2.17	18
Shenzhen 深圳市	Guangdong 广东省	2.12	16

10 Major Wholesalers 十家主要批发商	City 城市	Province 省	Telephone/Fax 电话/传真
China Ordins Corporation 中国兵工物资总公司	Beijing 北京市	Beijing 北京市	(010)68962929 (010)68962922
China Shougang International Trade & Engineering Corp. 中国首钢国际贸易工程公司	Beijing 北京市	Beijing 北京市	(010)88297572 (010)88297500
Tianjin Baosteel North Trade Co.,Ltd. 天津宝钢北方贸易有限公司	Tianjin 天津市	Tianjin 天津市	(022)28236341 (022)28267197
China Railway Goods & Materials Shenyang Company 中国铁路物资沈阳公司	Shenyang 沈阳市	Liaoning 辽宁省	(024)23506794 (024)23506622
Shanghai Hardware Minerals Import & Export Company 上海市五金矿产进出口公司	Shanghai 上海市	Shanghai 上海市	(021)63815858 (021)63806600
Baosteel Iron & Steel Trade Co.,Ltd. Shanghai Filiale 上海宝钢钢材贸易有限公司分公司	Shanghai 上海市	Shanghai 上海市	(021)68404611 (021)68404618
Jiangsu Foreign Trade Corpration 江苏省对外经贸股份有限公司	Nanjing 南京市	Jiangsu 江苏省	(025)3190088 (025)3190001
Nanjing Goods & Materials Industrial Group General Company 南京物资实业集团总公司	Nanjing 南京市	Jiangsu 江苏省	(025)4549090 (025)4408957
Zhejiang Metal Material Company 浙江省金属材料公司	Hangzhou 杭州市	Zhejiang 浙江省	(0571)85271168 (0571)85271111
Ma Steel International Trade & Economic Corp. 马钢国际经济贸易总公司	Maanshan 马鞍山市	Anhui 安徽省	(0555)2882092 (0555)2321079

3420: Cast Iron Pipe 铸铁管制造业

The industry accounts for 0.093% of the total revenue of China's industrial sector in 2002. The rate of return on assets is 2.86%. 78.96% of all firms in the industry made a profit while 21.04% had negative returns.The top province in terms of the industry's revenue is Zhejiang, accounting for 17.58% of the total revenue.
2002年本行业收入占全行业的 0.093%，资产利润率为 2.86%。78.96%的企业赢利，21.04%的企业亏损。收入最高的省为浙江省，占本行业的17.58%。

	Total number of firms 企业总数	Total number of employees 职工总数	Total revenue (Mil.RMB) 总销售收入（百万元）	Total profit (Mil.RMB) 总利润（百万元）	Return on assets 资产利润率（%）	Return on equity 权益利润率（%）	Labour productivity ('000 RMB/ worker) 劳动生产率（千元/人）	Debts/ assets 资产负债率（%）	Total assets (Mil.RMB) 总资产（百万元）
Industry Overall 行业总体	309	49,630	10,006	260	2.86	8.62	54.57	66.88	9,095

	Number of firms 企业个数	Average number of employees 平均职工人数	Average revenue ('000 RMB) 平均销售收入（千元）	Average profit ('000 RMB) 平均利润（千元）	Return on assets 资产利润率（%）	Return on equity 权益利润率（%）	Labour productivity ('000 RMB/ worker) 劳动生产率（千元/人）	Debts/ assets 资产负债率（%）	Average total assets ('000 RMB) 平均总资产（千元）
By ownership 产业所有权									
State-owned 国有	17	206	12,223	-300	-0.74	-5.12	22.22	85.57	40,646
Collective-owned 集体	84	146	32,803	1,121	5.57	13.71	59.15	59.39	20,136
Foreign & Overseas Chinese Funded 三资	34	172	62,804	1,150	1.49	4.67	88.57	68.00	76,966
By regional distribution 地区分布									
Central-North 华北	59	184	19,005	1,046	5.02	14.18	41.28	64.56	20,828
Beijing 北京	12	271	16,273	1,359	6.46	20.16	20.90	67.93	21,023
Tianjin 天津	4	85	17,563	433	5.63	21.71	167.88	74.08	7,685
Hebei 河北	21	144	22,932	2,014	11.37	38.72	59.14	70.63	17,709
Shanxi 山西	18	198	18,003	259	1.25	3.76	36.34	66.69	20,683
Inner Mongolia 内蒙古	4	162	12,535	-811	-1.61	-2.86	21.38	43.75	50,415
Northeast 东北	30	173	19,596	-52	-0.20	-0.90	28.28	78.10	26,452
Liaoning 辽宁	22	148	21,418	125	0.50	4.14	31.02	88.01	25,241
Jilin 吉林	2	112	490	-93	-1.02	-3.36	8.21	69.70	9,145
Heilongjiang 黑龙江	6	285	19,286	-689	-1.88	-4.06	25.66	53.78	36,662
Central-East 华东	102	167	54,117	1,739	4.67	12.59	79.86	62.90	37,241
Shanghai 上海	2	299	93,462	4,274	6.24	19.21	56.04	67.52	68,484
Jiangsu 江苏	34	165	45,652	1,569	5.64	21.92	65.78	74.26	27,802
Zhejiang 浙江	17	207	103,496	4,796	7.27	16.58	88.36	56.14	65,952
Anhui 安徽	3	216	69,835	-5,155	-4.31	-8.62	59.38	50.04	119,634
Fujian 福建	8	53	11,620	-605	-4.04	-9.26	56.01	56.38	14,968
Jiangxi 江西	1	90	7,643	90	1.77	10.20	27.69	82.63	5,079
Shandong 山东	37	166	46,252	1,464	4.87	13.64	94.79	64.27	30,039
Central-South 中南	81	148	28,371	243	0.76	2.72	50.04	72.05	31,983
Henan 河南	19	222	15,605	805	9.39	27.46	26.93	65.82	8,578
Hubei 湖北	10	219	26,343	919	1.59	7.71	48.54	79.32	57,638
Hunan 湖南	9	128	11,884	-487	-2.28	-5.28	25.73	56.82	21,365
Guangdong 广东	40	106	36,581	-28	-0.07	-0.25	70.53	72.33	40,313
Guangxi 广西	2	101	82,667	351	1.79	3.87	252.17	53.62	19,532
Hainan 海南	1	23	2,601				117.04	75.97	7,398
Southwest 西南	17	176	21,095	-30	-0.09	-0.27	35.43	64.86	31,479
Chongqing 重庆	6	194	30,010	390	0.81	2.01	36.95	59.82	48,225
Sichuan 四川	6	181	23,131	114	0.41	1.54	50.49	73.56	28,008
Guizhou 贵州	2	45	8,352	-218	-3.12	-5.27	42.71	40.83	6,991
Yunnan 云南	3	215	7,690	-1,030	-4.85	-16.21	6.26	70.09	21,251
Tibet 西藏									
Northwest 西北	20	81	6,014	148	1.99	3.62	30.74	45.07	7,431
Shaanxi 陕西	7	131	7,010	111	0.91	1.62	15.26	43.72	12,148
Gansu 甘肃	12	53	5,445	163	4.04	9.37	54.13	56.93	4,026
Qinghai 青海									
Ningxia 宁夏									
Xinjiang 新疆	1	60	5,878	226	1.48	1.74	20.48	15.01	15,275

Year 年份	Number of firms 企业个数	Rate of change 变化率(%)	Number of employees 职工人数(人)	Rate of change 变化率(%)	Total revenue (Mil. RMB) 总销售收入(百万元)	Rate of change 变化率(%)	Total profit (Mil RMB) 总利润(百万元)	Rate of change 变化率(%)
2000	305		50,896		8,071		184	
2001	334	9.51	54,453	6.99	10,303	27.65	405	120.11
2002	309	-7.49	49,630	-8.86	10,006	-2.88	260	-35.80

Major Products 主要产品	Output 产量	Unit 单位
Cast Iron Pipe 铸铁管	189	10,000 Tons 万吨

10 Main Firms with Maximal Revenue (year founded) 收入最大的十家主要企业(创办年份)	City 城市	Province 省	Telephone/fax 电话/传真	Number of employees 职工人数	Ownership 产业所有权	Revenue ('000 RMB) 销售收入(千元)	Profit('000 RMB) (rank) 利润(千元)(排名)	Total assets ('000 RMB) 总资产(千元)	Major products 主要产品
ZheJiang Yule Industry & Trade Group Company	Shaoxing	Zhejiang	(0575)2011808		Collective-owned				Heat Zinc-plating Steel Tube热
浙江虞乐工贸集团公司(1994)	绍兴市	浙江省	(0575)2011808	938	集体企业	901,355	51,509(1)	419,450	镀锌钢管
Zhejiang Weiling Metal Group Co., Ltd.	Hangzhou	Zhejiang	(0571)86684668		Private Owned				Steel Strip
浙江威陵金属集团有限公司(1996)	杭州市	浙江省	(0571)86681498	1,544	私营企业	600,595	17,014(4)	416,594	钢带
Wuxi Seamless Oil Special Pipe Co., Ltd.	Wuxi	Jiangsu	(0510)5226516		Foreign Funded				Steel Pipe For Pertroleum石油
无锡西姆莱斯石油专用管制造有限公司(1999)	无锡市	江苏省	(0510)5226516	485	外商投资	388,310	40,760(2)	423,091	专用钢管
Qingdao Northern Steel & Pipes Co., ltd.	Qingdao	Shandong	(0532)7809778		Foreign Funded				Cast Iorn Pipe
青岛北钢铸管有限公司(1992)	青岛市	山东省	(0532)7809228	610	外商投资	253,474	-	296,629	铸铁管
Dongguan Qianhua Hardware Factory Co., Ltd.	Dongguan	Guangdong	(0769)5539156		Overseas Chinese-funded				Cast Iorn Pipe
东莞谦华五金厂有限公司(1993)	东莞市	广东省	(0769)5539158	215	港澳台资	196,299	4,832(14)	93,430	铸铁管
Shanghai Shentong Pipeline Co., Ltd.	Shanghai	Shanghai	(021)56754727		Overseas Chinese-funded				Nodular Pipe离
上海申同管道有限公司(2000)	上海市	上海市	(021)56754727	560	港澳台资	175,354	8,139(8)	131,228	心球墨管
Saint-gobain Pipelines Co., Ltd.	Maanshan	Anhui	(0555)3503078		Foreign Funded				Cast Iorn Pipe
马鞍山市圣戈班管道系统有限公司(1999)	马鞍山市	安徽省	(0555)3503328	440	外商投资	159,845	-	325,799	铸铁管
Chongqing Iron and Steel Group Steel Tube Co., Ltd.	Chongqing	Chongqing	(023)62590618		State Enterprises				Common Pipe
重庆钢铁集团钢管有限责任公司(1966)	重庆市	重庆市	(023)62590757	760	国有独资	144,318	3,860(20)	180,668	普管
Dongguan Li Qun Metal Factory Co., Ltd.	Dongguan	Guangdong	(0769)8826038		Foreign Funded				Iorn Pipe
东莞力群金属厂有限公司(1995)	东莞市	广东省	(0769)8826056	150	外商投资	128,495	262(127)	202,449	铁管
Jinan Changhong High-Tech Compound Pipe Co., Ltd	Jinan	Shandong	(0531)7226788		Joint Stock				Special Cast Pipe
济南长虹高科技复合管有限责任公司(1995)	济南市	山东省		130	股份制	125,160	6,455(10)	16,654	特种铸管

Top 10 Cities by Revenue 销售收入排名前10位城市	Province 省	Market share 市场份额(%)	Number of firms 企业个数
Shaoxing 绍兴市	Zhejiang 浙江省	9.01	1
Hangzhou 杭州市	Zhejiang 浙江省	7.12	6
Wuxi 无锡市	Jiangsu 江苏省	6.13	12
Zibo 淄博市	Shandong 山东省	5.74	3
Dongguan 东莞市	Guangdong 广东省	5.28	5
Foshan 佛山市	Guangdong 广东省	3.70	9
Nanjing 南京市	Jiangsu 江苏省	3.37	7
Qingdao 青岛市	Shandong 山东省	3.30	7
Yancheng 盐城市	Jiangsu 江苏省	3.05	2
Baoding 保定市	Hebei 河北省	2.60	4

10 Major Wholesalers 十家主要批发商	City 城市	Province 省	Telephone/Fax 电话/传真
China Ordins Corporation	Beijing	Beijing	(010)68962929
中国兵工物资总公司	北京市	北京市	(010)68962922
China Shougang International Trade & Engineering Corp.	Beijing	Beijing	(010)88297572
中国首钢国际贸易工程公司	北京市	北京市	(010)88297500
Tianjin Baosteel North Trade Co.,Ltd.	Tianjin	Tianjin	(022)28236341
天津宝钢北方贸易有限公司	天津市	天津市	(022)28267197
China Railway Goods & Materials Shenyang Company	Shenyang	Liaoning	(024)23506794
中国铁路物资沈阳公司	沈阳市	辽宁省	(024)23506622
Shanghai Hardware Minerals Import & Export Company	Shanghai	Shanghai	(021)63815858
上海市五金矿产进出口公司	上海市	上海市	(021)63806600
Baosteel Iron & Steel Trade Co.,Ltd. Shanghai Filiale	Shanghai	Shanghai	(021)68404611
上海宝钢钢材贸易有限公司分公司	上海市	上海市	(021)68404618
Jiangsu Foreign Trade Corpration	Nanjing	Jiangsu	(025)3190088
江苏省对外经贸股份有限公司	南京市	江苏省	(025)3190001
Nanjing Goods & Materials Industrial Group General Company	Nanjing	Jiangsu	(025)4549090
南京物资实业集团总公司	南京市	江苏省	(025)4408957
Zhejiang Metal Material Company	Hangzhou	Zhejiang	(0571)85271168
浙江省金属材料公司	杭州市	浙江省	(0571)85271111
Ma Steel International Trade & Economic Corp.	Maanshan	Anhui	(0555)2882092
马钢国际经济贸易总公司	马鞍山市	安徽省	(0555)2321079

3431: Cutting Tools 切削工具制造业

The industry accounts for 0.081% of the total revenue of China's industrial sector in 2002. The rate of return on assets is 4.70%. 82.53% of all firms in the industry made a profit while 17.47% had negative returns.The top province in terms of the industry's revenue is Jiangsu, accounting for 42.55% of the total revenue.
2002年本行业收入占全行业的 0.081%，资产利润率为 4.70%。82.53%的企业赢利，17.47%的企业亏损。收入最高的省为江苏省，占本行业的42.55%。

	Total number of firms 企业总数	Total number of employees 职工总数	Total revenue (Mil.RMB) 总销售收入（百万元）	Total profit (Mil.RMB) 总利润（百万元）	Return on assets 资产利润率（%）	Return on equity 权益利润率（%）	Labour productivity ('000 RMB/ worker) 劳动生产率（千元/人）	Debts/ assets 资产负债率（%）	Total assets (Mil.RMB) 总资产（百万元）
Industry Overall 行业总体	292	79,108	8,701	574	4.70	13.75	37.26	65.83	12,212

	Number of firms 企业个数	Average number of employees 平均职工人数	Average revenue ('000 RMB) 平均销售收入（千元）	Average profit ('000 RMB) 平均利润（千元）	Return on assets 资产利润率（%）	Return on equity 权益利润率（%）	Labour productivity ('000 RMB/ worker) 劳动生产率（千元/人）	Debts/ assets 资产负债率（%）	Average total assets ('000 RMB) 平均总资产（千元）
By ownership 产业所有权									
State-owned 国有	46	487	18,611	-1,166	-1.40	-11.92	17.67	88.29	83,551
Collective-owned 集体	41	223	16,608	210	0.98	3.37	23.23	70.92	21,413
Foreign & Overseas Chinese Funded 三资	62	148	29,938	3,515	8.11	12.98	67.37	37.52	43,352
By regional distribution 地区分布									
Central-North 华北	44	204	21,750	1,691	4.04	11.51	40.80	64.92	41,897
Beijing 北京	6	114	4,163	87	0.22	7.27	7.09	97.02	39,953
Tianjin 天津	8	226	11,441	-1,427	-4.31	-30.41	22.80	85.83	33,128
Hebei 河北	25	168	31,867	3,889	10.23	17.68	71.61	42.13	38,014
Shanxi 山西	5	456	8,758	-2,384	-3.07	-22.94	8.35	86.62	77,671
Inner Mongolia 内蒙古									
Northeast 东北	24	360	17,386	-1,316	-2.06	-15.35	17.32	86.59	63,927
Liaoning 辽宁	13	119	12,843	258	1.27	3.49	37.93	63.79	20,395
Jilin 吉林	2	389	16,058	1,939	3.46	26.14	27.69	86.76	56,031
Heilongjiang 黑龙江	9	701	24,243	-4,313	-3.35	-40.89	11.01	91.80	128,561
Central-East 华东	162	248	36,441	2,582	7.19	17.31	45.77	58.50	35,927
Shanghai 上海	27	218	34,460	1,698	3.06	7.32	41.14	58.26	55,557
Jiangsu 江苏	66	324	56,095	4,188	10.57	28.18	57.98	62.49	39,628
Zhejiang 浙江	36	130	12,626	504	3.42	8.88	28.74	61.50	14,731
Anhui 安徽	9	101	15,498	653	6.68	10.60	42.52	36.98	9,769
Fujian 福建	9	87	12,132	1,414	7.09	8.83	43.65	19.70	19,944
Jiangxi 江西	5	145	7,576	-402	-1.05	-1.89	15.65	44.29	38,204
Shandong 山东	10	582	52,961	6,125	8.55	20.52	23.78	58.31	71,596
Central-South 中南	41	213	21,016	2,329	8.47	20.69	33.58	59.05	27,485
Henan 河南	6	228	8,123	-196	-0.68	-4.51	13.60	84.91	28,805
Hubei 湖北	7	179	25,055	503	3.75	11.98	53.25	68.68	13,405
Hunan 湖南	8	108	13,726	2,924	5.63	13.80	45.62	59.18	51,922
Guangdong 广东	18	276	27,778	3,799	15.71	29.82	32.27	47.33	24,191
Guangxi 广西	1	147	27,236	1,510	21.26	22.84	54.63	6.90	7,102
Hainan 海南	1	131	499	-137	-5.93	-27.13	0.77	78.13	2,309
Southwest 西南	15	518	26,304	1,061	1.38	5.52	24.65	74.93	76,659
Chongqing 重庆	2	228	27,496	2,477	6.33	10.08	27.65	37.19	39,139
Sichuan 四川	7	651	33,250	1,438	1.30	11.02	27.59	88.22	110,803
Guizhou 贵州	5	540	21,208	374	0.65	1.27	19.46	48.43	57,285
Yunnan 云南	1	63	781	-978	-10.23	-1,459.70	11.81	99.30	9,558
Tibet 西藏									
Northwest 西北	6	799	27,791	223	0.18	0.87	22.39	79.05	122,931
Shaanxi 陕西	3	1,367	50,454	58	0.03	0.15	23.94	82.28	222,256
Gansu 甘肃	1	89	878				5.29	100.00	18,984
Qinghai 青海	2	303	7,252	583	2.25	3.20	14.42	29.78	25,916
Ningxia 宁夏									
Xinjiang 新疆									

3431: Cutting Tools 切削工具制造业

Year 年份	Number of firms 企业个数	Rate of change 变化率(%)	Number of employees 职工人数(人)	Rate of change 变化率(%)	Total revenue (Mil. RMB) 总销售收入(百万元)	Rate of change 变化率(%)	Total profit (Mil RMB) 总利润(百万元)	Rate of change 变化率(%)
2000	260		72,113		5,609		141	
2001	276	6.15	74,873	3.83	6,448	14.96	239	69.50
2002	292	5.80	79,108	5.66	8,701	34.94	574	140.17

Major Products 主要产品	Output 产量	Unit 单位
Metal Cutting Tools 金属切削工具	186,305	10,000 Pieces 万件

10 Main Firms with Maximal Revenue (year founded) 收入最大的十家主要企业(创办年份)	City 城市	Province 省	Telephone/fax 电话/传真	Number of employees 职工人数	Ownership 产业所有权	Revenue ('000 RMB) 销售收入(千元)	Profit('000 RMB) (rank) 利润(千元)(排名)	Total assets ('000 RMB) 总资产(千元)	Major products 主要产品
Jiangsu Tiangong Tools Co., Ltd. 江苏天工工具股份有限公司(1984)	Zhenjiang 镇江市	Jiangsu 江苏省	(0511)6312323 (0511)6312403	4,750	Private Owned 私营企业	918,005	93,814(1)	554,142	Twist Drill 麻花钻
Jiangsu Feida Group Company 江苏飞达工具集团股份有限公司(1992)	Zhenjiang 镇江市	Jiangsu 江苏省	(0511)6312945 (0511)6312066	4,800	Private Enterprises 私营独资	883,313	89,163(2)	423,327	Twist Drill 麻花钻
Shandong Weida Machine Tool Group Corp. 山东威达机床工具集团总公司(1995)	Weihai 威海市	Shandong 山东省	(0631)8545158 (0631)8545388	3,205	Limited-Liability 有限公司	279,792	54,109(4)	278,053	Drill 钻头
G . F . S . Co., Ltd 上海正峰工业有限公司(1997)	Shanghai 上海市	Shanghai 上海市	(021)59159626 (021)59159626	822	Foreign Funded 外商投资	268,839	15,048(10)	297,047	Electric Tool 电动工具
Dangyang Dangong Industrial General Company 丹阳市丹工实业总公司(1965)	Zhenjiang 镇江市	Jiangsu 江苏省	(0511)63100029	1,089	Private Owned 私营企业	181,540	14,500(11)	157,610	Twist Drill 麻花钻
Shanghai Tools Works Co., Ltd 上海工具厂有限公司(1949)	Shanghai 上海市	Shanghai 上海市	(021)65386538 (021)65381198	1,752	State-owned 国有企业	180,547	811(83)	493,976	Metal Cutting Tool金属 切削工具
Chengdu Cheng Liang Group Company 成都成量集团公司(1957)	Chengdu 成都市	Sichuan 四川省	(028)83241923 (028)83241923	3,157	State-owned 国有企业	150,577	5,142(22)	576,939	Cutting Tool 切削工具
Yancheng Petroleum Machine Factory 盐城市石油机械厂(1976)	Yancheng 盐城市	Jiangsu 江苏省	(0515)8802237	85	Joint Stock 股份制	104,610	3,190(34)	10,510	Screw Dilling Tools 螺杆钻具
HarBin NO.1 Tool works 哈尔滨第一工具厂(1948)	Harbin 哈尔滨市	Heilongjiang 黑龙江省	(0451)8340440 (0451)8322331	3,357	State-owned 国有企业	103,820	-	706,373	Cutting Tool 刃具
Jiangsu Feng Yu Tools Co., Ltd. 江苏丰裕工具有限公司(1996)	Zhenjiang 镇江市	Jiangsu 江苏省	(0511)6311611 (0511)6318618	750	Private Owned 私营企业	98,630	248(150)	49,702	Twist Drill 麻花钻

Top 10 Cities by Revenue 销售收入排名前10位城市	Province 省	Market share 市场份额(%)	Number of firms 企业个数
Zhenjiang 镇江市	Jiangsu 江苏省	31.74	29
Shanghai 上海市	Shanghai 上海市	10.69	27
Weihai 威海市	Shandong 山东省	3.46	3
Yancheng 盐城市	Jiangsu 江苏省	3.12	4
Langfang 廊坊市	Hebei 河北省	2.92	6
Xingtai 邢台市	Hebei 河北省	2.53	9
Chengdu 成都市	Sichuan 四川省	2.28	4
Shijiazhuang 石家庄市	Hebei 河北省	2.17	5
Wuxi 无锡市	Jiangsu 江苏省	2.16	7
Harbin 哈尔滨市	Heilongjiang 黑龙江省	1.97	5

10 Major Wholesalers 十家主要批发商	City 城市	Province 省	Telephone/Fax 电话/传真
SU MEC 中设江苏机械设备进出口(集团)公司	Nanjing 南京市	Jiangsu 江苏省	(025)4511888 (025)4411772
China Poster Mobile Communications Equipment Co.,Ltd. 中邮普泰移动通信设备股份有限公司	Beijing 北京市	Beijing 北京市	(010)66426993 (010)66426837
Sino Kama Co., Ltd. 中泰凯马股份有限公司	Shanghai 上海市	Shanghai 上海市	(021)62031188 (021)62030851
China Huayuan Group Co.,Ltd. 中国华源集团有限公司	Shanghai 上海市	Shanghai 上海市	(021)62031188 (021)62032288
Zhejiang Crand Imp.& Exp.Co.,Ltd. 浙江远大进出口有限公司	Ningbo 宁波市	Zhejiang 浙江省	(0574)87720170 (0574)87723350
Shandong Machinery Import & Export Group Corporation 山东省机械进出口集团公司	Qingdao 青岛市	Shandong 山东省	(0532)2661628 (0532)2991655
Qingdao Haier International Trade Co.,Ltd. 青岛海尔国际贸易有限公司	Qingdao 青岛市	Shandong 山东省	(0532)8938337 (0532)8939494
Guangdong Machinery Import & Export Group Corporation 广东省机械进出口集团公司	Guangzhou 广州市	Guangdong 广东省	(020)87782168 (020)87771803
China National Machinery Equipment Import & Export Corporation 中国机械设备进出口总公司	Beijing 北京市	Beijing 北京市	(010)63474506 (010)63261865
Beijing Cellstar Co.,Ltd. 北京蜂星事达电讯有限公司	Beijing 北京市	Beijing 北京市	(010)64602050 (010)64672648

3434: Moulds 模具制造业

The industry accounts for 0.107% of the total revenue of China's industrial sector in 2002. The rate of return on assets is 4.39%. 83.02% of all firms in the industry made a profit while 16.98% had negative returns.The top province in terms of the industry's revenue is Guangdong, accounting for 37.00% of the total revenue.
2002年本行业收入占全行业的 0.107%，资产利润率为 4.39%。83.02%的企业赢利，16.98%的企业亏损。收入最高的省为广东省，占本行业的37.00%。

	Total number of firms 企业总数	Total number of employees 职工总数	Total revenue (Mil.RMB) 总销售收入 (百万元)	Total profit (Mil.RMB) 总利润 (百万元)	Return on assets 资产利润率 (%)	Return on equity 权益利润率 (%)	Labour productivity ('000 RMB/ worker) 劳动生产率 (千元/人)	Debts/ assets 资产负债率 (%)	Total assets (Mil.RMB) 总资产 (百万元)
Industry Overall 行业总体	524	85,411	11,494	685	4.39	9.61	44.85	54.34	·15,616

	Number of firms 企业个数	Average number of employees 平均职工人数	Average revenue ('000 RMB) 平均销售收入 (千元)	Average profit ('000 RMB) 平均利润 (千元)	Return on assets 资产利润率 (%)	Return on equity 权益利润率 (%)	Labour productivity ('000 RMB/ worker) 劳动生产率 (千元/人)	Debts/ assets 资产负债率 (%)	Average total assets ('000 RMB) 平均总资产 (千元)
By ownership 产业所有权									
State-owned 国有	62	132	6,488	143	0.62	1.86	26.05	66.88	23,108
Collective-owned 集体	52	121	21,950	1,319	7.83	20.39	60.29	61.60	16,848
Foreign & Overseas Chinese Funded 三资	175	238	30,977	1,808	3.57	6.92	43.73	48.40	50,631
By regional distribution 地区分布									
Central-North 华北	57	96	10,918	252	1.57	4.05	46.29	61.25	16,039
Beijing 北京	18	74	14,005	-542	-3.60	-10.55	51.99	65.88	15,036
Tianjin 天津	27	77	8,292	775	4.84	12.03	49.56	59.77	16,019
Hebei 河北	10	170	13,105	462	2.58	6.97	43.05	63.04	17,926
Shanxi 山西	1	307	15,303	-1,453	-5.28	-6.92	23.47	23.59	27,496
Inner Mongolia 内蒙古	1	42						85.36	4,310
Northeast 东北	23	123	15,100	866	3.49	6.94	38.87	49.63	24,793
Liaoning 辽宁	17	146	19,485	1,174	3.70	7.01	42.26	47.18	31,702
Jilin 吉林	4	58	2,653	302	9.13	24.80	19.78	63.21	3,309
Heilongjiang 黑龙江	2	57	2,722	-625	-6.91		3.71	112.83	9,033
Central-East 华东	259	140	21,074	1,346	5.04	11.78	51.10	57.23	26,722
Shanghai 上海	66	93	16,032	1,312	4.45	9.11	56.44	51.17	29,478
Jiangsu 江苏	48	199	32,220	849	1.89	5.45	51.21	65.42	45,041
Zhejiang 浙江	87	107	15,127	1,315	8.21	21.19	43.94	61.28	16,023
Anhui 安徽	6	124	9,912	151	0.93	2.39	29.57	61.28	16,312
Fujian 福建	15	300	43,641	4,303	10.11	15.81	67.79	36.07	42,564
Jiangxi 江西	4	47	4,806	100	1.08	1.45	28.88	25.04	9,205
Shandong 山东	33	172	24,366	1,246	6.36	16.52	47.18	61.49	19,580
Central-South 中南	163	215	29,006	1,654	4.27	8.41	40.91	49.25	38,760
Henan 河南	14	75	10,868	349	3.59	9.64	45.33	62.76	9,712
Hubei 湖北	11	228	22,573	3,501	9.61	15.16	51.49	36.60	36,424
Hunan 湖南	6	146	10,685	311	4.19	18.64	26.02	77.53	7,422
Guangdong 广东	131	233	32,464	1,712	3.92	7.77	40.46	49.57	43,716
Guangxi 广西	1	145	10,652				10.18	66.30	9,964
Hainan 海南									
Southwest 西南	10	324	23,700	3,434	5.41	13.09	41.50	58.71	63,523
Chongqing 重庆	2	93	5,402	-981	-1.96	-23.51	13.90	91.67	50,100
Sichuan 四川	8	382	28,274	4,538	6.78	14.29	43.18	52.53	66,879
Guizhou 贵州									
Yunnan 云南									
Tibet 西藏									
Northwest 西北	12	217	8,459	-153	-0.71	-3.08	18.66	76.84	21,466
Shaanxi 陕西	6	349	12,581	-180	-0.54	-3.74	18.90	85.66	33,620
Gansu 甘肃	4	88	3,788	20	0.25	0.40	18.07	36.92	7,878
Qinghai 青海									
Ningxia 宁夏	1	60	8,107	1	0.01	0.03	37.17	56.69	9,051
Xinjiang 新疆	1	99	2,769	-837	-5.47	-12.10	4.35	54.80	15,307

3434: Moulds 模具制造业

Year 年份	Number of firms 企业个数	Rate of change 变化率 (%)	Number of employees 职工人数 (人)	Rate of change 变化率 (%)	Total revenue (Mil. RMB) 总销售收入 (百万元)	Rate of change 变化率 (%)	Total profit (Mil RMB) 总利润 (百万元)	Rate of change 变化率 (%)
2000	359		55,986		6,473		452	
2001	457	27.30	70,339	25.64	8,792	35.83	375	-17.04
2002	524	14.66	85,411	21.43	11,494	30.73	685	82.67

Major Products 主要产品	Output 产量	Unit 单位
Mould 模具	1,470	10,000 Sets 万套

10 Main Firms with Maximal Revenue (year founded) 收入最大的十家主要企业（创办年份）	City 城市	Province 省	Telephone/fax 电话/传真	Number of employees 职工人数	Ownership 产业所有权	Revenue ('000 RMB) 销售收入 (千元)	Profit('000 RMB) (rank) 利润(千元) (排名)	Total assets ('000 RMB) 总资产 (千元)	Major products 主要产品
Heyuan Longkee Metal Products Co., Ltd.	Heyuan	Guangdong	(0762)3210519		Overseas Chinese-funded				Metal Mould
河源龙记金属制品有限公司(1998)	河源市	广东省	(0762)3210501	1,050	港澳台资	389,630	64,910(1)	626,775	金属模具
Jiangsu Huayuan Group Company	Wuxi	Jiangsu	(0510)6301454		Collective-owned				Electronics Plate-making
江苏省花元集团公司(1997)	无锡市	江苏省	(0510)6301271	1,580	集体企业	278,530	20,572(6)	315,726	电子制版
Zhuhai Yue Mao Science & Technology Industrial Co., Ltd.	Zhuhai	Guangdong	(0756)8682653		Limited-Liability				Mould
珠海市粤茂科技实业有限公司(1999)	珠海市	广东省		193	有限公司	186,615	3,690(52)	78,985	模具
Fujian SBS Zipper Science & Technology Co., ltd.	Quanzhou	Fujian	(0595)8283788		Overseas Chinese-funded				Mould
福建浔兴拉链科技股份有限公司(1992)	泉州市	福建省	(0595)8282502	1,580	港澳台资	168,200	11,119(11)	162,837	模具
Fujian Putian Xiefeng Mould Co., Ltd.	Putian	Fujian	(0594)2895960		Foreign Funded				Mould
福建省莆田协丰模具有限公司(1991)	莆田市	福建省	(0594)2897872	787	外商投资	165,215	37,813(2)	117,107	模具
Jiantao Laminose Board (Kunshan) Co.,Ltd.	Suzhou	Jiangsu	(0512)57440038		Overseas Chinese-funded				Copper-cladding Board
建滔积层板(昆山)有限公司(2001)	苏州市	江苏省	(0512)57450506	140	港澳台资	148,971	928(164)	212,325	覆铜板
Kaiping Yaqi Plastic Machinery Mould Factory	Jiangmen	Guangdong	(0750)2619988		Overseas Chinese-funded				Blow Bottling Machine
开平雅琪塑胶机械模具厂(1998)	江门市	广东省	(0750)2613178	300	港澳台资	147,800	1,026(151)	78,719	吹瓶机
Nanhai Huada Mould Plastics Co., Ltd.	Foshan	Guangdong	(0757)5688355		Private Owned				Mould
南海市华达模具塑料有限公司(1987)	佛山市	广东省	(0757)5667577	450	私营企业	141,996	5,263(37)	144,808	模具
Haier Century (Qingdoa) Precision Products Co., Ltd.	Qingdao	Shandong	(0532)7273032		Overseas Chinese-funded				Mould
海尔世纪（青岛）精密制品有限公司(2000)	青岛市	山东省	(0532)7273033	1,061	港澳台资	132,183	4,881(40)	142,124	模具
Liansheng (Panyu) Plastic & Hardware Mould Co., Ltd.	Guangzhou	Guangdong	(020)84928001		Overseas Chinese-funded				Mould
联盛(番禺)塑料五金模具有限公司(1993)	广州市	广东省	(020)84928002	2,765	港澳台资	131,384	7,304(24)	278,593	模具

Top 10 Cities by Revenue 销售收入排名前10位城市	Province 省	Market share 市场份额 (%)	Number of firms 企业个数
Shanghai 上海市	Shanghai 上海市	9.21	66
Guangzhou 广州市	Guangdong 广东省	7.43	33
Suzhou 苏州市	Jiangsu 江苏省	6.14	26
Shenzhen 深圳市	Guangdong 广东省	5.43	30
Foshan 佛山市	Guangdong 广东省	4.69	18
Wuxi 无锡市	Jiangsu 江苏省	4.61	6
Ningbo 宁波市	Zhejiang 浙江省	4.53	37
Taizhou 台州市	Zhejiang 浙江省	4.46	25
Dongguan 东莞市	Guangdong 广东省	4.30	10
Jieyang 揭阳市	Guangdong 广东省	4.02	8

10 Major Wholesalers 十家主要批发商	City 城市	Province 省	Telephone/Fax 电话/传真
SU MEC	Nanjing	Jiangsu	(025)4511888
中设江苏机械设备进出口（集团）公司	南京市	江苏省	(025)4411772
China Poster Mobile Communications Equipment Co.,Ltd.	Beijing	Beijing	(010)66426993
中邮普泰移动通信设备股份有限公司	北京市	北京市	(010)66426837
Sino Kama Co., Ltd.	Shanghai	Shanghai	(021)62031188
中泰凯马股份有限公司	上海市	上海市	(021)62030851
China Huayuan Group Co.,Ltd.	Shanghai	Shanghai	(021)62031188
中国华源集团有限公司	上海市	上海市	(021)62032288
Zhejiang Crand Imp.& Exp.Co.,Ltd.	Ningbo	Zhejiang	(0574)87720170
浙江远大进出口有限公司	宁波市	浙江省	(0574)87723350
Shandong Machinery Import & Export Group Corporation	Qingdao	Shandong	(0532)2661628
山东省机械进出口集团公司	青岛市	山东省	(0532)2991655
Qingdao Haier International Trade Co.,Ltd.	Qingdao	Shandong	(0532)8938337
青岛海尔国际贸易有限公司	青岛市	山东省	(0532)8939494
Guangdong Machinery Import & Export Group Corporation	Guangzhou	Guangdong	(020)87782168
广东省机械进出口集团公司	广州市	广东省	(020)87771803
China National Machinery Equipment Import & Export Corporation	Beijing	Beijing	(010)63474506
中国机械设备进出口总公司	北京市	北京市	(010)63261865
Beijing Cellstar Co.,Ltd.	Beijing	Beijing	(010)64602050
北京蜂星事达电讯有限公司	北京市	北京市	(010)64672648

3435: Hand Tools 手工具制造业

The industry accounts for 0.095% of the total revenue of China's industrial sector in 2002. The rate of return on assets is 3.87%. 79.11% of all firms in the industry made a profit while 20.89% had negative returns.The top province in terms of the industry's revenue is Zhejiang, accounting for 40.81% of the total revenue.
2002年本行业收入占全行业的 0.095%，资产利润率为 3.87%。79.11%的企业赢利，20.89%的企业亏损。收入最高的省为浙江省，占本行业的40.81%。

	Total number of firms 企业总数	Total number of employees 职工总数	Total revenue (Mil.RMB) 总销售收入（百万元）	Total profit (Mil.RMB) 总利润（百万元）	Return on assets 资产利润率（%）	Return on equity 权益利润率（%）	Labour productivity ('000 RMB/worker) 劳动生产率（千元/人）	Debts/assets 资产负债率（%）	Total assets (Mil.RMB) 总资产（百万元）
Industry Overall 行业总体	383	80,245	10,147	338	3.87	11.54	31.52	66.46	8,736

	Number of firms 企业个数	Average number of employees 平均职工人数	Average revenue ('000 RMB) 平均销售收入（千元）	Average profit ('000 RMB) 平均利润（千元）	Return on assets 资产利润率（%）	Return on equity 权益利润率（%）	Labour productivity ('000 RMB/worker) 劳动生产率（千元/人）	Debts/assets 资产负债率（%）	Average total assets ('000 RMB) 平均总资产（千元）
By ownership 产业所有权									
State-owned 国有	21	289	16,377	-984	-2.49	-15.26	12.86	83.70	39,570
Collective-owned 集体	65	223	44,503	780	2.43	10.03	31.79	75.76	32,051
Foreign & Overseas Chinese Funded 三资	69	271	40,155	2,224	6.20	14.14	42.93	56.15	35,857
By regional distribution 地区分布									
Central-North 华北	39	172	18,687	-303	-0.99	-4.30	6.84	76.92	30,503
Beijing 北京	6	122	5,185	-1,217	-7.36	-53.49	13.54	86.24	16,532
Tianjin 天津	15	149	34,962	-760	-1.75	-9.36	-15.05	81.32	43,458
Hebei 河北	11	226	10,417	696	2.57	6.46	21.75	60.17	27,036
Shanxi 山西	7	178	8,382	-109	-0.54	-3.69	12.43	85.32	20,162
Inner Mongolia 内蒙古									
Northeast 东北	5	89	4,649	-165	-2.28	-29.68	16.09	92.32	7,251
Liaoning 辽宁	2	42	4,978	-171	-5.38	-13.27	29.33	59.46	3,169
Jilin 吉林	3	121	4,429	-162	-1.62	-226.64	13.06	99.28	9,973
Heilongjiang 黑龙江									
Central-East 华东	279	213	29,794	977	4.34	12.20	35.76	64.40	22,505
Shanghai 上海	24	241	37,108	999	2.63	8.11	55.96	67.57	37,952
Jiangsu 江苏	69	216	22,507	384	2.19	7.69	28.10	71.49	17,525
Zhejiang 浙江	129	165	32,103	1,062	5.02	12.49	39.52	59.82	21,160
Anhui 安徽	2	145	4,222	-53	-1.28		10.83	112.42	4,136
Fujian 福建	7	65	11,490	305	2.90	4.65	59.46	37.60	10,510
Jiangxi 江西	2	125	6,990	131	2.89	3.35	14.11	13.77	4,538
Shandong 山东	46	354	35,325	1,802	6.20	18.61	30.82	66.70	29,089
Central-South 中南	48	227	20,129	1,699	8.64	25.03	28.05	65.47	19,657
Henan 河南	8	498	14,551	355	1.34		14.27	103.91	26,446
Hubei 湖北	10	120	11,264	6	0.06	68.29	30.46	99.91	8,634
Hunan 湖南	8	169	24,657	310	2.99	6.15	49.70	51.35	10,376
Guangdong 广东	22	199	24,541	3,462	13.54	25.94	33.25	47.81	25,574
Guangxi 广西									
Hainan 海南									
Southwest 西南	10	236	9,342	-501	-2.59	-13.73	16.61	81.12	19,324
Chongqing 重庆	2	538	14,792	-2,462	-4.58	-59.90	14.29	92.35	53,702
Sichuan 四川	7	175	8,337	-20	-0.18	-0.61	18.19	71.20	11,137
Guizhou 贵州									
Yunnan 云南	1	56	5,478	54	0.69	0.93	26.34	26.26	7,874
Tibet 西藏									
Northwest 西北	2	257	11,106	807	1.72	2.93	18.21	41.50	47,046
Shaanxi 陕西	1	164	10,204	804	14.11	56.38	20.34	74.97	5,698
Gansu 甘肃									
Qinghai 青海	1	350	12,008	810	0.92	1.51	17.21	39.34	88,394
Ningxia 宁夏									
Xinjiang 新疆									

3435: Hand Tools 手工具制造业

Year 年份	Number of firms 企业个数	Rate of change 变化率 (%)	Number of employees 职工人数 (人)	Rate of change 变化率 (%)	Total revenue (Mil. RMB) 总销售收入 (百万元)	Rate of change 变化率 (%)	Total profit (Mil RMB) 总利润 (百万元)	Rate of change 变化率 (%)
2000	335		85,409		8,144		211	
2001	351	4.78	80,148	-6.16	8,663	6.37	249	18.01
2002	383	9.12	80,245	0.12	10,147	17.13	338	35.74

Major Products 主要产品	Output 产量	Unit 单位
Hand Tools 手工工具	23	100,000,000 Pieces 亿把

10 Main Firms with Maximal Revenue (year founded) 收入最大的十家主要企业（创办年份）	City 城市	Province 省	Telephone/fax 电话/传真	Number of employees 职工人数	Ownership 产业所有权	Revenue ('000 RMB) 销售收入 (千元)	Profit('000 RMB) (rank) 利润(千元) (排名)	Total assets ('000 RMB) 总资产 (千元)	Major products 主要产品
Zhejiang Wanli Tools Group Company	Hangzhou	Zhejiang	(0571)86625088		Collective-owned				Hardware Tools
浙江万利工具集团公司(1995)	杭州市	浙江省	(0571)86624181	762	集体企业	947,210	6,500(16)	386,120	五金工具
Zhejiang Wanda Group Company	Hangzhou	Zhejiang	(0571)82301088		Collective-owned				Hardware Tools
浙江万达集团公司(1991)	杭州市	浙江省	(0571)82306333	2,257	集体企业	535,564	13,523(4)	378,905	五金工具
Wendeng Maxpower Tool Group Corp	Weihai	Shandong	(0631)8252421		Overseas Chinese-funded				Tools Manufacturing
文登威力工具集团公司(1968)	威海市	山东省	(0631)8258027	1,792	港澳台资	224,310	12,000(6)	148,147	工具制造
Tianjin Steel File Factory	Tianjin	Tianjin	(022)26390704		Collective-owned				File
天津市钢锉厂(1974)	天津市	天津市	(022)26390922	189	集体企业	215,870	10(233)	173,510	锉刀
Shandong Jinma Industrial Group Co., Ltd.	Rizhao	Shandong	(0633)8326948		Joint Stock				Hardware Tools
山东金马工业集团股份有限公司(1993)	日照市	山东省	(0633)8331979	1,839	股份制	200,536	6,964(13)	292,570	五金工具
TCT Co., Ltd .	Huizhou	Guangdong	(0752)6302586		Overseas Chinese-funded				Milling Tools
创国机械五金(惠州)有限公司(1998)	惠州市	广东省	(0752)6302587	800	港澳台资	169,309	69,398(1)	150,411	铣削工具
Wendeng Dongqi Tools Factory	Weihai	Shandong	(0631)8631047		Private Enterprises				Spanner
文登市东琦工具厂(1998)	威海市	山东省	(0631)8631047	180	私营独资	159,410	17,460(3)	24,410	扳手
Shanghai Xing Jie Ke Enterprise Co., Ltd.	Shanghai	Shanghai	(021)64890147		Foreign Funded				Hand Tools
上海星杰克企业有限公司(1996)	上海市	上海市		156	外商投资	141,451	-	37,595	手工具
Ningbo Paoshin Garden Tool Co., Ltd	Ningbo	Zhejiang	(0574)62988704		Overseas Chinese-funded				Gardening Scissor
宁波宝兴园艺设备有限公司(1993)	宁波市	浙江省	(0574)62900701	560	港澳台资	140,000	11,200(8)	89,960	园艺剪刀
Tajima Tool Co., ltd.	Shanghai	Shanghai	(021)57741298		Foreign Funded				Hand Tools
上海田岛工具有限公司(1995)	上海市	上海市	(021)57741284	528	外商投资	128,906	6,812(14)	143,987	手工工具

Top 10 Cities by Revenue 销售收入排名前10位城市	Province 省	Market share 市场份额 (%)	Number of firms 企业个数
Hangzhou 杭州市	Zhejiang 浙江省	21.96	36
Ningbo 宁波市	Zhejiang 浙江省	10.76	37
Shanghai 上海市	Shanghai 上海市	8.78	24
Tianjin 天津市	Tianjin 天津市	5.17	15
Jinhua 金华市	Zhejiang 浙江省	4.61	32
Weihai 威海市	Shandong 山东省	3.78	3
Yantai 烟台市	Shandong 山东省	3.37	7
Suzhou 苏州市	Jiangsu 江苏省	3.10	13
Rizhao 日照市	Shandong 山东省	2.66	4
Changzhou 常州市	Jiangsu 江苏省	2.65	13

10 Major Wholesalers 十家主要批发商	City 城市	Province 省	Telephone/Fax 电话/传真
SU MEC	Nanjing	Jiangsu	(025)4511888
中设江苏机械设备进出口（集团）公司	南京市	江苏省	(025)4411772
China Poster Mobile Communications Equipment Co.,Ltd.	Beijing	Beijing	(010)66426993
中邮普泰移动通信设备股份有限公司	北京市	北京市	(010)66426837
Sino Kama Co., Ltd.	Shanghai	Shanghai	(021)62031188
中泰凯马股份有限公司	上海市	上海市	(021)62030851
China Huayuan Group Co.,Ltd.	Shanghai	Shanghai	(021)62031188
中国华源集团有限公司	上海市	上海市	(021)62032288
Zhejiang Crand Imp.& Exp.Co.,Ltd.	Ningbo	Zhejiang	(0574)87720170
浙江远大进出口有限公司	宁波市	浙江省	(0574)87723350
Shandong Machinery Import & Export Group Corporation	Qingdao	Shandong	(0532)2661628
山东省机械进出口集团公司	青岛市	山东省	(0532)2991655
Qingdao Haier International Trade Co.,Ltd.	Qingdao	Shandong	(0532)8938337
青岛海尔国际贸易有限公司	青岛市	山东省	(0532)8939494
Guangdong Machinery Import & Export Group Corporation	Guangzhou	Guangdong	(020)87782168
广东省机械进出口集团公司	广州市	广东省	(020)87771803
China National Machinery Equipment Import & Export Corporation	Beijing	Beijing	(010)63474506
中国机械设备进出口总公司	北京市	北京市	(010)63261865
Beijing Cellstar Co.,Ltd.	Beijing	Beijing	(010)64602050
北京蜂星事达电讯有限公司	北京市	北京市	(010)64672648

3439: Other Tools 其他工具制造业

The industry accounts for 0.021% of the total revenue of China's industrial sector in 2002. The rate of return on assets is 8.34%. 89.41% of all firms in the industry made a profit while 10.59% had negative returns.The top province in terms of the industry's revenue is Zhejiang, accounting for 68.03% of the total revenue.
2002年本行业收入占全行业的 0.021%，资产利润率为 8.34%。89.41%的企业赢利，10.59%的企业亏损。收入最高的省为浙江省，占本行业的68.03%。

	Total number of firms 企业总数	Total number of employees 职工总数	Total revenue (Mil.RMB) 总销售收入（百万元）	Total profit (Mil.RMB) 总利润（百万元）	Return on assets 资产利润率（%）	Return on equity 权益利润率（%）	Labour productivity ('000 RMB/ worker) 劳动生产率（千元/人）	Debts/ assets 资产负债率（%）	Total assets (Mil.RMB) 总资产（百万元）
Industry Overall 行业总体	85	12,911	2,226	120	8.34	18.41	47.69	54.67	1,443

	Number of firms 企业个数	Average number of employees 平均职工人数	Average revenue ('000 RMB) 平均销售收入（千元）	Average profit ('000 RMB) 平均利润（千元）	Return on assets 资产利润率（%）	Return on equity 权益利润率（%）	Labour productivity ('000 RMB/ worker) 劳动生产率（千元/人）	Debts/ assets 资产负债率（%）	Average total assets ('000 RMB) 平均总资产（千元）
By ownership 产业所有权									
State-owned 国有	3	123	1,049	-1,101	-5.50		-0.33	116.76	20,019
Collective-owned 集体	9	148	11,189	199	1.84	4.33	27.01	57.46	10,826
Foreign & Overseas Chinese Funded 三资	28	193	37,095	2,608	10.96	20.98	55.04	47.75	23,790
By regional distribution 地区分布									
Central-North 华北	4	127	4,464	261	1.72	6.66	16.89	74.15	15,156
Beijing 北京	1	125	6,199	889	22.91	70.44	31.93	67.48	3,881
Tianjin 天津	2	42	428	-130	-2.24	-7.56	3.04	70.32	5,775
Hebei 河北									
Shanxi 山西	1	300	10,800	413	0.91	3.76	14.50	75.70	45,192
Inner Mongolia 内蒙古									
Northeast 东北	3	84	11,898	1,436	8.30	18.35	56.94	54.79	17,304
Liaoning 辽宁	1	113	24,378	4,266	16.17	22.18	98.71	27.10	26,381
Jilin 吉林	1	21	300	3	0.04	0.18	7.14	79.63	8,311
Heilongjiang 黑龙江	1	118	11,016	39	0.23	1.53	25.80	85.20	17,220
Central-East 华东	66	158	27,827	1,745	10.14	21.28	45.13	52.36	17,214
Shanghai 上海	14	95	15,396	350	3.07	5.44	38.32	43.56	11,378
Jiangsu 江苏	4	75	17,722	346	2.08	4.35	56.80	52.12	16,604
Zhejiang 浙江	45	185	33,648	2,400	12.55	27.85	46.80	54.96	19,133
Anhui 安徽									
Fujian 福建	1	75	14,957	866	16.28	32.12	50.20	49.33	5,321
Jiangxi 江西									
Shandong 山东	2	192	10,515	14	0.06	0.10	22.68	34.24	22,058
Central-South 中南	11	155	29,678	-34	-0.21	-0.51	69.54	59.52	16,446
Henan 河南	6	124	19,258	224	4.58	6.02	80.32	23.99	4,885
Hubei 湖北									
Hunan 湖南	1	282	2,848	-3,307	-7.58		-0.97	128.17	43,649
Guangdong 广东	4	169	52,015	398	1.47	2.52	87.11	41.41	26,988
Guangxi 广西									
Hainan 海南									
Southwest 西南	1	50	9,300	266	1.96	44.93	102.00	95.65	13,605
Chongqing 重庆	1	50	9,300	266	1.96	44.93	102.00	95.65	13,605
Sichuan 四川									
Guizhou 贵州									
Yunnan 云南									
Tibet 西藏									
Northwest 西北									
Shaanxi 陕西									
Gansu 甘肃									
Qinghai 青海									
Ningxia 宁夏									
Xinjiang 新疆									

Year 年份	Number of firms 企业个数	Rate of change 变化率 (%)	Number of employees 职工人数 (人)	Rate of change 变化率 (%)	Total revenue (Mil. RMB) 总销售收入 (百万元)	Rate of change 变化率 (%)	Total profit (Mil RMB) 总利润 (百万元)	Rate of change 变化率 (%)
2000	70		9,358		1,394		63	
2001	68	-2.86	11,011	17.66	1,541	10.55	103	63.49
2002	85	25.00	12,911	17.26	2,226	44.45	120	16.50

Major Products 主要产品	Output 产量	Unit 单位
Measuring Instrument 量具	2,685	10,000 Pieces 万件

10 Main Firms with Maximal Revenue (year founded) 收入最大的十家主要企业（创办年份）	City 城市	Province 省	Telephone/fax 电话/传真	Number of employees 职工人数	Ownership 产业所有权	Revenue ('000 RMB) 销售收入 (千元)	Profit('000 RMB) (rank) 利润(千元) (排名)	Total assets ('000 RMB) 总资产 (千元)	Major products 主要产品
Ningbo Longxing Group Company	Ningbo	Zhejiang	(0574)88218191		Joint Stock				Welding And Cutting Fire
宁波隆兴集团公司(1995)	宁波市	浙江省	(0574)88218191	973	股份制	180,386	17,935(1)	150,668	焊割炬
Ningbo Landa Measuring Tools Co.,Ltd.	Ningbo	Zhejiang	(0574)62724198		Foreign Funded				Steel Tape Measure
宁波蓝达工量具有限公司(2000)	宁波市	浙江省	(0574)62708477	820	外商投资	150,463	4,542(8)	57,867	钢卷尺
East Precision Measuring Tools Co., Ltd.	Jinhua	Zhejiang	(0579)2101488		Private Owned				Level Ruler
浙江东精工量具有限公司(1998)	金华市	浙江省	(0579)2101288	578	私营企业	121,680	6,320(6)	70,209	水平尺
Sihui Precise & Standard Hardware Products Co., Ltd.	Zhaoqing	Guangdong	(0758)3855345		Overseas Chinese-funded				Tape Measure
四会市精准五金制品有限公司(1999)	肇庆市	广东省	(0758)3855050	225	港澳台资	105,120	-	21,447	卷尺
Ningbo Jiangxin Hardware Measuring Instrument Co., Ltd.	Ningbo	Zhejiang	(0574)65055193		Overseas Chinese-funded				Steel Tape Measure
宁波江信五金工量具有限公司(1993)	宁波市	浙江省	(0574)62055500	351	港澳台资	89,526	2,317(15)	21,961	钢卷尺
Ningbo Xuli Metal Products Co.,Ltd.	Ningbo	Zhejiang	(0574)88488879		Foreign Funded				Straining Machine
宁波旭力金属制品有限公司(2000)	宁波市	浙江省	(0574)88488825	271	外商投资	61,678	17,391(2)	40,444	拉紧机
Ningbo Navite Coating Machinery Co.,Ltd.	Ningbo	Zhejiang	(0574)88447704		Limited-Liability				Spray Paint Gun
宁波成田涂装机械有限公司(1995)	宁波市	浙江省	(0574)88447692	125	有限公司	56,364	5,051(7)	19,815	喷漆枪
Jinhua Precision Tools Manufacturing Co., Ltd.	Jinhua	Zhejiang	(0579)2591247		Private Owned				worktable
金华市精工工具制造有限公司(1996)	金华市	浙江省	(0579)2591223	280	私营企业	54,550	3,520(11)	29,170	工作台
Shanghai Wei Ke Precise Moulding Co., Ltd.	Shanghai	Shanghai	(021)54297719		Foreign Funded				3571 Casting
上海维科精密模塑有限公司(2001)	上海市	上海市	(021)54295258	226	外商投资	40,920	4,044(10)	34,625	3571铸件
Guangzhou Cheng Fa Shingsat Metal & Plastic Co., ltd.	Guangzhou	Guangdong	(020)87871673		Overseas Chinese-funded				lock
广州成发五金塑胶有限公司(1993)	广州市	广东省	(020)87871113	260	港澳台资	40,650	1,840(17)	62,425	锁

Top 10 Cities by Revenue 销售收入排名前10位城市	Province 省	Market share 市场份额 (%)	Number of firms 企业个数
Ningbo 宁波市	Zhejiang 浙江省	47.58	25
Jinhua 金华市	Zhejiang 浙江省	13.48	12
Shanghai 上海市	Shanghai 上海市	9.68	14
Zhaoqing 肇庆市	Guangdong 广东省	7.04	2
Shangqiu 商丘市	Henan 河南省	5.19	6
Jiaxing 嘉兴市	Zhejiang 浙江省	3.58	3
Changzhou 常州市	Jiangsu 江苏省	2.52	3
Hangzhou 杭州市	Zhejiang 浙江省	1.93	4
Guangzhou 广州市	Guangdong 广东省	1.83	1
Taizhou 台州市	Zhejiang 浙江省	1.45	1

10 Major Wholesalers 十家主要批发商	City 城市	Province 省	Telephone/Fax 电话/传真
SU MEC	Nanjing	Jiangsu	(025)4511888
中设江苏机械设备进出口（集团）公司	南京市	江苏省	(025)4411772
China Poster Mobile Communications Equipment Co.,Ltd.	Beijing	Beijing	(010)66426993
中邮普泰移动通信设备股份有限公司	北京市	北京市	(010)66426837
Sino Kama Co., Ltd.	Shanghai	Shanghai	(021)62031188
中泰凯马股份有限公司	上海市	上海市	(021)62030851
China Huayuan Group Co.,Ltd.	Shanghai	Shanghai	(021)62031188
中国华源集团有限公司	上海市	上海市	(021)62032288
Zhejiang Crand Imp.& Exp.Co.,Ltd.	Ningbo	Zhejiang	(0574)87720170
浙江远大进出口有限公司	宁波市	浙江省	(0574)87723350
Shandong Machinery Import & Export Group Corporation	Qingdao	Shandong	(0532)2661628
山东省机械进出口集团公司	青岛市	山东省	(0532)2991655
Qingdao Haier International Trade Co.,Ltd.	Qingdao	Shandong	(0532)8938337
青岛海尔国际贸易有限公司	青岛市	山东省	(0532)8939494
Guangdong Machinery Import & Export Group Corporation	Guangzhou	Guangdong	(020)87782168
广东省机械进出口集团公司	广州市	广东省	(020)87771803
China National Machinery Equipment Import & Export Corporation	Beijing	Beijing	(010)63474506
中国机械设备进出口总公司	北京市	北京市	(010)63261865
Beijing Cellstar Co.,Ltd.	Beijing	Beijing	(010)64602050
北京蜂星事达电讯有限公司	北京市	北京市	(010)64672648

3441: Containers 集装箱制造业

The industry accounts for 0.170% of the total revenue of China's industrial sector in 2002. The rate of return on assets is 3.79%. 68.09% of all firms in the industry made a profit while 31.91% had negative returns.The top province in terms of the industry's revenue is Guangdong, accounting for 37.31% of the total revenue.
2002年本行业收入占全行业的 0.170%，资产利润率为 3.79%。68.09%的企业赢利，31.91%的企业亏损。收入最高的省为广东省，占本行业的37.31%。

	Total number of firms 企业总数	Total number of employees 职工总数	Total revenue (Mil.RMB) 总销售收入(百万元)	Total profit (Mil.RMB) 总利润(百万元)	Return on assets 资产利润率(%)	Return on equity 权益利润率(%)	Labour productivity ('000 RMB/worker) 劳动生产率(千元/人)	Debts/assets 资产负债率(%)	Total assets (Mil.RMB) 总资产(百万元)
Industry Overall 行业总体	47	30,441	18,254	558	3.79	12.29	124.07	69.13	14,722

	Number of firms 企业个数	Average number of employees 平均职工人数	Average revenue ('000 RMB) 平均销售收入（千元）	Average profit ('000 RMB) 平均利润(千元)	Return on assets 资产利润率(%)	Return on equity 权益利润率(%)	Labour productivity ('000 RMB/worker) 劳动生产率(千元/人)	Debts/assets 资产负债率(%)	Average total assets ('000 RMB) 平均总资产(千元)
By ownership 产业所有权									
State-owned 国有	2	588	42,385	2,782	4.98	37.76	11.20	86.81	55,843
Collective-owned 集体	1	78	13,182	408	5.26	14.33	19.28	63.30	7,757
Foreign & Overseas Chinese Funded 三资	35	758	494,014	14,712	3.75	12.17	132.77	69.22	392,573
By regional distribution 地区分布									
Central-North 华北	3	580	365,822	8,503	3.81	15.61	58.26	75.57	223,013
Beijing 北京									
Tianjin 天津	3	580	365,822	8,503	3.81	15.61	58.26	75.57	223,013
Hebei 河北									
Shanxi 山西									
Inner Mongolia 内蒙古									
Northeast 东北	2	783	329,142	-3,293	-0.95	-7.89	59.11	87.90	344,826
Liaoning 辽宁	2	783	329,142	-3,293	-0.95	-7.89	59.11	87.90	344,826
Jilin 吉林									
Heilongjiang 黑龙江									
Central-East 华东	32	543	301,846	13,189	5.06	13.62	111.02	62.86	260,701
Shanghai 上海	15	423	273,659	15,629	7.34	16.41	98.11	55.28	212,988
Jiangsu 江苏	9	769	314,628	8,426	2.64	10.35	76.80	74.52	319,696
Zhejiang 浙江									
Anhui 安徽									
Fujian 福建	2	353	222,846	1,584	0.82	2.09	84.23	60.93	193,884
Jiangxi 江西									
Shandong 山东	6	571	379,474	18,103	5.77	13.84	209.63	58.32	313,764
Central-South 中南	9	974	759,744	13,071	2.38	9.81	188.47	75.76	549,532
Henan 河南									
Hubei 湖北	1	212	26,964	-1,809	-4.96	-32.68	39.07	84.82	36,466
Hunan 湖南									
Guangdong 广东	8	1,069	851,342	14,931	2.43	10.01	192.17	75.69	613,665
Guangxi 广西									
Hainan 海南									
Southwest 西南									
Chongqing 重庆									
Sichuan 四川									
Guizhou 贵州									
Yunnan 云南									
Tibet 西藏									
Northwest 西北	1	980	1,080	-280	-0.37	-70.00	0.25	99.47	75,000
Shaanxi 陕西	1	980	1,080	-280	-0.37	-70.00	0.25	99.47	75,000
Gansu 甘肃									
Qinghai 青海									
Ningxia 宁夏									
Xinjiang 新疆									

3441: Containers 集装箱制造业

Year 年份	Number of firms 企业个数	Rate of change 变化率 (%)	Number of employees 职工人数 (人)	Rate of change 变化率 (%)	Total revenue (Mil. RMB) 总销售收入 (百万元)	Rate of change 变化率 (%)	Total profit (Mil RMB) 总利润 (百万元)	Rate of change 变化率 (%)
2000	50		39,294		19,668		684	
2001	46	-8.00	27,424	-30.21	14,664	-25.44	1,061	55.12
2002	47	2.17	30,441	11.00	18,254	24.48	558	-47.41

Major Products 主要产品	Output 产量	Unit 单位
Metal Container 金属集装箱	4,938	10,000 Stere 万立方米

10 Main Firms with Maximal Revenue (year founded) 收入最大的十家主要企业（创办年份）	City 城市	Province 省	Telephone/fax 电话/传真	Number of employees 职工人数	Ownership 产业所有权	Revenue ('000 RMB) 销售收入 (千元)	Profit('000 RMB) (rank) 利润(千元) (排名)	Total assets ('000 RMB) 总资产 (千元)	Major products 主要产品
Shunde Shun An Da Pacific Container Co.,Ltd. 顺德顺安达太平货柜有限公司(1991)	Foshan 佛山市	Guangdong 广东省	(0765)5330136 (0765)5666159	1,881	Overseas Chinese-funded 港澳台资	1,676,904	81,729(3)	1,172,318	Container 集装箱
Shenzhen Southern CIMC Containers Manufacture Co., Ltd. 深圳南方中集集装箱制造有限公司(1995)	Shenzhen 深圳市	Guangdong 广东省	(0755)26691131 (0755)26693975	2,500	Overseas Chinese-funded 港澳台资	1,615,821	51,841(4)	1,626,962	Container 集装箱
Xinhui CIMC Container Co., Ltd. 新会中集集装箱有限公司(1992)	Jiangmen 江门市	Guangdong 广东省	(0750)6248888 (0750)6248365	1,401	Foreign Funded 外商投资	1,185,490	11,710(15)	626,108	Container 集装箱
Shanghai CIMC Refrigerator Co., Ltd. 上海中集冷藏箱有限公司(1996)	Shanghai 上海市	Shanghai 上海市	(021)56010088 (021)56011111	1,006	Foreign Funded 外商投资	1,163,793	169,848(1)	679,523	Container 集装箱
Tianjin CIMC Northern Ocean Container Co., ltd. 天津中集北洋集装箱有限公司(1989)	Tianjin 天津市	Tianjin 天津市	(022)25211600 (022)25322021	1,222	Overseas Chinese-funded 港澳台资	833,193	30,850(8)	495,036	Container 集装箱
Shanghai CIMC Far-east Container Co.,Ltd. 上海中集远东集装箱有限公司(1992)	Shanghai 上海市	Shanghai 上海市	(021)58991280 (021)58991188	1,292	Overseas Chinese-funded 港澳台资	826,074	39,922(6)	458,916	Container 集装箱
Nantong CIMC Smooth Sail Container Co., Ltd. 南通中集顺达集装箱有限公司(1991)	Nantong 南通市	Jiangsu 江苏省	(0513)5562116 (0513)5564961	1,789	Foreign Funded 外商投资	790,312	11,421(16)	386,579	Container 集装箱
Qingdao Maersk Containetr Industry Co., Ltd. 青岛马士基集装箱工业有限公司(1998)	Qingdao 青岛市	Shandong 山东省	(0532)7725410 (0532)7725411	730	Foreign Funded 外商投资	746,219	6,952(18)	630,929	Container 集装箱
Qingdao CIMC Refrigerator Manufacture Co., Ltd. 青岛中集冷藏箱制造有限公司(1999)	Qingdao 青岛市	Shandong 山东省	(0532)2279978 (0532)2279978	939	Foreign Funded 外商投资	705,361	82,265(2)	507,082	Deepfreeze 冷藏箱
Qingdao CIMC Container Manufacture Co., Ltd. 青岛中集集装箱制造有限公司(1999)	Qingdao 青岛市	Shandong 山东省	(0532)2279565 (0532)2279528	1,052	Foreign Funded 外商投资	673,592	14,082(14)	587,207	Container 集装箱

Top 10 Cities by Revenue 销售收入排名前10位城市	Province 省	Market share 市场份额 (%)	Number of firms 企业个数
Shanghai 上海市	Shanghai 上海市	22.49	15
Qingdao 青岛市	Shandong 山东省	12.47	6
Jiangmen 江门市	Guangdong 广东省	11.53	2
Foshan 佛山市	Guangdong 广东省	9.19	1
Shenzhen 深圳市	Guangdong 广东省	9.11	2
Nantong 南通市	Jiangsu 江苏省	6.83	2
Tianjin 天津市	Tianjin 天津市	6.01	3
Huizhou 惠州市	Guangdong 广东省	4.77	1
Yangzhou 扬州市	Jiangsu 江苏省	4.26	2
Changzhou 常州市	Jiangsu 江苏省	3.62	1

10 Major Wholesalers 十家主要批发商	City 城市	Province 省	Telephone/Fax 电话/传真
SU MEC 中设江苏机械设备进出口（集团）公司	Nanjing 南京市	Jiangsu 江苏省	(025)4511888 (025)4411772
China Poster Mobile Communications Equipment Co.,Ltd. 中邮普泰移动通信设备股份有限公司	Beijing 北京市	Beijing 北京市	(010)66426993 (010)66426837
Sino Kama Co., Ltd. 中泰凯马股份有限公司	Shanghai 上海市	Shanghai 上海市	(021)62031188 (021)62030851
China Huayuan Group Co.,Ltd. 中国华源集团有限公司	Shanghai 上海市	Shanghai 上海市	(021)62031188 (021)62032288
Zhejiang Crand Imp.& Exp.Co.,Ltd. 浙江远大进出口有限公司	Ningbo 宁波市	Zhejiang 浙江省	(0574)87720170 (0574)87723350
Shandong Machinery Import & Export Group Corporation 山东省机械进出口集团公司	Qingdao 青岛市	Shandong 山东省	(0532)2661628 (0532)2991655
Qingdao Haier International Trade Co.,Ltd. 青岛海尔国际贸易有限公司	Qingdao 青岛市	Shandong 山东省	(0532)8938337 (0532)8939494
Guangdong Machinery Import & Export Group Corporation 广东省机械进出口集团公司	Guangzhou 广州市	Guangdong 广东省	(020)87782168 (020)87771803
China National Machinery Equipment Import & Export Corporation 中国机械设备进出口总公司	Beijing 北京市	Beijing 北京市	(010)63474506 (010)63261865
Beijing Cellstar Co.,Ltd. 北京蜂星事达电讯有限公司	Beijing 北京市	Beijing 北京市	(010)64602050 (010)64672648

3442: Metal Packing Goods and Containers

金属包装物品及容器制造业

The industry accounts for 0.224% of the total revenue of China's industrial sector in 2002. The rate of return on assets is 2.59%. 79.03% of all firms in the industry made a profit while 20.97% had negative returns.The top province in terms of the industry's revenue is Guangdong, accounting for 20.63% of the total revenue.
2002年本行业收入占全行业的 0.224%，资产利润率为 2.59%。79.03%的企业赢利，20.97%的企业亏损。收入最高的省为广东省，占本行业的20.63%。

	Total number of firms 企业总数	Total number of employees 职工总数	Total revenue (Mil.RMB) 总销售收入（百万元）	Total profit (Mil.RMB) 总利润（百万元）	Return on assets 资产利润率 (%)	Return on equity 权益利润率 (%)	Labour productivity ('000 RMB/ worker) 劳动生产率（千元/人）	Debts/ assets 资产负债率 (%)	Total assets (Mil.RMB) 总资产（百万元）
Industry Overall 行业总体	739	107,653	24,016	711	2.59	6.31	57.09	58.98	27,430

	Number of firms 企业个数	Average number of employees 平均职工人数	Average revenue ('000 RMB) 平均销售收入（千元）	Average profit ('000 RMB) 平均利润（千元）	Return on assets 资产利润率 (%)	Return on equity 权益利润率 (%)	Labour productivity ('000 RMB/ worker) 劳动生产率（千元/人）	Debts/ assets 资产负债率 (%)	Average total assets ('000 RMB) 平均总资产（千元）
By ownership 产业所有权									
State-owned 国有	62	138	21,515	-792	-1.86	-14.27	33.55	86.97	42,579
Collective-owned 集体	153	151	25,650	1,235	5.99	15.45	46.04	61.26	20,622
Foreign & Overseas Chinese Funded 三资	153	156	67,214	1,443	1.59	3.33	110.05	52.31	90,719
By regional distribution 地区分布									
Central-North 华北	117	125	30,704	1,309	4.19	10.30	52.03	59.32	31,243
Beijing 北京	26	162	63,384	2,440	2.99	6.98	80.64	57.18	81,634
Tianjin 天津	47	87	17,050	572	4.18	14.43	17.97	71.05	13,678
Hebei 河北	40	143	27,741	1,559	7.47	17.25	59.14	56.70	20,864
Shanxi 山西	3	131	8,254	82	0.50	0.97	22.32	48.37	16,338
Inner Mongolia 内蒙古	1	249	8,653	191	2.91	3.63	12.37	19.87	6,558
Northeast 东北	40	139	21,537	700	2.45	6.99	38.13	64.97	28,579
Liaoning 辽宁	29	136	24,591	595	1.75	4.89	42.14	64.14	33,935
Jilin 吉林	6	129	8,546	628	5.10	16.55	32.42	69.17	12,304
Heilongjiang 黑龙江	5	167	19,412	1,392	8.17	28.06	24.47	70.90	17,042
Central-East 华东	346	152	34,643	1,760	4.24	9.92	59.34	57.24	41,485
Shanghai 上海	65	153	39,786	1,960	3.33	7.59	62.46	56.12	58,866
Jiangsu 江苏	100	146	36,958	2,720	6.61	16.67	68.11	60.36	41,166
Zhejiang 浙江	85	122	25,081	1,092	4.02	8.96	47.26	55.19	27,191
Anhui 安徽	13	129	12,933	990	8.00	13.89	30.73	42.37	12,364
Fujian 福建	34	103	45,613	-94	-0.17	-0.37	103.80	53.37	53,722
Jiangxi 江西	12	170	13,294	287	1.65	4.85	31.92	66.06	17,420
Shandong 山东	37	283	45,787	2,797	5.44	13.35	51.14	59.26	51,439
Central-South 中南	179	152	38,264	-498	-1.25	-3.09	66.00	59.64	39,922
Henan 河南	19	113	13,345	555	4.42	11.03	27.85	59.92	12,558
Hubei 湖北	22	160	43,287	2,012	6.08	11.98	79.62	49.29	33,109
Hunan 湖南	8	162	17,655	-4,226	-23.54		23.74	154.94	17,952
Guangdong 广东	122	154	40,606	-1,257	-2.82	-6.55	66.17	57.00	44,655
Guangxi 广西	4	170	37,860	7,458	10.61	41.76	102.17	74.60	70,297
Hainan 海南	4	196	99,211	3,346	4.37	15.94	143.56	72.59	76,573
Southwest 西南	23	119	11,872	-647	-3.05	-14.45	35.67	78.86	21,186
Chongqing 重庆	4	151	10,691	-1,149	-6.47		8.64	111.93	17,771
Sichuan 四川	9	167	18,399	-1,022	-2.92	-13.38	51.34	78.17	34,984
Guizhou 贵州	4	45	2,905	97	1.96	3.44	22.14	42.94	4,929
Yunnan 云南	6	76	8,848	-247	-1.81	-4.70	25.13	61.37	13,605
Tibet 西藏									
Northwest 西北	34	143	13,342	726	3.83	10.28	31.85	62.76	18,964
Shaanxi 陕西	12	132	17,153	1,135	5.63	14.75	38.23	61.84	20,173
Gansu 甘肃	14	119	7,698	2	0.02	0.09	30.54	82.25	12,326
Qinghai 青海									
Ningxia 宁夏	1	60	17,600	366	1.41	21.62	70.87	93.49	26,022
Xinjiang 新疆	7	219	17,489	1,524	5.23	9.24	25.21	43.46	29,160

3442: Metal Packing Goods and Containers

金属包装物品及容器制造业

Year 年份	Number of firms 企业个数	Rate of change 变化率 (%)	Number of employees 职工人数 (人)	Rate of change 变化率 (%)	Total revenue (Mil. RMB) 总销售收入 (百万元)	Rate of change 变化率 (%)	Total profit (Mil RMB) 总利润 (百万元)	Rate of change 变化率 (%)
2000	690		127,069		24,496		445	
2001	724	4.93	114,699	-9.73	22,814	-6.87	556	24.94
2002	739	2.07	107,653	-6.14	24,016	5.27	711	27.88

Major Products 主要产品	Output 产量	Unit 单位
Metal Packing Good 金属制包装物品	65	10,000 Tons 万吨
Liquid Storage Tank From Metal 金属制液体贮藏罐	24	10,000 Tons 万吨

10 Main Firms with Maximal Revenue (year founded) 收入最大的十家主要企业（创办年份）	City 城市	Province 省	Telephone/fax 电话/传真	Number of employees 职工人数	Ownership 产业所有权	Revenue ('000 RMB) 销售收入 (千元)	Profit('000 RMB) (rank) 利润(千元) (排名)	Total assets ('000 RMB) 总资产 (千元)	Major products 主要产品
Sanshui Jianlibao Ftb Packaging Co., Ltd.	Foshan	Guangdong	(0757)7811828		Foreign Funded				Aluminiium Easy Open Can
三水健力宝富特容器有限公司(1992)	佛山市	广东省	(0757)7831888	509	外商投资	609,817	41,807(3)	686,735	铝质易拉罐
Shandong Huanri Group General Company	Yantai	Shandong	(0535)2335201		Collective-owned				Steel Cylinder
山东环日集团总公司(1984)	烟台市	山东省	(0535)2331262	2,056	集体企业	543,829	46,723(2)	451,329	钢瓶
Huadong Jar Making General Company	Zhenjiang	Jiangsu	(0511)5028970		State-owned				Easy Open Can
华东制罐有限公司(1985)	镇江市	江苏省	(0511)5623378	352	国有企业	428,654	24,890(10)	530,741	易拉罐
Coconut Palm Group Can-making Industry Co., Ltd.	Haikou	Hainan	(0898)66777124		Limited-Liability				Packing Can
椰树制罐工业有限公司(1997)	海口市	海南省	(0898)66773891	562	有限公司	349,681	13,048(22)	205,007	包装罐
Beijing Tian Hai Industry Co., Ltd.	Beijing	Beijing	(010)67383444		Foreign Funded				Steel Non-slot Gas-Cylinder
北京天海工业有限公司(1992)	北京市	北京市	(010)67367022	939	外商投资	300,977	4,440(58)	252,896	钢质无缝气瓶
Qingdao Kaituo Group Co., Ltd.	Qingdao	Shandong	(0532)7863407		Collective-owned				Deep Freezer Fittings
青岛开拓集团有限公司(1999)	青岛市	山东省	(0532)7867465	725	集体企业	291,210	19,662(14)	172,202	冰柜配件
Zhuhai Ftb Packaging Ltd.	Zhuhai	Guangdong	(0756)3331808		Overseas Chinese-funded				Aluminiium Easy Open Can
珠海富特波尔容器有限公司(1988)	珠海市	广东省	(0756)3331712	136	港澳台资	288,955	-	283,969	铝质易拉罐
Beijing Ftb Packaging Co., Ltd.	Beijing	Beijing	(010)61668288		Overseas Chinese-funded				Aluminiium Easy Open Can
北京富特波尔容器有限公司(1993)	北京市	北京市	(010)61667148	178	港澳台资	277,616	18,303(17)	451,341	铝质易拉罐
Taicang Corner Can Porduction Co., ltd .	Suzhou	Jiangsu	(0512)53456652		Overseas Chinese-funded				Empty Can
太仓兴达制罐有限公司(1993)	苏州市	江苏省	(0512)53458633	220	港澳台资	267,960	25,600(9)	463,980	空罐
Shanghai Huang Guan Packing Ltd. Company	Shanghai	Shanghai	(021)58995108		Overseas Chinese-funded				Bamboo Shoot Can
上海皇冠包装有限公司(1992)	上海市	上海市	(021)58995107	145	港澳台资	234,083	17,834(19)	143,464	笋罐

Top 10 Cities by Revenue 销售收入排名前10位城市	Province 省	Market share 市场份额 (%)	Number of firms 企业个数
Shanghai 上海市	Shanghai 上海市	10.77	65
Beijing 北京市	Beijing 北京市	6.86	26
Foshan 佛山市	Guangdong 广东省	6.82	30
Hangzhou 杭州市	Zhejiang 浙江省	4.13	34
Suzhou 苏州市	Jiangsu 江苏省	3.73	22
Shenzhen 深圳市	Guangdong 广东省	3.50	13
Tianjin 天津市	Tianjin 天津市	3.34	47
Qingdao 青岛市	Shandong 山东省	2.97	15
Wuxi 无锡市	Jiangsu 江苏省	2.85	20
Zhangzhou 漳州市	Fujian 福建省	2.75	16

10 Major Wholesalers 十家主要批发商	City 城市	Province 省	Telephone/Fax 电话/传真
SU MEC	Nanjing	Jiangsu	(025)4511888
中设江苏机械设备进出口（集团）公司	南京市	江苏省	(025)4411772
China Poster Mobile Communications Equipment Co.,Ltd.	Beijing	Beijing	(010)66426993
中邮普泰移动通信设备股份有限公司	北京市	北京市	(010)66426837
Sino Kama Co., Ltd.	Shanghai	Shanghai	(021)62031188
中泰凯马股份有限公司	上海市	上海市	(021)62030851
China Huayuan Group Co.,Ltd.	Shanghai	Shanghai	(021)62031188
中国华源集团有限公司	上海市	上海市	(021)62032288
Zhejiang Crand Imp.& Exp.Co.,Ltd.	Ningbo	Zhejiang	(0574)87720170
浙江远大进出口有限公司	宁波市	浙江省	(0574)87723350
Shandong Machinery Import & Export Group Corporation	Qingdao	Shandong	(0532)2661628
山东省机械进出口集团公司	青岛市	山东省	(0532)2991655
Qingdao Haier International Trade Co.,Ltd.	Qingdao	Shandong	(0532)8938337
青岛海尔国际贸易有限公司	青岛市	山东省	(0532)8939494
Guangdong Machinery Import & Export Group Corporation	Guangzhou	Guangdong	(020)87782168
广东省机械进出口集团公司	广州市	广东省	(020)87771803
China National Machinery Equipment Import & Export Corporation	Beijing	Beijing	(010)63474506
中国机械设备进出口总公司	北京市	北京市	(010)63261865
Beijing Cellstar Co.,Ltd.	Beijing	Beijing	(010)64602050
北京蜂星事达电讯有限公司	北京市	北京市	(010)64672648

3450: Metal Wire and Cable 金属丝绳及其制品业

The industry accounts for 0.287% of the total revenue of China's industrial sector in 2002. The rate of return on assets is 3.69%. 82.58% of all firms in the industry made a profit while 17.42% had negative returns.The top province in terms of the industry's revenue is Jiangsu, accounting for 28.13% of the total revenue.
2002年本行业收入占全行业的0.287%，资产利润率为3.69%。82.58%的企业赢利，17.42%的企业亏损。收入最高的省为江苏省，占本行业的28.13%。

	Total number of firms 企业总数	Total number of employees 职工总数	Total revenue (Mil.RMB) 总销售收入(百万元)	Total profit (Mil.RMB) 总利润(百万元)	Return on assets 资产利润率(%)	Return on equity 权益利润率(%)	Labour productivity ('000 RMB/worker) 劳动生产率(千元/人)	Debts/assets 资产负债率(%)	Total assets (Mil.RMB) 总资产(百万元)
Industry Overall 行业总体	884	157,987	30,736	1,214	3.69	10.32	53.35	64.22	32,889

	Number of firms 企业个数	Average number of employees 平均职工人数	Average revenue ('000 RMB) 平均销售收入(千元)	Average profit ('000 RMB) 平均利润(千元)	Return on assets 资产利润率(%)	Return on equity 权益利润率(%)	Labour productivity ('000 RMB/worker) 劳动生产率(千元/人)	Debts/assets 资产负债率(%)	Average total assets ('000 RMB) 平均总资产(千元)
By ownership 产业所有权									
State-owned 国有	63	285	60,424	-33	-0.03	-0.13	49.92	78.93	120,048
Collective-owned 集体	201	155	23,775	1,050	6.76	18.72	48.21	63.86	15,518
Foreign & Overseas Chinese Funded 三资	130	166	43,809	2,677	6.40	12.67	72.15	49.46	41,808
By regional distribution 地区分布									
Central-North 华北	228	182	27,376	675	1.95	9.09	45.13	78.52	34,566
Beijing 北京	11	130	41,876	2,886	7.26	17.66	80.97	58.88	39,732
Tianjin 天津	112	170	26,023	559	1.40	10.84	46.00	87.11	40,005
Hebei 河北	92	179	27,207	602	2.10	6.38	42.36	67.09	28,675
Shanxi 山西	5	414	18,814	114	0.54	2.35	17.89	76.94	21,092
Inner Mongolia 内蒙古	8	316	33,671	446	1.62	8.36	58.71	80.63	27,505
Northeast 东北	34	230	21,752	932	1.25	4.67	24.39	73.24	74,572
Liaoning 辽宁	27	254	25,696	1,109	1.96	7.04	26.06	72.20	56,674
Jilin 吉林	5	159	7,174	220	0.11	0.45	11.03	74.99	196,358
Heilongjiang 黑龙江	2	80	4,952	328	2.80	8.54	19.41	67.25	11,733
Central-East 华东	406	146	40,349	1,741	4.95	12.33	68.24	59.84	35,166
Shanghai 上海	65	87	28,739	1,790	6.94	15.03	71.08	53.84	25,808
Jiangsu 江苏	165	147	52,396	2,408	5.07	12.84	93.64	60.49	47,460
Zhejiang 浙江	80	135	38,145	942	4.24	12.11	50.46	65.02	22,236
Anhui 安徽	21	229	18,619	13	0.04	0.16	13.11	74.47	32,024
Fujian 福建	18	130	14,682	165	1.47	2.75	38.78	46.47	11,209
Jiangxi 江西	9	221	55,165	3,844	5.20	11.53	59.72	54.90	73,941
Shandong 山东	48	192	34,687	1,669	5.52	12.07	58.46	54.25	30,213
Central-South 中南	163	173	30,858	1,724	6.47	13.41	60.10	51.75	26,656
Henan 河南	41	187	24,149	976	4.96	17.80	44.46	72.16	19,699
Hubei 湖北	21	399	73,545	6,564	7.72	15.41	79.26	49.89	85,005
Hunan 湖南	12	108	19,349	309	2.81	9.22	48.01	69.49	10,992
Guangdong 广东	85	124	26,390	1,170	6.25	10.81	59.17	42.17	18,715
Guangxi 广西	2	144	8,288	32	0.39	0.68	20.43	43.13	8,126
Hainan 海南	2	35	1,685	4	0.05	0.09	9.97	40.76	6,553
Southwest 西南	31	382	41,129	199	0.33	0.88	27.01	62.02	59,541
Chongqing 重庆	10	322	37,304	-340	-0.81	-3.82	20.80	78.85	42,113
Sichuan 四川	12	149	23,268	-96	-0.68	-2.09	31.70	67.57	14,245
Guizhou 贵州	8	840	74,216	1,368	0.90	1.97	28.97	54.39	151,914
Yunnan 云南	1	107	29,031	-223	-0.58	-9.64	12.91	93.98	38,393
Tibet 西藏									
Northwest 西北	22	430	48,544	1,550	1.70	3.94	32.89	56.82	91,136
Shaanxi 陕西	5	350	42,669	3,012	3.37	7.03	38.54	52.05	89,416
Gansu 甘肃	11	78	15,093	224	3.32	5.67	75.44	41.53	6,738
Qinghai 青海	3	96	14,278	296	2.73	8.58	108.04	68.15	10,817
Ningxia 宁夏	1	6,159	595,046	14,621	1.03	2.50	22.04	58.66	1,415,376
Xinjiang 新疆	2	202	25,368	530	2.95	8.36	30.10	64.76	17,987

3450: Metal Wire and Cable 金属丝绳及其制品业

Year 年份	Number of firms 企业个数	Rate of change 变化率（%）	Number of employees 职工人数（人）	Rate of change 变化率（%）	Total revenue (Mil. RMB) 总销售收入（百万元）	Rate of change 变化率（%）	Total profit (Mil RMB) 总利润（百万元）	Rate of change 变化率（%）
2000	818		158,368		24,961		844	
2001	863	5.50	156,046	-1.47	25,945	3.94	969	14.81
2002	884	2.43	157,987	1.24	30,736	18.47	1,214	25.28

Major Products 主要产品	Output 产量	Unit 单位
Steel Wire Net 钢丝网	159,426	Ton 吨
Steel Wire 钢丝	169	10,000 Tons 万吨

10 Main Firms with Maximal Revenue (year founded) 收入最大的十家主要企业（创办年份）	City 城市	Province 省	Telephone/fax 电话/传真	Number of employees 职工人数	Ownership 产业所有权	Revenue ('000 RMB) 销售收入（千元）	Profit('000 RMB) (rank) 利润（千元）（排名）	Total assets ('000 RMB) 总资产（千元）	Major products 主要产品
Hubei Fuxing Science & Technology Stock Co., Ltd.	Xiaogan	Hubei	(0712)8740018		Joint Stock				Steel Wire
湖北福星科技股份有限公司(1985)	孝感市	湖北省	(0712)8740089	3,750	股份制	914,270	118,728(3)	1,087,950	钢丝
Zhejiang Yuanli Metal Products Group Co., Ltd.	Lishui	Zhejiang	(0578)8195008		Limited-Liability				Iron Wire & Iron Piton
浙江元立金属制品集团有限公司(1990)	丽水市	浙江省	(0578)8195035	1,450	有限公司	635,312	24,265(10)	478,149	铁丝铁钉
Ningxia Hengli Steel Iron Group Co., Ltd.	Shizuishan	Ningxia	(0952)3671293		State Enterprises				Rolled Steel
宁夏恒力钢铁集团有限公司(1959)	石嘴山市	宁夏	(0952)3681907	6,159	国有独资	595,046	14,621(20)	1,415,376	钢材
Zhejiang Suichang Suigang Metal Products Co., Ltd.	Lishui	Zhejiang	(0578)8185710		Limited-Liability				Iron Wire & Iron Piton
浙江遂昌遂钢金属制品有限公司(1998)	丽水市	浙江省	(0578)8195035	2,014	有限公司	416,724	168(377)	89,392	铁丝铁钉
Xinhua Metal Products Stock Co., Ltd.	Xinyu	Jiangxi	(0790)6460888		Overseas Chinese-funded				pc Stranded Steel Wire
新华金属制品股份有限公司(1986)	新余市	江西省	(0790)6460999	906	港澳台资	397,371	32,321(7)	489,125	pc钢铰线
Weihai Xingwei Industry Group Company	Weihai	Shandong	(0631)5765278		Collective-owned				Stranded Steel Wire
威海兴威工业集团公司(1995)	威海市	山东省	(0631)5764106	810	集体企业	366,810	21,020(13)	175,610	钢铰线
Jiangsu Jinyang Group Co., Ltd.	Wuxi	Jiangsu	(0510)8731337		Joint Stock				Stranded Steel Wire
江苏金羊集团有限公司(1984)	无锡市	江苏省	(0510)8731791	447	股份制	326,770	29,980(8)	424,770	钢铰线
Shanghai Shenjia Metal Products Co., Ltd.	Shanghai	Shanghai	(021)65181928		Overseas Chinese-funded				Steel Wire
上海申佳金属制品有限公司(1995)	上海市	上海市	(021)65195482	242	港澳台资	312,214	35,533(4)	347,873	钢丝
Hubei Tianye Co., Ltd.	Xianning	Hubei	(0715)6718035		Joint Stock				Steel Wire Rope
湖北田野股份有限公司(1993)	咸宁市	湖北省	(0715)6718003	818	股份制	283,569	32,783(6)	210,304	钢缆索
Beijing ORG-MC Metal Containers Co., Ltd.	Beijing	Beijing	(010)84970210		Foreign Funded				Three Slice Tear Tab Ends三
北京奥瑞金新美制罐有限公司(1997)	北京市	北京市	(010)84990071	357	外商投资	239,420	20,040(14)	210,768	片易拉罐

Top 10 Cities by Revenue 销售收入排名前10位城市	Province 省	Market share 市场份额（%）	Number of firms 企业个数
Wuxi 无锡市	Jiangsu 江苏省	14.76	31
Tianjin 天津市	Tianjin 天津市	9.48	112
Shanghai 上海市	Shanghai 上海市	6.08	65
Nantong 南通市	Jiangsu 江苏省	3.67	38
Taizhou 泰州市	Jiangsu 江苏省	3.46	18
Lishui 丽水市	Zhejiang 浙江省	3.45	3
Xiaogan 孝感市	Hubei 湖北省	3.31	5
Cangzhou 沧州市	Hebei 河北省	1.99	15
Hengshui 衡水市	Hebei 河北省	1.97	23
Shizuishan 石嘴山市	Ningxia 宁夏	1.94	1

10 Major Wholesalers 十家主要批发商	City 城市	Province 省	Telephone/Fax 电话/传真
SU MEC	Nanjing	Jiangsu	(025)4511888
中设江苏机械设备进出口（集团）公司	南京市	江苏省	(025)4411772
China Poster Mobile Communications Equipment Co.,Ltd.	Beijing	Beijing	(010)66426993
中邮普泰移动通信设备股份有限公司	北京市	北京市	(010)66426837
Sino Kama Co., Ltd.	Shanghai	Shanghai	(021)62031188
中泰凯马股份有限公司	上海市	上海市	(021)62030851
China Huayuan Group Co.,Ltd.	Shanghai	Shanghai	(021)62031188
中国华源集团有限公司	上海市	上海市	(021)62032288
Zhejiang Crand Imp.& Exp.Co.,Ltd.	Ningbo	Zhejiang	(0574)87720170
浙江远大进出口有限公司	宁波市	浙江省	(0574)87723350
Shandong Machinery Import & Export Group Corporation	Qingdao	Shandong	(0532)2661628
山东省机械进出口集团公司	青岛市	山东省	(0532)2991655
Qingdao Haier International Trade Co.,Ltd.	Qingdao	Shandong	(0532)8938337
青岛海尔国际贸易有限公司	青岛市	山东省	(0532)8939494
Guangdong Machinery Import & Export Group Corporation	Guangzhou	Guangdong	(020)87782168
广东省机械进出口集团公司	广州市	广东省	(020)87771803
China National Machinery Equipment Import & Export Corporation	Beijing	Beijing	(010)63474506
中国机械设备进出口总公司	北京市	北京市	(010)63261865
Beijing Cellstar Co.,Ltd.	Beijing	Beijing	(010)64602050
北京蜂星事达电讯有限公司	北京市	北京市	(010)64672648

3461: Metal Construction Hardware 建筑小五金制造业

The industry accounts for 0.047% of the total revenue of China's industrial sector in 2002. The rate of return on assets is 4.51%. 87.55% of all firms in the industry made a profit while 12.45% had negative returns.The top province in terms of the industry's revenue is Guangdong, accounting for 52.35% of the total revenue.
2002年本行业收入占全行业的 0.047%，资产利润率为 4.51%。87.55%的企业赢利，12.45%的企业亏损。收入最高的省为广东省，占本行业的52.35%。

	Total number of firms 企业总数	Total number of employees 职工总数	Total revenue (Mil.RMB) 总销售收入 (百万元)	Total profit (Mil.RMB) 总利润 (百万元)	Return on assets 资产利润率 (%)	Return on equity 权益利润率 (%)	Labour productivity ('000 RMB/ worker) 劳动生产率 (千元/人)	Debts/ assets 资产负债率 (%)	Total assets (Mil.RMB) 总资产 (百万元)
Industry Overall 行业总体	249	31,568	5,078	178	4.51	10.48	42.06	56.99	3,950

	Number of firms 企业个数	Average number of employees 平均职工人数	Average revenue ('000 RMB) 平均销售收入（千元)	Average profit ('000 RMB) 平均利润 (千元)	Return on assets 资产利润率 (%)	Return on equity 权益利润率 (%)	Labour productivity ('000 RMB/ worker) 劳动生产率 (千元/人)	Debts/ assets 资产负债率 (%)	Average total assets ('000 RMB) 平均总资产 (千元)
By ownership 产业所有权									
State-owned 国有	10	141	4,588	-80	-0.32	-1.73	15.06	81.79	25,424
Collective-owned 集体	35	104	16,065	385	2.66	6.95	40.98	61.76	14,508
Foreign & Overseas Chinese Funded 三资	67	197	28,912	1,357	4.60	9.37	38.69	50.95	29,515
By regional distribution 地区分布									
Central-North 华北	19	80	16,823	1,266	9.35	27.43	70.98	65.90	13,534
Beijing 北京	4	52	27,510	2,104	8.16	40.18	222.40	79.68	25,774
Tianjin 天津	11	80	16,851	1,284	16.03	39.77	58.84	59.69	8,010
Hebei 河北	3	111	7,402	398	2.49	6.30	26.72	60.56	16,018
Shanxi 山西	1	89	2,024	316	1.77	2.58	7.30	31.42	17,892
Inner Mongolia 内蒙古									
Northeast 东北	1	12	575	2	0.02	0.07	27.83	66.75	8,641
Liaoning 辽宁									
Jilin 吉林	1	12	575	2	0.02	0.07	27.83	66.75	8,641
Heilongjiang 黑龙江									
Central-East 华东	108	110	15,592	751	6.31	15.75	33.05	59.97	11,918
Shanghai 上海	24	114	16,657	557	4.18	10.30	33.69	59.37	13,319
Jiangsu 江苏	17	115	18,598	1,718	9.52	23.27	34.59	59.09	18,043
Zhejiang 浙江	52	110	15,283	560	6.40	14.78	31.55	56.68	8,751
Anhui 安徽									
Fujian 福建	6	105	12,371	251	1.70	4.68	26.22	63.80	14,803
Jiangxi 江西	1	47	3,652	253	7.38	11.48	81.28	35.74	3,428
Shandong 山东	8	93	11,928	961	6.78	27.12	40.97	74.99	14,177
Central-South 中南	117	140	25,283	627	3.61	7.43	48.67	51.46	17,392
Henan 河南	5	54	18,173	1,256	8.52	20.07	96.93	57.56	14,746
Hubei 湖北	6	147	30,133	1,443	25.07	60.06	61.99	58.26	5,756
Hunan 湖南	5	45	3,454	-9	-0.44	-2.28	20.58	80.68	1,953
Guangdong 广东	100	150	26,581	584	3.06	6.22	47.37	50.82	19,102
Guangxi 广西	1	30	11,072	66	1.00	12.20	81.33	91.77	6,575
Hainan 海南									
Southwest 西南	4	450	28,920	-131	-0.14	-0.50	16.90	70.92	90,506
Chongqing 重庆									
Sichuan 四川	3	425	21,476	-205	-0.24	-0.86	14.77	72.54	86,502
Guizhou 贵州									
Yunnan 云南	1	525	51,252	90	0.09	0.26	22.05	66.81	102,516
Tibet 西藏									
Northwest 西北									
Shaanxi 陕西									
Gansu 甘肃									
Qinghai 青海									
Ningxia 宁夏									
Xinjiang 新疆									

3461: Metal Construction Hardware 建筑小五金制造业

Year 年份	Number of firms 企业个数	Rate of change 变化率 (%)	Number of employees 职工人数 (人)	Rate of change 变化率 (%)	Total revenue (Mil. RMB) 总销售收入 (百万元)	Rate of change 变化率 (%)	Total profit (Mil RMB) 总利润 (百万元)	Rate of change 变化率 (%)
2000	178		27,580		3,394		33	
2001	213	19.66	28,855	4.62	4,719	39.04	128	287.88
2002	249	16.90	31,568	9.40	5,078	7.61	178	39.06

Major Products 主要产品	Output 产量	Unit 单位
Steel Nail 钢钉	20	10,000 Tons 万吨

10 Main Firms with Maximal Revenue (year founded) 收入最大的十家主要企业（创办年份）	City 城市	Province 省	Telephone/fax 电话/传真	Number of employees 职工人数	Ownership 产业所有权	Revenue ('000 RMB) 销售收入 (千元)	Profit('000 RMB) (rank) 利润(千元) (排名)	Total assets ('000 RMB) 总资产 (千元)	Major products 主要产品
Stanley (Zhongshan) Hardware Co., Ltd.	Zhongshan	Guangdong	(0760)2268632		Foreign Funded				Hinge
史丹利(中山)五金有限公司(1997)	中山市	广东省	(0760)2250190	899	外商投资	163,557	7,739(3)	205,379	铰链
Nam Wah Precision Product (Shenzhen) Co., Ltd.	Shenzhen	Guangdong	(0755)84898168		Overseas Chinese-funded				Hardware Fitting Parts
南精机电（深圳）有限公司(1992)	深圳市	广东省	(0755)84894843	635	港澳台资	102,102	6,336(5)	83,240	五金配件
Daguang Aluminium Decorative Materials Co., Ltd.	Guangzhou	Guangdong	(020)84788108		Private Enterprises				Aluminium Celling
大广铝业装饰材料有限公司(1992)	广州市	广东省	(020)84795188	394	私营独资	95,976	1,386(39)	114,255	铝天花
Beijing Roto Building Materials Co., Ltd.	Beijing	Beijing	(010)82950045		Foreign Funded				Building Hardware Components建
北京诺托建筑材料有限公司(1997)	北京市	北京市	(010)82920115	152	外商投资	84,372	8,910(2)	76,785	筑五金件
Dongguan Shilong Wantong Slide-Rail Manufacturing Factory	Dongguan	Guangdong	(0769)6110301		Overseas Chinese-funded				Drawn Rail
东莞市石龙万通滑轨制造厂(1997)	东莞市	广东省	(0769)6110302	436	港澳台资	77,622	2,619(21)	36,743	抽轨
Sanba Qianhui Hardware Co., Ltd.	Jiangmen	Guangdong	(0750)5851047		Private Enterprises				Hardware Collecting Components
三八乾慧五金有限公司(1985)	江门市	广东省		152	私营独资	75,810	73(161)	21,938	五金集件
Jiana (Tianjin) Hardware Industry Co., Ltd.	Tianjin	Tianjin	(022)26991832		Overseas Chinese-funded				Hardware
迦拿（天津）五金工业有限公司(1995)	天津市	天津市	(022)26992231	251	港澳台资	73,740	6,990(4)	30,190	五金
Zhongshan Jingsheng Hardware Co., Ltd.	Zhongshan	Guangdong	(0760)3408660		Private Owned				Door Hinge
中山市京盛五金有限公司(1998)	中山市	广东省	(0760)3408661	168	私营企业	72,240	1,450(38)	10,000	门铰
Guangzhou Panyu Lingshan Rongxing Metal Material Processing	Guangzhou	Guangdong	(020)34931788		Private Enterprises				Angle Iron
Factory 广州市番禺区灵山荣兴金属材料加工厂(2000)	广州市	广东省	(020)34931788	70	私营独资	66,082	-	12,517	角铁
Weiyang Building Hardware Co., Ltd.	Yangzhou	Jiangsu	(0514)7853013		Overseas Chinese-funded				Hinge
伟扬建筑五金有限公司(1987)	扬州市	江苏省	(0514)7887898	203	港澳台资	58,280	700(68)	25,960	合页

Top 10 Cities by Revenue 销售收入排名前10位城市	Province 省	Market share 市场份额 (%)	Number of firms 企业个数
Guangzhou 广州市	Guangdong 广东省	18.61	41
Zhongshan 中山市	Guangdong 广东省	9.39	12
Shanghai 上海市	Shanghai 上海市	7.87	24
Wenzhou 温州市	Zhejiang 浙江省	7.67	22
Jiangmen 江门市	Guangdong 广东省	7.26	9
Dongguan 东莞市	Guangdong 广东省	5.77	11
Shenzhen 深圳市	Guangdong 广东省	5.41	9
Tianjin 天津市	Tianjin 天津市	3.65	11
Hangzhou 杭州市	Zhejiang 浙江省	3.08	10
Huanggang 黄冈市	Hubei 湖北省	2.84	3

10 Major Wholesalers 十家主要批发商	City 城市	Province 省	Telephone/Fax 电话/传真
Xuzhou New Century Building Materials Decorative City	Xuzhou	Jiangsu	(0516)83666780
徐州市新世纪建材装饰城	徐州市	江苏省	(0516)63804485
Orienthome Co.,Ltd.	Beijing	Beijing	(010)63808294
东方家园有限公司	北京市	北京市	
Shanghai Jinkai Goods & Materials Co.,Ltd.	Shanghai	Shanghai	(021)52193967
上海金凯物资有限公司	上海市	上海市	
Guangzhou Building Materials Development Co.,Ltd.	Guangzhou	Guangdong	(020)83335062
广州市建材发展有限公司	广州市	广东省	(020)83341110
Guangxi Qiaofeng Goods & Materials Trade Co.,Ltd.	Nanning	Guangxi	(0771)2631539
广西侨丰物资贸易有限责任公司	南宁市	广西	(0771)2631539
Gansu Building Materials State-owned Assets Marketing Co.,Ltd.	Lanzhou	Gansu	(0931)8821359
甘肃建材国有资产经营有限责任公司	兰州市	甘肃省	(0931)8960243
Shanghai East Asia United Building Materials Co.,Ltd.	Shanghai	Shanghai	(021)33134520
上海东亚联合建材有限公司	上海市	上海市	(021)63216165
Shanghai Zhuzong Materials General Company	Shanghai	Shanghai	(021)32240030
上海住总物资总公司	上海市	上海市	(021)32240024
Guangdong Building Materials Company	Guangzhou	Guangdong	(020)83802713
广东省建材公司	广州市	广东省	(020)83817640
Guangdong Dongguan Hardware Minerals Import & Export Co.,Ltd	Dongguan	Guangdong	(0769)2227090
广东省东莞五金矿产进出口公司	东莞市	广东省	(0769)2221045

3463: Plumbing Parts 水暖管道零件制造业

The industry accounts for 0.130% of the total revenue of China's industrial sector in 2002. The rate of return on assets is 6.70%. 86.39% of all firms in the industry made a profit while 13.61% had negative returns.The top province in terms of the industry's revenue is Zhejiang, accounting for 21.41% of the total revenue.
2002年本行业收入占全行业的 0.130%，资产利润率为 6.70%。86.39%的企业赢利，13.61%的企业亏损。收入最高的省为浙江省，占本行业的21.41%。

	Total number of firms 企业总数	Total number of employees 职工总数	Total revenue (Mil.RMB) 总销售收入 (百万元)	Total profit (Mil.RMB) 总利润 (百万元)	Return on assets 资产利润率 (%)	Return on equity 权益利润率 (%)	Labour productivity ('000 RMB/ worker) 劳动生产率 (千元/人)	Debts/ assets 资产负债率 (%)	Total assets (Mil.RMB) 总资产 (百万元)
Industry Overall 行业总体	463	109,227	13,996	762	6.70	14.67	36.53	54.36	11,381

	Number of firms 企业个数	Average number of employees 平均职工人数	Average revenue ('000 RMB) 平均销售收入 (千元)	Average profit ('000 RMB) 平均利润 (千元)	Return on assets 资产利润率 (%)	Return on equity 权益利润率 (%)	Labour productivity ('000 RMB/ worker) 劳动生产率 (千元/人)	Debts/ assets 资产负债率 (%)	Average total assets ('000 RMB) 平均总资产 (千元)
By ownership 产业所有权									
State-owned 国有	20	141	8,904	-1,013	-5.38	-26.22	11.40	79.50	18,839
Collective-owned 集体	94	362	40,868	1,906	7.02	17.14	36.77	59.01	27,136
Foreign & Overseas Chinese Funded 三资	84	232	49,541	4,472	9.16	17.71	54.89	48.28	48,817
By regional distribution 地区分布									
Central-North 华北	107	434	35,981	1,834	5.65	12.59	25.64	55.13	32,473
Beijing 北京	20	77	23,727	4,539	13.52	22.11	94.69	38.86	33,582
Tianjin 天津	11	150	34,948	2,488	5.55	13.17	52.66	57.85	44,829
Hebei 河北	49	395	38,402	1,376	5.17	13.83	32.11	62.62	26,614
Shanxi 山西	27	885	41,086	395	1.06	2.36	14.09	54.96	37,251
Inner Mongolia 内蒙古									
Northeast 东北	30	147	15,070	789	4.66	11.45	38.23	59.33	16,949
Liaoning 辽宁	14	209	23,621	1,435	7.37	13.67	44.29	46.09	19,476
Jilin 吉林	13	99	6,857	157	1.13	8.83	23.79	87.18	13,851
Heilongjiang 黑龙江	3	66	10,757	513	2.76	4.20	42.88	34.16	18,584
Central-East 华东	223	173	28,896	1,918	9.65	19.00	46.36	49.20	19,874
Shanghai 上海	31	94	14,319	849	5.51	11.57	56.35	52.38	15,409
Jiangsu 江苏	26	108	25,024	793	3.69	8.30	73.86	55.47	21,464
Zhejiang 浙江	110	147	27,247	1,586	10.54	21.77	34.25	51.60	15,048
Anhui 安徽	1	226	2,311				3.30		3,211
Fujian 福建	19	282	34,594	3,005	7.15	10.67	37.17	32.94	42,001
Jiangxi 江西	1	350	46,188	3,050	13.59	24.12	38.63	43.66	22,443
Shandong 山东	35	310	47,037	4,179	15.95	34.55	60.28	53.83	26,204
Central-South 中南	82	186	36,606	1,339	4.17	10.40	49.36	59.90	32,107
Henan 河南	17	269	34,477	1,107	2.82	13.36	44.34	78.90	39,281
Hubei 湖北	2	405	20,603	116	0.36	0.63	21.76	43.35	32,523
Hunan 湖南	6	75	6,325	-135	-1.60	-54.44	59.44	97.06	8,433
Guangdong 广东	54	159	42,078	1,778	5.70	12.30	56.48	53.60	31,165
Guangxi 广西	3	279	21,393	-1,495	-2.69	-4.69	25.13	42.58	55,475
Hainan 海南									
Southwest 西南	9	193	9,550	192	1.16	1.83	17.18	36.63	16,508
Chongqing 重庆	3	133	13,139	462	1.57	1.97	36.89	20.14	29,437
Sichuan 四川	6	223	7,755	56	0.56	1.43	11.29	60.81	10,044
Guizhou 贵州									
Yunnan 云南									
Tibet 西藏									
Northwest 西北	12	231	13,547	254	1.65	11.15	20.74	85.17	15,358
Shaanxi 陕西	2	310	5,688	-725	-5.56		2.93	142.27	13,039
Gansu 甘肃	8	37	7,758	359	8.20	20.95	80.18	60.89	4,385
Qinghai 青海									
Ningxia 宁夏									
Xinjiang 新疆	2	924	44,564	811	1.32	6.58	17.09	80.00	61,572

3463: Plumbing Parts 水暖管道零件制造业

Year 年份	Number of firms 企业个数	Rate of change 变化率 (%)	Number of employees 职工人数 (人)	Rate of change 变化率 (%)	Total revenue (Mil. RMB) 总销售收入 (百万元)	Rate of change 变化率 (%)	Total profit (Mil RMB) 总利润 (百万元)	Rate of change 变化率 (%)
2000	375		99,695		8,699		294	
2001	418	11.47	104,464	4.78	10,550	21.28	503	71.09
2002	463	10.77	109,227	4.56	13,996	32.66	762	51.49

Major Products 主要产品	Output 产量	Unit 单位
Welded Steel Pipe 焊接钢管	701	10,000 Tons 万吨
Seamless Steel Pipe 无缝钢管	608	10,000 Tons 万吨

10 Main Firms with Maximal Revenue (year founded) 收入最大的十家主要企业（创办年份）	City 城市	Province 省	Telephone/fax 电话/传真	Number of employees 职工人数	Ownership 产业所有权	Revenue ('000 RMB) 销售收入 (千元)	Profit('000 RMB) (rank) 利润(千元) (排名)	Total assets ('000 RMB) 总资产 (千元)	Major products 主要产品
Zhejiang Maple Leaf Pipe Industry Co.,Ltd	Shaoxing	Zhejiang	(0575)7068897		Private Owned				Water-heating Pipeline Parts
浙江枫叶管业有限公司(1990)	绍兴市	浙江省	(0575)7061687	511	私营企业	543,945	49,803(3)	330,543	水暖管道零件
Tianyuan Radiator Group Company	Hengshui	Hebei	(0318)8462308		Collective-owned				Gray Cast Iron Radiator
天元散热器集团公司(1987)	衡水市	河北省	(0318)8462233	3,925	集体企业	482,234	6,537(23)	251,184	灰铸铁散热器
Ji'nan Meide Casting Co., Ltd.	Jinan	Shandong	(0531)7885015		Foreign Funded				Malleable Cast Iron Pipe Fittings
济南玫德铸造有限公司(玛钢股份)(1992)	济南市	山东省	(0531)7871021	3,188	外商投资	431,333	85,015(1)	357,271	玛钢管件
Moen Guangzhou Heating Equipment Co., ltd.	Guangzhou	Guangdong	(020)37084317		Foreign Funded				Water Supply & Heating Equipment
广州摩恩水暖器材有限公司(1995)	广州市	广东省	(020)37081050	229	外商投资	399,077	17,051(11)	261,655	水暖管件
Fujian Joyou Group Corportion	Quanzhou	Fujian	(0595)6141289		Collective-owned				Tap
福建省中宇集团公司(1995)	泉州市	福建省	(0595)6143389	1,920	集体企业	321,490	25,899(6)	324,080	水龙头
Shenqiu Xinya Group General Company	Zhoukou	Henan	(0394)5531307		Collective-owned				Water Supply & Heating Equipment
沈丘县新亚集团总公司(1980)	周口市	河南省	(0394)5531118	2,136	集体企业	307,550	15,992(13)	321,376	水暖器材
Shanxi Qingxu Yuanyue Radiator Co., Ltd.	Taiyuan	Shanxi	(0351)5960435		Private Owned				Heating Pieces
清徐垣跃暖气片有限公司(1998)	太原市	山西省	(0351)7951833	3,000	私营企业	295,093	-	106,506	暖气片
Guangzhou Panyu Seagull Lavatory Products Co., Ltd.	Guangzhou	Guangdong	(020)84896117		Overseas Chinese-funded				Water Supply & Heating Equipment
广州市番禺海鸥卫浴用品有限公司(1998)	广州市	广东省	(020)84893787	1,195	港澳台资	285,544	43,723(4)	191,264	水暖器材
Wendeng Valve Factory	Weihai	Shandong	(0631)8681026		Collective-owned				Valve
文登市阀门厂(1969)	威海市	山东省	(0631)8681027	184	集体企业	284,190	21,290(8)	33,340	阀门
Xiamen Hcg-lota Co., Ltd.	Xiamen	Fujian	(0592)6214485		Overseas Chinese-funded				Tap
和成路达(厦门)有限公司(2000)	厦门市	福建省	(0592)6226350	650	港澳台资	171,132	24,445(7)	134,899	水龙头

Top 10 Cities by Revenue 销售收入排名前10位城市	Province 省	Market share 市场份额 (%)	Number of firms 企业个数
Hengshui 衡水市	Hebei 河北省	8.49	8
Taizhou 台州市	Zhejiang 浙江省	6.87	42
Shaoxing 绍兴市	Zhejiang 浙江省	6.69	25
Jiangmen 江门市	Guangdong 广东省	6.45	29
Jinan 济南市	Shandong 山东省	6.32	6
Guangzhou 广州市	Guangdong 广东省	5.69	7
Taiyuan 太原市	Shanxi 山西省	5.66	9
Ningbo 宁波市	Zhejiang 浙江省	3.88	24
Beijing 北京市	Beijing 北京市	3.39	20
Shanghai 上海市	Shanghai 上海市	3.17	31

10 Major Wholesalers 十家主要批发商	City 城市	Province 省	Telephone/Fax 电话/传真
Xuzhou New Century Building Materials Decorative City	Xuzhou	Jiangsu	(0516)83666780
徐州市新世纪建材装饰城	徐州市	江苏省	(0516)63804485
Orienthome Co.,Ltd.	Beijing	Beijing	(010)63808294
东方家园有限公司	北京市	北京市	
Shanghai Jinkai Goods & Materials Co.,Ltd.	Shanghai	Shanghai	(021)52193967
上海金凯物资有限公司	上海市	上海市	
Guangzhou Building Materials Development Co.,Ltd.	Guangzhou	Guangdong	(020)83335062
广州市建材发展有限公司	广州市	广东省	(020)83341110
Guangxi Qiaofeng Goods & Materials Trade Co.,Ltd.	Nanning	Guangxi	(0771)2631539
广西侨丰物资贸易有限责任公司	南宁市	广西	(0771)2631539
Gansu Building Materials State-owned Assets Marketing Co.,Ltd.	Lanzhou	Gansu	(0931)8821359
甘肃建材国有资产经营有限责任公司	兰州市	甘肃省	(0931)8960243
Shanghai East Asia United Building Materials Co.,Ltd.	Shanghai	Shanghai	(021)33134520
上海东亚联合建材有限公司	上海市	上海市	(021)63216165
Shanghai Zhuzong Materials General Company	Shanghai	Shanghai	(021)32240030
上海住总物资总公司	上海市	上海市	(021)32240024
Guangdong Building Materials Company	Guangzhou	Guangdong	(020)83802713
广东省建材公司	广州市	广东省	(020)83817640
Guangdong Dongguan Hardware Minerals Import & Export Co.,Ltd	Dongguan	Guangdong	(0769)2227090
广东省东莞五金矿产进出口公司	东莞市	广东省	(0769)2221045

3465: Metal Doors and Windows 金属门窗制造业

The industry accounts for 0.148% of the total revenue of China's industrial sector in 2002. The rate of return on assets is 3.89%. 82.26% of all firms in the industry made a profit while 17.74% had negative returns.The top province in terms of the industry's revenue is Jiangsu, accounting for 13.94% of the total revenue.
2002年本行业收入占全行业的 0.148%，资产利润率为 3.89%。82.26%的企业赢利，17.74%的企业亏损。收入最高的省为江苏省，占本行业的13.94%。

	Total number of firms 企业总数	Total number of employees 职工总数	Total revenue (Mil.RMB) 总销售收入 (百万元)	Total profit (Mil.RMB) 总利润 (百万元)	Return on assets 资产利润率 (%)	Return on equity 权益利润率 (%)	Labour productivity ('000 RMB/ worker) 劳动生产率 (千元/人)	Debts/ assets 资产负债率 (%)	Total assets (Mil.RMB) 总资产 (百万元)
Industry Overall 行业总体	682	101,509	15,833	630	3.89	9.83	49.09	60.39	16,188

	Number of firms 企业个数	Average number of employees 平均职工人数	Average revenue ('000 RMB) 平均销售收入 (千元)	Average profit ('000 RMB) 平均利润 (千元)	Return on assets 资产利润率 (%)	Return on equity 权益利润率 (%)	Labour productivity ('000 RMB/ worker) 劳动生产率 (千元/人)	Debts/ assets 资产负债率 (%)	Average total assets ('000 RMB) 平均总资产 (千元)
By ownership 产业所有权									
State-owned 国有	84	116	7,079	-249	-1.72	-12.14	16.06	85.85	14,496
Collective-owned 集体	145	161	18,095	961	6.87	18.29	40.09	62.46	13,992
Foreign & Overseas Chinese Funded 三资	75	115	32,793	1,813	5.06	11.54	95.65	56.12	35,814
By regional distribution 地区分布									
Central-North 华北	135	165	18,174	1,098	4.47	11.13	43.72	59.85	24,586
Beijing 北京	81	189	16,754	759	3.34	8.72	41.34	61.74	22,743
Tianjin 天津	27	99	10,129	437	3.89	10.92	30.40	64.42	11,249
Hebei 河北	16	219	48,347	4,700	6.94	15.70	69.01	55.76	67,670
Shanxi 山西	7	74	4,253	221	4.02	8.22	16.93	51.09	5,495
Inner Mongolia 内蒙古	4	91	4,919	-428	-3.30	-7.82	35.85	57.82	12,987
Northeast 东北	58	217	33,858	1,948	4.16	10.51	45.62	60.43	46,835
Liaoning 辽宁	32	259	50,967	3,423	5.77	13.79	52.68	58.15	59,326
Jilin 吉林	11	69	7,787	77	1.12	3.33	52.54	66.35	6,865
Heilongjiang 黑龙江	15	237	16,477	173	0.35	1.02	27.69	65.66	49,499
Central-East 华东	256	152	27,614	1,232	5.49	14.04	50.09	60.93	22,452
Shanghai 上海	45	93	30,571	2,087	10.38	30.05	78.16	65.45	20,101
Jiangsu 江苏	72	172	30,649	1,037	4.37	11.23	45.00	61.08	23,724
Zhejiang 浙江	64	138	25,553	1,349	5.70	12.30	46.34	53.63	23,651
Anhui 安徽	11	174	6,505	287	3.06	8.57	14.34	64.34	9,397
Fujian 福建	12	67	10,911	340	1.81	4.17	57.43	56.54	18,739
Jiangxi 江西	5	193	42,905	3,547	7.92	17.55	76.99	54.89	44,807
Shandong 山东	47	207	30,519	755	3.32	10.73	51.59	69.08	22,749
Central-South 中南	118	122	25,207	111	0.56	1.42	67.03	60.78	19,976
Henan 河南	24	76	17,846	1,027	13.73	28.38	67.40	51.64	7,484
Hubei 湖北	20	218	43,532	1,226	4.22	13.81	60.29	69.47	29,080
Hunan 湖南	10	64	13,260	113	1.12	2.77	59.64	59.66	10,130
Guangdong 广东	57	120	22,367	-629	-2.70	-7.15	69.52	62.23	23,264
Guangxi 广西	6	112	44,325	-229	-0.84	-1.19	94.51	29.61	27,370
Hainan 海南	1	36	2,049	43	0.98	1.58	10.31	37.55	4,367
Southwest 西南	42	180	24,101	789	2.39	5.08	49.04	52.91	32,966
Chongqing 重庆	10	308	59,669	2,824	3.42	6.58	70.76	48.04	82,608
Sichuan 四川	20	146	13,919	155	1.08	2.71	42.01	60.04	14,297
Guizhou 贵州	3	79	11,066	104	0.64	1.28	38.55	50.06	16,187
Yunnan 云南	6	173	13,475	-689	-2.02	-5.33	38.19	62.03	34,016
Tibet 西藏	3	94	7,706	1,876	28.30	82.61	-66.16	65.74	6,630
Northwest 西北	73	80	4,926	98	1.08	3.91	26.25	72.38	9,084
Shaanxi 陕西	7	187	7,055	218	1.08	6.55	17.99	83.45	20,158
Gansu 甘肃	53	61	4,629	243	3.51	12.97	34.32	72.90	6,914
Qinghai 青海	4	112	3,244	-325	-5.87	-24.39	12.22	75.93	5,532
Ningxia 宁夏									
Xinjiang 新疆	9	94	5,767	-662	-4.46	-10.80	15.81	58.67	14,827

3465: Metal Doors and Windows 金属门窗制造业

Year 年份	Number of firms 企业个数	Rate of change 变化率 (%)	Number of employees 职工人数 (人)	Rate of change 变化率 (%)	Total revenue (Mil. RMB) 总销售收入 (百万元)	Rate of change 变化率 (%)	Total profit (Mil RMB) 总利润 (百万元)	Rate of change 变化率 (%)
2000	590		94,995		10,921		373	
2001	662	12.20	94,765	-0.24	14,814	35.65	573	53.62
2002	682	3.02	101,509	7.12	15,833	6.88	630	9.95

Major Products 主要产品	Output 产量	Unit 单位
Metal Products For Building 建筑用金属品	198	10,000 Tons 万吨

10 Main Firms with Maximal Revenue (year founded) 收入最大的十家主要企业（创办年份）	City 城市	Province 省	Telephone/fax 电话/传真	Number of employees 职工人数	Ownership 产业所有权	Revenue ('000 RMB) 销售收入 (千元)	Profit('000 RMB) (rank) 利润(千元) (排名)	Total assets ('000 RMB) 总资产 (千元)	Major products 主要产品
Chongqing Meixin (Group) Co., Ltd.	Chongqing	Chongqing	(023)62811586		Private Owned				Guard Against Theft Door
重庆美心（集团）有限公司(1995)	重庆市	重庆市	(023)62911231	2,042	私营企业	473,157	26,693(5)	544,739	防盗门
Yingkou Reynaers Aluminum Products Co., Ltd.	Yingkou	Liaoning	(0417)7265408		Foreign Funded				Aluminium Window & Door
营口瑞那斯铝业有限公司(1997)	营口市	辽宁省	(0417)7265082	400	外商投资	469,893	45,163(2)	433,984	铝门窗
Zhengfang Group Co., Ltd.	Nanjing	Jiangsu	(025)2755366		Limited-Liability				Door & Window Series
正方集团有限责任公司(1984)	南京市	江苏省	(025)2755828	3,092	有限公司	441,480	15,680(9)	265,500	门窗系列
Hebei Zhenhai Aluminium Industry Group Co., Ltd.	Cangzhou	Hebei	(0317)3223738		Private Owned				Aluminium Window & Door
河北振海铝业集团有限公司(1997)	沧州市	河北省	(0317)3222119	680	私营企业	427,655	46,456(1)	782,274	铝门窗
Panpan Group Co.,Ltd	Yingkou	Liaoning	(0417)5179104		Private Enterprises				Guard Against Theft Door
盼盼集团有限公司(1996)	营口市	辽宁省	(0417)5140658	3,100	私营独资	368,671	30,433(3)	485,790	防撬门
Zhejiang Buyang Group Co., Ltd.	Jinhua	Zhejiang	(0579)7271166		Private Owned				Guard Against Theft Door
浙江步阳集团有限公司(1998)	金华市	浙江省	(0579)7271226	1,200	私营企业	268,129	16,814(8)	183,381	防盗门
Beijing Dongya Aluminum Co.,Ltd	Beijing	Beijing	(010)69575102		Overseas Chinese-funded				Aluminium Materials
北京东亚铝业有限公司(1993)	北京市	北京市	(010)69571551	1,205	港澳台资	264,722	7,700(21)	294,292	铝型材
Pingguo Yazhou Aluminium Co., Ltd.	Baise	Guangxi	(0776)5608888		Private Enterprises				Aluminium Materials
平果亚洲铝业有限公司(2001)	百色市	广西	(0776)5608666	270	私营独资	234,291	-	120,314	铝型材
State-owned Wanfeng Radio Factory	Xiaogan	Hubei	(0712)2959508		State owned				Plastic & Steel Shapes
国营万峰无线电厂(1973)	孝感市	湖北省	(0712)2959588	1,530	国有企业	228,482	1,244(114)	266,365	塑钢型材
Weifang Dajiang Enterprise Group Co., Ltd.	Weifang	Shandong	(0536)4561356		Private Enterprises				Dajiang Furniture
潍坊市大江企业集团有限公司(1997)	潍坊市	山东省	(0536)4641201	3,250	私营独资	221,886	1,146(122)	183,019	大江家私

Top 10 Cities by Revenue 销售收入排名前10位城市	Province 省	Market share 市场份额 (%)	Number of firms 企业个数
Shanghai 上海市	Shanghai 上海市	8.69	45
Beijing 北京市	Beijing 北京市	8.57	81
Yingkou 营口市	Liaoning 辽宁省	8.16	9
Jinhua 金华市	Zhejiang 浙江省	6.21	18
Nanjing 南京市	Jiangsu 江苏省	5.96	15
Chongqing 重庆市	Chongqing 重庆市	3.77	10
Xiaogan 孝感市	Hubei 湖北省	3.49	6
Wuxi 无锡市	Jiangsu 江苏省	3.30	13
Cangzhou 沧州市	Hebei 河北省	2.70	1
Jinan 济南市	Shandong 山东省	2.41	10

10 Major Wholesalers 十家主要批发商	City 城市	Province 省	Telephone/Fax 电话/传真
Xuzhou New Century Building Materials Decorative City	Xuzhou	Jiangsu	(0516)83666780
徐州市新世纪建材装饰城	徐州市	江苏省	(0516)63804485
Orienthome Co.,Ltd.	Beijing	Beijing	(010)63808294
东方家园有限公司	北京市	北京市	
Shanghai Jinkai Goods & Materials Co.,Ltd.	Shanghai	Shanghai	(021)52193967
上海金凯物资有限公司	上海市	上海市	
Guangzhou Building Materials Development Co.,Ltd.	Guangzhou	Guangdong	(020)83335062
广州市建材发展有限公司	广州市	广东省	(020)83341110
Guangxi Qiaofeng Goods & Materials Trade Co.,Ltd.	Nanning	Guangxi	(0771)2631539
广西侨丰物资贸易有限责任公司	南宁市	广西	(0771)2631539
Gansu Building Materials State-owned Assets Marketing Co.,Ltd.	Lanzhou	Gansu	(0931)8821359
甘肃建材国有资产经营有限责任公司	兰州市	甘肃省	(0931)8960243
Shanghai East Asia United Building Materials Co.,Ltd.	Shanghai	Shanghai	(021)33134520
上海东亚联合建材有限公司	上海市	上海市	(021)63216165
Shanghai Zhuzong Materials General Company	Shanghai	Shanghai	(021)32240030
上海住总物资总公司	上海市	上海市	(021)32240024
Guangdong Building Materials Company	Guangzhou	Guangdong	(020)83802713
广东省建材公司	广州市	广东省	(020)83817640
Guangdong Dongguan Hardware Minerals Import & Export Co.,Ltd	Dongguan	Guangdong	(0769)2227090
广东省东莞五金矿产进出口公司	东莞市	广东省	(0769)2221045

3469: Other Metal Products For Construction 其他建筑用金属制品业

The industry accounts for 0.049% of the total revenue of China's industrial sector in 2002. The rate of return on assets is 4.72%. 84.55% of all firms in the industry made a profit while 15.45% had negative returns.The top province in terms of the industry's revenue is Guangdong, accounting for 19.26% of the total revenue.
2002年本行业收入占全行业的0.049%，资产利润率为4.72%。84.55%的企业赢利，15.45%的企业亏损。收入最高的省为广东省，占本行业的19.26%。

	Total number of firms 企业总数	Total number of employees 职工总数	Total revenue (Mil.RMB) 总销售收入（百万元）	Total profit (Mil.RMB) 总利润（百万元）	Return on assets 资产利润率（%）	Return on equity 权益利润率（%）	Labour productivity ('000 RMB/worker) 劳动生产率（千元/人）	Debts/assets 资产负债率（%）	Total assets (Mil.RMB) 总资产（百万元）
Industry Overall 行业总体	220	25,677	5,220	218	4.72	11.62	52.39	59.39	4,623

	Number of firms 企业个数	Average number of employees 平均职工人数	Average revenue ('000 RMB) 平均销售收入（千元）	Average profit ('000 RMB) 平均利润（千元）	Return on assets 资产利润率（%）	Return on equity 权益利润率（%）	Labour productivity ('000 RMB/worker) 劳动生产率（千元/人）	Debts/assets 资产负债率（%）	Average total assets ('000 RMB) 平均总资产（千元）
By ownership 产业所有权									
State-owned 国有	14	140	8,870	-366	-1.97	-47.66	11.08	95.87	18,612
Collective-owned 集体	38	103	17,982	782	4.78	10.27	70.19	53.45	16,370
Foreign & Overseas Chinese Funded 三资	39	168	46,441	2,443	5.21	11.59	68.60	55.00	46,844
By regional distribution 地区分布									
Central-North 华北	41	116	16,440	1,064	5.66	14.66	41.90	61.42	18,809
Beijing 北京	15	133	13,792	300	2.06	4.99	26.30	58.73	14,544
Tianjin 天津	20	80	19,821	1,817	8.07	25.07	79.78	67.83	22,526
Hebei 河北	5	177	13,646	558	3.17	4.79	21.00	33.90	17,609
Shanxi 山西									
Inner Mongolia 内蒙古	1	269	2,492	3	0.02	0.07	0.37	69.82	14,468
Northeast 东北	5	111	23,215	86	0.48	5.38	49.61	91.01	17,685
Liaoning 辽宁	4	133	27,564	88	0.41	4.47	45.20	90.84	21,493
Jilin 吉林									
Heilongjiang 黑龙江	1	24	5,816	76	3.10	104.11	147.17	97.03	2,455
Central-East 华东	119	96	22,835	1,035	5.16	12.14	62.00	57.49	20,041
Shanghai 上海	25	64	19,119	974	4.17	8.91	63.87	53.22	23,356
Jiangsu 江苏	42	66	20,312	708	5.65	23.82	74.66	76.28	12,532
Zhejiang 浙江	22	167	34,423	2,536	7.83	15.00	42.11	47.80	32,378
Anhui 安徽	1	42	2,563	3	0.09	100.00	23.19	99.91	3,190
Fujian 福建	11	147	19,497	-194	-0.68	-1.48	74.37	53.76	28,440
Jiangxi 江西	3	58	17,792	283	2.22	6.97	88.37	68.16	12,756
Shandong 山东	15	99	23,905	969	6.99	16.65	69.94	58.04	13,871
Central-South 中南	32	194	44,003	1,425	4.64	10.16	49.69	54.36	30,742
Henan 河南	1	62	23,451	1,654	11.14	27.84	105.02	60.00	14,854
Hubei 湖北	6	188	31,772	1,683	9.14	17.08	48.48	46.50	18,416
Hunan 湖南	4	381	46,529	1,599	5.82	13.78	24.63	57.78	27,475
Guangdong 广东	20	169	50,259	1,407	3.81	8.36	61.31	54.41	36,915
Guangxi 广西	1	98	2,735	-691	-6.78	-72.58	17.52	90.67	10,199
Hainan 海南									
Southwest 西南	18	130	14,688	614	4.38	8.72	41.43	49.76	14,008
Chongqing 重庆	9	88	10,031	611	7.93	13.96	35.03	43.23	7,709
Sichuan 四川	8	172	18,903	528	2.53	5.20	40.93	51.28	20,855
Guizhou 贵州									
Yunnan 云南	1	170	22,889	1,320	8.29	21.97	75.37	62.25	15,917
Tibet 西藏									
Northwest 西北	5	93	8,016	-1,116	-3.91		19.21	112.46	28,530
Shaanxi 陕西	2	108	8,006	-1,748	-6.08	-68.46	11.62	91.12	28,770
Gansu 甘肃	1	58	11,117	463	7.47	13.56	61.31	44.92	6,200
Qinghai 青海	1	16	60	-7	-0.92	-1.28	4.19	27.93	759
Ningxia 宁夏									
Xinjiang 新疆	1	178	12,890	-2,540	-3.25		16.01	134.34	78,150

3469: Other Metal Products For Construction 其他建筑用金属制品业

Year 年份	Number of firms 企业个数	Rate of change 变化率 (%)	Number of employees 职工人数 (人)	Rate of change 变化率 (%)	Total revenue (Mil. RMB) 总销售收入 (百万元)	Rate of change 变化率 (%)	Total profit (Mil RMB) 总利润 (百万元)	Rate of change 变化率 (%)
2000	150		18,557		4,452		91	
2001	202	34.67	25,658	38.27	4,610	3.55	150	64.84
2002	220	8.91	25,677	0.07	5,220	13.23	218	45.33

Major Products 主要产品	Output 产量	Unit 单位

10 Main Firms with Maximal Revenue (year founded) 收入最大的十家主要企业（创办年份）	City 城市	Province 省	Telephone/fax 电话/传真	Number of employees 职工人数	Ownership 产业所有权	Revenue ('000 RMB) 销售收入 (千元)	Profit('000 RMB) (rank) 利润(千元) (排名)	Total assets ('000 RMB) 总资产 (千元)	Major products 主要产品
Jiedong Experiment Area Taifengqiao Metal Products Co.,Ltd	Jieyang	Guangdong	(0663)3264579		Overseas Chinese-funded				Galvanized Pipe
揭东试验区泰丰侨金属制品有限公司(1993)	揭阳市	广东省	(0663)3264021	1,160	港澳台资	438,788	17,767(2)	358,134	镀锌管
Shanghai Huiya Aluminium Alloy Products Co., Ltd.	Shanghai	Shanghai	(021)57641772		Foreign Funded				Aluminium Alloy High Frame Floor
上海惠亚铝合金制品有限公司(1996)	上海市	上海市	(021)57645069	760	外商投资	208,031	3,973(12)	177,374	铝合金高架地板
Foshan Lanshi Astronavigation Stainless Steel Tube Manufacturing Co., Ltd.	Foshan	Guangdong	(0757)3311488		Limited-Liability				Stainless Steel Tube
佛山市澜石宇航不锈钢制管有限公司(1999)	佛山市	广东省	(0757)3313541	300	有限公司	207,766	1,550(41)	65,481	不锈钢管
Geze Industry (Tianjin) Co., Ltd.	Tianjin	Tianjin	(022)26973995		Foreign Funded				Door Closer
盖泽工业（天津）有限公司(1998)	天津市	天津市	(022)26972702	149	外商投资	131,360	18,870(1)	149,090	闭门器
Zhangjiagang Huaxia Traffic Facilities Materials Co., Ltd.	Suzhou	Jiangsu	(0512)58204795		Private Owned				Guardrail Kit
张家港市华夏交通设施材料有限公司(1994)	苏州市	江苏省	(0512)58204795	250	私营企业	130,010	3,390(19)	91,320	护栏套件
Ningbo Hardware Rigging Co., Ltd.	Ningbo	Zhejiang	(0574)87589247		Limited-Liability				Rigging
宁波五金索具有限公司(1956)	宁波市	浙江省	(0574)87589096	854	有限公司	127,510	10,832(4)	67,642	索具
Kunshan Hongyuan Machine Manufacturing Co., Ltd.	Suzhou	Jiangsu	(0512)57896086		Overseas Chinese-funded				Pull-rod
昆山鸿源机械制造有限公司(1998)	苏州市	江苏省	(0512)57897589	376	港澳台资	108,109	7,739(6)	68,775	拉杆
Hangzhou Xinfeng Steel Structure Co., Ltd.	Hangzhou	Zhejiang	(0571)82831136		Foreign Funded				Cold Pressing Shaping
杭州新峰钢结构有限公司(1994)	杭州市	浙江省	(0571)82821397	112	外商投资	104,002	10,490(5)	76,383	冷压成型
Jiangsu Hooverccor Ornaments Industrial Co., Ltd	Zhenjiang	Jiangsu	(0511)6632666		Private Enterprises				Glass Curtain Wall
江苏合发装饰实业有限公司(1995)	镇江市	江苏省	(0511)6632329	514	私营独资	83,205	452(86)	107,149	玻璃幕墙
Sichuan Telida Industrial Co., Ltd.	Ziyang	Sichuan	(0832)4580888		Private Owned				Aluminum Ceiling Materials
四川省特丽达实业有限公司(1995)	资阳市	四川省	(0832)4580888	180	私营企业	76,640	177(130)	44,973	铝质天花板材料

Top 10 Cities by Revenue 销售收入排名前10位城市	Province 省	Market share 市场份额 (%)	Number of firms 企业个数
Shanghai 上海市	Shanghai 上海市	9.16	25
Jieyang 揭阳市	Guangdong 广东省	8.57	2
Suzhou 苏州市	Jiangsu 江苏省	8.55	24
Tianjin 天津市	Tianjin 天津市	7.59	20
Zibo 淄博市	Shandong 山东省	4.49	6
Foshan 佛山市	Guangdong 广东省	4.42	3
Ningbo 宁波市	Zhejiang 浙江省	4.27	7
Hangzhou 杭州市	Zhejiang 浙江省	4.05	4
Beijing 北京市	Beijing 北京市	3.96	15
Taizhou 台州市	Zhejiang 浙江省	3.50	4

10 Major Wholesalers 十家主要批发商	City 城市	Province 省	Telephone/Fax 电话/传真
Xuzhou New Century Building Materials Decorative City	Xuzhou	Jiangsu	(0516)83666780
徐州市新世纪建材装饰城	徐州市	江苏省	(0516)63804485
Orienthome Co.,Ltd.	Beijing	Beijing	(010)63808294
东方家园有限公司	北京市	北京市	
Shanghai Jinkai Goods & Materials Co.,Ltd.	Shanghai	Shanghai	(021)52193967
上海金凯物资有限公司	上海市	上海市	
Guangzhou Building Materials Development Co.,Ltd.	Guangzhou	Guangdong	(020)83335062
广州市建材发展有限公司	广州市	广东省	(020)83341110
Guangxi Qiaofeng Goods & Materials Trade Co.,Ltd.	Nanning	Guangxi	(0771)2631539
广西侨丰物资贸易有限责任公司	南宁市	广西	(0771)2631539
Gansu Building Materials State-owned Assets Marketing Co.,Ltd.	Lanzhou	Gansu	(0931)8821359
甘肃建材国有资产经营有限责任公司	兰州市	甘肃省	(0931)8960243
Shanghai East Asia United Building Materials Co.,Ltd.	Shanghai	Shanghai	(021)33134520
上海东亚联合建材有限公司	上海市	上海市	(021)63216165
Shanghai Zhuzong Materials General Company	Shanghai	Shanghai	(021)32240030
上海住总物资总公司	上海市	上海市	(021)32240024
Guangdong Building Materials Company	Guangzhou	Guangdong	(020)83802713
广东省建材公司	广州市	广东省	(020)83817640
Guangdong Dongguan Hardware Minerals Import & Export Co.,Ltd	Dongguan	Guangdong	(0769)2227090
广东省东莞五金矿产进出口公司	东莞市	广东省	(0769)2221045

3470: Metal Surface Treatment and Heat Treatment

金属表面处理及热处理业

The industry accounts for 0.204% of the total revenue of China's industrial sector in 2002. The rate of return on assets is 5.95%. 88.02% of all firms in the industry made a profit while 11.98% had negative returns.The top province in terms of the industry's revenue is Guangdong, accounting for 28.80% of the total revenue.
2002年本行业收入占全行业的0.204%，资产利润率为5.95%。88.02%的企业赢利，11.98%的企业亏损。收入最高的省为广东省，占本行业的28.80%。

	Total number of firms 企业总数	Total number of employees 职工总数	Total revenue (Mil.RMB) 总销售收入(百万元)	Total profit (Mil.RMB) 总利润(百万元)	Return on assets 资产利润率(%)	Return on equity 权益利润率(%)	Labour productivity ('000 RMB/worker) 劳动生产率(千元/人)	Debts/assets 资产负债率(%)	Total assets (Mil.RMB) 总资产(百万元)
Industry Overall 行业总体	718	89,088	21,894	1,091	5.95	17.09	63.76	65.18	18,337

	Number of firms 企业个数	Average number of employees 平均职工人数	Average revenue ('000 RMB) 平均销售收入(千元)	Average profit ('000 RMB) 平均利润(千元)	Return on assets 资产利润率(%)	Return on equity 权益利润率(%)	Labour productivity ('000 RMB/worker) 劳动生产率(千元/人)	Debts/assets 资产负债率(%)	Average total assets ('000 RMB) 平均总资产(千元)
By ownership 产业所有权									
State-owned 国有	37	84	5,155	-216	-2.48	-7.11	19.93	65.15	8,741
Collective-owned 集体	166	135	23,815	1,024	7.27	19.32	47.62	62.39	14,096
Foreign & Overseas Chinese Funded 三资	127	148	65,261	4,368	6.40	18.77	101.40	65.93	68,281
By regional distribution 地区分布									
Central-North 华北	74	104	25,001	1,771	9.52	23.41	61.72	59.34	18,609
Beijing 北京	16	102	11,492	1,813	7.30	17.13	37.99	57.40	24,838
Tianjin 天津	40	98	21,370	1,220	8.90	24.37	38.35	63.49	13,714
Hebei 河北	17	121	47,677	3,133	12.40	28.12	127.36	55.90	25,263
Shanxi 山西	1	73	933				6.34	40.97	1,667
Inner Mongolia 内蒙古									
Northeast 东北	24	107	53,205	4,004	9.30	17.91	119.90	48.08	43,060
Liaoning 辽宁	18	114	63,404	5,030	9.53	18.53	134.84	48.58	52,800
Jilin 吉林	1	121	6,332	56	0.16	0.19	33.11	14.74	34,763
Heilongjiang 黑龙江	5	82	25,866	1,101	11.41	30.30	70.82	62.34	9,654
Central-East 华东	400	119	27,777	1,230	5.39	15.03	65.98	64.14	22,808
Shanghai 上海	99	93	18,591	1,216	8.75	19.20	55.40	54.44	13,898
Jiangsu 江苏	154	125	28,639	888	3.92	13.77	73.87	71.56	22,685
Zhejiang 浙江	111	128	20,619	1,047	6.78	18.29	38.96	62.94	15,446
Anhui 安徽	2	113	159,247	4,414	5.53	17.81	99.23	68.95	79,800
Fujian 福建	14	99	101,101	4,237	3.83	10.81	223.62	64.60	110,667
Jiangxi 江西									
Shandong 山东	20	162	41,869	2,515	6.06	12.04	97.62	49.70	41,517
Central-South 中南	199	144	37,288	1,840	5.68	19.30	59.28	70.59	32,414
Henan 河南	12	70	13,741	684	5.01	32.68	67.34	84.68	13,653
Hubei 湖北	10	127	59,251	7,713	20.32	35.28	118.60	42.42	37,967
Hunan 湖南	12	81	21,444	1,025	4.43	9.86	84.54	55.10	23,150
Guangdong 广东	160	158	39,411	1,682	4.82	17.82	55.58	72.94	34,878
Guangxi 广西	5	43	19,992	-116	-1.19	-3.10	-2.34	61.50	9,704
Hainan 海南									
Southwest 西南	18	142	12,005	283	1.61	4.70	21.02	65.73	17,540
Chongqing 重庆	10	152	7,594	148	1.81	5.63	13.75	67.93	8,189
Sichuan 四川	6	149	19,344	593	1.80	5.56	27.42	67.60	32,902
Guizhou 贵州	1	79	13,970	286	2.79	13.24	69.05	78.96	10,268
Yunnan 云南	1	60	10,120	-234	-0.90	-1.48	46.45	39.54	26,144
Tibet 西藏									
Northwest 西北	3	54	6,613	167	1.36	4.54	79.66	70.13	12,330
Shaanxi 陕西	2	69	9,056	185	1.08	3.52	88.86	69.46	17,206
Gansu 甘肃	1	25	1,728	132	5.12	24.49	28.92	79.10	2,579
Qinghai 青海									
Ningxia 宁夏									
Xinjiang 新疆									

3470: Metal Surface Treatment and Heat Treatment

金属表面处理及热处理业

Year 年份	Number of firms 企业个数	Rate of change 变化率 (%)	Number of employees 职工人数 (人)	Rate of change 变化率 (%)	Total revenue (Mil. RMB) 总销售收入 (百万元)	Rate of change 变化率 (%)	Total profit (Mil RMB) 总利润 (百万元)	Rate of change 变化率 (%)
2000	539		71,014		14,562		407	
2001	603	11.87	74,743	5.25	16,058	10.27	466	14.50
2002	718	19.07	89,088	19.19	21,894	36.34	1,091	134.12

Major Products 主要产品	Output 产量	Unit 单位

10 Main Firms with Maximal Revenue (year founded) 收入最大的十家主要企业（创办年份）	City 城市	Province 省	Telephone/fax 电话/传真	Number of employees 职工人数	Ownership 产业所有权	Revenue ('000 RMB) 销售收入 (千元)	Profit('000 RMB) (rank) 利润(千元) (排名)	Total assets ('000 RMB) 总资产 (千元)	Major products 主要产品
Dalian Pujin SteelPlate Co., Ltd.	Dalian	Liaoning	(0411)7515065		Foreign Funded				Galvanized Steel Sheet
大连浦金钢板有限公司(1995)	大连市	辽宁省	(0411)7514710	306	外商投资	872,652	90,719(2)	593,324	镀锌板
Zhejiang Kingland Group Co., Ltd.	Huzhou	Zhejiang	(0572)2065107		Joint Stock				Metal Pipe Materials & Works金属
浙江金洲集团股份有限公司(2000)	湖州市	浙江省	(0572)2066981	1,179	股份制	816,005	44,091(4)	733,601	管材管件
FuJian Tongya Tinplate Steel Co.,Ltd.	Zhangzhou	Fujian	(0596)6766266		Overseas Chinese-funded				Tinned Steel Plate
福建统一马口铁有限公司(1995)	漳州市	福建省	(0596)6765292	289	港澳台资	693,835	15,032(15)	1,039,932	镀锡钢板
Zhongshan Zhongyue Tinplate Industrial Co., Ltd.	Zhongshan	Guangdong	(0760)5596487		Overseas Chinese-funded				Plating Tinned Thin Steel Plate镀
中山中粤马口铁工业有限公司(1989)	中山市	广东省	(0760)5596252	300	港澳台资	630,131	105,576(1)	409,019	锡薄钢板
Guangzhou Pacific Tinplate Co., Ltd .	Guangzhou	Guangdong	(020)82220310		Foreign Funded				Tinplate
广州太平洋马口铁有限公司(1994)	广州市	广东省	(020)82221324	265	外商投资	511,189	39,565(5)	702,613	马口铁
Shunde Pohang Coated Steel Co.,Ltd.	Foshan	Guangdong	(0765)6657870		Foreign Funded				Galvanized Steel Sheet
顺德市浦项镀锌板有限公司(1997)	佛山市	广东省	(0765)6657760	168	外商投资	482,348	52,290(3)	393,781	镀锌钢板
Baosteel Yichang Huangshi Aluminized Steel Co.,Ltd.	Huangshi	Hubei	(0714)6359556		Overseas Chinese-funded				Galvanized Steel Sheet
宝钢益昌黄石镀铝薄板有限公司(1992)	黄石市	湖北省	(0714)6351726	320	港澳台资	473,519	37,018(7)	183,366	镀锌钢板
Jiangsu Tonya Tinplate Co., Ltd.	Wuxi	Jiangsu	(0510)5215096		Foreign Funded				Tinplate
江苏统一马口铁有限公司(1996)	无锡市	江苏省	(0510)5210124	259	外商投资	420,098	8,390(24)	989,314	马口铁
Zhangjiagang Huada Coating Co., Ltd.	Suzhou	Jiangsu	(0512)58387888		Private Owned				Colored Drawing Steel Sheet
张家港华达涂层有限公司(2001)	苏州市	江苏省	(0512)58387320	150	私营企业	383,344	5,259(36)	269,515	彩涂钢板
Fujian Kaiguan Steel Development Co., Ltd.	Zhangzhou	Fujian	(0596)6766251		Overseas Chinese-funded				Galvanized Steel Sheet
福建凯冠钢铁开发有限公司(1998)	漳州市	福建省	(0596)6766253	158	港澳台资	383,063	37,659(6)	236,661	镀锌钢铁

Top 10 Cities by Revenue 销售收入排名前10位城市	Province 省	Market share 市场份额 (%)	Number of firms 企业个数
Foshan 佛山市	Guangdong 广东省	9.89	22
Shanghai 上海市	Shanghai 上海市	8.41	99
Guangzhou 广州市	Guangdong 广东省	6.58	50
Zhangzhou 漳州市	Fujian 福建省	5.29	6
Suzhou 苏州市	Jiangsu 江苏省	5.22	43
Zhongshan 中山市	Guangdong 广东省	5.15	18
Wuxi 无锡市	Jiangsu 江苏省	4.60	22
Dalian 大连市	Liaoning 辽宁省	4.30	7
Tianjin 天津市	Tianjin 天津市	3.90	40
Huzhou 湖州市	Zhejiang 浙江省	3.85	3

10 Major Wholesalers 十家主要批发商	City 城市	Province 省	Telephone/Fax 电话/传真
SU MEC	Nanjing	Jiangsu	(025)4511888
中设江苏机械设备进出口（集团）公司	南京市	江苏省	(025)4411772
China Poster Mobile Communications Equipment Co.,Ltd.	Beijing	Beijing	(010)66426993
中邮普泰移动通信设备股份有限公司	北京市	北京市	(010)66426837
Sino Kama Co., Ltd.	Shanghai	Shanghai	(021)62031188
中泰凯马股份有限公司	上海市	上海市	(021)62030851
China Huayuan Group Co.,Ltd.	Shanghai	Shanghai	(021)62031188
中国华源集团有限公司	上海市	上海市	(021)62032288
Zhejiang Crand Imp.& Exp.Co.,Ltd.	Ningbo	Zhejiang	(0574)87720170
浙江远大进出口有限公司	宁波市	浙江省	(0574)87723350
Shandong Machinery Import & Export Group Corporation	Qingdao	Shandong	(0532)2661628
山东省机械进出口集团公司	青岛市	山东省	(0532)2991655
Qingdao Haier International Trade Co.,Ltd.	Qingdao	Shandong	(0532)8938337
青岛海尔国际贸易有限公司	青岛市	山东省	(0532)8939494
Guangdong Machinery Import & Export Group Corporation	Guangzhou	Guangdong	(020)87782168
广东省机械进出口集团公司	广州市	广东省	(020)87771803
China National Machinery Equipment Import & Export Corporation	Beijing	Beijing	(010)63474506
中国机械设备进出口总公司	北京市	北京市	(010)63261865
Beijing Cellstar Co.,Ltd.	Beijing	Beijing	(010)64602050
北京蜂星事达电讯有限公司	北京市	北京市	(010)64672648

3481: Enamel Products 日用搪瓷制造业

The industry accounts for 0.031% of the total revenue of China's industrial sector in 2002. The rate of return on assets is -0.90%. 69.34% of all firms in the industry made a profit while 30.66% had negative returns.The top province in terms of the industry's revenue is Shanghai, accounting for 20.20% of the total revenue.
2002年本行业收入占全行业的 0.031%，资产利润率为 -0.90%。69.34%的企业赢利，30.66%的企业亏损。收入最高的省为上海市，占本行业的20.20%。

	Total number of firms 企业总数	Total number of employees 职工总数	Total revenue (Mil.RMB) 总销售收入（百万元）	Total profit (Mil.RMB) 总利润（百万元）	Return on assets 资产利润率（%）	Return on equity 权益利润率（%）	Labour productivity ('000 RMB/ worker) 劳动生产率（千元/人）	Debts/ assets 资产负债率（%）	Total assets (Mil.RMB) 总资产（百万元）
Industry Overall 行业总体	137	32,211	3,312	-38	-0.90	-4.86	27.32	81.42	4,206

	Number of firms 企业个数	Average number of employees 平均职工人数	Average revenue ('000 RMB) 平均销售收入（千元）	Average profit ('000 RMB) 平均利润（千元）	Return on assets 资产利润率（%）	Return on equity 权益利润率（%）	Labour productivity ('000 RMB/ worker) 劳动生产率（千元/人）	Debts/ assets 资产负债率（%）	Average total assets ('000 RMB) 平均总资产（千元）
By ownership 产业所有权									
State-owned 国有	14	254	12,226	-3,340	-6.28		3.06	112.15	53,173
Collective-owned 集体	21	228	36,255	1,237	4.78	19.62	42.94	75.65	25,900
Foreign & Overseas Chinese Funded 三资	18	282	48,425	-1,463	-2.22	-7.30	55.33	69.56	65,840
By regional distribution 地区分布									
Central-North 华北	13	167	28,371	530	1.86	6.62	49.77	71.88	28,457
Beijing 北京	1	179	30,349	-7,915	-12.11	-16.20	44.59	25.26	65,355
Tianjin 天津	3	135	9,204	-382	-1.30	-74.85	-8.10	98.26	29,284
Hebei 河北	7	133	42,394	2,277	13.61	72.41	106.36	81.20	16,730
Shanxi 山西	2	324	7,054	2		0.01	5.79	68.24	49,810
Inner Mongolia 内蒙古									
Northeast 东北	5	287	11,604	-658	-1.55	-34.76	11.39	95.54	42,468
Liaoning 辽宁	4	235	11,501	-821	-2.02		14.72	103.79	40,570
Jilin 吉林									
Heilongjiang 黑龙江	1	496	12,018	-6	-0.01	-0.04	5.08	68.81	50,064
Central-East 华东	85	197	23,204	-3	-0.01	-0.07	32.00	80.45	26,424
Shanghai 上海	17	210	39,349	-545	-1.51	-10.12	55.56	85.13	36,220
Jiangsu 江苏	17	200	28,162	-318	-0.92	-3.99	37.41	77.04	34,701
Zhejiang 浙江	30	148	16,940	585	4.95	13.03	24.95	61.98	11,802
Anhui 安徽	4	215	9,796	-1,453	-4.18	-49.95	22.41	91.62	34,726
Fujian 福建	4	168	19,507	1,577	7.06	11.70	41.19	39.62	22,331
Jiangxi 江西	1	645	18,103	-1,509	-2.69	-97.86	4.21	97.25	56,108
Shandong 山东	12	261	15,098	-179	-0.53	-20.77	15.60	97.43	33,495
Central-South 中南	25	443	34,404	-682	-1.48	-5.55	20.27	73.37	46,121
Henan 河南	8	479	25,174	173	0.73	2.13	13.79	65.82	23,705
Hubei 湖北	2	305	14,178	339	4.07	8.39	38.56	51.50	8,330
Hunan 湖南	4	490	52,984	363	0.93	3.88	25.25	76.10	39,109
Guangdong 广东	9	400	42,572	-1,895	-2.68	-10.23	25.83	73.82	70,734
Guangxi 广西	2	540	17,632	-1,755	-2.28	-11.66	5.42	80.42	76,844
Hainan 海南									
Southwest 西南	6	102	6,370	-3,970	-11.86		-13.75	140.98	33,485
Chongqing 重庆	3	145	9,932	-7,461	-13.19		-18.64	146.99	56,548
Sichuan 四川									
Guizhou 贵州	1	5	954	-390	-1.87	-36.59	-365.80	94.89	20,866
Yunnan 云南	2	87	3,736	-525	-10.09		8.72	135.38	5,199
Tibet 西藏									
Northwest 西北	3	57	4,855	-136	-1.69	-9.47	21.72	82.19	8,048
Shaanxi 陕西									
Gansu 甘肃									
Qinghai 青海	1	25	589				3.20	111.59	6,732
Ningxia 宁夏									
Xinjiang 新疆	2	73	6,988	-204	-2.34	-8.01	24.89	70.82	8,706

3481: Enamel Products 日用搪瓷制造业

Year 年份	Number of firms 企业个数	Rate of change 变化率 (%)	Number of employees 职工人数 (人)	Rate of change 变化率 (%)	Total revenue (Mil. RMB) 总销售收入 (百万元)	Rate of change 变化率 (%)	Total profit (Mil RMB) 总利润 (百万元)	Rate of change 变化率 (%)
2000	115		37,170		2,529		-54	
2001	136	18.26	33,438	-10.04	3,281	29.74	18	-
2002	137	0.74	32,211	-3.67	3,312	0.94	-38	-

Major Products 主要产品	Output 产量	Unit 单位
Porcelain Enamel Products 搪瓷制品	13	10,000 Tons 万吨

10 Main Firms with Maximal Revenue (year founded) 收入最大的十家主要企业（创办年份）	City 城市	Province 省	Telephone/fax 电话/传真	Number of employees 职工人数	Ownership 产业所有权	Revenue ('000 RMB) 销售收入 (千元)	Profit('000 RMB) (rank) 利润(千元) (排名)	Total assets ('000 RMB) 总资产 (千元)	Major products 主要产品
Hebei Zhengzhong Porcelain Enamel Factory 河北正中搪瓷厂(1993)	Shijiazhuang 石家庄市	Hebei 河北省	(0311)8298445 (0311)8298445	160	Collective-owned 集体企业	217,834	10,700(1)	85,623	Bathtub Porcelain Glaze 浴盆瓷釉
Xinhui Giessdorf Health Care Bath Co., Ltd. 新会吉事多卫浴有限公司(1998)	Jiangmen 江门市	Guangdong 广东省	(0750)3677333 (0750)6817456	2,000	Overseas Chinese-funded 港澳台资	180,507	2,134(9)	252,886	Health Care Bath Products 卫浴产品
Hunan Wujiang Light Chemical Industry Group Co.,Ltd. 湖南五江轻化集团有限公司(1996)	Loudi 娄底市	Hunan 湖南省	(0738)4760352 (0738)4760218	1,500	Private Owned 私营企业	175,300	855(21)	125,910	Porcelain Enamel Products 搪瓷制品
Shanghai Jiuliting Industrial Company 上海九里亭实业公司(1993)	Shanghai 上海市	Shanghai 上海市	(021)57637280 (021)57637280	105	Collective-owned 集体企业	134,488	5,182(3)	69,184	Heat Preservation Oven 保温炉
Zhoukou Porcelain Enamel Factory 周口市搪瓷厂(1976)	Zhoukou 周口市	Henan 河南省	(0394)3197270 (0394)3197613	1,200	Joint Stock 股份制	84,214	130(66)	42,689	Daily Porcelain Enamel 日用搪瓷
Yinglian Lavatory Products(Dongguan) Co., Ltd. 英联卫浴器材(东莞)有限公司(1998)	Dongguan 东莞市	Guangdong 广东省	(0769)3387970 (0769)3388100	302	Foreign Funded 外商投资	81,348	-	108,505	Health Care Bath Products 卫浴产品
Shangqiu Metal And Porcelain Co., Ltd. 商丘市金瓷股份有限公司(1976)	Shangqiu 商丘市	Henan 河南省	(0370)2617088 (0370)2614815	1,091	Joint Stock 股份制	72,106	93(71)	69,519	Daily Porcelain Enamel 日用搪瓷
Linyi Luozhuang Hongsheng Porcelain Enamel Factory 临沂市罗庄区红盛搪瓷厂(1996)	Linyi 临沂市	Shandong 山东省	(0539)8271568 (0539)8271801	520	Collective-owned 集体企业	57,786	3,436(5)	19,756	Porcelain Enamel Products 搪瓷制品
Xuzhou Yingfa Porcelain Enamel Co., Ltd. 徐州营发搪瓷有限公司(1956)	Xuzhou 徐州市	Jiangsu 江苏省	(0516)7715452 (0516)7710454	464	Private Owned 私营企业	56,195	-	14,097	Daily Porcelain Enamel Products 搪瓷制品
Wuxi Porcelain Enamel Factory 无锡市搪瓷厂(1954)	Wuxi 无锡市	Jiangsu 江苏省	(0510)3702685 (0510)3702685	271	State-owned 国有企业	54,051	-	39,762	Daily Porcelain Enamel Products 搪瓷制品

Top 10 Cities by Revenue 销售收入排名前10位城市	Province 省	Market share 市场份额 (%)	Number of firms 企业个数
Shanghai 上海市	Shanghai 上海市	20.20	17
Shijiazhuang 石家庄市	Hebei 河北省	8.68	5
Jiangmen 江门市	Guangdong 广东省	6.74	3
Hangzhou 杭州市	Zhejiang 浙江省	6.63	11
Loudi 娄底市	Hunan 湖南省	5.45	2
Linyi 临沂市	Shandong 山东省	5.01	10
Wenzhou 温州市	Zhejiang 浙江省	3.10	8
Zhoukou 周口市	Henan 河南省	3.04	2
Nanjing 南京市	Jiangsu 江苏省	2.76	2
Zhenjiang 镇江市	Jiangsu 江苏省	2.67	3

10 Major Wholesalers 十家主要批发商	City 城市	Province 省	Telephone/Fax 电话/传真
Harbin ChinaSun Group Co., Ltd. 哈尔滨中央红集团股份有限公司	Harbin 哈尔滨市	Heilongjiang 黑龙江省	(0451)84885100 (0451)84885111
Guangzhou Yuexiu Enterprise (Group) Company 广州越秀企业（集团）公司	Guangzhou 广州市	Guangdong 广东省	(020)85597130 (020)85599018
China Reed Screen Imp. & Exp. Corp.Ltd. 中艺苇帘进出口有限责任公司	Beijing 北京市	Beijing 北京市	(010)65521133 (010)65513995
Hebei Xintai Foreign Trade Corp.ltd. 河北信泰对外贸易有限公司	Shijiazhuang 石家庄市	Hebei 河北省	(0311)7767908 (0311)7755347
Hebei Arts & Crafts Imp. & Exp. Corp. 河北省工艺品进出口公司	Shijiazhuang 石家庄市	Hebei 河北省	(0311)7764345 (0311)7755347
Shanghai Hengda Ceramic Building Materials Trade Market 上海恒大陶瓷建材交易市场	Shanghai 上海市	Shanghai 上海市	(021)58425842 (021)58427389
Hangzhou Local Product General Corporation 杭州市土特产总公司	Hangzhou 杭州市	Zhejiang 浙江省	(0571)87026301 (0571)87026323
Ningbo Zhonglin Foreign Trade Co.,Ltd. 宁波中蔺对外贸易有限公司	Ningbo 宁波市	Zhejiang 浙江省	(0574)87871797 (0574)87871790
Wuyi Local Products Daily Groceries Co.,Ltd. 武义县土产日用杂品有限责任公司	Jinhua 金华市	Zhejiang 浙江省	(0579)7623401 (0579)7623401
Guangdong Shunde Local Products Import & Export Company 广东省顺德土产进出口公司	Foshan 佛山市	Guangdong 广东省	(0765)6682839 (0765)6681441

3482: Aluminum Products 铝制品业

The industry accounts for 0.151% of the total revenue of China's industrial sector in 2002. The rate of return on assets is 3.07%. 80.29% of all firms in the industry made a profit while 19.71% had negative returns.The top province in terms of the industry's revenue is Guangdong, accounting for 35.95% of the total revenue.
2002年本行业收入占全行业的 0.151%，资产利润率为 3.07%。80.29%的企业赢利，19.71%的企业亏损。收入最高的省为广东省，占本行业的35.95%。

	Total number of firms 企业总数	Total number of employees 职工总数	Total revenue (Mil.RMB) 总销售收入（百万元）	Total profit (Mil.RMB) 总利润（百万元）	Return on assets 资产利润率 (%)	Return on equity 权益利润率 (%)	Labour productivity ('000 RMB/ worker) 劳动生产率（千元/人）	Debts/ assets 资产负债率 (%)	Total assets (Mil.RMB) 总资产（百万元）
Industry Overall 行业总体	487	74,870	16,183	501	3.07	7.48	54.69	58.91	16,297

	Number of firms 企业个数	Average number of employees 平均职工人数	Average revenue ('000 RMB) 平均销售收入（千元）	Average profit ('000 RMB) 平均利润（千元）	Return on assets 资产利润率 (%)	Return on equity 权益利润率 (%)	Labour productivity ('000 RMB/ worker) 劳动生产率（千元/人）	Debts/ assets 资产负债率 (%)	Average total assets ('000 RMB) 平均总资产（千元）
By ownership 产业所有权									
State-owned 国有	28	156	10,491	-763	-2.65	-20.68	25.79	87.21	28,851
Collective-owned 集体	78	137	20,724	791	5.16	14.75	46.49	65.01	15,325
Foreign & Overseas Chinese Funded 三资	93	261	67,774	1,827	2.38	5.23	57.49	54.40	76,631
By regional distribution 地区分布									
Central-North 华北	44	125	24,708	269	1.36	5.58	53.79	75.62	19,747
Beijing 北京	12	80	15,640	883	7.26	15.29	60.08	52.52	12,161
Tianjin 天津	16	176	15,087	5	0.02	0.10	19.75	81.97	28,736
Hebei 河北	13	67	48,751	300	1.99	7.17	198.50	72.18	15,061
Shanxi 山西	2	364	6,612	-1,082	-6.31		9.82	113.00	17,137
Inner Mongolia 内蒙古	1	150	11,102	-591	-1.79	-6.11	30.61	70.78	33,083
Northeast 东北	17	461	43,564	-14	-0.01	-0.03	15.29	56.80	117,827
Liaoning 辽宁	13	574	51,510	-1,256	-0.91	-2.00	12.84	54.65	138,450
Jilin 吉林	4	95	17,741	4,024	7.92	32.75	63.66	75.81	50,804
Heilongjiang 黑龙江									
Central-East 华东	192	152	32,015	1,553	4.73	11.28	48.92	58.03	32,818
Shanghai 上海	20	109	31,497	2,567	8.53	12.11	71.88	29.59	30,106
Jiangsu 江苏	52	98	25,141	802	3.89	10.77	60.79	63.86	20,603
Zhejiang 浙江	75	188	38,609	2,004	4.61	11.85	40.40	61.11	43,488
Anhui 安徽	4	82	8,326	186	1.19	2.95	16.88	59.72	15,679
Fujian 福建	9	163	42,598	1,417	3.10	8.99	68.97	65.54	45,762
Jiangxi 江西	5	132	11,193	1,165	7.07	19.33	26.12	63.45	16,483
Shandong 山东	27	197	31,154	1,319	4.40	9.69	49.91	54.56	29,966
Central-South 中南	195	139	37,531	876	2.79	6.73	71.60	58.62	31,464
Henan 河南	31	180	21,255	995	10.94	27.79	39.32	60.63	9,090
Hubei 湖北	14	191	46,373	4,500	14.47	34.01	87.16	57.46	31,098
Hunan 湖南	10	56	11,840	14	0.08	0.32	56.54	75.01	16,891
Guangdong 广东	135	131	43,094	599	1.57	3.67	80.48	57.08	38,015
Guangxi 广西	5	110	14,883	-773	-3.29		52.04	101.63	23,486
Hainan 海南									
Southwest 西南	26	140	20,625	313	1.34	3.65	51.40	63.17	23,268
Chongqing 重庆	5	113	12,683	-61	-0.39	-3.04	7.90	87.13	15,622
Sichuan 四川	13	145	26,873	514	2.08	5.81	81.50	64.13	24,654
Guizhou 贵州	6	128	17,786	647	2.07	4.36	32.17	52.56	31,276
Yunnan 云南	2	215	8,379	-1,059	-11.32	-24.15	10.88	53.10	9,351
Tibet 西藏									
Northwest 西北	13	127	27,205	933	3.17	5.69	76.29	44.32	29,468
Shaanxi 陕西	3	221	45,331	2,959	4.81	6.55	49.51	26.56	61,490
Gansu 甘肃	8	95	18,457	346	2.01	7.02	95.49	71.42	17,232
Qinghai 青海	1	170	44,050	450	0.82	1.20	88.76	31.87	54,922
Ningxia 宁夏									
Xinjiang 新疆	1	55	25,973	42	0.72	4.18	96.31	82.78	5,835

3482: Aluminum Products 铝制品业

Year 年份	Number of firms 企业个数	Rate of change 变化率 (%)	Number of employees 职工人数 (人)	Rate of change 变化率 (%)	Total revenue (Mil. RMB) 总销售收入 (百万元)	Rate of change 变化率 (%)	Total profit (Mil RMB) 总利润 (百万元)	Rate of change 变化率 (%)
2000	419		61,977		12,923		189	
2001	479	14.32	73,183	18.08	15,676	21.30	305	61.38
2002	487	1.67	74,870	2.31	16,183	3.23	501	64.26

Major Products 主要产品	Output 产量	Unit 单位
Daily Refined Aluminium Products 日用精铝制品	101,178	Ton 吨

10 Main Firms with Maximal Revenue (year founded) 收入最大的十家主要企业（创办年份）	City 城市	Province 省	Telephone/fax 电话/传真	Number of employees 职工人数	Ownership 产业所有权	Revenue ('000 RMB) 销售收入 (千元)	Profit('000 RMB) (rank) 利润(千元) (排名)	Total assets ('000 RMB) 总资产 (千元)	Major products 主要产品
Zhejiang Taizhou Aishida Electrical Appliance Co.,Ltd.	Taizhou	Zhejiang	(0576)6130388		Overseas Chinese-funded				Pressure Boiler
浙江台州爱仕达电器有限公司(1987)	台州市	浙江省	(0576)6130288	2,885	港澳台资	419,494	29,493(4)	296,876	高压锅
Huizhou Huangguan Jar Making Co.,Ltd	Huizhou	Guangdong	(0752)2381211		Overseas Chinese-funded				Aluminium Can
惠州皇冠制罐有限公司(1995)	惠州市	广东省	(0752)2275910	136	港澳台资	327,883	18,636(5)	450,130	铝罐
Ningbo Shuangyuan Co.,Ltd.	Ningbo	Zhejiang	(0574)87836129		Limited-Liability				Aluminium Sheet
宁波双圆有限公司(1958)	宁波市	浙江省	(0574)87832272	863	有限公司	262,602	12,548(10)	492,321	铝板
SuZhou Lopskig Aluminum Industrial Co.,Ltd.	Suzhou	Jiangsu	(0512)65493876		Overseas Chinese-funded				Aluminum Alloy Materials铝
苏州罗普斯金铝合金花格网有限公司(1993)	苏州市	江苏省	(0512)65491425	500	港澳台资	242,860	8,862(19)	174,560	合金型材
Wuhan Supor Pressure Cooker Co., Ltd.	Wuhan	Hubei	(027)84410039		Private Owned				Pressure Boiler
武汉苏泊尔压力锅有限公司(1998)	武汉市	湖北省	(027)84845536	420	私营企业	220,773	48,492(1)	103,840	压力锅
Zengcheng Rongyang Aluminium Materials Co., Ltd.	Guangzhou	Guangdong	(020)82633588		Overseas Chinese-funded				Aluminum Alloy Materials铝合
增城荣阳铝材有限公司(1998)	广州市	广东省	(020)82627828	524	港澳台资	220,566	-	203,957	金型材
Jin De Aluminium Mould Multiple-unit Pipe Co.,Ltd.	Shenyang	Liaoning	(024)86518888		Foreign Funded		7		uminiunm & Plastics Pipe
金德铝塑复合管有限公司(1999)	沈阳市	辽宁省	(024)86576666	6,000	外商投资	219,650	-	661,700	铝塑管
Shanghai United Jar Making Co., Ltd.	Shanghai	Shanghai	(021)57602801		Overseas Chinese-funded				Tear Tab Ends of Aluminium铝
上海联合制罐有限公司(1997)	上海市	上海市	(021)57601071	226	港澳台资	213,099	29,721(3)	293,386	质易拉罐
Tai'ao Aluminium Industry (Taishan) Co.,Ltd.	Jiangmen	Guangdong	(0750)5586383		Foreign Funded				Aluminum Materials
台澳铝业（台山）有限公司(2000)	江门市	广东省	(0750)5586393	600	外商投资	207,880	6,130(27)	282,916	铝型材
Taishan Taicheng Fucheng Aluminium Industry Co.,Ltd.	Jiangmen	Guangdong	(0750)5582588		Overseas Chinese-funded				Aluminiun Products
台山市台城镇富城铝业有限公司(1999)	江门市	广东省	(0750)5582585	360	港澳台资	189,229	-	132,815	铝制品

Top 10 Cities by Revenue 销售收入排名前10位城市	Province 省	Market share 市场份额 (%)	Number of firms 企业个数
Jiangmen 江门市	Guangdong 广东省	11.26	20
Foshan 佛山市	Guangdong 广东省	9.82	34
Taizhou 台州市	Zhejiang 浙江省	7.18	7
Ningbo 宁波市	Zhejiang 浙江省	6.01	33
Shanghai 上海市	Shanghai 上海市	3.89	20
Guangzhou 广州市	Guangdong 广东省	3.60	19
Suzhou 苏州市	Jiangsu 江苏省	3.31	11
Zhongshan 中山市	Guangdong 广东省	2.76	14
Baoding 保定市	Hebei 河北省	2.55	1
Huizhou 惠州市	Guangdong 广东省	2.51	3

10 Major Wholesalers 十家主要批发商	City 城市	Province 省	Telephone/Fax 电话/传真
Harbin ChinaSun Group Co., Ltd.	Harbin	Heilongjiang	(0451)84885100
哈尔滨中央红集团股份有限公司	哈尔滨市	黑龙江省	(0451)84885111
Guangzhou Yuexiu Enterprise (Group) Company	Guangzhou	Guangdong	(020)85597130
广州越秀企业（集团）公司	广州市	广东省	(020)85599018
China Reed Screen Imp. & Exp. Corp.Ltd.	Beijing	Beijing	(010)65521133
中艺苇帘进出口有限责任公司	北京市	北京市	(010)65513995
Hebei Xintai Foreign Trade Corp.ltd.	Shijiazhuang	Hebei	(0311)7767908
河北信泰对外贸易有限公司	石家庄市	河北省	(0311)7755347
Hebei Arts & Crafts Imp. & Exp. Corp.	Shijiazhuang	Hebei	(0311)7764345
河北省工艺品进出口公司	石家庄市	河北省	(0311)7755347
Shanghai Hengda Ceramic Building Materials Trade Market	Shanghai	Shanghai	(021)58425842
上海恒大陶瓷建材交易市场	上海市	上海市	(021)58427389
Hangzhou Local Product General Corporation	Hangzhou	Zhejiang	(0571)87026301
杭州市土特产总公司	杭州市	浙江省	(0571)87026323
Ningbo Zhonglin Foreign Trade Co.,Ltd.	Ningbo	Zhejiang	(0574)87871797
宁波中蔺对外贸易有限公司	宁波市	浙江省	(0574)87871790
Wuyi Local Products Daily Groceries Co.,Ltd.	Jinhua	Zhejiang	(0579)7623401
武义县土产日用杂品有限责任公司	金华市	浙江省	(0579)7623401
Guangdong Shunde Local Products Import & Export Company	Foshan	Guangdong	(0765)6682839
广东省顺德土产进出口公司	佛山市	广东省	(0765)6681441

3483: Stainless Steel Products 不锈钢制品业

The industry accounts for 0.211% of the total revenue of China's industrial sector in 2002. The rate of return on assets is 3.24%. 76.82% of all firms in the industry made a profit while 23.18% had negative returns.The top province in terms of the industry's revenue is Guangdong, accounting for 49.04% of the total revenue.
2002年本行业收入占全行业的0.211%，资产利润率为3.24%。76.82%的企业赢利，23.18%的企业亏损。收入最高的省为广东省，占本行业的49.04%。

	Total number of firms 企业总数	Total number of employees 职工总数	Total revenue (Mil.RMB) 总销售收入 (百万元)	Total profit (Mil.RMB) 总利润 (百万元)	Return on assets 资产利润率 (%)	Return on equity 权益利润率 (%)	Labour productivity ('000 RMB/ worker) 劳动生产率 (千元/人)	Debts/ assets 资产负债率 (%)	Total assets (Mil.RMB) 总资产 (百万元)
Industry Overall 行业总体	686	129,078	22,683	589	3.24	8.15	42.06	60.28	18,206

	Number of firms 企业个数	Average number of employees 平均职工人数	Average revenue ('000 RMB) 平均销售收入 (千元)	Average profit ('000 RMB) 平均利润 (千元)	Return on assets 资产利润率 (%)	Return on equity 权益利润率 (%)	Labour productivity ('000 RMB/ worker) 劳动生产率 (千元/人)	Debts/ assets 资产负债率 (%)	Average total assets ('000 RMB) 平均总资产 (千元)
By ownership 产业所有权									
State-owned 国有	8	74	1,608	-974	-2.41	-87.94	28.07	97.26	40,414
Collective-owned 集体	75	153	26,395	555	2.89	9.15	50.00	68.47	19,246
Foreign & Overseas Chinese Funded 三资	242	266	47,308	1,151	2.54	5.97	41.50	57.50	45,335
By regional distribution 地区分布									
Central-North 华北	69	197	19,785	444	1.28	4.78	32.87	73.28	34,754
Beijing 北京	8	74	16,069	-1,168	-1.74	-13.39	44.34	87.04	67,299
Tianjin 天津	38	215	20,501	717	2.03	6.85	29.91	70.37	35,321
Hebei 河北	20	228	21,534	546	2.23	6.75	36.32	66.92	24,456
Shanxi 山西	3	97	8,972	616	6.53	16.04	38.86	59.28	9,429
Inner Mongolia 内蒙古									
Northeast 东北	11	339	39,076	2,064	5.15	11.09	35.45	53.58	40,068
Liaoning 辽宁	8	396	51,202	3,149	6.46	14.77	39.65	56.28	48,773
Jilin 吉林	2	38	4,333	-847	-9.41	-11.63	26.63	19.12	9,004
Heilongjiang 黑龙江	1	485	11,547	-799	-2.45	-4.11	9.41	40.25	32,558
Central-East 华东	301	156	31,522	1,094	4.72	12.06	46.22	60.86	23,175
Shanghai 上海	62	178	37,998	903	2.75	7.41	46.40	62.97	32,878
Jiangsu 江苏	81	103	36,795	1,316	7.58	19.90	80.26	61.89	17,351
Zhejiang 浙江	102	139	27,192	1,301	6.49	15.83	37.99	58.99	20,046
Anhui 安徽	3	74	8,605	781	10.46	15.07	30.15	30.59	7,465
Fujian 福建	15	258	31,713	-16	-0.03	-0.07	42.50	54.32	51,870
Jiangxi 江西	2	87	5,995	309	4.65	6.95	23.39	33.05	6,644
Shandong 山东	36	255	24,020	870	4.65	14.11	30.26	67.06	18,704
Central-South 中南	298	214	37,723	679	2.55	5.74	41.55	55.67	26,675
Henan 河南									
Hubei 湖北	5	96	11,942	330	2.17	12.70	32.92	82.93	15,242
Hunan 湖南	3	62	15,169	92	1.28	7.85	56.17	83.65	7,197
Guangdong 广东	287	219	38,759	700	2.57	5.73	41.77	55.20	27,307
Guangxi 广西	1	321	9,876	-254	-3.84	-26.85	8.23	85.69	6,611
Hainan 海南	2	26	1,293	-207	-5.48		8.23	152.61	3,778
Southwest 西南	5	156	30,824	950	1.12	3.63	27.78	69.19	84,973
Chongqing 重庆	1	107	6,330	44	1.24	3.28	17.05	62.18	3,548
Sichuan 四川	4	169	36,948	1,177	1.12	3.63	29.48	69.25	105,329
Guizhou 贵州									
Yunnan 云南									
Tibet 西藏									
Northwest 西北	2	35	2,091	-179	-2.03	-28.58	20.50	92.90	8,793
Shaanxi 陕西									
Gansu 甘肃	2	35	2,091	-179	-2.03	-28.58	20.50	92.90	8,793
Qinghai 青海									
Ningxia 宁夏									
Xinjiang 新疆									

Year 年份	Number of firms 企业个数	Rate of change 变化率(%)	Number of employees 职工人数(人)	Rate of change 变化率(%)	Total revenue (Mil. RMB) 总销售收入(百万元)	Rate of change 变化率(%)	Total profit (Mil RMB) 总利润(百万元)	Rate of change 变化率(%)
2000	519		93,467		14,760		338	
2001	619	19.27	114,371	22.37	18,949	28.38	452	33.73
2002	686	10.82	129,078	12.86	22,683	19.71	589	30.31

Major Products 主要产品	Output 产量	Unit 单位
Daily Stainless Steel Products 日用不锈钢制品	414,983	Ton 吨

10 Main Firms with Maximal Revenue (year founded) 收入最大的十家主要企业(创办年份)	City 城市	Province 省	Telephone/fax 电话/传真	Number of employees 职工人数	Ownership 产业所有权	Revenue ('000 RMB) 销售收入(千元)	Profit('000 RMB) (rank) 利润(千元)(排名)	Total assets ('000 RMB) 总资产(千元)	Major products 主要产品
Xinhui Rixin Stainless Steel Material Factory Co., Ltd. 新会区日新不锈钢材料厂有限公司(1993)	Jiangmen 江门市	Guangdong 广东省	(0750)6101288 (0750)6138088	85	Overseas Chinese-funded 港澳台资	977,560	20,723(4)	220,457	Stainless Steel 不锈钢
Shanghai Xingxin Kitchen Utensils Co., Ltd. 上海兴信厨房用具有限公司(1994)	Shanghai 上海市	Shanghai 上海市	(021)69361967 (021)69361974	2,601	Overseas Chinese-funded 港澳台资	534,743	22,457(3)	379,853	Daily Stainless Steel日用不锈钢
Huizhou Hongli Hardware & Plastic Products Factory Co.,Ltd. 惠州宏利五金塑胶制品厂有限公司(1993)	Huizhou 惠州市	Guangdong 广东省	(0752)2600161 (0752)2601051	2,349	Overseas Chinese-funded 港澳台资	415,964	7,020(24)	410,270	Stainless Steel Tableware不锈钢餐厨具
Guangzhou Huadu Yongda Stainless Section Factory Co.,Ltd. 广州市花都永大不锈钢型材厂有限公司(1994)	Guangzhou 广州市	Guangdong 广东省	(020)86847851 (020)86847856	280	Overseas Chinese-funded 港澳台资	340,056	5,000(31)	280,128	Stainless Marerials Products不锈钢型材制品
Wuxi Xinde Stainless Steel Co., Ltd. 无锡市信德不锈钢有限公司(2000)	Wuxi 无锡市	Jiangsu 江苏省	(0510)2102788 (0510)2102908	15	Private Owned 私营企业	326,470	-	51,271	Stainless Steel 不锈钢
Shanghai Husheng Electronic Equipment Co., Ltd. 上海虎生电子电器有限公司(1995)	Shanghai 上海市	Shanghai 上海市	(021)64290660 (021)64290620	590	Overseas Chinese-funded 港澳台资	315,433	13,478(8)	183,574	Metal Tableware金属厨用具
Nanhai Yuexiui Qifeng Stainless Steel Products Co.,Ltd. 南海越秀旗峰不锈钢制品有限公司(1996)	Foshan 佛山市	Guangdong 广东省	(0757)5669192 (0757)5668198	1,250	Overseas Chinese-funded 港澳台资	224,835	7,135(23)	237,715	Stainless Steel Boiler 不锈钢煲
Foshan Gaoming Chengde Industrial Co., Ltd. 佛山市高明区诚德实业有限公司(2001)	Foshan 佛山市	Guangdong 广东省	(0757)8877111 (0757)8877222	397	Private Owned 私营企业	220,670	2,250(72)	37,703	Stainless Steel Products不锈钢制品
Meyer(ZhaoQing) Metal Products Co.,Ltd. 美亚(肇庆)金属制品有限公司(1991)	Zhaoqing 肇庆市	Guangdong 广东省	(0758)2770015 (0758)2770066	1,657	Overseas Chinese-funded 港澳台资	215,291	4,818(32)	187,192	Daily Stainless Steel Products日用不锈钢制品
Nanhai Guanyi Stainless Steel Products Co., Ltd. 南海冠益不锈钢制品有限公司(1993)	Foshan 佛山市	Guangdong 广东省	(0757)5227036 (0757)5111881	1,000	Foreign Funded 外商投资	203,281	12,491(9)	141,557	Stainless Steel Composite Underpan Cooker不锈钢复合底煲

Top 10 Cities by Revenue 销售收入排名前10位城市	Province 省	Market share 市场份额(%)	Number of firms 企业个数
Jiangmen 江门市	Guangdong 广东省	15.33	79
Shanghai 上海市	Shanghai 上海市	10.39	62
Yunfu 云浮市	Guangdong 广东省	8.84	22
Wuxi 无锡市	Jiangsu 江苏省	7.68	21
Foshan 佛山市	Guangdong 广东省	6.62	37
Ningbo 宁波市	Zhejiang 浙江省	5.53	52
Yangjiang 阳江市	Guangdong 广东省	4.17	43
Jinhua 金华市	Zhejiang 浙江省	3.74	24
Tianjin 天津市	Tianjin 天津市	3.43	38
Guangzhou 广州市	Guangdong 广东省	3.01	24

10 Major Wholesalers 十家主要批发商	City 城市	Province 省	Telephone/Fax 电话/传真
Harbin ChinaSun Group Co., Ltd. 哈尔滨中央红集团股份有限公司	Harbin 哈尔滨市	Heilongjiang 黑龙江省	(0451)84885100 (0451)84885111
Guangzhou Yuexiu Enterprise (Group) Company 广州越秀企业(集团)公司	Guangzhou 广州市	Guangdong 广东省	(020)85597130 (020)85599018
China Reed Screen Imp. & Exp. Corp.Ltd. 中艺苇帘进出口有限责任公司	Beijing 北京市	Beijing 北京市	(010)65521133 (010)65513995
Hebei Xintai Foreign Trade Corp.ltd. 河北信泰对外贸易有限公司	Shijiazhuang 石家庄市	Hebei 河北省	(0311)7767908 (0311)7755347
Hebei Arts & Crafts Imp. & Exp. Corp. 河北省工艺品进出口公司	Shijiazhuang 石家庄市	Hebei 河北省	(0311)7764345 (0311)7755347
Shanghai Hengda Ceramic Building Materials Trade Market 上海恒大陶瓷建材交易市场	Shanghai 上海市	Shanghai 上海市	(021)58425842 (021)58427389
Hangzhou Local Product General Corporation 杭州市土特产总公司	Hangzhou 杭州市	Zhejiang 浙江省	(0571)87026301 (0571)87026323
Ningbo Zhonglin Foreign Trade Co.,Ltd. 宁波中蔺对外贸易有限公司	Ningbo 宁波市	Zhejiang 浙江省	(0574)87871797 (0574)87871790
Wuyi Local Products Daily Groceries Co.,Ltd. 武义县土产日用杂品有限责任公司	Jinhua 金华市	Zhejiang 浙江省	(0579)7623401 (0579)7623401
Guangdong Shunde Local Products Import & Export Company 广东省顺德土产进出口公司	Foshan 佛山市	Guangdong 广东省	(0765)6682839 (0765)6681441

3484: Cutlery 刀剪制造业

The industry accounts for 0.024% of the total revenue of China's industrial sector in 2002. The rate of return on assets is 8.19%. 90.99% of all firms in the industry made a profit while 9.01% had negative returns.The top province in terms of the industry's revenue is Guangdong, accounting for 61.70% of the total revenue.
2002年本行业收入占全行业的0.024%，资产利润率为8.19%。90.99%的企业赢利，9.01%的企业亏损。收入最高的省为广东省，占本行业的61.70%。

	Total number of firms 企业总数	Total number of employees 职工总数	Total revenue (Mil.RMB) 总销售收入（百万元）	Total profit (Mil.RMB) 总利润（百万元）	Return on assets 资产利润率 (%)	Return on equity 权益利润率 (%)	Labour productivity ('000 RMB/worker) 劳动生产率（千元/人）	Debts/assets 资产负债率 (%)	Total assets (Mil.RMB) 总资产（百万元）
Industry Overall 行业总体	111	24,841	2,572	125	8.19	17.26	33.05	52.56	1,525

	Number of firms 企业个数	Average number of employees 平均职工人数	Average revenue ('000 RMB) 平均销售收入（千元）	Average profit ('000 RMB) 平均利润（千元）	Return on assets 资产利润率 (%)	Return on equity 权益利润率 (%)	Labour productivity ('000 RMB/worker) 劳动生产率（千元/人）	Debts/assets 资产负债率 (%)	Average total assets ('000 RMB) 平均总资产（千元）
By ownership 产业所有权									
State-owned 国有	3	294	14,068	-1		-0.01	28.36	65.89	15,269
Collective-owned 集体	4	60	14,111	647	7.05	49.81	134.74	85.84	9,169
Foreign & Overseas Chinese Funded 三资	16	460	44,583	2,936	8.12	17.66	27.01	54.01	36,152
By regional distribution 地区分布									
Central-North 华北	2	84	2,534	-79	-1.76		11.56	129.32	4,491
Beijing 北京									
Tianjin 天津	1	40	27	-681	-15.69			218.94	4,341
Hebei 河北	1	127	5,040	523	11.27	20.67	15.20	45.47	4,640
Shanxi 山西									
Inner Mongolia 内蒙古									
Northeast 东北	1	47	241	-170	-4.25		2.98	137.72	4,001
Liaoning 辽宁									
Jilin 吉林	1	47	241	-170	-4.25		2.98	137.72	4,001
Heilongjiang 黑龙江									
Central-East 华东	33	225	29,263	1,917	9.64	21.20	40.57	54.54	19,891
Shanghai 上海	7	164	35,768	3,489	8.65	17.72	82.07	51.15	40,314
Jiangsu 江苏	3	260	13,799	236	2.62	9.21	13.10	71.52	9,010
Zhejiang 浙江	20	248	21,435	934	5.98	14.50	26.24	58.75	15,617
Anhui 安徽									
Fujian 福建	1	131	5,030	153	4.55	9.37	17.59	51.38	3,359
Jiangxi 江西									
Shandong 山东	2	197	120,092	9,652	61.34	86.32	162.51	28.95	15,735
Central-South 中南	74	232	21,636	836	7.24	14.44	30.07	49.86	11,551
Henan 河南									
Hubei 湖北	1	170	13,980	3,796	17.06	25.61	127.80	33.40	22,253
Hunan 湖南									
Guangdong 广东	73	233	21,741	796	6.98	14.04	29.10	50.30	11,404
Guangxi 广西									
Hainan 海南									
Southwest 西南									
Chongqing 重庆									
Sichuan 四川									
Guizhou 贵州									
Yunnan 云南									
Tibet 西藏									
Northwest 西北	1	13	5	2	0.54	0.56	62.08	3.52	369
Shaanxi 陕西									
Gansu 甘肃	1	13	5	2	0.54	0.56	62.08	3.52	369
Qinghai 青海									
Ningxia 宁夏									
Xinjiang 新疆									

3484: Cutlery 刀剪制造业

Year 年份	Number of firms 企业个数	Rate of change 变化率 (%)	Number of employees 职工人数 (人)	Rate of change 变化率 (%)	Total revenue (Mil. RMB) 总销售收入 (百万元)	Rate of change 变化率 (%)	Total profit (Mil RMB) 总利润 (百万元)	Rate of change 变化率 (%)
2000	111		19,216		1,725		61	
2001	110	-0.90	20,750	7.98	2,128	23.36	101	65.57
2002	111	0.91	24,841	19.72	2,572	20.86	125	23.76

Major Products 主要产品	Output 产量	Unit 单位
Scissors 剪刀	21,836	10,000 Pieces 万把

10 Main Firms with Maximal Revenue (year founded) 收入最大的十家主要企业（创办年份）	City 城市	Province 省	Telephone/fax 电话/传真	Number of employees 职工人数	Ownership 产业所有权	Revenue ('000 RMB) 销售收入 (千元)	Profit('000 RMB) (rank) 利润(千元) (排名)	Total assets ('000 RMB) 总资产 (千元)	Major products 主要产品
Wendeng Daxing Metal Products Co., Ltd.	Weihai	Shandong	(0631)8545442		Foreign Funded				Nail Clippers
文登大星金属制品有限公司(1996)	威海市	山东省	(0631)8545452	150	外商投资	235,000	19,283(1)	19,320	指甲刀
Shanghai Shuangliren Hengkesi Co.,Ltd	Shanghai	Shanghai	(021)58410237		Foreign Funded				Kitchen Knife
上海双立人亨克斯有限公司(1995)	上海市	上海市	(021)64119588	434	外商投资	126,218	17,288(2)	136,053	菜刀
Zhongshan Qinglian Metal Products Co., Ltd.	Zhongshan	Guangdong	(0760)6652327		Overseas Chinese-funded				Scissors
中山庆琏金属制品有限公司(1994)	中山市	广东省	(0760)6653658	568	港澳台资	116,021	2,031(15)	109,634	剪刀
Yangjiang South Hardware & Plastic Products Co.,Ltd.	Yangjiang	Guangdong	(0662)3171143		Private Enterprises				Suit Knife
阳江市南方五金塑胶制品总厂(1998)	阳江市	广东省	(0662)3171012	415	私营独资	73,750	2,359(10)	24,738	套刀
Paiyi Daily-used Hardware Co, Ltd，Xiqiao	Foshan	Guangdong	(0757)6850417		Private Owned				Daily Use Hardware Products日用
南海市西樵牌一日用五金有限公司(1987)	佛山市	广东省	(0757)6850283	500	私营企业	66,938	2,058(14)	23,023	五金制品
Wenzhou Zhongqing Hardware Cutting Tool Co., Ltd.	Wenzhou	Zhejiang	(0577)88786644		Limited-Liability				Cutting Tool
温州市中轻五金刀具有限公司(1992)	温州市	浙江省	(0577)88781321	794	有限公司	66,038	1,939(18)	23,486	刀具
ZheJiang King Stone Cutlery Co.,Ltd.	Wenzhou	Zhejiang	(0577)65522024		Joint Stock				Cutting Tool
浙江金石刀具股份有限公司(1995)	温州市	浙江省	(0577)65520955	390	股份制	61,300	3,260(7)	36,846	刀具
Hangzhou Zhang Xiaoquan Group Co., Ltd.	Hangzhou	Zhejiang	(0571)88073733		Limited-Liability				Knife & Scissors
杭州张小泉集团有限公司(1995)	杭州市	浙江省	(0571)88068295	777	有限公司	56,521	3,072(8)	75,159	刀剪
Shanghai Beiyin Blade Tools Co., Ltd.	Shanghai	Shanghai	(021)57741465		Foreign Funded				Razor
上海贝印刃具有限公司(1995)	上海市	上海市	(021)57747470	221	外商投资	45,147	7,548(3)	60,820	剃刀
Ningbo Xingwei Plastic Products Co., Ltd.	Ningbo	Zhejiang	(0574)65181087		Private Owned				Art Design Knife
宁波兴伟塑料制品有限公司(1995)	宁波市	浙江省	(0574)65182083	188	私营企业	43,665	1,839(19)	17,666	美工刀

Top 10 Cities by Revenue 销售收入排名前10位城市	Province 省	Market share 市场份额 (%)	Number of firms 企业个数
Yangjiang 阳江市	Guangdong 广东省	45.45	60
Shanghai 上海市	Shanghai 上海市	9.73	7
Weihai 威海市	Shandong 山东省	9.14	1
Wenzhou 温州市	Zhejiang 浙江省	7.55	10
Zhongshan 中山市	Guangdong 广东省	5.27	2
Foshan 佛山市	Guangdong 广东省	3.93	3
Jinhua 金华市	Zhejiang 浙江省	2.40	4
Hangzhou 杭州市	Zhejiang 浙江省	2.20	1
Jiangmen 江门市	Guangdong 广东省	1.97	3
Guangzhou 广州市	Guangdong 广东省	1.83	2

10 Major Wholesalers 十家主要批发商	City 城市	Province 省	Telephone/Fax 电话/传真
Harbin ChinaSun Group Co., Ltd.	Harbin	Heilongjiang	(0451)84885100
哈尔滨中央红集团股份有限公司	哈尔滨市	黑龙江省	(0451)84885111
Guangzhou Yuexiu Enterprise (Group) Company	Guangzhou	Guangdong	(020)85597130
广州越秀企业（集团）公司	广州市	广东省	(020)85599018
China Reed Screen Imp. & Exp. Corp.Ltd.	Beijing	Beijing	(010)65521133
中艺苇帘进出口有限责任公司	北京市	北京市	(010)65513995
Hebei Xintai Foreign Trade Corp.ltd.	Shijiazhuang	Hebei	(0311)7767908
河北信泰对外贸易有限公司	石家庄市	河北省	(0311)7755347
Hebei Arts & Crafts Imp. & Exp. Corp.	Shijiazhuang	Hebei	(0311)7764345
河北省工艺品进出口公司	石家庄市	河北省	(0311)7755347
Shanghai Hengda Ceramic Building Materials Trade Market	Shanghai	Shanghai	(021)58425842
上海恒大陶瓷建材交易市场	上海市	上海市	(021)58427389
Hangzhou Local Product General Corporation	Hangzhou	Zhejiang	(0571)87026301
杭州市土特产总公司	杭州市	浙江省	(0571)87026323
Ningbo Zhonglin Foreign Trade Co.,Ltd.	Ningbo	Zhejiang	(0574)87871797
宁波中蔺对外贸易有限公司	宁波市	浙江省	(0574)87871790
Wuyi Local Products Daily Groceries Co.,Ltd.	Jinhua	Zhejiang	(0579)7623401
武义县土产日用杂品有限责任公司	金华市	浙江省	(0579)7623401
Guangdong Shunde Local Products Import & Export Company	Foshan	Guangdong	(0765)6682839
广东省顺德土产进出口公司	佛山市	广东省	(0765)6681441

3485: Locks 制锁业

The industry accounts for 0.072% of the total revenue of China's industrial sector in 2002. The rate of return on assets is 4.59%. 88.07% of all firms in the industry made a profit while 11.93% had negative returns.The top province in terms of the industry's revenue is Guangdong, accounting for 31.50% of the total revenue.
2002年本行业收入占全行业的 0.072%，资产利润率为 4.59%。88.07%的企业赢利，11.93%的企业亏损。收入最高的省为广东省，占本行业的31.50%。

	Total number of firms 企业总数	Total number of employees 职工总数	Total revenue (Mil.RMB) 总销售收入（百万元）	Total profit (Mil.RMB) 总利润（百万元）	Return on assets 资产利润率（%）	Return on equity 权益利润率（%）	Labour productivity ('000 RMB/ worker) 劳动生产率（千元/人）	Debts/ assets 资产负债率（%）	Total assets (Mil.RMB) 总资产（百万元）
Industry Overall 行业总体	285	69,537	7,698	270	4.59	9.54	30.18	51.87	5,887

	Number of firms 企业个数	Average number of employees 平均职工人数	Average revenue ('000 RMB) 平均销售收入（千元）	Average profit ('000 RMB) 平均利润（千元）	Return on assets 资产利润率（%）	Return on equity 权益利润率（%）	Labour productivity ('000 RMB/ worker) 劳动生产率（千元/人）	Debts/ assets 资产负债率（%）	Average total assets ('000 RMB) 平均总资产（千元）
By ownership 产业所有权									
State-owned 国有	11	92	3,547	-105	-1.23		6.81	107.46	8,518
Collective-owned 集体	43	267	14,881	394	1.98	4.15	17.08	52.23	19,873
Foreign & Overseas Chinese Funded 三资	43	339	52,709	2,944	6.31	9.40	40.67	32.85	46,656
By regional distribution 地区分布									
Central-North 华北	7	61	5,334	-1,343	-4.71	-26.28	22.27	82.07	28,493
Beijing 北京									
Tianjin 天津	6	53	4,653	-1,578	-4.86	-27.07	21.92	82.05	32,474
Hebei 河北	1	106	9,420	70	1.52	8.93	23.29	82.99	4,609
Shanxi 山西									
Inner Mongolia 内蒙古									
Northeast 东北	6	155	12,299	483	5.31	14.19	22.28	62.53	9,091
Liaoning 辽宁	5	109	13,676	678	8.23	20.83	30.51	60.50	8,236
Jilin 吉林									
Heilongjiang 黑龙江	1	384	5,412	-490	-3.67	-11.75	10.60	68.79	13,366
Central-East 华东	202	227	25,111	1,106	6.26	15.05	31.06	58.42	17,670
Shanghai 上海	17	133	26,907	2,843	13.47	25.00	43.68	46.13	21,108
Jiangsu 江苏	42	212	28,335	697	3.74	11.31	34.94	66.93	18,636
Zhejiang 浙江	115	159	16,115	553	5.22	11.13	27.73	53.08	10,591
Anhui 安徽	4	140	3,245	152	1.72	3.34	8.91	48.42	8,821
Fujian 福建	1	315	26,938	857	16.84	70.83	11.86	76.23	5,090
Jiangxi 江西									
Shandong 山东	23	680	66,599	3,510	6.90	18.30	32.08	62.29	50,845
Central-South 中南	63	340	39,386	803	2.59	4.08	29.25	36.54	31,003
Henan 河南	4	167	6,049	414	4.10	18.91	15.24	78.33	10,096
Hubei 湖北	1	120	12,949	50	0.42	1.32	35.61	68.01	11,826
Hunan 湖南	1	80	14,210	394	10.30	17.87	78.36	42.35	3,825
Guangdong 广东	56	362	43,302	869	2.57	3.97	29.88	35.27	33,809
Guangxi 广西	1	300	5,027	-195	-5.06		2.38	122.88	3,850
Hainan 海南									
Southwest 西南	4	149	7,218	745	3.14	5.24	19.95	40.04	23,694
Chongqing 重庆	1	374	22,568	3,105	4.68	6.36	31.41	26.41	66,325
Sichuan 四川									
Guizhou 贵州	1	40	90	17	0.09	0.66	-1.48	85.86	18,319
Yunnan 云南	2	91	3,107	-71	-1.40	-2.61	1.03	46.36	5,066
Tibet 西藏									
Northwest 西北	3	69	1,496	6	0.12		11.50	118.73	5,196
Shaanxi 陕西	1	88	2,468	6	0.08		8.52	174.55	7,171
Gansu 甘肃	2	60	1,010	6	0.14	0.49	13.71	71.18	4,209
Qinghai 青海									
Ningxia 宁夏									
Xinjiang 新疆									

3485: Locks 制锁业

Year 年份	Number of firms 企业个数	Rate of change 变化率 (%)	Number of employees 职工人数 (人)	Rate of change 变化率 (%)	Total revenue (Mil. RMB) 总销售收入 (百万元)	Rate of change 变化率 (%)	Total profit (Mil RMB) 总利润 (百万元)	Rate of change 变化率 (%)
2000	231		64,746		4,816		127	
2001	260	12.55	68,372	5.60	6,061	25.85	174	37.01
2002	285	9.62	69,537	1.70	7,698	27.01	270	55.17

Major Products 主要产品	Output 产量	Unit 单位
Lock 锁	123,024	10,000 Pieces 万把

10 Main Firms with Maximal Revenue (year founded) 收入最大的十家主要企业（创办年份）	City 城市	Province 省	Telephone/fax 电话/传真	Number of employees 职工人数	Ownership 产业所有权	Revenue ('000 RMB) 销售收入 (千元)	Profit('000 RMB) (rank) 利润(千元) (排名)	Total assets ('000 RMB) 总资产 (千元)	Major products 主要产品
Yantai Tri-Cirde Lock Industry Group Co., Ltd.	Yantai	Shandong	(0535)6254401		State Enterprises				Padlock
烟台三环锁业集团有限公司(1930)	烟台市	山东省	(0535)6244704	4,906	国有独资	522,443	6,127(9)	481,688	挂锁
Guli Security Products Co., Ltd.	Zhongshan	Guangdong	(0760)2102326		Foreign Funded				Ball Door Lock
固力保安制品有限公司(1996)	中山市	广东省	(0760)2100316	1,997	外商投资	214,182	2,331(28)	497,118	球形门锁
Wuxi Weida Lock Industry Co., Ltd.	Wuxi	Jiangsu	(0510)8789588		Private Owned				Core Inserted Door Lock
无锡市伟达锁业有限公司(1997)	无锡市	江苏省	(0510)8782168	460	私营企业	179,400	1,290(50)	125,020	插芯门锁
Yantai Tri-Circle Group Rushan Shuanglian Co.,Ltd.	Weihai	Shandong	(0631)6622640		Limited-Liability				Uranium Iron Padlock
烟台三环集团乳山双连有限公司(1974)	威海市	山东省	(0631)6623405	1,707	有限公司	173,424	6,187(8)	96,991	铀铁挂锁
Zhongshan Huafeng Lock Product Co., Ltd.	Zhongshan	Guangdong	(0760)2265895		Overseas Chinese-funded				Door Lock
中山市华锋制锁有限公司(1993)	中山市	广东省	(0760)2278063	1,500	港澳台资	148,349	2,219(31)	70,520	门锁
Yantai HUF Automotive Lock Co., Ltd.	Yantai	Shandong	(0535)6370518		Foreign Funded				Jata Sets Of Locks.Jata
烟台霍富汽车锁有限公司(1996)	烟台市	山东省	(0535)6378609	310	外商投资	145,451	46,065(1)	147,485	成套锁
Wujin Chenyang Industry Group Company	Changzhou	Jiangsu	(0519)3681056		Foreign Funded				Glass Tools
武进晨阳工业集团公司(1996)	常州市	江苏省	(0519)3681598	914	外商投资	123,400	140(166)	74,100	镜具
Fushing Industry Strial(Shanghai) CO.,Ltd.	Shanghai	Shanghai	(021)59100198		Overseas Chinese-funded				Door Lock
福兴工业（上海）有限公司(1995)	上海市	上海市	(021)59100273	465	港澳台资	105,290	16,309(3)	143,909	门锁
Zheiiang Baodean Lock Industry Co.,ltd.	Taizhou	Zhejiang	(0576)2881688		Limited-Liability				Lock
浙江保德安锁业有限公司(1995)	台州市	浙江省	(0576)2883868	805	有限公司	100,189	2,847(22)	44,554	锁
Rushan Rujia Lock Making Equipment Co., Ltd.	Weihai	Shandong	(0631)6422046		Limited-Liability				Lock Making Equipment
乳山市乳嘉造锁设备有限公司(1966)	威海市	山东省	(0631)6422088	236	有限公司	98,961	2,541(26)	10,242	造锁设备

Top 10 Cities by Revenue 销售收入排名前10位城市	Province 省	Market share 市场份额 (%)	Number of firms 企业个数
Yantai 烟台市	Shandong 山东省	13.31	10
Zhongshan 中山市	Guangdong 广东省	11.38	22
Wenzhou 温州市	Zhejiang 浙江省	10.19	40
Jiangmen 江门市	Guangdong 广东省	8.95	4
Shanghai 上海市	Shanghai 上海市	5.94	17
Wuxi 无锡市	Jiangsu 江苏省	5.66	10
Jinhua 金华市	Zhejiang 浙江省	4.59	25
Weihai 威海市	Shandong 山东省	4.41	5
Ningbo 宁波市	Zhejiang 浙江省	4.25	23
Guangzhou 广州市	Guangdong 广东省	3.31	9

10 Major Wholesalers 十家主要批发商	City 城市	Province 省	Telephone/Fax 电话/传真
Harbin ChinaSun Group Co., Ltd.	Harbin	Heilongjiang	(0451)84885100
哈尔滨中央红集团股份有限公司	哈尔滨市	黑龙江省	(0451)84885111
Guangzhou Yuexiu Enterprise (Group) Company	Guangzhou	Guangdong	(020)85597130
广州越秀企业（集团）公司	广州市	广东省	(020)85599018
China Reed Screen Imp. & Exp. Corp.Ltd.	Beijing	Beijing	(010)65521133
中艺苇帘进出口有限责任公司	北京市	北京市	(010)65513995
Hebei Xintai Foreign Trade Corp.ltd.	Shijiazhuang	Hebei	(0311)7767908
河北信泰对外贸易有限公司	石家庄市	河北省	(0311)7755347
Hebei Arts & Crafts Imp. & Exp. Corp.	Shijiazhuang	Hebei	(0311)7764345
河北省工艺品进出口公司	石家庄市	河北省	(0311)7755347
Shanghai Hengda Ceramic Building Materials Trade Market	Shanghai	Shanghai	(021)58425842
上海恒大陶瓷建材交易市场	上海市	上海市	(021)58427389
Hangzhou Local Product General Corporation	Hangzhou	Zhejiang	(0571)87026301
杭州市土特产总公司	杭州市	浙江省	(0571)87026323
Ningbo Zhonglin Foreign Trade Co.,Ltd.	Ningbo	Zhejiang	(0574)87871797
宁波中蔺对外贸易有限公司	宁波市	浙江省	(0574)87871790
Wuyi Local Products Daily Groceries Co.,Ltd.	Jinhua	Zhejiang	(0579)7623401
武义县土产日用杂品有限责任公司	金华市	浙江省	(0579)7623401
Guangdong Shunde Local Products Import & Export Company	Foshan	Guangdong	(0765)6682839
广东省顺德土产进出口公司	佛山市	广东省	(0765)6681441

3486: Cooking Utensils 炊事用具制造业

The industry accounts for 0.026% of the total revenue of China's industrial sector in 2002. The rate of return on assets is 3.90%. 82.93% of all firms in the industry made a profit while 17.07% had negative returns.The top province in terms of the industry's revenue is Guangdong, accounting for 40.27% of the total revenue.
2002年本行业收入占全行业的 0.026%，资产利润率为 3.90%。82.93%的企业赢利，17.07%的企业亏损。收入最高的省为广东省，占本行业的40.27%。

	Total number of firms 企业总数	Total number of employees 职工总数	Total revenue (Mil.RMB) 总销售收入 (百万元)	Total profit (Mil.RMB) 总利润 (百万元)	Return on assets 资产利润率 (%)	Return on equity 权益利润率 (%)	Labour productivity ('000 RMB/ worker) 劳动生产率 (千元/人)	Debts/ assets 资产负债率 (%)	Total assets (Mil.RMB) 总资产 (百万元)
Industry Overall 行业总体	164	23,117	2,797	111	3.90	10.63	38.96	63.32	2,850

	Number of firms 企业个数	Average number of employees 平均职工人数	Average revenue ('000 RMB) 平均销售收入 (千元)	Average profit ('000 RMB) 平均利润 (千元)	Return on assets 资产利润率 (%)	Return on equity 权益利润率 (%)	Labour productivity ('000 RMB/ worker) 劳动生产率 (千元/人)	Debts/ assets 资产负债率 (%)	Average total assets ('000 RMB) 平均总资产 (千元)
By ownership 产业所有权									
State-owned 国有	23	120	9,544	-145	-1.03	-3.84	22.03	73.30	14,127
Collective-owned 集体	33	133	19,624	1,087	4.76	26.42	60.71	82.00	22,855
Foreign & Overseas Chinese Funded 三资	21	230	35,016	1,455	4.73	8.70	40.33	45.68	30,775
By regional distribution 地区分布									
Central-North 华北	20	128	15,859	976	5.58	11.44	46.24	51.26	17,499
Beijing 北京	6	101	11,242	149	0.52	1.24	54.60	57.70	28,530
Tianjin 天津	9	102	18,351	1,106	7.90	14.69	58.47	46.18	13,996
Hebei 河北	5	205	16,912	1,733	16.40	28.52	30.33	42.49	10,568
Shanxi 山西									
Inner Mongolia 内蒙古									
Northeast 东北	4	274	43,334	444	0.86	2.46	37.79	64.92	51,553
Liaoning 辽宁	2	538	83,337	284	0.29	0.82	35.14	64.83	98,275
Jilin 吉林									
Heilongjiang 黑龙江	2	11	3,331	605	12.53	37.77	173.43	66.83	4,830
Central-East 华东	39	153	23,068	1,324	8.12	17.77	46.53	54.32	16,309
Shanghai 上海	4	122	24,763	260	1.26	2.22	40.34	43.44	20,668
Jiangsu 江苏	5	111	12,842	158	1.97	11.79	26.73	83.27	8,000
Zhejiang 浙江	16	103	15,758	820	7.36	18.82	38.48	60.86	11,131
Anhui 安徽	3	54	6,897	220	8.17	18.60	36.43	56.06	2,695
Fujian 福建	3	93	16,966	286	1.73	3.31	26.92	47.68	16,493
Jiangxi 江西									
Shandong 山东	8	354	51,587	4,396	12.66	25.50	58.63	50.33	34,716
Central-South 中南	73	163	18,506	528	2.53	8.53	36.37	70.35	20,888
Henan 河南	21	145	6,181	563	7.98	21.01	18.72	62.01	7,054
Hubei 湖北	2	25	10,465	-47	-1.25		192.04	134.13	3,769
Hunan 湖南	8	188	8,537	214	2.33	9.21	15.67	74.68	9,187
Guangdong 广东	40	177	28,166	628	1.96	6.58	48.09	70.20	32,039
Guangxi 广西	2	102	2,662	-8	-0.11		7.65	114.75	7,031
Hainan 海南									
Southwest 西南	7	82	4,005	-11	-0.15	-0.36	21.37	56.41	7,382
Chongqing 重庆									
Sichuan 四川	4	89	3,809	35	0.38	0.71	17.69	47.28	9,262
Guizhou 贵州	2	23	376	-154	-3.79	-19.38	9.04	80.43	4,048
Yunnan 云南	1	172	12,051	88	1.35	6.23	32.31	78.37	6,533
Tibet 西藏									
Northwest 西北	21	50	1,345	-15	-0.39	-0.85	18.56	54.23	3,851
Shaanxi 陕西	2	30	3,605	148	1.82	2.41	35.98	24.33	8,099
Gansu 甘肃	18	54	1,151	-34	-0.97	-2.50	17.46	61.21	3,500
Qinghai 青海	1	12	320	1	0.06	0.30	22.17	80.47	1,690
Ningxia 宁夏									
Xinjiang 新疆									

Year 年份	Number of firms 企业个数	Rate of change 变化率 (%)	Number of employees 职工人数 (人)	Rate of change 变化率 (%)	Total revenue (Mil. RMB) 总销售收入 (百万元)	Rate of change 变化率 (%)	Total profit (Mil RMB) 总利润 (百万元)	Rate of change 变化率 (%)
2000	157		23,096		2,173		109	
2001	154	-1.91	23,662	2.45	2,543	17.03	109	o
2002	164	6.49	23,117	-2.30	2,797	9.99	111	1.83

Major Products 主要产品	Output 产量	Unit 单位
Household Electric Roaster 家用电热烘烤器具	4,853	10,000 Units 万个
Microwave Oven 微波炉	2,271	10,000 Units 万台

10 Main Firms with Maximal Revenue (year founded) 收入最大的十家主要企业（创办年份）	City 城市	Province 省	Telephone/fax 电话/传真	Number of employees 职工人数	Ownership 产业所有权	Revenue ('000 RMB) 销售收入 (千元)	Profit('000 RMB) (rank) 利润(千元) (排名)	Total assets ('000 RMB) 总资产 (千元)	Major products 主要产品
Zhangqiu Cooker Machinery General Factory	Jinan	Shandong	(0531)3511279		Collective-owned				Kitchen Machinery
章丘市炊具机械总厂(1974)	济南市	山东省	(0531)3511279	995	集体企业	207,000	20,980(1)	76,980	炊具机械
Shenyang No.3523 Machinery Factory	Shenyang	Liaoning	(024)25824964		State-owned				Pressure Boiler
沈阳第三五二三机械厂(1938)	沈阳市	辽宁省	(024)25820314	1,025	国有企业	158,224	217(74)	190,870	压力锅
Guangdong South Hardware General Factory	Foshan	Guangdong	(0757)5932402		Collective-owned				Kitchen Utensils
广东南方五金总厂(1971)	佛山市	广东省	(0757)5936711	542	集体企业	120,726	-	496,122	厨具
Ji'nan Taidao Cooker Machinery Co., Ltd.	Jinan	Shandong	(0531)3511121		Overseas Chinese-funded				Kitchen Utensils
济南台岛炊事机械有限公司(1995)	济南市	山东省	(0531)3521777	323	港澳台资	73,600	8,830(2)	29,630	炊具
Zhejiang Tianxi Industrial Co., Ltd.	Lishui	Zhejiang	(0578)3153940		Private Owned				Pressure Boiler
浙江天喜实业有限公司(1996)	丽水市	浙江省	(0578)3155688	418	私营企业	68,100	2,020(15)	25,203	压力锅
Guangzhou Yidao Enterprise Co., Ltd.	Guangzhou	Guangdong	(020)84790933		Private Partnership				Oven
广州市意道企业有限公司(1996)	广州市	广东省	(020)84790618	560	私营合伙	61,330	288(66)	95,018	烤炉
Zhongshan Lihui Metal Product Co.,Ltd	Zhongshan	Guangdong	(0760)3378138		Overseas Chinese-funded				Barbecue
中山立辉金属制品有限公司(1995)	中山市	广东省	(0760)8201656	983	港澳台资	.58,866	3,910(7)	53,384	烧烤架
Nanhai Xiangzhao Metal ware Co., ltd.	Foshan	Guangdong	(0757)5441975		Limited-Liability				Barbecue Furnace
南海市祥兆金属制品有限公司(1999)	佛山市	广东省	(0757)5443418	140	有限公司	55,851	-	20,153	烧烤炉
Gaoming Songzhan Metal Co., Ltd.	Foshan	Guangdong	(0757)8918121		Overseas Chinese funded				Roast Furnace
高明淞湛金属有限公司(2000)	佛山市	广东省	(0757)8802881	120	港澳台资	54,183	903(36)	21,503	烧烤炉
Zaozhuang Duole Heating Equipment Co., Ltd.	Zaozhuang	Shandong	(0632)4511818		Joint Stock				Multipurpose Furmace
枣庄市多乐采暖设备有限责任公司(1970)	枣庄市	山东省	(0632)4514999	380	股份制	53,700	3,270(8)	13,000	多用炉

Top 10 Cities by Revenue 销售收入排名前10位城市	Province 省	Market share 市场份额 (%)	Number of firms 企业个数
Jinan 济南市	Shandong 山东省	10.53	3
Foshan 佛山市	Guangdong 广东省	10.15	7
Guangzhou 广州市	Guangdong 广东省	8.88	9
Zhongshan 中山市	Guangdong 广东省	7.44	7
Tianjin 天津市	Tianjin 天津市	5.90	9
Shenyang 沈阳市	Liaoning 辽宁省	5.66	1
Jiangmen 江门市	Guangdong 广东省	5.52	4
Zhuhai 珠海市	Guangdong 广东省	4.97	3
Shanghai 上海市	Shanghai 上海市	3.54	4
Jinhua 金华市	Zhejiang 浙江省	3.13	7

10 Major Wholesalers 十家主要批发商	City 城市	Province 省	Telephone/Fax 电话/传真
Harbin ChinaSun Group Co., Ltd.	Harbin	Heilongjiang	(0451)84885100
哈尔滨中央红集团股份有限公司	哈尔滨市	黑龙江省	(0451)84885111
Guangzhou Yuexiu Enterprise (Group) Company	Guangzhou	Guangdong	(020)85597130
广州越秀企业（集团）公司	广州市	广东省	(020)85599018
China Reed Screen Imp. & Exp. Corp.Ltd.	Beijing	Beijing	(010)65521133
中艺苇帘进出口有限责任公司	北京市	北京市	(010)65513995
Hebei Xintai Foreign Trade Corp.ltd.	Shijiazhuang	Hebei	(0311)7767908
河北信泰对外贸易有限公司	石家庄市	河北省	(0311)7755347
Hebei Arts & Crafts Imp. & Exp. Corp.	Shijiazhuang	Hebei	(0311)7764345
河北省工艺品进出口公司	石家庄市	河北省	(0311)7755347
Shanghai Hengda Ceramic Building Materials Trade Market	Shanghai	Shanghai	(021)58425842
上海恒大陶瓷建材交易市场	上海市	上海市	(021)58427389
Hangzhou Local Product General Corporation	Hangzhou	Zhejiang	(0571)87026301
杭州市土特产总公司	杭州市	浙江省	(0571)87026323
Ningbo Zhonglin Foreign Trade Co.,Ltd.	Ningbo	Zhejiang	(0574)87871797
宁波中蔺对外贸易有限公司	宁波市	浙江省	(0574)87871790
Wuyi Local Products Daily Groceries Co.,Ltd.	Jinhua	Zhejiang	(0579)7623401
武义县土产日用杂品有限责任公司	金华市	浙江省	(0579)7623401
Guangdong Shunde Local Products Import & Export Company	Foshan	Guangdong	(0765)6682839
广东省顺德土产进出口公司	佛山市	广东省	(0765)6681441

3487: Gas Utensils 燃气用具制造业

The industry accounts for 0.065% of the total revenue of China's industrial sector in 2002. The rate of return on assets is 2.14%. 77.27% of all firms in the industry made a profit while 22.73% had negative returns.The top province in terms of the industry's revenue is Guangdong, accounting for 34.53% of the total revenue.
2002年本行业收入占全行业的 0.065%，资产利润率为 2.14%。77.27%的企业赢利，22.73%的企业亏损。收入最高的省为广东省，占本行业的34.53%。

	Total number of firms 企业总数	Total number of employees 职工总数	Total revenue (Mil.RMB) 总销售收入（百万元）	Total profit (Mil.RMB) 总利润（百万元）	Return on assets 资产利润率（%）	Return on equity 权益利润率（%）	Labour productivity ('000 RMB/worker) 劳动生产率（千元/人）	Debts/assets 资产负债率（%）	Total assets (Mil.RMB) 总资产（百万元）
Industry Overall 行业总体	154	33,070	6,924	143	2.14	7.45	52.26	71.26	6,674

	Number of firms 企业个数	Average number of employees 平均职工人数	Average revenue ('000 RMB) 平均销售收入（千元）	Average profit ('000 RMB) 平均利润（千元）	Return on assets 资产利润率（%）	Return on equity 权益利润率（%）	Labour productivity ('000 RMB/worker) 劳动生产率（千元/人）	Debts/assets 资产负债率（%）	Average total assets ('000 RMB) 平均总资产（千元）
By ownership 产业所有权									
State-owned 国有	7	164	5,773	-2,220	-4.98		6.48	121.27	44,587
Collective-owned 集体	25	192	23,311	1,051	2.64	8.58	41.53	69.29	39,869
Foreign & Overseas Chinese Funded 三资	32	389	107,137	1,238	1.11	3.83	58.18	70.98	111,399
By regional distribution 地区分布									
Central-North 华北	15	129	35,895	836	2.49	20.75	69.43	88.01	33,614
Beijing 北京	7	150	41,981	552	1.14	8.14	31.63	86.02	48,477
Tianjin 天津	5	108	41,336	1,461	8.24	224.85	171.96	96.34	17,731
Hebei 河北	3	114	12,628	460	1.81	14.12	24.08	87.18	25,404
Shanxi 山西									
Inner Mongolia 内蒙古									
Northeast 东北	2	85	4,276	-1,093	-3.36		13.22	173.69	32,531
Liaoning 辽宁	2	85	4,276	-1,093	-3.36		13.22	173.69	32,531
Jilin 吉林									
Heilongjiang 黑龙江									
Central-East 华东	66	249	56,624	2,274	4.56	11.54	50.34	60.50	49,867
Shanghai 上海	12	189	56,931	2,070	2.60	5.12	59.57	49.12	79,484
Jiangsu 江苏	15	352	93,736	4,209	5.18	14.90	65.68	65.22	81,233
Zhejiang 浙江	33	222	41,184	1,851	6.83	16.59	36.67	58.87	27,112
Anhui 安徽									
Fujian 福建	1	283	83,693	1,357	14.49	56.85	82.41	74.51	9,364
Jiangxi 江西	1	173	2,435	-215	-0.37	-1.81	2.18	79.35	57,576
Shandong 山东	4	286	50,693	-34	-0.09	-1.57	48.10	94.46	39,329
Central-South 中南	61	217	41,870	-220	-0.51	-2.18	55.63	76.58	43,090
Henan 河南	1	80	6,650	525	21.47	81.40	31.20	73.62	2,445
Hubei 湖北	3	89	12,007	349	2.19	2.77	47.42	21.09	15,976
Hunan 湖南	3	232	40,062	2,236	4.17	6.74	78.51	38.07	53,559
Guangdong 广东	54	226	44,282	-402	-0.90	-4.55	54.66	80.24	44,767
Guangxi 广西									
Hainan 海南									
Southwest 西南	7	170	10,875	-652	-2.63		19.00	108.51	24,814
Chongqing 重庆	6	168	10,025	-344	-1.52		13.20	115.82	22,603
Sichuan 四川	1	187	15,980	-2,501	-6.57	-37.53	50.17	82.50	38,085
Guizhou 贵州									
Yunnan 云南									
Tibet 西藏									
Northwest 西北	3	30	3,248	169	4.44	10.32	52.03	56.99	3,809
Shaanxi 陕西	1	61	9,738	505	5.24	15.30	52.66	65.76	9,642
Gansu 甘肃	2	15	3	1	0.11	0.12	50.77	9.59	892
Qinghai 青海									
Ningxia 宁夏									
Xinjiang 新疆									

3487: Gas Utensils 燃气用具制造业

Year 年份	Number of firms 企业个数	Rate of change 变化率 (%)	Number of employees 职工人数 (人)	Rate of change 变化率 (%)	Total revenue (Mil. RMB) 总销售收入 (百万元)	Rate of change 变化率 (%)	Total profit (Mil RMB) 总利润 (百万元)	Rate of change 变化率 (%)
2000	161		41,843		6,070		112	
2001	163	1.24	40,134	-4.08	6,591	8.58	80	-28.57
2002	154	-5.52	33,070	-17.60	6,924	5.05	143	78.75

Major Products 主要产品	Output 产量	Unit 单位
Gas Instrument 燃气用具	1,330	10,000 Units 万台
Gas Water Heater 燃气热水器	244	10,000 Units 万台

10 Main Firms with Maximal Revenue (year founded) 收入最大的十家主要企业（创办年份）	City 城市	Province 省	Telephone/fax 电话/传真	Number of employees 职工人数	Ownership 产业所有权	Revenue ('000 RMB) 销售收入(千元)	Profit('000 RMB) (rank) 利润(千元)(排名)	Total assets ('000 RMB) 总资产(千元)	Major products 主要产品
Sakura Bath Kitchen Products (china) Co., Ltd .	Suzhou	Jiangsu	(0512)57710968		Foreign Funded				Water Heater
樱花卫厨(中国)有限公司(1994)	苏州市	江苏省	(0512)57707060	810	外商投资	511,485	58,070(1)	425,242	热水器
Zhongshan Vantage Gas Utensils Co., Ltd.	Zhongshan	Guangdong	(0760)2262981		Limited-Liability				Stove Utensils
中山华帝燃具有限公司(1992)	中山市	广东省	(0760)2264283	1,400	有限公司	458,310	33,569(2)	217,317	炉具
Shunde Vanward Electric Appliance Co.,Ltd.	Foshan	Guangdong	(0765)8982663		Overseas Chinese-funded				Antisepsis Cupboard
顺德万和电器有限公司(1995)	佛山市	广东省	(0765)8989938	1,300	港澳台资	332,322	238(77)	292,086	消毒柜
A.O Smith(China) Water Heater Co., Ltd.	Nanjing	Jiangsu	(025)5568000		Foreign Funded				Quick Gas Water Heater快速燃
南京艾欧史密斯热水器有限公司(1995)	南京市	江苏省	(025)5803100	760	外商投资	255,690	-	255,110	气热水器
Shaoxing Putian Electric Appliance Co., Ltd.	Shaoxing	Zhejiang	(0575)3081376		Private Owned				Gas Stove
绍兴市普田电器有限公司(1992)	绍兴市	浙江省	(0575)3081745	130	私营企业	234,988	13,501(5)	116,338	燃气灶
Hangzhou Panasonic Gas Appliance Co.,Ltd.	Hangzhou	Zhejiang	(0571)86910221		Foreign Funded				Gas Stove
杭州松下燃气具有限公司(1995)	杭州市	浙江省	(0571)86910230	384	外商投资	217,089	10,318(7)	174,784	燃气用具
Hangzhou Deyi Electric Industrial Co., Ltd.	Hangzhou	Zhejiang	(0571)82191888		Limited-Liability				Gas Stove
杭州德意电气实业有限公司(1995)	杭州市	浙江省	(0571)82191777	527	有限公司	216,772	16,933(3)	152,967	燃气用具
Zhongshan Chant Gas Appliance Co., Ltd.	Zhongshan	Guangdong	(0760)2111888		Overseas Chinese-funded				Gas Stove
中山长青燃气具有限公司(1994)	中山市	广东省	(0760)2111999	663	港澳台资	196,572	8,015(10)	133,352	燃气具
Longkou Tengxiang Gas Appliance Co., Ltd.	Yantai	Shandong	(0535)8911438		Limited-Liability				Kitchen Multipurpose Cupboard厨房灶
龙口市腾翔燃气具有限公司(1979)	烟台市	山东省		150	有限公司	170,496	6,900(12)	17,090	具多用柜
Jiangsu Guangmang Group	Taizhou	Jiangsu	(0523)4321088		Overseas Chinese-funded				Water Heater
江苏光芒集团公司(1975)	泰州市	江苏省	(0523)4321452	1,014	港澳台资	170,354	6,504(14)	115,414	热水器

Top 10 Cities by Revenue 销售收入排名前10位城市	Province 省	Market share 市场份额 (%)	Number of firms 企业个数
Zhongshan 中山市	Guangdong 广东省	15.95	30
Foshan 佛山市	Guangdong 广东省	14.10	12
Shanghai 上海市	Shanghai 上海市	9.87	12
Suzhou 苏州市	Jiangsu 江苏省	7.39	1
Hangzhou 杭州市	Zhejiang 浙江省	7.14	4
Ningbo 宁波市	Zhejiang 浙江省	5.86	15
Nanjing 南京市	Jiangsu 江苏省	5.69	5
Shaoxing 绍兴市	Zhejiang 浙江省	5.67	7
Beijing 北京市	Beijing 北京市	4.24	7
Yangzhou 扬州市	Jiangsu 江苏省	3.52	3

10 Major Wholesalers 十家主要批发商	City 城市	Province 省	Telephone/Fax 电话/传真
Harbin ChinaSun Group Co., Ltd.	Harbin	Heilongjiang	(0451)84885100
哈尔滨中央红集团股份有限公司	哈尔滨市	黑龙江省	(0451)84885111
Guangzhou Yuexiu Enterprise (Group) Company	Guangzhou	Guangdong	(020)85597130
广州越秀企业（集团）公司	广州市	广东省	(020)85599018
China Reed Screen Imp. & Exp. Corp.Ltd.	Beijing	Beijing	(010)65521133
中艺苇帘进出口有限责任公司	北京市	北京市	(010)65513995
Hebei Xintai Foreign Trade Corp.ltd.	Shijiazhuang	Hebei	(0311)7767908
河北信泰对外贸易有限公司	石家庄市	河北省	(0311)7755347
Hebei Arts & Crafts Imp. & Exp. Corp.	Shijiazhuang	Hebei	(0311)7764345
河北省工艺品进出口公司	石家庄市	河北省	(0311)7755347
Shanghai Hengda Ceramic Building Materials Trade Market	Shanghai	Shanghai	(021)58425842
上海恒大陶瓷建材交易市场	上海市	上海市	(021)58427389
Hangzhou Local Product General Corporation	Hangzhou	Zhejiang	(0571)87026301
杭州市土特产总公司	杭州市	浙江省	(0571)87026323
Ningbo Zhonglin Foreign Trade Co.,Ltd.	Ningbo	Zhejiang	(0574)87871797
宁波中蔺对外贸易有限公司	宁波市	浙江省	(0574)87871790
Wuyi Local Products Daily Groceries Co.,Ltd.	Jinhua	Zhejiang	(0579)7623401
武义县土产日用杂品有限责任公司	金华市	浙江省	(0579)7623401
Guangdong Shunde Local Products Import & Export Company	Foshan	Guangdong	(0765)6682839
广东省顺德土产进出口公司	佛山市	广东省	(0765)6681441

3488: Hair Cutting Equipment 理发用具制造业

The industry accounts for 0.015% of the total revenue of China's industrial sector in 2002. The rate of return on assets is 12.59%. 93.33% of all firms in the industry made a profit while 6.67% had negative returns.The top province in terms of the industry's revenue is Shanghai, accounting for 43.41% of the total revenue.
2002年本行业收入占全行业的0.015%，资产利润率为12.59%。93.33%的企业赢利，6.67%的企业亏损。收入最高的省为上海市，占本行业的43.41%。

	Total number of firms 企业总数	Total number of employees 职工总数	Total revenue (Mil.RMB) 总销售收入 (百万元)	Total profit (Mil.RMB) 总利润 (百万元)	Return on assets 资产利润率 (%)	Return on equity 权益利润率 (%)	Labour productivity ('000 RMB/ worker) 劳动生产率 (千元/人)	Debts/ assets 资产负债率 (%)	Total assets (Mil.RMB) 总资产 (百万元)
Industry Overall 行业总体	45	9,181	1,601	227	12.59	18.19	65.28	30.82	1,802

	Number of firms 企业个数	Average number of employees 平均职工人数	Average revenue ('000 RMB) 平均销售收入 (千元)	Average profit ('000 RMB) 平均利润 (千元)	Return on assets 资产利润率 (%)	Return on equity 权益利润率 (%)	Labour productivity ('000 RMB/ worker) 劳动生产率 (千元/人)	Debts/ assets 资产负债率 (%)	Average total assets ('000 RMB) 平均总资产 (千元)
By ownership 产业所有权									
State-owned 国有	4	219	8,212	4,744	6.07	11.39	6.26	46.68	78,131
Collective-owned 集体	1	285	27,265	430	1.36	1.69	26.69	19.86	31,720
Foreign & Overseas Chinese Funded 三资	13	325	78,312	13,667	16.45	20.44	108.42	19.56	83,103
By regional distribution 地区分布									
Central-North 华北	1	8		-555	-2.20	-4.34		49.23	25,196
Beijing 北京									
Tianjin 天津	1	8		-555	-2.20	-4.34		49.23	25,196
Hebei 河北									
Shanxi 山西									
Inner Mongolia 内蒙古									
Northeast 东北	2	133	16,844	4,813	7.80	27.79	99.60	71.94	61,712
Liaoning 辽宁	2	133	16,844	4,813	7.80	27.79	99.60	71.94	61,712
Jilin 吉林									
Heilongjiang 黑龙江									
Central-East 华东	33	173	38,445	6,449	15.07	19.96	83.46	24.51	42,792
Shanghai 上海	6	191	115,828	24,520	15.59	18.76	271.01	16.92	157,327
Jiangsu 江苏	2	92	6,478	5	0.04	0.25	14.24	85.54	13,941
Zhejiang 浙江	24	166	23,075	2,746	16.16	24.65	40.22	34.43	16,990
Anhui 安徽									
Fujian 福建									
Jiangxi 江西	1	402	6,950	-211	-0.65	-2.04	8.38	68.19	32,548
Shandong 山东									
Central-South 中南	9	354	33,186	547	2.04	3.70	29.92	44.79	26,803
Henan 河南									
Hubei 湖北									
Hunan 湖南									
Guangdong 广东	9	354	33,186	547	2.04	3.70	29.92	44.79	26,803
Guangxi 广西									
Hainan 海南									
Southwest 西南									
Chongqing 重庆									
Sichuan 四川									
Guizhou 贵州									
Yunnan 云南									
Tibet 西藏									
Northwest 西北									
Shaanxi 陕西									
Gansu 甘肃									
Qinghai 青海									
Ningxia 宁夏									
Xinjiang 新疆									

3488: Hair Cutting Equipment 理发用具制造业

Year 年份	Number of firms 企业个数	Rate of change 变化率 (%)	Number of employees 职工人数 (人)	Rate of change 变化率 (%)	Total revenue (Mil. RMB) 总销售收入 (百万元)	Rate of change 变化率 (%)	Total profit (Mil RMB) 总利润 (百万元)	Rate of change 变化率 (%)
2000	40		7,429		2,331		245	
2001	45	12.50	8,755	17.85	2,212	-5.11	325	32.65
2002	45	o	9,181	4.87	1,601	-27.62	227	-30.15

Major Products 主要产品	Output 产量	Unit 单位
Scissors 剪刀	21,836	10,000 Pieces 万把

10 Main Firms with Maximal Revenue (year founded) 收入最大的十家主要企业（创办年份）	City 城市	Province 省	Telephone/fax 电话/传真	Number of employees 职工人数	Ownership 产业所有权	Revenue ('000 RMB) 销售收入 (千元)	Profit('000 RMB) (rank) 利润(千元) (排名)	Total assets ('000 RMB) 总资产 (千元)	Major products 主要产品
Gillette (Shanghai) Co., Ltd.	Shanghai	Shanghai	(021)58498000		Foreign Funded				Shaving Blade
上海吉列有限公司(1992)	上海市	上海市	(021)58411724	369	外商投资	623,919	123,397(1)	692,353	刮脸刀片
Super Human Group Holding Co.,Ltd. Zhejiang	Jinhua	Zhejiang	(0579)7232490		Private Owned				Electric Shaver
浙江超人集团有限公司(1983)	金华市	浙江省	(0579)7232806	524	私营企业	163,200	17,250(4)	118,730	电须刀
Wahl Clipper(NingBo) limited	Ningbo	Zhejiang	(0574)88845763		Foreign Funded				Hairdressing Tool
华尔推剪（宁波）有限公司(1995)	宁波市	浙江省	(0574)88845097	676	外商投资	84,633	26,030(2)	80,302	理发用具
Guangzhou Panyu Xianhua Household Appliances Industrial	Guangzhou	Guangdong	(020)84993855		Overseas Chinese-funded				Shaver
Co., Ltd.广州市番禺显华家电实业有限公司(1995)	广州市	广东省	(020)84995904	942	港澳台资	62,468	-	63,340	剃毛器
YuyaoFine & Bruidgc Electrics Co.,Ltd.	Ningbo	Zhejiang	(0574)62823970		Overseas Chinese-funded				Electric Hair Dryer
余姚富一桥电器有限公司(1999)	宁波市	浙江省	(0574)62802531	250	港澳台资	42,171	7,866(6)	24,905	电吹风
ZhongShan Sanding Industrical Co.,Ltd.	Zhongshan	Guangdong	(0760)2109472		Limited-Liability				Motor-driven Haircut Scissors
中山市三鼎电器工业有限公司(1996)	中山市	广东省	(0760)2107015	296	有限公司	30,864	758(14)	29,809	电动理发剪
Shenmei Daily Use Products Co.,Ltd.	Shenyang	Liaoning	(024)88323848		Foreign Funded				Blade
沈美日用品有限公司(1983)	沈阳市	辽宁省	(024)88323680	63	外商投资	28,367	11,123(5)	65,071	刀片
Dongguan Yiliang Electrical Appliance Products Co., Ltd.	Dongguan	Guangdong	(0769)6635233		Overseas Chinese-funded				Water Heater
东莞毅良电器制品有限公司(1994)	东莞市	广东省	(0769)6635236	148	港澳台资	27,904	41(38)	22,136	热水器
Ningbo Yongfeng Blade Co., Ltd.	Ningbo	Zhejiang	(0574)87586184		Foreign Funded				No.74 Double-faced Blade
宁波永锋刀片有限公司(1985)	宁波市	浙江省	(0574)87586514	180	外商投资	24,874	5,262(7)	27,809	74号双面刀片
Shanghai Zhenbo Electric Co., ltd.	Shanghai	Shanghai	(021)67632323		Private Owned				Hairdressing Tool
上海真博电器有限公司(2000)	上海市	上海市	(021)67632525	182	私营企业	24,664	506(19)	15,925	理发工具

Top 10 Cities by Revenue 销售收入排名前10位城市	Province 省	Market share 市场份额 (%)	Number of firms 企业个数
Shanghai 上海市	Shanghai 上海市	43.41	6
Ningbo 宁波市	Zhejiang 浙江省	12.19	8
Wenzhou 温州市	Zhejiang 浙江省	10.32	13
Jinhua 金华市	Zhejiang 浙江省	10.19	1
Shenzhen 深圳市	Guangdong 广东省	4.88	2
Guangzhou 广州市	Guangdong 广东省	4.69	2
Jieyang 揭阳市	Guangdong 广东省	2.85	2
Foshan 佛山市	Guangdong 广东省	2.56	1
Zhongshan 中山市	Guangdong 广东省	1.93	1
Shenyang 沈阳市	Liaoning 辽宁省	1.77	1

10 Major Wholesalers 十家主要批发商	City 城市	Province 省	Telephone/Fax 电话/传真
Harbin ChinaSun Group Co., Ltd.	Harbin	Heilongjiang	(0451)84885100
哈尔滨中央红集团股份有限公司	哈尔滨市	黑龙江省	(0451)84885111
Guangzhou Yuexiu Enterprise (Group) Company	Guangzhou	Guangdong	(020)85597130
广州越秀企业（集团）公司	广州市	广东省	(020)85599018
China Reed Screen Imp. & Exp. Corp.Ltd.	Beijing	Beijing	(010)65521133
中艺苇帘进出口有限责任公司	北京市	北京市	(010)65513995
Hebei Xintai Foreign Trade Corp.ltd.	Shijiazhuang	Hebei	(0311)7767908
河北信泰对外贸易有限公司	石家庄市	河北省	(0311)7755347
Hebei Arts & Crafts Imp. & Exp. Corp.	Shijiazhuang	Hebei	(0311)7764345
河北省工艺品进出口公司	石家庄市	河北省	(0311)7755347
Shanghai Hengda Ceramic Building Materials Trade Market	Shanghai	Shanghai	(021)58425842
上海恒大陶瓷建材交易市场	上海市	上海市	(021)58427389
Hangzhou Local Product General Corporation	Hangzhou	Zhejiang	(0571)87026301
杭州市土特产总公司	杭州市	浙江省	(0571)87026323
Ningbo Zhonglin Foreign Trade Co.,Ltd.	Ningbo	Zhejiang	(0574)87871797
宁波中蔺对外贸易有限公司	宁波市	浙江省	(0574)87871790
Wuyi Local Products Daily Groceries Co.,Ltd.	Jinhua	Zhejiang	(0579)7623401
武义县土产日用杂品有限责任公司	金华市	浙江省	(0579)7623401
Guangdong Shunde Local Products Import & Export Company	Foshan	Guangdong	(0765)6682839
广东省顺德土产进出口公司	佛山市	广东省	(0765)6681441

3489: Other Household Metal Products 其他日用金属制品业

The industry accounts for 0.111% of the total revenue of China's industrial sector in 2002. The rate of return on assets is 4.11%. 83.67% of all firms in the industry made a profit while 16.33% had negative returns.The top province in terms of the industry's revenue is Guangdong, accounting for 50.43% of the total revenue.
2002年本行业收入占全行业的 0.111%，资产利润率为 4.11%。83.67%的企业赢利，16.33%的企业亏损。收入最高的省为广东省，占本行业的50.43%。

	Total number of firms 企业总数	Total number of employees 职工总数	Total revenue (Mil.RMB) 总销售收入 (百万元)	Total profit (Mil.RMB) 总利润 (百万元)	Return on assets 资产利润率 (%)	Return on equity 权益利润率 (%)	Labour productivity ('000 RMB/ worker) 劳动生产率 (千元/人)	Debts/ assets 资产负债率 (%)	Total assets (Mil.RMB) 总资产 (百万元)
Industry Overall 行业总体	502	94,347	11,953	413	4.11	8.66	39.55	52.56	10,054

	Number of firms 企业个数	Average number of employees 平均职工人数	Average revenue ('000 RMB) 平均销售收入（千元）	Average profit ('000 RMB) 平均利润 (千元)	Return on assets 资产利润率 (%)	Return on equity 权益利润率 (%)	Labour productivity ('000 RMB/ worker) 劳动生产率 (千元/人)	Debts/ assets 资产负债率 (%)	Average total assets ('000 RMB) 平均总资产 (千元)
By ownership 产业所有权									
State-owned 国有	16	82	7,793	-256	-1.98	-11.62	24.41	82.96	12,943
Collective-owned 集体	70	139	18,028	672	5.27	12.99	45.55	59.38	12,736
Foreign & Overseas Chinese Funded 三资	165	284	36,336	1,252	3.82	7.30	41.06	47.68	32,756
By regional distribution 地区分布									
Central-North 华北	26	99	12,005	394	2.32	6.99	78.98	66.82	16,976
Beijing 北京	12	109	11,091	155	0.66	1.85	43.96	64.16	23,411
Tianjin 天津	11	90	14,394	656	5.17	15.87	136.70	67.45	12,710
Hebei 河北	3	92	6,904	386	5.61	433.71	37.90	98.71	6,884
Shanxi 山西									
Inner Mongolia 内蒙古									
Northeast 东北	11	112	19,002	2,159	2.53	5.48	71.22	53.77	85,207
Liaoning 辽宁	4	151	18,632	2,105	8.47	14.60	90.46	41.94	24,842
Jilin 吉林	1	146	2,514	-1,630	-9.54		7.21	106.92	17,078
Heilongjiang 黑龙江	6	81	21,996	2,827	2.07	4.50	66.63	54.10	136,804
Central-East 华东	219	159	21,918	949	5.91	12.57	37.99	53.02	16,063
Shanghai 上海	58	89	19,134	922	7.30	15.18	52.51	51.95	12,633
Jiangsu 江苏	55	205	25,849	818	4.08	9.86	39.13	58.61	20,033
Zhejiang 浙江	54	127	17,456	835	6.95	14.91	31.74	53.38	12,013
Anhui 安徽	4	239	14,432	177	1.42	2.83	16.40	49.71	12,414
Fujian 福建	23	132	14,761	491	3.49	6.90	18.16	49.44	14,079
Jiangxi 江西	4	89	690	-99	-4.88	-10.31	3.03	52.69	2,020
Shandong 山东	21	343	44,091	2,504	8.05	15.04	44.69	46.47	31,093
Central-South 中南	244	227	27,157	707	3.36	6.82	38.15	50.69	21,043
Henan 河南	3	41	8,217	1,163	23.23	26.49	63.66	12.30	5,005
Hubei 湖北	13	143	25,051	993	4.95	12.67	74.84	60.92	20,057
Hunan 湖南	1	30	537	-58	-5.56	-11.81	41.33	52.97	1,044
Guangdong 广东	209	225	28,844	756	3.32	6.59	40.48	49.52	22,737
Guangxi 广西	18	356	13,719	-98	-1.66	-10.06	9.92	83.48	5,873
Hainan 海南									
Southwest 西南	1	157	5,295	-670	-10.35	-15.28	16.33	32.28	6,474
Chongqing 重庆									
Sichuan 四川									
Guizhou 贵州									
Yunnan 云南	1	157	5,295	-670	-10.35	-15.28	16.33	32.28	6,474
Tibet 西藏									
Northwest 西北	1	160	246	-730	-4.52	-146.88	4.21	96.92	16,157
Shaanxi 陕西									
Gansu 甘肃	1	160	246	-730	-4.52	-146.88	4.21	96.92	16,157
Qinghai 青海									
Ningxia 宁夏									
Xinjiang 新疆									

3489: Other Household Metal Products 其他日用金属制品业

Year 年份	Number of firms 企业个数	Rate of change 变化率(%)	Number of employees 职工人数(人)	Rate of change 变化率(%)	Total revenue (Mil. RMB) 总销售收入(百万元)	Rate of change 变化率(%)	Total profit (Mil RMB) 总利润(百万元)	Rate of change 变化率(%)
2000	381		74,559		9,316		228	
2001	412	8.14	84,413	13.22	10,140	8.85	376	64.91
2002	502	21.84	94,347	11.77	11,953	17.88	413	9.84

Major Products 主要产品	Output 产量	Unit 单位
	.	

10 Main Firms with Maximal Revenue (year founded) 收入最大的十家主要企业（创办年份）	City 城市	Province 省	Telephone/fax 电话/传真	Number of employees 职工人数	Ownership 产业所有权	Revenue ('000 RMB) 销售收入(千元)	Profit('000 RMB) (rank) 利润(千元)(排名)	Total assets ('000 RMB) 总资产(千元)	Major products 主要产品
Shenzhen Yijing Hardware Industrial Ltd.	Shenzhen	Guangdong	(0755)26626841		Overseas Chinese-funded				Hardware Fittings
深圳艺晶五金实业有限公司(1991)	深圳市	广东省	(0755)26623290	2,048	港澳台资	319,805	25,242(1)	439,735	五金配件
Jiangsu Wanma Metal Products Group Co.	Taizhou	Jiangsu	(0523)6552030		Collective-owned				Air-conditioner Plating Ware空
江苏万马金属制品集团公司(1995)	泰州市	江苏省	(0523)6567863	1,074	集体企业	267,717	3,075(39)	220,836	调钣金件
Shunde Taiming Metal Products Lmited.	Foshan	Guangdong	(0765)5332687		Overseas Chinese-funded				Drawer Slide
顺德市泰明金属制品厂有限公司(1989)	佛山市	广东省	(0765)5565909	2,100	港澳台资	246,503	810(129)	205,645	轴屉滑轨
Changzhou Qiaoyu Tourism Articles Co.,Ltd.	Changzhou	Jiangsu	(0519)3562888		Joint Stock				Sand Beach Chairs
常州侨裕旅游用品有限公司(1989)	常州市	江苏省	(0519)3561118	1,498	股份制	230,920	2,460(48)	154,350	沙滩椅
ShanDong Guoqiang Handware Products Group Co.,Ltd.	Dezhou	Shandong	(0534)6221915		Joint Stock				Hardware Components
乐陵市国强五金制品有限公司(1990)	德州市	山东省	(0534)6221935	1,750	股份制	229,497	14,497(6)	159,286	五金件
Weihai Changxing Knitting Equipment Co., Ltd.	Weihai	Shandong	(0631)8842030		Overseas Chinese-funded				Weaving Needle针
威海常兴针织器材有限公司(1992)	威海市	山东省	(0631)8842082	150	港澳台资	209,600	16,920(4)	17,000	织用机针
Haiyang Riyue Hardware Co., Ltd.	Yantai	Shandong	(0535)3222357		Limited-Liability				Hardware Fittings
海阳日月五金有限公司(1998)	烟台市	山东省	(0535)3228532	485	有限公司	170,800	13,000(7)	85,780	五金配件
Shanghai East Drogon Zipper Marking CO., Ltd.	Shanghai	Shanghai	(021)64591008		Overseas Chinese-funded				Slide Fastener
上海东龙拉链制造有限公司(1996)	上海市	上海市	(021)68016888	120	港澳台资	143,000	3,851(23)	60,708	拉链
Zhongshan Roadmate Daily Appliances Co., Ltd.	Zhongshan	Guangdong	(0760)2102828		Overseas Chinese-funded				Baby Barrow婴
中山乐美达日用制品有限公司(1993)	中山市	广东省	(0760)2102878	816	港澳台资	136,909	1,240(90)	106,270	儿手推车
Dongguan Housheng Hardware Plastic Cement Products	Dongguan	Guangdong	(0769)7734017		Overseas Chinese-funded				Steel Strip Slice
Co., Ltd.东莞厚升五金塑胶制品有限公司(1993)	东莞市	广东省	(0769)7735027	900	港澳台资	130,453	187(251)	58,592	铜带片

Top 10 Cities by Revenue 销售收入排名前10位城市	Province 省	Market share 市场份额(%)	Number of firms 企业个数
Guangzhou 广州市	Guangdong 广东省	11.52	39
Shenzhen 深圳市	Guangdong 广东省	10.47	18
Shanghai 上海市	Shanghai 上海市	9.28	58
Foshan 佛山市	Guangdong 广东省	8.43	38
Zhongshan 中山市	Guangdong 广东省	6.52	31
Dongguan 东莞市	Guangdong 广东省	4.17	19
Jiangmen 江门市	Guangdong 广东省	3.78	22
Changzhou 常州市	Jiangsu 江苏省	3.56	10
Taizhou 泰州市	Jiangsu 江苏省	2.64	3
Yantai 烟台市	Shandong 山东省	2.59	6

10 Major Wholesalers 十家主要批发商	City 城市	Province 省	Telephone/Fax 电话/传真
Harbin ChinaSun Group Co., Ltd.	Harbin	Heilongjiang	(0451)84885100
哈尔滨中央红集团股份有限公司	哈尔滨市	黑龙江省	(0451)84885111
Guangzhou Yuexiu Enterprise (Group) Company	Guangzhou	Guangdong	(020)85597130
广州越秀企业（集团）公司	广州市	广东省	(020)85599018
China Reed Screen Imp. & Exp. Corp.Ltd.	Beijing	Beijing	(010)65521133
中艺苇帘进出口有限责任公司	北京市	北京市	(010)65513995
Hebei Xintai Foreign Trade Corp.ltd.	Shijiazhuang	Hebei	(0311)7767908
河北信泰对外贸易有限公司	石家庄市	河北省	(0311)7755347
Hebei Arts & Crafts Imp. & Exp. Corp.	Shijiazhuang	Hebei	(0311)7764345
河北省工艺品进出口公司	石家庄市	河北省	(0311)7755347
Shanghai Hengda Ceramic Building Materials Trade Market	Shanghai	Shanghai	(021)58425842
上海恒大陶瓷建材交易市场	上海市	上海市	(021)58427389
Hangzhou Local Product General Corporation	Hangzhou	Zhejiang	(0571)87026301
杭州市土特产总公司	杭州市	浙江省	(0571)87026323
Ningbo Zhonglin Foreign Trade Co.,Ltd.	Ningbo	Zhejiang	(0574)87871797
宁波中蔺对外贸易有限公司	宁波市	浙江省	(0574)87871790
Wuyi Local Products Daily Groceries Co.,Ltd.	Jinhua	Zhejiang	(0579)7623401
武义县土产日用杂品有限责任公司	金华市	浙江省	(0579)7623401
Guangdong Shunde Local Products Import & Export Company	Foshan	Guangdong	(0765)6682839
广东省顺德土产进出口公司	佛山市	广东省	(0765)6681441

3491: Iron Farming Tools 铁制小农具制造业

The industry accounts for 0.013% of the total revenue of China's industrial sector in 2002. The rate of return on assets is 7.36%. 82.11% of all firms in the industry made a profit while 17.89% had negative returns.The top province in terms of the industry's revenue is Shandong, accounting for 20.14% of the total revenue.
2002年本行业收入占全行业的 0.013%，资产利润率为 7.36%。82.11%的企业赢利，17.89%的企业亏损。收入最高的省为山东省，占本行业的20.14%。

	Total number of firms 企业总数	Total number of employees 职工总数	Total revenue (Mil.RMB) 总销售收入(百万元)	Total profit (Mil.RMB) 总利润(百万元)	Return on assets 资产利润率(%)	Return on equity 权益利润率(%)	Labour productivity ('000 RMB/worker) 劳动生产率(千元/人)	Debts/assets 资产负债率(%)	Total assets (Mil.RMB) 总资产(百万元)
Industry Overall 行业总体	123	12,598	1,362	67	7.36	16.35	34.99	54.99	909

	Number of firms 企业个数	Average number of employees 平均职工人数	Average revenue ('000 RMB) 平均销售收入(千元)	Average profit ('000 RMB) 平均利润(千元)	Return on assets 资产利润率(%)	Return on equity 权益利润率(%)	Labour productivity ('000 RMB/worker) 劳动生产率(千元/人)	Debts/assets 资产负债率(%)	Average total assets ('000 RMB) 平均总资产(千元)
By ownership 产业所有权									
State-owned 国有	17	46	651	-140	-3.48	-12.18	8.50	71.47	4,032
Collective-owned 集体	30	108	15,920	990	12.65	25.35	56.92	50.10	7,830
Foreign & Overseas Chinese Funded 三资	15	151	15,051	766	6.52	16.80	22.29	61.21	11,754
By regional distribution 地区分布									
Central-North 华北	21	171	13,780	903	9.22	25.18	23.52	63.37	9,789
Beijing 北京	1	27	1,544	-192	-5.16	-20.38	13.78	74.70	3,723
Tianjin 天津	6	273	14,165	519	5.94	12.06	7.62	50.76	8,742
Hebei 河北	14	137	14,490	1,145	10.73	33.05	37.23	67.52	10,671
Shanxi 山西									
Inner Mongolia 内蒙古									
Northeast 东北	9	83	3,532	70	1.63	4.30	13.14	62.04	4,276
Liaoning 辽宁	6	61	4,090	145	3.35	5.66	19.52	40.89	4,327
Jilin 吉林	3	126	2,417	-80	-1.92		7.02	105.87	4,176
Heilongjiang 黑龙江									
Central-East 华东	31	120	18,161	723	8.10	18.17	53.57	55.43	8,932
Shanghai 上海									
Jiangsu 江苏	12	93	12,627	161	2.81	10.93	37.01	74.25	5,719
Zhejiang 浙江	9	116	14,381	397	3.83	10.46	28.36	63.37	10,356
Anhui 安徽	1	110	3,750	447	7.77	19.43	9.65	60.00	5,750
Fujian 福建									
Jiangxi 江西	1	210	3,931	-381	-3.99	-16.36	5.76	75.60	9,545
Shandong 山东	8	153	34,293	2,107	16.90	25.17	102.51	32.86	12,469
Central-South 中南	33	96	13,139	896	10.82	21.43	39.33	49.48	8,275
Henan 河南	8	97	12,142	455	12.24	22.85	30.14	46.42	3,718
Hubei 湖北									
Hunan 湖南	15	74	10,758	1,310	28.55	34.65	48.59	17.59	4,590
Guangdong 广东	8	113	19,340	782	6.38	13.76	46.67	53.60	12,249
Guangxi 广西	2	192	10,185	4	0.01	0.04	13.97	74.09	38,252
Hainan 海南									
Southwest 西南	6	133	4,183	-844	-7.84	-11.75	7.35	33.25	10,763
Chongqing 重庆									
Sichuan 四川	1	487	18,467	1			11.76	19.68	28,683
Guizhou 贵州									
Yunnan 云南	3	96	2,178	-1,694	-14.66	-26.98	0.42	45.67	11,553
Tibet 西藏	2	12	49	8	1.30	1.30	1.54		617
Northwest 西北	23	25	834	17	0.77	2.63	29.29	70.66	2,190
Shaanxi 陕西	1	3						57.03	2,765
Gansu 甘肃	19	22	637	9	0.49	2.54	34.57	80.76	1,798
Qinghai 青海	1	20	501	-139	-6.82	-9.33	5.65	26.92	2,039
Ningxia 宁夏	2	73	3,299	180	3.16	6.52	18.14	51.51	5,698
Xinjiang 新疆									

3491: Iron Farming Tools 铁制小农具制造业

Year 年份	Number of firms 企业个数	Rate of change 变化率 (%)	Number of employees 职工人数 (人)	Rate of change 变化率 (%)	Total revenue (Mil. RMB) 总销售收入 (百万元)	Rate of change 变化率 (%)	Total profit (Mil RMB) 总利润 (百万元)	Rate of change 变化率 (%)
2000	133		14,487		1,395		61	
2001	123	-7.52	13,928	-3.86	1,258	-9.82	70	14.75
2002	123	o	12,598	-9.55	1,362	8.27	67	-4.29

Major Products 主要产品	Output 产量	Unit 单位
Welding Rod 焊条	143	10,000 Tons 万吨

10 Main Firms with Maximal Revenue (year founded) 收入最大的十家主要企业（创办年份）	City 城市	Province 省	Telephone/fax 电话/传真	Number of employees 职工人数	Ownership 产业所有权	Revenue ('000 RMB) 销售收入 (千元)	Profit('000 RMB) (rank) 利润(千元) (排名)	Total assets ('000 RMB) 总资产 (千元)	Major products 主要产品
Shandong Gardening Tool General Factory	Yantai	Shandong	(0535)8623705		Collective-owned				Gardening Tools
山东省园艺工具总厂(1972)	烟台市	山东省	(0535)8623705	472	集体企业	189,710	11,140(1)	49,130	园艺工具
Tangshan Yinying Industrial Co., Ltd.	Tangshan	Hebei	(0315)4558334		Private Owned				Steel Shovel
唐山市银鹰实业有限公司(2001)	唐山市	河北省	(0315)4558104	200	私营企业	67,870	4,884(3)	60,176	钢锹
Rhinoceros Daily Use Articles(Zhongshan) Co.,Ltd.	Zhongshan	Guangdong	(0760)3371785		Overseas Chinese-funded				Gardening Tools
犀牛日用制品（中山）有限公司(1995)	中山市	广东省	(0760)2226464	250	港澳台资	47,197	2,559(6)	19,876	园艺工具
Tianjin Dead Stock Factory	Tianjin	Tianjin	(022)88520444		Collective-owned				Hoe & Sugarcane Knife锄
天津农具厂(1991)	天津市	天津市	(022)88521592	700	集体企业	40,000	2,150(7)	31,990	头甘蔗刀
Xingtang Jiangfeng Machinery Factory	Shijiazhuang	Hebei	(0311)2731227		Collective-owned				Plough
行唐县江峰机械厂(1990)	石家庄市	河北省		62	集体企业	27,100	2,900(5)	2,230	农用犁
Zhejiang Huatai Garden Tools Co., ltd.	Jinhua	Zhejiang	(0579)7623371		Private Owned				Gardening Tools
浙江华泰园艺工具有限公司(1999)	金华市	浙江省	(0579)7625266	190	私营企业	26,880	863(29)	21,815	园艺工具
Yankee Tools (Hangzhou) Inc.	Hangzhou	Zhejiang	(0571)87823896		Overseas Chinese-funded				Gardening Tools
杨信工具（杭州）有限公司(1999)	杭州市	浙江省	(0571)85222634	25	港澳台资	26,315	694(34)	22,283	园林工具
JiangSu Renmin Machines & Tools Co.,Ltd.	Changzhou	Jiangsu	(0519)7620085		Collective-owned				Saw And Sickle
江苏人民机具厂(1951)	常州市	江苏省	(0519)7623685	240	集体企业	24,220	720(33)	20,270	锯镰
GuiLin Electric Welding Factory	Guilin	Guangxi	(0773)3832227		Collective-owned				Electric Welding Rod
桂林市电焊条厂(1971)	桂林市	广西	(0773)3833202	299	集体企业	20,046	12(74)	66,611	电焊条
Tai Zhou Hyde Tools Co., Ltd.	Taizhou	Zhejiang	(0576)7788224		Foreign Funded				Gardening Tools
台州海德工具有限公司(1994)	台州市	浙江省	(0576)7785782	178	外商投资	19,808	128(61)	9,646	花园工具

Top 10 Cities by Revenue 销售收入排名前10位城市	Province 省	Market share 市场份额 (%)	Number of firms 企业个数
Yantai 烟台市	Shandong 山东省	15.12	2
Tangshan 唐山市	Hebei 河北省	10.57	9
Chenzhou 郴州市	Hunan 湖南省	9.41	11
Zhongshan 中山市	Guangdong 广东省	6.67	3
Tianjin 天津市	Tianjin 天津市	6.24	6
Jinhua 金华市	Zhejiang 浙江省	5.64	6
Lianyungang 连云港市	Jiangsu 江苏省	3.23	3
Changzhou 常州市	Jiangsu 江苏省	3.20	4
Kaifeng 开封市	Henan 河南省	3.09	1
Weihai 威海市	Shandong 山东省	2.57	1

10 Major Wholesalers 十家主要批发商	City 城市	Province 省	Telephone/Fax 电话/传真
Harbin ChinaSun Group Co., Ltd.	Harbin	Heilongjiang	(0451)84885100
哈尔滨中央红集团股份有限公司	哈尔滨市	黑龙江省	(0451)84885111
Guangzhou Yuexiu Enterprise (Group) Company	Guangzhou	Guangdong	(020)85597130
广州越秀企业（集团）公司	广州市	广东省	(020)85599018
China Reed Screen Imp. & Exp. Corp.Ltd.	Beijing	Beijing	(010)65521133
中艺苇帘进出口有限责任公司	北京市	北京市	(010)65513995
Hebei Xintai Foreign Trade Corp.ltd.	Shijiazhuang	Hebei	(0311)7767908
河北信泰对外贸易有限公司	石家庄市	河北省	(0311)7755347
Hebei Arts & Crafts Imp. & Exp. Corp.	Shijiazhuang	Hebei	(0311)7764345
河北省工艺品进出口公司	石家庄市	河北省	(0311)7755347
Shanghai Hengda Ceramic Building Materials Trade Market	Shanghai	Shanghai	(021)58425842
上海恒大陶瓷建材交易市场	上海市	上海市	(021)58427389
Hangzhou Local Product General Corporation	Hangzhou	Zhejiang	(0571)87026301
杭州市土特产总公司	杭州市	浙江省	(0571)87026323
Ningbo Zhonglin Foreign Trade Co.,Ltd.	Ningbo	Zhejiang	(0574)87871797
宁波中蔺对外贸易有限公司	宁波市	浙江省	(0574)87871790
Wuyi Local Products Daily Groceries Co.,Ltd	Jinhua	Zhejiang	(0579)7623401
武义县土产日用杂品有限责任公司	金华市	浙江省	(0579)7623401
Guangdong Shunde Local Products Import & Export Company	Foshan	Guangdong	(0765)6682839
广东省顺德土产进出口公司	佛山市	广东省	(0765)6681441

3495: Welding Rods 焊条制造业

The industry accounts for 0.063% of the total revenue of China's industrial sector in 2002. The rate of return on assets is 4.24%. 79.33% of all firms in the industry made a profit while 20.67% had negative returns.The top province in terms of the industry's revenue is Tianjin, accounting for 36.90% of the total revenue.
2002年本行业收入占全行业的0.063%，资产利润率为4.24%。79.33%的企业赢利，20.67%的企业亏损。收入最高的省为天津市，占本行业的36.90%。

	Total number of firms 企业总数	Total number of employees 职工总数	Total revenue (Mil.RMB) 总销售收入(百万元)	Total profit (Mil.RMB) 总利润(百万元)	Return on assets 资产利润率(%)	Return on equity 权益利润率(%)	Labour productivity ('000 RMB/worker) 劳动生产率(千元/人)	Debts/assets 资产负债率(%)	Total assets (Mil.RMB) 总资产(百万元)
Industry Overall 行业总体	150	27,091	6,756	247	4.24	11.80	55.65	64.11	5,828

	Number of firms 企业个数	Average number of employees 平均职工人数	Average revenue ('000 RMB) 平均销售收入(千元)	Average profit ('000 RMB) 平均利润(千元)	Return on assets 资产利润率(%)	Return on equity 权益利润率(%)	Labour productivity ('000 RMB/worker) 劳动生产率(千元/人)	Debts/assets 资产负债率(%)	Average total assets ('000 RMB) 平均总资产(千元)
By ownership 产业所有权									
State-owned 国有	7	78	2,217	-1,288	-4.81		3.54	163.01	26,771
Collective-owned 集体	35	166	21,879	772	3.94	13.50	36.50	70.83	19,620
Foreign & Overseas Chinese Funded 三资	25	125	58,811	5,100	10.26	20.41	150.30	49.76	49,726
By regional distribution 地区分布									
Central-North 华北	22	374	130,482	4,578	7.08	17.04	57.39	58.47	64,697
Beijing 北京	4	71	38,739	3,110	9.25	14.08	173.07	34.28	33,616
Tianjin 天津	9	732	276,964	9,918	7.99	18.96	54.18	57.86	124,106
Hebei 河北	7	145	19,589	-146	-0.95	-28.00	34.96	96.60	15,341
Shanxi 山西	1			-122	-0.60	-3.05		80.45	20,458
Inner Mongolia 内蒙古	1	344	85,859	163	0.37	0.67	89.49	44.77	44,076
Northeast 东北	9	189	60,953	2,600	3.87	10.03	128.26	61.39	67,151
Liaoning 辽宁	8	205	67,946	2,992	3.98	10.22	132.27	61.07	75,169
Jilin 吉林	1	60	5,005	-530	-17.62		18.67	124.93	3,008
Heilongjiang 黑龙江									
Central-East 华东	76	128	26,351	867	3.91	11.06	49.62	64.61	22,142
Shanghai 上海	13	156	43,918	2,352	5.39	10.66	72.33	49.45	43,656
Jiangsu 江苏	21	151	32,760	577	2.01	9.34	47.44	78.45	28,660
Zhejiang 浙江	16	88	18,592	664	4.88	14.69	47.09	66.80	13,611
Anhui 安徽	5	109	12,576	112	1.37	8.12	18.75	83.07	8,179
Fujian 福建	3	128	18,974	37	0.25	0.43	28.10	40.49	14,734
Jiangxi 江西	2	59	6,594	-287	-1.53	-5.12	28.25	70.04	18,691
Shandong 山东	16	131	19,582	778	7.19	20.00	45.81	64.06	10,821
Central-South 中南	34	137	19,441	-790	-2.37	-50.34	33.19	95.29	33,316
Henan 河南	6	109	11,160	176	2.36	16.85	39.43	85.96	7,457
Hubei 湖北	4	152	12,395	-7,876	-7.35		13.20	108.83	107,189
Hunan 湖南	10	191	37,177	837	2.08	5.75	44.31	63.79	40,192
Guangdong 广东	10	120	13,655	-448	-1.91		23.16	127.80	23,490
Guangxi 广西	4	75	9,036	-75	-1.33	-6.39	29.48	79.15	5,611
Hainan 海南									
Southwest 西南	5	342	122,857	17,704	10.72	14.27	88.87	24.92	165,210
Chongqing 重庆									
Sichuan 四川	3	486	119,597	13,708	5.98	7.90	71.25	24.27	229,201
Guizhou 贵州									
Yunnan 云南	2	126	127,747	23,698	34.23	47.64	191.16	28.15	69,224
Tibet 西藏									
Northwest 西北	4	255	14,595	-1,199	-3.03		25.90	101.34	39,580
Shaanxi 陕西									
Gansu 甘肃	3	307	12,746	-1,463	-3.63		21.85	107.25	40,273
Qinghai 青海									
Ningxia 宁夏	1	100	20,139	-404	-1.08	-6.09	63.16	82.30	37,498
Xinjiang 新疆									

Year 年份	Number of firms 企业个数	Rate of change 变化率 (%)	Number of employees 职工人数 (人)	Rate of change 变化率 (%)	Total revenue (Mil. RMB) 总销售收入 (百万元)	Rate of change 变化率 (%)	Total profit (Mil RMB) 总利润 (百万元)	Rate of change 变化率 (%)
2000	148		29,985		4,763		77	
2001	143	-3.38	28,407	-5.26	5,707	19.82	171	122.08
2002	150	4.90	27,091	-4.63	6,756	18.38	247	44.44

Major Products 主要产品	Output 产量	Unit 单位
Welding Rod 焊条	143	10,000 Tons 万吨

10 Main Firms with Maximal Revenue (year founded) 收入最大的十家主要企业（创办年份）	City 城市	Province 省	Telephone/fax 电话/传真	Number of employees 职工人数	Ownership 产业所有权	Revenue ('000 RMB) 销售收入 (千元)	Profit('000 RMB) (rank) 利润(千元) (排名)	Total assets ('000 RMB) 总资产 (千元)	Major products 主要产品
Tianjin Golden Bridge Welding Materials Co., ltd.	Tianjin	Tianjin	(022)24994924		Private Owned				Welding Rod
天津市金桥焊材有限公司(1998)	天津市	天津市	(022)24996812	1,000	私营企业	971,428	60,370(1)	284,140	焊条
Tianjin Daqiao Dasi Electric Welding Rod Co., Ltd.	Tianjin	Tianjin	(022)23971429		Limited-Liability				Electric Welding Rod
天津市大桥大寺电焊条有限公司(1988)	天津市	天津市	(022)23971429	1,800	有限公司	519,980	17,100(5)	120,870	电焊条
Jinzhou Jintai Welding & Metal Co.,Ltd.	Jinzhou	Liaoning	(0416)5179785		Foreign Funded				Electric Welding Rod
锦州锦泰金属工业有限公司(1995)	锦州市	辽宁省	(0416)5176907	500	外商投资	432,212	20,625(4)	412,506	电焊条
Sichuan Atlantic Welding Consumable Inc.	Zigong	Sichuan	(0813)5102109		Joint Stock				Electric Welding Rod
四川大西洋焊接材料股份有限公司(1999)	自贡市	四川省	(0813)5101216	1,130	股份制	288,511	32,236(3)	637,012	电焊条
Alpho Yunnan Tin Solder Co., Ltd.	Kunming	Yunnan	(0871)5633870		Foreign Funded				Solder
云南爱法焊料化工有限公司(1990)	昆明市	云南省	(0871)5634478	100	外商投资	199,380	43,094(2)	86,268	焊料
Zhenjiang Xingchen Group	Zhenjiang	Jiangsu	(0511)8422035		Collective-owned				Solder
镇江星辰集团公司(1986)	镇江市	江苏省	(0511)8425588	576	集体企业	116,164	6,150(12)	132,179	焊料
Taizhou Universe Welding Material Co.,Ltd.	Taizhou	Jiangsu	(0523)6564988		Joint Owned				Electric Welding Rod
泰州宇宙焊接材料有限公司(1992)	泰州市	江苏省	(0523)6559019	400	联营企业	108,964	-	112,500	电焊条
Zhuzhou Electric Welding Rod Co., Ltd.	Zhuzhou	Hunan	(0733)8413242		Joint Stock				Welding Rod
株洲电焊条股份有限公司(1958)	株洲市	湖南省	(0733)8414449	513	股份制	95,506	-	140,456	焊条
Sany Group Materials Industry Co.,Ltd.	Loudi	Hunan	(0738)4424763		Private Partnership				
三一集团材料工业有限公司	娄底市	湖南省	(0738)4424378	542	私营合伙	86,000	670(44)	144,600	
Inner mongolia Jining Ruitai Metal Ind.Co., ltd.	Wulanchabu	Inner Mongolia	(0474)8283366		Overseas Chinese-funded				Electric Welding Rod
内蒙古集宁瑞泰金属工业有限公司(1999)	乌兰察布	内蒙古	(0474)8284190	344	港澳台资	85,859	163(71)	44,076	电焊条

Top 10 Cities by Revenue 销售收入排名前10位城市	Province 省	Market share 市场份额 (%)	Number of firms 企业个数
Tianjin 天津市	Tianjin 天津市	36.90	9
Shanghai 上海市	Shanghai 上海市	8.45	13
Jinzhou 锦州市	Liaoning 辽宁省	7.06	3
Zigong 自贡市	Sichuan 四川省	4.27	1
Kunming 昆明市	Yunnan 云南省	3.78	2
Taizhou 泰州市	Jiangsu 江苏省	3.69	4
Zhuzhou 株洲市	Hunan 湖南省	3.07	3
Hangzhou 杭州市	Zhejiang 浙江省	2.98	10
Beijing 北京市	Beijing 北京市	2.29	4
Zhenjiang 镇江市	Jiangsu 江苏省	2.04	4

10 Major Wholesalers 十家主要批发商	City 城市	Province 省	Telephone/Fax 电话/传真
Yihua Kangqi Chemical Fibre Co.,Ltd.	Yangzhou	Jiangsu	(0514)3235499
仪化康祺化纤有限责任公司	扬州市	江苏省	(0514)3233847
Sinochem Guangdong Import & Export Company	Guangzhou	Guangdong	(020)86672288
中化广东进出口公司	广州市	广东省	(020)86507512
Sinochem Shanghai Import & Export Company	Shanghai	Shanghai	(021)63289888
中化上海进出口公司	上海市	上海市	(021)63283968
Sinochem Tianjin Import & Export Company	Tianjin	Tianjin	(022)23146216
中化天津进出口公司	天津市	天津市	(022)23146215
China Chemical Sales & Supply (North China) Corporation	Tianjin	Tianjin	(022)23011031
中国化工供销华北公司	天津市	天津市	(022)23011032
China Chemical Sales & Supply (North China) Corporation	Shanghai	Shanghai	(021)62103300
中国化工供销华东公司	上海市	上海市	(021)62515799
Nantong Chemical Light Industry Co.,Ltd.	Nantong	Jiangsu	(0513)5518397
南通化工轻工股份有限公司	南通市	江苏省	(0513)5512735
Taizhou Heshun Plastics Co.,Ltd.	Taizhou	Zhejiang	(0576)2510220
台州市和顺塑料有限公司	台州市	浙江省	(0576)2510160
China Petroleum Technology Development Corporation	Beijing	Beijing	(010)84080722
中国石油技术开发公司	北京市	北京市	(010)84080800
China National Chemical Fiber Corporation	Beijing	Beijing	(010)65816699
中国化纤总公司	北京市	北京市	(010)65813483

3499: Other Metal Products 其他类未包括的金属制品业

The industry accounts for 0.140% of the total revenue of China's industrial sector in 2002. The rate of return on assets is 6.62%. 82.83% of all firms in the industry made a profit while 17.17% had negative returns.The top province in terms of the industry's revenue is Guangdong, accounting for 31.22% of the total revenue.
2002年本行业收入占全行业的 0.140%，资产利润率为 6.62%。82.83%的企业赢利，17.17%的企业亏损。收入最高的省为广东省，占本行业的31.22%。

	Total number of firms 企业总数	Total number of employees 职工总数	Total revenue (Mil.RMB) 总销售收入 (百万元)	Total profit (Mil.RMB) 总利润 (百万元)	Return on assets 资产利润率 (%)	Return on equity 权益利润率 (%)	Labour productivity ('000 RMB/ worker) 劳动生产率 (千元/人)	Debts/ assets 资产负债率 (%)	Total assets (Mil.RMB) 总资产 (百万元)
Industry Overall 行业总体	501	79,959	15,054	972	6.62	13.68	54.07	51.60	14,682

	Number of firms 企业个数	Average number of employees 平均职工人数	Average revenue ('000 RMB) 平均销售收入 (千元)	Average profit ('000 RMB) 平均利润 (千元)	Return on assets 资产利润率 (%)	Return on equity 权益利润率 (%)	Labour productivity ('000 RMB/ worker) 劳动生产率 (千元/人)	Debts/ assets 资产负债率 (%)	Average total assets ('000 RMB) 平均总资产 (千元)
By ownership 产业所有权									
State-owned 国有	42	219	36,172	5,435	8.33	11.94	84.02	30.28	65,279
Collective-owned 集体	116	139	16,195	637	4.87	12.24	37.37	60.23	13,083
Foreign & Overseas Chinese Funded 三资	131	207	53,807	3,704	7.06	14.46	64.76	51.15	52,433
By regional distribution 地区分布									
Central-North 华北	74	145	14,863	945	4.75	11.10	37.73	57.21	19,907
Beijing 北京	16	57	7,273	533	5.86	12.09	45.09	51.57	9,103
Tianjin 天津	29	85	18,114	1,341	9.36	23.58	82.86	60.30	14,328
Hebei 河北	23	146	16,357	305	1.10	3.02	36.35	63.55	27,782
Shanxi 山西	5	596	13,906	-117	-0.40	-1.46	9.64	72.54	29,198
Inner Mongolia 内蒙古	1	998	12,491	16,091	12.67	13.21	7.51	4.08	126,982
Northeast 东北	22	275	34,955	430	0.68	1.00	45.05	32.14	63,097
Liaoning 辽宁	14	368	50,335	1,038	1.14	1.55	49.56	26.66	91,126
Jilin 吉林	6	88	3,980	-627	-6.08		13.95	117.23	10,302
Heilongjiang 黑龙江	2	185	20,222	-658	-2.60	-7.75	26.86	66.45	25,276
Central-East 华东	230	160	30,679	2,542	8.25	16.49	59.09	50.00	30,829
Shanghai 上海	67	127	30,128	4,375	15.20	26.21	87.46	42.00	28,785
Jiangsu 江苏	73	186	39,387	3,373	8.91	16.69	64.18	46.64	37,866
Zhejiang 浙江	22	144	26,894	1,095	4.09	19.09	36.71	78.57	26,766
Anhui 安徽	16	77	6,156	129	1.98	4.36	26.22	54.59	6,485
Fujian 福建	19	182	28,625	-1,840	-4.43	-7.15	49.53	38.03	41,549
Jiangxi 江西	1	230	24,733	-953	-2.23	-4.00	34.27	44.09	42,663
Shandong 山东	32	206	28,238	1,721	6.31	20.73	34.84	69.58	27,290
Central-South 中南	140	161	39,902	2,056	7.07	16.69	57.60	57.65	29,086
Henan 河南	6	66	14,227	569	9.98	23.02	90.62	56.65	5,700
Hubei 湖北	15	97	13,859	455	5.24	16.77	44.52	68.77	8,683
Hunan 湖南	8	61	12,165	708	5.30	8.58	52.46	38.15	13,337
Guangdong 广东	108	184	43,518	2,281	7.75	16.72	55.15	53.68	29,454
Guangxi 广西	2	50	5,028	-147	-4.16	-7.28	52.87	42.94	3,537
Hainan 海南	1	267	485,652	25,829	4.21	20.59	272.63	79.53	612,810
Southwest 西南	24	130	18,687	699	3.08	7.38	45.24	58.20	22,658
Chongqing 重庆	10	103	12,846	161	1.69	5.48	35.41	69.08	9,479
Sichuan 四川	7	142	32,486	2,177	5.50	11.25	84.95	51.12	39,598
Guizhou 贵州	1	31					-11.29	92.52	28,885
Yunnan 云南	5	206	18,350	-2	-0.01	-0.02	19.55	56.86	27,911
Tibet 西藏	1	16	881	-57	-1.69	-39.86	-27.56	95.76	3,369
Northwest 西北	11	68	8,581	311	2.99	9.52	45.19	68.62	10,411
Shaanxi 陕西	5	72	9,663	322	2.49	8.14	46.77	69.41	12,924
Gansu 甘肃	5	17	1,190	90	5.64	15.36	60.54	63.27	1,592
Qinghai 青海									
Ningxia 宁夏									
Xinjiang 新疆	1	300	40,127	1,363	3.25	10.29	38.83	68.41	41,940

3499: Other Metal Products 其他类未包括的金属制品业

Year 年份	Number of firms 企业个数	Rate of change 变化率 (%)	Number of employees 职工人数 (人)	Rate of change 变化率 (%)	Total revenue (Mil. RMB) 总销售收入 (百万元)	Rate of change 变化率 (%)	Total profit (Mil RMB) 总利润 (百万元)	Rate of change 变化率 (%)
2000	465		69,145		12,610		703	
2001	466	0.22	71,466	3.36	12,245	-2.89	752	6.97
2002	501	7.51	79,959	11.88	15,054	22.94	972	29.26

Major Products 主要产品	Output 产量	Unit 单位

10 Main Firms with Maximal Revenue (year founded) 收入最大的十家主要企业（创办年份）	City 城市	Province 省	Telephone/fax 电话/传真	Number of employees 职工人数	Ownership 产业所有权	Revenue ('000 RMB) 销售收入 (千元)	Profit('000 RMB) (rank) 利润(千元) (排名)	Total assets ('000 RMB) 总资产 (千元)	Major products 主要产品
Shanghai Mint 上海造币厂(1933)	Shanghai 上海市	Shanghai 上海市	(021)52900000 (021)52901922	1,578	State-owned 国有企业	519,612	136,312(1)	717,072	Coin 造币
Shenyang Mint 沈阳造币厂(1900)	Shenyang 沈阳市	Liaoning 辽宁省	(024)24313906 (024)24832001	1,537	State-owned 国有企业	390,035	708(168)	752,378	Coin 硬币
Nanjing Mint 南京造币厂(1990)	Nanjing 南京市	Jiangsu 江苏省	(025)2282820 (025)2281511	2,025	State-owned 国有企业	366,150	69,600(2)	690,130	Coin 硬币
Nanjing Zhenrong Group Co., Ltd. 南京振容集团有限公司(1995)	Nanjing 南京市	Jiangsu 江苏省	(025)6130664 (025)6131879	950	Joint Stock 股份制	278,120	5,200(37)	89,160	Metal Packing Materials 金属制包装物品
Shunde Xingpu Steel Processing Co., ltd. 顺德市星浦钢材加工有限公司(1997)	Foshan 佛山市	Guangdong 广东省	(0765)6330413 (0765)6661107	100	Foreign Funded 外商投资	277,393	22,427(12)	219,977	Steel Piece 钢件
Guangzhou Shenshan Wufeng Steel Tube Factory 广州神山五丰钢管厂(1993)	Guangzhou 广州市	Guangdong 广东省	(020)86060840 (020)86060841	280	Collective-owned 集体企业	240,513	2,212(80)	71,463	Steel Tube 钢管
Shenzhen Chunyuan Iron & Steel Industry Co., Ltd. 深圳春源钢铁工业有限公司(1994)	Shenzhen 深圳市	Guangdong 广东省	(0755)84890719 (0755)84890740	210	Overseas Chinese-funded 港澳台资	233,137	30,297(8)	221,395	Cold Rolling Silicon Steel Products 冷轧硅钢制品
Topper Silicon Steel (Shenzhen) Co., ltd. 优钢铁芯（深圳）有限公司(1994)	Shenzhen 深圳市	Guangdong 广东省	(0755)27235005 (0755)27235446	310	Overseas Chinese-funded 港澳台资	197,122	387(225)	110,757	Silicon Steel Plate 矽钢片
Quanxin Metal Products (Kunshan) Co., Ltd. 泉新金属制品(昆山)有限公司(1997)	Suzhou 苏州市	Jiangsu 江苏省	(0512)57301048 (0512)57301049	320	Foreign Funded 外商投资	192,356	31,187(7)	188,671	Aluminium Tube 铝管
Amtek (Suzhou) Precision Engineering Ltd. 安特(苏州)精密机械有限公司(1997)	Suzhou 苏州市	Jiangsu 江苏省	(0512)67630083 (0512)67614655	452	Foreign Funded 外商投资	163,117	32,075(6)	220,017	Pressing Piece 冲压件

Top 10 Cities by Revenue 销售收入排名前10位城市	Province 省	Market share 市场份额 (%)	Number of firms 企业个数
Shanghai 上海市	Shanghai 上海市	13.41	67
Suzhou 苏州市	Jiangsu 江苏省	8.04	28
Foshan 佛山市	Guangdong 广东省	6.53	27
Guangzhou 广州市	Guangdong 广东省	6.20	14
Nanjing 南京市	Jiangsu 江苏省	4.93	5
Shenzhen 深圳市	Guangdong 广东省	4.17	12
Zhongshan 中山市	Guangdong 广东省	4.10	16
Dongguan 东莞市	Guangdong 广东省	3.63	9
Tianjin 天津市	Tianjin 天津市	3.49	29
Haikou 海口市	Hainan 海南省	3.23	1

10 Major Wholesalers 十家主要批发商	City 城市	Province 省	Telephone/Fax 电话/传真
Yihua Kangqi Chemical Fibre Co.,Ltd. 仪化康祺化纤有限责任公司	Yangzhou 扬州市	Jiangsu 江苏省	(0514)3235499 (0514)3233847
Sinochem Guangdong Import & Export Company 中化广东进出口公司	Guangzhou 广州市	Guangdong 广东省	(020)86672288 (020)86507512
Sinochem Shanghai Import & Export Company 中化上海进出口公司	Shanghai 上海市	Shanghai 上海市	(021)63289888 (021)63283968
Sinochem Tianjin Import & Export Company 中化天津进出口公司	Tianjin 天津市	Tianjin 天津市	(022)23146216 (022)23146215
China Chemical Sales & Supply (North China) Corporation 中国化工供销华北公司	Tianjin 天津市	Tianjin 天津市	(022)23011031 (022)23011032
China Chemical Sales & Supply (North China) Corporation 中国化工供销华东公司	Shanghai 上海市	Shanghai 上海市	(021)62103300 (021)62515799
Nantong Chemical Light Industry Co.,Ltd. 南通化工轻工股份有限公司	Nantong 南通市	Jiangsu 江苏省	(0513)5518397 (0513)5512735
Taizhou Heshun Plastics Co.,Ltd. 台州市和顺塑料有限公司	Taizhou 台州市	Zhejiang 浙江省	(0576)2510220 (0576)2510160
China Petroleum Technology Development Corporation 中国石油技术开发公司	Beijing 北京市	Beijing 北京市	(010)84080722 (010)84080800
China National Chemical Fiber Corporation 中国化纤总公司	Beijing 北京市	Beijing 北京市	(010)65816699 (010)65813483

3511: Boilers 锅炉制造业

The industry accounts for 0.176% of the total revenue of China's industrial sector in 2002. The rate of return on assets is 1.73%. 75.47% of all firms in the industry made a profit while 24.53% had negative returns.The top province in terms of the industry's revenue is Jiangsu, accounting for 21.58% of the total revenue.
2002年本行业收入占全行业的 0.176%，资产利润率为 1.73%。75.47%的企业赢利，24.53%的企业亏损。收入最高的省为江苏省，占本行业的21.58%。

	Total number of firms 企业总数	Total number of employees 职工总数	Total revenue (Mil.RMB) 总销售收入(百万元)	Total profit (Mil.RMB) 总利润(百万元)	Return on assets 资产利润率(%)	Return on equity 权益利润率(%)	Labour productivity ('000 RMB/ worker) 劳动生产率(千元/人)	Debts/ assets 资产负债率(%)	Total assets (Mil.RMB) 总资产(百万元)
Industry Overall 行业总体	481	139,685	18,904	576	1.73	5.83	40.98	70.33	33,329

	Number of firms 企业个数	Average number of employees 平均职工人数	Average revenue ('000 RMB) 平均销售收入（千元）	Average profit ('000 RMB) 平均利润(千元)	Return on assets 资产利润率(%)	Return on equity 权益利润率(%)	Labour productivity ('000 RMB/ worker) 劳动生产率(千元/人)	Debts/ assets 资产负债率(%)	Average total assets ('000 RMB) 平均总资产(千元)
By ownership 产业所有权									
State-owned 国有	78	382	26,718	-1,524	-1.56	-7.52	22.91	79.22	97,534
Collective-owned 集体	94	249	20,500	985	3.69	9.21	30.34	59.95	26,717
Foreign & Overseas Chinese Funded 三资	36	268	63,685	3,232	3.54	7.80	65.36	54.57	91,241
By regional distribution 地区分布									
Central-North 华北	92	235	26,125	874	1.75	4.68	40.86	62.64	49,940
Beijing 北京	25	212	31,751	728	1.11	3.51	45.10	68.50	65,774
Tianjin 天津	25	132	31,919	2,089	5.42	9.39	88.82	42.25	38,515
Hebei 河北	23	294	18,709	169	0.38	1.05	25.19	64.18	44,964
Shanxi 山西	12	410	27,229	1,010	1.63	5.13	30.78	68.14	61,849
Inner Mongolia 内蒙古	7	190	7,809	-863	-2.86	-16.97	21.53	83.12	30,124
Northeast 东北	84	326	29,849	358	0.52	1.94	29.13	73.20	68,810
Liaoning 辽宁	36	251	16,089	505	1.09	5.35	31.61	79.56	46,138
Jilin 吉林	24	208	5,326	11	0.06	0.17	11.61	65.94	19,427
Heilongjiang 黑龙江	24	555	75,010	484	0.32	1.11	34.02	71.23	152,202
Central-East 华东	199	266	50,308	2,453	3.66	11.29	54.68	67.56	66,978
Shanghai 上海	26	287	81,371	201	0.18	1.18	57.12	84.61	111,117
Jiangsu 江苏	72	267	56,652	4,668	6.59	15.53	55.05	57.56	70,802
Zhejiang 浙江	28	143	31,721	1,215	2.89	7.61	48.31	62.07	42,092
Anhui 安徽	8	186	7,895	-229	-0.91	-3.58	21.62	74.55	25,107
Fujian 福建	1	645	61,895	403	0.29	1.12	41.56	74.27	140,084
Jiangxi 江西	3	846	90,083	-2,260	-0.99	-3.41	43.81	71.04	228,918
Shandong 山东	61	289	41,529	1,983	3.86	12.32	59.52	68.68	51,403
Central-South 中南	58	350	36,756	579	0.62	1.99	33.30	69.00	93,779
Henan 河南	16	289	13,006	179	0.54	2.54	19.75	78.73	33,018
Hubei 湖北	11	748	91,251	867	0.30	0.95	38.76	68.69	291,275
Hunan 湖南	15	229	17,385	-13	-0.04	-0.28	27.43	83.94	29,663
Guangdong 广东	13	207	46,477	2,237	2.82	6.12	53.99	53.97	79,377
Guangxi 广西	3	440	18,336	-2,565	-3.35	-31.88	19.71	89.50	76,664
Hainan 海南									
Southwest 西南	20	527	75,680	-2,325	-1.65	-15.36	33.36	89.27	140,966
Chongqing 重庆	5	195	14,255	-2,146	-4.55		16.43	100.37	47,200
Sichuan 四川	13	704	110,057	-2,747	-1.43	-14.17	36.35	89.91	192,191
Guizhou 贵州	1	147	2,164	-383	-1.43	-2.84	5.72	49.45	26,697
Yunnan 云南	1	256	9,432	330	0.57	0.87	6.85	34.73	58,154
Tibet 西藏									
Northwest 西北	28	248	12,019	-338	-0.69	-3.03	17.62	77.16	48,850
Shaanxi 陕西	10	275	13,758	9	0.02	0.07	18.09	76.93	49,919
Gansu 甘肃	14	211	9,705	-518	-1.63	-5.67	19.46	71.28	31,815
Qinghai 青海									
Ningxia 宁夏	1	150	18,022	575	0.66	0.90	16.06	26.84	87,513
Xinjiang 新疆	3	365	15,025	-953	-0.85	-54.36	11.69	98.43	111,893

3511: Boilers 锅炉制造业

Year 年份	Number of firms 企业个数	Rate of change 变化率 (%)	Number of employees 职工人数 (人)	Rate of change 变化率 (%)	Total revenue (Mil. RMB) 总销售收入 (百万元)	Rate of change 变化率 (%)	Total profit (Mil RMB) 总利润 (百万元)	Rate of change 变化率 (%)
2000	410		149,892		12,749		120	
2001	433	5.61	139,640	-6.84	14,403	12.97	81	-32.50
2002	481	11.09	139,685	0.03	18,904	31.25	576	611.11

Major Products 主要产品	Output 产量	Unit 单位
Industrial Boiler 工业锅炉	92,411	vaporation Ton 蒸发量吨
Power Station Boiler 电站锅炉	88,198	vaporation Ton 蒸发量吨

10 Main Firms with Maximal Revenue (year founded) 收入最大的十家主要企业（创办年份）	City 城市	Province 省	Telephone/fax 电话/传真	Number of employees 职工人数	Ownership 产业所有权	Revenue ('000 RMB) 销售收入 (千元)	Profit('000 RMB) (rank) 利润(千元) (排名)	Total assets ('000 RMB) 总资产 (千元)	Major products 主要产品
Wuxi Huaguang Boiler Group Co., Ltd.	Wuxi	Jiangsu	(0510)5215556		Limited-Liability				Power Station Boiler
无锡华光锅炉股份有限公司(2000)	无锡市	江苏省	(0510)5215605	4,195	有限公司	1,513,951	243,652(1)	2,035,065	电站锅炉
Harbin Boiler Co., Ltd.	Harbin	Heilongjiang	(0451)2198888		Limited-Liability				Power Station Boiler
哈尔滨锅炉有限责任公司(1957)	哈尔滨市	黑龙江省	(0451)2681689	5,006	有限公司	1,463,047	7,900(18)	2,917,285	电站锅炉
Dongfang Boiler (Group) Co.,Ltd.	Zigong	Sichuan	(0831)4733754		Joint Stock				Power Station Boiler
东方锅炉（集团 ）股份有限公司(1989)	自贡市	四川省	(0831)2203200	3,354	股份制	1,073,920	5,750(23)	1,854,990	电站锅炉
Wuhan Boiler Group Co., ltd.	Wuhan	Hubei	(027)87657153		State-owned				Power Station Boiler
武汉锅炉集团有限公司(1995)	武汉市	湖北省	(027)87883938	5,296	国有企业	767,030	1,790(73)	2,798,530	电站锅炉
Wujin Dazhong Steel Co., ltd.	Changzhou	Jiangsu	(0519)8779333		Foreign Funded				Wire
武进大众钢铁有限公司(1999)	常州市	江苏省	(0519)8772347	894	外商投资	641,630	47,050(2)	482,130	线材
Babcock & Wilcox Beijing Co.,Ltd.	Beijing	Beijing	(010)68862244		Foreign Funded				Boiler
北京巴布科克·威尔科克斯有限公司(1986)	北京市	北京市	(010)68861336	2,070	外商投资	538,560	15,791(7)	808,580	锅炉
Hangzhou Boiler Group Co., Ltd.	Hangzhou	Zhejiang	(0571)85387288		Limited-Liability				Boiler
杭州锅炉集团有限公司(1955)	杭州市	浙江省	(0571)85377420	473	有限公司	320,161	13,889(9)	518,568	锅炉
Jiangxi Boiler Chemical Petroleum Machinery Joint Co.,Ltd.	Nanchang	Jiangxi	(0791)5232225		Limited-Liability				Boiler
江西锅炉化工石油机械联合有限责任公司(1958)	南昌市	江西省	(0791)5232225	1,725	有限公司	247,143	251(182)	560,571	锅炉
Shandong Shuilongwang Group Co., Ltd.	Jinan	Shandong	(0531)7488068		Collective-owned				Refrigerator
山东水龙王集团有限公司(1996)	济南市	山东省	(0531)7488118	1,555	集体企业	210,200	17,922(6)	136,910	制冷机
Sichuan Boiler Factory	Chengdu	Sichuan	(028)84479318		State-owned				Power Station Boiler
四川锅炉厂(1975)	成都市	四川省	(028)82938000	2,469	国有企业	190,980	-	380,000	电站锅炉

Top 10 Cities by Revenue 销售收入排名前10位城市	Province 省	Market share 市场份额 (%)	Number of firms 企业个数
Wuxi 无锡市	Jiangsu 江苏省	11.36	22
Shanghai 上海市	Shanghai 上海市	11.19	26
Harbin 哈尔滨市	Heilongjiang 黑龙江省	9.06	11
Zigong 自贡市	Sichuan 四川省	6.42	7
Jinan 济南市	Shandong 山东省	5.49	15
Changzhou 常州市	Jiangsu 江苏省	5.22	11
Wuhan 武汉市	Hubei 湖北省	4.54	7
Tianjin 天津市	Tianjin 天津市	4.22	25
Beijing 北京市	Beijing 北京市	4.20	25
Hangzhou 杭州市	Zhejiang 浙江省	3.61	14

10 Major Wholesalers 十家主要批发商	City 城市	Province 省	Telephone/Fax 电话/传真
SU MEC	Nanjing	Jiangsu	(025)4511888
中设江苏机械设备进出口（集团）公司	南京市	江苏省	(025)4411772
China Poster Mobile Communications Equipment Co.,Ltd.	Beijing	Beijing	(010)66426993
中邮普泰移动通信设备股份有限公司	北京市	北京市	(010)66426837
Sino Kama Co., Ltd.	Shanghai	Shanghai	(021)62031188
中泰凯马股份有限公司	上海市	上海市	(021)62030851
China Huayuan Group Co.,Ltd.	Shanghai	Shanghai	(021)62031188
中国华源集团有限公司	上海市	上海市	(021)62032288
Zhejiang Crand Imp.& Exp.Co.,Ltd.	Ningbo	Zhejiang	(0574)87720170
浙江远大进出口有限公司	宁波市	浙江省	(0574)87723350
Shandong Machinery Import & Export Group Corporation	Qingdao	Shandong	(0532)2661628
山东省机械进出口集团公司	青岛市	山东省	(0532)2991655
Qingdao Haier International Trade Co.,Ltd.	Qingdao	Shandong	(0532)8938337
青岛海尔国际贸易有限公司	青岛市	山东省	(0532)8939494
Guangdong Machinery Import & Export Group Corporation	Guangzhou	Guangdong	(020)87782168
广东省机械进出口集团公司	广州市	广东省	(020)87771803
China National Machinery Equipment Import & Export Corporation	Beijing	Beijing	(010)63474506
中国机械设备进出口总公司	北京市	北京市	(010)63261865
Beijing Cellstar Co.,Ltd.	Beijing	Beijing	(010)64602050
北京蜂星事达电讯有限公司	北京市	北京市	(010)64672648

3512: Internal Combustion Engines 内燃机制造业

The industry accounts for 0.358% of the total revenue of China's industrial sector in 2002. The rate of return on assets is 2.61%. 61.34% of all firms in the industry made a profit while 38.66% had negative returns.The top province in terms of the industry's revenue is Jiangsu, accounting for 31.71% of the total revenue.
2002年本行业收入占全行业的0.358%，资产利润率为2.61%。61.34%的企业赢利，38.66%的企业亏损。收入最高的省为江苏省，占本行业的31.71%。

	Total number of firms 企业总数	Total number of employees 职工总数	Total revenue (Mil.RMB) 总销售收入（百万元）	Total profit (Mil.RMB) 总利润（百万元）	Return on assets 资产利润率（%）	Return on equity 权益利润率（%）	Labour productivity ('000 RMB/ worker) 劳动生产率（千元/人）	Debts/ assets 资产负债率（%）	Total assets (Mil.RMB) 总资产（百万元）
Industry Overall 行业总体	194	146,954	38,445	1,411	2.61	6.68	62.70	60.86	54,000

	Number of firms 企业个数	Average number of employees 平均职工人数	Average revenue ('000 RMB) 平均销售收入（千元）	Average profit ('000 RMB) 平均利润（千元）	Return on assets 资产利润率（%）	Return on equity 权益利润率（%）	Labour productivity ('000 RMB/ worker) 劳动生产率（千元/人）	Debts/ assets 资产负债率（%）	Average total assets ('000 RMB) 平均总资产（千元）
By ownership 产业所有权									
State-owned 国有	58	1,022	259,883	3,415	1.00	4.79	50.76	79.09	340,548
Collective-owned 集体	12	201	18,445	1,191	4.81	15.67	22.99	69.28	24,734
Foreign & Overseas Chinese Funded 三资	26	740	377,170	30,966	6.41	9.96	171.10	35.70	483,444
By regional distribution 地区分布									
Central-North 华北	16	735	107,656	-14,272	-3.66	-18.93	46.07	80.66	389,903
Beijing 北京	4	809	32,991	-73,485	-14.09		1.52	138.07	521,355
Tianjin 天津	3	861	306,542	2,434	0.27	0.47	115.50	43.41	918,000
Hebei 河北	7	793	95,408	8,765	4.71	14.15	42.74	66.75	186,256
Shanxi 山西	2	196	1,526	-1,537	-3.23	-37.48	3.29	91.39	47,617
Inner Mongolia 内蒙古									
Northeast 东北	7	1,574	747,485	57,986	6.41	14.50	112.91	55.81	905,158
Liaoning 辽宁	6	1,333	855,579	73,089	8.78	21.33	154.00	58.83	832,038
Jilin 吉林	1	3,022	98,923	-32,634	-2.43	-4.38	4.20	44.60	1,343,875
Heilongjiang 黑龙江									
Central-East 华东	91	756	228,445	7,163	2.67	6.16	61.04	56.66	268,464
Shanghai 上海	6	1,216	443,102	28,123	5.00	7.57	107.98	33.96	562,235
Jiangsu 江苏	47	671	259,339	6,834	2.44	5.91	58.65	58.70	279,940
Zhejiang 浙江	12	376	94,953	2,714	2.02	5.70	61.09	64.63	134,676
Anhui 安徽	5	1,182	119,891	11,544	3.06	5.07	27.09	39.67	377,421
Fujian 福建	2	569	124,345	935	0.78	2.48	52.83	68.68	120,585
Jiangxi 江西	3	653	30,410	-652	-0.76	-3.04	11.20	74.98	85,768
Shandong 山东	16	1,024	241,387	4,482	1.84	6.66	63.50	72.39	243,623
Central-South 中南	55	655	131,443	5,956	2.88	7.46	63.36	61.46	207,047
Henan 河南	9	1,001	30,671	-3,501	-1.67	-6.18	8.10	72.91	209,024
Hubei 湖北	10	340	92,867	6,737	5.98	12.56	168.98	52.36	112,643
Hunan 湖南	14	498	16,319	-5,147	-5.74	-41.31	7.08	86.10	89,626
Guangdong 广东	7	553	50,799	-299	-0.27	-0.64	24.66	57.44	109,182
Guangxi 广西	15	854	362,707	24,390	5.75	12.87	116.53	55.31	424,058
Hainan 海南									
Southwest 西南	20	553	150,683	13,764	6.42	13.57	76.47	52.70	214,484
Chongqing 重庆	10	431	91,890	3,393	2.40	5.79	70.28	58.63	141,663
Sichuan 四川	6	592	177,048	20,644	8.31	22.92	76.83	63.72	248,338
Guizhou 贵州									
Yunnan 云南	4	801	258,119	29,371	8.49	13.02	84.40	34.74	345,755
Tibet 西藏									
Northwest 西北	5	1,662	91,640	-4,162	-1.58	-16.62	12.26	90.49	263,550
Shaanxi 陕西	4	1,981	95,414	-5,370	-1.82	-27.93	11.46	93.49	295,444
Gansu 甘肃									
Qinghai 青海									
Ningxia 宁夏	1	387	76,543	666	0.49	1.38	28.51	64.43	135,972
Xinjiang 新疆									

3512: Internal Combustion Engines 内燃机制造业

Year 年份	Number of firms 企业个数	Rate of change 变化率 (%)	Number of employees 职工人数 (人)	Rate of change 变化率 (%)	Total revenue (Mil. RMB) 总销售收入 (百万元)	Rate of change 变化率 (%)	Total profit (Mil RMB) 总利润 (百万元)	Rate of change 变化率 (%)
2000	191		215,640		27,593		600	
2001	188	-1.57	188,780	-12.46	27,798	0.74	111	-81.50
2002	194	3.19	146,954	-22.16	38,445	38.30	1,411	1,171.17

Major Products 主要产品	Output 产量	Unit 单位
Internal-combustion Engine 内燃机	28,433	10,000 KW 万千瓦

10 Main Firms with Maximal Revenue (year founded) 收入最大的十家主要企业（创办年份）	City 城市	Province 省	Telephone/fax 电话/传真	Number of employees 职工人数	Ownership 产业所有权	Revenue ('000 RMB) 销售收入 (千元)	Profit('000 RMB) (rank) 利润(千元) (排名)	Total assets ('000 RMB) 总资产 (千元)	Major products 主要产品
China FAW Wuxi Diesel Engine Factory	Wuxi	Jiangsu	(0510)5014990		State-owned				Diesel Engine
一汽无锡柴油机厂(1943)	无锡市	江苏省	(0510)5016785	4,647	国有企业	5,376,311	272,043(2)	3,266,471	柴油机
Weifang Diesel Engine Works	Weifang	Shandong	(0536)8197078		State-owned				WD15 Diesel EngineWD15
潍坊柴油机厂(1946)	潍坊市	山东省	(0536)8231074	8,047	国有企业	2,713,466	61,297(9)	2,043,071	柴油机
China FAW Dalian Diesel Engine Factory	Dalian	Liaoning	(0411)3631588		State-owned				Diesel Engine
中国第一汽车集团大连柴油机厂(1951)	大连市	辽宁省	(0411)3632495	2,288	国有企业	2,375,393	183,818(4)	1,517,018	柴油机
Shanghai Diesel Engine Co.,Ltd.	Shanghai	Shanghai	(021)65745656		Foreign Funded				Internal-combustion Engine
上海柴油机股份有限公司(1993)	上海市	上海市	(021)65749845	4,655	外商投资	1,721,344	149,635(5)	2,165,956	内燃机
Dongfeng Chaoyang Diesel Engine Company	Chaoyang	Liaoning	(0421)2720221		State Enterprises				Diesel Engine
东风朝阳柴油机有限责任公司(1960)	朝阳市	辽宁省	(0421)2720131	3,088	国有独资	1,382,673	56,629(11)	1,265,323	柴油机
Changchai Co.,Ltd.	Changzhou	Jiangsu	(0519)6603656		Joint Stock				Diesel Engine
常柴股份有限公司(1913)	常州市	江苏省	(0519)6670765	4,355	股份制	1,373,650	-	2,183,920	柴油机
Jiangsu Jiangdong Group Co., Ltd.	Yancheng	Jiangsu	(0515)8311495		State Enterprises				Diesel Engine
江苏江动集团有限公司(1945)	盐城市	江苏省	(0515)8322986	3,229	国有独资	1,150,480	1,000(56)	2,206,540	柴油机
Kunming Yunnei Power Co.,ltd.	Kunming	Yunnan	(0871)5633185		Joint Stock				Diesel Engine
昆明云内动力股份有限公司(1958)	昆明市	云南省	(0871)5633176	1,513	股份制	927,037	120,693(7)	1,108,827	柴油机
Hudong Heavy-duty Machinery Stock Co., Ltd.	Shanghai	Shanghai	(021)58713222		Joint Stock				Internal combustion Engine
沪东重机股份有限公司(1998)	上海市	上海市	(021)58462023	2,197	股份制	863,550	19,999(18)	1,132,288	内燃机
Jiangsu Linhai Dongli Machinery Group Company	Taizhou	Jiangsu	(0523)6551888		State-owned				Motorcycle
江苏林海动力机械集团公司(1956)	泰州市	江苏省	(0523)6601839	1,387	国有企业	700,000	40,800(13)	1,258,000	摩托车

Top 10 Cities by Revenue 销售收入排名前10位城市	Province 省	Market share 市场份额 (%)	Number of firms 企业个数
Wuxi 无锡市	Jiangsu 江苏省	15.29	7
Yulin 玉林市	Guangxi 广西	9.21	2
Weifang 潍坊市	Shandong 山东省	7.22	5
Shanghai 上海市	Shanghai 上海市	6.92	6
Changzhou 常州市	Jiangsu 江苏省	6.30	19
Dalian 大连市	Liaoning 辽宁省	6.21	3
Liuzhou 柳州市	Guangxi 广西	4.47	6
Chaoyang 朝阳市	Liaoning 辽宁省	3.60	1
Shenyang 沈阳市	Liaoning 辽宁省	3.55	2
Taizhou 泰州市	Jiangsu 江苏省	3.50	5

10 Major Wholesalers 十家主要批发商	City 城市	Province 省	Telephone/Fax 电话/传真
SU MEC	Nanjing	Jiangsu	(025)4511888
中设江苏机械设备进出口（集团）公司	南京市	江苏省	(025)4411772
China Poster Mobile Communications Equipment Co.,Ltd.	Beijing	Beijing	(010)66426993
中邮普泰移动通信设备股份有限公司	北京市	北京市	(010)66426837
Sino Kama Co., Ltd.	Shanghai	Shanghai	(021)62031188
中泰凯马股份有限公司	上海市	上海市	(021)62030851
China Huayuan Group Co.,Ltd.	Shanghai	Shanghai	(021)62031188
中国华源集团有限公司	上海市	上海市	(021)62032288
Zhejiang Crand Imp.& Exp.Co.,Ltd.	Ningbo	Zhejiang	(0574)87720170
浙江远大进出口有限公司	宁波市	浙江省	(0574)87723350
Shandong Machinery Import & Export Group Corporation	Qingdao	Shandong	(0532)2661628
山东省机械进出口集团公司	青岛市	山东省	(0532)2991655
Qingdao Haier International Trade Co.,Ltd.	Qingdao	Shandong	(0532)8938337
青岛海尔国际贸易有限公司	青岛市	山东省	(0532)8939494
Guangdong Machinery Import & Export Group Corporation	Guangzhou	Guangdong	(020)87782168
广东省机械进出口集团公司	广州市	广东省	(020)87771803
China National Machinery Equipment Import & Export Corporation	Beijing	Beijing	(010)63474506
中国机械设备进出口总公司	北京市	北京市	(010)63261865
Beijing Cellstar Co.,Ltd.	Beijing	Beijing	(010)64602050
北京蜂星事达电讯有限公司	北京市	北京市	(010)64672648

3513: Steam Turbines 汽轮机制造业

The industry accounts for 0.049% of the total revenue of China's industrial sector in 2002. The rate of return on assets is 0.07%. 78.13% of all firms in the industry made a profit while 21.88% had negative returns.The top province in terms of the industry's revenue is Shanghai, accounting for 29.57% of the total revenue.
2002年本行业收入占全行业的0.049%，资产利润率为0.07%。78.13%的企业赢利，21.88%的企业亏损。收入最高的省为上海市，占本行业的29.57%。

	Total number of firms 企业总数	Total number of employees 职工总数	Total revenue (Mil.RMB) 总销售收入（百万元）	Total profit (Mil.RMB) 总利润（百万元）	Return on assets 资产利润率（%）	Return on equity 权益利润率（%）	Labour productivity ('000 RMB/ worker) 劳动生产率（千元/人）	Debts/ assets 资产负债率（%）	Total assets (Mil.RMB) 总资产（百万元）
Industry Overall 行业总体	32	36,004	5,291	10	0.07	0.21	42.13	64.12	13,454

	Number of firms 企业个数	Average number of employees 平均职工人数	Average revenue ('000 RMB) 平均销售收入（千元）	Average profit ('000 RMB) 平均利润（千元）	Return on assets 资产利润率（%）	Return on equity 权益利润率（%）	Labour productivity ('000 RMB/ worker) 劳动生产率（千元/人）	Debts/ assets 资产负债率（%）	Average total assets ('000 RMB) 平均总资产（千元）
By ownership 产业所有权									
State-owned 国有	4	2,378	257,561	2,422	0.28	0.87	42.52	67.99	867,385
Collective-owned 集体	10	359	25,350	754	2.37	6.22	26.15	61.93	31,872
Foreign & Overseas Chinese Funded 三资	4	1,563	374,643	-27,078	-2.99	-8.75	49.29	65.78	904,137
By regional distribution 地区分布									
Central-North 华北									
Beijing 北京									
Tianjin 天津									
Hebei 河北									
Shanxi 山西									
Inner Mongolia 内蒙古									
Northeast 东北	6	1,248	121,450	-508	-0.11	-0.31	16.09	64.40	465,727
Liaoning 辽宁	1	182	9,328	-4,436	-6.95	-439.64	-4.05	98.42	63,828
Jilin 吉林									
Heilongjiang 黑龙江	5	1,461	143,875	277	0.05	0.14	16.59	63.61	546,107
Central-East 华东	19	958	186,368	454	0.12	0.30	54.99	61.39	394,795
Shanghai 上海	7	938	223,515	-14,974	-2.86	-8.29	52.59	65.43	522,887
Jiangsu 江苏	5	866	145,485	4,517	1.36	3.99	53.32	65.87	331,257
Zhejiang 浙江	2	1,456	263,864	27,605	4.86	8.55	72.62	43.14	567,602
Anhui 安徽	1	630	105,163	1,190	2.92	14.99	40.33	80.51	40,715
Fujian 福建									
Jiangxi 江西									
Shandong 山东	4	940	154,017	8,617	3.42	8.37	49.90	59.16	252,176
Central-South 中南	5	295	30,210	219	0.24	0.50	28.07	52.48	92,080
Henan 河南	2	488	52,612	767	0.68	1.14	28.42	40.91	113,390
Hubei 湖北	1	86	10,000	1,425	30.32	39.36	43.69	22.98	4,700
Hunan 湖南									
Guangdong 广东	2	208	17,913	-932	-0.81	-2.30	23.99	64.55	114,460
Guangxi 广西									
Hainan 海南									
Southwest 西南	2	4,423	435,178	1,636	0.12	0.46	40.05	73.37	1,349,122
Chongqing 重庆									
Sichuan 四川	2	4,423	435,178	1,636	0.12	0.46	40.05	73.37	1,349,122
Guizhou 贵州									
Yunnan 云南									
Tibet 西藏									
Northwest 西北									
Shaanxi 陕西									
Gansu 甘肃									
Qinghai 青海									
Ningxia 宁夏									
Xinjiang 新疆									

3513: Steam Turbines 汽轮机制造业

Year 年份	Number of firms 企业个数	Rate of change 变化率 (%)	Number of employees 职工人数 (人)	Rate of change 变化率 (%)	Total revenue (Mil. RMB) 总销售收入 (百万元)	Rate of change 变化率 (%)	Total profit (Mil RMB) 总利润 (百万元)	Rate of change 变化率 (%)
2000	32		36,286		3,878		100	
2001	32	o	37,314	2.83	4,137	6.68	-1	-
2002	32	o	36,004	-3.51	5,291	27.89	10	-

Major Products 主要产品	Output 产量	Unit 单位
Power Station Steam Turbine 电站汽轮机	1,667	10,000 KW 万千瓦

10 Main Firms with Maximal Revenue (year founded) 收入最大的十家主要企业（创办年份）	City 城市	Province 省	Telephone/fax 电话/传真	Number of employees 职工人数	Ownership 产业所有权	Revenue ('000 RMB) 销售收入 (千元)	Profit('000 RMB) (rank) 利润(千元) (排名)	Total assets ('000 RMB) 总资产 (千元)	Major products 主要产品
Harbin Steam Turbine Co.,Ltd.	Harbin	Heilongjiang	(0451)82952888		Limited-Liability				Power Station Steam Turbine电
哈尔滨市汽轮机厂有限责任公司(1958)	哈尔滨市	黑龙江省		5,560	有限公司	667,758	2,905(8)	2,438,702	站汽轮机
Qingdao Jieneng Electrician-Engrneerring And Electron Group	Qingdao	Shandong	(0532)4851291		State Enterprises				Steam Turbine
Co., Ltd.青岛捷能电工电子有限责任公司(1999)	青岛市	山东省	(0532)4858036	3,370	国有独资	550,000	27,150(2)	977,980	汽轮机
Nanjing Steam Turbine Electromotor (Group) Co., Ltd.	Nanjing	Jiangsu	(025)5503750		State Enterprises				Steam Turbine
南京汽轮电机(集团)有限责任公司(1956)	南京市	江苏省	(025)5502858	3,013	国有独资	519,330	10,150(3)	1,196,840	汽轮机
Hangzhou Steam Turbine Power Group Co., Ltd.	Hangzhou	Zhejiang	(0571)85780114		State Enterprises				Steam Turbine
杭州汽轮动力集团有限公司(1958)	杭州市	浙江省	(0571)85780008	2,751	国有独资	514,973	54,754(1)	1,126,992	汽轮机
Bengbu Zhenchong Anli Engineering Machinery Co., Ltd.	Bengbu	Anhui	(0552)4928778		Limited-Liability				Autocrane
蚌埠市振冲安利工程机械有限公司(2000)	蚌埠市	安徽省	(0552)4928470	630	有限公司	105,163	1,190(13)	40,715	起重机
Laiyang Steam Turbine Fittings Factory	Yantai	Shandong	(0535)7560021		Collective-owned				Steam Turbine Fittings汽
莱阳市汽轮机配件厂(1978)	烟台市	山东省	(0535)7560021	130	集体企业	51,076	6,500(5)	12,339	轮机配件
Wuxi Electric Instrument Complete Set Of Factory	Wuxi	Jiangsu	(0510)3316786		Joint Stock				Steam Turbine Fittings汽
无锡市电力仪表成套厂(1987)	无锡市	江苏省	(0510)3311872	250	股份制	36,227	7,155(4)	27,782	轮机叶片
Zhongzhou Steam Turbine Factory	Sanmenxia	Henan	(0398)8835559		State-owned				Auxiliary Machinery Of Steam Turbine汽
中州汽轮机厂(1983)	三门峡市	河南省	(0398)8835552	476	国有企业	31,354	595(18)	206,227	轮机辅机
Shanghai Yida Machinery Factory	Shanghai	Shanghai	(021)64901946		Joint Owned				Steam Turbine Fittings汽
上海益达机械厂(1994)	上海市	上海市	(021)64902028	125	联营企业	30,716	2,054(10)	41,697	轮机配件
Dongfang Steam Turbine Factory Industry Company	Deyang	Sichuan	(0838)6355607		Collective-owned				Steam Turbine Fittings汽
东方汽轮机厂工业公司(1983)	德阳市	四川省	(0838)6302533	803	集体企业	27,710	371(20)	28,017	轮机部套

Top 10 Cities by Revenue 销售收入排名前10位城市	Province 省	Market share 市场份额 (%)	Number of firms 企业个数
Shanghai 上海市	Shanghai 上海市	29.57	7
Deyang 德阳市	Sichuan 四川省	16.45	2
Harbin 哈尔滨市	Heilongjiang 黑龙江省	13.60	5
Qingdao 青岛市	Shandong 山东省	10.53	2
Nanjing 南京市	Jiangsu 江苏省	10.22	2
Hangzhou 杭州市	Zhejiang 浙江省	9.73	1
Wuxi 无锡市	Jiangsu 江苏省	3.37	2
Bengbu 蚌埠市	Anhui 安徽省	1.99	1
Zhengzhou 郑州市	Henan 河南省	1.40	1
Yantai 烟台市	Shandong 山东省	1.11	2

10 Major Wholesalers 十家主要批发商	City 城市	Province 省	Telephone/Fax 电话/传真
SU MEC	Nanjing	Jiangsu	(025)4511888
中设江苏机械设备进出口（集团）公司	南京市	江苏省	(025)4411772
China Poster Mobile Communications Equipment Co.,Ltd.	Beijing	Beijing	(010)66426993
中邮普泰移动通信设备股份有限公司	北京市	北京市	(010)66426837
Sino Kama Co., Ltd.	Shanghai	Shanghai	(021)62031188
中泰凯马股份有限公司	上海市	上海市	(021)62030851
China Huayuan Group Co.,Ltd.	Shanghai	Shanghai	(021)62031188
中国华源集团有限公司	上海市	上海市	(021)62032288
Zhejiang Crand Imp.& Exp.Co.,Ltd.	Ningbo	Zhejiang	(0574)87720170
浙江远大进出口有限公司	宁波市	浙江省	(0574)87723350
Shandong Machinery Import & Export Group Corporation	Qingdao	Shandong	(0532)2661628
山东省机械进出口集团公司	青岛市	山东省	(0532)2991655
Qingdao Haier International Trade Co.,Ltd.	Qingdao	Shandong	(0532)8938337
青岛海尔国际贸易有限公司	青岛市	山东省	(0532)8939494
Guangdong Machinery Import & Export Group Corporation	Guangzhou	Guangdong	(020)87782168
广东省机械进出口集团公司	广州市	广东省	(020)87771803
China National Machinery Equipment Import & Export Corporation	Beijing	Beijing	(010)63474506
中国机械设备进出口总公司	北京市	北京市	(010)63261865
Beijing Cellstar Co.,Ltd.	Beijing	Beijing	(010)64602050
北京蜂星事达电讯有限公司	北京市	北京市	(010)64672648

3514: Hydraulic Turbines 水轮机制造业

The industry accounts for 0.004% of the total revenue of China's industrial sector in 2002. The rate of return on assets is -2.76%. 69.57% of all firms in the industry made a profit while 30.43% had negative returns.The top province in terms of the industry's revenue is Zhejiang, accounting for 34.46% of the total revenue.
2002年本行业收入占全行业的0.004%，资产利润率为 -2.76%。69.57%的企业赢利，30.43%的企业亏损。收入最高的省为浙江省，占本行业的34.46%。

	Total number of firms 企业总数	Total number of employees 职工总数	Total revenue (Mil.RMB) 总销售收入 (百万元)	Total profit (Mil.RMB) 总利润 (百万元)	Return on assets 资产利润率 (%)	Return on equity 权益利润率 (%)	Labour productivity ('000 RMB/ worker) 劳动生产率 (千元/人)	Debts/ assets 资产负债率 (%)	Total assets (Mil.RMB) 总资产 (百万元)
Industry Overall 行业总体	23	5,299	410	-27	-2.76	-10.95	20.86	74.78	978

	Number of firms 企业个数	Average number of employees 平均职工人数	Average revenue ('000 RMB) 平均销售收入（千元）	Average profit ('000 RMB) 平均利润 (千元)	Return on assets 资产利润率 (%)	Return on equity 权益利润率 (%)	Labour productivity ('000 RMB/ worker) 劳动生产率 (千元/人)	Debts/ assets 资产负债率 (%)	Average total assets ('000 RMB) 平均总资产 (千元)
By ownership 产业所有权									
State-owned 国有	10	179	8,565	-501	-2.52	-14.87	15.64	83.05	19,859
Collective-owned 集体									
Foreign & Overseas Chinese Funded 三资	2	170	61,023	-14,943	-7.47	-37.45	-57.24	80.06	200,082
By regional distribution 地区分布									
Central-North 华北	1	162	1,429	-431	-4.19		3.10	147.33	10,292
Beijing 北京									
Tianjin 天津									
Hebei 河北	1	162	1,429	-431	-4.19		3.10	147.33	10,292
Shanxi 山西									
Inner Mongolia 内蒙古									
Northeast 东北									
Liaoning 辽宁									
Jilin 吉林									
Heilongjiang 黑龙江									
Central-East 华东	10	239	29,984	-2,194	-3.45	-12.49	19.54	72.35	63,551
Shanghai 上海	2	170	61,023	-14,943	-7.47	-37.45	-57.24	80.06	200,082
Jiangsu 江苏	1	66	7,018	103	1.80	3.87	31.86	53.37	5,713
Zhejiang 浙江	3	443	47,061	2,616	3.94	10.04	38.92	60.72	66,348
Anhui 安徽									
Fujian 福建	3	164	6,262	-120	-1.48	-2.62	16.09	43.66	8,097
Jiangxi 江西	1	160	10,812	352	5.59	25.67	27.09	78.22	6,294
Shandong 山东									
Central-South 中南	9	225	8,170	-156	-0.55	-2.08	26.76	73.65	28,476
Henan 河南	1	506	16,564	2,091	3.95	11.07	59.82	64.31	52,937
Hubei 湖北									
Hunan 湖南	1	267	3,849				10.82	35.52	11,975
Guangdong 广东	4	165	7,770	-377	-1.77	-6.28	19.15	71.84	21,341
Guangxi 广西	3	198	7,346	-662	-1.87	-11.77	14.21	84.09	35,337
Hainan 海南									
Southwest 西南	3	241	11,627	-1,077	-4.25	-38.72	12.70	89.03	25,365
Chongqing 重庆	2	269	8,108	-1,766	-5.91	-65.64	8.31	91.00	29,877
Sichuan 四川	1	186	18,664	300	1.84	10.11	25.39	81.85	16,341
Guizhou 贵州									
Yunnan 云南									
Tibet 西藏									
Northwest 西北									
Shaanxi 陕西									
Gansu 甘肃									
Qinghai 青海									
Ningxia 宁夏									
Xinjiang 新疆									

3514: Hydraulic Turbines 水轮机制造业

Year 年份	Number of firms 企业个数	Rate of change 变化率 (%)	Number of employees 职工人数 (人)	Rate of change 变化率 (%)	Total revenue (Mil. RMB) 总销售收入 (百万元)	Rate of change 变化率 (%)	Total profit (Mil RMB) 总利润 (百万元)	Rate of change 变化率 (%)
2000	28		10,465		598		-34	
2001	22	-21.43	5,337	-49.00	374	-37.46	-24	29.41
2002	23	4.55	5,299	-0.71	410	9.63	-27	-12.50

Major Products 主要产品	Output 产量	Unit 单位
Hydraulic Turbine of Power Station 电站水轮机	75	10,000 KW 万千瓦

10 Main Firms with Maximal Revenue (year founded) 收入最大的十家主要企业（创办年份）	City 城市	Province 省	Telephone/fax 电话/传真	Number of employees 职工人数	Ownership 产业所有权	Revenue ('000 RMB) 销售收入 (千元)	Profit('000 RMB) (rank) 利润(千元) (排名)	Total assets ('000 RMB) 总资产 (千元)	Major products 主要产品
ShangHai Hydro Power Equipment Co.,	Shanghai	Shanghai	(021)64625765		Foreign Funded				Hydraulic Turbine
上海希科水电设备有限公司(1994)	上海市	上海市	(021)64308330	320	外商投资	119,958	-	398,869	水轮机
Zhejiang Jinlun Electromechanical Industrial Co., Ltd.	Jinhua	Zhejiang	(0579)2342297		Joint Stock				Hydraulic Turbine
浙江金轮机电实业有限公司(1958)	金华市	浙江省	(0579)2341066	600	股份制	59,122	5154(1)	122,773	水轮机
Zhejiang Linhai Machinery Co., Ltd.	Taizhou	Zhejiang	(0576)5135971		State Enterprises				Hydraulic Turbine
浙江临海机械有限公司(1956)	台州市	浙江省	(0576)5135408	409	国有独资	55,447	1,480(3)	51,739	水轮机
Leqing Machinery Factory	Wenzhou	Zhejiang	(0577)62522885		State-owned				Hydraulic Turbine
乐清市机械厂(1956)	温州市	浙江省	(0577)62522116	321	国有企业	26,613	1,215(4)	24,532	水轮机
Yibin Fuyuan Power Equipment Co., Ltd.	Yibin	Sichuan	(0831)4625906		Limited-Liability				Hydraulic Turbine
宜宾富源发电设备有限公司(1958)	宜宾市	四川省	(0831)4623949	186	有限公司	18,664	300(7)	16,341	水轮机
Guangdong Luoding Hydraulic Turbine Factory Co., Ltd.	Yunfu	Guangdong	(0766)3730242		State-owned				Hydraulic Turbine
广东省罗定市水轮机厂有限公司(1958)	云浮市	广东省	(0766)3722388	242	国有企业	17,449	296(8)	18,256	水轮机
Fangcheng Yuzhou Bearing Co., Ltd.	Nanyang	Henan	(0377)7233584		Limited-Liability				Bearing
方城县裕州轴承有限公司(1998)	南阳市	河南省	(0377)7232482	506	有限公司	16,564	2,091(2)	52,937	轴承
Jiangxi Lotus Hydraulic Turbine Factory Co., Ltd.	Pingxiang	Jiangxi	(0799)7221100		Private Owned				Hydraulic Turbine
江西省莲花水轮机厂有限公司(1958)	萍乡市	江西省	(0799)7223039	160	私营企业	10,812	352(6)	6,294	水轮机
Zhenghe Hydraulic Turbine Manufacturing Co., Ltd.	Nanping	Fujian	(0599)3321428		Joint Stock				Hydraulic Turbine
政和水轮机制造有限责任公司(1958)	南平市	福建省	(0599)3321428	238	股份制	10,738	204(9)	14,766	水轮机
Chongqing Zhongzhou Hydraulic Turbine Manufacturing	Chongqing	Chongqing	(023)54400108		State-owned				Hydraulic Turbine
Co., Ltd.重庆市忠州水轮机制造有限责任公司(2000)	重庆市	重庆市	(023)54400179	220	国有企业	10,072	-	29,971	水轮机

Top 10 Cities by Revenue 销售收入排名前10位城市	Province 省	Market share 市场份额 (%)	Number of firms 企业个数
Shanghai 上海市	Shanghai 上海市	29.79	2
Jinhua 金华市	Zhejiang 浙江省	14.43	1
Taizhou 台州市	Zhejiang 浙江省	13.53	1
Wenzhou 温州市	Zhejiang 浙江省	6.50	1
Yibin 宜宾市	Sichuan 四川省	4.56	1
Yunfu 云浮市	Guangdong 广东省	4.26	1
Nanyang 南阳市	Henan 河南省	4.04	1
Chongqing 重庆市	Chongqing 重庆市	3.96	2
Pingxiang 萍乡市	Jiangxi 江西省	2.64	1
Nanping 南平市	Fujian 福建省	2.62	1

10 Major Wholesalers 十家主要批发商	City 城市	Province 省	Telephone/Fax 电话/传真
SU MEC	Nanjing	Jiangsu	(025)4511888
中设江苏机械设备进出口（集团）公司	南京市	江苏省	(025)4411772
China Poster Mobile Communications Equipment Co.,Ltd.	Beijing	Beijing	(010)66426993
中邮普泰移动通信设备股份有限公司	北京市	北京市	(010)66426837
Sino Kama Co., Ltd.	Shanghai	Shanghai	(021)62031188
中泰凯马股份有限公司	上海市	上海市	(021)62030851
China Huayuan Group Co.,Ltd.	Shanghai	Shanghai	(021)62031188
中国华源集团有限公司	上海市	上海市	(021)62032288
Zhejiang Crand Imp.& Exp.Co.,Ltd.	Ningbo	Zhejiang	(0574)87720170
浙江远大进出口有限公司	宁波市	浙江省	(0574)87723350
Shandong Machinery Import & Export Group Corporation	Qingdao	Shandong	(0532)2661628
山东省机械进出口集团公司	青岛市	山东省	(0532)2991655
Qingdao Haier International Trade Co.,Ltd.	Qingdao	Shandong	(0532)8938337
青岛海尔国际贸易有限公司	青岛市	山东省	(0532)8939494
Guangdong Machinery Import & Export Group Corporation	Guangzhou	Guangdong	(020)87782168
广东省机械进出口集团公司	广州市	广东省	(020)87771803
China National Machinery Equipment Import & Export Corporation	Beijing	Beijing	(010)63474506
中国机械设备进出口总公司	北京市	北京市	(010)63261865
Beijing Cellstar Co.,Ltd.	Beijing	Beijing	(010)64602050
北京蜂星事达电讯有限公司	北京市	北京市	(010)64672648

3515: Internal-combustion Engine Parts 内燃机零部件及配件制造业

The industry accounts for 0.124% of the total revenue of China's industrial sector in 2002. The rate of return on assets is 3.46%. 77.60% of all firms in the industry made a profit while 22.40% had negative returns.The top province in terms of the industry's revenue is Jiangsu, accounting for 38.53% of the total revenue.
2002年本行业收入占全行业的 0.124%，资产利润率为 3.46%。77.60%的企业赢利，22.40%的企业亏损。收入最高的省为江苏省，占本行业的38.53%。

	Total number of firms 企业总数	Total number of employees 职工总数	Total revenue (Mil.RMB) 总销售收入 (百万元)	Total profit (Mil.RMB) 总利润 (百万元)	Return on assets 资产利润率 (%)	Return on equity 权益利润率 (%)	Labour productivity ('000 RMB/ worker) 劳动生产率 (千元/人)	Debts/ assets 资产负债率 (%)	Total assets (Mil.RMB) 总资产 (百万元)
Industry Overall 行业总体	384	128,347	13,282	601	3.46	10.26	31.81	66.28	17,383

	Number of firms 企业个数	Average number of employees 平均职工人数	Average revenue ('000 RMB) 平均销售收入 (千元)	Average profit ('000 RMB) 平均利润 (千元)	Return on assets 资产利润率 (%)	Return on equity 权益利润率 (%)	Labour productivity ('000 RMB/ worker) 劳动生产率 (千元/人)	Debts/ assets 资产负债率 (%)	Average total assets ('000 RMB) 平均总资产 (千元)
By ownership 产业所有权									
State-owned 国有	68	435	20,642	-405	-0.69	-2.88	17.02	76.01	58,646
Collective-owned 集体	56	171	34,991	2,075	11.22	33.96	69.60	66.97	18,503
Foreign & Overseas Chinese Funded 三资	24	267	58,234	9,229	13.60	22.08	70.49	38.43	67,882
By regional distribution 地区分布									
Central-North 华北	28	429	24,779	778	1.08	4.24	9.82	74.47	71,865
Beijing 北京	5	141	40,674	8,517	23.64	44.68	-4.54	47.09	36,027
Tianjin 天津	2	32	3,654	-17	-0.30	-0.44	17.78	30.64	5,625
Hebei 河北	14	621	27,454	-1,253	-1.11	-5.33	8.72	79.24	113,230
Shanxi 山西	6	285	14,932	-347	-1.46	-5.58	21.99	73.89	23,790
Inner Mongolia 内蒙古	1	827	9,190	-1,152	-1.24	-2.61	7.89	52.44	92,860
Northeast 东北	16	418	33,423	-59	-0.09	-0.20	17.76	56.70	68,700
Liaoning 辽宁	14	438	35,979	-32	-0.04	-0.10	18.13	56.30	75,256
Jilin 吉林									
Heilongjiang 黑龙江	2	278	15,530	-249	-1.09	-3.19	13.66	65.82	22,803
Central-East 华东	262	302	39,521	2,137	5.58	15.14	40.02	63.16	38,323
Shanghai 上海	19	165	39,309	3,442	9.79	15.94	63.96	38.57	35,160
Jiangsu 江苏	128	325	39,981	2,073	5.04	14.34	36.89	64.84	41,099
Zhejiang 浙江	27	172	20,163	659	2.67	6.04	30.87	55.82	24,691
Anhui 安徽	21	327	19,228	-149	-0.57	-1.39	18.09	58.76	26,064
Fujian 福建	3	155	13,621	463	4.40	7.01	30.14	37.15	10,506
Jiangxi 江西	5	312	7,785	32	0.12	0.48	10.74	74.58	25,789
Shandong 山东	59	355	58,679	3,612	7.78	24.59	54.27	68.35	46,397
Central-South 中南	53	362	23,558	733	1.72	6.43	25.46	73.30	42,710
Henan 河南	16	357	20,300	309	0.70	2.23	23.09	68.68	44,202
Hubei 湖北	12	290	38,477	4,536	11.39	23.15	55.05	50.80	39,819
Hunan 湖南	12	430	13,473	-1,416	-3.33	-118.98	12.11	97.20	42,506
Guangdong 广东	5	255	16,119	1,114	4.17	10.11	26.74	58.71	26,687
Guangxi 广西	8	448	27,475	-1,135	-2.09	-11.57	19.31	81.96	54,385
Hainan 海南									
Southwest 西南	15	444	25,978	303	0.30	0.73	24.48	59.48	102,267
Chongqing 重庆	2	689	64,844	3,522	2.70	5.52	47.47	51.15	130,502
Sichuan 四川	8	373	25,057	-26	-0.03	-0.05	25.85	43.19	93,993
Guizhou 贵州	1	1,264	28,955				3.96	88.00	392,277
Yunnan 云南	4	259	7,643	-574	-1.78	-11.55	15.02	84.55	32,196
Tibet 西藏									
Northwest 西北	10	456	6,028	-2,285	-5.27		5.33	112.27	43,364
Shaanxi 陕西	3	541	2,408	-6,447	-7.73		2.68	132.12	83,423
Gansu 甘肃	6	456	8,590	-373	-1.33	-8.52	7.76	84.36	27,956
Qinghai 青海	1	201	1,516	-1,273	-8.14	-135.43	-6.33	93.99	15,631
Ningxia 宁夏									
Xinjiang 新疆									

3515: Internal-combustion Engine Parts 内燃机零部件及配件制造业

Year 年份	Number of firms 企业个数	Rate of change 变化率 (%)	Number of employees 职工人数 (人)	Rate of change 变化率 (%)	Total revenue (Mil. RMB) 总销售收入 (百万元)	Rate of change 变化率 (%)	Total profit (Mil RMB) 总利润 (百万元)	Rate of change 变化率 (%)
2000	390		175,487		13,486		415	
2001	379	-2.82	134,375	-23.43	11,053	-18.04	391	-5.78
2002	384	1.32	128,347	-4.49	13,282	20.17	601	53.71

Major Products 主要产品	Output 产量	Unit 单位

10 Main Firms with Maximal Revenue (year founded) 收入最大的十家主要企业（创办年份）	City 城市	Province 省	Telephone/fax 电话/传真	Number of employees 职工人数	Ownership 产业所有权	Revenue ('000 RMB) 销售收入 (千元)	Profit('000 RMB) (rank) 利润(千元) (排名)	Total assets ('000 RMB) 总资产 (千元)	Major products 主要产品
Shandong Crank Shaft General Factory	Weihai	Shandong	(0631)8982137		State-owned				Crank Shaft
山东曲轴总厂(1956)	威海市	山东省	(0631)8451761	1,816	国有企业	380,529	32,005(5)	643,312	曲轴
JiangSu Changdong Machinery Co., Ltd.	Changzhou	Jiangsu	(0519)6261071		Joint Stock				Diesel Engine
江苏常动机械有限公司(1956)	常州市	江苏省	(0519)6261413	2,533	股份制	354,880	21,160(8)	266,470	柴油机
Shandong Yongjia Cylinder Lid Group Corporation	Yantai	Shandong	(0535)8322174		Overseas Chinese-funded				Cylinder Cover
山东永嘉缸盖集团公司(1994)	烟台市	山东省	(0535)8323736	563	港澳台资	292,000	29,700(7)	120,000	缸盖
Nantong Wanli Machinery Group Co., Ltd.	Nantong	Jiangsu	(0513)8812363		Limited-Liability				Internal-combustion Engine Fittings
南通万力机械集团有限公司(1949)	南通市	江苏省	(0513)8812623	1,092	有限公司	267,887	12,395(16)	157,861	内燃机配件
Wendeng Electromechanical Equipment Factory	Weihai	Shandong	(0631)8727032		Collective-owned				Hydraulic Pressure Oil Cylinder
文登市机电设备厂(1984)	威海市	山东省	(0631)8727065	160	集体企业	261,140	16,930(11)	17,280	液压油缸
Shandong Molong Petroleum Machinery Group Co.,Ltd.	Weifang	Shandong	(0536)5101565		Collective-owned				Petroleum Machinery Fittings
山东墨龙石油机械股份有限公司(1985)	潍坊市	山东省	(0536)5100888	1,010	集体企业	250,900	30,360(6)	283,660	石油机械配件
Shangyu Dongli Machinery Co., Ltd.	Shaoxing	Zhejiang	(0575)2015819		Limited-Liability				Internal-combustion Engine Crank Shaft
上虞动力机械有限公司(1958)	绍兴市	浙江省	(0575)2015819	459	有限公司	240,204	13,706(14)	203,110	内燃机曲轴
Shanghai Pudong Yiwei Fuel Injiection Equipment Co., Ltd.	Shanghai	Shanghai	(021)58713907		Limited-Liability				Internal-combustion Engine Fittings
上海浦东伊维燃油喷射有限公司(1995)	上海市	上海市	(021)58712914	902	有限公司	233,476	35,628(4)	301,111	内燃机配件
Changzhou Internal-combustion Engine Co., Ltd.	Changzhou	Jiangsu	(0519)8679588		Limited-Liability				Diesel Engine
常州内燃机有限公司(1992)	常州市	江苏省	(0519)8679588	480	有限公司	230,690	20,420(9)	229,490	柴油机
Shijiazhuang JinGang Internal-combustion Engine Parts Group	Shijiazhuang	Hebei	(0311)5054066		State Enterprises				Piston
Co., Ltd.石家庄金刚内燃机零部件集团有限公司(1958)	石家庄市	河北省	(0311)5051008	3,858	国有独资	225,946	-	1,054,531	活塞

Top 10 Cities by Revenue 销售收入排名前10位城市	Province 省	Market share 市场份额 (%)	Number of firms 企业个数
Changzhou 常州市	Jiangsu 江苏省	12.10	31
Yantai 烟台市	Shandong 山东省	11.92	23
Weihai 威海市	Shandong 山东省	6.31	5
Wuxi 无锡市	Jiangsu 江苏省	5.75	17
Shanghai 上海市	Shanghai 上海市	5.62	19
Yangzhou 扬州市	Jiangsu 江苏省	5.16	20
Nantong 南通市	Jiangsu 江苏省	4.44	10
Yancheng 盐城市	Jiangsu 江苏省	3.21	14
Nanjing 南京市	Jiangsu 江苏省	2.81	14
Zibo 淄博市	Shandong 山东省	2.57	6

10 Major Wholesalers 十家主要批发商	City 城市	Province 省	Telephone/Fax 电话/传真
SU MEC	Nanjing	Jiangsu	(025)4511888
中设江苏机械设备进出口（集团）公司	南京市	江苏省	(025)4411772
China Poster Mobile Communications Equipment Co.,Ltd.	Beijing	Beijing	(010)66426993
中邮普泰移动通信设备股份有限公司	北京市	北京市	(010)66426837
Sino Kama Co., Ltd.	Shanghai	Shanghai	(021)62031188
中泰凯马股份有限公司	上海市	上海市	(021)62030851
China Huayuan Group Co.,Ltd.	Shanghai	Shanghai	(021)62031188
中国华源集团有限公司	上海市	上海市	(021)62032288
Zhejiang Crand Imp.& Exp.Co.,Ltd.	Ningbo	Zhejiang	(0574)87720170
浙江远大进出口有限公司	宁波市	浙江省	(0574)87723350
Shandong Machinery Import & Export Group Corporation	Qingdao	Shandong	(0532)2661628
山东省机械进出口集团公司	青岛市	山东省	(0532)2991655
Qingdao Haier International Trade Co.,Ltd.	Qingdao	Shandong	(0532)8938337
青岛海尔国际贸易有限公司	青岛市	山东省	(0532)8939494
Guangdong Machinery Import & Export Group Corporation	Guangzhou	Guangdong	(020)87782168
广东省机械进出口集团公司	广州市	广东省	(020)87771803
China National Machinery Equipment Import & Export Corporation	Beijing	Beijing	(010)63474506
中国机械设备进出口总公司	北京市	北京市	(010)63261865
Beijing Cellstar Co.,Ltd.	Beijing	Beijing	(010)64602050
北京蜂星事达电讯有限公司	北京市	北京市	(010)64672648

3519: Other Boiler and Power Generation Equipment

其他锅炉及原动机制造业

The industry accounts for 0.011% of the total revenue of China's industrial sector in 2002. The rate of return on assets is 4.40%. 80.00% of all firms in the industry made a profit while 20.00% had negative returns. The top province in terms of the industry's revenue is Jiangsu, accounting for 52.11% of the total revenue.
2002年本行业收入占全行业的 0.011%，资产利润率为 4.40%。80.00%的企业赢利，20.00%的企业亏损。收入最高的省为江苏省，占本行业的52.11%。

	Total number of firms 企业总数	Total number of employees 职工总数	Total revenue (Mil.RMB) 总销售收入 (百万元)	Total profit (Mil.RMB) 总利润 (百万元)	Return on assets 资产利润率 (%)	Return on equity 权益利润率 (%)	Labour productivity ('000 RMB/worker) 劳动生产率 (千元/人)	Debts/assets 资产负债率 (%)	Total assets (Mil.RMB) 总资产 (百万元)
Industry Overall 行业总体	45	7,869	1,175	71	4.40	10.34	49.91	57.48	1,608

	Number of firms 企业个数	Average number of employees 平均职工人数	Average revenue ('000 RMB) 平均销售收入 (千元)	Average profit ('000 RMB) 平均利润 (千元)	Return on assets 资产利润率 (%)	Return on equity 权益利润率 (%)	Labour productivity ('000 RMB/worker) 劳动生产率 (千元/人)	Debts/assets 资产负债率 (%)	Average total assets ('000 RMB) 平均总资产 (千元)
By ownership 产业所有权									
State-owned 国有	6	239	26,797	-5,510	-9.89	-45.30	30.49	78.16	55,697
Collective-owned 集体	13	97	11,075	805	7.18	28.50	37.34	74.79	11,209
Foreign & Overseas Chinese Funded 三资	4	163	22,002	760	1.73	2.60	35.55	33.67	43,978
By regional distribution 地区分布									
Central-North 华北	9	145	20,119	1,399	5.28	8.78	36.63	39.82	26,472
Beijing 北京	2	175	13,885	1,003	6.34	18.00	29.52	64.78	15,820
Tianjin 天津	4	196	28,998	1,530	3.78	5.88	31.42	35.66	40,454
Hebei 河北	2	41	10,743	1,081	18.94	30.32	75.68	37.52	5,704
Shanxi 山西	1	90	15,825	2,300	6.89	10.96	73.98	37.14	33,385
Inner Mongolia 内蒙古									
Northeast 东北	6	170	10,222	353	4.05	10.25	11.69	60.47	8,705
Liaoning 辽宁	3	94	9,913	477	4.60	16.72	11.51	72.47	10,361
Jilin 吉林									
Heilongjiang 黑龙江	3	246	10,531	229	3.24	5.67	11.76	42.82	7,049
Central-East 华东	11	243	61,617	7,756	11.61	26.08	88.44	55.47	66,782
Shanghai 上海									
Jiangsu 江苏	4	461	153,034	20,578	13.41	27.96	115.63	52.05	153,497
Zhejiang 浙江	1	40	5,224	-58	-1.39	-2.95	23.60	52.79	4,160
Anhui 安徽	1	78	3,937	18	0.29	0.46	19.63	36.85	6,234
Fujian 福建									
Jiangxi 江西									
Shandong 山东	5	143	11,299	609	2.76	11.36	29.39	75.68	22,043
Central-South 中南	4	63	3,956	521	5.35	18.97	44.69	71.82	9,735
Henan 河南	1	97	2,438	17	0.13		56.80	101.81	12,838
Hubei 湖北									
Hunan 湖南									
Guangdong 广东	3	51	4,462	688	7.91	18.43	37.06	57.07	8,700
Guangxi 广西									
Hainan 海南									
Southwest 西南	3	252	14,366	156	0.34	0.78	37.76	57.06	46,492
Chongqing 重庆									
Sichuan 四川	3	252	14,366	156	0.34	0.78	37.76	57.06	46,492
Guizhou 贵州									
Yunnan 云南									
Tibet 西藏									
Northwest 西北	12	155	16,294	-2,658	-7.89	-26.23	30.48	69.90	33,670
Shaanxi 陕西	3	135	7,049	-312	-1.51	-4.16	22.38	63.71	20,686
Gansu 甘肃	7	176	23,405	-4,329	-9.94	-40.93	36.76	75.72	43,559
Qinghai 青海									
Ningxia 宁夏									
Xinjiang 新疆	2	112	5,271	-325	-1.75	-2.60	10.48	32.44	18,534

3519: Other Boiler and Power Generation Equipment
其他锅炉及原动机制造业

Year 年份	Number of firms 企业个数	Rate of change 变化率（%）	Number of employees 职工人数（人）	Rate of change 变化率（%）	Total revenue (Mil. RMB) 总销售收入（百万元）	Rate of change 变化率（%）	Total profit (Mil RMB) 总利润（百万元）	Rate of change 变化率（%）
2000	51		9,922		1,123		45	
2001	52	1.96	10,551	6.34	1,133	0.89	35	-22.22
2002	45	-13.46	7,869	-25.42	1,175	3.71	71	102.86

Major Products 主要产品	Output 产量	Unit 单位

10 Main Firms with Maximal Revenue (year founded) 收入最大的十家主要企业（创办年份）	City 城市	Province 省	Telephone/fax 电话/传真	Number of employees 职工人数	Ownership 产业所有权	Revenue ('000 RMB) 销售收入（千元）	Profit('000 RMB) (rank) 利润(千元)(排名)	Total assets ('000 RMB) 总资产（千元）	Major products 主要产品
Gansu Electric Power Industry Bureau Lanzhou Electric Power Repair & Building Factory 甘肃省电力工业局兰州电力修造厂(1966)	Lanzhou 兰州市	Gansu 甘肃省	(0931)2336124 (0931)2310639	1,008	State-owned 国有企业	150,221	-	286,899	Electric Dust Catcher 电除尘器
Jiangsu Xingguang Electricity Generationg Equipment Co.,Ltd. 江苏星光发电设备有限公司(1971)	Taizhou 泰州市	Jiangsu 江苏省	(0523)7791067 (0523)7791002	80	Private Owned 私营企业	41,030	260(20)	10,470	Diesel Engine Dynamotor Set柴油发电机组
Ji'nan Huangtai Industry Gas Stove Factory 济南市黄台工业煤气炉厂(1978)	Jinan 济南市	Shandong 山东省	(0531)6954021 (0531)6944757	321	Collective-owned 集体企业	37,593	2,610(3)	43,091	Gas Happenfurnace煤气发生炉
Tianjin Huaneng Group Energy Equipment Factory 天津华能集团能源设备厂(1987)	Tianjin 天津市	Tianjin 天津市	(022)29138133 (022)29131710	428	Collective-owned 集体企业	34,645	2,618(2)	37,525	Energy Sources Equipment 能源设备
Marunaka(TianJin) Machinery Manufacturing Center Co., Ltd. 丸仲（天津）机械制造中心有限公司(1993)	Tianjin 天津市	Tianjin 天津市	(022)24992501 (022)24994272	112	Foreign Funded 外商投资	34,321	1,509(10)	51,887	Light Industry Machinery 轻工机械
Tianjin Mikuni Co.Ltd. 天津三国有限公司(1994)	Tianjin 天津市	Tianjin 天津市	(022)23973920 (022)23972281	192	Foreign Funded 外商投资	25,845	-	58,445	Motor Fittings摩托车配件
Beijing Tegao Heat-exchanging Equipment Co., Ltd. 北京特高换热设备有限公司(1997)	Beijing 北京市	Beijing 北京市	(010)69575820 (010)69575810	170	Foreign Funded 外商投资	17,803	1,908(9)	19,157	Heat Exchanger 热交换器
Hualong Machinery Manufacturing Co., Ltd. 华龙机械制造有限公司(1971)	Suihua 绥化市	Heilongjiang 黑龙江省	(0455)7712929 (0455)7714259	480	Private Owned 私营企业	15,871	401(15)	8,026	Weaving Machine fittings 纺机配件
Shanxi Huaiqi Machinery Co., Ltd. 山西华奇机械有限公司(1990)	Taiyuan 太原市	Shanxi 山西省	(0351)4377526 (0351)4377526	90	Private Owned 私营企业	15,825	2,300(5)	33,385	Inermediate Frequency Induction Water Oven中频感应热水炉
Shannxi Baishi Co., Ltd. 陕西白狮股份有限公司(1956)	Weinan 渭南市	Shannxi 陕西省	(0913)2193933 (0913)2192467	138	Joint Stock 股份制	15,679	858(12)	31,613	Tea Oven 茶水炉

Top 10 Cities by Revenue 销售收入排名前10位城市	Province 省	Market share 市场份额（%）	Number of firms 企业个数
Wuxi 无锡市	Jiangsu 江苏省	47.61	2
Lanzhou 兰州市	Gansu 甘肃省	13.61	4
Tianjin 天津市	Tianjin 天津市	9.87	4
Leshan 乐山市	Sichuan 四川省	3.67	3
Taizhou 泰州市	Jiangsu 江苏省	3.49	1
Jinan 济南市	Shandong 山东省	3.20	1
Beijing 北京市	Beijing 北京市	2.36	2
Weinan 渭南市	Shannxi 陕西省	1.80	3
Suihua 绥化市	Heilongjiang 黑龙江省	1.35	1
Taiyuan 太原市	Shanxi 山西省	1.35	1

10 Major Wholesalers 十家主要批发商	City 城市	Province 省	Telephone/Fax 电话/传真
SU MEC 中设江苏机械设备进出口（集团）公司	Nanjing 南京市	Jiangsu 江苏省	(025)4511888 (025)4411772
China Poster Mobile Communications Equipment Co.,Ltd. 中邮普泰移动通信设备股份有限公司	Beijing 北京市	Beijing 北京市	(010)66426993 (010)66426837
Sino Kama Co., Ltd. 中泰凯马股份有限公司	Shanghai 上海市	Shanghai 上海市	(021)62031188 (021)62030851
China Huayuan Group Co.,Ltd. 中国华源集团有限公司	Shanghai 上海市	Shanghai 上海市	(021)62031188 (021)62032288
Zhejiang Crand Imp.& Exp.Co.,Ltd. 浙江远大进出口有限公司	Ningbo 宁波市	Zhejiang 浙江省	(0574)87720170 (0574)87723350
Shandong Machinery Import & Export Group Corporation 山东省机械进出口集团公司	Qingdao 青岛市	Shandong 山东省	(0532)2661628 (0532)2991655
Qingdao Haier International Trade Co.,Ltd. 青岛海尔国际贸易有限公司	Qingdao 青岛市	Shandong 山东省	(0532)8938337 (0532)8939494
Guangdong Machinery Import & Export Group Corporation 广东省机械进出口集团公司	Guangzhou 广州市	Guangdong 广东省	(020)87782168 (020)87771803
China National Machinery Equipment Import & Export Corporation 中国机械设备进出口总公司	Beijing 北京市	Beijing 北京市	(010)63474506 (010)63261865
Beijing Cellstar Co.,Ltd. 北京蜂星事达电讯有限公司	Beijing 北京市	Beijing 北京市	(010)64602050 (010)64672648

3521: Metal Cutting Machine Tools 金属切削机床制造业

The industry accounts for 0.177% of the total revenue of China's industrial sector in 2002. The rate of return on assets is 0.87%. 76.89% of all firms in the industry made a profit while 23.11% had negative returns.The top province in terms of the industry's revenue is Liaoning, accounting for 17.60% of the total revenue.
2002年本行业收入占全行业的 0.177%，资产利润率为 0.87%。76.89%的企业赢利，23.11%的企业亏损。收入最高的省为辽宁省，占本行业的17.60%。

	Total number of firms 企业总数	Total number of employees 职工总数	Total revenue (Mil.RMB) 总销售收入（百万元）	Total profit (Mil.RMB) 总利润（百万元）	Return on assets 资产利润率 (%)	Return on equity 权益利润率 (%)	Labour productivity ('000 RMB/ worker) 劳动生产率（千元/人）	Debts/ assets 资产负债率 (%)	Total assets (Mil.RMB) 总资产（百万元）
Industry Overall 行业总体	411	187,487	18,959	385	0.87	2.87	32.73	69.59	44,100

	Number of firms 企业个数	Average number of employees 平均职工人数	Average revenue ('000 RMB) 平均销售收入（千元）	Average profit ('000 RMB) 平均利润（千元）	Return on assets 资产利润率 (%)	Return on equity 权益利润率 (%)	Labour productivity ('000 RMB/ worker) 劳动生产率（千元/人）	Debts/ assets 资产负债率 (%)	Average total assets ('000 RMB) 平均总资产（千元）
By ownership 产业所有权									
State-owned 国有	150	593	33,500	-686	-0.56	-3.01	21.05	81.31	121,946
Collective-owned 集体	31	148	30,259	1,203	9.67	22.26	59.22	56.54	12,440
Foreign & Overseas Chinese Funded 三资	57	182	40,470	3,615	6.04	11.31	66.16	46.55	59,821
By regional distribution 地区分布									
Central-North 华北	39	413	37,320	660	0.66	1.86	27.71	64.45	99,665
Beijing 北京	12	457	66,141	895	0.47	1.03	42.27	53.90	189,220
Tianjin 天津	11	236	18,912	256	0.50	2.06	25.66	75.54	50,700
Hebei 河北	13	506	29,044	969	1.43	8.04	19.64	82.27	67,971
Shanxi 山西	3	481	25,398	-130	-0.22	-0.93	12.90	76.02	58,323
Inner Mongolia 内蒙古									
Northeast 东北	29	1,003	126,621	2,824	0.85	4.57	35.50	81.51	334,132
Liaoning 辽宁	19	1,023	175,609	2,509	0.61	2.27	47.38	73.04	409,267
Jilin 吉林	3	242	6,898	-530	-1.70	-6.91	10.53	75.46	31,245
Heilongjiang 黑龙江	7	1,277	44,964	5,117	1.97		11.68	118.05	260,005
Central-East 华东	220	317	35,690	750	1.18	3.66	35.80	67.65	63,405
Shanghai 上海	41	213	33,392	1,265	1.77	8.06	45.80	78.09	71,676
Jiangsu 江苏	58	401	45,776	-377	-0.44	-1.32	37.29	66.57	85,731
Zhejiang 浙江	53	201	30,407	1,667	4.67	11.00	43.44	57.56	35,701
Anhui 安徽	14	353	18,683	121	0.29	1.65	18.03	82.49	41,909
Fujian 福建	12	250	20,254	818	2.36	3.65	30.91	35.47	34,706
Jiangxi 江西	9	348	15,209	-190	-0.33	-1.70	16.28	80.36	56,793
Shandong 山东	33	483	47,717	1,119	1.40	3.97	33.31	64.61	79,742
Central-South 中南	69	379	25,309	76	0.12	0.43	19.67	73.38	65,516
Henan 河南	11	564	45,396	350	0.46	1.99	38.46	77.11	76,665
Hubei 湖北	19	482	18,001	-667	-0.66	-2.60	12.79	74.62	101,142
Hunan 湖南	14	196	9,604	-1,396	-4.48	-19.22	15.93	76.69	31,162
Guangdong 广东	20	237	28,764	1,364	3.13	10.26	10.11	69.47	43,548
Guangxi 广西	5	657	39,045	1,263	1.41	4.07	20.24	65.45	89,682
Hainan 海南									
Southwest 西南	32	740	75,592	3,577	1.70	4.22	41.43	59.72	210,190
Chongqing 重庆	6	802	39,022	1,081	1.30	7.35	18.78	82.34	83,319
Sichuan 四川	12	647	137,056	10,762	3.28	7.06	84.49	53.50	327,804
Guizhou 贵州	5	939	23,370	-2,607	-2.89		12.64	115.32	90,209
Yunnan 云南	9	711	47,031	-904	-0.44	-0.94	27.38	53.24	204,607
Tibet 西藏									
Northwest 西北	22	1,037	82,484	-357	-0.15	-0.43	29.30	66.00	242,163
Shaanxi 陕西	12	998	87,944	970	0.38	0.95	35.75	59.77	252,865
Gansu 甘肃	3	1,171	30,096	-3,146	-2.92	-25.55	8.47	88.57	107,732
Qinghai 青海	4	1,200	103,323	2,158	0.74	1.44	29.01	48.75	292,944
Ningxia 宁夏	3	843	85,245	-6,229	-2.34		28.27	105.84	266,078
Xinjiang 新疆									

3521: Metal Cutting Machine Tools 金属切削机床制造业

Year 年份	Number of firms 企业个数	Rate of change 变化率 (%)	Number of employees 职工人数 (人)	Rate of change 变化率 (%)	Total revenue (Mil. RMB) 总销售收入 (百万元)	Rate of change 变化率 (%)	Total profit (Mil RMB) 总利润 (百万元)	Rate of change 变化率 (%)
2000	358		218,909		12,707		246	
2001	392	9.50	193,380	-11.66	16,803	32.23	669	171.95
2002	411	4.85	187,487	-3.05	18,959	12.83	385	-42.45

Major Products 主要产品	Output 产量	Unit 单位
Metal Cutting Machine Tool 金属切削机床	23	10,000 Units 万台

10 Main Firms with Maximal Revenue (year founded) 收入最大的十家主要企业（创办年份）	City 城市	Province 省	Telephone/fax 电话/传真	Number of employees 职工人数	Ownership 产业所有权	Revenue ('000 RMB) 销售收入（千元）	Profit('000 RMB) (rank) 利润(千元)(排名)	Total assets ('000 RMB) 总资产（千元）	Major products 主要产品
Dalian Machine Tool Group Co., Ltd.	Dalian	Liaoning	(0411)3631851		State Enterprises				Ordinary Lathe
大连机床集团有限责任公司(1997)	大连市	辽宁省	(0411)3631305	5,688	国有独资	1,895,955	11,548(15)	2,726,409	普通车床
Shenyang Machine Tool (Group) Co.,Ltd.	Shenyang	Liaoning	(024)25878003		Joint Stock				Metal Cutting Machine Tool金属
沈阳机床股份有限公司(1993)	沈阳市	辽宁省	(024)25878762	7,802	股份制	1,158,642	46,529(3)	3,983,080	切削机床
Wuxi Kaiyuan Machine Tool Group Co., Ltd.	Wuxi	Jiangsu	(0510)5802978		Limited-Liability				Metal Cutting Machine Tool金属
无锡开源机床集团有限公司(1948)	无锡市	江苏省	(0510)5807314	4,378	有限公司	615,548	32,632(4)	1,028,687	切削机床
Qinchuan Machine Tool Group Co., Ltd.	Baoji	Shannxi	(0917)3370665		State-owned				Metal Cutting Machine Tool金属
秦川机床集团有限公司(1965)	宝鸡市	陕西省	(0917)3390960	2,980	国有企业	512,000	12,500(14)	1,250,000	切削机床
Nanjing Machine Tool (Group)Co., Ltd.	Nanjing	Jiangsu	(025)3229290		State-owned				Nc Machine Tool
南京机床(集团)有限公司(1995)	南京市	江苏省	(025)3229290	4,337	国有企业	430,200	8,540(24)	1,199,610	数控机床
Qinghai Huading Industrial Co., Ltd.	Xining	Qinghai	(0971)8224981		Joint Stock				Machine Tool
青海华鼎实业股份有限公司(1998)	西宁市	青海省	(0971)8224981	2,373	股份制	339,982	19,400(9)	694,491	机床
Henan Xinji Stock Co., Ltd.	Xinxiang	Henan	(0373)5031255		Joint Stock				Metal Cutting Machine Tool金属
河南新机股份有限公司(1954)	新乡市	河南省	(0373)5032246	1,985	股份制	290,348	3,328(54)	308,492	切削机床
Baoji Machine Tool Factory	Baoji	Shannxi	(0917)3415688		State-owned				CS6140 Lathe Series.CS6140
宝鸡机床厂(1965)	宝鸡市	陕西省	(0917)3412327	1,664	国有企业	255,919	12,591(13)	464,302	系列车床
Suzhou Sanguang Group Co., Ltd.	Suzhou	Jiangsu	(0512)65231449		Foreign Funded				DK7740 Line Incising Machine Tool线
苏州三光集团有限公司(1995)	苏州市	江苏省	(0512)65231449	464	外商投资	254,962	28,381(5)	231,390	切割机床
Beijing No.1 Machine Tool Plant	Beijing	Beijing	(010)65671155		State-owned				Machine Tool
北京第一机床厂(1949)	北京市	北京市	(010)65680715	2,044	国有企业	236,064	197(190)	883,516	机床

Top 10 Cities by Revenue 销售收入排名前10位城市	Province 省	Market share 市场份额 (%)	Number of firms 企业个数
Dalian 大连市	Liaoning 辽宁省	10.75	3
Shanghai 上海市	Shanghai 上海市	7.22	41
Shenyang 沈阳市	Liaoning 辽宁省	6.47	9
Chengdu 成都市	Sichuan 四川省	4.73	6
Hangzhou 杭州市	Zhejiang 浙江省	4.55	20
Baoji 宝鸡市	Shannxi 陕西省	4.47	5
Wuxi 无锡市	Jiangsu 江苏省	4.41	13
Beijing 北京市	Beijing 北京市	4.19	12
Zigong 自贡市	Sichuan 四川省	3.76	3
Nanjing 南京市	Jiangsu 江苏省	3.28	10

10 Major Wholesalers 十家主要批发商	City 城市	Province 省	Telephone/Fax 电话/传真
SU MEC	Nanjing	Jiangsu	(025)4511888
中设江苏机械设备进出口（集团）公司	南京市	江苏省	(025)4411772
China Poster Mobile Communications Equipment Co.,Ltd.	Beijing	Beijing	(010)66426993
中邮普泰移动通信设备股份有限公司	北京市	北京市	(010)66426837
Sino Kama Co., Ltd.	Shanghai	Shanghai	(021)62031188
中泰凯马股份有限公司	上海市	上海市	(021)62030851
China Huayuan Group Co.,Ltd.	Shanghai	Shanghai	(021)62031188
中国华源集团有限公司	上海市	上海市	(021)62032288
Zhejiang Crand Imp.& Exp.Co.,Ltd.	Ningbo	Zhejiang	(0574)87720170
浙江远大进出口有限公司	宁波市	浙江省	(0574)87723350
Shandong Machinery Import & Export Group Corporation	Qingdao	Shandong	(0532)2661628
山东省机械进出口集团公司	青岛市	山东省	(0532)2991655
Qingdao Haier International Trade Co.,Ltd.	Qingdao	Shandong	(0532)8938337
青岛海尔国际贸易有限公司	青岛市	山东省	(0532)8939494
Guangdong Machinery Import & Export Group Corporation	Guangzhou	Guangdong	(020)87782168
广东省机械进出口集团公司	广州市	广东省	(020)87771803
China National Machinery Equipment Import & Export Corporation	Beijing	Beijing	(010)63474506
中国机械设备进出口总公司	北京市	北京市	(010)63261865
Beijing Cellstar Co.,Ltd.	Beijing	Beijing	(010)64602050
北京蜂星事达电讯有限公司	北京市	北京市	(010)64672648

3523: Forging and Pressing Equipment 锻压设备制造业

The industry accounts for 0.061% of the total revenue of China's industrial sector in 2002. The rate of return on assets is 2.01%. 79.82% of all firms in the industry made a profit while 20.18% had negative returns.The top province in terms of the industry's revenue is Jiangsu, accounting for 31.74% of the total revenue.
2002年本行业收入占全行业的0.061%，资产利润率为2.01%。79.82%的企业赢利，20.18%的企业亏损。收入最高的省为江苏省，占本行业的31.74%。

	Total number of firms 企业总数	Total number of employees 职工总数	Total revenue (Mil.RMB) 总销售收入 (百万元)	Total profit (Mil.RMB) 总利润 (百万元)	Return on assets 资产利润率 (%)	Return on equity 权益利润率 (%)	Labour productivity ('000 RMB/ worker) 劳动生产率 (千元/人)	Debts/ assets 资产负债率 (%)	Total assets (Mil.RMB) 总资产 (百万元)
Industry Overall 行业总体	218	61,444	6,505	207	2.01	6.39	33.62	68.54	10,285

	Number of firms 企业个数	Average number of employees 平均职工人数	Average revenue ('000 RMB) 平均销售收入 (千元)	Average profit ('000 RMB) 平均利润 (千元)	Return on assets 资产利润率 (%)	Return on equity 权益利润率 (%)	Labour productivity ('000 RMB/ worker) 劳动生产率 (千元/人)	Debts/ assets 资产负债率 (%)	Average total assets ('000 RMB) 平均总资产 (千元)
By ownership 产业所有权									
State-owned 国有	43	391	22,169	-973	-1.44	-9.30	16.98	84.53	67,616
Collective-owned 集体	23	137	17,734	524	3.98	9.36	39.62	57.44	13,154
Foreign & Overseas Chinese Funded 三资	20	152	40,491	3,944	6.50	13.21	70.86	50.79	60,664
By regional distribution 地区分布									
Central-North 华北	21	281	16,838	-794	-1.61	-6.54	21.04	75.43	49,360
Beijing 北京	2	86	18,077	1,389	17.85	42.66	86.74	58.16	7,780
Tianjin 天津	9	188	17,735	263	0.43	1.89	36.56	77.11	60,756
Hebei 河北	6	327	21,476	470	2.23	8.34	30.31	73.22	21,051
Shanxi 山西	4	518	7,241	-6,157	-7.08	-27.61	-5.93	74.36	86,974
Inner Mongolia 内蒙古									
Northeast 东北	13	247	6,634	-1,495	-4.50		13.15	112.04	33,198
Liaoning 辽宁	9	244	7,008	-1,640	-4.81		14.81	108.79	34,130
Jilin 吉林	1	373	11,330	16	0.03		13.09	109.58	57,913
Heilongjiang 黑龙江	3	215	3,946	-1,562	-7.05		7.52	129.21	22,165
Central-East 华东	132	281	36,612	1,340	2.85	8.31	41.29	65.73	47,035
Shanghai 上海	13	227	36,039	-54	-0.07	-0.28	41.59	72.95	72,632
Jiangsu 江苏	54	243	38,233	1,496	4.33	14.90	44.40	70.91	34,502
Zhejiang 浙江	21	201	34,802	3,192	7.41	15.23	57.00	51.32	43,048
Anhui 安徽	11	206	22,212	640	1.91	4.56	27.08	58.17	33,592
Fujian 福建	5	140	27,522	789	2.10	2.90	54.37	27.68	37,630
Jiangxi 江西	2	515	4,300	-71	-0.41		0.99	152.83	17,418
Shandong 山东	26	493	45,319	727	0.99	3.06	37.90	67.55	73,260
Central-South 中南	39	265	25,800	1,804	3.70	12.38	28.28	70.08	48,709
Henan 河南	8	228	7,488	-114	-0.71	-57.53	13.00	98.77	16,107
Hubei 湖北	11	396	34,137	820	0.96	4.18	27.84	77.06	85,472
Hunan 湖南	4	277	16,609	-406	-1.06	-2.36	13.29	55.24	38,355
Guangdong 广东	13	191	36,709	4,994	10.65	25.55	49.30	58.32	46,907
Guangxi 广西	3	193	9,049	-345	-1.54	-3.66	18.43	58.05	22,466
Hainan 海南									
Southwest 西南	8	388	17,943	-423	-0.87	-1.82	14.75	52.36	48,697
Chongqing 重庆	3	333	20,358	328	0.61	0.95	25.80	35.70	53,381
Sichuan 四川	3	592	24,258	-1,566	-2.98	-6.50	9.68	54.06	52,478
Guizhou 贵州	1	153	5,120	1,562	2.87	5.82	7.94	50.62	54,346
Yunnan 云南	1	179	4,580	-1,228	-6.96		9.21	193.59	17,655
Tibet 西藏									
Northwest 西北	5	353	16,595	-217	-0.34	-0.72	16.24	52.66	63,837
Shaanxi 陕西	4	201	7,860	-311	-1.91	-4.70	12.13	59.32	16,282
Gansu 甘肃	1	960	51,537	160	0.06	0.13	19.68	50.96	254,059
Qinghai 青海									
Ningxia 宁夏									
Xinjiang 新疆									

3523: Forging and Pressing Equipment 锻压设备制造业

Year 年份	Number of firms 企业个数	Rate of change 变化率 (%)	Number of employees 职工人数 (人)	Rate of change 变化率 (%)	Total revenue (Mil. RMB) 总销售收入 (百万元)	Rate of change 变化率 (%)	Total profit (Mil RMB) 总利润 (百万元)	Rate of change 变化率 (%)
2000	191		65,545		5,053		142	
2001	211	10.47	63,894	-2.52	5,312	5.13	122	-14.08
2002	218	3.32	61,444	-3.83	6,505	22.46	207	69.67

Major Products 主要产品	Output 产量	Unit 单位
Forging & Pressing Equipment 锻压设备	36	10,000 Tons 万吨

10 Main Firms with Maximal Revenue (year founded) 收入最大的十家主要企业（创办年份）	City 城市	Province 省	Telephone/ fax 电话/传真	Number of employees 职工人数	Ownership 产业所有权	Revenue ('000 RMB) 销售收入 (千元)	Profit('000 RMB) (rank) 利润(千元) (排名)	Total assets ('000 RMB) 总资产 (千元)	Major products 主要产品
Ji'nan No.2 Machine Tool Group Co.,Ltd.	Jinan	Shandong	(0531)7963311		State Enterprises				Forging And Pressing Equipment
济南二机床集团有限公司(1937)	济南市	山东省	(0531)7961014	5,109	国有独资	462,260	11,911(6)	1,142,126	锻压设备
Jiangsu Yangli Forging Press Machine Tool Co., Ltd.	Yangzhou	Jiangsu	(0514)7461251		Private Owned				Pressure Machinery
江苏扬力锻压机床有限公司(1966)	扬州市	江苏省	(0514)7461090	1,510	私营企业	314,400	14,103(5)	299,060	压力机械
Nanjing Zhouyu Machine Tool Manufacturing Co., Ltd.	Nanjing	Jiangsu	(025)4165989		Private Owned				Plate Shearing & Press Braking Machinery
南京周宇机床制造有限公司(1998)	南京市	江苏省	(025)4165989	180	私营企业	165,100	7,200(14)	28,200	剪折机械
Nanjing Juwei Machinery Manufacturing Co., Ltd.	Nanjing	Jiangsu	(025)4165888		Private Owned				Plate Shearing & Press Braking Machinery
南京巨威机械制造有限公司(1970)	南京市	江苏省	(025)4165588	170	私营企业	152,950	7,010(15)	36,410	剪折机械
Guangdong Forging And Pressing Machine Tool Factory	Foshan	Guangdong	(0765)2634745		Limited-Liability				Mechanical Press Machine机
Co., Ltd.广东锻压机床厂有限公司(1958)	佛山市	广东省	(0765)2621475	650	有限公司	130,913	7,372(11)	194,149	械压力机
Huzhou Machine Tool Factory Co., Ltd.	Huzhou	Zhejiang	(0572)2024561		Limited-Liability				Hydraulic Press Machine
湖州机床厂有限公司(1996)	湖州市	浙江省	(0572)2023920	845	有限公司	129,302	7,334(12)	159,738	液压机
Jinfeng (China) Machinery Industry Co., Ltd.	Ningbo	Zhejiang	(0574)86303359		Foreign Funded				Forging And Pressing Equipment
金丰(中国)机械工业有限公司(1994)	宁波市	浙江省	(0574)86303709	286	外商投资	118,912	16,368(3)	274,908	锻压设备
Jiangyin Machinery ManufactureCo.,Lcd.	Wuxi	Jiangsu	(0510)6883331		Limited-Liability				Weaving Machinery
江阴市机械制造有限公司(1997)	无锡市	江苏省	(0510)6891584	553	有限公司	109,997	9,300(8)	153,524	纺织机械
Hubei Sanhuan Forging Press Machine Tool Co., Ltd.	Huangshi	Hubei	(0714)6330998		State-owned				Forging And Pressing Equipment
湖北三环锻压机床有限公司(1958)	黄石市	湖北省	(0714)6333212	837	国有企业	106,306	3,337(19)	307,112	锻压设备
Jiangsu Jinfangyuan Group Yangzhou Forging And Pressing Machine	Yangzhou	Jiangsu	(0514)7501129		Limited-Liability				Mechanical Press Machine机
Tool Co., Ltd.江苏金方圆集团扬州锻压机床有限公司(1958)	扬州市	江苏省	(0514)7501570	525	有限公司	100,128	4,022(26)	74,145	械压力机

Top 10 Cities by Revenue 销售收入排名前10位城市	Province 省	Market share 市场份额 (%)	Number of firms 企业个数
Yangzhou 扬州市	Jiangsu 江苏省	11.54	13
Nanjing 南京市	Jiangsu 江苏省	7.99	8
Jinan 济南市	Shandong 山东省	7.51	2
Shanghai 上海市	Shanghai 上海市	7.20	13
Wuxi 无锡市	Jiangsu 江苏省	4.18	11
Ningbo 宁波市	Zhejiang 浙江省	3.66	6
Foshan 佛山市	Guangdong 广东省	3.41	4
Shaoxing 绍兴市	Zhejiang 浙江省	3.32	7
Nantong 南通市	Jiangsu 江苏省	3.20	12
Xuzhou 徐州市	Jiangsu 江苏省	2.76	2

10 Major Wholesalers 十家主要批发商	City 城市	Province 省	Telephone/Fax 电话/传真
SU MEC	Nanjing	Jiangsu	(025)4511888
中设江苏机械设备进出口（集团）公司	南京市	江苏省	(025)4411772
China Poster Mobile Communications Equipment Co.,Ltd.	Beijing	Beijing	(010)66426993
中邮普泰移动通信设备股份有限公司	北京市	北京市	(010)66426837
Sino Kama Co., Ltd.	Shanghai	Shanghai	(021)62031188
中泰凯马股份有限公司	上海市	上海市	(021)62030851
China Huayuan Group Co.,Ltd.	Shanghai	Shanghai	(021)62031188
中国华源集团有限公司	上海市	上海市	(021)62032288
Zhejiang Crand Imp.& Exp.Co.,Ltd.	Ningbo	Zhejiang	(0574)87720170
浙江远大进出口有限公司	宁波市	浙江省	(0574)87723350
Shandong Machinery Import & Export Group Corporation	Qingdao	Shandong	(0532)2661628
山东省机械进出口集团公司	青岛市	山东省	(0532)2991655
Qingdao Haier International Trade Co.,Ltd.	Qingdao	Shandong	(0532)8938337
青岛海尔国际贸易有限公司	青岛市	山东省	(0532)8939494
Guangdong Machinery Import & Export Group Corporation	Guangzhou	Guangdong	(020)87782168
广东省机械进出口集团公司	广州市	广东省	(020)87771803
China National Machinery Equipment Import & Export Corporation	Beijing	Beijing	(010)63474506
中国机械设备进出口总公司	北京市	北京市	(010)63261865
Beijing Cellstar Co.,Ltd.	Beijing	Beijing	(010)64602050
北京蜂星事达电讯有限公司	北京市	北京市	(010)64672648

3525: Casting Machinery 铸造机械制造业

The industry accounts for 0.023% of the total revenue of China's industrial sector in 2002. The rate of return on assets is 3.38%. 83.57% of all firms in the industry made a profit while 16.43% had negative returns.The top province in terms of the industry's revenue is Shandong, accounting for 25.27% of the total revenue.
2002年本行业收入占全行业的0.023%，资产利润率为3.38%。83.57%的企业赢利，16.43%的企业亏损。收入最高的省为山东省，占本行业的25.27%。

	Total number of firms 企业总数	Total number of employees 职工总数	Total revenue (Mil.RMB) 总销售收入（百万元）	Total profit (Mil.RMB) 总利润（百万元）	Return on assets 资产利润率（%）	Return on equity 权益利润率（%）	Labour productivity ('000 RMB/worker) 劳动生产率（千元/人）	Debts/assets 资产负债率（%）	Total assets (Mil.RMB) 总资产（百万元）
Industry Overall 行业总体	140	27,547	2,452	98	3.38	8.39	29.17	59.73	2,905

	Number of firms 企业个数	Average number of employees 平均职工人数	Average revenue ('000 RMB) 平均销售收入（千元）	Average profit ('000 RMB) 平均利润（千元）	Return on assets 资产利润率（%）	Return on equity 权益利润率（%）	Labour productivity ('000 RMB/worker) 劳动生产率（千元/人）	Debts/assets 资产负债率（%）	Average total assets ('000 RMB) 平均总资产（千元）
By ownership 产业所有权									
State-owned 国有	15	280	15,806	-2,053	-4.45	-21.54	17.71	79.34	46,144
Collective-owned 集体	42	241	17,687	717	4.02	10.51	23.83	61.78	17,838
Foreign & Overseas Chinese Funded 三资	17	101	23,461	3,702	13.28	20.51	70.98	35.27	27,882
By regional distribution 地区分布									
Central-North 华北	23	295	9,224	-71	-0.32	-0.74	11.41	56.66	22,063
Beijing 北京	6	127	12,064	-1,027	-4.08	-5.48	28.68	25.56	25,160
Tianjin 天津	2	100	17,360	2,480	29.77	67.12	65.70	55.64	8,330
Hebei 河北	9	427	7,819	-241	-0.75	-3.48	7.59	78.46	32,142
Shanxi 山西	6	332	5,779	291	3.45	4.61	6.71	25.20	8,426
Inner Mongolia 内蒙古									
Northeast 东北	13	194	8,504	196	1.40	5.39	16.43	73.93	13,950
Liaoning 辽宁	9	171	9,018	98	0.58	2.59	20.69	77.61	16,968
Jilin 吉林	3	103	5,067	320	6.50	30.84	13.16	78.92	4,927
Heilongjiang 黑龙江	1	679	14,191	702	5.06	7.03	8.26	27.98	13,864
Central-East 华东	64	172	22,288	1,149	5.37	13.89	39.15	61.34	21,396
Shanghai 上海	11	136	25,748	5,713	17.60	31.30	62.55	43.77	32,462
Jiangsu 江苏	20	189	21,669	663	3.84	11.24	30.40	65.84	17,269
Zhejiang 浙江	5	101	12,742	474	5.82	19.74	29.02	70.50	8,142
Anhui 安徽	1	51	5,145	180	4.76	7.76	40.20	38.62	3,780
Fujian 福建	2	51	7,848	687	21.22	28.29	58.20	24.97	3,235
Jiangxi 江西	1	142	5,500	369	11.68	15.50	19.13	24.63	3,159
Shandong 山东	24	205	25,823	-287	-1.12	-3.64	39.98	69.15	25,532
Central-South 中南	28	108	13,777	624	5.53	9.78	46.15	43.42	11,284
Henan 河南	14	101	14,905	667	5.29	9.08	56.25	41.79	12,615
Hubei 湖北	4	120	10,033	452	5.05	7.11	44.10	28.98	8,961
Hunan 湖南									
Guangdong 广东	9	82	12,363	616	6.20	12.30	41.75	49.58	9,933
Guangxi 广西	1	400	25,672	786	5.57	14.52	20.84	61.62	14,100
Hainan 海南									
Southwest 西南	8	437	34,348	991	1.85	5.07	29.18	63.46	53,565
Chongqing 重庆	1	50	3,468	19	0.36	1.05	29.14	65.48	5,258
Sichuan 四川	5	628	51,568	1,910	2.42	6.20	30.36	61.05	79,067
Guizhou 贵州									
Yunnan 云南	2	151	6,739	-819	-5.87	-207.08	16.85	97.17	13,962
Tibet 西藏									
Northwest 西北	4	174	10,614	-421	-1.65	-4.46	16.84	63.02	25,475
Shaanxi 陕西	2	220	18,778	126	0.56	0.70	23.26	20.17	22,456
Gansu 甘肃	1	220	3,289	-1,873	-3.73		5.38	103.43	50,260
Qinghai 青海									
Ningxia 宁夏									
Xinjiang 新疆	1	37	1,610	-61	-0.91	-1.72	8.81	47.14	6,727

3525: Casting Machinery 铸造机械制造业

Year 年份	Number of firms 企业个数	Rate of change 变化率 (%)	Number of employees 职工人数 (人)	Rate of change 变化率 (%)	Total revenue (Mil. RMB) 总销售收入 (百万元)	Rate of change 变化率 (%)	Total profit (Mil RMB) 总利润 (百万元)	Rate of change 变化率 (%)
2000	96		25,699		3,373		136	
2001	125	30.21	25,561	-0.54	2,156	-36.08	66	-51.47
2002	140	12.00	27,547	7.77	2,452	13.73	98	48.48

Major Products 主要产品	Output 产量	Unit 单位
Casting Machinery 铸造机械	19,441	Unit 台
Casting 铸件	775	10,000 Tons 万吨

10 Main Firms with Maximal Revenue (year founded) 收入最大的十家主要企业（创办年份）	City 城市	Province 省	Telephone/fax 电话/传真	Number of employees 职工人数	Ownership 产业所有权	Revenue ('000 RMB) 销售收入 (千元)	Profit('000 RMB) (rank) 利润(千元) (排名)	Total assets ('000 RMB) 总资产 (千元)	Major products 主要产品
Qingdao Casting Machinery Group Company	Qingdao	Shandong	(0532)3832156		State-owned				Foundry Machinery
青岛铸造机械集团公司(1952)	青岛市	山东省	(0532)3835495	1,236	国有企业	107,447	-	312,176	铸造机械
ShangHai Atech Machinery Co.,Ltd.	Shanghai	Shanghai	(021)37643539		Overseas Chinese-funded				Clod Storage Die-casting Machine冷
上海一达机械有限公司(1995)	上海市	上海市	(021)37643555	213	港澳台资	73,969	25,551(1)	104,655	室压铸机
Dezhou Changhong Machinery Manufacturing Co., Ltd.	Dezhou	Shandong	(0534)2356745		Limited-Liability				Casting
德州长虹机械制造有限公司(1998)	德州市	山东省	(0534)2358346	233	有限公司	65,449	4,063(7)	36,493	铸件
Jiangning Lukou Machinery Factory	Nanjing	Jiangsu	(025)2770693		Private Enterprises				Ironed Cap
江宁区禄口机械厂(1967)	南京市	江苏省	(025)2770693	196	私营独资	62,710	1,970(20)	14,180	铁帽
Qingdao Tiantai Machinery Co., Ltd.	Qingdao	Shandong	(0532)6383130		Overseas Chinese-funded				Foundry Machinery
青岛天泰机械有限公司(1992)	青岛市	山东省	(0532)6383666	320	港澳台资	61,000	3,640(10)	24,410	铸造机械
Gongyi Xinda Hydraulic Press Machinery Co., Ltd.	Zhengzhou	Henan	(0371)4352387		Joint Stock				Machine
巩义市信达液压机械有限公司(1958)	郑州市	河南省	(0371)4351191	130	股份制	56,672	1,553(24)	5,865	机械
Shanghai Die-casting Machine Factory	Shanghai	Shanghai	(021)57822541		State-owned				Foundry Machinery
上海压铸机厂(1945)	上海市	上海市	(021)57820229	222	国有企业	49,713	164(79)	39,892	铸造机械
Qixian Huangdong Machinery Factory	Hebi	Henan	(0392)7888868		Collective-owned				Ball Segment
淇县黄洞机械厂(1975)	鹤壁市	河南省		105	集体企业	49,686	3,519(11)	5,930	球段
Shanghai Haili Casting Co., Ltd.	Shanghai	Shanghai	(021)57319182		Limited-Liability				Engine Parts机
上海海立铸造有限公司(1991)	上海市	上海市	(021)57321183	360	有限公司	44,979	5,484(4)	55,550	械零部件
Shanghai Chunri Machinery Industry Co., Ltd.	Shanghai	Shanghai	(021)59742888		Overseas Chinese-funded				Forging Machine
上海春日机械工业有限公司(1999)	上海市	上海市	(021)59742882	108	港澳台资	40,220	5,066(5)	64,509	注锻机

Top 10 Cities by Revenue 销售收入排名前10位城市	Province 省	Market share 市场份额 (%)	Number of firms 企业个数
Qingdao 青岛市	Shandong 山东省	13.47	13
Shanghai 上海市	Shanghai 上海市	11.55	11
Chengdu 成都市	Sichuan 四川省	10.31	4
Yancheng 盐城市	Jiangsu 江苏省	4.77	4
Wuxi 无锡市	Jiangsu 江苏省	4.68	6
Weihai 威海市	Shandong 山东省	3.76	2
Dezhou 德州市	Shandong 山东省	3.46	3
Beijing 北京市	Beijing 北京市	2.95	6
Nanjing 南京市	Jiangsu 江苏省	2.56	1
Zhengzhou 郑州市	Henan 河南省	2.51	2

10 Major Wholesalers 十家主要批发商	City 城市	Province 省	Telephone/Fax 电话/传真
SU MEC	Nanjing	Jiangsu	(025)4511888
中设江苏机械设备进出口（集团）公司	南京市	江苏省	(025)4411772
China Poster Mobile Communications Equipment Co.,Ltd.	Beijing	Beijing	(010)66426993
中邮普泰移动通信设备股份有限公司	北京市	北京市	(010)66426837
Sino Kama Co., Ltd.	Shanghai	Shanghai	(021)62031188
中泰凯马股份有限公司	上海市	上海市	(021)62030851
China Huayuan Group Co.,Ltd.	Shanghai	Shanghai	(021)62031188
中国华源集团有限公司	上海市	上海市	(021)62032288
Zhejiang Crand Imp.& Exp.Co.,Ltd.	Ningbo	Zhejiang	(0574)87720170
浙江远大进出口有限公司	宁波市	浙江省	(0574)87723350
Shandong Machinery Import & Export Group Corporation	Qingdao	Shandong	(0532)2661628
山东省机械进出口集团公司	青岛市	山东省	(0532)2991655
Qingdao Haier International Trade Co.,Ltd.	Qingdao	Shandong	(0532)8938337
青岛海尔国际贸易有限公司	青岛市	山东省	(0532)8939494
Guangdong Machinery Import & Export Group Corporation	Guangzhou	Guangdong	(020)87782168
广东省机械进出口集团公司	广州市	广东省	(020)87771803
China National Machinery Equipment Import & Export Corporation	Beijing	Beijing	(010)63474506
中国机械设备进出口总公司	北京市	北京市	(010)63261865
Beijing Cellstar Co.,Ltd.	Beijing	Beijing	(010)64602050
北京蜂星事达电讯有限公司	北京市	北京市	(010)64672648

3526: Machine Tools Parts 机床附件制造业

The industry accounts for 0.015% of the total revenue of China's industrial sector in 2002. The rate of return on assets is 1.52%. 74.07% of all firms in the industry made a profit while 25.93% had negative returns.The top province in terms of the industry's revenue is Shandong, accounting for 27.08% of the total revenue.
2002年本行业收入占全行业的0.015%，资产利润率为1.52%。74.07%的企业赢利，25.93%的企业亏损。收入最高的省为山东省，占本行业的27.08%。

	Total number of firms 企业总数	Total number of employees 职工总数	Total revenue (Mil.RMB) 总销售收入 (百万元)	Total profit (Mil.RMB) 总利润 (百万元)	Return on assets 资产利润率 (%)	Return on equity 权益利润率 (%)	Labour productivity ('000 RMB/ worker) 劳动生产率 (千元/人)	Debts/ assets 资产负债率 (%)	Total assets (Mil.RMB) 总资产 (百万元)
Industry Overall 行业总体	108	20,278	1,633	42	1.52	4.16	27.62	63.53	2,739

	Number of firms 企业个数	Average number of employees 平均职工人数	Average revenue ('000 RMB) 平均销售收入（千元）	Average profit ('000 RMB) 平均利润 (千元)	Return on assets 资产利润率 (%)	Return on equity 权益利润率 (%)	Labour productivity ('000 RMB/ worker) 劳动生产率 (千元/人)	Debts/ assets 资产负债率 (%)	Average total assets ('000 RMB) 平均总资产 (千元)
By ownership 产业所有权									
State-owned 国有	28	230	9,601	-473	-1.74	-6.44	15.13	72.89	27,083
Collective-owned 集体	20	106	11,413	216	2.68	9.03	34.45	70.27	8,062
Foreign & Overseas Chinese Funded 三资	16	109	22,312	2,463	5.79	10.53	66.30	45.03	42,575
By regional distribution 地区分布									
Central-North 华北	18	281	12,155	-1,305	-2.98	-10.65	21.20	71.99	43,732
Beijing 北京	6	70	6,835	-133	-1.15	-2.20	32.65	47.59	11,534
Tianjin 天津	6	168	9,434	-1,154	-2.42	-9.47	30.82	74.47	47,725
Hebei 河北	4	105	7,097	353	4.25	6.75	28.45	37.08	8,302
Shanxi 山西	1	323	4,495	-1,122	-4.42		6.46	152.43	25,402
Inner Mongolia 内蒙古	1	2,895	88,285	-16,047	-4.30	-15.50	16.79	72.25	373,005
Northeast 东北	8	131	7,026	88	0.62	1.67	15.68	62.71	14,091
Liaoning 辽宁	5	127	7,606	-234	-1.59	-5.69	18.40	72.12	14,758
Jilin 吉林	3	137	6,059	625	4.81	8.73	11.47	44.88	12,981
Heilongjiang 黑龙江									
Central-East 华东	60	194	19,721	1,149	4.64	10.03	32.26	53.76	24,780
Shanghai 上海	12	85	12,190	1,052	4.09	10.16	48.59	59.76	25,718
Jiangsu 江苏	16	121	23,607	2,333	12.63	18.90	57.20	33.17	18,473
Zhejiang 浙江	11	176	19,269	1,307	7.21	13.25	36.48	45.62	18,134
Anhui 安徽	1	58	1,378	1	0.03	0.06	15.41	57.34	3,938
Fujian 福建									
Jiangxi 江西	2	282	1,835	-317	-2.54	-3.61	3.52	29.58	12,462
Shandong 山东	18	340	24,569	291	0.80	2.20	23.18	63.62	36,349
Central-South 中南	15	94	9,992	101	0.62	2.35	37.84	73.58	16,187
Henan 河南	4	106	15,927	460	2.91	10.56	46.00	72.48	15,830
Hubei 湖北	4	92	2,827	251	1.78	15.12	17.31	88.20	14,067
Hunan 湖南	3	96	5,285	-51	-0.77	-2.36	17.23	67.39	6,571
Guangdong 广东	4	81	14,754	-296	-1.14	-3.52	68.64	67.47	25,876
Guangxi 广西									
Hainan 海南									
Southwest 西南	3	234	2,566	-2,065	-8.77		1.17	132.38	23,560
Chongqing 重庆									
Sichuan 四川	1	311	5,648	-4,024	-8.38		-0.13	136.95	48,035
Guizhou 贵州	1	303	378	-1,872	-10.42		0.47	139.23	17,962
Yunnan 云南	1	87	1,672	-300	-6.40	-15.73	8.29	59.29	4,684
Tibet 西藏									
Northwest 西北	4	109	4,368	36	0.37	1.83	16.85	79.96	9,656
Shaanxi 陕西									
Gansu 甘肃	4	109	4,368	36	0.37	1.83	16.85	79.96	9,656
Qinghai 青海									
Ningxia 宁夏									
Xinjiang 新疆									

3526: Machine Tools Parts 机床附件制造业

Year 年份	Number of firms 企业个数	Rate of change 变化率 (%)	Number of employees 职工人数 (人)	Rate of change 变化率 (%)	Total revenue (Mil. RMB) 总销售收入 (百万元)	Rate of change 变化率 (%)	Total profit (Mil RMB) 总利润 (百万元)	Rate of change 变化率 (%)
2000	92		24,946		1,502		55	
2001	107	16.30	27,127	8.74	1,529	1.80	77	40.00
2002	108	0.93	20,278	-25.25	1,633	6.80	42	-45.45

Major Products 主要产品	Output 产量	Unit 单位
Gear 齿轮	180,440	Ton 吨

10 Main Firms with Maximal Revenue (year founded) 收入最大的十家主要企业（创办年份）	City 城市	Province 省	Telephone/fax 电话/传真	Number of employees 职工人数	Ownership 产业所有权	Revenue ('000 RMB) 销售收入 (千元)	Profit('000 RMB) (rank) 利润(千元) (排名)	Total assets ('000 RMB) 总资产 (千元)	Major products 主要产品
Jacobs Chuck Manufacturing (Suzhou) Co., Ltd.	Suzhou	Jiangsu	(0512)67616165		Foreign Funded				Drills
捷可勃斯夹头(苏州)有限公司(1996)	苏州市	江苏省	(0512)67612066	414	外商投资	144,644	29,589(1)	180,494	钻具
Taizhou San'ou Drill Chunk Manufacturing Co., Ltd.	Taizhou	Zhejiang	(0576)2512227		Limited-Liability				Drills Collet
台州市三鸥钻夹头制造有限公司(1998)	台州市	浙江省	(0576)2512198	1,120	有限公司	80,136	4,207(4)	96,026	钻夹头
Yangzhou Jinyun Plate Welding Machinery Co., Ltd.	Yangzhou	Jiangsu	(0514)7511318		Private Owned				Shield
扬州金运钣焊机械有限公司(1987)	扬州市	江苏省	(0514)7511318	40	私营企业	57,830	1,000(19)	16,487	护罩
Yantai Universal Machine Tool Accessory Co.,Ltd.	Yantai	Shandong	(0535)6535511		State-owned				Mechanical Graduation Head机
烟台环球机床附件有限公司(1950)	烟台市	山东省	(0535)6530527	1,453	国有企业	48,158	-	233,474	械分度头
Jiyang Tongda Machinery Factory	Jinan	Shandong	(0531)4520030		Private Enterprises				Machine Tool Fittings
济阳县通达机械厂(1973)	济南市	山东省		174	私营独资	45,760	2,180(7)	3,310	机床配件
Henan Yingyang Forging And Pressing Machinery Equipment	Zhengzhou	Henan	(0371)4859033		Collective-owned				Punch
Factory河南省荥阳市锻压机械设备厂(1996)	郑州市	河南省	(0371)4859626	148	集体企业	44,725	747(27)	4,266	冲压机
YanTai No.2 Machine Tool Accessories Factory	Yantai	Shandong	(0535)6245230		State-owned				Chuck
烟台第二机床附件厂(1966)	烟台市	山东省	(0535)6242469	453	国有企业	32,197	-	43,875	卡盘
Linqing Hongxin Machine Tool Co., Ltd.	Liaocheng	Shandong	(0635)2319769		Joint Stock				Multifunction Magnetic Cupule多功能
临清宏鑫机床有限责任公司(1955)	聊城市	山东省	(0635)2319753	359	股份制	30,660	1,502(10)	26,669	磁力吸盘
Yongjia Liubian Machinery Lubricating Co., Ltd.	Wenzhou	Zhejiang	(0577)67357733		Foreign Funded				Strength Of The Hand Pump
永嘉县流遍机械润滑有限公司(1995)	温州市	浙江省	(0577)67352180	108	外商投资	28,248	5,481(3)	23,899	手动泵
Mogan Rolling Mill (Shanghai)Co., Ltd.	Shanghai	Shanghai	(021)34073293		Foreign Funded				Rolling Machine
摩根轧机配件(上海)有限公司(1997)	上海市	上海市	(021)34073324	101	外商投资	28,176	9,139(2)	82,478	轧机

Top 10 Cities by Revenue 销售收入排名前10位城市	Province 省	Market share 市场份额 (%)	Number of firms 企业个数
Yantai 烟台市	Shandong 山东省	13.53	7
Suzhou 苏州市	Jiangsu 江苏省	10.07	3
Shanghai 上海市	Shanghai 上海市	8.96	12
Taizhou 台州市	Zhejiang 浙江省	6.25	2
Huhhot 呼和浩特市	Inner Mongolia 内蒙古	5.41	1
Yangzhou 扬州市	Jiangsu 江苏省	3.54	1
Tianjin 天津市	Tianjin 天津市	3.47	6
Nanjing 南京市	Jiangsu 江苏省	3.44	3
Taian 泰安市	Shandong 山东省	3.26	2
Jinan 济南市	Shandong 山东省	2.80	1

10 Major Wholesalers 十家主要批发商	City 城市	Province 省	Telephone/Fax 电话/传真
SU MEC	Nanjing	Jiangsu	(025)4511888
中设江苏机械设备进出口（集团）公司	南京市	江苏省	(025)4411772
China Poster Mobile Communications Equipment Co.,Ltd.	Beijing	Beijing	(010)66426993
中邮普泰移动通信设备股份有限公司	北京市	北京市	(010)66426837
Sino Kama Co., Ltd.	Shanghai	Shanghai	(021)62031188
中泰凯马股份有限公司	上海市	上海市	(021)62030851
China Huayuan Group Co.,Ltd.	Shanghai	Shanghai	(021)62031188
中国华源集团有限公司	上海市	上海市	(021)62032288
Zhejiang Crand Imp.& Exp.Co.,Ltd.	Ningbo	Zhejiang	(0574)87720170
浙江远大进出口有限公司	宁波市	浙江省	(0574)87723350
Shandong Machinery Import & Export Group Corporation	Qingdao	Shandong	(0532)2661628
山东省机械进出口集团公司	青岛市	山东省	(0532)2991655
Qingdao Haier International Trade Co.,Ltd.	Qingdao	Shandong	(0532)8938337
青岛海尔国际贸易有限公司	青岛市	山东省	(0532)8939494
Guangdong Machinery Import & Export Group Corporation	Guangzhou	Guangdong	(020)87782168
广东省机械进出口集团公司	广州市	广东省	(020)87771803
China National Machinery Equipment Import & Export Corporation	Beijing	Beijing	(010)63474506
中国机械设备进出口总公司	北京市	北京市	(010)63261865
Beijing Cellstar Co.,Ltd.	Beijing	Beijing	(010)64602050
北京蜂星事达电讯有限公司	北京市	北京市	(010)64672648

3529: Other Metal Processing Machinery 其他金属加工机械制造业

The industry accounts for 0.073% of the total revenue of China's industrial sector in 2002. The rate of return on assets is 3.14%. 80.54% of all firms in the industry made a profit while 19.46% had negative returns.The top province in terms of the industry's revenue is Shandong, accounting for 20.47% of the total revenue.
2002年本行业收入占全行业的0.073%，资产利润率为3.14%。80.54%的企业赢利，19.46%的企业亏损。收入最高的省为山东省，占本行业的20.47%。

	Total number of firms 企业总数	Total number of employees 职工总数	Total revenue (Mil.RMB) 总销售收入（百万元）	Total profit (Mil.RMB) 总利润（百万元）	Return on assets 资产利润率（%）	Return on equity 权益利润率（%）	Labour productivity ('000 RMB/ worker) 劳动生产率（千元/人）	Debts/ assets 资产负债率（%）	Total assets (Mil.RMB) 总资产（百万元）
Industry Overall 行业总体	334	56,606	7,834	305	3.14	6.89	43.16	54.45	9,730

	Number of firms 企业个数	Average number of employees 平均职工人数	Average revenue ('000 RMB) 平均销售收入（千元）	Average profit ('000 RMB) 平均利润（千元）	Return on assets 资产利润率（%）	Return on equity 权益利润率（%）	Labour productivity ('000 RMB/ worker) 劳动生产率（千元/人）	Debts/ assets 资产负债率（%）	Average total assets ('000 RMB) 平均总资产（千元）
By ownership 产业所有权									
State-owned 国有	67	274	18,072	-249	-0.42	-0.78	24.48	46.24	59,559
Collective-owned 集体	69	145	16,170	659	5.22	18.90	34.14	72.36	12,614
Foreign & Overseas Chinese Funded 三资	45	120	39,601	2,699	7.65	17.58	85.42	56.49	35,290
By regional distribution 地区分布									
Central-North 华北	62	127	11,253	208	1.32	3.66	22.57	63.87	15,765
Beijing 北京	16	60	16,537	536	3.74	12.86	70.11	70.95	14,332
Tianjin 天津	32	42	6,357	547	17.54	38.47	8.66	54.40	3,119
Hebei 河北	4	259	10,683	-544	-1.16	-2.18	22.26	46.66	46,838
Shanxi 山西	7	461	17,854	-1,068	-2.16	-8.33	15.11	74.10	49,497
Inner Mongolia 内蒙古	3	439	20,665	-1,166	-3.06	-6.82	20.48	55.18	38,165
Northeast 东北	26	347	35,941	557	0.47	0.72	42.88	34.58	118,775
Liaoning 辽宁	19	188	13,105	41	0.21	0.93	30.82	77.77	20,154
Jilin 吉林	5	996	134,065	2,670	0.50	0.69	53.30	28.19	535,975
Heilongjiang 黑龙江	2	227	7,569	170	1.34	3.17	23.76	57.65	12,674
Central-East 华东	163	155	30,466	1,442	5.84	16.70	59.22	65.02	24,693
Shanghai 上海	46	84	18,266	700	3.96	8.80	72.44	54.96	17,671
Jiangsu 江苏	52	139	27,184	889	4.09	14.38	54.78	71.57	21,729
Zhejiang 浙江	26	177	33,072	2,693	8.16	19.82	41.69	58.82	32,993
Anhui 安徽	8	189	7,425	-784	-4.87		12.85	110.95	16,095
Fujian 福建	2	257	16,579	892	3.65	7.18	37.83	49.12	24,434
Jiangxi 江西	3	469	52,054	-542	-0.69	-3.23	18.03	78.53	78,261
Shandong 山东	26	238	61,677	3,568	11.43	30.30	91.72	62.28	31,228
Central-South 中南	49	147	16,943	642	3.17	8.76	33.75	63.79	20,231
Henan 河南	9	247	22,621	1,151	3.58	12.06	27.05	70.30	32,127
Hubei 湖北	6	115	7,890	450	6.07	16.89	25.14	64.06	7,419
Hunan 湖南	9	177	9,383	634	4.33	13.56	19.46	68.06	14,633
Guangdong 广东	23	113	21,506	554	2.44	6.00	51.62	59.31	22,715
Guangxi 广西	2	45	89	-40	-2.25	-3.30	0.71	31.65	1,776
Hainan 海南									
Southwest 西南	15	228	18,374	756	3.03	6.05	21.48	49.90	24,944
Chongqing 重庆	3	299	27,352	869	1.76	2.95	29.17	40.25	49,369
Sichuan 四川	9	219	19,137	983	4.56	9.46	21.67	51.85	21,580
Guizhou 贵州	3	181	7,106	-40	-0.38	-2.21	8.06	82.91	10,612
Yunnan 云南									
Tibet 西藏									
Northwest 西北	19	198	6,866				16.64	62.12	14,398
Shaanxi 陕西	1	179	10,318	110	0.16	0.20	16.92	19.30	68,296
Gansu 甘肃	18	200	6,674	-6	-0.06	-0.23	16.62	76.36	11,404
Qinghai 青海									
Ningxia 宁夏									
Xinjiang 新疆									

3529: Other Metal Processing Machinery 其他金属加工机械制造业

Year 年份	Number of firms 企业个数	Rate of change 变化率 (%)	Number of employees 职工人数 (人)	Rate of change 变化率 (%)	Total revenue (Mil. RMB) 总销售收入 (百万元)	Rate of change 变化率 (%)	Total profit (Mil RMB) 总利润 (百万元)	Rate of change 变化率 (%)
2000	325		68,712		5,908		165	
2001	352	8.31	61,873	-9.95	7,222	22.24	253	53.33
2002	334	-5.11	56,606	-8.51	7,834	8.47	305	20.55

Major Products 主要产品	Output 产量	Unit 单位

10 Main Firms with Maximal Revenue (year founded) 收入最大的十家主要企业（创办年份）	City 城市	Province 省	Telephone/fax 电话/传真	Number of employees 职工人数	Ownership 产业所有权	Revenue ('000 RMB) 销售收入 (千元)	Profit('000 RMB) (rank) 利润(千元) (排名)	Total assets ('000 RMB) 总资产 (千元)	Major products 主要产品
Rongcheng Daming Group Co., Ltd.	Weihai	Shandong	(0631)7771103		Joint Stock				Guard Against Theft Door
荣成大明集团有限公司(1996)	威海市	山东省	(0631)7771200	447	股份制	260,050	23,140(2)	52,030	防盗门
Qingdao INI Machinery Co.,Ltd.	Qingdao	Shandong	(0532)5261680		Foreign Funded				Forging and Casting
青岛爱恩耐机械有限公司(2000)	青岛市	山东省	(0532)5261677	40	外商投资	240,303	3,581(31)	98,193	铸锻件
Qingdao Zangnan Paper Products Machinery Factory	Qingdao	Shandong	(0532)4161036		Joint Stock				Package Machinery
青岛市藏南纸制品机械厂(1966)	青岛市	山东省	(0532)4161008	810	股份制	187,000	5,120(17)	30,500	包装机械
Katsushiro Machinery(ShanDong) Co.,Ltd.	Jining	Shandong	(0537)2363102		Foreign Funded				Steel Plate & Cutting Plate Materials钢
胜代机械（山东）有限公司(1997)	济宁市	山东省	(0537)2369206	206	外商投资	170,206	33,195(1)	118,939	板切板件
China Nucleus Industry General Company No.720 Factory	Nanchang	Jiangxi	(0791)3708901		State-owned				Filter
中国核工业总公司七二0厂(1969)	南昌市	江西省	(0791)3708720	1,209	国有企业	148,897	-	159,587	过滤机
Jiaonan Gaogezhuang Paper Board Box Equipment Factory	Qingdao	Shandong	(0532)4166188		Collective-owned				Single-side Corrugated Units单面
胶南市高戈庄纸箱设备厂(1975)	青岛市	山东省	(0532)4166075	552	集体企业	137,001	2,972(35)	16,670	瓦楞机组
Henan Yingwei Dongfeng Machinery Manufacturing Co., Ltd.	Nanyang	Henan	(0377)3297066		Foreign Funded				Liquided Gas Steel Bottle液
河南英威东风机械制造有限公司(1995)	南阳市	河南省		982	外商投资	127,519	9,938(7)	146,712	化气钢瓶
Xiaoshan Welding Machinery Manufacturing Factory	Hangzhou	Zhejiang	(0571)82610868		Private Enterprises				Building Machinery
杭州萧山焊接机械制造厂(1990)	杭州市	浙江省	(0571)82614456	120	私营独资	117,606	6,729(11)	83,343	建筑机械
Qingdao D & D Electric Machinery Technologies Co.,Ltd Machinery	Qingdao	Shandong	(0532)8377812		Private Owned				Bench Drill
Manufacturing Branch青岛地恩地机电科技股份有限公司机械制造分公司(1997)	青岛市	山东省	(0532)8374255	340	私营企业	100,000	1,220(73)	87,281	台钻
Changchun Saloon Car Muffler Factory	Changchun	Jilin	(0431)5383849		State-owned				
长春轿车消车消声器厂(1965)	长春市	吉林省	(0431)5304807	675	国有企业	78,581	1,100(78)	106,412	

Top 10 Cities by Revenue 销售收入排名前10位城市	Province 省	Market share 市场份额 (%)	Number of firms 企业个数
Shanghai 上海市	Shanghai 上海市	10.73	46
Qingdao 青岛市	Shandong 山东省	10.47	11
Wuxi 无锡市	Jiangsu 江苏省	7.12	16
Songyuan 松原市	Jilin 吉林省	6.97	1
Hangzhou 杭州市	Zhejiang 浙江省	5.31	10
Guangzhou 广州市	Guangdong 广东省	3.83	11
Weihai 威海市	Shandong 山东省	3.52	2
Beijing 北京市	Beijing 北京市	3.38	16
Ningbo 宁波市	Zhejiang 浙江省	2.95	6
Yangzhou 扬州市	Jiangsu 江苏省	2.92	6

10 Major Wholesalers 十家主要批发商	City 城市	Province 省	Telephone/Fax 电话/传真
SU MEC	Nanjing	Jiangsu	(025)4511888
中设江苏机械设备进出口（集团）公司	南京市	江苏省	(025)4411772
China Poster Mobile Communications Equipment Co.,Ltd.	Beijing	Beijing	(010)66426993
中邮普泰移动通信设备股份有限公司	北京市	北京市	(010)66426837
Sino Kama Co., Ltd.	Shanghai	Shanghai	(021)62031188
中泰凯马股份有限公司	上海市	上海市	(021)62030851
China Huayuan Group Co.,Ltd.	Shanghai	Shanghai	(021)62031188
中国华源集团有限公司	上海市	上海市	(021)62032288
Zhejiang Crand Imp.& Exp.Co.,Ltd.	Ningbo	Zhejiang	(0574)87720170
浙江远大进出口有限公司	宁波市	浙江省	(0574)87723350
Shandong Machinery Import & Export Group Corporation	Qingdao	Shandong	(0532)2661628
山东省机械进出口集团公司	青岛市	山东省	(0532)2991655
Qingdao Haier International Trade Co.,Ltd.	Qingdao	Shandong	(0532)8938337
青岛海尔国际贸易有限公司	青岛市	山东省	(0532)8939494
Guangdong Machinery Import & Export Group Corporation	Guangzhou	Guangdong	(020)87782168
广东省机械进出口集团公司	广州市	广东省	(020)87771803
China National Machinery Equipment Import & Export Corporation	Beijing	Beijing	(010)63474506
中国机械设备进出口总公司	北京市	北京市	(010)63261865
Beijing Cellstar Co.,Ltd.	Beijing	Beijing	(010)64602050
北京蜂星事达电讯有限公司	北京市	北京市	(010)64672648

3531: Hoisting and Conveying Equipment 起重运输设备制造业

The industry accounts for 0.487% of the total revenue of China's industrial sector in 2002. The rate of return on assets is 4.42%. 74.65% of all firms in the industry made a profit while 25.35% had negative returns.The top province in terms of the industry's revenue is Jiangsu, accounting for 25.46% of the total revenue.
2002年本行业收入占全行业的 0.487%，资产利润率为 4.42%。74.65%的企业赢利，25.35%的企业亏损。收入最高的省为江苏省，占本行业的25.46%。

	Total number of firms 企业总数	Total number of employees 职工总数	Total revenue (Mil.RMB) 总销售收入(百万元)	Total profit (Mil.RMB) 总利润(百万元)	Return on assets 资产利润率(%)	Return on equity 权益利润率(%)	Labour productivity ('000 RMB/worker) 劳动生产率(千元/人)	Debts/assets 资产负债率(%)	Total assets (Mil.RMB) 总资产(百万元)
Industry Overall 行业总体	635	211,934	52,273	2,788	4.42	13.40	60.08	66.99	63,039

	Number of firms 企业个数	Average number of employees 平均职工人数	Average revenue ('000 RMB) 平均销售收入(千元)	Average profit ('000 RMB) 平均利润(千元)	Return on assets 资产利润率(%)	Return on equity 权益利润率(%)	Labour productivity ('000 RMB/worker) 劳动生产率(千元/人)	Debts/assets 资产负债率(%)	Average total assets ('000 RMB) 平均总资产(千元)
By ownership 产业所有权									
State-owned 国有	119	449	41,832	-2,524	-2.62	-14.58	22.51	82.04	96,375
Collective-owned 集体	98	175	29,838	1,169	4.93	16.44	56.05	70.03	23,733
Foreign & Overseas Chinese Funded 三资	82	398	257,108	25,191	8.59	21.28	164.12	59.66	293,382
By regional distribution 地区分布									
Central-North 华北	65	377	68,387	1,030	1.01	4.31	45.31	76.58	101,996
Beijing 北京	17	344	69,117	-6,127	-4.81	-22.65	50.27	78.76	127,303
Tianjin 天津	22	308	108,956	7,632	8.89	32.62	81.11	72.76	85,882
Hebei 河北	20	467	41,584	336	0.29	1.11	26.90	73.74	115,814
Shanxi 山西	4	505	7,433	-653	-1.66		5.29	153.52	39,436
Inner Mongolia 内蒙古	2	268	5,861	-470	-0.92	-1.73	10.68	46.87	51,089
Northeast 东北	47	324	44,726	-35	-0.05	-0.32	36.71	84.89	74,228
Liaoning 辽宁	30	275	57,334	1,344	1.63	5.95	59.71	72.68	82,626
Jilin 吉林	9	331	32,542	-42	-0.08	-0.42	19.94	81.41	53,515
Heilongjiang 黑龙江	8	499	11,150	-5,202	-7.88		1.69	145.35	66,035
Central-East 华东	348	336	105,058	7,292	6.49	17.52	73.21	62.97	112,434
Shanghai 上海	81	315	144,489	14,849	6.77	17.49	103.23	61.29	219,281
Jiangsu 江苏	105	383	126,742	5,219	5.19	18.20	65.63	71.46	100,495
Zhejiang 浙江	88	212	59,270	5,926	13.53	27.79	79.31	51.32	43,803
Anhui 安徽	13	517	106,075	8,850	6.97	9.89	69.04	29.51	126,935
Fujian 福建	8	293	166,717	-842	-0.37	-1.52	90.38	76.01	230,310
Jiangxi 江西	7	700	37,257	-939	-0.54	-1.95	16.87	72.09	172,290
Shandong 山东	46	402	73,028	3,558	7.24	20.89	56.36	65.33	49,127
Central-South 中南	131	287	62,331	2,112	2.59	6.68	59.33	61.20	81,490
Henan 河南	35	260	23,908	178	0.47	1.59	35.34	70.43	37,962
Hubei 湖北	16	468	25,054	-1,153	-1.64	-4.65	21.72	64.80	70,510
Hunan 湖南	25	276	43,052	-439	-0.43	-0.99	36.35	56.40	102,077
Guangdong 广东	50	248	113,453	6,079	5.64	13.42	116.68	57.99	107,817
Guangxi 广西	5	341	35,756	-819	-1.49		28.80	109.31	55,117
Hainan 海南									
Southwest 西南	26	463	26,693	-952	-1.29	-15.25	18.30	91.55	73,927
Chongqing 重庆	11	229	18,001	-1,605	-5.21	-29.92	16.70	82.60	30,821
Sichuan 四川	10	856	46,967	-601	-0.47		19.84	110.63	127,200
Guizhou 贵州	2	131	7,303	92	0.81	2.03	17.10	59.98	11,245
Yunnan 云南	3	231	3,909	-426	-0.44	-0.56	5.71	20.45	96,191
Tibet 西藏									
Northwest 西北	18	318	17,027	-3,690	-5.55		10.26	105.52	66,442
Shaanxi 陕西	6	422	26,747	-3,671	-4.22		11.96	118.00	86,985
Gansu 甘肃	3	201	4,504	-635	-4.99	-9.95	9.01	49.86	12,728
Qinghai 青海									
Ningxia 宁夏	6	353	15,433	-3,678	-3.83		4.03	102.06	96,043
Xinjiang 新疆	3	160	13,299	-6,807	-34.26	-98.53	30.30	65.23	19,869

3531: Hoisting and Conveying Equipment 起重运输设备制造业

Year 年份	Number of firms 企业个数	Rate of change 变化率 (%)	Number of employees 职工人数 (人)	Rate of change 变化率 (%)	Total revenue (Mil. RMB) 总销售收入 (百万元)	Rate of change 变化率 (%)	Total profit (Mil RMB) 总利润 (百万元)	Rate of change 变化率 (%)
2000	494		217,753		30,716		1,088	
2001	561	13.56	213,111	-2.13	41,180	34.07	2,044	87.87
2002	635	13.19	211,934	-0.55	52,273	26.94	2,788	36.40

Major Products 主要产品	Output 产量	Unit 单位
Hoisting Equipment 起重设备	77	10,000 Tons 万吨

10 Main Firms with Maximal Revenue (year founded) 收入最大的十家主要企业（创办年份）	City 城市	Province 省	Telephone/fax 电话/传真	Number of employees 职工人数	Ownership 产业所有权	Revenue ('000 RMB) 销售收入 (千元)	Profit('000 RMB) (rank) 利润(千元) (排名)	Total assets ('000 RMB) 总资产 (千元)	Major products 主要产品
Xuzhou Construction Machinery Group Co., Ltd. 徐州工程机械集团有限公司(1989)	Xuzhou 徐州市	Jiangsu 江苏省	(0516)5756044 (0516)7739999	18,890	State Enterprises 国有独资	7,698,050	152,020(5)	5,414,820	Autocrane汽车起重机
Shanghai Mitsubishi Elevator Co., Ltd. 上海三菱电梯有限公司(1987)	Shanghai 上海市	Shanghai 上海市	(021)64303030 (021)64300932	1,745	Foreign Funded 外商投资	3,689,703	781,858(1)	4,709,616	Lift & Elevator 电梯
Shanghai Zhenhua Port Machinery Group Co., Ltd. 上海振华港口机械集团股份有限公司(1992)	Shanghai 上海市	Shanghai 上海市	(021)58396666 (021)58399555	8,690	Overseas Chinese-funded 港澳台资	3,255,427	221,436(2)	5,435,181	Hoisting Equipment 起重设备
Otis Elevator Co., Ltd. 奥的斯电梯有限公司(1984)	Tianjin 天津市	Tianjin 天津市	(022)28225342 (022)28301256	3,141	Foreign Funded 外商投资	2,055,998	151,238(6)	1,304,926	Lift & Elevator 电梯
Guangdong Taishan Machinery Group Co.,Ltd. 广东省台山市机械集团公司(1992)	Jiangmen 江门市	Guangdong 广东省	(0750)5523440 (0750)5527064	3,242	State-owned 国有企业	1,603,429	-	711,070	Steel Bottle 钢瓶
Hangzhou Xizi Otis Elevator Co., Ltd. 杭州西子奥的斯电梯有限公司(1997)	Hangzhou 杭州市	Zhejiang 浙江省	(0571)85140888 (0571)85145692	1,024	Foreign Funded 外商投资	1,216,437	202,423(3)	756,316	Lift & Elevator 电梯
Jiangsu Tongrun M & E Co., Ltd. 江苏通润机电集团有限公司(1955)	Suzhou 苏州市	Jiangsu 江苏省	(0512)52880518 (0512)52881282	1,545	Limited-Liability 有限公司	975,390	103,550(9)	905,390	Jack 千斤顶
Guangzhou Otis Elevator Co., Ltd. 广州奥的斯电梯有限公司(1993)	Guangzhou 广州市	Guangdong 广东省	(020)86071060 (020)86071061	1,031	Foreign Funded 外商投资	870,906	41,357(15)	565,969	Lift & Elevator 电梯
Suzhou Schindler Elevator Co., ltd. 苏州迅达电梯有限公司(1990)	Suzhou 苏州市	Jiangsu 江苏省	(0512)67232429 (0512)67231127	929	Foreign Funded 外商投资	689,301	49,010(13)	615,656	Lift & Elevator 电梯
Hunan Puyuan Group Co., Ltd. 湖南省浦沅集团有限公司(1973)	Changsha 长沙市	Hunan 湖南省	(0731)5667200 (0731)5582657	3,091	State Enterprises 国有独资	680,389	6,265(52)	1,178,399	Autocrane汽车起重机

Top 10 Cities by Revenue 销售收入排名前10位城市	Province 省	Market share 市场份额 (%)	Number of firms 企业个数
Shanghai 上海市	Shanghai 上海市	22.39	81
Xuzhou 徐州市	Jiangsu 江苏省	14.77	4
Hangzhou 杭州市	Zhejiang 浙江省	5.86	33
Suzhou 苏州市	Jiangsu 江苏省	5.78	26
Guangzhou 广州市	Guangdong 广东省	5.63	16
Tianjin 天津市	Tianjin 天津市	4.59	22
Jiangmen 江门市	Guangdong 广东省	3.12	4
Weihai 威海市	Shandong 山东省	2.75	7
Beijing 北京市	Beijing 北京市	2.25	17
Hefei 合肥市	Anhui 安徽省	2.09	6

10 Major Wholesalers 十家主要批发商	City 城市	Province 省	Telephone/Fax 电话/传真
SU MEC 中设江苏机械设备进出口（集团）公司	Nanjing 南京市	Jiangsu 江苏省	(025)4511888 (025)4411772
China Poster Mobile Communications Equipment Co.,Ltd. 中邮普泰移动通信设备股份有限公司	Beijing 北京市	Beijing 北京市	(010)66426993 (010)66426837
Sino Kama Co., Ltd. 中泰凯马股份有限公司	Shanghai 上海市	Shanghai 上海市	(021)62031188 (021)62030851
China Huayuan Group Co.,Ltd. 中国华源集团有限公司	Shanghai 上海市	Shanghai 上海市	(021)62031188 (021)62032288
Zhejiang Crand Imp.& Exp.Co.,Ltd. 浙江远大进出口有限公司	Ningbo 宁波市	Zhejiang 浙江省	(0574)87720170 (0574)87723350
Shandong Machinery Import & Export Group Corporation 山东省机械进出口集团公司	Qingdao 青岛市	Shandong 山东省	(0532)2661628 (0532)2991655
Qingdao Haier International Trade Co.,Ltd. 青岛海尔国际贸易有限公司	Qingdao 青岛市	Shandong 山东省	(0532)8938337 (0532)8939494
Guangdong Machinery Import & Export Group Corporation 广东省机械进出口集团公司	Guangzhou 广州市	Guangdong 广东省	(020)87782168 (020)87771803
China National Machinery Equipment Import & Export Corporation 中国机械设备进出口总公司	Beijing 北京市	Beijing 北京市	(010)63474506 (010)63261865
Beijing Cellstar Co.,Ltd. 北京蜂星事达电讯有限公司	Beijing 北京市	Beijing 北京市	(010)64602050 (010)64672648

3532: Mining Vehicles 工矿车辆制造业

The industry accounts for 0.046% of the total revenue of China's industrial sector in 2002. The rate of return on assets is 5.20%. 59.57% of all firms in the industry made a profit while 40.43% had negative returns.The top province in terms of the industry's revenue is Shandong, accounting for 47.80% of the total revenue.
2002年本行业收入占全行业的 0.046%，资产利润率为 5.20%。59.57%的企业赢利，40.43%的企业亏损。收入最高的省为山东省，占本行业的47.80%。

	Total number of firms 企业总数	Total number of employees 职工总数	Total revenue (Mil.RMB) 总销售收入 (百万元)	Total profit (Mil.RMB) 总利润 (百万元)	Return on assets 资产利润率 (%)	Return on equity 权益利润率 (%)	Labour productivity ('000 RMB/ worker) 劳动生产率 (千元/人)	Debts/ assets 资产负债率 (%)	Total assets (Mil.RMB) 总资产 (百万元)
Industry Overall 行业总体	47	20,862	4,880	183	5.20	13.38	60.02	61.13	3,520

	Number of firms 企业个数	Average number of employees 平均职工人数	Average revenue ('000 RMB) 平均销售收入 (千元)	Average profit ('000 RMB) 平均利润 (千元)	Return on assets 资产利润率 (%)	Return on equity 权益利润率 (%)	Labour productivity ('000 RMB/ worker) 劳动生产率 (千元/人)	Debts/ assets 资产负债率 (%)	Average total assets ('000 RMB) 平均总资产 (千元)
By ownership 产业所有权									
State-owned 国有	13	432	9,642	-1,980	-3.32	-12.06	6.26	72.49	59,704
Collective-owned 集体	9	227	24,137	1,478	8.55	19.07	24.71	55.19	17,296
Foreign & Overseas Chinese Funded 三资	2	98	12,436	73	0.57	0.89	42.94	35.84	12,711
By regional distribution 地区分布									
Central-North 华北	7	228	9,801	-808	-6.27	-76.76	16.91	91.83	12,882
Beijing 北京	1	272	11,124	12	0.06	36.36	19.39	99.83	19,784
Tianjin 天津	1	113	4,834	-781	-11.48		13.96	109.51	6,804
Hebei 河北									
Shanxi 山西	5	243	10,529	-977	-7.68	-61.22	16.63	87.45	12,717
Inner Mongolia 内蒙古									
Northeast 东北	3	279	6,044	248	0.51		4.97	105.47	48,588
Liaoning 辽宁									
Jilin 吉林	2	229	8,302	518	0.81		9.98	101.44	64,198
Heilongjiang 黑龙江	1	380	1,527	-292	-1.68		-1.06	135.21	17,369
Central-East 华东	15	691	170,655	2,655	3.60	16.26	62.53	77.89	73,858
Shanghai 上海	1	97	16,405	-1,545	-6.39	-27.83	34.65	77.05	24,189
Jiangsu 江苏	2	89	9,146	290	2.19	3.88	36.43	43.43	13,214
Zhejiang 浙江	2	99	13,693	140	0.93	5.84	26.30	84.11	15,037
Anhui 安徽	1	353	14,579	-8	-0.03	-0.91	14.00	96.80	27,498
Fujian 福建	2	281	75,295	6,308	13.88	21.16	43.44	34.39	45,446
Jiangxi 江西									
Shandong 山东	7	1,282	333,225	3,987	3.07	17.53	67.25	82.48	129,828
Central-South 中南	11	407	187,666	14,461	9.83	19.01	116.12	48.31	147,167
Henan 河南	5	179	7,050	-8	-0.08	-1.28	21.19	94.08	11,120
Hubei 湖北									
Hunan 湖南	2	262	9,699	28	0.19	0.54	12.24	64.79	14,707
Guangdong 广东	1	75	14,861	-352	-1.79	-2.54	63.44	29.45	19,649
Guangxi 广西	2	1,458	993,827	79,697	10.59	19.86	167.44	46.68	752,663
Hainan 海南	1	71	7,162	20	0.23	0.31	26.17	26.52	8,850
Southwest 西南	6	405	9,307	-1,530	-2.46	-4.41	7.17	44.28	62,306
Chongqing 重庆	2	62	4,273	14	0.29	0.51	20.65	42.67	4,757
Sichuan 四川	1	314	2,285	-588	-7.15	-23.79	2.98	69.93	8,221
Guizhou 贵州	3	663	15,003	-2,874	-2.42	-4.30	6.99	43.73	118,700
Yunnan 云南									
Tibet 西藏									
Northwest 西北	5	231	22,722	-343	-0.94	-2.18	30.51	57.11	36,693
Shaanxi 陕西	3	344	28,371	-1,382	-2.59	-5.85	22.10	55.81	53,443
Gansu 甘肃	2	62	14,249	1,216	10.51	31.06	100.58	66.17	11,569
Qinghai 青海									
Ningxia 宁夏									
Xinjiang 新疆									

3532: Mining Vehicles 工矿车辆制造业

Year 年份	Number of firms 企业个数	Rate of change 变化率 (%)	Number of employees 职工人数 (人)	Rate of change 变化率 (%)	Total revenue (Mil. RMB) 总销售收入 (百万元)	Rate of change 变化率 (%)	Total profit (Mil RMB) 总利润 (百万元)	Rate of change 变化率 (%)
2000	44		22,196		2,544		-7	
2001	51	15.91	20,442	-7.90	3,487	37.07	54	-
2002	47	-7.84	20,862	2.05	4,880	39.95	183	238.89

Major Products 主要产品	Output 产量	Unit 单位
Plant & Mining Vehicle 工矿车辆	13,470	130

10 Main Firms with Maximal Revenue (year founded) 收入最大的十家主要企业（创办年份）	City 城市	Province 省	Telephone/fax 电话/传真	Number of employees 职工人数	Ownership 产业所有权	Revenue ('000 RMB) 销售收入 (千元)	Profit('000 RMB) (rank) 利润(千元) (排名)	Total assets ('000 RMB) 总资产 (千元)	Major products 主要产品
Qingdao Taifa Group Co.,Ltd.	Qingdao	Shandong	(0532)3195509		Joint Stock				Handcart
青岛泰发集团股份有限公司(1997)	青岛市	山东省	(0532)3191088	7,000	股份制	2,101,233	31,048(2)	659,052	手推车
Guangxi Liugong Machinery Co.,Ltd.	Liuzhou	Guangxi	(0772)3886054		Joint Stock				Loading Machine
广西柳工机械股份有限公司(1958)	柳州市	广西	(0772)3691147	2,537	股份制	1,733,680	145,684(1)	1,426,827	装载机
Liuzhou Liugong Small-type Loader Co., Ltd.	Liuzhou	Guangxi	(0772)3886503		Limited-Liability				Gear
柳州柳工小型装载机有限公司(1988)	柳州市	广西	(0772)3886512	379	有限公司	253,974	13,709(3)	78,499	齿轮
Qingdao Xinghua Group Co., Ltd.	Qingdao	Shandong	(0532)5173088		Private Owned				Handcart
青岛市星华集团有限公司(1998)	青岛市	山东省	(0532)3191067	600	私营企业	154,533	2,883(5)	83,472	手推车
Xiamen Engineering Machinery Brake Factory	Xiamen	Fujian	(0592)6314768		Collective-owned				Engineering Mechanical Arrester工程机
厦门工程机械制动器厂(1971)	厦门市	福建省	(0592)6041021	494	集体企业	106,307	12,137(4)	54,461	械制动器
Liupanshui Coal Mine Machinery Factory	Liupanshui	Guizhou	(0858)5323682		State-owned				Explosion-protection Electric Engine
六盘水煤机厂(1966)	六盘水市	贵州省	(0858)5323682	1,354	国有企业	39,477	-	103,301	爆电机车
Yantai Engineering Works	Yantai	Shandong	(0535)6531315		State-owned				2110 Loading Machine.2110
烟台工程机械厂(1981)	烟台市	山东省	(0535)6530964	403	国有企业	20,915	-	108,405	装载机
Shanxi Pingyao Plant & Mining Electric Locomotive Factory	Jinzhong	Shanxi	(0354)5650887		State-owned				Electric Locomotive Of Plant & Mining工
山西省平遥工矿电机车厂(1968)	晋中市	山西省	(0354)5655268	723	国有企业	20,175	-	43,166	矿电机车
Qingdao Dalu Vehicles Manufacturing Co., Ltd.	Qingdao	Shandong	(0532)3191027		Others				Handcart
青岛大卢车辆制造有限公司(2000)	青岛市	山东省	(0532)3193738	104	其他企业	18,882	6(22)	15,895	手推车
Mengjin Matun Forging Factory	Luoyang	Henan	(0379)7899125		Private Enterprises				Road Roller Fittings轧
孟津县麻屯锻造厂(2001)	洛阳市	河南省	(0379)7899125	135	私营独资	16,928	320(14)	3,800	路机配件

Top 10 Cities by Revenue 销售收入排名前10位城市	Province 省	Market share 市场份额 (%)	Number of firms 企业个数
Qingdao 青岛市	Shandong 山东省	47.01	5
Liuzhou 柳州市	Guangxi 广西	40.73	2
Xiamen 厦门市	Fujian 福建省	2.18	1
Xi'an 西安市	Shannxi 陕西省	1.70	1
Quanzhou 泉州市	Fujian 福建省	0.91	1
Liupanshui 六盘水市	Guizhou 贵州省	0.81	1
Lanzhou 兰州市	Gansu 甘肃省	0.58	1
Yantai 烟台市	Shandong 山东省	0.43	1
Datong 大同市	Shanxi 山西省	0.42	2
Jinzhong 晋中市	Shanxi 山西省	0.41	1

10 Major Wholesalers 十家主要批发商	City 城市	Province 省	Telephone/Fax 电话/传真
SU MEC	Nanjing	Jiangsu	(025)4511888
中设江苏机械设备进出口（集团）公司	南京市	江苏省	(025)4411772
China Poster Mobile Communications Equipment Co.,Ltd.	Beijing	Beijing	(010)66426993
中邮普泰移动通信设备股份有限公司	北京市	北京市	(010)66426837
Sino Kama Co., Ltd.	Shanghai	Shanghai	(021)62031188
中泰凯马股份有限公司	上海市	上海市	(021)62030851
China Huayuan Group Co.,Ltd.	Shanghai	Shanghai	(021)62031188
中国华源集团有限公司	上海市	上海市	(021)62032288
Zhejiang Crand Imp.& Exp.Co.,Ltd.	Ningbo	Zhejiang	(0574)87720170
浙江远大进出口有限公司	宁波市	浙江省	(0574)87723350
Shandong Machinery Import & Export Group Corporation	Qingdao	Shandong	(0532)2661628
山东省机械进出口集团公司	青岛市	山东省	(0532)2991655
Qingdao Haier International Trade Co.,Ltd.	Qingdao	Shandong	(0532)8938337
青岛海尔国际贸易有限公司	青岛市	山东省	(0532)8939494
Guangdong Machinery Import & Export Group Corporation	Guangzhou	Guangdong	(020)87782168
广东省机械进出口集团公司	广州市	广东省	(020)87771803
China National Machinery Equipment Import & Export Corporation	Beijing	Beijing	(010)63474506
中国机械设备进出口总公司	北京市	北京市	(010)63261865
Beijing Cellstar Co.,Ltd.	Beijing	Beijing	(010)64602050
北京蜂星事达电讯有限公司	北京市	北京市	(010)64672648

3533: Pumps 泵制造业

The industry accounts for 0.141% of the total revenue of China's industrial sector in 2002. The rate of return on assets is 3.92%. 81.61% of all firms in the industry made a profit while 18.39% had negative returns.The top province in terms of the industry's revenue is Zhejiang, accounting for 20.15% of the total revenue.
2002年本行业收入占全行业的0.141%，资产利润率为3.92%。81.61%的企业赢利，18.39%的企业亏损。收入最高的省为浙江省，占本行业的20.15%。

	Total number of firms 企业总数	Total number of employees 职工总数	Total revenue (Mil.RMB) 总销售收入（百万元）	Total profit (Mil.RMB) 总利润（百万元）	Return on assets 资产利润率（%）	Return on equity 权益利润率（%）	Labour productivity ('000 RMB/ worker) 劳动生产率（千元/人）	Debts/ assets 资产负债率（%）	Total assets (Mil.RMB) 总资产（百万元）
Industry Overall 行业总体	598	121,056	15,086	814	3.92	9.78	36.31	59.93	20,753

	Number of firms 企业个数	Average number of employees 平均职工人数	Average revenue ('000 RMB) 平均销售收入（千元）	Average profit ('000 RMB) 平均利润（千元）	Return on assets 资产利润率（%）	Return on equity 权益利润率（%）	Labour productivity ('000 RMB/ worker) 劳动生产率（千元/人）	Debts/ assets 资产负债率（%）	Average total assets ('000 RMB) 平均总资产（千元）
By ownership 产业所有权									
State-owned 国有	92	285	11,962	-164	-0.51	-2.26	15.55	77.32	31,988
Collective-owned 集体	85	189	20,171	1,237	6.06	15.52	38.34	60.95	20,403
Foreign & Overseas Chinese Funded 三资	69	155	45,804	3,708	7.12	14.88	64.53	52.16	52,089
By regional distribution 地区分布									
Central-North 华北	67	271	21,745	1,477	3.69	10.01	29.31	63.11	39,979
Beijing 北京	6	123	13,182	-427	-0.79	-1.75	13.56	54.75	53,947
Tianjin 天津	13	259	26,209	2,051	4.02	14.29	36.58	71.86	51,008
Hebei 河北	31	292	26,213	2,133	5.35	12.99	33.06	58.82	39,881
Shanxi 山西	12	318	14,734	705	2.37	6.69	19.87	64.62	29,779
Inner Mongolia 内蒙古	5	237	9,543	56	0.29	1.44	20.23	80.04	19,625
Northeast 东北	55	233	17,354	211	0.41	1.55	25.61	73.56	51,497
Liaoning 辽宁	42	255	20,857	239	0.39	1.54	27.23	74.84	61,567
Jilin 吉林	7	143	3,064	-691	-3.98	-15.80	10.12	74.83	17,376
Heilongjiang 黑龙江	6	183	9,505	1,066	5.12	9.44	23.89	45.77	20,815
Central-East 华东	357	162	28,306	1,808	5.98	13.37	45.57	55.29	30,248
Shanghai 上海	57	130	39,180	2,446	5.83	11.97	65.72	51.32	41,993
Jiangsu 江苏	77	193	28,942	1,498	4.47	10.58	40.97	57.73	33,489
Zhejiang 浙江	143	106	21,259	1,708	7.85	15.48	46.53	49.31	21,772
Anhui 安徽	15	190	15,377	289	0.95	2.81	29.61	66.08	30,298
Fujian 福建	12	183	24,180	574	4.17	10.55	24.36	60.48	13,767
Jiangxi 江西	7	219	12,930	129	0.48	1.64	23.24	70.57	26,582
Shandong 山东	46	302	43,308	2,922	7.05	18.66	47.80	62.23	41,458
Central-South 中南	86	262	25,749	799	2.01	4.75	32.73	57.63	39,712
Henan 河南	23	204	11,218	131	0.70	3.00	25.63	76.48	18,643
Hubei 湖北	16	439	37,590	1,993	5.11	13.12	28.29	61.05	39,004
Hunan 湖南	19	259	28,219	725	1.00	1.77	33.62	43.61	72,490
Guangdong 广东	24	209	33,114	1,062	3.00	8.43	48.40	64.38	35,384
Guangxi 广西	3	277	7,839	-1,812	-4.03	-22.90	11.41	82.40	44,959
Hainan 海南	1	29	582	6	0.65	2.19	4.38	70.31	923
Southwest 西南	18	334	15,144	110	0.31	0.74	19.00	57.93	35,135
Chongqing 重庆	2	675	39,088	3,063	3.60	5.41	28.17	33.40	85,002
Sichuan 四川	11	285	14,873	-5	-0.02	-0.05	18.24	65.43	31,915
Guizhou 贵州	2	205	5,948	39	0.30	0.82	12.05	63.18	12,942
Yunnan 云南	3	369	6,308	-1,389	-4.88	-18.95	12.52	74.27	28,492
Tibet 西藏									
Northwest 西北	15	243	5,482	-891	-3.38	-35.28	12.13	90.43	26,383
Shaanxi 陕西	8	279	4,556	-940	-3.57	-87.58	11.72	95.92	26,287
Gansu 甘肃	5	189	4,302	-1,461	-5.75	-166.35	10.63	96.54	25,407
Qinghai 青海									
Ningxia 宁夏									
Xinjiang 新疆	2	232	12,132	728	2.49	5.84	17.18	57.34	29,203

Year 年份	Number of firms 企业个数	Rate of change 变化率 (%)	Number of employees 职工人数 (人)	Rate of change 变化率 (%)	Total revenue (Mil. RMB) 总销售收入 (百万元)	Rate of change 变化率 (%)	Total profit (Mil RMB) 总利润 (百万元)	Rate of change 变化率 (%)
2000	529		136,750		10,587		328	
2001	569	7.56	125,861	-7.96	12,334	16.50	513	56.40
2002	598	5.10	121,056	-3.82	15,086	22.31	814	58.67

Major Products 主要产品	Output 产量	Unit 单位
Pump 泵	1,745	10,000 Units 万台

10 Main Firms with Maximal Revenue (year founded) 收入最大的十家主要企业（创办年份）	City 城市	Province 省	Telephone/fax 电话/传真	Number of employees 职工人数	Ownership 产业所有权	Revenue ('000 RMB) 销售收入（千元）	Profit('000 RMB) (rank) 利润（千元）（排名）	Total assets ('000 RMB) 总资产（千元）	Major products 主要产品
Shanghai Kaiquan Water Supply Project Co., Ltd. 上海凯泉给水工程有限公司(1994)	Shanghai 上海市	Shanghai 上海市	(021)56505666 (021)56502616	380	Limited-Liability 有限公司	298,893	3,668(59)	170,846	Water Supply Equipment 给水设备
Bosch Automotive Products (Suzhou) Co., Ltd. 博世汽车部件（苏州）有限公司(2000)	Suzhou 苏州市	Jiangsu 江苏省	(0512)62568989 (0512)62561818	154	Foreign Funded 外商投资	268,290	8,279(29)	490,760	Engine 发动机
Jiangsu Yatai Pump Group Company 江苏亚太泵业集团公司(1988)	Taizhou 泰州市	Jiangsu 江苏省	(0523)7633148 (0523)7625252	818	State-owned 国有企业	249,339	22,784(9)	192,172	Hidden Dirt Pump 潜污泵
Eaton Fluid Power (ShangHai) Co.,Ltd. 伊顿流体动力(上海)有限公司(1998)	Shanghai 上海市	Shanghai 上海市	(021)50460011 (021)50460767	73	Foreign Funded 外商投资	245,206	36,550(1)	164,636	Pump 泵
Hunan Tianyi Science & Technology Co., Ltd. 湖南省天一科技股份有限公司(1998)	Yueyang 岳阳市	Hunan 湖南省	(0730)6289536 (0730)6289548	1,053	Joint Stock 股份制	234,016	25,080(6)	768,358	Pump 泵
ShanDong Boshan Pump Science And Technology Co.,Ltd. 山东博泵科技股份有限公司(1929)	Zibo 淄博市	Shandong 山东省	(0533)4183532 (0533)4182018	2,169	Joint Stock 股份制	220,026	25,065(7)	272,684	Industrial Pump 工业泵
ShanDong ShuangLun Group Co., Ltd. 山东双轮集团股份有限公司(1952)	Weihai 威海市	Shandong 山东省	(0631)5280571 (0631)5231322	1,059	Joint Stock 股份制	203,920	14,860(13)	280,038	Pump 泵
Grondfos Pumps (Suzhou) Co., Ltd. 格兰富水泵(苏州)有限公司(1996)	Suzhou 苏州市	Jiangsu 江苏省	(0512)67617832 (0512)67618167	205	Foreign Funded 外商投资	202,006	8,945(26)	287,339	Water Pump 水泵
KSB ShangHai Pump Co., Ltd. 上海凯士比泵有限公司(1995)	Shanghai 上海市	Shanghai 上海市	(021)64302888 (021)64301504	870	Foreign Funded 外商投资	192,947	3,045(74)	316,092	Pump 泵
Shenyang Pump Co., Ltd. 沈阳水泵股份有限公司(1998)	Shenyang 沈阳市	Liaoning 辽宁省	(024)25546045 (024)25546850	2,139	Joint Stock 股份制	168,688	-	1,232,815	Pump 泵

Top 10 Cities by Revenue 销售收入排名前10位城市	Province 省	Market share 市场份额 (%)	Number of firms 企业个数
Shanghai 上海市	Shanghai 上海市	14.80	57
Taizhou 台州市	Zhejiang 浙江省	9.77	75
Zibo 淄博市	Shandong 山东省	5.35	14
Wenzhou 温州市	Zhejiang 浙江省	4.05	30
Suzhou 苏州市	Jiangsu 江苏省	3.87	9
Weihai 威海市	Shandong 山东省	3.74	6
Taizhou 泰州市	Jiangsu 江苏省	3.65	17
Wuxi 无锡市	Jiangsu 江苏省	3.35	15
Shenyang 沈阳市	Liaoning 辽宁省	2.89	14
Shiyan 十堰市	Hubei 湖北省	2.54	1

10 Major Wholesalers 十家主要批发商	City 城市	Province 省	Telephone/Fax 电话/传真
SU MEC 中设江苏机械设备进出口（集团）公司	Nanjing 南京市	Jiangsu 江苏省	(025)4511888 (025)4411772
China Poster Mobile Communications Equipment Co.,Ltd. 中邮普泰移动通信设备股份有限公司	Beijing 北京市	Beijing 北京市	(010)66426993 (010)66426837
Sino Kama Co., Ltd. 中泰凯马股份有限公司	Shanghai 上海市	Shanghai 上海市	(021)62031188 (021)62030851
China Huayuan Group Co.,Ltd. 中国华源集团有限公司	Shanghai 上海市	Shanghai 上海市	(021)62031188 (021)62032288
Zhejiang Crand Imp.& Exp.Co.,Ltd. 浙江远大进出口有限公司	Ningbo 宁波市	Zhejiang 浙江省	(0574)87720170 (0574)87723350
Shandong Machinery Import & Export Group Corporation 山东省机械进出口集团公司	Qingdao 青岛市	Shandong 山东省	(0532)2661628 (0532)2991655
Qingdao Haier International Trade Co.,Ltd. 青岛海尔国际贸易有限公司	Qingdao 青岛市	Shandong 山东省	(0532)8938337 (0532)8939494
Guangdong Machinery Import & Export Group Corporation 广东省机械进出口集团公司	Guangzhou 广州市	Guangdong 广东省	(020)87782168 (020)87771803
China National Machinery Equipment Import & Export Corporation 中国机械设备进出口总公司	Beijing 北京市	Beijing 北京市	(010)63474506 (010)63261865
Beijing Cellstar Co.,Ltd. 北京蜂星事达电讯有限公司	Beijing 北京市	Beijing 北京市	(010)64602050 (010)64672648

3534: Fans 风机制造业

The industry accounts for 0.064% of the total revenue of China's industrial sector in 2002. The rate of return on assets is 3.83%. 86.63% of all firms in the industry made a profit while 13.37% had negative returns.The top province in terms of the industry's revenue is Shandong, accounting for 18.87% of the total revenue.
2002年本行业收入占全业的0.064%，资产利润率为3.83%。86.63%的企业赢利，13.37%的企业亏损。收入最高的省为山东省，占本行业的18.87%。

	Total number of firms 企业总数	Total number of employees 职工总数	Total revenue (Mil.RMB) 总销售收入（百万元）	Total profit (Mil.RMB) 总利润（百万元）	Return on assets 资产利润率（%）	Return on equity 权益利润率（%）	Labour productivity ('000 RMB/ worker) 劳动生产率（千元/人）	Debts/ assets 资产负债率（%）	Total assets (Mil.RMB) 总资产（百万元）
Industry Overall 行业总体	187	45,188	6,890	398	3.83	9.62	47.26	60.13	10,376

	Number of firms 企业个数	Average number of employees 平均职工人数	Average revenue ('000 RMB) 平均销售收入（千元）	Average profit ('000 RMB) 平均利润（千元）	Return on assets 资产利润率（%）	Return on equity 权益利润率（%）	Labour productivity ('000 RMB/ worker) 劳动生产率（千元/人）	Debts/ assets 资产负债率（%）	Average total assets ('000 RMB) 平均总资产（千元）
By ownership 产业所有权									
State-owned 国有	27	456	55,185	1,698	1.22	4.81	43.71	74.56	138,906
Collective-owned 集体	28	207	40,170	3,191	11.23	25.31	62.75	55.63	28,413
Foreign & Overseas Chinese Funded 三资	17	151	33,928	3,519	6.79	15.13	63.99	55.14	51,845
By regional distribution 地区分布									
Central-North 华北	27	169	18,479	1,021	5.11	15.06	44.01	66.07	19,984
Beijing 北京	5	164	13,006	227	0.90	2.16	44.67	58.36	25,205
Tianjin 天津	8	176	17,797	-17	-0.07	-0.24	51.58	72.63	24,875
Hebei 河北	8	169	28,493	3,294	16.54	40.25	50.30	58.90	19,911
Shanxi 山西	5	157	11,314	56	0.79	4.10	25.40	80.65	7,084
Inner Mongolia 内蒙古	1	200	7,008	-63	-0.32	-1.66	18.68	80.91	19,836
Northeast 东北	13	490	71,123	-336	-0.21	-0.77	42.42	72.58	159,730
Liaoning 辽宁	8	642	98,523	-534	-0.26	-1.00	42.43	74.35	209,158
Jilin 吉林	4	251	32,233	126	0.13	0.41	50.18	67.28	93,838
Heilongjiang 黑龙江	1	229	7,480	-602	-2.16	-3.46	8.21	37.61	27,879
Central-East 华东	98	190	38,316	2,999	6.81	13.93	59.35	51.13	44,048
Shanghai 上海	18	207	28,845	1,602	3.06	9.21	55.88	66.80	52,421
Jiangsu 江苏	31	153	24,108	721	3.32	12.01	40.34	72.37	21,740
Zhejiang 浙江	22	128	51,988	5,946	9.53	12.90	99.86	26.13	62,410
Anhui 安徽	1	180	12,274	29	0.38	0.73	21.08	47.54	7,612
Fujian 福建	3	137	10,650	618	3.20	5.67	32.62	43.48	19,292
Jiangxi 江西									
Shandong 山东	23	292	56,540	4,782	8.72	19.66	60.42	55.63	54,814
Central-South 中南	26	259	26,398	665	1.69	4.43	29.97	61.82	39,279
Henan 河南	3	620	9,401	-151	-0.53	-1.73	8.31	69.42	28,569
Hubei 湖北	5	282	18,233	-391	-0.64	-3.68	21.23	82.64	61,199
Hunan 湖南	4	340	46,896	1,048	1.89	4.52	50.52	58.19	55,422
Guangdong 广东	12	146	30,790	1,378	4.81	8.50	48.46	43.46	28,657
Guangxi 广西	2	175	4,952	-517	-1.62	-4.40	7.77	63.28	31,987
Hainan 海南									
Southwest 西南	10	405	30,306	901	0.98	1.70	23.23	41.96	91,504
Chongqing 重庆	3	679	51,541	2,964	1.43	2.07	23.35	31.04	207,374
Sichuan 四川	5	388	28,281	80	0.15	0.43	23.97	64.66	52,483
Guizhou 贵州	2	34	3,517	-143	-0.94	-3.06	-1.24	69.35	15,253
Yunnan 云南									
Tibet 西藏									
Northwest 西北	13	377	55,532	4,194	3.62	15.41	54.38	76.52	115,915
Shaanxi 陕西	6	670	113,536	8,695	3.73	16.63	61.73	77.60	233,339
Gansu 甘肃	2	102	2,985	1	0.01	0.01	12.60	60.85	9,513
Qinghai 青海									
Ningxia 宁夏	1	401	10,440	844	2.21	5.04	15.21	56.17	38,192
Xinjiang 新疆	4	69	6,073	378	3.05	9.45	34.90	67.73	12,410

3534: Fans 风机制造业

Year 年份	Number of firms 企业个数	Rate of change 变化率 (%)	Number of employees 职工人数 (人)	Rate of change 变化率 (%)	Total revenue (Mil. RMB) 总销售收入 (百万元)	Rate of change 变化率 (%)	Total profit (Mil RMB) 总利润 (百万元)	Rate of change 变化率 (%)
2000	171		71,984		4,834		256	
2001	171		43,765	-39.20	5,676	17.42	292	14.06
2002	187	9.36	45,188	3.25	6,890	21.39	398	36.30

Major Products 主要产品	Output 产量	Unit 单位
Air Blower 风机	76	10,000 Units 万台

10 Main Firms with Maximal Revenue (year founded) 收入最大的十家主要企业（创办年份）	City 城市	Province 省	Telephone/fax 电话/传真	Number of employees 职工人数	Ownership 产业所有权	Revenue ('000 RMB) 销售收入 (千元)	Profit('000 RMB) (rank) 利润(千元) (排名)	Total assets ('000 RMB) 总资产 (千元)	Major products 主要产品
Zhejiang Shangfeng Indevstrial Holdings Ltd.	Shaoxing	Zhejiang	(0575)2365905		Joint Stock				Blower
浙江上风实业股份有限公司(1993)	绍兴市	浙江省	(0575)2366328	934	股份制	862,371	113,410(1)	1,096,665	风机
Shaanxi Blower (Group) Co., Ltd.	Xi'an	Shannxi	(029)3931400		State-owned				Blower
陕西鼓风机（集团）有限公司(1970)	西安市	陕西省	(029)3931422	3,424	国有企业	591,190	50,873(2)	1,240,765	风机
Wendeng Ventilator Factory	Weihai	Shandong	(0631)8731032		Collective-owned				Blower
文登市风机厂(1958)	威海市	山东省	(0631)8731098	385	集体企业	395,440	35,680(3)	67,620	风机
Howsen Power Ltd.	Weihai	Shandong	(0631)5927212		Overseas Chinese-funded				Blower
豪顿华工程有限公司(1996)	威海市	山东省	(0631)5926087	355	港澳台资	207,585	24,440(4)	361,356	风机
Shanghai Blower Co., Ltd.	Shanghai	Shanghai	(021)56650577		Limited-Liability				Blower
上海鼓风机厂有限公司(1947)	上海市	上海市	(021)56651514	1,289	有限公司	195,121	671(59)	535,852	风机
Shandong Zhangqiu Blower Factory	Jinan	Shandong	(0531)3250002		Collective-owned				Blower
山东省章丘鼓风机厂(1968)	济南市	山东省	(0531)3214543	1,143	集体企业	167,480	16,850(5)	246,864	风机
Shanggu Nanjing Blower Co., Ltd.	Nanjing	Jiangsu	(025)2417387		Collective Owned				Fanner
上鼓南京风机有限公司(1998)	南京市	江苏省	(025)2413872	360	集体企业	125,170	260(98)	16,590	通风机
Yantai Blower Factory	Yantai	Shandong	(0535)6798298		Collective-owned				Blower
烟台市风机厂(1978)	烟台市	山东省	(0535)6798658	680	集体企业	119,520	9,560(8)	66,180	风机
Chongqing General Industry (Group) Co., Ltd.	Chongqing	Chongqing	(023)67661064		State Enterprises				Blower
重庆通用工业（集团）有限责任公司(1938)	重庆市	重庆市	(023)67661064	1,558	国有独资	119,499	8,492(10)	602,687	风机
Guangdong Zhaoqing Deton Co.,Ltd.	Zhaoqing	Guangdong	(0758)7731821		Private Partnership				Blower
广东肇庆德通有限公司(1997)	肇庆市	广东省	(0758)7731251	270	私营合伙	109,579	1,068(48)	115,571	风机

Top 10 Cities by Revenue 销售收入排名前10位城市	Province 省	Market share 市场份额 (%)	Number of firms 企业个数
Shaoxing 绍兴市	Zhejiang 浙江省	14.77	9
Xi'an 西安市	Shannxi 陕西省	9.76	4
Weihai 威海市	Shandong 山东省	8.75	2
Shenyang 沈阳市	Liaoning 辽宁省	8.33	4
Shanghai 上海市	Shanghai 上海市	7.54	18
Jinan 济南市	Shandong 山东省	3.76	6
Zhaoqing 肇庆市	Guangdong 广东省	2.93	3
Yingkou 营口市	Liaoning 辽宁省	2.73	2
Wuxi 无锡市	Jiangsu 江苏省	2.65	9
Zibo 淄博市	Shandong 山东省	2.65	4

10 Major Wholesalers 十家主要批发商	City 城市	Province 省	Telephone/Fax 电话/传真
SU MEC	Nanjing	Jiangsu	(025)4511888
中设江苏机械设备进出口（集团）公司	南京市	江苏省	(025)4411772
China Poster Mobile Communications Equipment Co.,Ltd.	Beijing	Beijing	(010)66426993
中邮普泰移动通信设备股份有限公司	北京市	北京市	(010)66426837
Sino Kama Co., Ltd.	Shanghai	Shanghai	(021)62031188
中泰凯马股份有限公司	上海市	上海市	(021)62030851
China Huayuan Group Co.,Ltd.	Shanghai	Shanghai	(021)62031188
中国华源集团有限公司	上海市	上海市	(021)62032288
Zhejiang Crand Imp.& Exp.Co.,Ltd.	Ningbo	Zhejiang	(0574)87720170
浙江远大进出口有限公司	宁波市	浙江省	(0574)87723350
Shandong Machinery Import & Export Group Corporation	Qingdao	Shandong	(0532)2661628
山东省机械进出口集团公司	青岛市	山东省	(0532)2991655
Qingdao Haier International Trade Co.,Ltd.	Qingdao	Shandong	(0532)8938337
青岛海尔国际贸易有限公司	青岛市	山东省	(0532)8939494
Guangdong Machinery Import & Export Group Corporation	Guangzhou	Guangdong	(020)87782168
广东省机械进出口集团公司	广州市	广东省	(020)87771803
China National Machinery Equipment Import & Export Corporation	Beijing	Beijing	(010)63474506
中国机械设备进出口总公司	北京市	北京市	(010)63261865
Beijing Cellstar Co.,Ltd.	Beijing	Beijing	(010)64602050
北京蜂星事达电讯有限公司	北京市	北京市	(010)64672648

3535: Air Compressors and Separation Equipment

气体压缩机及气体分离设备制造业

The industry accounts for 0.078% of the total revenue of China's industrial sector in 2002. The rate of return on assets is 3.02%. 71.83% of all firms in the industry made a profit while 28.17% had negative returns.The top province in terms of the industry's revenue is Jiangsu, accounting for 24.10% of the total revenue.
2002年本行业收入占全行业的 0.078%，资产利润率为 3.02%。71.83%的企业赢利，28.17%的企业亏损。收入最高的省为江苏省，占本行业的24.10%。

	Total number of firms 企业总数	Total number of employees 职工总数	Total revenue (Mil.RMB) 总销售收入（百万元）	Total profit (Mil.RMB) 总利润（百万元）	Return on assets 资产利润率（%）	Return on equity 权益利润率（%）	Labour productivity ('000 RMB/ worker) 劳动生产率（千元/人）	Debts/ assets 资产负债率（%）	Total assets (Mil.RMB) 总资产（百万元）
Industry Overall 行业总体	142	48,787	8,315	405	3.02	9.04	46.88	66.58	13,402

	Number of firms 企业个数	Average number of employees 平均职工人数	Average revenue ('000 RMB) 平均销售收入（千元）	Average profit ('000 RMB) 平均利润（千元）	Return on assets 资产利润率（%）	Return on equity 权益利润率（%）	Labour productivity ('000 RMB/ worker) 劳动生产率（千元/人）	Debts/ assets 资产负债率（%）	Average total assets ('000 RMB) 平均总资产（千元）
By ownership 产业所有权									
State-owned 国有	24	590	32,407	-3,165	-2.67	-21.76	10.47	87.72	118,473
Collective-owned 集体	16	175	20,452	-166	-0.57	-1.07	25.41	46.60	29,047
Foreign & Overseas Chinese Funded 三资	33	206	109,537	9,846	7.58	16.46	170.39	53.94	129,849
By regional distribution 地区分布									
Central-North 华北	14	330	22,167	-374	-1.02	-6.24	18.10	83.63	36,566
Beijing 北京	5	191	47,523	1,326	2.64	8.60	63.38	69.25	50,153
Tianjin 天津	4	73	6,109	349	3.27	17.39	21.88	81.18	10,655
Hebei 河北	3	846	11,017	-4,003	-7.02	-342.92	4.08	97.95	57,059
Shanxi 山西	2	417	7,617	-625	-2.64		7.48	110.16	23,677
Inner Mongolia 内蒙古									
Northeast 东北	8	558	36,033	-5,353	-2.48	-29.68	16.39	91.63	215,434
Liaoning 辽宁	6	400	42,378	-2,240	-0.98	-5.07	27.70	80.67	228,625
Jilin 吉林									
Heilongjiang 黑龙江	2	1,030	17,000	-14,691	-8.35		3.21	134.38	175,861
Central-East 华东	90	270	65,296	3,417	4.18	10.86	64.82	61.48	81,692
Shanghai 上海	28	146	66,484	3,789	4.70	13.56	121.61	65.31	80,535
Jiangsu 江苏	27	334	74,222	3,746	4.12	8.95	62.42	53.95	90,927
Zhejiang 浙江	22	279	62,184	3,309	4.51	11.97	56.77	62.31	73,351
Anhui 安徽	3	529	24,186	-1,182	-1.26	-3.35	13.15	62.56	94,169
Fujian 福建	3	210	34,244	293	0.98	3.22	30.46	69.68	30,016
Jiangxi 江西	3	368	28,014	140	0.34	0.94	27.68	63.69	41,187
Shandong 山东	4	446	95,926	7,431	5.58	22.27	55.62	74.93	133,109
Central-South 中南	17	506	54,842	3,732	2.98	8.39	33.53	64.44	125,067
Henan 河南	3	1,054	97,350	140	0.06	0.19	25.90	67.95	226,895
Hubei 湖北									
Hunan 湖南	3	322	5,208	-1,214	-4.18	-14.67	7.37	71.52	29,058
Guangdong 广东	6	267	55,046	2,873	4.16	8.19	95.34	49.16	69,029
Guangxi 广西	5	574	58,871	9,884	5.23	16.34	16.26	67.96	188,823
Hainan 海南									
Southwest 西南	6	847	67,746	756	0.45	2.02	13.43	77.76	168,244
Chongqing 重庆	1	725	50,144	1,157	1.01	1.96	20.85	48.20	114,132
Sichuan 四川	5	872	71,266	675	0.38	2.04	12.19	81.53	179,067
Guizhou 贵州									
Yunnan 云南									
Tibet 西藏									
Northwest 西北	7	240	71,521	11,069	11.41	17.69	116.45	35.50	97,000
Shaanxi 陕西	7	240	71,521	11,069	11.41	17.69	116.45	35.50	97,000
Gansu 甘肃									
Qinghai 青海									
Ningxia 宁夏									
Xinjiang 新疆									

3535: Air Compressors and Separation Equipment

气体压缩机及气体分离设备制造业

Year 年份	Number of firms 企业个数	Rate of change 变化率 (%)	Number of employees 职工人数 (人)	Rate of change 变化率 (%)	Total revenue (Mil. RMB) 总销售收入 (百万元)	Rate of change 变化率 (%)	Total profit (Mil RMB) 总利润 (百万元)	Rate of change 变化率 (%)
2000	136		61,389		5,919		108	
2001	141	3.68	61,467	0.13	6,968	17.72	206	90.74
2002	142	0.71	48,787	-20.63	8,315	19.33	405	96.60

Major Products 主要产品	Output 产量	Unit 单位
Gas Compressor 气体压缩机	808,715	Unit 台

10 Main Firms with Maximal Revenue (year founded) 收入最大的十家主要企业（创办年份）	City 城市	Province 省	Telephone/fax 电话/传真	Number of employees 职工人数	Ownership 产业所有权	Revenue ('000 RMB) 销售收入 (千元)	Profit('000 RMB) (rank) 利润(千元) (排名)	Total assets ('000 RMB) 总资产 (千元)	Major products 主要产品
Hangzhou Oxygen Making Machine Group Co.,Ltd. 杭州制氧机集团有限公司(1950)	Hangzhou 杭州市	Zhejiang 浙江省	(0571)85372001 (0571)85373773	3,870	Limited-Liability 有限公司	1,028,308	57,290(4)	1,283,673	Compressor and Inner Engine压缩机及内机
Emerson Electric （SuZhou）Co.,Ltd. 艾默生电气（苏州）有限公司(2000)	Suzhou 苏州市	Jiangsu 江苏省	(0512)62575505 (0512)62575506	530	Foreign Funded 外商投资	603,311	54,882(5)	758,034	Compressor 压缩机
Fusheng Industrial (Shanghai) Company Co., Ltd. 复盛实业(上海)有限公司(1995)	Shanghai 上海市	Shanghai 上海市	(021)57686868 (021)57686688	361	Overseas Chinese-funded 港澳台资	358,055	41,979(7)	384,061	Compressor 压缩机
Shanghai Zanussi Electrical Appliance Machinery Co.,Ltd. 上海扎努西电器机械有限公司(1998)	Shanghai 上海市	Shanghai 上海市	(021)50481048 (021)50481115	791	Foreign Funded 外商投资	326,109	-	623,103	Household Refrigerator Compressor家用冰箱压缩机
Shandong Weifang Shengjian Group 山东省潍坊生建集团(1951)	Weifang 潍坊市	Shandong 山东省	(0536)8181191 (0536)8181062	1,286	State-owned 国有企业	311,294	18,150(9)	469,736	Gas Compressor气体压缩机
Shanghai Ingersoll-Rand Compressor Co., Ltd. 上海英格索兰压缩机有限公司(1990)	Shanghai 上海市	Shanghai 上海市	(021)64302631 (021)64302196	303	Foreign Funded 外商投资	301,388	71,047(2)	239,246	Gas Compressor气体压缩机
Kaifeng Air Separation Group Co., Ltd. 开封空分集团有限公司(1965)	Kaifeng 开封市	Henan 河南省	(0378)2925977 (0378)2921298	2,753	State Enterprises 国有独资	257,767	105(75)	614,732	Gas Separate Equipment气体分离设备
Zhongshan Fusheng Electromechanical Co., Ltd. 中山复盛机电有限公司(1995)	Zhongshan 中山市	Guangdong 广东省	(0760)5591551 (0760)5591552	510	Overseas Chinese-funded 港澳台资	240,539	18,185(8)	342,626	Air Compressor of A Type.A型空气压缩机
Shenyang Gas Compressor Co., Ltd. 沈阳气体压缩机股份有限公司(1930)	Shenyang 沈阳市	Liaoning 辽宁省	(024)25875111 (024)25852167	1,688	Joint Stock 股份制	183,437	-	1,126,363	Gas Compressor气体压缩机
Shanghai Youjiali Liquid Helium Co., ltd. 上海尤嘉利液氦有限公司(1994)	Shanghai 上海市	Shanghai 上海市	(021)36120519 (021)36120519	14	Overseas Chinese-funded 港澳台资	130,992	714(46)	11,297	Gas Fulling 气体充装

Top 10 Cities by Revenue 销售收入排名前10位城市	Province 省	Market share 市场份额 (%)	Number of firms 企业个数
Shanghai 上海市	Shanghai 上海市	22.39	28
Hangzhou 杭州市	Zhejiang 浙江省	14.57	9
Suzhou 苏州市	Jiangsu 江苏省	9.35	7
Wuxi 无锡市	Jiangsu 江苏省	7.34	3
Xi'an 西安市	Shannxi 陕西省	5.88	5
Weifang 潍坊市	Shandong 山东省	3.74	1
Ziyang 资阳市	Sichuan 四川省	3.72	2
Liuzhou 柳州市	Guangxi 广西	3.54	5
Kaifeng 开封市	Henan 河南省	3.32	2
Nanjing 南京市	Jiangsu 江苏省	3.12	4

10 Major Wholesalers 十家主要批发商	City 城市	Province 省	Telephone/Fax 电话/传真
SU MEC 中设江苏机械设备进出口（集团）公司	Nanjing 南京市	Jiangsu 江苏省	(025)4511888 (025)4411772
China Poster Mobile Communications Equipment Co.,Ltd. 中邮普泰移动通信设备股份有限公司	Beijing 北京市	Beijing 北京市	(010)66426993 (010)66426837
Sino Kama Co., Ltd. 中泰凯马股份有限公司	Shanghai 上海市	Shanghai 上海市	(021)62031188 (021)62030851
China Huayuan Group Co.,Ltd. 中国华源集团有限公司	Shanghai 上海市	Shanghai 上海市	(021)62031188 (021)62032288
Zhejiang Crand Imp.& Exp.Co.,Ltd. 浙江远大进出口有限公司	Ningbo 宁波市	Zhejiang 浙江省	(0574)87720170 (0574)87723350
Shandong Machinery Import & Export Group Corporation 山东省机械进出口集团公司	Qingdao 青岛市	Shandong 山东省	(0532)2661628 (0532)2991655
Qingdao Haier International Trade Co.,Ltd. 青岛海尔国际贸易有限公司	Qingdao 青岛市	Shandong 山东省	(0532)8938337 (0532)8939494
Guangdong Machinery Import & Export Group Corporation 广东省机械进出口集团公司	Guangzhou 广州市	Guangdong 广东省	(020)87782168 (020)87771803
China National Machinery Equipment Import & Export Corporation 中国机械设备进出口总公司	Beijing 北京市	Beijing 北京市	(010)63474306 (010)63261865
Beijing Cellstar Co.,Ltd. 北京蜂星事达电讯有限公司	Beijing 北京市	Beijing 北京市	(010)64602050 (010)64672648

3536: Refrigeration Equipment 冷冻设备制造业

The industry accounts for 0.198% of the total revenue of China's industrial sector in 2002. The rate of return on assets is 6.33%. 78.69% of all firms in the industry made a profit while 21.31% had negative returns.The top province in terms of the industry's revenue is Shanghai, accounting for 27.50% of the total revenue.
2002年本行业收入占全行业的0.198%，资产利润率为6.33%。78.69%的企业赢利，21.31%的企业亏损。收入最高的省为上海市，占本行业的27.50%。

	Total number of firms 企业总数	Total number of employees 职工总数	Total revenue (Mil.RMB) 总销售收入（百万元）	Total profit (Mil.RMB) 总利润（百万元）	Return on assets 资产利润率（%）	Return on equity 权益利润率（%）	Labour productivity ('000 RMB/ worker) 劳动生产率（千元/人）	Debts/ assets 资产负债率（%）	Total assets (Mil.RMB) 总资产（百万元）
Industry Overall 行业总体	244	63,060	21,238	1,773	6.33	14.04	103.15	54.92	28,013

	Number of firms 企业个数	Average number of employees 平均职工人数	Average revenue ('000 RMB) 平均销售收入（千元）	Average profit ('000 RMB) 平均利润（千元）	Return on assets 资产利润率（%）	Return on equity 权益利润率（%）	Labour productivity ('000 RMB/ worker) 劳动生产率（千元/人）	Debts/ assets 资产负债率（%）	Average total assets ('000 RMB) 平均总资产（千元）
By ownership 产业所有权									
State-owned 国有	27	184	17,792	-345	-0.64	-2.13	25.86	69.96	53,963
Collective-owned 集体	27	281	100,752	11,743	8.69	18.73	98.42	53.58	135,088
Foreign & Overseas Chinese Funded 三资	77	209	102,405	11,112	8.37	16.75	170.28	50.06	132,820
By regional distribution 地区分布									
Central-North 华北	15	117	42,601	1,871	1.38	4.07	86.14	66.07	135,597
Beijing 北京	10	83	22,074	1,320	3.39	6.67	74.73	49.20	38,962
Tianjin 天津	3	247	93,751	-9,937	-2.15	-7.99	25.81	73.06	461,803
Hebei 河北	2	93	68,514	22,336	17.25	37.56	377.07	54.07	129,464
Shanxi 山西									
Inner Mongolia 内蒙古									
Northeast 东北	12	1,325	401,430	25,306	4.30	9.40	86.73	54.27	588,432
Liaoning 辽宁	9	1,555	515,208	32,357	4.39	9.31	94.36	52.85	737,116
Jilin 吉林									
Heilongjiang 黑龙江	3	637	60,099	4,153	2.92	12.33	30.82	76.35	142,380
Central-East 华东	154	216	84,159	8,033	8.29	17.43	120.47	52.45	96,946
Shanghai 上海	68	171	85,897	9,811	10.10	18.32	172.60	44.88	97,161
Jiangsu 江苏	37	273	87,014	7,722	6.70	16.37	80.48	59.07	115,289
Zhejiang 浙江	35	201	73,266	6,222	9.59	20.42	102.54	53.04	64,899
Anhui 安徽	2	95	22,691	1,579	8.39	15.96	52.22	47.44	18,822
Fujian 福建	1	70	11,069	943	7.78	11.73	27.23	33.63	12,117
Jiangxi 江西									
Shandong 山东	11	377	116,290	5,665	3.59	10.10	106.55	64.44	157,800
Central-South 中南	57	204	48,324	3,612	5.31	13.07	82.50	59.39	68,045
Henan 河南	10	189	25,444	-1,351	-2.49	-9.03	40.19	72.40	54,181
Hubei 湖北	8	237	40,457	2,406	3.08	5.04	49.00	38.79	78,041
Hunan 湖南	2	689	78,630	1,661	0.68	1.75	28.70	60.95	243,515
Guangdong 广东	33	173	60,254	5,982	9.07	24.01	131.23	62.21	65,946
Guangxi 广西	4	199	7,685	-139	-1.13	-1.79	7.03	36.95	12,291
Hainan 海南									
Southwest 西南	5	102	13,182	-268	-1.28	-3.77	27.74	66.10	21,021
Chongqing 重庆	2	137	12,440	-1,038	-2.37	-5.46	18.69	56.65	43,829
Sichuan 四川	1	44	10,850	1,245	45.96	62.25	81.59	26.17	2,709
Guizhou 贵州	1	165	29,814	-435	-3.73	-56.06	30.80	93.35	11,661
Yunnan 云南	1	26	368	-77	-2.50		12.46	266.95	3,080
Tibet 西藏									
Northwest 西北	1	50	633	-40	-0.97	-66.67	6.14	98.55	4,141
Shaanxi 陕西	1	50	633	-40	-0.97	-66.67	6.14	98.55	4,141
Gansu 甘肃									
Qinghai 青海									
Ningxia 宁夏									
Xinjiang 新疆									

3536: Refrigeration Equipment 冷冻设备制造业

Year 年份	Number of firms 企业个数	Rate of change 变化率 (%)	Number of employees 职工人数 (人)	Rate of change 变化率 (%)	Total revenue (Mil. RMB) 总销售收入 (百万元)	Rate of change 变化率 (%)	Total profit (Mil RMB) 总利润 (百万元)	Rate of change 变化率 (%)
2000	178		57,167		14,149		946	
2001	184	3.37	52,405	-8.33	16,003	13.10	1,325	40.06
2002	244	32.61	63,060	20.33	21,238	32.71	1,773	33.81

Major Products 主要产品	Output 产量	Unit 单位
Refrigerating & Air Conditioning Equipment 制冷空调设备	855,243	Unit 台(套)
Cold Storage Processing Equipment 冷藏加工设备	74,003	Unit 台(套、座)

10 Main Firms with Maximal Revenue (year founded) 收入最大的十家主要企业（创办年份）	City 城市	Province 省	Telephone/fax 电话/传真	Number of employees 职工人数	Ownership 产业所有权	Revenue ('000 RMB) 销售收入 (千元)	Profit('000 RMB) (rank) 利润(千元) (排名)	Total assets ('000 RMB) 总资产 (千元)	Major products 主要产品
Dalian Bingshan Group Co., Ltd. 大连冰山集团有限公司(1988)	Dalian 大连市	Liaoning 辽宁省	(0411)6653081 (0411)6641470	12,639	Limited-Liability 有限公司	4,539,000	288,470(1)	6,490,226	Refrigeration Equipment 制冷设备
Shanghai Hitachi Electrical Co.,Ltd. 上海日立电器有限公司(1993)	Shanghai 上海市	Shanghai 上海市	(021)50554560 (021)58991084	2,482	Foreign Funded 外商投资	1,859,892	174,045(3)	2,110,488	Refrigerating & Air Conditioner Equipment 制冷空调设备
Yantai Moon Group Co., Ltd. 烟台冰轮集团有限公司(1995)	Yantai 烟台市	Shandong 山东省	(0535)6243451 (0535)6252302	3,173	State Enterprises 国有独资	1,045,751	49,013(10)	1,499,198	Refrigeration Equipment 制冷设备
Zhejiang Chunhui Group Co., Ltd. 浙江春晖集团有限公司(1966)	Shaoxing 绍兴市	Zhejiang 浙江省	(0575)2164484 (0575)2150888	1,610	Private Owned 私营企业	824,583	85,317(5)	531,510	Refrigeration Equipment 制冷设备
York GuangZhou Air Conditioning And Refrigeration Co.,Ltd. 约克广州空调冷冻设备有限公司(1995)	Qingyuan 清远市	Guangdong 广东省	(0763)4681111 (0763)4681115	831	Foreign Funded 外商投资	770,411	65,130(8)	529,817	Wind Cold And Hot Pump 风冷热泵
Shanghai Hezhong Carrier Air Conditioning Equipment Co.,Ltd 上海合众开利空调设备有限公司(1987)	Shanghai 上海市	Shanghai 上海市	(021)65661188 (021)65695404	311	Foreign Funded 外商投资	394,400	102,037(4)	267,215	Refrigeration Equipment 制冷设备
Shanghai Tonghui Carrier Air-Conditioning Equipment Co.,Ltd 上海通惠开利空调设备有限公司(1987)	Shanghai 上海市	Shanghai 上海市	(021)57420683 (021)57420685	337	Foreign Funded 外商投资	343,719	80,919(6)	193,587	Refrigerating & Air Conditioner Equipment 制冷空调设备
Shanghai Yileng Carrier Air Conditioning Equipment Co., Ltd. 上海一冷开利空调设备有限公司(1995)	Shanghai 上海市	Shanghai 上海市	(021)56805680 (021)56803051	433	Foreign Funded 外商投资	305,077	30,222(17)	301,906	Refrigerating & Air Conditioner Equipment 制冷空调设备
Zanussi Electricity Machinery Tianjin Compressor Co., Ltd. 扎努西电气机械天津压缩机有限公司(1993)	Tianjin 天津市	Tianjin 天津市	(022)24211737 (022)24302568	624	Foreign Funded 外商投资	274,606	-	1,047,941	Refrigerating Installation 冷冻设备
Shanghai Senlin Electrical Appliance Co., Ltd. 上海森林电器有限公司(1995)	Shanghai 上海市	Shanghai 上海市	(021)58996222 (021)58996146	1,119	Overseas Chinese-funded 港澳台资	269,132	-	921,178	Refrigerating & Air Conditioner Equipment 制冷空调设备

Top 10 Cities by Revenue 销售收入排名前10位城市	Province 省	Market share 市场份额 (%)	Number of firms 企业个数
Shanghai 上海市	Shanghai 上海市	27.50	68
Dalian 大连市	Liaoning 辽宁省	21.67	4
Shaoxing 绍兴市	Zhejiang 浙江省	9.18	15
Wuxi 无锡市	Jiangsu 江苏省	7.54	5
Yantai 烟台市	Shandong 山东省	4.95	2
Qingyuan 清远市	Guangdong 广东省	3.78	2
Suzhou 苏州市	Jiangsu 江苏省	3.26	11
Guangzhou 广州市	Guangdong 广东省	1.86	12
Zhuhai 珠海市	Guangdong 广东省	1.59	6
Jiaxing 嘉兴市	Zhejiang 浙江省	1.43	1

10 Major Wholesalers 十家主要批发商	City 城市	Province 省	Telephone/Fax 电话/传真
SU MEC 中设江苏机械设备进出口（集团）公司	Nanjing 南京市	Jiangsu 江苏省	(025)4511888 (025)4411772
China Poster Mobile Communications Equipment Co.,Ltd. 中邮普泰移动通信设备股份有限公司	Beijing 北京市	Beijing 北京市	(010)66426993 (010)66426837
Sino Kama Co., Ltd. 中泰凯马股份有限公司	Shanghai 上海市	Shanghai 上海市	(021)62031188 (021)62030851
China Huayuan Group Co.,Ltd. 中国华源集团有限公司	Shanghai 上海市	Shanghai 上海市	(021)62031188 (021)62032288
Zhejiang Crand Imp.& Exp.Co.,Ltd. 浙江远大进出口有限公司	Ningbo 宁波市	Zhejiang 浙江省	(0574)87720170 (0574)87723350
Shandong Machinery Import & Export Group Corporation 山东省机械进出口集团公司	Qingdao 青岛市	Shandong 山东省	(0532)2661628 (0532)2991655
Qingdao Haier International Trade Co.,Ltd. 青岛海尔国际贸易有限公司	Qingdao 青岛市	Shandong 山东省	(0532)8938337 (0532)8939494
Guangdong Machinery Import & Export Group Corporation 广东省机械进出口集团公司	Guangzhou 广州市	Guangdong 广东省	(020)87782168 (020)87771803
China National Machinery Equipment Import & Export Corporation 中国机械设备进出口总公司	Beijing 北京市	Beijing 北京市	(010)63474506 (010)63261865
Beijing Cellstar Co.,Ltd. 北京蜂星事达电讯有限公司	Beijing 北京市	Beijing 北京市	(010)64602050 (010)64672648

3537: Pneumatic Tools 风动工具制造业

The industry accounts for 0.010% of the total revenue of China's industrial sector in 2002. The rate of return on assets is 2.41%. 82.76% of all firms in the industry made a profit while 17.24% had negative returns.The top province in terms of the industry's revenue is Guangxi, accounting for 27.86% of the total revenue.
2002年本行业收入占全行业的 0.010%，资产利润率为 2.41%。82.76%的企业赢利，17.24%的企业亏损。收入最高的省为广西，占本行业的27.86%。

	Total number of firms 企业总数	Total number of employees 职工总数	Total revenue (Mil.RMB) 总销售收入 (百万元)	Total profit (Mil.RMB) 总利润 (百万元)	Return on assets 资产利润率 (%)	Return on equity 权益利润率 (%)	Labour productivity ('000 RMB/ worker) 劳动生产率 (千元/人)	Debts/ assets 资产负债率 (%)	Total assets (Mil.RMB) 总资产 (百万元)
Industry Overall 行业总体	29	9,443	1,027	63	2.41	5.84	27.82	58.78	2,617

	Number of firms 企业个数	Average number of employees 平均职工人数	Average revenue ('000 RMB) 平均销售收入 (千元)	Average profit ('000 RMB) 平均利润 (千元)	Return on assets 资产利润率 (%)	Return on equity 权益利润率 (%)	Labour productivity ('000 RMB/ worker) 劳动生产率 (千元/人)	Debts/ assets 资产负债率 (%)	Average total assets ('000 RMB) 平均总资产 (千元)
By ownership 产业所有权									
State-owned 国有	6	659	18,356	-5,723	-7.21		9.07	108.38	79,358
Collective-owned 集体	1	10	6,432	238	8.93	8.93	156.70		2,665
Foreign & Overseas Chinese Funded 三资	9	164	28,953	1,544	5.31	8.87	47.11	40.14	29,084
By regional distribution 地区分布									
Central-North 华北	2	723	12,499	-16,740	-18.13		1.21	147.05	92,310
Beijing 北京	1	93	13,623	797	5.98	8.55	59.11	30.10	13,337
Tianjin 天津									
Hebei 河北	1	1,353	11,374	-34,276	-20.01		-2.76	156.16	171,282
Shanxi 山西									
Inner Mongolia 内蒙古									
Northeast 东北	5	414	25,424	-45	-0.04	-0.24	23.35	82.17	102,910
Liaoning 辽宁	3	606	37,881	-98	-0.06	-0.33	25.22	82.02	167,813
Jilin 吉林	1	213	6,599	101	1.56	15.66	9.76	90.05	6,483
Heilongjiang 黑龙江	1	42	6,875	-30	-0.65	-5.17	11.48	87.47	4,629
Central-East 华东	15	246	28,961	1,201	3.73	10.04	36.87	62.81	32,156
Shanghai 上海	5	126	25,307	1,389	6.69	12.09	52.10	44.71	20,774
Jiangsu 江苏	3	371	37,233	970	1.40	5.55	28.89	74.84	69,433
Zhejiang 浙江	3	177	20,478	1,045	7.01	20.96	22.90	66.56	14,908
Anhui 安徽									
Fujian 福建	1	59	10,509	118	1.79	3.58	46.66	49.96	6,587
Jiangxi 江西	1	1,167	27,828	13	0.01	0.03	15.77	55.09	98,475
Shandong 山东	2	97	48,206	2,443	23.97	69.30	196.33	65.41	10,190
Central-South 中南	5	435	85,675	15,673	5.51	8.81	33.91	37.53	284,662
Henan 河南									
Hubei 湖北	1	364	120,217	1,693	4.09	5.37	120.86	23.83	41,402
Hunan 湖南	1	666	15,296	38	0.07	0.27	9.02	75.20	56,169
Guangdong 广东	1	41	6,593	65	1.93	3.54	33.59	45.56	3,369
Guangxi 广西	2	552	143,135	38,285	5.79	9.09	20.27	36.33	661,186
Hainan 海南									
Southwest 西南	1	50	6,045	81	0.85	3.19	23.36	73.32	9,512
Chongqing 重庆									
Sichuan 四川	1	50	6,045	81	0.85	3.19	23.36	73.32	9,512
Guizhou 贵州									
Yunnan 云南									
Tibet 西藏									
Northwest 西北	1	10	6,432	238	8.93	8.93	156.70		2,665
Shaanxi 陕西	1	10	6,432	238	8.93	8.93	156.70		2,665
Gansu 甘肃									
Qinghai 青海									
Ningxia 宁夏									
Xinjiang 新疆									

3537: Pneumatic Tools 风动工具制造业

Year 年份	Number of firms 企业个数	Rate of change 变化率 (%)	Number of employees 职工人数 (人)	Rate of change 变化率 (%)	Total revenue (Mil. RMB) 总销售收入 (百万元)	Rate of change 变化率 (%)	Total profit (Mil RMB) 总利润 (百万元)	Rate of change 变化率 (%)
2000	37		11,285		611		-21	
2001	33	-10.81	11,517	2.06	907	48.45	69	-
2002	29	-12.12	9,443	-18.01	1,027	13.23	63	-8.70

Major Products 主要产品	Output 产量	Unit 单位
Pneumatic Tools 风动工具	14	10,000 Units 万台

10 Main Firms with Maximal Revenue (year founded) 收入最大的十家主要企业（创办年份）	City 城市	Province 省	Telephone/fax 电话/传真	Number of employees 职工人数	Ownership 产业所有权	Revenue ('000 RMB) 销售收入 (千元)	Profit('000 RMB) (rank) 利润(千元) (排名)	Total assets ('000 RMB) 总资产 (千元)	Major products 主要产品
LiuZhou WuLing Motors Co.,Ltd.	Liuzhou	Guangxi	(0772)3750455		State Enterprises				Automobile
柳州五菱汽车有限责任公司(1999)	柳州市	广西	(0772)3750018	847	国有独资	250,084	74246(1)	1,267,665	汽车
Shenyang Rock Drilling Co., Ltd.	Shenyang	Liaoning	(024)25874511		Joint Stock				Pneumatic Tools
沈阳凿岩机械股份有限公司(1955)	沈阳市	辽宁省		1,762	股份制	110,438	-	486,271	气动工具
Longkou Pneumatic Tool Factory	Yantai	Shandong	(0535)8911351		Joint Stock				Gas Trigger
龙口市风动工具厂(1952)	烟台市	山东省	(0535)8911252	150	股份制	85,000	4,730(3)	13,720	气扳机
Shanghai Hyphon Tool Co., Ltd.	Shanghai	Shanghai	(021)59593069		Overseas Chinese-funded				Pneumatic Tools
上海海峰工具有限公司(1993)	上海市	上海市	(021)59596923	273	港澳台资	60,998	5,940(2)	49,541	风动工具
ChangZhou Superay Tools Co.,Ltd.	Changzhou	Jiangsu	(0519)2321003		Overseas Chinese-funded				Pneumatic Tools
常州特辉工具有限公司(1993)	常州市	江苏省	(0519)2321001	343	港澳台资	53,330	2,460(4)	66,350	风动工具
Nanjing Engineering Machinery Factory	Nanjing	Jiangsu	(025)5503433		State-owned				Gas Pickax
南京工程机械厂(1952)	南京市	江苏省	(025)5502508	715	国有企业	52,430	150(14)	133,050	气镐
Shanghai Kangbao Electromechanical Co., Ltd.	Shanghai	Shanghai	(021)54711137		Foreign Funded				Air Compressor
上海康保机电有限公司(2001)	上海市	上海市	(021)64357915	50	外商投资	33,505	2,150(6)	23,283	空压机
NingBo Lis Industrial Co., Ltd.	Ningbo	Zhejiang	(0574)88474153		Private Owned				Pneumatic Tools
宁波李氏实业有限公司(1995)	宁波市	浙江省	(0574)88474153	286	私营企业	31,854	1,776(7)	16,317	风动工具
Jiangxi Yichun Pneumatic Tool Works	Yichun	Jiangxi	(0795)3251431		State-owned				Rock Drill
江西省宜春风动工具厂(1960)	宜春市	江西省	(0795)3251518	1,167	国有企业	27,828	13(22)	98,475	凿岩机
Ningbo Gaofeng Toll Co., Ltd.	Ningbo	Zhejiang	(0574)86061995		Overseas Chinese-funded				Pneumatic Tools
宁波高峰工具有限公司(1998)	宁波市	浙江省	(0574)86062554	190	港澳台资	24,960	1,269(9)	21,780	风动工具

Top 10 Cities by Revenue 销售收入排名前10位城市	Province 省	Market share 市场份额 (%)	Number of firms 企业个数
Liuzhou 柳州市	Guangxi 广西	24.34	1
Shanghai 上海市	Shanghai 上海市	12.32	5
Wuhan 武汉市	Hubei 湖北省	11.70	1
Shenyang 沈阳市	Liaoning 辽宁省	10.78	2
Yantai 烟台市	Shandong 山东省	8.27	1
Ningbo 宁波市	Zhejiang 浙江省	5.98	3
Changzhou 常州市	Jiangsu 江苏省	5.19	1
Nanjing 南京市	Jiangsu 江苏省	5.10	1
Guilin 桂林市	Guangxi 广西	3.52	1
Yichun 宜春市	Jiangxi 江西省	2.71	1

10 Major Wholesalers 十家主要批发商	City 城市	Province 省	Telephone/Fax 电话/传真
SU MEC	Nanjing	Jiangsu	(025)4511888
中设江苏机械设备进出口（集团）公司	南京市	江苏省	(025)4411772
China Poster Mobile Communications Equipment Co.,Ltd.	Beijing	Beijing	(010)66426993
中邮普泰移动通信设备股份有限公司	北京市	北京市	(010)66426837
Sino Kama Co., Ltd.	Shanghai	Shanghai	(021)62031188
中泰凯马股份有限公司	上海市	上海市	(021)62030851
China Huayuan Group Co.,Ltd.	Shanghai	Shanghai	(021)62031188
中国华源集团有限公司	上海市	上海市	(021)62032288
Zhejiang Crand Imp.& Exp.Co.,Ltd.	Ningbo	Zhejiang	(0574)87720170
浙江远大进出口有限公司	宁波市	浙江省	(0574)87723350
Shandong Machinery Import & Export Group Corporation	Qingdao	Shandong	(0532)2661628
山东省机械进出口集团公司	青岛市	山东省	(0532)2991655
Qingdao Haier International Trade Co.,Ltd.	Qingdao	Shandong	(0532)8938337
青岛海尔国际贸易有限公司	青岛市	山东省	(0532)8939494
Guangdong Machinery Import & Export Group Corporation	Guangzhou	Guangdong	(020)87782168
广东省机械进出口集团公司	广州市	广东省	(020)87771803
China National Machinery Equipment Import & Export Corporation	Beijing	Beijing	(010)63474506
中国机械设备进出口总公司	北京市	北京市	(010)63261865
Beijing Cellstar Co.,Ltd.	Beijing	Beijing	(010)64602050
北京蜂星事达电讯有限公司	北京市	北京市	(010)64672648

3538: Electric Tools 电动工具制造业

The industry accounts for 0.127% of the total revenue of China's industrial sector in 2002. The rate of return on assets is 6.28%. 82.95% of all firms in the industry made a profit while 17.05% had negative returns.The top province in terms of the industry's revenue is Jiangsu, accounting for 42.39% of the total revenue.
2002年本行业收入占全行业的 0.127%，资产利润率为 6.28%。82.95%的企业赢利，17.05%的企业亏损。收入最高的省为江苏省，占本行业的42.39%。

	Total number of firms 企业总数	Total number of employees 职工总数	Total revenue (Mil.RMB) 总销售收入（百万元）	Total profit (Mil.RMB) 总利润（百万元）	Return on assets 资产利润率 (%)	Return on equity 权益利润率 (%)	Labour productivity ('000 RMB/ worker) 劳动生产率（千元/人）	Debts/ assets 资产负债率 (%)	Total assets (Mil.RMB) 总资产（百万元）
Industry Overall 行业总体	258	58,855	13,625	716	6.28	14.43	57.87	56.50	11,412

	Number of firms 企业个数	Average number of employees 平均职工人数	Average revenue ('000 RMB) 平均销售收入（千元）	Average profit ('000 RMB) 平均利润（千元）	Return on assets 资产利润率 (%)	Return on equity 权益利润率 (%)	Labour productivity ('000 RMB/ worker) 劳动生产率（千元/人）	Debts/ assets 资产负债率 (%)	Average total assets ('000 RMB) 平均总资产（千元）
By ownership 产业所有权									
State-owned 国有	15	286	13,170	-1,197	-2.48	-38.75	16.22	93.59	48,213
Collective-owned 集体	13	162	23,293	146	0.93	2.81	36.57	66.95	15,738
Foreign & Overseas Chinese Funded 三资	60	271	102,192	6,749	7.70	13.88	97.77	44.54	87,688
By regional distribution 地区分布									
Central-North 华北	8	268	11,358	-824	-1.94		13.91	100.52	42,553
Beijing 北京	1	38	6	1,175	23.92	29.19		18.04	4,912
Tianjin 天津	3	162	4,674	277	0.99		27.13	107.60	27,994
Hebei 河北	3	347	23,603	-1,932	-3.15		10.88	104.61	61,241
Shanxi 山西									
Inner Mongolia 内蒙古	1	580	6,025	-2,797	-4.12	-30.84	9.16	86.63	67,808
Northeast 东北	2	1,015	168,988	5,114	2.43	4.78	44.90	49.20	210,565
Liaoning 辽宁	1	1,788	309,039	10,226	2.90	6.28	44.55	53.72	352,015
Jilin 吉林	1	242	28,937	1			47.48	26.19	69,114
Heilongjiang 黑龙江									
Central-East 华东	228	215	53,470	3,087	7.60	17.24	62.55	55.91	40,619
Shanghai 上海	15	197	41,408	1,135	2.62	8.30	57.71	68.48	43,392
Jiangsu 江苏	54	271	106,946	8,201	12.85	22.50	101.47	42.87	63,809
Zhejiang 浙江	145	197	36,648	1,755	5.60	14.63	44.69	61.70	31,321
Anhui 安徽									
Fujian 福建	3	196	60,177	438	0.68	1.20	70.23	43.77	64,931
Jiangxi 江西	3	156	4,060	-2,495	-5.20		13.69	102.95	47,955
Shandong 山东	8	207	36,038	-534	-1.50	-6.59	46.68	77.21	35,550
Central-South 中南	16	256	55,889	605	0.86	1.59	45.45	45.96	70,301
Henan 河南	4	242	8,019	-91	-1.06	-6.62	8.93	83.92	8,528
Hubei 湖北	1	122	40,000	266	2.37	8.22	98.48	71.16	11,220
Hunan 湖南	2	63	1,356	-305	-1.67	-5.67	9.85	70.50	18,225
Guangdong 广东	9	320	91,049	1,153	1.00	1.76	57.03	43.59	115,893
Guangxi 广西									
Hainan 海南									
Southwest 西南	4	418	27,636	-213	-0.32	-1.39	23.62	76.88	66,147
Chongqing 重庆	1	45	1,800	125	5.16	9.27	7.22	44.39	2,424
Sichuan 四川	2	450	47,636	376	0.41	1.38	35.92	70.09	91,078
Guizhou 贵州	1	725	13,471	-1,727	-2.16	-32.39	9.36	93.34	80,009
Yunnan 云南									
Tibet 西藏									
Northwest 西北									
Shaanxi 陕西									
Gansu 甘肃									
Qinghai 青海									
Ningxia 宁夏									
Xinjiang 新疆									

3538: Electric Tools 电动工具制造业

Year 年份	Number of firms 企业个数	Rate of change 变化率 (%)	Number of employees 职工人数 (人)	Rate of change 变化率 (%)	Total revenue (Mil. RMB) 总销售收入 (百万元)	Rate of change 变化率 (%)	Total profit (Mil RMB) 总利润 (百万元)	Rate of change 变化率 (%)
2000	172		41,532		10,227		601	
2001	211	22.67	49,142	18.32	10,313	0.84	512	-14.81
2002	258	22.27	58,855	19.77	13,625	32.11	716	39.84

Major Products 主要产品	Output 产量	Unit 单位
Electric Tools 电动工具	9,332	10,000 Units 万台

10 Main Firms with Maximal Revenue (year founded) 收入最大的十家主要企业（创办年份）	City 城市	Province 省	Telephone/fax 电话/传真	Number of employees 职工人数	Ownership 产业所有权	Revenue ('000 RMB) 销售收入 (千元)	Profit('000 RMB) (rank) 利润(千元)(排名)	Total assets ('000 RMB) 总资产 (千元)	Major products 主要产品
Makita (China) Co.,Ltd.	Suzhou	Jiangsu	(0512)57707710		Foreign Funded				Electromotion Tools
牧田(中国)有限公司(1974)	苏州市	江苏省	(0512)57713623	1,226	外商投资	1,160,014	117,501(2)	1,040,766	电动工具
Jiangsu Jinding Electric Tools Group Co.,Ltd.	Changzhou	Jiangsu	(0519)3341245		Private Owned				Electromotion Tools
江苏金鼎电动工具有限公司(1970)	常州市	江苏省	(0519)3341245	3,396	私营企业	938,020	49,060(3)	379,600	电动工具
Ningbo Economic Technology Development Zone Zhongqiang Electric	Ningbo	Zhejiang	(0574)86227880		Limited-Liability				Electromotion Tools
Tool Co., Ltd.宁波经济技术开发区中强电动工具有限公司(1993)	宁波市	浙江省	(0574)86227351	1,794	有限公司	449,634	23,520(5)	379,459	电动工具
SuZhou Taihu Industrial Co.,Ltd.	Suzhou	Jiangsu	(0512)65272518		Limited-Liability				Electromotion Tools
苏州太湖企业有限公司(1994)	苏州市	江苏省	(0512)65272512	2,000	有限公司	441,510	36,400(4)	525,040	电动工具
RYOBI (Dalian) Machine Tool Co., Ltd.	Dalian	Liaoning	(0411)7621111		Foreign Funded				Electromotion Tools
利优比（大连）机器有限公司(1994)	大连市	辽宁省	(0411)7623142	1,788	外商投资	309,039	10,226(14)	352,015	电动工具
Zhejiang Huafeng Electric Tools Co., Ltd.	Jinhua	Zhejiang	(0579)2911996		Limited-Liability				Electromotion Tools
浙江华丰电动工具有限公司(1988)	金华市	浙江省	(0579)2911967	1,129	有限公司	252,869	9,294(16)	168,172	电动工具
Hilfi (China) Co., Ltd.	Zhanjiang	Guangdong	(0759)3383968		Overseas Chinese-funded				Electric Drill
喜利得(中国)有限公司(1995)	湛江市	广东省	(0759)3383978	210	港澳台资	242,934	16,719(6)	578,410	电钻
Yongkang Jiahe Tools Co., Ltd.	Jinhua	Zhejiang	(0579)7230602		Private Owned				Electromotion Tools
永康市嘉禾工具有限公司(1997)	金华市	浙江省	(0579)7230600	1,137	私营企业	242,838	6,715(23)	147,123	电动工具
Hangzhou Bosch Power Tools Co.Ltd	Hangzhou	Zhejiang	(0571)88850987		Foreign Funded				Electromotion Tools
杭州博世电动工具有限公司(1996)	杭州市	浙江省	(0571)88862159	336	外商投资	195,633	1,575(72)	143,302	电动工具
Shanghai Hitachi Power Tools Co.,Ltd.	Shanghai	Shanghai	(021)64300041		Foreign Funded				Electromotion Tools
上海日立电动工具有限公司(1991)	上海市	上海市	(021)64301835	1,022	外商投资	190,550	-	342,928	电动工具

Top 10 Cities by Revenue 销售收入排名前10位城市	Province 省	Market share 市场份额 (%)	Number of firms 企业个数
Suzhou 苏州市	Jiangsu 江苏省	23.20	8
Jinhua 金华市	Zhejiang 浙江省	18.66	79
Ningbo 宁波市	Zhejiang 浙江省	11.86	39
Changzhou 常州市	Jiangsu 江苏省	8.92	13
Nantong 南通市	Jiangsu 江苏省	6.11	23
Shanghai 上海市	Shanghai 上海市	4.56	15
Hangzhou 杭州市	Zhejiang 浙江省	3.27	8
Dalian 大连市	Liaoning 辽宁省	2.27	1
Nanjing 南京市	Jiangsu 江苏省	2.13	4
Wenzhou 温州市	Zhejiang 浙江省	2.00	10

10 Major Wholesalers 十家主要批发商	City 城市	Province 省	Telephone/Fax 电话/传真
SU MEC	Nanjing	Jiangsu	(025)4511888
中设江苏机械设备进出口（集团）公司	南京市	江苏省	(025)4411772
China Poster Mobile Communications Equipment Co.,Ltd.	Beijing	Beijing	(010)66426993
中邮普泰移动通信设备股份有限公司	北京市	北京市	(010)66426837
Sino Kama Co., Ltd.	Shanghai	Shanghai	(021)62031188
中泰凯马股份有限公司	上海市	上海市	(021)62030851
China Huayuan Group Co.,Ltd.	Shanghai	Shanghai	(021)62031188
中国华源集团有限公司	上海市	上海市	(021)62032288
Zhejiang Crand Imp.& Exp.Co.,Ltd.	Ningbo	Zhejiang	(0574)87720170
浙江远大进出口有限公司	宁波市	浙江省	(0574)87723350
Shandong Machinery Import & Export Group Corporation	Qingdao	Shandong	(0532)2661628
山东省机械进出口集团公司	青岛市	山东省	(0532)2991655
Qingdao Haier International Trade Co.,Ltd.	Qingdao	Shandong	(0532)8938337
青岛海尔国际贸易有限公司	青岛市	山东省	(0532)8939494
Guangdong Machinery Import & Export Group Corporation	Guangzhou	Guangdong	(020)87782168
广东省机械进出口集团公司	广州市	广东省	(020)87771803
China National Machinery Equipment Import & Export Corporation	Beijing	Beijing	(010)63474506
中国机械设备进出口总公司	北京市	北京市	(010)63261865
Beijing Cellstar Co.,Ltd.	Beijing	Beijing	(010)64602050
北京蜂星事达电讯有限公司	北京市	北京市	(010)64672648

3539: Other General Equipment 其他通用设备制造业

The industry accounts for 0.059% of the total revenue of China's industrial sector in 2002. The rate of return on assets is 4.00%. 85.19% of all firms in the industry made a profit while 14.81% had negative returns.The top province in terms of the industry's revenue is Jiangsu, accounting for 28.53% of the total revenue.
2002年本行业收入占全行业的 0.059%，资产利润率为 4.00%。85.19%的企业赢利，14.81%的企业亏损。收入最高的省为江苏省，占本行业的28.53%。

	Total number of firms 企业总数	Total number of employees 职工总数	Total revenue (Mil.RMB) 总销售收入 (百万元)	Total profit (Mil.RMB) 总利润 (百万元)	Return on assets 资产利润率 (%)	Return on equity 权益利润率 (%)	Labour productivity ('000 RMB/ worker) 劳动生产率 (千元/人)	Debts/ assets 资产负债率 (%)	Total assets (Mil.RMB) 总资产 (百万元)
Industry Overall 行业总体	243	49,154	6,295	407	4.00	9.77	40.58	59.04	10,180

	Number of firms 企业个数	Average number of employees 平均职工人数	Average revenue ('000 RMB) 平均销售收入 (千元)	Average profit ('000 RMB) 平均利润 (千元)	Return on assets 资产利润率 (%)	Return on equity 权益利润率 (%)	Labour productivity ('000 RMB/ worker) 劳动生产率 (千元/人)	Debts/ assets 资产负债率 (%)	Average total assets ('000 RMB) 平均总资产 (千元)
By ownership 产业所有权									
State-owned 国有	36	336	15,337	-1,105	-1.52	-5.04	16.13	69.88	72,759
Collective-owned 集体	28	243	24,740	920	3.36	9.44	35.70	64.38	27,336
Foreign & Overseas Chinese Funded 三资	28	145	55,381	10,141	15.67	26.45	126.29	40.76	64,724
By regional distribution 地区分布									
Central-North 华北	26	273	52,561	8,673	11.81	23.18	62.34	49.06	73,460
Beijing 北京	3	115	32,361	1,046	2.91	5.80	101.55	49.81	35,957
Tianjin 天津	11	267	89,513	19,371	17.16	30.28	113.73	43.33	112,892
Hebei 河北	9	352	23,675	858	1.59	4.41	16.93	63.94	53,933
Shanxi 山西	3	217	23,932	520	2.08	3.90	30.11	46.65	24,961
Inner Mongolia 内蒙古									
Northeast 东北	19	285	21,350	-899	-0.96	-4.09	22.82	76.50	93,539
Liaoning 辽宁	10	293	25,634	-731	-1.11	-4.48	20.03	75.20	65,777
Jilin 吉林	7	134	15,975	2,507	4.61	18.75	50.63	75.41	54,371
Heilongjiang 黑龙江	2	772	18,742	-13,663	-3.70	-16.99	11.26	78.23	369,440
Central-East 华东	149	171	24,993	1,280	4.80	11.71	44.50	59.00	26,647
Shanghai 上海	20	99	15,944	1,641	9.29	17.75	58.47	47.63	17,658
Jiangsu 江苏	54	229	33,255	1,069	3.08	8.47	39.34	63.60	34,671
Zhejiang 浙江	40	136	17,769	1,231	4.57	9.56	40.99	52.22	26,942
Anhui 安徽	2	323	13,268	-2,691	-6.08		9.52	106.23	44,268
Fujian 福建	4	136	21,672	4,671	15.53	24.95	47.89	37.74	30,065
Jiangxi 江西	2	28	142	-67	-4.72	-13,300.00	7.29	99.96	1,409
Shandong 山东	27	165	29,078	1,398	8.28	21.32	62.09	61.14	16,875
Central-South 中南	34	229	17,984	302	0.49	1.12	29.74	55.87	61,032
Henan 河南	9	161	6,809	63	0.81	3.27	14.02	75.07	7,695
Hubei 湖北	9	307	27,503	788	2.09	5.13	34.84	59.13	37,632
Hunan 湖南	5	133	8,008	-267	-2.39	-4.45	16.91	46.27	11,154
Guangdong 广东	8	300	28,952	489	0.25	0.55	39.48	53.37	191,651
Guangxi 广西	3	166	10,335	7	0.03	0.15	17.40	80.75	26,058
Hainan 海南									
Southwest 西南	9	257	15,787	257	0.98	2.23	20.71	56.14	26,346
Chongqing 重庆	3	545	27,734	475	0.96	1.97	20.38	51.39	49,647
Sichuan 四川	5	105	10,639	178	1.12	3.34	23.84	66.49	15,930
Guizhou 贵州									
Yunnan 云南	1	158	5,682				13.79	42.41	8,524
Tibet 西藏									
Northwest 西北	6	173	7,553	-748	-2.13	-3.40	13.61	37.29	35,038
Shaanxi 陕西	5	178	7,927	-761	-1.98	-3.05	13.77	35.14	38,493
Gansu 甘肃	1	149	5,686	-680	-3.83	-9.72	12.65	60.62	17,765
Qinghai 青海									
Ningxia 宁夏									
Xinjiang 新疆									

3539: Other General Equipment 其他通用设备制造业

Year 年份	Number of firms 企业个数	Rate of change 变化率(%)	Number of employees 职工人数(人)	Rate of change 变化率(%)	Total revenue (Mil. RMB) 总销售收入(百万元)	Rate of change 变化率(%)	Total profit (Mil RMB) 总利润(百万元)	Rate of change 变化率(%)
2000	248		60,552		4,677		121	
2001	263	6.05	57,837	-4.48	5,462	16.78	173	42.98
2002	243	-7.60	49,154	-15.01	6,295	15.25	407	135.26

Major Products 主要产品	Output 产量	Unit 单位

10 Main Firms with Maximal Revenue (year founded) 收入最大的十家主要企业（创办年份）	City 城市	Province 省	Telephone/fax 电话/传真	Number of employees 职工人数	Ownership 产业所有权	Revenue ('000 RMB) 销售收入(千元)	Profit('000 RMB) (rank) 利润(千元)(排名)	Total assets ('000 RMB) 总资产(千元)	Major products 主要产品
SEW Eurodrive (Tianjing) Co., Ltd.	Tianjin	Tianjin	(022)25322612		Foreign Funded				Speed-down Machine
SEW传动设备(天津)有限公司(1997)	天津市	天津市	(022)25322611	473	外商投资	430,272	171,111(1)	503,338	减速机
Taixing Speed Reducer Co., Ltd.	Taizhou	Jiangsu	(0523)7541046		Joint Stock				Speed-down Machine
泰星减速机股份有限公司(1984)	泰州市	江苏省	(0523)7635683	1,890	股份制	344,022	17,541(4)	248,647	减速机
JiangSu Tailong Decelerator Michinery Co.,Ltd.	Taizhou	Jiangsu	(0523)7668008		Collective-owned				Speed-down Machine
江苏省泰隆减速机股份有限公司(1970)	泰州市	江苏省	(0523)7665426	2,108	集体企业	237,833	8,863(8)	199,755	减速机
Qingdao Jiaonan Feichao Speed Reducer Stock Co.,Ltd.	Qingdao	Shandong	(0532)2151018		Joint Stock				Speed-down Machine
青岛市胶南飞超减速机股份有限公司(1956)	青岛市	山东省	(0532)2151938	290	股份制	138,200	3,750(24)	26,434	减速机
Tianjin Speed Reducer Co..,Ltd	Tianjin	Tianjin	(022)24328924		Joint Owned				Speed-down Machine
天津减速机股份有限公司(1957)	天津市	天津市	(022)24328568	1,167	联营企业	115,890	844(71)	157,381	减速机
Wuxi Hualian Welding and Cutting Equipment Factory	Wuxi	Jiangsu	(0510)5384577		Private Enterprises				H Tape Steel Production Line.H型
无锡华联焊割设备厂(1994)	无锡市	江苏省	(0510)5381880	260	私营独资	111,230	1,920(39)	57,668	钢生产线
Guangzhou Guangzhong Enterprise Group Co., Ltd.	Guangzhou	Guangdong	(020)84369817		State Enterprises				Chemical Equipment
广州广重企业集团有限公司(1948)	广州市	广东省	(020)84366767	1,172	国有独资	110,703	1,156(56)	1,245,893	化工设备
Sumitomo (SHI) CycLo Driven (China)Co., Ltd.	Tianjin	Tianjin	(022)24993501		Foreign Funded				Speed-down Machine
住友重机械减速机（中国）有限公司(1995)	天津市	天津市	(022)24993507	282	外商投资	106,145	1,396(48)	159,928	减速机
Hangzhou Wanjie Speed Reducer Co., Ltd.	Hangzhou	Zhejiang	(0571)82992222		Private Owned				Speed-down Machine
杭州万杰减速机有限公司(1996)	杭州市	浙江省	(0571)82993333	240	私营企业	98,704	8,492(9)	59,349	减速机
Flender Power Transmission (Tianjin) Co., Ltd.	Tianjin	Tianjin	(022)26972063		Foreign Funded				Speed-down Machine
弗兰德机电传动（天津）有限公司(1996)	天津市	天津市	(022)26972061	131	外商投资	93,300	4,920(17)	106,430	减速机

Top 10 Cities by Revenue 销售收入排名前10位城市	Province 省	Market share 市场份额 (%)	Number of firms 企业个数
Tianjin 天津市	Tianjin 天津市	15.64	11
Taizhou 泰州市	Jiangsu 江苏省	9.94	5
Wuxi 无锡市	Jiangsu 江苏省	6.13	13
Shanghai 上海市	Shanghai 上海市	5.07	20
Wenzhou 温州市	Zhejiang 浙江省	4.47	19
Qingdao 青岛市	Shandong 山东省	4.11	8
Hangzhou 杭州市	Zhejiang 浙江省	3.97	9
Changzhou 常州市	Jiangsu 江苏省	3.82	10
Wuhan 武汉市	Hubei 湖北省	2.80	4
Zibo 淄博市	Shandong 山东省	2.59	7

10 Major Wholesalers 十家主要批发商	City 城市	Province 省	Telephone/Fax 电话/传真
SU MEC	Nanjing	Jiangsu	(025)4511888
中设江苏机械设备进出口（集团）公司	南京市	江苏省	(025)4411772
China Poster Mobile Communications Equipment Co.,Ltd.	Beijing	Beijing	(010)66426993
中邮普泰移动通信设备股份有限公司	北京市	北京市	(010)66426837
Sino Kama Co., Ltd.	Shanghai	Shanghai	(021)62031188
中泰凯马股份有限公司	上海市	上海市	(021)62030851
China Huayuan Group Co.,Ltd.	Shanghai	Shanghai	(021)62031188
中国华源集团有限公司	上海市	上海市	(021)62032288
Zhejiang Crand Imp.& Exp.Co.,Ltd.	Ningbo	Zhejiang	(0574)87720170
浙江远大进出口有限公司	宁波市	浙江省	(0574)87723350
Shandong Machinery Import & Export Group Corporation	Qingdao	Shandong	(0532)2661628
山东省机械进出口集团公司	青岛市	山东省	(0532)2991655
Qingdao Haier International Trade Co.,Ltd.	Qingdao	Shandong	(0532)8938337
青岛海尔国际贸易有限公司	青岛市	山东省	(0532)8939494
Guangdong Machinery Import & Export Group Corporation	Guangzhou	Guangdong	(020)87782168
广东省机械进出口集团公司	广州市	广东省	(020)87771803
China National Machinery Equipment Import & Export Corporation	Beijing	Beijing	(010)63474506
中国机械设备进出口总公司	北京市	北京市	(010)63261865
Beijing Cellstar Co.,Ltd.	Beijing	Beijing	(010)64602050
北京蜂星事达电讯有限公司	北京市	北京市	(010)64672648

3541: Bearings 轴承制造业

The industry accounts for 0.254% of the total revenue of China's industrial sector in 2002. The rate of return on assets is 3.16%. 82.09% of all firms in the industry made a profit while 17.91% had negative returns.The top province in terms of the industry's revenue is Zhejiang, accounting for 27.70% of the total revenue.
2002年本行业收入占全行业的0.254%，资产利润率为3.16%。82.09%的企业赢利，17.91%的企业亏损。收入最高的省为浙江省，占本行业的27.70%。

	Total number of firms 企业总数	Total number of employees 职工总数	Total revenue (Mil.RMB) 总销售收入（百万元）	Total profit (Mil.RMB) 总利润（百万元）	Return on assets 资产利润率 (%)	Return on equity 权益利润率 (%)	Labour productivity ('000 RMB/worker) 劳动生产率（千元/人）	Debts/assets 资产负债率 (%)	Total assets (Mil.RMB) 总资产（百万元）
Industry Overall 行业总体	698	268,704	27,195	1,443	3.16	8.19	33.09	61.48	45,725

	Number of firms 企业个数	Average number of employees 平均职工人数	Average revenue ('000 RMB) 平均销售收入（千元）	Average profit ('000 RMB) 平均利润（千元）	Return on assets 资产利润率 (%)	Return on equity 权益利润率 (%)	Labour productivity ('000 RMB/worker) 劳动生产率（千元/人）	Debts/assets 资产负债率 (%)	Average total assets ('000 RMB) 平均总资产（千元）
By ownership 产业所有权									
State-owned 国有	93	620	29,375	-1,638	-1.45	-6.41	18.04	77.37	112,859
Collective-owned 集体	91	189	16,098	1,226	5.67	16.43	31.52	65.47	21,613
Foreign & Overseas Chinese Funded 三资	93	325	71,060	7,144	7.22	12.27	69.73	41.15	98,931
By regional distribution 地区分布									
Central-North 华北	36	428	20,142	-59	-0.10	-0.41	27.91	75.74	59,695
Beijing 北京	5	607	72,891	938	0.73	1.80	78.16	59.35	127,883
Tianjin 天津	4	43	4,764	-1,174	-3.75	-815.28	-2.71	99.54	31,275
Hebei 河北	21	362	13,023	313	0.76	3.93	21.21	80.58	40,989
Shanxi 山西	5	897	13,626	-1,736	-1.69	-10.02	7.04	83.12	102,668
Inner Mongolia 内蒙古	1	100						32.92	10,390
Northeast 东北	51	903	74,861	3,141	1.51	3.06	26.91	50.48	207,429
Liaoning 辽宁	36	717	80,366	3,963	2.25	4.38	37.24	48.73	176,446
Jilin 吉林	6	830	23,769	193	0.19	0.71	19.48	73.42	102,106
Heilongjiang 黑龙江	9	1,693	86,906	1,815	0.45	0.90	11.84	49.66	401,573
Central-East 华东	474	271	37,130	2,718	5.96	13.83	43.46	56.90	45,612
Shanghai 上海	43	331	74,604	6,411	5.73	10.12	73.42	43.38	111,917
Jiangsu 江苏	114	293	37,101	2,431	5.76	13.80	40.23	58.21	42,171
Zhejiang 浙江	232	231	32,468	2,625	7.79	19.46	41.60	59.96	33,681
Anhui 安徽	15	341	28,770	286	0.52	2.62	37.73	80.22	55,267
Fujian 福建	14	315	34,387	3,476	5.44	7.87	44.79	30.91	63,889
Jiangxi 江西	8	158	6,042	-364	-1.47	-6.16	13.47	76.10	24,712
Shandong 山东	48	345	34,754	1,592	3.37	12.21	33.92	72.36	47,183
Central-South 中南	99	504	34,904	-20	-0.03	-0.12	20.00	77.33	69,226
Henan 河南	43	797	49,594	1,002	0.95	3.19	19.47	70.20	105,300
Hubei 湖北	22	264	17,051	-445	-1.17	-24.22	28.31	95.16	37,986
Hunan 湖南	12	205	11,764	-21	-0.05		22.07	113.55	45,429
Guangdong 广东	18	300	41,434	1,345	3.28	7.34	17.42	55.35	41,011
Guangxi 广西	4	480	15,218	-14,792	-28.66		8.98	144.35	51,616
Hainan 海南									
Southwest 西南	20	570	44,993	1,102	1.20	5.01	33.65	76.10	92,088
Chongqing 重庆	4	774	151,455	10,945	5.25	13.99	89.47	62.47	208,437
Sichuan 四川	9	244	14,710	-480	-1.54	-4.87	20.20	68.35	31,132
Guizhou 贵州	4	1,174	27,008	-3,980	-2.87		8.10	108.45	138,567
Yunnan 云南	3	470	17,873	-502	-0.87	-1.76	17.13	50.77	57,853
Tibet 西藏									
Northwest 西北	18	969	38,727	-1,279	-0.86	-4.24	14.61	79.75	149,007
Shaanxi 陕西	3	685	11,931	-7,842	-6.51		7.51	104.45	120,479
Gansu 甘肃	8	959	27,036	-177	-0.15	-0.98	7.46	84.97	120,426
Qinghai 青海									
Ningxia 宁夏	6	1,200	70,712	315	0.15	0.49	24.07	69.70	211,731
Xinjiang 新疆	1	520	20,728	30	0.03	0.10	17.11	65.92	86,883

3541: Bearings 轴承制造业

Year 年份	Number of firms 企业个数	Rate of change 变化率 (%)	Number of employees 职工人数 (人)	Rate of change 变化率 (%)	Total revenue (Mil. RMB) 总销售收入 (百万元)	Rate of change 变化率 (%)	Total profit (Mil RMB) 总利润 (百万元)	Rate of change 变化率 (%)
2000	576		292,888		22,151		656	
2001	643	11.63	278,358	-4.96	23,771	7.31	898	36.89
2002	698	8.55	268,704	-3.47	27,195	14.40	1,443	60.69

Major Products 主要产品	Output 产量	Unit 单位
Bearing 轴承	37	100,000,000 Sets 亿套

10 Main Firms with Maximal Revenue (year founded) 收入最大的十家主要企业（创办年份）	City 城市	Province 省	Telephone/fax 电话/传真	Number of employees 职工人数	Ownership 产业所有权	Revenue ('000 RMB) 销售收入 (千元)	Profit('000 RMB) (rank) 利润(千元) (排名)	Total assets ('000 RMB) 总资产 (千元)	Major products 主要产品
Shanghai MINEBER Electronics & Hi-Tech Components Co., Ltd.上海美蓓亚精密机电有限公司(1994)	Shanghai 上海市	Shanghai 上海市	(021)59290113 (021)59290260	5,268	Foreign Funded 外商投资	1,887,113	221,877(1)	2,996,271	Bearing 轴承
Wafangdian Bearing Group Co.,Ltd. 瓦房店轴承集团有限责任公司(1938)	Dalian 大连市	Liaoning 辽宁省	(0411)5509888 (0411)5500585	13,689	State Enterprises 国有独资	1,848,301	59,633(2)	3,899,327	Bearing 轴承
Luoyang Bearing Group Corp. 洛阳轴承集团公司(1957)	Luoyang 洛阳市	Henan 河南省	(0379)4986116 (0379)4922784	24,346	State Enterprises 国有独资	1,482,199	11,001(38)	3,358,947	Bearing 轴承
C & U GROUP Co.,Ltd. 人本集团有限公司(1997)	Wenzhou 温州市	Zhejiang 浙江省	(0577)86554123 (0577)86555014	2,483	Private Owned 私营企业	718,204	43,814(5)	724,570	Bearing 轴承
Harbin Bearing Group Corp. 哈尔滨轴承集团公司(1950)	Harbin 哈尔滨市	Heilongjiang 黑龙江省	(0451)55115011 (0451)55663704	11,269	State-owned 国有企业	608,663	29,940(10)	3,174,067	Bearing 轴承
Jiangsu Hongtai Electromechanical Co., Ltd. 江苏鸿泰机电股份有限公司(1966)	Taizhou 泰州市	Jiangsu 江苏省	(0523)6135020 (0523)6131724	1,189	Joint Stock 股份制	342,364	14,383(33)	138,472	Table Vice 台虎钳
Huanchi Group Co.,Ltd. 环驰集团有限公司(2000)	Ningbo 宁波市	Zhejiang 浙江省	(0574)63199858 (0574)63197123	2,439	Private Owned 私营企业	290,911	20,340(20)	462,776	Minitype Bearing 微型轴承
Kunshan NSK Co., Ltd. 昆山恩斯克有限公司(1997)	Suzhou 苏州市	Jiangsu 江苏省	(0520)57715654 (0520)57715689	710	Foreign Funded 外商投资	272,935	27,151(14)	648,193	Bearing 轴承
Xibei Bearing Group Co.,Ltd. 西北轴承股份有限公司(1996)	Yinchuan 银川市	Ningxia 宁夏	(0951)2021581 (0951)2036747	5,036	Joint Stock 股份制	265,919	-	990,304	Bearing 轴承
Cixing Group Co., Ltd. 慈兴集团有限公司(2000)	Ningbo 宁波市	Zhejiang 浙江省	(0574)63106524 (0574)63100564	1,315	Private Owned 私营企业	245,214	47,187(4)	388,076	Bearing 轴承

Top 10 Cities by Revenue 销售收入排名前10位城市	Province 省	Market share 市场份额 (%)	Number of firms 企业个数
Ningbo 宁波市	Zhejiang 浙江省	12.03	123
Shanghai 上海市	Shanghai 上海市	11.80	43
Dalian 大连市	Liaoning 辽宁省	9.70	22
Luoyang 洛阳市	Henan 河南省	6.84	17
Shaoxing 绍兴市	Zhejiang 浙江省	6.41	38
Wuxi 无锡市	Jiangsu 江苏省	3.96	35
Changzhou 常州市	Jiangsu 江苏省	3.41	27
Wenzhou 温州市	Zhejiang 浙江省	3.08	8
Suzhou 苏州市	Jiangsu 江苏省	3.03	10
Harbin 哈尔滨市	Heilongjiang 黑龙江省	2.69	5

10 Major Wholesalers 十家主要批发商	City 城市	Province 省	Telephone/Fax 电话/传真
SU MEC 中设江苏机械设备进出口（集团）公司	Nanjing 南京市	Jiangsu 江苏省	(025)4511888 (025)4411772
China Poster Mobile Communications Equipment Co.,Ltd. 中邮普泰移动通信设备股份有限公司	Beijing 北京市	Beijing 北京市	(010)66426993 (010)66426837
Sino Kama Co., Ltd. 中泰凯马股份有限公司	Shanghai 上海市	Shanghai 上海市	(021)62031188 (021)62030851
China Huayuan Group Co.,Ltd. 中国华源集团有限公司	Shanghai 上海市	Shanghai 上海市	(021)62031188 (021)62032288
Zhejiang Crand Imp.& Exp.Co.,Ltd. 浙江远大进出口有限公司	Ningbo 宁波市	Zhejiang 浙江省	(0574)87720170 (0574)87723350
Shandong Machinery Import & Export Group Corporation 山东省机械进出口集团公司	Qingdao 青岛市	Shandong 山东省	(0532)2661628 (0532)2991655
Qingdao Haier International Trade Co.,Ltd. 青岛海尔国际贸易有限公司	Qingdao 青岛市	Shandong 山东省	(0532)8938337 (0532)8939494
Guangdong Machinery Import & Export Group Corporation 广东省机械进出口集团公司	Guangzhou 广州市	Guangdong 广东省	(020)87782168 (020)87771803
China National Machinery Equipment Import & Export Corporation 中国机械设备进出口总公司	Beijing 北京市	Beijing 北京市	(010)63474506 (010)63261865
Beijing Cellstar Co.,Ltd. 北京蜂星事达电讯有限公司	Beijing 北京市	Beijing 北京市	(010)64602050 (010)64672648

3542: Valves 阀门制造业

The industry accounts for 0.138% of the total revenue of China's industrial sector in 2002. The rate of return on assets is 4.09%. 87.86% of all firms in the industry made a profit while 12.14% had negative returns.The top province in terms of the industry's revenue is Zhejiang, accounting for 37.99% of the total revenue.
2002年本行业收入占全行业的 0.138%，资产利润率为 4.09%。87.86%的企业赢利，12.14%的企业亏损。收入最高的省为浙江省，占本行业的37.99%。

	Total number of firms 企业总数	Total number of employees 职工总数	Total revenue (Mil.RMB) 总销售收入 (百万元)	Total profit (Mil.RMB) 总利润 (百万元)	Return on assets 资产利润率 (%)	Return on equity 权益利润率 (%)	Labour productivity ('000 RMB/ worker) 劳动生产率 (千元/人)	Debts/ assets 资产负债率 (%)	Total assets (Mil.RMB) 总资产 (百万元)
Industry Overall 行业总体	659	111,678	14,854	724	4.09	9.82	37.84	58.34	17,704

	Number of firms 企业个数	Average number of employees 平均职工人数	Average revenue ('000 RMB) 平均销售收入 (千元)	Average profit ('000 RMB) 平均利润 (千元)	Return on assets 资产利润率 (%)	Return on equity 权益利润率 (%)	Labour productivity ('000 RMB/ worker) 劳动生产率 (千元/人)	Debts/ assets 资产负债率 (%)	Average total assets ('000 RMB) 平均总资产 (千元)
By ownership 产业所有权									
State-owned 国有	58	328	23,909	-665	-1.16	-6.09	22.13	80.90	57,159
Collective-owned 集体	76	166	20,631	962	6.92	15.54	35.33	55.44	13,900
Foreign & Overseas Chinese Funded 三资	90	185	37,032	2,432	6.85	14.03	52.83	51.16	35,482
By regional distribution 地区分布									
Central-North 华北	59	237	23,714	1,013	3.09	8.34	33.21	63.00	32,826
Beijing 北京	10	104	32,542	2,304	4.93	10.42	110.77	52.71	46,774
Tianjin 天津	26	152	17,497	265	1.07	2.29	33.41	53.18	24,781
Hebei 河北	17	445	31,868	1,636	4.54	18.32	25.65	75.25	36,077
Shanxi 山西	5	261	15,326	570	1.66	7.26	17.69	77.18	34,418
Inner Mongolia 内蒙古	1	115	400	-815	-2.08	-30.32	-4.48	93.16	39,270
Northeast 东北	43	172	17,005	295	0.85	2.58	33.72	66.85	34,588
Liaoning 辽宁	34	189	18,163	179	0.51	1.45	31.90	65.01	35,327
Jilin 吉林	3	131	8,014	322	1.09	2.65	10.07	58.93	29,599
Heilongjiang 黑龙江	6	98	14,936	940	2.86	15.54	69.37	81.61	32,895
Central-East 华东	461	141	22,566	1,097	5.18	11.70	42.93	55.73	21,178
Shanghai 上海	48	120	21,842	889	3.65	10.51	53.11	65.25	24,354
Jiangsu 江苏	99	163	27,377	924	3.82	8.60	46.93	55.59	24,182
Zhejiang 浙江	263	117	21,456	1,307	7.08	14.30	44.17	50.51	18,464
Anhui 安徽	11	338	16,084	282	0.84	2.89	19.17	70.88	33,540
Fujian 福建	11	105	11,084	585	5.25	10.72	40.91	51.00	11,142
Jiangxi 江西	2	156	5,015	-231	-3.11	-8.67	10.63	64.12	7,409
Shandong 山东	27	258	25,643	698	2.25	6.82	34.27	66.99	31,033
Central-South 中南	70	240	25,981	1,554	3.24	7.04	33.22	53.98	47,970
Henan 河南	33	303	31,391	700	2.32	7.29	32.34	68.18	30,193
Hubei 湖北	14	185	20,705	2,050	3.30	5.56	33.79	40.69	62,194
Hunan 湖南	8	198	17,712	1,374	6.39	15.98	30.44	60.03	21,508
Guangdong 广东	14	170	24,406	3,391	3.65	7.41	41.69	50.70	92,847
Guangxi 广西	1	240	9,541	-1,500	-7.94	-61.07	-1.78	87.01	18,900
Hainan 海南									
Southwest 西南	19	236	18,636	2,172	5.94	15.17	28.99	60.82	36,553
Chongqing 重庆	5	240	16,847	392	6.80	19.12	16.35	64.46	5,762
Sichuan 四川	12	247	21,694	3,314	6.46	16.15	36.22	59.98	51,293
Guizhou 贵州	1	115	3,830	-486	-2.07		-6.23	105.52	23,517
Yunnan 云南	1	192	5,692	24	0.09	0.14	17.31	36.86	26,653
Tibet 西藏									
Northwest 西北	7	595	21,164	-543	-0.82	-14.69	9.45	94.42	66,267
Shaanxi 陕西	3	342	21,575	238	0.49	1.84	18.55	73.53	48,898
Gansu 甘肃	4	785	20,856	-1,130	-1.42		6.48	104.08	79,295
Qinghai 青海									
Ningxia 宁夏									
Xinjiang 新疆									

Year 年份	Number of firms 企业个数	Rate of change 变化率 (%)	Number of employees 职工人数 (人)	Rate of change 变化率 (%)	Total revenue (Mil. RMB) 总销售收入 (百万元)	Rate of change 变化率 (%)	Total profit (Mil RMB) 总利润 (百万元)	Rate of change 变化率 (%)
2000	518		112,461		10,894		403	
2001	595	14.86	110,241	-1.97	12,613	15.78	580	43.92
2002	659	10.76	111,678	1.30	14,854	17.77	724	24.83

Major Products 主要产品	Output 产量	Unit 单位
Valve 阀门	76	10,000 Tons 万吨

10 Main Firms with Maximal Revenue (year founded) 收入最大的十家主要企业（创办年份）	City 城市	Province 省	Telephone/fax 电话/传真	Number of employees 职工人数	Ownership 产业所有权	Revenue ('000 RMB) 销售收入 (千元)	Profit('000 RMB) (rank) 利润(千元) (排名)	Total assets ('000 RMB) 总资产 (千元)	Major products 主要产品
SUFA Technology Industry Co.,Ltd.CNNC	Suzhou	Jiangsu	(0512)67533655		State-owned				Pipeline Valve
中核苏阀科技实业股份有限公司(1952)	苏州市	江苏省	(0512)67532587	1,539	国有企业	274,115	-	643,900	管道阀门
Ningbo Amico Copper Valves Manufacturing Inc.	Ningbo	Zhejiang	(0574)87676118		Foreign Funded				Valve
宁波埃美柯铜阀门有限公司(1986)	宁波市	浙江省	(0574)87359048	784	外商投资	226,222	11,011(11)	119,708	阀门
Zhejiang Best & Honest Electromechanical Co.,Ltd.	Taizhou	Zhejiang	(0576)7101230		Joint Stock				Valve
浙江博民机电股份有限公司(1998)	台州市	浙江省	(0576)7101229	328	股份制	211,139	4,249(47)	85,955	阀门
NingBo Huacheng Valve Co.,Ltd.	Ningbo	Zhejiang	(0574)65273166		Foreign Funded				Copper Valve
宁波华成阀门有限公司(1993)	宁波市	浙江省	(0574)65572800	350	外商投资	152,415	18,028(7)	100,650	铜阀门
Zhejiang Tefulong Group Co., Ltd.	Wenzhou	Zhejiang	(0577)86533555		Limited-Liability				Valve
特福隆集团有限公司(1998)	温州市	浙江省	(0577)86554281	220	有限公司	151,611	13,650(8)	190,347	阀门
Henan Shangdie Valve Co., Ltd.	Zhengzhou	Henan	(0371)8919888		Joint Stock				Butterfly Valve蝶阀
河南上蝶阀门股份有限公司(1969)	郑州市	河南省	(0371)8919991	550	股份制	148,000	1,280(125)	88,500	系列产品
Wenzhou Tingyu Group Co.,Ltd.	Wenzhou	Zhejiang	(0577)88620035		Private Owned				Valve
温州挺宇集团有限公司(1996)	温州市	浙江省	(0577)88620230	203	私营企业	132,819	5,527(36)	82,832	阀门
TianJin Tanggu Watts Valve Co.,Ltd.	Tianjin	Tianjin	(022)65727711		Foreign Funded				Medium & Low Pressure Valve中
天津塘沽瓦特斯阀门有限公司(1994)	天津市	天津市	(022)25718857	650	外商投资	129,985	-	217,584	低压阀门
Jiangsu Tongshan Shenglong Valve Factory	Xuzhou	Jiangsu	(0516)3240039		Joint Stock				Low Pressure Valve
铜山县盛龙阀门厂(1993)	徐州市	江苏省	(0516)3240039	650	股份制	125,000	7,380(22)	78,340	低压阀门
Suzhou Neway Machinery Co., Ltd.	Suzhou	Jiangsu	(0512)65350358		Foreign Funded				Valve
苏州纽威机械有限公司(1997)	苏州市	江苏省	(0512)65352090	318	外商投资	120,994	25,987(4)	131,167	阀门

Top 10 Cities by Revenue 销售收入排名前10位城市	Province 省	Market share 市场份额 (%)	Number of firms 企业个数
Taizhou 台州市	Zhejiang 浙江省	14.03	93
Wenzhou 温州市	Zhejiang 浙江省	13.35	101
Ningbo 宁波市	Zhejiang 浙江省	7.84	42
Shanghai 上海市	Shanghai 上海市	7.06	48
Yancheng 盐城市	Jiangsu 江苏省	7.05	30
Zhengzhou 郑州市	Henan 河南省	4.38	18
Suzhou 苏州市	Jiangsu 江苏省	3.88	10
Tianjin 天津市	Tianjin 天津市	3.06	26
Shijiazhuang 石家庄市	Hebei 河北省	2.56	8
Beijing 北京市	Beijing 北京市	2.19	10

10 Major Wholesalers 十家主要批发商	City 城市	Province 省	Telephone/Fax 电话/传真
SU MEC	Nanjing	Jiangsu	(025)4511888
中设江苏机械设备进出口（集团）公司	南京市	江苏省	(025)4411772
China Poster Mobile Communications Equipment Co.,Ltd.	Beijing	Beijing	(010)66426993
中邮普泰移动通信设备股份有限公司	北京市	北京市	(010)66426837
Sino Kama Co., Ltd.	Shanghai	Shanghai	(021)62031188
中泰凯马股份有限公司	上海市	上海市	(021)62030851
China Huayuan Group Co.,Ltd.	Shanghai	Shanghai	(021)62031188
中国华源集团有限公司	上海市	上海市	(021)62032288
Zhejiang Crand Imp.& Exp.Co.,Ltd.	Ningbo	Zhejiang	(0574)87720170
浙江远大进出口有限公司	宁波市	浙江省	(0574)87723350
Shandong Machinery Import & Export Group Corporation	Qingdao	Shandong	(0532)2661628
山东省机械进出口集团公司	青岛市	山东省	(0532)2991655
Qingdao Haier International Trade Co.,Ltd.	Qingdao	Shandong	(0532)8938337
青岛海尔国际贸易有限公司	青岛市	山东省	(0532)8939494
Guangdong Machinery Import & Export Group Corporation	Guangzhou	Guangdong	(020)87782168
广东省机械进出口集团公司	广州市	广东省	(020)87771803
China National Machinery Equipment Import & Export Corporation	Beijing	Beijing	(010)63474506
中国机械设备进出口总公司	北京市	北京市	(010)63261865
Beijing Cellstar Co.,Ltd.	Beijing	Beijing	(010)64602050
北京蜂星事达电讯有限公司	北京市	北京市	(010)64672648

3561: Hydraulic Equipment 液压件及液力件制造业

The industry accounts for 0.084% of the total revenue of China's industrial sector in 2002. The rate of return on assets is 3.65%. 81.96% of all firms in the industry made a profit while 18.04% had negative returns.The top province in terms of the industry's revenue is Shandong, accounting for 17.71% of the total revenue.
2002年本行业收入占全行业的 0.084%，资产利润率为 3.65%。81.96%的企业赢利，18.04%的企业亏损。收入最高的省为山东省，占本行业的17.71%。

	Total number of firms 企业总数	Total number of employees 职工总数	Total revenue (Mil.RMB) 总销售收入(百万元)	Total profit (Mil.RMB) 总利润(百万元)	Return on assets 资产利润率(%)	Return on equity 权益利润率(%)	Labour productivity ('000 RMB/ worker) 劳动生产率(千元/人)	Debts/ assets 资产负债率(%)	Total assets (Mil.RMB) 总资产(百万元)
Industry Overall 行业总体	316	77,143	9,049	459	3.65	9.82	39.41	62.82	12,565

	Number of firms 企业个数	Average number of employees 平均职工人数	Average revenue ('000 RMB) 平均销售收入（千元）	Average profit ('000 RMB) 平均利润(千元)	Return on assets 资产利润率(%)	Return on equity 权益利润率(%)	Labour productivity ('000 RMB/ worker) 劳动生产率(千元/人)	Debts/ assets 资产负债率(%)	Average total assets ('000 RMB) 平均总资产(千元)
By ownership 产业所有权									
State-owned 国有	60	429	26,221	182	0.27	1.08	20.72	74.53	66,527
Collective-owned 集体	43	184	22,184	505	3.64	11.46	38.00	68.22	13,872
Foreign & Overseas Chinese Funded 三资	32	134	44,820	4,007	7.55	13.58	106.91	44.41	53,072
By regional distribution 地区分布									
Central-North 华北	43	415	32,350	303	0.34	0.84	25.91	59.81	89,878
Beijing 北京	11	398	42,825	-222	-0.21	-0.47	23.90	54.73	104,146
Tianjin 天津	13	247	28,547	1,477	2.29	4.26	39.73	46.28	64,583
Hebei 河北	9	224	10,986	-1,460	-3.60		15.28	104.19	40,570
Shanxi 山西	8	1,018	53,473	432	0.23	0.59	23.45	60.98	186,297
Inner Mongolia 内蒙古	2	53	11,098	2,971	24.70	34.34	81.07	28.07	12,026
Northeast 东北	26	344	24,468	979	2.19	9.78	28.78	77.57	44,589
Liaoning 辽宁	23	268	27,399	1,288	2.68	11.64	41.16	76.94	47,975
Jilin 吉林	2	241	693	-956	-3.68	-38.65	2.73	90.48	25,959
Heilongjiang 黑龙江	1	2,306	4,613	-2,267	-56.92	-331.43	1.13	82.83	3,983
Central-East 华东	179	210	32,329	2,130	6.61	16.48	49.88	59.91	32,248
Shanghai 上海	28	117	31,826	1,980	5.93	10.85	72.57	45.36	33,403
Jiangsu 江苏	60	173	24,692	1,082	4.46	17.48	46.16	74.48	24,245
Zhejiang 浙江	47	173	27,459	2,403	10.27	23.25	50.96	55.83	23,398
Anhui 安徽	5	279	24,768	1,055	2.92	6.22	38.90	53.07	36,152
Fujian 福建	5	335	66,895	8,534	18.34	35.55	61.41	48.42	46,533
Jiangxi 江西	3	351	20,876	-593	-1.53	-6.64	16.44	76.93	38,698
Shandong 山东	31	379	51,699	3,285	5.81	14.25	48.72	59.24	56,554
Central-South 中南	49	191	20,870	612	2.20	5.96	37.63	63.01	27,762
Henan 河南	11	213	18,530	211	1.01	2.50	42.23	59.57	20,873
Hubei 湖北	14	176	17,982	524	2.54	9.26	37.66	72.56	20,625
Hunan 湖南	9	300	17,645	69	0.20	0.76	20.18	74.32	35,118
Guangdong 广东	13	132	30,980	1,503	3.78	7.85	60.07	51.85	39,761
Guangxi 广西	2	52	2,756	90	1.98	17.03	14.86	88.35	4,512
Hainan 海南									
Southwest 西南	12	194	13,293	598	2.30	214.98	28.52	98.93	26,019
Chongqing 重庆	1	132	5,631	-217	-3.57	-19.85	8.05	82.00	6,071
Sichuan 四川	9	233	16,852	849	2.53	30,568.00	30.98	99.99	33,560
Guizhou 贵州	2	48	1,106	-126	-6.11	-11.31	2.80	45.97	2,054
Yunnan 云南									
Tibet 西藏									
Northwest 西北	7	143	7,598	271	1.98	5.10	23.29	61.24	13,706
Shaanxi 陕西	3	162	7,901	135	0.86	2.31	16.50	62.74	15,737
Gansu 甘肃	2	166	2,655	583	7.61	17.85	9.79	57.35	7,652
Qinghai 青海	1	96	17,333	243	1.06	3.17	104.44	66.52	22,901
Ningxia 宁夏	1	88	6,841	83	0.79	1.54	23.13	48.73	10,526
Xinjiang 新疆									

3561: Hydraulic Equipment 液压件及液力件制造业

Year 年份	Number of firms 企业个数	Rate of change 变化率 (%)	Number of employees 职工人数 (人)	Rate of change 变化率 (%)	Total revenue (Mil. RMB) 总销售收入 (百万元)	Rate of change 变化率 (%)	Total profit (Mil RMB) 总利润 (百万元)	Rate of change 变化率 (%)
2000	275		73,579		5,607		209	
2001	288	4.73	76,225	3.60	7,366	31.37	312	49.28
2002	316	9.72	77,143	1.20	9,049	22.85	459	47.12

Major Products 主要产品	Output 产量	Unit 单位
Hydraulic Component 液压元件	2,165	10,000 Pieces 万件
Hydraulic Parts 液力件	30	10,000 Pieces 万件

10 Main Firms with Maximal Revenue (year founded) 收入最大的十家主要企业（创办年份）	City 城市	Province 省	Telephone/fax 电话/传真	Number of employees 职工人数	Ownership 产业所有权	Revenue ('000 RMB) 销售收入(千元)	Profit('000 RMB) (rank) 利润(千元)(排名)	Total assets ('000 RMB) 总资产(千元)	Major products 主要产品
Shandong Binzhou Bohai Piston Co., Ltd.	Binzhou	Shandong	(0543)3325288		Joint Stock				Piston
山东滨州渤海活塞股份有限公司(1951)	滨州市	山东省	(0543)3325305	2,533	股份制	627,325	47,015(1)	863,549	活塞
Beijing Coal Mine Machinery Factory	Beijing	Beijing	(010)69313201		State-owned				Hydraulic Pressure Bracket
北京煤矿机械厂(1961)	北京市	北京市	(010)69311624	2,622	国有企业	272,849	-	516,194	液压支架
Shanghai Teijin Seiki Co.,Ltd.	Shanghai	Shanghai	(021)57741831		Foreign Funded				Engineering Hydraulic Pressure Components工
上海帝人制机有限公司(1996)	上海市	上海市	(021)57741347	85	外商投资	245,073	16,504(5)	157,126	程液压件
Rongcheng High Pressure Pump Valve Factory	Weihai	Shandong	(0631)7661151		Joint Stock				High Pressure Valve
荣成市高压泵阀厂(1958)	威海市	山东省	(0631)7661152	100	股份制	204,610	15,420(7)	35,120	高压泵阀
Shanxi Pingyang Machinery Factory	Linfen	Shanxi	(0357)4252501		State-owned				Hydraulic Pressure Bracket
山西平阳机械厂(1964)	临汾市	山西省	(0357)4253701	3,724	国有企业	148,276	589(124)	416,858	液压支架
Fenghua Hydraulic Pressure Machinery Factory	Ningbo	Zhejiang	(0574)88637854		Collective-owned				Cricoid Jack轮
奉化液压机械厂(1987)	宁波市	浙江省	(0574)88637997	472	集体企业	146,169	2,217(51)	58,970	式千斤顶
Beijing Huade Hydraulic Pressure Industry Group Co., Ltd.	Beijing	Beijing	(010)67881998		Limited-Liability				Hydraulic Pressure Valve
北京华德液压工业集团有限责任公司(1979)	北京市	北京市	(010)67882009	1,344	有限公司	144,483	1,835(63)	566,474	液压阀
Xiamen Yinhua Machinery Factory	Xiamen	Fujian	(0592)7023454		State-owned				Hydrocylinder
厦门银华机械厂(1975)	厦门市	福建省	(0592)7033357	651	国有企业	137,937	8,603(14)	120,254	油缸
Hua Boluo (Tianjin) Industry Co., Ltd.	Tianjin	Tianjin	(022)26971640		Foreign Funded				Motor Carburettor摩托
华博罗（天津）工业有限公司(1995)	天津市	天津市	(022)26970217	550	外商投资	122,790	7,090(17)	168,230	车化油器
Shandong Runguang Hydraulic Pressure Science & Technology	Weifang	Shandong	(0536)3296445		Private Owned				Gear Pump
Co., Ltd.山东润光液压科技股份有限公司(1966)	潍坊市	山东省	(0536)3296410	1,060	私营企业	105,685	3,079(38)	152,426	齿轮泵

Top 10 Cities by Revenue 销售收入排名前10位城市	Province 省	Market share 市场份额 (%)	Number of firms 企业个数
Shanghai 上海市	Shanghai 上海市	9.85	28
Binzhou 滨州市	Shandong 山东省	6.93	1
Beijing 北京市	Beijing 北京市	5.21	11
Ningbo 宁波市	Zhejiang 浙江省	4.71	14
Jiaxing 嘉兴市	Zhejiang 浙江省	4.15	16
Tianjin 天津市	Tianjin 天津市	4.10	13
Dalian 大连市	Liaoning 辽宁省	3.51	8
Nanjing 南京市	Jiangsu 江苏省	3.48	10
Weihai 威海市	Shandong 山东省	3.28	2
Wuxi 无锡市	Jiangsu 江苏省	3.11	8

10 Major Wholesalers 十家主要批发商	City 城市	Province 省	Telephone/Fax 电话/传真
SU MEC	Nanjing	Jiangsu	(025)4511888
中设江苏机械设备进出口（集团）公司	南京市	江苏省	(025)4411772
China Poster Mobile Communications Equipment Co.,Ltd.	Beijing	Beijing	(010)66426993
中邮普泰移动通信设备股份有限公司	北京市	北京市	(010)66426837
Sino Kama Co., Ltd.	Shanghai	Shanghai	(021)62031188
中泰凯马股份有限公司	上海市	上海市	(021)62030851
China Huayuan Group Co.,Ltd.	Shanghai	Shanghai	(021)62031188
中国华源集团有限公司	上海市	上海市	(021)62032288
Zhejiang Crand Imp.& Exp.Co.,Ltd.	Ningbo	Zhejiang	(0574)87720170
浙江远大进出口有限公司	宁波市	浙江省	(0574)87723350
Shandong Machinery Import & Export Group Corporation	Qingdao	Shandong	(0532)2661628
山东省机械进出口集团公司	青岛市	山东省	(0532)2991655
Qingdao Haier International Trade Co.,Ltd.	Qingdao	Shandong	(0532)8938337
青岛海尔国际贸易有限公司	青岛市	山东省	(0532)8939494
Guangdong Machinery Import & Export Group Corporation	Guangzhou	Guangdong	(020)87782168
广东省机械进出口集团公司	广州市	广东省	(020)87771003
China National Machinery Equipment Import & Export Corporation	Beijing	Beijing	(010)63474506
中国机械设备进出口总公司	北京市	北京市	(010)63261865
Beijing Cellstar Co.,Ltd.	Beijing	Beijing	(010)64602050
北京蜂星事达电讯有限公司	北京市	北京市	(010)64672648

3562: Pneumatic Components 气动元件制造业

The industry accounts for 0.030% of the total revenue of China's industrial sector in 2002. The rate of return on assets is 9.19%. 87.50% of all firms in the industry made a profit while 12.50% had negative returns.The top province in terms of the industry's revenue is Jiangsu, accounting for 25.66% of the total revenue.
2002年本行业收入占全行业的 0.030%，资产利润率为 9.19%。87.50%的企业赢利，12.50%的企业亏损。收入最高的省为江苏省，占本行业的25.66%。

	Total number of firms 企业总数	Total number of employees 职工总数	Total revenue (Mil.RMB) 总销售收入 (百万元)	Total profit (Mil.RMB) 总利润 (百万元)	Return on assets 资产利润率 (%)	Return on equity 权益利润率 (%)	Labour productivity ('000 RMB/worker) 劳动生产率 (千元/人)	Debts/assets 资产负债率 (%)	Total assets (Mil.RMB) 总资产 (百万元)
Industry Overall 行业总体	120	19,836	3,195	357	9.19	14.94	59.81	38.47	3,880

	Number of firms 企业个数	Average number of employees 平均职工人数	Average revenue ('000 RMB) 平均销售收入 (千元)	Average profit ('000 RMB) 平均利润 (千元)	Return on assets 资产利润率 (%)	Return on equity 权益利润率 (%)	Labour productivity ('000 RMB/worker) 劳动生产率 (千元/人)	Debts/assets 资产负债率 (%)	Average total assets ('000 RMB) 平均总资产 (千元)
By ownership 产业所有权									
State-owned 国有	9	125	5,819	-412	-2.29	-6.72	8.43	65.88	17,974
Collective-owned 集体	13	147	17,175	1,514	11.35	20.52	37.23	44.69	13,343
Foreign & Overseas Chinese Funded 三资	24	221	71,279	12,349	13.59	17.56	119.09	22.57	90,851
By regional distribution 地区分布									
Central-North 华北	18	160	47,178	5,571	7.03	8.64	109.58	18.59	79,224
Beijing 北京	6	246	95,624	13,711	6.57	7.81	159.38	15.95	208,792
Tianjin 天津	5	64	15,850	1,166	28.32	40.27	24.69	29.67	4,117
Hebei 河北	6	134	30,640	1,826	8.18	13.40	84.64	38.93	22,313
Shanxi 山西	1	286	12,374	1,231	6.54	10.51	17.41	37.81	18,826
Inner Mongolia 内蒙古									
Northeast 东北	3	186	5,908	120	1.00	2.33	10.77	57.18	12,012
Liaoning 辽宁	2	112	6,954	303	4.77	13.18	23.79	63.82	6,357
Jilin 吉林	1	333	3,816	-246	-1.05	-2.27	2.01	53.55	23,323
Heilongjiang 黑龙江									
Central-East 华东	78	161	24,743	3,064	12.11	23.27	53.22	47.96	25,309
Shanghai 上海	7	104	50,820	8,514	12.42	21.69	168.66	42.74	68,544
Jiangsu 江苏	30	153	27,330	4,494	23.16	48.05	62.19	51.81	19,407
Zhejiang 浙江	24	137	14,995	775	4.46	9.00	29.11	50.39	17,377
Anhui 安徽	1	215	39,457	3,960	19.65	28.03	46.53	29.88	20,150
Fujian 福建	4	181	17,317	1,524	7.29	10.28	51.96	29.13	20,912
Jiangxi 江西	1	190	15,850	-80	-0.36	-3.57	20.39	90.00	22,448
Shandong 山东	11	257	24,532	1,457	4.35	8.46	40.16	48.62	33,522
Central-South 中南	18	184	21,193	894	3.82	9.70	56.72	60.65	23,435
Henan 河南	4	84	16,617	480	9.96	59.00	43.13	83.11	4,818
Hubei 湖北	1	60	12,638	89	0.63	1.07	298.57	40.57	14,058
Hunan 湖南	3	256	7,944	25	0.45	0.64	12.41	30.54	5,522
Guangdong 广东	10	215	27,854	1,401	3.77	9.81	67.93	61.59	37,194
Guangxi 广西									
Hainan 海南									
Southwest 西南	3	169	5,558	282	3.92	4.82	13.87	18.57	7,191
Chongqing 重庆	1	209	5,051	823	7.81	9.25	10.54	15.63	10,542
Sichuan 四川	1	178	9,038	12	0.13	0.15	23.57	10.92	9,136
Guizhou 贵州	1	120	2,586	11	0.58	2.05	5.28	71.73	1,896
Yunnan 云南									
Tibet 西藏									
Northwest 西北									
Shaanxi 陕西									
Gansu 甘肃									
Qinghai 青海									
Ningxia 宁夏									
Xinjiang 新疆									

Year 年份	Number of firms 企业个数	Rate of change 变化率 (%)	Number of employees 职工人数 (人)	Rate of change 变化率 (%)	Total revenue (Mil. RMB) 总销售收入 (百万元)	Rate of change 变化率 (%)	Total profit (Mil RMB) 总利润 (百万元)	Rate of change 变化率 (%)
2000	90		17,227		2,342		249	
2001	112	24.44	18,322	6.36	2,479	5.85	220	-11.65
2002	120	7.14	19,836	8.26	3,195	28.88	357	62.27

Major Products 主要产品	Output 产量	Unit 单位
Valve 阀门	76	10,000 Tons 万吨

10 Main Firms with Maximal Revenue (year founded) 收入最大的十家主要企业（创办年份）	City 城市	Province 省	Telephone/fax 电话/传真	Number of employees 职工人数	Ownership 产业所有权	Revenue ('000 RMB) 销售收入 (千元)	Profit('000 RMB) (rank) 利润(千元) (排名)	Total assets ('000 RMB) 总资产 (千元)	Major products 主要产品
SMC (China) Co.,Ltd.	Beijing	Beijing	(010)67885566		Foreign Funded				Pneumatic Components
SMC（中国）有限公司(1994)	北京市	北京市	(010)67881837	861	外商投资	322,586	38,080(4)	900,302	气动元件
Pall Filter (BeiJing) Co.,Ltd.	Beijing	Beijing	(010)84584011		Foreign Funded				Filter
颇尔过滤器(北京)有限公司(1993)	北京市	北京市	(010)85484001	341	外商投资	204,050	43,755(3)	201,434	过滤器
Festo (China) Ltd.	Shanghai	Shanghai	(021)58549001		Foreign Funded				Pneumatic Components
费斯托(中国)有限公司(1993)	上海市	上海市	(021)58540300	104	外商投资	196,427	44,806(2)	227,097	气动元件
Guangzhou Airpac Automation Industry Co., Ltd.	Guangzhou	Guangdong	(020)36470863		Overseas Chinese-funded				Air Compressor Components
广州健良自动化工业有限公司(1998)	广州市	广东省	(020)36470665	467	港澳台资	115,912	7,141(7)	73,870	空压元件
Shijiazhuang Honglin Internal-combustion Engine Fittings	Shijiazhuang	Hebei	(0311)3522201		Private Owned				Air Valve
Co.,Ltd.石家庄市弘林内燃机配件有限公司(1986)	石家庄市	河北省	(0311)3522201	120	私营企业	68,545	1,387(29)	3,970	气门
Ji'nan Hua'neng Pneumatics Components Corp.	Jinan	Shandong	(0531)8963993		State Owned				Pneumatic Components
济南华能气动元器件公司(1956)	济南市	山东省	(0531)8964275	901	国有企业	66,274	160(78)	145,568	气动元件
Ningbo Mikuni Machinery & Electronics Co., Ltd,	Ningbo	Zhejiang	(0574)63652485		Foreign Funded				BSV Magnet Valve
宁波三国机械电子有限公司(1995)	宁波市	浙江省	(0574)63652143	301	外商投资	62,705	10,095(6)	64,395	BSV电磁阀
Ji'nan Ruiyuan Pneumatic Engineering Ltd. Company	Jinan	Shandong	(0531)7481878		Private Owned				Pneumatic Components
济南瑞原气动工程有限公司(2000)	济南市	山东省	(0531)7481878	30	私营企业	50,000	3,240(16)	6,100	气动元件
Shanghai Ranco Controller Co., Ltd.	Shanghai	Shanghai	(021)59758242		Foreign Funded				4 Item Commutator Valve四
上海兰柯控制器有限公司(1994)	上海市	上海市	(021)59758441	84	外商投资	45,124	-	81,957	通换向阀
Ningbo Easun Science & Technology Co., Ltd.	Ningbo	Zhejiang	(0574)63025039		Foreign Funded				Pneumatic Components
宁波亿日科技实业有限公司(2001)	宁波市	浙江省	(0574)63024823	587	外商投资	40,050	90(86)	37,686	气动元件

Top 10 Cities by Revenue 销售收入排名前10位城市	Province 省	Market share 市场份额 (%)	Number of firms 企业个数
Beijing 北京市	Beijing 北京市	17.96	6
Changzhou 常州市	Jiangsu 江苏省	12.30	5
Shanghai 上海市	Shanghai 上海市	11.13	7
Ningbo 宁波市	Zhejiang 浙江省	6.58	12
Wuxi 无锡市	Jiangsu 江苏省	4.64	10
Jinan 济南市	Shandong 山东省	4.07	3
Guangzhou 广州市	Guangdong 广东省	3.93	2
Yangzhou 扬州市	Jiangsu 江苏省	2.93	4
Suzhou 苏州市	Jiangsu 江苏省	2.65	4
Tianjin 天津市	Tianjin 天津市	2.48	5

10 Major Wholesalers 十家主要批发商	City 城市	Province 省	Telephone/Fax 电话/传真
SU MEC	Nanjing	Jiangsu	(025)4511888
中设江苏机械设备进出口（集团）公司	南京市	江苏省	(025)4411772
China Poster Mobile Communications Equipment Co.,Ltd.	Beijing	Beijing	(010)66426993
中邮普泰移动通信设备股份有限公司	北京市	北京市	(010)66426837
Sino Kama Co., Ltd.	Shanghai	Shanghai	(021)62031188
中泰凯马股份有限公司	上海市	上海市	(021)62030851
China Huayuan Group Co.,Ltd.	Shanghai	Shanghai	(021)62031188
中国华源集团有限公司	上海市	上海市	(021)62032288
Zhejiang Crand Imp.& Exp.Co.,Ltd.	Ningbo	Zhejiang	(0574)87720170
浙江远大进出口有限公司	宁波市	浙江省	(0574)87723350
Shandong Machinery Import & Export Group Corporation	Qingdao	Shandong	(0532)2661628
山东省机械进出口集团公司	青岛市	山东省	(0532)2991655
Qingdao Haier International Trade Co.,Ltd.	Qingdao	Shandong	(0532)8938337
青岛海尔国际贸易有限公司	青岛市	山东省	(0532)8939494
Guangdong Machinery Import & Export Group Corporation	Guangzhou	Guangdong	(020)87782168
广东省机械进出口集团公司	广州市	广东省	(020)87771803
China National Machinery Equipment Import & Export Corporation	Beijing	Beijing	(010)63474506
中国机械设备进出口总公司	北京市	北京市	(010)63261865
Beijing Cellstar Co.,Ltd.	Beijing	Beijing	(010)64602050
北京蜂星事达电讯有限公司	北京市	北京市	(010)64672648

3563: Gaskets, Seals and Related Products 密封件制造业

The industry accounts for 0.027% of the total revenue of China's industrial sector in 2002. The rate of return on assets is 9.50%. 90.53% of all firms in the industry made a profit while 9.47% had negative returns.The top province in terms of the industry's revenue is Jiangsu, accounting for 42.43% of the total revenue.
2002年本行业收入占全行业的0.027%，资产利润率为9.50%。90.53%的企业赢利，9.47%的企业亏损。收入最高的省为江苏省，占本行业的42.43%。

	Total number of firms 企业总数	Total number of employees 职工总数	Total revenue (Mil.RMB) 总销售收入（百万元）	Total profit (Mil.RMB) 总利润（百万元）	Return on assets 资产利润率（%）	Return on equity 权益利润率（%）	Labour productivity ('000 RMB/worker) 劳动生产率（千元/人）	Debts/assets 资产负债率（%）	Total assets (Mil.RMB) 总资产（百万元）
Industry Overall 行业总体	95	13,714	2,924	251	9.50	19.40	59.90	51.05	2,638

	Number of firms 企业个数	Average number of employees 平均职工人数	Average revenue ('000 RMB) 平均销售收入（千元）	Average profit ('000 RMB) 平均利润（千元）	Return on assets 资产利润率（%）	Return on equity 权益利润率（%）	Labour productivity ('000 RMB/worker) 劳动生产率（千元/人）	Debts/assets 资产负债率（%）	Average total assets ('000 RMB) 平均总资产（千元）
By ownership 产业所有权									
State-owned 国有	7	39	570	112	2.61	6.52	4.89	60.07	4,287
Collective-owned 集体	17	220	61,937	4,581	13.83	26.53	63.00	47.85	33,112
Foreign & Overseas Chinese Funded 三资	15	183	55,928	7,404	10.73	20.03	91.51	46.45	69,024
By regional distribution 地区分布									
Central-North 华北	9	87	21,001	3,811	14.85	24.70	64.32	39.88	25,659
Beijing 北京	2	70	24,792	1,366	3.75	5.36	175.38	30.06	36,410
Tianjin 天津	6	94	22,068	5,151	20.61	37.91	42.06	45.64	24,995
Hebei 河北	1	76	7,021	658	8.08	10.32	26.46	21.65	8,139
Shanxi 山西									
Inner Mongolia 内蒙古									
Northeast 东北	6	199	32,483	2,066	4.31	10.61	28.50	59.43	47,986
Liaoning 辽宁	4	235	41,501	3,285	4.91	12.19	31.01	59.71	66,864
Jilin 吉林									
Heilongjiang 黑龙江	2	127	14,447	-371	-3.63	-8.21	19.19	55.83	10,230
Central-East 华东	64	156	36,796	3,040	10.27	21.53	67.68	52.28	29,598
Shanghai 上海	5	111	77,656	12,957	13.68	23.84	260.78	42.59	94,693
Jiangsu 江苏	21	234	59,087	3,299	9.02	21.01	53.04	57.06	36,575
Zhejiang 浙江	25	103	15,084	1,556	9.07	18.01	55.99	49.61	17,143
Anhui 安徽	3	54	4,675	197	4.76	18.23	27.55	73.88	4,138
Fujian 福建	1	330	33,746	124	0.29	0.71	21.02	58.67	42,361
Jiangxi 江西									
Shandong 山东	9	163	33,441	2,324	12.35	31.92	79.30	61.30	18,818
Central-South 中南	9	91	6,579	149	1.68	3.69	20.96	54.50	8,892
Henan 河南	4	69	5,135	211	2.86	4.93	24.16	41.98	7,373
Hubei 湖北									
Hunan 湖南	2	78	2,614	60	0.50	0.94	10.78	46.74	11,893
Guangdong 广东	3	128	11,149	127	1.42	5.74	22.77	75.19	8,918
Guangxi 广西									
Hainan 海南									
Southwest 西南	3	216	20,044	-48	-0.17	-0.25	35.65	30.96	28,528
Chongqing 重庆	1	559	41,337	-1,856	-3.50	-5.90	14.57	40.61	52,971
Sichuan 四川	2	44	9,398	856	5.25	6.19	169.55	15.29	16,306
Guizhou 贵州									
Yunnan 云南									
Tibet 西藏									
Northwest 西北	4	69	16,497	2,013	13.54	22.19	72.77	38.98	14,863
Shaanxi 陕西	2	99	31,136	3,958	14.48	22.46	93.15	35.50	27,323
Gansu 甘肃	2	39	1,857	69	2.85	13.25	20.62	78.48	2,402
Qinghai 青海									
Ningxia 宁夏									
Xinjiang 新疆									

3563: Gaskets, Seals and Related Products 密封件制造业

Year 年份	Number of firms 企业个数	Rate of change 变化率 (%)	Number of employees 职工人数 (人)	Rate of change 变化率 (%)	Total revenue (Mil. RMB) 总销售收入 (百万元)	Rate of change 变化率 (%)	Total profit (Mil RMB) 总利润 (百万元)	Rate of change 变化率 (%)
2000	95		10,853		1,597		150	
2001	104	9.47	14,576	34.30	2,170	35.88	191	27.33
2002	95	-8.65	13,714	-5.91	2,924	34.75	251	31.41

Major Products 主要产品	Output 产量	Unit 单位
Seal Part 密封件	138,552	10,000 Pieces 万件

10 Main Firms with Maximal Revenue (year founded) 收入最大的十家主要企业 (创办年份)	City 城市	Province 省	Telephone/fax 电话/传真	Number of employees 职工人数	Ownership 产业所有权	Revenue ('000 RMB) 销售收入 (千元)	Profit('000 RMB) (rank) 利润(千元) (排名)	Total assets ('000 RMB) 总资产 (千元)	Major products 主要产品
Shanghai Saic-Metzeler Sealing Systems Co., Ltd.	Shanghai	Shanghai	(021)59221580		Foreign Funded				Rubber Airproof Parts橡
上海申雅密封件有限公司(1995)	上海市	上海市	(021)59221520	383	外商投资	340,371	62,498(1)	420,748	胶密封件
Yixing Hokkai Head Co.,Ltd.	Wuxi	Jiangsu	(0510)7842935		Foreign Funded				6000T Punch.6000T
宜兴北海封头有限公司(1995)	无锡市	江苏省	(0510)7841678	325	外商投资	122,680	2,950(16)	203,670	冲压机
Zhejiang Cathay Packing &Sealing Co., ltd.	Hangzhou	Zhejiang	(0571)82322193		Private Enterprises				Airproofing Parts
浙江国泰密封材料股份有限公司(1985)	杭州市	浙江省	(0571)82321234	406	私营独资	97,882	9,806(4)	141,549	密封件
CHIYODA Electronic Manufacturing (Dalian) Co., Ltd.	Dalian	Liaoning	(0411)7654010		Foreign Funded				Airproofing Gasket
千代达电子制造（大连）有限公司(1994)	大连市	辽宁省	(0411)7653446	279	外商投资	76,520	4,580(12)	68,296	密封垫
Dandong Colossus Group Co.,Ltd.	Dandong	Liaoning	(0415)6221005		Private Enterprises				Machinery Airproofing
丹东克隆集团有限公司(1988)	丹东市	辽宁省	(0415)6225536	494	私营独资	72,437	7,288(7)	176,617	机械密封
Shandong Wuhao Automobile Seal Parts Co., Ltd.	Dezhou	Shandong	(0534)6394286		Collective-owned				Automobile Airproofing Parts汽
山东武豪汽车密封件有限公司(1998)	德州市	山东省	(0534)6392258	192	集体企业	71,462	7,347(6)	29,565	车密封件
Bagshing Precision Products (Tianjin) Co.,Ltd.	Tianjin	Tianjin	(022)24996388		Foreign Funded				Airproofing Parts
万新精密制品（天津）有限公司(1998)	天津市	天津市	(022)24995940	298	外商投资	70,109	16,091(3)	71,907	密封件
Penglai Petrifaction Fittings Co.,Ltd.	Yantai	Shandong	(0535)5891434		Private Owned				Fasteners
蓬莱石化配件有限公司(2000)	烟台市	山东省		376	私营企业	62,840	2,480(20)	40,520	紧固件
Xi'an Yonghua Group Company Limited	Xi'an	Shannxi	(029)6499400		Private Enterprises				Machinery Airproofing
西安永华集团公司(1998)	西安市	陕西省	(029)6499252	75	私营独资	45,251	2,893(17)	17,128	机械密封
Chongqing Yifeng High Pressure Container Co., Ltd.	Chongqing	Chongqing	(023)46287625		State Enterprises				Steel Gas Bottle
重庆益峰高压容器有限责任公司(2001)	重庆市	重庆市	(023)46287026	559	国有独资	41,337	-	52,971	钢质汽瓶

Top 10 Cities by Revenue 销售收入排名前10位城市	Province 省	Market share 市场份额 (%)	Number of firms 企业个数
Wuxi 无锡市	Jiangsu 江苏省	35.11	9
Shanghai 上海市	Shanghai 上海市	13.28	5
Tianjin 天津市	Tianjin 天津市	4.53	6
Wenzhou 温州市	Zhejiang 浙江省	4.41	8
Nantong 南通市	Jiangsu 江苏省	4.17	2
Hangzhou 杭州市	Zhejiang 浙江省	4.13	3
Yantai 烟台市	Shandong 山东省	3.76	3
Ningbo 宁波市	Zhejiang 浙江省	2.77	7
Dandong 丹东市	Liaoning 辽宁省	2.75	2
Dalian 大连市	Liaoning 辽宁省	2.62	1

10 Major Wholesalers 十家主要批发商	City 城市	Province 省	Telephone/Fax 电话/传真
SU MEC	Nanjing	Jiangsu	(025)4511888
中设江苏机械设备进出口（集团）公司	南京市	江苏省	(025)4411772
China Poster Mobile Communications Equipment Co.,Ltd.	Beijing	Beijing	(010)66426993
中邮普泰移动通信设备股份有限公司	北京市	北京市	(010)66426837
Sino Kama Co., Ltd.	Shanghai	Shanghai	(021)62031188
中泰凯马股份有限公司	上海市	上海市	(021)62030851
China Huayuan Group Co.,Ltd.	Shanghai	Shanghai	(021)62031188
中国华源集团有限公司	上海市	上海市	(021)62032288
Zhejiang Crand Imp.& Exp.Co.,Ltd.	Ningbo	Zhejiang	(0574)87720170
浙江远大进出口有限公司	宁波市	浙江省	(0574)87723350
Shandong Machinery Import & Export Group Corporation	Qingdao	Shandong	(0532)2661628
山东省机械进出口集团公司	青岛市	山东省	(0532)2991655
Qingdao Haier International Trade Co.,Ltd.	Qingdao	Shandong	(0532)8938337
青岛海尔国际贸易有限公司	青岛市	山东省	(0532)8939494
Guangdong Machinery Import & Export Group Corporation	Guangzhou	Guangdong	(020)87782168
广东省机械进出口集团公司	广州市	广东省	(020)87771803
China National Machinery Equipment Import & Export Corporation	Beijing	Beijing	(010)63474506
中国机械设备进出口总公司	北京市	北京市	(010)63261865
Beijing Cellstar Co.,Ltd.	Beijing	Beijing	(010)64602050
北京蜂星事达电讯有限公司	北京市	北京市	(010)64672648

3564: Powder Metallurgical Products 粉末冶金制品业

The industry accounts for 0.055% of the total revenue of China's industrial sector in 2002. The rate of return on assets is 6.01%. 80.93% of all firms in the industry made a profit while 19.07% had negative returns.The top province in terms of the industry's revenue is Zhejiang, accounting for 49.39% of the total revenue.
2002年本行业收入占全行业的 0.055%，资产利润率为 6.01%。80.93%的企业赢利，19.07%的企业亏损。收入最高的省为浙江省，占本行业的49.39%。

	Total number of firms 企业总数	Total number of employees 职工总数	Total revenue (Mil.RMB) 总销售收入（百万元）	Total profit (Mil.RMB) 总利润（百万元）	Return on assets 资产利润率（%）	Return on equity 权益利润率（%）	Labour productivity ('000 RMB/ worker) 劳动生产率（千元/人）	Debts/ assets 资产负债率（%）	Total assets (Mil.RMB) 总资产（百万元）
Industry Overall 行业总体	194	42,865	5,871	549	6.01	13.77	47.54	56.34	9,129

	Number of firms 企业个数	Average number of employees 平均职工人数	Average revenue ('000 RMB) 平均销售收入（千元）	Average profit ('000 RMB) 平均利润（千元）	Return on assets 资产利润率（%）	Return on equity 权益利润率（%）	Labour productivity ('000 RMB/ worker) 劳动生产率（千元/人）	Debts/ assets 资产负债率（%）	Average total assets ('000 RMB) 平均总资产（千元）
By ownership 产业所有权									
State-owned 国有	23	128	7,304	-338	-1.81	-8.01	24.36	77.40	18,706
Collective-owned 集体	32	460	60,295	8,889	11.45	29.43	44.33	61.09	77,625
Foreign & Overseas Chinese Funded 三资	25	192	41,081	4,472	7.09	14.55	97.49	51.26	63,048
By regional distribution 地区分布									
Central-North 华北	14	213	17,193	677	2.12	7.42	34.54	71.40	31,913
Beijing 北京	5	254	27,347	1,273	2.36	7.90	46.75	70.12	53,967
Tianjin 天津	1	70	6,400	100	2.09	4.90	40.29	57.32	4,780
Hebei 河北	2	134	8,410	73	0.54	1.03	26.28	47.56	13,423
Shanxi 山西	6	230	13,457	478	1.97	9.23	24.62	78.64	24,220
Inner Mongolia 内蒙古									
Northeast 东北	5	147	15,263	883	4.92	17.00	76.88	71.07	17,953
Liaoning 辽宁	2	227	31,897	2,161	7.13	18.21	104.15	60.84	30,296
Jilin 吉林	3	93	4,174	31	0.32	4.19	32.50	92.31	9,724
Heilongjiang 黑龙江									
Central-East 华东	121	242	35,846	4,111	7.24	15.46	52.04	53.16	56,767
Shanghai 上海	14	102	16,191	2,099	12.93	24.28	53.06	46.73	16,228
Jiangsu 江苏	30	182	27,759	1,652	4.40	11.51	59.24	61.78	37,562
Zhejiang 浙江	51	359	56,852	8,081	8.42	17.24	53.56	51.18	96,015
Anhui 安徽	4	259	18,695	1,774	6.50	15.89	28.49	59.09	27,287
Fujian 福建	10	149	16,661	-742	-2.29	-5.92	38.29	61.31	32,383
Jiangxi 江西	3	96	9,308	442	8.04	28.58	31.88	71.88	5,504
Shandong 山东	9	142	12,129	592	3.16	5.30	38.07	40.42	18,728
Central-South 中南	44	180	23,286	330	1.17	3.45	36.71	66.14	28,300
Henan 河南	9	113	16,484	960	8.47	26.86	40.12	68.48	11,340
Hubei 湖北	13	172	13,467	366	1.63	6.35	27.16	74.38	22,491
Hunan 湖南	4	53	6,792	-158	-3.49		55.31	177.95	4,527
Guangdong 广东	16	267	41,931	160	0.31	0.79	41.11	60.67	51,125
Guangxi 广西	2	86	1,558	-393	-5.37	-11.37	8.46	52.78	7,323
Hainan 海南									
Southwest 西南	8	225	23,542	2,900	4.93	12.21	34.61	59.60	58,767
Chongqing 重庆	4	280	38,340	5,218	6.29	14.60	42.74	56.93	82,990
Sichuan 四川	2	164	15,166	1,987	4.20	7.42	39.25	43.49	47,355
Guizhou 贵州	1	287	2,431	-1,579	-3.81		3.46	117.25	41,422
Yunnan 云南	1	64	2,211	-69	-3.38	-11.69	8.39	71.12	2,043
Tibet 西藏									
Northwest 西北	2	78	1,628	-63	-1.55	-4.39	11.07	64.72	4,038
Shaanxi 陕西									
Gansu 甘肃	2	78	1,628	-63	-1.55	-4.39	11.07	64.72	4,038
Qinghai 青海									
Ningxia 宁夏									
Xinjiang 新疆									

3564: Powder Metallurgical Products 粉末冶金制品业

Year 年份	Number of firms 企业个数	Rate of change 变化率 (%)	Number of employees 职工人数 (人)	Rate of change 变化率 (%)	Total revenue (Mil. RMB) 总销售收入 (百万元)	Rate of change 变化率 (%)	Total profit (Mil RMB) 总利润 (百万元)	Rate of change 变化率 (%)
2000	162		38,995		4,486		470	
2001	183	12.96	41,942	7.56	5,046	12.48	482	2.55
2002	194	6.01	42,865	2.20	5,871	16.35	549	13.90

Major Products 主要产品	Output 产量	Unit 单位
Powder Metallurgy Products 粉末冶金制品	28	10,000 Tons 万吨

10 Main Firms with Maximal Revenue (year founded) 收入最大的十家主要企业（创办年份）	City 城市	Province 省	Telephone/fax 电话/传真	Number of employees 职工人数	Ownership 产业所有权	Revenue ('000 RMB) 销售收入 (千元)	Profit('000 RMB) (rank) 利润(千元)(排名)	Total assets ('000 RMB) 总资产 (千元)	Major products 主要产品
Dong Magnet Co., Ltd. of Hengdian Group	Jinhua	Zhejiang	(0579)6551359		Collective-owned				Permanent Magnetism Iron Oxygen Ball永
横店集团东磁有限公司(1980)	金华市	浙江省	(0579)6551157	9,161	集体企业	1,316,757	240,369(1)	1,842,972	磁铁氧球
Ningbo Yunsheng Group Co.,Ltd.	Ningbo	Zhejiang	(0574)87761128		Joint Stock				Magnetical Materials
宁波韵升（集团）股份有限公司(1994)	宁波市	浙江省	(0574)87776466	1,402	股份制	522,482	76,627(2)	1,585,565	磁性材料
JIiangmen Power Metallurgy Co., Ltd.	Jiangmen	Guangdong	(0750)3532142		Limited-Liability				Iron & Copper Base Part铁
江门市粉末冶金厂有限公司(1975)	江门市	广东省	(0750)3558344	1,474	有限公司	342,131	5,627(11)	343,664	铜基零件
Yangzhou Prorite Iindustry Co., Ltd.	Yangzhou	Jiangsu	(0514)7880887		Overseas Chinese-funded				Bearing
扬州保来得工业有限公司(1994)	扬州市	江苏省	(0514)7880884	417	港澳台资	251,510	27,279(4)	435,212	轴承
Ningbo Dongmu New Materials Stock Co., Ltd.	Ningbo	Zhejiang	(0574)87833776		Foreign Funded				Powder Metallurgy Product粉末
宁波东睦新材料股份有限公司(1994)	宁波市	浙江省	(0574)87831133	592	外商投资	203,594	42,555(3)	299,677	冶金制品
Chongqing Huafu Industry Co., ltd.	Chongqing	Chongqing	(023)65220533		Joint Stock				Powder Metallurgy Product粉末
重庆华孚工业股份有限公司(1954)	重庆市	重庆市	(023)65219459	629	股份制	101,913	18,840(5)	238,577	冶金制品
Nanjing Yuhuatai Xishan Mineral Powder Sintering Factory	Nanjing	Jiangsu	(025)2809769		Collective-owned				Sinter Mine
南京市雨花台区西善矿粉烧结厂(1992)	南京市	江苏省		710	集体企业	81,160	1,820(34)	52,740	烧结矿
Shunde Magnetic Electricity Co., Ltd.	Foshan	Guangdong	(0765)5383211		Limited-Liability				Magnet
顺德市磁电有限公司(1986)	佛山市	广东省	(0765)5574333	812	有限公司	63,014	-	98,899	磁铁
Dongguan Xiute Electronics Co., Ltd.	Dongguan	Guangdong	(0769)7773572		Overseas Chinese funded				Magnet
东莞秀特电子有限公司(1993)	东莞市	广东省	(0769)7773574	315	港澳台资	60,712	1,680(37)	103,779	磁铁
Ningbo Mingzhou Dongmu Powder Metallurgy Co., Ltd.	Ningbo	Zhejiang	(0574)88234707		Foreign Funded				Powder Metallurgy
宁波明州东睦粉末冶金有限公司(2000)	宁波市	浙江省	(0574)88236942	182	外商投资	57,934	5,294(12)	125,805	粉末冶金

Top 10 Cities by Revenue 销售收入排名前10位城市	Province 省	Market share 市场份额 (%)	Number of firms 企业个数
Jinhua 金华市	Zhejiang 浙江省	28.97	17
Ningbo 宁波市	Zhejiang 浙江省	17.30	17
Jiangmen 江门市	Guangdong 广东省	6.30	2
Yangzhou 扬州市	Jiangsu 江苏省	4.88	2
Nanjing 南京市	Jiangsu 江苏省	3.94	7
Shanghai 上海市	Shanghai 上海市	3.86	14
Foshan 佛山市	Guangdong 广东省	2.72	7
Chongqing 重庆市	Chongqing 重庆市	2.61	4
Beijing 北京市	Beijing 北京市	2.33	5
Wuxi 无锡市	Jiangsu 江苏省	2.16	8

10 Major Wholesalers 十家主要批发商	City 城市	Province 省	Telephone/Fax 电话/传真
SU MEC	Nanjing	Jiangsu	(025)4511888
中设江苏机械设备进出口（集团）公司	南京市	江苏省	(025)4411772
China Poster Mobile Communications Equipment Co.,Ltd.	Beijing	Beijing	(010)66426993
中邮普泰移动通信设备股份有限公司	北京市	北京市	(010)66426837
Sino Kama Co., Ltd.	Shanghai	Shanghai	(021)62031188
中泰凯马股份有限公司	上海市	上海市	(021)62030851
China Huayuan Group Co.,Ltd.	Shanghai	Shanghai	(021)62031188
中国华源集团有限公司	上海市	上海市	(021)62032288
Zhejiang Crand Imp.& Exp.Co.,Ltd.	Ningbo	Zhejiang	(0574)87720170
浙江远大进出口有限公司	宁波市	浙江省	(0574)87723350
Shandong Machinery Import & Export Group Corporation	Qingdao	Shandong	(0532)2661628
山东省机械进出口集团公司	青岛市	山东省	(0532)2991655
Qingdao Haier International Trade Co.,Ltd.	Qingdao	Shandong	(0532)8938337
青岛海尔国际贸易有限公司	青岛市	山东省	(0532)8939494
Guangdong Machinery Import & Export Group Corporation	Guangzhou	Guangdong	(020)87782168
广东省机械进出口集团公司	广州市	广东省	(020)87771803
China National Machinery Equipment Import & Export Corporation	Beijing	Beijing	(010)63474506
中国机械设备进出口总公司	北京市	北京市	(010)63261865
Beijing Cellstar Co.,Ltd.	Beijing	Beijing	(010)64602050
北京蜂星事达电讯有限公司	北京市	北京市	(010)64672648

3565: Fasteners 紧固件制造业

The industry accounts for 0.100% of the total revenue of China's industrial sector in 2002. The rate of return on assets is 3.97%. 86.22% of all firms in the industry made a profit while 13.78% had negative returns.The top province in terms of the industry's revenue is Zhejiang, accounting for 40.14% of the total revenue.
2002年本行业收入占全行业的 0.100%，资产利润率为 3.97%。86.22%的企业赢利，13.78%的企业亏损。收入最高的省为浙江省，占本行业的40.14%。

	Total number of firms 企业总数	Total number of employees 职工总数	Total revenue (Mil.RMB) 总销售收入 (百万元)	Total profit (Mil.RMB) 总利润 (百万元)	Return on assets 资产利润率 (%)	Return on equity 权益利润率 (%)	Labour productivity ('000 RMB/ worker) 劳动生产率 (千元/人)	Debts/ assets 资产负债率 (%)	Total assets (Mil.RMB) 总资产 (百万元)
Industry Overall 行业总体	508	71,263	10,715	453	3.97	9.77	43.63	59.36	11,426

	Number of firms 企业个数	Average number of employees 平均职工人数	Average revenue ('000 RMB) 平均销售收入 (千元)	Average profit ('000 RMB) 平均利润 (千元)	Return on assets 资产利润率 (%)	Return on equity 权益利润率 (%)	Labour productivity ('000 RMB/ worker) 劳动生产率 (千元/人)	Debts/ assets 资产负债率 (%)	Average total assets ('000 RMB) 平均总资产 (千元)
By ownership 产业所有权									
State-owned 国有	55	194	6,583	-863	-2.62	-15.04	10.78	82.60	32,992
Collective-owned 集体	74	149	20,062	1,135	6.70	20.19	56.10	66.80	16,937
Foreign & Overseas Chinese Funded 三资	87	148	37,008	2,313	5.01	8.44	71.64	40.69	46,186
By regional distribution 地区分布									
Central-North 华北	37	147	15,513	634	3.00	13.38	70.08	77.59	21,122
Beijing 北京	2	533	6,980	-7,103	-6.23	-66.71	0.82	90.66	113,981
Tianjin 天津	18	112	24,237	2,026	11.09	32.63	172.21	66.02	18,278
Hebei 河北	14	152	8,593	85	0.54	2.99	15.27	81.79	15,528
Shanxi 山西	3	77	1,151	-1	-0.03	-0.08	5.43	65.11	2,392
Inner Mongolia 内蒙古									
Northeast 东北	13	256	18,407	188	0.44	0.95	18.07	54.18	43,315
Liaoning 辽宁	7	291	26,844	411	0.55	1.14	21.81	52.02	75,409
Jilin 吉林	3	82	1,340	-61	-1.00	-7.51	8.47	86.67	6,060
Heilongjiang 黑龙江	3	347	15,789	-82	-1.44	-10.76	12.99	86.66	5,685
Central-East 华东	358	132	23,643	1,206	5.98	13.47	47.86	55.63	20,182
Shanghai 上海	48	137	24,590	1,089	3.85	7.55	47.31	49.06	28,313
Jiangsu 江苏	75	143	29,431	998	5.47	15.13	50.81	63.82	18,238
Zhejiang 浙江	196	117	21,946	1,378	7.23	15.01	48.90	51.83	19,068
Anhui 安徽	2	55	5,082	51	0.61	4.23	27.95	85.65	8,313
Fujian 福建	7	115	17,467	1,588	6.27	8.95	46.71	29.92	25,332
Jiangxi 江西	7	236	6,133	-910	-6.28		4.17	140.71	14,505
Shandong 山东	23	195	26,072	1,293	6.39	22.44	53.14	71.52	20,230
Central-South 中南	73	121	14,776	-64	-0.22	-0.53	34.10	58.58	29,247
Henan 河南	18	130	8,933	287	2.44	6.81	21.73	64.15	11,767
Hubei 湖北	12	109	6,435	-439	-0.91	-2.42	26.97	62.54	48,431
Hunan 湖南	5	173	6,203	-1,003	-4.39		11.72	115.22	22,865
Guangdong 广东	35	117	22,737	94	0.28	0.55	49.61	49.71	33,683
Guangxi 广西	3	77	4,617	-951	-5.84	-18.93	7.88	69.15	16,282
Hainan 海南									
Southwest 西南	20	268	15,855	-37	-0.12	-1.34	17.64	90.77	29,922
Chongqing 重庆	5	332	17,543	676	2.01		9.97	107.82	33,575
Sichuan 四川	12	225	16,249	-244	-0.91	-12.12	23.22	92.45	26,694
Guizhou 贵州	3	333	11,464	-397	-1.08	-2.70	15.32	59.89	36,745
Yunnan 云南									
Tibet 西藏									
Northwest 西北	7	157	5,965	159	0.90	1.69	11.36	46.81	17,618
Shaanxi 陕西									
Gansu 甘肃	6	120	3,590	-29	-0.23	-0.46	9.53	49.80	12,502
Qinghai 青海									
Ningxia 宁夏									
Xinjiang 新疆	1	377	20,217	1,283	2.66	4.59	14.87	42.16	48,317

3565: Fasteners 紧固件制造业

Year 年份	Number of firms 企业个数	Rate of change 变化率 (%)	Number of employees 职工人数 (人)	Rate of change 变化率 (%)	Total revenue (Mil. RMB) 总销售收入 (百万元)	Rate of change 变化率 (%)	Total profit (Mil RMB) 总利润 (百万元)	Rate of change 变化率 (%)
2000	445		72,838		8,830		312	
2001	457	2.70	70,754	-2.86	8,765	-0.74	331	6.09
2002	508	11.16	71,263	0.72	10,715	22.25	453	36.86

Major Products 主要产品	Output 产量	Unit 单位
Standard Fastener 标准紧固件	101	10,000 Tons 万吨

10 Main Firms with Maximal Revenue (year founded) 收入最大的十家主要企业（创办年份）	City 城市	Province 省	Telephone/ fax 电话/传真	Number of employees 职工人数	Ownership 产业所有权	Revenue ('000 RMB) 销售收入 (千元)	Profit('000 RMB) (rank) 利润(千元) (排名)	Total assets ('000 RMB) 总资产 (千元)	Major products 主要产品
GEM-YEAR Industrial Co., Ltd.	Jiaxing	Zhejiang	(0573)4185001		Overseas Chinese-funded				Fasteners
晋亿实业有限公司(1995)	嘉兴市	浙江省	(0573)4184567	1,431	港澳台资	703,834	84,180(1)	969,838	紧固件
Changshu Standard Parts Factory	Suzhou	Jiangsu	(0512)52811688		Joint Stock				Standard Fastener标
常熟市标准件厂(1966)	苏州市	江苏省	(0512)52811984	850	股份制	414,950	10,013(9)	362,813	准紧固件
Tianjin Xianda Automobile Industrial Trading Company	Tianjin	Tianjin	(022)27990035		Collective-owned				Automobile Fitting Part
天津市先达汽车工贸公司(1992)	天津市	天津市	(022)27993704	319	集体企业	240,750	22,270(2)	135,930	汽车配件
Nanjing Jiahe Hardware Machinery Co., Ltd.	Nanjing	Jiangsu	(025)2642296		Overseas Chinese-funded				Standard Fastener标
南京佳和五金机械有限公司(1994)	南京市	江苏省	(025)2642857	780	港澳台资	202,370	12,700(4)	45,750	准紧固件
Zhejiang Zhapugang Standard Piece Industrial Co., Ltd.	Jiaxing	Zhejiang	(0573)5581127		Private Owned				Bolt
浙江省乍浦港标准件实业有限公司(1993)	嘉兴市	浙江省	(0573)5520333	626	私营企业	178,780	4,935(23)	145,198	螺栓
Dongming Industrial (Jiaxing) Co., Ltd.	Jiaxing	Zhejiang	(0573)2203125		Overseas Chinese-funded				Nut
东明实业(嘉兴)有限公司(1998)	嘉兴市	浙江省	(0573)2207588	280	港澳台资	177,991	16,885(3)	291,738	螺帽
Nanjing Jiafuxin Machinery Co., Ltd.	Nanjing	Jiangsu	(025)2642296		Overseas Chinese-funded				Standard Fastener标
南京佳富鑫机械有限公司(1994)	南京市	江苏省	(025)2642857	614	港澳台资	168,960	10,640(7)	31,040	准紧固件
Chunyu (Dongguan) Hardware Co., Ltd.	Dongguan	Guangdong	(0769)3310921		Overseas Chinese-funded				Nut
春雨（东莞）五金制品有限公司(1998)	东莞市	广东省	(0769)3181001	350	港澳台资	142,863	-	607,226	螺帽
Zhejiang Haili Standard Parts Co., ltd.	Quzhou	Zhejiang	(0570)2932888		Private Owned				Electric Circuitry Fastener电力线
浙江海力标准件有限公司(2000)	衢州市	浙江省	(0570)2932333	479	私营企业	99,367	6,807(15)	75,991	路紧固件
Zibo High Strength Screw Bolt Factory Boshan Antisepis Pump	Zibo	Shandong	(0533)4200119		Collective-owned				Fence Bolt
Factory 淄博高强度螺栓厂博山防腐电泵厂(1970)	淄博市	山东省	(0533)4201143	848	集体企业	98,903	3,249(34)	80,007	护栏栓

Top 10 Cities by Revenue 销售收入排名前10位城市	Province 省	Market share 市场份额 (%)	Number of firms 企业个数
Jiaxing 嘉兴市	Zhejiang 浙江省	15.12	32
Shanghai 上海市	Shanghai 上海市	11.02	48
Ningbo 宁波市	Zhejiang 浙江省	10.37	53
Wenzhou 温州市	Zhejiang 浙江省	7.32	63
Suzhou 苏州市	Jiangsu 江苏省	6.97	14
Tianjin 天津市	Tianjin 天津市	4.07	18
Nanjing 南京市	Jiangsu 江苏省	3.57	4
Yancheng 盐城市	Jiangsu 江苏省	2.67	9
Hangzhou 杭州市	Zhejiang 浙江省	2.59	17
Wuxi 无锡市	Jiangsu 江苏省	2.50	12

10 Major Wholesalers 十家主要批发商	City 城市	Province 省	Telephone/Fax 电话/传真
SU MEC	Nanjing	Jiangsu	(025)4511888
中设江苏机械设备进出口（集团）公司	南京市	江苏省	(025)4411772
China Poster Mobile Communications Equipment Co.,Ltd.	Beijing	Beijing	(010)66426993
中邮普泰移动通信设备股份有限公司	北京市	北京市	(010)66426837
Sino Kama Co., Ltd.	Shanghai	Shanghai	(021)62031188
中泰凯马股份有限公司	上海市	上海市	(021)62030851
China Huayuan Group Co.,Ltd.	Shanghai	Shanghai	(021)62031188
中国华源集团有限公司	上海市	上海市	(021)62032288
Zhejiang Crand Imp.& Exp.Co.,Ltd.	Ningbo	Zhejiang	(0574)87720170
浙江远大进出口有限公司	宁波市	浙江省	(0574)87723350
Shandong Machinery Import & Export Group Corporation	Qingdao	Shandong	(0532)2661628
山东省机械进出口集团公司	青岛市	山东省	(0532)2991655
Qingdao Haier International Trade Co.,Ltd.	Qingdao	Shandong	(0532)8938337
青岛海尔国际贸易有限公司	青岛市	山东省	(0532)8939494
Guangdong Machinery Import & Export Group Corporation	Guangzhou	Guangdong	(020)87782168
广东省机械进出口集团公司	广州市	广东省	(020)87771803
China National Machinery Equipment Import & Export Corporation	Beijing	Beijing	(010)63474506
中国机械设备进出口总公司	北京市	北京市	(010)63261865
Beijing Cellstar Co.,Ltd.	Beijing	Beijing	(010)64602050
北京蜂星事达电讯有限公司	北京市	北京市	(010)64672648

3566: Springs 弹簧制造业

The industry accounts for 0.039% of the total revenue of China's industrial sector in 2002. The rate of return on assets is 6.35%. 87.50% of all firms in the industry made a profit while 12.50% had negative returns.The top province in terms of the industry's revenue is Shandong, accounting for 48.93% of the total revenue.
2002年本行业收入占全行业的 0.039%，资产利润率为 6.35%。87.50%的企业赢利，12.50%的企业亏损。收入最高的省为山东省，占本行业的48.93%。

	Total number of firms 企业总数	Total number of employees 职工总数	Total revenue (Mil.RMB) 总销售收入（百万元）	Total profit (Mil.RMB) 总利润（百万元）	Return on assets 资产利润率（%）	Return on equity 权益利润率（%）	Labour productivity ('000 RMB/worker) 劳动生产率（千元/人）	Debts/assets 资产负债率（%）	Total assets (Mil.RMB) 总资产（百万元）
Industry Overall 行业总体	144	23,795	4,136	219	6.35	14.76	49.78	56.98	3,455

	Number of firms 企业个数	Average number of employees 平均职工人数	Average revenue ('000 RMB) 平均销售收入（千元）	Average profit ('000 RMB) 平均利润（千元）	Return on assets 资产利润率（%）	Return on equity 权益利润率（%）	Labour productivity ('000 RMB/worker) 劳动生产率（千元/人）	Debts/assets 资产负债率（%）	Average total assets ('000 RMB) 平均总资产（千元）
By ownership 产业所有权									
State-owned 国有	11	505	72,563	488	0.58	1.49	27.53	61.20	84,174
Collective-owned 集体	23	122	11,223	381	3.24	9.76	28.07	66.85	11,765
Foreign & Overseas Chinese Funded 三资	25	124	25,480	1,919	5.17	9.84	60.55	47.42	37,093
By regional distribution 地区分布									
Central-North 华北	16	138	14,106	500	4.60	13.96	35.07	67.05	10,873
Beijing 北京	3	107	10,498	460	3.98	10.26	25.65	61.14	11,552
Tianjin 天津	5	88	11,683	923	12.37	49.17	59.49	74.83	7,459
Hebei 河北	4	111	6,341	340	7.44	16.49	18.85	54.89	4,570
Shanxi 山西	2	131	5,075	-287	-6.15		13.44	113.48	4,665
Inner Mongolia 内蒙古	2	373	50,138	611	1.64	4.44	41.94	63.07	37,206
Northeast 东北	8	116	10,675	781	4.10	12.49	31.63	67.15	19,019
Liaoning 辽宁	4	138	14,379	1,016	6.01	18.43	31.63	67.39	16,913
Jilin 吉林	2	135	6,845	168	0.96	2.16	21.54	55.70	17,563
Heilongjiang 黑龙江	2	54	7,099	922	3.73	14.92	56.86	74.98	24,687
Central-East 华东	84	198	39,482	2,148	7.21	16.50	55.50	56.33	29,816
Shanghai 上海	13	93	22,626	1,170	3.81	7.76	76.22	50.93	30,698
Jiangsu 江苏	23	133	18,526	1,186	8.13	23.80	39.32	65.83	14,586
Zhejiang 浙江	32	136	15,305	1,186	8.19	14.14	34.13	42.11	14,494
Anhui 安徽	1	206	3,354	-117	-2.06	-21.59	8.11	90.46	5,683
Fujian 福建	2	203	25,801	520	1.17	3.91	21.46	70.07	44,340
Jiangxi 江西	1	200	27,745	2,380	25.79	46.48	59.24	44.53	9,230
Shandong 山东	12	600	168,649	8,058	8.04	20.04	74.92	59.87	100,214
Central-South 中南	27	125	15,255	806	3.91	8.14	33.78	51.98	20,607
Henan 河南	4	154	8,197	281	4.17	15.17	14.53	72.50	6,726
Hubei 湖北	4	81	6,973	444	4.89	44.62	28.81	89.03	9,073
Hunan 湖南	3	89	6,943	7	0.11	0.22	32.69	49.22	6,542
Guangdong 广东	16	136	20,649	1,177	3.98	7.66	40.10	48.09	29,597
Guangxi 广西									
Hainan 海南									
Southwest 西南	5	93	17,859	585	5.20	17.23	81.44	69.82	11,242
Chongqing 重庆	2	126	5,254	-1,171	-8.30	-38.06	30.47	78.19	14,109
Sichuan 四川	3	71	26,262	1,755	18.81	48.70	141.22	61.39	9,332
Guizhou 贵州									
Yunnan 云南									
Tibet 西藏									
Northwest 西北	4	50	1,862	-10	-0.31	-2.87	19.20	89.06	3,032
Shaanxi 陕西	1	38	4,323	3	0.04		45.92	102.15	6,878
Gansu 甘肃	3	54	1,042	-14	-0.78	-2.78	12.93	71.91	1,749
Qinghai 青海									
Ningxia 宁夏									
Xinjiang 新疆									

3566: Springs 弹簧制造业

Year 年份	Number of firms 企业个数	Rate of change 变化率(%)	Number of employees 职工人数(人)	Rate of change 变化率(%)	Total revenue (Mil. RMB) 总销售收入(百万元)	Rate of change 变化率(%)	Total profit (Mil RMB) 总利润(百万元)	Rate of change 变化率(%)
2000	119		14,555		1,528		87	
2001	132	10.92	18,863	29.60	2,376	55.50	125	43.68
2002	144	9.09	23,795	26.15	4,136	74.07	219	75.20

Major Products 主要产品	Output 产量	Unit 单位

10 Main Firms with Maximal Revenue (year founded) 收入最大的十家主要企业（创办年份）	City 城市	Province 省	Telephone/fax 电话/传真	Number of employees 职工人数	Ownership 产业所有权	Revenue ('000 RMB) 销售收入(千元)	Profit('000 RMB) (rank) 利润(千元)(排名)	Total assets ('000 RMB) 总资产(千元)	Major products 主要产品
Shandong Laidong Gas Engine Co., ltd.	Yantai	Shandong	(0535)7293371		State-owned				Spring
山东莱动内燃机有限公司(1943)	烟台市	山东省	(0535)7211177	4,730	国有企业	768,677	6,912(6)	860,626	弹簧
Shangdong Wendeng Shuangli Plate Spring Co., Ltd.	Weihai	Shandong	(0631)8761078		Joint Stock				Armor Plate Spring
山东省文登市双力板簧有限公司(1954)	威海市	山东省	(0631)8767199	480	股份制	629,180	43,180(1)	44,770	钢板弹簧
Weihai Lianyi Plate Spring Co., Ltd.	Weihai	Shandong	(0631)6711052		Joint Stock				Plate Spring
威海联谊板簧有限公司(1975)	威海市	山东省	(0631)6711052	163	股份制	282,999	19,895(2)	22,512	板簧
Qingdao Shuaichao Industrial Co., Ltd.	Qingdao	Shandong	(0532)4833328		Private Owned				Spring
青岛帅潮实业有限公司(2000)	青岛市	山东省	(0532)4832028	116	私营企业	104,424	8,941(4)	90,782	弹簧
Shanghai Dongfeng Hardware Co., Ltd.	Shanghai	Shanghai	(021)64780789		Overseas Chinese-funded				Fastener Spring紧
上海东丰五金有限公司(1993)	上海市	上海市	(021)64190761	141	港澳台资	90,280	1,481(34)	91,751	固件弹簧
Weifang Hongwei Steel Factory	Weifang	Shandong	(0536)8801095		Private Enterprises				Spring Steel Plate
潍坊市宏伟钢厂(2000)	潍坊市	山东省	(0536)8801095	793	私营独资	80,300	3,000(19)	64,200	弹簧钢板
Guangzhou Huade Automobile Spring Co., Ltd.	Guangzhou	Guangdong	(020)82708000		Overseas Chinese-funded				Spring
广州华德汽车弹簧有限公司(1993)	广州市	广东省	(020)82979172	211	港澳台资	63,903	3,727(11)	122,585	弹簧
Dongguan KENT Spring Co., Ltd.	Dongguan	Guangdong	(0769)5538535		Foreign Funded				Spring
东莞奄美弹簧有限公司(1994)	东莞市	广东省	(0769)5537055	360	外商投资	61,365	4,742(10)	74,537	弹簧
KERN LIEBERS (TAICANG) Spring Co.,Ltd.	Suzhou	Jiangsu	(0812)53578996		Foreign Funded				Spring
太仓克恩-里伯斯弹簧有限公司(1993)	苏州市	江苏省	(0812)53578997	90	外商投资	59,480	17,780(3)	73,430	弹簧
Zhejiang Zhuji Spring General Factory Co., Ltd.	Shaoxing	Zhejiang	(0575)7071857		Private Enterprises				Spring
浙江省诸暨弹簧总厂有限公司(1974)	绍兴市	浙江省	(0575)7071577	320	私营独资	50,761	6,204(7)	56,768	弹簧

Top 10 Cities by Revenue 销售收入排名前10位城市	Province 省	Market share 市场份额(%)	Number of firms 企业个数
Weihai 威海市	Shandong 山东省	22.05	2
Yantai 烟台市	Shandong 山东省	18.58	1
Shaoxing 绍兴市	Zhejiang 浙江省	7.89	18
Shanghai 上海市	Shanghai 上海市	7.11	13
Qingdao 青岛市	Shandong 山东省	3.37	3
Weifang 潍坊市	Shandong 山东省	3.00	3
Changzhou 常州市	Jiangsu 江苏省	2.80	8
Guangzhou 广州市	Guangdong 广东省	2.67	4
Baotou 包头市	Inner Mongolia 内蒙古	2.42	2
Hangzhou 杭州市	Zhejiang 浙江省	2.31	7

10 Major Wholesalers 十家主要批发商	City 城市	Province 省	Telephone/Fax 电话/传真
SU MEC	Nanjing	Jiangsu	(025)4511888
中设江苏机械设备进出口（集团）公司	南京市	江苏省	(025)4411772
China Poster Mobile Communications Equipment Co.,Ltd.	Beijing	Beijing	(010)66426993
中邮普泰移动通信设备股份有限公司	北京市	北京市	(010)66426837
Sino Kama Co., Ltd.	Shanghai	Shanghai	(021)62031188
中泰凯马股份有限公司	上海市	上海市	(021)62030851
China Huayuan Group Co.,Ltd.	Shanghai	Shanghai	(021)62031188
中国华源集团有限公司	上海市	上海市	(021)62032288
Zhejiang Crand Imp.& Exp.Co.,Ltd.	Ningbo	Zhejiang	(0574)87720170
浙江远大进出口有限公司	宁波市	浙江省	(0574)87723350
Shandong Machinery Import & Export Group Corporation	Qingdao	Shandong	(0532)2661628
山东省机械进出口集团公司	青岛市	山东省	(0532)2991655
Qingdao Haier International Trade Co.,Ltd.	Qingdao	Shandong	(0532)8938337
青岛海尔国际贸易有限公司	青岛市	山东省	(0532)8939494
Guangdong Machinery Import & Export Group Corporation	Guangzhou	Guangdong	(020)87782168
广东省机械进出口集团公司	广州市	广东省	(020)87771803
China National Machinery Equipment Import & Export Corporation	Beijing	Beijing	(010)63474506
中国机械设备进出口总公司	北京市	北京市	(010)63261865
Beijing Cellstar Co.,Ltd.	Beijing	Beijing	(010)64602050
北京蜂星事达电讯有限公司	北京市	北京市	(010)64672648

3567: Chains 链条制造业

The industry accounts for 0.029% of the total revenue of China's industrial sector in 2002. The rate of return on assets is 3.92%. 81.89% of all firms in the industry made a profit while 18.11% had negative returns.The top province in terms of the industry's revenue is Zhejiang, accounting for 41.83% of the total revenue.
2002年本行业收入占全行业的0.029%，资产利润率为3.92%。81.89%的企业赢利，18.11%的企业亏损。收入最高的省为浙江省，占本行业的41.83%。

	Total number of firms 企业总数	Total number of employees 职工总数	Total revenue (Mil.RMB) 总销售收入（百万元）	Total profit (Mil.RMB) 总利润（百万元）	Return on assets 资产利润率（%）	Return on equity 权益利润率（%）	Labour productivity ('000 RMB/ worker) 劳动生产率（千元/人）	Debts/ assets 资产负债率（%）	Total assets (Mil.RMB) 总资产（百万元）
Industry Overall 行业总体	127	30,192	3,164	132	3.92	12.01	28.96	67.40	3,363

	Number of firms 企业个数	Average number of employees 平均职工人数	Average revenue ('000 RMB) 平均销售收入（千元）	Average profit ('000 RMB) 平均利润（千元）	Return on assets 资产利润率（%）	Return on equity 权益利润率（%）	Labour productivity ('000 RMB/ worker) 劳动生产率（千元/人）	Debts/ assets 资产负债率（%）	Average total assets ('000 RMB) 平均总资产（千元）
By ownership 产业所有权									
State-owned 国有	12	174	7,884	-245	-0.97	-97.54	17.25	99.00	25,164
Collective-owned 集体	18	466	37,775	1,544	4.08	14.66	23.32	72.17	37,850
Foreign & Overseas Chinese Funded 三资	12	303	53,760	2,897	4.75	9.47	46.88	49.91	61,048
By regional distribution 地区分布									
Central-North 华北	9	669	50,916	2,885	5.76	19.89	24.59	71.04	50,078
Beijing 北京									
Tianjin 天津	3	95	7,823	593	17.33	50.14	10.84	65.43	3,423
Hebei 河北	6	956	72,462	4,030	5.49	19.04	25.28	71.17	73,406
Shanxi 山西									
Inner Mongolia 内蒙古									
Northeast 东北	6	244	10,558	-95	-0.26	-1.87	17.17	86.27	37,070
Liaoning 辽宁	4	221	13,548	626	1.43	5.16	29.44	72.38	43,893
Jilin 吉林	1	186	2,999	-256	-5.84	-5.84	2.00		4,384
Heilongjiang 黑龙江	1	395	6,158	-2,820	-6.64		-3.08	152.62	42,464
Central-East 华东	91	206	26,483	1,218	4.87	13.32	33.75	63.43	24,993
Shanghai 上海	7	137	16,949	2,037	14.45	31.93	32.68	54.73	14,096
Jiangsu 江苏	21	209	31,932	1,275	4.98	14.47	39.99	65.60	25,607
Zhejiang 浙江	42	246	31,509	1,490	4.67	11.88	32.43	60.70	31,915
Anhui 安徽	14	145	10,789	178	1.26	4.11	25.81	69.23	14,113
Fujian 福建									
Jiangxi 江西									
Shandong 山东	7	148	20,901	673	4.71	32.74	37.02	85.60	14,274
Central-South 中南	18	139	9,945	-75	-0.45	-2.33	23.34	80.92	16,766
Henan 河南	4	145	4,239	-35	-0.29		25.01	113.07	12,323
Hubei 湖北	4	79	10,916	450	6.14		39.75	114.51	7,330
Hunan 湖南	5	143	5,489	-285	-1.54	-6.87	14.11	77.59	18,499
Guangdong 广东	4	165	19,107	-425	-1.92	-4.60	25.94	58.30	22,145
Guangxi 广西	1	232	14,520	122	0.29	1.15	17.74	74.80	42,102
Hainan 海南									
Southwest 西南	2	255	9,195	-1,594	-5.82	-24.85	5.63	76.56	27,370
Chongqing 重庆	1	360	15,264	77	0.25	0.71	10.96	64.51	30,761
Sichuan 四川	1	150	3,126	-3,265	-13.62	-170.76	-7.16	92.03	23,978
Guizhou 贵州									
Yunnan 云南									
Tibet 西藏									
Northwest 西北	1	937	34,878	50	0.08	0.15	7.38	43.81	59,293
Shaanxi 陕西									
Gansu 甘肃	1	937	34,878	50	0.08	0.15	7.38	43.81	59,293
Qinghai 青海									
Ningxia 宁夏									
Xinjiang 新疆									

3567: Chains 链条制造业

Year 年份	Number of firms 企业个数	Rate of change 变化率 (%)	Number of employees 职工人数 (人)	Rate of change 变化率 (%)	Total revenue (Mil. RMB) 总销售收入 (百万元)	Rate of change 变化率 (%)	Total profit (Mil RMB) 总利润 (百万元)	Rate of change 变化率 (%)
2000	127		30,379		2,640		15	
2001	134	5.51	29,830	-1.81	2,793	5.80	30	100.00
2002	127	-5.22	30,192	1.21	3,164	13.28	132	340.00

Major Products 主要产品	Output 产量	Unit 单位
Industrial Chain 工业链条	182,858	Ton 吨

10 Main Firms with Maximal Revenue (year founded) 收入最大的十家主要企业（创办年份）	City 城市	Province 省	Telephone/fax 电话/传真	Number of employees 职工人数	Ownership 产业所有权	Revenue ('000 RMB) 销售收入 (千元)	Profit('000 RMB) (rank) 利润(千元) (排名)	Total assets ('000 RMB) 总资产 (千元)	Major products 主要产品
Hebei Guanghua Enterprise Group Company 河北省光华企业集团公司(1993)	Shijiazhuang 石家庄市	Hebei 河北省	(0311)5053794 (0311)5083614	2,890	Collective-owned 集体企业	313,800	27920(1)	267,327	Chain Wheel 链轮
Zhejiang Hengjiu Machinery Co.,Ltd 浙江恒久机械集团有限公司(1989)	Shaoxing 绍兴市	Zhejiang 浙江省	(0575)7215625 (0575)7214388	1,137	Overseas Chinese-funded 港澳台资	223,180	15,800(2)	223,954	Industrial Chain 工业链条
Hangzhou Donghua Electromechanical Equipment Group Co., Ltd.杭州东华机电器材集团有限公司(1995)	Hangzhou 杭州市	Zhejiang 浙江省	(0571)85144908 (0571)85147178	1,875	Limited-Liability 有限公司	182,141	4,502(9)	159,288	Chain 链条
Hangzhou Ziqiang Chain Transmission Co., ltd. 杭州自强链传动有限公司(1999)	Hangzhou 杭州市	Zhejiang 浙江省	(0571)86210506 (0571)86210512	745	Private Owned 私营企业	133,388	7,057(5)	113,332	Industrial Chain 工业链条
Suzhou Guimeng Chain (Taicang) Co.,Ltd 苏州桂盟链条(太仓)有限公司(1996)	Suzhou 苏州市	Jiangsu 江苏省	(0512)53457988 (0512)53450286	532	Overseas Chinese-funded 港澳台资	130,060	9,880(4)	101,710	Motobicycle Chain摩托车链条
Nantong Haixun Industrial Co.,Ltd 南通海迅实业有限公司(1994)	Nantong 南通市	Jiangsu 江苏省	(0513)8343841 (0513)8915005	135	Limited-Liability 有限公司	100,543	2,991(14)	33,680	Iron Chain 铁链
Hangzhou Xuefeng Chain Co.,Ltd 杭州雪峰链条有限公司(1993)	Hangzhou 杭州市	Zhejiang 浙江省	(0571)82464236 (0571)82462322	486	Overseas Chinese-funded 港澳台资	94,694	3,367(12)	77,759	Tyre Chain 防滑链
Nanjing Meishan Chain Factory 南京梅山链条厂(2000)	Nanjing 南京市	Jiangsu 江苏省	(025)2809701 (025)2802459	850	Private Enterprises 私营独资	83,160	6,060(7)	30,900	Torus Chain For Mine矿用圆环链
Suzhou Universal Chain Transmission Co.,Ltd. 苏州环球链传动有限公司(1992)	Suzhou 苏州市	Jiangsu 江苏省	(0512)67232385 (0512)67232366	460	Overseas Chinese-funded 港澳台资	79,150	448(45)	104,702	Chain 链条
Huzhou Shuangshi Chain Transmission Co.,Ltd 湖州双狮链传动有限公司(1998)	Huzhou 湖州市	Zhejiang 浙江省	(0572)3489058 (0572)3489388	739	Limited-Liability 有限公司	69,682	148(66)	73,365	Industrial Chain 工业链条

Top 10 Cities by Revenue 销售收入排名前10位城市	Province 省	Market share 市场份额 (%)	Number of firms 企业个数
Hangzhou 杭州市	Zhejiang 浙江省	23.19	24
Shaoxing 绍兴市	Zhejiang 浙江省	10.00	4
Shijiazhuang 石家庄市	Hebei 河北省	9.92	1
Suzhou 苏州市	Jiangsu 江苏省	9.67	9
Nantong 南通市	Jiangsu 江苏省	4.36	5
Nanjing 南京市	Jiangsu 江苏省	3.92	3
Shanghai 上海市	Shanghai 上海市	3.75	7
Jinhua 金华市	Zhejiang 浙江省	3.74	6
Huzhou 湖州市	Zhejiang 浙江省	3.57	4
Yantai 烟台市	Shandong 山东省	2.47	1

10 Major Wholesalers 十家主要批发商	City 城市	Province 省	Telephone/Fax 电话/传真
SU MEC 中设江苏机械设备进出口（集团）公司	Nanjing 南京市	Jiangsu 江苏省	(025)4511888 (025)4411772
China Poster Mobile Communications Equipment Co.,Ltd. 中邮普泰移动通信设备股份有限公司	Beijing 北京市	Beijing 北京市	(010)66426993 (010)66426837
Sino Kama Co., Ltd. 中泰凯马股份有限公司	Shanghai 上海市	Shanghai 上海市	(021)62031188 (021)62030851
China Huayuan Group Co.,Ltd. 中国华源集团有限公司	Shanghai 上海市	Shanghai 上海市	(021)62031188 (021)62032288
Zhejiang Crand Imp.& Exp.Co.,Ltd. 浙江远大进出口有限公司	Ningbo 宁波市	Zhejiang 浙江省	(0574)87720170 (0574)87723350
Shandong Machinery Import & Export Group Corporation 山东省机械进出口集团公司	Qingdao 青岛市	Shandong 山东省	(0532)2661628 (0532)2991655
Qingdao Haier International Trade Co.,Ltd. 青岛海尔国际贸易有限公司	Qingdao 青岛市	Shandong 山东省	(0532)8938337 (0532)8939494
Guangdong Machinery Import & Export Group Corporation 广东省机械进出口集团公司	Guangzhou 广州市	Guangdong 广东省	(020)87782168 (020)87771803
China National Machinery Equipment Import & Export Corporation 中国机械设备进出口总公司	Beijing 北京市	Beijing 北京市	(010)63474506 (010)63261865
Beijing Cellstar Co.,Ltd. 北京蜂星事达电讯有限公司	Beijing 北京市	Beijing 北京市	(010)64602050 (010)64672648

3568: Gears 齿轮制造业

The industry accounts for 0.058% of the total revenue of China's industrial sector in 2002. The rate of return on assets is 4.53%. 80.65% of all firms in the industry made a profit while 19.35% had negative returns.The top province in terms of the industry's revenue is Jiangsu, accounting for 25.79% of the total revenue.
2002年本行业收入占全行业的0.058%，资产利润率为4.53%。80.65%的企业赢利，19.35%的企业亏损。收入最高的省为江苏省，占本行业的25.79%。

	Total number of firms 企业总数	Total number of employees 职工总数	Total revenue (Mil.RMB) 总销售收入（百万元）	Total profit (Mil.RMB) 总利润（百万元）	Return on assets 资产利润率（%）	Return on equity 权益利润率（%）	Labour productivity ('000 RMB/worker) 劳动生产率（千元/人）	Debts/assets 资产负债率（%）	Total assets (Mil.RMB) 总资产（百万元）
Industry Overall 行业总体	186	52,657	6,245	359	4.53	12.82	37.10	64.71	7,935

	Number of firms 企业个数	Average number of employees 平均职工人数	Average revenue ('000 RMB) 平均销售收入（千元）	Average profit ('000 RMB) 平均利润（千元）	Return on assets 资产利润率（%）	Return on equity 权益利润率（%）	Labour productivity ('000 RMB/worker) 劳动生产率（千元/人）	Debts/assets 资产负债率（%）	Average total assets ('000 RMB) 平均总资产（千元）
By ownership 产业所有权									
State-owned 国有	32	389	27,110	-325	-0.57	-2.24	22.53	74.67	57,427
Collective-owned 集体	23	183	27,160	2,317	11.62	37.87	46.58	69.31	19,935
Foreign & Overseas Chinese Funded 三资	19	278	41,634	2,359	4.37	10.43	29.01	58.13	53,979
By regional distribution 地区分布									
Central-North 华北	14	186	16,822	1,026	5.68	13.65	33.87	58.39	18,060
Beijing 北京	5	97	10,864	2,176	21.45	57.84	44.25	62.91	10,145
Tianjin 天津	5	92	6,455	128	1.22	2.61	16.86	53.06	10,485
Hebei 河北	4	413	37,230	708	1.89	4.59	35.55	58.73	37,424
Shanxi 山西									
Inner Mongolia 内蒙古									
Northeast 东北	6	314	25,179	1,642	3.70	10.17	32.01	63.57	44,336
Liaoning 辽宁	4	185	21,423	1,647	4.70	11.72	47.86	59.89	35,037
Jilin 吉林	1	1,142	65,379	3,265	2.63	8.05	21.75	67.31	124,122
Heilongjiang 黑龙江	1							92.63	1,750
Central-East 华东	115	252	33,311	1,550	4.01	10.73	42.51	62.65	38,698
Shanghai 上海	3	98	11,185	687	5.26	26.68	56.96	80.30	13,078
Jiangsu 江苏	46	238	35,005	1,591	3.55	8.06	47.02	55.96	44,801
Zhejiang 浙江	30	201	25,249	1,332	5.50	13.74	33.27	59.99	24,214
Anhui 安徽	5	340	16,304	336	0.94	2.15	19.11	56.04	35,545
Fujian 福建	8	196	36,993	1,800	4.39	12.15	55.42	63.84	40,950
Jiangxi 江西	6	531	39,763	-26	-0.03	-0.14	31.80	80.12	93,358
Shandong 山东	17	313	47,852	2,775	8.45	31.83	53.02	73.46	32,844
Central-South 中南	26	284	27,089	815	2.04	8.81	16.93	76.87	40,012
Henan 河南	10	250	30,435	1,808	5.29	16.29	47.98	67.53	34,182
Hubei 湖北	6	76	12,745	846	6.16	25.52	22.56	75.88	13,737
Hunan 湖南	6	377	26,250	200	0.46	3.34	26.67	86.18	43,284
Guangdong 广东	1	600	114,627	6,194	4.61	11.89	-137.37	61.26	134,443
Guangxi 广西	2	546	6,043	-5,690	-7.09	-106.37	0.72	93.33	80,211
Hainan 海南	1	481	39,282	2,030	3.30	18.43	33.76	82.09	61,499
Southwest 西南	22	394	23,629	-445	-0.82	-3.32	16.30	75.19	54,035
Chongqing 重庆	7	201	14,251	252	0.90	3.09	22.48	70.95	28,083
Sichuan 四川	10	636	38,333	-454	-0.54	-2.04	15.76	73.71	84,529
Guizhou 贵州	2	224	4,871	-2,845	-9.62		1.07	131.12	29,576
Yunnan 云南	3	149	9,001	-437	-1.49	-3.85	19.76	61.23	29,248
Tibet 西藏									
Northwest 西北	3	1,032	267,685	48,396	19.71	36.22	98.58	45.58	245,535
Shaanxi 陕西	2	1,520	400,983	72,595	20.00	36.76	100.13	45.58	362,888
Gansu 甘肃	1	56	1,090				14.63	45.89	10,830
Qinghai 青海									
Ningxia 宁夏									
Xinjiang 新疆									

3568: Gears 齿轮制造业

Year 年份	Number of firms 企业个数	Rate of change 变化率 (%)	Number of employees 职工人数 (人)	Rate of change 变化率 (%)	Total revenue (Mil. RMB) 总销售收入 (百万元)	Rate of change 变化率 (%)	Total profit (Mil RMB) 总利润 (百万元)	Rate of change 变化率 (%)
2000	151		52,328		3,660		63	
2001	160	5.96	52,961	1.21	4,394	20.05	111	76.19
2002	186	16.25	52,657	-0.57	6,245	42.13	359	223.42

Major Products 主要产品	Output 产量	Unit 单位
Gear 齿轮	180,440	Ton 吨

10 Main Firms with Maximal Revenue (year founded) 收入最大的十家主要企业（创办年份）	City 城市	Province 省	Telephone/fax 电话/传真	Number of employees 职工人数	Ownership 产业所有权	Revenue ('000 RMB) 销售收入 (千元)	Profit('000 RMB) (rank) 利润(千元) (排名)	Total assets ('000 RMB) 总资产 (千元)	Major products 主要产品
Shaanxi Fast Gear Co., Ltd.	Xi'an	Shannxi	(029)4625500		Limited-Liability				Automobile Variable Speed Case
陕西法士特汽车齿轮有限责任公司(1970)	西安市	陕西省	(029)4623110	2,984	有限公司	801,569	145,185(1)	718,131	汽车变速箱
Shandong Yinglun Machinery Co., Ltd.	Yantai	Shandong	(0535)8332876		Overseas Chinese-funded				Gear
山东鹰轮机械有限公司(1985)	烟台市	山东省	(0535)8332060	801	港澳台资	264,250	22,470(3)	66,660	齿轮
Jiangsu Airship Co.,Ltd.	Taizhou	Jiangsu	(0523)8754729		Joint Stock				Gear
江苏飞船股份有限公司(1958)	泰州市	江苏省	(0523)8751899	1,115	股份制	260,041	26,761(2)	322,349	齿轮
Changzhou Feitian Group Company (Chanzhou Gear Works)	Changzhou	Jiangsu	(0519)8812631		State-owned				Gear
常州飞天集团公司(常州齿轮厂)(1958)	常州市	江苏省	(0519)8822742	1,447	国有企业	190,050	350(90)	430,430	齿轮
Zhejiang Wuyi Hengyou Electromechanical Co.,Ltd.	Jinhua	Zhejiang	(0579)7612284		Private Owned				Electric Hammer Gear
浙江武义恒友机电有限公司(1988)	金华市	浙江省	(0579)7612004	909	私营企业	181,330	4,479(16)	84,331	电锤齿轮
Huanghe Pump Machince Co., Ltd.	Zhengzhou	Henan	(0371)4460511		Collective-owned				Casting
黄河泵业(1996)	郑州市	河南省	(0371)7933361	716	集体企业	177,097	16,012(4)	127,464	铸钢件
Sichuan Gear Factory	Chengdu	Sichuan	(028)85100019		State-owned				Gear Fittings
四川齿轮厂(1958)	成都市	四川省	(028)85167042	2,698	国有企业	170,000	50(120)	329,069	齿轮配件
Xiamen Gear Manufactacture Factory	Xiamen	Fujian	(0592)5859033		State-owned				Gear
厦门齿轮厂(1979)	厦门市	福建省	(0592)5859031	450	国有企业	142,882	5,061(12)	102,387	齿轮
Haomeng Vehicle Materials (Shenzhen) Co., Ltd.	Shenzhen	Guangdong	(0755)27705090		Overseas Chinese-funded				Bicycle Chains
浩盟车料（深圳）有限公司(1993)	深圳市	广东省	(0755)27705094	600	港澳台资	114,627	6,194(10)	134,443	曲杯链轮
Henan Yiyang Gear Ltd. Company	Yiyang	Hunan	(0737)4219448		Joint Stock				Automobile Variable Speed Case
河南益阳齿轮股份有限公司(1997)	益阳市	湖南省	(0737)4224744	1,320	股份制	90,362	525(71)	189,114	汽车变速箱

Top 10 Cities by Revenue 销售收入排名前10位城市	Province 省	Market share 市场份额 (%)	Number of firms 企业个数
Xi'an 西安市	Shannxi 陕西省	12.84	2
Changzhou 常州市	Jiangsu 江苏省	9.68	22
Taizhou 泰州市	Jiangsu 江苏省	6.92	6
Yantai 烟台市	Shandong 山东省	6.26	3
Taizhou 台州市	Zhejiang 浙江省	4.53	12
Jinhua 金华市	Zhejiang 浙江省	4.52	7
Suzhou 苏州市	Jiangsu 江苏省	3.70	7
Chengdu 成都市	Sichuan 四川省	3.69	2
Zhengzhou 郑州市	Henan 河南省	3.45	3
Nanchang 南昌市	Jiangxi 江西省	3.23	1

10 Major Wholesalers 十家主要批发商	City 城市	Province 省	Telephone/Fax 电话/传真
SU MEC	Nanjing	Jiangsu	(025)4511888
中设江苏机械设备进出口（集团）公司	南京市	江苏省	(025)4411772
China Poster Mobile Communications Equipment Co.,Ltd.	Beijing	Beijing	(010)66426993
中邮普泰移动通信设备股份有限公司	北京市	北京市	(010)66426837
Sino Kama Co., Ltd.	Shanghai	Shanghai	(021)62031188
中泰凯马股份有限公司	上海市	上海市	(021)62030851
China Huayuan Group Co.,Ltd.	Shanghai	Shanghai	(021)62031188
中国华源集团有限公司	上海市	上海市	(021)62032288
Zhejiang Crand Imp.& Exp.Co.,Ltd.	Ningbo	Zhejiang	(0574)87720170
浙江远大进出口有限公司	宁波市	浙江省	(0574)87723350
Shandong Machinery Import & Export Group Corporation	Qingdao	Shandong	(0532)2661628
山东省机械进出口集团公司	青岛市	山东省	(0532)2991655
Qingdao Haier International Trade Co.,Ltd.	Qingdao	Shandong	(0532)8938337
青岛海尔国际贸易有限公司	青岛市	山东省	(0532)8939494
Guangdong Machinery Import & Export Group Corporation	Guangzhou	Guangdong	(020)87782168
广东省机械进出口集团公司	广州市	广东省	(020)87771803
China National Machinery Equipment Import & Export Corporation	Beijing	Beijing	(010)63474306
中国机械设备进出口总公司	北京市	北京市	(010)63261865
Beijing Cellstar Co.,Ltd.	Beijing	Beijing	(010)64602050
北京蜂星事达电讯有限公司	北京市	北京市	(010)64672648

3569: Other General Parts 其他类未包括的通用零部件制造业

The industry accounts for 0.112% of the total revenue of China's industrial sector in 2002. The rate of return on assets is 5.89%. 82.52% of all firms in the industry made a profit while 17.48% had negative returns.The top province in terms of the industry's revenue is Jiangsu, accounting for 26.93% of the total revenue.
2002年本行业收入占全行业的 0.112%，资产利润率为 5.89%。82.52%的企业赢利，17.48%的企业亏损。收入最高的省为江苏省，占本行业的26.93%。

	Total number of firms 企业总数	Total number of employees 职工总数	Total revenue (Mil.RMB) 总销售收入 (百万元)	Total profit (Mil.RMB) 总利润 (百万元)	Return on assets 资产利润率 (%)	Return on equity 权益利润率 (%)	Labour productivity ('000 RMB/ worker) 劳动生产率 (千元/人)	Debts/ assets 资产负债率 (%)	Total assets (Mil.RMB) 总资产 (百万元)
Industry Overall 行业总体	429	74,448	12,054	710	5.89	15.12	46.70	61.03	12,057

	Number of firms 企业个数	Average number of employees 平均职工人数	Average revenue ('000 RMB) 平均销售收入 (千元)	Average profit ('000 RMB) 平均利润 (千元)	Return on assets 资产利润率 (%)	Return on equity 权益利润率 (%)	Labour productivity ('000 RMB/ worker) 劳动生产率 (千元/人)	Debts/ assets 资产负债率 (%)	Average total assets ('000 RMB) 平均总资产 (千元)
By ownership 产业所有权									
State-owned 国有	58	151	12,527	-164	-0.52	-1.62	28.83	67.92	31,624
Collective-owned 集体	79	169	16,954	1,024	7.33	18.32	31.77	59.96	13,966
Foreign & Overseas Chinese Funded 三资	64	144	44,462	2,895	6.95	17.06	88.22	59.24	41,627
By regional distribution 地区分布									
Central-North 华北	56	105	8,378	429	4.27	8.13	27.44	47.54	10,066
Beijing 北京	12	39	5,200	-28	-0.30	-0.43	45.32	30.08	9,403
Tianjin 天津	20	93	9,588	526	8.68	16.18	34.76	46.37	6,059
Hebei 河北	19	149	9,738	726	5.08	10.63	22.64	52.24	14,290
Shanxi 山西	5	143	5,992	16	0.14	0.37	15.55	61.91	11,630
Inner Mongolia 内蒙古									
Northeast 东北	37	224	16,267	128	0.45	1.36	16.06	67.12	28,761
Liaoning 辽宁	33	241	17,079	-93	-0.32	-1.05	15.10	69.78	29,480
Jilin 吉林	3	70	9,579	2,488	14.88	25.29	43.47	41.16	16,721
Heilongjiang 黑龙江	1	125	9,529	358	0.87	1.35	31.17	35.77	41,163
Central-East 华东	250	182	34,412	2,449	7.85	19.39	54.23	59.52	31,206
Shanghai 上海	30	108	32,137	2,584	7.83	23.74	70.81	67.03	33,003
Jiangsu 江苏	80	204	40,572	3,092	8.09	17.67	54.48	54.22	38,210
Zhejiang 浙江	65	153	30,595	2,895	8.79	21.07	57.90	58.27	32,923
Anhui 安徽	14	165	12,000	-5	-0.04	-0.11	17.17	67.99	14,816
Fujian 福建	12	113	17,737	468	2.96	5.53	53.90	46.58	15,841
Jiangxi 江西	7	195	15,675	-714	-2.30	-6.68	28.76	65.52	30,974
Shandong 山东	42	264	45,566	2,350	9.87	33.33	56.63	70.39	23,819
Central-South 中南	65	162	28,985	888	2.84	7.58	51.75	62.61	31,339
Henan 河南	11	313	14,194	-728	-1.83	-5.92	17.85	69.00	39,717
Hubei 湖北	7	118	21,416	873	10.71	30.43	77.88	64.81	8,148
Hunan 湖南	7	131	8,952	280	3.80	15.23	15.72	75.05	7,371
Guangdong 广东	30	135	38,265	3,141	9.58	24.34	83.15	60.64	32,785
Guangxi 广西	10	133	36,738	-3,654	-7.19	-17.72	52.48	59.41	50,793
Hainan 海南									
Southwest 西南	11	322	42,430	872	1.76	8.57	42.61	79.48	49,619
Chongqing 重庆	3	547	116,848	3,195	2.09	10.09	72.13	79.27	152,673
Sichuan 四川	8	238	14,524	2	0.01	0.08	17.16	80.58	10,973
Guizhou 贵州									
Yunnan 云南									
Tibet 西藏									
Northwest 西北	10	55	2,949	172	3.86	8.28	20.07	53.39	4,447
Shaanxi 陕西	3	68	4,645	100	2.10	7.86	20.85	73.25	4,772
Gansu 甘肃	5	47	1,153	-5	-0.18	-0.32	13.39	42.75	2,627
Qinghai 青海									
Ningxia 宁夏									
Xinjiang 新疆	2	56	4,893	720	8.46	15.36	32.70	44.90	8,511

3569: Other General Parts 其他类未包括的通用零部件制造业

Year 年份	Number of firms 企业个数	Rate of change 变化率 (%)	Number of employees 职工人数 (人)	Rate of change 变化率 (%)	Total revenue (Mil. RMB) 总销售收入 (百万元)	Rate of change 变化率 (%)	Total profit (Mil RMB) 总利润 (百万元)	Rate of change 变化率 (%)
2000	363		63,698		7,800		376	
2001	356	-1.93	70,572	10.79	9,665	23.91	544	44.68
2002	429	20.51	74,448	5.49	12,054	24.72	710	30.51

Major Products 主要产品	Output 产量	Unit 单位

10 Main Firms with Maximal Revenue (year founded) 收入最大的十家主要企业（创办年份）	City 城市	Province 省	Telephone/fax 电话/传真	Number of employees 职工人数	Ownership 产业所有权	Revenue ('000 RMB) 销售收入 (千元)	Profit('000 RMB) (rank) 利润(千元) (排名)	Total assets ('000 RMB) 总资产 (千元)	Major products 主要产品
Zhejiang Sanhua Group Co., Ltd.	Shaoxing	Zhejiang	(0575)6221859		Joint Stock				Refrigerator Fittings冷
浙江三花集团有限公司(2000)	绍兴市	浙江省	(0575)6227971	3,009	股份制	1,154,711	135,369(1)	1,380,884	冻机配件
Jiangsu Changfa Refrigeration Stock Co., Ltd.	Changzhou	Jiangsu	(0519)6239060		Limited-Liability				Refrigeration Equipment
江苏常发制冷股份有限公司(1992)	常州市	江苏省	(0519)6232918	3,430	有限公司	989,370	116,910(2)	982,290	制冷器材
Liaocheng Zhengjia Bearing Hold Unit Group Company	Liaocheng	Shandong	(0635)8635017		Private Partnership				Hold Unit
聊城市郑家轴承保持器集团公司(2001)	聊城市	山东省		2,600	私营合伙	420,000	7,500(19)	271,910	保持器
Nanjing Highspeed & Accurate Gear Co., Ltd.	Nanjing	Jiangsu	(025)2415583		Joint Stock				Plant & Mining Accessories
南京高精齿轮股份有限公司(2001)	南京市	江苏省	(025)2412731	1,095	股份制	346,700	27,240(5)	337,470	工矿配件
Wendeng Zhaowen Absorber Co., Ltd.	Weihai	Shandong	(0631)8761099		Overseas Chinese-funded				Shock Absorber
文登兆文减震器有限公司(1990)	威海市	山东省	(0631)8761067	380	港澳台资	337,800	17,360(10)	37,560	减震器
Chongqing Gearbox Co., Ltd.	Chongqing	Chongqing	(023)47211114		State-owned				Gear Case
重庆齿轮箱有限责任公司(1974)	重庆市	重庆市	(023)47211128	1,315	国有企业	306,606	8,871(15)	450,961	齿轮箱
Amtek (Huizhou) Industries Co., Ltd.	Huizhou	Guangdong	(0752)2609511		Foreign Funded				Precision Metal Punching精密
安特(惠州)工业有限公司(1993)	惠州市	广东省	(0752)2601124	688	外商投资	212,348	50,687(3)	207,197	金属冲压
Jiangsu Baixin Group Co., Ltd.	Taizhou	Jiangsu	(0523)8331266		Joint Stock				Corrugation Compensator波
江苏百新集团有限公司(1983)	泰州市	江苏省	(0523)8331090	717	股份制	153,499	6,096(24)	99,304	纹补偿器
Shanghai Guiwu Electrical ApplianceCo., Ltd.	Shanghai	Shanghai	(021)57741533		Foreign Funded				Washing Machine Parts洗
上海龟屋电器有限公司(1995)	上海市	上海市	(021)57741823	299	外商投资	152,200	11,221(12)	126,402	衣机零件
Hongguang VP (Taicang) Company	Suzhou	Jiangsu	(0520)53459088		Overseas Chinese-funded				Bicycle Parts自
宏光车料(太仓)有限公司(1997)	苏州市	江苏省	(0520)53457792	125	港澳台资	125,410	25,740(6)	106,340	行车零件

Top 10 Cities by Revenue 销售收入排名前10位城市	Province 省	Market share 市场份额 (%)	Number of firms 企业个数
Shaoxing 绍兴市	Zhejiang 浙江省	11.15	10
Changzhou 常州市	Jiangsu 江苏省	9.75	5
Shanghai 上海市	Shanghai 上海市	8.00	30
Weihai 威海市	Shandong 山东省	6.69	5
Liaocheng 聊城市	Shandong 山东省	6.15	19
Suzhou 苏州市	Jiangsu 江苏省	4.15	12
Nanjing 南京市	Jiangsu 江苏省	3.48	8
Ningbo 宁波市	Zhejiang 浙江省	3.10	29
Liuzhou 柳州市	Guangxi 广西	3.05	10
Taizhou 泰州市	Jiangsu 江苏省	2.91	11

10 Major Wholesalers 十家主要批发商	City 城市	Province 省	Telephone/Fax 电话/传真
SU MEC	Nanjing	Jiangsu	(025)4511888
中设江苏机械设备进出口（集团）公司	南京市	江苏省	(025)4411772
China Poster Mobile Communications Equipment Co.,Ltd.	Beijing	Beijing	(010)66426993
中邮普泰移动通信设备股份有限公司	北京市	北京市	(010)66426837
Sino Kama Co., Ltd.	Shanghai	Shanghai	(021)62031188
中泰凯马股份有限公司	上海市	上海市	(021)62030851
China Huayuan Group Co.,Ltd.	Shanghai	Shanghai	(021)62031188
中国华源集团有限公司	上海市	上海市	(021)62032288
Zhejiang Crand Imp.& Exp.Co.,Ltd.	Ningbo	Zhejiang	(0574)87720170
浙江远大进出口有限公司	宁波市	浙江省	(0574)87723350
Shandong Machinery Import & Export Group Corporation	Qingdao	Shandong	(0532)2661628
山东省机械进出口集团公司	青岛市	山东省	(0532)2991655
Qingdao Haier International Trade Co.,Ltd.	Qingdao	Shandong	(0532)8938337
青岛海尔国际贸易有限公司	青岛市	山东省	(0532)8939494
Guangdong Machinery Import & Export Group Corporation	Guangzhou	Guangdong	(020)87782168
广东省机械进出口集团公司	广州市	广东省	(020)87771803
China National Machinery Equipment Import & Export Corporation	Beijing	Beijing	(010)63474506
中国机械设备进出口总公司	北京市	北京市	(010)63261865
Beijing Cellstar Co.,Ltd.	Beijing	Beijing	(010)64602050
北京蜂星事达电讯有限公司	北京市	北京市	(010)64672648

3571: Castings 铸件制造业

The industry accounts for 0.355% of the total revenue of China's industrial sector in 2002. The rate of return on assets is 4.54%. 86.92% of all firms in the industry made a profit while 13.08% had negative returns.The top province in terms of the industry's revenue is Jiangsu, accounting for 20.82% of the total revenue.
2002年本行业收入占全行业的0.355%，资产利润率为4.54%。86.92%的企业赢利，13.08%的企业亏损。收入最高的省为江苏省，占本行业的20.82%。

	Total number of firms 企业总数	Total number of employees 职工总数	Total revenue (Mil.RMB) 总销售收入（百万元）	Total profit (Mil.RMB) 总利润（百万元）	Return on assets 资产利润率（%）	Return on equity 权益利润率（%）	Labour productivity ('000 RMB/ worker) 劳动生产率（千元/人）	Debts/ assets 资产负债率（%）	Total assets (Mil.RMB) 总资产（百万元）
Industry Overall 行业总体	1782	285,664	38,031	1,582	4.54	11.72	39.92	61.30	34,865

	Number of firms 企业个数	Average number of employees 平均职工人数	Average revenue ('000 RMB) 平均销售收入（千元）	Average profit ('000 RMB) 平均利润（千元）	Return on assets 资产利润率（%）	Return on equity 权益利润率（%）	Labour productivity ('000 RMB/ worker) 劳动生产率（千元/人）	Debts/ assets 资产负债率（%）	Average total assets ('000 RMB) 平均总资产（千元）
By ownership 产业所有权									
State-owned 国有	116	185	11,462	-842	-1.97	-9.55	21.95	79.35	42,694
Collective-owned 集体	436	177	20,890	947	6.67	17.59	37.05	62.10	14,212
Foreign & Overseas Chinese Funded 三资	159	195	36,940	2,300	5.10	10.05	61.09	49.20	45,050
By regional distribution 地区分布									
Central-North 华北	300	166	17,744	1,044	5.40	13.18	36.89	59.05	19,341
Beijing 北京	27	188	21,346	367	1.66	4.08	37.18	59.34	22,126
Tianjin 天津	69	118	20,625	2,367	9.98	19.90	55.25	49.87	23,734
Hebei 河北	158	156	16,921	1,161	7.68	19.34	39.59	60.31	15,127
Shanxi 山西	37	219	14,502	-1,029	-4.28	-12.61	22.10	66.02	24,028
Inner Mongolia 内蒙古	9	433	12,651	-612	-1.91	-8.96	11.81	78.68	32,019
Northeast 东北	120	205	16,885	528	1.76	5.80	17.67	69.71	30,065
Liaoning 辽宁	100	213	16,775	423	1.30	4.47	14.54	70.89	32,508
Jilin 吉林	9	85	14,567	1,859	7.32	12.04	65.63	39.17	25,392
Heilongjiang 黑龙江	11	239	19,780	393	3.36	57.72	28.94	94.17	11,680
Central-East 华东	903	150	23,221	1,052	5.61	13.83	45.65	59.45	18,754
Shanghai 上海	87	156	24,399	1,211	4.06	10.08	49.20	59.76	29,847
Jiangsu 江苏	296	143	26,751	735	3.35	8.62	51.64	61.11	21,919
Zhejiang 浙江	194	113	17,044	1,271	9.28	21.97	42.43	57.76	13,692
Anhui 安徽	50	252	20,084	1,058	3.79	9.08	28.34	58.19	27,891
Fujian 福建	57	76	14,049	545	7.28	11.70	47.43	37.80	7,485
Jiangxi 江西	24	106	15,308	818	7.51	22.53	38.14	66.67	10,892
Shandong 山东	195	198	27,941	1,419	8.90	22.29	45.56	60.09	15,954
Central-South 中南	347	162	23,837	761	4.06	10.79	43.67	62.40	18,747
Henan 河南	109	186	23,492	1,329	8.91	20.88	42.32	57.31	14,906
Hubei 湖北	54	175	27,217	1,110	7.39	21.72	51.68	65.97	15,023
Hunan 湖南	43	139	14,408	63	0.36	2.84	32.12	87.23	17,334
Guangdong 广东	125	137	24,492	459	1.95	4.90	44.11	60.13	23,485
Guangxi 广西	15	236	36,580	-57	-0.22	-0.41	47.38	45.32	25,575
Hainan 海南	1	65	11,479	-5	-0.10	-0.60	42.62	82.61	4,778
Southwest 西南	61	201	15,566	-211	-0.97	-2.46	22.99	60.55	21,775
Chongqing 重庆	13	213	13,512	-46	-0.30	-0.57	17.68	47.78	15,550
Sichuan 四川	31	202	19,344	-158	-0.72	-1.42	29.76	49.03	21,813
Guizhou 贵州	8	133	5,564	-536	-3.39	-9.98	10.78	66.01	15,806
Yunnan 云南	9	241	14,413	-344	-0.96	-10.04	16.21	90.48	35,940
Tibet 西藏									
Northwest 西北	51	130	9,644	90	0.67	2.46	27.66	72.69	13,465
Shaanxi 陕西	16	157	8,148	55	0.41	1.52	17.79	72.91	13,193
Gansu 甘肃	30	76	6,913	153	2.74	6.03	33.00	54.55	5,570
Qinghai 青海	1	94	333	-102	-5.11	-11.36	7.07	55.01	1,996
Ningxia 宁夏	1	989	117,747	17,174	8.79	21.00	53.89	58.12	195,284
Xinjiang 新疆	3	259	12,009	-5,973	-16.11		12.95	125.43	37,079

3571: Castings 铸件制造业

Year 年份	Number of firms 企业个数	Rate of change 变化率 (%)	Number of employees 职工人数 (人)	Rate of change 变化率 (%)	Total revenue (Mil. RMB) 总销售收入 (百万元)	Rate of change 变化率 (%)	Total profit (Mil RMB) 总利润 (百万元)	Rate of change 变化率 (%)
2000	1548		271,906		27,045		1,148	
2001	1623	4.84	268,421	-1.28	30,680	13.44	1,255	9.32
2002	1782	9.80	285,664	6.42	38,031	23.96	1,582	26.06

Major Products 主要产品	Output 产量	Unit 单位
Casting 铸件	775	10,000 Tons 万吨

10 Main Firms with Maximal Revenue (year founded) 收入最大的十家主要企业（创办年份）	City 城市	Province 省	Telephone/fax 电话/传真	Number of employees 职工人数	Ownership 产业所有权	Revenue ('000 RMB) 销售收入(千元)	Profit('000 RMB) (rank) 利润(千元)(排名)	Total assets ('000 RMB) 总资产(千元)	Major products 主要产品
Jiangsu Tieben Cast Steel Co., Ltd. 江苏铁本钢铁有限公司(1996)	Changzhou 常州市	Jiangsu 江苏省	(0519)3739672 (0519)3732439	1,358	Limited-Liability 有限公司	1,001,840	24,850(8)	981,450	Steel-making 炼钢
Jimo Shanqian New International Group Company 即墨市山前新国际集团公司(1993)	Qingdao 青岛市	Shandong 山东省	(0532)7525968 (0532)7525868	1,140	Private Partnership 私营合伙	408,220	12,810(23)	96,400	Pipe Fittings 管件
Kolbenschmidt Pierburg Shanghai Nonferrous Components Co.,Ltd.上海皮尔博格有色零部件有限公司(2001)	Shanghai 上海市	Shanghai 上海市	(021)52817808 (021)52807675	881	Foreign Funded 外商投资	361,107	27,221(6)	371,620	Nonferrous Metal Casting 有色铸件
Tianjin New Weisan Industrial Co., Ltd. 天津新伟祥工业有限公司(1995)	Tianjin 天津市	Tianjin 天津市	(022)82289920 (022)82288638	250	Overseas Chinese-funded 港澳台资	254,740	52,400(2)	302,010	Casting 铸件
Bo'ai Automobile Fitting Part Manufacturing Co., Ltd. 博爱县汽车配件制造有限公司(1975)	Jiaozuo 焦作市	Henan 河南省	(0391)8685573 (0391)8685576	506	Collective-owned 集体企业	252,816	17,700(13)	34,956	Belt Pulley 皮带轮
Guangdong Shaoguan Foundry & Forging Group Co., Ltd. 广东省韶铸集团有限公司(1969)	Shaoguan 韶关市	Guangdong 广东省	(0751)8857507 (0751)8853784	1,680	State Enterprises 国有独资	249,062	162(740)	617,252	Casting Materials 铸钢件
Ji'nan Huanggang Group Co., Ltd. 济南黄岗集团有限责任公司(1996)	Jinan 济南市	Shandong 山东省	(0531)5971174 (0531)5987868	745	Collective-owned 集体企业	233,149	6,014(63)	106,466	Casting Materials 铸件
Shanghai Sandmann Foundry Co.,Ltd. 上海圣德曼铸造有限公司(2000)	Shanghai 上海市	Shanghai 上海市	(021)59579841 (021)59573565	865	Foreign Funded 外商投资	226,039	783(436)	340,427	Iron Casting 钢铁铸件
Haicheng Dejin Foundry Co.,Ltd. 海城市德金铸业有限公司(1990)	Anshan 鞍山市	Liaoning 辽宁省	(0412)3548197	120	Limited-Liability 有限公司	194,500	19,400(11)	33,900	Global Iron 球铁
Gaoyao Modern Metal & Industry Co.,Ltd 高要鸿图工业有限公司(1988)	Zhaoqing 肇庆市	Guangdong 广东省	(0758)8391957 (0758)8392249	568	Overseas Chinese-funded 港澳台资	194,080	19,899(10)	255,335	Aluminium Alloy Stempressing Casting 铝合金模压铸件

Top 10 Cities by Revenue 销售收入排名前10位城市	Province 省	Market share 市场份额 (%)	Number of firms 企业个数
Shanghai 上海市	Shanghai 上海市	5.58	87
Changzhou 常州市	Jiangsu 江苏省	5.20	46
Tianjin 天津市	Tianjin 天津市	3.74	69
Ningbo 宁波市	Zhejiang 浙江省	3.44	63
Wuxi 无锡市	Jiangsu 江苏省	3.24	47
Weifang 潍坊市	Shandong 山东省	2.70	51
Taizhou 泰州市	Jiangsu 江苏省	2.35	35
Jiaozuo 焦作市	Henan 河南省	2.14	24
Qingdao 青岛市	Shandong 山东省	2.08	15
Nanjing 南京市	Jiangsu 江苏省	1.99	35

10 Major Wholesalers 十家主要批发商	City 城市	Province 省	Telephone/Fax 电话/传真
SU MEC 中设江苏机械设备进出口（集团）公司	Nanjing 南京市	Jiangsu 江苏省	(025)4511888 (025)4411772
China Poster Mobile Communications Equipment Co.,Ltd. 中邮普泰移动通信设备股份有限公司	Beijing 北京市	Beijing 北京市	(010)66426993 (010)66426837
Sino Kama Co., Ltd. 中泰凯马股份有限公司	Shanghai 上海市	Shanghai 上海市	(021)62031188 (021)62030851
China Huayuan Group Co.,Ltd. 中国华源集团有限公司	Shanghai 上海市	Shanghai 上海市	(021)62031188 (021)62032288
Zhejiang Crand Imp.& Exp.Co.,Ltd. 浙江远大进出口有限公司	Ningbo 宁波市	Zhejiang 浙江省	(0574)87720170 (0574)87723350
Shandong Machinery Import & Export Group Corporation 山东省机械进出口集团公司	Qingdao 青岛市	Shandong 山东省	(0532)2661628 (0532)2991655
Qingdao Haier International Trade Co.,Ltd. 青岛海尔国际贸易有限公司	Qingdao 青岛市	Shandong 山东省	(0532)8938337 (0532)8939494
Guangdong Machinery Import & Export Group Corporation 广东省机械进出口集团公司	Guangzhou 广州市	Guangdong 广东省	(020)87782168 (020)87771803
China National Machinery Equipment Import & Export Corporation 中国机械设备进出口总公司	Beijing 北京市	Beijing 北京市	(010)63474506 (010)63261865
Beijing Cellstar Co.,Ltd. 北京蜂星事达电讯有限公司	Beijing 北京市	Beijing 北京市	(010)64602050 (010)64672648

3572: Forgings 锻件制造业

The industry accounts for 0.073% of the total revenue of China's industrial sector in 2002. The rate of return on assets is 2.87%. 87.07% of all firms in the industry made a profit while 12.93% had negative returns.The top province in terms of the industry's revenue is Jiangsu, accounting for 20.66% of the total revenue.
2002年本行业收入占全行业的0.073%，资产利润率为2.87%。87.07%的企业赢利，12.93%的企业亏损。收入最高的省为江苏省，占本行业的20.66%。

	Total number of firms 企业总数	Total number of employees 职工总数	Total revenue (Mil.RMB) 总销售收入 (百万元)	Total profit (Mil.RMB) 总利润 (百万元)	Return on assets 资产利润率 (%)	Return on equity 权益利润率 (%)	Labour productivity ('000 RMB/ worker) 劳动生产率 (千元/人)	Debts/ assets 资产负债率 (%)	Total assets (Mil.RMB) 总资产 (百万元)
Industry Overall 行业总体	317	55,786	7,844	244	2.87	7.92	40.03	63.77	8,508

	Number of firms 企业个数	Average number of employees 平均职工人数	Average revenue ('000 RMB) 平均销售收入 (千元)	Average profit ('000 RMB) 平均利润 (千元)	Return on assets 资产利润率 (%)	Return on equity 权益利润率 (%)	Labour productivity ('000 RMB/ worker) 劳动生产率 (千元/人)	Debts/ assets 资产负债率 (%)	Average total assets ('000 RMB) 平均总资产 (千元)
By ownership 产业所有权									
State-owned 国有	27	629	62,070	134	0.11	0.35	21.77	68.11	119,630
Collective-owned 集体	64	93	14,456	953	10.68	26.07	50.04	59.04	8,926
Foreign & Overseas Chinese Funded 三资	17	138	36,246	1,236	2.37	5.25	79.07	54.89	52,232
By regional distribution 地区分布									
Central-North 华北	35	182	22,680	1,684	9.99	25.71	26.19	61.13	16,857
Beijing 北京	2	58	6,441	687	13.62	54.57	23.54	75.03	5,043
Tianjin 天津	10	152	28,732	3,923	25.52	56.93	26.99	55.17	15,372
Hebei 河北	6	174	14,199	362	2.78	7.12	29.82	60.90	12,983
Shanxi 山西	16	213	24,245	1,019	4.91	13.00	25.98	62.24	20,765
Inner Mongolia 内蒙古	1	288	20,495	-131	-0.82	-6.65	12.42	87.72	16,051
Northeast 东北	35	103	12,058	-1,050	-6.62	-19.33	26.35	65.75	15,862
Liaoning 辽宁	28	104	11,801	-1,357	-7.90	-25.53	22.18	69.07	17,187
Jilin 吉林	5	120	15,883	230	1.78	2.98	46.53	40.13	12,912
Heilongjiang 黑龙江	2	45	6,103	50	1.07	3.82	26.27	72.12	4,689
Central-East 华东	183	131	23,840	902	4.60	12.82	54.00	64.08	19,590
Shanghai 上海	24	96	26,337	1,129	3.71	9.40	63.22	60.48	30,388
Jiangsu 江苏	76	114	21,325	511	2.67	7.77	52.60	65.61	19,141
Zhejiang 浙江	37	106	17,468	776	4.78	12.74	42.91	62.51	16,244
Anhui 安徽	3	301	27,505	512	1.00	4.38	28.75	77.08	50,967
Fujian 福建	6	71	8,153	280	2.70	5.61	46.67	51.83	10,346
Jiangxi 江西	4	178	14,617	17	0.06	0.42	28.89	85.15	27,257
Shandong 山东	33	213	38,597	2,035	14.11	34.83	65.08	59.49	14,423
Central-South 中南	41	339	36,194	1,086	1.79	4.25	33.62	57.84	60,589
Henan 河南	7	637	59,710	2,084	1.53	3.39	23.93	54.93	136,526
Hubei 湖北	13	427	53,818	1,939	2.32	4.85	50.62	52.04	83,431
Hunan 湖南	7	259	20,039	-598	-2.80		14.55	127.89	21,356
Guangdong 广东	13	109	15,694	664	3.38	6.73	30.75	49.80	19,652
Guangxi 广西	1	646	22,049	265	0.68	2.69	14.06	74.69	38,880
Hainan 海南									
Southwest 西南	14	318	39,055	846	2.19	10.72	29.85	79.53	38,547
Chongqing 重庆	7	532	67,125	1,340	2.03	9.85	26.94	79.37	65,918
Sichuan 四川	5	92	14,587	399	3.16	14.26	70.21	77.84	12,621
Guizhou 贵州	2	133	1,977	235	3.10	36.44	0.99	91.49	7,565
Yunnan 云南									
Tibet 西藏									
Northwest 西北	9	396	26,127	39	0.05	0.16	22.47	71.19	83,746
Shaanxi 陕西	3	856	56,584	-241	-0.11	-0.38	23.07	72.10	229,004
Gansu 甘肃	5	43	3,319	-6	-0.13	-0.26	32.33	50.80	4,610
Qinghai 青海	1	785	48,798	1,102	2.52	7.78	17.83	67.56	43,659
Ningxia 宁夏									
Xinjiang 新疆									

3572: Forgings 锻件制造业

Year 年份	Number of firms 企业个数	Rate of change 变化率(%)	Number of employees 职工人数(人)	Rate of change 变化率(%)	Total revenue (Mil. RMB) 总销售收入(百万元)	Rate of change 变化率(%)	Total profit (Mil RMB) 总利润(百万元)	Rate of change 变化率(%)
2000	248		61,348		5,882		-64	
2001	291	17.34	63,621	3.71	7,261	23.44	17	-
2002	317	8.93	55,786	-12.32	7,844	8.03	244	1,335.29

Major Products 主要产品	Output 产量	Unit 单位
Forging Materials 锻件	153	10,000 Tons 万吨

10 Main Firms with Maximal Revenue (year founded) 收入最大的十家主要企业(创办年份)	City 城市	Province 省	Telephone/fax 电话/传真	Number of employees 职工人数	Ownership 产业所有权	Revenue ('000 RMB) 销售收入(千元)	Profit('000 RMB) (rank) 利润(千元)(排名)	Total assets ('000 RMB) 总资产(千元)	Major products 主要产品
Shandong Guangfu Iron And Steel Group Co., Ltd. 山东广富钢铁有限公司(1999)	Binzhou 滨州市	Shandong 山东省	(0543)4571093 (0543)4575686	835	Private Owned 私营企业	461,973	18,275(2)	99,496	Rolled Steel 钢材
Henan Zhongyuan Special Steel Factory 河南中原特殊钢厂(1984)	Jiaozuo 焦作市	Henan 河南省	(0391)6099018 (0391)6099019	3,444	State-owned 国有企业	324,980	14,210(3)	722,850	Forging Materials 锻材锻件
Wuhan Heavy Casting Forge Co.,Ltd. 武汉重工铸锻有限责任公司(1967)	Wuhan 武汉市	Hubei 湖北省	(027)68861992 (027)86434069	3,786	Limited-Liability 有限公司	308,549	6,014(13)	710,159	Forging Materials 锻件
Chongqing Heavy-Duty Casting & Forging Plant 重庆重型铸锻厂(1979)	Chongqing 重庆市	Chongqing 重庆市	(023)68541510 (023)68541015	2,213	State-owned 国有企业	302,264	6,950(9)	367,591	Forged Steel Piece 锻钢件
Jiangsu Asian Star Anchor Chain Co.Ltd. 江苏亚星锚链有限公司(1976)	Taizhou 泰州市	Jiangsu 江苏省	(0523)4682291 (0523)4681390	634	Private Owned 私营企业	194,288	3,549(24)	167,958	Marine Ahchor Chain & Accessories船用锚链及附件
Shanghai Guoxing Metal Product Co., Ltd. 上海国兴金属制品有限公司(1992)	Shanghai 上海市	Shanghai 上海市	(021)69778027 (021)69778086	430	Overseas Chinese-funded 港澳台资	192,487	6,684(10)	156,463	Aluminium Alloy Rim铝合金轮圈
Hubei Shenli Forging Co., Ltd. 湖北神力锻造有限责任公司(1997)	Shiyan 十堰市	Hubei 湖北省	(0719)5221454	260	State-owned 国有企业	113,951	6,104(12)	176,045	Forging Materials 锻件
Hubei Tri-ring Forging Co., Ltd. 湖北三环锻造有限公司(1961)	Xiangfan 襄樊市	Hubei 湖北省	(0710)7232310 (0710)7241753	696	Joint Stock 股份制	102,699	5,101(18)	157,477	redirector 转向节
Tianjin Tianzhong Axle Building Co., Ltd. 天津天重车轴制造有限公司(1999)	Tianjin 天津市	Tianjin 天津市	(022)26623351 (022)26623351	226	Collective-owned 集体企业	99,640	26,100(1)	27,740	Train Axis 火车轴
Wuxi Hongda Heavy-duty Forging And Pressing Plant 无锡宏达重型锻压厂(1998)	Wuxi 无锡市	Jiangsu 江苏省	(0510)5952557 (0510)5953536	215	Joint Stock 股份制	95,200	2,560(33)	67,940	Forging Materials 锻件

Top 10 Cities by Revenue 销售收入排名前10位城市	Province 省	Market share 市场份额(%)	Number of firms 企业个数
Shanghai 上海市	Shanghai 上海市	8.06	24
Jinan 济南市	Shandong 山东省	6.55	13
Chongqing 重庆市	Chongqing 重庆市	5.99	7
Binzhou 滨州市	Shandong 山东省	5.89	1
Wuxi 无锡市	Jiangsu 江苏省	4.47	16
Jiaozuo 焦作市	Henan 河南省	4.14	1
Wuhan 武汉市	Hubei 湖北省	3.96	2
Taizhou 泰州市	Jiangsu 江苏省	3.73	5
Tianjin 天津市	Tianjin 天津市	3.66	10
Changzhou 常州市	Jiangsu 江苏省	3.58	20

10 Major Wholesalers 十家主要批发商	City 城市	Province 省	Telephone/Fax 电话/传真
SU MEC 中设江苏机械设备进出口(集团)公司	Nanjing 南京市	Jiangsu 江苏省	(025)4511888 (025)4411772
China Poster Mobile Communications Equipment Co.,Ltd. 中邮普泰移动通信设备股份有限公司	Beijing 北京市	Beijing 北京市	(010)66426993 (010)66426837
Sino Kama Co., Ltd. 中泰凯马股份有限公司	Shanghai 上海市	Shanghai 上海市	(021)62031188 (021)62030851
China Huayuan Group Co.,Ltd. 中国华源集团有限公司	Shanghai 上海市	Shanghai 上海市	(021)62031188 (021)62032288
Zhejiang Crand Imp.& Exp.Co.,Ltd. 浙江远大进出口有限公司	Ningbo 宁波市	Zhejiang 浙江省	(0574)87720170 (0574)87723350
Shandong Machinery Import & Export Group Corporation 山东省机械进出口集团公司	Qingdao 青岛市	Shandong 山东省	(0532)2661628 (0532)2991655
Qingdao Haier International Trade Co.,Ltd. 青岛海尔国际贸易有限公司	Qingdao 青岛市	Shandong 山东省	(0532)8938337 (0532)8939494
Guangdong Machinery Import & Export Group Corporation 广东省机械进出口集团公司	Guangzhou 广州市	Guangdong 广东省	(020)87782168 (020)87771803
China National Machinery Equipment Import & Export Corporation 中国机械设备进出口总公司	Beijing 北京市	Beijing 北京市	(010)63174506 (010)63261865
Beijing Cellstar Co.,Ltd. 北京蜂星事达电讯有限公司	Beijing 北京市	Beijing 北京市	(010)64602050 (010)64672648

3590: Other General Machinery 其他普通机械制造业

The industry accounts for 0.082% of the total revenue of China's industrial sector in 2002. The rate of return on assets is 3.49%. 82.14% of all firms in the industry made a profit while 17.86% had negative returns.The top province in terms of the industry's revenue is Jiangsu, accounting for 24.25% of the total revenue.
2002年本行业收入占全行业的0.082%，资产利润率为3.49%。82.14%的企业赢利，17.86%的企业亏损。收入最高的省为江苏省，占本行业的24.25%。

	Total number of firms 企业总数	Total number of employees 职工总数	Total revenue (Mil.RMB) 总销售收入 (百万元)	Total profit (Mil.RMB) 总利润 (百万元)	Return on assets 资产利润率 (%)	Return on equity 权益利润率 (%)	Labour productivity ('000 RMB/ worker) 劳动生产率 (千元/人)	Debts/ assets 资产负债率 (%)	Total assets (Mil.RMB) 总资产 (百万元)
Industry Overall 行业总体	364	60,869	8,756	401	3.49	8.85	42.85	60.62	11,504

	Number of firms 企业个数	Average number of employees 平均职工人数	Average revenue ('000 RMB) 平均销售收入（千元）	Average profit ('000 RMB) 平均利润 (千元)	Return on assets 资产利润率 (%)	Return on equity 权益利润率 (%)	Labour productivity ('000 RMB/ worker) 劳动生产率 (千元/人)	Debts/ assets 资产负债率 (%)	Average total assets ('000 RMB) 平均总资产 (千元)
By ownership 产业所有权									
State-owned 国有	79	255	23,076	222	0.41	1.29	26.00	68.36	54,322
Collective-owned 集体	47	159	29,870	1,695	4.72	9.29	51.97	49.19	35,901
Foreign & Overseas Chinese Funded 三资	41	126	28,141	2,580	7.68	14.77	66.80	48.01	33,599
By regional distribution 地区分布									
Central-North 华北	51	210	18,179	524	1.75	4.99	27.79	64.90	29,930
Beijing 北京	17	93	14,220	2,302	12.98	19.99	57.15	35.07	17,729
Tianjin 天津	10	43	6,431	677	9.60	45.37	32.00	78.84	7,054
Hebei 河北	14	190	14,182	-1,149	-3.43	-18.32	23.99	81.30	33,545
Shanxi 山西	9	413	35,401	90	0.14	0.44	27.93	69.32	65,827
Inner Mongolia 内蒙古	1	2,329	103,918	-3,883	-4.20	-6.98	11.30	39.86	92,445
Northeast 东北	38	183	15,117	389	1.21	2.75	21.06	56.18	32,286
Liaoning 辽宁	28	168	16,840	729	2.07	4.07	26.79	49.08	35,220
Jilin 吉林	4	265	1,833	-2,099	-6.43		3.30	105.09	32,660
Heilongjiang 黑龙江	6	198	15,930	462	2.52	6.59	14.24	61.81	18,343
Central-East 华东	168	162	33,101	2,023	5.33	11.77	58.24	54.69	37,928
Shanghai 上海	15	99	20,706	2,370	8.82	17.20	40.38	48.70	26,864
Jiangsu 江苏	66	151	32,171	2,002	5.76	10.23	63.35	43.71	34,775
Zhejiang 浙江	41	140	27,085	1,649	7.06	17.40	58.01	59.40	23,348
Anhui 安徽	10	192	9,244	-1,606	-9.23	-466.42	9.79	98.02	17,403
Fujian 福建	13	172	31,341	1,876	7.44	15.07	40.43	50.65	25,211
Jiangxi 江西	1	80	6,300	200	6.13	6.64	25.88	7.67	3,260
Shandong 山东	22	259	68,655	4,365	4.34	11.55	77.97	62.40	100,516
Central-South 中南	83	140	16,106	329	1.57	5.66	37.88	72.25	20,951
Henan 河南	20	230	22,109	282	1.01	3.50	27.12	71.23	27,967
Hubei 湖北	9	109	10,618	254	2.77	11.49	45.46	75.88	9,161
Hunan 湖南	10	120	10,655	-14	-0.12	-0.38	23.73	67.33	11,146
Guangdong 广东	39	116	17,553	547	2.25	8.30	53.34	72.84	24,264
Guangxi 广西	5	71	1,591	-358	-4.55	-21.38	7.03	78.72	7,880
Hainan 海南									
Southwest 西南	17	228	16,393	-484	-1.47	-27.11	28.23	94.57	32,881
Chongqing 重庆	2	92	6,886	-55	-0.82		40.90	113.45	6,659
Sichuan 四川	7	285	28,564	-91	-0.17	-0.71	39.39	76.09	53,320
Guizhou 贵州	7	237	9,116	-1,044	-4.35		13.65	134.41	23,986
Yunnan 云南	1	38	1,147	-180	-3.98	-27.44	14.97	85.48	4,519
Tibet 西藏									
Northwest 西北	7	77	11,125	92	0.80	1.13	60.60	28.84	11,518
Shaanxi 陕西	1	216	29,047	73	0.32	0.32	77.76		22,645
Gansu 甘肃	3	56	8,865	246	2.51	3.85	63.38	34.93	9,811
Qinghai 青海	1	3	66	12	1.97	2.40	18.67	18.03	610
Ningxia 宁夏									
Xinjiang 新疆	2	76	11,085	-88	-0.63	-1.17	33.77	46.04	13,970

3590: Other General Machinery 其他普通机械制造业

Year 年份	Number of firms 企业个数	Rate of change 变化率 (%)	Number of employees 职工人数 (人)	Rate of change 变化率 (%)	Total revenue (Mil. RMB) 总销售收入 (百万元)	Rate of change 变化率 (%)	Total profit (Mil RMB) 总利润 (百万元)	Rate of change 变化率 (%)
2000	351		80,663		6,680		177	
2001	390	11.11	72,050	-10.68	7,864	17.72	252	42.37
2002	364	-6.67	60,869	-15.52	8,756	11.34	401	59.13

Major Products 主要产品	Output 产量	Unit 单位
Handling Machinery 装卸机械	4,897	Unit 台
Plant & Mining Accessories 工矿配件	46	10,000 Tons 万吨

10 Main Firms with Maximal Revenue (year founded) 收入最大的十家主要企业（创办年份）	City 城市	Province 省	Telephone/fax 电话/传真	Number of employees 职工人数	Ownership 产业所有权	Revenue ('000 RMB) 销售收入 (千元)	Profit('000 RMB) (rank) 利润(千元) (排名)	Total assets ('000 RMB) 总资产 (千元)	Major products 主要产品
Jiangyin Xiagang Changjiang Ship Dismantling Factory 江阴市夏港长江拆船厂(1998)	Wuxi 无锡市	Jiangsu 江苏省	(0510)6165399 (0510)6166107	535	Collective-owned 集体企业	487,429	38,180(2)	767,392	Hulk Dismantling 拆解废船
Fuzhou University Automation-Tech Co., Ltd. 福州福大自动化科技有限公司(2000)	Fuzhou 福州市	Fujian 福建省	(0591)3792094 (0591)3713795	220	Limited-Liability 有限公司	189,672	6,411(14)	45,818	Electric Project 电气工程
Hangzhou Hengda Steel Structure Industrial Co., Ltd. 杭州恒达钢构实业有限公司(1995)	Hangzhou 杭州市	Zhejiang 浙江省	(0571)82617618 (0571)82615618	154	Private Owned 私营企业	187,403	12,413(9)	110,039	Environment Protecting Equipment 环保设备
Wuxi CSI Vibration Isolator Co., Ltd. 无锡中策减震器有限公司(1993)	Wuxi 无锡市	Jiangsu 江苏省	(0510)5016071 (0510)5017584	650	Foreign Funded 外商投资	164,114	26,883(3)	307,615	Automobile Shock Absorber汽车减震器
State-Owned Hongshan Machinery Factory 国营红山机械厂(1970)	Yuncheng 运城市	Shanxi 山西省	(0359)6821569 (0359)6821456	1,574	State-owned 国有企业	161,272	2,963(42)	358,411	Bridge Shell Assembly 桥壳总成
Jiangsu Xinlong Chemical Machinery Group Company 盐城鑫龙化机集团公司(1986)	Yancheng 盐城市	Jiangsu 江苏省	(0515)8661188 (0515)8661998	253	Collective-owned 集体企业	114,190	7,940(11)	66,690	Chemical Fibre Machinery 化纤机械
Sanmenxia Hydraulic Machinery Co., Ltd. 水利部三门峡水工机械厂(1957)	Sanmenxia 三门峡市	Henan 河南省	(0398)2926102 (0398)2821732	1,385	State-owned 国有企业	112,867	-	189,098	Metal Structural Parts金属结构件
Shanghai Fushen Freezing Machinery Co., Ltd. 上海富申冷机有限公司(1990)	Shanghai 上海市	Shanghai 上海市	(021)56503555 (021)56502266	155	Overseas Chinese-funded 港澳台资	107,154	5,434(18)	98,068	Refrigerator 冷柜
Zhangjiagang Zhongyuan Tube Manufacturing Co., Ltd. 张家港市中原制管有限公司(1994)	Suzhou 苏州市	Jiangsu 江苏省	(0512)58337888 (0512)58371628	230	Private Owned 私营企业	102,234	1,155(85)	81,750	Electrothermal Tube 电热管
Beijing JD Mechanical & Electronic System Research Center 北京精雕机电系统研究中心(1994)	Beijing 北京市	Beijing 北京市	(010)68482139	292	Private Owned 私营企业	100,211	16,410(6)	54,194	Fine-carve Machine 精雕机

Top 10 Cities by Revenue 销售收入排名前10位城市	Province 省	Market share 市场份额 (%)	Number of firms 企业个数
Wuxi 无锡市	Jiangsu 江苏省	10.20	15
Yantai 烟台市	Shandong 山东省	9.61	2
Suzhou 苏州市	Jiangsu 江苏省	6.02	21
Hangzhou 杭州市	Zhejiang 浙江省	5.68	12
Shanghai 上海市	Shanghai 上海市	3.55	15
Jinan 济南市	Shandong 山东省	3.15	6
Fuzhou 福州市	Fujian 福建省	2.91	4
Shaoxing 绍兴市	Zhejiang 浙江省	2.89	8
Beijing 北京市	Beijing 北京市	2.76	17
Shenyang 沈阳市	Liaoning 辽宁省	2.68	12

10 Major Wholesalers 十家主要批发商	City 城市	Province 省	Telephone/Fax 电话/传真
SU MEC 中设江苏机械设备进出口（集团）公司	Nanjing 南京市	Jiangsu 江苏省	(025)4511888 (025)4411772
China Poster Mobile Communications Equipment Co.,Ltd. 中邮普泰移动通信设备股份有限公司	Beijing 北京市	Beijing 北京市	(010)66426993 (010)66426837
Sino Kama Co., Ltd. 中泰凯马股份有限公司	Shanghai 上海市	Shanghai 上海市	(021)62031188 (021)62030851
China Huayuan Group Co.,Ltd. 中国华源集团有限公司	Shanghai 上海市	Shanghai 上海市	(021)62031188 (021)62032288
Zhejiang Crand Imp.& Exp.Co.,Ltd. 浙江远大进出口有限公司	Ningbo 宁波市	Zhejiang 浙江省	(0574)87720170 (0574)87723350
Shandong Machinery Import & Export Group Corporation 山东省机械进出口集团公司	Qingdao 青岛市	Shandong 山东省	(0532)2661628 (0532)2991655
Qingdao Haier International Trade Co.,Ltd. 青岛海尔国际贸易有限公司	Qingdao 青岛市	Shandong 山东省	(0532)8938337 (0532)8939494
Guangdong Machinery Import & Export Group Corporation 广东省机械进出口集团公司	Guangzhou 广州市	Guangdong 广东省	(020)87782168 (020)87771803
China National Machinery Equipment Import & Export Corporation 中国机械设备进出口总公司	Beijing 北京市	Beijing 北京市	(010)63474506 (010)63261865
Beijing Cellstar Co.,Ltd. 北京蜂星事达电讯有限公司	Beijing 北京市	Beijing 北京市	(010)64602050 (010)64672648

3611: Mining Equipment 矿山设备制造业

The industry accounts for 0.128% of the total revenue of China's industrial sector in 2002. The rate of return on assets is -0.25%. 69.66% of all firms in the industry made a profit while 30.34% had negative returns.The top province in terms of the industry's revenue is Henan, accounting for 14.97% of the total revenue.
2002年本行业收入占全行业的 0.128%，资产利润率为 -0.25%。69.66%的企业赢利，30.34%的企业亏损。收入最高的省为河南省，占本行业的14.97%。

	Total number of firms 企业总数	Total number of employees 职工总数	Total revenue (Mil.RMB) 总销售收入 (百万元)	Total profit (Mil.RMB) 总利润 (百万元)	Return on assets 资产利润率 (%)	Return on equity 权益利润率 (%)	Labour productivity ('000 RMB/ worker) 劳动生产率 (千元/人)	Debts/ assets 资产负债率 (%)	Total assets (Mil.RMB) 总资产 (百万元)
Industry Overall 行业总体	356	164,914	13,758	-80	-0.25	-0.97	22.29	74.05	31,711

	Number of firms 企业个数	Average number of employees 平均职工人数	Average revenue ('000 RMB) 平均销售收入 (千元)	Average profit ('000 RMB) 平均利润 (千元)	Return on assets 资产利润率 (%)	Return on equity 权益利润率 (%)	Labour productivity ('000 RMB/ worker) 劳动生产率 (千元/人)	Debts/ assets 资产负债率 (%)	Average total assets ('000 RMB) 平均总资产 (千元)
By ownership 产业所有权									
State-owned 国有	113	704	36,725	-2,028	-1.76	-10.69	14.77	83.58	115,533
Collective-owned 集体	70	245	27,254	812	4.07	16.07	31.23	74.69	19,963
Foreign & Overseas Chinese Funded 三资	13	179	112,648	2,503	2.58	8.54	113.19	69.74	96,884
By regional distribution 地区分布									
Central-North 华北	57	624	51,916	568	0.41	1.14	21.63	64.42	139,551
Beijing 北京	2	168	10,503	534	2.36	13.86	19.85	82.95	22,592
Tianjin 天津	6	153	62,659	3,538	3.43	13.57	44.80	74.71	103,059
Hebei 河北	22	473	49,655	1,420	2.05	8.39	32.36	75.64	69,430
Shanxi 山西	23	1,015	62,386	-658	-0.27	-0.67	15.62	60.49	246,960
Inner Mongolia 内蒙古	4	133	8,749	-1,513	-7.26	-12.11	36.56	40.07	20,836
Northeast 东北	51	529	38,995	-670	-0.41	-1.55	22.78	73.40	162,662
Liaoning 辽宁	23	624	61,418	-1,392	-0.51	-1.71	27.35	69.93	270,560
Jilin 吉林	17	410	17,319	243	0.45	3.55	16.72	87.24	53,709
Heilongjiang 黑龙江	11	516	25,609	-570	-0.54	-2.87	18.70	81.14	105,437
Central-East 华东	120	383	38,989	377	0.64	2.83	25.15	77.40	58,809
Shanghai 上海	14	451	117,518	591	0.34	1.68	34.07	79.55	171,660
Jiangsu 江苏	25	244	22,857	181	0.51	1.91	33.06	73.17	35,318
Zhejiang 浙江	26	242	30,584	411	0.87	3.21	37.83	73.00	47,487
Anhui 安徽	9	776	14,153	-2,430	-4.52		4.26	114.61	53,787
Fujian 福建	3	138	8,304	-738	-2.84	-5.41	16.81	47.45	25,939
Jiangxi 江西	8	353	13,745	-215	-0.46	-3.84	12.92	88.02	46,630
Shandong 山东	35	487	40,129	1,357	2.97	9.17	25.11	67.63	45,752
Central-South 中南	96	396	30,353	-377	-0.65	-3.06	22.90	78.85	58,252
Henan 河南	49	509	42,033	101	0.13	0.56	24.43	76.91	77,783
Hubei 湖北	13	139	21,081	-195	-0.86	-3.05	48.47	71.96	22,833
Hunan 湖南	18	322	18,013	-754	-1.78	-34.81	19.63	94.89	42,360
Guangdong 广东	8	239	15,720	-1,618	-5.61	-14.37	15.44	60.95	28,824
Guangxi 广西	8	439	16,281	-1,510	-2.46	-13.39	8.39	81.62	61,366
Hainan 海南									
Southwest 西南	19	433	30,730	-2,637	-3.78	-20.72	16.20	81.76	69,787
Chongqing 重庆	1	157	34,967	2,438	5.72	16.20	104.83	64.70	42,627
Sichuan 四川	9	361	31,674	262	0.42	1.35	20.83	69.01	62,751
Guizhou 贵州	2	95	1,412	39	0.66	0.82	2.97	19.07	5,797
Yunnan 云南	7	662	37,287	-7,853	-7.78	-129.76	10.50	94.01	100,995
Tibet 西藏									
Northwest 西北	13	783	48,720	-2,853	-2.50	-21.62	12.95	88.45	114,275
Shaanxi 陕西	3	658	23,657	-8,949	-11.44		11.65	144.17	78,245
Gansu 甘肃	4	630	30,767	490	0.61	2.60	11.03	76.45	80,027
Qinghai 青海									
Ningxia 宁夏	4	1,335	107,624	-2,472	-1.15	-5.92	14.91	80.61	215,295
Xinjiang 新疆	2	171	4,416	-1,158	-3.33	-7.04	4.04	52.75	34,774

3611: Mining Equipment 矿山设备制造业

Year 年份	Number of firms 企业个数	Rate of change 变化率 (%)	Number of employees 职工人数 (人)	Rate of change 变化率 (%)	Total revenue (Mil. RMB) 总销售收入 (百万元)	Rate of change 变化率 (%)	Total profit (Mil RMB) 总利润 (百万元)	Rate of change 变化率 (%)
2000	338		190,059		9,922		-280	
2001	336	-0.59	159,016	-16.33	10,794	8.79	-198	29.29
2002	356	5.95	164,914	3.71	13,758	27.46	-80	59.60

Major Products 主要产品	Output 产量	Unit 单位
Mine Equipment 矿山设备	48	10,000 Tons 万吨

10 Main Firms with Maximal Revenue (year founded) 收入最大的十家主要企业（创办年份）	City 城市	Province 省	Telephone/fax 电话/传真	Number of employees 职工人数	Ownership 产业所有权	Revenue ('000 RMB) 销售收入 (千元)	Profit('000 RMB) (rank) 利润(千元) (排名)	Total assets ('000 RMB) 总资产 (千元)	Major products 主要产品
Taiyuan Heavy Machinery Group Co., Ltd.	Taiyuan	Shanxi	(0351)6360028		State Enterprises				Excavating Equipment
太原重型机械集团有限公司	太原市	山西省	(0351)6360527	9,873	国有独资	901,646	5,000(15)	3,602,791	挖掘设备
Shanghai Jianshe Luqiao Machinery Equipment Co., Ltd.	Shanghai	Shanghai	(021)63134136		Overseas Chinese-funded				Mine Equipment
上海建设路桥机械设备有限公司(1989)	上海市	上海市	(021)63133936	933	港澳台资	799,769	11,577(4)	417,361	矿山设备
Citic Heavy Machinery Company Ltd.	Luoyang	Henan	(0379)4088114		State-owned				Plant & Mining Accessories
中信重型机械公司(1958)	洛阳市	河南省	(0379)4214680	9,962	国有企业	756,950	-	1,887,540	工矿备件
Shenyang Heavy Machinery Group Co., Ltd.	Shenyang	Liaoning	(024)25875435		State Enterprises				Mine Equipment
沈阳重型机械集团有限责任公司(1937)	沈阳市	辽宁省	(024)25851610	3,857	国有独资	507,570	-	3,446,479	矿山设备
Zhangjiakou Coal Mine Machinery Co., Ltd.	Zhangjiakou	Hebei	(0313)2056273		State-owned				Mine Equipment
张家口煤矿机械有限公司(1949)	张家口市	河北省	(0313)2017708	4,684	国有企业	396,200	3,300(21)	856,970	矿山设备
Ningxia Xibei Benniu Industrial Group Co.,Ltd.	Shizuishan	Ningxia	(0952)2174449		State Enterprises				Blow Board Feeding Machine刮
宁夏西北奔牛实业集团有限公司(1970)	石嘴山市	宁夏	(0952)2174600	2,827	国有独资	311,730	5,100(14)	508,430	板输送机
Zhengzhou Coal Mine Machinery Group Co., Ltd.	Zhengzhou	Henan	(0371)7628482		State-owned				Mine Equipment
郑州煤矿机械集团有限公司(1959)	郑州市	河南省	(0371)7631369	3,395	国有企业	266,880	15,960(2)	683,910	矿山设备
Shanghai Heavy Machinery Plant	Shanghai	Shanghai	(021)54721141		State-owned				Mining Equipment
上海重型机器厂(1934)	上海市	上海市	(021)54721132	3,226	国有企业	261,141	500(107)	1,406,617	采矿设备
Asiatrak (Tianjin) Co., ltd.	Tianjin	Tianjin	(022)25760808		Foreign Funded				Pedrail & Fittings履
亚实履带(天津)有限公司(1997)	天津市	天津市	(022)25760606	330	外商投资	233,376	-	390,729	带及配件
Taiyuan Mine Group Company	Taiyuan	Shanxi	(0351)3041515		State Enterprises				Mine Equipment
太原矿山集团公司	太原市	山西省	(0351)3041194	5,469	国有独资	204,159	105(142)	864,253	矿山设备

Top 10 Cities by Revenue 销售收入排名前10位城市	Province 省	Market share 市场份额 (%)	Number of firms 企业个数
Shanghai 上海市	Shanghai 上海市	11.96	14
Taiyuan 太原市	Shanxi 山西省	9.08	5
Shenyang 沈阳市	Liaoning 辽宁省	8.55	12
Luoyang 洛阳市	Henan 河南省	6.25	6
Zhengzhou 郑州市	Henan 河南省	5.24	17
Zhangjiakou 张家口市	Hebei 河北省	4.00	8
Weifang 潍坊市	Shandong 山东省	3.71	4
Shizuishan 石嘴山市	Ningxia 宁夏	3.13	4
Quzhou 衢州市	Zhejiang 浙江省	2.82	4
Tianjin 天津市	Tianjin 天津市	2.73	6

10 Major Wholesalers 十家主要批发商	City 城市	Province 省	Telephone/Fax 电话/传真
SU MEC	Nanjing	Jiangsu	(025)4511888
中设江苏机械设备进出口（集团）公司	南京市	江苏省	(025)4411772
China Poster Mobile Communications Equipment Co.,Ltd.	Beijing	Beijing	(010)66426993
中邮普泰移动通信设备股份有限公司	北京市	北京市	(010)66426837
Sino Kama Co., Ltd.	Shanghai	Shanghai	(021)62031188
中泰凯马股份有限公司	上海市	上海市	(021)62030851
China Huayuan Group Co.,Ltd.	Shanghai	Shanghai	(021)62031188
中国华源集团有限公司	上海市	上海市	(021)62032288
Zhejiang Crand Imp.& Exp.Co.,Ltd.	Ningbo	Zhejiang	(0574)87720170
浙江远大进出口有限公司	宁波市	浙江省	(0574)87723350
Shandong Machinery Import & Export Group Corporation	Qingdao	Shandong	(0532)2661628
山东省机械进出口集团公司	青岛市	山东省	(0532)2991655
Qingdao Haier International Trade Co.,Ltd.	Qingdao	Shandong	(0532)8938337
青岛海尔国际贸易有限公司	青岛市	山东省	(0532)8939494
Guangdong Machinery Import & Export Group Corporation	Guangzhou	Guangdong	(020)87782168
广东省机械进出口集团公司	广州市	广东省	(020)87771803
China National Machinery Equipment Import & Export Corporation	Beijing	Beijing	(010)63474506
中国机械设备进出口总公司	北京市	北京市	(010)63261865
Beijing Cellstar Co.,Ltd.	Beijing	Beijing	(010)64602050
北京蜂星事达电讯有限公司	北京市	北京市	(010)64672648

3613: Metallurgy Equipment 冶金工业专用设备制造业

The industry accounts for 0.097% of the total revenue of China's industrial sector in 2002. The rate of return on assets is 0.22%. 76.13% of all firms in the industry made a profit while 23.87% had negative returns.The top province in terms of the industry's revenue is Liaoning, accounting for 17.56% of the total revenue.
2002年本行业收入占全行业的0.097%，资产利润率为0.22%。76.13%的企业赢利，23.87%的企业亏损。收入最高的省为辽宁省，占本行业的17.56%。

	Total number of firms 企业总数	Total number of employees 职工总数	Total revenue (Mil.RMB) 总销售收入（百万元）	Total profit (Mil.RMB) 总利润（百万元）	Return on assets 资产利润率（%）	Return on equity 权益利润率（%）	Labour productivity ('000 RMB/ worker) 劳动生产率（千元/人）	Debts/ assets 资产负债率（%）	Total assets (Mil.RMB) 总资产（百万元）
Industry Overall 行业总体	155	101,315	10,407	54	0.22	0.71	27.60	69.08	24,436

	Number of firms 企业个数	Average number of employees 平均职工人数	Average revenue ('000 RMB) 平均销售收入（千元）	Average profit ('000 RMB) 平均利润（千元）	Return on assets 资产利润率（%）	Return on equity 权益利润率（%）	Labour productivity ('000 RMB/ worker) 劳动生产率（千元/人）	Debts/ assets 资产负债率（%）	Average total assets ('000 RMB) 平均总资产（千元）
By ownership 产业所有权									
State-owned 国有	37	1,312	86,862	-2,758	-1.09	-4.21	16.60	74.10	252,954
Collective-owned 集体	21	206	19,848	958	4.32	15.54	28.67	72.19	22,156
Foreign & Overseas Chinese Funded 三资	13	272	39,768	2,073	2.91	9.31	47.34	68.71	71,152
By regional distribution 地区分布									
Central-North 华北	31	611	50,656	1,512	1.14	3.71	30.85	69.22	132,212
Beijing 北京	8	296	58,866	2,600	2.40	7.05	76.45	66.01	108,550
Tianjin 天津	3	351	2,756	-1,396	-3.99	-78.79	-2.04	94.93	34,975
Hebei 河北	19	803	56,591	1,588	0.97	3.17	26.28	69.30	163,253
Shanxi 山西									
Inner Mongolia 内蒙古	1	249	15,911	91	0.39	1.04	15.58	62.69	23,449
Northeast 东北	15	1,552	191,926	699	0.12	0.39	27.34	68.10	560,119
Liaoning 辽宁	11	999	166,139	2,144	0.52	1.52	39.97	65.52	408,994
Jilin 吉林	2	43	841	-267	-1.85	-5.74	27.46	67.81	14,453
Heilongjiang 黑龙江	2	6,105	524,839	-6,280	-0.32	-1.12	15.97	71.10	1,936,975
Central-East 华东	68	251	41,879	1,546	2.80	7.00	44.78	60.02	55,249
Shanghai 上海	14	238	43,655	2,697	4.07	7.01	42.56	41.98	66,325
Jiangsu 江苏	33	270	54,294	1,822	2.90	7.65	54.65	62.07	62,794
Zhejiang 浙江	12	201	17,172	-929	-3.12	-9.82	25.64	68.26	29,779
Anhui 安徽									
Fujian 福建	2	77	15,209	213	1.38	13.94	36.26	90.11	15,414
Jiangxi 江西	1	98	6,192	369	2.68	8.27	26.06	67.57	13,757
Shandong 山东	6	354	33,698	2,925	4.96	31.06	30.00	84.04	59,038
Central-South 中南	26	465	38,645	-845	-1.20	-10.04	25.18	88.00	70,137
Henan 河南	12	147	37,453	1,552	5.22	22.26	70.87	76.57	29,749
Hubei 湖北	5	862	50,297	-1,415	-1.19	-4.15	18.77	71.38	119,255
Hunan 湖南	7	843	33,755	-4,970	-4.13		12.70	105.79	120,324
Guangdong 广东	2	54	33,784	641	4.57	9.68	216.18	52.76	14,017
Guangxi 广西									
Hainan 海南									
Southwest 西南	10	2,007	156,423	-4,677	-0.99	-2.92	18.23	66.07	472,695
Chongqing 重庆	1	1,006	55,051	517	0.47	0.71	17.24	33.62	109,216
Sichuan 四川	6	2,774	229,006	-1,056	-0.17	-0.46	19.18	63.87	635,090
Guizhou 贵州	1	344	6,522	-2,178	-8.14	-109.01	11.09	92.53	26,753
Yunnan 云南	2	1,038	64,309	-19,385	-4.97	-25.41	12.27	80.45	390,222
Tibet 西藏									
Northwest 西北	5	1,982	108,165	-8,010	-2.46	-13.80	14.35	82.17	325,677
Shaanxi 陕西	4	2,047	131,760	-9,136	-2.42	-12.80	16.88	81.13	378,206
Gansu 甘肃	1	1,723	13,787	-3,509	-3.04	-72.61	2.36	95.82	115,560
Qinghai 青海									
Ningxia 宁夏									
Xinjiang 新疆									

3613: Metallurgy Equipment 冶金工业专用设备制造业

Year 年份	Number of firms 企业个数	Rate of change 变化率(%)	Number of employees 职工人数(人)	Rate of change 变化率(%)	Total revenue (Mil. RMB) 总销售收入(百万元)	Rate of change 变化率(%)	Total profit (Mil RMB) 总利润(百万元)	Rate of change 变化率(%)
2000	145		114,492		6,798		-234	
2001	152	4.83	103,946	-9.21	7,981	17.40	-289	-23.50
2002	155	1.97	101,315	-2.53	10,407	30.40	54	-

Major Products 主要产品	Output 产量	Unit 单位
Smelting Equipment 冶炼设备	100,155	Ton 吨
Metal Rolling Equipment 金属轧制设备	85,367	Ton 吨

10 Main Firms with Maximal Revenue (year founded) 收入最大的十家主要企业（创办年份）	City 城市	Province 省	Telephone/fax 电话/传真	Number of employees 职工人数	Ownership 产业所有权	Revenue ('000 RMB) 销售收入(千元)	Profit('000 RMB) (rank) 利润(千元)(排名)	Total assets ('000 RMB) 总资产(千元)	Major products 主要产品
Dalian Heavy Industry Crane Group Co., Ltd.	Dalian	Liaoning	(0411)4604201		State Enterprises				Metal Smelting Equipment金属
大连重工起重集团有限公司(2001)	大连市	辽宁省	(0411)4604760	6,621	国有独资	1,529,786	17,014(4)	3,663,144	冶炼设备
China National Erzhong Group Co.	Deyang	Sichuan	(0838)2341192		State-owned				Metallurgy Equipment
中国第二重型机械集团公司(1965)	德阳市	四川省	(0838)2201998	12,801	国有企业	1,056,954	4,377(15)	3,295,563	冶金设备
China First Heavy Industries (CFHI)_	Qiqihar	Heilongjiang	(0452)6809001		State Enterprises				Metal Rolling Equipment金属
中国第一重型机械集团公司(1960)	齐齐哈尔市	黑龙江省	(0452)6806777	11,889	国有独资	1,042,150	-	3,864,653	轧制设备
Xingtai Machinery Mill Roll (Group) Corporation	Xingtai	Hebei	(0319)2116436		State Enterprises				Metallurgy Roller
邢台机械轧辊（集团）有限公司(1959)	邢台市	河北省	(0319)2022061	6,690	国有独资	509,463	17,630(3)	1,892,893	冶金轧辊
Baoshan Steel & Iron Group Changzhou Metallurgical	Changzhou	Jiangsu	(0519)3258888		State-owned				Metallurgy Equipment
Machinery Works 宝钢集团常州冶金机械厂(1962)	常州市	江苏省	(0519)3260460	2,358	国有企业	287,140	2,590(26)	543,110	冶金设备
Wuxi Huaye Iron & Steel Co., Ltd.	Wuxi	Jiangsu	(0510)3260888		Limited-Liability				Strip Steel
无锡华业钢铁有限公司(2000)	无锡市	江苏省		243	有限公司	260,370	16,510(6)	122,280	带钢
Shannxi Forging & Rolling Equipment Works	Weinan	Shannxi	(0913)8622049		State-owned				Metal Rolling Equipment金属
陕西压延设备厂(1970)	渭南市	陕西省	(0913)8622000	3,422	国有企业	254,869	1,405(39)	505,899	轧制设备
Xi'an Metallurgy Machine Co., Ltd.	Xi'an	Shannxi	(029)4619222		State Enterprises				Metallurgy Equipment Spare Parts冶金
西安冶金机械有限公司(1958)	西安市	陕西省	(029)4619333	2,927	国有独资	216,195	3,437(19)	562,331	设备备件
Shenyang Metallurgy Machine Co., Ltd	Shenyang	Liaoning	(024)25873017		Limited-Liability				Metallurgy Equipment
沈阳冶金机械有限公司(2001)	沈阳市	辽宁省	(024)25875415	3,301	有限公司	186,369	2,308(31)	698,216	冶金设备
Shanghai Heavy Mining Machinery Company (Headquarter)	Shanghai	Shanghai	(021)63044076		State-owned				Smelting Equipment
上海重型矿山机械公司(本部)(1992)	上海市	上海市	(021)63022932	91	国有企业	173,430	3,850(18)	176,806	冶炼设备

Top 10 Cities by Revenue 销售收入排名前10位城市	Province 省	Market share 市场份额(%)	Number of firms 企业个数
Dalian 大连市	Liaoning 辽宁省	15.09	4
Deyang 德阳市	Sichuan 四川省	10.91	2
Qiqihar 齐齐哈尔市	Heilongjiang 黑龙江省	10.09	2
Wuxi 无锡市	Jiangsu 江苏省	6.20	13
Shanghai 上海市	Shanghai 上海市	5.87	14
Xingtai 邢台市	Hebei 河北省	5.28	5
Changzhou 常州市	Jiangsu 江苏省	4.59	8
Beijing 北京市	Beijing 北京市	4.53	8
Zhengzhou 郑州市	Henan 河南省	3.54	8
Nanjing 南京市	Jiangsu 江苏省	2.94	2

10 Major Wholesalers 十家主要批发商	City 城市	Province 省	Telephone/Fax 电话/传真
SU MEC	Nanjing	Jiangsu	(025)4511888
中设江苏机械设备进出口（集团）公司	南京市	江苏省	(025)4411772
China Poster Mobile Communications Equipment Co.,Ltd.	Beijing	Beijing	(010)66426993
中邮普泰移动通信设备股份有限公司	北京市	北京市	(010)66426837
Sino Kama Co., Ltd.	Shanghai	Shanghai	(021)62031188
中泰凯马股份有限公司	上海市	上海市	(021)62030851
China Huayuan Group Co.,Ltd.	Shanghai	Shanghai	(021)62031188
中国华源集团有限公司	上海市	上海市	(021)62032288
Zhejiang Crand Imp.& Exp.Co.,Ltd.	Ningbo	Zhejiang	(0574)87720170
浙江远大进出口有限公司	宁波市	浙江省	(0574)87723350
Shandong Machinery Import & Export Group Corporation	Qingdao	Shandong	(0532)2661628
山东省机械进出口集团公司	青岛市	山东省	(0532)2991655
Qingdao Haier International Trade Co.,Ltd.	Qingdao	Shandong	(0532)8938337
青岛海尔国际贸易有限公司	青岛市	山东省	(0532)8939494
Guangdong Machinery Import & Export Group Corporation	Guangzhou	Guangdong	(020)87782168
广东省机械进出口集团公司	广州市	广东省	(020)87771803
China National Machinery Equipment Import & Export Corporation	Beijing	Beijing	(010)63474506
中国机械设备进出口总公司	北京市	北京市	(010)63261865
Beijing Cellstar Co.,Ltd.	Beijing	Beijing	(010)64602050
北京蜂星事达电讯有限公司	北京市	北京市	(010)64672648

3615: Electric Engineering Equipment 电工专用设备制造业

The industry accounts for 0.016% of the total revenue of China's industrial sector in 2002. The rate of return on assets is 6.20%. 82.61% of all firms in the industry made a profit while 17.39% had negative returns.The top province in terms of the industry's revenue is Beijing, accounting for 35.43% of the total revenue.
2002年本行业收入占全行业的0.016%，资产利润率为6.20%。82.61%的企业赢利，17.39%的企业亏损。收入最高的省为北京市，占本行业的35.43%。

	Total number of firms 企业总数	Total number of employees 职工总数	Total revenue (Mil.RMB) 总销售收入(百万元)	Total profit (Mil.RMB) 总利润(百万元)	Return on assets 资产利润率(%)	Return on equity 权益利润率(%)	Labour productivity ('000 RMB/ worker) 劳动生产率(千元/人)	Debts/ assets 资产负债率(%)	Total assets (Mil.RMB) 总资产(百万元)
Industry Overall 行业总体	46	9,757	1,763	169	6.20	15.79	65.51	60.75	2,728

	Number of firms 企业个数	Average number of employees 平均职工人数	Average revenue ('000 RMB) 平均销售收入(千元)	Average profit ('000 RMB) 平均利润(千元)	Return on assets 资产利润率(%)	Return on equity 权益利润率(%)	Labour productivity ('000 RMB/ worker) 劳动生产率(千元/人)	Debts/ assets 资产负债率(%)	Average total assets ('000 RMB) 平均总资产(千元)
By ownership 产业所有权									
State-owned 国有	6	179	12,522	463	1.02	6.59	28.52	84.58	45,541
Collective-owned 集体	5	82	7,646	452	5.52	10.64	31.07	48.10	8,176
Foreign & Overseas Chinese Funded 三资	6	85	33,212	1,242	4.36	14.01	110.81	68.88	28,479
By regional distribution 地区分布									
Central-North 华北	8	138	83,971	21,384	21.96	38.28	277.47	42.65	97,398
Beijing 北京	4	156	156,115	40,948	22.70	37.89	429.16	40.08	180,379
Tianjin 天津									
Hebei 河北	4	121	11,827	1,820	12.62	49.90	82.94	74.70	14,417
Shanxi 山西									
Inner Mongolia 内蒙古									
Northeast 东北	2	677	11,091	-3,763	-6.82	-23.74	-2.19	71.26	55,158
Liaoning 辽宁	2	677	11,091	-3,763	-6.82	-23.74	-2.19	71.26	55,158
Jilin 吉林									
Heilongjiang 黑龙江									
Central-East 华东	27	155	33,697	1,314	2.89	7.96	61.00	63.68	45,457
Shanghai 上海	13	200	40,570	1,656	2.74	7.86	51.12	65.09	60,399
Jiangsu 江苏	4	131	21,365	363	1.37	2.56	51.30	46.50	26,489
Zhejiang 浙江	3	62	9,609	461	4.28	9.81	42.31	56.40	10,769
Anhui 安徽	6	134	41,638	1,505	3.00	8.97	101.16	66.54	50,132
Fujian 福建									
Jiangxi 江西									
Shandong 山东	1	70	18,300	2,070	66.99	739.29	89.47	90.94	3,090
Central-South 中南	5	80	10,290	692	1.78	5.20	72.93	65.79	38,886
Henan 河南	1	50	9,715	782	15.64	18.02	63.82	13.20	5,000
Hubei 湖北	3	75	8,183	333	0.75	2.80	87.03	73.11	44,183
Hunan 湖南									
Guangdong 广东	1	128	17,186	1,680	2.95	6.33	51.80	53.36	56,881
Guangxi 广西									
Hainan 海南									
Southwest 西南	4	679	26,851	-8,336	-8.00	-41.65	18.69	80.80	104,222
Chongqing 重庆	1	175	5,666	69	1.27	3.47	11.05	63.37	5,432
Sichuan 四川	2	1,248	50,554	-16,708	-8.15	-42.88	19.09	81.00	205,047
Guizhou 贵州	1	45	631	1	0.07	0.70	26.60	89.52	1,364
Yunnan 云南									
Tibet 西藏									
Northwest 西北									
Shaanxi 陕西									
Gansu 甘肃									
Qinghai 青海									
Ningxia 宁夏									
Xinjiang 新疆									

3615: Electric Engineering Equipment 电工专用设备制造业

Year 年份	Number of firms 企业个数	Rate of change 变化率 (%)	Number of employees 职工人数 (人)	Rate of change 变化率 (%)	Total revenue (Mil. RMB) 总销售收入 (百万元)	Rate of change 变化率 (%)	Total profit (Mil RMB) 总利润 (百万元)	Rate of change 变化率 (%)
2000	40		9,233		1,317		161	
2001	36	-10.00	7,142	-22.65	1,022	-22.40	81	-49.69
2002	46	27.78	9,757	36.61	1,763	72.50	169	108.64

Major Products 主要产品	Output 产量	Unit 单位
Electric Wire & Cable Manufacturing Special Equipment 电线电缆制造专用设备	18,517	Ton 吨

10 Main Firms with Maximal Revenue (year founded) 收入最大的十家主要企业（创办年份）	City 城市	Province 省	Telephone/fax 电话/传真	Number of employees 职工人数	Ownership 产业所有权	Revenue ('000 RMB) 销售收入 (千元)	Profit('000 RMB) (rank) 利润(千元) (排名)	Total assets ('000 RMB) 总资产 (千元)	Major products 主要产品
Shanghai Electric Power Repair & Making General Factory Co. 上海电力修造总厂有限公司(1956)	Shanghai 上海市	Shanghai 上海市	(021)63130227 (021)63130757	735	Limited-Liability 有限公司	247,075	2,508(7)	293,644	Industrial Pump 工业泵
Hefei Walsin Electric Industry Co.,Ltd. 合肥华新电工有限公司(1996)	Hefei 合肥市	Anhui 安徽省	(0551)3812605 (0551)3812207	106	Overseas Chinese-funded 港澳台资	74,967	522(21)	49,130	Special Electrician's Equipment电工专用设备
Hefei Shenma Cable Machinery Corporation 合肥神马电缆机械股份有限公司(1999)	Hefei 合肥市	Anhui 安徽省	(0551)3812605 (0551)3812207	116	Joint Stock 股份制	68,489	333(22)	60,054	Special Electrician's Equipment电工专用设备
Dingtian Science & Technology Co.,Ltd. 鼎天科技股份有限公司(1966)	Deyang 德阳市	Sichuan 四川省	(0838)2826888 (0838)2821408	2,367	Joint Stock 股份制	57,183	-	370,662	Special Electrician's Equipment电工专用设备
Wuxi Huadong Electric Power Equipment Co., Ltd. 无锡市华东电力设备有限公司(1983)	Wuxi 无锡市	Jiangsu 江苏省	(0510)3231794 (0510)3235831	200	Private Enterprises 私营独资	48,400	2,390(8)	54,360	Circumgyrating Filter Mesh 旋转滤网
Shanghai Nextrom Machinery Manufacture Co., Ltd. 上海耐世隆机器制造有限公司(1995)	Shanghai 上海市	Shanghai 上海市	(021)58419988 (021)58411778	40	Foreign Funded 外商投资	46,021	4,623(5)	34,079	Cable Manufacturing Machine电缆制造机械
Haite Electric Industry Equipment Co., Ltd. 成都海特电工设备厂(1993)	Chengdu 成都市	Sichuan 四川省	(028)85802412 (028)85807815	128	Limited-Liability 有限公司	43,925	1,709(11)	39,431	Electrician Mechanical Equipment电工机械设备
Anhui Jiyuan Electric Network Technology Co., Ltd. 安徽继远电网技术有限责任公司(1996)	Hefei 合肥市	Anhui 安徽省	(0551)3605888 (0551)3605888	57	Limited-Liability 有限公司	40,820	7,510(3)	54,110	Transform Power Complex Automatic System变电综合自动化系统
Hefei Shenma Electrician Co., Ltd. 合肥神马电工股份有限公司(1958)	Hefei 合肥市	Anhui 安徽省	(0551)5523932 (0551)5523932	139	Joint Stock 股份制	25,019	17(30)	58,814	Cable Special Equipment电缆专用设备
Huahai Electrification Co., Ltd. 华海电器化有限公司(1990)	Suzhou 宿州市	Anhui 安徽省	(0557)6021100	135	State Enterprises 国有独资	21,522	633(19)	31,346	Electric Wire 电线

Top 10 Cities by Revenue 销售收入排名前10位城市	Province 省	Market share 市场份额 (%)	Number of firms 企业个数
Beijing 北京市	Beijing 北京市	35.43	4
Shanghai 上海市	Shanghai 上海市	29.92	13
Hefei 合肥市	Anhui 安徽省	11.87	4
Deyang 德阳市	Sichuan 四川省	3.24	1
Wuxi 无锡市	Jiangsu 江苏省	2.88	2
Chengdu 成都市	Sichuan 四川省	2.49	1
Suzhou 宿州市	Anhui 安徽省	1.22	1
Nantong 南通市	Jiangsu 江苏省	1.20	1
Tangshan 唐山市	Hebei 河北省	1.17	2
Wuhu 芜湖市	Anhui 安徽省	1.08	1

10 Major Wholesalers 十家主要批发商	City 城市	Province 省	Telephone/Fax 电话/传真
SU MEC 中设江苏机械设备进出口（集团）公司	Nanjing 南京市	Jiangsu 江苏省	(025)4511888 (025)4411772
China Poster Mobile Communications Equipment Co.,Ltd. 中邮普泰移动通信设备股份有限公司	Beijing 北京市	Beijing 北京市	(010)66426993 (010)66426837
Sino Kama Co., Ltd. 中泰凯马股份有限公司	Shanghai 上海市	Shanghai 上海市	(021)62031188 (021)62030851
China Huayuan Group Co.,Ltd. 中国华源集团有限公司	Shanghai 上海市	Shanghai 上海市	(021)62031188 (021)62032288
Zhejiang Crand Imp.& Exp.Co.,Ltd. 浙江远大进出口有限公司	Ningbo 宁波市	Zhejiang 浙江省	(0574)87720170 (0574)87723350
Shandong Machinery Import & Export Group Corporation 山东省机械进出口集团公司	Qingdao 青岛市	Shandong 山东省	(0532)2661628 (0532)2991655
Qingdao Haier International Trade Co.,Ltd. 青岛海尔国际贸易有限公司	Qingdao 青岛市	Shandong 山东省	(0532)8938337 (0532)8939494
Guangdong Machinery Import & Export Group Corporation 广东省机械进出口集团公司	Guangzhou 广州市	Guangdong 广东省	(020)87782168 (020)87771803
China National Machinery Equipment Import & Export Corporation 中国机械设备进出口总公司	Beijing 北京市	Beijing 北京市	(010)63474506 (010)63261865
Beijing Cellstar Co.,Ltd. 北京蜂星事达电讯有限公司	Beijing 北京市	Beijing 北京市	(010)64602050 (010)64672648

3617: Electronics Equipment 电子工业专用设备制造业

The industry accounts for 0.038% of the total revenue of China's industrial sector in 2002. The rate of return on assets is 4.70%. 80.72% of all firms in the industry made a profit while 19.28% had negative returns.The top province in terms of the industry's revenue is Jiangsu, accounting for 24.01% of the total revenue.
2002年本行业收入占全行业的 0.038%，资产利润率为 4.70%。80.72%的企业赢利，19.28%的企业亏损。收入最高的省为江苏省，占本行业的24.01%。

	Total number of firms 企业总数	Total number of employees 职工总数	Total revenue (Mil.RMB) 总销售收入 (百万元)	Total profit (Mil.RMB) 总利润 (百万元)	Return on assets 资产利润率 (%)	Return on equity 权益利润率 (%)	Labour productivity ('000 RMB/ worker) 劳动生产率 (千元/人)	Debts/ assets 资产负债率 (%)	Total assets (Mil.RMB) 总资产 (百万元)
Industry Overall 行业总体	83	25,308	4,124	280	4.70	11.68	60.64	59.79	5,969

	Number of firms 企业个数	Average number of employees 平均职工人数	Average revenue ('000 RMB) 平均销售收入 (千元)	Average profit ('000 RMB) 平均利润 (千元)	Return on assets 资产利润率 (%)	Return on equity 权益利润率 (%)	Labour productivity ('000 RMB/ worker) 劳动生产率 (千元/人)	Debts/ assets 资产负债率 (%)	Average total assets ('000 RMB) 平均总资产 (千元)
By ownership 产业所有权									
State-owned 国有	13	408	35,572	2,599	3.80	11.32	48.24	66.45	68,449
Collective-owned 集体	11	278	49,896	4,208	12.27	29.55	54.74	58.49	34,305
Foreign & Overseas Chinese Funded 三资	22	333	56,648	3,097	4.15	9.18	59.47	54.81	74,694
By regional distribution 地区分布									
Central-North 华北	14	207	75,747	8,148	8.76	22.57	133.63	61.18	92,993
Beijing 北京	8	233	117,415	13,913	9.83	25.28	180.62	61.13	141,589
Tianjin 天津	3	181	21,696	712	3.46	8.63	67.27	59.95	20,599
Hebei 河北	2	105	11,351	231	1.07	2.43	33.47	55.91	21,542
Shanxi 山西	1	280	33,349	165	0.26	0.77	24.78	66.67	64,312
Inner Mongolia 内蒙古									
Northeast 东北	7	128	17,803	1,933	6.95	12.58	45.88	44.72	27,809
Liaoning 辽宁	4	159	22,098	2,519	9.48	18.38	48.92	48.40	26,563
Jilin 吉林	1	60	7,617	364	3.56	18.60	39.55	80.84	10,216
Heilongjiang 黑龙江	2	100	14,305	1,546	3.95	6.08	38.10	35.00	39,099
Central-East 华东	35	244	47,213	2,831	5.50	14.44	52.75	61.94	51,514
Shanghai 上海	10	219	31,364	1,132	3.69	9.22	25.23	59.99	30,685
Jiangsu 江苏	13	341	76,163	5,209	5.74	17.11	60.59	66.49	90,820
Zhejiang 浙江	6	95	9,296	1,092	4.45	8.30	41.94	46.37	24,541
Anhui 安徽									
Fujian 福建									
Jiangxi 江西									
Shandong 山东	6	221	48,822	2,247	8.01	15.20	76.63	47.26	28,042
Central-South 中南	18	365	43,870	2,759	3.67	7.45	56.47	50.74	75,201
Henan 河南	3	184	6,300	-409	-2.32	-47.12	15.14	95.08	17,646
Hubei 湖北	4	236	4,941	-1,714	-2.69	-6.75	13.57	60.11	63,678
Hunan 湖南	2	171	24,770	4,870	15.96	21.95	58.80	27.29	30,512
Guangdong 广东	9	526	77,939	5,335	4.87	9.27	69.64	47.39	109,438
Guangxi 广西									
Hainan 海南									
Southwest 西南	4	376	22,368	-4,771	-4.66	-36.45	25.77	87.23	102,492
Chongqing 重庆	1	114	23,328	1,259	2.83	6.67	83.25	57.61	44,517
Sichuan 四川	1	1,276	65,650	-14,500	-4.47	-23.35	22.75	80.86	324,410
Guizhou 贵州	2	57	248	-2,922	-14.24		1.81	169.71	20,521
Yunnan 云南									
Tibet 西藏									
Northwest 西北	5	984	81,537	4,636	2.56	6.07	50.27	57.84	181,072
Shaanxi 陕西	5	984	81,537	4,636	2.56	6.07	50.27	57.84	181,072
Gansu 甘肃									
Qinghai 青海									
Ningxia 宁夏									
Xinjiang 新疆									

3617: Electronics Equipment 电子工业专用设备制造业

Year 年份	Number of firms 企业个数	Rate of change 变化率 (%)	Number of employees 职工人数 (人)	Rate of change 变化率 (%)	Total revenue (Mil. RMB) 总销售收入 (百万元)	Rate of change 变化率 (%)	Total profit (Mil RMB) 总利润 (百万元)	Rate of change 变化率 (%)
2000	74		23,760		2,232		104	
2001	84	13.51	23,154	-2.55	3,672	64.52	95	-8.65
2002	83	-1.19	25,308	9.30	4,124	12.31	280	194.74

Major Products 主要产品	Output 产量	Unit 单位
Numerical Controlling Machine Tool 数控机床	24,803	Unit 台

10 Main Firms with Maximal Revenue (year founded) 收入最大的十家主要企业（创办年份）	City 城市	Province 省	Telephone/fax 电话/传真	Number of employees 职工人数	Ownership 产业所有权	Revenue ('000 RMB) 销售收入 (千元)	Profit('000 RMB) (rank) 利润(千元) (排名)	Total assets ('000 RMB) 总资产 (千元)	Major products 主要产品
Beijing Sifang Jibao Automation Co., Ltd. 北京四方继保自动化有限公司(1994)	Beijing 北京市	Beijing 北京市	(010)62961515 (010)62981004	423	Limited-Liability 有限公司	570,378	66,717(1)	657,691	CSL2000 Transformer Station.CSL2000变电站
Jiangsu Sujing Group Co., Ltd. 江苏苏净州集团有限公司(1970)	Suzhou 苏州市	Jiangsu 江苏省	(0512)67232660 (0512)65338132	746	Limited-Liability 有限公司	327,625	41,139(2)	482,933	Air Purifier空气净化设备
Shaanxi Baoguang Vacuum Electronic Apparatus Co., Ltd. 陕西宝光真空电器股份有限公司(1997)	Baoji 宝鸡市	Shannxi 陕西省	(0917)3561172 (0917)3561391	1,443	Joint Stock 股份制	250,190	16,650(5)	484,810	Electrical Vacuum Component电真空器件
Beijing Qixing Huachuang Electronics Co.,Ltd. 北京七星华创电子股份有限公司(2001)	Beijing 北京市	Beijing 北京市	(010)64353493 (010)84566380	719	State-owned 国有企业	220,080	29,811(3)	303,791	Electronic Special Equipment电子专用设备
Shandong Tongyu Co.,Ltd. 山东通裕集团有限公司(1995)	Dezhou 德州市	Shandong 山东省	(0534)7520689 (0534)7521470	600	Collective-owned 集体企业	194,360	14,256(6)	106,629	Forging Materials锻件
Wuxi ULTrasound Electronic Equipment Co., Ltd. 无锡市超声电子设备有限公司(1998)	Wuxi 无锡市	Jiangsu 江苏省	(0510)3708951 (0510)3700395	530	Limited-Liability 有限公司	182,630	2,355(22)	53,906	Supersonic Cleaner超声清洗机
Xinrui Electronics (Shenzhen) Co., Ltd. 信瑞电子（深圳）有限公司(1995)	Shenzhen 深圳市	Guangdong 广东省	(0755)25260902 (0755)25557915	296	Overseas Chinese-funded 港澳台资	154,952	7,100(12)	97,963	UPS.不间断电源
Jiangsu Yunagyang Group 江苏远洋集团(1988)	Xuzhou 徐州市	Jiangsu 江苏省	(0516)7055306 (0516)7055306	1,450	Collective-owned 集体企业	146,000	13,360(8)	56,670	Magnetic Matrial磁性材料
Elite Electronic Material (kunshan) Co., Ltd. 台光电子材料(昆山)有限公司(1998)	Suzhou 苏州市	Jiangsu 江苏省	(0512)57663671 (0512)57663737	231	Overseas Chinese-funded 港澳台资	136,090	-	295,984	Substrates基板
Northwest Machine Factory 西北机器厂(1940)	Baoji 宝鸡市	Shannxi 陕西省	(0917)8551709 (0917)8551749	2,866	State-owned 国有企业	101,787	2,890(18)	246,598	Electrical Vacuum Component Equipment电真空器件设备

Top 10 Cities by Revenue 销售收入排名前10位城市	Province 省	Market share 市场份额 (%)	Number of firms 企业个数
Beijing 北京市	Beijing 北京市	22.78	8
Shenzhen 深圳市	Guangdong 广东省	13.81	5
Suzhou 苏州市	Jiangsu 江苏省	12.09	5
Baoji 宝鸡市	Shannxi 陕西省	8.64	3
Shanghai 上海市	Shanghai 上海市	7.60	10
Dezhou 德州市	Shandong 山东省	5.08	2
Wuxi 无锡市	Jiangsu 江苏省	4.43	1
Xuzhou 徐州市	Jiangsu 江苏省	3.54	1
Guangzhou 广州市	Guangdong 广东省	3.20	4
Changzhou 常州市	Jiangsu 江苏省	2.41	1

10 Major Wholesalers 十家主要批发商	City 城市	Province 省	Telephone/Fax 电话/传真
SU MEC 中设江苏机械设备进出口（集团）公司	Nanjing 南京市	Jiangsu 江苏省	(025)4511888 (025)4411772
China Poster Mobile Communications Equipment Co.,Ltd. 中邮普泰移动通信设备股份有限公司	Beijing 北京市	Beijing 北京市	(010)66426993 (010)66426837
Sino Kama Co., Ltd. 中泰凯马股份有限公司	Shanghai 上海市	Shanghai 上海市	(021)62031188 (021)62030851
China Huayuan Group Co.,Ltd. 中国华源集团有限公司	Shanghai 上海市	Shanghai 上海市	(021)62031188 (021)62032288
Zhejiang Crand Imp.& Exp.Co.,Ltd. 浙江远大进出口有限公司	Ningbo 宁波市	Zhejiang 浙江省	(0574)87720170 (0574)87723350
Shandong Machinery Import & Export Group Corporation 山东省机械进出口集团公司	Qingdao 青岛市	Shandong 山东省	(0532)2661628 (0532)2991655
Qingdao Haier International Trade Co.,Ltd. 青岛海尔国际贸易有限公司	Qingdao 青岛市	Shandong 山东省	(0532)8938337 (0532)8939494
Guangdong Machinery Import & Export Group Corporation 广东省机械进出口集团公司	Guangzhou 广州市	Guangdong 广东省	(020)87782168 (020)87771803
China National Machinery Equipment Import & Export Corporation 中国机械设备进出口总公司	Beijing 北京市	Beijing 北京市	(010)63474506 (010)63261865
Beijing Cellstar Co.,Ltd. 北京蜂星事达电讯有限公司	Beijing 北京市	Beijing 北京市	(010)64602050 (010)64672648

3619: Other Special Electromechanical Equipment

其他机电工业专用设备制造业

The industry accounts for 0.024% of the total revenue of China's industrial sector in 2002. The rate of return on assets is 8.84%. 82.42% of all firms in the industry made a profit while 17.58% had negative returns.The top province in terms of the industry's revenue is Beijing, accounting for 25.44% of the total revenue.
2002年本行业收入占全行业的0.024%，资产利润率为8.84%。82.42%的企业赢利，17.58%的企业亏损。收入最高的省为北京市，占本行业的25.44%。

	Total number of firms 企业总数	Total number of employees 职工总数	Total revenue (Mil.RMB) 总销售收入 (百万元)	Total profit (Mil.RMB) 总利润 (百万元)	Return on assets 资产利润率 (%)	Return on equity 权益利润率 (%)	Labour productivity ('000 RMB/ worker) 劳动生产率 (千元/人)	Debts/ assets 资产负债率 (%)	Total assets (Mil.RMB) 总资产 (百万元)
Industry Overall 行业总体	91	13,913	2,611	251	8.84	17.85	50.89	50.47	2,836

	Number of firms 企业个数	Average number of employees 平均职工人数	Average revenue ('000 RMB) 平均销售收入（千元）	Average profit ('000 RMB) 平均利润 (千元)	Return on assets 资产利润率 (%)	Return on equity 权益利润率 (%)	Labour productivity ('000 RMB/ worker) 劳动生产率 (千元/人)	Debts/ assets 资产负债率 (%)	Average total assets ('000 RMB) 平均总资产 (千元)
By ownership 产业所有权									
State-owned 国有	14	225	11,087	-300	-0.76	-2.19	16.36	65.12	39,343
Collective-owned 集体	6	335	15,218	291	2.44	5.41	30.58	54.97	11,932
Foreign & Overseas Chinese Funded 三资	21	114	67,288	10,759	18.90	31.43	132.15	39.86	56,914
By regional distribution 地区分布									
Central-North 华北	19	149	38,583	7,367	17.72	33.97	94.99	47.84	41,576
Beijing 北京	9	124	73,803	14,935	19.79	35.85	224.69	44.80	75,472
Tianjin 天津	7	78	6,622	186	1.44	5.06	14.33	71.55	12,897
Hebei 河北	2	547	8,452	239	4.13	10.08	5.27	58.98	5,770
Shanxi 山西									
Inner Mongolia 内蒙古	1	65	5,607	3,779	42.51	56.76	46.57	25.11	8,890
Northeast 东北	7	129	69,120	10,658	15.90	21.99	141.33	27.71	67,039
Liaoning 辽宁	7	129	69,120	10,658	15.90	21.99	141.33	27.71	67,039
Jilin 吉林									
Heilongjiang 黑龙江									
Central-East 华东	41	92	20,103	832	6.34	17.12	57.88	62.96	13,124
Shanghai 上海	3	73	17,494	2,451	14.82	24.67	76.56	39.93	16,542
Jiangsu 江苏	23	100	24,304	489	3.38	10.96	60.82	69.18	14,463
Zhejiang 浙江	8	82	14,220	542	5.03	11.67	40.36	56.92	10,781
Anhui 安徽	1	91	2,458				10.85	50.87	3,981
Fujian 福建	2	87	7,925	178	2.10	3.90	22.64	46.16	8,486
Jiangxi 江西									
Shandong 山东	4	91	20,167	2,713	22.33	58.00	88.35	61.49	12,145
Central-South 中南	20	219	20,780	114	0.44	1.15	11.18	61.54	25,713
Henan 河南	6	352	19,615	128	0.50	1.76	32.60	71.41	25,308
Hubei 湖北									
Hunan 湖南	4	217	16,789	-1,860	-6.02	-23.85	39.55	74.77	30,907
Guangdong 广东	7	157	30,116	1,230	3.78	7.11	-55.19	46.83	32,550
Guangxi 广西	3	98	6,650	112	3.08	16.36	21.65	81.18	3,649
Hainan 海南									
Southwest 西南	3	153	18,998	-149	-0.23	-0.86	22.79	73.05	63,948
Chongqing 重庆	1	42	3,022	15	0.21	20.27	13.62	98.96	7,089
Sichuan 四川	1	369	33,646	-857	-0.89	-3.68	6.83	75.75	95,969
Guizhou 贵州									
Yunnan 云南	1	47	20,325	395	0.44	1.39	156.21	68.06	88,787
Tibet 西藏									
Northwest 西北	1	1,564	97,495	245	0.07	0.12	21.52	38.48	332,712
Shaanxi 陕西	1	1,564	97,495	245	0.07	0.12	21.52	38.48	332,712
Gansu 甘肃									
Qinghai 青海									
Ningxia 宁夏									
Xinjiang 新疆									

3619: Other Special Electromechanical Equipment

其他机电工业专用设备制造业

Year 年份	Number of firms 企业个数	Rate of change 变化率 (%)	Number of employees 职工人数 (人)	Rate of change 变化率 (%)	Total revenue (Mil. RMB) 总销售收入 (百万元)	Rate of change 变化率 (%)	Total profit (Mil RMB) 总利润 (百万元)	Rate of change 变化率 (%)
2000	108		20,226		2,117		129	
2001	114	5.56	17,722	-12.38	2,720	28.48	155	20.16
2002	91	-20.18	13,913	-21.49	2,611	-4.01	251	61.94

Major Products 主要产品	Output 产量	Unit 单位
Feeding Machinery 给料机械	6,888	Unit 台
Conveying Machinery 输送机械	72	10,000 Meters 万米

10 Main Firms with Maximal Revenue (year founded) 收入最大的十家主要企业（创办年份）	City 城市	Province 省	Telephone/fax 电话/传真	Number of employees 职工人数	Ownership 产业所有权	Revenue ('000 RMB) 销售收入 (千元)	Profit('000 RMB) (rank) 利润(千元) (排名)	Total assets ('000 RMB) 总资产 (千元)	Major products 主要产品
Mitsubishi Electric Dalian Mechinery Co.,Ltd.	Dalian	Liaoning	(0411)7613073		Foreign Funded				Discharge Processing Machine
三菱电机大连机器有限公司(1994)	大连市	辽宁省	(0411)7613007	525	外商投资	389,249	62,661(2)	340,773	放电加工机
Beijing-Fanuc Mech Co., ltd.	Beijing	Beijing	(010)62985923		Foreign Funded				Numerical Control System
北京发那科机电有限公司(1993)	北京市	北京市	(010)62984741	100	外商投资	380,934	108,345(1)	293,801	数控系统
Siemens Factory Automation Engineering Co., Ltd.	Beijing	Beijing	(010)64610005		Foreign Funded				Electric Tank
西门子工厂自动化工程有限公司(1993)	北京市	北京市	(010)64632976	257	外商投资	195,547	14,370(3)	122,732	电柜
Copartner Electric Wire & Cable (Shenzhen) MFG Co.,Ltd.	Shenzhen	Guangdong	(0755)27312988		Overseas Chinese-funded				Electric Wire & Cable
联颖电线电缆（深圳）有限公司(1993)	深圳市	广东省	(0755)27312681	528	港澳台资	136,926	7,463(5)	144,109	电线电缆
Nanjing Hengfengyuan Industrial Co., Ltd.	Nanjing	Jiangsu	(025)2890666		Private Owned				Drawbench Whole Set Equipment
南京恒丰园实业有限责任公司(1996)	南京市	江苏省		171	私营企业	111,030	660(29)	15,940	拉丝机成套设备
Xi'an Nuclear Equipment Manufactring Co.,Ltd.	Xi'an	Shannxi	(029)6158888		State Enterprises				Store Jar Series
西安核设备有限公司(1970)	西安市	陕西省	(029)6158398	1,564	国有独资	97,495	245(47)	332,712	贮罐系列
Suzhou Xinzhi Electromechanical Industry Co., Ltd.	Suzhou	Jiangsu	(0512)66363920		Foreign Funded				Electromechanical Equipment
苏州新智机电工业有限公司(1995)	苏州市	江苏省	(0512)66261353	105	外商投资	39,480	2,110(16)	46,630	机电设备
Beijing MECC Hydraulic Co.,ltd.	Beijing	Beijing	(010)69277416		Limited-Liability				Hydraulic Pressure Equipment
北京中冶迈克液压有限责任公司(1995)	北京市	北京市	(010)67155550	210	有限公司	37,624	564(32)	19,898	液压设备
Wujiang Jinxiao Air conditioning Purification Co., Ltd	Suzhou	Jiangsu	(0512)63203222		Private Owned				Colored Steel Sheet
吴江市金晓空调净化有限公司(1994)	苏州市	江苏省	(0512)63202714	140	私营企业	35,840	716(28)	36,851	彩钢板
Hunan Electric Power Equipment General Factory	Zhuzhou	Hunan	(0733)8468007		State-owned				Oil Isolation Pump
湖南省电力设备总厂(1958)	株洲市	湖南省	(0733)8468000	434	国有企业	33,498	-	77,004	油隔离泵

Top 10 Cities by Revenue 销售收入排名前10位城市	Province 省	Market share 市场份额 (%)	Number of firms 企业个数
Beijing 北京市	Beijing 北京市	25.44	9
Dalian 大连市	Liaoning 辽宁省	16.48	3
Wuxi 无锡市	Jiangsu 江苏省	9.11	11
Nanjing 南京市	Jiangsu 江苏省	5.42	3
Shenzhen 深圳市	Guangdong 广东省	5.24	1
Suzhou 苏州市	Jiangsu 江苏省	4.45	5
Xi'an 西安市	Shannxi 陕西省	3.73	1
Guangzhou 广州市	Guangdong 广东省	2.58	4
Huaian 淮安市	Jiangsu 江苏省	2.22	3
Yantai 烟台市	Shandong 山东省	2.09	2

10 Major Wholesalers 十家主要批发商	City 城市	Province 省	Telephone/Fax 电话/传真
SU MEC	Nanjing	Jiangsu	(025)4511888
中设江苏机械设备进出口（集团）公司	南京市	江苏省	(025)4411772
China Poster Mobile Communications Equipment Co.,Ltd.	Beijing	Beijing	(010)66426993
中邮普泰移动通信设备股份有限公司	北京市	北京市	(010)66426837
Sino Kama Co., Ltd.	Shanghai	Shanghai	(021)62031188
中泰凯马股份有限公司	上海市	上海市	(021)62030851
China Huayuan Group Co.,Ltd.	Shanghai	Shanghai	(021)62031188
中国华源集团有限公司	上海市	上海市	(021)62032288
Zhejiang Crand Imp.& Exp.Co.,Ltd.	Ningbo	Zhejiang	(0574)87720170
浙江远大进出口有限公司	宁波市	浙江省	(0574)87723350
Shandong Machinery Import & Export Group Corporation	Qingdao	Shandong	(0532)2661628
山东省机械进出口集团公司	青岛市	山东省	(0532)2991655
Qingdao Haier International Trade Co.,Ltd.	Qingdao	Shandong	(0532)8938337
青岛海尔国际贸易有限公司	青岛市	山东省	(0532)8939494
Guangdong Machinery Import & Export Group Corporation	Guangzhou	Guangdong	(020)87782168
广东省机械进出口集团公司	广州市	广东省	(020)87771803
China National Machinery Equipment Import & Export Corporation	Beijing	Beijing	(010)63474506
中国机械设备进出口总公司	北京市	北京市	(010)63261865
Beijing Cellstar Co.,Ltd.	Beijing	Beijing	(010)64602050
北京蜂星事达电讯有限公司	北京市	北京市	(010)64672648

3621: Petroleum Special Equipment 石油工业专用设备制造业

The industry accounts for 0.100% of the total revenue of China's industrial sector in 2002. The rate of return on assets is 3.32%. 78.90% of all firms in the industry made a profit while 21.10% had negative returns.The top province in terms of the industry's revenue is Hubei, accounting for 16.65% of the total revenue.
2002年本行业收入占全行业的 0.100%，资产利润率为 3.32%。78.90%的企业赢利，21.10%的企业亏损。收入最高的省为湖北省，占本行业的16.65%。

	Total number of firms 企业总数	Total number of employees 职工总数	Total revenue (Mil.RMB) 总销售收入（百万元）	Total profit (Mil.RMB) 总利润（百万元）	Return on assets 资产利润率（%）	Return on equity 权益利润率（%）	Labour productivity ('000 RMB/ worker) 劳动生产率（千元/人）	Debts/ assets 资产负债率（%）	Total assets (Mil.RMB) 总资产（百万元）
Industry Overall 行业总体	218	80,405	10,721	558	3.32	8.46	41.66	60.75	16,815

	Number of firms 企业个数	Average number of employees 平均职工人数	Average revenue ('000 RMB) 平均销售收入（千元）	Average profit ('000 RMB) 平均利润（千元）	Return on assets 资产利润率（%）	Return on equity 权益利润率（%）	Labour productivity ('000 RMB/ worker) 劳动生产率（千元/人）	Debts/ assets 资产负债率（%）	Average total assets ('000 RMB) 平均总资产（千元）
By ownership 产业所有权									
State-owned 国有	43	756	67,645	-2,236	-1.43	-4.12	28.34	65.22	155,932
Collective-owned 集体	32	209	39,266	3,716	10.77	21.83	61.73	50.67	34,502
Foreign & Overseas Chinese Funded 三资	20	201	69,120	11,841	11.51	19.40	105.38	40.64	102,850
By regional distribution 地区分布									
Central-North 华北	36	268	60,047	5,850	7.27	16.74	69.75	56.60	80,514
Beijing 北京	6	205	49,941	6,094	8.19	17.48	90.36	53.13	74,369
Tianjin 天津	9	223	61,843	11,921	19.87	44.97	79.18	55.80	59,984
Hebei 河北	19	256	62,584	3,505	4.07	8.35	76.47	51.26	86,108
Shanxi 山西	2	773	58,186	70	0.05	1.08	19.99	95.35	138,186
Inner Mongolia 内蒙古									
Northeast 东北	47	227	21,036	578	1.20	3.87	28.75	69.04	48,299
Liaoning 辽宁	18	304	27,863	-661	-0.83	-3.19	26.81	73.88	79,312
Jilin 吉林	12	317	19,064	469	1.37	4.65	19.80	70.56	34,273
Heilongjiang 黑龙江	17	83	15,200	1,968	7.76	16.02	60.39	51.55	25,362
Central-East 华东	64	214	34,337	2,710	6.52	17.15	45.89	61.99	41,584
Shanghai 上海	8	135	26,508	-52	-0.12	-0.50	49.77	76.07	43,721
Jiangsu 江苏	33	199	41,325	4,519	10.95	24.61	62.47	55.51	41,272
Zhejiang 浙江	6	154	16,504	1,175	4.84	19.40	36.79	75.05	24,274
Anhui 安徽									
Fujian 福建									
Jiangxi 江西	2	877	26,401	-1,039	-1.27	-5.91	12.90	78.50	81,745
Shandong 山东	15	227	31,329	1,319	3.09	7.90	32.21	60.91	42,701
Central-South 中南	27	517	98,084	3,319	4.31	7.45	68.46	42.10	76,932
Henan 河南	10	294	55,526	1,187	2.96	7.18	143.51	58.76	40,083
Hubei 湖北	12	739	148,743	5,475	5.52	7.51	51.63	26.50	99,229
Hunan 湖南									
Guangdong 广东	5	431	61,619	2,410	2.48	7.43	35.46	66.61	97,116
Guangxi 广西									
Hainan 海南									
Southwest 西南	14	389	50,742	3,104	5.70	19.55	47.41	70.83	54,435
Chongqing 重庆	3	287	15,508	-1,970	-7.58	-23.97	6.06	68.37	25,976
Sichuan 四川	9	363	69,079	5,487	8.48	33.30	72.85	74.52	64,676
Guizhou 贵州	1	1,274	41,310	10	0.01	0.02	11.67	50.60	99,290
Yunnan 云南	1	42	840	-25	-0.89	-8.28	0.88	89.20	2,796
Tibet 西藏									
Northwest 西北	30	898	67,133	469	0.23	0.64	19.53	64.15	204,853
Shaanxi 陕西	14	336	51,188	1,329	1.64	16.97	50.56	90.37	81,267
Gansu 甘肃	13	1,655	92,190	-1,072	-0.29	-0.69	12.12	57.98	370,068
Qinghai 青海									
Ningxia 宁夏									
Xinjiang 新疆	3	242	32,957	3,134	4.77	13.01	37.88	63.31	65,656

3621: Petroleum Special Equipment 石油工业专用设备制造业

Year 年份	Number of firms 企业个数	Rate of change 变化率 (%)	Number of employees 职工人数 (人)	Rate of change 变化率 (%)	Total revenue (Mil. RMB) 总销售收入 (百万元)	Rate of change 变化率 (%)	Total profit (Mil RMB) 总利润 (百万元)	Rate of change 变化率 (%)
2000	193		97,719		5,966		77	
2001	219	13.47	79,530	-18.61	8,434	41.37	424	450.65
2002	218	-0.46	80,405	1.10	10,721	27.12	558	31.60

Major Products 主要产品	Output 产量	Unit 单位
Drilling & Mining Equipment for Oil 石油钻采设备	174,460	Ton 吨
Refining Equipment 炼油设备	38,991	Ton 吨

10 Main Firms with Maximal Revenue (year founded) 收入最大的十家主要企业（创办年份）	City 城市	Province 省	Telephone/fax 电话/传真	Number of employees 职工人数	Ownership 产业所有权	Revenue ('000 RMB) 销售收入 (千元)	Profit('000 RMB) (rank) 利润(千元) (排名)	Total assets ('000 RMB) 总资产 (千元)	Major products 主要产品
Hubei Zhensheng (Group) Co., Ltd.	Jingzhou	Hubei	(0716)2204198		Joint Stock				Pressure Container
湖北振声（集团）股份有限公司(1997)	荆州市	湖北省	(0716)2872002	3,392	股份制	810,910	57,175(4)	325,680	压力容器
SINOPEC Jingmen Petrochemistry General Factory	Jingmen	Hubei	(0724)2211501		State-owned				Petroleum Equipment Servicing 石油
中国石化集团荆门石化总厂(1970)	荆门市	湖北省		4,054	国有企业	794,256	10(150)	693,247	设备维修
Baoji Petroleum Machinery Co.,Ltd.	Baoji	Shannxi	(0917)3215599		State-owned				Drilling & Oil Extraction Equipment 石油
宝鸡石油机械有限责任公司(1938)	宝鸡市	陕西省	(0917)3213839	2,871	国有企业	601,539	20,141(10)	946,731	钻采设备
Lanzhou Lanshi National Oil Wall Petroleum Engineering	Lanzhou	Gansu	(0931)2350029		Foreign Funded				Drilling & Oil Extraction Equipment 石油
Co., Ltd.兰州兰石国民油井石油工程有限公司(2001)	兰州市	甘肃省	(0931)2350029	1,163	外商投资	457,487	122,511(1)	486,793	钻采设备
Tianjin Rongheng Group Co.,Ltd	Tianjin	Tianjin	(022)69192201		Joint Stock				Pump Products
天津市荣亨集团股份有限公司(1983)	天津市	天津市	(022)69192201	960	股份制	371,420	60,630(3)	233,820	泵类产品
Lanzhou Petrolem & Chemical Machinery General Works	Lanzhou	Gansu	(0931)2336277		Limited-Liability				Drilling & Mining Equipment
兰州石油化工机器总厂(1958)	兰州市	甘肃省	(0931)2339794	6,185	有限公司	277,433	-	1,442,894	钻采设备
OCTG Steel Tube Co., Ltd.	Cangzhou	Hebei	(0317)2571059		Overseas Chinese-funded				Screwed Weld Steel Pipe 螺
华油钢管有限公司(2001)	沧州市	河北省	(0317)4125333	785	港澳台资	251,292	23,756(9)	399,765	旋焊钢管
Bobai NKK Drill Pipe Co.,Ltd.	Cangzhou	Hebei	(0317)2571931		Foreign Funded				Drill Stem
渤海能克钻杆有限公司(1997)	沧州市	河北省	(0317)4028121	187	外商投资	185,018	34,284(5)	257,298	钻杆
PetroChina Lanzhou Oil Refining Chemical Industry General	Lanzhou	Gansu	(0931)7935114		State-owned				Oil Refining Equipment
Factory 中国石油天然气集团公司兰州炼油化工总厂(1958)	兰州市	甘肃省	(0931)7932503	7,983	国有企业	156,940	-	2,120,170	炼化设备
Gansu Lanke Petroleum Chemical Equipment Co.,Ltd.	Lanzhou	Gansu	(0931)2337150		Collective-owned				Oil Refining Equipment
甘肃蓝科石化设备有限责任公司(1995)	兰州市	甘肃省	(0931)7663346	490	集体企业	126,620	5,835(29)	61,627	炼油设备

Top 10 Cities by Revenue 销售收入排名前10位城市	Province 省	Market share 市场份额 (%)	Number of firms 企业个数
Lanzhou 兰州市	Gansu 甘肃省	11.09	11
Jingzhou 荆州市	Hubei 湖北省	8.98	4
Jingmen 荆门市	Hubei 湖北省	7.41	1
Cangzhou 沧州市	Hebei 河北省	5.95	7
Baoji 宝鸡市	Shannxi 陕西省	5.86	5
Deyang 德阳市	Sichuan 四川省	5.30	6
Tianjin 天津市	Tianjin 天津市	5.19	9
Taizhou 泰州市	Jiangsu 江苏省	5.08	2
Puyang 濮阳市	Henan 河南省	3.11	3
Beijing 北京市	Beijing 北京市	2.80	6

10 Major Wholesalers 十家主要批发商	City 城市	Province 省	Telephone/Fax 电话/传真
SU MEC	Nanjing	Jiangsu	(025)4511888
中设江苏机械设备进出口（集团）公司	南京市	江苏省	(025)4411772
China Poster Mobile Communications Equipment Co.,Ltd.	Beijing	Beijing	(010)66426993
中邮普泰移动通信设备股份有限公司	北京市	北京市	(010)66426837
Sino Kama Co., Ltd.	Shanghai	Shanghai	(021)62031188
中泰凯马股份有限公司	上海市	上海市	(021)62030851
China Huayuan Group Co.,Ltd.	Shanghai	Shanghai	(021)62031188
中国华源集团有限公司	上海市	上海市	(021)62032288
Zhejiang Crand Imp.& Exp.Co.,Ltd.	Ningbo	Zhejiang	(0574)87720170
浙江远大进出口有限公司	宁波市	浙江省	(0574)87723350
Shandong Machinery Import & Export Group Corporation	Qingdao	Shandong	(0532)2661628
山东省机械进出口集团公司	青岛市	山东省	(0532)2991655
Qingdao Haier International Trade Co.,Ltd.	Qingdao	Shandong	(0532)8938337
青岛海尔国际贸易有限公司	青岛市	山东省	(0532)8939494
Guangdong Machinery Import & Export Group Corporation	Guangzhou	Guangdong	(020)87782168
广东省机械进出口集团公司	广州市	广东省	(020)87771803
China National Machinery Equipment Import & Export Corporation	Beijing	Beijing	(010)63474506
中国机械设备进出口总公司	北京市	北京市	(010)63261865
Beijing Cellstar Co.,Ltd.	Beijing	Beijing	(010)64602050
北京蜂星事达电讯有限公司	北京市	北京市	(010)64672648

3622: Chemical Equipment 化学工业专用设备制造业

The industry accounts for 0.045% of the total revenue of China's industrial sector in 2002. The rate of return on assets is 1.01%. 72.12% of all firms in the industry made a profit while 27.88% had negative returns.The top province in terms of the industry's revenue is Jiangsu, accounting for 22.06% of the total revenue.
2002年本行业收入占全行业的0.045%，资产利润率为1.01%。72.12%的企业赢利，27.88%的企业亏损。收入最高的省为江苏省，占本行业的22.06%。

	Total number of firms 企业总数	Total number of employees 职工总数	Total revenue (Mil.RMB) 总销售收入（百万元）	Total profit (Mil.RMB) 总利润（百万元）	Return on assets 资产利润率（%）	Return on equity 权益利润率（%）	Labour productivity ('000 RMB/ worker) 劳动生产率（千元/人）	Debts/ assets 资产负债率（%）	Total assets (Mil.RMB) 总资产（百万元）
Industry Overall 行业总体	208	49,709	4,789	89	1.01	3.67	30.07	72.51	8,856

	Number of firms 企业个数	Average number of employees 平均职工人数	Average revenue ('000 RMB) 平均销售收入（千元）	Average profit ('000 RMB) 平均利润（千元）	Return on assets 资产利润率（%）	Return on equity 权益利润率（%）	Labour productivity ('000 RMB/ worker) 劳动生产率（千元/人）	Debts/ assets 资产负债率（%）	Average total assets ('000 RMB) 平均总资产（千元）
By ownership 产业所有权									
State-owned 国有	50	445	17,233	-2,756	-3.78	-23.31	11.15	83.77	72,828
Collective-owned 集体	37	155	30,570	1,358	7.72	24.74	64.82	68.82	17,598
Foreign & Overseas Chinese Funded 三资	14	63	22,161	938	4.01	8.08	86.70	50.41	23,391
By regional distribution 地区分布									
Central-North 华北	35	272	19,766	-319	-0.47	-1.89	20.71	75.09	67,781
Beijing 北京	8	444	29,182	-425	-0.24	-0.88	26.08	73.08	178,288
Tianjin 天津	14	127	12,292	389	2.44	5.53	19.56	55.85	15,924
Hebei 河北	11	241	21,956	358	0.81	4.53	22.92	82.17	44,352
Shanxi 山西	2	774	22,367	-8,578	-7.29	-79.46	5.93	90.82	117,619
Inner Mongolia 内蒙古									
Northeast 东北	20	398	41,030	86	0.10	0.38	30.42	74.13	87,804
Liaoning 辽宁	16	435	45,950	1,424	1.43	5.20	31.67	72.58	99,848
Jilin 吉林	3	32	890	-1	-0.04	-18.18	10.54	99.77	3,229
Heilongjiang 黑龙江	1	909	82,738	-21,055	-14.15	-130.27	23.02	89.14	148,823
Central-East 华东	100	153	25,304	1,408	4.92	13.10	52.79	62.45	28,626
Shanghai 上海	14	161	19,581	-722	-1.84	-5.90	49.28	68.78	39,166
Jiangsu 江苏	47	149	22,479	2,003	8.36	23.39	47.64	64.26	23,967
Zhejiang 浙江	19	76	8,933	265	2.19	5.57	31.23	60.60	12,071
Anhui 安徽	4	235	16,889	1,001	3.52	8.47	27.33	58.50	28,449
Fujian 福建	1	664	70,061	6,630	1.77	4.03	17.93	56.19	375,610
Jiangxi 江西	1	182	48,395	953	4.78	5.31	22.18	10.03	19,941
Shandong 山东	14	201	60,288	2,868	8.94	22.20	98.30	59.72	32,080
Central-South 中南	37	296	14,648	-495	-1.49	-6.04	16.12	75.30	33,215
Henan 河南	13	398	15,474	-83	-0.38	-1.20	12.80	68.49	22,100
Hubei 湖北	8	151	7,404	10	0.06	0.40	15.70	84.04	14,981
Hunan 湖南	7	443	13,513	-1,816	-2.85	-15.94	9.35	82.15	63,802
Guangdong 广东	8	155	23,371	-320	-0.76	-2.42	50.75	68.53	42,042
Guangxi 广西	1	210		-2,049	-5.27	-24.75	-3.35	78.70	38,871
Hainan 海南									
Southwest 西南	11	386	18,094	-1,439	-4.18		17.20	105.91	34,382
Chongqing 重庆	2	294	12,879	-2,260	-6.00		21.32	103.08	37,686
Sichuan 四川	7	459	21,675	-1,583	-5.27		17.04	128.86	30,022
Guizhou 贵州									
Yunnan 云南	1	423	21,072	-227	-0.25	-0.57	13.55	55.96	91,198
Tibet 西藏	1	21	484				0.48	70.10	1,485
Northwest 西北	5	346	1,088	-1,586	-3.08	-24.00	-1.38	87.18	51,549
Shaanxi 陕西	3	213	828	-196	-0.93	-8.44	-8.28	89.00	21,117
Gansu 甘肃	2	547	1,479	-3,671	-3.78	-28.15	2.65	86.59	97,197
Qinghai 青海									
Ningxia 宁夏									
Xinjiang 新疆									

Year 年份	Number of firms 企业个数	Rate of change 变化率(%)	Number of employees 职工人数(人)	Rate of change 变化率(%)	Total revenue (Mil. RMB) 总销售收入(百万元)	Rate of change 变化率(%)	Total profit (Mil RMB) 总利润(百万元)	Rate of change 变化率(%)
2000	210		65,176		4,166		-32	
2001	209	-0.48	56,315	-13.60	4,301	3.24	23	-
2002	208	-0.48	49,709	-11.73	4,789	11.35	89	286.96

Major Products 主要产品	Output 产量	Unit 单位
Chemical Equipment 化工设备	203,701	Ton 吨

10 Main Firms with Maximal Revenue (year founded) 收入最大的十家主要企业（创办年份）	City 城市	Province 省	Telephone/fax 电话/传真	Number of employees 职工人数	Ownership 产业所有权	Revenue ('000 RMB) 销售收入(千元)	Profit('000 RMB) (rank) 利润(千元)(排名)	Total assets ('000 RMB) 总资产(千元)	Major products 主要产品
Zibo Chemical Equipment Plant 淄博市化工设备厂(1977)	Zibo 淄博市	Shandong 山东省	(0533)2980280 (0533)2980710	300	Collective-owned 集体企业	273,560	12,340(4)	56,220	Glass Lining Retort玻璃反应罐
Jinxi Chemical Machinery(Group) Co.,Ltd. 锦西化工机械（集团）有限责任公司(1939)	Huludao 葫芦岛市	Liaoning 辽宁省	(0429)2980409 (0429)2980551	3,233	Limited-Liability 有限公司	193,177	3,358(16)	771,255	Oil Refining Equipment炼油化工设备
Alfa Laval Plate Heat Exchanger Co.Ltd. 阿法拉伐板式换热器有限公司(1993)	Wuxi 无锡市	Jiangsu 江苏省	(0510)6561280 (0510)6561600	161	Private Partnership 私营合伙	160,840	74,530(1)	173,320	Patch Heater,Band Heater热片、热圈
Beijing Chemical Industry Machinery Factory 北京化工机械厂(1966)	Beijing 北京市	Beijing 北京市	(010)67712634 (010)67749829	1,535	State-owned 国有企业	143,077	197(93)	567,545	Chemical Equipment 化工设备
Anshan Chemical Equipment Manufacturing Co.,ltd. 鞍山市化工设备制造有限公司(1993)	Anshan 鞍山市	Liaoning 辽宁省	(0412)8920892 (0412)8921881	103	Collective-owned 集体企业	87,800	7,960(6)	37,740	Chemical Equipment 化工设备
Daqing Petrochemical Machinery Factory 大庆石油化工机械厂(2002)	Daqing 大庆市	Heilongjiang 黑龙江省	(0459)6759237 (0459)6243363	909	State-owned 国有企业	82,738	-	148,823	Oil Refining Equipment 炼化设备
Xin'ao Group Shijiazhuang Chemical Industry Machinery Co., Ltd.新奥集团石家庄化工机械股份有限公司(1970)	Shijiazhuang 石家庄市	Hebei 河北省	(0311)7776901 (0311)7753981	740	Joint Stock 股份制	77,489	442(71)	111,407	Liquefaction Gas Welds Steel Bottle液化气体焊接钢瓶
Zibo Taiji Industry Enamel Co.,Ltd. 淄博太极工业搪瓷有限公司(1995)	Zibo 淄博市	Shandong 山东省	(0533)2837618 (0533)2837619	320	Private Owned 私营企业	70,540	4,610(10)	20,740	Chemical Equipment & Parts化工设备及配件
Nanjing Petroleum Chemical Equipment Repair & Making Factory 南京石油化工设备修造厂(1991)	Nanjing 南京市	Jiangsu 江苏省	(025)2412555 (025)2411935	260	Joint Owned 联营企业	59,850	3,390(15)	8,680	Chemical Equipment 化工设备
Yangzhou Jinyuan Chemical Industry Environment Protecting Equipment General Factory 扬州金圆化工环保设备总厂(1986)	Yangzhou 扬州市	Jiangsu 江苏省	(0514)7233546 (0514)7212081	292	Private Enterprises 私营独资	58,870	1,641(25)	55,010	Aluminium Mould Electric Mist Eliminator铝塑电除雾器

Top 10 Cities by Revenue 销售收入排名前10位城市	Province 省	Market share 市场份额(%)	Number of firms 企业个数
Zibo 淄博市	Shandong 山东省	14.84	8
Wuxi 无锡市	Jiangsu 江苏省	8.71	20
Panjin 盘锦市	Liaoning 辽宁省	6.56	2
Shanghai 上海市	Shanghai 上海市	5.72	14
Beijing 北京市	Beijing 北京市	4.87	8
Yangzhou 扬州市	Jiangsu 江苏省	4.30	4
Huludao 葫芦岛市	Liaoning 辽宁省	4.14	2
Tianjin 天津市	Tianjin 天津市	3.59	14
Chengdu 成都市	Sichuan 四川省	2.56	5
Nanjing 南京市	Jiangsu 江苏省	2.35	5

10 Major Wholesalers 十家主要批发商	City 城市	Province 省	Telephone/Fax 电话/传真
SU MEC 中设江苏机械设备进出口（集团）公司	Nanjing 南京市	Jiangsu 江苏省	(025)4511888 (025)4411772
China Poster Mobile Communications Equipment Co.,Ltd. 中邮普泰移动通信设备股份有限公司	Beijing 北京市	Beijing 北京市	(010)66426993 (010)66426837
Sino Kama Co., Ltd. 中泰凯马股份有限公司	Shanghai 上海市	Shanghai 上海市	(021)62031188 (021)62030851
China Huayuan Group Co.,Ltd. 中国华源集团有限公司	Shanghai 上海市	Shanghai 上海市	(021)62031188 (021)62032288
Zhejiang Crand Imp.& Exp.Co.,Ltd. 浙江远大进出口有限公司	Ningbo 宁波市	Zhejiang 浙江省	(0574)87720170 (0574)87723350
Shandong Machinery Import & Export Group Corporation 山东省机械进出口集团公司	Qingdao 青岛市	Shandong 山东省	(0532)2661628 (0532)2991655
Qingdao Haier International Trade Co.,Ltd. 青岛海尔国际贸易有限公司	Qingdao 青岛市	Shandong 山东省	(0532)8938337 (0532)8939494
Guangdong Machinery Import & Export Group Corporation 广东省机械进出口集团公司	Guangzhou 广州市	Guangdong 广东省	(020)87782168 (020)87771803
China National Machinery Equipment Import & Export Corporation 中国机械设备进出口总公司	Beijing 北京市	Beijing 北京市	(010)63474506 (010)63261865
Beijing Cellstar Co.,Ltd. 北京蜂星事达电讯有限公司	Beijing 北京市	Beijing 北京市	(010)64602050 (010)64672648

3623: Special Chemical Fibre Equipment

化学纤维工业专用设备制造业

The industry accounts for 0.008% of the total revenue of China's industrial sector in 2002. The rate of return on assets is 1.60%. 80.65% of all firms in the industry made a profit while 19.35% had negative returns.The top province in terms of the industry's revenue is Jiangsu, accounting for 35.12% of the total revenue.
2002年本行业收入占全行业的 0.008%，资产利润率为 1.60%。80.65%的企业赢利，19.35%的企业亏损。收入最高的省为江苏省，占本行业的35.12%。

	Total number of firms 企业总数	Totai number of employees 职工总数	Total revenue (Mil.RMB) 总销售收入 (百万元)	Total profit (Mil.RMB) 总利润 (百万元)	Return on assets 资产利润率 (%)	Return on equity 权益利润率 (%)	Labour productivity ('000 RMB/ worker) 劳动生产率 (千元/人)	Debts/ assets 资产负债率 (%)	Total assets (Mil.RMB) 总资产 (百万元)
Industry Overall 行业总体	31	3,637	824	16	1.60	5.60	48.16	71.45	1,020

	Number of firms 企业个数	Average number of employees 平均职工人数	Average revenue ('000 RMB) 平均销售收入 (千元)	Average profit ('000 RMB) 平均利润 (千元)	Return on assets 资产利润率 (%)	Return on equity 权益利润率 (%)	Labour productivity ('000 RMB/ worker) 劳动生产率 (千元/人)	Debts/ assets 资产负债率 (%)	Average total assets ('000 RMB) 平均总资产 (千元)
By ownership 产业所有权									
State-owned 国有	4	90	21,752	138	0.48	3.86	23.99	87.66	28,925
Collective-owned 集体	2	163	16,831	-5,133	-17.77	-75.16	5.18	76.35	28,878
Foreign & Overseas Chinese Funded 三资	5	65	27,763	2,319	8.01	27.98	60.09	71.37	28,950
By regional distribution 地区分布									
Central-North 华北	7	90	34,340	3,056	6.98	16.38	82.75	57.37	43,758
Beijing 北京	6	57	24,070	2,342	7.45	16.07	62.42	53.62	31,422
Tianjin 天津									
Hebei 河北	1	285	95,964	7,339	6.23	17.02	107.22	63.38	117,774
Shanxi 山西									
Inner Mongolia 内蒙古									
Northeast 东北	4	126	31,722	-1,741	-4.36	-30.63	26.99	85.76	39,905
Liaoning 辽宁	4	126	31,722	-1,741	-4.36	-30.63	26.99	85.76	39,905
Jilin 吉林									
Heilongjiang 黑龙江									
Central-East 华东	16	136	21,615	30	0.09	0.47	38.73	79.68	31,681
Shanghai 上海									
Jiangsu 江苏	12	153	24,107	-672	-1.87	-12.58	36.52	85.10	35,819
Zhejiang 浙江	4	85	14,139	2,135	11.08	21.93	50.70	49.46	19,266
Anhui 安徽									
Fujian 福建									
Jiangxi 江西									
Shandong 山东									
Central-South 中南	3	61	36,767	628	5.70	6.12	137.59	6.84	11,015
Henan 河南	2	55	24,580	749	7.89	7.89	56.69		9,493
Hubei 湖北									
Hunan 湖南									
Guangdong 广东	1	75	61,140	386	2.75	3.27	255.17	16.07	14,060
Guangxi 广西									
Hainan 海南									
Southwest 西南	1	148	346	-501	-3.66	-12.55	0.55	70.82	13,682
Chongqing 重庆									
Sichuan 四川	1	148	346	-501	-3.66	-12.55	0.55	70.82	13,682
Guizhou 贵州									
Yunnan 云南									
Tibet 西藏									
Northwest 西北									
Shaanxi 陕西									
Gansu 甘肃									
Qinghai 青海									
Ningxia 宁夏									
Xinjiang 新疆									

3623: Special Chemical Fibre Equipment
化学纤维工业专用设备制造业

Year 年份	Number of firms 企业个数	Rate of change 变化率 (%)	Number of employees 职工人数 (人)	Rate of change 变化率 (%)	Total revenue (Mil. RMB) 总销售收入 (百万元)	Rate of change 变化率 (%)	Total profit (Mil RMB) 总利润 (百万元)	Rate of change 变化率 (%)
2000	15		4,850		719		23	
2001	20	33.33	4,107	-15.32	621	-13.63	45	95.65
2002	31	55.00	3,637	-11.44	824	32.69	16	-64.44

Major Products 主要产品	Output 产量	Unit 单位

10 Main Firms with Maximal Revenue (year founded) 收入最大的十家主要企业（创办年份）	City 城市	Province 省	Telephone/fax 电话/传真	Number of employees 职工人数	Ownership 产业所有权	Revenue ('000 RMB) 销售收入 (千元)	Profit('000 RMB) (rank) 利润(千元) (排名)	Total assets ('000 RMB) 总资产 (千元)	Major products 主要产品
Dalian High & New Garden Synthetic Fibre Installation Center 大连高新园区合成纤维特种装备中心(2000)	Dalian 大连市	Liaoning 辽宁省	(0411)4601071	140	State-owned 国有企业	82,753	1,033(10)	93,116	Chemical Fibre Equipment 化纤设备
Zhangjiagang Chemical Industry Machinery Co., Ltd. 张家港市化工机械有限公司(1998)	Suzhou 苏州市	Jiangsu 江苏省	(0512)58771511 (0512)58770850	435	Limited-Liability 有限公司	70,258	3,240(5)	135,754	Vacuum Drying Machine 真空干燥机
Puning Zhanlong Qiusheng Chemical Fibre Co., Ltd. 普宁市占陇秋盛化纤有限公司(2000)	Jieyang 揭阳市	Guangdong 广东省	(0663)2342004 (0663)2338004	75	Private Partnership 私营合伙	61,140	386(14)	14,060	Chemical Fibre Equipment 化纤设备
Beijing Zhongli Chemical Fibre Machinery Co.,Ltd. 北京中丽化纤机械有限公司(1995)	Beijing 北京市	Beijing 北京市	(010)65927110 (010)65927112	77	Foreign Funded 外商投资	55,071	312(16)	49,710	Terylene FDY Series 涤纶FDY系列
Beijing Bamage Machinery Co.,Ltd. 北京巴马格机械有限公司(1992)	Beijing 北京市	Beijing 北京市	(010)65302128 (010)65019014	80	Overseas Chinese-funded 港澳台资	52,669	10,292(1)	58,857	Mechanical Equipment 机械设备
Zhangjiagang Gangying Industrial Co., Ltd. 张家港市港鹰实业有限公司(1958)	Suzhou 苏州市	Jiangsu 江苏省	(0512)58741072 (0512)58982012	542	Private Owned 私营企业	47,803	-	123,626	Synthetic Fibre Equipment 合成纤维设备
Changshu Feilong Non-woven Equipment Co., Ltd. 常熟市飞龙无纺设备有限公司(1997)	Suzhou 苏州市	Jiangsu 江苏省	(0512)52585179 (0512)52583888	182	Private Owned 私营企业	38,698	-	37,953	Non-woven Mechanical Equipment 无纺机械设备
Ninghai Precision Industry Machinery Factory 宁海县精工机械厂(1999)	Ningbo 宁波市	Zhejiang 浙江省	(0574)65198067 (0574)65198899	198	Private Enterprises 私营独资	31,757	3,898(4)	48,666	Chemical Fibre Special Equipment 化学纤维专用设备
Zhangjiagang Yili Machinery Co., Ltd. 张家港亿利机械有限公司(1990)	Suzhou 苏州市	Jiangsu 江苏省	(0512)58578518 (0512)58570805	73	Private Owned 私营企业	21,729	619(11)	22,945	Plastic Processing Machine 塑机
Changshu Chemical Fibre Equipment Factory 常熟市化纤设备厂(1952)	Suzhou 苏州市	Jiangsu 江苏省	(0512)52671662 (0512)52671340	120	Joint Stock 股份制	14,839	97(20)	10,731	Chemical Fibre Equipment 化纤设备

Top 10 Cities by Revenue 销售收入排名前10位城市	Province 省	Market share 市场份额 (%)	Number of firms 企业个数
Suzhou 苏州市	Jiangsu 江苏省	33.13	11
Beijing 北京市	Beijing 北京市	17.53	6
Dalian 大连市	Liaoning 辽宁省	14.32	3
Langfang 廊坊市	Hebei 河北省	11.65	1
Jieyang 揭阳市	Guangdong 广东省	7.42	1
Anyang 安阳市	Henan 河南省	5.97	1
Ningbo 宁波市	Zhejiang 浙江省	4.63	2
Changzhou 常州市	Jiangsu 江苏省	1.99	1
Hangzhou 杭州市	Zhejiang 浙江省	1.59	1
Shenyang 沈阳市	Liaoning 辽宁省	1.08	1

10 Major Wholesalers 十家主要批发商	City 城市	Province 省	Telephone/Fax 电话/传真
SU MEC 中设江苏机械设备进出口（集团）公司	Nanjing 南京市	Jiangsu 江苏省	(025)4511888 (025)4411772
China Poster Mobile Communications Equipment Co.,Ltd. 中邮普泰移动通信设备股份有限公司	Beijing 北京市	Beijing 北京市	(010)66426993 (010)66426837
Sino Kama Co., Ltd. 中泰凯马股份有限公司	Shanghai 上海市	Shanghai 上海市	(021)62031188 (021)62030851
China Huayuan Group Co.,Ltd. 中国华源集团有限公司	Shanghai 上海市	Shanghai 上海市	(021)62031188 (021)62032288
Zhejiang Crand Imp.& Exp.Co.,Ltd. 浙江远大进出口有限公司	Ningbo 宁波市	Zhejiang 浙江省	(0574)87720170 (0574)87723350
Shandong Machinery Import & Export Group Corporation 山东省机械进出口集团公司	Qingdao 青岛市	Shandong 山东省	(0532)2661628 (0532)2991655
Qingdao Haier International Trade Co.,Ltd. 青岛海尔国际贸易有限公司	Qingdao 青岛市	Shandong 山东省	(0532)8938337 (0532)8939494
Guangdong Machinery Import & Export Group Corporation 广东省机械进出口集团公司	Guangzhou 广州市	Guangdong 广东省	(020)87782168 (020)87771803
China National Machinery Equipment Import & Export Corporation 中国机械设备进出口总公司	Beijing 北京市	Beijing 北京市	(010)63474506 (010)63261865
Beijing Cellstar Co.,Ltd. 北京蜂星事达电讯有限公司	Beijing 北京市	Beijing 北京市	(010)64602050 (010)64672648

3624: Rubber Equipment 橡胶工业专用设备制造业

The industry accounts for 0.018% of the total revenue of China's industrial sector in 2002. The rate of return on assets is 3.39%. 78.95% of all firms in the industry made a profit while 21.05% had negative returns.The top province in terms of the industry's revenue is Jiangsu, accounting for 29.68% of the total revenue.
2002年本行业收入占全行业的0.018%，资产利润率为3.39%。78.95%的企业赢利，21.05%的企业亏损。收入最高的省为江苏省，占本行业的29.68%。

	Total number of firms 企业总数	Total number of employees 职工总数	Total revenue (Mil.RMB) 总销售收入 (百万元)	Total profit (Mil.RMB) 总利润 (百万元)	Return on assets 资产利润率 (%)	Return on equity 权益利润率 (%)	Labour productivity ('000 RMB/ worker) 劳动生产率 (千元/人)	Debts/ assets 资产负债率 (%)	Total assets (Mil.RMB) 总资产 (百万元)
Industry Overall 行业总体	57	12,394	1,954	95	3.39	11.41	47.38	70.28	2,797

	Number of firms 企业个数	Average number of employees 平均职工人数	Average revenue ('000 RMB) 平均销售收入（千元）	Average profit ('000 RMB) 平均利润 (千元)	Return on assets 资产利润率 (%)	Return on equity 权益利润率 (%)	Labour productivity ('000 RMB/ worker) 劳动生产率 (千元/人)	Debts/ assets 资产负债率 (%)	Average total assets ('000 RMB) 平均总资产 (千元)
By ownership 产业所有权									
State-owned 国有	11	331	37,113	-508	-0.58	-5.94	37.73	90.25	87,764
Collective-owned 集体	9	161	16,990	599	1.87	4.09	32.96	54.21	31,968
Foreign & Overseas Chinese Funded 三资	8	111	21,415	2,127	5.20	11.50	81.22	54.74	40,881
By regional distribution 地区分布									
Central-North 华北	6	205	31,277	2,542	5.08	30.97	50.34	83.60	50,030
Beijing 北京	1	77	20,340	1,609	5.89	137.64	231.29	95.72	27,328
Tianjin 天津	4	257	39,733	3,408	5.12	28.96	39.48	82.34	66,611
Hebei 河北									
Shanxi 山西									
Inner Mongolia 内蒙古	1	126	8,388	9	0.14	0.90	28.46	84.39	6,405
Northeast 东北	2	151	20,647	7,895	33.79	94.78	66.05	64.35	23,365
Liaoning 辽宁	2	151	20,647	7,895	33.79	94.78	66.05	64.35	23,365
Jilin 吉林									
Heilongjiang 黑龙江									
Central-East 华东	35	172	35,889	1,813	4.60	11.69	56.51	60.66	39,444
Shanghai 上海	7	137	22,418	1,477	2.91	6.67	55.93	56.42	50,802
Jiangsu 江苏	9	221	64,463	2,296	3.63	9.39	61.66	61.34	63,237
Zhejiang 浙江	5	89	21,953	1,642	13.76	29.27	56.63	53.00	11,936
Anhui 安徽									
Fujian 福建	3	169	39,805	5,440	6.43	17.60	69.11	63.48	84,618
Jiangxi 江西	1	50	13,881	749	5.58	6.75	85.06	17.37	13,430
Shandong 山东	10	206	27,597	718	5.58	19.84	47.99	71.89	12,882
Central-South 中南	13	318	34,234	-9	-0.01	-0.05	39.20	79.12	81,640
Henan 河南	1	147	6,479	-375	-3.77	-34.28	9.14	89.01	9,954
Hubei 湖北	1	54	1,232	-352	-4.73		55.76	125.51	7,436
Hunan 湖南	2	579	53,728	-1,164	-0.67	-2.98	23.61	77.47	173,490
Guangdong 广东	5	334	28,070	-231	-0.27	-1.76	31.43	84.76	86,460
Guangxi 广西	4	276	47,380	1,023	1.55	5.23	70.47	70.40	66,162
Hainan 海南									
Southwest 西南	1	720	24,324	484	5.85	68.75	5.25	91.49	8,271
Chongqing 重庆									
Sichuan 四川	1	720	24,324	484	5.85	68.75	5.25	91.49	8,271
Guizhou 贵州									
Yunnan 云南									
Tibet 西藏									
Northwest 西北									
Shaanxi 陕西									
Gansu 甘肃									
Qinghai 青海									
Ningxia 宁夏									
Xinjiang 新疆									

Year 年份	Number of firms 企业个数	Rate of change 变化率 (%)	Number of employees 职工人数 (人)	Rate of change 变化率 (%)	Total revenue (Mil. RMB) 总销售收入 (百万元)	Rate of change 变化率 (%)	Total profit (Mil RMB) 总利润 (百万元)	Rate of change 变化率 (%)
2000	61		19,483		1,501		-15	
2001	54	-11.48	15,047	-22.77	1,591	6.00	22	-
2002	57	5.56	12,394	-17.63	1,954	22.82	95	331.82

Major Products 主要产品	Output 产量	Unit 单位

10 Main Firms with Maximal Revenue (year founded) 收入最大的十家主要企业(创办年份)	City 城市	Province 省	Telephone/fax 电话/传真	Number of employees 职工人数	Ownership 产业所有权	Revenue ('000 RMB) 销售收入(千元)	Profit('000 RMB) (rank) 利润(千元)(排名)	Total assets ('000 RMB) 总资产(千元)	Major products 主要产品
Jiangsu Double Elephants Group	Wuxi	Jiangsu	(0510)8993888		Joint Stock				Rubber & Plastic Machine
江苏双象集团有限公司(1985)	无锡市	江苏省	(0510)8990983	992	股份制	459,850	16,100(2)	422,780	橡塑机
Tianjin Saixiang Science & Technology Co., Ltd.	Tianjin	Tianjin	(022)26745881		Joint Stock				Rubber & Plastic Machinery
天津赛象科技股份有限公司(1995)	天津市	天津市	(022)26743885	855	股份制	151,235	14,333(4)	182,458	橡塑机械
Qingdao Yadong Rubber Machine Group Co., Ltd.	Qingdao	Shandong	(0532)3121117		Private Owned				Rubber Machine
青岛亚东橡机集团有限公司(1994)	青岛市	山东省	(0532)3121116	725	私营企业	130,571	3,013(9)	44,637	橡机
Yiyang Rubber & Plastics Machinery Group Co., Ltd.	Yiyang	Hunan	(0737)4299404		State-owned				Opening Mixing Mill
益阳橡胶塑料机械集团有限公司(1971)	益阳市	湖南省	(0737)4298888	1,116	国有企业	102,579	-	343,108	离炼机
Seyen Machinery (Shanghai) Co.,Ltd.	Shanghai	Shanghai	(021)59760916		Foreign Funded				Rubber Machinery
上海精元机械有限公司(1996)	上海市	上海市	(021)59767067	325	外商投资	72,782	7,034(5)	213,037	橡胶机械
Shaoxing Junma Machinery Co.,Ltd.	Shaoxing	Zhejiang	(0575)4361365		Private Owned				Rubber Machinery
绍兴县骏马机械制造有限公司(1996)	绍兴市	浙江省	(0575)4360812	120	私营企业	59,241	5,151(6)	14,673	橡胶机械
Weihai Light Industry Machinery Factory	Weihai	Shandong	(0631)5225259		State-owned				Rubber Machinery
威海轻工机械厂(1967)	威海市	山东省	(0631)5225259	135	国有企业	49,381	1,184(18)	6,540	橡胶机械
Guangdong Zhanjiang Machinery Factory	Zhanjiang	Guangdong	(0759)2194855		State-owned				Rubber Spacial Equipment橡胶
广东省湛江机械厂(1952)	湛江市	广东省	(0759)2198471	924	国有企业	44,201	-	208,507	专用设备
Shantou Far East Light Chemical Industry Equipment Co.,Ltd.	Shantou	Guangdong	(0754)5763289		Collective-owned				Plastic Composition Units塑料
汕头市远东轻化装备有限公司(1982)	汕头市	广东省	(0754)5762555	298	集体企业	44,061	3,017(8)	105,575	复合机组
Wuxi NO.1 Rubber & Plastic Machinery Co.,Ltd.	Wuxi	Jiangsu	(0510)3757148		Private Owned				Rubber Machinery
无锡市第一橡塑机械有限公司(2001)	无锡市	江苏省	(0510)3750600	200	私营企业	30,370	1,420(16)	16,340	橡胶机械

Top 10 Cities by Revenue 销售收入排名前10位城市	Province 省	Market share 市场份额 (%)	Number of firms 企业个数
Wuxi 无锡市	Jiangsu 江苏省	26.71	4
Qingdao 青岛市	Shandong 山东省	10.18	7
Guilin 桂林市	Guangxi 广西	9.70	4
Tianjin 天津市	Tianjin 天津市	8.13	4
Shanghai 上海市	Shanghai 上海市	8.03	7
Sanming 三明市	Fujian 福建省	5.81	1
Yiyang 益阳市	Hunan 湖南省	5.25	1
Shantou 汕头市	Guangdong 广东省	4.51	2
Shaoxing 绍兴市	Zhejiang 浙江省	3.97	2
Weihai 威海市	Shandong 山东省	2.53	1

10 Major Wholesalers 十家主要批发商	City 城市	Province 省	Telephone/Fax 电话/传真
SU MEC	Nanjing	Jiangsu	(025)4511888
中设江苏机械设备进出口(集团)公司	南京市	江苏省	(025)4411772
China Poster Mobile Communications Equipment Co.,Ltd.	Beijing	Beijing	(010)66426993
中邮普泰移动通信设备股份有限公司	北京市	北京市	(010)66426837
Sino Kama Co., Ltd.	Shanghai	Shanghai	(021)62031188
中泰凯马股份有限公司	上海市	上海市	(021)62030851
China Huayuan Group Co.,Ltd.	Shanghai	Shanghai	(021)62031188
中国华源集团有限公司	上海市	上海市	(021)62032288
Zhejiang Crand Imp.& Exp.Co.,Ltd.	Ningbo	Zhejiang	(0574)87720170
浙江远大进出口有限公司	宁波市	浙江省	(0574)87723350
Shandong Machinery Import & Export Group Corporation	Qingdao	Shandong	(0532)2661628
山东省机械进出口集团公司	青岛市	山东省	(0532)2991655
Qingdao Haier International Trade Co.,Ltd.	Qingdao	Shandong	(0532)8938337
青岛海尔国际贸易有限公司	青岛市	山东省	(0532)8939494
Guangdong Machinery Import & Export Group Corporation	Guangzhou	Guangdong	(020)87782168
广东省机械进出口集团公司	广州市	广东省	(020)87771803
China National Machinery Equipment Import & Export Corporation	Beijing	Beijing	(010)63474506
中国机械设备进出口总公司	北京市	北京市	(010)63261865
Beijing Cellstar Co.,Ltd.	Beijing	Beijing	(010)64602050
北京蜂星事达电讯有限公司	北京市	北京市	(010)64672648

3625: Plastics Equipment 塑料工业专用设备制造业

The industry accounts for 0.099% of the total revenue of China's industrial sector in 2002. The rate of return on assets is 7.98%. 88.37% of all firms in the industry made a profit while 11.63% had negative returns.The top province in terms of the industry's revenue is Zhejiang, accounting for 44.83% of the total revenue.
2002年本行业收入占全行业的0.099%，资产利润率为7.98%。88.37%的企业赢利，11.63%的企业亏损。收入最高的省为浙江省，占本行业的44.83%。

	Total number of firms 企业总数	Total number of employees 职工总数	Total revenue (Mil.RMB) 总销售收入（百万元）	Total profit (Mil.RMB) 总利润（百万元）	Return on assets 资产利润率（%）	Return on equity 权益利润率（%）	Labour productivity ('000 RMB/worker) 劳动生产率（千元/人）	Debts/assets 资产负债率（%）	Total assets (Mil.RMB) 总资产（百万元）
Industry Overall 行业总体	215	41,382	10,579	1,043	7.98	20.47	74.09	61.03	13,069

	Number of firms 企业个数	Average number of employees 平均职工人数	Average revenue ('000 RMB) 平均销售收入（千元）	Average profit ('000 RMB) 平均利润（千元）	Return on assets 资产利润率（%）	Return on equity 权益利润率（%）	Labour productivity ('000 RMB/worker) 劳动生产率（千元/人）	Debts/assets 资产负债率（%）	Average total assets ('000 RMB) 平均总资产（千元）
By ownership 产业所有权									
State-owned 国有	15	304	15,238	-1,214	-1.84	-7.37	12.48	75.10	66,132
Collective-owned 集体	21	264	36,719	1,539	2.68	7.82	39.88	65.73	57,409
Foreign & Overseas Chinese Funded 三资	64	157	65,407	7,529	11.47	26.71	119.83	57.07	65,657
By regional distribution 地区分布									
Central-North 华北	13	203	21,294	318	0.50	1.73	46.57	71.30	64,272
Beijing 北京	2	443	60,100	-3,131	-1.13	-4.52	36.56	74.97	276,910
Tianjin 天津	4	92	9,338	1,650	7.08	23.12	86.83	69.38	23,314
Hebei 河北	4	149	22,453	1,431	5.52	12.11	82.63	54.40	25,917
Shanxi 山西	3	264	9,822	-642	-2.27	-7.60	11.88	70.10	28,265
Inner Mongolia 内蒙古									
Northeast 东北	5	128	15,415	4,192	18.52	33.13	39.78	44.11	22,637
Liaoning 辽宁	4	150	16,906	5,237	20.53	39.73	38.58	48.33	25,509
Jilin 吉林	1	40	9,452	11	0.10	0.10	57.80	5.47	11,148
Heilongjiang 黑龙江									
Central-East 华东	143	188	55,227	5,620	9.36	22.66	81.26	58.68	60,021
Shanghai 上海	17	167	35,560	3,057	4.96	11.52	63.45	56.94	61,628
Jiangsu 江苏	27	168	36,872	1,450	3.46	10.69	52.30	67.63	41,882
Zhejiang 浙江	79	161	60,028	7,577	11.95	28.56	96.43	58.14	63,383
Anhui 安徽	1	20	5,100	612	17.00	24.48	67.55	30.56	3,600
Fujian 福建	2	130	14,553	3,022	19.18	46.68	39.88	58.90	15,753
Jiangxi 江西									
Shandong 山东	17	387	89,470	6,310	7.87	17.35	81.25	54.62	80,128
Central-South 中南	51	213	45,120	4,297	6.45	18.29	66.95	64.74	66,626
Henan 河南	4	333	12,324	-557	-2.36		12.99	118.03	23,573
Hubei 湖北	6	394	21,572	-1,388	-1.97	-5.83	13.78	66.23	70,546
Hunan 湖南	2	79	3,745	-150	-1.32	-274.31	25.35	99.52	11,298
Guangdong 广东	34	169	59,192	7,030	9.90	23.72	111.98	58.28	71,028
Guangxi 广西	5	254	20,473	-1,803	-2.04	-14.00	24.00	85.45	88,561
Hainan 海南									
Southwest 西南	3	92	8,948	-1,740	-3.73	-11.65	-1.56	67.94	46,605
Chongqing 重庆									
Sichuan 四川	2	116	9,619	-1,800	-3.00	-8.40	3.16	64.33	60,076
Guizhou 贵州									
Yunnan 云南	1	44	7,606	-1,621	-8.24	-82.66	-26.36	90.03	19,662
Tibet 西藏									
Northwest 西北									
Shaanxi 陕西									
Gansu 甘肃									
Qinghai 青海									
Ningxia 宁夏									
Xinjiang 新疆									

3625: Plastics Equipment 塑料工业专用设备制造业

Year 年份	Number of firms 企业个数	Rate of change 变化率(%)	Number of employees 职工人数(人)	Rate of change 变化率(%)	Total revenue (Mil. RMB) 总销售收入(百万元)	Rate of change 变化率(%)	Total profit (Mil RMB) 总利润(百万元)	Rate of change 变化率(%)
2000	170		39,790		6,644		574	
2001	185	8.82	41,451	4.17	7,471	12.45	589	2.61
2002	215	16.22	41,382	-0.17	10,579	41.60	1,043	77.08

Major Products 主要产品	Output 产量	Unit 单位
Plastic Processing Equipment 塑料加工设备	300,480	Ton 吨

10 Main Firms with Maximal Revenue (year founded) 收入最大的十家主要企业（创办年份）	City 城市	Province 省	Telephone/fax 电话/传真	Number of employees 职工人数	Ownership 产业所有权	Revenue ('000 RMB) 销售收入(千元)	Profit('000 RMB) (rank) 利润(千元)(排名)	Total assets ('000 RMB) 总资产(千元)	Major products 主要产品
Ningbo Haitian Co.,Ltd. 宁波海天股份有限公司(1966)	Ningbo 宁波市	Zhejiang 浙江省	(0574)86177006 (0574)86181763	1,266	Joint Stock 股份制	1,360,707	224,394(1)	1,444,618	Plastic Processing Machinery塑料加工机械
Ningbo Dagang Hai Tian Machinery Co., Ltd. 宁波大港海天机械有限公司(2001)	Ningbo 宁波市	Zhejiang 浙江省	(0574)86177145 (0574)86181881	483	Overseas Chinese-funded 港澳台资	583,640	123,702(2)	378,860	Plastic-injection Machine 注塑机
Shandong Huaguan Group Co., Ltd. 山东华冠集团有限责任公司(1966)	Laiwu 莱芜市	Shandong 山东省	(0634)6256052 (0634)6215934	2,537	Limited-Liability 有限公司	501,112	30,322(6)	646,422	Plastic Rubber Machinery塑料橡胶机械
Shunde Zhende Plastics Machinery Co., Ltd. 顺德市震德塑料机械厂有限公司(1985)	Foshan 佛山市	Guangdong 广东省	(0765)2338728 (0765)2632335	763	Overseas Chinese-funded 港澳台资	460,372	120,730(3)	476,168	Plastic-injection Moulding Machine塑料注射成型机
Shenzhen Zhenxiong Machinery Co., Ltd. 深圳震雄机械有限公司(1996)	Shenzhen 深圳市	Guangdong 广东省	(0755)27326943 (0755)84137875	403	Overseas Chinese-funded 港澳台资	299,684	42,120(5)	489,959	Plastic-injection Machine 注塑机
Zhejiang Shenda Plastics Machinery Co., Ltd. 浙江申达塑料机械有限公司(1993)	Hangzhou 杭州市	Zhejiang 浙江省	(0571)87091051 (0571)87091046	597	Overseas Chinese-funded 港澳台资	169,980	537(113)	222,920	Plastic Industrial Special Equipment塑料工业专用设备
Ningbo Yongtai Industrial Company 宁波永泰实业公司(1994)	Ningbo 宁波市	Zhejiang 浙江省	(0574)87760558 (0574)87770232	602	Collective-owned 集体企业	154,804	13,980(16)	222,391	Plastic-injection Machine 注塑机
Hangzhou Huaxing Group Company 杭州华兴集团公司(1993)	Hangzhou 杭州市	Zhejiang 浙江省	(0571)88542017 (0571)88541050	483	Collective-owned 集体企业	145,620	4,060(42)	176,300	Plastic-injection Machinery 注塑机械
Taishan Hoptake Machine Factory 台山市合德机器厂(1991)	Jiangmen 江门市	Guangdong 广东省	(0730)3377871 (0750)5577871	248	Overseas Chinese-funded 港澳台资	145,217	-	37,622	Plastic Bag Machinery & Parts塑胶袋机械及零配件
Jiangsu Keya Chemical Equipment Corporation 江苏科亚化工装备有限公司(1993)	Nanjing 南京市	Jiangsu 江苏省	(025)2630877 (025)2611188	222	Overseas Chinese-funded 港澳台资	140,540	2,120(64)	42,910	Chemical Industry Machinery 化工机械

Top 10 Cities by Revenue 销售收入排名前10位城市	Province 省	Market share 市场份额(%)	Number of firms 企业个数
Ningbo 宁波市	Zhejiang 浙江省	33.90	37
Foshan 佛山市	Guangdong 广东省	7.22	10
Shanghai 上海市	Shanghai 上海市	5.71	17
Yantai 烟台市	Shandong 山东省	5.09	7
Hangzhou 杭州市	Zhejiang 浙江省	4.77	12
Laiwu 莱芜市	Shandong 山东省	4.74	1
Dongguan 东莞市	Guangdong 广东省	4.11	5
Shenzhen 深圳市	Guangdong 广东省	3.74	4
Zhoushan 舟山市	Zhejiang 浙江省	3.23	10
Wuxi 无锡市	Jiangsu 江苏省	2.66	7

10 Major Wholesalers 十家主要批发商	City 城市	Province 省	Telephone/Fax 电话/传真
SU MEC 中设江苏机械设备进出口（集团）公司	Nanjing 南京市	Jiangsu 江苏省	(025)4511888 (025)4411772
China Poster Mobile Communications Equipment Co.,Ltd. 中邮普泰移动通信设备股份有限公司	Beijing 北京市	Beijing 北京市	(010)66426993 (010)66426837
Sino Kama Co., Ltd. 中泰凯马股份有限公司	Shanghai 上海市	Shanghai 上海市	(021)62031188 (021)62030851
China Huayuan Group Co.,Ltd. 中国华源集团有限公司	Shanghai 上海市	Shanghai 上海市	(021)62031188 (021)62032288
Zhejiang Crand Imp.& Exp.Co.,Ltd. 浙江远大进出口有限公司	Ningbo 宁波市	Zhejiang 浙江省	(0574)87720170 (0574)87723350
Shandong Machinery Import & Export Group Corporation 山东省机械进出口集团公司	Qingdao 青岛市	Shandong 山东省	(0532)2661628 (0532)2991655
Qingdao Haier International Trade Co.,Ltd. 青岛海尔国际贸易有限公司	Qingdao 青岛市	Shandong 山东省	(0532)8938337 (0532)8939494
Guangdong Machinery Import & Export Group Corporation 广东省机械进出口集团公司	Guangzhou 广州市	Guangdong 广东省	(020)87782168 (020)87771803
China National Machinery Equipment Import & Export Corporation 中国机械设备进出口总公司	Beijing 北京市	Beijing 北京市	(010)63474506 (010)63261865
Beijing Cellstar Co.,Ltd. 北京蜂星事达电讯有限公司	Beijing 北京市	Beijing 北京市	(010)64602050 (010)64672648

3626: Lumber Equipment 木材工业专用设备制造业

The industry accounts for 0.035% of the total revenue of China's industrial sector in 2002. The rate of return on assets is 5.10%. 76.47% of all firms in the industry made a profit while 23.53% had negative returns.The top province in terms of the industry's revenue is Shandong, accounting for 55.49% of the total revenue.
2002年本行业收入占全行业的 0.035%，资产利润率为 5.10%。76.47%的企业赢利，23.53%的企业亏损。收入最高的省为山东省，占本行业的55.49%。

	Total number of firms 企业总数	Total number of employees 职工总数	Total revenue (Mil.RMB) 总销售收入 (百万元)	Total profit (Mil.RMB) 总利润 (百万元)	Return on assets 资产利润率 (%)	Return on equity 权益利润率 (%)	Labour productivity ('000 RMB/ worker) 劳动生产率 (千元/人)	Debts/ assets 资产负债率 (%)	Total assets (Mil.RMB) 总资产 (百万元)
Industry Overall 行业总体	68	19,613	3,757	170	5.10	18.75	51.31	72.81	3,336

	Number of firms 企业个数	Average number of employees 平均职工人数	Average revenue ('000 RMB) 平均销售收入 (千元)	Average profit ('000 RMB) 平均利润 (千元)	Return on assets 资产利润率 (%)	Return on equity 权益利润率 (%)	Labour productivity ('000 RMB/ worker) 劳动生产率 (千元/人)	Debts/ assets 资产负债率 (%)	Average total assets ('000 RMB) 平均总资产 (千元)
By ownership 产业所有权									
State-owned 国有	15	287	7,997	-1,711	-3.05	-22.67	9.56	86.55	56,135
Collective-owned 集体	11	194	47,561	2,951	20.62	53.49	65.86	61.46	14,311
Foreign & Overseas Chinese Funded 三资	6	148	31,971	1,994	8.58	14.79	53.26	41.99	23,236
By regional distribution 地区分布									
Central-North 华北	3	69	18,557	1,967	21.94	44.03	97.48	50.17	8,966
Beijing 北京	1	15	152	105	2.56	4.71	6.00	45.55	4,097
Tianjin 天津									
Hebei 河北	2	96	27,759	2,898	25.42	51.88	104.66	51.00	11,400
Shanxi 山西									
Inner Mongolia 内蒙古									
Northeast 东北	11	297	7,549	-798	-1.68	-13.03	9.08	87.10	47,461
Liaoning 辽宁	2	125	5,742	-727	-2.60		22.46	106.74	27,923
Jilin 吉林	1	1,199	26,091	-2,580	-2.60		6.22	106.62	99,059
Heilongjiang 黑龙江	8	228	5,684	-594	-1.29	-6.11	9.13	78.84	45,895
Central-East 华东	38	304	82,512	4,525	7.85	25.07	66.87	68.69	57,647
Shanghai 上海	7	218	70,953	2,226	2.40	12.67	45.79	81.03	92,588
Jiangsu 江苏	13	243	38,730	1,849	3.36	7.72	40.38	56.54	55,077
Zhejiang 浙江	2	184	18,340	881	3.38	24.74	33.27	86.35	26,080
Anhui 安徽									
Fujian 福建	3	41	4,430	306	8.45	16.17	85.87	47.73	3,617
Jiangxi 江西	2	38	245	-40	-0.85		6.88	103.33	4,631
Shandong 山东	11	573	189,529	11,796	17.20	54.23	87.56	68.28	68,565
Central-South 中南	12	224	33,280	1,481	8.32	32.18	55.51	74.14	17,790
Henan 河南	5	218	34,828	1,550	6.60	31.24	55.00	78.86	23,475
Hubei 湖北	2	353	70,765	2,288	13.68	47.53	85.07	71.22	16,720
Hunan 湖南									
Guangdong 广东	3	174	20,604	1,491	15.52	51.66	37.41	69.96	9,611
Guangxi 广西	2	186	10,942	483	2.86	7.98	26.39	64.22	16,917
Hainan 海南									
Southwest 西南	3	368	24,732	-5,282	-5.17	-20.71	24.56	75.06	102,232
Chongqing 重庆									
Sichuan 四川	2	397	27,312	-6,933	-7.57	-35.40	27.61	78.60	91,524
Guizhou 贵州									
Yunnan 云南	1	312	19,571	-1,980	-1.60	-5.30	16.81	69.80	123,649
Tibet 西藏									
Northwest 西北	1	777	9,550	-935	-1.22	-10.60	8.92	88.51	76,748
Shaanxi 陕西	1	777	9,550	-935	-1.22	-10.60	8.92	88.51	76,748
Gansu 甘肃									
Qinghai 青海									
Ningxia 宁夏									
Xinjiang 新疆									

3626: Lumber Equipment 木材工业专用设备制造业

Year 年份	Number of firms 企业个数	Rate of change 变化率 (%)	Number of employees 职工人数 (人)	Rate of change 变化率 (%)	Total revenue (Mil. RMB) 总销售收入 (百万元)	Rate of change 变化率 (%)	Total profit (Mil RMB) 总利润 (百万元)	Rate of change 变化率 (%)
2000	75		28,444		3,718		180	
2001	74	-1.33	24,844	-12.66	3,406	-8.39	129	-28.33
2002	68	-8.11	19,613	-21.06	3,757	10.31	170	31.78

Major Products 主要产品	Output 产量	Unit 单位

10 Main Firms with Maximal Revenue (year founded) 收入最大的十家主要企业（创办年份）	City 城市	Province 省	Telephone/fax 电话/传真	Number of employees 职工人数	Ownership 产业所有权	Revenue ('000 RMB) 销售收入 (千元)	Profit('000 RMB) (rank) 利润(千元)(排名)	Total assets ('000 RMB) 总资产 (千元)	Major products 主要产品
Weihai Qiquan Woodworking Machinery Co.,Ltd. 威海齐全木机集团有限公司(1978)	Weihai 威海市	Shandong 山东省	(0631)5584136 (0631)5584044	1,100	Limited-Liability 有限公司	455,870	26,689(2)	72,573	2P1.2P2 Woodworking Planer.2P1、2P2 木工刨床
Shandong Xing Wang Group Co.,Ltd. 山东星王集团有限公司(1963)	Weihai 威海市	Shandong 山东省	(0631)5382085 (0631)5382231	1,091	Collective-owned 集体企业	339,710	23,050(3)	90,750	Wood Processing Machinery木材加工机械
Shanghai Manmade Board Machiney Co.,Ltd. 上海人造板机器厂有限公司(1952)	Shanghai 上海市	Shanghai 上海市	(021)59577480 (021)59572568	914	Limited-Liability 有限公司	257,223	4,380(7)	469,619	Wood Processing Machinery木材加工机械
Sufoma Co.,Ltd. 苏福马股份有限公司(1998)	Suzhou 苏州市	Jiangsu 江苏省	(0512)67534811 (0512)67534072	598	Joint Stock 股份制	199,514	17,000(4)	406,753	Manmade Board Equipment人造板设备
Shanghai Jiecheng Baihe Wood Working Machinery Co., Ltd. 上海捷成白鹤木工机械有限公司(1994)	Shanghai 上海市	Shanghai 上海市	(021)59740552 (021)59741747	221	Joint Owned 联营企业	102,558	3,878(9)	70,269	Wood Processing Machinery木材加工机械
Gongyi Veneer Equipment General Factory 巩义市胶合板设备总厂(1993)	Zhengzhou 郑州市	Henan 河南省	(0371)4351258 (0371)4365635	92	Collective-owned 集体企业	60,246	5,236(6)	3,889	Veneer Equipment胶合板设备
Renqiu Yongmao Woodwork Machinery Co., Ltd. 任丘市永茂木工机械有限公司(1994)	Cangzhou 沧州市	Hebei 河北省	(0317)2692288 (0317)2692157	140	Foreign Funded 外商投资	55,518	5,796(5)	19,860	Woodwork Machinery 木工机械
Shanghai Ping'an Woodwork Products Co., Ltd. 上海平安木制品有限公司(1992)	Shanghai 上海市	Shanghai 上海市	(021)62200003 (021)52635037	155	Foreign Funded 外商投资	37,263	3,123(11)	11,630	Wooden Handicrafts木制工艺品
Homag Machine (Shanghai) Co., Ltd. 豪德机械上海有限公司(1993)	Shanghai 上海市	Shanghai 上海市	(021)57740970 (021)57740977	102	Foreign Funded 外商投资	35,641	2,867(13)	58,580	Milling Machine 铣床
Rongcheng Huada Machine Tool Co., Ltd. 荣成华达机床有限公司(1998)	Weihai 威海市	Shandong 山东省	(0631)7631161 (0631)7631161	220	Limited-Liability 有限公司	33,530	2,980(12)	21,910	Agricutural Machinery Fittings 农机配件

Top 10 Cities by Revenue 销售收入排名前10位城市	Province 省	Market share 市场份额 (%)	Number of firms 企业个数
Weihai 威海市	Shandong 山东省	53.11	6
Shanghai 上海市	Shanghai 上海市	13.22	7
Suzhou 苏州市	Jiangsu 江苏省	8.04	5
Zhengzhou 郑州市	Henan 河南省	4.34	3
Zhenjiang 镇江市	Jiangsu 江苏省	2.15	1
Yancheng 盐城市	Jiangsu 江苏省	1.84	4
Foshan 佛山市	Guangdong 广东省	1.65	3
Cangzhou 沧州市	Hebei 河北省	1.48	2
Yantai 烟台市	Shandong 山东省	1.30	2

10 Major Wholesalers 十家主要批发商	City 城市	Province 省	Telephone/Fax 电话/传真
SU MEC 中设江苏机械设备进出口（集团）公司	Nanjing 南京市	Jiangsu 江苏省	(025)4511888 (025)4411772
China Poster Mobile Communications Equipment Co.,Ltd. 中邮普泰移动通信设备股份有限公司	Beijing 北京市	Beijing 北京市	(010)66426993 (010)66426837
Sino Kama Co., Ltd. 中泰凯马股份有限公司	Shanghai 上海市	Shanghai 上海市	(021)62031188 (021)62030851
China Huayuan Group Co.,Ltd. 中国华源集团有限公司	Shanghai 上海市	Shanghai 上海市	(021)62031188 (021)62032288
Zhejiang Crand Imp.& Exp.Co.,Ltd. 浙江远大进出口有限公司	Ningbo 宁波市	Zhejiang 浙江省	(0574)87720170 (0574)87723350
Shandong Machinery Import & Export Group Corporation 山东省机械进出口集团公司	Qingdao 青岛市	Shandong 山东省	(0532)2661628 (0532)2991655
Qingdao Haier International Trade Co.,Ltd. 青岛海尔国际贸易有限公司	Qingdao 青岛市	Shandong 山东省	(0532)8938337 (0532)8939494
Guangdong Machinery Import & Export Group Corporation 广东省机械进出口集团公司	Guangzhou 广州市	Guangdong 广东省	(020)87782168 (020)87771803
China National Machinery Equipment Import & Export Corporation 中国机械设备进出口总公司	Beijing 北京市	Beijing 北京市	(010)63474506 (010)63261865
Beijing Cellstar Co.,Ltd. 北京蜂星事达电讯有限公司	Beijing 北京市	Beijing 北京市	(010)64602050 (010)64672648

3627: Printing Equipment 印刷工业专用设备制造业

The industry accounts for 0.049% of the total revenue of China's industrial sector in 2002. The rate of return on assets is 4.14%. 78.77% of all firms in the industry made a profit while 21.23% had negative returns.The top province in terms of the industry's revenue is Shanghai, accounting for 36.18% of the total revenue.
2002年本行业收入占全行业的 0.049%，资产利润率为 4.14%。78.77%的企业赢利，21.23%的企业亏损。收入最高的省为上海市，占本行业的36.18%。

	Total number of firms 企业总数	Total number of employees 职工总数	Total revenue (Mil.RMB) 总销售收入 (百万元)	Total profit (Mil.RMB) 总利润 (百万元)	Return on assets 资产利润率 (%)	Return on equity 权益利润率 (%)	Labour productivity ('000 RMB/ worker) 劳动生产率 (千元/人)	Debts/ assets 资产负债率 (%)	Total assets (Mil.RMB) 总资产 (百万元)
Industry Overall 行业总体	146	36,146	5,205	426	4.14	8.36	55.21	50.47	10,303

	Number of firms 企业个数	Average number of employees 平均职工人数	Average revenue ('000 RMB) 平均销售收入 (千元)	Average profit ('000 RMB) 平均利润 (千元)	Return on assets 资产利润率 (%)	Return on equity 权益利润率 (%)	Labour productivity ('000 RMB/ worker) 劳动生产率 (千元/人)	Debts/ assets 资产负债率 (%)	Average total assets ('000 RMB) 平均总资产 (千元)
By ownership 产业所有权									
State-owned 国有	17	338	14,679	-788	-0.55	-1.10	11.83	50.10	143,314
Collective-owned 集体	12	116	10,163	123	0.92	2.42	25.76	62.00	13,398
Foreign & Overseas Chinese Funded 三资	46	200	53,008	5,587	7.82	16.10	95.95	51.44	71,450
By regional distribution 地区分布									
Central-North 华北	22	376	55,973	5,259	2.94	4.86	54.77	39.54	178,879
Beijing 北京	12	443	79,598	7,857	2.77	4.35	70.47	36.50	284,159
Tianjin 天津	5	100	39,163	4,836	7.98	15.99	64.59	50.13	60,629
Hebei 河北	4	323	17,104	-216	-0.61	-2.12	30.18	71.07	35,252
Shanxi 山西	1	1,160	12,001	-1,906	-2.34	-8.59	5.99	72.71	81,283
Inner Mongolia 内蒙古									
Northeast 东北	9	305	23,704	-296	-0.38	-1.42	32.86	73.36	78,457
Liaoning 辽宁	7	192	24,072	1,010	1.95	4.93	60.07	60.38	51,682
Jilin 吉林	1	732	26,342	115	0.12	0.20	7.73	42.41	98,556
Heilongjiang 黑龙江	1	673	18,488	-9,848	-4.01		5.87	104.88	245,787
Central-East 华东	89	205	36,740	3,435	6.77	14.64	69.77	53.79	50,773
Shanghai 上海	28	246	67,268	7,843	8.88	17.36	97.10	48.86	88,369
Jiangsu 江苏	22	190	22,169	73	0.28	0.90	37.31	69.09	26,313
Zhejiang 浙江	24	107	12,296	698	3.70	9.13	35.11	59.45	18,852
Anhui 安徽									
Fujian 福建	3	165	17,094	-1,181	-2.18	-3.57	66.83	39.05	54,230
Jiangxi 江西	3	368	53,900	7,980	9.99	25.72	178.32	61.16	79,898
Shandong 山东	9	341	43,392	5,257	7.75	17.65	43.07	56.11	67,860
Central-South 中南	17	222	14,515	169	0.45	1.29	22.44	65.24	37,493
Henan 河南									
Hubei 湖北	3	145	19,714	132	0.51	1.22	36.84	58.39	25,909
Hunan 湖南	4	504	7,392	-1,051	-2.13	-4.87	8.09	56.14	49,211
Guangdong 广东	9	109	16,697	1,647	5.86	10.57	49.76	44.55	28,111
Guangxi 广西	1	349	7,773	-8,153	-7.42		10.70	134.08	109,808
Hainan 海南									
Southwest 西南	5	89	16,811	929	3.14	5.71	66.48	45.08	29,609
Chongqing 重庆	3	66	13,320	1,063	4.29	5.36	37.69	19.99	24,799
Sichuan 四川	1	202	26,423	717	1.35	4.35	80.09	68.99	53,132
Guizhou 贵州									
Yunnan 云南	1	45	17,671	740	3.61	13.94	132.04	74.13	20,513
Tibet 西藏									
Northwest 西北	4	657	40,019	56	0.06	0.15	23.95	59.63	89,263
Shaanxi 陕西	3	713	48,123	501	0.53	1.29	26.36	58.88	94,097
Gansu 甘肃	1	490	15,708	-1,280	-1.71	-4.56	13.43	62.48	74,762
Qinghai 青海									
Ningxia 宁夏									
Xinjiang 新疆									

3627: Printing Equipment 印刷工业专用设备制造业

Year 年份	Number of firms 企业个数	Rate of change 变化率（%）	Number of employees 职工人数（人）	Rate of change 变化率（%）	Total revenue (Mil. RMB) 总销售收入（百万元）	Rate of change 变化率（%）	Total profit (Mil RMB) 总利润（百万元）	Rate of change 变化率（%）
2000	116		37,115		3,598		219	
2001	138	18.97	38,512	3.76	4,527	25.82	269	22.83
2002	146	5.80	36,146	-6.14	5,205	14.98	426	58.36

Major Products 主要产品	Output 产量	Unit 单位
Printing Machine 印刷机	56,412	Ton 吨
Binding Machinery 装订机械	6,910	Ton 吨

10 Main Firms with Maximal Revenue (year founded) 收入最大的十家主要企业（创办年份）	City 城市	Province 省	Telephone/fax 电话/传真	Number of employees 职工人数	Ownership 产业所有权	Revenue ('000 RMB) 销售收入（千元）	Profit('000 RMB) (rank) 利润（千元）（排名）	Total assets ('000 RMB) 总资产（千元）	Major products 主要产品
Beiren Printing Machinery Co.,Ltd 北人印刷机械股份有限公司(1993)	Beijing 北京市	Beijing 北京市	(010)67737711 (010)67714032	3,193	Joint Stock 股份制	688,623	81,109(1)	1,520,643	Single-color Offset Printing Machine单色胶印机
Shanghai Goss Printing Equipment Co.,Ltd. 上海高斯印刷设备有限公司(1994)	Shanghai 上海市	Shanghai 上海市	(021)52804762 (021)52808772	766	Foreign Funded 外商投资	301,617	48,844(2)	473,097	Printing Machine 印刷机械
Shanghai Guanghua Printing Machinery Co., Ltd. 上海光华印刷机械有限公司(1992)	Shanghai 上海市	Shanghai 上海市	(021)56681572 (021)56684176	703	Foreign Funded 外商投资	200,241	13,030(13)	193,301	Printing Machine 印刷机械
Shanghai Yahua Printing Machinery Co., Ltd. 上海亚华印刷机械有限公司(1998)	Shanghai 上海市	Shanghai 上海市	(021)64045160 (021)64041244	529	Overseas Chinese-funded 港澳台资	180,345	18,647(6)	170,332	Printing Machine 印刷机械
Shanghai Shenweida Machinery Co., Ltd. 上海申威达机械有限公司(1991)	Shanghai 上海市	Shanghai 上海市	(021)58891376 (021)58810161	626	Overseas Chinese-funded 港澳台资	172,095	17,939(7)	210,630	Printing Machine 印刷机械
Shanghai Purlux Machinery Co.,Ltd. 上海紫光机械有限公司(1993)	Shanghai 上海市	Shanghai 上海市	(021)63018426 (021)63010910	574	Foreign Funded 外商投资	165,535	27,013(3)	201,113	Printing Machine 印刷机械
Jingdezhen Printing Packing Machinery Co.,Ltd. 景德镇印刷包装机械有限公司(1958)	Jingdezhen 景德镇市	Jiangxi 江西省	(0798)8446341 (0798)8441654	897	Limited-Liability 有限公司	155,678	23,954(5)	204,708	Printing Machine 印刷机械
Lintec (Tianjin) Industrial Co.,Ltd. 琳得科(天津)实业有限公司(1993)	Tianjin 天津市	Tianjin 天津市	(022)87610012 (022)27030922	184	Foreign Funded 外商投资	121,791	15,716(8)	168,875	Printing Machine 印刷机
Shaanxi Beiren Printing Machinery Co., Ltd. 陕西北人印刷机械有限责任公司(1967)	Weinan 渭南市	Shannxi 陕西省	(0913)2189401 (0913)2189416	1,633	Limited-Liability 有限公司	114,767	2,453(31)	202,994	Assembling Set Gravure Printing Machine机组式凹印机
Shanghai Purple Machinery Co., Ltd. 上海紫宏机械有限公司(1998)	Shanghai 上海市	Shanghai 上海市	(021)64786150 (021)64198920	220	Foreign Funded 外商投资	74,168	13,045(12)	92,268	Printing Special Machine印刷专业设备

Top 10 Cities by Revenue 销售收入排名前10位城市	Province 省	Market share 市场份额（%）	Number of firms 企业个数
Shanghai 上海市	Shanghai 上海市	36.18	28
Beijing 北京市	Beijing 北京市	18.35	12
Tianjin 天津市	Tianjin 天津市	3.76	5
Jingdezhen 景德镇市	Jiangxi 江西省	2.99	1
Nantong 南通市	Jiangsu 江苏省	2.91	2
Wenzhou 温州市	Zhejiang 浙江省	2.89	11
Weihai 威海市	Shandong 山东省	2.68	2
Taizhou 泰州市	Jiangsu 江苏省	2.64	5
Weinan 渭南市	Shannxi 陕西省	2.20	1
Weifang 潍坊市	Shandong 山东省	2.09	2

10 Major Wholesalers 十家主要批发商	City 城市	Province 省	Telephone/Fax 电话/传真
SU MEC 中设江苏机械设备进出口（集团）公司	Nanjing 南京市	Jiangsu 江苏省	(025)4511888 (025)4411772
China Poster Mobile Communications Equipment Co.,Ltd. 中邮普泰移动通信设备股份有限公司	Beijing 北京市	Beijing 北京市	(010)66426993 (010)66426837
Sino Kama Co., Ltd. 中泰凯马股份有限公司	Shanghai 上海市	Shanghai 上海市	(021)62031188 (021)62030851
China Huayuan Group Co.,Ltd. 中国华源集团有限公司	Shanghai 上海市	Shanghai 上海市	(021)62031188 (021)62032288
Zhejiang Crand Imp.& Exp.Co.,Ltd. 浙江远大进出口有限公司	Ningbo 宁波市	Zhejiang 浙江省	(0574)87720170 (0574)87723350
Shandong Machinery Import & Export Group Corporation 山东省机械进出口集团公司	Qingdao 青岛市	Shandong 山东省	(0532)2661628 (0532)2991655
Qingdao Haier International Trade Co.,Ltd. 青岛海尔国际贸易有限公司	Qingdao 青岛市	Shandong 山东省	(0532)8938337 (0532)8939494
Guangdong Machinery Import & Export Group Corporation 广东省机械进出口集团公司	Guangzhou 广州市	Guangdong 广东省	(020)87782168 (020)87771803
China National Machinery Equipment Import & Export Corporation 中国机械设备进出口总公司	Beijing 北京市	Beijing 北京市	(010)63474506 (010)63261865
Beijing Cellstar Co.,Ltd. 北京蜂星事达电讯有限公司	Beijing 北京市	Beijing 北京市	(010)64602050 (010)64672648

3628: Pharmaceutical Equipment 制药工业专用设备制造业

The industry accounts for 0.016% of the total revenue of China's industrial sector in 2002. The rate of return on assets is 5.53%. 86.08% of all firms in the industry made a profit while 13.92% had negative returns.The top province in terms of the industry's revenue is Jiangsu, accounting for 20.17% of the total revenue.
2002年本行业收入占全行业的0.016%，资产利润率为5.53%。86.08%的企业赢利，13.92%的企业亏损。收入最高的省为江苏省，占本行业的20.17%。

	Total number of firms 企业总数	Total number of employees 职工总数	Total revenue (Mil.RMB) 总销售收入（百万元）	Total profit (Mil.RMB) 总利润（百万元）	Return on assets 资产利润率（%）	Return on equity 权益利润率（%）	Labour productivity ('000 RMB/ worker) 劳动生产率（千元/人）	Debts/ assets 资产负债率（%）	Total assets (Mil.RMB) 总资产（百万元）
Industry Overall 行业总体	79	13,286	1,758	125	5.53	15.78	42.57	64.95	2,255

	Number of firms 企业个数	Average number of employees 平均职工人数	Average revenue ('000 RMB) 平均销售收入（千元）	Average profit ('000 RMB) 平均利润（千元）	Return on assets 资产利润率（%）	Return on equity 权益利润率（%）	Labour productivity ('000 RMB/ worker) 劳动生产率（千元/人）	Debts/ assets 资产负债率（%）	Average total assets ('000 RMB) 平均总资产（千元）
By ownership 产业所有权									
State-owned 国有	13	212	16,593	-720	-1.73	-21.32	19.65	91.89	41,672
Collective-owned 集体	7	96	8,779	399	3.11	8.99	34.89	65.42	12,849
Foreign & Overseas Chinese Funded 三资	4	125	36,367	6,199	15.65	23.94	103.87	34.63	39,615
By regional distribution 地区分布									
Central-North 华北	6	142	38,977	5,198	12.11	19.15	84.27	36.76	42,914
Beijing 北京	4	146	51,477	7,554	12.81	19.65	101.67	34.80	58,954
Tianjin 天津	1	173	10,003	-599	-4.51	-33.02	45.62	86.33	13,267
Hebei 河北	1	95	17,953	1,571	18.70	21.64	47.49	13.57	8,400
Shanxi 山西									
Inner Mongolia 内蒙古									
Northeast 东北	5	262	30,198	1,644	2.22	6.57	37.47	66.21	74,060
Liaoning 辽宁	3	339	30,527	1,134	1.05	4.22	28.44	75.04	107,729
Jilin 吉林	1	150	39,662	2,300	15.23	15.89	83.60	4.17	15,100
Heilongjiang 黑龙江	1	145	19,745	2,520	7.87	8.40	53.09	6.28	32,011
Central-East 华东	47	150	22,888	1,945	8.75	21.72	49.81	59.69	22,216
Shanghai 上海	8	191	38,880	6,384	13.06	32.91	62.80	60.31	48,866
Jiangsu 江苏	16	164	22,162	872	4.59	14.82	46.10	69.01	18,988
Zhejiang 浙江	15	107	18,604	1,461	10.74	19.69	53.85	45.46	13,602
Anhui 安徽	1	211	12,876	74	0.37	0.64	25.27	41.30	19,805
Fujian 福建									
Jiangxi 江西	2	167	4,437	-217	-1.11	-1.94	14.14	42.75	19,582
Shandong 山东	5	146	21,860	965	5.59	18.41	50.38	69.66	17,282
Central-South 中南	17	186	15,676	360	1.43	4.01	27.68	64.34	25,138
Henan 河南	1	152	9,549	725	7.47	22.94	20.64	67.44	9,709
Hubei 湖北	3	80	3,980	37	0.56		13.14	103.59	6,653
Hunan 湖南	11	212	20,868	667	2.31	6.96	32.76	66.88	28,923
Guangdong 广东	2	220	7,729	-1,030	-2.59	-4.62	11.10	43.93	39,761
Guangxi 广西									
Hainan 海南									
Southwest 西南	2	208	9,106	-2,751	-7.23		2.00	130.94	38,040
Chongqing 重庆	2	208	9,106	-2,751	-7.23		2.00	130.94	38,040
Sichuan 四川									
Guizhou 贵州									
Yunnan 云南									
Tibet 西藏									
Northwest 西北	2	256	6,300	-3,358	-8.47		11.74	159.89	39,666
Shaanxi 陕西	1	426	6,950	-6,059	-8.16		7.48	166.23	74,265
Gansu 甘肃	1	85	5,650	-657	-12.97	-39.29	33.08	67.00	5,067
Qinghai 青海									
Ningxia 宁夏									
Xinjiang 新疆									

3628: Pharmaceutical Equipment 制药工业专用设备制造业

Year 年份	Number of firms 企业个数	Rate of change 变化率(%)	Number of employees 职工人数(人)	Rate of change 变化率(%)	Total revenue (Mil. RMB) 总销售收入(百万元)	Rate of change 变化率(%)	Total profit (Mil RMB) 总利润(百万元)	Rate of change 变化率(%)
2000	52		11,292		936		35	
2001	65	25.00	13,413	18.78	1,268	35.47	51	45.71
2002	79	21.54	13,286	-0.95	1,758	38.64	125	145.10

Major Products 主要产品	Output 产量	Unit 单位
Pharmacy Special Equipment 制药工业专用设备	15,364	Ton 吨

10 Main Firms with Maximal Revenue (year founded) 收入最大的十家主要企业(创办年份)	City 城市	Province 省	Telephone/fax 电话/传真	Number of employees 职工人数	Ownership 产业所有权	Revenue ('000 RMB) 销售收入(千元)	Profit('000 RMB) (rank) 利润(千元)(排名)	Total assets ('000 RMB) 总资产(千元)	Major products 主要产品
Beijing Ruituo Bioengineering Equipment Co., Ltd.	Beijing	Beijing	(010)61085076		Private Owned				Filtering Equipment
北京锐拓生物工程设备有限公司(2001)	北京市	北京市	(010)61085075	122	私营企业	89,302	11,209(4)	96,155	过滤设备
Shanghai TianXiang & Chentai Pharmaceutical Machinery	Shanghai	Shanghai	(021)62300800		Foreign Funded				Pharmacy Machinery
Co.,Ltd 上海天祥健台制药机械有限公司(1992)	上海市	上海市	(021)62303648	283	外商投资	69,790	12,139(2)	66,830	制药机械
Wenzhou Pharmaceutical Mechanical Equipment Factory	Wenzhou	Zhejiang	(0577)88912789		Joint Stock				High Efficient Capsule Machine高
温州市制药设备厂(1993)	温州市	浙江省	(0577)88912420	411	股份制	67,128	2,173(14)	38,169	效包衣机
Changsha Zhengzhong Medicine Machiney Factory	Changsha	Hunan	(0731)8809862		State-owned				Pharmacy Machinery
长沙正中药机厂(1998)	长沙市	湖南省	(0731)8809862	511	国有企业	65,058	866(29)	124,462	制药机械
Shanghai Yuandong Pharmacy Machinery General Factory Jinqiao	Shanghai	Shanghai	(021)58995186		Joint Owned				Freeze-dry Equipment
Branch Company 上海远东制药机械总厂金桥分厂(1995)	上海市	上海市	(021)58991944	390	联营企业	60,692	48(62)	59,050	冻干设备
Beijing Tianli Deeply Freezing Equipment Stock Co.,Ltd.	Beijing	Beijing	(010)64392868		Overseas Chinese-funded				Freeze-dry Machine
北京天利深冷设备股份有限公司(1993)	北京市	北京市	(010)64392556	123	港澳台资	55,790	11,888(3)	65,390	冻干机
Hengyang Qianshan Pharmaceutical Machinery Co.,Ltd.	Hengyang	Hunan	(0734)8217388		Private Owned				Transfusion Automasiam Product Line输液
衡阳市千山制药机械有限公司(1998)	衡阳市	湖南省	(0734)8217388	680	私营企业	52,504	1,250(22)	35,402	生产自动线
Dandong Jinwan Group Co., Ltd.	Dandong	Liaoning	(0415)4153004		Joint Stock				Filling Machine
丹东金丸集团有限公司(1998)	丹东市	辽宁省	(0415)3133208	380	股份制	50,170	2,800(9)	115,098	充填机
Shanghai Huadong Pharmacy Machinery Co., Ltd.	Shanghai	Shanghai	(021)58108108		Private Owned				Pharmacy Machinery
上海华东制药机械有限公司(1994)	上海市	上海市	(021)58109090	95	私营企业	49,360	32,203(1)	29,900	制药机械
Jilin Huadong Pharmacy Equipment Co., Ltd.	Changchun	Jilin	(0431)4549299		Private Owned				
吉林省华通制药设备有限公司(1999)	长春市	吉林省	(0431)4549499	150	私营企业	39,662	2,300(12)	15,100	

Top 10 Cities by Revenue 销售收入排名前10位城市	Province 省	Market share 市场份额 (%)	Number of firms 企业个数
Shanghai 上海市	Shanghai 上海市	17.69	8
Wenzhou 温州市	Zhejiang 浙江省	14.11	13
Beijing 北京市	Beijing 北京市	11.71	4
Changsha 长沙市	Hunan 湖南省	7.57	7
Wuxi 无锡市	Jiangsu 江苏省	6.74	2
Taizhou 泰州市	Jiangsu 江苏省	4.08	1
Changzhou 常州市	Jiangsu 江苏省	4.03	7
Suzhou 苏州市	Jiangsu 江苏省	3.36	4
Hengyang 衡阳市	Hunan 湖南省	3.16	2
Weifang 潍坊市	Shandong 山东省	2.97	1

10 Major Wholesalers 十家主要批发商	City 城市	Province 省	Telephone/Fax 电话/传真
SU MEC	Nanjing	Jiangsu	(025)4511888
中设江苏机械设备进出口（集团）公司	南京市	江苏省	(025)4411772
China Poster Mobile Communications Equipment Co.,Ltd.	Beijing	Beijing	(010)66426993
中邮普泰移动通信设备股份有限公司	北京市	北京市	(010)66426837
Sino Kama Co., Ltd.	Shanghai	Shanghai	(021)62031188
中泰凯马股份有限公司	上海市	上海市	(021)62030851
China Huayuan Group Co.,Ltd.	Shanghai	Shanghai	(021)62031188
中国华源集团有限公司	上海市	上海市	(021)62032288
Zhejiang Crand Imp.& Exp.Co.,Ltd.	Ningbo	Zhejiang	(0574)87720170
浙江远大进出口有限公司	宁波市	浙江省	(0574)87723350
Shandong Machinery Import & Export Group Corporation	Qingdao	Shandong	(0532)2661628
山东省机械进出口集团公司	青岛市	山东省	(0532)2991655
Qingdao Haier International Trade Co.,Ltd.	Qingdao	Shandong	(0532)8938337
青岛海尔国际贸易有限公司	青岛市	山东省	(0532)8939494
Guangdong Machinery Import & Export Group Corporation	Guangzhou	Guangdong	(020)87782168
广东省机械进出口集团公司	广州市	广东省	(020)87771803
China National Machinery Equipment Import & Export Corporation	Beijing	Beijing	(010)63474506
中国机械设备进出口总公司	北京市	北京市	(010)63261865
Beijing Cellstar Co.,Ltd.	Beijing	Beijing	(010)64602050
北京蜂星事达电讯有限公司	北京市	北京市	(010)64672648

3629: Constructing Material and Other Non-metal Mineral Products
建材及其他非金属矿物制品专用设备制造业

The industry accounts for 0.043% of the total revenue of China's industrial sector in 2002. The rate of return on assets is -0.06%. 73.56% of all firms in the industry made a profit while 26.44% had negative returns.The top province in terms of the industry's revenue is Jiangsu, accounting for 24.33% of the total revenue.
2002年本行业收入占全行业的 0.043%，资产利润率为 -0.06%。73.56%的企业赢利，26.44%的企业亏损。收入最高的省为江苏省，占本行业的24.33%。

	Total number of firms 企业总数	Total number of employees 职工总数	Total revenue (Mil.RMB) 总销售收入（百万元）	Total profit (Mil.RMB) 总利润（百万元）	Return on assets 资产利润率（%）	Return on equity 权益利润率（%）	Labour productivity ('000 RMB/ worker) 劳动生产率（千元/人）	Debts/ assets 资产负债率（%）	Total assets (Mil.RMB) 总资产（百万元）
Industry Overall 行业总体	174	41,639	4,642	-6	-0.06	-0.27	31.74	77.36	9,444

	Number of firms 企业个数	Average number of employees 平均职工人数	Average revenue ('000 RMB) 平均销售收入（千元）	Average profit ('000 RMB) 平均利润（千元）	Return on assets 资产利润率（%）	Return on equity 权益利润率（%）	Labour productivity ('000 RMB/ worker) 劳动生产率（千元/人）	Debts/ assets 资产负债率（%）	Average total assets ('000 RMB) 平均总资产（千元）
By ownership 产业所有权									
State-owned 国有	46	327	18,878	-1,927	-2.45	-44.49	15.93	94.50	78,755
Collective-owned 集体	22	137	16,028	808	7.02	20.17	34.63	65.21	11,521
Foreign & Overseas Chinese Funded 三资	14	125	44,146	1,634	3.16	11.58	106.42	72.66	51,650
By regional distribution 地区分布									
Central-North 华北	23	261	29,864	1,163	1.58	4.76	40.82	66.76	73,450
Beijing 北京	6	144	18,303	2,455	3.83	4.85	72.70	20.95	64,080
Tianjin 天津	2	143	128,059	10,750	6.09	37.60	261.84	83.80	176,487
Hebei 河北	12	364	25,400	-795	-1.07	-5.22	23.34	79.41	74,019
Shanxi 山西	3	160	5,379	21	0.10	0.35	10.86	72.48	21,221
Inner Mongolia 内蒙古									
Northeast 东北	7	621	33,694	-13,279	-7.90		-1.82	105.82	168,112
Liaoning 辽宁	6	723	39,279	-15,475	-7.89		-1.89	105.83	196,079
Jilin 吉林	1	6	185	-99	-31.83	-61.88	49.17	48.55	311
Heilongjiang 黑龙江									
Central-East 华东	81	193	25,141	758	2.38	14.88	42.44	84.00	31,855
Shanghai 上海	8	260	36,279	1,369	3.20		43.22	149.95	42,829
Jiangsu 江苏	42	172	26,888	630	2.05	5.63	54.09	63.60	30,723
Zhejiang 浙江	4	91	11,867	182	1.14	2.52	29.29	54.62	15,906
Anhui 安徽	3	108	6,193	376	2.41	5.42	25.46	55.48	15,609
Fujian 福建	3	187	14,745	1,292	7.84	12.83	37.22	38.89	16,475
Jiangxi 江西	2	217	9,070	-258	-0.89	-3.83	10.31	76.78	28,995
Shandong 山东	19	247	25,710	990	2.58	89.93	29.99	97.13	38,389
Central-South 中南	45	201	27,227	-1		-0.01	33.78	68.77	54,643
Henan 河南	12	116	24,912	1,294	7.20	21.36	71.20	66.32	17,990
Hubei 湖北	9	413	11,673	-1,974	-3.22	-40.47	8.34	92.04	61,307
Hunan 湖南	7	230	10,622	-2,661	-6.44	-39.63	12.46	83.74	41,311
Guangdong 广东	15	142	49,367	1,395	1.50	3.47	71.38	56.70	92,701
Guangxi 广西	2	86	3,179	-60	-1.02	-5.32	13.48	80.77	5,813
Hainan 海南									
Southwest 西南	9	449	22,258	-601	-0.63	-1.40	17.39	55.29	96,067
Chongqing 重庆	1	100	7,260	180	19.52	23.32	18.90	16.27	922
Sichuan 四川	5	504	27,115	-65	-0.06	-0.13	19.68	56.73	117,975
Guizhou 贵州									
Yunnan 云南	3	475	19,163	-1,754	-1.92	-4.03	13.22	52.33	91,269
Tibet 西藏									
Northwest 西北	9	283	28,570	487	0.65	5.67	17.28	88.53	74,869
Shaanxi 陕西	7	288	30,552	81	0.10	1.34	14.09	92.82	84,201
Gansu 甘肃	1	50	27,754	2,663	51.98	83.01	189.54	37.38	5,123
Qinghai 青海									
Ningxia 宁夏	1	483	15,514	1,151	1.45	3.62	12.76	59.95	79,290
Xinjiang 新疆									

3629: Constructing Material and Other Non-metal Mineral Products

建材及其他非金属矿物制品专用设备制造业

Year 年份	Number of firms 企业个数	Rate of change 变化率 (%)	Number of employees 职工人数 (人)	Rate of change 变化率 (%)	Total revenue (Mil. RMB) 总销售收入 (百万元)	Rate of change 变化率 (%)	Total profit (Mil RMB) 总利润 (百万元)	Rate of change 变化率 (%)
2000	193		55,968		3,178		-73	
2001	174	-9.84	44,794	-19.96	3,520	10.76	-87	-19.18
2002	174		41,639	-7.04	4,642	31.88	-6	93.10

Major Products 主要产品	Output 产量	Unit 单位
Cement Equipment 水泥设备	168,834	Ton 吨

10 Main Firms with Maximal Revenue (year founded) 收入最大的十家主要企业（创办年份）	City 城市	Province 省	Telephone/fax 电话/传真	Number of employees 职工人数	Ownership 产业所有权	Revenue ('000 RMB) 销售收入 (千元)	Profit('000 RMB) (rank) 利润(千元) (排名)	Total assets ('000 RMB) 总资产 (千元)	Major products 主要产品
Foshan Eagle Brand Equipment Complete Set Co., Ltd.	Foshan	Guangdong	(0757)3963605		Overseas Chinese-funded				Ceramic Furnace
佛山市鹰牌设备配套有限公司(1995)	佛山市	广东省	(0757)2271664	345	港澳台资	241,119	3,753(13)	347,658	陶瓷窑炉
Guangdong Keda Electromechanical Co., Ltd.	Foshan	Guangdong	(0765)3832998		Private Owned				Ceramic Machinery
广东科达机电股份有限公司(1996)	佛山市	广东省	(0765)3312955	498	私营企业	216,830	3,617(14)	493,773	陶瓷机械
Tangshan Cement Machinery Factory	Tangshan	Hebei	(0315)3271311		State-owned				Cement Equipment
唐山水泥机械厂(1910)	唐山市	河北省	(0315)3271128	2,123	国有企业	150,098	-	463,302	水泥设备
Xi'an Mining Machinery Factory	Xi'an	Shannxi	(029)4265702		Joint Stock				Cement Equipment
西安矿山机械厂(1965)	西安市	陕西省	(029)4265604	489	股份制	149,707	18,971(2)	184,459	水泥设备
Shanghai Xinjian Machinery Factory	Shanghai	Shanghai	(021)58801888		State-owned				Cement Equipment
上海新建机器厂(1955)	上海市	上海市	(021)58801119	940	国有企业	121,871	2,995(19)	139,277	水泥设备
Zhangjiagang Potain Construction Machinery Co.,Ltd.	Suzhou	Jiangsu	(0520)58780088		Foreign Funded				Tower Hoist
张家港波坦建筑机械有限公司(1995)	苏州市	江苏省	(0520)58780098	238	外商投资	112,418	4,065(11)	128,174	塔吊
Jiangsu Pengfei Industrial Co., Ltd.	Nantong	Jiangsu	(0513)8755312		Joint Stock				Ball Milling Machine
江苏鹏飞实业股份有限公司(1955)	南通市	江苏省	(0513)8755315	433	股份制	96,258	1,625(25)	139,920	球磨机
Shandong Boxing Huaxing Enterprise Group Company	Binzhou	Shandong	(0543)2321531		State-owned				Sawing Stone Machine
山东省博兴县华兴企业集团公司(1995)	滨州市	山东省	(0543)2321531	417	国有企业	89,762	8,206(5)	140,144	锯石机
Chaozhong Group Co.,Ltd.	Chaoyang	Liaoning	(0421)2810501		State Enterprises				Cement Equipment
朝重集团有限责任公司(1995)	朝阳市	辽宁省	(0421)2819131	2,164	国有独资	[illegible]0,000	-	532,804	水泥设备
Zhongtian Shiming (Xuzhou) Heavy Co., Ltd.	Xuzhou	Jiangsu	(0516)5755950		Joint Stock				Cement Equipment
中天仕名（徐州）重型有限公司(1970)	徐州市	江苏省	(0516)5755950	471	股份制	81,780	-	157,490	水泥设备

Top 10 Cities by Revenue 销售收入排名前10位城市	Province 省	Market share 市场份额 (%)	Number of firms 企业个数
Foshan 佛山市	Guangdong 广东省	14.03	5
Shanghai 上海市	Shanghai 上海市	6.25	8
Suzhou 苏州市	Jiangsu 江苏省	5.70	6
Tianjin 天津市	Tianjin 天津市	5.52	2
Nantong 南通市	Jiangsu 江苏省	5.00	6
Tangshan 唐山市	Hebei 河北省	4.65	5
Xi'an 西安市	Shannxi 陕西省	4.06	5
Chaoyang 朝阳市	Liaoning 辽宁省	3.57	3
Xuzhou 徐州市	Jiangsu 江苏省	3.18	6
Taizhou 泰州市	Jiangsu 江苏省	2.64	2

10 Major Wholesalers 十家主要批发商	City 城市	Province 省	Telephone/Fax 电话/传真
SU MEC	Nanjing	Jiangsu	(025)4511888
中设江苏机械设备进出口（集团）公司	南京市	江苏省	(025)4411772
China Poster Mobile Communications Equipment Co.,Ltd.	Beijing	Beijing	(010)66426993
中邮普泰移动通信设备股份有限公司	北京市	北京市	(010)66426837
Sino Kama Co., Ltd.	Shanghai	Shanghai	(021)62031188
中泰凯马股份有限公司	上海市	上海市	(021)62030851
China Huayuan Group Co.,Ltd.	Shanghai	Shanghai	(021)62031188
中国华源集团有限公司	上海市	上海市	(021)62032288
Zhejiang Crand Imp.& Exp.Co.,Ltd.	Ningbo	Zhejiang	(0574)87720170
浙江远大进出口有限公司	宁波市	浙江省	(0574)87723350
Shandong Machinery Import & Export Group Corporation	Qingdao	Shandong	(0532)2661628
山东省机械进出口集团公司	青岛市	山东省	(0532)2991655
Qingdao Haier International Trade Co.,Ltd.	Qingdao	Shandong	(0532)8938337
青岛海尔国际贸易有限公司	青岛市	山东省	(0532)8939494
Guangdong Machinery Import & Export Group Corporation	Guangzhou	Guangdong	(020)87782168
广东省机械进出口集团公司	广州市	广东省	(020)87771803
China National Machinery Equipment Import & Export Corporation	Beijing	Beijing	(010)63474506
中国机械设备进出口总公司	北京市	北京市	(010)63261865
Beijing Cellstar Co.,Ltd.	Beijing	Beijing	(010)64602050
北京蜂星事达电讯有限公司	北京市	北京市	(010)64672648

3631: Food, Beverage and Tobacco Equipment

食品、饮料、烟草工业专用设备制造业

The industry accounts for 0.058% of the total revenue of China's industrial sector in 2002. The rate of return on assets is 2.58%. 76.36% of all firms in the industry made a profit while 23.64% had negative returns.The top province in terms of the industry's revenue is Shanghai, accounting for 16.68% of the total revenue.
2002年本行业收入占全行业的0.058%，资产利润率为2.58%。76.36%的企业赢利，23.64%的企业亏损。收入最高的省为上海市，占本行业的16.68%。

	Total number of firms 企业总数	Total number of employees 职工总数	Total revenue (Mil.RMB) 总销售收入 (百万元)	Total profit (Mil.RMB) 总利润 (百万元)	Return on assets 资产利润率 (%)	Return on equity 权益利润率 (%)	Labour productivity ('000 RMB/ worker) 劳动生产率 (千元/人)	Debts/ assets 资产负债率 (%)	Total assets (Mil.RMB) 总资产 (百万元)
Industry Overall 行业总体	220	48,878	6,221	301	2.58	6.53	44.55	60.46	11,667

	Number of firms 企业个数	Average number of employees 平均职工人数	Average revenue ('000 RMB) 平均销售收入（千元）	Average profit ('000 RMB) 平均利润 (千元)	Return on assets 资产利润率 (%)	Return on equity 权益利润率 (%)	Labour productivity ('000 RMB/ worker) 劳动生产率 (千元/人)	Debts/ assets 资产负债率 (%)	Average total assets ('000 RMB) 平均总资产 (千元)
By ownership 产业所有权									
State-owned 国有	35	385	34,498	657	0.78	2.33	36.71	66.73	84,738
Collective-owned 集体	28	142	31,657	2,200	7.72	17.60	60.64	56.16	28,502
Foreign & Overseas Chinese Funded 三资	28	135	34,675	2,322	5.86	12.56	81.27	53.32	39,592
By regional distribution 地区分布									
Central-North 华北	25	270	22,694	486	0.99	3.32	29.39	70.22	49,139
Beijing 北京	7	100	11,528	830	4.38	9.76	44.77	55.15	18,951
Tianjin 天津	3	305	54,296	1,445	1.61	5.04	61.36	68.15	90,006
Hebei 河北	13	353	22,155	46	0.08	0.29	21.10	72.78	58,450
Shanxi 山西									
Inner Mongolia 内蒙古	2	269	17,878	706	2.14	10.45	25.74	79.53	32,976
Northeast 东北	5	152	20,819	878	6.43	30.27	46.09	78.75	13,644
Liaoning 辽宁	1	130	3,470	330	5.16	6.37	9.59	19.06	6,400
Jilin 吉林	2	117	42,272	2,146	13.58	48.57	118.01	72.04	15,797
Heilongjiang 黑龙江	2	198	8,041	-117	-0.77	-48.24	15.50	98.40	15,114
Central-East 华东	98	158	28,084	2,165	4.63	9.20	56.99	49.67	46,761
Shanghai 上海	19	215	54,617	3,906	2.68	4.67	92.77	42.61	145,729
Jiangsu 江苏	28	121	25,766	2,293	9.22	23.57	56.78	60.88	24,871
Zhejiang 浙江	27	99	17,307	1,533	8.45	18.38	53.81	54.02	18,140
Anhui 安徽	4	277	18,635	813	1.98	6.04	17.98	67.20	41,060
Fujian 福建	4	80	13,336	1,141	6.64	8.56	26.05	22.42	17,186
Jiangxi 江西									
Shandong 山东	16	243	24,871	1,532	6.21	21.73	35.36	71.41	24,659
Central-South 中南	63	217	29,516	530	1.03	2.75	48.31	62.63	51,654
Henan 河南	15	341	28,219	990	1.93	4.96	31.70	61.14	51,301
Hubei 湖北	7	148	20,156	539	2.07	8.59	38.77	75.90	26,029
Hunan 湖南	6	289	74,355	3,545	3.72	7.16	116.13	48.14	95,409
Guangdong 广东	30	164	26,576	-370	-0.68	-2.13	47.47	67.92	53,977
Guangxi 广西	5	168	10,341	920	4.15	8.10	26.36	48.72	22,153
Hainan 海南									
Southwest 西南	22	475	39,985	2,620	2.57	6.91	36.23	62.85	102,097
Chongqing 重庆	1	723	24,477	1,505	1.40	3.16	22.44	55.65	107,344
Sichuan 四川	2	147	48,863	1,005	1.66	2.30	109.59	27.90	60,572
Guizhou 贵州	1	19		-53	-1.48	-8.53	-0.84	82.66	3,581
Yunnan 云南	18	523	42,081	3,010	2.69	7.75	35.07	65.30	111,892
Tibet 西藏									
Northwest 西北	7	257	8,350	-2,620	-6.38		13.48	143.20	41,088
Shaanxi 陕西	5	339	11,604	-3,625	-6.52		13.54	145.72	55,585
Gansu 甘肃	2	54	215	-108	-2.23	-7.66	12.46	70.90	4,844
Qinghai 青海									
Ningxia 宁夏									
Xinjiang 新疆									

3631: Food, Beverage and Tobacco Equipment
食品、饮料、烟草工业专用设备制造业

Year 年份	Number of firms 企业个数	Rate of change 变化率 (%)	Number of employees 职工人数 (人)	Rate of change 变化率 (%)	Total revenue (Mil. RMB) 总销售收入 (百万元)	Rate of change 变化率 (%)	Total profit (Mil RMB) 总利润 (百万元)	Rate of change 变化率 (%)
2000	214		62,044		5,098		187	
2001	217	1.40	49,648	-19.98	5,436	6.63	190	1.60
2002	220	1.38	48,878	-1.55	6,221	14.44	301	58.42

Major Products 主要产品	Output 产量	Unit 单位
Tobacco Processing Machinery 烟草加工机械	4,304	Unit 台(条、组)

10 Main Firms with Maximal Revenue (year founded) 收入最大的十家主要企业（创办年份）	City 城市	Province 省	Telephone/fax 电话/传真	Number of employees 职工人数	Ownership 产业所有权	Revenue ('000 RMB) 销售收入(千元)	Profit('000 RMB) (rank) 利润(千元)(排名)	Total assets ('000 RMB) 总资产(千元)	Major products 主要产品
Shanghai Tobacco Machinery Co., Ltd.	Shanghai	Shanghai	(021)50312600		State-owned				Tobacco Industry Special Equipment烟草工
上海烟草工业机械有限责任公司(1952)	上海市	上海市	(021)58992585	1,196	国有企业	370,226	35,062(1)	796,507	业专用设备
Changde Tobacco Machinery Co.,Ltd.	Changde	Hunan	(0736)7178000		Limited-Liability				Corrugated Set
常德烟草机械有限责任公司(1970)	常德市	湖南省	(0736)7178888	1,054	有限公司	262,450	20,250(4)	490,120	卷接机组
Yunnan Kunchuan Second Machinery Co., Ltd.	Kunming	Yunnan	(0871)7232873		Limited-Liability				Tobacco Shredding Machine烟草
云南昆船第二机械有限公司(1979)	昆明市	云南省	(0871)7232835	1,980	有限公司	257,423	24,628(3)	463,863	制丝设备
Qinhuangdao Tobacco Machinery Co., Ltd.	Qinhuangdao	Hebei	(0335)3064935		State-owned				Tobacco Machinery
秦皇岛烟草机械有限责任公司(1969)	秦皇岛市	河北省	(0335)3063426	1,502	国有企业	172,859	3,938(28)	476,284	烟草机械
Shanghai Light Industry Installation (Group) Co., Ltd.	Shanghai	Shanghai	(021)63027299		Limited-Liability				Cold Drinks Machinery
上海轻工装备(集团)有限公司(1950)	上海市	上海市	(021)63042404	480	有限公司	169,001	723(75)	1,072,946	冷饮机械
Satake Manufacturing(Suzhou)Co.,Ltd.	Suzhou	Jiangsu	(0512)65368225		Foreign Funded				Grain Processing Machinery粮食
佐竹机械(苏州)有限公司(1998)	苏州市	江苏省	(0512)65365922	215	外商投资	167,516	34,690(2)	158,081	加工机械
Xuchang Tobacco Machinery Co., Ltd.	Xuchang	Henan	(0374)3266911		State-owned				Cigaret Roller Equipment卷烟
许昌烟草机械有限责任公司(1966)	许昌市	河南省	(0374)3266977	1,353	国有企业	148,150	3,920(29)	367,000	机械设备
Yunnan Kunchuan First Machinery Co.,Ltd.	Kunming	Yunnan	(0871)7231840		Limited-Liability				Tobacco Machinery
云南昆船第一机械有限公司(1975)	昆明市	云南省	(0871)7231757	2,075	有限公司	144,549	974(66)	509,073	烟草机械
Sinmag Machinery (Wuxi) Co., Ltd.	Wuxi	Jiangsu	(0510)3771247		Overseas Chinese-funded				Food Mechanical Oven食品
新麦机械(无锡)有限公司(1994)	无锡市	江苏省	(0510)3774360	230	港澳台资	120,820	19,470(5)	85,480	机械烤炉
Guangdong Laida Industrial (Group) Company	Shantou	Guangdong	(0661)8603234		Private Owned				Beer Filling Production Whole Set Equipment啤酒生
广东莱达实业（集团）公司(1978)	汕头市	广东省	(0661)8824220	633	私营企业	105,300	250(113)	349,930	产成套设备

Top 10 Cities by Revenue 销售收入排名前10位城市	Province 省	Market share 市场份额 (%)	Number of firms 企业个数
Shanghai 上海市	Shanghai 上海市	16.68	19
Kunming 昆明市	Yunnan 云南省	11.75	13
Changde 常德市	Hunan 湖南省	4.89	3
Guangzhou 广州市	Guangdong 广东省	4.79	10
Suzhou 苏州市	Jiangsu 江苏省	4.17	6
Ningbo 宁波市	Zhejiang 浙江省	3.83	12
Xuchang 许昌市	Henan 河南省	3.36	3
Zhanjiang 湛江市	Guangdong 广东省	3.00	9
Qinhuangdao 秦皇岛市	Hebei 河北省	2.91	3
Wuxi 无锡市	Jiangsu 江苏省	2.86	4

10 Major Wholesalers 十家主要批发商	City 城市	Province 省	Telephone/Fax 电话/传真
SU MEC	Nanjing	Jiangsu	(025)4511888
中设江苏机械设备进出口（集团）公司	南京市	江苏省	(025)4411772
China Poster Mobile Communications Equipment Co.,Ltd.	Beijing	Beijing	(010)66426993
中邮普泰移动通信设备股份有限公司	北京市	北京市	(010)66426837
Sino Kama Co., Ltd.	Shanghai	Shanghai	(021)62031188
中泰凯马股份有限公司	上海市	上海市	(021)62030851
China Huayuan Group Co.,Ltd.	Shanghai	Shanghai	(021)62031188
中国华源集团有限公司	上海市	上海市	(021)62032288
Zhejiang Crand Imp.& Exp.Co.,Ltd.	Ningbo	Zhejiang	(0574)87720170
浙江远大进出口有限公司	宁波市	浙江省	(0574)87723350
Shandong Machinery Import & Export Group Corporation	Qingdao	Shandong	(0532)2661628
山东省机械进出口集团公司	青岛市	山东省	(0532)2991655
Qingdao Haier International Trade Co.,Ltd.	Qingdao	Shandong	(0532)8938337
青岛海尔国际贸易有限公司	青岛市	山东省	(0532)8939494
Guangdong Machinery Import & Export Group Corporation	Guangzhou	Guangdong	(020)87782168
广东省机械进出口集团公司	广州市	广东省	(020)87771803
China National Machinery Equipment Import & Export Corporation	Beijing	Beijing	(010)63474506
中国机械设备进出口总公司	北京市	北京市	(010)63261865
Beijing Cellstar Co.,Ltd.	Beijing	Beijing	(010)64602050
北京蜂星事达电讯有限公司	北京市	北京市	(010)64672648

3632: Grain and Cooking Oil Equipment 粮油工业专用设备制造业

The industry accounts for 0.033% of the total revenue of China's industrial sector in 2002. The rate of return on assets is 1.33%. 69.11% of all firms in the industry made a profit while 30.89% had negative returns.The top province in terms of the industry's revenue is Henan, accounting for 24.90% of the total revenue.
2002年本行业收入占全行业的0.033%，资产利润率为1.33%。69.11%的企业赢利，30.89%的企业亏损。收入最高的省为河南省，占本行业的24.90%。

	Total number of firms 企业总数	Total number of employees 职工总数	Total revenue (Mil.RMB) 总销售收入 (百万元)	Total profit (Mil.RMB) 总利润 (百万元)	Return on assets 资产利润率 (%)	Return on equity 权益利润率 (%)	Labour productivity ('000 RMB/ worker) 劳动生产率 (千元/人)	Debts/ assets 资产负债率 (%)	Total assets (Mil.RMB) 总资产 (百万元)
Industry Overall 行业总体	246	45,396	3,556	66	1.33	3.21	28.25	58.59	4,932

	Number of firms 企业个数	Average number of employees 平均职工人数	Average revenue ('000 RMB) 平均销售收入 (千元)	Average profit ('000 RMB) 平均利润 (千元)	Return on assets 资产利润率 (%)	Return on equity 权益利润率 (%)	Labour productivity ('000 RMB/ worker) 劳动生产率 (千元/人)	Debts/ assets 资产负债率 (%)	Average total assets ('000 RMB) 平均总资产 (千元)
By ownership 产业所有权									
State-owned 国有	101	163	5,422	-309	-1.87	-6.09	11.39	69.23	16,467
Collective-owned 集体	30	240	30,640	976	3.63	6.94	53.90	47.71	26,906
Foreign & Overseas Chinese Funded 三资	6	168	24,714	398	0.74	1.22	59.58	39.07	53,574
By regional distribution 地区分布									
Central-North 华北	21	194	12,316	879	6.20	18.71	27.53	66.89	14,192
Beijing 北京	1	25	8,375	417	4.91	12.25	296.56	59.88	8,486
Tianjin 天津	2	177	137	-250	-3.34	-7.27	0.97	54.06	7,489
Hebei 河北	15	232	15,744	1,236	7.11	22.39	28.43	68.25	17,384
Shanxi 山西	3	72	4,608	3	0.06	0.14	25.23	59.49	4,598
Inner Mongolia 内蒙古									
Northeast 东北	21	160	6,495	52	0.24	0.69	17.20	65.48	21,538
Liaoning 辽宁	7	189	12,302	621	2.12	5.13	28.73	58.61	29,272
Jilin 吉林	12	159	3,595	-37	-0.19	-0.65	8.00	70.82	19,552
Heilongjiang 黑龙江	2	62	3,568	-1,413	-22.13	-98.85	35.46	77.61	6,383
Central-East 华东	67	216	22,715	225	0.83	1.91	29.41	56.36	26,906
Shanghai 上海	1	194	48,828				62.68	77.03	136,298
Jiangsu 江苏	21	185	25,518	144	0.48	0.89	43.71	46.72	30,277
Zhejiang 浙江	7	77	9,413	672	6.31	14.45	48.40	56.31	10,650
Anhui 安徽	5	325	4,641	-85	-0.52	-1.28	7.20	59.44	16,379
Fujian 福建	6	78	1,174	-141	-2.23	-5.80	4.98	61.53	6,326
Jiangxi 江西	3	178	4,450	-9	-0.04	-0.10	8.61	65.22	26,152
Shandong 山东	24	300	34,488	359	1.14	2.79	27.50	59.22	31,574
Central-South 中南	103	173	14,264	308	1.67	3.89	33.51	57.24	18,500
Henan 河南	39	231	22,703	830	3.52	7.68	45.50	54.11	23,556
Hubei 湖北	23	164	11,031	36	0.23	0.48	25.47	52.17	15,803
Hunan 湖南	19	110	9,560	111	0.89	2.44	23.53	63.54	12,471
Guangdong 广东	11	144	11,393	275	1.19	3.84	22.43	68.88	23,017
Guangxi 广西	10	132	1,707	-649	-5.07	-12.37	4.46	58.99	12,800
Hainan 海南	1	88	6,024	-110	-2.11	-6.79	22.16	68.94	5,216
Southwest 西南	18	118	5,093	-1	-0.01	-0.04	19.49	64.68	9,733
Chongqing 重庆	1	8	268	51	7.72	9.24	8.88	16.49	661
Sichuan 四川	9	206	9,925	234	1.58	3.25	22.09	51.38	14,840
Guizhou 贵州	5	28	114	-176	-4.86	-31.29	3.06	84.46	3,614
Yunnan 云南	3	43	502	-436	-5.71		1.17	128.09	7,632
Tibet 西藏									
Northwest 西北	16	221	4,920	-41	-0.22	-0.53	13.51	58.35	18,658
Shaanxi 陕西	7	315	8,467	18	0.06	0.12	16.22	47.06	29,938
Gansu 甘肃	7	172	1,432	-136	-1.43	-6.22	5.74	77.08	9,533
Qinghai 青海									
Ningxia 宁夏									
Xinjiang 新疆	2	59	4,711	85	0.76		42.47	108.57	11,117

3632: Grain and Cooking Oil Equipment 粮油工业专用设备制造业

Year 年份	Number of firms 企业个数	Rate of change 变化率 (%)	Number of employees 职工人数 (人)	Rate of change 变化率 (%)	Total revenue (Mil. RMB) 总销售收入 (百万元)	Rate of change 变化率 (%)	Total profit (Mil RMB) 总利润 (百万元)	Rate of change 变化率 (%)
2000	308		65,134		3,768		64	
2001	294	-4.55	57,642	-11.50	4,404	16.88	118	84.38
2002	246	-16.33	45,396	-21.24	3,556	-19.26	66	-44.07

Major Products 主要产品	Output 产量	Unit 单位
Cereal & Oilseed Processing Machinery 粮食加工机械	56	10,000 Units 万台

10 Main Firms with Maximal Revenue (year founded) 收入最大的十家主要企业（创办年份）	City 城市	Province 省	Telephone/fax 电话/传真	Number of employees 职工人数	Ownership 产业所有权	Revenue ('000 RMB) 销售收入 (千元)	Profit('000 RMB) (rank) 利润(千元)(排名)	Total assets ('000 RMB) 总资产 (千元)	Major products 主要产品
Jiangsu Jinggu Rice Machine Co., Ltd.	Zhenjiang	Jiangsu	(0511)6346492		Private Enterprises				Rice Machine
丹阳晶谷米机集团公司(1993)	镇江市	江苏省	(0511)6342340	875	私营独资	160,000	1,089(28)	195,920	米机
GuangDong Hengli Hushan Machinery Tecnology Co.Ltd.	Weihai	Shandong	(0631)7431234		Joint Stock				Cereal & Oilseed Starch Making Machinery粮
山东恒力虎山机械科技有限责任公司(2000)	威海市	山东省	(0631)7431072	1,012	股份制	154,690	17,240(1)	49,970	油制粉机
Kaifeng Second Grain Machinery Factory	Kaifeng	Henan	(0378)8991438		Collective-owned				Vibrating Screen
开封第二粮机厂(1976)	开封市	河南省	(0378)8993123	1,100	集体企业	153,681	5,806(5)	97,149	振动筛
Qingdao Haichi Industrial Co., Ltd.	Qingdao	Shandong	(0532)2846050		Limited-Liability				Cereal & Oilseed Processing Machinery粮食
青岛海驰实业有限公司(1999)	青岛市	山东省	(0532)2807767	113	有限公司	105,154	13(113)	33,129	加工机械
Wuxi Buhler Machine Manufacturing Co.,Ltd.	Wuxi	Jiangsu	(0510)5756641		Foreign Funded				Starch Making Machine
无锡布勒机械制造有限公司(1994)	无锡市	江苏省	(0510)5755277	591	外商投资	80,315	1,056(31)	162,374	制粉机械
Zibo Huantai Jintai Alloy Roller Co.,Ltd.	Zibo	Shandong	(0533)8880068		Private Enterprises				Alloy Roller
淄博桓台金泰轧辊有限公司(1976)	淄博市	山东省	(0533)8880066	188	私营独资	79,013	2,797(10)	25,920	合金轧辊
Shandong Tongtai Group Co.,Ltd.	Rizhao	Shandong	(0633)8286807		Joint Stock				Cereal & Oilseed Processing Machinery粮食
山东同泰集团股份有限公司(1937)	日照市	山东省	(0633)8285655	1,065	股份制	69,867	1,625(18)	101,997	加工机械
Hebei Huangpai Machinery Co., Ltd.	Shijiazhuang	Hebei	(0311)4221504		State-owned				Cereal & Oilseed Processing Machinery粮食
河北皇牌机械有限公司(1958)	石家庄市	河北省	(0311)4220503	1,391	国有企业	58,001	8,400(3)	43,456	加工机械
Danyang Grind Mill Equipment Factory	Zhenjiang	Jiangsu	(0511)6612721		Private Enterprises				Paddy Pounder
丹阳市碾米设备厂(1962)	镇江市	江苏省	(0511)6611732	201	私营独资	53,695	-	10,332	碾米机
Shanghai Suncue Mahchinery Co., Ltd.	Shanghai	Shanghai	(021)62211839		Foreign Funded				Corn Drying Machine谷
上海三久机械有限公司(1996)	上海市	上海市	(021)62211848	194	外商投资	48,828	-	136,298	物烘干机

Top 10 Cities by Revenue 销售收入排名前10位城市	Province 省	Market share 市场份额 (%)	Number of firms 企业个数
Weihai 威海市	Shandong 山东省	9.55	2
Zhengzhou 郑州市	Henan 河南省	9.47	3
Luohe 漯河市	Henan 河南省	7.04	14
Zhenjiang 镇江市	Jiangsu 江苏省	6.01	2
Kaifeng 开封市	Henan 河南省	4.35	2
Wuxi 无锡市	Jiangsu 江苏省	3.74	3
Shijiazhuang 石家庄市	Hebei 河北省	3.53	6
Jining 济宁市	Shandong 山东省	3.32	5
Zibo 淄博市	Shandong 山东省	3.04	3
Qingdao 青岛市	Shandong 山东省	3.03	2

10 Major Wholesalers 十家主要批发商	City 城市	Province 省	Telephone/Fax 电话/传真
SU MEC	Nanjing	Jiangsu	(025)4511888
中设江苏机械设备进出口（集团）公司	南京市	江苏省	(025)4411772
China Poster Mobile Communications Equipment Co.,Ltd.	Beijing	Beijing	(010)66426993
中邮普泰移动通信设备股份有限公司	北京市	北京市	(010)66426837
Sino Kama Co., Ltd.	Shanghai	Shanghai	(021)62031188
中泰凯马股份有限公司	上海市	上海市	(021)62030851
China Huayuan Group Co.,Ltd.	Shanghai	Shanghai	(021)62031188
中国华源集团有限公司	上海市	上海市	(021)62032288
Zhejiang Crand Imp.& Exp.Co.,Ltd.	Ningbo	Zhejiang	(0574)87720170
浙江远大进出口有限公司	宁波市	浙江省	(0574)87723350
Shandong Machinery Import & Export Group Corporation	Qingdao	Shandong	(0532)2661628
山东省机械进出口集团公司	青岛市	山东省	(0532)2991655
Qingdao Haier International Trade Co.,Ltd.	Qingdao	Shandong	(0532)8938337
青岛海尔国际贸易有限公司	青岛市	山东省	(0532)8939494
Guangdong Machinery Import & Export Group Corporation	Guangzhou	Guangdong	(020)87782168
广东省机械进出口集团公司	广州市	广东省	(020)87771803
China National Machinery Equipment Import & Export Corporation	Beijing	Beijing	(010)63474506
中国机械设备进出口总公司	北京市	北京市	(010)63261865
Beijing Cellstar Co.,Ltd.	Beijing	Beijing	(010)64602050
北京蜂星事达电讯有限公司	北京市	北京市	(010)64672648

3633: Animal Feed Equipment 饲料工业专用设备制造业

The industry accounts for 0.011% of the total revenue of China's industrial sector in 2002. The rate of return on assets is 1.57%. 79.31% of all firms in the industry made a profit while 20.69% had negative returns.The top province in terms of the industry's revenue is Jiangsu, accounting for 82.01% of the total revenue.
2002年本行业收入占全行业的0.011%，资产利润率为1.57%。79.31%的企业赢利，20.69%的企业亏损。收入最高的省为江苏省，占本行业的82.01%。

	Total number of firms 企业总数	Total number of employees 职工总数	Total revenue (Mil.RMB) 总销售收入(百万元)	Total profit (Mil.RMB) 总利润(百万元)	Return on assets 资产利润率(%)	Return on equity 权益利润率(%)	Labour productivity ('000 RMB/ worker) 劳动生产率(千元/人)	Debts/ assets 资产负债率(%)	Total assets (Mil.RMB) 总资产(百万元)
Industry Overall 行业总体	29	4,918	1,156	19	1.57	4.43	75.25	64.59	1,221

	Number of firms 企业个数	Average number of employees 平均职工人数	Average revenue ('000 RMB) 平均销售收入(千元)	Average profit ('000 RMB) 平均利润(千元)	Return on assets 资产利润率(%)	Return on equity 权益利润率(%)	Labour productivity ('000 RMB/ worker) 劳动生产率(千元/人)	Debts/ assets 资产负债率(%)	Average total assets ('000 RMB) 平均总资产(千元)
By ownership 产业所有权									
State-owned 国有	10	155	51,062	-1,330	-2.28	-6.06	127.71	62.42	58,429
Collective-owned 集体	2	171	9,300	701	8.92	11.02	26.85	19.10	7,855
Foreign & Overseas Chinese Funded 三资	5	51	18,755	2,080	5.13	13.23	174.28	61.23	40,550
By regional distribution 地区分布									
Central-North 华北	5	116	6,600	877	5.34	15.11	25.93	64.67	16,416
Beijing 北京									
Tianjin 天津									
Hebei 河北	4	124	7,942	1,096	7.39	16.34	28.36	54.77	14,829
Shanxi 山西	1	86	1,232				11.92	90.46	22,766
Inner Mongolia 内蒙古									
Northeast 东北									
Liaoning 辽宁									
Jilin 吉林									
Heilongjiang 黑龙江									
Central-East 华东	8	328	124,234	1,696	1.48	4.14	115.05	64.15	114,285
Shanghai 上海	1	73	45,802	8,506	5.53	16.05	403.97	65.57	153,885
Jiangsu 江苏	7	364	135,438	724	0.67	1.84	106.77	63.87	108,628
Zhejiang 浙江									
Anhui 安徽									
Fujian 福建									
Jiangxi 江西									
Shandong 山东									
Central-South 中南	10	91	8,890	103	0.60	1.77	41.98	66.37	17,221
Henan 河南	3	20	2,373	207	22.70	34.77	13.93	34.71	910
Hubei 湖北	1	142	5,349	231	3.18	3.18	33.46		7,275
Hunan 湖南	1	54	6,425	102	3.54	22.72	47.70	84.43	2,884
Guangdong 广东	3	59	17,443	31	0.07	0.29	135.18	74.94	41,489
Guangxi 广西	2	239	8,839	-10	-0.05	-0.11	12.81	50.60	17,427
Hainan 海南									
Southwest 西南	4	158	7,441	62	0.83	1.85	17.95	55.22	7,451
Chongqing 重庆									
Sichuan 四川	4	158	7,441	62	0.83	1.85	17.95	55.22	7,451
Guizhou 贵州									
Yunnan 云南									
Tibet 西藏									
Northwest 西北	2	88	5,272	-40	-0.34	-1.76	23.27	80.45	11,508
Shaanxi 陕西	2	88	5,272	-40	-0.34	-1.76	23.27	80.45	11,508
Gansu 甘肃									
Qinghai 青海									
Ningxia 宁夏									
Xinjiang 新疆									

3633: Animal Feed Equipment 饲料工业专用设备制造业

Year 年份	Number of firms 企业个数	Rate of change 变化率 (%)	Number of employees 职工人数 (人)	Rate of change 变化率 (%)	Total revenue (Mil. RMB) 总销售收入 (百万元)	Rate of change 变化率 (%)	Total profit (Mil RMB) 总利润 (百万元)	Rate of change 变化率 (%)
2000	38		7,678		980		45	
2001	29	-23.68	5,841	-23.93	960	-2.04	34	-24.44
2002	29		4,918	-15.80	1,156	20.42	19	-44.12

Major Products 主要产品	Output 产量	Unit 单位
Feed Processing Machinery 饲料加工机械	126,094	Unit 台

10 Main Firms with Maximal Revenue (year founded) 收入最大的十家主要企业（创办年份）	City 城市	Province 省	Telephone/fax 电话/传真	Number of employees 职工人数	Ownership 产业所有权	Revenue ('000 RMB) 销售收入 (千元)	Profit('000 RMB) (rank) 利润(千元) (排名)	Total assets ('000 RMB) 总资产 (千元)	Major products 主要产品
Jiangsu Zhengchang Group Co.,Ltd. 江苏正昌集团公司(1997)	Changzhou 常州市	Jiangsu 江苏省	(0519)7309850 (0519)7309831	861	State-owned 国有企业	455,060	-	385,750	Feedstuff Machinery 饲料机械
Jiangsu Muyang Group Co.,Ltd. 江苏牧羊集团有限公司(1968)	Yangzhou 扬州市	Jiangsu 江苏省	(0514)7848888 (0514)7848777	1,061	Limited-Liability 有限公司	364,316	18,695(1)	334,596	Grinding Machine 粉碎机
Sheyang Huaya Electromechanical Manufacture Company 射阳县华亚机电制造公司(1993)	Yangzhou 盐城市	Jiangsu 江苏省	(0515)2732049	98	Joint Stock 股份制	77,610	610(7)	6,100	Grinding Machine 粉碎机
Shanghai Shende Machinery Co.,Ltd. 上海申德机械有限公司(1992)	Shanghai 上海市	Shanghai 上海市	(021)57745781 (021)57745786	73	Foreign Funded 外商投资	45,802	8,506(2)	153,885	Pressing Roller 压辊
Huaiji First Agricutural Machinery Factory 怀集县农机一厂(1956)	Zhaoqing 肇庆市	Guangdong 广东省	(0758)5553566 (0758)5553566	35	State-owned 国有企业	24,250	969(5)	10,537	Feedstuff Machinery 饲料机械
Guangxi Jingda Machinery Co.,Ltd. 广西金达机械股份有限公司(1994)	Yulin 玉林市	Guangxi 广西	(0775)6223323 (0775)6224617	437	Joint Stock 股份制	17,453	-	27,548	Feed Grinder Machine饲料粉碎机
Zhongshan Soon Strong Machinery Tech Co.,Ltd. 中山申川机械科技有限公司(2001)	Zhongshan 中山市	Guangdong 广东省	(0760)6507818 (0760)6507816	30	Overseas Chinese-funded 港澳台资	14,178	-	19,023	Feedstuff Processing Machinery饲料加工设备
CPM Machinery (wuxi) Co., Ltd. 希彼埃姆机械(无锡)有限公司(1998)	Wuxi 无锡市	Jiangsu 江苏省	(0510)5280487 (0510)5282429	20	Foreign Funded 外商投资	11,418	193(11)	12,172	Pressing Roller 压辊
Huayin Agricultural Machinery Repair & Making Factory 华阴市农业机械修造厂(1970)	Weinan 渭南市	Shannxi 陕西省	(0913)4616811	120	State-owned 国有企业	10,276	19(19)	4,672	Agricultural Machinery 农业机械
Sichuan Peng'an Tianfu Machine Co.,Ltd. 四川蓬安天府机器有限责任公司(1970)	Nanchong 南充市	Sichuan 四川省	(0817)8621044 (0817)8620727	160	Limited-Liability 有限公司	9,308	8(20)	7,683	9FQ Grinder Machine 9FQ粉碎机

Top 10 Cities by Revenue 销售收入排名前10位城市	Province 省	Market share 市场份额 (%)	Number of firms 企业个数
Changzhou 常州市	Jiangsu 江苏省	39.36	1
Yangzhou 扬州市	Jiangsu 江苏省	31.51	1
Yancheng 盐城市	Jiangsu 江苏省	6.71	1
Shanghai 上海市	Shanghai 上海市	3.96	1
Zhaoqing 肇庆市	Guangdong 广东省	3.30	2
Taizhou 泰州市	Jiangsu 江苏省	2.05	1
Yulin 玉林市	Guangxi 广西	1.51	1
Suzhou 苏州市	Jiangsu 江苏省	1.38	2
Nanchong 南充市	Sichuan 四川省	1.37	2
Shijiazhuang 石家庄市	Hebei 河北省	1.28	2

10 Major Wholesalers 十家主要批发商	City 城市	Province 省	Telephone/Fax 电话/传真
SU MEC 中设江苏机械设备进出口（集团）公司	Nanjing 南京市	Jiangsu 江苏省	(025)4511888 (025)4411772
China Poster Mobile Communications Equipment Co.,Ltd. 中邮普泰移动通信设备股份有限公司	Beijing 北京市	Beijing 北京市	(010)66426993 (010)66426837
Sino Kama Co., Ltd. 中泰凯马股份有限公司	Shanghai 上海市	Shanghai 上海市	(021)62031188 (021)62030851
China Huayuan Group Co.,Ltd. 中国华源集团有限公司	Shanghai 上海市	Shanghai 上海市	(021)62031188 (021)62032288
Zhejiang Crand Imp.& Exp.Co.,Ltd. 浙江远大进出口有限公司	Ningbo 宁波市	Zhejiang 浙江省	(0574)87720170 (0574)87723350
Shandong Machinery Import & Export Group Corporation 山东省机械进出口集团公司	Qingdao 青岛市	Shandong 山东省	(0532)2661628 (0532)2991655
Qingdao Haier International Trade Co.,Ltd. 青岛海尔国际贸易有限公司	Qingdao 青岛市	Shandong 山东省	(0532)8938337 (0532)8939494
Guangdong Machinery Import & Export Group Corporation 广东省机械进出口集团公司	Guangzhou 广州市	Guangdong 广东省	(020)87782168 (020)87771803
China National Machinery Equipment Import & Export Corporation 中国机械设备进出口总公司	Beijing 北京市	Beijing 北京市	(010)63474506 (010)63261865
Beijing Cellstar Co.,Ltd. 北京蜂星事达电讯有限公司	Beijing 北京市	Beijing 北京市	(010)64602050 (010)64672648

3634: Special Packing Equipment 包装工业专用设备制造业

The industry accounts for 0.033% of the total revenue of China's industrial sector in 2002. The rate of return on assets is 4.29%. 84.35% of all firms in the industry made a profit while 15.65% had negative returns.The top province in terms of the industry's revenue is Hubei, accounting for 32.70% of the total revenue.
2002年本行业收入占全行业的0.033%，资产利润率为4.29%。84.35%的企业赢利，15.65%的企业亏损。收入最高的省为湖北省，占本行业的32.70%。

	Total number of firms 企业总数	Total number of employees 职工总数	Total revenue (Mil.RMB) 总销售收入（百万元）	Total profit (Mil.RMB) 总利润（百万元）	Return on assets 资产利润率（%）	Return on equity 权益利润率（%）	Labour productivity ('000 RMB/worker) 劳动生产率（千元/人）	Debts/assets 资产负债率（%）	Total assets (Mil.RMB) 总资产（百万元）
Industry Overall 行业总体	115	20,740	3,505	208	4.29	8.97	52.41	52.20	4,857

	Number of firms 企业个数	Average number of employees 平均职工人数	Average revenue ('000 RMB) 平均销售收入（千元）	Average profit ('000 RMB) 平均利润（千元）	Return on assets 资产利润率（%）	Return on equity 权益利润率（%）	Labour productivity ('000 RMB/worker) 劳动生产率（千元/人）	Debts/assets 资产负债率（%）	Average total assets ('000 RMB) 平均总资产（千元）
By ownership 产业所有权									
State-owned 国有	12	329	26,206	115	0.18	0.87	24.19	79.41	63,954
Collective-owned 集体	11	172	9,757	-1,082	-6.92	-33.49	19.77	79.34	15,638
Foreign & Overseas Chinese Funded 三资	25	143	29,585	2,789	9.06	17.62	66.09	48.57	30,777
By regional distribution 地区分布									
Central-North 华北	15	146	15,059	533	2.34	5.12	39.95	54.28	22,764
Beijing 北京	4	195	26,316	503	1.12	2.22	49.71	49.59	44,979
Tianjin 天津	4	68	6,937	300	3.52	13.74	48.21	74.36	8,525
Hebei 河北	7	162	13,268	682	3.75	8.43	31.26	55.51	18,205
Shanxi 山西									
Inner Mongolia 内蒙古									
Northeast 东北	7	169	11,392	204	1.11	3.58	27.90	68.96	18,386
Liaoning 辽宁	5	153	12,912	188	0.92	3.02	32.58	69.46	20,352
Jilin 吉林	2	209	7,591	245	1.82	5.53	19.33	67.09	13,474
Heilongjiang 黑龙江									
Central-East 华东	53	164	25,150	1,375	4.77	11.77	47.61	59.43	28,813
Shanghai 上海	6	109	22,507	2,097	8.88	18.81	86.06	52.78	23,602
Jiangsu 江苏	16	236	30,953	1,076	2.74	8.88	34.10	69.11	39,225
Zhejiang 浙江	18	117	17,071	1,963	7.78	15.24	51.97	48.92	25,212
Anhui 安徽	1	216	6,209	-9,055	-53.78	-481.14	8.39	88.82	16,837
Fujian 福建	2	75	9,816	2,190	16.40	21.56	36.17	23.94	13,352
Jiangxi 江西	1	33						34.81	15,438
Shandong 山东	9	196	41,060	1,382	5.08	13.14	63.76	61.36	27,230
Central-South 中南	37	226	49,875	3,392	4.47	8.47	64.92	47.17	75,829
Henan 河南	3	201	12,513	263	1.59	5.57	18.67	71.41	16,510
Hubei 湖北	8	469	143,280	11,086	5.22	7.44	87.30	29.78	212,341
Hunan 湖南	4	129	12,297	116	0.65	1.79	29.75	63.81	17,991
Guangdong 广东	22	159	27,836	1,616	3.61	14.26	54.08	74.70	44,793
Guangxi 广西									
Hainan 海南									
Southwest 西南	1	74	6,740	572	1.88	3.23	23.65	41.83	30,472
Chongqing 重庆									
Sichuan 四川	1	74	6,740	572	1.88	3.23	23.65	41.83	30,472
Guizhou 贵州									
Yunnan 云南									
Tibet 西藏									
Northwest 西北	2	112	7,171	-92	-0.79	-3.08	31.41	74.41	11,597
Shaanxi 陕西	1	152	13,776	444	3.09	17.63	27.70	82.45	14,349
Gansu 甘肃	1	72	566	-627	-7.09	-18.35	39.24	61.37	8,845
Qinghai 青海									
Ningxia 宁夏									
Xinjiang 新疆									

3634: Special Packing Equipment 包装工业专用设备制造业

Year 年份	Number of firms 企业个数	Rate of change 变化率 (%)	Number of employees 职工人数 (人)	Rate of change 变化率 (%)	Total revenue (Mil. RMB) 总销售收入 (百万元)	Rate of change 变化率 (%)	Total profit (Mil RMB) 总利润 (百万元)	Rate of change 变化率 (%)
2000	98		23,083		2,440		174	
2001	110	12.24	20,768	-10.03	3,171	29.96	226	29.89
2002	115	4.55	20,740	-0.13	3,505	10.53	208	-7.96

Major Products 主要产品	Output 产量	Unit 单位
Packing Machinery 包装机械	102,052	Unit 台
Binding Machinery 装订机械	6,910	Ton 吨

10 Main Firms with Maximal Revenue (year founded) 收入最大的十家主要企业（创办年份）	City 城市	Province 省	Telephone/fax 电话/传真	Number of employees 职工人数	Ownership 产业所有权	Revenue ('000 RMB) 销售收入 (千元)	Profit('000 RMB) (rank) 利润(千元) (排名)	Total assets ('000 RMB) 总资产 (千元)	Major products 主要产品
Jingshan Light Industrial Machinery Co., Ltd.	Jingmen	Hubei	(0724)722294		Joint Stock				Carton Packing Machinery纸箱
京山县轻机集团公司(1997)	荆门市	湖北省	(0724)7551496	2,345	股份制	1,083,288	86,794(1)	1,540,368	包装机械
China Light Industry Machinery General Company Nanjing Light Industry	Nanjing	Jiangsu	(025)4497408		State-owned				Packing Machinery
Machinery Factory中国轻工业机械总公司南京轻工机械厂(1969)	南京市	江苏省	(025)4600331	1,374	国有企业	185,150	6,270(4)	332,570	包装机械
Linx （Guangzhou) Packaging Equipment Co.,Ltd.	Guangzhou	Guangdong	(020)82218945		Overseas Chinese-funded				Packing Machinery
领新达嘉（广州）包装设备有限公司(1994)	广州市	广东省	(020)82221889	290	港澳台资	132,464	22,501(2)	62,486	包装机
Qingdao Huachi Packing Machinery Co., Ltd.	Qingdao	Shandong	(0532)7142109		Limited-Liability				Packing Machinery
青岛华池包装机械有限公司(1955)	青岛市	山东省	(0532)7142188	270	有限公司	118,801	1,800(27)	39,313	包装机械
Zhongshan Quanlifa Machinery Co., Ltd.	Zhongshan	Guangdong	(0760)3116801		Overseas Chinese-funded				Plastic-injection Machine
中山全立发机械有限公司(1992)	中山市	广东省	(0760)3116806	260	港澳台资	95,625	4,260(8)	90,395	注塑机
Guangzhou Tech-long Group Packing Machinery Co.,Ltd.	Guangzhou	Guangdong	(020)82266688		Private Owned				Packing Machinery
广州达意隆包装机械有限公司(1999)	广州市	广东省	(020)82266911	200	私营企业	66,204	3,463(12)	101,548	包装机械
Nantong Cotton Machinery Co., Ltd.	Nantong	Jiangsu	(0513)5544125		Limited-Liability				Cotton Packer棉
南通棉花机械有限公司(1952)	南通市	江苏省	(0513)5544125	527	有限公司	51,833	4,264(7)	65,906	花打包机
Shanghai Arenco Machinery Co., Ltd.	Shanghai	Shanghai	(021)58995190		Foreign Funded				Packing Machinery
上海阿仁科机械有限公司(1992)	上海市	上海市	(021)58995291	256	外商投资	50,085	6,105(5)	50,492	包装机械
Guangdong Zhaoqing Jialong Package Machinery Group	Zhaoqing	Guangdong	(0758)2233120		Limited-Liability				Single Side Corrugated Set单面
Co.,Ltd.广东肇庆嘉隆包装机械制造有限公司(1969)	肇庆市	广东省	(0738)2230133	418	有限公司	47,320	2,192(24)	331,663	瓦楞机组
Jiangsu Huayu Pranting & Besmearing Equipment	Nantong	Jiangsu	(0513)2545701		Limited-Liability				Roasting Room
Co.,Ltd.江苏华宇印涂设备集团有限公司(1972)	南通市	江苏省	(0513)2545703	445	有限公司	44,726	3,076(16)	41,516	烘房

Top 10 Cities by Revenue 销售收入排名前10位城市	Province 省	Market share 市场份额 (%)	Number of firms 企业个数
Jingmen 荆门市	Hubei 湖北省	30.92	2
Guangzhou 广州市	Guangdong 广东省	6.99	4
Nanjing 南京市	Jiangsu 江苏省	5.28	1
Qingdao 青岛市	Shandong 山东省	5.19	4
Wenzhou 温州市	Zhejiang 浙江省	5.07	13
Zhongshan 中山市	Guangdong 广东省	5.01	4
Shanghai 上海市	Shanghai 上海市	3.85	6
Beijing 北京市	Beijing 北京市	3.00	4
Liaocheng 聊城市	Shandong 山东省	3.00	2
Nantong 南通市	Jiangsu 江苏省	2.90	3

10 Major Wholesalers 十家主要批发商	City 城市	Province 省	Telephone/Fax 电话/传真
SU MEC	Nanjing	Jiangsu	(025)4511888
中设江苏机械设备进出口（集团）公司	南京市	江苏省	(025)4411772
China Poster Mobile Communications Equipment Co.,Ltd.	Beijing	Beijing	(010)66426993
中邮普泰移动通信设备股份有限公司	北京市	北京市	(010)66426837
Sino Kama Co., Ltd.	Shanghai	Shanghai	(021)62031188
中泰凯马股份有限公司	上海市	上海市	(021)62030851
China Huayuan Group Co.,Ltd.	Shanghai	Shanghai	(021)62031188
中国华源集团有限公司	上海市	上海市	(021)62032288
Zhejiang Crand Imp.& Exp.Co.,Ltd.	Ningbo	Zhejiang	(0574)87720170
浙江远大进出口有限公司	宁波市	浙江省	(0574)87723350
Shandong Machinery Import & Export Group Corporation	Qingdao	Shandong	(0532)2661628
山东省机械进出口集团公司	青岛市	山东省	(0532)2991655
Qingdao Haier International Trade Co.,Ltd.	Qingdao	Shandong	(0532)8938337
青岛海尔国际贸易有限公司	青岛市	山东省	(0532)8939494
Guangdong Machinery Import & Export Group Corporation	Guangzhou	Guangdong	(020)87782168
广东省机械进出口集团公司	广州市	广东省	(020)87771803
China National Machinery Equipment Import & Export Corporation	Beijing	Beijing	(010)63474506
中国机械设备进出口总公司	北京市	北京市	(010)63261865
Beijing Cellstar Co.,Ltd.	Beijing	Beijing	(010)64602050
北京蜂星事达电讯有限公司	北京市	北京市	(010)64672648

3635: Special Textile, Garment, Leather Processing Equipment

纺织、服装、皮革工业专用设备制造业

The industry accounts for 0.258% of the total revenue of China's industrial sector in 2002. The rate of return on assets is 4.67%. 82.09% of all firms in the industry made a profit while 17.91% had negative returns.The top province in terms of the industry's revenue is Jiangsu, accounting for 28.91% of the total revenue.
2002年本行业收入占全行业的0.258%，资产利润率为4.67%。82.09%的企业赢利，17.91%的企业亏损。收入最高的省为江苏省，占本行业的28.91%。

	Total number of firms 企业总数	Total number of employees 职工总数	Total revenue (Mil.RMB) 总销售收入（百万元）	Total profit (Mil.RMB) 总利润（百万元）	Return on assets 资产利润率（%）	Return on equity 权益利润率（%）	Labour productivity ('000 RMB/ worker) 劳动生产率（千元/人）	Debts/ assets 资产负债率（%）	Total assets (Mil.RMB) 总资产（百万元）
Industry Overall 行业总体	564	162,704	27,666	1,571	4.67	12.77	46.76	63.40	33,632

	Number of firms 企业个数	Average number of employees 平均职工人数	Average revenue ('000 RMB) 平均销售收入（千元）	Average profit ('000 RMB) 平均利润（千元）	Return on assets 资产利润率（%）	Return on equity 权益利润率（%）	Labour productivity ('000 RMB/ worker) 劳动生产率（千元/人）	Debts/ assets 资产负债率（%）	Average total assets ('000 RMB) 平均总资产（千元）
By ownership 产业所有权									
State-owned 国有	74	487	42,552	1,218	1.36	6.29	24.49	78.43	89,822
Collective-owned 集体	54	172	33,062	2,666	10.58	23.43	41.91	54.84	25,200
Foreign & Overseas Chinese Funded 三资	88	250	66,532	3,338	3.75	8.32	70.30	54.88	88,961
By regional distribution 地区分布									
Central-North 华北	58	462	56,356	3,249	3.17	7.67	26.03	58.61	102,382
Beijing 北京	8	300	90,692	7,900	5.38	14.51	111.45	62.92	146,870
Tianjin 天津	25	194	26,055	1,562	4.14	15.52	-9.80	73.30	37,707
Hebei 河北	13	419	18,791	520	0.88	1.94	14.93	54.90	59,436
Shanxi 山西	12	1,177	137,286	6,620	2.61	5.59	28.07	53.34	253,989
Inner Mongolia 内蒙古									
Northeast 东北	9	244	21,146	-107	-0.15	-0.55	34.85	72.59	71,464
Liaoning 辽宁	9	244	21,146	-107	-0.15	-0.55	34.85	72.59	71,464
Jilin 吉林									
Heilongjiang 黑龙江									
Central-East 华东	411	227	51,150	3,060	5.80	15.63	60.98	62.86	52,723
Shanghai 上海	56	231	48,807	308	0.43	1.22	59.04	64.62	71,692
Jiangsu 江苏	186	190	43,007	3,004	8.17	22.63	61.36	63.91	36,783
Zhejiang 浙江	109	193	56,731	4,874	8.38	18.45	76.84	54.60	58,196
Anhui 安徽	9	245	14,745	61	0.21	1.39	22.51	84.78	28,920
Fujian 福建	11	202	32,051	2,969	7.21	14.27	46.47	49.49	41,191
Jiangxi 江西	5	146	3,380	-264	-0.46	-3.31	19.64	86.11	57,359
Shandong 山东	35	542	102,984	3,387	3.42	12.21	51.82	72.01	99,126
Central-South 中南	75	479	40,293	1,742	2.87	7.88	30.58	63.57	60,713
Henan 河南	27	571	46,314	1,166	1.66	4.36	24.84	61.94	70,299
Hubei 湖北	14	534	32,834	1,034	1.65	6.34	29.53	73.91	62,522
Hunan 湖南	11	796	49,982	3,342	4.39	15.68	18.36	72.02	76,163
Guangdong 广东	22	188	34,564	2,225	5.27	10.43	81.05	49.44	42,184
Guangxi 广西	1	180	1,630	-987	-6.94	-23.09	2.63	69.97	14,231
Hainan 海南									
Southwest 西南	3	275	11,456	421	1.27	2.97	23.04	57.19	33,131
Chongqing 重庆	2	381	17,185	632	1.41	3.59	24.98	60.77	44,926
Sichuan 四川	1	64						23.55	9,543
Guizhou 贵州									
Yunnan 云南									
Tibet 西藏									
Northwest 西北	8	447	15,976	-723	-0.79		6.16	110.39	91,106
Shaanxi 陕西	7	434	16,923	-468	-0.50		6.22	116.24	93,652
Gansu 甘肃	1	536	9,350	-2,505	-3.42	-8.15	5.79	58.04	73,284
Qinghai 青海									
Ningxia 宁夏									
Xinjiang 新疆									

3635: Special Textile, Garment, Leather Processing Equipment

纺织、服装、皮革工业专用设备制造业

Year 年份	Number of firms 企业个数	Rate of change 变化率 (%)	Number of employees 职工人数 (人)	Rate of change 变化率 (%)	Total revenue (Mil. RMB) 总销售收入 (百万元)	Rate of change 变化率 (%)	Total profit (Mil RMB) 总利润 (百万元)	Rate of change 变化率 (%)
2000	483		174,637		19,593		826	
2001	513	6.21	161,933	-7.27	20,453	4.39	905	9.56
2002	564	9.94	162,704	0.48	27,666	35.27	1,571	73.59

Major Products 主要产品	Output 产量	Unit 单位
Cotton Weaving Equipment 棉纺织设备	278,738	Ton 吨
Dyeing & Finishing Machinery & Equipment 染整机械设备	55,523	Ton 吨

10 Main Firms with Maximal Revenue (year founded) 收入最大的十家主要企业（创办年份）	City 城市	Province 省	Telephone/fax 电话/传真	Number of employees 职工人数	Ownership 产业所有权	Revenue ('000 RMB) 销售收入 (千元)	Profit('000 RMB) (rank) 利润(千元) (排名)	Total assets ('000 RMB) 总资产 (千元)	Major products 主要产品
Qingdao Spark Textile Machinery & Textile Group Co.,Ltd.	Qingdao	Shandong	(0532)3131057		Joint Stock				Weaving Machine
青岛星火纺机纺织集团股份有限公司(1997)	青岛市	山东省	(0532)3133960	1,676	股份制	1,106,530	47,675(8)	646,507	纺织机械
Wuxi Hongyuan Group Co.,Ltd.	Wuxi	Jiangsu	(0510)5804827		State Enterprises				Chemical Fibre Equipment
无锡宏源集团有限责任公司(1997)	无锡市	江苏省	(0510)5807923	2,073	国有独资	1,028,820	52,800(5)	1,008,617	化纤设备
Yuci Branch of Jingwei Textile Machinery Co., Ltd.	Jinzhong	Shanxi	(0354)2492010		Overseas Chinese-funded				Spinning Frame
经纬纺织机械股份有限公司榆次分公司(1954)	晋中市	山西省	(0354)2425428	4,769	港澳台资	1,024,688	55,289(4)	1,674,604	细纱机
Zhejiang Golden Eagle Co.,Ltd.	Zhoushan	Zhejiang	(0580)8021189		Joint Stock				Weaving Machine Whole Set Equipment纺机
浙江金鹰股份有限公司(1994)	舟山市	浙江省	(0580)8020228	4,557	股份制	731,458	85,574(2)	891,901	成套设备
Shanghai No.2 Textile Machinery Co., Ltd.	Shanghai	Shanghai	(021)65318888		Foreign Funded				Spinning Mechanical Equipment纺纱
上海二纺机股份有限公司(1944)	上海市	上海市	(021)65421963	2,235	外商投资	615,761	7,848(50)	1,301,206	机械设备
Qingdao Hongda Textile Machinery Co.,Ltd.	Qingdao	Shandong	(0532)4892719		Limited-Liability				Waste Silk Card
青岛宏大纺织机械有限责任公司(1920)	青岛市	山东省	(0532)4857541	1,442	有限公司	606,716	30,255(13)	464,463	梳棉机
Zhengzhou Weaving Machinery Co.,Ltd.	Zhengzhou	Henan	(0371)3585788		State-owned				Weaving Machine
郑州纺织机械股份有限公司(1949)	郑州市	河南省	(0371)3935814	5,072	国有企业	523,778	21,613(27)	1,000,714	纺织机械
China Weaving Machinery Co., Ltd.	Shanghai	Shanghai	(021)65432970		Overseas Chinese-funded				Tatting Machine
中国纺织机械股份有限公司(1992)	上海市	上海市	(021)65455130	1,860	港澳台资	504,496	7,047(58)	553,882	有梭织机
Marzoli Dongtai Textile Machinery Co.,Ltd.	Yancheng	Jiangsu	(0515)5212538		Foreign Funded				Weaving Machine Whole Set Equipment纺机
马佐里东台纺机有限公司(2000)	盐城市	江苏省	(0515)5226303	1,284	外商投资	476,830	36,540(11)	408,990	成套设备
China Textil Science Academe Machinery Facoty	Beijing	Beijing	(010)65015397		State-owned				Weaving Special Fittings纺织机械
中国纺科科学研究院机械厂(1970)	北京市	北京市	(010)65024425	755	国有企业	434,020	26,862(14)	459,331	专用配件

Top 10 Cities by Revenue 销售收入排名前10位城市	Province 省	Market share 市场份额 (%)	Number of firms 企业个数
Shaoxing 绍兴市	Zhejiang 浙江省	12.60	31
Qingdao 青岛市	Shandong 山东省	10.38	13
Shanghai 上海市	Shanghai 上海市	9.88	56
Wuxi 无锡市	Jiangsu 江苏省	8.52	57
Suzhou 苏州市	Jiangsu 江苏省	7.14	33
Jinzhong 晋中市	Shanxi 山西省	5.95	12
Yancheng 盐城市	Jiangsu 江苏省	4.81	16
Hangzhou 杭州市	Zhejiang 浙江省	4.44	33
Changzhou 常州市	Jiangsu 江苏省	3.78	32
Zhengzhou 郑州市	Henan 河南省	3.58	10

10 Major Wholesalers 十家主要批发商	City 城市	Province 省	Telephone/Fax 电话/传真
SU MEC	Nanjing	Jiangsu	(025)4511888
中设江苏机械设备进出口（集团）公司	南京市	江苏省	(025)4411772
China Poster Mobile Communications Equipment Co.,Ltd.	Beijing	Beijing	(010)66426993
中邮普泰移动通信设备股份有限公司	北京市	北京市	(010)66426837
Sino Kama Co., Ltd.	Shanghai	Shanghai	(021)62031188
中泰凯马股份有限公司	上海市	上海市	(021)62030851
China Huayuan Group Co.,Ltd.	Shanghai	Shanghai	(021)62031188
中国华源集团有限公司	上海市	上海市	(021)62032288
Zhejiang Crand Imp.& Exp.Co.,Ltd.	Ningbo	Zhejiang	(0574)87720170
浙江远大进出口有限公司	宁波市	浙江省	(0574)87723350
Shandong Machinery Import & Export Group Corporation	Qingdao	Shandong	(0532)2661628
山东省机械进出口集团公司	青岛市	山东省	(0532)2991655
Qingdao Haier International Trade Co.,Ltd.	Qingdao	Shandong	(0532)8938337
青岛海尔国际贸易有限公司	青岛市	山东省	(0532)8939494
Guangdong Machinery Import & Export Group Corporation	Guangzhou	Guangdong	(020)87782168
广东省机械进出口集团公司	广州市	广东省	(020)87771803
China National Machinery Equipment Import & Export Corporation	Beijing	Beijing	(010)63474306
中国机械设备进出口总公司	北京市	北京市	(010)63261865
Beijing Cellstar Co.,Ltd.	Beijing	Beijing	(010)64602050
北京蜂星事达电讯有限公司	北京市	北京市	(010)64672648

3636: Special Electricity Light Source Equipment
电光源工业专用设备制造业

The industry accounts for 0.005% of the total revenue of China's industrial sector in 2002. The rate of return on assets is 2.12%. 93.75% of all firms in the industry made a profit while 6.25% had negative returns.The top province in terms of the industry's revenue is Guangdong, accounting for 39.14% of the total revenue.
2002年本行业收入占全行业的0.005%，资产利润率为2.12%。93.75%的企业赢利，6.25%的企业亏损。收入最高的省为广东省，占本行业的39.14%。

	Total number of firms 企业总数	Total number of employees 职工总数	Total revenue (Mil.RMB) 总销售收入(百万元)	Total profit (Mil.RMB) 总利润(百万元)	Return on assets 资产利润率(%)	Return on equity 权益利润率(%)	Labour productivity ('000 RMB/worker) 劳动生产率(千元/人)	Debts/assets 资产负债率(%)	Total assets (Mil.RMB) 总资产(百万元)
Industry Overall 行业总体	32	7,769	561	17	2.12	6.10	23.31	65.28	813

	Number of firms 企业个数	Average number of employees 平均职工人数	Average revenue ('000 RMB) 平均销售收入（千元)	Average profit ('000 RMB) 平均利润(千元)	Return on assets 资产利润率(%)	Return on equity 权益利润率(%)	Labour productivity ('000 RMB/worker) 劳动生产率(千元/人)	Debts/assets 资产负债率(%)	Average total assets ('000 RMB) 平均总资产(千元)
By ownership 产业所有权									
State-owned 国有	6	303	9,950	-82	-0.15	-1.01	13.28	85.03	54,520
Collective-owned 集体	4	100	9,814	504	5.40	8.96	28.43	39.67	9,329
Foreign & Overseas Chinese Funded 三资	8	352	24,717	615	2.03	4.05	24.92	49.76	30,247
By regional distribution 地区分布									
Central-North 华北	5	73	9,942	258	3.96	8.33	46.23	52.53	6,523
Beijing 北京	4	81	11,191	185	2.53	5.21	48.48	51.43	7,303
Tianjin 天津	1	40	4,950	550	16.18	42.64	28.00	62.06	3,400
Hebei 河北									
Shanxi 山西									
Inner Mongolia 内蒙古									
Northeast 东北	3	122	11,274	927	2.92	8.34	38.37	65.02	31,755
Liaoning 辽宁	3	122	11,274	927	2.92	8.34	38.37	65.02	31,755
Jilin 吉林									
Heilongjiang 黑龙江									
Central-East 华东	9	198	20,302	886	5.73	17:51	30.96	67.27	15,452
Shanghai 上海	2	35	10,795	98	1.68	7.46	250.04	77.53	5,851
Jiangsu 江苏	6	267	25,523	1,269	6.37	20.52	22.46	68.98	19,931
Zhejiang 浙江	1	107	7,990	161	2.07	2.78	17.05	25.47	7,782
Anhui 安徽									
Fujian 福建									
Jiangxi 江西									
Shandong 山东									
Central-South 中南	12	343	21,758	375	1.05	3.34	20.28	68.66	35,761
Henan 河南	2	381	14,824	211	0.85	2.24	19.88	62.06	24,789
Hubei 湖北									
Hunan 湖南	1	122	11,890	-917	-0.69		36.58	113.73	132,529
Guangdong 广东	9	360	24,395	555	2.02	3.73	19.76	45.81	27,448
Guangxi 广西									
Hainan 海南									
Southwest 西南	2	539	14,085	36	0.07	0.17	9.28	57.94	49,911
Chongqing 重庆									
Sichuan 四川	1	132	8,210	21	0.42	0.83	30.66	49.28	4,982
Guizhou 贵州	1	946	19,960	50	0.05	0.13	6.30	58.39	94,840
Yunnan 云南									
Tibet 西藏									
Northwest 西北	1	60	5,476	629	3.59	5.39	25.47	33.52	17,543
Shaanxi 陕西	1	60	5,476	629	3.59	5.39	25.47	33.52	17,543
Gansu 甘肃									
Qinghai 青海									
Ningxia 宁夏									
Xinjiang 新疆									

3636: Special Electricity Light Source Equipment

电光源工业专用设备制造业

Year 年份	Number of firms 企业个数	Rate of change 变化率 (%)	Number of employees 职工人数 (人)	Rate of change 变化率 (%)	Total revenue (Mil. RMB) 总销售收入 (百万元)	Rate of change 变化率 (%)	Total profit (Mil RMB) 总利润 (百万元)	Rate of change 变化率 (%)
2000	34		6,404		463		16	
2001	29	-14.71	5,391	-15.82	537	15.98	-11	
2002	32	10.34	7,769	44.11	561	4.47	17	

Major Products 主要产品	Output 产量	Unit 单位
Lamp Bulb 灯泡	560,704	10,000 Units 万只
Lamps & Lanterns 灯具	10	100,000,000 Units 亿只

10 Main Firms with Maximal Revenue (year founded) 收入最大的十家主要企业（创办年份）	City 城市	Province 省	Telephone/fax 电话/传真	Number of employees 职工人数	Ownership 产业所有权	Revenue ('000 RMB) 销售收入(千元)	Profit('000 RMB) (rank) 利润(千元)(排名)	Total assets ('000 RMB) 总资产(千元)	Major products 主要产品
Jianfa Electrical Appliance Products (Shenzhen) Co., Ltd. 建发电器制品（深圳）有限公司(1992)	Shenzhen 深圳市	Guangdong 广东省	(0755)27495391 (0755)27495394	1,975	Overseas Chinese-funded 港澳台资	82,689	1,575(5)	91,053	Emergency Lamp 应急灯
Taizhou Xin'gang Lighting Electrical Appliance Co., Ltd. 泰州市新港照明电器有限公司(1996)	Taizhou 泰州市	Jiangsu 江苏省	(0523)6983066 (0523)6982943	428	Private Owned 私营企业	53,570	2,693(1)	34,574	Power-saving Lampwick Pole节能灯芯柱
POOKIN INTERNATONAL LINGHTING CO., LTD. 普今照明集团有限公司(1998)	Changzhou 常州市	Jiangsu 江苏省	(0519)5100066 (0519)5100099	120	Foreign Funded 外商投资	42,850	1,910(2)	31,360	Power-saving Lamps And Lanterns 节能灯具
Guangzhou Xinge-Yangguang Electricity Co., Ltd. 广州新格扬光电气有限公司(1995)	Guangzhou 广州市	Guangdong 广东省	(020)87981638 (020)87981638	184	Private Enterprises 私营独资	22,110	1,040(8)	19,094	Lamps & Lanterns 灯具
Shanghai Luoman Electric Linght Source Co., Ltd. 上海罗曼电光源有限公司(1994)	Shanghai 上海市	Shanghai 上海市	(021)65031217 (021)65031706	69	Overseas Chinese-funded 港澳台资	21,590	196(16)	11,701	Metal Halide Lamp金属卤化物灯
He'nan Xinxiang Lightning Machinery Factory 河南省新乡市电光机械厂(1964)	Xinxiang 新乡市	Henan 河南省	(0373)2621301 (0373)2621301	636	State-owned 国有企业	20,446	276(14)	47,985	General Lamp Linkage Line普灯联动线
Guiyang Miner's Lamp Factory 贵阳矿灯厂(1966)	Guiyang 贵阳市	Guizhou 贵州省	(0851)3871326 (0851)3871326	946	State-owned 国有企业	19,960	50(24)	94,840	Miner's Lamp 矿灯
Zhongshan Hetian Plastic Electron Products Factory Co.,Ltd. 中山贺田塑胶电子制品厂有限公司(1997)	Zhongshan 中山市	Guangdong 广东省	(0760)6685593 (0760)6683543	289	Overseas Chinese-funded 港澳台资	19,715	-	31,445	Solar Energy Lamp Electronic Toy太阳能电子玩具
Beijing Donghu Electric Engineering Project Installment Department 北京市东湖电气工程安装处(1984)	Beijing 北京市	Beijing 北京市	(010)64722388 (010)64722388	187	Collective-owned 集体企业	16,687	117(21)	14,580	Impracticable under 10,000 battles Circuit10千伏以下架空线路
Dalian Marine Electrical Equipment Co.,Ltd. 大连市船用电器有限公司(1997)	Dalian 大连市	Liaoning 辽宁省	(0411)3635148 (0411)3629574	103	Collective-owned 集体企业	12,051	1,160(7)	13,229	Electric Appliance Of Ship 船用电器

Top 10 Cities by Revenue 销售收入排名前10位城市	Province 省	Market share 市场份额 (%)	Number of firms 企业个数
Shenzhen 深圳市	Guangdong 广东省	16.01	2
Zhongshan 中山市	Guangdong 广东省	14.79	3
Changzhou 常州市	Jiangsu 江苏省	14.74	3
Taizhou 泰州市	Jiangsu 江苏省	9.55	1
Beijing 北京市	Beijing 北京市	7.98	4
Guangzhou 广州市	Guangdong 广东省	3.94	1
Shanghai 上海市	Shanghai 上海市	3.85	2
Xinxiang 新乡市	Henan 河南省	3.64	1
Guiyang 贵阳市	Guizhou 贵州省	3.56	1
Anshan 鞍山市	Liaoning 辽宁省	3.53	1

10 Major Wholesalers 十家主要批发商	City 城市	Province 省	Telephone/Fax 电话/传真
SU MEC 中设江苏机械设备进出口（集团）公司	Nanjing 南京市	Jiangsu 江苏省	(025)4511888 (025)4411772
China Poster Mobile Communications Equipment Co.,Ltd. 中邮普泰移动通信设备股份有限公司	Beijing 北京市	Beijing 北京市	(010)66426993 (010)66426837
Sino Kama Co., Ltd. 中泰凯马股份有限公司	Shanghai 上海市	Shanghai 上海市	(021)62031188 (021)62030851
China Huayuan Group Co.,Ltd. 中国华源集团有限公司	Shanghai 上海市	Shanghai 上海市	(021)62031188 (021)62032288
Zhejiang Crand Imp.& Exp.Co.,Ltd. 浙江远大进出口有限公司	Ningbo 宁波市	Zhejiang 浙江省	(0574)87720170 (0574)87723350
Shandong Machinery Import & Export Group Corporation 山东省机械进出口集团公司	Qingdao 青岛市	Shandong 山东省	(0532)2661628 (0532)2991655
Qingdao Haier International Trade Co.,Ltd. 青岛海尔国际贸易有限公司	Qingdao 青岛市	Shandong 山东省	(0532)8938337 (0532)8939494
Guangdong Machinery Import & Export Group Corporation 广东省机械进出口集团公司	Guangzhou 广州市	Guangdong 广东省	(020)87782168 (020)87771803
China National Machinery Equipment Import & Export Corporation 中国机械设备进出口总公司	Beijing 北京市	Beijing 北京市	(010)63474306 (010)63261865
Beijing Cellstar Co.,Ltd. 北京蜂星事达电讯有限公司	Beijing 北京市	Beijing 北京市	(010)64602050 (010)64672648

3638: Paper-making Equipment 制浆、造纸工业专用设备制造业

The industry accounts for 0.032% of the total revenue of China's industrial sector in 2002. The rate of return on assets is 1.91%. 75.52% of all firms in the industry made a profit while 24.48% had negative returns.The top province in terms of the industry's revenue is Henan, accounting for 23.74% of the total revenue.
2002年本行业收入占全行业的 0.032%，资产利润率为 1.91%。75.52%的企业赢利，24.48%的企业亏损。收入最高的省为河南省，占本行业的23.74%。

	Total number of firms 企业总数	Total number of employees 职工总数	Total revenue (Mil.RMB) 总销售收入（百万元）	Total profit (Mil.RMB) 总利润（百万元）	Return on assets 资产利润率（%）	Return on equity 权益利润率（%）	Labour productivity ('000 RMB/ worker) 劳动生产率（千元/人）	Debts/ assets 资产负债率（%）	Total assets (Mil.RMB) 总资产（百万元）
Industry Overall 行业总体	143	35,981	3,473	107	1.91	7.35	30.79	74.07	5,599

	Number of firms 企业个数	Average number of employees 平均职工人数	Average revenue ('000 RMB) 平均销售收入（千元）	Average profit ('000 RMB) 平均利润（千元）	Return on assets 资产利润率（%）	Return on equity 权益利润率（%）	Labour productivity ('000 RMB/ worker) 劳动生产率（千元/人）	Debts/ assets 资产负债率（%）	Average total assets ('000 RMB) 平均总资产（千元）
By ownership 产业所有权									
State-owned 国有	23	335	12,138	-1,513	-2.56	-30.65	11.57	91.65	59,141
Collective-owned 集体	34	227	25,409	1,757	10.30	26.05	39.08	60.47	17,068
Foreign & Overseas Chinese Funded 三资	15	236	37,827	1,056	2.02	5.24	40.95	61.46	52,333
By regional distribution 地区分布									
Central-North 华北	11	241	16,256	-929	-2.06	-24.94	17.19	91.75	45,139
Beijing 北京									
Tianjin 天津	8	296	17,975	-102	-0.18	-1.47	14.22	87.77	56,711
Hebei 河北	2	57	16,279	1,350	24.66	47.49	103.06	48.07	5,475
Shanxi 山西	1	175	2,464	-12,100	-37.94		1.85	163.43	31,893
Inner Mongolia 内蒙古									
Northeast 东北	17	218	14,743	162	0.53	5.28	20.91	89.99	30,659
Liaoning 辽宁	14	236	17,612	201	0.55	5.68	22.21	90.34	36,639
Jilin 吉林	2	190	1,665	2	0.06	0.31	10.21	79.72	3,169
Heilongjiang 黑龙江	1	23	737	-63	-3.26	-4.61	11.30	29.32	1,934
Central-East 华东	67	229	26,762	842	1.94	5.91	32.28	67.16	43,367
Shanghai 上海	7	211	32,778	817	2.25	14.65	27.64	84.60	36,251
Jiangsu 江苏	21	153	25,250	-14	-0.04	-0.13	41.47	67.40	33,119
Zhejiang 浙江	8	87	14,043	630	5.06	22.47	41.28	77.50	12,461
Anhui 安徽	3	178	20,909	2,560	2.57	8.40	59.03	69.35	99,468
Fujian 福建	4	114	13,329	929	7.16	11.98	32.77	40.25	12,978
Jiangxi 江西									
Shandong 山东	24	373	33,540	1,440	2.29	6.36	27.43	63.92	62,762
Central-South 中南	39	267	24,338	1,161	4.31	20.81	34.91	79.28	26,930
Henan 河南	31	262	26,602	1,759	7.86	19.11	38.54	58.84	22,361
Hubei 湖北	4	277	21,638	291	0.80	11.19	28.72	92.83	36,185
Hunan 湖南	1	415	15,751	-4,982	-5.46		18.71	163.30	91,178
Guangdong 广东	1	60	5,426	310	9.16	10.75	26.07	14.77	3,385
Guangxi 广西	2	355	8,391	-2,861	-4.86		13.35	119.74	58,892
Hainan 海南									
Southwest 西南	5	446	24,680	-208	-0.29	-1.39	34.32	79.54	72,980
Chongqing 重庆									
Sichuan 四川	4	437	25,968	-280	-0.42	-1.53	42.75	72.34	65,877
Guizhou 贵州	1	484	19,529	78	0.08	4.41	3.85	98.25	101,390
Yunnan 云南									
Tibet 西藏									
Northwest 西北	4	413	44,565	3,386	5.20	12.03	30.28	56.79	65,131
Shaanxi 陕西	4	413	44,565	3,386	5.20	12.03	30.28	56.79	65,131
Gansu 甘肃									
Qinghai 青海									
Ningxia 宁夏									
Xinjiang 新疆									

3638: Paper-making Equipment 制浆、造纸工业专用设备制造业

Year 年份	Number of firms 企业个数	Rate of change 变化率 (%)	Number of employees 职工人数 (人)	Rate of change 变化率 (%)	Total revenue (Mil. RMB) 总销售收入 (百万元)	Rate of change 变化率 (%)	Total profit (Mil RMB) 总利润 (百万元)	Rate of change 变化率 (%)
2000	132		42,193		2,784		42	
2001	126	-4.55	35,643	-15.52	2,899	4.13	73	73.81
2002	143	13.49	35,981	0.95	3,473	19.80	107	46.58

Major Products 主要产品	Output 产量	Unit 单位
Paper Making Machinery 造纸机械	12,818	Unit 台

10 Main Firms with Maximal Revenue (year founded) 收入最大的十家主要企业（创办年份）	City 城市	Province 省	Telephone/fax 电话/传真	Number of employees 职工人数	Ownership 产业所有权	Revenue ('000 RMB) 销售收入 (千元)	Profit('000 RMB) (rank) 利润(千元) (排名)	Total assets ('000 RMB) 总资产 (千元)	Major products 主要产品
Shangdong Haitian Light Industry Textile Co., Ltd.	Zibo	Shandong	(0533)6680181		Joint Stock				Paper Making Machinery
山东海天轻纺有限公司(1992)	淄博市	山东省	(0533)6680181	987	股份制	176,050	8,556(4)	163,213	造纸机械
Shandong Hengxing Group Co., Ltd.	Zibo	Shandong	(0533)6556018		Limited-Liability				Paper Making Machinery
恒星集团有限公司(1995)	淄博市	山东省	(0533)6556285	1,566	有限公司	169,436	9,585(2)	687,406	造纸机械
Valmet Xi'an Paper Mechinery Co.,Ltd.	Xi'an	Shannxi	(029)4514931		Foreign Funded				Papermaking Industry Special Equipment造纸工
维美德西安造纸机械有限公司(1989)	西安市	陕西省	(029)4622820	1,206	外商投资	149,065	8,178(5)	180,153	业专用设备
Zhangjiagang Siegind Machinery Equipment Manufacturing	Suzhou	Jiangsu	(0520)58620295		Overseas Chinese-funded				Platform Sawing Band Machine台
Co., Ltd.张家港斯依格机械设备制造有限公司(1992)	苏州市	江苏省	(0520)58628128	650	港澳台资	130,002	3,000(18)	57,444	式带锯机
Qinyang Paper Making Equipment Factory	Jiaozuo	Henan	(0391)5690920		Collective-owned				Paper Making Machine
沁阳市造纸设备厂(1968)	焦作市	河南省	(0391)5690920	490	集体企业	94,860	7,030(7)	34,680	纸机
Liaoyang Paper Machinery Co.,Ltd.	Liaoyang	Liaoning	(0419)3132329		Joint Stock				Paper Making Machinery
辽阳造纸机械股份有限公司(1935)	辽阳市	辽宁省	(0419)3132877	1,325	股份制	90,874	-	258,894	造纸机械
Jining Huayi Light Industry Co.Ltd.	Jining	Shandong	(0537)2233060		Limited-Liability				Paper Making Machinery
济宁华一轻工机械有限公司(1965)	济宁市	山东省	(0537)2231221	452	有限公司	63,561	6,208(11)	82,454	造纸机械
Kunshan Zhong Lian First Paper Machinery Factory	Suzhou	Jiangsu	(0512)57550379		Joint Stock				Paper Making Machinery
昆山市中联第一造纸机械厂(1980)	苏州市	江苏省	(0512)57554942	289	股份制	63,010	6,541(8)	100,195	造纸机械
Shandong Second Linght Industry Machinery Co.,Ltd.	Liaocheng	Shandong	(0635)8221107		Joint Stock				Paper Making Machinery
山东省第二轻工业机械厂(1967)	聊城市	山东省	(0635)8221985	731	股份制	62,560	49(81)	79,959	造纸设备
Qinyang Xianfeng Machinery Factory	Jiaozuo	Henan	(0391)5033011		Collective-owned				Paper Making Machinery
沁阳市险峰机械厂(1954)	焦作市	河南省	(0391)5031284	350	集体企业	61,440	2,840(20)	18,870	造纸机

Top 10 Cities by Revenue 销售收入排名前10位城市	Province 省	Market share 市场份额 (%)	Number of firms 企业个数
Jiaozuo 焦作市	Henan 河南省	19.55	23
Zibo 淄博市	Shandong 山东省	12.39	5
Suzhou 苏州市	Jiangsu 江苏省	9.39	8
Shanghai 上海市	Shanghai 上海市	6.61	7
Xi'an 西安市	Shannxi 陕西省	4.95	3
Liaoyang 辽阳市	Liaoning 辽宁省	4.42	4
Tianjin 天津市	Tianjin 天津市	4.14	8
Wuxi 无锡市	Jiangsu 江苏省	3.25	6
Dandong 丹东市	Liaoning 辽宁省	2.36	8
Leshan 乐山市	Sichuan 四川省	1.90	2

10 Major Wholesalers 十家主要批发商	City 城市	Province 省	Telephone/Fax 电话/传真
SU MEC	Nanjing	Jiangsu	(025)4511888
中设江苏机械设备进出口（集团）公司	南京市	江苏省	(025)4411772
China Poster Mobile Communications Equipment Co.,Ltd.	Beijing	Beijing	(010)66426993
中邮普泰移动通信设备股份有限公司	北京市	北京市	(010)66426837
Sino Kama Co., Ltd.	Shanghai	Shanghai	(021)62031188
中泰凯马股份有限公司	上海市	上海市	(021)62030851
China Huayuan Group Co.,Ltd.	Shanghai	Shanghai	(021)62031188
中国华源集团有限公司	上海市	上海市	(021)62032288
Zhejiang Crand Imp.& Exp.Co.,Ltd.	Ningbo	Zhejiang	(0574)87720170
浙江远大进出口有限公司	宁波市	浙江省	(0574)87723350
Shandong Machinery Import & Export Group Corporation	Qingdao	Shandong	(0532)2661628
山东省机械进出口集团公司	青岛市	山东省	(0532)2991655
Qingdao Haier International Trade Co.,Ltd.	Qingdao	Shandong	(0532)8938337
青岛海尔国际贸易有限公司	青岛市	山东省	(0532)8939494
Guangdong Machinery Import & Export Group Corporation	Guangzhou	Guangdong	(020)87782168
广东省机械进出口集团公司	广州市	广东省	(020)87771803
China National Machinery Equipment Import & Export Corporation	Beijing	Beijing	(010)63474506
中国机械设备进出口总公司	北京市	北京市	(010)63261865
Beijing Cellstar Co.,Ltd.	Beijing	Beijing	(010)64602050
北京蜂星事达电讯有限公司	北京市	北京市	(010)64672648

3639: Special Daily Chemical Processing Equipment

日用化学工业专用设备制造业

The industry accounts for 0.009% of the total revenue of China's industrial sector in 2002. The rate of return on assets is 3.02%. 77.14% of all firms in the industry made a profit while 22.86% had negative returns.The top province in terms of the industry's revenue is Henan, accounting for 49.04% of the total revenue.
2002年本行业收入占全行业的 0.009%，资产利润率为 3.02%。77.14%的企业赢利，22.86%的企业亏损。收入最高的省为河南省，占本行业的49.04%。

	Total number of firms 企业总数	Total number of employees 职工总数	Total revenue (Mil.RMB) 总销售收入（百万元）	Total profit (Mil.RMB) 总利润（百万元）	Return on assets 资产利润率（%）	Return on equity 权益利润率（%）	Labour productivity ('000 RMB/worker) 劳动生产率（千元/人）	Debts/assets 资产负债率（%）	Total assets (Mil.RMB) 总资产（百万元）
Industry Overall 行业总体	35	11,616	994	44	3.02	8.15	26.83	63.01	1,470

	Number of firms 企业个数	Average number of employees 平均职工人数	Average revenue ('000 RMB) 平均销售收入（千元）	Average profit ('000 RMB) 平均利润（千元）	Return on assets 资产利润率（%）	Return on equity 权益利润率（%）	Labour productivity ('000 RMB/worker) 劳动生产率（千元/人）	Debts/assets 资产负债率（%）	Average total assets ('000 RMB) 平均总资产（千元）
By ownership 产业所有权									
State-owned 国有	5	100	6,154	291	3.22	7.49	19.73	57.09	9,063
Collective-owned 集体	5	87	7,542	9	0.14	0.60	37.27	76.82	6,301
Foreign & Overseas Chinese Funded 三资	5	173	15,604	1,576	7.19	11.42	47.28	36.99	21,903
By regional distribution 地区分布									
Central-North 华北	3	81	4,033	200	3.20	5.82	17.84	45.01	6,251
Beijing 北京	1	104	8,820	949	9.29	15.30	41.82	39.29	10,219
Tianjin 天津	2	70	1,640	-175	-4.09	-8.50	-0.10	51.87	4,268
Hebei 河北									
Shanxi 山西									
Inner Mongolia 内蒙古									
Northeast 东北									
Liaoning 辽宁									
Jilin 吉林									
Heilongjiang 黑龙江									
Central-East 华东	16	108	22,642	802	3.85	13.15	64.55	70.74	20,855
Shanghai 上海	4	58	12,748	961	6.01	15.35	94.81	60.83	15,989
Jiangsu 江苏	7	119	31,491	987	3.86	12.86	72.02	69.97	25,553
Zhejiang 浙江									
Anhui 安徽	2	169	14,813	113	0.80	3.78	18.00	78.92	14,195
Fujian 福建									
Jiangxi 江西									
Shandong 山东	3	109	20,409	619	2.97	14.41	72.26	79.36	20,818
Central-South 中南	10	879	56,001	2,946	3.03	8.17	20.18	62.86	97,077
Henan 河南	2	3,794	243,667	11,897	2.76	8.30	18.98	66.76	431,485
Hubei 湖北									
Hunan 湖南									
Guangdong 广东	8	151	9,084	708	5.25	7.68	27.76	31.61	13,475
Guangxi 广西									
Hainan 海南									
Southwest 西南	3	82	2,053	-67	-3.40	-10.98	1.45	69.03	1,960
Chongqing 重庆	1	75	452	-299	-14.86		7.85	109.39	2,012
Sichuan 四川	1	171	5,707	99	4.70	7.15	-1.36	34.28	2,106
Guizhou 贵州	1	1						64.47	1,762
Yunnan 云南									
Tibet 西藏									
Northwest 西北	3	201	17,749	552	1.17	2.25	29.53	47.90	47,104
Shaanxi 陕西	2	163	13,454	-12	-0.02	-0.04	25.73	43.90	54,527
Gansu 甘肃	1	278	26,341	1,679	5.20	13.50	33.98	61.44	32,259
Qinghai 青海									
Ningxia 宁夏									
Xinjiang 新疆									

3639: Special Daily Chemical Processing Equipment

日用化学工业专用设备制造业

Year 年份	Number of firms 企业个数	Rate of change 变化率 (%)	Number of employees 职工人数 (人)	Rate of change 变化率 (%)	Total revenue (Mil. RMB) 总销售收入 (百万元)	Rate of change 变化率 (%)	Total profit (Mil RMB) 总利润 (百万元)	Rate of change 变化率 (%)
2000	24		3,869		424		20	
2001	36	50.00	4,877	26.05	621	46.46	12	-40.00
2002	35	-2.78	11,616	138.18	994	60.06	44	266.67

Major Products 主要产品	Output 产量	Unit 单位

10 Main Firms with Maximal Revenue (year founded) 收入最大的十家主要企业（创办年份）	City 城市	Province 省	Telephone/fax 电话/传真	Number of employees 职工人数	Ownership 产业所有权	Revenue ('000 RMB) 销售收入 (千元)	Profit('000 RMB) (rank) 利润(千元) (排名)	Total assets ('000 RMB) 总资产 (千元)	Major products 主要产品
Henan Huanyu Power Source Co., Ltd.	Xinxiang	Henan	(0373)2688002		Joint Stock				Battery
河南环宇电源股份有限公司(2001)	新乡市	河南省	(0373)2688001	5,900	股份制	448,479	32,999(1)	460,045	电池
Jiangsu Xuebao Daily Chemistry Co., Ltd.	Wuxi	Jiangsu	(0510)6284448		Private Owned				Polishing Liquid
江苏雪豹日化有限公司(1993)	无锡市	江苏省	(0510)6282882	280	私营企业	146,369	3,614(3)	118,541	上光液
Zhengzhou Oil & Fat Chemistry Group Co., Ltd.	Zhengzhou	Henan	(0371)3944257		State Enterprises				Washing Things
郑州油脂化学集团有限责任公司(1954)	郑州市	河南省	(0371)3944170	1,688	国有独资	38,854	-	402,925	洗涤用品
Ningjin Hongfa Chemical Industry Ink Co., Ltd.	Dezhou	Shandong	(0534)5916666		Private Enterprises				Printing Ink
宁津县宏发化工油墨有限公司(1999)	德州市	山东省	(0534)5916666	60	私营独资	29,500	1,990(5)	3,900	油墨
Bengbu Fukang Battery Co.,Ltd.	Bengbu	Anhui	(0552)4922358		Private Owned				Dry Cell
蚌埠福康电池有限公司(1996)	蚌埠市	安徽省	(0552)4923709	257	私营企业	28,476	99(23)	25,631	干电池
Shanghai Anfu Chemical Fertilizer Co., Ltd.	Shanghai	Shanghai	(021)64501216		Overseas Chinese-funded				Chemical Equipment
上海安富化肥有限公司(2002)	上海市	上海市	(021)64500497	30	港澳台资	27,534	4,166(2)	25,783	化工设备
Shandong Zibo Disheng Power Source Co., Ltd.	Zibo	Shandong	(0533)5287777		Private Enterprises				Battery
山东淄博迪生电源有限公司(1994)	淄博市	山东省	(0533)5283333	214	私营独资	26,566	209(17)	48,233	电池
Dongguan PENC Chemical Industry Machinery Co., Ltd.	Dongguan	Guangdong	(0769)8862545		Overseas Chinese-funded				Metallurgy Industry Special Equipment冶金工
东莞市庞思化工机械有限公司(1992)	东莞市	广东省	(0769)8862092	122	港澳台资	21,213	501(13)	38,255	业专用设备
Yangzhou Tongchuang Chemical Equipment Installation	Yangzhou	Jiangsu	(0514)7281152		Collective-owned				Equipment Assembling
Co.,Ltd.扬州同创化工设备安装有限责任公司(1966)	扬州市	江苏省	(0514)7282419	238	集体企业	16,998	142(20)	8,714	设备安装
Shanghai Baili Industrial Co., Ltd.	Shanghai	Shanghai	(021)65430853		Collective-owned				Daily Use Chemical Special Equipment日用化
上海白丽实业有限公司(1995)	上海市	上海市	(021)65195406	35	集体企业	9,923	102(22)	6,567	工专用设备

Top 10 Cities by Revenue 销售收入排名前10位城市	Province 省	Market share 市场份额 (%)	Number of firms 企业个数
Xinxiang 新乡市	Henan 河南省	45.13	1
Wuxi 无锡市	Jiangsu 江苏省	16.41	3
Shanghai 上海市	Shanghai 上海市	5.13	4
Zhengzhou 郑州市	Henan 河南省	3.91	1
Bengbu 蚌埠市	Anhui 安徽省	2.98	2
Dezhou 德州市	Shandong 山东省	2.97	1
Xi'an 西安市	Shannxi 陕西省	2.71	2
Zibo 淄博市	Shandong 山东省	2.67	1
Lanzhou 兰州市	Gansu 甘肃省	2.65	1
Dongguan 东莞市	Guangdong 广东省	2.13	1

10 Major Wholesalers 十家主要批发商	City 城市	Province 省	Telephone/Fax 电话/传真
SU MEC	Nanjing	Jiangsu	(025)4511888
中设江苏机械设备进出口（集团）公司	南京市	江苏省	(025)4411772
China Poster Mobile Communications Equipment Co.,Ltd.	Beijing	Beijing	(010)66426993
中邮普泰移动通信设备股份有限公司	北京市	北京市	(010)66426837
Sino Kama Co., Ltd.	Shanghai	Shanghai	(021)62031188
中泰凯马股份有限公司	上海市	上海市	(021)62030851
China Huayuan Group Co.,Ltd.	Shanghai	Shanghai	(021)62031188
中国华源集团有限公司	上海市	上海市	(021)62032288
Zhejiang Crand Imp.& Exp.Co.,Ltd.	Ningbo	Zhejiang	(0574)87720170
浙江远大进出口有限公司	宁波市	浙江省	(0574)87723350
Shandong Machinery Import & Export Group Corporation	Qingdao	Shandong	(0532)2661628
山东省机械进出口集团公司	青岛市	山东省	(0532)2991655
Qingdao Haier International Trade Co.,Ltd.	Qingdao	Shandong	(0532)8938337
青岛海尔国际贸易有限公司	青岛市	山东省	(0532)8939494
Guangdong Machinery Import & Export Group Corporation	Guangzhou	Guangdong	(020)87782168
广东省机械进出口集团公司	广州市	广东省	(020)87771803
China National Machinery Equipment Import & Export Corporation	Beijing	Beijing	(010)63474506
中国机械设备进出口总公司	北京市	北京市	(010)63261865
Beijing Cellstar Co.,Ltd.	Beijing	Beijing	(010)64602050
北京蜂星事达电讯有限公司	北京市	北京市	(010)64672648

3641: Tractors 拖拉机制造业

The industry accounts for 0.127% of the total revenue of China's industrial sector in 2002. The rate of return on assets is -1.30%. 59.59% of all firms in the industry made a profit while 40.41% had negative returns.The top province in terms of the industry's revenue is Henan, accounting for 32.84% of the total revenue.
2002年本行业收入占全行业的 0.127%，资产利润率为 -1.30%。59.59%的企业赢利，40.41%的企业亏损。收入最高的省为河南省，占本行业的32.84%。

	Total number of firms 企业总数	Total number of employees 职工总数	Total revenue (Mil.RMB) 总销售收入（百万元）	Total profit (Mil.RMB) 总利润（百万元）	Return on assets 资产利润率 (%)	Return on equity 权益利润率 (%)	Labour productivity ('000 RMB/ worker) 劳动生产率（千元/人）	Debts/ assets 资产负债率 (%)	Total assets (Mil.RMB) 总资产（百万元）
Industry Overall 行业总体	146	103,714	13,615	-262	-1.30	-4.44	28.09	70.69	20,138

	Number of firms 企业个数	Average number of employees 平均职工人数	Average revenue ('000 RMB) 平均销售收入（千元）	Average profit ('000 RMB) 平均利润（千元）	Return on assets 资产利润率 (%)	Return on equity 权益利润率 (%)	Labour productivity ('000 RMB/ worker) 劳动生产率（千元/人）	Debts/ assets 资产负债率 (%)	Average total assets ('000 RMB) 平均总资产（千元）
By ownership 产业所有权									
State-owned 国有	34	1,025	89,408	-5,966	-4.23	-19.04	16.42	77.80	141,195
Collective-owned 集体	10	187	24,754	997	4.00	17.70	34.88	77.39	24,917
Foreign & Overseas Chinese Funded 三资	3	1,207	274,440	-7,241	-3.35	-7.42	32.63	54.76	215,854
By regional distribution 地区分布									
Central-North 华北	11	937	39,510	-11,914	-5.64		4.90	102.20	211,181
Beijing 北京									
Tianjin 天津	3	774	85,305	-10,985	-11.85	-51.44	9.08	76.96	92,685
Hebei 河北	4	1,434	22,751	-22,398	-5.35		-3.16	115.65	418,591
Shanxi 山西	2	882	7,756	-4,521	-5.40	-41.13	1.05	86.86	83,673
Inner Mongolia 内蒙古	2	246	36,092	264	0.26	0.42	93.06	38.61	101,614
Northeast 东北	8	697	26,983	-5,777	-4.95	-17.93	4.63	72.37	116,629
Liaoning 辽宁	1	671	37,772	-4,598	-7.48	-58.67	15.18	87.25	61,450
Jilin 吉林	1	1,190	930	-5,356	-8.93	-38.71	-1.21	76.93	59,980
Heilongjiang 黑龙江	6	619	29,527	-6,044	-4.47	-15.36	4.59	70.91	135,267
Central-East 华东	71	471	78,656	-635	-0.79	-2.69	37.29	70.53	80,061
Shanghai 上海	3	399	155,614	1,937	2.15	3.30	54.40	34.75	89,977
Jiangsu 江苏	13	502	80,985	-1,215	-1.27	-5.21	34.11	75.68	96,011
Zhejiang 浙江	15	338	103,446	2,315	3.73	9.25	62.00	59.70	62,089
Anhui 安徽	5	387	67,115	940	0.91	2.01	30.38	54.84	103,269
Fujian 福建	6	337	17,614	-925	-2.96	-14.34	17.22	79.34	31,216
Jiangxi 江西	2	100	26,869	-129	-1.72	-36.19	34.08	95.26	7,519
Shandong 山东	27	610	74,751	-2,545	-2.73	-12.55	33.01	78.24	93,194
Central-South 中南	38	1,184	148,156	563	0.24	0.61	30.22	60.63	236,281
Henan 河南	16	2,332	279,484	1,602	0.33	0.78	30.98	57.83	486,252
Hubei 湖北	3	343	8,759	-2,945	-4.84		4.26	103.63	60,839
Hunan 湖南	5	326	113,169	2,382	3.96		64.74	101.17	60,116
Guangdong 广东	4	333	27,246	-1,670	-3.05	-56.64	12.96	94.61	54,704
Guangxi 广西	9	354	42,407	-188	-0.42	-0.81	19.79	47.98	44,422
Hainan 海南	1	485	75,405	1,061	1.09	2.37	26.06	53.82	96,913
Southwest 西南	13	478	116,659	149	0.19	0.73	31.44	74.16	78,501
Chongqing 重庆									
Sichuan 四川	6	650	226,324	2,728	2.54	9.72	45.22	73.84	107,259
Guizhou 贵州	1	201	1,820	-5,944	-5.37		-28.35	121.29	110,617
Yunnan 云南	6	353	26,133	-1,415	-3.19	-7.14	11.73	55.38	44,391
Tibet 西藏									
Northwest 西北	5	644	46,775	-12,597	-5.25	-28.43	11.23	81.52	239,752
Shaanxi 陕西	2	443	3,170	-3,930	-6.88		0.59	132.66	57,082
Gansu 甘肃	1	910	164,922	-23,415	-4.93	-25.33	39.91	80.54	475,070
Qinghai 青海									
Ningxia 宁夏	1	452	10,694	-4,980	-6.89	-40.13	-12.17	82.83	72,253
Xinjiang 新疆	1	971	51,919	-26,728	-4.97	-17.36	4.96	71.34	537,272

3641: Tractors 拖拉机制造业

Year 年份	Number of firms 企业个数	Rate of change 变化率 (%)	Number of employees 职工人数 (人)	Rate of change 变化率 (%)	Total revenue (Mil. RMB) 总销售收入 (百万元)	Rate of change 变化率 (%)	Total profit (Mil RMB) 总利润 (百万元)	Rate of change 变化率 (%)
2000	134		151,870		13,521		-355	
2001	134	o	131,375	-13.50	12,963	-4.13	-237	33.24
2002	146	8.96	103,714	-21.06	13,615	5.03	-262	-10.55

Major Products 主要产品	Output 产量	Unit 单位
Large & Medium Tractor 大中型拖拉机	45,354	Unit 台
Small Tractor 小型拖拉机	185	10,000 Units 万台

10 Main Firms with Maximal Revenue (year founded) 收入最大的十家主要企业（创办年份）	City 城市	Province 省	Telephone/fax 电话/传真	Number of employees 职工人数	Ownership 产业所有权	Revenue ('000 RMB) 销售收入 (千元)	Profit('000 RMB) (rank) 利润(千元) (排名)	Total assets ('000 RMB) 总资产 (千元)	Major products 主要产品
Yituo International ,Ltd. 中国一拖集团有限公司(1959)	Luoyang 洛阳市	Henan 河南省	(0379)4968011 (0379)4242683	26,844	State Enterprises 国有独资	2,875,961	10,834(4)	6,520,017	Tractor 拖拉机
Cheng Du Wang Pai Motor Co.,Ltd. 成都王牌车辆股份有限公司(1987)	Chengdu 成都市	Sichuan 四川省	(028)83672111 (028)83672794	2,086	Joint Stock 股份制	715,005	9,707(6)	356,808	Loading Automobile 载货汽车
Linhai Baoma Machinery Co., Ltd. 临海市宝马机械有限公司(1998)	Taizhou 台州市	Zhejiang 浙江省	(0576)5122395 (0576)5125956	750	Private Owned 私营企业	540,430	12,950(3)	164,060	Tractor 拖拉机
Shandong Changlin Machinery Group Stock Co., Ltd. 山东常林机械集团股份有限公司(1993)	Linyi 临沂市	Shandong 山东省	(0539)6212942 (0539)6261668	3,306	State-owned 国有企业	509,289	36,260(1)	415,459	Walking Tractor手扶拖拉机
Shanghai Niuhelan Agricultural Machinery Co., Ltd. 上海纽荷兰农业机械有限公司(2002)	Shanghai 上海市	Shanghai 上海市	(021)55584500 (021)55057774	1,111	Foreign Funded 外商投资	456,245	4,656(14)	260,191	Tractor 拖拉机
Kaifeng Kaituo Tractor Factory 开封淯川拖拉机制造厂(1997)	Kaifeng 开封市	Henan 河南省	(0378)7260014 (0378)7266515	620	Joint Stock 股份制	341,157	6,356(11)	96,851	Agricultural Four-wheel Tractor农用四轮拖拉机
Changzhou Tractor Factory of Dongfeng Agricultural Machinery Group 东风农机集团公司(常州拖拉机厂)(1952)	Changzhou 常州市	Jiangsu 江苏省	(0519)3260424 (0519)3260225	1,615	State-owned 国有企业	298,560	-	495,700	Walking Tractor手扶拖拉机
Zhejiang Sifang Group Company 浙江四方集团公司(1961)	Jinhua 金华市	Zhejiang 浙江省	(0579)7155922 (0579)7155293	1,952	State-owned 国有企业	263,849	1,656(22)	329,327	Tractor 拖拉机
John Deere Tiantuo Ltd. Company 约翰·迪尔天拖有限公司(2000)	Tianjin 天津市	Tianjin 天津市	(022)83691775 (022)83691532	1,967	Foreign Funded 外商投资	239,654	-	250,861	Large & Medium Type Tractor大中型拖拉机
Frist Tractor Qingjiang Tractor Co., Ltd. 一拖清江拖拉机有限公司(1998)	Huaian 淮安市	Jiangsu 江苏省	(0517)3932141 (0517)3942371	1,510	Limited-Liability 有限公司	232,129	2,047(20)	263,183	Large & Medium Type Tractor大中型拖拉机

Top 10 Cities by Revenue 销售收入排名前10位城市	Province 省	Market share 市场份额 (%)	Number of firms 企业个数
Luoyang 洛阳市	Henan 河南省	21.12	1
Chengdu 成都市	Sichuan 四川省	6.03	4
Kaifeng 开封市	Henan 河南省	5.74	4
Xinxiang 新乡市	Henan 河南省	5.29	1
Weifang 潍坊市	Shandong 山东省	4.82	12
Jinhua 金华市	Zhejiang 浙江省	4.65	5
Taizhou 台州市	Zhejiang 浙江省	3.97	1
Linyi 临沂市	Shandong 山东省	3.95	2
Changsha 长沙市	Hunan 湖南省	3.90	1
Ziyang 资阳市	Sichuan 四川省	3.80	1

10 Major Wholesalers 十家主要批发商	City 城市	Province 省	Telephone/Fax 电话/传真
SU MEC 中设江苏机械设备进出口（集团）公司	Nanjing 南京市	Jiangsu 江苏省	(025)4511888 (025)4411772
China Poster Mobile Communications Equipment Co.,Ltd. 中邮普泰移动通信设备股份有限公司	Beijing 北京市	Beijing 北京市	(010)66426993 (010)66426837
Sino Kama Co., Ltd. 中泰凯马股份有限公司	Shanghai 上海市	Shanghai 上海市	(021)62031188 (021)62030851
China Huayuan Group Co.,Ltd. 中国华源集团有限公司	Shanghai 上海市	Shanghai 上海市	(021)62031188 (021)62032288
Zhejiang Crand Imp.& Exp.Co.,Ltd. 浙江远大进出口有限公司	Ningbo 宁波市	Zhejiang 浙江省	(0574)87720170 (0574)87723350
Shandong Machinery Import & Export Group Corporation 山东省机械进出口集团公司	Qingdao 青岛市	Shandong 山东省	(0532)2661628 (0532)2991655
Qingdao Haier International Trade Co.,Ltd. 青岛海尔国际贸易有限公司	Qingdao 青岛市	Shandong 山东省	(0532)8938337 (0532)8939494
Guangdong Machinery Import & Export Group Corporation 广东省机械进出口集团公司	Guangzhou 广州市	Guangdong 广东省	(020)87782168 (020)87771803
China National Machinery Equipment Import & Export Corporation 中国机械设备进出口总公司	Beijing 北京市	Beijing 北京市	(010)63474506 (010)63261865
Beijing Cellstar Co.,Ltd. 北京蜂星事达电讯有限公司	Beijing 北京市	Beijing 北京市	(010)64602050 (010)64672648

3642: Mechanized Farm Tools 机械化农机具制造业

The industry accounts for 0.089% of the total revenue of China's industrial sector in 2002. The rate of return on assets is 2.55%. 70.90% of all firms in the industry made a profit while 29.10% had negative returns.The top province in terms of the industry's revenue is Shandong, accounting for 43.80% of the total revenue.
2002年本行业收入占全行业的 0.089%，资产利润率为 2.55%。70.90%的企业赢利，29.10%的企业亏损。收入最高的省为山东省，占本行业的43.80%。

	Total number of firms 企业总数	Total number of employees 职工总数	Total revenue (Mil.RMB) 总销售收入（百万元）	Total profit (Mil.RMB) 总利润（百万元）	Return on assets 资产利润率 (%)	Return on equity 权益利润率 (%)	Labour productivity ('000 RMB/ worker) 劳动生产率（千元/人）	Debts/ assets 资产负债率 (%)	Total assets (Mil.RMB) 总资产（百万元）
Industry Overall 行业总体	354	72,098	9,586	265	2.55	8.10	34.52	68.59	10,397

	Number of firms 企业个数	Average number of employees 平均职工人数	Average revenue ('000 RMB) 平均销售收入（千元）	Average profit ('000 RMB) 平均利润（千元）	Return on assets 资产利润率 (%)	Return on equity 权益利润率 (%)	Labour productivity ('000 RMB/ worker) 劳动生产率（千元/人）	Debts/ assets 资产负债率 (%)	Average total assets ('000 RMB) 平均总资产（千元）
By ownership 产业所有权									
State-owned 国有	144	180	5,996	-608	-3.10	-141.52	9.35	97.81	19,631
Collective-owned 集体	63	133	26,792	1,808	11.52	26.59	57.75	56.66	15,689
Foreign & Overseas Chinese Funded 三资	10	239	78,488	7,629	9.60	17.44	77.88	44.94	79,431
By regional distribution 地区分布									
Central-North 华北	37	220	20,540	415	1.33	3.45	31.12	61.40	31,138
Beijing 北京	5	70	9,175	188	2.15	18.52	38.62	88.39	8,736
Tianjin 天津	2	136	57,661	5,790	13.83	77.57	110.26	82.18	41,872
Hebei 河北	20	211	18,354	57	0.19	0.55	21.96	65.96	30,517
Shanxi 山西	9	342	24,600	188	0.44	0.81	37.30	45.84	42,748
Inner Mongolia 内蒙古	1	223	10,300				11.01	71.01	29,619
Northeast 东北	47	230	13,258	-517	-1.56	-9.72	17.13	83.93	33,110
Liaoning 辽宁	11	68	5,477	288	2.56	5.20	24.50	50.71	11,256
Jilin 吉林	11	186	7,430	279	1.27	4.32	24.43	70.48	21,865
Heilongjiang 黑龙江	25	320	19,245	-1,222	-2.56	-25.89	14.58	90.10	47,674
Central-East 华东	102	275	57,631	2,478	5.78	14.13	45.69	59.07	42,853
Shanghai 上海	4	433	40,094	2,353	3.59	11.52	36.47	68.81	65,492
Jiangsu 江苏	32	214	32,474	1,737	5.15	18.98	34.62	72.88	33,734
Zhejiang 浙江	12	130	27,355	1,400	8.45	16.64	48.52	49.19	16,562
Anhui 安徽	10	189	5,452	-401	-2.96	-38.77	11.70	92.36	13,529
Fujian 福建	4	72	9,477	150	2.25	7.70	44.93	70.72	6,669
Jiangxi 江西	7	357	8,437	219	2.22	4.66	7.79	52.40	9,858
Shandong 山东	33	400	127,243	5,238	6.65	13.69	64.34	51.44	78,783
Central-South 中南	112	164	19,016	766	4.45	15.69	37.76	71.63	17,203
Henan 河南	66	166	19,874	1,107	6.18	34.03	39.70	81.84	17,913
Hubei 湖北	7	375	81,538	2,476	6.56	9.81	66.55	33.12	37,729
Hunan 湖南	18	157	9,743	68	0.69	2.15	22.17	67.83	9,890
Guangdong 广东	6	79	7,130	247	1.26	5.84	27.23	78.36	19,533
Guangxi 广西	14	102	1,739	-524	-4.11	-10.72	4.89	61.68	12,750
Hainan 海南	1	56	4,880	-20	-0.30	-0.48	18.18	37.03	6,589
Southwest 西南	15	58	2,017	-126	-2.23	-6.25	9.77	64.40	5,683
Chongqing 重庆	1	71	6,590	209	3.40	12.97	19.18	73.82	6,153
Sichuan 四川	5	63	3,273	193	3.23	6.11	19.50	47.19	5,996
Guizhou 贵州	1	19	207	-21	-1.60	-2.02	4.16	20.67	1,311
Yunnan 云南	6	68	1,029	-520	-7.61	-48.00	2.11	84.14	6,826
Tibet 西藏	2	27	465	33	0.96	1.23	0.33	21.66	3,426
Northwest 西北	41	145	4,006	-1,536	-4.82	-30.68	11.69	84.28	31,854
Shaanxi 陕西	13	193	2,519	-951	-3.93		6.25	107.24	24,209
Gansu 甘肃	17	110	3,432	120	1.13	6.85	14.28	83.52	10,635
Qinghai 青海	1	85	2,250	-236	-2.82	-19.72	6.61	85.68	8,357
Ningxia 宁夏	1	60	5,404	564	23.62	216.92	31.73	89.11	2,388
Xinjiang 新疆	9	156	7,278	-5,887	-6.63	-26.92	17.47	75.39	88,860

3642: Mechanized Farm Tools 机械化农机具制造业

Year 年份	Number of firms 企业个数	Rate of change 变化率 (%)	Number of employees 职工人数 (人)	Rate of change 变化率 (%)	Total revenue (Mil. RMB) 总销售收入 (百万元)	Rate of change 变化率 (%)	Total profit (Mil RMB) 总利润 (百万元)	Rate of change 变化率 (%)
2000	469		115,267		9,993		184	
2001	399	-14.93	83,635	-27.44	8,983	-10.11	119	-35.33
2002	354	-11.28	72,098	-13.79	9,586	6.71	265	122.69

Major Products 主要产品	Output 产量	Unit 单位
Harvesting Machinery 收获机械	231,508	Unit 台
Field Work Machinery 场上作业机械	16	10,000 Units 万台

10 Main Firms with Maximal Revenue (year founded) 收入最大的十家主要企业（创办年份）	City 城市	Province 省	Telephone/fax 电话/传真	Number of employees 职工人数	Ownership 产业所有权	Revenue ('000 RMB) 销售收入 (千元)	Profit('000 RMB) (rank) 利润(千元) (排名)	Total assets ('000 RMB) 总资产 (千元)	Major products 主要产品
Shandong Juli Co.,Ltd. 山东巨力集团有限公司(1994)	Weifang 潍坊市	Shandong 山东省	(0536)8555878 (0536)8555822	2,950	Limited-Liability 有限公司	1,875,940	63,180(1)	1,205,380	Tricycle Agricultural Transporter三轮农用运输车
Shandong Wuzheng Agricultural Vehicle Co., Ltd. 山东五征农用车有限公司(2000)	Rizhao 日照市	Shandong 山东省	(0633)5321166 (0633)5323562	1,528	Limited-Liability 有限公司	998,289	28,576(4)	216,522	Agricultural Tricycle农用三轮车
Hubei Jiahua Machinery Stock. Co., Ltd. 湖北省佳华机械股份有限公司(1997)	Jingzhou 荆州市	Hubei 湖北省	(0716)2423691 (0716)2422691	2,055	Joint Stock 股份制	549,820	17050(8)	245,020	Harvester 收割机
Wendeng NO.1 General Machinery Factory 文登市第一通用机械厂(1948)	Weihai 威海市	Shandong 山东省	(0631)8561097	158	Collective-owned 集体企业	387,770	35,330(3)	37,330	Amplitude Modulation Plough 调幅犁
Yangma Agricutural Machinery (China) Co., Ltd. 洋马农机（中国）有限公司(1998)	Wuxi 无锡市	Jiangsu 江苏省	(0510)5216877 (0510)5212550	265	Foreign Funded 外商投资	206,665	17,201(7)	160,168	Joint Harvester联合收割机
KUBOTA Agricultural Machinery (Suzhou) Co., Ltd. 久保田农业机械（苏州）有限公司(2000)	Suzhou 苏州市	Jiangsu 江苏省	(0512)67163122 (0512)67163344	119	Foreign Funded 外商投资	186,431	44,079(2)	106,162	Joint Harvester联合收割机
Zhengzhou BaiYun Electromechanical Equipment Co., Ltd. 郑州白云机电装备股份有限公司(1958)	Zhengzhou 郑州市	Henan 河南省	(0371)6781936 (0371)6781936	655	Collective-owned 集体企业	166,267	25,237(5)	200,931	Joint Harvester联合收割机
Linyi Huasheng Enterprise Group General Company 临沂华盛企业集团总公司(1994)	Linyi 临沂市	Shandong 山东省	(0539)8312250 (0539)8241427	920	State-owned 国有企业	108,409	2,776(27)	244,652	Machinery Farm Machine & Tool机械化农机具
Tianjin Xinshan Agricutural Cropper Co.,Ltd. 天津新山农业收获机械制造有限公司(1995)	Tianjin 天津市	Tianjin 天津市	(022)28933265 (022)28933265	133	Joint Stock 股份制	107,090	11,430(9)	53,290	Xinjiang-2 Harvester新疆-2收割机
Zhejiang Liulin Machinery Co., Ltd. 浙江柳林机械有限公司(1997)	Taizhou 台州市	Zhejiang 浙江省	(0576)2664185 (0576)2662955	280	Limited-Liability 有限公司	100,391	6,870(17)	31,700	Harvester 收割机

Top 10 Cities by Revenue 销售收入排名前10位城市	Province 省	Market share 市场份额 (%)	Number of firms 企业个数
Weifang 潍坊市	Shandong 山东省	19.87	4
Rizhao 日照市	Shandong 山东省	10.47	2
Zhengzhou 郑州市	Henan 河南省	6.06	8
Jingzhou 荆州市	Hubei 湖北省	5.74	1
Weihai 威海市	Shandong 山东省	5.35	2
Jiamusi 佳木斯市	Heilongjiang 黑龙江省	3.22	4
Shijiazhuang 石家庄市	Hebei 河北省	2.84	8
Suzhou 苏州市	Jiangsu 江苏省	2.65	4
Wuxi 无锡市	Jiangsu 江苏省	2.65	4
Taizhou 台州市	Zhejiang 浙江省	2.57	5

10 Major Wholesalers 十家主要批发商	City 城市	Province 省	Telephone/Fax 电话/传真
SU MEC 中设江苏机械设备进出口（集团）公司	Nanjing 南京市	Jiangsu 江苏省	(025)4511888 (025)4411772
China Poster Mobile Communications Equipment Co.,Ltd. 中邮普泰移动通信设备股份有限公司	Beijing 北京市	Beijing 北京市	(010)66426993 (010)66426837
Sino Kama Co., Ltd. 中泰凯马股份有限公司	Shanghai 上海市	Shanghai 上海市	(021)62031188 (021)62030851
China Huayuan Group Co.,Ltd. 中国华源集团有限公司	Shanghai 上海市	Shanghai 上海市	(021)62031188 (021)62032288
Zhejiang Crand Imp.& Exp.Co.,Ltd. 浙江远大进出口有限公司	Ningbo 宁波市	Zhejiang 浙江省	(0574)87720170 (0574)87723350
Shandong Machinery Import & Export Group Corporation 山东省机械进出口集团公司	Qingdao 青岛市	Shandong 山东省	(0532)2661628 (0532)2991655
Qingdao Haier International Trade Co.,Ltd. 青岛海尔国际贸易有限公司	Qingdao 青岛市	Shandong 山东省	(0532)8938337 (0532)8939494
Guangdong Machinery Import & Export Group Corporation 广东省机械进出口集团公司	Guangzhou 广州市	Guangdong 广东省	(020)87782168 (020)87771803
China National Machinery Equipment Import & Export Corporation 中国机械设备进出口总公司	Beijing 北京市	Beijing 北京市	(010)63474506 (010)63261865
Beijing Cellstar Co.,Ltd. 北京蜂星事达电讯有限公司	Beijing 北京市	Beijing 北京市	(010)64602050 (010)64672648

3644: Animal Husbandry Machinery 畜牧机械制造业

The industry accounts for 0.003% of the total revenue of China's industrial sector in 2002. The rate of return on assets is 4.24%. 80.00% of all firms in the industry made a profit while 20.00% had negative returns.The top province in terms of the industry's revenue is Shanghai, accounting for 48.75% of the total revenue.
2002年本行业收入占全行业的0.003%，资产利润率为4.24%。80.00%的企业赢利，20.00%的企业亏损。收入最高的省为上海市，占本行业的48.75%。

	Total number of firms 企业总数	Total number of employees 职工总数	Total revenue (Mil.RMB) 总销售收入（百万元）	Total profit (Mil.RMB) 总利润（百万元）	Return on assets 资产利润率（%）	Return on equity 权益利润率（%）	Labour productivity ('000 RMB/ worker) 劳动生产率（千元/人）	Debts/ assets 资产负债率（%）	Total assets (Mil.RMB) 总资产（百万元）
Industry Overall 行业总体	25	3,646	337	21	4.24	13.59	23.79	68.77	496

	Number of firms 企业个数	Average number of employees 平均职工人数	Average revenue ('000 RMB) 平均销售收入（千元）	Average profit ('000 RMB) 平均利润（千元）	Return on assets 资产利润率（%）	Return on equity 权益利润率（%）	Labour productivity ('000 RMB/ worker) 劳动生产率（千元/人）	Debts/ assets 资产负债率（%）	Average total assets ('000 RMB) 平均总资产（千元）
By ownership 产业所有权									
State-owned 国有	10	167	3,454	15	0.12	0.54	9.85	77.42	12,011
Collective-owned 集体	1	339	13,445	1		0.01	17.97	52.39	23,341
Foreign & Overseas Chinese Funded 三资	4	72	40,576	3,486	9.26	31.09	113.44	70.20	37,629
By regional distribution 地区分布									
Central-North 华北	8	189	11,928	-145	-0.54	-2.36	18.47	76.94	26,690
Beijing 北京	1	89	5,152	4	0.04	0.10	17.87	58.98	10,080
Tianjin 天津	3	83	20,719	856	3.66	67.75	59.26	94.60	23,401
Hebei 河北	1	110	7,500	250	2.83	10.80	19.55	73.83	8,841
Shanxi 山西	2	213	2,473	-2,112	-5.70	-18.22	1.61	68.72	37,050
Inner Mongolia 内蒙古	1	639	15,667	238	0.47	1.50	13.76	68.54	50,299
Northeast 东北	1	311	12,974	50	0.24	0.32	11.87	24.77	20,664
Liaoning 辽宁	1	311	12,974	50	0.24	0.32	11.87	24.77	20,664
Jilin 吉林									
Heilongjiang 黑龙江									
Central-East 华东	11	132	19,383	1,970	8.92	25.59	31.55	65.15	22,091
Shanghai 上海	4	79	41,122	3,408	9.24	26.33	91.53	64.91	36,890
Jiangsu 江苏	2	299	9,064	3,572	22.47	67.88	8.07	66.89	15,893
Zhejiang 浙江									
Anhui 安徽									
Fujian 福建	1	38	5,883	582	6.52	10.14	63.79	35.69	8,924
Jiangxi 江西	2	57	1,022	-94	-0.65	-5.04	-0.68	87.18	14,468
Shandong 山东	2	198	11,335	248	1.92	3.84	25.48	49.92	12,900
Central-South 中南	1	36	2,700	325	28.56	101.88	102.08	71.97	1,138
Henan 河南	1	36	2,700	325	28.56	101.88	102.08	71.97	1,138
Hubei 湖北									
Hunan 湖南									
Guangdong 广东									
Guangxi 广西									
Hainan 海南									
Southwest 西南	1	63							
Chongqing 重庆									
Sichuan 四川	1	63							
Guizhou 贵州									
Yunnan 云南									
Tibet 西藏									
Northwest 西北	3	89	4,358	58	0.98	3.37	20.49	71.05	5,941
Shaanxi 陕西	2	75	4,565	86	1.92	4.12	22.71	53.39	4,480
Gansu 甘肃									
Qinghai 青海									
Ningxia 宁夏									
Xinjiang 新疆	1	118	3,945	2	0.02	0.20	17.68	88.91	8,862

3644: Animal Husbandry Machinery 畜牧机械制造业

Year 年份	Number of firms 企业个数	Rate of change 变化率 (%)	Number of employees 职工人数 (人)	Rate of change 变化率 (%)	Total revenue (Mil. RMB) 总销售收入 (百万元)	Rate of change 变化率 (%)	Total profit (Mil RMB) 总利润 (百万元)	Rate of change 变化率 (%)
2000	27		5,703		152		-7	
2001	25	-7.41	4,813	-15.61	192	26.32	-3	57.14
2002	25	o	3,646	-24.25	337	75.52	21	-

Major Products 主要产品	Output 产量	Unit 单位
Feed Processing Machinery 饲料加工机械	126,094	Unit 台

10 Main Firms with Maximal Revenue (year founded) 收入最大的十家主要企业（创办年份）	City 城市	Province 省	Telephone/fax 电话/传真	Number of employees 职工人数	Ownership 产业所有权	Revenue ('000 RMB) 销售收入 (千元)	Profit('000 RMB) (rank) 利润(千元) (排名)	Total assets ('000 RMB) 总资产 (千元)	Major products 主要产品
Delaval (Shanghai) Milk Machinery Co., ltd.	Shanghai	Shanghai	(021)32051155		Foreign Funded				Milking Machine
利拉伐（上海）乳业机械有限公司(2000)	上海市	上海市	(021)62849422	46	外商投资	86,119	8,705(1)	65,009	挤奶设备
Shanghai Milk Products Machinery Factory Co., Ltd.	Shanghai	Shanghai	(021)54770117		Limited-Liability				Milk Products Machinery
上海乳品机械厂有限公司(1964)	上海市	上海市	(021)54770117	146	有限公司	52,061	2,188(5)	54,831	乳品机械
Tianjin Zhengda Machinery Co.,Ltd.	Tianjin	Tianjin	(022)25325237		Foreign Funded				Livestock Raising Machinery
天津正大机械有限公司(1992)	天津市	天津市	(022)25327511	171	外商投资	47,539	7,119(3)	41,825	畜牧机械
Jiangyin SAT Air Treament Co., Ltd.	Wuxi	Jiangsu	(0510)6607998		Private Owned				Wet Curtain
江阴三特空气处理设备有限公司(1998)	无锡市	江苏省	(0510)6605978	45	私营企业	18,120	7,143(2)	12,928	湿帘
Inner mongolia Hailar Animal Husbandry Machinery Factory	Hulunbeier	ıner Mongol	(0470)8334822		State-owned				Farming Raising Machinery
内蒙古海拉尔牧业机械总厂(1949)	呼伦贝尔市	内蒙古	(0470)8333569	639	国有企业	15,667	238(11)	50,299	农牧机械
Shanghai Shijing Livestock Raising Equipment Co., Ltd.	Shanghai	Shanghai	(021)57686148		Foreign Funded				Incubator
上海石井畜牧设备有限公司(1997)	上海市	上海市	(021)57686150	32	外商投资	14,664	2,401(4)	18,483	孵化器
Liaoning Fengcheng Dongfeng Machinery Factory	Dandong	Liaoning	(0415)8123976		Joint Stock				Farming Machine
辽宁凤城东风机械厂(1953)	丹东市	辽宁省	(0415)8122268	311	股份制	12,974	50(13)	20,664	农用机械
Xi' an Animal Husbandry Machinery & Dairy Equipment	Xi'an	Shannxi	(029)6602073		State-owned				Hay Cutter Machine
Factory 西安市畜牧乳品机械厂(1952)	西安市	陕西省	(029)6601682	104	国有企业	8,363	175(12)	6,314	铡草机
Mindong Wuyi Electromechanical Equipment Co.,Ltd.	Ningde	Fujian	(0593)6583029		Private Owned				Grass Cutter Machine
闽东五一机电有限公司(1995)	宁德市	福建省	(0593)6560198	38	私营企业	5,883	582(6)	8,924	割草机
Beijing Livestock Machinery Chang	Beijing	Beijing	(010)67994037		State-owned				Poultry Feeding Mechine
北京市畜牧机械厂(1978)	北京市	北京市	(010)67991383	89	国有企业	5,152	4(14)	10,080	养禽设备

Top 10 Cities by Revenue 销售收入排名前10位城市	Province 省	Market share 市场份额 (%)	Number of firms 企业个数
Shanghai 上海市	Shanghai 上海市	48.75	4
Tianjin 天津市	Tianjin 天津市	18.42	3
Wuxi 无锡市	Jiangsu 江苏省	5.37	1
Hulunbeier 呼伦贝尔市	Inner Mongolia 内蒙古	4.64	1
Binzhou 滨州市	Shandong 山东省	3.99	1
Dandong 丹东市	Liaoning 辽宁省	3.85	1
Linyi 临沂市	Shandong 山东省	2.73	1
Xi'an 西安市	Shannxi 陕西省	2.48	1
Tangshan 唐山市	Hebei 河北省	2.22	1
Ningde 宁德市	Fujian 福建省	1.74	1

10 Major Wholesalers 十家主要批发商	City 城市	Province 省	Telephone/Fax 电话/传真
SU MEC	Nanjing	Jiangsu	(025)4511888
中设江苏机械设备进出口（集团）公司	南京市	江苏省	(025)4411772
China Poster Mobile Communications Equipment Co.,Ltd.	Beijing	Beijing	(010)66426993
中邮普泰移动通信设备股份有限公司	北京市	北京市	(010)66426837
Sino Kama Co., Ltd.	Shanghai	Shanghai	(021)62031188
中泰凯马股份有限公司	上海市	上海市	(021)62030851
China Huayuan Group Co.,Ltd.	Shanghai	Shanghai	(021)62031188
中国华源集团有限公司	上海市	上海市	(021)62032288
Zhejiang Crand Imp.& Exp.Co.,Ltd.	Ningbo	Zhejiang	(0574)87720170
浙江远大进出口有限公司	宁波市	浙江省	(0574)87723350
Shandong Machinery Import & Export Group Corporation	Qingdao	Shandong	(0532)2661628
山东省机械进出口集团公司	青岛市	山东省	(0532)2991655
Qingdao Haier International Trade Co.,Ltd.	Qingdao	Shandong	(0532)8938337
青岛海尔国际贸易有限公司	青岛市	山东省	(0532)8939494
Guangdong Machinery Import & Export Group Corporation	Guangzhou	Guangdong	(020)87782168
广东省机械进出口集团公司	广州市	广东省	(020)87771803
China National Machinery Equipment Import & Export Corporation	Beijing	Beijing	(010)63474506
中国机械设备进出口总公司	北京市	北京市	(010)63261865
Beijing Cellstar Co.,Ltd.	Beijing	Beijing	(010)64602050
北京蜂星事达电讯有限公司	北京市	北京市	(010)64672648

3645: Fishery Machinery 渔业机械制造业

The industry accounts for 0.005% of the total revenue of China's industrial sector in 2002. The rate of return on assets is 2.51%. 68.97% of all firms in the industry made a profit while 31.03% had negative returns.The top province in terms of the industry's revenue is Jiangsu, accounting for 43.24% of the total revenue.
2002年本行业收入占全行业的 0.005%，资产利润率为 2.51%。68.97%的企业赢利，31.03%的企业亏损。收入最高的省为江苏省，占本行业的43.24%。

	Total number of firms 企业总数	Total number of employees 职工总数	Total revenue (Mil.RMB) 总销售收入 (百万元)	Total profit (Mil.RMB) 总利润 (百万元)	Return on assets 资产利润率 (%)	Return on equity 权益利润率 (%)	Labour productivity ('000 RMB/ worker) 劳动生产率 (千元/人)	Debts/ assets 资产负债率 (%)	Total assets (Mil.RMB) 总资产 (百万元)
Industry Overall 行业总体	29	5,443	528	16	2.51	8.48	29.88	70.38	638

	Number of firms 企业个数	Average number of employees 平均职工人数	Average revenue ('000 RMB) 平均销售收入 (千元)	Average profit ('000 RMB) 平均利润 (千元)	Return on assets 资产利润率 (%)	Return on equity 权益利润率 (%)	Labour productivity ('000 RMB/ worker) 劳动生产率 (千元/人)	Debts/ assets 资产负债率 (%)	Average total assets ('000 RMB) 平均总资产 (千元)
By ownership 产业所有权									
State-owned 国有	7	75	1,780	-183	-1.39	-4.71	5.49	70.45	13,161
Collective-owned 集体	6	215	12,857	498	2.23	5.35	21.56	58.27	22,318
Foreign & Overseas Chinese Funded 三资									
By regional distribution 地区分布									
Central-North 华北	1	150	15,589	555	1.15	3.20	20.79	64.19	48,416
Beijing 北京	1	150	15,589	555	1.15	3.20	20.79	64.19	48,416
Tianjin 天津									
Hebei 河北									
Shanxi 山西									
Inner Mongolia 内蒙古									
Northeast 东北	1	1,050	59,933	5,963	5.22	35.59	20.94	85.34	114,265
Liaoning 辽宁									
Jilin 吉林	1	1,050	59,933	5,963	5.22	35.59	20.94	85.34	114,265
Heilongjiang 黑龙江									
Central-East 华东	19	185	20,497	296	1.33	4.12	32.07	67.70	22,183
Shanghai 上海	1	109	3,116	-1,033	-3.49	-11.76	6.52	70.37	29,639
Jiangsu 江苏	10	151	22,815	108	0.65	3.83	42.48	83.06	16,575
Zhejiang 浙江	4	237	29,574	1,135	3.63	7.92	33.19	54.14	31,249
Anhui 安徽									
Fujian 福建									
Jiangxi 江西									
Shandong 山东	4	235	9,971	259	1.02	2.46	17.21	58.49	25,275
Central-South 中南	8	92	7,836	487	7.19	20.68	34.01	65.26	6,778
Henan 河南	2	105	13,315	1,007	20.69	26.45	40.69	21.79	4,865
Hubei 湖北	1	48	5,833	140	3.15	7.95	40.65	60.44	4,451
Hunan 湖南	1	15	800	-1	-0.02		11.93	124.06	6,601
Guangdong 广东	3	100	9,809	632	6.27	15.62	47.73	59.85	10,082
Guangxi 广西									
Hainan 海南	1	162		-153	-4.79			134.12	3,195
Southwest 西南									
Chongqing 重庆									
Sichuan 四川									
Guizhou 贵州									
Yunnan 云南									
Tibet 西藏									
Northwest 西北									
Shaanxi 陕西									
Gansu 甘肃									
Qinghai 青海									
Ningxia 宁夏									
Xinjiang 新疆									

Year 年份	Number of firms 企业个数	Rate of change 变化率 (%)	Number of employees 职工人数 (人)	Rate of change 变化率 (%)	Total revenue (Mil. RMB) 总销售收入 (百万元)	Rate of change 变化率 (%)	Total profit (Mil RMB) 总利润 (百万元)	Rate of change 变化率 (%)
2000	20		4,465		678		23	
2001	29	45.00	6,873	53.93	851	25.52	17	-26.09
2002	29	o	5,443	-20.81	528	-37.96	16	-5.88

Major Products 主要产品	Output 产量	Unit 单位
Knitting Machinery Equipment 针织机械设备	28,222	Ton 吨

10 Main Firms with Maximal Revenue (year founded) 收入最大的十家主要企业（创办年份）	City 城市	Province 省	Telephone/fax 电话/传真	Number of employees 职工人数	Ownership 产业所有权	Revenue ('000 RMB) 销售收入 (千元)	Profit('000 RMB) (rank) 利润(千元) (排名)	Total assets ('000 RMB) 总资产 (千元)	Major products 主要产品
Zhejiang Sensen Industrial Co., Ltd.	Zhoushan	Zhejiang	(0580)8080129		Private Owned				Oxygen Adding Machine
浙江森森实业有限公司(1985)	舟山市	浙江省	(0580)8080127	660	私营企业	91,620	3,730(2)	62,030	增氧机
Changchun Zhucheng Group Co., Ltd.	Changchun	Jilin	(0431)7915999		Joint Stock				
长春铸诚集团有限责任公司(1998)	长春市	吉林省	(0431)2627666	1,050	股份制	59,933	5,963(1)	114,265	
Jiangsu Jianghai Machinery Co., Ltd.	Suzhou	Jiangsu	(0512)58211248		Limited-Liability				Knitting Equipment
江苏江海机械有限公司(1967)	苏州市	江苏省	(0512)58223109	501	有限公司	33,880	-	82,230	针织设备
Shunde Jinshunda Machinery Co., Ltd.	Foshan	Guangdong	(0765)2227080		Limited-Liability				Fishing Pond Oxygen Adding Machine鱼
顺德市金顺达机械有限公司(1972)	佛山市	广东省	(0765)2227080	228	有限公司	27,866	2,119(3)	15,089	塘增氧机
Shandong Dapeng Group Co., Ltd.	Jining	Shandong	(0537)7332132		Collective-owned				Light Body Board Door
山东大鹏集团有限责任公司(1976)	济宁市	山东省	(0537)7332132	792	集体企业	27,480	674(9)	57,308	轻体板门
Zhoushan Putuo Gear Box Co., ltd.	Zhoushan	Zhejiang	(0580)3695369		Private Owned				170 Marine Gear Kase.170船
舟山市普陀齿轮箱有限公司(2000)	舟山市	浙江省	(0580)3695369	87	私营企业	18,773	808(7)	21,701	用齿轮箱
Yuzhou Fishing Industrial Machinery Factory	Xuchang	Henan	(0374)8711088		Collective-owned				Fishery Machinery
禹州市渔业机械厂(1969)	许昌市	河南省	(0374)8711019	125	集体企业	16,450	1,365(5)	6,950	渔业机械
Wuxi Taihu Fishing Machinery Factory	Wuxi	Jiangsu	(0510)5515168		Collective-owned				Fishery Machinery
无锡市太湖渔机厂(1978)	无锡市	江苏省	(0510)5505886	170	集体企业	14,784	215(15)	25,860	渔业机械
Nantong Eastern Ship Equipment Manufacturing Co., Ltd.	Nantong	Jiangsu	(0513)3711126		Private Enterprises				Colander For Ship
南通东方船用设备制造有限公司(1998)	南通市	江苏省	(0513)3714389	45	私营独资	10,450	760(8)	7,071	船用滤器
Zhenzhou Zhongmu Environmental protection Equipment	Zhengzhou	Henan	(0371)2292044		Collective-owned				Weaving Cleaning Dirt Machine纺织除尘
Factory 郑州市中牟环保设备厂(1996)	郑州市	河南省	(0371)2292098	84	集体企业	10,180	648(11)	2,780	空调设备

Top 10 Cities by Revenue 销售收入排名前10位城市	Province 省	Market share 市场份额 (%)	Number of firms 企业个数
Zhoushan 舟山市	Zhejiang 浙江省	20.92	2
Lianyungang 连云港市	Jiangsu 江苏省	18.15	2
Changchun 长春市	Jilin 吉林省	11.36	1
Huaian 淮安市	Jiangsu 江苏省	8.65	1
Suzhou 苏州市	Jiangsu 江苏省	7.50	2
Foshan 佛山市	Guangdong 广东省	5.28	1
Jining 济宁市	Shandong 山东省	5.21	1
Wuxi 无锡市	Jiangsu 江苏省	3.88	2
Xuchang 许昌市	Henan 河南省	3.12	1
Beijing 北京市	Beijing 北京市	2.95	1

10 Major Wholesalers 十家主要批发商	City 城市	Province 省	Telephone/Fax 电话/传真
SU MEC	Nanjing	Jiangsu	(025)4511888
中设江苏机械设备进出口（集团）公司	南京市	江苏省	(025)4411772
China Poster Mobile Communications Equipment Co.,Ltd.	Beijing	Beijing	(010)66426993
中邮普泰移动通信设备股份有限公司	北京市	北京市	(010)66426837
Sino Kama Co., Ltd.	Shanghai	Shanghai	(021)62031188
中泰凯马股份有限公司	上海市	上海市	(021)62030851
China Huayuan Group Co.,Ltd.	Shanghai	Shanghai	(021)62031188
中国华源集团有限公司	上海市	上海市	(021)62032288
Zhejiang Crand Imp.& Exp.Co.,Ltd.	Ningbo	Zhejiang	(0574)87720170
浙江远大进出口有限公司	宁波市	浙江省	(0574)87723350
Shandong Machinery Import & Export Group Corporation	Qingdao	Shandong	(0532)2661628
山东省机械进出口集团公司	青岛市	山东省	(0532)2991655
Qingdao Haier International Trade Co.,Ltd.	Qingdao	Shandong	(0532)8938337
青岛海尔国际贸易有限公司	青岛市	山东省	(0532)8939494
Guangdong Machinery Import & Export Group Corporation	Guangzhou	Guangdong	(020)87782168
广东省机械进出口集团公司	广州市	广东省	(020)87771803
China National Machinery Equipment Import & Export Corporation	Beijing	Beijing	(010)63474506
中国机械设备进出口总公司	北京市	北京市	(010)63261865
Beijing Cellstar Co.,Ltd.	Beijing	Beijing	(010)64602050
北京蜂星事达电讯有限公司	北京市	北京市	(010)64672648

3646: Irrigation Equipment 水利机械制造业

The industry accounts for 0.008% of the total revenue of China's industrial sector in 2002. The rate of return on assets is -2.33%. 72.41% of all firms in the industry made a profit while 27.59% had negative returns.The top province in terms of the industry's revenue is Jiangsu, accounting for 28.70% of the total revenue.
2002年本行业收入占全行业的0.008%，资产利润率为 -2.33%。72.41%的企业赢利，27.59%的企业亏损。收入最高的省为江苏省，占本行业的28.70%。

	Total number of firms 企业总数	Total number of employees 职工总数	Total revenue (Mil.RMB) 总销售收入 (百万元)	Total profit (Mil.RMB) 总利润 (百万元)	Return on assets 资产利润率 (%)	Return on equity 权益利润率 (%)	Labour productivity ('000 RMB/ worker) 劳动生产率 (千元/人)	Debts/ assets 资产负债率 (%)	Total assets (Mil.RMB) 总资产 (百万元)
Industry Overall 行业总体	58	10,649	852	-37	-2.33	-7.64	25.79	69.50	1,570

	Number of firms 企业个数	Average number of employees 平均职工人数	Average revenue ('000 RMB) 平均销售收入（千元）	Average profit ('000 RMB) 平均利润 (千元)	Return on assets 资产利润率 (%)	Return on equity 权益利润率 (%)	Labour productivity ('000 RMB/ worker) 劳动生产率 (千元/人)	Debts/ assets 资产负债率 (%)	Average total assets ('000 RMB) 平均总资产 (千元)
By ownership 产业所有权									
State-owned 国有	19	242	11,048	-2,461	-6.50	-22.76	16.64	71.42	37,832
Collective-owned 集体	5	97	10,124	244	3.10	5.73	22.67	45.80	7,872
Foreign & Overseas Chinese Funded 三资	3	82	30,490	-1,208	-4.07	-24.64	-19.79	83.48	29,682
By regional distribution 地区分布									
Central-North 华北	8	129	8,416	360	3.09	15.06	25.40	79.46	11,621
Beijing 北京	1	25	5,011	-17	-0.37	-3.36	5.72	88.92	4,565
Tianjin 天津	1	4	75				1.00	80.92	2,091
Hebei 河北	4	166	13,921	1,034	11.25	33.09	36.92	66.01	9,190
Shanxi 山西	2	172	3,279	-621	-2.51	-21.79	4.85	88.50	24,776
Inner Mongolia 内蒙古									
Northeast 东北	6	47	5,227	160	3.58	16.55	43.72	78.36	4,472
Liaoning 辽宁	3	41	6,030	25	0.42	1.45	57.84	70.73	5,985
Jilin 吉林	2	47	2,138	115	3.17		36.13	100.28	3,616
Heilongjiang 黑龙江	1	67	8,994	656	39.83	114.89	28.55	65.33	1,647
Central-East 华东	17	195	23,345	261	1.04	3.18	45.72	67.33	25,067
Shanghai 上海	1	133	67,449	-639	-1.49	-8.43	25.64	82.32	42,878
Jiangsu 江苏	8	253	30,572	312	0.87	2.74	59.30	68.03	35,666
Zhejiang 浙江									
Anhui 安徽	1	161	7,553	43	0.25	0.61	27.61	58.84	17,074
Fujian 福建									
Jiangxi 江西									
Shandong 山东	7	143	11,042	362	3.13	7.58	23.82	58.68	11,551
Central-South 中南	20	244	16,027	-2,227	-5.11	-17.33	14.01	70.51	43,565
Henan 河南	12	295	18,202	-3,314	-7.18	-33.66	15.05	78.65	46,131
Hubei 湖北	2	144	5,695	14	0.10	1.31	15.56	92.67	14,601
Hunan 湖南	2	234	16,036	-1,239	-1.87	-4.32	17.60	56.74	66,281
Guangdong 广东	2	181	27,843	-907	-1.71	-4.38	3.61	60.91	52,947
Guangxi 广西	1	174	1,680	-330	-0.71	-0.89	6.60	19.44	46,171
Hainan 海南	1	64	1,302	-184	-4.71	-24.40	1.89	80.69	3,905
Southwest 西南	3	270	7,385	-153	-0.64	-1.96	15.53	67.21	23,792
Chongqing 重庆									
Sichuan 四川	2	319	7,785	33	0.16	0.45	14.79	65.60	20,957
Guizhou 贵州									
Yunnan 云南	1	171	6,585	-524	-1.78	-5.83	18.29	69.50	29,462
Tibet 西藏									
Northwest 西北	4	81	3,490	37	0.18	0.42	10.96	57.75	20,348
Shaanxi 陕西	3	71	4,653	49	0.22	0.43	16.65	49.41	22,146
Gansu 甘肃									
Qinghai 青海									
Ningxia 宁夏	1	110						94.80	14,954
Xinjiang 新疆									

Year 年份	Number of firms 企业个数	Rate of change 变化率 (%)	Number of employees 职工人数 (人)	Rate of change 变化率 (%)	Total revenue (Mil. RMB) 总销售收入 (百万元)	Rate of change 变化率 (%)	Total profit (Mil RMB) 总利润 (百万元)	Rate of change 变化率 (%)
2000	53		12,181		650		-1	
2001	56	5.66	11,343	-6.88	761	17.08	-	-
2002	58	3.57	10,649	-6.12	852	11.96	-37	-

Major Products 主要产品	Output 产量	Unit 单位
Water Conservancy Project Machinery 水工机械	44,134	Ton 吨
Pump 泵	1,745	10,000 Units 万台

10 Main Firms with Maximal Revenue (year founded) 收入最大的十家主要企业（创办年份）	City 城市	Province 省	Telephone/fax 电话/传真	Number of employees 职工人数	Ownership 产业所有权	Revenue ('000 RMB) 销售收入(千元)	Profit('000 RMB) (rank) 利润(千元)(排名)	Total assets ('000 RMB) 总资产(千元)	Major products 主要产品
Jiangsu Tianyu Water Supply & Sewage Equipment Co.,ltd. 江苏天雨环保集团有限公司(1968)	Yangzhou 扬州市	Jiangsu 江苏省	(0514)6162875 (0514)6161445	730	Private Owned 私营企业	110,012	2,769(2)	80,677	Strobe 闸门
Shanghai Hanhua Water -Treatment Equipment & Project Co.,Ltd. 上海汉华水处理工程有限公司(1998)	Shanghai 上海市	Shanghai 上海市	(021)52271100 (021)52271178	133	Overseas Chinese-funded 港澳台资	67,449	-	42,878	Water Processor 水处理机
Henan Shangcheng Kaiyuan Enviromental Protection Equipment Co., Ltd.河南省商城县开源环保工程设备有限公司(1970)	Xinyang 信阳市	Henan 河南省	(0376)7923366 (0376)7867009	432	Joint Stock 股份制	57,557	3,214(1)	65,597	Dirt Cleaner 除污机
Guangdong Jianghai Electromechanical Equipment Co., Ltd. 广东江海机电工程有限公司(1960)	Guangzhou 广州市	Guangdong 广东省	(020)87631217 (020)87711772	299	State-owned 国有企业	32,684	708(10)	77,446	Hydraulic Turbine Speed Governor水轮机调速器
Guangdong Yasheng Water Conservancy Machinery Co.,Ltd. 山东亚盛水利机械有限公司(2000)	Weifang 潍坊市	Shandong 山东省	(0536)2330266 (0536)2334888	180	Private Owned 私营企业	29,590	1,430(4)	15,719	Water Conservancy Machinery 水利机械
Huanghua Wuyi Machinery Ltd. Company 黄骅市五一机械有限公司(1958)	Cangzhou 沧州市	Hebei 河北省	(0317)5223049 (0317)5222323	370	Limited-Liability 有限公司	25,901	1,849(3)	28,891	Head Stock Gear 启闭机
Changsha Tianxin District Jinlong Water Supply Equipment Factory 长沙市天心区金龙给水设备厂(1996)	Changsha 长沙市	Hunan 湖南省	(0731)5143285 (0731)5828222	174	Collective-owned 集体企业	25,000	180(21)	15,460	High Building Water Pump高楼送水器
Jiangsu Water Conservancy Machine Manufacturing Factory 江苏省水利机械厂(1958)	Yangzhou 扬州市	Jiangsu 江苏省	(0514)7231821 (0514)7220050	680	State-owned 国有企业	23,146	-	62,482	Water Conservancy Desilting Machinery水利清淤机械
OMEX International (Shenzhen) Co.,Ltd. 欧美科实业（深圳）有限公司(1996)	Shenzhen 深圳市	Guangdong 广东省	(0755)82091899 (0755)82096002	62	Overseas Chinese-funded 港澳台资	23,001	-	28,448	Water Processing Machine水处理设备
Wujin Second Water Machinery Facory 国营武进第二水机厂(1998)	Changzhou 常州市	Jiangsu 江苏省	(0519)8780298	89	Limited-Liability 有限公司	16,350	250(17)	8,650	Water Drinking Machine 饮水机

Top 10 Cities by Revenue 销售收入排名前10位城市	Province 省	Market share 市场份额 (%)	Number of firms 企业个数
Yangzhou 扬州市	Jiangsu 江苏省	20.34	5
Zhengzhou 郑州市	Henan 河南省	13.46	5
Xinyang 信阳市	Henan 河南省	10.62	3
Shanghai 上海市	Shanghai 上海市	7.91	1
Changzhou 常州市	Jiangsu 江苏省	7.32	2
Weifang 潍坊市	Shandong 山东省	4.71	2
Guangzhou 广州市	Guangdong 广东省	3.84	1
Changsha 长沙市	Hunan 湖南省	3.76	2
Cangzhou 沧州市	Hebei 河北省	3.04	1
Shenzhen 深圳市	Guangdong 广东省	2.70	1

10 Major Wholesalers 十家主要批发商	City 城市	Province 省	Telephone/Fax 电话/传真
SU MEC 中设江苏机械设备进出口（集团）公司	Nanjing 南京市	Jiangsu 江苏省	(025)4511888 (025)4411772
China Poster Mobile Communications Equipment Co.,Ltd. 中邮普泰移动通信设备股份有限公司	Beijing 北京市	Beijing 北京市	(010)66426993 (010)66426837
Sino Kama Co., Ltd. 中泰凯马股份有限公司	Shanghai 上海市	Shanghai 上海市	(021)62031188 (021)62030851
China Huayuan Group Co.,Ltd. 中国华源集团有限公司	Shanghai 上海市	Shanghai 上海市	(021)62031188 (021)62032288
Zhejiang Crand Imp.& Exp.Co.,Ltd. 浙江远大进出口有限公司	Ningbo 宁波市	Zhejiang 浙江省	(0574)87720170 (0574)87723350
Shandong Machinery Import & Export Group Corporation 山东省机械进出口集团公司	Qingdao 青岛市	Shandong 山东省	(0532)2661628 (0532)2991655
Qingdao Haier International Trade Co.,Ltd. 青岛海尔国际贸易有限公司	Qingdao 青岛市	Shandong 山东省	(0532)8938337 (0532)8939494
Guangdong Machinery Import & Export Group Corporation 广东省机械进出口集团公司	Guangzhou 广州市	Guangdong 广东省	(020)87782168 (020)87771803
China National Machinery Equipment Import & Export Corporation 中国机械设备进出口总公司	Beijing 北京市	Beijing 北京市	(010)63474506 (010)63261865
Beijing Cellstar Co.,Ltd. 北京蜂星事达电讯有限公司	Beijing 北京市	Beijing 北京市	(010)64602050 (010)64672648

3647: Tractor Parts 拖拉机配件制造业

The industry accounts for 0.055% of the total revenue of China's industrial sector in 2002. The rate of return on assets is 2.32%. 73.28% of all firms in the industry made a profit while 26.72% had negative returns.The top province in terms of the industry's revenue is Shandong, accounting for 45.33% of the total revenue.
2002年本行业收入占全行业的 0.055%，资产利润率为 2.32%。73.28%的企业赢利，26.72%的企业亏损。收入最高的省为山东省，占本行业的45.33%。

	Total number of firms 企业总数	Total number of employees 职工总数	Total revenue (Mil.RMB) 总销售收入 (百万元)	Total profit (Mil.RMB) 总利润 (百万元)	Return on assets 资产利润率 (%)	Return on equity 权益利润率 (%)	Labour productivity ('000 RMB/ worker) 劳动生产率 (千元/人)	Debts/ assets 资产负债率 (%)	Total assets (Mil.RMB) 总资产 (百万元)
Industry Overall 行业总体	232	62,640	5,899	125	2.32	8.14	31.40	71.48	5,382

	Number of firms 企业个数	Average number of employees 平均职工人数	Average revenue ('000 RMB) 平均销售收入 (千元)	Average profit ('000 RMB) 平均利润 (千元)	Return on assets 资产利润率 (%)	Return on equity 权益利润率 (%)	Labour productivity ('000 RMB/ worker) 劳动生产率 (千元/人)	Debts/ assets 资产负债率 (%)	Average total assets ('000 RMB) 平均总资产 (千元)
By ownership 产业所有权									
State-owned 国有	59	313	10,420	-462	-1.62	-10.19	12.03	84.06	28,419
Collective-owned 集体	66	244	25,994	1,066	7.27	17.53	35.18	58.54	14,667
Foreign & Overseas Chinese Funded 三资	2	296	29,027	1,226	4.62	6.29	27.06	26.54	26,532
By regional distribution 地区分布									
Central-North 华北	18	95	4,713	-140	-1.21	-4.91	22.91	75.36	11,525
Beijing 北京	1	105	820	-2,778	-21.88	-113.06	2.46	80.64	12,694
Tianjin 天津	5	89	8,637	100	1.12	2.99	56.50	62.77	8,933
Hebei 河北	8	71	3,988	-28	-0.22	-1.27	15.56	82.72	12,693
Shanxi 山西	4	148	2,232	-2	-0.02	-0.06	8.36	70.18	12,138
Inner Mongolia 内蒙古									
Northeast 东北	14	685	32,271	-83	-0.13	-0.63	16.23	79.88	65,176
Liaoning 辽宁	5	1,022	82,645	2,854	2.00	7.53	27.25	73.49	142,937
Jilin 吉林	3	122	4,546	-7	-0.06	-0.15	16.16	57.33	11,067
Heilongjiang 黑龙江	6	686	4,154	-2,568	-9.36		2.56	112.20	27,429
Central-East 华东	129	248	30,987	904	4.31	13.68	39.05	68.49	20,987
Shanghai 上海	6	134	8,227	-42	-0.42	-1.66	18.58	74.58	9,824
Jiangsu 江苏	45	183	25,189	378	2.77	11.82	30.47	76.60	13,657
Zhejiang 浙江	6	72	12,842	572	6.77	19.56	33.57	65.36	8,446
Anhui 安徽	4	150	10,781	-421	-2.68	-7.06	25.70	61.98	15,686
Fujian 福建	2	87	4,664	218	8.93	42.81	24.91	79.15	2,437
Jiangxi 江西	4	232	2,759	-948	-4.30		5.07	105.37	22,021
Shandong 山东	62	337	43,128	1,638	5.56	15.46	45.34	64.07	29,476
Central-South 中南	56	289	20,971	322	1.35	3.82	29.96	64.71	23,924
Henan 河南	36	287	25,416	673	2.82	8.39	41.25	66.40	23,845
Hubei 湖北	8	412	6,514	-652	-3.67	-22.57	8.18	83.75	17,761
Hunan 湖南	6	168	2,536	-90	-0.99	-3.64	6.09	72.70	9,093
Guangdong 广东	2	273	15,056	-591	-2.24	-3.87	19.64	42.01	26,357
Guangxi 广西	4	259	40,497	190	0.33	0.66	15.38	50.11	57,994
Hainan 海南									
Southwest 西南	6	195	25,947	-259	-1.58	-40.87	11.30	96.14	16,432
Chongqing 重庆									
Sichuan 四川	1	40	1,764	-1,737	-21.93	-95.39	1.10	77.01	7,921
Guizhou 贵州	2	96	3,666	-391	-3.92	-18.83	11.61	79.21	9,987
Yunnan 云南	3	313	48,862	321	1.36		11.67	103.07	23,565
Tibet 西藏									
Northwest 西北	9	212	3,895	-499	-3.86		11.15	125.52	12,922
Shaanxi 陕西	3	309	4,488	-1,485	-6.59		9.77	161.13	22,527
Gansu 甘肃	5	168	4,221	292	4.14	10.33	13.77	59.92	7,051
Qinghai 青海									
Ningxia 宁夏									
Xinjiang 新疆	1	143	485	-1,493	-11.09		4.75	118.56	13,464

Year 年份	Number of firms 企业个数	Rate of change 变化率 (%)	Number of employees 职工人数 (人)	Rate of change 变化率 (%)	Total revenue (Mil. RMB) 总销售收入 (百万元)	Rate of change 变化率 (%)	Total profit (Mil RMB) 总利润 (百万元)	Rate of change 变化率 (%)
2000	338		94,206		7,582		218	
2001	266	-21.30	69,814	-25.89	5,465	-27.92	141	-35.32
2002	232	-12.78	62,640	-10.28	5,899	7.94	125	-11.35

Major Products 主要产品	Output 产量	Unit 单位
Agricultural Transport Machinery 农业运输机械	263	10,000 Vehicles 万辆

10 Main Firms with Maximal Revenue (year founded) 收入最大的十家主要企业（创办年份）	City 城市	Province 省	Telephone/fax 电话/传真	Number of employees 职工人数	Ownership 产业所有权	Revenue ('000 RMB) 销售收入 (千元)	Profit('000 RMB) (rank) 利润(千元)(排名)	Total assets ('000 RMB) 总资产 (千元)	Major products 主要产品
Shandong Shuangxing Group Co.,Ltd.	Weihai	Shandong	(0631)7741178		Joint Stock				Fender Tile
山东双兴集团有限公司(1998)	威海市	山东省	(0631)7741203	918	股份制	645,050	5,200(11)	175,180	挡泥瓦
Wendeng Wenfeng Vechicle General Fatory	Weihai	Shandong	(0631)8561030		Collective-owned				Automobile & Tractor Fittings汽车拖
山东省文登市车辆总厂(1993)	威海市	山东省	(0631)8564418	500	集体企业	395,470	28,070(1)	39,450	拉机配件
Kaifeng Hongda Yoke Group Co.,Ltd.	Kaifeng	Henan	(0378)6681307		State Enterprises				Shifting Yoke
开封宏达拨叉集团有限公司(1951)	开封市	河南省	(0378)6681307	702	国有独资	294,528	1,149(41)	92,658	拨叉
Dandong No.518 Internal-combustion Engine Fittings Co.,Ltd.	Dandong	Liaoning	(0415)6158361		State Enterprises				Internal-combustion Engine Parts内
丹东市五一八内燃机配件有限责任公司(1952)	丹东市	辽宁省	(0415)6155758	2,258	国有独资	275,265	12,800(2)	441,449	燃机零件
Shandong Huijin Co., Ltd.	Laiwu	Shandong	(0634)6650264		Collective-owned				Automobil For and Back Bridge Assembly汽车
山东汇金股份有限公司(1998)	莱芜市	山东省	(0634)6650061	3,000	集体企业	180,675	6,196(9)	160,800	前后桥总成
Jiangsu Zhonghuan Machinery Factory	Yancheng	Jiangsu	(0515)8335935		Joint Stock				Crank Shaft
江苏中环机械股份有限公司(1986)	盐城市	江苏省	(0515)8227306	695	股份制	154,070	6,680(7)	78,470	曲轴
Henan Zhongzhou Group Co.,Ltd.	Jiaozuo	Henan	(0391)3933051		State-owned				Agricultural Machinery Decoration Bearing农
河南中轴集团有限公司(1997)	焦作市	河南省	(0391)3938456	2,702	国有企业	148,855	10,206(4)	351,462	机花件轴
Jiangsu Feidaer Group Co., Ltd.	Yancheng	Jiangsu	(0515)6212683		Joint Stock				Rotary Tillage Knife Series旋
江苏飞达尔集团有限公司(1974)	盐城市	江苏省	(0515)6212718	715	股份制	145,020	1,120(43)	47,560	耕刀系列
Hechi Vehicle Co., Ltd.	Hechi	Guangxi	(0778)2308673		State-owned				Small Four-wheel Tractor小四
河池车辆有限责任公司(1958)	河池市	广西	(0778)2286013	631	国有企业	137,023	719(52)	158,611	轮拖拉机
Longkou Dongxing Machinery General Company	Yantai	Shandong	(0535)8619061		Collective-owned				Tractor Inner Fittings
龙口市东兴机械总公司(1986)	烟台市	山东省	(0535)8619061	998	集体企业	121,390	7,880(6)	33,890	拖内配件

Top 10 Cities by Revenue 销售收入排名前10位城市	Province 省	Market share 市场份额 (%)	Number of firms 企业个数
Weihai 威海市	Shandong 山东省	20.10	6
Yancheng 盐城市	Jiangsu 江苏省	10.32	8
Weifang 潍坊市	Shandong 山东省	8.76	21
Kaifeng 开封市	Henan 河南省	5.02	2
Laiwu 莱芜市	Shandong 山东省	4.87	7
Dandong 丹东市	Liaoning 辽宁省	4.67	1
Xuchang 许昌市	Henan 河南省	3.94	6
Taian 泰安市	Shandong 山东省	3.79	6
Yantai 烟台市	Shandong 山东省	3.73	6
Huaian 淮安市	Jiangsu 江苏省	3.20	10

10 Major Wholesalers 十家主要批发商	City 城市	Province 省	Telephone/Fax 电话/传真
SU MEC	Nanjing	Jiangsu	(025)4511888
中设江苏机械设备进出口（集团）公司	南京市	江苏省	(025)4411772
China Poster Mobile Communications Equipment Co.,Ltd.	Beijing	Beijing	(010)66426993
中邮普泰移动通信设备股份有限公司	北京市	北京市	(010)66426837
Sino Kama Co., Ltd.	Shanghai	Shanghai	(021)62031188
中泰凯马股份有限公司	上海市	上海市	(021)62030851
China Huayuan Group Co.,Ltd.	Shanghai	Shanghai	(021)62031188
中国华源集团有限公司	上海市	上海市	(021)62032288
Zhejiang Crand Imp.& Exp.Co.,Ltd.	Ningbo	Zhejiang	(0574)87720170
浙江远大进出口有限公司	宁波市	浙江省	(0574)87723350
Shandong Machinery Import & Export Group Corporation	Qingdao	Shandong	(0532)2661628
山东省机械进出口集团公司	青岛市	山东省	(0532)2991655
Qingdao Haier International Trade Co.,Ltd.	Qingdao	Shandong	(0532)8938337
青岛海尔国际贸易有限公司	青岛市	山东省	(0532)8939494
Guangdong Machinery Import & Export Group Corporation	Guangzhou	Guangdong	(020)87782168
广东省机械进出口集团公司	广州市	广东省	(020)87771803
China National Machinery Equipment Import & Export Corporation	Beijing	Beijing	(010)63474506
中国机械设备进出口总公司	北京市	北京市	(010)63261865
Beijing Cellstar Co.,Ltd.	Beijing	Beijing	(010)64602050
北京蜂星事达电讯有限公司	北京市	北京市	(010)64672648

3649: Other Farming, Forestry, Husbandry, and Fishery Machinery

其他农、林、牧、渔、水利业机械制造业

The industry accounts for 0.183% of the total revenue of China's industrial sector in 2002. The rate of return on assets is 4.22%. 74.90% of all firms in the industry made a profit while 25.10% had negative returns.The top province in terms of the industry's revenue is Shandong, accounting for 69.67% of the total revenue.
2002年本行业收入占全行业的 0.183%，资产利润率为 4.22%。74.90%的企业赢利，25.10%的企业亏损。收入最高的省为山东省，占本行业的69.67%。

	Total number of firms 企业总数	Total number of employees 职工总数	Total revenue (Mil.RMB) 总销售收入（百万元）	Total profit (Mil.RMB) 总利润（百万元）	Return on assets 资产利润率（%）	Return on equity 权益利润率（%）	Labour productivity ('000 RMB/ worker) 劳动生产率（千元/人）	Debts/ assets 资产负债率（%）	Total assets (Mil.RMB) 总资产（百万元）
Industry Overall 行业总体	247	94,284	19,672	635	4.22	13.19	56.90	68.03	15,056

	Number of firms 企业个数	Average number of employees 平均职工人数	Average revenue ('000 RMB) 平均销售收入（千元）	Average profit ('000 RMB) 平均利润（千元）	Return on assets 资产利润率（%）	Return on equity 权益利润率（%）	Labour productivity ('000 RMB/ worker) 劳动生产率（千元/人）	Debts/ assets 资产负债率（%）	Average total assets ('000 RMB) 平均总资产（千元）
By ownership 产业所有权									
State-owned 国有	55	263	19,783	754	1.51	7.54	28.14	79.98	49,929
Collective-owned 集体	42	235	31,517	960	5.03	13.84	45.23	63.64	19,084
Foreign & Overseas Chinese Funded 三资	3	70	5,959	251	2.15	3.88	18.92	44.65	11,692
By regional distribution 地区分布									
Central-North 华北	14	226	11,225	183	0.67	2.72	19.50	75.40	27,358
Beijing 北京	3	21	662	-324	-12.55		14.84	112.31	2,581
Tianjin 天津									
Hebei 河北	7	350	21,420	1,276	3.58	13.42	23.56	73.29	35,604
Shanxi 山西	1	140					15.58	80.49	6,237
Inner Mongolia 内蒙古	3	170	1,739	-1,800	-4.51	-19.73	1.66	77.15	39,933
Northeast 东北	8	238	36,267	-875	-2.06	-7.18	59.31	71.32	42,453
Liaoning 辽宁	1	1,035	249,832	-7,380	-2.66	-10.08	99.85	73.60	277,357
Jilin 吉林	4	51	1,662	-17	-0.31	-0.67	32.81	52.80	5,478
Heilongjiang 黑龙江	3	221	11,218	151	1.12	3.27	4.14	65.73	13,450
Central-East 华东	117	573	148,448	5,369	5.26	15.32	66.42	65.65	101,990
Shanghai 上海	2	29	23,863	546	1.88	5.81	125.33	67.62	29,005
Jiangsu 江苏	21	193	41,764	-1,618	-3.44	-72.67	68.34	95.27	47,035
Zhejiang 浙江	17	319	84,921	4,706	6.91	16.22	90.76	57.39	68,106
Anhui 安徽	13	342	82,757	2,519	1.33	4.01	73.07	66.90	190,000
Fujian 福建	8	82	17,685	-899	-0.94	-96.10	35.14	99.02	95,825
Jiangxi 江西	6	182	12,803	-41	-0.21	-0.40	12.22	48.12	19,639
Shandong 山东	50	1,026	274,116	11,114	8.72	20.94	64.60	58.36	127,496
Central-South 中南	74	249	20,115	315	1.38	4.54	34.59	69.52	22,757
Henan 河南	45	276	19,203	708	3.39	8.56	37.18	60.38	20,885
Hubei 湖北	7	390	56,187	-1,014	-1.71	-9.97	46.15	82.90	59,431
Hunan 湖南	8	127	9,546	360	3.52	9.82	20.81	64.12	10,207
Guangdong 广东	5	168	12,190	-108	-0.43	-1.79	19.53	76.08	25,239
Guangxi 广西	5	124	16,460	-346	-1.94	-10.78	13.78	82.01	17,813
Hainan 海南	4	202	2,856	-516	-6.60		4.65	118.52	7,814
Southwest 西南	21	124	12,866	-592	-2.52		24.94	104.05	23,501
Chongqing 重庆									
Sichuan 四川	11	146	21,380	-383	-1.33		36.67	100.12	28,831
Guizhou 贵州	4	51	2,940	-740	-5.40		10.03	125.30	13,698
Yunnan 云南	6	134	3,876	-877	-4.33		5.25	104.71	20,264
Tibet 西藏									
Northwest 西北	13	89	7,502	50	0.29	2.15	31.03	86.56	17,179
Shaanxi 陕西	3	119	14,820	197	2.53	16.77	64.81	84.91	7,801
Gansu 甘肃	4	57	530	-16	-0.08	-0.33	18.76	76.80	21,253
Qinghai 青海									
Ningxia 宁夏	2	78	3,828	-314	-3.04	-378.31	12.34	99.20	10,329
Xinjiang 新疆	4	105	10,823	187	0.79	11.32	15.91	93.00	23,563

3649: Other Farming, Forestry, Husbandry, and Fishery Machinery

其他农、林、牧、渔、水利业机械制造业

Year 年份	Number of firms 企业个数	Rate of change 变化率 (%)	Number of employees 职工人数 (人)	Rate of change 变化率 (%)	Total revenue (Mil. RMB) 总销售收入 (百万元)	Rate of change 变化率 (%)	Total profit (Mil RMB) 总利润 (百万元)	Rate of change 变化率 (%)
2000	274		108,324		19,931		400	
2001	246	-10.22	94,087	-13.14	16,257	-18.43	334	-16.50
2002	247	0.41	94,284	0.21	19,672	21.01	635	90.12

Major Products 主要产品	Output 产量	Unit 单位

10 Main Firms with Maximal Revenue (year founded) 收入最大的十家主要企业（创办年份）	City 城市	Province 省	Telephone/fax 电话/传真	Number of employees 职工人数	Ownership 产业所有权	Revenue ('000 RMB) 销售收入 (千元)	Profit('000 RMB) (rank) 利润(千元) (排名)	Total assets ('000 RMB) 总资产 (千元)	Major products 主要产品
Shandong Shifeng (Group) Co.,Ltd.	Liaocheng	Shandong	(0635)3953153		Limited-Liability				Agricultural Tricycle农
山东时风（集团）有限责任公司(1993)	聊城市	山东省	(0635)3953153	25,652	有限公司	6,781,953	408,880(1)	1,847,574	用三轮车
Shandong Shuangli Group Co., Ltd.	Liaocheng	Shandong	(0635)8335402		Joint Stock				Agricultural Transporter农
山东双力集团股份有限公司(1994)	聊城市	山东省	(0635)8335607	3,179	股份制	1,060,000	9,500(6)	1,058,970	用运输车
Anhui Feicai (Group) Co., Ltd.	Xuancheng	Anhui	(0563)2612679		State Enterprises				Tricycle Agricultural Transporter三轮农
安徽飞彩(集团)有限公司(1970)	宣城市	安徽省	(0563)2612555	2,806	国有独资	863,622	27,923(4)	2,295,807	用运输车
Hangzhou Advance Gear Case Group Co.,Ltd.	Hangzhou	Zhejiang	(0571)82673888		State-owned				Marine Gear Case船
杭州前进齿轮箱集团公司(1965)	杭州市	浙江省	(0571)82675966	3,628	国有企业	786,975	70,040(2)	841,518	用齿轮箱
Hangzhou Hanggua Electromechanical Co., Ltd.	Hangzhou	Zhejiang	(0571)87091110		Limited-Liability				Agricultural Transporter农
杭州杭桂机电有限公司(2000)	杭州市	浙江省	(0571)87322311	365	有限公司	445,398	4,377(19)	124,546	用运输车
Rifa Vehicles Manufacturing Co., Ltd.	Rizhao	Shandong	(0633)5411159		Limited-Liability				Agricultural Transporter农
日发车辆制造有限公司(1986)	日照市	山东省	(0633)8254612	1,050	有限公司	285,066	7,475(8)	296,915	用运输车
Shenyang Tianling Machinery Co., Ltd.	Shenyang	Liaoning	(024)89757367		Private Owned				Agricultural Automobile
沈阳天菱机械有限责任公司(2000)	沈阳市	辽宁省	(024)89757466	1,035	私营企业	249,832	-	277,357	农用汽车
shandong Heibao Group Co., Ltd.	Weihai	Shandong	(0631)8352146		Joint Stock				Agricultural Transporter农
山东黑豹股份有限公司(1980)	威海市	山东省	(0631)8352228	2,131	股份制	234,258	2,729(24)	753,920	用运输车
First Tractor Company Dongfang Industrial Company	Luoyang	Henan	(0379)4971642		Collective owned				Agricultural Automobile Machine Fittings农用汽车工
一拖公司东方实业公司(1979)	洛阳市	河南省	(0379)4971642	3,822	集体企业	216,651	1,016(42)	234,539	程机械配件
Beijing Automobile Futian Vehicle Co., Ltd.Agriculture Installation Kuiwe	Weifang	Shandong	(0536)8806279		Joint Stock				Agricultural Transporter
Kuiwen Factory北汽福田车辆股份有限公司农业装备奎文厂(2001)	潍坊市	山东省	(0536)8806279	276	股份制	184,501	3,116(22)	41,865	农用车

Top 10 Cities by Revenue 销售收入排名前10位城市	Province 省	Market share 市场份额 (%)	Number of firms 企业个数
Liaocheng 聊城市	Shandong 山东省	40.16	7
Weifang 潍坊市	Shandong 山东省	21.61	16
Hangzhou 杭州市	Zhejiang 浙江省	6.54	4
Xuancheng 宣城市	Anhui 安徽省	4.69	5
Rizhao 日照市	Shandong 山东省	3.82	9
Nanjing 南京市	Jiangsu 江苏省	3.35	12
Xuchang 许昌市	Henan 河南省	2.55	33
Weihai 威海市	Shandong 山东省	2.12	4
Shenyang 沈阳市	Liaoning 辽宁省	1.27	1
Luoyang 洛阳市	Henan 河南省	1.10	1

10 Major Wholesalers 十家主要批发商	City 城市	Province 省	Telephone/Fax 电话/传真
SU MEC	Nanjing	Jiangsu	(025)4511888
中设江苏机械设备进出口（集团）公司	南京市	江苏省	(025)4411772
China Poster Mobile Communications Equipment Co.,Ltd.	Beijing	Beijing	(010)66426993
中邮普泰移动通信设备股份有限公司	北京市	北京市	(010)66426837
Sino Kama Co., Ltd.	Shanghai	Shanghai	(021)62031188
中泰凯马股份有限公司	上海市	上海市	(021)62030851
China Huayuan Group Co.,Ltd.	Shanghai	Shanghai	(021)62031188
中国华源集团有限公司	上海市	上海市	(021)62032288
Zhejiang Crand Imp.& Exp.Co.,Ltd.	Ningbo	Zhejiang	(0574)87720170
浙江远大进出口有限公司	宁波市	浙江省	(0574)87723350
Shandong Machinery Import & Export Group Corporation	Qingdao	Shandong	(0532)2661628
山东省机械进出口集团公司	青岛市	山东省	(0532)2991655
Qingdao Haier International Trade Co.,Ltd.	Qingdao	Shandong	(0532)8938337
青岛海尔国际贸易有限公司	青岛市	山东省	(0532)8939494
Guangdong Machinery Import & Export Group Corporation	Guangzhou	Guangdong	(020)87782168
广东省机械进出口集团公司	广州市	广东省	(020)87771803
China National Machinery Equipment Import & Export Corporation	Beijing	Beijing	(010)63474506
中国机械设备进出口总公司	北京市	北京市	(010)63261865
Beijing Cellstar Co.,Ltd.	Beijing	Beijing	(010)64602050
北京蜂星事达电讯有限公司	北京市	北京市	(010)64672648

3651: Surgical Apparatus and Instruments 手术器械制造业

The industry accounts for 0.021% of the total revenue of China's industrial sector in 2002. The rate of return on assets is 7.63%. 94.64% of all firms in the industry made a profit while 5.36% had negative returns.The top province in terms of the industry's revenue is Jiangsu, accounting for 65.24% of the total revenue.
2002年本行业收入占全行业的0.021%，资产利润率为7.63%。94.64%的企业赢利，5.36%的企业亏损。收入最高的省为江苏省，占本行业的65.24%。

	Total number of firms 企业总数	Total number of employees 职工总数	Total revenue (Mil.RMB) 总销售收入（百万元）	Total profit (Mil.RMB) 总利润（百万元）	Return on assets 资产利润率 (%)	Return on equity 权益利润率 (%)	Labour productivity ('000 RMB/ worker) 劳动生产率（千元/人）	Debts/ assets 资产负债率 (%)	Total assets (Mil.RMB) 总资产（百万元）
Industry Overall 行业总体	56	15,323	2,266	177	7.63	18.52	45.93	58.80	2,315

	Number of firms 企业个数	Average number of employees 平均职工人数	Average revenue ('000 RMB) 平均销售收入（千元）	Average profit ('000 RMB) 平均利润（千元）	Return on assets 资产利润率 (%)	Return on equity 权益利润率 (%)	Labour productivity ('000 RMB/ worker) 劳动生产率（千元/人）	Debts/ assets 资产负债率 (%)	Average total assets ('000 RMB) 平均总资产（千元）
By ownership 产业所有权									
State-owned 国有	9	240	18,930	537	1.85	7.88	39.15	76.47	28,954
Collective-owned 集体	7	117	38,145	3,846	17.31	51.67	86.42	66.50	22,219
Foreign & Overseas Chinese Funded 三资	7	172	20,736	1,677	3.69	8.78	38.91	57.94	45,416
By regional distribution 地区分布									
Central-North 华北	10	120	10,469	582	2.34	7.48	29.18	68.68	24,826
Beijing 北京	2	83	13,761	623	11.17	22.27	20.50	49.86	5,578
Tianjin 天津	8	129	9,646	572	1.93	6.34	30.58	69.56	29,638
Hebei 河北									
Shanxi 山西									
Inner Mongolia 内蒙古									
Northeast 东北	2	84	6,604	-1,839	-4.26		16.76	104.23	43,169
Liaoning 辽宁	2	84	6,604	-1,839	-4.26		16.76	104.23	43,169
Jilin 吉林									
Heilongjiang 黑龙江									
Central-East 华东	35	367	56,194	4,801	9.23	20.88	47.92	55.82	52,039
Shanghai 上海	11	280	35,573	2,873	6.75	14.94	45.63	54.81	42,551
Jiangsu 江苏	13	672	113,720	9,429	10.09	24.14	50.18	58.19	93,423
Zhejiang 浙江	9	106	9,404	1,252	10.08	18.93	33.46	46.72	12,413
Anhui 安徽									
Fujian 福建									
Jiangxi 江西									
Shandong 山东	2	34	6,252	1,294	9.55	10.04	64.34	4.89	13,552
Central-South 中南	7	130	24,185	893	4.30	9.17	52.71	53.15	20,781
Henan 河南	1	226	5,896	53	0.10	0.23	20.21	56.33	52,055
Hubei 湖北									
Hunan 湖南									
Guangdong 广东	5	121	31,062	794	4.97	11.30	56.84	56.03	15,982
Guangxi 广西	1	82	8,090	2,227	16.49	21.64	111.85	23.80	13,502
Hainan 海南									
Southwest 西南	1	198	10,773	63	0.56	0.97	11.75	42.73	11,299
Chongqing 重庆									
Sichuan 四川	1	198	10,773	63	0.56	0.97	11.75	42.73	11,299
Guizhou 贵州									
Yunnan 云南									
Tibet 西藏									
Northwest 西北	1	17	1,377	109	6.08	40.22	36.71	84.88	1,792
Shaanxi 陕西	1	17	1,377	109	6.08	40.22	36.71	84.88	1,792
Gansu 甘肃									
Qinghai 青海									
Ningxia 宁夏									
Xinjiang 新疆									

3651: Surgical Apparatus and Instruments 手术器械制造业

Year 年份	Number of firms 企业个数	Rate of change 变化率 (%)	Number of employees 职工人数 (人)	Rate of change 变化率 (%)	Total revenue (Mil. RMB) 总销售收入 (百万元)	Rate of change 变化率 (%)	Total profit (Mil RMB) 总利润 (百万元)	Rate of change 变化率 (%)
2000	46		15,536		1,787		75	
2001	55	19.57	13,958	-10.16	2,037	13.99	130	73.33
2002	56	1.82	15,323	9.78	2,266	11.24	177	36.15

Major Products 主要产品	Output 产量	Unit 单位
Medical Apparatuses & Equipment 医疗仪器设备	31	100,000,000 Yuan 亿元
Operating Apparatuses 手术器械	3	100,000,000 Yuan 亿元

10 Main Firms with Maximal Revenue (year founded) 收入最大的十家主要企业（创办年份）	City 城市	Province 省	Telephone/fax 电话/传真	Number of employees 职工人数	Ownership 产业所有权	Revenue ('000 RMB) 销售收入 (千元)	Profit('000 RMB) (rank) 利润(千元) (排名)	Total assets ('000 RMB) 总资产 (千元)	Major products 主要产品
Jiangsu Hongbao Group Co.,Ltd.	Suzhou	Jiangsu	(0520)5876008		Limited-Liability				Operating Apparatuses
江苏宏宝集团有限公司(1964)	苏州市	江苏省	(0520)58760569	3,754	有限公司	761,330	44,030(1)	550,980	手术器械
Jiangsu Jinlu Group Co., Ltd.	Suzhou	Jiangsu	(0512)58550752		Joint Stock				Medical Apparatuses
江苏金鹿集团有限公司(1965)	苏州市	江苏省	(0512)58550492	1,968	股份制	242,930	29,330(2)	237,680	医疗器械
Shanghai Operating Apparatuses Factory	Shanghai	Shanghai	(021)65289166		State-owned				Operating Apparatuses
上海手术器械厂(1950)	上海市	上海市	(021)65287200	1,283	国有企业	128,375	7,396(6)	106,250	手术器械
Guangzhou Panyu Huaxin Science & Technology Co., Ltd.	Guangzhou	Guangdong	(020)84763998		Private Owned				Medical Treatment Expendable
广州市番禺区华鑫科技有限公司(1999)	广州市	广东省	(020)34763169	150	私营企业	90,228	1,570(19)	41,519	医疗消耗品
Suzhou Medical Instrument Factory	Suzhou	Jiangsu	(0512)67770273		Joint Stock				Eyes Operating Apparatuses
苏州医疗器械厂(1956)	苏州市	江苏省	(0512)67284889	798	股份制	89,693	9,070(5)	171,486	手术器械
Shanghai Meihua Medical Instrument Co., ltd	Shanghai	Shanghai	(021)59148099		Foreign Funded				Medical Treatment Apparatuses
上海美华医疗器具股份有限公司(2001)	上海市	上海市	(021)59148142	180	外商投资	51,296	7,014(8)	71,759	医疗器具
Shanghai Shuangge Industrial Co., Ltd.	Shanghai	Shanghai	(021)67104888		Private Owned				Plastic Medical Treatment Apparatuses
上海双鸽实业有限公司(2000)	上海市	上海市	(021)67104666	720	私营企业	50,120	9,795(4)	105,912	医疗器械
Yangjiang Jiangcheng Medical Apparatuses Factory	Yangjiang	Guangdong	(0662)3262661		Private Enterprises				Cosmetology Tools
阳江市江城区医疗器械厂(1999)	阳江市	广东省	(0662)3253715	180	私营独资	34,980	2,045(17)	12,420	美容工具
Huaiyi Medical Instrument Co.,Ltd.	Huaian	Jiangsu	(0517)3806541		Others				Operation Blade
淮阴医疗器械有限公司(2000)	淮安市	江苏省	(0517)3806511	454	其他企业	34,905	3,335(10)	29,468	手术刀片
Tianjin Medical Apparatuses Industry Company	Tianjin	Tianjin	(022)24347817		State-owned				Orthopedics Apparatus
天津市医疗器械工业公司(1973)	天津市	天津市	(022)24347820	450	国有企业	24,305	405(33)	60,287	骨科器械

Top 10 Cities by Revenue 销售收入排名前10位城市	Province 省	Market share 市场份额 (%)	Number of firms 企业个数
Suzhou 苏州市	Jiangsu 江苏省	50.29	5
Shanghai 上海市	Shanghai 上海市	17.27	11
Wuxi 无锡市	Jiangsu 江苏省	9.99	2
Guangzhou 广州市	Guangdong 广东省	4.49	2
Tianjin 天津市	Tianjin 天津市	3.41	8
Ningbo 宁波市	Zhejiang 浙江省	2.00	5
Yangjiang 阳江市	Guangdong 广东省	1.54	1
Huaian 淮安市	Jiangsu 江苏省	1.54	1
Taizhou 泰州市	Jiangsu 江苏省	1.22	1
Beijing 北京市	Beijing 北京市	1.21	2

10 Major Wholesalers 十家主要批发商	City 城市	Province 省	Telephone/Fax 电话/传真
Johnson & Johnson Medical (China) Ltd.	Shanghai	Shanghai	(021)62826988
强生(中国)医疗器材有限公司	上海市	上海市	(021)62825073
China New Era Co., Ltd.	Beijing	Beijing	(010)82803388
中国新时代公司	北京市	北京市	(010)82803688
Beijing Kanglian Medicine Appliances Developing & Marketing Company	Beijing	Beijing	(010)68977301
北京市康联医药器械开发经营公司	北京市	北京市	(010)68975345
Shanghai Medical Instruments Wholesale Department	Shanghai	Shanghai	(021)63219999
上海市医疗器械批发部	上海市	上海市	(021)63210456
Jiangsu Medicines Company	Nanjing	Jiangsu	(025)3232715
江苏省药材公司	南京市	江苏省	(025)3232715
Suzhou Medical Health Products Import & Export Company	Suzhou	Jiangsu	(0512)68627233
苏州市医药保健品进出口公司	苏州市	江苏省	(0512)68621176
Jiangsu Nantong Medicine Co.,Ltd.	Nantong	Jiangsu	(0513)5513093
江苏省南通医药股份有限公司	南通市	江苏省	(0513)5527814
Zhejiang Jiashan Medicine General Company	Jiaxing	Zhejiang	(0573)4026343
浙江省嘉善县医药总公司	嘉兴市	浙江省	(0573)4026344
Hefei Pharmaceutical Medical Apparatuses Company	Hefei	Anhui	(0551)4296721
合肥市药品医疗器械公司	合肥市	安徽省	(0551)4296402
Fuzhou Medical Instruments Stock & Supply Station	Fuzhou	Fujian	(0591)3258409
福州医疗器械采购供应站	福州市	福建省	(0591)3258413

3652: Medical Apparatus and Equipment 医疗仪器、设备制造业

The industry accounts for 0.076% of the total revenue of China's industrial sector in 2002. The rate of return on assets is 9.23%. 78.57% of all firms in the industry made a profit while 21.43% had negative returns.The top province in terms of the industry's revenue is Beijing, accounting for 31.75% of the total revenue.
2002年本行业收入占全行业的0.076%，资产利润率为9.23%。78.57%的企业赢利，21.43%的企业亏损。收入最高的省为北京市，占本行业的31.75%。

	Total number of firms 企业总数	Total number of employees 职工总数	Total revenue (Mil.RMB) 总销售收入(百万元)	Total profit (Mil.RMB) 总利润(百万元)	Return on assets 资产利润率(%)	Return on equity 权益利润率(%)	Labour productivity ('000 RMB/ worker) 劳动生产率(千元/人)	Debts/ assets 资产负债率(%)	Total assets (Mil.RMB) 总资产(百万元)
Industry Overall 行业总体	210	33,450	8,146	941	9.23	19.24	105.19	52.03	10,192

	Number of firms 企业个数	Average number of employees 平均职工人数	Average revenue ('000 RMB) 平均销售收入(千元)	Average profit ('000 RMB) 平均利润(千元)	Return on assets 资产利润率(%)	Return on equity 权益利润率(%)	Labour productivity ('000 RMB/ worker) 劳动生产率(千元/人)	Debts/ assets 资产负债率(%)	Average total assets ('000 RMB) 平均总资产(千元)
By ownership 产业所有权									
State-owned 国有	47	201	23,093	1,348	2.76	6.44	40.24	57.23	48,894
Collective-owned 集体	13	144	9,829	998	4.75	9.88	32.95	51.90	21,004
Foreign & Overseas Chinese Funded 三资	47	122	87,022	11,445	15.41	31.44	339.97	50.99	74,278
By regional distribution 地区分布									
Central-North 华北	48	124	57,946	11,085	17.69	36.73	276.11	51.83	62,649
Beijing 北京	27	130	95,781	19,427	20.08	39.73	444.79	49.46	96,729
Tianjin 天津	15	94	9,542	452	2.66	8.39	36.05	68.28	16,976
Hebei 河北	6	169	8,696	130	0.55	1.63	27.27	66.06	23,469
Shanxi 山西									
Inner Mongolia 内蒙古									
Northeast 东北	7	174	57,628	10,121	10.17	21.43	159.54	52.55	99,524
Liaoning 辽宁	4	223	100,566	17,518	10.33	20.67	217.00	50.03	169,613
Jilin 吉林	1	177	260	-270	-4.13		3.38	144.50	6,540
Heilongjiang 黑龙江	2	75	436	523	8.95		2.86	147.31	5,838
Central-East 华东	95	175	35,896	2,346	6.22	13.07	57.68	52.44	37,741
Shanghai 上海	43	168	32,057	2,371	6.61	13.35	53.92	50.48	35,876
Jiangsu 江苏	26	144	42,964	636	2.49	6.95	72.14	64.20	25,569
Zhejiang 浙江	11	106	27,669	4,992	15.62	30.90	99.38	49.44	31,955
Anhui 安徽	3	77	31,904	5,216	13.63	23.42	223.43	41.80	38,268
Fujian 福建	6	151	26,050	1,954	9.42	13.37	43.26	29.50	20,741
Jiangxi 江西									
Shandong 山东	6	565	59,706	3,676	2.80	5.95	28.00	52.88	131,189
Central-South 中南	42	149	27,894	2,380	4.85	9.04	88.96	46.33	49,048
Henan 河南	4	163	22,669	2,283	6.85	11.36	55.08	39.68	33,322
Hubei 湖北	9	151	36,589	3,823	10.18	20.63	92.22	50.67	37,565
Hunan 湖南	3	59	7,346	329	6.06	35.95	21.87	83.13	5,421
Guangdong 广东	22	173	31,794	2,225	3.44	6.49	99.28	47.07	64,783
Guangxi 广西	4	69	7,515	1,618	4.40	6.38	53.42	31.08	36,782
Hainan 海南									
Southwest 西南	11	168	16,864	684	1.44	4.11	48.77	64.85	47,365
Chongqing 重庆	4	186	26,578	1,082	1.60	5.72	23.92	71.95	67,443
Sichuan 四川	6	158	12,882	507	1.27	3.13	76.04	59.36	39,861
Guizhou 贵州	1	162	1,900	151	1.25	1.47	3.36	14.99	12,078
Yunnan 云南									
Tibet 西藏									
Northwest 西北	7	220	27,704	1,079	2.34	6.52	51.79	64.05	46,008
Shaanxi 陕西	4	306	47,359	1,964	2.55	7.08	63.34	64.00	77,009
Gansu 甘肃	2	149	1,492	-157	-2.59	-9.93	5.76	73.88	6,035
Qinghai 青海									
Ningxia 宁夏									
Xinjiang 新疆	1	21	1,509	7	0.36	0.41	29.71	11.45	1,948

3652: Medical Apparatus and Equipment 医疗仪器、设备制造业

Year 年份	Number of firms 企业个数	Rate of change 变化率 (%)	Number of employees 职工人数 (人)	Rate of change 变化率 (%)	Total revenue (Mil. RMB) 总销售收入 (百万元)	Rate of change 变化率 (%)	Total profit (Mil RMB) 总利润 (百万元)	Rate of change 变化率 (%)
2000	186		28,906		4,941		425	
2001	192	3.23	32,012	10.75	6,901	39.67	717	68.71
2002	210	9.38	33,450	4.49	8,146	18.04	941	31.24

Major Products 主要产品	Output 产量	Unit 单位
Medical Apparatuses & Equipment 医疗仪器设备	31	100,000,000 Yuan 亿元
Operating Apparatuses 手术器械	3	100,000,000 Yuan 亿元

10 Main Firms with Maximal Revenue (year founded) 收入最大的十家主要企业（创办年份）	City 城市	Province 省	Telephone/fax 电话/传真	Number of employees 职工人数	Ownership 产业所有权	Revenue ('000 RMB) 销售收入 (千元)	Profit('000 RMB) (rank) 利润(千元) (排名)	Total assets ('000 RMB) 总资产 (千元)	Major products 主要产品
Hangwei GE Medical System Co.,Ltd.	Beijing	Beijing	(010)67881880		Foreign Funded				Medical Video Equipment医学
航卫通用电气医疗系统有限公司(1991)	北京市	北京市	(010)67871798	230	外商投资	1,698,862	326,900(1)	886,948	影象设备
Rexton(suzhou) Hearing System Co.,Ltd.	Suzhou	Jiangsu	(0512)67613201		Foreign Funded				Audition Appliance and Fittings听力器
力斯顿听力技术(苏州)有限公司(1995)	苏州市	江苏省	(0512)67615149	513	外商投资	432,861	945(83)	93,594	械及配件
Shenyang Neusoft Digital Medical System Co.,Ltd.	Shenyang	Liaoning	(024)83665010		Limited-Liability				CT Equipment
沈阳东软数字医疗系统股份有限公司(1998)	沈阳市	辽宁省	(024)23782711	481	有限公司	359,753	68,929(3)	406,570	CT机
Beijing Wandong Medical Equipment Co.,Ltd.	Beijing	Beijing	(010)65682238		Joint Stock				500MAX Ray Machine.500max
北京万东医疗装备股份有限公司(1997)	北京市	北京市	(010)65681151	997	股份制	347,055	41,050(4)	565,635	射线机
Shandong Xinhua Medical Instrument Co.,Ltd.	Zibo	Shandong	(0533)2282093		State-owned				One-off Syringe & Puncture Apparatuses一次性注
山东新华医械集团(1943)	淄博市	山东省	(0533)2183211	1,930	国有企业	299,377	19,984(7)	674,416	射穿刺器械
Yangzhou Zhonghui Group Company	Yangzhou	Jiangsu	(0514)6290788		Private Enterprises				B Ultrasound Wave Machine
扬州中惠集团公司(1995)	扬州市	江苏省	(0514)6290758	300	私营独资	141,838	4,272(39)	56,113	B超
Shenzhen Anke High-tech Co.,Ltd.	Shenzhen	Guangdong	(0755)26688889		Foreign Funded				MRI System核磁共振
深圳安科高技术股份有限公司(1986)	深圳市	广东省	(0755)26695307	281	外商投资	138,601	5,895(32)	313,635	成像系统
Wuhan Chutian Laser Group Co., Ltd.	Wuhan	Hubei	(027)87454912		Joint Stock				Laser Machinery激
武汉楚天激光集团股份有限公司(1994)	武汉市	湖北省	(027)87561282	202	股份制	132,134	16,918(9)	76,895	光机机械
Beijing Jing Jing Medical Equipment Co., Ltd.	Beijing	Beijing	(010)67870022		Overseas Chinese-funded				Blood Reclaim Machine血
北京京精医疗设备有限公司(2000)	北京市	北京市	(010)67879961	143	港澳台资	126,134	86,039(2)	302,121	液回收机
Shanghai Medical Apparatuses Factory	Shanghai	Shanghai	(021)65430919		State-owned				Medical Apparatuses
上海医疗器械厂(1949)	上海市	上海市	(021)65439380	737	国有企业	113,087	2,313(58)	176,896	医疗器械

Top 10 Cities by Revenue 销售收入排名前10位城市	Province 省	Market share 市场份额 (%)	Number of firms 企业个数
Beijing 北京市	Beijing 北京市	31.75	27
Shanghai 上海市	Shanghai 上海市	16.92	43
Suzhou 苏州市	Jiangsu 江苏省	5.77	4
Shenyang 沈阳市	Liaoning 辽宁省	4.94	4
Zibo 淄博市	Shandong 山东省	3.68	1
Wuxi 无锡市	Jiangsu 江苏省	3.62	3
Shenzhen 深圳市	Guangdong 广东省	3.20	5
Zhuhai 珠海市	Guangdong 广东省	2.86	5
Ningbo 宁波市	Zhejiang 浙江省	2.75	5
Wuhan 武汉市	Hubei 湖北省	2.14	7

10 Major Wholesalers 十家主要批发商	City 城市	Province 省	Telephone/Fax 电话/传真
Johnson & Johnson Medical (China) Ltd.	Shanghai	Shanghai	(021)62826988
强生(中国)医疗器材有限公司	上海市	上海市	(021)62825073
China New Era Co., Ltd.	Beijing	Beijing	(010)82803388
中国新时代公司	北京市	北京市	(010)82803688
Beijing Kanglian Medicine Appliances Developing & Marketing Company	Beijing	Beijing	(010)68977301
北京市康联医药器械开发经营公司	北京市	北京市	(010)68975345
Shanghai Medical Instruments Wholesale Department	Shanghai	Shanghai	(021)63219999
上海市医疗器械批发部	上海市	上海市	(021)63210456
Jiangsu Medicines Company	Nanjing	Jiangsu	(025)3232715
江苏省药材公司	南京市	江苏省	(025)3232715
Suzhou Medical Health Products Import & Export Company	Suzhou	Jiangsu	(0512)68627233
苏州市医药保健品进出口公司	苏州市	江苏省	(0512)68621176
Jiangsu Nantong Medicine Co.,Ltd.	Nantong	Jiangsu	(0513)5513093
江苏省南通医药股份有限公司	南通市	江苏省	(0513)5527814
Zhejiang Jiashan Medicine General Company	Jiaxing	Zhejiang	(0573)4026343
浙江省嘉善县医药总公司	嘉兴市	浙江省	(0573)4026344
Hefei Pharmaceutical Medical Apparatuses Company	Hefei	Anhui	(0551)4296721
合肥市药品医疗器械公司	合肥市	安徽省	(0551)4296402
Fuzhou Medical Instruments Stock & Supply Station	Fuzhou	Fujian	(0591)3258409
福州医疗器械采购供应站	福州市	福建省	(0591)3258413

3653: Diagnostic Products 诊断用品制造业

The industry accounts for 0.030% of the total revenue of China's industrial sector in 2002. The rate of return on assets is 6.07%. 80.72% of all firms in the industry made a profit while 19.28% had negative returns.The top province in terms of the industry's revenue is Liaoning, accounting for 27.30% of the total revenue.
2002年本行业收入占全行业的0.030%，资产利润率为6.07%。80.72%的企业赢利，19.28%的企业亏损。收入最高的省为辽宁省，占本行业的27.30%。

	Total number of firms 企业总数	Total number of employees 职工总数	Total revenue (Mil.RMB) 总销售收入（百万元）	Total profit (Mil.RMB) 总利润（百万元）	Return on assets 资产利润率 (%)	Return on equity 权益利润率 (%)	Labour productivity ('000 RMB/ worker) 劳动生产率（千元/人）	Debts/ assets 资产负债率 (%)	Total assets (Mil.RMB) 总资产（百万元）
Industry Overall 行业总体	83	23,844	3,193	177	6.07	12.21	39.92	50.29	2,918

	Number of firms 企业个数	Average number of employees 平均职工人数	Average revenue ('000 RMB) 平均销售收入（千元）	Average profit ('000 RMB) 平均利润（千元）	Return on assets 资产利润率 (%)	Return on equity 权益利润率 (%)	Labour productivity ('000 RMB/ worker) 劳动生产率（千元/人）	Debts/ assets 资产负债率 (%)	Average total assets ('000 RMB) 平均总资产（千元）
By ownership 产业所有权									
State-owned 国有	7	370	7,598	-1,526	-3.80	-263.76	10.68	98.56	40,155
Collective-owned 集体	13	202	10,481	260	2.13	5.90	19.17	63.95	12,197
Foreign & Overseas Chinese Funded 三资	18	313	77,040	3,824	7.76	12.72	57.92	39.02	49,287
By regional distribution 地区分布									
Central-North 华北	6	160	11,178	2,245	8.34	16.65	67.52	49.95	26,930
Beijing 北京	4	127	16,620	3,555	13.11	18.24	127.61	28.14	27,119
Tianjin 天津	1	15	224	-283	-3.88		0.13	134.74	7,291
Hebei 河北	1	440	363	-469	-1.02	-8.60	0.57	88.09	45,814
Shanxi 山西									
Inner Mongolia 内蒙古									
Northeast 东北	3	786	291,708	9,407	6.58	10.23	77.70	35.67	142,963
Liaoning 辽宁	2	1,131	435,743	14,256	7.17	11.27	80.49	36.37	198,854
Jilin 吉林	1	96	3,638	-289	-0.93	-1.27	11.83	26.75	31,182
Heilongjiang 黑龙江									
Central-East 华东	55	239	32,143	2,420	7.73	14.62	42.43	47.17	31,321
Shanghai 上海	8	199	51,321	3,990	8.30	13.47	57.22	38.33	48,042
Jiangsu 江苏	15	173	29,274	630	4.00	11.16	51.96	64.10	15,742
Zhejiang 浙江	23	277	34,033	3,421	9.07	17.70	42.25	48.74	37,714
Anhui 安徽	1	222	3,692	91	2.67	12.21	8.33	78.10	3,402
Fujian 福建	2	85	13,796	5,555	11.68	21.32	123.01	45.24	47,575
Jiangxi 江西	4	470	21,887	385	1.33	1.84	15.84	27.58	28,872
Shandong 山东	2	163	8,303	151	1.46	4.17	32.24	65.06	10,366
Central-South 中南	12	306	32,399	920	4.03	8.28	28.70	51.24	22,807
Henan 河南	1	156	20,151	720	13.90	16.40	22.24	15.25	5,180
Hubei 湖北	2	83	1,808	-230	-1.99	-4.76	7.39	58.25	11,551
Hunan 湖南	3	298	12,339	-314	-7.51	-15.76	14.41	52.31	4,183
Guangdong 广东	6	410	54,667	1,954	5.04	10.34	35.73	51.29	38,809
Guangxi 广西									
Hainan 海南									
Southwest 西南	4	349	14,369	245	1.35	3.15	13.73	57.22	18,147
Chongqing 重庆	1	140	6,972	-149	-1.06		25.86	147.36	14,065
Sichuan 四川	3	418	16,835	376	1.93	2.99	12.37	35.55	19,508
Guizhou 贵州									
Yunnan 云南									
Tibet 西藏									
Northwest 西北	3	769	12,090	-3,237	-3.76	-51.00	9.23	92.63	86,188
Shaanxi 陕西	1	620	6,140	-3,112	-6.93	-28.46	6.50	75.65	44,900
Gansu 甘肃	2	843	15,065	-3,300	-3.09	-81.38	10.23	96.20	106,832
Qinghai 青海									
Ningxia 宁夏									
Xinjiang 新疆									

3653: Diagnostic Products 诊断用品制造业

Year 年份	Number of firms 企业个数	Rate of change 变化率 (%)	Number of employees 职工人数 (人)	Rate of change 变化率 (%)	Total revenue (Mil. RMB) 总销售收入 (百万元)	Rate of change 变化率 (%)	Total profit (Mil RMB) 总利润 (百万元)	Rate of change 变化率 (%)
2000	69		21,582		2,581		94	
2001	73	5.80	20,397	-5.49	3,029	17.36	100	6.38
2002	83	13.70	23,844	16.90	3,193	5.41	177	77.00

Major Products 主要产品	Output 产量	Unit 单位
Diagnostic Article 诊断用品	21	100,000,000 Yuan 亿元

10 Main Firms with Maximal Revenue (year founded) 收入最大的十家主要企业（创办年份）	City 城市	Province 省	Telephone/fax 电话/传真	Number of employees 职工人数	Ownership 产业所有权	Revenue ('000 RMB) 销售收入 (千元)	Profit('000 RMB) (rank) 利润(千元) (排名)	Total assets ('000 RMB) 总资产 (千元)	Major products 主要产品
Omron (Dalian) Co.,Ltd. 欧姆龙（大连）有限公司(1993)	Dalian 大连市	Liaoning 辽宁省	(0411)7614222 (0411)7628494	1,585	Foreign Funded 外商投资	753,726	19,985(3)	268,269	Blood-pressure Meter 血压计
Shuangge Group Co.,Ltd. 双鸽集团有限公司(1984)	Taizhou 台州市	Zhejiang 浙江省	(0576)4066588 (0576)4066666	1,229	Limited-Liability 有限公司	301,371	64,803(1)	456,072	Injector 注射器
ONBO Electronic (Shenzhen) Co., Ltd. 鸿邦电子（深圳）有限公司(1992)	Shenzhen 深圳市	Guangdong 广东省	(0755)28120227 (0755)28121104	1,630	Foreign Funded 外商投资	213,912	10,994(6)	136,705	Clinical Thermometer 体温计
Shanghai Kindly Enterprise Development Co., ltd. 上海康德莱企业发展有限公司(1995)	Shanghai 上海市	Shanghai 上海市	(021)59144059 (021)59118500	73	Private Owned 私营企业	187,363	2,152(11)	147,002	One-off Injector一次性注射器
Jiangsu Yuyue Medical Equipment Co.,Ltd. 江苏鱼跃医疗设备有限公司(1984)	Zhenjiang 镇江市	Jiangsu 江苏省	(0511)6523507 (0511)6963281	420	Private Owned 私营企业	126,930	1,021(21)	39,713	Medical Stethoscope医用听诊器
JMS Dalian Medical Supply Co.,Ltd. 大连JMS医疗器具有限公司(1988)	Dalian 大连市	Liaoning 辽宁省	(0411)7611733 (0411)7612300	677	Foreign Funded 外商投资	117,759	8,526(7)	129,439	Transfusion Set 输液器
Yancheng Infusion Appliances Factory 盐城市输液厂(1997)	Yancheng 盐城市	Jiangsu 江苏省	(0515)6410028 (0515)6410028	142	Private Owned 私营企业	66,550	1,100(20)	6,220	One-off Transfusion Set一次性输液器
Zhejiang KangKang Medical Apparatuses Co., Ltd. 浙江康康医疗器械有限公司(1995)	Taizhou 台州市	Zhejiang 浙江省	(0576)7418033 (0576)7418066	402	Private Owned 私营企业	55,832	1,589(16)	38,045	One-off Transfusion Set一次性输液器
Yangzhou Yada Industrial Group Corp. 扬州市亚达实业有限公司(1981)	Yangzhou 扬州市	Jiangsu 江苏省	(0514)7481420 (0514)7481848	154	Foreign Funded 外商投资	48,910	1,164(19)	11,981	Diagnose Articles 诊断用品
Zhejiang Lingyang Medical Apparatuses Co., Ltd. 浙江灵洋医疗器械有限公司(1987)	Taizhou 台州市	Zhejiang 浙江省	(0576)5881147 (0576)5881588	900	Private Owned 私营企业	45,982	1,955(13)	43,379	Transfusion Set 输液器

Top 10 Cities by Revenue 销售收入排名前10位城市	Province 省	Market share 市场份额 (%)	Number of firms 企业个数
Dalian 大连市	Liaoning 辽宁省	27.30	2
Taizhou 台州市	Zhejiang 浙江省	14.47	6
Shanghai 上海市	Shanghai 上海市	12.86	8
Shenzhen 深圳市	Guangdong 广东省	6.70	1
Wenzhou 温州市	Zhejiang 浙江省	6.56	8
Zhenjiang 镇江市	Jiangsu 江苏省	4.31	2
Yangzhou 扬州市	Jiangsu 江苏省	2.97	4
Jiangmen 江门市	Guangdong 广东省	2.73	1
Suzhou 苏州市	Jiangsu 江苏省	2.64	3
Nanchang 南昌市	Jiangxi 江西省	2.40	3

10 Major Wholesalers 十家主要批发商	City 城市	Province 省	Telephone/Fax 电话/传真
Johnson & Johnson Medical (China) Ltd. 强生(中国)医疗器材有限公司	Shanghai 上海市	Shanghai 上海市	(021)62826988 (021)62825073
China New Era Co., Ltd. 中国新时代公司	Beijing 北京市	Beijing 北京市	(010)82803388 (010)82803688
Beijing Kanglian Medicine Appliances Developing & Marketing Company 北京市康联医药器械开发经营公司	Beijing 北京市	Beijing 北京市	(010)68977301 (010)68975345
Shanghai Medical Instruments Wholesale Department 上海市医疗器械批发部	Shanghai 上海市	Shanghai 上海市	(021)63219999 (021)63210456
Jiangsu Medicines Company 江苏省药材公司	Nanjing 南京市	Jiangsu 江苏省	(025)3232715 (025)3232715
Suzhou Medical Health Products Import & Export Company 苏州市医药保健品进出口公司	Suzhou 苏州市	Jiangsu 江苏省	(0512)68627233 (0512)68621176
Jiangsu Nantong Medicine Co.,Ltd. 江苏省南通医药股份有限公司	Nantong 南通市	Jiangsu 江苏省	(0513)5513093 (0513)5527814
Zhejiang Jiashan Medicine General Company 浙江省嘉善县医药总公司	Jiaxing 嘉兴市	Zhejiang 浙江省	(0573)4026343 (0573)4026344
Hefei Pharmaceutical Medical Apparatuses Company 合肥市药品医疗器械公司	Hefei 合肥市	Anhui 安徽省	(0551)4296721 (0551)4296402
Fuzhou Medical Instruments Stock & Supply Station 福州医疗器械采购供应站	Fuzhou 福州市	Fujian 福建省	(0591)3258409 (0591)3258413

3654: Medical Materials and Utilities 医用材料及医疗用品制造业

The industry accounts for 0.073% of the total revenue of China's industrial sector in 2002. The rate of return on assets is 7.11%. 84.34% of all firms in the industry made a profit while 15.66% had negative returns.The top province in terms of the industry's revenue is Shanghai, accounting for 19.66% of the total revenue.
2002年本行业收入占全行业的 0.073%，资产利润率为 7.11%。84.34%的企业赢利，15.66%的企业亏损。收入最高的省为上海市，占本行业的19.66%。

	Total number of firms 企业总数	Total number of employees 职工总数	Total revenue (Mil.RMB) 总销售收入 (百万元)	Total profit (Mil.RMB) 总利润 (百万元)	Return on assets 资产利润率 (%)	Return on equity 权益利润率 (%)	Labour productivity ('000 RMB/ worker) 劳动生产率 (千元/人)	Debts/ assets 资产负债率 (%)	Total assets (Mil.RMB) 总资产 (百万元)
Industry Overall 行业总体	281	57,081	7,844	641	7.11	13.09	55.39	45.68	9,018

	Number of firms 企业个数	Average number of employees 平均职工人数	Average revenue ('000 RMB) 平均销售收入 (千元)	Average profit ('000 RMB) 平均利润 (千元)	Return on assets 资产利润率 (%)	Return on equity 权益利润率 (%)	Labour productivity ('000 RMB/ worker) 劳动生产率 (千元/人)	Debts/ assets 资产负债率 (%)	Average total assets ('000 RMB) 平均总资产 (千元)
By ownership 产业所有权									
State-owned 国有	26	95	7,497	589	5.37	14.06	29.63	61.82	10,981
Collective-owned 集体	39	198	15,245	261	2.10	8.04	19.98	73.95	12,442
Foreign & Overseas Chinese Funded 三资	69	247	52,415	5,744	10.19	18.34	99.18	44.41	56,357
By regional distribution 地区分布									
Central-North 华北	38	123	23,533	4,477	15.84	31.88	121.10	50.31	28,266
Beijing 北京	14	124	39,377	9,049	20.60	42.00	263.78	50.96	43,938
Tianjin 天津	13	160	20,209	3,012	15.77	24.98	41.61	36.84	19,091
Hebei 河北	5	99	7,592	432	4.19	24.68	20.83	83.03	10,306
Shanxi 山西	5	59	4,687	-39	-0.28	-0.64	19.52	56.31	13,818
Inner Mongolia 内蒙古	1	85	18,842	2,322	2.58	6.39	95.42	59.67	90,156
Northeast 东北	7	269	19,649	31	0.02	0.02	32.77	4.29	153,659
Liaoning 辽宁	2	170	755				5.03	102.89	7,884
Jilin 吉林	2	118	11,585	32	0.08	0.11	25.99	25.62	37,167
Heilongjiang 黑龙江	3	436	37,621	52	0.02	0.02	41.21	1.10	328,504
Central-East 华东	175	215	31,812	2,190	6.82	13.95	53.19	51.16	32,138
Shanghai 上海	27	257	57,118	4,173	6.64	13.12	61.11	49.43	62,886
Jiangsu 江苏	61	172	24,889	625	3.48	9.90	37.56	64.86	17,984
Zhejiang 浙江	43	117	19,623	2,617	9.94	15.03	64.14	33.86	26,322
Anhui 安徽	13	159	6,467	148	1.94	7.78	14.67	75.11	7,642
Fujian 福建	6	152	64,803	3,300	6.93	14.66	428.64	52.72	47,617
Jiangxi 江西	9	426	21,703	1,258	5.36	10.90	20.07	50.79	23,460
Shandong 山东	16	519	62,170	5,429	7.89	17.71	43.43	55.45	68,822
Central-South 中南	51	219	22,423	1,585	7.93	15.52	41.72	48.90	19,996
Henan 河南	12	73	6,283	184	2.34	4.16	29.24	43.86	7,881
Hubei 湖北	17	328	25,732	775	5.13	11.21	27.51	54.22	15,108
Hunan 湖南	3	354	29,758	537	2.46	4.69	28.25	47.52	21,823
Guangdong 广东	18	201	29,546	3,515	10.55	20.10	69.66	47.50	33,310
Guangxi 广西	1	42	9,616	583	17.54	43.83	124.69	59.99	3,324
Hainan 海南									
Southwest 西南	6	170	13,649	1,093	3.35	10.19	57.33	67.13	32,624
Chongqing 重庆	1	75	2,386	-4,155	-15.02		-35.73	252.77	27,665
Sichuan 四川	2	256	27,228	2,295	5.87	15.53	85.38	62.23	39,114
Guizhou 贵州	1	155	5,028	99	1.21	1.79	10.38	32.47	8,204
Yunnan 云南	2	139	10,011	3,012	7.38	8.42	56.96	12.41	40,824
Tibet 西藏									
Northwest 西北	4	177	5,022	57	0.79	6.73	10.36	88.20	7,117
Shaanxi 陕西	1	250	4,443	-318	-1.97	-17.46	5.33	88.74	16,168
Gansu 甘肃	3	152	5,214	181	4.42	35.35	13.11	87.49	4,100
Qinghai 青海									
Ningxia 宁夏									
Xinjiang 新疆									

3654: Medical Materials and Utilities 医用材料及医疗用品制造业

Year 年份	Number of firms 企业个数	Rate of change 变化率 (%)	Number of employees 职工人数 (人)	Rate of change 变化率 (%)	Total revenue (Mil. RMB) 总销售收入 (百万元)	Rate of change 变化率 (%)	Total profit (Mil RMB) 总利润 (百万元)	Rate of change 变化率 (%)
2000	232		50,812		5,531		253	
2001	256	10.34	56,865	11.91	6,428	16.22	584	130.83
2002	281	9.77	57,081	0.38	7,844	22.03	641	9.76

Major Products 主要产品	Output 产量	Unit 单位

10 Main Firms with Maximal Revenue (year founded) 收入最大的十家主要企业（创办年份）	City 城市	Province 省	Telephone/fax 电话/传真	Number of employees 职工人数	Ownership 产业所有权	Revenue ('000 RMB) 销售收入 (千元)	Profit('000 RMB) (rank) 利润(千元) (排名)	Total assets ('000 RMB) 总资产 (千元)	Major products 主要产品
Beijing Bausch & Lomb Eyecare Co., Ltd.	Beijing	Beijing	(010)67768585		Foreign Funded				1aterials & Articles for Medicine
北京博士伦眼睛护理产品有限公司(1991)	北京市	北京市	(010)67111601	544	外商投资	360,911	104,871(1)	423,702	医用材料及医疗用品
Shanghai Jinquanshan Medical Apparatuses Inc.	Shanghai	Shanghai	(021)67727466		Overseas Chinese-funded				PVC Gloves
上海金泉山医疗器材有限公司(1998)	上海市	上海市	(021)67725858	1,451	港澳台资	352,567	8,121(18)	312,504	PVC手套
Teyumo Medical Products (Hangzhou) Co.,Ltd.	Hangzhou	Zhejiang	(0571)86910212		Foreign Funded				Medical Articles
泰尔茂医疗用品（杭州）有限公司(1995)	杭州市	浙江省	(0571)86910293	622	外商投资	283,504	70,912(2)	487,540	医疗用品
GN Resoud (China) Co., Ltd.	Xiamen	Fujian	(0592)5607188		Foreign Funded				Audiphone
瑞声达听力技术（中国）有限公司(1987)	厦门市	福建省	(0592)6023540	518	外商投资	267,999	4,864(30)	190,218	助听器
Shanghai Johnson& Johnson Co.,Ltd.	Shanghai	Shanghai	(021)64302410		Foreign Funded				Medical Treatment Materials
上海强生有限公司(1988)	上海市	上海市	(021)64302579	213	外商投资	215,111	30,598(5)	197,735	医用材料
Jiangsu Likang Group Corp.	Suzhou	Jiangsu	(0512)63242142		Collective-owned				Gauze
江苏利康集团公司(1980)	苏州市	江苏省	(0512)63241262	1,316	集体企业	176,697	208(146)	72,440	纱布
Shanghai Jintengshan Plastic Cement Enterprise Co.,Ltd.	Shanghai	Shanghai	(021)67725678		Overseas Chinese-funded				PVC Gloves
上海金藤山塑胶企业有限公司(1995)	上海市	上海市	(021)67725858	795	港澳台资	174,793	8,047(19)	125,445	PVC手套
Tianjian Hanaco Medical Co.,Ltd.	Tianjin	Tianjin	(022)66204551		Foreign Funded				Transfusion Set
天津市哈娜好医材有限公司(1986)	天津市	天津市	(022)66200803	1,278	外商投资	129,680	15,885(9)	90,052	输液器
Shanghai Jinbaoshan Plastic Cement Enterprise Co., Ltd.	Shanghai	Shanghai	(021)67727466		Overseas Chinese-funded				PVC Gloves
上海金宝山塑胶企业有限公司(1992)	上海市	上海市	(021)67725858	530	港澳台资	116,064	5,028(29)	108,442	PVC手套
Zhuhai Economical Special Zone Viop Bioenergy Science & Technology	Zhuhai	Guangdong	(0756)8135135		Foreign Funded				Medical Apparatuses
Co.,Ltd.珠海经特区天年生物工程科技有限公司(1992)	珠海市	广东省	(0756)8888756	280	外商投资	109,772	32,022(4)	127,325	医疗器械

Top 10 Cities by Revenue 销售收入排名前10位城市	Province 省	Market share 市场份额 (%)	Number of firms 企业个数
Shanghai 上海市	Shanghai 上海市	19.66	27
Beijing 北京市	Beijing 北京市	7.03	14
Zibo 淄博市	Shandong 山东省	5.96	3
Suzhou 苏州市	Jiangsu 江苏省	5.70	13
Changzhou 常州市	Jiangsu 江苏省	4.95	16
Weihai 威海市	Shandong 山东省	4.53	1
Hangzhou 杭州市	Zhejiang 浙江省	4.20	6
Xiamen 厦门市	Fujian 福建省	3.42	1
Tianjin 天津市	Tianjin 天津市	3.35	13
Shengzhixiaxingzhengdanwei 省直辖行政单位	Hubei 湖北省	3.14	7

10 Major Wholesalers 十家主要批发商	City 城市	Province 省	Telephone/Fax 电话/传真
Johnson & Johnson Medical (China) Ltd.	Shanghai	Shanghai	(021)62826988
强生(中国)医疗器材有限公司	上海市	上海市	(021)62825073
China New Era Co., Ltd.	Beijing	Beijing	(010)82803388
中国新时代公司	北京市	北京市	(010)82803688
Beijing Kanglian Medicine Appliances Developing & Marketing Company	Beijing	Beijing	(010)68977301
北京市康联医药器械开发经营公司	北京市	北京市	(010)68975345
Shanghai Medical Instruments Wholesale Department	Shanghai	Shanghai	(021)63219999
上海市医疗器械批发部	上海市	上海市	(021)63210456
Jiangsu Medicines Company	Nanjing	Jiangsu	(025)3232715
江苏省药材公司	南京市	江苏省	(025)3232715
Suzhou Medical Health Products Import & Export Company	Suzhou	Jiangsu	(0512)68627233
苏州市医药保健品进出口公司	苏州市	江苏省	(0512)68621176
Jiangsu Nantong Medicine Co.,Ltd.	Nantong	Jiangsu	(0513)5513093
江苏省南通医药股份有限公司	南通市	江苏省	(0513)5527814
Zhejiang Jiashan Medicine General Company	Jiaxing	Zhejiang	(0573)4026343
浙江省嘉善县医药总公司	嘉兴市	浙江省	(0573)4026344
Hefei Pharmaceutical Medical Apparatuses Company	Hefei	Anhui	(0551)4296721
合肥市药品医疗器械公司	合肥市	安徽省	(0551)4296402
Fuzhou Medical Instruments Stock & Supply Station	Fuzhou	Fujian	(0591)3258409
福州医疗器械采购供应站	福州市	福建省	(0591)3258413

3655: Artificial Limb, Orthopaedic Equipment 假肢、矫形器制造业

The industry accounts for 0.005% of the total revenue of China's industrial sector in 2002. The rate of return on assets is 2.41%. 54.55% of all firms in the industry made a profit while 45.45% had negative returns.The top province in terms of the industry's revenue is Guangdong, accounting for 34.90% of the total revenue.
2002年本行业收入占全行业的 0.005%，资产利润率为 2.41%。54.55%的企业赢利，45.45%的企业亏损。收入最高的省为广东省，占本行业的34.90%。

	Total number of firms 企业总数	Total number of employees 职工总数	Total revenue (Mil.RMB) 总销售收入（百万元）	Total profit (Mil.RMB) 总利润（百万元）	Return on assets 资产利润率（%）	Return on equity 权益利润率（%）	Labour productivity ('000 RMB/ worker) 劳动生产率（千元/人）	Debts/ assets 资产负债率（%）	Total assets (Mil.RMB) 总资产（百万元）
Industry Overall 行业总体	33	3,641	494	20	2.41	4.37	65.70	44.73	833

	Number of firms 企业个数	Average number of employees 平均职工人数	Average revenue ('000 RMB) 平均销售收入（千元）	Average profit ('000 RMB) 平均利润（千元）	Return on assets 资产利润率（%）	Return on equity 权益利润率（%）	Labour productivity ('000 RMB/ worker) 劳动生产率（千元/人）	Debts/ assets 资产负债率（%）	Average total assets ('000 RMB) 平均总资产（千元）
By ownership 产业所有权									
State-owned 国有	22	104	8,539	341	1.89	3.62	28.25	47.86	18,043
Collective-owned 集体									
Foreign & Overseas Chinese Funded 三资	7	146	26,703	-145	-0.31	-0.52	73.91	41.53	47,508
By regional distribution 地区分布									
Central-North 华北	9	101	22,328	2,385	10.17	16.70	157.94	39.12	23,464
Beijing 北京	4	121	26,745	1,344	4.95	7.60	93.76	34.89	27,181
Tianjin 天津	4	80	22,402	3,256	14.40	24.59	304.36	41.44	22,616
Hebei 河北									
Shanxi 山西	1	107	4,362	3,065	25.57	63.84	9.17	59.94	11,986
Inner Mongolia 内蒙古									
Northeast 东北	5	63	1,533	-20	-0.40	-0.52	7.73	22.12	5,051
Liaoning 辽宁									
Jilin 吉林	2	106	2,238	-81	-1.84	-2.71	4.61	31.87	4,364
Heilongjiang 黑龙江	3	35	1,063	20	0.36	0.43	13.95	16.97	5,509
Central-East 华东	10	94	8,704	-304	-1.05	-1.74	43.44	39.77	29,033
Shanghai 上海	3	88	13,699	-523	-0.91	-1.54	113.47	40.99	57,661
Jiangsu 江苏	3	102	9,957	-467	-2.01	-3.53	22.09	43.09	23,279
Zhejiang 浙江	1	76	2,103	249	3.28	5.65	1.16	41.92	7,588
Anhui 安徽	1	59	2,043	-9	-0.17	-0.19	20.58	9.02	5,330
Fujian 福建									
Jiangxi 江西	1	45	1,118	-244	-3.33	-6.01	6.58	44.62	7,335
Shandong 山东	1	193	10,804	-66	-0.24	-0.33	14.07	27.64	27,258
Central-South 中南	5	213	36,390	301	0.63	1.47	45.92	57.04	47,693
Henan 河南	1	102	6,724	235	1.65	2.60	22.67	36.41	14,229
Hubei 湖北									
Hunan 湖南	1	89	2,919	-121	-0.66	-2.40	11.42	72.33	18,209
Guangdong 广东	3	291	57,436	464	0.68	1.58	52.15	57.11	68,676
Guangxi 广西									
Hainan 海南									
Southwest 西南	2	116	5,677	307	1.74	2.92	8.35	40.35	17,606
Chongqing 重庆									
Sichuan 四川	1	125	8,441	541	2.45	3.80	12.45	35.44	22,049
Guizhou 贵州	1	107	2,913	72	0.55	1.06	3.57	48.56	13,163
Yunnan 云南									
Tibet 西藏									
Northwest 西北	2	88	2,372	-171	-1.04	-2.45	8.23	57.47	16,394
Shaanxi 陕西	1	142	4,743	-342	-1.30	-3.00	10.20	56.51	26,216
Gansu 甘肃									
Qinghai 青海									
Ningxia 宁夏	1	34						61.29	6,572
Xinjiang 新疆									

3655: Artificial Limb, Orthopaedic Equipment 假肢、矫形器制造业

Year 年份	Number of firms 企业个数	Rate of change 变化率（%）	Number of employees 职工人数（人）	Rate of change 变化率（%）	Total revenue (Mil. RMB) 总销售收入（百万元）	Rate of change 变化率（%）	Total profit (Mil RMB) 总利润（百万元）	Rate of change 变化率（%）
2000	32		3,165		176		2	
2001	34	6.25	3,698	16.84	415	135.80	25	1,150.00
2002	33	-2.94	3,641	-1.54	494	19.04	20	-20.00

Major Products 主要产品	Output 产量	Unit 单位

10 Main Firms with Maximal Revenue (year founded) 收入最大的十家主要企业（创办年份）	City 城市	Province 省	Telephone/fax 电话/传真	Number of employees 职工人数	Ownership 产业所有权	Revenue ('000 RMB) 销售收入（千元）	Profit('000 RMB) (rank) 利润（千元）（排名）	Total assets ('000 RMB) 总资产（千元）	Major products 主要产品
Tianjin New Technology Industry Garden Lide Medical Equipment	Tianjin	Tianjin	(022)27355416		Private Owned				Curing Machine
Co., Ltd.天津新技术产业园区利德医用设备有限公司(1995)	天津市	天津市	(022)27355295	195	私营企业	77,171	12,556(1)	45,558	治疗仪
Rpoon Medical Sports Products Co.,Ltd.	Foshan	Guangdong	(0757)5448866		Overseas Chinese-funded				Oxter Walking Stick
南海良润医疗运动器材有限公司(1994)	佛山市	广东省	(0757)5443535	440	港澳台资	68,109	50(16)	59,087	腋下拐
Beijing Ottobock Orthopaedic Industry Co., ltd.	Beijing	Beijing	(010)61568861		Foreign Funded				Artificial Limb Rectifier
北京奥托博克假肢矫形器工业有限公司(1993)	北京市	北京市	(010)69575026	210	外商投资	56,443	2,883(3)	60,945	假肢矫形器
Beijing Tianyifu Medical Apparatus Co., Ltd.	Beijing	Beijing	(010)60998016		Private Owned				Medical Apparatuses
北京天义福医疗器材有限公司(1998)	北京市	北京市	(010)60998016	110	私营企业	39,157	1,115(7)	22,755	医疗器材
Weichuang Medical Apparatuses (Shanghai) Co., Ltd.	Shanghai	Shanghai	(021)38954600		Foreign Funded				PTCA Ball Shell Pipe.PTCA
微创医疗器械(上海)有限公司(1998)	上海市	上海市	(021)50801305	101	外商投资	16,832	-	90,350	球壳导管
Shanghai Prosthetic & Orthopaedic Co., Ltd.	Shanghai	Shanghai	(021)62172513		State-owned				Artificial Limb Rectifier
上海假肢厂有限公司(1965)	上海市	上海市	(021)62534972	145	国有企业	15,698	2,010(4)	31,887	假肢矫形器
Suzhou Detai Medical Healthy Devices Co., Ltd.	Suzhou	Jiangsu	(0520)53458488		Overseas Chinese-funded				Protect Cover
苏州得泰医疗卫生用品有限公司(1994)	苏州市	江苏省	(0520)53458119	200	港澳台资	15,470	480(10)	48,200	护套
Oticon Audition Technology (Nanjing) Co., Ltd.	Nanjing	Jiangsu	(025)4611998		Foreign Funded				Audiphone
奥迪康听力技术（南京）有限公司(1998)	南京市	江苏省	(025)4610217	37	外商投资	13,540	-	19,030	助听器
Shandong Artificial limb Orthotics Rehabilitation Center	Jinan	Shandong	(0531)8933584		State owned				Artificial Limb
山东假肢矫形康复中心(1950)	济南市	山东省	(0531)8950655	193	国有企业	10,804	-	27,258	假肢
Sichuan Disability Rehabilitation Center	Chengdu	Sichuan	(028)85439186		State-owned				Artificial Limb
四川省肢体伤残康复中心(1950)	成都市	四川省	(028)85439830	125	国有企业	8,441	541(9)	22,049	假肢

Top 10 Cities by Revenue 销售收入排名前10位城市	Province 省	Market share 市场份额（%）	Number of firms 企业个数
Beijing 北京市	Beijing 北京市	21.67	4
Shantou 汕头市	Guangdong 广东省	20.28	1
Tianjin 天津市	Tianjin 天津市	18.15	4
Foshan 佛山市	Guangdong 广东省	13.80	1
Shanghai 上海市	Shanghai 上海市	8.32	3
Suzhou 苏州市	Jiangsu 江苏省	3.13	1
Nanjing 南京市	Jiangsu 江苏省	2.74	1
Jinan 济南市	Shandong 山东省	2.19	1
Chengdu 成都市	Sichuan 四川省	1.71	1
Zhengzhou 郑州市	Henan 河南省	1.36	1

10 Major Wholesalers 十家主要批发商	City 城市	Province 省	Telephone/Fax 电话/传真
Johnson & Johnson Medical (China) Ltd.	Shanghai	Shanghai	(021)62826988
强生(中国)医疗器材有限公司	上海市	上海市	(021)62825073
China New Era Co., Ltd.	Beijing	Beijing	(010)82803388
中国新时代公司	北京市	北京市	(010)82803688
Beijing Kanglian Medicine Appliances Developing & Marketing Company	Beijing	Beijing	(010)68977301
北京市康联医药器械开发经营公司	北京市	北京市	(010)68975345
Shanghai Medical Instruments Wholesale Department	Shanghai	Shanghai	(021)63219999
上海市医疗器械批发部	上海市	上海市	(021)63210456
Jiangsu Medicines Company	Nanjing	Jiangsu	(025)3232715
江苏省药材公司	南京市	江苏省	(025)3232715
Suzhou Medical Health Products Import & Export Company	Suzhou	Jiangsu	(0512)68627233
苏州市医药保健品进出口公司	苏州市	江苏省	(0512)68621176
Jiangsu Nantong Medicine Co.,Ltd.	Nantong	Jiangsu	(0513)5513093
江苏省南通医药股份有限公司	南通市	江苏省	(0513)5527814
Zhejiang Jiashan Medicine General Company	Jiaxing	Zhejiang	(0573)4026343
浙江省嘉善县医药总公司	嘉兴市	浙江省	(0573)4026344
Hefei Pharmaceutical Medical Apparatuses Company	Hefei	Anhui	(0551)4296721
合肥市药品医疗器械公司	合肥市	安徽省	(0551)4296402
Fuzhou Medical Instruments Stock & Supply Station	Fuzhou	Fujian	(0591)3258409
福州医疗器械采购供应站	福州市	福建省	(0591)3258413

3671: Construction Machinery 建筑机械制造业

The industry accounts for 0.292% of the total revenue of China's industrial sector in 2002. The rate of return on assets is 5.36%. 73.74% of all firms in the industry made a profit while 26.26% had negative returns.The top province in terms of the industry's revenue is Shandong, accounting for 27.16% of the total revenue.
2002年本行业收入占全行业的0.292%，资产利润率为5.36%。73.74%的企业赢利，26.26%的企业亏损。收入最高的省为山东省，占本行业的27.16%。

	Total number of firms 企业总数	Total number of employees 职工总数	Total revenue (Mil.RMB) 总销售收入（百万元）	Total profit (Mil.RMB) 总利润（百万元）	Return on assets 资产利润率 (%)	Return on equity 权益利润率 (%)	Labour productivity ('000 RMB/ worker) 劳动生产率（千元/人）	Debts/ assets 资产负债率 (%)	Total assets (Mil.RMB) 总资产（百万元）
Industry Overall 行业总体	297	122,900	31,364	2,023	5.36	15.41	65.91	65.20	37,716

	Number of firms 企业个数	Average number of employees 平均职工人数	Average revenue ('000 RMB) 平均销售收入（千元）	Average profit ('000 RMB) 平均利润（千元）	Return on assets 资产利润率 (%)	Return on equity 权益利润率 (%)	Labour productivity ('000 RMB/ worker) 劳动生产率（千元/人）	Debts/ assets 资产负债率 (%)	Average total assets ('000 RMB) 平均总资产（千元）
By ownership 产业所有权									
State-owned 国有	71	453	50,040	-2,761	-2.63	-21.22	25.47	87.60	104,948
Collective-owned 集体	40	162	28,042	1,544	7.73	19.45	65.51	60.28	19,976
Foreign & Overseas Chinese Funded 三资	38	305	290,416	34,389	15.44	34.51	239.78	55.25	222,666
By regional distribution 地区分布									
Central-North 华北	34	372	35,897	-682	-0.82	-2.29	12.73	64.32	83,436
Beijing 北京	11	116	13,080	-584	-1.51	-3.54	36.02	57.35	38,713
Tianjin 天津	7	498	69,135	-2,367	-1.75	-3.96	-4.39	55.79	135,342
Hebei 河北	11	613	51,808	1,122	0.95	3.13	18.68	69.48	117,668
Shanxi 山西	5	225	4,559	-2,506	-7.40	-74.50	3.71	90.06	33,849
Inner Mongolia 内蒙古									
Northeast 东北	21	605	28,342	-11,724	-10.42		7.43	140.59	112,545
Liaoning 辽宁	13	479	38,553	-16,831	-13.38		10.13	160.02	125,760
Jilin 吉林	5	1,084	8,260	-5,228	-4.28	-117.41	3.07	96.35	122,145
Heilongjiang 黑龙江	3	353	17,564	-421	-1.07		13.88	100.24	39,279
Central-East 华东	138	390	154,295	12,245	8.61	19.13	96.27	54.98	142,185
Shanghai 上海	9	366	81,441	2,770	3.03	5.92	56.79	48.72	91,308
Jiangsu 江苏	43	278	110,415	5,904	7.31	18.71	72.88	60.92	80,765
Zhejiang 浙江	19	125	18,684	954	5.44	13.71	47.25	60.34	17,541
Anhui 安徽	8	281	300,178	51,232	22.53	38.81	289.78	41.95	227,410
Fujian 福建	20	407	200,657	7,787	5.73	11.03	106.74	48.05	135,908
Jiangxi 江西	3	828	174,718	20,196	3.82	7.17	77.24	46.71	528,395
Shandong 山东	36	648	236,616	21,297	8.64	21.24	98.51	59.31	246,416
Central-South 中南	67	318	63,616	6,976	7.72	17.59	68.31	56.07	90,312
Henan 河南	24	320	34,755	624	1.34	3.25	31.46	58.76	46,571
Hubei 湖北	14	227	29,228	-510	-1.22	-8.24	30.50	85.24	41,924
Hunan 湖南	7	895	317,201	60,214	13.35	24.85	145.54	46.29	451,183
Guangdong 广东	15	137	30,989	1,067	2.49	7.49	59.13	66.74	42,820
Guangxi 广西	7	303	47,673	3,157	4.05	11.01	39.37	63.22	77,958
Hainan 海南									
Southwest 西南	22	544	130,391	6,197	3.30	16.84	65.59	80.41	187,849
Chongqing 重庆	2	382	6,530	-4,046	-10.88		-8.07	112.73	37,180
Sichuan 四川	13	553	198,712	11,537	4.28	19.89	98.15	78.48	269,586
Guizhou 贵州	3	983	77,347	879	0.65	5.28	24.76	87.64	134,602
Yunnan 云南	4	266	10,060	-2,047	-5.46	-54.26	11.58	89.93	37,474
Tibet 西藏									
Northwest 西北	15	700	74,975	-78	-0.04	-0.15	40.64	71.55	180,705
Shaanxi 陕西	8	939	120,258	262	0.09	0.35	49.75	73.86	284,236
Gansu 甘肃	3	419	9,753	-411	-1.17	-5.73	11.61	79.55	35,097
Qinghai 青海	2	484	49,631	4,108	4.63	9.40	26.95	50.74	88,673
Ningxia 宁夏									
Xinjiang 新疆	2	381	17,023	-5,126	-6.66	-15.12	16.12	55.98	77,021

3671: Construction Machinery 建筑机械制造业

Year 年份	Number of firms 企业个数	Rate of change 变化率(%)	Number of employees 职工人数(人)	Rate of change 变化率(%)	Total revenue (Mil. RMB) 总销售收入(百万元)	Rate of change 变化率(%)	Total profit (Mil RMB) 总利润(百万元)	Rate of change 变化率(%)
2000	274		131,443		17,946		1,034	
2001	261	-4.74	120,908	-8.01	20,335	13.31	1,158	11.99
2002	297	13.79	122,900	1.65	31,364	54.24	2,023	74.70

Major Products 主要产品	Output 产量	Unit 单位
Concrete Machinery 混凝土机械	73,951	Unit 台
Scraping & Conveying Machinery 铲土运输机械	58,131	Unit 台

10 Main Firms with Maximal Revenue (year founded) 收入最大的十家主要企业（创办年份）	City 城市	Province 省	Telephone/fax 电话/传真	Number of employees 职工人数	Ownership 产业所有权	Revenue ('000 RMB) 销售收入(千元)	Profit('000 RMB) (rank) 利润(千元)(排名)	Total assets ('000 RMB) 总资产(千元)	Major products 主要产品
Hefei Hitachi Excavators Co.,Ltd. 合肥日立挖掘机有限公司(1995)	Hefei 合肥市	Anhui 安徽省	(0551)3813907 (0551)3813378	640	Foreign Funded 外商投资	2,188,227	406,697(1)	1,445,388	Hydraulic Pressure Digging Machine 液压挖掘机
Komatsu Shantui Construction Machinery Co.,Ltd. 小松山推工程机械有限公司(1995)	Jining 济宁市	Shandong 山东省	(0537)2360036 (0537)2360083	433	Foreign Funded 外商投资	2,083,753	333,421(2)	1,182,055	Hydraulic Pressure Digging Machine 液压挖掘机
Daewoo Heavy Industry (Yantai) Co.,Ltd. 大宇重工业（烟台）有限公司(1996)	Yantai 烟台市	Shandong 山东省	(0535)6382000 (0535)6382004	697	Foreign Funded 外商投资	1,820,438	147,752(6)	1,866,014	Hydraulic Pressure Digging Machine 液压挖掘机
Sany Heavy Industry Co., Ltd. 三一重工股份有限公司(1994)	Changsha 长沙市	Hunan 湖南省	(0731)4031748 (0731)4031999	2,861	Joint Stock 股份制	1,316,416	258,778(3)	1,299,985	Concrete Machinery 砼机械
Shandong Linyi Engineering Machinery Co., Ltd. 山东临沂工程机械股份有限公司(1994)	Linyi 临沂市	Shandong 山东省	(0539)8315782 (0539)8109193	3,417	Joint Stock 股份制	1,212,070	37,544(14)	1,465,463	Loading Machine 装载机
Changlin Co.,Ltd. 常林股份有限公司(1958)	Changzhou 常州市	Jiangsu 江苏省	(0519)6781230 (0519)6750025	1,205	Joint Stock 股份制	1,000,980	42,000(11)	890,770	Loading Machine 装载机
Fujian Longyan Engineering Machinery (Group) Co., Ltd. 福建龙岩工程机械（集团）有限公司(1993)	Longyan 龙岩市	Fujian 福建省	(0597)2522188 (0597)2520988	298	Private Owned 私营企业	847,437	15,224(23)	275,204	Wheel Loading Machine 轮式装载机
Shantui Construction Machinery Co.,Ltd. 山推工程机械股份有限公司(1993)	Jining 济宁市	Shandong 山东省	(0537)2909644 (0537)2315986	3,833	Joint Stock 股份制	804,232	152,097(5)	1,406,770	Bulldozer 推土机
Shandong Engineering Machinery Factory 山东工程机械厂(1958)	Weifang 潍坊市	Shandong 山东省	(0536)3818232 (0536)3818628	1,644	State-owned 国有企业	650,572	3,624(58)	701,577	Loading Machine 装载机
Fangyuan Group Co.,Ltd. 方圆集团(1970)	Yantai 烟台市	Shandong 山东省	(0535)3221111 (0535)3221660	3,248	Limited-Liability 有限公司	562,104	38,623(12)	633,974	Mixer Ingredient Pump 搅拌机配料机泵

Top 10 Cities by Revenue 销售收入排名前10位城市	Province 省	Market share 市场份额(%)	Number of firms 企业个数
Changzhou 常州市	Jiangsu 江苏省	11.04	7
Jining 济宁市	Shandong 山东省	9.77	5
Chengdu 成都市	Sichuan 四川省	8.05	10
Yantai 烟台市	Shandong 山东省	7.85	6
Hefei 合肥市	Anhui 安徽省	7.62	5
Changsha 长沙市	Hunan 湖南省	6.50	4
Xiamen 厦门市	Fujian 福建省	6.22	6
Linyi 临沂市	Shandong 山东省	4.38	4
Longyan 龙岩市	Fujian 福建省	2.89	2
Weifang 潍坊市	Shandong 山东省	2.54	4

10 Major Wholesalers 十家主要批发商	City 城市	Province 省	Telephone/Fax 电话/传真
SU MEC 中设江苏机械设备进出口（集团）公司	Nanjing 南京市	Jiangsu 江苏省	(025)4511888 (025)4411772
China Poster Mobile Communications Equipment Co.,Ltd. 中邮普泰移动通信设备股份有限公司	Beijing 北京市	Beijing 北京市	(010)66426993 (010)66426837
Sino Kama Co., Ltd. 中泰凯马股份有限公司	Shanghai 上海市	Shanghai 上海市	(021)62031188 (021)62030851
China Huayuan Group Co.,Ltd. 中国华源集团有限公司	Shanghai 上海市	Shanghai 上海市	(021)62031188 (021)62032288
Zhejiang Crand Imp.& Exp.Co.,Ltd. 浙江远大进出口有限公司	Ningbo 宁波市	Zhejiang 浙江省	(0574)87720170 (0574)87723350
Shandong Machinery Import & Export Group Corporation 山东省机械进出口集团公司	Qingdao 青岛市	Shandong 山东省	(0532)2661628 (0532)2991655
Qingdao Haier International Trade Co.,Ltd. 青岛海尔国际贸易有限公司	Qingdao 青岛市	Shandong 山东省	(0532)8938337 (0532)8939494
Guangdong Machinery Import & Export Group Corporation 广东省机械进出口集团公司	Guangzhou 广州市	Guangdong 广东省	(020)87782168 (020)87771803
China National Machinery Equipment Import & Export Corporation 中国机械设备进出口总公司	Beijing 北京市	Beijing 北京市	(010)63474506 (010)63261865
Beijing Cellstar Co.,Ltd. 北京蜂星事达电讯有限公司	Beijing 北京市	Beijing 北京市	(010)64602050 (010)64672648

3672: Geology Equipment 地质专用设备制造业

The industry accounts for 0.008% of the total revenue of China's industrial sector in 2002. The rate of return on assets is 1.36%. 72.09% of all firms in the industry made a profit while 27.91% had negative returns.The top province in terms of the industry's revenue is Jiangsu, accounting for 30.32% of the total revenue.
2002年本行业收入占全行业的 0.008%，资产利润率为 1.36%。72.09%的企业赢利，27.91%的企业亏损。收入最高的省为江苏省，占本行业的30.32%。

	Total number of firms 企业总数	Total number of employees 职工总数	Total revenue (Mil.RMB) 总销售收入（百万元）	Total profit (Mil.RMB) 总利润（百万元）	Return on assets 资产利润率（%）	Return on equity 权益利润率（%）	Labour productivity ('000 RMB/worker) 劳动生产率（千元/人）	Debts/assets 资产负债率（%）	Total assets (Mil.RMB) 总资产（百万元）
Industry Overall 行业总体	43	15,134	853	28	1.36	5.49	20.67	75.27	2,034

	Number of firms 企业个数	Average number of employees 平均职工人数	Average revenue ('000 RMB) 平均销售收入（千元）	Average profit ('000 RMB) 平均利润（千元）	Return on assets 资产利润率（%）	Return on equity 权益利润率（%）	Labour productivity ('000 RMB/worker) 劳动生产率（千元/人）	Debts/assets 资产负债率（%）	Average total assets ('000 RMB) 平均总资产（千元）
By ownership 产业所有权									
State-owned 国有	34	339	14,832	241	0.54	2.61	15.36	79.46	44,986
Collective-owned 集体	1	87	63,720	3,593	26.73	96.69	365.61	72.36	13,443
Foreign & Overseas Chinese Funded 三资	2	75	21,592	2,040	26.24	37.92	85.58	30.80	7,774
By regional distribution 地区分布									
Central-North 华北	11	540	27,031	680	0.85	4.15	16.11	79.66	80,520
Beijing 北京	3	100	19,503	545	1.41	5.80	30.62	75.65	38,604
Tianjin 天津	2	181	7,670	-847	-3.50	-8.04	18.55	56.42	24,154
Hebei 河北	4	1,217	55,148	2,169	1.30	7.05	16.18	81.50	166,364
Shanxi 山西	1	250	1,780	-1,072	-2.33	-25.68	2.17	90.91	45,916
Inner Mongolia 内蒙古	1	161	1,127	-59	-0.58	-1.61	2.98	64.16	10,233
Northeast 东北	5	233	4,696	-832	-6.14	-48.72	7.87	87.40	13,551
Liaoning 辽宁	1	311	3,693	-3,340	-20.20		-1.15	110.25	16,534
Jilin 吉林	2	134	3,105	-435	-3.65	-12.04	10.52	69.65	11,890
Heilongjiang 黑龙江	2	294	6,788	25	0.18	1.66	11.43	89.02	13,721
Central-East 华东	13	306	31,015	1,080	2.25	7.05	38.15	68.01	47,899
Shanghai 上海									
Jiangsu 江苏	6	299	43,132	1,687	3.31	10.13	54.82	67.36	50,993
Zhejiang 浙江	2	231	25,667	98	0.39	0.98	32.10	60.51	25,312
Anhui 安徽	1	390	1,937	-767	-3.39		7.29	104.66	22,635
Fujian 福建	1	89	1,757	105	0.85	1.74	4.48	50.93	12,292
Jiangxi 江西									
Shandong 山东	3	415	29,790	1,462	1.90	5.90	28.49	67.83	77,058
Central-South 中南	8	309	10,303	1,252	3.81	18.95	13.72	79.87	32,837
Henan 河南	1	276	2,366	7	0.04	0.10	5.48	56.27	16,405
Hubei 湖北	2	218	7,967	70	0.60	2.59	12.51	77.03	11,756
Hunan 湖南	3	511	18,042	3,210	5.00	32.65	15.51	84.67	64,139
Guangdong 广东	1	201	4,675	-377	-1.33	-4.10	6.26	67.66	28,438
Guangxi 广西	1	28	5,325	620	32.29	38.27	69.54	15.63	1,920
Hainan 海南									
Southwest 西南	2	444	16,456	110	0.27	0.45	20.28	39.57	40,465
Chongqing 重庆	1	823	30,255	150	0.22	0.37	21.06	41.26	68,209
Sichuan 四川									
Guizhou 贵州									
Yunnan 云南	1	64	2,656	70	0.55	0.79	10.30	30.46	12,721
Tibet 西藏									
Northwest 西北	4	173	3,517	-3	-0.01	-0.08	6.34	88.36	28,532
Shaanxi 陕西	1	335	5,978	52	0.07	0.79	2.76	91.49	76,895
Gansu 甘肃	1	218	4,846	76	0.38	2.86	7.31	86.74	20,048
Qinghai 青海	1	52	1,485	-95	-0.66	-2.82	20.94	76.56	14,363
Ningxia 宁夏	1	85	1,759	-44	-1.56	-6.17	9.02	74.73	2,821
Xinjiang 新疆									

3672: Geology Equipment 地质专用设备制造业

Year 年份	Number of firms 企业个数	Rate of change 变化率 (%)	Number of employees 职工人数 (人)	Rate of change 变化率 (%)	Total revenue (Mil. RMB) 总销售收入 (百万元)	Rate of change 变化率 (%)	Total profit (Mil RMB) 总利润 (百万元)	Rate of change 变化率 (%)
2000	39		12,984		512		11	
2001	41	5.13	12,691	-2.26	683	33.40	17	54.55
2002	43	4.88	15,134	19.25	853	24.89	28	64.71

Major Products 主要产品	Output 产量	Unit 单位

10 Main Firms with Maximal Revenue (year founded) 收入最大的十家主要企业（创办年份）	City 城市	Province 省	Telephone/fax 电话/传真	Number of employees 职工人数	Ownership 产业所有权	Revenue ('000 RMB) 销售收入(千元)	Profit('000 RMB) (rank) 利润(千元)(排名)	Total assets ('000 RMB) 总资产(千元)	Major products 主要产品
Shijiazhuang Coal Mining Machinery Co., Ltd.	Shijiazhuang	Hebei	(0311)5916222		State Enterprises				Geological Drilling Rig
石家庄煤矿机械有限责任公司(1940)	石家庄市	河北省	(0311)5052437	2,273	国有独资	118,172	6,026(2)	261,778	地质钻机
Wuxi Drilling Tools Factory	Wuxi	Jiangsu	(0510)5406441		State-owned				Geology Tools
国土资源部无锡钻探工具厂(1958)	无锡市	江苏省	(0510)5407347	453	国有企业	92,096	2,204(7)	136,145	地质工具
Zhangjiakou Exploration Machinery General Factory	Zhangjiakou	Hebei	(0313)4080494		State-owned				Driller
张家口探矿机械总厂(1953)	张家口市	河北省	(0313)4061039	2,251	国有企业	68,634	-	372,443	钻机
Shandong Yanggu Rock Drilling Tools Co.,Ltd.	Liaocheng	Shandong	(0635)6511658		Limited-Liability				Rock Drill
阳谷凿岩钎具厂(1996)	聊城市	山东省	(0635)6511880	410	有限公司	48,085	3,712(3)	105,664	钎具
Beijing Huanding Science & Technology Co., Ltd.	Beijing	Beijing	(010)69724846		Joint Stock				Petroleum & Natural Gas Prospecting Equipment石油天燃
北京环鼎科技有限责任公司(1999)	北京市	北京市	(010)89740972	105	股份制	47,980	1,108(9)	76,739	气勘察设备
Wuxi Jinjie Tongyong Engineer Machinery Prant	Wuxi	Jiangsu	(0510)5013094		Foreign Funded				Driller
无锡金杰通用工程机械有限公司(1985)	无锡市	江苏省	(0510)5280099	108	外商投资	33,490	2,810(5)	2,404	钻机
Lianyungang Huanghai Machinery Factory	Lianyungang	Jiangsu	(0518)5806405		State-owned				Rock-heart Driller
连云港黄海机械厂(1995)	连云港市	江苏省	(0518)5801232	704	国有企业	30,798	178(15)	99,300	岩心钻机
Chongqing Mine Prospecting Machinery Factory	Chongqing	Chongqing	(023)65404314		State-owned				Geology Engineering Driller地质
重庆探矿机械厂(1966)	重庆市	重庆市	(023)65311658	823	国有企业	30,255	150(16)	68,209	工程钻机
Shandong Geology Prospecting Machinery Plant	Jinan	Shandong	(0531)8937431		State-owned				Engineering Construction Driller工程
山东省地质探矿机械厂(1959)	济南市	山东省	(0531)8939010	598	国有企业	30,067	635(10)	77,308	施工钻机
Jiangsu Wuxi Mine Prospecting Machinery General Factory	Wuxi	Jiangsu	(0510)5025731		State-owned				Drilling Machine & Fittings钻探机
江苏省无锡探矿机械总厂(1956)	无锡市	江苏省	(0510)5013426	398	国有企业	28,997	67(23)	41,524	械及配件

Top 10 Cities by Revenue 销售收入排名前10位城市	Province 省	Market share 市场份额 (%)	Number of firms 企业个数
Wuxi 无锡市	Jiangsu 江苏省	19.25	4
Shijiazhuang 石家庄市	Hebei 河北省	16.59	2
Lianyungang 连云港市	Jiangsu 江苏省	11.08	2
Zhangjiakou 张家口市	Hebei 河北省	8.04	1
Beijing 北京市	Beijing 北京市	6.86	3
Liaocheng 聊城市	Shandong 山东省	5.63	1
Hangzhou 杭州市	Zhejiang 浙江省	4.62	1
Hengyang 衡阳市	Hunan 湖南省	4.38	1
Chongqing 重庆市	Chongqing 重庆市	3.55	1
Jinan 济南市	Shandong 山东省	3.52	1

10 Major Wholesalers 十家主要批发商	City 城市	Province 省	Telephone/Fax 电话/传真
SU MEC	Nanjing	Jiangsu	(025)4511888
中设江苏机械设备进出口（集团）公司	南京市	江苏省	(025)4411772
China Poster Mobile Communications Equipment Co.,Ltd.	Beijing	Beijing	(010)66426993
中邮普泰移动通信设备股份有限公司	北京市	北京市	(010)66426837
Sino Kama Co., Ltd.	Shanghai	Shanghai	(021)62031188
中泰凯马股份有限公司	上海市	上海市	(021)62030851
China Huayuan Group Co.,Ltd.	Shanghai	Shanghai	(021)62031188
中国华源集团有限公司	上海市	上海市	(021)62032288
Zhejiang Crand Imp.& Exp.Co.,Ltd.	Ningbo	Zhejiang	(0574)87720170
浙江远大进出口有限公司	宁波市	浙江省	(0574)87723350
Shandong Machinery Import & Export Group Corporation	Qingdao	Shandong	(0532)2661628
山东省机械进出口集团公司	青岛市	山东省	(0532)2991655
Qingdao Haier International Trade Co.,Ltd.	Qingdao	Shandong	(0532)8938337
青岛海尔国际贸易有限公司	青岛市	山东省	(0532)8939494
Guangdong Machinery Import & Export Group Corporation	Guangzhou	Guangdong	(020)87782168
广东省机械进出口集团公司	广州市	广东省	(020)87771803
China National Machinery Equipment Import & Export Corporation	Beijing	Beijing	(010)63474506
中国机械设备进出口总公司	北京市	北京市	(010)63261865
Beijing Cellstar Co.,Ltd.	Beijing	Beijing	(010)64602050
北京蜂星事达电讯有限公司	北京市	北京市	(010)64672648

3674: Sewing Machine 缝纫机制造业

The industry accounts for 0.080% of the total revenue of China's industrial sector in 2002. The rate of return on assets is 7.44%. 82.84% of all firms in the industry made a profit while 17.16% had negative returns.The top province in terms of the industry's revenue is Zhejiang, accounting for 37.46% of the total revenue.
2002年本行业收入占全行业的 0.080%，资产利润率为 7.44%。82.84%的企业赢利，17.16%的企业亏损。收入最高的省为浙江省，占本行业的37.46%。

	Total number of firms 企业总数	Total number of employees 职工总数	Total revenue (Mil.RMB) 总销售收入 (百万元)	Total profit (Mil.RMB) 总利润 (百万元)	Return on assets 资产利润率 (%)	Return on equity 权益利润率 (%)	Labour productivity ('000 RMB/ worker) 劳动生产率 (千元/人)	Debts/ assets 资产负债率 (%)	Total assets (Mil.RMB) 总资产 (百万元)
Industry Overall 行业总体	169	39,021	8,547	703	7.44	16.82	60.80	55.76	9,447

	Number of firms 企业个数	Average number of employees 平均职工人数	Average revenue ('000 RMB) 平均销售收入 (千元)	Average profit ('000 RMB) 平均利润 (千元)	Return on assets 资产利润率 (%)	Return on equity 权益利润率 (%)	Labour productivity ('000 RMB/ worker) 劳动生产率 (千元/人)	Debts/ assets 资产负债率 (%)	Average total assets ('000 RMB) 平均总资产 (千元)
By ownership 产业所有权									
State-owned 国有	11	177	3,306	-1,482	-3.57	-172.02	-2.07	97.93	41,511
Collective-owned 集体	14	272	32,900	1,950	6.55	21.36	36.23	69.35	29,794
Foreign & Overseas Chinese Funded 三资	38	244	91,896	8,227	7.99	14.19	75.88	43.72	102,980
By regional distribution 地区分布									
Central-North 华北	19	175	67,371	7,901	13.95	27.70	76.24	49.64	56,632
Beijing 北京									
Tianjin 天津	17	162	47,221	5,341	11.79	24.14	57.07	51.17	45,316
Hebei 河北	2	281	238,647	29,657	19.41	35.81	170.59	45.80	152,814
Shanxi 山西									
Inner Mongolia 内蒙古									
Northeast 东北	3	234	18,848	693	2.42	6.04	50.37	59.96	28,682
Liaoning 辽宁	3	234	18,848	693	2.42	6.04	50.37	59.96	28,682
Jilin 吉林									
Heilongjiang 黑龙江									
Central-East 华东	120	230	42,054	2,830	5.91	16.76	57.67	64.72	47,875
Shanghai 上海	30	210	39,166	1,032	1.24	3.82	47.66	67.52	83,241
Jiangsu 江苏	22	240	26,815	1,279	5.15	15.71	31.66	67.20	24,818
Zhejiang 浙江	63	235	50,821	4,434	10.80	27.54	74.49	60.78	41,045
Anhui 安徽									
Fujian 福建	1	78	7,463	400	15.56	30.51	41.40	49.01	2,571
Jiangxi 江西									
Shandong 山东	4	292	18,095	205	0.72	3.88	17.31	81.31	28,341
Central-South 中南	17	223	61,292	2,573	4.12	7.98	42.43	48.37	62,406
Henan 河南	3	288	7,647	53	0.38	1.11	22.16	66.07	14,182
Hubei 湖北	1	470	39,103	3	0.03	0.11	38.70	77.10	11,907
Hunan 湖南	4	142	8,900	868	2.19	7.81	30.31	72.03	39,703
Guangdong 广东	9	210	104,925	4,455	4.73	8.25	56.24	42.65	94,182
Guangxi 广西									
Hainan 海南									
Southwest 西南	1	464	35,124	2,492	6.31	13.90	27.14	54.62	39,512
Chongqing 重庆	1	464	35,124	2,492	6.31	13.90	27.14	54.62	39,512
Sichuan 四川									
Guizhou 贵州									
Yunnan 云南									
Tibet 西藏									
Northwest 西北	9	347	120,783	18,317	11.45	16.31	101.66	29.80	159,958
Shaanxi 陕西	9	347	120,783	18,317	11.45	16.31	101.66	29.80	159,958
Gansu 甘肃									
Qinghai 青海									
Ningxia 宁夏									
Xinjiang 新疆									

Year 年份	Number of firms 企业个数	Rate of change 变化率 (%)	Number of employees 职工人数 (人)	Rate of change 变化率 (%)	Total revenue (Mil. RMB) 总销售收入 (百万元)	Rate of change 变化率 (%)	Total profit (Mil RMB) 总利润 (百万元)	Rate of change 变化率 (%)
2000	129		35,601		6,261		435	
2001	164	27.13	37,718	5.95	7,274	16.18	577	32.64
2002	169	3.05	39,021	3.45	8,547	17.50	703	21.84

Major Products 主要产品	Output 产量	Unit 单位
Sewing Machine 缝纫机	691	10,000 Sets 万架

10 Main Firms with Maximal Revenue (year founded) 收入最大的十家主要企业（创办年份）	City 城市	Province 省	Telephone/fax 电话/传真	Number of employees 职工人数	Ownership 产业所有权	Revenue ('000 RMB) 销售收入(千元)	Profit('000 RMB) (rank) 利润(千元)(排名)	Total assets ('000 RMB) 总资产(千元)	Major products 主要产品
Feiyue Group Co., ltd.	Taizhou	Zhejiang	(0576)8155828		Limited-Liability				Industrial Sewing Machine工
飞跃集团有限公司(1986)	台州市	浙江省	(0576)8155800	1,672	有限公司	1,126,679	95,231(1)	876,851	业缝纫机
Zhuhai Brother Industries Co.,Ltd.	Zhuhai	Guangdong	(0756)8610174		Overseas Chinese-funded				Household Sewing Machine家
珠海兄弟工业有限公司(1991)	珠海市	广东省	(0756)8610134	644	港澳台资	513,370	19,665(12)	162,108	用缝纫机
Xi 'An Brother Standard Industry Co.,Ltd.	Xi'an	Shannxi	(029)8316684		Foreign Funded				Sewing Machine
西安兄弟标准工业有限公司(1995)	西安市	陕西省	(029)8314514	368	外商投资	399,475	77,391(3)	350,207	缝纫机
China Jemsy Sewing Machine Industrial Corp	Taizhou	Zhejiang	(0576)8201981		Joint Stock				Industrial Sewing Machine工
宝石缝纫机实业公司(1993)	台州市	浙江省	(0576)8202667	1,009	股份制	380,240	52,025(6)	263,488	业缝纫机
Joge Sewing Machine Co.,Ltd.	Taizhou	Zhejiang	(0576)7338213		Joint Stock				Sewing Machine
中捷缝纫机股份有限公司(1994)	台州市	浙江省	(0576)7332587	948	股份制	314,615	40,165(7)	303,940	缝纫机
Tianma Sewing Machine Manufacturing Co.,Ltd.	Tianjin	Tianjin	(022)27539904		Foreign Funded				High Speed Whipstitch Machine高
天马缝纫机制造有限公司(1988)	天津市	天津市	(022)27539903	201	外商投资	303,730	60,580(5)	174,711	速包缝机
Shanggong Group Co.,Ltd.	Shanghai	Shanghai	(021)68407700		Overseas Chinese-funded				Sewing Machine
上工股份有限公司(1965)	上海市	上海市	(021)63302939	1,321	港澳台资	293,893	9,485(16)	1,054,622	缝纫机
China Standard Sewing Machine Company Shanghai Huigong Sewing Machine	Shanghai	Shanghai	(021)64954311		Collective-owned				Sewing machine
No.3 Factory中国标准缝纫机公司上海惠工缝纫机三厂(1991)	上海市	上海市	(021)64853208	486	集体企业	235,380	23,824(11)	182,715	缝纫机械
Zhejinag Jack Sewing Machine Co., Ltd.	Taizhou	Zhejiang	(0576)8177795		Private Owned				Industrial Sewing Machine工
浙江杰克缝纫机有限公司(1995)	台州市	浙江省	(0576)8177758	665	私营企业	218,559	11,718(13)	78,767	业缝纫机
Gaolin Electromechanical Industrial (Shenzhen) Co., Ltd.	Shenzhen	Guangdong	(0755)27120592		Foreign Funded				Industrial Sewing Machine工
高林机电实业（深圳）有限公司(1996)	深圳市	广东省	(0755)27120594	430	外商投资	212,406	27,211(9)	361,693	业缝纫机

Top 10 Cities by Revenue 销售收入排名前10位城市	Province 省	Market share 市场份额 (%)	Number of firms 企业个数
Taizhou 台州市	Zhejiang 浙江省	26.17	13
Shanghai 上海市	Shanghai 上海市	13.75	30
Xi'an 西安市	Shannxi 陕西省	12.65	8
Tianjin 天津市	Tianjin 天津市	9.39	17
Zhuhai 珠海市	Guangdong 广东省	7.92	6
Suzhou 苏州市	Jiangsu 江苏省	5.75	14
Langfang 廊坊市	Hebei 河北省	5.58	1
Ningbo 宁波市	Zhejiang 浙江省	5.27	24
Lishui 丽水市	Zhejiang 浙江省	3.77	12
Shenzhen 深圳市	Guangdong 广东省	2.49	1

10 Major Wholesalers 十家主要批发商	City 城市	Province 省	Telephone/Fax 电话/传真
SU MEC	Nanjing	Jiangsu	(025)4511888
中设江苏机械设备进出口（集团）公司	南京市	江苏省	(025)4411772
China Poster Mobile Communications Equipment Co.,Ltd.	Beijing	Beijing	(010)66426993
中邮普泰移动通信设备股份有限公司	北京市	北京市	(010)66426837
Sino Kama Co., Ltd.	Shanghai	Shanghai	(021)62031188
中泰凯马股份有限公司	上海市	上海市	(021)62030851
China Huayuan Group Co.,Ltd.	Shanghai	Shanghai	(021)62031188
中国华源集团有限公司	上海市	上海市	(021)62032288
Zhejiang Crand Imp.& Exp.Co.,Ltd.	Ningbo	Zhejiang	(0574)87720170
浙江远大进出口有限公司	宁波市	浙江省	(0574)87723350
Shandong Machinery Import & Export Group Corporation	Qingdao	Shandong	(0532)2661628
山东省机械进出口集团公司	青岛市	山东省	(0532)2991655
Qingdao Haier International Trade Co.,Ltd.	Qingdao	Shandong	(0532)8938337
青岛海尔国际贸易有限公司	青岛市	山东省	(0532)8939494
Guangdong Machinery Import & Export Group Corporation	Guangzhou	Guangdong	(020)87782168
广东省机械进出口集团公司	广州市	广东省	(020)87771803
China National Machinery Equipment Import & Export Corporation	Beijing	Beijing	(010)63474506
中国机械设备进出口总公司	北京市	北京市	(010)63261865
Beijing Cellstar Co.,Ltd.	Beijing	Beijing	(010)64602050
北京蜂星事达电讯有限公司	北京市	北京市	(010)64672648

3675: Commerce, Food, and Service Machinery

商业、饮食业、服务业专用机械制造业

The industry accounts for 0.012% of the total revenue of China's industrial sector in 2002. The rate of return on assets is 6.09%. 69.64% of all firms in the industry made a profit while 30.36% had negative returns.The top province in terms of the industry's revenue is Guangdong, accounting for 41.41% of the total revenue.
2002年本行业收入占全行业的0.012%，资产利润率为6.09%。69.64%的企业赢利，30.36%的企业亏损。收入最高的省为广东省，占本行业的41.41%。

	Total number of firms 企业总数	Total number of employees 职工总数	Total revenue (Mil.RMB) 总销售收入(百万元)	Total profit (Mil.RMB) 总利润(百万元)	Return on assets 资产利润率(%)	Return on equity 权益利润率(%)	Labour productivity ('000 RMB/worker) 劳动生产率(千元/人)	Debts/assets 资产负债率(%)	Total assets (Mil.RMB) 总资产(百万元)
Industry Overall 行业总体	56	7,791	1,283	83	6.09	13.26	51.76	54.06	1,360

	Number of firms 企业个数	Average number of employees 平均职工人数	Average revenue ('000 RMB) 平均销售收入(千元)	Average profit ('000 RMB) 平均利润(千元)	Return on assets 资产利润率(%)	Return on equity 权益利润率(%)	Labour productivity ('000 RMB/worker) 劳动生产率(千元/人)	Debts/assets 资产负债率(%)	Average total assets ('000 RMB) 平均总资产(千元)
By ownership 产业所有权									
State-owned 国有	13	107	1,616	-327	-2.30	-6.23	3.02	63.07	14,220
Collective-owned 集体	9	77	21,641	821	13.76	19.66	87.85	30.01	5,967
Foreign & Overseas Chinese Funded 三资	7	123	24,537	-347	-1.17	-3.88	10.82	69.97	29,787
By regional distribution 地区分布									
Central-North 华北	13	154	12,707	330	1.79	6.62	17.12	72.97	18,433
Beijing 北京	5	37	4,948	126	2.61	4.80	35.35	45.56	4,812
Tianjin 天津	5	139	17,693	930	7.19	14.70	-2.06	51.09	12,929
Hebei 河北	3	372	17,329	-330	-0.66	-4.94	26.02	86.71	50,310
Shanxi 山西									
Inner Mongolia 内蒙古									
Northeast 东北	6	119	11,164	1,116	3.94	6.99	32.99	43.63	28,341
Liaoning 辽宁	3	74	10,516	1,794	5.01	7.49	47.00	33.19	35,844
Jilin 吉林	1	108	14,395	881	3.00	16.80	45.79	82.12	29,335
Heilongjiang 黑龙江	2	193	10,520	217	1.31	2.31	21.28	43.45	16,590
Central-East 华东	12	185	31,004	1,651	4.90	11.11	54.19	55.89	33,691
Shanghai 上海	2	115	17,610	-1,942	-3.65	-12.42	37.73	70.65	53,254
Jiangsu 江苏	4	225	44,970	4,218	7.59	15.24	63.04	50.19	55,553
Zhejiang 浙江									
Anhui 安徽									
Fujian 福建									
Jiangxi 江西									
Shandong 山东	6	182	26,159	1,137	9.03	18.74	50.36	51.84	12,595
Central-South 中南	20	109	31,408	2,400	9.73	18.38	96.21	47.07	24,671
Henan 河南	10	108	5,587	251	2.59	7.49	19.35	65.45	9,701
Hubei 湖北	1	287	31,757	155	0.78	1.20	37.74	35.39	19,950
Hunan 湖南									
Guangdong 广东	8	98	66,402	5,655	12.54	22.35	226.60	43.89	45,091
Guangxi 广西									
Hainan 海南	1	40	9,315	100	0.64	0.81	32.95	21.60	15,726
Southwest 西南	4	152	11,220	864	7.47	15.60	21.05	52.11	11,566
Chongqing 重庆	1	58	11,753	-1,014	-7.26	-13.62	36.95	46.67	13,959
Sichuan 四川	1	212	30,239	4,364	24.64	83.41	47.13	70.45	17,708
Guizhou 贵州	1	281	2,720	149	1.26	1.79	2.16	29.74	11,814
Yunnan 云南	1	55	168	-43	-1.55	-3.65	0.33	57.71	2,783
Tibet 西藏									
Northwest 西北	1	60	5,552	612	9.29	23.88	29.58	61.09	6,587
Shaanxi 陕西	1	60	5,552	612	9.29	23.88	29.58	61.09	6,587
Gansu 甘肃									
Qinghai 青海									
Ningxia 宁夏									
Xinjiang 新疆									

3675: Commerce, Food, and Service Machinery

商业、饮食业、服务业专用机械制造业

Year 年份	Number of firms 企业个数	Rate of change 变化率 (%)	Number of employees 职工人数 (人)	Rate of change 变化率 (%)	Total revenue (Mil. RMB) 总销售收入 (百万元)	Rate of change 变化率 (%)	Total profit (Mil RMB) 总利润 (百万元)	Rate of change 变化率 (%)
2000	64		10,928		930		41	
2001	60	-6.25	10,417	-4.68	1,093	17.53	11	-73.17
2002	56	-6.67	7,791	-25.21	1,283	17.38	83	654.55

Major Products 主要产品	Output 产量	Unit 单位
Cereal & Oilseed Processing Machinery 粮食加工机械	56	10,000 Units 万台

10 Main Firms with Maximal Revenue (year founded) 收入最大的十家主要企业（创办年份）	City 城市	Province 省	Telephone/fax 电话/传真	Number of employees 职工人数	Ownership 产业所有权	Revenue ('000 RMB) 销售收入 (千元)	Profit('000 RMB) (rank) 利润(千元)(排名)	Total assets ('000 RMB) 总资产 (千元)	Major products 主要产品
Shenzhen New Era Drinking Water Sci& Tech Co., Ltd. 深圳新世纪饮水科技有限公司(1992)	Shenzhen 深圳市	Guangdong 广东省	(0755)83868277 (0755)83300584	84	Limited-Liability 有限公司	306,467	18,658(2)	150,642	Drinking Water Machine 饮用水机
Jiangsu Sea lion Machinery Group Corp. 江苏海狮机械集团有限公司(1970)	Suzhou 苏州市	Jiangsu 江苏省	(0512)58660864 (0512)58660927	560	Limited-Liability 有限公司	122,560	15,250(3)	191,730	Washing Machinery 洗涤机械
Shandong Longkou Cooking Machine Factory 山东省龙口市炊事机械厂(1962)	Yantai 烟台市	Shandong 山东省	(0535)8591152 (0535)8591152	292	Collective-owned 集体企业	68,000	3,690(8)	13,990	Noodle Press Machine 压面机
Shenzhen Xiongzhen Science & Technology Co., Ltd. 深圳市雄震科技有限公司(1998)	Shenzhen 深圳市	Guangdong 广东省	(0755)26780055 (0755)26798025	140	Private Owned 私营企业	67,192	24,977(1)	134,509	Auto Selling Machine 自动售卖机
Taishan Fucheng Guangming Hardware Factory 台山市附城光明五金厂(1989)	Jiangmen 江门市	Guangdong 广东省	(0750)5656082 (0750)5669929	139	Private Enterprises 私营独资	55,350	229(29)	15,664	Capsular Jack Fittings 千斤顶配件
Tianjin Dingjia Machinery Co., Ltd. 天津顶嘉机械有限公司(1996)	Tianjin 天津市	Tianjin 天津市	(022)25327914 (022)25237913	92	Overseas Chinese-funded 港澳台资	49,310	6,651(4)	52,206	Food Machinery 食品机械
Longkou Welfare Metal Products Factory 龙口市福利金属制品厂(1987)	Yantai 烟台市	Shandong 山东省	(0535)8559197 (0535)8559197	95	Collective-owned 集体企业	43,440	1,425(11)	8,900	Noodle Press Machine 压面机
Langfang Tongyong Machinery Co., Ltd. 廊坊通用机械有限公司(1983)	Langfang 廊坊市	Hebei 河北省	(0316)2680547 (0316)2682249	536	Limited-Liability 有限公司	36,539	1,835(10)	94,033	Colloid Mill 胶体磨
Sichuan Yongguan Supermarket Equipment Co., ltd. 四川永冠超市设备有限公司(2000)	Chengdu 成都市	Sichuan 四川省	(028)87514342 (028)87515818	212	Limited Liability 有限公司	30,239	4,364(7)	17,708	Supermarket Equipment 超市设备
Changzhou Shule Kitchen Co., Ltd. 常州市墅乐厨具有限公司(1996)	Changzhou 常州市	Jiangsu 江苏省	(0519)3431042 (0519)3431183	220	Joint Stock 股份制	29,420	540(21)	17,620	Noodles Machine 摇面机

Top 10 Cities by Revenue 销售收入排名前10位城市	Province 省	Market share 市场份额 (%)	Number of firms 企业个数
Shenzhen 深圳市	Guangdong 广东省	31.48	3
Yantai 烟台市	Shandong 山东省	11.34	3
Suzhou 苏州市	Jiangsu 江苏省	9.55	1
Jiangmen 江门市	Guangdong 广东省	7.93	2
Tianjin 天津市	Tianjin 天津市	6.90	5
Changzhou 常州市	Jiangsu 江苏省	4.47	3
Langfang 廊坊市	Hebei 河北省	2.85	1
Shanghai 上海市	Shanghai 上海市	2.75	2
Wuhan 武汉市	Hubei 湖北省	2.48	1
Chengdu 成都市	Sichuan 四川省	2.36	1

10 Major Wholesalers 十家主要批发商	City 城市	Province 省	Telephone/Fax 电话/传真
SU MEC 中设江苏机械设备进出口（集团）公司	Nanjing 南京市	Jiangsu 江苏省	(025)4511888 (025)4411772
China Poster Mobile Communications Equipment Co.,Ltd. 中邮普泰移动通信设备股份有限公司	Beijing 北京市	Beijing 北京市	(010)66426993 (010)66426837
Sino Kama Co., Ltd. 中泰凯马股份有限公司	Shanghai 上海市	Shanghai 上海市	(021)62031188 (021)62030851
China Huayuan Group Co.,Ltd. 中国华源集团有限公司	Shanghai 上海市	Shanghai 上海市	(021)62031188 (021)62032288
Zhejiang Crand Imp.& Exp.Co.,Ltd. 浙江远大进出口有限公司	Ningbo 宁波市	Zhejiang 浙江省	(0574)87720170 (0574)87723350
Shandong Machinery Import & Export Group Corporation 山东省机械进出口集团公司	Qingdao 青岛市	Shandong 山东省	(0532)2661628 (0532)2991655
Qingdao Haier International Trade Co.,Ltd. 青岛海尔国际贸易有限公司	Qingdao 青岛市	Shandong 山东省	(0532)8938337 (0532)8939494
Guangdong Machinery Import & Export Group Corporation 广东省机械进出口集团公司	Guangzhou 广州市	Guangdong 广东省	(020)87782168 (020)87771803
China National Machinery Equipment Import & Export Corporation 中国机械设备进出口总公司	Beijing 北京市	Beijing 北京市	(010)63474506 (010)63261865
Beijing Cellstar Co.,Ltd. 北京蜂星事达电讯有限公司	Beijing 北京市	Beijing 北京市	(010)64602050 (010)64672648

3676: Postal Service Machinery 邮政机械及器材制造业

The industry accounts for 0.005% of the total revenue of China's industrial sector in 2002. The rate of return on assets is 1.62%. 57.14% of all firms in the industry made a profit while 42.86% had negative returns.The top province in terms of the industry's revenue is Fujian, accounting for 35.24% of the total revenue.
2002年本行业收入占全行业的 0.005%，资产利润率为 1.62%。57.14%的企业赢利，42.86%的企业亏损。收入最高的省为福建省，占本行业的35.24%。

	Total number of firms 企业总数	Total number of employees 职工总数	Total revenue (Mil.RMB) 总销售收入（百万元）	Total profit (Mil.RMB) 总利润（百万元）	Return on assets 资产利润率（%）	Return on equity 权益利润率（%）	Labour productivity ('000 RMB/worker) 劳动生产率（千元/人）	Debts/assets 资产负债率（%）	Total assets (Mil.RMB) 总资产（百万元）
Industry Overall 行业总体	21	3,042	495	9	1.62	3.49	52.98	53.53	542

	Number of firms 企业个数	Average number of employees 平均职工人数	Average revenue ('000 RMB) 平均销售收入（千元）	Average profit ('000 RMB) 平均利润（千元）	Return on assets 资产利润率（%）	Return on equity 权益利润率（%）	Labour productivity ('000 RMB/worker) 劳动生产率（千元/人）	Debts/assets 资产负债率（%）	Average total assets ('000 RMB) 平均总资产（千元）
By ownership 产业所有权									
State-owned 国有	10	207	17,868	-1,220	-4.30	-10.38	32.97	58.61	28,388
Collective-owned 集体	3	85	4,306	-68	-0.54		13.00	121.39	12,533
Foreign & Overseas Chinese Funded 三资	2	64	88,880	6,184	8.71	10.95	252.94	20.41	70,991
By regional distribution 地区分布									
Central-North 华北	4	212	12,552	-3,062	-16.21	-27.61	18.01	41.28	18,892
Beijing 北京	1	43	7,110	-4,247	-15.43	-15.43	0.23		27,520
Tianjin 天津	3	268	14,365	-2,667	-16.65	-47.48	18.96	64.93	16,016
Hebei 河北									
Shanxi 山西									
Inner Mongolia 内蒙古									
Northeast 东北									
Liaoning 辽宁									
Jilin 吉林									
Heilongjiang 黑龙江									
Central-East 华东	12	151	34,210	1,785	5.32	9.95	78.09	46.51	33,532
Shanghai 上海	1	195	13,752	527	1.03	1.87	86.27	44.88	51,234
Jiangsu 江苏	3	118	20,970	43	0.15	0.27	50.95	43.26	28,510
Zhejiang 浙江	2	111	8,656	279	2.78	3.95	36.12	29.73	10,036
Anhui 安徽	1	140	18,062	542	3.07	6.35	24.33	51.69	17,678
Fujian 福建	2	78	87,292	8,141	13.67	18.77	217.18	27.16	59,535
Jiangxi 江西	1	33	10,698	100	1.26	10.18	88.12	87.63	7,941
Shandong 山东	2	356	56,604	1,639	3.25	11.66	82.25	72.12	50,430
Central-South 中南	4	77	5,011	-49	-0.37		13.72	115.83	13,347
Henan 河南									
Hubei 湖北	1	180	4,450	102	1.47		8.88	155.10	6,960
Hunan 湖南	1	14	703	-219	-3.52	-5.31	12.07	33.75	6,229
Guangdong 广东	2	56	7,445	-40	-0.20		21.69	121.74	20,100
Guangxi 广西									
Hainan 海南									
Southwest 西南	1	80	14,686	-175	-1.64	-25.11	4.89	93.48	10,697
Chongqing 重庆									
Sichuan 四川	1	80	14,686	-175	-1.64	-25.11	4.89	93.48	10,697
Guizhou 贵州									
Yunnan 云南									
Tibet 西藏									
Northwest 西北									
Shaanxi 陕西									
Gansu 甘肃									
Qinghai 青海									
Ningxia 宁夏									
Xinjiang 新疆									

3676: Postal Service Machinery 邮政机械及器材制造业

Year 年份	Number of firms 企业个数	Rate of change 变化率 (%)	Number of employees 职工人数 (人)	Rate of change 变化率 (%)	Total revenue (Mil. RMB) 总销售收入 (百万元)	Rate of change 变化率 (%)	Total profit (Mil RMB) 总利润 (百万元)	Rate of change 变化率 (%)
2000	21		3,819		428		19	
2001	20	-4.76	3,621	-5.18	527	23.13	29	52.63
2002	21	5.00	3,042	-15.99	495	-6.07	9	-68.97

Major Products 主要产品	Output 产量	Unit 单位

10 Main Firms with Maximal Revenue (year founded) 收入最大的十家主要企业（创办年份）	City 城市	Province 省	Telephone/fax 电话/传真	Number of employees 职工人数	Ownership 产业所有权	Revenue ('000 RMB) 销售收入 (千元)	Profit('000 RMB) (rank) 利润(千元) (排名)	Total assets ('000 RMB) 总资产 (千元)	Major products 主要产品
Longkou Pengfei Communication Equipment Co., Ltd. 龙口市鹏飞通讯设备有限公司(1985)	Yantai 烟台市	Shandong 山东省	(0535)8581228 (0535)8581356	190	Limited-Liability 有限公司	70,008	6,830(2)	30,105	Junction Box 分线箱
Ji'Nan Putian Communications Equipment Factory 济南普天通信设备厂(1958)	Jinan 济南市	Shandong 山东省	(0531)3256008 (0531)3256530	521	State-owned 国有企业	43,200	-	70,754	Refitted Vehicle 改装汽车
Tianjin Putian Communication Equipment Factory 天津普天通信设备厂(1953)	Tianjin 天津市	Tianjin 天津市	(022)24312435 (022)24312174	620	State-owned 国有企业	38,668	-	45,914	Postal Bags 邮袋
Jiangsu Postal Printing Factory 江苏省邮电印刷厂(1970)	Changzhou 常州市	Jiangsu 江苏省	(0519)6750338 (0519)6757809	213	State-owned 国有企业	37,290	-	65,620	Residence Letter & Newspaper Box住宅信报箱
Liyang Xinhua Electromechanical Equipment Manufacturing Co., Ltd.溧阳市新华机电设备制造有限公司(1994)	Changzhou 常州市	Jiangsu 江苏省	(0519)7871800 (0519)7871188	90	Private Owned 私营企业	20,120	670(3)	6,370	
Ma'anshan Circuit Equipment Company 马鞍山市线路器材公司(1979)	Maanshan 马鞍山市	Anhui 安徽省	(0555)2222935 (0555)2217209	140	Joint Stock 股份制	18,062	542(4)	17,678	Postal Circuitry Equipment邮电线路器材
Shanghai Postal Service General Technology Equipment Company 上海邮政通用技术设备公司(1992)	Shanghai 上海市	Shanghai 上海市	(021)65489096 (021)65480805	195	State-owned 国有企业	13,752	527(5)	51,234	Postal Machinery Equipment邮政械及器材
Jiangxi Postal Service Machinery Factory 江西省邮政机械厂(1978)	Nanchang 南昌市	Jiangxi 江西省	(0791)6105519 (0791)3849660	33	State-owned 国有企业	10,698	100(10)	7,941	Postal Newspaper and Periodical Stand邮政报刊亭
Guangzhou Panyu Qiaojianhua Post And Telecommunication Equipment Factory广州市番禺区市桥建华邮电器材厂(1965)	Guangzhou 广州市	Guangdong 广东省	(020)84876450 (020)84892461	72	Collective-owned 集体企业	8,490	-	35,465	Pyrocondensation Bushing 热缩套管
Ningbo Guomai Postal Service Equipment Co., Ltd. 宁波国脉邮政器材有限公司(1994)	Ningbo 宁波市	Zhejiang 浙江省	(0574)65272288 (0574)65273118	75	Private Enterprises 私营独资	6,011	485(6)	6,151	Single-house Information Box单户信息箱

Top 10 Cities by Revenue 销售收入排名前10位城市	Province 省	Market share 市场份额 (%)	Number of firms 企业个数
Fuzhou 福州市	Fujian 福建省	35.24	2
Yantai 烟台市	Shandong 山东省	14.13	1
Changzhou 常州市	Jiangsu 江苏省	11.59	2
Jinan 济南市	Shandong 山东省	8.72	1
Tianjin 天津市	Tianjin 天津市	8.70	3
Maanshan 马鞍山市	Anhui 安徽省	3.65	1
Guangzhou 广州市	Guangdong 广东省	3.01	2
Chengdu 成都市	Sichuan 四川省	2.96	1
Shanghai 上海市	Shanghai 上海市	2.78	1
Jiaxing 嘉兴市	Zhejiang 浙江省	2.28	1

10 Major Wholesalers 十家主要批发商	City 城市	Province 省	Telephone/Fax 电话/传真
SU MEC 中设江苏机械设备进出口（集团）公司	Nanjing 南京市	Jiangsu 江苏省	(025)4511888 (025)4411772
China Poster Mobile Communications Equipment Co.,Ltd. 中邮普泰移动通信设备股份有限公司	Beijing 北京市	Beijing 北京市	(010)66426993 (010)66426837
Sino Kama Co., Ltd. 中泰凯马股份有限公司	Shanghai 上海市	Shanghai 上海市	(021)62031188 (021)62030851
China Huayuan Group Co.,Ltd. 中国华源集团有限公司	Shanghai 上海市	Shanghai 上海市	(021)62031188 (021)62032288
Zhejiang Crand Imp.& Exp.Co.,Ltd. 浙江远大进出口有限公司	Ningbo 宁波市	Zhejiang 浙江省	(0574)87720170 (0574)87723350
Shandong Machinery Import & Export Group Corporation 山东省机械进出口集团公司	Qingdao 青岛市	Shandong 山东省	(0532)2661628 (0532)2991655
Qingdao Haier International Trade Co.,Ltd. 青岛海尔国际贸易有限公司	Qingdao 青岛市	Shandong 山东省	(0532)8938337 (0532)8939494
Guangdong Machinery Import & Export Group Corporation 广东省机械进出口集团公司	Guangzhou 广州市	Guangdong 广东省	(020)87782168 (020)87771803
China National Machinery Equipment Import & Export Corporation 中国机械设备进出口总公司	Beijing 北京市	Beijing 北京市	(010)63474506 (010)63261865
Beijing Cellstar Co.,Ltd. 北京蜂星事达电讯有限公司	Beijing 北京市	Beijing 北京市	(010)64602050 (010)64672648

3677: Environmental Protection Machinery 环境保护机械制造业

The industry accounts for 0.060% of the total revenue of China's industrial sector in 2002. The rate of return on assets is 3.50%. 85.37% of all firms in the industry made a profit while 14.63% had negative returns.The top province in terms of the industry's revenue is Zhejiang, accounting for 32.22% of the total revenue.
2002年本行业收入占全行业的 0.060%，资产利润率为 3.50%。85.37%的企业赢利，14.63%的企业亏损。收入最高的省为浙江省，占本行业的32.22%。

	Total number of firms 企业总数	Total number of employees 职工总数	Total revenue (Mil.RMB) 总销售收入（百万元）	Total profit (Mil.RMB) 总利润（百万元）	Return on assets 资产利润率（%）	Return on equity 权益利润率（%）	Labour productivity ('000 RMB/ worker) 劳动生产率（千元/人）	Debts/ assets 资产负债率（%）	Total assets (Mil.RMB) 总资产（百万元）
Industry Overall 行业总体	246	30,353	6,484	447	3.50	6.49	68.27	46.09	12,779

	Number of firms 企业个数	Average number of employees 平均职工人数	Average revenue ('000 RMB) 平均销售收入（千元）	Average profit ('000 RMB) 平均利润（千元）	Return on assets 资产利润率（%）	Return on equity 权益利润率（%）	Labour productivity ('000 RMB/ worker) 劳动生产率（千元/人）	Debts/ assets 资产负债率（%）	Average total assets ('000 RMB) 平均总资产（千元）
By ownership 产业所有权									
State-owned 国有	17	176	20,589	-426	-0.88	-4.94	33.03	82.18	48,354
Collective-owned 集体	30	127	20,029	1,689	8.26	23.03	55.69	64.11	20,445
Foreign & Overseas Chinese Funded 三资	42	92	25,110	2,361	5.91	10.04	100.37	41.19	39,977
By regional distribution 地区分布									
Central-North 华北	31	113	17,498	1,362	3.08	6.12	51.18	49.68	44,249
Beijing 北京	16	100	20,988	3,078	5.23	7.63	72.09	31.41	58,815
Tianjin 天津	5	36	5,388	52	0.57	2.51	6.52	77.46	9,258
Hebei 河北	8	200	22,333	-919	-1.97	-22.00	38.39	91.03	46,538
Shanxi 山西	2	55	513	24	0.40	5.45	5.19	92.70	6,035
Inner Mongolia 内蒙古									
Northeast 东北	17	197	15,444	793	0.35	0.53	70.35	32.41	223,401
Liaoning 辽宁	14	213	14,892	625	0.24	0.35	71.85	32.24	262,859
Jilin 吉林	3	122	18,023	1,577	4.02	6.45	58.20	37.77	39,267
Heilongjiang 黑龙江									
Central-East 华东	158	123	31,452	2,334	5.41	11.07	72.98	51.11	43,128
Shanghai 上海	20	81	15,934	420	2.25	4.22	70.27	46.80	18,685
Jiangsu 江苏	80	93	20,068	1,157	5.77	12.38	61.09	53.41	20,060
Zhejiang 浙江	30	175	69,644	4,749	5.91	12.80	91.80	53.82	80,332
Anhui 安徽	7	174	23,485	3,098	6.18	15.42	49.91	59.95	50,156
Fujian 福建	7	225	57,898	7,869	4.59	6.98	104.32	34.20	171,314
Jiangxi 江西	1	82	14,490	460	3.10	8.42	54.78	63.26	14,860
Shandong 山东	13	178	28,608	3,704	5.60	14.29	61.57	60.84	66,206
Central-South 中南	35	102	18,924	624	3.17	9.29	60.81	65.81	19,661
Henan 河南	9	183	22,352	542	1.70	11.06	44.02	84.59	31,823
Hubei 湖北	10	62	10,554	676	5.91	9.03	55.79	34.53	11,435
Hunan 湖南	3	78	6,624	128	0.73	1.51	32.47	51.88	17,602
Guangdong 广东	9	89	13,269	-247	-1.37	-4.53	29.54	69.67	17,987
Guangxi 广西	4	65	54,086	3,012	16.57	28.84	301.21	42.54	18,177
Hainan 海南									
Southwest 西南	3	80	6,646	323	3.94	5.95	44.38	33.74	8,189
Chongqing 重庆									
Sichuan 四川	2	107	5,010	332	3.15	4.87	33.10	35.43	10,535
Guizhou 贵州									
Yunnan 云南	1	28	9,920	305	8.72	11.41	130.21	23.56	3,498
Tibet 西藏									
Northwest 西北	2	115	13,747	-15	-0.04	-0.06	39.37	40.23	41,099
Shaanxi 陕西									
Gansu 甘肃	2	115	13,747	-15	-0.04	-0.06	39.37	40.23	41,099
Qinghai 青海									
Ningxia 宁夏									
Xinjiang 新疆									

3677: Environmental Protection Machinery 环境保护机械制造业

Year 年份	Number of firms 企业个数	Rate of change 变化率 (%)	Number of employees 职工人数 (人)	Rate of change 变化率 (%)	Total revenue (Mil. RMB) 总销售收入 (百万元)	Rate of change 变化率 (%)	Total profit (Mil RMB) 总利润 (百万元)	Rate of change 变化率 (%)
2000	186		31,658		4,990		407	
2001	221	18.82	33,718	6.51	5,891	18.06	430	5.65
2002	246	11.31	30,353	-9.98	6,484	10.07	447	3.95

Major Products 主要产品	Output 产量	Unit 单位
Preventing Equipment for Air Pollution 大气污染防治设备	142,999	Ton 吨

10 Main Firms with Maximal Revenue (year founded) 收入最大的十家主要企业（创办年份）	City 城市	Province 省	Telephone/fax 电话/传真	Number of employees 职工人数	Ownership 产业所有权	Revenue ('000 RMB) 销售收入 (千元)	Profit('000 RMB) (rank) 利润(千元) (排名)	Total assets ('000 RMB) 总资产 (千元)	Major products 主要产品
Tianjie Group Co., Ltd. 天洁集团有限公司(1995)	Shaoxing 绍兴市	Zhejiang 浙江省	(0575)7051717 (0575)7052108	826	Joint Stock 股份制	562,592	45,194(2)	331,358	Environment Protecting Equipment环保设备机械
Zhejiang Feida Electromechanical Group Corpration. 浙江菲达机电集团有限公司(1995)	Shaoxing 绍兴市	Zhejiang 浙江省	(0575)7212511 (0575)7214695	1,326	State Enterprises 国有独资	418,901	39,523(3)	980,234	Electric Dust Remover 电除尘器
Guilin Reecat Environment Industry Co., Ltd. 桂林利凯特环保实业有限公司(1991)	Guilin 桂林市	Guangxi 广西	(0773)5857335	60	Overseas Chinese-funded 港澳台资	188,470	11,800(10)	48,120	
Jiangsu Pengyao Group Co., Ltd. 江苏鹏鹞集团有限公司(1984)	Wuxi 无锡市	Jiangsu 江苏省	(0510)7062960 (0510)7061990	400	Joint Stock 股份制	168,080	14,000(8)	119,750	Water Quality Pollution Prevention and Cure Equipment水质污染防治设备
Xuanhua Metallurgy Environment Protecting Equipment Manufacturing Factory 宣化冶金环保设备制造厂(1965)	Zhangjiakou 张家口市	Hebei 河北省	(0313)3067141 (0313)3067734	597	State-owned 国有企业	97,960	-	257,980	Electric Dust Remover 电除尘器
Fujian Fengquan Group Co., Ltd. 福建丰泉集团有限公司(1996)	Fuzhou 福州市	Fujian 福建省	(0591)7808809 (0591)7856177	402	Limited-Liability 有限公司	90,610	15,671(6)	139,556	Incinerator 焚烧炉
Haining Jiehua Group 海宁洁华集团(1998)	Jiaxing 嘉兴市	Zhejiang 浙江省	(0573)7855220 (0573)7855220	346	Limited-Liability 有限公司	88,505	15,046(7)	83,793	Dust Remover 除尘设备
Anqiu Wenrui Machine Manufacturing Co., Ltd. 安丘汶瑞机械制造有限公司(1958)	Weifang 潍坊市	Shandong 山东省	(0536)4361881 (0536)4362807	719	Foreign Funded 外商投资	81,232	10,902(14)	161,455	Environment Protecting Equipment 环保设备
Beijing Greencool New Type Refrigeration Engineering Co., Ltd.北京格林柯尔新型制冷剂换装工程有限公司(2001)	Beijing 北京市	Beijing 北京市	(010)63012255	36	Foreign Funded 外商投资	79,510	51,292(1)	120,765	Refrigeration Pharmaceutical Equipment制冷剂设备
Nantong Huaxin Environment Protecting Equipment Engineering Co., Ltd.南通华新环保设备工程有限公司(1995)	Nantong 南通市	Jiangsu 江苏省	(0513)2560219 (0513)2560220	250	Foreign Funded 外商投资	75,505	4,150(27)	31,309	Environment Protecting Machinery环境保护机械

Top 10 Cities by Revenue 销售收入排名前10位城市	Province 省	Market share 市场份额 (%)	Number of firms 企业个数
Shaoxing 绍兴市	Zhejiang 浙江省	24.94	13
Wuxi 无锡市	Jiangsu 江苏省	16.05	49
Beijing 北京市	Beijing 北京市	5.18	16
Shanghai 上海市	Shanghai 上海市	4.91	20
Longyan 龙岩市	Fujian 福建省	4.56	5
Guilin 桂林市	Guangxi 广西	3.08	2
Suzhou 苏州市	Jiangsu 江苏省	2.58	8
Pingdingshan 平顶山市	Henan 河南省	2.31	2
Hangzhou 杭州市	Zhejiang 浙江省	2.17	8
Yangzhou 扬州市	Jiangsu 江苏省	1.94	9

10 Major Wholesalers 十家主要批发商	City 城市	Province 省	Telephone/Fax 电话/传真
SU MEC 中设江苏机械设备进出口（集团）公司	Nanjing 南京市	Jiangsu 江苏省	(025)4511888 (025)4411772
China Poster Mobile Communications Equipment Co.,Ltd. 中邮普泰移动通信设备股份有限公司	Beijing 北京市	Beijing 北京市	(010)66426993 (010)66426837
Sino Kama Co., Ltd. 中泰凯马股份有限公司	Shanghai 上海市	Shanghai 上海市	(021)62031188 (021)62030851
China Huayuan Group Co.,Ltd. 中国华源集团有限公司	Shanghai 上海市	Shanghai 上海市	(021)62031188 (021)62032288
Zhejiang Crand Imp.& Exp.Co.,Ltd. 浙江远大进出口有限公司	Ningbo 宁波市	Zhejiang 浙江省	(0574)87720170 (0574)87723350
Shandong Machinery Import & Export Group Corporation 山东省机械进出口集团公司	Qingdao 青岛市	Shandong 山东省	(0532)2661628 (0532)2991655
Qingdao Haier International Trade Co.,Ltd. 青岛海尔国际贸易有限公司	Qingdao 青岛市	Shandong 山东省	(0532)8938337 (0532)8939494
Guangdong Machinery Import & Export Group Corporation 广东省机械进出口集团公司	Guangzhou 广州市	Guangdong 广东省	(020)87782168 (020)87771803
China National Machinery Equipment Import & Export Corporation 中国机械设备进出口总公司	Beijing 北京市	Beijing 北京市	(010)63474506 (010)63261865
Beijing Cellstar Co.,Ltd. 北京蜂星事达电讯有限公司	Beijing 北京市	Beijing 北京市	(010)64602050 (010)64672648

3678: Security and Fire-fighting Equipment
社会公共安全设备及器材制造业

The industry accounts for 0.041% of the total revenue of China's industrial sector in 2002. The rate of return on assets is 5.72%. 86.02% of all firms in the industry made a profit while 13.98% had negative returns.The top province in terms of the industry's revenue is Jiangsu, accounting for 19.68% of the total revenue.
2002年本行业收入占全行业的0.041%，资产利润率为5.72%。86.02%的企业赢利，13.98%的企业亏损。收入最高的省为江苏省，占本行业的19.68%。

	Total number of firms 企业总数	Total number of employees 职工总数	Total revenue (Mil.RMB) 总销售收入 (百万元)	Total profit (Mil.RMB) 总利润 (百万元)	Return on assets 资产利润率 (%)	Return on equity 权益利润率 (%)	Labour productivity ('000 RMB/worker) 劳动生产率 (千元/人)	Debts/assets 资产负债率 (%)	Total assets (Mil.RMB) 总资产 (百万元)
Industry Overall 行业总体	186	28,801	4,414	319	5.72	13.67	59.26	58.12	5,577

	Number of firms 企业个数	Average number of employees 平均职工人数	Average revenue ('000 RMB) 平均销售收入 (千元)	Average profit ('000 RMB) 平均利润 (千元)	Return on assets 资产利润率 (%)	Return on equity 权益利润率 (%)	Labour productivity ('000 RMB/worker) 劳动生产率 (千元/人)	Debts/assets 资产负债率 (%)	Average total assets ('000 RMB) 平均总资产 (千元)
By ownership 产业所有权									
State-owned 国有	28	250	20,409	1,232	2.79	9.95	31.38	71.93	44,121
Collective-owned 集体	23	155	34,007	1,706	4.69	12.04	76.29	61.06	36,376
Foreign & Overseas Chinese Funded 三资	26	121	21,588	3,353	9.52	15.50	47.28	38.55	35,213
By regional distribution 地区分布									
Central-North 华北	31	131	19,098	3,546	10.27	17.59	125.70	41.61	34,528
Beijing 北京	11	70	13,761	1,108	6.55	12.64	53.76	48.17	16,909
Tianjin 天津	13	136	10,421	2,335	6.40	8.91	25.20	28.12	36,468
Hebei 河北	4	241	67,051	16,583	20.01	37.30	417.36	46.36	82,871
Shanxi 山西	2	173	12,066	185	0.55	11.37	44.51	95.14	33,465
Inner Mongolia 内蒙古	1	221	12,858	675	5.68	9.94	32.36	42.89	11,885
Northeast 东北	13	165	11,886	584	2.07	17.68	31.90	88.29	28,188
Liaoning 辽宁	8	163	10,753	779	2.45	24.71	32.65	90.10	31,857
Jilin 吉林	2	70	30,424	982	8.59	41.49	165.49	79.29	11,429
Heilongjiang 黑龙江	3	234	2,550	-203	-0.69	-4.71	3.85	85.41	29,574
Central-East 华东	99	167	26,291	1,549	5.36	14.24	46.89	62.39	28,907
Shanghai 上海	14	123	30,199	2,550	5.87	15.37	100.55	61.81	43,440
Jiangsu 江苏	26	188	33,419	1,486	5.22	13.83	52.13	62.25	28,473
Zhejiang 浙江	38	117	20,011	968	4.63	12.29	37.52	62.30	20,886
Anhui 安徽	5	244	31,965	1,240	5.39	13.06	45.56	58.73	23,001
Fujian 福建	6	340	35,595	4,767	9.79	22.13	29.35	55.75	48,687
Jiangxi 江西	4	111	8,788	158	1.98	8.18	37.36	75.79	7,959
Shandong 山东	6	295	23,690	1,129	2.41	8.36	27.11	71.15	46,791
Central-South 中南	32	129	23,045	1,286	5.78	12.11	63.48	52.29	22,261
Henan 河南	4	80	11,402	533	5.17	30.50	47.15	83.04	10,297
Hubei 湖北	3	73	5,662	94	0.93	1.70	17.98	45.01	10,102
Hunan 湖南	3	204	12,964	1,553	5.72	9.44	28.62	39.46	27,167
Guangdong 广东	18	147	33,869	1,859	6.31	13.14	70.60	52.01	29,479
Guangxi 广西	4	84	6,581	156	2.17	5.08	116.19	57.40	7,181
Hainan 海南									
Southwest 西南	4	112	12,896	110	0.45	1.13	20.42	60.02	24,259
Chongqing 重庆	1	190	23,848	42	0.10	0.17	23.35	38.40	40,920
Sichuan 四川	2	70	5,244	31	0.27	1.87	22.98	85.45	11,397
Guizhou 贵州									
Yunnan 云南	1	118	17,247	334	1.00	3.25	12.65	69.19	33,322
Tibet 西藏									
Northwest 西北	7	211	39,434	974	1.45	3.20	54.64	54.65	67,008
Shaanxi 陕西	6	231	45,806	1,134	1.45	3.21	57.64	54.64	77,994
Gansu 甘肃	1	91	1,200	12	1.10	2.64	8.87	58.41	1,094
Qinghai 青海									
Ningxia 宁夏									
Xinjiang 新疆									

3678: Security and Fire-fighting Equipment

社会公共安全设备及器材制造业

Year 年份	Number of firms 企业个数	Rate of change 变化率 (%)	Number of employees 职工人数 (人)	Rate of change 变化率 (%)	Total revenue (Mil. RMB) 总销售收入 (百万元)	Rate of change 变化率 (%)	Total profit (Mil RMB) 总利润 (百万元)	Rate of change 变化率 (%)
2000	187		36,378		3,734		323	
2001	183	-2.14	29,514	-18.87	3,857	3.29	295	-8.67
2002	186	1.64	28,801	-2.42	4,414	14.44	319	8.14

Major Products 主要产品	Output 产量	Unit 单位

10 Main Firms with Maximal Revenue (year founded) 收入最大的十家主要企业（创办年份）	City 城市	Province 省	Telephone/fax 电话/传真	Number of employees 职工人数	Ownership 产业所有权	Revenue ('000 RMB) 销售收入 (千元)	Profit('000 RMB) (rank) 利润(千元) (排名)	Total assets ('000 RMB) 总资产 (千元)	Major products 主要产品
Gulf Safety Technology Co., Ltd. 海湾安全技术股份有限公司(1993)	Qinhuangdao 秦皇岛市	Hebei 河北省	(0335)8502311 (0335)8051972	735	Joint Stock 股份制	236,655	60,940(1)	285,417	Detector 探测器
Zhejiang Jindun Fire Fighting Equipment Co., Ltd. 浙江金盾消防器材有限公司(1998)	Shaoxing 绍兴市	Zhejiang 浙江省	(0575)2031248 (0575)2031752	490	Private Owned 私营企业	214,858	14,610(5)	105,343	Fire Fighting Equipment 消防器材
Zhuhai Qianshan Dixin Safety & Guard Equipment Products Factory珠海市前山迪信安保器材制品厂(1995)	Zhuhai 珠海市	Guangdong 广东省	(0756)8622618 (0756)8622328	445	Collective-owned 集体企业	210,829	1,910(38)	13,800	DS820 DS820
Shanghai Songjiang Electronic Instrument Plant 上海市松江电子仪器厂(1986)	Shanghai 上海市	Shanghai 上海市	(021)57820515 (021)57713647	490	Collective-owned 集体企业	174,091	14,023(6)	348,772	Fire Detector火灾探测器
Fujian Yong'an Machinery Factory 福建永安机械厂(1962)	Sanming 三明市	Fujian 福建省	(0598)3838611 (0598)3837006	1,393	State-owned 国有企业	115,608	12,589(8)	149,634	Dried Powder Fire Extinguisher干粉灭火器
Xi'an System Sensor Electronics Co.,Ltd. 西安盛赛尔电子有限公司(1995)	Xi'an 西安市	Shannxi 陕西省	(029)5246253 (029)5246259	168	Foreign Funded 外商投资	112,170	22,980(3)	102,784	Fire Detector火灾探测器
Taizhou Hongbao Kaili Fire-Fighting Equipment Factory 泰州市鸿宝凯利消防器材厂(1983)	Taizhou 泰州市	Jiangsu 江苏省	(0523)6131739 (0523)6131567	83	Private Partnership 私营合伙	108,754	8,877(11)	43,121	Fire Fighting Costume 消防服装
Jiangsu Jing'an Fire Fighting Appliance Manufacturing Co.,Ltd. 江苏京安消防设备制造有限公司(1999)	Nanjing 南京市	Jiangsu 江苏省	(025)2806408 (025)2801833	500	Limited-Liability 有限公司	87,810	2,100(34)	31,810	Fireproof Door 防火门
Shandong Tianhe Enterprise Co., Ltd. 山东省天河企业有限公司(1951)	Linyi 临沂市	Shandong 山东省	(0539)8365112 (0539)8352540	944	State owned 国有企业	86,000	3,537(20)	143,049	Fire Engine 消防车
Fujian Tianguang Fire-Fighting Equipment Co., Ltd. 福建省天广消防器材有限公司(1996)	Quanzhou 泉州市	Fujian 福建省	(0595)6392888 (0595)6385228	410	Collective-owned 集体企业	67,116	14,944(4)	70,041	Fire Fighting Equipment消防器材产品

Top 10 Cities by Revenue 销售收入排名前10位城市	Province 省	Market share 市场份额 (%)	Number of firms 企业个数
Nanjing 南京市	Jiangsu 江苏省	10.92	7
Shanghai 上海市	Shanghai 上海市	9.58	14
Ningbo 宁波市	Zhejiang 浙江省	5.90	16
Qinhuangdao 秦皇岛市	Hebei 河北省	5.36	1
Zhuhai 珠海市	Guangdong 广东省	5.12	3
Xi'an 西安市	Shannxi 陕西省	5.04	5
Shaoxing 绍兴市	Zhejiang 浙江省	5.00	2
Taizhou 泰州市	Jiangsu 江苏省	3.98	5
Guangzhou 广州市	Guangdong 广东省	3.77	5
Beijing 北京市	Beijing 北京市	3.43	11

10 Major Wholesalers 十家主要批发商	City 城市	Province 省	Telephone/Fax 电话/传真
SU MEC 中设江苏机械设备进出口（集团）公司	Nanjing 南京市	Jiangsu 江苏省	(025)4511888 (025)4411772
China Poster Mobile Communications Equipment Co.,Ltd. 中邮普泰移动通信设备股份有限公司	Beijing 北京市	Beijing 北京市	(010)66426993 (010)66426837
Sino Kama Co., Ltd. 中泰凯马股份有限公司	Shanghai 上海市	Shanghai 上海市	(021)62031188 (021)62030851
China Huayuan Group Co.,Ltd. 中国华源集团有限公司	Shanghai 上海市	Shanghai 上海市	(021)62031188 (021)62032288
Zhejiang Crand Imp.& Exp.Co.,Ltd. 浙江远大进出口有限公司	Ningbo 宁波市	Zhejiang 浙江省	(0574)87720170 (0574)87723350
Shandong Machinery Import & Export Group Corporation 山东省机械进出口集团公司	Qingdao 青岛市	Shandong 山东省	(0532)2661628 (0532)2991655
Qingdao Haier International Trade Co.,Ltd. 青岛海尔国际贸易有限公司	Qingdao 青岛市	Shandong 山东省	(0532)8938337 (0532)8939494
Guangdong Machinery Import & Export Group Corporation 广东省机械进出口集团公司	Guangzhou 广州市	Guangdong 广东省	(020)87782168 (020)87771803
China National Machinery Equipment Import & Export Corporation 中国机械设备进出口总公司	Beijing 北京市	Beijing 北京市	(010)63474506 (010)63261865
Beijing Cellstar Co.,Ltd. 北京蜂星事达电讯有限公司	Beijing 北京市	Beijing 北京市	(010)64602050 (010)64672648

3679: Other Special Equipment 其他类未包括的专用设备制造业

The industry accounts for 0.068% of the total revenue of China's industrial sector in 2002. The rate of return on assets is 2.69%. 80.97% of all firms in the industry made a profit while 19.03% had negative returns.The top province in terms of the industry's revenue is Jiangsu, accounting for 17.88% of the total revenue.
2002年本行业收入占全行业的 0.068%，资产利润率为 2.69%。80.97%的企业赢利，19.03%的企业亏损。收入最高的省为江苏省，占本行业的17.88%。

	Total number of firms 企业总数	Total number of employees 职工总数	Total revenue (Mil.RMB) 总销售收入（百万元）	Total profit (Mil.RMB) 总利润（百万元）	Return on assets 资产利润率（%）	Return on equity 权益利润率（%）	Labour productivity ('000 RMB/worker) 劳动生产率（千元/人）	Debts/assets 资产负债率（%）	Total assets (Mil.RMB) 总资产（百万元）
Industry Overall 行业总体	247	48,451	7,283	285	2.69	7.07	46.32	62.00	10,624

	Number of firms 企业个数	Average number of employees 平均职工人数	Average revenue ('000 RMB) 平均销售收入（千元）	Average profit ('000 RMB) 平均利润（千元）	Return on assets 资产利润率（%）	Return on equity 权益利润率（%）	Labour productivity ('000 RMB/worker) 劳动生产率（千元/人）	Debts/assets 资产负债率（%）	Average total assets ('000 RMB) 平均总资产（千元）
By ownership 产业所有权									
State-owned 国有	40	333	27,733	-2,118	-3.35	-14.27	20.95	76.56	63,327
Collective-owned 集体	34	125	21,049	793	3.80	9.30	65.14	59.14	20,870
Foreign & Overseas Chinese Funded 三资	54	166	31,640	1,729	4.37	9.95	51.35	56.06	39,553
By regional distribution 地区分布									
Central-North 华北	47	180	34,808	1,716	3.26	12.90	63.74	74.76	52,711
Beijing 北京	18	236	57,080	2,608	2.72	12.20	78.81	77.73	95,974
Tianjin 天津	10	83	20,364	2,303	9.02	18.72	140.00	51.81	25,537
Hebei 河北	17	154	23,076	636	2.63	9.82	31.62	73.27	24,227
Shanxi 山西	2	394	6,299	-66	-0.16	-1.78	8.99	91.09	41,335
Inner Mongolia 内蒙古									
Northeast 东北	21	165	15,685	-1,108	-2.29	-5.84	23.39	60.84	48,504
Liaoning 辽宁	12	201	13,715	-3,262	-4.65	-13.15	10.13	64.65	70,177
Jilin 吉林	4	166	18,411	1,101	8.67	14.59	26.68	40.61	12,698
Heilongjiang 黑龙江	5	79	18,233	2,293	9.12	16.14	98.59	43.49	25,135
Central-East 华东	120	176	29,034	1,617	4.42	9.93	52.99	55.47	36,574
Shanghai 上海	24	65	17,039	1,069	5.25	14.41	70.76	63.54	20,347
Jiangsu 江苏	41	183	31,756	1,972	5.62	11.07	60.04	49.26	35,100
Zhejiang 浙江	23	168	42,622	2,237	5.27	12.41	71.01	57.50	42,418
Anhui 安徽	3	770	37,144	7,813	4.09	7.22	37.32	43.39	191,042
Fujian 福建	7	142	16,416	236	0.94	3.00	39.27	68.81	25,286
Jiangxi 江西	2	108	4,756	166	5.11	5.98	9.31	14.48	3,249
Shandong 山东	20	232	27,846	537	1.47	4.36	33.46	66.20	36,458
Central-South 中南	42	229	35,486	2,350	5.08	11.22	39.82	54.71	46,249
Henan 河南	13	250	42,434	5,323	8.33	18.83	48.43	55.77	63,926
Hubei 湖北	8	347	44,928	2,430	6.09	10.45	38.15	41.73	39,902
Hunan 湖南	2	110	36,332	151	2.21	4.00	78.13	44.80	6,846
Guangdong 广东	18	180	28,148	568	1.32	3.21	31.77	59.01	43,145
Guangxi 广西	1	140		-460	-24.21	-144.20		83.21	1,900
Hainan 海南									
Southwest 西南	10	342	23,971	-6,393	-12.75	-202.36	26.85	93.70	50,149
Chongqing 重庆	1	463	24,834	1,333	1.46	2.28	31.58	35.72	91,042
Sichuan 四川	6	138	16,641	294	0.95	2.19	51.25	56.54	30,852
Guizhou 贵州	3	709	38,344	-22,341	-29.74		16.31	147.65	75,112
Yunnan 云南									
Tibet 西藏									
Northwest 西北	7	340	14,776	-121	-0.29	-0.58	12.77	50.05	42,153
Shaanxi 陕西	3	583	23,092	86	0.12	0.20	10.42	39.40	72,337
Gansu 甘肃	3	157	8,780	-373	-2.99	-33.30	21.48	91.03	12,500
Qinghai 青海									
Ningxia 宁夏									
Xinjiang 新疆	1	159	7,816	14	0.03	0.11	12.81	69.12	40,563

3679: Other Special Equipment 其他类未包括的专用设备制造业

Year 年份	Number of firms 企业个数	Rate of change 变化率 (%)	Number of employees 职工人数 (人)	Rate of change 变化率 (%)	Total revenue (Mil. RMB) 总销售收入 (百万元)	Rate of change 变化率 (%)	Total profit (Mil RMB) 总利润 (百万元)	Rate of change 变化率 (%)
2000	246		53,188		5,768		167	
2001	233	-5.28	48,653	-8.53	6,729	16.66	297	77.84
2002	247	6.01	48,451	-0.42	7,283	8.23	285	-4.04

Major Products 主要产品	Output 产量	Unit 单位
Cotton Weaving Equipment 棉纺织设备	278,738	Ton 吨
Cutton Processing Equipment 棉花加工设备	10,746	Unit 台

10 Main Firms with Maximal Revenue (year founded) 收入最大的十家主要企业（创办年份）	City 城市	Province 省	Telephone/fax 电话/传真	Number of employees 职工人数	Ownership 产业所有权	Revenue ('000 RMB) 销售收入 (千元)	Profit('000 RMB) (rank) 利润(千元) (排名)	Total assets ('000 RMB) 总资产 (千元)	Major products 主要产品
Zhejiang Hangxiao Steel Structure Co., ltd.	Hangzhou	Zhejiang	(0571)82645988		Joint Stock				Steel Structure Components
浙江杭萧钢构股份有限公司(1995)	杭州市	浙江省	(0571)82645977	779	股份制	510,550	36,750(3)	352,510	钢结构件
BeiJing Power Equipment General Factory	Beijing	Beijing	(010)69352050		State-owned				Miling Coal Machine
北京电力设备总厂(1953)	北京市	北京市	(010)69352288	1,816	国有企业	444,922	3,055(31)	932,391	磨煤机
Beijing Tsing Solar Co.,Ltd.	Beijing	Beijing	(010)69766832		Limited-Liability				High Efficient Energy Saving Equipment高效
北京清华阳光太阳能设备有限责任公司(1998)	北京市	北京市	(010)69768072	705	有限公司	220,338	18,605(6)	86,244	节能设备
Qing Dao Huatian Hand Truck Co., Ltd.	Qingdao	Shandong	(0532)3196507		Foreign Funded				Handcart
青岛华天车辆有限公司(2000)	青岛市	山东省	(0532)3195157	1,300	外商投资	205,800	2,643(38)	115,140	手推车
Jiangsu Haifeng Electrical Machinery Group Co., Ltd.	Nantong	Jiangsu	(0513)2673040		Joint Stock				Dehydration Warehouse
江苏海峰电力机械集团股份有限公司(1986)	南通市	江苏省	(0513)2673129	250	股份制	173,510	6,680(12)	78,770	脱水仓
Tacgima Machinery (China) Co.,ltd.	Jieyang	Guangdong	(0663)8886688		Overseas Chinese-funded				Embroidery machinery
田岛机械(中国)有限公司(2001)	揭阳市	广东省	(0663)8885507	170	港澳台资	153,148	1,830(48)	149,693	绣花机械
Luoyang North Glass Technology Co., Ltd.	Luoyang	Henan	(0379)4332058		Joint Stock				
洛阳北方玻璃技术股份有限公司(1995)	洛阳市	河南省	(0379)4331810	530	股份制	143,946	41,814(2)	180,888	
Shandong Cotton Machinery Company	Jinan	Shandong	(0531)5704882		Collective-owned				Cotton Equipment
山东棉花机械公司(1955)	济南市	山东省	(0531)5704882	451	集体企业	135,626	6,038(14)	158,842	棉花机械
Tianjin Dingsheng Engineering Machinery Co., Ltd.	Tianjin	Tianjin	(022)26554005		Limited-Liability				Engineering Mechinery
天津市鼎盛工程机械有限公司(1998)	天津市	天津市	(022)26370033	400	有限公司	124,689	17,928(7)	196,917	工程机械
Zhongsahn Rongnan Machinery Industry Co., Ltd.	Zhongshan	Guangdong	(0760)3133500		Overseas Chinese-funded				Disabled Person Recovering Assistant Equipment残疾人康
中山荣南机械工业有限公司(2001)	中山市	广东省	(0760)3133506	850	港澳台资	111,788	-	129,595	复铺助器械

Top 10 Cities by Revenue 销售收入排名前10位城市	Province 省	Market share 市场份额 (%)	Number of firms 企业个数
Beijing 北京市	Beijing 北京市	14.11	18
Hangzhou 杭州市	Zhejiang 浙江省	8.31	8
Shanghai 上海市	Shanghai 上海市	5.61	24
Wuxi 无锡市	Jiangsu 江苏省	5.23	13
Zhengzhou 郑州市	Henan 河南省	4.45	7
Yancheng 盐城市	Jiangsu 江苏省	3.91	3
Jinan 济南市	Shandong 山东省	3.03	8
Wuhan 武汉市	Hubei 湖北省	2.97	3
Nantong 南通市	Jiangsu 江苏省	2.93	5
Qingdao 青岛市	Shandong 山东省	2.83	1

10 Major Wholesalers 十家主要批发商	City 城市	Province 省	Telephone/Fax 电话/传真
SU MEC	Nanjing	Jiangsu	(025)4511888
中设江苏机械设备进出口（集团）公司	南京市	江苏省	(025)4411772
China Poster Mobile Communications Equipment Co.,Ltd.	Beijing	Beijing	(010)66426993
中邮普泰移动通信设备股份有限公司	北京市	北京市	(010)66426837
Sino Kama Co., Ltd.	Shanghai	Shanghai	(021)62031188
中泰凯马股份有限公司	上海市	上海市	(021)62030851
China Huayuan Group Co.,Ltd.	Shanghai	Shanghai	(021)62031188
中国华源集团有限公司	上海市	上海市	(021)62032288
Zhejiang Crand Imp.& Exp.Co.,Ltd.	Ningbo	Zhejiang	(0574)87720170
浙江远大进出口有限公司	宁波市	浙江省	(0574)87723350
Shandong Machinery Import & Export Group Corporation	Qingdao	Shandong	(0532)2661628
山东省机械进出口集团公司	青岛市	山东省	(0532)2991655
Qingdao Haier International Trade Co.,Ltd.	Qingdao	Shandong	(0532)8938337
青岛海尔国际贸易有限公司	青岛市	山东省	(0532)8939494
Guangdong Machinery Import & Export Group Corporation	Guangzhou	Guangdong	(020)87782168
广东省机械进出口集团公司	广州市	广东省	(020)87771803
China National Machinery Equipment Import & Export Corporation	Beijing	Beijing	(010)63474506
中国机械设备进出口总公司	北京市	北京市	(010)63261865
Beijing Cellstar Co.,Ltd.	Beijing	Beijing	(010)64602050
北京蜂星事达电讯有限公司	北京市	北京市	(010)64672648

3714: Rolling Stock Accessories 机车车辆配件制造业

The industry accounts for 0.040% of the total revenue of China's industrial sector in 2002. The rate of return on assets is 2.68%. 84.47% of all firms in the industry made a profit while 15.53% had negative returns.The top province in terms of the industry's revenue is Jiangsu, accounting for 12.66% of the total revenue.
2002年本行业收入占全行业的 0.040%，资产利润率为 2.68%。84.47%的企业赢利，15.53%的企业亏损。收入最高的省为江苏省，占本行业的12.66%。

	Total number of firms 企业总数	Total number of employees 职工总数	Total revenue (Mil.RMB) 总销售收入 (百万元)	Total profit (Mil.RMB) 总利润 (百万元)	Return on assets 资产利润率 (%)	Return on equity 权益利润率 (%)	Labour productivity ('000 RMB/ worker) 劳动生产率 (千元/人)	Debts/ assets 资产负债率 (%)	Total assets (Mil.RMB) 总资产 (百万元)
Industry Overall 行业总体	161	66,267	4,278	166	2.68	6.55	21.96	59.04	6,182

	Number of firms 企业个数	Average number of employees 平均职工人数	Average revenue ('000 RMB) 平均销售收入 (千元)	Average profit ('000 RMB) 平均利润 (千元)	Return on assets 资产利润率 (%)	Return on equity 权益利润率 (%)	Labour productivity ('000 RMB/ worker) 劳动生产率 (千元/人)	Debts/ assets 资产负债率 (%)	Average total assets ('000 RMB) 平均总资产 (千元)
By ownership 产业所有权									
State-owned 国有	41	469	29,263	401	0.55	1.31	22.84	58.30	73,594
Collective-owned 集体	53	658	31,205	902	3.37	10.61	13.22	68.19	26,721
Foreign & Overseas Chinese Funded 三资	11	143	38,060	5,021	8.78	14.19	114.80	38.16	57,201
By regional distribution 地区分布									
Central-North 华北	27	523	40,933	2,582	3.34	6.88	34.91	51.43	77,276
Beijing 北京	9	580	33,767	1,811	2.19	5.33	24.32	59.02	82,844
Tianjin 天津	3	1,166	68,736	824	0.45	0.84	41.29	46.82	184,215
Hebei 河北	6	479	31,872	1,219	3.34	7.09	21.43	52.95	36,525
Shanxi 山西	9	280	44,873	4,848	7.67	14.03	63.36	45.36	63,230
Inner Mongolia 内蒙古									
Northeast 东北	42	336	22,048	113	0.34	0.86	21.22	59.98	32,920
Liaoning 辽宁	16	313	27,661	512	2.67	7.77	23.95	65.71	19,211
Jilin 吉林	17	190	13,757	390	1.74	5.20	26.60	66.51	22,410
Heilongjiang 黑龙江	9	656	27,730	-1,119	-1.45	-3.14	15.98	53.86	77,144
Central-East 华东	41	242	26,280	1,705	4.77	12.05	30.33	60.47	35,773
Shanghai 上海	1	31	7,600	3,136	37.31	51.99	67.13	28.24	8,406
Jiangsu 江苏	19	253	28,512	1,743	5.19	10.46	30.62	50.42	33,594
Zhejiang 浙江	4	111	22,837	1,956	6.33	17.83	61.55	64.47	30,875
Anhui 安徽	5	158	12,579	487	3.74	6.82	19.56	45.13	13,029
Fujian 福建	1	67	14,180	2,449	14.30	23.56	69.76	39.29	17,123
Jiangxi 江西	1	686	103,786	1,920	1.87	3.14	42.08	40.51	102,868
Shandong 山东	10	310	25,593	1,902	3.72	17.92	24.33	79.25	51,137
Central-South 中南	34	606	21,625	527	2.61	9.75	9.30	73.20	20,171
Henan 河南	10	161	8,004	39	0.46	1.57	12.73	70.83	8,583
Hubei 湖北	3	4,395	9,950	-173	-1.21		0.58	110.03	14,259
Hunan 湖南	15	334	36,114	1,145	3.72	14.17	28.36	73.73	30,765
Guangdong 广东	5	105	13,643	316	2.07	4.86	34.78	57.31	15,250
Guangxi 广西	1	257	15,457	-710	-3.65	-7.62	11.30	52.17	19,468
Hainan 海南									
Southwest 西南	10	438	32,283	305	0.77	1.68	27.75	54.26	39,659
Chongqing 重庆	3	252	17,155	60	0.35	0.64	14.21	45.85	17,200
Sichuan 四川	6	592	44,206	478	0.84	1.89	30.14	55.68	57,170
Guizhou 贵州									
Yunnan 云南	1	76	6,127				50.76	28.46	1,975
Tibet 西藏									
Northwest 西北	7	447	15,859	72	0.31	2.51	15.48	87.67	23,432
Shaanxi 陕西	5	486	14,060	-97	-0.47		14.67	108.47	20,739
Gansu 甘肃	2	352	20,355	496	1.64	3.42	18.27	51.92	30,165
Qinghai 青海									
Ningxia 宁夏									
Xinjiang 新疆									

3714: Rolling Stock Accessories 机车车辆配件制造业

Year 年份	Number of firms 企业个数	Rate of change 变化率 (%)	Number of employees 职工人数 (人)	Rate of change 变化率 (%)	Total revenue (Mil. RMB) 总销售收入 (百万元)	Rate of change 变化率 (%)	Total profit (Mil RMB) 总利润 (百万元)	Rate of change 变化率 (%)
2000	141		58,962		3,948		157	
2001	144	2.13	57,637	-2.25	4,710	19.30	154	-1.91
2002	161	11.81	66,267	14.97	4,278	-9.17	166	7.79

Major Products 主要产品	Output 产量	Unit 单位

10 Main Firms with Maximal Revenue (year founded) 收入最大的十家主要企业（创办年份）	City 城市	Province 省	Telephone/fax 电话/传真	Number of employees 职工人数	Ownership 产业所有权	Revenue ('000 RMB) 销售收入 (千元)	Profit('000 RMB) (rank) 利润(千元) (排名)	Total assets ('000 RMB) 总资产 (千元)	Major products 主要产品
Datong ABC Costing Co.,Ltd. 大同爱碧玺铸造有限公司(1996)	Datong 大同市	Shanxi 山西省	(0352)5199263 (0352)5199111	392	Foreign Funded 外商投资	266,619	42,097(1)	401,602	Casting Steel Wheel 铸钢车轮
Zhuzhou Lince Group Co., Ltd. 株洲联诚集团有限责任公司(1971)	Zhuzhou 株洲市	Hunan 湖南省	(0733)8499460 (0733)8431017	2,254	Collective-owned 集体企业	209,347	3,778(9)	201,918	Auxiliary Electric Machine 辅助电机
China Nan Che Group QisHuyan Locomotive Vehicle Technics Institute中国南车集团戚墅堰机车车辆工艺研究所(1959)	Changzhou 常州市	Jiangsu 江苏省	(0519)5054011	1,137	State-owned 国有企业	199,130	15,370(4)	279,300	Piston Ring 活塞环
Tianjin Locomotive Vehicles Machinery Factory 天津机车车辆机械厂(1912)	Tianjin 天津市	Tianjin 天津市	(022)26270268 (022)26271234	3,450	State-owned 国有企业	178,517	23(112)	527,685	Booster 增压器
Dalian Locomotive Vehicle Factory Fittings Branch 大连机车车辆工厂配件分厂(1980)	Dalian 大连市	Liaoning 辽宁省	(0411)4644530 (0411)4644530	1,736	Collective-owned 集体企业	162,523	6(118)	73,517	Locomotive Fittings 机车配件
Beijing Nankou Locomotive Vehicle Factory 北京南口机车车辆机械厂(1906)	Beijing 北京市	Beijing 北京市	(010)69771260 (010)69771809	2,888	State-owned 国有企业	119,821	33(109)	466,171	Locomotive Vehicles Fittings机车车辆配件
Nanchang Railway Bureau Nanchang Machinery Fatory 南昌铁路局南昌机械厂(1958)	Nanchang 南昌市	Jiangxi 江西省	(0791)7022458	686	State-owned 国有企业	103,786	1,920(23)	102,868	Railway Vehicles Fittings铁路机车车辆配件
Tangshan Huada General Company 唐山华达总公司(1986)	Tangshan 唐山市	Hebei 河北省	(0315)3238114	1,666	Collective-owned 集体企业	87,607	1,509(30)	96,866	Buffer 缓冲器
Qiqihar Jinche Industry Company 齐齐哈尔市金车工业公司(1900)	Qiqihar 齐齐哈尔市	Heilongjiang 黑龙江省	(0452)2938430 (0452)2311439	1,256	Collective-owned 集体企业	73,748	1,398(28)	27,596	Railway Wangon Parts铁路货车配件
Changchun Passenger Bus Factory Industry Company Railway Passenger Bus Door & Window Factory长春客车厂工业公司铁路客车门窗厂(1970)	Changchun 长春市	Jilin 吉林省	(0431)7902296 (0431)7903584	353	Collective-owned 集体企业	54,351	704(50)	64,377	Concentrator 浓缩机

Top 10 Cities by Revenue 销售收入排名前10位城市	Province 省	Market share 市场份额 (%)	Number of firms 企业个数
Zhuzhou 株洲市	Hunan 湖南省	12.66	15
Dalian 大连市	Liaoning 辽宁省	7.86	9
Beijing 北京市	Beijing 北京市	7.10	9
Datong 大同市	Shanxi 山西省	6.56	2
Changzhou 常州市	Jiangsu 江苏省	5.63	6
Tianjin 天津市	Tianjin 天津市	4.82	3
Changchun 长春市	Jilin 吉林省	4.59	9
Ziyang 资阳市	Sichuan 四川省	4.09	3
Nanjing 南京市	Jiangsu 江苏省	4.07	6
Qingdao 青岛市	Shandong 山东省	3.30	5

10 Major Wholesalers 十家主要批发商	City 城市	Province 省	Telephone/Fax 电话/传真
SU MEC 中设江苏机械设备进出口（集团）公司	Nanjing 南京市	Jiangsu 江苏省	(025)4511888 (025)4411772
China Poster Mobile Communications Equipment Co.,Ltd. 中邮普泰移动通信设备股份有限公司	Beijing 北京市	Beijing 北京市	(010)66426993 (010)66426837
Sino Kama Co., Ltd. 中泰凯马股份有限公司	Shanghai 上海市	Shanghai 上海市	(021)62031188 (021)62030851
China Huayuan Group Co.,Ltd. 中国华源集团有限公司	Shanghai 上海市	Shanghai 上海市	(021)62031188 (021)62032288
Zhejiang Crand Imp.& Exp.Co.,Ltd. 浙江远大进出口有限公司	Ningbo 宁波市	Zhejiang 浙江省	(0574)87720170 (0574)87723350
Shandong Machinery Import & Export Group Corporation 山东省机械进出口集团公司	Qingdao 青岛市	Shandong 山东省	(0532)2661628 (0532)2991655
Qingdao Haier International Trade Co.,Ltd. 青岛海尔国际贸易有限公司	Qingdao 青岛市	Shandong 山东省	(0532)8938337 (0532)8939494
Guangdong Machinery Import & Export Group Corporation 广东省机械进出口集团公司	Guangzhou 广州市	Guangdong 广东省	(020)87782168 (020)87771803
China National Machinery Equipment Import & Export Corporation 中国机械设备进出口总公司	Beijing 北京市	Beijing 北京市	(010)63474506 (010)63261865
Beijing Cellstar Co.,Ltd. 北京蜂星事达电讯有限公司	Beijing 北京市	Beijing 北京市	(010)64602050 (010)64672648

3715: Railway Traffic Signal Equipment 铁路信号设备制造业

The industry accounts for 0.007% of the total revenue of China's industrial sector in 2002. The rate of return on assets is 3.86%. 79.17% of all firms in the industry made a profit while 20.83% had negative returns.The top province in terms of the industry's revenue is Shannxi, accounting for 35.38% of the total revenue.
2002年本行业收入占全行业的 0.007%，资产利润率为 3.86%。79.17%的企业赢利，20.83%的企业亏损。收入最高的省为陕西省，占本行业的35.38%。

	Total number of firms 企业总数	Total number of employees 职工总数	Total revenue (Mil.RMB) 总销售收入（百万元）	Total profit (Mil.RMB) 总利润（百万元）	Return on assets 资产利润率（%）	Return on equity 权益利润率（%）	Labour productivity ('000 RMB/ worker) 劳动生产率（千元/人）	Debts/ assets 资产负债率（%）	Total assets (Mil.RMB) 总资产（百万元）
Industry Overall 行业总体	24	7,302	719	45	3.86	7.41	38.11	47.95	1,163

	Number of firms 企业个数	Average number of employees 平均职工人数	Average revenue ('000 RMB) 平均销售收入（千元）	Average profit ('000 RMB) 平均利润（千元）	Return on assets 资产利润率（%）	Return on equity 权益利润率（%）	Labour productivity ('000 RMB/ worker) 劳动生产率（千元/人）	Debts/ assets 资产负债率（%）	Average total assets ('000 RMB) 平均总资产（千元）
By ownership 产业所有权									
State-owned 国有	13	451	32,399	916	1.46	2.70	29.45	45.78	62,626
Collective-owned 集体	2	260	20,832	532	5.73	10.89	19.96	47.44	9,292
Foreign & Overseas Chinese Funded 三资	2	113	60,763	12,174	13.19	23.73	297.59	44.42	92,293
By regional distribution 地区分布									
Central-North 华北	8	198	20,044	630	1.81	3.34	41.24	45.82	34,772
Beijing 北京	5	62	7,517	228	1.57	3.83	34.59	59.01	14,531
Tianjin 天津	2	515	48,669	1,406	1.43	2.51	45.90	42.97	98,088
Hebei 河北	1	245	25,430	1,085	11.60	11.98	30.02	3.17	9,351
Shanxi 山西									
Inner Mongolia 内蒙古									
Northeast 东北	4	425	35,214	772	1.22	2.39	31.98	49.00	63,317
Liaoning 辽宁	2	734	67,880	2,184	1.85	3.25	37.08	42.97	117,973
Jilin 吉林	1	99	1,426	-690	-7.16		5.11	113.19	9,641
Heilongjiang 黑龙江	1	134	3,672	-589	-7.67		-4.13	153.80	7,682
Central-East 华东	8	124	20,448	1,962	9.87	23.90	51.18	58.69	19,866
Shanghai 上海	3	106	22,709	4,108	17.07	46.36	90.30	63.19	24,072
Jiangsu 江苏									
Zhejiang 浙江	4	129	21,287	895	4.61	11.22	34.04	58.94	19,429
Anhui 安徽									
Fujian 福建									
Jiangxi 江西	1	161	10,310	-214	-2.38	-2.99	28.40	20.38	8,999
Shandong 山东									
Central-South 中南									
Henan 河南									
Hubei 湖北									
Hunan 湖南									
Guangdong 广东									
Guangxi 广西									
Hainan 海南									
Southwest 西南									
Chongqing 重庆									
Sichuan 四川									
Guizhou 贵州									
Yunnan 云南									
Tibet 西藏									
Northwest 西北	4	756	63,632	5,261	4.46	8.11	35.62	45.03	118,037
Shaanxi 陕西	4	756	63,632	5,261	4.46	8.11	35.62	45.03	118,037
Gansu 甘肃									
Qinghai 青海									
Ningxia 宁夏									
Xinjiang 新疆									

3715: Railway Traffic Signal Equipment 铁路信号设备制造业

Year 年份	Number of firms 企业个数	Rate of change 变化率(%)	Number of employees 职工人数(人)	Rate of change 变化率(%)	Total revenue (Mil. RMB) 总销售收入(百万元)	Rate of change 变化率(%)	Total profit (Mil RMB) 总利润(百万元)	Rate of change 变化率(%)
2000	22		7,902		409		25	
2001	23	4.55	7,519	-4.85	633	54.77	41	64.00
2002	24	4.35	7,302	-2.89	719	13.59	45	9.76

Major Products 主要产品	Output 产量	Unit 单位

10 Main Firms with Maximal Revenue (year founded) 收入最大的十家主要企业（创办年份）	City 城市	Province 省	Telephone/fax 电话/传真	Number of employees 职工人数	Ownership 产业所有权	Revenue ('000 RMB) 销售收入(千元)	Profit('000 RMB) (rank) 利润(千元)(排名)	Total assets ('000 RMB) 总资产(千元)	Major products 主要产品
Shenyang Railway Signal Factory 沈阳铁路信号工厂(1937)	Shenyang 沈阳市	Liaoning 辽宁省	(024)25872609 (024)25879167	1,194	State-owned 国有企业	119,526	4,388(4)	226,713	Signal Relay信号继电器
Tian Jing Railway Signol Factory 天津铁路信号工厂(1939)	Tianjin 天津市	Tianjin 天津市	(022)26189522 (022)24393390	938	State-owned 国有企业	97,337	2,811(6)	196,175	Motor-driven Point Switch电动转辙机
Siemens Signal Co., Ltd. 西门子信号有限公司(1995)	Xi'an 西安市	Shannxi 陕西省	(029)6522777 (029)6529348	178	Foreign Funded 外商投资	94,076	15,160(1)	167,204	Point Switch 转辙机
Ningbo Honggang Railroad Signal Equipment Factory 宁波鸿钢铁路信号设备厂(1999)	Ningbo 宁波市	Zhejiang 浙江省	(0574)88027367 (0574)88027677	67	Joint Stock 股份制	29,190	2,330(7)	14,958	Aluminium Alloy Signal Organization铝合金信号机构
Shanghai Tieda Telecommunications Equipment Co., Ltd. 上海铁大电信设备有限公司(1992)	Shanghai 上海市	Shanghai 上海市	(021)50801893 (021)50801893	100	Limited-Liability 有限公司	28,898	3,138(5)	35,175	Network Monitor Station网络监测站
Shanghai Xin'gantong Communication Equipment Co.,ltd. 上海新干通通信设备有限公司(1999)	Shanghai 上海市	Shanghai 上海市	(021)66531912 (021)66531921	48	Overseas Chinese-funded 港澳台资	27,449	9,187(2)	17,382	Railway Communication Equipment铁路通信设备
Hebei Nanpi Railway Signal Equipment Factory 河北省南皮铁路信号器材厂(1986)	Cangzhou 沧州市	Hebei 河北省	(0317)8851566 (0317)8855568	245	Collective-owned 集体企业	25,430	1,085(9)	9,351	Railway Signal Equipment铁路信号器材
Xi'an Railway Signal Factory Electric Fittings Factory 西安铁路信号工厂电器配件厂(1989)	Xi'an 西安市	Shannxi 陕西省	(029)3235522 (029)2327154	100	State-owned 国有企业	18,444	399(11)	12,651	Railway Signal Equipment铁路信号器材
Shenyang Railway Equipment Factory 沈阳铁路器材厂(1977)	Shenyang 沈阳市	Liaoning 辽宁省	(024)23831792 (024)62071228	274	Collective-owned 集体企业	16,233	-	9,232	Railway Equipment 铁路器材
Xi'an Railway Branch Bureau Xi'an Electric Service Equipment Factory 西安铁路分局西安电务器材厂(1969)	Xi'an 西安市	Shannxi 陕西省	(029)2327516 (029)2229727	150	State-owned 国有企业	10,097	9(17)	12,997	Railway Special Electronic Equipment电物器材

Top 10 Cities by Revenue 销售收入排名前10位城市	Province 省	Market share 市场份额（%）	Number of firms 企业个数
Xi'an 西安市	Shannxi 陕西省	35.38	4
Shenyang 沈阳市	Liaoning 辽宁省	18.87	2
Tianjin 天津市	Tianjin 天津市	13.53	2
Ningbo 宁波市	Zhejiang 浙江省	9.96	2
Shanghai 上海市	Shanghai 上海市	9.47	3
Beijing 北京市	Beijing 北京市	5.22	5
Cangzhou 沧州市	Hebei 河北省	3.54	1
Nanchang 南昌市	Jiangxi 江西省	1.43	1
Taizhou 台州市	Zhejiang 浙江省	1.24	1
Jinhua 金华市	Zhejiang 浙江省	0.64	1

10 Major Wholesalers 十家主要批发商	City 城市	Province 省	Telephone/Fax 电话/传真
SU MEC 中设江苏机械设备进出口（集团）公司	Nanjing 南京市	Jiangsu 江苏省	(025)4511888 (025)4411772
China Poster Mobile Communications Equipment Co.,Ltd. 中邮普泰移动通信设备股份有限公司	Beijing 北京市	Beijing 北京市	(010)66426993 (010)66426837
Sino Kama Co., Ltd. 中泰凯马股份有限公司	Shanghai 上海市	Shanghai 上海市	(021)62031188 (021)62030851
China Huayuan Group Co.,Ltd. 中国华源集团有限公司	Shanghai 上海市	Shanghai 上海市	(021)62031188 (021)62032288
Zhejiang Crand Imp.& Exp.Co.,Ltd. 浙江远大进出口有限公司	Ningbo 宁波市	Zhejiang 浙江省	(0574)87720170 (0574)87723350
Shandong Machinery Import & Export Group Corporation 山东省机械进出口集团公司	Qingdao 青岛市	Shandong 山东省	(0532)2661628 (0532)2991655
Qingdao Haier International Trade Co.,Ltd. 青岛海尔国际贸易有限公司	Qingdao 青岛市	Shandong 山东省	(0532)8938337 (0532)8939494
Guangdong Machinery Import & Export Group Corporation 广东省机械进出口集团公司	Guangzhou 广州市	Guangdong 广东省	(020)87782168 (020)87771803
China National Machinery Equipment Import & Export Corporation 中国机械设备进出口总公司	Beijing 北京市	Beijing 北京市	(010)63474506 (010)63261865
Beijing Cellstar Co.,Ltd. 北京蜂星事达电讯有限公司	Beijing 北京市	Beijing 北京市	(010)64602050 (010)64672648

3716: Special Railway Equipment 铁路专用设备制造业

The industry accounts for 0.018% of the total revenue of China's industrial sector in 2002. The rate of return on assets is 2.70%. 92.00% of all firms in the industry made a profit while 8.00% had negative returns.The top province in terms of the industry's revenue is Hebei, accounting for 30.77% of the total revenue.
2002年本行业收入占全行业的0.018%，资产利润率为2.70%。92.00%的企业赢利，8.00%的企业亏损。收入最高的省为河北省，占本行业的30.77%。

	Total number of firms 企业总数	Total number of employees 职工总数	Total revenue (Mil.RMB) 总销售收入（百万元）	Total profit (Mil.RMB) 总利润（百万元）	Return on assets 资产利润率（%）	Return on equity 权益利润率（%）	Labour productivity ('000 RMB/ worker) 劳动生产率（千元/人）	Debts/ assets 资产负债率（%）	Total assets (Mil.RMB) 总资产（百万元）
Industry Overall 行业总体	25	13,520	1,942	96	2.70	7.60	46.70	64.51	3,565

	Number of firms 企业个数	Average number of employees 平均职工人数	Average revenue ('000 RMB) 平均销售收入（千元）	Average profit ('000 RMB) 平均利润（千元）	Return on assets 资产利润率（%）	Return on equity 权益利润率（%）	Labour productivity ('000 RMB/ worker) 劳动生产率（千元/人）	Debts/ assets 资产负债率（%）	Average total assets ('000 RMB) 平均总资产（千元）
By ownership 产业所有权									
State-owned 国有	8	362	68,205	2,596	1.92	8.38	56.66	77.06	135,048
Collective-owned 集体	2	112	19,902	1,166	5.45		64.29	123.14	21,397
Foreign & Overseas Chinese Funded 三资	2	44	21,096	2,818	8.23	16.12	118.70	48.95	34,237
By regional distribution 地区分布									
Central-North 华北	9	685	76,742	3,064	1.99	4.36	39.16	54.26	153,716
Beijing 北京	5	142	13,952	1,193	3.68	7.70	40.84	52.22	32,398
Tianjin 天津	2	65	11,722	1,464	18.12	34.80	48.85	47.93	8,081
Hebei 河北	2	2,664	298,738	9,344	1.55	3.42	38.70	54.62	602,645
Shanxi 山西									
Inner Mongolia 内蒙古									
Northeast 东北	1	461	41,708	201	0.40	0.92	7.08	56.42	50,230
Liaoning 辽宁									
Jilin 吉林									
Heilongjiang 黑龙江	1	461	41,708	201	0.40	0.92	7.08	56.42	50,230
Central-East 华东	8	109	19,372	1,204	6.33	39.71	47.14	84.05	19,012
Shanghai 上海									
Jiangsu 江苏	3	141	19,190	477	3.76	12.61	25.21	70.18	12,677
Zhejiang 浙江	1	143	15,180	756	3.24	12.95	39.44	74.97	23,326
Anhui 安徽									
Fujian 福建									
Jiangxi 江西	1	117	6,732	187	6.73		26.71	100.00	2,777
Shandong 山东	3	61	25,165	2,419	8.25	102.54	116.64	91.95	29,320
Central-South 中南	1	417	28,909	8	0.02	0.03	30.04	35.88	39,548
Henan 河南	1	417	28,909	8	0.02	0.03	30.04	35.88	39,548
Hubei 湖北									
Hunan 湖南									
Guangdong 广东									
Guangxi 广西									
Hainan 海南									
Southwest 西南	4	458	124,010	6,254	2.64	14.32	84.58	81.59	237,176
Chongqing 重庆									
Sichuan 四川	3	253	31,803	1,672	4.24	13.78	50.48	69.26	39,488
Guizhou 贵州									
Yunnan 云南	1	1,074	400,628	20,000	2.41	14.47	108.69	83.35	830,239
Tibet 西藏									
Northwest 西北	2	1,887	264,854	16,858	3.40	8.72	47.21	61.01	495,699
Shaanxi 陕西	2	1,887	264,854	16,858	3.40	8.72	47.21	61.01	495,699
Gansu 甘肃									
Qinghai 青海									
Ningxia 宁夏									
Xinjiang 新疆									

3716: Special Railway Equipment 铁路专用设备制造业

Year 年份	Number of firms 企业个数	Rate of change 变化率 (%)	Number of employees 职工人数 (人)	Rate of change 变化率 (%)	Total revenue (Mil. RMB) 总销售收入 (百万元)	Rate of change 变化率 (%)	Total profit (Mil RMB) 总利润 (百万元)	Rate of change 变化率 (%)
2000	18		14,165		1,480		76	
2001	24	33.33	14,458	2.07	1,676	13.24	122	60.53
2002	25	4.17	13,520	-6.49	1,942	15.87	96	-21.31

Major Products 主要产品	Output 产量	Unit 单位
Metal Container 金属集装箱	4,938	10,000 Stere 万立方米
Metal Structure Products 金属结构制品	252	10,000 Tons 万吨

10 Main Firms with Maximal Revenue (year founded) 收入最大的十家主要企业（创办年份）	City 城市	Province 省	Telephone/ fax 电话/传真	Number of employees 职工人数	Ownership 产业所有权	Revenue ('000 RMB) 销售收入 (千元)	Profit('000 RMB) (rank) 利润(千元) (排名)	Total assets ('000 RMB) 总资产 (千元)	Major products 主要产品
China Railway Shanghaiguan Bridge Group Co.,Ltd. 中铁山桥集团有限公司(1894)	Qinhuangdao 秦皇岛市	Hebei 河北省	(0335)5151185 (0335)5153186	5,256	Limited-Liability 有限公司	590,210	18,160(3)	1,174,720	Girder Steel & Steel Structure钢梁钢结构
China Railway Construction Co. Kunming Machinery Plant 中国铁道建筑总公司昆明机械厂(1954)	Kunming 昆明市	Yunnan 云南省	(0871)3911613 (0871)3911799	1,074	State-owned 国有企业	400,628	20,000(2)	830,239	Large-type Ac Motor Clear Riddle Machine大型清筛机
China Railway Baoqiao Tianyuan Industrial Development Co., Ltd.中铁宝桥天元实业发展有限公司(1988)	Baoji 宝鸡市	Shannxi 陕西省	(0917)3578622 (0917)3554363	638	Limited-Liability 有限公司	58,640	129(19)	63,344	Girder Steel & Steel Structure钢梁钢结构
Shifang Railway-Helper Machinery Co.Ltd. 什邡瑞邦机械有限责任公司(1967)	Deyang 德阳市	Sichuan 四川省	(0838)8280282 (0838)8280282	185	Limited-Liability 有限公司	42,550	3,279(5)	32,792	Railway Special Equipment铁路专用设备器材机械
Haju Industry General Company Qiqiha'er Engineering Machinery Factory 哈局工业总公司齐齐哈尔工务机械厂(1958)	Qiqihar 齐齐哈尔市	Heilongjiang 黑龙江省	(0452)2923323 (0452)2925255	461	State-owned 国有企业	41,708	201(17)	50,230	Switch Series Products道岔系列产品
Qingdao Alstom Railway Equipment Co.Ltd. 青岛阿尔斯通铁路设备有限公司(1999)	Qingdao 青岛市	Shandong 山东省	(0532)4991605 (0532)4992102	16	Foreign Funded 外商投资	34,926	5,107(4)	37,903	Assembly Shock Absorber组装减震器
Zibo Braking Equipment Factory 淄博制动设备厂(1991)	Zibo 淄博市	Shandong 山东省	(0533)2778202	106	Collective-owned 集体企业	33,071	2,144(10)	40,016	Braking Equipment & Parts制动设备及配件
Meishan Vehicles Factory Sanshan Industrial Company 眉山车辆厂三山实业公司(1998)	Meishan 眉山市	Sichuan 四川省	(0833)8502639 (0833)8502568	307	State-owned 国有企业	31,921	-	71,375	Special Railway Equipment铁路专用设备
Zhengzhou Railway Bureau Engineering Machinery Factory 郑州铁路局工务机械厂(1950)	Zhengzhou 郑州市	Henan 河南省	(0371)8322555 (0371)8322555	417	State-owned 国有企业	28,909	8(22)	39,548	Orbit Vehicle 轨道车
Guanghan Kefeng Electron Cooporation Ltd. 广汉科峰电子有限责任公司(2000)	Deyang 德阳市	Sichuan 四川省	(0838)5302858 (0838)5302858	267	Limited-Liability 有限公司	20,939	2,177(9)	14,298	Infrared Bearing Temperature Detector红外线轴温探测仪

Top 10 Cities by Revenue 销售收入排名前10位城市	Province 省	Market share 市场份额 (%)	Number of firms 企业个数
Qinhuangdao 秦皇岛市	Hebei 河北省	30.39	1
Baoji 宝鸡市	Shannxi 陕西省	27.28	2
Kunming 昆明市	Yunnan 云南省	20.63	1
Beijing 北京市	Beijing 北京市	3.59	5
Deyang 德阳市	Sichuan 四川省	3.27	2
Changzhou 常州市	Jiangsu 江苏省	2.96	3
Qingdao 青岛市	Shandong 山东省	2.18	2
Qiqihar 齐齐哈尔市	Heilongjiang 黑龙江省	2.15	1
Zibo 淄博市	Shandong 山东省	1.70	1
Meishan 眉山市	Sichuan 四川省	1.64	1

10 Major Wholesalers 十家主要批发商	City 城市	Province 省	Telephone/Fax 电话/传真
SU MEC 中设江苏机械设备进出口（集团）公司	Nanjing 南京市	Jiangsu 江苏省	(025)4511888 (025)4411772
China Poster Mobile Communications Equipment Co.,Ltd. 中邮普泰移动通信设备股份有限公司	Beijing 北京市	Beijing 北京市	(010)66426993 (010)66426837
Sino Kama Co., Ltd. 中泰凯马股份有限公司	Shanghai 上海市	Shanghai 上海市	(021)62031188 (021)62030851
China Huayuan Group Co.,Ltd. 中国华源集团有限公司	Shanghai 上海市	Shanghai 上海市	(021)62031188 (021)62032288
Zhejiang Crand Imp.& Exp.Co.,Ltd. 浙江远大进出口有限公司	Ningbo 宁波市	Zhejiang 浙江省	(0574)87720170 (0574)87723350
Shandong Machinery Import & Export Group Corporation 山东省机械进出口集团公司	Qingdao 青岛市	Shandong 山东省	(0532)2661628 (0532)2991655
Qingdao Haier International Trade Co.,Ltd. 青岛海尔国际贸易有限公司	Qingdao 青岛市	Shandong 山东省	(0532)8938337 (0532)8939494
Guangdong Machinery Import & Export Group Corporation 广东省机械进出口集团公司	Guangzhou 广州市	Guangdong 广东省	(020)87782168 (020)87771803
China National Machinery Equipment Import & Export Corporation 中国机械设备进出口总公司	Beijing 北京市	Beijing 北京市	(010)63474506 (010)63261865
Beijing Cellstar Co.,Ltd. 北京蜂星事达电讯有限公司	Beijing 北京市	Beijing 北京市	(010)64602050 (010)64672648

3717: Special Railway Equipment 铁路专用器材制造业

The industry accounts for 0.010% of the total revenue of China's industrial sector in 2002. The rate of return on assets is 0.27%. 79.31% of all firms in the industry made a profit while 20.69% had negative returns.The top province in terms of the industry's revenue is Liaoning, accounting for 23.80% of the total revenue.
2002年本行业收入占全行业的 0.010%，资产利润率为 0.27%。79.31%的企业赢利，20.69%的企业亏损。收入最高的省为辽宁省，占本行业的23.80%。

	Total number of firms 企业总数	Total number of employees 职工总数	Total revenue (Mil.RMB) 总销售收入（百万元）	Total profit (Mil.RMB) 总利润（百万元）	Return on assets 资产利润率（%）	Return on equity 权益利润率（%）	Labour productivity ('000 RMB/ worker) 劳动生产率（千元/人）	Debts/ assets 资产负债率（%）	Total assets (Mil.RMB) 总资产（百万元）
Industry Overall 行业总体	58	12,430	1,087	5	0.27	0.69	25.57	61.13	1,683

	Number of firms 企业个数	Average number of employees 平均职工人数	Average revenue ('000 RMB) 平均销售收入（千元）	Average profit ('000 RMB) 平均利润（千元）	Return on assets 资产利润率（%）	Return on equity 权益利润率（%）	Labour productivity ('000 RMB/ worker) 劳动生产率（千元/人）	Debts/ assets 资产负债率（%）	Average total assets ('000 RMB) 平均总资产（千元）
By ownership 产业所有权									
State-owned 国有	32	265	22,619	-295	-0.80	-1.91	23.35	58.02	36,837
Collective-owned 集体	8	227	15,778	452	2.16	10.60	22.75	79.63	20,913
Foreign & Overseas Chinese Funded 三资	1	85	10,469	1,213	8.30	17.44	34.85	52.42	14,616
By regional distribution 地区分布									
Central-North 华北	10	232	21,232	537	1.76	6.12	35.71	71.22	30,490
Beijing 北京	4	150	8,440	163	0.91	5.87	22.21	84.51	17,973
Tianjin 天津	1	42	4,556	172	6.18	12.52	37.00	50.66	2,785
Hebei 河北	3	422	31,815	1,167	2.47	9.58	27.84	74.25	47,301
Shanxi 山西	2	207	39,280	522	1.18	2.70	79.27	56.17	44,159
Inner Mongolia 内蒙古									
Northeast 东北	15	224	18,365	-682	-2.46	-6.81	15.57	63.84	27,710
Liaoning 辽宁	13	236	19,900	-711	-2.43	-6.60	15.11	63.15	29,254
Jilin 吉林	1	160	1,329	-1,039	-11.12	-53.28	5.01	79.13	9,344
Heilongjiang 黑龙江	1	139	15,454	51	0.20	0.62	37.91	68.49	26,002
Central-East 华东	15	146	15,887	393	1.80	3.05	28.58	40.92	21,840
Shanghai 上海									
Jiangsu 江苏	4	63	11,071	94	0.90	1.93	46.40	53.11	10,341
Zhejiang 浙江	5	47	7,859	761	9.49	27.54	53.04	65.54	8,021
Anhui 安徽	2	700	63,121	16	0.02	0.02	17.26	29.91	104,779
Fujian 福建	1	58	7,334	46	0.58	1.66	103.98	64.80	7,878
Jiangxi 江西	1	34	1,158	-813	-41.69		5.97	126.36	1,950
Shandong 山东	2	108	9,994	1,227	9.17	21.91	37.88	58.12	13,374
Central-South 中南	9	169	12,903	213	1.33	5.40	17.04	75.29	15,932
Henan 河南	6	186	12,880	219	1.13	5.45	14.62	79.21	19,290
Hubei 湖北	1	194	17,252	264	2.80	7.70	24.23	63.67	9,440
Hunan 湖南									
Guangdong 广东									
Guangxi 广西	2	104	10,796	170	1.86	4.27	23.35	56.42	9,102
Hainan 海南									
Southwest 西南	4	259	19,814	223	0.42	0.97	24.29	57.05	53,366
Chongqing 重庆									
Sichuan 四川	4	259	19,814	223	0.42	0.97	24.29	57.05	53,366
Guizhou 贵州									
Yunnan 云南									
Tibet 西藏									
Northwest 西北	5	400	33,112	136	0.24	0.71	34.42	65.64	55,643
Shaanxi 陕西	3	383	46,164	1,557	2.91	5.89	51.55	50.57	53,445
Gansu 甘肃	1	595	12,653	-536	-0.69		10.19	105.62	77,167
Qinghai 青海									
Ningxia 宁夏									
Xinjiang 新疆	1	258	14,417	-3,455	-8.49	-16.70	14.03	49.18	40,710

3717: Special Railway Equipment 铁路专用器材制造业

Year 年份	Number of firms 企业个数	Rate of change 变化率 (%)	Number of employees 职工人数 (人)	Rate of change 变化率 (%)	Total revenue (Mil. RMB) 总销售收入 (百万元)	Rate of change 变化率 (%)	Total profit (Mil RMB) 总利润 (百万元)	Rate of change 变化率 (%)
2000	63		21,158		1,286		-	
2001	52	-17.46	14,435	-31.78	1,055	-17.96	-5	-
2002	58	11.54	12,430	-13.89	1,087	3.03	5	-

Major Products 主要产品	Output 产量	Unit 单位

10 Main Firms with Maximal Revenue (year founded) 收入最大的十家主要企业（创办年份）	City 城市	Province 省	Telephone/fax 电话/传真	Number of employees 职工人数	Ownership 产业所有权	Revenue ('000 RMB) 销售收入 (千元)	Profit('000 RMB) (rank) 利润(千元) (排名)	Total assets ('000 RMB) 总资产 (千元)	Major products 主要产品
Anhui Chaohu Casting Factory Co.,Ltd. 安徽省巢湖铸造厂有限责任公司(1959)	Chaohu 巢湖市	Anhui 安徽省	(0565)2317032 (0565)2317588	1,360	State-owned 国有企业	126,241	32(35)	181,883	Railway Buckle Items 铁路扣件
Baoji Line Parts Works Of Elelctrification Engineering Bureau,Minstry Of Railways铁道部电气化工程局宝鸡器材厂(1958)	Baoji 宝鸡市	Shannxi 陕西省	(0917)3432524 (0917)3432524	国有企业	State-owned 国有企业	120,459	2516(2)	130,633	Contact Net 接触网
Beijing Railway Bureau Taiyuan Electric Service Equipment Factory 北京铁路局太原电务器材厂	Taiyuan 太原市	Shanxi 山西省	(0351)2642668 (0351)2642138	353	State-owned 国有企业	74,489	1,035(10)	64,464	Railway Communication Equipment 铁路通信器材
Longchang Railway Materials Factory 隆昌工务器材厂(1971)	Neijiang 内江市	Sichuan 四川省	(0832)3944559 (0832)3944703	734	State-owned 国有企业	54,533	104(27)	111,640	Railway Buckle Items 铁路扣件
Cangzhou Kaida Railway Electrification Equipment Manufacturing Co.,Ltd.凯达铁路电器化制造有限公司(1998)	Cangzhou 沧州市	Hebei 河北省	(0317)3841518 (0317)3841158	270	Private Owned 私营企业	53,100	3,300(1)	25,100	Contact Net Parts 接触网零部件
Zhengzhou Railway Special-purpose Equipment General Factory郑州铁路专用器材总厂(1993)	Zhengzhou 郑州市	Henan 河南省	(0371)8907695 (0371)8907666	365	Collective-owned 集体企业	33,069	-	81,520	Transformer Tank 变压器箱
Shenyang Railway Branch Bureau Shenyang Engineering Equipment Factory 沈阳铁路分局沈阳工务器材厂(1956)	Shenyang 沈阳市	Liaoning 辽宁省	(024)25851758 (024)25853283	430	State-owned 国有企业	30,439	-	21,868	Sand Rammer 捣固机
Tangshan Railway Switch Factory 唐山铁路道岔厂(1989)	Tangshan 唐山市	Hebei 河北省	(0315)2038675 (0315)2010046	550	Joint Owned 联营企业	25,743	200(21)	102,532	Switch 道岔
Railway Department Academy of Sciences Locomotive Vehicle Research Institute Daxing Daxing Testing Factory铁道部科学院机机辆研究所大兴实验工厂(1986)	Beijing 北京市	Beijing 北京市	(010)80281340 (010)80281343	247	Collective-owned 集体企业	24,770	584(12)	35,620	Braking Tray 制动盘
Jurong Electromagnetic Wire Co., Ltd. 句容电磁线公司(1998)	Zhenjiang 镇江市	Jiangsu 江苏省	(0511)7831228 (0511)7831111	98	Private Owned 私营企业	22,042	-	16,835	Paper Wrapped Wire 纸包线

Top 10 Cities by Revenue 销售收入排名前10位城市	Province 省	Market share 市场份额 (%)	Number of firms 企业个数
Chaohu 巢湖市	Anhui 安徽省	11.61	1
Baoji 宝鸡市	Shannxi 陕西省	11.08	1
Shenyang 沈阳市	Liaoning 辽宁省	10.95	8
Anshan 鞍山市	Liaoning 辽宁省	7.47	2
Taiyuan 太原市	Shanxi 山西省	6.85	1
Neijiang 内江市	Sichuan 四川省	5.02	1
Cangzhou 沧州市	Hebei 河北省	4.88	1
Zhengzhou 郑州市	Henan 河南省	4.15	3
Jinzhou 锦州市	Liaoning 辽宁省	4.01	1
Beijing 北京市	Beijing 北京市	3.11	4

10 Major Wholesalers 十家主要批发商	City 城市	Province 省	Telephone/Fax 电话/传真
SU MEC 中设江苏机械设备进出口（集团）公司	Nanjing 南京市	Jiangsu 江苏省	(025)4511888 (025)4411772
China Poster Mobile Communications Equipment Co.,Ltd. 中邮普泰移动通信设备股份有限公司	Beijing 北京市	Beijing 北京市	(010)66426993 (010)66426837
Sino Kama Co., Ltd. 中泰凯马股份有限公司	Shanghai 上海市	Shanghai 上海市	(021)62031188 (021)62030851
China Huayuan Group Co.,Ltd. 中国华源集团有限公司	Shanghai 上海市	Shanghai 上海市	(021)62031188 (021)62032288
Zhejiang Crand Imp.& Exp.Co.,Ltd. 浙江远大进出口有限公司	Ningbo 宁波市	Zhejiang 浙江省	(0574)87720170 (0574)87723350
Shandong Machinery Import & Export Group Corporation 山东省机械进出口集团公司	Qingdao 青岛市	Shandong 山东省	(0532)2661628 (0532)2991655
Qingdao Haier International Trade Co.,Ltd. 青岛海尔国际贸易有限公司	Qingdao 青岛市	Shandong 山东省	(0532)8938337 (0532)8939494
Guangdong Machinery Import & Export Group Corporation 广东省机械进出口集团公司	Guangzhou 广州市	Guangdong 广东省	(020)87782168 (020)87771803
China National Machinery Equipment Import & Export Corporation 中国机械设备进出口总公司	Beijing 北京市	Beijing 北京市	(010)63474506 (010)63261865
Beijing Cellstar Co.,Ltd. 北京蜂星事达电讯有限公司	Beijing 北京市	Beijing 北京市	(010)64602050 (010)64672648

3719: Other Railroad Transporting Equipment 其他铁路运输设备制造业

The industry accounts for 0.011% of the total revenue of China's industrial sector in 2002. The rate of return on assets is 1.83%. 79.31% of all firms in the industry made a profit while 20.69% had negative returns.The top province in terms of the industry's revenue is Hubei, accounting for 28.09% of the total revenue.
2002年本行业收入占全行业的 0.011%，资产利润率为 1.83%。79.31%的企业赢利，20.69%的企业亏损。收入最高的省为湖北省，占本行业的28.09%。

	Total number of firms 企业总数	Total number of employees 职工总数	Total revenue (Mil.RMB) 总销售收入（百万元）	Total profit (Mil.RMB) 总利润（百万元）	Return on assets 资产利润率 (%)	Return on equity 权益利润率 (%)	Labour productivity ('000 RMB/ worker) 劳动生产率（千元/人）	Debts/ assets 资产负债率 (%)	Total assets (Mil.RMB) 总资产（百万元）
Industry Overall 行业总体	29	13,260	1,183	33	1.83	5.43	23.22	66.38	1,827

	Number of firms 企业个数	Average number of employees 平均职工人数	Average revenue ('000 RMB) 平均销售收入（千元）	Average profit ('000 RMB) 平均利润（千元）	Return on assets 资产利润率 (%)	Return on equity 权益利润率 (%)	Labour productivity ('000 RMB/ worker) 劳动生产率（千元/人）	Debts/ assets 资产负债率 (%)	Average total assets ('000 RMB) 平均总资产（千元）
By ownership 产业所有权									
State-owned 国有	10	805	28,971	-1,101	-1.04	-2.89	12.38	64.15	106,336
Collective-owned 集体	7	202	14,486	619	3.83	15.37	21.79	75.06	16,142
Foreign & Overseas Chinese Funded 三资	1	300	132,095	20,000	11.81	32.10	172.20	63.20	169,331
By regional distribution 地区分布									
Central-North 华北	5	407	29,519	1,243	3.74	13.22	23.80	71.71	33,236
Beijing 北京	1	425	31,556	5,955	16.17	119.12	29.98	86.42	36,818
Tianjin 天津									
Hebei 河北	3	304	17,431	-228	-0.64	-2.07	23.98	69.19	35,687
Shanxi 山西	1	697	63,749	943	4.23	10.45	19.80	59.52	22,303
Inner Mongolia 内蒙古									
Northeast 东北	8	289	21,722	1,075	3.52	6.29	25.24	44.12	30,563
Liaoning 辽宁	2	645	50,967	1,420	1.86	2.61	27.33	28.63	76,179
Jilin 吉林	4	170	14,919	1,435	7.29	27.27	27.26	73.25	19,677
Heilongjiang 黑龙江	2	171	6,082	8	0.11	0.22	13.30	49.04	6,722
Central-East 华东	9	204	41,291	2,727	6.70	15.81	64.69	57.64	40,730
Shanghai 上海	1	119	7,459	-1,830	-5.79	-7.22	-4.55	19.78	31,585
Jiangsu 江苏	2	235	46,878	995	3.03	4.22	62.58	28.36	32,890
Zhejiang 浙江									
Anhui 安徽									
Fujian 福建									
Jiangxi 江西									
Shandong 山东	6	208	45,067	4,064	9.06	29.44	72.11	69.23	44,868
Central-South 中南	5	973	74,904	-175	-0.11	-0.44	9.26	74.34	156,022
Henan 河南									
Hubei 湖北	3	1,521	110,793	162	0.07	0.28	6.99	75.54	240,143
Hunan 湖南	1	130	28,120	323	1.83	12.38	79.65	85.20	17,625
Guangdong 广东	1	173	14,020	-1,686	-4.01	-7.88	16.29	49.14	42,054
Guangxi 广西									
Hainan 海南									
Southwest 西南	1	90	16,396	250	3.49	6.79	42.67	48.66	7,168
Chongqing 重庆									
Sichuan 四川	1	90	16,396	250	3.49	6.79	42.67	48.66	7,168
Guizhou 贵州									
Yunnan 云南									
Tibet 西藏									
Northwest 西北	1	2,127	99,457	-5,381	-2.05	-7.52	15.83	72.77	262,697
Shaanxi 陕西	1	2,127	99,457	-5,381	-2.05	-7.52	15.83	72.77	262,697
Gansu 甘肃									
Qinghai 青海									
Ningxia 宁夏									
Xinjiang 新疆									

3719: Other Railroad Transporting Equipment 其他铁路运输设备制造业

Year 年份	Number of firms 企业个数	Rate of change 变化率 (%)	Number of employees 职工人数 (人)	Rate of change 变化率 (%)	Total revenue (Mil. RMB) 总销售收入 (百万元)	Rate of change 变化率 (%)	Total profit (Mil RMB) 总利润 (百万元)	Rate of change 变化率 (%)
2000	17		6,655		445		-3	
2001	25	47.06	7,757	16.56	701	57.53	4	-
2002	29	16.00	13,260	70.94	1,183	68.76	33	725.00

Major Products 主要产品	Output 产量	Unit 单位
Handling Machinery 装卸机械	4,897	Unit 台

10 Main Firms with Maximal Revenue (year founded) 收入最大的十家主要企业（创办年份）	City 城市	Province 省	Telephone/fax 电话/传真	Number of employees 职工人数	Ownership 产业所有权	Revenue ('000 RMB) 销售收入 (千元)	Profit('000 RMB) (rank) 利润(千元) (排名)	Total assets ('000 RMB) 总资产 (千元)	Major products 主要产品
Qingdao Ultimate Transportation Equipment Co.,Ltd. 青岛欧特美交通设备有限公司(1999)	Qingdao 青岛市	Shandong 山东省	(0532)8704332 (0532)8704338	300	Foreign Funded 外商投资	132,095	20,000(1)	169,331	Sliding Door 塞拉门
Qingdao SiFang Engine Hongda Industry & Trade Co., Ltd. 青岛四机宏达工贸有限公司(1999)	Qingdao 青岛市	Shandong 山东省	(0532)7805418 (0532)7801445	486	Limited-Liability 有限公司	103,750	1,100(10)	59,066	Locomotive Fittings 机车配件
China Railway Bus Co.,Ltd. 中铁宝工有限责任公司(1955)	Baoji 宝鸡市	Shannxi 陕西省	(0917)2864634	2,127	State-owned 国有企业	99,457	-	262,697	Orbit Vehicle 轨道车
China Northern Locomotive Rolling Group Corporation Shenyang Kailway Brake Factory中国北车集团沈阳铁道制动机厂(1942)	Shenyang 沈阳市	Liaoning 辽宁省	(024)25874953 (024)25862114	1,063	State-owned 国有企业	90,028	2,753(5)	141,375	Air Distributed Valve for Wagon货车空气分配阀
Wuxi Dongjiang Railway Fittings Factory 无锡市东绛铁路配件厂(1989)	Wuxi 无锡市	Jiangsu 江苏省	(0510)5061562 (0510)5061562	300	Joint Stock 股份制	67,856	1,150(9)	59,330	Metal Ripple Tube金属波纹管
Yongji Railway Casting Co., Ltd. 永济铁路铸造有限责任公司(1998)	Yuncheng 运城市	Shanxi 山西省	(0359)8072301 (0359)8072301	697	Limited-Liability 有限公司	63,749	943(11)	22,303	Ferrous Metal Smelting黑色金属冶炼
Beijing Railway Bureau Baoding Engineering Equipment Factory 北京铁路局保定工务器材厂(1971)	Baoding 保定市	Hebei 河北省	(0312)7942058 (0312)7942458	392	State-owned 国有企业	34,457	88(16)	83,374	Quench Orbit 淬火轨
Beijing Yinqiao Electric Motor Factory 北京银桥电机厂(1996)	Beijing 北京市	Beijing 北京市	(010)60733119 (010)60731146	425	Joint Stock 股份制	31,556	5,955(2)	36,818	Resistance Braking 电阻制动
Zixing Shunxing Railway Circuit Equipment Factory 资兴市顺兴铁道线路器材厂。(1993)	Chenzhou 郴州市	Hunan 湖南省	(0735)3372406 (0735)3372406	130	Collective-owned 集体企业	28,120	323(13)	17,625	Railway Control Board 铁道控板
Changchun Changlong Passenger Bus New Type Decorative Materials Co., Ltd.长春市长龙客车新型装饰材料有限公司(2000)	Changchun 长春市	Jilin 吉林省	(0431)2659441 (0431)2659421	84	Joint Stock 股份制	18,020	1,190(8)	10,280	

Top 10 Cities by Revenue 销售收入排名前10位城市	Province 省	Market share 市场份额 (%)	Number of firms 企业个数
Xiangfan 襄樊市	Hubei 湖北省	27.64	2
Qingdao 青岛市	Shandong 山东省	22.44	5
Shenyang 沈阳市	Liaoning 辽宁省	8.61	2
Baoji 宝鸡市	Shannxi 陕西省	8.40	1
Wuxi 无锡市	Jiangsu 江苏省	5.73	1
Yuncheng 运城市	Shanxi 山西省	5.39	1
Changchun 长春市	Jilin 吉林省	4.30	3
Baoding 保定市	Hebei 河北省	3.01	2
Beijing 北京市	Beijing 北京市	2.67	1
Chenzhou 郴州市	Hunan 湖南省	2.38	1

10 Major Wholesalers 十家主要批发商	City 城市	Province 省	Telephone/Fax 电话/传真
SU MEC 中设江苏机械设备进出口（集团）公司	Nanjing 南京市	Jiangsu 江苏省	(025)4511888 (025)4411772
China Poster Mobile Communications Equipment Co.,Ltd. 中邮普泰移动通信设备股份有限公司	Beijing 北京市	Beijing 北京市	(010)66426993 (010)66426837
Sino Kama Co., Ltd. 中泰凯马股份有限公司	Shanghai 上海市	Shanghai 上海市	(021)62031188 (021)62030851
China Huayuan Group Co.,Ltd. 中国华源集团有限公司	Shanghai 上海市	Shanghai 上海市	(021)62031188 (021)62032288
Zhejiang Crand Imp.& Exp.Co.,Ltd. 浙江远大进出口有限公司	Ningbo 宁波市	Zhejiang 浙江省	(0574)87720170 (0574)87723350
Shandong Machinery Import & Export Group Corporation 山东省机械进出口集团公司	Qingdao 青岛市	Shandong 山东省	(0532)2661628 (0532)2991655
Qingdao Haier International Trade Co.,Ltd. 青岛海尔国际贸易有限公司	Qingdao 青岛市	Shandong 山东省	(0532)8938337 (0532)8939494
Guangdong Machinery Import & Export Group Corporation 广东省机械进出口集团公司	Guangzhou 广州市	Guangdong 广东省	(020)87782168 (020)87771803
China National Machinery Equipment Import & Export Corporation 中国机械设备进出口总公司	Beijing 北京市	Beijing 北京市	(010)63474506 (010)63261865
Beijing Cellstar Co.,Ltd. 北京蜂星事达电讯有限公司	Beijing 北京市	Beijing 北京市	(010)64602050 (010)64672648

3721: Trucks 载重汽车制造业

The industry accounts for 1.166% of the total revenue of China's industrial sector in 2002. The rate of return on assets is 3.71%. 67.90% of all firms in the industry made a profit while 32.10% had negative returns.The top province in terms of the industry's revenue is Jilin, accounting for 39.43% of the total revenue.
2002年本行业收入占全行业的 1.166%，资产利润率为 3.71%。67.90%的企业赢利，32.10%的企业亏损。收入最高的省为吉林省，占本行业的39.43%。

	Total number of firms 企业总数	Total number of employees 职工总数	Total revenue (Mil.RMB) 总销售收入 (百万元)	Total profit (Mil.RMB) 总利润 (百万元)	Return on assets 资产利润率 (%)	Return on equity 权益利润率 (%)	Labour productivity ('000 RMB/ worker) 劳动生产率 (千元/人)	Debts/ assets 资产负债率 (%)	Total assets (Mil.RMB) 总资产 (百万元)
Industry Overall 行业总体	81	271,446	125,112	6,060	3.71	9.71	110.90	61.79	163,281
	Number of firms 企业个数	Average number of employees 平均职工人数	Average revenue ('000 RMB) 平均销售收入（千元）	Average profit ('000 RMB) 平均利润 (千元)	Return on assets 资产利润率 (%)	Return on equity 权益利润率 (%)	Labour productivity ('000 RMB/ worker) 劳动生产率 (千元/人)	Debts/ assets 资产负债率 (%)	Average total assets ('000 RMB) 平均总资产 (千元)
By ownership 产业所有权									
State-owned 国有	28	4,695	2,074,495	27,774	1.00	3.32	105.09	69.91	2,777,272
Collective-owned 集体	3	521	362,826	39,936	22.25	60.48	266.58	63.21	179,472
Foreign & Overseas Chinese Funded 三资	9	2,831	1,040,246	55,967	4.19	12.68	80.97	66.94	1,335,184
By regional distribution 地区分布									
Central-North 华北	16	1,662	573,374	15,734	2.42	6.31	44.18	61.73	651,378
Beijing 北京	6	3,445	1,335,937	28,038	2.62	8.72	45.71	69.93	1,069,317
Tianjin 天津	2	84	6,659	-184	-1.81	-4.14	11.60	56.37	10,194
Hebei 河北	2	431	105,148	21,889	9.16	21.43	89.31	57.25	238,938
Shanxi 山西	3	1,026	47,583	370	0.13	0.27	6.73	50.47	276,987
Inner Mongolia 内蒙古	3	604	264,001	12,997	1.46	2.72	71.91	46.42	892,310
Northeast 东北	9	10,632	5,524,612	131,545	2.19	7.55	128.04	71.04	6,015,265
Liaoning 辽宁	2	55	17,445	-1,035	-2.32	-3.70	80.68	37.29	44,634
Jilin 吉林	6	15,307	8,221,182	231,198	2.59	8.45	133.39	69.29	8,910,448
Heilongjiang 黑龙江	1	3,740	359,527	-201,219	-34.37		-1.76	236.15	585,434
Central-East 华东	21	2,827	1,189,389	18,630	1.22	3.21	101.00	61.81	1,521,031
Shanghai 上海	1	37	49,998	612	1.73	6.00	788.49	71.12	35,301
Jiangsu 江苏	4	3,683	1,733,617	-36,065	-1.19	-2.41	95.34	50.44	3,020,243
Zhejiang 浙江	1	2,373	953,271	22,265	2.50	6.95	77.58	64.11	891,955
Anhui 安徽	3	947	651,729	8,299	1.85	2.93	128.52	36.79	448,445
Fujian 福建	4	399	20,963	-8,301	-5.51	-60.99	23.66	90.96	150,508
Jiangxi 江西	3	5,920	1,905,973	136,154	5.89	14.24	75.37	58.66	2,312,927
Shandong 山东	5	4,005	1,856,496	22,490	1.12	5.34	131.65	79.03	2,009,454
Central-South 中南	18	3,490	1,666,090	214,945	8.03	19.84	119.09	59.53	2,677,257
Henan 河南	2	1,393	612,199	22,700	2.64	12.69	105.17	79.21	860,208
Hubei 湖北	5	10,078	4,985,240	763,142	10.14	21.67	130.99	53.21	7,524,917
Hunan 湖南	6	301	87,281	907	0.63		34.62	100.51	143,207
Guangdong 广东	4	1,241	88,814	-33,961	-2.05	-15.22	18.82	86.51	1,654,578
Guangxi 广西	1	2,867	2,960,086	138,311	10.11	21.28	150.43	52.50	1,368,071
Hainan 海南									
Southwest 西南	15	1,289	594,106	16,525	1.46	2.39	103.67	38.93	1,134,213
Chongqing 重庆	5	1,933	1,297,512	58,516	2.15	3.08	174.68	30.26	2,726,875
Sichuan 四川	4	789	234,950	-2,208	-1.78	-7.95	34.82	77.58	123,931
Guizhou 贵州	2	239	17,650	-13,005	-3.26	-35.47	-10.42	90.81	398,751
Yunnan 云南	4	1,509	362,232	-2,465	-0.47	-1.41	35.00	66.55	521,398
Tibet 西藏									
Northwest 西北	2	3,828	1,169,036	58,276	7.40	18.50	156.09	60.01	787,854
Shaanxi 陕西	2	3,828	1,169,036	58,276	7.40	18.50	156.09	60.01	787,854
Gansu 甘肃									
Qinghai 青海									
Ningxia 宁夏									
Xinjiang 新疆									

Year 年份	Number of firms 企业个数	Rate of change 变化率 (%)	Number of employees 职工人数 (人)	Rate of change 变化率 (%)	Total revenue (Mil. RMB) 总销售收入 (百万元)	Rate of change 变化率 (%)	Total profit (Mil RMB) 总利润 (百万元)	Rate of change 变化率 (%)
2000	79		314,917		79,943		819	
2001	76	-3.80	276,157	-12.31	94,086	17.69	3,292	301.95
2002	81	6.58	271,446	-1.71	125,112	32.98	6,060	84.08

Major Products 主要产品	Output 产量	Unit 单位
Truck 载货汽车	125	10,000 Vehicles 万辆

10 Main Firms with Maximal Revenue (year founded) 收入最大的十家主要企业（创办年份）	City 城市	Province 省	Telephone/fax 电话/传真	Number of employees 职工人数	Ownership 产业所有权	Revenue ('000 RMB) 销售收入 (千元)	Profit('000 RMB) (rank) 利润(千元) (排名)	Total assets ('000 RMB) 总资产 (千元)	Major products 主要产品
Beijing Foton Automobile Co.,Ltd. 北京福田车辆股份有限公司(1996)	Beijing 北京市	Beijing 北京市	(010)80716401 (010)80716402	13,470	Joint Stock 股份制	7,576,138	190,295(5)	3,305,802	Agricultural Vehicle 农用车
China Heavy Automobile Group Company 中国重型汽车集团公司(1983)	Jinan 济南市	Shandong 山东省	(0531)5582114 (0531)5952412	15,087	State Enterprises 国有独资	7,473,542	28,251(15)	8,860,890	Camion 载重汽车
Nanjing Automobile (Group) Co., Ltd. 南京汽车集团有限公司(1947)	Nanjing 南京市	Jiangsu 江苏省	(025)3437788 (025)3433526	14,065	State-owned 国有企业	6,724,610	-	11,982,420	Truck 载货汽车
Jiangling Motors Co .,Ltd 江铃汽车集团公司(1991)	Nanchang 南昌市	Jiangxi 江西省	(0791)5232888 (0791)5231032	16,078	Foreign Funded 外商投资	5,509,315	408,329(4)	6,493,083	Wushiling Series五十铃系列
Qingling Automobile Group Co.,Ltd. 庆铃汽车（集团）有限公司(1994)	Chongqing 重庆市	Chongqing 重庆市	(023)65262233 (023)68830397	4,413	State Enterprises 国有独资	3,909,453	163,709(6)	11,402,476	Automobile Parts汽车零部件
Chongqing Heavy Automobile Group Co., Ltd. 重庆重型汽车集团有限责任公司(1965)	Chongqing 重庆市	Chongqing 重庆市	(023)49638863 (023)49639833	4,403	State Enterprises 国有独资	2,213,839	105,126(9)	1,963,980	Red Rock Heavy Automobile红岩重型汽车
Shaanxi Automobile Group Co., Ltd. 陕西汽车集团有限责任公司(1975)	Xi'an 西安市	Shannxi 陕西省	(029)2527591 (029)2527664	6,510	Limited-Liability 有限公司	1,883,547	95,484(10)	1,411,270	Automobile 汽车
Anhui Jianghuai Automobile Co.,Ltd. 合肥江淮汽车有限公司(1996)	Hefei 合肥市	Anhui 安徽省	(0551)3415133 (0551)3415133	1,979	Foreign Funded 外商投资	1,773,631	30,176(14)	641,161	Light Truck轻型载货汽车
FAW Group Hongta Yunnan Automobile Manufacturing Co., Ltd. 一汽红塔云南汽车制造有限公司(1997)	Qujing 曲靖市	Yunnan 云南省	(0874)3140718 (0874)3141990	3,032	Limited-Liability 有限公司	1,109,750	20,642(18)	1,160,728	Truck 载货汽车
Qingdao Special Type Automobile Group 青岛特种汽车集团公司(1993)	Qingdao 青岛市	Shandong 山东省	(0532)7869236 (0532)7860388	1,439	Collective-owned 集体企业	1,049,266	119,689(8)	516,188	Half Trailer 半挂车

Top 10 Cities by Revenue 销售收入排名前10位城市	Province 省	Market share 市场份额 (%)	Number of firms 企业个数
Changchun 长春市	Jilin 吉林省	39.24	4
Shiyan 十堰市	Hubei 湖北省	14.90	1
Beijing 北京市	Beijing 北京市	6.41	6
Jinan 济南市	Shandong 山东省	5.97	1
Nanjing 南京市	Jiangsu 江苏省	5.52	3
Chongqing 重庆市	Chongqing 重庆市	5.19	5
Xiangfan 襄樊市	Hubei 湖北省	4.92	1
Nanchang 南昌市	Jiangxi 江西省	4.43	2
Liuzhou 柳州市	Guangxi 广西	2.37	1
Xi'an 西安市	Shannxi 陕西省	1.51	1

10 Major Wholesalers 十家主要批发商	City 城市	Province 省	Telephone/Fax 电话/传真
Tianjin Automobile Xiali Sale Co.,Ltd. 天津汽车夏利销售有限公司	Tianjin 天津市	Tianjin 天津市	(022)28010071 (022)88370861
SAIC-Volkswagen Sales Co.,Ltd. Tianjin Sale Service Center 上海上汽大众汽车销售有限公司天津销售服务中心	Tianjin 天津市	Tianjin 天津市	(022)25321428 (022)25321057
Faw Car Sale Co.,Ltd. 一汽轿车销售有限公司	Changchun 长春市	Jilin 吉林省	(0431)5981943 (0431)5977611
Nanjing Langchi Group Co.,Ltd. 南京朗驰集团有限公司	Nanjing 南京市	Jiangsu 江苏省	(025)5532000 (025)5532012
JMC Sale General Co., Ltd. 江西江铃汽车销售总公司	Nanchang 南昌市	Jiangxi 江西省	(0791)5232888 (0791)5231032
Guangdong Goods & Materials Automobile Trade Corporation 广东物资集团汽车贸易公司	Guangzhou 广州市	Guangdong 广东省	(020)86329072 (020)86329056
Changchun Automobile Trade City Development Group Co., Ltd. 长春汽车贸易城开发集团股份有限公司	Changchun 长春市	Jilin 吉林省	(0431)7619450 (0431)7619748
Zhejiang Yuantong Automobile Co.,Ltd. 浙江元通汽车有限公司	Hangzhou 杭州市	Zhejiang 浙江省	(0571)88283398 (0571)88283798
Qingdao Qingqi Automobile Sale Co.,Ltd. 青岛青汽汽车销售有限公司	Qingdao 青岛市	Shandong 山东省	(0532)4913560 (0532)4913564
Shanxi Electromechanical Equipment General Company 山西省机电设备总公司	Taiyuan 太原市	Shanxi 山西省	(0351)4042445 (0351)4044137

3722: Buses 客车制造业

The industry accounts for 0.378% of the total revenue of China's industrial sector in 2002. The rate of return on assets is 2.03%. 59.55% of all firms in the industry made a profit while 40.45% had negative returns.The top province in terms of the industry's revenue is Liaoning, accounting for 24.27% of the total revenue.
2002年本行业收入占全行业的 0.378%，资产利润率为 2.03%。59.55%的企业赢利，40.45%的企业亏损。收入最高的省为辽宁省，占本行业的24.27%。

	Total number of firms 企业总数	Total number of employees 职工总数	Total revenue (Mil.RMB) 总销售收入（百万元）	Total profit (Mil.RMB) 总利润（百万元）	Return on assets 资产利润率（%）	Return on equity 权益利润率（%）	Labour productivity ('000 RMB/ worker) 劳动生产率（千元/人）	Debts/ assets 资产负债率（%）	Total assets (Mil.RMB) 总资产（百万元）
Industry Overall 行业总体	89	81,757	40,519	936	2.03	6.54	97.34	68.99	46,105

	Number of firms 企业个数	Average number of employees 平均职工人数	Average revenue ('000 RMB) 平均销售收入（千元）	Average profit ('000 RMB) 平均利润（千元）	Return on assets 资产利润率（%）	Return on equity 权益利润率（%）	Labour productivity ('000 RMB/ worker) 劳动生产率（千元/人）	Debts/ assets 资产负债率（%）	Average total assets ('000 RMB) 平均总资产（千元）
By ownership 产业所有权									
State-owned 国有	27	856	158,476	922	0.36	1.37	41.06	73.47	253,633
Collective-owned 集体	4	483	85,638	855	0.83	1.61	32.20	48.03	102,497
Foreign & Overseas Chinese Funded 三资	15	958	846,264	26,978	3.76	7.85	236.79	52.12	718,091
By regional distribution 地区分布									
Central-North 华北	10	940	266,158	-8,749	-1.76	-8.82	26.81	80.02	496,495
Beijing 北京	4	735	402,267	9,823	2.61	5.76	67.03	54.72	376,660
Tianjin 天津	2	833	7,444	-17,658	-4.66		-3.90	119.35	378,572
Hebei 河北	3	1,271	343,333	-30,339	-3.69	-25.03	15.91	85.25	822,011
Shanxi 山西	1	978	7,621	-451	-0.19	-0.49	0.71	60.53	235,138
Inner Mongolia 内蒙古									
Northeast 东北	10	1,893	985,314	-37,922	-2.52	-18.00	74.39	85.99	1,504,425
Liaoning 辽宁	8	2,237	1,229,006	-45,226	-2.45	-17.46	78.51	85.95	1,843,890
Jilin 吉林	1	283	4,341	-7,618	-7.99	-35.86	-6.18	77.73	95,397
Heilongjiang 黑龙江	1	753	16,750	-9,790	-4.95	-70.80	6.66	93.01	197,739
Central-East 华东	31	811	527,677	24,478	5.34	11.11	153.99	51.94	458,617
Shanghai 上海	1	1,229	402,870	-39,895	-6.88	-14.90	18.28	53.81	579,699
Jiangsu 江苏	12	1,100	423,561	15,043	2.92	6.05	59.07	51.71	515,267
Zhejiang 浙江	7	333	149,268	17,322	11.22	45.25	71.71	75.20	154,325
Anhui 安徽	4	1,318	1,221,241	26,164	2.92	6.09	144.75	52.09	896,840
Fujian 福建	2	994	2,403,144	193,271	14.69	24.79	1,059.84	40.76	1,315,789
Jiangxi 江西	1	155	11,531	709	8.41	21.29	21.85	60.51	8,432
Shandong 山东	4	239	31,182	1,261	3.44	17.15	29.41	79.95	36,649
Central-South 中南	23	913	421,220	19,775	5.00	15.00	85.72	66.65	395,389
Henan 河南	3	544	65,623	-43	-0.02	-0.10	34.12	79.52	218,466
Hubei 湖北	6	1,642	781,964	6,131	1.15	4.51	77.46	74.60	535,220
Hunan 湖南	6	668	526,810	66,678	13.03	36.80	171.09	64.59	511,677
Guangdong 广东	7	420	91,595	-8,017	-5.44	-16.53	16.19	67.10	147,457
Guangxi 广西	1	2,561	997,380	74,220	6.60	11.31	96.80	41.68	1,124,970
Hainan 海南									
Southwest 西南	13	477	146,113	15,028	7.50	14.70	99.80	48.98	200,366
Chongqing 重庆	2	153	44,834	-161	-0.37	-2.64	54.87	85.88	43,251
Sichuan 四川	8	485	192,814	24,883	9.04	16.74	133.85	46.00	275,347
Guizhou 贵州	2	733	122,414	5,745	4.71	8.53	54.16	44.72	121,864
Yunnan 云南	1	542	22,456	-14,866	-20.72		4.63	110.28	71,746
Tibet 西藏									
Northwest 西北	2	555	29,435	-3,256	-3.62	-128.80	9.32	97.19	89,876
Shaanxi 陕西									
Gansu 甘肃	1	746	8,864	-7,100	-5.87		2.00	102.63	121,045
Qinghai 青海									
Ningxia 宁夏									
Xinjiang 新疆	1	364	50,005	588	1.00	7.14	24.30	85.96	58,706

3722: Buses 客车制造业

Year 年份	Number of firms 企业个数	Rate of change 变化率(%)	Number of employees 职工人数(人)	Rate of change 变化率(%)	Total revenue (Mil. RMB) 总销售收入(百万元)	Rate of change 变化率(%)	Total profit (Mil RMB) 总利润(百万元)	Rate of change 变化率(%)
2000	94		98,594		22,792		804	
2001	93	-1.06	93,656	-5.01	33,440	46.72	882	9.70
2002	89	-4.30	81,757	-12.71	40,519	21.17	936	6.12

Major Products 主要产品	Output 产量	Unit 单位
Highway Passenger Bus 公路客车	92	10,000 Vehicles 万辆

10 Main Firms with Maximal Revenue (year founded) 收入最大的十家主要企业(创办年份)	City 城市	Province 省	Telephone/fax 电话/传真	Number of employees 职工人数	Ownership 产业所有权	Revenue ('000 RMB) 销售收入(千元)	Profit('000 RMB) (rank) 利润(千元)(排名)	Total assets ('000 RMB) 总资产(千元)	Major products 主要产品
Jinbei Automobile Co.,Ltd. 金杯汽车股份有限公司(1984)	Shenyang 沈阳市	Liaoning 辽宁省	(024)23745249 (024)23745250	10,730	Joint Stock 股份制	8,671,748	-	12,988,949	Light Bus 轻型客车
South East (Fujian) Automobile Industry Co.,Ltd. 东南(福建)汽车工业有限公司(1995)	Fuzhou 福州市	Fujian 福建省	(0591)2766566 (0591)2766568	1,715	Overseas Chinese-funded 港澳台资	4,769,069	382,153(2)	2,607,606	Southeast Light Bus-Delika东南轻型客车-得利卡
Anhui Jianghuai Automobile Co., Ltd. 安徽江淮汽车股份有限公司(1999)	Hefei 合肥市	Anhui 安徽省	(0551)3415133 (0551)3415133	1,615	Foreign Funded 外商投资	3,460,853	145,652(3)	1,800,000	Passenger Bus 客车
Changfeng Group Co.,Ltd. 长丰(集团)有限责任公司(1996)	Yongzhou 永州市	Hunan 湖南省	(0746)8315976 (0746)8456629	2,217	State Enterprises 国有独资	2,920,640	399,061(1)	2,559,874	Automobile 汽车
China Sanjiang Aerospace Industrial Group General Co.,Ltd. 中国三江航天工业集团总公司(1969)	Wuhan 武汉市	Hubei 湖北省	(027)83562114 (027)83816164	7,611	State-owned 国有企业	1,956,565	20,569(14)	1,889,480	Light Bus 轻型客车
Kinglong United Automobile Industry(Suzhou)Co.,Ltd. 金龙联合汽车工业(苏州)有限公司(1999)	Suzhou 苏州市	Jiangsu 江苏省	(0512)65512566 (0512)65341469	752	Limited-Liability 有限公司	1,492,996	103,858(6)	450,272	Passenger Bus 客车
Jiangsu Yaxing Motor Coach Co.,Ltd. 江苏亚星客车集团有限公司(1996)	Yangzhou 扬州市	Jiangsu 江苏省	(0514)7882999 (0514)7861136	4,609	State Enterprises 国有独资	1,401,460	27,000(12)	2,288,626	Passenger Bus 客车
Beijing Foton Environmental Protection Engine Co.,Ltd. 北京福田环保动力股份有限公司(1999)	Beijing 北京市	Beijing 北京市	(010)69733311	1,762	Joint Stock 股份制	1,310,483	20,014(15)	813,363	Automobile 汽车
Liaoning Huanghai Auto (Group) Co.,Ltd. 辽宁黄海汽车(集团)有限责任公司(1951)	Dandong 丹东市	Liaoning 辽宁省	(0415)6272338 (0415)6220602	4,465	State Enterprises 国有独资	958,860	10,034(17)	695,423	Passenger Bus 客车
Anhui Ankai Auto Co., Ltd. 安徽安凯汽车股份有限公司(1966)	Hefei 合肥市	Anhui 安徽省	(0551)4844828 (0551)4844888	2,821	State Enterprises 国有独资	844,740	-	1,442,780	Passenger Bus 客车

Top 10 Cities by Revenue 销售收入排名前10位城市	Province 省	Market share 市场份额(%)	Number of firms 企业个数
Shenyang 沈阳市	Liaoning 辽宁省	21.78	6
Hefei 合肥市	Anhui 安徽省	12.04	3
Fuzhou 福州市	Fujian 福建省	11.77	1
Yongzhou 永州市	Hunan 湖南省	7.22	2
Shiyan 十堰市	Hubei 湖北省	5.22	1
Yichang 宜昌市	Hubei 湖北省	4.83	1
Beijing 北京市	Beijing 北京市	3.97	4
Yangzhou 扬州市	Jiangsu 江苏省	3.71	4
Suzhou 苏州市	Jiangsu 江苏省	3.70	2
Chengdu 成都市	Sichuan 四川省	3.67	6

10 Major Wholesalers 十家主要批发商	City 城市	Province 省	Telephone/Fax 电话/传真
Tianjin Automobile Xiali Sale Co.,Ltd. 天津汽车夏利销售有限公司	Tianjin 天津市	Tianjin 天津市	(022)28010071 (022)88370861
SAIC-Volkswagen Sales Co.,Ltd. Tianjin Sale Service Center 上海上汽大众汽车销售有限公司天津销售服务中心	Tianjin 天津市	Tianjin 天津市	(022)25321428 (022)25321057
Faw Car Sale Co.,Ltd. 一汽轿车销售有限公司	Changchun 长春市	Jilin 吉林省	(0431)5981943 (0431)5977611
Nanjing Langchi Group Co.,Ltd. 南京朗驰集团有限公司	Nanjing 南京市	Jiangsu 江苏省	(025)5532000 (025)5532012
JMC Sale General Co., Ltd. 江西江铃汽车销售总公司	Nanchang 南昌市	Jiangxi 江西省	(0791)5232888 (0791)5231032
Guangdong Goods & Materials Automobile Trade Corporation 广东物资集团汽车贸易公司	Guangzhou 广州市	Guangdong 广东省	(020)86329072 (020)86329056
Changchun Automobile Trade City Development Group Co., Ltd. 长春汽车贸易城开发集团股份有限公司	Changchun 长春市	Jilin 吉林省	(0431)7619450 (0431)7619748
Zhejiang Yuantong Automobile Co.,Ltd. 浙江元通汽车有限公司	Hangzhou 杭州市	Zhejiang 浙江省	(0571)88283398 (0571)88283798
Qingdao Qingqi Automobile Sale Co.,Ltd. 青岛青汽汽车销售有限公司	Qingdao 青岛市	Shandong 山东省	(0532)4913560 (0532)4913564
Shanxi Electromechanical Equipment General Company 山西省机电设备总公司	Taiyuan 太原市	Shanxi 山西省	(0351)4042445 (0351)4044137

3723: Cars 小轿车制造业

The industry accounts for 1.255% of the total revenue of China's industrial sector in 2002. The rate of return on assets is 15.44%. 76.19% of all firms in the industry made a profit while 23.81% had negative returns.The top province in terms of the industry's revenue is Shanghai, accounting for 40.75% of the total revenue.
2002年本行业收入占全行业的 1.255%，资产利润率为 15.44%。76.19%的企业赢利，23.81%的企业亏损。收入最高的省为上海市，占本行业的40.75%。

	Total number of firms 企业总数	Total number of employees 职工总数	Total revenue (Mil.RMB) 总销售收入（百万元）	Total profit (Mil.RMB) 总利润（百万元）	Return on assets 资产利润率（%）	Return on equity 权益利润率（%）	Labour productivity ('000 RMB/ worker) 劳动生产率（千元/人）	Debts/ assets 资产负债率（%）	Total assets (Mil.RMB) 总资产（百万元）
Industry Overall 行业总体	21	59,994	134,559	17,813	15.44	28.62	717.87	46.05	115,349

	Number of firms 企业个数	Average number of employees 平均职工人数	Average revenue ('000 RMB) 平均销售收入（千元）	Average profit ('000 RMB) 平均利润（千元）	Return on assets 资产利润率（%）	Return on equity 权益利润率（%）	Labour productivity ('000 RMB/ worker) 劳动生产率（千元/人）	Debts/ assets 资产负债率（%）	Average total assets ('000 RMB) 平均总资产（千元）
By ownership 产业所有权									
State-owned 国有	1	1,075	3,313,757	289,159	10.74	24.78	926.00	56.64	2,691,402
Collective-owned 集体									
Foreign & Overseas Chinese Funded 三资	11	3,230	10,389,321	1,500,145	18.48	31.42	949.62	41.16	8,115,993
By regional distribution 地区分布									
Central-North 华北	4	4,380	1,654,626	-398,549	-9.88	-32.17	246.89	69.29	4,034,654
Beijing 北京	2	2,085	734,864	-127,493	-6.14	-13.42	50.37	54.20	2,074,820
Tianjin 天津	2	6,676	2,574,387	-669,605	-11.17	-43.83	308.28	74.51	5,994,488
Hebei 河北									
Shanxi 山西									
Inner Mongolia 内蒙古									
Northeast 东北	1	6,184	30,280,958	5,355,450	31.22	49.77	1,220.02	37.27	17,152,533
Liaoning 辽宁									
Jilin 吉林	1	6,184	30,280,958	5,355,450	31.22	49.77	1,220.02	37.27	17,152,533
Heilongjiang 黑龙江									
Central-East 华东	8	2,855	7,759,196	1,126,680	17.57	29.15	859.45	39.73	6,412,580
Shanghai 上海	2	7,024	27,414,124	4,040,186	18.47	28.54	1,219.03	35.29	21,879,029
Jiangsu 江苏	2	694	710,280	8,776	1.37	8.49	186.09	83.83	638,784
Zhejiang 浙江	2	1,855	752,756	6,510	0.81	2.64	122.91	69.24	802,532
Anhui 安徽	1	3,532	4,295,491	902,176	19.42	47.67	504.06	59.25	4,644,563
Fujian 福建									
Jiangxi 江西									
Shandong 山东	1	160	23,760	320	2.08	2.41	49.00	13.65	15,390
Central-South 中南	6	1,862	5,325,444	803,721	17.34	34.74	964.92	50.10	4,636,309
Henan 河南									
Hubei 湖北	3	2,039	3,163,671	185,115	4.07	12.32	562.04	66.96	4,547,385
Hunan 湖南									
Guangdong 广东	2	1,989	9,573,948	1,988,912	34.64	48.47	1,595.11	28.54	5,742,148
Guangxi 广西									
Hainan 海南	1	1,075	3,313,757	289,159	10.74	24.78	926.00	56.64	2,691,402
Southwest 西南	1	1,282	3,012,037	215,100	11.69	17.63	541.58	33.74	1,840,787
Chongqing 重庆	1	1,282	3,012,037	215,100	11.69	17.63	541.58	33.74	1,840,787
Sichuan 四川									
Guizhou 贵州									
Yunnan 云南									
Tibet 西藏									
Northwest 西北	1	1,001	621,086	726	0.07	0.15	98.52	54.89	1,098,405
Shaanxi 陕西	1	1,001	621,086	726	0.07	0.15	98.52	54.89	1,098,405
Gansu 甘肃									
Qinghai 青海									
Ningxia 宁夏									
Xinjiang 新疆									

3723: Cars 小轿车制造业

Year 年份	Number of firms 企业个数	Rate of change 变化率(%)	Number of employees 职工人数(人)	Rate of change 变化率(%)	Total revenue (Mil. RMB) 总销售收入(百万元)	Rate of change 变化率(%)	Total profit (Mil RMB) 总利润(百万元)	Rate of change 变化率(%)
2000	16		63,849		75,935		7,000	
2001	17	6.25	58,148	-8.93	93,373	22.96	10,845	54.93
2002	21	23.53	59,994	3.17	134,559	44.11	17,813	64.25

Major Products 主要产品	Output 产量	Unit 单位
Saloon Car 轿车	106	10,000 Vehicles 万辆

10 Main Firms with Maximal Revenue (year founded) 收入最大的十家主要企业（创办年份）	City 城市	Province 省	Telephone/fax 电话/传真	Number of employees 职工人数	Ownership 产业所有权	Revenue ('000 RMB) 销售收入(千元)	Profit('000 RMB) (rank) 利润(千元)(排名)	Total assets ('000 RMB) 总资产(千元)	Major products 主要产品
Shanghai Volkswagen Automobile Co.,Ltd.	Shanghai	Shanghai	(021)59561888		Foreign Funded				Small Sedan
上海大众汽车有限公司(1985)	上海市	上海市	(021)59572815	10,652	外商投资	36,265,280	4,787,366(2)	29,628,900	小轿车
China Faw Group Volkswagen Automobile Co.,Ltd.	Changchun	Jilin	(0431)5990253		Foreign Funded				Automobile
一汽一大众汽车有限公司(1996)	长春市	吉林省	(0431)5990130	6,184	外商投资	30,280,958	5,355,450(1)	17,152,533	汽车
Shanghai General Motors Co.,Ltd.	Shanghai	Shanghai	(021)28902890		Foreign Funded				Sedan
上海通用汽车有限公司(1997)	上海市	上海市	(021)50319099	3,396	外商投资	18,562,967	3,293,006(3)	14,129,158	轿车
Guangzhou Honda Automobile Co.,Ltd.	Guangzhou	Guangdong	(020)82277789		Foreign Funded				Guangzhou Yage
广州本田汽车有限公司(1998)	广州市	广东省	(020)82270620	2,274	外商投资	13,631,731	2,799,856(4)	6,126,251	广州雅阁
Dongfeng Peugeot Citroen Automobile Co.,Ltd.	Wuhan	Hubei	(027)84299114		Foreign Funded				Sedan
神龙汽车有限公司(1992)	武汉市	湖北省	(027)84874312	5,270	外商投资	9,384,595	541,092(7)	13,456,763	轿车
Tianjin Auto Industry (Group)Co.,Ltd.	Tianjin	Tianjin	(022)23316066		State Enterprises				Xiali Sedan
天津汽车工业（集团）有限公司(1995)	天津市	天津市	(022)23310858	12,706	国有独资	4,802,023	-	10,504,977	夏利轿车
Beijing Jeep Co.,Ltd.	Beijing	Beijing	(010)67712233		Foreign Funded				Light Cross-country Vehicle轻型
北京吉普汽车有限公司(1984)	北京市	北京市	(010)67711363	3,502	外商投资	1,271,762	-	2,139,761	越野汽车
Jiangsu Dongfeng Yueda Kia Automobile Co.,Ltd.	Yancheng	Jiangsu	(0515)8333808		Foreign Funded				Sedan
江苏东风悦达起亚汽车有限公司(1992)	盐城市	江苏省	(0515)8333601	885	外商投资	1,234,170	12,790(11)	1,150,970	轿车
Zhejiang Haoqing Automobile Manufacturing Co.,Ltd.	Taizhou	Zhejiang	(0576)5121444		Limited-Liability				Sedan
浙江豪情汽车制造有限公司(1996)	台州市	浙江省	(0576)5121555	1,750	有限公司	749,860	9,060(12)	649,180	轿车
Byd Auto Co.,Ltd.	Xi'an	Shannxi	(029)3290920		Limited-Liability				Automobile
比亚迪汽车有限责任公司(1997)	西安市	陕西省	(029)3235687	1,001	有限公司	621,086	726(15)	1,098,405	汽车

Top 10 Cities by Revenue 销售收入排名前10位城市	Province 省	Market share 市场份额(%)	Number of firms 企业个数
Shanghai 上海市	Shanghai 上海市	40.75	2
Changchun 长春市	Jilin 吉林省	22.50	1
Guangzhou 广州市	Guangdong 广东省	14.23	2
Wuhan 武汉市	Hubei 湖北省	6.98	2
Tianjin 天津市	Tianjin 天津市	3.83	2
Wuhu 芜湖市	Anhui 安徽省	3.19	1
Haikou 海口市	Hainan 海南省	2.46	1
Chongqing 重庆市	Chongqing 重庆市	2.24	1
Beijing 北京市	Beijing 北京市	1.09	2
Yancheng 盐城市	Jiangsu 江苏省	0.92	1

10 Major Wholesalers 十家主要批发商	City 城市	Province 省	Telephone/Fax 电话/传真
Tianjin Automobile Xiali Sale Co.,Ltd.	Tianjin	Tianjin	(022)28010071
天津汽车夏利销售有限公司	天津市	天津市	(022)88370861
SAIC-Volkswagen Sales Co.,Ltd. Tianjin Sale Service Center	Tianjin	Tianjin	(022)25321428
上海上汽大众汽车销售有限公司天津销售服务中心	天津市	天津市	(022)25321057
Faw Car Sale Co.,Ltd.	Changchun	Jilin	(0431)5981943
一汽轿车销售有限公司	长春市	吉林省	(0431)5977611
Nanjing Langchi Group Co.,Ltd.	Nanjing	Jiangsu	(025)5532000
南京朗驰集团有限公司	南京市	江苏省	(025)5532012
JMC Sale General Co., Ltd.	Nanchang	Jiangxi	(0791)5232888
江西江铃汽车销售总公司	南昌市	江西省	(0791)5231032
Guangdong Goods & Materials Automobile Trade Corporation	Guangzhou	Guangdong	(020)86329072
广东物资集团汽车贸易公司	广州市	广东省	(020)86329056
Changchun Automobile Trade City Development Group Co., Ltd.	Changchun	Jilin	(0431)7619450
长春汽车贸易城开发集团股份有限公司	长春市	吉林省	(0431)7619748
Zhejiang Yuantong Automobile Co.,Ltd.	Hangzhou	Zhejiang	(0571)88283398
浙江元通汽车有限公司	杭州市	浙江省	(0571)88283798
Qingdao Qingqi Automobile Sale Co.,Ltd.	Qingdao	Shandong	(0532)4913560
青岛青汽汽车销售有限公司	青岛市	山东省	(0532)4913564
Shanxi Electromechanical Equipment General Company	Taiyuan	Shanxi	(0351)4042445
山西省机电设备总公司	太原市	山西省	(0351)4044137

3724: Minicar 微型汽车制造业

The industry accounts for 0.143% of the total revenue of China's industrial sector in 2002. The rate of return on assets is 7.12%. 66.67% of all firms in the industry made a profit while 33.33% had negative returns.The top province in terms of the industry's revenue is Chongqing, accounting for 45.03% of the total revenue.
2002年本行业收入占全行业的 0.143%，资产利润率为 7.12%。66.67%的企业赢利，33.33%的企业亏损。收入最高的省为重庆市，占本行业的45.03%。

	Total number of firms 企业总数	Total number of employees 职工总数	Total revenue (Mil.RMB) 总销售收入（百万元）	Total profit (Mil.RMB) 总利润（百万元）	Return on assets 资产利润率（%）	Return on equity 权益利润率（%）	Labour productivity ('000 RMB/worker) 劳动生产率（千元/人）	Debts/assets 资产负债率（%）	Total assets (Mil.RMB) 总资产（百万元）
Industry Overall 行业总体	24	23,093	15,377	1,028	7.12	20.17	209.89	64.72	14,442

	Number of firms 企业个数	Average number of employees 平均职工人数	Average revenue ('000 RMB) 平均销售收入（千元）	Average profit ('000 RMB) 平均利润（千元）	Return on assets 资产利润率（%）	Return on equity 权益利润率（%）	Labour productivity ('000 RMB/worker) 劳动生产率（千元/人）	Debts/assets 资产负债率（%）	Average total assets ('000 RMB) 平均总资产（千元）
By ownership 产业所有权									
State-owned 国有	1	332	46,434	-2,839	-1.96		-0.10	102.45	144,798
Collective-owned 集体	5	1,276	270,767	1,170	0.54	1.89	52.30	71.38	216,654
Foreign & Overseas Chinese Funded 三资	1	4,080	3,773,066	54,743	2.57	7.98	160.88	67.80	2,131,297
By regional distribution 地区分布									
Central-North 华北	3	236	53,212	-6,713	-10.49	-571.32	49.54	98.16	63,967
Beijing 北京									
Tianjin 天津	2	184	57,166	-7,878	-22.72		49.77	216.93	34,666
Hebei 河北	1	340	45,304	-4,384	-3.58	-5.18	49.29	30.98	122,568
Shanxi 山西									
Inner Mongolia 内蒙古									
Northeast 东北	2	2,957	615,217	10,829	2.15	5.60	52.97	61.53	502,810
Liaoning 辽宁									
Jilin 吉林									
Heilongjiang 黑龙江	2	2,957	615,217	10,829	2.15	5.60	52.97	61.53	502,810
Central-East 华东	11	414	283,048	10,992	3.31	9.68	356.66	65.85	332,405
Shanghai 上海									
Jiangsu 江苏	2	90	430,290	8,010	2.12	4.78	5,458.21	55.70	378,065
Zhejiang 浙江	1	60	7,679	18	0.42	1.50	23.95	72.15	4,323
Anhui 安徽	3	888	580,153	30,768	8.23	36.35	197.50	77.36	373,809
Fujian 福建	1	65	10,138	652	1.00	1.09	135.17	8.65	65,466
Jiangxi 江西	1	208	66,073	7,120	1.64	4.20	146.02	60.87	433,314
Shandong 山东	3	457	142,865	1,600	0.38	1.12	57.21	66.36	425,264
Central-South 中南	5	986	774,773	10,676	2.31	7.64	135.89	69.81	463,012
Henan 河南	2	118	21,009	630	3.66	9.10	44.30	59.84	17,232
Hubei 湖北									
Hunan 湖南									
Guangdong 广东	2	306	29,390	-1,311	-1.76		4.58	100.78	74,650
Guangxi 广西	1	4,080	3,773,066	54,743	2.57	7.98	160.88	67.80	2,131,297
Hainan 海南									
Southwest 西南	3	2,331	2,333,208	283,956	11.71	30.89	315.50	62.08	2,424,197
Chongqing 重庆	1	6,553	6,924,590	894,400	12.92	28.58	341.70	54.78	6,920,530
Sichuan 四川									
Guizhou 贵州	2	221	37,517	-21,267	-12.08		-73.78	205.68	176,030
Yunnan 云南									
Tibet 西藏									
Northwest 西北									
Shaanxi 陕西									
Gansu 甘肃									
Qinghai 青海									
Ningxia 宁夏									
Xinjiang 新疆									

Year 年份	Number of firms 企业个数	Rate of change 变化率 (%)	Number of employees 职工人数 (人)	Rate of change 变化率 (%)	Total revenue (Mil. RMB) 总销售收入 (百万元)	Rate of change 变化率 (%)	Total profit (Mil RMB) 总利润 (百万元)	Rate of change 变化率 (%)
2000	25		33,555		13,341		157	
2001	31	24.00	29,834	-11.09	13,752	3.08	76	-51.59
2002	24	-22.58	23,093	-22.60	15,377	11.82	1,028	1,252.63

Major Products 主要产品	Output 产量	Unit 单位
Automobile 汽车	348	10,000 Vehicles 万辆

10 Main Firms with Maximal Revenue (year founded) 收入最大的十家主要企业（创办年份）	City 城市	Province 省	Telephone/fax 电话/传真	Number of employees 职工人数	Ownership 产业所有权	Revenue ('000 RMB) 销售收入（千元）	Profit('000 RMB) (rank) 利润(千元)(排名)	Total assets ('000 RMB) 总资产（千元）	Major products 主要产品
Chongqing Chang'an Automobile Co.,Ltd. 重庆长安汽车股份有限公司(1996)	Chongqing 重庆市	Chongqing 重庆市	(023)67590114 (023)67870261	6,553	Joint Stock 股份制	6,924,590	894,400(1)	6,920,530	Minitype Automobile 微型汽车
SAIC-GM-WULING Automobile Co.,Ltd. 上汽通用五菱汽车股份有限公司(1999)	Liuzhou 柳州市	Guangxi 广西	(0772)3750189 (0772)3711150	4,080	Foreign Funded 外商投资	3,773,066	54,743(3)	2,131,297	Minitype Automobile 微型汽车
Jiangxi Changhe Automobile Co.,Ltd. Hefei Branch 江西昌河汽车股份有限公司合肥分公司(1999)	Hefei 合肥市	Anhui 安徽省	(0551)5842344 (0551)5842250	2,375	Joint Stock 股份制	1,655,487	92,242(2)	821,815	Minitype Automobile 微型汽车
Hafei Industrial & Commercial Company 哈尔滨哈飞实业总公司(1979)	Harbin 哈尔滨市	Heilongjiang 黑龙江省	(0451)86501680 (0451)86501631	5,438	Collective-owned 集体企业	977,741	33,613(4)	880,689	Minitype Automobile 微型车
Nanjing Chang'an Automobile Co.,Ltd. 南京长安汽车有限公司(2000)	Nanjing 南京市	Jiangsu 江苏省	(025)5504558 (025)5501748	83	Limited-Liability 有限公司	851,510	16,070(6)	747,810	Minitype Automobile 微型汽车
Rongcheng Huatai Automobile Co.,Ltd. 荣成市华泰汽车有限公司(2000)	Weihai 威海市	Shandong 山东省	(0631)7558999 (0631)7558619	476	Private Owned 私营企业	254,993	21,679(5)	806,730	SQ6470W Light Bus.SQ6470W 轻型客车
Harbin Hafei Industrial & Commercial Company Automobile Manufacturing Factory 哈尔滨哈飞实业汽车制造厂(1999)	Harbin 哈尔滨市	Heilongjiang 黑龙江省	(0451)6501680 (0451)6501631	476	Collective-owned 集体企业	252,692	-	124,930	Minitype Automobile 微型汽车
Shandong Rusan Yulong Vehicles Co.,Ltd. 山东乳山玉龙车辆有限公司(1998)	Weihai 威海市	Shandong 山东省	(0631)6752578 (0631)6752282	655	Joint Stock 股份制	158,608	5,305(8)	220,972	Internal-conbustion Engine Connecting Rod 内燃机连杆
Wuhu Tongbao Bus Co.,Ltd. 芜湖通宝客车有限公司(2000)	Wuhu 芜湖市	Anhui 安徽省	(0553)5853168 (0553)5853168	230	Private Owned 私营企业	84,973	63(13)	8,031	Minitype Automobile 微型汽车
Guizhou Yunque Automobile Co.,Ltd. 贵州云雀汽车有限责任公司(1996)	Anshun 安顺市	Guizhou 贵州省	(0853)3412620 (0853)3412623	141	Limited-Liability 有限公司	66,845	-	341,130	Minitype Automobile 微型汽车

Top 10 Cities by Revenue 销售收入排名前10位城市	Province 省	Market share 市场份额 (%)	Number of firms 企业个数
Chongqing 重庆市	Chongqing 重庆市	45.03	1
Liuzhou 柳州市	Guangxi 广西	24.54	1
Hefei 合肥市	Anhui 安徽省	10.77	1
Harbin 哈尔滨市	Heilongjiang 黑龙江省	8.00	2
Nanjing 南京市	Jiangsu 江苏省	5.60	2
Weihai 威海市	Shandong 山东省	2.69	2
Tianjin 天津市	Tianjin 天津市	0.74	2
Wuhu 芜湖市	Anhui 安徽省	0.55	1
Anshun 安顺市	Guizhou 贵州省	0.43	1
Jiujiang 九江市	Jiangxi 江西省	0.43	1

10 Major Wholesalers 十家主要批发商	City 城市	Province 省	Telephone/Fax 电话/传真
Tianjin Automobile Xiali Sale Co.,Ltd. 天津汽车夏利销售有限公司	Tianjin 天津市	Tianjin 天津市	(022)28010071 (022)88370861
SAIC-Volkswagen Sales Co.,Ltd. Tianjin Sale Service Center 上海上汽大众汽车销售有限公司天津销售服务中心	Tianjin 天津市	Tianjin 天津市	(022)25321428 (022)25321057
Faw Car Sale Co.,Ltd. 一汽轿车销售有限公司	Changchun 长春市	Jilin 吉林省	(0431)5981943 (0431)5977611
Nanjing Langchi Group Co.,Ltd. 南京朗驰集团有限公司	Nanjing 南京市	Jiangsu 江苏省	(025)5532000 (025)5532012
JMC Sale General Co., Ltd. 江西江铃汽车销售总公司	Nanchang 南昌市	Jiangxi 江西省	(0791)5232888 (0791)5231032
Guangdong Goods & Materials Automobile Trade Corporation 广东物资集团汽车贸易公司	Guangzhou 广州市	Guangdong 广东省	(020)86329072 (020)86329056
Changchun Automobile Trade City Development Group Co., Ltd. 长春汽车贸易城开发集团股份有限公司	Changchun 长春市	Jilin 吉林省	(0431)7619450 (0431)7619748
Zhejiang Yuantong Automobile Co.,Ltd. 浙江元通汽车有限公司	Hangzhou 杭州市	Zhejiang 浙江省	(0571)88283398 (0571)88283798
Qingdao Qingqi Automobile Sale Co.,Ltd. 青岛青汽汽车销售有限公司	Qingdao 青岛市	Shandong 山东省	(0532)4913560 (0532)4913564
Shanxi Electromechanical Equipment General Company 山西省机电设备总公司	Taiyuan 太原市	Shanxi 山西省	(0351)4042445 (0351)4044137

3725: Special and Refitted Vehicles 特种车辆及改装汽车制造业

The industry accounts for 0.531% of the total revenue of China's industrial sector in 2002. The rate of return on assets is 4.91%. 69.48% of all firms in the industry made a profit while 30.52% had negative returns.The top province in terms of the industry's revenue is Shandong, accounting for 30.64% of the total revenue.
2002年本行业收入占全行业的0.531%，资产利润率为4.91%。69.48%的企业赢利，30.52%的企业亏损。收入最高的省为山东省，占本行业的30.64%。

	Total number of firms 企业总数	Total number of employees 职工总数	Total revenue (Mil.RMB) 总销售收入 (百万元)	Total profit (Mil.RMB) 总利润 (百万元)	Return on assets 资产利润率 (%)	Return on equity 权益利润率 (%)	Labour productivity ('000 RMB/ worker) 劳动生产率 (千元/人)	Debts/ assets 资产负债率 (%)	Total assets (Mil.RMB) 总资产 (百万元)
Industry Overall 行业总体	308	147,314	56,960	2,258	4.91	14.11	81.45	65.21	45,986

	Number of firms 企业个数	Average number of employees 平均职工人数	Average revenue ('000 RMB) 平均销售收入 (千元)	Average profit ('000 RMB) 平均利润 (千元)	Return on assets 资产利润率 (%)	Return on equity 权益利润率 (%)	Labour productivity ('000 RMB/ worker) 劳动生产率 (千元/人)	Debts/ assets 资产负债率 (%)	Average total assets ('000 RMB) 平均总资产 (千元)
By ownership 产业所有权									
State-owned 国有	98	486	203,849	10,163	7.42	27.11	69.16	72.62	136,918
Collective-owned 集体	28	247	74,301	1,350	2.58	5.49	101.57	52.95	52,233
Foreign & Overseas Chinese Funded 三资	29	264	191,738	8,435	6.67	16.35	203.84	59.20	126,427
By regional distribution 地区分布									
Central-North 华北	50	365	156,889	5,809	4.55	12.74	86.98	64.28	127,672
Beijing 北京	22	408	149,391	1,957	1.45	3.95	61.12	63.22	134,794
Tianjin 天津	5	221	44,162	3,084	4.50	9.07	28.76	50.45	68,591
Hebei 河北	21	378	204,128	10,717	7.87	24.57	124.81	67.98	136,224
Shanxi 山西	1	160	3,374	3	0.05	0.09	8.44	43.05	6,107
Inner Mongolia 内蒙古	1	102	47,000	6,900	3.31	6.90	174.15	52.01	208,370
Northeast 东北	25	261	30,314	-986	-1.86	-6.22	58.15	70.12	53,074
Liaoning 辽宁	12	254	17,622	-845	-1.46	-3.97	22.02	63.12	57,733
Jilin 吉林	8	286	51,358	-1,981	-3.05	-10.66	121.98	71.37	64,905
Heilongjiang 黑龙江	5	235	27,106	269	1.17		27.77	106.76	22,966
Central-East 华东	108	600	305,109	16,528	7.74	22.55	109.14	65.69	213,668
Shanghai 上海	14	343	75,563	-3,963	-3.12	-13.68	38.12	77.20	127,044
Jiangsu 江苏	26	655	277,180	7,965	3.13	8.43	97.34	62.85	254,351
Zhejiang 浙江	10	135	44,755	8,238	15.08	24.99	95.33	39.66	54,632
Anhui 安徽	14	729	195,895	7,356	3.14	9.71	59.07	67.69	234,363
Fujian 福建	5	477	786,661	31,883	9.32	36.23	489.40	74.29	342,212
Jiangxi 江西	3	337	36,820	917	0.72	1.99	34.53	64.04	128,291
Shandong 山东	36	779	484,815	35,718	14.68	41.66	117.68	64.77	243,362
Central-South 中南	78	391	143,208	2,915	2.51	7.14	65.35	64.83	116,043
Henan 河南	10	938	398,471	17,820	5.05	12.36	88.60	59.15	352,982
Hubei 湖北	34	389	106,807	181	0.20	0.62	47.52	68.55	92,450
Hunan 湖南	12	191	51,226	2,885	5.98	17.85	48.90	66.48	48,211
Guangdong 广东	18	237	67,873	-1,556	-2.24	-6.56	65.83	65.85	69,422
Guangxi 广西	4	332	429,416	9,098	6.62	27.62	105.44	76.05	137,535
Hainan 海南									
Southwest 西南	35	615	90,055	-917	-0.68	-1.58	35.88	56.90	134,961
Chongqing 重庆	9	1,194	210,709	-1,218	-0.34	-0.62	36.22	44.11	353,702
Sichuan 四川	18	485	63,567	-208	-0.29	-1.73	37.61	83.33	72,204
Guizhou 贵州	4	338	9,953	-1,304	-3.77	-35.92	8.47	89.51	34,620
Yunnan 云南	4	172	17,888	-3,047	-11.93	-47.48	62.61	74.88	25,542
Tibet 西藏									
Northwest 西北	12	478	90,286	1,009	0.85	6.48	34.04	86.88	118,692
Shaanxi 陕西	6	525	31,712	-1,107	-1.30		22.05	101.61	85,333
Gansu 甘肃									
Qinghai 青海									
Ningxia 宁夏									
Xinjiang 新疆	6	430	148,861	3,124	2.05	9.61	48.67	78.61	152,052

3725: Special and Refitted Vehicles 特种车辆及改装汽车制造业

Year 年份	Number of firms 企业个数	Rate of change 变化率 (%)	Number of employees 职工人数 (人)	Rate of change 变化率 (%)	Total revenue (Mil. RMB) 总销售收入 (百万元)	Rate of change 变化率 (%)	Total profit (Mil RMB) 总利润 (百万元)	Rate of change 变化率 (%)
2000	299		169,896		27,316		504	
2001	278	-7.02	156,328	-7.99	33,347	22.08	625	24.01
2002	308	10.79	147,314	-5.77	56,960	70.81	2,258	261.28

Major Products 主要产品	Output 产量	Unit 单位
Refitted Automobile 改装汽车	41	10,000 Vehicles 万辆

10 Main Firms with Maximal Revenue (year founded) 收入最大的十家主要企业（创办年份）	City 城市	Province 省	Telephone/fax 电话/传真	Number of employees 职工人数	Ownership 产业所有权	Revenue ('000 RMB) 销售收入 (千元)	Profit('000 RMB) (rank) 利润(千元) (排名)	Total assets ('000 RMB) 总资产 (千元)	Major products 主要产品
China Faw Group Qingdao Auto Factory	Qingdao	Shandong	(0532)4913615		State-owned				Medium-type Diesel Oil Truck中型柴油
一汽解放青岛汽车厂(1956)	青岛市	山东省	(0532)4816687	3,818	国有企业	10,322,913	1,021,000(1)	2,997,120	载货汽车
Zhengzhou Yutong Bus Co.,Ltd.	Zhengzhou	Henan	(0371)6806170		Joint Stock				Passenger Bus
郑州宇通客车股份有限公司(1993)	郑州市	河南省	(0371)6806000	1,999	股份制	2,742,713	162,971(2)	1,734,811	客车
Baoding Great Wall Automobile Co.,Ltd.	Baoding	Hebei	(0312)2192907		Joint Stock				CC1021s Light Bus & Truck.CC1021s轻
保定长城汽车股份有限公司(1974)	保定市	河北省	(0312)2192809	2,553	股份制	2,304,594	132,849(3)	1,203,305	型客货车
Xiamen Kinglong United Automobile Industry Co.,Ltd.	Xiamen	Fujian	(0592)5052608		Foreign Funded				Jinglong Passenger Bus
厦门金龙联合汽车工业有限公司(1989)	厦门市	福建省	(0592)5716502	1,343	外商投资	2,008,952	80,439(7)	1,002,486	金龙客车
Xiamen Golden Dragon Van Co., Ltd.	Xiamen	Fujian	(0592)5608908		Overseas Chinese-funded				Refitted Passenger Bus
厦门金龙旅行车有限公司(1992)	厦门市	福建省	(0592)6032726	988	港澳台资	1,917,971	79,070(8)	691,010	改装客车
Beiqi Foton Auto Stock Co.,Ltd. Huairou Automobile Factory	Beijing	Beijing	(010)69623284		Joint Stock				Automobile
北汽福田车辆股份有限公司怀柔汽车厂(1996)	北京市	北京市	(010)69643280	3,551	股份制	1,618,106	38,556(14)	1,236,356	汽车
China Faw Group Liuzhou Special Type Auto Factory	Liuzhou	Guangxi	(0772)3124119		State-owned				Load Automobile
中国第一汽车集团柳州特种汽车厂(1972)	柳州市	广西	(0772)3125476	484	国有企业	1,519,455	34,603(15)	382,797	载重汽车
Beiqi Foton Auto Stock Co., Ltd. Weifang Agri-Etuipment Branch	Weifang	Shandong	(0536)7606645		Joint Stock				Joint Harvester联
Branch.北汽福田汽车股份有限公司潍坊农业装备分公司(1998)	潍坊市	山东省	(0536)7602137	2,530	股份制	1,440,000	65,300(9)	412,369	合收割机
Hubei Tri-ring Special Truck Co.,Ltd.	Shiyan	Hubei	(0719)8782079		State-owned				Refitted Vehicle
湖北三环专用汽车有限公司(1983)	十堰市	湖北省	(0719)8781306	2,019	国有企业	1,384,046	23,957(21)	450,920	改装汽车
China Faw Group Shandong Special Automobile Works	Yantai	Shandong	(0535)5643073		State Owned				Refitted Vehicle
一汽山东汽车改装厂(1968)	烟台市	山东省	(0535)5641724	1,147	国有企业	1,345,570	85,830(6)	396,200	改装汽车

Top 10 Cities by Revenue 销售收入排名前10位城市	Province 省	Market share 市场份额 (%)	Number of firms 企业个数
Qingdao 青岛市	Shandong 山东省	19.01	7
Xiamen 厦门市	Fujian 福建省	6.89	2
Baoding 保定市	Hebei 河北省	6.29	6
Beijing 北京市	Beijing 北京市	5.77	22
Zhengzhou 郑州市	Henan 河南省	5.60	3
Suzhou 苏州市	Jiangsu 江苏省	5.58	7
Nanjing 南京市	Jiangsu 江苏省	4.61	8
Chongqing 重庆市	Chongqing 重庆市	3.33	9
Shiyan 十堰市	Hubei 湖北省	3.01	5
Liuzhou 柳州市	Guangxi 广西	2.95	2

10 Major Wholesalers 十家主要批发商	City 城市	Province 省	Telephone/Fax 电话/传真
Tianjin Automobile Xiali Sale Co.,Ltd.	Tianjin	Tianjin	(022)28010071
天津汽车夏利销售有限公司	天津市	天津市	(022)88370861
SAIC-Volkswagen Sales Co.,Ltd. Tianjin Sale Service Center	Tianjin	Tianjin	(022)25321428
上海上汽大众汽车销售有限公司天津销售服务中心	天津市	天津市	(022)25321057
Faw Car Sale Co.,Ltd.	Changchun	Jilin	(0431)5981943
一汽轿车销售有限公司	长春市	吉林省	(0431)5977611
Nanjing Langchi Group Co.,Ltd.	Nanjing	Jiangsu	(025)5532000
南京朗驰集团有限公司	南京市	江苏省	(025)5532012
JMC Sale General Co., Ltd.	Nanchang	Jiangxi	(0791)5232888
江西江铃汽车销售总公司	南昌市	江西省	(0791)5231032
Guangdong Goods & Materials Automobile Trade Corporation	Guangzhou	Guangdong	(020)86329072
广东物资集团汽车贸易公司	广州市	广东省	(020)86329056
Changchun Automobile Trade City Development Group Co., Ltd.	Changchun	Jilin	(0431)7619450
长春汽车贸易城开发集团股份有限公司	长春市	吉林省	(0431)7619748
Zhejiang Yuantong Automobile Co.,Ltd.	Hangzhou	Zhejiang	(0571)88283398
浙江元通汽车有限公司	杭州市	浙江省	(0571)88283798
Qingdao Qingqi Automobile Sale Co.,Ltd.	Qingdao	Shandong	(0532)4913560
青岛青汽汽车销售有限公司	青岛市	山东省	(0532)4913564
Shanxi Electromechanical Equipment General Company	Taiyuan	Shanxi	(0351)4042445
山西省机电设备总公司	太原市	山西省	(0351)4044137

3726: Automobile Body 汽车车身制造业

The industry accounts for 0.074% of the total revenue of China's industrial sector in 2002. The rate of return on assets is 7.76%. 74.55% of all firms in the industry made a profit while 25.45% had negative returns.The top province in terms of the industry's revenue is Shanghai, accounting for 19.33% of the total revenue.
2002年本行业收入占全行业的 0.074%，资产利润率为 7.76%。74.55%的企业赢利，25.45%的企业亏损。收入最高的省为上海市，占本行业的19.33%。

	Total number of firms 企业总数	Total number of employees 职工总数	Total revenue (Mil.RMB) 总销售收入（百万元）	Total profit (Mil.RMB) 总利润（百万元）	Return on assets 资产利润率（%）	Return on equity 权益利润率（%）	Labour productivity ('000 RMB/ worker) 劳动生产率（千元/人）	Debts/ assets 资产负债率（%）	Total assets (Mil.RMB) 总资产（百万元）
Industry Overall 行业总体	110	30,421	7,958	453	7.76	22.25	65.90	65.11	5,831

	Number of firms 企业个数	Average number of employees 平均职工人数	Average revenue ('000 RMB) 平均销售收入（千元）	Average profit ('000 RMB) 平均利润（千元）	Return on assets 资产利润率（%）	Return on equity 权益利润率（%）	Labour productivity ('000 RMB/ worker) 劳动生产率（千元/人）	Debts/ assets 资产负债率（%）	Average total assets ('000 RMB) 平均总资产（千元）
By ownership 产业所有权									
State-owned 国有	19	287	18,675	-472	-0.94	-3.93	12.06	76.13	50,307
Collective-owned 集体	20	183	25,306	594	3.27	17.87	37.56	81.70	18,147
Foreign & Overseas Chinese Funded 三资	9	290	146,002	20,174	12.58	26.29	205.65	52.16	160,407
By regional distribution 地区分布									
Central-North 华北	21	260	20,323	-1,057	-2.28	-8.15	18.19	72.00	46,268
Beijing 北京	5	119	16,330	184	1.07	1.83	19.16	41.54	17,221
Tianjin 天津	3	162	30,831	-2,296	-4.21		76.19	102.55	54,479
Hebei 河北	10	350	16,280	-1,642	-2.48	-7.40	11.06	66.47	66,146
Shanxi 山西	3	294	29,946	65	0.32	4.73	13.80	93.20	20,211
Inner Mongolia 内蒙古									
Northeast 东北	13	224	42,587	932	2.64	14.62	42.06	81.96	35,328
Liaoning 辽宁	4	84	18,709	-141	-0.36	-1.84	8.93	80.47	39,158
Jilin 吉林	8	313	59,838	1,585	4.34	25.74	47.71	83.13	36,491
Heilongjiang 黑龙江	1	74	85				0.14	71.78	10,699
Central-East 华东	33	248	132,403	7,189	9.98	30.51	115.61	67.29	72,049
Shanghai 上海	2	145	769,132	47,525	21.67	48.46	556.30	55.29	219,359
Jiangsu 江苏	5	465	186,295	2,039	1.37	10.17	48.30	86.51	148,679
Zhejiang 浙江	7	135	60,682	3,233	8.45	29.29	124.38	71.17	38,272
Anhui 安徽	3	235	102,078	1,553	4.49	18.77	127.86	76.10	34,617
Fujian 福建	2	112	130,829	35,710	26.50	34.99	947.66	24.27	134,767
Jiangxi 江西									
Shandong 山东	14	264	64,779	2,377	6.01	19.01	68.51	68.41	39,586
Central-South 中南	37	344	63,999	6,645	14.77	38.22	60.46	61.35	44,989
Henan 河南	4	498	157,766	9,375	13.47	67.43	49.15	80.02	69,594
Hubei 湖北	6	176	8,858	-338	-2.42	-8.57	17.88	71.73	13,970
Hunan 湖南	19	366	43,386	1,877	5.57	13.19	28.79	57.79	33,711
Guangdong 广东	5	443	167,060	34,922	27.96	63.19	201.67	55.75	124,891
Guangxi 广西	3	166	8,037	44	0.35	0.76	10.72	53.63	12,481
Hainan 海南									
Southwest 西南	5	210	47,149	-3,928	-5.61	-7.53	63.49	25.42	69,971
Chongqing 重庆									
Sichuan 四川	4	164	42,220	1,333	7.22	25.45	98.54	71.65	18,478
Guizhou 贵州	1	393	66,866	-24,974	-9.05	-10.41	4.91	13.04	275,944
Yunnan 云南									
Tibet 西藏									
Northwest 西北	1	86	4,497	-776	-9.67		9.06	133.44	8,023
Shaanxi 陕西									
Gansu 甘肃									
Qinghai 青海									
Ningxia 宁夏									
Xinjiang 新疆	1	86	4,497	-776	-9.67		9.06	133.44	8,023

3726: Automobile Body 汽车车身制造业

Year 年份	Number of firms 企业个数	Rate of change 变化率 (%)	Number of employees 职工人数 (人)	Rate of change 变化率 (%)	Total revenue (Mil. RMB) 总销售收入 (百万元)	Rate of change 变化率 (%)	Total profit (Mil RMB) 总利润 (百万元)	Rate of change 变化率 (%)
2000	79		19,131		2,615		67	
2001	91	15.19	24,650	28.85	5,203	98.97	201	200.00
2002	110	20.88	30,421	23.41	7,958	52.95	453	125.37

Major Products 主要产品	Output 产量	Unit 单位

10 Main Firms with Maximal Revenue (year founded) 收入最大的十家主要企业（创办年份）	City 城市	Province 省	Telephone/fax 电话/传真	Number of employees 职工人数	Ownership 产业所有权	Revenue ('000 RMB) 销售收入 (千元)	Profit('000 RMB) (rank) 利润(千元) (排名)	Total assets ('000 RMB) 总资产 (千元)	Major products 主要产品
Shanghai Pudong China Faw Group Qingdao Special Automobile Factory 上海浦东一汽青岛专用车厂(2000)	Shanghai 上海市	Shanghai 上海市	(021)58137635 (021)58137431	217	Joint Owned 联营企业	1,527,029	95,853(2)	421,491	Half Trailer 半挂
Zhumadian Huajun Vehicle Co.,Ltd. 驻马店市华骏车辆有限公司(1952)	Zhumadian 驻马店市	Henan 河南省	(0396)2917590 (0396)2914384	1,542	Joint Stock 股份制	620,668	36,087(4)	167,618	Special Vehicle 专用车辆
Shunde Fuhua Engineering Machine Manufacturing Co.,Ltd. 顺德富华工程机械制造有限公司(1997)	Foshan 佛山市	Guangdong 广东省	(0765)5665828 (0765)5665005	738	Foreign Funded 外商投资	493,812	164,623(1)	394,795	Half Trailer Axle Assembly 半挂车车轴总成
China Faw Group Huaiyin Special Automobile Manufacturing Factory 一汽淮阴专用汽车制造厂(1958)	Huaian 淮安市	Jiangsu 江苏省	(0517)3750801 (0517)3761875	530	Joint Owned 联营企业	349,086	2,775(26)	149,256	Half Trailer 半挂车
Yangzhou Zhongji Tonghua Special Automobile Co.,Ltd. 扬州中集通华专用车股份有限公司(1991)	Yangzhou 扬州市	Jiangsu 江苏省	(0514)7873005 (0514)7873290	373	Foreign Funded 外商投资	316,124	13,259(7)	228,440	Half Trailer 半挂车
Anhui Fuyang Automotive Industry Co.,Ltd. 安徽省阜阳市汽车工业有限责任公司(1971)	Fuyang 阜阳市	Anhui 安徽省	(0558)2210139 (0558)2328310	545	Limited-Liability 有限公司	273,780	3,791(20)	80,305	Refitted Vehicle Series Semitrailer 改装汽车系列半挂
Hunan Tongxin Industrial & Commercial Co.,Ltd. 湖南同心实业股份有限公司(1984)	Changsha 长沙市	Hunan 湖南省	(0731)6292069 (0731)6290047	1,800	Joint Stock 股份制	253,771	8,365(10)	169,163	1030 Cab Assembly. 1030驾驶室总成
Liangshan Tongya Automobile Manufacturing Co.,Ltd. 梁山通亚汽车制造有限公司(1984)	Jining 济宁市	Shandong 山东省	(0537)7768888 (0537)7762553	586	Private Owned 私营企业	242,190	8,040(11)	119,830	Trailer 挂车
Nanhai Fudi Auto Co.,Ltd. 南海市福迪汽车有限公司(2001)	Foshan 佛山市	Guangdong 广东省	(0757)6251062 (0757)6251071	725	Limited-Liability 有限公司	192,219	4,376(18)	89,538	Automobile Fittings 汽车配件
Liangshan Dongyue Traffic Machinery Manufacturing Co.,Ltd. 梁山东岳交通机械制造有限公司(1986)	Jining 济宁市	Shandong 山东省	(0537)7762104 (0537)7762018	400	Private Owned 私营企业	153,720	5,360(15)	74,600	Trailer 挂车

Top 10 Cities by Revenue 销售收入排名前10位城市	Province 省	Market share 市场份额 (%)	Number of firms 企业个数
Shanghai 上海市	Shanghai 上海市	19.33	2
Foshan 佛山市	Guangdong 广东省	9.80	3
Changsha 长沙市	Hunan 湖南省	9.75	16
Zhumadian 驻马店市	Henan 河南省	7.84	2
Jining 济宁市	Shandong 山东省	5.70	5
Huaian 淮安市	Jiangsu 江苏省	4.39	1
Yangzhou 扬州市	Jiangsu 江苏省	3.97	1
Fuyang 阜阳市	Anhui 安徽省	3.44	1
Xiamen 厦门市	Fujian 福建省	3.29	2
Siping 四平市	Jilin 吉林省	3.21	4

10 Major Wholesalers 十家主要批发商	City 城市	Province 省	Telephone/Fax 电话/传真
Tianjin Automobile Xiali Sale Co.,Ltd. 天津汽车夏利销售有限公司	Tianjin 天津市	Tianjin 天津市	(022)28010071 (022)88370861
SAIC-Volkswagen Sales Co.,Ltd. Tianjin Sale Service Center 上海上汽大众汽车销售有限公司天津销售服务中心	Tianjin 天津市	Tianjin 天津市	(022)25321428 (022)25321057
Faw Car Sale Co.,Ltd. 一汽轿车销售有限公司	Changchun 长春市	Jilin 吉林省	(0431)5981943 (0431)5977611
Nanjing Langchi Group Co.,Ltd. 南京朗驰集团有限公司	Nanjing 南京市	Jiangsu 江苏省	(025)5532000 (025)5532012
JMC Sale General Co., Ltd. 江西江铃汽车销售总公司	Nanchang 南昌市	Jiangxi 江西省	(0791)5232888 (0791)5231032
Guangdong Goods & Materials Automobile Trade Corporation 广东物资集团汽车贸易公司	Guangzhou 广州市	Guangdong 广东省	(020)86329072 (020)86329056
Changchun Automobile Trade City Development Group Co., Ltd. 长春汽车贸易城开发集团股份有限公司	Changchun 长春市	Jilin 吉林省	(0431)7619450 (0431)7619748
Zhejiang Yuantong Automobile Co.,Ltd. 浙江元通汽车有限公司	Hangzhou 杭州市	Zhejiang 浙江省	(0571)88283398 (0571)88283798
Qingdao Qingqi Automobile Sale Co.,Ltd. 青岛青汽汽车销售有限公司	Qingdao 青岛市	Shandong 山东省	(0532)4913560 (0532)4913564
Shanxi Electromechanical Equipment General Company 山西省机电设备总公司	Taiyuan 太原市	Shanxi 山西省	(0351)4042445 (0351)4044137

3727: Automobile Parts 汽车零部件及配件制造业

The industry accounts for 1.729% of the total revenue of China's industrial sector in 2002. The rate of return on assets is 7.96%. 85.24% of all firms in the industry made a profit while 14.76% had negative returns.The top province in terms of the industry's revenue is Shanghai, accounting for 19.52% of the total revenue.
2002年本行业收入占全行业的 1.729%，资产利润率为 7.96%。85.24%的企业赢利，14.76%的企业亏损。收入最高的省为上海市，占本行业的19.52%。

	Total number of firms 企业总数	Total number of employees 职工总数	Total revenue (Mil.RMB) 总销售收入 (百万元)	Total profit (Mil.RMB) 总利润 (百万元)	Return on assets 资产利润率 (%)	Return on equity 权益利润率 (%)	Labour productivity ('000 RMB/ worker) 劳动生产率 (千元/人)	Debts/ assets 资产负债率 (%)	Total assets (Mil.RMB) 总资产 (百万元)
Industry Overall 行业总体	2968	837,432	185,484	16,520	7.96	16.85	64.52	52.78	207,601

	Number of firms 企业个数	Average number of employees 平均职工人数	Average revenue ('000 RMB) 平均销售收入 (千元)	Average profit ('000 RMB) 平均利润 (千元)	Return on assets 资产利润率 (%)	Return on equity 权益利润率 (%)	Labour productivity ('000 RMB/ worker) 劳动生产率 (千元/人)	Debts/ assets 资产负债率 (%)	Average total assets ('000 RMB) 平均总资产 (千元)
By ownership 产业所有权									
State-owned 国有	360	454	58,135	1,499	1.78	6.43	35.77	72.33	84,304
Collective-owned 集体	464	244	54,370	3,334	6.13	14.45	49.39	57.55	54,356
Foreign & Overseas Chinese Funded 三资	541	277	125,195	17,974	14.39	24.16	138.72	40.43	124,911
By regional distribution 地区分布									
Central-North 华北	344	220	38,390	2,852	5.29	12.01	55.83	55.97	53,938
Beijing 北京	75	197	38,216	4,230	7.78	19.87	62.06	60.86	54,399
Tianjin 天津	134	176	32,856	584	1.31	2.52	45.65	48.11	44,596
Hebei 河北	115	228	40,247	4,591	8.13	17.10	68.29	52.44	56,435
Shanxi 山西	15	600	79,783	3,905	3.38	17.11	42.75	80.27	115,642
Inner Mongolia 内蒙古	5	427	22,420	-168	-0.31	-1.92	27.58	84.02	54,884
Northeast 东北	293	413	81,977	6,738	7.18	19.76	56.15	63.66	93,856
Liaoning 辽宁	94	441	95,647	8,166	7.07	25.58	55.07	72.36	115,501
Jilin 吉林	169	397	80,725	6,718	7.85	17.43	60.60	54.94	85,528
Heilongjiang 黑龙江	30	414	46,192	2,377	3.26	14.91	35.70	78.15	72,946
Central-East 华东	1,475	228	66,568	6,412	9.27	16.94	82.45	45.30	69,186
Shanghai 上海	290	245	124,881	16,589	10.93	16.23	158.76	32.67	151,794
Jiangsu 江苏	300	238	61,057	4,115	7.95	18.23	64.21	56.41	51,783
Zhejiang 浙江	528	178	50,159	3,977	8.34	17.16	61.68	51.39	47,680
Anhui 安徽	67	316	40,736	3,485	6.50	18.00	48.52	63.87	53,585
Fujian 福建	92	166	36,532	4,583	11.19	18.51	72.98	39.56	40,955
Jiangxi 江西	39	269	31,383	880	2.34	7.23	48.87	67.70	37,688
Shandong 山东	159	332	61,989	3,919	7.34	19.91	64.59	63.15	53,404
Central-South 中南	615	359	68,024	6,065	8.15	18.83	56.41	56.70	74,394
Henan 河南	87	341	41,902	2,130	4.90	14.55	44.53	66.31	43,454
Hubei 湖北	270	433	76,237	4,971	6.28	14.02	54.31	55.20	79,140
Hunan 湖南	70	360	45,390	5,247	5.07	15.94	42.68	68.22	103,562
Guangdong 广东	111	277	104,837	15,008	16.80	32.16	93.96	47.74	89,313
Guangxi 广西	76	238	36,644	2,234	4.95	11.50	44.81	56.95	45,125
Hainan 海南	1	110	5,872	-341	-3.09	-12.85	42.02	75.98	11,049
Southwest 西南	214	357	36,412	1,649	2.75	8.86	35.44	68.96	59,994
Chongqing 重庆	99	374	38,959	2,278	3.87	14.18	35.05	72.70	58,851
Sichuan 四川	85	331	33,762	1,187	2.15	6.60	38.65	67.40	55,169
Guizhou 贵州	14	530	55,326	2,691	2.17	4.45	34.12	51.22	123,818
Yunnan 云南	16	239	18,173	-696	-1.89	-55.33	18.20	96.59	36,857
Tibet 西藏									
Northwest 西北	27	288	16,473	878	2.62	9.46	20.42	72.35	33,569
Shaanxi 陕西	15	327	22,319	1,767	4.90	13.80	25.20	64.49	36,056
Gansu 甘肃	8	173	2,119	-451	-3.86	-41.18	7.17	90.62	11,672
Qinghai 青海	1	502	22,740	-4,854	-5.17	-31.96	15.60	83.81	93,817
Ningxia 宁夏	1	428	8,300	18	0.03	0.17	4.52	81.14	56,863
Xinjiang 新疆	2	278	31,002	2,830	4.66	23.68	27.75	80.33	60,725

Year 年份	Number of firms 企业个数	Rate of change 变化率 (%)	Number of employees 职工人数 (人)	Rate of change 变化率 (%)	Total revenue (Mil. RMB) 总销售收入 (百万元)	Rate of change 变化率 (%)	Total profit (Mil RMB) 总利润 (百万元)	Rate of change 变化率 (%)
2000	2496		755,000		108,760		7,904	
2001	2724	9.13	776,776	2.88	138,784	27.61	11,265	42.52
2002	2968	8.96	837,432	7.81	185,484	33.65	16,520	46.65

Major Products 主要产品	Output 产量	Unit 单位

10 Main Firms with Maximal Revenue (year founded) 收入最大的十家主要企业（创办年份）	City 城市	Province 省	Telephone/fax 电话/传真	Number of employees 职工人数	Ownership 产业所有权	Revenue ('000 RMB) 销售收入 (千元)	Profit('000 RMB) (rank) 利润(千元) (排名)	Total assets ('000 RMB) 总资产 (千元)	Major products 主要产品
WanXxang Group Co.,Ltd. 万向集团公司(1990)	Hangzhou 杭州市	Zhejiang 浙江省	(0571)82832999 (0571)82833999	13,727	Collective-owned 集体企业	11,826,469	750,923(2)	11,291,194	Automobile Parts汽车零部件
Wuxi Weifu Group Co.,Ltd. 无锡威孚集团有限公司(1958)	Wuxi 无锡市	Jiangsu 江苏省	(0510)2708345 (0510)2702740	8,420	State-owned 国有企业	4,220,668	175,964(17)	3,386,806	High Pressure Oil Pump Assembly高压油泵总成
Dongfeng Honda Engine Co.,Ltd. 东风本田发动机有限公司(1998)	Guangzhou 广州市	Guangdong 广东省	(020)82277789 (020)82271675	712	Foreign Funded 外商投资	4,148,012	1,208,438(1)	2,621,533	Sedan Engine轿车发动机
Shanghai Huizhong Auto Manufacturing Co.,Ltd. 上海汇众汽车制造有限公司(1997)	Shanghai 上海市	Shanghai 上海市	(021)58201188 (021)58204570	7,666	Overseas Chinese-funded 港澳台资	3,896,415	185,231(15)	2,955,700	Santana Front Suspension Assembly桑车前悬挂总成
China Faw Group Changchun Fou-ring Auto Stock Co.,Ltd. 长春一汽四环汽车股份有限公司(1993)	Changchun 长春市	Jilin 吉林省	(0431)7629116 (0431)7629092	7,149	Joint Stock 股份制	3,240,838	169,720(19)	1,928,298	Others Special Automobile其它专用车
Shenyang Xingyuandong Automobile Parts Co.,Ltd. 沈阳兴远东汽车零部件有限公司(1998)	Shenyang 沈阳市	Liaoning 辽宁省	(024)23787385	698	Foreign Funded 外商投资	3,038,256	299,310(6)	543,789	Automobile Parts汽车零部件
Shanghai Yanfeng Johnson Controls Seating Co.,Ltd. 上海延锋江森座椅有限公司(1997)	Shanghai 上海市	Shanghai 上海市	(021)68121818 (021)68121919	1,348	Foreign Funded 外商投资	2,196,456	268,064(7)	980,971	Controls Seating Assembly座椅总成
Dongfeng Vehicle Axle Co.,Ltd. Xiangfan Factory 东风车桥公司襄樊工厂(1949)	Xiangfan 襄樊市	Hubei 湖北省	(0710)3451853 (0710)3458574	3,161	Joint Stock 股份制	2,113,419	401,462(5)	853,889	Automobile Parts汽车零部件
United Automobile Electronic Systems Co.,Ltd. 联合汽车电子有限公司(1995)	Shanghai 上海市	Shanghai 上海市	(021)58992288 (021)58995244	1,099	Foreign Funded 外商投资	1,938,280	700,002(3)	2,760,152	Engine Electropult System发动机电喷系统
Shanghai Automobile Co.,Ltd. 上海汽车股份有限公司(1925)	Shanghai 上海市	Shanghai 上海市	(021)50803808 (021)50803780	3,760	Joint Stock 股份制	1,735,771	265,682(8)	8,187,295	Gearbox Assembly变速器总成

Top 10 Cities by Revenue 销售收入排名前10位城市	Province 省	Market share 市场份额 (%)	Number of firms 企业个数
Shanghai 上海市	Shanghai 上海市	19.52	290
Hangzhou 杭州市	Zhejiang 浙江省	7.70	70
Changchun 长春市	Jilin 吉林省	6.08	81
Shiyan 十堰市	Hubei 湖北省	5.79	90
Guangzhou 广州市	Guangdong 广东省	3.34	37
Ningbo 宁波市	Zhejiang 浙江省	2.89	163
Wuxi 无锡市	Jiangsu 江苏省	2.82	35
Shenyang 沈阳市	Liaoning 辽宁省	2.50	26
Tianjin 天津市	Tianjin 天津市	2.37	134
Chongqing 重庆市	Chongqing 重庆市	2.08	99

10 Major Wholesalers 十家主要批发商	City 城市	Province 省	Telephone/Fax 电话/传真
Faw Trade General Company 一汽贸易总公司	Changchun 长春市	Jilin 吉林省	(0431)5904147 (0431)5909761
Shanghai Automobile Import & Export Company 上海汽车进出口公司	Shanghai 上海市	Shanghai 上海市	(021)22011717 (021)22011789
Shiyan Ronghua Dongfeng Automobile Monopoly Co.,Ltd. 十堰荣华东风汽车专营有限公司	Shiyan 十堰市	Hubei 湖北省	(0719)8669242 (0719)8689666
Shenzhen Automobile Industry & Trade General Company 深圳市汽车工业贸易总公司	Shenzhen 深圳市	Guangdong 广东省	(0755)83617079 (0755)83346186
Shanghai Volkswagen Automobile (Tianjin) Co.,Ltd. 上海大众汽车（天津）有限公司	Tianjin 天津市	Tianjin 天津市	(022)25320000 (022)25320532
Shanghai Dongfang Automobile Fittings City Co.,Ltd. 上海东方汽配城有限公司	Shanghai 上海市	Shanghai 上海市	(021)59185910 (021)59184868
Zhejiang Aotong Automobile Co.,Ltd. 浙江奥通汽车有限公司	Hangzhou 杭州市	Zhejiang 浙江省	(0571)85368000 (0571)85365099
Runhua Group Co.,Ltd. 润华集团股份有限公司	Jinan 济南市	Shandong 山东省	(0531)7519704 (0531)7983746
Shenzhen Motors Ind.Import & Export Co. 深圳市汽车工业进出口公司	Shenzhen 深圳市	Guangdong 广东省	(0755)83626234 (0755)26711560
Shenzhen Dongfeng Real Estate Co.,Ltd. 深圳东风置业有限公司	Shenzhen 深圳市	Guangdong 广东省	(0755)83210279 (0755)83257208

3731: Motorcycles 摩托车整车制造业

The industry accounts for 0.349% of the total revenue of China's industrial sector in 2002. The rate of return on assets is -0.14%. 72.69% of all firms in the industry made a profit while 27.31% had negative returns.The top province in terms of the industry's revenue is Guangdong, accounting for 27.11% of the total revenue.
2002•••••••••• 0.349%•••••• -0.14%•72.69%•••••27.31%•••••••••••••••••••27.11%•

	Total number of firms 企业总数	Total number of employees 职工总数	Total revenue (Mil.RMB) 总销售收入(百万元)	Total profit (Mil.RMB) 总利润(百万元)	Return on assets 资产利润率(%)	Return on equity 权益利润率(%)	Labour productivity ('000 RMB/worker) 劳动生产率(千元/人)	Debts/assets 资产负债率(%)	Total assets (Mil.RMB) 总资产(百万元)
Industry Overall 行业总体	216	107,158	37,386	-64	-0.14	-0.46	86.03	68.68	44,424

	Number of firms 企业个数	Average number of employees 平均职工人数	Average revenue ('000 RMB) 平均销售收入(千元)	Average profit ('000 RMB) 平均利润(千元)	Return on assets 资产利润率(%)	Return on equity 权益利润率(%)	Labour productivity ('000 RMB/worker) 劳动生产率(千元/人)	Debts/assets 资产负债率(%)	Average total assets ('000 RMB) 平均总资产(千元)
By ownership 产业所有权									
State-owned 国有	19	708	55,904	-1,740	-0.71	-2.27	18.60	68.90	246,245
Collective-owned 集体	24	247	65,196	447	0.63	2.43	65.16	74.05	70,752
Foreign & Overseas Chinese Funded 三资	31	870	438,425	-2			117.95	67.49	425,769
By regional distribution 地区分布									
Central-North 华北	22	452	174,688	1,600	1.07	3.41	70.17	68.71	149,819
Beijing 北京	1	50	6,980	830	42.89	102.47	46.60	58.14	1,935
Tianjin 天津	11	806	291,760	-1,364	-0.48	-1.68	56.27	71.23	281,628
Hebei 河北	9	105	68,366	5,396	28.15	36.52	190.48	22.93	19,169
Shanxi 山西	1	93	11,498	817	3.45	12.87	189.19	73.18	23,666
Inner Mongolia 内蒙古									
Northeast 东北	1	2,516	166,911	-220,000	-22.48	-74.44	5.71	69.81	978,746
Liaoning 辽宁									
Jilin 吉林	1	2,516	166,911	-220,000	-22.48	-74.44	5.71	69.81	978,746
Heilongjiang 黑龙江									
Central-East 华东	82	507	167,848	2,325	0.95	3.22	87.79	70.47	244,356
Shanghai 上海	3	1,104	599,740	9,932	3.31	23.86	132.29	86.15	300,480
Jiangsu 江苏	24	326	141,336	1,469	1.41	3.91	102.07	63.82	103,927
Zhejiang 浙江	25	505	224,399	8,164	3.15	6.36	102.48	50.51	259,340
Anhui 安徽	2	102	81,271	-2,809	-3.39	-5.83	702.33	41.77	82,769
Fujian 福建	3	390	139,880	-10,232	-4.85		139.07	104.95	211,133
Jiangxi 江西	7	119	5,864	-1,833	-8.21	-28.30	14.50	70.98	22,319
Shandong 山东	18	866	129,944	-1,631	-0.32	-1.87	51.28	82.93	511,271
Central-South 中南	76	457	169,888	1,525	0.91	2.61	92.69	65.37	168,476
Henan 河南	22	296	43,857	243	0.41	0.75	29.24	45.43	59,026
Hubei 湖北	3	254	62,140	247	0.31		77.56	102.55	80,314
Hunan 湖南	7	693	102,798	-12,264	-6.04	-10.19	31.17	40.75	203,070
Guangdong 广东	41	508	247,184	4,841	2.18	6.92	117.59	68.53	222,334
Guangxi 广西									
Hainan 海南	3	606	302,020	-930	-0.38	-13.76	205.49	97.21	242,500
Southwest 西南	34	539	197,085	-5,456	-2.54	-8.27	89.20	69.23	214,519
Chongqing 重庆	31	562	213,453	-5,735	-2.49	-8.06	92.64	69.13	230,558
Sichuan 四川	2	177	34,177	791	2.92	10.05	50.44	70.98	27,132
Guizhou 贵州	1	571	15,491	-9,308	-10.11	-42.04	8.36	75.96	92,104
Yunnan 云南									
Tibet 西藏									
Northwest 西北	1	25		-17	-0.12			148.44	13,826
Shaanxi 陕西	1	25		-17	-0.12			148.44	13,826
Gansu 甘肃									
Qinghai 青海									
Ningxia 宁夏									
Xinjiang 新疆									

3731: Motorcycles 摩托车整车制造业

Year 年份	Number of firms 企业个数	Rate of change 变化率 (%)	Number of employees 职工人数 (人)	Rate of change 变化率 (%)	Total revenue (Mil. RMB) 总销售收入 (百万元)	Rate of change 变化率 (%)	Total profit (Mil RMB) 总利润 (百万元)	Rate of change 变化率 (%)
2000	233		106,469		36,076		418	
2001	240	3.00	101,837	-4.35	34,003	-5.75	31	-92.58
2002	216	10.00	107,158	5.23	37,386	9.95	-64	

Major Products 主要产品	Output 产量	Unit 单位
Motorcycle 摩托车	1,150	10,000 Vehicles 万辆

10 Main Firms with Maximal Revenue (year founded) 收入最大的十家主要企业 (创办年份)	City 城市	Province 省	Telephone/fax 电话/传真	Number of employees 职工人数	Ownership 产业所有权	Revenue ('000 RMB) 销售收入 (千元)	Profit('000 RMB) (rank) 利润(千元) (排名)	Total assets ('000 RMB) 总资产 (千元)	Major products 主要产品
Jiangmen DachangJiang Group Co., Ltd.	Jiangmen	Guangdong	(0750)3221511		Foreign Funded				Motorcycle
江门市大长江集团有限公司(1999)	江门市	广东省	(0750)3228480	3,300	外商投资	3,197,946	298,325(1)	2,141,886	摩托车
Qianjiang Goup Co.,Ltd.	Taizhou	Zhejiang	(0576)6139140		State Enterprises				Double-wheeled Motorcycle
钱江集团有限公司(1952)	台州市	浙江省	(0576)6111045	3,914	国有独资	2,744,313	153,818(2)	3,858,883	二轮摩托车
Sundiro Honda Motorcycle Co., Ltd.	Tianjin	Tianjin	(022)88251925		Foreign Funded				Motorcycle
新大洲本田摩托有限公司(2001)	天津市	天津市	(022)88253562	6,335	外商投资	2,588,361	12,032(10)	2,403,127	摩托车
Wuyang-Honda Motors(Guangzhou) Co.,Ltd.	Guangzhou	Guangdong	(020)84182436		Foreign Funded				Double-wheeled Motorcycle
五羊-本田摩托（广州）有限公司(1992)	广州市	广东省	(020)84186548	2,181	外商投资	1,708,953	6,123(22)	1,167,516	二轮摩托车
Sundiro Honda Motorcycle Co., Ltd. Shanghai Branch	Shanghai	Shanghai	(021)59799999		Foreign Funded				Motorcycle
新大洲本田摩托有限公司上海分公司(2001)	上海市	上海市		1,956	外商投资	1,322,850	24,540(5)	561,094	摩托车
Guangdong Kingtown Group Guangzhou Tianma Motorcycle Co., Ltd.	Guangzhou	Guangdong	(020)87982688		Limited-Liability				Motorcycle
广东精通集团广州天马摩托车有限公司(1998)	广州市	广东省	(020)87981676	2,380	有限公司	1,298,520	6,512(20)	310,526	摩托车
Mpa Motorcyde Co.Ltd. Huizhou	Huizhou	Guangdong	(0752)3650888		Foreign Funded				MCT Motorcycle
惠州玛骐摩托车有限公司(1993)	惠州市	广东省	(0752)3650776	905	外商投资	640,732	-	690,897	MCT摩托车
Xingyue Group Co.,Ltd.	Jinhua	Zhejiang	(0579)7516622		Private Owned				Motorcycle
星月集团有限公司(1995)	金华市	浙江省	(0579)7512370	2,829	私营企业	633,321	33,172(4)	426,632	摩托车
Luoyang Northern EK Chor Motorcycle Co.,Ltd.	Luoyang	Henan	(0379)4937083		Foreign Funded				Motorcycle
洛阳北方易初摩托车有限公司(1992)	洛阳市	河南省	(0379)4180016	2,282	外商投资	587,416	2,975(39)	528,621	摩托车
Zhejiang Zhongnan Construction Group Co.,Ltd.	Hangzhou	Zhejiang	(0571)86624508		Collective-owned				Motorcycle
浙江中南建设集团公司(1984)	杭州市	浙江省	(0571)86624038	738	集体企业	561,110	10,158(13)	624,301	摩托车

Top 10 Cities by Revenue 销售收入排名前10位城市	Province 省	Market share 市场份额 (%)	Number of firms 企业个数
Chongqing 重庆市	Chongqing 重庆市	17.70	31
Guangzhou 广州市	Guangdong 广东省	14.56	23
Taizhou 台州市	Zhejiang 浙江省	9.21	14
Jiangmen 江门市	Guangdong 广东省	8.95	5
Tianjin 天津市	Tianjin 天津市	8.58	11
Wuxi 无锡市	Jiangsu 江苏省	6.82	13
Shanghai 上海市	Shanghai 上海市	4.81	3
Jinan 济南市	Shandong 山东省	4.78	5
Luoyang 洛阳市	Henan 河南省	2.39	14

10 Major Wholesalers 十家主要批发商	City 城市	Province 省	Telephone/Fax 电话/传真
Nanjing Jincheng Group Motor Sale Co.,Ltd.	Nanjing	Jiangsu	(025)4593388
南京金城集团摩托车销售有限公司	南京市	江苏省	(025)4603816
Zhejiang Xinzhongyi Trade Co.,Ltd.	Shaoxing	Zhejiang	(0575)7381888
浙江新中义商贸股份有限公司	绍兴市	浙江省	(0575)7381848
Chongqing Construction Sale Co.,Ltd.	Chongqing	Chongqing	(023)68813741
重庆建设销售有限责任公司	重庆市	重庆市	(023)68434994
Nanjing Jincheng Group Import & Export Co.,Ltd.	Nanjing	Jiangsu	(025)4593388
南京金城集团进出口有限公司	南京市	江苏省	(025)4591758
Changzhou Haojue Motor Sale Co.,Ltd.	Changzhou	Jiangsu	(0519)5125905
常州豪爵摩托车销售有限公司	常州市	江苏省	(0519)5125906
Ji'nan Qingqi Suzuki Motorcycle Co., Ltd.	Jinan	Shandong	(0531)8876861
济南轻骑铃木摩托车有限公司	济南市	山东省	(0531)8876862
Ji'nan Qingqi Sales Co., Ltd.	Jinan	Shandong	(0531)8877430
济南轻骑销售有限公司	济南市	山东省	(0531)8877413
Fujian Shishi Changjiang Industrial Co.,Ltd.	Quanzhou	Fujian	(0595)8783669
福建省石狮市长江实业有限公司	泉州市	福建省	(0595)8784151
Shandong Jincheng Motor Sales Co., Ltd.	Jinan	Shandong	(0531)8024174
山东金城摩托车销售有限公司	济南市	山东省	(0531)8021054
Jialing Group Foreign Trade Development Co.,Ltd.	Chongqing	Chongqing	(023)65190114
嘉陵集团对外贸易发展有限公司	重庆市	重庆市	(023)65193234

3732: Motorcycle Parts and Accessories 摩托车零部件及配件制造业

The industry accounts for 0.324% of the total revenue of China's industrial sector in 2002. The rate of return on assets is 2.37%. 82.08% of all firms in the industry made a profit while 17.92% had negative returns.The top province in terms of the industry's revenue is Chongqing, accounting for 39.56% of the total revenue.
2002年本行业收入占全行业的0.324%，资产利润率为2.37%。82.08%的企业赢利，17.92%的企业亏损。收入最高的省为重庆市，占本行业的39.56%。

	Total number of firms 企业总数	Total number of employees 职工总数	Total revenue (Mil.RMB) 总销售收入（百万元）	Total profit (Mil.RMB) 总利润（百万元）	Return on assets 资产利润率（%）	Return on equity 权益利润率（%）	Labour productivity ('000 RMB/ worker) 劳动生产率（千元/人）	Debts/ assets 资产负债率（%）	Total assets (Mil.RMB) 总资产（百万元）
Industry Overall 行业总体	971	219,445	34,762	827	2.37	6.29	37.18	62.32	34,901

	Number of firms 企业个数	Average number of employees 平均职工人数	Average revenue ('000 RMB) 平均销售收入（千元）	Average profit ('000 RMB) 平均利润（千元）	Return on assets 资产利润率（%）	Return on equity 权益利润率（%）	Labour productivity ('000 RMB/ worker) 劳动生产率（千元/人）	Debts/ assets 资产负债率（%）	Average total assets ('000 RMB) 平均总资产（千元）
By ownership 产业所有权									
State-owned 国有	41	529	33,131	-4,410	-4.34	-22.13	13.92	80.39	101,667
Collective-owned 集体	118	208	24,907	584	2.71	9.93	35.57	72.77	21,581
Foreign & Overseas Chinese Funded 三资	140	199	48,607	1,265	1.93	3.69	54.18	47.68	65,465
By regional distribution 地区分布									
Central-North 华北	17	284	18,830	-1,567	-3.08	-8.24	19.69	62.66	50,906
Beijing 北京	1	3	28	162	55.48	182.02	1.00	69.52	292
Tianjin 天津	8	215	23,198	-1,663	-2.17	-5.15	21.06	57.83	76,578
Hebei 河北	7	176	17,022	1,405	8.51	14.20	43.21	40.03	16,499
Shanxi 山西									
Inner Mongolia 内蒙古	1	1,881	15,350	-23,330	-17.03		3.06	103.31	136,991
Northeast 东北									
Liaoning 辽宁									
Jilin 吉林									
Heilongjiang 黑龙江									
Central-East 华东	497	175	29,287	1,360	4.58	11.07	44.90	58.58	29,664
Shanghai 上海	26	152	51,382	1,632	2.81	5.11	64.90	44.99	58,010
Jiangsu 江苏	132	175	34,851	897	2.39	6.04	52.66	60.52	37,588
Zhejiang 浙江	240	152	24,313	1,519	6.48	15.82	39.85	59.05	23,439
Anhui 安徽	2	580	22,971	-296	-1.09	-3.73	11.61	70.79	27,135
Fujian 福建	42	147	17,213	902	4.70	10.56	46.71	55.54	19,207
Jiangxi 江西	14	242	27,154	250	0.89	2.63	47.81	66.24	28,180
Shandong 山东	41	315	39,879	2,677	7.88	21.65	40.43	63.60	33,961
Central-South 中南	172	203	29,800	-166	-0.41	-1.20	32.76	65.76	40,348
Henan 河南	33	316	20,842	-1,118	-2.78	-20.59	12.41	86.48	40,158
Hubei 湖北	6	620	79,175	1,027	1.48	5.05	55.67	70.60	69,249
Hunan 湖南	6	78	9,306	-1,774	-4.36	-5.30	5.70	17.64	40,639
Guangdong 广东	118	166	31,941	132	0.33	0.88	39.22	62.88	40,429
Guangxi 广西	2	82	7,828	-746	-6.59	-130.56	67.23	94.96	11,319
Hainan 海南	7	77	17,452	-173	-0.75	-1.19	46.18	36.89	23,147
Southwest 西南	283	327	52,141	730	1.67	4.76	32.52	64.83	43,613
Chongqing 重庆	260	307	52,898	863	2.20	6.82	32.45	67.76	39,249
Sichuan 四川	19	642	50,977	-940	-0.84	-1.71	33.86	50.63	111,331
Guizhou 贵州	4	137	8,500	-34	-0.61	-2.24	12.05	72.98	5,615
Yunnan 云南									
Tibet 西藏									
Northwest 西北	2	52	2,295	-36	-0.69	-2.35	19.97	70.45	5,194
Shaanxi 陕西	1	31	135	-82	-2.88	-5.41	3.06	46.64	2,843
Gansu 甘肃	1	72	4,455	10	0.13	0.64	27.25	79.43	7,544
Qinghai 青海									
Ningxia 宁夏									
Xinjiang 新疆									

3732: Motorcycle Parts and Accessories 摩托车零部件及配件制造业

Year 年份	Number of firms 企业个数	Rate of change 变化率 (%)	Number of employees 职工人数 (人)	Rate of change 变化率 (%)	Total revenue (Mil. RMB) 总销售收入 (百万元)	Rate of change 变化率 (%)	Total profit (Mil RMB) 总利润 (百万元)	Rate of change 变化率 (%)
2000	843		191,494		24,919		526	
2001	942	11.74	207,418	8.32	29,987	20.34	551	4.75
2002	971	3.08	219,445	5.80	34,762	15.92	827	50.09

Major Products 主要产品	Output 产量	Unit 单位
Internal-combustion Engine 内燃机	28,433	10,000 KW 万千瓦

10 Main Firms with Maximal Revenue (year founded) 收入最大的十家主要企业（创办年份）	City 城市	Province 省	Telephone/ fax 电话/ 传真	Number of employees 职工人数	Ownership 产业所有权	Revenue ('000 RMB) 销售收入 (千元)	Profit('000 RMB) (rank) 利润(千元) (排名)	Total assets ('000 RMB) 总资产 (千元)	Major products 主要产品
Chongqing Lifan Industrial & Commercial (Group) Co.,Ltd. 重庆力帆实业（集团）有限公司(1997)	Chongqing 重庆市	Chongqing 重庆市	(023)65200162 (023)65215679	2,863	Private Owned 私营企业	3,804,004	69,952(2)	1,510,874	Motorcycle 摩托车
Chongqing Zongshen Motorcycle Science & Technology Group Co.,Ltd.重庆宗申摩托车科技集团有限公司(1992)	Chongqing 重庆市	Chongqing 重庆市	(023)66372668 (023)66372804	2,482	Private Owned 私营企业	1,718,486	32,515(4)	1,219,938	Motorcycle Engine摩托车发动机
Zhejiang Wanfeng Auto Group Co.,Ltd. 浙江万丰奥特集团有限公司(1998)	Shaoxing 绍兴市	Zhejiang 浙江省	(0575)6296295 (0575)6297550	2,488	Limited-Liability 有限公司	905,280	128,100(1)	1,014,930	Motorcycle Aluminium wheel摩托车铝轮
Shanghai Toyo Denso Electronic Equipment Co.,Ltd. 上海东洋电装有限公司(1992)	Shanghai 上海市	Shanghai 上海市	(021)57741332 (021)57741346	1,163	Foreign Funded 外商投资	607,432	22,394(6)	385,068	Motorcycle Fittings摩托车配件
Chongqing Yujiang Die-casting Co.,Ltd. 重庆市渝江压铸有限公司(1993)	Chongqing 重庆市	Chongqing 重庆市	(023)67683966 (023)67661327	3,022	Private Owned 私营企业	423,655	18,131(10)	287,991	Motorcycle Parts摩托车零部件
Jiangsu Gangyang Co.,Ltd. 江苏罡阳股份有限公司(1958)	Taizhou 泰州市	Jiangsu 江苏省	(0523)8764556	1,136	Joint Stock 股份制	281,242	16,890(11)	289,060	Motorcycle Fittings摩托车配件
Nanjing Jingbin Carburettor Co.,Ltd. 南京京滨化油器有限公司(1997)	Nanjing 南京市	Jiangsu 江苏省	(025)7152306 (025)7152800	720	Foreign Funded 外商投资	272,190	7,560(27)	338,750	Motor Carburettor摩托车化油器
Jiangmen United Engine Co.,Ltd. 江门联和发动机有限公司(1994)	Jiangmen 江门市	Guangdong 广东省	(0750)6801888 (0750)6802908	522	Overseas Chinese-funded 港澳台资	260,849	1,106(188)	274,293	Motorcycle Fittings摩托车配件
Nanjing Zhongding Motor Brake Factory 南京中鼎摩托车制动器厂(1997)	Nanjing 南京市	Jiangsu 江苏省	(025)6800147	450	Private Owned 私营企业	235,410	8,830(23)	18,310	Motorcycle Fittings 摩车配件
Zhejiang Hongqiao Power Manufacture Co.,Ltd. 浙江虹桥动力制造有限公司(1996)	Wenzhou 温州市	Zhejiang 浙江省	(0577)62336005 (0577)62336893	493	Limited-Liability 有限公司	221,320	8,122(26)	195,105	Motorcycle 摩托车

Top 10 Cities by Revenue 销售收入排名前10位城市	Province 省	Market share 市场份额 (%)	Number of firms 企业个数
Chongqing 重庆市	Chongqing 重庆市	39.56	260
Taizhou 台州市	Zhejiang 浙江省	5.89	104
Guangzhou 广州市	Guangdong 广东省	5.34	55
Shanghai 上海市	Shanghai 上海市	3.84	26
Wuxi 无锡市	Jiangsu 江苏省	3.61	37
Shaoxing 绍兴市	Zhejiang 浙江省	3.11	9
Wenzhou 温州市	Zhejiang 浙江省	2.74	41
Jiangmen 江门市	Guangdong 广东省	2.60	25
Nanjing 南京市	Jiangsu 江苏省	2.50	11
Jinhua 金华市	Zhejiang 浙江省	2.03	21

10 Major Wholesalers 十家主要批发商	City 城市	Province 省	Telephone/Fax 电话/传真
Faw Trade General Company 一汽贸易总公司	Changchun 长春市	Jilin 吉林省	(0431)5904147 (0431)5909761
Shanghai Automobile Import & Export Company 上海汽车进出口公司	Shanghai 上海市	Shanghai 上海市	(021)22011717 (021)22011789
Shiyan Ronghua Dongfeng Automobile Monopoly Co.,Ltd. 十堰荣华东风汽车专营有限公司	Shiyan 十堰市	Hubei 湖北省	(0719)8669242 (0719)8689666
Shenzhen Automobile Industry & Trade General Company 深圳市汽车工业贸易总公司	Shenzhen 深圳市	Guangdong 广东省	(0755)83617079 (0755)83346186
Shanghai Volkswagen Automobile (Tianjin) Co.,Ltd. 上海大众汽车（天津）有限公司	Tianjin 天津市	Tianjin 天津市	(022)25320000 (022)25320532
Shanghai Dongfang Automobile Fittings City Co.,Ltd. 上海东方汽配城有限公司	Shanghai 上海市	Shanghai 上海市	(021)59185910 (021)59184868
Zhejiang Aotong Automobile Co.,Ltd. 浙江奥通汽车有限公司	Hangzhou 杭州市	Zhejiang 浙江省	(0571)85368000 (0571)85365099
Runhua Group Co.,Ltd. 润华集团股份有限公司	Jinan 济南市	Shandong 山东省	(0531)7519704 (0531)7983746
Shenzhen Motors Ind.Import & Export Co. 深圳市汽车工业进出口公司	Shenzhen 深圳市	Guangdong 广东省	(0755)83626234 (0755)26711560
Shenzhen Dongfeng Real Estate Co.,Ltd. 深圳东风置业有限公司	Shenzhen 深圳市	Guangdong 广东省	(0755)83210279 (0755)83257208

3740: Bicycles 自行车制造业

The industry accounts for 0.211% of the total revenue of China's industrial sector in 2002. The rate of return on assets is 2.85%. 76.33% of all firms in the industry made a profit while 23.67% had negative returns.The top province in terms of the industry's revenue is Guangdong, accounting for 30.97% of the total revenue.
2002年本行业收入占全行业的 0.211%，资产利润率为 2.85%。76.33%的企业赢利，23.67%的企业亏损。收入最高的省为广东省，占本行业的30.97%。

	Total number of firms 企业总数	Total number of employees 职工总数	Total revenue (Mil.RMB) 总销售收入 (百万元)	Total profit (Mil.RMB) 总利润 (百万元)	Return on assets 资产利润率 (%)	Return on equity 权益利润率 (%)	Labour productivity ('000 RMB/ worker) 劳动生产率 (千元/人)	Debts/ assets 资产负债率 (%)	Total assets (Mil.RMB) 总资产 (百万元)
Industry Overall 行业总体	490	117,850	22,618	684	2.85	12.41	41.17	77.08	24,033

	Number of firms 企业个数	Average number of employees 平均职工人数	Average revenue ('000 RMB) 平均销售收入（千元）	Average profit ('000 RMB) 平均利润 (千元)	Return on assets 资产利润率 (%)	Return on equity 权益利润率 (%)	Labour productivity ('000 RMB/ worker) 劳动生产率 (千元/人)	Debts/ assets 资产负债率 (%)	Average total assets ('000 RMB) 平均总资产 (千元)
By ownership 产业所有权									
State-owned 国有	27	205	3,106	-2,549	-3.00		-1.48	109.29	84,966
Collective-owned 集体	63	170	22,903	440	2.36	8.87	40.87	73.39	18,665
Foreign & Overseas Chinese Funded 三资	156	354	87,309	4,016	4.65	14.97	53.35	68.94	86,381
By regional distribution 地区分布									
Central-North 华北	105	181	25,111	1,046	4.51	41.67	31.89	89.18	23,204
Beijing 北京									
Tianjin 天津	88	174	26,426	1,241	5.11	46.46	31.98	89.00	24,272
Hebei 河北	15	243	20,745	42	0.21	2.19	31.51	90.51	20,032
Shanxi 山西	2								
Inner Mongolia 内蒙古									
Northeast 东北	2	173	8,720	-3,365	-4.46		-0.87	110.86	75,400
Liaoning 辽宁	2	173	8,720	-3,365	-4.46		-0.87	110.86	75,400
Jilin 吉林									
Heilongjiang 黑龙江									
Central-East 华东	273	208	46,271	1,446	3.02	8.94	43.53	66.21	47,852
Shanghai 上海	37	276	88,717	1,568	1.12	3.80	45.39	70.60	140,287
Jiangsu 江苏	118	228	53,564	2,159	4.87	11.57	50.10	57.86	44,285
Zhejiang 浙江	99	151	27,114	751	3.45	11.50	36.68	70.04	21,790
Anhui 安徽	1	386	4,783	-2,367	-22.93	-281.79	4.72	91.86	10,322
Fujian 福建	3	240	7,895	-794	-2.25		5.18	125.53	35,251
Jiangxi 江西	2	113	6,709	519	0.75		22.78	114.22	69,506
Shandong 山东	13	257	23,296	872	4.82	13.16	29.79	63.35	18,092
Central-South 中南	100	409	72,411	1,837	2.23	23.93	42.55	90.70	82,525
Henan 河南	11	171	16,863	144	0.31		10.53	104.69	46,887
Hubei 湖北	2	116	15,423	946	4.22	20.36	52.60	79.28	22,419
Hunan 湖南									
Guangdong 广东	84	455	83,381	2,160	2.40	24.28	44.64	90.11	89,932
Guangxi 广西	3	198	6,926	-395	-0.86	-3.35	5.33	74.27	45,878
Hainan 海南									
Southwest 西南	4	84	13,285	479	4.63	10.26	61.96	54.85	10,335
Chongqing 重庆									
Sichuan 四川	4	84	13,285	479	4.63	10.26	61.96	54.85	10,335
Guizhou 贵州									
Yunnan 云南									
Tibet 西藏									
Northwest 西北	6	93	6,320	69	0.47	0.68	29.92	31.04	14,643
Shaanxi 陕西	4	115	8,245	98	0.47	0.68	31.72	30.15	20,618
Gansu 甘肃	2	51	2,471	12	0.43	0.77	21.74	44.73	2,694
Qinghai 青海									
Ningxia 宁夏									
Xinjiang 新疆									

3740: Bicycles 自行车制造业

Year 年份	Number of firms 企业个数	Rate of change 变化率 (%)	Number of employees 职工人数 (人)	Rate of change 变化率 (%)	Total revenue (Mil. RMB) 总销售收入 (百万元)	Rate of change 变化率 (%)	Total profit (Mil RMB) 总利润 (百万元)	Rate of change 变化率 (%)
2000	377		97,574		18,886		511	
2001	443	17.51	116,444	19.34	19,091	1.09	307	-39.92
2002	490	10.61	117,850	1.21	22,618	18.47	684	122.80

Major Products 主要产品	Output 产量	Unit 单位
Bicycle 自行车	3,570	10,000 Vehicles 万辆

10 Main Firms with Maximal Revenue (year founded) 收入最大的十家主要企业（创办年份）	City 城市	Province 省	Telephone/fax 电话/传真	Number of employees 职工人数	Ownership 产业所有权	Revenue ('000 RMB) 销售收入 (千元)	Profit('000 RMB) (rank) 利润(千元) (排名)	Total assets ('000 RMB) 总资产 (千元)	Major products 主要产品
Giant (China) Co.,Ltd.	Suzhou	Jiangsu	(0512)57709888		Foreign Funded				Bicycle
捷安特(中国)有限公司(1992)	苏州市	江苏省	(0512)57709688	1,820	外商投资	1,367,881	87,836(2)	781,786	自行车
Shunde Tianren Tandems Spares of Bike Products Co.,Ltd.	Foshan	Guangdong	(0765)5638946		Overseas Chinese-funded				Bicycle
顺德天任车料有限公司(1992)	佛山市	广东省	(0765)5635408	3,000	港澳台资	995,417	3,647(47)	293,716	自行车
Phoenix Co.,Ltd.	Shanghai	Shanghai	(021)65950100		Overseas Chinese-funded				Bicycle
凤凰股份有限公司(1958)	上海市	上海市	(021)65645357	2,382	港澳台资	636,710	9,509(16)	1,654,813	自行车
Shanghai Great Phoenix Bicycle Co.,Ltd.	Shanghai	Shanghai	(021)58670118		Foreign Funded				Bicycle
上海巨凤自行车有限公司(1993)	上海市	上海市		857	外商投资	472,467	40,766(5)	277,754	自行车
Jiantai Rubber (Shenzhen) Co.,Ltd.	Shenzhen	Guangdong	(0755)28095282		Overseas Chinese-funded				Tyre
建泰橡胶（深圳）有限公司(1990)	深圳市	广东省	(0755)28115123	1,860	港澳台资	423,104	61,338(4)	914,795	轮胎
Aidiya (Dongguan) Bicycle Co.,Ltd.	Dongguan	Guangdong	(0769)5812521		Foreign Funded				Bicycle
爱地雅（东莞）自行车有限公司(1997)	东莞市	广东省	(0769)5821508	150	外商投资	407,501	15,240(11)	130,612	自行车
Shanghai Permanent Co.,Ltd.	Shanghai	Shanghai	(021)65131177		Overseas Chinese-funded				Bicycle
上海永久股份有限公司(1940)	上海市	上海市	(021)65139966	984	港澳台资	368,782	68,494(3)	413,058	自行车
Huiyang Jindawei Industry Co.,Ltd	Huizhou	Guangdong	(0752)3866000		Foreign Funded				Bicycle Fore & back Yoke自行
惠阳金达伟工业有限公司(1999)	惠州市	广东省	(0752)3866020	990	外商投资	317,430	6,091(27)	185,889	车前后叉
Shenzhen Bao'an Bicycle Co.,Ltd.	Shenzhen	Guangdong	(0755)27722011		Overseas Chinese-funded				Bicycle
深圳保安自行车有限公司(1990)	深圳市	广东省	(0755)27204447	1,000	港澳台资	311,220	9,097(18)	184,278	自行车
Guangzhou Huanqiu Bicycle Industry Co.,Ltd.	Guangzhou	Guangdong	(020)82215097		Overseas Chinese-funded				Bicycle
广州环球自行车工业有限公司(1990)	广州市	广东省	(020)82229702	500	港澳台资	306,269	7,389(23)	186,068	自行车

Top 10 Cities by Revenue 销售收入排名前10位城市	Province 省	Market share 市场份额 (%)	Number of firms 企业个数
Suzhou 苏州市	Jiangsu 江苏省	15.38	41
Shanghai 上海市	Shanghai 上海市	14.51	37
Shenzhen 深圳市	Guangdong 广东省	13.94	37
Tianjin 天津市	Tianjin 天津市	10.28	88
Foshan 佛山市	Guangdong 广东省	5.89	9
Hangzhou 杭州市	Zhejiang 浙江省	5.61	49
Guangzhou 广州市	Guangdong 广东省	5.59	21
Changzhou 常州市	Jiangsu 江苏省	4.99	28
Ningbo 宁波市	Zhejiang 浙江省	3.13	21
Huizhou 惠州市	Guangdong 广东省	2.93	7

10 Major Wholesalers 十家主要批发商	City 城市	Province 省	Telephone/Fax 电话/传真
China Chemical Industry Supply & Sale (Group) General Company	Beijing	Beijing	(010)64238623
中国化工供销(集团)总公司	北京市	北京市	(010)64238623
China Chemical Industry Import & Export General Company	Beijing	Beijing	(010)88078888
中国化工进出口总公司	北京市	北京市	(010)88078890
Tianjin Bridge Group Welding Materials Supply & Sale Co., Ltd.	Tianjin	Tianjin	(022)83968861
天津大桥集团电焊条供销有限公司	天津市	天津市	(022)83968865
Taizhou Xingwei Chunlan Chain Stores Co., Ltd.	Taizhou	Jiangsu	(0523)6611200
泰州星威春兰连锁店有限公司	泰州市	江苏省	(0523)6224181
Taizhou Chunlan Sale Company	Taizhou	Jiangsu	(0523)6611200
泰州春兰销售公司	泰州市	江苏省	(0523)6224181
Shandong Tri-Union Co., Ltd.	Jinan	Shandong	(0531)6086351
山东三联有限责任公司	济南市	山东省	(0531)6093103
Haier Electrical Appliances Co.,Ltd.	Qingdao	Shandong	(0532)8939175
海尔集团电器产业有限公司	青岛市	山东省	(0532)8938086
Guangzhou Haier Industry & Trade Co.,Ltd.	Guangzhou	Guangdong	(020)87397315
广州海尔工贸有限公司	广州市	广东省	(020)87374302
Huizhou TCL Electrical Appliances Sales Co.,Ltd.	Huizhou	Guangdong	(0752)2289885
惠州市TCL电器销售有限公司	惠州市	广东省	(0752)2280690
Guangdong Hardware Minerals Import & Export Group Company	Guangzhou	Guangdong	(020)87752204
广东省五金矿产进出口集团公司	广州市	广东省	(020)87752205

3761: Ocean Shipping Boats 海洋运输船制造业

The industry accounts for 0.217% of the total revenue of China's industrial sector in 2002. The rate of return on assets is -0.03%. 67.12% of all firms in the industry made a profit while 32.88% had negative returns.The top province in terms of the industry's revenue is Shanghai, accounting for 31.63% of the total revenue.
2002年本行业收入占全行业的0.217%，资产利润率为-0.03%。67.12%的企业赢利，32.88%的企业亏损。收入最高的省为上海市，占本行业的31.63%。

	Total number of firms 企业总数	Total number of employees 职工总数	Total revenue (Mil.RMB) 总销售收入（百万元）	Total profit (Mil.RMB) 总利润（百万元）	Return on assets 资产利润率（%）	Return on equity 权益利润率（%）	Labour productivity ('000 RMB/ worker) 劳动生产率（千元/人）	Debts/ assets 资产负债率（%）	Total assets (Mil.RMB) 总资产（百万元）
Industry Overall 行业总体	73	107,731	23,312	-19	-0.03	-0.19	58.92	86.83	74,476

	Number of firms 企业个数	Average number of employees 平均职工人数	Average revenue ('000 RMB) 平均销售收入（千元）	Average profit ('000 RMB) 平均利润（千元）	Return on assets 资产利润率（%）	Return on equity 权益利润率（%）	Labour productivity ('000 RMB/ worker) 劳动生产率（千元/人）	Debts/ assets 资产负债率（%）	Average total assets ('000 RMB) 平均总资产（千元）
By ownership 产业所有权									
State-owned 国有	30	1,398	186,388	-2,469	-0.41	-4.53	46.64	90.88	597,403
Collective-owned 集体	9	338	23,800	8	0.02	0.24	26.84	92.00	39,791
Foreign & Overseas Chinese Funded 三资	10	856	471,638	16,860	2.10	8.34	55.66	74.86	804,649
By regional distribution 地区分布									
Central-North 华北	4	1,725	142,667	-5,964	-1.68	-5.23	26.22	67.93	355,429
Beijing 北京									
Tianjin 天津	4	1,725	142,667	-5,964	-1.68	-5.23	26.22	67.93	355,429
Hebei 河北									
Shanxi 山西									
Inner Mongolia 内蒙古									
Northeast 东北	5	4,011	698,823	-36,418	-0.79	-5.19	89.18	84.87	4,636,907
Liaoning 辽宁	5	4,011	698,823	-36,418	-0.79	-5.19	89.18	84.87	4,636,907
Jilin 吉林									
Heilongjiang 黑龙江									
Central-East 华东	52	1,218	281,742	2,760	0.38	3.23	57.04	88.33	731,791
Shanghai 上海	12	2,595	614,395	1,537	0.09	0.75	47.11	88.11	1,730,091
Jiangsu 江苏	14	862	274,978	10,185	1.72	25.56	91.48	93.26	591,123
Zhejiang 浙江	8	402	109,201	1,671	0.87	5.35	71.18	83.82	193,165
Anhui 安徽	3	1,511	212,814	-10,601	-2.34		40.24	107.47	452,490
Fujian 福建	4	984	194,539	1,946	0.26	1.37	90.66	81.36	761,260
Jiangxi 江西	3	1,231	75,627	-9,519	-4.34		21.41	142.72	219,164
Shandong 山东	8	597	113,886	2,713	0.90	2.22	41.04	59.41	301,379
Central-South 中南	12	1,452	383,058	3,633	0.37	3.11	43.91	88.12	984,742
Henan 河南									
Hubei 湖北	3	2,418	396,458	13,264	0.57	12.27	90.36	95.31	2,307,159
Hunan 湖南									
Guangdong 广东	6	1,287	546,315	2,920	0.42	1.92	11.99	78.02	693,174
Guangxi 广西	3	817	43,143	-4,570	-1.86	-8.29	7.03	77.55	245,462
Hainan 海南									
Southwest 西南									
Chongqing 重庆									
Sichuan 四川									
Guizhou 贵州									
Yunnan 云南									
Tibet 西藏									
Northwest 西北									
Shaanxi 陕西									
Gansu 甘肃									
Qinghai 青海									
Ningxia 宁夏									
Xinjiang 新疆									

Year 年份	Number of firms 企业个数	Rate of change 变化率 (%)	Number of employees 职工人数 (人)	Rate of change 变化率 (%)	Total revenue (Mil. RMB) 总销售收入 (百万元)	Rate of change 变化率 (%)	Total profit (Mil RMB) 总利润 (百万元)	Rate of change 变化率 (%)
2000	64		119,061		19,657		-113	
2001	66	3.13	109,232	-8.26	20,199	2.76	29	-
2002	73	10.61	107,731	-1.37	23,312	15.41	-19	-

Major Products 主要产品	Output 产量	Unit 单位
Civil Steel-made Ship 民用钢质船舶	547	10,000 Synthetic Tons 万综合吨

10 Main Firms with Maximal Revenue (year founded) 收入最大的十家主要企业（创办年份）	City 城市	Province 省	Telephone/fax 电话/传真	Number of employees 职工人数	Ownership 产业所有权	Revenue ('000 RMB) 销售收入 (千元)	Profit('000 RMB) (rank) 利润(千元) (排名)	Total assets ('000 RMB) 总资产 (千元)	Major products 主要产品
Jiangnan Shipyard (Group)Co.,Ltd.	Shanghai	Shanghai	(021)63151818		State Enterprises				Steel Ship
江南造船(集团)有限责任公司(1865)	上海市	上海市	(021)63134743	10,895	国有独资	3,137,659	12,389(9)	8,281,354	金属船舶
Hudong Zhonghua Shipbuilding (Group) Co., Ltd.	Shanghai	Shanghai	(021)58713222		State Enterprises				Steel Ship
沪东中华造船（集团）有限公司(1928)	上海市	上海市	(021)58712603	10,274	国有独资	2,875,329	35,860(3)	8,832,106	金属船舶
Guangzhou Shipyard International Co., Ltd.	Guangzhou	Guangdong	(020)81891712		Overseas Chinese-funded				Ship
广州广船国际股份有限公司(1993)	广州市	广东省	(020)81891575	4,335	港澳台资	2,418,628	19,892(5)	3,158,636	船舶
Dalian Shipyard Heavy Industry Co.,Ltd.	Dalian	Liaoning	(0411)2637627		Limited-Liability				Civil Steel Ship民用
大连造船重工有限责任公司(1898)	大连市	辽宁省	(0411)2633461	6,450	有限公司	1,674,763	-	5,224,505	钢质船舶
Wuchang Shipbuilding Factory	Wuhan	Hubei	(027)68887710		State-owned				Ship Manufacturing & Repairing船舶
武昌造船厂(1934)	武汉市	湖北省	(027)88314876	6,795	国有企业	1,173,509	38,580(2)	6,898,318	制造修理
Dalian New Shipbuilding Heavy Industry Co.,Ltd.	Dalian	Liaoning	(0411)4482888		Limited-Liability				Civil Steel Ship民用
大连新船重工有限责任公司(1990)	大连市	辽宁省	(0411)4417540	4,495	有限公司	1,161,374	1,683(23)	7,024,385	钢质船舶
Nantong Cosco KHI Ship Engineering Co.Ltd.	Nantong	Jiangsu	(0513)3500666		Foreign Funded				Ocean Transportation Ship海洋
南通中远川崎船舶工程有限公司(1999)	南通市	江苏省	(0513)3514349	976	外商投资	1,150,960	119,208(1)	2,855,334	运输船舶
Jiangsu New Centry Shipbuilding Co., Ltd.	Taizhou	Jiangsu	(0523)4211337		Joint Stock				Civil Steel Ship民用
江苏新世纪造船股份有限公司(1971)	泰州市	江苏省	(0523)4211573	2,022	股份制	1,011,312	22,091(4)	1,872,571	钢质船舶
Guangzhou Huangpu Shipyard	Guangzhou	Guangdong	(020)82502110		State-owned				Ship Manufacturing & Repairing船舶
广州黄埔造船厂(1851)	广州市	广东省	(020)82201387	2,868	国有企业	815,444	-	899,540	制造修理
Shanghai Shipyard	Shanghai	Shanghai	(021)58790451		State-owned				Steel Ship
上海船厂(1862)	上海市	上海市	(021)58401840	5,555	国有企业	796,464	8,000(10)	2,817,962	金属船舶

Top 10 Cities by Revenue 销售收入排名前10位城市	Province 省	Market share 市场份额 (%)	Number of firms 企业个数
Shanghai 上海市	Shanghai 上海市	31.63	12
Guangzhou 广州市	Guangdong 广东省	13.97	5
Dalian 大连市	Liaoning 辽宁省	12.80	4
Taizhou 泰州市	Jiangsu 江苏省	5.98	3
Nantong 南通市	Jiangsu 江苏省	5.35	4
Wuhan 武汉市	Hubei 湖北省	5.03	1
Yantai 烟台市	Shandong 山东省	2.78	3
Wuhu 芜湖市	Anhui 安徽省	2.74	3
Xiamen 厦门市	Fujian 福建省	2.55	1
Tianjin 天津市	Tianjin 天津市	2.45	4

10 Major Wholesalers 十家主要批发商	City 城市	Province 省	Telephone/Fax 电话/传真
SU MEC	Nanjing	Jiangsu	(025)4511888
中设江苏机械设备进出口（集团）公司	南京市	江苏省	(025)4411772
China Poster Mobile Communications Equipment Co.,Ltd.	Beijing	Beijing	(010)66426993
中邮普泰移动通信设备股份有限公司	北京市	北京市	(010)66426837
Sino Kama Co., Ltd.	Shanghai	Shanghai	(021)62031188
中泰凯马股份有限公司	上海市	上海市	(021)62030851
China Huayuan Group Co.,Ltd.	Shanghai	Shanghai	(021)62031788
中国华源集团有限公司	上海市	上海市	(021)62032288
Zhejiang Crand Imp.& Exp.Co.,Ltd.	Ningbo	Zhejiang	(0574)87720170
浙江远大进出口有限公司	宁波市	浙江省	(0574)87723350
Shandong Machinery Import & Export Group Corporation	Qingdao	Shandong	(0532)2661628
山东省机械进出口集团公司	青岛市	山东省	(0532)2991655
Qingdao Haier International Trade Co.,Ltd.	Qingdao	Shandong	(0532)8938337
青岛海尔国际贸易有限公司	青岛市	山东省	(0532)8939494
Guangdong Machinery Import & Export Group Corporation	Guangzhou	Guangdong	(020)87782168
广东省机械进出口集团公司	广州市	广东省	(020)87771803
China National Machinery Equipment Import & Export Corporation	Beijing	Beijing	(010)63474506
中国机械设备进出口总公司	北京市	北京市	(010)63261865
Beijing Cellstar Co.,Ltd.	Beijing	Beijing	(010)64602050
北京蜂星事达电讯有限公司	北京市	北京市	(010)64672648

3762: Waterway Shipping Boats 内河船制造业

The industry accounts for 0.033% of the total revenue of China's industrial sector in 2002. The rate of return on assets is -1.65%. 73.74% of all firms in the industry made a profit while 26.26% had negative returns.The top province in terms of the industry's revenue is Jiangsu, accounting for 44.39% of the total revenue.
2002年本行业收入占全行业的0.033%，资产利润率为-1.65%。73.74%的企业赢利，26.26%的企业亏损。收入最高的省为江苏省，占本行业的44.39%。

	Total number of firms 企业总数	Total number of employees 职工总数	Total revenue (Mil.RMB) 总销售收入（百万元）	Total profit (Mil.RMB) 总利润（百万元）	Return on assets 资产利润率（%）	Return on equity 权益利润率（%）	Labour productivity ('000 RMB/ worker) 劳动生产率（千元/人）	Debts/ assets 资产负债率（%）	Total assets (Mil.RMB) 总资产（百万元）
Industry Overall 行业总体	99	29,638	3,552	-86	-1.65	-10.42	29.42	84.17	5,239

	Number of firms 企业个数	Average number of employees 平均职工人数	Average revenue ('000 RMB) 平均销售收入（千元）	Average profit ('000 RMB) 平均利润（千元）	Return on assets 资产利润率（%）	Return on equity 权益利润率（%）	Labour productivity ('000 RMB/ worker) 劳动生产率（千元/人）	Debts/ assets 资产负债率（%）	Average total assets ('000 RMB) 平均总资产（千元）
By ownership 产业所有权									
State-owned 国有	32	530	52,996	-2,598	-2.34	-18.06	23.31	87.05	111,098
Collective-owned 集体	12	278	50,631	-138	-0.63	-5.43	38.17	88.38	21,853
Foreign & Overseas Chinese Funded 三资	4	98	29,733	-2,865	-4.71	-27.11	79.27	82.62	60,796
By regional distribution 地区分布									
Central-North 华北									
Beijing 北京									
Tianjin 天津									
Hebei 河北									
Shanxi 山西									
Inner Mongolia 内蒙古									
Northeast 东北	2	117	7,546	507	2.47	4.99	8.77	50.53	20,515
Liaoning 辽宁									
Jilin 吉林	1	42	640	2	0.06	0.12	3.10	45.97	3,178
Heilongjiang 黑龙江	1	192	14,451	1,011	2.67	5.44	10.02	50.91	37,852
Central-East 华东	58	213	33,472	485	1.32	6.35	38.23	79.18	36,660
Shanghai 上海									
Jiangsu 江苏	31	244	50,859	528	0.93	6.47	50.41	85.54	56,430
Zhejiang 浙江	3	64	7,432	-145	-1.04	-2.39	16.36	56.62	13,995
Anhui 安徽	8	208	9,501	84	0.52	1.15	12.46	54.82	16,125
Fujian 福建	5	59	5,305	347	5.27	8.79	29.39	40.09	6,581
Jiangxi 江西	3	178	3,481	2	0.02	0.02	11.23	24.99	13,499
Shandong 山东	8	264	28,685	1,224	7.39	15.49	25.03	52.30	16,567
Central-South 中南	31	364	43,892	-2,353	-3.06	-17.41	28.43	82.44	77,008
Henan 河南	2	348	64,031	530	12.09	37.56	42.90	67.82	4,385
Hubei 湖北	7	805	79,342	-4,944	-3.56	-17.16	18.63	79.27	139,013
Hunan 湖南	4	314	13,769	-1,016	-1.22	-3.01	17.16	59.54	83,494
Guangdong 广东	17	193	35,487	-1,961	-3.47	-48.42	41.61	92.83	56,511
Guangxi 广西	1	436	18,840	-1,996	-1.80	-18.87	65.11	90.45	110,744
Hainan 海南									
Southwest 西南	8	719	29,305	-5,322	-6.22		13.31	107.72	85,529
Chongqing 重庆	5	1,048	42,563	-8,081	-6.50		13.18	107.84	124,258
Sichuan 四川	2	204	9,103	-1,091	-4.50		15.24	119.86	24,241
Guizhou 贵州	1	106	3,416	11	0.08	0.20	12.08	61.81	14,463
Yunnan 云南									
Tibet 西藏									
Northwest 西北									
Shaanxi 陕西									
Gansu 甘肃									
Qinghai 青海									
Ningxia 宁夏									
Xinjiang 新疆									

3762: Waterway Shipping Boats 内河船制造业

Year 年份	Number of firms 企业个数	Rate of change 变化率 (%)	Number of employees 职工人数 (人)	Rate of change 变化率 (%)	Total revenue (Mil. RMB) 总销售收入 (百万元)	Rate of change 变化率 (%)	Total profit (Mil RMB) 总利润 (百万元)	Rate of change 变化率 (%)
2000	108		35,749		2,798		-227	
2001	95	-12.04	32,383	-9.42	3,300	17.94	-200	11.89
2002	99	4.21	29,638	-8.48	3,552	7.64	-86	57.00

Major Products 主要产品	Output 产量	Unit 单位
Civil Steel-made Ship 民用钢质船舶	547	10,000 Synthetic Tons 万综合吨

10 Main Firms with Maximal Revenue (year founded) 收入最大的十家主要企业（创办年份）	City 城市	Province 省	Telephone/fax 电话/传真	Number of employees 职工人数	Ownership 产业所有权	Revenue ('000 RMB) 销售收入 (千元)	Profit('000 RMB) (rank) 利润(千元) (排名)	Total assets ('000 RMB) 总资产 (千元)	Major products 主要产品
Jinling Ship Factory,Changjiang Shipping Grop China	Nanjing	Jiangsu	(025)8785115		State-owned				Steel Ship
中国长江航运集团金陵船厂(1952)	南京市	江苏省	(025)8781075	2,426	国有企业	870,010	6,080(1)	1,190,690	金属船舶
Guangzhou Panyu Ship Dismantling & Steel Rolling Co.,Ltd.	Guangzhou	Guangdong	(020)84844611		Collective-owned				Old Ship Dismantling
广州市番禺区拆船轧钢公司(1980)	广州市	广东省	(020)84861712	492	集体企业	269,728	-	145,644	旧船拆解
Jingjiang SUMFC Shiping Project Co.,Ltd.	Taizhou	Jiangsu	(0523)4633191		Joint Stock				Civil Steel Ship民用
靖江苏美达船舶工程有限公司(1973)	泰州市	江苏省	(0523)4630661	616	股份制	130,125	2,051(6)	175,248	钢质船舶
Jiangsu Wuxi Ship Factory	Wuxi	Jiangsu	(0510)3708456		Joint Owned				Civil Ship
江苏省无锡船厂(1956)	无锡市	江苏省	(0510)3703627	976	联营企业	100,622	300(30)	163,218	民用船舶
Changjiang Shipping Group China Co.,Ltd. Yichang	Yichang	Hubei	(0717)6271304		State-owned				Ship
Ship Factory 中国长江航运集团宜昌船厂(1956)	宜昌市	湖北省	(0717)6271058	1,221	国有企业	78,290	-	217,310	船舶
Chongqing Dongfeng Ship Industry Co.,Ltd.	Chongqing	Chongqing	(023)67780390		State-owned				Steel Ship
重庆东风船舶工业公司(1928)	重庆市	重庆市	(023)67782332	2,278	国有企业	67,725	-	129,722	钢质船舶
Guangdong New China Shipyard Co.,Ltd.	Guangzhou	Guangdong	(020)84215663		State Enterprises				Freshwater Ship
广东新中国船厂有限公司(1963)	广州市	广东省	(020)84219621	584	国有独资	61,488	-	145,296	内河船
Chongqing Shipbuilding Factory	Chongqing	Chongqing	(023)62490016		State-owned				Civil Ship
重庆造船厂(1976)	重庆市	重庆市	(023)62490888	959	国有企业	54,174	-	202,172	民用船舶
Wuhan Zhongnan Industrial General Co.,Ltd	Wuhan	Hubei	(027)86730191		Collective-owned				Freshwater Ship
武汉市中南实业总公司(1994)	武汉市	湖北省	(027)86730191	368	集体企业	51,333	213(34)	36,529	内河船
Zaozhuang Taigang Fada Group Company	Zaozhuang	Shandong	(0632)6611553		Collective-owned				Ship Manufacture
枣庄市台港发达集团公司(1995)	枣庄市	山东省	(0632)6611821	620	集体企业	49,964	3,113(3)	22,687	造船

Top 10 Cities by Revenue 销售收入排名前10位城市	Province 省	Market share 市场份额 (%)	Number of firms 企业个数
Nanjing 南京市	Jiangsu 江苏省	28.52	7
Guangzhou 广州市	Guangdong 广东省	12.90	7
Wuhan 武汉市	Hubei 湖北省	11.19	2
Taizhou 泰州市	Jiangsu 江苏省	6.40	6
Chongqing 重庆市	Chongqing 重庆市	5.99	5
Zaozhuang 枣庄市	Shandong 山东省	5.06	4
Xinyang 信阳市	Henan 河南省	3.61	2
Yangzhou 扬州市	Jiangsu 江苏省	3.48	7
Yichang 宜昌市	Hubei 湖北省	3.02	3
Wuxi 无锡市	Jiangsu 江苏省	2.83	1

10 Major Wholesalers 十家主要批发商	City 城市	Province 省	Telephone/Fax 电话/传真
SU MEC	Nanjing	Jiangsu	(025)4511888
中设江苏机械设备进出口（集团）公司	南京市	江苏省	(025)4411772
China Poster Mobile Communications Equipment Co.,Ltd.	Beijing	Beijing	(010)66426993
中邮普泰移动通信设备股份有限公司	北京市	北京市	(010)66426837
Sino Kama Co., Ltd.	Shanghai	Shanghai	(021)62031188
中泰凯马股份有限公司	上海市	上海市	(021)62030851
China Huayuan Group Co.,Ltd.	Shanghai	Shanghai	(021)62031188
中国华源集团有限公司	上海市	上海市	(021)62032288
Zhejiang Crand Imp.& Exp.Co.,Ltd.	Ningbo	Zhejiang	(0574)87720170
浙江远大进出口有限公司	宁波市	浙江省	(0574)87723350
Shandong Machinery Import & Export Group Corporation	Qingdao	Shandong	(0532)2661628
山东省机械进出口集团公司	青岛市	山东省	(0532)2991655
Qingdao Haier International Trade Co.,Ltd.	Qingdao	Shandong	(0532)8938337
青岛海尔国际贸易有限公司	青岛市	山东省	(0532)8939494
Guangdong Machinery Import & Export Group Corporation	Guangzhou	Guangdong	(020)87782168
广东省机械进出口集团公司	广州市	广东省	(020)87771803
China National Machinery Equipment Import & Export Corporation	Beijing	Beijing	(010)63474506
中国机械设备进出口总公司	北京市	北京市	(010)63261865
Beijing Cellstar Co.,Ltd.	Beijing	Beijing	(010)64602050
北京蜂星事达电讯有限公司	北京市	北京市	(010)64672648

3763: Fishing Vessel 渔轮制造业

The industry accounts for 0.019% of the total revenue of China's industrial sector in 2002. The rate of return on assets is 5.72%. 87.76% of all firms in the industry made a profit while 12.24% had negative returns.The top province in terms of the industry's revenue is Zhejiang, accounting for 53.34% of the total revenue.
2002年本行业收入占全行业的 0.019%，资产利润率为 5.72%。87.76%的企业赢利，12.24%的企业亏损。收入最高的省为浙江省，占本行业的53.34%。

	Total number of firms 企业总数	Total number of employees 职工总数	Total revenue (Mil.RMB) 总销售收入(百万元)	Total profit (Mil.RMB) 总利润(百万元)	Return on assets 资产利润率(%)	Return on equity 权益利润率(%)	Labour productivity ('000 RMB/worker) 劳动生产率(千元/人)	Debts/assets 资产负债率(%)	Total assets (Mil.RMB) 总资产(百万元)
Industry Overall 行业总体	49	10,190	2,036	96	5.72	23.89	45.07	76.06	1,682

	Number of firms 企业个数	Average number of employees 平均职工人数	Average revenue ('000 RMB) 平均销售收入（千元）	Average profit ('000 RMB) 平均利润（千元）	Return on assets 资产利润率(%)	Return on equity 权益利润率(%)	Labour productivity ('000 RMB/worker) 劳动生产率(千元/人)	Debts/assets 资产负债率(%)	Average total assets ('000 RMB) 平均总资产(千元)
By ownership 产业所有权									
State-owned 国有	5	535	24,628	-76	-0.11	-0.68	14.93	84.10	69,656
Collective-owned 集体	3	211	33,660	2,271	6.67	24.55	46.57	72.85	34,066
Foreign & Overseas Chinese Funded 三资	2	242	26,033	582	2.68	6.27	12.20	57.31	21,727
By regional distribution 地区分布									
Central-North 华北	1	632	10,084	-361	-0.57	-2.52	9.50	77.51	63,801
Beijing 北京									
Tianjin 天津	1	632	10,084	-361	-0.57	-2.52	9.50	77.51	63,801
Hebei 河北									
Shanxi 山西									
Inner Mongolia 内蒙古									
Northeast 东北	4	398	15,473	-225	-0.43	-1.62	10.25	73.60	52,635
Liaoning 辽宁	3	518	20,631	-300	-0.43	-1.66	10.50	73.98	69,390
Jilin 吉林	1	39						39.72	2,369
Heilongjiang 黑龙江									
Central-East 华东	37	185	47,320	2,529	8.63	29.64	56.69	70.89	29,313
Shanghai 上海									
Jiangsu 江苏	2	221	9,449	-600	-2.80		18.09	128.00	21,461
Zhejiang 浙江	23	89	47,227	2,240	12.06	35.13	90.02	65.68	18,584
Anhui 安徽									
Fujian 福建	3	78	8,350	33	2.16	3.18	34.57	32.18	1,543
Jiangxi 江西									
Shandong 山东	9	459	68,964	4,792	7.08	24.25	45.50	70.82	67,731
Central-South 中南	7	159	30,492	554	1.20	22.80	43.50	94.73	46,147
Henan 河南									
Hubei 湖北									
Hunan 湖南									
Guangdong 广东	6	178	35,574	646	1.20	22.80	39.46	94.73	53,839
Guangxi 广西									
Hainan 海南	1	42					146.43		
Southwest 西南									
Chongqing 重庆									
Sichuan 四川									
Guizhou 贵州									
Yunnan 云南									
Tibet 西藏									
Northwest 西北									
Shaanxi 陕西									
Gansu 甘肃									
Qinghai 青海									
Ningxia 宁夏									
Xinjiang 新疆									

3763: Fishing Vessel 渔轮制造业

Year 年份	Number of firms 企业个数	Rate of change 变化率 (%)	Number of employees 职工人数 (人)	Rate of change 变化率 (%)	Total revenue (Mil. RMB) 总销售收入 (百万元)	Rate of change 变化率 (%)	Total profit (Mil RMB) 总利润 (百万元)	Rate of change 变化率 (%)
2000	46		10,074		1,145		42	
2001	50	8.70	10,394	3.18	1,558	36.07	55	30.95
2002	49	-2.00	10,190	-1.96	2,036	30.68	96	74.55

Major Products 主要产品	Output 产量	Unit 单位

10 Main Firms with Maximal Revenue (year founded) 收入最大的十家主要企业（创办年份）	City 城市	Province 省	Telephone/fax 电话/传真	Number of employees 职工人数	Ownership 产业所有权	Revenue ('000 RMB) 销售收入 (千元)	Profit('000 RMB) (rank) 利润(千元) (排名)	Total assets ('000 RMB) 总资产 (千元)	Major products 主要产品
Taizhou Hongguan Shipbuilding Co.,Ltd. 台州市宏冠造船有限公司(1995)	Taizhou 台州市	Zhejiang 浙江省	(0576)5289103 (0576)5289516	800	Limited-Liability 有限公司	500,020	30,001(1)	155,900	Fishing Boat&Sand Ship 渔船挖沙船
Rongcheng Huanghai Shipbuilding Co.,Ltd. 荣成市黄海造船有限公司(1944)	Weihai 威海市	Shandong 山东省	(0631)7381878 (0631)7381613	1,286	Limited-Liability 有限公司	213,660	15,880(2)	202,550	Steel Fish-ship 钢质渔轮
Rongcheng Haida Shipbuilding Co.,Ltd. 荣成市海达造船有限公司(1998)	Weihai 威海市	Shandong 山东省	(0631)7668060	617	Limited-Liability 有限公司	139,886	10,654(3)	61,031	Fishing Boat 渔船
Wenling Songmen Xianfeng Ship Repairing & Building Factory 温岭市松门先锋船舶修造厂(1989)	Taizhou 台州市	Zhejiang 浙江省	(0576)6662034 (0576)6662034	73	Joint Stock 股份制	114,000	1,910(8)	39,660	Fishing Vessel 渔轮
Rushan Shipbuilding Factory 乳山市造船厂(1951)	Weihai 威海市	Shandong 山东省	(0631)6761055 (0631)6761988	532	Joint Stock 股份制	76,291	1,373(13)	104,125	Fishing Boat 渔船
Rongcheng Shipbuilding Industry Co.,Ltd. 荣成市造船工业有限公司(1953)	Weihai 威海市	Shandong 山东省	(0631)7381744 (0631)7381744	720	Limited-Liability 有限公司	69,008	4,510(7)	97,423	Ship 船舶
Wenling Jiaoshan Ship Repair & Manufacturing Factory 温岭市礁山船舶修造厂(2000)	Taizhou 台州市	Zhejiang 浙江省	(0576)6628538 (0576)6628478	76	Joint Stock 股份制	56,000	1,020(17)	18,300	Fishing Vessel 渔轮
Zhuhai Xiangzhou Ship Repair & Manufacturing Factory 珠海市香洲船舶修造厂(1992)	Zhuhai 珠海市	Guangdong 广东省	(0756)3314770 (0756)3314811	121	State-owned 国有企业	51,005	1,715(11)	44,302	Ship 船舶
Wenling Ship Repair & Making Industrial Co.,Ltd. 温岭市船舶修造实业公司(1993)	Taizhou 台州市	Zhejiang 浙江省	(0576)6501131	190	Collective-owned 集体企业	50,780	563(22)	12,399	Fishing Vessel 渔轮
CNFC Dalian Fishing Vessel Co., 中国水产大连渔轮公司(1907)	Dalian 大连市	Liaoning 辽宁省	(0411)2542721 (0411)2542049	1,363	State-owned 国有企业	43,148	-	190,475	Fishing Vessel 渔轮

Top 10 Cities by Revenue 销售收入排名前10位城市	Province 省	Market share 市场份额 (%)	Number of firms 企业个数
Taizhou 台州市	Zhejiang 浙江省	53.34	23
Weihai 威海市	Shandong 山东省	30.17	8
Guangzhou 广州市	Guangdong 广东省	4.95	2
Dalian 大连市	Liaoning 辽宁省	3.03	2
Zhuhai 珠海市	Guangdong 广东省	2.50	1
Foshan 佛山市	Guangdong 广东省	1.75	1
Shanwei 汕尾市	Guangdong 广东省	1.27	2
Ningde 宁德市	Fujian 福建省	1.23	3
Nantong 南通市	Jiangsu 江苏省	0.61	1
Tianjin 天津市	Tianjin 天津市	0.50	1

10 Major Wholesalers 十家主要批发商	City 城市	Province 省	Telephone/Fax 电话/传真
SU MEC 中设江苏机械设备进出口（集团）公司	Nanjing 南京市	Jiangsu 江苏省	(025)4511888 (025)4411772
China Poster Mobile Communications Equipment Co.,Ltd. 中邮普泰移动通信设备股份有限公司	Beijing 北京市	Beijing 北京市	(010)66426993 (010)66426837
Sino Kama Co., Ltd. 中泰凯马股份有限公司	Shanghai 上海市	Shanghai 上海市	(021)62031188 (021)62030851
China Huayuan Group Co.,Ltd. 中国华源集团有限公司	Shanghai 上海市	Shanghai 上海市	(021)62031188 (021)62032288
Zhejiang Crand Imp.& Exp.Co.,Ltd. 浙江远大进出口有限公司	Ningbo 宁波市	Zhejiang 浙江省	(0574)87720170 (0574)87723350
Shandong Machinery Import & Export Group Corporation 山东省机械进出口集团公司	Qingdao 青岛市	Shandong 山东省	(0532)2661628 (0532)2991655
Qingdao Haier International Trade Co.,Ltd. 青岛海尔国际贸易有限公司	Qingdao 青岛市	Shandong 山东省	(0532)8938337 (0532)8939494
Guangdong Machinery Import & Export Group Corporation 广东省机械进出口集团公司	Guangzhou 广州市	Guangdong 广东省	(020)87782168 (020)87771803
China National Machinery Equipment Import & Export Corporation 中国机械设备进出口总公司	Beijing 北京市	Beijing 北京市	(010)63474506 (010)63261865
Beijing Cellstar Co.,Ltd. 北京蜂星事达电讯有限公司	Beijing 北京市	Beijing 北京市	(010)64602050 (010)64672648

3764: Shipping Machinery and Equipment 船舶机械设备制造业

The industry accounts for 0.047% of the total revenue of China's industrial sector in 2002. The rate of return on assets is 2.61%. 85.54% of all firms in the industry made a profit while 14.46% had negative returns.The top province in terms of the industry's revenue is Jiangsu, accounting for 43.73% of the total revenue.
2002年本行业收入占全行业的 0.047%，资产利润率为 2.61%。85.54%的企业赢利，14.46%的企业亏损。收入最高的省为江苏省，占本行业的43.73%。

	Total number of firms 企业总数	Total number of employees 职工总数	Total revenue (Mil.RMB) 总销售收入(百万元)	Total profit (Mil.RMB) 总利润(百万元)	Return on assets 资产利润率(%)	Return on equity 权益利润率(%)	Labour productivity ('000 RMB/ worker) 劳动生产率(千元/人)	Debts/ assets 资产负债率(%)	Total assets (Mil.RMB) 总资产(百万元)
Industry Overall 行业总体	83	37,506	5,048	199	2.61	8.55	43.72	69.48	7,633

	Number of firms 企业个数	Average number of employees 平均职工人数	Average revenue ('000 RMB) 平均销售收入（千元）	Average profit ('000 RMB) 平均利润(千元)	Return on assets 资产利润率(%)	Return on equity 权益利润率(%)	Labour productivity ('000 RMB/ worker) 劳动生产率(千元/人)	Debts/ assets 资产负债率(%)	Average total assets ('000 RMB) 平均总资产(千元)
By ownership 产业所有权									
State-owned 国有	20	881	88,480	955	0.48	2.21	34.29	78.17	197,562
Collective-owned 集体	11	431	26,158	864	4.11	21.36	17.63	80.78	21,035
Foreign & Overseas Chinese Funded 三资	11	161	37,973	5,153	9.64	19.28	93.30	50.01	53,474
By regional distribution 地区分布									
Central-North 华北	4	88	10,759	779	3.48	12.03	27.96	71.11	22,422
Beijing 北京									
Tianjin 天津	2	43	12,652	2,801	11.87	18.41	26.80	35.49	23,588
Hebei 河北	2	133	8,867	-1,243	-5.85		28.34	110.63	21,257
Shanxi 山西									
Inner Mongolia 内蒙古									
Northeast 东北	13	516	46,347	1,363	1.66	7.12	28.38	76.74	82,277
Liaoning 辽宁	12	517	49,166	1,470	1.69	7.60	29.93	77.72	86,815
Jilin 吉林									
Heilongjiang 黑龙江	1	501	12,510	75	0.27	0.45	9.17	40.24	27,824
Central-East 华东	48	321	64,054	3,335	4.29	11.04	61.46	61.16	77,797
Shanghai 上海	8	123	14,503	910	5.62	9.97	38.27	43.65	16,208
Jiangsu 江苏	27	291	81,758	3,921	4.32	10.54	85.93	58.98	90,673
Zhejiang 浙江	4	313	83,169	10,342	10.32	19.51	102.63	47.10	100,230
Anhui 安徽	3	393	42,396	691	0.89	3.49	30.00	74.53	77,770
Fujian 福建									
Jiangxi 江西	3	676	41,303	1,106	1.11	9.52	17.27	88.33	99,560
Shandong 山东	3	697	55,783	48	0.06	0.22	16.27	70.20	74,510
Central-South 中南	15	801	80,088	990	0.63	3.15	36.06	79.84	156,005
Henan 河南	2	1,899	92,599	196	0.09	0.73	10.18	88.33	230,231
Hubei 湖北	8	851	115,578	1,720	0.81	3.97	53.23	79.63	212,516
Hunan 湖南									
Guangdong 广东	3	172	5,077	74	0.80	3.43	9.15	76.56	9,235
Guangxi 广西	2	443	38,134	239	0.31	0.73	30.64	57.04	75,896
Hainan 海南									
Southwest 西南	3	1,015	42,274	1,178	0.89	2.66	19.90	66.70	133,048
Chongqing 重庆	3	1,015	42,274	1,178	0.89	2.66	19.90	66.70	133,048
Sichuan 四川									
Guizhou 贵州									
Yunnan 云南									
Tibet 西藏									
Northwest 西北									
Shaanxi 陕西									
Gansu 甘肃									
Qinghai 青海									
Ningxia 宁夏									
Xinjiang 新疆									

3764: Shipping Machinery and Equipment 船舶机械设备制造业

Year 年份	Number of firms 企业个数	Rate of change 变化率 (%)	Number of employees 职工人数 (人)	Rate of change 变化率 (%)	Total revenue (Mil. RMB) 总销售收入 (百万元)	Rate of change 变化率 (%)	Total profit (Mil RMB) 总利润 (百万元)	Rate of change 变化率 (%)
2000	72		47,354		4,167		46	
2001	68	-5.56	40,213	-15.08	4,728	13.46	124	169.57
2002	83	22.06	37,506	-6.73	5,048	6.77	199	60.48

Major Products 主要产品	Output 产量	Unit 单位
Internal-combustion Engine 内燃机	28,433	10,000 KW 万千瓦

10 Main Firms with Maximal Revenue (year founded) 收入最大的十家主要企业（创办年份）	City 城市	Province 省	Telephone/fax 电话/传真	Number of employees 职工人数	Ownership 产业所有权	Revenue ('000 RMB) 销售收入 (千元)	Profit('000 RMB) (rank) 利润(千元) (排名)	Total assets ('000 RMB) 总资产 (千元)	Major products 主要产品
Jiangyin Zhenhua Port Machinery Co.,Ltd. Jiangyin Branch 江阴市振华港口机械有限公司江阴分公司(1993)	Wuxi 无锡市	Jiangsu 江苏省	(0510)6853818 (0510)6853758	512	Joint Owned 联营企业	1,200,000	72,800(1)	818,988	Crane 起重机
Dalian Marine Diesel Engine Factory 大连船用柴油机厂(1984)	Dalian 大连市	Liaoning 辽宁省	(0411)4414701 (0411)4417499	1,152	State-owned 国有企业	271,054	2,002(22)	639,602	Low-speed Marine Diesel Engine低速船用柴油机
Yichang Marine Diesel Engine Factory 宜昌船舶柴油机厂(1983)	Yichang 宜昌市	Hubei 湖北省	(0717)6469159 (0717)6469152	1,433	State-owned 国有企业	225,308	2,617(16)	410,684	Diesel Engine 柴油机
Nanjing Lvzhou Machine Works 南京绿洲机器厂(1960)	Nanjing 南京市	Jiangsu 江苏省	(025)6700476 (025)6700325	2,323	State-owned 国有企业	218,000	3,080(12)	433,430	Marine Deck Machinery船用甲板机械
Zhenjiang CME Co.,Ltd. 镇江中船设备有限公司(2001)	Zhenjiang 镇江市	Jiangsu 江苏省	(0511)4511316 (0511)4511210	1,217	State Enterprises 国有独资	198,200	6,770(5)	331,790	Moderate-Speed Diesel Engine中速柴油机
Zhengmao Group Co.,Ltd. 正茂集团有限责任公司(1994)	Zhenjiang 镇江市	Jiangsu 江苏省	(0511)4511775 (0511)4511893	616	Limited-Liability 有限公司	183,370	-	445,340	Ahchor Chain 锚链
Hangzhou Fada Gear Case Co.,Ltd. 杭州发达齿轮箱有限公司(1988)	Hangzhou 杭州市	Zhejiang 浙江省	(0571)82464211 (0571)82462179	450	Private Owned 私营企业	169,762	5,916(7)	76,390	Marine Gear Case船用齿轮箱
Sansung Heavy Industry(Ningbo) Co.,Ltd. 三星重工业(宁波)有限公司(1995)	Ningbo 宁波市	Zhejiang 浙江省	(0574)86226688 (0574)86224275	678	Foreign Funded 外商投资	151,430	34,302(2)	310,082	Ship 船舶
Wuhan Nanhua High Speed Ship Engineering Co.,Ltd. 武汉南华高速船舶工程有限公司(1995)	Wuhan 武汉市	Hubei 湖北省	(027)88116904 (027)88118878	554	Foreign Funded 外商投资	97,137	1,176(31)	85,594	High-Speed Ship 高速船舶
Bohai Heavy Industry Ship Repair & Manufacturing General Company 渤海重工船舶修造总公司(1976)	Huludao 葫芦岛市	Liaoning 辽宁省	(0429)2793713 (0429)2793705	1,935	Collective-owned 集体企业	89,445	304(46)	155,398	Bridge-type Autocrane桥式门座起重机

Top 10 Cities by Revenue 销售收入排名前10位城市	Province 省	Market share 市场份额 (%)	Number of firms 企业个数
Wuxi 无锡市	Jiangsu 江苏省	25.49	5
Wuhan 武汉市	Hubei 湖北省	10.89	2
Dalian 大连市	Liaoning 辽宁省	9.34	10
Zhenjiang 镇江市	Jiangsu 江苏省	8.80	5
Nanjing 南京市	Jiangsu 江苏省	4.66	3
Yichang 宜昌市	Hubei 湖北省	4.46	1
Luoyang 洛阳市	Henan 河南省	3.67	2
Hangzhou 杭州市	Zhejiang 浙江省	3.36	1
Ningbo 宁波市	Zhejiang 浙江省	3.23	3
Chongqing 重庆市	Chongqing 重庆市	2.51	3

10 Major Wholesalers 十家主要批发商	City 城市	Province 省	Telephone/Fax 电话/传真
SU MEC 中设江苏机械设备进出口（集团）公司	Nanjing 南京市	Jiangsu 江苏省	(025)4511888 (025)4411772
China Poster Mobile Communications Equipment Co.,Ltd. 中邮普泰移动通信设备股份有限公司	Beijing 北京市	Beijing 北京市	(010)66426993 (010)66426837
Sino Kama Co., Ltd. 中泰凯马股份有限公司	Shanghai 上海市	Shanghai 上海市	(021)62031188 (021)62030851
China Huayuan Group Co.,Ltd. 中国华源集团有限公司	Shanghai 上海市	Shanghai 上海市	(021)62031188 (021)62032288
Zhejiang Crand Imp.& Exp.Co.,Ltd. 浙江远大进出口有限公司	Ningbo 宁波市	Zhejiang 浙江省	(0574)87720170 (0574)87723350
Shandong Machinery Import & Export Group Corporation 山东省机械进出口集团公司	Qingdao 青岛市	Shandong 山东省	(0532)2661628 (0532)2991655
Qingdao Haier International Trade Co.,Ltd. 青岛海尔国际贸易有限公司	Qingdao 青岛市	Shandong 山东省	(0532)8938337 (0532)8939494
Guangdong Machinery Import & Export Group Corporation 广东省机械进出口集团公司	Guangzhou 广州市	Guangdong 广东省	(020)87782168 (020)87771803
China National Machinery Equipment Import & Export Corporation 中国机械设备进出口总公司	Beijing 北京市	Beijing 北京市	(010)63474506 (010)63261865
Beijing Cellstar Co.,Ltd. 北京蜂星事达电讯有限公司	Beijing 北京市	Beijing 北京市	(010)64602050 (010)64672648

3793: Road Traffic Mark 公路标志制造业

The industry accounts for 0.013% of the total revenue of China's industrial sector in 2002. The rate of return on assets is 4.86%. 80.33% of all firms in the industry made a profit while 19.67% had negative returns.The top province in terms of the industry's revenue is Shanxi, accounting for 13.47% of the total revenue.
2002年本行业收入占全行业的 0.013%，资产利润率为 4.86%。80.33%的企业赢利，19.67%的企业亏损。收入最高的省为山西省，占本行业的13.47%。

	Total number of firms 企业总数	Total number of employees 职工总数	Total revenue (Mil.RMB) 总销售收入（百万元）	Total profit (Mil.RMB) 总利润（百万元）	Return on assets 资产利润率（%）	Return on equity 权益利润率（%）	Labour productivity ('000 RMB/worker) 劳动生产率（千元/人）	Debts/assets 资产负债率（%）	Total assets (Mil.RMB) 总资产（百万元）
Industry Overall 行业总体	61	7,394	1,342	72	4.86	14.98	62.24	67.56	1,482

	Number of firms 企业个数	Average number of employees 平均职工人数	Average revenue ('000 RMB) 平均销售收入（千元）	Average profit ('000 RMB) 平均利润（千元）	Return on assets 资产利润率（%）	Return on equity 权益利润率（%）	Labour productivity ('000 RMB/worker) 劳动生产率（千元/人）	Debts/assets 资产负债率（%）	Average total assets ('000 RMB) 平均总资产（千元）
By ownership 产业所有权									
State-owned 国有	11	173	24,374	170	0.48	1.76	32.69	72.57	35,316
Collective-owned 集体	16	106	9,546	1,103	7.11	17.38	39.02	59.10	15,521
Foreign & Overseas Chinese Funded 三资	6	89	31,574	2,789	8.76	30.17	81.60	70.97	31,835
By regional distribution 地区分布									
Central-North 华北	9	178	30,500	451	1.36	6.43	50.09	78.79	33,092
Beijing 北京	2	72	3,753	30	0.75	2.01	11.45	62.74	3,943
Tianjin 天津									
Hebei 河北	4	92	19,635	-43	-0.35		62.69	135.31	12,004
Shanxi 山西	2	532	90,391	969	0.85	3.01	49.49	71.60	113,405
Inner Mongolia 内蒙古	1	30	7,673	2,235	14.78	17.51	103.17	15.60	15,123
Northeast 东北	4	119	11,982	430	4.53	6.85	35.46	33.89	9,498
Liaoning 辽宁	2	99	9,951	153	2.11	7.78	48.28	72.88	7,227
Jilin 吉林									
Heilongjiang 黑龙江	2	140	14,014	708	6.02	6.68	26.44	9.94	11,769
Central-East 华东	26	71	15,180	455	2.29	8.35	56.45	72.58	19,864
Shanghai 上海	5	76	13,840	809	3.24	13.28	53.35	75.58	24,929
Jiangsu 江苏	7	64	18,076	101	0.46	3.85	63.72	88.08	22,059
Zhejiang 浙江	5	76	14,650	159	0.66	2.04	59.20	67.76	24,245
Anhui 安徽	1	109	30,107	1,962	6.69	14.76	76.94	54.67	29,313
Fujian 福建	1	10	5,340	-14	-0.22	-0.66	43.20	65.81	6,250
Jiangxi 江西	2	55	8,953	1,735	21.88	26.50	66.34	17.44	7,927
Shandong 山东	5	82	14,471	171	1.32	3.39	41.10	61.17	12,951
Central-South 中南	16	163	23,545	2,063	7.36	17.46	55.05	57.82	28,008
Henan 河南	5	99	26,427	2,236	7.24	23.88	64.05	69.68	30,880
Hubei 湖北	2	107	25,923	208	3.27	15.07	230.16	78.28	6,340
Hunan 湖南	1	93	5,923	76	0.83	2.61	117.14	68.20	9,151
Guangdong 广东	5	292	31,048	2,432	6.30	13.01	19.13	51.57	38,604
Guangxi 广西	2	140	14,552	4,450	11.66	20.97	83.25	44.41	38,165
Hainan 海南	1	65	2,469	273	10.75	41.68	5.63	74.20	2,539
Southwest 西南	4	168	29,512	1,525	5.29	18.30	77.05	71.11	28,839
Chongqing 重庆									
Sichuan 四川	2	293	57,195	3,110	9.54	52.70	81.61	81.89	32,584
Guizhou 贵州	2	43	1,830	-60	-0.24	-0.56	45.65	57.11	25,094
Yunnan 云南									
Tibet 西藏									
Northwest 西北	2	94	65,193	7,668	23.07	53.71	337.53	57.05	33,242
Shaanxi 陕西									
Gansu 甘肃									
Qinghai 青海									
Ningxia 宁夏									
Xinjiang 新疆	2	94	65,193	7,668	23.07	53.71	337.53	57.05	33,242

Year 年份	Number of firms 企业个数	Rate of change 变化率 (%)	Number of employees 职工人数 (人)	Rate of change 变化率 (%)	Total revenue (Mil. RMB) 总销售收入 (百万元)	Rate of change 变化率 (%)	Total profit (Mil RMB) 总利润 (百万元)	Rate of change 变化率 (%)
2000	41		5,466		942		93	
2001	53	29.27	5,675	3.82	1,021	8.39	41	-55.91
2002	61	15.09	7,394	30.29	1,342	31.44	72	75.61

Major Products 主要产品	Output 产量	Unit 单位
Metal Structure Products 金属结构制品	252	10,000 Tons 万吨

10 Main Firms with Maximal Revenue (year founded) 收入最大的十家主要企业（创办年份）	City 城市	Province 省	Telephone/fax 电话/传真	Number of employees 职工人数	Ownership 产业所有权	Revenue ('000 RMB) 销售收入(千元)	Profit('000 RMB) (rank) 利润(千元)(排名)	Total assets ('000 RMB) 总资产(千元)	Major products 主要产品
State-owned Shanxi Punching Factory	Yuncheng	Shanxi	(0359)6555037		State-owned				Pipe Parts Processing
国营山西冲压厂(1970)	运城市	山西省	(0359)6555038	951	国有企业	151,821	1,811(15)	182,350	管件加工
Xinjiang Traffic Development Co., Ltd.	Changji	Xinjiang	(0994)6869502		Limited-Liability				Guardrail
新疆交通发展有限公司(1997)	昌吉州	新疆		158	有限公司	121,500	11200(1)	52,260	护栏
Zhengzhou Tianshi Highway Engineering Technology Development	Zhengzhou	Henan	(0371)2586366		Foreign Funded				Road Materials
Co.,Ltd.郑州天时高速公路工程技术开发有限公司(2000)	郑州市	河南省	(0371)2586366	57	外商投资	76,033	8,194(4)	66,489	道路材料
Foshan Sanshui Jing'an Communication & Traffic Facilities	Foshan	Guangdong	(0757)7755116		Overseas Chinese-funded				Traffic Light
Co.,Ltd.佛山市三水京安通讯交通设施有限公司(1993)	佛山市	广东省	(0757)7727838	220	港澳台资	71,916	8,283(3)	60,125	交通灯
Jingjiang Xunda Traffic Facilities Engineering Co.,Ltd.	Taizhou	Jiangsu	(0523)4836148		Private Owned				Protect Fence
靖江市迅达交通设施工程有限公司(1998)	泰州市	江苏省	(0523)4859248	168	私营企业	69,087	1,912(13)	31,112	隔离栅
Sichuan Lanling (Group) Co.,Ltd.	Chengdu	Sichuan	(028)87510657		Limited-Liability				Traffic Facilities
四川蓝灵（集团）有限责任公司(1999)	成都市	四川省	(028)87510657	516	有限公司	54,279	3,308(8)	61,977	交通设施
Guangzhou Highway Industrial Development Co.,Ltd.	Guangzhou	Guangdong	(020)87705285		State-owned				Highway Traffic Sign公路
广州市公路实业发展公司(1979)	广州市	广东省	(020)87706149	242	国有企业	46,261	2,975(9)	45,001	交通标志
Zibo Zhoucun Huayang Traffic Equipment Co.,Ltd.	Zibo	Shandong	(0533)6811585		Private Owned				Glistening Sign
淄博市周村华洋交通器材有限公司(1984)	淄博市	山东省	(0533)6811503	180	私营企业	36,430	576(25)	10,454	反光标志
Henan Modern Traffic Engineering Co.Ltd.	Jiaozuo	Henan	(0391)6102792		Private Owned				Steel For Protection
河南现代交通工程有限公司(2000)	焦作市	河南省	(0391)6101735	120	私营企业	32,826	3,602(6)	49,192	护钢
Shanghai Traffic University Tianchang Traffic Equipment	Chuzhou	Anhui	(0550)7038619		Collective Owned				Traffic Safety Sign交通
Factory 上海交通大学天长交通器材厂(1988)	滁州市	安徽省	(0550)7024968	109	集体企业	30,107	1,962(12)	29,313	安全标志

Top 10 Cities by Revenue 销售收入排名前10位城市	Province 省	Market share 市场份额 (%)	Number of firms 企业个数
Yuncheng 运城市	Shanxi 山西省	11.31	1
Changji 昌吉州	Xinjiang 新疆	9.05	1
Chengdu 成都市	Sichuan 四川省	8.52	2
Zhengzhou 郑州市	Henan 河南省	6.17	2
Taizhou 泰州市	Jiangsu 江苏省	5.97	2
Guangzhou 广州市	Guangdong 广东省	5.63	3
Foshan 佛山市	Guangdong 广东省	5.36	1
Shanghai 上海市	Shanghai 上海市	5.16	5
Tangshan 唐山市	Hebei 河北省	4.44	1
Huangshi 黄石市	Hubei 湖北省	3.71	1

10 Major Wholesalers 十家主要批发商	City 城市	Province 省	Telephone/Fax 电话/传真
SU MEC	Nanjing	Jiangsu	(025)4511888
中设江苏机械设备进出口（集团）公司	南京市	江苏省	(025)4411772
China Poster Mobile Communications Equipment Co.,Ltd.	Beijing	Beijing	(010)66426993
中邮普泰移动通信设备股份有限公司	北京市	北京市	(010)66426837
Sino Kama Co., Ltd.	Shanghai	Shanghai	(021)62031188
中泰凯马股份有限公司	上海市	上海市	(021)62030851
China Huayuan Group Co.,Ltd.	Shanghai	Shanghai	(021)62031188
中国华源集团有限公司	上海市	上海市	(021)62032288
Zhejiang Crand Imp.& Exp.Co.,Ltd.	Ningbo	Zhejiang	(0574)87720170
浙江远大进出口有限公司	宁波市	浙江省	(0574)87723350
Shandong Machinery Import & Export Group Corporation	Qingdao	Shandong	(0532)2661628
山东省机械进出口集团公司	青岛市	山东省	(0532)2991655
Qingdao Haier International Trade Co.,Ltd.	Qingdao	Shandong	(0532)8938337
青岛海尔国际贸易有限公司	青岛市	山东省	(0532)8939494
Guangdong Machinery Import & Export Group Corporation	Guangzhou	Guangdong	(020)87782168
广东省机械进出口集团公司	广州市	广东省	(020)87771803
China National Machinery Equipment Import & Export Corporation	Beijing	Beijing	(010)63474506
中国机械设备进出口总公司	北京市	北京市	(010)63261865
Beijing Cellstar Co.,Ltd.	Beijing	Beijing	(010)64602050
北京蜂星事达电讯有限公司	北京市	北京市	(010)64672648

4011: Generators 发电机制造业

The industry accounts for 0.083% of the total revenue of China's industrial sector in 2002. The rate of return on assets is 0.44%. 77.56% of all firms in the industry made a profit while 22.44% had negative returns.The top province in terms of the industry's revenue is Sichuan, accounting for 14.52% of the total revenue.
2002年本行业收入占全行业的 0.083%，资产利润率为 0.44%。77.56%的企业赢利，22.44%的企业亏损。收入最高的省为四川省，占本行业的14.52%。

	Total number of firms 企业总数	Total number of employees 职工总数	Total revenue (Mil.RMB) 总销售收入（百万元）	Total profit (Mil.RMB) 总利润（百万元）	Return on assets 资产利润率（%）	Return on equity 权益利润率（%）	Labour productivity ('000 RMB/ worker) 劳动生产率（千元/人）	Debts/ assets 资产负债率（%）	Total assets (Mil.RMB) 总资产（百万元）
Industry Overall 行业总体	156	71,461	8,953	99	0.44	1.35	36.41	67.27	22,387

	Number of firms 企业个数	Average number of employees 平均职工人数	Average revenue ('000 RMB) 平均销售收入（千元）	Average profit ('000 RMB) 平均利润（千元）	Return on assets 资产利润率（%）	Return on equity 权益利润率（%）	Labour productivity ('000 RMB/ worker) 劳动生产率（千元/人）	Debts/ assets 资产负债率（%）	Average total assets ('000 RMB) 平均总资产（千元）
By ownership 产业所有权									
State-owned 国有	28	743	60,090	2,460	1.22	3.75	32.01	67.43	201,585
Collective-owned 集体	18	150	21,499	514	2.22	7.75	42.72	71.41	23,189
Foreign & Overseas Chinese Funded 三资	26	245	68,619	-1,663	-1.40	-3.62	70.12	61.37	118,943
By regional distribution 地区分布									
Central-North 华北	12	412	71,238	-4,065	-1.93	-5.61	43.77	65.68	211,156
Beijing 北京	5	478	133,882	1,623	0.54	1.11	105.64	51.74	302,277
Tianjin 天津	4	532	35,642	-14,303	-5.97	-48.74	-26.48	87.76	239,727
Hebei 河北	1	80	1,138	2	0.02	0.24	2.65	91.52	9,913
Shanxi 山西	1	183	38,346	278	0.69	1.58	101.50	56.09	40,134
Inner Mongolia 内蒙古	1	170	3,400	35	0.26	0.81	9.49	68.03	13,539
Northeast 东北	6	1,307	140,254	1,221	0.23	0.87	29.87	73.61	533,597
Liaoning 辽宁	3	217	12,628	47	0.10	0.13	31.85	22.79	47,441
Jilin 吉林	1	336	8,966	-2	-0.01	-0.02	3.60	38.22	21,051
Heilongjiang 黑龙江	2	3,429	397,338	3,595	0.24	1.00	30.97	76.23	1,519,104
Central-East 华东	85	263	47,562	1,090	1.27	3.26	46.90	61.11	85,917
Shanghai 上海	14	151	60,730	-1,358	-1.23	-2.63	85.98	53.09	110,208
Jiangsu 江苏	20	216	40,975	1,243	2.80	8.68	45.35	67.68	44,309
Zhejiang 浙江	12	324	42,502	1,190	1.33	2.95	42.65	54.81	89,351
Anhui 安徽	3	211	15,550	-214	-1.09	-4.49	20.10	75.65	19,593
Fujian 福建	18	190	30,734	693	0.75	1.97	43.84	61.90	92,054
Jiangxi 江西	4	602	117,392	8,264	4.33	8.28	35.88	47.65	190,737
Shandong 山东	14	398	56,687	1,977	2.09	9.21	45.93	77.30	94,496
Central-South 中南	39	327	36,837	882	1.12	5.52	47.90	79.67	78,556
Henan 河南	6	240	14,795	-301	-0.51	-3.38	19.39	84.92	59,074
Hubei 湖北	7	809	99,208	4,282	1.76	9.16	70.32	80.74	242,817
Hunan 湖南	5	347	17,015	71	0.18	1.58	17.71	88.82	40,231
Guangdong 广东	17	162	22,892	578	1.91	5.73	36.86	66.61	30,213
Guangxi 广西	4	289	44,789	-987	-1.34	-8.18	45.31	83.63	73,684
Hainan 海南									
Southwest 西南	10	1,859	144,889	752	0.14	0.38	21.60	61.64	519,602
Chongqing 重庆	1	1,999	35,953	-35,185	-10.57		-3.19	113.74	332,934
Sichuan 四川	6	2,481	216,624	6,584	0.86	2.00	24.95	56.74	762,842
Guizhou 贵州									
Yunnan 云南	3	569	37,731	1,066	1.12	5.43	21.43	79.43	95,345
Tibet 西藏									
Northwest 西北	4	1,245	82,156	1,393	0.51	3.55	18.20	85.58	272,151
Shaanxi 陕西	1	488		-804	-1.25	-1.56		20.01	64,392
Gansu 甘肃	2	2,205	132,722	90	0.02	0.26	17.35	92.41	455,756
Qinghai 青海									
Ningxia 宁夏									
Xinjiang 新疆	1	81	63,180	6,197	5.50	17.06	174.02	67.77	112,702

4011: Generators 发电机制造业

Year 年份	Number of firms 企业个数	Rate of change 变化率 (%)	Number of employees 职工人数 (人)	Rate of change 变化率 (%)	Total revenue (Mil. RMB) 总销售收入 (百万元)	Rate of change 变化率 (%)	Total profit (Mil RMB) 总利润 (百万元)	Rate of change 变化率 (%)
2000	144		90,428		7,891		34	
2001	145	0.69	74,848	-17.23	7,141	-9.50	-234	-
2002	156	7.59	71,461	-4.53	8,953	25.37	99	-

Major Products 主要产品	Output 产量	Unit 单位
Power Equipment 发电设备	2,121	10,000 KW 万千瓦
Steam Turbine Generator 汽轮发电机	1,766	10,000 KW 万千瓦

10 Main Firms with Maximal Revenue (year founded) 收入最大的十家主要企业（创办年份）	City 城市	Province 省	Telephone/fax 电话/传真	Number of employees 职工人数	Ownership 产业所有权	Revenue ('000 RMB) 销售收入 (千元)	Profit('000 RMB) (rank) 利润(千元) (排名)	Total assets ('000 RMB) 总资产 (千元)	Major products 主要产品
Dongfang Electromotor Co.,Ltd. 东方电机股份有限公司(1993)	Deyang 德阳市	Sichuan 四川省	(0838)2410228 (0838)2409408	6,428	Joint Stock 股份制	939,037	18,629(5)	2,860,708	Water Turbine Generator水轮发电机组
Harbin Electromotor Co.,Ltd. 哈尔滨电机厂有限责任公司(1951)	Harbin 哈尔滨市	Heilongjiang 黑龙江省	(0451)2102625 (0451)2102630	6,658	Limited-Liability 有限公司	794,155	7,207(10)	3,031,132	Electricity Generating Equipment 发电设备
Wuhan Steam Turbine Generator Factory 武汉汽轮发电机厂(1959)	Wuhan 武汉市	Hubei 湖北省	(027)87801035 (027)87801455	4,788	State-owned 国有企业	608,476	32,808(2)	1,585,738	Steam Turbine Generator汽轮发电机组
Beijing Steam Turbine Electromotor Co., Ltd. 北京汽轮电机有限责任公司(2000)	Beijing 北京市	Beijing 北京市	(010)68639675 (010)68639675	2,070	Limited-Liability 有限公司	523,431	1,058(40)	1,396,429	Generator 发电机
Shanghai Steam Turbine Generator Co., Ltd. 上海汽轮发电机有限公司(1995)	Shanghai 上海市	Shanghai 上海市	(021)64638221 (021)64620368	880	Foreign Funded 外商投资	501,919	-	1,065,792	Generator 发电机
Tsinghua Tellhow Sci-Tech Co., Ltd. 清华泰豪科技股份有限公司(1996)	Nanchang 南昌市	Jiangxi 江西省	(0791)8105588 (0791)8107788	1,008	Joint Stock 股份制	381,441	31,496(3)	635,668	Generator 发电机
Shandong Qilu Motor Manufacturing Co.,Ltd. 山东齐鲁电机制造有限公司(1959)	Jinan 济南市	Shandong 山东省	(0531)8582613 (0531)8582633	1,190	State-owned 国有企业	296,699	17,719(6)	634,134	Steam Turbine Generator汽轮发电机组
General Electric Asia Water & Electricity Equipment Co.,Ltd. 通用电器亚州水电设备有限公司(1996)	Hangzhou 杭州市	Zhejiang 浙江省	(0571)82621898 (0571)82655630	1,063	Foreign Funded 外商投资	199,658	2,489(22)	398,056	Generator 发电机
Guilin NEC Wireless Communication Co.,Ltd. 桂林NEC无线通信有限公司(1996)	Guilin 桂林市	Guangxi 广西	(0773)5825588 (0773)5825958	68	Foreign Funded 外商投资	128,552	8,586(8)	124,971	
Yangzhou Yingtai Electromotor Group Co.,Ltd. 扬州英泰电机集团有限公司(1995)	Yangzhou 扬州市	Jiangsu 江苏省	(0514)6591014 (0514)6591317	398	Overseas Chinese-funded 港澳台资	98,580	2,300(25)	45,662	Diesel Turbine Generator柴油发电机组

Top 10 Cities by Revenue 销售收入排名前10位城市	Province 省	Market share 市场份额 (%)	Number of firms 企业个数
Deyang 德阳市	Sichuan 四川省	11.84	2
Shanghai 上海市	Shanghai 上海市	9.50	14
Harbin 哈尔滨市	Heilongjiang 黑龙江省	8.87	1
Beijing 北京市	Beijing 北京市	7.48	5
Wuhan 武汉市	Hubei 湖北省	6.88	2
Nanchang 南昌市	Jiangxi 江西省	4.35	2
Hangzhou 杭州市	Zhejiang 浙江省	4.35	6
Fuzhou 福州市	Fujian 福建省	3.98	10
Jinan 济南市	Shandong 山东省	3.38	2
Yangzhou 扬州市	Jiangsu 江苏省	2.94	9

10 Major Wholesalers 十家主要批发商	City 城市	Province 省	Telephone/Fax 电话/传真
SU MEC 中设江苏机械设备进出口（集团）公司	Nanjing 南京市	Jiangsu 江苏省	(025)4511888 (025)4411772
China Poster Mobile Communications Equipment Co.,Ltd. 中邮普泰移动通信设备股份有限公司	Beijing 北京市	Beijing 北京市	(010)66426993 (010)66426837
Sino Kama Co., Ltd. 中泰凯马股份有限公司	Shanghai 上海市	Shanghai 上海市	(021)62031188 (021)62030851
China Huayuan Group Co.,Ltd. 中国华源集团有限公司	Shanghai 上海市	Shanghai 上海市	(021)62031188 (021)62032288
Zhejiang Crand Imp.& Exp.Co.,Ltd. 浙江远大进出口有限公司	Ningbo 宁波市	Zhejiang 浙江省	(0574)87720170 (0574)87723350
Shandong Machinery Import & Export Group Corporation 山东省机械进出口集团公司	Qingdao 青岛市	Shandong 山东省	(0532)2661628 (0532)2991655
Qingdao Haier International Trade Co.,Ltd. 青岛海尔国际贸易有限公司	Qingdao 青岛市	Shandong 山东省	(0532)8938337 (0532)8939494
Guangdong Machinery Import & Export Group Corporation 广东省机械进出口集团公司	Guangzhou 广州市	Guangdong 广东省	(020)87782168 (020)87771803
China National Machinery Equipment Import & Export Corporation 中国机械设备进出口总公司	Beijing 北京市	Beijing 北京市	(010)63474506 (010)63261865
Beijing Cellstar Co.,Ltd. 北京蜂星事达电讯有限公司	Beijing 北京市	Beijing 北京市	(010)64602050 (010)64672648

4012: Motors 电动机制造业

The industry accounts for 0.168% of the total revenue of China's industrial sector in 2002. The rate of return on assets is 2.05%. 78.49% of all firms in the industry made a profit while 21.51% had negative returns.The top province in terms of the industry's revenue is Jiangsu, accounting for 16.77% of the total revenue.
2002年本行业收入占全行业的 0.168%，资产利润率为 2.05%。78.49%的企业赢利，21.51%的企业亏损。收入最高的省为江苏省，占本行业的16.77%。

	Total number of firms 企业总数	Total number of employees 职工总数	Total revenue (Mil.RMB) 总销售收入（百万元）	Total profit (Mil.RMB) 总利润（百万元）	Return on assets 资产利润率 (%)	Return on equity 权益利润率 (%)	Labour productivity ('000 RMB/worker) 劳动生产率（千元/人）	Debts/assets 资产负债率 (%)	Total assets (Mil.RMB) 总资产（百万元）
Industry Overall 行业总体	451	156,419	18,029	573	2.05	5.96	34.59	65.53	27,913

	Number of firms 企业个数	Average number of employees 平均职工人数	Average revenue ('000 RMB) 平均销售收入（千元）	Average profit ('000 RMB) 平均利润（千元）	Return on assets 资产利润率 (%)	Return on equity 权益利润率 (%)	Labour productivity ('000 RMB/worker) 劳动生产率（千元/人）	Debts/assets 资产负债率 (%)	Average total assets ('000 RMB) 平均总资产（千元）
By ownership 产业所有权									
State-owned 国有	87	528	40,472	-1,476	-1.33	-5.12	20.91	74.10	111,335
Collective-owned 集体	36	163	17,548	698	3.09	8.55	33.48	63.84	22,574
Foreign & Overseas Chinese Funded 三资	54	307	63,543	4,884	7.59	14.26	67.13	46.76	64,327
By regional distribution 地区分布									
Central-North 华北	37	556	53,160	609	0.57	1.68	35.13	65.78	106,113
Beijing 北京	5	434	51,019	822	1.28	2.34	38.15	45.06	64,065
Tianjin 天津	13	265	33,657	-149	-0.20	-0.52	50.90	61.60	74,119
Hebei 河北	11	533	44,600	961	1.16	4.37	31.74	73.46	82,888
Shanxi 山西	7	1,225	108,852	1,356	0.57	1.83	31.92	68.73	237,345
Inner Mongolia 内蒙古	1	534	21,710	300	0.43	0.83	9.60	47.97	69,118
Northeast 东北	29	451	40,524	-1,418	-1.15	-3.72	27.84	68.99	122,874
Liaoning 辽宁	16	548	58,016	-2,018	-1.22	-3.57	32.49	65.74	165,018
Jilin 吉林	3	183	3,207	-22	-0.49	-0.71	2.65	30.73	4,410
Heilongjiang 黑龙江	10	376	23,731	-878	-0.96	-4.59	20.66	78.97	90,982
Central-East 华东	256	283	43,239	2,306	4.68	12.76	45.07	63.29	49,246
Shanghai 上海	39	368	62,851	1,506	1.56	4.61	43.46	66.25	96,802
Jiangsu 江苏	75	284	40,316	2,441	5.95	15.26	40.12	61.04	41,067
Zhejiang 浙江	73	155	35,639	3,350	9.63	18.39	61.22	47.62	34,780
Anhui 安徽	14	391	27,644	352	0.91	3.70	32.16	75.32	38,617
Fujian 福建	24	234	47,776	1,545	5.01	18.09	77.24	72.29	30,832
Jiangxi 江西	6	477	38,355	793	0.85	2.85	28.76	70.33	93,675
Shandong 山东	25	459	49,154	2,288	4.18	17.91	34.78	76.68	54,806
Central-South 中南	101	364	28,179	64	0.11	0.32	20.82	64.00	55,978
Henan 河南	21	332	21,538	911	1.94	9.33	19.79	79.19	46,877
Hubei 湖北	9	413	19,970	-301	-0.64	-2.84	15.24	77.29	46,657
Hunan 湖南	20	836	57,611	529	0.37	0.81	17.54	54.76	144,615
Guangdong 广东	41	166	19,393	-422	-1.74	-4.52	29.76	61.42	24,195
Guangxi 广西	10	249	26,677	-329	-0.90	-7.47	29.53	87.94	36,521
Hainan 海南									
Southwest 西南	15	343	27,246	428	1.03	8.27	25.18	87.49	41,399
Chongqing 重庆	8	339	32,043	1,953	4.79	15.47	31.45	69.01	40,743
Sichuan 四川	5	316	15,219	-1,791	-4.36		15.14	127.63	41,120
Guizhou 贵州									
Yunnan 云南	2	426	38,131	-123	-0.27	-0.73	23.84	62.54	44,719
Tibet 西藏									
Northwest 西北	13	652	43,303	-894	-0.75	-2.70	19.51	72.05	118,579
Shaanxi 陕西	8	622	52,189	-83	-0.07	-0.21	26.42	63.74	110,407
Gansu 甘肃	2	380	4,842	245	0.87		6.32	110.01	28,081
Qinghai 青海									
Ningxia 宁夏	2	914	50,578	-91	-0.06	-0.47	14.48	88.24	164,060
Xinjiang 新疆	1	910	34,592	-11,271	-4.11	-14.50	2.82	71.64	273,993

Year 年份	Number of firms 企业个数	Rate of change 变化率 (%)	Number of employees 职工人数 (人)	Rate of change 变化率 (%)	Total revenue (Mil. RMB) 总销售收入 (百万元)	Rate of change 变化率 (%)	Total profit (Mil RMB) 总利润 (百万元)	Rate of change 变化率 (%)
2000	413		183,348		13,460		117	
2001	432	4.60	167,747	-8.51	16,487	22.49	473	304.27
2002	451	4.40	156,419	-6.75	18,029	9.35	573	21.14

Major Products 主要产品	Output 产量	Unit 单位
AC Motor 交流电动机	7,005	10,000 KW 万千瓦

10 Main Firms with Maximal Revenue (year founded) 收入最大的十家主要企业（创办年份）	City 城市	Province 省	Telephone/fax 电话/传真	Number of employees 职工人数	Ownership 产业所有权	Revenue ('000 RMB) 销售收入 (千元)	Profit('000 RMB) (rank) 利润(千元) (排名)	Total assets ('000 RMB) 总资产 (千元)	Major products 主要产品
Zhejiang Wolong Group Co.,Ltd. 浙江卧龙控股集团有限公司(1984)	Shaoxing 绍兴市	Zhejiang 浙江省	(0575)2019460 (0575)2019783	1,600	Joint Stock 股份制	932,506	98,879(1)	1,012,000	AC Electromotor交流电动机
Yongji Electromotor Factory 永济电机厂(1969)	Yuncheng 运城市	Shanxi 山西省	(0359)8075182 (0359)8022090	5,667	State-owned 国有企业	624,121	6,758(28)	1,076,886	Electromotor 电机
Mabuchi Electromotor (Jiangsu) Co.,Ltd. 华渊电机(江苏)有限公司(1995)	Suzhou 苏州市	Jiangsu 江苏省	(0512)63451111 (0512)63450438	4,396	Overseas Chinese-funded 港澳台资	479,162	90,471(2)	556,570	Electromotor 电机
Shanghai United Electromotor (Group) Co.,Ltd. 上海联合电机（集团）有限公司(2000)	Shanghai 上海市	Shanghai 上海市	(021)62538434 (021)32181462	4,210	State Enterprises 国有独资	420,920	8,100(21)	787,500	Electromotor 电动机
Jiangsu Qingjiang Electromotor Co.,Ltd. 江苏清江电机股份有限公司(1958)	Huaian 淮安市	Jiangsu 江苏省	(0517)3933481 (0517)3942307	1,734	Joint Stock 股份制	339,227	6,780(27)	295,770	AC Electromotor交流电动机
Nanyang Explosion-proof Group Co.,Ltd. 南阳防爆集团有限公司(1971)	Nanyang 南阳市	Henan 河南省	(0377)3258320 (0377)3224273	2,269	State Enterprises 国有独资	324,910	21,015(7)	409,197	Explosion-proof Motor 防爆电机
Shanghai ABB Electromotor Co.,Ltd. 上海ABB电机有限公司(1996)	Shanghai 上海市	Shanghai 上海市	(021)57781362 (021)57781364	675	Foreign Funded 外商投资	255,485	57,195(3)	160,412	Electromotor 电动机
Shenyang Electromotor Co.,Ltd. 沈阳电机股份有限公司(1950)	Shenyang 沈阳市	Liaoning 辽宁省	(024)2552155 (024)25820928	2,200	Joint Stock 股份制	241,604	-	826,478	AC Electromotor交流电动机
Shanghai Anchuan Electromotor Co.,Ltd. 上海安川电动机有限公司(1995)	Shanghai 上海市	Shanghai 上海市	(021)59510067 (021)59510467	250	Foreign Funded 外商投资	240,451	21,163(6)	169,801	Electromotor 电动机
Beijing B.j. Electric Motor Co.,Ltd. 北京毕捷电机股份有限公司(2001)	Beijing 北京市	Beijing 北京市	(010)64382312 (010)64382311	1,615	Joint Stock 股份制	224,240	3,210(52)	243,446	Electromotor 电动机

Top 10 Cities by Revenue 销售收入排名前10位城市	Province 省	Market share 市场份额 (%)	Number of firms 企业个数
Shanghai 上海市	Shanghai 上海市	13.60	39
Shaoxing 绍兴市	Zhejiang 浙江省	6.57	10
Ningde 宁德市	Fujian 福建省	5.66	18
Xiangtan 湘潭市	Hunan 湖南省	4.07	2
Suzhou 苏州市	Jiangsu 江苏省	3.77	7
Yuncheng 运城市	Shanxi 山西省	3.46	1
Taizhou 台州市	Zhejiang 浙江省	3.42	29
Dalian 大连市	Liaoning 辽宁省	3.35	8
Weihai 威海市	Shandong 山东省	3.32	5
Wuxi 无锡市	Jiangsu 江苏省	3.04	21

10 Major Wholesalers 十家主要批发商	City 城市	Province 省	Telephone/Fax 电话/传真
SU MEC 中设江苏机械设备进出口（集团）公司	Nanjing 南京市	Jiangsu 江苏省	(025)4511888 (025)4411772
China Poster Mobile Communications Equipment Co.,Ltd. 中邮普泰移动通信设备股份有限公司	Beijing 北京市	Beijing 北京市	(010)66426993 (010)66426837
Sino Kama Co., Ltd. 中泰凯马股份有限公司	Shanghai 上海市	Shanghai 上海市	(021)62031188 (021)62030851
China Huayuan Group Co.,Ltd. 中国华源集团有限公司	Shanghai 上海市	Shanghai 上海市	(021)62031188 (021)62032288
Zhejiang Crand Imp.& Exp.Co.,Ltd. 浙江远大进出口有限公司	Ningbo 宁波市	Zhejiang 浙江省	(0574)87720170 (0574)87723350
Shandong Machinery Import & Export Group Corporation 山东省机械进出口集团公司	Qingdao 青岛市	Shandong 山东省	(0532)2661628 (0532)2991655
Qingdao Haier International Trade Co.,Ltd. 青岛海尔国际贸易有限公司	Qingdao 青岛市	Shandong 山东省	(0532)8938337 (0532)8939494
Guangdong Machinery Import & Export Group Corporation 广东省机械进出口集团公司	Guangzhou 广州市	Guangdong 广东省	(020)87782168 (020)87771803
China National Machinery Equipment Import & Export Corporation 中国机械设备进出口总公司	Beijing 北京市	Beijing 北京市	(010)63474506 (010)63261865
Beijing Cellstar Co.,Ltd. 北京蜂星事达电讯有限公司	Beijing 北京市	Beijing 北京市	(010)64602050 (010)64672648

4013: Min-motors 微电机制造业

The industry accounts for 0.156% of the total revenue of China's industrial sector in 2002. The rate of return on assets is 6.65%. 81.47% of all firms in the industry made a profit while 18.53% had negative returns.The top province in terms of the industry's revenue is Guangdong, accounting for 26.70% of the total revenue.
2002年本行业收入占全行业的 0.156%，资产利润率为 6.65%。81.47%的企业赢利，18.53%的企业亏损。收入最高的省为广东省，占本行业的26.70%。

	Total number of firms 企业总数	Total number of employees 职工总数	Total revenue (Mil.RMB) 总销售收入 (百万元)	Total profit (Mil.RMB) 总利润 (百万元)	Return on assets 资产利润率 (%)	Return on equity 权益利润率 (%)	Labour productivity ('000 RMB/ worker) 劳动生产率 (千元/人)	Debts/ assets 资产负债率 (%)	Total assets (Mil.RMB) 总资产 (百万元)
Industry Overall 行业总体	313	113,024	16,679	925	6.65	14.53	41.74	54.22	13,904

	Number of firms 企业个数	Average number of employees 平均职工人数	Average revenue ('000 RMB) 平均销售收入 (千元)	Average profit ('000 RMB) 平均利润 (千元)	Return on assets 资产利润率 (%)	Return on equity 权益利润率 (%)	Labour productivity ('000 RMB/ worker) 劳动生产率 (千元/人)	Debts/ assets 资产负债率 (%)	Average total assets ('000 RMB) 平均总资产 (千元)
By ownership 产业所有权									
State-owned 国有	19	326	15,761	-1,293	-2.65	-12.13	13.69	78.19	48,863
Collective-owned 集体	37	590	43,556	1,873	5.20	9.70	21.10	46.38	36,016
Foreign & Overseas Chinese Funded 三资	98	525	93,045	5,670	8.13	14.75	47.03	44.91	69,753
By regional distribution 地区分布									
Central-North 华北	23	165	18,073	1,124	3.66	11.73	20.93	68.84	30,749
Beijing 北京	4	147	15,806	3,512	12.42	24.48	25.86	49.28	28,280
Tianjin 天津	16	150	19,584	1,381	4.88	18.44	20.76	73.56	28,316
Hebei 河北	3	268	13,039	-3,430	-7.30	-23.82	17.86	69.37	47,020
Shanxi 山西									
Inner Mongolia 内蒙古									
Northeast 东北	13	1,182	247,971	32,871	17.39	26.13	54.02	33.45	189,054
Liaoning 辽宁	10	1,441	316,994	43,219	18.87	26.70	56.96	29.34	229,032
Jilin 吉林	1	108						109.68	64,333
Heilongjiang 黑龙江	2	423	26,841	-2,433	-4.72	-20.74	10.78	77.23	51,524
Central-East 华东	184	247	43,218	1,292	3.63	10.26	50.41	64.67	35,646
Shanghai 上海	18	331	45,333	1,788	3.96	6.44	41.43	38.51	45,149
Jiangsu 江苏	64	290	45,153	1,430	3.80	12.67	42.10	69.97	37,594
Zhejiang 浙江	75	182	32,534	163	0.53	1.50	54.26	64.71	30,898
Anhui 安徽	11	236	35,737	3,800	11.98	30.08	50.77	60.17	31,721
Fujian 福建	5	104	10,991	247	2.63	8.12	52.73	67.63	9,384
Jiangxi 江西	2	56	975	-20	-0.28	-3.15	28.59	91.20	7,207
Shandong 山东	9	449	150,702	6,535	9.60	48.27	88.85	80.11	68,055
Central-South 中南	85	553	58,325	2,720	5.92	11.27	31.61	47.45	45,918
Henan 河南	4	141	25,225	3,121	11.34	17.57	60.48	35.42	27,513
Hubei 湖北	3	181	113,115	27,367	21.54	44.44	302.52	51.54	127,083
Hunan 湖南	6	146	10,574	83	0.57	2.47	19.34	76.86	14,603
Guangdong 广东	72	626	61,861	1,890	4.09	7.67	28.23	46.60	46,168
Guangxi 广西									
Hainan 海南									
Southwest 西南	6	203	20,078	478	1.11	2.06	23.12	46.17	43,024
Chongqing 重庆	3	156	22,087	34	0.39	3.08	30.48	87.23	8,732
Sichuan 四川	1	87	5,010	66	0.67	0.81	13.63	17.88	9,878
Guizhou 贵州	2	331	24,598	1,350	1.22	2.12	19.14	42.58	111,035
Yunnan 云南									
Tibet 西藏									
Northwest 西北	2	97	4,576	-11	-0.12	-1.08	21.87	89.13	9,357
Shaanxi 陕西	2	97	4,576	-11	-0.12	-1.08	21.87	89.13	9,357
Gansu 甘肃									
Qinghai 青海									
Ningxia 宁夏									
Xinjiang 新疆									

Year 年份	Number of firms 企业个数	Rate of change 变化率 (%)	Number of employees 职工人数 (人)	Rate of change 变化率 (%)	Total revenue (Mil. RMB) 总销售收入 (百万元)	Rate of change 变化率 (%)	Total profit (Mil RMB) 总利润 (百万元)	Rate of change 变化率 (%)
2000	253		99,433		13,878		787	
2001	285	12.65	98,829	-0.61	14,370	3.55	928	17.92
2002	313	9.82	113,024	14.36	16,679	16.07	925	-0.32

Major Products 主要产品	Output 产量	Unit 单位

10 Main Firms with Maximal Revenue (year founded) 收入最大的十家主要企业（创办年份）	City 城市	Province 省	Telephone/fax 电话/传真	Number of employees 职工人数	Ownership 产业所有权	Revenue ('000 RMB) 销售收入 (千元)	Profit('000 RMB) (rank) 利润(千元) (排名)	Total assets ('000 RMB) 总资产 (千元)	Major products 主要产品
NIDEC (Dalian) Co.,Ltd.	Dalian	Liaoning	(0411)7310202		Foreign Funded				Mini-motor
日本电产（大连）有限公司(1992)	大连市	辽宁省	(0411)7314979	4,119	外商投资	1,918,653	188,646(2)	827,957	微电机
Zhuhai Panasonic Motor Co.,Ltd.	Zhuhai	Guangdong	(0756)2263111		Foreign Funded				Miniature Motor
珠海松下马达有限公司(1993)	珠海市	广东省	(0756)2263116	3,621	外商投资	1,041,062	8,964(23)	463,074	微型马达
Weihai Hengda Electromotor Group Co., Ltd.	Weihai	Shandong	(0631)8731029		Collective-owned				Electromotor
威海恒大电机集团公司(1997)	威海市	山东省	(0631)8732288	839	集体企业	640,510	40,670(6)	147,250	电动机
Japan NIDEC Shibaura(Zhejiang) Co., Ltd.	Jiaxing	Zhejiang	(0573)5092551		Foreign Funded				Plastic Packing Non-brush Electric Motor塑封直
日本电产芝浦(浙江)有限公司(1996)	嘉兴市	浙江省	(0573)5092512	1,977	外商投资	636,460	-	649,633	流无刷电机
Jiangsu Jinfeida Power Tools Co.,Ltd.	Yangzhou	Jiangsu	(0514)4732424		Limited-Liability				Electric Motor
江苏金飞达电动工具有限公司(1958)	扬州市	江苏省	(0514)4732069	1,697	有限公司	404,959	5,993(31)	180,541	电机
Zhangqiu Haier Electrc Motor Co., Ltd.	Jinan	Shandong	(0531)3250848		Limited-Liability				Washing Machine Electromotor洗
章丘海尔电机有限公司(1958)	济南市	山东省	(0531)3232775	1,209	有限公司	310,759	3,590(46)	200,206	衣机电机
Wuhan Jinglun Electronic Co.,Ltd.	Wuhan	Hubei	(027)87921111		Private Owned				Public-phone Fee-Counter公用电
武汉精伦电子股份有限公司(1994)	武汉市	湖北省	(027)87921316	362	私营企业	306,761	81,302(3)	343,178	话计费器
Taishan Xiangda Electrical Co., Ltd.	Jiangmen	Guangdong	(0750)5619388		Overseas Chinese-funded				Synchronization Electromotor
台山市祥达电器厂有限公司(1995)	江门市	广东省	(0750)5617688	480	港澳台资	249,687	349(148)	193,797	同步电机
Weiling (Wuhu)Electric Motor Manufacturing Co., Ltd.	Wuhu	Anhui	(0553)5847808		Overseas Chinese-funded				Electromotor
威灵(芜湖)电机制造有限公司(1999)	芜湖市	安徽省	(0553)5846876	621	港澳台资	239,329	49,663(5)	130,357	电机
Zhejiang Jeano Motor Co., Ltd.	Jiaxing	Zhejiang	(0573)8573988		Private Owned				Electromotor
浙江京马电机有限公司(1979)	嘉兴市	浙江省	(0573)8571799	598	私营企业	226,562	22,537(11)	146,421	电机

Top 10 Cities by Revenue 销售收入排名前10位城市	Province 省	Market share 市场份额 (%)	Number of firms 企业个数
Dalian 大连市	Liaoning 辽宁省	18.91	5
Zhuhai 珠海市	Guangdong 广东省	6.73	6
Weihai 威海市	Shandong 山东省	5.95	6
Jiaxing 嘉兴市	Zhejiang 浙江省	5.17	2
Shanghai 上海市	Shanghai 上海市	4.89	18
Taizhou 泰州市	Jiangsu 江苏省	4.82	7
Changzhou 常州市	Jiangsu 江苏省	4.76	21
Shenzhen 深圳市	Guangdong 广东省	4.03	9
Jiangmen 江门市	Guangdong 广东省	3.66	7
Zhongshan 中山市	Guangdong 广东省	3.47	13

10 Major Wholesalers 十家主要批发商	City 城市	Province 省	Telephone/Fax 电话/传真
SU MEC	Nanjing	Jiangsu	(025)4511888
中设江苏机械设备进出口（集团）公司	南京市	江苏省	(025)4411772
China Poster Mobile Communications Equipment Co.,Ltd.	Beijing	Beijing	(010)66426993
中邮普泰移动通信设备股份有限公司	北京市	北京市	(010)66426837
Sino Kama Co., Ltd.	Shanghai	Shanghai	(021)62031188
中泰凯马股份有限公司	上海市	上海市	(021)62030851
China Huayuan Group Co.,Ltd.	Shanghai	Shanghai	(021)62031188
中国华源集团有限公司	上海市	上海市	(021)62032288
Zhejiang Crand Imp.& Exp.Co.,Ltd.	Ningbo	Zhejiang	(0574)87720170
浙江远大进出口有限公司	宁波市	浙江省	(0574)87723350
Shandong Machinery Import & Export Group Corporation	Qingdao	Shandong	(0532)2661628
山东省机械进出口集团公司	青岛市	山东省	(0532)2991655
Qingdao Haier International Trade Co.,Ltd.	Qingdao	Shandong	(0532)8938337
青岛海尔国际贸易有限公司	青岛市	山东省	(0532)8939494
Guangdong Machinery Import & Export Group Corporation	Guangzhou	Guangdong	(020)87782168
广东省机械进出口集团公司	广州市	广东省	(020)87771803
China National Machinery Equipment Import & Export Corporation	Beijing	Beijing	(010)63474506
中国机械设备进出口总公司	北京市	北京市	(010)63261865
Beijing Cellstar Co.,Ltd.	Beijing	Beijing	(010)64602050
北京蜂星事达电讯有限公司	北京市	北京市	(010)64672648

4021: Transformers 变压器制造业

The industry accounts for 0.285% of the total revenue of China's industrial sector in 2002. The rate of return on assets is 3.33%. 79.51% of all firms in the industry made a profit while 20.49% had negative returns.The top province in terms of the industry's revenue is Guangdong, accounting for 26.65% of the total revenue.
2002年本行业收入占全行业的 0.285%，资产利润率为 3.33%。79.51%的企业赢利，20.49%的企业亏损。收入最高的省为广东省，占本行业的26.65%。

	Total number of firms 企业总数	Total number of employees 职工总数	Total revenue (Mil.RMB) 总销售收入 (百万元)	Total profit (Mil.RMB) 总利润 (百万元)	Return on assets 资产利润率 (%)	Return on equity 权益利润率 (%)	Labour productivity ('000 RMB/ worker) 劳动生产率 (千元/人)	Debts/ assets 资产负债率 (%)	Total assets (Mil.RMB) 总资产 (百万元)
Industry Overall 行业总体	571	144,714	30,530	1,294	3.33	9.03	57.95	63.16	38,897

	Number of firms 企业个数	Average number of employees 平均职工人数	Average revenue ('000 RMB) 平均销售收入 (千元)	Average profit ('000 RMB) 平均利润 (千元)	Return on assets 资产利润率 (%)	Return on equity 权益利润率 (%)	Labour productivity ('000 RMB/ worker) 劳动生产率 (千元/人)	Debts/ assets 资产负债率 (%)	Average total assets ('000 RMB) 平均总资产 (千元)
By ownership 产业所有权									
State-owned 国有	84	253	27,048	-1,356	-1.80	-6.86	26.03	73.75	75,271
Collective-owned 集体	81	141	19,770	1,177	5.33	17.11	47.38	68.84	22,088
Foreign & Overseas Chinese Funded 三资	124	369	84,017	3,363	4.28	10.24	56.86	58.16	78,509
By regional distribution 地区分布									
Central-North 华北	64	246	38,992	1,642	2.08	5.14	33.99	59.42	78,765
Beijing 北京	19	117	17,357	463	1.36	2.91	49.19	53.33	34,095
Tianjin 天津	17	139	28,172	1,864	4.29	10.39	41.08	58.76	43,497
Hebei 河北	15	516	98,579	4,548	2.19	5.29	36.32	58.66	208,095
Shanxi 山西	8	292	17,547	38	0.08	0.33	13.70	77.25	50,218
Inner Mongolia 内蒙古	5	213	13,541	-787	-3.01	-6.97	14.05	56.78	26,113
Northeast 东北	56	248	33,442	-1,015	-1.32	-4.25	28.02	68.94	76,813
Liaoning 辽宁	36	283	41,479	-1,341	-1.33	-4.31	27.35	69.20	100,990
Jilin 吉林	9	144	12,328	-739	-2.90	-10.97	41.01	73.56	25,497
Heilongjiang 黑龙江	11	216	24,418	-173	-0.44	-1.22	23.77	64.28	39,676
Central-East 华东	215	228	60,087	3,111	4.76	12.92	76.59	63.15	65,361
Shanghai 上海	24	250	69,305	3,154	3.70	8.79	68.83	57.88	85,171
Jiangsu 江苏	75	221	59,699	2,711	4.87	14.30	75.64	65.97	55,683
Zhejiang 浙江	40	212	60,443	4,395	8.18	17.68	70.52	53.70	53,699
Anhui 安徽	16	174	45,031	568	1.11	3.07	86.49	63.99	51,273
Fujian 福建	7	140	22,560	830	3.10	6.99	60.61	55.61	26,772
Jiangxi 江西	9	205	35,567	773	1.53	10.90	49.20	85.92	50,369
Shandong 山东	44	283	71,856	4,370	4.55	13.18	88.87	65.45	95,985
Central-South 中南	167	303	59,839	2,760	4.56	12.14	55.39	62.41	60,498
Henan 河南	21	184	19,907	1,055	4.21	16.72	34.30	74.83	25,063
Hubei 湖北	17	144	15,679	124	0.52	2.63	43.24	80.37	24,044
Hunan 湖南	19	187	33,731	2,318	4.65	12.14	69.72	61.70	49,860
Guangdong 广东	104	377	78,247	3,089	4.22	10.97	54.91	61.49	73,142
Guangxi 广西	4	265	53,735	5,398	7.68	30.04	82.81	74.43	70,267
Hainan 海南	2	249	157,501	24,858	14.94	22.55	156.13	33.75	166,411
Southwest 西南	47	202	33,901	245	0.43	1.53	44.39	72.04	57,281
Chongqing 重庆	11	196	47,378	-1,110	-1.18	-5.23	43.41	77.54	94,433
Sichuan 四川	20	176	22,440	-281	-0.76	-2.36	39.09	67.69	36,847
Guizhou 贵州	6	250	30,678	1,946	5.04	18.05	46.20	72.05	38,580
Yunnan 云南	10	234	43,930	1,766	2.58	8.14	52.08	68.35	68,501
Tibet 西藏									
Northwest 西北	22	264	75,318	4,764	3.87	8.60	81.10	54.95	123,030
Shaanxi 陕西	9	214	15,092	-257	-0.59	-1.76	25.43	66.22	43,221
Gansu 甘肃	5	187	25,241	-213	-0.56	-2.14	40.84	74.03	38,346
Qinghai 青海	1	54	3,316	210	1.31	3.49	57.22	62.34	15,976
Ningxia 宁夏	2	328	36,585	2,104	3.36	13.89	-28.79	75.80	62,591
Xinjiang 新疆	5	448	263,696	20,753	5.23	10.36	178.43	49.53	396,954

4021: Transformers 变压器制造业

Year 年份	Number of firms 企业个数	Rate of change 变化率 (%)	Number of employees 职工人数 (人)	Rate of change 变化率 (%)	Total revenue (Mil. RMB) 总销售收入 (百万元)	Rate of change 变化率 (%)	Total profit (Mil RMB) 总利润 (百万元)	Rate of change 变化率 (%)
2000	487		148,106		21,734		784	
2001	528	8.42	143,424	-3.16	25,361	16.69	774	-1.28
2002	571	8.14	144,714	0.90	30,530	20.38	1,294	67.18

Major Products 主要产品	Output 产量	Unit 单位
Transformer 变压器	29,606	10,000 Kilovolt-ampere 万千伏安

10 Main Firms with Maximal Revenue (year founded) 收入最大的十家主要企业（创办年份）	City 城市	Province 省	Telephone/fax 电话/传真	Number of employees 职工人数	Ownership 产业所有权	Revenue ('000 RMB) 销售收入(千元)	Profit('000 RMB) (rank) 利润(千元)(排名)	Total assets ('000 RMB) 总资产(千元)	Major products 主要产品
Xinjiang Tbea Electric Apparatus Stock Co.,Ltd.	Changji	Xinjiang	(0994)2726688		Joint Stock				Electric Power Transformer
新疆特变电工股份有限公司(1993)	昌吉州	新疆	(0994)2723615	1,682	股份制	1,218,850	95,500(1)	1,833,484	电力变压器
Qingdao Transformer Group Co.,Ltd.	Qingdao	Shandong	(0532)7716888		Limited-Liability				Transformer
青岛变压器集团有限公司(1995)	青岛市	山东省	(0532)7711588	1,951	有限公司	1,026,362	78,000(2)	1,244,397	变压器
Shunde Special Transformer Works	Foshan	Guangdong	(0765)2627411		Joint Stock				Dry-type Transformer
顺德市特种变压器厂(1990)	佛山市	广东省	(0765)2629923	1,125	股份制	762,943	20,069(18)	1,087,299	干式变压器
Jiangsu Huapeng Group Co.,Ltd.	Changzhou	Jiangsu	(0519)7302414		Joint Stock				Electromotor
江苏华朋集团有限公司(1967)	常州市	江苏省	(0519)7300072	1,432	股份制	585,490	39,550(7)	461,770	电动机
Hongzhou Qianjiang Electric Group Stock Co.,Ltd.	Hangzhou	Zhejiang	(0571)82583178		Joint Stock				Electric Power Transformer
杭州钱江电气集团股份有限公司(1976)	杭州市	浙江省	(0571)82582108	675	股份制	435,652	30,602(10)	368,705	电力变压器
Changzhou Toshiba Transformer Co.,Ltd.	Changzhou	Jiangsu	(0519)3256041		Foreign Funded				Electric Power Transformer
常州东芝变压器有限公司(1997)	常州市	江苏省	(0519)3256008	303	外商投资	422,260	14,060(27)	527,480	电力变压器
Hefei ABB Transformer Co., Ltd.	Hefei	Anhui	(0551)5135313		Foreign Funded				Electric Power Transformer
合肥ABB变压器有限公司(1992)	合肥市	安徽省	(0551)5130360	511	外商投资	381,336	557(227)	388,989	电力变压器
Chint Group Complete Equipment Manufacturing Co.,Ltd.	Wenzhou	Zhejiang	(0577)86555555		Limited-Liability				High&Low Voltage Power Cabinet
正泰集团成套设备制造有限公司(1998)	温州市	浙江省	(0577)86528136	1,283	有限公司	369,516	17,713(21)	252,062	高低压开关柜
Tbea Hengyang Transformer CO.,Ltd.	Hengyang	Hunan	(0734)8498414		Joint Stock				Transformer
特变电工衡阳变压器有限公司(1958)	衡阳市	湖南省	(0734)8400443	985	股份制	360,066	37,239(8)	542,913	变压器
Shandong Modern Dachi Electric Co.,Ltd.	Heze	Shandong	(0530)8651616		Joint Stock				Transformer
山东现代达驰电工电气股份有限公司(1999)	荷泽市	山东省	(0530)8651679	636	股份制	352,329	35,636(9)	293,004	变压器

Top 10 Cities by Revenue 销售收入排名前10位城市	Province 省	Market share 市场份额 (%)	Number of firms 企业个数
Shenzhen 深圳市	Guangdong 广东省	10.35	28
Changzhou 常州市	Jiangsu 江苏省	5.68	17
Shanghai 上海市	Shanghai 上海市	5.45	24
Qingdao 青岛市	Shandong 山东省	4.32	10
Baoding 保定市	Hebei 河北省	4.32	3
Foshan 佛山市	Guangdong 广东省	4.25	10
Changji 昌吉州	Xinjiang 新疆	3.99	1
Guangzhou 广州市	Guangdong 广东省	3.58	15
Wenzhou 温州市	Zhejiang 浙江省	3.01	13
Dongguan 东莞市	Guangdong 广东省	2.46	16

10 Major Wholesalers 十家主要批发商	City 城市	Province 省	Telephone/Fax 电话/传真
SU MEC	Nanjing	Jiangsu	(025)4511888
中设江苏机械设备进出口（集团）公司	南京市	江苏省	(025)4411772
China Poster Mobile Communications Equipment Co.,Ltd.	Beijing	Beijing	(010)66426993
中邮普泰移动通信设备股份有限公司	北京市	北京市	(010)66426837
Sino Kama Co., Ltd.	Shanghai	Shanghai	(021)62031188
中泰凯马股份有限公司	上海市	上海市	(021)62030851
China Huayuan Group Co.,Ltd.	Shanghai	Shanghai	(021)62031188
中国华源集团有限公司	上海市	上海市	(021)62032288
Zhejiang Crand Imp.& Exp.Co.,Ltd.	Ningbo	Zhejiang	(0574)87720170
浙江远大进出口有限公司	宁波市	浙江省	(0574)87723350
Shandong Machinery Import & Export Group Corporation	Qingdao	Shandong	(0532)2661628
山东省机械进出口集团公司	青岛市	山东省	(0532)2991655
Qingdao Haier International Trade Co.,Ltd.	Qingdao	Shandong	(0532)8938337
青岛海尔国际贸易有限公司	青岛市	山东省	(0532)8939494
Guangdong Machinery Import & Export Group Corporation	Guangzhou	Guangdong	(020)87782168
广东省机械进出口集团公司	广州市	广东省	(020)87771803
China National Machinery Equipment Import & Export Corporation	Beijing	Beijing	(010)63474506
中国机械设备进出口总公司	北京市	北京市	(010)63261865
Beijing Cellstar Co.,Ltd.	Beijing	Beijing	(010)64602050
北京蜂星事达电讯有限公司	北京市	北京市	(010)64672648

4022: Rectifiers 整流器制造业

The industry accounts for 0.020% of the total revenue of China's industrial sector in 2002. The rate of return on assets is 3.86%. 71.93% of all firms in the industry made a profit while 28.07% had negative returns.The top province in terms of the industry's revenue is Jiangsu, accounting for 64.08% of the total revenue.
2002年本行业收入占全行业的 0.020%，资产利润率为 3.86%。71.93%的企业赢利，28.07%的企业亏损。收入最高的省为江苏省，占本行业的64.08%。

	Total number of firms 企业总数	Total number of employees 职工总数	Total revenue (Mil.RMB) 总销售收入（百万元）	Total profit (Mil.RMB) 总利润（百万元）	Return on assets 资产利润率（%）	Return on equity 权益利润率（%）	Labour productivity ('000 RMB/ worker) 劳动生产率（千元/人）	Debts/ assets 资产负债率（%）	Total assets (Mil.RMB) 总资产（百万元）
Industry Overall 行业总体	57	10,013	2,145	102	3.86	14.45	59.96	73.30	2,639

	Number of firms 企业个数	Average number of employees 平均职工人数	Average revenue ('000 RMB) 平均销售收入（千元）	Average profit ('000 RMB) 平均利润（千元）	Return on assets 资产利润率（%）	Return on equity 权益利润率（%）	Labour productivity ('000 RMB/ worker) 劳动生产率（千元/人）	Debts/ assets 资产负债率（%）	Average total assets ('000 RMB) 平均总资产（千元）
By ownership 产业所有权									
State-owned 国有	11	162	10,493	633	1.42	13.31	27.33	89.33	44,577
Collective-owned 集体	10	136	13,398	-485	-1.98	-6.23	28.19	68.12	24,424
Foreign & Overseas Chinese Funded 三资	14	251	109,723	6,466	6.96	23.95	110.94	70.95	92,915
By regional distribution 地区分布									
Central-North 华北	10	168	17,498	1,914	3.94	10.95	77.67	64.03	48,557
Beijing 北京	5	117	9,151	-1,488	-6.13	-13.17	25.74	53.41	24,263
Tianjin 天津	2	195	13,673	-74	-0.13	-1.31	31.22	90.12	56,751
Hebei 河北	3	237	33,961	8,908	10.66	24.99	145.82	57.35	83,585
Shanxi 山西									
Inner Mongolia 内蒙古									
Northeast 东北	7	153	17,037	-147	-0.57	-1.72	22.89	66.73	25,592
Liaoning 辽宁	3	116	13,866	52	0.29	0.85	28.44	66.12	17,950
Jilin 吉林									
Heilongjiang 黑龙江	4	182	19,415	-295	-0.94	-2.85	20.23	66.98	31,324
Central-East 华东	26	205	65,960	3,499	5.83	22.19	75.66	73.71	59,961
Shanghai 上海	5	201	30,366	2,048	3.40	28.22	28.77	87.97	60,323
Jiangsu 江苏	8	349	171,815	8,367	6.39	23.52	109.78	72.81	130,868
Zhejiang 浙江	4	68	9,751	1,994	18.27	28.49	54.85	35.87	10,910
Anhui 安徽	1	36	779	-1,272	-6.86	-7.11	5.22	3.60	18,554
Fujian 福建	2	73	8,789	349	8.15	20.61	45.56	60.46	4,283
Jiangxi 江西	1	312	34,047	82	0.10	0.96	57.14	89.72	83,402
Shandong 山东	5	154	19,439	1,260	11.20	20.24	37.24	44.65	11,253
Central-South 中南	12	150	10,712	-596	-1.80	-12.81	22.16	85.99	33,189
Henan 河南	1								
Hubei 湖北									
Hunan 湖南	4	67	3,682	83	0.53	4.16	23.30	87.27	15,681
Guangdong 广东	5	151	13,211	1,627	13.12	33.35	15.63	60.65	12,401
Guangxi 广西	2	391	23,881	-7,811	-5.71	-66.69	28.08	91.44	136,769
Hainan 海南									
Southwest 西南									
Chongqing 重庆									
Sichuan 四川									
Guizhou 贵州									
Yunnan 云南									
Tibet 西藏									
Northwest 西北	2	63	3,599	-70	-0.83	-3.07	15.53	73.06	8,411
Shaanxi 陕西	2	63	3,599	-70	-0.83	-3.07	15.53	73.06	8,411
Gansu 甘肃									
Qinghai 青海									
Ningxia 宁夏									
Xinjiang 新疆									

4022: Rectifiers 整流器制造业

Year 年份	Number of firms 企业个数	Rate of change 变化率 (%)	Number of employees 职工人数 (人)	Rate of change 变化率 (%)	Total revenue (Mil. RMB) 总销售收入 (百万元)	Rate of change 变化率 (%)	Total profit (Mil RMB) 总利润 (百万元)	Rate of change 变化率 (%)
2000	53		12,804		1,966		92	
2001	42	-20.75	7,705	-39.82	838	-57.38	34	-63.04
2002	57	35.71	10,013	29.95	2,145	155.97	102	200.00

Major Products 主要产品	Output 产量	Unit 单位

10 Main Firms with Maximal Revenue (year founded) 收入最大的十家主要企业（创办年份）	City 城市	Province 省	Telephone/fax 电话/传真	Number of employees 职工人数	Ownership 产业所有权	Revenue ('000 RMB) 销售收入 (千元)	Profit('000 RMB) (rank) 利润(千元) (排名)	Total assets ('000 RMB) 总资产 (千元)	Major products 主要产品
Cutler-Hammer(Suzhou) Electric Motor Co.,Ltd. 卡特拉-汉莫(苏州)电器有限公司(1996)	Suzhou 苏州市	Jiangsu 江苏省	(0512)67163728 (0512)67169535	72	Foreign Funded 外商投资	73,969	20,978(3)	130,960	Breaker 断路器
Smartem Electric Technologies (China) Co.,Ltd. 迈特电子(中国)有限公司(1996)	Shanghai 上海市	Shanghai 上海市	(021)64808118 (021)64809898	132	Foreign Funded 外商投资	67,869	-	35,112	Electronic Ballast电子镇流器
Yangzhou Hongyang Electronics Co.,Ltd. 扬州虹扬电子有限公司(1992)	Yangzhou 扬州市	Jiangsu 江苏省	(0514)7651952 (0514)7651951	650	Overseas Chinese-funded 港澳台资	59,992	1,250(16)	45,090	Bridge Rectifier桥式整流器
Mudanjiang No.1 Transformer Factory 牡丹江第一互感器厂(1984)	Mudanjiang 牡丹江市	Heilongjiang 黑龙江省	(0453)6483069 (0453)6481843	274	Collective-owned 集体企业	47,843	200(25)	62,627	Transformer 互感器
Jiangsu Dazhong Electric Appliance Co.,Ltd. 江苏大众电器有限公司(1994)	Taizhou 泰州市	Jiangsu 江苏省	(0523)6242047 (0523)6226348	150	Private Owned 私营企业	36,838	969(18)	32,796	Silicon Rectifier 硅整流器
Shanghai Electric (Group) Shanghai Transformer Factory 上海电气（集团）上海互感器厂(2000)	Shanghai 上海市	Shanghai 上海市	(021)64307400 (021)64307400	116	State-owned 国有企业	35,879	8,277(4)	40,964	Transformer 互感器
Jiujiang Rectifier Factory 九江整流器厂(1968)	Jiujiang 九江市	Jiangxi 江西省	(0792)8113060 (0792)8221773	312	State-owned 国有企业	34,047	82(31)	83,402	Silicon Rectifier Equipment硅整流设备
Ningjin Wanliang High Efficiency Energy-saving Heat-exchanger Co.,Ltd. Co.,Ltd.宁津县万良高效节能换热器有限公司(1979)	Dezhou 德州市	Shandong 山东省	(0534)5551028 (0534)5551789	240	Private Owned 私营企业	31,300	2,300(9)	9,800	Heat Exchanger 换热器
Shijiazhuang Guoyao Electronic Science & Technology Development Co.,Ltd.石家庄国耀电子科技发展有限公司(1998)	Shijiazhuang 石家庄市	Hebei 河北省	(0311)5086524 (0311)5070345	210	Private Owned 私营企业	25,466	5,970(5)	41,324	Stabilized Voltage Supply 稳压电源
Shenzhen Frecom Electronics Co.,Ltd. 深圳市福瑞康电子有限公司(1999)	Shenzhen 深圳市	Guangdong 广东省	(0755)26984326 (0755)26983344	345	Private Owned 私营企业	21,147	5,263(6)	22,152	Transformer 变压器

Top 10 Cities by Revenue 销售收入排名前10位城市	Province 省	Market share 市场份额 (%)	Number of firms 企业个数
Suzhou 苏州市	Jiangsu 江苏省	58.87	4
Shanghai 上海市	Shanghai 上海市	7.08	5
Shijiazhuang 石家庄市	Hebei 河北省	4.71	2
Mudanjiang 牡丹江市	Heilongjiang 黑龙江省	3.62	4
Yangzhou 扬州市	Jiangsu 江苏省	2.80	1
Dezhou 德州市	Shandong 山东省	2.55	2
Beijing 北京市	Beijing 北京市	2.13	5
Liuzhou 柳州市	Guangxi 广西	1.84	1
Shenzhen 深圳市	Guangdong 广东省	1.80	2
Taizhou 泰州市	Jiangsu 江苏省	1.72	1

10 Major Wholesalers 十家主要批发商	City 城市	Province 省	Telephone/Fax 电话/传真
SU MEC 中设江苏机械设备进出口（集团）公司	Nanjing 南京市	Jiangsu 江苏省	(025)4511888 (025)4411772
China Poster Mobile Communications Equipment Co.,Ltd. 中邮普泰移动通信设备股份有限公司	Beijing 北京市	Beijing 北京市	(010)66426993 (010)66426837
Sino Kama Co., Ltd. 中泰凯马股份有限公司	Shanghai 上海市	Shanghai 上海市	(021)62031188 (021)62030851
China Huayuan Group Co.,Ltd. 中国华源集团有限公司	Shanghai 上海市	Shanghai 上海市	(021)62031188 (021)62032288
Zhejiang Crand Imp.& Exp.Co.,Ltd. 浙江远大进出口有限公司	Ningbo 宁波市	Zhejiang 浙江省	(0574)87720170 (0574)87723350
Shandong Machinery Import & Export Group Corporation 山东省机械进出口集团公司	Qingdao 青岛市	Shandong 山东省	(0532)2661628 (0532)2991655
Qingdao Haier International Trade Co.,Ltd. 青岛海尔国际贸易有限公司	Qingdao 青岛市	Shandong 山东省	(0532)8938337 (0532)8939494
Guangdong Machinery Import & Export Group Corporation 广东省机械进出口集团公司	Guangzhou 广州市	Guangdong 广东省	(020)87782168 (020)87771803
China National Machinery Equipment Import & Export Corporation 中国机械设备进出口总公司	Beijing 北京市	Beijing 北京市	(010)63474506 (010)63261865
Beijing Cellstar Co.,Ltd. 北京蜂星事达电讯有限公司	Beijing 北京市	Beijing 北京市	(010)64602050 (010)64672648

4023: Capacitors 电容器制造业

The industry accounts for 0.049% of the total revenue of China's industrial sector in 2002. The rate of return on assets is 3.09%. 75.76% of all firms in the industry made a profit while 24.24% had negative returns.The top province in terms of the industry's revenue is Jiangsu, accounting for 37.57% of the total revenue.
2002年本行业收入占全行业的 0.049%，资产利润率为 3.09%。75.76%的企业赢利，24.24%的企业亏损。收入最高的省为江苏省，占本行业的37.57%。

	Total number of firms 企业总数	Total number of employees 职工总数	Total revenue (Mil.RMB) 总销售收入（百万元）	Total profit (Mil.RMB) 总利润（百万元）	Return on assets 资产利润率（%）	Return on equity 权益利润率（%）	Labour productivity ('000 RMB/ worker) 劳动生产率（千元/人）	Debts/ assets 资产负债率（%）	Total assets (Mil.RMB) 总资产（百万元）
Industry Overall 行业总体	132	27,181	5,248	190	3.09	7.38	56.98	58.20	6,169

	Number of firms 企业个数	Average number of employees 平均职工人数	Average revenue ('000 RMB) 平均销售收入（千元）	Average profit ('000 RMB) 平均利润（千元）	Return on assets 资产利润率（%）	Return on equity 权益利润率（%）	Labour productivity ('000 RMB/ worker) 劳动生产率（千元/人）	Debts/ assets 资产负债率（%）	Average total assets ('000 RMB) 平均总资产（千元）
By ownership 产业所有权									
State-owned 国有	4	473	56,011	165	0.15	1.45	37.33	89.58	109,012
Collective-owned 集体	11	121	8,389	102	0.98	3.95	19.05	75.20	10,419
Foreign & Overseas Chinese Funded 三资	63	237	48,377	551	0.94	1.91	63.62	50.93	58,859
By regional distribution 地区分布									
Central-North 华北	5	101	11,681	-842	-4.04	-16.63	-2.15	75.68	20,826
Beijing 北京	2	23	7,240	162	2.48	5.50	140.13	54.91	6,509
Tianjin 天津	3	154	14,642	-1,512	-4.98	-23.31	-16.03	78.65	30,372
Hebei 河北									
Shanxi 山西									
Inner Mongolia 内蒙古									
Northeast 东北	9	254	40,956	3,020	5.65	19.26	37.86	70.65	53,417
Liaoning 辽宁	6	293	50,203	3,853	6.57	24.13	40.51	72.77	58,647
Jilin 吉林									
Heilongjiang 黑龙江	3	176	22,461	1,352	3.15	8.96	29.02	64.85	42,956
Central-East 华东	82	196	42,688	1,581	3.48	7.65	62.67	54.52	45,428
Shanghai 上海	13	113	30,558	2,346	5.63	10.44	85.54	46.06	41,671
Jiangsu 江苏	30	298	65,721	373	0.50	1.27	62.89	60.65	74,615
Zhejiang 浙江	22	117	25,586	2,755	10.55	20.34	64.08	48.14	26,108
Anhui 安徽	1	87	11,716	291	4.06	20.82	24.29	80.51	7,173
Fujian 福建	6	120	14,974	-2,889	-15.45	-26.61	48.96	41.93	18,693
Jiangxi 江西	1	123	10,201	590	4.21	4.21	17.58		14,000
Shandong 山东	9	243	50,764	4,866	18.46	30.70	53.26	39.86	26,358
Central-South 中南	32	243	38,536	981	1.86	4.84	55.40	61.59	52,747
Henan 河南	1	258	10,517	28	0.12	1.79	26.57	93.35	23,484
Hubei 湖北	3	147	3,030	-181	-2.24	-7.26	5.15	69.16	8,079
Hunan 湖南	2	98	4,078	-276	-2.58		23.44	148.76	10,684
Guangdong 广东	24	214	41,012	1,322	2.65	5.36	68.03	50.69	49,976
Guangxi 广西	2	873	110,558	370	0.18	1.27	38.70	86.10	209,689
Hainan 海南									
Southwest 西南	1	32	1,235	-627	-7.87	-256.97	3.47	96.94	7,962
Chongqing 重庆	1	32	1,235	-627	-7.87	-256.97	3.47	96.94	7,962
Sichuan 四川									
Guizhou 贵州									
Yunnan 云南									
Tibet 西藏									
Northwest 西北	3	162	28,642	2,362	4.34	10.16	48.78	57.25	54,395
Shaanxi 陕西	3	162	28,642	2,362	4.34	10.16	48.78	57.25	54,395
Gansu 甘肃									
Qinghai 青海									
Ningxia 宁夏									
Xinjiang 新疆									

Year 年份	Number of firms 企业个数	Rate of change 变化率(%)	Number of employees 职工人数(人)	Rate of change 变化率(%)	Total revenue (Mil. RMB) 总销售收入(百万元)	Rate of change 变化率(%)	Total profit (Mil RMB) 总利润(百万元)	Rate of change 变化率(%)
2000	111		26,110		3,620		176	
2001	110	-0.90	25,359	-2.88	3,925	8.43	137	-22.16
2002	132	20.00	27,181	7.18	5,248	33.71	190	38.69

Major Products 主要产品	Output 产量	Unit 单位

10 Main Firms with Maximal Revenue (year founded) 收入最大的十家主要企业（创办年份）	City 城市	Province 省	Telephone/fax 电话/传真	Number of employees 职工人数	Ownership 产业所有权	Revenue ('000 RMB) 销售收入(千元)	Profit('000 RMB) (rank) 利润(千元)(排名)	Total assets ('000 RMB) 总资产(千元)	Major products 主要产品
Fujitsu Media Devices (Suzhou) Co.,Ltd. 富士通多媒体部品(苏州)有限公司(1996)	Suzhou 苏州市	Jiangsu 江苏省	(0512)67612423 (0512)67617076	729	Foreign Funded 外商投资	280,944	-	364,439	Capacitor 电容器
Jinzhou Electric Power Capacitor Co.,Ltd. 锦州电力电容器有限责任公司(1965)	Jinzhou 锦州市	Liaoning 辽宁省	(0416)3155426 (0416)3148272	1,088	Limited-Liability 有限公司	263,727	25,288(3)	281,415	Capacitor 电容器
Guilin Electric Power Capacitor General Factory 桂林电力电容器总厂(1972)	Guilin 桂林市	Guangxi 广西	(0773)5892593 (0773)5215669	1,187	State-owned 国有企业	220,954	1,330(33)	267,193	Electric Power Capacitor电力电容器
Wuxi Power Capacitor Co.,Ltd. 无锡市电力电容器有限公司(1970)	Wuxi 无锡市	Jiangsu 江苏省	(0510)5212525 (0510)3703710	494	Joint Stock 股份制	207,138	26,295(2)	236,350	Electric Power Capacitor电力电容器
Lelon Electronics (Huidong) Industry Co.,Ltd. 立隆电子(惠东)工业有限公司(1997)	Huizhou 惠州市	Guangdong 广东省	(0752)8768200 (0752)8769198	365	Overseas Chinese-funded 港澳台资	152,159	2,330(27)	148,708	Aluminium Electrolysis Capacitor铝电解电容器
Zhejiang Zhuji Wufeng Capacitor Co.,Ltd. 浙江省诸暨市五峰电容器有限公司(1992)	Shaoxing 绍兴市	Zhejiang 浙江省	(0575)7951688 (0575)7951188	295	Limited-Liability 有限公司	150,810	7,029(11)	56,821	Capacitor 电容器
Wendeng Dahao Electronics Co.,Ltd. 文登大浩电子有限公司(1998)	Weihai 威海市	Shandong 山东省	(0631)8571688 (0631)8571698	240	Foreign Funded 外商投资	145,000	14,500(5)	16,270	Capacitor 电容器
Ningbo Bicai Industry Co.Ltd. 宁波碧彩实业有限公司(1995)	Ningbo 宁波市	Zhejiang 浙江省	(0574)88473777 (0574)88345777	331	Limited-Liability 有限公司	111,520	31,613(1)	121,878	Capacitor 电容器
Renhua Fengbin Science & Technology (Renhua) Co.,Ltd. 仁化县丰宾科技(仁化)有限)公司(1999)	Shaoguan 韶关市	Guangdong 广东省	(0751)6291867 (0751)6291868	110	Overseas Chinese-funded 港澳台资	109,765	3,071(23)	83,569	Pure Foil 正箔
Gaoyou Shengda Electronics Co.,Ltd. 高邮市升达电子有限公司(1981)	Yangzhou 扬州市	Jiangsu 江苏省	(0514)4611081 (0514)4061305	759	Limited-Liability 有限公司	88,378	876(39)	112,470	Aluminium Electrolysis Capacitor铝电解电容器

Top 10 Cities by Revenue 销售收入排名前10位城市	Province 省	Market share 市场份额 (%)	Number of firms 企业个数
Suzhou 苏州市	Jiangsu 江苏省	23.72	10
Shenzhen 深圳市	Guangdong 广东省	7.60	6
Shanghai 上海市	Shanghai 上海市	7.57	13
Wuxi 无锡市	Jiangsu 江苏省	6.09	8
Weihai 威海市	Shandong 山东省	5.62	2
Jinzhou 锦州市	Liaoning 辽宁省	5.14	2
Huizhou 惠州市	Guangdong 广东省	5.00	4
Guilin 桂林市	Guangxi 广西	4.21	2
Shaoxing 绍兴市	Zhejiang 浙江省	3.88	4
Ningbo 宁波市	Zhejiang 浙江省	3.04	5

10 Major Wholesalers 十家主要批发商	City 城市	Province 省	Telephone/Fax 电话/传真
SU MEC 中设江苏机械设备进出口（集团）公司	Nanjing 南京市	Jiangsu 江苏省	(025)4511888 (025)4411772
China Poster Mobile Communications Equipment Co.,Ltd. 中邮普泰移动通信设备股份有限公司	Beijing 北京市	Beijing 北京市	(010)66426993 (010)66426837
Sino Kama Co., Ltd. 中泰凯马股份有限公司	Shanghai 上海市	Shanghai 上海市	(021)62031188 (021)62030851
China Huayuan Group Co.,Ltd. 中国华源集团有限公司	Shanghai 上海市	Shanghai 上海市	(021)62031188 (021)62032288
Zhejiang Crand Imp.& Exp.Co.,Ltd. 浙江远大进出口有限公司	Ningbo 宁波市	Zhejiang 浙江省	(0574)87720170 (0574)87723350
Shandong Machinery Import & Export Group Corporation 山东省机械进出口集团公司	Qingdao 青岛市	Shandong 山东省	(0532)2661628 (0532)2991655
Qingdao Haier International Trade Co.,Ltd. 青岛海尔国际贸易有限公司	Qingdao 青岛市	Shandong 山东省	(0532)8938337 (0532)8939494
Guangdong Machinery Import & Export Group Corporation 广东省机械进出口集团公司	Guangzhou 广州市	Guangdong 广东省	(020)87782168 (020)87771803
China National Machinery Equipment Import & Export Corporation 中国机械设备进出口总公司	Beijing 北京市	Beijing 北京市	(010)63474506 (010)63261865
Beijing Cellstar Co.,Ltd. 北京蜂星事达电讯有限公司	Beijing 北京市	Beijing 北京市	(010)64602050 (010)64672648

4024: Switches and Control Equipment 开关控制设备制造业

The industry accounts for 0.378% of the total revenue of China's industrial sector in 2002. The rate of return on assets is 5.61%. 83.65% of all firms in the industry made a profit while 16.35% had negative returns.The top province in terms of the industry's revenue is Zhejiang, accounting for 20.23% of the total revenue.
2002年本行业收入占全行业的 0.378%，资产利润率为 5.61%。83.65%的企业赢利，16.35%的企业亏损。收入最高的省为浙江省，占本行业的20.23%。

	Total number of firms 企业总数	Total number of employees 职工总数	Total revenue (Mil.RMB) 总销售收入 (百万元)	Total profit (Mil.RMB) 总利润 (百万元)	Return on assets 资产利润率 (%)	Return on equity 权益利润率 (%)	Labour productivity ('000 RMB/ worker) 劳动生产率 (千元/人)	Debts/ assets 资产负债率 (%)	Total assets (Mil.RMB) 总资产 (百万元)
Industry Overall 行业总体	942	200,154	40,511	3,026	5.61	14.12	60.79	60.29	53,958

	Number of firms 企业个数	Average number of employees 平均职工人数	Average revenue ('000 RMB) 平均销售收入（千元）	Average profit ('000 RMB) 平均利润 (千元)	Return on assets 资产利润率 (%)	Return on equity 权益利润率 (%)	Labour productivity ('000 RMB/ worker) 劳动生产率 (千元/人)	Debts/ assets 资产负债率 (%)	Average total assets ('000 RMB) 平均总资产 (千元)
By ownership 产业所有权									
State-owned 国有	106	421	51,350	-517	-0.39	-1.26	30.08	69.31	134,011
Collective-owned 集体	188	169	25,511	1,103	4.17	12.09	42.73	65.54	26,478
Foreign & Overseas Chinese Funded 三资	155	187	72,121	11,098	16.48	33.01	122.41	50.08	67,359
By regional distribution 地区分布									
Central-North 华北	118	150	38,751	5,560	12.53	29.05	82.91	56.86	44,374
Beijing 北京	56	152	54,535	8,275	13.38	29.58	127.75	54.79	61,868
Tianjin 天津	32	96	31,777	5,638	19.07	41.55	72.75	54.10	29,565
Hebei 河北	21	169	18,714	777	2.92	8.08	34.09	63.83	26,585
Shanxi 山西	8	304	10,274	-966	-3.68	-24.61	11.69	85.04	26,248
Inner Mongolia 内蒙古	1	125	26,592	3,685	6.45	14.91	55.65	56.76	57,143
Northeast 东北	80	204	28,295	-113	-0.21	-0.79	35.95	73.21	53,227
Liaoning 辽宁	60	207	31,880	-217	-0.36	-1.37	39.07	73.48	59,763
Jilin 吉林	11	111	9,659	2	0.01	0.03	25.02	73.68	25,465
Heilongjiang 黑龙江	9	300	27,176	443	1.02	3.43	26.53	70.40	43,586
Central-East 华东	502	176	45,177	4,112	8.21	18.81	77.37	56.35	50,063
Shanghai 上海	100	148	51,348	3,557	6.06	16.42	89.07	63.10	58,702
Jiangsu 江苏	106	197	46,051	3,804	7.01	18.41	76.57	61.95	54,305
Zhejiang 浙江	212	170	38,649	3,651	9.10	16.61	63.28	45.22	40,129
Anhui 安徽	12	174	24,165	29	0.06	0.15	54.26	61.54	50,671
Fujian 福建	18	216	138,845	25,795	19.15	43.50	245.46	55.98	134,726
Jiangxi 江西	6	199	11,090	251	1.44	5.65	16.47	74.42	17,341
Shandong 山东	48	196	33,611	1,353	3.49	10.36	58.23	66.31	38,764
Central-South 中南	161	234	34,506	1,709	3.46	8.16	48.55	57.56	49,351
Henan 河南	34	269	38,624	1,636	1.78	5.00	60.79	64.46	92,051
Hubei 湖北	12	102	20,829	602	2.61	5.09	65.42	48.78	23,070
Hunan 湖南	16	188	21,484	766	2.03	4.84	33.11	57.94	37,682
Guangdong 广东	87	257	38,276	2,397	6.03	12.40	40.03	51.33	39,723
Guangxi 广西	11	167	28,335	-754	-1.75	-4.57	105.79	61.72	43,076
Hainan 海南	1	26	6,819	-177	-2.82	-21.02	27.81	86.59	6,278
Southwest 西南	40	291	31,754	-69	-0.15	-0.45	37.67	67.70	47,729
Chongqing 重庆	6	302	19,064	-2,991	-5.39	-97.20	20.04	94.45	55,471
Sichuan 四川	18	420	50,047	289	0.48	1.20	44.98	60.33	60,721
Guizhou 贵州	6	75	5,843	68	0.99	3.37	16.64	70.54	6,808
Yunnan 云南	10	182	21,988	956	2.16	6.27	29.95	65.52	44,252
Tibet 西藏									
Northwest 西北	41	700	101,705	1,030	0.45	1.38	35.76	67.64	231,155
Shaanxi 陕西	13	1,452	257,838	1,956	0.33	0.94	39.49	64.91	591,611
Gansu 甘肃	15	557	37,975	25	0.03	0.16	25.31	84.30	98,031
Qinghai 青海									
Ningxia 宁夏	3	139	27,254	3,713	8.90	16.45	72.03	45.88	41,702
Xinjiang 新疆	10	105	16,662	530	2.78	7.60	37.55	63.49	19,084

4024: Switches and Control Equipment 开关控制设备制造业

Year 年份	Number of firms 企业个数	Rate of change 变化率 (%)	Number of employees 职工人数 (人)	Rate of change 变化率 (%)	Total revenue (Mil. RMB) 总销售收入 (百万元)	Rate of change 变化率 (%)	Total profit (Mil RMB) 总利润 (百万元)	Rate of change 变化率 (%)
2000	760		200,799		31,569		2,107	
2001	823	8.29	186,621	-7.06	32,280	2.25	2,163	2.66
2002	942	14.46	200,154	7.25	40,511	25.50	3,026	39.90

Major Products 主要产品	Output 产量	Unit 单位
Low Voltage Switch Board 低压开关板	3,328,264	Piece 面
High Voltage Switch Board 高压开关板	218,038	Piece 面

10 Main Firms with Maximal Revenue (year founded) 收入最大的十家主要企业（创办年份）	City 城市	Province 省	Telephone/fax 电话/传真	Number of employees 职工人数	Ownership 产业所有权	Revenue ('000 RMB) 销售收入 (千元)	Profit('000 RMB) (rank) 利润(千元) (排名)	Total assets ('000 RMB) 总资产 (千元)	Major products 主要产品
Xi'an Electric Machinery Manufacturing Co.,Ltd.	Xi'an	Shannxi	(029)4261041		State-owned				High Voltage Breaker高
西安电力机械制造公司(1958)	西安市	陕西省	(029)4242679	14,415	国有企业	3,175,410	57,348(15)	6,995,093	压断路器
Xiamen ABB Switch Co.,Ltd.	Xiamen	Fujian	(0592)6026033		Foreign Funded				High Voltage Switch Board高
厦门ＡＢＢ开关有限公司(1992)	厦门市	福建省	(0592)6030505	339	外商投资	1,080,169	302,760(1)	758,753	压开关板
Jiangsu Changjiang Electric Appliance Group Corporation	Zhenjiang	Jiangsu	(0511)8411200		Limited-Liability				Switch Cabinet
江苏长江电器集团有限公司(1965)	镇江市	江苏省	(0511)8411211	2,259	有限公司	878,208	46,183(18)	1,587,655	开关柜
People Group Electric Appliance Co.,Ltd.	Wenzhou	Zhejiang	(0577)62738888		Limited-Liability				Contact Implement
人民电器集团有限公司(1996)	温州市	浙江省	(0577)62730608	1,295	有限公司	740,549	69,515(11)	331,164	接触器
Ningbo Tian'an Group Co.,Ltd.	Ningbo	Zhejiang	(0574)65728118		Joint Stock				High Voltage Switch Board高
宁波天安集团股份有限公司(1996)	宁波市	浙江省	(0574)65700217	1,407	股份制	651,818	111,993(5)	969,089	压开关板
Schneider(Beijing) Medium Voltage Electric Appliance Co.,Ltd	Beijing	Beijing	(010)67889191		Foreign Funded				High Voltage Switch Board高
施耐德（北京）中压电器有限公司(1997)	北京市	北京市	(010)67880521	176	外商投资	639,850	179,085(3)	299,826	压开关板
Shenyang High Voltage Switchgear Co.,Ltd.	Shenyang	Liaoning	(024)25877911		Limited-Liability				High Voltage Isolator Switch
沈阳高压开关有限责任公司(1937)	沈阳市	辽宁省	(024)25849863	3,163	有限公司	553,690	15,210(36)	1,258,740	隔离开关
Shanghai Schneider Distribution Electric Appliance Co.,Ltd.	Shanghai	Shanghai	(021)58122222		Foreign Funded				M Switch
上海施耐德配电电器有限公司(1995)	上海市	上海市	(021)58120985	157	外商投资	499,200	98,485(6)	350,990	M开关
Changshu Switch Factory	Suzhou	Jiangsu	(0512)52840991		Joint Stock				Plastic Shell Breaker塑
常熟开关厂(1974)	苏州市	江苏省	(0512)52841606	1,265	股份制	466,682	148,382(4)	462,836	壳断路器
Fuzhou Tianyu Electric Co.,Ltd.	Fuzhou	Fujian	(0591)7916470		Joint Stock				Transformer
福州天宇电气股份有限公司(1996)	福州市	福建省	(0591)7916449	1,266	股份制	450,787	25,000(24)	684,313	变压器

Top 10 Cities by Revenue 销售收入排名前10位城市	Province 省	Market share 市场份额 (%)	Number of firms 企业个数
Shanghai 上海市	Shanghai 上海市	12.68	100
Wenzhou 温州市	Zhejiang 浙江省	10.36	123
Xi'an 西安市	Shannxi 陕西省	8.07	9
Beijing 北京市	Beijing 北京市	7.54	56
Xiamen 厦门市	Fujian 福建省	4.43	7
Ningbo 宁波市	Zhejiang 浙江省	4.29	32
Hangzhou 杭州市	Zhejiang 浙江省	3.81	23
Zhenjiang 镇江市	Jiangsu 江苏省	3.71	13
Suzhou 苏州市	Jiangsu 江苏省	2.59	17
Shenyang 沈阳市	Liaoning 辽宁省	2.57	24

10 Major Wholesalers 十家主要批发商	City 城市	Province 省	Telephone/Fax 电话/传真
SU MEC	Nanjing	Jiangsu	(025)4511888
中设江苏机械设备进出口（集团）公司	南京市	江苏省	(025)4411772
China Poster Mobile Communications Equipment Co.,Ltd.	Beijing	Beijing	(010)66426993
中邮普泰移动通信设备股份有限公司	北京市	北京市	(010)66426837
Sino Kama Co., Ltd.	Shanghai	Shanghai	(021)62031188
中泰凯马股份有限公司	上海市	上海市	(021)62030851
China Huayuan Group Co.,Ltd.	Shanghai	Shanghai	(021)62031188
中国华源集团有限公司	上海市	上海市	(021)62032288
Zhejiang Crand Imp.& Exp.Co.,Ltd.	Ningbo	Zhejiang	(0574)87720170
浙江远大进出口有限公司	宁波市	浙江省	(0574)87723350
Shandong Machinery Import & Export Group Corporation	Qingdao	Shandong	(0532)2661628
山东省机械进出口集团公司	青岛市	山东省	(0532)2991655
Qingdao Haier International Trade Co.,Ltd.	Qingdao	Shandong	(0532)8938337
青岛海尔国际贸易有限公司	青岛市	山东省	(0532)8939494
Guangdong Machinery Import & Export Group Corporation	Guangzhou	Guangdong	(020)87782168
广东省机械进出口集团公司	广州市	广东省	(020)87771803
China National Machinery Equipment Import & Export Corporation	Beijing	Beijing	(010)63171506
中国机械设备进出口总公司	北京市	北京市	(010)63261865
Beijing Cellstar Co.,Ltd.	Beijing	Beijing	(010)64602050
北京蜂星事达电讯有限公司	北京市	北京市	(010)64672648

4027: Electronic Equipment Parts 电器设备元件制造业

The industry accounts for 0.156% of the total revenue of China's industrial sector in 2002. The rate of return on assets is 7.28%. 82.94% of all firms in the industry made a profit while 17.06% had negative returns.The top province in terms of the industry's revenue is Zhejiang, accounting for 44.89% of the total revenue.
2002年本行业收入占全行业的0.156%，资产利润率为7.28%。82.94%的企业赢利，17.06%的企业亏损。收入最高的省为浙江省，占本行业的44.89%。

	Total number of firms 企业总数	Total number of employees 职工总数	Total revenue (Mil.RMB) 总销售收入(百万元)	Total profit (Mil.RMB) 总利润(百万元)	Return on assets 资产利润率(%)	Return on equity 权益利润率(%)	Labour productivity ('000 RMB/ worker) 劳动生产率(千元/人)	Debts/ assets 资产负债率(%)	Total assets (Mil.RMB) 总资产(百万元)
Industry Overall 行业总体	428	96,029	16,687	1,268	7.28	15.24	47.52	52.25	17,420

	Number of firms 企业个数	Average number of employees 平均职工人数	Average revenue ('000 RMB) 平均销售收入(千元)	Average profit ('000 RMB) 平均利润(千元)	Return on assets 资产利润率(%)	Return on equity 权益利润率(%)	Labour productivity ('000 RMB/ worker) 劳动生产率(千元/人)	Debts/ assets 资产负债率(%)	Average total assets ('000 RMB) 平均总资产(千元)
By ownership 产业所有权									
State-owned 国有	38	174	12,463	-112	-0.28	-0.95	23.90	70.54	40,185
Collective-owned 集体	69	132	13,998	1,104	6.98	17.73	37.27	60.63	15,823
Foreign & Overseas Chinese Funded 三资	94	271	53,711	3,503	6.68	13.02	43.42	48.73	52,470
By regional distribution 地区分布									
Central-North 华北	51	157	15,213	611	2.26	6.53	34.19	65.31	26,990
Beijing 北京	14	174	23,600	875	1.90	6.40	50.30	70.28	46,031
Tianjin 天津	23	143	12,667	508	2.27	5.30	26.23	57.13	22,343
Hebei 河北	10	131	9,332	600	4.27	12.44	33.32	65.66	14,041
Shanxi 山西	2	368	17,760	548	2.90	8.18	16.79	64.49	18,874
Inner Mongolia 内蒙古	2	120	12,655	67	0.33	3.34	37.86	89.96	20,003
Northeast 东北	10	209	11,627	-615	-2.51	-19.93	14.27	87.43	24,543
Liaoning 辽宁	7	166	12,763	-801	-3.01	-107.95	16.07	97.21	26,568
Jilin 吉林	2	212	9,819	384	1.63	4.77	14.89	65.85	23,561
Heilongjiang 黑龙江	1	508	7,292	-1,310	-10.62	-13.70	9.63	22.50	12,338
Central-East 华东	256	234	49,245	4,591	11.10	21.61	57.58	48.65	41,376
Shanghai 上海	36	202	48,529	4,985	10.19	23.05	63.63	55.77	48,903
Jiangsu 江苏	53	192	36,553	2,177	6.94	14.73	28.44	52.93	31,396
Zhejiang 浙江	125	258	59,928	5,799	12.63	22.45	68.88	43.73	45,902
Anhui 安徽	7	162	32,604	4,300	16.04	30.34	65.67	47.13	26,804
Fujian 福建	11	206	47,769	5,297	17.19	26.12	68.64	34.19	30,817
Jiangxi 江西	2	104	11,253	691	8.59	13.59	44.88	36.82	8,046
Shandong 山东	22	304	29,781	2,997	7.43	20.83	35.98	64.33	40,331
Central-South 中南	85	192	30,227	920	2.40	5.31	34.33	54.90	38,382
Henan 河南	13	124	14,243	1,260	8.17	17.28	37.79	52.73	15,419
Hubei 湖北	4	78	8,132	-1,166	-4.57	-11.97	33.71	61.85	25,545
Hunan 湖南	10	108	9,643	-311	-2.65	-7.80	33.20	65.97	11,730
Guangdong 广东	50	245	43,750	1,429	2.64	5.72	34.75	53.89	54,186
Guangxi 广西	6	154	10,822	-184	-1.02	-3.17	28.31	67.82	18,011
Hainan 海南	2	77	1,372	-393	-3.12	-5.76	10.20	45.82	12,587
Southwest 西南	10	658	34,607	-2,023	-1.36	-2.64	18.88	48.40	148,288
Chongqing 重庆	4	228	35,958	1,510	4.01	12.54	32.58	68.03	37,662
Sichuan 四川	3	32	13,149	-40	-0.20	-0.28	168.91	28.79	19,756
Guizhou 贵州	3	1,859	54,264	-8,716	-2.05	-3.87	14.06	46.99	424,321
Yunnan 云南									
Tibet 西藏									
Northwest 西北	16	191	17,020	602	2.09	7.21	40.04	70.98	28,754
Shaanxi 陕西	10	130	10,354	734	4.75	11.10	40.12	57.25	15,473
Gansu 甘肃	5	347	33,606	473	0.78	3.53	40.40	77.92	60,687
Qinghai 青海									
Ningxia 宁夏									
Xinjiang 新疆	1	25	755	-80	-4.19	-22.10	11.00	81.05	1,910

4027: Electronic Equipment Parts 电器设备元件制造业

Year 年份	Number of firms 企业个数	Rate of change 变化率 (%)	Number of employees 职工人数 (人)	Rate of change 变化率 (%)	Total revenue (Mil. RMB) 总销售收入 (百万元)	Rate of change 变化率 (%)	Total profit (Mil RMB) 总利润 (百万元)	Rate of change 变化率 (%)
2000	375		88,598		12,393		786	
2001	397	5.87	89,239	0.72	13,351	7.73	868	10.43
2002	428	7.81	96,029	7.61	16,687	24.99	1,268	46.08

Major Products 主要产品	Output 产量	Unit 单位
Mutual Inducor 互感器	90	10,000 Units 万台

10 Main Firms with Maximal Revenue (year founded) 收入最大的十家主要企业（创办年份）	City 城市	Province 省	Telephone/fax 电话/传真	Number of employees 职工人数	Ownership 产业所有权	Revenue ('000 RMB) 销售收入 (千元)	Profit('000 RMB) (rank) 利润(千元) (排名)	Total assets ('000 RMB) 总资产 (千元)	Major products 主要产品
Chint Group Co.,Ltd. 正泰集团公司(1994)	Wenzhou 温州市	Zhejiang 浙江省	(0577)62777777 (0577)62775888	4,011	Joint Stock 股份制	1,777,898	247,658(1)	948,202	Component of Low Voltage Electric Equipment低压电器元件
Delixi Group Co.,Ltd. 德力西集团有限公司(1993)	Wenzhou 温州市	Zhejiang 浙江省	(0577)62723888 (0577)62725559	4,215	Limited-Liability 有限公司	1,331,912	136,040(2)	809,586	Low Voltage Electric Equipment 低压电器
Tengen Group Co.,Ltd. 天正集团有限公司(1997)	Wenzhou 温州市	Zhejiang 浙江省	(0577)62761028 (0577)62776888	1,921	Limited-Liability 有限公司	875,770	75,880(3)	399,200	Low-pressure Electric and Element低压电气及元件
Delta Electronics Industry (Dongguan) Co.,Ltd. 台达电子工业（东莞）有限公司(1998)	Dongguan 东莞市	Guangdong 广东省	(0769)6329008 (0769)6631589	855	Foreign Funded 外商投资	685,039	34,829(6)	585,316	Electronic Products 电子产品
Foshan Tongbao Co.,Ltd. 佛山通宝股份有限公司(1993)	Foshan 佛山市	Guangdong 广东省	(0757)2298522 (0757)2231574	1,506	Overseas Chinese-funded 港澳台资	505,137	21,181(13)	769,500	Temperature Controller温度控制器
Great Wall Electric Group Co.,Ltd. 长城电器集团有限公司(1988)	Wenzhou 温州市	Zhejiang 浙江省	(0577)62722888 (0577)62727095	2,013	Joint Stock 股份制	498,590	48,725(5)	321,890	Low Voltage Electric Equipment 低压电器
Shanghai MWB Transformer Co.,Ltd. 上海MWB互感器有限公司(1993)	Shanghai 上海市	Shanghai 上海市	(021)54720088 (021)54723898	276	Foreign Funded 外商投资	283,554	59,612(4)	336,589	Transformer 互感器
Shanghai People Electric Apparatus Works 上海人民电器厂(1914)	Shanghai 上海市	Shanghai 上海市	(021)56653680 (021)56650609	1,518	Joint Stock 股份制	281,548	11,000(22)	289,508	Air Switch 空气开关
Sino-Japan Electric Heat (Xiamen) Co.,Ltd. 中日电热(厦门)有限公司(1990)	Xiamen 厦门市	Fujian 福建省	(0592)6211270 (0592)6214280	1,192	Overseas Chinese-funded 港澳台资	276,281	33,553(7)	132,526	Electrothermal Tube 电热管
Enjiasheng (Lianyungang) Electronic Co.,Ltd. 恩佳升(连云港)电子有限公司(1997)	Lianyungang 连云港市	Jiangsu 江苏省	(0518)5151452 (0518)5151454	1,142	Foreign Funded 外商投资	253,656	23,461(12)	167,071	ABS Sensor.ABS传感器

Top 10 Cities by Revenue 销售收入排名前10位城市	Province 省	Market share 市场份额 (%)	Number of firms 企业个数
Wenzhou 温州市	Zhejiang 浙江省	37.63	71
Shanghai 上海市	Shanghai 上海市	10.47	36
Dongguan 东莞市	Guangdong 广东省	4.98	8
Suzhou 苏州市	Jiangsu 江苏省	4.86	21
Foshan 佛山市	Guangdong 广东省	4.15	12
Ningbo 宁波市	Zhejiang 浙江省	3.60	33
Xiamen 厦门市	Fujian 福建省	2.51	6
Wuxi 无锡市	Jiangsu 江苏省	2.24	9
Beijing 北京市	Beijing 北京市	1.98	14
Tianjin 天津市	Tianjin 天津市	1.75	23

10 Major Wholesalers 十家主要批发商	City 城市	Province 省	Telephone/Fax 电话/传真
SU MEC 中设江苏机械设备进出口（集团）公司	Nanjing 南京市	Jiangsu 江苏省	(025)4511888 (025)4411772
China Poster Mobile Communications Equipment Co.,Ltd. 中邮普泰移动通信设备股份有限公司	Beijing 北京市	Beijing 北京市	(010)66426993 (010)66426837
Sino Kama Co., Ltd. 中泰凯马股份有限公司	Shanghai 上海市	Shanghai 上海市	(021)62031188 (021)62030851
China Huayuan Group Co.,Ltd. 中国华源集团有限公司	Shanghai 上海市	Shanghai 上海市	(021)62031188 (021)62032288
Zhejiang Crand Imp.& Exp.Co.,Ltd. 浙江远大进出口有限公司	Ningbo 宁波市	Zhejiang 浙江省	(0574)87720170 (0574)87723350
Shandong Machinery Import & Export Group Corporation 山东省机械进出口集团公司	Qingdao 青岛市	Shandong 山东省	(0532)2661628 (0532)2991655
Qingdao Haier International Trade Co.,Ltd. 青岛海尔国际贸易有限公司	Qingdao 青岛市	Shandong 山东省	(0532)8938337 (0532)8939494
Guangdong Machinery Import & Export Group Corporation 广东省机械进出口集团公司	Guangzhou 广州市	Guangdong 广东省	(020)87782168 (020)87771803
China National Machinery Equipment Import & Export Corporation 中国机械设备进出口总公司	Beijing 北京市	Beijing 北京市	(010)63474506 (010)63261865
Beijing Cellstar Co.,Ltd. 北京蜂星事达电讯有限公司	Beijing 北京市	Beijing 北京市	(010)64602050 (010)64672648

4029:Other Electricity Transmission, Distribution & Control Equipment

其他输配电及控制设备制造业

The industry accounts for 0.193% of the total revenue of China's industrial sector in 2002. The rate of return on assets is 6.40%. 80.82% of all firms in the industry made a profit while 19.18% had negative returns.The top province in terms of the industry's revenue is Jiangsu, accounting for 32.21% of the total revenue.
2002年本行业收入占全行业的 0.193%，资产利润率为 6.40%。80.82%的企业赢利，19.18%的企业亏损。收入最高的省为江苏省，占本行业的32.21%。

	Total number of firms 企业总数	Total number of employees 职工总数	Total revenue (Mil.RMB) 总销售收入(百万元)	Total profit (Mil.RMB) 总利润(百万元)	Return on assets 资产利润率(%)	Return on equity 权益利润率(%)	Labour productivity ('000 RMB/worker) 劳动生产率(千元/人)	Debts/assets 资产负债率(%)	Total assets (Mil.RMB) 总资产(百万元)
Industry Overall 行业总体	485	88,812	20,671	1,840	6.40	15.32	70.86	58.25	28,765

	Number of firms 企业个数	Average number of employees 平均职工人数	Average revenue ('000 RMB) 平均销售收入（千元）	Average profit ('000 RMB) 平均利润(千元)	Return on assets 资产利润率(%)	Return on equity 权益利润率(%)	Labour productivity ('000 RMB/worker) 劳动生产率(千元/人)	Debts/assets 资产负债率(%)	Average total assets ('000 RMB) 平均总资产(千元)
By ownership 产业所有权									
State-owned 国有	46	291	117,551	7,751	3.24	8.21	135.41	60.54	239,414
Collective-owned 集体	96	188	24,886	1,318	4.51	16.52	38.12	72.72	29,247
Foreign & Overseas Chinese Funded 三资	68	212	53,401	4,310	9.15	21.74	51.36	57.88	47,078
By regional distribution 地区分布									
Central-North 华北	46	130	49,122	5,959	13.41	34.65	102.98	61.31	44,456
Beijing 北京	15	147	69,687	9,284	12.43	33.67	183.71	63.08	74,676
Tianjin 天津	24	118	45,538	5,171	16.14	39.44	59.02	59.07	32,032
Hebei 河北	4	157	27,027	2,663	8.59	18.08	59.42	52.49	30,990
Shanxi 山西	2	116	3,274	33	0.25	5.23	9.97	95.29	13,213
Inner Mongolia 内蒙古	1	82	6,764	69	1.22	2.49	34.30	51.14	5,678
Northeast 东北	41	258	30,525	2,054	3.60	10.45	41.42	65.60	57,118
Liaoning 辽宁	24	173	28,892	3,135	8.08	19.03	67.04	57.56	38,815
Jilin 吉林	6	136	18,980	719	2.22	4.49	51.95	50.63	32,435
Heilongjiang 黑龙江	11	510	40,387	422	0.38	1.48	20.89	74.16	110,513
Central-East 华东	273	151	38,000	3,346	7.51	17.43	71.20	56.95	44,587
Shanghai 上海	49	133	35,497	1,827	4.07	10.61	63.08	61.70	44,938
Jiangsu 江苏	140	172	47,565	4,880	8.88	21.09	77.56	57.88	54,949
Zhejiang 浙江	46	130	21,677	1,788	7.91	13.25	48.51	40.29	22,601
Anhui 安徽	6	82	11,356	414	3.86	6.84	50.35	43.55	10,720
Fujian 福建	8	62	15,207	1,544	9.96	20.33	46.97	51.01	15,500
Jiangxi 江西	1	117	26,003	184	0.59	4.08	76.84	85.47	31,071
Shandong 山东	23	148	33,159	1,893	4.28	10.03	87.94	57.39	44,277
Central-South 中南	90	265	65,524	5,318	4.34	10.53	81.76	58.80	122,576
Henan 河南	12	473	292,936	22,841	3.58	9.02	212.51	60.34	638,770
Hubei 湖北	19	140	41,229	6,043	8.90	15.92	147.88	44.13	67,931
Hunan 湖南	7	176	28,130	657	1.60	4.46	38.66	64.09	41,004
Guangdong 广东	48	287	28,325	1,442	4.27	11.98	15.27	64.34	33,763
Guangxi 广西	3	91	9,653	5,512	16.60	26.21	327.79	36.65	33,198
Hainan 海南	1	256	13,160	-634	-0.92	-1.60	22.79	42.40	68,701
Southwest 西南	21	199	23,239	1,073	3.17	7.68	30.25	58.69	33,806
Chongqing 重庆	8	189	25,041	1,570	4.36	15.05	19.26	71.03	36,012
Sichuan 四川	9	219	27,718	1,003	2.63	5.78	41.26	54.57	38,153
Guizhou 贵州	3	157	9,694	143	0.64	0.96	23.64	33.19	22,356
Yunnan 云南	1	220	9,148	521	4.58	5.78	21.52	20.77	11,375
Tibet 西藏									
Northwest 西北	14	219	28,636	4,814	14.52	20.08	75.95	27.68	33,153
Shaanxi 陕西	11	256	35,122	6,141	15.00	20.28	82.30	26.03	40,943
Gansu 甘肃	1	30	3,561	23	0.64	2.30	53.77	72.40	3,619
Qinghai 青海									
Ningxia 宁夏									
Xinjiang 新疆	2	116	5,504	-87	-1.72	-11.31	1.50	84.83	5,071

4029: Other Electricity Transmission, Distribution & Control Equipment

其他输配电及控制设备制造业

Year 年份	Number of firms 企业个数	Rate of change 变化率 (%)	Number of employees 职工人数 (人)	Rate of change 变化率 (%)	Total revenue (Mil. RMB) 总销售收入 (百万元)	Rate of change 变化率 (%)	Total profit (Mil RMB) 总利润 (百万元)	Rate of change 变化率 (%)
2000	431		85,767		14,024		873	
2001	495	14.85	89,565	4.43	17,948	27.98	1,393	59.56
2002	485	-2.02	88,812	-0.84	20,671	15.17	1,840	32.09

Major Products 主要产品	Output 产量	Unit 单位
High Voltage Circuit-breaker 高压断路器	14	10,000 Units 万台

10 Main Firms with Maximal Revenue (year founded) 收入最大的十家主要企业（创办年份）	City 城市	Province 省	Telephone/fax 电话/传真	Number of employees 职工人数	Ownership 产业所有权	Revenue ('000 RMB) 销售收入 (千元)	Profit('000 RMB) (rank) 利润(千元) (排名)	Total assets ('000 RMB) 总资产 (千元)	Major products 主要产品
Xuji Group Co.,Ltd. 许继集团有限公司(1996)	Xuchang 许昌市	Henan 河南省	(0374)3212285 (0374)3212282	4,862	State-owned 国有企业	3,429,581	274788(2)	7,510,965	Relay 继电器
Nanjing Electric Power Automation Equipment General Factory 国家电力公司南京电力自动化设备总厂(1940)	Nanjing 南京市	Jiangsu 江苏省	(025)3421394 (025)3419872	1,625	State-owned 国有企业	921,190	27,600(14)	1,474,850	Relay Protection Series继电保护系列
Nari-relay Electric Engineering & Technial Co., Ltd. 南京南瑞继保营销有限公司(2001)	Nanjing 南京市	Jiangsu 江苏省	(025)2100686 (025)2100686	102	Limited-Liability 有限公司	673,390	126,810(3)	483,630	Electric Power Automatic Control Equipment电力自动化控制设备
Nari-relays Jibao Electric Co., Ltd. 南京南瑞继保电气有限公司(1995)	Nanjing 南京市	Jiangsu 江苏省	(025)2100695 (025)2100695	265	Limited-Liability 有限公司	528,730	275,830(1)	630,790	Electric Power Automatic Control Equipment电力自动化控制设备
Nari Group Corporation 南京南瑞集团公司(1992)	Nanjing 南京市	Jiangsu 江苏省	(025)3429900 (025)3427142	1,043	State-owned 国有企业	505,030	57,910(6)	822,800	Electric Network Control Automation System电网调度自动化系统
Siemens Electricity Drives Co., Ltd. 西门子电气传动有限公司(1995)	Tianjin 天津市	Tianjin 天津市	(022)84397088 (022)24977210	164	Foreign Funded 外商投资	390,517	53,822(7)	270,133	Frequency Conversion & Timing Equipment变频调速装置
Suzhou Futai Electronics Co., Ltd. 苏州福泰电子有限公司(1998)	Suzhou 苏州市	Jiangsu 江苏省	(0512)63456992 (0512)63456997	2,285	Overseas Chinese-funded 港澳台资	372,300	34,660(12)	210,400	Inductance Instrument 电感器
Acheng Relay Group Co., Ltd. 阿城继电器集团有限公司(1946)	Harbin 哈尔滨市	Heilongjiang 黑龙江省	(0451)53709000 (0451)53701318	3,971	State Enterprises 国有独资	268,553	120(288)	1,033,309	Relay 继电器
Yantai Huadong Transformer Co., Ltd. 烟台华东变压器有限公司(1997)	Yantai 烟台市	Shandong 山东省	(0535)6385198 (0535)6385197	475	Foreign Funded 外商投资	246,171	7,306(42)	130,011	High Voltage Transformer高压变压器
Shanghai Dongxing Electric Power Industrial Co., Ltd. 上海东兴电力实业有限公司(1989)	Shanghai 上海市	Shanghai 上海市	(021)64500150 (021)64528828	603	Limited-Liability 有限公司	243,614	5,712(55)	151,862	Electricity Station Equipment Examining & Repairing电站设备检修

Top 10 Cities by Revenue 销售收入排名前10位城市	Province 省	Market share 市场份额 (%)	Number of firms 企业个数
Xuchang 许昌市	Henan 河南省	16.59	1
Nanjing 南京市	Jiangsu 江苏省	16.04	21
Shanghai 上海市	Shanghai 上海市	8.41	49
Zhenjiang 镇江市	Jiangsu 江苏省	5.49	68
Tianjin 天津市	Tianjin 天津市	5.29	24
Beijing 北京市	Beijing 北京市	5.06	15
Wenzhou 温州市	Zhejiang 浙江省	3.66	30
Wuhan 武汉市	Hubei 湖北省	3.58	14
Suzhou 苏州市	Jiangsu 江苏省	2.61	10
Guangzhou 广州市	Guangdong 广东省	2.56	12

10 Major Wholesalers 十家主要批发商	City 城市	Province 省	Telephone/Fax 电话/传真
SU MEC 中设江苏机械设备进出口（集团）公司	Nanjing 南京市	Jiangsu 江苏省	(025)4511888 (025)4411772
China Poster Mobile Communications Equipment Co.,Ltd. 中邮普泰移动通信设备股份有限公司	Beijing 北京市	Beijing 北京市	(010)66426993 (010)66126837
Sino Kama Co., Ltd. 中泰凯马股份有限公司	Shanghai 上海市	Shanghai 上海市	(021)62031188 (021)62030851
China Huayuan Group Co.,Ltd. 中国华源集团有限公司	Shanghai 上海市	Shanghai 上海市	(021)62031188 (021)62032288
Zhejiang Crand Imp.& Exp.Co.,Ltd. 浙江远大进出口有限公司	Ningbo 宁波市	Zhejiang 浙江省	(0574)87720170 (0574)87723350
Shandong Machinery Import & Export Group Corporation 山东省机械进出口集团公司	Qingdao 青岛市	Shandong 山东省	(0532)2661628 (0532)2991655
Qingdao Haier International Trade Co.,Ltd. 青岛海尔国际贸易有限公司	Qingdao 青岛市	Shandong 山东省	(0532)8938337 (0532)8939494
Guangdong Machinery Import & Export Group Corporation 广东省机械进出口集团公司	Guangzhou 广州市	Guangdong 广东省	(020)87782168 (020)87771803
China National Machinery Equipment Import & Export Corporation 中国机械设备进出口总公司	Beijing 北京市	Beijing 北京市	(010)63474506 (010)63261865
Beijing Cellstar Co.,Ltd. 北京蜂星事达电讯有限公司	Beijing 北京市	Beijing 北京市	(010)64602050 (010)64672648

4041: Wire and Cable 电线电缆制造业

The industry accounts for 1.102% of the total revenue of China's industrial sector in 2002. The rate of return on assets is 4.43%. 83.68% of all firms in the industry made a profit while 16.32% had negative returns.The top province in terms of the industry's revenue is Jiangsu, accounting for 20.88% of the total revenue.
2002年本行业收入占全行业的 1.102%，资产利润率为 4.43%。83.68%的企业赢利，16.32%的企业亏损。收入最高的省为江苏省，占本行业的20.88%。

	Total number of firms 企业总数	Total number of employees 职工总数	Total revenue (Mil.RMB) 总销售收入 (百万元)	Total profit (Mil.RMB) 总利润 (百万元)	Return on assets 资产利润率 (%)	Return on equity 权益利润率 (%)	Labour productivity ('000 RMB/ worker) 劳动生产率 (千元/人)	Debts/ assets 资产负债率 (%)	Total assets (Mil.RMB) 总资产 (百万元)
Industry Overall 行业总体	2034	377,495	118,242	5,304	4.43	10.89	80.89	59.29	119,670

	Number of firms 企业个数	Average number of employees 平均职工人数	Average revenue ('000 RMB) 平均销售收入 (千元)	Average profit ('000 RMB) 平均利润 (千元)	Return on assets 资产利润率 (%)	Return on equity 权益利润率 (%)	Labour productivity ('000 RMB/ worker) 劳动生产率 (千元/人)	Debts/ assets 资产负债率 (%)	Average total assets ('000 RMB) 平均总资产 (千元)
By ownership 产业所有权									
State-owned 国有	107	376	51,600	-2,105	-1.94	-12.02	28.80	83.87	108,554
Collective-owned 集体	413	171	51,742	2,898	7.46	19.72	82.92	62.20	38,862
Foreign & Overseas Chinese Funded 三资	321	266	75,850	3,116	3.72	7.57	78.26	50.81	83,700
By regional distribution 地区分布									
Central-North 华北	261	177	45,475	3,567	7.15	17.25	70.98	58.57	49,911
Beijing 北京	25	110	23,927	1,224	3.86	9.12	63.83	57.62	31,673
Tianjin 天津	78	200	52,395	5,240	8.81	22.72	67.05	61.23	59,496
Hebei 河北	138	151	48,842	3,818	8.31	18.42	92.15	54.87	45,922
Shanxi 山西	11	396	22,767	-2,745	-4.35	-12.45	15.95	65.04	63,048
Inner Mongolia 内蒙古	9	308	21,488	-564	-0.90	-3.19	27.54	71.72	62,622
Northeast 东北	115	373	36,996	64	0.09	0.61	19.05	84.48	67,202
Liaoning 辽宁	85	386	37,025	-333	-0.54	-2.65	12.97	79.72	61,984
Jilin 吉林	13	213	23,122	397	0.62	1.80	67.69	65.32	63,720
Heilongjiang 黑龙江	17	430	47,460	1,793	1.87		27.92	109.57	95,951
Central-East 华东	1,006	172	71,882	3,740	5.45	12.49	109.51	56.37	68,655
Shanghai 上海	186	135	51,074	2,889	5.49	11.56	88.86	52.52	52,619
Jiangsu 江苏	317	170	77,873	3,300	4.59	11.27	121.17	59.27	71,921
Zhejiang 浙江	274	153	68,511	3,758	5.45	12.38	101.45	55.99	68,979
Anhui 安徽	85	134	41,913	1,729	3.92	9.44	76.58	58.46	44,068
Fujian 福建	26	280	71,298	2,429	2.97	7.34	91.92	59.52	81,733
Jiangxi 江西	21	205	47,007	440	0.87	2.26	37.16	61.33	50,410
Shandong 山东	97	296	133,531	9,591	8.73	18.39	145.86	52.51	109,807
Central-South 中南	510	176	45,967	1,190	2.72	6.92	67.11	60.78	43,824
Henan 河南	119	162	37,886	1,326	3.08	8.88	56.45	65.29	43,030
Hubei 湖北	62	179	40,836	824	1.53	3.61	82.58	57.69	53,887
Hunan 湖南	39	139	31,466	1,231	4.11	10.77	52.43	61.83	29,944
Guangdong 广东	270	189	52,995	1,268	2.87	7.07	67.51	59.31	44,094
Guangxi 广西	15	160	50,381	73	0.16	0.44	103.55	64.34	47,198
Hainan 海南	5	87	22,212	1,334	6.19	19.51	79.64	68.26	21,549
Southwest 西南	100	187	47,077	-132	-0.25	-0.56	56.15	55.07	53,013
Chongqing 重庆	26	152	42,762	1,565	4.62	16.34	93.36	71.71	33,850
Sichuan 四川	55	200	48,974	-1,303	-2.06	-3.85	48.35	46.66	63,391
Guizhou 贵州	7	112	30,421	609	1.57	6.55	39.45	76.01	38,791
Yunnan 云南	12	250	57,448	1,126	2.04	6.50	40.07	68.66	55,261
Tibet 西藏									
Northwest 西北	42	176	39,394	228	0.44	1.15	63.22	62.01	52,280
Shaanxi 陕西	21	139	35,396	442	0.90	2.43	76.62	62.81	48,854
Gansu 甘肃	11	325	51,754	-78	-0.12	-0.29	50.91	60.26	66,708
Qinghai 青海	1	191	18,896	338	2.14	8.60	31.43	75.14	15,803
Ningxia 宁夏	2	143	55,407	2,987	7.41	29.89	82.29	75.21	40,317
Xinjiang 新疆	7	58	30,321	-738	-1.52	-3.77	76.53	59.67	48,513

Year 年份	Number of firms 企业个数	Rate of change 变化率(%)	Number of employees 职工人数(人)	Rate of change 变化率(%)	Total revenue (Mil. RMB) 总销售收入(百万元)	Rate of change 变化率(%)	Total profit (Mil RMB) 总利润(百万元)	Rate of change 变化率(%)
2000	1709		341,268		96,776		4,013	
2001	1899	11.12	345,281	1.18	111,078	14.78	6,254	55.84
2002	2034	7.11	377,495	9.33	118,242	6.45	5,304	-15.19

Major Products 主要产品	Output 产量	Unit 单位
Communication Cable 通讯电缆	4,213	10,000 Km 万公里
Electrical Wire 电线	1,626	10,000 Km 万公里

10 Main Firms with Maximal Revenue (year founded) 收入最大的十家主要企业（创办年份）	City 城市	Province 省	Telephone/fax 电话/传真	Number of employees 职工人数	Ownership 产业所有权	Revenue ('000 RMB) 销售收入(千元)	Profit('000 RMB) (rank) 利润(千元)(排名)	Total assets ('000 RMB) 总资产(千元)	Major products 主要产品
Shandong Luneng Taishan Cable Co., Ltd. 山东鲁能泰山电缆股份有限公司(1998)	Taian 泰安市	Shandong 山东省	(0538)7238609 (0538)8539810	4,220	Joint Stock 股份制	1,771,882	179,379(3)	2,903,544	Electric Power Cable 电力电缆
Hengtong Group Co.,Ltd. 亨通集团公司(1991)	Suzhou 苏州市	Jiangsu 江苏省	(0512)63800103 (0512)63801518	1,978	Collective-owned 集体企业	1,602,927	107,880(8)	1,551,878	Cable 电缆
Jiangsu Far East Group Co., Ltd. 江苏远东集团有限公司(1990)	Wuxi 无锡市	Jiangsu 江苏省	(0512)63270177 (0512)7241200	1,969	Limited-Liability 有限公司	1,515,180	65,500(16)	792,720	Electrical Wire & Cable 电线电缆
Nanjing Huaxin Photoelectric Co., Ltd. 南京华新光电股份有限公司(1993)	Nanjing 南京市	Jiangsu 江苏省	(025)5567572 (025)5567573	128	Foreign Funded 外商投资	1,487,990	38,710(33)	420,570	Copper Pole 铜杆
Zhejiang Fuchunjiang Commucation Group Co., Ltd. 浙江富春江通信集团有限公司(1996)	Hangzhou 杭州市	Zhejiang 浙江省	(0571)63371406 (0571)63372476	1,134	Limited-Liability 有限公司	1,301,485	69,030(15)	1,402,369	Communication Cable 通信电缆
Wanda Group Stock Co., Ltd. 万达集团股份有限公司(1994)	Dongying 东营市	Shandong 山东省	(0546)2063989 (0546)2061318	2,516	Joint Stock 股份制	1,291,438	121,002(6)	790,922	Electrical Wire 电线
Qingdao Hanhe Cable Group Co.,Ltd. 青岛汉缆集团有限公司(1982)	Qingdao 青岛市	Shandong 山东省	(0532)8817759 (0532)8817462	1,288	Collective-owned 集体企业	1,150,293	75,975(14)	633,892	Electrical Wire 电线
Hangzhou Futong Group Co.,lLtd. 杭州富通集团有限公司(1994)	Hangzhou 杭州市	Zhejiang 浙江省	(0571)63322660 (0571)63326488	1,569	Private Owned 私营企业	1,087,646	84,573(12)	2,095,290	Electrical Wire & Cable 电线电缆
Jiaozuo Yellow River Group Company 焦作黄河集团公司(1991)	Jiaozuo 焦作市	Henan 河南省	(0391)7566400	2,450	Collective-owned 集体企业	1,010,000	86,820(11)	265,000	Cable 电缆
Andrew Telecommunication (China) Co., Ltd. 安德鲁电信器材（苏州）有限公司(1998)	Suzhou 苏州市	Jiangsu 江苏省	(0512)67610069 (0512)67615220	705	Foreign Funded 外商投资	800,793	145,235(4)	738,212	Cable 电缆

Top 10 Cities by Revenue 销售收入排名前10位城市	Province 省	Market share 市场份额(%)	Number of firms 企业个数
Shanghai 上海市	Shanghai 上海市	8.03	186
Hangzhou 杭州市	Zhejiang 浙江省	7.12	78
Suzhou 苏州市	Jiangsu 江苏省	6.72	68
Wuxi 无锡市	Jiangsu 江苏省	5.44	74
Tianjin 天津市	Tianjin 天津市	3.46	78
Weihai 威海市	Shandong 山东省	2.70	7
Ningbo 宁波市	Zhejiang 浙江省	2.50	40
Dongguan 东莞市	Guangdong 广东省	2.22	47
Yangzhou 扬州市	Jiangsu 江苏省	2.10	34
Changzhou 常州市	Jiangsu 江苏省	2.09	43

10 Major Wholesalers 十家主要批发商	City 城市	Province 省	Telephone/Fax 电话/传真
SU MEC 中设江苏机械设备进出口（集团）公司	Nanjing 南京市	Jiangsu 江苏省	(025)4511888 (025)4411772
China Poster Mobile Communications Equipment Co.,Ltd. 中邮普泰移动通信设备股份有限公司	Beijing 北京市	Beijing 北京市	(010)66426993 (010)66426837
Sino Kama Co., Ltd. 中泰凯马股份有限公司	Shanghai 上海市	Shanghai 上海市	(021)62031188 (021)62030851
China Huayuan Group Co.,Ltd. 中国华源集团有限公司	Shanghai 上海市	Shanghai 上海市	(021)62031188 (021)62032288
Zhejiang Crand Imp.& Exp.Co.,Ltd. 浙江远大进出口有限公司	Ningbo 宁波市	Zhejiang 浙江省	(0574)87720170 (0574)87723350
Shandong Machinery Import & Export Group Corporation 山东省机械进出口集团公司	Qingdao 青岛市	Shandong 山东省	(0532)2661628 (0532)2991655
Qingdao Haier International Trade Co.,Ltd. 青岛海尔国际贸易有限公司	Qingdao 青岛市	Shandong 山东省	(0532)8938337 (0532)8939494
Guangdong Machinery Import & Export Group Corporation 广东省机械进出口集团公司	Guangzhou 广州市	Guangdong 广东省	(020)87782168 (020)87771803
China National Machinery Equipment Import & Export Corporation 中国机械设备进出口总公司	Beijing 北京市	Beijing 北京市	(010)63474506 (010)63261865
Beijing Cellstar Co.,Ltd. 北京蜂星事达电讯有限公司	Beijing 北京市	Beijing 北京市	(010)64602050 (010)64672648

4043: Insulated Products 绝缘制品业

The industry accounts for 0.051% of the total revenue of China's industrial sector in 2002. The rate of return on assets is 4.47%. 80.85% of all firms in the industry made a profit while 19.15% had negative returns.The top province in terms of the industry's revenue is Jiangsu, accounting for 22.50% of the total revenue.
2002年本行业收入占全行业的 0.051%，资产利润率为 4.47%。80.85%的企业赢利，19.15%的企业亏损。收入最高的省为江苏省，占本行业的22.50%。

	Total number of firms 企业总数	Total number of employees 职工总数	Total revenue (Mil.RMB) 总销售收入（百万元）	Total profit (Mil.RMB) 总利润（百万元）	Return on assets 资产利润率（%）	Return on equity 权益利润率（%）	Labour productivity ('000 RMB/ worker) 劳动生产率（千元/人）	Debts/ assets 资产负债率（%）	Total assets (Mil.RMB) 总资产（百万元）
Industry Overall 行业总体	188	28,849	5,454	284	4.47	12.23	55.83	63.48	6,352

	Number of firms 企业个数	Average number of employees 平均职工人数	Average revenue ('000 RMB) 平均销售收入（千元）	Average profit ('000 RMB) 平均利润（千元）	Return on assets 资产利润率（%）	Return on equity 权益利润率（%）	Labour productivity ('000 RMB/ worker) 劳动生产率（千元/人）	Debts/ assets 资产负债率（%）	Average total assets ('000 RMB) 平均总资产（千元）
By ownership 产业所有权									
State-owned 国有	17	172	11,005	-1,611	-4.26		19.83	113.07	37,818
Collective-owned 集体	44	116	19,125	1,040	6.72	18.67	53.07	64.02	15,484
Foreign & Overseas Chinese Funded 三资	39	227	50,995	3,059	4.73	10.17	67.92	53.47	64,631
By regional distribution 地区分布									
Central-North 华北	18	168	20,218	-483	-1.31	-6.84	37.18	80.84	36,849
Beijing 北京	6	130	15,292	-276	-0.90	-4.28	36.94	79.04	30,704
Tianjin 天津	5	169	23,456	-1,698	-2.92	-19.72	19.01	85.22	58,243
Hebei 河北	6	184	25,644	317	1.20	5.29	60.99	77.36	26,495
Shanxi 山西	1	290	1,023	-450	-1.56	-4.76	0.08	67.29	28,872
Inner Mongolia 内蒙古									
Northeast 东北	8	164	12,374	-449	-1.83		36.35	114.57	24,517
Liaoning 辽宁	3	38	15,842	2,125	17.18	31.06	275.47	44.70	12,370
Jilin 吉林	1	11	338	175	3.51	8.65	27.09	59.47	4,991
Heilongjiang 黑龙江	4	298	12,782	-2,535	-6.58		13.74	133.18	38,510
Central-East 华东	111	116	28,961	1,903	7.24	18.03	74.50	59.84	26,284
Shanghai 上海	12	72	17,749	1,510	8.29	30.28	78.52	72.61	18,213
Jiangsu 江苏	44	111	27,890	1,224	4.50	14.40	76.09	68.73	27,186
Zhejiang 浙江	31	111	23,942	1,451	5.57	11.48	49.65	51.49	26,062
Anhui 安徽	2	38	17,285	452	3.46	5.16	44.75	32.83	13,046
Fujian 福建	2	41	18,990	6,313	21.28	49.16	337.23	56.72	29,670
Jiangxi 江西	1	216	22,054	6,275	10.37	14.09	17.96	26.42	60,522
Shandong 山东	19	173	49,354	3,922	13.58	28.88	95.07	53.00	28,889
Central-South 中南	36	221	22,815	625	1.85	4.83	23.65	61.79	33,850
Henan 河南	14	111	12,263	550	3.46	9.41	29.11	63.21	15,868
Hubei 湖北	4	210	13,404	371	2.99	5.12	18.96	41.53	12,391
Hunan 湖南	3	158	5,350	-197	-0.80	-100.34	12.48	99.20	24,445
Guangdong 广东	15	338	38,666	927	1.59	3.93	23.79	59.43	58,237
Guangxi 广西									
Hainan 海南									
Southwest 西南	6	421	132,310	10,665	6.80	19.68	95.58	65.46	156,943
Chongqing 重庆									
Sichuan 四川	5	453	156,844	13,657	8.05	22.63	105.90	64.42	169,594
Guizhou 贵州									
Yunnan 云南	1	260	9,643	-4,298	-4.59	-18.27	5.68	74.89	93,687
Tibet 西藏									
Northwest 西北	9	130	17,956	-204	-0.44	-0.71	53.20	37.66	46,052
Shaanxi 陕西	4	198	31,639	-1,270	-1.54	-2.32	56.77	33.95	82,690
Gansu 甘肃	4	78	6,048	-153	-0.91	-2.09	39.92	56.20	16,702
Qinghai 青海									
Ningxia 宁夏									
Xinjiang 新疆	1	65	10,856	3,857	22.83	36.22	73.48	36.98	16,897

4043: Insulated Products 绝缘制品业

Year 年份	Number of firms 企业个数	Rate of change 变化率 (%)	Number of employees 职工人数 (人)	Rate of change 变化率 (%)	Total revenue (Mil. RMB) 总销售收入 (百万元)	Rate of change 变化率 (%)	Total profit (Mil RMB) 总利润 (百万元)	Rate of change 变化率 (%)
2000	182		26,056		5,160		178	
2001	170	-6.59	23,722	-8.96	5,047	-2.19	195	9.55
2002	188	10.59	28,849	21.61	5,454	8.06	284	45.64

Major Products 主要产品	Output 产量	Unit 单位
Insulation Products 绝缘制品	325,045	Ton 吨

10 Main Firms with Maximal Revenue (year founded) 收入最大的十家主要企业（创办年份）	City 城市	Province 省	Telephone/fax 电话/传真	Number of employees 职工人数	Ownership 产业所有权	Revenue ('000 RMB) 销售收入 (千元)	Profit('000 RMB) (rank) 利润(千元) (排名)	Total assets ('000 RMB) 总资产 (千元)	Major products 主要产品
Sichuan Dongcai Enterprise Group Company	Mianyang	Sichuan	(0816)2282713		Joint Stock				Insulation Products
四川东材企业集团公司(1994)	绵阳市	四川省	(0816)2283860	1,619	股份制	400,638	20,975(3)	536,146	绝缘制品
Zigong Sediver Toughened Glass Insulator Co., Ltd.	Zigong	Sichuan	(0813)3302749		Foreign Funded				Toughened Glass Insulation
自贡塞迪维尔钢化玻璃绝缘子有限公司(1994)	自贡市	四川省	(0813)3302615	167	外商投资	272,052	31,280(1)	223,226	钢化玻璃绝缘子
Longkou Electrical Appliance Insulating Material Factory	Yantai	Shandong	(0535)8581236		Private Partnership				Insulation Tube
龙口市电器绝缘材料厂(1974)	烟台市	山东省	(0535)8581938	200	私营合伙	264,390	10,630(9)	13,290	绝缘管
International Laminated Material Co., Ltd.	Hangzhou	Zhejiang	(0571)63723641		Foreign Funded				FR－4 Copper Clad Board.
国际层压板材有限公司(1990)	杭州市	浙江省	(0571)63714407	175	外商投资	148,734	1,052(62)	157,573	FR－4覆铜板
Jingjiang Yahua Pressure Sensitiveglue Co., Ltd.	Taizhou	Jiangsu	(0523)4859452		Limited-Liability				Colour Fire-proof Adhesive Tape
靖江市亚华压敏胶有限公司(1991)	泰州市	江苏省	(0523)4815704	420	有限公司	146,300	14,560(5)	204,462	彩色阻燃胶带
Hangzhou Hongshen Electrical Apparatus Co., Ltd.	Hangzhou	Zhejiang	(0571)82699208		Limited-Liability				Insulation Material
杭州红申电器有限公司(1997)	杭州市	浙江省	(0571)82609578	477	有限公司	117,002	21,146(2)	132,584	绝缘材料
Jiantao (Fogang) Insulation Material Co., Ltd.	Qingyuan	Guangdong	(0763)4286941		Overseas Chinese-funded				Copper Clad Board Plywood Base Paper
建滔（佛冈）绝缘材料有限公司(1999)	清远市	广东省	(0763)4293558	94	港澳台资	113,649	5,430(17)	190,054	覆铜箔积层板基纸
Changzhou Electrical Insulation Main Works	Changzhou	Jiangsu	(0519)6601625		Limited-Liability				Polyester Pellicle
常州绝缘材料总厂(1958)	常州市	江苏省	(0519)6622333	365	有限公司	108,570	520(79)	108,360	聚酯薄膜
Zhucheng Sida Industry & Trade Co.,Ltd.	Weifang	Shandong	(0536)6213175		Joint Stock				Glass Cloth-Board
诸城市四达工贸股份有限公司(1993)	潍坊市	山东省	(0536)6111058	525	股份制	90,296	12,905(7)	83,320	玻璃布板
Shaanxi Shengyi Huadian Science & Technology Co.,Ltd.	Xianyang	Shannxi	(0910)3342318		Overseas Chinese-funded				Copper Clad Board
陕西生益华电科技有限公司(2000)	咸阳市	陕西省	(0910)3342328	446	港澳台资	89,641	-	246,552	履铜板

Top 10 Cities by Revenue 销售收入排名前10位城市	Province 省	Market share 市场份额 (%)	Number of firms 企业个数
Yantai 烟台市	Shandong 山东省	12.24	10
Mianyang 绵阳市	Sichuan 四川省	7.35	1
Zigong 自贡市	Sichuan 四川省	6.49	2
Hangzhou 杭州市	Zhejiang 浙江省	6.05	10
Wuxi 无锡市	Jiangsu 江苏省	4.55	8
Yangzhou 扬州市	Jiangsu 江苏省	4.28	5
Taizhou 泰州市	Jiangsu 江苏省	4.16	7
Shanghai 上海市	Shanghai 上海市	3.90	12
Suzhou 苏州市	Jiangsu 江苏省	3.70	5
Ningbo 宁波市	Zhejiang 浙江省	3.60	8

10 Major Wholesalers 十家主要批发商	City 城市	Province 省	Telephone/Fax 电话/传真
SU MEC	Nanjing	Jiangsu	(025)4511888
中设江苏机械设备进出口（集团）公司	南京市	江苏省	(025)4411772
China Poster Mobile Communications Equipment Co.,Ltd.	Beijing	Beijing	(010)66426993
中邮普泰移动通信设备股份有限公司	北京市	北京市	(010)66426837
Sino Kama Co., Ltd.	Shanghai	Shanghai	(021)62031188
中泰凯马股份有限公司	上海市	上海市	(021)62030851
China Huayuan Group Co.,Ltd.	Shanghai	Shanghai	(021)62031188
中国华源集团有限公司	上海市	上海市	(021)62032288
Zhejiang Crand Imp.& Exp.Co.,Ltd.	Ningbo	Zhejiang	(0574)87720170
浙江远大进出口有限公司	宁波市	浙江省	(0574)87723350
Shandong Machinery Import & Export Group Corporation	Qingdao	Shandong	(0532)2661628
山东省机械进出口集团公司	青岛市	山东省	(0532)2991655
Qingdao Haier International Trade Co.,Ltd.	Qingdao	Shandong	(0532)8938337
青岛海尔国际贸易有限公司	青岛市	山东省	(0532)8939494
Guangdong Machinery Import & Export Group Corporation	Guangzhou	Guangdong	(020)87782168
广东省机械进出口集团公司	广州市	广东省	(020)87771803
China National Machinery Equipment Import & Export Corporation	Beijing	Beijing	(010)63474506
中国机械设备进出口总公司	北京市	北京市	(010)63261865
Beijing Cellstar Co.,Ltd.	Beijing	Beijing	(010)64602050
北京蜂星事达电讯有限公司	北京市	北京市	(010)64672648

4045: Storage Batteries 蓄电池制造业

The industry accounts for 0.132% of the total revenue of China's industrial sector in 2002. The rate of return on assets is 5.26%. 80.07% of all firms in the industry made a profit while 19.93% had negative returns.The top province in terms of the industry's revenue is Guangdong, accounting for 27.57% of the total revenue.
2002年本行业收入占全行业的 0.132%，资产利润率为 5.26%。80.07%的企业赢利，19.93%的企业亏损。收入最高的省为广东省，占本行业的27.57%。

	Total number of firms 企业总数	Total number of employees 职工总数	Total revenue (Mil.RMB) 总销售收入(百万元)	Total profit (Mil.RMB) 总利润(百万元)	Return on assets 资产利润率(%)	Return on equity 权益利润率(%)	Labour productivity ('000 RMB/ worker) 劳动生产率(千元/人)	Debts/ assets 资产负债率(%)	Total assets (Mil.RMB) 总资产(百万元)
Industry Overall 行业总体	276	75,109	14,203	1,029	5.26	10.98	55.59	52.10	19,566

	Number of firms 企业个数	Average number of employees 平均职工人数	Average revenue ('000 RMB) 平均销售收入（千元)	Average profit ('000 RMB) 平均利润(千元)	Return on assets 资产利润率(%)	Return on equity 权益利润率(%)	Labour productivity ('000 RMB/ worker) 劳动生产率(千元/人)	Debts/ assets 资产负债率(%)	Average total assets ('000 RMB) 平均总资产(千元)
By ownership 产业所有权									
State-owned 国有	15	431	28,501	440	0.66	1.55	27.38	57.56	66,802
Collective-owned 集体	41	158	25,902	1,350	5.31	12.84	52.74	58.63	25,402
Foreign & Overseas Chinese Funded 三资	72	354	97,443	5,959	5.53	12.32	77.15	55.10	107,737
By regional distribution 地区分布									
Central-North 华北	39	276	52,389	1,626	1.42	3.89	32.83	63.37	114,239
Beijing 北京	1	85	13,491	51	1.13	1.84	37.51	38.31	4,495
Tianjin 天津	9	396	109,447	75	0.03	0.07	9.82	65.48	293,172
Hebei 河北	25	269	40,028	2,315	3.45	9.02	44.25	61.72	67,074
Shanxi 山西	3	52	6,433	413	4.13	11.12	56.67	62.85	9,986
Inner Mongolia 内蒙古	1	216	24,675	3,559	3.37	5.45	38.50	38.06	105,472
Northeast 东北	10	391	109,213	14,516	7.34	19.61	107.43	62.58	197,798
Liaoning 辽宁	6	453	92,039	7,056	3.46	11.76	84.64	70.60	204,070
Jilin 吉林	2	242	19,217	-1,465	-5.91	-92.05	19.63	93.58	24,771
Heilongjiang 黑龙江	2	353	250,731	52,879	15.02	28.05	255.47	46.44	352,012
Central-East 华东	115	219	50,422	4,248	8.66	17.81	80.60	51.39	49,052
Shanghai 上海	10	164	65,912	10,934	10.58	15.74	152.82	32.76	103,314
Jiangsu 江苏	31	172	51,122	4,606	9.22	21.52	104.96	57.17	49,965
Zhejiang 浙江	27	231	43,192	3,662	7.98	18.48	49.59	56.79	45,873
Anhui 安徽	9	143	15,753	613	4.23	21.30	41.70	80.15	14,509
Fujian 福建	14	373	50,324	868	1.74	3.28	42.65	47.02	49,881
Jiangxi 江西	5	84	12,589	50	0.46	1.24	64.34	63.03	10,949
Shandong 山东	19	270	77,850	6,292	12.76	27.63	119.74	53.81	49,297
Central-South 中南	98	325	50,396	3,354	4.68	8.09	37.61	42.08	71,612
Henan 河南	9	395	25,124	-800	-2.06	-7.41	13.93	72.23	38,868
Hubei 湖北	15	230	39,956	3,129	4.91	11.54	76.70	57.45	63,720
Hunan 湖南	11	211	13,435	202	0.80	4.00	23.42	80.04	25,259
Guangdong 广东	61	361	64,184	4,699	5.36	8.26	37.05	35.05	87,641
Guangxi 广西	2	270	25,178	45	0.10	0.27	27.41	62.41	44,220
Hainan 海南									
Southwest 西南	14	239	23,634	224	0.66	1.63	51.08	59.34	33,826
Chongqing 重庆	4	285	35,590	167	0.31	0.70	42.58	55.59	53,640
Sichuan 四川	9	182	15,241	-10	-0.05	-0.19	26.61	74.85	19,764
Guizhou 贵州	1	568	51,348	2,556	3.15	4.87	138.72	35.25	81,119
Yunnan 云南									
Tibet 西藏									
Northwest 西北									
Shaanxi 陕西									
Gansu 甘肃									
Qinghai 青海									
Ningxia 宁夏									
Xinjiang 新疆									

4045: Storage Batteries 蓄电池制造业

Year 年份	Number of firms 企业个数	Rate of change 变化率 (%)	Number of employees 职工人数 (人)	Rate of change 变化率 (%)	Total revenue (Mil. RMB) 总销售收入 (百万元)	Rate of change 变化率 (%)	Total profit (Mil RMB) 总利润 (百万元)	Rate of change 变化率 (%)
2000	239		78,189		10,366		841	
2001	266	11.30	73,295	-6.26	11,549	11.41	761	-9.51
2002	276	3.76	75,109	2.47	14,203	22.98	1,029	35.22

Major Products 主要产品	Output 产量	Unit 单位
Accumulator 蓄电池	3,222	10,000 Kilovolt-ampere-hou 万千伏安时

10 Main Firms with Maximal Revenue (year founded) 收入最大的十家主要企业（创办年份）	City 城市	Province 省	Telephone/fax 电话/传真	Number of employees 职工人数	Ownership 产业所有权	Revenue ('000 RMB) 销售收入(千元)	Profit('000 RMB) (rank) 利润(千元)(排名)	Total assets ('000 RMB) 总资产(千元)	Major products 主要产品
Shenzhen BYD Co., Ltd.	Shenzhen	Guangdong	(0755)84218888		Limited-Liability				NI-Cd Battery
深圳市比亚迪实业有限公司(1995)	深圳市	广东省	(0755)84202222	9,800	有限公司	1,101,753	255,180(1)	2,565,907	镍镉电池
Weihai Wenlong Battery Co.,Ltd.	Weihai	Shandong	(0631)8846898		Foreign Funded				Battery
威海文隆电池有限公司(1991)	威海市	山东省	(0631)8842068	306	外商投资	816,160	74,300(4)	118,886	电池
Guangyu Storage Battery Co.,Ltd.	Harbin	Heilongjiang	(0451)6677970		Joint Stock				Lead-acid Battery铅
光宇蓄电池有限公司(1997)	哈尔滨市	黑龙江省	(0451)6678032	536	股份制	493,205	105,795(2)	697,491	酸蓄电池
Jiangsu Longyuan Shuangdeng Power Supply Co., Ltd.	Taizhou	Jiangsu	(0523)8529866		Overseas Chinese-funded				Storage Battery
江苏隆源双登电源有限公司(1999)	泰州市	江苏省	(0523)8521244	825	港澳台资	410,311	57,983(5)	494,158	蓄电池
Tianjin Tongyee Industurial Co.,Ltd.	Tianjin	Tianjin	(022)25325681		Overseas Chinese-funded				Storage Battery
天津统一工业有限公司(1994)	天津市	天津市	(022)25324523	961	港澳台资	408,041	3,701(40)	603,165	蓄电池
Shenyang Pananisonic Storage Battery Co.,Ltd.	Shenyang	Liaoning	(024)25818921		Foreign Funded				Airproof（Lead-acid）Battery密封(铅酸)
沈阳松下蓄电池有限公司(1994)	沈阳市	辽宁省	(024)25818910	1,386	外商投资	335,938	36,789(7)	352,639	蓄电池
Guangdong Panyu Hengda Storage Battery General Plant	Guangzhou	Guangdong	(020)84868024		Collective-owned				Storage Battery
广东省番禺恒达蓄电池总厂(1988)	广州市	广东省	(020)84863889	288	集体企业	238,010	10,084(20)	212,934	蓄田池
Tianjin Lan-Tian Sanyo Energy Co.,Ltd.	Tianjin	Tianjin	(022)83710596		Foreign Funded				Nickel-metal Hydride Battery
天津蓝天三祥电源有限公司(1999)	天津市	天津市	(022)83710371	593	外商投资	234,756	10,490(18)	350,161	镍氢电池
Hangzhou Narada Battery Co., Ltd.	Hangzhou	Zhejiang	(0571)85123388		Foreign Funded				Lead-acid Battery铅
杭州南都电源集团有限公司(1994)	杭州市	浙江省	(0571)85128965	396	外商投资	223,766	13,516(17)	307,769	酸蓄电池
BB Battery Co., Ltd.	Chaozhou	Guangdong	(0768)7601001		Overseas Chinese-funded				Lead-acid Battery铅
美美电池有限公司(1995)	潮州市	广东省	(0768)7601469	1,297	港澳台资	182,919	4,133(34)	159,747	酸蓄电池

Top 10 Cities by Revenue 销售收入排名前10位城市	Province 省	Market share 市场份额 (%)	Number of firms 企业个数
Shenzhen 深圳市	Guangdong 广东省	9.85	6
Tianjin 天津市	Tianjin 天津市	6.94	9
Weihai 威海市	Shandong 山东省	5.75	1
Zhuhai 珠海市	Guangdong 广东省	5.64	7
Shanghai 上海市	Shanghai 上海市	4.64	10
Baoding 保定市	Hebei 河北省	4.63	7
Quanzhou 泉州市	Fujian 福建省	3.94	8
Hangzhou 杭州市	Zhejiang 浙江省	3.75	8
Guangzhou 广州市	Guangdong 广东省	3.73	12
Shenyang 沈阳市	Liaoning 辽宁省	3.57	4

10 Major Wholesalers 十家主要批发商	City 城市	Province 省	Telephone/Fax 电话/传真
SU MEC	Nanjing	Jiangsu	(025)4511888
中设江苏机械设备进出口（集团）公司	南京市	江苏省	(025)4411772
China Poster Mobile Communications Equipment Co.,Ltd.	Beijing	Beijing	(010)66426993
中邮普泰移动通信设备股份有限公司	北京市	北京市	(010)66426837
Sino Kama Co., Ltd.	Shanghai	Shanghai	(021)62031188
中泰凯马股份有限公司	上海市	上海市	(021)62030851
China Huayuan Group Co.,Ltd.	Shanghai	Shanghai	(021)62031188
中国华源集团有限公司	上海市	上海市	(021)62032288
Zhejiang Crand Imp.& Exp.Co.,Ltd.	Ningbo	Zhejiang	(0574)87720170
浙江远大进出口有限公司	宁波市	浙江省	(0574)87723350
Shandong Machinery Import & Export Group Corporation	Qingdao	Shandong	(0532)2661628
山东省机械进出口集团公司	青岛市	山东省	(0532)2991655
Qingdao Haier International Trade Co.,Ltd.	Qingdao	Shandong	(0532)8938337
青岛海尔国际贸易有限公司	青岛市	山东省	(0532)8939494
Guangdong Machinery Import & Export Group Corporation	Guangzhou	Guangdong	(020)87782168
广东省机械进出口集团公司	广州市	广东省	(020)87771803
China National Machinery Equipment Import & Export Corporation	Beijing	Beijing	(010)63474506
中国机械设备进出口总公司	北京市	北京市	(010)63261865
Beijing Cellstar Co.,Ltd.	Beijing	Beijing	(010)64602050
北京蜂星事达电讯有限公司	北京市	北京市	(010)64672648

4046: Dry Cells 干电池制造业

The industry accounts for 0.111% of the total revenue of China's industrial sector in 2002. The rate of return on assets is 6.07%. 79.41% of all firms in the industry made a profit while 20.59% had negative returns.The top province in terms of the industry's revenue is Guangdong, accounting for 48.26% of the total revenue.
2002年本行业收入占全行业的 0.111%，资产利润率为 6.07%。79.41%的企业赢利，20.59%的企业亏损。收入最高的省为广东省，占本行业的48.26%。

	Total number of firms 企业总数	Total number of employees 职工总数	Total revenue (Mil.RMB) 总销售收入(百万元)	Total profit (Mil.RMB) 总利润(百万元)	Return on assets 资产利润率(%)	Return on equity 权益利润率(%)	Labour productivity ('000 RMB/worker) 劳动生产率(千元/人)	Debts/assets 资产负债率(%)	Total assets (Mil.RMB) 总资产(百万元)
Industry Overall 行业总体	170	66,065	11,861	756	6.07	15.48	49.75	60.79	12,449

	Number of firms 企业个数	Average number of employees 平均职工人数	Average revenue ('000 RMB) 平均销售收入（千元）	Average profit ('000 RMB) 平均利润（千元）	Return on assets 资产利润率(%)	Return on equity 权益利润率(%)	Labour productivity ('000 RMB/worker) 劳动生产率(千元/人)	Debts/assets 资产负债率(%)	Average total assets ('000 RMB) 平均总资产（千元）
By ownership 产业所有权									
State-owned 国有	20	632	23,123	-939	-1.52	-13.98	11.16	89.16	61,971
Collective-owned 集体	15	174	26,139	593	1.97	5.41	45.64	63.48	30,025
Foreign & Overseas Chinese Funded 三资	47	409	126,756	12,082	10.09	18.77	95.20	46.23	119,729
By regional distribution 地区分布									
Central-North 华北	9	348	73,705	8,319	8.05	23.87	51.18	66.27	103,337
Beijing 北京									
Tianjin 天津	4	319	129,032	18,856	14.65	29.30	104.36	50.00	128,683
Hebei 河北	4	465	36,806	-139	-0.14	-1.04	14.70	86.89	101,931
Shanxi 山西	1	1						62.77	7,580
Inner Mongolia 内蒙古									
Northeast 东北	2	153	44,200	12,000	14.98	34.87	122.71	57.05	80,121
Liaoning 辽宁	1	67						270.05	4,594
Jilin 吉林									
Heilongjiang 黑龙江	1	239	88,400	24,000	15.42	31.31	157.11	50.76	155,647
Central-East 华东	70	309	62,017	6,775	10.48	21.19	65.34	50.53	64,627
Shanghai 上海	24	257	54,211	3,306	5.97	13.23	59.93	54.89	55,393
Jiangsu 江苏	12	173	19,259	149	1.02	5.05	27.80	79.86	14,613
Zhejiang 浙江	21	249	55,666	7,474	13.20	30.36	75.56	56.52	56,615
Anhui 安徽	3	160	1,391	-745	-3.86	-35.21	2.42	89.04	19,311
Fujian 福建	3	1,318	375,623	74,465	14.82	21.80	111.98	32.03	502,471
Jiangxi 江西	1	321	21,074				13.22	90.44	5,845
Shandong 山东	6	562	81,319	2,499	5.79	27.49	41.80	78.95	43,166
Central-South 中南	79	412	79,768	2,318	3.16	9.32	46.76	66.11	73,371
Henan 河南	2	3,395	61,337	-8,638	-3.67	-127.77	3.08	97.13	235,361
Hubei 湖北	4	142	28,664	3,659	3.83	11.97	82.13	67.99	95,529
Hunan 湖南	5	225	17,284	-113	-0.20	-0.64	18.20	68.92	56,927
Guangdong 广东	63	340	90,849	2,884	4.12	11.03	63.59	62.66	70,029
Guangxi 广西	4	631	62,940	1,200	1.98	5.19	28.29	61.89	60,602
Hainan 海南	1	127	2,670	-153	-3.32	-37.23	4.55	91.07	4,605
Southwest 西南	8	990	56,222	114	0.09	0.33	18.65	71.60	123,873
Chongqing 重庆	2	1,597	110,807	6,720	4.03	9.69	20.34	58.47	166,924
Sichuan 四川	2	607	32,872	-4,307	-2.25	-23.86	13.21	90.59	191,708
Guizhou 贵州	1	1,358	55,050	1,066	1.06	2.06	19.05	48.65	100,707
Yunnan 云南	3	718	35,789	-1,659	-2.88	-9.05	18.97	68.22	57,671
Tibet 西藏									
Northwest 西北	2	264	8,114	-800	-3.37	-10.81	11.04	68.81	23,707
Shaanxi 陕西									
Gansu 甘肃									
Qinghai 青海									
Ningxia 宁夏									
Xinjiang 新疆	2	264	8,114	-800	-3.37	-10.81	11.04	68.81	23,707

Year 年份	Number of firms 企业个数	Rate of change 变化率 (%)	Number of employees 职工人数 (人)	Rate of change 变化率 (%)	Total revenue (Mil. RMB) 总销售收入 (百万元)	Rate of change 变化率 (%)	Total profit (Mil RMB) 总利润 (百万元)	Rate of change 变化率 (%)
2000	156		66,825		9,306		388	
2001	177	13.46	76,574	14.59	11,626	24.93	478	23.20
2002	170	-3.95	66,065	-13.72	11,861	2.02	756	58.16

Major Products 主要产品	Output 产量	Unit 单位
Dry Battery(Converting into No.1 Battery) 干电池（折一号电池）	187	100,000,000 Units 亿只

10 Main Firms with Maximal Revenue (year founded) 收入最大的十家主要企业（创办年份）	City 城市	Province 省	Telephone/fax 电话/传真	Number of employees 职工人数	Ownership 产业所有权	Revenue ('000 RMB) 销售收入 (千元)	Profit('000 RMB) (rank) 利润(千元) (排名)	Total assets ('000 RMB) 总资产 (千元)	Major products 主要产品
Guangzhou Tigerhead Battery Group Co., Ltd.	Guangzhou	Guangdong	(020)85525623		Limited-Liability				Battery
广州市虎头电池集团有限公司(2000)	广州市	广东省	(020)85524224	2,410	有限公司	1,259,145	12,360(16)	666,789	电池
Fujian Nanping Nanfu Battery Co., Ltd.	Nanping	Fujian	(0599)8710716		Overseas Chinese-funded				Battery
南平南孚电池有限公司(1988)	南平市	福建省	(0599)8735117	1,163	港澳台资	717,513	185,759(1)	881,665	电池
Shenzhen Sanyang Huaqiang Energy Co.,Ltd.	Shenzhen	Guangdong	(0755)84193063		Overseas Chinese-funded				Charging Battery
深圳三洋华强能源有限公司(1995)	深圳市	广东省	(0755)84192460	1,080	港澳台资	535,867	6,572(29)	202,382	充电电池
Zhongyin (Ningbo) Battery & Electrical Appaliance Co.,Ltd.	Ningbo	Zhejiang	(0574)87491115		Overseas Chinese-funded				Battery
中银（宁波）电池有限公司(1993)	宁波市	浙江省	(0574)87462372	916	港澳台资	414,149	74,338(2)	389,530	电池
Xiamen Three Circles Co., Ltd.	Xiamen	Fujian	(0592)2215959		State Enterprises				Battery
厦门三圈日化有限公司(1996)	厦门市	福建省	(0592)2221193	2,609	国有独资	379,652	35,222(5)	614,358	电池
Duracell (China) Co.,Ltd.Dongguan Factory	Dongguan	Guangdong	(0769)2403615		Foreign Funded				Battery
金霸王(中国)有限公司东莞工厂(1994)	东莞市	广东省	(0769)2403614	313	外商投资	378,783	49,996(4)	639,793	电池
Huizhou Desay Energy Science & Technology Co.,Ltd.	Huizhou	Guangdong	(0752)2382998		Overseas Chinese-funded				Alkali Manganese Battery
惠州市德赛能源科技有限公司(1999)	惠州市	广东省	(0752)2286936	515	港澳台资	302,158	4,018(36)	181,149	碱锰电池
Linyi Huatai Battery Co.,Ltd.	Linyi	Shandong	(0539)8710999		Overseas Chinese-funded				Dry battery
临沂市华太电池有限公司(1993)	临沂市	山东省	(0539)8711237	1,106	港澳台资	271,155	7,985(25)	65,732	干电池
Huizhou Power Pack Battery Co.,Ltd.	Huizhou	Guangdong	(0752)2292383		Overseas Chinese-funded				Battery
惠州市超霸电池有限公司(1993)	惠州市	广东省	(0752)2291043	1,323	港澳台资	264,090	30,889(7)	110,050	电池
ShangHai Baixiang Tian'e Battery Co.Ltd.	Shanghai	Shanghai	(021)63012665		Limited-Liability				Battery
上海白象天鹅电池有限公司(1999)	上海市	上海市	(021)63010814	870	有限公司	236,951	8,133(23)	137,480	电池

Top 10 Cities by Revenue 销售收入排名前10位城市	Province 省	Market share 市场份额 (%)	Number of firms 企业个数
Guangzhou 广州市	Guangdong 广东省	14.39	17
Huizhou 惠州市	Guangdong 广东省	11.47	11
Shanghai 上海市	Shanghai 上海市	10.97	24
Dongguan 东莞市	Guangdong 广东省	7.58	7
Ningbo 宁波市	Zhejiang 浙江省	7.15	10
Nanping 南平市	Fujian 福建省	6.05	1
Shenzhen 深圳市	Guangdong 广东省	4.71	3
Tianjin 天津市	Tianjin 天津市	4.35	4
Linyi 临沂市	Shandong 山东省	3.40	3
Xiamen 厦门市	Fujian 福建省	3.20	1

10 Major Wholesalers 十家主要批发商	City 城市	Province 省	Telephone/Fax 电话/传真
SU MEC	Nanjing	Jiangsu	(025)4511888
中设江苏机械设备进出口（集团）公司	南京市	江苏省	(025)4411772
China Poster Mobile Communications Equipment Co.,Ltd.	Beijing	Beijing	(010)66426993
中邮普泰移动通信设备股份有限公司	北京市	北京市	(010)66426837
Sino Kama Co., Ltd.	Shanghai	Shanghai	(021)62031188
中泰凯马股份有限公司	上海市	上海市	(021)62030851
China Huayuan Group Co.,Ltd.	Shanghai	Shanghai	(021)62031188
中国华源集团有限公司	上海市	上海市	(021)62032288
Zhejiang Crand Imp.& Exp.Co.,Ltd.	Ningbo	Zhejiang	(0574)87720170
浙江远大进出口有限公司	宁波市	浙江省	(0574)87723350
Shandong Machinery Import & Export Group Corporation	Qingdao	Shandong	(0532)2661628
山东省机械进出口集团公司	青岛市	山东省	(0532)2991655
Qingdao Haier International Trade Co.,Ltd.	Qingdao	Shandong	(0532)8938337
青岛海尔国际贸易有限公司	青岛市	山东省	(0532)8939494
Guangdong Machinery Import & Export Group Corporation	Guangzhou	Guangdong	(020)87782168
广东省机械进出口集团公司	广州市	广东省	(020)87771803
China National Machinery Equipment Import & Export Corporation	Beijing	Beijing	(010)63474506
中国机械设备进出口总公司	北京市	北京市	(010)63261865
Beijing Cellstar Co.,Ltd.	Beijing	Beijing	(010)64602050
北京蜂星事达电讯有限公司	北京市	北京市	(010)64672648

4049: Other Electric Engineering Equipment 其他电工器材制造业

The industry accounts for 0.101% of the total revenue of China's industrial sector in 2002. The rate of return on assets is 6.95%. 86.38% of all firms in the industry made a profit while 13.62% had negative returns.The top province in terms of the industry's revenue is Guangdong, accounting for 33.34% of the total revenue.
2002年本行业收入占全行业的 0.101%，资产利润率为 6.95%。86.38%的企业赢利，13.62%的企业亏损。收入最高的省为广东省，占本行业的33.34%。

	Total number of firms 企业总数	Total number of employees 职工总数	Total revenue (Mil.RMB) 总销售收入 (百万元)	Total profit (Mil.RMB) 总利润 (百万元)	Return on assets 资产利润率 (%)	Return on equity 权益利润率 (%)	Labour productivity ('000 RMB/ worker) 劳动生产率 (千元/人)	Debts/ assets 资产负债率 (%)	Total assets (Mil.RMB) 总资产 (百万元)
Industry Overall 行业总体	257	48,651	10,843	655	6.95	15.55	58.93	55.29	9,429

	Number of firms 企业个数	Average number of employees 平均职工人数	Average revenue ('000 RMB) 平均销售收入 (千元)	Average profit ('000 RMB) 平均利润 (千元)	Return on assets 资产利润率 (%)	Return on equity 权益利润率 (%)	Labour productivity ('000 RMB/ worker) 劳动生产率 (千元/人)	Debts/ assets 资产负债率 (%)	Average total assets ('000 RMB) 平均总资产 (千元)
By ownership 产业所有权									
State-owned 国有	19	167	26,493	44	0.13	0.51	46.55	74.32	33,414
Collective-owned 集体	38	146	28,307	1,292	8.73	21.55	53.91	59.50	14,803
Foreign & Overseas Chinese Funded 三资	54	424	104,874	8,282	8.96	18.78	59.75	52.29	92,433
By regional distribution 地区分布									
Central-North 华北	18	128	45,578	1,189	3.34	6.09	78.82	45.19	35,614
Beijing 北京	4	298	103,183	714	0.60	1.07	50.61	44.07	118,847
Tianjin 天津	6	33	9,701	-255	-2.95	-12.02	65.16	75.43	8,617
Hebei 河北	7	110	49,189	2,873	19.46	28.29	137.53	31.22	14,762
Shanxi 山西	1	139	5,140	-35	-0.33	-2.11	13.45	84.38	10,624
Inner Mongolia 内蒙古									
Northeast 东北	23	93	16,073	-79	-0.48	-1.36	61.92	64.56	16,514
Liaoning 辽宁	14	90	16,037	898	5.50	12.14	66.76	54.71	16,332
Jilin 吉林	3	31	2,193	4	0.15	1.43	29.48	89.22	2,813
Heilongjiang 黑龙江	6	128	23,098	-2,402	-10.10	-47.79	57.93	78.88	23,790
Central-East 华东	145	184	38,157	2,030	6.25	15.39	50.53	59.42	32,501
Shanghai 上海	23	103	43,420	2,681	5.68	12.45	77.62	54.37	47,177
Jiangsu 江苏	55	186	37,453	1,165	3.75	10.04	48.53	62.60	31,037
Zhejiang 浙江	45	208	35,810	2,226	8.27	22.87	40.09	63.83	26,905
Anhui 安徽	1	85	19,323	232	2.07	22.57	28.16	90.84	11,218
Fujian 福建	6	219	57,221	4,535	14.54	39.25	113.50	62.95	31,191
Jiangxi 江西	2	41	3,919	26	0.55	1.90	25.31	71.37	4,677
Shandong 山东	13	255	37,866	3,156	8.17	15.31	43.09	46.63	38,619
Central-South 中南	61	269	65,562	5,597	9.63	19.01	71.02	49.36	58,149
Henan 河南	8	51	32,201	1,797	14.15	48.55	171.57	70.86	12,704
Hubei 湖北	4	96	14,586	255	1.37	2.45	100.30	44.10	18,642
Hunan 湖南	3	203	20,515	1,499	5.29	15.65	31.30	66.17	28,316
Guangdong 广东	45	329	80,333	7,150	9.82	18.95	69.81	48.16	72,800
Guangxi 广西	1	184	6,825	-221	-2.23		15.06	120.27	9,929
Hainan 海南									
Southwest 西南	5	129	8,933	316	4.95	11.28	15.53	56.16	6,389
Chongqing 重庆									
Sichuan 四川	5	129	8,933	316	4.95	11.28	15.53	56.16	6,389
Guizhou 贵州									
Yunnan 云南									
Tibet 西藏									
Northwest 西北	5	92	15,134	-320	-1.37	-22.88	63.79	94.01	23,378
Shaanxi 陕西	4	99	18,917	-401	-1.37	-22.83	72.37	93.99	29,208
Gansu 甘肃	1	65					11.63	125.45	55
Qinghai 青海									
Ningxia 宁夏									
Xinjiang 新疆									

Year 年份	Number of firms 企业个数	Rate of change 变化率 (%)	Number of employees 职工人数 (人)	Rate of change 变化率 (%)	Total revenue (Mil. RMB) 总销售收入 (百万元)	Rate of change 变化率 (%)	Total profit (Mil RMB) 总利润 (百万元)	Rate of change 变化率 (%)
2000	227		38,715		9,748		358	
2001	247	8.81	45,782	18.25	8,609	-11.68	474	32.40
2002	257	4.05	48,651	6.27	10,843	25.95	655	38.19

Major Products 主要产品	Output 产量	Unit 单位

10 Main Firms with Maximal Revenue (year founded) 收入最大的十家主要企业（创办年份）	City 城市	Province 省	Telephone/fax 电话/传真	Number of employees 职工人数	Ownership 产业所有权	Revenue ('000 RMB) 销售收入 (千元)	Profit('000 RMB) (rank) 利润(千元) (排名)	Total assets ('000 RMB) 总资产 (千元)	Major products 主要产品
Tyco Electronics NTP Guangdong Co.,Ltd.	Foshan	Guangdong	(0765)8381368		Foreign Funded				Electronic Equipment Connector
顺德泰科电子有限公司(1995)	佛山市	广东省	(0765)8381456	1,961	外商投资	785,962	207,844(1)	570,864	电器连接器
Shanghai Xingtehao Industury Co.,Ltd.	Shanghai	Shanghai	(021)64063051		Overseas Chinese-funded				Electric Tool
上海星特浩企业有限公司(1996)	上海市	上海市	(021)64063257	525	港澳台资	373,906	34,668(3)	668,082	电动工具
Sanyo Energy (Beijing) Co., Ltd.	Beijing	Beijing	(010)67873434		Foreign Funded				Lithium-ion Cell
三洋能源（北京）有限公司(2000)	北京市	北京市	(010)67873438	847	外商投资	373,283	-	391,794	锂离子电池
Clipsal Electric (Huizhou) Industry Co.,Ltd.	Huizhou	Guangdong	(0752)2227555		Overseas Chinese-funded				Lighting Switch
奇胜电器（惠州）工业有限公司(1987)	惠州市	广东省	(0752)2224294	1,109	港澳台资	363,340	-	328,715	照明开关
Cixi HongYi Electric Co., Ltd.	Ningbo	Zhejiang	(0574)63668266		Overseas Chinese-funded				European Style Socket
慈溪宏一电子有限公司(1994)	宁波市	浙江省	(0574)63668745	1,268	港澳台资	356,894	36,249(2)	148,575	欧式插座
TCL International Electric (Huizhou) Co., Ltd.	Huizhou	Guangdong	(0752)2529999		Overseas Chinese-funded				Electric Switch
ＴＣＬ国际电工(惠州)有限公司(1993)	惠州市	广东省	(0752)2288000	2,460	港澳台资	319,574	25,000(5)	177,402	电器开关
Scud (Fujian)Electronics Co., Ltd.	Fuzhou	Fujian	(0591)3997550		Overseas Chinese-funded				Battery
飞毛腿(福建)电子有限公司(1998)	福州市	福建省	(0591)3989999	983	港澳台资	289,655	24,186(6)	144,859	电池
Suzhou Industrial Park Kingyou Metal Products Co.,Ltd.	Suzhou	Jiangsu	(0512)62710288		Private Owned				Silicon Steel Plate
苏州工业园区金月金属制品有限公司(1997)	苏州市	江苏省	(0512)62710988	31	私营企业	263,089	5,579(21)	128,104	矽钢片
Ningbo Kaifeng Electric Co.,Ltd.	Ningbo	Zhejiang	(0574)63653730		Foreign Funded				Electrical Source Connector
宁波凯峰电器有限公司(1997)	宁波市	浙江省	(0574)63668899	1,739	外商投资	240,490	12,779(12)	166,852	电源连接器
Zhuhai Yuancheng Electronics Co., Ltd.	Zhuhai	Guangdong	(0756)8897254		Foreign Funded				Stabilized Voltage Power Supply Board
珠海缘成电子有限公司(1995)	珠海市	广东省	(0756)88975605	946	外商投资	235,630	2,752(43)	57,579	稳压电源板

Top 10 Cities by Revenue 销售收入排名前10位城市	Province 省	Market share 市场份额 (%)	Number of firms 企业个数
Foshan 佛山市	Guangdong 广东省	12.00	10
Ningbo 宁波市	Zhejiang 浙江省	9.86	20
Shanghai 上海市	Shanghai 上海市	9.21	23
Huizhou 惠州市	Guangdong 广东省	9.16	5
Suzhou 苏州市	Jiangsu 江苏省	7.27	13
Yangzhou 扬州市	Jiangsu 江苏省	5.71	14
Guangzhou 广州市	Guangdong 广东省	3.97	10
Beijing 北京市	Beijing 北京市	3.81	4
Hangzhou 杭州市	Zhejiang 浙江省	3.43	17
Fuzhou 福州市	Fujian 福建省	3.06	4

10 Major Wholesalers 十家主要批发商	City 城市	Province 省	Telephone/Fax 电话/传真
SU MEC	Nanjing	Jiangsu	(025)4511888
中设江苏机械设备进出口（集团）公司	南京市	江苏省	(025)4411772
China Poster Mobile Communications Equipment Co.,Ltd.	Beijing	Beijing	(010)66426993
中邮普泰移动通信设备股份有限公司	北京市	北京市	(010)66426837
Sino Kama Co., Ltd.	Shanghai	Shanghai	(021)62031188
中泰凯马股份有限公司	上海市	上海市	(021)62030851
China Huayuan Group Co.,Ltd.	Shanghai	Shanghai	(021)62031188
中国华源集团有限公司	上海市	上海市	(021)62032288
Zhejiang Crand Imp.& Exp.Co.,Ltd.	Ningbo	Zhejiang	(0574)87720170
浙江远大进出口有限公司	宁波市	浙江省	(0574)87723350
Shandong Machinery Import & Export Group Corporation	Qingdao	Shandong	(0532)2661628
山东省机械进出口集团公司	青岛市	山东省	(0532)2991655
Qingdao Haier International Trade Co.,Ltd.	Qingdao	Shandong	(0532)8938337
青岛海尔国际贸易有限公司	青岛市	山东省	(0532)8939494
Guangdong Machinery Import & Export Group Corporation	Guangzhou	Guangdong	(020)87782168
广东省机械进出口集团公司	广州市	广东省	(020)87771803
China National Machinery Equipment Import & Export Corporation	Beijing	Beijing	(010)63474506
中国机械设备进出口总公司	北京市	北京市	(010)63261865
Beijing Cellstar Co.,Ltd.	Beijing	Beijing	(010)64602050
北京蜂星事达电讯有限公司	北京市	北京市	(010)64672648

4061: Washing Machines 洗衣机制造业

The industry accounts for 0.135% of the total revenue of China's industrial sector in 2002. The rate of return on assets is -0.26%. 75.51% of all firms in the industry made a profit while 24.49% had negative returns.The top province in terms of the industry's revenue is Jiangsu, accounting for 37.95% of the total revenue.
2002年本行业收入占全行业的 0.135%，资产利润率为 -0.26%。75.51%的企业赢利，24.49%的企业亏损。收入最高的省为江苏省，占本行业的37.95%。

	Total number of firms 企业总数	Total number of employees 职工总数	Total revenue (Mil.RMB) 总销售收入（百万元）	Total profit (Mil.RMB) 总利润（百万元）	Return on assets 资产利润率 (%)	Return on equity 权益利润率 (%)	Labour productivity ('000 RMB/ worker) 劳动生产率（千元/人）	Debts/ assets 资产负债率 (%)	Total assets (Mil.RMB) 总资产（百万元）
Industry Overall 行业总体	98	44,581	14,511	-53	-0.26	-0.67	73.55	61.23	20,390

	Number of firms 企业个数	Average number of employees 平均职工人数	Average revenue ('000 RMB) 平均销售收入（千元）	Average profit ('000 RMB) 平均利润（千元）	Return on assets 资产利润率 (%)	Return on equity 权益利润率 (%)	Labour productivity ('000 RMB/ worker) 劳动生产率（千元/人）	Debts/ assets 资产负债率 (%)	Average total assets ('000 RMB) 平均总资产（千元）
By ownership 产业所有权									
State-owned 国有	6	1,329	737,442	3,466	0.35	0.71	128.10	50.46	990,722
Collective-owned 集体	8	346	42,249	1,329	1.76	11.19	36.89	84.23	75,322
Foreign & Overseas Chinese Funded 三资	16	768	305,050	3,384	0.83	1.91	99.01	56.66	409,018
By regional distribution 地区分布									
Central-North 华北	5	515	18,048	-6,660	-4.08	-17.48	6.93	76.69	163,430
Beijing 北京	1	694	38,249	303	0.08	0.33	5.08	76.47	389,744
Tianjin 天津	2	110	3,151	-14,746	-19.68	-3,237.32	-13.81	99.39	74,942
Hebei 河北	1	751	29,810	1,229	1.35	2.28	14.61	40.84	91,021
Shanxi 山西	1	912	15,879	-5,340	-2.86	-12.14	6.98	76.42	186,500
Inner Mongolia 内蒙古									
Northeast 东北	2	746	50,064	-9,355	-6.07	-40.65	29.94	85.05	153,993
Liaoning 辽宁	1	1,132	23,539	-12,864	-11.36		16.33	106.71	113,244
Jilin 吉林	1	360	76,589	-5,846	-3.00	-10.90	72.73	72.46	194,742
Heilongjiang 黑龙江									
Central-East 华东	65	493	178,926	-232	-0.09	-0.22	84.30	59.05	257,762
Shanghai 上海	5	167	79,819	-12,626	-10.46		9.51	125.79	120,720
Jiangsu 江苏	14	731	393,297	5,758	1.22	2.45	118.52	50.12	471,119
Zhejiang 浙江	40	227	65,612	3,402	4.76	10.54	69.89	54.88	71,512
Anhui 安徽	3	1,762	572,754	13,828	1.31	2.58	125.17	49.13	1,052,602
Fujian 福建									
Jiangxi 江西									
Shandong 山东	3	2,206	460,723	-70,041	-5.94	-25.31	27.97	76.53	1,178,990
Central-South 中南	24	323	108,621	956	1.03	2.81	65.47	63.34	92,829
Henan 河南	2	61	13,900	503	3.41	6.21	75.72	45.06	14,752
Hubei 湖北	5	360	71,574	1,056	1.27	7.07	33.40	82.06	83,308
Hunan 湖南	1	110	4,235				194.09	153.42	13,571
Guangdong 广东	14	399	156,789	1,051	0.86	2.05	71.58	58.31	122,806
Guangxi 广西	2	68	10,977	967	3.95	11.90	125.12	66.81	24,494
Hainan 海南									
Southwest 西南	2	360	41,709	-4,559	-3.22		10.41	103.22	141,409
Chongqing 重庆	1	650	83,418	-8,071	-4.27	-10.81	12.22	60.45	188,815
Sichuan 四川									
Guizhou 贵州	1	70		-1,046	-1.11		-6.43	189.14	94,002
Yunnan 云南									
Tibet 西藏									
Northwest 西北									
Shaanxi 陕西									
Gansu 甘肃									
Qinghai 青海									
Ningxia 宁夏									
Xinjiang 新疆									

4061: Washing Machines 洗衣机制造业

Year 年份	Number of firms 企业个数	Rate of change 变化率 (%)	Number of employees 职工人数 (人)	Rate of change 变化率 (%)	Total revenue (Mil. RMB) 总销售收入 (百万元)	Rate of change 变化率 (%)	Total profit (Mil RMB) 总利润 (百万元)	Rate of change 变化率 (%)
2000	76		42,567		13,265		333	
2001	97	27.63	41,536	-2.42	12,261	-7.57	131	-60.66
2002	98	1.03	44,581	7.33	14,511	18.35	-53	-

Major Products 主要产品	Output 产量	Unit 单位
Household Washing Machine 家用洗衣机	1,587	10,000 Units 万台

10 Main Firms with Maximal Revenue (year founded) 收入最大的十家主要企业（创办年份）	City 城市	Province 省	Telephone/fax 电话/传真	Number of employees 职工人数	Ownership 产业所有权	Revenue ('000 RMB) 销售收入 (千元)	Profit('000 RMB) (rank) 利润(千元) (排名)	Total assets ('000 RMB) 总资产 (千元)	Major products 主要产品
Jiangsu Littleswan Group Co.,Ltd. 江苏小天鹅集团有限公司(1995)	Wuxi 无锡市	Jiangsu 江苏省	(0510)3704003 (0510)3704031	7,527	State-owned 国有企业	4,413,055	21,950(6)	5,772,380	Washing Machine 洗衣机
Hefei Royalstar Group Co., Ltd. 合肥荣事达集团有限责任公司(1997)	Hefei 合肥市	Anhui 安徽省	(0551)5318332 (0551)5318332	5,117	Foreign Funded 外商投资	1,511,150	33,817(3)	3,034,515	Hosehold Washing Machine家用洗衣机
Shandong Xiaoya Group Co., Ltd. 山东小鸭集团有限责任公司(1984)	Jinan 济南市	Shandong 山东省	(0531)8696666 (0531)8696009	6,218	State Enterprises 国有独资	1,357,791	-	3,446,668	Hosehold Washing Machine家用洗衣机
Jinling Electrical Co., Ltd. 金羚电器有限公司(1994)	Jiangmen 江门市	Guangdong 广东省	(0750)3811611 (0750)3817625	1,672	Overseas Chinese-funded 港澳台资	1,020,877	-	1,036,190	Washing Machine 洗衣机
Hangzhou Panasonic Household Appliances Co., Ltd. 杭州松下家用电器有限公司(1992)	Hangzhou 杭州市	Zhejiang 浙江省	(0571)88077124 (0571)88078471	1,359	Foreign Funded 外商投资	789,253	42,136(1)	565,225	Washing Machine 洗衣机
Nanjing LG Panda Electrical Appliance Co. Ltd. 南京乐金熊猫电器有限公司(1995)	Nanjing 南京市	Jiangsu 江苏省	(025)4879998 (025)4879998	533	Foreign Funded 外商投资	659,290	35,540(2)	427,340	Full Automatic Washing Machine全自动洗衣机
Shunde Haier Electrical Appliance Co., Ltd. 顺德海尔电器有限公司(1997)	Foshan 佛山市	Guangdong 广东省	(0765)8386278 (0765)8892383	466	Limited-Liability 有限公司	555,746	27,968(4)	260,417	Washing Machine 洗衣机
Hefei Haier Washing Machine Co., Ltd. 合肥海尔洗衣机有限公司(2001)	Hefei 合肥市	Anhui 安徽省	(0551)3813768 (0551)3521616	98	Limited-Liability 有限公司	201,971	7,588(14)	119,433	Washing Machine 洗衣机
Zhaoqing Duanzhou Automation Meter No.2 Factory Co., Ltd. 肇庆市端州区自动化仪表二厂有限公司(1970)	Zhaoqing 肇庆市	Guangdong 广东省	(0758)2233627 (0758)2280652	250	Limited-Liability 有限公司	139,360	13,326(10)	94,385	Washing Machine Clutch洗衣机离合器
Taishan Huafu Electronics Co.,Ltd. 台山市华富电子有限公司(1993)	Jiangmen 江门市	Guangdong 广东省	(0750)5613618 (0750)5616828	133	Overseas Chinese-funded 港澳台资	126,419	837(39)	40,529	Washing Machine Computer Board洗衣机电脑板

Top 10 Cities by Revenue 销售收入排名前10位城市	Province 省	Market share 市场份额 (%)	Number of firms 企业个数
Wuxi 无锡市	Jiangsu 江苏省	32.66	9
Hefei 合肥市	Anhui 安徽省	11.81	2
Jinan 济南市	Shandong 山东省	9.36	1
Ningbo 宁波市	Zhejiang 浙江省	9.07	24
Jiangmen 江门市	Guangdong 广东省	8.29	3
Hangzhou 杭州市	Zhejiang 浙江省	7.14	7
Nanjing 南京市	Jiangsu 江苏省	5.11	3
Foshan 佛山市	Guangdong 广东省	3.83	1
Shanghai 上海市	Shanghai 上海市	2.75	5
Taizhou 台州市	Zhejiang 浙江省	1.07	4

10 Major Wholesalers 十家主要批发商	City 城市	Province 省	Telephone/Fax 电话/传真
China Chemical Industry Supply & Sale (Group) General Company 中国化工供销(集团)总公司	Beijing 北京市	Beijing 北京市	(010)64238623 (010)64238623
China Chemical Industry Import & Export General Company 中国化工进出口总公司	Beijing 北京市	Beijing 北京市	(010)88078888 (010)88078890
Tianjin Bridge Group Welding Materials Supply & Sale Co., Ltd. 天津大桥集团电焊条供销有限公司	Tianjin 天津市	Tianjin 天津市	(022)83968861 (022)83968865
Taizhou Xingwei Chunlan Chain Stores Co., Ltd. 泰州星威春兰连锁店有限公司	Taizhou 泰州市	Jiangsu 江苏省	(0523)6611200 (0523)6224181
Taizhou Chunlan Sale Company 泰州春兰销售公司	Taizhou 泰州市	Jiangsu 江苏省	(0523)6611200 (0523)6224181
Shandong Tri-Union Co., Ltd. 山东三联有限责任公司	Jinan 济南市	Shandong 山东省	(0531)6086351 (0531)6093103
Haier Electrical Appliances Co.,Ltd. 海尔集团电器产业有限公司	Qingdao 青岛市	Shandong 山东省	(0532)8939175 (0532)8938086
Guangzhou Haier Industry & Trade Co.,Ltd. 广州海尔工贸有限公司	Guangzhou 广州市	Guangdong 广东省	(020)87397315 (020)87374302
Huizhou TCL Electrical Appliances Sales Co.,Ltd. 惠州市TCL电器销售有限公司	Huizhou 惠州市	Guangdong 广东省	(0752)2289885 (0752)2280690
Guangdong Hardware Minerals Import & Export Group Company 广东省五金矿产进出口集团公司	Guangzhou 广州市	Guangdong 广东省	(020)87752204 (020)87752205

4062: Vacuums Cleaner 吸尘器制造业

The industry accounts for 0.050% of the total revenue of China's industrial sector in 2002. The rate of return on assets is 9.72%. 89.74% of all firms in the industry made a profit while 10.26% had negative returns.The top province in terms of the industry's revenue is Jiangsu, accounting for 51.67% of the total revenue.
2002年本行业收入占全行业的 0.050%，资产利润率为 9.72%。89.74%的企业赢利，10.26%的企业亏损。收入最高的省为江苏省，占本行业的51.67%。

	Total number of firms 企业总数	Total number of employees 职工总数	Total revenue (Mil.RMB) 总销售收入（百万元）	Total profit (Mil.RMB) 总利润（百万元）	Return on assets 资产利润率（%）	Return on equity 权益利润率（%）	Labour productivity ('000 RMB/ worker) 劳动生产率（千元/人）	Debts/ assets 资产负债率（%）	Total assets (Mil.RMB) 总资产（百万元）
Industry Overall 行业总体	39	12,324	5,393	470	9.72	24.63	112.63	60.55	4,839

	Number of firms 企业个数	Average number of employees 平均职工人数	Average revenue ('000 RMB) 平均销售收入（千元）	Average profit ('000 RMB) 平均利润（千元）	Return on assets 资产利润率（%）	Return on equity 权益利润率（%）	Labour productivity ('000 RMB/ worker) 劳动生产率（千元/人）	Debts/ assets 资产负债率（%）	Average total assets ('000 RMB) 平均总资产（千元）
By ownership 产业所有权									
State-owned 国有	2	125	5,481	-17,119	-50.42		8.19	164.65	33,950
Collective-owned 集体	1	303	42,060	3,090	8.56	13.59	84.26	37.03	36,110
Foreign & Overseas Chinese Funded 三资	21	376	187,954	17,054	12.01	31.05	142.31	61.32	142,005
By regional distribution 地区分布									
Central-North 华北	4	105	23,375	-3,099	-3.75	-23.33	60.27	83.93	82,652
Beijing 北京									
Tianjin 天津	4	105	23,375	-3,099	-3.75	-23.33	60.27	83.93	82,652
Hebei 河北									
Shanxi 山西									
Inner Mongolia 内蒙古									
Northeast 东北	1	90	8,957	11	0.13		31.98	120.92	8,768
Liaoning 辽宁	1	90	8,957	11	0.13		31.98	120.92	8,768
Jilin 吉林									
Heilongjiang 黑龙江									
Central-East 华东	27	343	170,242	16,841	12.59	25.34	129.60	50.32	133,776
Shanghai 上海	3	276	31,458	-6,464	-12.97		209.08	103.84	49,850
Jiangsu 江苏	11	353	253,352	26,586	17.44	31.18	192.61	44.07	152,420
Zhejiang 浙江	12	355	139,434	14,881	10.21	21.27	59.90	52.01	145,806
Anhui 安徽									
Fujian 福建									
Jiangxi 江西									
Shandong 山东	1	303	42,060	3,090	8.56	13.59	84.26	37.03	36,110
Central-South 中南	7	364	99,168	3,993	3.15	44.06	62.32	92.85	126,800
Henan 河南									
Hubei 湖北									
Hunan 湖南									
Guangdong 广东	7	364	99,168	3,993	3.15	44.06	62.32	92.85	126,800
Guangxi 广西									
Hainan 海南									
Southwest 西南									
Chongqing 重庆									
Sichuan 四川									
Guizhou 贵州									
Yunnan 云南									
Tibet 西藏									
Northwest 西北									
Shaanxi 陕西									
Gansu 甘肃									
Qinghai 青海									
Ningxia 宁夏									
Xinjiang 新疆									

4062: Vacuums Cleaner 吸尘器制造业

Year 年份	Number of firms 企业个数	Rate of change 变化率 (%)	Number of employees 职工人数 (人)	Rate of change 变化率 (%)	Total revenue (Mil. RMB) 总销售收入 (百万元)	Rate of change 变化率 (%)	Total profit (Mil RMB) 总利润 (百万元)	Rate of change 变化率 (%)
2000	34		7,040		2,775		221	
2001	31	-8.82	10,394	47.64	3,441	24.00	282	27.60
2002	39	25.81	12,324	18.57	5,393	56.73	470	66.67

Major Products 主要产品	Output 产量	Unit 单位
Vaccum Cleaner 吸尘器	1,517	10,000 Units 万台

10 Main Firms with Maximal Revenue (year founded) 收入最大的十家主要企业（创办年份）	City 城市	Province 省	Telephone/fax 电话/传真	Number of employees 职工人数	Ownership 产业所有权	Revenue ('000 RMB) 销售收入 (千元)	Profit('000 RMB) (rank) 利润(千元) (排名)	Total assets ('000 RMB) 总资产 (千元)	Major products 主要产品
Ningbo Fuda Electric Appliance Co.,Ltd.	Ningbo	Zhejiang	(0574)62812534		Joint Stock				Dust Collector
宁波富达电器股份有限公司(1989)	宁波市	浙江省	(0574)62818088	1,486	股份制	787,333	109,999(1)	1,192,427	吸尘器
Suzhou Jinlaike Cleaning Utensils Co.,Ltd.	Suzhou	Jiangsu	(0512)68253085		Overseas Chinese-funded				Dust Collector
苏州金莱克清洁器具有限公司(2000)	苏州市	江苏省	(0512)68253076	450	港澳台资	773,846	86,213(2)	307,332	吸尘器
Hangzhi Machinery & Electronics Co.,Ltd.	Hangzhou	Zhejiang	(0571)88072428		Foreign Funded				Dust Collector
杭芝机电有限公司(1991)	杭州市	浙江省		1,037	外商投资	357,179	11,426(12)	180,629	吸尘器
Suzhou Chunfei Household Appliances Co., Ltd.	Suzhou	Jiangsu	(0512)68253516		Foreign Funded				Household Dust Collector
苏州春飞家用电器有限公司(1996)	苏州市	江苏省	(0512)68253457	347	外商投资	356,769	31,631(6)	196,773	用吸尘器
TEK Electrical (Suzhou) Co., Ltd.	Suzhou	Jiangsu	(0512)65611855		Overseas Chinese-funded				Dust Collector
泰怡凯电器(苏州)有限公司(1998)	苏州市	江苏省	(0512)65614671	800	港澳台资	301,080	8,233(13)	153,094	吸尘器
Sanyo Electronic Home Appliances(Suzhou)Co., Ltd.	Suzhou	Jiangsu	(0512)66213246		Foreign Funded				Dust Collector
三洋家用电器(苏州)有限公司(1995)	苏州市	江苏省	(0512)66212945	553	外商投资	237,908	35,520(5)	326,884	吸尘器
Shunde Beiyao Town Xianhua Multimedia Products Co.,Ltd.	Foshan	Guangdong	(0765)6655813		Overseas Chinese-funded				Dust Collector
顺德市北窖镇蚬华多媒体制品有限公司(1995)	佛山市	广东省	(0765)6656727	322	港澳台资	211,549	12,060(10)	608,431	吸尘机
Zhongshan Longde Electric Industires Co.Ltd.	Zhongshan	Guangdong	(0760)3408581		Private Owned				Dust Collector
中山市龙的电器实业有限公司(1999)	中山市	广东省	(0760)3408648	568	私营企业	166,234	1,090(25)	92,141	吸尘器
Ningbo Fujia Electric Co.,Ltd.	Ningbo	Zhejiang	(0574)62814646		Overseas Chinese-funded				Dust Collector
宁波富佳电器有限公司(1997)	宁波市	浙江省	(0574)62814626	480	港澳台资	164,001	7,960(14)	145,904	吸尘器
Jiangsu Chunhua Electric Group Co.,Ltd.	Suzhou	Jiangsu	(0512)67539580		Joint Stock				Dust Collector
江苏春花电器集团股份有限公司(1959)	苏州市	江苏省	(0512)67516078	561	股份制	120,209	1,549(24)	146,536	吸尘器

Top 10 Cities by Revenue 销售收入排名前10位城市	Province 省	Market share 市场份额 (%)	Number of firms 企业个数
Suzhou 苏州市	Jiangsu 江苏省	50.83	10
Ningbo 宁波市	Zhejiang 浙江省	19.79	5
Hangzhou 杭州市	Zhejiang 浙江省	9.10	5
Zhongshan 中山市	Guangdong 广东省	3.99	2
Foshan 佛山市	Guangdong 广东省	3.92	1
Dongguan 东莞市	Guangdong 广东省	2.26	2
Shanghai 上海市	Shanghai 上海市	1.75	3
Tianjin 天津市	Tianjin 天津市	1.73	4
Taizhou 台州市	Zhejiang 浙江省	1.59	1
Wuxi 无锡市	Jiangsu 江苏省	0.84	1

10 Major Wholesalers 十家主要批发商	City 城市	Province 省	Telephone/Fax 电话/传真
China Chemical Industry Supply & Sale (Group) General Company	Beijing	Beijing	(010)64238623
中国化工供销(集团)总公司	北京市	北京市	(010)64238623
China Chemical Industry Import & Export General Company	Beijing	Beijing	(010)88078888
中国化工进出口总公司	北京市	北京市	(010)88078890
Tianjin Bridge Group Welding Materials Supply & Sale Co., Ltd.	Tianjin	Tianjin	(022)83968861
天津大桥集团电焊条供销有限公司	天津市	天津市	(022)83968865
Taizhou Xingwei Chunlan Chain Stores Co., Ltd.	Taizhou	Jiangsu	(0523)6611200
泰州星威春兰连锁店有限公司	泰州市	江苏省	(0523)6224181
Taizhou Chunlan Sale Company	Taizhou	Jiangsu	(0523)6611200
泰州春兰销售公司	泰州市	江苏省	(0523)6224181
Shandong Tri-Union Co., Ltd.	Jinan	Shandong	(0531)6086351
山东三联有限责任公司	济南市	山东省	(0531)6093103
Haier Electrical Appliances Co.,Ltd.	Qingdao	Shandong	(0532)8939175
海尔集团电器产业有限公司	青岛市	山东省	(0532)8938086
Guangzhou Haier Industry & Trade Co.,Ltd.	Guangzhou	Guangdong	(020)87397315
广州海尔工贸有限公司	广州市	广东省	(020)87374302
Huizhou TCL Electrical Appliances Sales Co.,Ltd.	Huizhou	Guangdong	(0752)2289885
惠州市TCL电器销售有限公司	惠州市	广东省	(0752)2280690
Guangdong Hardware Minerals Import & Export Group Company	Guangzhou	Guangdong	(020)87752204
广东省五金矿产进出口集团公司	广州市	广东省	(020)87752205

4063: Refrigerators 电冰箱制造业

The industry accounts for 0.543% of the total revenue of China's industrial sector in 2002. The rate of return on assets is 2.93%. 81.40% of all firms in the industry made a profit while 18.60% had negative returns.The top province in terms of the industry's revenue is Shandong, accounting for 60.70% of the total revenue.
2002年本行业收入占全行业的 0.543%，资产利润率为 2.93%。81.40%的企业赢利，18.60%的企业亏损。收入最高的省为山东省，占本行业的60.70%。

	Total number of firms 企业总数	Total number of employees 职工总数	Total revenue (Mil.RMB) 总销售收入 (百万元)	Total profit (Mil.RMB) 总利润 (百万元)	Return on assets 资产利润率 (%)	Return on equity 权益利润率 (%)	Labour productivity ('000 RMB/ worker) 劳动生产率 (千元/人)	Debts/ assets 资产负债率 (%)	Total assets (Mil.RMB) 总资产 (百万元)
Industry Overall 行业总体	86	76,960	58,204	1,685	2.93	6.75	180.28	56.61	57,511

	Number of firms 企业个数	Average number of employees 平均职工人数	Average revenue ('000 RMB) 平均销售收入 (千元)	Average profit ('000 RMB) 平均利润 (千元)	Return on assets 资产利润率 (%)	Return on equity 权益利润率 (%)	Labour productivity ('000 RMB/ worker) 劳动生产率 (千元/人)	Debts/ assets 资产负债率 (%)	Average total assets ('000 RMB) 平均总资产 (千元)
By ownership 产业所有权									
State-owned 国有	9	554	95,997	496	0.13	0.42	77.81	69.05	378,531
Collective-owned 集体	20	1,379	1,802,323	53,544	4.00	8.09	270.26	50.55	1,338,557
Foreign & Overseas Chinese Funded 三资	16	1,016	596,807	28,621	5.12	11.38	141.59	54.95	558,479
By regional distribution 地区分布									
Central-North 华北	10	249	70,341	-1,092	-1.08	-2.25	49.81	51.93	100,897
Beijing 北京	4	473	121,473	-3,066	-1.79	-3.79	53.13	52.70	170,918
Tianjin 天津	6	99	36,254	224	0.41	0.83	39.26	50.32	54,216
Hebei 河北									
Shanxi 山西									
Inner Mongolia 内蒙古									
Northeast 东北	3	466	115,515	65	0.02	0.10	50.83	81.99	360,480
Liaoning 辽宁	2	499	173,272	98	0.04	0.07	71.21	37.93	234,221
Jilin 吉林	1	400						115.66	613,000
Heilongjiang 黑龙江									
Central-East 华东	47	997	953,997	32,222	3.91	8.43	220.66	53.60	823,513
Shanghai 上海	3	178	34,367	-10,876	-13.02	-61.74	21.97	78.92	83,566
Jiangsu 江苏	11	438	352,719	16,951	8.56	17.90	216.53	52.16	197,945
Zhejiang 浙江	20	380	101,315	1,346	0.83	2.22	68.94	62.66	162,509
Anhui 安徽	4	1,536	661,490	52,006	4.47	10.33	185.90	56.77	1,164,575
Fujian 福建									
Jiangxi 江西	2	1,705	427,396	13,009	0.85	2.16	105.64	60.76	1,536,940
Shandong 山东	7	3,478	5,046,828	157,096	4.35	8.84	298.12	50.85	3,613,520
Central-South 中南	18	1,184	610,960	12,766	1.57	4.22	143.51	62.68	811,398
Henan 河南	3	1,792	817,557	29,703	3.17	6.87	54.99	53.88	937,966
Hubei 湖北	2	439	95,926	5,056	2.04	3.41	119.58	40.10	247,756
Hunan 湖南	2	968	395,403	12,049	2.32	12.40	90.48	81.30	519,640
Guangdong 广东	10	1,295	754,391	10,647	1.04	2.91	191.21	64.28	1,024,334
Guangxi 广西	1	168	18,045	4	0.03	0.15	36.36	80.21	13,125
Hainan 海南									
Southwest 西南	5	436	181,323	490	0.46	0.92	74.02	50.50	107,667
Chongqing 重庆	1	242	8,145	-6,584	-12.88		7.16	131.48	51,118
Sichuan 四川	2	476	132,097	-5,569	-3.57	-6.07	88.77	41.25	156,058
Guizhou 贵州	2	494	317,138	10,086	11.52	20.33	76.21	43.33	87,551
Yunnan 云南									
Tibet 西藏									
Northwest 西北	3	912	137,519	-17,060	-3.25	-8.56	44.36	61.98	524,140
Shaanxi 陕西	2	1,361	205,899	-25,617	-3.26	-8.58	44.33	62.01	785,765
Gansu 甘肃	1	14	760	53	5.96	6.02	49.07	1.12	890
Qinghai 青海									
Ningxia 宁夏									
Xinjiang 新疆									

4063: Refrigerators 电冰箱制造业

Year 年份	Number of firms 企业个数	Rate of change 变化率 (%)	Number of employees 职工人数 (人)	Rate of change 变化率 (%)	Total revenue (Mil. RMB) 总销售收入 (百万元)	Rate of change 变化率 (%)	Total profit (Mil RMB) 总利润 (百万元)	Rate of change 变化率 (%)
2000	96		95,233		48,805		718	
2001	96	o	78,881	-17.17	51,641	5.81	352	-50.97
2002	86	-10.42	76,960	-2.44	58,204	12.71	1,685	378.69

Major Products 主要产品	Output 产量	Unit 单位
Domestic Refrigerator 家用电冰箱	1,599	10,000 Units 万台
Freezor 冷冻箱	465	10,000 Units 万台

10 Main Firms with Maximal Revenue (year founded) 收入最大的十家主要企业（创办年份）	City 城市	Province 省	Telephone/fax 电话/传真	Number of employees 职工人数	Ownership 产业所有权	Revenue ('000 RMB) 销售收入 (千元)	Profit('000 RMB) (rank) 利润(千元) (排名)	Total assets ('000 RMB) 总资产 (千元)	Major products 主要产品
Haier Group Corporation	Qingdao	Shandong	(0532)8938233		Collective-owned				Househoud Electric Appliance
海尔集团公司(1980)	青岛市	山东省	(0532)8938666	18,131	集体企业	30,268,225	1,025,330(1)	19,581,263	家电
Guangdong Kelon Electrical Holding Co., Ltd.	Foshan	Guangdong	(0765)8362811		Joint Stock				Refrigerator
广东科龙电器股份有限公司(1997)	佛山市	广东省	(0765)8361661	8,375	股份制	6,157,194	127,543(4)	7,766,009	电冰箱
Qingdao Aucma Group General Company	Qingdao	Shandong	(0532)6765688		Collective-owned				Deep Freezer
青岛澳柯玛集团总公司(1989)	青岛市	山东省	(0532)6765199	5,731	集体企业	4,916,683	71,905(6)	5,572,075	冷柜
Henan Xinfei Electric Co.,Ltd.	Xinxiang	Henan	(0373)3381616		Foreign Funded				Refrigerator
河南新飞电器有限公司(1994)	新乡市	河南省	(0373)3384788	4,551	外商投资	2,451,001	89,831(5)	2,700,658	电冰箱
Hefei Meiling Group Co.,Ltd.	Hefei	Anhui	(0551)2869344		State Enterprises				Refrigerator
合肥美菱集团控股有限公司(1951)	合肥市	安徽省	(0551)2880605	4,091	国有独资	1,538,854	28,344(9)	3,846,714	电冰箱
Anhui BSA Cooling Appliances Co., Ltd.	Chuzhou	Anhui	(0550)3052731		Foreign Funded				Refrigerator
安徽博西华制冷有限公司(1996)	滁州市	安徽省	(0550)3054873	1,362	外商投资	857,859	155,585(2)	544,001	电冰箱
Xingxing Group Co., Ltd.	Taizhou	Zhejiang	(0576)8022911		Limited-Liability				Refrigerator
星星集团有限公司(1999)	台州市	浙江省	(0576)8022918	2,590	有限公司	852,894	25,313(11)	1,261,293	电冰箱
Jingdezhen Huayi Electrical Appliance General Company	Jingdezhen	Jiangxi	(0798)8470113		State-owned				Refrigerator
景德镇华意电器总公司(1988)	景德镇市	江西省	(0798)8441779	2,300	国有企业	704,000	25,910(10)	2,659,373	电冰箱
Guizhou Haier Electrical Appliance Co.,Ltd.	Zunyi	Guizhou	(0852)8690888		Limited-Liability				Household Refrigerator家
贵州海尔电器有限公司(1997)	遵义市	贵州省	(0852)8690898	788	有限公司	601,046	20,058(13)	149,188	用电冰箱
China Refrigeration Industry Co., Ltd.	Guangzhou	Guangdong	(020)37241668		Overseas Chinese-funded				Household Refrigerator家
中国雪柜实业有限公司(1988)	广州市	广东省	(020)37241181	904	港澳台资	365,729	-	1,000,339	用电冰箱

Top 10 Cities by Revenue 销售收入排名前10位城市	Province 省	Market share 市场份额 (%)	Number of firms 企业个数
Qingdao 青岛市	Shandong 山东省	60.53	5
Foshan 佛山市	Guangdong 广东省	11.05	3
Suzhou 苏州市	Jiangsu 江苏省	4.76	4
Xinxiang 新乡市	Henan 河南省	4.21	1
Hefei 合肥市	Anhui 安徽省	3.07	3
Guangzhou 广州市	Guangdong 广东省	1.78	5
Taizhou 台州市	Zhejiang 浙江省	1.71	3
Chuzhou 滁州市	Anhui 安徽省	1.47	1
Changsha 长沙市	Hunan 湖南省	1.36	2
Taizhou 泰州市	Jiangsu 江苏省	1.23	1

10 Major Wholesalers 十家主要批发商	City 城市	Province 省	Telephone/Fax 电话/传真
China Chemical Industry Supply & Sale (Group) General Company	Beijing	Beijing	(010)64238623
中国化工供销(集团)总公司	北京市	北京市	(010)64238623
China Chemical Industry Import & Export General Company	Beijing	Beijing	(010)88078888
中国化工进出口总公司	北京市	北京市	(010)88078890
Tianjin Bridge Group Welding Materials Supply & Sale Co., Ltd.	Tianjin	Tianjin	(022)83968861
天津大桥集团电焊条供销有限公司	天津市	天津市	(022)83968865
Taizhou Xingwei Chunlan Chain Stores Co., Ltd.	Taizhou	Jiangsu	(0523)6611200
泰州星威春兰连锁店有限公司	泰州市	江苏省	(0523)6224181
Taizhou Chunlan Sale Company	Taizhou	Jiangsu	(0523)6611200
泰州春兰销售公司	泰州市	江苏省	(0523)6224181
Shandong Tri-Union Co., Ltd.	Jinan	Shandong	(0531)6086351
山东三联有限责任公司	济南市	山东省	(0531)6093103
Haier Electrical Appliances Co.,Ltd.	Qingdao	Shandong	(0532)8939175
海尔集团电器产业有限公司	青岛市	山东省	(0532)8938086
Guangzhou Haier Industry & Trade Co.,Ltd.	Guangzhou	Guangdong	(020)87397315
广州海尔工贸有限公司	广州市	广东省	(020)87374302
Huizhou TCL Electrical Appliances Sales Co.,Ltd.	Huizhou	Guangdong	(0752)2289885
惠州市TCL电器销售有限公司	惠州市	广东省	(0752)2280690
Guangdong Hardware Minerals Import & Export Group Company	Guangzhou	Guangdong	(020)87752204
广东省五金矿产进出口集团公司	广州市	广东省	(020)87752205

4064: Electric Fans 电风扇制造业

The industry accounts for 0.102% of the total revenue of China's industrial sector in 2002. The rate of return on assets is 2.06%. 74.84% of all firms in the industry made a profit while 25.16% had negative returns.The top province in terms of the industry's revenue is Guangdong, accounting for 75.53% of the total revenue.
2002年本行业收入占全行业的 0.102%，资产利润率为 2.06%。74.84%的企业赢利，25.16%的企业亏损。收入最高的省为广东省，占本行业的75.53%。

	Total number of firms 企业总数	Total number of employees 职工总数	Total revenue (Mil.RMB) 总销售收入（百万元）	Total profit (Mil.RMB) 总利润（百万元）	Return on assets 资产利润率 (%)	Return on equity 权益利润率 (%)	Labour productivity ('000 RMB/ worker) 劳动生产率（千元/人）	Debts/ assets 资产负债率 (%)	Total assets (Mil.RMB) 总资产（百万元）
Industry Overall 行业总体	155	50,789	10,962	165	2.06	5.66	59.80	63.58	7,989

	Number of firms 企业个数	Average number of employees 平均职工人数	Average revenue ('000 RMB) 平均销售收入（千元）	Average profit ('000 RMB) 平均利润（千元）	Return on assets 资产利润率 (%)	Return on equity 权益利润率 (%)	Labour productivity ('000 RMB/ worker) 劳动生产率（千元/人）	Debts/ assets 资产负债率 (%)	Average total assets ('000 RMB) 平均总资产（千元）
By ownership 产业所有权									
State-owned 国有	7	214	9,892	-146	-0.42	-1.96	12.42	78.65	34,927
Collective-owned 集体	29	505	123,312	787	1.04	5.43	87.53	80.77	75,341
Foreign & Overseas Chinese Funded 三资	31	534	116,991	1,994	2.24	4.49	53.88	50.09	88,976
By regional distribution 地区分布									
Central-North 华北	1	14	3,590	-70	-2.34	-3.23	281.43	27.42	2,990
Beijing 北京									
Tianjin 天津	1	14	3,590	-70	-2.34	-3.23	281.43	27.42	2,990
Hebei 河北									
Shanxi 山西									
Inner Mongolia 内蒙古									
Northeast 东北									
Liaoning 辽宁									
Jilin 吉林									
Heilongjiang 黑龙江									
Central-East 华东	43	225	59,957	1,322	3.22	8.34	79.64	61.33	41,024
Shanghai 上海	6	202	17,980	1,517	4.62	12.33	20.32	62.52	32,836
Jiangsu 江苏	15	238	45,256	1,974	5.08	10.53	60.38	51.76	38,851
Zhejiang 浙江	17	90	21,701	646	3.01	6.83	43.61	56.01	21,488
Anhui 安徽	1	443	23,483	-6,370	-4.96	-175.00	-1.71	97.17	128,523
Fujian 福建	2	300	20,530	-3,606	-6.07	-11.48	27.69	47.16	59,418
Jiangxi 江西	1	160	1,953	-266	-1.78	-2.04	8.79	12.45	14,905
Shandong 山东	1	2,160	1,356,000	21,020	5.89	24.19	206.78	75.64	356,700
Central-South 中南	106	381	78,409	1,034	1.81	5.01	55.56	63.84	57,077
Henan 河南	2	80	2,241	-117	-1.81		15.67	170.69	6,445
Hubei 湖北									
Hunan 湖南	3	46	4,120	6	0.10	0.48	33.50	79.19	6,326
Guangdong 广东	99	401	83,634	1,121	1.87	5.04	56.22	62.81	59,788
Guangxi 广西	2	198	7,376	-582	-1.17		13.70	108.31	49,657
Hainan 海南									
Southwest 西南	4	129	9,712	-1,270	-4.76	-88.12	17.90	94.60	26,696
Chongqing 重庆	3	155	4,620	-1,880	-5.56	-186.97	3.38	97.03	33,793
Sichuan 四川	1	50	24,987	558	10.33	20.29	153.26	49.09	5,402
Guizhou 贵州									
Yunnan 云南									
Tibet 西藏									
Northwest 西北	1	196	29,780	3,583	5.49	11.16	47.29	50.79	65,256
Shaanxi 陕西	1	196	29,780	3,583	5.49	11.16	47.29	50.79	65,256
Gansu 甘肃									
Qinghai 青海									
Ningxia 宁夏									
Xinjiang 新疆									

4064: Electric Fans 电风扇制造业

Year 年份	Number of firms 企业个数	Rate of change 变化率 (%)	Number of employees 职工人数 (人)	Rate of change 变化率 (%)	Total revenue (Mil. RMB) 总销售收入 (百万元)	Rate of change 变化率 (%)	Total profit (Mil RMB) 总利润 (百万元)	Rate of change 变化率 (%)
2000	144		65,292		19,895		499	
2001	142	-1.39	49,520	-24.16	10,133	-49.07	86	-82.77
2002	155	9.15	50,789	2.56	10,962	8.18	165	91.86

Major Products 主要产品	Output 产量	Unit 单位
Domestic Electric Fan 家用电风扇	9,056	10,000 Units 万台

10 Main Firms with Maximal Revenue (year founded) 收入最大的十家主要企业（创办年份）	City 城市	Province 省	Telephone/fax 电话/传真	Number of employees 职工人数	Ownership 产业所有权	Revenue ('000 RMB) 销售收入 (千元)	Profit('000 RMB) (rank) 利润(千元) (排名)	Total assets ('000 RMB) 总资产 (千元)	Major products 主要产品
Airmate Electrical (Shenzhen) Co., Ltd.	Shenzhen	Guangdong	(0755)27643218		Overseas Chinese-funded				Electric Fan
艾美特电器（深圳）有限公司(1991)	深圳市	广东省	(0755)27642263	3,000	港澳台资	497,927	3,442(12)	286,291	电风扇
Shunde Xianhua Electrical Appliance Co., Ltd	Foshan	Guangdong	(0765)6655118		Collective-owned				Ceiling Electric Fan
顺德市蚬华电器有限公司(1987)	佛山市	广东省	(0765)6656811	3,046	集体企业	431,192	6,562(8)	419,037	吊扇
Guangdong Matsushita Ecology Systems Co.,Ltd	Foshan	Guangdong	(0765)8391633		Foreign Funded				Ceiling Electric Fan
广东松下环境系统有限公司(1993)	佛山市	广东省	(0765)8392405	1,305	外商投资	387,454	37,892(1)	259,047	吊扇
Zhongshan Weihe Electrical Appliance Manufacturing Co.,Ltd.	Zhongshan	Guangdong	(0760)8552001		Private Enterprises				Electric Fan
中山市威禾电器制造有限公司(1998)	中山市	广东省	(0760)8552018	155	私营独资	359,200	2,982(16)	172,629	风扇
Huiyang Yuangao Electrical Appliance Co., Ltd.	Huizhou	Guangdong	(0752)3892551		Overseas Chinese-funded				High-grade Ceiling Electric Fan
惠阳源高电器有限公司(1994)	惠州市	广东省	(0752)3892558	998	港澳台资	336,190	1,352(27)	195,323	高级吊扇
Shunde Guizhou No.1 Electronics Fan Factory	Foshan	Guangdong	(0765)8896783		Collective-owned				Electric Fan
顺德市桂洲第一风扇厂(1980)	佛山市	广东省	(0765)8889207	2,276	集体企业	304,010	1,332(29)	229,676	电风扇
Shunde Jinke Electrical Appliance Co., Ltd.	Foshan	Guangdong	(0765)3833399		Private Owned				Electric Fan
顺德市金科电器有限公司(1999)	佛山市	广东省	(0765)3352299	2,268	私营企业	265,874	248(72)	247,035	电风扇
Jiangmen Jinling Household Elec.ApplianceCo.,Ltd.	Jiangmen	Guangdong	(0750)3786266		Collective-owned				Electric Fan
江门市金羚家用电器有限公司(1981)	江门市	广东省	(0750)3351237	811	集体企业	263,181	898(35)	299,243	电风扇
Xinhui Baoli Electrical Appliance Co.,Ltd.	Jiangmen	Guangdong	(0750)6696830		Limited-Liability				Electric Fan
新会区宝力电器有限公司(2002)	江门市	广东省	(0750)6696318	989	有限公司	261,662	21,070(3)	221,134	电风扇
Zhongshan Ganglian Huakai Electrical Appliance Products Co.,Ltd.	Zhongshan	Guangdong	(0760)5601191		Private Owned				Electric Fan
中山市港联华凯电器制品有限公司(1995)	中山市	广东省	(0760)5600564	2,465	私营企业	231,179	24,988(2)	127,575	电风扇

Top 10 Cities by Revenue 销售收入排名前10位城市	Province 省	Market share 市场份额 (%)	Number of firms 企业个数
Jiangmen 江门市	Guangdong 广东省	24.23	31
Foshan 佛山市	Guangdong 广东省	18.66	24
Zhongshan 中山市	Guangdong 广东省	14.02	22
Yantai 烟台市	Shandong 山东省	12.37	1
Shenzhen 深圳市	Guangdong 广东省	8.25	7
Dongguan 东莞市	Guangdong 广东省	4.19	4
Huizhou 惠州市	Guangdong 广东省	3.07	1
Ningbo 宁波市	Zhejiang 浙江省	2.82	12
Suzhou 苏州市	Jiangsu 江苏省	2.66	7
Yangzhou 扬州市	Jiangsu 江苏省	2.13	1

10 Major Wholesalers 十家主要批发商	City 城市	Province 省	Telephone/Fax 电话/传真
China Chemical Industry Supply & Sale (Group) General Company	Beijing	Beijing	(010)64238623
中国化工供销(集团)总公司	北京市	北京市	(010)64238623
China Chemical Industry Import & Export General Company	Beijing	Beijing	(010)88078888
中国化工进出口总公司	北京市	北京市	(010)88078890
Tianjin Bridge Group Welding Materials Supply & Sale Co., Ltd.	Tianjin	Tianjin	(022)83968861
天津大桥集团电焊条供销有限公司	天津市	天津市	(022)83968865
Taizhou Xingwei Chunlan Chain Stores Co., Ltd.	Taizhou	Jiangsu	(0523)6611200
泰州星威春兰连锁店有限公司	泰州市	江苏省	(0523)6224181
Taizhou Chunlan Sale Company	Taizhou	Jiangsu	(0523)6611200
泰州春兰销售公司	泰州市	江苏省	(0523)6224181
Shandong Tri-Union Co., Ltd.	Jinan	Shandong	(0531)6086351
山东三联有限责任公司	济南市	山东省	(0531)6093103
Haier Electrical Appliances Co.,Ltd.	Qingdao	Shandong	(0532)8939175
海尔集团电器产业有限公司	青岛市	山东省	(0532)8938086
Guangzhou Haier Industry & Trade Co.,Ltd.	Guangzhou	Guangdong	(020)87397315
广州海尔工贸有限公司	广州市	广东省	(020)87374302
Huizhou TCL Electrical Appliances Sales Co.,Ltd.	Huizhou	Guangdong	(0752)2289885
惠州市TCL电器销售有限公司	惠州市	广东省	(0752)2280690
Guangdong Hardware Minerals Import & Export Group Company	Guangzhou	Guangdong	(020)87752204
广东省五金矿产进出口集团公司	广州市	广东省	(020)87752205

4065: Air Conditioners 空调器制造业

The industry accounts for 0.631% of the total revenue of China's industrial sector in 2002. The rate of return on assets is 5.60%. 79.54% of all firms in the industry made a profit while 20.46% had negative returns.The top province in terms of the industry's revenue is Guangdong, accounting for 49.35% of the total revenue.
2002年本行业收入占全行业的0.631%，资产利润率为5.60%。79.54%的企业赢利，20.46%的企业亏损。收入最高的省为广东省，占本行业的49.35%。

	Total number of firms 企业总数	Total number of employees 职工总数	Total revenue (Mil.RMB) 总销售收入（百万元）	Total profit (Mil.RMB) 总利润（百万元）	Return on assets 资产利润率（%）	Return on equity 权益利润率（%）	Labour productivity ('000 RMB/ worker) 劳动生产率（千元/人）	Debts/ assets 资产负债率（%）	Total assets (Mil.RMB) 总资产（百万元）
Industry Overall 行业总体	259	113,088	67,702	3,589	5.60	13.43	179.72	58.29	64,063

	Number of firms 企业个数	Average number of employees 平均职工人数	Average revenue ('000 RMB) 平均销售收入（千元）	Average profit ('000 RMB) 平均利润（千元）	Return on assets 资产利润率（%）	Return on equity 权益利润率（%）	Labour productivity ('000 RMB/ worker) 劳动生产率（千元/人）	Debts/ assets 资产负债率（%）	Average total assets ('000 RMB) 平均总资产（千元）
By ownership 产业所有权									
State-owned 国有	10	114	3,767	-235	-0.68	-2.10	18.03	67.75	34,604
Collective-owned 集体	18	227	54,413	1,867	2.85	7.15	62.44	60.13	65,495
Foreign & Overseas Chinese Funded 三资	90	459	343,245	17,820	5.86	14.73	166.57	60.20	304,000
By regional distribution 地区分布									
Central-North 华北	27	267	230,458	5,636	2.79	8.29	49.34	66.37	202,132
Beijing 北京	13	196	43,260	2,269	2.56	6.25	78.93	59.06	88,680
Tianjin 天津	12	368	468,572	10,005	2.80	8.87	31.40	68.44	357,284
Hebei 河北	2	114	18,566	1,304	15.07	26.06	66.05	42.18	8,653
Shanxi 山西									
Inner Mongolia 内蒙古									
Northeast 东北	10	515	204,907	31,863	8.79	15.08	135.82	41.72	362,630
Liaoning 辽宁	6	573	255,629	39,252	9.20	15.90	134.90	42.15	426,837
Jilin 吉林	1	286	345,140	73,165	22.74	36.64	404.99	37.94	321,790
Heilongjiang 黑龙江	3	474	56,719	3,319	1.34	2.30	83.97	41.86	247,830
Central-East 华东	126	376	177,847	13,067	7.24	15.06	160.39	51.94	180,530
Shanghai 上海	13	508	589,973	24,252	5.66	13.23	177.88	57.25	428,804
Jiangsu 江苏	45	274	100,895	6,396	4.29	6.42	244.83	33.08	148,958
Zhejiang 浙江	38	472	166,311	16,097	9.18	22.65	85.24	59.47	175,308
Anhui 安徽	7	346	345,049	56,003	16.58	45.19	609.63	63.31	337,798
Fujian 福建	3	51	39,838	960	4.93	8.46	190.39	41.75	19,465
Jiangxi 江西									
Shandong 山东	20	395	67,206	1,842	2.66	7.98	46.40	66.66	69,224
Central-South 中南	87	598	420,926	16,916	4.65	12.52	222.60	62.87	363,781
Henan 河南	3	135	39,094	4,527	16.06	29.54	65.64	45.63	28,180
Hubei 湖北	4	646	430,260	39,743	13.76	32.74	142.49	57.97	288,842
Hunan 湖南	5	443	265,888	41,776	11.19	13.80	209.37	18.89	373,316
Guangdong 广东	73	637	457,711	14,918	3.83	11.28	229.91	66.05	389,481
Guangxi 广西	2	161	19,938	595	1.08	2.14	98.02	49.76	55,175
Hainan 海南									
Southwest 西南	8	162	49,718	989	1.78	7.51	70.80	76.28	55,507
Chongqing 重庆	3	160	60,568	-181	-0.20	-0.85	107.25	76.97	92,511
Sichuan 四川	5	163	43,207	1,691	5.08	20.42	49.39	75.13	33,304
Guizhou 贵州									
Yunnan 云南									
Tibet 西藏									
Northwest 西北	1	68	3,340	-7,467	-5.37		12.47	114.09	138,951
Shaanxi 陕西	1	68	3,340	-7,467	-5.37		12.47	114.09	138,951
Gansu 甘肃									
Qinghai 青海									
Ningxia 宁夏									
Xinjiang 新疆									

Year 年份	Number of firms 企业个数	Rate of change 变化率 (%)	Number of employees 职工人数 (人)	Rate of change 变化率 (%)	Total revenue (Mil. RMB) 总销售收入 (百万元)	Rate of change 变化率 (%)	Total profit (Mil RMB) 总利润 (百万元)	Rate of change 变化率 (%)
2000	195		81,145		42,973		2,607	
2001	248	27.18	110,895	36.66	68,998	60.56	3,947	51.40
2002	259	4.44	113,088	1.98	67,702	-1.88	3,589	-9.07

Major Products 主要产品	Output 产量	Unit 单位
Room Air Conditioner 房间空气调节器	3,135	10,000 Units 万台

10 Main Firms with Maximal Revenue (year founded) 收入最大的十家主要企业（创办年份）	City 城市	Province 省	Telephone/fax 电话/传真	Number of employees 职工人数	Ownership 产业所有权	Revenue ('000 RMB) 销售收入 (千元)	Profit('000 RMB) (rank) 利润(千元) (排名)	Total assets ('000 RMB) 总资产 (千元)	Major products 主要产品
Gree Electric Appliances Inc of zhuhai 珠海格力电器股份有限公司(1988)	Zhuhai 珠海市	Guangdong 广东省	(0756)8614883 (0756)8614998	5,575	Joint Stock 股份制	7,029,691	349,361(3)	7,087,852	Household Air Conditioner家用空调器
LG Electronics (TianJin) Appliances Co., Ltd. 乐金电子（天津）电器有限公司(1995)	Tianjin 天津市	Tianjin 天津市	(022)26903300 (022)26991331	2,548	Foreign Funded 外商投资	5,111,520	150,017(9)	3,492,699	Air Conditioner 空调机
Panasonic.Wanbao (Guangzhou)Air-Conditioner Co.,Ltd. 松下.万宝(广州)空调器有限公司(1993)	Guangzhou 广州市	Guangdong 广东省	(020)84778123 (020)84716787	2,590	Foreign Funded 外商投资	2,542,067	73,413(14)	1,085,489	Air Conditioner 空调器
Guangdong Zhigao Air-conditioner Co., Ltd. 广东志高空调有限公司(1997)	Foshan 佛山市	Guangdong 广东省	(0757)5682383 (0757)5662764	2,200	Private Owned 私营企业	2,456,578	53,179(18)	925,272	Air Conditioner 空调机
Shanghai Sharp Electronics Co., Ltd. 上海夏普电器有限公司(1992)	Shanghai 上海市	Shanghai 上海市	(021)58341111 (021)50311923	2,003	Foreign Funded 外商投资	1,857,126	5,969(45)	1,936,465	Household Air Conditioner家用空调器
Jiangsu Chunlan Refrigeration Equipment Co.,Ltd. 江苏春兰制冷设备股份有限公司(1988)	Taizhou 泰州市	Jiangsu 江苏省	(0523)6663710 (0523)6228134	2,451	Joint Stock 股份制	1,660,060	168,790(8)	3,950,000	Room Air Conditioner房间空调器
Matsushita-Wanbao (Guangzhou) Compressor Co.,Ltd. 松下.万宝(广州)压缩机有限公司(1993)	Guangzhou 广州市	Guangdong 广东省	(020)84778123 (020)84716787	3,920	Foreign Funded 外商投资	1,602,008	94,313(11)	2,052,909	Air Conditioner Compressor空调器用压缩机
Guangdong Midea Group Wuhu Refrigeration Equipment Co.,Ltd.广东美的集团芜湖制冷设备有限公司(1998)	Wuhu 芜湖市	Anhui 安徽省	(0553)5840802 (0553)5843888	1,297	Overseas Chinese-funded 港澳台资	1,507,816	319,067(4)	910,226	Room Air Conditioner房间空调器
Fujitsu General (Shanghai) Co.,Ltd. 富士通将军(上海)有限公司(1994)	Shanghai 上海市	Shanghai 上海市	(021)59161476 (021)59162476	512	Foreign Funded 外商投资	1,491,393	-	891,603	Air Conditioner 空调器
Broad Firing Machinery Co.,Ltd. 远大直燃机有限公司(1992)	Changsha 长沙市	Hunan 湖南省	(0731)4086688 (0731)4614673	1,599	Private Owned 私营企业	1,268,110	206,410(7)	1,741,960	Air Conditioner 空调器

Top 10 Cities by Revenue 销售收入排名前10位城市	Province 省	Market share 市场份额 (%)	Number of firms 企业个数
Foshan 佛山市	Guangdong 广东省	21.94	17
Shanghai 上海市	Shanghai 上海市	11.33	13
Zhuhai 珠海市	Guangdong 广东省	10.38	1
Guangzhou 广州市	Guangdong 广东省	10.07	23
Tianjin 天津市	Tianjin 天津市	8.31	12
Ningbo 宁波市	Zhejiang 浙江省	4.87	14
Taizhou 泰州市	Jiangsu 江苏省	2.98	13
Zhongshan 中山市	Guangdong 广东省	2.63	15
Wuhu 芜湖市	Anhui 安徽省	2.34	4
Shenyang 沈阳市	Liaoning 辽宁省	2.08	5

10 Major Wholesalers 十家主要批发商	City 城市	Province 省	Telephone/Fax 电话/传真
China Chemical Industry Supply & Sale (Group) General Company 中国化工供销(集团)总公司	Beijing 北京市	Beijing 北京市	(010)64238623 (010)64238623
China Chemical Industry Import & Export General Company 中国化工进出口总公司	Beijing 北京市	Beijing 北京市	(010)88078888 (010)88078890
Tianjin Bridge Group Welding Materials Supply & Sale Co., Ltd. 天津大桥集团电焊条供销有限公司	Tianjin 天津市	Tianjin 天津市	(022)83968861 (022)83968865
Taizhou Xingwei Chunlan Chain Stores Co., Ltd. 泰州星威春兰连锁店有限公司	Taizhou 泰州市	Jiangsu 江苏省	(0523)6611200 (0523)6224181
Taizhou Chunlan Sale Company 泰州春兰销售公司	Taizhou 泰州市	Jiangsu 江苏省	(0523)6611200 (0523)6224181
Shandong Tri-Union Co., Ltd. 山东三联有限责任公司	Jinan 济南市	Shandong 山东省	(0531)6086351 (0531)6093103
Haier Electrical Appliances Co.,Ltd. 海尔集团电器产业有限公司	Qingdao 青岛市	Shandong 山东省	(0532)8939175 (0532)8938086
Guangzhou Haier Industry & Trade Co.,Ltd. 广州海尔工贸有限公司	Guangzhou 广州市	Guangdong 广东省	(020)87397315 (020)87374302
Huizhou TCL Electrical Appliances Sales Co.,Ltd. 惠州市TCL电器销售有限公司	Huizhou 惠州市	Guangdong 广东省	(0752)2289885 (0752)2280690
Guangdong Hardware Minerals Import & Export Group Company 广东省五金矿产进出口集团公司	Guangzhou 广州市	Guangdong 广东省	(020)87752204 (020)87752205

4066: Lampblack Releasing Equipment 排油烟机制造业

The industry accounts for 0.037% of the total revenue of China's industrial sector in 2002. The rate of return on assets is 4.35%. 77.55% of all firms in the industry made a profit while 22.45% had negative returns.The top province in terms of the industry's revenue is Zhejiang, accounting for 42.76% of the total revenue.
2002年本行业收入占全行业的 0.037%，资产利润率为 4.35%。77.55%的企业赢利，22.45%的企业亏损。收入最高的省为浙江省，占本行业的42.76%。

	Total number of firms 企业总数	Total number of employees 职工总数	Total revenue (Mil.RMB) 总销售收入（百万元）	Total profit (Mil.RMB) 总利润（百万元）	Return on assets 资产利润率（%）	Return on equity 权益利润率（%）	Labour productivity ('000 RMB/ worker) 劳动生产率（千元/人）	Debts/ assets 资产负债率（%）	Total assets (Mil.RMB) 总资产（百万元）
Industry Overall 行业总体	49	13,396	4,013	152	4.35	9.50	70.30	54.24	3,495

	Number of firms 企业个数	Average number of employees 平均职工人数	Average revenue ('000 RMB) 平均销售收入（千元）	Average profit ('000 RMB) 平均利润（千元）	Return on assets 资产利润率（%）	Return on equity 权益利润率（%）	Labour productivity ('000 RMB/ worker) 劳动生产率（千元/人）	Debts/ assets 资产负债率（%）	Average total assets ('000 RMB) 平均总资产（千元）
By ownership 产业所有权									
State-owned 国有	1	17	655	27	0.85	3.94	32.18	78.43	3,176
Collective-owned 集体	3	128	17,659	4,065	18.07	20.83	54.13	13.23	22,493
Foreign & Overseas Chinese Funded 三资	11	244	135,735	1,050	1.24	2.91	68.29	57.52	84,907
By regional distribution 地区分布									
Central-North 华北	1	17	655	27	0.85	3.94	32.18	78.43	3,176
Beijing 北京	1	17	655	27	0.85	3.94	32.18	78.43	3,176
Tianjin 天津									
Hebei 河北									
Shanxi 山西									
Inner Mongolia 内蒙古									
Northeast 东北									
Liaoning 辽宁									
Jilin 吉林									
Heilongjiang 黑龙江									
Central-East 华东	35	326	98,614	4,725	5.73	12.01	75.67	52.29	82,449
Shanghai 上海	9	203	146,949	3,638	5.83	12.17	75.34	52.06	62,360
Jiangsu 江苏	4	284	93,825	4,053	5.23	9.38	95.92	44.22	77,464
Zhejiang 浙江	20	404	85,790	5,866	6.23	13.27	73.74	53.03	94,120
Anhui 安徽									
Fujian 福建									
Jiangxi 江西									
Shandong 山东	2	189	18,926	-444	-0.67	-1.75	57.64	61.68	66,113
Central-South 中南	13	151	43,143	-1,039	-2.23	-6.09	39.36	63.40	46,627
Henan 河南									
Hubei 湖北	1	145	8,985	-2,184	-10.76	-464.68	20.45	97.68	20,288
Hunan 湖南	1	69	3,053	8	0.38	0.41	15.28	7.58	2,097
Guangdong 广东	11	159	49,892	-1,030	-1.94	-5.16	41.88	62.41	53,069
Guangxi 广西									
Hainan 海南									
Southwest 西南									
Chongqing 重庆									
Sichuan 四川									
Guizhou 贵州									
Yunnan 云南									
Tibet 西藏									
Northwest 西北									
Shaanxi 陕西									
Gansu 甘肃									
Qinghai 青海									
Ningxia 宁夏									
Xinjiang 新疆									

4066: Lampblack Releasing Equipment 排油烟机制造业

Year 年份	Number of firms 企业个数	Rate of change 变化率 (%)	Number of employees 职工人数 (人)	Rate of change 变化率 (%)	Total revenue (Mil. RMB) 总销售收入 (百万元)	Rate of change 变化率 (%)	Total profit (Mil RMB) 总利润 (百万元)	Rate of change 变化率 (%)
2000	32		13,632		2,738		186	
2001	34	6.25	10,594	-22.29	2,212	-19.21	123	-33.87
2002	49	44.12	13,396	26.45	4,013	81.42	152	23.58

Major Products 主要产品	Output 产量	Unit 单位
Oil-Smoke Exhausting Machine 排油烟机	341	10,000 Units 万台

10 Main Firms with Maximal Revenue (year founded) 收入最大的十家主要企业（创办年份）	City 城市	Province 省	Telephone/fax 电话/传真	Number of employees 职工人数	Ownership 产业所有权	Revenue ('000 RMB) 销售收入 (千元)	Profit('000 RMB) (rank) 利润(千元) (排名)	Total assets ('000 RMB) 总资产 (千元)	Major products 主要产品
Shanghai Panasonic Microwave Oven Co., Ltd. 上海松下微波炉有限公司(1994)	Shanghai 上海市	Shanghai 上海市	(021)50800705 (021)50801117	970	Foreign Funded 外商投资	1,064,897	30,883(3)	334,517	Microwave Oven 微波炉
Shuaikang Group Co.,Ltd. 帅康集团有限公司(1996)	Ningbo 宁波市	Zhejiang 浙江省	(0574)62241695 (0574)62241447	3,315	Limited-Liability 有限公司	738,219	32,911(2)	835,023	Inhale Smoke Absorber吸 排油烟机
Ningbo Fotile Kitchen Ware Co.,Ltd. 宁波方太厨具有限公司(1995)	Ningbo 宁波市	Zhejiang 浙江省	(0574)63013593 (0574)63028021	1,811	Limited-Liability 有限公司	403,185	58,257(1)	306,196	Smoke Absorber 油烟机
Guangdong Xinde Science & Technology Group Co., Ltd. 广东新的科技集团有限公司(1998)	Foshan 佛山市	Guangdong 广东省	(0765)6666999 (0765)6671686	729	Private Owned 私营企业	359,237	2,986(9)	344,820	Smoke Absorber 抽油烟机
Hangzhou Robam Industrial Group Co., Ltd. 杭州老板实业集团有限公司(1979)	Hangzhou 杭州市	Zhejiang 浙江省	(0571)86281532 (0571)86281535	550	Private Owned 私营企业	200,490	10,040(6)	138,992	Smoke Absorber 排油烟机
Nanjing Flaminia Electrical Appliance Co., Ltd. 南京法拉米尼亚电器有限公司(1996)	Nanjing 南京市	Jiangsu 江苏省	(025)2190149 (025)2195124	205	Foreign Funded 外商投资	81,470	3,580(8)	79,200	Smoke Absorber 油烟机
Zhongshan Haika Electrical Appliance Co., Ltd. 中山市海卡电器有限公司(2000)	Zhongshan 中山市	Guangdong 广东省	(0760)2121368 (0760)2120032	160	Private Owned 私营企业	63,861	468(22)	38,493	Smoke Absorber 抽油烟机
ZheJiang Dibei Electrical Machinery Group Co.,Ltd. 浙江迪贝机电集团有限公司(1985)	Shaoxing 绍兴市	Zhejiang 浙江省	(0575)3045892 (0575)3045887	560	Private Owned 私营企业	63,254	1,622(15)	134,898	Smoke Absorber 排油烟机
Jiangsu Jintian Kitchen Utensils Co., Ltd. 江苏金田厨具有限公司(1987)	Nantong 南通市	Jiangsu 江苏省	(0513)6482171 (0513)2518301	132	Overseas Chinese-funded 港澳台资	53,240	1,085(18)	28,273	Doff Smoke Absorber脱 排油烟器
Yantai Dipper Conditioner Co., Ltd. 烟台迪帕迩空调有限公司(1996)	Yantai 烟台市	Shandong 山东省	(0535)6302601 (0535)6302610	179	Overseas Chinese-funded 港澳台资	34,990	-	113,146	Air Conditioner 空调器

Top 10 Cities by Revenue 销售收入排名前10位城市	Province 省	Market share 市场份额 (%)	Number of firms 企业个数
Ningbo 宁波市	Zhejiang 浙江省	33.50	9
Shanghai 上海市	Shanghai 上海市	32.96	9
Foshan 佛山市	Guangdong 广东省	11.03	6
Hangzhou 杭州市	Zhejiang 浙江省	6.31	4
Wuxi 无锡市	Jiangsu 江苏省	5.35	1
Shaoxing 绍兴市	Zhejiang 浙江省	2.69	6
Zhongshan 中山市	Guangdong 广东省	2.30	4
Nanjing 南京市	Jiangsu 江苏省	2.03	1
Nantong 南通市	Jiangsu 江苏省	1.33	1
Yantai 烟台市	Shandong 山东省	0.87	1

10 Major Wholesalers 十家主要批发商	City 城市	Province 省	Telephone/Fax 电话/传真
China Chemical Industry Supply & Sale (Group) General Company 中国化工供销(集团)总公司	Beijing 北京市	Beijing 北京市	(010)64238623 (010)64238623
China Chemical Industry Import & Export General Company 中国化工进出口总公司	Beijing 北京市	Beijing 北京市	(010)88078888 (010)88078890
Tianjin Bridge Group Welding Materials Supply & Sale Co., Ltd. 天津大桥集团电焊条供销有限公司	Tianjin 天津市	Tianjin 天津市	(022)83968861 (022)83968865
Taizhou Xingwei Chunlan Chain Stores Co., Ltd. 泰州星威春兰连锁店有限公司	Taizhou 泰州市	Jiangsu 江苏省	(0523)6611200 (0523)6224181
Taizhou Chunlan Sale Company 泰州春兰销售公司	Taizhou 泰州市	Jiangsu 江苏省	(0523)6611200 (0523)6224181
Shandong Tri-Union Co., Ltd. 山东三联有限责任公司	Jinan 济南市	Shandong 山东省	(0531)6086351 (0531)6093103
Haier Electrical Appliances Co.,Ltd. 海尔集团电器产业有限公司	Qingdao 青岛市	Shandong 山东省	(0532)8939175 (0532)8938086
Guangzhou Haier Industry & Trade Co.,Ltd. 广州海尔工贸有限公司	Guangzhou 广州市	Guangdong 广东省	(020)87397315 (020)87374302
Huizhou TCL Electrical Appliances Sales Co.,Ltd. 惠州市TCL电器销售有限公司	Huizhou 惠州市	Guangdong 广东省	(0752)2289885 (0752)2280690
Guangdong Hardware Minerals Import & Export Group Company 广东省五金矿产进出口集团公司	Guangzhou 广州市	Guangdong 广东省	(020)87752204 (020)87752205

4069: Other Household Electrical Appliances 其他日用电器制造业

The industry accounts for 0.375% of the total revenue of China's industrial sector in 2002. The rate of return on assets is 6.50%. 83.00% of all firms in the industry made a profit while 17.00% had negative returns.The top province in terms of the industry's revenue is Guangdong, accounting for 60.72% of the total revenue.
2002年本行业收入占全行业的 0.375%，资产利润率为 6.50%。83.00%的企业赢利，17.00%的企业亏损。收入最高的省为广东省，占本行业的60.72%。

	Total number of firms 企业总数	Total number of employees 职工总数	Total revenue (Mil.RMB) 总销售收入 (百万元)	Total profit (Mil.RMB) 总利润 (百万元)	Return on assets 资产利润率 (%)	Return on equity 权益利润率 (%)	Labour productivity ('000 RMB/ worker) 劳动生产率 (千元/人)	Debts/ assets 资产负债率 (%)	Total assets (Mil.RMB) 总资产 (百万元)
Industry Overall 行业总体	594	180,074	40,233	2,194	6.50	17.49	66.45	62.82	33,729

	Number of firms 企业个数	Average number of employees 平均职工人数	Average revenue ('000 RMB) 平均销售收入 (千元)	Average profit ('000 RMB) 平均利润 (千元)	Return on assets 资产利润率 (%)	Return on equity 权益利润率 (%)	Labour productivity ('000 RMB/ worker) 劳动生产率 (千元/人)	Debts/ assets 资产负债率 (%)	Average total assets ('000 RMB) 平均总资产 (千元)
By ownership 产业所有权									
State-owned 国有	18	143	12,701	119	0.45	2.07	17.90	78.28	26,505
Collective-owned 集体	52	225	27,481	464	0.95	4.21	27.15	77.36	48,619
Foreign & Overseas Chinese Funded 三资	172	532	106,096	7,428	8.41	18.53	81.48	54.62	88,344
By regional distribution 地区分布									
Central-North 华北	27	155	33,680	1,810	4.31	10.77	55.79	59.98	41,979
Beijing 北京	11	185	29,119	3,431	6.27	13.43	73.67	53.29	54,716
Tianjin 天津	13	135	42,910	557	1.43	4.38	43.48	67.25	38,830
Hebei 河北	3	133	10,405	1,296	14.54	54.37	18.86	73.26	8,916
Shanxi 山西									
Inner Mongolia 内蒙古									
Northeast 东北	6	268	16,662	-3,741	-6.74	-91.57	19.07	92.64	55,538
Liaoning 辽宁	1	727	35,203	-22,414	-9.83		7.89	108.50	228,039
Jilin 吉林	1	15	3,375	-165	-1.38	-1.81	253.33	23.69	11,917
Heilongjiang 黑龙江	4	217	15,349	33	0.14	0.38	24.39	62.70	23,318
Central-East 华东	270	226	50,654	3,875	8.24	18.14	88.59	54.56	47,014
Shanghai 上海	43	203	65,014	4,576	6.41	13.91	79.28	53.93	71,434
Jiangsu 江苏	47	154	47,635	4,195	7.97	20.01	81.02	60.19	52,656
Zhejiang 浙江	136	196	32,103	2,184	7.43	18.79	39.43	60.44	29,384
Anhui 安徽	5	170	14,575	559	2.05	3.72	27.10	44.92	27,271
Fujian 福建	13	938	245,206	25,744	14.63	24.06	225.78	39.17	175,917
Jiangxi 江西									
Shandong 山东	26	199	39,056	682	2.44	5.53	55.27	55.90	27,997
Central-South 中南	282	389	88,862	3,891	5.87	18.27	55.82	67.86	66,258
Henan 河南	6	529	44,023	1,772	2.67	6.84	23.93	60.99	66,422
Hubei 湖北	9	212	37,536	657	0.70	1.48	86.09	52.65	93,764
Hunan 湖南									
Guangdong 广东	264	393	92,533	4,123	6.28	19.93	56.68	68.51	65,678
Guangxi 广西	3	302	9,517	-2,612	-7.58		4.88	109.16	34,444
Hainan 海南									
Southwest 西南	6	322	71,672	3,955	3.82	8.35	86.51	54.29	103,645
Chongqing 重庆									
Sichuan 四川	4	368	83,957	6,420	5.28	9.62	111.11	45.14	121,672
Guizhou 贵州	2	229	47,102	-973	-1.44	-11.24	7.27	87.19	67,593
Yunnan 云南									
Tibet 西藏									
Northwest 西北	3	613	19,356	157	0.18	10.96	11.48	98.36	87,399
Shaanxi 陕西									
Gansu 甘肃	3	613	19,356	157	0.18	10.96	11.48	98.36	87,399
Qinghai 青海									
Ningxia 宁夏									
Xinjiang 新疆									

4069: Other Household Electrical Appliances 其他日用电器制造业

Year 年份	Number of firms 企业个数	Rate of change 变化率(%)	Number of employees 职工人数(人)	Rate of change 变化率(%)	Total revenue (Mil. RMB) 总销售收入(百万元)	Rate of change 变化率(%)	Total profit (Mil RMB) 总利润(百万元)	Rate of change 变化率(%)
2000	479		133,056		30,892		1,411	
2001	567	18.37	161,325	21.25	36,296	17.49	1,499	6.24
2002	594	4.76	180,074	11.62	40,233	10.85	2,194	46.36

Major Products 主要产品	Output 产量	Unit 单位
Household Electric Roaster 家用电热烘烤器具	4,853	10,000 Units 万个
Microwave Oven 微波炉	2,271	10,000 Units 万台

10 Main Firms with Maximal Revenue (year founded) 收入最大的十家主要企业（创办年份）	City 城市	Province 省	Telephone/fax 电话/传真	Number of employees 职工人数	Ownership 产业所有权	Revenue ('000 RMB) 销售收入(千元)	Profit('000 RMB) (rank) 利润(千元)(排名)	Total assets ('000 RMB) 总资产(千元)	Major products 主要产品
Guangdong Galanz Group Corporation 广东格兰仕集团公司(1992)	Foshan 佛山市	Guangdong 广东省	(0765)8886389 (0765)8889628	11,200	Joint Stock 股份制	8,623,786	321,374(2)	3,758,028	Microwave Oven 微波炉
Shunde Xinbao Electrical Appliance Co., Ltd. 顺德市新宝电器有限公司(1996)	Foshan 佛山市	Guangdong 广东省	(0765)5333662 (0765)5562533	4,330	Overseas Chinese-funded 港澳台资	1,008,970	120,594(4)	449,337	Electric Hot Water Pot 电热水壶
Personal Care Company of Zhuhai SEZ, Ltd. 珠海经济特区飞利浦家庭电器有限公司(1990)	Zhuhai 珠海市	Guangdong 广东省	(0756)7621898 (0756)7621000	890	Foreign Funded 外商投资	757,061	129,903(3)	560,447	Electric Shaver 电须刨
Shunde Whirlpool Electrical Appliances Co., Ltd. 顺德惠而浦家电制品有限公司(1988)	Foshan 佛山市	Guangdong 广东省	(0765)6656922 (0765)6656931	1,647	Foreign Funded 外商投资	748,384	2,498(98)	829,215	Microwave Oven 微波炉
Tsannkuen China (shanghai) Enerprise Co., Ltd. 上海灿坤实业有限公司(1995)	Shanghai 上海市	Shanghai 上海市	(021)69593232 (021)69591674	2,423	Foreign Funded 外商投资	678,391	10,571(33)	782,624	Domestic Appliance Produsts 日用电器
Shenzhen Original Electric Machinery Co., Ltd. 深圳王利电机有限公司(1992)	Shenzhen 深圳市	Guangdong 广东省	(0755)27620888 (0755)27620777	2,803	Foreign Funded 外商投资	512,624	117,114(5)	445,521	Relayer 继电器
Jhiaphua Electric Appliances (Shenzhen) Co., Ltd. 捷家宝电器（深圳）有限公司(1997)	Shenzhen 深圳市	Guangdong 广东省	(0755)27608818 (0755)27647392	6,930	Overseas Chinese-funded 港澳台资	491,266	9,296(36)	720,796	Home Electrical Appliance 家庭电器
Guangdong Dehao Runda Elec-Tech International Co.,Ltd. 广东德豪润达电气股份有限公司(1996)	Zhuhai 珠海市	Guangdong 广东省	(0756)8677585 (0756)8676764	1,382	Joint Stock 股份制	479,047	75,504(8)	413,316	Bread Machine 面包机
Panasonic Electric Industry Wanbao (Guangzhou) Co., Ltd. 松下电工万宝电器(广州)有限公司(1993)	Guangzhou 广州市	Guangdong 广东省	(020)84770333 (020)84770333	698	Foreign Funded 外商投资	448,631	35,186(11)	414,751	Electric Shaving Razor 电须刀
Shangwu Electrical Industry (Shenzhen) Co.,Ltd. 上屋电业（深圳）有限公司(1997)	Shenzhen 深圳市	Guangdong 广东省	(0755)27644042 (0755)27644901	1,557	Overseas Chinese-funded 港澳台资	396,199	32,018(13)	145,293	Household Small Electrical Appliance家用小电器

Top 10 Cities by Revenue 销售收入排名前10位城市	Province 省	Market share 市场份额(%)	Number of firms 企业个数
Foshan 佛山市	Guangdong 广东省	32.48	59
Shenzhen 深圳市	Guangdong 广东省	8.84	27
Ningbo 宁波市	Zhejiang 浙江省	7.96	76
Xiamen 厦门市	Fujian 福建省	7.39	4
Shanghai 上海市	Shanghai 上海市	6.95	43
Guangzhou 广州市	Guangdong 广东省	5.28	33
Zhongshan 中山市	Guangdong 广东省	3.47	47
Zhuhai 珠海市	Guangdong 广东省	3.27	7
Jiangmen 江门市	Guangdong 广东省	2.91	34
Suzhou 苏州市	Jiangsu 江苏省	2.70	14

10 Major Wholesalers 十家主要批发商	City 城市	Province 省	Telephone/Fax 电话/传真
China Chemical Industry Supply & Sale (Group) General Company 中国化工供销(集团)总公司	Beijing 北京市	Beijing 北京市	(010)64238623 (010)64238623
China Chemical Industry Import & Export General Company 中国化工进出口总公司	Beijing 北京市	Beijing 北京市	(010)88078888 (010)88078890
Tianjin Bridge Group Welding Materials Supply & Sale Co., Ltd. 天津大桥集团电焊条供销有限公司	Tianjin 天津市	Tianjin 天津市	(022)83968861 (022)83968865
Taizhou Xingwei Chunlan Chain Stores Co., Ltd. 泰州星威春兰连锁店有限公司	Taizhou 泰州市	Jiangsu 江苏省	(0523)6611200 (0523)6224181
Taizhou Chunlan Sale Company 泰州春兰销售公司	Taizhou 泰州市	Jiangsu 江苏省	(0523)6611200 (0523)6224181
Shandong Tri-Union Co., Ltd. 山东三联有限责任公司	Jinan 济南市	Shandong 山东省	(0531)6086351 (0531)6093103
Haier Electrical Appliances Co.,Ltd. 海尔集团电器产业有限公司	Qingdao 青岛市	Shandong 山东省	(0532)8939175 (0532)8938086
Guangzhou Haier Industry & Trade Co.,Ltd. 广州海尔工贸有限公司	Guangzhou 广州市	Guangdong 广东省	(020)87397315 (020)87374302
Huizhou TCL Electrical Appliances Sales Co.,Ltd. 惠州市TCL电器销售有限公司	Huizhou 惠州市	Guangdong 广东省	(0752)2289885 (0752)2280690
Guangdong Hardware Minerals Import & Export Group Company 广东省五金矿产进出口集团公司	Guangzhou 广州市	Guangdong 广东省	(020)87752204 (020)87752205

4071: Light Bulbs 电光源制造业

The industry accounts for 0.122% of the total revenue of China's industrial sector in 2002. The rate of return on assets is 4.77%. 79.03% of all firms in the industry made a profit while 20.97% had negative returns.The top province in terms of the industry's revenue is Guangdong, accounting for 28.22% of the total revenue.
2002年本行业收入占全行业的 0.122%，资产利润率为 4.77%。79.03%的企业赢利，20.97%的企业亏损。收入最高的省为广东省，占本行业的28.22%。

	Total number of firms 企业总数	Total number of employees 职工总数	Total revenue (Mil.RMB) 总销售收入（百万元）	Total profit (Mil.RMB) 总利润（百万元）	Return on assets 资产利润率（%）	Return on equity 权益利润率（%）	Labour productivity ('000 RMB/ worker) 劳动生产率（千元/人）	Debts/ assets 资产负债率（%）	Total assets (Mil.RMB) 总资产（百万元）
Industry Overall 行业总体	329	118,106	13,122	741	4.77	9.08	33.83	47.47	15,534

	Number of firms 企业个数	Average number of employees 平均职工人数	Average revenue ('000 RMB) 平均销售收入（千元）	Average profit ('000 RMB) 平均利润（千元）	Return on assets 资产利润率（%）	Return on equity 权益利润率（%）	Labour productivity ('000 RMB/ worker) 劳动生产率（千元/人）	Debts/ assets 资产负债率（%）	Average total assets ('000 RMB) 平均总资产（千元）
By ownership 产业所有权									
State-owned 国有	24	266	10,643	-423	-0.77	-3.09	13.06	75.06	54,897
Collective-owned 集体	20	384	19,983	742	3.38	10.30	17.73	67.14	21,919
Foreign & Overseas Chinese Funded 三资	91	521	78,528	5,422	5.73	9.07	50.69	36.75	94,559
By regional distribution 地区分布									
Central-North 华北	15	272	24,628	-193	-0.39	-0.82	29.33	52.01	48,897
Beijing 北京	5	200	40,205	-305	-0.45	-0.68	62.62	33.29	67,609
Tianjin 天津	3	122	6,212	-1,416	-2.05	-7.05	-0.95	70.94	69,103
Hebei 河北	5	417	24,955	575	1.89	5.64	21.65	66.41	30,356
Shanxi 山西	2	315	12,493	5	0.02	0.06	19.46	58.03	18,162
Inner Mongolia 内蒙古									
Northeast 东北	10	321	11,025	-355	-0.83	-3.69	21.90	77.46	42,717
Liaoning 辽宁	8	342	10,819	-518	-1.22	-6.17	15.53	80.18	42,407
Jilin 吉林	2	236	11,850	298	0.68	2.05	58.85	66.95	43,958
Heilongjiang 黑龙江									
Central-East 华东	223	318	38,210	1,825	4.79	10.28	32.29	53.40	38,095
Shanghai 上海	26	422	95,843	2,810	3.11	8.74	60.73	64.39	90,308
Jiangsu 江苏	67	224	23,167	1,191	5.32	11.82	33.74	55.00	22,391
Zhejiang 浙江	101	238	29,827	2,063	7.73	15.38	30.40	49.75	26,688
Anhui 安徽	4	182	9,503	39	0.14	0.55	15.93	74.83	28,440
Fujian 福建	11	686	64,178	3,199	2.87	4.84	17.68	40.60	111,340
Jiangxi 江西	4	571	17,661	120	0.41	0.89	11.92	53.88	29,284
Shandong 山东	10	1,039	64,954	1,006	2.03	3.56	20.78	42.97	49,585
Central-South 中南	72	459	53,533	4,736	6.21	9.29	42.59	33.14	76,286
Henan 河南	8	145	6,442	140	1.14		15.73	114.38	12,247
Hubei 湖北	3	337	8,899	-248	-4.16	-65.35	14.90	93.63	5,966
Hunan 湖南	4	551	15,871	90	1.14		5.78	109.69	7,937
Guangdong 广东	56	498	66,127	6,186	6.59	9.34	48.85	29.39	93,827
Guangxi 广西	1	776	9,541	-6,121	-6.75		-1.49	123.94	90,660
Hainan 海南									
Southwest 西南	7	545	21,647	45	0.17	0.88	19.75	80.45	26,030
Chongqing 重庆	2	81	8,985	732	8.19	24.31	32.81	66.33	8,936
Sichuan 四川	4	685	31,759	17	0.06	0.27	25.30	79.28	31,179
Guizhou 贵州	1	918	6,523	-1,218	-3.07	-32.26	0.89	90.47	39,626
Yunnan 云南									
Tibet 西藏									
Northwest 西北	2	1,510	57,775	-627	-0.62	-2.78	10.60	77.81	101,625
Shaanxi 陕西	1	3,009	114,946	23	0.01	0.05	10.34	74.75	190,485
Gansu 甘肃	1	10	603	-1,277	-10.00		89.70	123.35	12,765
Qinghai 青海									
Ningxia 宁夏									
Xinjiang 新疆									

Year 年份	Number of firms 企业个数	Rate of change 变化率 (%)	Number of employees 职工人数 (人)	Rate of change 变化率 (%)	Total revenue (Mil. RMB) 总销售收入 (百万元)	Rate of change 变化率 (%)	Total profit (Mil RMB) 总利润 (百万元)	Rate of change 变化率 (%)
2000	303		120,554		11,725		580	
2001	320	5.61	113,644	-5.73	12,670	8.06	729	25.69
2002	329	2.81	118,106	3.93	13,122	3.57	741	1.65

Major Products 主要产品	Output 产量	Unit 单位
Lamp Bulb 灯泡	560,704	10,000 Units 万只

10 Main Firms with Maximal Revenue (year founded) 收入最大的十家主要企业（创办年份）	City 城市	Province 省	Telephone/fax 电话/传真	Number of employees 职工人数	Ownership 产业所有权	Revenue ('000 RMB) 销售收入 (千元)	Profit('000 RMB) (rank) 利润(千元) (排名)	Total assets ('000 RMB) 总资产 (千元)	Major products 主要产品
Foshan Electrical Appliance Lighting Co., Ltd. 佛山电器照明股份有限公司(1958)	Foshan 佛山市	Guangdong 广东省	(0575)2813838 (0575)2816276	2,610	Overseas Chinese-funded 港澳台资	956,153	235,628(1)	2,398,876	Light Bulb 灯炮
Zhejiang Yanqom Co., Ltd. 浙江阳光控股有限公司(1975)	Shaoxing 绍兴市	Zhejiang 浙江省	(0575)2013368 (0575)2015355	3,539	Joint Stock 股份制	908,900	131,510(2)	1,024,528	Fluorescent Lamp Tube 荧光灯管
Philips & Yaming Lighting Co., Ltd. 飞利浦亚明照明有限公司(1994)	Shanghai 上海市	Shanghai 上海市	(021)59154075 (021)59150242	1,615	Foreign Funded 外商投资	559,863	34,354(5)	563,118	Common Lamp Bulb 普通灯泡
Osram Foshan Lighting Co., Ltd. 欧司朗佛山照明有限公司(1995)	Foshan 佛山市	Guangdong 广东省	(0757)6482111 (0757)5569040	1,730	Foreign Funded 外商投资	536,842	36,928(4)	650,717	Power-saving Lamp 节能灯
Shanghai Zhenxin Electronics Engineering Co., Ltd. 上海振欣电子工程有限公司(1995)	Shanghai 上海市	Shanghai 上海市	(021)57610451 (021)57619961	1,300	Foreign Funded 外商投资	473,629	25,817(7)	171,358	Power-saving Lamp 节能灯
Heshan Gonghe Yinyu Light Decorations Factory 鹤山市共和银雨灯饰厂(1991)	Jiangmen 江门市	Guangdong 广东省	(0750)8300790 (0750)8300799	8,000	Overseas Chinese-funded 港澳台资	466,940	9,364(19)	487,259	Light Decorations 灯饰
GE Lighting Co., Ltd. 通用电气照明有限公司(1994)	Shanghai 上海市	Shanghai 上海市	(021)59125060 (021)52341156	4,569	Foreign Funded 外商投资	436,671	-	760,042	Electro-optic Source 电光源
Zhongyu Electrical Appliance (Shenzhen) Co.,Ltd. 中裕电器（深圳）有限公司(1991)	Shenzhen 深圳市	Guangdong 广东省	(0755)28617666 (0755)28617166	960	Overseas Chinese-funded 港澳台资	371,806	5,264(29)	85,712	Christmas Lamp 圣诞灯
Shanghai Xiangshan Industrial Co., Ltd. 上海翔山实业有限责任公司(1992)	Shanghai 上海市	Shanghai 上海市	(021)59204789 (021)69203739	254	Collective Owned 集体企业	228,404	5,092(31)	156,923	Lamps & Lanterns 灯具
Xiamen Topstar Lighting Co.,Ltd. 厦门通士达照明有限公司(2000)	Xiamen 厦门市	Fujian 福建省	(0592)6518188 (0592)6512626	1,557	Foreign Funded 外商投资	200,388	16,225(9)	241,026	Compacted Electronic Power-saving Lamp 紧凑型电子节能灯

Top 10 Cities by Revenue 销售收入排名前10位城市	Province 省	Market share 市场份额 (%)	Number of firms 企业个数
Shanghai 上海市	Shanghai 上海市	18.99	26
Foshan 佛山市	Guangdong 广东省	13.47	19
Shaoxing 绍兴市	Zhejiang 浙江省	8.61	14
Hangzhou 杭州市	Zhejiang 浙江省	6.06	28
Jiangmen 江门市	Guangdong 广东省	5.41	8
Shenzhen 深圳市	Guangdong 广东省	4.56	8
Xiamen 厦门市	Fujian 福建省	3.38	3
Yantai 烟台市	Shandong 山东省	3.00	3
Nanjing 南京市	Jiangsu 江苏省	2.74	13
Suzhou 苏州市	Jiangsu 江苏省	2.15	10

10 Major Wholesalers 十家主要批发商	City 城市	Province 省	Telephone/Fax 电话/传真
China Chemical Industry Supply & Sale (Group) General Company 中国化工供销(集团)总公司	Beijing 北京市	Beijing 北京市	(010)64238623 (010)64238623
China Chemical Industry Import & Export General Company 中国化工进出口总公司	Beijing 北京市	Beijing 北京市	(010)88078888 (010)88078890
Tianjin Bridge Group Welding Materials Supply & Sale Co., Ltd. 天津大桥集团电焊条供销有限公司	Tianjin 天津市	Tianjin 天津市	(022)83968861 (022)83968865
Taizhou Xingwei Chunlan Chain Stores Co., Ltd. 泰州星威春兰连锁店有限公司	Taizhou 泰州市	Jiangsu 江苏省	(0523)6611200 (0523)6224181
Taizhou Chunlan Sale Company 泰州春兰销售公司	Taizhou 泰州市	Jiangsu 江苏省	(0523)6611200 (0523)6224181
Shandong Tri-Union Co., Ltd. 山东三联有限责任公司	Jinan 济南市	Shandong 山东省	(0531)6086351 (0531)6093103
Haier Electrical Appliances Co.,Ltd. 海尔集团电器产业有限公司	Qingdao 青岛市	Shandong 山东省	(0532)8939175 (0532)8938086
Guangzhou Haier Industry & Trade Co.,Ltd. 广州海尔工贸有限公司	Guangzhou 广州市	Guangdong 广东省	(020)87397315 (020)87374302
Huizhou TCL Electrical Appliances Sales Co.,Ltd. 惠州市TCL电器销售有限公司	Huizhou 惠州市	Guangdong 广东省	(0752)2289885 (0752)2280690
Guangdong Hardware Minerals Import & Export Group Company 广东省五金矿产进出口集团公司	Guangzhou 广州市	Guangdong 广东省	(020)87752204 (020)87752205

4072: Lamp Sockets 灯头、灯座制造业

The industry accounts for 0.024% of the total revenue of China's industrial sector in 2002. The rate of return on assets is 2.68%. 71.08% of all firms in the industry made a profit while 28.92% had negative returns.The top province in terms of the industry's revenue is Guangdong, accounting for 54.28% of the total revenue.
2002年本行业收入占全行业的 0.024%，资产利润率为 2.68%。71.08%的企业赢利，28.92%的企业亏损。收入最高的省为广东省，占本行业的54.28%。

	Total number of firms 企业总数	Total number of employees 职工总数	Total revenue (Mil.RMB) 总销售收入（百万元）	Total profit (Mil.RMB) 总利润（百万元）	Return on assets 资产利润率（%）	Return on equity 权益利润率（%）	Labour productivity ('000 RMB/ worker) 劳动生产率（千元/人）	Debts/ assets 资产负债率（%）	Total assets (Mil.RMB) 总资产（百万元）
Industry Overall 行业总体	83	24,526	2,547	49	2.68	8.23	26.01	67.49	1,830

	Number of firms 企业个数	Average number of employees 平均职工人数	Average revenue ('000 RMB) 平均销售收入（千元）	Average profit ('000 RMB) 平均利润（千元）	Return on assets 资产利润率（%）	Return on equity 权益利润率（%）	Labour productivity ('000 RMB/ worker) 劳动生产率（千元/人）	Debts/ assets 资产负债率（%）	Average total assets ('000 RMB) 平均总资产（千元）
By ownership 产业所有权									
State-owned 国有	8	320	11,307	-785	-3.70		9.58	102.56	21,199
Collective-owned 集体	9	196	21,787	303	3.64	15.94	31.84	77.18	8,340
Foreign & Overseas Chinese Funded 三资	25	482	53,286	1,128	3.24	9.44	24.71	65.67	34,828
By regional distribution 地区分布									
Central-North 华北	6	148	12,362	1,143	8.28	19.92	23.06	58.45	13,804
Beijing 北京									
Tianjin 天津	5	146	13,623	1,377	9.22	20.38	24.69	54.76	14,935
Hebei 河北									
Shanxi 山西	1	160	6,057	-28	-0.34	-4.42	15.64	92.22	8,149
Inner Mongolia 内蒙古									
Northeast 东北	2	137	11,938	805	3.10	6.02	21.68	48.55	25,986
Liaoning 辽宁	2	137	11,938	805	3.10	6.02	21.68	48.55	25,986
Jilin 吉林									
Heilongjiang 黑龙江									
Central-East 华东	45	235	21,912	591	3.08	8.79	26.42	65.00	19,200
Shanghai 上海	7	273	27,952	-423	-1.21	-3.73	34.76	67.51	34,869
Jiangsu 江苏	17	324	33,054	1,033	4.22	10.95	25.57	61.47	24,479
Zhejiang 浙江	15	108	11,318	914	10.57	23.94	33.21	55.85	8,649
Anhui 安徽									
Fujian 福建	2	70	12,131	189	3.20	8.84	56.51	63.84	5,894
Jiangxi 江西	3	453	5,136	-1,029	-5.60		2.90	100.50	18,383
Shandong 山东	1	26	19,011	1,001	14.06	65.08	238.46	78.40	7,122
Central-South 中南	26	453	54,221	594	2.12	8.30	26.76	74.43	27,989
Henan 河南	1	22		-394	-1.68			130.51	23,476
Hubei 湖北	2	127	8,547	654	14.14	27.74	34.44	49.02	4,625
Hunan 湖南	1	50	10,270	836	6.30	7.74	43.66	18.55	13,262
Guangdong 广东	22	521	62,836	622	2.01	7.70	26.57	73.93	30,987
Guangxi 广西									
Hainan 海南									
Southwest 西南	3	150	15,056	-415	-1.29	-3.08	29.52	58.19	32,292
Chongqing 重庆	2	130	11,723	-1,629	-7.71		3.40	112.78	21,119
Sichuan 四川	1	189	21,721	2,012	3.68	4.38	65.47	15.99	54,638
Guizhou 贵州									
Yunnan 云南									
Tibet 西藏									
Northwest 西北	1	562	7,656	-283	-4.24	-5.89	6.43	28.10	6,680
Shaanxi 陕西	1	562	7,656	-283	-4.24	-5.89	6.43	28.10	6,680
Gansu 甘肃									
Qinghai 青海									
Ningxia 宁夏									
Xinjiang 新疆									

4072: Lamp Sockets 灯头、灯座制造业

Year 年份	Number of firms 企业个数	Rate of change 变化率 (%)	Number of employees 职工人数 (人)	Rate of change 变化率 (%)	Total revenue (Mil. RMB) 总销售收入 (百万元)	Rate of change 变化率 (%)	Total profit (Mil RMB) 总利润 (百万元)	Rate of change 变化率 (%)
2000	71		16,190		1,604		2	
2001	79	11.27	19,044	17.63	1,927	20.14	20	900.00
2002	83	5.06	24,526	28.79	2,547	32.17	49	145.00

Major Products 主要产品	Output 产量	Unit 单位

10 Main Firms with Maximal Revenue (year founded) 收入最大的十家主要企业（创办年份）	City 城市	Province 省	Telephone/fax 电话/传真	Number of employees 职工人数	Ownership 产业所有权	Revenue ('000 RMB) 销售收入 (千元)	Profit('000 RMB) (rank) 利润(千元) (排名)	Total assets ('000 RMB) 总资产 (千元)	Major products 主要产品
Dongguan Dong Li Electronics Co., Ltd.	Dongguan	Guangdong	(0769)7723276		Overseas Chinese-funded				
东莞东力电子有限公司(1993)	东莞市	广东省	(0769)7722120	6,500	港澳台资	424,749	8,811(1)	294,339	
Taishan International Electrical Appliance Factory Co., Ltd.	Jiangmen	Guangdong	(0750)5578766		Overseas Chinese-funded				Light Decorations
台山市国际电器厂有限公司(1993)	江门市	广东省	(0750)5578678	890	港澳台资	354,118	-	120,180	灯饰
Jiangsu Bright Group Co., Ltd.	Yancheng	Jiangsu	(0515)8590361		Limited-Liability				Direction Neon Light
江苏伯乐达集团有限公司(1984)	盐城市	江苏省	(0515)8590599	1,121	有限公司	145,270	7,500(2)	140,790	指示氖灯
Zhongshan Jinwei Light Decorations Electric Equipment Factor	Zhongshan	Guangdong	(0760)3117210		Private Enterprises				Light Decorations for Illuminating Appliance
中山市金威灯饰电器厂(1992)	中山市	广东省	(0760)3116281	480	私营独资	110,500	962(22)	20,387	照明电器灯饰
Nanhai Xiqiao Datong Wanshun Cable Electrical Appliance Factory	Foshan	Guangdong	(0757)6853900		Private Enterprises				Plug & Switch
南海市西樵大同万顺电缆电器制造厂(1992)	佛山市	广东省	(0757)6853238	167	私营独资	61,000	2,139(11)	6,180	插头开关
Shanghai Jia Bao Guangming Lamp Cap Co., Ltd.	Shanghai	Shanghai	(021)59516628		Joint Stock				Lamp Holder
上海嘉宝光明灯头有限公司(1971)	上海市	上海市	(021)59511312	893	股份制	60,520	-	82,547	灯头
Jiangsu Huaming Industrial Company	Taizhou	Jiangsu	(0523)4832394		State-owned				Lamp Holder
江苏华明实业公司(1971)	泰州市	江苏省	(0523)4838837	921	国有企业	55,147	308(38)	39,108	灯头
Zhenjiang Xingguang Electrical Applaince Co.,Ltd.	Zhenjiang	Jiangsu	(0511)8789992		Private Owned				Power-saving Lamp
镇江星光电器有限公司(1999)	镇江市	江苏省	(0511)8789992	140	私营企业	51,020	120(49)	9,054	节能灯
Clipsal Lighting (Huizhou) Co., Ltd.	Huizhou	Guangdong	(0752)2606028		Overseas Chinese-funded				Lamp Holder
奇胜照明(惠州)有限公司(2002)	惠州市	广东省	(0752)2606018	95	港澳台资	43,187		14,789	灯头
Shangyu Jiasheng Lighting Material Co.,Ltd.	Shaoxing	Zhejiang	(0575)2672845		Private Owned				Aluminium Lamp Holder
上虞市佳盛照明材料有限公司(1987)	绍兴市	浙江省	(0575)2672086	318	私营企业	42,483	3,256(6)	38,930	铝灯头

Top 10 Cities by Revenue 销售收入排名前10位城市	Province 省	Market share 市场份额 (%)	Number of firms 企业个数
Dongguan 东莞市	Guangdong 广东省	19.10	4
Jiangmen 江门市	Guangdong 广东省	18.78	3
Shanghai 上海市	Shanghai 上海市	7.68	7
Zhenjiang 镇江市	Jiangsu 江苏省	7.55	4
Zhongshan 中山市	Guangdong 广东省	6.90	5
Yancheng 盐城市	Jiangsu 江苏省	5.70	1
Foshan 佛山市	Guangdong 广东省	5.63	6
Changzhou 常州市	Jiangsu 江苏省	3.61	5
Huizhou 惠州市	Guangdong 广东省	3.54	3
Wenzhou 温州市	Zhejiang 浙江省	3.26	10

10 Major Wholesalers 十家主要批发商	City 城市	Province 省	Telephone/Fax 电话/传真
China Chemical Industry Supply & Sale (Group) General Company	Beijing	Beijing	(010)64238623
中国化工供销(集团)总公司	北京市	北京市	(010)64238623
China Chemical Industry Import & Export General Company	Beijing	Beijing	(010)88078888
中国化工进出口总公司	北京市	北京市	(010)88078890
Tianjin Bridge Group Welding Materials Supply & Sale Co., Ltd.	Tianjin	Tianjin	(022)83968861
天津大桥集团电焊条供销有限公司	天津市	天津市	(022)83968865
Taizhou Xingwei Chunlan Chain Stores Co., Ltd.	Taizhou	Jiangsu	(0523)6611200
泰州星威春兰连锁店有限公司	泰州市	江苏省	(0523)6224181
Taizhou Chunlan Sale Company	Taizhou	Jiangsu	(0523)6611200
泰州春兰销售公司	泰州市	江苏省	(0523)6224181
Shandong Tri-Union Co., Ltd.	Jinan	Shandong	(0531)6086351
山东三联有限责任公司	济南市	山东省	(0531)6093103
Haier Electrical Appliances Co.,Ltd.	Qingdao	Shandong	(0532)8939175
海尔集团电器产业有限公司	青岛市	山东省	(0532)8938086
Guangzhou Haier Industry & Trade Co.,Ltd.	Guangzhou	Guangdong	(020)87397315
广州海尔工贸有限公司	广州市	广东省	(020)87374302
Huizhou TCL Electrical Appliances Sales Co.,Ltd.	Huizhou	Guangdong	(0752)2289885
惠州市TCL电器销售有限公司	惠州市	广东省	(0752)2280690
Guangdong Hardware Minerals Import & Export Group Company	Guangzhou	Guangdong	(020)87752204
广东省五金矿产进出口集团公司	广州市	广东省	(020)87752205

4073: Lamps and Lanterns 灯具制造业

The industry accounts for 0.201% of the total revenue of China's industrial sector in 2002. The rate of return on assets is 6.20%. 85.36% of all firms in the industry made a profit while 14.64% had negative returns.The top province in terms of the industry's revenue is Guangdong, accounting for 40.97% of the total revenue.
2002年本行业收入占全行业的0.201%，资产利润率为6.20%。85.36%的企业赢利，14.64%的企业亏损。收入最高的省为广东省，占本行业的40.97%。

	Total number of firms 企业总数	Total number of employees 职工总数	Total revenue (Mil.RMB) 总销售收入（百万元）	Total profit (Mil.RMB) 总利润（百万元）	Return on assets 资产利润率（%）	Return on equity 权益利润率（%）	Labour productivity ('000 RMB/ worker) 劳动生产率（千元/人）	Debts/ assets 资产负债率（%）	Total assets (Mil.RMB) 总资产（百万元）
Industry Overall 行业总体	690	141,885	21,517	1,017	6.20	14.85	35.82	58.23	16,391

	Number of firms 企业个数	Average number of employees 平均职工人数	Average revenue ('000 RMB) 平均销售收入（千元）	Average profit ('000 RMB) 平均利润（千元）	Return on assets 资产利润率（%）	Return on equity 权益利润率（%）	Labour productivity ('000 RMB/ worker) 劳动生产率（千元/人）	Debts/ assets 资产负债率（%）	Average total assets ('000 RMB) 平均总资产（千元）
By ownership 产业所有权									
State-owned 国有	18	232	10,735	18	0.06	0.16	16.70	64.90	31,988
Collective-owned 集体	54	191	35,181	1,316	5.72	17.75	41.38	67.76	23,000
Foreign & Overseas Chinese Funded 三资	233	296	44,252	2,388	6.48	14.27	36.76	54.63	36,876
By regional distribution 地区分布									
Central-North 华北	33	147	36,895	3,014	7.79	13.23	49.73	41.13	38,707
Beijing 北京	16	187	49,540	4,101	7.68	12.07	45.75	36.34	53,366
Tianjin 天津	9	116	26,560	2,369	8.32	17.00	48.81	51.03	28,457
Hebei 河北	6	118	29,339	2,008	7.71	15.60	72.32	50.62	26,059
Shanxi 山西	1	59	5,180	189	5.39	6.41	17.64	15.96	3,509
Inner Mongolia 内蒙古	1	60	4,638	299	3.99	10.84	28.83	63.23	7,503
Northeast 东北	7	151	11,201	438	2.67	3.50	29.79	23.72	16,390
Liaoning 辽宁	6	96	11,631	492	2.79	3.64	52.34	23.35	17,641
Jilin 吉林									
Heilongjiang 黑龙江	1	480	8,618	113	1.27	1.77	2.69	28.11	8,880
Central-East 华东	355	180	31,345	1,898	8.42	22.21	40.45	62.07	22,530
Shanghai 上海	72	136	31,976	2,577	12.58	28.97	50.86	56.59	20,490
Jiangsu 江苏	71	215	33,346	2,446	10.79	31.46	36.91	65.70	22,666
Zhejiang 浙江	177	157	28,723	1,371	6.21	16.89	39.73	63.23	22,075
Anhui 安徽	5	915	56,977	4,270	6.00	24.26	20.31	75.25	71,142
Fujian 福建	14	236	25,528	578	2.35	4.93	27.70	52.28	24,576
Jiangxi 江西	3	106	4,501	184	2.99	7.37	15.87	59.48	6,175
Shandong 山东	13	222	55,216	3,212	14.51	28.84	80.17	49.69	22,136
Central-South 中南	288	247	31,364	833	3.49	8.27	30.82	57.80	23,893
Henan 河南	6	358	23,068	194	0.44	3.31	18.21	86.73	44,038
Hubei 湖北	5	97	8,681	139	0.43	0.71	62.03	39.93	32,572
Hunan 湖南	6	143	6,076	65	1.87	4.48	12.48	58.26	3,496
Guangdong 广东	271	249	32,526	877	3.70	8.61	31.23	57.07	23,739
Guangxi 广西									
Hainan 海南									
Southwest 西南	6	112	9,792	65	0.39	0.72	44.01	46.73	16,801
Chongqing 重庆	4	94	10,577	84	0.43	0.68	30.11	37.47	19,511
Sichuan 四川	2	148	8,221	28	0.24	1.12	61.72	78.50	11,380
Guizhou 贵州									
Yunnan 云南									
Tibet 西藏									
Northwest 西北	1	230	2,163	19	0.10	0.12	1.98	16.88	19,257
Shaanxi 陕西	1	230	2,163	19	0.10	0.12	1.98	16.88	19,257
Gansu 甘肃									
Qinghai 青海									
Ningxia 宁夏									
Xinjiang 新疆									

Year 年份	Number of firms 企业个数	Rate of change 变化率 (%)	Number of employees 职工人数 (人)	Rate of change 变化率 (%)	Total revenue (Mil. RMB) 总销售收入 (百万元)	Rate of change 变化率 (%)	Total profit (Mil RMB) 总利润 (百万元)	Rate of change 变化率 (%)
2000	381		85,084		13,065		635	
2001	531	39.37	109,120	28.25	16,164	23.72	773	21.73
2002	690	29.94	141,885	30.03	21,517	33.12	1,017	31.57

Major Products 主要产品	Output 产量	Unit 单位
Lamps & Lanterns 灯具	10	100,000,000 Units 亿只

10 Main Firms with Maximal Revenue (year founded) 收入最大的十家主要企业（创办年份）	City 城市	Province 省	Telephone/fax 电话/传真	Number of employees 职工人数	Ownership 产业所有权	Revenue ('000 RMB) 销售收入 (千元)	Profit('000 RMB) (rank) 利润(千元) (排名)	Total assets ('000 RMB) 总资产 (千元)	Major products 主要产品
BEIJING MATSUSHITA ELECTRIC WORKS,LTD	Beijing	Beijing	(010)67881179		Foreign Funded				Lighting Lamps & Lanterns
北京松下电工有限公司(1993)	北京市	北京市	(010)67881177	1,160	外商投资	507,650	40,821(5)	433,326	照明灯具
Shanghai Dongsheng Electric Co., Ltd.	Shanghai	Shanghai	(021)56863636		Joint Stock				Others Lamps & Lanterns
上海东升电子股份有限公司(1992)	上海市	上海市	(021)56862609	1,000	股份制	466,926	29,708(7)	261,650	其他灯具
Weihai Jintong Lamp and Lanterns Co.,Ltd.	Weihai	Shandong	(0631)5584021		Collective-owned				Lamps & Lanterns
威海金通灯具有限公司(1984)	威海市	山东省	(0631)5584166	680	集体企业	433,790	26,160(8)	74,138	灯具
Zhejiang Suilun Industrial Co.,Ltd.	Jiaxing	Zhejiang	(0573)5844158		Private Owned				Lamps & Lanterns
浙江穗轮实业有限公司(2000)	嘉兴市	浙江省	(0573)5844228	1,713	私营企业	341,780	6,020(26)	214,060	灯具
Philips & Yaming Linghting Co., Ltd.	Shanghai	Shanghai	(021)59103624		Foreign Funded				Lamps & Lanterns
飞利浦亚明灯具有限公司(1995)	上海市	上海市	(021)59103378	129	外商投资	323,492	32,617(6)	152,819	灯具
Suzhou Changrong Lighting Decorations Co., Ltd.	Suzhou	Jiangsu	(0520)53810111		Overseas Chinese-funded				Lamps & Lanterns
苏州长荣灯饰有限公司(1993)	苏州市	江苏省	(0520)53812226	860	港澳台资	263,520	54,910(2)	195,720	灯具
Jiaojiang Festival Decoration Lamp Jointly-operated General Factory	Taizhou	Zhejiang	(0576)8204916		Collective-owned				Festival Decoration Lamp
椒江节日灯联营总厂(1984)	台州市	浙江省	(0576)8201156	1,291	集体企业	232,692	8,816(21)	323,872	节日灯
Jiadianbao Electric Equipment (Shenzhen) Co.,Ltd.	Shenzhen	Guangdong	(0755)27938666		Overseas Chinese-funded				Lamps & Lanterns
家电宝电器(深圳)有限公司(1992)	深圳市	广东省	(0755)27938555	2,053	港澳台资	226,588	1,005(174)	248,287	灯具
Guangzhou Jiufo Electrical Appliance Industrial Co., Ltd.	Guangzhou	Guangdong	(020)87811438		Limited Liability				Fluorescent Lamp Lamps & Lanterns
广州市九佛电器实业有限公司(1986)	广州市	广东省	(020)87811073	1,026	有限公司	206,487	-	122,091	荧光灯灯具
Anhui Shilin Electrical Lighting Co.,Ltd.	Lu'an	Anhui	(0564)5418571		Private Owned				Bulb
安徽世林电光源有限公司(1997)	六安市	安徽省	(0564)5411007	3,800	私营企业	194,576	13,874(14)	210,223	灯泡

Top 10 Cities by Revenue 销售收入排名前10位城市	Province 省	Market share 市场份额 (%)	Number of firms 企业个数
Zhongshan 中山市	Guangdong 广东省	11.00	86
Shanghai 上海市	Shanghai 上海市	10.70	72
Ningbo 宁波市	Zhejiang 浙江省	8.06	63
Taizhou 台州市	Zhejiang 浙江省	7.79	61
Guangzhou 广州市	Guangdong 广东省	5.66	38
Shenzhen 深圳市	Guangdong 广东省	4.96	26
Dongguan 东莞市	Guangdong 广东省	4.93	29
Jiangmen 江门市	Guangdong 广东省	4.63	21
Foshan 佛山市	Guangdong 广东省	4.47	39
Changzhou 常州市	Jiangsu 江苏省	4.45	15

10 Major Wholesalers 十家主要批发商	City 城市	Province 省	Telephone/Fax 电话/传真
China Chemical Industry Supply & Sale (Group) General Company	Beijing	Beijing	(010)64238623
中国化工供销(集团)总公司	北京市	北京市	(010)64238623
China Chemical Industry Import & Export General Company	Beijing	Beijing	(010)88078888
中国化工进出口总公司	北京市	北京市	(010)88078890
Tianjin Bridge Group Welding Materials Supply & Sale Co., Ltd.	Tianjin	Tianjin	(022)83968861
天津大桥集团电焊条供销有限公司	天津市	天津市	(022)83968865
Taizhou Xingwei Chunlan Chain Stores Co., Ltd.	Taizhou	Jiangsu	(0523)6611200
泰州星威春兰连锁店有限公司	泰州市	江苏省	(0523)6224181
Taizhou Chunlan Sale Company	Taizhou	Jiangsu	(0523)6611200
泰州春兰销售公司	泰州市	江苏省	(0523)6224181
Shandong Tri-Union Co., Ltd.	Jinan	Shandong	(0531)6086351
山东三联有限责任公司	济南市	山东省	(0531)6093103
Haier Electrical Appliances Co.,Ltd.	Qingdao	Shandong	(0532)8939175
海尔集团电器产业有限公司	青岛市	山东省	(0532)8938086
Guangzhou Haier Industry & Trade Co.,Ltd.	Guangzhou	Guangdong	(020)87397315
广州海尔工贸有限公司	广州市	广东省	(020)87374302
Huizhou TCL Electrical Appliances Sales Co.,Ltd.	Huizhou	Guangdong	(0752)2289885
惠州市TCL电器销售有限公司	惠州市	广东省	(0752)2280690
Guangdong Hardware Minerals Import & Export Group Company	Guangzhou	Guangdong	(020)87752204
广东省五金矿产进出口集团公司	广州市	广东省	(020)87752205

4074: Lamp Appliance Accessories 灯用电器附件制造业

The industry accounts for 0.046% of the total revenue of China's industrial sector in 2002. The rate of return on assets is 9.73%. 90.55% of all firms in the industry made a profit while 9.45% had negative returns.The top province in terms of the industry's revenue is Guangdong, accounting for 41.38% of the total revenue.
2002年本行业收入占全行业的 0.046%，资产利润率为 9.73%。90.55%的企业赢利，9.45%的企业亏损。收入最高的省为广东省，占本行业的41.38%。

	Total number of firms 企业总数	Total number of employees 职工总数	Total revenue (Mil.RMB) 总销售收入 (百万元)	Total profit (Mil.RMB) 总利润 (百万元)	Return on assets 资产利润率 (%)	Return on equity 权益利润率 (%)	Labour productivity ('000 RMB/ worker) 劳动生产率 (千元/人)	Debts/ assets 资产负债率 (%)	Total assets (Mil.RMB) 总资产 (百万元)
Industry Overall 行业总体	127	26,544	4,962	321	9.73	19.36	44.28	49.72	3,299

	Number of firms 企业个数	Average number of employees 平均职工人数	Average revenue ('000 RMB) 平均销售收入（千元）	Average profit ('000 RMB) 平均利润 (千元)	Return on assets 资产利润率 (%)	Return on equity 权益利润率 (%)	Labour productivity ('000 RMB/ worker) 劳动生产率 (千元/人)	Debts/ assets 资产负债率 (%)	Average total assets ('000 RMB) 平均总资产 (千元)
By ownership 产业所有权									
State-owned 国有	10	104	6,302	-158	-1.61	-10.93	14.90	85.27	9,834
Collective-owned 集体	9	230	7,722	306	2.57	7.15	13.68	64.06	11,915
Foreign & Overseas Chinese Funded 三资	45	383	84,901	5,801	11.13	20.89	49.22	46.71	52,113
By regional distribution 地区分布									
Central-North 华北	8	114	11,604	763	4.64	11.97	31.13	61.21	16,433
Beijing 北京	3	228	19,954	1,210	3.42	9.37	20.41	63.51	35,374
Tianjin 天津	3	32	4,638	331	7.96	15.43	59.84	48.45	4,156
Hebei 河北	1	108	14,334	1,477	33.57	86.88	68.53	61.36	4,400
Shanxi 山西									
Inner Mongolia 内蒙古	1	27	4,726	8	0.09	0.19	51.81	51.14	8,472
Northeast 东北	4	82	5,537	91	0.25	0.55	19.32	53.91	36,199
Liaoning 辽宁	2	49	9,467	177	3.61	7.61	35.39	52.63	4,908
Jilin 吉林	1	5	720	-3	-0.30	-42.86	103.80	99.30	1,005
Heilongjiang 黑龙江	1	225	2,496	14	0.01	0.02	10.44	53.66	133,977
Central-East 华东	73	181	37,705	3,448	12.24	21.27	52.19	42.46	28,172
Shanghai 上海	15	215	54,133	5,233	12.38	19.56	51.69	36.69	42,254
Jiangsu 江苏	15	164	28,951	2,176	16.74	36.58	50.11	54.24	12,997
Zhejiang 浙江	32	113	15,339	1,200	10.37	19.61	38.15	47.11	11,571
Anhui 安徽	1	58	6,288	570	24.05	83.82	29.76	71.31	2,370
Fujian 福建	5	258	55,648	7,517	7.16	12.08	63.01	40.75	105,020
Jiangxi 江西	1	241	2,117	-164	-0.83	-124.24	3.98	99.33	19,654
Shandong 山东	4	583	182,177	16,045	20.68	34.68	76.35	40.37	77,588
Central-South 中南	35	333	59,321	1,952	7.56	20.09	37.77	62.38	25,821
Henan 河南	1	14	27	23	4.40	4.40	-0.93		523
Hubei 湖北									
Hunan 湖南	2	278	9,572	191	1.37	2.11	15.50	35.39	13,946
Guangdong 广东	31	356	66,240	2,339	8.52	24.09	39.11	64.62	27,441
Guangxi 广西									
Hainan 海南	1	68	3,650	-4,601	-18.67	-22.41	11.16	16.72	24,650
Southwest 西南	2	108	5,290	-1,557	-22.49		15.78	100.62	6,921
Chongqing 重庆									
Sichuan 四川	1	110	8,051	1	0.02	0.08	28.71	70.67	4,071
Guizhou 贵州									
Yunnan 云南	1	105	2,528	-3,114	-31.87		2.23	113.10	9,770
Tibet 西藏									
Northwest 西北	5	40	1,643	-452	-4.68	-12.77	33.08	63.32	9,650
Shaanxi 陕西	1	42	6,327	-2,221	-5.57	-12.97	93.12	57.05	39,862
Gansu 甘肃	4	39	473	-10	-0.46	-6.78	16.91	93.15	2,097
Qinghai 青海									
Ningxia 宁夏									
Xinjiang 新疆									

4074: Lamp Appliance Accessories 灯用电器附件制造业

Year 年份	Number of firms 企业个数	Rate of change 变化率 (%)	Number of employees 职工人数 (人)	Rate of change 变化率 (%)	Total revenue (Mil. RMB) 总销售收入 (百万元)	Rate of change 变化率 (%)	Total profit (Mil RMB) 总利润 (百万元)	Rate of change 变化率 (%)
2000	104		22,534		3,958		222	
2001	115	10.58	23,693	5.14	4,532	14.50	286	28.83
2002	127	10.43	26,544	12.03	4,962	9.49	321	12.24

Major Products 主要产品	Output 产量	Unit 单位

10 Main Firms with Maximal Revenue (year founded) 收入最大的十家主要企业（创办年份）	City 城市	Province 省	Telephone/fax 电话/传真	Number of employees 职工人数	Ownership 产业所有权	Revenue ('000 RMB) 销售收入 (千元)	Profit('000 RMB) (rank) 利润(千元) (排名)	Total assets ('000 RMB) 总资产 (千元)	Major products 主要产品
Qingdao Hosiden Electronics Co., Ltd. 青岛星电电子有限公司(1992)	Qingdao 青岛市	Shandong 山东省	(0532)4911164 (0532)4817832	1,571	Foreign Funded 外商投资	344,202	21,139(5)	189,074	Earphone 耳机
Philips Lighting Electronics (Shanghai) Co., Ltd. 飞利浦照明电子（上海）有限公司(1993)	Shanghai 上海市	Shanghai 上海市	(021)64855330 (021)46853915	625	Foreign Funded 外商投资	340,120	29,437(3)	281,345	Electric Appliance Fittings for Lamp灯用电器附件
Wendeng Sanji Electronics Co., Ltd. 文登三吉电子有限公司(1992)	Weihai 威海市	Shandong 山东省	(0631)8898082 (0631)8898342	450	Foreign Funded 外商投资	314,830	43,820(1)	59,570	Transformer 变压器
Extralight(guangzhou) Electrical Co.,Ltd. 广州雅耀电器有限公司(1992)	Guangzhou 广州市	Guangdong 广东省	(020)84733932 (020)84734000	537	Overseas Chinese-funded 港澳台资	224,278	7,238(12)	78,097	Lamps & Lanterns 灯具
Nanjing Fangjiang Lighting Electrical Appliance Co., Ltd. 南京方将照明电器有限公司(1992)	Nanjing 南京市	Jiangsu 江苏省	(025)2416464 (025)2422463	951	Overseas Chinese-funded 港澳台资	216,960	9,370(10)	46,860	Start Light Machine 启辉器
Shanghai Gold Lighting Co., Ltd. 上海光达照明有限公司(1994)	Shanghai 上海市	Shanghai 上海市	(021)56300561 (021)61504686	286	Limited-Liability 有限公司	179,554	6,070(15)	75,498	Electronic Ballast电子镇流器
Philips Lighting Electronics (Xiamen) Co., Ltd. 飞利浦照明电子（厦门）有限公司(1999)	Xiamen 厦门市	Fujian 福建省	(0592)5774192 (0592)5774191	205	Foreign Funded 外商投资	138,258	21,265(4)	86,977	Electrical Appliance Accessories for Lamp灯用电器附件
Taishan Cheuk Tang Products Co.,Ltd. 台山卓藤钢材制品有限公司(1992)	Jiangmen 江门市	Guangdong 广东省	(0750)5411495 (0750)5411998	75	Overseas Chinese-funded 港澳台资	79,380	330(68)	28,110	Silicon Steel Slice 硅钢片
Ningbo Self Electronics Co., Ltd. 宁波赛尔富电子有限公司(1997)	Ningbo 宁波市	Zhejiang 浙江省	(0574)88213456 (0574)88214326	304	Private Owned 私营企业	63,842	18,920(6)	55,613	Lamps & Lanterns Transformer灯具用变压器
Wenzhou Feidiao Electrical Appliance Co.,Ltd. 温州飞雕电器有限公司(1995)	Wenzhou 温州市	Zhejiang 浙江省	(0577)86525993 (0577)86525240	645	Overseas Chinese-funded 港澳台资	62,417	1,190(39)	34,370	Wall Switch 墙壁开关

Top 10 Cities by Revenue 销售收入排名前10位城市	Province 省	Market share 市场份额 (%)	Number of firms 企业个数
Guangzhou 广州市	Guangdong 广东省	26.61	10
Shanghai 上海市	Shanghai 上海市	16.36	15
Qingdao 青岛市	Shandong 山东省	7.91	2
Weihai 威海市	Shandong 山东省	6.34	1
Foshan 佛山市	Guangdong 广东省	5.36	4
Wenzhou 温州市	Zhejiang 浙江省	5.11	20
Nanjing 南京市	Jiangsu 江苏省	4.89	4
Xiamen 厦门市	Fujian 福建省	3.01	2
Jiangmen 江门市	Guangdong 广东省	2.89	5
Ningbo 宁波市	Zhejiang 浙江省	2.73	4

10 Major Wholesalers 十家主要批发商	City 城市	Province 省	Telephone/Fax 电话/传真
China Chemical Industry Supply & Sale (Group) General Company 中国化工供销(集团)总公司	Beijing 北京市	Beijing 北京市	(010)64238623 (010)64238623
China Chemical Industry Import & Export General Company 中国化工进出口总公司	Beijing 北京市	Beijing 北京市	(010)88078888 (010)88078890
Tianjin Bridge Group Welding Materials Supply & Sale Co., Ltd. 天津大桥集团电焊条供销有限公司	Tianjin 天津市	Tianjin 天津市	(022)83968861 (022)83968865
Taizhou Xingwei Chunlan Chain Stores Co., Ltd. 泰州星威春兰连锁店有限公司	Taizhou 泰州市	Jiangsu 江苏省	(0523)6611200 (0523)6224181
Taizhou Chunlan Sale Company 泰州春兰销售公司	Taizhou 泰州市	Jiangsu 江苏省	(0523)6611200 (0523)6224181
Shandong Tri-Union Co., Ltd. 山东三联有限责任公司	Jinan 济南市	Shandong 山东省	(0531)6086351 (0531)6093103
Haier Electrical Appliances Co.,Ltd. 海尔集团电器产业有限公司	Qingdao 青岛市	Shandong 山东省	(0532)8939175 (0532)8938086
Guangzhou Haier Industry & Trade Co.,Ltd. 广州海尔工贸有限公司	Guangzhou 广州市	Guangdong 广东省	(020)87397315 (020)87374302
Huizhou TCL Electrical Appliances Sales Co.,Ltd. 惠州市TCL电器销售有限公司	Huizhou 惠州市	Guangdong 广东省	(0752)2289885 (0752)2280690
Guangdong Hardware Minerals Import & Export Group Company 广东省五金矿产进出口集团公司	Guangzhou 广州市	Guangdong 广东省	(020)87752204 (020)87752205

4079: Other Lighting Equipment 其他照明器具制造业

The industry accounts for 0.022% of the total revenue of China's industrial sector in 2002. The rate of return on assets is 1.60%. 87.50% of all firms in the industry made a profit while 12.50% had negative returns.The top province in terms of the industry's revenue is Guangdong, accounting for 46.75% of the total revenue.
2002年本行业收入占全行业的0.022%，资产利润率为1.60%。87.50%的企业赢利，12.50%的企业亏损。收入最高的省为广东省，占本行业的46.75%。

	Total number of firms 企业总数	Total number of employees 职工总数	Total revenue (Mil.RMB) 总销售收入 (百万元)	Total profit (Mil.RMB) 总利润 (百万元)	Return on assets 资产利润率 (%)	Return on equity 权益利润率 (%)	Labour productivity ('000 RMB/ worker) 劳动生产率 (千元/人)	Debts/ assets 资产负债率 (%)	Total assets (Mil.RMB) 总资产 (百万元)
Industry Overall 行业总体	96	22,221	2,381	37	1.60	3.94	30.57	59.30	2,295

	Number of firms 企业个数	Average number of employees 平均职工人数	Average revenue ('000 RMB) 平均销售收入（千元）	Average profit ('000 RMB) 平均利润 (千元)	Return on assets 资产利润率 (%)	Return on equity 权益利润率 (%)	Labour productivity ('000 RMB/ worker) 劳动生产率 (千元/人)	Debts/ assets 资产负债率 (%)	Average total assets ('000 RMB) 平均总资产 (千元)
By ownership 产业所有权									
State-owned 国有	2	1,789	258,796	5,287	1.41	5.56	48.66	74.68	375,255
Collective-owned 集体	14	298	21,257	408	2.07	5.92	19.38	65.00	19,702
Foreign & Overseas Chinese Funded 三资	23	166	30,836	-96	-0.32	-0.58	51.59	43.99	29,649
By regional distribution 地区分布									
Central-North 华北	2	58	11,634	950	6.48	21.57	65.83	69.96	14,651
Beijing 北京	1	50	16,267	1,049	5.00	13.69	118.72	63.46	20,971
Tianjin 天津	1	66	7,000	850	10.20	74.56	25.76	86.31	8,330
Hebei 河北									
Shanxi 山西									
Inner Mongolia 内蒙古									
Northeast 东北	3	374	35,154	-2,225	-3.31		34.93	113.13	67,261
Liaoning 辽宁									
Jilin 吉林	3	374	35,154	-2,225	-3.31		34.93	113.13	67,261
Heilongjiang 黑龙江									
Central-East 华东	58	154	16,283	831	8.18	16.35	26.76	49.96	10,161
Shanghai 上海	3	407	15,803	592	4.61	24.92	6.64	81.49	12,823
Jiangsu 江苏	15	113	19,726	1,318	10.17	16.78	57.82	39.36	12,956
Zhejiang 浙江	36	149	15,635	743	8.94	21.44	23.84	58.33	8,311
Anhui 安徽	1	400	7,780	-763	-12.11		7.21	157.86	6,303
Fujian 福建	3	85	10,152	236	1.39	1.45	8.16	4.15	17,006
Jiangxi 江西									
Shandong 山东									
Central-South 中南	28	387	45,281	-21	-0.04	-0.09	35.51	54.43	49,719
Henan 河南	1	812	16,629				1.41	98.94	7,666
Hubei 湖北	2	201	36,583	-16,717	-20.32	-29.64	68.17	31.45	82,285
Hunan 湖南	1	557	37,779	1,394	3.88	5.57	28.78	30.36	35,955
Guangdong 广东	23	360	48,391	1,364	2.71	6.42	39.83	57.75	50,325
Guangxi 广西	1	788	27,289	72	0.27	0.98	13.35	72.24	26,486
Hainan 海南									
Southwest 西南	3	279	9,162	-2,028	-9.21	-47.65	5.85	80.68	22,027
Chongqing 重庆									
Sichuan 四川	2	346	11,913	-3,069	-9.88	-53.37	5.96	81.48	31,053
Guizhou 贵州	1	145	3,659	55	1.38	4.34	5.34	68.15	3,975
Yunnan 云南									
Tibet 西藏									
Northwest 西北	2	195	6,070	10	0.12	0.21	10.39	40.54	8,030
Shaanxi 陕西									
Gansu 甘肃	2	195	6,070	10	0.12	0.21	10.39	40.54	8,030
Qinghai 青海									
Ningxia 宁夏									
Xinjiang 新疆									

4079: Other Lighting Equipment 其他照明器具制造业

Year 年份	Number of firms 企业个数	Rate of change 变化率 (%)	Number of employees 职工人数 (人)	Rate of change 变化率 (%)	Total revenue (Mil. RMB) 总销售收入 (百万元)	Rate of change 变化率 (%)	Total profit (Mil RMB) 总利润 (百万元)	Rate of change 变化率 (%)
2000	99		25,043		2,610		120	
2001	95	-4.04	22,759	-9.12	2,428	-6.97	75	-37.50
2002	96	1.05	22,221	-2.36	2,381	-1.94	37	-50.67

Major Products 主要产品	Output 产量	Unit 单位

10 Main Firms with Maximal Revenue (year founded) 收入最大的十家主要企业（创办年份）	City 城市	Province 省	Telephone/fax 电话/传真	Number of employees 职工人数	Ownership 产业所有权	Revenue ('000 RMB) 销售收入 (千元)	Profit('000 RMB) (rank) 利润(千元)(排名)	Total assets ('000 RMB) 总资产 (千元)	Major products 主要产品
Guangzhou Flashlight Industrial Corporation	Guangzhou	Guangdong	(020)81814971		State-owned				Electric Torch
广州市电筒工业公司(1921)	广州市	广东省	(020)81813591	2,723	国有企业	431,043	18,263(1)	562,306	手电筒
Guangzhou Flashlight Industrial Co.,Ltd.	Guangzhou	Guangdong	(020)36346304		Collective-owned				Illuminating Appliance
江高镇沙溪电器照明厂(1994)	广州市	广东省	(020)36346690	1,314	集体企业	133,301	1,430(15)	88,376	照明器具
Thorn Lighting (Guang zhou) Co., Ltd.	Guangzhou	Guangdong	(020)82241706		Foreign Funded				Lamp Holder
索恩照明（广州）有限公司(1996)	广州市	广东省	(020)82245777	123	外商投资	101,453	6,495(3)	56,576	灯盒
Siping Moly-b Metal Material General Factory	Siping	Jilin	(0434)3388043		State-owned				Tungsten Wire
四平环球钨钼有限公司(1970)	四平市	吉林省	(0434)3387116	855	国有企业	86,548	-	188,204	钨丝
Jiangmen Kinglite Electlonics Lighting Factory Co., Ltd.	Jiangmen	Guangdong	(0750)3390181		Private Owned				Emergency Lamp
江门市金莱特电器灯饰厂有限公司(2000)	江门市	广东省	(0750)3392033	170	私营企业	84,463	640(34)	14,769	应急灯
Chinese-foreign Joint Venture Suzhou Sanyo Electromechanical Co., Ltd.中外合资苏州三洋机电有限公司(1994)	Suzhou 苏州市	Jiangsu 江苏省	(0512)66211858 (0512)66211238	130	Foreign Funded 外商投资	62,188	14,253(2)	74,190	Lighting Set of Bicycle自行车摩电灯
GP Precision Parts (Huizhou) Co., Ltd.	Huizhou	Guangdong	(0752)2382189		Overseas Chinese-funded				Flashlight
惠州金山精密部件有限公司(1986)	惠州市	广东省	(0752)2260144	544	港澳台资	60,286	2,085(6)	33,498	电筒
Ningbo Tenglong Electromechanical Co.,Ltd.	Ningbo	Zhejiang	(0574)88432118		Overseas Chinese-funded				Flashlight
宁波腾龙机电有限公司(1993)	宁波市	浙江省	(0574)88431167	484	港澳台资	44,502	697(32)	20,141	电筒
Dongguan Anyu Electrical Appliance Products Co.,Ltd.	Dongguan	Guangdong	(0769)7727246		Overseas Chinese-funded				Flashlight
东莞安宇电器制品有限公司(1994)	东莞市	广东省	(0769)7727247	330	港澳台资	43,341	531(38)	30,829	电筒
Guangzhou Mingfa Plastic Cement Electrical Appliance Products Co.,Ltd. 广州明发塑胶电器制品厂有限公司(1992)	Guangzhou 广州市	Guangdong 广东省	(020)86414044 (020)86418899	175	Overseas Chinese-funded 港澳台资	42,043	1,300(18)	27,980	Electric Torch 手电筒

Top 10 Cities by Revenue 销售收入排名前10位城市	Province 省	Market share 市场份额 (%)	Number of firms 企业个数
Guangzhou 广州市	Guangdong 广东省	33.93	9
Ningbo 宁波市	Zhejiang 浙江省	14.20	25
Shaoxing 绍兴市	Zhejiang 浙江省	7.08	8
Siping 四平市	Jilin 吉林省	4.02	2
Suzhou 苏州市	Jiangsu 江苏省	3.74	2
Jiangmen 江门市	Guangdong 广东省	3.55	1
Jingzhou 荆州市	Hubei 湖北省	3.07	1
Huizhou 惠州市	Guangdong 广东省	2.53	1
Dongguan 东莞市	Guangdong 广东省	2.36	2
Nanjing 南京市	Jiangsu 江苏省	2.32	1

10 Major Wholesalers 十家主要批发商	City 城市	Province 省	Telephone/Fax 电话/传真
China Chemical Industry Supply & Sale (Group) General Company	Beijing	Beijing	(010)64238623
中国化工供销(集团)总公司	北京市	北京市	(010)64238623
China Chemical Industry Import & Export General Company	Beijing	Beijing	(010)88078888
中国化工进出口总公司	北京市	北京市	(010)88078890
Tianjin Bridge Group Welding Materials Supply & Sale Co., Ltd.	Tianjin	Tianjin	(022)83968861
天津大桥集团电焊条供销有限公司	天津市	天津市	(022)83968865
Taizhou Xingwei Chunlan Chain Stores Co., Ltd.	Taizhou	Jiangsu	(0523)6611200
泰州星威春兰连锁店有限公司	泰州市	江苏省	(0523)6224181
Taizhou Chunlan Sale Company	Taizhou	Jiangsu	(0523)6611200
泰州春兰销售公司	泰州市	江苏省	(0523)6224181
Shandong Tri-Union Co., Ltd.	Jinan	Shandong	(0531)6086351
山东三联有限责任公司	济南市	山东省	(0531)6093103
Haier Electrical Appliances Co.,Ltd.	Qingdao	Shandong	(0532)8939175
海尔集团电器产业有限公司	青岛市	山东省	(0532)8938086
Guangzhou Haier Industry & Trade Co.,Ltd.	Guangzhou	Guangdong	(020)87397315
广州海尔工贸有限公司	广州市	广东省	(020)87374302
Huizhou TCL Electrical Appliances Sales Co.,Ltd.	Huizhou	Guangdong	(0752)2289885
惠州市TCL电器销售有限公司	惠州市	广东省	(0752)2280690
Guangdong Hardware Minerals Import & Export Group Company	Guangzhou	Guangdong	(020)87752204
广东省五金矿产进出口集团公司	广州市	广东省	(020)87752205

4091: Electric Welding Machines 电焊机制造业

The industry accounts for 0.023% of the total revenue of China's industrial sector in 2002. The rate of return on assets is 7.61%. 80.43% of all firms in the industry made a profit while 19.57% had negative returns.The top province in terms of the industry's revenue is Shandong, accounting for 27.43% of the total revenue.
2002年本行业收入占全行业的0.023%，资产利润率为7.61%。80.43%的企业赢利，19.57%的企业亏损。收入最高的省为山东省，占本行业的27.43%。

	Total number of firms 企业总数	Total number of employees 职工总数	Total revenue (Mil.RMB) 总销售收入（百万元）	Total profit (Mil.RMB) 总利润（百万元）	Return on assets 资产利润率（%）	Return on equity 权益利润率（%）	Labour productivity ('000 RMB/worker) 劳动生产率（千元/人）	Debts/assets 资产负债率（%）	Total assets (Mil.RMB) 总资产（百万元）
Industry Overall 行业总体	92	14,940	2,494	207	7.61	17.24	57.46	55.84	2,718

	Number of firms 企业个数	Average number of employees 平均职工人数	Average revenue ('000 RMB) 平均销售收入（千元）	Average profit ('000 RMB) 平均利润（千元）	Return on assets 资产利润率（%）	Return on equity 权益利润率（%）	Labour productivity ('000 RMB/worker) 劳动生产率（千元/人）	Debts/assets 资产负债率（%）	Average total assets ('000 RMB) 平均总资产（千元）
By ownership 产业所有权									
State-owned 国有	20	147	6,137	-602	-2.51	-14.05	14.59	82.14	23,987
Collective-owned 集体	8	272	91,672	3,717	8.64	13.90	126.65	37.83	43,004
Foreign & Overseas Chinese Funded 三资	11	157	44,882	3,472	6.79	14.21	39.36	52.26	51,170
By regional distribution 地区分布									
Central-North 华北	15	154	31,570	7,680	16.66	33.89	115.45	50.84	46,099
Beijing 北京	5	112	15,239	1,851	7.70	13.80	63.28	44.21	24,035
Tianjin 天津	4	95	4,016	74	0.44	1.75	17.05	74.97	16,819
Hebei 河北	5	274	76,258	21,130	20.96	41.26	164.03	49.20	100,808
Shanxi 山西	1								
Inner Mongolia 内蒙古									
Northeast 东北	3	57	21,236	2,683	10.29	13.36	225.89	23.00	26,072
Liaoning 辽宁	2	37	3,249	39	0.79	1.82	17.53	56.71	4,889
Jilin 吉林									
Heilongjiang 黑龙江	1	97	57,212	7,971	11.65	14.24	384.85	18.19	68,439
Central-East 华东	52	157	30,271	1,390	5.74	12.47	59.01	53.94	24,202
Shanghai 上海	16	104	14,414	603	2.96	6.98	41.08	57.61	20,363
Jiangsu 江苏	14	148	31,678	1,942	6.42	18.59	47.13	65.45	30,227
Zhejiang 浙江	11	148	13,285	604	3.62	7.32	29.22	50.53	16,688
Anhui 安徽	2	106	2,375	-339	-5.18	-8.49	8.49	39.02	6,539
Fujian 福建	3	265	15,719	89	1.67	4.56	10.46	63.48	5,340
Jiangxi 江西	2	75	8,878	233	8.96	24.49	37.55	63.42	2,602
Shandong 山东	4	413	171,045	7,185	9.85	15.22	153.07	35.26	72,908
Central-South 中南	14	226	19,476	743	2.20	5.64	5.30	60.96	33,729
Henan 河南	2	226	4,064	-44	-0.30	-0.77	9.95	60.46	14,460
Hubei 湖北	1	104	15,118	928	3.73	5.35	51.38	30.36	24,904
Hunan 湖南	3	117	5,195	-255	-1.48	-12.19	10.25	87.89	17,250
Guangdong 广东	8	283	29,229	1,290	2.82	6.91	1.49	59.27	45,829
Guangxi 广西									
Hainan 海南									
Southwest 西南	6	161	13,879	-290	-0.85	-5.54	45.80	84.65	34,071
Chongqing 重庆									
Sichuan 四川	5	164	15,175	-358	-0.92	-7.32	50.45	87.37	38,734
Guizhou 贵州									
Yunnan 云南	1	146	7,399	52	0.48	0.75	19.76	35.53	10,755
Tibet 西藏									
Northwest 西北	2	78	13,598	1,351	20.86	57.55	63.40	63.75	6,476
Shaanxi 陕西									
Gansu 甘肃	2	78	13,598	1,351	20.86	57.55	63.40	63.75	6,476
Qinghai 青海									
Ningxia 宁夏									
Xinjiang 新疆									

Year 年份	Number of firms 企业个数	Rate of change 变化率 (%)	Number of employees 职工人数 (人)	Rate of change 变化率 (%)	Total revenue (Mil. RMB) 总销售收入 (百万元)	Rate of change 变化率 (%)	Total profit (Mil RMB) 总利润 (百万元)	Rate of change 变化率 (%)
2000	84		16,789		2,171		130	
2001	86	2.38	13,626	-18.84	2,239	3.13	183	40.77
2002	92	6.98	14,940	9.64	2,494	11.39	207	13.11

Major Products 主要产品	Output 产量	Unit 单位
Electric Welder 电焊机	212,536	Unit 台

10 Main Firms with Maximal Revenue (year founded) 收入最大的十家主要企业（创办年份）	City 城市	Province 省	Telephone/fax 电话/传真	Number of employees 职工人数	Ownership 产业所有权	Revenue ('000 RMB) 销售收入(千元)	Profit('000 RMB) (rank) 利润(千元)(排名)	Total assets ('000 RMB) 总资产(千元)	Major products 主要产品
Shandong Yanshan Group General Company 山东燕山集团有限公司(1998)	Jinan 济南市	Shandong 山东省	(0531)8934043 (0531)8934043	1,300	Collective-owned 集体企业	560,000	23,600(2)	253,600	Electric Welder 电焊机
Tiantai Welding Material (Kunshan) Co., Ltd. 天泰焊材(昆山)有限公司(1999)	Suzhou 苏州市	Jiangsu 江苏省	(0512)57446669 (0512)57446535	309	Overseas Chinese-funded 港澳台资	155,381	4,930(9)	194,506	Welding Material 焊材
Ridong Electronics Development (Shenzhen) Co., Ltd. 日东电子发展（深圳）有限公司(1997)	Shenzhen 深圳市	Guangdong 广东省	(0755)27393550 (0755)27396321	580	Overseas Chinese-funded 港澳台资	83,678	5,237(7)	132,498	Pofeng Welding Material波峰焊系列
Shenzhen Baoshan Iron & Steel Corporation Atlantic Electric Welding Rod Co., Ltd. 深圳市宝钢大西洋电焊条有限公司(1985)	Shenzhen 深圳市	Guangdong 广东省	(0755)82431310 (0755)82260601	206	State Owned 国有企业	74,035	5,449(6)	78,441	Electric Welding Rod 电焊条
OBARA (Nanjing) Machinery & Electric Co., Ltd. 小原(南京)机电有限公司(1994)	Nanjing 南京市	Jiangsu 江苏省	(025)2104395 (025)2104305	154	Foreign Funded 外商投资	63,250	15,640(3)	69,650	Jointing Complete Sets of Equipment焊接成套设备
Mudanjiang OTC Welding Machine Co., Ltd. 牡丹江欧地希焊接机有限公司(1998)	Mudanjiang 牡丹江市	Heilongjiang 黑龙江省	(0453)6500690 (0453)6500336	97	Foreign Funded 外商投资	57,212	7,971(4)	68,439	Electric Welder 电焊机
Beijing Times Science & Technology Co., Ltd. 北京时代科技股份有限公司(2000)	Beijing 北京市	Beijing 北京市	(010)62961055 (010)62980728	183	Joint Stock 股份制	55,657	7,829(5)	84,841	Electric Welder 电焊机
Kaierda Electric Welding Machine Co., Ltd. 凯尔达电焊机有限公司(1992)	Wenzhou 温州市	Zhejiang 浙江省	(0577)62515256 (0577)62517677	338	Limited-Liability 有限公司	42,880	2,796(12)	55,096	Electric Welder 电焊机
Shanghai Electric Welding Machine Works 上海电焊机厂(1953)	Shanghai 上海市	Shanghai 上海市	(021)65030866 (021)65026145	556	State-owned 国有企业	37,561	-	118,396	Electric Welder 电焊机
Nantong Sanjiu Welding Equipment Co., Ltd. 南通三九焊接设备有限公司(1960)	Nantong 南通市	Jiangsu 江苏省	(0513)3549501 (0513)3519614	315	Limited-Liability 有限公司	37,083	242(48)	57,008	AC Electric Welding Machine交流电焊机

Top 10 Cities by Revenue 销售收入排名前10位城市	Province 省	Market share 市场份额 (%)	Number of firms 企业个数
Jinan 济南市	Shandong 山东省	22.66	2
Tangshan 唐山市	Hebei 河北省	13.80	2
Shanghai 上海市	Shanghai 上海市	9.25	16
Shenzhen 深圳市	Guangdong 广东省	6.32	2
Suzhou 苏州市	Jiangsu 江苏省	6.23	1
Weihai 威海市	Shandong 山东省	4.58	1
Wenzhou 温州市	Zhejiang 浙江省	4.00	6
Nantong 南通市	Jiangsu 江苏省	3.34	3
Nanjing 南京市	Jiangsu 江苏省	3.07	3
Beijing 北京市	Beijing 北京市	3.05	5

10 Major Wholesalers 十家主要批发商	City 城市	Province 省	Telephone/Fax 电话/传真
SU MEC 中设江苏机械设备进出口（集团）公司	Nanjing 南京市	Jiangsu 江苏省	(025)4511888 (025)4411772
China Poster Mobile Communications Equipment Co.,Ltd. 中邮普泰移动通信设备股份有限公司	Beijing 北京市	Beijing 北京市	(010)66426993 (010)66426837
Sino Kama Co., Ltd. 中泰凯马股份有限公司	Shanghai 上海市	Shanghai 上海市	(021)62031188 (021)62030851
China Huayuan Group Co.,Ltd. 中国华源集团有限公司	Shanghai 上海市	Shanghai 上海市	(021)62031188 (021)62032288
Zhejiang Crand Imp.& Exp.Co.,Ltd. 浙江远大进出口有限公司	Ningbo 宁波市	Zhejiang 浙江省	(0574)87720170 (0574)87723350
Shandong Machinery Import & Export Group Corporation 山东省机械进出口集团公司	Qingdao 青岛市	Shandong 山东省	(0532)2661628 (0532)2991655
Qingdao Haier International Trade Co.,Ltd. 青岛海尔国际贸易有限公司	Qingdao 青岛市	Shandong 山东省	(0532)8938337 (0532)8939494
Guangdong Machinery Import & Export Group Corporation 广东省机械进出口集团公司	Guangzhou 广州市	Guangdong 广东省	(020)87782168 (020)87771803
China National Machinery Equipment Import & Export Corporation 中国机械设备进出口总公司	Beijing 北京市	Beijing 北京市	(010)63474506 (010)63261865
Beijing Cellstar Co.,Ltd. 北京蜂星事达电讯有限公司	Beijing 北京市	Beijing 北京市	(010)64602050 (010)64672648

4092: Industrial Electric Furnaces 工业用电炉制造业

The industry accounts for 0.011% of the total revenue of China's industrial sector in 2002. The rate of return on assets is 0.61%. 73.81% of all firms in the industry made a profit while 26.19% had negative returns.The top province in terms of the industry's revenue is Beijing, accounting for 50.12% of the total revenue.
2002年本行业收入占全行业的0.011%，资产利润率为0.61%。73.81%的企业赢利，26.19%的企业亏损。收入最高的省为北京市，占本行业的50.12%。

	Total number of firms 企业总数	Total number of employees 职工总数	Total revenue (Mil.RMB) 总销售收入 (百万元)	Total profit (Mil.RMB) 总利润 (百万元)	Return on assets 资产利润率 (%)	Return on equity 权益利润率 (%)	Labour productivity ('000 RMB/ worker) 劳动生产率 (千元/人)	Debts/ assets 资产负债率 (%)	Total assets (Mil.RMB) 总资产 (百万元)
Industry Overall 行业总体	42	12,481	1,178	16	0.61	3.55	27.25	82.75	2,653

	Number of firms 企业个数	Average number of employees 平均职工人数	Average revenue ('000 RMB) 平均销售收入 (千元)	Average profit ('000 RMB) 平均利润 (千元)	Return on assets 资产利润率 (%)	Return on equity 权益利润率 (%)	Labour productivity ('000 RMB/ worker) 劳动生产率 (千元/人)	Debts/ assets 资产负债率 (%)	Average total assets ('000 RMB) 平均总资产 (千元)
By ownership 产业所有权									
State-owned 国有	11	773	64,423	537	0.30	2.11	25.14	85.70	178,174
Collective-owned 集体	4	263	16,419	35	0.11	0.56	19.03	80.41	31,489
Foreign & Overseas Chinese Funded 三资	4	88	15,031	89	0.43	1.13	55.17	62.08	20,761
By regional distribution 地区分布									
Central-North 华北	5	1,108	124,949	3,111	0.93	5.04	33.95	81.63	336,075
Beijing 北京	2	2,602	295,307	6,451	0.80	4.48	36.45	82.16	807,411
Tianjin 天津	1	130	15,999	3,268	11.32	112.81	-55.98	89.97	28,874
Hebei 河北	2	103	9,067	-308	-1.68	-3.49	27.54	51.89	18,341
Shanxi 山西									
Inner Mongolia 内蒙古									
Northeast 东北	5	547	23,889	-988	-1.79		10.98	113.69	55,041
Liaoning 辽宁	2	912	30,005	92	0.26		7.46	135.17	34,953
Jilin 吉林	1	470	34,629	39	0.05	0.25	24.04	81.67	84,299
Heilongjiang 黑龙江	2	220	12,403	-2,581	-4.27		11.61	123.60	60,502
Central-East 华东	24	117	13,360	99	0.46	1.89	30.16	75.52	21,426
Shanghai 上海	3	182	7,532	-574	-1.34	-7.67	3.51	82.55	42,861
Jiangsu 江苏	17	101	14,823	274	1.69	6.71	37.29	74.82	16,229
Zhejiang 浙江	2	84	18,751	425	1.31	2.86	61.92	54.08	32,403
Anhui 安徽									
Fujian 福建									
Jiangxi 江西	2	188	4,278	-705	-3.13	-33.49	22.11	90.64	22,474
Shandong 山东									
Central-South 中南	6	170	11,976	625	3.49	8.91	23.08	60.84	17,909
Henan 河南	1	76	1,126	-92	-2.13		6.53	127.98	4,325
Hubei 湖北									
Hunan 湖南	2	343	13,749	946	2.30	5.41	14.93	57.56	41,203
Guangdong 广东	3	86	14,411	650	9.41	23.43	49.70	59.87	6,908
Guangxi 广西									
Hainan 海南									
Southwest 西南	1	200	6,956	-950	-2.88	-22.32	5.93	87.08	32,951
Chongqing 重庆	1	200	6,956	-950	-2.88	-22.32	5.93	87.08	32,951
Sichuan 四川									
Guizhou 贵州									
Yunnan 云南									
Tibet 西藏									
Northwest 西北	1	180	34,692	447	1.06	3.10	70.01	65.93	42,317
Shaanxi 陕西	1	180	34,692	447	1.06	3.10	70.01	65.93	42,317
Gansu 甘肃									
Qinghai 青海									
Ningxia 宁夏									
Xinjiang 新疆									

4092: Industrial Electric Furnaces 工业用电炉制造业

Year 年份	Number of firms 企业个数	Rate of change 变化率(%)	Number of employees 职工人数(人)	Rate of change 变化率(%)	Total revenue (Mil. RMB) 总销售收入(百万元)	Rate of change 变化率(%)	Total profit (Mil RMB) 总利润(百万元)	Rate of change 变化率(%)
2000	44		8,056		458		-19	
2001	40	-9.09	12,872	59.78	1,113	143.01	2	
2002	42	5.00	12,481	-3.04	1,178	5.84	16	700.00

Major Products 主要产品	Output 产量	Unit 单位
Industrial Electric Furnace 工业用电炉	7,541	Unit 台

10 Main Firms with Maximal Revenue (year founded) 收入最大的十家主要企业（创办年份）	City 城市	Province 省	Telephone/fax 电话/传真	Number of employees 职工人数	Ownership 产业所有权	Revenue ('000 RMB) 销售收入(千元)	Profit('000 RMB) (rank) 利润(千元)(排名)	Total assets ('000 RMB) 总资产(千元)	Major products 主要产品
Jinzhou Electric Furnace Co.,Ltd. 锦州电炉有限责任公司(1949)	Jinzhou 锦州市	Liaoning 辽宁省	(0416)3495183 (0416)3495183	1,784	State-owned 国有企业	57,154	154(23)	68,127	Electric Furnace 电炉
Wuxi Electric Furnace Works 无锡电炉厂(1966)	Wuxi. 无锡市	Jiangsu 江苏省	(0510)5807660 (0510)5807660	386	Collective-owned 集体企业	41,944	474(12)	48,398	Industry Electric Furnace 工业电炉
Xi'an Delian Electric Power Equipment Co.,Ltd. 西安德联电力设备公司(1994)	Xi'an 西安市	Shannxi 陕西省	(029)6252109 (029)6275399	180	Limited-Liability 有限公司	34,692	447(15)	42,317	Electric Heat Equipment 电热设备
Nanjing Sheshan Electric Furnace Factory 南京摄炉（集团）有限公司(1995)	Nanjing 南京市	Jiangsu 江苏省	(025)5761318 (025)5761587	236	Limited-Liability 有限公司	32,150	1,100(5)	22,460	Industry Electric Furnace 工 业用电炉
Jiashan San Yung Electric Furnace Industries Co., Ltd. 嘉善三永电炉工业有限公司(1999)	Jiaxing 嘉兴市	Zhejiang 浙江省	(0573)4184395 (0573)4181317	99	Foreign Funded 外商投资	30,556	454(14)	57,777	Industry Electric Furnace 工 业用电炉
Harbin Songjiang Electric Furnace Works 哈尔滨市松江电炉厂(1952)	Harbin 哈尔滨市	Heilongjiang 黑龙江省	(0451)4301475 (0451)4307219	339	State-owned 国有企业	23,480	-	107,310	Industry Electric Furnace 工 业用电炉
Jiangsu Huaneng Metallurgical Power Machinery General Plant 江苏华能冶金电力机械有限公司(1958)	Taizhou 泰州市	Jiangsu 江苏省	(0523)8541183 (0523)8541188	93	Joint Stock 股份制	17,617	303(19)	17,716	Electric Furnace Bottom Stick 电炉底棍
Wuxi Xishan Transformer Electric Furnace Works 无锡市锡山变压器电炉厂(1992)	Wuxi 无锡市	Jiangsu 江苏省	(0510)3781247 (0510)3781247	80	Private Enterprises 私营独资	17,240	320(18)	8,140	Electric Furnace 电炉
Nanjing Guangying Furnace Industry Co.,Ltd. 南京光英炉业有限公司(1998)	Nanjing 南京市	Jiangsu 江苏省	(025)3213006 (025)4124058	45	Joint Owned 联营企业	16,070	240(22)	9,850	Industry Boiler 工业锅炉
Tianjin Jinneng Power and Electronic Co.,Ltd. 天津市金能电力电子有限公司(1995)	Tianjin 天津市	Tianjin 天津市	(022)88243818 (022)88243818	130	Limited-Liability 有限公司	15,999	3,268(2)	28,874	High Frequency Inductiong Calefaction Equipment高频感 应加热设备

Top 10 Cities by Revenue 销售收入排名前10位城市	Province 省	Market share 市场份额(%)	Number of firms 企业个数
Beijing 北京市	Beijing 北京市	50.12	2
Wuxi 无锡市	Jiangsu 江苏省	7.98	5
Nanjing 南京市	Jiangsu 江苏省	6.03	5
Jinzhou 锦州市	Liaoning 辽宁省	5.09	2
Taizhou 泰州市	Jiangsu 江苏省	3.98	4
Guangzhou 广州市	Guangdong 广东省	3.13	2
Xi'an 西安市	Shannxi 陕西省	2.94	1
Changchun 长春市	Jilin 吉林省	2.94	1
Jiaxing 嘉兴市	Zhejiang 浙江省	2.59	1
Suzhou 苏州市	Jiangsu 江苏省	2.32	2

10 Major Wholesalers 十家主要批发商	City 城市	Province 省	Telephone/Fax 电话/传真
SU MEC 中设江苏机械设备进出口（集团）公司	Nanjing 南京市	Jiangsu 江苏省	(025)4511888 (025)4411772
China Poster Mobile Communications Equipment Co.,Ltd. 中邮普泰移动通信设备股份有限公司	Beijing 北京市	Beijing 北京市	(010)66426993 (010)66426837
Sino Kama Co., Ltd. 中泰凯马股份有限公司	Shanghai 上海市	Shanghai 上海市	(021)62031188 (021)62030851
China Huayuan Group Co.,Ltd. 中国华源集团有限公司	Shanghai 上海市	Shanghai 上海市	(021)62031188 (021)62032288
Zhejiang Crand Imp.& Exp.Co.,Ltd. 浙江远大进出口有限公司	Ningbo 宁波市	Zhejiang 浙江省	(0574)87720170 (0574)87723350
Shandong Machinery Import & Export Group Corporation 山东省机械进出口集团公司	Qingdao 青岛市	Shandong 山东省	(0532)2661628 (0532)2991655
Qingdao Haier International Trade Co.,Ltd. 青岛海尔国际贸易有限公司	Qingdao 青岛市	Shandong 山东省	(0532)8938337 (0532)8939494
Guangdong Machinery Import & Export Group Corporation 广东省机械进出口集团公司	Guangzhou 广州市	Guangdong 广东省	(020)87782168 (020)87771803
China National Machinery Equipment Import & Export Corporation 中国机械设备进出口总公司	Beijing 北京市	Beijing 北京市	(010)63474506 (010)63261865
Beijing Cellstar Co.,Ltd. 北京蜂星事达电讯有限公司	Beijing 北京市	Beijing 北京市	(010)64602050 (010)64672648

4099: Other Electric Machinery 其他类未包括的电气机械制造业

The industry accounts for 0.044% of the total revenue of China's industrial sector in 2002. The rate of return on assets is 7.58%. 77.21% of all firms in the industry made a profit while 22.79% had negative returns.The top province in terms of the industry's revenue is Shanghai, accounting for 27.32% of the total revenue.
2002年本行业收入占全行业的 0.044%，资产利润率为 7.58%。77.21%的企业赢利，22.79%的企业亏损。收入最高的省为上海市，占本行业的27.32%。

	Total number of firms 企业总数	Total number of employees 职工总数	Total revenue (Mil.RMB) 总销售收入 (百万元)	Total profit (Mil.RMB) 总利润 (百万元)	Return on assets 资产利润率 (%)	Return on equity 权益利润率 (%)	Labour productivity ('000 RMB/ worker) 劳动生产率 (千元/人)	Debts/ assets 资产负债率 (%)	Total assets (Mil.RMB) 总资产 (百万元)
Industry Overall 行业总体	136	18,464	4,679	488	7.58	13.41	91.88	43.49	6,446

	Number of firms 企业个数	Average number of employees 平均职工人数	Average revenue ('000 RMB) 平均销售收入 (千元)	Average profit ('000 RMB) 平均利润 (千元)	Return on assets 资产利润率 (%)	Return on equity 权益利润率 (%)	Labour productivity ('000 RMB/ worker) 劳动生产率 (千元/人)	Debts/ assets 资产负债率 (%)	Average total assets ('000 RMB) 平均总资产 (千元)
By ownership 产业所有权									
State-owned 国有	16	151	15,475	-1,618	-3.59	-9.90	24.28	63.75	45,059
Collective-owned 集体	14	103	20,279	1,192	9.59	22.84	70.65	57.99	12,427
Foreign & Overseas Chinese Funded 三资	30	173	73,524	7,664	10.70	20.42	175.75	47.59	71,634
By regional distribution 地区分布									
Central-North 华北	15	135	22,665	4,626	7.41	15.18	52.90	51.21	62,454
Beijing 北京	6	113	37,776	13,708	11.42	19.57	140.59	41.64	120,016
Tianjin 天津	5	82	9,094	-204	-1.07	-2.96	30.79	63.80	19,106
Hebei 河北	3	312	22,616	-3,944	-9.76	-530.06	-1.05	98.16	40,396
Shanxi 山西	1								
Inner Mongolia 内蒙古									
Northeast 东北	7	166	28,286	877	3.31	8.60	44.39	61.58	26,533
Liaoning 辽宁	5	165	21,548	781	2.28	5.83	19.56	60.82	34,165
Jilin 吉林	2	167	45,131	1,119	15.01	50.45	105.97	70.26	7,454
Heilongjiang 黑龙江									
Central-East 华东	62	140	42,364	5,772	9.24	14.15	106.29	34.68	62,439
Shanghai 上海	15	197	85,228	13,980	8.93	11.29	156.17	20.86	156,475
Jiangsu 江苏	21	135	22,418	535	1.50	3.79	49.62	60.33	35,538
Zhejiang 浙江	10	118	16,279	876	5.78	11.10	46.60	47.90	15,161
Anhui 安徽	3	47	24,778	3,231	14.94	29.71	340.29	49.72	21,627
Fujian 福建	5	147	89,195	20,869	24.17	50.53	182.78	52.18	86,351
Jiangxi 江西	1	101	6,658	-659	-10.52	-37.57	23.80	72.00	6,264
Shandong 山东	7	109	26,802	2,113	12.00	26.79	110.54	55.23	17,618
Central-South 中南	37	137	33,553	827	2.92	7.38	98.22	60.40	28,280
Henan 河南	3	89	23,676	809	8.41	22.78	104.11	63.07	9,616
Hubei 湖北	5	61	9,577	184	0.82	2.61	59.96	68.72	22,609
Hunan 湖南	7	86	18,791	504	2.73	5.08	72.87	46.32	18,478
Guangdong 广东	22	177	45,045	1,078	3.06	7.94	104.74	61.44	35,233
Guangxi 广西									
Hainan 海南									
Southwest 西南	8	140	27,179	2,451	8.76	20.32	85.81	56.90	27,984
Chongqing 重庆									
Sichuan 四川	8	140	27,179	2,451	8.76	20.32	85.81	56.90	27,984
Guizhou 贵州									
Yunnan 云南									
Tibet 西藏									
Northwest 西北	7	57	7,954	672	2.58	6.29	50.77	58.92	26,023
Shaanxi 陕西	3	63	8,895	1,556	4.41	8.15	65.25	45.85	35,266
Gansu 甘肃	2	49	10,363	110	0.34	1.28	58.23	73.78	32,655
Qinghai 青海									
Ningxia 宁夏	1	88	7,727	4	0.04	0.58	25.01	92.59	9,336
Xinjiang 新疆	1	28	541	-189	-11.03		8.18	116.63	1,714

4099: Other Electric Machinery 其他类未包括的电气机械制造业

Year 年份	Number of firms 企业个数	Rate of change 变化率 (%)	Number of employees 职工人数 (人)	Rate of change 变化率 (%)	Total revenue (Mil. RMB) 总销售收入 (百万元)	Rate of change 变化率 (%)	Total profit (Mil RMB) 总利润 (百万元)	Rate of change 变化率 (%)
2000	114		14,718		3,062		321	
2001	127	11.40	18,455	25.39	3,450	12.67	275	-14.33
2002	136	7.09	18,464	0.05	4,679	35.62	488	77.45

Major Products 主要产品	Output 产量	Unit 单位
Electrician's Instrument & Meter 电工仪器仪表	5,817	10,000 Units(Sets) 万台(套)

10 Main Firms with Maximal Revenue (year founded) 收入最大的十家主要企业（创办年份）	City 城市	Province 省	Telephone/fax 电话/传真	Number of employees 职工人数	Ownership 产业所有权	Revenue ('000 RMB) 销售收入 (千元)	Profit('000 RMB) (rank) 利润(千元) (排名)	Total assets ('000 RMB) 总资产 (千元)	Major products 主要产品
Shanghai Xiaomi Automobile Lamp Co., Ltd. 上海小糸车灯有限公司(1989)	Shanghai 上海市	Shanghai 上海市	(021)69520114 (021)59162899	720	Foreign Funded 外商投资	731,210	86,291(2)	646,706	Lamps and Lanterns for Santana桑塔纳系列灯具
Shunming Electronics (Fuzhou) Co.,Ltd. 顺明电子(福州)有限公司(1995)	Fuzhou 福州市	Fujian 福建省	(0591)3970650 (0591)3970659	141	Overseas Chinese-funded 港澳台资	241,015	97,982(1)	279,404	Kinescope Parts显像管零配件
Fuzhou Development Zone Hongji Electronics Co.,Ltd. 福州开发区宏吉电子有限公司(1997)	Fuzhou 福州市	Fujian 福建省	(0591)3971202 (0591)3971203	313	Overseas Chinese-funded 港澳台资	186,815	16,695(6)	94,781	Face Plate 面盘
Shenzhen Jiejiade Cash Automation Treatment Equipment Co., Ltd. 深圳捷佳德现金自动化处理设备有限公司(1998)	Shenzhen 深圳市	Guangdong 广东省	(0755)83427667 (0755)83413189	120	Foreign Funded 外商投资	152,116	8,976(9)	122,640	Bank Automated Equipment银行自动化设备
Guangzhou Elevator Group Fittings Co.,Ltd. 广州电梯集团配件有限公司(1998)	Guangzhou 广州市	Guangdong 广东省	(020)84795888 (020)84795898	315	Limited-Liability 有限公司	142,560	13,644(7)	70,858	Elevator Fittings 电梯配件
Taishan Aida Electricl Co., Ltd. 台山市爱达电器厂有限公司(1991)	Jiangmen 江门市	Guangdong 广东省	(0750)5619838 (0750)5615315	136	Overseas Chinese-funded 港澳台资	141,060	1,258(35)	59,508	Microwave Oven 微波炉
Shenghai Aerospace Automobile Electromechanical Co., Ltd. 上海航天汽车机电股份有限公司(1998)	Shanghai 上海市	Shanghai 上海市	(021)64828985 (021)64822300	660	Joint Stock 股份制	131,515	79,339(4)	1,291,417	Direct Current Electric Motor 直流电机
Arai (Zhongshan) Air Conditioners Manifacturing Co., Ltd. 荒井制作所（中山）空调器材有限公司(1994)	Zhongshan 中山市	Guangdong 广东省	(0760)6659067 (0760)6653497	387	Foreign Funded 外商投资	111,785	-	53,627	Air Conditioner Tube空调器配管
Nanjing Dongda Science & Technology Industrial (Group) General Company 南京东大科技实业(集团)总公司(1992)	Nanjing 南京市	Jiangsu 江苏省	(025)3792746 (025)7713019	271	State-owned 国有企业	110,000	600(52)	174,460	Micro electronics Component微电子元器件
Shanghai Siyuan Electricity Co.,Ltd. 上海思源电气股份有限公司(1993)	Shanghai 上海市	Shanghai 上海市	(021)64420909 (021)64896584	205	Joint Stock 股份制	102,813	32,487(5)	131,903	Electricity Automated Equipment电力自动化设备

Top 10 Cities by Revenue 销售收入排名前10位城市	Province 省	Market share 市场份额 (%)	Number of firms 企业个数
Shanghai 上海市	Shanghai 上海市	27.32	15
Fuzhou 福州市	Fujian 福建省	9.44	3
Shenzhen 深圳市	Guangdong 广东省	8.34	8
Beijing 北京市	Beijing 北京市	4.84	6
Jiangmen 江门市	Guangdong 广东省	4.05	2
Chengdu 成都市	Sichuan 四川省	4.03	6
Guangzhou 广州市	Guangdong 广东省	3.78	4
Zhongshan 中山市	Guangdong 广东省	3.45	3
Nanjing 南京市	Jiangsu 江苏省	2.97	4
Nantong 南通市	Jiangsu 江苏省	2.65	4

10 Major Wholesalers 十家主要批发商	City 城市	Province 省	Telephone/Fax 电话/传真
SU MEC 中设江苏机械设备进出口（集团）公司	Nanjing 南京市	Jiangsu 江苏省	(025)4511888 (025)4411772
China Poster Mobile Communications Equipment Co.,Ltd. 中邮普泰移动通信设备股份有限公司	Beijing 北京市	Beijing 北京市	(010)66426993 (010)66426837
Sino Kama Co., Ltd. 中泰凯马股份有限公司	Shanghai 上海市	Shanghai 上海市	(021)62031188 (021)62030851
China Huayuan Group Co.,Ltd. 中国华源集团有限公司	Shanghai 上海市	Shanghai 上海市	(021)62031188 (021)62032288
Zhejiang Crand Imp.& Exp.Co.,Ltd. 浙江远大进出口有限公司	Ningbo 宁波市	Zhejiang 浙江省	(0574)87720170 (0574)87723350
Shandong Machinery Import & Export Group Corporation 山东省机械进出口集团公司	Qingdao 青岛市	Shandong 山东省	(0532)2661628 (0532)2991655
Qingdao Haier International Trade Co.,Ltd. 青岛海尔国际贸易有限公司	Qingdao 青岛市	Shandong 山东省	(0532)8938337 (0532)8939494
Guangdong Machinery Import & Export Group Corporation 广东省机械进出口集团公司	Guangzhou 广州市	Guangdong 广东省	(020)87782168 (020)87771803
China National Machinery Equipment Import & Export Corporation 中国机械设备进出口总公司	Beijing 北京市	Beijing 北京市	(010)63474506 (010)63261865
Beijing Cellstar Co.,Ltd. 北京蜂星事达电讯有限公司	Beijing 北京市	Beijing 北京市	(010)64602050 (010)64672648

4111: Transmission Equipment 传输设备制造业

The industry accounts for 0.278% of the total revenue of China's industrial sector in 2002. The rate of return on assets is 4.20%. 79.52% of all firms in the industry made a profit while 20.48% had negative returns.The top province in terms of the industry's revenue is Zhejiang, accounting for 22.05% of the total revenue.
2002年本行业收入占全行业的 0.278%，资产利润率为 4.20%。79.52%的企业赢利，20.48%的企业亏损。收入最高的省为浙江省，占本行业的22.05%。

	Total number of firms 企业总数	Total number of employees 职工总数	Total revenue (Mil.RMB) 总销售收入(百万元)	Total profit (Mil.RMB) 总利润(百万元)	Return on assets 资产利润率(%)	Return on equity 权益利润率(%)	Labour productivity ('000 RMB/worker) 劳动生产率(千元/人)	Debts/assets 资产负债率(%)	Total assets (Mil.RMB) 总资产(百万元)
Industry Overall 行业总体	166	59,118	29,868	1,979	4.20	8.77	142.00	52.06	47,076

	Number of firms 企业个数	Average number of employees 平均职工人数	Average revenue ('000 RMB) 平均销售收入(千元)	Average profit ('000 RMB) 平均利润(千元)	Return on assets 资产利润率(%)	Return on equity 权益利润率(%)	Labour productivity ('000 RMB/worker) 劳动生产率(千元/人)	Debts/assets 资产负债率(%)	Average total assets ('000 RMB) 平均总资产(千元)
By ownership 产业所有权									
State-owned 国有	27	762	198,200	21,821	5.38	9.41	100.74	42.82	405,398
Collective-owned 集体	11	144	25,851	2,923	6.90	15.61	57.94	55.82	42,386
Foreign & Overseas Chinese Funded 三资	55	226	181,490	8,927	4.45	9.41	218.28	52.77	200,783
By regional distribution 地区分布									
Central-North 华北	23	239	124,411	18,645	9.27	17.73	126.83	47.74	201,223
Beijing 北京	15	171	156,132	26,086	10.17	18.07	192.94	43.73	256,547
Tianjin 天津	2	736	44,690	8	0.01	0.03	22.74	77.85	137,257
Hebei 河北	5	101	27,991	4,308	12.98	46.19	181.78	71.90	33,189
Shanxi 山西	1	953	290,139	16,000	4.71	11.00	80.03	57.14	339,463
Inner Mongolia 内蒙古									
Northeast 东北	3	83	86,743	2,621	5.90	18.05	75.76	67.33	44,439
Liaoning 辽宁	3	83	86,743	2,621	5.90	18.05	75.76	67.33	44,439
Jilin 吉林									
Heilongjiang 黑龙江									
Central-East 华东	46	452	293,370	8,305	1.74	3.97	144.28	56.19	477,618
Shanghai 上海	11	304	163,120	10,173	4.74	10.86	91.23	56.38	214,700
Jiangsu 江苏	18	372	267,485	8,224	1.47	7.59	164.07	80.58	557,650
Zhejiang 浙江	9	1,011	731,843	10,943	1.07	1.52	165.86	29.78	1,027,258
Anhui 安徽	1	51	11,284	405	1.14	1.28	85.67	10.57	35,479
Fujian 福建	2	196	58,310	3,024	8.43	14.48	57.80	41.82	35,891
Jiangxi 江西	2	187	16,710	125	0.71	2.54	43.37	72.02	17,579
Shandong 山东	3	278	46,019	5,638	9.23	24.40	52.18	62.17	61,090
Central-South 中南	64	334	165,642	12,950	4.97	9.38	174.29	46.99	260,292
Henan 河南	5	577	347,775	14,214	8.18	22.77	210.45	64.09	173,837
Hubei 湖北	28	422	219,610	22,120	5.25	8.74	192.70	39.88	420,936
Hunan 湖南									
Guangdong 广东	26	218	91,227	5,188	4.39	10.31	121.27	57.41	118,179
Guangxi 广西	5	202	68,244	689	0.37	2.77	153.45	86.63	186,129
Hainan 海南									
Southwest 西南	22	318	96,431	13,849	10.91	25.43	112.12	57.08	126,913
Chongqing 重庆	5	145	86,840	10,770	7.91	21.74	153.92	63.60	136,104
Sichuan 四川	15	370	108,556	16,464	12.56	27.91	118.55	55.01	131,094
Guizhou 贵州									
Yunnan 云南	2	358	29,470	1,940	2.67	5.89	19.85	54.62	72,574
Tibet 西藏									
Northwest 西北	8	526	66,090	3,391	3.04	6.02	39.99	49.57	111,692
Shaanxi 陕西	8	526	66,090	3,391	3.04	6.02	39.99	49.57	111,692
Gansu 甘肃									
Qinghai 青海									
Ningxia 宁夏									
Xinjiang 新疆									

4111: Transmission Equipment 传输设备制造业

Year 年份	Number of firms 企业个数	Rate of change 变化率 (%)	Number of employees 职工人数 (人)	Rate of change 变化率 (%)	Total revenue (Mil. RMB) 总销售收入 (百万元)	Rate of change 变化率 (%)	Total profit (Mil RMB) 总利润 (百万元)	Rate of change 变化率 (%)
2000	145		63,407		27,554		2,574	
2001	155	6.90	67,708	6.78	34,198	24.11	3,493	35.70
2002	166	7.10	59,118	-12.69	29,868	-12.66	1,979	-43.34

Major Products 主要产品	Output 产量	Unit 单位
Optical Communication Equipment 光通信设备	64,474	Set 部
Carrier Communication Equipment 载波通信设备	4,176	Set 部

10 Main Firms with Maximal Revenue (year founded) 收入最大的十家主要企业（创办年份）	City 城市	Province 省	Telephone/fax 电话/传真	Number of employees 职工人数	Ownership 产业所有权	Revenue ('000 RMB) 销售收入 (千元)	Profit('000 RMB) (rank) 利润(千元) (排名)	Total assets ('000 RMB) 总资产 (千元)	Major products 主要产品
Panda Electronics Group Co., Ltd. 熊猫电子集团有限公司(1936)	Nanjing 南京市	Jiangsu 江苏省	(025)4800855 (025)4805030	4,250	Limited-Liability 有限公司	4,245,270	120,860(5)	8,708,470	Radio Communication Equipment无线电通信设备
Zhejiang Eastern Communication Group Co., Ltd. 普天东方通信集团有限公司(1995)	Hangzhou 杭州市	Zhejiang 浙江省	(0571)88865262 (0571)88865263	4,993	Limited-Liability 有限公司	4,015,297	9,094(41)	8,098,640	Wave Carrier Telecommunication Equipment载波通信设备
Hangzhou Motorola Cellulau Equipment Co., Ltd. 杭州摩托罗拉移动电信设备有限公司(1996)	Hangzhou 杭州市	Zhejiang 浙江省	(0571)86912888 (0571)86910302	1,557	Foreign Funded 外商投资	2,216,974	28,704(23)	618,791	Transmission Equipment 传输设备
State-owned Liaoyuan Radio Works 国营燎原无线电厂(1958)	Xinxiang 新乡市	Henan 河南省	(0373)3381760 (0373)3368143	2,789	State-owned 国有企业	1,717,742	68,184(7)	844,687	Exceed Shortwave Communication to Space超短波对空通讯台
Yangtze Optical Fibre and CalbeCo., Ltd. 长飞光纤光缆有限公司(1990)	Wuhan 武汉市	Hubei 湖北省	(027)87802543 (027)87802536	787	Foreign Funded 外商投资	1,148,588	126,625(3)	2,610,416	Optical Fiber & Optical Cable 光纤光缆
Shanghai Post & Telecommunications Equipment Co., Ltd. 上海邮电通信设备股份有限公司(1993)	Shanghai 上海市	Shanghai 上海市	(021)64360900 (021)64333435	1,452	Foreign Funded 外商投资	881,448	64,603(10)	1,305,616	Wiring and Distributing-branch Equipment配线分线设备
Guangzhou Siemens Transmission System Co., Ltd. Guangzhou 西门子（广州）传输系统有限公司(1993)	Guangzhou 广州市	Guangdong 广东省	(020)85686168 (020)85686420	200	Foreign Funded 外商投资	806,943	53,033(13)	421,807	SDH System SDH系统
Wuhan Zhongyuan Electronics Group Co.,Ltd. (710 Plant) 武汉中原电子集团有限公司（710厂）(1949)	Wuhan 武汉市	Hubei 湖北省	(027)82731501 (027)82724212	2,854	State Enterprises 国有独资	609,332	65,981(9)	924,097	Mobile Communication Equipment移动通信设备
Wuhan Changjiang Communication Industry Co.,Ltd. 武汉长江通信产业股份有限公司(1996)	Wuhan 武汉市	Hubei 湖北省	(027)8740741 (027)87407417	86	Joint Stock 股份制	413,648	52,116(14)	1,084,063	Optic Communications 光通信
Longmarch Launch Vehicle Technology Co., Ltd. 长征火箭技术股份有限公司(1990)	Wuhan 武汉市	Hubei 湖北省	(027)85487710 (027)85487727	1,231	Joint Stock 股份制	403,607	120,902(4)	692,319	Rocket Measure & Control Equipment火箭测控设备

Top 10 Cities by Revenue 销售收入排名前10位城市	Province 省	Market share 市场份额 (%)	Number of firms 企业个数
Hangzhou 杭州市	Zhejiang 浙江省	21.77	4
Wuhan 武汉市	Hubei 湖北省	20.43	25
Nanjing 南京市	Jiangsu 江苏省	15.42	7
Beijing 北京市	Beijing 北京市	7.84	15
Guangzhou 广州市	Guangdong 广东省	6.35	10
Shanghai 上海市	Shanghai 上海市	6.01	11
Xinxiang 新乡市	Henan 河南省	5.75	1
Chengdu 成都市	Sichuan 四川省	5.18	13
Chongqing 重庆市	Chongqing 重庆市	1.45	5
Guilin 桂林市	Guangxi 广西	1.14	5

10 Major Wholesalers 十家主要批发商	City 城市	Province 省	Telephone/Fax 电话/传真
SU MEC 中设江苏机械设备进出口（集团）公司	Nanjing 南京市	Jiangsu 江苏省	(025)4511888 (025)4411772
China Poster Mobile Communications Equipment Co.,Ltd. 中邮普泰移动通信设备股份有限公司	Beijing 北京市	Beijing 北京市	(010)66426993 (010)66426837
Sino Kama Co., Ltd. 中泰凯马股份有限公司	Shanghai 上海市	Shanghai 上海市	(021)62031188 (021)62030851
China Huayuan Group Co.,Ltd. 中国华源集团有限公司	Shanghai 上海市	Shanghai 上海市	(021)62031188 (021)62032288
Zhejiang Crand Imp.& Exp.Co.,Ltd. 浙江远大进出口有限公司	Ningbo 宁波市	Zhejiang 浙江省	(0574)87720170 (0574)87723350
Shandong Machinery Import & Export Group Corporation 山东省机械进出口集团公司	Qingdao 青岛市	Shandong 山东省	(0532)2661628 (0532)2991655
Qingdao Haier International Trade Co.,Ltd. 青岛海尔国际贸易有限公司	Qingdao 青岛市	Shandong 山东省	(0532)8938337 (0532)8939494
Guangdong Machinery Import & Export Group Corporation 广东省机械进出口集团公司	Guangzhou 广州市	Guangdong 广东省	(020)87782168 (020)87771803
China National Machinery Equipment Import & Export Corporation 中国机械设备进出口总公司	Beijing 北京市	Beijing 北京市	(010)63474506 (010)63261865
Beijing Cellstar Co.,Ltd. 北京蜂星事达电讯有限公司	Beijing 北京市	Beijing 北京市	(010)64602050 (010)64672648

4112: Switching Equipment 交换设备制造业

The industry accounts for 0.567% of the total revenue of China's industrial sector in 2002. The rate of return on assets is 3.81%. 76.26% of all firms in the industry made a profit while 23.74% had negative returns.The top province in terms of the industry's revenue is Guangdong, accounting for 57.78% of the total revenue.
2002年本行业收入占全行业的 0.567%，资产利润率为 3.81%。76.26%的企业赢利，23.74%的企业亏损。收入最高的省为广东省，占本行业的57.78%。

	Total number of firms 企业总数	Total number of employees 职工总数	Total revenue (Mil.RMB) 总销售收入（百万元）	Total profit (Mil.RMB) 总利润（百万元）	Return on assets 资产利润率 (%)	Return on equity 权益利润率 (%)	Labour productivity ('000 RMB/ worker) 劳动生产率（千元/人）	Debts/ assets 资产负债率 (%)	Total assets (Mil.RMB) 总资产（百万元）
Industry Overall 行业总体	139	68,674	60,856	3,119	3.81	9.15	302.14	58.41	81,977

	Number of firms 企业个数	Average number of employees 平均职工人数	Average revenue ('000 RMB) 平均销售收入（千元）	Average profit ('000 RMB) 平均利润（千元）	Return on assets 资产利润率 (%)	Return on equity 权益利润率 (%)	Labour productivity ('000 RMB/ worker) 劳动生产率（千元/人）	Debts/ assets 资产负债率 (%)	Average total assets ('000 RMB) 平均总资产（千元）
By ownership 产业所有权									
State-owned 国有	18	402	53,660	-3,379	-2.38	-7.30	9.50	67.41	142,097
Collective-owned 集体	3	239	58,317	-7,617	-2.42	-14.95	24.16	83.83	315,033
Foreign & Overseas Chinese Funded 三资	42	353	586,701	20,952	3.20	8.52	504.07	62.45	654,644
By regional distribution 地区分布									
Central-North 华北	20	310	288,900	7,394	1.85	5.99	362.75	69.07	399,284
Beijing 北京	14	336	380,313	19,182	3.68	12.26	348.68	69.96	520,940
Tianjin 天津	2	369	99,250	-65,125	-33.75	-79.92	-9.74	57.77	192,974
Hebei 河北	3	148	83,479	4,002	5.51	10.30	1,388.80	46.54	72,644
Shanxi 山西	1	317	4,686	-2,424	-2.73		0.26	100.16	88,639
Inner Mongolia 内蒙古									
Northeast 东北	9	314	40,546	-894	-0.92	-2.08	33.56	55.61	96,808
Liaoning 辽宁	7	147	41,478	3,749	5.16	10.45	95.53	50.58	72,626
Jilin 吉林	2	896	37,283	-17,145	-9.45	-25.30	-2.14	62.65	181,445
Heilongjiang 黑龙江									
Central-East 华东	61	254	295,177	13,783	3.94	9.02	344.77	56.27	349,414
Shanghai 上海	13	499	665,895	21,421	2.31	5.10	376.22	54.78	927,978
Jiangsu 江苏	15	204	447,367	25,139	8.39	23.33	780.10	64.06	299,747
Zhejiang 浙江	21	142	34,258	2,187	5.51	13.73	57.34	59.83	39,660
Anhui 安徽	1	20	498	-1,841	-2.75		18.65	111.56	66,903
Fujian 福建	3	378	60,780	3,319	4.59	8.97	52.91	48.82	72,320
Jiangxi 江西	2	104	21,194	3,743	15.16	25.48	69.54	40.50	24,691
Shandong 山东	6	264	282,335	20,611	3.45	6.94	162.51	50.34	598,031
Central-South 中南	39	1,031	908,932	54,717	4.35	10.13	313.29	57.10	1,259,222
Henan 河南	2	1,499	122,874	-17,134	-2.84	-8.51	2.03	66.64	603,491
Hubei 湖北									
Hunan 湖南	3	84	11,932	4,846	7.87	17.65	55.70	55.42	61,574
Guangdong 广东	33	1,112	1,065,467	65,361	4.53	10.49	342.79	56.84	1,444,171
Guangxi 广西	1	273	6,380	-3,201	-5.30	-22.61	3.64	76.54	60,343
Hainan 海南									
Southwest 西南	6	357	37,625	-3,333	-2.85	-7.52	12.59	62.06	116,768
Chongqing 重庆	2	812	74,305	-11,094	-3.95	-10.23	1.40	61.37	280,617
Sichuan 四川	4	130	19,285	548	1.57	4.47	47.62	64.82	34,843
Guizhou 贵州									
Yunnan 云南									
Tibet 西藏									
Northwest 西北	4	454	258,226	6,164	1.24	4.25	243.93	70.95	498,768
Shaanxi 陕西	4	454	258,226	6,164	1.24	4.25	243.93	70.95	498,768
Gansu 甘肃									
Qinghai 青海									
Ningxia 宁夏									
Xinjiang 新疆									

4112: Switching Equipment 交换设备制造业

Year 年份	Number of firms 企业个数	Rate of change 变化率 (%)	Number of employees 职工人数 (人)	Rate of change 变化率 (%)	Total revenue (Mil. RMB) 总销售收入 (百万元)	Rate of change 变化率 (%)	Total profit (Mil RMB) 总利润 (百万元)	Rate of change 变化率 (%)
2000	178		85,045		63,771		7,449	
2001	145	-18.54	69,076	-18.78	84,704	32.83	8,138	9.25
2002	139	-4.14	68,674	-0.58	60,856	-28.15	3,119	-61.67

Major Products 主要产品	Output 产量	Unit 单位
Spc Exchange 程控交换机	5,861	10,000 Lines 万线
Digital Spc Exchange 数字程控交换机	5,766	10,000 Lines 万线

10 Main Firms with Maximal Revenue (year founded) 收入最大的十家主要企业（创办年份）	City 城市	Province 省	Telephone/fax 电话/传真	Number of employees 职工人数	Ownership 产业所有权	Revenue ('000 RMB) 销售收入 (千元)	Profit('000 RMB) (rank) 利润(千元) (排名)	Total assets ('000 RMB) 总资产 (千元)	Major products 主要产品
Huawei Technologies Co., Ltd.	Shenzhen	Guangdong	(0755)26540808		Limited-Liability				Programme-controlled Exchanger 程
华为技术有限公司(1987)	深圳市	广东省	(0755)28560772	21,483	有限公司	17,214,203	1,246,145(1)	23,828,057	控交换机
Shenzhen Zhongxing Communication Corporation	Shenzhen	Guangdong	(0755)26770000		Joint Stock				Exchanger Products
深圳市中兴通讯股份有限公司(1997)	深圳市	广东省	(0755)26771999	7,856	股份制	11,009,240	738,195(2)	12,405,770	交换产品
Shanghai Bell Alcatel Co.,Ltd.	Shanghai	Shanghai	(021)58541240		Foreign Funded				Programme-controlled Phone Exchanger 程控
上海贝尔阿尔卡特股份有限公司(1983)	上海市	上海市	(021)58540791	4,632	外商投资	7,363,477	239,778(4)	10,557,950	电话交换设
Nanjing Ericsson Panda Communication Co., Ltd.	Nanjing	Jiangsu	(025)2101188		Foreign Funded				Programme-controlled Exchanger 程
南京爱立信熊猫通信有限公司(1992)	南京市	江苏省	(025)2101199	395	外商投资	5,410,460	279,160(3)	3,062,590	控交换机
Guangzhou Jinpeng Group Co.,Ltd.	Guangzhou	Guangdong	(020)85571601		State Owned				Moving Programme-controlled Exchanger 移动程
广州金鹏集团有限公司(1998)	广州市	广东省	(020)85520076	464	国有企业	1,844,770	19,005(16)	2,778,722	控交换机
Qingdao Lucent Technologies Co.,Ltd.	Qingdao	Shandong	(0532)6768104		Foreign Funded				PHS
青岛朗讯科技通讯企业有限公司(2000)	青岛市	山东省	(0532)6768156	120	外商投资	1,196,306	46,448(9)	1,550,796	phs
Jiangsu Fujitsu Communication Technology Co.,Ltd.	Suzhou	Jiangsu	(0512)68250097		Foreign Funded				Programme-controlled Exchanger 程
江苏富士通通信技术有限公司(1994)	苏州市	江苏省	(0512)68253090	643	外商投资	516,137	17,196(19)	751,254	控交换机
Guangzhou Suntek Technology Co.,Ltd.	Guangzhou	Guangdong	(020)85521741		Limited-Liability				Computer Engineering 计
广州新太科技有限公司(1997)	广州市	广东省	(020)85533364	708	有限公司	449,987	32,802(10)	1,231,604	算机工程
Macat Group Telecommunications Equipment Co.,Ltd.	Huizhou	Guangdong	(0752)2119631		Limited-Liability				Telephone
麦科特集团电信设备有限公司(1993)	惠州市	广东省	(0752)2119631	642	有限公司	391,287	8,033(31)	260,764	电话机
Shanghai Bell Samsung Mobile Communication Co.,Ltd.	Shanghai	Shanghai	(021)50504900		Foreign Funded				Electronic Communication
上海贝尔三星移动通信有限公司(2001)	上海市	上海市	(021)50551233	118	外商投资	378,886	-	583,045	电子通信

Top 10 Cities by Revenue 销售收入排名前10位城市	Province 省	Market share 市场份额 (%)	Number of firms 企业个数
Shenzhen 深圳市	Guangdong 广东省	47.28	18
Shanghai 上海市	Shanghai 上海市	14.22	13
Nanjing 南京市	Jiangsu 江苏省	9.47	5
Beijing 北京市	Beijing 北京市	8.75	14
Foshan 佛山市	Guangdong 广东省	4.97	2
Guangzhou 广州市	Guangdong 广东省	4.76	10
Qingdao 青岛市	Shandong 山东省	2.21	3
Xi'an 西安市	Shannxi 陕西省	1.70	4
Suzhou 苏州市	Jiangsu 江苏省	1.23	7
Huizhou 惠州市	Guangdong 广东省	0.69	2

10 Major Wholesalers 十家主要批发商	City 城市	Province 省	Telephone/Fax 电话/传真
SU MEC	Nanjing	Jiangsu	(025)4511888
中设江苏机械设备进出口（集团）公司	南京市	江苏省	(025)4411772
China Poster Mobile Communications Equipment Co.,Ltd.	Beijing	Beijing	(010)66426993
中邮普泰移动通信设备股份有限公司	北京市	北京市	(010)66426837
Sino Kama Co., Ltd.	Shanghai	Shanghai	(021)62031188
中泰凯马股份有限公司	上海市	上海市	(021)62030851
China Huayuan Group Co.,Ltd.	Shanghai	Shanghai	(021)62031188
中国华源集团有限公司	上海市	上海市	(021)62032288
Zhejiang Crand Imp.& Exp.Co.,Ltd.	Ningbo	Zhejiang	(0574)87720170
浙江远大进出口有限公司	宁波市	浙江省	(0574)87723350
Shandong Machinery Import & Export Group Corporation	Qingdao	Shandong	(0532)2661628
山东省机械进出口集团公司	青岛市	山东省	(0532)2991655
Qingdao Haier International Trade Co.,Ltd.	Qingdao	Shandong	(0532)8938337
青岛海尔国际贸易有限公司	青岛市	山东省	(0532)8939494
Guangdong Machinery Import & Export Group Corporation	Guangzhou	Guangdong	(020)87782168
广东省机械进出口集团公司	广州市	广东省	(020)87771803
China National Machinery Equipment Import & Export Corporation	Beijing	Beijing	(010)63474506
中国机械设备进出口总公司	北京市	北京市	(010)63261865
Beijing Cellstar Co.,Ltd.	Beijing	Beijing	(010)64602050
北京蜂星事达电讯有限公司	北京市	北京市	(010)64672648

4113: Communication Terminal Equipment 通信终端设备制造业

The industry accounts for 1.287% of the total revenue of China's industrial sector in 2002. The rate of return on assets is 10.36%. 74.78% of all firms in the industry made a profit while 25.22% had negative returns.The top province in terms of the industry's revenue is Tianjin, accounting for 35.99% of the total revenue.
2002年本行业收入占全行业的 1.287%，资产利润率为 10.36%。74.78%的企业赢利，25.22%的企业亏损。收入最高的省为天津市，占本行业的35.99%。

	Total number of firms 企业总数	Total number of employees 职工总数	Total revenue (Mil.RMB) 总销售收入（百万元）	Total profit (Mil.RMB) 总利润（百万元）	Return on assets 资产利润率 (%)	Return on equity 权益利润率 (%)	Labour productivity ('000 RMB/ worker) 劳动生产率（千元/人）	Debts/ assets 资产负债率 (%)	Total assets (Mil.RMB) 总资产（百万元）
Industry Overall 行业总体	226	127,354	138,044	9,268	10.36	22.03	287.51	52.96	89,426

	Number of firms 企业个数	Average number of employees 平均职工人数	Average revenue ('000 RMB) 平均销售收入（千元）	Average profit ('000 RMB) 平均利润（千元）	Return on assets 资产利润率 (%)	Return on equity 权益利润率 (%)	Labour productivity ('000 RMB/ worker) 劳动生产率（千元/人）	Debts/ assets 资产负债率 (%)	Average total assets ('000 RMB) 平均总资产（千元）
By ownership 产业所有权									
State-owned 国有	29	329	45,006	1,205	1.65	6.93	42.73	76.18	72,959
Collective-owned 集体	7	416	50,852	8,472	18.94	48.03	49.07	60.57	44,734
Foreign & Overseas Chinese Funded 三资	117	767	1,010,528	70,769	12.24	26.16	356.65	53.20	578,048
By regional distribution 地区分布									
Central-North 华北	34	627	1,707,041	113,036	10.92	17.77	877.98	38.57	1,035,455
Beijing 北京	11	301	630,772	29,063	8.23	21.09	253.81	60.99	353,258
Tianjin 天津	18	963	2,759,917	165,952	9.84	15.33	982.01	35.83	1,686,545
Hebei 河北									
Shanxi 山西	4	106	8,884	-850	-2.77	-5.50	23.03	49.73	30,715
Inner Mongolia 内蒙古	1	242	1,386,845	539,803	64.34	94.73	3,457.32	32.08	838,963
Northeast 东北	7	244	57,199	5,015	2.64	5.56	124.27	52.43	189,590
Liaoning 辽宁	4	217	70,512	8,615	10.53	25.20	173.84	58.20	81,795
Jilin 吉林	3	280	39,448	214	0.06	0.13	72.93	50.54	333,317
Heilongjiang 黑龙江									
Central-East 华东	76	419	551,279	43,123	11.81	36.94	271.10	68.04	365,251
Shanghai 上海	21	542	797,669	61,625	12.72	34.58	348.71	63.20	484,372
Jiangsu 江苏	13	260	147,951	670	0.61	2.74	-14.95	77.77	110,130
Zhejiang 浙江	25	360	740,258	72,151	13.57	48.30	425.82	71.90	531,619
Anhui 安徽									
Fujian 福建	12	448	153,724	5,342	4.59	11.10	43.44	58.61	116,318
Jiangxi 江西	1	1,606	237,097	12,784	6.52	43.93	59.53	85.16	196,173
Shandong 山东	4	283	658,645	23,466	7.37	20.01	495.55	63.15	318,285
Central-South 中南	95	702	378,026	21,138	9.32	22.82	125.84	59.17	226,850
Henan 河南	1								
Hubei 湖北	5	456	52,431	3,970	3.44	11.43	46.51	69.89	115,369
Hunan 湖南	6	133	7,256	-642	-2.19		18.98	106.62	29,346
Guangdong 广东	80	790	443,960	24,748	9.57	23.07	129.81	58.50	258,471
Guangxi 广西	2	62	14,147	2,306	13.08	25.07	154.44	47.82	17,627
Hainan 海南	1	229	61,738	7,722	9.10	20.95	177.13	56.57	84,876
Southwest 西南	9	217	83,642	6,064	7.08	11.72	139.56	39.56	85,636
Chongqing 重庆	1	38	22,175	2,111	21.17	27.40	554.26	22.75	9,973
Sichuan 四川	6	282	61,555	9,191	9.43	13.00	136.20	27.45	97,423
Guizhou 贵州	2	109	180,637	-1,343	-1.52	-7.89	93.37	80.67	88,108
Yunnan 云南									
Tibet 西藏									
Northwest 西北	5	771	208,330	9,922	1.76	2.96	101.21	40.43	562,517
Shaanxi 陕西	1	325	22,209	2,571	10.48	18.94	60.14	44.67	24,535
Gansu 甘肃	3	1,124	339,194	15,881	1.72	2.87	109.82	39.86	921,553
Qinghai 青海	1	160	1,860	-604	-2.58		3.12	102.59	23,392
Ningxia 宁夏									
Xinjiang 新疆									

4113: Communication Terminal Equipment 通信终端设备制造业

Year 年份	Number of firms 企业个数	Rate of change 变化率 (%)	Number of employees 职工人数 (人)	Rate of change 变化率 (%)	Total revenue (Mil. RMB) 总销售收入 (百万元)	Rate of change 变化率 (%)	Total profit (Mil RMB) 总利润 (百万元)	Rate of change 变化率 (%)
2000	129		64,416		28,306		1,173	
2001	188	45.74	108,948	69.13	129,071	355.98	10,672	809.80
2002	226	20.21	127,354	16.89	138,044	6.95	9,268	-13.16

Major Products 主要产品	Output 产量	Unit 单位
Mobile Telephone Set 移动电话机	11,960	10,000 Sets 万部
Telephone Single Set 电话单机	11,149	10,000 Sets 万部

10 Main Firms with Maximal Revenue (year founded) 收入最大的十家主要企业（创办年份）	City 城市	Province 省	Telephone/ fax 电话/传真	Number of employees 职工人数	Ownership 产业所有权	Revenue ('000 RMB) 销售收入 (千元)	Profit('000 RMB) (rank) 利润(千元) (排名)	Total assets ('000 RMB) 总资产 (千元)	Major products 主要产品
MOTOROLA (China) Electronics Co., Ltd. 摩托罗拉(中国)电子有限公司(1992)	Tianjin 天津市	Tianjin 天津市	(022)25325050 (022)25328301	12,177	Foreign Funded 外商投资	45,332,047	2,867,120(1)	27,073,564	Mobile Communication Equipment 移动通信设备
Siemens Shanghai Mobile Communication Co., Ltd. 上海西门子移动通信有限公司(1993)	Shanghai 上海市	Shanghai 上海市	(021)58541688 (021)50550946	2,724	Foreign Funded 外商投资	10,718,931	679,053(4)	4,831,348	Mobile Telephone移动电话机
Dongguang Nokia Mobile Telephone Co., Ltd. 东莞诺基亚移动电话有限公司(1995)	Dongguan 东莞市	Guangdong 广东省	(0769)2402844 (0769)2400401	801	Foreign Funded 外商投资	10,295,139	464,099(6)	2,576,413	Mobile Telephone 手机
UT Starcom (Hangzhou) Telecommunications Co.,Ltd. UT斯达康(杭州)通讯有限公司(1993)	Hangzhou 杭州市	Zhejiang 浙江省	(0571)88862342 (0571)88862328	1,628	Foreign Funded 外商投资	7,093,907	1,401,345(2)	6,056,172	Communication Products 通信产品
Huizhou TCL Mobile Communication Co., Ltd. 惠州TCL移动通信有限公司(1999)	Huizhou 惠州市	Guangdong 广东省	(0752)2611133 (0752)2611800	3,190	Foreign Funded 外商投资	6,921,698	1,288,349(3)	4,067,596	Digital Mobile Telephone 数字移动电话
Ningbo Bird Co.,Ltd. 宁波市波导股份有限公司(1999)	Ningbo 宁波市	Zhejiang 浙江省	(0574)88918941 (0574)88927489	2,950	Joint Stock 股份制	6,233,575	254,673(9)	2,989,278	Mobile Telephone 手机
Hangzhou Motorola Communication Equipment Co., Ltd. 杭州摩托罗拉移动通信设备有限公司(1996)	Hangzhou 杭州市	Zhejiang 浙江省	(0571)86698888 (0571)86698866	600	Foreign Funded 外商投资	4,427,815	105,006(10)	2,847,418	Communication Products 通信产品
China Kejian Co., Ltd. 中国科健股份有限公司(1984)	Shenzhen 深圳市	Guangdong 广东省	(0755)82910417 (0755)26695940	1,200	Joint Stock 股份制	3,251,410	29,156(23)	1,445,038	GSM Mobile Telephone GSM手机
Tianjin Sansung Communication Technology Co.,Ltd. 天津三星通信技术有限公司(2001)	Tianjin 天津市	Tianjin 天津市	(022)83969600 (022)83966747	408	Foreign Funded 外商投资	2,446,700	36,560(17)	1,093,349	Mobile Telephone 手机
Guangzhou Soutec(Group) Technology Co., Ltd. 广州南方高科有限公司(1999)	Guangzhou 广州市	Guangdong 广东省	(020)82340308 (020)82340208	431	Limited-Liability 有限公司	1,820,104	49,785(14)	775,954	Digital Mobile Telephone 数字移动手机

Top 10 Cities by Revenue 销售收入排名前10位城市	Province 省	Market share 市场份额 (%)	Number of firms 企业个数
Tianjin 天津市	Tianjin 天津市	35.99	18
Shanghai 上海市	Shanghai 上海市	12.13	21
Hangzhou 杭州市	Zhejiang 浙江省	8.67	7
Shenzhen 深圳市	Guangdong 广东省	8.10	31
Dongguan 东莞市	Guangdong 广东省	7.73	8
Huizhou 惠州市	Guangdong 广东省	6.57	10
Beijing 北京市	Beijing 北京市	5.03	11
Ningbo 宁波市	Zhejiang 浙江省	4.66	11
Guangzhou 广州市	Guangdong 广东省	2.11	14
Nanjing 南京市	Jiangsu 江苏省	1.15	3

10 Major Wholesalers 十家主要批发商	City 城市	Province 省	Telephone/Fax 电话/传真
SU MEC 中设江苏机械设备进出口（集团）公司	Nanjing 南京市	Jiangsu 江苏省	(025)4511888 (025)4411772
China Poster Mobile Communications Equipment Co.,Ltd. 中邮普泰移动通信设备股份有限公司	Beijing 北京市	Beijing 北京市	(010)66426993 (010)66426837
Sino Kama Co., Ltd. 中泰凯马股份有限公司	Shanghai 上海市	Shanghai 上海市	(021)62031188 (021)62030851
China Huayuan Group Co.,Ltd. 中国华源集团有限公司	Shanghai 上海市	Shanghai 上海市	(021)62031188 (021)62032288
Zhejiang Crand Imp.& Exp.Co.,Ltd. 浙江远大进出口有限公司	Ningbo 宁波市	Zhejiang 浙江省	(0574)87720170 (0574)87723350
Shandong Machinery Import & Export Group Corporation 山东省机械进出口集团公司	Qingdao 青岛市	Shandong 山东省	(0532)2661628 (0532)2991655
Qingdao Haier International Trade Co.,Ltd. 青岛海尔国际贸易有限公司	Qingdao 青岛市	Shandong 山东省	(0532)8938337 (0532)8939494
Guangdong Machinery Import & Export Group Corporation 广东省机械进出口集团公司	Guangzhou 广州市	Guangdong 广东省	(020)87782168 (020)87771803
China National Machinery Equipment Import & Export Corporation 中国机械设备进出口总公司	Beijing 北京市	Beijing 北京市	(010)63474506 (010)63261865
Beijing Cellstar Co.,Ltd. 北京蜂星事达电讯有限公司	Beijing 北京市	Beijing 北京市	(010)64602050 (010)64672648

4119: Other Communication Equipment 其他通信设备制造业

The industry accounts for 0.550% of the total revenue of China's industrial sector in 2002. The rate of return on assets is 7.76%. 73.07% of all firms in the industry made a profit while 26.93% had negative returns.The top province in terms of the industry's revenue is Beijing, accounting for 52.82% of the total revenue.
2002年本行业收入占全行业的0.550%，资产利润率为7.76%。73.07%的企业赢利，26.93%的企业亏损。收入最高的省为北京市，占本行业的52.82%。

	Total number of firms 企业总数	Total number of employees 职工总数	Total revenue (Mil.RMB) 总销售收入（百万元）	Total profit (Mil.RMB) 总利润（百万元）	Return on assets 资产利润率（%）	Return on equity 权益利润率（%）	Labour productivity ('000 RMB/ worker) 劳动生产率（千元/人）	Debts/ assets 资产负债率（%）	Total assets (Mil.RMB) 总资产（百万元）
Industry Overall 行业总体	349	90,128	59,028	3,567	7.76	16.21	104.82	52.13	45,967

	Number of firms 企业个数	Average number of employees 平均职工人数	Average revenue ('000 RMB) 平均销售收入（千元）	Average profit ('000 RMB) 平均利润（千元）	Return on assets 资产利润率（%）	Return on equity 权益利润率（%）	Labour productivity ('000 RMB/ worker) 劳动生产率（千元/人）	Debts/ assets 资产负债率（%）	Average total assets ('000 RMB) 平均总资产（千元）
By ownership 产业所有权									
State-owned 国有	38	511	59,953	1,652	1.67	4.88	30.77	65.87	99,163
Collective-owned 集体	25	89	19,524	1,317	4.96	13.00	46.81	61.89	26,574
Foreign & Overseas Chinese Funded 三资	112	347	432,737	24,581	10.36	22.35	175.54	53.64	237,244
By regional distribution 地区分布									
Central-North 华北	46	263	697,250	33,603	9.82	19.71	229.48	50.20	342,285
Beijing 北京	35	305	890,829	44,615	10.42	20.47	254.53	49.07	427,984
Tianjin 天津	6	159	115,508	-7,093	-7.84	-51.18	-37.15	84.68	90,462
Hebei 河北	3	109	52,552	8,864	21.44	38.52	204.82	44.35	41,352
Shanxi 山西	1	101	41,293	787	0.92	1.40	244.45	34.86	85,992
Inner Mongolia 内蒙古	1	33	2,490	-612	-4.77	-18.29	20.73	73.93	12,836
Northeast 东北	5	99	3,076	83	0.54	1,725.00	17.70	99.97	15,391
Liaoning 辽宁	3	140	3,244	191	0.91		18.05	102.35	21,111
Jilin 吉林	2	39	2,824	-80	-1.17	-10.57	15.81	88.89	6,811
Heilongjiang 黑龙江									
Central-East 华东	177	198	75,244	3,456	4.40	9.19	97.00	52.11	78,514
Shanghai 上海	34	133	68,330	860	0.94	1.87	123.64	50.01	91,815
Jiangsu 江苏	53	279	142,059	7,215	6.85	15.03	124.73	54.40	105,265
Zhejiang 浙江	51	163	31,484	1,946	3.54	8.18	55.03	56.72	55,006
Anhui 安徽	2	78	75,890	2,962	8.11	19.69	34.99	58.80	36,500
Fujian 福建	17	137	29,590	2,545	7.40	15.13	63.54	51.09	34,399
Jiangxi 江西	5	320	91,227	2,693	1.91	3.07	92.72	37.90	141,068
Shandong 山东	15	220	49,946	2,546	3.72	6.55	70.61	43.31	68,523
Central-South 中南	92	363	130,472	14,050	10.32	22.82	87.40	54.77	136,138
Henan 河南	10	255	26,311	2,196	4.12	9.05	29.41	54.47	53,294
Hubei 湖北	18	287	83,861	7,627	6.11	13.43	92.16	54.55	124,916
Hunan 湖南	8	284	20,169	423	1.12	2.97	30.56	62.26	37,716
Guangdong 广东	53	416	188,616	21,261	12.19	26.60	103.21	54.15	174,366
Guangxi 广西	3	461	24,283	1,052	1.58	6.32	18.00	75.04	66,715
Hainan 海南									
Southwest 西南	21	228	59,202	4,367	3.12	5.99	35.72	47.88	139,752
Chongqing 重庆	2	589	97,137	8,780	6.10	9.74	46.40	37.33	143,827
Sichuan 四川	17	168	55,600	3,823	2.63	5.11	29.43	48.41	145,101
Guizhou 贵州	2	383	51,883	4,575	5.07	11.93	42.72	57.48	90,207
Yunnan 云南									
Tibet 西藏									
Northwest 西北	8	538	46,744	3,058	3.10	7.79	40.41	60.15	98,509
Shaanxi 陕西	7	516	47,651	3,336	3.28	8.21	44.57	60.02	101,565
Gansu 甘肃	1	690	40,392	1,115	1.45	3.74	18.64	61.37	77,117
Qinghai 青海									
Ningxia 宁夏									
Xinjiang 新疆									

4119: Other Communication Equipment 其他通信设备制造业

Year 年份	Number of firms 企业个数	Rate of change 变化率 (%)	Number of employees 职工人数 (人)	Rate of change 变化率 (%)	Total revenue (Mil. RMB) 总销售收入 (百万元)	Rate of change 变化率 (%)	Total profit (Mil RMB) 总利润 (百万元)	Rate of change 变化率 (%)
2000	354		106,466		96,590		9,917	
2001	360	1.69	95,957	-9.87	46,631	-51.72	4,739	-52.21
2002	349	-3.06	90,128	-6.07	59,028	26.59	3,567	-24.73

Major Products 主要产品	Output 产量	Unit 单位
Beep Pager BP机	85	10,000 Sets 万部

10 Main Firms with Maximal Revenue (year founded) 收入最大的十家主要企业（创办年份）	City 城市	Province 省	Telephone/ fax 电话/传真	Number of employees 职工人数	Ownership 产业所有权	Revenue ('000 RMB) 销售收入 (千元)	Profit('000 RMB) (rank) 利润(千元) (排名)	Total assets ('000 RMB) 总资产 (千元)	Major products 主要产品
Beijing Ericsson Putian Mobile Communication Co., Ltd.	Beijing	Beijing	(010)64571188		Foreign Funded				Mobile Telephone
北京爱立信普天移动通信有限公司(1995)	北京市	北京市	(010)64575729	815	外商投资	4,968,060	170,097(5)	2,631,699	手机
Silitek Electronic (Guangzhou) Co., Ltd.	Guangzhou	Guangdong	(020)82373688		Foreign Funded				Multi-function Affair Machine多功
旭丽电子（广州）有限公司(2000)	广州市	广东省	(020)82373688	3,950	外商投资	3,046,729	21,151(29)	1,477,056	能事务机
Beijing Matsushita Communications Equipment Co., Ltd.	Beijing	Beijing	(010)80480000		Foreign Funded				Mobile Telephone
北京松下通信设备有限公司(1992)	北京市	北京市	(010)80486660	789	外商投资	2,257,752	58,629(11)	1,001,360	移动电话
Nokia (Suzhou) Telecom Communications Co., Ltd.	Suzhou	Jiangsu	(0512)67616166		Foreign Funded				Communication Equipment
诺基亚（苏州）电信有限公司(1998)	苏州市	江苏省	(0512)67616216	400	外商投资	1,856,624	105,780(8)	1,181,095	通讯设备
Suzhou Benq Electronic Technique Co.,Ltd.	Suzhou	Jiangsu	(0512)66651888		Foreign Funded				Communication Products
苏州明基电子信息技术有限公司(2000)	苏州市	江苏省	(0512)66651999	730	外商投资	1,711,383	62,074(10)	476,797	通讯产品
Wuxi Miehua Group Company	Wuxi	Jiangsu	(0510)5807345		State-owned				Inner Core
无锡梅花电子集团公司(1985)	无锡市	江苏省	(0510)5801575	3,509	国有企业	877,234	7,513(61)	510,658	机芯
Dawm Telecom Group Co.,Ltd.	Hangzhou	Zhejiang	(0571)87796133		Limited-Liability				Posts and Telecommunications Cable邮电
东冠集团有限公司(1995)	杭州市	浙江省	(0571)86616429	3,020	有限公司	674,048	20,187(31)	1,002,830	通信电缆
Flextronics Science (Changzhou) Co.,Ltd.	Changzhou	Jiangsu	(0519)5117000		Foreign Funded				Electronic Products
卡特门-瑞福科技（常州）有限公司(1999)	常州市	江苏省	(0519)5100778	537	外商投资	634,830	45,800(16)	321,490	电子产品
Comba Telecom Systems (Guangzhou) Co.,Ltd.	Guangzhou	Guangdong	(020)82225788		Overseas Chinese-funded				Mobile Communication Equipment 数字移动
京信通信系统（广州）有限公司(1997)	广州市	广东省	(020)82001126	676	港澳台资	633,960	393,259(3)	877,783	通讯设备
Nanjing Putian Communication Co., Ltd.	Nanjing	Jiangsu	(025)2418518		Foreign Funded				Wiring and Branch Wiring Products配线
南京普天通信股份有限公司(1958)	南京市	江苏省	(025)2416518	1,795	外商投资	630,540	-	1,006,070	分线产品

Top 10 Cities by Revenue 销售收入排名前10位城市	Province 省	Market share 市场份额 (%)	Number of firms 企业个数
Beijing 北京市	Beijing 北京市	52.82	35
Guangzhou 广州市	Guangdong 广东省	9.34	13
Suzhou 苏州市	Jiangsu 江苏省	7.27	19
Shenzhen 深圳市	Guangdong 广东省	5.53	19
Shanghai 上海市	Shanghai 上海市	3.94	34
Wuhan 武汉市	Hubei 湖北省	2.56	18
Hangzhou 杭州市	Zhejiang 浙江省	1.80	19
Nanjing 南京市	Jiangsu 江苏省	1.72	13
Wuxi 无锡市	Jiangsu 江苏省	1.62	2
Chengdu 成都市	Sichuan 四川省	1.53	13

10 Major Wholesalers 十家主要批发商	City 城市	Province 省	Telephone/Fax 电话/传真
SU MEC	Nanjing	Jiangsu	(025)4511888
中设江苏机械设备进出口（集团）公司	南京市	江苏省	(025)4411772
China Poster Mobile Communications Equipment Co.,Ltd.	Beijing	Beijing	(010)66426993
中邮普泰移动通信设备股份有限公司	北京市	北京市	(010)66426837
Sino Kama Co., Ltd.	Shanghai	Shanghai	(021)62031188
中泰凯马股份有限公司	上海市	上海市	(021)62030851
China Huayuan Group Co.,Ltd.	Shanghai	Shanghai	(021)62031188
中国华源集团有限公司	上海市	上海市	(021)62032288
Zhejiang Crand Imp.& Exp.Co.,Ltd.	Ningbo	Zhejiang	(0574)87720170
浙江远大进出口有限公司	宁波市	浙江省	(0574)87723350
Shandong Machinery Import & Export Group Corporation	Qingdao	Shandong	(0532)2661628
山东省机械进出口集团公司	青岛市	山东省	(0532)2991655
Qingdao Haier International Trade Co.,Ltd.	Qingdao	Shandong	(0532)8938337
青岛海尔国际贸易有限公司	青岛市	山东省	(0532)8939494
Guangdong Machinery Import & Export Group Corporation	Guangzhou	Guangdong	(020)87782168
广东省机械进出口集团公司	广州市	广东省	(020)87771803
China National Machinery Equipment Import & Export Corporation	Beijing	Beijing	(010)63474506
中国机械设备进出口总公司	北京市	北京市	(010)63261865
Beijing Cellstar Co.,Ltd.	Beijing	Beijing	(010)64602050
北京蜂星事达电讯有限公司	北京市	北京市	(010)64672648

4130: Broadcast and Television Equipment 广播电视设备制造业

The industry accounts for 0.038% of the total revenue of China's industrial sector in 2002. The rate of return on assets is 2.12%. 75.22% of all firms in the industry made a profit while 24.78% had negative returns.The top province in terms of the industry's revenue is Guangdong, accounting for 31.97% of the total revenue.
2002年本行业收入占全行业的 0.038%，资产利润率为 2.12%。75.22%的企业赢利，24.78%的企业亏损。收入最高的省为广东省，占本行业的31.97%。

	Total number of firms 企业总数	Total number of employees 职工总数	Total revenue (Mil.RMB) 总销售收入（百万元）	Total profit (Mil.RMB) 总利润（百万元）	Return on assets 资产利润率（%）	Return on equity 权益利润率（%）	Labour productivity ('000 RMB/ worker) 劳动生产率（千元/人）	Debts/ assets 资产负债率（%）	Total assets (Mil.RMB) 总资产（百万元）
Industry Overall 行业总体	113	23,998	4,082	121	2.12	5.79	50.75	63.37	5,694

	Number of firms 企业个数	Average number of employees 平均职工人数	Average revenue ('000 RMB) 平均销售收入（千元）	Average profit ('000 RMB) 平均利润（千元）	Return on assets 资产利润率（%）	Return on equity 权益利润率（%）	Labour productivity ('000 RMB/ worker) 劳动生产率（千元/人）	Debts/ assets 资产负债率（%）	Average total assets ('000 RMB) 平均总资产（千元）
By ownership 产业所有权									
State-owned 国有	20	172	16,290	-1,489	-1.91	-229.20	24.41	99.17	77,965
Collective-owned 集体	7	116	34,709	784	5.62	24.73	61.77	77.28	13,957
Foreign & Overseas Chinese Funded 三资	30	314	62,469	1,438	3.06	5.85	63.53	47.79	47,083
By regional distribution 地区分布									
Central-North 华北	21	233	38,136	2,967	3.43	6.24	48.40	45.01	86,427
Beijing 北京	16	282	47,370	3,795	3.41	6.15	50.27	44.50	111,158
Tianjin 天津	2	106	18,421	1,847	16.59	30.33	33.37	45.32	11,136
Hebei 河北	2	50	3,005	-827	-14.99		32.14	135.53	5,517
Shanxi 山西									
Inner Mongolia 内蒙古	1	80	93	-469	-15.01	-16.93	2.89	11.33	3,125
Northeast 东北	5	187	19,968	-1,253	-1.21	-6.42	70.95	81.22	103,857
Liaoning 辽宁	1	498	41,880	-4,590	-1.08	-13.30	13.39	91.87	424,500
Jilin 吉林	1	75	9,600	683	3.72	5.46	46.76	31.99	18,381
Heilongjiang 黑龙江	3	121	16,121	-786	-3.09	-4.67	154.90	33.89	25,467
Central-East 华东	50	154	30,901	1,054	3.50	9.05	54.79	61.29	30,103
Shanghai 上海	9	101	22,495	-44	-0.22	-0.43	29.61	48.13	19,937
Jiangsu 江苏	10	232	68,488	1,832	4.00	14.56	98.65	72.51	45,761
Zhejiang 浙江	25	160	24,949	1,152	3.64	8.77	38.71	58.54	31,700
Anhui 安徽	2	76	12,198	2,828	15.99	34.54	64.58	53.70	17,684
Fujian 福建									
Jiangxi 江西	1	172	204	-210	-2.22	-3.62	0.32	38.80	9,480
Shandong 山东	3	56	3,126	175	1.71	4.05	15.83	57.75	10,256
Central-South 中南	28	308	50,208	965	2.88	5.88	48.25	51.00	33,493
Henan 河南	2	334	8,665	234	1.12	4.60	15.02	75.61	20,868
Hubei 湖北	1	131	21,800	870	2.43	5.00	74.51	51.48	35,855
Hunan 湖南	4	65	13,308	486	5.35	21.49	57.92	75.12	9,085
Guangdong 广东	19	394	68,679	1,246	2.93	5.75	50.60	49.01	42,474
Guangxi 广西	2	41	4,277	30	0.36	0.52	31.44	32.10	8,444
Hainan 海南									
Southwest 西南	7	91	23,787	2,412	9.86	32.55	82.79	69.70	24,457
Chongqing 重庆									
Sichuan 四川	5	119	33,280	3,950	13.35	24.16	89.05	44.76	29,594
Guizhou 贵州	1	34	110	-2,861	-12.32		-4.88	228.59	23,229
Yunnan 云南	1	9							
Tibet 西藏									
Northwest 西北	2	591	32,066	-15,918	-4.27		19.12	113.89	372,937
Shaanxi 陕西	2	591	32,066	-15,918	-4.27		19.12	113.89	372,937
Gansu 甘肃									
Qinghai 青海									
Ningxia 宁夏									
Xinjiang 新疆									

4130: Broadcast and Television Equipment 广播电视设备制造业

Year 年份	Number of firms 企业个数	Rate of change 变化率 (%)	Number of employees 职工人数 (人)	Rate of change 变化率 (%)	Total revenue (Mil. RMB) 总销售收入 (百万元)	Rate of change 变化率 (%)	Total profit (Mil RMB) 总利润 (百万元)	Rate of change 变化率 (%)
2000	96		23,217		3,313		162	
2001	99	3.13	23,215	-0.01	3,493	5.43	56	-65.43
2002	113	14.14	23,998	3.37	4,082	16.86	121	116.07

Major Products 主要产品	Output 产量	Unit 单位
CATV Antenna 电缆电视（有线电视）天线	1,036	10,000 sets 万付
Vidicon & Application Television 摄像机及应用电视	23	10,000 Sets 万部

10 Main Firms with Maximal Revenue (year founded) 收入最大的十家主要企业（创办年份）	City 城市	Province 省	Telephone/fax 电话/传真	Number of employees 职工人数	Ownership 产业所有权	Revenue ('000 RMB) 销售收入(千元)	Profit('000 RMB) (rank) 利润(千元)(排名)	Total assets ('000 RMB) 总资产(千元)	Major products 主要产品
Regent Electionic (Shuzhou) Co., Ltd. 峻凌电子(苏州)有限公司(1999)	Suzhou 苏州市	Jiangsu 江苏省	(0512)63401633 (0512)36401631	596	Overseas Chinese-funded 港澳台资	459,030	12680(3)	257,810	CD-ROM CD-ROM
Jebsee Electronic(Shen Zhen) Co., Ltd. 全一电子（深圳）有限公司(1990)	Shenzhen 深圳市	Guangdong 广东省	(0755)27475888 (0755)27475468	2,100	Overseas Chinese-funded 港澳台资	272,433	3,817(14)	231,299	Antenna 天线
Shantou SEZ Tokyo Parts Co., Ltd. 汕头经济特区东京元件有限公司(1988)	Shantou 汕头市	Guangdong 广东省	(0754)8261188 (0754)8261281	1,946	Foreign Funded 外商投资	263,310	1,249(26)	98,626	Circle Loop 中周线圈
Zhejiang 001 Electronics Group Co.,Ltd. 浙江001电子集团有限公司(1995)	Quzhou 衢州市	Zhejiang 浙江省	(0570)7015888 (0570)7015888	880	Overseas Chinese-funded 港澳台资	172,599	6,711(8)	200,931	Electronic Products 电子产品
Beijing BBEF Electronics Group Co., Ltd. 北京北广电子集团有限责任公司(1950)	Beijing 北京市	Beijing 北京市	(010)62018844 (010)62018409	979	Limited-Liability 有限公司	149,699	9,274(7)	848,393	Broadcast & Tv Equipment 广播电视设备
Zhongshan Taifeng Electromechanical Co., Ltd. 中山市泰峰电气有限公司(1981)	Zhongshan 中山市	Guangdong 广东省	(0760)2611945 (0760)2601891	395	Private Enterprises 私营独资	137,268	6,275(9)	116,658	Transformer 互感器
Good Mind Electionics (Shen Zhen) Co., Ltd. 格第电子（深圳）有限公司(1992)	Shenzhen 深圳市	Guangdong 广东省	(0755)27091917 (0755)27091918	1,035	Foreign Funded 外商投资	105,879	705(33)	67,553	Satellite Receiving System Equipment 卫星接收系统器材
Jiaxing Zhongfa Antenna Industrial Co., Ltd. 嘉兴市中法天线实业有限公司(1996)	Jiaxing 嘉兴市	Zhejiang 浙江省	(0573)3131666 (0573)3131310	726	Private Owned 私营企业	97,230	310(53)	37,830	Pull-rod Threads 拉杆开线
Beijing BBEF Digital Radio & TV Co., Ltd 北京北广数字广播电视股份有限公司(2001)	Beijing 北京市	Beijing 北京市	(010)64315255 (010)64315255	423	State-owned 国有企业	96,646	2,054(20)	116,258	Television Transmitter 电视发射机
Sichuan Digital Telemedia Co., Ltd. 四川迪佳通电子有限公司(2001)	Mianyang 绵阳市	Sichuan 四川省	(0816)2468044 (0816)2469375	29	Foreign Funded 外商投资	76,446	301(54)	40,241	Digital Satellite Receiver 数字卫星接收机

Top 10 Cities by Revenue 销售收入排名前10位城市	Province 省	Market share 市场份额 (%)	Number of firms 企业个数
Beijing 北京市	Beijing 北京市	18.57	16
Suzhou 苏州市	Jiangsu 江苏省	11.24	1
Zhongshan 中山市	Guangdong 广东省	10.38	10
Shenzhen 深圳市	Guangdong 广东省	9.57	4
Shantou 汕头市	Guangdong 广东省	7.90	3
Quzhou 衢州市	Zhejiang 浙江省	5.09	2
Shanghai 上海市	Shanghai 上海市	4.96	9
Hangzhou 杭州市	Zhejiang 浙江省	4.07	13
Jiaxing 嘉兴市	Zhejiang 浙江省	3.63	4
Jiangmen 江门市	Guangdong 广东省	3.58	1

10 Major Wholesalers 十家主要批发商	City 城市	Province 省	Telephone/Fax 电话/传真
SU MEC 中设江苏机械设备进出口（集团）公司	Nanjing 南京市	Jiangsu 江苏省	(025)4511888 (025)4411772
China Poster Mobile Communications Equipment Co.,Ltd. 中邮普泰移动通信设备股份有限公司	Beijing 北京市	Beijing 北京市	(010)66426993 (010)66426837
Sino Kama Co., Ltd. 中泰凯马股份有限公司	Shanghai 上海市	Shanghai 上海市	(021)62031188 (021)62030851
China Huayuan Group Co.,Ltd. 中国华源集团有限公司	Shanghai 上海市	Shanghai 上海市	(021)62031188 (021)62032288
Zhejiang Crand Imp.& Exp.Co.,Ltd. 浙江远大进出口有限公司	Ningbo 宁波市	Zhejiang 浙江省	(0574)87720170 (0574)87723350
Shandong Machinery Import & Export Group Corporation 山东省机械进出口集团公司	Qingdao 青岛市	Shandong 山东省	(0532)2661628 (0532)2991655
Qingdao Haier International Trade Co.,Ltd. 青岛海尔国际贸易有限公司	Qingdao 青岛市	Shandong 山东省	(0532)8938337 (0532)8939494
Guangdong Machinery Import & Export Group Corporation 广东省机械进出口集团公司	Guangzhou 广州市	Guangdong 广东省	(020)87782168 (020)87771803
China National Machinery Equipment Import & Export Corporation 中国机械设备进出口总公司	Beijing 北京市	Beijing 北京市	(010)63474506 (010)63261865
Beijing Cellstar Co.,Ltd. 北京蜂星事达电讯有限公司	Beijing 北京市	Beijing 北京市	(010)64602050 (010)64672648

4141: Computers 电子计算机整机制造业

The industry accounts for 1.522% of the total revenue of China's industrial sector in 2002. The rate of return on assets is 6.78%. 70.77% of all firms in the industry made a profit while 29.23% had negative returns.The top province in terms of the industry's revenue is Guangdong, accounting for 44.52% of the total revenue.
2002年本行业收入占全行业的 1.522%，资产利润率为 6.78%。70.77%的企业赢利，29.23%的企业亏损。收入最高的省为广东省，占本行业的44.52%。

	Total number of firms 企业总数	Total number of employees 职工总数	Total revenue (Mil.RMB) 总销售收入 (百万元)	Total profit (Mil.RMB) 总利润 (百万元)	Return on assets 资产利润率 (%)	Return on equity 权益利润率 (%)	Labour productivity ('000 RMB/ worker) 劳动生产率 (千元/人)	Debts/ assets 资产负债率 (%)	Total assets (Mil.RMB) 总资产 (百万元)
Industry Overall 行业总体	130	96,737	163,240	5,690	6.78	28.02	253.23	75.82	83,975

	Number of firms 企业个数	Average number of employees 平均职工人数	Average revenue ('000 RMB) 平均销售收入 (千元)	Average profit ('000 RMB) 平均利润 (千元)	Return on assets 资产利润率 (%)	Return on equity 权益利润率 (%)	Labour productivity ('000 RMB/ worker) 劳动生产率 (千元/人)	Debts/ assets 资产负债率 (%)	Average total assets ('000 RMB) 平均总资产 (千元)
By ownership 产业所有权									
State-owned 国有	20	606	177,678	1,684	0.61	2.94	50.69	79.41	277,679
Collective-owned 集体	1	958	386,410	22,310	44.97	52.72	179.19	14.69	49,610
Foreign & Overseas Chinese Funded 三资	49	1,286	2,914,537	96,973	8.31	55.69	299.33	85.08	1,166,950
By regional distribution 地区分布									
Central-North 华北	30	498	709,516	35,390	8.66	18.41	234.08	52.97	408,771
Beijing 北京	16	625	1,288,954	65,093	9.38	19.54	336.48	51.99	693,975
Tianjin 天津	11	74	15,593	352	0.95	2.89	-15.15	67.28	37,275
Hebei 河北									
Shanxi 山西	1	4,046	129,948	16		0.01	11.12	63.21	645,427
Inner Mongolia 内蒙古	2	39	180,379	8,160	15.68	25.29	1,282.61	37.99	52,035
Northeast 东北	7	950	857,448	10,937	1.71	7.60	122.03	77.43	637,927
Liaoning 辽宁	4	1,451	1,378,134	7,317	0.72	3.86	126.71	81.30	1,014,420
Jilin 吉林									
Heilongjiang 黑龙江	3	281	163,199	15,764	11.60	18.99	89.74	38.93	135,937
Central-East 华东	53	620	1,138,794	38,836	6.50	32.56	315.45	80.05	597,722
Shanghai 上海	19	461	983,523	25,127	4.54	34.28	72.37	86.76	553,448
Jiangsu 江苏	16	979	1,052,143	-9,080	-1.53	-14.14	284.49	89.19	593,780
Zhejiang 浙江	4	89	78,722	6,985	12.38	37.25	180.44	66.75	56,400
Anhui 安徽	2	355	399,403	7,674	6.45	22.23	220.78	70.97	118,927
Fujian 福建	4	755	4,542,805	393,185	18.58	75.38	902.15	75.36	2,116,541
Jiangxi 江西	1	34	2,770	40	0.41	0.78	4.65	47.22	9,676
Shandong 山东	7	617	792,455	15,735	4.04	6.61	539.44	38.85	389,140
Central-South 中南	30	1,339	2,469,938	78,722	7.48	41.82	234.35	82.11	1,052,226
Henan 河南	1	60	23,051	2,034	9.07	18.82	46.70	51.80	22,429
Hubei 湖北	6	285	230,930	9,442	6.29	14.34	234.27	56.14	150,095
Hunan 湖南	1	35	8,800	571	6.67	12.23	76.91	45.48	8,565
Guangdong 广东	21	1,825	3,460,915	109,642	7.52	43.98	235.08	82.91	1,458,757
Guangxi 广西									
Hainan 海南	1	48	1,504	-75	-5.61	-7.77	6.21	27.88	1,338
Southwest 西南	6	203	160,031	19,059	4.81	10.68	228.06	54.99	396,621
Chongqing 重庆									
Sichuan 四川	4	247	238,916	29,797	5.15	10.36	280.25	50.29	578,845
Guizhou 贵州	2	115	2,260	-2,417	-7.51		3.13	224.07	32,173
Yunnan 云南									
Tibet 西藏									
Northwest 西北	4	232	134,383	4,429	1.09	3.58	149.64	69.44	405,218
Shaanxi 陕西	4	232	134,383	4,429	1.09	3.58	149.64	69.44	405,218
Gansu 甘肃									
Qinghai 青海									
Ningxia 宁夏									
Xinjiang 新疆									

Year 年份	Number of firms 企业个数	Rate of change 变化率(%)	Number of employees 职工人数(人)	Rate of change 变化率(%)	Total revenue (Mil. RMB) 总销售收入(百万元)	Rate of change 变化率(%)	Total profit (Mil RMB) 总利润(百万元)	Rate of change 变化率(%)
2000	139		61,012		65,731		3,630	
2001	130	-6.47	83,060	36.14	97,021	47.60	3,696	1.82
2002	130		96,737	16.47	163,240	68.25	5,690	53.95

Major Products 主要产品	Output 产量	Unit 单位
Computer 电子计算机	26,622	Set 部
Microcomputer 微型电子计算机	1,464	10,000 Sets 万部

10 Main Firms with Maximal Revenue (year founded) 收入最大的十家主要企业(创办年份)	City 城市	Province 省	Telephone/fax 电话/传真	Number of employees 职工人数	Ownership 产业所有权	Revenue ('000 RMB) 销售收入(千元)	Profit('000 RMB) (rank) 利润(千元)(排名)	Total assets ('000 RMB) 总资产(千元)	Major products 主要产品
Great Wall Interational Infarmation Products(Shenzhen) Co.,Ltd.长城国际信息产品（深圳）有限公司(1994)	Shenzhen 深圳市	Guangdong 广东省	(0755)26728151 (0755)26728060	1,970	Foreign Funded 外商投资	15,580,514	1,274,373(2)	5,400,300	Microcomputer 微机
Shunde Shunda Mitac Computer Co., Ltd. 顺德市顺达电脑厂有限公司(1993)	Foshan 佛山市	Guangdong 广东省	(0765)7753168 (0765)7759246	5,759	Overseas Chinese-funded 港澳台资	9,229,019	6,368(37)	4,312,805	Computer Main Engine 电脑主机
Benq Communication & Muliimedia Co., Ltd. 明基电通信息技术有限公司(1993)	Suzhou 苏州市	Jiangsu 江苏省	(0512)68251233 (0512)68259121	6,540	Overseas Chinese-funded 港澳台资	8,768,287	63,983(14)	3,402,665	Computer Display 显示器
Compal Electronics Techonology(Kunshan) Co.,Ltd. 人保电子科技(昆山)有限公司(1999)	Suzhou 苏州市	Jiangsu 江苏省	(0512)57355000 (0512)57355200	3,298	Foreign Funded 外商投资	5,141,679	-	2,123,890	Computer 电脑
Langchao Group Co., Ltd. 浪潮集团有限公司(1988)	Jinan 济南市	Shandong 山东省	(0531)8932888 (0531)8935880	2,522	State Enterprises 国有独资	4,084,679	82,723(12)	2,097,472	Langchao Computer浪潮电子计算机
Shanghai HP Co., Ltd. 上海惠普有限公司(1998)	Shanghai 上海市	Shanghai 上海市	(021)28982998 (021)28982188	166	Foreign Funded 外商投资	4,054,449	263,667(6)	1,544,067	Computer 计算机
Dyere (Shanghai) Co.,Ltd. 英业达（上海）有限公司(2000)	Shanghai 上海市	Shanghai 上海市	(021)54261366 (021)54261297	1,800	Foreign Funded 外商投资	2,971,234	-	2,349,149	Notepad电脑笔记本
Global Trigem Computer (Shenyang)Co.,Ltd. 三宝电脑(沈阳)有限公司(1999)	Shenyang 沈阳市	Liaoning 辽宁省	(024)23743000 (024)23743333	1,217	Foreign Funded 外商投资	2,823,677	11,967(29)	808,461	Computer 计算机
Changbai Computer Group Co.,Ltd. 长白计算机集团公司(1982)	Shenyang 沈阳市	Liaoning 辽宁省	(024)23988207 (024)23988213	4,176	State-owned 国有企业	2,659,793	17,203(22)	3,182,922	Microcomputer微型计算机
Huiyang Taiyangcheng Electronics Industry Co.,Ltd. 惠阳市太阳城电子工业有限公司(1998)	Huizhou 惠州市	Guangdong 广东省	(0752)3500450 (0752)3500417	957	Overseas Chinese-funded 港澳台资	2,338,744	133,493(8)	421,051	Computer 电脑

Top 10 Cities by Revenue 销售收入排名前10位城市	Province 省	Market share 市场份额 (%)	Number of firms 企业个数
Shenzhen 深圳市	Guangdong 广东省	34.33	9
Beijing 北京市	Beijing 北京市	12.63	16
Shanghai 上海市	Shanghai 上海市	11.45	19
Xiamen 厦门市	Fujian 福建省	10.83	2
Suzhou 苏州市	Jiangsu 江苏省	9.80	9
Foshan 佛山市	Guangdong 广东省	5.65	1
Shenyang 沈阳市	Liaoning 辽宁省	3.37	3
Jinan 济南市	Shandong 山东省	3.14	3
Huizhou 惠州市	Guangdong 广东省	2.30	3
Zhongshan 中山市	Guangdong 广东省	1.43	3

10 Major Wholesalers 十家主要批发商	City 城市	Province 省	Telephone/Fax 电话/传真
SU MEC 中设江苏机械设备进出口（集团）公司	Nanjing 南京市	Jiangsu 江苏省	(025)4511888 (025)4411772
China Poster Mobile Communications Equipment Co.,Ltd. 中邮普泰移动通信设备股份有限公司	Beijing 北京市	Beijing 北京市	(010)66426993 (010)66426837
Sino Kama Co., Ltd. 中泰凯马股份有限公司	Shanghai 上海市	Shanghai 上海市	(021)62031188 (021)62030851
China Huayuan Group Co.,Ltd. 中国华源集团有限公司	Shanghai 上海市	Shanghai 上海市	(021)62031188 (021)62032288
Zhejiang Crand Imp.& Exp.Co.,Ltd. 浙江远大进出口有限公司	Ningbo 宁波市	Zhejiang 浙江省	(0574)87720170 (0574)87723350
Shandong Machinery Import & Export Group Corporation 山东省机械进出口集团公司	Qingdao 青岛市	Shandong 山东省	(0532)2661628 (0532)2991655
Qingdao Haier International Trade Co.,Ltd. 青岛海尔国际贸易有限公司	Qingdao 青岛市	Shandong 山东省	(0532)8938337 (0532)8939494
Guangdong Machinery Import & Export Group Corporation 广东省机械进出口集团公司	Guangzhou 广州市	Guangdong 广东省	(020)87782168 (020)87771803
China National Machinery Equipment Import & Export Corporation 中国机械设备进出口总公司	Beijing 北京市	Beijing 北京市	(010)63474506 (010)63261865
Beijing Cellstar Co.,Ltd. 北京蜂星事达电讯有限公司	Beijing 北京市	Beijing 北京市	(010)64602050 (010)64672648

4143: Computer Peripherals 电子计算机外部设备制造业

The industry accounts for 1.407% of the total revenue of China's industrial sector in 2002. The rate of return on assets is 4.89%. 72.43% of all firms in the industry made a profit while 27.57% had negative returns.The top province in terms of the industry's revenue is Guangdong, accounting for 45.65% of the total revenue.
2002年本行业收入占全行业的 1.407%，资产利润率为 4.89%。72.43%的企业赢利，27.57%的企业亏损。收入最高的省为广东省，占本行业的45.65%。

	Total number of firms 企业总数	Total number of employees 职工总数	Total revenue (Mil.RMB) 总销售收入（百万元）	Total profit (Mil.RMB) 总利润（百万元）	Return on assets 资产利润率（%）	Return on equity 权益利润率（%）	Labour productivity ('000 RMB/worker) 劳动生产率（千元/人）	Debts/assets 资产负债率（%）	Total assets (Mil.RMB) 总资产（百万元）
Industry Overall 行业总体	399	219,933	150,931	4,763	4.89	13.40	135.15	63.55	97,506

	Number of firms 企业个数	Average number of employees 平均职工人数	Average revenue ('000 RMB) 平均销售收入（千元）	Average profit ('000 RMB) 平均利润（千元）	Return on assets 资产利润率（%）	Return on equity 权益利润率（%）	Labour productivity ('000 RMB/worker) 劳动生产率（千元/人）	Debts/assets 资产负债率（%）	Average total assets ('000 RMB) 平均总资产（千元）
By ownership 产业所有权									
State-owned 国有	18	244	97,882	1,483	0.69	1.76	178.43	60.54	213,530
Collective-owned 集体	15	1,017	74,539	2,850	2.93	5.20	15.77	43.69	97,377
Foreign & Overseas Chinese Funded 三资	254	660	515,994	15,714	5.62	18.23	145.59	69.18	279,659
By regional distribution 地区分布									
Central-North 华北	55	307	231,729	10,982	4.61	14.93	132.26	69.11	238,091
Beijing 北京	35	249	169,557	11,513	3.84	12.09	159.87	68.26	299,963
Tianjin 天津	17	427	396,710	11,711	8.23	29.79	111.90	72.38	142,354
Hebei 河北	2	156	18,144	913	2.48	5.19	32.04	52.25	36,802
Shanxi 山西	1	569	30,231	144	0.14	1.39	23.00	89.89	102,691
Inner Mongolia 内蒙古									
Northeast 东北	13	726	328,883	8,458	1.33	3.45	111.16	61.45	636,584
Liaoning 辽宁	10	865	368,598	9,041	2.69	4.41	98.40	39.00	336,074
Jilin 吉林	1	175	24,659	6,500	7.14	11.61	72.70	38.46	91,000
Heilongjiang 黑龙江	2	308	282,421	6,526	0.27	1.20	301.21	77.52	2,411,928
Central-East 华东	147	450	416,680	18,193	7.75	22.06	218.93	64.86	234,662
Shanghai 上海	39	374	328,833	22,893	12.55	33.53	175.55	62.58	182,459
Jiangsu 江苏	55	596	559,689	18,906	6.57	20.90	226.92	68.58	287,891
Zhejiang 浙江	10	229	32,391	3,740	5.32	14.25	48.50	62.68	70,310
Anhui 安徽	4	98	12,154	822	2.59	3.34	95.58	22.54	31,715
Fujian 福建	24	540	650,290	27,947	7.07	19.18	306.30	63.13	395,133
Jiangxi 江西	1	58	11,655	1,824	45.78	59.14	59.10	22.59	3,984
Shandong 山东	14	220	118,099	2,034	2.32	4.56	117.61	49.16	87,731
Central-South 中南	173	684	409,432	7,405	3.36	8.78	98.00	61.66	220,056
Henan 河南	1	35	5,337	79	2.64	4.93	-8.69	46.53	2,994
Hubei 湖北	9	189	107,714	864	1.10	2.20	220.02	49.93	78,456
Hunan 湖南	6	245	158,108	12,919	4.26	5.29	107.34	19.44	302,989
Guangdong 广东	156	737	441,669	7,654	3.36	9.36	96.11	64.09	227,681
Guangxi 广西	1	62	7,957	1,581	6.49	7.27	97.34	10.72	24,354
Hainan 海南									
Southwest 西南	10	913	182,059	10,378	3.07	7.04	39.59	56.34	337,587
Chongqing 重庆	2	1,051	78,420	3,975	1.37	4.88	21.75	71.83	289,313
Sichuan 四川	7	826	174,591	7,387	2.49	6.77	29.19	63.27	297,026
Guizhou 贵州									
Yunnan 云南	1	1,240	441,608	44,119	6.14	8.06	118.29	23.81	718,065
Tibet 西藏									
Northwest 西北	1	45	6,061	-9,622	-4.96	-8.66	48.51	42.72	194,074
Shaanxi 陕西	1	45	6,061	-9,622	-4.96	-8.66	48.51	42.72	194,074
Gansu 甘肃									
Qinghai 青海									
Ningxia 宁夏									
Xinjiang 新疆									

4143: Computer Peripherals 电子计算机外部设备制造业

Year 年份	Number of firms 企业个数	Rate of change 变化率 (%)	Number of employees 职工人数 (人)	Rate of change 变化率 (%)	Total revenue (Mil. RMB) 总销售收入 (百万元)	Rate of change 变化率 (%)	Total profit (Mil RMB) 总利润 (百万元)	Rate of change 变化率 (%)
2000	272		126,113		76,302		3,362	
2001	322	18.38	166,950	32.38	110,839	45.26	3,668	9.10
2002	399	23.91	219,933	31.74	150,931	36.17	4,763	29.85

Major Products 主要产品	Output 产量	Unit 单位
Display 显示器	5,226	10,000 Sets 万部
Printer 打印机	2,409	10,000 Sets 万部

10 Main Firms with Maximal Revenue (year founded) 收入最大的十家主要企业（创办年份）	City 城市	Province 省	Telephone/fax 电话/传真	Number of employees 职工人数	Ownership 产业所有权	Revenue ('000 RMB) 销售收入 (千元)	Profit('000 RMB) (rank) 利润(千元) (排名)	Total assets ('000 RMB) 总资产 (千元)	Major products 主要产品
AOC Electronic (Fujian) Co., Ltd. 冠捷电子（福建）有限公司(1992)	Fuzhou 福州市	Fujian 福建省	(0591)5285555 (0591)5285447	6,000	Overseas Chinese-funded 港澳台资	10,250,579	448,435(2)	4,238,635	Computer Display 电脑显示器
Xijie Internation Technology (Wuxi) Co., Ltd. 希捷国际科技（无锡）有限公司(1995)	Wuxi 无锡市	Jiangsu 江苏省	(0510)5282828 (0510)5282864	4,029	Foreign Funded 外商投资	10,236,474	515,239(1)	3,806,873	Hard Disk Driver硬磁盘驱动器
Elite Computer System (Shen Zhen) Co.,Ltd. 鑫茂科技（深圳）有限公司(1998)	Shenzhen 深圳市	Guangdong 广东省	(0755)25261698 (0755)25260850	6,436	Foreign Funded 外商投资	7,710,322	19,724(52)	445,291	Computer Cabinet电脑高机柜
Compal Electronics(China) Co.,Ltd. 仁宝电脑工业(中国)有限公司(1997)	Suzhou 苏州市	Jiangsu 江苏省	(0512)57713333 (0512)57703001	2,424	Foreign Funded 外商投资	6,299,323	20,476(50)	1,865,032	Display 显示器
Shenzhen kafa Technology Co., Ltd. 深圳开发科技股份有限公司(1985)	Shenzhen 深圳市	Guangdong 广东省	(0755)83275000 (0755)83275054	4,488	Joint Stock 股份制	5,415,560	101,060(10)	5,057,580	Computer Peripheral 计算机外部设备
Dongguan Samsung Electric Motor Co.,Ltd. 东莞三星电机有限公司(1992)	Dongguan 东莞市	Guangdong 广东省	(0769)3305000 (0769)3305001	6,811	Foreign Funded 外商投资	4,809,035	146,252(8)	1,513,616	Floppy Disk Driver 软盘驱动器
Hewlett Packard Computer Produts (Shanghai) Co., Ltd. 惠普计算机产品(上海)有限公司(1995)	Shanghai 上海市	Shanghai 上海市	(021)50481088 (021)50480982	53	Foreign Funded 外商投资	4,347,466	297,406(4)	1,022,835	Colour Ink-Jetting Printer 彩色喷墨打印机
Ameitek Computer(Shen Zhen)Co., Ltd. 才众电脑（深圳）有限公司(1994)	Shenzhen 深圳市	Guangdong 广东省	(0755)25261110 (0755)25260355	2,150	Foreign Funded 外商投资	3,980,389	12,317(70)	860,876	Computer Main Board 电脑主机板
MSI Computer(Shenzhen) Co.,Ltd. 恩斯迈电子（深圳）有限公司(2000)	Shenzhen 深圳市	Guangdong 广东省	(0755)28101899 (0755)27628305	4,500	Overseas Chinese-funded 港澳台资	3,828,955	13,349(64)	1,262,009	Computer Main Board 微机主机板
EMC Proview Technology Co.,Ltd. 唯冠科技（深圳）有限公司(1995)	Shenzhen 深圳市	Guangdong 广东省	(0755)25261512 (0755)25261565	2,422	Overseas Chinese-funded 港澳台资	3,575,101	73,000(17)	936,975	Color Display 彩色显示器

Top 10 Cities by Revenue 销售收入排名前10位城市	Province 省	Market share 市场份额 (%)	Number of firms 企业个数
Shenzhen 深圳市	Guangdong 广东省	28.44	59
Suzhou 苏州市	Jiangsu 江苏省	10.93	26
Fuzhou 福州市	Fujian 福建省	10.07	15
Shanghai 上海市	Shanghai 上海市	8.50	39
Dongguan 东莞市	Guangdong 广东省	7.00	43
Wuxi 无锡市	Jiangsu 江苏省	6.87	8
Zhuhai 珠海市	Guangdong 广东省	5.23	15
Tianjin 天津市	Tianjin 天津市	4.47	17
Beijing 北京市	Beijing 北京市	3.93	35
Dalian 大连市	Liaoning 辽宁省	2.20	5

10 Major Wholesalers 十家主要批发商	City 城市	Province 省	Telephone/Fax 电话/传真
SU MEC 中设江苏机械设备进出口（集团）公司	Nanjing 南京市	Jiangsu 江苏省	(025)4511888 (025)4411772
China Poster Mobile Communications Equipment Co.,Ltd. 中邮普泰移动通信设备股份有限公司	Beijing 北京市	Beijing 北京市	(010)66426993 (010)66426837
Sino Kama Co., Ltd. 中泰凯马股份有限公司	Shanghai 上海市	Shanghai 上海市	(021)62031188 (021)62030851
China Huayuan Group Co.,Ltd. 中国华源集团有限公司	Shanghai 上海市	Shanghai 上海市	(021)62031188 (021)62032288
Zhejiang Crand Imp.& Exp.Co.,Ltd. 浙江远大进出口有限公司	Ningbo 宁波市	Zhejiang 浙江省	(0574)87720170 (0574)87723350
Shandong Machinery Import & Export Group Corporation 山东省机械进出口集团公司	Qingdao 青岛市	Shandong 山东省	(0532)2661628 (0532)2991655
Qingdao Haier International Trade Co.,Ltd. 青岛海尔国际贸易有限公司	Qingdao 青岛市	Shandong 山东省	(0532)8938337 (0532)8939494
Guangdong Machinery Import & Export Group Corporation 广东省机械进出口集团公司	Guangzhou 广州市	Guangdong 广东省	(020)87782168 (020)87771803
China National Machinery Equipment Import & Export Corporation 中国机械设备进出口总公司	Beijing 北京市	Beijing 北京市	(010)63474506 (010)63261865
Beijing Cellstar Co.,Ltd. 北京蜂星事达电讯有限公司	Beijing 北京市	Beijing 北京市	(010)64602050 (010)64672648

4151: Vacuum Tubes 电真空器件制造业

The industry accounts for 0.490% of the total revenue of China's industrial sector in 2002. The rate of return on assets is 3.71%. 74.07% of all firms in the industry made a profit while 25.93% had negative returns.The top province in terms of the industry's revenue is Guangdong, accounting for 21.41% of the total revenue.
2002年本行业收入占全行业的 0.490%，资产利润率为 3.71%。74.07%的企业赢利，25.93%的企业亏损。收入最高的省为广东省，占本行业的21.41%。

	Total number of firms 企业总数	Total number of employees 职工总数	Total revenue (Mil.RMB) 总销售收入（百万元）	Total profit (Mil.RMB) 总利润（百万元）	Return on assets 资产利润率（%）	Return on equity 权益利润率（%）	Labour productivity ('000 RMB/ worker) 劳动生产率（千元/人）	Debts/ assets 资产负债率（%）	Total assets (Mil.RMB) 总资产（百万元）
Industry Overall 行业总体	108	104,122	52,553	3,141	3.71	8.38	127.04	55.70	84,566

	Number of firms 企业个数	Average number of employees 平均职工人数	Average revenue ('000 RMB) 平均销售收入（千元）	Average profit ('000 RMB) 平均利润（千元）	Return on assets 资产利润率（%）	Return on equity 权益利润率（%）	Labour productivity ('000 RMB/ worker) 劳动生产率（千元/人）	Debts/ assets 资产负债率（%）	Average total assets ('000 RMB) 平均总资产（千元）
By ownership 产业所有权									
State-owned 国有	23	1,320	205,385	12,730	2.23	6.60	51.93	66.22	570,627
Collective-owned 集体	4	237	41,114	170	0.43		73.06	132.27	39,107
Foreign & Overseas Chinese Funded 三资	40	1,187	1,038,513	60,858	4.35	10.15	217.31	57.21	1,400,523
By regional distribution 地区分布									
Central-North 华北	18	922	548,013	34,620	3.54	7.24	175.74	51.15	978,505
Beijing 北京	7	1,068	616,648	41,975	4.22	6.77	125.22	37.72	995,503
Tianjin 天津	10	408	411,218	25,198	4.23	8.94	345.94	52.68	595,549
Hebei 河北	1	5,046	1,435,534	77,355	1.65	5.35	112.94	69.18	4,689,092
Shanxi 山西									
Inner Mongolia 内蒙古									
Northeast 东北	4	531	35,565	-1,829	-1.54	-55.53	43.46	97.22	118,594
Liaoning 辽宁	4	531	35,565	-1,829	-1.54	-55.53	43.46	97.22	118,594
Jilin 吉林									
Heilongjiang 黑龙江									
Central-East 华东	55	771	387,738	21,990	3.79	8.72	116.42	56.57	580,515
Shanghai 上海	12	511	641,349	49,631	4.78	9.07	290.18	47.29	1,038,362
Jiangsu 江苏	24	966	309,996	3,773	0.79	2.00	67.53	60.57	478,648
Zhejiang 浙江	7	335	56,848	8,205	8.14	23.82	63.58	65.85	100,854
Anhui 安徽	1	70	5,020	640	4.61	71.11	25.99	93.52	13,890
Fujian 福建	2	3,142	2,645,455	214,877	6.70	19.00	195.82	64.74	3,208,075
Jiangxi 江西	2	533	23,512	-2,218	-1.39	-2.53	23.88	45.07	159,769
Shandong 山东	7	470	64,091	5,702	7.60	44.70	54.82	82.99	74,982
Central-South 中南	23	1,183	812,664	50,232	3.96	9.08	161.89	56.40	1,269,240
Henan 河南	4	1,233	830,267	46,351	2.11	6.61	190.33	68.02	2,191,661
Hubei 湖北	2	901	61,171	210	0.17	0.33	34.98	49.08	124,818
Hunan 湖南	5	1,273	799,139	39,277	3.03	7.11	138.25	57.32	1,294,712
Guangdong 广东	12	1,177	937,681	64,427	5.64	10.99	178.81	48.67	1,141,890
Guangxi 广西									
Hainan 海南									
Southwest 西南	5	840	70,287	1,177	0.48	1.11	52.56	56.37	243,908
Chongqing 重庆	1	135	26,959	589	1.04	3.34	225.37	68.75	56,368
Sichuan 四川	3	1,340	108,143	2,482	0.64	1.40	47.33	53.95	386,124
Guizhou 贵州	1	45	50	-2,152	-44.82		1.22	497.02	4,801
Yunnan 云南									
Tibet 西藏									
Northwest 西北	3	3,867	726,144	51,438	3.73	8.98	56.66	58.49	1,379,276
Shaanxi 陕西	2	5,011	1,079,849	77,146	3.91	8.67	64.81	54.87	1,972,835
Gansu 甘肃	1	1,578	18,735	23	0.01		4.86	132.79	192,159
Qinghai 青海									
Ningxia 宁夏									
Xinjiang 新疆									

4151: Vacuum Tubes 电真空器件制造业

Year 年份	Number of firms 企业个数	Rate of change 变化率（%）	Number of employees 职工人数（人）	Rate of change 变化率（%）	Total revenue (Mil. RMB) 总销售收入（百万元）	Rate of change 变化率（%）	Total profit (Mil RMB) 总利润（百万元）	Rate of change 变化率（%）
2000	105		119,271		53,304		5,710	
2001	104	-0.95	108,156	-9.32	47,095	-11.65	1,764	-69.11
2002	108	3.85	104,122	-3.73	52,553	11.59	3,141	78.06

Major Products 主要产品	Output 产量	Unit 单位
Colour Tube 彩色显象管	7,049	10,000 Units 万只
Black and White Tube 黑白显象管	489	10,000 Units 万只

10 Main Firms with Maximal Revenue (year founded) 收入最大的十家主要企业（创办年份）	City 城市	Province 省	Telephone/fax 电话/传真	Number of employees 职工人数	Ownership 产业所有权	Revenue ('000 RMB) 销售收入（千元）	Profit('000 RMB) (rank) 利润（千元）（排名）	Total assets ('000 RMB) 总资产（千元）	Major products 主要产品
CPTF Optronics Co., Ltd.	Fuzhou	Fujian	(0591)3971357		Foreign Funded				Colour Kinescope彩
华映光电股份有限公司(1994)	福州市	福建省	(0591)3970489	6,037	外商投资	5,264,545	428,083(2)	6,390,580	色显示管
Shenzhen Samsung Sdi Co.,Ltd.	Shenzhen	Guangdong	(0755)83357000		Overseas Chinese-funded				Colour Kinescope彩
深圳三星电管有限公司(1996)	深圳市	广东省	(0755)83367008	2,093	港澳台资	4,699,312	513,948(1)	3,965,389	色显像管
Huafei Colour Displays Systems Co., Ltd.	Nanjing	Jiangsu	(025)5421166		Foreign Funded				Colour Kinescope彩
华飞彩色显示系统有限公司(1988)	南京市	江苏省	(025)5417470	6,003	外商投资	3,873,780	-	6,040,580	色显像管
LG Philips Dawn Electronics Co., Ltd.	Changsha	Hunan	(0731)4063522		Foreign Funded				Colour Kinescope彩
乐金飞利浦曙光电子有限公司(1994)	长沙市	湖南省	(0731)4063997	4,213	外商投资	3,823,418	195,385(5)	5,405,291	色显示管
Tianjin Samsung Display International Co., Ltd.	Tianjin	Tianjin	(022)82129971		Foreign Funded				Colour Kinescope彩
天津三星视界有限公司(1998)	天津市	天津市	(022)82129984	1,392	外商投资	3,552,408	274,016(3)	4,292,700	色显像管
Henan Anyang Color Picture Tube Glass Bulb Co., Ltd.	Anyang	Henan	(0372)3932916		Overseas Chinese-funded				54CM Colour Kinescope Glass Shell54CM彩色显
河南安阳彩色显像管玻壳有限公司(1987)	安阳市	河南省	(0372)3932808	3,284	港澳台资	2,885,620	110,890(11)	7,658,830	像管玻壳
Irico Color Picture Tube Plant	Xianyang	Shannxi	(0910)3334433		State-owned				Colour Kinescope彩
彩虹彩色显像管总厂(1982)	咸阳市	陕西省	(0910)3313762	9,982	国有企业	2,154,013	153,844(7)	3,939,509	色显象管
Shenzhen Seg Hitachi Colour Display Devices Co.,Ltd.	Shenzhen	Guangdong	(0755)83350777		Foreign Funded				54CM Colour Kinescope 54CM彩
深圳赛格日立彩色显示器件有限公司(1989)	深圳市	广东省	(0755)83355850	2,790	外商投资	1,940,260	101,928(13)	2,423,413	色显像管
Shanghai Solecotron Electronics Glass Co.,Ltd	Shanghai	Shanghai	(021)64531688		Foreign Funded				Colour Kinescope彩色显
上海旭电子玻璃有限公司(1996)	上海市	上海市	(021)64776126	476	外商投资	1,903,061	208,075(4)	3,767,101	像管玻壳
Samsung Electronics (Suzhou)Semiconductor Co.,Ltd.	Suzhou	Jiangsu	(0512)67611121		Foreign Funded				TC RC Electron Device .TC RC
三星电子(苏州)半导体有限公司(1996)	苏州市	江苏省	(0512)67611432	890	外商投资	1,231,764	91,926(14)	619,114	电子器件

Top 10 Cities by Revenue 销售收入排名前10位城市	Province 省	Market share 市场份额（%）	Number of firms 企业个数
Shenzhen 深圳市	Guangdong 广东省	14.79	6
Shanghai 上海市	Shanghai 上海市	14.64	12
Nanjing 南京市	Jiangsu 江苏省	10.29	8
Fuzhou 福州市	Fujian 福建省	10.02	1
Beijing 北京市	Beijing 北京市	8.21	7
Tianjin 天津市	Tianjin 天津市	7.82	10
Changsha 长沙市	Hunan 湖南省	7.55	2
Anyang 安阳市	Henan 河南省	6.29	3
Xianyang 咸阳市	Shannxi 陕西省	4.10	1
Dongguan 东莞市	Guangdong 广东省	3.85	1

10 Major Wholesalers 十家主要批发商	City 城市	Province 省	Telephone/Fax 电话/传真
SU MEC	Nanjing	Jiangsu	(025)4511888
中设江苏机械设备进出口（集团）公司	南京市	江苏省	(025)4411772
China Poster Mobile Communications Equipment Co.,Ltd.	Beijing	Beijing	(010)66426993
中邮普泰移动通信设备股份有限公司	北京市	北京市	(010)66426837
Sino Kama Co., Ltd.	Shanghai	Shanghai	(021)62031188
中泰凯马股份有限公司	上海市	上海市	(021)62030851
China Huayuan Group Co.,Ltd.	Shanghai	Shanghai	(021)62031188
中国华源集团有限公司	上海市	上海市	(021)62032288
Zhejiang Crand Imp.& Exp.Co.,Ltd.	Ningbo	Zhejiang	(0574)87720170
浙江远大进出口有限公司	宁波市	浙江省	(0574)87723350
Shandong Machinery Import & Export Group Corporation	Qingdao	Shandong	(0532)2661628
山东省机械进出口集团公司	青岛市	山东省	(0532)2991655
Qingdao Haier International Trade Co.,Ltd.	Qingdao	Shandong	(0532)8938337
青岛海尔国际贸易有限公司	青岛市	山东省	(0532)8939494
Guangdong Machinery Import & Export Group Corporation	Guangzhou	Guangdong	(020)87782168
广东省机械进出口集团公司	广州市	广东省	(020)87771803
China National Machinery Equipment Import & Export	Beijing	Beijing	(010)63474506
Corporation 中国机械设备进出口总公司	北京市	北京市	(010)63261865
Beijing Cellstar Co.,Ltd.	Beijing	Beijing	(010)64602050
北京蜂星事达电讯有限公司	北京市	北京市	(010)64672648

4153: Semi-conductor Devices 半导体器件制造业

The industry accounts for 0.277% of the total revenue of China's industrial sector in 2002. The rate of return on assets is 1.04%. 74.28% of all firms in the industry made a profit while 25.72% had negative returns.The top province in terms of the industry's revenue is Shanghai, accounting for 37.11% of the total revenue.
2002年本行业收入占全行业的0.277%，资产利润率为1.04%。74.28%的企业赢利，25.72%的企业亏损。收入最高的省为上海市，占本行业的37.11%。

	Total number of firms 企业总数	Total number of employees 职工总数	Total revenue (Mil.RMB) 总销售收入 (百万元)	Total profit (Mil.RMB) 总利润 (百万元)	Return on assets 资产利润率 (%)	Return on equity 权益利润率 (%)	Labour productivity ('000 RMB/ worker) 劳动生产率 (千元/人)	Debts/ assets 资产负债率 (%)	Total assets (Mil.RMB) 总资产 (百万元)
Industry Overall 行业总体	311	111,020	29,709	342	1.04	2.90	55.23	64.02	32,698

	Number of firms 企业个数	Average number of employees 平均职工人数	Average revenue ('000 RMB) 平均销售收入 (千元)	Average profit ('000 RMB) 平均利润 (千元)	Return on assets 资产利润率 (%)	Return on equity 权益利润率 (%)	Labour productivity ('000 RMB/ worker) 劳动生产率 (千元/人)	Debts/ assets 资产负债率 (%)	Average total assets ('000 RMB) 平均总资产 (千元)
By ownership 产业所有权									
State-owned 国有	57	280	19,691	-940	-1.35	-21.54	20.44	93.74	69,684
Collective-owned 集体	7	131	17,583	1,407	9.01	15.47	31.96	41.74	15,613
Foreign & Overseas Chinese Funded 三资	162	429	147,637	211	0.16	0.40	57.30	58.45	128,076
By regional distribution 地区分布									
Central-North 华北	40	278	42,211	3,548	4.29	8.45	59.76	49.26	82,770
Beijing 北京	13	203	24,047	3,270	5.43	8.78	52.03	38.15	60,242
Tianjin 天津	18	319	59,096	4,165	3.74	7.85	68.42	52.41	111,446
Hebei 河北	7	291	43,208	3,494	6.21	12.28	65.67	49.41	56,229
Shanxi 山西	2	349	4,830	4	0.01	0.02	0.47	67.60	64,003
Inner Mongolia 内蒙古									
Northeast 东北	22	390	59,271	26	0.01	0.05	45.87	72.39	171,526
Liaoning 辽宁	17	293	43,102	-716	-0.76	-2.82	24.40	73.13	94,436
Jilin 吉林	2	946	152,965	1,000	0.12	0.45	91.44	72.62	812,607
Heilongjiang 黑龙江	3	570	88,432	3,576	1.98	6.47	58.02	69.46	180,977
Central-East 华东	148	295	117,939	-2,851	-3.02	-10.63	42.13	71.56	94,275
Shanghai 上海	43	346	256,424	-12,869	-7.54	-34.71	11.33	78.27	170,619
Jiangsu 江苏	51	299	67,061	1,219	1.60	4.37	62.27	63.36	76,082
Zhejiang 浙江	22	165	26,094	1,280	3.12	7.77	40.05	59.79	41,001
Anhui 安徽	3	134	9,746	10	0.04	0.14	88.91	68.32	22,200
Fujian 福建	12	357	85,691	1,546	2.63	6.61	36.81	60.22	58,812
Jiangxi 江西									
Shandong 山东	17	307	81,001	1,327	2.13	7.84	73.19	72.88	62,448
Central-South 中南	87	446	89,083	5,781	5.93	11.73	71.67	49.45	97,502
Henan 河南	6	182	12,226	313	0.66	1.43	20.48	53.82	47,373
Hubei 湖北	6	120	8,860	-1,289	-2.22	-25.60	28.77	91.33	58,088
Hunan 湖南	4	104	1,643	-102	-0.49		27.98	125.14	20,598
Guangdong 广东	67	532	112,354	7,664	6.80	12.48	74.14	45.51	112,716
Guangxi 广西	3	291	29,685	-1,379	-1.92	-12.21	92.12	84.25	71,718
Hainan 海南	1	18	390	-119	-30.43		13.61	349.36	391
Southwest 西南	10	621	134,651	13,767	5.46	16.48	67.14	66.87	252,200
Chongqing 重庆	1	55	12,104	1,451	14.60	22.58	29.47	35.37	9,941
Sichuan 四川	6	816	207,491	22,960	6.23	17.36	78.06	64.11	368,451
Guizhou 贵州	2	510	26,084	-1,353	-1.31	-34.17	17.91	96.16	103,015
Yunnan 云南	1	244	37,292	1,165	1.22	4.22	62.38	71.04	95,320
Tibet 西藏									
Northwest 西北	4	668	41,244	-4,889	-2.98		13.94	107.62	164,125
Shaanxi 陕西	3	470	20,686	-9,518	-7.43		-0.79	129.97	128,167
Gansu 甘肃	1	1,261	102,920	9,000	3.31	13.80	30.41	76.02	272,000
Qinghai 青海									
Ningxia 宁夏									
Xinjiang 新疆									

4153: Semi-conductor Devices 半导体器件制造业

Year 年份	Number of firms 企业个数	Rate of change 变化率 (%)	Number of employees 职工人数 (人)	Rate of change 变化率 (%)	Total revenue (Mil. RMB) 总销售收入 (百万元)	Rate of change 变化率 (%)	Total profit (Mil RMB) 总利润 (百万元)	Rate of change 变化率 (%)
2000	236		83,510		12,683		794	
2001	275	16.53	91,379	9.42	15,964	25.87	630	-20.65
2002	311	13.09	111,020	21.49	29,709	86.10	342	-45.71

Major Products 主要产品	Output 产量	Unit 单位
Semiconductor Discrete Device 半导体分立器件	593	100,000,000 Units 亿只

10 Main Firms with Maximal Revenue (year founded) 收入最大的十家主要企业（创办年份）	City 城市	Province 省	Telephone/fax 电话/传真	Number of employees 职工人数	Ownership 产业所有权	Revenue ('000 RMB) 销售收入 (千元)	Profit('000 RMB) (rank) 利润(千元) (排名)	Total assets ('000 RMB) 总资产 (千元)	Major products 主要产品
Philips Electronic Components (Shanghai)Co.,Ltd. 飞利浦电子元件(上海)有限公司(1996)	Shanghai 上海市	Shanghai 上海市	(021)50481188 (021)50481199	2,596	Foreign Funded 外商投资	5,759,359	-	2,264,758	Liquid Crystal Display液晶显示器
Leshan Radio Co.,Ltd. 乐山无线电股份有限公司(1970)	Leshan 乐山市	Sichuan 四川省	(0833)2150051 (0833)2132212	2,754	Joint Stock 股份制	982,949	85,354(2)	1,616,553	Diode & Audion 二、三极管
Shenzhen STS Microelectronics Co.,Ltd. 深圳赛意法微电子有限公司(1994)	Shenzhen 深圳市	Guangdong 广东省	(0755)83590950 (0755)83591400	1,370	Foreign Funded 外商投资	689,407	146,006(1)	1,845,463	Semiconductor Discrete Device 半导体分立器件
Xiamen Fujitsu Electrochemical Co.,Ltd. 厦门富士电气化学有限公司(1994)	Xiamen 厦门市	Fujian 福建省	(0592)6030576 (0592)6030579	1,615	Foreign Funded 外商投资	688,964	-	376,936	Power Source Supply Machine电源供应器
Shanghai Schlumberger Intelligent Card Technologies Co.,Ltd. 上海斯伦贝谢智能卡技术有限公司(2000)	Shanghai 上海市	Shanghai 上海市	(021)58547475 (021)58546299	148	Foreign Funded 外商投资	593,477	30,000(16)	332,149	Intelligence Cards Module IC电话卡
Ricoh International (Shanghai) Co.,Ltd. 理光国际(上海)有限公司(1996)	Shanghai 上海市	Shanghai 上海市	(021)50460698 (021)50460690	296	Foreign Funded 外商投资	512,362	2,241(91)	197,396	Electrograph Parts 传真机零部件
Zhuhai Eastcon Peace Smart Card Co., Ltd. 珠海东信和平智能卡股份有限公司(1998)	Zhuhai 珠海市	Guangdong 广东省	(0756)8682900 (0756)8682800	663	Joint Stock 股份制	491,217	36,098(8)	314,214	Mobile Telephone SIM Card 移动电话用SIM卡
Fuzhun Precision Industry (Shenzhen) Co., Ltd. 富准精密工业（深圳）有限公司(1998)	Shenzhen 深圳市	Guangdong 广东省	(0755)27231888 (0755)27231888	1,500	Foreign Funded 外商投资	488,675	23,600(21)	238,250	Computer Heat Sink 电脑用散热片
Nitto Denko (shanghai Pudong) Co., Ltd. 日东电工(上海浦东新区)有限公司(1995)	Shanghai 上海市	Shanghai 上海市	(021)58663802 (021)58663710	768	Foreign Funded 外商投资	444,950	33,080(11)	219,784	Adhesive Tape 胶带
Infineon Technologies AG(Wuxi) Co.,Ltd. 英飞凌科技（无锡）有限公司(1995)	Wuxi 无锡市	Jiangsu 江苏省	(0510)5282096 (0510)5282432	633	Foreign Funded 外商投资	423,009	31,223(13)	300,837	Photoelectricity Coupling Device 光电藕合器

Top 10 Cities by Revenue 销售收入排名前10位城市	Province 省	Market share 市场份额 (%)	Number of firms 企业个数
Shanghai 上海市	Shanghai 上海市	37.11	43
Shenzhen 深圳市	Guangdong 广东省	8.89	19
Suzhou 苏州市	Jiangsu 江苏省	4.81	10
Zhongshan 中山市	Guangdong 广东省	4.49	5
Tianjin 天津市	Tianjin 天津市	3.58	18
Wuxi 无锡市	Jiangsu 江苏省	3.39	12
Leshan 乐山市	Sichuan 四川省	3.31	1
Xiamen 厦门市	Fujian 福建省	3.31	9
Dongguan 东莞市	Guangdong 广东省	3.23	11
Qingdao 青岛市	Shandong 山东省	2.90	3

10 Major Wholesalers 十家主要批发商	City 城市	Province 省	Telephone/Fax 电话/传真
SU MEC 中设江苏机械设备进出口（集团）公司	Nanjing 南京市	Jiangsu 江苏省	(025)4511888 (025)4411772
China Poster Mobile Communications Equipment Co.,Ltd. 中邮普泰移动通信设备股份有限公司	Beijing 北京市	Beijing 北京市	(010)66426993 (010)66426837
Sino Kama Co., Ltd. 中泰凯马股份有限公司	Shanghai 上海市	Shanghai 上海市	(021)62031188 (021)62030851
China Huayuan Group Co.,Ltd. 中国华源集团有限公司	Shanghai 上海市	Shanghai 上海市	(021)62031188 (021)62032288
Zhejiang Crand Imp.& Exp.Co.,Ltd. 浙江远大进出口有限公司	Ningbo 宁波市	Zhejiang 浙江省	(0574)87720170 (0574)87723350
Shandong Machinery Import & Export Group Corporation 山东省机械进出口集团公司	Qingdao 青岛市	Shandong 山东省	(0532)2661628 (0532)2991655
Qingdao Haier International Trade Co.,Ltd. 青岛海尔国际贸易有限公司	Qingdao 青岛市	Shandong 山东省	(0532)8938337 (0532)8939494
Guangdong Machinery Import & Export Group Corporation 广东省机械进出口集团公司	Guangzhou 广州市	Guangdong 广东省	(020)87782168 (020)87771803
China National Machinery Equipment Import & Export Corporation 中国机械设备进出口总公司	Beijing 北京市	Beijing 北京市	(010)63474506 (010)63261865
Beijing Cellstar Co.,Ltd. 北京蜂星事达电讯有限公司	Beijing 北京市	Beijing 北京市	(010)64602050 (010)64672648

4155: Integrated Circuit 集成电路制造业

The industry accounts for 0.288% of the total revenue of China's industrial sector in 2002. The rate of return on assets is -0.42%. 75.98% of all firms in the industry made a profit while 24.02% had negative returns.The top province in terms of the industry's revenue is Guangdong, accounting for 34.72% of the total revenue.
2002年本行业收入占全行业的 0.288%，资产利润率为 -0.42%。75.98%的企业赢利，24.02%的企业亏损。收入最高的省为广东省，占本行业的34.72%。

	Total number of firms 企业总数	Total number of employees 职工总数	Total revenue (Mil.RMB) 总销售收入 (百万元)	Total profit (Mil.RMB) 总利润 (百万元)	Return on assets 资产利润率 (%)	Return on equity 权益利润率 (%)	Labour productivity ('000 RMB/ worker) 劳动生产率 (千元/人)	Debts/ assets 资产负债率 (%)	Total assets (Mil.RMB) 总资产 (百万元)
Industry Overall 行业总体	179	74,203	30,919	-204	-0.42	-0.89	126.28	52.73	48,317

	Number of firms 企业个数	Average number of employees 平均职工人数	Average revenue ('000 RMB) 平均销售收入 (千元)	Average profit ('000 RMB) 平均利润 (千元)	Return on assets 资产利润率 (%)	Return on equity 权益利润率 (%)	Labour productivity ('000 RMB/ worker) 劳动生产率 (千元/人)	Debts/ assets 资产负债率 (%)	Average total assets ('000 RMB) 平均总资产 (千元)
By ownership 产业所有权									
State-owned 国有	10	1,033	110,093	-4,508	-1.67	-4.44	39.53	62.52	270,609
Collective-owned 集体	6	97	7,977	271	4.19	13.93	22.61	69.94	6,468
Foreign & Overseas Chinese Funded 三资	107	470	243,078	-5,121	-1.34	-2.85	151.68	53.14	383,012
By regional distribution 地区分布									
Central-North 华北	26	286	95,468	-5,901	-4.42	-10.60	86.94	58.32	133,576
Beijing 北京	11	395	147,275	-18,444	-6.80	-17.15	92.45	60.38	271,405
Tianjin 天津	6	183	37,051	620	1.83	4.74	25.21	61.40	33,878
Hebei 河北	9	222	71,092	5,083	16.09	24.56	108.95	34.46	31,584
Shanxi 山西									
Inner Mongolia 内蒙古									
Northeast 东北	4	110	55,627	6,001	17.65	47.10	167.23	62.52	33,994
Liaoning 辽宁	2	163	75,661	11,732	23.78	61.75	179.39	61.49	49,342
Jilin 吉林	1	56	62,892	154	0.57	2.43	239.29	76.72	27,218
Heilongjiang 黑龙江	1	60	8,294	387	3.84	5.84	34.12	34.26	10,075
Central-East 华东	78	467	221,650	-6,054	-1.26	-2.63	158.72	52.22	480,953
Shanghai 上海	26	460	223,078	-37,912	-3.83	-7.76	187.47	50.70	991,127
Jiangsu 江苏	30	593	330,430	10,977	3.50	8.78	167.26	60.12	313,300
Zhejiang 浙江	13	232	83,432	13,818	9.71	14.39	132.31	32.51	142,237
Anhui 安徽									
Fujian 福建	5	537	87,807	1,739	2.38	4.43	58.93	46.40	73,169
Jiangxi 江西	1	600	6,695	-1,978	-9.46	-113.42	3.35	91.66	20,916
Shandong 山东	3	130	15,133	-717	-1.95	-8.28	18.81	76.40	36,728
Central-South 中南	67	385	161,499	6,007	5.91	11.76	109.03	49.70	101,578
Henan 河南									
Hubei 湖北									
Hunan 湖南	1	964	28,853	-3,259	-2.67	-30.15	11.90	91.14	121,986
Guangdong 广东	64	382	167,747	6,331	6.19	11.89	114.09	47.96	102,319
Guangxi 广西	1	165	10,194	212	0.52	6.91	18.90	92.55	41,162
Hainan 海南	1	243	45,587	298	0.32	19.93	47.15	98.41	94,197
Southwest 西南	3	854	28,585	-1,001	-1.21	-9.88	16.46	87.78	82,929
Chongqing 重庆									
Sichuan 四川	3	854	28,585	-1,001	-1.21	-9.88	16.46	87.78	82,929
Guizhou 贵州									
Yunnan 云南									
Tibet 西藏									
Northwest 西北	1	1,509	19,300	-1,500	-1.08		6.09	127.76	138,700
Shaanxi 陕西									
Gansu 甘肃	1	1,509	19,300	-1,500	-1.08		6.09	127.76	138,700
Qinghai 青海									
Ningxia 宁夏									
Xinjiang 新疆									

4155: Integrated Circuit 集成电路制造业

Year 年份	Number of firms 企业个数	Rate of change 变化率 (%)	Number of employees 职工人数 (人)	Rate of change 变化率 (%)	Total revenue (Mil. RMB) 总销售收入 (百万元)	Rate of change 变化率 (%)	Total profit (Mil RMB) 总利润 (百万元)	Rate of change 变化率 (%)
2000	172		71,475		26,027		1,769	
2001	155	-9.88	63,781	-10.76	22,329	-14.21	-402	
2002	179	15.48	74,203	16.34	30,919	38.47	-204	-

Major Products 主要产品	Output 产量	Unit 单位
Semiconductor Integrated Circuit 半导体集成电路	963,101	10,000 Blocks 万块
Large Scale Semiconductor Integrated Circuit 大规模半导体集成电路	413,240	10,000 Blocks 万块

10 Main Firms with Maximal Revenue (year founded) 收入最大的十家主要企业（创办年份）	City 城市	Province 省	Telephone/fax 电话/传真	Number of employees 职工人数	Ownership 产业所有权	Revenue ('000 RMB) 销售收入 (千元)	Profit('000 RMB) (rank) 利润(千元) (排名)	Total assets ('000 RMB) 总资产 (千元)	Major products 主要产品
Solectron (Suzhou)Technology Co., Ltd. 旭电(苏州)科技有限公司(1996)	Suzhou 苏州市	Jiangsu 江苏省	(0512)67612300 (0512)67630971	2,714	Foreign Funded 外商投资	5,538,436	276,660(1)	2,662,363	Electronic Circuit Board 电子线路板
Shanghai Huahong NEC Electronics Co., Ltd. 上海华虹NEC电子有限公司(1997)	Shanghai 上海市	Shanghai 上海市	(021)50310909 (021)58344909	924	Foreign Funded 外商投资	1,459,040	-	6,124,658	LSI 大规模集成电路
China Resources Microelectronics(holdings) limited. 无锡华润微电子有限公司(1989)	Wuxi 无锡市	Jiangsu 江苏省	(0510)5807123 (0510)5804647	3,913	State-owned 国有企业	871,708	-	1,803,609	Integrated Circuit 集成电路
Kaiping Elec & Eltek Co.,Ltd. 开平依利安达电子有限公司(1992)	Jiangmen 江门市	Guangdong 广东省	(0750)2218428 (0750)2210993	2,322	Foreign Funded 外商投资	790,597	105,925(5)	786,410	Printed Circuit Board 印刷线路板
Intel Products (Shanghai) Co., Ltd. 英特尔产品（上海）有限公司(2001)	Shanghai 上海市	Shanghai 上海市	(021)50481818 (021)50481212	1,440	Foreign Funded 外商投资	706,289	130,941(3)	1,972,962	Writable Memorizer 快擦写存储器
Jiangsu Changjiang Electronics Technology Co., Ltd. 江苏长电科技股份有限公司(1972)	Wuxi 无锡市	Jiangsu 江苏省	(0510)6856417 (0510)6854550	1,896	Joint Stock 股份制	681,581	73,656(6)	750,957	Integrated Circuit 集成电路
Huiyang Tecswise Circuits Co., Ltd. 惠阳科惠电路有限公司(1995)	Huizhou 惠州市	Guangdong 广东省	(0752)3500078 (0752)3500306	1,278	Overseas Chinese-funded 港澳台资	678,241	39,144(16)	297,440	Printed Circuit Board 印刷线路板
Shanghai Advanced Semiconductor Manufacturing Co.,Ltd. 上海先进半导体制造有限公司(1992)	Shanghai 上海市	Shanghai 上海市	(021)64851900 (021)64851056	769	Foreign Funded 外商投资	643,503	184,288(2)	1,124,026	LSI 大规模集成电路
ChipPAC (Shanghai) Co. Ltd. 金朋(上海)有限公司(1994)	Shanghai 上海市	Shanghai 上海市	(021)59765858 (021)59763838	1,960	Foreign Funded 外商投资	561,029	13,926(28)	1,183,298	Electronic Products 电子产品
Dongguan Changping Maiyuan Anmeishi Electronic Products Factory 东莞常平麦园安美时电子制品厂(1997)	Dongguan 东莞市	Guangdong 广东省	(0769)3394581 (0769)3394582	200	Overseas Chinese-funded 港澳台资	519,398	15,807(24)	20,662	Electronic Circuit Board 电子电路板

Top 10 Cities by Revenue 销售收入排名前10位城市	Province 省	Market share 市场份额 (%)	Number of firms 企业个数
Suzhou 苏州市	Jiangsu 江苏省	24.72	21
Shanghai 上海市	Shanghai 上海市	18.76	26
Dongguan 东莞市	Guangdong 广东省	13.22	10
Huizhou 惠州市	Guangdong 广东省	8.76	12
Wuxi 无锡市	Jiangsu 江苏省	5.66	4
Beijing 北京市	Beijing 北京市	5.24	11
Jiangmen 江门市	Guangdong 广东省	4.35	5
Guangzhou 广州市	Guangdong 广东省	3.46	11
Shenzhen 深圳市	Guangdong 广东省	3.43	11
Cangzhou 沧州市	Hebei 河北省	2.04	8

10 Major Wholesalers 十家主要批发商	City 城市	Province 省	Telephone/Fax 电话/传真
SU MEC 中设江苏机械设备进出口（集团）公司	Nanjing 南京市	Jiangsu 江苏省	(025)4511888 (025)4411772
China Poster Mobile Communications Equipment Co.,Ltd. 中邮普泰移动通信设备股份有限公司	Beijing 北京市	Beijing 北京市	(010)66426993 (010)66426837
Sino Kama Co., Ltd. 中泰凯马股份有限公司	Shanghai 上海市	Shanghai 上海市	(021)62031188 (021)62030851
China Huayuan Group Co.,Ltd. 中国华源集团有限公司	Shanghai 上海市	Shanghai 上海市	(021)62031188 (021)62032288
Zhejiang Crand Imp.& Exp.Co.,Ltd. 浙江远大进出口有限公司	Ningbo 宁波市	Zhejiang 浙江省	(0574)87720170 (0574)87723350
Shandong Machinery Import & Export Group Corporation 山东省机械进出口集团公司	Qingdao 青岛市	Shandong 山东省	(0532)2661628 (0532)2991655
Qingdao Haier International Trade Co.,Ltd. 青岛海尔国际贸易有限公司	Qingdao 青岛市	Shandong 山东省	(0532)8938337 (0532)8939494
Guangdong Machinery Import & Export Group Corporation 广东省机械进出口集团公司	Guangzhou 广州市	Guangdong 广东省	(020)87782168 (020)87771803
China National Machinery Equipment Import & Export Corporation 中国机械设备进出口总公司	Beijing 北京市	Beijing 北京市	(010)63474506 (010)63261865
Beijing Cellstar Co.,Ltd. 北京蜂星事达电讯有限公司	Beijing 北京市	Beijing 北京市	(010)64602050 (010)64672648

4160: Electronic Components 电子元件制造业

The industry accounts for 1.381% of the total revenue of China's industrial sector in 2002. The rate of return on assets is 3.96%. 76.52% of all firms in the industry made a profit while 23.48% had negative returns.The top province in terms of the industry's revenue is Guangdong, accounting for 39.89% of the total revenue.
2002年本行业收入占全行业的 1.381%，资产利润率为 3.96%。76.52%的企业赢利，23.48%的企业亏损。收入最高的省为广东省，占本行业的39.89%。

	Total number of firms 企业总数	Total number of employees 职工总数	Total revenue (Mil.RMB) 总销售收入（百万元）	Total profit (Mil.RMB) 总利润（百万元）	Return on assets 资产利润率 (%)	Return on equity 权益利润率 (%)	Labour productivity ('000 RMB/ worker) 劳动生产率（千元/人）	Debts/ assets 资产负债率 (%)	Total assets (Mil.RMB) 总资产（百万元）
Industry Overall 行业总体	2019	765,343	148,103	6,772	3.96	8.64	49.46	54.21	171,203

	Number of firms 企业个数	Average number of employees 平均职工人数	Average revenue ('000 RMB) 平均销售收入（千元）	Average profit ('000 RMB) 平均利润（千元）	Return on assets 资产利润率 (%)	Return on equity 权益利润率 (%)	Labour productivity ('000 RMB/ worker) 劳动生产率（千元/人）	Debts/ assets 资产负债率 (%)	Average total assets ('000 RMB) 平均总资产（千元）
By ownership 产业所有权									
State-owned 国有	120	372	40,041	-171	-0.16	-0.72	28.58	78.44	110,232
Collective-owned 集体	113	372	22,364	565	2.36	7.90	20.48	70.15	23,963
Foreign & Overseas Chinese Funded 三资	1,064	445	104,791	4,494	4.75	9.88	55.50	51.95	94,700
By regional distribution 地区分布									
Central-North 华北	232	302	66,239	903	1.07	2.40	42.98	55.54	84,638
Beijing 北京	65	223	52,118	1,927	1.85	3.13	58.39	41.06	104,413
Tianjin 天津	122	359	91,860	408	0.46	1.14	42.27	59.25	87,783
Hebei 河北	28	279	20,413	532	0.99	7.48	28.30	86.72	53,475
Shanxi 山西	11	218	10,333	1,527	3.35	12.72	22.20	73.68	45,611
Inner Mongolia 内蒙古	6	277	14,571	469	2.00	7.98	26.30	74.90	23,425
Northeast 东北	41	500	111,402	2,655	1.18	2.28	55.72	48.56	225,919
Liaoning 辽宁	33	453	135,917	6,632	4.60	9.43	70.10	51.22	144,101
Jilin 吉林	5	1,042	15,305	-21,980	-2.46	-4.47	17.44	44.87	892,451
Heilongjiang 黑龙江	3	115	1,890	-29	-0.20		10.28	133.29	15,029
Central-East 华东	980	322	60,688	3,523	5.18	10.51	49.84	50.73	68,043
Shanghai 上海	136	291	104,123	5,111	4.53	9.13	64.02	50.33	112,762
Jiangsu 江苏	369	289	51,605	2,462	4.07	8.65	51.47	52.99	60,540
Zhejiang 浙江	239	262	33,066	3,060	7.32	15.11	39.68	51.51	41,778
Anhui 安徽	40	234	28,176	1,423	2.67	6.89	38.35	61.27	53,320
Fujian 福建	81	546	96,340	5,946	6.50	12.51	46.70	48.00	91,430
Jiangxi 江西	17	772	51,937	3,281	2.79	4.68	25.22	40.34	117,561
Shandong 山东	98	406	87,290	5,340	6.99	13.01	61.64	46.25	76,378
Central-South 中南	699	451	87,177	3,706	4.22	9.77	48.58	56.87	87,920
Henan 河南	17	335	37,763	835	1.03	3.95	25.64	74.03	81,330
Hubei 湖北	29	155	15,740	1,818	6.68	14.90	46.86	55.14	27,202
Hunan 湖南	30	225	18,672	-138	-0.39	-1.34	28.28	71.24	35,696
Guangdong 广东	617	479	95,750	4,062	4.35	9.92	49.53	56.17	93,419
Guangxi 广西	6	382	33,423	3,576	3.74	9.83	46.44	61.98	95,648
Hainan 海南									
Southwest 西南	48	523	58,208	4,653	3.66	7.48	65.40	51.12	127,292
Chongqing 重庆	5	172	29,048	-837	-2.01		41.45	145.29	41,680
Sichuan 四川	35	443	51,143	4,971	6.06	16.78	64.32	63.91	82,084
Guizhou 贵州	7	1,238	122,398	8,624	2.02	2.95	70.28	31.73	427,928
Yunnan 云南	1	84	1,966	-6,812	-20.55		7.94	103.47	33,153
Tibet 西藏									
Northwest 西北	19	1,008	261,228	9,821	2.32	7.32	53.66	68.35	424,006
Shaanxi 陕西	17	1,075	288,290	10,943	2.41	7.60	54.62	68.27	453,528
Gansu 甘肃									
Qinghai 青海									
Ningxia 宁夏	1	777	55,194	550	0.17	0.59	35.18	71.73	330,016
Xinjiang 新疆	1	116	7,201	23	0.14	0.23	27.42	38.16	16,112

4160: Electronic Components 电子元件制造业

Year 年份	Number of firms 企业个数	Rate of change 变化率 (%)	Number of employees 职工人数 (人)	Rate of change 变化率 (%)	Total revenue (Mil. RMB) 总销售收入 (百万元)	Rate of change 变化率 (%)	Total profit (Mil RMB) 总利润 (百万元)	Rate of change 变化率 (%)
2000	1598		656,554		99,382		6,548	
2001	1787	11.83	677,220	3.15	115,145	15.86	5,318	-18.78
2002	2019	12.98	765,343	13.01	148,103	28.62	6,772	27.34

Major Products 主要产品	Output 产量	Unit 单位
Electronic Component 电子元件	4,055	100,000,000 Units 亿只

10 Main Firms with Maximal Revenue (year founded) 收入最大的十家主要企业（创办年份）	City 城市	Province 省	Telephone/fax 电话/传真	Number of employees 职工人数	Ownership 产业所有权	Revenue ('000 RMB) 销售收入 (千元)	Profit('000 RMB) (rank) 利润(千元) (排名)	Total assets ('000 RMB) 总资产 (千元)	Major products 主要产品
Shenzhen Hailiang Storage Equipment Co., Ltd. 深圳海量存储设备有限公司(1995)	Shenzhen 深圳市	Guangdong 广东省	(0755)26633866 (0755)26630846	3,166	Foreign Funded 外商投资	4,200,009	131,976(5)	779,586	Magnetism Resistance & Magnetic Head 磁阻磁头
Shinwa Industries(China) Co., Ltd. 信华精机有限公司(1986)	Huizhou 惠州市	Guangdong 广东省	(0752)2602373 (0752)2602401	3,511	Overseas Chinese-funded 港澳台资	3,873,708	165,916(3)	842,995	Household Auto Audio Special-purpose Inner Works汽车音响机芯
Flextronics Technology (Zhuhai) Co., Ltd. 伟创力科技（珠海）有限公司(1996)	Zhuhai 珠海市	Guangdong 广东省	(0756)5553068 (0756)5535564	2,119	Foreign Funded 外商投资	3,779,856	60,325(24)	2,145,511	PCBACircuit Plate PCBA线路板
Flextronics MFG(Shang Hai) Co., Ltd. 伟创力电子制造(上海)有限公司(1997)	Shanghai 上海市	Shanghai 上海市	(021)50644678 (021)50480408	2,500	Foreign Funded 外商投资	3,080,771	110,072(8)	1,356,959	Handset Electronics Circuit Board手机电子电路板
Irico Display Devices Co., Ltd. 彩虹显示器件股份有限公司(1992)	Xi'an 西安市	Shannxi 陕西省	(029)8214034 (029)8214864	4,045	Joint Stock 股份制	2,827,432	190,082(1)	2,363,318	Colour Kinescope彩色显像管
Tianjin Samsung Electric Motro Co., Ltd. 天津三星电机有限公司(1994)	Tianjin 天津市	Tianjin 天津市	(022)28301307 (022)28316600	5,738	Foreign Funded 外商投资	2,693,434	155,017(4)	1,529,673	Video Recorder Memory Drum录相机磁鼓
TDK Xiamen Co., Ltd. 厦门TDK有限公司(1994)	Xiamen 厦门市	Fujian 福建省	(0592)6150333 (0592)6150323	8,374	Foreign Funded 外商投资	1,601,085	86,329(12)	1,313,101	Capacitor 电容器
Samsung Tech-Electric Motor (Tianjin) Co., Ltd. 三星高新电机（天津）有限公司(2001)	Tianjin 天津市	Tianjin 天津市	(022)23979000 (022)23962532	3,013	Foreign Funded 外商投资	1,307,510	-	812,726	New Type Electric Component新型电子元件
Fenghua Advanced Technology Group Co., Ltd. 广东风华高新科技集团有限公司(1984)	Zhaoqing 肇庆市	Guangdong 广东省	(0758)2847084 (0758)2865223	6,067	State Enterprises 国有独资	1,244,488	3,402(414)	5,836,153	Electric Component 电子元件
Tianjin Mitsumi Electric Motor Co., Ltd. 天津三美电机有限公司(1992)	Tianjin 天津市	Tianjin 天津市	(022)24371221 (022)24375407	2,875	Foreign Funded 外商投资	1,226,622	57,036(27)	1,030,698	Electronic Tuner电子调谐器

Top 10 Cities by Revenue 销售收入排名前10位城市	Province 省	Market share 市场份额 (%)	Number of firms 企业个数
Shenzhen 深圳市	Guangdong 广东省	9.77	137
Shanghai 上海市	Shanghai 上海市	9.56	136
Huizhou 惠州市	Guangdong 广东省	7.74	57
Tianjin 天津市	Tianjin 天津市	7.57	122
Zhuhai 珠海市	Guangdong 广东省	5.91	74
Dongguan 东莞市	Guangdong 广东省	5.08	87
Suzhou 苏州市	Jiangsu 江苏省	4.91	105
Guangzhou 广州市	Guangdong 广东省	4.61	94
Xiamen 厦门市	Fujian 福建省	3.81	41
Wuxi 无锡市	Jiangsu 江苏省	2.56	57

10 Major Wholesalers 十家主要批发商	City 城市	Province 省	Telephone/Fax 电话/传真
SU MEC 中设江苏机械设备进出口（集团）公司	Nanjing 南京市	Jiangsu 江苏省	(025)4511888 (025)4411772
China Poster Mobile Communications Equipment Co.,Ltd. 中邮普泰移动通信设备股份有限公司	Beijing 北京市	Beijing 北京市	(010)66426993 (010)66426837
Sino Kama Co., Ltd. 中泰凯马股份有限公司	Shanghai 上海市	Shanghai 上海市	(021)62031188 (021)62030851
China Huayuan Group Co.,Ltd. 中国华源集团有限公司	Shanghai 上海市	Shanghai 上海市	(021)62031188 (021)62032288
Zhejiang Crand Imp.& Exp.Co.,Ltd. 浙江远大进出口有限公司	Ningbo 宁波市	Zhejiang 浙江省	(0574)87720170 (0574)87723350
Shandong Machinery Import & Export Group Corporation 山东省机械进出口集团公司	Qingdao 青岛市	Shandong 山东省	(0532)2661628 (0532)2991655
Qingdao Haier International Trade Co.,Ltd. 青岛海尔国际贸易有限公司	Qingdao 青岛市	Shandong 山东省	(0532)8938337 (0532)8939494
Guangdong Machinery Import & Export Group Corporation 广东省机械进出口集团公司	Guangzhou 广州市	Guangdong 广东省	(020)87782168 (020)87771803
China National Machinery Equipment Import & Export Corporation 中国机械设备进出口总公司	Beijing 北京市	Beijing 北京市	(010)63474506 (010)63261865
Beijing Cellstar Co.,Ltd. 北京蜂星事达电讯有限公司	Beijing 北京市	Beijing 北京市	(010)64602050 (010)64672648

4171: Television Sets 电视机制造业

The industry accounts for 1.346% of the total revenue of China's industrial sector in 2002. The rate of return on assets is 3.48%. 67.04% of all firms in the industry made a profit while 32.96% had negative returns.The top province in terms of the industry's revenue is Guangdong, accounting for 28.95% of the total revenue.
2002年本行业收入占全行业的 1.346%，资产利润率为 3.48%。67.04%的企业赢利，32.96%的企业亏损。收入最高的省为广东省，占本行业的28.95%。

	Total number of firms 企业总数	Total number of employees 职工总数	Total revenue (Mil.RMB) 总销售收入（百万元）	Total profit (Mil.RMB) 总利润（百万元）	Return on assets 资产利润率（%）	Return on equity 权益利润率（%）	Labour productivity ('000 RMB/ worker) 劳动生产率（千元/人）	Debts/ assets 资产负债率（%）	Total assets (Mil.RMB) 总资产（百万元）
Industry Overall 行业总体	267	211,581	144,363	3,823	3.48	9.03	158.27	61.47	109,812

	Number of firms 企业个数	Average number of employees 平均职工人数	Average revenue ('000 RMB) 平均销售收入（千元）	Average profit ('000 RMB) 平均利润（千元）	Return on assets 资产利润率（%）	Return on equity 权益利润率（%）	Labour productivity ('000 RMB/ worker) 劳动生产率（千元/人）	Debts/ assets 资产负债率（%）	Average total assets ('000 RMB) 平均总资产（千元）
By ownership 产业所有权									
State-owned 国有	20	393	270,292	9,168	3.24	10.22	85.89	68.33	283,245
Collective-owned 集体	13	287	73,884	670	1.03	3.81	49.03	73.06	65,252
Foreign & Overseas Chinese Funded 三资	107	876	660,730	21,114	5.52	21.11	191.99	73.88	382,806
By regional distribution 地区分布									
Central-North 华北	25	380	318,942	20,943	11.75	25.51	280.54	53.94	178,249
Beijing 北京	5	454	278,806	7,855	4.23	5.05	81.45	16.22	185,526
Tianjin 天津	16	354	307,361	23,326	11.93	38.17	383.36	68.75	195,553
Hebei 河北									
Shanxi 山西	3	147	49,761	38	0.07	0.16	15.60	52.36	50,894
Inner Mongolia 内蒙古	1	1,138	1,512,468	110,966	44.91	49.31	268.74	8.91	247,062
Northeast 东北	11	1,590	1,120,874	47,455	5.29	11.12	153.63	52.41	896,574
Liaoning 辽宁	6	2,473	1,977,658	88,313	5.70	11.59	176.88	50.81	1,549,408
Jilin 吉林	4	403	52,572	-1,780	-2.07	-38.16	58.97	94.59	86,197
Heilongjiang 黑龙江	1	1,037	253,384	-760	-0.34	-0.75	-31.86	53.96	221,078
Central-East 华东	107	648	625,104	19,496	4.71	12.96	181.57	63.64	413,668
Shanghai 上海	18	1,023	691,938	37,094	5.14	10.06	112.26	48.88	721,388
Jiangsu 江苏	37	506	579,615	9,486	2.77	9.75	204.54	71.64	342,933
Zhejiang 浙江	26	279	77,167	2,394	1.87	4.67	44.38	59.91	127,773
Anhui 安徽	6	444	282,808	5,151	3.51	10.42	217.24	66.30	146,649
Fujian 福建	7	1,359	1,657,204	96,381	9.18	56.48	331.69	83.75	1,049,880
Jiangxi 江西	3	548	19,018	-198	-0.35		22.94	328.23	56,856
Shandong 山东	10	1,114	1,762,482	30,022	4.37	8.77	233.54	50.15	686,728
Central-South 中南	109	643	383,459	3,479	1.36	5.23	164.32	74.06	256,617
Henan 河南	2	58	2,161	-402	-2.03		8.57	188.04	19,755
Hubei 湖北	1	65	1,439	-665	-1.10	-1.57	51.63	29.91	60,413
Hunan 湖南	1	135		-3,506	-2.57		-39.04	182.94	136,363
Guangdong 广东	105	665	398,012	3,659	1.39	5.22	165.07	73.46	264,143
Guangxi 广西									
Hainan 海南									
Southwest 西南	9	4,348	1,633,414	22,629	0.96	1.80	86.27	46.85	2,361,459
Chongqing 重庆	1	382	21,689	2,340	2.44	4.70	36.87	48.01	95,728
Sichuan 四川	4	9,386	3,543,804	52,060	1.01	1.85	87.23	45.42	5,162,193
Guizhou 贵州	4	303	125,955	-1,728	-1.36		72.16	104.48	127,157
Yunnan 云南									
Tibet 西藏									
Northwest 西北	6	998	112,681	18,006	5.38	11.72	107.46	54.07	334,506
Shaanxi 陕西	5	1,014	135,119	22,847	6.00	11.81	126.85	49.22	380,859
Gansu 甘肃	1	918	492	-6,200	-6.03		0.41	144.03	102,743
Qinghai 青海									
Ningxia 宁夏									
Xinjiang 新疆									

4171: Television Sets 电视机制造业

Year 年份	Number of firms 企业个数	Rate of change 变化率 (%)	Number of employees 职工人数 (人)	Rate of change 变化率 (%)	Total revenue (Mil. RMB) 总销售收入 (百万元)	Rate of change 变化率 (%)	Total profit (Mil RMB) 总利润 (百万元)	Rate of change 变化率 (%)
2000	179		179,865		101,655		2,859	
2001	232	29.61	175,004	-2.70	108,998	7.22	1,676	-41.38
2002	267	15.09	211,581	20.90	144,363	32.45	3,823	128.10

Major Products 主要产品	Output 产量	Unit 单位
Colour Television Set 彩色电视机	5,447	10,000 Sets 万部
Black & White Television Set 黑白电视机	651	10,000 Sets 万部

10 Main Firms with Maximal Revenue (year founded) 收入最大的十家主要企业（创办年份）	City 城市	Province 省	Telephone/fax 电话/传真	Number of employees 职工人数	Ownership 产业所有权	Revenue ('000 RMB) 销售收入 (千元)	Profit('000 RMB) (rank) 利润(千元) (排名)	Total assets ('000 RMB) 总资产 (千元)	Major products 主要产品
Hisense GroupCo., Ltd.	Qingdao	Shandong	(0532)3878888		State Enterprises				Television Set
海信集团有限公司(1979)	青岛市	山东省	(0532)3872882	7,828	国有独资	14,842,785	252,364(5)	5,700,263	电视机
Sichuan Changhong Electronics Group Co.,Ltd.	Mianyang	Sichuan	(0816)2411114		Joint Stock				Television Set
四川长虹电子集团公司(1958)	绵阳市	四川省	(0816)2418518	32,908	股份制	13,405,853	183,952(7)	18,898,498	电视机
Konka Group Co., Ltd.	Shenzhen	Guangdong	(0755)26608866		Joint Stock				Color Television
康佳集团股份有限公司(1980)	深圳市	广东省	(0755)26600082	2,349	股份制	8,248,983	55,632(19)	7,133,521	彩电
Dalian Daxian Group Co., Ltd.	Dalian	Liaoning	(0411)7407788		State Enterprises				Television Set
大连大显集团有限公司(1995)	大连市	辽宁省	(0411)7407522	10,162	国有独资	7,307,465	288,216(3)	5,926,697	电视机
Xianmen Overseas Chinese Electronic Co., Ltd.	Xiamen	Fujian	(0592)5687327		Overseas Chinese-funded				Colour Television Set彩
厦门华侨电子企业有限公司(1985)	厦门市	福建省	(0592)6021331	4,881	港澳台资	6,488,391	61,560(17)	3,841,767	色电视机
Changzhou Xinke Digital Technology Co., Ltd.	Changzhou	Jiangsu	(0519)6551751		Limited-Liability				DVD、VCD
常州市新科数字技术有限公司(1998)	常州市	江苏省	(0519)5125050	5,080	有限公司	5,470,350	84,400(14)	4,172,140	DVD、VCD
Suzhou Philips Electronics Co., Ltd.	Suzhou	Jiangsu	(0512)68251042		Foreign Funded				Colour Television Set彩
苏州飞利浦消费电子有限公司(1994)	苏州市	江苏省	(0512)68410237	2,130	外商投资	5,266,243	168,093(9)	2,010,308	色电视机
TCL King Electric Appliances (Huizhou) Co., Ltd.	Huizhou	Guangdong	(0752)2601888		Overseas Chinese-funded				Colour Television Set彩
ＴＣＬ王牌电器（惠州）有限公司(1994)	惠州市	广东省	(0752)2600999	4,399	港澳台资	4,225,086	180,178(8)	3,928,869	色电视机
Shenzhen Sanyo Huaqiang Laser & Electron Co., Ltd.	Shenzhen	Guangdong	(0755)83316198		Foreign Funded				Laser Head 激
深圳三洋华强激光电子有限公司(1993)	深圳市	广东省	(0755)83319131	7,000	外商投资	4,094,720	33,578(26)	337,018	光拾音头
China Hualu Group Co., Ltd.	Dalian	Liaoning	(0411)4790599		State Enterprises				DVD
中国华录集团有限公司(2000)	大连市	辽宁省	(0411)4791956	2,663	国有独资	3,811,452	241,692(6)	2,990,221	DVD

Top 10 Cities by Revenue 销售收入排名前10位城市	Province 省	Market share 市场份额 (%)	Number of firms 企业个数
Shenzhen 深圳市	Guangdong 广东省	15.99	29
Qingdao 青岛市	Shandong 山东省	10.44	3
Mianyang 绵阳市	Sichuan 四川省	9.29	1
Shanghai 上海市	Shanghai 上海市	8.63	18
Dalian 大连市	Liaoning 辽宁省	7.71	3
Xiamen 厦门市	Fujian 福建省	7.62	3
Suzhou 苏州市	Jiangsu 江苏省	5.83	8
Huizhou 惠州市	Guangdong 广东省	4.66	8
Changzhou 常州市	Jiangsu 江苏省	4.51	7
Dongguan 东莞市	Guangdong 广东省	3.85	11

10 Major Wholesalers 十家主要批发商	City 城市	Province 省	Telephone/Fax 电话/传真
SU MEC	Nanjing	Jiangsu	(025)4511888
中设江苏机械设备进出口（集团）公司	南京市	江苏省	(025)4411772
China Poster Mobile Communications Equipment Co.,Ltd.	Beijing	Beijing	(010)66426993
中邮普泰移动通信设备股份有限公司	北京市	北京市	(010)66426837
Sino Kama Co., Ltd.	Shanghai	Shanghai	(021)62031188
中泰凯马股份有限公司	上海市	上海市	(021)62030851
China Huayuan Group Co.,Ltd.	Shanghai	Shanghai	(021)62031188
中国华源集团有限公司	上海市	上海市	(021)62032288
Zhejiang Crand Imp.& Exp.Co.,Ltd.	Ningbo	Zhejiang	(0574)87720170
浙江远大进出口有限公司	宁波市	浙江省	(0574)87723350
Shandong Machinery Import & Export Group Corporation	Qingdao	Shandong	(0532)2661628
山东省机械进出口集团公司	青岛市	山东省	(0532)2991655
Qingdao Haier International Trade Co.,Ltd.	Qingdao	Shandong	(0532)8938337
青岛海尔国际贸易有限公司	青岛市	山东省	(0532)8939494
Guangdong Machinery Import & Export Group Corporation	Guangzhou	Guangdong	(020)87782168
广东省机械进出口集团公司	广州市	广东省	(020)87771803
China National Machinery Equipment Import & Export Corporation	Beijing	Beijing	(010)63474506
中国机械设备进出口总公司	北京市	北京市	(010)63261865
Beijing Cellstar Co.,Ltd.	Beijing	Beijing	(010)64602050
北京蜂星事达电讯有限公司	北京市	北京市	(010)64672648

4172: Radio Receivers and Sound Recorders Equipment

收音机、录音机制造业

The industry accounts for 0.357% of the total revenue of China's industrial sector in 2002. The rate of return on assets is 5.59%. 72.56% of all firms in the industry made a profit while 27.44% had negative returns.The top province in terms of the industry's revenue is Guangdong, accounting for 76.68% of the total revenue.
2002年本行业收入占全行业的 0.357%，资产利润率为 5.59%。72.56%的企业赢利，27.44%的企业亏损。收入最高的省为广东省，占本行业的76.68%。

	Total number of firms 企业总数	Total number of employees 职工总数	Total revenue (Mil.RMB) 总销售收入 (百万元)	Total profit (Mil.RMB) 总利润 (百万元)	Return on assets 资产利润率 (%)	Return on equity 权益利润率 (%)	Labour productivity ('000 RMB/ worker) 劳动生产率 (千元/人)	Debts/ assets 资产负债率 (%)	Total assets (Mil.RMB) 总资产 (百万元)
Industry Overall 行业总体	277	136,401	38,337	1,209	5.59	13.07	55.47	57.24	21,629

	Number of firms 企业个数	Average number of employees 平均职工人数	Average revenue ('000 RMB) 平均销售收入 (千元)	Average profit ('000 RMB) 平均利润 (千元)	Return on assets 资产利润率 (%)	Return on equity 权益利润率 (%)	Labour productivity ('000 RMB/ worker) 劳动生产率 (千元/人)	Debts/ assets 资产负债率 (%)	Average total assets ('000 RMB) 平均总资产 (千元)
By ownership 产业所有权									
State-owned 国有	14	207	20,010	-607	-1.03	-3.70	16.71	72.15	58,928
Collective-owned 集体	9	802	29,317	241	1.27	2.01	14.29	36.60	18,930
Foreign & Overseas Chinese Funded 三资	169	605	207,811	6,509	6.33	14.44	65.94	56.13	102,755
By regional distribution 地区分布									
Central-North 华北	8	323	170,155	5,550	7.23	31.28	34.26	76.88	76,741
Beijing 北京	1	495	900,494	54,360	25.89	47.89	111.71	45.93	209,932
Tianjin 天津	7	298	65,821	-1,423	-2.46	-34.99	15.88	92.96	57,714
Hebei 河北									
Shanxi 山西									
Inner Mongolia 内蒙古									
Northeast 东北	3	149	12,319	520	1.60	7.82	27.91	79.55	32,498
Liaoning 辽宁	1	146	1,945	-1,514	-3.38		1.75	101.04	44,805
Jilin 吉林	2	150	17,506	1,537	5.83	15.06	40.64	61.28	26,344
Heilongjiang 黑龙江									
Central-East 华东	89	320	83,842	4,018	5.65	11.41	46.65	50.48	71,121
Shanghai 上海	21	414	151,805	4,836	4.53	6.89	46.72	34.17	106,701
Jiangsu 江苏	22	340	64,713	3,030	4.10	11.79	46.45	65.22	73,928
Zhejiang 浙江	28	166	22,455	1,729	9.39	22.77	33.49	58.74	18,402
Anhui 安徽									
Fujian 福建	13	506	164,149	10,855	7.65	16.32	56.59	53.15	141,980
Jiangxi 江西	3	230	16,059	-61	-0.37	-26.57	52.55	98.60	16,345
Shandong 山东	2	187	19,738	32	0.12	0.40	26.35	70.12	26,300
Central-South 中南	175	593	168,149	4,770	5.82	14.29	59.18	59.30	81,997
Henan 河南									
Hubei 湖北	2	51	12,008	221	0.16	0.38	128.13	58.77	141,782
Hunan 湖南	1	40		320	1.73			137.53	18,534
Guangdong 广东	170	606	172,923	4,927	5.98	14.59	59.40	58.98	82,322
Guangxi 广西	2	244	2,551	-1,773	-6.73		3.16	120.05	26,327
Hainan 海南									
Southwest 西南	2	596	25,675	-14,796	-12.44	-26.10	0.14	52.35	118,965
Chongqing 重庆	1	85	11,938	-505	-4.05	-15.50	10.12	73.88	12,478
Sichuan 四川	1	1,107	39,411	-29,086	-12.90	-26.41	-0.62	51.16	225,452
Guizhou 贵州									
Yunnan 云南									
Tibet 西藏									
Northwest 西北									
Shaanxi 陕西									
Gansu 甘肃									
Qinghai 青海									
Ningxia 宁夏									
Xinjiang 新疆									

4172: Radio Receivers and Sound Recorders Equipment

收音机、录音机制造业

Year 年份	Number of firms 企业个数	Rate of change 变化率(%)	Number of employees 职工人数(人)	Rate of change 变化率(%)	Total revenue (Mil. RMB) 总销售收入(百万元)	Rate of change 变化率(%)	Total profit (Mil RMB) 总利润(百万元)	Rate of change 变化率(%)
2000	274		154,565		45,125		1,223	
2001	258	-5.84	129,095	-16.48	35,376	-21.60	245	-79.97
2002	277	7.36	136,401	5.66	38,337	8.37	1,209	393.47

Major Products 主要产品	Output 产量	Unit 单位
Recorder 录放音机	5,915	10,000 Sets 万部
Combination Audio 组合音响	4,716	10,000 Sets 万部

10 Main Firms with Maximal Revenue (year founded) 收入最大的十家主要企业（创办年份）	City 城市	Province 省	Telephone/fax 电话/传真	Number of employees 职工人数	Ownership 产业所有权	Revenue ('000 RMB) 销售收入(千元)	Profit('000 RMB) (rank) 利润(千元)(排名)	Total assets ('000 RMB) 总资产(千元)	Major products 主要产品
LG Electronics（Huizhou）Inc. 乐金电子(惠州)有限公司(1993)	Huizhou 惠州市	Guangdong 广东省	(0752)2600944 (0752)2600945	1,768	Foreign Funded 外商投资	7,819,977	65,171(5)	1,747,187	Radio 收音机
Huizhou Samsung Electronics Co.,Ltd. 惠州三星电子有限公司(1992)	Huizhou 惠州市	Guangdong 广东省	(0752)3897777 (0752)3897000	1,738	Foreign Funded 外商投资	3,337,036	320,699(1)	1,044,821	Desk Sounder 台式音响
Sanyo Electric(Shekou)Co., Ltd. 三洋电机（蛇口）有限公司(1983)	Shenzhen 深圳市	Guangdong 广东省	(0755)26691616 (0755)26691621	4,034	Overseas Chinese-funded 港澳台资	2,203,753	79,014(3)	786,730	Radio 收音机
Huiyang Dongwei Electronics Co., Ltd. 惠阳东威电子制品有限公司(1997)	Huizhou 惠州市	Guangdong 广东省	(0752)3338408 (0752)3338519	1,900	Overseas Chinese-funded 港澳台资	1,646,474	14,062(19)	597,073	Sounder 音箱
Shanghai Pioneer Electroacoustic Equipment Co.,Ltd. 上海先锋电声器材有限公司(1993)	Shanghai 上海市	Shanghai 上海市	(021)69133300 (021)69133049	3,541	Foreign Funded 外商投资	1,107,703	49,245(8)	786,437	Sounder Equipment 扬声器
Zhuhai Tenko Electronics Co.,Ltd. 珠海天虎电子有限公司(1993)	Zhuhai 珠海市	Guangdong 广东省	(0756)8682768 (0756)8682479	1,289	Overseas Chinese-funded 港澳台资	952,941	-	96,398	Electronic Recorder 电子收放机
Dadong-Zegna (Dongguan) Electronics Co.,Ltd. 大东骏通(东莞)电子有限公司(1994)	Dongguan 东莞市	Guangdong 广东省	(0769)3391483 (0769)3393927	4,908	Overseas Chinese-funded 港澳台资	767,982	4,566(37)	344,164	Combination Audio 组合音响
Xiamen Panasonic Audio Co., Ltd. 厦门松下音响有限公司(1993)	Xiamen 厦门市	Fujian 福建省	(0592)6037819 (0592)6030587	1,453	Foreign Funded 外商投资	760,636	77,766(4)	462,649	Radio 收音机
Nanjing Malata Audio-visual Co.,Ltd. 南靖县万利达视听有限公司(1995)	Zhangzhou 漳州市	Fujian 福建省	(0596)7663858 (0596)7663733	2,137	Overseas Chinese-funded 港澳台资	738,999	52,509(7)	972,696	Laser Video Disc Player 激光视盘机
Siemens VDO Automotive (Huizhou) Co., Ltd. 西门子威迪欧汽车电子（惠州）有限公司(1986)	Huizhou 惠州市	Guangdong 广东省	(0752)2289088 (0752)2270289	662	Foreign Funded 外商投资	719,885	115,746(2)	422,278	Philip Automobile Radio 飞利浦汽车收放机

Top 10 Cities by Revenue 销售收入排名前10位城市	Province 省	Market share 市场份额 (%)	Number of firms 企业个数
Huizhou 惠州市	Guangdong 广东省	43.07	29
Shenzhen 深圳市	Guangdong 广东省	13.37	31
Dongguan 东莞市	Guangdong 广东省	11.41	48
Shanghai 上海市	Shanghai 上海市	8.32	21
Zhuhai 珠海市	Guangdong 广东省	3.41	6
Xiamen 厦门市	Fujian 福建省	3.20	7
Guangzhou 广州市	Guangdong 广东省	2.63	23
Beijing 北京市	Beijing 北京市	2.35	1
Zhangzhou 漳州市	Fujian 福建省	1.94	2
Zhongshan 中山市	Guangdong 广东省	1.83	16

10 Major Wholesalers 十家主要批发商	City 城市	Province 省	Telephone/Fax 电话/传真
SU MEC 中设江苏机械设备进出口（集团）公司	Nanjing 南京市	Jiangsu 江苏省	(025)4511888 (025)4411772
China Poster Mobile Communications Equipment Co.,Ltd. 中邮普泰移动通信设备股份有限公司	Beijing 北京市	Beijing 北京市	(010)66426993 (010)66426837
Sino Kama Co., Ltd. 中泰凯马股份有限公司	Shanghai 上海市	Shanghai 上海市	(021)62031188 (021)62030851
China Huayuan Group Co.,Ltd. 中国华源集团有限公司	Shanghai 上海市	Shanghai 上海市	(021)62031188 (021)62032288
Zhejiang Crand Imp.& Exp.Co.,Ltd. 浙江远大进出口有限公司	Ningbo 宁波市	Zhejiang 浙江省	(0574)87720170 (0574)87723350
Shandong Machinery Import & Export Group Corporation 山东省机械进出口集团公司	Qingdao 青岛市	Shandong 山东省	(0532)2661628 (0532)2991655
Qingdao Haier International Trade Co.,Ltd. 青岛海尔国际贸易有限公司	Qingdao 青岛市	Shandong 山东省	(0532)8938337 (0532)8939494
Guangdong Machinery Import & Export Group Corporation 广东省机械进出口集团公司	Guangzhou 广州市	Guangdong 广东省	(020)87782168 (020)87771803
China National Machinery Equipment Import & Export Corporation 中国机械设备进出口总公司	Beijing 北京市	Beijing 北京市	(010)63474506 (010)63261865
Beijing Cellstar Co.,Ltd. 北京蜂星事达电讯有限公司	Beijing 北京市	Beijing 北京市	(010)64602050 (010)64672648

4173: Electronic Calculators 电子计算器制造业

The industry accounts for 0.144% of the total revenue of China's industrial sector in 2002. The rate of return on assets is 6.26%. 80.95% of all firms in the industry made a profit while 19.05% had negative returns.The top province in terms of the industry's revenue is Guangdong, accounting for 63.73% of the total revenue.
2002年本行业收入占全行业的0.144%，资产利润率为6.26%。80.95%的企业赢利，19.05%的企业亏损。收入最高的省为广东省，占本行业的63.73%。

	Total number of firms 企业总数	Total number of employees 职工总数	Total revenue (Mil.RMB) 总销售收入(百万元)	Total profit (Mil.RMB) 总利润(百万元)	Return on assets 资产利润率(%)	Return on equity 权益利润率(%)	Labour productivity ('000 RMB/worker) 劳动生产率(千元/人)	Debts/assets 资产负债率(%)	Total assets (Mil.RMB) 总资产(百万元)
Industry Overall 行业总体	63	49,143	15,405	598	6.26	12.54	78.31	50.11	9,563

	Number of firms 企业个数	Average number of employees 平均职工人数	Average revenue ('000 RMB) 平均销售收入(千元)	Average profit ('000 RMB) 平均利润(千元)	Return on assets 资产利润率(%)	Return on equity 权益利润率(%)	Labour productivity ('000 RMB/worker) 劳动生产率(千元/人)	Debts/assets 资产负债率(%)	Average total assets ('000 RMB) 平均总资产(千元)
By ownership 产业所有权									
State-owned 国有	1	251	88	-1		-0.02	0.22	86.68	43,578
Collective-owned 集体	4	2,759	68,593	7,605	6.57	7.68	9.70	14.38	115,659
Foreign & Overseas Chinese Funded 三资	42	821	243,786	11,643	7.33	14.59	88.29	49.74	158,744
By regional distribution 地区分布									
Central-North 华北	3	349	492,620	76,987	12.74	23.18	341.80	45.02	604,132
Beijing 北京	3	349	492,620	76,987	12.74	23.18	341.80	45.02	604,132
Tianjin 天津									
Hebei 河北									
Shanxi 山西									
Inner Mongolia 内蒙古									
Northeast 东北	1	140	14,608	191	1.20	1.94	22.00	38.32	15,928
Liaoning 辽宁	1	140	14,608	191	1.20	1.94	22.00	38.32	15,928
Jilin 吉林									
Heilongjiang 黑龙江									
Central-East 华东	23	629	172,988	4,440	4.05	8.85	116.06	54.26	109,656
Shanghai 上海	3	217	60,417	-6,067	-5.69	-15.40	82.02	63.06	106,617
Jiangsu 江苏	8	553	288,613	9,977	6.28	15.01	163.47	58.14	158,793
Zhejiang 浙江	5	122	69,860	3,046	5.33	12.89	190.41	58.67	57,169
Anhui 安徽									
Fujian 福建	7	1,256	162,754	3,609	3.91	6.55	89.59	40.32	92,293
Jiangxi 江西									
Shandong 山东									
Central-South 中南	35	956	281,281	7,187	4.86	9.70	52.29	49.94	148,014
Henan 河南	1	307	26,652	1,632	6.28	15.14	14.39	58.55	26,006
Hubei 湖北									
Hunan 湖南									
Guangdong 广东	34	975	288,770	7,351	4.85	9.68	52.64	49.89	151,602
Guangxi 广西									
Hainan 海南									
Southwest 西南	1	20	88,666	13,563	42.47	76.56	2,886.70	44.53	31,939
Chongqing 重庆									
Sichuan 四川	1	20	88,666	13,563	42.47	76.56	2,886.70	44.53	31,939
Guizhou 贵州									
Yunnan 云南									
Tibet 西藏									
Northwest 西北									
Shaanxi 陕西									
Gansu 甘肃									
Qinghai 青海									
Ningxia 宁夏									
Xinjiang 新疆									

4173: Electronic Calculators 电子计算器制造业

Year 年份	Number of firms 企业个数	Rate of change 变化率 (%)	Number of employees 职工人数 (人)	Rate of change 变化率 (%)	Total revenue (Mil. RMB) 总销售收入 (百万元)	Rate of change 变化率 (%)	Total profit (Mil RMB) 总利润 (百万元)	Rate of change 变化率 (%)
2000	51		31,600		6,837		118	
2001	59	15.69	30,155	-4.57	9,504	39.01	187	58.47
2002	63	6.78	49,143	62.97	15,405	62.09	598	219.79

Major Products 主要产品	Output 产量	Unit 单位
Electronic Calculator 电子计算器	13,297	10,000 Units 万台

10 Main Firms with Maximal Revenue (year founded) 收入最大的十家主要企业（创办年份）	City 城市	Province 省	Telephone/fax 电话/传真	Number of employees 职工人数	Ownership 产业所有权	Revenue ('000 RMB) 销售收入 (千元)	Profit('000 RMB) (rank) 利润(千元) (排名)	Total assets ('000 RMB) 总资产 (千元)	Major products 主要产品
Dongguan Founder Technology Computer Co., Ltd. 东莞市方正科技电脑有限公司(1998)	Dongguan 东莞市	Guangdong 广东省	(0769)6116111 (0769)6116222	700	Limited-Liability 有限公司	3,598,541	8,436(15)	661,998	Computer Fittings 计算机配件
Ambit Microsystems Corporation 国基电子中山有限公司(1998)	Zhongshan 中山市	Guangdong 广东省	(0760)3381357 (0760)3382117	1,419	Overseas Chinese-funded 港澳台资	1,947,511	18,648(9)	996,056	Network Card MODEM 上网卡MODEM
Arima Computer (Jiangsu)Co., Ltd. 华宇电脑(江苏)有限公司(1999)	Suzhou 苏州市	Jiangsu 江苏省	(0512)63409898 (0512)63409700	1,079	Foreign Funded 外商投资	1,685,104	35,034(4)	609,810	Computer 电脑
Namtei Electronic(Shen Zhen)Co., Ltd. 南太电子（深圳）有限公司(1989)	Shenzhen 深圳市	Guangdong 广东省	(0755)7495818 (0755)7494014	1,751	Overseas Chinese-funded 港澳台资	1,459,240	80,689(2)	1,048,208	Liquid Crystal Display Module 液晶显示模块
NCR(BeiJing)Financial Equipment System Co., Ltd. 安迅（北京）金融设备系统有限公司(1997)	Beijing 北京市	Beijing 北京市	(010)67885500 (010)67884636	195	Overseas Chinese-funded 港澳台资	1,086,085	219,417(1)	734,747	Automatic Teller Machine ATM自动柜员机
Hypercom Electronics Manufacturing(Shenzhen) Co., Ltd. 海博通电子制造（深圳）有限公司(1998)	Shenzhen 深圳市	Guangdong 广东省	(0755)25179534 (0755)25736356	240	Overseas Chinese-funded 港澳台资	445,387	42,085(3)	165,911	Punching card machine 刷卡机
Jiangsu Yinhe Electronics Co., Ltd. 江苏银河电子股份有限公司(1975)	Suzhou 苏州市	Jiangsu 江苏省	(0512)58443440 (0512)58441550	600	Joint Stock 股份制	394,940	23,680(8)	310,630	Computer Machine Case 电脑机箱
Dongguan Chang'an Quanzhi Electronics Works 东莞长安权智电子厂(1993)	Dongguan 东莞市	Guangdong 广东省	(0769)5548000 (0769)5546993	2,902	Foreign Funded 外商投资	369,232	33,198(5)	287,262	Transducer 翻译机
ACER INFORMATION SERVICES(Zhongshan)CO., LTD. 中山宏基讯息有限公司(1999)	Zhongshan 中山市	Guangdong 广东省	(0760)3382940 (0760)3382944	57	Overseas Chinese-funded 港澳台资	324,766	24,018(7)	111,187	Large, Medium and Miniature Computer大中及微型计算机
Fujian Sunway Electronics Industrial Co., Ltd. 福建省新威电子工业有限公司(1989)	Putian 莆田市	Fujian 福建省	(0594)3793988 (0594)3791613	3,600	Overseas Chinese-funded 港澳台资	287,834	8,640(14)	443,689	Electronic Watch 电子表

Top 10 Cities by Revenue 销售收入排名前10位城市	Province 省	Market share 市场份额 (%)	Number of firms 企业个数
Dongguan 东莞市	Guangdong 广东省	27.59	6
Zhongshan 中山市	Guangdong 广东省	16.42	7
Shenzhen 深圳市	Guangdong 广东省	16.25	11
Suzhou 苏州市	Jiangsu 江苏省	14.91	7
Beijing 北京市	Beijing 北京市	9.59	3
Putian 莆田市	Fujian 福建省	7.11	6
Guangzhou 广州市	Guangdong 广东省	2.22	7
Hangzhou 杭州市	Zhejiang 浙江省	2.13	3
Shanghai 上海市	Shanghai 上海市	1.18	3
Shanwei 汕尾市	Guangdong 广东省	0.75	1

10 Major Wholesalers 十家主要批发商	City 城市	Province 省	Telephone/Fax 电话/传真
SU MEC 中设江苏机械设备进出口（集团）公司	Nanjing 南京市	Jiangsu 江苏省	(025)4511888 (025)4411772
China Poster Mobile Communications Equipment Co.,Ltd. 中邮普泰移动通信设备股份有限公司	Beijing 北京市	Beijing 北京市	(010)66426993 (010)66426837
Sino Kama Co., Ltd. 中泰凯马股份有限公司	Shanghai 上海市	Shanghai 上海市	(021)62031188 (021)62030851
China Huayuan Group Co.,Ltd. 中国华源集团有限公司	Shanghai 上海市	Shanghai 上海市	(021)62031188 (021)62032288
Zhejiang Crand Imp.& Exp.Co.,Ltd. 浙江远大进出口有限公司	Ningbo 宁波市	Zhejiang 浙江省	(0574)87720170 (0574)87723350
Shandong Machinery Import & Export Group Corporation 山东省机械进出口集团公司	Qingdao 青岛市	Shandong 山东省	(0532)2661628 (0532)2991655
Qingdao Haier International Trade Co.,Ltd. 青岛海尔国际贸易有限公司	Qingdao 青岛市	Shandong 山东省	(0532)8938337 (0532)8939494
Guangdong Machinery Import & Export Group Corporation 广东省机械进出口集团公司	Guangzhou 广州市	Guangdong 广东省	(020)87782168 (020)87771803
China National Machinery Equipment Import & Export Corporation 中国机械设备进出口总公司	Beijing 北京市	Beijing 北京市	(010)63474506 (010)63261865
Beijing Cellstar Co.,Ltd. 北京蜂星事达电讯有限公司	Beijing 北京市	Beijing 北京市	(010)64602050 (010)64672648

4190: Other Electronic Equipment 其他电子设备制造业

The industry accounts for 0.229% of the total revenue of China's industrial sector in 2002. The rate of return on assets is 6.72%. 79.60% of all firms in the industry made a profit while 20.40% had negative returns.The top province in terms of the industry's revenue is Guangdong, accounting for 23.09% of the total revenue.
2002年本行业收入占全行业的 0.229%，资产利润率为 6.72%。79.60%的企业赢利，20.40%的企业亏损。收入最高的省为广东省，占本行业的23.09%。

	Total number of firms 企业总数	Total number of employees 职工总数	Total revenue (Mil.RMB) 总销售收入（百万元）	Total profit (Mil.RMB) 总利润（百万元）	Return on assets 资产利润率（%）	Return on equity 权益利润率（%）	Labour productivity ('000 RMB/ worker) 劳动生产率（千元/人）	Debts/ assets 资产负债率（%）	Total assets (Mil.RMB) 总资产（百万元）
Industry Overall 行业总体	505	110,432	24,546	2,366	6.72	14.01	72.66	52.02	35,210

	Number of firms 企业个数	Average number of employees 平均职工人数	Average revenue ('000 RMB) 平均销售收入（千元）	Average profit ('000 RMB) 平均利润（千元）	Return on assets 资产利润率（%）	Return on equity 权益利润率（%）	Labour productivity ('000 RMB/ worker) 劳动生产率（千元/人）	Debts/ assets 资产负债率（%）	Average total assets ('000 RMB) 平均总资产（千元）
By ownership 产业所有权									
State-owned 国有	45	173	19,363	-366	-0.67	-2.77	31.72	75.98	54,999
Collective-owned 集体	11	231	31,848	931	3.70	9.99	28.21	62.98	25,168
Foreign & Overseas Chinese Funded 三资	201	275	68,164	6,272	7.99	16.72	77.68	52.20	78,465
By regional distribution 地区分布									
Central-North 华北	102	129	49,288	7,146	8.03	14.52	154.73	44.70	88,987
Beijing 北京	76	130	58,287	8,812	9.70	17.09	179.10	43.23	90,811
Tianjin 天津	19	122	26,281	2,637	2.51	4.81	93.45	47.96	105,271
Hebei 河北	5	54	7,004	560	5.80	14.05	96.73	58.75	9,660
Shanxi 山西	1	268	5,614				7.65	81.07	56,141
Inner Mongolia 内蒙古	1	434	57,570	6,244	8.86	21.32	53.30	58.44	70,468
Northeast 东北	35	206	68,724	6,005	4.28	8.24	143.19	48.05	140,301
Liaoning 辽宁	24	178	66,401	4,715	3.66	6.93	150.08	47.16	128,722
Jilin 吉林	6	423	132,626	16,198	5.46	10.86	150.98	49.74	296,737
Heilongjiang 黑龙江	5	79	3,195	-38	-0.46	-0.80	18.59	42.42	8,158
Central-East 华东	194	207	49,885	1,936	3.08	7.25	62.65	57.54	62,834
Shanghai 上海	16	207	54,585	1,862	2.25	5.50	65.49	59.03	82,610
Jiangsu 江苏	62	187	47,733	2,221	4.31	11.63	67.16	62.93	51,530
Zhejiang 浙江	50	130	25,891	1,625	7.69	16.56	48.61	53.59	21,148
Anhui 安徽	8	139	25,977	3,096	3.82	6.43	85.89	40.69	81,147
Fujian 福建	32	213	45,886	3,875	8.52	15.96	41.34	46.64	45,493
Jiangxi 江西	1	139	5,010	-1,986	-7.43		11.02	116.94	26,745
Shandong 山东	25	426	114,766	-801	-0.45	-1.11	77.31	59.81	179,361
Central-South 中南	159	303	44,937	6,592	13.15	27.84	49.40	52.76	50,133
Henan 河南	10	104	25,234	6,003	10.11	18.54	57.20	45.44	59,358
Hubei 湖北	16	138	31,493	2,807	4.52	7.73	89.13	41.59	62,134
Hunan 湖南	7	143	93,087	19,229	21.15	50.14	231.97	57.82	90,915
Guangdong 广东	119	366	47,632	6,791	14.23	31.40	42.69	54.67	47,708
Guangxi 广西	6	58	8,462	107	1.13	7.08	81.30	84.04	9,496
Hainan 海南	1	20	18,056	-128	-1.00	-1.30	154.90	23.11	12,820
Southwest 西南	11	111	13,798	-380	-0.52	-1.67	66.39	68.97	73,266
Chongqing 重庆	4	123	5,016	-3,720	-6.49		7.36	106.45	57,335
Sichuan 四川	4	148	24,545	-215	-0.19	-0.35	98.39	45.43	111,923
Guizhou 贵州	1	71	675	-2,921	-11.72		-28.06	203.98	24,918
Yunnan 云南	2	32	16,430	7,241	13.93	31.17	332.68	55.32	51,991
Tibet 西藏									
Northwest 西北	4	134	34,740	1,888	2.95	5.80	-39.47	49.06	63,943
Shaanxi 陕西	4	134	34,740	1,888	2.95	5.80	-39.47	49.06	63,943
Gansu 甘肃									
Qinghai 青海									
Ningxia 宁夏									
Xinjiang 新疆									

Year 年份	Number of firms 企业个数	Rate of change 变化率 (%)	Number of employees 职工人数 (人)	Rate of change 变化率 (%)	Total revenue (Mil. RMB) 总销售收入 (百万元)	Rate of change 变化率 (%)	Total profit (Mil RMB) 总利润 (百万元)	Rate of change 变化率 (%)
2000	464		110,667		25,995		2,416	
2001	486	4.74	109,731	-0.85	24,927	-4.11	1,993	-17.51
2002	505	3.91	110,432	0.64	24,546	-1.53	2,366	18.72

Major Products 主要产品	Output 产量	Unit 单位

10 Main Firms with Maximal Revenue (year founded) 收入最大的十家主要企业（创办年份）	City 城市	Province 省	Telephone/fax 电话/传真	Number of employees 职工人数	Ownership 产业所有权	Revenue ('000 RMB) 销售收入 (千元)	Profit('000 RMB) (rank) 利润(千元) (排名)	Total assets ('000 RMB) 总资产 (千元)	Major products 主要产品
Shenyang Neusoft Group Co.,Ltd.	Shenyang	Liaoning	(024)23783000		Foreign Funded				Safety Products
沈阳东软软件股份有限公司(1991)	沈阳市	辽宁省	(024)23782700	853	外商投资	1,014,149	123,096(5)	1,808,235	安全产品
Kunshan Younger Optics Co.,Ltd.	Suzhou	Jiangsu	(0512)57353850		Foreign Funded				Apheliotropic Plate
昆山扬明光学有限公司(2001)	苏州市	江苏省	(0512)57353860	558	外商投资	875,477	-	448,335	背光板
BYD Co.,Ltd.	Shenzhen	Guangdong	(0755)84202555		Limited-Liability				Lithium Sarcenet Battery锂
深圳市比亚迪股份有限公司(1998)	深圳市	广东省	(0755)84202222	7,400	有限公司	862,104	368,869(1)	1,122,507	里子电池
TYCO Electronics AMP Qingdao Co.,Ltd.	Qingdao	Shandong	(0532)4938888		Foreign Funded				Connector
青岛安普泰科电子有限公司(1996)	青岛市	山东省	(0532)4938600	1,651	外商投资	766,769	48,103(11)	641,116	连接器
Jielishi Multilayer Circuit Plate (Zhongshan) Co., Ltd.	Zhongshan	Guangdong	(0760)2277760		Overseas Chinese-funded				Circuit Plate
皆利士多层线路板（中山）有限公司(1999)	中山市	广东省	(0760)2252045	3,568	港澳台资	746,866	294,837(2)	486,657	线路板
Xiamen Doowell Co.,Ltd.	Xiamen	Fujian	(0592)6517401		Foreign Funded				Amusement Instrument Thread
厦门多威电子有限公司(1992)	厦门市	福建省	(0592)6517402	1,704	外商投资	728,139	52,477(8)	494,002	游乐器线
XiMens VDO Automobile (changchun) Co., Ltd.	Changchun	Jilin	(0431)5176888		Foreign Funded				
西门子VDO汽车(长春)电子有限公司(1995)	长春市	吉林省	(0431)5176333	285	外商投资	396,242	84,225(6)	327,056	
Fuding Precision Components (Shenzhen) Co., Ltd.	Shenzhen	Guangdong	(0755)27904888		Overseas Chinese-funded				Computer Connector电脑
富顶精密组件（深圳）有限公司(1995)	深圳市	广东省	(0755)27901391	3,500	港澳台资	370,617	13,721(33)	189,783	用接插件
Microteck Computer Technology (Wujiang) Co.,Ltd.	Suzhou	Jiangsu	(0512)63401290		Overseas Chinese-funded				Display
全友电脑科技(吴江)有限公司(1999)	苏州市	江苏省	(0512)63401293	407	港澳台资	354,480	14,700(31)	290,311	显示器
Hunan Changhai Digital Science & Technology Development Group	Changsha	Hunan	(0731)4015886		Private Owned				Digital Language Laboratory 数字化语
Co.,Ltd.湖南长海数码科技发展股份有限公司(1993)	长沙市	湖南省	(0731)4015858	418	私营企业	336,126	49,823(9)	271,230	言实验室

Top 10 Cities by Revenue 销售收入排名前10位城市	Province 省	Market share 市场份额 (%)	Number of firms 企业个数
Beijing 北京市	Beijing 北京市	18.05	76
Shenzhen 深圳市	Guangdong 广东省	9.21	42
Suzhou 苏州市	Jiangsu 江苏省	8.69	23
Shenyang 沈阳市	Liaoning 辽宁省	5.62	12
Xiamen 厦门市	Fujian 福建省	3.77	6
Jinan 济南市	Shandong 山东省	3.73	7
Shanghai 上海市	Shanghai 上海市	3.56	16
Qingdao 青岛市	Shandong 山东省	3.49	6
Zhongshan 中山市	Guangdong 广东省	3.39	9
Guangzhou 广州市	Guangdong 广东省	3.38	19

10 Major Wholesalers 十家主要批发商	City 城市	Province 省	Telephone/Fax 电话/传真
SU MEC	Nanjing	Jiangsu	(025)4511888
中设江苏机械设备进出口（集团）公司	南京市	江苏省	(025)4411772
China Poster Mobile Communications Equipment Co.,Ltd.	Beijing	Beijing	(010)66426993
中邮普泰移动通信设备股份有限公司	北京市	北京市	(010)66426837
Sino Kama Co., Ltd.	Shanghai	Shanghai	(021)62031188
中泰凯马股份有限公司	上海市	上海市	(021)62030851
China Huayuan Group Co.,Ltd.	Shanghai	Shanghai	(021)62031188
中国华源集团有限公司	上海市	上海市	(021)62032288
Zhejiang Crand Imp.& Exp.Co.,Ltd.	Ningbo	Zhejiang	(0574)87720170
浙江远大进出口有限公司	宁波市	浙江省	(0574)87723350
Shandong Machinery Import & Export Group Corporation	Qingdao	Shandong	(0532)2661628
山东省机械进出口集团公司	青岛市	山东省	(0532)2991655
Qingdao Haier International Trade Co.,Ltd.	Qingdao	Shandong	(0532)8938337
青岛海尔国际贸易有限公司	青岛市	山东省	(0532)8939494
Guangdong Machinery Import & Export Group Corporation	Guangzhou	Guangdong	(020)87782168
广东省机械进出口集团公司	广州市	广东省	(020)87771803
China National Machinery Equipment Import & Export	Beijing	Beijing	(010)63474506
Corporation 中国机械设备进出口总公司	北京市	北京市	(010)63261865
Beijing Cellstar Co.,Ltd.	Beijing	Beijing	(010)64602050
北京蜂星事达电讯有限公司	北京市	北京市	(010)64672648

4211: Industrial Automation Equipment 工业自动化仪表制造业

The industry accounts for 0.116% of the total revenue of China's industrial sector in 2002. The rate of return on assets is 4.47%. 77.71% of all firms in the industry made a profit while 22.29% had negative returns.The top province in terms of the industry's revenue is Beijing, accounting for 24.33% of the total revenue.
2002年本行业收入占全行业的 0.116%，资产利润率为 4.47%。77.71%的企业赢利，22.29%的企业亏损。收入最高的省为北京市，占本行业的24.33%。

	Total number of firms 企业总数	Total number of employees 职工总数	Total revenue (Mil.RMB) 总销售收入 (百万元)	Total profit (Mil.RMB) 总利润 (百万元)	Return on assets 资产利润率 (%)	Return on equity 权益利润率 (%)	Labour productivity ('000 RMB/ worker) 劳动生产率 (千元/人)	Debts/ assets 资产负债率 (%)	Total assets (Mil.RMB) 总资产 (百万元)
Industry Overall 行业总体	314	62,583	12,390	795	4.47	11.03	59.85	59.44	17,764

	Number of firms 企业个数	Average number of employees 平均职工人数	Average revenue ('000 RMB) 平均销售收入（千元）	Average profit ('000 RMB) 平均利润 (千元)	Return on assets 资产利润率 (%)	Return on equity 权益利润率 (%)	Labour productivity ('000 RMB/ worker) 劳动生产率 (千元/人)	Debts/ assets 资产负债率 (%)	Average total assets ('000 RMB) 平均总资产 (千元)
By ownership 产业所有权									
State-owned 国有	67	148	9,165	-135	-0.41	-1.58	21.17	74.17	33,237
Collective-owned 集体	27	290	34,341	1,600	3.94	7.46	35.08	47.15	40,602
Foreign & Overseas Chinese Funded 三资	78	164	76,144	6,169	8.84	19.33	130.18	54.26	69,768
By regional distribution 地区分布									
Central-North 华北	84	173	50,574	3,884	7.13	14.07	73.24	49.30	54,465
Beijing 北京	39	147	77,293	6,960	9.20	16.39	127.56	43.88	75,683
Tianjin 天津	33	201	28,788	622	1.62	4.12	35.05	60.68	38,400
Hebei 河北	8	240	34,961	4,422	10.55	21.32	51.40	50.52	41,924
Shanxi 山西	4	60	1,020	-262	-5.01		4.95	104.97	5,219
Inner Mongolia 内蒙古									
Northeast 东北	34	145	16,116	443	1.21	3.68	45.39	67.06	36,528
Liaoning 辽宁	24	159	17,087	626	1.44	3.97	43.27	63.90	43,600
Jilin 吉林	2	252	26,386	445	1.17		38.73	104.71	38,009
Heilongjiang 黑龙江	8	76	10,637	-107	-0.71	-2.44	64.15	70.83	14,943
Central-East 华东	111	158	36,486	2,784	6.60	15.43	72.64	57.25	42,208
Shanghai 上海	33	186	65,059	4,544	6.89	15.95	106.68	56.82	65,968
Jiangsu 江苏	29	129	33,640	2,632	7.22	19.30	86.86	62.59	36,461
Zhejiang 浙江	25	138	21,442	1,679	5.24	10.67	41.58	50.90	32,039
Anhui 安徽	3	209	13,860	1,037	2.29	6.25	35.08	63.34	45,226
Fujian 福建	6	109	13,438	1,539	8.89	18.72	39.88	52.53	17,318
Jiangxi 江西									
Shandong 山东	15	196	17,946	1,896	6.93	16.26	35.33	57.37	27,350
Central-South 中南	58	149	21,427	2,214	7.04	18.43	57.37	61.81	31,453
Henan 河南	7	203	7,986	-259	-1.39	-13.10	14.52	89.38	18,626
Hubei 湖北	17	169	9,856	-6	-0.04	-0.16	17.58	76.77	15,045
Hunan 湖南	6	140	7,222	643	5.73	37.83	15.37	84.85	11,225
Guangdong 广东	25	132	37,398	4,672	8.86	20.24	113.95	56.22	52,740
Guangxi 广西	2	100	19,951	4,828	18.96	27.51	179.72	31.08	25,459
Hainan 海南	1	12	1,132	17	1.25	1.81	-9.58	31.28	1,365
Southwest 西南	18	554	93,143	1,160	0.77	2.67	51.64	71.06	150,126
Chongqing 重庆	11	661	136,613	3,972	2.14	7.97	65.95	73.15	185,696
Sichuan 四川	3	738	51,985	-5,702	-3.06	-10.28	12.63	70.22	186,225
Guizhou 贵州	3	93	4,272	-1,240	-8.34	-22.69	20.21	63.27	14,871
Yunnan 云南	1	199	5,059	-1,983	-3.52	-3.90	6.30	9.82	56,325
Tibet 西藏									
Northwest 西北	9	773	69,418	-549	-0.18	-0.50	24.70	63.62	303,968
Shaanxi 陕西	8	521	22,276	-4,300	-3.73	-15.08	3.40	75.23	115,132
Gansu 甘肃									
Qinghai 青海									
Ningxia 宁夏	1	2,788	446,552	29,453	1.62	3.84	56.53	57.73	1,814,659
Xinjiang 新疆									

4211: Industrial Automation Equipment 工业自动化仪表制造业

Year 年份	Number of firms 企业个数	Rate of change 变化率(%)	Number of employees 职工人数(人)	Rate of change 变化率(%)	Total revenue (Mil. RMB) 总销售收入(百万元)	Rate of change 变化率(%)	Total profit (Mil RMB) 总利润(百万元)	Rate of change 变化率(%)
2000	287		72,154		7,441		353	
2001	301	4.88	75,003	3.95	11,910	60.06	733	107.65
2002	314	4.32	62,583	-16.56	12,390	4.03	795	8.46

Major Products 主要产品	Output 产量	Unit 单位
Automatic Instrument, Meter & System 自动化仪表及系统	4,116	10,000 Units(Sets) 万台(套)

10 Main Firms with Maximal Revenue (year founded) 收入最大的十家主要企业（创办年份）	City 城市	Province 省	Telephone/fax 电话/传真	Number of employees 职工人数	Ownership 产业所有权	Revenue ('000 RMB) 销售收入(千元)	Profit('000 RMB) (rank) 利润(千元)(排名)	Total assets ('000 RMB) 总资产(千元)	Major products 主要产品
Foxconn Fuhon Precision Component (Beijing) Co., Ltd. 富士康精密组件（北京）有限公司(2001)	Beijing 北京市	Beijing 北京市	(010)67879988 (010)67879988	781	Foreign Funded 外商投资	1,544,217	176,301(1)	751,502	New Type instrument Components & Parts新型仪表元器件
Chongqing Chuanyi Instrumentation Co., Ltd. 重庆川仪总厂有限公司(1966)	Chongqing 重庆市	Chongqing 重庆市	(023)68862766 (023)68216674	3,142	State Enterprises 国有独资	863,490	36,473(2)	917,672	Industry Automation Meter工业自动化仪表
Shanghai Automation Instrumentation Co., Ltd. 上海自动化仪表股份有限公司(1989)	Shanghai 上海市	Shanghai 上海市	(021)62521870 (021)62801680	3,053	Foreign Funded 外商投资	479,738	10,256(23)	765,042	Automation Meter System 自动化仪表系统
Shanghai Foxboro CO.,Ltd. 上海福克斯波罗有限公司(1982)	Shanghai 上海市	Shanghai 上海市	(021)64362380 (021)64700447	392	Foreign Funded 外商投资	330,509	27,249(7)	236,418	I/A Intelligentized Control I/A智能化控制
Shanghai Hi-Tech Control System Co., Ltd. 海得控制系统公司(1994)	Shanghai 上海市	Shanghai 上海市	(021)64401020 (021)64401504	130	Joint Stock 股份制	258,500	21,957(11)	95,686	Industry Automation Equipment 工业自动化设备
Beijing Yanhua Xingye Electronic&Science Technology Co.,Ltd.北京研华兴业电子科技有限公司(1994)	Beijing 北京市	Beijing 北京市	(010)62984346 (010)62984341	125	Foreign Funded 外商投资	241,070	6,437(40)	89,263	Industry Control Products 工控产品
Tianjin Dazhan Group Co., Ltd. 天津大站集团有限公司(1992)	Tianjin 天津市	Tianjin 天津市	(022)28618611 (022)28618611	2,400	Collective-owned 集体企业	223,370	4,000(50)	261,830	Valve Water-heating Pipe Parts 阀门水暖管件
Chongqing Naide Industry Co., Ltd. 重庆耐德工业股份有限公司(1958)	Chongqing 重庆市	Chongqing 重庆市	(023)67855563 (023)67871271	517	Joint Stock 股份制	206,797	9,256(29)	274,322	Industry Automation Meter 工业自动化仪表
Shanghai Omron Automation System Co., Ltd.. 上海欧姆龙自动化系统有限公司(1994)	Shanghai 上海市	Shanghai 上海市	(021)50504535 (021)58542658	158	Foreign Funded 外商投资	188,492	34,007(3)	161,780	Program Controller 可编程序控制器
Ningbo Donghai Group Co., Ltd. 宁波东海集团有限公司(1997)	Ningbo 宁波市	Zhejiang 浙江省	(0574)88426871 (0574)88426658	898	Private Owned 私营企业	185,909	12,580(18)	258,570	Water Meter 水表

Top 10 Cities by Revenue 销售收入排名前10位城市	Province 省	Market share 市场份额 (%)	Number of firms 企业个数
Beijing 北京市	Beijing 北京市	24.33	39
Shanghai 上海市	Shanghai 上海市	17.33	33
Chongqing 重庆市	Chongqing 重庆市	12.13	11
Tianjin 天津市	Tianjin 天津市	7.67	33
Wuxi 无锡市	Jiangsu 江苏省	4.54	13
Wuzhong 吴忠市	Ningxia 宁夏	3.60	1
Shenzhen 深圳市	Guangdong 广东省	2.53	8
Ningbo 宁波市	Zhejiang 浙江省	2.27	8
Guangzhou 广州市	Guangdong 广东省	2.21	5
Nanjing 南京市	Jiangsu 江苏省	2.00	5

10 Major Wholesalers 十家主要批发商	City 城市	Province 省	Telephone/Fax 电话/传真
SU MEC 中设江苏机械设备进出口（集团）公司	Nanjing 南京市	Jiangsu 江苏省	(025)4511888 (025)4411772
China Poster Mobile Communications Equipment Co.,Ltd. 中邮普泰移动通信设备股份有限公司	Beijing 北京市	Beijing 北京市	(010)66426993 (010)66426837
Sino Kama Co., Ltd. 中泰凯马股份有限公司	Shanghai 上海市	Shanghai 上海市	(021)62031188 (021)62030851
China Huayuan Group Co.,Ltd. 中国华源集团有限公司	Shanghai 上海市	Shanghai 上海市	(021)62031188 (021)62032288
Zhejiang Crand Imp.& Exp.Co.,Ltd. 浙江远大进出口有限公司	Ningbo 宁波市	Zhejiang 浙江省	(0574)87720170 (0574)87723350
Shandong Machinery Import & Export Group Corporation 山东省机械进出口集团公司	Qingdao 青岛市	Shandong 山东省	(0532)2661628 (0532)2991655
Qingdao Haier International Trade Co.,Ltd. 青岛海尔国际贸易有限公司	Qingdao 青岛市	Shandong 山东省	(0532)8938337 (0532)8939494
Guangdong Machinery Import & Export Group Corporation 广东省机械进出口集团公司	Guangzhou 广州市	Guangdong 广东省	(020)87782168 (020)87771803
China National Machinery Equipment Import & Export Corporation 中国机械设备进出口总公司	Beijing 北京市	Beijing 北京市	(010)63474506 (010)63261865
Beijing Cellstar Co.,Ltd. 北京蜂星事达电讯有限公司	Beijing 北京市	Beijing 北京市	(010)64602050 (010)64672648

4212: Electrical Instruments and Meters 电工仪器、仪表制造业

The industry accounts for 0.086% of the total revenue of China's industrial sector in 2002. The rate of return on assets is 4.66%. 75.72% of all firms in the industry made a profit while 24.28% had negative returns.The top province in terms of the industry's revenue is Zhejiang, accounting for 37.91% of the total revenue.
2002年本行业收入占全行业的 0.086%，资产利润率为 4.66%。75.72%的企业赢利，24.28%的企业亏损。收入最高的省为浙江省，占本行业的37.91%。

	Total number of firms 企业总数	Total number of employees 职工总数	Total revenue (Mil.RMB) 总销售收入 (百万元)	Total profit (Mil.RMB) 总利润 (百万元)	Return on assets 资产利润率 (%)	Return on equity 权益利润率 (%)	Labour productivity ('000 RMB/ worker) 劳动生产率 (千元/人)	Debts/ assets 资产负债率 (%)	Total assets (Mil.RMB) 总资产 (百万元)
Industry Overall 行业总体	173	46,012	9,243	557	4.66	12.14	55.49	61.62	11,941

	Number of firms 企业个数	Average number of employees 平均职工人数	Average revenue ('000 RMB) 平均销售收入 (千元)	Average profit ('000 RMB) 平均利润 (千元)	Return on assets 资产利润率 (%)	Return on equity 权益利润率 (%)	Labour productivity ('000 RMB/ worker) 劳动生产率 (千元/人)	Debts/ assets 资产负债率 (%)	Average total assets ('000 RMB) 平均总资产 (千元)
By ownership 产业所有权									
State-owned 国有	23	572	39,961	-2,822	-2.58	-10.89	24.56	76.28	109,219
Collective-owned 集体	9	120	17,154	168	1.35	3.21	46.69	57.86	12,442
Foreign & Overseas Chinese Funded 三资	32	204	72,098	4,189	6.27	14.65	107.64	57.20	66,805
By regional distribution 地区分布									
Central-North 华北	16	212	36,575	1,886	4.30	10.23	50.17	57.93	43,823
Beijing 北京	8	160	60,503	4,272	8.06	16.24	104.62	50.38	53,011
Tianjin 天津	4	372	18,144	-1,208	-2.45	-8.18	6.93	70.04	49,286
Hebei 河北	3	176	8,629	276	1.14	3.25	46.59	65.09	24,323
Shanxi 山西	1	97	2,711				15.22	100.03	6,968
Inner Mongolia 内蒙古									
Northeast 东北	11	309	34,500	654	1.30	3.39	48.19	61.67	50,369
Liaoning 辽宁	5	107	30,264	2,607	6.36	11.71	115.65	45.71	41,006
Jilin 吉林	2	761	11,637	-3,150	-6.26	-39.71	3.30	84.24	50,332
Heilongjiang 黑龙江	4	335	51,227	115	0.18	0.54	72.17	65.70	62,092
Central-East 华东	97	213	58,462	3,986	7.47	18.49	62.93	59.58	53,320
Shanghai 上海	17	57	24,780	1,118	7.76	20.17	76.11	61.52	14,408
Jiangsu 江苏	24	189	54,789	3,127	6.62	16.67	75.51	60.27	47,220
Zhejiang 浙江	35	295	100,104	8,387	9.45	21.95	72.85	56.95	88,744
Anhui 安徽	4	106	7,860	-618	-6.20	-12.34	18.22	49.78	9,967
Fujian 福建	3	89	18,435	198	2.34	10.34	74.96	77.38	8,454
Jiangxi 江西	3	474	12,654	-2,121	-4.69	-127.49	12.47	96.32	45,210
Shandong 山东	11	246	27,844	659	1.49	4.08	31.43	63.50	44,265
Central-South 中南	33	325	53,854	3,092	3.03	8.30	53.97	63.46	101,909
Henan 河南	6	699	58,588	6,643	3.13	7.48	31.44	58.25	212,582
Hubei 湖北	3	111	47,588	1,450	2.39	4.37	146.50	45.22	60,637
Hunan 湖南	8	363	51,171	4,110	3.84	13.65	47.21	71.88	107,109
Guangdong 广东	14	202	56,520	1,017	1.52	4.33	86.16	64.89	66,864
Guangxi 广西	1	437	25,826	-2,849	-3.49		5.61	104.51	81,583
Hainan 海南	1	17	56,406	13,568	43.69	44.16	838.29	1.05	31,052
Southwest 西南	8	372	34,996	6,739	6.96	13.11	43.20	46.91	96,793
Chongqing 重庆	3	248	64,795	18,992	10.22	16.93	139.78	39.62	185,803
Sichuan 四川	2	55	10,603	520	6.69	14.80	65.51	54.79	7,764
Guizhou 贵州	1	1,780	22,577	-1,486	-1.00	-3.04	4.66	67.27	149,204
Yunnan 云南	2	172	20,900	-1,310	-5.02	-14.03	26.65	64.23	26,102
Tibet 西藏									
Northwest 西北	8	610	68,813	-2,924	-1.70	-6.77	43.66	74.92	172,097
Shaanxi 陕西	4	730	130,725	-3,110	-1.02	-2.56	68.80	60.14	305,311
Gansu 甘肃	4	490	6,901	-2,738	-7.04		6.18	190.91	38,884
Qinghai 青海									
Ningxia 宁夏									
Xinjiang 新疆									

4212: Electrical Instruments and Meters 电工仪器、仪表制造业

Year 年份	Number of firms 企业个数	Rate of change 变化率 (%)	Number of employees 职工人数 (人)	Rate of change 变化率 (%)	Total revenue (Mil. RMB) 总销售收入 (百万元)	Rate of change 变化率 (%)	Total profit (Mil RMB) 总利润 (百万元)	Rate of change 变化率 (%)
2000	170		55,198		8,779		660	
2001	192	12.94	50,313	-8.85	9,126	3.95	555	-15.91
2002	173	-9.90	46,012	-8.55	9,243	1.28	557	0.36

Major Products 主要产品	Output 产量	Unit 单位
Electrician's Instrument & Meter 电工仪器仪表	5,817	10,000 Units(Sets) 万台(套)

10 Main Firms with Maximal Revenue (year founded) 收入最大的十家主要企业（创办年份）	City 城市	Province 省	Telephone/fax 电话/传真	Number of employees 职工人数	Ownership 产业所有权	Revenue ('000 RMB) 销售收入 (千元)	Profit('000 RMB) (rank) 利润(千元) (排名)	Total assets ('000 RMB) 总资产 (千元)	Major products 主要产品
Holley Group Co., Ltd. 华立集团有限公司(1970)	Hangzhou 杭州市	Zhejiang 浙江省	(0571)88900710 (0571)88052408	3,986	Limited-Liability 有限公司	2,302,604	168,722(1)	1,981,333	Electrician's Meter 电工仪表
Ningbo Samsung Science & Technology Co., Ltd. 宁波三星科技股份有限公司(2001)	Ningbo 宁波市	Zhejiang 浙江省	(0574)88220158 (0574)88220158	2,046	Joint Stock 股份制	564,326	96,904(2)	344,845	Electric Energy Meter 电能表
Xi'an Gaoke (Group) Co.,Ltd. 西安高科(集团)公司(1992)	Xi'an 西安市	Shannxi 陕西省	(029)8229104 (029)8235111	2,308	State-owned 国有企业	471,904	-	1,084,653	Thick Film Circuit 厚膜电路
Jiansu Linyang Electronics Co., Ltd. 江苏林洋电子有限公司(1995)	Nantong 南通市	Jiangsu 江苏省	(0513)3329751 (0513)3310816	600	Overseas Chinese-funded 港澳台资	320,582	13,423(10)	221,735	Single-phase Electronic Watch 单相电子表
Goldtron Electronics(Shen Zhen)Co., Ltd. 鸿城电子（深圳）有限公司(1994)	Shenzhen 深圳市	Guangdong 广东省	(0755)28557432 (0755)28557074	600	Foreign Funded 外商投资	303,358	405(69)	129,365	Scanner 扫描仪
Beijing Rosemount Far East Instrument Co., Ltd. 北京远东罗斯蒙特仪表有限公司(1995)	Beijing 北京市	Beijing 北京市	(010)64282233 (010)64281512	129	Foreign Funded 外商投资	254,291	20,155(8)	91,751	Industry Sensor工业用传感器
Shanghai Lianneng Meter Co.,Ltd. 上海联能仪表有限公司(2001)	Shanghai 上海市	Shanghai 上海市	(021)58833441 (021)50879160	152	Limited-Liability 有限公司	203,271	6,283(16)	84,495	Kilowatt-hour Meter 电度表
Henan Star Hi-Tech Co., Ltd. 河南思达高科技股份有限公司(1996)	Zhengzhou 郑州市	Henan 河南省	(0371)7982832 (0371)7980780	1,092	Joint Stock 股份制	181,860	40,614(5)	766,002	Complete Sets Instrument & Meter for Electricity 电力配套仪器
Chongqing Holly Holding Co., Ltd. 重庆华立控股股份有限公司(1993)	Chongqing 重庆市	Chongqing 重庆市	(023)67750888 (023)67755788	529	Joint Stock 股份制	177,913	57,059(3)	341,190	Electrican's Instrument & Meter 电工仪器仪表
Harbin Electrical Measuring Instrument Co., Ltd. 哈尔滨电表仪器股份有限公司(1956)	Harbin 哈尔滨市	Heilongjiang 黑龙江省	(0451)6662848 (0451)6662765	1,008	State-owned 国有企业	171,284	214(84)	207,240	Electronic Instrument & Meter电子仪器仪表

Top 10 Cities by Revenue 销售收入排名前10位城市	Province 省	Market share 市场份额 (%)	Number of firms 企业个数
Hangzhou 杭州市	Zhejiang 浙江省	26.49	12
Ningbo 宁波市	Zhejiang 浙江省	6.81	5
Xi'an 西安市	Shannxi 陕西省	5.66	4
Beijing 北京市	Beijing 北京市	5.24	8
Shenzhen 深圳市	Guangdong 广东省	5.19	4
Suzhou 苏州市	Jiangsu 江苏省	4.70	5
Shanghai 上海市	Shanghai 上海市	4.56	17
Wuxi 无锡市	Jiangsu 江苏省	3.85	6
Nantong 南通市	Jiangsu 江苏省	3.47	1
Changsha 长沙市	Hunan 湖南省	3.06	5

10 Major Wholesalers 十家主要批发商	City 城市	Province 省	Telephone/Fax 电话/传真
SU MEC 中设江苏机械设备进出口（集团）公司	Nanjing 南京市	Jiangsu 江苏省	(025)4511888 (025)4411772
China Poster Mobile Communications Equipment Co.,Ltd. 中邮普泰移动通信设备股份有限公司	Beijing 北京市	Beijing 北京市	(010)66426993 (010)66426837
Sino Kama Co., Ltd. 中泰凯马股份有限公司	Shanghai 上海市	Shanghai 上海市	(021)62031188 (021)62030851
China Huayuan Group Co.,Ltd. 中国华源集团有限公司	Shanghai 上海市	Shanghai 上海市	(021)62031188 (021)62032288
Zhejiang Crand Imp.& Exp.Co.,Ltd. 浙江远大进出口有限公司	Ningbo 宁波市	Zhejiang 浙江省	(0574)87720170 (0574)87723350
Shandong Machinery Import & Export Group Corporation 山东省机械进出口集团公司	Qingdao 青岛市	Shandong 山东省	(0532)2661628 (0532)2991655
Qingdao Haier International Trade Co.,Ltd. 青岛海尔国际贸易有限公司	Qingdao 青岛市	Shandong 山东省	(0532)8938337 (0532)8939494
Guangdong Machinery Import & Export Group Corporation 广东省机械进出口集团公司	Guangzhou 广州市	Guangdong 广东省	(020)87782168 (020)87771803
China National Machinery Equipment Import & Export Corporation 中国机械设备进出口总公司	Beijing 北京市	Beijing 北京市	(010)63474506 (010)63261865
Beijing Cellstar Co.,Ltd. 北京蜂星事达电讯有限公司	Beijing 北京市	Beijing 北京市	(010)64602050 (010)64672648

4213: Optical Instruments 光学仪器制造业

The industry accounts for 0.084% of the total revenue of China's industrial sector in 2002. The rate of return on assets is 1.38%. 78.17% of all firms in the industry made a profit while 21.83% had negative returns.The top province in terms of the industry's revenue is Guangdong, accounting for 20.96% of the total revenue.
2002年本行业收入占全行业的0.084%，资产利润率为 1.38%。78.17%的企业赢利，21.83%的企业亏损。收入最高的省为广东省，占本行业的20.96%。

	Total number of firms 企业总数	Total number of employees 职工总数	Total revenue (Mil.RMB) 总销售收入（百万元）	Total profit (Mil.RMB) 总利润（百万元）	Return on assets 资产利润率（%）	Return on equity 权益利润率（%）	Labour productivity ('000 RMB/worker) 劳动生产率（千元/人）	Debts/assets 资产负债率（%）	Total assets (Mil.RMB) 总资产（百万元）
Industry Overall 行业总体	197	84,666	8,963	206	1.38	3.12	30.28	55.83	14,992

	Number of firms 企业个数	Average number of employees 平均职工人数	Average revenue ('000 RMB) 平均销售收入（千元）	Average profit ('000 RMB) 平均利润（千元）	Return on assets 资产利润率（%）	Return on equity 权益利润率（%）	Labour productivity ('000 RMB/worker) 劳动生产率（千元/人）	Debts/assets 资产负债率（%）	Average total assets ('000 RMB) 平均总资产（千元）
By ownership 产业所有权									
State-owned 国有	38	814	52,341	-648	-0.44	-1.47	20.07	69.76	145,806
Collective-owned 集体	13	156	35,145	870	4.29	10.36	56.38	58.56	20,259
Foreign & Overseas Chinese Funded 三资	70	367	53,292	-232	-0.42	-0.89	33.75	52.89	55,127
By regional distribution 地区分布									
Central-North 华北	25	203	16,795	3,454	4.68	7.23	29.16	35.24	73,793
Beijing 北京	14	248	22,059	5,831	5.04	7.08	38.86	28.79	115,677
Tianjin 天津	8	148	13,350	754	3.58	12.13	8.10	70.48	21,055
Hebei 河北	2	107	1,916	-292	-3.96		14.84	115.59	7,353
Shanxi 山西	1	218	411	-723	-1.71		3.10	114.33	42,187
Inner Mongolia 内蒙古									
Northeast 东北	9	739	79,027	6,913	4.50	8.89	34.46	49.44	153,773
Liaoning 辽宁	5	420	84,438	13,057	17.59	24.06	59.25	26.89	74,214
Jilin 吉林	4	1,138	72,262	-766	-0.30	-0.72	23.01	57.71	253,223
Heilongjiang 黑龙江									
Central-East 华东	79	353	47,808	3,107	5.00	10.52	43.17	52.47	62,165
Shanghai 上海	11	182	49,866	941	2.29	6.02	50.38	61.94	41,052
Jiangsu 江苏	24	473	53,577	2,993	3.76	8.28	42.88	54.54	79,563
Zhejiang 浙江	24	271	28,453	4,611	12.36	25.00	34.35	50.56	37,302
Anhui 安徽	2	116	4,909	281	2.02	4.41	17.83	54.21	13,931
Fujian 福建	11	159	25,258	2,997	7.67	16.84	43.86	54.47	39,089
Jiangxi 江西	1	4,548	440,855	640	0.07	0.15	27.73	50.52	869,794
Shandong 山东	6	252	88,508	3,076	5.64	8.67	123.13	34.88	54,512
Central-South 中南	44	574	57,659	-3,863	-4.93	-12.22	20.84	59.63	78,348
Henan 河南	6	564	40,614	550	0.74	2.10	11.63	64.99	74,868
Hubei 湖北	7	492	31,929	-1,041	-1.00	-2.62	18.91	61.98	104,446
Hunan 湖南	4	558	43,636	1,525	1.66	3.75	29.34	55.88	92,090
Guangdong 广东	26	606	72,274	-6,534	-9.11	-21.71	22.31	58.05	71,763
Guangxi 广西	1	464	16,147	-2,213	-6.75	-19.98	11.74	66.22	32,784
Hainan 海南									
Southwest 西南	36	396	25,347	-475	-0.74	-3.28	23.30	77.54	64,586
Chongqing 重庆	11	404	26,690	-4,922	-8.52		16.06	116.13	57,751
Sichuan 四川	6	372	14,442	-602	-0.66	-9.64	14.65	93.17	91,460
Guizhou 贵州	3	409	15,871	986	2.64	3.56	21.54	25.90	37,387
Yunnan 云南	16	398	30,289	2,355	3.66	7.48	31.74	51.01	64,307
Tibet 西藏									
Northwest 西北	4	1,371	151,509	-137	-0.05	-0.11	22.30	55.61	269,998
Shaanxi 陕西	4	1,371	151,509	-137	-0.05	-0.11	22.30	55.61	269,998
Gansu 甘肃									
Qinghai 青海									
Ningxia 宁夏									
Xinjiang 新疆									

Year 年份	Number of firms 企业个数	Rate of change 变化率 (%)	Number of employees 职工人数 (人)	Rate of change 变化率 (%)	Total revenue (Mil. RMB) 总销售收入 (百万元)	Rate of change 变化率 (%)	Total profit (Mil RMB) 总利润 (百万元)	Rate of change 变化率 (%)
2000	143		81,433		7,055		314	
2001	168	17.48	77,027	-5.41	6,262	-11.24	249	-20.70
2002	197	17.26	84,666	9.92	8,963	43.13	206	-17.27

Major Products 主要产品	Output 产量	Unit 单位
Optical Instrument 光学仪器	695	10,000 Units 万台

10 Main Firms with Maximal Revenue (year founded) 收入最大的十家主要企业（创办年份）	City 城市	Province 省	Telephone/fax 电话/传真	Number of employees 职工人数	Ownership 产业所有权	Revenue ('000 RMB) 销售收入 (千元)	Profit('000 RMB) (rank) 利润(千元) (排名)	Total assets ('000 RMB) 总资产 (千元)	Major products 主要产品
Sicong Opto-electronic Co., Ltd.	Xi'an	Shannxi	(029)2521712		State Enterprises				Infrared Temperature Measuring Machine
西安北方光电有限公司(1956)	西安市	陕西省	(029)2526666	4,645	国有独资	589,680	-	986,450	红外测温仪
Jiangxi Phenix Optical Instrument General Factory	Shangrao	Jiangxi	(0793)8260731		State-owned				Optical Instrument
江西凤凰光学仪器总厂(1968)	上饶市	江西省	(0793)8250249	4,548	国有企业	440,855	640(92)	869,794	光学仪器
Dezhou Huangming Solar Energy Vacuum Pipe Co., Ltd.	Dezhou	Shandong	(0534)2561921		Private Enterprises				Vacuum Tube
德州皇明太阳能真空管有限公司(2000)	德州市	山东省	(0534)2561120	280	私营独资	334,611	2,140(45)	132,249	真空管
Konica (Dalian) Co., Ltd.	Dalian	Liaoning	(0411)7622575		Foreign Funded				CD Lens
柯尼卡（大连）有限公司(1995)	大连市	辽宁省	(0411)7621379	1,066	外商投资	315,395	46,892(3)	274,779	CD镜片
Suzhou Banxiaozi Electronics Co., Ltd.	Suzhou	Jiangsu	(0512)68257409		Foreign Funded				Liquid Crystal Display Base Plate Glass
苏州板硝子电子有限公司(1996)	苏州市	江苏省	(0512)62855045	1,107	外商投资	282,601	5,187(21)	330,846	液晶显示基板玻璃
ZheJiang Sunny Group Co., Ltd.	Ningbo	Zhejiang	(0574)62538080		Limited-Liability				Electric Parts
浙江舜宇集团有限公司(1984)	宁波市	浙江省	(0574)62538111	2,344	有限公司	280,221	74,345(1)	394,508	电器元件
Jilin Dongguang Precision Machinery Co.,Ltd.	Changchun	Jilin	(0431)5173591		State-owned				Optical Instrument
吉林东光精密机械厂(1963)	长春市	吉林省	(0431)5172269	3,591	国有企业	242,340	300(114)	824,980	光学仪器
Henan Pingyuan Optics Electronic Instrument Works	Jiaozuo	Henan	(0391)2633258		State-owned				Electromechanical Products
河南平原光学电子仪器厂(1965)	焦作市	河南省	(0391)2625782	2,375	国有企业	169,962	1,062(73)	417,995	机电产品
Nanhai Xiangwang Optical Electric Product Co.,Ltd	Foshan	Guangdong	(0757)5445504		Overseas Chinese-funded				Telescope
南海祥旺光学电子制品有限公司(1994)	佛山市	广东省	(0757)5443326	2,831	港澳台资	157,998	-	173,132	望远镜
Ditto Denko (Shenzhen) Co.,Ltd.	Shenzhen	Guangdong	(0755)27390757		Overseas Chinese-funded				Lean towards the slide
新日东电工(深圳)有限公司(1993)	深圳市	广东省	(0755)27396965	3,215	港澳台资	150,151	2,780(34)	74,863	偏光片

Top 10 Cities by Revenue 销售收入排名前10位城市	Province 省	Market share 市场份额 (%)	Number of firms 企业个数
Dongguan 东莞市	Guangdong 广东省	8.84	5
Xi'an 西安市	Shannxi 陕西省	6.76	4
Ningbo 宁波市	Zhejiang 浙江省	6.33	15
Shanghai 上海市	Shanghai 上海市	6.12	11
Kunming 昆明市	Yunnan 云南省	5.41	16
Suzhou 苏州市	Jiangsu 江苏省	5.09	4
Nanjing 南京市	Jiangsu 江苏省	5.05	8
Shangrao 上饶市	Jiangxi 江西省	4.92	1
Dezhou 德州市	Shandong 山东省	3.73	1
Foshan 佛山市	Guangdong 广东省	3.58	6

10 Major Wholesalers 十家主要批发商	City 城市	Province 省	Telephone/Fax 电话/传真
SU MEC	Nanjing	Jiangsu	(025)4511888
中设江苏机械设备进出口（集团）公司	南京市	江苏省	(025)4411772
China Poster Mobile Communications Equipment Co.,Ltd.	Beijing	Beijing	(010)66426993
中邮普泰移动通信设备股份有限公司	北京市	北京市	(010)66426837
Sino Kama Co., Ltd.	Shanghai	Shanghai	(021)62031188
中泰凯马股份有限公司	上海市	上海市	(021)62030851
China Huayuan Group Co.,Ltd.	Shanghai	Shanghai	(021)62031188
中国华源集团有限公司	上海市	上海市	(021)62032288
Zhejiang Crand Imp.& Exp.Co.,Ltd.	Ningbo	Zhejiang	(0574)87720170
浙江远大进出口有限公司	宁波市	浙江省	(0574)87723350
Shandong Machinery Import & Export Group Corporation	Qingdao	Shandong	(0532)2661628
山东省机械进出口集团公司	青岛市	山东省	(0532)2991655
Qingdao Haier International Trade Co.,Ltd.	Qingdao	Shandong	(0532)8938337
青岛海尔国际贸易有限公司	青岛市	山东省	(0532)8939494
Guangdong Machinery Import & Export Group Corporation	Guangzhou	Guangdong	(020)87782168
广东省机械进出口集团公司	广州市	广东省	(020)87771803
China National Machinery Equipment Import & Export	Beijing	Beijing	(010)63474506
Corporation 中国机械设备进出口总公司	北京市	北京市	(010)63261865
Beijing Cellstar Co.,Ltd.	Beijing	Beijing	(010)64602050
北京蜂星事达电讯有限公司	北京市	北京市	(010)64672648

4214: Timing Instruments 计时仪器制造业

The industry accounts for 0.008% of the total revenue of China's industrial sector in 2002. The rate of return on assets is 3.30%. 84.21% of all firms in the industry made a profit while 15.79% had negative returns.The top province in terms of the industry's revenue is Zhejiang, accounting for 70.74% of the total revenue.
2002年本行业收入占全行业的 0.008%，资产利润率为 3.30%。84.21%的企业赢利，15.79%的企业亏损。收入最高的省为浙江省，占本行业的70.74%。

	Total number of firms 企业总数	Total number of employees 职工总数	Total revenue (Mil.RMB) 总销售收入（百万元）	Total profit (Mil.RMB) 总利润（百万元）	Return on assets 资产利润率（%）	Return on equity 权益利润率（%）	Labour productivity ('000 RMB/ worker) 劳动生产率（千元/人）	Debts/ assets 资产负债率（%）	Total assets (Mil.RMB) 总资产（百万元）
Industry Overall 行业总体	38	9,557	833	34	3.30	7.10	30.62	53.49	1,039

	Number of firms 企业个数	Average number of employees 平均职工人数	Average revenue ('000 RMB) 平均销售收入（千元）	Average profit ('000 RMB) 平均利润（千元）	Return on assets 资产利润率（%）	Return on equity 权益利润率（%）	Labour productivity ('000 RMB/ worker) 劳动生产率（千元/人）	Debts/ assets 资产负债率（%）	Average total assets ('000 RMB) 平均总资产（千元）
By ownership 产业所有权									
State-owned 国有	1	24	2,210	73	1.01	1.05	129.04	3.82	7,227
Collective-owned 集体	5	281	12,835	1,410	6.17	17.33	18.74	64.40	22,857
Foreign & Overseas Chinese Funded 三资	10	280	29,233	420	1.13	2.43	37.58	53.45	37,167
By regional distribution 地区分布									
Central-North 华北	2	263	5,195	-144	-0.35	-0.60	13.53	41.15	40,495
Beijing 北京	1	24	2,210	73	1.01	1.05	129.04	3.82	7,227
Tianjin 天津									
Hebei 河北	1	501	8,180	-360	-0.49	-0.88	8.00	44.81	73,762
Shanxi 山西									
Inner Mongolia 内蒙古									
Northeast 东北	1	40	42,756	-142	-2.31	-3.64	244.40	36.58	6,149
Liaoning 辽宁	1	40	42,756	-142	-2.31	-3.64	244.40	36.58	6,149
Jilin 吉林									
Heilongjiang 黑龙江									
Central-East 华东	30	239	22,984	1,260	4.65	9.23	29.47	49.61	27,101
Shanghai 上海	4	58	14,040	-145	-0.66	-1.20	58.07	44.37	21,846
Jiangsu 江苏	1	108	5,070				12.96	67.22	4,790
Zhejiang 浙江	24	280	24,559	1,381	5.17	11.57	26.24	55.32	26,712
Anhui 安徽									
Fujian 福建									
Jiangxi 江西									
Shandong 山东	1	124	38,878	5,222	6.55	7.15	165.56	8.46	79,773
Central-South 中南	5	362	18,106	-609	-2.20	-13.86	35.41	84.16	27,747
Henan 河南									
Hubei 湖北									
Hunan 湖南	1	21	1,721	-585	-8.74	-83.45	163.33	89.52	6,692
Guangdong 广东	4	448	22,203	-615	-1.86	-11.57	33.90	83.89	33,011
Guangxi 广西									
Hainan 海南									
Southwest 西南									
Chongqing 重庆									
Sichuan 四川									
Guizhou 贵州									
Yunnan 云南									
Tibet 西藏									
Northwest 西北									
Shaanxi 陕西									
Gansu 甘肃									
Qinghai 青海									
Ningxia 宁夏									
Xinjiang 新疆									

4214: Timing Instruments 计时仪器制造业

Year 年份	Number of firms 企业个数	Rate of change 变化率 (%)	Number of employees 职工人数 (人)	Rate of change 变化率 (%)	Total revenue (Mil. RMB) 总销售收入 (百万元)	Rate of change 变化率 (%)	Total profit (Mil RMB) 总利润 (百万元)	Rate of change 变化率 (%)
2000	34		9,729		1,072		78	
2001	37	8.82	10,524	8.17	1,062	-0.93	38	-51.28
2002	38	2.70	9,557	-9.19	833	-21.56	34	-10.53

Major Products 主要产品	Output 产量	Unit 单位

10 Main Firms with Maximal Revenue (year founded) 收入最大的十家主要企业（创办年份）	City 城市	Province 省	Telephone/fax 电话/传真	Number of employees 职工人数	Ownership 产业所有权	Revenue ('000 RMB) 销售收入 (千元)	Profit('000 RMB) (rank) 利润(千元) (排名)	Total assets ('000 RMB) 总资产 (千元)	Major products 主要产品
Hangzhou Westlake Timer Factory	Hangzhou	Zhejiang	(0571)88211788		Private Enterprises				Timer
杭州西湖定时器厂(1987)	杭州市	浙江省	(0571)88211985	1,000	私营独资	74,966	772(9)	34,350	定时器
Yingzhou Hengda Electronichanical Co.,Ltd.	Ningbo	Zhejiang	(0574)88330888		Private Owned				Timer
鄞县恒达电器有限公司(1994)	宁波市	浙江省	(0574)88330999	305	私营企业	65,890	14,546(1)	54,860	定时器
NINGBO MING JONG ELECTRIC INDUSTRIES CO.,LTD.	Ningbo	Zhejiang	(0574)86181000		Overseas Chinese-funded				Timer
宁波名钟机电工业有限公司(1993)	宁波市	浙江省	(0574)86177601	655	港澳台资	60,094	3,946(4)	68,968	定时器
Hangzhou Fudan Time Control Si-tech Co.Ltd.	Hangzhou	Zhejiang	(0571)86497511		Limited-Liability				Timer
杭州复旦时控科技有限公司(1987)	杭州市	浙江省	(0571)86496865	772	有限公司	50,423	1,526(7)	111,416	定时器
Shenyang Holley Electric Energy Watch Co., Ltd.	Shenyang	Liaoning	(024)22927779		Limited-Liability				Timer
沈阳华立电能表有限公司(1998)	沈阳市	辽宁省	(024)22907778	40	有限公司	42,756	-	6,149	定时器
Invensys Weihai Controls Co.,Ltd.	Weihai	Shandong	(0631)5233541		Foreign Funded				Electric Energy Meter
威海英维思控制器有限公司(1997)	威海市	山东省	(0631)5233325	124	外商投资	38,878	5,222(3)	79,773	电能表
Dongguan Automatic Viton Co., Ltd.	Dongguan	Guangdong	(0769)7712264		Overseas Chinese-funded				Program Controller 程
东莞艺美达电子有限公司(1992)	东莞市	广东省	(0769)7791715	625	港澳台资	33,710	-	28,359	序控制器
Jinyi Electronics (Shenzhen) Co., Ltd.	Shenzhen	Guangdong	(0755)27268415		Foreign Funded				Time Controller 时
金毅电子（深圳）有限公司(1995)	深圳市	广东省		165	外商投资	30,106	281(19)	25,108	间控制器
Cixi Sijia Electric Works	Ningbo	Zhejiang	(0574)63550818		Private Enterprises				Timer
慈溪市斯佳电器厂(1991)	宁波市	浙江省	(0574)63550308	297	私营独资	27,253	638(11)	19,788	定时器
Ningbo Timer General Works	Ningbo	Zhejiang	(0574)87373998		Collective-owned				Timer
宁波定时器总厂(1958)	宁波市	浙江省	(0574)87332644	295	集体企业	21,506	150(26)	40,255	定时器

Top 10 Cities by Revenue 销售收入排名前10位城市	Province 省	Market share 市场份额 (%)	Number of firms 企业个数
Ningbo 宁波市	Zhejiang 浙江省	40.48	14
Hangzhou 杭州市	Zhejiang 浙江省	24.63	7
Shanghai 上海市	Shanghai 上海市	6.74	4
Shenzhen 深圳市	Guangdong 广东省	5.59	2
Shenyang 沈阳市	Liaoning 辽宁省	5.13	1
Dongguan 东莞市	Guangdong 广东省	5.07	2
Weihai 威海市	Shandong 山东省	4.67	1
Jinhua 金华市	Zhejiang 浙江省	2.86	1
Wenzhou 温州市	Zhejiang 浙江省	2.06	1
Cangzhou 沧州市	Hebei 河北省	0.98	1

10 Major Wholesalers 十家主要批发商	City 城市	Province 省	Telephone/Fax 电话/传真
SU MEC	Nanjing	Jiangsu	(025)4511888
中设江苏机械设备进出口（集团）公司	南京市	江苏省	(025)4411772
China Poster Mobile Communications Equipment Co.,Ltd.	Beijing	Beijing	(010)66426993
中邮普泰移动通信设备股份有限公司	北京市	北京市	(010)66426837
Sino Kama Co., Ltd.	Shanghai	Shanghai	(021)62031188
中泰凯马股份有限公司	上海市	上海市	(021)62030851
China Huayuan Group Co.,Ltd.	Shanghai	Shanghai	(021)62031188
中国华源集团有限公司	上海市	上海市	(021)62032288
Zhejiang Crand Imp.& Exp.Co.,Ltd.	Ningbo	Zhejiang	(0574)87720170
浙江远大进出口有限公司	宁波市	浙江省	(0574)87723350
Shandong Machinery Import & Export Group Corporation	Qingdao	Shandong	(0532)2661628
山东省机械进出口集团公司	青岛市	山东省	(0532)2991655
Qingdao Haier International Trade Co.,Ltd.	Qingdao	Shandong	(0532)8938337
青岛海尔国际贸易有限公司	青岛市	山东省	(0532)8939494
Guangdong Machinery Import & Export Group Corporation	Guangzhou	Guangdong	(020)87782168
广东省机械进出口集团公司	广州市	广东省	(020)87771803
China National Machinery Equipment Import & Export	Beijing	Beijing	(010)63474506
Corporation 中国机械设备进出口总公司	北京市	北京市	(010)63261865
Beijing Cellstar Co.,Ltd.	Beijing	Beijing	(010)64602050
北京蜂星事达电讯有限公司	北京市	北京市	(010)64672648

4215: Analytical Equipment 分析仪器制造业

The industry accounts for 0.013% of the total revenue of China's industrial sector in 2002. The rate of return on assets is 4.21%. 72.58% of all firms in the industry made a profit while 27.42% had negative returns.The top province in terms of the industry's revenue is Shanghai, accounting for 51.20% of the total revenue.
2002年本行业收入占全行业的0.013%，资产利润率为4.21%。72.58%的企业赢利，27.42%的企业亏损。收入最高的省为上海市，占本行业的51.20%。

	Total number of firms 企业总数	Total number of employees 职工总数	Total revenue (Mil.RMB) 总销售收入（百万元）	Total profit (Mil.RMB) 总利润（百万元）	Return on assets 资产利润率（%）	Return on equity 权益利润率（%）	Labour productivity ('000 RMB/ worker) 劳动生产率（千元/人）	Debts/ assets 资产负债率（%）	Total assets (Mil.RMB) 总资产（百万元）
Industry Overall 行业总体	62	9,468	1,440	87	4.21	10.92	45.97	61.46	2,079

	Number of firms 企业个数	Average number of employees 平均职工人数	Average revenue ('000 RMB) 平均销售收入（千元）	Average profit ('000 RMB) 平均利润（千元）	Return on assets 资产利润率（%）	Return on equity 权益利润率（%）	Labour productivity ('000 RMB/ worker) 劳动生产率（千元/人）	Debts/ assets 资产负债率（%）	Average total assets ('000 RMB) 平均总资产（千元）
By ownership 产业所有权									
State-owned 国有	13	96	5,461	-722	-3.36	-13.25	19.71	74.61	21,473
Collective-owned 集体	4	240	17,618	305	0.98	2.71	48.19	63.84	31,114
Foreign & Overseas Chinese Funded 三资	12	70	48,913	3,218	7.30	17.76	152.69	58.87	44,061
By regional distribution 地区分布									
Central-North 华北	16	79	7,937	54	0.26	1.29	38.05	79.75	20,806
Beijing 北京	10	89	9,110	-122	-0.47	-2.53	30.01	81.42	26,046
Tianjin 天津	3	47	4,287	-744	-5.94	-54.07	16.87	89.01	12,532
Hebei 河北	3	76	7,675	1,442	12.42	29.10	82.62	57.31	11,611
Shanxi 山西									
Inner Mongolia 内蒙古									
Northeast 东北	6	58	7,129	616	4.60	15.04	48.85	69.40	13,389
Liaoning 辽宁	5	68	8,554	752	4.69	15.30	49.98	69.34	16,036
Jilin 吉林	1	7	4	-63	-41.18		-6.14	100.00	153
Heilongjiang 黑龙江									
Central-East 华东	26	221	43,176	3,067	6.26	14.03	52.58	55.38	48,991
Shanghai 上海	3	846	245,790	13,983	5.59	13.45	62.38	58.48	250,292
Jiangsu 江苏	3	131	19,980	3,421	11.45	18.03	61.35	36.50	29,874
Zhejiang 浙江	14	119	17,878	2,108	8.42	17.63	58.21	52.23	25,038
Anhui 安徽	1	110	3,600	750	30.00	57.69	10.22	48.00	2,500
Fujian 福建	1	92	2,391	-748	-7.55	-14.54	11.77	48.05	9,905
Jiangxi 江西									
Shandong 山东	4	237	17,244	-501	-2.85	-7.78	21.67	63.40	17,585
Central-South 中南	12	123	10,600	-17	-0.06	-0.18	41.06	65.92	27,361
Henan 河南	1	168	4,587	11	0.10	1.07	10.52	91.00	11,394
Hubei 湖北	3	138	5,441	-169	-1.05	-8.72	10.97	87.93	16,088
Hunan 湖南	2	67	9,497	716	12.47	24.20	55.93	48.45	5,740
Guangdong 广东	5	81	11,406	-394	-0.92	-2.48	38.20	62.68	42,645
Guangxi 广西	1	350	30,261	829	1.89	4.24	88.95	55.57	43,972
Hainan 海南									
Southwest 西南	2	318	10,349	1,684	5.32	11.63	11.62	54.23	31,626
Chongqing 重庆									
Sichuan 四川	2	318	10,349	1,684	5.32	11.63	11.62	54.23	31,626
Guizhou 贵州									
Yunnan 云南									
Tibet 西藏									
Northwest 西北									
Shaanxi 陕西									
Gansu 甘肃									
Qinghai 青海									
Ningxia 宁夏									
Xinjiang 新疆									

4215: Analytical Equipment 分析仪器制造业

Year 年份	Number of firms 企业个数	Rate of change 变化率 (%)	Number of employees 职工人数 (人)	Rate of change 变化率 (%)	Total revenue (Mil. RMB) 总销售收入 (百万元)	Rate of change 变化率 (%)	Total profit (Mil RMB) 总利润 (百万元)	Rate of change 变化率 (%)
2000	32		7,913		801		16	
2001	40	25.00	8,084	2.16	1,031	28.71	80	400.00
2002	62	55.00	9,468	17.12	1,440	39.67	87	8.75

Major Products 主要产品	Output 产量	Unit 单位
Composition Analytical Instrument 成分分析仪器	51,035	Unit 台

10 Main Firms with Maximal Revenue (year founded) 收入最大的十家主要企业（创办年份）	City 城市	Province 省	Telephone/fax 电话/传真	Number of employees 职工人数	Ownership 产业所有权	Revenue ('000 RMB) 销售收入 (千元)	Profit('000 RMB) (rank) 利润(千元) (排名)	Total assets ('000 RMB) 总资产 (千元)	Major products 主要产品
Shanghai Precison & Scientific Insturment Co., Ltd. 上海精密科学仪器有限公司(1992)	Shanghai 上海市	Shanghai 上海市	(021)64957636 (021)64950892	2,235	State Enterprises 国有独资	288,334	16,244(3)	409,840	Composition Analytical Instrument 成分分析仪
Hangzhou Xianfeng Electronic Technology Co., Ltd. 杭州先锋电子技术有限公司(1991)	Hangzhou 杭州市	Zhejiang 浙江省	(0571)85363612 (0571)85363612	81	Private Owned 私营企业	61,371	16,300(2)	54,244	Intelligent Gas Meter 智能燃气表
SHIMADZU Insturment (Suzhou) Co.,Ltd. 岛津仪器(苏州)有限公司(1999)	Suzhou 苏州市	Jiangsu 江苏省	(0512)66651966 (0512)66651965	52	Foreign Funded 外商投资	40,862	8,742(4)	55,423	Analytical Instrument 分析仪器
Guilin Medical Electronic Instrument Factory 桂林市医疗电子仪器厂(1970)	Guilin 桂林市	Guangxi 广西	(0773)2699368 (0773)2693847	350	Collective-owned 集体企业	30,261	829(20)	43,972	Emiction Analysis Implement 尿液分析仪
Shandong Gaomi Caihong Analytical Instruments Co.,Ltd. 高密彩虹分析仪器有限公司(1955)	Weifang 潍坊市	Shandong 山东省	(0536)2322197 (0536)2323953	501	Limited-Liability 有限公司	28,012	706(24)	24,566	Analytical Instrument 分析仪器
Foshan Analytical Instrument Factory 佛山分析仪器厂(1970)	Foshan 佛山市	Guangdong 广东省	(0757)3815504 (0757)3815506	255	State-owned 国有企业	27,617	-	152,923	Automobile Exhaust Analysis Appearance 汽车排气分析仪
Beijing Beifenruili Analytic Instrument (Group) Co.,Ltd. 北京北分瑞利分析仪器(集团)有限责任公司(1965)	Beijing 北京市	Beijing 北京市	(010)62457772 (010)62456592	396	Limited-Liability 有限公司	22,970	-	162,525	Analytical Instrument 分析仪器
Shanghai Sako Instrument Co., Ltd. 上海三科仪器有限公司(1993)	Shanghai 上海市	Shanghai 上海市	(021)64873364 (021)64879966	58	Overseas Chinese-funded 港澳台资	20,372	565(26)	5,582	Double-wave Long Enzyme Analytical Instrument双波长酶标仪
Wenzhou Fuma Meter Factory 温州市富马仪表厂(1992)	Wenzhou 温州市	Zhejiang 浙江省	(0577)86373726 (0577)86882360	84	Joint Stock 股份制	16,899	1,191(15)	22,866	Flowmeter 流量计
Dalian Rigo Instrument Co., Ltd. 大连离合仪器有限公司(1994)	Dalian 大连市	Liaoning 辽宁省	(0411)4301808 (0411)4301808	86	Foreign Funded 外商投资	14,599	3,217(8)	12,295	Petroleum Analytical Instrument石油分析仪器

Top 10 Cities by Revenue 销售收入排名前10位城市	Province 省	Market share 市场份额 (%)	Number of firms 企业个数
Shanghai 上海市	Shanghai 上海市	51.20	3
Wenzhou 温州市	Zhejiang 浙江省	9.83	8
Beijing 北京市	Beijing 北京市	6.33	10
Hangzhou 杭州市	Zhejiang 浙江省	4.67	2
Suzhou 苏州市	Jiangsu 江苏省	2.84	1
Dalian 大连市	Liaoning 辽宁省	2.61	4
Guilin 桂林市	Guangxi 广西	2.10	1
Taizhou 台州市	Zhejiang 浙江省	2.09	3
Weifang 潍坊市	Shandong 山东省	1.94	1
Foshan 佛山市	Guangdong 广东省	1.92	1

10 Major Wholesalers 十家主要批发商	City 城市	Province 省	Telephone/Fax 电话/传真
SU MEC 中设江苏机械设备进出口（集团）公司	Nanjing 南京市	Jiangsu 江苏省	(025)4511888 (025)4411772
China Poster Mobile Communications Equipment Co.,Ltd. 中邮普泰移动通信设备股份有限公司	Beijing 北京市	Beijing 北京市	(010)66426993 (010)66426837
Sino Kama Co., Ltd. 中泰凯马股份有限公司	Shanghai 上海市	Shanghai 上海市	(021)62031188 (021)62030851
China Huayuan Group Co.,Ltd. 中国华源集团有限公司	Shanghai 上海市	Shanghai 上海市	(021)62031188 (021)62032288
Zhejiang Crand Imp.& Exp.Co.,Ltd. 浙江远大进出口有限公司	Ningbo 宁波市	Zhejiang 浙江省	(0574)87720170 (0574)87723350
Shandong Machinery Import & Export Group Corporation 山东省机械进出口集团公司	Qingdao 青岛市	Shandong 山东省	(0532)2661628 (0532)2991655
Qingdao Haier International Trade Co.,Ltd. 青岛海尔国际贸易有限公司	Qingdao 青岛市	Shandong 山东省	(0532)8938337 (0532)8939494
Guangdong Machinery Import & Export Group Corporation 广东省机械进出口集团公司	Guangzhou 广州市	Guangdong 广东省	(020)87782168 (020)87771803
China National Machinery Equipment Import & Export Corporation 中国机械设备进出口总公司	Beijing 北京市	Beijing 北京市	(010)63474506 (010)63261865
Beijing Cellstar Co.,Ltd. 北京蜂星事达电讯有限公司	Beijing 北京市	Beijing 北京市	(010)64602050 (010)64672648

4216: Testing Equipment 试验机制造业

The industry accounts for 0.008% of the total revenue of China's industrial sector in 2002. The rate of return on assets is 1.80%. 82.61% of all firms in the industry made a profit while 17.39% had negative returns.The top province in terms of the industry's revenue is Shandong, accounting for 26.37% of the total revenue.
2002年本行业收入占全行业的 0.008%，资产利润率为 1.80%。82.61%的企业赢利，17.39%的企业亏损。收入最高的省为山东省，占本行业的26.37%。

	Total number of firms 企业总数	Total number of employees 职工总数	Total revenue (Mil.RMB) 总销售收入 (百万元)	Total profit (Mil.RMB) 总利润 (百万元)	Return on assets 资产利润率 (%)	Return on equity 权益利润率 (%)	Labour productivity ('000 RMB/ worker) 劳动生产率 (千元/人)	Debts/ assets 资产负债率 (%)	Total assets (Mil.RMB) 总资产 (百万元)
Industry Overall 行业总体	46	10,478	835	25	1.80	8.54	26.14	78.91	1,406

	Number of firms 企业个数	Average number of employees 平均职工人数	Average revenue ('000 RMB) 平均销售收入（千元）	Average profit ('000 RMB) 平均利润 (千元)	Return on assets 资产利润率 (%)	Return on equity 权益利润率 (%)	Labour productivity ('000 RMB/ worker) 劳动生产率 (千元/人)	Debts/ assets 资产负债率 (%)	Average total assets ('000 RMB) 平均总资产 (千元)
By ownership 产业所有权									
State-owned 国有	10	295	14,832	-1,035	-3.42		11.76	107.02	30,254
Collective-owned 集体									
Foreign & Overseas Chinese Funded 三资	6	150	21,236	2,904	9.83	18.39	59.26	46.57	29,557
By regional distribution 地区分布									
Central-North 华北	6	143	13,804	1,000	4.81	14.39	22.83	66.58	20,797
Beijing 北京	2	70	12,147	1,066	13.66	19.52	33.47	30.01	7,802
Tianjin 天津	1	42	10,325	3,167	23.32	117.91	73.33	80.23	13,583
Hebei 河北	3	225	16,069	234	0.73	2.50	17.50	70.61	31,865
Shanxi 山西									
Inner Mongolia 内蒙古									
Northeast 东北	7	201	11,126	144	0.39	1.81	10.08	78.59	37,048
Liaoning 辽宁	5	144	12,904	359	0.92	4.74	13.54	80.66	39,165
Jilin 吉林	2	345	6,682	-394	-1.24	-4.47	6.45	72.22	31,758
Heilongjiang 黑龙江									
Central-East 华东	21	261	24,421	1,457	4.07	13.55	35.63	69.94	35,769
Shanghai 上海	7	117	17,507	1,634	7.02	17.80	59.29	60.52	23,254
Jiangsu 江苏	8	158	16,255	1,087	5.74	31.47	36.48	81.77	18,942
Zhejiang 浙江	2	221	19,997	1,825	5.99	10.02	39.61	40.14	30,434
Anhui 安徽									
Fujian 福建									
Jiangxi 江西									
Shandong 山东	4	738	55,062	1,705	1.81	6.99	28.11	74.07	93,994
Central-South 中南	8	131	12,317	38	0.33	1.32	31.43	74.68	11,285
Henan 河南	1	32	2,386	4	0.09	0.22	36.00	57.06	4,287
Hubei 湖北	2	83	4,412	-774	-5.30	-15.57	35.37	65.94	14,593
Hunan 湖南	1	118	8,602	-191	-1.50	-4.13	33.03	63.55	12,701
Guangdong 广东	2	338	35,636	824	5.08		28.20	101.55	16,220
Guangxi 广西	2	27	3,727	194	3.32	5.59	53.59	40.47	5,835
Hainan 海南									
Southwest 西南									
Chongqing 重庆									
Sichuan 四川									
Guizhou 贵州									
Yunnan 云南									
Tibet 西藏									
Northwest 西北	4	421	15,801	-3,148	-7.00		7.07	127.43	44,997
Shaanxi 陕西									
Gansu 甘肃	2	389	15,117	-3,740	-6.81		8.28	125.69	54,903
Qinghai 青海									
Ningxia 宁夏	2	454	16,486	-2,556	-7.28		6.04	130.16	35,090
Xinjiang 新疆									

Year 年份	Number of firms 企业个数	Rate of change 变化率 (%)	Number of employees 职工人数 (人)	Rate of change 变化率 (%)	Total revenue (Mil. RMB) 总销售收入 (百万元)	Rate of change 变化率 (%)	Total profit (Mil RMB) 总利润 (百万元)	Rate of change 变化率 (%)
2000	31		12,112		626		9	
2001	43	38.71	11,254	-7.08	829	32.43	23	155.56
2002	46	6.98	10,478	-6.90	835	0.72	25	8.70

Major Products 主要产品	Output 产量	Unit 单位
Testing Equipment 试验机	1	10,000 Units 万台

10 Main Firms with Maximal Revenue (year founded) 收入最大的十家主要企业（创办年份）	City 城市	Province 省	Telephone/fax 电话/传真	Number of employees 职工人数	Ownership 产业所有权	Revenue ('000 RMB) 销售收入 (千元)	Profit('000 RMB) (rank) 利润(千元) (排名)	Total assets ('000 RMB) 总资产 (千元)	Major products 主要产品
Zhongshan Baite Electrical Appliance Co., Ltd. 中山市百特电器有限公司(1994)	Zhongshan 中山市	Guangdong 广东省	(0760)3388168 (0760)2355466	480	Private Owned 私营企业	60,177	1,644(11)	13,424	Financial Machines 金融机具
Wuxi Jianyi Instrument &Machinery Co., Ltd. 无锡建仪仪器机械有限公司(1958)	Wuxi 无锡市	Jiangsu 江苏省	(0510)5456223 (0510)5456168	513	Private Owned 私营企业	48,729	2,345(9)	64,140	NYL-2000D Pressure Testing Machine NYL-2000D压力试验机
Schenck-Shanghai Testing Machinery Co.,Ltd. 上海申克试验机有限公司(1991)	Shanghai 上海市	Shanghai 上海市	(021)63246355 (021)63240519	376	Foreign Funded 外商投资	48,020	1,383(12)	73,273	Dynamic-Balance Testing Machine 动平衡试验机
Shangdong Laizhou Testing Instrument Co., Ltd. 山东莱州市试验机总厂(1948)	Yantai 烟台市	Shandong 山东省	(0535)2207900 (0535)2213954	806	State-owned 国有企业	40,279	1,271(13)	36,286	Sclerometer 硬度计
Tangshan Baichuan Intelligence Machine Co., Ltd. 唐山百川智能机器有限公司(1998)	Tangshan 唐山市	Hebei 河北省	(0315)3173501 (0315)3173500	166	Private Owned 私营企业	31,844	728(18)	36,622	Internal-combustion Engine Test-Bed 内燃机车试验台
Zhejiang Jingyuan Mechanical Equipment Co., Ltd. 浙江竞远机械设备有限公司(1995)	Jinhua 金华市	Zhejiang 浙江省	(0579)2272911 (0579)2271161	365	Foreign Funded 外商投资	31,274	3,448(4)	56,600	Testing Machine 试验机
Suzhou Testing Instrument General Factory 苏州试验仪器总厂(1956)	Suzhou 苏州市	Jiangsu 江苏省	(0512)68292821 (0512)68272243	258	Joint Stock 股份制	29,556	1,058(16)	40,996	Testing Machine 试验机
Weihai Testing Machinery Manufacturing Co., Ltd. 威海市试验机械制造有限公司(1977)	Weihai 威海市	Shandong 山东省	(0631)5322997 (0631)5320878	260	Joint Stock 股份制	24,020	2,340(10)	15,590	Universal Materials Testing Machine万能材料试验机
Ji'nan Testing Instrument & Equipment Factory 济南市试验仪器设备厂(1980)	Jinan 济南市	Shandong 山东省	(0531)7983383 (0531)7983383	58	Joint Stock 股份制	20,390	2,569(7)	6,839	Impacting Testing Machine 冲击试验机
Beijing Railway Scientific Instrument Equipment Factory 北京铁道科学仪器设备厂(1972)	Beijing 北京市	Beijing 北京市	(010)62256316 (010)62256316	91	State-owned 国有企业	17,039	878(17)	9,473	Probe Head 探头

Top 10 Cities by Revenue 销售收入排名前10位城市	Province 省	Market share 市场份额 (%)	Number of firms 企业个数
Jinan 济南市	Shandong 山东省	18.67	2
Shanghai 上海市	Shanghai 上海市	14.67	7
Zhongshan 中山市	Guangdong 广东省	7.20	1
Wuxi 无锡市	Jiangsu 江苏省	5.83	1
Dandong 丹东市	Liaoning 辽宁省	5.60	3
Yantai 烟台市	Shandong 山东省	4.82	1
Tangshan 唐山市	Hebei 河北省	3.81	1
Jinhua 金华市	Zhejiang 浙江省	3.74	1
Tianshui 天水市	Gansu 甘肃省	3.62	2
Suzhou 苏州市	Jiangsu 江苏省	3.54	1

10 Major Wholesalers 十家主要批发商	City 城市	Province 省	Telephone/Fax 电话/传真
SU MEC 中设江苏机械设备进出口（集团）公司	Nanjing 南京市	Jiangsu 江苏省	(025)4511888 (025)4411772
China Poster Mobile Communications Equipment Co.,Ltd. 中邮普泰移动通信设备股份有限公司	Beijing 北京市	Beijing 北京市	(010)66426993 (010)66426837
Sino Kama Co., Ltd. 中泰凯马股份有限公司	Shanghai 上海市	Shanghai 上海市	(021)62031188 (021)62030851
China Huayuan Group Co.,Ltd. 中国华源集团有限公司	Shanghai 上海市	Shanghai 上海市	(021)62031188 (021)62032288
Zhejiang Crand Imp.& Exp.Co.,Ltd. 浙江远大进出口有限公司	Ningbo 宁波市	Zhejiang 浙江省	(0574)87720170 (0574)87723350
Shandong Machinery Import & Export Group Corporation 山东省机械进出口集团公司	Qingdao 青岛市	Shandong 山东省	(0532)2661628 (0532)2991655
Qingdao Haier International Trade Co.,Ltd. 青岛海尔国际贸易有限公司	Qingdao 青岛市	Shandong 山东省	(0532)8938337 (0532)8939494
Guangdong Machinery Import & Export Group Corporation 广东省机械进出口集团公司	Guangzhou 广州市	Guangdong 广东省	(020)87782168 (020)87771803
China National Machinery Equipment Import & Export Corporation 中国机械设备进出口总公司	Beijing 北京市	Beijing 北京市	(010)63474506 (010)63261865
Beijing Cellstar Co.,Ltd. 北京蜂星事达电讯有限公司	Beijing 北京市	Beijing 北京市	(010)64602050 (010)64672648

4217: Laboratory Instruments and Equipment
实验室仪器及装置制造业

The industry accounts for 0.004% of the total revenue of China's industrial sector in 2002. The rate of return on assets is 2.78%. 73.91% of all firms in the industry made a profit while 26.09% had negative returns.The top province in terms of the industry's revenue is Jiangsu, accounting for 26.44% of the total revenue.
2002年本行业收入占全行业的0.004%，资产利润率为2.78%。73.91%的企业赢利，26.09%的企业亏损。收入最高的省为江苏省，占本行业的26.44%。

	Total number of firms 企业总数	Total number of employees 职工总数	Total revenue (Mil.RMB) 总销售收入（百万元）	Total profit (Mil.RMB) 总利润（百万元）	Return on assets 资产利润率 (%)	Return on equity 权益利润率 (%)	Labour productivity ('000 RMB/ worker) 劳动生产率（千元/人）	Debts/ assets 资产负债率 (%)	Total assets (Mil.RMB) 总资产（百万元）
Industry Overall 行业总体	23	3,356	437	14	2.78	7.72	42.25	63.95	519

	Number of firms 企业个数	Average number of employees 平均职工人数	Average revenue ('000 RMB) 平均销售收入（千元）	Average profit ('000 RMB) 平均利润（千元）	Return on assets 资产利润率 (%)	Return on equity 权益利润率 (%)	Labour productivity ('000 RMB/ worker) 劳动生产率（千元/人）	Debts/ assets 资产负债率 (%)	Average total assets ('000 RMB) 平均总资产（千元）
By ownership 产业所有权									
State-owned 国有	11	132	7,689	-96	-0.35	-1.52	23.40	76.88	27,305
Collective-owned 集体	2	84	40,027	3,277	48.16	98.23	218.92	50.97	6,803
Foreign & Overseas Chinese Funded 三资	2	52	6,510	163	2.20	3.21	45.17	31.53	7,414
By regional distribution 地区分布									
Central-North 华北	6	164	11,414	661	2.51	4.73	31.09	47.03	26,363
Beijing 北京	4	230	15,598	958	2.51	4.71	30.89	46.61	38,095
Tianjin 天津	2	32	3,046	67	2.29	5.48	34.06	58.10	2,899
Hebei 河北									
Shanxi 山西									
Inner Mongolia 内蒙古									
Northeast 东北	2	75	12,437	44	0.82	1.16	24.94	29.24	5,377
Liaoning 辽宁	2	75	12,437	44	0.82	1.16	24.94	29.24	5,377
Jilin 吉林									
Heilongjiang 黑龙江									
Central-East 华东	7	138	33,418	1,900	10.75	15.97	74.06	32.70	17,674
Shanghai 上海	3	197	12,412	882	5.10	9.39	28.24	45.67	17,286
Jiangsu 江苏	1	100	115,480	3,800	9.30	10.99	154.40	15.37	40,850
Zhejiang 浙江	1	50	5,170	155	1.33	1.75	29.44	23.77	11,649
Anhui 安徽									
Fujian 福建	1	101	6,670	246	2.54	4.58	47.23	44.46	9,678
Jiangxi 江西									
Shandong 山东	1	126	69,370	6,450	66.63	103.04	264.79	35.33	9,680
Central-South 中南	7	138	11,333	-857	-3.13	-173.47	20.78	98.20	27,420
Henan 河南									
Hubei 湖北	2	41	5,883	54	1.75		46.30	109.21	3,094
Hunan 湖南	3	186	9,297	-2,166	-4.78		5.34	112.90	45,361
Guangdong 广东	2	163	19,837	194	0.78	1.80	40.94	56.54	24,837
Guangxi 广西									
Hainan 海南									
Southwest 西南	1	290	30,162	3,109	8.98	34.33	54.06	73.84	34,612
Chongqing 重庆	1	290	30,162	3,109	8.98	34.33	54.06	73.84	34,612
Sichuan 四川									
Guizhou 贵州									
Yunnan 云南									
Tibet 西藏									
Northwest 西北									
Shaanxi 陕西									
Gansu 甘肃									
Qinghai 青海									
Ningxia 宁夏									
Xinjiang 新疆									

4217: Laboratory Instruments and Equipment

实验室仪器及装置制造业

Year 年份	Number of firms 企业个数	Rate of change 变化率 (%)	Number of employees 职工人数 (人)	Rate of change 变化率 (%)	Total revenue (Mil. RMB) 总销售收入 (百万元)	Rate of change 变化率 (%)	Total profit (Mil RMB) 总利润 (百万元)	Rate of change 变化率 (%)
2000	27		4,429		298		-9	
2001	30	11.11	3,545	-19.96	404	35.57	19	-
2002	23	-23.33	3,356	-5.33	437	8.17	14	-26.32

Major Products 主要产品	Output 产量	Unit 单位

10 Main Firms with Maximal Revenue (year founded) 收入最大的十家主要企业（创办年份）	City 城市	Province 省	Telephone/fax 电话/传真	Number of employees 职工人数	Ownership 产业所有权	Revenue ('000 RMB) 销售收入（千元）	Profit('000 RMB) (rank) 利润（千元）（排名）	Total assets ('000 RMB) 总资产（千元）	Major products 主要产品
Nanjing Aeronautical University Yihang Science & Technology 南京航大意航科技股份有限公司(2000)	Nanjing 南京市	Jiangsu 江苏省	(025)4820099 (025)4807203	100	Limited-Liability 有限公司	115,480	3,800(2)	40,850	Motor-driven Rotating Platform 电动转台
Rongcheng Testing Instrument Factory 荣成实验仪器厂(1991)	Weihai 威海市	Shandong 山东省	(0631)7681110	126	Collective-owned 集体企业	69,370	6450(1)	9,680	Ergometer 测力机
Beijing Instrument Factory 北京仪器厂(1954)	Beijing 北京市	Beijing 北京市	(010)65813041 (010)65813041	554	State-owned 国有企业	45,675	3,023(4)	129,180	Vacuum Coating Machine真空镀膜机
Chongqing Yinhe Testing Instrument Co., Ltd. 重庆银河实验仪器有限公司(1966)	Chongqing 重庆市	Chongqing 重庆市	(023)68242995 (023)68242993	290	Limited-Liability 有限公司	30,162	3,109(3)	34,612	Dry Box 干燥箱
Kerric Lab Equipment Development Factory 三水市科艺实验室设备研制厂(2000)	Foshan 佛山市	Guangdong 广东省	(0757)7238778 (0757)7238778	70	Private Partnership 私营合伙	28,253	-	28,396	Experiment Equipment 实验设备
Sanshui Longsea Xiandai Lab Equipment Co.Ltd 长沙长海现代实验室设备有限公司(2001)	Changsha 长沙市	Hunan 湖南省	(0731)4015894 (0731)4015856	246	Private Owned 私营企业	21,528	-	9,870	Laboratory Equipment实验室设备
Liaoyang Yuda Teaching Equipment Co., Ltd. 辽阳育达教学设备有限公司(1999)	Liaoyang 辽阳市	Liaoning 辽宁省	(0419)2191103 (0419)2191108	120	Private Owned 私营企业	20,300	650(8)	6,543	Physics Laboratory Equipment物理实验室设备
Beijing Photoelectricity Equipment Factory 北京光电设备厂(1986)	Beijing 北京市	Beijing 北京市	(010)68033263 (010)68033263	314	State-owned 国有企业	8,507	142(13)	17,202	Laboratory Equipment & Fittings实验室设备及装置
Shanghai Renshi Electronics Co., Ltd. 上海任氏电子有限公司(1993)	Shanghai 上海市	Shanghai 上海市	(021)57619599 (021)57619598	75	Foreign Funded 外商投资	8,447	888(6)	10,616	Acid-Alkalinity Instrument酸碱值测控仪器
Qinghua University Science & Education Instrument Factory 清华大学科教仪器厂(1998)	Beijing 北京市	Beijing 北京市	(010)62782245 (010)62785777	46	State-owned 国有企业	8,045	719(7)	5,472	Teaching Instrument 教学仪器

Top 10 Cities by Revenue 销售收入排名前10位城市	Province 省	Market share 市场份额 (%)	Number of firms 企业个数
Nanjing 南京市	Jiangsu 江苏省	26.44	1
Weihai 威海市	Shandong 山东省	15.88	1
Beijing 北京市	Beijing 北京市	14.28	4
Shanghai 上海市	Shanghai 上海市	8.53	3
Chongqing 重庆市	Chongqing 重庆市	6.91	1
Foshan 佛山市	Guangdong 广东省	6.47	1
Changsha 长沙市	Hunan 湖南省	6.39	3
Liaoyang 辽阳市	Liaoning 辽宁省	4.65	1
Huanggang 黄冈市	Hubei 湖北省	2.69	2
Shaoguan 韶关市	Guangdong 广东省	2.61	1

10 Major Wholesalers 十家主要批发商	City 城市	Province 省	Telephone/Fax 电话/传真
SU MEC 中设江苏机械设备进出口（集团）公司	Nanjing 南京市	Jiangsu 江苏省	(025)4511888 (025)4411772
China Poster Mobile Communications Equipment Co.,Ltd. 中邮普泰移动通信设备股份有限公司	Beijing 北京市	Beijing 北京市	(010)66426993 (010)66426837
Sino Kama Co., Ltd. 中泰凯马股份有限公司	Shanghai 上海市	Shanghai 上海市	(021)62031188 (021)62030851
China Huayuan Group Co.,Ltd. 中国华源集团有限公司	Shanghai 上海市	Shanghai 上海市	(021)62031188 (021)62032288
Zhejiang Crand Imp.& Exp.Co.,Ltd. 浙江远大进出口有限公司	Ningbo 宁波市	Zhejiang 浙江省	(0574)87720170 (0574)87723350
Shandong Machinery Import & Export Group Corporation 山东省机械进出口集团公司	Qingdao 青岛市	Shandong 山东省	(0532)2661628 (0532)2991655
Qingdao Haier International Trade Co.,Ltd. 青岛海尔国际贸易有限公司	Qingdao 青岛市	Shandong 山东省	(0532)8938337 (0532)8939494
Guangdong Machinery Import & Export Group Corporation 广东省机械进出口集团公司	Guangzhou 广州市	Guangdong 广东省	(020)87782168 (020)87771803
China National Machinery Equipment Import & Export Corporation中国机械设备进出口总公司	Beijing 北京市	Beijing 北京市	(010)63474506 (010)63261865
Beijing Cellstar Co.,Ltd. 北京蜂星事达电讯有限公司	Beijing 北京市	Beijing 北京市	(010)64602050 (010)64672648

4218: General Meter Parts and Equipment

通用仪器仪表元件、器件制造业

The industry accounts for 0.018% of the total revenue of China's industrial sector in 2002. The rate of return on assets is 6.31%. 83.05% of all firms in the industry made a profit while 16.95% had negative returns.The top province in terms of the industry's revenue is Hunan, accounting for 26.82% of the total revenue.
2002年本行业收入占全行业的0.018%，资产利润率为6.31%。83.05%的企业赢利，16.95%的企业亏损。收入最高的省为湖南省，占本行业的26.82%。

	Total number of firms 企业总数	Total number of employees 职工总数	Total revenue (Mil.RMB) 总销售收入（百万元）	Total profit (Mil.RMB) 总利润（百万元）	Return on assets 资产利润率（%）	Return on equity 权益利润率（%）	Labour productivity ('000 RMB/ worker) 劳动生产率（千元/人）	Debts/ assets 资产负债率（%）	Total assets (Mil.RMB) 总资产（百万元）
Industry Overall 行业总体	59	10,743	1,893	160	6.31	14.37	57.22	56.06	2,532

	Number of firms 企业个数	Average number of employees 平均职工人数	Average revenue ('000 RMB) 平均销售收入（千元）	Average profit ('000 RMB) 平均利润（千元）	Return on assets 资产利润率（%）	Return on equity 权益利润率（%）	Labour productivity ('000 RMB/ worker) 劳动生产率（千元/人）	Debts/ assets 资产负债率（%）	Average total assets ('000 RMB) 平均总资产（千元）
By ownership 产业所有权									
State-owned 国有	6	339	117,042	12,252	5.34	12.49	106.79	57.25	229,462
Collective-owned 集体	3	42	3,940	150	2.56	4.67	23.47	45.29	5,865
Foreign & Overseas Chinese Funded 三资	15	208	32,521	2,598	7.14	10.42	59.94	31.44	36,368
By regional distribution 地区分布									
Central-North 华北	5	139	13,431	60	0.29	0.58	93.70	50.20	20,615
Beijing 北京	3	50	7,572	425	6.93	9.52	49.33	27.18	6,131
Tianjin 天津	2	274	22,220	-488	-1.15	-2.57	105.87	55.20	42,342
Hebei 河北									
Shanxi 山西									
Inner Mongolia 内蒙古									
Northeast 东北	1	38						100.34	50,119
Liaoning 辽宁	1	38						100.34	50,119
Jilin 吉林									
Heilongjiang 黑龙江									
Central-East 华东	47	169	23,748	1,815	8.17	18.19	41.46	55.09	22,224
Shanghai 上海	7	228	29,828	1,723	4.32	10.70	37.94	59.60	39,847
Jiangsu 江苏	17	172	22,046	1,940	8.39	15.97	36.65	47.44	23,115
Zhejiang 浙江	11	82	8,739	678	10.73	25.20	31.98	57.42	6,322
Anhui 安徽									
Fujian 福建	3	142	14,010	-856	-4.84	-5.71	19.29	15.26	17,706
Jiangxi 江西									
Shandong 山东	9	236	43,826	3,931	14.15	47.03	59.21	69.90	27,774
Central-South 中南	3	648	191,811	7,572	1.89	4.68	107.88	59.63	401,001
Henan 河南									
Hubei 湖北	2	524	33,954	-1,480	-1.77		24.68	101.73	83,722
Hunan 湖南	1	897	507,525	25,677	2.48	5.26	205.09	52.82	1,035,560
Guangdong 广东									
Guangxi 广西									
Hainan 海南									
Southwest 西南	1	30	126,334	50,790	41.30	49.30	226.00	16.21	122,969
Chongqing 重庆	1	30	126,334	50,790	41.30	49.30	226.00	16.21	122,969
Sichuan 四川									
Guizhou 贵州									
Yunnan 云南									
Tibet 西藏									
Northwest 西北	2	36	3,800	350	8.78	20.31	38.44	56.78	3,988
Shaanxi 陕西	1	37	7,200	700	13.44	33.65	53.00	60.08	5,210
Gansu 甘肃	1	35	399				23.06	50.56	2,765
Qinghai 青海									
Ningxia 宁夏									
Xinjiang 新疆									

4218: General Meter Parts and Equipment

通用仪器仪表元件、器件制造业

Year 年份	Number of firms 企业个数	Rate of change 变化率 (%)	Number of employees 职工人数 (人)	Rate of change 变化率 (%)	Total revenue (Mil. RMB) 总销售收入 (百万元)	Rate of change 变化率 (%)	Total profit (Mil RMB) 总利润 (百万元)	Rate of change 变化率 (%)
2000	55		10,064		1,952		90	
2001	64	16.36	11,102	10.31	1,795	-8.04	113	25.56
2002	59	-7.81	10,743	-3.23	1,893	5.46	160	41.59

Major Products 主要产品	Output 产量	Unit 单位
Meter Component 仪表元件	5	100,000,000 Pieces 亿件

10 Main Firms with Maximal Revenue (year founded) 收入最大的十家主要企业（创办年份）	City 城市	Province 省	Telephone/fax 电话/传真	Number of employees 职工人数	Ownership 产业所有权	Revenue ('000 RMB) 销售收入 (千元)	Profit('000 RMB) (rank) 利润(千元) (排名)	Total assets ('000 RMB) 总资产 (千元)	Major products 主要产品
Zhuzhou Times Electric Group 株洲时代集团公司(1959)	Zhuzhou 株洲市	Hunan 湖南省	(0733)8498353 (0733)8432946	897	State-owned 国有企业	507,525	25677(2)	1,035,560	Locomotive Electronic Cupboard机车电子柜
Rongcheng Yuxiang Industrial Co., Ltd. 荣成宇翔实业有限公司(1985)	Weihai 威海市	Shandong 山东省	(0631)7411163 (0631)7411260	326	mited-Liability 有限公司	241,500	19,280(3)	32,040	Gas Meter 煤气表
Sam Electrical Appliance (Nantong)Co., Ltd. 山姆电器(南通)有限公司(1995)	Nantong 南通市	Jiangsu 江苏省	(0513)5601590 (0513)5541136	522	Foreign Funded 外商投资	85,959	4,330(9)	83,218	Aim Mirror 瞄准镜
Qingdao Hakin Meter(Group)Co.,LTD. 青岛华青仪表（集团）有限公司(1998)	Qingdao 青岛市	Shandong 山东省	(0532)5870388 (0532)3391888	500	'rivate Owned 私营企业	79,716	13,518(5)	81,589	Meter 仪表
Shanghai Alloy Co., Ltd. 上海合金有限公司(1952)	Shanghai 上海市	Shanghai 上海市	(021)69987188 (021)69987188	545	ate Enterprises 国有独资	77,869	142(32)	150,231	Brass Wires 康铜丝
Xiangfan Meter Component Factory 襄樊市仪表元件厂(1966)	Xiangfan 襄樊市	Hubei 湖北省	(0710)3502754 (0710)3500847	750	State-owned 国有企业	64,750	2,430(12)	80,300	Transistor & Module 晶闸管及其模块
Suzhou Mir Mechatronic Elements Co., Ltd. 苏州凯旋机电元件有限公司(1994)	Suzhou 苏州市	Jiangsu 江苏省	(0512)65241958 (0512)65241951	134	oreign Funded 外商投资	47,846	4,432(8)	62,674	Mould 模具
Celtron Science & Technology (Tianjin) Co.,Ltd. 世铨科技(天津)有限公司(1993)	Tianjin 天津市	Tianjin 天津市	(022)28352466 (022)28357261	415	oreign Funded 外商投资	39,637	1,462(16)	64,969	Sensor 传感器
Fuqing Zhaohe Chenghong Electronics Co., Ltd. 福清昭和成鸿电子有限公司(2000)	Fuzhou 福州市	Fujian 福建省	(0591)5377787 (0591)5377737	138	oreign Funded 外商投资	27,096	-	28,714	Instrument & Meter 仪器仪表
Shanghai Xiangming Equipment Box Co., Ltd. 上海祥明仪表机箱有限公司(1996)	Shanghai 上海市	Shanghai 上海市	(021)56680929 (021)56502794	350	'rivate Owned 私营企业	23,838	4,210(10)	20,568	Instrument & Meter Casing 仪表仪器机箱

Top 10 Cities by Revenue 销售收入排名前10位城市	Province 省	Market share 市场份额 (%)	Number of firms 企业个数
Zhuzhou 株洲市	Hunan 湖南省	26.82	1
Weihai 威海市	Shandong 山东省	12.76	1
Shanghai 上海市	Shanghai 上海市	11.03	7
Suzhou 苏州市	Jiangsu 江苏省	7.42	5
Chongqing 重庆市	Chongqing 重庆市	6.67	1
Nantong 南通市	Jiangsu 江苏省	4.83	2
Qingdao 青岛市	Shandong 山东省	4.38	2
Xiangfan 襄樊市	Hubei 湖北省	3.59	2
Nanjing 南京市	Jiangsu 江苏省	3.19	1
Tianjin 天津市	Tianjin 天津市	2.35	2

10 Major Wholesalers 十家主要批发商	City 城市	Province 省	Telephone/Fax 电话/传真
SU MEC 中设江苏机械设备进出口（集团）公司	Nanjing 南京市	Jiangsu 江苏省	(025)4511888 (025)4411772
China Poster Mobile Communications Equipment Co.,Ltd. 中邮普泰移动通信设备股份有限公司	Beijing 北京市	Beijing 北京市	(010)66426993 (010)66426837
Sino Kama Co., Ltd. 中泰凯马股份有限公司	Shanghai 上海市	Shanghai 上海市	(021)62031188 (021)62030851
China Huayuan Group Co.,Ltd. 中国华源集团有限公司	Shanghai 上海市	Shanghai 上海市	(021)62031188 (021)62032288
Zhejiang Crand Imp.& Exp.Co.,Ltd. 浙江远大进出口有限公司	Ningbo 宁波市	Zhejiang 浙江省	(0574)87720170 (0574)87723350
Shandong Machinery Import & Export Group Corporation 山东省机械进出口集团公司	Qingdao 青岛市	Shandong 山东省	(0532)2661628 (0532)2991655
Qingdao Haier International Trade Co.,Ltd. 青岛海尔国际贸易有限公司	Qingdao 青岛市	Shandong 山东省	(0532)8938337 (0532)8939494
Guangdong Machinery Import & Export Group Corporation 广东省机械进出口集团公司	Guangzhou 广州市	Guangdong 广东省	(020)87782168 (020)87771803
China National Machinery Equipment Import & Export Corporation 中国机械设备进出口总公司	Beijing 北京市	Beijing 北京市	(010)63474506 (010)63261865
Beijing Cellstar Co.,Ltd. 北京蜂星事达电讯有限公司	Beijing 北京市	Beijing 北京市	(010)64602050 (010)64672648

4219: Other General Meters 其他通用仪表制造业

The industry accounts for 0.023% of the total revenue of China's industrial sector in 2002. The rate of return on assets is 6.24%. 90.00% of all firms in the industry made a profit while 10.00% had negative returns.The top province in terms of the industry's revenue is Zhejiang, accounting for 41.53% of the total revenue.
2002年本行业收入占全行业的0.023%，资产利润率为6.24%。90.00%的企业赢利，10.00%的企业亏损。收入最高的省为浙江省，占本行业的41.53%。

	Total number of firms 企业总数	Total number of employees 职工总数	Total revenue (Mil.RMB) 总销售收入(百万元)	Total profit (Mil.RMB) 总利润(百万元)	Return on assets 资产利润率(%)	Return on equity 权益利润率(%)	Labour productivity ('000 RMB/ worker) 劳动生产率(千元/人)	Debts/ assets 资产负债率(%)	Total assets (Mil.RMB) 总资产(百万元)
Industry Overall 行业总体	100	14,589	2,439	183	6.24	15.43	52.45	59.55	2,935

	Number of firms 企业个数	Average number of employees 平均职工人数	Average revenue ('000 RMB) 平均销售收入（千元）	Average profit ('000 RMB) 平均利润(千元)	Return on assets 资产利润率(%)	Return on equity 权益利润率(%)	Labour productivity ('000 RMB/ worker) 劳动生产率(千元/人)	Debts/ assets 资产负债率(%)	Average total assets ('000 RMB) 平均总资产(千元)
By ownership 产业所有权									
State-owned 国有	8	102	6,438	108	0.82	4.27	18.17	80.88	13,287
Collective-owned 集体	14	191	23,538	2,522	8.58	24.70	30.41	65.25	29,386
Foreign & Overseas Chinese Funded 三资	13	80	22,665	595	2.23	4.07	50.89	45.26	26,729
By regional distribution 地区分布									
Central-North 华北	9	68	20,105	2,279	7.19	16.52	145.17	56.50	31,713
Beijing 北京	7	77	24,174	2,860	7.35	17.00	153.35	56.78	38,933
Tianjin 天津	1	26	6,490				185.88	98.67	5,470
Hebei 河北	1	48	5,240	490	6.60	7.75	30.94	14.82	7,420
Shanxi 山西									
Inner Mongolia 内蒙古									
Northeast 东北	9	164	19,652	2,083	5.78	12.72	46.16	54.54	36,020
Liaoning 辽宁	7	185	22,475	2,457	6.05	13.49	47.53	55.12	40,586
Jilin 吉林									
Heilongjiang 黑龙江	2	88	9,773	773	3.85	7.78	36.07	50.49	20,042
Central-East 华东	71	162	27,536	1,941	6.25	15.86	48.57	60.62	31,068
Shanghai 上海	5	206	51,105	5,154	8.00	29.99	69.65	73.31	64,395
Jiangsu 江苏	16	175	35,128	1,653	4.71	11.57	46.41	59.28	35,078
Zhejiang 浙江	45	146	22,506	1,794	6.81	16.71	49.20	59.23	26,333
Anhui 安徽									
Fujian 福建	2	131	15,022	206	0.83	2.08	50.32	60.27	24,905
Jiangxi 江西	1	680	73,920	4,015	4.95	8.17	24.21	39.44	81,113
Shandong 山东	2	68	10,355	221	6.59	19.11	20.79	65.50	3,352
Central-South 中南	6	124	17,375	1,066	6.34	17.52	58.25	63.80	16,808
Henan 河南	1	245	34,089	1,069	4.18	14.40	89.22	70.94	25,552
Hubei 湖北									
Hunan 湖南	2	77	3,077	-50	-0.74	-4.56	8.45	83.86	6,790
Guangdong 广东	3	115	21,335	1,808	8.79	20.18	58.49	56.44	20,572
Guangxi 广西									
Hainan 海南									
Southwest 西南	4	60	5,152	-78	-1.84	-3.20	25.62	42.56	4,257
Chongqing 重庆	3	58	1,896	37	1.28	3.11	12.78	58.82	2,892
Sichuan 四川									
Guizhou 贵州	1	67	14,922	-424	-5.08	-6.83	58.97	25.66	8,349
Yunnan 云南									
Tibet 西藏									
Northwest 西北	1	30	1,101				17.47	68.17	1,200
Shaanxi 陕西									
Gansu 甘肃	1	30	1,101				17.47	68.17	1,200
Qinghai 青海									
Ningxia 宁夏									
Xinjiang 新疆									

4219: Other General Meters 其他通用仪表制造业

Year 年份	Number of firms 企业个数	Rate of change 变化率 (%)	Number of employees 职工人数 (人)	Rate of change 变化率 (%)	Total revenue (Mil. RMB) 总销售收入 (百万元)	Rate of change 变化率 (%)	Total profit (Mil RMB) 总利润 (百万元)	Rate of change 变化率 (%)
2000	65		12,644		3,048		76	
2001	71	9.23	8,218	-35.00	954	-68.70	62	-18.42
2002	100	40.85	14,589	77.52	2,439	155.66	183	195.16

Major Products 主要产品	Output 产量	Unit 单位

10 Main Firms with Maximal Revenue (year founded) 收入最大的十家主要企业（创办年份）	City 城市	Province 省	Telephone/fax 电话/传真	Number of employees 职工人数	Ownership 产业所有权	Revenue ('000 RMB) 销售收入 (千元)	Profit('000 RMB) (rank) 利润(千元) (排名)	Total assets ('000 RMB) 总资产 (千元)	Major products 主要产品
Ningbo Water Meter Co., Ltd. 宁波水表股份有限公司(1958)	Ningbo 宁波市	Zhejiang 浙江省	(0574)87332931 (0574)87376630	970	Joint Stock 股份制	160,201	22,217(2)	120,733	Flux Meter &Parts 流量仪表及零件
Dandong Dongfa Group Co.,Ltd. 丹东东发集团有限公司(1998)	Dandong 丹东市	Liaoning 辽宁省	(0415)2823402 (0415)2825588	871	Private Owned 私营企业	116,269	13,635(4)	178,497	Gas Meter 煤气表
Hangzhou Hualong Electronic Technique Co., Ltd. 杭州华隆电子技术有限公司(1996)	Hangzhou 杭州市	Zhejiang 浙江省	(0571)88858598 (0571)86714201	253	Limited-Liability 有限公司	85,205	14,770(3)	59,361	Industry Kilowatt-hour Meter 工业用电度表
Jiangsu Changheng Group Automatic Controller Factory 江苏常恒集团自动控制器厂(1993)	Changzhou 常州市	Jiangsu 江苏省	(0519)5718007 (0519)5718375	598	Collective-owned 集体企业	71,150	9,060(7)	125,460	Temperature Controller 温控器
Zhejiang Feiyue Meter Co.,Ltd. 浙江飞跃仪器仪表有限公司(1996)	Wenzhou 温州市	Zhejiang 浙江省	(0577)62787111 (0577)62785577	300	Limited-Liability 有限公司	67,438	3,486(15)	58,500	Kilowatt-hour Meter 电度表
Beijing Kedong Power Control System Co.,Ltd. 北京科东电力控制系统有限责任公司(1995)	Beijing 北京市	Beijing 北京市	(010)62913201 (010)62935006	182	Limited-Liability 有限公司	56,413	11,165(5)	58,887	Electricity Automation Controlling 电力自动化控制
Hengdian Group Linix Motor Co.,Ltd. 横店集团联宜电机有限公司(1968)	Jinhua 金华市	Zhejiang 浙江省	(0579)6633503 (0579)6630757	446	Limited-Liability 有限公司	50,038	5,710(11)	90,699	yySeries Control Mini-motor yy系列控制微电机
Beijing Daheng Electronics Co.,Ltd. 北京大恒电气有限责任公司(1998)	Beijing 北京市	Beijing 北京市	(010)62628380 (010)82678033	112	Limited-Liability 有限公司	49,185	992(35)	64,272	Transducer 变频器
Jiangsu Changheng Group Appliance Products Factory 江苏常恒集团器件制品厂(1992)	Changzhou 常州市	Jiangsu 江苏省	(0519)5718118 (0519)5712153	358	Collective owned 集体企业	45,980	860(36)	77,330	KSD Defender,KSD 保护器
Zhejiang Qiujing Meter Co., Ltd. 浙江求精仪表有限公司(1997)	Wenzhou 温州市	Zhejiang 浙江省	(0577)62789070 (0577)62778099	235	Private Owned 私营企业	42,349	5,904(10)	42,876	Kilowatt-hour Meter 电度表

Top 10 Cities by Revenue 销售收入排名前10位城市	Province 省	Market share 市场份额 (%)	Number of firms 企业个数
Ningbo 宁波市	Zhejiang 浙江省	14.69	17
Hangzhou 杭州市	Zhejiang 浙江省	11.00	7
Shanghai 上海市	Shanghai 上海市	10.48	5
Wenzhou 温州市	Zhejiang 浙江省	10.41	15
Suzhou 苏州市	Jiangsu 江苏省	7.93	4
Changzhou 常州市	Jiangsu 江苏省	7.82	3
Beijing 北京市	Beijing 北京市	6.94	7
Huaian 淮安市	Jiangsu 江苏省	6.22	7
Dandong 丹东市	Liaoning 辽宁省	4.77	1
Jinhua 金华市	Zhejiang 浙江省	3.60	2

10 Major Wholesalers 十家主要批发商	City 城市	Province 省	Telephone/Fax 电话/传真
SU MEC 中设江苏机械设备进出口（集团）公司	Nanjing 南京市	Jiangsu 江苏省	(025)4511888 (025)4411772
China Poster Mobile Communications Equipment Co.,Ltd. 中邮普泰移动通信设备股份有限公司	Beijing 北京市	Beijing 北京市	(010)66426993 (010)66426837
Sino Kama Co., Ltd. 中泰凯马股份有限公司	Shanghai 上海市	Shanghai 上海市	(021)62031188 (021)62030851
China Huayuan Group Co.,Ltd. 中国华源集团有限公司	Shanghai 上海市	Shanghai 上海市	(021)62031188 (021)62032288
Zhejiang Crand Imp.& Exp.Co.,Ltd. 浙江远大进出口有限公司	Ningbo 宁波市	Zhejiang 浙江省	(0574)87720170 (0574)87723350
Shandong Machinery Import & Export Group Corporation 山东省机械进出口集团公司	Qingdao 青岛市	Shandong 山东省	(0532)2661628 (0532)2991655
Qingdao Haier International Trade Co.,Ltd. 青岛海尔国际贸易有限公司	Qingdao 青岛市	Shandong 山东省	(0532)8938337 (0532)8939494
Guangdong Machinery Import & Export Group Corporation 广东省机械进出口集团公司	Guangzhou 广州市	Guangdong 广东省	(020)87782168 (020)87771803
China National Machinery Equipment Import & Export Corporation 中国机械设备进出口总公司	Beijing 北京市	Beijing 北京市	(010)63474506 (010)63261865
Beijing Cellstar Co.,Ltd. 北京蜂星事达电讯有限公司	Beijing 北京市	Beijing 北京市	(010)64602050 (010)64672648

4221: Environment Protecting Meters and Equipment
环境保护仪器仪表制造业

The industry accounts for 0.009% of the total revenue of China's industrial sector in 2002. The rate of return on assets is 4.96%. 86.11% of all firms in the industry made a profit while 13.89% had negative returns.The top province in terms of the industry's revenue is Hubei, accounting for 16.30% of the total revenue.
2002年本行业收入占全行业的0.009%，资产利润率为4.96%。86.11%的企业赢利，13.89%的企业亏损。收入最高的省为湖北省，占本行业的16.30%。

	Total number of firms 企业总数	Total number of employees 职工总数	Total revenue (Mil.RMB) 总销售收入 (百万元)	Total profit (Mil.RMB) 总利润 (百万元)	Return on assets 资产利润率 (%)	Return on equity 权益利润率 (%)	Labour productivity ('000 RMB/ worker) 劳动生产率 (千元/人)	Debts/ assets 资产负债率 (%)	Total assets (Mil.RMB) 总资产 (百万元)
Industry Overall 行业总体	36	5,011	916	77	4.96	10.40	54.50	52.25	1,551

	Number of firms 企业个数	Average number of employees 平均职工人数	Average revenue ('000 RMB) 平均销售收入（千元)	Average profit ('000 RMB) 平均利润 (千元)	Return on assets 资产利润率 (%)	Return on equity 权益利润率 (%)	Labour productivity ('000 RMB/ worker) 劳动生产率 (千元/人)	Debts/ assets 资产负债率 (%)	Average total assets ('000 RMB) 平均总资产 (千元)
By ownership 产业所有权									
State-owned 国有	7	158	4,873	-325	-1.59	-4.43	11.59	63.99	20,384
Collective-owned 集体	2	50	25,176	2,561	62.58	106.69	82.69	41.34	4,093
Foreign & Overseas Chinese Funded 三资	13	121	33,719	2,982	5.88	13.84	81.24	57.53	50,728
By regional distribution 地区分布									
Central-North 华北	11	129	16,233	-1,058	-3.00	-6.98	20.33	57.04	35,263
Beijing 北京	7	98	17,685	-1,992	-5.14	-12.40	21.55	58.56	38,788
Tianjin 天津	2	273	20,784	582	4.50	6.62	10.61	31.97	12,909
Hebei 河北	1	126	5,171	86	0.10	0.26	34.04	60.93	83,547
Shanxi 山西	1	64	8,024	1,062	15.15	26.96	63.02	43.79	7,008
Inner Mongolia 内蒙古									
Northeast 东北	4	212	12,963	1,580	9.94	32.85	39.09	69.75	15,893
Liaoning 辽宁	4	212	12,963	1,580	9.94	32.85	39.09	69.75	15,893
Jilin 吉林									
Heilongjiang 黑龙江									
Central-East 华东	12	87	29,123	4,140	8.98	20.17	99.41	55.49	46,121
Shanghai 上海	3	47	23,177	3,530	14.04	20.19	90.11	30.49	25,153
Jiangsu 江苏	3	77	26,866	3,964	7.51	50.60	96.14	85.17	52,813
Zhejiang 浙江	4	126	25,235	3,753	8.14	17.01	66.48	52.13	46,093
Anhui 安徽									
Fujian 福建									
Jiangxi 江西									
Shandong 山东	2	83	49,202	6,091	9.01	14.83	212.65	39.25	67,588
Central-South 中南	6	104	28,312	2,772	4.75	7.28	89.80	34.75	58,376
Henan 河南									
Hubei 湖北	4	101	37,328	4,046	4.89	7.39	117.98	33.77	82,647
Hunan 湖南	1	187	15,096	357	2.29	4.41	33.55	48.04	15,564
Guangdong 广东	1	34	5,461	90	2.19	6.00	66.00	63.44	4,103
Guangxi 广西									
Hainan 海南									
Southwest 西南	3	360	55,335	5,338	8.18	20.07	47.91	59.26	65,274
Chongqing 重庆	1	363	27,773	2,007	3.92	11.92	21.64	67.07	51,143
Sichuan 四川	2	359	69,116	7,004	9.68	22.26	61.20	56.50	72,340
Guizhou 贵州									
Yunnan 云南									
Tibet 西藏									
Northwest 西北									
Shaanxi 陕西									
Gansu 甘肃									
Qinghai 青海									
Ningxia 宁夏									
Xinjiang 新疆									

4221: Environment Protecting Meters and Equipment

环境保护仪器仪表制造业

Year 年份	Number of firms 企业个数	Rate of change 变化率 (%)	Number of employees 职工人数 (人)	Rate of change 变化率 (%)	Total revenue (Mil. RMB) 总销售收入 (百万元)	Rate of change 变化率 (%)	Total profit (Mil RMB) 总利润 (百万元)	Rate of change 变化率 (%)
2000	31		3,760		568		65	
2001	30	-3.23	4,408	17.23	808	42.25	71	9.23
2002	36	20.00	5,011	13.68	916	13.37	77	8.45

Major Products 主要产品	Output 产量	Unit 单位

10 Main Firms with Maximal Revenue (year founded) 收入最大的十家主要企业（创办年份）	City 城市	Province 省	Telephone/fax 电话/传真	Number of employees 职工人数	Ownership 产业所有权	Revenue ('000 RMB) 销售收入(千元)	Profit('000 RMB) (rank) 利润(千元)(排名)	Total assets ('000 RMB) 总资产(千元)	Major products 主要产品
Qingdao Qianshao Brown&sharpe Co.,Ltd. 青岛前哨朗普测量技术有限公司(1993)	Qingdao 青岛市	Shandong 山东省	(0532)8702188 (0532)4856427	150	Foreign Funded 外商投资	90,939	11,994(2)	121,268	Three Coordinates Measuring Instrument三坐标测量仪器
Sichuan Danfu Refrigeration Compressor Co., Ltd. 四川丹甫制冷压缩机有限责任公司(1997)	Meishan 眉山市	Sichuan 四川省	(0833)8926009 (0833)8926346	616	Limited-Liability 有限公司	89,860	2,230(12)	69,229	Compressor 压缩机
Kunshan Byland Water Treatment Co., Ltd. 昆山半岛水处理有限公司(1995)	Suzhou 苏州市	Jiangsu 江苏省	(0512)57641881 (0512)57641883	150	Overseas Chinese-funded 港澳台资	63,810	11,290(5)	147,120	Machinery Hot Water Treatment机械热水处理
Beijing Fortune Draeger Safely Equipment Co., Ltd. 北京吉祥德尔格安全设备有限公司(1996)	Beijing 北京市	Beijing 北京市	(010)80498000 (010)80498005	64	Foreign Funded 外商投资	39,706	3,130(9)	36,805	Gas Monitoring & Protection Equipment气体监测及防护设备
Beijing Acorp Electromechanical Engineering Co., Ltd. 北京阿科普机电工程有限公司(1992)	Beijing 北京市	Beijing 北京市	(010)68223399 (010)68288347	67	Overseas Chinese-funded 港澳台资	39,434	2,192(13)	52,504	Environment Protection Instrument & Meter环境保护仪器仪表
Hayward Industrial Products (Shanghai)CO.,LTD. 恒维工业过滤(上海)有限公司(1997)	Shanghai 上海市	Shanghai 上海市	(021)58666161 (021)58661238	42	Foreign Funded 外商投资	35,999	7,347(7)	39,227	Strainer 过滤器
Shenyang Daxibi-Dongyu Environmental Monitoring Equipment Co., Ltd. 沈阳大西比-东宇环境监测仪器有限公司(2000)	Shenyang 沈阳市	Liaoning 辽宁省	(024)24501840 (024)24515551	77	Foreign Funded 外商投资	35,658	8,716(6)	31,471	Air Monitoring Instrument空气监测仪器
Tornex Industry & Trading (Shanghai)Co., Ltd. 统能克斯工贸(上海)有限公司(1995)	Shanghai 上海市	Shanghai 上海市	(021)50480302 (021)50643330	53	Foreign Funded 外商投资	29,513	3,182(8)	32,123	TORNEX Series.TORNEX系列
Chongqing Sida Testing Instrument Factory 重庆四达实验仪器厂(1989)	Chongqing 重庆市	Chongqing 重庆市	(023)67530510 (023)67510330	363	Joint Stock 股份制	27,773	2,007(15)	51,143	Environment Testing Equipment环境试验设备
Tianjin Wuqing NO.1 Environmental Protection Equipment Factory 天津市武清县第一环境保护设备厂(1976)	Tianjin 天津市	Tianjin 天津市	(022)29347007 (022)29538696	60	Collective-owned 集体企业	22,550	2,620(10)	1,350	Dust-cleaning Apparatus 除尘设备

Top 10 Cities by Revenue 销售收入排名前10位城市	Province 省	Market share 市场份额 (%)	Number of firms 企业个数
Wuhan 武汉市	Hubei 湖北省	16.30	4
Beijing 北京市	Beijing 北京市	13.52	7
Qingdao 青岛市	Shandong 山东省	10.75	2
Meishan 眉山市	Sichuan 四川省	9.81	1
Jinhua 金华市	Zhejiang 浙江省	8.21	1
Shanghai 上海市	Shanghai 上海市	7.59	3
Suzhou 苏州市	Jiangsu 江苏省	6.97	1
Chengdu 成都市	Sichuan 四川省	5.28	1
Shenyang 沈阳市	Liaoning 辽宁省	4.95	2
Tianjin 天津市	Tianjin 天津市	4.54	2

10 Major Wholesalers 十家主要批发商	City 城市	Province 省	Telephone/Fax 电话/传真
SU MEC 中设江苏机械设备进出口（集团）公司	Nanjing 南京市	Jiangsu 江苏省	(025)4511888 (025)4411772
China Poster Mobile Communications Equipment Co.,Ltd. 中邮普泰移动通信设备股份有限公司	Beijing 北京市	Beijing 北京市	(010)66426993 (010)66426837
Sino Kama Co., Ltd. 中泰凯马股份有限公司	Shanghai 上海市	Shanghai 上海市	(021)62031188 (021)62030851
China Huayuan Group Co.,Ltd. 中国华源集团有限公司	Shanghai 上海市	Shanghai 上海市	(021)62031188 (021)62032288
Zhejiang Crand Imp.& Exp.Co.,Ltd. 浙江远大进出口有限公司	Ningbo 宁波市	Zhejiang 浙江省	(0574)87720170 (0574)87723350
Shandong Machinery Import & Export Group Corporation 山东省机械进出口集团公司	Qingdao 青岛市	Shandong 山东省	(0532)2661628 (0532)2991655
Qingdao Haier International Trade Co.,Ltd. 青岛海尔国际贸易有限公司	Qingdao 青岛市	Shandong 山东省	(0532)8938337 (0532)8939494
Guangdong Machinery Import & Export Group Corporation 广东省机械进出口集团公司	Guangzhou 广州市	Guangdong 广东省	(020)87782168 (020)87771803
China National Machinery Equipment Import & Export Corporation 中国机械设备进出口总公司	Beijing 北京市	Beijing 北京市	(010)63474506 (010)63261865
Beijing Cellstar Co.,Ltd. 北京蜂星事达电讯有限公司	Beijing 北京市	Beijing 北京市	(010)64602050 (010)64672648

4222: Motor Meters and Instruments 汽车仪器仪表制造业

The industry accounts for 0.023% of the total revenue of China's industrial sector in 2002. The rate of return on assets is 9.14%. 83.33% of all firms in the industry made a profit while 16.67% had negative returns.The top province in terms of the industry's revenue is Shanghai, accounting for 28.64% of the total revenue.
2002年本行业收入占全行业的 0.023%，资产利润率为 9.14%。83.33%的企业赢利，16.67%的企业亏损。收入最高的省为上海市，占本行业的28.64%。

	Total number of firms 企业总数	Total number of employees 职工总数	Total revenue (Mil.RMB) 总销售收入 (百万元)	Total profit (Mil.RMB) 总利润 (百万元)	Return on assets 资产利润率 (%)	Return on equity 权益利润率 (%)	Labour productivity ('000 RMB/ worker) 劳动生产率 (千元/人)	Debts/ assets 资产负债率 (%)	Total assets (Mil.RMB) 总资产 (百万元)
Industry Overall 行业总体	48	13,192	2,515	293	9.14	15.93	66.85	42.66	3,210

	Number of firms 企业个数	Average number of employees 平均职工人数	Average revenue ('000 RMB) 平均销售收入（千元）	Average profit ('000 RMB) 平均利润 (千元)	Return on assets 资产利润率 (%)	Return on equity 权益利润率 (%)	Labour productivity ('000 RMB/ worker) 劳动生产率 (千元/人)	Debts/ assets 资产负债率 (%)	Average total assets ('000 RMB) 平均总资产 (千元)
By ownership 产业所有权									
State-owned 国有	4	768	50,528	1,152	0.72	1.98	34.12	63.57	159,834
Collective-owned 集体	3	99	7,631	374	4.99	16.55	30.58	69.87	7,494
Foreign & Overseas Chinese Funded 三资	16	378	108,484	14,851	13.41	20.86	98.64	35.73	110,783
By regional distribution 地区分布									
Central-North 华北	5	173	9,337	-2,237	-6.55	-10.82	18.21	39.45	34,136
Beijing 北京	3	38	5,740	360	13.38	32.09	67.99	58.30	2,693
Tianjin 天津	2	376	14,733	-6,133	-7.54	-12.27	10.58	38.51	81,302
Hebei 河北									
Shanxi 山西									
Inner Mongolia 内蒙古									
Northeast 东北	3	144	35,039	4,627	7.87	17.39	63.57	54.77	58,829
Liaoning 辽宁	1	320	47,542	7,965	12.65	23.96	50.33	47.19	62,947
Jilin 吉林									
Heilongjiang 黑龙江	2	56	28,788	2,958	5.21	12.70	101.38	58.97	56,770
Central-East 华东	29	239	61,322	8,277	11.84	18.79	91.39	36.98	69,893
Shanghai 上海	9	260	80,054	10,174	12.78	18.70	99.61	31.68	79,638
Jiangsu 江苏	3	173	14,718	1,667	4.99	7.90	29.69	36.82	33,410
Zhejiang 浙江	12	224	42,534	3,240	6.83	9.96	58.00	31.41	47,414
Anhui 安徽	4	325	124,128	25,502	16.13	31.03	174.96	48.02	158,121
Fujian 福建									
Jiangxi 江西									
Shandong 山东	1	87	6,789	2,558	30.14	48.09	22.70	37.33	8,487
Central-South 中南	5	421	73,751	9,356	18.06	32.39	48.38	44.24	51,815
Henan 河南									
Hubei 湖北	1	168	7,969	518	4.58	81.70	30.54	94.39	11,305
Hunan 湖南									
Guangdong 广东	3	595	117,032	15,231	19.69	34.00	51.82	42.08	77,340
Guangxi 广西	1	153	9,687	570	3.62	6.05	27.76	40.17	15,752
Hainan 海南									
Southwest 西南	5	557	42,482	779	0.68	1.67	37.11	59.29	114,367
Chongqing 重庆	1	65	22,426	1,129	2.79	3.62	80.72	22.92	40,477
Sichuan 四川	4	680	47,496	691	0.52	1.37	36.07	62.06	132,840
Guizhou 贵州									
Yunnan 云南									
Tibet 西藏									
Northwest 西北	1	78	3,991	-128	-2.45	-4.34	6.86	43.54	5,218
Shaanxi 陕西									
Gansu 甘肃	1	78	3,991	-128	-2.45	-4.34	6.86	43.54	5,218
Qinghai 青海									
Ningxia 宁夏									
Xinjiang 新疆									

4222: Motor Meters and Instruments 汽车仪器仪表制造业

Year 年份	Number of firms 企业个数	Rate of change 变化率 (%)	Number of employees 职工人数 (人)	Rate of change 变化率 (%)	Total revenue (Mil. RMB) 总销售收入 (百万元)	Rate of change 变化率 (%)	Total profit (Mil RMB) 总利润 (百万元)	Rate of change 变化率 (%)
2000	30		9,002		1,772		195	
2001	40	33.33	10,916	21.26	1,885	6.38	218	11.79
2002	48	20.00	13,192	20.85	2,515	33.42	293	34.40

Major Products 主要产品	Output 产量	Unit 单位
Automobile Instrument & Meter 汽车仪器仪表	1,277	10,000 Units 万台

10 Main Firms with Maximal Revenue (year founded) 收入最大的十家主要企业（创办年份）	City 城市	Province 省	Telephone/fax 电话/传真	Number of employees 职工人数	Ownership 产业所有权	Revenue ('000 RMB) 销售收入 (千元)	Profit('000 RMB) (rank) 利润(千元) (排名)	Total assets ('000 RMB) 总资产 (千元)	Major products 主要产品
Siemens VDO Automotive (Wuhu) Co., Ltd.	Wuhu	Anhui	(0553)5844088		Foreign Funded				Automobile Combination Meter
西门子威迪欧汽车电子(芜湖)有限公司(1995)	芜湖市	安徽省	(0553)5844288	234	外商投资	402,881	91,690(1)	323,587	汽车组合仪表
Visteon Electronimics (Shangfai) Co., Ltd.	Shanghai	Shanghai	(021)57741278		Foreign Funded				Automobile Instrument & Meter
伟世通电子(上海)有限公司(1994)	上海市	上海市	(021)57741271	147	外商投资	321,525	64,533(2)	314,528	汽车仪器仪表
Shanghai Delco Electronic Instrument Co., Ltd.	Shanghai	Shanghai	(021)59666140		Foreign Funded				Automobile Instrument & Meter
上海德科电子仪表有限公司(1996)	上海市	上海市	(021)59666583	1,178	外商投资	280,720	23,327(4)	274,272	汽车仪器仪表
Huanan Yazaki (Shandou) Automobile Parts Co., Ltd.	Shantou	Guangdong	(0754)7882122		Foreign Funded				Automobile Fittings
华南矢崎(汕头)汽车配件有限公司(2001)	汕头市	广东省	(0754)7882322	1,560	外商投资	263,597	23,950(3)	146,924	汽车配件
Magneti Marelli Automobile Meter Co.,Ltd.	Guangzhou	Guangdong	(020)86601808		Foreign Funded				Automobile Meter
广州马瑞利汽车仪表有限公司(1996)	广州市	广东省	(020)86610838	165	外商投资	81,634	21,372(5)	80,453	汽车仪表
Shangyu Meter Component Factory	Shaoxing	Zhejiang	(0575)2031251		Private Owned				Counter
上虞市仪表元件厂(1997)	绍兴市	浙江省	(0575)2031925	200	私营企业	74,002	7,069(11)	19,130	计数器
Zhejiang Automobile Meter Factory	Shaoxing	Zhejiang	(0575)5181187		Limited-Liability				Automobile Single Meter
浙江汽车仪表厂(1975)	绍兴市	浙江省	(0575)5182593	367	有限公司	55,911	7,137(10)	67,629	汽车单表
Anhui Sanlian Science & Technology Co., Ltd.	Hefei	Anhui	(0551)5319313		Joint Stock				Electronic Police
安徽三联科技股份有限公司(1998)	合肥市	安徽省	(0551)5319277	180	股份制	48,169	13,590(6)	105,197	电子警察
Shanghai Liangbiao Intelligence Terminal Co., Ltd.	Shanghai	Shanghai	(021)64855045		Joint Stock				Taxi Counter Meter
上海良标智能终端股份有限公司(1999)	上海市	上海市	(021)64852348	320	股份制	48,011	1,275(19)	64,756	出租汽车计价表
Liaoyang Jinxing Automobile Inside Ornaments Co., Ltd.	Liaoyang	Liaoning	(0419)3303562		Overseas Chinese-funded				Automobile Meter Plate
辽阳市金兴汽车内饰件有限公司(1998)	辽阳市	辽宁省	(0419)3303545	320	港澳台资	47,542	7,965(9)	62,947	汽车仪表板

Top 10 Cities by Revenue 销售收入排名前10位城市	Province 省	Market share 市场份额 (%)	Number of firms 企业个数
Shanghai 上海市	Shanghai 上海市	28.64	9
Wuhu 芜湖市	Anhui 安徽省	17.53	2
Shaoxing 绍兴市	Zhejiang 浙江省	13.62	3
Shantou 汕头市	Guangdong 广东省	10.48	1
Chengdu 成都市	Sichuan 四川省	7.55	4
Guangzhou 广州市	Guangdong 广东省	3.48	2
Ningbo 宁波市	Zhejiang 浙江省	2.35	3
Harbin 哈尔滨市	Heilongjiang 黑龙江省	2.29	2
Taizhou 台州市	Zhejiang 浙江省	2.17	3
Hefei 合肥市	Anhui 安徽省	1.92	1

10 Major Wholesalers 十家主要批发商	City 城市	Province 省	Telephone/Fax 电话/传真
SU MEC	Nanjing	Jiangsu	(025)4511888
中设江苏机械设备进出口（集团）公司	南京市	江苏省	(025)4411772
China Poster Mobile Communications Equipment Co.,Ltd.	Beijing	Beijing	(010)66426993
中邮普泰移动通信设备股份有限公司	北京市	北京市	(010)66426837
Sino Kama Co., Ltd.	Shanghai	Shanghai	(021)62031188
中泰凯马股份有限公司	上海市	上海市	(021)62030851
China Huayuan Group Co.,Ltd.	Shanghai	Shanghai	(021)62031188
中国华源集团有限公司	上海市	上海市	(021)62032288
Zhejiang Crand Imp.& Exp.Co.,Ltd.	Ningbo	Zhejiang	(0574)87720170
浙江远大进出口有限公司	宁波市	浙江省	(0574)87723350
Shandong Machinery Import & Export Group Corporation	Qingdao	Shandong	(0532)2661628
山东省机械进出口集团公司	青岛市	山东省	(0532)2991655
Qingdao Haier International Trade Co.,Ltd.	Qingdao	Shandong	(0532)8938337
青岛海尔国际贸易有限公司	青岛市	山东省	(0532)8939494
Guangdong Machinery Import & Export Group Corporation	Guangzhou	Guangdong	(020)87782168
广东省机械进出口集团公司	广州市	广东省	(020)87771803
China National Machinery Equipment Import & Export Corporation	Beijing	Beijing	(010)63474506
中国机械设备进出口总公司	北京市	北京市	(010)63261865
Beijing Cellstar Co.,Ltd.	Beijing	Beijing	(010)64602050
北京蜂星事达电讯有限公司	北京市	北京市	(010)64672648

4225: Geology, Prospecting, Mining, and Earthquake Detection Instruments

地质勘探、开采、地震专用仪器制造业

The industry accounts for 0.008% of the total revenue of China's industrial sector in 2002. The rate of return on assets is 1.16%. 82.14% of all firms in the industry made a profit while 17.86% had negative returns.The top province in terms of the industry's revenue is Shannxi, accounting for 29.53% of the total revenue.
2002年本行业收入占全行业的 0.008%，资产利润率为 1.16%。82.14%的企业赢利，17.86%的企业亏损。收入最高的省为陕西省，占本行业的29.53%。

	Total number of firms 企业总数	Total number of employees 职工总数	Total revenue (Mil.RMB) 总销售收入（百万元）	Total profit (Mil.RMB) 总利润（百万元）	Return on assets 资产利润率 (%)	Return on equity 权益利润率 (%)	Labour productivity ('000 RMB/ worker) 劳动生产率（千元/人）	Debts/ assets 资产负债率 (%)	Total assets (Mil.RMB) 总资产（百万元）
Industry Overall 行业总体	28	6,897	884	28	1.16	3.85	35.11	69.87	2,392

	Number of firms 企业个数	Average number of employees 平均职工人数	Average revenue ('000 RMB) 平均销售收入（千元）	Average profit ('000 RMB) 平均利润（千元）	Return on assets 资产利润率 (%)	Return on equity 权益利润率 (%)	Labour productivity ('000 RMB/ worker) 劳动生产率（千元/人）	Debts/ assets 资产负债率 (%)	Average total assets ('000 RMB) 平均总资产（千元）
By ownership 产业所有权									
State-owned 国有	11	406	33,818	-3,805	-2.46	-11.18	21.47	77.97	154,503
Collective-owned 集体	3	291	23,540	866	2.40	4.79	30.04	49.76	36,012
Foreign & Overseas Chinese Funded 三资	4	96	38,650	8,804	12.96	21.72	98.96	40.33	67,944
By regional distribution 地区分布									
Central-North 华北	7	236	35,013	4,477	6.68	18.72	54.46	64.31	67,009
Beijing 北京	2	304	9,424	-17	-0.02	-0.05	10.65	67.43	104,425
Tianjin 天津	4	146	21,026	2,842	11.31	30.96	76.22	63.45	25,117
Hebei 河北	1	462	142,143	20,007	12.52	31.93	84.58	60.78	159,748
Shanxi 山西									
Inner Mongolia 内蒙古									
Northeast 东北	3	429	39,248	2,632	3.02	16.60	33.33	81.82	87,210
Liaoning 辽宁	2	604	51,782	3,214	2.62	15.96	26.11	83.62	122,895
Jilin 吉林									
Heilongjiang 黑龙江	1	79	14,182	1,467	9.26	20.10	143.67	53.93	15,840
Central-East 华东	9	127	15,973	305	1.31	3.07	37.49	57.40	23,365
Shanghai 上海	3	127	26,430	-330	-0.72	-1.75	57.25	58.95	45,878
Jiangsu 江苏	2	278	11,155	75	0.38	0.88	18.54	56.78	19,830
Zhejiang 浙江	3	55	11,028	1,007	11.54	20.26	52.61	43.04	8,727
Anhui 安徽									
Fujian 福建									
Jiangxi 江西									
Shandong 山东	1	46	9,077	566	8.31	55.33	48.30	84.97	6,807
Central-South 中南	5	72	19,533	4,768	9.28	15.09	12.10	38.53	51,388
Henan 河南									
Hubei 湖北	2	93	6,691	46	0.50	1.25	23.23	59.85	9,048
Hunan 湖南									
Guangdong 广东	3	58	28,095	7,916	9.94	15.76	0.19	36.91	79,614
Guangxi 广西									
Hainan 海南									
Southwest 西南	2	210	6,581	2	0.01	0.02	12.38	61.98	18,422
Chongqing 重庆	1	418	13,162	3	0.01	0.02	12.41	61.98	36,843
Sichuan 四川									
Guizhou 贵州									
Yunnan 云南	1	1							
Tibet 西藏									
Northwest 西北	2	1,018	133,468	-19,049	-3.29	-15.59	27.92	78.88	578,802
Shaanxi 陕西	1	2,007	261,190	-38,430	-3.36	-16.37	27.44	79.50	1,145,010
Gansu 甘肃									
Qinghai 青海									
Ningxia 宁夏									
Xinjiang 新疆	1	28	5,746	333	2.64	3.44	62.18	23.14	12,593

4225: Geology, Prospecting, Mining, and Earthquake Detection Instruments

地质勘探、开采、地震专用仪器制造业

Year 年份	Number of firms 企业个数	Rate of change 变化率 (%)	Number of employees 职工人数 (人)	Rate of change 变化率 (%)	Total revenue (Mil. RMB) 总销售收入 (百万元)	Rate of change 变化率 (%)	Total profit (Mil RMB) 总利润 (百万元)	Rate of change 变化率 (%)
2000	23		8,994		524		18	
2001	27	17.39	7,248	-19.41	698	33.21	51	183.33
2002	28	3.70	6,897	-4.84	884	26.65	28	-45.10

Major Products 主要产品	Output 产量	Unit 单位
Geology Prospecting, Drilling & Earthquake Special Instrument & Met 地质勘探、钻采	10,498	Unit 台

10 Main Firms with Maximal Revenue (year founded) 收入最大的十家主要企业（创办年份）	City 城市	Province 省	Telephone/fax 电话/传真	Number of employees 职工人数	Ownership 产业所有权	Revenue ('000 RMB) 销售收入 (千元)	Profit('000 RMB) (rank) 利润(千元) (排名)	Total assets ('000 RMB) 总资产 (千元)	Major products 主要产品
Hebei Junfeng Physical Prospecting Equipment Co., Ltd.	Baoding	Hebei	(0312)8648355		Limited-Liability				Cymoscope
河北俊峰物探装备有限公司(1998)	保定市	河北省	(0312)8648441	462	有限公司	142,143	20,007(2)	159,748	检波器
Fushun Coal Mine Safety Instrument General Factory	Fushun	Liaoning	(0413)7684207		State-owned				Coal Mine Safety Instrument 煤矿
抚顺煤矿安全仪器总厂(1953)	抚顺市	辽宁省	(0413)7676559	771	国有企业	60,104	5,417(5)	177,484	安全仪器
Shanghai ShengKai Science Engineering Co., Ltd.	Shanghai	Shanghai	(021)64290476		Joint Stock				Geological Prospecting Special-purpose Instrument 地质勘
上海神开科技工程有限公司(1993)	上海市	上海市	(021)34030004	125	股份制	57,880	7,120(4)	64,398	探专用仪器
Tianjin Becker Electornic Co., Ltd.	Tianjin	Tianjin	(022)24344560		Foreign Funded				Monitor System
天津贝克电气有限公司(1993)	天津市	天津市		34	外商投资	35,395	7,990(3)	34,740	监控系统
Tianjin Selt Survey Equipment Co., Ltd.	Tianjin	Tianjin	(022)24666113		Foreign Funded				Water Level
天津市赛特测机有限公司(1992)	天津市	天津市	(022)24669581	174	外商投资	29,680	2,640(6)	26,480	水准仪
China Petroleum Shanghai Instrument Co., Ltd.	Shanghai	Shanghai	(021)59113961		Limited-Liability				Compositive Copy-well Instrument 综合
上海中油石油仪器制造有限公司(2000)	上海市	上海市	(021)59113963	50	有限公司	17,850	417(14)	14,442	录井仪
7Desai Electronic Instrument Co.,Ltd.	Daqing	Heilongjiang	(0459)5693930		Collective-owned				Combined Sound Wave Measure Well Instrument 组合
大庆高新技术产业开发区德赛电子仪器公司(1992)	大庆市	黑龙江省	(0459)6868568	79	集体企业	14,182	1,467(8)	15,840	生波测井仪
Chongqing Geology Instrument Factory	Chongqing	Chongqing	(023)65291574		State-owned				Earthquake Special Instrument 地震
重庆地质仪器厂(1969)	重庆市	重庆市	(023)65291750	418	国有企业	13,162	3(21)	36,843	专用仪器
Nanjing Soil Instrument Factory	Nanjing	Jiangsu	(025)4862412		Collective-owned				Construction Equipment
南京土壤仪器厂(1958)	南京市	江苏省	(025)4865546	357	集体企业	12,980	120(18)	23,890	土工仪器
Wuhan Haiwang Electromechanical Engineering Technology Cc	Wuhan	Hubei	(027)88041811		Limited-Liability				Compensation Neutron Well Mesure Instrument 补偿
武汉海王机电工程技术公司(2001)	武汉市	湖北省	(027)88041815	105	有限公司	12,036	270(16)	13,080	中子测井仪

Top 10 Cities by Revenue 销售收入排名前10位城市	Province 省	Market share 市场份额 (%)	Number of firms 企业个数
Xi'an 西安市	Shannxi 陕西省	29.53	1
Baoding 保定市	Hebei 河北省	16.07	1
Tianjin 天津市	Tianjin 天津市	9.51	4
Shenzhen 深圳市	Guangdong 广东省	9.16	1
Shanghai 上海市	Shanghai 上海市	8.97	3
Fushun 抚顺市	Liaoning 辽宁省	6.80	1
Panjin 盘锦市	Liaoning 辽宁省	4.91	1
Shaoxing 绍兴市	Zhejiang 浙江省	3.74	3
Nanjing 南京市	Jiangsu 江苏省	2.52	2
Beijing 北京市	Beijing 北京市	2.13	2

10 Major Wholesalers 十家主要批发商	City 城市	Province 省	Telephone/Fax 电话/传真
SU MEC	Nanjing	Jiangsu	(025)4511888
中设江苏机械设备进出口（集团）公司	南京市	江苏省	(025)4411772
China Poster Mobile Communications Equipment Co.,Ltd.	Beijing	Beijing	(010)66426993
中邮普泰移动通信设备股份有限公司	北京市	北京市	(010)66426837
Sino Kama Co., Ltd.	Shanghai	Shanghai	(021)62031188
中泰凯马股份有限公司	上海市	上海市	(021)62030851
China Huayuan Group Co.,Ltd.	Shanghai	Shanghai	(021)62031188
中国华源集团有限公司	上海市	上海市	(021)62032288
Zhejiang Crand Imp.& Exp.Co.,Ltd.	Ningbo	Zhejiang	(0574)87720170
浙江远大进出口有限公司	宁波市	浙江省	(0574)87723350
Shandong Machinery Import & Export Group Corporation	Qingdao	Shandong	(0532)2661628
山东省机械进出口集团公司	青岛市	山东省	(0532)2991655
Qingdao Haier International Trade Co.,Ltd.	Qingdao	Shandong	(0532)8938337
青岛海尔国际贸易有限公司	青岛市	山东省	(0532)8939494
Guangdong Machinery Import & Export Group Corporation	Guangzhou	Guangdong	(020)87782168
广东省机械进出口集团公司	广州市	广东省	(020)87771803
China National Machinery Equipment Import & Export	Beijing	Beijing	(010)63474506
Corporation 中国机械设备进出口总公司	北京市	北京市	(010)63261865
Beijing Cellstar Co.,Ltd.	Beijing	Beijing	(010)64602050
北京蜂星事达电讯有限公司	北京市	北京市	(010)64672648

4227: Instructional Instruments 教学仪器制造业

The industry accounts for 0.009% of the total revenue of China's industrial sector in 2002. The rate of return on assets is 7.07%. 82.46% of all firms in the industry made a profit while 17.54% had negative returns.The top province in terms of the industry's revenue is Jiangsu, accounting for 53.51% of the total revenue.
2002年本行业收入占全行业的 0.009%，资产利润率为 7.07%。82.46%的企业赢利，17.54%的企业亏损。收入最高的省为江苏省，占本行业的53.51%。

	Total number of firms 企业总数	Total number of employees 职工总数	Total revenue (Mil.RMB) 总销售收入 (百万元)	Total profit (Mil.RMB) 总利润 (百万元)	Return on assets 资产利润率 (%)	Return on equity 权益利润率 (%)	Labour productivity ('000 RMB/ worker) 劳动生产率 (千元/人)	Debts/ assets 资产负债率 (%)	Total assets (Mil.RMB) 总资产 (百万元)
Industry Overall 行业总体	57	4,952	944	60	7.07	13.95	74.46	49.27	850

	Number of firms 企业个数	Average number of employees 平均职工人数	Average revenue ('000 RMB) 平均销售收入 (千元)	Average profit ('000 RMB) 平均利润 (千元)	Return on assets 资产利润率 (%)	Return on equity 权益利润率 (%)	Labour productivity ('000 RMB/ worker) 劳动生产率 (千元/人)	Debts/ assets 资产负债率 (%)	Average total assets ('000 RMB) 平均总资产 (千元)
By ownership 产业所有权									
State-owned 国有	26	57	3,815	-48	-0.59	-1.12	23.91	47.76	8,147
Collective-owned 集体	8	58	7,893	338	5.55	12.29	43.69	54.86	6,084
Foreign & Overseas Chinese Funded 三资	2	240	229,425	24,770	19.05	33.64	427.91	43.37	130,047
By regional distribution 地区分布									
Central-North 华北	11	48	1,856	88	2.49	5.74	9.26	56.62	3,536
Beijing 北京									
Tianjin 天津	7	24	1,089	161	6.27	10.58	2.78	40.73	2,572
Hebei 河北	3	59	3,503	150	4.69	20.58	19.97	77.19	3,195
Shanxi 山西	1	180	2,292	-611	-5.40	-15.22	4.90	64.49	11,308
Inner Mongolia 内蒙古									
Northeast 东北	2	108	6,614	-4,133	-13.48	-24.43	19.81	44.82	30,662
Liaoning 辽宁	2	108	6,614	-4,133	-13.48	-24.43	19.81	44.82	30,662
Jilin 吉林									
Heilongjiang 黑龙江									
Central-East 华东	31	108	26,146	2,078	10.14	19.35	94.00	47.61	20,502
Shanghai 上海	4	109	6,436	-67	-0.35	-0.56	39.32	37.13	19,006
Jiangsu 江苏	5	140	101,062	10,225	18.79	33.05	312.44	43.13	54,406
Zhejiang 浙江	18	94	13,640	652	4.87	10.42	40.49	53.29	13,399
Anhui 安徽	1	60	10,507	656	7.06	27.15	47.23	74.01	9,296
Fujian 福建	2	103	6,985	255	1.99	5.46	20.25	63.62	12,830
Jiangxi 江西									
Shandong 山东	1	245	9,466	665	5.84	10.92	11.41	46.53	11,391
Central-South 中南	9	75	9,715	310	2.85	7.01	60.55	59.28	10,863
Henan 河南	2	56	7,205	1,003	25.12	49.23	39.87	48.97	3,991
Hubei 湖北	3	80	9,701	243	3.15	7.80	39.96	59.65	7,733
Hunan 湖南	1	18	5,436	-728	-10.98	-16.92	195.06	35.09	6,629
Guangdong 广东	3	103	12,828	261	1.31	3.55	76.13	63.19	19,987
Guangxi 广西									
Hainan 海南									
Southwest 西南	2	86	5,721	188	3.03	6.51	18.91	53.36	6,196
Chongqing 重庆	1	160	10,210	338	3.12	7.68	18.89	59.36	10,834
Sichuan 四川									
Guizhou 贵州									
Yunnan 云南	1	11	1,232	38	2.44	2.76	19.18	11.62	1,557
Tibet 西藏									
Northwest 西北	2	10	681	-71	-3.30	-7.04	65.40	53.09	2,134
Shaanxi 陕西									
Gansu 甘肃	2	10	681	-71	-3.30	-7.04	65.40	53.09	2,134
Qinghai 青海									
Ningxia 宁夏									
Xinjiang 新疆									

Year 年份	Number of firms 企业个数	Rate of change 变化率 (%)	Number of employees 职工人数 (人)	Rate of change 变化率 (%)	Total revenue (Mil. RMB) 总销售收入 (百万元)	Rate of change 变化率 (%)	Total profit (Mil RMB) 总利润 (百万元)	Rate of change 变化率 (%)
2000	60		5,651		452		19	
2001	57	-5.00	4,660	-17.54	589	30.31	4	-78.95
2002	57		4,952	6.27	944	60.27	60	1,400.00

Major Products 主要产品	Output 产量	Unit 单位
Electric Teaching Instrument 电教设备	56,803	Unit 台

10 Main Firms with Maximal Revenue (year founded) 收入最大的十家主要企业 (创办年份)	City 城市	Province 省	Telephone/fax 电话/传真	Number of employees 职工人数	Ownership 产业所有权	Revenue ('000 RMB) 销售收入 (千元)	Profit('000 RMB) (rank) 利润(千元) (排名)	Total assets ('000 RMB) 总资产 (千元)	Major products 主要产品
Suzhou Matsushita Communication Industry Co., Ltd.	Suzhou	Jiangsu	(0512)68255606		Foreign Funded				Language Learning System 语言
苏州松下通信工业有限公司(1995)	苏州市	江苏省	(0512)68255811	376	外商投资	449,552	48,540(1)	248,904	学习系统
Fangyuan Scientific & Technological Eterprise Co.,Ltd.	Hangzhou	Zhejiang	(0571)87977846		Limited-Liability				Teaching Instrument
浙江大学方圆科技产业有限公司(1998)	杭州市	浙江省	(0571)87993716	249	有限公司	47,478	835(12)	59,065	教学仪器
Zhejiang Three Peacefuls Scientific Educational Machine Co., Ltd.	Wenzhou	Zhejiang	(0577)67391668		Joint Stock				Teaching Instrument
浙江三和科教仪器有限公司(1995)	温州市	浙江省	(0577)67391008	180	股份制	37,286	3,254(2)	28,389	教学仪器
Jiangmen Education Instrument Factory	Jiangmen	Guangdong	(0750)3332886		Others				Teaching Instrument
江门市教学仪器厂(1978)	江门市	广东省	(0750)3352592	280	其他企业	36,729	693(14)	43,967	教学仪器
Xinghua Shuguang Education Instrument Factory	Taizhou	Jiangsu	(0523)3511618		Collective-owned				Teaching Making Materials 教学
兴化市曙光教学仪器厂(1992)	泰州市	江苏省	(0523)3511999	150	集体企业	28,900	940(10)	10,790	制作材料
Jingzhou Xinke Education Instrument Co., Ltd.	Jingzhou	Hubei	(0716)8474579		Private Owned				Teaching Instrument
荆州新科教学仪器有限公司(1999)	荆州市	湖北省	(0716)8474579	80	私营企业	18,021	180(31)	3,210	教学仪器
Zhejiang Yalong Teaching Instrument Co., Ltd.	Wenzhou	Zhejiang	(0577)67314901		Private Owned				Teachig Products
浙江亚龙教仪有限公司(1992)	温州市	浙江省	(0577)67314678	152	私营企业	15,911	702(13)	30,484	教学产品
Science & Education Instruments of Ecnu	Shanghai	Shanghai	(021)52811134		State-owned				Teaching Instrument
华东师范大学科教仪器厂(1958)	上海市	上海市	(021)52811134	150	国有企业	11,646	1,257(4)	31,646	教学仪器
Quanzhou Heshi Educational Audiovisuals Co., Ltd.	Quanzhou	Fujian	(0595)2033668		Private Owned				WX Series Wireless Earphone WX系列
泉州市河市电教设备有限公司(1986)	泉州市	福建省	(0595)2036660	142	私营企业	11,523	500(20)	17,009	无线耳机
Bengbu Education Instrument Factory	Bengbu	Anhui	(0552)3017191		State-owned				Electrical Source
蚌埠市教学仪器厂(1971)	蚌埠市	安徽省	(0552)3028700	60	国有企业	10,507	656(17)	9,296	电源

Top 10 Cities by Revenue 销售收入排名前10位城市	Province 省	Market share 市场份额 (%)	Number of firms 企业个数
Suzhou 苏州市	Jiangsu 江苏省	47.60	1
Hangzhou 杭州市	Zhejiang 浙江省	13.37	6
Wenzhou 温州市	Zhejiang 浙江省	9.31	6
Jiangmen 江门市	Guangdong 广东省	3.89	1
Taizhou 泰州市	Jiangsu 江苏省	3.06	1
Shanghai 上海市	Shanghai 上海市	2.73	4
Jingzhou 荆州市	Hubei 湖北省	1.91	1
Ningbo 宁波市	Zhejiang 浙江省	1.69	2
Quanzhou 泉州市	Fujian 福建省	1.48	2
Zhengzhou 郑州市	Henan 河南省	1.29	1

10 Major Wholesalers 十家主要批发商	City 城市	Province 省	Telephone/Fax 电话/传真
King Paper Source Trade (shanghai) Co.,Ltd.	Shanghai	Shanghai	(021)62720808
金纸源贸易(上海)有限公司	上海市	上海市	(021)62720909
China National Paper & Pulp Corpration	Beijing	Beijing	(010)67780346
中国纸张纸浆进出口公司	北京市	北京市	(010)67747294
Sinar Mas Linjiang Paper Industry Trade (Beijing) Co.,Ltd.	Beijing	Beijing	(010)65666688
金光林浆纸业贸易(北京)有限公司	北京市	北京市	(010)65669599
Sinar Mas Paper Industry (Xishan) Co.,Ltd.	Wuxi	Jiangsu	(0510)8251188
金光纸业(锡山)有限公司	无锡市	江苏省	(0510)8250906
China Printing Materials General Company	Beijing	Beijing	(010)63442905
中国印刷物资总公司	北京市	北京市	(010)63442900
TSS Eortune Co., ltd.	Tianjin	Tianjin	(022)28131350
天津同鑫进出口有限公司	天津市	天津市	(022)28131353
Wenzhou Import & Export Corpration	Wenzhou	Zhejiang	(0577)88862681
温州市进出口公司	温州市	浙江省	(0577)88844557
Sinar Mas Paper Industry (Xiamen) Co.,Ltd.	Xiamen	Fujian	(0592)2962018
金光纸业(厦门)有限公司	厦门市	福建省	(0592)2962010
Sinar Mas Paper Industry (Shenzhen) Co.,Ltd.	Shenzhen	Guangdong	(0755)83516701
金光纸业(深圳)有限公司	深圳市	广东省	(0755)83516773
Jieyang Ocean Shipping Supply Group Co.,Ltd.	Jieyang	Guangdong	(0663)8239634
揭阳市外轮供应集团有限公司	揭阳市	广东省	(0663)8236186

4230: Electric Measuring Instruments 电子测量仪器制造业

The industry accounts for 0.026% of the total revenue of China's industrial sector in 2002. The rate of return on assets is 4.31%. 82.08% of all firms in the industry made a profit while 17.92% had negative returns.The top province in terms of the industry's revenue is Beijing, accounting for 30.46% of the total revenue.
2002年本行业收入占全行业的 0.026%，资产利润率为 4.31%。82.08%的企业赢利，17.92%的企业亏损。收入最高的省为北京市，占本行业的30.46%。

	Total number of firms 企业总数	Total number of employees 职工总数	Total revenue (Mil.RMB) 总销售收入 (百万元)	Total profit (Mil.RMB) 总利润 (百万元)	Return on assets 资产利润率 (%)	Return on equity 权益利润率 (%)	Labour productivity ('000 RMB/ worker) 劳动生产率 (千元/人)	Debts/ assets 资产负债率 (%)	Total assets (Mil.RMB) 总资产 (百万元)
Industry Overall 行业总体	106	19,285	2,814	175	4.31	11.12	42.39	61.30	4,063

	Number of firms 企业个数	Average number of employees 平均职工人数	Average revenue ('000 RMB) 平均销售收入 (千元)	Average profit ('000 RMB) 平均利润 (千元)	Return on assets 资产利润率 (%)	Return on equity 权益利润率 (%)	Labour productivity ('000 RMB/ worker) 劳动生产率 (千元/人)	Debts/ assets 资产负债率 (%)	Average total assets ('000 RMB) 平均总资产 (千元)
By ownership 产业所有权									
State-owned 国有	24	219	7,718	-87	-0.23	-4.34	12.75	94.63	37,194
Collective-owned 集体	11	227	34,938	368	0.84	2.68	37.68	68.55	43,603
Foreign & Overseas Chinese Funded 三资	22	167	56,662	4,054	7.20	14.77	73.79	51.26	56,330
By regional distribution 地区分布									
Central-North 华北	35	118	28,567	647	1.40	3.92	37.26	64.22	46,166
Beijing 北京	24	111	35,705	302	0.59	1.50	54.81	60.44	50,716
Tianjin 天津	7	107	16,032	1,518	4.26	16.96	-8.18	74.89	35,644
Hebei 河北	2	121	4,410	43	0.15		21.46	132.98	28,993
Shanxi 山西	1	300	21,040	4,800	5.68	9.90	26.61	42.68	84,551
Inner Mongolia 内蒙古	1	167	848	-100	-1.52	-2.10	1.74	27.80	6,580
Northeast 东北	9	101	16,361	1,555	5.22	9.31	64.90	43.95	29,786
Liaoning 辽宁	8	106	16,856	1,511	4.66	8.23	65.77	43.37	32,442
Jilin 吉林									
Heilongjiang 黑龙江	1	60	12,402	1,901	22.25	57.78	52.63	61.49	8,543
Central-East 华东	34	204	34,547	3,446	10.16	22.26	58.03	54.34	33,914
Shanghai 上海	7	98	25,132	2,637	7.58	12.96	90.62	41.47	34,776
Jiangsu 江苏	12	243	54,500	7,509	15.88	37.03	80.33	57.12	47,281
Zhejiang 浙江	6	201	21,160	900	4.88	12.22	36.87	60.01	18,421
Anhui 安徽	3	387	12,247	-768	-2.93	-6.71	12.02	56.31	26,191
Fujian 福建									
Jiangxi 江西									
Shandong 山东	6	159	30,162	918	3.60	8.87	49.41	59.42	25,527
Central-South 中南	20	184	16,439	802	4.16	6.75	27.11	38.30	19,254
Henan 河南	3	73	440	-24	-0.63	-13.42	2.54	95.31	3,762
Hubei 湖北	8	74	10,554	897	5.18	8.02	60.21	35.39	17,320
Hunan 湖南	1	21	500	-1,649	-47.66		-28.90	311.13	3,460
Guangdong 广东	7	405	33,843	1,449	4.41	6.60	21.38	33.19	32,868
Guangxi 广西	1	25	5,635	438	25.87	39.04	160.08	33.73	1,693
Hainan 海南									
Southwest 西南	3	387	39,923	712	0.62	1.34	73.77	53.42	114,174
Chongqing 重庆									
Sichuan 四川	3	387	39,923	712	0.62	1.34	73.77	53.42	114,174
Guizhou 贵州									
Yunnan 云南									
Tibet 西藏									
Northwest 西北	5	498	8,687	592	0.99		7.16	126.56	59,769
Shaanxi 陕西	2	147	5,061	-655	-1.51		10.13	111.94	43,256
Gansu 甘肃	1	1,602	23,440	-4,980	-3.55		7.85	151.43	140,260
Qinghai 青海									
Ningxia 宁夏	2	297	4,937	4,625	12.83	299.13	3.83	95.71	36,037
Xinjiang 新疆									

4230: Electric Measuring Instruments 电子测量仪器制造业

Year 年份	Number of firms 企业个数	Rate of change 变化率 (%)	Number of employees 职工人数 (人)	Rate of change 变化率 (%)	Total revenue (Mil. RMB) 总销售收入 (百万元)	Rate of change 变化率 (%)	Total profit (Mil RMB) 总利润 (百万元)	Rate of change 变化率 (%)
2000	79		21,330		1,962		195	
2001	89	12.66	18,447	-13.52	1,978	0.82	222	13.85
2002	106	19.10	19,285	4.54	2,814	42.26	175	-21.17

Major Products 主要产品	Output 产量	Unit 单位

10 Main Firms with Maximal Revenue (year founded) 收入最大的十家主要企业（创办年份）	City 城市	Province 省	Telephone/fax 电话/传真	Number of employees 职工人数	Ownership 产业所有权	Revenue ('000 RMB) 销售收入 (千元)	Profit('000 RMB) (rank) 利润(千元) (排名)	Total assets ('000 RMB) 总资产 (千元)	Major products 主要产品
Tektronix (Yangzhong) Co., Ltd.	Zhenjiang	Jiangsu	(0511)8324976		Foreign Funded				Oscillograph
泰克(扬中)有限公司(1999)	镇江市	江苏省		94	外商投资	181,722	43,597(1)	72,294	示波器
Time Group Inc.	Beijing	Beijing	(010)62980818		Collective-owned				Detecting Instrument
时代集团公司(1984)	北京市	北京市	(010)62980728	365	集体企业	180,906	1,058(42)	310,045	检测仪器
Gaojin Electronics (Shenzhen) Co., Ltd.	Shenzhen	Guangdong	(0755)28458590		Overseas Chinese-funded				Electronic Clock
高劲电子（深圳）有限公司(1995)	深圳市	广东省	(0755)28458594	1,300	港澳台资	111,034	542(48)	69,749	电子钟表
Shanghai Heraeus Electro-nite Co., Ltd.	Shanghai	Shanghai	(021)54798896		Foreign Funded				Sensor
上海贺利氏电测骑士有限公司(1995)	上海市	上海市	(021)54798826	185	外商投资	82,391	6,030(11)	126,889	传感器
Jiangsu Xiou Electronics Co., Ltd.	Nantong	Jiangsu	(0513)3348888		Private Owned				Electronic Fire Meter
江苏西欧电子有限公司(1999)	南通市	江苏省	(0513)3348888	132	私营企业	72,912	1,417(34)	41,760	电子火表
Jiangsu Yangzhong Electronic Instrument Fatory	Zhenjiang	Jiangsu	(0511)8322022		State-owned				Electronic Measuring Instrument电子
江苏扬中电子仪器厂(1970)	镇江市	江苏省	(0511)8323149	355	国有企业	68,186	1,238(39)	84,447	测量仪器
Beijing Sartorius Instrument & System Engineering Co., Ltd.	Beijing	Beijing	(010)64392846		Foreign Funded				Electronic Balance
北京赛多利斯仪器系统有限公司(1995)	北京市	北京市	(010)64392726	62	外商投资	67,975	11,296(4)	54,843	电子天平
Hongze Right Electronic Equipment Co., Ltd.	Huaian	Jiangsu	(0517)7222718		Limited-Liability				Electronic Measuring Instrument电子
洪泽县瑞特电子设备有限公司(1998)	淮安市	江苏省	(0517)7222761	497	有限公司	61,922	8,102(6)	61,641	测量仪器
Ningbo Zhongce Electron Co., Ltd.	Ningbo	Zhejiang	(0574)87333183		Overseas Chinese-funded				Electronic Measuring Instrument电子
宁波中策电子有限公司(1956)	宁波市	浙江省	(0574)87334525	467	港澳台资	61,274	2,570(21)	52,760	测量仪器
Changzhou Secei Optoelectronics Equipment Co., Ltd.	Changzhou	Jiangsu	(0519)6973926		Limited-Liability				Laser Range Finder 激光
常州二电仪光电子装备有限公司(原二电仪)(1958)	常州市	江苏省	(0519)6960452	427	有限公司	55,160	9,060(5)	55,560	测距仪

Top 10 Cities by Revenue 销售收入排名前10位城市	Province 省	Market share 市场份额 (%)	Number of firms 企业个数
Beijing 北京市	Beijing 北京市	30.46	24
Zhenjiang 镇江市	Jiangsu 江苏省	10.74	3
Shenzhen 深圳市	Guangdong 广东省	6.59	5
Shanghai 上海市	Shanghai 上海市	6.25	7
Weihai 威海市	Shandong 山东省	4.69	1
Tianjin 天津市	Tianjin 天津市	3.99	7
Chengdu 成都市	Sichuan 四川省	3.82	2
Nanjing 南京市	Jiangsu 江苏省	3.18	2
Changzhou 常州市	Jiangsu 江苏省	2.68	2
Wuhan 武汉市	Hubei 湖北省	2.63	6

10 Major Wholesalers 十家主要批发商	City 城市	Province 省	Telephone/Fax 电话/传真
SU MEC	Nanjing	Jiangsu	(025)4511888
中设江苏机械设备进出口（集团）公司	南京市	江苏省	(025)4411772
China Poster Mobile Communications Equipment Co.,Ltd.	Beijing	Beijing	(010)66426993
中邮普泰移动通信设备股份有限公司	北京市	北京市	(010)66426837
Sino Kama Co., Ltd.	Shanghai	Shanghai	(021)62031188
中泰凯马股份有限公司	上海市	上海市	(021)62030851
China Huayuan Group Co.,Ltd.	Shanghai	Shanghai	(021)62031188
中国华源集团有限公司	上海市	上海市	(021)62032288
Zhejiang Crand Imp.& Exp.Co.,Ltd.	Ningbo	Zhejiang	(0574)87720170
浙江远大进出口有限公司	宁波市	浙江省	(0574)87723350
Shandong Machinery Import & Export Group Corporation	Qingdao	Shandong	(0532)2661628
山东省机械进出口集团公司	青岛市	山东省	(0532)2991655
Qingdao Haier International Trade Co.,Ltd.	Qingdao	Shandong	(0532)8938337
青岛海尔国际贸易有限公司	青岛市	山东省	(0532)8939494
Guangdong Machinery Import & Export Group Corporation	Guangzhou	Guangdong	(020)87782168
广东省机械进出口集团公司	广州市	广东省	(020)87771803
China National Machinery Equipment Import & Export	Beijing	Beijing	(010)63474306
Corporation 中国机械设备进出口总公司	北京市	北京市	(010)63261865
Beijing Cellstar Co.,Ltd.	Beijing	Beijing	(010)64602050
北京蜂星事达电讯有限公司	北京市	北京市	(010)64672648

4241: Transmission Measurement and Calibration Instruments
传递标准用计量仪器制造业

The industry accounts for 0.004% of the total revenue of China's industrial sector in 2002. The rate of return on assets is 5.41%. 90.00% of all firms in the industry made a profit while 10.00% had negative returns.The top province in terms of the industry's revenue is Anhui, accounting for 27.35% of the total revenue.
2002年本行业收入占全行业的 0.004%，资产利润率为 5.41%。90.00%的企业赢利，10.00%的企业亏损。收入最高的省为安徽省，占本行业的27.35%。

	Total number of firms 企业总数	Total number of employees 职工总数	Total revenue (Mil.RMB) 总销售收入（百万元）	Total profit (Mil.RMB) 总利润（百万元）	Return on assets 资产利润率（%）	Return on equity 权益利润率（%）	Labour productivity ('000 RMB/ worker) 劳动生产率（千元/人）	Debts/ assets 资产负债率（%）	Total assets (Mil.RMB) 总资产（百万元）
Industry Overall 行业总体	20	2,585	422	31	5.41	9.48	48.31	42.90	573

	Number of firms 企业个数	Average number of employees 平均职工人数	Average revenue ('000 RMB) 平均销售收入（千元）	Average profit ('000 RMB) 平均利润（千元）	Return on assets 资产利润率（%）	Return on equity 权益利润率（%）	Labour productivity ('000 RMB/ worker) 劳动生产率（千元/人）	Debts/ assets 资产负债率（%）	Average total assets ('000 RMB) 平均总资产（千元）
By ownership 产业所有权									
State-owned 国有	2	39	1,035	-179	-12.96		10.25	104.89	1,382
Collective-owned 集体	6	182	37,436	1,876	6.61	18.90	57.86	65.04	28,387
Foreign & Overseas Chinese Funded 三资	3	231	33,530	3,732	3.97	4.88	41.86	18.75	94,041
By regional distribution 地区分布									
Central-North 华北	4	175	20,907	588	0.92	1.21	28.86	23.98	64,173
Beijing 北京	2	261	32,629	634	0.55	0.68	29.29	18.89	115,483
Tianjin 天津	2	89	9,185	543	4.22	13.92	27.58	69.67	12,863
Hebei 河北									
Shanxi 山西									
Inner Mongolia 内蒙古									
Northeast 东北									
Liaoning 辽宁									
Jilin 吉林									
Heilongjiang 黑龙江									
Central-East 华东	13	135	21,891	1,734	7.90	21.20	47.51	62.73	21,947
Shanghai 上海	2	102	15,915	4,467	24.42	36.76	45.54	33.58	18,293
Jiangsu 江苏	4	148	14,572	-348	-2.44	-4.64	20.33	47.53	14,280
Zhejiang 浙江	4	72	9,163	311	5.45	13.67	27.32	60.14	5,712
Anhui 安徽	1	420	115,310	6,470	6.91	28.70	89.33	75.92	93,600
Fujian 福建	1	101	4,023	14	0.45	1.23	15.70	63.84	3,139
Jiangxi 江西									
Shandong 山东	1	155	38,478	7,265	10.09	37.70	98.41	73.24	72,019
Central-South 中南	2	52	26,449	3,060	21.57	25.94	199.94	16.87	14,187
Henan 河南	1	20	41,020	4,850	104.12	349.42	611.65	70.20	4,658
Hubei 湖北	1	84	11,877	1,269	5.35	5.72	101.92	6.40	23,716
Hunan 湖南									
Guangdong 广东									
Guangxi 广西									
Hainan 海南									
Southwest 西南									
Chongqing 重庆									
Sichuan 四川									
Guizhou 贵州									
Yunnan 云南									
Tibet 西藏									
Northwest 西北	1	24	555	2	0.08	0.10	17.58	16.97	2,422
Shaanxi 陕西									
Gansu 甘肃	1	24	555	2	0.08	0.10	17.58	16.97	2,422
Qinghai 青海									
Ningxia 宁夏									
Xinjiang 新疆									

4241: Transmission Measurement and Calibration Instruments

传递标准用计量仪器制造业

Year 年份	Number of firms 企业个数	Rate of change 变化率(%)	Number of employees 职工人数(人)	Rate of change 变化率(%)	Total revenue (Mil. RMB) 总销售收入(百万元)	Rate of change 变化率(%)	Total profit (Mil RMB) 总利润(百万元)	Rate of change 变化率(%)
2000	16		2,375		389		18	
2001	22	37.50	1,960	-17.47	308	-20.82	15	-16.67
2002	20	-9.09	2,585	31.89	422	37.01	31	106.67

Major Products 主要产品	Output 产量	Unit 单位

10 Main Firms with Maximal Revenue (year founded) 收入最大的十家主要企业(创办年份)	City 城市	Province 省	Telephone/fax 电话/传真	Number of employees 职工人数	Ownership 产业所有权	Revenue ('000 RMB) 销售收入(千元)	Profit('000 RMB) (rank) 利润(千元)(排名)	Total assets ('000 RMB) 总资产(千元)	Major products 主要产品
Anhui Shitai Gas Meter General Factory	Chizhou	Anhui	(0556)6411088		Collective-owned				Gas Meter
安徽省石台县煤气仪表总厂(1985)	池州市	安徽省	(0556)6411088	420	集体企业	115,310	6470(3)	93,600	煤气仪表
Beijing Changkong Industrial Co.,Ltd.	Beijing	Beijing	(010)89700799		ɛas Chinese-funded				Automation Metering Oiling Equipment 自动计量
北京长空工业有限公司(1994)	北京市	北京市	(010)89700788	502	港澳台资	63,347	1,225(7)	228,602	加油设备
Qixian Social Welfare Electric Wire Factory	Hebi	Henan	(0392)7280209		Collective-owned				Electrical Wire
淇县社会福利电线厂(1990)	鹤壁市	河南省		20	集体企业	41,020	4,850(4)	4,658	电线
Weihai Sunfull Electronics & Sensor Co., Ltd.	Weihai	Shandong	(0631)5689258		mited-Liability				Earthquake Cymoscope 地
威海双丰电子有限公司(1996)	威海市	山东省	(0631)5689261	155	有限公司	38,478	7,265(2)	72,019	震检波器
Wuxi Water Meter Factory	Wuxi	Jiangsu	(0510)5100803		ıllective-owned				Water Meter
无锡市水表厂(1976)	无锡市	江苏省	(0510)5114313	185	集体企业	26,041	96(13)	11,890	水表
Minol Meters Shanghai Co., Ltd.	Shanghai	Shanghai	(021)57744789		oreign Funded				Water Meter
米诺测量仪表上海有限公司(2002)	上海市	上海市	(021)57744790	106	外商投资	25,367	8,703(1)	29,804	水表
Tianjin Water Supply Equipment Complete Set Co.,Ltd.	Tianjin	Tianjin	(022)27365255		ıllective-owned				Water Meter
天津市给水设备配套公司(1993)	天津市	天津市	(022)27362819	121	集体企业	18,212	1,486(5)	25,326	水表
Cixi New Type Copper Products Factory	Ningbo	Zhejiang	(0574)63578248		vate Enterprises				Copper Water Meter Fittings 铜
慈溪市新型铜制品厂(1992)	宁波市	浙江省	(0574)63576222	155	私营独资	16,789	520(8)	12,544	水表配件
Ningbo Yonggang Instrument & Equipment Co., Ltd.	Ningbo	Zhejiang	(0574)63578508		'rivate Owned				Water Meter
慈溪市甬港仪表电器有限公司(1994)	宁波市	浙江省		65	私营企业	10,867	222(11)	4,298	水表
Shanghai Huamao Machine Tool Accessories Co., Ltd.	Shanghai	Shanghai	(021)58814365		mited-Liability				Gap gauge
上海华茂机床附件有限公司(2001)	上海市	上海市	(021)58396139	97	有限公司	6,463	230(10)	6,781	塞尺

Top 10 Cities by Revenue 销售收入排名前10位城市	Province 省	Market share 市场份额(%)	Number of firms 企业个数
Chizhou 池州市	Anhui 安徽省	27.35	1
Beijing 北京市	Beijing 北京市	15.48	2
Hebi 鹤壁市	Henan 河南省	9.73	1
Weihai 威海市	Shandong 山东省	9.13	1
Ningbo 宁波市	Zhejiang 浙江省	8.69	4
Shanghai 上海市	Shanghai 上海市	7.55	2
Wuxi 无锡市	Jiangsu 江苏省	6.18	1
Nanjing 南京市	Jiangsu 江苏省	4.75	1
Tianjin 天津市	Tianjin 天津市	4.36	2
Wuhan 武汉市	Hubei 湖北省	2.82	1

10 Major Wholesalers 十家主要批发商	City 城市	Province 省	Telephone/Fax 电话/传真
SU MEC	Nanjing	Jiangsu	(025)4511888
中设江苏机械设备进出口(集团)公司	南京市	江苏省	(025)4411772
China Poster Mobile Communications Equipment Co.,Ltd.	Beijing	Beijing	(010)66426993
中邮普泰移动通信设备股份有限公司	北京市	北京市	(010)66426837
Sino Kama Co., Ltd.	Shanghai	Shanghai	(021)62031188
中泰凯马股份有限公司	上海市	上海市	(021)62030851
China Huayuan Group Co.,Ltd.	Shanghai	Shanghai	(021)62031188
中国华源集团有限公司	上海市	上海市	(021)62032288
Zhejiang Crand Imp.& Exp.Co.,Ltd.	Ningbo	Zhejiang	(0574)87720170
浙江远大进出口有限公司	宁波市	浙江省	(0574)87723350
Shandong Machinery Import & Export Group Corporation	Qingdao	Shandong	(0532)2661628
山东省机械进出口集团公司	青岛市	山东省	(0532)2991655
Qingdao Haier International Trade Co.,Ltd.	Qingdao	Shandong	(0532)8938337
青岛海尔国际贸易有限公司	青岛市	山东省	(0532)8939494
Guangdong Machinery Import & Export Group Corporation	Guangzhou	Guangdong	(020)87782168
广东省机械进出口集团公司	广州市	广东省	(020)87771803
China National Machinery Equipment Import & Export	Beijing	Beijing	(010)63474506
Corporation 中国机械设备进出口总公司	北京市	北京市	(010)63261865
Beijing Cellstar Co.,Ltd.	Beijing	Beijing	(010)64602050
北京蜂星事达电讯有限公司	北京市	北京市	(010)64672648

4242: Measuring Instruments 量具量仪制造业

The industry accounts for 0.012% of the total revenue of China's industrial sector in 2002. The rate of return on assets is 0.93%. 77.78% of all firms in the industry made a profit while 22.22% had negative returns.The top province in terms of the industry's revenue is Shanghai, accounting for 24.31% of the total revenue.
2002年本行业收入占全行业的 0.012%，资产利润率为 0.93%。77.78%的企业赢利，22.22%的企业亏损。收入最高的省为上海市，占本行业的24.31%。

	Total number of firms 企业总数	Total number of employees 职工总数	Total revenue (Mil.RMB) 总销售收入（百万元）	Total profit (Mil.RMB) 总利润（百万元）	Return on assets 资产利润率 (%)	Return on equity 权益利润率 (%)	Labour productivity ('000 RMB/worker) 劳动生产率（千元/人）	Debts/assets 资产负债率 (%)	Total assets (Mil.RMB) 总资产（百万元）
Industry Overall 行业总体	54	19,691	1,329	22	0.93	3.48	19.85	73.42	2,344

	Number of firms 企业个数	Average number of employees 平均职工人数	Average revenue ('000 RMB) 平均销售收入（千元）	Average profit ('000 RMB) 平均利润（千元）	Return on assets 资产利润率 (%)	Return on equity 权益利润率 (%)	Labour productivity ('000 RMB/worker) 劳动生产率（千元/人）	Debts/assets 资产负债率 (%)	Average total assets ('000 RMB) 平均总资产（千元）
By ownership 产业所有权									
State-owned 国有	12	613	40,193	-443	-0.43	-2.39	16.22	82.13	103,847
Collective-owned 集体	7	187	10,043	501	4.37	8.77	19.15	50.14	11,465
Foreign & Overseas Chinese Funded 三资	7	231	29,440	495	1.46	2.18	42.59	33.08	33,895
By regional distribution 地区分布									
Central-North 华北	7	152	6,593	274	3.28	12.33	13.04	73.41	8,368
Beijing 北京	2	51	962	-132	-5.34	-12.47	6.58	57.16	2,471
Tianjin 天津	3	193	9,415	592	13.36	60.59	13.03	77.94	4,433
Hebei 河北	2	192	7,991	204	1.01	3.87	14.77	73.90	20,167
Shanxi 山西									
Inner Mongolia 内蒙古									
Northeast 东北	3	1,386	56,434	885	0.39	3.68	11.18	89.30	224,902
Liaoning 辽宁	1	35	6,965	1,742	41.85	57.70	79.63	27.46	4,162
Jilin 吉林									
Heilongjiang 黑龙江	2	2,061	81,168	457	0.14	1.32	10.60	89.69	335,272
Central-East 华东	31	254	24,706	273	0.81	2.36	24.03	65.55	33,606
Shanghai 上海	7	230	46,148	530	0.92	3.39	28.90	72.82	57,472
Jiangsu 江苏	7	190	20,973	69	0.28	0.50	35.80	42.55	24,348
Zhejiang 浙江	7	126	14,562	451	3.24	10.80	31.86	69.99	13,912
Anhui 安徽	1	287	10,715	-58	-0.12	-0.23	37.74	49.25	48,844
Fujian 福建	2	431	34,193	82	0.29	0.65	22.02	55.81	28,563
Jiangxi 江西	3	471	9,417	-1,135	-3.49	-21.54	3.03	83.78	32,491
Shandong 山东	4	371	21,688	1,105	2.63	7.81	22.02	66.37	42,056
Central-South 中南	10	305	20,779	739	2.10	5.40	33.43	61.14	35,216
Henan 河南	4	321	11,396	353	1.62	4.20	21.48	61.36	21,744
Hubei 湖北									
Hunan 湖南	2	68	17,088	1,274	9.65	30.13	52.68	67.99	13,202
Guangdong 广东	2	151	15,022	-2,845	-10.93	-22.04	34.26	50.39	26,014
Guangxi 广西	2	663	48,993	4,562	4.88	13.23	42.83	63.06	93,378
Hainan 海南									
Southwest 西南	1	2,216	88,347	1,178	1.68	12.08	13.73	86.13	70,302
Chongqing 重庆									
Sichuan 四川									
Guizhou 贵州	1	2,216	88,347	1,178	1.68	12.08	13.73	86.13	70,302
Yunnan 云南									
Tibet 西藏									
Northwest 西北	2	669	25,714	33	0.05	0.22	6.92	79.68	73,033
Shaanxi 陕西	1	472	12,811	12	0.06	0.19	9.84	70.97	21,250
Gansu 甘肃									
Qinghai 青海	1	865	38,617	54	0.04	0.23	5.32	81.17	124,815
Ningxia 宁夏									
Xinjiang 新疆									

4242: Measuring Instruments 量具量仪制造业

Year 年份	Number of firms 企业个数	Rate of change 变化率 (%)	Number of employees 职工人数 (人)	Rate of change 变化率 (%)	Total revenue (Mil. RMB) 总销售收入 (百万元)	Rate of change 变化率 (%)	Total profit (Mil RMB) 总利润 (百万元)	Rate of change 变化率 (%)
2000	59		21,239		1,181		-28	
2001	59		23,201	9.24	1,287	8.98	3	
2002	54	-8.47	19,691	-15.13	1,329	3.26	22	633.33

Major Products 主要产品	Output 产量	Unit 单位
Measuring Instrument 量具	2,685	10,000 Pieces 万件
Measuring Apparatus 量仪	11	10,000 Pieces 万件

10 Main Firms with Maximal Revenue (year founded) 收入最大的十家主要企业（创办年份）	City 城市	Province 省	Telephone/fax 电话/传真	Number of employees 职工人数	Ownership 产业所有权	Revenue ('000 RMB) 销售收入 (千元)	Profit('000 RMB) (rank) 利润(千元) (排名)	Total assets ('000 RMB) 总资产 (千元)	Major products 主要产品
Shanghai Water Supply Equipment & Engineering Co.	Shanghai	Shanghai	(021)56959993		State-owned				Water Meter
上海自来水给水设备工程公司(1958)	上海市	上海市	(021)56050884	706	国有企业	212,303	502(19)	149,443	水表
Harbin Measuring And Cutting Tool Works	Harbin	Heilongjiang	(0451)2623021		State-owned				Measuring Blade Tool
哈尔滨量具刃具厂(1955)	哈尔滨市	黑龙江省	(0451)2623555	4,100	国有企业	150,622	262(27)	655,708	量刃具
Amekai Meter (Xiamen) Co., Ltd.	Xiamen	Fujian	(0592)6030566		Foreign Funded				Pressure Gauge
艾美凯仪表（厦门）有限公司(1994)	厦门市	福建省	(0592)6030570	778	外商投资	62,377	20(40)	53,514	压力表
Shanghai Measuring And Cutting Tools Works	Shanghai	Shanghai	(021)67696101		State-owned				Measuring Instrument
上海量具刃具厂(1958)	上海市	上海市	(021)67696131	538	国有企业	56,160	70(35)	219,385	量具
Zhejiang Tianqiu Inplement-Measuring Tool Co.,Ltd.	Jinhua	Zhejiang	(0579)2170357		Private Owned				Measuring Instrument
浙江天球工量具实业有限公司(1995)	金华市	浙江省	(0579)2172088	219	私营企业	55,004	1,030(13)	31,492	工量具
Ji'nan Dongxing Precision Meastrement Co., Ltd.	Jinan	Shandong	(0531)5929906		Foreign Funded				Precision Measuring Instrument
济南东星精密仪器有限公司(1992)	济南市	山东省	(0531)8917779	100	外商投资	46,996	2,134(4)	14,713	精密量仪
Wuxi Xigong Measuring Instrument Co., Ltd.	Wuxi	Jiangsu	(0510)8732938		Limited-Liability				Measuring Instrument
无锡锡工量具有限公司(1975)	无锡市	江苏省	(0510)8731804	400	有限公司	42,280	-	22,620	量具
Jingjiang Measuring Tool Co., Ltd.	Taizhou	Jiangsu	(0523)4543330		Overseas Chinese-funded				Measuring Instrument
靖江市量具有限公司(1958)	泰州市	江苏省	(0523)4543311	386	港澳台资	31,647	660(16)	29,453	量具
Sanmenxia Zhongyuan Measuring Instrument Co., Ltd.	Sanmenxia	Henan	(0398)2821913		Joint Stock				Pneumatic Measuring Instrument
三门峡中原量仪股份有限公司(1966)	三门峡市	河南省	(0398)2821510	925	股份制	30,531	159(31)	60,756	气动量仪
Hongkong Risevchain Industries(zhuhai) Co.,Ltd.	Zhuhai	Guangdong	(0756)8881939		Overseas Chinese-funded				Ribbon
香港宏正工业（珠海）有限公司(1989)	珠海市	广东省	(0756)8881693	230	港澳台资	30,025	287(26)	39,617	钢卷尺

Top 10 Cities by Revenue 销售收入排名前10位城市	Province 省	Market share 市场份额 (%)	Number of firms 企业个数
Shanghai 上海市	Shanghai 上海市	24.31	7
Harbin 哈尔滨市	Heilongjiang 黑龙江省	12.22	2
Guilin 桂林市	Guangxi 广西	7.37	2
Guiyang 贵阳市	Guizhou 贵州省	6.65	1
Xiamen 厦门市	Fujian 福建省	4.69	1
Jinhua 金华市	Zhejiang 浙江省	4.37	2
Wuxi 无锡市	Jiangsu 江苏省	4.28	2
Jinan 济南市	Shandong 山东省	3.54	1
Taizhou 泰州市	Jiangsu 江苏省	3.48	2
Suzhou 苏州市	Jiangsu 江苏省	3.29	3

10 Major Wholesalers 十家主要批发商	City 城市	Province 省	Telephone/Fax 电话/传真
SU MEC	Nanjing	Jiangsu	(025)4511888
中设江苏机械设备进出口（集团）公司	南京市	江苏省	(025)4411772
China Poster Mobile Communications Equipment Co.,Ltd.	Beijing	Beijing	(010)66426993
中邮普泰移动通信设备股份有限公司	北京市	北京市	(010)66426837
Sino Kama Co., Ltd.	Shanghai	Shanghai	(021)62031188
中泰凯马股份有限公司	上海市	上海市	(021)62030851
China Huayuan Group Co.,Ltd.	Shanghai	Shanghai	(021)62031188
中国华源集团有限公司	上海市	上海市	(021)62032288
Zhejiang Crand Imp.& Exp.Co.,Ltd.	Ningbo	Zhejiang	(0574)87720170
浙江远大进出口有限公司	宁波市	浙江省	(0574)87723350
Shandong Machinery Import & Export Group Corporation	Qingdao	Shandong	(0532)2661628
山东省机械进出口集团公司	青岛市	山东省	(0532)2991655
Qingdao Haier International Trade Co.,Ltd.	Qingdao	Shandong	(0532)8938337
青岛海尔国际贸易有限公司	青岛市	山东省	(0532)8939494
Guangdong Machinery Import & Export Group Corporation	Guangzhou	Guangdong	(020)87782168
广东省机械进出口集团公司	广州市	广东省	(020)87771803
China National Machinery Equipment Import & Export	Beijing	Beijing	(010)63474506
Corporation 中国机械设备进出口总公司	北京市	北京市	(010)63261865
Beijing Cellstar Co.,Ltd.	Beijing	Beijing	(010)64602050
北京蜂星事达电讯有限公司	北京市	北京市	(010)64672648

4243: Scales 衡器制造业

The industry accounts for 0.026% of the total revenue of China's industrial sector in 2002. The rate of return on assets is 7.52%. 74.29% of all firms in the industry made a profit while 25.71% had negative returns.The top province in terms of the industry's revenue is Jiangsu, accounting for 23.98% of the total revenue.
2002年本行业收入占全行业的 0.026%，资产利润率为 7.52%。74.29%的企业赢利，25.71%的企业亏损。收入最高的省为江苏省，占本行业的23.98%。

	Total number of firms 企业总数	Total number of employees 职工总数	Total revenue (Mil.RMB) 总销售收入（百万元）	Total profit (Mil.RMB) 总利润（百万元）	Return on assets 资产利润率（%）	Return on equity 权益利润率（%）	Labour productivity ('000 RMB/ worker) 劳动生产率（千元/人）	Debts/ assets 资产负债率（%）	Total assets (Mil.RMB) 总资产（百万元）
Industry Overall 行业总体	105	19,119	2,791	221	7.52	16.38	49.14	54.06	2,941

	Number of firms 企业个数	Average number of employees 平均职工人数	Average revenue ('000 RMB) 平均销售收入（千元）	Average profit ('000 RMB) 平均利润（千元）	Return on assets 资产利润率（%）	Return on equity 权益利润率（%）	Labour productivity ('000 RMB/ worker) 劳动生产率（千元/人）	Debts/ assets 资产负债率（%）	Average total assets ('000 RMB) 平均总资产（千元）
By ownership 产业所有权									
State-owned 国有	14	108	1,965	-438	-2.34	-25.24	3.51	90.71	18,661
Collective-owned 集体	15	223	16,154	443	3.65	14.32	22.42	74.52	12,126
Foreign & Overseas Chinese Funded 三资	25	210	59,950	7,719	14.48	24.59	99.46	41.10	53,294
By regional distribution 地区分布									
Central-North 华北	14	189	10,320	-620	-2.43	-9.28	16.88	73.85	25,560
Beijing 北京	7	87	13,027	-155	-0.84	-1.46	47.78	42.50	18,490
Tianjin 天津	2	262	7,043	-702	-2.32	-51.56	10.82	95.50	30,261
Hebei 河北	3	364	6,856	-1,920	-4.62	-103.30	4.15	95.53	41,546
Shanxi 山西	2	211	9,320	-219	-1.01	-4.04	12.58	74.91	21,629
Inner Mongolia 内蒙古									
Northeast 东北	7	94	4,667	-796	-3.68	-81.77	12.86	95.49	21,617
Liaoning 辽宁	7	94	4,667	-796	-3.68	-81.77	12.86	95.49	21,617
Jilin 吉林									
Heilongjiang 黑龙江									
Central-East 华东	50	178	37,531	3,855	11.24	22.87	69.64	50.84	34,280
Shanghai 上海	9	101	39,070	3,822	9.44	14.75	98.67	36.00	40,498
Jiangsu 江苏	14	196	47,794	8,843	20.75	44.31	91.55	53.17	42,616
Zhejiang 浙江	11	138	16,037	1,231	7.73	16.95	40.71	54.41	15,933
Anhui 安徽									
Fujian 福建	5	88	12,065	24	0.12	0.41	20.35	69.47	19,583
Jiangxi 江西	1	192	6,040	18	0.08	0.12	10.13	33.56	23,095
Shandong 山东	10	309	61,303	2,085	4.57	10.18	66.58	55.14	45,664
Central-South 中南	27	223	25,047	1,564	6.62	11.41	39.68	42.01	23,648
Henan 河南	10	223	14,078	733	4.56	9.62	20.20	52.62	16,088
Hubei 湖北	1	80	5,018	251	2.96	7.17	32.79	58.65	8,470
Hunan 湖南	3	74	4,583	3	0.02	0.03	-6.15	49.32	18,295
Guangdong 广东	12	279	42,512	2,884	8.49	13.25	57.07	35.89	33,961
Guangxi 广西	1	151	6,582	37	0.55	2.50	12.30	78.01	6,730
Hainan 海南									
Southwest 西南	3	218	13,377	12	0.06	0.15	28.53	58.01	18,671
Chongqing 重庆	1	245	8,711	-662	-4.31	-13.37	11.24	67.80	15,373
Sichuan 四川	1	92	24,472	1,501	5.25	13.21	141.42	60.26	28,599
Guizhou 贵州									
Yunnan 云南	1	317	6,949	-803	-6.67	-11.15	9.14	40.17	12,040
Tibet 西藏									
Northwest 西北	4	58	5,121	134	2.30	3,77	39.72	39.01	5,819
Shaanxi 陕西	1	83	5,621	15	0.39	2.23	32.24	82.52	3,845
Gansu 甘肃	2	53	1,052	1	0.02	0.07	12.45	71.99	2,419
Qinghai 青海									
Ningxia 宁夏									
Xinjiang 新疆	1	44	12,758	519	3.56	4.26	119.52	16.62	14,595

4243: Scales 衡器制造业

Year 年份	Number of firms 企业个数	Rate of change 变化率 (%)	Number of employees 职工人数 (人)	Rate of change 变化率 (%)	Total revenue (Mil. RMB) 总销售收入 (百万元)	Rate of change 变化率 (%)	Total profit (Mil RMB) 总利润 (百万元)	Rate of change 变化率 (%)
2000	91		18,382		2,037		126	
2001	99	8.79	17,856	-2.86	2,391	17.38	188	49.21
2002	105	6.06	19,119	7.07	2,791	16.73	221	17.55

Major Products 主要产品	Output 产量	Unit 单位
Ground Scale 地上衡	12,581	Unit 台
Platform Scale 台秤	2,196	10,000 Units 万台

10 Main Firms with Maximal Revenue (year founded) 收入最大的十家主要企业（创办年份）	City 城市	Province 省	Telephone/fax 电话/传真	Number of employees 职工人数	Ownership 产业所有权	Revenue ('000 RMB) 销售收入 (千元)	Profit('000 RMB) (rank) 利润(千元) (排名)	Total assets ('000 RMB) 总资产 (千元)	Major products 主要产品
Mettler-Toledo (Changzhou) Weigh Equipment System Co.,Ltd 梅特勒-托利多(常州)称重设备系统有限公司(1987)	Changzhou 常州市	Jiangsu 江苏省	(0519)6642040 (0519)6641991	513	Foreign Funded 外商投资	435,050	104,750(1)	354,050	Electronic Weighing Apparatus 电子衡器
Shanghai Teraoka Electronic Co., Ltd. 上海寺冈电子有限公司(1993)	Shanghai 上海市	Shanghai 上海市	(021)57234888 (021)57234090	242	Foreign Funded 外商投资	217,762	37,360(2)	147,003	Weighing Apparatus 衡器
Ji'nan Jinzhong Electronic Scale Co., Ltd. 济南金钟电子衡器股份有限公司(1955)	Jinan 济南市	Shandong 山东省	(0531)2974544 (0531)2971352	738	Joint Stock 股份制	168,057	5,750(7)	219,589	Weigh Sensor 称重传感器
Dongguan Tanita Health Equipment Co., Ltd. 东莞百利达健康器材有限公司(1994)	Dongguan 东莞市	Guangdong 广东省	(0769)2403204 (0769)2407443	480	Foreign Funded 外商投资	136,987	12,910(4)	115,106	Fat Scale 脂肪磅
Shandong Taishan Scale Co., Ltd. 山东泰山衡器股份有限公司(1994)	Taian 泰安市	Shandong 山东省	(0538)8613390 (0538)8611210	829	Joint Stock 股份制	68,659	74(54)	109,486	Weighing Apparatus 衡器
Chashi Electronics Industrial (Shenzhen) Co., Ltd. 查氏电子实业（深圳）有限公司(1996)	Shenzhen 深圳市	Guangdong 广东省	(0755)28708755 (0755)28708754	823	Overseas Chinese-funded 港澳台资	49,909	458(36)	69,455	Electronic Small Scale 电子小磅称
Shanghai Yamato Scale Co., Ltd. 上海大和衡器有限公司(1990)	Shanghai 上海市	Shanghai 上海市	(021)58970037 (021)58973737	240	Foreign Funded 外商投资	48,024	-	128,839	Electronic Price Computing Scale 电子计价称
Penglai Balance Fittings Factory 蓬莱市天平配件厂(1976)	Yantai 烟台市	Shandong 山东省	(0535)5711235 (0535)5711235	75	Collective-owned 集体企业	46,679	1,630(17)	3,850	Poise 砝码
Dongguan Panaview Metal Products Co., Ltd 东莞柏威金属制品有限公司(1994)	Dongguan 东莞市	Guangdong 广东省	(0769)8835933 (0769)8835966	330	Overseas Chinese-funded 港澳台资	46,380	257(43)	12,916	Machinery Scale 机械磅
Beijing Tedea-Huntleight Electronics Co., Ltd. 北京特迪亚-亨特利电子有限公司(1994)	Beijing 北京市	Beijing 北京市	(010)67881604 (010)67881576	170	Foreign Funded 外商投资	40,030	3,601(11)	38,160	Sensor 传感器

Top 10 Cities by Revenue 销售收入排名前10位城市	Province 省	Market share 市场份额 (%)	Number of firms 企业个数
Changzhou 常州市	Jiangsu 江苏省	17.35	5
Shanghai 上海市	Shanghai 上海市	12.60	9
Weihai 威海市	Shandong 山东省	8.38	1
Zhongshan 中山市	Guangdong 广东省	8.09	5
Dongguan 东莞市	Guangdong 广东省	6.57	2
Jinan 济南市	Shandong 山东省	6.39	2
Beijing 北京市	Beijing 北京市	3.27	7
Xuzhou 徐州市	Jiangsu 江苏省	3.06	2
Jinhua 金华市	Zhejiang 浙江省	2.92	5
Shenzhen 深圳市	Guangdong 广东省	2.80	2

10 Major Wholesalers 十家主要批发商	City 城市	Province 省	Telephone/Fax 电话/传真
SU MEC 中设江苏机械设备进出口（集团）公司	Nanjing 南京市	Jiangsu 江苏省	(025)4511888 (025)4411772
China Poster Mobile Communications Equipment Co.,Ltd. 中邮普泰移动通信设备股份有限公司	Beijing 北京市	Beijing 北京市	(010)66426993 (010)66426837
Sino Kama Co., Ltd. 中泰凯马股份有限公司	Shanghai 上海市	Shanghai 上海市	(021)62031188 (021)62030851
China Huayuan Group Co.,Ltd. 中国华源集团有限公司	Shanghai 上海市	Shanghai 上海市	(021)62031188 (021)62032288
Zhejiang Crand Imp.& Exp.Co.,Ltd. 浙江远大进出口有限公司	Ningbo 宁波市	Zhejiang 浙江省	(0574)87720170 (0574)87723350
Shandong Machinery Import & Export Group Corporation 山东省机械进出口集团公司	Qingdao 青岛市	Shandong 山东省	(0532)2661628 (0532)2991655
Qingdao Haier International Trade Co.,Ltd. 青岛海尔国际贸易有限公司	Qingdao 青岛市	Shandong 山东省	(0532)8938337 (0532)8939494
Guangdong Machinery Import & Export Group Corporation 广东省机械进出口集团公司	Guangzhou 广州市	Guangdong 广东省	(020)87782168 (020)87771803
China National Machinery Equipment Import & Export Corporation 中国机械设备进出口总公司	Beijing 北京市	Beijing 北京市	(010)63474506 (010)63261865
Beijing Cellstar Co.,Ltd. 北京蜂星事达电讯有限公司	Beijing 北京市	Beijing 北京市	(010)64602050 (010)64672648

4254: Cameras 照机机及器材制造业

The industry accounts for 0.191% of the total revenue of China's industrial sector in 2002. The rate of return on assets is 5.35%. 76.00% of all firms in the industry made a profit while 24.00% had negative returns.The top province in terms of the industry's revenue is Guangdong, accounting for 60.51% of the total revenue.
2002年本行业收入占全行业的 0.191%，资产利润率为 5.35%。76.00%的企业赢利，24.00%的企业亏损。收入最高的省为广东省，占本行业的60.51%。

	Total number of firms 企业总数	Total number of employees 职工总数	Total revenue (Mil.RMB) 总销售收入（百万元）	Total profit (Mil.RMB) 总利润（百万元）	Return on assets 资产利润率（%）	Return on equity 权益利润率（%）	Labour productivity ('000 RMB/ worker) 劳动生产率（千元/人）	Debts/ assets 资产负债率（%）	Total assets (Mil.RMB) 总资产（百万元）
Industry Overall 行业总体	100	54,877	20,453	703	5.35	10.92	58.76	51.05	13,145

	Number of firms 企业个数	Average number of employees 平均职工人数	Average revenue ('000 RMB) 平均销售收入（千元）	Average profit ('000 RMB) 平均利润（千元）	Return on assets 资产利润率（%）	Return on equity 权益利润率（%）	Labour productivity ('000 RMB/ worker) 劳动生产率（千元/人）	Debts/ assets 资产负债率（%）	Average total assets ('000 RMB) 平均总资产（千元）
By ownership 产业所有权									
State-owned 国有	14	422	5,747	-2,589	-3.77		4.61	112.16	68,655
Collective-owned 集体	3	1,122	34,104	2,067	21.56	43.70	9.49	50.67	9,590
Foreign & Overseas Chinese Funded 三资	66	622	295,766	10,830	6.94	13.29	74.43	47.76	156,027
By regional distribution 地区分布									
Central-North 华北	13	290	136,509	5,414	6.12	16.71	64.96	63.35	88,412
Beijing 北京	7	181	129,624	5,998	6.94	20.50	53.09	66.12	86,378
Tianjin 天津	6	417	144,543	4,732	5.21	13.12	70.96	60.29	90,785
Hebei 河北									
Shanxi 山西									
Inner Mongolia 内蒙古									
Northeast 东北	4	959	36,194	2,278	5.18	81.35	16.06	93.63	43,985
Liaoning 辽宁	4	959	36,194	2,278	5.18	81.35	16.06	93.63	43,985
Jilin 吉林									
Heilongjiang 黑龙江									
Central-East 华东	45	280	135,194	7,564	7.12	13.28	97.30	46.44	106,301
Shanghai 上海	22	269	147,347	5,110	4.76	10.07	87.58	52.76	107,398
Jiangsu 江苏	9	319	193,995	3,194	1.76	2.87	143.22	38.55	181,321
Zhejiang 浙江	9	183	21,160	618	2.36	3.96	24.11	40.34	26,186
Anhui 安徽									
Fujian 福建	4	490	218,704	49,257	40.12	70.31	131.08	42.94	122,782
Jiangxi 江西	1	200	30,880	-3,377	-5.44	-15.16	-0.54	64.11	62,089
Shandong 山东									
Central-South 中南	35	843	353,632	9,123	5.02	8.88	56.32	43.53	181,910
Henan 河南									
Hubei 湖北	1	69	885	-653	-2.02	-37.81	2.88	94.64	32,248
Hunan 湖南									
Guangdong 广东	34	866	364,007	9,411	5.05	8.90	56.44	43.27	186,312
Guangxi 广西									
Hainan 海南									
Southwest 西南	1	1,850	35,060	-14,490	-7.54		2.59	148.84	192,060
Chongqing 重庆	1	1,850	35,060	-14,490	-7.54		2.59	148.84	192,060
Sichuan 四川									
Guizhou 贵州									
Yunnan 云南									
Tibet 西藏									
Northwest 西北	2	1,655	18,617	-10,918	-4.58		7.50	112.78	238,445
Shaanxi 陕西									
Gansu 甘肃	2	1,655	18,617	-10,918	-4.58		7.50	112.78	238,445
Qinghai 青海									
Ningxia 宁夏									
Xinjiang 新疆									

4254: Cameras 照相机及器材制造业

Year 年份	Number of firms 企业个数	Rate of change 变化率(%)	Number of employees 职工人数(人)	Rate of change 变化率(%)	Total revenue (Mil. RMB) 总销售收入(百万元)	Rate of change 变化率(%)	Total profit (Mil RMB) 总利润(百万元)	Rate of change 变化率(%)
2000	83		44,786		15,768		660	
2001	91	9.64	51,369	14.70	16,844	6.82	457	-30.76
2002	100	9.89	54,877	6.83	20,453	21.43	703	53.83

Major Products 主要产品	Output 产量	Unit 单位
Camera 照相机	4,810	10,000 Units 万台

10 Main Firms with Maximal Revenue (year founded) 收入最大的十家主要企业（创办年份）	City 城市	Province 省	Telephone/fax 电话/传真	Number of employees 职工人数	Ownership 产业所有权	Revenue ('000 RMB) 销售收入(千元)	Profit('000 RMB) (rank) 利润(千元)(排名)	Total assets ('000 RMB) 总资产(千元)	Major products 主要产品
Canon Zhuhai Co.,Ltd.	Zhuhai	Guangdong	(0756)8888101		Foreign Funded				Camera
佳能珠海有限公司(1990)	珠海市	广东省	(0756)8114744	5,139	外商投资	4,271,478	139,155(2)	1,585,538	照相机
Olympus(Shenzhen) Industrial Co., Ltd.	Shenzhen	Guangdong	(0755)26980118		Foreign Funded				Camera
奥林巴斯深圳工业有限公司(1991)	深圳市	广东省	(0755)26980784	4,980	外商投资	1,574,257	73,566(3)	1,041,333	照相机
Kodak Electronics (Shanghai)Co., Ltd.	Shanghai	Shanghai	(021)50321010		Foreign Funded				Digital Camera 数
柯达电子(上海)有限公司(1995)	上海市	上海市	(021)50327018	893	外商投资	1,205,482	60,271(4)	480,811	码照相机
Olympus (Beijing) Science & Technology Co., Ltd.	Beijing	Beijing	(010)82111943		Foreign Funded				Camera
奥林巴斯（北京）科技有限公司(2001)	北京市	北京市	(010)82112856	4	外商投资	823,478	37,281(5)	366,201	照相机
Fujifilm Imageing Systems (Suzhou)Co., Ltd.	Suzhou	Jiangsu	(0512)68251188		Foreign Funded				Digital Camera 数
苏州富士胶片映像元器件有限公司(1997)	苏州市	江苏省	(0512)68257122	268	外商投资	810,560	8,470(17)	622,473	码照相机
Shanghai MINOLTA Products Co., Ltd.	Shanghai	Shanghai	(021)57741620		Foreign Funded				Camera & Equipment照相
上海美能达光学仪器有限公司(1995)	上海市	上海市	(021)57741554	1,274	外商投资	746,430	11,759(13)	255,944	机及器材
KaDak (Xiamen) Co., Ltd.	Xiamen	Fujian	(0592)6517890		Foreign Funded				One-off Camera一
柯达（厦门）有限公司(2000)	厦门市	福建省	(0592)6805002	546	外商投资	709,491	185,386(1)	342,704	次性相机
Tianjin Samsung Opotoelectrics Co., Ltd.	Tianjin	Tianjin	(022)27619212		Foreign Funded				Camera &Fittings照相
天津三星光电子有限公司(1994)	天津市	天津市	(022)27618864	730	外商投资	683,441	18,043(8)	292,823	机及配件
Tamron Optical(Fuoshan) Co., Ltd.	Foshan	Guangdong	(0757)2982223		Foreign Funded				Camera Video Camera Lens 照相机摄
腾龙光学(佛山)有限公司(1997)	佛山市	广东省	(0757)2203442	753	外商投资	544,737	32,507(6)	207,432	像机镜头
Suzhou Fujifilm Film Machine Co., Ltd.	Suzhou	Jiangsu	(0512)68251188		Foreign Funded				Camera
苏州富士胶片映像机器有限公司(1995)	苏州市	江苏省	(0512)68257122	1,385	外商投资	334,630	17,080(9)	726,275	照相机

Top 10 Cities by Revenue 销售收入排名前10位城市	Province 省	Market share 市场份额(%)	Number of firms 企业个数
Zhuhai 珠海市	Guangdong 广东省	23.09	4
Foshan 佛山市	Guangdong 广东省	19.54	5
Shanghai 上海市	Shanghai 上海市	15.85	22
Shenzhen 深圳市	Guangdong 广东省	8.42	8
Suzhou 苏州市	Jiangsu 江苏省	8.34	5
Beijing 北京市	Beijing 北京市	4.44	7
Xiamen 厦门市	Fujian 福建省	4.28	4
Dongguan 东莞市	Guangdong 广东省	4.27	3
Tianjin 天津市	Tianjin 天津市	4.24	6
Huizhou 惠州市	Guangdong 广东省	2.53	3

10 Major Wholesalers 十家主要批发商	City 城市	Province 省	Telephone/Fax 电话/传真
SU MEC	Nanjing	Jiangsu	(025)4511888
中设江苏机械设备进出口（集团）公司	南京市	江苏省	(025)4411772
China Poster Mobile Communications Equipment Co.,Ltd.	Beijing	Beijing	(010)66426993
中邮普泰移动通信设备股份有限公司	北京市	北京市	(010)66426837
Sino Kama Co., Ltd.	Shanghai	Shanghai	(021)62031188
中泰凯马股份有限公司	上海市	上海市	(021)62030851
China Huayuan Group Co.,Ltd.	Shanghai	Shanghai	(021)62031188
中国华源集团有限公司	上海市	上海市	(021)62032288
Zhejiang Crand Imp.& Exp.Co.,Ltd.	Ningbo	Zhejiang	(0574)87720170
浙江远大进出口有限公司	宁波市	浙江省	(0574)87723350
Shandong Machinery Import & Export Group Corporation	Qingdao	Shandong	(0532)2661628
山东省机械进出口集团公司	青岛市	山东省	(0532)2991655
Qingdao Haier International Trade Co.,Ltd.	Qingdao	Shandong	(0532)8938337
青岛海尔国际贸易有限公司	青岛市	山东省	(0532)8939494
Guangdong Machinery Import & Export Group Corporation	Guangzhou	Guangdong	(020)87782168
广东省机械进出口集团公司	广州市	广东省	(020)87771803
China National Machinery Equipment Import & Export	Beijing	Beijing	(010)63474506
Corporation 中国机械设备进出口总公司	北京市	北京市	(010)63261863
Beijing Cellstar Co.,Ltd.	Beijing	Beijing	(010)64602050
北京蜂星事达电讯有限公司	北京市	北京市	(010)64672648

4256: Copiers 复印机制造业

The industry accounts for 0.136% of the total revenue of China's industrial sector in 2002. The rate of return on assets is 10.40%. 84.21% of all firms in the industry made a profit while 15.79% had negative returns.The top province in terms of the industry's revenue is Guangdong, accounting for 58.34% of the total revenue.
2002年本行业收入占全行业的 0.136%，资产利润率为 10.40%。84.21%的企业赢利，15.79%的企业亏损。收入最高的省为广东省，占本行业的58.34%。

	Total number of firms 企业总数	Total number of employees 职工总数	Total revenue (Mil.RMB) 总销售收入 (百万元)	Total profit (Mil.RMB) 总利润 (百万元)	Return on assets 资产利润率 (%)	Return on equity 权益利润率 (%)	Labour productivity ('000 RMB/ worker) 劳动生产率 (千元/人)	Debts/ assets 资产负债率 (%)	Total assets (Mil.RMB) 总资产 (百万元)
Industry Overall 行业总体	38	21,286	14,591	741	10.40	21.69	109.35	52.03	7,122

	Number of firms 企业个数	Average number of employees 平均职工人数	Average revenue ('000 RMB) 平均销售收入（千元）	Average profit ('000 RMB) 平均利润 (千元)	Return on assets 资产利润率 (%)	Return on equity 权益利润率 (%)	Labour productivity ('000 RMB/ worker) 劳动生产率 (千元/人)	Debts/ assets 资产负债率 (%)	Average total assets ('000 RMB) 平均总资产 (千元)
By ownership 产业所有权									
State-owned 国有	5	364	24,531	-5,542	-3.44	-122.42	17.78	97.19	160,883
Collective-owned 集体	2	1,232	14,983	-667	-4.25	-120.96	6.76	96.48	15,675
Foreign & Overseas Chinese Funded 三资	26	566	521,442	28,316	13.62	24.87	140.53	45.23	207,841
By regional distribution 地区分布									
Central-North 华北	5	183	21,043	-509	-0.72	-2.21	38.78	67.43	70,735
Beijing 北京									
Tianjin 天津	5	183	21,043	-509	-0.72	-2.21	38.78	67.43	70,735
Hebei 河北									
Shanxi 山西									
Inner Mongolia 内蒙古									
Northeast 东北									
Liaoning 辽宁									
Jilin 吉林									
Heilongjiang 黑龙江									
Central-East 华东	15	549	377,082	24,549	10.83	19.07	143.21	43.22	226,749
Shanghai 上海	6	316	221,766	22,012	16.47	29.92	160.13	44.93	133,620
Jiangsu 江苏	7	699	508,105	32,011	12.21	19.86	143.39	38.52	262,146
Zhejiang 浙江	1	102	4,970	378	9.37	25.10	15.86	62.67	4,034
Anhui 安徽									
Fujian 福建									
Jiangxi 江西									
Shandong 山东	1	1,347	763,925	11,703	1.54	3.25	128.39	52.67	760,461
Central-South 中南	18	674	490,557	20,852	11.15	27.40	91.68	59.32	187,072
Henan 河南									
Hubei 湖北	1	142	287,022	1,351	0.74	1.73	576.57	57.06	182,336
Hunan 湖南									
Guangdong 广东	16	690	532,040	24,168	13.29	29.56	92.75	55.03	181,823
Guangxi 广西	1	953	30,373	-12,713	-4.61		7.00	106.01	275,805
Hainan 海南									
Southwest 西南									
Chongqing 重庆									
Sichuan 四川									
Guizhou 贵州									
Yunnan 云南									
Tibet 西藏									
Northwest 西北									
Shaanxi 陕西									
Gansu 甘肃									
Qinghai 青海									
Ningxia 宁夏									
Xinjiang 新疆									

4256: Copiers 复印机制造业

Year 年份	Number of firms 企业个数	Rate of change 变化率 (%)	Number of employees 职工人数 (人)	Rate of change 变化率 (%)	Total revenue (Mil. RMB) 总销售收入 (百万元)	Rate of change 变化率 (%)	Total profit (Mil RMB) 总利润 (百万元)	Rate of change 变化率 (%)
2000	32		15,063		11,043		467	
2001	32		14,500	-3.74	12,208	10.55	578	23.77
2002	38	18.75	21,286	46.80	14,591	19.52	741	28.20

Major Products 主要产品	Output 产量	Unit 单位
Duplicating Machinery 复印机械	2,073,193	Unit 台

10 Main Firms with Maximal Revenue (year founded) 收入最大的十家主要企业（创办年份）	City 城市	Province 省	Telephone/fax 电话/传真	Number of employees 职工人数	Ownership 产业所有权	Revenue ('000 RMB) 销售收入 (千元)	Profit('000 RMB) (rank) 利润(千元) (排名)	Total assets ('000 RMB) 总资产 (千元)	Major products 主要产品
Ricon(Shenzhen)Industry Development Co.,Ltd.	Shenzhen	Guangdong	(0755)83360885		Foreign Funded				Duplicator
理光(深圳)工业公司(1991)	深圳市	广东省	(0755)83264609	2,578	外商投资	3,531,087	190,415(1)	1,157,862	复印机
Sharp Office Work Equipment (Changshu)Co., Ltd.	Suzhou	Jiangsu	(0512)52856404		Foreign Funded				Duplicator
夏普办公设备(常熟)有限公司(1995)	苏州市	江苏省	(0512)52856037	1,163	外商投资	2,628,521	183,331(2)	1,058,726	复印机
Toshiba Copying Machine (Shenzhen)Co., Ltd.	Shenzhen	Guangdong	(0755)27311901		Foreign Funded				Duplicator
东芝复印机(深圳)有限公司(1993)	深圳市	广东省	(0755)27311909	830	外商投资	1,378,679	74,578(5)	480,718	复印机
Weihai Beiyang Electricity Group Co., Ltd.	Weihai	Shandong	(0631)5231031		Joint Stock				Heat Sensitive Printing Head Picture Sensor热敏打印头
威海北洋电气集团股份有限公司(1988)	威海市	山东省		1,347	股份制	763,925	11,703(9)	760,461	图像传感器
Shanghai Fuji Xerox Co., Ltd.	Shanghai	Shanghai	(021)64300480		Foreign Funded				Duplicator
上海富士施乐复印机有限公司(1987)	上海市	上海市	(021)64300119	469	外商投资	742,426	93,607(4)	468,308	复印机
Shanghai Sinei Elect Co., Ltd.	Shanghai	Shanghai	(021)59159324		Foreign Funded				Duplicator
上海三荣电器有限公司(1994)	上海市	上海市	(021)59155844	505	外商投资	410,499	4,278(14)	169,534	复印机
Wuhan Minolta Office Automation Equipments Co., Ltd.	Wuhan	Hubei	(027)83560400		Foreign Funded				Duplicator
武汉美能达办公机器有限公司(1995)	武汉市	湖北省	(027)83560400	142	外商投资	287,022	1,351(20)	182,336	复印机
Chuangmei Craft (Changshu)Co., Ltd.	Suzhou	Jiangsu	(0512)52682743		Foreign Funded				Duplicator
创美工艺(常熟)有限公司(1993)	苏州市	江苏省	(0512)52682139	609	外商投资	257,000	15,330(7)	121,473	复印机
Xingguang Resin Products (Kunshan)Co., Ltd	Suzhou	Jiangsu	(0512)57641220		Foreign Funded				printer
星光树脂制品(昆山)有限公司(1993)	苏州市	江苏省	(0512)57641211	640	外商投资	237,770	3,080(16)	221,000	打印机
Gestener (Zhanjiang) Co., Ltd.	Zhanjiang	Guangdong	(0759)3367195		Overseas Chinese-funded				Duplicator
基士得耶湛江有限公司(1994)	湛江市	广东省	(0759)3367215	54	港澳台资	198,304	6,004(12)	119,198	复印机

Top 10 Cities by Revenue 销售收入排名前10位城市	Province 省	Market share 市场份额 (%)	Number of firms 企业个数
Shenzhen 深圳市	Guangdong 广东省	55.70	6
Suzhou 苏州市	Jiangsu 江苏省	24.38	7
Shanghai 上海市	Shanghai 上海市	9.12	6
Weihai 威海市	Shandong 山东省	5.74	1
Wuhan 武汉市	Hubei 湖北省	1.97	1
Zhanjiang 湛江市	Guangdong 广东省	1.37	2
Tianjin 天津市	Tianjin 天津市	0.72	5
Dongguan 东莞市	Guangdong 广东省	0.62	4
Guangzhou 广州市	Guangdong 广东省	0.50	2
Guilin 桂林市	Guangxi 广西	0.21	1

10 Major Wholesalers 十家主要批发商	City 城市	Province 省	Telephone/Fax 电话/传真
SU MEC	Nanjing	Jiangsu	(025)4511888
中设江苏机械设备进出口（集团）公司	南京市	江苏省	(025)4411772
China Poster Mobile Communications Equipment Co.,Ltd.	Beijing	Beijing	(010)66426993
中邮普泰移动通信设备股份有限公司	北京市	北京市	(010)66426837
Sino Kama Co., Ltd.	Shanghai	Shanghai	(021)62031188
中泰凯马股份有限公司	上海市	上海市	(021)62030851
China Huayuan Group Co.,Ltd.	Shanghai	Shanghai	(021)62031188
中国华源集团有限公司	上海市	上海市	(021)62032288
Zhejiang Crand Imp.& Exp.Co.,Ltd.	Ningbo	Zhejiang	(0574)87720170
浙江远大进出口有限公司	宁波市	浙江省	(0574)87723350
Shandong Machinery Import & Export Group Corporation	Qingdao	Shandong	(0532)2661628
山东省机械进出口集团公司	青岛市	山东省	(0532)2991655
Qingdao Haier International Trade Co.,Ltd.	Qingdao	Shandong	(0532)8938337
青岛海尔国际贸易有限公司	青岛市	山东省	(0532)8939494
Guangdong Machinery Import & Export Group Corporation	Guangzhou	Guangdong	(020)87782168
广东省机械进出口集团公司	广州市	广东省	(020)87771803
China National Machinery Equipment Import & Export Corporation 中国机械设备进出口总公司	Beijing	Beijing	(010)63474506
	北京市	北京市	(010)63261865
Beijing Cellstar Co.,Ltd.	Beijing	Beijing	(010)64602050
北京蜂星事达电讯有限公司	北京市	北京市	(010)64672648

4259: Other Educational and Office Machinery

其他文化、办公用机械制造业

The industry accounts for 0.012% of the total revenue of China's industrial sector in 2002. The rate of return on assets is 4.78%. 69.23% of all firms in the industry made a profit while 30.77% had negative returns.The top province in terms of the industry's revenue is Jiangsu, accounting for 36.38% of the total revenue.
2002年本行业收入占全行业的0.012%，资产利润率为4.78%。69.23%的企业赢利，30.77%的企业亏损。收入最高的省为江苏省，占本行业的36.38%。

	Total number of firms 企业总数	Total number of employees 职工总数	Total revenue (Mil.RMB) 总销售收入(百万元)	Total profit (Mil.RMB) 总利润(百万元)	Return on assets 资产利润率(%)	Return on equity 权益利润率(%)	Labour productivity ('000 RMB/worker) 劳动生产率(千元/人)	Debts/assets 资产负债率(%)	Total assets (Mil.RMB) 总资产(百万元)
Industry Overall 行业总体	39	6,144	1,328	52	4.78	9.92	54.35	51.79	1,083

	Number of firms 企业个数	Average number of employees 平均职工人数	Average revenue ('000 RMB) 平均销售收入(千元)	Average profit ('000 RMB) 平均利润(千元)	Return on assets 资产利润率(%)	Return on equity 权益利润率(%)	Labour productivity ('000 RMB/worker) 劳动生产率(千元/人)	Debts/assets 资产负债率(%)	Average total assets ('000 RMB) 平均总资产(千元)
By ownership 产业所有权									
State-owned 国有	4	54	1,395	-624	-6.03	-10.50	0.33	42.54	10,332
Collective-owned 集体	2	119	15,467	436	1.35	6.24	31.73	78.34	32,208
Foreign & Overseas Chinese Funded 三资	12	229	67,732	3,570	6.15	11.27	71.82	45.45	58,067
By regional distribution 地区分布									
Central-North 华北	8	94	24,903	941	3.68	6.66	71.61	44.77	25,585
Beijing 北京	7	100	28,247	1,501	5.48	9.72	78.95	43.56	27,367
Tianjin 天津	1	50	1,499	-2,981	-22.73	-60.33	-30.88	62.33	13,115
Hebei 河北									
Shanxi 山西									
Inner Mongolia 内蒙古									
Northeast 东北	2	71	15,019	221	2.13	6.23	114.42	65.81	10,374
Liaoning 辽宁	2	71	15,019	221	2.13	6.23	114.42	65.81	10,374
Jilin 吉林									
Heilongjiang 黑龙江									
Central-East 华东	16	194	42,321	2,049	6.28	13.19	49.15	52.39	32,620
Shanghai 上海	5	138	26,563	4,841	17.58	26.66	50.45	34.07	27,536
Jiangsu 江苏	6	307	80,550	986	1.85	4.89	56.03	62.16	53,334
Zhejiang 浙江	3	110	10,970	860	10.42	13.91	33.84	25.05	8,253
Anhui 安徽									
Fujian 福建	1	193	25,579	184	0.57	1.04	9.56	45.46	32,346
Jiangxi 江西									
Shandong 山东	1	45	2,538	-104	-1.46	-25.49	29.02	94.28	7,138
Central-South 中南	12	164	34,384	914	3.38	7.43	55.46	54.48	27,007
Henan 河南	2	92	24,297	1,208	23.76	60.92	75.46	61.00	5,085
Hubei 湖北	2	75	17,533	-907	-4.01	-21.85	26.77	81.65	22,619
Hunan 湖南									
Guangdong 广东	8	204	41,118	1,295	3.86	7.66	55.84	49.66	33,585
Guangxi 广西									
Hainan 海南									
Southwest 西南									
Chongqing 重庆									
Sichuan 四川									
Guizhou 贵州									
Yunnan 云南									
Tibet 西藏									
Northwest 西北	1	189	9,434	41	0.37	0.71	14.52	48.18	11,073
Shaanxi 陕西	1	189	9,434	41	0.37	0.71	14.52	48.18	11,073
Gansu 甘肃									
Qinghai 青海									
Ningxia 宁夏									
Xinjiang 新疆									

4259: Other Educational and Office Machinery

其他文化、办公用机械制造业

Year 年份	Number of firms 企业个数	Rate of change 变化率 (%)	Number of employees 职工人数 (人)	Rate of change 变化率 (%)	Total revenue (Mil. RMB) 总销售收入 (百万元)	Rate of change 变化率 (%)	Total profit (Mil RMB) 总利润 (百万元)	Rate of change 变化率 (%)
2000	36		11,468		6,037		264	
2001	39	8.33	11,262	-1.80	6,589	9.14	500	89.39
2002	39		6,144	-45.44	1,328	-79.85	52	-89.60

Major Products 主要产品	Output 产量	Unit 单位
Printer 打印机	2,409	10,000 Sets 万部
Electrograph 传真机	288	10,000 Sets 万部

10 Main Firms with Maximal Revenue (year founded) 收入最大的十家主要企业（创办年份）	City 城市	Province 省	Telephone/fax 电话/传真	Number of employees 职工人数	Ownership 产业所有权	Revenue ('000 RMB) 销售收入 (千元)	Profit('000 RMB) (rank) 利润(千元) (排名)	Total assets ('000 RMB) 总资产 (千元)	Major products 主要产品
Avision (Shzhou) Co., Ltd.	Suzhou	Jiangsu	(0512)62565888		Foreign Funded				Scanner
虹光精密工业(苏州)有限公司(1999)	苏州市	江苏省	(0512)62560115	1,113	外商投资	398,041	4,035(5)	269,465	扫描仪
Gestener Office Equipment (China) Co., Ltd.	Beijing	Beijing	(010)67713117		Foreign Funded				Plate-making Machin
基士得耶办公设备（中国）有限公司(1993)	北京市	北京市	(010)67713117	138	外商投资	100,194	1,874(10)	93,853	制版机
Shanghai Kalu Stationery Co., Ltd.	Shanghai	Shanghai	(021)57857288		Foreign Funded				Punch
上海咖路文具有限公司(1996)	上海市	上海市	(021)57857362	197	外商投资	66,382	18,536(1)	72,354	打孔机
Liguang Electronic Technique (Beijing)Co., Ltd.	Beijing	Beijing	(010)88797580		Foreign Funded				
理光电子技术(北京)有限公司(1995)	北京市	北京市	(010)88797572	58	外商投资	46,778	7,268(2)	33,633	
Zhongshan Readboy Electronics Co., Ltd.	Zhongshan	Guangdong	(0760)3378088		Private Owned				Children's studying machine 儿
中山市读书郎电子有限公司(1999)	中山市	广东省	(0760)3378295	160	私营企业	41,085	1,985(9)	9,136	童学习机
Wuxi Mengyang Automobile Electrical Appliance Factory	Wuxi	Jiangsu	(0510)5105562		Private Enterprises				Collector
无锡市梦阳汽车电器厂(1989)	无锡市	江苏省	(0510)5100416	300	私营独资	36,219	708(12)	11,359	整流子
Wuhan Huazhao Documents Communication System Co., Ltd.	Wuhan	Hubei	(027)87413219		Foreign Funded				Facsimile Machine
武汉华昭施乐文件通信系统有限公司(1994)	武汉市	湖北省	(027)87808483	82	外商投资	34,745	-	36,248	传真机
Xilekang Electromechanical (Shanghai) Co., Ltd.	Shanghai	Shanghai	(021)59752800		Foreign Funded				Packing Machinery
喜乐康机电（上海）有限公司(1994)	上海市	上海市	(021)59753553	127	外商投资	31,814	5,278(4)	19,107	包装机械
Shenyang Shenfeifei Shilan Files Books Apparel Co., Ltd.	Shenyang	Liaoning	(024)86518494		Limited-Liability				Filing Cabinet
沈阳沈飞飞世兰档案图书装具有限公司(1989)	沈阳市	辽宁省	(024)86526656	132	有限公司	26,007	462(17)	20,183	档案柜
Xiamen Oute Electronics Co., Ltd.	Xiamen	Fujian	(0592)5283152		Foreign Funded				Sensitization Drum Cleanliness Spatula 感光鼓
厦门欧特电子有限公司(2001)	厦门市	福建省	(0592)5280079	193	外商投资	25,579	184(20)	32,346	用清洁刮

Top 10 Cities by Revenue 销售收入排名前10位城市	Province 省	Market share 市场份额 (%)	Number of firms 企业个数
Suzhou 苏州市	Jiangsu 江苏省	30.31	2
Beijing 北京市	Beijing 北京市	14.88	7
Huizhou 惠州市	Guangdong 广东省	11.88	2
Shanghai 上海市	Shanghai 上海市	10.00	5
Shenzhen 深圳市	Guangdong 广东省	5.55	1
Wuxi 无锡市	Jiangsu 江苏省	3.80	2
Luohe 漯河市	Henan 河南省	3.66	1
Guangzhou 广州市	Guangdong 广东省	3.43	2
Zhongshan 中山市	Guangdong 广东省	3.09	1
Wuhan 武汉市	Hubei 湖北省	2.64	2

10 Major Wholesalers 十家主要批发商	City 城市	Province 省	Telephone/Fax 电话/传真
King Paper Source Trade (shanghai) Co.,Ltd.	Shanghai	Shanghai	(021)62720808
金纸源贸易（上海）有限公司	上海市	上海市	(021)62720909
China National Paper & Pulp Corpration	Beijing	Beijing	(010)67780346
中国纸张纸浆进出口公司	北京市	北京市	(010)67747294
Sinar Mas Linjiang Paper Industry Trade (Beijing) Co.,Ltd.	Beijing	Beijing	(010)65666688
金光林浆纸业贸易(北京)有限公司	北京市	北京市	(010)65669599
Sinar Mas Paper Industry (Xishan) Co.,Ltd.	Wuxi	Jiangsu	(0510)8251188
金光纸业(锡山)有限公司	无锡市	江苏省	(0510)8250906
China Printing Materials General Company	Beijing	Beijing	(010)63442905
中国印刷物资总公司	北京市	北京市	(010)63442900
TSS Eortune Co., ltd.	Tianjin	Tianjin	(022)28131350
天津同鑫进出口有限公司	天津市	天津市	(022)28131353
Wenzhou Import & Export Corpration	Wenzhou	Zhejiang	(0577)88862681
温州市进出口公司	温州市	浙江省	(0577)88844557
Sinar Mas Paper Industry (Xiamen) Co.,Ltd.	Xiamen	Fujian	(0592)2962018
金光纸业（厦门）有限公司	厦门市	福建省	(0592)2962010
Sinar Mas Paper Industry (Shenzhen) Co.,Ltd.	Shenzhen	Guangdong	(0755)83516701
金光纸业（深圳）有限公司	深圳市	广东省	(0755)83516773
Jieyang Ocean Shipping Supply Group Co.,Ltd.	Jieyang	Guangdong	(0663)8239634
揭阳市外轮供应集团有限公司	揭阳市	广东省	(0663)8236186

4260: Clocks and Watches 钟表制造业

The industry accounts for 0.074% of the total revenue of China's industrial sector in 2002. The rate of return on assets is 1.04%. 66.54% of all firms in the industry made a profit while 33.46% had negative returns.The top province in terms of the industry's revenue is Guangdong, accounting for 66.91% of the total revenue.
2002年本行业收入占全行业的 0.074%，资产利润率为 1.04%。66.54%的企业赢利，33.46%的企业亏损。收入最高的省为广东省，占本行业的66.91%。

	Total number of firms 企业总数	Total number of employees 职工总数	Total revenue (Mil.RMB) 总销售收入 (百万元)	Total profit (Mil.RMB) 总利润 (百万元)	Return on assets 资产利润率 (%)	Return on equity 权益利润率 (%)	Labour productivity ('000 RMB/ worker) 劳动生产率 (千元/人)	Debts/ assets 资产负债率 (%)	Total assets (Mil.RMB) 总资产 (百万元)
Industry Overall 行业总体	260	86,298	7,918	104	1.04	2.94	28.85	64.46	9,959

	Number of firms 企业个数	Average number of employees 平均职工人数	Average revenue ('000 RMB) 平均销售收入 (千元)	Average profit ('000 RMB) 平均利润 (千元)	Return on assets 资产利润率 (%)	Return on equity 权益利润率 (%)	Labour productivity ('000 RMB/ worker) 劳动生产率 (千元/人)	Debts/ assets 资产负债率 (%)	Average total assets ('000 RMB) 平均总资产 (千元)
By ownership 产业所有权									
State-owned 国有	39	231	7,140	-725	-1.24		10.14	100.75	58,267
Collective-owned 集体	26	304	31,285	-101	-0.48	-2.19	29.24	78.03	21,106
Foreign & Overseas Chinese Funded 三资	144	381	37,179	511	1.47	2.99	32.84	50.88	34,771
By regional distribution 地区分布									
Central-North 华北	22	207	19,018	248	0.45	1.78	38.32	74.76	55,222
Beijing 北京	4	275	35,596	1,210	2.33	8.08	33.85	71.17	51,957
Tianjin 天津	16	186	15,524	-6	-0.01	-0.04	41.66	72.90	58,404
Hebei 河北	2	234	13,814	363	1.00		27.61	108.99	36,292
Shanxi 山西									
Inner Mongolia 内蒙古									
Northeast 东北	7	377	16,058	-2,848	-3.39		18.37	124.66	84,001
Liaoning 辽宁	5	432	19,877	-3,588	-3.61		19.85	131.10	99,313
Jilin 吉林									
Heilongjiang 黑龙江	2	239	6,511	-997	-2.18	-21.05	11.66	89.64	45,722
Central-East 华东	72	270	24,939	627	2.10	7.88	26.77	73.34	29,808
Shanghai 上海	9	197	21,869	1,211	3.01	9.46	32.62	68.13	40,184
Jiangsu 江苏	6	332	24,370	-793	-3.89	-11.68	16.22	66.68	20,362
Zhejiang 浙江	12	168	14,128	274	1.70	3.00	20.94	43.32	16,125
Anhui 安徽									
Fujian 福建	31	194	24,599	1,088	8.61	15.19	41.10	43.32	12,635
Jiangxi 江西	3	433	6,453	73	0.29	0.39	4.58	26.05	25,089
Shandong 山东	11	578	45,558	159	0.17	6.06	21.26	97.12	91,083
Central-South 中南	156	379	35,826	476	1.24	2.65	29.54	53.11	38,289
Henan 河南	4	424	4,488	-57	-0.15	-4.69	4.99	96.72	37,045
Hubei 湖北	4	756	61,409	-1,599	-4.22		36.20	105.85	37,867
Hunan 湖南	1	315	4,512	-2,112	-6.34	-86.03	0.91	92.63	33,303
Guangdong 广东	145	361	36,535	579	1.51	3.04	30.68	50.45	38,475
Guangxi 广西	2	818	11,558	-545	-1.78	-2.84	11.71	37.47	30,610
Hainan 海南									
Southwest 西南	3	194	947	-298	-2.46	-21.25	2.10	88.44	12,148
Chongqing 重庆	1	49	433	-421	-14.99		5.80	154.43	2,809
Sichuan 四川	1	314	309	-526	-2.87	-30.04	0.99	90.43	18,306
Guizhou 贵州	1	220	2,099	52	0.34	1.30	2.86	73.97	15,328
Yunnan 云南									
Tibet 西藏									
Northwest 西北									
Shaanxi 陕西									
Gansu 甘肃									
Qinghai 青海									
Ningxia 宁夏									
Xinjiang 新疆									

Year 年份	Number of firms 企业个数	Rate of change 变化率 (%)	Number of employees 职工人数 (人)	Rate of change 变化率 (%)	Total revenue (Mil. RMB) 总销售收入 (百万元)	Rate of change 变化率 (%)	Total profit (Mil RMB) 总利润 (百万元)	Rate of change 变化率 (%)
2000	254		86,166		6,655		-21	
2001	254		78,748	-8.61	8,102	21.74	143	
2002	260	2.36	86,298	9.59	7,918	-2.27	104	-27.27

Major Products 主要产品	Output 产量	Unit 单位
Clock 表	18,392	10,000 Units 万只
Watch 钟	17,962	10,000 Units 万只

10 Main Firms with Maximal Revenue (year founded) 收入最大的十家主要企业 （创办年份）	City 城市	Province 省	Telephone/ fax 电话/ 传真	Number of employees 职工 人数	Ownership 产业所有权	Revenue ('000 RMB) 销售收入 (千元)	Profit('000 RMB) (rank) 利润(千元) (排名)	Total assets ('000 RMB) 总资产 (千元)	Major products 主要 产品
Flextronics Ind.(Shenzhen)Co., Ltd.	Shenzhen	Guangdong	(0755)27497333		Foreign Funded				PCBA Circuit Plate.PCBA
伟创力实业（深圳）有限公司(1994)	深圳市	广东省	(0755)27497222	1,657	外商投资	813,299	7,502(9)	380,284	线路板
Zhuhai New Pearl Watchmaking Co., Ltd.	Zhuhai	Guangdong	(0756)8134199		Foreign Funded				Watch Core
珠海新明珠表业有限公司(1996)	珠海市	广东省	(0756)8111882	1,436	外商投资	398,363	10,079(7)	123,404	表芯
Hubei Fuyuan Watch Industry Co., Ltd.	Huanggang	Hubei	(0713)6222888		Overseas Chinese-funded				Clock
湖北富源表业有限公司(1992)	黄冈市	湖北省	(0713)6227888	2,098	港澳台资	227,008	307(87)	19,637	钟表
Zhaoqing Liheng Plastic Cement Hardware Electron Factory	Zhaoqing	Guangdong	(0758)2874393		Collective-owned				Electronic Watch
肇庆市力恒塑胶五金电子厂(1992)	肇庆市	广东省	(0758)2878198	371	集体企业	190,140	90(125)	35,284	电子表
Panyu Pearl Clock Factory	Guangzhou	Guangdong	(020)84785850		Overseas Chinese-funded				Quartz Clock
番禺明珠星钟厂(1996)	广州市	广东省	(020)84781118	1,780	港澳台资	180,089	3,802(16)	98,240	石英钟
Yantai Polaris Clock & Watch Group Company	Yantai	Shandong	(0535)6226207		State Owned				Clock
烟台北极星钟表集团公司(1987)	烟台市	山东省	(0535)6215205	2,924	国有企业	174,641	-	470,167	钟
Fuzhou Reida Electronics Co., Ltd.	Fuzhou	Fujian	(0591)3856301		Overseas Chinese-funded				Quartz Clock
福州瑞达电子有限公司(1993)	福州市	福建省	(0591)3767111	400	港澳台资	168,549	7,363(10)	72,707	石英钟
Shenzhen Fiyta(Group) Holdings Co.Ltd.	Shenzhen	Guangdong	(0755)83217888		Joint Stock				FIYTA Wristwatch飞
深圳市飞亚达（集团）股份有限公司(1990)	深圳市	广东省	(0755)83348369	1,526	股份制	155,599	14,107(4)	665,030	亚达手表
Longhai Huayi (Longhai) Clocks & Watches CO.,LTD	Zhangzhou	Fujian	(0596)6650214		Private Owned				Quartz Watch Core石
龙海市华艺钟表有限公司(1995)	漳州市	福建省	(0596)6650590	550	私营企业	152,405	14,700(2)	49,997	石英钟机芯
Univesal Industrial Development (Shenzhen) Co., Ltd.	Shenzhen	Guangdong	(0755)27555778		Overseas Chinese-funded				Wristwatch
环球实业发展（深圳）有限公司(1991)	深圳市	广东省	(0755)27555678	1,900	港澳台资	126,783	3,329(19)	96,920	手表

Top 10 Cities by Revenue 销售收入排名前10位城市	Province 省	Market share 市场份额 (%)	Number of firms 企业个数
Shenzhen 深圳市	Guangdong 广东省	27.42	47
Guangzhou 广州市	Guangdong 广东省	11.94	26
Zhuhai 珠海市	Guangdong 广东省	7.40	8
Zhangzhou 漳州市	Fujian 福建省	5.38	15
Dongguan 东莞市	Guangdong 广东省	4.42	17
Yantai 烟台市	Shandong 山东省	3.81	4
Fuzhou 福州市	Fujian 福建省	3.28	7
Tianjin 天津市	Tianjin 天津市	3.14	16
Huanggang 黄冈市	Hubei 湖北省	3.07	2
Foshan 佛山市	Guangdong 广东省	2.63	9

10 Major Wholesalers 十家主要批发商	City 城市	Province 省	Telephone/Fax 电话/传真
King Paper Source Trade (shanghai) Co.,Ltd.	Shanghai	Shanghai	(021)62720808
金纸源贸易（上海）有限公司	上海市	上海市	(021)62720909
China National Paper & Pulp Corpration	Beijing	Beijing	(010)67780346
中国纸张纸浆进出口公司	北京市	北京市	(010)67747294
Sinar Mas Linjiang Paper Industry Trade (Beijing) Co.,Ltd.	Beijing	Beijing	(010)65666688
金光林浆纸业贸易(北京)有限公司	北京市	北京市	(010)65669599
Sinar Mas Paper Industry (Xishan) Co.,Ltd.	Wuxi	Jiangsu	(0510)8251188
金光纸业(锡山)有限公司	无锡市	江苏省	(0510)8250906
China Printing Materials General Company	Beijing	Beijing	(010)63442905
中国印刷物资总公司	北京市	北京市	(010)63442900
TSS Eortune Co., ltd.	Tianjin	Tianjin	(022)28131350
天津同鑫进出口有限公司	天津市	天津市	(022)28131353
Wenzhou Import & Export Corpration	Wenzhou	Zhejiang	(0577)88862681
温州市进出口公司	温州市	浙江省	(0577)88844557
Sinar Mas Paper Industry (Xiamen) Co.,Ltd.	Xiamen	Fujian	(0592)2962018
金光纸业（厦门）有限公司	厦门市	福建省	(0592)2962010
Sinar Mas Paper Industry (Shenzhen) Co.,Ltd.	Shenzhen	Guangdong	(0755)83516701
金光纸业（深圳）有限公司	深圳市	广东省	(0755)83516773
Jieyang Ocean Shipping Supply Group Co.,Ltd.	Jieyang	Guangdong	(0663)8239634
揭阳市外轮供应集团有限公司	揭阳市	广东省	(0663)8236186

4290: Other Meters 其他仪器仪表制造业

The industry accounts for 0.019% of the total revenue of China's industrial sector in 2002. The rate of return on assets is 9.22%. 70.24% of all firms in the industry made a profit while 29.76% had negative returns.The top province in terms of the industry's revenue is Shanghai, accounting for 34.69% of the total revenue.
2002年本行业收入占全行业的0.019%，资产利润率为9.22%。70.24%的企业赢利，29.76%的企业亏损。收入最高的省为上海市，占本行业的34.69%。

	Total number of firms 企业总数	Total number of employees 职工总数	Total revenue (Mil.RMB) 总销售收入（百万元）	Total profit (Mil.RMB) 总利润（百万元）	Return on assets 资产利润率 (%)	Return on equity 权益利润率 (%)	Labour productivity ('000 RMB/ worker) 劳动生产率（千元/人）	Debts/ assets 资产负债率 (%)	Total assets (Mil.RMB) 总资产（百万元）
Industry Overall 行业总体	84	12,181	2,058	281	9.22	17.98	55.23	48.71	3,049

	Number of firms 企业个数	Average number of employees 平均职工人数	Average revenue ('000 RMB) 平均销售收入（千元）	Average profit ('000 RMB) 平均利润（千元）	Return on assets 资产利润率 (%)	Return on equity 权益利润率 (%)	Labour productivity ('000 RMB/ worker) 劳动生产率（千元/人）	Debts/ assets 资产负债率 (%)	Average total assets ('000 RMB) 平均总资产（千元）
By ownership 产业所有权									
State-owned 国有	17	93	7,067	-138	-0.54	-3.72	23.89	85.46	25,486
Collective-owned 集体	11	130	9,117	219	1.12	2.19	5.60	48.91	19,548
Foreign & Overseas Chinese Funded 三资	23	123	49,202	10,101	14.13	23.97	142.90	41.07	71,506
By regional distribution 地区分布									
Central-North 华北	15	120	14,968	1,649	4.75	14.58	27.75	67.40	34,700
Beijing 北京	6	78	14,888	1,859	12.35	16.11	34.04	23.33	15,047
Tianjin 天津	3	94	5,452	157	0.88	2.15	-49.72	59.21	17,855
Hebei 河北	4	257	29,570	3,402	3.77	17.80	46.59	78.82	90,226
Shanxi 山西	2	9	275	-250	-3.17	-23.09	3.33	86.28	7,878
Inner Mongolia 内蒙古									
Northeast 东北	4	49	6,405	153	2.85	4.95	21.10	42.45	5,374
Liaoning 辽宁	3	61	8,407	200	2.84	4.88	21.67	41.85	7,029
Jilin 吉林	1	11	400	14	3.41	12.84	11.73	73.41	410
Heilongjiang 黑龙江									
Central-East 华东	39	204	36,725	6,538	14.87	28.08	73.40	47.03	43,957
Shanghai 上海	12	251	59,483	15,383	19.36	35.88	77.53	46.04	79,438
Jiangsu 江苏	11	190	13,872	728	3.55	11.94	26.55	70.30	20,533
Zhejiang 浙江	6	80	21,180	446	2.58	7.81	62.10	67.01	17,304
Anhui 安徽	1	68	14,435	1,641	8.41	112.78	53.78	92.55	19,521
Fujian 福建	4	198	67,859	16,350	32.73	41.89	254.17	21.87	49,960
Jiangxi 江西	2	513	41,585	-5,416	-11.22	-16.14	31.23	30.50	48,287
Shandong 山东	3	161	23,256	1,167	3.03	5.18	56.82	41.40	38,478
Central-South 中南	20	79	15,147	259	0.77	1.18	13.58	35.21	33,802
Henan 河南	2	38	4,620	607	12.43	18.90	47.45	34.25	4,884
Hubei 湖北	6	78	11,412	310	3.12	8.52	64.10	63.35	9,929
Hunan 湖南	1	17	2,047	57	2.08	12.23	40.18	82.99	2,739
Guangdong 广东	11	93	20,289	187	0.34	0.50	-12.42	32.23	54,905
Guangxi 广西									
Hainan 海南									
Southwest 西南	3	190	20,855	-1,114	-3.84	-17.09	17.60	77.52	28,995
Chongqing 重庆	1	299	60,148	-685	-1.06	-4.18	31.64	74.56	64,359
Sichuan 四川	1	236	2,083	-2,410	-16.94	-255.57	1.32	93.37	14,229
Guizhou 贵州	1	35	333	-247	-2.94	-11.03	7.51	73.33	8,398
Yunnan 云南									
Tibet 西藏									
Northwest 西北	3	30	3,315	-309	-3.11	-5.72	45.38	45.63	9,932
Shaanxi 陕西	2	39	4,783	-465	-3.17	-5.78	47.75	45.25	14,672
Gansu 甘肃	1	12	380	3	0.66	2.19	30.17	69.76	453
Qinghai 青海									
Ningxia 宁夏									
Xinjiang 新疆									

Year 年份	Number of firms 企业个数	Rate of change 变化率 (%)	Number of employees 职工人数 (人)	Rate of change 变化率 (%)	Total revenue (Mil. RMB) 总销售收入 (百万元)	Rate of change 变化率 (%)	Total profit (Mil RMB) 总利润 (百万元)	Rate of change 变化率 (%)
2000	83		14,101		1,525		102	
2001	74	-10.84	12,010	-14.83	1,431	-6.16	86	-15.69
2002	84	13.51	12,181	1.42	2,058	43.82	281	226.74

Major Products 主要产品	Output 产量	Unit 单位
Film Machinery 电影机械	6,497	Unit 台

10 Main Firms with Maximal Revenue (year founded) 收入最大的十家主要企业（创办年份）	City 城市	Province 省	Telephone/fax 电话/传真	Number of employees 职工人数	Ownership 产业所有权	Revenue ('000 RMB) 销售收入 (千元)	Profit('000 RMB) (rank) 利润(千元) (排名)	Total assets ('000 RMB) 总资产 (千元)	Major products 主要产品
Diebold Finance Equipment Co., Ltd.	Shanghai	Shanghai	(021)58545678		Foreign Funded				Automatic Teller Machine ATM自
迪堡金融设备有限公司(1993)	上海市	上海市	(021)58544351	189	外商投资	452,684	154,784(1)	669,126	动柜员机
Xiamen Imaje Jinling Paint Sign Machine Co., Ltd	Xiamen	Fujian	(0592)6021964		Foreign Funded				Paint Sign Machine
厦门依玛士一金陵喷码机有限公司(1992)	厦门市	福建省	(0592)6021965	142	外商投资	143,905	23,916(3)	58,524	喷码机
Thermaster Electronic(Xiamen)Co.,Ltd.	Xiamen	Fujian	(0592)6025275		Foreign Funded				Thermostat
厦门升明电子有限公司(1997)	厦门市	福建省	(0592)5623726	555	外商投资	107,592	35,537(2)	129,519	恒温器
Jiangxi Sida Electronics Co., Ltd.	Jiujiang	Jiangxi	(0792)6825656		Limited-Liability				Ammeter
江西思达电子有限公司(2000)	九江市	江西省	(0792)6820557	394	有限公司	80,492	-	15,540	电表
Beijing Taike Xianfeng Science & Technology Co., Ltd.	Beijing	Beijing	(010)67874159		Limited-Liability				IC Card
北京泰科先锋科技有限公司(2000)	北京市	北京市	(010)67874159	51	有限公司	72,941	10,315(6)	22,527	Ic卡
Shenzhen Star Meter Co., Ltd.	Shenzhen	Guangdong	(0755)26546858		Overseas Chinese-funded				Single-phase Electronic Ammeter 单相电子
深圳思达仪表有限公司(1993)	深圳市	广东省	(0755)26546787	80	港澳台资	60,943	11,904(5)	77,848	式电度表
Qianwei Kromschorder Meters(Chongqing)Co.Ltd.	Chongqing	Chongqing	(023)67619956		Foreign Funded				Gas Meter
重庆前卫克罗姆有限责任公司(2000)	重庆市	重庆市	(023)67619960	299	外商投资	60,148	-	64,359	煤气表
Shanghai Gas Meter Indtrument Co., Ltd.	Shanghai	Shanghai	(021)63222311		Joint Stock				Household Gas Meter 家用
上海煤气表具股份有限公司(1953)	上海市	上海市	(021)63220858	703	股份制	51,700	-	84,929	燃气表
Shijiazhuang Changtong Electrical Appliance Co., Ltd.	Shijiazhuang	Hebei	(0311)5316349		Private Enterprises				Electric Energy Meter
石家庄市长通电器有限公司(1980)	石家庄市	河北省	(0311)5316999	160	私营独资	37,974	3,050(14)	24,107	电能表
Yantai WIO Telecommunications Equipment Co., Ltd.	Yantai	Shandong	(0535)6373377		Limited-Liability				Optical Cable Communication Equipment 光
烟台十维电信设备有限公司(1998)	烟台市	山东省	(0535)6373311	106	有限公司	30,951	3,657(13)	77,831	通信设备

Top 10 Cities by Revenue 销售收入排名前10位城市	Province 省	Market share 市场份额 (%)	Number of firms 企业个数
Shanghai 上海市	Shanghai 上海市	34.69	12
Xiamen 厦门市	Fujian 福建省	12.22	2
Shenzhen 深圳市	Guangdong 广东省	5.84	4
Beijing 北京市	Beijing 北京市	4.34	6
Jiujiang 九江市	Jiangxi 江西省	3.91	1
Langfang 廊坊市	Hebei 河北省	3.66	2
Hangzhou 杭州市	Zhejiang 浙江省	3.65	2
Chongqing 重庆市	Chongqing 重庆市	2.92	1
Wuhan 武汉市	Hubei 湖北省	2.17	4
Changzhou 常州市	Jiangsu 江苏省	2.08	2

10 Major Wholesalers 十家主要批发商	City 城市	Province 省	Telephone/Fax 电话/传真
SU MEC	Nanjing	Jiangsu	(025)4511888
中设江苏机械设备进出口（集团）公司	南京市	江苏省	(025)4411772
China Poster Mobile Communications Equipment Co.,Ltd.	Beijing	Beijing	(010)66426993
中邮普泰移动通信设备股份有限公司	北京市	北京市	(010)66426837
Sino Kama Co., Ltd.	Shanghai	Shanghai	(021)62031188
中泰凯马股份有限公司	上海市	上海市	(021)62030851
China Huayuan Group Co.,Ltd.	Shanghai	Shanghai	(021)62031188
中国华源集团有限公司	上海市	上海市	(021)62032288
Zhejiang Crand Imp.& Exp.Co.,Ltd.	Ningbo	Zhejiang	(0574)87720170
浙江远大进出口有限公司	宁波市	浙江省	(0574)87723350
Shandong Machinery Import & Export Group Corporation	Qingdao	Shandong	(0532)2661628
山东省机械进出口集团公司	青岛市	山东省	(0532)2991655
Qingdao Haier International Trade Co.,Ltd.	Qingdao	Shandong	(0532)8938337
青岛海尔国际贸易有限公司	青岛市	山东省	(0532)8939494
Guangdong Machinery Import & Export Group Corporation	Guangzhou	Guangdong	(020)87782168
广东省机械进出口集团公司	广州市	广东省	(020)87771803
China National Machinery Equipment Import & Export	Beijing	Beijing	(010)63474506
Corporation 中国机械设备进出口总公司	北京市	北京市	(010)63261865
Beijing Cellstar Co.,Ltd.	Beijing	Beijing	(010)64602050
北京蜂星事达电讯有限公司	北京市	北京市	(010)64672648

4311: Sculpture Handicraft 雕塑工艺品制造业

The industry accounts for 0.071% of the total revenue of China's industrial sector in 2002. The rate of return on assets is 6.03%. 91.83% of all firms in the industry made a profit while 8.17% had negative returns.The top province in terms of the industry's revenue is Fujian, accounting for 51.69% of the total revenue.
2002年本行业收入占全行业的0.071%，资产利润率为6.03%。91.83%的企业赢利，8.17%的企业亏损。收入最高的省为福建省，占本行业的51.69%。

	Total number of firms 企业总数	Total number of employees 职工总数	Total revenue (Mil.RMB) 总销售收入 (百万元)	Total profit (Mil.RMB) 总利润 (百万元)	Return on assets 资产利润率 (%)	Return on equity 权益利润率 (%)	Labour productivity ('000 RMB/ worker) 劳动生产率 (千元/人)	Debts/ assets 资产负债率 (%)	Total assets (Mil.RMB) 总资产 (百万元)
Industry Overall 行业总体	416	79,189	7,636	304	6.03	10.97	27.42	45.02	5,040

	Number of firms 企业个数	Average number of employees 平均职工人数	Average revenue ('000 RMB) 平均销售收入 (千元)	Average profit ('000 RMB) 平均利润 (千元)	Return on assets 资产利润率 (%)	Return on equity 权益利润率 (%)	Labour productivity ('000 RMB/ worker) 劳动生产率 (千元/人)	Debts/ assets 资产负债率 (%)	Average total assets ('000 RMB) 平均总资产 (千元)
By ownership 产业所有权									
State-owned 国有	13	76	5,459	158	1.82	5.99	22.55	69.53	8,642
Collective-owned 集体	37	143	22,461	574	6.14	11.99	35.91	48.76	9,341
Foreign & Overseas Chinese Funded 三资	168	286	23,999	764	4.81	9.25	23.23	48.06	15,907
By regional distribution 地区分布									
Central-North 华北	6	81	7,363	831	2.90	4.79	32.36	39.40	28,606
Beijing 北京	3	51	1,187	-216	-4.04	-21.75	10.45	81.43	5,348
Tianjin 天津									
Hebei 河北	2	26	13,152	934	36.68	331.79	162.02	88.95	2,547
Shanxi 山西									
Inner Mongolia 内蒙古	1	280	14,310	3,765	2.50	3.75	20.79	33.25	150,501
Northeast 东北	1	92	8,091	1,967	8.73	12.73	36.29	31.44	22,541
Liaoning 辽宁									
Jilin 吉林									
Heilongjiang 黑龙江	1	92	8,091	1,967	8.73	12.73	36.29	31.44	22,541
Central-East 华东	331	180	17,125	741	6.81	11.81	25.88	42.29	10,872
Shanghai 上海	14	140	16,470	563	3.57	6.89	24.45	48.12	15,745
Jiangsu 江苏	15	121	43,790	518	5.44	15.15	49.07	64.10	9,524
Zhejiang 浙江	34	115	9,880	535	8.82	19.37	25.75	54.46	6,061
Anhui 安徽	2	147	9,850	778	15.25	21.43	29.90	28.84	5,102
Fujian 福建	253	183	15,599	682	8.36	14.22	25.58	41.22	8,160
Jiangxi 江西	5	638	46,404	6,640	4.23	6.25	18.49	32.29	156,844
Shandong 山东	8	288	30,843	506	2.37	6.18	24.71	61.62	21,302
Central-South 中南	69	269	27,653	777	4.50	9.68	32.57	53.45	17,256
Henan 河南	24	112	19,862	738	14.41	105.75	79.42	86.37	5,124
Hubei 湖北	5	148	9,764	347	5.01	13.01	27.56	61.52	6,936
Hunan 湖南	1	30	979	1	0.03	0.08	8.67	55.90	3,009
Guangdong 广东	39	388	35,425	876	3.32	6.54	24.53	49.24	26,411
Guangxi 广西									
Hainan 海南									
Southwest 西南	3	17	93	-132	-10.74	-17.28	1.13	37.82	1,232
Chongqing 重庆									
Sichuan 四川									
Guizhou 贵州									
Yunnan 云南									
Tibet 西藏	3	17	93	-132	-10.74	-17.28	1.13	37.82	1,232
Northwest 西北	6	52	1,100	-226	-2.58	-7.37	9.97	64.96	8,752
Shaanxi 陕西	2	62	917	68	0.84	2.17	4.19	61.20	8,093
Gansu 甘肃	4	47	1,192	-373	-4.11	-12.31	13.73	66.64	9,082
Qinghai 青海									
Ningxia 宁夏									
Xinjiang 新疆									

4311: Sculpture Handicraft 雕塑工艺品制造业

Year 年份	Number of firms 企业个数	Rate of change 变化率 (%)	Number of employees 职工人数 (人)	Rate of change 变化率 (%)	Total revenue (Mil. RMB) 总销售收入 (百万元)	Rate of change 变化率 (%)	Total profit (Mil RMB) 总利润 (百万元)	Rate of change 变化率 (%)
2000	384		97,874		6,693,528		298,784	
2001	409	6.51	87,463	-10.64	6,737	-99.90	272	-99.91
2002	416	1.71	79,189	-9.46	7,636	13.34	304	11.76

Major Products 主要产品	Output 产量	Unit 单位
Industrial Arts Products 工艺美术制品	432	100,000,000 yuan 亿元

10 Main Firms with Maximal Revenue (year founded) 收入最大的十家主要企业（创办年份）	City 城市	Province 省	Telephone/fax 电话/传真	Number of employees 职工人数	Ownership 产业所有权	Revenue ('000 RMB) 销售收入 (千元)	Profit('000 RMB) (rank) 利润(千元) (排名)	Total assets ('000 RMB) 总资产 (千元)	Major products 主要产品
Guangzhou Xinlin Technology Co., Ltd. 广州鑫林工艺有限公司(1992)	Guangzhou 广州市	Guangdong 广东省	(020)87993098 (020)87993114	2,571	Overseas Chinese-funded 港澳台资	268,550	13,090(2)	410,566	Industrial Art Products 工艺美术品
Gudai (Taishan) Gifts Factory 古代(台山)礼品厂(1990)	Jiangmen 江门市	Guangdong 广东省	(0750)5571978 (0750)5571036	357	Overseas Chinese-funded 港澳台资	210,307	929(93)	47,539	Boli Ornaments Gifts波丽装饰礼品
Guangzhou Fumincheng Technology Co., Ltd. 广州富敏城工艺有限公司(1992)	Guangzhou 广州市	Guangdong 广东省	(020)87980051 (020)87980057	947	Overseas Chinese-funded 港澳台资	155,540	7,440(5)	115,486	Industrial Art Products 工艺美术品
Quanzhou Jianwen Handicraft Co., Ltd. 泉州建文艺品有限公司(1997)	Quanzhou 泉州市	Fujian 福建省	(0595)2631687 (0595)2631822	3,000	Foreign Funded 外商投资	128,005	4,500(9)	58,960	Resin Products 树脂制品
Guangzhou Dexin Technology Co., Ltd. 广州得鑫工艺有限公司(1995)	Guangzhou 广州市	Guangdong 广东省	(020)87993098 (020)87993114	880	Overseas Chinese-funded 港澳台资	126,730	6,130(6)	51,725	Industrial Art Products 工艺美术品
Guangzhou Yifeng Wood Co., Ltd. 广州义丰木业有限公司(1993)	Guangzhou 广州市	Guangdong 广东省	(020)87912548 (020)87912467	545	Overseas Chinese-funded 港澳台资	96,447	4,822(7)	54,376	Craftwork 工艺品
Quanzhou Lianqun Building Materials Co., Ltd. 泉州联群建材有限公司(1999)	Quanzhou 泉州市	Fujian 福建省	(0595)7682728 (0595)7689701	249	Foreign Funded 外商投资	73,249	1,040(85)	30,880	Gravestone 墓碑
Fuqing Yuansheng Light Industrial Products Co., Ltd. 福清元升轻工制品有限公司(1992)	Fuzhou 福州市	Fujian 福建省	(0591)5567801 (0591)5567804	1,280	Overseas Chinese-funded 港澳台资	70,071	11,007(3)	197,504	Boli Products 波丽制品
Boshi (Panyu) Art China Co., Ltd. 博仕(番禺)陶瓷有限公司(1993)	Guangzhou 广州市	Guangdong 广东省	(020)84929612 (020)84929632	1,527	Overseas Chinese-funded 港澳台资	69,940	790(104)	24,574	Industrial Art Pottery 工艺美术陶瓷
Quanzhou Nanyang Handicraft Co., Ltd. 泉州南洋艺品有限公司(1997)	Quanzhou 泉州市	Fujian 福建省	(0595)2630819 (0595)2634819	1,621	Overseas Chinese-funded 港澳台资	69,748	2,180(30)	20,543	Resin Arts and Crafts 树脂工艺品

Top 10 Cities by Revenue 销售收入排名前10位城市	Province 省	Market share 市场份额 (%)	Number of firms 企业个数
Quanzhou 泉州市	Fujian 福建省	44.26	217
Guangzhou 广州市	Guangdong 广东省	11.05	14
Nanjing 南京市	Jiangsu 江苏省	6.22	5
Nanyang 南阳市	Henan 河南省	5.61	17
Fuzhou 福州市	Fujian 福建省	4.53	17
Jiangmen 江门市	Guangdong 广东省	3.04	4
Shanghai 上海市	Shanghai 上海市	3.02	14
Yingtan 鹰潭市	Jiangxi 江西省	2.65	2
Taizhou 台州市	Zhejiang 浙江省	2.15	13
Qingdao 青岛市	Shandong 山东省	1.71	3

10 Major Wholesalers 十家主要批发商	City 城市	Province 省	Telephone/Fax 电话/传真
China National Arts & Crafts Import & Export Corporation 中国工艺品进出口总公司	Beijing 北京市	Beijing 北京市	(010)65521133 (010)65531143
Shanghai Arts & Crafts Import & Export Co.,Ltd. 上海市工艺品进出口有限公司	Shanghai 上海市	Shanghai 上海市	(021)65222888 (021)65221898
Shandong Arts & Crafts Import & Export (Group) Co.,Ltd. 山东工艺品进出口（集团）股份有限公司	Qingdao 青岛市	Shandong 山东省	(0532)5021355 (0532)5021168
Zhejiang Arts & Crafts Import & Export Co.,Ltd. 浙江省工艺品进出口有限公司	Hangzhou 杭州市	Zhejiang 浙江省	(0571)87063393 (0571)87063838
Shanghai Shenhua Import & Export Co., Ltd. 上海申华进出口有限公司	Shanghai 上海市	Shanghai 上海市	(021)63177063 (021)63173819
China Hunan Arts & Crafts Import & Export Corporation 湖南省工艺品进出口公司	Changsha 长沙市	Hunan 湖南省	(0731)2284632 (0731)2287869
Guangdong Arts and Crafts Import & Export (Group) Corporation 广东省工艺品进出口（集团）公司	Guangzhou 广州市	Guangdong 广东省	(020)83193388 (020)83343614
Guangdong Nanhai Handicrafts Import & Export Co.,Ltd. 广东南海工艺品进出口有限公司	Foshan 佛山市	Guangdong 广东省	(0757)6220536 (0757)6220225
Tianjin Handicrafts Import & Export Group Co.,Ltd. 天津工艺品进出口集团有限公司	Tianjin 天津市	Tianjin 天津市	(022)23310080 (022)23317828
Taizhou International Trade Co.,Ltd. 台州市国际贸易有限公司	Taizhou 台州市	Zhejiang 浙江省	(0576)8811680 (0576)8882427

4312: Metal Arts And Crafts Articles 金属工艺品制造业

The industry accounts for 0.035% of the total revenue of China's industrial sector in 2002. The rate of return on assets is 6.04%. 83.23% of all firms in the industry made a profit while 16.77% had negative returns.The top province in terms of the industry's revenue is Jiangsu, accounting for 32.78% of the total revenue.
2002年本行业收入占全行业的 0.035%，资产利润率为 6.04%。83.23%的企业赢利，16.77%的企业亏损。收入最高的省为江苏省，占本行业的32.78%。

	Total number of firms 企业总数	Total number of employees 职工总数	Total revenue (Mil.RMB) 总销售收入（百万元）	Total profit (Mil.RMB) 总利润（百万元）	Return on assets 资产利润率 (%)	Return on equity 权益利润率 (%)	Labour productivity ('000 RMB/ worker) 劳动生产率（千元/人）	Debts/ assets 资产负债率 (%)	Total assets (Mil.RMB) 总资产（百万元）
Industry Overall 行业总体	167	32,571	3,716	166	6.04	13.60	32.66	55.61	2,754

	Number of firms 企业个数	Average number of employees 平均职工人数	Average revenue ('000 RMB) 平均销售收入（千元）	Average profit ('000 RMB) 平均利润（千元）	Return on assets 资产利润率 (%)	Return on equity 权益利润率 (%)	Labour productivity ('000 RMB/ worker) 劳动生产率（千元/人）	Debts/ assets 资产负债率 (%)	Average total assets ('000 RMB) 平均总资产（千元）
By ownership 产业所有权									
State-owned 国有	11	133	6,938	-600	-5.53	-1,770.51	22.29	99.69	10,854
Collective-owned 集体	21	142	17,107	939	11.06	24.42	35.92	54.71	8,488
Foreign & Overseas Chinese Funded 三资	46	237	22,794	939	5.59	11.94	29.25	53.19	16,804
By regional distribution 地区分布									
Central-North 华北	25	152	14,913	702	6.42	17.90	26.59	64.15	10,947
Beijing 北京	10	159	14,421	650	5.67	58.40	27.47	90.30	11,464
Tianjin 天津	3	276	37,715	964	5.61	12.99	26.78	56.82	17,182
Hebei 河北	10	87	10,493	873	13.42	18.28	32.68	26.61	6,504
Shanxi 山西	1	289	8,440	150	0.57	1.07	20.07	46.83	26,379
Inner Mongolia 内蒙古	1	230	2,103	-701	-4.37	-23.69	4.90	81.57	16,058
Northeast 东北	2	306	3,962	-535	-8.64	-13.95	4.51	38.06	6,190
Liaoning 辽宁	1	400	5,517	371	7.01	10.88	5.64	35.58	5,293
Jilin 吉林									
Heilongjiang 黑龙江	1	211	2,407	-1,441	-20.33	-33.84	2.36	39.92	7,087
Central-East 华东	90	200	25,590	1,401	7.06	16.05	35.73	55.98	19,826
Shanghai 上海	8	56	14,814	1,906	11.66	19.15	64.65	39.08	16,346
Jiangsu 江苏	22	303	55,370	3,579	8.23	18.22	47.24	54.84	43,505
Zhejiang 浙江	46	189	15,462	660	5.84	13.59	25.31	57.05	11,310
Anhui 安徽	1	130	19,020	1,907	18.63	29.23	39.47	36.25	10,236
Fujian 福建	6	106	11,339	-122	-1.17	-3.18	37.76	63.21	10,431
Jiangxi 江西	2	300	10,933	-1,607	-6.93	-67.43	9.36	89.72	23,186
Shandong 山东	5	176	29,253	744	6.53	23.50	52.56	72.23	11,397
Central-South 中南	45	205	21,304	492	3.58	7.38	31.88	51.52	13,751
Henan 河南	2	57	6,688	491	7.56	40.12	42.89	81.16	6,490
Hubei 湖北	2	37	9,856	429	16.87	18.94	97.82	10.94	2,540
Hunan 湖南	1	90	3,854	137	6.85	9.36	48.68	26.84	2,001
Guangdong 广东	38	213	23,841	514	3.33	6.92	33.54	51.90	15,428
Guangxi 广西	1	860	15,580	650	5.70	7.51	7.62	24.12	11,400
Hainan 海南	1	6	212				14.33	18.36	1,100
Southwest 西南	3	57	6,891	321	2.85	5.29	47.16	46.21	11,269
Chongqing 重庆									
Sichuan 四川	1	70	1,694	-514	-4.17	-24.31	15.26	82.87	12,339
Guizhou 贵州									
Yunnan 云南	1	85	18,808	1,495	8.89	12.81	79.46	30.62	16,823
Tibet 西藏	1	16	170	-19	-0.41	-0.43	15.13	5.27	4,646
Northwest 西北	2	353	26,307	283	1.84	4.37	18.03	57.84	15,324
Shaanxi 陕西	2	353	26,307	283	1.84	4.37	18.03	57.84	15,324
Gansu 甘肃									
Qinghai 青海									
Ningxia 宁夏									
Xinjiang 新疆									

4312: Metal Arts And Crafts Articles 金属工艺品制造业

Year 年份	Number of firms 企业个数	Rate of change 变化率(%)	Number of employees 职工人数(人)	Rate of change 变化率(%)	Total revenue (Mil. RMB) 总销售收入(百万元)	Rate of change 变化率(%)	Total profit (Mil RMB) 总利润(百万元)	Rate of change 变化率(%)
2000	115		26,103		2,548,340		107,466	
2001	154	33.91	28,700	9.95	3,033	-99.88	146	-99.86
2002	167	8.44	32,571	13.49	3,716	22.52	166	13.70

Major Products 主要产品	Output 产量	Unit 单位

10 Main Firms with Maximal Revenue (year founded) 收入最大的十家主要企业（创办年份）	City 城市	Province 省	Telephone/fax 电话/传真	Number of employees 职工人数	Ownership 产业所有权	Revenue ('000 RMB) 销售收入(千元)	Profit('000 RMB) (rank) 利润(千元)(排名)	Total assets ('000 RMB) 总资产(千元)	Major products 主要产品
Nanjing Gold Foil Group CO.,Ltd.	Nanjing	Jiangsu	(025)2123772		Limited-Liability				GoldLeaf
南京金箔集团有限责任公司(1955)	南京市	江苏省	(025)2281516	2,891	有限公司	598,020	58,830(1)	680,780	金箔
Changzhou HongLin Metal Material Co., Ltd.	Changzhou	Jiangsu	(0519)6751313		Private Owned				Metal Materials
常州市洪林金属材料有限公司(2000)	常州市	江苏省		93	私营企业	123,520	1,090(33)	34,140	金属材料
Guangzhou ChangHong Ornaments Co., Ltd.	Guangzhou	Guangdong	(020)87888679		Overseas Chinese-funded				Metal Craftwork 金
广州长弘饰品有限公司(1999)	广州市	广东省	(020)87888667	330	港澳台资	90,820	3,260(11)	46,567	属工艺品
Xuzhou Pengju Snapdragon Handicraft Co., Ltd.	Xuzhou	Jiangsu	(0516)4561032		Private Enterprises				Craftwork Casting 工
徐州鹏举金鱼草工艺品有限公司(1992)	徐州市	江苏省	(0516)4563296	650	私营独资	76,130	1,100(32)	33,960	艺品铸件
Heshan Yayao Gelang Hardware Industrial Co., Ltd.	Jiangmen	Guangdong	(0750)8288289		Private Owned				Handware Arts and Crafts
鹤山市雅瑶隔朗五金实业有限公司(1998)	江门市	广东省	(0750)8288089	800	私营企业	62,280	140(101)	27,569	五金工艺
Zhejiang Zhengyi Handicraft Co., Ltd.	Wenzhou	Zhejiang	(0577)62316125		Joint Stock				Metal Candleholder Decrorations 金属
浙江正怡工艺品有限公司(1993)	温州市	浙江省	(0577)62322230	462	股份制	61,785	1,875(17)	30,031	烛台饰品
Kotat Yuya Pins Factory China Fuhusi Road Nan'an Town Gaoyao	Zhaoqing	Guangdong	(0758)8396010		Overseas Chinese-funded				Copper & Iron Badge
Guangdong China 南岸镇佑亚五金厂(1998)	肇庆市	广东省	(0758)8396010	487	港澳台资	59,060	1,110(31)	15,087	铜铁徽章
Kunshan Toptree Decoration Co., Ltd.	Suzhou	Jiangsu	(0520)57790052		Foreign Funded				Scutcheon
昆山高树饰品有限公司(1992)	苏州市	江苏省	(0520)57791152	570	外商投资	51,792	13,075(2)	35,924	标牌
Tianjin Hanchang Handcrafts Co., Ltd.	Tianjin	Tianjin	(022)24930765		Foreign Funded				Craftwork
天津韩昌工艺有限公司(1995)	天津市	天津市	(022)24957004	138	外商投资	51,310	-	23,865	工艺品
Guangzhou Panyu Color Arts Jewellery Products Co., Ltd.	Guangzhou	Guangdong	(020)84929346		Overseas Chinese-funded				Copper Ornament Watch
广州番禺彩艺首饰制品有限公司(1994)	广州市	广东省	(020)84926346	195	港澳台资	46,239	4,661(8)	17,282	铜首饰表

Top 10 Cities by Revenue 销售收入排名前10位城市	Province 省	Market share 市场份额 (%)	Number of firms 企业个数
Nanjing 南京市	Jiangsu 江苏省	22.14	5
Jiangmen 江门市	Guangdong 广东省	6.54	10
Wenzhou 温州市	Zhejiang 浙江省	6.45	12
Guangzhou 广州市	Guangdong 广东省	6.40	7
Foshan 佛山市	Guangdong 广东省	5.19	7
Taizhou 台州市	Zhejiang 浙江省	4.94	13
Xuzhou 徐州市	Jiangsu 江苏省	4.00	6
Beijing 北京市	Beijing 北京市	3.88	10
Changzhou 常州市	Jiangsu 江苏省	3.32	1
Shanghai 上海市	Shanghai 上海市	3.19	8

10 Major Wholesalers 十家主要批发商	City 城市	Province 省	Telephone/Fax 电话/传真
China National Arts & Crafts Import & Export Corporation	Beijing	Beijing	(010)65521133
中国工艺品进出口总公司	北京市	北京市	(010)65531143
Shanghai Arts & Crafts Import & Export Co.,Ltd.	Shanghai	Shanghai	(021)65222888
上海市工艺品进出口有限公司	上海市	上海市	(021)65221898
Shandong Arts & Crafts Import & Export (Group) Co.,Ltd.	Qingdao	Shandong	(0532)5021355
山东工艺品进出口（集团）股份有限公司	青岛市	山东省	(0532)5021168
Zhejiang Arts & Crafts Import & Export Co.,Ltd.	Hangzhou	Zhejiang	(0571)87063393
浙江省工艺品进出口有限公司	杭州市	浙江省	(0571)87063838
Shanghai Shenhua Import & Export Co., Ltd.	Shanghai	Shanghai	(021)63177063
上海申华进出口有限公司	上海市	上海市	(021)63173819
China Hunan Arts & Crafts Import & Export Corporation	Changsha	Hunan	(0731)2284632
湖南省工艺品进出口公司	长沙市	湖南省	(0731)2287869
Guangdong Arts and Crafts Import & Export (Group) Corporation	Guangzhou	Guangdong	(020)83193388
广东省工艺品进出口（集团）公司	广州市	广东省	(020)83343614
Guangdong Nanhai Handicrafts Import & Export Co.,Ltd.	Foshan	Guangdong	(0757)6220536
广东南海工艺品进出口有限公司	佛山市	广东省	(0757)6220225
Tianjin Handicrafts Import & Export Group Co.,Ltd.	Tianjin	Tianjin	(022)23310080
天津工艺品进出口集团有限公司	天津市	天津市	(022)23317828
Taizhou International Trade Co.,Ltd.	Taizhou	Zhejiang	(0576)8811680
台州市国际贸易有限公司	台州市	浙江省	(0576)8882427

4313: Lacquerwork Arts And Crafts Articles 漆器工艺品制造业

The industry accounts for 0.002% of the total revenue of China's industrial sector in 2002. The rate of return on assets is 0.77%. 78.79% of all firms in the industry made a profit while 21.21% had negative returns.The top province in terms of the industry's revenue is Fujian, accounting for 62.48% of the total revenue.
2002年本行业收入占全行业的 0.002%，资产利润率为 0.77%。78.79%的企业赢利，21.21%的企业亏损。收入最高的省为福建省，占本行业的62.48%。

	Total number of firms 企业总数	Total number of employees 职工总数	Total revenue (Mil.RMB) 总销售收入 (百万元)	Total profit (Mil.RMB) 总利润 (百万元)	Return on assets 资产利润率 (%)	Return on equity 权益利润率 (%)	Labour productivity ('000 RMB/ worker) 劳动生产率 (千元/人)	Debts/ assets 资产负债率 (%)	Total assets (Mil.RMB) 总资产 (百万元)
Industry Overall 行业总体	33	5,415	267	3	0.77	1.53	18.12	49.82	358

	Number of firms 企业个数	Average number of employees 平均职工人数	Average revenue ('000 RMB) 平均销售收入 (千元)	Average profit ('000 RMB) 平均利润 (千元)	Return on assets 资产利润率 (%)	Return on equity 权益利润率 (%)	Labour productivity ('000 RMB/ worker) 劳动生产率 (千元/人)	Debts/ assets 资产负债率 (%)	Average total assets ('000 RMB) 平均总资产 (千元)
By ownership 产业所有权									
State-owned 国有	7	112	1,805	-293	-2.66	-8.96	9.19	70.34	11,035
Collective-owned 集体	8	142	4,305	-12	-0.13	-0.43	12.39	70.73	9,531
Foreign & Overseas Chinese Funded 三资	9	200	9,185	144	2.00	3.20	8.69	37.44	7,195
By regional distribution 地区分布									
Central-North 华北	3	151	3,030	-90	-0.51	-4.56	13.48	88.74	17,451
Beijing 北京	2	144	3,776	-137	-0.62	-5.10	17.00	87.88	22,083
Tianjin 天津									
Hebei 河北									
Shanxi 山西	1	164	1,540	4	0.05	0.73	7.30	93.34	8,187
Inner Mongolia 内蒙古									
Northeast 东北									
Liaoning 辽宁									
Jilin 吉林									
Heilongjiang 黑龙江									
Central-East 华东	22	210	11,103	141	1.14	2.00	18.45	43.04	12,405
Shanghai 上海	1	35	8,410	128	9.06	20.38	57.40	55.56	1,413
Jiangsu 江苏	2	325	14,665	10	0.06	0.24	10.39	76.77	17,910
Zhejiang 浙江									
Anhui 安徽									
Fujian 福建	15	211	11,132	165	1.24	1.84	20.73	32.58	13,303
Jiangxi 江西	1	15	14,253				132.33	70.58	1,924
Shandong 山东	3	255	8,430	161	1.41	4.24	11.90	66.68	11,400
Central-South 中南	1	15	2,500				74.13	56.27	1,946
Henan 河南									
Hubei 湖北									
Hunan 湖南	1	15	2,500				74.13	56.27	1,946
Guangdong 广东									
Guangxi 广西									
Hainan 海南									
Southwest 西南	2	63	2,469	37	1.04	1.38	15.28	25.09	3,567
Chongqing 重庆									
Sichuan 四川									
Guizhou 贵州	2	63	2,469	37	1.04	1.38	15.28	25.09	3,567
Yunnan 云南									
Tibet 西藏									
Northwest 西北	5	39	1,289	-34	-0.71	-1.39	18.49	48.88	4,825
Shaanxi 陕西									
Gansu 甘肃	5	39	1,289	-34	-0.71	-1.39	18.49	48.88	4,825
Qinghai 青海									
Ningxia 宁夏									
Xinjiang 新疆									

4313: Lacquerwork Arts And Crafts Articles 漆器工艺品制造业

Year 年份	Number of firms 企业个数	Rate of change 变化率 (%)	Number of employees 职工人数 (人)	Rate of change 变化率 (%)	Total revenue (Mil. RMB) 总销售收入 (百万元)	Rate of change 变化率 (%)	Total profit (Mil RMB) 总利润 (百万元)	Rate of change 变化率 (%)
2000	31		5,938		290,911		-203	
2001	36	16.13	6,799	14.50	316	-99.89	1	
2002	33	-8.33	5,415	-20.36	267	-15.51	3	200.00

Major Products 主要产品	Output 产量	Unit 单位

10 Main Firms with Maximal Revenue (year founded) 收入最大的十家主要企业（创办年份）	City 城市	Province 省	Telephone/fax 电话/传真	Number of employees 职工人数	Ownership 产业所有权	Revenue ('000 RMB) 销售收入 (千元)	Profit('000 RMB) (rank) 利润(千元) (排名)	Total assets ('000 RMB) 总资产 (千元)	Major products 主要产品
Xianyong Liguang Lacquerware Technology Co., Ltd. 仙游县鲤光漆器工艺有限公司(1997)	Putian 莆田市	Fujian 福建省	(0594)8293599 (0594)8296666	212	Joint Stock 股份制	26,200	-	13,840	Lacquer Handicraft 漆器工艺品
Yangzhou Lacquerware Factory 扬州漆器厂(1955)	Yangzhou 扬州市	Jiangsu 江苏省	(0514)7347338 (0514)7340265	549	Collective-owned 集体企业	17,680	20(14)	27,659	Lacquer Handicraft漆器工艺品
Putian Shanli Industrial Co.,Ltd. 莆田市山立实业公司(1995)	Putian 莆田市	Fujian 福建省	(0594)7698998 (0594)7699998	76	Private Owned 私营企业	14,628	215(7)	11,618	Lacquer Handicraft 漆器工艺品
Taicang Precision Wooden lacquerwork Co., Ltd. 太仓精工漆木器有限公司(1996)	Suzhou 苏州市	Jiangsu 江苏省	(0512)53410232 (0512)53414046	101	Foreign Funded 外商投资	11,650	-	8,160	Lacquer Handicraft 漆器工艺品
Xianyong Jianhua Craftwork Co., Ltd. 仙游县建华工艺品有限公司(2001)	Putian 莆田市	Fujian 福建省	(0594)7396177 (0594)7396177	56	Private Owned 私营企业	10,440	193(8)	1,570	Lacquering Plate 漆盘
Xianyong Nanlin Craftwork Industrial Co., Ltd. 仙游南林工艺实业有限公司(2003)	Putian 莆田市	Fujian 福建省	(0594)8690778 (0594)8696653	282	Overseas Chinese-funded 港澳台资	9,975	603(3)	5,161	Woodwork 木制品
Xianyong Qianglong Wood Craftwork Co., Ltd. 仙游县强龙木工艺品有限公司(1998)	Putian 莆田市	Fujian 福建省	(0594)7397681 (0594)7396537	56	Overseas Chinese-funded 港澳台资	9,938	332(6)	4,610	Lacquer Handicraft 漆器工艺品
Xianyong Craftwork Quality Goods Co., Ltd. 仙游工艺精品有限公司(1993)	Putian 莆田市	Fujian 福建省	(0594)8295831 (0594)8599583	88	Foreign Funded 外商投资	9,652	497(4)	12,048	wooden fish 木鱼
Xianyong Nanshuo Toy Co.,Ltd. 仙游南硕玩具有限公司(1998)	Putian 莆田市	Fujian 福建省	(0594)8690080 (0594)8699653	232	Overseas Chinese funded 港澳台资	8,845	46(13)	6,120	Woodwork 木制品
Shanghai Ningbo Handicrafts Co.,Ltd. 上海宁博工艺品有限公司(2001)	Shanghai 上海市	Shanghai 上海市	(021)64889143 (021)64927325	35	Private Partnership 私营合伙	8,410	128(9)	1,413	Craftwork 工艺品

Top 10 Cities by Revenue 销售收入排名前10位城市	Province 省	Market share 市场份额 (%)	Number of firms 企业个数
Putian 莆田市	Fujian 福建省	58.66	11
Yangzhou 扬州市	Jiangsu 江苏省	6.62	1
Nanchang 南昌市	Jiangxi 江西省	5.33	1
Jining 济宁市	Shandong 山东省	4.73	1
Suzhou 苏州市	Jiangsu 江苏省	4.36	1
Shanghai 上海市	Shanghai 上海市	3.15	1
Zhangzhou 漳州市	Fujian 福建省	3.09	1
Beijing 北京市	Beijing 北京市	2.83	2
Weifang 潍坊市	Shandong 山东省	2.57	1
Weihai 威海市	Shandong 山东省	2.16	1

10 Major Wholesalers 十家主要批发商	City 城市	Province 省	Telephone/Fax 电话/传真
China National Arts & Crafts Import & Export Corporation 中国工艺品进出口总公司	Beijing 北京市	Beijing 北京市	(010)65521133 (010)65531143
Shanghai Arts & Crafts Import & Export Co.,Ltd. 上海市工艺品进出口有限公司	Shanghai 上海市	Shanghai 上海市	(021)65222888 (021)65221898
Shandong Arts & Crafts Import & Export (Group) Co.,Ltd. 山东工艺品进出口（集团）股份有限公司	Qingdao 青岛市	Shandong 山东省	(0532)5021355 (0532)5021168
Zhejiang Arts & Crafts Import & Export Co.,Ltd. 浙江省工艺品进出口有限公司	Hangzhou 杭州市	Zhejiang 浙江省	(0571)87063393 (0571)87063838
Shanghai Shenhua Import & Export Co., Ltd. 上海申华进出口有限公司	Shanghai 上海市	Shanghai 上海市	(021)63177063 (021)63173819
China Hunan Arts & Crafts Import & Export Corporation 湖南省工艺品进出口公司	Changsha 长沙市	Hunan 湖南省	(0731)2284632 (0731)2287869
Guangdong Arts and Crafts Import & Export (Group) Corporation 广东省工艺品进出口（集团）公司	Guangzhou 广州市	Guangdong 广东省	(020)83193388 (020)83343614
Guangdong Nanhai Handicrafts Import & Export Co.,Ltd. 广东南海工艺品进出口有限公司	Foshan 佛山市	Guangdong 广东省	(0757)6220536 (0757)6220225
Tianjin Handicrafts Import & Export Group Co.,Ltd. 天津工艺品进出口集团有限公司	Tianjin 天津市	Tianjin 天津市	(022)23310080 (022)23317828
Taizhou International Trade Co.,Ltd. 台州市国际贸易有限公司	Taizhou 台州市	Zhejiang 浙江省	(0576)8811680 (0576)8882427

4314: Flower And Birds Painting 花画工艺品制造业

The industry accounts for 0.033% of the total revenue of China's industrial sector in 2002. The rate of return on assets is 3.23%. 83.33% of all firms in the industry made a profit while 16.67% had negative returns.The top province in terms of the industry's revenue is Guangdong, accounting for 71.49% of the total revenue.
2002年本行业收入占全行业的0.033%，资产利润率为3.23%。83.33%的企业赢利，16.67%的企业亏损。收入最高的省为广东省，占本行业的71.49%。

	Total number of firms 企业总数	Total number of employees 职工总数	Total revenue (Mil.RMB) 总销售收入 (百万元)	Total profit (Mil.RMB) 总利润 (百万元)	Return on assets 资产利润率 (%)	Return on equity 权益利润率 (%)	Labour productivity ('000 RMB/ worker) 劳动生产率 (千元/人)	Debts/ assets 资产负债率 (%)	Total assets (Mil.RMB) 总资产 (百万元)
Industry Overall 行业总体	138	44,814	3,588	81	3.23	6.33	20.38	48.96	2,492

	Number of firms 企业个数	Average number of employees 平均职工人数	Average revenue ('000 RMB) 平均销售收入 (千元)	Average profit ('000 RMB) 平均利润 (千元)	Return on assets 资产利润率 (%)	Return on equity 权益利润率 (%)	Labour productivity ('000 RMB/ worker) 劳动生产率 (千元/人)	Debts/ assets 资产负债率 (%)	Average total assets ('000 RMB) 平均总资产 (千元)
By ownership 产业所有权									
State-owned 国有	6	179	4,487	557	6.49	17.66	12.49	63.26	8,579
Collective-owned 集体	22	268	17,696	475	2.49	8.92	18.78	72.09	19,099
Foreign & Overseas Chinese Funded 三资	84	397	32,387	517	2.44	4.29	20.32	43.11	21,158
By regional distribution 地区分布									
Central-North 华北	5	135	6,501	1,016	19.73	28.75	21.15	31.35	5,146
Beijing 北京	2	159	6,304	2,184	29.94	42.81	24.14	30.08	7,294
Tianjin 天津	2	104	5,661	173	8.05	21.43	16.09	62.45	2,144
Hebei 河北	1	151	8,575	366	5.34	6.25	21.83	14.60	6,855
Shanxi 山西									
Inner Mongolia 内蒙古									
Northeast 东北	9	147	19,674	561	4.93	10.75	37.75	54.17	11,394
Liaoning 辽宁	9	147	19,674	561	4.93	10.75	37.75	54.17	11,394
Jilin 吉林									
Heilongjiang 黑龙江									
Central-East 华东	37	318	21,428	901	3.98	8.68	19.90	54.11	22,636
Shanghai 上海	3	60	5,460	165	3.49	4.88	34.17	28.51	4,723
Jiangsu 江苏	4	74	3,781	-12	-0.26	-0.52	32.23	50.63	4,684
Zhejiang 浙江	8	183	23,140	837	8.84	22.32	24.05	60.38	9,468
Anhui 安徽	1	63	942	3	0.24	0.30	12.71	17.93	1,238
Fujian 福建	7	767	43,634	1,320	2.70	3.91	20.06	30.92	48,904
Jiangxi 江西	3	530	19,017	1,342	20.39	34.76	7.51	41.34	6,580
Shandong 山东	11	256	19,344	1,176	3.54	15.06	22.39	76.50	33,235
Central-South 中南	87	357	29,714	426	2.43	4.50	19.81	46.08	17,541
Henan 河南									
Hubei 湖北	1	167	10,898	808	20.09	26.81	15.23	25.06	4,022
Hunan 湖南	1	180	9,420				18.14	91.24	12,894
Guangdong 广东	85	361	30,174	426	2.40	4.43	19.84	45.75	17,755
Guangxi 广西									
Hainan 海南									
Southwest 西南									
Chongqing 重庆									
Sichuan 四川									
Guizhou 贵州									
Yunnan 云南									
Tibet 西藏									
Northwest 西北									
Shaanxi 陕西									
Gansu 甘肃									
Qinghai 青海									
Ningxia 宁夏									
Xinjiang 新疆									

4314: Flower And Birds Painting 花画工艺品制造业

Year 年份	Number of firms 企业个数	Rate of change 变化率 (%)	Number of employees 职工人数 (人)	Rate of change 变化率 (%)	Total revenue (Mil. RMB) 总销售收入 (百万元)	Rate of change 变化率 (%)	Total profit (Mil RMB) 总利润 (百万元)	Rate of change 变化率 (%)
2000	125		44,150		3,469,519		89,640	
2001	121	-3.20	38,301	-13.25	3,066	-99.91	77	-99.91
2002	138	14.05	44,814	17.00	3,588	17.03	81	5.19

Major Products 主要产品	Output 产量	Unit 单位

10 Main Firms with Maximal Revenue (year founded) 收入最大的十家主要企业（创办年份）	City 城市	Province 省	Telephone/fax 电话/传真	Number of employees 职工人数	Ownership 产业所有权	Revenue ('000 RMB) 销售收入 (千元)	Profit('000 RMB) (rank) 利润(千元) (排名)	Total assets ('000 RMB) 总资产 (千元)	Major products 主要产品
Zhongshan Huatai Handicrafts Co., Ltd.	Zhongshan	Guangdong	(0760)7726286		Overseas Chinese-funded				Silk Flower
中山华泰工艺制品有限公司(1994)	中山市	广东省	(0760)7726888	1,200	港澳台资	210,787	5,247(3)	209,048	丝花
Xiamen JinPeng Artificial Flowers Co., Ltd.	Xiamen	Fujian	(0592)7101226		Overseas Chinese-funded				Artificial Flower
厦门金鹏人造花有限公司(1989)	厦门市	福建省	(0592)7310563	4,000	港澳台资	143,832	6,000(1)	146,743	人造花
Sanshui Fuyang Artificial Flowers Co., Ltd.	Foshan	Guangdong	(0757)7831393		Overseas Chinese-funded				Plastic Artificial Flower塑
三水市富洋人造花有限公司(1993)	佛山市	广东省	(0757)7831176	1,200	港澳台资	133,649	710(37)	18,877	料人造花
Sanshui Dacheng Craftwork Co., Ltd.	Foshan	Guangdong	(0757)7736338		Overseas Chinese-funded				Plastic Cloth Tree Flower塑
三水市大成工艺有限公司(1993)	佛山市	广东省	(0757)7736338	882	港澳台资	127,482	211(71)	15,843	料布树花
Sanshui Xinan Yifu Artificial Flower Co., Ltd.	Foshan	Guangdong	(0757)7731383		Overseas Chinese-funded				Plastic Cloth Tree Flower塑
三水市西南溢富人造花有限公司(1996)	佛山市	广东省	(0757)7705540	770	港澳台资	80,254	111(85)	21,509	胶布树花
Sanshui Huawen Man-made Silk & Velvet Flower Co., Ltd.	Foshan	Guangdong	(0757)7319268		Private Owned				Artificial Silk Flower
三水市华文人造绢花有限公司(1996)	佛山市	广东省	(0757)7319268	705	私营企业	76,800	1,240(21)	12,065	人造绢花
Kaiping Weili Artificial Flower Factory	Jiangmen	Guangdong	(0750)2612892		Overseas Chinese-funded				Terylene Flower
开平威利人造花厂(1993)	江门市	广东省	(0750)2612763	417	港澳台资	76,000	-	29,124	涤纶花
Doumen Qingyi Craftwork Factory	Zhuhai	Guangdong	(0756)5229668		Overseas Chinese-funded				Artificial Flower
斗门区庆怡工艺厂(1999)	珠海市	广东省	(0756)5229613	100	港澳台资	67,000	400(53)	12,623	人造花
Zhuhai Doumen Xinlongchang Silk Flower Factory	Zhuhai	Guangdong	(0756)5229484		Overseas Chinese-funded				Artificial Silk Flower
珠海市斗门新龙昌丝花厂(1994)	珠海市	广东省	(0756)5229484	40	港澳台资	65,850	421(32)	22,000	人造丝花
Doumen Fulai Silk Flower Factory	Zhuhai	Guangdong	(0756)5229484		Overseas Chinese-funded				Artificial Silk Flower
斗门区富来丝花厂(1997)	珠海市	广东省	(0756)5229541	50	港澳台资	65,602	439(51)	6,310	人造丝花

Top 10 Cities by Revenue 销售收入排名前10位城市	Province 省	Market share 市场份额 (%)	Number of firms 企业个数
Foshan 佛山市	Guangdong 广东省	19.59	11
Zhuhai 珠海市	Guangdong 广东省	12.63	12
Zhongshan 中山市	Guangdong 广东省	10.65	6
Jiangmen 江门市	Guangdong 广东省	8.70	11
Guangzhou 广州市	Guangdong 广东省	6.00	13
Xiamen 厦门市	Fujian 福建省	5.02	2
Zhaoqing 肇庆市	Guangdong 广东省	4.55	6
Zaozhuang 枣庄市	Shandong 山东省	2.83	2
Taizhou 台州市	Zhejiang 浙江省	2.79	1
Shenyang 沈阳市	Liaoning 辽宁省	2.68	4

10 Major Wholesalers 十家主要批发商	City 城市	Province 省	Telephone/Fax 电话/传真
China National Arts & Crafts Import & Export Corporation	Beijing	Beijing	(010)65521133
中国工艺品进出口总公司	北京市	北京市	(010)65531143
Shanghai Arts & Crafts Import & Export Co.,Ltd.	Shanghai	Shanghai	(021)65222888
上海市工艺品进出口有限公司	上海市	上海市	(021)65221898
Shandong Arts & Crafts Import & Export (Group) Co.,Ltd.	Qingdao	Shandong	(0532)5021355
山东工艺品进出口（集团）股份有限公司	青岛市	山东省	(0532)5021168
Zhejiang Arts & Crafts Import & Export Co.,Ltd.	Hangzhou	Zhejiang	(0571)87063393
浙江省工艺品进出口有限公司	杭州市	浙江省	(0571)87063838
Shanghai Shenhua Import & Export Co., Ltd.	Shanghai	Shanghai	(021)63177063
上海申华进出口有限公司	上海市	上海市	(021)63173819
China Hunan Arts & Crafts Import & Export Corporation	Changsha	Hunan	(0731)2284632
湖南省工艺品进出口公司	长沙市	湖南省	(0731)2287869
Guangdong Arts and Crafts Import & Export (Group) Corporation	Guangzhou	Guangdong	(020)83193388
广东省工艺品进出口（集团）公司	广州市	广东省	(020)83343614
Guangdong Nanhai Handicrafts Import & Export Co.,Ltd.	Foshan	Guangdong	(0757)6220536
广东南海工艺品进出口有限公司	佛山市	广东省	(0757)6220225
Tianjin Handicrafts Import & Export Group Co.,Ltd.	Tianjin	Tianjin	(022)23310080
天津工艺品进出口集团有限公司	天津市	天津市	(022)23317828
Taizhou International Trade Co.,Ltd.	Taizhou	Zhejiang	(0576)8811680
台州市国际贸易有限公司	台州市	浙江省	(0576)8882427

4315: Bamboo,Rattan,Palm,Hasty handicraft 竹、藤、棕、草工艺品制造业

The industry accounts for 0.090% of the total revenue of China's industrial sector in 2002. The rate of return on assets is 7.02%. 90.00% of all firms in the industry made a profit while 10.00% had negative returns.The top province in terms of the industry's revenue is Zhejiang, accounting for 29.26% of the total revenue.
2002年本行业收入占全行业的 0.090%，资产利润率为 7.02%。90.00%的企业赢利，10.00%的企业亏损。收入最高的省为浙江省，占本行业的29.26%。

	Total number of firms 企业总数	Total number of employees 职工总数	Total revenue (Mil.RMB) 总销售收入(百万元)	Total profit (Mil.RMB) 总利润(百万元)	Return on assets 资产利润率(%)	Return on equity 权益利润率(%)	Labour productivity ('000 RMB/ worker) 劳动生产率(千元/人)	Debts/ assets 资产负债率(%)	Total assets (Mil.RMB) 总资产(百万元)
Industry Overall 行业总体	520	102,094	9,649	336	7.02	14.84	28.58	52.70	4,790

	Number of firms 企业个数	Average number of employees 平均职工人数	Average revenue ('000 RMB) 平均销售收入（千元)	Average profit ('000 RMB) 平均利润(千元)	Return on assets 资产利润率(%)	Return on equity 权益利润率(%)	Labour productivity ('000 RMB/ worker) 劳动生产率(千元/人)	Debts/ assets 资产负债率(%)	Average total assets ('000 RMB) 平均总资产(千元)
By ownership 产业所有权									
State-owned 国有	3	40	2,410	-590	-14.95		-3.49	119.67	3,948
Collective-owned 集体	61	262	23,961	792	7.98	16.63	25.98	52.00	9,920
Foreign & Overseas Chinese Funded 三资	167	245	24,655	881	7.55	16.50	32.59	54.23	11,666
By regional distribution 地区分布									
Central-North 华北	3	91	6,323	710	27.15	49.71	25.42	45.38	2,616
Beijing 北京	1	4	436	-4	-0.49	-1.27	33.00	61.43	814
Tianjin 天津	1	120	9,050	2,110	77.57	133.54	31.42	41.91	2,720
Hebei 河北	1	150	9,482	25	0.58	1.04	20.43	44.54	4,315
Shanxi 山西									
Inner Mongolia 内蒙古									
Northeast 东北	4	125	5,510	108	1.55	6.06	15.59	74.46	6,995
Liaoning 辽宁	4	125	5,510	108	1.55	6.06	15.59	74.46	6,995
Jilin 吉林									
Heilongjiang 黑龙江									
Central-East 华东	372	177	17,647	611	6.46	14.44	30.74	55.29	9,465
Shanghai 上海	3	32	7,496	424	15.00	23.55	56.25	36.29	2,826
Jiangsu 江苏	11	197	22,401	390	2.95	11.20	28.18	73.62	13,205
Zhejiang 浙江	208	148	13,572	409	4.59	10.83	25.42	57.65	8,917
Anhui 安徽	11	459	19,478	963	7.55	15.81	15.20	52.26	12,762
Fujian 福建	69	263	26,942	1,067	10.09	18.96	39.74	46.82	10,580
Jiangxi 江西	2	49	4,264	256	8.60	11.15	22.03	22.88	2,972
Shandong 山东	68	139	20,456	764	8.17	18.24	39.52	55.20	9,353
Central-South 中南	136	258	22,181	771	8.69	15.75	24.80	44.85	8,873
Henan 河南	8	628	27,584	3,219	37.19	68.07	13.58	45.37	8,655
Hubei 湖北	1	48	4,870	20	0.72	0.93	34.08	23.20	2,789
Hunan 湖南	3	127	15,827	238	3.26	19.93	37.47	83.65	7,313
Guangdong 广东	97	232	24,410	648	6.40	11.57	29.53	44.67	10,126
Guangxi 广西	27	261	13,918	573	11.85	19.70	16.89	39.88	4,835
Hainan 海南									
Southwest 西南	4	107	6,393	357	6.01	10.63	22.93	43.42	5,933
Chongqing 重庆	1	138	8,580	356	4.24	6.91	8.87	38.60	8,389
Sichuan 四川	3	97	5,663	357	6.98	12.94	29.62	46.06	5,115
Guizhou 贵州									
Yunnan 云南									
Tibet 西藏									
Northwest 西北	1	30	1,200				26.90	61.94	2,583
Shaanxi 陕西									
Gansu 甘肃	1	30	1,200				26.90	61.94	2,583
Qinghai 青海									
Ningxia 宁夏									
Xinjiang 新疆									

4315: Bamboo,Rattan,Palm,Hasty handicraft 竹、藤、棕、草工艺品制造业

Year 年份	Number of firms 企业个数	Rate of change 变化率(%)	Number of employees 职工人数(人)	Rate of change 变化率(%)	Total revenue (Mil. RMB) 总销售收入(百万元)	Rate of change 变化率(%)	Total profit (Mil RMB) 总利润(百万元)	Rate of change 变化率(%)
2000	272		65,501		5,340,202		161,680	
2001	431	58.46	99,417	51.78	7,499	-99.86	226	-99.86
2002	520	20.65	102,094	2.69	9,649	28.67	336	48.67

Major Products 主要产品	Output 产量	Unit 单位
Industrial Arts Products 工艺美术制品	432	100,000,000 yuan 亿元

10 Main Firms with Maximal Revenue (year founded) 收入最大的十家主要企业（创办年份）	City 城市	Province 省	Telephone/fax 电话/传真	Number of employees 职工人数	Ownership 产业所有权	Revenue ('000 RMB) 销售收入(千元)	Profit('000 RMB) (rank) 利润(千元)(排名)	Total assets ('000 RMB) 总资产(千元)	Major products 主要产品
Minhou Minxing Knitting Products Co., Ltd.	Fuzhou	Fujian	(0591)2951252		Overseas Chinese-funded				Ironwork Basket
闽侯闽兴编织品有限公司(1990)	福州市	福建省	(0591)2955835	926	港澳台资	342,100	26,185(1)	72,018	铁花篮
Shandong Laizhou Handicrafts Group Co., Ltd.	Yantai	Shandong	(0535)2213239		Limited-Liability				Straw Handicrafts草
山东省莱州工艺品集团有限责任公司(1950)	烟台市	山东省	(0535)2211655	777	有限公司	204,753	4,129(15)	102,632	制工艺品
Anhui Qingfahu Handicrafts Co.,Ltd.	Lu'an	Anhui	(0564)6281048		Foreign Funded				Willow & Wicker Products
安徽省庆发湖工艺品有限公司(1993)	六安市	安徽省	(0564)6281087	3,000	外商投资	141,987	7,432(4)	87,823	柳制品
Changle Fudeng Handicrafts Co., Ltd.	Fuzhou	Fujian	(0591)8811886		Overseas Chinese-funded				Craftwork
长乐市富登工艺品有限公司(2001)	福州市	福建省	(0591)8810608	1,600	港澳台资	116,223	-	67,791	工艺品
Zhejiang Fanrong Industrial Co.,Ltd.	Taizhou	Zhejiang	(0576)4899554		Collective-owned				Wooden Handicrafts 木
浙江繁荣实业公司(1993)	台州市	浙江省	(0576)4899924	1,324	集体企业	114,136	1,974(37)	59,905	制工艺品
Anxi Yingfa Furniture Decorating Co.,Ltd.	Quanzhou	Fujian	(0595)3256193		Foreign Funded				Bamboo & Rattan Handicrafts 竹
安溪县英发家具装饰有限公司(1990)	泉州市	福建省	(0595)3231158	1,200	外商投资	109,158	5,857(10)	22,976	藤工艺品
Weihai Dahua Wood Industry Co., Ltd.	Weihai	Shandong	(0631)5757730		Foreign Funded				Wooden Products
威海大华木业有限公司(1992)	威海市	山东省	(0631)5757307	760	外商投资	100,610	6,300(8)	62,866	木制品
Nanshan Metal Plastic Products (Huzhou) Industrial Co., Ltd.	Huzhou	Zhejiang	(0572)5900288		Overseas Chinese-funded				Torch
南山金属塑料制品（湖州）实业有限公司(1998)	湖州市	浙江省	(0572)5900279	380	港澳台资	97,800	3,500(19)	47,400	火炬
Guangdong Deqing Decheng kangzhou Craftwork Factory	Zhaoqing	Guangdong	(0758)7731098		Private Enterprises				Rattan Products
广东省德庆县德城镇康州工艺厂(1976)	肇庆市	广东省	(0758)7732200	219	私营独资	93,215	492(141)	33,984	藤制品
Gaozhou Xingfa Technology Co., Ltd.	Maoming	Guangdong	(0668)6132171		Overseas Chinese-funded				Craftwork
高州兴发工艺有限公司(1999)	茂名市	广东省	(0668)6130498	650	港澳台资	92,674	685(107)	23,323	工艺品

Top 10 Cities by Revenue 销售收入排名前10位城市	Province 省	Market share 市场份额 (%)	Number of firms 企业个数
Taizhou 台州市	Zhejiang 浙江省	17.45	127
Fuzhou 福州市	Fujian 福建省	11.97	32
Maoming 茂名市	Guangdong 广东省	7.21	34
Zhaoqing 肇庆市	Guangdong 广东省	6.01	16
Quanzhou 泉州市	Fujian 福建省	5.93	19
Huzhou 湖州市	Zhejiang 浙江省	3.70	24
Ningbo 宁波市	Zhejiang 浙江省	3.61	20
Linyi 临沂市	Shandong 山东省	3.54	27
Heze 荷泽市	Shandong 山东省	2.73	11
Yantai 烟台市	Shandong 山东省	2.68	5

10 Major Wholesalers 十家主要批发商	City 城市	Province 省	Telephone/Fax 电话/传真
China National Arts & Crafts Import & Export Corporation	Beijing	Beijing	(010)65521133
中国工艺品进出口总公司	北京市	北京市	(010)65531143
Shanghai Arts & Crafts Import & Export Co.,Ltd.	Shanghai	Shanghai	(021)65222888
上海市工艺品进出口有限公司	上海市	上海市	(021)65221898
Shandong Arts & Crafts Import & Export (Group) Co.,Ltd.	Qingdao	Shandong	(0532)5021355
山东工艺品进出口（集团）股份有限公司	青岛市	山东省	(0532)5021168
Zhejiang Arts & Crafts Import & Export Co.,Ltd.	Hangzhou	Zhejiang	(0571)87063393
浙江省工艺品进出口有限公司	杭州市	浙江省	(0571)87063838
Shanghai Shenhua Import & Export Co., Ltd.	Shanghai	Shanghai	(021)63177063
上海申华进出口有限公司	上海市	上海市	(021)63173819
China Hunan Arts & Crafts Import & Export Corporation	Changsha	Hunan	(0731)2284632
湖南省工艺品进出口公司	长沙市	湖南省	(0731)2287869
Guangdong Arts and Crafts Import & Export (Group) Corporation	Guangzhou	Guangdong	(020)83193388
广东省工艺品进出口（集团）公司	广州市	广东省	(020)83343614
Guangdong Nanhai Handicrafts Import & Export Co.,Ltd.	Foshan	Guangdong	(0757)6220536
广东南海工艺品进出口有限公司	佛山市	广东省	(0757)6220225
Tianjin Handicrafts Import & Export Group Co.,Ltd.	Tianjin	Tianjin	(022)23310080
天津工艺品进出口集团有限公司	天津市	天津市	(022)23317828
Taizhou International Trade Co.,Ltd.	Taizhou	Zhejiang	(0576)8811680
台州市国际贸易有限公司	台州市	浙江省	(0576)8882427

4316: Drawnwork and Embroidery Craftwork 抽纱刺绣工艺品制造业

The industry accounts for 0.086% of the total revenue of China's industrial sector in 2002. The rate of return on assets is 3.58%. 81.02% of all firms in the industry made a profit while 18.98% had negative returns.The top province in terms of the industry's revenue is Shandong, accounting for 40.99% of the total revenue.
2002年本行业收入占全行业的 0.086%，资产利润率为 3.58%。81.02%的企业赢利，18.98%的企业亏损。收入最高的省为山东省，占本行业的40.99%。

	Total number of firms 企业总数	Total number of employees 职工总数	Total revenue (Mil.RMB) 总销售收入 (百万元)	Total profit (Mil.RMB) 总利润 (百万元)	Return on assets 资产利润率 (%)	Return on equity 权益利润率 (%)	Labour productivity ('000 RMB/ worker) 劳动生产率 (千元/人)	Debts/ assets 资产负债率 (%)	Total assets (Mil.RMB) 总资产 (百万元)
Industry Overall 行业总体	374	77,406	9,181	260	3.58	10.81	33.64	66.86	7,257

	Number of firms 企业个数	Average number of employees 平均职工人数	Average revenue ('000 RMB) 平均销售收入 (千元)	Average profit ('000 RMB) 平均利润 (千元)	Return on assets 资产利润率 (%)	Return on equity 权益利润率 (%)	Labour productivity ('000 RMB/ worker) 劳动生产率 (千元/人)	Debts/ assets 资产负债率 (%)	Average total assets ('000 RMB) 平均总资产 (千元)
By ownership 产业所有权									
State-owned 国有	21	156	10,835	-119	-1.03	-5.22	15.20	80.27	11,588
Collective-owned 集体	60	234	35,904	619	1.98	7.60	43.71	73.89	31,185
Foreign & Overseas Chinese Funded 三资	98	185	24,228	1,036	4.61	10.79	36.51	57.27	22,463
By regional distribution 地区分布									
Central-North 华北	21	138	7,323	165	2.04	6.81	15.17	70.01	8,076
Beijing 北京	5	98	2,993	-22	-0.60	-0.83	7.34	28.10	3,687
Tianjin 天津	2	149	12,012	592	3.37		18.18	118.23	17,535
Hebei 河北	14	150	8,199	171	2.06	5.43	16.58	62.10	8,292
Shanxi 山西									
Inner Mongolia 内蒙古									
Northeast 东北	5	180	11,738	-205	-1.08	-184.17	17.23	99.41	18,877
Liaoning 辽宁	5	180	11,738	-205	-1.08	-184.17	17.23	99.41	18,877
Jilin 吉林									
Heilongjiang 黑龙江									
Central-East 华东	286	228	27,953	829	3.87	11.50	35.01	66.40	21,439
Shanghai 上海	23	129	26,971	1,605	6.02	12.96	70.02	53.54	26,649
Jiangsu 江苏	84	122	24,879	476	3.15	8.71	55.01	63.81	15,123
Zhejiang 浙江	59	135	19,711	703	4.58	12.20	32.43	62.45	15,342
Anhui 安徽	4	2,135	73,066	2,282	12.29	23.74	9.12	48.26	18,574
Fujian 福建	6	201	10,974	174	0.57	1.20	14.93	52.89	30,797
Jiangxi 江西									
Shandong 山东	110	311	34,212	986	3.52	12.75	33.73	72.42	28,035
Central-South 中南	59	137	15,989	256	1.80	5.27	31.59	65.90	14,228
Henan 河南	10	123	9,972	594	9.06	26.87	19.16	66.27	6,553
Hubei 湖北	4	140	6,627	176	3.71	6.41	31.42	42.10	4,751
Hunan 湖南	9	201	11,124	174	1.98	6.13	15.05	67.70	8,795
Guangdong 广东	36	125	19,917	191	1.02	3.02	41.67	66.32	18,772
Guangxi 广西									
Hainan 海南									
Southwest 西南	1	320	28,837	5,297	25.20	88.37	18.02	71.49	21,021
Chongqing 重庆	1	320	28,837	5,297	25.20	88.37	18.02	71.49	21,021
Sichuan 四川									
Guizhou 贵州									
Yunnan 云南									
Tibet 西藏									
Northwest 西北	2	16	728	36	5.44	10.17	40.16	46.47	652
Shaanxi 陕西									
Gansu 甘肃	2	16	728	36	5.44	10.17	40.16	46.47	652
Qinghai 青海									
Ningxia 宁夏									
Xinjiang 新疆									

4316: Drawnwork and Embroidery Craftwork 抽纱刺绣工艺品制造业

Year 年份	Number of firms 企业个数	Rate of change 变化率（%）	Number of employees 职工人数（人）	Rate of change 变化率（%）	Total revenue (Mil. RMB) 总销售收入（百万元）	Rate of change 变化率（%）	Total profit (Mil RMB) 总利润（百万元）	Rate of change 变化率（%）
2000	309		84,659		6,886,504		190,499	
2001	345	11.65	94,207	11.28	7,830	-99.89	216	-99.89
2002	374	8.41	77,406	-17.83	9,181	17.25	260	20.37

Major Products 主要产品	Output 产量	Unit 单位
Industrial Arts Products 工艺美术制品	432	100,000,000 yuan 亿元

10 Main Firms with Maximal Revenue (year founded) 收入最大的十家主要企业（创办年份）	City 城市	Province 省	Telephone/fax 电话/传真	Number of employees 职工人数	Ownership 产业所有权	Revenue ('000 RMB) 销售收入（千元）	Profit('000 RMB) (rank) 利润(千元)（排名）	Total assets ('000 RMB) 总资产（千元）	Major products 主要产品
Shandong Yunlong Embroidery Industry Co.,Ltd 山东云龙绣品工业公司(1981)	Weihai 威海市	Shandong 山东省	(0631)8353307 (0631)8356276	1,583	Collective-owned 集体企业	510,927	12,200(4)	202,010	Industiral Art Products 工艺美术品
Shanghai Jiali Wool Embroidery Factory 上海佳丽绒绣厂(1992)	Shanghai 上海市	Shanghai 上海市	(021)65650002 (021)55670423	226	Collective-owned 集体企业	332,474	7,334(9)	133,675	Floss Embroidery Products 绒绣制品
Zhaoyuan Jinxiu Household Textile Co., Ltd 招远锦绣家用纺织品有限责任公司(1988)	Yantai 烟台市	Shandong 山东省	(0535)8216553 (0535)8213183	1,254	Limited-Liability 有限公司	200,163	11,507(5)	102,324	Drawnwork Embroidered Handicraft 抽纱刺绣工艺品
Qingdao Lace Weaving Co., Ltd. 青岛荣花边有限公司(1993)	Qingdao 青岛市	Shandong 山东省	(0532)7612888 (0532)7893875	1,038	Foreign Funded 外商投资	187,115	16,707(1)	267,710	Lace Weaving 花边
Wendeng Hualong Embroidery Co., Ltd. 文登市华龙绣品有限公司(1993)	Weihai 威海市	Shandong 山东省	(0631)8480623 (0631)8989866	977	Overseas Chinese-funded 港澳台资	150,932	8,019(6)	177,219	Drawnwork 抽纱
Qingdao Arts & Crafts Group Co.,Ltd. 青岛工艺美术集团公司(1992)	Qingdao 青岛市	Shandong 山东省	(0532)4853575 (0532)4857091	1,611	Collective-owned 集体企业	136,649	256(150)	299,605	Drawnwork Embroidered Handicraft抽纱刺绣工艺品
Anhui Swan Textile Products (Group)Co., Ltd. 安徽省天鹅纺织制品(集团)有限公司(1999)	Anqing 安庆市	Anhui 安徽省	(0556)2185217 (0556)2180581	4,200	Private Enterprises 私营独资	135,000	2,950(24)	42,960	Crafts Quilt 工艺被
Tiantang Textile Art Products General Factory 天堂纺织工艺制品总厂(1991)	Anqing 安庆市	Anhui 安徽省	(0556)2173430 (0556)2173430	3,655	Joint Stock 股份制	127,800	5,290(11)	24,890	Crafts Quilt 工艺被
China Drawnwork Shanghai Factory NO.3 Import & Export Co.,Ltd. 中国抽纱上海进出口公司三厂(1982)	Ningbo 宁波市	Zhejiang 浙江省	(0574)87804639 (0574)87807948	526	State-owned 国有企业	116,746	103(196)	64,088	Drawnwork Embroidered Handicraft抽纱刺绣工艺品
Weihai Yiyuan Embroidery Group Co., Ltd. 威海市艺源绣业集团有限公司(1955)	Weihai 威海市	Shandong 山东省	(0631)8452564 (0631)8451486	862	Collective-owned 集体企业	110,995	2,055(36)	91,416	Drawnwork Products 抽纱制品

Top 10 Cities by Revenue 销售收入排名前10位城市	Province 省	Market share 市场份额（%）	Number of firms 企业个数
Weihai 威海市	Shandong 山东省	13.08	18
Nantong 南通市	Jiangsu 江苏省	11.02	39
Qingdao 青岛市	Shandong 山东省	7.55	25
Shanghai 上海市	Shanghai 上海市	6.76	23
Weifang 潍坊市	Shandong 山东省	6.39	17
Yantai 烟台市	Shandong 山东省	6.12	17
Jinhua 金华市	Zhejiang 浙江省	5.03	18
Suzhou 苏州市	Jiangsu 江苏省	4.46	26
Yancheng 盐城市	Jiangsu 江苏省	4.26	11
Rizhao 日照市	Shandong 山东省	3.42	11

10 Major Wholesalers 十家主要批发商	City 城市	Province 省	Telephone/Fax 电话/传真
China National Arts & Crafts Import & Export Corporation 中国工艺品进出口总公司	Beijing 北京市	Beijing 北京市	(010)65521133 (010)65531143
Shanghai Arts & Crafts Import & Export Co.,Ltd. 上海市工艺品进出口有限公司	Shanghai 上海市	Shanghai 上海市	(021)65222888 (021)65221898
Shandong Arts & Crafts Import & Export (Group) Co.,Ltd. 山东工艺品进出口（集团）股份有限公司	Qingdao 青岛市	Shandong 山东省	(0532)5021355 (0532)5021168
Zhejiang Arts & Crafts Import & Export Co.,Ltd. 浙江省工艺品进出口有限公司	Hangzhou 杭州市	Zhejiang 浙江省	(0571)87063393 (0571)87063838
Shanghai Shenhua Import & Export Co., Ltd. 上海申华进出口有限公司	Shanghai 上海市	Shanghai 上海市	(021)63177063 (021)63173819
China Hunan Arts & Crafts Import & Export Corporation 湖南省工艺品进出口公司	Changsha 长沙市	Hunan 湖南省	(0731)2284632 (0731)2287869
Guangdong Arts and Crafts Import & Export (Group) Corporation 广东省工艺品进出口（集团）公司	Guangzhou 广州市	Guangdong 广东省	(020)83193388 (020)83343614
Guangdong Nanhai Handicrafts Import & Export Co.,Ltd. 广东南海工艺品进出口有限公司	Foshan 佛山市	Guangdong 广东省	(0757)6220536 (0757)6220225
Tianjin Handicrafts Import & Export Group Co.,Ltd. 天津工艺品进出口集团有限公司	Tianjin 天津市	Tianjin 天津市	(022)23310080 (022)23317828
Taizhou International Trade Co.,Ltd. 台州市国际贸易有限公司	Taizhou 台州市	Zhejiang 浙江省	(0576)8811680 (0576)8882427

4317: Carpet 地毯制造业

The industry accounts for 0.072% of the total revenue of China's industrial sector in 2002. The rate of return on assets is 4.49%. 84.57% of all firms in the industry made a profit while 15.43% had negative returns.The top province in terms of the industry's revenue is Shandong, accounting for 34.05% of the total revenue.
2002年本行业收入占全行业的 0.072%，资产利润率为 4.49%。84.57%的企业赢利，15.43%的企业亏损。收入最高的省为山东省，占本行业的34.05%。

	Total number of firms 企业总数	Total number of employees 职工总数	Total revenue (Mil.RMB) 总销售收入(百万元)	Total profit (Mil.RMB) 总利润(百万元)	Return on assets 资产利润率(%)	Return on equity 权益利润率(%)	Labour productivity ('000 RMB/ worker) 劳动生产率(千元/人)	Debts/ assets 资产负债率(%)	Total assets (Mil.RMB) 总资产(百万元)
Industry Overall 行业总体	363	118,452	7,746	405	4.49	15.80	20.67	71.60	9,022

	Number of firms 企业个数	Average number of employees 平均职工人数	Average revenue ('000 RMB) 平均销售收入（千元）	Average profit ('000 RMB) 平均利润(千元)	Return on assets 资产利润率(%)	Return on equity 权益利润率(%)	Labour productivity ('000 RMB/ worker) 劳动生产率(千元/人)	Debts/ assets 资产负债率(%)	Average total assets ('000 RMB) 平均总资产(千元)
By ownership 产业所有权									
State-owned 国有	30	191	6,232	-777	-2.84		8.74	126.64	27,346
Collective-owned 集体	87	340	18,548	745	3.08	14.74	20.15	79.08	24,163
Foreign & Overseas Chinese Funded 三资	63	382	35,274	2,360	6.21	16.51	29.25	62.36	37,987
By regional distribution 地区分布									
Central-North 华北	106	349	18,072	1,140	4.94	35.75	12.10	86.19	23,091
Beijing 北京	7	153	25,099	-382	-1.13	-3.62	41.75	68.81	33,833
Tianjin 天津	68	292	16,403	1,116	5.15	73.62	6.65	93.00	21,678
Hebei 河北	27	494	21,897	1,807	7.70	39.82	17.99	80.66	23,455
Shanxi 山西									
Inner Mongolia 内蒙古	4	690	8,333	-302	-1.17	-3.13	11.33	62.78	25,847
Northeast 东北	6	603	16,408	-655	-1.28	-4.79	10.23	73.19	50,999
Liaoning 辽宁	2	239	4,383	-730	-3.81	-14.38	0.78	73.49	19,141
Jilin 吉林	2	235	2,536	-60	-0.22	-4.71	29.55	95.38	27,550
Heilongjiang 黑龙江	2	1,336	42,305	-1,176	-1.11	-3.39	8.53	67.39	106,307
Central-East 华东	150	373	30,383	1,726	5.94	15.43	27.11	61.53	29,060
Shanghai 上海	7	351	65,744	4,828	4.25	10.31	67.87	58.76	113,602
Jiangsu 江苏	42	219	24,678	1,590	7.66	19.50	34.46	60.70	20,740
Zhejiang 浙江	16	190	19,538	1,578	10.33	32.82	29.07	68.54	15,285
Anhui 安徽	1	215	8,200	1,200	25.53	41.38	20.51	38.30	4,700
Fujian 福建	2	481	50,076	3,765	6.17	11.71	21.57	47.27	60,993
Jiangxi 江西	2	41	1,238	-72	-1.86		22.49	113.77	3,871
Shandong 山东	80	499	32,966	1,556	5.38	14.41	22.94	62.67	28,922
Central-South 中南	38	287	21,927	482	1.65	7.14	27.66	76.89	29,204
Henan 河南	26	313	21,377	1,273	5.61	20.22	28.31	72.26	22,683
Hubei 湖北	4	208	19,306	271	0.88	2.08	26.41	57.71	30,778
Hunan 湖南	1	92	7,204	60	0.65	0.78	20.70	16.24	9,200
Guangdong 广东	7	264	27,573	-2,273	-4.10	-48.05	25.72	91.46	55,380
Guangxi 广西									
Hainan 海南									
Southwest 西南	17	126	10,094	535	4.06	10.65	25.23	61.90	13,181
Chongqing 重庆	2	234	39,626	3,682	11.39	44.16	48.06	74.20	32,316
Sichuan 四川	1	803	77,142	94	0.12	0.84	31.74	86.10	80,544
Guizhou 贵州									
Yunnan 云南									
Tibet 西藏	14	62	1,087	117	2.07	2.84	6.98	27.12	5,636
Northwest 西北	46	192	3,690	34	0.28	1.29	10.35	78.65	12,504
Shaanxi 陕西	3	122	1,053	-87	-0.94		17.07	112.97	9,245
Gansu 甘肃	38	150	3,708	35	0.29	1.60	13.79	82.03	12,303
Qinghai 青海	3	801	7,379	440	2.11	3.28	2.71	35.74	20,914
Ningxia 宁夏	1	260	839	-176	-2.73		-0.50	101.10	6,457
Xinjiang 新疆	1	137	2,674	-649	-6.05	-30.61	4.12	80.23	10,723

Year 年份	Number of firms 企业个数	Rate of change 变化率 (%)	Number of employees 职工人数 (人)	Rate of change 变化率 (%)	Total revenue (Mil. RMB) 总销售收入 (百万元)	Rate of change 变化率 (%)	Total profit (Mil RMB) 总利润 (百万元)	Rate of change 变化率 (%)
2000	342		108,546		6,372,422		235,357	
2001	345	0.88	110,745	2.03	6,739	-99.89	267	-99.89
2002	363	5.22	118,452	6.96	7,746	14.94	405	51.69

Major Products 主要产品	Output 产量	Unit 单位
Industrial Arts Products 工艺美术制品	432	100,000,000 yuan 亿元

10 Main Firms with Maximal Revenue (year founded) 收入最大的十家主要企业（创办年份）	City 城市	Province 省	Telephone/fax 电话/传真	Number of employees 职工人数	Ownership 产业所有权	Revenue ('000 RMB) 销售收入 (千元)	Profit('000 RMB) (rank) 利润(千元) (排名)	Total assets ('000 RMB) 总资产 (千元)	Major products 主要产品
Laizhou Xiaohe Handicrafts Co., Ltd.	Yantai	Shandong	(0535)2812275		Foreign Funded				Artistic Tapestry
莱州小河工艺品有限公司(1996)	烟台市	山东省	(0535)2812191	1,200	外商投资	373,610	29,870(2)	5,390	工艺挂毯
Weihai Shanhua Carpet Group Co., Ltd.	Weihai	Shandong	(0631)5219988		Limited-Liability				Carpet
威海市山花地毯集团有限公司(1982)	威海市	山东省	(0631)5233009	1,450	有限公司	277,893	30,389(1)	385,652	蔟绒地毯
Shanghai Automobile Carpet General Factory	Shanghai	Shanghai	(021)67727091		Joint Owned				Saloon Car Carpet
上海汽车地毯总厂(1985)	上海市	上海市	(021)67727989	919	联营企业	264,375	26,365(3)	489,279	轿车地毯
Weihai Carpet Factory NO.1	Weihai	Shandong	(0631)5225880		Collective-owned				Wilton Machine-weaved Carpet 威尔顿
威海地毯一厂(1958)	威海市	山东省	(0631)5226887	1,271	集体企业	202,088	8,006(14)	233,233	机织地毯
Hebei Xingtai Nangong Hua'ao Leather & Fur Co., Ltd.	Xingtai	Hebei	(0319)5306216		Foreign Funded				Big Carpet
河北省邢台市南宫市华澳皮毛有限公司(1987)	邢台市	河北省	(0319)5306527	500	外商投资	142,640	18,968(4)	34,211	大毯
Yangxin Ruixin Woollen Products Co., Ltd.	Binzhou	Shandong	(0543)8451888		Foreign Funded				Wool Glue Carries Carpet羊毛
阳信瑞鑫毛制品有限公司(1998)	滨州市	山东省	(0543)8451388	8,200	外商投资	124,197	1,302(74)	65,713	股背地毯
Shandong Linqing Lianchuang Industrial Co., Ltd.	Liaocheng	Shandong	(0635)2341767		Foreign Funded				Carpet
山东临清联创实业有限公司(1994)	聊城市	山东省	(0635)2340363	538	外商投资	120,515	6,120(21)	57,720	地毯
Tianjin Longxing Group Co., Ltd.	Tianjin	Tianjin	(022)28275093		State Enterprises				Carpet
天津市隆兴集团有限公司(1999)	天津市	天津市	(022)28275092	414	国有独资	93,817	-	231,263	地毯
Henan Zhenping Carpet Group Industry Co.,Ltd.	Nanyang	Henan	(0377)5921727		Collective-owned				Carpet
河南省镇平县地毯集团工业公司(1980)	南阳市	河南省	(0377)5923497	1,395	集体企业	92,273	15,486(5)	212,095	地毯
Yantai Jiamei Carpet Co., Ltd.	Yantai	Shandong	(0535)4712081		Collective-owned				Carpet
烟台佳美地毯有限公司(1999)	烟台市	山东省	(0535)4712218	360	集体企业	89,366	6,605(19)	10,812	地毯

Top 10 Cities by Revenue 销售收入排名前10位城市	Province 省	Market share 市场份额 (%)	Number of firms 企业个数
Tianjin 天津市	Tianjin 天津市	14.40	68
Weihai 威海市	Shandong 山东省	7.06	4
Dezhou 德州市	Shandong 山东省	6.98	19
Yantai 烟台市	Shandong 山东省	6.67	9
Shanghai 上海市	Shanghai 上海市	5.94	7
Suzhou 苏州市	Jiangsu 江苏省	3.92	6
Nanyang 南阳市	Henan 河南省	3.58	18
Binzhou 滨州市	Shandong 山东省	3.24	8
Changzhou 常州市	Jiangsu 江苏省	2.78	9
Xingtai 邢台市	Hebei 河北省	2.77	6

10 Major Wholesalers 十家主要批发商	City 城市	Province 省	Telephone/Fax 电话/传真
China National Arts & Crafts Import & Export Corporation	Beijing	Beijing	(010)65521133
中国工艺品进出口总公司	北京市	北京市	(010)65531143
Shanghai Arts & Crafts Import & Export Co.,Ltd.	Shanghai	Shanghai	(021)65222888
上海市工艺品进出口有限公司	上海市	上海市	(021)65221898
Shandong Arts & Crafts Import & Export (Group) Co.,Ltd.	Qingdao	Shandong	(0532)5021355
山东工艺品进出口（集团）股份有限公司	青岛市	山东省	(0532)5021168
Zhejiang Arts & Crafts Import & Export Co.,Ltd.	Hangzhou	Zhejiang	(0571)87063393
浙江省工艺品进出口有限公司	杭州市	浙江省	(0571)87063838
Shanghai Shenhua Import & Export Co., Ltd.	Shanghai	Shanghai	(021)63177063
上海申华进出口有限公司	上海市	上海市	(021)63173819
China Hunan Arts & Crafts Import & Export Corporation	Changsha	Hunan	(0731)2284632
湖南省工艺品进出口公司	长沙市	湖南省	(0731)2287869
Guangdong Arts and Crafts Import & Export (Group) Corporation	Guangzhou	Guangdong	(020)83193388
广东省工艺品进出口（集团）公司	广州市	广东省	(020)83343614
Guangdong Nanhai Handicrafts Import & Export Co.,Ltd.	Foshan	Guangdong	(0757)6220536
广东南海工艺品进出口有限公司	佛山市	广东省	(0757)6220225
Tianjin Handicrafts Import & Export Group Co.,Ltd.	Tianjin	Tianjin	(022)23310080
天津工艺品进出口集团有限公司	天津市	天津市	(022)23317828
Taizhou International Trade Co.,Ltd.	Taizhou	Zhejiang	(0576)8811680
台州市国际贸易有限公司	台州市	浙江省	(0576)8882427

4318: Jewelry 首饰制造业

The industry accounts for 0.124% of the total revenue of China's industrial sector in 2002. The rate of return on assets is 4.39%. 74.47% of all firms in the industry made a profit while 25.53% had negative returns.The top province in terms of the industry's revenue is Guangdong, accounting for 43.25% of the total revenue.
2002年本行业收入占全行业的 0.124%，资产利润率为 4.39%。74.47%的企业赢利，25.53%的企业亏损。收入最高的省为广东省，占本行业的43.25%。

	Total number of firms 企业总数	Total number of employees 职工总数	Total revenue (Mil.RMB) 总销售收入 (百万元)	Total profit (Mil.RMB) 总利润 (百万元)	Return on assets 资产利润率 (%)	Return on equity 权益利润率 (%)	Labour productivity ('000 RMB/ worker) 劳动生产率 (千元/人)	Debts/ assets 资产负债率 (%)	Total assets (Mil.RMB) 总资产 (百万元)
Industry Overall 行业总体	235	74,000	13,283	492	4.39	9.05	47.91	51.48	11,196

	Number of firms 企业个数	Average number of employees 平均职工人数	Average revenue ('000 RMB) 平均销售收入（千元)	Average profit ('000 RMB) 平均利润 (千元)	Return on assets 资产利润率 (%)	Return on equity 权益利润率 (%)	Labour productivity ('000 RMB/ worker) 劳动生产率 (千元/人)	Debts/ assets 资产负债率 (%)	Average total assets ('000 RMB) 平均总资产 (千元)
By ownership 产业所有权									
State-owned 国有	12	120	84,675	-342	-1.62	-6.31	-391.97	74.37	21,122
Collective-owned 集体	40	177	41,766	415	1.24	4.54	58.40	72.73	33,511
Foreign & Overseas Chinese Funded 三资	104	447	63,582	3,609	6.77	11.90	54.99	43.11	53,304
By regional distribution 地区分布									
Central-North 华北	15	137	29,610	-1,013	-3.96	-14.60	33.44	72.87	25,589
Beijing 北京	8	125	15,839	-2,091	-12.12	-74.08	46.03	83.64	17,252
Tianjin 天津	3	110	29,881	93	0.31	0.83	22.05	62.97	30,203
Hebei 河北	2	198	82,224	556	1.51	5.85	15.49	74.11	36,687
Shanxi 山西	2	164	31,672	69	0.17	0.48	28.02	64.55	40,919
Inner Mongolia 内蒙古									
Northeast 东北	7	260	10,399	783	5.15	8.34	18.75	38.23	15,206
Liaoning 辽宁	3	103	10,464	1,616	10.38	18.86	40.51	44.96	15,562
Jilin 吉林	2	42	7,336	119	0.82	1.11	80.41	26.30	14,494
Heilongjiang 黑龙江	2	715	13,365	199	1.29	2.13	10.46	39.26	15,383
Central-East 华东	97	262	55,911	2,854	6.50	14.99	77.69	56.66	43,920
Shanghai 上海	14	207	116,733	2,251	2.54	9.13	125.27	72.24	88,795
Jiangsu 江苏	19	198	35,919	944	3.36	8.89	51.24	62.24	28,126
Zhejiang 浙江	23	261	80,230	6,428	9.73	16.79	53.65	42.02	66,034
Anhui 安徽	2	160	3,981	-13	-0.03	-0.18	16.27	83.23	42,166
Fujian 福建	10	215	32,727	-442	-1.54	-3.80	346.98	59.41	28,658
Jiangxi 江西	2	77	27,228	7,837	9.72	14.53	54.76	33.14	80,637
Shandong 山东	27	373	32,284	2,529	15.82	37.80	33.07	58.15	15,989
Central-South 中南	105	401	64,451	1,356	2.95	6.25	28.47	52.72	45,919
Henan 河南	3	72	17,361	-549	-2.86	-13.27	4.06	78.44	19,183
Hubei 湖北	7	167	37,574	370	0.82	1.75	134.15	52.85	44,822
Hunan 湖南	1	55	2,451	-100	-0.53	-1.41	15.40	62.41	18,806
Guangdong 广东	77	505	74,601	1,689	3.89	8.88	24.23	56.22	43,425
Guangxi 广西	5	172	54,847	390	0.56	4.43	16.64	87.25	69,007
Hainan 海南	12	83	35,941	801	1.29	1.59	86.55	18.63	61,885
Southwest 西南	5	156	4,649	-82	-0.72	-1.10	8.24	34.29	11,429
Chongqing 重庆	1	120	4,926	-364	-2.03	-3.14	19.50	35.55	17,966
Sichuan 四川	2	59	8,088	-96	-0.83	-1.88	18.62	56.00	11,589
Guizhou 贵州									
Yunnan 云南									
Tibet 西藏	2	272	1,071	72	0.90	0.91	3.52	1.44	8,000
Northwest 西北	6	304	91,961	13,750	5.26	7.50	145.51	29.84	261,193
Shaanxi 陕西	4	349	111,000	20,139	5.49	7.57	163.22	27.45	366,774
Gansu 甘肃									
Qinghai 青海	2	213	53,885	971	1.94	5.54	87.31	64.96	50,032
Ningxia 宁夏									
Xinjiang 新疆									

4318: Jewelry 首饰制造业

Year 年份	Number of firms 企业个数	Rate of change 变化率 (%)	Number of employees 职工人数 (人)	Rate of change 变化率 (%)	Total revenue (Mil. RMB) 总销售收入 (百万元)	Rate of change 变化率 (%)	Total profit (Mil RMB) 总利润 (百万元)	Rate of change 变化率 (%)
2000	210		58,418		12,525,850		430,029	
2001	222	5.71	67,827	16.11	12,158	-99.90	385	-99.91
2002	235	5.86	74,000	9.10	13,283	9.25	492	27.79

Major Products 主要产品	Output 产量	Unit 单位

10 Main Firms with Maximal Revenue (year founded) 收入最大的十家主要企业（创办年份）	City 城市	Province 省	Telephone/fax 电话/传真	Number of employees 职工人数	Ownership 产业所有权	Revenue ('000 RMB) 销售收入(千元)	Profit('000 RMB) (rank) 利润(千元)(排名)	Total assets ('000 RMB) 总资产(千元)	Major products 主要产品
Conghua Donglin Diamond Co., Ltd.	Guangzhou	Guangdong	(020)87862050		Overseas Chinese-funded				Diamond Jewelry
从化东麟钻石有限公司(1992)	广州市	广东省	(020)87861048	5,380	港澳台资	1,466,460	58,910(3)	323,780	钻石首饰
Zhejiang Sun & Moon Jewellery Group Co., Ltd.	Shaoxing	Zhejiang	(0575)4025665		Overseas Chinese-funded				Golden Jewelry
浙江日月首饰集团有限公司(1995)	绍兴市	浙江省	(0575)4021062	780	港澳台资	1,103,817	80,138(2)	795,404	黄金首饰
Shanghai Laofengxiang Co., Ltd.	Shanghai	Shanghai	(021)64833388		Limited-Liability				Jewelry
上海老凤祥有限公司(1996)	上海市	上海市	(021)64084932	1,420	有限公司	878,849	18,783(5)	768,721	首饰
Shenzhen Cuilv Jewellery Co., Ltd.	Shenzhen	Guangdong	(0755)25261399		State-owned				Jewelry
深圳市翠绿珠宝首饰有限公司(1996)	深圳市	广东省	(0755)25260612	680	国有企业	589,482	2,287(40)	114,322	首饰
Xi'an Cuibao Jewellery Group Co.,Ltd.	Xi'an	Shannxi	(029)3282058		Overseas Chinese-funded				Gemmy Jewelry
西安翠宝首饰集团公司(1988)	西安市	陕西省	(029)3282058	592	港澳台资	351,129	81,763(1)	1,284,529	镶嵌首饰
Shenzhen Jinsheng Jewellery Co., Ltd.	Shenzhen	Guangdong	(0755)25261075		State-owned				Golden Jewelry
深圳市金森珠宝首饰有限公司(1995)	深圳市	广东省	(0755)25261665	13	国有企业	335,289	973(68)	11,843	黄金首饰
Zhejiang Ruan's Pearl Jewellery Co., Ltd.	Shaoxing	Zhejiang	(0575)7686662		Foreign Funded				Pearl Jewelry 珍
浙江阮仕珍珠首饰有限公司(1999)	绍兴市	浙江省	(0575)7681798	88	外商投资	278,032	36,291(4)	124,737	珠首饰品
	Foshan	Guangdong	(0757)2243038		Limited-Liability				Golden Jewelry & Artificial Flower 金饰品及
佛山市工艺总厂有限公司(1970)	佛山市	广东省	(0757)2286797	626	有限公司	265,922	2,977(34)	135,693	人造花卉
Conghua Yongzhao Diamond Factory	Guangzhou	Guangdong	(020)87861228		Overseas Chinese-funded				Diamond Jewelry
从化市永钊钻石厂(1991)	广州市	广东省	(020)87861208	896	港澳台资	264,870	7,880(11)	53,210	钻石首饰
Shanghai Laochenghuangmiao Gold &Silver Jewellery Factory	Shanghai	Shanghai	(021)58726081		Joint Stock				Jewelry
上海老城隍庙金银珠宝首饰厂(1997)	上海市	上海市	(021)58455841	57	股份制	258,678	6,025(18)	46,771	首饰

Top 10 Cities by Revenue 销售收入排名前10位城市	Province 省	Market share 市场份额 (%)	Number of firms 企业个数
Guangzhou 广州市	Guangdong 广东省	18.08	25
Shenzhen 深圳市	Guangdong 广东省	12.59	18
Shanghai 上海市	Shanghai 上海市	12.30	14
Shaoxing 绍兴市	Zhejiang 浙江省	12.02	8
Foshan 佛山市	Guangdong 广东省	4.71	7
Qingdao 青岛市	Shandong 山东省	3.92	17
Xi'an 西安市	Shannxi 陕西省	2.91	2
Fuzhou 福州市	Fujian 福建省	2.13	4
Guilin 桂林市	Guangxi 广西	1.96	3
Yantai 烟台市	Shandong 山东省	1.94	4

10 Major Wholesalers 十家主要批发商	City 城市	Province 省	Telephone/Fax 电话/传真
China National Arts & Crafts Import & Export Corporation	Beijing	Beijing	(010)65521133
中国工艺品进出口总公司	北京市	北京市	(010)65531143
Shanghai Arts & Crafts Import & Export Co.,Ltd.	Shanghai	Shanghai	(021)65222888
上海市工艺品进出口有限公司	上海市	上海市	(021)65221898
Shandong Arts & Crafts Import & Export (Group) Co.,Ltd.	Qingdao	Shandong	(0532)5021355
山东工艺品进出口（集团）股份有限公司	青岛市	山东省	(0532)5021168
Zhejiang Arts & Crafts Import & Export Co.,Ltd.	Hangzhou	Zhejiang	(0571)87063393
浙江省工艺品进出口有限公司	杭州市	浙江省	(0571)87063838
Shanghai Shenhua Import & Export Co., Ltd.	Shanghai	Shanghai	(021)63177063
上海申华进出口有限公司	上海市	上海市	(021)63173819
China Hunan Arts & Crafts Import & Export Corporation	Changsha	Hunan	(0731)2284632
湖南省工艺品进出口公司	长沙市	湖南省	(0731)2287869
Guangdong Arts and Crafts Import & Export (Group) Corporation	Guangzhou	Guangdong	(020)83193388
广东省工艺品进出口（集团）公司	广州市	广东省	(020)83343614
Guangdong Nanhai Handicrafts Import & Export Co.,Ltd.	Foshan	Guangdong	(0757)6220536
广东南海工艺品进出口有限公司	佛山市	广东省	(0757)6220225
Tianjin Handicrafts Import & Export Group Co.,Ltd.	Tianjin	Tianjin	(022)23310080
天津工艺品进出口集团有限公司	天津市	天津市	(022)23317828
Taizhou International Trade Co.,Ltd.	Taizhou	Zhejiang	(0576)8811680
台州市国际贸易有限公司	台州市	浙江省	(0576)8882427

4319: Other Industrial Artworks 其他工艺美术品制造业

The industry accounts for 0.206% of the total revenue of China's industrial sector in 2002. The rate of return on assets is 6.93%. 85.57% of all firms in the industry made a profit while 14.43% had negative returns.The top province in terms of the industry's revenue is Guangdong, accounting for 18.07% of the total revenue.
2002年本行业收入占全行业的 0.206%，资产利润率为 6.93%。85.57%的企业赢利，14.43%的企业亏损。收入最高的省为广东省，占本行业的18.07%。

	Total number of firms 企业总数	Total number of employees 职工总数	Total revenue (Mil.RMB) 总销售收入 (百万元)	Total profit (Mil.RMB) 总利润 (百万元)	Return on assets 资产利润率 (%)	Return on equity 权益利润率 (%)	Labour productivity ('000 RMB/ worker) 劳动生产率 (千元/人)	Debts/ assets 资产负债率 (%)	Total assets (Mil.RMB) 总资产 (百万元)
Industry Overall 行业总体	998	278,536	22,117	928	6.93	15.90	25.81	56.43	13,394

	Number of firms 企业个数	Average number of employees 平均职工人数	Average revenue ('000 RMB) 平均销售收入 (千元)	Average profit ('000 RMB) 平均利润 (千元)	Return on assets 资产利润率 (%)	Return on equity 权益利润率 (%)	Labour productivity ('000 RMB/ worker) 劳动生产率 (千元/人)	Debts/ assets 资产负债率 (%)	Average total assets ('000 RMB) 平均总资产 (千元)
By ownership 产业所有权									
State-owned 国有	22	147	13,527	339	1.94	6.24	15.45	68.88	17,450
Collective-owned 集体	192	261	25,302	777	7.94	15.00	36.69	47.07	9,785
Foreign & Overseas Chinese Funded 三资	308	370	29,455	1,398	6.81	16.14	26.33	57.80	20,528
By regional distribution 地区分布									
Central-North 华北	45	409	24,444	2,800	18.61	32.57	33.60	42.86	15,045
Beijing 北京	4	105	7,937	1,076	8.64	12.74	34.35	32.16	12,448
Tianjin 天津	24	361	29,808	3,899	21.14	36.62	56.96	42.27	18,442
Hebei 河北	16	537	20,640	1,755	16.51	32.04	11.43	48.46	10,629
Shanxi 山西									
Inner Mongolia 内蒙古	1	731	22,614	34	0.23	0.34	16.66	32.05	14,579
Northeast 东北	27	217	12,407	230	2.34	7.81	15.60	70.06	9,826
Liaoning 辽宁	23	215	13,316	263	2.60	7.11	15.92	63.44	10,125
Jilin 吉林	2	119	3,610	-226	-3.77	-63.52	13.52	94.07	5,984
Heilongjiang 黑龙江	2	345	10,759	301	2.94		14.03	131.40	10,230
Central-East 华东	472	267	25,404	890	6.78	15.13	29.08	55.19	13,134
Shanghai 上海	18	167	25,727	-114	-0.52	-1.62	46.62	67.91	21,929
Jiangsu 江苏	77	225	24,472	475	5.78	15.70	26.94	63.21	8,230
Zhejiang 浙江	144	173	21,314	1,053	6.56	15.41	31.02	57.42	16,047
Anhui 安徽	5	157	8,405	287	7.97	16.96	14.01	52.98	3,594
Fujian 福建	116	431	17,945	677	6.27	11.31	13.30	44.53	10,789
Jiangxi 江西	39	273	12,768	548	6.50	10.74	16.37	39.48	8,436
Shandong 山东	73	267	54,141	1,819	10.52	24.95	73.73	57.82	17,281
Central-South 中南	439	286	19,566	828	5.93	14.25	22.02	58.40	13,974
Henan 河南	54	331	42,499	3,169	12.66	32.44	34.74	60.99	25,034
Hubei 湖北	5	255	10,292	107	1.20	3.06	22.53	60.76	8,948
Hunan 湖南	171	264	10,067	282	4.86	11.95	17.24	59.33	5,805
Guangdong 广东	184	279	21,722	726	4.07	9.43	21.33	56.81	17,826
Guangxi 广西	20	416	20,817	149	0.80	2.29	24.08	64.91	18,485
Hainan 海南	5	316	21,714	1,452	7.60	12.68	26.64	40.06	19,108
Southwest 西南	6	231	14,456	1,996	15.27	40.80	24.93	62.57	13,069
Chongqing 重庆	1	230	26,496	9,850	26.34	59.66	44.59	55.86	37,398
Sichuan 四川	3	371	19,394	748	6.44	25.55	21.61	74.78	11,606
Guizhou 贵州	1	3	1,666	-188	-18.80		6.67	200.00	1,000
Yunnan 云南									
Tibet 西藏	1	43	393	71	1.37	1.40	6.70	2.62	5,200
Northwest 西北	9	118	1,626	-44	-1.00	-4.08	7.89	75.57	4,426
Shaanxi 陕西	3	270	4,074	3	0.04	0.71	6.39	93.64	5,947
Gansu 甘肃	5	50	482	-81	-1.90	-4.73	12.94	59.83	4,262
Qinghai 青海									
Ningxia 宁夏									
Xinjiang 新疆	1	6						94.74	684

4319: Other Industrial Artworks 其他工艺美术品制造业

Year 年份	Number of firms 企业个数	Rate of change 变化率(%)	Number of employees 职工人数(人)	Rate of change 变化率(%)	Total revenue (Mil. RMB) 总销售收入(百万元)	Rate of change 变化率(%)	Total profit (Mil RMB) 总利润(百万元)	Rate of change 变化率(%)
2000	766		222,246		16,967,783		571,717	
2001	859	12.14	224,578	1.05	17,970	-99.89	595	-99.90
2002	998	16.18	278,536	24.03	22,117	23.08	928	55.97

Major Products 主要产品	Output 产量	Unit 单位
Industrial Arts Products 工艺美术制品	432	100,000,000 yuan 亿元

10 Main Firms with Maximal Revenue (year founded) 收入最大的十家主要企业(创办年份)	City 城市	Province 省	Telephone/fax 电话/传真	Number of employees 职工人数	Ownership 产业所有权	Revenue ('000 RMB) 销售收入(千元)	Profit('000 RMB) (rank) 利润(千元)(排名)	Total assets ('000 RMB) 总资产(千元)	Major products 主要产品
Qingdao Feilong Technics Group Company	Qingdao	Shandong	(0532)8281688		Collective-owned				Jym Cap
青岛飞龙工艺品集团公司(1971)	青岛市	山东省	(0532)8280065	3,540	集体企业	1,694,200	5,500(27)	218,330	球帽
Henan Rebecca Hair Products Co., Ltd.	Xuchang	Henan	(0374)5137605		Joint Stock				Craftwork Hair
河南瑞贝卡发制品股份有限公司(1993)	许昌市	河南省	(0374)5134939	4,280	股份制	393,105	49,271(3)	344,808	工艺发条
Xuchang Longzheng Hair Products Co., Ltd.	Xuchang	Henan	(0374)3183045		Overseas Chinese-funded				Hair Products
许昌龙正发制品有限公司(1995)	许昌市	河南省	(0374)3183266	850	港澳台资	257,383	19,763(9)	97,467	发制品
Zhejiang Zhuquang Electrical Appliance (Group)Co.,Ltd.	Taizhou	Zhejiang	(0576)2430713		Limited-Liability				VL Festival Decoration Lamp
浙江珠光电器(集团)有限公司(1994)	台州市	浙江省	(0576)2430724	501	有限公司	190,747	1,890(95)	323,268	VL节日灯
Tianjin Shin Sung Arts Crafts & Beauty Products Co., Ltd.	Tianjin	Tianjin	(022)88539451		Foreign Funded				Craftwork Nail
天津新晟工艺美容用品有限公司(1998)	天津市	天津市	(022)88538028	2,222	外商投资	180,959	58,883(1)	167,710	工艺指甲
Shanghai Arts & Crafts General Company Substance	Shanghai	Shanghai	(021)64080473		State-owned				Industrial Arts Products 工
上海工艺美术总公司实体(1988)	上海市	上海市	(021)64834297	353	国有企业	173,413	780(212)	144,053	艺美术品
Qingdao Kingking Applied Chemistry Co., Ltd.	Qingdao	Shandong	(0532)5718989		Overseas Chinese-funded				Glass Products
青岛金王应用化学股份有限公司(1997)	青岛市	山东省	(0532)5718686	620	港澳台资	170,206	20,878(7)	146,730	玻璃制品
Zhejiang Wangbin Decorative Materials Factory	Jinhua	Zhejiang	(0579)5322875		Private Enterprises				Line
浙江王斌装饰材料有限公司(2001)	金华市	浙江省	(0579)5311230	992	私营独资	165,490	23,239(5)	162,433	线条
Wendeng Export Fireworks Factory	Weihai	Shandong	(0631)8631139		Collective-owned				Firework
文登市出口礼花厂(1981)	威海市	山东省	(0631)8631139	120	集体企业	156,730	17,190(10)	27,000	烟花
Tianjin Gaoli-Yana Handicrafts Co., Ltd.	Tianjin	Tianjin	(022)84871092		Foreign Funded				Wig
天津高丽亚那工艺品有限公司(1993)	天津市	天津市	(022)84871790	1,500	外商投资	150,253	9,990(15)	42,448	假发

Top 10 Cities by Revenue 销售收入排名前10位城市	Province 省	Market share 市场份额(%)	Number of firms 企业个数
Qingdao 青岛市	Shandong 山东省	12.55	32
Xuchang 许昌市	Henan 河南省	9.64	46
Taizhou 台州市	Zhejiang 浙江省	6.06	64
Quanzhou 泉州市	Fujian 福建省	5.55	79
Changsha 长沙市	Hunan 湖南省	4.08	106
Guangzhou 广州市	Guangdong 广东省	3.99	33
Yancheng 盐城市	Jiangsu 江苏省	3.85	28
Tianjin 天津市	Tianjin 天津市	3.23	24
Jinhua 金华市	Zhejiang 浙江省	2.97	20
Shantou 汕头市	Guangdong 广东省	2.78	42

10 Major Wholesalers 十家主要批发商	City 城市	Province 省	Telephone/Fax 电话/传真
China National Arts & Crafts Import & Export Corporation	Beijing	Beijing	(010)65521133
中国工艺品进出口总公司	北京市	北京市	(010)65531143
Shanghai Arts & Crafts Import & Export Co.,Ltd.	Shanghai	Shanghai	(021)65222888
上海市工艺品进出口有限公司	上海市	上海市	(021)65221898
Shandong Arts & Crafts Import & Export (Group) Co.,Ltd.	Qingdao	Shandong	(0532)5021355
山东工艺品进出口（集团）股份有限公司	青岛市	山东省	(0532)5021168
Zhejiang Arts & Crafts Import & Export Co.,Ltd.	Hangzhou	Zhejiang	(0571)87063393
浙江省工艺品进出口有限公司	杭州市	浙江省	(0571)87063838
Shanghai Shenhua Import & Export Co., Ltd.	Shanghai	Shanghai	(021)63177063
上海申华进出口有限公司	上海市	上海市	(021)63173819
China Hunan Arts & Crafts Import & Export Corporation	Changsha	Hunan	(0731)2284632
湖南省工艺品进出口公司	长沙市	湖南省	(0731)2287869
Guangdong Arts and Crafts Import & Export (Group) Corporation	Guangzhou	Guangdong	(020)83193388
广东省工艺品进出口（集团）公司	广州市	广东省	(020)83343614
Guangdong Nanhai Handicrafts Import & Export Co.,Ltd.	Foshan	Guangdong	(0757)6220536
广东南海工艺品进出口有限公司	佛山市	广东省	(0757)6220225
Tianjin Handicrafts Import & Export Group Co.,Ltd.	Tianjin	Tianjin	(022)23310080
天津工艺品进出口集团有限公司	天津市	天津市	(022)23317828
Taizhou International Trade Co.,Ltd.	Taizhou	Zhejiang	(0576)8811680
台州市国际贸易有限公司	台州市	浙江省	(0576)8882427

4351: Mirrors 制镜业

The industry accounts for 0.006% of the total revenue of China's industrial sector in 2002. The rate of return on assets is 3.99%. 77.42% of all firms in the industry made a profit while 22.58% had negative returns.The top province in terms of the industry's revenue is Zhejiang, accounting for 32.55% of the total revenue.
2002年本行业收入占全行业的 0.006%，资产利润率为 3.99%。77.42%的企业赢利，22.58%的企业亏损。收入最高的省为浙江省，占本行业的32.55%。

	Total number of firms 企业总数	Total number of employees 职工总数	Total revenue (Mil.RMB) 总销售收入 (百万元)	Total profit (Mil.RMB) 总利润 (百万元)	Return on assets 资产利润率 (%)	Return on equity 权益利润率 (%)	Labour productivity ('000 RMB/ worker) 劳动生产率 (千元/人)	Debts/ assets 资产负债率 (%)	Total assets (Mil.RMB) 总资产 (百万元)
Industry Overall 行业总体	31	4,957	659	27	3.99	8.18	39.12	51.18	668

	Number of firms 企业个数	Average number of employees 平均职工人数	Average revenue ('000 RMB) 平均销售收入（千元）	Average profit ('000 RMB) 平均利润 (千元)	Return on assets 资产利润率 (%)	Return on equity 权益利润率 (%)	Labour productivity ('000 RMB/ worker) 劳动生产率 (千元/人)	Debts/ assets 资产负债率 (%)	Average total assets ('000 RMB) 平均总资产 (千元)
By ownership 产业所有权									
State-owned 国有	2	55	908	-55	-2.24	-9.74	4.67	77.05	2,438
Collective-owned 集体	3	277	7,120	-292	-1.00	-4.42	8.29	77.35	29,198
Foreign & Overseas Chinese Funded 三资	11	205	22,057	294	1.35	2.35	32.82	42.58	21,744
By regional distribution 地区分布									
Central-North 华北	6	82	12,178	505	3.30	6.82	56.36	51.59	15,304
Beijing 北京	3	27	9,793	723	5.69	9.95	212.15	42.82	12,712
Tianjin 天津	1	40	6,260	300	3.93	4.89	38.50	19.53	7,630
Hebei 河北	2	186	18,713	281	1.22	3.41	24.70	64.17	23,027
Shanxi 山西									
Inner Mongolia 内蒙古									
Northeast 东北									
Liaoning 辽宁									
Jilin 吉林									
Heilongjiang 黑龙江									
Central-East 华东	12	148	29,338	1,547	4.72	8.99	52.59	47.52	32,780
Shanghai 上海	2	22	3,592	2	0.04	0.07	29.66	36.88	3,349
Jiangsu 江苏	2	123	20,725	100	0.91	1.53	44.61	40.66	11,030
Zhejiang 浙江	4	171	53,608	4,509	6.88	13.59	76.86	49.35	65,491
Anhui 安徽									
Fujian 福建									
Jiangxi 江西	2	41	4,071	144	2.72	5.93	38.43	54.11	5,293
Shandong 山东	2	358	40,425	19	0.04	0.07	35.14	43.96	46,028
Central-South 中南	9	261	23,291	542	3.90	9.69	27.34	59.76	13,895
Henan 河南	4	334	32,327	1,130	9.34	155.85	30.83	94.01	12,090
Hubei 湖北									
Hunan 湖南	2	23	5,426	-199	-1.51	-6.71	130.76	77.47	13,125
Guangdong 广东	3	322	23,155	251	1.49	1.81	17.68	17.72	16,816
Guangxi 广西									
Hainan 海南									
Southwest 西南	1	171	18,963	326	0.71	1.54	36.44	53.92	45,814
Chongqing 重庆									
Sichuan 四川	1	171	18,963	326	0.71	1.54	36.44	53.92	45,814
Guizhou 贵州									
Yunnan 云南									
Tibet 西藏									
Northwest 西北	3	60	1,693	-38	-0.96	-3.00	15.49	68.10	3,976
Shaanxi 陕西	1	105	685	-114	-2.60	-12.75	3.00	79.61	4,385
Gansu 甘肃	2	37	2,197				33.22	61.40	3,771
Qinghai 青海									
Ningxia 宁夏									
Xinjiang 新疆									

Year 年份	Number of firms 企业个数	Rate of change 变化率(%)	Number of employees 职工人数(人)	Rate of change 变化率(%)	Total revenue (Mil. RMB) 总销售收入(百万元)	Rate of change 变化率(%)	Total profit (Mil RMB) 总利润(百万元)	Rate of change 变化率(%)
2000	25		3,946		345,292		8,636	
2001	32	28.00	4,529	14.77	642	-99.81	27	-99.69
2002	31	-3.13	4,957	9.45	659	2.65	27	

Major Products 主要产品	Output 产量	Unit 单位

10 Main Firms with Maximal Revenue (year founded) 收入最大的十家主要企业(创办年份)	City 城市	Province 省	Telephone/fax 电话/传真	Number of employees 职工人数	Ownership 产业所有权	Revenue ('000 RMB) 销售收入(千元)	Profit('000 RMB) (rank) 利润(千元)(排名)	Total assets ('000 RMB) 总资产(千元)	Major products 主要产品
Qingdao Bogo Optical Co., Ltd. 青岛宝库光学有限公司(1995)	Qingdao 青岛市	Shandong 山东省	(0532)7795771 (0532)7795708	660	Foreign Funded 外商投资	76,686	-	85,485	Swimming Glasses 泳镜
Junyuhe Glass Products Co., Ltd. 浚玉鹤玻璃制品有限责任公司(1998)	Hebi 鹤壁市	Hunan 湖南省	(0392)5820073	650	Limited-Liability 有限公司	120,040	5150(2)	3,802	Wall Mirreo 壁镜
PineField (Shenzhen) Wooden Products Co., Ltd. 奔辉（深圳）木制品有限公司(1989)	Shenzhen 深圳市	Guangdong 广东省	(0755)27740750 (0755)27740758	750	Overseas Chinese-funded 港澳台资	52,941	663(7)	23,478	Phtologh Frame 相框
Xinji Huaming Glasses Co., Ltd. 辛集华明眼镜有限公司(1992)	Shijiazhuang 石家庄市	Hebei 河北省	(0311)3962888 (0311)3962745	300	Overseas Chinese-funded 港澳台资	27,050	202(14)	31,455	Glasses Lens 眼镜片
Wuxi Marcati Optics Co., Ltd. 无锡梦卡迪光学有限公司(1995)	Wuxi 无锡市	Jiangsu 江苏省	(0510)8791629 (0510)2766538	145	Overseas Chinese-funded 港澳台资	23,620	-	12,850	Lens 镜片
Sichuan Longchang Glass Co.,Ltd. 四川省隆昌玻璃镜公司(1957)	Neijiang 内江市	Sichuan 四川省	(0832)3954100 (0832)39598312	171	Collective-owned 集体企业	18,963	326(11)	45,814	Civil Mirror 民用镜
Donghai Dongfang Mirror Making Factory 东海县东方制镜厂(1997)	Lianyungang 连云港市	Jiangsu 江苏省	(0518)7889825 (0518)7298799	100	Private Enterprises 私营独资	17,830	330(10)	9,210	Decorated Mirror 装簧镜
Hangzhou Qianjiang Cosmetology Cupboard Co., Ltd. 杭州钱江美容柜有限公司(1985)	Hangzhou 杭州市	Zhejiang 浙江省	(0571)82522807 (0571)82522185	50	Limited-Liability 有限公司	13,870	687(6)	18,142	Mirror Making 制镜
Beijing Jubo Photoelectricity Co., Ltd. 北京巨玻光电有限公司(1991)	Beijing 北京市	Beijing 北京市	(010)67113670 (010)67117117	21	Foreign Funded 外商投资	13,381	1,132(3)	8,072	Optical Film-plating Materials 光学镀膜材料
Qinhuangdao Qinguan Radian Mirror Co., Ltd. 秦皇岛秦冠弧度镜有限公司(1992)	Qinhuangdao 秦皇岛市	Hebei 河北省	(0335)3410694 (0335)3410461	71	Overseas Chinese-funded 港澳台资	10,375	360(9)	14,599	Car Backing Mirror 倒车镜

Top 10 Cities by Revenue 销售收入排名前10位城市	Province 省	Market share 市场份额(%)	Number of firms 企业个数
Hangzhou 杭州市	Zhejiang 浙江省	31.27	3
Hebi 鹤壁市	Henan 河南省	18.22	1
Qingdao 青岛市	Shandong 山东省	11.64	1
Shenzhen 深圳市	Guangdong 广东省	9.06	2
Beijing 北京市	Beijing 北京市	4.46	3
Shijiazhuang 石家庄市	Hebei 河北省	4.11	1
Wuxi 无锡市	Jiangsu 江苏省	3.59	1
Neijiang 内江市	Sichuan 四川省	2.88	1
Lianyungang 连云港市	Jiangsu 江苏省	2.71	1
Qinhuangdao 秦皇岛市	Hebei 河北省	1.57	1

10 Major Wholesalers 十家主要批发商	City 城市	Province 省	Telephone/Fax 电话/传真
King Paper Source Trade (shanghai) Co.,Ltd. 金纸源贸易（上海）有限公司	Shanghai 上海市	Shanghai 上海市	(021)62720808 (021)62720909
China National Paper & Pulp Corpration 中国纸张纸浆进出口公司	Beijing 北京市	Beijing 北京市	(010)67780346 (010)67747294
Sinar Mas Linjiang Paper Industry Trade (Beijing) Co.,Ltd. 金光林浆纸业贸易(北京)有限公司	Beijing 北京市	Beijing 北京市	(010)65666688 (010)65669599
Sinar Mas Paper Industry (Xishan) Co.,Ltd. 金光纸业(锡山)有限公司	Wuxi 无锡市	Jiangsu 江苏省	(0510)8251188 (0510)8250906
China Printing Materials General Company 中国印刷物资总公司	Beijing 北京市	Beijing 北京市	(010)63442905 (010)63442900
TSS Eortune Co., ltd. 天津同鑫进出口有限公司	Tianjin 天津市	Tianjin 天津市	(022)28131350 (022)28131353
Wenzhou Import & Export Corpration 温州市进出口公司	Wenzhou 温州市	Zhejiang 浙江省	(0577)88862681 (0577)88844557
Sinar Mas Paper Industry (Xiamen) Co.,Ltd. 金光纸业（厦门）有限公司	Xiamen 厦门市	Fujian 福建省	(0592)2962018 (0592)2962010
Sinar Mas Paper Industry (Shenzhen) Co.,Ltd. 金光纸业（深圳）有限公司	Shenzhen 深圳市	Guangdong 广东省	(0755)83516701 (0755)83516773
Jieyang Ocean Shipping Supply Group Co.,Ltd. 揭阳市外轮供应集团有限公司	Jieyang 揭阳市	Guangdong 广东省	(0663)8239634 (0663)8236186

4353: Eye Glasses 眼镜制造业

The industry accounts for 0.054% of the total revenue of China's industrial sector in 2002. The rate of return on assets is 14.67%. 85.59% of all firms in the industry made a profit while 14.41% had negative returns.The top province in terms of the industry's revenue is Zhejiang, accounting for 32.92% of the total revenue.
2002年本行业收入占全行业的0.054%，资产利润率为 14.67%。85.59%的企业赢利，14.41%的企业亏损。收入最高的省为浙江省，占本行业的32.92%。

	Total number of firms 企业总数	Total number of employees 职工总数	Total revenue (Mil.RMB) 总销售收入 (百万元)	Total profit (Mil.RMB) 总利润 (百万元)	Return on assets 资产利润率 (%)	Return on equity 权益利润率 (%)	Labour productivity ('000 RMB/ worker) 劳动生产率 (千元/人)	Debts/ assets 资产负债率 (%)	Total assets (Mil.RMB) 总资产 (百万元)
Industry Overall 行业总体	229	63,953	5,786	882	14.67	28.97	29.45	49.35	6,013

	Number of firms 企业个数	Average number of employees 平均职工人数	Average revenue ('000 RMB) 平均销售收入 (千元)	Average profit ('000 RMB) 平均利润 (千元)	Return on assets 资产利润率 (%)	Return on equity 权益利润率 (%)	Labour productivity ('000 RMB/ worker) 劳动生产率 (千元/人)	Debts/ assets 资产负债率 (%)	Average total assets ('000 RMB) 平均总资产 (千元)
By ownership 产业所有权									
State-owned 国有	4	32	2,661	-456	-10.41	-98.01	24.17	89.38	4,382
Collective-owned 集体	7	300	18,525	53	0.45	0.66	12.66	32.01	11,659
Foreign & Overseas Chinese Funded 三资	123	318	30,434	6,687	18.61	35.29	32.80	47.27	35,937
By regional distribution 地区分布									
Central-North 华北	8	58	6,268	-380	-3.19	-5.64	24.35	43.47	11,938
Beijing 北京	5	77	9,976	-384	-2.51	-3.99	30.61	37.11	15,295
Tianjin 天津	3	27	90	-375	-5.91	-19.08	-5.76	69.04	6,343
Hebei 河北									
Shanxi 山西									
Inner Mongolia 内蒙古									
Northeast 东北	3	256	36,891	4,053	6.91	10.43	45.65	33.80	58,678
Liaoning 辽宁	3	256	36,891	4,053	6.91	10.43	45.65	33.80	58,678
Jilin 吉林									
Heilongjiang 黑龙江									
Central-East 华东	162	274	24,608	1,033	4.36	9.50	30.35	54.17	23,727
Shanghai 上海	11	172	40,880	2,998	6.28	12.62	174.76	50.28	47,762
Jiangsu 江苏	16	299	31,375	2,208	6.37	15.19	37.26	58.10	34,695
Zhejiang 浙江	107	226	17,802	631	4.62	10.29	23.47	55.12	13,661
Anhui 安徽									
Fujian 福建	26	509	42,705	1,201	2.44	5.25	20.25	53.57	49,313
Jiangxi 江西									
Shandong 山东	2	195	9,825	191	1.97	2.35	12.25	16.11	9,688
Central-South 中南	53	328	27,268	13,253	42.54	70.68	24.19	39.81	31,155
Henan 河南	1	60	1,748	-2	-0.11	-0.12	9.37	11.36	1,893
Hubei 湖北									
Hunan 湖南									
Guangdong 广东	52	333	27,759	13,508	42.59	70.80	24.24	39.85	31,717
Guangxi 广西									
Hainan 海南									
Southwest 西南	1	820	192,410	3,560	1.49	2.98	81.23	50.13	239,680
Chongqing 重庆									
Sichuan 四川	1	820	192,410	3,560	1.49	2.98	81.23	50.13	239,680
Guizhou 贵州									
Yunnan 云南									
Tibet 西藏									
Northwest 西北	2	38	501	-37	-1.04	-14.72	15.32	92.92	3,504
Shaanxi 陕西									
Gansu 甘肃	2	38	501	-37	-1.04	-14.72	15.32	92.92	3,504
Qinghai 青海									
Ningxia 宁夏									
Xinjiang 新疆									

Year 年份	Number of firms 企业个数	Rate of change 变化率 (%)	Number of employees 职工人数 (人)	Rate of change 变化率 (%)	Total revenue (Mil. RMB) 总销售收入 (百万元)	Rate of change 变化率 (%)	Total profit (Mil RMB) 总利润 (百万元)	Rate of change 变化率 (%)
2000	168		43,305		4,399,875		189,809	
2001	221	31.55	57,225	32.14	5,363	-99.88	224	-99.88
2002	229	3.62	63,953	11.76	5,786	7.89	882	293.75

Major Products 主要产品	Output 产量	Unit 单位
Glasses 眼镜	58,341	10,000 Pairs 万付

10 Main Firms with Maximal Revenue (year founded) 收入最大的十家主要企业（创办年份）	City 城市	Province 省	Telephone/fax 电话/传真	Number of employees 职工人数	Ownership 产业所有权	Revenue ('000 RMB) 销售收入(千元)	Profit('000 RMB) (rank) 利润(千元)(排名)	Total assets ('000 RMB) 总资产(千元)	Major products 主要产品
Chengdu Jinghua Group Co.,Ltd. 成都晶华集团(1993)	Chengdu 成都市	Sichuan 四川省	(028)4868058 (028)88431988	820	Private Partnership 私营合伙	192,410	3,560(15)	239,680	Optics Lens 光学镜片
Zhijiang Tide Optical Co., Ltd. 浙江泰恒光学有限公司(1996)	Wenzhou 温州市	Zhejiang 浙江省	(0577)86761288 (0577)86767601	2,435	Limited-Liability 有限公司	185,306	7,795(8)	303,497	Glasses 眼镜
Shanghai Weikon Optics Co., Ltd. 上海卫康光学有限公司(1992)	Shanghai 上海市	Shanghai 上海市	(021)58420251 (021)58423331	630	Foreign Funded 外商投资	179,763	57,482(2)	125,303	Glasses 眼镜
Roring Industry (Xiamen) Co., Ltd. 来明工业(厦门)有限公司(1989)	Xiamen 厦门市	Fujian 福建省	(0592)6216191 (0592)6210138	1,986	Overseas Chinese-funded 港澳台资	154,624	20,379(4)	218,018	Glasses 眼镜
Chaoyang Matian Glasses Co., Ltd. 潮阳马田眼镜有限公司(1999)	Shantou 汕头市	Guangdong 广东省	(0661)2251782 (0661)2251523	1,200	Private Owned 私营企业	150,600	1,300(38)	23,000	Glasses 眼镜
Hoya (Guangzhou)Optics Co.,Ltd. 豪雅（广州）光学有限公司(1996)	Guangzhou 广州市	Guangdong 广东省	(020)82223999 (020)82221142	380	Foreign Funded 外商投资	124,623	4,368(14)	150,536	Resin lens 树脂镜片
II-VI Optics SIN 贰陆光学(苏州)有限公司(1996)	Suzhou 苏州市	Jiangsu 江苏省	(0512)67619295 (0512)67615049	172	Foreign Funded 外商投资	111,849	29,197(3)	63,783	Infrared Optics Lens 红外光学镜片
Chengyi Optics (Xiamen) Co., Ltd. 诚益光学（厦门）有限公司(1990)	Xiamen 厦门市	Fujian 福建省	(0592)5516018 (0592)5516028	1,300	Overseas Chinese-funded 港澳台资	107,284	3,395(17)	147,754	Glasses 眼镜
Zhenjiang Wanxin Option Glasses Co., Ltd 镇江万新光学眼镜有限公司(1989)	Zhenjiang 镇江市	Jiangsu 江苏省	(0511)6802427 (0511)6802007	1,008	Overseas Chinese-funded 港澳台资	96,736	1,093(51)	89,176	Metal Glasses Frame 金属眼镜架
Jiangsu Dongfang Optics Co., Ltd. 江苏东方光学有限公司(1993)	Zhenjiang 镇江市	Jiangsu 江苏省	(0511)6802005 (0511)6802006	1,660	Overseas Chinese-funded 港澳台资	93,575	1,621(31)	97,388	Glasses Frame 眼镜架

Top 10 Cities by Revenue 销售收入排名前10位城市	Province 省	Market share 市场份额 (%)	Number of firms 企业个数
Wenzhou 温州市	Zhejiang 浙江省	30.19	97
Xiamen 厦门市	Fujian 福建省	16.66	22
Guangzhou 广州市	Guangdong 广东省	12.68	26
Shanghai 上海市	Shanghai 上海市	7.77	11
Zhenjiang 镇江市	Jiangsu 江苏省	4.86	10
Shenzhen 深圳市	Guangdong 广东省	3.97	7
Dongguan 东莞市	Guangdong 广东省	3.86	10
Suzhou 苏州市	Jiangsu 江苏省	3.50	4
Chengdu 成都市	Sichuan 四川省	3.33	1
Shantou 汕头市	Guangdong 广东省	2.60	1

10 Major Wholesalers 十家主要批发商	City 城市	Province 省	Telephone/Fax 电话/传真
King Paper Source Trade (shanghai) Co.,Ltd. 金纸源贸易（上海）有限公司	Shanghai 上海市	Shanghai 上海市	(021)62720808 (021)62720909
China National Paper & Pulp Corpration 中国纸张纸浆进出口公司	Beijing 北京市	Beijing 北京市	(010)67780346 (010)67747294
Sinar Mas Linjiang Paper Industry Trade (Beijing) Co.,Ltd. 金光林浆纸业贸易(北京)有限公司	Beijing 北京市	Beijing 北京市	(010)65666688 (010)65669599
Sinar Mas Paper Industry (Xishan) Co.,Ltd. 金光纸业(锡山)有限公司	Wuxi 无锡市	Jiangsu 江苏省	(0510)8251188 (0510)8250906
China Printing Materials General Company 中国印刷物资总公司	Beijing 北京市	Beijing 北京市	(010)63442905 (010)63442900
TSS Eortune Co., ltd. 天津同鑫进出口有限公司	Tianjin 天津市	Tianjin 天津市	(022)28131350 (022)28131353
Wenzhou Import & Export Corpration 温州市进出口公司	Wenzhou 温州市	Zhejiang 浙江省	(0577)88862681 (0577)88844557
Sinar Mas Paper Industry (Xiamen) Co.,Ltd. 金光纸业（厦门）有限公司	Xiamen 厦门市	Fujian 福建省	(0592)2962018 (0592)2962010
Sinar Mas Paper Industry (Shenzhen) Co.,Ltd. 金光纸业（深圳）有限公司	Shenzhen 深圳市	Guangdong 广东省	(0755)83516701 (0755)83516773
Jieyang Ocean Shipping Supply Group Co.,Ltd. 揭阳市外轮供应集团有限公司	Jieyang 揭阳市	Guangdong 广东省	(0663)8239634 (0663)8236186

4355: Umbrellas 制伞业

The industry accounts for 0.044% of the total revenue of China's industrial sector in 2002. The rate of return on assets is 3.16%. 75.14% of all firms in the industry made a profit while 24.86% had negative returns.The top province in terms of the industry's revenue is Zhejiang, accounting for 40.85% of the total revenue.
2002年本行业收入占全行业的 0.044%，资产利润率为 3.16%。75.14%的企业赢利，24.86%的企业亏损。收入最高的省为浙江省，占本行业的40.85%。

	Total number of firms 企业总数	Total number of employees 职工总数	Total revenue (Mil.RMB) 总销售收入 (百万元)	Total profit (Mil.RMB) 总利润 (百万元)	Return on assets 资产利润率 (%)	Return on equity 权益利润率 (%)	Labour productivity ('000 RMB/ worker) 劳动生产率 (千元/人)	Debts/ assets 资产负债率 (%)	Total assets (Mil.RMB) 总资产 (百万元)
Industry Overall 行业总体	181	38,788	4,741	122	3.16	7.78	36.00	59.41	3,862

	Number of firms 企业个数	Average number of employees 平均职工人数	Average revenue ('000 RMB) 平均销售收入 (千元)	Average profit ('000 RMB) 平均利润 (千元)	Return on assets 资产利润率 (%)	Return on equity 权益利润率 (%)	Labour productivity ('000 RMB/ worker) 劳动生产率 (千元/人)	Debts/ assets 资产负债率 (%)	Average total assets ('000 RMB) 平均总资产 (千元)
By ownership 产业所有权									
State-owned 国有	3	170	1,173	-861	-7.14		-0.60	150.82	12,054
Collective-owned 集体	8	235	30,019	1,069	3.02	10.44	59.74	71.11	35,436
Foreign & Overseas Chinese Funded 三资	93	236	29,649	430	1.57	3.48	37.77	54.89	27,332
By regional distribution 地区分布									
Central-North 华北	1	165	15,591	19	0.35	2.74	31.36	87.21	5,426
Beijing 北京	1	165	15,591	19	0.35	2.74	31.36	87.21	5,426
Tianjin 天津									
Hebei 河北									
Shanxi 山西									
Inner Mongolia 内蒙古									
Northeast 东北									
Liaoning 辽宁									
Jilin 吉林									
Heilongjiang 黑龙江									
Central-East 华东	143	217	27,323	741	3.38	8.56	36.15	60.55	21,938
Shanghai 上海	18	106	21,889	-593	-2.05	-5.76	51.70	64.45	28,981
Jiangsu 江苏	5	183	25,196	944	9.35	23.66	37.97	60.50	10,100
Zhejiang 浙江	65	214	29,795	1,170	5.08	18.86	33.00	73.09	23,044
Anhui 安徽	1	95	4,940	360	28.35	36.00	11.17	21.26	1,270
Fujian 福建	50	277	28,517	718	3.50	5.74	37.60	39.03	20,502
Jiangxi 江西	2	44	2,079	-231	-16.57		14.64	243.29	1,394
Shandong 山东	2	116	7,746	42	0.22	1.18	22.08	81.47	18,978
Central-South 中南	36	209	22,228	360	1.82	3.99	35.61	54.44	19,821
Henan 河南									
Hubei 湖北	1	97	599				17.87	14.17	4,488
Hunan 湖南									
Guangdong 广东	34	206	23,455	444	2.21	4.64	38.01	52.31	20,045
Guangxi 广西	1	402	2,112	-2,120	-7.70		-2.00	113.60	27,532
Hainan 海南									
Southwest 西南	1	128	18,152	2,930	52.81	70.52	28.93	25.11	5,548
Chongqing 重庆									
Sichuan 四川	1	128	18,152	2,930	52.81	70.52	28.93	25.11	5,548
Guizhou 贵州									
Yunnan 云南									
Tibet 西藏									
Northwest 西北									
Shaanxi 陕西									
Gansu 甘肃									
Qinghai 青海									
Ningxia 宁夏									
Xinjiang 新疆									

Year 年份	Number of firms 企业个数	Rate of change 变化率 (%)	Number of employees 职工人数 (人)	Rate of change 变化率 (%)	Total revenue (Mil. RMB) 总销售收入 (百万元)	Rate of change 变化率 (%)	Total profit (Mil RMB) 总利润 (百万元)	Rate of change 变化率 (%)
2000	137		29,984		3,089,191		71,016	
2001	145	5.84	33,065	10.28	3,894	-99.87	125	-99.82
2002	181	24.83	38,788	17.31	4,741	21.75	122	-2.40

Major Products 主要产品	Output 产量	Unit 单位
Umbrella 伞	13,150	10,000 Pieces 万把

10 Main Firms with Maximal Revenue (year founded) 收入最大的十家主要企业（创办年份）	City 城市	Province 省	Telephone/fax 电话/传真	Number of employees 职工人数	Ownership 产业所有权	Revenue ('000 RMB) 销售收入（千元）	Profit('000 RMB) (rank) 利润(千元)（排名）	Total assets ('000 RMB) 总资产（千元）	Major products 主要产品
Zhejiang Taizhou Yada Industrial Co.,Ltd. 浙江省台州亚达实业有限公司(1988)	Taizhou 台州市	Zhejiang 浙江省	(0576)3119693 (0576)3117555	1,959	Private Partnership 私营合伙	310,468	12,613(3)	166,179	Sun Umbrella 太阳伞
Xiamen Futai Umbrella Co., Ltd. 厦门福太伞业有限公司(1990)	Xiamen 厦门市	Fujian 福建省	(0592)6210181 (0592)6227181	1,702	Overseas Chinese-funded 港澳台资	227,863	17,700(1)	200,799	Umbrella 雨伞
Hangzhou Paradise Umbrella Group Co., Ltd. 杭州天堂伞业集团有限公司(1997)	Hangzhou 杭州市	Zhejiang 浙江省	(0571)85283333 (0571)85183111	1,874	Private Enterprises 私营独资	213,847	10,057(5)	153,217	Sun Umbrella 晴雨伞
Taizhou Yongqiang Arts & Crafes Co., Ltd. 台州永强工艺品有限公司(1995)	Taizhou 台州市	Zhejiang 浙江省	(0576)5282303 (0576)5282515	701	Foreign Funded 外商投资	211,675	5,155(9)	235,340	Sun umbrella 太阳伞
Shaoxing Jinding Umbrella Co., Ltd. 绍兴市金鼎伞业有限公司(1993)	Shaoxing 绍兴市	Zhejiang 浙江省	(0575)2065138 (0575)2065017	361	Private Owned 私营企业	135,000	14,597(2)	47,221	Umbrella 雨伞
Zhejiang Zhengte Industrial Co., Ltd. 浙江正特实业有限公司(1996)	Taizhou 台州市	Zhejiang 浙江省	(0576)5962553 (0576)5962555	772	Limited-Liability 有限公司	122,671	3,072(14)	47,200	Aluminum Alloy Sun Umbrella铝合金太阳伞
Wenzhou Conch Industry Group Co., Ltd. 温州市海螺工业集团公司(1995)	Wenzhou 温州市	Zhejiang 浙江省	(0577)86531962 (0577)86531961	765	Collective-owned 集体企业	105,086	5,989(7)	205,938	Umbrella 晴雨伞
Jinjiang Hengshun Western Umbrella Co., Ltd. 晋江市恒顺洋伞有限公司(1995)	Quanzhou 泉州市	Fujian 福建省	(0595)5585256 (0595)5581002	560	Overseas Chinese-funded 港澳台资	91,116	6,129(6)	28,972	Umbrella 雨伞
Ningbo Wanhui Fallow Articles Co., Ltd. 宁波万汇休闲用品有限公司(2000)	Ningbo 宁波市	Zhejiang 浙江省	(0574)88240520	350	Foreign Funded 外商投资	87,390	503(56)	62,197	Fallow Umbrella 休闲伞
Fuxing Umbrella Industry Co., Ltd. 富兴伞业有限公司(1988)	Quanzhou 泉州市	Fujian 福建省	(0595)5587435 (0595)5585190	600	Overseas Chinese-funded 港澳台资	66,730	4,671(11)	71,466	Umbrella 雨伞

Top 10 Cities by Revenue 销售收入排名前10位城市	Province 省	Market share 市场份额 (%)	Number of firms 企业个数
Taizhou 台州市	Zhejiang 浙江省	16.89	13
Quanzhou 泉州市	Fujian 福建省	10.73	22
Zhangzhou 漳州市	Fujian 福建省	10.00	18
Xiamen 厦门市	Fujian 福建省	9.13	9
Shanghai 上海市	Shanghai 上海市	8.31	18
Shaoxing 绍兴市	Zhejiang 浙江省	6.43	15
Hangzhou 杭州市	Zhejiang 浙江省	5.84	6
Shenzhen 深圳市	Guangdong 广东省	5.79	11
Ningbo 宁波市	Zhejiang 浙江省	3.35	3
Jinhua 金华市	Zhejiang 浙江省	3.08	11

10 Major Wholesalers 十家主要批发商	City 城市	Province 省	Telephone/Fax 电话/传真
Harbin ChinaSun Group Co., Ltd. 哈尔滨中央红集团股份有限公司	Haerbin 哈尔滨市	Heilongjiang 黑龙江省	(0451)84885100 (0451)84885111
Guangzhou Yuexiu Enterprise (Group) Company 广州越秀企业（集团）公司	Guangzhou 广州市	Guangdong 广东省	(020)85597130 (020)85599018
China Reed Screen Imp. & Exp. Corp.Ltd. 中艺苇帘进出口有限责任公司	Beijing 北京市	Beijing 北京市	(010)65521133 (010)65513995
Hebei Xintai Foreign Trade Corp.ltd. 河北信泰对外贸易有限公司	Shijiazhuang 石家庄市	Hebei 河北省	(0311)7767908 (0311)7755347
Hebei Arts & Crafts Imp. & Exp. Corp. 河北省工艺品进出口公司	Shijiazhuang 石家庄市	Hebei 河北省	(0311)7764345 (0311)7755347
Shanghai Hengda Ceramic Building Materials Trade Market 上海恒大陶瓷建材交易市场	Shanghai 上海市	Shanghai 上海市	(021)58425842 (021)58427389
Hangzhou Local Product General Corporation 杭州市土特产总公司	Hangzhou 杭州市	Zhejiang 浙江省	(0571)87026301 (0571)87026323
Ningbo Zhonglin Foreign Trade Co.,Ltd. 宁波中蔺对外贸易有限公司	Ningbo 宁波市	Zhejiang 浙江省	(0574)87871797 (0574)87871790
Wuyi Local Products Daily Groceries Co.,Ltd. 武义县土产日用杂品有限责任公司	Jinhua 金华市	Zhejiang 浙江省	(0579)7623401 (0579)7623401
Guangdong Shunde Local Products Import & Export Company 广东省顺德土产进出口公司	Foshan 佛山市	Guangdong 广东省	(0765)6682839 (0765)6681441

4357: Bristle Processing And Brush 鬃毛加工及制刷业

The industry accounts for 0.027% of the total revenue of China's industrial sector in 2002. The rate of return on assets is 5.32%. 88.55% of all firms in the industry made a profit while 11.45% had negative returns.The top province in terms of the industry's revenue is Jiangsu, accounting for 31.58% of the total revenue.
2002年本行业收入占全行业的0.027%，资产利润率为5.32%。88.55%的企业赢利，11.45%的企业亏损。收入最高的省为江苏省，占本行业的31.58%。

	Total number of firms 企业总数	Total number of employees 职工总数	Total revenue (Mil.RMB) 总销售收入（百万元）	Total profit (Mil.RMB) 总利润（百万元）	Return on assets 资产利润率 (%)	Return on equity 权益利润率 (%)	Labour productivity ('000 RMB/ worker) 劳动生产率（千元/人）	Debts/ assets 资产负债率 (%)	Total assets (Mil.RMB) 总资产（百万元）
Industry Overall 行业总体	166	28,300	2,850	99	5.32	14.16	26.84	62.40	1,855

	Number of firms 企业个数	Average number of employees 平均职工人数	Average revenue ('000 RMB) 平均销售收入（千元）	Average profit ('000 RMB) 平均利润（千元）	Return on assets 资产利润率 (%)	Return on equity 权益利润率 (%)	Labour productivity ('000 RMB/ worker) 劳动生产率（千元/人）	Debts/ assets 资产负债率 (%)	Average total assets ('000 RMB) 平均总资产（千元）
By ownership 产业所有权									
State-owned 国有	10	63	2,707	-645	-4.94		9.11	153.67	13,058
Collective-owned 集体	28	191	18,394	501	3.55	11.65	23.18	69.56	14,118
Foreign & Overseas Chinese Funded 三资	45	218	22,995	1,112	7.13	13.23	29.52	46.14	15,601
By regional distribution 地区分布									
Central-North 华北	24	165	15,294	1,094	11.03	18.79	22.50	41.26	9,911
Beijing 北京	3	160	17,949	758	3.57	5.22	22.34	31.63	21,210
Tianjin 天津	8	103	14,668	1,922	25.36	44.37	36.16	42.84	7,577
Hebei 河北	13	205	15,067	661	7.57	13.97	18.30	45.82	8,740
Shanxi 山西									
Inner Mongolia 内蒙古									
Northeast 东北	2	650	30,253	2,931	6.55		11.35	156.28	44,762
Liaoning 辽宁	1	1,174	50,505	7,577	19.21	31.53	12.31	39.08	39,452
Jilin 吉林									
Heilongjiang 黑龙江	1	125	10,000	-1,716	-3.43		2.38	248.62	50,072
Central-East 华东	88	165	18,197	610	6.51	16.83	29.60	61.33	9,370
Shanghai 上海	2	135	6,906	500	7.15	8.11	19.33	11.81	6,994
Jiangsu 江苏	49	173	18,366	449	5.40	16.31	27.89	66.87	8,315
Zhejiang 浙江	14	131	14,477	688	7.57	16.13	30.74	53.03	9,088
Anhui 安徽	7	70	2,858	286	7.79	31.05	14.85	74.90	3,670
Fujian 福建	4	80	13,378	527	5.83	11.10	35.18	47.45	9,028
Jiangxi 江西	1	527	55,922	2,350	7.74	64.52	17.36	88.00	30,360
Shandong 山东	11	240	32,318	1,325	7.93	17.61	39.82	54.98	16,709
Central-South 中南	33	168	17,626	338	2.48	5.28	32.48	53.09	13,630
Henan 河南	16	158	14,886	611	5.26	11.63	30.06	54.83	11,634
Hubei 湖北	1	85	6,669	22	0.29	1.09	31.62	73.19	7,542
Hunan 湖南	2	169	9,511	71	0.82	1.75	23.65	53.09	8,658
Guangdong 广东	13	162	21,214	40	0.38	0.80	30.47	52.25	10,535
Guangxi 广西	1	481	42,005	670	0.66	1.30	60.32	49.57	101,824
Hainan 海南									
Southwest 西南	16	174	13,905	55	0.37	1.22	13.54	69.56	14,742
Chongqing 重庆	6	211	16,702	-576	-3.06	-33.54	9.09	90.88	18,809
Sichuan 四川	10	152	12,226	433	3.52	7.05	17.26	50.01	12,302
Guizhou 贵州									
Yunnan 云南									
Tibet 西藏									
Northwest 西北	3	54	5,616	307	5.35	14.45	45.53	62.97	5,737
Shaanxi 陕西									
Gansu 甘肃	3	54	5,616	307	5.35	14.45	45.53	62.97	5,737
Qinghai 青海									
Ningxia 宁夏									
Xinjiang 新疆									

4357: Bristle Processing And Brush 鬃毛加工及制刷业

Year 年份	Number of firms 企业个数	Rate of change 变化率 (%)	Number of employees 职工人数 (人)	Rate of change 变化率 (%)	Total revenue (Mil. RMB) 总销售收入 (百万元)	Rate of change 变化率 (%)	Total profit (Mil RMB) 总利润 (百万元)	Rate of change 变化率 (%)
2000	137		26,428		2,385,653		45,230	
2001	150	9.49	27,096	2.53	2,513	-99.89	89	-99.80
2002	166	10.67	28,300	4.44	2,850	13.41	99	11.24

Major Products 主要产品	Output 产量	Unit 单位

10 Main Firms with Maximal Revenue (year founded) 收入最大的十家主要企业（创办年份）	City 城市	Province 省	Telephone/fax 电话/传真	Number of employees 职工人数	Ownership 产业所有权	Revenue ('000 RMB) 销售收入 (千元)	Profit('000 RMB) (rank) 利润(千元) (排名)	Total assets ('000 RMB) 总资产 (千元)	Major products 主要产品
Zaozhuang Zhengtong Brush-making Co., Ltd.	Zaozhuang	Shandong	(0632)7561198		Private Owned				Brush
枣庄市正通制刷有限公司(1980)	枣庄市	山东省	(0632)7561711	624	私营企业	78,060	4,210(4)	31,260	刷子
Qingdao Qianxiang Hair Products Co., Ltd.	Qingdao	Shandong	(0532)8809485		Foreign Funded				Curly Hair
青岛乾祥发制品有限公司(1999)	青岛市	山东省	(0532)8809845	23	外商投资	75,739	820(40)	30,276	曲发
Huai'an Xinghuai Bristle Products Co., Ltd.	Huaian	Jiangsu	(0517)5720144		Private Enterprises				Poached Bristle
淮安市兴淮猪鬃制品有限公司(1996)	淮安市	江苏省	(0517)5720558	622	私营独资	60,510	2,132(15)	12,000	水煮鬃
Zhongyuan Bristle Processing Group Co., Ltd.	Xinyang	Henan	(0376)7922655		Collective-owned				Bristle
中原制鬃集团有限公司(1955)	信阳市	河南省	(0376)7923333	912	集体企业	60,100	1,500(23)	114,472	猪鬃
Wuxi Shengfa Brush Co., Ltd.	Wuxi	Jiangsu	(0510)2626725		Overseas Chinese-funded				Paintbrush
无锡盛发制刷有限公司(1992)	无锡市	江苏省	(0510)2607524	79	港澳台资	58,202	6,636(3)	17,209	漆刷
Taizhou Jianghai Bristle Products Factory	Taizhou	Jiangsu	(0523)6559838		Collective-owned				Bristle
泰州市江海鬃制品厂(1991)	泰州市	江苏省	(0523)6558213	500	集体企业	55,061	106(100)	50,382	猪鬃
Cangzhou Baosheng Brush Co., Ltd.	Cangzhou	Hebei	(0317)4317079		Foreign Funded				Cosmetic Brush
沧州宝胜制刷有限公司(1995)	沧州市	河北省	(0317)4125804	600	外商投资	52,944	2,574(8)	15,621	化妆刷
Gaoyou Huayu Rabbit Hair Factory	Yangzhou	Jiangsu	(0514)4232056		Private Enterprises				Rabbit Hair Processing
高邮市华宇兔毛厂(1978)	扬州市	江苏省		138	私营独资	51,711	20(124)	5,225	兔毛加工
Yingkou Cosmetic Applicators Corp.	Yingkou	Liaoning	(0417)6271649		Foreign Funded				Cosmetic Brush 化
营口化妆用具有限公司(1989)	营口市	辽宁省	(0417)6271632	1,174	外商投资	50,505	7,377(1)	39,452	妆用毛刷
Chongqing Guhua Livestock Products Co., Ltd.	Chongqing	Chongqing	(023)48655834		Foreign Funded				Bristle
重庆古华蓄产有限公司(1992)	重庆市	重庆市	(023)48653486	624	外商投资	48,432	207(82)	53,017	猪鬃

Top 10 Cities by Revenue 销售收入排名前10位城市	Province 省	Market share 市场份额 (%)	Number of firms 企业个数
Yangzhou 扬州市	Jiangsu 江苏省	9.20	18
Zhenjiang 镇江市	Jiangsu 江苏省	8.90	17
Taizhou 泰州市	Jiangsu 江苏省	5.12	6
Qingdao 青岛市	Shandong 山东省	5.11	2
Ningbo 宁波市	Zhejiang 浙江省	5.08	9
Jiangmen 江门市	Guangdong 广东省	4.49	2
Zaozhuang 枣庄市	Shandong 山东省	4.45	3
Tianjin 天津市	Tianjin 天津市	4.12	8
Chongqing 重庆市	Chongqing 重庆市	3.52	6
Cangzhou 沧州市	Hebei 河北省	3.47	6

10 Major Wholesalers 十家主要批发商	City 城市	Province 省	Telephone/Fax 电话/传真
Harbin ChinaSun Group Co., Ltd.	Haerbin	Heilongjiang	(0451)84885100
哈尔滨中央红集团股份有限公司	哈尔滨市	黑龙江省	(0451)84885111
Guangzhou Yuexiu Enterprise (Group) Company	Guangzhou	Guangdong	(020)85597130
广州越秀企业（集团）公司	广州市	广东省	(020)85599018
China Reed Screen Imp. & Exp. Corp.Ltd.	Beijing	Beijing	(010)65521133
中艺苇帘进出口有限责任公司	北京市	北京市	(010)65513995
Hebei Xintai Foreign Trade Corp.ltd.	Shijiazhuang	Hebei	(0311)7767908
河北信泰对外贸易有限公司	石家庄市	河北省	(0311)7755347
Hebei Arts & Crafts Imp. & Exp. Corp.	Shijiazhuang	Hebei	(0311)7764345
河北省工艺品进出口公司	石家庄市	河北省	(0311)7755347
Shanghai Hengda Ceramic Building Materials Trade Market	Shanghai	Shanghai	(021)58425842
上海恒大陶瓷建材交易市场	上海市	上海市	(021)58427389
Hangzhou Local Product General Corporation	Hangzhou	Zhejiang	(0571)87026301
杭州市土特产总公司	杭州市	浙江省	(0571)87026323
Ningbo Zhonglin Foreign Trade Co.,Ltd.	Ningbo	Zhejiang	(0574)87871797
宁波中蔺对外贸易有限公司	宁波市	浙江省	(0574)87871790
Wuyi Local Products Daily Groceries Co.,Ltd.	Jinhua	Zhejiang	(0579)7623401
武义县土产日用杂品有限责任公司	金华市	浙江省	(0579)7623401
Guangdong Shunde Local Products Import & Export Company	Foshan	Guangdong	(0765)6682839
广东省顺德土产进出口公司	佛山市	广东省	(0765)6681441

4392: Other puroducts For Live and Use 生活用其他产品制造业

The industry accounts for 0.108% of the total revenue of China's industrial sector in 2002. The rate of return on assets is 4.45%. 83.94% of all firms in the industry made a profit while 16.06% had negative returns.The top province in terms of the industry's revenue is Zhejiang, accounting for 25.45% of the total revenue.
2002年本行业收入占全行业的 0.108%，资产利润率为 4.45%。83.94%的企业赢利，16.06%的企业亏损。收入最高的省为浙江省，占本行业的25.45%。

	Total number of firms 企业总数	Total number of employees 职工总数	Total revenue (Mil.RMB) 总销售收入(百万元)	Total profit (Mil.RMB) 总利润(百万元)	Return on assets 资产利润率(%)	Return on equity 权益利润率(%)	Labour productivity ('000 RMB/ worker) 劳动生产率(千元/人)	Debts/ assets 资产负债率(%)	Total assets (Mil.RMB) 总资产(百万元)
Industry Overall 行业总体	554	96,721	11,531	572	4.45	8.20	37.35	45.79	12,862

	Number of firms 企业个数	Average number of employees 平均职工人数	Average revenue ('000 RMB) 平均销售收入（千元）	Average profit ('000 RMB) 平均利润（千元）	Return on assets 资产利润率(%)	Return on equity 权益利润率(%)	Labour productivity ('000 RMB/ worker) 劳动生产率(千元/人)	Debts/ assets 资产负债率(%)	Average total assets ('000 RMB) 平均总资产(千元)
By ownership 产业所有权									
State-owned 国有	44	48	1,773	-138	-2.58	-18.34	10.19	85.92	5,328
Collective-owned 集体	60	127	18,042	986	7.24	20.00	43.09	63.78	13,610
Foreign & Overseas Chinese Funded 三资	171	248	30,472	1,547	3.80	6.18	43.47	38.56	40,743
By regional distribution 地区分布									
Central-North 华北	52	134	19,764	1,059	5.54	11.98	42.28	53.76	19,113
Beijing 北京	21	70	11,973	-739	-5.12	-13.08	32.26	60.88	14,438
Tianjin 天津	10	117	21,312	2,177	15.06	63.05	47.53	76.12	14,460
Hebei 河北	10	192	34,094	3,916	35.75	52.98	55.62	32.52	10,954
Shanxi 山西	11	220	20,204	876	2.21	4.15	35.19	46.73	39,685
Inner Mongolia 内蒙古									
Northeast 东北	18	133	22,981	1,158	2.02	2.61	130.86	22.42	57,297
Liaoning 辽宁	9	155	37,155	2,031	1.96	2.38	199.03	17.73	103,821
Jilin 吉林	3	148	15,157	667	4.76	11.65	37.28	59.17	14,019
Heilongjiang 黑龙江	6	92	5,632	95	1.03	3.96	33.55	73.94	9,150
Central-East 华东	323	175	19,676	999	5.28	10.46	31.60	49.51	18,922
Shanghai 上海	10	146	24,080	1,217	5.10	10.86	33.87	53.08	23,875
Jiangsu 江苏	44	148	23,924	1,323	7.50	17.81	43.82	57.90	17,649
Zhejiang 浙江	171	148	17,164	933	6.29	13.57	30.67	53.63	14,830
Anhui 安徽	4	80	2,860	40	1.34	3.01	17.09	55.57	2,952
Fujian 福建	59	224	18,678	1,283	5.93	8.68	29.19	31.68	21,637
Jiangxi 江西	14	276	9,992	-66	-0.78	-1.61	8.78	51.26	8,396
Shandong 山东	21	272	41,585	852	1.55	3.34	43.02	53.58	54,990
Central-South 中南	121	227	28,142	1,442	4.24	7.63	40.26	44.44	34,041
Henan 河南	11	164	39,023	1,907	7.01	8.87	75.13	20.98	27,212
Hubei 湖北	10	207	25,404	779	8.96	18.44	37.07	51.41	8,695
Hunan 湖南	8	65	2,499	7	0.05		12.84	102.29	14,085
Guangdong 广东	84	254	31,297	1,730	4.15	7.30	40.53	43.09	41,655
Guangxi 广西	7	235	10,388	48	0.28	1.68	12.67	83.43	17,149
Hainan 海南	1	57	218	14	1.47	1.61	1.14	8.40	952
Southwest 西南	10	102	10,567	-453	-2.58	-4.54	32.71	43.09	17,525
Chongqing 重庆	3	97	12,544	118	1.04	4.75	23.88	77.99	11,325
Sichuan 四川	2	133	14,292	-2,406	-5.85	-6.41	37.34	8.73	41,114
Guizhou 贵州	2	208	19,321	51	0.19	0.78	36.95	75.99	27,177
Yunnan 云南									
Tibet 西藏	3	16	270	-57	-3.64	-4.10	24.16	11.28	1,566
Northwest 西北	30	83	7,460	104	0.73	1.31	33.56	44.45	14,342
Shaanxi 陕西	6	74	9,250	19	0.15	0.21	69.91	26.22	12,491
Gansu 甘肃	22	91	7,562	141	0.89	1.71	26.14	48.27	15,914
Qinghai 青海									
Ningxia 宁夏									
Xinjiang 新疆	2	28	975	-47	-1.80	-3.62	11.00	50.38	2,614

4392: Other puroducts For Live and Use 生活用其他产品制造业

Year 年份	Number of firms 企业个数	Rate of change 变化率(%)	Number of employees 职工人数(人)	Rate of change 变化率(%)	Total revenue (Mil. RMB) 总销售收入(百万元)	Rate of change 变化率(%)	Total profit (Mil RMB) 总利润(百万元)	Rate of change 变化率(%)
2000	492		77,089		10,497,179		459,135	
2001	513	4.27	91,893	19.20	11,332	-99.89	527	-99.89
2002	554	7.99	96,721	5.25	11,531	1.76	572	8.54

Major Products 主要产品	Output 产量	Unit 单位

10 Main Firms with Maximal Revenue (year founded) 收入最大的十家主要企业（创办年份）	City 城市	Province 省	Telephone/fax 电话/传真	Number of employees 职工人数	Ownership 产业所有权	Revenue ('000 RMB) 销售收入(千元)	Profit('000 RMB) (rank) 利润(千元)(排名)	Total assets ('000 RMB) 总资产(千元)	Major products 主要产品
Baoji Handicrafts (Shenzhen) Co., Ltd.	Shenzhen	Guangdong	(0755)84166378		Overseas Chinese-funded				Plastic Christmas Tree
宝吉工艺品（深圳）有限公司(1988)	深圳市	广东省	(0755)84166278	6,000	港澳台资	461,112	16,247(8)	924,730	塑料圣诞树
YKK Zipper (Shen Zhang) Co., Ltd.	Shenzhen	Guangdong	(0755)27377486		Overseas Chinese-funded				Slide Fastener
吉田拉链（深圳）有限公司(1995)	深圳市	广东省	(0755)27377486	720	港澳台资	304,061	65,002(1)	728,654	拉链
Heng'an (Luohe) Linying Hygiene Articles For Use Co., Ltd.	Luohe	Henan	(0395)8863284		Foreign Funded				An'erle Feminine Napkins Series
恒安(漯河)临颍卫生用品有限公司(1994)	漯河市	河南省	(0395)8862323	248	外商投资	271,425	11,469(10)	175,465	安尔乐卫生巾系列
Xinle Electric Blanket Group Co.,Ltd.	Shijiazhuang	Hebei	(0311)8581319		Collective-owned				Electric Carpet & Fittings
新乐市电热毯集团(1992)	石家庄市	河北省	(0311)8651889	900	集体企业	181,500	19,945(5)	13,000	电热毯及配件
Changshu Libao Decorative Materials Co.,Ltd.	Suzhou	Jiangsu	(0520)52571624		Private Owned				PVC Affix
常熟市力宝装璜材料有限责任公司(1984)	苏州市	江苏省	(0520)52572333	459	私营企业	172,233	29,425(3)	116,257	pvc粘贴
Yangzhou Huayang Solar Energy Water Heater Co., Ltd.	Yangzhou	Jiangsu	(0514)7551925		Limited-Liability				Solar Energy Water Heater
扬州市华扬太阳能热水器有限公司(1997)	扬州市	江苏省	(0514)7552123	458	有限公司	149,559	5,592(25)	52,973	太阳能热水器
Apulijia (Zhongshan) Co.,Ltd.	Zhongshan	Guangdong	(0760)6650417		Foreign Funded				Baby-Car
阿普丽佳（中山）有限公司(1994)	中山市	广东省	(0760)6650134	308	外商投资	142,900	2,680(45)	54,897	婴儿车
Taishan Yuda Handicrafts Designing Co., Ltd.	Jiangmen	Guangdong	(0750)5576828		Foreign Funded				Human Body Model
台山市宇达工艺品设计有限公司(1997)	江门市	广东省	(0750)5576868	332	外商投资	132,028	-	26,863	人体模特
Shanxi Guangsheng Medicine Packaging Co., Ltd.	Jinzhong	Shanxi	(0354)6635441		Joint Stock				Medical hollow glue pill
山西广生医药包装股份有限公司(1983)	晋中市	山西省	(0354)6635444	1,200	股份制	102,331	8,273(14)	227,329	药用空心胶丸
Hangzhou Hengfeng Leather Products Co., Ltd.	Hangzhou	Zhejiang	(0571)88096782		Foreign Funded				Fishing Appliance
杭州恒丰皮革制品有限公司(1995)	杭州市	浙江省	(0571)88191510	320	外商投资	100,257	1,035(101)	42,344	钓鱼用具

Top 10 Cities by Revenue 销售收入排名前10位城市	Province 省	Market share 市场份额(%)	Number of firms 企业个数
Wenzhou 温州市	Zhejiang 浙江省	10.30	96
Shenzhen 深圳市	Guangdong 广东省	8.45	13
Quanzhou 泉州市	Fujian 福建省	5.44	28
Ningbo 宁波市	Zhejiang 浙江省	4.69	20
Dezhou 德州市	Shandong 山东省	3.17	5
Zhongshan 中山市	Guangdong 广东省	3.06	13
Jinhua 金华市	Zhejiang 浙江省	2.81	16
Foshan 佛山市	Guangdong 广东省	2.81	15
Luohe 漯河市	Henan 河南省	2.74	2
Taizhou 台州市	Zhejiang 浙江省	2.65	3

10 Major Wholesalers 十家主要批发商	City 城市	Province 省	Telephone/Fax 电话/传真
Harbin ChinaSun Group Co., Ltd.	Haerbin	Heilongjiang	(0451)84885100
哈尔滨中央红集团股份有限公司	哈尔滨市	黑龙江省	(0451)84885111
Guangzhou Yuexiu Enterprise (Group) Company	Guangzhou	Guangdong	(020)85597130
广州越秀企业（集团）公司	广州市	广东省	(020)85599018
China Reed Screen Imp. & Exp. Corp.Ltd.	Beijing	Beijing	(010)65521133
中艺苇帘进出口有限责任公司	北京市	北京市	(010)65513995
Hebei Xintai Foreign Trade Corp.ltd.	Shijiazhuang	Hebei	(0311)7767908
河北信泰对外贸易有限公司	石家庄市	河北省	(0311)7755347
Hebei Arts & Crafts Imp. & Exp. Corp.	Shijiazhuang	Hebei	(0311)7764345
河北省工艺品进出口公司	石家庄市	河北省	(0311)7755347
Shanghai Hengda Ceramic Building Materials Trade Market	Shanghai	Shanghai	(021)58425842
上海恒大陶瓷建材交易市场	上海市	上海市	(021)58427389
Hangzhou Local Product General Corporation	Hangzhou	Zhejiang	(0571)87026301
杭州市土特产总公司	杭州市	浙江省	(0571)87026323
Ningbo Zhonglin Foreign Trade Co.,Ltd.	Ningbo	Zhejiang	(0574)87871797
宁波中蔺对外贸易有限公司	宁波市	浙江省	(0574)87871790
Wuyi Local Products Daily Groceries Co.,Ltd.	Jinhua	Zhejiang	(0579)7623401
武义县土产日用杂品有限责任公司	金华市	浙江省	(0579)7623401
Guangdong Shunde Local Products Import & Export Company	Foshan	Guangdong	(0765)6682839
广东省顺德土产进出口公司	佛山市	广东省	(0765)6681441

4411: Thermal Power Generation 火力发电业

The industry accounts for 3.082% of the total revenue of China's industrial sector in 2002. The rate of return on assets is 3.95%. 74.52% of all firms in the industry made a profit while 25.48% had negative returns.The top province in terms of the industry's revenue is Guangdong, accounting for 14.62% of the total revenue.
2002年本行业收入占全行业的3.082%，资产利润率为3.95%。74.52%的企业赢利，25.48%的企业亏损。收入最高的省为广东省，占本行业的14.62%。

	Total number of firms 企业总数	Total number of employees 职工总数	Total revenue (Mil.RMB) 总销售收入(百万元)	Total profit (Mil.RMB) 总利润(百万元)	Return on assets 资产利润率(%)	Return on equity 权益利润率(%)	Labour productivity ('000 RMB/worker) 劳动生产率(千元/人)	Debts/assets 资产负债率(%)	Total assets (Mil.RMB) 总资产(百万元)
Industry Overall 行业总体	1091	821,812	330,606	32,451	3.95	10.14	196.86	61.10	822,533

	Number of firms 企业个数	Average number of employees 平均职工人数	Average revenue ('000 RMB) 平均销售收入（千元）	Average profit ('000 RMB) 平均利润（千元）	Return on assets 资产利润率(%)	Return on equity 权益利润率(%)	Labour productivity ('000 RMB/worker) 劳动生产率(千元/人)	Debts/assets 资产负债率(%)	Average total assets ('000 RMB) 平均总资产(千元)
By ownership 产业所有权									
State-owned 国有	393	939	278,694	14,586	2.51	7.91	123.91	68.21	580,166
Collective-owned 集体	67	295	53,297	5,120	4.84	12.96	72.22	62.66	105,802
Foreign & Overseas Chinese Funded 三资	249	434	343,302	59,112	6.47	12.96	485.62	50.06	913,004
By regional distribution 地区分布									
Central-North 华北	177	768	355,609	39,202	4.73	14.48	199.67	67.34	828,934
Beijing 北京	13	607	265,149	77,763	7.11	10.72	224.08	33.69	1,094,180
Tianjin 天津	10	480	464,743	26,930	1.96	10.56	494.84	81.45	1,375,052
Hebei 河北	61	752	587,108	66,121	8.49	18.29	254.70	53.57	778,677
Shanxi 山西	58	727	246,080	31,113	4.75	22.43	171.61	78.81	654,695
Inner Mongolia 内蒙古	35	1,007	136,063	-5,127	-0.54	-3.08	115.99	82.48	950,712
Northeast 东北	113	1,564	442,122	8,467	0.75	1.98	117.08	62.29	1,132,946
Liaoning 辽宁	49	1,043	312,961	18,728	1.98	4.62	172.86	57.06	943,719
Jilin 吉林	16	1,290	281,323	-41,618	-4.75	-34.12	64.16	86.08	876,250
Heilongjiang 黑龙江	48	2,187	627,573	14,686	1.04	2.66	100.34	60.93	1,411,682
Central-East 华东	341	643	296,137	36,448	5.36	11.63	254.39	53.87	679,401
Shanghai 上海	13	1,204	1,137,605	197,525	8.94	14.77	550.71	39.49	2,209,965
Jiangsu 江苏	93	412	228,842	35,770	6.32	10.97	278.52	42.43	566,408
Zhejiang 浙江	80	362	220,823	26,498	5.94	12.89	352.86	53.96	446,410
Anhui 安徽	22	1,267	470,490	20,984	2.11	6.30	157.96	66.48	993,625
Fujian 福建	20	389	416,092	52,678	4.20	12.29	552.33	65.84	1,254,649
Jiangxi 江西	8	816	368,237	-7,837	-0.63	-2.57	183.67	75.37	1,239,873
Shandong 山东	105	898	244,067	28,210	5.13	12.15	173.96	57.74	549,388
Central-South 中南	308	512	278,382	37,392	5.51	13.51	278.71	59.24	678,906
Henan 河南	89	861	242,567	21,812	3.44	10.10	170.26	65.91	633,442
Hubei 湖北	31	464	239,982	7,057	0.82	3.16	191.70	73.94	856,236
Hunan 湖南	18	796	236,688	2,504	0.32	1.56	122.60	79.24	774,905
Guangdong 广东	154	280	313,958	57,598	8.90	17.43	568.22	48.97	647,379
Guangxi 广西	13	549	241,114	21,910	3.02	8.72	206.52	65.36	725,614
Hainan 海南	3	679	323,110	52,245	5.05	7.64	194.38	33.91	1,035,226
Southwest 西南	67	899	248,577	12,170	1.42	3.65	145.23	60.99	855,605
Chongqing 重庆	10	387	198,833	14,426	2.21	2.94	341.79	24.93	653,915
Sichuan 四川	31	717	51,209	3,236	1.99	8.10	145.68	75.43	162,629
Guizhou 贵州	13	851	748,329	28,435	1.20	3.24	200.13	62.90	2,363,607
Yunnan 云南	11	2,073	303,903	18,311	1.35	4.25	86.69	68.22	1,356,556
Tibet 西藏	2	127	3,820	-136	-0.28	-0.36	-22.70	21.97	47,946
Northwest 西北	85	847	168,523	-2,414	-0.41	-2.21	76.08	81.31	584,521
Shaanxi 陕西	37	756	160,905	4,939	0.83	5.23	84.45	84.05	592,202
Gansu 甘肃	18	922	193,867	-3,014	-0.48	-2.55	78.35	81.05	624,805
Qinghai 青海	2	1,136	416,080	18,754	1.09	3.25	182.29	66.62	1,727,374
Ningxia 宁夏	6	1,632	291,844	-18,188	-2.98	-14.96	40.87	80.11	610,976
Xinjiang 新疆	22	698	104,460	-11,912	-2.79	-14.73	65.09	81.09	427,535

4411: Thermal Power Generation 火力发电业

Year 年份	Number of firms 企业个数	Rate of change 变化率 (%)	Number of employees 职工人数 (人)	Rate of change 变化率 (%)	Total revenue (Mil. RMB) 总销售收入 (百万元)	Rate of change 变化率 (%)	Total profit (Mil RMB) 总利润 (百万元)	Rate of change 变化率 (%)
2000	1081		1,101,563		261,918		23,173	
2001	1080	-0.09	803,079	-27.10	306,735	17.11	27,140	17.12
2002	1091	1.02	821,812	2.33	330,606	7.78	32,451	19.57

Major Products 主要产品	Output 产量	Unit 单位
Themal Power 火电	13,288	100,000,000 KWH 亿千瓦小时

10 Main Firms with Maximal Revenue (year founded) 收入最大的十家主要企业 (创办年份)	City 城市	Province 省	Telephone/fax 电话/传真	Number of employees 职工人数	Ownership 产业所有权	Revenue ('000 RMB) 销售收入 (千元)	Profit('000 RMB) (rank) 利润(千元) (排名)	Total assets ('000 RMB) 总资产 (千元)	Major products 主要产品
Heilongjiang Electric Power Co., Ltd.	Harbin	Heilongjiang	(0451)3682222		State Enterprises				Electricity
黑龙江省电力有限公司(1949)	哈尔滨市	黑龙江省	(0451)3682331	52,279	国有独资	12,619,517	301,778(33)	29,201,574	电力
Daqing Petroleum Managemeng Bureau	Daqing	Heilongjiang	(0459)5996155		State-owned				Electricity
大庆石油管理局(1958)	大庆市	黑龙江省	(0459)5999156	16,610	国有企业	10,215,000	131,072(71)	11,945,300	电力
Zhangjiakou Power of Beijing Datang Power Co., Ltd.	Zhangjiakou	Hebei	(0313)8603035		Joint Stock				Thermal Power
北京大唐发电股份有限公司张家口发电厂(1988)	张家口市	河北省	(0313)8603084	2,413	股份制	9,439,720	260,554(41)	6,690,096	火电
Guangdong Guanghe Electric Power Co., Ltd.	Dongguan	Guangdong	(020)8512786		Overseas Chinese-funded				Electricity
广东广合电力有限公司(1996)	东莞市	广东省	(020)37650795	676	港澳台资	4,673,403	913,810(3)	7,026,183	电力
Guangdong Zhuhai Power Factory Co., Ltd.	Zhuhai	Guangdong	(0756)3363978		Overseas Chinese-funded				Electricity
广东省珠海发电厂有限公司(1996)	珠海市	广东省	(0756)3365691	350	港澳台资	3,529,495	1,135,425(1)	10,703,594	电力
Shanghai Electric Power Co., Ltd.	Shanghai	Shanghai	(021)64721060		Joint Stock				Thermal Power
上海电力股份有限公司(1998)	上海市	上海市	(021)64723578	6,220	股份制	3,220,216	480,492(18)	7,159,465	火力发电
Zhejiang Beilun Power Generation Co., Ltd.	Ningbo	Zhejiang	(0574)86892176		Limited-Liability				Thermal Power
浙江北仑发电有限公司(1997)	宁波市	浙江省	(0574)86889396	16	有限公司	3,198,676	633,276(9)	7,716,844	火力发电
Matou Electric Power Generating General Factory	Handan	Hebei	(0310)6272142		State-owned				Thermal Power
马头发电总厂(1968)	邯郸市	河北省	(0310)6272064	2,730	国有企业	2,802,655	77,358(109)	420,518	火力发电
CINOPEC Qilu Co. Thermoelectricity Company	Zibo	Shandong	(0533)7588637		State-owned				Thermal Power
中国石化集团齐鲁石油化工公司(1984)	淄博市	山东省	(0533)7580777	20,800	国有企业	2,698,160	-	6,579,889	火力发电
Broadcasting & Television Group Company Shandou Power	Shantou	Guangdong	(0754)8307920		State-owned				Electricity
Supply Branch Co. 广电集团公司汕头供电分公司(2000)	汕头市	广东省	(0754)8250122	2,155	国有企业	2,621,458	-	3,139,120	电力

Top 10 Cities by Revenue 销售收入排名前10位城市	Province 省	Market share 市场份额 (%)	Number of firms 企业个数
Harbin 哈尔滨市	Heilongjiang 黑龙江省	4.74	10
Shanghai 上海市	Shanghai 上海市	4.47	13
Zhangjiakou 张家口市	Hebei 河北省	3.50	2
Daqing 大庆市	Heilongjiang 黑龙江省	3.23	2
Dongguan 东莞市	Guangdong 广东省	3.01	14
Guangzhou 广州市	Guangdong 广东省	2.99	32
Ningbo 宁波市	Zhejiang 浙江省	2.53	18
Guiyang 贵阳市	Guizhou 贵州省	2.30	3
Handan 邯郸市	Hebei 河北省	2.09	12
Foshan 佛山市	Guangdong 广东省	1.60	15

10 Major Wholesalers 十家主要批发商	City 城市	Province 省	Telephone/Fax 电话/传真

4412: Hydro Power Generation 水力发电业

The industry accounts for 0.427% of the total revenue of China's industrial sector in 2002. The rate of return on assets is 2.28%. 64.54% of all firms in the industry made a profit while 35.46% had negative returns.The top province in terms of the industry's revenue is Sichuan, accounting for 18.35% of the total revenue.
2002年本行业收入占全行业的0.427%，资产利润率为2.28%。64.54%的企业赢利，35.46%的企业亏损。收入最高的省为四川省，占本行业的18.35%。

	Total number of firms 企业总数	Total number of employees 职工总数	Total revenue (Mil.RMB) 总销售收入 (百万元)	Total profit (Mil.RMB) 总利润 (百万元)	Return on assets 资产利润率 (%)	Return on equity 权益利润率 (%)	Labour productivity ('000 RMB/ worker) 劳动生产率 (千元/人)	Debts/ assets 资产负债率 (%)	Total assets (Mil.RMB) 总资产 (百万元)
Industry Overall 行业总体	1788	328,988	45,768	6,482	2.28	7.08	94.91	67.82	284,511

	Number of firms 企业个数	Average number of employees 平均职工人数	Average revenue ('000 RMB) 平均销售收入 (千元)	Average profit ('000 RMB) 平均利润 (千元)	Return on assets 资产利润率 (%)	Return on equity 权益利润率 (%)	Labour productivity ('000 RMB/ worker) 劳动生产率 (千元/人)	Debts/ assets 资产负债率 (%)	Average total assets ('000 RMB) 平均总资产 (千元)
By ownership 产业所有权									
State-owned 国有	1,220	171	15,767	2,102	2.55	6.94	74.26	63.30	82,567
Collective-owned 集体	73	96	16,180	1,603	4.04	6.91	58.15	41.55	39,692
Foreign & Overseas Chinese Funded 三资	33	80	21,574	4,066	2.99	5.99	172.61	50.13	136,175
By regional distribution 地区分布									
Central-North 华北	51	116	8,156	225	0.16	0.42	48.82	60.95	137,011
Beijing 北京	1	875	9,856	699	0.12	0.40	3.26	69.43	569,684
Tianjin 天津									
Hebei 河北	28	77	2,515	-11	-0.07	-0.20	7.73	64.45	15,757
Shanxi 山西	19	112	17,116	583	0.31	0.77	90.27	59.50	187,441
Inner Mongolia 内蒙古	3	255	3,500				100.99	60.45	805,100
Northeast 东北	56	187	28,295	4,890	3.10	12.17	117.71	74.48	157,514
Liaoning 辽宁	15	249	13,302	1,340	1.98	2.39	52.45	17.26	67,851
Jilin 吉林	26	191	48,234	10,112	3.84	20.85	193.41	81.59	263,522
Heilongjiang 黑龙江	15	119	8,727	-612	-0.97	-6.23	43.19	84.50	63,431
Central-East 华东	383	147	26,825	5,601	4.74	13.41	131.84	64.67	118,219
Shanghai 上海									
Jiangsu 江苏	4	72	15,816	-1,528	-1.01	-3.84	100.56	73.80	151,742
Zhejiang 浙江	93	105	42,268	9,271	6.06	20.20	254.77	69.97	152,877
Anhui 安徽	16	191	16,283	-1,643	-1.72	-6.20	45.37	72.32	95,751
Fujian 福建	164	168	31,912	7,786	5.28	12.78	156.89	58.67	147,372
Jiangxi 江西	106	148	7,414	365	0.81	3.35	28.74	75.71	44,833
Shandong 山东									
Central-South 中南	675	180	22,333	3,335	2.36	5.63	79.41	58.05	141,249
Henan 河南	18	261	16,085	239	0.15	0.23	50.17	31.49	154,371
Hubei 湖北	94	267	46,070	7,719	2.33	5.15	110.49	54.75	331,005
Hunan 湖南	150	214	24,111	3,448	2.62	9.54	78.36	72.54	131,536
Guangdong 广东	239	137	15,546	1,365	1.32	2.98	54.50	55.84	103,567
Guangxi 广西	139	166	20,479	4,443	4.28	9.63	89.71	55.58	103,824
Hainan 海南	35	113	7,879	1,716	2.37	4.80	72.08	50.62	72,451
Southwest 西南	429	241	34,472	4,359	2.01	7.99	102.64	74.81	216,570
Chongqing 重庆	27	468	51,884	1,780	0.76	2.28	44.31	66.84	235,781
Sichuan 四川	169	304	49,697	6,510	1.80	9.94	112.90	81.93	362,674
Guizhou 贵州	76	196	21,439	4,731	3.65	16.75	138.68	66.06	129,635
Yunnan 云南	99	223	32,809	3,649	2.85	8.62	95.55	66.90	127,943
Tibet 西藏	58	45	1,920	16	0.03	0.03	37.10	1.63	47,105
Northwest 西北	194	160	18,714	-359	-0.20	-0.97	63.88	79.58	181,304
Shaanxi 陕西	44	96	10,475	-1,320	-1.43	-3.13	57.35	54.36	92,372
Gansu 甘肃	81	110	10,234	1,979	3.28	10.16	51.35	67.74	60,402
Qinghai 青海	36	122	37,543	-3,650	-0.66	-6.07	182.18	89.15	554,553
Ningxia 宁夏	3	671	40,973	3,490	2.72	44.37	22.87	93.87	128,302
Xinjiang 新疆	30	382	28,878	-1,696	-0.87	-3.27	37.87	73.45	195,577

Year 年份	Number of firms 企业个数	Rate of change 变化率 (%)	Number of employees 职工人数 (人)	Rate of change 变化率 (%)	Total revenue (Mil. RMB) 总销售收入 (百万元)	Rate of change 变化率 (%)	Total profit (Mil RMB) 总利润 (百万元)	Rate of change 变化率 (%)
2000	1780		327,554		36,808		4,534	
2001	1763	-0.96	328,642	0.33	40,731	10.66	4,897	8.01
2002	1788	1.42	328,988	0.11	45,768	12.37	6,482	32.37

Major Products 主要产品	Output 产量	Unit 单位
Hydroelectricity 水电	2,465	100,000,000 KWH 亿千瓦小时

10 Main Firms with Maximal Revenue (year founded) 收入最大的十家主要企业（创办年份）	City 城市	Province 省	Telephone/fax 电话/传真	Number of employees 职工人数	Ownership 产业所有权	Revenue ('000 RMB) 销售收入（千元）	Profit('000 RMB) (rank) 利润(千元)（排名）	Total assets ('000 RMB) 总资产（千元）	Major products 主要产品
Ertan Hydropower Development Co., Ltd.	Panzhihua	Sichuan	(0812)3331555		Limited-Liability				Hydropower
二滩水电开发有限责任公司(1998)	攀枝花市	四川省	(0812)3331900	525	有限公司	2,500,384	-	25,470,295	水电
Huadong Tianhuangping Pumping Water & Power Accumulatic	Huzhou	Zhejiang	(0572)5041845		Limited-Liability				Pumping Water & Power Accumulation Machine Set抽
Co., Ltd. 华东天荒坪抽水蓄能有限责任公司(1998)	湖州市	浙江省	(0572)5041884	141	有限公司	1,517,000	180,270(10)	5,516,000	水蓄能机组
Hunan Wuqiangxi Hydropower Factory	Huaihua	Hunan	(0745)4712276		State-owned				Hydropower
湖南省五强溪水力发电厂(1994)	怀化市	湖南省	(0745)4712323	598	国有企业	1,277,260	365,860(4)	6,389,340	水力发电
Yellow River Upper Reaches Hydropower Development	Xining	Qinghai	(0971)6174821		State Enterprises				Electricity
Co.,Ltd.黄河上游水电开发有限责任公司(1999)	西宁市	青海省	(0971)6174808	440	国有独资	1,123,862	-	18,611,351	电力
Gongzui Hydropower General Factory	Leshan	Sichuan	(0833)3493053		State-owned				Electricity
龚嘴水力发电总厂	乐山市	四川省	(0833)3493096	1,466	国有企业	878,292	593,935(2)	3,206,131	电力
Guizhou Wujiang Hydropower Development Co., Ltd.	Guiyang	Guizhou	(0851)5784589		State-owned				Hydropower
贵州乌江水电开发有限责任公司(1996)	贵阳市	贵州省	(0851)5784555	1,635	国有企业	724,700	284,800(6)	6,783,400	水电
Hanjiang Water Conservancy Hydropower (Group) Co., Ltd.	Shiyan	Hubei	(0719)5375671		State Enterprises				Hydropower
汉江水利水电（集团）有限责任公司(1968)	十堰市	湖北省	(0719)5375671	3,506	国有独资	693,606	85,865(15)	2,788,057	水力发电
Guangdong Power Storage Generating Electricity Co., Ltd.	Guangzhou	Guangdong	(020)87518168		Joint Owned				Electricity
广东蓄能发电有限公司(1988)	广州市	广东省	(020)87568499	268	联营企业	688,019	132,794(12)	6,151,752	电力
Yunnan South China Manwan Power Plant	Lincang	Yunnan	(0883)3814001		State-owned				Hydropower
云南华南漫湾发电厂(1993)	临沧	云南省	(0883)3814023	472	国有企业	685,099	212,848(9)	2,485,192	水电
Yunnan Lubuge Generating Power General Plant	Qujing	Yunnan	(0874)8257328		State-owned				Hydropower
云南省鲁布革发电总厂(1977)	曲靖市	云南省	(0874)8213993	443	国有企业	465,332	6,975(128)	703,366	水力发电

Top 10 Cities by Revenue 销售收入排名前10位城市	Province 省	Market share 市场份额 (%)	Number of firms 企业个数
Yichang 宜昌市	Hubei 湖北省	5.62	10
Panzhihua 攀枝花市	Sichuan 四川省	5.56	3
Fuzhou 福州市	Fujian 福建省	3.93	17
Huaihua 怀化市	Hunan 湖南省	3.76	34
Leshan 乐山市	Sichuan 四川省	3.41	20
Huzhou 湖州市	Zhejiang 浙江省	3.33	3
Chongqing 重庆市	Chongqing 重庆市	3.06	27
Xining 西宁市	Qinghai 青海省	2.51	2
Hechi 河池市	Guangxi 广西	2.01	17
Shiyan 十堰市	Hubei 湖北省	1.98	18

10 Major Wholesalers 十家主要批发商	City 城市	Province 省	Telephone/Fax 电话/传真

4419: Other Electricity generation 其他电业

The industry accounts for 0.009% of the total revenue of China's industrial sector in 2002. The rate of return on assets is 0.84%. 77.78% of all firms in the industry made a profit while 22.22% had negative returns.The top province in terms of the industry's revenue is Shandong, accounting for 14.37% of the total revenue.
2002年本行业收入占全行业的 0.009%，资产利润率为 0.84%。77.78%的企业赢利，22.22%的企业亏损。收入最高的省为山东省，占本行业的14.37%。

	Total number of firms 企业总数	Total number of employees 职工总数	Total revenue (Mil.RMB) 总销售收入（百万元）	Total profit (Mil.RMB) 总利润（百万元）	Return on assets 资产利润率（%）	Return on equity 权益利润率（%）	Labour productivity ('000 RMB/worker) 劳动生产率（千元/人）	Debts/assets 资产负债率（%）	Total assets (Mil.RMB) 总资产（百万元）
Industry Overall 行业总体	45	4,988	923	39	0.84	1.96	191.45	57.28	4,595

	Number of firms 企业个数	Average number of employees 平均职工人数	Average revenue ('000 RMB) 平均销售收入（千元）	Average profit ('000 RMB) 平均利润（千元）	Return on assets 资产利润率（%）	Return on equity 权益利润率（%）	Labour productivity ('000 RMB/worker) 劳动生产率（千元/人）	Debts/assets 资产负债率（%）	Average total assets ('000 RMB) 平均总资产（千元）
By ownership 产业所有权									
State-owned 国有	19	112	12,947	-290	-0.37	-0.82	48.94	54.93	78,572
Collective-owned 集体	2	489	48,280	2,818	3.60	5.21	502.18	30.86	78,192
Foreign & Overseas Chinese Funded 三资	1	36	25,291	5,051	4.38	5.22	257.72	16.15	115,449
By regional distribution 地区分布									
Central-North 华北	5	31	5,280	1,874	1.92	3.70	428.42	47.99	97,417
Beijing 北京	1	74	5,166	-187	-0.81	-0.87	72.70	7.22	23,127
Tianjin 天津									
Hebei 河北	2	21	10,617	4,780	9.32	13.54	404.90	31.16	51,283
Shanxi 山西									
Inner Mongolia 内蒙古	2	20					1,128.10	55.38	180,696
Northeast 东北	9	85	14,416	1,192	1.23	3.40	118.19	63.70	96,588
Liaoning 辽宁	6	55	9,470	850	0.92	1.97	77.76	53.58	92,826
Jilin 吉林	3	145	24,309	1,875	1.80	9.87	148.95	81.74	104,110
Heilongjiang 黑龙江									
Central-East 华东	10	107	31,331	2,902	3.69	6.79	165.63	45.60	78,598
Shanghai 上海	1	266	55,243	4,103	4.04	4.43	95.01	8.83	101,558
Jiangsu 江苏	1	36	25,291	5,051	4.38	5.22	257.72	16.15	115,449
Zhejiang 浙江	4	68	21,517	876	1.21	3.65	128.76	66.73	72,157
Anhui 安徽									
Fujian 福建	2	16	7,018	1,460	2.71	9.74	173.94	72.19	53,913
Jiangxi 江西									
Shandong 山东	2	233	66,338	6,722	7.79	11.98	219.91	34.97	86,262
Central-South 中南	9	223	33,856	-418	-0.26	-0.60	40.66	56.95	161,315
Henan 河南	2	576	51,423	1,902	0.85	1.68	33.06	49.22	222,473
Hubei 湖北	1	61	40,660	1,330	1.23	2.05	197.51	39.70	107,767
Hunan 湖南	1	565	75,972	4,549	1.39	3.14	13.45	55.77	327,209
Guangdong 广东	4	53	19,793	-2,490	-2.06	-9.30	99.21	77.84	120,782
Guangxi 广西									
Hainan 海南	1	18	6,058	-3,490	-3.93	-4.24	162.50	7.35	88,786
Southwest 西南	5	90	6,823	18	0.06	0.07	43.09	14.15	30,181
Chongqing 重庆									
Sichuan 四川									
Guizhou 贵州									
Yunnan 云南									
Tibet 西藏	5	90	6,823	18	0.06	0.07	43.09	14.15	30,181
Northwest 西北	7	77	16,401	-982	-0.81	-3.25	963.35	75.07	121,361
Shaanxi 陕西									
Gansu 甘肃	2	13	5	2	0.54	0.56	17,698.19	3.52	369
Qinghai 青海	1	78	11,966	91	0.51	0.59	43.87	13.31	17,772
Ningxia 宁夏									
Xinjiang 新疆	4	109	25,707	-1,743	-0.84	-3.56	129.90	76.45	207,754

4419: Other Electricity generation 其他电业

Year 年份	Number of firms 企业个数	Rate of change 变化率 (%)	Number of employees 职工人数 (人)	Rate of change 变化率 (%)	Total revenue (Mil. RMB) 总销售收入 (百万元)	Rate of change 变化率 (%)	Total profit (Mil RMB) 总利润 (百万元)	Rate of change 变化率 (%)
2000	34		3,634		1,062		2	
2001	41	20.59	6,043	66.29	718	-32.39	35	-
2002	45	9.76	4,988	-17.46	923	28.55	39	11.43

Major Products 主要产品	Output 产量	Unit 单位
Generating Electricity Volume 发电量	16,024	100,000,000 KWH 亿千瓦小时
Nuclear power 核电	259	100,000,000 KWH 亿千瓦小时

10 Main Firms with Maximal Revenue (year founded) 收入最大的十家主要企业（创办年份）	City 城市	Province 省	Telephone/fax 电话/传真	Number of employees 职工人数	Ownership 产业所有权	Revenue ('000 RMB) 销售收入 (千元)	Profit('000 RMB) (rank) 利润(千元) (排名)	Total assets ('000 RMB) 总资产 (千元)	Major products 主要产品
Shandong Huipu Waste Rock Electric Power Co., Ltd. 山东惠普矸石电力股份有限公司(1988)	Taian 泰安市	Shandong 山东省	(0538)7332218 (0538)7331503	450	Joint Stock 股份制	125,120	11,080(2)	132,620	Coal Waste Rock Generating Electricity煤矸石发电
Pingdingshan Hongxiang Thermoelectricity Co., Ltd. 平顶山鸿翔热电有限责任公司(1992)	Pingdingshan 平顶山市	Henan 河南省	(0375)3933311 (0375)3822000	965	Collective-owned 集体企业	96,555	5,633(4)	156,014	Others Electricity Indusry 其它电业
Huayuan Jinyuan Electric Power Group 花垣县金垣电力集团(2000)	Xiangxi 湘西州	Hunan 湖南省	(0743)7227215 (0743)7222957	565	State-owned 国有企业	75,972	4,549(7)	327,209	Electricity Generating & Supply 发供电
Shanghai Electric Power Transformer Repair & Making Factory Co., Ltd. 上海电力变压器修造厂有限公司(2001)	Shanghai 上海市	Shanghai 上海市	(021)56770352 (021)56770352	266	Limited-Liability 有限公司	55,243	4,103(8)	101,558	Transforming Device Repair & Making 输配电设备修造
Tongyu Wind Power Factory 通榆县风力发电厂(1999)	Baicheng 白城市	Jilin 吉林省	(0436)4798098 (0436)4798099	8	Joint Stock 股份制	54,000	5,560(5)	274,000	
Wuhan Power Station Engineering Complete Sets Co.,Ltd. 武汉电站工程配套公司(1992)	Wuhan 武汉市	Hubei 湖北省	(027)82789605 (027)82842659	61	Joint Stock 股份制	40,660	1,330(16)	107,767	Electricity Complete Sets 电力配套
Xinjiang Tianfeng Power Co., Ltd. 新疆天风发电股份有限公司(1997)	Urumchi 乌鲁木齐市	Xinjiang 新疆	(0991)2921305 (0991)2920278	14	Limited-Liability 有限公司	40,525	20,455(1)	231,262	Wind Power 风力发电
Nan'ao Zhenneng Wind Power Co., Ltd. 南澳县振能风电有限公司(1994)	Shantou 汕头市	Guangdong 广东省	(0754)6808733 (0754)6808733	56	State-owned 国有企业	36,391	-	304,316	Wind Power 风力发电
Xinjiang Changji Thermoelectricity Co., Ltd. 新疆昌吉热电有限责任公司(1997)	Changji 昌吉州	Xinjiang 新疆	(0994)2723049 (0994)2723049	302	Limited-Liability 有限公司	32,325	-	214,012	Electricity 电力
Nan'ao Wind Energy Development General Co.,Ltd. 南澳县风能开发总公司(1989)	Shantou 汕头市	Guangdong 广东省	(0754)6812459 (0754)6805707	70	State-owned 国有企业	31,237	-	108,294	Electricity 电力

Top 10 Cities by Revenue 销售收入排名前10位城市	Province 省	Market share 市场份额 (%)	Number of firms 企业个数
Taian 泰安市	Shandong 山东省	13.55	1
Pingdingshan 平顶山市	Henan 河南省	10.46	1
Xiangxi 湘西州	Hunan 湖南省	8.23	1
Ulumuqi 乌鲁木齐市	Xinjiang 新疆	7.64	3
Shantou 汕头市	Guangdong 广东省	7.33	2
Baicheng 白城市	Jilin 吉林省	7.01	2
Hangzhou 杭州市	Zhejiang 浙江省	6.00	2
Shanghai 上海市	Shanghai 上海市	5.98	1
Wuhan 武汉市	Hubei 湖北省	4.40	1
Lasa 拉萨市	Tibet 西藏	3.70	1

10 Major Wholesalers 十家主要批发商	City 城市	Province 省	Telephone/Fax 电话/传真

4420: Transmission and Distribution Of Electricity 电力供应业

The industry accounts for 4.621% of the total revenue of China's industrial sector in 2002. The rate of return on assets is 1.46%. 79.10% of all firms in the industry made a profit while 20.90% had negative returns.The top province in terms of the industry's revenue is Guangdong, accounting for 15.80% of the total revenue.
2002年本行业收入占全行业的 4.621%，资产利润率为 1.46%。79.10%的企业赢利，20.90%的企业亏损。收入最高的省为广东省，占本行业的15.80%。

	Total number of firms 企业总数	Total number of employees 职工总数	Total revenue (Mil.RMB) 总销售收入 (百万元)	Total profit (Mil.RMB) 总利润 (百万元)	Return on assets 资产利润率 (%)	Return on equity 权益利润率 (%)	Labour productivity ('000 RMB/ worker) 劳动生产率 (千元/人)	Debts/ assets 资产负债率 (%)	Total assets (Mil.RMB) 总资产 (百万元)
Industry Overall 行业总体	1675	1,068,028	495,617	14,753	1.46	3.66	104.02	60.03	1,009,008

	Number of firms 企业个数	Average number of employees 平均职工人数	Average revenue ('000 RMB) 平均销售收入（千元）	Average profit ('000 RMB) 平均利润 (千元)	Return on assets 资产利润率 (%)	Return on equity 权益利润率 (%)	Labour productivity ('000 RMB/ worker) 劳动生产率 (千元/人)	Debts/ assets 资产负债率 (%)	Average total assets ('000 RMB) 平均总资产 (千元)
By ownership 产业所有权									
State-owned 国有	1,446	671	312,401	9,401	1.50	3.73	107.44	59.92	628,126
Collective-owned 集体	22	64	32,074	1,270	6.43	16.42	124.43	60.84	19,750
Foreign & Overseas Chinese Funded 三资	8	123	164,299	15,682	3.41	8.14	214.70	58.13	460,214
By regional distribution 地区分布									
Central-North 华北	248	603	259,996	7,793	1.49	4.51	108.93	66.85	521,461
Beijing 北京	1	9,434	4,627,550	496,645	1.93		377.13	100.00	25,748,320
Tianjin 天津	13	1,243	769,844	2,505	0.16	0.36	57.36	55.83	1,585,712
Hebei 河北	118	571	272,407	7,749	2.12	4.99	115.16	57.41	364,869
Shanxi 山西	27	1,077	306,381	8,420	0.74	1.92	71.20	61.59	1,143,211
Inner Mongolia 内蒙古	89	309	105,924	2,942	2.90	7.33	71.87	60.48	101,556
Northeast 东北	191	447	224,986	1,325	0.27	0.80	89.52	65.77	486,091
Liaoning 辽宁	61	743	514,948	11,131	0.89	2.25	132.49	60.56	1,253,308
Jilin 吉林	44	473	209,338	-9,333	-3.85	-67.00	52.84	94.25	242,463
Heilongjiang 黑龙江	86	224	27,321	-176	-0.27	-1.49	28.15	82.24	66,549
Central-East 华东	400	799	501,841	14,674	1.62	3.66	128.72	55.78	906,935
Shanghai 上海	2	7,148	10,825,519	351,326	1.19	1.63	364.26	27.07	29,585,268
Jiangsu 江苏	3	17,196	16,133,541	250,909	1.00	2.34	239.25	57.41	25,147,167
Zhejiang 浙江	62	540	738,030	12,344	1.16	2.38	215.10	51.19	1,061,193
Anhui 安徽	64	440	121,166	17,910	8.47	70.75	104.18	88.03	211,488
Fujian 福建	71	425	152,769	12,269	2.98	22.26	122.11	86.59	411,096
Jiangxi 江西	81	691	112,395	1,317	0.39	1.19	54.63	66.92	334,231
Shandong 山东	117	904	489,075	13,035	1.65	3.96	63.23	58.39	791,216
Central-South 中南	437	655	290,469	12,009	2.20	5.33	103.03	58.70	545,459
Henan 河南	129	810	243,731	4,322	1.01	3.05	73.42	67.04	429,958
Hubei 湖北	41	987	145,230	47,356	6.81	118.49	61.22	94.25	695,237
Hunan 湖南	65	562	75,602	6,293	1.40	30.09	76.90	95.36	450,774
Guangdong 广东	96	659	815,468	21,599	2.01	2.89	217.26	30.41	1,073,680
Guangxi 广西	85	402	66,275	2,370	1.02	4.79	64.96	78.77	232,877
Hainan 海南	21	343	33,647	3,094	2.92	5.31	77.23	45.05	106,108
Southwest 西南	251	486	127,325	3,074	0.75	2.15	90.83	65.16	410,766
Chongqing 重庆	21	1,283	321,654	14,405	1.55	5.06	78.75	69.45	932,005
Sichuan 四川	84	542	204,041	2,518	0.37	1.15	91.19	67.69	679,776
Guizhou 贵州	65	312	38,195	506	0.61	1.52	72.04	59.87	82,955
Yunnan 云南	75	372	73,593	3,053	1.11	2.52	117.06	55.95	275,236
Tibet 西藏	6	205	10,362	-693	-1.05	-1.74	55.77	39.44	65,736
Northwest 西北	148	714	192,811	4,579	0.82	2.00	52.04	59.02	558,110
Shaanxi 陕西	45	575	256,379	10,261	1.84	5.05	65.77	63.61	558,406
Gansu 甘肃	54	963	156,230	-402	-0.08	-0.24	32.69	66.80	501,647
Qinghai 青海	8	1,023	325,794	150	0.01	0.01	75.60	37.56	1,641,517
Ningxia 宁夏	8	1,000	492,187	18,398	1.70	3.46	61.23	51.05	1,084,982
Xinjiang 新疆	33	352	61,173	2,706	1.04	2.74	85.27	61.93	259,731

4420: Transmission and Distribution Of Electricity 电力供应业

Year 年份	Number of firms 企业个数	Rate of change 变化率 (%)	Number of employees 职工人数 (人)	Rate of change 变化率 (%)	Total revenue (Mil. RMB) 总销售收入 (百万元)	Rate of change 变化率 (%)	Total profit (Mil RMB) 总利润 (百万元)	Rate of change 变化率 (%)
2000	1627		1,067,080		364,720		15,082	
2001	1676	3.01	1,046,414	-1.94	404,139	10.81	17,478	15.89
2002	1675	-0.06	1,068,028	2.07	495,617	22.64	14,753	-15.59

Major Products 主要产品	Output 产量	Unit 单位
Power Supply Volume 供电量	16,164	100,000,000 KWH 亿千瓦小时

10 Main Firms with Maximal Revenue (year founded) 收入最大的十家主要企业（创办年份）	City 城市	Province 省	Telephone/fax 电话/传真	Number of employees 职工人数	Ownership 产业所有权	Revenue ('000 RMB) 销售收入 (千元)	Profit('000 RMB) (rank) 利润(千元) (排名)	Total assets ('000 RMB) 总资产 (千元)	Major products 主要产品
Jiangsu Electric Power Company	Nanjing	Jiangsu	(025)3300300		State-owned				Electricity Generation
江苏省电力公司(1950)	南京市	江苏省	(025)5082304	51,312	国有企业	48,266,486	723,746(5)	74,974,260	发电
Shandong Electric Power Group Co.	Jinan	Shandong	(0531)6932222		State-owned				Electricity
山东电力集团公司	济南市	山东省	(0531)6035970	30,386	国有企业	35,296,512	944657(2)	60,884,734	电力
Zhejiang Electric Power Company	Hangzhou	Zhejiang	(0571)85162314		State-owned				Electricity
浙江省电力公司(1958)	杭州市	浙江省	(0571)51212419	293	国有企业	32,983,906	783,189(4)	13,026,542	电力
Liaoning Electric Power Company	Shenyang	Liaoning	(024)23112404		State Enterprises				Thermal Power
辽宁省电力有限公司(1999)	沈阳市	辽宁省	(024)23853810		国有独资	23,394,510	553,330(8)	53,848,350	火力发电
Shanghai Electric Power Company	Shanghai	Shanghai	(021)63291010		State-owned				Electricity Generation
上海市电力公司(1986)	上海市	上海市	(021)63297330	14,159	国有企业	21,613,870	702,080(6)	59,098,060	发电
Henan Electric Power Company	Zhengzhou	Henan	(0371)7903193		State-owned				Electricity
河南省电力公司(1956)	郑州市	河南省	(0371)7903194	43,648	国有企业	20,483,207	315,634(16)	44,624,763	电力
Guangdong Electric Power Group Co.,Ltd. Dongguan Power Supply	Dongguan	Guangdong	(0769)2462988		State-owned				Electricity
Branch Co. 广东省电力集团有限公司东莞供电分公司(1958)	东莞市	广东省	(0769)2462292	945	国有企业	13,944,813	397,552(12)	9,392,295	电力
Sichuan Electric Power Company	Chengdu	Sichuan	(028)86661888		State-owned				Electricity
四川省电力公司(1950)	成都市	四川省	(028)84441794		国有企业	13,442,065	47,575(58)	48,148,105	电力
China Broadcasting & Television Group Foshan Power Supply	Foshan	Guangdong	(0757)3331218		State-owned				Electricity
Branch 广电集团有限公司佛山供电分公司(1913)	佛山市	广东省	(0757)3803669	1,919	国有企业	11,386,746	243,596(17)	11,940,309	电力
Tianjin Electric Power Company	Tianjin	Tianjin	(022)24406133		State-owned				Electricity
天津市电力公司(1906)	天津市	天津市	(022)24406965	12,029	国有企业	8,021,074	72,044(44)	17,674,882	电力

Top 10 Cities by Revenue 销售收入排名前10位城市	Province 省	Market share 市场份额 (%)	Number of firms 企业个数
Nanjing 南京市	Jiangsu 江苏省	9.74	1
Shandong 山东省	Shandong 山东省	7.12	1
Hangzhou 杭州市	Zhejiang 浙江省	6.66	6
Liaoning 辽宁省	Liaoning 辽宁省	4.72	1
Zhengzhou 郑州市	Henan 河南省	4.44	8
Shanghai 上海市	Shanghai 上海市	4.37	2
Chengdu 成都市	Sichuan 四川省	2.93	15
Guangzhou 广州市	Guangdong 广东省	2.90	1
Dongguan 东莞市	Guangdong 广东省	2.81	1
Foshan 佛山市	Guangdong 广东省	2.33	2

10 Major Wholesalers 十家主要批发商	City 城市	Province 省	Telephone/Fax 电话/传真

4430: Steam and Hot Water Production and Supply
蒸汽、热水生产和供应业

The industry accounts for 0.125% of the total revenue of China's industrial sector in 2002. The rate of return on assets is 0.46%. 54.94% of all firms in the industry made a profit while 45.06% had negative returns.The top province in terms of the industry's revenue is Liaoning, accounting for 25.55% of the total revenue.
2002年本行业收入占全行业的 0.125%，资产利润率为 0.46%。54.94%的企业赢利，45.06%的企业亏损。收入最高的省为辽宁省，占本行业的25.55%。

	Total number of firms 企业总数	Total number of employees 职工总数	Total revenue (Mil.RMB) 总销售收入（百万元）	Total profit (Mil.RMB) 总利润（百万元）	Return on assets 资产利润率（%）	Return on equity 权益利润率（%）	Labour productivity ('000 RMB/worker) 劳动生产率（千元/人）	Debts/assets 资产负债率（%）	Total assets (Mil.RMB) 总资产（百万元）
Industry Overall 行业总体	344	104,876	13,425	258	0.46	0.94	42.51	51.11	55,947

	Number of firms 企业个数	Average number of employees 平均职工人数	Average revenue ('000 RMB) 平均销售收入（千元）	Average profit ('000 RMB) 平均利润（千元）	Return on assets 资产利润率（%）	Return on equity 权益利润率（%）	Labour productivity ('000 RMB/worker) 劳动生产率（千元/人）	Debts/assets 资产负债率（%）	Average total assets ('000 RMB) 平均总资产（千元）
By ownership 产业所有权									
State-owned 国有	222	248	27,174	-419	-0.43	-1.04	35.57	58.46	97,090
Collective-owned 集体	14	177	26,997	561	1.03	1.76	41.80	41.65	54,521
Foreign & Overseas Chinese Funded 三资	7	401	68,856	11,793	5.04	8.69	73.70	42.08	234,195
By regional distribution 地区分布									
Central-North 华北	76	366	50,226	1,404	0.50	0.78	53.27	35.75	280,276
Beijing 北京	14	543	109,673	2,920	0.41	0.49	65.08	15.66	712,896
Tianjin 天津	21	141	26,507	709	0.84	1.24	88.93	32.48	84,595
Hebei 河北	17	505	58,554	1,268	0.39	0.88	44.37	55.30	322,919
Shanxi 山西	7	241	27,312	-611	-0.45	-2.66	54.38	83.00	134,955
Inner Mongolia 内蒙古	17	411	31,675	1,982	1.08	2.32	35.94	53.21	182,917
Northeast 东北	135	394	42,944	674	0.43	1.16	33.11	62.89	156,430
Liaoning 辽宁	67	428	51,206	1,367	0.69	1.91	33.24	63.97	198,354
Jilin 吉林	36	343	34,144	485	0.39	0.96	34.09	59.92	125,523
Heilongjiang 黑龙江	32	382	35,546	-565	-0.55	-1.46	31.82	62.57	103,421
Central-East 华东	57	208	43,335	1,109	0.93	2.27	59.37	58.79	118,693
Shanghai 上海	5	68	31,248	4,199	4.54	6.24	198.58	27.20	92,412
Jiangsu 江苏	13	175	31,605	2,203	3.04	11.06	74.03	72.50	72,397
Zhejiang 浙江	4	198	50,033	-2,026	-1.91	-4.36	45.95	56.17	105,914
Anhui 安徽	5	268	47,060	1,544	1.75	5.86	61.83	70.13	88,229
Fujian 福建	5	84	15,572	-1,358	-2.27	-4.61	39.60	50.77	59,850
Jiangxi 江西									
Shandong 山东	25	267	55,588	830	0.49	1.20	49.64	58.84	167,928
Central-South 中南	16	346	41,937	1,688	0.92	1.93	35.92	52.58	184,227
Henan 河南	6	297	38,998	-2,046	-0.93	-2.36	49.35	60.47	219,413
Hubei 湖北	4	405	50,338	1,756	0.95	1.59	29.52	40.15	184,787
Hunan 湖南	1	665	55,892	-3,974	-3.49	-14.02	26.60	75.14	114,023
Guangdong 广东	3	52	24,311	958	2.88	4.60	155.26	37.50	33,317
Guangxi 广西	2	658	53,417	16,679	4.92	9.69	16.19	49.24	339,018
Hainan 海南									
Southwest 西南	3	191	8,902	255	0.92	2.44	14.55	62.21	27,677
Chongqing 重庆	2	149	7,976	626	3.38	5.32	19.01	36.38	18,496
Sichuan 四川	1	275	10,756	-485	-1.05	-6.19	9.72	82.97	46,040
Guizhou 贵州									
Yunnan 云南									
Tibet 西藏									
Northwest 西北	57	103	11,281	-539	-0.82	-1.91	51.65	56.82	65,477
Shaanxi 陕西	4	82	4,250	-992	-1.59	-5.85	33.15	72.87	62,543
Gansu 甘肃	8	81	4,013	-63	-0.40	-0.64	20.57	37.18	15,545
Qinghai 青海	4	60	1,641	-624	-7.80	-34.12	15.74	77.13	7,999
Ningxia 宁夏	10	131	12,803	-19	-0.02	-0.05	42.28	52.65	82,525
Xinjiang 新疆	31	108	14,817	-761	-0.94	-2.21	65.63	57.31	80,658

4430: Steam and Hot Water Production and Supply

蒸汽、热水生产和供应业

Year 年份	Number of firms 企业个数	Rate of change 变化率 (%)	Number of employees 职工人数 (人)	Rate of change 变化率 (%)	Total revenue (Mil. RMB) 总销售收入 (百万元)	Rate of change 变化率 (%)	Total profit (Mil RMB) 总利润 (百万元)	Rate of change 变化率 (%)
2000	300		98,495		9,787		307	
2001	310	3.33	108,121	9.77	10,529	7.58	141	-54.07
2002	344	10.97	104,876	-3.00	13,425	27.50	258	82.98

Major Products 主要产品	Output 产量	Unit 单位
Heat Supply Volume 供热量	15	100,000,000 Million KJ 亿百万千焦

10 Main Firms with Maximal Revenue (year founded) 收入最大的十家主要企业（创办年份）	City 城市	Province 省	Telephone/fax 电话/传真	Number of employees 职工人数	Ownership 产业所有权	Revenue ('000 RMB) 销售收入 (千元)	Profit('000 RMB) (rank) 利润(千元) (排名)	Total assets ('000 RMB) 总资产 (千元)	Major products 主要产品
Beijing Heating Power Group Co., Ltd.	Beijing	Beijing	(010)84551872		State Enterprises				Steam & Hot Water
北京市热力集团有限责任公司(1958)	北京市	北京市	(010)84551870	4,189	国有独资	1,220,188	27,646(7)	8,641,520	蒸汽热水
Dalian Thermoelectricity Group Co., Ltd.	Dalian	Liaoning	(0411)4422999		Limited-Liability				Heat Supply
大连市热电集团有限公司(2000)	大连市	辽宁省	(0411)4438670	1,726	有限公司	667,151	2,943(35)	3,447,928	供热
Shenyang Huitian Thermoelectricity Stock Co., Ltd.	Shenyang	Liaoning	(024)22939482		Joint Stock				Heat Supply
沈阳惠天热电股份有限公司(1980)	沈阳市	辽宁省	(024)22939739	4,847	股份制	561,965	23,735(10)	1,870,539	供暖
Weihai Thermoelectricity Factory	Weihai	Shandong	(0631)5800399		State-owned				Power Generation
威海热电厂(1981)	威海市	山东省	(0631)5800399	381	国有企业	470,234	38,023(3)	611,889	发电
Shijiazhuang Dongfang Thermoelectric Co., Ltd.	Shijiazhuang	Hebei	(0311)5053391		State Enterprises				Steam & Hot Water
石家庄东方热电燃气集团有限公司(1998)	石家庄市	河北省	(0311)5053924	2,507	国有独资	452,246	45,317(2)	3,069,909	蒸汽热水
Chifeng Fulong Public Group Co., Ltd.	Chifeng	InnerMongolia	(0476)8239805		State Enterprises				Heat Supply
赤峰富龙公用集团有限责任公司(1975)	赤峰市	内蒙古	(0476)8240049	2,410	国有独资	211,550	28,901(6)	1,796,190	供热
Qingdao Thermoelectricity Group Co., Ltd.	Qingdao	Shandong	(0532)5653495		State Enterprises				Heat Supply
青岛热电集团有限公司(1993)	青岛市	山东省	(0532)5669594	820	国有独资	200,219	4,872(26)	579,427	供热
Jinzhou Thermoelectricity General Company	Jinzhou	Liaoning	(0416)2812672		State-owned				Heat Supply
锦州热电总公司(1983)	锦州市	辽宁省	(0416)2815415	1,571	国有企业	190,306	531(83)	696,562	供热
Tangshan Heating Power General Company	Tangshan	Hebei	(0315)2821305		State-owned				Steam & Hot Water
唐山市热力总公司(1978)	唐山市	河北省	(0315)2813106	2,562	国有企业	185,621	2,761(36)	649,783	蒸气热水
Taiyuan Heating Power Company	Taiyuan	Shanxi	(0351)4158803		State-owned				
太原市热力公司	太原市	山西省	(0351)4158803	541	国有企业	149,130	2,660(41)	740,290	

Top 10 Cities by Revenue 销售收入排名前10位城市	Province 省	Market share 市场份额 (%)	Number of firms 企业个数
Beijing 北京市	Beijing 北京市	11.44	14
Shenyang 沈阳市	Liaoning 辽宁省	8.12	12
Dalian 大连市	Liaoning 辽宁省	7.46	8
Tianjin 天津市	Tianjin 天津市	4.15	21
Weihai 威海市	Shandong 山东省	3.99	3
Changchun 长春市	Jilin 吉林省	3.37	9
Shijiazhuang 石家庄市	Hebei 河北省	3.37	1
Jinzhou 锦州市	Liaoning 辽宁省	2.38	4
Qingdao 青岛市	Shandong 山东省	2.23	4
Harbin 哈尔滨市	Heilongjiang 黑龙江省	2.20	6

10 Major Wholesalers 十家主要批发商	City 城市	Province 省	Telephone/Fax 电话/传真

4510: Gas Production 煤气生产业

The industry accounts for 0.066% of the total revenue of China's industrial sector in 2002. The rate of return on assets is -0.91%. 51.92% of all firms in the industry made a profit while 48.08% had negative returns.The top province in terms of the industry's revenue is Tianjin, accounting for 16.22% of the total revenue.
2002年本行业收入占全行业的 0.066%，资产利润率为 -0.91%。51.92%的企业赢利，48.08%的企业亏损。收入最高的省为天津市，占本行业的16.22%。

	Total number of firms 企业总数	Total number of employees 职工总数	Total revenue (Mil.RMB) 总销售收入 (百万元)	Total profit (Mil.RMB) 总利润 (百万元)	Return on assets 资产利润率 (%)	Return on equity 权益利润率 (%)	Labour productivity ('000 RMB/ worker) 劳动生产率 (千元/人)	Debts/ assets 资产负债率 (%)	Total assets (Mil.RMB) 总资产 (百万元)
Industry Overall 行业总体	52	48,950	7,050	-189	-0.91	-2.03	18.10	55.15	20,785

	Number of firms 企业个数	Average number of employees 平均职工人数	Average revenue ('000 RMB) 平均销售收入 (千元)	Average profit ('000 RMB) 平均利润 (千元)	Return on assets 资产利润率 (%)	Return on equity 权益利润率 (%)	Labour productivity ('000 RMB/ worker) 劳动生产率 (千元/人)	Debts/ assets 资产负债率 (%)	Average total assets ('000 RMB) 平均总资产 (千元)
By ownership 产业所有权									
State-owned 国有	31	1,156	125,670	-1,618	-0.41	-0.96	22.73	57.60	396,031
Collective-owned 集体	3	109	21,627	1,567	25.29	29.65	39.90	14.71	6,195
Foreign & Overseas Chinese Funded 三资	7	170	154,848	6,520	4.61	16.44	36.87	71.96	141,429
By regional distribution 地区分布									
Central-North 华北	14	1,008	118,665	-1,090	-0.29	-0.99	12.82	71.02	379,144
Beijing 北京	1	80	10,080	-1,851	-2.42	-6.48	85.90	62.71	76,636
Tianjin 天津	5	735	228,719	1,976	0.34	0.90	6.33	62.10	581,736
Hebei 河北	3	761	46,659	-1,359	-0.39	-1.13	17.91	65.99	352,564
Shanxi 山西	4	1,628	60,251	-4,864	-2.17		12.17	118.99	223,872
Inner Mongolia 内蒙古	1	1,564	126,658	239	0.06	0.11	19.62	41.09	369,524
Northeast 东北	6	1,193	95,724	-2,550	-0.79	-1.31	51.61	39.77	322,385
Liaoning 辽宁	4	1,643	123,761	-3,825	-0.81	-1.31	6.70	38.65	474,743
Jilin 吉林									
Heilongjiang 黑龙江	2	295	39,650				552.60	100.00	17,670
Central-East 华东	16	980	193,670	-10,611	-1.88	-3.42	6.90	44.95	563,862
Shanghai 上海	3	1,689	329,778	-69,585	-7.66	-9.64	14.99	20.53	908,445
Jiangsu 江苏	3	338	356,941	11,952	4.90	8.29	56.93	40.88	243,899
Zhejiang 浙江	1	2,015	234,174	10,128	0.71	1.44	-0.82	50.93	1,433,100
Anhui 安徽	3	690	67,997	-3,665	-1.55	-2.41	23.73	35.60	235,678
Fujian 福建	1	190	7,598	-1,980	-2.07	-2.24	17.04	7.54	95,556
Jiangxi 江西	2	297	12,684	-4,415	-6.31	-21.90	15.63	71.19	69,976
Shandong 山东	3	1,573	189,142	4,936	0.46	1.37	-18.13	66.11	1,063,041
Central-South 中南	11	729	97,867	670	0.22	0.42	18.54	48.95	309,518
Henan 河南	2	68	23,625	2,125	26.50	28.26	65.63	6.23	8,020
Hubei 湖北	2	1,049	51,955	-6,047	-1.81	-3.93	5.82	53.97	334,359
Hunan 湖南	2	1,162	61,048	-6,461	-3.07	-6.86	5.18	55.25	210,479
Guangdong 广东	5	692	160,656	5,627	1.22	2.29	33.39	46.63	459,795
Guangxi 广西									
Hainan 海南									
Southwest 西南	3	1,310	213,026	1,370	0.37		19.77	107.85	370,539
Chongqing 重庆									
Sichuan 四川	1	352	11,881	101	0.41	0.69	12.80	41.62	24,918
Guizhou 贵州	1	1,699	285,703	4,537	0.76		29.58	171.60	595,087
Yunnan 云南	1	1,879	341,494	-528	-0.11	-0.16	12.20	34.05	491,611
Tibet 西藏									
Northwest 西北	2	31	81	-17	-0.72	-2.61	14.90	72.41	2,363
Shaanxi 陕西	1	51	161	-34	-0.73	-2.69	0.82	73.04	4,684
Gansu 甘肃	1	10					86.70	2.38	42
Qinghai 青海									
Ningxia 宁夏									
Xinjiang 新疆									

4510: Gas Production 煤气生产业

Year 年份	Number of firms 企业个数	Rate of change 变化率 (%)	Number of employees 职工人数 (人)	Rate of change 变化率 (%)	Total revenue (Mil. RMB) 总销售收入 (百万元)	Rate of change 变化率 (%)	Total profit (Mil RMB) 总利润 (百万元)	Rate of change 变化率 (%)
2000	53		63,828		5,542		-203	
2001	56	5.66	52,419	-17.87	5,593	0.92	-37	-
2002	52	-7.14	48,950	-6.62	7,050	26.05	-189	-

Major Products 主要产品	Output 产量	Unit 单位
Coke 焦炭	11,237	10,000 Tons 万吨
Coal Gas 煤气	1,317	100,000,000 Stere 亿立方米

10 Main Firms with Maximal Revenue (year founded) 收入最大的十家主要企业(创办年份)	City 城市	Province 省	Telephone/fax 电话/传真	Number of employees 职工人数	Ownership 产业所有权	Revenue ('000 RMB) 销售收入(千元)	Profit('000 RMB) (rank) 利润(千元)(排名)	Total assets ('000 RMB) 总资产(千元)	Major products 主要产品
YPC-PANVA ENERGY CO.,LTD.	Nanjing	Jiangsu	(025)8393717		Overseas Chinese-funded				Liuefied Petroleum Gas
扬子石化百江能源有限公司(1999)	南京市	江苏省	(025)8392237	132	港澳台资	571,260	12,030(6)	96,180	液化石油气
Tianjin No.3 Gas Factory	Tianjin	Tianjin	(022)24367546		State-owned				Coke
天津市第三煤气厂(2001)	天津市	天津市	(022)24367547	1,375	国有企业	531,648	-	1,850,060	焦炭
Shanghai Pudong Gas-making (Group)Co., Ltd.	Shanghai	Shanghai	(021)68466898		State Enterprises				Gas
上海浦东煤气制气有限公司(1987)	上海市	上海市	(021)68467161	2,581	国有独资	527,635	-	979,084	煤气
Guangzhou Gas Co.Ltd.	Guangzhou	Guangdong	(020)87302186		State-owned				Gas
广州市煤气公司(1983)	广州市	广东省	(020)87302178	2,585	国有企业	508,953	13,005(5)	1,979,812	煤气
Jiangsu Jiangdong Chemical Co.,Ltd.	Changzhou	Jiangsu	(0519)8811413		State-owned				Gas
江苏江东化工股份有限公司(1952)	常州市	江苏省	(0519)8820786	782	国有企业	472,130	20,740(2)	613,860	燃气
Tianjin NO.2 Gas Factory	Tianjin	Tianjin	(022)26321775		State-owned				Coke Oven Gas
天津市第二煤气厂(1987)	天津市	天津市	(022)26321773	1,972	国有企业	425,401	24,228(1)	632,332	焦炉煤气
Kunming Coking & Gas Factory	Kunming	Yunnan	(0871)6263211		State-owned				Gas
昆明焦化制气厂(1986)	昆明市	云南省	(0871)6263298	1,879	国有企业	341,494	-	491,611	煤气
Shanghai Wusong Gas &Gas-making Co., Ltd.	Shanghai	Shanghai	(021)56826666		State Enterprises				Gas
上海吴淞煤气制气有限公司(1939)	上海市	上海市	(021)56820123	2,026	国有独资	335,196	-	480,820	煤气
Guiyang Gas Source Factory	Guiyang	Guizhou	(0851)2561170		State-owned				Coke
贵阳煤气气源厂(1994)	贵阳市	贵州省	(0851)2561986	1,699	国有企业	285,703	4,537(11)	595,087	焦炭
Panyu Delta Petrochemical Industry Co., Ltd.	Guangzhou	Guangdong	(020)84581073		Overseas Chinese-funded				Liuefied Petroleum Gas液化
番禺三角洲石油化工有限公司(1992)	广州市	广东省	(020)84581849	258	港澳台资	242,563	1,676(16)	44,230	石油气

Top 10 Cities by Revenue 销售收入排名前10位城市	Province 省	Market share 市场份额 (%)	Number of firms 企业个数
Tianjin 天津市	Tianjin 天津市	16.22	5
Shanghai 上海市	Shanghai 上海市	14.03	3
Guangzhou 广州市	Guangdong 广东省	11.09	3
Nanjing 南京市	Jiangsu 江苏省	8.10	1
Qingdao 青岛市	Shandong 山东省	7.24	1
Changzhou 常州市	Jiangsu 江苏省	6.70	1
Kunming 昆明市	Yunnan 云南省	4.84	1
Guiyang 贵阳市	Guizhou 贵州省	4.05	1
Dalian 大连市	Liaoning 辽宁省	3.50	1
Hangzhou 杭州市	Zhejiang 浙江省	3.32	1

10 Major Wholesalers 十家主要批发商	City 城市	Province 省	Telephone/Fax 电话/传真

4520: Gas Supply 煤气供应业

The industry accounts for 0.235% of the total revenue of China's industrial sector in 2002. The rate of return on assets is 0.17%. 58.12% of all firms in the industry made a profit while 41.88% had negative returns.The top province in terms of the industry's revenue is Guangdong, accounting for 26.36% of the total revenue.
2002年本行业收入占全行业的 0.235%，资产利润率为 0.17%。58.12%的企业赢利，41.88%的企业亏损。收入最高的省为广东省，占本行业的26.36%。

	Total number of firms 企业总数	Total number of employees 职工总数	Total revenue (Mil.RMB) 总销售收入 (百万元)	Total profit (Mil.RMB) 总利润 (百万元)	Return on assets 资产利润率 (%)	Return on equity 权益利润率 (%)	Labour productivity ('000 RMB/ worker) 劳动生产率 (千元/人)	Debts/ assets 资产负债率 (%)	Total assets (Mil.RMB) 总资产 (百万元)
Industry Overall 行业总体	277	98,181	25,231	84	0.17	0.30	45.06	44.37	50,429

	Number of firms 企业个数	Average number of employees 平均职工人数	Average revenue ('000 RMB) 平均销售收入 (千元)	Average profit ('000 RMB) 平均利润 (千元)	Return on assets 资产利润率 (%)	Return on equity 权益利润率 (%)	Labour productivity ('000 RMB/ worker) 劳动生产率 (千元/人)	Debts/ assets 资产负债率 (%)	Average total assets ('000 RMB) 平均总资产 (千元)
By ownership 产业所有权									
State-owned 国有	159	434	50,216	-1,914	-1.19	-2.55	21.91	53.37	161,095
Collective-owned 集体	8	66	35,410	1,602	9.87	19.34	175.84	48.94	16,225
Foreign & Overseas Chinese Funded 三资	42	116	180,626	1,416	1.09	2.63	129.58	58.45	129,542
By regional distribution 地区分布									
Central-North 华北	33	687	149,498	-1,022	-0.26	-0.34	41.98	23.89	395,298
Beijing 北京	6	1,377	504,432	12,223	0.91	0.98	110.07	7.41	1,346,229
Tianjin 天津	8	694	110,850	-11,608	-3.14	-5.62	-60.86	44.13	369,741
Hebei 河北	13	544	37,697	-2,160	-1.72	-4.69	19.03	63.26	125,361
Shanxi 山西	4	250	4,299	-1,160	-2.82	-5.12	5.20	44.85	41,088
Inner Mongolia 内蒙古	2	390	256,394	9,262	8.60	17.19	308.47	49.99	107,746
Northeast 东北	36	560	43,978	-1,822	-1.19	-2.41	22.55	50.69	153,221
Liaoning 辽宁	18	608	44,411	-739	-0.66	-1.24	19.38	47.11	112,777
Jilin 吉林	12	581	53,374	-3,118	-1.17	-2.50	32.30	53.26	266,599
Heilongjiang 黑龙江	6	374	23,885	-2,477	-5.18	-9.86	7.73	47.45	47,795
Central-East 华东	69	387	103,385	-993	-0.46	-0.83	49.99	45.26	217,919
Shanghai 上海	5	1,134	591,661	3,321	0.30	0.48	116.62	36.33	1,096,976
Jiangsu 江苏	17	478	79,976	-2,841	-1.14	-2.43	40.04	53.08	249,100
Zhejiang 浙江	11	107	85,996	2,044	3.06	4.60	55.72	33.54	66,831
Anhui 安徽	12	266	38,159	-1,100	-1.17	-2.12	21.02	44.82	94,003
Fujian 福建	7	273	112,394	-3,894	-1.87	-3.76	67.80	50.32	208,682
Jiangxi 江西	4	141	4,806	-632	-1.38	-2.99	10.48	54.04	45,964
Shandong 山东	13	464	46,602	-1,253	-0.90	-1.96	13.00	54.04	139,154
Central-South 中南	62	194	136,509	1,112	0.84	2.30	76.68	63.29	131,835
Henan 河南	11	506	65,972	5,909	2.63	6.84	22.53	61.52	224,603
Hubei 湖北	4	355	73,953	468	0.49	1.27	81.36	61.18	94,641
Hunan 湖南	4	176	23,319	-1,833	-4.73	-9.08	14.14	47.88	38,742
Guangdong 广东	32	97	207,850	350	0.29	0.91	183.91	68.02	121,009
Guangxi 广西	4	134	19,831	-2,576	-1.89	-4.92	43.19	61.62	136,478
Hainan 海南	7	98	88,321	1,218	1.13	2.28	113.26	50.20	107,343
Southwest 西南	66	196	42,350	2,824	2.42	5.09	50.93	52.58	116,879
Chongqing 重庆	10	314	87,073	2,778	1.77	3.06	42.00	42.12	156,626
Sichuan 四川	51	155	33,967	3,090	3.22	6.79	63.06	52.54	95,906
Guizhou 贵州	3	362	27,808	-1,820	-0.89	-5.80	16.33	84.69	204,921
Yunnan 云南	2	421	54,325	3,230	1.01	1.92	14.93	47.68	320,879
Tibet 西藏									
Northwest 西北	11	339	29,285	-319	-0.37	-0.68	28.09	45.28	85,822
Shaanxi 陕西	3	663	58,231	-1,719	-0.89	-1.91	29.44	53.47	193,252
Gansu 甘肃	1	240	42,105	430	2.53	8.58	66.82	70.48	16,978
Qinghai 青海									
Ningxia 宁夏	1	382	17,382	2,682	4.84	5.82	2.81	16.78	55,357
Xinjiang 新疆	6	187	14,659	-243	-0.50	-0.75	26.04	32.94	48,659

Year 年份	Number of firms 企业个数	Rate of change 变化率 (%)	Number of employees 职工人数 (人)	Rate of change 变化率 (%)	Total revenue (Mil. RMB) 总销售收入 (百万元)	Rate of change 变化率 (%)	Total profit (Mil RMB) 总利润 (百万元)	Rate of change 变化率 (%)
2000	247		96,231		17,923		-166	
2001	264	6.88	94,713	-1.58	19,637	9.56	-39	-
2002	277	4.92	98,181	3.66	25,231	28.49	84	-

Major Products 主要产品	Output 产量	Unit 单位
Coal Gas 煤气	1,317	100,000,000 Stere 亿立方米
Liquefied Petroleum Gas 液化石油气	1,190	10,000 Tons 万吨

10 Main Firms with Maximal Revenue (year founded) 收入最大的十家主要企业（创办年份）	City 城市	Province 省	Telephone/fax 电话/传真	Number of employees 职工人数	Ownership 产业所有权	Revenue ('000 RMB) 销售收入 (千元)	Profit('000 RMB) (rank) 利润(千元) (排名)	Total assets ('000 RMB) 总资产 (千元)	Major products 主要产品
Beijing Gas Group Co., Ltd.	Beijing	Beijing	(010)65125509		State Enterprises				Gas
北京市燃气集团有限责任公司(1999)	北京市	北京市	(010)65126086	5,012	国有独资	2,684,571	62,716(2)	7,237,861	燃气
Zhuhai Jiufeng Ake Energy Co., Ltd.	Zhuhai	Guangdong	(0756)7268384		Overseas Chinese-funded				Liuefied Petroleum Gas
珠海九丰阿科能源有限公司(1997)	珠海市	广东省	(0756)7268000	138	港澳台资	2,007,780	52,973(5)	471,230	液化石油气
Caltex Ocean Gas Energy Co., Ltd.	Shantou	Guangdong	(0754)3580061		Foreign Funded				Liuefied Petroleum Gas
加德士海洋燃气能源有限公司(2000)	汕头市	广东省	(0754)3582286	113	外商投资	1,911,991	-	1,156,537	液化石油气
Shanghai Dazhong Gas Co., Ltd.	Shanghai	Shanghai	(021)62311001		Limited-Liability				Gas
上海大众燃气有限公司(2001)	上海市	上海市	(021)62318471	1,913	有限公司	985,850	15,193(13)	1,464,439	燃气
Shanghai Gas Shibei Sale Co., Ltd.	Shanghai	Shanghai	(021)63222333		State Enterprises				Gas
上海燃气市北销售有限公司(1865)	上海市	上海市	(021)63222311	1,866	国有独资	944,326	1,290(67)	1,844,487	燃气
Ocean Petroleum (Yangjiang)Industorial Co., Ltd.	Yangjiang	Guangdong	(0662)3100006		Foreign Funded				Oil & Gas Wharf
海洋石油(阳江)实业有限公司(1995)	阳江市	广东省	(0662)3167167	127	外商投资	803,739	9,864(20)	187,035	油气码头
Shanghai Gas Pudong Sale Co., Ltd.	Shanghai	Shanghai	(021)58995588		State Enterprises				Gas
上海燃气浦东销售有限公司(1995)	上海市	上海市	(021)50550173	508	国有独资	691,069	1,682(59)	1,278,238	燃气
Wushenqi Natural Gas Co.,Ltd.	Eerduosi	ıner Mongol	(0477)7214007		State-owned				Natural Gas
乌审旗天然气公司(1998)	鄂尔多斯市	内蒙古		150	国有企业	498,931	22,960(7)	128,830	天然气
Tianjin Gas Group Co., Ltd.	Tianjin	Tianjin	(022)23318515		State owned				Gas
天津燃气集团有限公司(2000)	天津市	天津市	(022)23342929	3,849	国有企业	495,395	-	2,276,816	煤气
Chendu Gas General Company	Chengdu	Sichuan	(028)87777343		State-owned				Gas
成都市煤气总公司(1967)	成都市	四川省	(028)87776326	1,379	国有企业	465,733	947(76)	1,540,024	煤气

Top 10 Cities by Revenue 销售收入排名前10位城市	Province 省	Market share 市场份额 (%)	Number of firms 企业个数
Beijing 北京市	Beijing 北京市	12.00	6
Shanghai 上海市	Shanghai 上海市	11.72	5
Zhuhai 珠海市	Guangdong 广东省	8.60	2
Shantou 汕头市	Guangdong 广东省	7.58	1
Tianjin 天津市	Tianjin 天津市	3.51	8
Chongqing 重庆市	Chongqing 重庆市	3.45	10
Yangjiang 阳江市	Guangdong 广东省	3.19	1
Chaozhou 潮州市	Guangdong 广东省	2.81	6
Chengdu 成都市	Sichuan 四川省	2.75	8
Zhanjiang 湛江市	Guangdong 广东省	2.21	7

10 Major Wholesalers 十家主要批发商	City 城市	Province 省	Telephone/Fax 电话/传真

4610: Purification Of Tap Water 自来水生产业

The industry accounts for 0.205% of the total revenue of China's industrial sector in 2002. The rate of return on assets is 0.09%. 55.74% of all firms in the industry made a profit while 44.26% had negative returns.The top province in terms of the industry's revenue is Guangdong, accounting for 14.29% of the total revenue.
2002年本行业收入占全行业的0.205%，资产利润率为0.09%。55.74%的企业赢利，44.26%的企业亏损。收入最高的省为广东省，占本行业的14.29%。

	Total number of firms 企业总数	Total number of employees 职工总数	Total revenue (Mil.RMB) 总销售收入(百万元)	Total profit (Mil.RMB) 总利润(百万元)	Return on assets 资产利润率(%)	Return on equity 权益利润率(%)	Labour productivity ('000 RMB/ worker) 劳动生产率(千元/人)	Debts/ assets 资产负债率(%)	Total assets (Mil.RMB) 总资产(百万元)
Industry Overall 行业总体	1367	279,841	21,952	108	0.09	0.15	39.00	43.22	123,703

	Number of firms 企业个数	Average number of employees 平均职工人数	Average revenue ('000 RMB) 平均销售收入(千元)	Average profit ('000 RMB) 平均利润(千元)	Return on assets 资产利润率(%)	Return on equity 权益利润率(%)	Labour productivity ('000 RMB/ worker) 劳动生产率(千元/人)	Debts/ assets 资产负债率(%)	Average total assets ('000 RMB) 平均总资产(千元)
By ownership 产业所有权									
State-owned 国有	1,176	200	12,286	-395	-0.57	-1.04	30.60	45.22	69,072
Collective-owned 集体	66	132	24,216	1,742	1.63	3.04	84.82	46.35	106,814
Foreign & Overseas Chinese Funded 三资	19	152	62,335	15,638	5.85	11.62	134.15	49.66	267,372
By regional distribution 地区分布									
Central-North 华北	117	219	19,325	1,382	1.45	2.42	48.35	40.01	95,290
Beijing 北京	4	189	114,775	38,642	10.10	24.70	262.87	59.11	382,514
Tianjin 天津	6	474	120,332	-3,206	-0.40	-0.61	171.88	33.62	794,206
Hebei 河北	36	325	20,890	903	0.90	1.48	30.33	39.05	100,082
Shanxi 山西	47	111	3,306	-28	-0.21	-0.33	16.80	35.50	13,079
Inner Mongolia 内蒙古	24	215	7,187	-200	-0.76	-1.57	21.64	51.70	26,497
Northeast 东北	125	352	22,685	-262	-0.24	-0.35	34.13	30.46	108,188
Liaoning 辽宁	39	516	34,426	-765	-0.48	-0.70	29.27	30.95	158,929
Jilin 吉林	27	391	29,137	-834	-0.52	-0.76	38.74	31.58	160,354
Heilongjiang 黑龙江	59	225	11,972	332	0.65	0.91	37.84	27.84	50,775
Central-East 华东	411	202	18,115	120	0.10	0.20	44.09	47.82	117,074
Shanghai 上海	21	510	73,541	3,676	0.74	1.62	52.95	54.53	499,807
Jiangsu 江苏	66	233	23,011	-46	-0.03	-0.05	49.20	46.52	172,747
Zhejiang 浙江	89	124	20,351	-85	-0.07	-0.14	91.64	45.76	115,478
Anhui 安徽	51	208	12,144	-6	-0.01	-0.02	32.99	37.97	64,175
Fujian 福建	60	152	13,009	162	0.19	0.29	50.43	33.98	83,616
Jiangxi 江西	71	151	4,201	-100	-0.49	-0.95	15.06	47.90	20,237
Shandong 山东	53	293	16,471	-368	-0.31	-0.76	22.94	58.59	117,285
Central-South 中南	396	229	17,542	-169	-0.19	-0.31	37.08	39.75	91,075
Henan 河南	72	311	13,083	-54	-0.10	-0.16	20.25	36.08	52,238
Hubei 湖北	80	271	16,320	-375	-0.47	-0.77	23.03	39.42	80,604
Hunan 湖南	73	198	12,163	-48	-0.09	-0.17	30.22	43.88	50,925
Guangdong 广东	98	194	32,013	2			83.20	37.64	191,358
Guangxi 广西	65	167	9,068	-135	-0.31	-0.60	34.45	48.47	43,870
Hainan 海南	8	292	10,547	-2,609	-3.91	-12.26	7.81	68.13	66,779
Southwest 西南	205	124	9,718	123	0.21	0.43	38.01	50.85	57,960
Chongqing 重庆	20	285	27,587	2,611	2.20	4.90	41.71	55.03	118,605
Sichuan 四川	88	135	9,519	-228	-0.35	-0.70	33.00	50.39	65,890
Guizhou 贵州	32	81	2,738	-1	-0.01	-0.01	13.32	56.82	21,361
Yunnan 云南	64	81	7,618	-161	-0.35	-0.69	55.36	49.03	45,449
Tibet 西藏	1	190	27,539	3,360	2.82	2.82	103.91		119,219
Northwest 西北	113	96	4,174	-256	-0.98	-1.98	15.88	50.55	26,242
Shaanxi 陕西	42	103	2,818	-289	-2.29	-4.25	9.38	46.08	12,606
Gansu 甘肃	22	89	2,679	-271	-1.31	-4.41	12.83	70.24	20,626
Qinghai 青海	7	53	1,389	-260	-3.86	-9.75	-53.91	60.42	6,741
Ningxia 宁夏	6	223	12,596	-263	-0.35	-0.51	19.05	32.65	76,227
Xinjiang 新疆	36	79	5,808	-208	-0.51	-1.04	35.66	51.33	41,044

Year 年份	Number of firms 企业个数	Rate of change 变化率 (%)	Number of employees 职工人数 (人)	Rate of change 变化率 (%)	Total revenue (Mil. RMB) 总销售收入 (百万元)	Rate of change 变化率 (%)	Total profit (Mil RMB) 总利润 (百万元)	Rate of change 变化率 (%)
2000	1409		289,354		20,632		744	
2001	1338	-5.04	283,384	-2.06	20,629	-0.01	619	-16.80
2002	1367	2.17	279,841	-1.25	21,952	6.41	108	-82.55

Major Products 主要产品	Output 产量	Unit 单位
Running Water Manufacturing Volume 自来水生产量	350	100,000,000 Tons 亿吨

10 Main Firms with Maximal Revenue (year founded) 收入最大的十家主要企业（创办年份）	City 城市	Province 省	Telephone/fax 电话/传真	Number of employees 职工人数	Ownership 产业所有权	Revenue ('000 RMB) 销售收入 (千元)	Profit('000 RMB) (rank) 利润(千元) (排名)	Total assets ('000 RMB) 总资产 (千元)	Major products 主要产品
Shenzhen Water Affairs (Group)Co., Ltd. 深圳市自来水（集团）有限公司(1962)	Shenzhen 深圳市	Guangdong 广东省	(0755)82137888 (0755)82137882	1,425	State Enterprises 国有独资	691,950	-	6,303,381	Tap Water 自来水
Shanghai Tape Water Shibei Co., Ltd. 上海市自来水市北有限公司(2000)	Shanghai 上海市	Shanghai 上海市	(021)55150088 (021)65087172	4,044	State Enterprises 国有独资	621,473	17,342(13)	3,887,838	Tap Water 自来水
Shanghai Tape Water Shinan Company 上海市自来水市南公司(2000)	Shanghai 上海市	Shanghai 上海市	(021)63215577	3,504	State Enterprises 国有独资	478,351	27,302(7)	3,454,523	Tap Water 自来水
Changchun Water Affairs Company 长春市自来水公司(1932)	Changchun 长春市	Jilin 吉林省	(0431)8978370 (0431)8978370	3,245	State-owned 国有企业	467,329	-	2,699,317	Tap Water 自来水
Dalian Water Supply Group Company 大连市自来水集团有限公司(1879)	Dalian 大连市	Liaoning 辽宁省	(0411)3644644 (0411)3633305	2,653	State-owned 国有企业	451,330	-	2,474,460	Tap Water 自来水
Wuhan Water Supply Company 武汉市自来水公司(1909)	Wuhan 武汉市	Hubei 湖北省	(027)83882346 (027)83873749	5,440	State-owned 国有企业	445,594	-	1,793,147	Tap Water 自来水
Tianjin Water Supply Group Company 天津市自来水集团有限公司(1898)	Tianjin 天津市	Tianjin 天津市	(022)23393887	1,718	State Enterprises 国有独资	427,614	-	3,215,995	Tap Water 自来水
Hangzhou Water Supply General Company 杭州市自来水总公司(1931)	Hangzhou 杭州市	Zhejiang 浙江省	(0571)87815788 (0571)87829689	1,528	State-owned 国有企业	353,836	9,302(26)	2,549,354	Tap Water 自来水
Chengdu Water Supply General Company 成都市自来水总公司(1965)	Chengdu 成都市	Sichuan 四川省	(028)87763122 (028)87776876	1,595	State-owned 国有企业	291,103	-	2,536,803	Tap Water 自来水
Kunming Water Supply General Company 昆明市自来水总公司(1918)	Kunming 昆明市	Yunnan 云南省	(0871)3135610 (0871)3193405	1,686	State-owned 国有企业	276,764	1,606(102)	1,563,048	Tap Water 自来水

Top 10 Cities by Revenue 销售收入排名前10位城市	Province 省	Market share 市场份额 (%)	Number of firms 企业个数
Shanghai 上海市	Shanghai 上海市	7.04	21
Shenzhen 深圳市	Guangdong 广东省	4.71	11
Wuhan 武汉市	Hubei 湖北省	3.34	12
Tianjin 天津市	Tianjin 天津市	3.29	6
Changchun 长春市	Jilin 吉林省	2.53	4
Chongqing 重庆市	Chongqing 重庆市	2.51	20
Hangzhou 杭州市	Zhejiang 浙江省	2.51	12
Dalian 大连市	Liaoning 辽宁省	2.24	4
Beijing 北京市	Beijing 北京市	2.09	4
Harbin 哈尔滨市	Heilongjiang 黑龙江省	1.89	7

10 Major Wholesalers 十家主要批发商	City 城市	Province 省	Telephone/Fax 电话/传真

4620: Supply Of Tap Water 自来水供应业

The industry accounts for 0.126% of the total revenue of China's industrial sector in 2002. The rate of return on assets is 0.55%. 56.13% of all firms in the industry made a profit while 43.87% had negative returns.The top province in terms of the industry's revenue is Guangdong, accounting for 32.82% of the total revenue.
2002年本行业收入占全行业的0.126%，资产利润率为0.55%。56.13%的企业赢利，43.87%的企业亏损。收入最高的省为广东省，占本行业的32.82%。

	Total number of firms 企业总数	Total number of employees 职工总数	Total revenue (Mil.RMB) 总销售收入（百万元）	Total profit (Mil.RMB) 总利润（百万元）	Return on assets 资产利润率（%）	Return on equity 权益利润率（%）	Labour productivity ('000 RMB/worker) 劳动生产率（千元/人）	Debts/assets 资产负债率（%）	Total assets (Mil.RMB) 总资产（百万元）
Industry Overall 行业总体	1053	174,100	13,512	366	0.55	0.92	35.53	39.81	66,437

	Number of firms 企业个数	Average number of employees 平均职工人数	Average revenue ('000 RMB) 平均销售收入（千元）	Average profit ('000 RMB) 平均利润（千元）	Return on assets 资产利润率（%）	Return on equity 权益利润率（%）	Labour productivity ('000 RMB/worker) 劳动生产率（千元/人）	Debts/assets 资产负债率（%）	Average total assets ('000 RMB) 平均总资产（千元）
By ownership 产业所有权									
State-owned 国有	907	168	10,626	-50	-0.09	-0.14	29.83	38.14	56,575
Collective-owned 集体	75	71	20,772	1,660	3.01	7.59	101.35	60.34	55,133
Foreign & Overseas Chinese Funded 三资	5	372	67,603	4,300	0.82	1.22	85.79	33.20	526,621
By regional distribution 地区分布									
Central-North 华北	158	164	14,275	42	0.05	0.07	34.86	28.90	88,787
Beijing 北京	6	611	216,523	8,361	0.53	0.71	124.07	25.32	1,567,383
Tianjin 天津	7	38	2,862				118.20	6.42	8,097
Hebei 河北	50	153	6,389	-622	-1.98	-4.53	14.28	56.41	31,494
Shanxi 山西	50	167	9,359	-220	-0.44	-0.58	26.49	24.39	50,031
Inner Mongolia 内蒙古	45	134	3,308	-32	-0.30	-0.46	14.64	34.66	10,913
Northeast 东北	86	314	15,243	-490	-0.74	-1.43	22.40	48.06	65,972
Liaoning 辽宁	33	544	33,801	-379	-0.26	-0.49	26.55	46.62	146,145
Jilin 吉林	28	190	4,531	-669	-3.97	-9.30	16.79	57.32	16,874
Heilongjiang 黑龙江	25	148	2,743	-434	-2.87	-6.34	10.35	54.75	15,133
Central-East 华东	189	212	15,774	601	0.67	1.11	33.56	39.59	89,286
Shanghai 上海	7	280	57,585	939	0.23	0.33	88.71	30.32	410,079
Jiangsu 江苏	21	357	27,754	2,176	1.11	1.75	32.19	36.99	196,846
Zhejiang 浙江	27	136	20,104	1,619	1.51	2.85	69.78	46.99	107,260
Anhui 安徽	16	142	4,486	-379	-2.46	-4.43	21.66	44.59	15,432
Fujian 福建	22	121	11,627	1,040	1.68	3.66	60.57	54.13	61,915
Jiangxi 江西	17	269	16,566	2,162	3.40	5.14	32.12	33.82	63,537
Shandong 山东	79	220	10,677	-455	-0.84	-1.39	18.06	39.86	54,249
Central-South 中南	294	167	18,538	1,097	1.53	2.53	51.68	39.32	71,555
Henan 河南	54	198	4,278	-250	-1.56	-2.49	13.77	37.52	16,031
Hubei 湖北	29	165	4,931	-203	-1.02	-1.97	15.82	48.30	19,940
Hunan 湖南	38	184	9,721	-13	-0.02	-0.04	31.18	35.86	50,836
Guangdong 广东	127	163	34,920	2,713	2.13	3.45	94.30	38.26	127,197
Guangxi 广西	34	94	3,618	-126	-0.58	-1.26	20.97	54.38	21,985
Hainan 海南	12	221	12,419	171	0.27	0.55	27.28	50.88	63,327
Southwest 西南	165	85	3,960	-24	-0.10	-0.23	23.71	58.85	24,773
Chongqing 重庆	18	92	5,698	-148	-0.52	-1.40	30.33	63.07	28,683
Sichuan 四川	45	122	4,872	-7	-0.03	-0.06	22.76	56.71	27,693
Guizhou 贵州	54	90	4,131	122	0.41	1.21	21.95	65.86	29,677
Yunnan 云南	41	44	2,379	-199	-1.29	-2.53	25.31	49.10	15,447
Tibet 西藏	7	31	1,566	87	0.68	0.74	23.57	7.49	12,746
Northwest 西北	161	112	5,343	-188	-0.64	-1.25	25.68	48.81	29,409
Shaanxi 陕西	58	142	7,936	-346	-0.99	-1.88	32.45	47.27	34,854
Gansu 甘肃	31	163	6,450	-215	-0.44	-0.85	16.38	47.60	48,325
Qinghai 青海	22	78	3,859	191	0.80	2.08	30.28	61.45	23,797
Ningxia 宁夏	6	97	2,304	-150	-1.14	-2.14	13.50	46.47	13,116
Xinjiang 新疆	44	55	2,302	-155	-1.11	-2.08	21.79	46.35	13,931

4620: Supply Of Tap Water 自来水供应业

Year 年份	Number of firms 企业个数	Rate of change 变化率 (%)	Number of employees 职工人数 (人)	Rate of change 变化率 (%)	Total revenue (Mil. RMB) 总销售收入 (百万元)	Rate of change 变化率 (%)	Total profit (Mil RMB) 总利润 (百万元)	Rate of change 变化率 (%)
2000	999		149,148		10,174		183	
2001	1060	6.11	168,253	12.81	11,779	15.78	290	58.47
2002	1053	-0.66	174,100	3.48	13,512	14.71	366	26.21

Major Products 主要产品	Output 产量	Unit 单位
Running Water Manufacturing Volume 自来水生产量	350	100,000,000 Tons 亿吨

10 Main Firms with Maximal Revenue (year founded) 收入最大的十家主要企业 （创办年份）	City 城市	Province 省	Telephone/ fax 电话/ 传真	Number of employees 职工人数	Ownership 产业所有权	Revenue ('000 RMB) 销售收入 (千元)	Profit('000 RMB) (rank) 利润(千元) (排名)	Total assets ('000 RMB) 总资产 (千元)	Major products 主要产品
Beijing Waterworks Group Company	Beijing	Beijing	(010)66410088		State-owned				Tap Water
北京市自来水集团有限责任公司(1910)	北京市	北京市	(010)66419830	2,778	国有企业	1,180,150	45,014(3)	8,893,329	自来水
Guangzhou Water Supply Company	Guangzhou	Guangdong	(020)81816951		State-owned				Tap Water
广州市自来水公司(1908)	广州市	广东省	(020)81058114	4,910	国有企业	1,177,566	31,406(7)	4,503,614	自来水
Shenyang Water Supply General Company	Shenyang	Liaoning	(024)22824682		State-owned				Tap Water
沈阳市自来水总公司(1915)	沈阳市	辽宁省	(024)22717506	6,564	国有企业	413,078	-	1,648,402	自来水
Xi'an Water Supply Company	Xi'an	Shannxi	(029)8625044		State-owned				Tap Water
西安市自来水公司(1952)	西安市	陕西省	(029)8621420	2,832	国有企业	305,788	10,459(18)	1,367,172	自来水
Nanjing Water Supply General Company	Nanjing	Jiangsu	(025)4402716		State-owned				Tap Water
南京市自来水总公司(1933)	南京市	江苏省	(025)4455060	2,751	国有企业	290,000	-	2,402,690	自来水
Shanghai Pudong Vivendi Water Supply Co., Ltd.	Shanghai	Shanghai	(021)58811366		Foreign Funded				Tap Water
上海浦东威望迪自来水有限公司(2000)	上海市	上海市	(021)58732661	1,467	外商投资	272,303	2,977(46)	2,406,120	自来水
Dalian Water Supply Company	Dalian	Liaoning	(0411)3634665		State-owned				Tap Water
大连市供水公司(1997)	大连市	辽宁省	(0411)3624098	315	国有企业	227,504	6,674(28)	1,105,067	自来水
Qingdao Water Supply Group Company	Qingdao	Shandong	(0532)2864210		State Enterprises				Tap Water
青岛市自来水集团有限公司(1901)	青岛市	山东省	(0532)2964180	1,957	国有独资	217,965	-	1,035,864	自来水
Nanchang Water Industry Group Co.,Ltd.	Nanchang	Jiangxi	(0791)5234708		State Enterprises				Tap Water
南昌水业集团有限责任公司(1937)	南昌市	江西省	(0791)5234681	1,742	国有独资	201,032	40,164(4)	799,672	自来水
Taiyuan Water Supply Company	Taiyuan	Shanxi	(0351)3030067		State-owned				Tap Water
太原市自来水公司	太原市	山西省	(0351)3031371	1,827	国有企业	193,500	21,003(10)	767,532	自来水

Top 10 Cities by Revenue 销售收入排名前10位城市	Province 省	Market share 市场份额 (%)	Number of firms 企业个数
Beijing 北京市	Beijing 北京市	9.61	6
Guangzhou 广州市	Guangdong 广东省	9.41	8
Dongguan 东莞市	Guangdong 广东省	7.25	29
Foshan 佛山市	Guangdong 广东省	5.53	20
Shenzhen 深圳市	Guangdong 广东省	3.18	8
Shenyang 沈阳市	Liaoning 辽宁省	3.14	4
Shanghai 上海市	Shanghai 上海市	2.98	7
Xi'an 西安市	Shannxi 陕西省	2.27	2
Dalian 大连市	Liaoning 辽宁省	2.27	3
Nanjing 南京市	Jiangsu 江苏省	2.19	2

10 Major Wholesalers 十家主要批发商	City 城市	Province 省	Telephone/Fax 电话/传真

Index

索引

Alphabetical Index

D

E

F

G

H

I

T

U

V

W

Y

笔画索引

五画

六画

七画

八画

九画

十画

十一画

十二画

十三画

十四画

十五画

十六画

十七画

十八画

图书在版编目（CIP）数据

中国市场年鉴.2004 / 高余先.主编
北京：外文出版社，2003.10
ISBN 7-119-03448-0

Ⅰ.中...　Ⅱ.高...　Ⅲ. 企业-概况-中国-2004-年鉴-英、汉
Ⅳ.F279.24-54

中国版本图书馆 CIP 数据核字(2003)第 086375 号

外文出版社网址：
http://www.flp.com.cn
外文出版社电子信箱：
info@flp.com.cn
sales@flp.com.cn

中国市场年鉴 2004

编　译　北京华通人市场信息有限责任公司
网　址：http://www.acmr.com.cn
电子信箱：cdc@acmr.com.cn
编　委　高余先　谢贵枝　蒋兴荣
林昭辉　唐洪芳　曹丽娜
技术负责　刘纪文

责任编辑　刘承忠
封面设计　王　博
出 版 者　外文出版社
社　址　北京市百万庄大街 24 号　　**邮政编码**　100037
印　刷　北京恒智彩印有限公司
开　本　大 16 开　　**字　数**　1020 千字
版　次　2004 年第 1 版第 1 次印刷　　**印　张**　67
装　别　精
书　号　ISBN 7-119-03448-0/Z・654（外）
国内定价　1500.00 元